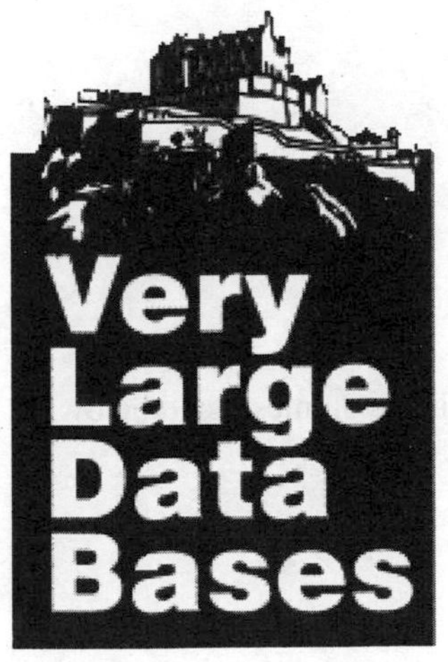

Proceedings
of the
Twenty-fifth
International Conference
on
Very Large Data Bases

Edinburgh, Scotland
7-10th September 1999

Editors:

Malcolm Atkinson
Maria E. Orlowska
Patrick Valduriez
Stan Zdonik
Michael Brodie

Ordering Information

Morgan Kaufmann Publishers is the exclusive world-wide distributor for the VLDB proceedings volumes listed below:

	ISBN
1999 Edinburgh, Scotland	1-55860-615-7
1998 New York, USA	1-55860-566-5
1997 Athens, Greece	1-55860-470-7
1996 Mumbai (Bombay), India	1-55860-382-4
1995 Zurich, Switzerland	1-55860-379-4
1994 Santiago, Chile	1-55860-153-8
1993 Dublin, Ireland	1-55860-152-X
1992 Vancouver, Canada	1-55860-151-1
1991 Barcelona, Spain	1-55860-150-3
1990 Brisbane, Australia	1-55860-149-X
1989 Amsterdam, The Netherlands	1-55860-101-5
1988 Los Angeles, USA	0-934613-75-3
1987 Brighton, United Kingdom	0-934613-46-X
1985 Stockholm, Sweden	0-934613-17-6
1984 Singapore	0-934613-16-8
1983 Florence, Italy	0-934613-15-X
1995-1999 5-year set	1-55860-626-2 ($185.00)
1987-1999 13-year set	1-55860-627-0 ($400.00)

Prices are $50.00 per copy for the 1999 volume, $40.00 per copy for all other volumes.

Shipping is free from Morgan Kaufmann within the U.S on prepaid orders. International shipping costs are $7 per volume via DHL/regular mail combination, or $20.00 per volume via international overnight courier. Morgan Kaufmann U.S. accepts credit card payments: the buyer should provide card number, expiration date, and name as it appears on the card for Visa, MasterCard, or American Express credit cards. Morgan Kaufmann also accepts cheque payments in U.S. dollars only; cheques must be drawn on a U.S. bank.

Order from	Morgan Kaufmann Publishers
By Mail:	Morgan Kaufmann Publishers Attention: Order Fulfilment Department 6277 Sea Harbor Drive Orlando, FL 32887 USA
By Phone:	800-745-7323 (from within US \& Canada) and 407-345-3800 (international)
By Fax:	800-874-6418 or 407-345-4060
By Email:	orders@mkp.com
By Web:	http://www.mkp.com

VLDB 1999 ISBN 1-55860-615-7
ISSN 0730-9317

Conference Organisers

General Conference Chair	Keith Jeffery, CLRC Rutherford Appleton Lab.
Organisation Chair	Jessie Kennedy, Napier University
Programme Chair	Malcolm Atkinson, University of Glasgow
Regional Programme Chairs	
Asia and Australia	Maria Orlowaska, University of Queensland
Europe and Africa	Patrick Valduriez, INRIA
North and South America	Stan Zdonik, Brown University
Industrial Programme Chair	Michael Brodie, GTE Laboratories
Panel & Demonstrations Chair	Ron Morrison, University of St Andrews
Tutorial Programme Chair	Carole Goble, University of Manchester
Organising Committee	
Exhibitions	Lachlan MacKinnon, Heriot-Watt University
Local Arrangements	Albert Burger, Heriot-Watt University
Proceedings Production	Peter Barclay, Napier University
Publicity Chair	Mary Garvey, University of Wolverhampton
Secretary	Jon Kerridge, Napier University
Social Programme	Alex Gray, University of Wales, Cardiff
Treasurer	Mike Jackson, University of Wolverhampton

Programme Committees

Programme Committee Members **Asia and Australia**

Chair Maria E Orlowska, University of Queensland, Australia
David Abel, CSIRO, Australia
David Cheung, The University of Hong Kong, Hong Kong
Alan Fekete, University of Sydney, Australia
Joseph Fong, City University of Hong Kong, Hong Kong
Yahiko Kambayashi, Kyoto University, Japan
Kamal Karlapalem, Hong Kong University of Science & Technology, Hong Kong
Hiroyuki Kitagawa, University of Tsukuba, Japan
Masaru Kitsuregawa, University of Tokyo, Japan
Dik Lee, Hong Kong University of Science & Technology, Hong Kong
Xuemin Lin, University of New South Wales, Australia
Tok Wang Ling, National University of Singapore, Singapore
Hongjun Lu, National University of Singapore, Singapore
Ramamohanarao (Rao) Kotagiri, The University of Melbourne, Australia
Akifumi Makinouchi, Kyushu University, Japan
Shojiro Nishio, Osaka University, Japan
Beng Chin Ooi, National University of Singapore, Singapore
Dimitris Papadias, Hong Kong University of Science & Technology, Hong Kong
Ron Sacks-Davis, RMIT Multimedia Database Systems, Australia
Rodney Topor, Griffith University, Australia
Kyu-Young Whang, Korea Advanced Institute of Science and Technology, Korea

Programme Committees Continued

Programme Committee Members **Europe and Africa**

Chair Patrick Valduriez, INRIA, France
Serge Abiteboul, INRIA, France
Gustavo Alonso, ETH Zurich, Switzerland
Elena Baralis, Politecnico di Torino, Italy
David Bell, University of Ulster, Northern Ireland
Sonia Berman, Cape Town University, South Africa
Elisa Bertino, Politecnico di Milano, Italy
Catriel Beeri, University of Jerusalem, Israel
Kjell Bratbergsengen, University of Trondheim, Norway
Michael Bohlen, Aalborg University, Denmark
Alex Buchmann, University of Darmstadt, Germany
Richard Connor, University of Glasgow, Scotland
Oscar Diaz, University of the Basque Country, Spain
Jean Ferrie, University of Montpellier, France
Dana Florescu, INRIA, France
Piero Fraternali, Politecnico di Milano, Italy
Theo Haerder, University of Kaiserslautern, Germany
Yannis Ioannidis, University of Athens, Greece
Matthias Jarke, RWTH Aachen, Germany
Genevieve Jomier, University of Paris 9, France
Leonid Kalinichenko, Russian Academy of Sciences, Russia
Nabil Kamel, American University in Cairo, Egypt
Daniel Keim, University of Munich, Germany
Martin Kersten, CWI, the Netherlands
Guido Moerkotte, University of Mannheim, Germany
Giansalvatore Mecca, Universita della Basilicata, Italy
Michele Missikoff, IASI-CNR, Italy
Alain Pirotte, University of Louvain, Belgium
Philippe Pucheral, University of Versailles, France
Oded Shmueli, Technion Israel Institute of Technology, Israel
Stefano Spaccapietra, EPF Lausanne, Switzerland
Anthony Tomasic, INRIA, France
Ozgur Ulusoy, Bilken University, Turkey
Yannis Vassiliou, National Technical University of Athens, Greece

Programme Committees Continued

Programme Committee Members **North and South America**

Chair Stan Zdonik, Brown University, USA

Swarup Acharya, Bell Labs, USA
Rafael Alonso, Sarnoff Labs, USA
Jose Blakely, Microsoft, USA
Anthony Bonner, University of Toronto, Canada
Alex Brodsky, George Mason University, USA
Michael Carey, IBM Almaden Research Center, USA
Mariano Consens, University of Waterloo, Canada
Isabel Cruz, Worcester Polytechnic Institute, USA
Susan Davidson, University of Pennsylvania, USA
Laurent Daynes, Sun Labs, USA
David DeWitt, University of Wisconsin at Madison, USA
Umesh Dayal, HP Labs, USA
Pam Drew, The Boeing Company, USA
Max Egenhofer, University of Maine, USA
Michael Franklin, University of Maryland, USA
Dina Goldin, University of Massachusets at Boston, USA
Nat Goodman, Compaq Corp., USA
Joe Hellerstein, University of California at Berkeley, USA
Rick Hull, Lucent Technology, USA
Tomasz Imielinski, Rutgers University, USA
Roger King, University of Colorado at Boulder, USA
Dennis McLeod, USC, USA
Stuart Madnick, MIT Sloan School, USA
Dave Maier, Oregon Graduate Institute, USA
Alberto Mendelzon, University of Toronto, Canada
Gail Mitchell, GTE Labs, USA
Pat O'Neil, University of Massachusetts at Boston, USA
Frank Olken, Lawrence Berkeley National Lab, USA
M. Tamer Özsu, University of Alberta, Canada
Xiaolei Qian, Securesoft, USA
Ken Ross, Columbia University, USA
Elke Rundensteiner, Worcester Polytechnic Institute, USA
Betty Salzberg, Northeastern University, USA
Len Shapiro, Portland State University, USA
Nandit Soparkar, University of Michigan, USA
Praveen Seshadri, Cornell University, USA
Rick Snodgrass, University of Arizona, USA
Jacob Stein, Sybase, USA
Jeff Ullman, Stanford University, USA
Bennet Vance, IBM Almaden Research Center, USA
Yelana Yesha, NASA, CESDIS and UMBC, USA

Additional Reviewers

Abdulghane A.
Abileah S.
Al-Halimi R.
Albert J.
Avadhanam S.
Baradaram N.
Barish G.
Barrera R.
Barta A.
Bettini C.
Blott S.
Bordia A.
Bouganim L.
Budiarto
Buneman P.
Burkowski F.
Camara G.
Cao Q.
Cart M.
Catania B.
Celis P.
Cetintemel U.
Chandan K.
Chang L.
Chen L.
Cho W-S.
Chrisopoulos A.
Chuan Wu M.
Cicekli N.
Claypool K.
Cosar A.
Crabtree J.
Crestana V.
Dayal V.
Delcambre L.
Desai S.
Ding L.
Dogac A.
Dunkel B.
Finance B.
Flewelling D.
Fonseca F.
Formica A.
Fox N.
Freire J.
Fujikawa K.
Galindo-Legaria C.
Gardarin G.
Garofalakis M.
Gibbons P.
Gorafalakis M.
Goyal R.
Graefe G.
Gravano L.
Guerrini G.
Gupta H.
Haas L.
Hara T.
Hatanaka A.
Heiler S.
Heinz S.
Hinneburg A.
Hornsby K.
Ishii H.
Ishikawa Y.
Jagadish H.
James K.
Jensen P.
Joseph A.
Kalnis P.
Karagoz P.
Katayama K.
Kemme B.
Khan L.
Köller A.
Kolahdouzan M.
Kornacker M.
Kothuri R.
Kuo L.
Lee W-C.
Lee S.Y.
Lei Y.
Li C.
Liebig C.
Liefke H.
Liu H.
Loeser H.
Loukopoulos T.
Lynch C.
Mahnke W.
Mamoulis N.
Mantzourogiannis M.
Marder U.
Martinez J.
Merialdo P.
Mihaila G.
Mishra N.
Miyazaki J.
Monties S
Morishima A.
Muslea I.
Nakano M.
Nayak N.
Nierman A.
Nestorov S.
Ngu A.
Ohmori T.
Okada A.
Oria V.
Orlowski M.
Palpanas T.
Pant G.
Park C-M.
Park Y.C.
Patel B.
Pizzicannella R.
Plazanet C.
Poosala V.
Psaila G.
Rafiei D.
Ramer A.
Rao J.
Rastogi R.
Reddy K.
Reza M.
Ritter N.
Rochat P.
Safar M.
Sahuguet A.
Satoh T.
Seshradi S.
Sellis T.
Shapiro W.
Sharma J.
Shepherd J.
Shi X.
Shimojo S.
Simeon J.
Snider T.
Stefanidis A.
Steiert H-P
Stroe D.
Subramanian S.
Suciu D.
Surjanto B.
Takakura H.
Tamassia R.
Tan K.L.
Tandon A.
Tatbul N.
Teisseire M.
Teorey T.
Theodoridis Y.
Thom J.
Toman D.
Tompa F.
Toroslu I.
Vassalos V.
Voruganti K.
Wallace C.
Wang C.
Wang Y.
Wang K.
Weddell G.
Williams H.
Wong R.
Yang J.
Yeh L.
Yesha Y.
Yokota H.
Yu Y.
Yu J.X.
Zaman K.
Zhang N.
Zhang X.
Zhao W.
Zhao Y.
Zimmerman J.
Zjang X.
Zou C.

Sponsors

Principal Sponsor

ORACLE®

Sponsors

Contributors

Organising and Supporting Bodies

NAPIER UNIVERSITY
EDINBURGH

Lothian and
Edinburgh
Enterprise
Limited

UNIVERSITY
of
GLASGOW

VLDB Endowment

Board of Trustees

Preface

The Twenty-fifth International Conference on Very Large Data Bases (VLDB99) was held in Edinburgh, Scotland from the 7th to the 10th September 1999. This book contains all of the material prepared for VLDB99 and as such represents a valuable compendium of current database research, challenges and applications.

These proceedings contain 51 papers that were selected from the 387 submitted papers, three solicited industrial sessions, the ten-year award paper, an extended abstract of one of the two keynote talks, an overview of the panel session and eight selected demonstration descriptions. This provides a total of 77 high-quality papers contributed by 206 authors. It therefore provides excellent insights into:

- recent achievements in database research,
- pressing problems facing the users of databases that will challenge researchers for the coming years, and
- effective techniques for building and using databases.

The conference also included five tutorials:

From Semistructured Data to XML	Dan Suciu, AT&T Labs, USA
A Database Centric Update on CORBA	Sean Baker, IONA Technologies, Ireland
Design and Perception in Information Visualisation	Matthew Chalmers, University of Glasgow, Scotland
Using SQL/J for enterprise database applications: access, procedures and storage	Brian Becker, Oracle Corporation
Metasearch Engines: Solutions and Challenges	Clement Yu, U. of Illinois at Chicago, USA Weiyi Meng, SUNY at Binghamton, USA

A collection of these tutorials is available from the organisers as a separate book.

The papers and tutorials show that there continues to be interest and progress in all of the traditional database topics: optimisation, caching, data model extension, and interaction with programming languages. Sophisticated decision support, based on OLAP, provokes progress in optimisation and approximation. The significance of the large volume of data held as text attracts attention, particularly as XML promises to offer a common notation, so that the real issues of extracting information can be addressed. The interaction with networks is addressed from two points of view: what must databases do to contribute to their management and how can databases be used in conjunction with expanding networks. Considerable practical progress in extending relations towards an object-oriented capability is reported. The integration of databases with information retrieval is demonstrated.

Our ten-year award celebrates the significant contribution of the ARIES algorithm for logging and recovery, and the contribution of Mohan in continuing to develop this widely applicable research topic. The algorithm was first published at VLDB89 in conjunction with its application to nested transactions *ARIES/NT: A Recovery Method Based on Write-Ahead Logging for Nested Transactions*, K. Rothermel and C. Mohan. The programme committee therefore chose to recognise both C. Mohan, IBM Fellow (and currently Visiting Scientist at INRIA) and K. Rothermel, Universität Stuttgart with the ten-year award and to invite Mohan to give the opening talk at the conference in recognition of his sustained contributions.

Sadly, this year we had to include two obituaries. One, for Peter Stocker, recognising many years of contribution to database research and to VLDB conferences. The other, for Cheng Hian Goh, whose potential for such contributions, evidenced by being an author of two of this year's selected papers, was abruptly terminated by his sudden death.

Under the direction of Malcolm Atkinson, the Programme Committees have done a tremendous job in attracting the largest number of submissions and in maintaining the quality of VLDB as evidenced by these proceedings. The three regional programme committee chairs, Maria E. Orlowska, Patrick Valduriez and Stan Zdonik, and the industrial programme committee chair, Michael Brodie, would like to thank all of their programme committee members who worked so hard and conscientiously to review all of the submitted papers on a very tight schedule. Over one thousand reviews had to be produced in a month. The North and South America region had a particularly arduous task, with 17 papers to review per programme committee member. These programme committee members, in particular, will join us in thanking the 180 colleagues who assisted with the task of reviewing. The processing of this workload was supported by the Puma / Predator system, supplied by Praveen Sesandri, Cornell University. Ela Hunt, Stewart Macneill and Karen Renaud, at the University of Glasgow ran the web site and databases, supported the reviewers and regional chairs and "kept the show on the road". We greatly appreciate their combined efforts. Kathy Humphry helped with many of the tasks that followed paper selection, and Stewart Macneill processed all of the proceedings into its final digital form. Peter Barclay managed the printing, publishing and production process, while Mary Garvey diverted her artistic talents from publicity to prepare the cover.

The conference itself however includes more than is reflected in the proceedings and behind the scene work of several people deserve particular note. Many people in the organising committee under Jessie Kennedy's leadership have committed many hours of careful work preparing for the conference and running it. Mike Jackson, the treasurer believed we could afford the EICC when it didn't even exist and controlled our budget and cash flow when temptations arose. Mary Garvey deserves two thank you mentions as she did the job of at least two people: maintaining the VLDB web site and Publicity. When she agreed to undertake publicity, the web site was another little add-on, however she has done a tremendous job with the web pages, which devoured many of her evenings. Peter Barclay did a thorough job of negotiating with the printers and getting the proceedings delivered on time. A first for VLDB was the demonstrations selected and organised by Ron Morrison. The excellent selection of tutorials was managed by Carole Goble and the exhibition was organised by Lachlan MacKinnon while Albert Burger helped with local arrangements. With the assistance of Jenny Siegel, Jon Kerridge acted secretary with the proviso that he'd metamorphose into Jessie should she not last the pace, although we're not sure how convincing he'd have been! Jon did a stalwart job of technical manager responsible for the student helpers who aided the smooth running of the conference. Alex Gray's expertise and enthusiasm for Scottish culture and dance enhanced the social programme, an important aspect of any international conference.

From the outset the VLDB endowment under the leadership of Peter Lockeman and subsequently John Mylopolous were very supportive of the Scottish bid, for which we would like to thank them. Although the VLDB committees undertook a lot of work, the conference wouldn't have been possible without the help of our professional conference organisers, Clansman Monarch, whose professional support was much appreciated. Conferences like VLDB would be much less viable without the support of the industrial sponsors whose contributions were gratefully received.

If you collect these proceedings as a VLDB99 delegate we thank you for coming, welcome you and hope that you will enjoy both Edinburgh and the Conference. If you are reading them after the conference then we hope they will prove beneficial to your research or business.

Jessie Kennedy & Malcolm Atkinson

Obituary

In Memory of Cheng Hian GOH (1965 - 1999)

Cheng Hian Goh passed away on 1 April 1999 at the age of 33. He is survived by his wife Soh Mui Lee and two sons, Emmanuel and Gabriel, to whom we all send our deepest condolences.

Cheng Hian received his PhD in Information Technologies from the Massachusetts Institute of Technology in Feb 1997. Prior to undertaking his PhD studies, Cheng Hian received both a BSc (First Class Honors) and a MSc both in Computer Science from the National University of Singapore where he received numerous awards. He joined the Department of Computer Science, National University of Singapore as an Assistant Professor in November 1996.

He was totally dedicated to his work— teaching as well as research. He enjoyed preparing his lecture notes, and would spend much time in organizing them. He believed in giving his students the best. As a young database researcher, he demonstrated his research capability and made major contributions to the field as testified by his publications in ICDE'97, VLDB'98, ICDE'99, VLDB'99, etc.

He did not stop working/thinking about his research until he was forced to stop by his ill health. Towards his last days, he continued to guide his research students in the hospital. He also completed and co-authored several manuscripts. The submitted versions of his two papers that appear in the proceedings were in fact finalized with his co-authors when he was in hospital.

His last public appearance was at the ER'98 conference (Nov 98) held in Singapore. Despite his weak health, he shared his vision on Information Retrieval in the WWW as a member of a panel on Internet Applications, and as a speaker in the NSF-NSTB sponsored workshop on Databases and the Internet.

Cheng Hian was a very sociable person, and often sought the company of friends. As such, he was loved by those who came in contact with him. He would often go the extra mile to help his friends and colleagues. He was a great person, and had touched the lives of many. We suddenly realized that there are many things that we will never do together again. We'll miss him sorely, and his laughter, and his smile...

Stuart Madnick, Michael Siegel (MIT, USA), Stephane Bressan, Mong Li Lee, Sin Yeung Lee, Tok Wang Ling, Beng Chin Ooi, Kian Lee Tan, and Ke Wang (NUS, Singapore), Hongjun Lu (UST, Hong Kong)

Obituary

In memory of Peter M. Stocker (1927-98)

We regret to record the passing of Peter Stocker, a UK data base pioneer and a trustee of the VLDB Endowment (1984-91). He died suddenly and unexpectedly on 25th November 1998, aged 71, and was mourned by many. He was the founding Professor of Computing at the University of East Anglia and sometime Pro-Vice Chancellor.

Peter trained at Manchester University in the early days of mainframe computers. He took part in the early IFIP Working Conferences on Data Base Management, which were very influential at the dawn of our subject. Later (1982) he organised a very successful international summer school at the University of East Anglia on "Data Bases: Role and Structure".

He is probably best known, first for his pioneering work on self-organising databases, and then on distributed databases and conceptual schema languages. He led an early UK distributed database consortium in the Proteus project. He was an active member of the VLDB Endowment and served on numerous programme committees. In particular, he was Programme Committee co-chair for VLDB'87, when it was first held in the UK.

However, he was also a genuine polymath and his able mind enabled him to make insightful comments in any technical discussion. More than this, Peter was a good friend to many; he had a wonderful impish sense of humour which enabled him to negotiate successfully the most tricky of situations. He was also an inspiring leader and seminar speaker, who had a strong influence on the development of database research in the UK.

He found time to play and follow cricket, to cook for his friends and students and to listen to music. Apart from his children and grandchildren, of whom he was fiercely proud, his main non-academic interest was his garden (and that of his daughter, Anne, in Suffolk). Here he built up a large collection of varied and unusual plants.

Contents

Author Index

Repeating History Beyond ARIES

C. Mohan

IBM Almaden Research Center
650 Harry Road, K01/B1
San Jose, CA 95120, USA
mohan@almaden.ibm.com
www.almaden.ibm.com/u/mohan/

Abstract

In this paper, I describe first the background behind the development of the original ARIES recovery method, and its significant impact on the commercial world and the research community. Next, I provide a brief introduction to the various concurrency control and recovery methods in the ARIES family of algorithms. Subsequently, I discuss some of the recent developments affecting the transaction management area and what these mean for the future. In ARIES, the concept of *repeating history* turned out to be an important paradigm. As I examine where transaction management is headed in the world of the internet, I observe history repeating itself in the sense of requirements that used to be considered significant in the mainframe world (e.g., performance, availability and reliability) now becoming important requirements of the broader information technology community as well.

1. Introduction

Transaction management is one of the most important functionalities provided by a database management system (DBMS). Over the years, several techniques have been developed to deal with the two most important aspects of transaction management, namely, concurrency control and recovery (CC&R). The transaction abstraction with its ACID (atomicity, consistency, isolation and durability) properties [HaRe83] has been supported by DBMSs to let users designate the scope of their atomic and isolated database interactions. Over the last two decades, several CC&R techniques have been developed and a small subset of them have been implemented in products and prototypes [BeHG87, BeNe97, Elmag92, GrRe93, JaKe97, KuHs98, Kumar95].

Proceedings of the 25th VLDB Conference, Edinburgh, Scotland. 1999.

In this paper, I describe the background behind the invention of the ARIES (*Algorithms for Recovery and Isolation Exploiting Semantics*) family of CC&R algorithms, and the significant impact that these algorithms have had on the research community and the commercial world (section 2). In section 3, I briefly summarize some of the ARIES algorithms and discuss their implementation status. This presentation also gives a roadmap across the numerous papers that focus on ARIES and related work. The rest of this paper discusses some of the recent developments in transaction processing and distributed computing in general (section 4). Based on these observations, I speculate on what is likely to happen in the next few years (section 5).

2. Background and Impact

In the Starburst project [HCLMW90], which was started in the mid-80s at IBM's Almaden Research Center as the R* distributed DBMS project [MoLO86] was ending, we focussed on building a brand new relational DBMS with extensibility as the primary objective. Some of us treated this new project as a golden opportunity and decided to revisit many of the assumptions and conclusions of IBM's very influential System R RDBMS project [CABGK81] in the area of transaction management. We also decided to learn from the accumulated experiences with the IBM RDBMS products DB2/MVS [HaJa84] and SQL/DS [ChGY81], which, by then, had undergone customer usage for a few years. In particular, we decided to examine more closely the different approaches to database recovery adopted by these products – write-ahead logging (WAL) in DB2/MVS and shadow paging in SQL/DS.

While the System R researchers concluded [CABGK81] that WAL is better than shadow paging, they did not succeed in producing a recovery method that supported fine-granularity (e.g., record level) locking while still allowing the flexible management of variable length records as in System R. This was the primary reason behind DB2/MVS being released in 1984 with only a page as the smallest granularity of locking. Even though IBM's hierarchical DBMS IMS supported record level locking

[GaKi85, Ober80, Ober98a, Ober98b, PeSt83], it was unsatisfactory since it was doing very physical (e.g., byte-range) logging and locking that resulted in inflexible storage management and the need for frequent offline data reorganizations. We decided to aim for the best of both worlds! Since most of us were not IBMers during the System R days, we were able to look at the problems with a fresh perspective.

At a time when the research community had wrongly come to the conclusion that everything about CC&R was well understood and that there was no need for any additional work to be done, we had to be courageous to try to justify spending time on examining not only the paltry documentation but also the code of System R, SQL/DS, DB2/MVS and even IMS to try to understand everything about how their CC&R worked. Finding significant design bugs in System R ten years after the release of the product version of it (SQL/DS) was not considered, by some colleagues, to be a worthwhile exercise! In retrospect, such investigations proved to be extremely educative, insightful and invaluable. Almost all of the knowledge that we gained through these investigations have been documented extensively in the ARIES collection of papers cited here.

The original ARIES work, which was done in the mid-80s and publicly documented in a research report form in 1989 [MHLPS92], led to the establishment of the IBM Data Base Technology Institute (DBTI). This umbrella organization, which encompassed many database research and product groups within IBM, gave us, the IBM researchers, numerous opportunities to interact with IBM's DBMS customers and product developers. We were able to learn from them about important unsolved problems, and drawbacks of solutions and features implemented in different DBMS products and prototypes.

The basic ARIES algorithm summarized in Section 3.2 has been extended by us and others in numerous ways. We describe some of the extensions in the following subsections. Because of its generality and its extensive flexibility, ARIES has been implemented not only in DBMSs but also in persistent object systems, recoverable file systems, messaging and queuing systems, and transaction-based operating systems. Various approaches have been taken to formalize subsets of ARIES [Kuo96, LoTu95, MaRa97]. Extensions to ARIES have been proposed to exploit operation semantics [Billa96], provide high availability [BGHJ92] and support the client-server context [FZTCD92]. Simulation and analytical studies of ARIES's performance have been done [JhKh92, VuDo90].

Many of the algorithms summarized in this paper have been implemented to varying degrees in numerous products and research prototypes like Starburst extensible DBMS [HCLMW90], OS/2 Extended Edition Database Manager [ChMy88], DB2/390 [JMNT97], DB2 UDB for Unix, Windows and OS/2, Encina transaction processing monitor and recoverable file system, Microsoft SQL Server and NT file system, Gamma database machine [DGSBH90], EXODUS extensible DBMS [FZTCD92], Shore persistent object system [CDFHM94], Paradise GIS system, PREDATOR object-relational DBMS, MQSeries transactional messaging and queuing product [MoDi94], SQL/DS [ChGY81], ADSTAR Distributed Storage Manager (ADSM) [CaRH95], Lotus Domino/Notes R5 [Mohan99], QuickSilver distributed operating system [CMSW93], and VM Shared File System [StNC91]. There are likely to be many other implementations about which I am unaware.

ARIES has been covered in many database textbooks and tutorials (e.g., [RaCh96, Ramak98, Weihl95]). A cursory search on the web reveals that ARIES is being taught in university courses at Austin, Ben Gurion, Berkeley, Cornell, Duke, Ioannina, Maryland, Pittsburgh, Rensselaer, Seoul, Stanford, Trier and Wisconsin. At Cornell, based on earlier work at Wisconsin, a system called Mars has been developed for educational purposes. It is a recovery simulator that is used to explain and explore ARIES. It includes visualization features.

IBM obtained European patents [HLMPS94] on the basic ARIES recovery method. However, due to some fumbling by lawyers, after many years it gave up on trying to get the corresponding US patent! Subsequently, it let the European patents also lapse. IBM did obtain in the US and elsewhere patents on most of the other ARIES-related locking and recovery methods (for details, see www.almaden.ibm.com/u/mohan/aries_papers.html).

3. The ARIES Family of Algorithms

This section summarizes some of the CC&R algorithms that belong to the ARIES (*Algorithms for Recovery and Isolation Exploiting Semantics*) family. These algorithms support very high concurrency via fine-granularity locking, operation logging, efficient recovery, and flexible storage and buffer management. They relate to nested transactions, index management, hashing, cheap techniques for reducing or eliminating locking while guaranteeing consistency, fast restart recovery and interactions between query processing and concurrency control. While the recovery techniques are based on write-ahead logging, many of the concurrency control techniques that have been developed are applicable to systems using other recovery methods also (e.g., shadow paging).

3.1 Recovery Methods

There are two general approaches to recovery: the *write-ahead logging* (***WAL***) approach [Gray78, MHLPS92] and the *shadow-page technique* [GMBLL81, MHLPS92]. WAL is the recovery method of choice in most systems, even though the shadow-page technique of System R is used in some systems, possibly in a limited form (e.g., for managing long fields or BLOBs). In WAL systems, an updated page is written back to the same disk location from which it was read. That is, *in-place updating* is done on disk. The *WAL protocol* asserts that the log records representing changes to some data must already be on stable storage *before* the changed data is allowed to replace the previous version of that data on disk.

Each log record is assigned, by the log manager, a unique *log sequence number (LSN)* at the time the record is written to the log. The LSNs are assigned in ascending sequence. Typically, they are the logical addresses of the corresponding log records [Crus84]. At times, version numbers or timestamps are also used as LSNs [Borr84, MoNP90]. On finishing the logging of an update to a page, in many systems whose recovery is based on WAL, the LSN of the log record corresponding to the *latest* update to the page is placed in a field in the page header. Hence, knowing the LSN of a page allows the system to correlate the state of the page with respect to those logged updates relating to that page. That is, at the time of recovery, given a log record, the LSN of the database page referenced in the log record and the LSN of the log record can be compared to determine unambiguously whether or not that log record's update is already reflected in that page. The buffer manager, in order to enforce the WAL protocol, uses the LSN associated with a modified page to ensure that the log has been forced to disk up to that LSN *before* it writes that page to disk.

With the shadow-page technique, as it is implemented in System R and SQL/DS, the *first* time a (logical) page is modified after a checkpoint, a new *physical* page is associated with it on disk. Later, when the page (the *current* version) is written to disk, it is written to the new location. The old physical page (the ***shadow*** version) associated with the (logical) page is not discarded until the next checkpoint. Restart recovery occurs from the *shadow* version of the page if a system failure should occur. With shadow paging, checkpoints tend to be very expensive and disruptive. This is because a checkpoint is taken only when all activities in the data manager have been quiesced to an *action-consistent* state. After quiescing, all the modified pages in the buffer pool and the log are written to disk. Then, the shadow version is discarded and the current version is also made the new shadow version. As a result of all these synchronous actions by the checkpointing process, restart recovery always happens from the internally consistent, *shadow* version of the database.

Even when the shadow-page technique is used for recovery, logging of updates is still performed. Commercially, the WAL approach has been much more widely adopted than the shadow-page technique. Very detailed comparisons between the two methods are given in [MHLPS92]. In this paper, whenever I discuss recovery methods, I assume that it is based on WAL. The concurrency protocols that I discuss are applicable also to systems that use the shadow-page technique.

In the following, I summarize the original ARIES algorithm and its variants ARIES-RRH and ARIES/NT. I also discuss the adaptation of ARIES for the shared disks and client-server environments, and for the management of semi-structured data in Lotus Domino/Notes.

3.2 ARIES

The aim of this section is to provide a brief overview of the original ARIES recovery method which was developed for the flat (i.e., unnested) transaction model [MHLPS92].

3.2.1 Logging

Like other recovery methods, ARIES also guarantees the atomicity and durability properties of transactions [HaRe83]. In order to provide these guarantees, ARIES keeps track of the changes made to the database by using a log. It implements the WAL protocol. All updates to all pages are logged. Changes to each page may be logged in a logical fashion. That is, not every byte that was changed on the page needs to be logged. ARIES uses an LSN on every database page to track the page's state. Every time a page is updated and a log record is written, the LSN of the log record is placed in the ***page_LSN*** field of the updated page. Tagging every page with an LSN allows ARIES to precisely track, for restart/media recovery purposes, the state of a page with respect to logged updates for that page.

In addition to logging, on a per-affected-page basis, update activities performed during forward (i.e., normal) processing of transactions, ARIES also logs, typically using ***compensation log records*** (***CLRs***), updates performed during partial or total rollbacks of transactions during both normal and restart *undo* processing. For example, if the original log record (***nonCLR***) described the deletion of record R10 on page P1, the CLR written during the undo of that log record would describe the insertion of R10 on P1. As a result of writing CLRs and updating the page_LSN field with the LSNs of the CLRs also, as far as recovery is concerned, the state of a page is always viewed as evolving forward, even when some original updates are being undone.

ARIES allows the support of even semantically-rich lock modes like *increment/decrement* [BaRa87] that permit multiple transactions to update the same data concurrently.

This is the kind of feature that requires a recovery method to (1) support *operation* logging (i.e., logging the quantity by which a field's value was decremented or incremented, rather than logging the before and after values of the field as in IMS), (2) avoid erroneous attempts to undo or redo some actions unnecessarily by precisely tracking the state of a page using the LSN concept, and (3) write CLRs.

Unlike in earlier recovery methods, in ARIES, CLRs have the property that they are redo-only log records. By appropriate *chaining* of the CLRs to log records written during forward processing, a bounded amount of logging is ensured during rollbacks, even in the face of repeated failures during restart recovery or of nested rollbacks.[1] This is to be contrasted with what happens in IMS [PeSt83], which may undo the same nonCLR multiple times, and in AS/400 [ClCo89], DB2/MVS V1 and NonStop SQL, which, in addition to undoing the same nonCLR multiple times, may also undo CLRs one or more times (see [MHLPS92] for examples). In the past, these have caused severe problems in real-life situations.

When the undo of a log record causes a CLR to be written, the CLR is made to point, via the ***UndoNxtLSN*** field of the CLR, to the *predecessor* of the log record being undone. The latter information is readily available since every log record, including a CLR, contains a pointer (***PrevLSN***) to the most recent preceding log record written by the same transaction. Thus, during rollback, the UndoNxtLSN field of the *most recently written CLR* keeps track of the progress of rollback. It tells the system from where to continue the rollback of the transaction, if a system failure were to interrupt the completion of the rollback or if a nested rollback were to be performed. It lets the system bypass those log records that had already been undone.

Since CLRs can describe what actions are actually performed during the undo of an original action, the undo action need not be, in terms of which page(s) is affected, the exact inverse of the action that is being compensated (i.e., ***logical undo*** is made possible). This allows very high concurrency to be supported. For example, in a B^+-tree, a key inserted on page 10 by one transaction may be moved to page 20 by another transaction *before* the key insertion is committed, as we permit in ARIES/IM [Mohan95b, MoLe92] (see [Mohan93a] for the description of ARIES/LHS which also exploits this feature). Now, if the first transaction were to roll back, then the key will be located on page 20 by retraversing the tree and deleted from there. A CLR will be written to describe the key deletion on page 20. This enables ***page-oriented redo***, which is very efficient, during restart and media recovery [MHLPS92].

3.2.2 Restart Recovery

When restarting the transaction system after an abnormal termination, recovery processing in ARIES involves making three passes (*analysis, redo* and *undo*) over the log. In order to make this processing efficient, periodically during normal processing, ARIES takes checkpoints. The checkpoint log records identify the transactions that are active, their states, and the addresses of their most recently written log records, and also the modified data (***dirty*** data) that is in the buffer pool. During restart recovery, ARIES first scans the log from the last checkpoint to the end of the log. During this ***analysis pass***, information about dirty data and transactions that were in progress at the time of the checkpoint is brought up to date as of the end of the log. The analysis pass, using the dirty data information, determines the starting point (***RedoLSN***) for the log scan of the immediately following redo pass. The analysis pass also determines the list of transactions to be rolled back in the undo pass. For each in-progress transaction, the LSN of the most recently written log record will also be determined.

Next, during the ***redo pass***, ARIES ***repeats history*** with respect to those updates logged on stable storage but whose effects on the database pages did not get reflected on disk before the system failure. This is done for the updates of ALL transactions, *including the updates of those transactions that had neither committed nor reached the in-doubt state of two-phase commit by the time of the crash* (i.e., even the missing updates of the so-called ***loser*** transactions are redone).

The process of repeating history essentially reestablishes the state of the database as of the time of the failure. A log record's update is redone if the affected page's page_LSN is *less than* the log record's LSN. The redo pass also obtains the locks needed to protect the uncommitted updates of those distributed transactions which will remain in the *in-doubt* (*prepared*) state [MoLO86] at the end of restart recovery. In contrast, in the recovery methods of System R [GMBLL81] and DB2 V1 [Crus84], only the missing updates of terminated and in-doubt transactions (the ***nonloser*** transactions) are redone during the redo pass. This is called the ***selective redo*** paradigm. In [MHLPS92], we show why this paradigm leads to problems when fine-granularity (i.e., smaller than page-granularity) locking is to be supported with WAL.

The next pass is the ***undo pass*** during which all loser transactions' updates are rolled back, in reverse

[1] A *nested rollback* is said to have occurred if a partial rollback were to be later followed by a total rollback or another partial rollback whose point of termination is an *earlier* point in the transaction than the point of termination of the first rollback.

chronological order, in a single sweep of the log. This is done by continually taking the maximum of the LSNs of the next log record to be processed for each of the yet-to-be-completely-undone loser transactions, until no loser transaction remains to be undone. Unlike during the redo pass, during the undo pass (as well as during normal undo), performing undos is not a conditional operation. That is, ARIES does *not* compare the page_LSN of the affected page to the LSN of the log record to decide whether or not to undo the update. Once a log record is processed for a transaction, the next record to process for that transaction is determined by looking at the PrevLSN or the UndoNxtLSN field of the record, depending on whether it is a nonCLR or a CLR, respectively.

3.2.3 Nested Top Actions

There are times when we would like some changes of a transaction to be committed irrespective of whether later on the transaction as a whole commits or not. We do need the *atomicity* property for these changes themselves. A few of the many situations where this is very useful are: for performing page splits and page deletes in indexes [Mohan95b, MoLe92], for relocating records in a hash-based storage method [Mohan93a], and for allowing out-of-current-transaction PUTs and GETs in a transactional messaging system [MoDi94]. ARIES supports this via the concept of ***nested top actions (NTAs)***. The desired effect is accomplished by writing a ***dummy CLR*** at the end of the NTA. The dummy CLR has as its UndoNxtLSN the LSN of the most recent log record written by the current transaction just before it started the NTA.. Thus, the dummy CLR lets ARIES bypass the log records of the NTA if the transaction were to be rolled back *after* the completion of the NTA..

ARIES's repeating history feature ensures that the NTA's changes would be redone, if necessary, after a system failure even though they may be changes performed by a loser transaction. If a system failure were to occur before the dummy CLR is written, then the NTA will be undone since the NTA's log records are written as undo-redo (as opposed to redo-only) log records. This provides the desired atomicity property for the NTA itself.

3.2.4 Concurrency Control

While locks are acquired on data at the desired granularity to assure *logical* consistency of the accessed data, latches[2] on pages are acquired both during forward and undo processing to assure *physical* consistency of the data, when a page is being examined. Deadlocks involving latches alone, or latches and locks are avoided by ensuring that the following rules are obeyed:

1. Restricting the number of page latches held simultaneously to 2 [MoHa94].
2. Ordering the latches hierarchically and if they are requested unconditionally then ordering the requests to obey the hierarchy restriction.
3. Avoiding requesting a lock unconditionally while holding a latch.

No locks have to be acquired during transaction rollback, thereby preventing rolling back transactions from ever getting involved in deadlocks (contrast this with what happens in System R and R* [GMBLL81, MoLO86]).

ARIES supports selective and deferred restart [Mohan93c], fuzzy image copies (archive dumps) and efficient media recovery [MoNa93], and high-concurrency lock modes (e.g., increment/decrement), which exploit the semantics of the operations and which require the ability to do operation logging. It is flexible with respect to the kinds of buffer management policies (e.g., *steal*, *no-force*, etc. [HaRe83]) that can be implemented and the characteristics of the stored data. Efficient storage management can be done for varying length objects [MoHa94]. In the interest of efficiency, page-oriented redos and, in the interest of high concurrency, logical undos are supported. Opportunities also exist for exploiting parallelism during restart recovery. Algorithms for supporting the above features are summarized in [MHLPS92] and detailed in the other cited papers. Algorithms for creating remote site backups for recovering from disasters are presented in [MoTO93].

Even though CLRs have been written by many systems for a long time, [MHLPS92] was the first paper to explain the rationale behind writing them, and to point out the numerous advantages of writing them and not undoing their updates. In [MHLPS92], besides presenting a new recovery method, by way of motivation for our work, we also describe some previously unpublished aspects of recovery in System R (e.g., how partial rollbacks are handled). That paper also shows why the following System R paradigms for logging and recovery, which were based on the shadow page technique, had to be changed in the context of WAL.

- Selective redo
- Undo pass preceding redo pass
- No logging of updates performed during transaction rollback (i.e., no writing of CLRs)
- No logging of index updates and space management information changes

[2] A latch is like a semaphore. Compared to a lock, acquiring and releasing a latch is very cheap in terms of instructions executed [MHLPS92, Mohan90a, Mohan90b]. Readers of a page acquire a share (S) latch on the page before reading it, while updaters acquire an exclusive (X) latch.

- No tracking of page state on page itself to relate it to logged updates (i.e., no LSNs on pages)

With our ARIES work, we also showed why it is very important to consider concurrency control, recovery and storage management together to produce high concurrency and high performance CC&R methods.

3.3 ARIES for Shared Disks

With multiple computer systems, there are two approaches to providing scalability in DBMSs. One is the shared disks (SD) architecture and the other is the shared nothing (SN) architecture. SN has been implemented in Tandem's NonStop SQL, NCR's Teradata DBMS and IBM's DB2 Parallel Edition. SD has been implemented in IBM's IMS, DEC's Rdb, Oracle and, more recently, in IBM's DB2/390. The introduction of record level locking and support for SD was done in the same release of DB2/390. This necessitated enhancements to ARIES to deal with the fact that multiple instances of DB2, each with its own buffer pool, had concurrent read and write accesses to the same set of data on the shared disks. To make matters even more interesting, in addition to the shared disks, as in previous systems, in the S/390 Parallel Sysplex environment, we also had to deal with a page-addressable store (called *Coupling Facility*) that is shared by the S/390 machines running DB2 [IBM97].

As we designed for the SD environment, the hardware and software environment that we had to deal with kept changing: from centralized lock manager to distributed lock manager, from special-purpose hardware to general-purpose hardware running specialized software, from a software-only global lock manager to a hybrid lock manager, and so on. Our papers [JMNT97, MoNa91, MoNa92a, MoNa92b, MoNP90] document some of the alternatives in this environment for locking, logging, recovery, etc. What was implemented is described in [JMNT97]. Each DB2 instance writes its log records to its own local log, but the local logs are asynchronously merged for media recovery purposes [MoNa93]. The failure possibilities here are much more complex than in a single system environment.

3.4 ARIES/CSA

In the typical client-server environment, as exemplified by the object-oriented DBMSs, the client DBMS software directly operates on the database pages even though the disks containing the database are managed by only the server. The server ships the database pages to the clients and handles global locking across clients. Clients might cache pages across transaction commits. ARIES/CSA (*ARIES for the Client Server Architecture*) [MoNa94] supports such an environment. Here, the clients produce log records when they perform their updates and send them to the server at appropriate times. They generate LSNs locally rather than letting the log manager assign them. The server manages the log disk. It writes into a single log the log records received from the different clients. In many such ways, the CS environment differs from the SD environment of the last section in which the sharing systems have a peer-peer relationship. While we did not implement ARIES/CSA, a different version of ARIES designed for the client server environment has been implemented in EXODUS [FZTCD92].

3.5 ARIES for Semi-Structured Data

Since its first release in 1989, long before the topic became fashionable in the database and web research communities, Lotus Notes had been targeted for the management of semi-structured data. A few years ago, Notes was enabled for the internet. At that time, the product name was changed so that *Domino* represents the server and *Notes* the client. Database functionality is almost identical in Domino and Notes. Through the joint efforts of Lotus's subsidiary Iris Associates and IBM Almaden's Dominotes project, one of the major features implemented in the latest release (R5) of Lotus Domino/Notes is a traditional DBMS-style, log-based recovery scheme [Mohan99]. Since Notes had not been designed originally with this type of recovery in mind, accomplishing this required significant design work. Enhancements had to be made to ARIES to deal with the fact that storage management in Notes is done in an unconventional way, as described below.

A Notes database in its entirety is stored in a single operating system file in a location and machine architecture independent format. Some of the data structures in the file are paginated while others are just byte-streams. Over time, these data structures might also be moved around in arbitrary ways. Since some of the data structures might contain attachments like audio, video, etc., logging had to be made optional at the data structure level also. At the granularity of a database, logging can be turned on or off by the user. Notes users also frequently move or replicate databases by doing file copying via the operating system. This can cause a logged version of a database to be overlaid with an older or newer version of that database from another system. Accommodating all these complications has required changes to the analysis and redo passes of ARIES. For example, the modified analysis pass gathers some extra information that is used during the redo pass to skip processing some log records whose LSNs might have normally been compared with LSNs on corresponding database pages. In the future, we will write a paper describing the resulting variant of ARIES called ARIES/SSD (ARIES for Semi-Structured Data).

3.6 ARIES-RRH

ARIES-RRH (*Algorithm for Recovery and Isolation Exploiting Semantics with Restricted Repeating of History*) [MoPi91] is an enhanced version of the original ARIES recovery method. The ARIES-RRH enhancements relate to the amount of redo of updates that needs to be performed at the time of system restart in order to bring the database to a consistent state. They try to minimize the extent of repeating of history that needs to be performed.

As described earlier, the *repeating history* paradigm of ARIES includes redoing the missing updates of even those transactions that are to be rolled back later in the undo pass of restart. The latter may lead to some wasted work being done. We illustrated in the ARIES paper why repeating history was required to support fine-granularity (e.g., record) locking. [MoPi91] further analyzed this paradigm and proposed more efficient handling of redos, especially when the smallest granularity of locking is *not* less than a page, by combining the paradigm of *selective redo* from DB2/MVS V1 [Crus84] with the original ARIES algorithm. Even for data for which fine-granularity locking is being done, it is not always the case that all the unapplied but logged changes need to be redone. ARIES-RRH, which incorporates these changes, still retains all the good properties of ARIES - avoiding undo of CLRs, single pass media recovery, NTAs, etc. The ARIES-RRH enhancements should result in a reduction in the number of I/Os and in the amount of CPU processing during the redo and undo passes of restart. This should improve the availability of the system by allowing processing of new transactions to begin earlier than with the original ARIES algorithm [Mohan93c].

ARIES-RRH requires that, for each page, *all* updates logged at least up to the point of the *most recent* committed[3] or *in-doubt* update for that page be redone, if those updates are not already present in the page. The latter is as usual determined by comparing the LSN of the page with the LSNs of the relevant log records. For data for which page or coarser granularity of locking is being used, this rule implies that all loser transactions' logged but missing updates need not be redone, as was the case with DB2 V1 [Crus84]. It turns out that following this rule alone is not sufficient since some loser transaction might have already been rolling back when a system failure happened and as a result some CLRs might have been written which survived the system failure. Some of the pages affected by those CLRs' updates might not have been written back to disk after those undos were performed. Since those pages might have been written to disk after the *original* updates (i.e., the ones which the CLRs compensated) were performed on them, we need to ensure that the corresponding CLRs' updates are also redone, even though they belong to a loser transaction and they may not be followed by any nonloser transactions' updates for the affected pages. To be able to figure out when such a condition is true, given a CLR and the page affected by it, if the page's LSN is *less than* the CLR's LSN, then we need to know if the page contains the original log record's (nonCLR's) update. Comparing the UndoNxtLSN of the CLR with the LSN of the page is not sufficient for this purpose since the page LSN being greater than UndoNxtLSN does not necessarily mean that the original update is present in the page (see [MoPi91] for an example). What is needed is the LSN of the original (nonCLR) log record. So, the contents of a CLR are enhanced to also include a field called ***UndoneLSN*** which is the LSN of the log record which the CLR compensated.

Now, the rule for handling a CLR can be stated as follows: The update of a CLR must be redone if the LSN of the affected page is *greater than or equal to* the UndoneLSN of the CLR and is *less than* the LSN of the CLR. It should be noted that a rule like this was not needed in DB2 V1 since (1) DB2's recovery method performed the undo of CLRs' updates and (2) CLRs did not have the UndoNxtLSN pointer and hence DB2 did not bypass processing of already undone nonCLR log records.

Since, with ARIES-RRH, history is not being completely repeated, the handling of undos also needs to be changed to be a *conditional* one like in DB2 V1. That is, during undo, when a nonCLR is encountered, the undo of that log record's update should be performed only if the page's LSN is *greater than or equal to* the log record's LSN. A surprising requirement is that, irrespective of whether the undo has to performed or not, a CLR must always be written as if the undo was performed (see [MoPi91] for the explanation of why this is the case).

With the flexibility offered via operation logging and the support for semantically-rich modes of locking by ARIES and ARIES-RRH, this is the best that can be done in terms of reducing the extent of repeating of history for loser transactions' updates. Of course, if only physical logging and locking are supported (as in IMS), then the missing updates of loser transactions for a given page that even *precede* the updates of nonloser transactions for the same page need not be redone. ARIES-RRH does not compromise on the original ARIES algorithm's properties of never undoing a CLR's updates and never undoing the same nonCLR's updates more than once. [MoPi91] also explains the fundamental reasons behind why certain existing recovery algorithms work correctly in the face of

---

[3] Conceptually, we treat a transaction which terminated after rolling back completely as a transaction which performed a partial rollback to its beginning and then committed.

failures during restart recovery or during media recovery. The ARIES-RRH work has led to a better understanding of the fundamental interactions between concurrency control and recovery methods. So far ARIES-RRH has not been implemented.

3.7 ARIES/NT

ARIES/NT (*Algorithm for Recovery and Isolation Exploiting Semantics for Nested Transactions*) [RoMo89] is an extension of the ARIES algorithm which was originally designed for the single-level transaction model. ARIES/NT applies to a very general model of nested transactions [HaRo87, HaRo93], which includes partial rollbacks of subtransactions, upward and downward inheritance of locks, and concurrent execution of ancestor and descendent subtransactions. The adopted system architecture encompasses aspects of distributed database management also.

We will briefly summarize here the extensions that were made to the original ARIES recovery method to obtain ARIES/NT. In both ARIES and ARIES/NT, all log records written by the same transaction are linked via a so-called ***backward chain (BW-chain)*** using the PrevLSN pointers. In addition, in ARIES/NT, the BW-chains of *committed* subtransactions are linked to the BW-chains of their parents to reflect the transaction trees on the log. When a subtransaction T commits, a *c-committed* log record, which contains a pointer to the last record of T's BW-chain, is written to the BW-chain of T's parent. Consequently, the BW-chain of an *in-progress* transaction together with the chains of its *committed* inferiors form a tree structure, which is called the transaction's ***backward chain tree (BWC-tree)***. Since the parent/child relationships of committed subtransactions are stored on the log, subtransactions can be forgotten after their commit. The analysis pass need not collect data about committed subtransactions, thereby simplifying recovery.

Because our very general model of nested transactions allows upward and downward inheritance of locks, and concurrent execution of ancestor and descendent subtransactions, when a (sub)transaction is to be rolled back, the actions of that (sub)transaction and its (committed or active) inferiors must be rolled back in reverse chronological order. Like ARIES, ARIES/NT logs updates performed during rollback by means of CLRs. A CLR is also used to keep track how much of a (sub)transaction *and* its committed inferiors has already been rolled back, and how much more remains to be undone. This is achieved by recording in a CLR a *set of pointers*, each of which points to the next log record to be processed in the BW-chain of the (sub)transaction or a committed inferior during undo.

As in ARIES, in ARIES/NT also, restart processing starts with an analysis pass, continues with a redo pass and ends with an undo pass. Redo processing of ARIES/NT works in exactly the same way as in ARIES, while the algorithms of the analysis and undo passes have been modified to support tree-structured log contents. In ARIES/NT, the UndoNxtLSN field of a CLR contains a set of log addresses rather than a single LSN as in the original ARIES algorithm.

So far ARIES/NT has not been implemented. Basic features of ARIES/NT have been adapted in [Lomet92] to support recovery in multi-level systems. [Dombr95] presents modifications to ARIES/NT to support advanced transactions.

3.8 Index Management

Even though concurrency in search structures (e.g., B^+-tree indexes) had been discussed frequently in the literature, the problem of providing recovery from transaction and system failures when transactions consist of multiple search structure operations received very little attention until the late 80s. [MoLe92], in its original research report form, was the first paper to provide a comprehensive treatment of concurrency control and recovery for index management in transaction systems. [Mohan90a] was the first paper to document in detail the System R key-value locking algorithms and to explain the rationale behind their design features. That paper also enhanced those algorithms to vastly improve their concurrency and performance characteristics. In spite of these efforts and publications by a few others (e.g., [LoSa92]), index CC&R are not well understood by the research community. They are not taught sufficiently in database courses or discussed enough in database textbooks.

In this section, I summarize the two algorithms, ARIES/KVL [Mohan90a] and ARIES/IM [MoLe92], that we developed. A transaction may perform any number of nonindex and index operations, including range scans. Both serializable (*repeatable read*) and, optionally, nonserializable (*cursor stability*) executions of transactions are supported. To present them, I assume a tree architecture in which all the indexes on the data (e.g., a relational table) contain only the key values and record identifiers (RIDs) of records containing those key values. The ***RID*** of a record identifies the record's location in a set of data pages. All the leaf pages of an index contain ***index entries*** in the form of ***key-value,RID*** pairs. In most systems, when a nonunique index contains duplicate instances of a key value, the key value is stored *only once in each leaf page* where it appears. The single value is followed by as many RIDs as would fit on that page.

In ARIES/KVL, the object of locking is a key value, whereas in ARIES/IM, it is the individual index entry. This should make a difference only in the case of nonunique indexes. Apart from that difference, ARIES/IM does what is called ***data-only locking***. That is, an index entry is locked by locking the underlying data whose key is the one in the index entry to be locked. This means that if record locking is being done, then the lock will be on the RID; with page locking, it will be on the pageID part of the RID. In contrast, in ARIES/KVL, the index locks are different from the data locks. There are some performance and concurrency tradeoffs involved in choosing between these two approaches (see [Mohan95b, MoLe92] for detailed comparisons). ARIES/KVL's ***index-specific key value locking*** would be necessary where the records are stored in the index itself and an index entry contains the corresponding record, instead of a RID, as in NonStop SQL. It could also potentially lead to higher concurrency compared to the data-only locking feature of ARIES/IM, but with an increase in the locking overhead. It is possible to retain ARIES/IM's idea of locking individual index entries and still perform index-specific locking by taking the lock name as obtained in the case of data-only locking and prefixing that lock name with the index ID to make it specific to this index entry, as explained in [Mohan95b, MoLe92].

There are many problems involved in supporting recoverable, concurrent modifications to an index tree. Some of the questions to be answered are:

1. How to log the changes to the index so that, during recovery after a system failure, the missing updates can be reapplied efficiently?
2. If an ***SMO*** (**structure modification operation** - page split/deletion operation) were to be in progress at the time of a system failure and some of the effects of that SMO had already been reflected in the disk version of the database, how to ensure the restoration of the structural consistency of the tree during restart?
3. How to update index pages with minimal interference to concurrent accessors of the tree?
4. If a transaction were to roll back after successfully completing an SMO, how to ensure that it does not undo the SMO, since doing so might result in the loss of some updates performed by other transactions in the intervening period to the pages affected by the SMO?
5. How to detect that a key that had been inserted by a transaction T1 in page P1 had been moved, by a subsequent SMO by T2, to P2 so that if T1 were to roll back, then P2 is accessed and the key is deleted?
6. How to detect that a key that had been deleted by T1 from P1 no longer belongs on P1 but only on P2 due to subsequent SMOs by other transactions, so that if T1 were to roll back, then P2 is accessed and the key is inserted in it?
7. How to avoid a deadlock involving a transaction that is rolling back so that no special logic is needed to handle a deadlock involving only rolling back transactions?
8. How to support different granularities of locking and what to designate as the objects of locking?
9. How to lock the *not found* condition efficiently to guarantee repeatable read (i.e., the *phantom problem* - see [EGLT76])?
10. How to guarantee that in a unique index if a key value were to be deleted by one transaction, then no other transaction is permitted to insert the same key value before the former transaction commits?
11. How to let tree traversals go on even as an SMO is in progress and still ensure that the traversing transactions are able to recover if they run into the effects of the SMO that is still in progress?

3.8.1 ARIES/KVL

ARIES/KVL (*Algorithm for Recovery and Isolation Exploiting Semantics using Key-Value Locking*) [Mohan90a] is a method for concurrency control in B^+-tree indexes. The concurrent executions permitted by the locking protocols are correct logging and recovery are made possible. ARIES/KVL supports very high concurrency during tree traversals, structure modifications, and other operations. Unlike in System R, in ARIES/KVL, when one transaction is waiting for a lock on a key value in a given index page, reads and modifications of that page by other transactions are allowed. Further, transactions that are rolling back will never get into deadlocks. ARIES/KVL's locking rules differ depending on whether the index is a unique index or a nonunique index. Compared to System R, ARIES/KVL, by also using for key value locking the IX and SIX lock modes which were intended originally for table level locking, is able to exploit the semantics of the operations to improve concurrency. These techniques are also applicable to the concurrency control of links-based storage and access structures.

During a key lookup (Fetch) call, even if the requested key value is not found, the next key value is locked to make sure that the requested key does not suddenly appear (due to an insert by another transaction) before the current transaction *terminates* and prevent repeatable read from being possible. For the protection of the reader, if the value being inserted in not already present in the index, then an inserting transaction has to *check*, via an *instant* lock call, the lock on the next higher key value. Thus, a lock on a key value is really a ***range lock*** on the range of keys spanning the values from the *preceding* key value that is currently present in the index to the locked key value. For this range-locking protocol to work, the inserting transaction must check the lock on the *next key value*, *before* it does the insert of a given key value. The mode of Insert's next key value lock request must be such that it is incompatible with the S lock acquired by Fetch.

Since the deletion of the only instance of a certain key value would result in the key value disappearing from the index, a way is needed to communicate to readers (and inserters in the case of a unique index) the existence of an uncommitted deletion of that key value. By convention, under these conditions, the deleting transaction acquires a lock on the next key value. This is another reason why a reader needs to check the next key value lock when Fetch does not find the requested key value. The mode of Delete's next key value lock request must be such that it is incompatible with the S lock acquired by Fetch. Whereas the next key lock during an insert is only a check (instant lock), the one during deletion must be a lock which is held until commit.

Some of our ARIES/KVL enhancements over the original System R index concurrency control algorithms have been implemented in SQL/DS and the VM Shared File System.

3.8.2 ARIES/IM

ARIES/IM (*Algorithm for Recovery and Isolation Exploiting Semantics for Index Management*) [MoLe92] is a method for controlling concurrency and logging changes to index data stored in B$^+$-trees. ARIES/IM's recovery features are based on ARIES. ARIES/IM supports very high concurrency by

1. not locking the index data per se (i.e., keys),
2. locking the underlying record data in data pages only (e.g., at the record level),
3. not acquiring commit duration locks on index pages even during index structure modification operations (SMOs) like page splits and page deletions,
4. allowing retrievals, inserts, and deletes to go on concurrently with even an SMO, and
5. optionally, supporting degree 2 consistency of locking (cursor stability).

Even if a transaction which performed an SMO were to roll back, if all the effects of the SMO had been propagated successfully up the tree before the rollback is initiated, then the SMO is not undone. This is accomplished by doing the following:

1. Performing the SMO as an NTA.
2. If an insert requires a page split, all the actions relating to that split (the leaf-level actions, the propagation up the tree and the writing of the dummy CLR) are completed *before* the insert which necessitated the split is performed.
3. If the deletion of a key necessitates a page deletion (because the page became empty), the key deletion is first performed and logged and then all the actions relating to that page deletion are completed. The dummy CLR will point to the key deletion log record.

If the transaction were to rollback after completing the SMO, the dummy CLR lets it bypass the log records relating to the SMO. At the same time, it is ensured that the insert/delete operation causing the SMO is undone, on a rollback.

To restore the structural consistency of the tree, partially completed SMOs are undone in a page-oriented fashion. At the time of restart recovery, no special processing is performed to determine which indexes are structurally inconsistent. There is no special handling of such indexes.

During restart, any necessary redos of the index changes are always performed in a page-oriented fashion (i.e., without traversing the index tree) and, during normal processing and restart, undos are performed in a page-oriented fashion whenever possible. The protocols used during normal processing are such that if a system failure were to occur any time, then, during the subsequent restart, any incomplete SMO would be undone and thereby the structural consistency of the tree would be restored, *before* any necessary logical undo is attempted. This is done without resorting to any special restart processing.

Most of the ARIES/IM features were first implemented in the OS/2 Extended Edition Database Manager [ChMy88], which in its far enhanced form is now called DB2/UDB for Windows, Unix and OS/2. It was for that product that ARIES/IM was designed originally. Since the concurrency control techniques of ARIES/IM have general applicability, some of those techniques have also been incorporated in SQL/DS and the VM Shared File System even though those systems are based on System R which uses the shadow-page technique for recovery. ARIES/IM supports page-oriented media recovery for indexes - i.e., dumps of indexes can be taken and when there is a problem in reading a page (because, e.g., a crash had occurred when that page was being written [Mohan95a]), the page can be loaded from the last dump and then, by rolling forward using the log, the page can be brought up-to-date. Details concerning media recovery, deferred restart, etc. are presented in [MHLPS92].

Since ARIES/IM is able to handle deletion of empty pages, performing the merge of partially filled leaf pages requires only simple extensions to our method. ARIES/IM has been extended and implemented to handle the shared disks (*data sharing*, in the IMS terminology [PeSt83]) environment [JMNT97, MoNa91, MoNa92a, MoNa92b, MoNP90], in which multiple instances of DB2/390 access and modify the same database. We have developed ways to improve concurrency even further by reducing the negative implications of next index entry locking. This was done for DB2/390 by doing logical, rather than physical, deletion of keys (see [Mohan90b] for an outline of our solution). ARIES/IM and KVL ideas in conjunction with logical key deletions have been adapted in [KoMH97] for use with a generalized search tree (GiST). Adaptation of the ARIES/IM and KVL ideas to a hierarchy of indexes in a distributed database context is presented in [ChMo96]. The concurrency control implications of using multiple indexes in accessing a single table's records are presented in [MHWC90, Mohan90b, Mohan92a].

3.9 ARIES/LHS

Even though extendible hashing has been studied for a long time, very little has been reported in the literature on the concurrency control of multiple transactions simultaneously accessing such structures. Whatever little has appeared is usually based on a very simplified notion of a transaction. Generally, each transaction is assumed to consist of only one action (insert, delete, or retrieval) against the search structure.

The problems associated with guaranteeing serializability become much more complicated when one considers transactions consisting of multiple actions. Some papers deal with only extendible hashing, rather than the more complicated linear hashing. In any case, none of the papers deals with the problem of providing recovery from transaction and system failures for a general model of transactions with fine-granularity locking. Some of the concurrent activities permitted by the algorithms in the literature will cause inconsistencies when one considers failures and recovery. The interactions between concurrency control and logging (and recovery) with multiaction transactions are quite subtle. ARIES/LHS (*ARIES for Linear Hashing with Separators*) [Mohan93a] deals with the concurrency control and recovery aspects of multiaction transactions accessing dynamic hashing-based storage structures.

Larson proposed a dynamic hashing algorithm called *Linear Hashing with Separators* (LHS) that, given a unique primary key value, uses a table in memory to allow the retrieval of the corresponding record in the file in one page access to secondary storage [Lars88]. Larson considers LHS to be the first practical method offering one-access retrieval for large dynamic files. He did not discuss the impact of concurrent operations by different users, some of whom are reading the file while others are performing operations like inserts, deletes, updates, file expansions or file contractions which can cause relocations of records. ARIES/LHS is a method for controlling such concurrent operations with fine-granularity (e.g., record) locking, while guaranteeing serializability. ARIES/LHS prevents rolling back transactions from getting involved in deadlocks. It also includes recovery techniques for handling transaction and system failures, while allowing multiple operations in each transaction. To provide high concurrency and efficient recovery using write-ahead logging, ARIES/LHS exploits the power of the ARIES recovery method (e.g., the concept of NTAs and the ability to support logical undos). The impact of the LHS storage method on range queries and prefetching of data is discussed in [Mohan93a]. ARIES/LHS handles varying length records and updates of records also. So far ARIES/LHS has not been implemented.

3.10 Commit_LSN

Fine-granularity (e.g., record) locking is very helpful in increasing the level of concurrency that can be supported by reducing contention amongst transactions for access to data. The drawback of fine-granularity locking is that for those transactions that access large number of records, the number of locks that need to be acquired may increase dramatically compared to the situation with, for example, page locking. If, for those transactions which only need to determine that some piece of data is in the committed state the system could somehow avoid locking, then we can have the benefits of fine-granularity locking for transactions which access few records and at the same time avoid the drawbacks of such a locking granularity for transactions that access numerous records for reading. A method for avoiding locking is expected to be useful very often since in most databases, at any given time, most of the data is in the committed state.

The Commit_LSN method proposed in [Mohan90b] is one such idea. It is a novel and simple method for determining if a piece of data is in the committed state in a transaction processing system. This method is a much cheaper alternative to the locking approach used in the past for this purpose. The method takes advantage of the LSN concept. As described before, in transaction systems using WAL, an LSN is recorded in each page of the database to relate the state of the page to the log of update actions for that page.

The crux of the Commit_LSN method is to use this LSN information and information about the currently active update transactions to come to some conclusions about whether or not all the data on a given page is in the committed state, *without resorting to locking*. This is done by comparing the page's LSN with the information about the *oldest* update transaction still executing in the system. The crucial fact that makes our method accomplish its objectives is that no page with an LSN value that is *less than* the LSN (call it *Commit_LSN*) of the

Begin_Transaction log record of the *oldest* executing update transaction could have any uncommitted data. The Commit_LSN method applies whether the lowest granularity of locking is a page or something finer than that (e.g., record).

This simple new method reduces locking and latching. In addition, the method may also increase the level of concurrency that could be supported. It also benefits update transactions by reducing the cost of fine-granularity locking when contention is not present for data on a page. Many non-trivial applications of this method are discussed in detail in [Mohan90b]. In order to apply the Commit_LSN method, extensions have been proposed for those systems in which (1) LSNs are not associated with pages (AS/400, SQL/DS, System R), (2) LSNs are used only partially (IMS), and/or (3) not all objects' changes are logged (AS/400, SQL/DS, System R).

The Commit_LSN method's steps at the time of a page access are:

1. Find out Commit_LSN from the recovery manager or access it in shared storage. Note that it is not *necessary* for the transaction to obtain the latest value of Commit_LSN before every page access, as long as it is done at least once before the first page access. While an out of date Commit_LSN does not cause any inconsistencies, it may increase the number of times locks have to be obtained.
2. Latch the page in share (S) mode.
3. If page_LSN < Commit_LSN, then conclude that all data on the page is in the committed state; otherwise, do locking as usual and determine whether data of interest is committed or not.

Instead of having one **global** Commit_LSN that covers all objects, transactions can benefit further by computing an **object-specific Commit_LSN** that is specific to the object (e.g., file or table) to be accessed. In this way, a long-running update transaction that accesses some other objects and keeps the global Commit_LSN quite a bit in the past will not unduly restrict the applicability of the Commit_LSN method to the object of interest.

The Commit_LSN concept has turned out to be very useful in practice. It has been fully implemented in DB2/390 and partially in DB2/UDB for Windows, Unix and OS/2. Its performance advantages have been especially beneficial in the shared disks context of DB2/390. It has been exploited for providing fast restart capabilities in [Mohan93c]. Processing of new transactions can be done even while the redo and undo passes of restart recovery are in progress.

3.11 Query Processing and Locking Concerns

Traditionally, starting from the System R days, work on query processing has generally ignored considerations relating to concurrency control in making query execution choices during query optimization. Typically, concurrency control related actions are taken by the data manager (the RSS component in the case of System R) and the query optimization related actions are taken by the upper parts of the system (RDS component in the case of System R). In [Mohan92a], I have given numerous examples to illustrate why it is important to consider locking related issues while planning query executions. While it is sometimes merely a performance advantage to take such an integrated view, at other times even the correctness of query executions depends on such an approach. Some of the issues to consider are: isolation levels (repeatable read, dirty read, cursor stability), access path selection (table scan, index scan, index AND/ORing [MHWC90]), Commit_LSN optimization [Mohan90b], locking granularity (record, page, table), and high concurrency as a query optimization criterion. Our ideas are implemented in the DB2 family.

4. Transactions in the Internet Age[4]

In the last few years, there have been many significant developments in the transaction processing (TP) and distributed computing (DC) areas. Many areas of computing have influenced the recent trends in TP and DC: client-server computing, database management, object-oriented programming, groupware, internet and processor architectures, to name a few. The emergence of the worldwide web and Java has also had a dramatic influence on TP and DC.

Opening up the information resources of enterprises to customers and business partners for internet (web) access has changed the data access patterns of the DBMSs and file systems storing such information. This change has dramatically increased the requirements on TP systems with regard to attributes like availability, reliability, performance and ease of use. In this sense, history is repeating itself! What used to be considered high-end requirements in the context of mainframe computing by large enterprises are now becoming the requirements of small and medium enterprises also when they choose to web-enable their TP applications. Globalization and mergers of enterprises are also important driving factors.

Permitting data access from heterogeneous hardware and software environments has become a necessity. Legacy TP systems like CICS and IMS have been internet enabled.

---

[4] The slides of a long talk that expands on this section can be found at www.almaden.ibm.com/u/mohan/tp_dc.pdf

Windows NT has had to provide support for IBM SNA network protocols for distributed program to program communication and two-phase commit of distributed transactions involving mainframe and PC environments. With web enablement, enterprises are now able to provide better customer service and also reduce costs by eliminating certain intermediaries (e.g., distributors, call center operators) who are necessary in traditional ways of doing business. Network-centric computing is now a reality and, to remain competitive, organizations have to adapt their information systems to support it. When an enterprise's customers directly interface to that enterprise's TP systems their performance and usability expectations are more demanding than when they go through other trained people (e.g., customer service representatives) in that enterprise to get some services. Web-enabling a TP application is not merely an issue of purchasing the appropriate web gateway software. Some basic aspects of the TP application might have to be redesigned.

Electronic commerce (e-commerce) is taking off, especially with respect to business to business (B2B) interactions more than business to consumer (B2C) transactions. Of course, opening up traditional TP systems to doing full blown e-commerce, which would potentially involve performing multiple database updates originating from browsers as part of a single distributed transaction, as opposed to only information retrieval style accesses across the web, requires addressing a number of issues relating to security, client failures, payment systems, etc. Advanced transaction models like sagas, flex transactions, etc. [Elmag92] will have a key role to play. It is my belief that product-level support for such concepts will finally appear in the next few years in workflow management systems, rather than as extensions to traditional TP monitors.

While 2 tier distributed computing (client-server) was quite popular a few years ago, of late, 3 tier computing (caused by the addition of some middleware software running in a mid-tier machine) is being embraced more widely. Enterprises have become disillusioned with the difficulties and costs involved in realizing the often-trumpeted major benefits (e.g., cost reductions) of client-server computing with exclusively (non-mainframe) Unix/PC-based servers. This has resulted in the resurgence of the mainframe and the emergence of the concept *of server consolidations*. The latter refers to the replacement of a large collection of Unix/PC servers with a cluster consisting of a small number of CMOS-based, air-cooled mainframes like, for example, the IBM S/390. IMS, CICS and DB2 have been enhanced to support the shared disks S/390 cluster environment with valuable features like workload balancing and single system image [IBM97]. Modifying those systems to support the clustered environment, with a coupling facility (an intelligent shared store with sophisticated capabilities) in the midst of the sharing systems, has required the development of several innovative solutions for problems relating to global lock management, buffer coherency, logging, recovery and performance [JMNT97].

Asynchronous program to program communication in the form of transaction-based persistent messaging has become quite popular. IBM's MQSeries, for example, is a very successful product in this arena. MQSeries includes its own non-DBMS-based persistent storage mechanism, using an extended version of ARIES, for managing the messages [MoDi94]. Oracle, on the other hand, has recently introduced some messaging functionality directly in its RDBMS itself so that the messages are also managed by the Oracle DBMS. Such an approach requires enhancing the concurrency control protocols and isolation level support of the DBMS to meet the different consistency and performance requirements of a transactional messaging system. This is an area to which the research community has not paid enough attention. Concepts like publish-subscribe are currently very popular in the commercial world and they deserve to be researched.

In general, TP and DC standardization activities have become more widespread. The belief (and hope!) is that object technology is the right approach for improving software productivity and for reusing/integrating existing legacy TP applications by adding OO wrappers to those applications. Recently, many commercial implementations of OMG's Object Transaction Services (OTS) have become available. It is not yet clear how widely and quickly such products will be used in production TP applications and what their performance characteristics would be in comparison with applications built using traditional, procedural TP technologies. More recently, OTS has been extended to the Java world via Java Transaction Services (JTS). Enterprise Java Beans have also been proposed as a way of exploiting Java on the server side for building component-based TP applications. Performance and industrial-strength attributes like robustness are some of the major concerns with respect to such technologies.

In the last few years there have many debates in the TP and DC communities on the appropriate paradigms for program to program communications, and the role of TP monitors in the world of web servers and feature-rich RDBMSs. Many performance-enhancing features like support for threads which used to be present for a long time only in TP monitors like CICS and IMS/DC have now become widely available in RDBMSs like Oracle. TP monitors have traditionally been deeply involved in application and data management. RDBMSs have gone from managing only data to managing programs also (via triggers, stored procedures, etc.). Web servers and some

CORBA Object Request Brokers (ORBs) have also taken on many of the attributes of TP monitors. We are seeing the emergence of the so-called *Application Servers,* which are not too different from classical TP monitors enhanced with support for the web and, possibly, object technology.

Emergence of specialized Online Analytical Processing (OLAP) DBMSs like RedBrick and Arbor's ESSBASE has allowed huge data warehouses to be built and queried efficiently. Many algorithms and tools have been developed by vendors for extracting warehouse data from operational TP systems. Specialized indexes and massive data handling features have been developed for use in managing warehouse data. Only now researchers are beginning to address these issues. In contrast to what the research community focussed on with respect to replicated data algorithms, log-based asynchronous replication has been the more favored choice for implementation in RDBMS products.

One of the significant developments of the last few years is the widespread trend towards outsourcing of information technology (IT) operations by organizations whose core business is not computer related (e.g., Kodak). This is the result of (1) difficulties encountered by such organizations in managing networks of heterogeneous systems and (2) those organizations' desire to reduce their IT costs by letting computing professionals of companies like EDS and IBM Global Services do the job. A related trend is that many organizations have stopped developing their own TP application software. Instead, they buy packaged applications (e.g., for enterprise resource planning (ERP)) from vendors like SAP and PeopleSoft. The ERP vendors have been causing some significant enhancements to be made in the functionality of DBMSs that they rely on for storing their data.

Many businesses are also reengineering their supply chains by integrating their applications with those of their partners, suppliers and customers in order to improve their operational costs and time to market. Much of this integration is expected to happen in the near future using the internet rather than via private networks as was the case in the past with electronic data interchange (EDI). Workflow management systems are expected to play a big role in this transformation of way of doing business.

The industrial and academic research communities working on TP and DC have not always focussed on the problems that are of great interest in the commercial world. This has led to some very innovative technology being developed directly by product developers themselves.

5. Conclusions

In this paper, I repeated first the history of the evolution of the popular ARIES family of concurrency control and recovery (CC&R) algorithms. I also discussed the significant impact that those algorithms have had on the research and commercial worlds. With a view towards providing a roadmap across the numerous related papers, I provided a brief summary of most of the ARIES CC&R algorithms. While some researchers might have ignored certain aspects of CC&R as being engineering work, rather than science, by focussing on the details and deciding to pay attention to the practical experiences from the past, we were able to make some fundamental contributions to the area of transaction management. We were lucky to be working in an environment where this was possible.

I expect DBMSs to be enhanced in the future with features that allow higher concurrency and improved data availability to accommodate the demanding requirements of the internet world. Parallelism will be exploited to reduce the time taken to perform operations like data backups, index build, etc. Systems will be designed to be self tuning and manageable by less-qualified people. Transactions will be everywhere, in the least expected places in our daily lives. Designing systems with industrial-strength attributes like performance, reliability and availability in mind from the beginning will be crucial for such systems to be successful in real-life usage. Most of the related problems discussed in [Mohan93d] have not been addressed sufficiently so far by database researchers.

In this paper, I did not intend to do an exhaustive survey of CC&R work in the research literature. Many papers have been written in the last few years on application recovery, semantics-based CC&R protocols (especially in the object-oriented context), theories on an integrated view of recovery and concurrency control, sophisticated indexing protocols using numerous lock modes, etc. As it is usually the case, most of the proposed algorithms have not been implemented. Nor have the designs been spelt out in most cases in enough detail for others to implement them without the need for substantial additional design work.

Acknowledgements I would like to acknowledge the contributions of the following (past/present) colleagues of mine who have collaborated with me on some of the work that I have summarized here: Ron Barber, Dick Dievendorff, Don Haderle, Dave Herbert, Russ Holden, Jeff Josten, Tina Lee, Frank Levine, Bruce Lindsay, Bob Lyle, Inderpal Narang, Andrew Peterson, Hamid Pirahesh, Kurt Rothermel, Peter Schwarz, Amit Somani, Jim Teng, Kent Treiber, Julie Watts, Steve Watts and Markos Zaharioudakis. I would also like thank the people in the different product and research groups everywhere that have adopted our research results, and have brought out products or prototypes incorporating them. I highly appreciate the strong encouragement that I received from non-IBMers like David DeWitt, Theo Haerder, Mike Carey (now an IBMer), Paris Kanellakis, Andreas Reuter, Dave Lomet and Betty Salzberg. I would also like to acknowledge the cooperation of managers like Pat Selinger, Bob Yost, Laura Haas and Irv Traiger for tolerating my unconventional way of working at IBM Research and for letting me publish. My wife Kalpana Mohan deserves special thanks for her acceptance of my long working hours and frequent travels.

6. References

[BaRa87] Badrinath, B., Ramamritham, K. *Semantics-Based Concurrency Control: Beyond Commutativity*, **Proc. 3rd International Conference on Data Engineering**, February 1987.

[BeHG87] Bernstein, P., Hadzilacos, V., Goodman, N. **Concurrency Control and Recovery in Database Systems**, Addison-Wesley, 1987.

[BeNe97] Bernstein, P., Newcomer, E. **Principles of Transaction Processing for the Systems Professional**, Morgan Kaufmann, 1997.

[BGHJ92] Bhide, A., Goyal, A., Hsiao, H., Jhingran, A. *An Efficient Scheme for Providing High Availability*, **Proc. ACM SIGMOD International Conference on Management of Data**, San Diego, June 1992.

[Billa96] Billard, D. *Recovery of Transactions Exploiting Operation Semantics: Beyond ARIES*, **Proc. International Workshop on Advanced Transaction Models and Architectures (ATMA)**, Goa, August 1996.

[Borr84] Borr, A. *Robustness to Crash in a Distributed Database: A Non Shared-Memory Multi-Processor Approach*, **Proc. 10th International Conference on Very Large Data Bases**, Singapore, August 1984.

[CABGK81] Chamberlin, D., Astrahan, M., Blasgen, M., Gray, J., King, F., Lindsay, B., Lorie, R., Mehl, J., Price, T., Putzolu, F., Selinger, P., Schkolnick, M., Slutz, D., Traiger, I., Wade, B., Yost, R. *A History and Evaluation of System R*, **Communications of the ACM**, Vol. 24, No. 10, October 1981.

[CaRH95] Cabrera, L.-F., Rees, R., Hineman, W. *Applying Database Technology in the ADSM Mass Storage System*, **Proc. 21st International Conference on Very Large Data Bases**, Zurich, September 1995.

[CDFHM94] Carey, M., DeWitt, D., Franklin, M., Hall, N., McAuliffe, M., Naughton, J., Schuh, D., Solomon, M., Tan, C., Tsatalos, O., White, S., Zwilling, M. *Shoring Up Persistent Applications*, **Proc. ACM SIGMOD International Conference on Management of Data**, Minneapolis, May 1994.

[ChGY81] Chamberlin, D., Gilbert, A., Yost, R. *A History of System R and SQL/Data System*, **Proc. 7th International Conference on Very Large Data Bases**, Cannes, September 1981.

[ChMo96] Choy, D., Mohan, C. *Locking Protocols for Two-Tier Indexing of Partitioned Data*, **Proc. International Workshop on Advanced Transaction Models and Architectures**, Goa, August 1996.

[ChMy88] Chang, P.Y., Myre, W.W. *OS/2 EE Database Manager Overview and Technical Highlights*, **IBM Systems Journal**, Vol. 27, No. 2, 1988.

[ClCo89] Clark, B.E., Corrigan, M.J. *Application System/400 Performance Characteristics*, **IBM Systems Journal**, Vol. 28, No. 3, 1989.

[CMSW93] Cabrera, L.-F., McPherson, J., Schwarz, P., Wyllie, J. *Implementing Atomicity in Two Systems: Techniques, Tradeoffs*, and Experience, **IEEE Transactions on Software Engineering**, Vol. 19, No. 10, October 1993.

[Crus84] Crus, R. *Data Recovery in IBM Database 2*, **IBM Systems Journal**, Vol. 23, No. 2, 1984.

[DGSBH90] DeWitt, D., Ghandeharizadeh, S., Schneider, D., Bricker, A., Hsiao, H.-I, Rasmussen, R. *The Gamma Database Machine Project*, **IEEE Transactions on Knowledge and Data Engineering**, Vol. 2, No. 1, March 1990.

[Dombr95] Dombrowska, H. *ARIES/NT Modification for Advanced Transactions Support*, **Proc. International Symposium on Advances in Databases and Information Systems (ADBIS'95)**, Moscow, 1995.

[EGLT76] Eswaran, K.P., Gray, J., Lorie, R., Traiger, I. *The Notion of Consistency and Predicate Locks in a Database System*, **Communications of the ACM**, Vol. 19, No. 11, November 1976.

[Elmag92] Elmagarmid, A. (Ed.), **Database Transaction Models for Advanced Applications**, Morgan Kaufmann, 1992.

[FZTCD92] Franklin, M., Zwilling, M., Tan, C.K., Carey, M., DeWitt, D. *Crash Recovery in Client-Server EXODUS*, **Proc. ACM SIGMOD International Conference on Management of Data**, San Diego, June 1992.

[GaKi85] Gawlick, D., Kinkade, D. *Varieties of Concurrency Control in IMS/VS Fast Path*, **Database Engineering**, Vol. 8, No. 2, June 1985.

[GMBLL81] Gray, J., McJones, P., Blasgen, M., Lindsay, B., Lorie, R., Price, T., Putzolu, F., Traiger, I. *The Recovery Manager of the System R Database Manager*, **ACM Computing Surveys**, Vol. 13, No. 2, June 1981.

[GrRe93] Gray, J., Reuter, A. **Transaction Processing: Concepts and Techniques**, Morgan Kaufmann, 1993.

[HaJa84] Haderle, D., Jackson, R. *IBM Database 2 Overview*, **IBM Systems Journal**, Vol. 23, No. 2, 1984.

[HaRe83] Haerder, T., Reuter, A. *Principles of Transaction Oriented Database Recovery - A Taxonomy*, **Computing Surveys**, Vol. 15, No. 4, December 1983.

[HaRo87] Haerder, T., Rothermel, K. *Concepts for Transaction Recovery in Nested Transactions*, **Proc. ACM-SIGMOD International Conference on Management of Data**, San Francisco, May 1987.

[HaRo93] Haerder, T., Rothermel, K. *Concurrency Control Issues in Nested Transactions*, **VLDB Journal**, Vol. 2, No. 1, 1993.

[HCLMW90] Haas, L., Chang, W., Lohman, G., McPherson, J., Wilms, P., Lapis, G., Lindsay, B., Pirahesh, H., Carey, M., Shekita, E. *Starburst Mid-Flight: As the Dust Clears*, **IEEE Transactions on Knowledge and Data Engineering**, Vol. 2, No. 1, March 1990.

[HLMPS94] Haderle, D., Lindsay, B., Mohan, C., Pirahesh, H., Schwarz, P. *Method for Managing Subpage Concurrency Control and Partial Transaction Rollback in a Transaction-Oriented System of the Write-Ahead Logging Type*, **United**

Kingdom and France Patent 0,295,424, Germany Patent 3,889,254,508, IBM, April 1994.

[IBM97] Special Issue on IBM's S/390 Parallel Sysplex Cluster, **IBM Systems Journal**, Vol. 36, No. 2, 1997.

[JaKe97] Jajodia, S., Kerschberg, L. (Eds.) **Advanced Transaction Models and Architectures**, Kluwer Academic Publishers, 1997.

[JhKh92] Jhingran, A., Khedkar, P. *Analysis of Recovery in a Database System Using a Write-Ahead Log Protocol*, **Proc. ACM SIGMOD International Conference on Management of Data**, San Diego, June 1992.

[JMNT97] Josten, J., Mohan, C., Narang, I., Teng, J. *DB2's Use of the Coupling Facility for Data Sharing*, **IBM Systems Journal**, Vol. 36, No. 2, 1997.

[KoMH97] Kornacker, M., Mohan, C., Hellerstein, J. *Concurrency and Recovery in Generalized Search Trees*, **Proc. ACM SIGMOD International Conference on Management of Data**, Tucson, May 1997.

[KuHs98] Kumar, V., Hsu, M. (Eds.) **Recovery Mechanisms in Database Systems**, Prentice Hall, 1998.

[Kumar95] Kumar, V. (Ed.) **Performance of Concurrency Control Mechanisms in Centralized Database Systems**, Prentice Hall, 1995.

[Kuo96] Kuo, D. *Model and Verification of a Data Manager Based on ARIES,* **ACM Transactions on Database Systems**, Vol. 21, No. 4, December 1996.

[Lars88] Larson, P.-A. *Linear Hashing with Separators - A Dynamic Hashing Scheme Achieving One-Access Retrieval*, **ACM Transactions on Database Systems**, Vol. 13, No. 3, September 1988.

[Lomet92] Lomet, D. *MLR: A Recovery Method for Multi-Level Systems*, **Proc. ACM SIGMOD International Conference on Management of Data**, San Diego, June 1992.

[LoSa92] Lomet, D., Salzberg, B. *Access Method Concurrency with Recovery*, **Proc. ACM SIGMOD International Conference on Management of Data**, San Diego, June 1992.

[LoTu95] Lomet, D., Tuttle, M. *Redo Recovery after System Crashes*, **Proc. 21st International Conference on Very Large Data Bases**, Zurich, September 1995.

[MaRa97] Martin, C., Ramamritham, K. *Toward Formalizing Recovery of (Advanced) Transactions*, Chapter 8 in [JaKe97].

[MHLPS92] Mohan, C., Haderle, D., Lindsay, B., Pirahesh, H., Schwarz, P. *ARIES: A Transaction Recovery Method Supporting Fine-Granularity Locking and Partial Rollbacks Using Write-Ahead Logging*, **ACM Transactions on Database Systems**, Vol. 17, No. 1, March 1992. Reprinted in **Readings in Database Systems**, 3rd Edition, M. Stonebraker, J. Hellerstein (Eds.), Morgan Kaufmann Publishers, 1998. Reprinted in **Recovery Mechanisms In Database Systems**, V. Kumar, M. Hsu (Eds.), Prentice Hall, 1998. Also available as IBM Research Report RJ6649, IBM Almaden Research Center, January 1989; Revised November 1990.

[MHWC90] Mohan, C., Haderle, D., Wang, Y., Cheng, J. *Single Table Access Using Multiple Indexes: Optimization, Execution and Concurrency Control Techniques*, **Proc. International Conference on Extending Data Base Technology**, Venice, March 1990. A longer version of this paper is available as IBM Research Report RJ7341, IBM Almaden Research Center, March 1990.

[MoDi94] Mohan, C., Dievendorff, R. *Recent Work on Distributed Commit Protocols, and Recoverable Messaging and Queuing*, **Data Engineering**, Vol. 17, No. 1, March 1994.

[MoHa94] Mohan, C., Haderle, D. *Algorithms for Flexible Space Management in Transaction Systems Supporting Fine-Granularity Locking*, **Proc. 4th International Conference on Extending Database Technology**, Cambridge, March 1994. A longer version of this paper is available as IBM Research Report RJ9732, IBM Almaden Research Center, March 1994.

[Mohan90a] Mohan, C. *ARIES/KVL: A Key-Value Locking Method for Concurrency Control of Multiaction Transactions Operating on B-Tree Indexes*, **Proc. 16th International Conference on Very Large Data Bases**, Brisbane, August 1990. Another version of this paper is available as IBM Research Report RJ7008, IBM Almaden Research Center, September 1989.

[Mohan90b] Mohan, C. *Commit_LSN: A Novel and Simple Method for Reducing Locking and Latching in Transaction Processing Systems*, **Proc. 16th International Conference on Very Large Data Bases**, Brisbane, August 1990. A slightly revised version is reprinted in **Performance of Concurrency Control Mechanisms in Centralized Database Systems**, V. Kumar (Ed.), Prentice Hall, 1995.

[Mohan92a] Mohan, C. *Interactions Between Query Optimization and Concurrency Control*, **Proc. 2nd International Workshop on Research Issues on Data Engineering: Transaction and Query Processing**, Tempe, February 1992.

[Mohan92b] Mohan, C. *Less Optimism About Optimistic Concurrency Control*, **Proc. 2nd International Workshop on Research Issues on Data Engineering: Transaction and Query Processing**, Tempe, February 1992.

[Mohan93a] Mohan, C. *ARIES/LHS: A Concurrency Control and Recovery Method Using Write-Ahead Logging for Linear Hashing with Separators*, **Proc. 9th International Conference on Data Engineering**, Vienna, April 1993. A longer version of this paper is available as IBM Research Report RJ8682, IBM Almaden Research Center, March 1992.

[Mohan93b] Mohan, C. *IBM's Relational DBMS Products: Features and Technologies*, **Proc. ACM SIGMOD International Conference on Management of Data**, Washington, D.C., May 1993.

[Mohan93c] Mohan, C. *A Cost-Effective Method for Providing Improved Data Availability* During *DBMS Restart Recovery After a Failure*, **Proc. 19th International Conference on Very Large Data Bases**, Dublin, August 1993.

[Mohan93d] Mohan, C. *A Survey of DBMS Research Issues in Supporting Very Large Tables*, Invited Paper, **Proc. 4th International Conference on Foundations of Data Organization and Algorithms**, Evanston, October 1993. LNCS Volume 730, D. Lomet (Ed.), Springer-Verlag, 1993.

[Mohan95a] Mohan, C. *Disk Read-Write Optimizations and Data Integrity in Transaction Systems Using Write-Ahead Logging*, **Proc. 11th International Conference on Data Engineering, Taipei, March 1995.**

[Mohan95b] Mohan, C. *Concurrency Control and Recovery Methods for B^+-Tree Indexes: ARIES/KVL and ARIES/IM*, In **Performance of Concurrency Control Mechanisms in Centralized Database Systems**, V. Kumar (Ed.), Prentice Hall, 1995.

[Mohan99] Mohan, C. *A Database Perspective on Lotus Domino/Notes*, **Proc. ACM SIGMOD International Conference on Management of Data**, Philadelphia, June 1999. Slides at www.almaden.ibm.com/u/mohan/domino_sigmod99.pdf

[MoLe92] Mohan, C., Levine, F. *ARIES/IM: An Efficient and High Concurrency Index Management Method Using Write-Ahead Logging*, **Proc. ACM SIGMOD International Conference on Management of Data**, San Diego, June 1992. A longer version is available as IBM Research Report RJ6846, IBM Almaden Research Center, August 1989.

[MoLO86] Mohan, C., Lindsay, B., Obermarck, R. *Transaction Management in the R* Distributed Data Base Management System*, **ACM Transactions on Database Systems**, Vol. 11, No. 4, December 1986.

[MoNa91] Mohan, C., Narang, I. *Recovery and Coherency-Control Protocols for Fast Intersystem Page Transfer and Fine-Granularity Locking in a Shared Disks Transaction Environment*, **Proc. 17th International Conference on Very Large Data Bases**, Barcelona, September 1991. A longer version is available as IBM Research Report RJ8017, IBM Almaden Research Center, March 1991.

[MoNa92a] Mohan, C., Narang, I. *Efficient Locking and Caching of Data in the Multisystem Shared Disks Transaction Environment*, **Proc. 3rd International Conference on Extending Database Technology**, Vienna, March 1992.

[MoNa92b] Mohan, C., Narang, I. *Data Base Recovery in Shared Disks and Client-Server Architectures*, **Proc. 12th International Conference on Distributed Computing Systems**, Yokohama, June 1992.

[MoNa92c] Mohan, C., Narang, I. *Algorithms for Creating Indexes for Very Large Tables Without Quiescing Updates*, **Proc. ACM SIGMOD International Conference on Management of Data**, San Diego, June 1992.

[MoNa93] Mohan, C., Narang, I. *An Efficient and Flexible Method for Archiving a Data Base*, **Proc. ACM SIGMOD International Conference on Management of Data**, Washington, D.C., May 1993. A *corrected* version of this paper is available as IBM Research Report RJ9733, IBM Almaden Research Center, March 1993.

[MoNa94] Mohan, C., Narang, I. *ARIES/CSA: A Method for Database Recovery in Client-Server Architectures*, **Proc. ACM SIGMOD International Conference on Management of Data**, Minneapolis, May 1994.

[MoNP90] Mohan, C., Narang, I., Palmer, J. *A Case Study of Problems in Migrating to Distributed Computing: Page Recovery Using Multiple Logs in the Shared Disks Environment*, IBM Research Report RJ7343, IBM Almaden Research Center, March 1990.

[MoPi91] Mohan, C., Pirahesh, H. *ARIES-RRH: Restricted Repeating of History in the ARIES Transaction Recovery Method*, **Proc. 7th International Conference on Data Engineering**, Kobe, April 1991.

[MoPL92] Mohan, C., Pirahesh, H., Lorie, R. *Efficient and Flexible Methods for Transient Versioning of Records to Avoid Locking by Read-Only Transactions*, **Proc. ACM SIGMOD International Conference on Management of Data**, San Diego, June 1992.

[MoTO93] Mohan, C., Treiber, K., Obermarck, R. *Algorithms for the Management of Remote Backup Data Bases for Disaster Recovery*, **Proc. 9th International Conference on Data Engineering**, Vienna, April 1993. A longer version of this paper is available as IBM Research Report RJ7885, IBM Almaden Research Center, December 1990; Revised June 1991.

[Ober80] Obermarck, R. *IMS/VS Program Isolation Feature*, **IBM Research Report RJ2879**, IBM San Jose Research Laboratory, July 1980.

[Ober98a] Obermarck, R. *IMS/360 and IMS/VS Recovery: Historical Recollections*, In [KuHs98].

[Ober98b] Obermarck, R. *Logging and Recovery in Commercial Systems*, In [KuHs98].

[PeSt83] Peterson, R., Strickland, J.P. *Log Write-Ahead Protocols and IMS/VS Logging*, **Proc. 2nd ACM SIGACT-SIGMOD Symposium on Principles of Database Systems**, Atlanta, March 1983.

[RaCh96] Ramamritham, K., Chrysanthis, P. **Advances in Concurrency Control and Transaction Processing - An Executive Briefing**, Computer Society Press, 1996.

[Ramak98] Ramakrishnan, R. **Database Management Systems**, WCB/McGraw-Hill, 1998.

[RoMo89] Rothermel, K., Mohan, C. *ARIES/NT: A Recovery Method Based on Write-Ahead Logging for Nested Transactions*, **Proc. 15th International Conference on Very Large Data Bases**, Amsterdam, August 1989. A longer version of this paper is available as IBM Research Report RJ6650, IBM Almaden Research Center, January 1989.

[StNC91] Stone, R., Nettleship, T., Curtiss, J. *VM/ESA CMS Shared File System*, **IBM Systems Journal**, Vol. 30, No. 1, 1991.

[VuDo90] Vural, S., Dogac, A. *A Performance Analysis of the ARIES Recovery Method Through Simulation*, **Proc. 5th International Conference on Computer and Information Sciences**, Cappadocia, November 1990.

[Weihl95] Weihl, W. *Transaction Processing Techniques*, Chapter 13 in **Distributed Systems**, S. Mullender (Ed.), 2nd Edition, ACM Press, 1995.

Online Feedback for Nested Aggregate Queries with Multi-Threading[†]

Kian-Lee Tan Cheng Hian Goh[‡] Beng Chin Ooi
Dept. of Computer Science, National University of Singapore

Abstract

In this paper, we study the progressive evaluation of nested queries with aggregates (i.e., the inner query block is an aggregate query), where users are provided progressively with (approximate) answers as the inner query block is being evaluated. We propose an incremental evaluation strategy to present answers that are certainly in the final answer space first, before presenting those whose validity may be affected as the inner query aggregates are refined. We also propose a *multi-threaded model* in evaluating such queries: the outer query is assigned to a thread, and the inner query is assigned to another thread. The time-sliced across the two subqueries is *nondeterministic* in the sense that the user controls the relative rate at which these subqueries are being evaluated. We implemented a prototype system using JAVA, and evaluated our system. Our results show the effectiveness of the proposed mechanisms in providing online feedback that reduce the initial waiting time of users significantly without sacrificing on the quality of the answers.

1 Introduction

Database management systems are increasingly being employed to support end users in their decision making. Such users have a three-fold requirement: (1) the answers are summary data that characterize the datasets or are derived from or based on summary data, (2) imprecise answers can be tolerated, i.e., "approximately correct" answers suffice, and (3) the answers must be obtained quickly [7]. As such, database support for efficient computation of summary statistics in the form of aggregation queries becomes very important.

Traditionally, aggregation queries are evaluated under a *blocking execution model* (i.e., all data are examined and all operations are performed before a final answer is returned) to obtain precise answers. However, with greater availability of large volumes of data, this is not only computationally expensive, but users would find the waiting time unacceptable. Recently, Hellerstein et. al. [7] proposed a promising approach called *online aggregation* to meet the users requirements. Instead of presenting a final answer to the user (after a long period of waiting), an aggregation query is evaluated progressively: as soon as some data are evaluated, approximate answers with their respective running confidence intervals are presented; as more data are examined, the answers and their corresponding running confidence intervals are refined. In so doing, users are occupied with approximate answers and can terminate the evaluation prematurely if these answers suffice for their decision making. However, the work is restricted to simple non-nested queries.

Nesting of query blocks is a very interesting and powerful feature of SQL. In fact, it has been noted that the nested form is often easier for users to formulate and to understand [12]. Existing research (on nested queries) has sought methods of reducing the evaluation costs, typically by transforming a nested query into a logically equivalent form that can be evaluated more efficiently [2, 3, 10]. However, the class of *nested queries with aggregates* is especially interesting. First, such queries are commonly encountered. For example, to list employees who are *high-earners* where "high-earners" are defined as a certain factor of the average salaries of employees, requires a nested query with an average function. As another example, to list departments whose budgets are less than a factor of the average salaries of employees in those departments is another nested query involving the average function. Second, nested queries with aggregates cannot typically be expressed in a single query without nesting. Third, while some nested queries are transformed into non-nested forms that can be optimized into and eval-

[†]This work is partially supported by the University Research Grant RP982694.

[‡]Deceased on 1 April 1999.

Proceedings of the 25th VLDB Conference, Edinburgh, Scotland, 1999.

uated as a single plan, nested queries with aggregates still require multiple separate queries. To employ the traditional blocking execution model (i.e., the inner query block is processed before the outer block is processed) to evaluate such nested queries would frustrate the users if they are forced to wait without feedback.

In this paper, we present a novel approach for providing rapid online feedback for evaluating nested queries with aggregates (i.e., nested query where the inner query block is an aggregate query). For simplicity, we restrict our discussion to single-level nesting; the principles discussed can be easily generalized to multiple levels of nesting. Our technique is similar but goes beyond the online aggregation approach presented in [7]. Processing nested queries with aggregates online pose several interesting challenges that non-nested queries do not offer. First, it is not clear what forms the answers to a query and how the results should be interpreted, given that the inner query is an aggregate query. Furthermore, the outer query may or may not involve another aggregate, and the outer and the inner query blocks may or may not be correlated. Second, it is not clear how processing of the query can be *optimally* time-sliced across the outer and inner subqueries. This paper presents our solutions to these two issues. For the first problem, the answer space to the query begins with a superset of the final answers and is refined as the aggregates from the inner query block are refined. For the intermediary answers to be meaningful, they have to be interpreted with the aggregates from the inner query. We also propose an incremental evaluation strategy to present answers that are certainly in the final answer space first, before presenting those whose validity may be affected as the inner query aggregates are refined. For the second problem, we propose a *multi-threaded evaluation model* where the different query blocks are evaluated concurrently in a multi-threaded fashion. The time-sliced across the two query blocks is *nondeterministic* in the sense that the user controls the relative rate at which these subqueries are being evaluated. We implemented a prototype system using JAVA, and evaluated our system. Our results show the effectiveness of the proposed mechanisms in reducing the initial waiting time without sacrificing on the quality of the answers.

The remainder of this paper is organized as follows. In the next section, we present an overview of the proposed approach, together with issues that need to be addressed. In Section 3, we present a multi-threaded model for evaluating nested-queries with aggregates. Sections 4 and 5 present the various mechanisms and algorithms that are needed for the evaluation of the inner and outer query blocks respectively. Section 6 present the design, implementation and evaluation of a prototype system. In Section 7, we review some related work, and finally, we conclude in Section 8.

2 Motivation and Overview

In this section, we shall present an overview of the proposed approach with an example to reiterate the motivation behind online aggregation, i.e., to provide fast response of (approximate) answers to users. Before that, we shall review the two types of nested queries with aggregates that are relevant to our work.

2.1 Types of Nested Queries with Aggregates

In [10], Kim presented a classification of nested query types, two of which involve aggregates in the inner query block. For illustration, we shall use the example of a large admissions database that records information on persons (of different nationalities) applying to graduate business schools. The database has the following schema:

```
applicant(pid,city,income,gmat)
location(city,country)
```

In the relation `applicant`, we assume that an individual is uniquely identified by `pid`, resides in `city`, earns an annual salary given by `income`, and has a GMAT-score of `gmat`. The relation `location` identifies the country which a given city is in.

2.1.1 Type-A Nesting

A nested query is said to be of `Type-A` nesting if the inner query block Q has no correlation with the outer query block (i.e., it does not contain a join predicate that references a relation in the outer query block) and if the `SELECT` clause of Q consists of an aggregate function over a column in an inner relation. An example is the query that asks for applicants that earn a salary greater than 60,000 and have GMAT scores higher than the average score of applicants from the states. The SQL expression of this query is given by the left expression of Figure 1.

Traditionally, this query is evaluated in two steps. In the first step, the inner query block is computed to determine the average GMAT score of US applicants. In the second step, the outer query is evaluated with the inner query block being replaced by its answer. Unfortunately, step 1 is time consuming as the system needs to examine all result tuples in (`applicant` $\bowtie$ `location`) to compute the average function. Thus, it takes a long period of time before the answers to the (outer) query are returned to the user. This is frustrating to users, and new mode of computing such queries is desirable.

2.1.2 Type JA Nesting

`Type JA` nesting is present when the inner query block and outer query block are correlated (i.e., the `WHERE` clause of the inner query block contains a join predicate that references a relation of an outer query block),

Type-A query

```
SELECT a1.pid, a1.salary
FROM applicant a1
WHERE a1.salary > 60000
AND a1.gmat >
    (SELECT avg(a.gmat)
     FROM applicant a, location l
     WHERE a.city = l.city
     AND l.country = ''USA'');
```

Type-JA query

```
SELECT a1.pid, a1.salary
FROM applicant a1
WHERE a1.salary > 60000
AND a1.gmat >
      (SELECT avg(a2.gmat)
       FROM applicant a2, location l
       WHERE a1.city = a2.city
       AND a2.city = l.city
       AND l.country = ''USA'');
```

Figure 1: SQL expressions of sample Type-A and Type-JA queries.

and the inner **SELECT** clause consists of an aggregate function over an inner relation. An example is the query that asks for applicants that earn a salary greater than 60,000 and have GMAT scores higher than the average score of applicants from the same US city (see the right expression of Figure 1). This query can be evaluated efficiently by transforming it into the following two queries [10]:

Inner Query:

```
(SELECT city, avg(a.gmat)
 FROM application a, location l
 WHERE a.city = l.city
 AND l.country = ''USA''
 GROUP BY city);
```

Outer Query:

```
SELECT a.pid, a.salary
FROM applicant a, tmpAgg t
WHERE a.salary > 60000
AND a.city = t.c1
AND a.gmat > t.c2
```

where `tmpAgg` is the temporary relation for the inner query, and `c1` and `c2` are the first and second columns in `tmpAgg` respectively.

Again, under the traditional query evaluation model, the inner query will be completely evaluated before the outer query can proceed. This may be unacceptable to users as the evaluation of the inner query will take a long time.

2.2 Overview of Multi-threaded and Online Evaluation of Nested Queries

The proposed approach works as follows. Instead of blocking the execution of the outer query block (until the inner query block completes), the outer query block is allowed to proceed as soon as the inner query block produces some estimates for its answers. In other words, the inner query block will be evaluated progressively to provide estimates quickly so that the outer query block can proceed to be evaluated (progressively). In this way, users can have rapid feedback (i.e., approximate answers) to their nested queries. Subsequently, both query blocks can be evaluated concurrently: as the inner query estimates are refined *progressively*, the answers to the outer query block are also refined based on the inner query block's refined aggregates.

The proposed user interface is shown in Figure 2. The interface will appear (almost) immediately after the user submits the query and can begin to display output as soon as the system has examined sufficient data to compute an estimate for the inner query. The interface consists of two panels. The right panel displays the result of the inner subquery: the current estimates of the aggregations together with the confidence and intervals that reflect the probabilistic estimates of the proximity of the current running aggregates to the final aggregate values. This result is updated regularly as more samples are examined. The % done and status bar display provide an indication of the amount of processing remaining before the computation of the aggregates completes. The left panel displays the output of the query, the result of which should be interpreted together with the current running aggregates. The **Stop** button in the right panel allows us to terminate the sampling process in computing the aggregates. The **Next** button in the left panel will retrieve the next answer set that satisfies the query. We note that terminating the aggregate computation does not necessarily mean termination of the query as we can still retrieve answers based on the current estimated aggregate values. For example, Figure 2(a) shows a sample display of the `Type A` nesting query in Section 2.1.1. From the right panel, we note that 10% of the work on the inner query has been performed, and the current running average for GMAT scores is 500 ± 12.6 at 95% confidence. From the left panel, the user can browse through the answer tuples that are retrieved based on the current estimate. In fact, for all the answer tuples that are displayed, the GMAT scores are much higher than the estimate, so much so that the user can be quite certain that these tuples will eventually be in the answer space. This

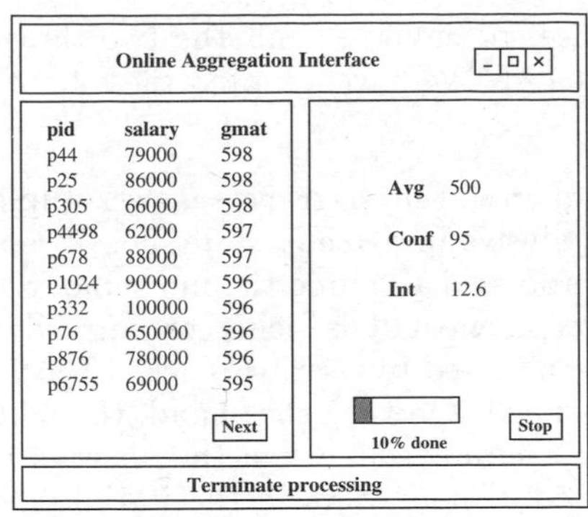

(a) Type A nesting.

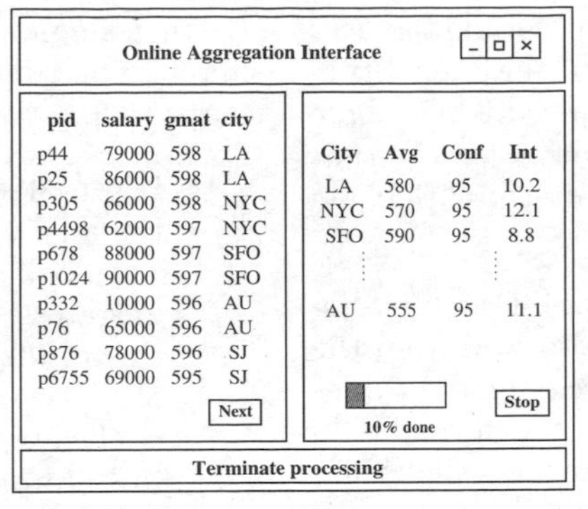

(b) Type JA nesting.

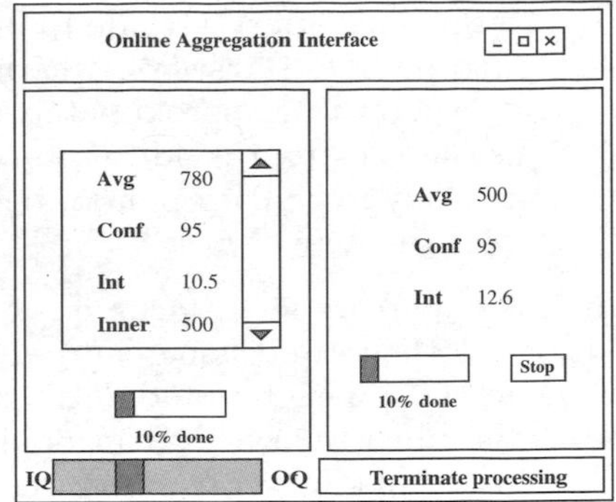

(c) Outer block with aggregate.

Figure 2: An online nested aggregation interface.

clearly demonstrates the advantage of the proposed approach: *correct results can be returned to the user quickly compared to the traditional blocking execution model.* We shall defer the discussion on how we deal with over- or under- estimation of the inner running aggregates when we look at the evaluation strategies.

As another example, consider the `Type JA` nesting query in Section 2.1.2. The sample display is shown in Figure 2(b). Again, from the right panel, the user can know the running average GMAT scores for the various US cities. The result displayed on the left panel shows those tuples that satisfy the query conditions using the inner query block's running averages.

We note that besides the targeted attributes, the answers include the additional attributes involved in the aggregation (`gmat` for the `Type A` nesting example, and `(city, gmat)` for the `Type JA` nesting example). This additional information allows the user to know which answer tuples are likely to be correct, and which are "approximately" correct (in the sense that future refinement may remove them from the final answer space).

The final example, which is more complex, is essentially a `Type A` nested query with aggregate function in the other query. The query

```
SELECT avg(a1.gmat)
FROM applicant a1
WHERE a1.salary > 60000
AND a1.gmat >
    (SELECT avg(a.gmat)
     FROM applicant a, location l
     WHERE a.city = l.city
     AND country = ''USA'');
```

asks for the average GMAT score of applicants that earn a salary greater than 60,000 and have GMAT scores higher than the average score of applicants from the states. The desired interface with sample results is shown in Figure 2(c). The display on the right panel is similar to the earlier examples. The left panel is essentially similar to the right panel, except that the results are presented differently. There is also the % done and status bar display to indicate the amount of processing remaining before the computation of the outer aggregate completes. We have also introduced a sliding bar to allow users to control the relative rate at which the two query blocks should be evaluated. Instead of displaying only one single aggregate that is based on the current estimate, the interface allows the user to view multiple average values based on different estimates from the inner query block. For example, the value shown represents the query's average when the inner query's average is 500. The confidence and interval represent the proximity of the average (of the query) at 95% confidence given that the inner query aggregate is actually 500. By clicking the up arrow at the top of the *scrollbar*, we will get the answer (query's average with the confidence and interval) for the case when the inner query's average is 499. Similarly, by clicking the down arrow at the bottom of the scrollbar, the answer with the inner query's average being 501 will be displayed. Such an approach allows the user to have a feel of what the average would be had the estimate change (as a result of refining the running aggregate for the inner query).

From the above discussion, we have identified a number of issues that have to be addressed to realize the proposed online evaluation of nested queries:

1. How can we interleave the execution of the inner and outer query blocks, i.e., how can we optimally timeslice the processing time across the two query blocks?

2. **Inner query block**. How much work must be done for the inner query block before the outer query block can proceed to be evaluated? How can the confidences and intervals be determined?

3. **Outer query block**. What are the *answer spaces* of a query (result of the outer query block)? The answer space of a query is the set of answer tuples relevant to the query. Since the inner query results are progressively refined, the answer spaces also change (as the outer query is evaluated based

on the inner query's results). How should the user interpret these answers, whether they are likely to be correct or approximately correct? Are there mechanisms to provide users with answers that are likely to be correct first, before those that are approximately correct?

In this paper, we shall focus on issues 1 and 3. Solutions to the second issue can be borrowed from the work in [4, 7], i.e., by randomly accessing the tuples from the inner query, we can apply the formulas in [4, 5, 7] to obtain the running aggregates and their confidence intervals.

3 A Multi-Threaded Nested Query Evaluation Model

Traditionally, query processing is performed under a *sequential* (or single-threaded) model, i.e., one task has to be completed before the next can be initiated. In other words, for nested queries with aggregates, the inner query has to be evaluated completely before the other query can be evaluated. Even if we can interleave multiple tasks (e.g., sample data from inner subquery, evaluate outer query, sample more data from inner subquery, evaluate outer query, etc.), the sequential model would make it cumbersome to facilitate the features discussed in Section 2.

In this section, we propose that the nested query be evaluated using a multi-threaded model. Under the multi-threaded model, two threads are used to evaluate the nested query in a concurrent fashion — thread `IQ` for the inner query block and thread `OQ` for the outer query block:

- Thread `IQ` evaluates the inner query block in phases. In the first phase, the estimates and their corresponding confidence intervals are obtained. In subsequent phases, these are refined.
- Thread `OQ` also evaluates the outer query block in phases (the number of phases is not the same as that of thread `IQ`). In the first phase, some answers are produced quickly based on the estimates obtained from thread `IQ`. Subsequent phases refine the answer spaces and produce refined answers or more answers.

The two threads operate in a *producer/consumer* relationship, where thread `IQ` produces some estimates of the inner query block (with increasing accuracy), which are then consumed by thread `OQ` in its evaluation of the outer query block. We note that the two threads have to be synchronized only once — when thread `IQ` must produce some estimates before thread `OQ` can begin evaluating the outer query. Subsequently, both threads operate concurrently and there is no need to synchronize between the two as thread `OQ` can use the current running aggregates from the inner query block to proceed.

In a single processor environment, the two threads have to be time-sliced. We have adopted the following approach:

- For nested queries that retrieve answer tuples, thread `IQ` is always in a *ready state*, i.e., it is always being processed to refine the inner block aggregates (except when it is being preempted by thread `OQ`, terminated by user or blocked because of I/O operations). On the other hand, thread `OQ` is always *suspended* except when the answers are to be produced. This occurs in the initial phase to produce the first answer set quickly, and subsequently, when the user requests for more answer tuples. In these instances, thread `OQ` resumes processing with a higher priority than thread `IQ`. This allows it to preempt thread `IQ` so that it can return answer tuples to the user rapidly.
- For nested queries that return aggregate values, both threads share equal time-slice by default. However, users may tune the time-slice by adjusting a sliding bar at the user interface (see Figure 2(c)).

In both the above cases, the evaluation of the outer query is "controlled" by the user. Thus, the allocation of time-slice between the two query blocks is essentially nondeterministic. In fact, the answers returned may also vary in the sense that the outer query may be based on different refined estimates at different time. In other words, for a user who takes a longer time to browse through each set of answers, each subsequent answer set will be based on a more accurate estimates (as more data are examined in the inner query). On the contrary, for a user that browses through the answers quickly, most of the answers are based on estimates that are more "crude".

4 Evaluation of Inner Query

In this section, we present the mechanisms and algorithms employed in evaluating the inner query in order to support the proposed online feedback approach.

The inner query is evaluated in phases, each of which produces a set of answer tuples from which the running aggregates can be estimated. At the end of each phase, the updated running aggregates will be reflected in the user interface as well as being passed to the outer query. We note that the aggregates are computed cumulatively. In other words, suppose there are k phases, and phase i ($1 \leq i \leq k$) produces t_i answer tuples; then, the aggregates at phase i are computed from $\sum_{j=1}^{i} t_j$ answer tuples. Moreover, the first phase is the most critical in the sense that sufficient answer tuples must be produced before meaningful estimates can be obtained. For subsequent phases, since the aggregates are computed cumulatively, the number of answer tuples is less of a concern.

There are two issues concerning the inner query evaluation:

1. For the inner query to provide meaningful running aggregates, mechanisms to generate or access random answer tuples (from which the aggregates are computed) are needed. Randomness is crucial since any biases may lead to poor estimates of the aggregate which are far from the actual aggregate values. In this paper, our focus is not on developing such strategies, and hence we opt to employ existing techniques. To access data randomly from a relation, we can employ the *heap scan* for heap files [7], *index scan* when there is no correlation between the attributes being aggregated and the indexed attribute [7] and the pseudo-random sampling schemes for B^+-trees [13]. For join queries, the ripple join algorithms [5] can be applied.

2. For the result (of the full query) to be useful, the estimate for the aggregate has to be meaningful. The proximity of the running aggregate to the actual value can be expressed in terms of a running confidence interval. The width of such a confidence interval serves as a measure of the precision of the estimator. Furthermore, we need to be able to determine the number of samples for the aggregate to be meaningful. In this paper, we restrict our work to *large-sample* confidence intervals based on the *central limit theorems* (CLT's) which contain the final answer μ with a probability approximately equal to p. [4, 7] provided the formulas and efficient methods to do so. In particular, given a confidence parameter p and a confidence interval half-width ϵ_n, let n denotes the size of a random sample required for constructing a large-sample confidence interval for μ that meets the given specification. Then $\epsilon_n^2 = \frac{z_p^2 s^2}{n}$ (see [4, 7]) where z_p is the $(p+1)/2$ quantile of Φ (the cumulative distribution function of an $N(0,1)$ random variable), so that $\Phi(z_p) = (p+1)/2$, and s is the sample variance.

5 Evaluation of Outer Query

In this section, we present the mechanisms and algorithms that the proposed approach adopt in evaluating the outer query. We shall present the evaluation strategies for outer queries without aggregates first, followed by outer queries with aggregates.

5.1 Outer Query Block Without Aggregate

Queries whose outer query blocks do not involve an aggregate operation are of the form:

```
SELECT target-list FROM relation-list
WHERE qualification
AND R.A op (inner query with aggregate);
```

where `R` is one of the relations in `relation-list` and `A` is an attribute of `R`, and `op` is one of the operations $>$, $\geq$, $<$, $\leq$, $=$. The sample queries in Section 2.1.1 and Section 2.1.2 are examples of queries in this category.

Traditionally, there is only one answer space (i.e., one unique set of tuples) to the query and the answers are the correct answers. However, under the multi-threaded evaluation model, the answers are based on estimates. Furthermore, as the estimates are refined, the answers may change. We shall first discuss the answer spaces and their interpretations before presenting the evaluation strategies.

5.1.1 Type-A Nested Query

Consider first the case when the nested query is of `Type-A` nesting. Let the set of running aggregates produced for the inner query block in the course of evaluating the nested query be $\overline{\mu}_1 \pm \delta_1$, $\overline{\mu}_2 \pm \delta_2$, ..., $\overline{\mu}_n \pm \delta_n$, where $\overline{\mu}_i \pm \delta_i$ is the running aggregate for phase i, and $\overline{\mu}_n$ is the final (actual) aggregate (and $\delta_n = 0$). Further, let the corresponding answer spaces be $\mathcal{A}_1, \mathcal{A}_2, \ldots, \mathcal{A}_n$.

Answer Space and Its Interpretation

Since $\overline{\mu_i}$ may take on different value in different phases, the answer space $\mathcal{A}_i$ is not likely to be the same as $\mathcal{A}_j$, for $i \neq j$. However, if the tuples of the relations are randomly accessed, we can expect the overlap in the answer spaces to be significant. We note that the concept of answer space is only a logical one and not all answers will be retrieved for the user at a single phase (recall that we only display a set of tuples each time). More specifically, suppose the current running aggregate is $\overline{\mu} - \delta \leq \mu \leq \overline{\mu} + \delta$. Then the corresponding answer space is given as follows.

- If the operation is "$>$" (or "$\geq$") (i.e., `R.A > aggregate` or `R.A` $\geq$ `aggregate`), the answer space includes tuples that satisfy the condition `R.A` $> \overline{\mu} - \delta - \epsilon$ (or `R.A` $\geq \overline{\mu} - \delta - \epsilon$) for some predetermined $\epsilon \geq 0$. In other words, the answer space should (hopefully) contain a superset of the final answers. In this way, we hope not to miss any answer should the actual aggregate be out of the range bound by the running aggregate.

- Similarly, if the operation is "$<$" (or "$\leq$"), the answer space includes tuples that satisfy the condition `R.A` $< \overline{\mu} + \delta + \epsilon$ (or `R.A` $\leq \overline{\mu} + \delta + \epsilon$) for some predetermined ϵ.

- Finally, if the operation is "$=$", the answer space will include all tuples that satisfy the condition $\overline{\mu} - \delta - \epsilon <$ `R.A` $< \overline{\mu} + \delta + \epsilon$.

As the estimate is refined, the current answer space is also refined accordingly — tuples retrieved that no longer satisfy the query will be removed; on the other hand, if too few tuples are in the current set, then a remainder query may have to be generated to retrieve the remaining tuples.

For the tuples to be useful, the user must have some means of ascertaining its quality, i.e., whether it is likely to be correct (in the final answer set), approximately correct (most likely to be in) or likely to be incorrect (likely to be out). Our approach is to include the attribute `R.A` in the target list (if it is not already user specified). In this way, the user knows exactly the value of `R.A`, and hence can take note of those tuples that are "fuzzy".[1] For example, if the operation is $>$, and the estimate has running aggregate of 150 ± 3, and an answer tuple has `R.A = 200`, then the user can be quite sure that this tuple will be in the final answer. Note that if the data are accessed randomly, it is unlikely for the estimator to be way out of the actual aggregate value.

Evaluation Strategy

Since answers are returned in sets (say 10 tuples each time), we propose that answer tuples that are most likely to be correct are returned to the users first. In this way, the users are likely to be browsing through correct answers (while the inner aggregates are being refined), and hopefully by the time they browse answer tuples that are towards the end of the answer space, the actual inner aggregates would have been computed and no (or few) poor quality answers are returned to users. Moreover, as argued in [7], it is not uncommon for users to terminate prematurely (i.e., before all tuples are retrieved), in which case, browsing correct answers at the initial phases would be highly desirable.

Let the running aggregate be $\overline{\mu} \pm \delta$. Let the nested predicate be `R.A > aggregate`. Furthermore, let the maximum value of `R.A` be `V`. This value is available in the DBMS statistics. The proposed approach splits the answer space into k partitions, each covering a range of $P = \lceil \frac{V-(\overline{\mu}+\delta+\epsilon)}{k} \rceil$. In other words, records in the range $[V - P,\ V]$ are in partition 1, records in the range $[V - 2P,\ V - P)$ are in partition 2, and records in the range $[V - kP,\ V - (k-1)P)$ are in partition k. The proposed algorithm returns answers in order of the partition number, i.e., answers are obtained from partition 1, followed by partition 2, and so on. The algorithmic description of the strategy is shown in Figure 3.[2] The algorithm is highly abstracted. The routine **OuterThreadWithoutAggregate** is invoked whenever the user requests for more records (or when the very first set of results is to be displayed). It first obtains the current running aggregate, i.e., $\mu \pm \delta$ (routine **getRunningAggregate()**), and set ϵ to a fraction of the aggregate. Then, it calls the **next()** iterator multiple times (10 in the figure) to display a set of (10) records. The **next()** iterator is the cruz of the algorithm. It returns a record (according to the partition order) each time when invoked. It essentially comprises two fragments. The first fragment evaluates the outer query, returns answer tuples from partition 1, and produces the other partitions (lines 2-14). This is achieved by using another iterator **getNextResult()** that evaluates the outer query based on conventional algorithm, Note that only records that are in the answer space will be returned (for example, if `R.A > aggregate`, then the answers must be greater than $\overline{\mu} - \delta - \epsilon$). The answer tuple from **getNextResult()** is either returned (being an output of **next()**) if it belongs to partition 1 or written to the appropriate partition. The second fragment retrieves answer tuples from the partitions, beginning from partition 2 (lines 15-22). Since the inner query aggregate value may change, the tuples in the partitions have to be checked again with the corresponding running aggregate at the time when it is invoked. We note that if the inner query completes before the outer query completes, then $\delta = 0$ and $\epsilon = 0$.

When the nested predicates involve the operations $>$, $\geq$, $<$, $\leq$, the above strategy can be applied. However, for "=", we adopt the simple strategy of just presenting all tuples whose `R.A` values fall in the range $[\overline{\mu} - \delta - \epsilon,\ \overline{\mu} + \delta + \epsilon]$. This is because the number of tuples are not expected to be many (compared with those involving inequalities). Moreover, it is not common to have nested predicates with the = operation.

A final note before we leave this section: it is "fine" for a displayed answer to fall out of the final answer space as the user would have the value of `R.A` for him to know the validity of the tuple.

5.1.2 Type-JA Nested Query

For `Type-JA` nested queries, the answer spaces, their interpretations and the evaluation strategy are essentially similar to `Type-A` nested queries. However, in each phase, we have multiple answer subspaces each associated with one of the running aggregate values in the inner query block (and multiple ϵ values). Moreover, the target list will include the pair (join attribute, aggregate value) so that user can assess the validity of the answer tuples (see Figure 2(b) for an example).

5.2 Outer Query Block With Aggregate

This category of queries has the form:

```
SELECT aggregate FROM relation-list
WHERE qualification
AND R.A op (inner query with aggregate);
```

[1] Alternatively, we can determine some statistical measures to reflect the confidence intervals of the answer tuples. This method is, in our opinion, less useful since the user is still not clear which tuples are valid.

[2] For ease of presentation, we have omitted the case when a remainder query is needed.

```
1. OuterThreadWithoutAggregate() {
2.     getRunningAggregate(μ̄, δ, ε)
3.     for (i = 0; i < 10; i++) {
4.         r = next()
5.         if r ≠ ∅
6.             display(r)
7.         else
8.             exit()
9.         }
10.    }
11. }
```

```
1. next() {
2.     while (more) {
3.         r = getNextResult(μ̄, δ, ε)
4.         if r = ∅ {
5.             more = false
6.             i = 2
7.         } else {
8.             j = determinePartition(r)
9.             if j = 1
10.                return(r)
11.            else
12.                cacheAnswer(r, P_j)
13.        }
14.    }
15.    while j ≤ n {
16.        r = getNextPartition(P_j, μ̄, δ, ε)
17.        if r = ∅
18.            j++
19.        else
20.            return(r)
21.    }
22.    if j > n return(∅)
23. }
```

Figure 3: Algorithm for Type-A query without aggregates.

where the outermost query involves an aggregate operation, `R` is one of the relations in `relation-list` and `A` is an attribute of `R`, and `op` is one of the operations $>$, $\geq$, $<$, $\leq$, $=$.

Traditionally, there is only one single answer tuple. Under the new query evaluation model, the outer query produces a set of answer tuples, each of which is a running aggregate, based on the inner query estimates. Consider first `Type-A` nested queries. Suppose the current running aggregate is $\bar{\mu} - \delta \leq \mu \leq \bar{\mu} + \delta$. Then, we compute the running aggregate of the outer query for a number of distinct values in the range $[\bar{\mu} - \delta - \epsilon, \bar{\mu} + \delta + \epsilon]$, for some predetermined ϵ. For example, let $\epsilon = 2$. If the inner query's running aggregate is 500 ± 3, then we can compute 11 running aggregates of the outer query: the first assumes that the actual aggregate value of the inner query is 495, the second for 496, and so on. Thus, the user can have quick feedback on what the outer-aggregate (with its confidence and interval) would be should the inner estimates be refined.

Figure 4 shows an abstracted algorithm. After determining the current running aggregate of the inner query block, the algorithm proceeds to obtain sample result tuples of the outer query (lines 6-9). This is again achieved with the help of the **next()** iterator. The **next()** here is similar to the one used in routine **OuterThreadWithoutAggregate()** except that the result tuples are generated using random access methods and ripple join algorithms (rather than conventional algorithms in iterator **getNextResult()**). The *stopping criterion* depends on how much timeslice is allocated for the thread. Next, assuming that there are n_{agg} aggregates to be computed for the outer query, the aggregates and their confidences and intervals are determined. Two points to note: first, if the inner query block completes execution, then $\delta_{iq} = 0$, $\epsilon = 0$ and n_{agg} will be reset to 1; second, the loop from lines 12-16 is only logical (for ease of presentation) in the sense that the actual implementation exploits the fact that the computation of the aggregates and the corresponding confidences and intervals at a later iteration can reuse results from earlier computation. Thus, evaluating multiple running aggregates is not that costly.

`Type-JA` nested queries are also interpreted and evaluated in a similar manner. The only complexity comes from the fact that the outer query involves an additional join operation.

6 Implementation and Evaluation

To study and validate the effectiveness of the proposed approach, we implemented the proposed approach. In this section, we shall present our findings. We use the initial response time (i.e., the time when the first answer set is presented) as the metric for comparison. The initial response time is taken to be the average value over multiple runs of the same experiment.

```
OuterThreadWithAggregate() {
    getRunningAggregate(μ̄_iq, δ_iq, ε)
    l_min = μ̄_iq − δ_iq − ε
    l_max = μ̄_iq + δ_iq + ε
    currSample = ∅
    repeat
        r = next()
        currSample = currSample ∪ r
    until stopping criterion or r = ∅
    if δ_iq = 0
        n_agg = 1
    for (i = 0; i < n_agg; i++) {
        m_i = l_min + (i + 1) * (l_max − l_min) / n_agg
        computeConfIntervals(μ̄_oq, δ_oq, conf, m_i)
        display(μ̄_oq, δ_oq, conf, m_i )
    }
```

Figure 4: Algorithm for outer query with an aggregate.

6.1 Implementation and Experimental Setup

The proposed approach is implemented in Java on a SUN UltraSparc2 workstation. Java is the language of choice mainly because of its powerful graphical user interface components and its support for multithreading. The current implementation consists of basic components necessary to facilitate online feedback: an access method that retrieves data randomly, a hash-based ripple join algorithm, a statistical analysis routine for efficiently computing the confidence and interval of an aggregate, and the proposed incremental evaluation strategy. The current system only supports the average function.

We use the example database in Section 2. The database has the following two self-explanatory tables:

```
applicant(pid, fname, lname, live_in, income, gmat)
location(cityid, city, country, region, description)
```

Here, `pid` and `cityid` are keys of the respective tables, and `live_in` is a foreign key (and hence has the same domain as `cityid`). The `applicant` table has 1,000,000 tuples and are generated as follows: `eno` is set by counting 1 to 1,000,000, `income` is randomly picked from [10000,60000], `gmat` is generated using a normal distribution with mean of 550 and is restricted to the range [200,800]. The domain of `live_in` is the same as that of `location.cityid` and will be described shortly. We have fixed 50% of the applicants to be from the US. `fname` and `lname` are simply padded with "garbage" characters to ensure that the `applicant` table is 200 bytes long.

The `location` table contains 10,000 tuples, and is generated in a similar manner as `applicant`: `cityid` is set from 1 to 10,000; `region` is randomly distributed in [1,100] to reflect the region of a country (e.g., Asia, US, Europe, Australia); and `city`, `country`, and `description` are padded with dummy characters to make up a 200-byte location tuple.

6.2 Experiment 1: Outer Queries Without Aggregates

In our first set of experiments, we study nested queries whose outer queries do not involve aggregates. The experiments are evaluated with the incremental strategy partitioning the answer tuples into two partitions. In all experiments, we set ϵ to be 1% of the estimated aggregate from the inner query block.

For the first experiment, we examine a `Type-A` nested query that selects the pid of applicants whose salary is greater than 59500 and the GMAT score is greater than the average GMAT-score of applicants from the US region. The resultant answer space has about 5000 tuples. Figure 5(a) shows the half-width of the confidence interval over the initial response time of the query. We note that the half-width is measured in terms of percentage with respect to the estimated aggregate value. As shown in the figure, the conventional blocking model takes more than 700 sec before the first set of tuples starts to appear on the display. For the proposed approach, the half-width of the interval is obtained with 99% confidence, and the evaluation of the `applicant` table in the outer query is based on a sequential scan of the table. We note that for the proposed approach, we can have the first set of tuples appearing as early as 10 sec when the half-width is about 8% of the estimated aggregate. As shown, even if we were to wait till the half-width is about 1% before we start evaluating the outer query, the first set of tuples would appear before 100 sec, which is far shorter than that of the conventional approach. Our investigation also shows that the answer tuples retrieved from partition 1 are all correct answers, i.e., they are in the final answer space. Thus, the result demonstrates that the proposed approach can provide quick and correct answers to users.

We also study the effect of user browsing time. As users take longer time to browse the result, subsequent requests will be based on better running aggregates. On the other hand, a shorter browsing time will imply that the results are likely to be based on running aggregates generated by fewer samples. We study three different user browsing time, t = 5, 10, and 20 sec, i.e., after every 10 tuples are retrieved, the user waits for t sec before requesting for the next set of tuples. Figure 5(b) shows the result of the experiment. As shown, in almost all cases, by the time the user has browsed through 20 answer sets, the half-width is already reduced to 1%. Moreover, these 20 answer sets are all from partition 1 which contains all correct answers.

Finally, we also study the effect of number of partitions on the incremental strategy. In this experiment, we fixed the half-width to be 5%, i.e., the outer

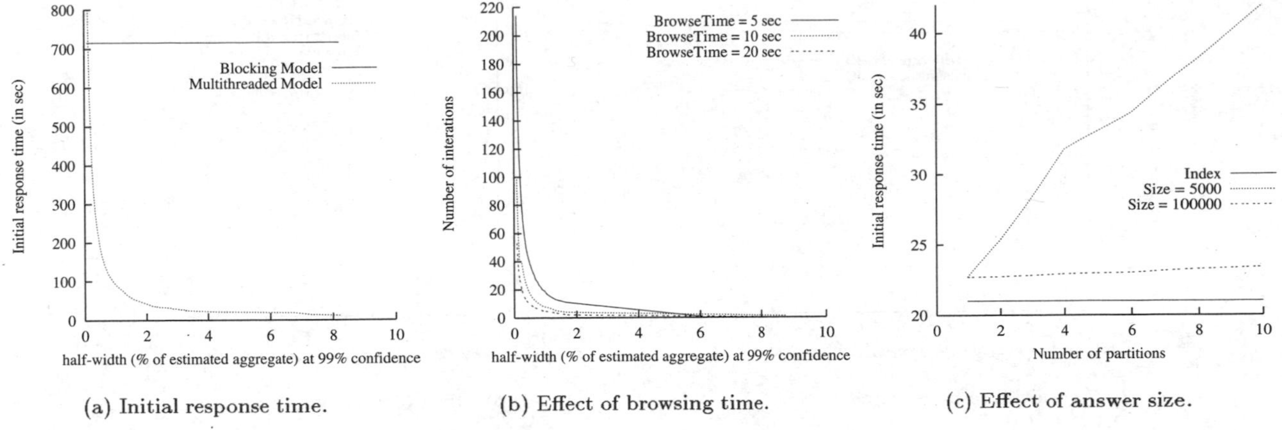

(a) Initial response time.

(b) Effect of browsing time.

(c) Effect of answer size.

Figure 5: Type-A nested query where the outer query does not involve an aggregate.

query will be evaluated only after the half-width for the aggregate of the inner query has reached 5% of the estimated aggregate value. We vary the number of partitions from 1 to 10. The result is shown in Figure 5(c). We shall look at the curve with result size of 5000 tuples. As shown, it turns out that the number of partitions can be crucial (when the number of answer tuples is small, i.e., 5000 out of 1000000 tuples). For small number of partitions, the proportion of answer tuples falling into these partitions is large. As a result, it takes a shorter time to find a set of tuples in an arbitrary partition (as table `applicant` is sequentially scanned). On the contrary, for large number of partitions, each partition contains a small number of answer tuples; and hence finding a set of tuples in a partition will take a longer time (more tuples in `applicant` has to be scanned before we can obtain a set of tuples). The same figure also shows another curve with result size of 100000 tuples. This is produced by changing the selection predicate on salary to retrieve applicants who earn greater than 50000. However, we note that the number of partitions is hardly a factor in this case. The reason is because for large answer sizes, it does not take a long time to find a set of tuples to display. On the contrary, when the answer size is small, it will take a longer time to produce a set of tuples, and the time will be lengthened with smaller number of partitions. Thus, depending on the answer size, different number of partitions may be employed for optimal performance. We have also included a third curve which shows the initial response time had the `applicant` table been indexed. The response time to produce the first set of tuples is the same regardless of the answer size, and is clearly better than sequentially scanning the `applicant` table.

We also repeated the experiment for a `Type-JA` nested query. The query selects the pid of US applicants whose salary is greater than 50000 and the GMAT score is greater than the average GMAT-score of applicants from the same US city. Figure 6(a) shows the half-width of the confidence interval over the initial response time of the query for one city only (since the inner query generates an estimate for a city, there will be as many half-width as the number of cities). In our work, all cities have about the same number of matching tuples, and so, one is sufficient to serve as a representative example. As before, the half-width is measured in terms of percentage with respect to the estimated aggregate value. Once again, the conventional blocking model takes a long time before the first tuple is produced. However, we note that the initial response time is also slightly above 700 sec despite that the query is more complex now. The reason for this is because the number of US cities is about 100, and the intermediate results are being stored in the main memory instead of writing out to disk. To produce the first answer set to the query is thus not much slower than the case without a join operation.

For the proposed approach, the half-width of the interval is obtained with 99% confidence, and the evaluation of the outer query is based on a conventional hash-based join of the table (with the incremental strategy). We note that the proposed approach remains effective. The first set of tuples starts to appear at about 20 sec when the half-width is about 10% of the estimated aggregate. If we had picked a half-width of 1% before evaluating the outer query, the first set of tuples would appear at about 200 sec. While this is 10 times as much compared to the first experiment, it is still much shorter than that of the conventional approach. The initial response time is higher (compared to the first experiment) because the inner query is generating a set of estimates, and each has to have sufficient samples before the estimate can be meaningful. As in the earlier experiment, we note that all answers in the first partition are correct answers.

We also study the effect of user browsing time by using three different user browsing time, $t = 5$, 10, and 20 sec. Figure 5(b) shows the result of the experiment. As shown, if the user browsing time is low (i.e., 5 sec), it will take about 60 answer sets before the half-width is reduced to 1%. On the other hand, when the brows-

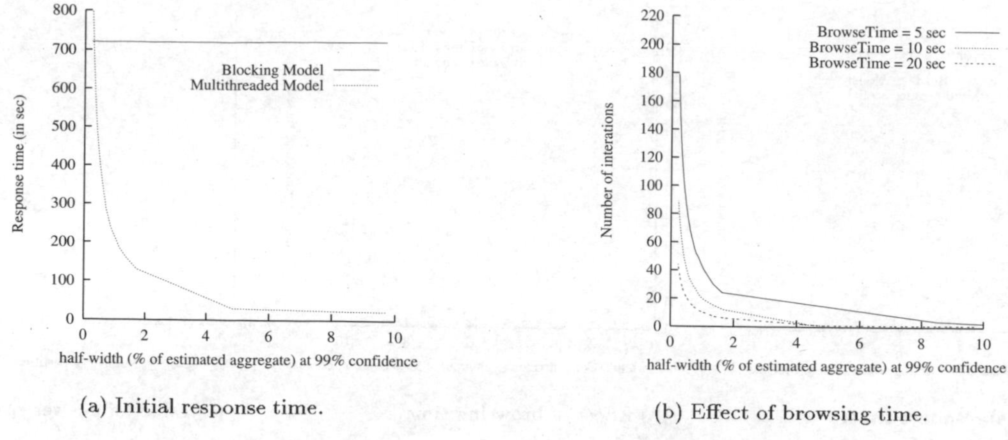

(a) Initial response time.

(b) Effect of browsing time.

Figure 6: Type-JA nested query where the outer query does not involve an aggregate.

ing time is 20 sec, it takes fewer than 20 answer sets before the half-width dropped to 1%. In any case, the number of answer sets is small in all cases. Again, all the 20 answer sets contain the correct answers.

From the experiments, it is clear that the multi-threaded model proposed can provide quick answers to users without sacrificing on the quality of the initial answers.

6.3 Experiment 2: Outer Queries With Aggregates

In this experiment, we study the performance of the proposed approach for outer queries with aggregates. We shall evaluate the `Type-A` nested query that finds the average GMAT score of applicants whose salary is greater than 50000 and has GMAT score greater than the average GMAT-score of applicants from the US region. For this experiment, we also set ϵ to be 1% of the inner query's running aggregate. Figure 7 shows the result of this experiment. In this study, we use the default of equal time being allocated to each query block. In the figure, the number of iterations represents the number of timeslice that has been expended on each thread.

Our first observation (see Figure 7(a)) is that the proposed approach can provide very fast feedback to the user compared to the traditional blocking model. The traditional model requires evaluating both the inner and outer query blocks completely before producing the final answer tuple. Because of the large table sizes, this takes up a total of almost 1400 sec. On the contrary, the proposed approach starts to produce the first estimate on the 8th iteration which has an initial time of 11 sec only!

Figure 7(b) and Figure 7(c) show the half-widths of the inner and outer query running aggregates at 99% confidence respectively. From the figures, we note that the half-widths drop rapidly. Within 200 iterations (which is about 200 sec from Figure 7(a)), the half-width for the inner query has reduced to less than 1% while that of the outer query has dropped to less than 0.1% (this is only for one value of the outer query; the result is similar for other values). This results clearly show that the proposed approach is a promising alternative to the conventional blocking model: it can produce reasonably good answers to users quickly.

7 Related Work

In [7], Hellerstein et. al. proposed modifications to database engine to support online aggregation. These include techniques to randomly access data, to evaluate operations (such as join and sort) without blocking, to incorporate statistical analysis [4], etc. For complex aggregate queries involving joins, the authors also proposed a new family of join algorithms, called *ripple joins* [5]. Experimental studies showed that online aggregation is promising and can reduce the initial response time. Moreover, the confidence intervals converge in a reasonable time. However, these work focused on non-nested queries.

To facilitate online aggregation, it is important that records be accessed in random order and that the running aggregate be computed meaningfully for it to be useful. Sampling from base relations provide a means of randomly accessing records [8, 9]. In [13], Olken studied the methods to access records randomly from B^+-trees and hash files, and how random samples can be obtained from relational operations and from select-project-join queries.

When records are accessed in a random order, the running aggregate can be viewed as a statistical estimator of the final result. As such, the precision of the running aggregate to the final result can be expressed in terms of a running confidence intervals. In [4, 7], formulas for running confidence intervals in the case of single table and multi-table **AVG**, **COUNT**, **SUM**, **VARIANCE** and **STDEV** queries with join and selection predicates are presented together with methods to compute these formulas efficiently. Duplicate elimination with **GROUP-BY** operations are also considered.

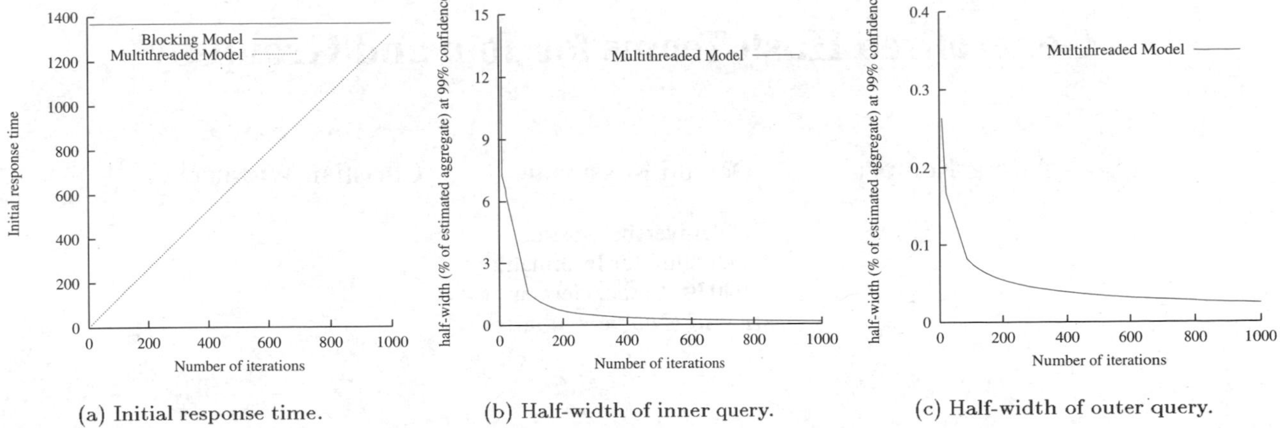

(a) Initial response time. (b) Half-width of inner query. (c) Half-width of outer query.

Figure 7: Type-A nested query where the outer query involves an aggregate.

Several earlier work [6, 8, 9, 11] have also addressed the issue of obtaining confidence intervals.

There has also been some work on *fast-first* query processing, that returns the first few answers to users quickly. These work largely focused on developing pipelined join methods or cost models that can predict the cost to obtain the first few rows of a query result set [1, 15], and aim to minimize initial response time. More recently, Tan et. al. [14] studied how a query can be rewritten into subqueries so that users can obtain the answers to the first subquery quickly.

8 Conclusion

In this paper, we have proposed a mechanism to provide rapid feedback to users issuing nested queries with aggregates. The proposed approach evaluates a nested query progressively using a multi-threaded evaluation model: as soon as the inner query produces estimates to its aggregates, the outer query is evaluated to produce approximate answers to users; as the inner query's estimates are refined, the approximate answers are refined too. We have implemented a prototype system using JAVA, and evaluated our system. Our results showed that the proposed mechanisms can provide rapid online feedback without sacrificing much on the quality of the answers.

References

[1] R. Bayardo and D. Miranker. Processing queries for the first few answers. In *CIKM'96*, Rockville, MD, 1996.

[2] U. Dayal. Of nests and trees: A unified approach of processing queries that contain nested subqueries, aggregates, and quantifiers. In *VLDB'87*, pages 197–208, Brighton, England, September 1987.

[3] R. Ganski and H.K.T. Wong. Optimization of nested sql queries revisited. In *SIGMOD'87*, pages 23–33, June 1987.

[4] P. J. Haas. Large-sample and deterministic confidence intervals for online aggregation. In *SSDBM'96*, pages 51–63, 1997.

[5] P. J. Haas and J. M. Hellerstein. Ripple joins for online aggregation. In *SIGMOD'99*, Philadelphia, June 1999.

[6] P.J. Haas, J.F. Naughton, S. Seshadri, and A.N. Swami. Selectivity and cost estimation for joins based on random sampling. *Journal of Computer and System Sciences*, 52(3), June 1996.

[7] J. M. Hellerstein, P. J. Haas, and H. J. Wang. Online aggregation. In *SIGMOD'97*, pages 171–182, June 1997.

[8] W.C. Hou, G. Ozsoyoglua, and B.K. Taneja. Statistical estimators for relational algebra expressions. In *PODS'88*, pages 276–287, Austin, March 1988.

[9] W.C. Hou, G. Ozsoyoglua, and B.K. Taneja. Processing aggregate relational queries with hard time constraints. In *PODS'89*, pages 68–77, Portland, May 1989.

[10] W. Kim. On optimizing an sql-like nested query. *ACM Transactions on Database Systmes*, 7(3), September 1982.

[11] R.J. Lipton, J.F. Naughton, D.A. Schneider, and S. Seshadri. Efficient sampling strategies for relational database operations. *Theoretical Computer Science*, 116, 1993.

[12] G.M. Lohman, D. Daniels, L.M. Haas, R. Kistler, and P.G. Selinger. Optimization of nested queries in a distributed relational database. In *VLDB'84*, pages 403–415, Singapore, June 1984.

[13] F. Olken. *Random Sampling from Databases*. PhD thesis, University of California, Berkeley, 1993.

[14] K. L. Tan, C. H. Goh, and B. C. Ooi. On getting some answers quickly, and then more later. In *ICDE'99*, Sydney, Australia, March 1999.

[15] A. N. Wilschut and P. M. G. Apers. Dataflow query execution in parallel main-memory environment. In *PDIS'91*, pages 68–77, Miami Beach, December 1991.

Generalized Hash Teams for Join and Group-by*

Alfons Kemper Donald Kossmann Christian Wiesner

Universität Passau
Lehrstuhl für Informatik
94030 Passau, Germany
⟨lastname⟩@*db.fmi.uni-passau.de*

Abstract

We propose a new class of algorithms that can be used to speed up the execution of multi-way join queries or of queries that involve one or more joins and a group-by. These new evaluation techniques allow to perform several hash-based operations (join and grouping) in one pass without repartitioning intermediate results. These techniques work particularly well for joining hierarchical structures, e.g., for evaluating functional join chains along key/foreign-key relationships. The idea is to generalize the concept of hash teams as proposed by Graefe et.al [GBC98] by indirectly partitioning the input data. Indirect partitioning means to partition the input data on an attribute that is not directly needed for the next hash-based operation, and it involves the construction of bitmaps to approximate the partitioning for the attribute that is needed in the next hash-based operation. Our performance experiments show that such generalized hash teams perform significantly better than conventional strategies for many common classes of decision support queries.

1 Introduction

Decision support is emerging as one of the most important database applications. Managers of large businesses, for example, want to study the development of *sales* for certain *products* by *region*, and they expect the database system to return the relevant information within seconds or at most few minutes.

Decision support typically involves the execution of complex queries with join and group-by operations. To support these kinds of queries, database vendors have significantly extended their query processors and researchers have just recently developed a large variety of new query processing techniques; e.g., the use of bitmap indices, special joins that exploit bitmap join indices, new join methods [HWM98, CKK98], or multi-query optimization for decision support to name just a few. In addition, a whole new industry, data warehouses, has appeared with products that materialize (i.e., pre-compute) query results and cache the results of queries. Furthermore, the TPC-D benchmark [TPC95] has been proposed in order to evaluate the performance of a database product for decision support queries.

In this work, we present a new class of algorithms that can be used to speed up the execution of decision support queries that involve one or more joins and a group-by operation. The idea is to partition the input data and, then, carry out all join and group-by operations in one pass. To make this possible, we propose to construct bitmaps in the partitioning phase of a table and use these bitmaps in the partitioning phase of other tables. The advantage of our approach is that a great deal of disk IO can be saved, if the data base and intermediate query results do not fit into the available main memory: only one partitioning step per table is required, rather than partitioning the inputs of every join and group-by operation individually, as done by conventional query execution engines today. Due to the use of bitmaps, however, our approach might suffer from so-called *false drops* in the partitioning phase and result in overall increased disk IO and CPU cost in certain cases. A query optimizer should, therefore, enumerate query evaluation plans based on our new approach in addition to traditional query evaluation plans, and we will give formulae that can be used by an optimizer in order to decide when to use our approach.

Our approach can be seen as a generalization of hash teams, as proposed in [Gra94, GBC98]. Our technique adopts the main idea of hash teams to partition base data once and carry out joins in one pass afterwards. Hash teams, however, can only be applied if all the joins within a team are carried out using the same join/group-by columns. Our approach, on the other hand, can be applied to any kind of (equi) join, and it works best for joining hierarchical structures, e.g., for evaluating functional join chains along key/foreign-key relationships. We, therefore, refer to our approach as *generalized hash teams*.

The remainder of this paper is organized as follows:

*This work was partially supported by the German National Research Council DFG Ke 401/7-1

Proceedings of the 25th VLDB Conference, Edinburgh, Scotland, 1999.

In Section 2 we introduce the use of generalized hash teams by way of a simple binary join followed by a grouping/aggregation. Section 3 provides more details on implementing generalized hash teams. In Section 4 the application of generalized hash teams for multi-way joins with or without a subsequent grouping is described. In Section 5 the number of false drops resulting from the indirect, bitmap-based partitioning is analyzed. In Section 6 a few representative decision support queries are benchmarked. Section 7 compares our work to other related proposals, and Section 8 concludes this paper with a summary.

2 Binary Joins with Aggregation

In this section, we will show how generalized hash teams work for queries that involve one join and one group-by operation. We will, furthermore, present a simplified variant, called *partition nested loops*. As a running example, we will use the following query which asks for the total *Value* of all *Orders* grouped by the *Customer City*.

> *Query 1*: **select** c.City, **sum**(o.Value)
> **from** Customer c, Order o
> **where** c.C# = o.C#
> **group by** c.City;

2.1 Generalized Hash Teams

The traditional (state-of-the-art) plan to execute our example query is shown in Figure 1. This plan uses hashing in order to execute the join and the group-by operation. This plan would first partition (abbreviated *ptn* in the figures) both the *Customer* and the *Order* tables by *C#* such that either all the *Customer* or all the *Order* partitions fit in memory; that is, this plan would carry out a (grace or hybrid) hash join between these two tables [Sha86]. After that, the traditional plan would use hashing (possibly with early aggregation [Lar97]) to group the results of the join by *City*. If there are more *Cities* than fit into main memory, this group-by operation would, again, involve partitioning such that every partition can be aggregated in memory. In all, there are three partitioning steps in this traditional plan, incurring IO costs to write and read the *Customer* table, the *Order* table, and the result of the join. As an alternative, *sorting*, rather than *hashing*, can be used for the join and/or the group by. In many cases, sorting has higher (CPU) cost than hashing; in any case, however, a traditional plan based on sorting would also involve IO costs to write and read the *Customer* table, the *Order* table, and the result of the join.

Figure 2 shows a plan that makes use of generalized hash teams in order to execute our example query. Like the traditional plan shown in Figure 1, this plan is based on hashing to execute the join and the group-by operation. The trick, however, is that the *Customer* table is partitioned by *City*, rather than by *C#*, so that the result of the join is partitioned by *City* as well and the group-by operation does not require an additional partitioning step. To make this work, this plan generates bitmaps while partitioning the *Customer* table. These bitmaps indicate in which partition every *Customer* tuple is inserted and these bitmaps are

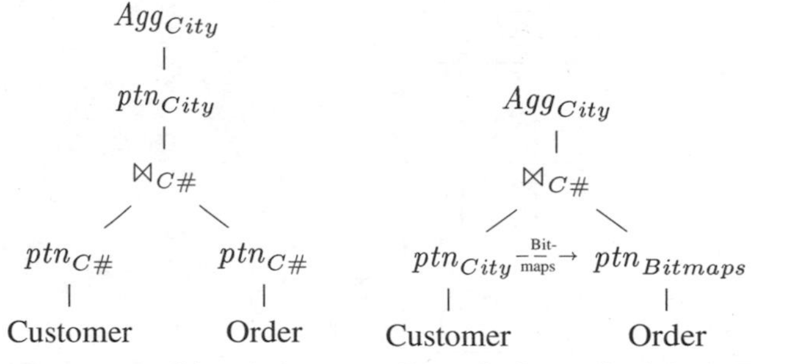

Figure 1: Traditional Plan

Figure 2: Generalized Hash Team

used to partition the *Order* table so that *Order* tuples and matching *Customer* tuples can be found in corresponding *Order* and *Customer* partitions. That is, the *Order* table is partitioned *indirectly* using the bitmaps.

To make this clearer, let us look at Figure 3 which illustrates the whole process in more detail. The figure shows a small example extension of the *Customer* table and how this *Customer* table is partitioned by *City* into three partitions: the first partition contains all *Customers* located in PA and M, the second partition contains all *Customers* located in B and HH, and the third partition contains all *Customers* located in NYC and LA. Just as in a traditional (grace or hybrid) hash join, the goal is to generate partitions that fit into main memory, and database statistics would be used for this purpose. Corresponding to every partition, there is one bitmap that keeps track of the *C#*'s stored in the partition; in this small example, there are three bitmaps of length ten each. If a *Customer* tuple is inserted into a partition, the 1 + (*C#* `mod 10`)'th bit of the corresponding bitmap is set. So, the fourth and sixth bit of the first bitmap are set because the first partition contains *Customer* tuples with *C#* = 5, 13, 25, and 23. Likewise, the first, third, seventh, and tenth bit are set in the second bitmap.

The next step is to partition the *Order* table using the bitmaps. To see how, let us look at the first *Order* tuple which refers to *Customer* 4. This *Order* is placed into the third *Order* partition because the bit at position $1 + (C\# \text{ mod } 10) = 5$ of the third bitmap is set. Likewise, the second *Order* which refers to *Customer* 9 is placed into the second partition, and the third *Order* which refers to *Customer* 25 is placed into the first partition. Following this approach, all *Orders* which refer to *Customers* stored in the first *Customer* partition are placed into the first *Order* partition, and the equivalent holds for *Orders* referring to *Customers* of the second and third *Customer* partitions. Thus, the query result can be computed by joining in memory the first *Order* partition with the first *Customer* partition, thereby immediately carrying out the aggregation in memory, and then doing the same procedure with the second and third *Order* and *Customer* partitions.

It is important to notice that in certain cases, *Order* tuples must be placed into two or even more *Order* partitions. In Figure 3, for instance, *Order* 10 (highlighted by bold face) is placed into the first and third *Order* partitions because this *Order* refers to *Customer* 3 and the fourth bit of

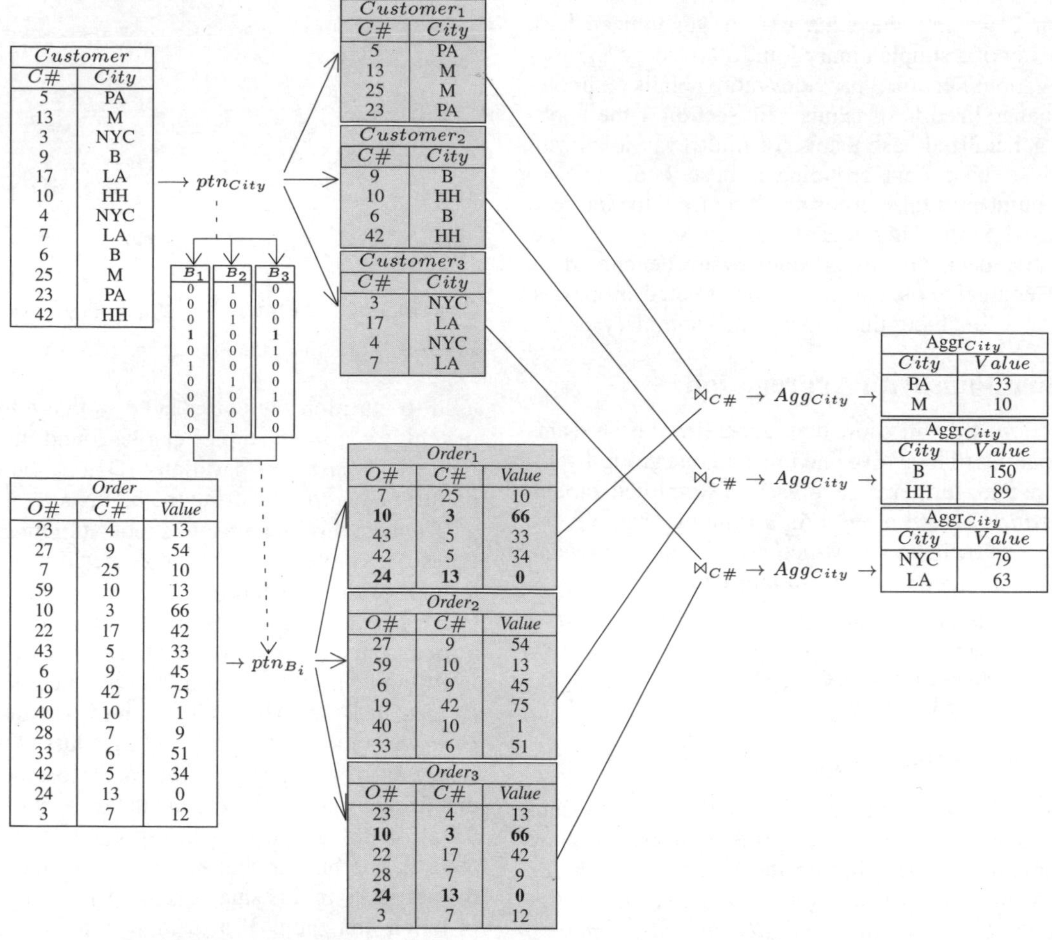

Figure 3: Example Execution of a Generalized Hash Team

the first and third bitmaps are set. We refer to the accidental placement of *Order* 10 in the first *Order* partition as a *false drop*. False drops do not jeopardize the correctness of the overall approach for regular joins because they are filtered out in the join phase[1], but false drops do impact the performance: the more false drops, the higher the IO cost to partition and re-read the *Orders*. The number of false drops depends on the length of the bitmaps, and we will give formulae that can be used in a cost model of a query optimizer in Section 5. Furthermore, *Order* duplicates occur if *Customer* tuples with the same *C#* are placed into different *Customer* partitions. Such a situation does not arise in our example query because *C#* is the key of the *Customer* table. In general, such situations cannot arise if there is a functional dependency between the join attribute (i.e., *C#*) and the partitioning attribute (i.e., *City*). In the absence of such a functional dependency, *Orders* must be duplicated in order to find their join partners in the different *Customer* partitions. In the remainder of this paper, we will assume that such a functional dependency exists or that there is at least a strong correlation between the join and partitioning attributes, and we recommend not to use generalized hash teams in other cases. One example, in which generalized hash teams are not appropriate, according to this criterion, would be a query in which the key of the group-by operation involves a column of the *Order* table, e.g., *OrderDate*.

To summarize, generalized hash teams save disk IO costs for partitioning intermediate query results if these intermediate results do not fit into the available main memory. On the negative side, generalized hash teams require additional main memory for the bitmaps in the partitioning phase, they might involve additional disk IO due to false drops, and they involve additional CPU costs to construct and use the bitmaps. Also, the application of generalized hash teams should be limited to situations in which a functional dependency can be inferred from the join attributes to the partitioning attributes. The optimizer of a database system should, therefore, be extended to enumerate generalized hash team plans (where applicable) in addition to traditional query plans.

2.2 Partition Nested Loop Joins

We now turn to another (novel) approach to execute our example query; we refer to this approach as *partition nested loops*. As with generalized hash teams, the key idea is to partition the *Customers* by *City* before the join so that the

[1] Outer joins cannot always filter out false drops so that generalized hash teams are not directly applicable for all outer join queries.

group-by operation does not require an additional partitioning step. In this approach, however, the join is carried out as a (blockwise hashed) nested loop join rather than using a (grace or hybrid) hash join, and the partition nested loop join approach is somewhat simpler than generalized hash teams because no bitmaps need to be constructed.

In detail, partition nested loop joins work as follows for our example query:

1. partition the *Customer* table by *City* into memory-sized partitions (as for generalized hash teams or any traditional hash join, if *City* were the join column)

2. read the *Order* table, project out the relevant columns (i.e., *C#* and *Value*), apply *Order* predicates (if any), and write the *reduced Order* table to disk

3. read the first *Customer* partition into memory and build a main-memory hash table on the *C#* column. Read the *reduced Order* table from disk and find the *Orders* that refer to the *Customers* of the first partition using the main-memory *C#* hash table. Carry out the aggregation on the fly. (Details on this step can be found in Section 3.2.)

4. repeat Step 3 for the second, third, fourth, and so on *Customer* partition.

Step 2 and Step 3 for the first *Customer* partition can be carried out together in order to save disk IO costs. If no or only marginal selections and projections are applicable on the *Order* table, then Step 2 can be omitted altogether and Step 3 is carried out using the full *Order* table.

The tradeoffs between generalized hash teams and partition nested loop joins are fairly much the same as between (grace and hybrid) hash joins and blockwise nested loop joins; see, e.g., [HR96, HCLS97]. If the *Customer* table is large and must be partitioned into many partitions, partition nested loop joins are likely to perform poorly for re-reading the reduced *Order* table many times. On the other hand, partition nested loop joins might perform better than generalized hash teams if it can be expected that there are many false drops. Also, of course, generalized hash teams require more main memory for the bitmaps in the partitioning phase. This additional main memory, however, is really only needed in the partitioning phase which usually requires much less main memory than the join phase (or the group-by operation). So, the bitmaps can be stored in the *extra* space which is allocated for the join but not needed during the partitioning phase so that the overall main memory requirements of the join and the whole query do not increase.

3 Implementation Details

In this section we will describe the indirect partitioning of generalized hashed teams and the actual execution (join and grouping phase) of generalized hash teams and partition nested-loop joins in more detail.

3.1 Fine-Tuning the Indirect Partitioning Phase

We will use our *Customer* and *Order* example schema to illustrate this discussion. In the initial partitioning step the *Customer* table (abbreviated *C*) is partitioned according to the *City*-attribute into n partitions $C_1, \dots, C_n$. For this purpose some partitioning (hash) function p is needed that maps *City*-values into $\{1, \dots, n\}$. For each partition C_i a separate bitmap B_i of length b is maintained to approximate the partitioning of the *C#* values. These bitmaps are initialized to 0. For setting and probing these bitmaps a second hash function, say h is needed that maps *C#* values into $\{1, \dots, b\}$. Now, consider a particular element $c \in C$: it is inserted into the i*-th* partition C_i for $i = p(c.City)$ and the k*-th* bit of B_i is set where $k = h(c.C\#)$. So, the first partitioning of C is done as follows:

```
forall c ∈ C do
  i := p(c.City);
  k := h(c.C#);
  insert c into C_i;
  B_i[k] := 1;
od
```

Having partitioned C into $C_1, \dots, C_n$ the n bitmaps $B_1, \dots, B_n$ approximate the partitioning function for *Customer* on *C#*. Then, when partitioning the *Order* table (abbreviated *O*) into $O_1, \dots, O_n$ any element o has to be inserted into partition O_i if the $h(o.C\#)$*-th* bit of the i*-th* bitmap B_i is set. Due to false drops, it is possible that an *Order* o is placed into more than one partition. Thus, the partitioning function for *Orders* is as follows:

```
forall o ∈ O do
  k := h(o.C#);
  forall i ∈ {1, ..., n} do
    if (B_i[k] = 1) insert o into O_i;
  od
od
```

We can tune this basic partitioning code in two ways: First, we can identify those *O*-objects for which the inner loop can be exited early. Second, we can increase the cache locality when accessing the bitmaps.

Short-Cuts in the Inner Partitioning Loop

There are two kinds of objects for which the inner partitioning loop can be entirely bypassed or exited early:

1. *Objects Without Join Partner*: For those $o \in O$ that definitely do not have a join partner in C we need not execute the inner loop at all. We will compute a separate bitmap, called *used*, to identify those objects. (This kind of bitmap has also been proposed to speed up traditional hash join operations [Bra84].)

2. *Objects Without Collisions*: For those $o \in O$ that are definitely not inserted into more than one partition (i.e., objects that won't drop into a false partition) we can exit the inner loop as soon as they are inserted into some partition C_i. Again, we maintain a separate bitmap, *collision*, for identifying these objects.

The *used* bitmap can easily be computed as follows:

$$used := B_1 \mid B_2 \mid \ldots \mid B_n$$

where | denotes the componentwise *or* operation.

The *coll* bitmap is set at position k if two (or more) bitmaps B_i and B_j are set at position k, that is:

$$coll[k] := \begin{cases} 1 & : \text{ if there exists } i \neq j \in \{1, \ldots, n\} \\ & \quad \text{such that } B_i[k] = B_j[k] = 1 \\ 0 & : \text{ otherwise} \end{cases}$$

In our system, both bitmaps are actually computed during the partitioning of the *Customer* table. For our example the two auxiliary bitmaps are shown below:

used	*coll*	B_1	B_2	B_3
1	0	0	1	0
0	0	0	0	0
1	0	0	1	0
1	1	1	0	1
1	0	0	0	1
1	0	1	0	0
1	0	0	1	0
1	0	0	0	1
0	0	0	0	0
1	0	0	1	0

The tuned partitioning pseudo code for the *Orders* then looks as follows:

```
forall o ∈ O do
  k := h(o.C#);
  if (used[k] = 0) // definitely no join partner, proceed
                      with next o ∈ O
    continue;
  if (coll[k] = 0) // no collisions
    forall i ∈ {1,...,n} do
      if (B_i[k] = 1)
        { insert o into O_i;
          break; } // this was the one and only, proceed
                      with next o ∈ O
    od
  else // collisions and false drops
    forall i ∈ {1,...,n} do
      if (B_i[k] = 1)
        insert o into O_i;
    od
od
```

Increasing Locality on Bitmaps

We can also tune the storage structure of the bitmaps in order to increase cache locality. We observe that the code for partitioning O accesses sequentially the *k-th* position of every bitmap, *used, coll*, $B_1, \ldots, B_n$. This observation allows us to achieve higher cache locality. Let's view the $n+2$ bitmaps of length b as a two-dimensional array with $n+2$ columns and b rows. To achieve higher cache locality we store this array in a single bitmap B of length $(n+2) * b$ by mapping the two-dimensional array in *row major sequence* into a one-dimensional vector. Then, the only bitmap B contains the elements in the following order

$$\begin{aligned} B = [\quad & u[1],\ c[1],\ B_1[1], B_2[1], \ldots, B_n[1], \ldots \\ & u[k],\ c[k],\ B_1[k], B_2[k], \ldots, B_n[k], \ldots \\ & u[b],\ c[b],\ B_1[b], B_2[b], \ldots, B_n[b] \quad] \end{aligned}$$

That is, $u[k]$ is found at position $B[(k-1)*(n+2)+1]$, $c[k]$ at $B[(k-1)*(n+2)+2]$, and $B_i[k]$ at $B[(k-1)*(n+2)+2+i]$. This way, the inner partitioning loop for the *Orders* can typically be carried out with a single processor cache miss. The resulting organization is illustrated below:

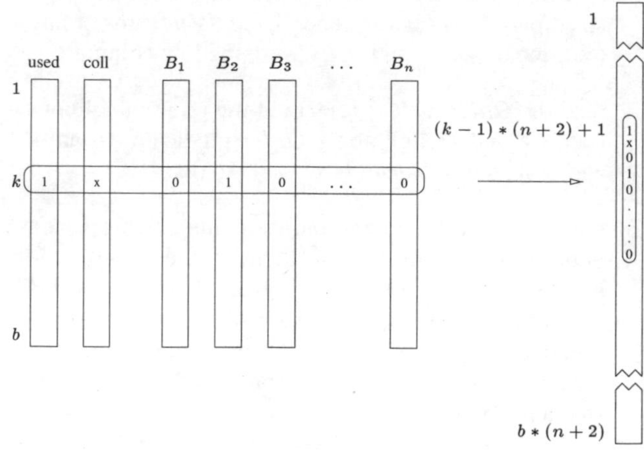

3.2 Teaming up the Hash Join and the Aggregation

The bitmap-based partitioning of O and C is the prerequisite for teaming up the hash join and the grouping/aggregation operator such that the join operator can directly deliver its result tuples to the aggregation operator—without having to repartition the data and write it to disk. The straight-forward implementation requires two separate hash tables: one hash table on $C_i.C\#$ for performing the join with the probe input O_i and a second hash table on $C_i.City$ for grouping/aggregating the join result. These two operators have to be managed by a so-called "team manager"—as it was called in [GBC98]—such that they switch to the next partition synchronously.

We will now devise a further optimization which is based on combining the join and the aggregation operator such that they share a common hash table on the build input C. This is illustrated in Figure 4. Let us first concentrate on the build phase during which the hash table for the *i-th* partition C_i is constructed—shown in Figure 4(a). While loading the partition C_i, two hash tables are maintained: one hash table called *HT_Join* on the join column $C_i.C\#$ and a second, temporary hash table, called *tmp_HT*, on the grouping column $C_i.City$. Both hash tables contain pointers into the *Hasharea* in which the group entries of the join/aggregation query are constructed. That is, the *Hasharea* will contain one entry for every *City* value of partition C_i. Let's look at a particular build input tuple $c \in C_i$ of the form $c = [C\# = 23, City = PA]$ and trace how it is installed in the hash tables and the hash area. First, its $C\#$ value, 23, is inserted into the *HT_Join* hash table; second, the aggregation tuple for its *City* value, *PA*,

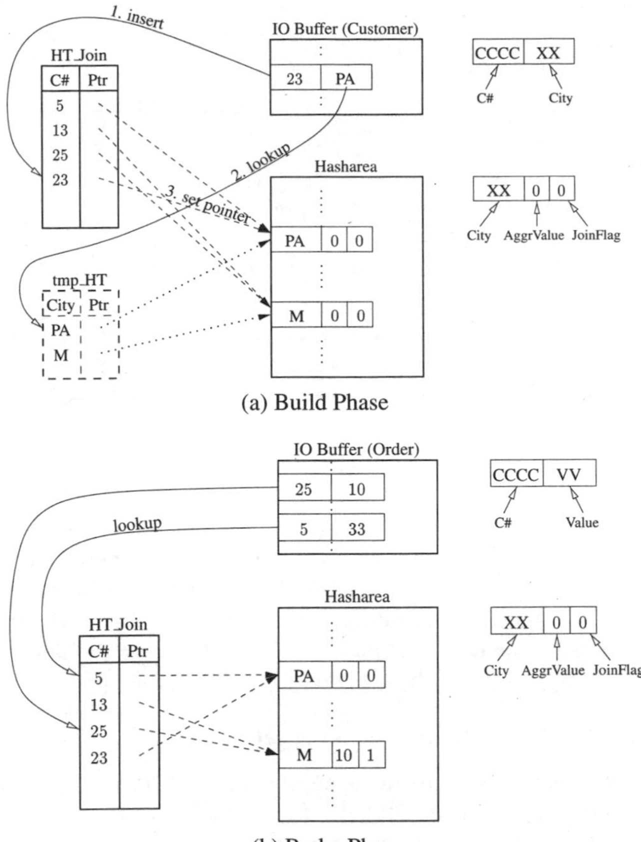

(a) Build Phase

(b) Probe Phase

Figure 4: Implementation of the Hash Tables

is looked up via the *tmp_HT* hash table. If this was the first C_i tuple with *City=PA*, a new group entry is installed in the *Hasharea* and the corresponding pointer is inserted into the *tmp_HT*. Third, the pointer to this group entry of the *Hasharea* is installed in the *HT_Join* hash table. After inserting all tuples of the current build input partition C_i, the probe phase with partition O_i of the probe input starts—shown in Figure 4(b). Let's now trace the *Order* tuple [$C\# = 25$, $Value = 10$]: The *HT_Join* hash table is inspected and the pointer to the group entry in the *Hasharea* is traversed. The *Value* is added to the *AggrValue* and the *JoinFlag* is set to indicate that the group entry "has found" a join partner (otherwise it would be discarded from the result when flushing the *Hasharea* of the *i-th* partition). After the current probe partition is exhausted, the result tuples are retrieved ("flushed") from the *Hasharea* and the computation of the next *Customer/Order* partitions starts.

While this organization sounds complicated at first glance, it is very easy to implement. The advantages are that a great deal of main memory is saved because long strings with, say, *City* names need only be stored once in the *Hasharea* rather than for each *Customer* individually, and that a great deal of CPU costs is saved in many cases because hashing by *City* is carried out once for every *Customer* rather than once for every tuple of the result of the *Customer* ⋈ *Order*. This organization can be used for generalized hash teams as well as for partition nested-loop joins.

4 Multi-Way Joins

Generalized hash teams and partition nested-loop joins can also be applied to multi-way joins. In the following, we will discuss this for generalized hash teams. (For partition nested-loop joins the tradeoffs are similar so we will omit the discussion for brevity.) For illustration, let us look at the following SQL query:

Query 2: **select** c.City, **sum**(l.Price)
from Customer c, Order o, Lineitem l
where c.C# = o.C# **and** l.O# = o.O#
group by c.City;

This is a three-way (functional) join of *Customer*, *Order*, and *Lineitem* followed by a grouping on the *City* attribute of *Customer*. Generalized hash teams are applicable by partitioning the *Customer* table by *City*, thereby constructing bitmaps in order to guide the partitioning of the *Order* table, as in the binary case described in Section 2. While partitioning the *Order* table another set of bitmaps is constructed and this set of bitmaps is then used to partition the *Lineitem* table. After that, corresponding *Customer, Order*, and *Lineitem* partitions can be joined and the result can be aggregated in one pass in memory. After partitioning, the join can be carried out in any particular order. Figure 5 shows two possible join orders for our example; the polygons surround a team of three operators. In the first plan, the *Customer-Order* join is carried out first; in the second plan, the *Order-Lineitem* join is carried out first. One of the arguments of the first join serves as the probe input of the whole team. In our example query *Lineitem* is the best choice as the probe input, because of its high cardinality, so that the second plan of Figure 5 would be better than the first plan.

It should be noted that the memory requirements of generalized hash teams increase with the number of operations that are teamed up. In our example, if *Lineitem* is chosen as probe input we need to keep information of all *Orders*, *Customers*, and *Cities* of a partition in memory as part of executing the team. (Our special organization described in Section 3.2, however, does help to reduce the memory requirements.) In the partitioning phase, memory for two sets of bitmaps are required: While partitioning the *Orders*, the *Customer* bitmaps must be probed and the *Order* bitmaps must be constructed; when partitioning the *Lineitems*, only the *Order* bitmaps are relevant (the *Customer* bitmaps can be discarded at that point).

This Query 2 is a "classical" case for employing generalized hash teams because the join/grouping columns form a hierarchy as can be derived from the functional dependencies

$$City \leftarrow C\# \leftarrow O\#$$

This hierarchy of the relations is illustrated in Figure 6. Indirect partitioning works particularly well for such hierarchical structures because, conceptually, the *cross-relation*

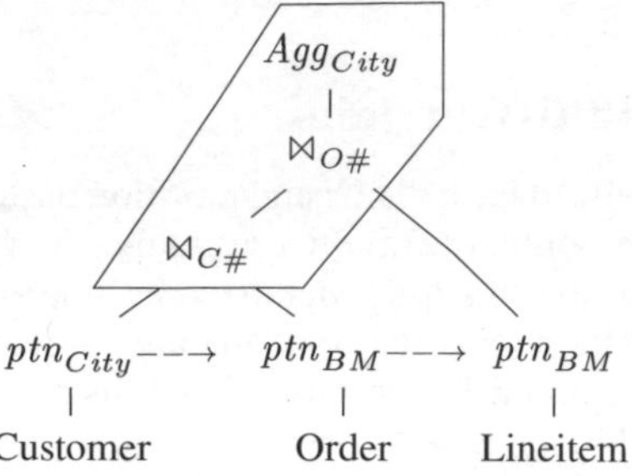

(a) *Customer* or *Order* as Probe Input of the Team

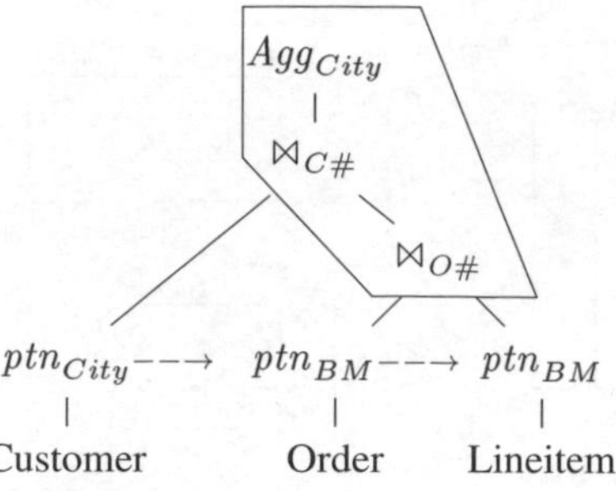

(b) *Order* or *Lineitem* as Probe Input

Figure 5: Alternative Query Evaluation Teams For The Three-Way Join

partitions (denoted as *Partition 1*, *Partition 2*, and *Partition 3*, and indicated by the shading) do not overlap. That is, as part of the partitioning, all matching tuples of all relations could be placed into a single cross-relation partition, and we are able to "team up" the two joins and the group-by operators. This way, we save the cost of two re-partitioning steps that would be carried out in a conventional hash-join/hash-aggregation plan (one for the second join and one for the aggregation). Of course, in practice, the partitions do overlap due to false drops resulting in extra cost, but this extra cost is usually much smaller than the cost of the additional partitioning steps carried out by a conventional plan. We should stress that the generalized hash team technique does not require disjoint cross-relation partitions for correctness—it has only performance relevance. Therefore, it could be applied to non-hierarchical cross-relation partitions. However, the performance gain will decrease as more tuples need to be inserted into multiple partitions.

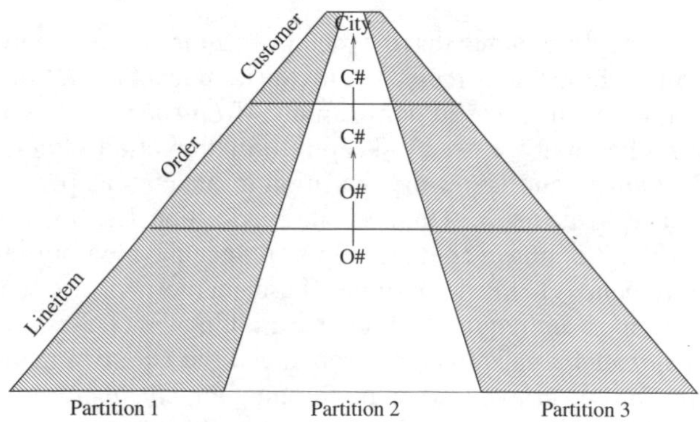

Figure 6: Indirectly Partitioning a Hierarchical Structure

5 False Drop Analysis

In this section, we will devise formulae in order to estimate the number of false drops that occur when executing generalized hash teams. These formulae can be used during query optimization in order to decide whether generalized hash teams are beneficial to execute parts of a query or whether traditional join techniques or partition nested-loop joins are more favorable. In addition to these formulae, the optimizer must be extended by formulae that estimate the overall cost of generalized hash teams (based on our false drop analysis) and by enumeration rules that generate plans with generalized hash teams. These extensions, however, are straightforward and/or are virtually the same as the extensions made in Microsoft's latest SQL Server product to integrate ordinary hash teams [GBC98].

5.1 Binary Joins and Aggregation

We begin and estimate the number of false drops for binary joins such as the Customer-Order query of Section 2. (We will consider multi-way joins in the next subsection.) To re-iterate, Figure 7 shows how false drops occur. The figure shows that the ▲ *Customer* and the ■ *Customer* are assigned to different partitions but have the same hash value for setting the bitmaps. As a result, all *Orders* that refer to the ▲ *Customer* will produce one false drop because they will be (accidently) copied into the second partition. Likewise, all the *Orders* that refer to the ■ *Customer* will produce a false drop because they will accidently be copied into the first partition. If there were another *Customer* with the same hash value, i, and stored in the third partition (not shown), then all the *Orders* referring to the ▲, ■, or this third *Customer* would produce two false drops. *Orders* which refer to the ● and □ *Customers*, on the other hand, do not produce any false drops: these two *Customers* have the same hash value, but they are stored in the same *Customer* partition.

Statistically, the number of false drops can be estimated fairly easily; similar formulae have, e.g., been devised in [Car75, HM97].

To simplify the discussion, we will assume that the join is a functional join and that there is a referential integrity constraint so that every *Order* refers to exactly one *Customer* in the join. (These assumptions can easily be relaxed for cases in which there is e. g. a predicate that restricts the *Customers* participating in the join.) Furthermore, we will use n to denote the number of partitions, b for the length of every bitmap, c for the number of *Customers*, and o for the number of *Orders*. Under these assumptions, an *Order* must be placed into at least one partition, and it is falsely

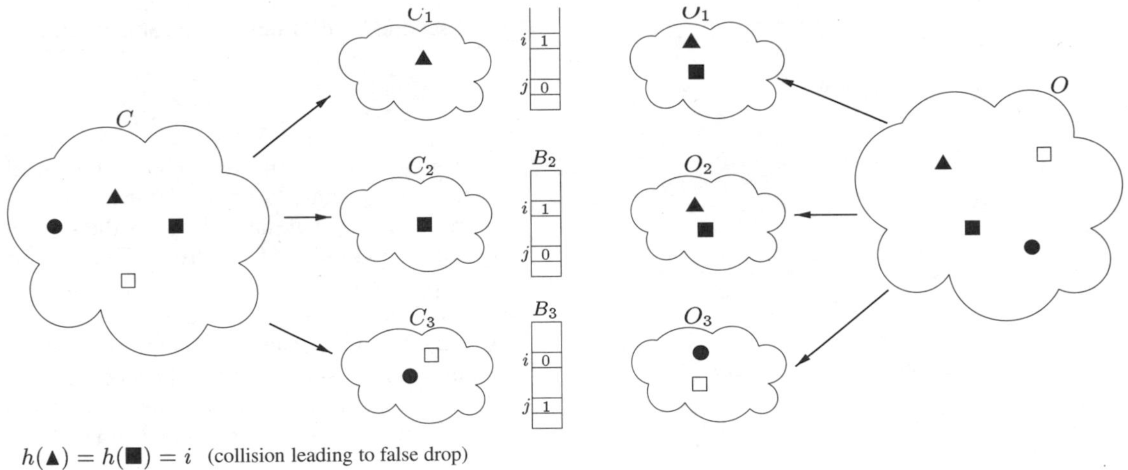

Figure 7: False Drops in Binary Joins

copied into one of the other $n-1$ partitions, if one of the other $c-1$ *Customers* to which the *Order* does not refer has set the corresponding bit in the bitmap of that partition. Putting it differently, the probability of a false drop for an *Order* in a partition is:

$$1 - \left(1 - \frac{1}{n*b}\right)^{c-1}$$

(Here, $\frac{1}{n*b}$ is the probability that a *Customer* sets the relevant bit; $1 - \frac{1}{n*b}$ is the probability that a *Customer* does not set the relevant bit; $(1 - \frac{1}{n*b})^{c-1}$ is the probability that none of the $c-1$ *Customers* sets the relevant bit; and finally, $1 - (1 - \frac{1}{n*b})^{c-1}$ is the probability that at least one of the $c-1$ *Customers* sets the relevant bit.)

In all, the number of false drops for all *Orders* considering all of the $n-1$ "critical" partitions can be estimated as follows:

$$o * (n-1) * \left(1 - \left(1 - \frac{1}{n*b}\right)^{c-1}\right) \quad (1)$$

It should be noted that this formula (and the actual number of false drops) is independent of skew between *Orders* and *Customers*; that is, if some *Customers* generate more *Orders* than others, this fact will (statistically) not affect the number of false drops. This formula does assume that the hash function used to hash the *C#* spreads evenly; if not, the number of false drops will obviously be higher. The formula also assumes that the *Customers* are partitioned evenly into partitions (this is the partitioning function applied to the *City* attribute). If the partitioning function is skewed, the number of false drops *decreases*. To see why, consider again Figure 7 in which *Orders* referring to the □ and ● Customers do not produce false drops because these two *Customers* are placed into the same partition. In the extreme case in which all *Customers* are placed into the same *Customer* partition, no false drops at all occur. (This extreme case, however, is obviously not desirable for other reasons.)

Unfortunately, Formula (1) cannot be used in a practical query optimizer. If c and b are large, which they usually are, computing the result of this formula with reasonable accuracy is prohibitively expensive. Also, computing the (standard) approximation using $e^{\frac{x}{y}}$ for $(1 - \frac{1}{y})^x$ is prohibitively expensive. We, therefore, propose to use the following very simple approximation in order to estimate the number of false drops in a query optimizer:

$$o * (n-1) * \frac{c-1}{n*b} \quad (2)$$

This formula simply estimates the probability that the relevant bit in a "critical" partition is set by one of the other $c-1$ *Customers* as $\frac{c-1}{n*b}$. The simplification consists in assuming that no two customers set the same bit in a bitmap. This formula is conservative: it can be shown that $\frac{c-1}{n*b} > 1 - (1 - \frac{1}{n*b})^{c-1}$. Thus, a query optimizer using this formula will overestimate the number of false drops and will use generalized hash teams cautiously. For Query 1 of Section 2, we measured how accurate this approximate formula is depending on the amount of memory available to execute a query, and we show the results in Figure 8. (The amount of available main memory determines n and b; we present details of our experimental environment in Section 6, the database cardinalities are summarized in Table 1, Page 10.) We see that the estimates of the approximate formula are quite precise compared to the actual number of false drops measured while executing the query. Only for small memory sizes (and correspondingly short bitmaps, i.e., small b), the approximate formula visibly overestimates the number of false drops.

5.2 Multi-way Joins

We now turn to multi-way join queries. Estimating the number of false drops is complicated in this case, and we have not yet found a statistically precise formula. Even if we did, such a formula would, again, probably be prohibitively expensive to compute. We, therefore, concen-

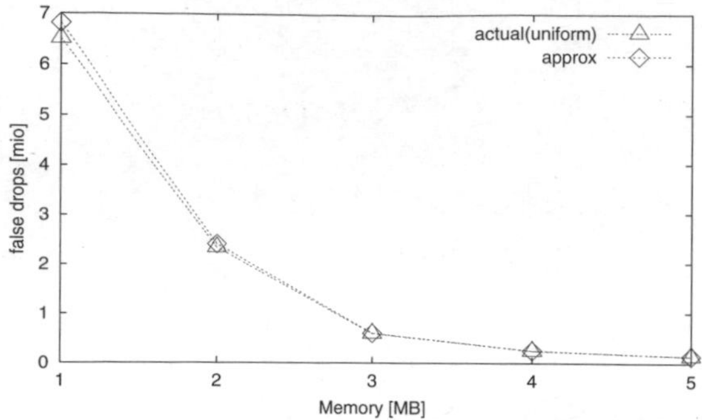

Figure 8: False Drops for Query 1

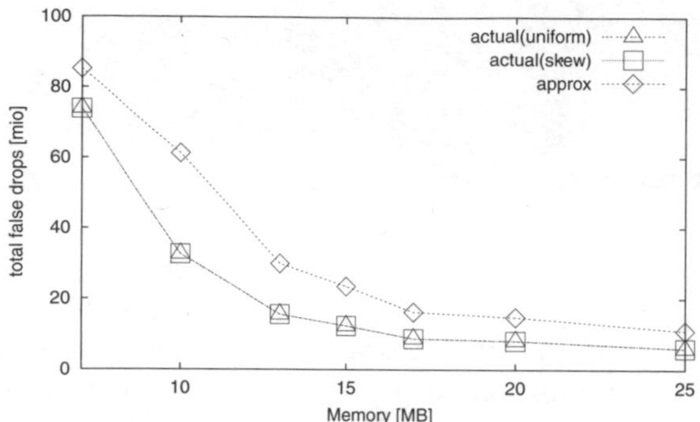

Figure 9: False Drops for Query 2

trate on a very simple approximate formula that can be implemented and evaluated by a query optimizer with very little effort. We will, furthermore, concentrate on Query 2 of Section 4, as an example, and note that our results can easily be generalized to other queries.

First of all we note that there are *Order* and *Lineitem* false drops when using generalized hash teams for our three-way join example query. The *Order* false drops can be computed using exactly the same (approximate or exact) formulae described in the previous subsection. Second, we note that the *Lineitem* false drops can occur in one of two ways:

1. *Orders* placed into different *Order* partitions can have the same *O#* hash value; all *Lineitems* referring to such *Orders* produce false drops. This is the same phenomenon as depicted in Figure 7, just transposed to the *Order-Lineitem* join.

2. False Drop Propagation: If an *Order* produces a false drop, all the *Lineitems* that refer to that *Order* produce a false drop as well. Consider, as an example, again Figure 7. All *Lineitems* that refer to an *Order* which in turn refers to the ▲ *Customer* are (falsely) copied into the second *Lineitem* partition.

The first kind of false drop can be approximated using Formula (2). Using l as the number of *Lineitems* and b_o as the length of the *Order* bitmaps, we get:

$$l * (n-1) * \frac{o-1}{n * b_o} \qquad (3)$$

The second kind of false drop can be estimated as

$$f_o * \frac{l}{o} \qquad (4)$$

where f_o is the estimated number of *Order* false drops, estimated using again Formula (2). In all, we approximate the number of *Lineitem* false drops as the sum of the number of these two kinds of false drops. This is again a conservative approach that overestimates the number of false drops and makes the optimizer be overly cautious to use generalized hash teams because this approach assumes that there is no *overlap* between the two kinds of false drops. (Modeling the number of false drops precisely, this overlap would have to be subtracted from the estimated total number of false drops.)

Again, we would like to note that the number of false drops is (statistically) independent of skew. The number of false drops is also independent of the join order within the generalized hash team. As stated in Section 4, joins can freely be ordered within a team, but the partitioning order is fixed and false drops only occur in the partitioning phase. The number of false drops, however, does depend on the quality of the hash function used to set the bitmaps and on the partitioning function used to partition the first relation (i.e., *Customer* in our examples).

To measure the accuracy of our approximate formula for multi-way joins, we ran Query 2 from Section 4 and compared the actual number of false drops with the estimated number of false drops. For these experiments, we used two different database instances: (a) *uniform* with *Orders* referring to *Customers* using a uniform distribution, and (b) *skewed* with *Orders* referring to *Customers* according to a 80-20 self-similar distribution as defined in [GSE$^+$94]. Figure 9 shows the total number of false drops for each case. We see that our approximations overestimates the number of false drops significantly in some cases; however, for the purpose of query optimization the approximations seems to be accurate enough. Furthermore, we see that the actual number of false drops is independent of skew, as expected.

6 Experimental Results

In this section, we will present experimental results conducted using an experimental implementation of generalized hash teams, partition nested loop joins, and traditional (hash-based) ways to carry out joins and aggregation. We will present the running times of our examples, Query 1 and 2, using a synthetic *Customer-Order-Lineitem* database.

6.1 Experimental Environment

We integrated our implementation of generalized hash teams and partition nested-loops into an experimental query engine that is based on the iterator model [Gra93]. That query engine also provides iterators for traditional (hash-based) joins and aggregation. All code is written in

Table	*Tuple Width*	*Cardinality*	*Size in MB*
Customer	88 bytes	750,000	66 MB
Order	112 bytes	7,500,000	840 MB
Lineitem	72 bytes	30,000,000	2,160 MB

Table 1: Database Characteristics

C++. We installed the query engine on a Sun UltraSPARC station with a 167 MHz processor, 512 MB of main memory, and running Solaris 2.6. In all experiments, we varied the amount of main memory available for query processing. We used relatively small memory sizes in order to simulate a multi-user environment in which many queries run concurrently an only little main memory is available for each query. We made use of Solaris' *direct IO* feature in order to avoid caching at the operating system level. The database was stored on a 9 GB Seagate Barracuda disk drive and another 9 GB Barracuda disk drive was used to store intermediate query results.

Our test database is characterized in Table 1. It consists of a *Customer, Order*, and *Lineitem* table with the usual TPC-D-style schema [TPC95]. The cardinalities of the tables are set according to the TPC-D specifications at a scaling factor of five. In some experiments, however, we varied the cardinality of the *Order* table in order to demonstrate the scalability of the approaches along that dimension. We generated random tuples using a uniform distribution wherever appropriate. That is, the *Customer.City* fields are uniformly distributed among 75,000 cities, the *Orders* referred uniformly to *Customers*, and *Lineitems* referred uniformly to *Orders*. As stated in Section 5, we also experimented with skewed databases, but we will not show the results here because they were identical with the results obtained using such a uniform database. The *C#* and *O#* fields, the keys of the tables, are also generated randomly, rather than just sequentially. A database with sequential *C#* and *O#*[2] would have made the use of generalized hash teams even more attractive because absolutely no false drops would occur in such a database if $b \geq c$ and $b_o \geq o$.

As benchmark queries, we used Query 1 and 2 from Sections 2 and 4. These are just two example queries for which generalized hash teams and, to some extent, partition nested loops are useful. Of course, many other examples can be found and it is just as easy to find example queries for which our new approaches are not useful (e.g., grouping by an attribute of the *Order* table). In all cases, we used the best possible plans (including the join order) and the best possible main memory allocation for each group of operators that run concurrently in a plan. Every operator (e.g., scan or partitioning) that reads and writes data to disk gets memory so that blocks of at least 64K are read and written to disk in order to avoid excessive random IO. For generalized hash teams, this minimum allocation was given to the partitioning operators and the rest of the available memory was used for the bitmaps in the partitioning phase. For the traditional plans (in particular if early aggregation was used), memory allocation was somewhat trickier because it is difficult to decide how much memory to allocate to the partitioning phase of the group-by which runs concurrently with the last join—again, we experimented with different configurations and report the best results.

[2]This is not unrealistic in practice because keys are typically generated sequentially by the application or database system.

6.2 Running Time of Query 1

Figure 10 shows the running time of Query 1 using generalized hash teams, partition nested loop joins, and two traditional plans that use an ordinary hash join and hash aggregation to execute the query. The difference between the two traditional plans is that early aggregation (as described in [Lar97]) is effected in one of the two plans. Early aggregation reduces the size of the intermediate results that must be written to disk in the partitioning phase of the group-by operator. We observe that, as expected, generalized hash teams and partition nested loop joins significantly outperform the traditional plans in the whole range of main memory sizes. The traditional plans perform particularly poorly if there is only little memory available—in this case, the IO costs of the join and group-by operators are very high because many small partitions must be created and thus, the benefits of saving the partitioning step for the group-by operation is high. Note that for small memory size, the number of false drops is also particularly high for generalized hash teams (Figure 8), but the extra cost due to false drops is much lower than the cost of an extra partitioning step. Increasing the size of the memory, the advantages of our new approaches get smaller, but only for very large memory sizes, when the join and/or group-by can completely be carried out in memory, the traditional plans would perform as well as our new approaches. For Query 1, generalized hash teams and partition nested loop joins have almost the same performance; in this case, processing false drops is as expensive as re-reading the reduced *Order* table for all memory sizes.

6.3 Running Time of Query 2

Figure 11 shows the running time of Query 2 for various different plans. Again, generalized hash teams are the overall winner. In this case, however, generalized hash teams are only beneficial if a certain amount of memory is available. (Recall from Section 4 that the memory requirements increase with the number of operations that participate in the team.) For the traditional plans, the best memory configuration involves carrying out the whole group-by in memory so that early aggregation does not improve the running time in these experiments. The traditional plans loose here because they require re-partitioning for the second join (i.e., the join with *Lineitem*). For Query 2, we studied two plans that make use of partition nested loops: the *PNL O, L* plan which carries out partition nested loops for both joins, and the *PNL L* plan which carries out a (traditional) hash join for *Customer* $\bowtie$ *Order* and partition nested loops for the join with *Lineitem*. Both plans show poor performance if there is only little memory available, for re-reading the reduced *Lineitem* and *Order* (for PNL O, L) tables several

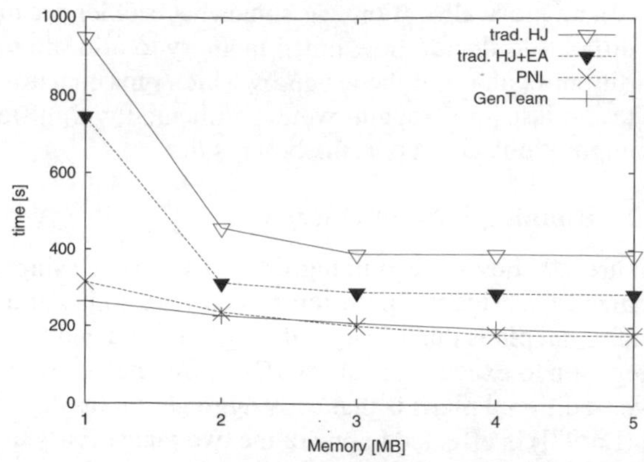

Figure 10: Response Time Query 1 [secs]

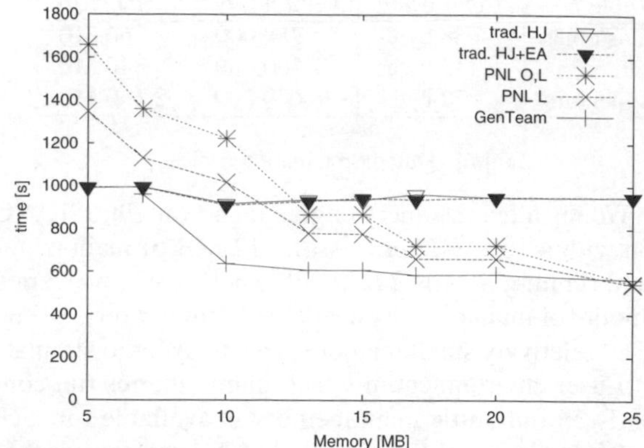

Figure 11: Response Time Query 2 [secs]

times, but both plans become better the more memory is available. All other plans, in contrast, are fairly flat. Beyond 25 MB of memory (not shown), the partition nested loop join plans flatten out as well and show the same performance as generalized hash teams.

7 Related Work

The use of bitmaps is becoming increasingly popular to support decision support queries. In the database context, bitmaps have been used to speed-up the execution of joins in distributed [Bab79, VG84] as well as centralized systems [Bra84]. In these proposals so-called Bloom-filters [Blo70] are used to filter out tuples without join partners. [HM97] use bitmap signatures for processing joins involving predicates on nested sets. Also, bitmap indexing is a well-known concept; see, e.g., the early work on signature files [CS89] or the bitmap indices in Model 204 [O'N87]. Indexing attribute values via bitmaps [OQ97, CI98, WB98] and bitmap join indices [GO95] have recently received renewed attention in the context of query processing for data warehouses. To the best of our knowledge, however, so far nobody has used bitmaps for indirectly partitioning arguments of hash joins (or grouping operators).

The most relevant related work are hash teams, which were proposed in [GBC98]. As stated in the introduction, our work extends hash teams so that they become applicable in situations in which the columns of the join and group-by operations are not the same. Sort/merge-joins and sort-based aggregations can also be used to execute join/group-by queries. Like regular hash teams, such sort-based query techniques are only attractive if the columns of at least some of the join and group-by operations are the same. Generalized hash teams, on the other hand, are applicable and attractive for a much wider spectrum of queries.

Furthermore, there have been a couple of proposals to integrate join and group-by processing and for special multi-way join operators [Ull89, RRS91, CM95]. In [CKK98] we devised a technique for combining sorting and hash join processing. The techniques proposed in that work, however, differ significantly from the approach proposed in this paper, and they would not perform as well as generalized hash teams in the situations described in this paper.

Another line of related work are approaches to optimize queries with group-by operations [YL94, CS94]. Our example *Customer-Order* query, for instance, could be implemented by grouping the *Order* table by *C#* before the join and then grouping the result of the join by *City*. In this particular example, such a strategy would not be beneficial because it would involve the execution of an additional expensive group-by operation without reducing the cost of the other operations substantially. In general, however, generalized hash teams and early group-by processing can be used independently, and they can, in particular, both be used together to speed-up certain decision support queries.

8 Conclusion

Graefe et. al. [GBC98] developed a new hash-based processing technique called *hash teams* which was integrated into Microsoft's SQL Server product. This technique allows to "team up" several join (and grouping operators) that are based on the *same* column. This way intermediate re-partitioning is avoided in quite the same way that re-sorting intermediate join results is avoided in sort/merge-joins.

[GBC98]'s technique requires that all operators of a team are based on the same column. In this work, we proposed generalized hash teams which allow to "team up" join and grouping operators even if they are based on different columns. This, of course, makes generalized hash teams applicable for a much larger class of queries. The key idea is indirect partitioning: A relation is partitioned on an attribute that is used in a later operation and bitmaps are constructed in order to guide the partitioning of other relations which are involved in the next operation. This technique can (in theory) be applied to an arbitrary number of relations and join and group-by operations; in practice, however, the number of operations that participate in a team is limited by the available memory needed to execute the team (as in traditional hash teams) and to construct the bitmaps.

In this paper, we presented details of such *generalized*

hash teams and carried out experiments demonstrating the usefulness of the approach for certain classes of decision support queries. We also presented formulae that can be used by a query optimizer in order to cost out plans with generalized hash teams and thus decide when they are beneficial. Furthermore, we described and evaluated another new algorithm which we called *partition nested loops* and that can, in some sense, be seen as a simplified variant of generalized hash teams. In our experiments, however, we could not find cases in which partition nested loops outperform generalized hash teams, but we did find cases in which partition nested loops perform much worse.

Acknowledgements

We would like to thank Christoph Pesch for his help on the estimation of the false drops.

References

[Bab79] E. Babb. Implementing a relational database by means of specialized hardware. *ACM Trans. on Database Systems*, 4(1):1–29, March 1979.

[Blo70] B. Bloom. Space/time trade-offs in hash coding with allowable errors. *Communications of the ACM*, 13:422–426, 1970.

[Bra84] K. Bratbergsengen. Hashing methods and relational algebra operations. In *Proc. of the Conf. on Very Large Data Bases (VLDB)*, pages 323–333, Singapore, Singapore, 1984.

[Car75] A. F. Cardenas. Analysis and performance of inverted data base structures. *Communications of the ACM*, 18(5):253–263, May 1975.

[CI98] C.-Y. Chan and Y. Ioannidis. Bitmap index design and evaluation. In *Proc. of the ACM SIGMOD Conf. on Management of Data*, pages 355–366, Seattle, WA, USA, June 1998.

[CKK98] J. Claussen, A. Kemper, and D. Kossmann. Order-preserving hash joins: Sorting (almost) for free. Technical Report MIP-9810, Universität Passau, 94030 Passau, Germany, August 1998.

[CM95] S. Cluet and G. Moerkotte. Efficient evaluation of aggregates on bulk types. In *Proc. Int. Workshop on Database Programming Languages*, Gubbio, Italy, Sept 1995.

[CS89] W. W. Chang and H.-J. Schek. A signature access method for the starburst database system. In *Proc. of the Conf. on Very Large Data Bases (VLDB)*, pages 145–153, Amsterdam, Netherlands, 1989.

[CS94] S. Chaudhuri and K. Shim. Including group-by in query optimization. In *Proc. of the Conf. on Very Large Data Bases (VLDB)*, pages 354–366, Santiago, Chile, September 1994.

[GBC98] G. Graefe, R. Bunker, and S. Cooper. Hash joins and hash teams in Microsoft SQL Server. In *Proc. of the Conf. on Very Large Data Bases (VLDB)*, pages 86–97, New York, USA, August 1998.

[GO95] G. Graefe and P. O'Neil. Multi-table joins through bitmapped join indices. *ACM SIGMOD Record*, 24(3):8–11, Oct 1995.

[Gra93] G. Graefe. Query evaluation techniques for large databases. *ACM Computing Surveys*, 25(2):73–170, June 1993.

[Gra94] G. Graefe. Sort-Merge-Join: An idea whose time has(h) passed? In *Proc. IEEE Conf. on Data Engineering*, pages 406–417, Houston, TX, USA, 1994.

[GSE+94] J. Gray, P. Sundaresan, S. Englert, K. Baclawski, and P. Weinberger. Quickly generating billion-record synthetic databases. In *Proc. of the ACM SIGMOD Conf. on Management of Data*, pages 243–252, Minneapolis, MI, USA, May 1994.

[HCLS97] L. Haas, M. Carey, M. Livny, and A. Shukla. Seeking the truth about *ad hoc* join costs. *The VLDB Journal*, 6(3):241–256, 1997.

[HM97] S. Helmer and G. Moerkotte. Evaluation of main memory join algorithms for joins with subset join predicates. In *Proc. of the Conf. on Very Large Data Bases (VLDB)*, pages 386–395, Athens, Greece, August 1997.

[HR96] E. Harris and K. Ramamohanarao. Join algorithm costs revisited. *The VLDB Journal*, 5(1):64–84, 1996.

[HWM98] S. Helmer, T. Westmann, and G. Moerkotte. Diag-Join: An opportunistic join algorithm for 1:N relationships. In *Proc. of the Conf. on Very Large Data Bases (VLDB)*, pages 98–109, New York, USA, August 1998.

[Lar97] P. A. Larson. Grouping and duplicate elimination: Benefits of early aggregation. Microsoft Technical Report, Jan 1997. `http://www.research.microsoft.com/~palarson/`.

[O'N87] P. O'Neil. Model 204 architecture and performance. In *Proc. of the 2nd Intl. Workshop on High Performance Transaction Systems*, Springer Verlag, Lecture Notes in Computer Science LNCS#359, pages 40–59, Asilomar, CA, USA, 1987.

[OQ97] P. O'Neil and D. Quass. Improved query performance with variant indexes. In *Proc. of the ACM SIGMOD Conf. on Management of Data*, pages 38–49, Tucson, AZ, USA, May 1997.

[RRS91] A. Rosenthal, C. Rich, and M. Scholl. Reducing duplicate work in relational join(s): a modular approach using nested relations. Technical report, ETH Zürich, 1991.

[Sha86] L. Shapiro. Join processing in database systems with large main memories. *ACM Trans. on Database Systems*, 11(9):239–264, September 1986.

[TPC95] Transaction Processing Performance Council TPC. TPC benchmark D (decision support). Standard Specification 1.0, Transaction Processing Performance Council (TPC), May 1995. `http://www.tpc.org/`.

[Ull89] J. Ullman. *Principles of Database and Knowledge-Base Systems*, volume II. Computer Science Press, Woodland Hills, CA, 1989.

[VG84] P. Valduriez and G. Gardarin. Join and semijoin algorithms for a multiprocessor database machine. *ACM Trans. on Database Systems*, 9(1):133–161, March 1984.

[WB98] M.-C. Wu and A. Buchmann. Encoded bitmap indexing for data warehouses. In *Proc. IEEE Conf. on Data Engineering*, pages 220–230, Orlando, FL, USA, 1998.

[YL94] W. Yan and P. A. Larson. Performing group-by before join. In *Proc. IEEE Conf. on Data Engineering*, pages 89–100, Houston, TX, USA, 1994.

Explaining differences in multidimensional aggregates

Sunita Sarawagi*

School of Information Technology
Indian Institute of Technology, Bombay
Mumbai 400076, INDIA
sunita@cs.berkeley.edu

Abstract

Our goal is to enhance multidimensional database systems with advanced mining primitives. Current Online Analytical Processing (OLAP) products provide a minimal set of basic aggregate operators like sum and average and a set of basic navigational operators like drill-downs and roll-ups. These operators have to be driven entirely by the analyst's intuition. Such ad hoc exploration gets tedious and error-prone as data dimensionality and size increases. In earlier work we presented one such advanced primitive where we premined OLAP data for exceptions, summarized the exceptions at appropriate levels, and used them to lead the analyst to the interesting regions.

In this paper we present a second enhancement: a single operator that lets the analyst get summarized reasons for drops or increases observed at an aggregated level. This eliminates the need to manually drill-down for such reasons. We develop an information theoretic formulation for expressing the reasons that is compact and easy to interpret. We design a dynamic programming algorithm that requires only one pass of the data improving significantly over our initial greedy algorithm that required multiple passes. In addition, the algorithm uses a small amount of memory independent of the data size. This allows easy integration with existing OLAP products. We illustrate with our prototype on the DB2/UDB ROLAP product with the Excel Pivot-table frontend. Experiments on this prototype using the OLAP data benchmark demonstrate (1) scalability of our algorithm as the size and dimensionality of the cube increases and (2) feasibility of getting interactive answers even with modest hardware resources.

1 Introduction

Online Analytical Processing (OLAP) [Cod93, CD97] products [Arb, Sof] were developed to help analysts do decision support on historic transactional data. Logically, they expose a multidimensional view of the data with categorical attributes like Products and Stores forming the *dimensions* and numeric attributes like Sales and Revenue forming the *measures* or cells of the multidimensional cube. Dimensions usually have associated with them *hierarchies* that specify aggregation levels. For instance, *store name* → *city* → *state* is a hierarchy on the Store dimension and *UPC code* → *type* → *category* is a hierarchy on the Product dimension. The measure attributes are aggregated to various levels of detail of the combination of dimension attributes using functions like sum, average, max, min, count and variance. For exploring the multidimensional data cube there are navigational operators like select, drill-down, roll-up and pivot conforming to the multidimensional view of data. In the past most of the effort has been spent on expediting these simple operations so that the user can interactively invoke sequences of these operations. A typical such analysis sequence proceeds as follows: the user starts from an aggregated level, inspects the entries visually maybe aided by some graphical tools, selects subsets to inspect further based on some intuitive hypothesis or needs, drills down to more detail, inspects the entries again and either rolls up to some less detailed view or drills down further and so on.

---

*Part of the work was done when the author was at IBM Almaden Research Center, USA

Proceedings of the 25th VLDB Conference, Edinburgh, Scotland, 1999.

The above form of manual exploration can get tedious and error-prone for large datasets that commonly appear in real-life. For instance, a typical OLAP dataset has five to seven dimensions, an average of three levels hierarchy on each dimension and aggregates more than a million rows [Cou]. The analyst could potentially overlook significant discoveries due to the heavy reliance on intuition and visual inspection.

This paper is part of our continued work on taking OLAP to the next stage of interactive analysis where we automate much of the manual effort spent in analysis. Recent work in this direction attempt to enhance OLAP products with known mining primitives: decision tree classifiers to find the factors affecting profitability of products is used by Information discovery Inc [Dis] and Cognos [Cor97a], clustering customers based on buying patterns to create new hierarchies is used in Pilot Software [Sof]; and association rules at multiple levels of aggregation to find progressively detailed correlation between members of a dimension is suggested by Han et al [HF95]. In all these cases, the approach has been to take existing mining algorithms and integrate them within OLAP products. Our approach is different in that we first investigate how and why analysts currently explore the data cube and next automate them using new or previously known operators. Unlike the batch processing of existing mining algorithms we wish to enable interactive invocation so that an analyst can use them seamlessly with the existing simple operations.

In [SAM98] we presented one such operation that was motivated with the observation that a significant reason why analysts explore to detailed levels is to search for abnormalities or exceptions in detailed data. We proposed methods for finding exceptions and used them to guide the analysts to the interesting regions.

In this paper we seek to automate another area where analysts spend significant manual effort exploring the data: namely, exploring reasons for why a certain aggregated quantity is lower or higher in one cell compared to another. For example, a busy executive looking at the annual reports might quickly wish to find the main reasons why sales dropped from the third to the fourth quarter in a region. Instead of digging through heaps of data manually, he could invoke our new DIFF operator which in a single step will do all the digging for him and return the main reasons in a compact form that he can easily assimilate.

We explore techniques for *defining* how to answer these form of "why" queries, *algorithms* for efficiently answering them in an ad hoc setting and system issue in integrating such a capability with existing OLAP products.

Product	Platform	Geography	Year
Product name (67)	Platform name (43)	Geography (4)	Year (5)
Prod_Category (14)	Plat_Type (6)		
Prod_Group (3)	Plat_User (2)		

Figure 1: Dimensions and hierarchies of the software revenue data. The number in brackets indicate the size of that level of the dimension.

Plat_User	(All)
Prod_Category	(All)
Product	(All)
Plat_Type	(All)
Prod_Group	(All)
Platform	(All)

Sum of Revenue	Year				
Geography	1990	1991	1992	1993	1994
Asia/Pacific	1440.24	1946.82	3453.56	5576.35	6309.88
Rest of World	2170.02	2154.14	4577.42	5203.84	5510.09
United States	6545.49	7524.29	10946.87	13545.42	15817.18
Western Europe	4551.90	6061.23	10053.19	12577.50	13501.03

Figure 2: Total revenue by geography and year. The two boxes with dark boundaries ('Rest of World', year 1990 and 1991) indicate the two values being compared.

1.1 Contents

We first demonstrate the use of the new DIFF operator using a real-life dataset. Next in Section 2 we discuss ways of formulating the answers. In Section 3 we present algorithms for efficiently finding the best answer based on our formulation. In Section 4 we describe our overall system architecture and present experimental results.

1.2 Illustration

Consider the dataset shown in Figure 1 with four dimensions Product, Platform, Geography and Time and a three level hierarchy on the Product and Platform dimension. This is real-life dataset obtained from International Data Corporation (IDC) [Cor97b] about the total yearly revenue in millions of dollars for different software products from 1990 to 1994. We will use this dataset as a running example in the paper.

Suppose a user is exploring the cube at the Geography×Year plane as shown in Figure 2. He notices a steady increase in revenue in all cases except when going from 1990 to 1991 in 'Rest of the World'.

With the existing tools the user has to find the reason for this drop by manually drilling down to the numerous different planes underneath it, inspecting the entries for big drops and drilling down further. This process can get rather tedious especially for the typically larger real-life datasets. We propose to use the new operator for finding the answer to this question in one step. The user simply highlights the two cells and invokes our "DIFF" module. The result as shown in Figure 3 is a list of at most 10 rows (the number 10

PRODUCT	PLAT_U	PLAT_T	PLATFORM	YEAR_1990	YEAR_1991	RATIO	ERROR
(All)-	(All)-	(All)	(All)	1620.02	1820.05	1.12	34.07
Operating Systems	Multi	(All)-	(All)	253.52	197.86	0.78	23.35
Operating Systems	Multi	Other M.	Multiuser Mainframe IBM	97.76	1.54	0.02	0.00
Operating Systems	Single	Wn16	(All)	94.26	10.73	0.11	0.00
*Middleware & Oth.I	Multi	Other M.	Multiuser Mainframe IBM	101.45	9.55	0.09	0.00
EDA	Multi	Unix M.	(All)	0.36	76.44	211.74	0.00
EDA	Single	Unix S.	(All)	0.06	13.49	210.78	0.00
EDA	Single	Wn16	(All)	1.80	10.89	6.04	0.00

Figure 3: Reasons for the drop in revenue marked in Figure 2.

Geography	(All)				
Plat_User	(All)				
Prod_Group	Soln				
Sum of Revenue	Year				
Prod_Category	1990	1991	1992	1993	1994
Cross Ind. Apps	1974.57	2484.20	4563.57	7407.35	8149.86
Home software				293.91	574.89
Other Apps	843.31	1172.44	3436.45		
Vertical Apps	898.06	1460.83	2826.90	7947.05	8663.39

Figure 4: Total revenue for different categories in product group "Soln". We are comparing the revenues in year 1992 and 1993 for product category "Vertical Apps".

is configurable by user) that concisely explain the reasons for the drop. In the figure the first row shows that after discounting the rows explicitly mentioned below it as indicated by the "-" symbol after (All), the overall revenue actually increased by 10%. The next four rows (rows second through fifth) identify entries that were largely responsible for the large drop. For instance, for "Operating systems" on "Multiuser Mainframe IBM" the revenue decreased from 97 to 1.5, a factor of 60 reduction and for "Operating systems" and all platforms of type "Wn16" the total revenue dropped from 94.3 to 10.7. The last three rows show cases where the revenue showed significantly more than the 10% overall increase indicated by the first row. The role of the RATIO and ERROR columns in Figure 3 will be explained in Section 2.

Similarly, a user might be interested in exploring reasons for sudden increases. In Figure 4 we show the total revenue for different categories in the Product group 'Soln'. The user wants to understand the reason for the sudden increase in revenue of "Vertical Apps" from 2826 in 1992 to 7947 in 1993 — almost a factor of three increase. For the answer he can again invoke the DIFF operator instead of doing multiple drill downs and selection steps on the huge amount of detailed data. The result is the set of rows shown in Figure 5. From the first row of the answer, we understand that overall the revenue increased by a modest 30% after discounting the rows underneath it. The next set of rows indicate that the main increase is due to product categories Manufacturing-Process, Other vertical Apps, Manufacturing-Discrete and Health care in various geographies and platforms. The last two rows indicate the two cases where there was actually a drop that is significant compared to the 30% overall increase indicated by the first row.

These form of answers helps the user to quickly grasp the major findings in detail data by simply glancing at the few rows returned.

2 Problem Formulation

In this section we discuss different formulations for summarizing the answer for the observed difference.

The user poses the question by pointing at two aggregated quantities v_a and v_b in the data cube and wishes to know why one is greater or smaller than the other. Both v_a and v_b are formed by aggregating one or more dimensions. Let C_a and C_b denote the two subcubes formed by expanding the common aggregated dimensions of v_a and v_b. For example, in Figure 2 v_a denotes the revenue for cell (All platforms, All products, 'Rest of world', 1990) and v_b denotes the total revenue for cell (All platforms, All products, 'Rest of world', 1991), C_a denotes the two-dimensional subcube with dimension $<$ Platform, Product $>$ for Year=1990 and Geography='Rest of world' and C_b denotes the two-dimensional subcube with the same set of dimensions for Year=1991 and Geography='Rest of world'. In this example, the two cells differ in only one dimension. We can equally well handle cases where the two cells differ in more than one dimension as long as we have some common dimensions on which both the cells are aggregated. The answer $\mathcal{A}$ consists of a set of rows that best explains the observed increase or decrease at the aggregated level. There is a limit N (configurable by the user) on the size of $\mathcal{A}$. The user sets this limit based on the number of rows the user is willing to inspect. We expect the value of N to be small around a dozen or so.

A simple approach is to show the large changes in detailed data sorted by the magnitude of the change (detail-N approach). The obvious problem with this simple solution is that the user could still be left with a large number of entries to eye-ball. In Figure 6 we show the first 10 rows obtained by this method for the difference query in Figure 4. This detail-N approach explains only 900 out of the total difference of about 5000. In contrast, with the answer in Figure 5 we could

PRODUCT	GEOGRAPHY	PLAT_TYPE	PLATFORM	YEAR_1992	YEAR_1993	RATIO	ERROR
(All)-	(All)-	(All)-	(All)	2113.0	2763.5	1.3	200.0
Manufacturing - Process	(All)	(All)	(All)	25.9	702.5	27.1	250.0
Other Vertical Apps	(All)-	(All)-	(All)	20.3	1858.4	91.4	251.0
Other Vertical Apps	United States	Unix S.	(All)	8.1	77.5	9.6	0.0
Other Vertical Apps	Western Europ	Unix S.	(All)	7.3	96.3	13.2	0.0
Manufacturing - Discrete	(All)	(All)	(All)		1135.2		0.0
Health Care	(All)-	(All)-	(All)-	6.9	820.4	118.2	98.0
Health Care	United States	Other M.	Multiuser Mai	1.5	10.6	6.9	0.0
Banking/Finance	United States	Other M.	(All)	341.3	239.3	0.7	60.0
Mechanical CAD	United States	(All)	(All)	327.8	243.4	0.7	34.0

Figure 5: Reasons for the increase in revenue marked in Figure 4.

PRODUCT	GEOGRAPHY	PLATFORM	YEAR_1992	YEAR_1993	RATIO
Other Vertical Apps	Western Europe	Multiuser Minicomputer OpenVMS		99.9	
Other Vertical Apps	Asia/Pacific	Single-user MAC OS		92.5	
Other Vertical Apps	Rest of World	Multiuser Mainframe IBM		88.1	
Other Vertical Apps	Western Europe	Single-user UNIX	7.3	96.3	13.2
Other Vertical Apps	United States	Multiuser Minicomputer Other		97.2	
Other Vertical Apps	United States	Multiuser Minicomputer OS/400		99.5	
Other Vertical Apps	Asia/Pacific	Multiuser Minicomputer OS/400		99.6	
EDA	Western Europe	Multiuser UNIX	192.6	277.8	1.4
Manufacturing - Discrete	United States	Multiuser Mainframe IBM		88.4	
Health Care	United States	Multiuser Minicomputer Other		88.2	

Figure 6: The top ten rows of the detail-N approach.

Product	Manufacturing - Process	
Geography	(All)	
Sum of Revenue	Year	
Plat_Type	1992	1993
Other M.	9.86	472.84
Other S.	0.02	21.88
Unix M.	7.45	105.09
Unix S.	1.31	16.89
Wn16	3.27	85.38
Wn32		0.38

Figure 7: Summarizing rows with similar change.

explain more than 4500 of the total difference. The main idea behind this more compact representation is summarizing rows with similar changes. In Figure 5 we have only one row from the detailed level the rest are all from summarized levels. By aggregating over Platforms and Geography with similar change, a more compact representation of the change is obtained. For instance, in Figure 7 we show the details along different "Platforms" for the second row in the answer in Figure 5 ("Manufacturing Process", ALL, ALL). Notice that all the different platform types show similar (though not exact) increase when going from 1992 to 1993. Hence, instead of listing them separately in the answer, we list a common parent of all these rows. The parent's ratio, shown as the RATIO column in Figures 3 and 5, is assumed to hold for all its children. The error incurred in making this assumption is indicated by the last column in the figures. In these experiments the error was calculated by taking a square root of the sum of squares of error of each detailed row. Notice that in both cases, this quantity is a small percent of the absolute difference of the values compared.

The compaction can be done in several different ways. The challenge is in choosing a method that on the one hand gives higher weightage to changes of larger magnitude but on the other hand allows summarization of rows which have almost similar changes. If we report everything at the most detailed level the error due to summarization is 0 but the coverage is also limited. Whereas if we aggregate heavily we can perhaps explain more of the change but the error due to summarization will also be high. We developed a information theoretic model for cleanly capturing these tradeoffs.

2.1 The model

Imagine a sender wishing to transmit the subcube C_b to a user (receiver) who already knows about subcube C_a. The sender could transmit the entire subcube C_b but that would be highly redundant because we expect a strong correlation between the values of corresponding cells in C_a and C_b. A more efficient method is to send a compact summary of the difference. The N-row answer $\mathcal{A}$ is such a summary. $\mathcal{A}$ consists of rows from not only detailed but also aggregated levels of the cube. With each aggregated row in the answer, we associate a ratio r that indicates to the user that everything underneath that row had the same ratio unless explicitly mentioned otherwise. For instance, in Figure 5 all Geography and Platforms for product category Health-Care are assumed to have a ratio of 118 except for those in 'United States' and Platform 'Multi-user mainframe'. We need to find $\mathcal{A}$ such that a user reconstructing C_b from C_a and $\mathcal{A}$ will incur the smallest amount of error. Intuitively, we can achieve this by listing rows that are significantly different than their parents and aggregating rows that are similar such that the error due to summarization is minimized. In information theory this error is characterized as the *number of bits* needed to transmit C_b to the user that already has C_a and $\mathcal{A}$. The number of bits are calculated using the classical Shannon's [CT91] information theorem which states that data $\vec{x}$ can be encoded using a model M that the sender and receiver have agreed on in $L(\vec{x}|M) \approx -\log \Pr[\vec{x}|M]$ bits where $\Pr[\vec{x}|M]$ denotes the probability of observing $\vec{x}$ given the model. In our case, data $\vec{x}$ is C_b, the model is C_a and $\mathcal{A}$ and the number of bits is calculated as follows:

For each detailed row v in C_b
  If it already appears in $\mathcal{A}$
    the probability is 1 and $\text{cost}(v) = 0$.
  Else,
    Find its most immediate parent $p \in \mathcal{A}$
    Let r be the ratio associated with p
    The expected value v_b of row v in C_b is rv_a.
    Assume a suitable probability distribution (as discussed in Section 2.1.1) centered around rv_a
    $\text{cost}(v) = -\log \Pr[v_b|rv_a]$.
  Increment the total number of bits by $\text{cost}(v)$

The ratio r associated with any $p \in \mathcal{A}$ is calculated as follows. When no child of p is in $\mathcal{A}$ then the ratio r is p_b/p_a. When a child of p is included in $\mathcal{A}$ we remove the contribution of the child to further refine the estimate of the ratio for children not included in $\mathcal{A}$.

The goal of the sender is then to pick an answer $\mathcal{A}$ that minimizes the total data transmission cost $-\log \Pr[C_b|C_a, \mathcal{A}]$.

In the above cost formulation we have ignored the cost of transmitting the answer set of size N since we assume that it is a user supplied parameter. We can easily include the cost of transmitting $\mathcal{A}$ by assuming a suitable model for transmitting each of its rows. One such model is to sum up the number of bits needed to transmit each attribute of each row as follows: For each attribute find the cardinality of the corresponding dimension of C_a. Since C_a is known to the user we only need to transmit an index of the required member. The number of bits needed for the index is: $\log(n_i+1)$ where n_i denotes the cardinality of the ith dimension of cube C_a and "+1" is to add the possibility of sending "(All)". Once the number of bits needed for calculating an answer set of size N is known, we can select the value of N that leads to minimum total number of bits. Such an approach would be particularly useful when the user is at a loss about picking the value of the parameter N. In such a case, the algorithm could start with a suitably large value of N and finally chop the answer at a value of N for which the total cost is minimized.

2.1.1 Probability function

We use the probability distribution function as a means to convert the difference between the actual value v_b and the expected value rv_a into number of bits. In real-life it is hard to find a probability distribution function that the data follows perfectly. We found that it is not critical to choose a perfect model for the data. In choosing a function we only need to make sure that changes that are significant (contribute large amounts to the total) get more number of bits for the same ratio and rows with slightly different ratios can be easily summarized. For instance, if one row changes from 1 to 10 and another from 100 to 1000, the second change should be considered more interesting even though the ratio of change is the same. However, simply looking at magnitude is not enough because large numbers with even slightly different ratios would have large difference and it should still be possible to summarize them to enable inclusion of other changes that could be slightly smaller in magnitude but have much larger ratios.

For measures representing counts such as "total units sold" the Poisson distribution (with mean rv_a) provides a good approximation because we can think of each transaction as contributing a count of 1 or 0 to the measure independently of other transactions and thus forming a binomial distribution which we can approximate to Poisson when the number of transactions is large [Ham77]. For other measures, the normal distribution is often a safe choice and is used extensively in business analysis when more specific information about the data is lacking [Ham77].

2.1.2 Missing values

Another important issue closely tied to the choice of the probability distribution function is the treatment of missing values. These are cells that are empty in subcube C_a but not in C_b and vice versa. For example, for the cubes in Figure 2 there were products that were sold in 1990 but were discontinued in 1991. In most datasets we considered missing values occurred in abundance, hence it is important to handle them well.

One option is to treat a missing value like a very small constant close to zero. The trick is to choose a good value of the constant. Choosing too small a replacement for the missing values in C_a will imply a large ratio and even small magnitude numbers will be reported as interesting. Also rows with missing values in C_a and different values v_b in C_b will have different ratios. For instance, for a product newly introduced in

1991 all platforms will have a missing value in 1990. By replacing that value with the same constant we will get different ratios for different platforms and thus cannot easily summarize them into a single row.

A better solution is to replace all missing values as a constant fraction F of the other value i.e., if v_a is missing than replace v_a with v_b/F. The main issue then is picking the right ratio. Too large a ratio will cause even small values of v_b to appear surprising as shown in the example below for N = 3. When F = 10000 the answer picked is this.

(All)-	(All)-	749	719
Western Europe	(All)-	-	3
Western Europe	Multiuser UNIX	96	5

The second row in the answer (where v_a is missing and v_b is 3) is clearly an inferior choice compared to the row below:

United States	Multiuser Mainframe IBM	60	12

We handle missing values in a special manner. Whenever we are summarizing rows all of which have missing values of v_a we assume an ideal summarization and assign a cost of 0 due to error. Otherwise, we assume a suitably small value of v_a depending on the data distribution. For Poisson distribution we use the Laplace correction [Lap95] and assign $v_a = 1/(v_b+1)$. For normal distribution we let $v_a = 0$ but use a variance of $v_b/2$.

2.2 Alternative formulations

We considered a few other alternatives in addition to the detail-N formulation discussed earlier and the information theoretic approach that we finally used.

The first alternative was based on the same structure of the answer but used a different objective function. It was formulated as a bicriteria optimization problem by associating each aggregated row with two quantities: a contribution term c that indicated what percent of the observed increase or decrease is explained by that row and a sum of squares of error term e that measured how much the ratio of its excluded children tuples differed from its ratio. The goal then was to find an answer with high total contribution and low total error. This alternative turned out to be unsatisfactory for several reasons. First, it was hard to formalize the goal. One way was to let the user place a bound on the error and choose an answer that maximizes total contribution within that error bound. But then it was unclear how the user would specify a good error bound. Second, choosing a row based on high contribution did not allow compact summarization of the form: "except for a single tuple t revenue for all others dropped uniformly by x%" because tuple t actually has a negative contribution and its role in the answer is to correct the error of its parent.

The second alternative we considered used a different structure of the answer. Instead of a flat set of rows it output a tiny decision tree where tuples with similar ratios were grouped within the same node of the tree. The problem with this approach is that the tree attempts to describe the entire data rather than pick out key summaries as we do in the present approach. This causes the description length to increase.

3 Algorithm

Finding an efficient algorithm for this problem is challenging because we wish to use the DIFF operator interactively and it is impossible to exhaustively solve in advance for all possible pair of cells that the user might possibly ask. Also to allow easy integration with existing OLAP engines we did not want to use special purpose storage structures or indices.

3.1 Greedy algorithm

The first cut greedy algorithm that we designed was as follows:

Compute all possible aggregates on concatenation of
  C_a and C_b i.e., cube($C_a|C_b$).
Initialize $\mathcal{A}$ with the top-most row of cube($C_a|C_b$).
This forms the first row of $\mathcal{A}$ as shown in Figure 3.
For i = 2 to N
  add to $\mathcal{A}$ the row from cube($C_a|C_b$) which
  leads to greatest reduction in number of bits.

There are two main problems with the above greedy algorithm. First, it requires as many passes of the data as the answer size N. Second, there are some common cases where it fails to get the optimal answer. We illustrate two such cases.

Consider the table in Figure 8 showing the revenues for different product categories for the data in Figure 1. We want to find the reasons for the revenue jumping from 9.2 million in 1992 to 287 million in 1994 for the category "System mgmt." . Suppose $N = 3$ for this example. The answer returned by the greedy algorithm is shown in Figure 10. According to the topmost row of the answer all Products except 'Storage Management' and 'Automated Operations' have a ratio of 16.3 between their values in 1992 and 1994. In Figure 9 we show the data at the next level of detail by drilling down to the Product dimension. We notice that for most products v_a is missing. Hence, the ratio of 16.3 introduces error for most Products like "Security Management" for which the ratio is almost infinity. A more forward looking algorithm could single out the only two products 'Performance Management' and 'Problem Management' for which the ratio is finite with the result that the final ratio of the top-row would be infinite as shown in Figure 11. With this solution, the total error is close to zero according to our model for handling missing values (Section 2.1.2). The greedy algorithm fails because it cannot predict the final ratio of the top-most row after removing the contribution of its divergent children tuples that finally

Platform	(All)		
Geography	(All)		
Product	(All)		
Sum of Revenue	Year		
Category	1992	1993	1994
Develop. tools	912.100	1287.070	1793.076
Info. tools	5.807	6.705	33.420
Office Apps	38.405	53.991	97.821
System mgmt.	9.233		278.612

Figure 8: Comparing revenues in 1992 and 1994 for Product Category 'System mgmt.'

Category	System mgmt.	
Platform	(All)	
Geography	(All)	
Sum of Revenue	Year	
Product	1992	1994
Automated Operations		59.108
Change & Configuration Mgmt.		27.905
Performance Management	5.515	66.565
Problem Management	3.718	35.897
Resource Accounting		11.421
Security Management		18.265
Storage Management		59.451

Figure 9: Details along different Products of 'System mgmt.' category.

PRODUCT	PLATFORM	GEOGRAPHY	YEAR_1992	YEAR_1994	RATIO
(All)-	(All)	(All)	9.8	160.1	16.3
Storage Management	(All)	(All)		59.5	
Automated Operations	(All)	(All)		59.1	

Figure 10: Answer returned by the greedy algorithm for the query in figure 8.

PRODUCT	PLATFORM	GEOGRAPHY	YEAR_1992	YEAR_1994	RATIO
(All)-	(All)	(All)		176.2	
Performance Management	(All)	(All)	5.5	66.6	12.1
Problem Management	(All)	(All)	3.7	35.9	9.7

Figure 11: A better solution to the difference query in Figure 8.

get included in the answer. This illustrates a failure of the algorithm even in the simple case of a single level of aggregation.

The next case illustrates the failure of the greedy algorithm even when the final ratio can somehow be magically predicted. This example is on a synthetic dataset with a two level hierarchy on a single dimension as shown in Figure 12. The topmost member m has optimal ratio 1 and the next intermediate level has three members m_1, m_2, m_3 with ratios 2, 1, 1 respectively. m_1 has one large child m_{11} with ratio 1 and several smaller children with ratio 2.5. Initially, $\mathcal{A}$ consists of just the topmost row with ratio 1. The reduction in the number of bits with adding m_1 to $\mathcal{A}$ is very small because of cancellations as follows: The predicted ratio for the children of m_1 changes from 1 to 2.0. While this helps the several small members with ratio 2.5, the benefit is canceled because for the large child m_{11} the error increases. The reduction in error with including any member with ratio 1 is 0. The reduction with including any of the other children of m_1 with ratio 2.5 is small but that is the best reduction possible and the final answer will include two of these children. However, the optimal answer consists of m_1 and its single divergent element m_{11} with ratio 1. This example indicates that another shortcoming of the greedy algorithm is its top-down approach to

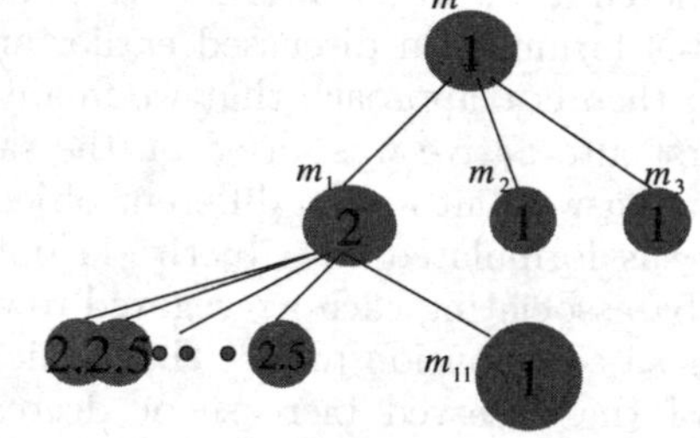

Figure 12: An example where greedy algorithm fails.

processing.

These two examples of the failure of the greedy solution should help the reader appreciate the difficult areas of the problem and it lead us to the dynamic programming algorithm described next.

3.2 Dynamic programming algorithm

The dynamic programming algorithm eliminates the above bad cases and is optimal under some assumptions elaborated next. We present the algorithm in three stages for ease of exposition. First, we discuss the case of a single dimension with no hierarchies. Next, we introduce hierarchies on that dimension and finally extend to the general case of multiple dimensions with hierarchies.

3.2.1 Single dimension with no hierarchies

In this case the subcube C_b consists of a one-dimensional array of T real-values. The basic premise behind the dynamic programming formulation is that we can decompose the set of tuples T into two subsets T' and $T - T'$, find the optimal solution for each of them separately and combine them to get the final answer for the full set T. Let $D(T, n, r)$ denote the total cost (number of bits) for T tuples, answer size n and final ratio of top-most row in $\mathcal{A}$ as r. Then,

$$D(T, n, r) = \min_{0 \leq m \leq n} (D(T - T', n - m, r) + D(T', m, r)) \quad (1)$$

This property enables us to design a bottom-up algorithm. We scan the tuples in $C_a|C_b$ at the detailed level sequentially while maintaining the best solution for slots from $n = 0$ to $n = N$. Assume that we magically know the best value of r. Let T_i denote the first i tuples scanned so far. When a new $(i + 1)$th tuple t_{i+1} is scanned we update the solution for all $(N + 1)$ slots using the equation above with $T' = t_{i+1}$. Thus, the solution for the slot n of the first $(i + 1)$th tuples is updated as

$$D(T_{i+1}, n, r) = \min \quad (D(T_i, n - 1, r) + D(t_{i+1}, 1, r), \\ D(T_i, n, r) + D(t_{i+1}, 0, r))$$

By the cost function in Section 2.1 $D(t_{i+1}, 1, r) = 0$ and $D(t_{i+1}, 0, r) = -\log \Pr[v_b | r v_a]$.

The best value of r is found by simultaneously solving for different guesses of r and refining those guesses as we progress. At start, we know (as part of the query parameters) the global ratio r_g when none of the tuples are included in the answer. We start with a fixed number R of the ratios around this value from $r_g/2$ to $2r_g$. We maintain a histogram of r values that is updated as tuples arrive. Periodically, from the histogram we pick $R - 1$ different r values by dropping up to N extreme values and using the average over the middle r values. We then select the R most distinct values from the R previous values and the $R - 1$ new values and use that to update the guess. When the algorithm ends, we pick the solution corresponding to that value of r which has the smallest cost. Thus, the final solution is:

$$D(T, N) = \min_{1 \leq i \leq R} D(T, N, r_i)$$

3.2.2 Single dimension with hierarchies

We now generalize to the case where there is a L level hierarchy on a dimension. For any intermediate hierarchy, we have the option of including in the answer the aggregated tuple at that level. When we include an aggregate tuple $agg(T)$, the ratio of all its children not in the answer is equal to the ratio induced by $agg(T)$ instead of the outer global ratio r. The updated cost equation is thus:

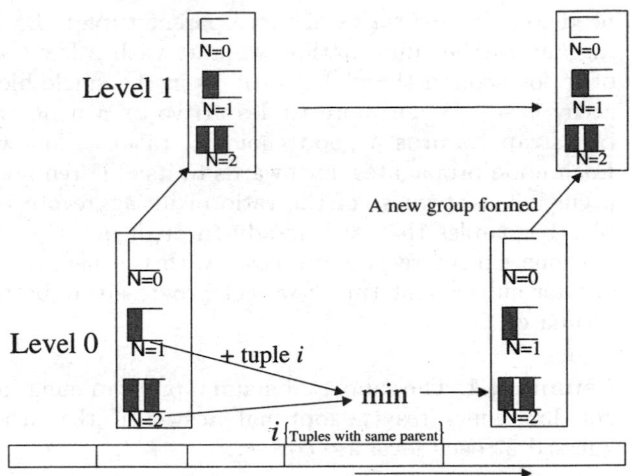

Figure 13: State of the dynamic programming algorithm for $N = 2$ and $L = 2$ and $R = 1$.

$$D(T, N, r) = \min(\text{cost } \textit{excluding} \text{ the aggregate tuple}, \\ \text{cost } \textit{including} \text{ the aggregate tuple})$$

$$D(T, N, r) = \min(D(T, N, r) \text{ from equation (1)}, \\ \min_{\forall r'} (D(T, N - 1, r') + agg(T))) \quad (2)$$

The algorithm maintains L different nodes one for each of the L levels of hierarchy. Each node stores partial solutions for the $N + 1$ slots as described for the case of a single hierarchy. In Figure 13 we show an example state where the answer size $N = 2$ and the number of levels of the hierarchy $L = 2$. The tuples in $C_a|C_b$ are then scanned in an order such that all tuples within the same hierarchy appear together. The tuples are first passed to the bottom-most (most detailed) node of the hierarchy. This node updates its solution using Equation 1 until it gets a tuple that is not a member of the current hierarchy. When that happens it finds the final best solution using Equation 2, passes the solution to the node above it and re-initializes its state for the next member of the hierarchy. The next non-leaf node on getting a new solution from a node below it updates its solution using the same procedure. Thus, data is pipelined from one level to the next up the hierarchy. At each level we find the best solution for the group of tuples that have the same parent at that level of hierarchy. The final answer is stored in the top-most node after all the tuples are scanned.

Next we discuss how to choose values for the ratios for internal nodes. We need to allow for the possibility that a node's aggregate tuple may not be included. Instead *any* of its parent up to the root could become its immediate parent in the final answer. Hence, we need to solve for ratios of those parent tuples. Lacking any further information we start with a fixed set of ratios around the global ratio as in the single hierarchy case. When more tuples arrive at a node, we bootstrap towards a good choice of ratio as follows: Each node propagates downwards to its children node a current best guess of the ratio of its aggregate tuple. For tuples that are already through nothing can be done except re-evaluate costs with the new ratios but for subsequent tuples we get progressively better estimates.

Lemma 3.1 The above dynamic programming algorithm generates the optimal answer if the ratios guessed at each level are correct.

PROOF. The proof of optimality follows directly from Equation 2 since the algorithm is a straight implementation of that equation with different ways of decomposing the tuples into subsets. The optimality of a dynamic programming algorithm is not affected by how and in how many parts we decompose the tuples as long as we can find the optimal solution in each part separately and combine them optimally. For $L = 1$ the decomposition is such that the new tuple becomes the T' in the equation and the size of T' is 1 always. For $L \geq 1$, we decompose tuples based on the boundaries of the hierarchy and T' consists of all children of the most recent value at that level of the hierarchy. ■

3.2.3 Multiple dimensions

In the general case we have multiple dimensions with one or more levels of hierarchies on each of the dimensions. We extend to multiple dimensions by preordering the levels of dimension and applying the solution of Section 3.2.1. The goal is to pick an ordering that will minimize the total number of bits. Intuitively, a good order is one where levels that show more similarity (in terms of ratio) are aggregated earlier. For example, for the queries in Figure 2 and Figure 4 on the data shown in Figure 1 we found the different levels of the platform dimension to be more similar than different levels of the product dimension. Therefore, we aggregated on platform first. We formalize this intuition by framing in the same information theoretic terms. For each level of each dimension, we calculate the total number of bits needed if all tuples at that level were summarized to their parent tuple in the next level. For each level l of dimension d we first aggregate the values to that level. Let T_{ld} denote the set of aggregated tuples at that level. We next estimate the error incurred if each tuple $t \in T_{ld}$ is approximated by the ratio induced by its parent tuple at level $l - 1$ as follows:

$$B_{ld} = \sum_{t \in T_{ld}} D(t, 0, r_{\text{parent(t)}})$$

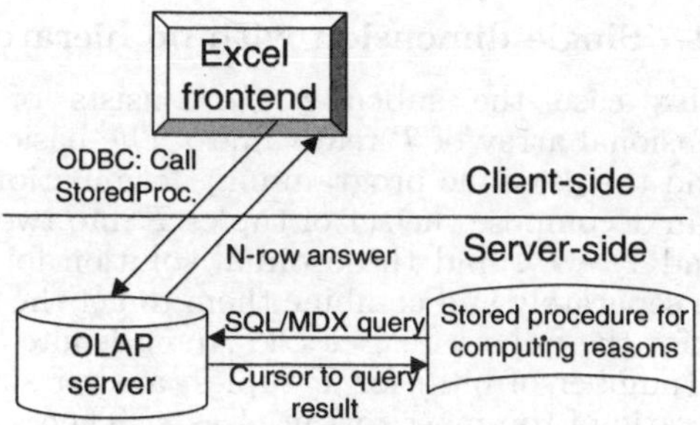

Figure 14: Our prototype.

Finally, we sort the levels of the dimension on B_{ld} with the smallest value corresponding to the lowermost level. Of course, in the final order the more detailed levels have to be below the less detailed level of the same hierarchy irrespective of the order specified by B_{ld}. The intuition behind this form of ordering is that, if the tuples within a level are similar, the parent tuple will be a good summary for those tuples and the number of bits needed to transmit those tuples to a receiver who already knows the parent tuple will be small. In contrast, if the children of a tuple are very divergent a larger number of bits will be needed to transmit them.

4 Implementation

4.1 Integrating with OLAP products

Our current prototype is based on IBM's DB2/UDB database (version 5.2) that we view as a ROLAP engine. We use SQL to access data such that partial processing is done inside the DBMS. In Figure 14 we show the architecture for our prototype. Our algorithm is packaged as a stored procedure that resides on the server side. The client (Microsoft Excel in our case) uses ODBC embedded in Visual Basic for invoking the stored procedure. The N row-answer is stored in the database and accessed by the client using ODBC. The stored procedure generates a giant SQL statement that subsets only the relevant part of the data cube. The query involves selecting the specified values at the specified aggregation level and sorting the data such that the stored procedure does not have to do any intermediate caching of the results. In Figure 15 we show the example SQL statement for the difference query in Figure 2. The data is assumed to be laid out in a star schema [CD97].

The stored procedure is a rather light-weight attachment to the main server. The indexing and query processing capability of the server is used to do most of the heavy-weight processing. Thus, the stored procedure itself does not use any extra disk space and the amount of memory it consumes is independent of the number of rows. It is $O(NLR)$ where N denotes the maximum answer size, L denotes the number of levels of hierarchy and R denotes the number of distinct

```
with subset(productId, platformId, year, revenue) as
   select productId, platformId, year, revenue from cube
   where geographyId = (select geographyId from geography where name = 'Rest of World')
with cube-A(productId, platformId, v_a, v_b) as
     select productId, platformId, revenue, 0 from subset
     where year = 1990
with cube-B(productId, platformId, v_a, v_b) as
     select productId, platformId, 0, revenue from subset
     where year = 1991
select prod_groupId, prod_categoryId, productId, plat_userId, plat_typeId,
   platformId, sum(v_a), sum(v_b)
   from (select * from cube-A) union all (select * from cube-B)
   group by prod_groupId, prod_categoryId, productId, plat_userId, plat_typeId, platformId
   order by prod_groupId, prod_categoryId, productId, plat_userId, plat_typeId, platformId
```

Figure 15: SQL query submitted to the OLAP server.

ratio values tried by the algorithm. This architecture is thus highly scalable in terms of resource requirements. We are also building a second prototype using the emerging OLE DB for OLAP [Mic98b] standard for integrating with any OLAP engine that supports the API.

4.2 Performance evaluation

In this section we present an experimental evaluation on our prototype to demonstrate the (1) feasibility of getting interactive answers on typical OLAP systems and the (2) scalability of our algorithm as the size and dimensionality of the cube increases.

All the experiments were done on a IBM PC with a 333 MHz Intel processor, 128 MB of memory and running Windows NT 4.0. We used thc following datasets.

Software revenue data: This is a small dataset but is interesting because it is real-life data about the revenues of different software products from 1990 to 1994. We discussed this dataset earlier in Section 1.2 and repeat the schema here for convenience. The numbers within bracket denote the cardinality of that level.

Product	Platform	Geography	Year
Product name (67)	Platform name (43)	Geography (4)	Year (5)
Prod_Category (14)	Plat_Type (6)		
Prod_Group (3)	Plat_User (2)		

OLAP Council benchmark [Cou]: This dataset was designed by the olap council to serve as a benchmark for comparing performance of different OLAP products. It has 1.36 million total non-zero entries and four dimensions: Product with a seven hierarchy, Customer with a three level hierarchy, Channel with no hierarchy and Time with a four level hierarchy as shown in the figure below.

Product	Customer	Channel	Time
Code (9000)	Store (900)	Channel (9)	Month (17)
Class (900)	Retailer (90)		Quarter (7)
Group (90)			Year (2)
Family (20)			
Line (7)			
Divison (2)			

Grocery sales data: This is a demo dataset obtained from the Microsoft DSS product [Mic98a]. It has 250 thousand total non-zero entries and consists of five dimensions with hierarchies as shown below.

Store	Customer	Product	Promotion	Time
Name (24)	City (109)	Name (1560)	Media type (14)	Month (24)
State (10)	State (13)	Subcategory (102)		Quarter (8)
Country (3)	Country (2)	Category (45)		Year (2)
		Department (22)		
		Family (3)		

We establish the computational feasibility of answering online why queries. Unlike conventional data mining algorithms, we intend this tool to be used in an interactive manner hence the processing time for each query should be bounded. In most cases, although the entire cube can be very large, the subset of the cube actually involved in the processing is rather small. When that is not true we bound the processing time by limiting the level of detail from which we start. When the server is first initialized it collects statistics of the number of tuples at various levels of detail and uses that to determine the level of detail from which the processing should start.

The queries for our experiments are generated by randomly selecting two cells from different levels of aggregation of the cube. There are three main attributes of the workload that affect processing time:

- The number of tuples in the query result (size of $C_a|C_b$).
- The total number of levels in $C_a|C_b$ that determines the number of nodes (L) in the dynamic programming algorithm.
- The answer size N that determines the number

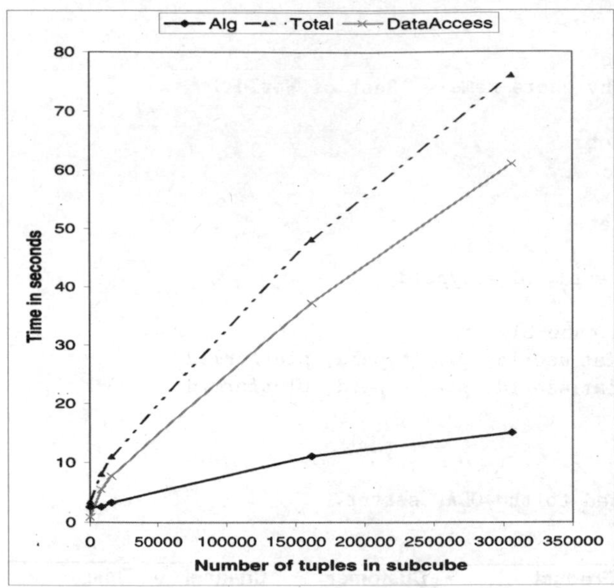

Figure 16: Total time taken as a function of subcube size

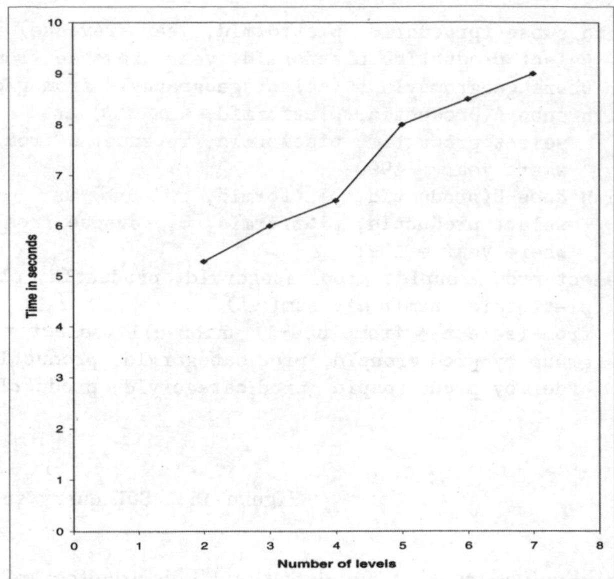

Figure 17: Total time taken versus number of levels in the answer

of slots per node. The default value of N in our experiments was 10.

We report on experimental results with varying values of each of these three parameters in the next three sections.

4.2.1 Number of tuples

We chose ten arbitrary queries within two levels of aggregation from the top. In Figure 16 we plot the total time in seconds for each query sorted by the number of non-zero tuples in the subcube $(C_a|C_b)$.

We show three graphs: The first one denotes the data access time which includes the time from the issue of the query to returning the relevant tuples to the stored procedures. The second curve denotes the time spent in the stored procudure for finding the answer. The third curve denotes the sum of these two times. From Figure 16 we can make the following observations:

- The total time taken for finding the answer is less than a minute for most cases. Even for the subcube with quarter million entries the total time is only slightly over a minute.
- Only a small fraction $< 20\%$ of the total time is spent in the stored procedure that implements the DIFF operator. The majority of the time is spent in subseting the relevant data from the database and passing to the stored procedure. This implies that if we used a server better optimized for answering OLAP queries the processing time could be even further reduced.
- The subset of the data actually relevant to the query is often very small even for fairly large sized datasets. For example, the OLAP-benchmark dataset has 1.37 million total tuples but the largest size of the subcube involving two comparisons along the month dimension is only 81 thousand for which the total processing time is only 8 seconds.

4.2.2 Number of levels

In Figure 17 we show the processing time as a function of the number of levels of aggregation. As we increase the number of levels, for a fixed total number of tuples, we expect the processing time to increase, although at a slower than linear rate because significantly more work is done at lower levels than higher levels of the node. The exact complexity depends also on the fanout of each node of the hierarchy. In Figure 17 we observe that as the number of levels is increased from 2 to 7 the processing time increases from 6 to 9 seconds for a fixed query size of 70 thousand tuples. This is a small increase compared to the total data access time of 40 seconds.

4.2.3 Result size N

In Figure 18 we show the processing time as a function of the answer size N for two different queries: query 1 with 8 thousand tuples and query 2 with 15 thousand tuples. As the value of N is increased from 10 to 100 the processing time increases from 2.7 to 6 seconds for query 1 and 3.1 to 9 seconds for query 2. When we add the data access time to the total processing time, this amounts to less than a factor of 2 increase in total time. The dynamic-programming algorithm has a $O(N^2)$ dependence on N but other fixed overheads

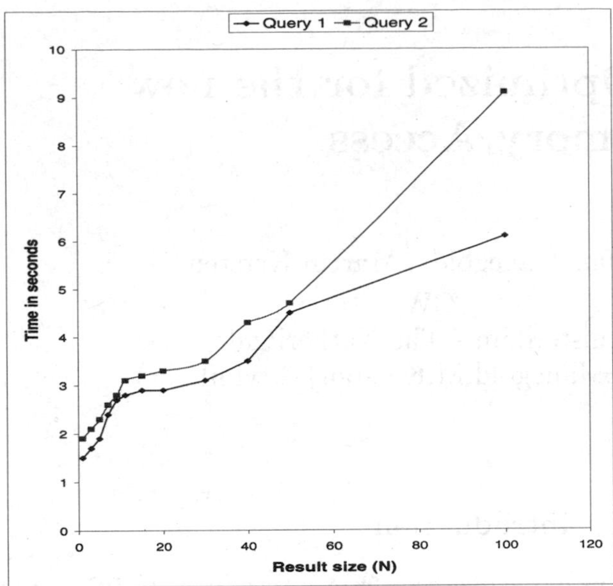

Figure 18: Total time taken as a function of result size(N)

dominant the total processing time more than the core algorithm. That explains why even when we increase N from 1 to 100, the processing time increases by less than a factor of 5.

5 Conclusion

In this paper we introduced a new operator for enhancing existing multidimensional OLAP products with more automated tools for analysis. The new operator allows a user to obtain in one step summarized reasons for changes observed at the aggregated level.

Our formulation of the operator allows *key* reasons to be conveyed to the user using a very small number of rows that (s)he can quickly assimilate. By casting in information theoretic terms, we obtained a clean objective function that could be optimized for getting the best answer. We designed a dynamic programming algorithm that optimizes this function using a single pass of the data and consuming very little memory. This algorithm is significantly better than our initial greedy algorithm both in terms of performance and quality of answer.

We prototyped the operator on the DB2/OLAP server using an excel front-end. Our design enables most of the heavy-weight processing involving index-lookups and sorts to be pushed inside the OLAP server. The extension code needed to support the operator does relatively smaller amount of work. Our design goal was to enable interactive use of the new operator and we demonstrated through experiments on the prototype. Experiment using the industry OLAP benchmark indicate that even when the subcubes defined by the DIFF query includes a quarter million tuples we can process them in a minute. Our experiments also show the scalability of our algorithm as the number of tuples, number of levels of hierarchy and the answer size increases.

In future we wish to design more operators of this nature so as to automate more of the existing tedious and error-prone manual discovery process in multidimensional data.

References

[Arb] Arbor Software Corporation, Sunnyvale, CA. *Multidimensional Analysis: Converting Corporate Data into Strategic Information.* `http://www.arborsoft.com`.

[CD97] S. Chaudhuri and U. Dayal. An overview of data warehouse and OLAP technology. *ACM SIGMOD Record*, March 1997.

[Cod93] E. F. Codd. Providing OLAP (on-line analytical processing) to user-analysts: An IT mandate. Technical report, E. F. Codd and Associates, 1993.

[Cor97a] Cognos Software Corporation. Power play 5, special edition. `http://www.cognos.com/powercubes/index.html`, 1997.

[Cor97b] International Data Corporation. `http://www.idc.com`, 1997.

[Cou] The OLAP Council. The OLAP benchmark. `http://www.olapcouncil.org`.

[CT91] Thomas M Cover and Joy A Thomas. *Elements of Information Theory.* John Wiley and Sons, Inc., 1991.

[Dis] Information Discovery. `http://www.datamine.inter.net/`.

[Ham77] M. Hamurg. *Statistical analysis for decision making.* Harcourt Brace Jovanovich, Inc, New York, 1977.

[HF95] J. Han and Y. Fu. Discovery of multiple-level association rules from large databases. In *Proc. of the 21st Int'l Conference on Very Large Databases*, Zurich, Switzerland, September 1995.

[Lap95] P-S Laplace. *Philosophical Essays on Probabilities.* Springer-Verlag, New York, 1995. Translated by A. I. Dale from the 5th French edition of 1825.

[Mic98a] Microsoft corporation. *Microsoft decision support services version 1.0*, 1998.

[Mic98b] Microsoft Corporation, `http://www.microsoft.com/data/oledb/olap/spec/`. *OLE DB for OLAP version 1.0 Specification.*, 1998.

[SAM98] Sunita Sarawagi, Rakesh Agrawal, and Nimrod Megiddo. Discovery-driven exploration of OLAP data cubes. In *Proc. of the 6th Int'l Conference on Extending Database Technology (EDBT)*, Valencia, Spain, 1998. expanded version available from `http://www.almaden.ibm.com/cs/quest`.

[Sof] Pilot Software. Decision support suite. `http://www.pilotsw.com`.

Database Architecture Optimized for the new Bottleneck: Memory Access

Peter Boncz*
Data Distilleries B.V.
Amsterdam · The Netherlands
P.Boncz@ddi.nl

Stefan Manegold Martin Kersten
CWI
Amsterdam · The Netherlands
{S.Manegold,M.Kersten}@cwi.nl

Abstract

In the past decade, advances in speed of commodity CPUs have far out-paced advances in memory latency. Main-memory access is therefore increasingly a performance bottleneck for many computer applications, including database systems. In this article, we use a simple scan test to show the severe impact of this bottleneck. The insights gained are translated into guidelines for database architecture; in terms of both data structures and algorithms. We discuss how vertically fragmented data structures optimize cache performance on sequential data access. We then focus on equi-join, typically a random-access operation, and introduce radix algorithms for partitioned hash-join. The performance of these algorithms is quantified using a detailed analytical model that incorporates memory access cost. Experiments that validate this model were performed on the Monet database system. We obtained exact statistics on events like TLB misses, L1 and L2 cache misses, by using hardware performance counters found in modern CPUs. Using our cost model, we show how the carefully tuned memory access pattern of our radix algorithms make them perform well, which is confirmed by experimental results.

*This work was carried out when the author was at the University of Amsterdam, supported by SION grant 612-23-431

Proceedings of the 25th VLDB Conference, Edinburgh, Scotland, 1999.

1 Introduction

Custom hardware – from workstations to PCs – has been experiencing tremendous improvements in the past decades. Unfortunately, this growth has not been equally distributed over all aspects of hardware performance and capacity. Figure 1 shows that the speed of commercial microprocessors has been increasing roughly 70% every year, while the speed of commodity DRAM has improved by little more than 50% over the past decade [Mow94]. Part of the reason for this is that there is a direct tradeoff between capacity and speed in DRAM chips, and the highest priority has been for increasing capacity. The result is that from the perspective of the processor, memory has been getting slower at a dramatic rate. This affects all computer systems, making it increasingly difficult to achieve high processor efficiencies.

Three aspects of memory performance are of interest: bandwidth, latency, and address translation. The only way to reduce effective memory latency for appli-

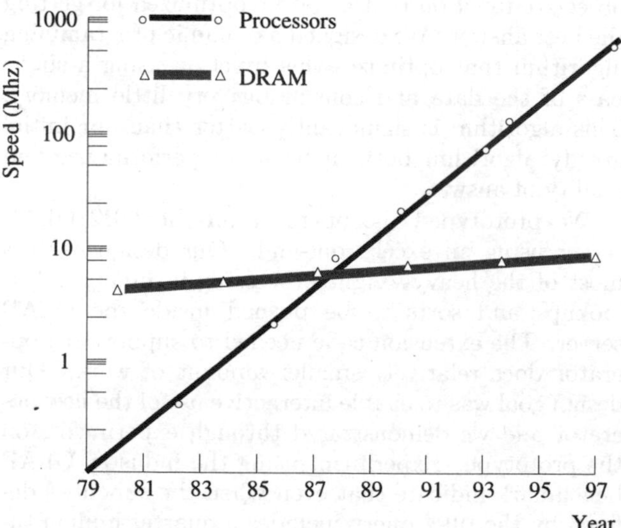

Figure 1: Hardware trends in DRAM and CPU speed

cations has been to incorporate *cache memories* in the memory subsystem. Fast and more expensive SRAM memory chips found their way to computer boards, to be used as L2 caches. Due to the ever-rising CPU clock-speeds, the time to bridge the physical distance between such chips and the CPU became a problem; so modern CPUs come with an on-chip L1 cache (see Figure 2). This physical distance is actually a major complication for designs trying to reduce main-memory latency. The new DRAM standards Rambus [htt96] and SLDRAM [htt97] therefore concentrate on fixing the memory bandwidth bottleneck [McC95], rather than the latency problem.

Cache memories can reduce the memory latency only when the requested data is found in the cache. This mainly depends on the memory access pattern of the application. Thus, unless special care is taken, memory latency becomes an increasing performance bottleneck, preventing applications – including database systems – from fully exploiting the power of modern hardware.

Besides memory latency and memory bandwidth, translation of logical virtual memory addresses to physical page addresses can also have severe impact on memory access performance. The Memory Management Unit (MMU) of all modern CPUs has a Translation Lookaside Buffer (TLB), a kind of cache that holds the translation for (typically) the 64 most recently used pages. If a logical address is found in the TLB, the translation has no additional cost. Otherwise, a *TLB miss* occurs. A TLB miss is handled by trapping to a routine in the operating system kernel, that translates the address and places it in the TLB. Depending on the implementation and hardware architecture, TLB misses can be more costly even than a main memory access.

1.1 Overview

In this article we investigate the effect of memory access cost on database performance, by looking in detail at the main-memory cost of typical database applications. Our research group has studied large main-memory database systems for the past 10 years. This research started in the PRISMA project [AvdBF+92], focusing on massive parallelism, and is now centered around Monet [BQK96, BWK98]; a high-performance system targeted to query-intensive application areas like OLAP and Data Mining. For the research presented here, we use Monet as our experimentation platform.

The rest of this paper is organized as follows: In Section 2, we analyze the impact of memory access costs on basic database operations. We show that, unless special care is taken, a database server running even a simple sequential scan on a table will spend 95% of its cycles waiting for memory to be accessed. This memory access bottleneck is even more difficult to avoid in more complex database operations like sorting, aggregation and join, that exhibit a random access pattern.

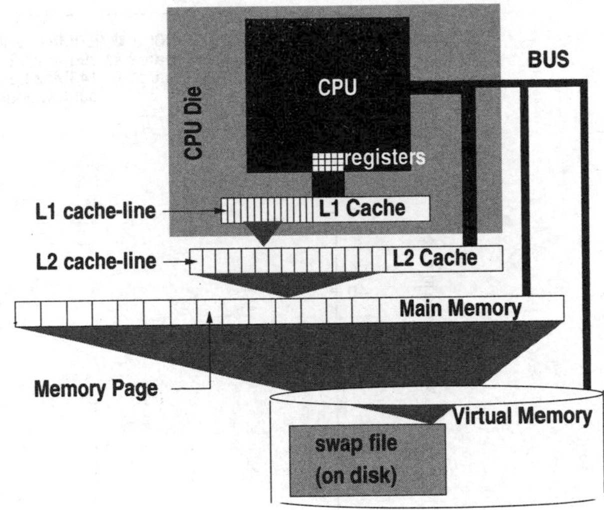

Figure 2: Hierarchical Memory System

In Section 3, we discuss the consequences of this bottleneck for data structures and algorithms to be used in database systems. We identify vertical fragmentation as the solution for database data structures that leads to optimal memory cache usage. Concerning query processing algorithms, we focus on equi-join, and introduce new radix-algorithms for partitioned hash-join. We analyze the properties of these algorithms with a detailed analytical model, that quantifies query cost in terms of CPU cycles, TLB misses, and cache misses. This model enables us to show how our algorithms achieve better performance by having a carefully tuned memory access pattern.

Finally, we evaluate our findings and conclude that the hard data obtained in our experiments justify the basic architectural choices of the Monet system, which back in 1992 were mostly based on intuition.

2 Initial Experiment

In this section, we demonstrate the severe impact of memory access cost on the performance of elementary database operations. Figure 3 shows results of a simple scan test on a number of popular workstations of the past decade. In this test, we sequentially scan an in-memory buffer, by iteratively reading one byte with a varying stride, i.e. the offset between two subsequently accessed memory addresses. This experiment mimics what happens if a database server performs a read-only scan of a one-byte column in an in-memory table with a certain record-width (the stride); as would happen in a selection on a column with zero selectivity or in a simple aggregation (e.g. Max or Sum). The Y-axis in Figure 3 shows the cost of 200,000 iterations in elapsed time, and the X-axis shows the stride used. We made sure that the buffer was in memory, but not in any of the memory caches.

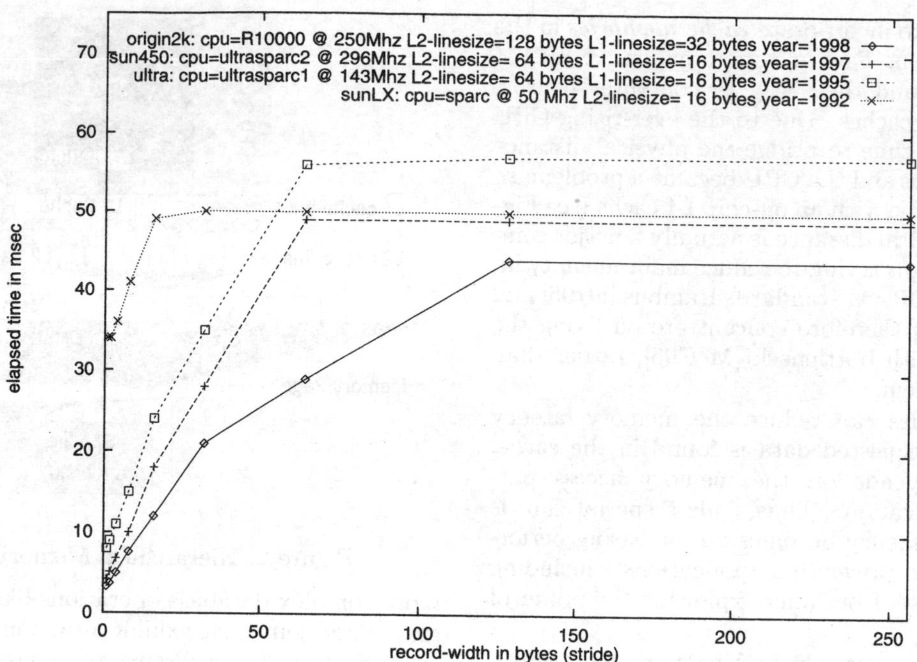

Figure 3: Reality Check: simple in-memory scan of 200,000 tuples

When the stride is small, successive iterations in the scan read bytes that are near to each other in memory, hitting the same cache line. The number of L1 and L2 cache misses is therefore low. The L1 miss rate reaches its maximum of one miss per iteration as soon as the stride reaches the size of an L1 cache line (16 to 32 bytes). Only the L2 miss rate increases further, until the stride exceeds the size of an L2 cache line (16 to 128 bytes). Then, it is certain that every memory read is a cache miss. Performance cannot become any worse and stays constant.

The following model describes—depending on the stride s—the execution costs per iteration of our experiment in terms of pure CPU costs (including data accesses in the on-chip L1 cache) and additional costs due to L2 cache accesses and main-memory accesses:

$$T(s) = T_{CPU} + T_{L2}(s) + T_{Mem}(s)$$

with

$$T_{L2}(s) = M_{L1}(s) * l_{L2}, \quad M_{L1}(s) = \min\left(\frac{s}{LS_{L1}}, 1\right)$$
$$T_{Mem}(s) = M_{L2}(s) * l_{Mem}, \quad M_{L2}(s) = \min\left(\frac{s}{LS_{L2}}, 1\right)$$

and M_x, LS_x, l_x denoting the number of cache misses, the cache line sizes and the (cache) memory access latencies for each level, respectively.

While all machines exhibit the same pattern of performance degradation with decreasing data locality, Figure 3 clearly shows that the penalty for poor memory cache usage has dramatically increased in the last six years. The CPU speed has improved by almost an order of magnitude, but the memory access latencies have hardly changed. In fact, we must draw the sad conclusion that if no attention is paid in query processing to data locality, all advances in CPU power are neutralized due to the memory access bottleneck. The considerable growth of memory bandwidth—reflected in the growing cache line sizes[1]—does not solve the problem if data locality is low.

This trend of improvement in bandwidth but standstill in latency [htt96, htt97] is expected to continue, with no real solutions in sight. The work in [Mow94] has proposed to hide memory latency behind CPU work by issuing *prefetch* instructions, before data is going to be accessed. The effectiveness of this technique for database applications is, however, limited due to the fact that the amount of CPU work per memory access tends to be small in database operations (e.g., the CPU work in our select-experiment requires only 4 cycles on the Origin2000). Another proposal [MKW+98] has been to make the caching system of a computer configurable, allowing the programmer to give a "cache-hint" by specifying the memory-access stride that is going to be used on a region. Only the specified data would then be fetched; hence optimizing bandwidth usage. Such a proposal has not yet been considered for custom hardware, however, let alone in OS and compiler tools that would need to provide the possibility to incorporate such hints for user-programs.

[1] In one memory fetch, the Origin2000 gets 128 bytes, whereas the Sun LX gets only 16; an improvement of factor 8.

3 Architectural Consequences

In the previous sections we have shown that it is less and less appropriate to think of the main memory of a computer system as "random access" memory. In this section, we analyze the consequences for both data structures and algorithms used in database systems.

3.1 Data Structures

The default physical tuple representation is a consecutive byte sequence, which must always be accessed by the bottom operators in a query evaluation tree (typically selections or projections). In the case of sequential scan, we have seen that performance is strongly determined by the record-width (the position on the X-axis of Figure 3). This width quickly becomes too large, hence performance decreases (e.g., an Item tuple, as shown in Figure 4, occupies at least 80 bytes on relational systems). To achieve better performance, a smaller stride is needed, and for this purpose we recommend using **vertically decomposed** data structures.

Monet uses the Decomposed Storage Model [CK85], storing each column of a relational table in a separate binary table, called a Binary Association Table (BAT). A BAT is represented in memory as an array of fixed-size two-field records [OID,value], or Binary UNits (BUN). Their width is typically 8 bytes.

In the case of the Origin2000 machine, we deduce from Figure 3 that a scan-selection on a table with stride 8 takes 10 CPU cycles per iteration, whereas a stride of 1 takes only 4 cycles. In other words, in a simple range-select, there is so little CPU work per tuple (4 cycles) that the memory access cost for a stride of 8 still weighs quite heavily (6 cycles). Therefore we have found it useful in Monet to apply two space optimizations that further reduce the per-tuple memory requirements in BATs:

virtual-OIDs Generally, when decomposing a relational table, we get an identical system-generated column of OIDs in all decomposition BATs, which is *dense and ascending* (e.g. 1000, 1001, ..., 1007). In such BATs, Monet computes the OID-values on-the-fly when they are accessed using positional lookup of the BUN, and avoids allocating the 4-byte OID field. This is called a "virtual-OID" or VOID column. Apart from reducing memory requirements by half, this optimization is also beneficial when joins or semi-joins are performed on OID columns.[2] When one of the join columns is VOID, Monet uses positional lookup instead of e.g., hash-lookup; effectively eliminating all join cost.

[2]The projection phase in query processing typically leads in Monet to additional "tuple-reconstruction" joins on OID columns, that are caused by the fact that tuples are decomposed into multiple BATs.

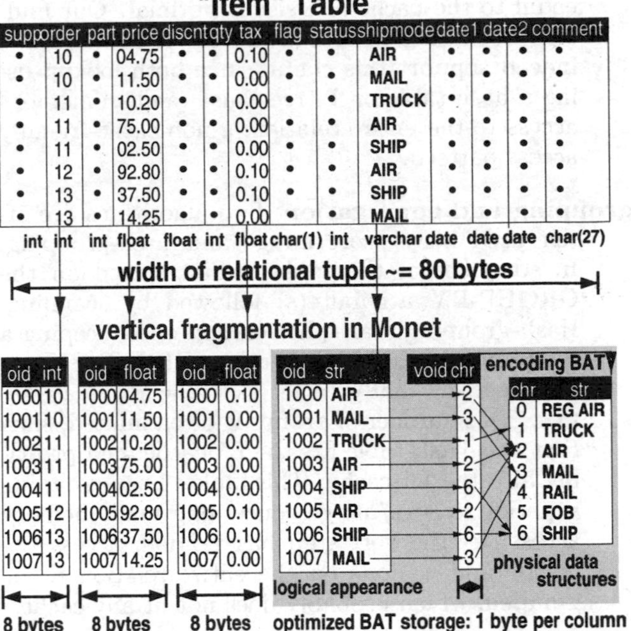

Figure 4: Vertically Decomposed Storage in BATs

byte-encodings Database columns often have a low domain cardinality. For such columns, Monet uses fixed-size encodings in 1- or 2-byte integer values. This simple technique was chosen because it does not require decoding effort when the values are used (e.g., a selection on a string "MAIL" can be re-mapped to a selection on a byte with value 3). A more complex scheme (e.g., using bit-compression) might yield even more memory savings, but the decoding-step required whenever values are accessed can quickly become counterproductive due to extra CPU effort. Even if decoding would just cost a handful of cycles for each tuple, this would more than double the amount of CPU effort in simple database operations, like the range-select from our experiment.

Figure 4 shows that when applying both techniques; the storage needed for 1 BUN in the "shipmode" column is reduced from 8 bytes to just one.

3.2 Query Processing Algorithms

We now shortly discuss the effect of the memory access bottleneck on the design of algorithms for common query processing operators.

selections If the selectivity is low; most data needs to be visited and this is best done with a scan-select (it has optimal data locality). For higher selectivities, Lehman and Carey [LC86] concluded that the T-tree and bucket-chained hash-table were the best data structures for accelerating selections in main-memory databases. The work in [Ron98] reports, however, that a B-tree with a block-size equal to the cache line size is optimal. Our findings about the increased impact of cache misses indeed support this claim, since both lookup using a hash-table or T-tree cause random memory access to the entire relation; a non cache-friendly access pattern.

grouping and aggregation Two algorithms are often used here: sort/merge and hash-grouping. In sort/merge, the table is first sorted on the GROUP-BY attribute(s) followed by scanning. Hash-grouping scans the relation once, keeping a temporary hash-table where the GROUP-BY values are a key that give access to the aggregate totals. This number of groups is often limited, such that this hash-table fits the L2 cache, and probably also the L1 cache. This makes hash-grouping superior to sort/merge concerning main-memory access; as the sort step has random access behavior and is done on the entire relation to be grouped, which probably does not fit any cache.

equi-joins Hash-join has long been the preferred main-memory join algorithm. It first builds a hash table on the smaller relation (the inner relation). The outer relation is then scanned; and for each tuple a hash-lookup is done to find the matching tuples. If this inner relation plus the hash table does not fit in any memory cache, a performance problem occurs, due to the random access pattern. Merge-join is not a viable alternative as it requires sorting on both relations first, which would cause random access over even a larger memory region.

Consequently, we identify join as the most problematic operator, therefore we investigate possible alternatives that can get optimal performance out of a hierarchical memory system.

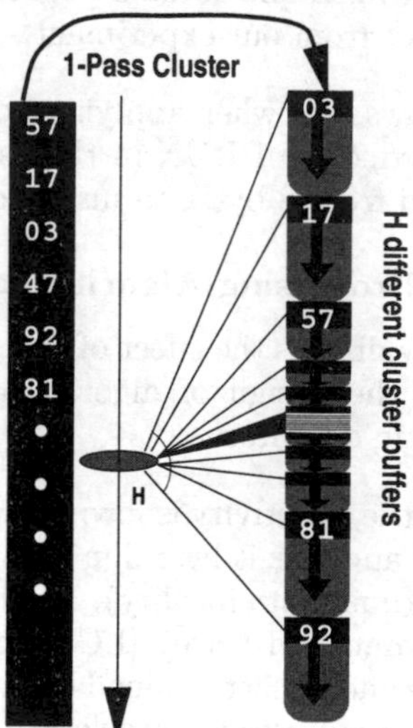

Figure 5: Straightforward clustering algorithm

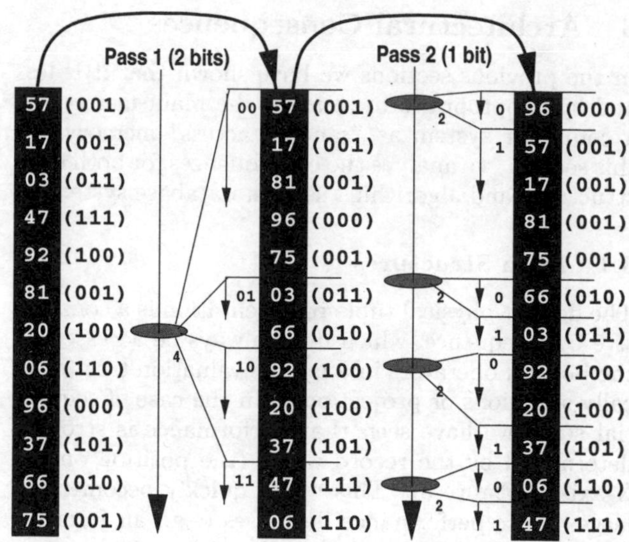

Figure 6: 2-pass/3-bit Radix Cluster (lower bits indicated between parentheses)

3.3 Clustered Hash-Join

Shatdahl et al. [SKN94] showed that a main-memory variant of Grace Join, in which both relations are first partitioned on hash-number into H separate *clusters*, that each fit the memory cache, performs better than normal bucket-chained hash join. This work employs a straightforward clustering-algorithm that simply scans the relation to be clustered once, inserting each scanned tuple in one of the clusters, as depicted in Figure 5. This constitutes a random access pattern that writes into H separate locations. If H exceeds the number available cache lines (L1 or L2), *cache trashing* occurs, or if H exceeds the number of TLB entries, the number of TLB misses will explode. Both factors will severely degrade overall join performance.

As an improvement over this straightforward algorithm, we propose a clustering algorithm that has a cache-friendly memory access pattern, even for high values of H.

3.3.1 Radix Algorithms

The **radix-cluster** algorithm splits a relation into H clusters using multiple passes (see Fig. 6). Radix-clustering on the lower B bits of the integer hash-value of a column is done in P sequential passes, in which each pass clusters tuples on B_p bits, starting with the leftmost bits ($\sum_1^P B_p = B$). The number of clusters created by the radix-cluster is $H = \prod_1^P H_p$, where each pass subdivides each cluster into $H_p = 2^{B_p}$ new ones. When the algorithm starts, the entire relation is considered as one cluster, and is subdivided in $H_1 = 2^{B_1}$ clusters. The next pass takes these clusters and subdivides each in $H_2 = 2^{B_2}$ new ones, yielding $H_1 * H_2$ clusters in total, etc.. Note that with $P = 1$, radix-cluster behaves like the straightforward algorithm.

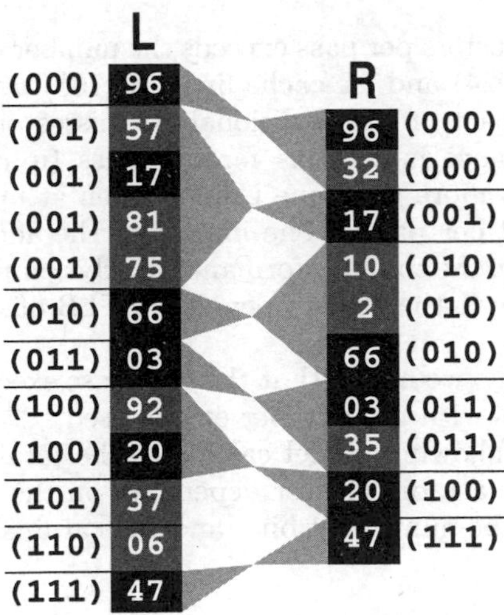

Figure 7: Joining 3-bit Radix-Clustered Inputs (black tuples hit)

The interesting property of the radix-cluster is that the number of randomly accessed regions H_x can be kept low; while still a high overall number of H clusters can be achieved using multiple passes. More specifically, if we keep $H_x = 2^{B_x}$ smaller than the number of cache lines, we avoid cache trashing altogether.

After radix-clustering a column on B bits, all tuples that have the same B lowest bits in its column hash-value, appear consecutively in the relation, typically forming chunks of $C/2^B$ tuples. It is therefore not strictly necessary to store the cluster boundaries in some additional data structure; an algorithm scanning a radix-clustered relation can determine the cluster boundaries by looking at these lower B "radix-bits". This allows very fine clusterings without introducing overhead by large boundary structures. It is interesting to note that a radix-clustered relation is in fact *ordered* on radix-bits. When using this algorithm in the partitioned hash-join, we exploit this property, by performing a merge step on the radix-bits of both radix-clustered relations to get the pairs of clusters that should be hash-joined with each other.

The alternative **radix-join** algorithm, also proposed here, makes use of the very fine clustering capabilities of radix-cluster. If the number of clusters H is high, the radix-clustering has brought the potentially matching tuples near to each other. As chunk sizes are small, a simple nested loop is then sufficient to filter out the matching tuples. Radix-join is similar to hash-join in the sense that the number H should be tuned to be the relation cardinality C divided by a small constant; just like the length of the bucket-chain in a hash-table. If this constant gets down to 1, radix-join degenerates to sort/merge-join, with radix-sort [Knu68] employed in the sorting phase.

```
partitioned-hashjoin(L, R, H):
  radix-cluster(L,H)
  radix-cluster(R,H)
  FOREACH cluster IN [1..H]
    hash-join(L[c], R[c])
radix-join(L, R, H):
  radix-cluster(L,H)
  radix-cluster(R,H)
  FOREACH cluster IN [1..H]
    nested-loop(L[c], R[c])
```

Figure 8: Join Algorithms Employed

3.4 Quantitative Assessment

The radix-cluster algorithm presented in the previous section provides three tuning parameters:

1. the number of bits used for clustering (B), implying the number of clusters $H = 2^B$,
2. the number of passes used during clustering (P),
3. the number of bits used per clustering pass (B_p).

In the following, we present an exhaustive series of experiments to analyze the performance impact of different settings of these parameters. After establishing which parameters settings are optimal for radix-clustering a relation on B bits, we turn our attention to the performance of the join algorithms with varying values of B. Finally, these two experiments are combined to gain insight in overall join performance.

3.4.1 Experimental Setup

In our experiments, we use binary relations (BATs) of 8 bytes wide tuples and varying cardinalities, consisting of uniformly distributed unique random numbers. In the join-experiments, the join hit-rate is one, and the result of a join is a BAT that contains the [OID,OID] combinations of matching tuples (i.e., a join-index [Val87]). Subsequent tuple reconstruction is cheap in Monet, and equal for all algorithms, so just like in [SKN94] we do not include it in our comparison.

The experiments were carried out with an Origin2000 machine on one 250Mhz MIPS R10000 processor. This system has 32Kb of L1 cache, consisting of 1024 lines of 32 bytes, 4MB of L2 cache, consisting of 32,768 lines of 128 bytes, and sufficient main memory to hold all data structures. Further, this system uses a page size of 16Kb and has 64 TLB entries. We used the hardware event counters of the MIPS R10000 CPU [Sil97] to get exact data on the number of cycles, TLB misses, L1 misses and L2 misses during these experiments.[3] Using the data from the experiments, we formulate an analytical main-memory cost model, that quantifies query cost in terms of these hardware events.

[3]The Intel Pentium family, SUN UltraSparc, and DEC Alpha provide similar counters.

3.4.2 Radix Cluster

To analyze the impact of all three parameters (B, P, B_p) on radix clustering, we conduct two series of experiments, keeping one parameter fixed and varying the remaining two.

First, we conduct experiments with various numbers of bits and passes, distributing the bits evenly across the passes. The points in Figure 9 depict the results for a BAT of 8M tuples—the remaining cardinalities ($\leq$ 64M) behave the same way. Up to 6 bits, using just one pass yields the best performance (cf. "millisecs"). Then, as the number of clusters to be filled concurrently exceeds the number of TLB entries (64), the number of TLB misses increases tremendously (cf. "TLB misses"), decreasing the performance. With more than 6 bits, two passes perform better than one. The costs of an additional pass are more than compensated by having significantly less TLB misses in each pass using half the number of bits. Analogously, three passes should be used with more than 12 bits, and four passes with more than 18 bits. Thus, the number of clusters per pass is limited to at most the number of TLB entries. A second more moderate increase in TLB misses occurs when the number of clusters exceeds the number of L2 cache lines, a behavior which we cannot really explain.

Similarly, the number of L1 cache misses and L2 cache misses significantly increases whenever the number of clusters per pass exceeds the number of L1 cache lines (1024) and L2 cache lines (32,768), respectively. The impact of the additional L2 misses on the total performance is obvious for one pass (it doesn't occur with more than one pass, as then at most 13 bits are used per pass). The impact of the additional L1 misses on the total performance nearly completely vanishes due to the heavier penalty of TLB misses and L2 misses.

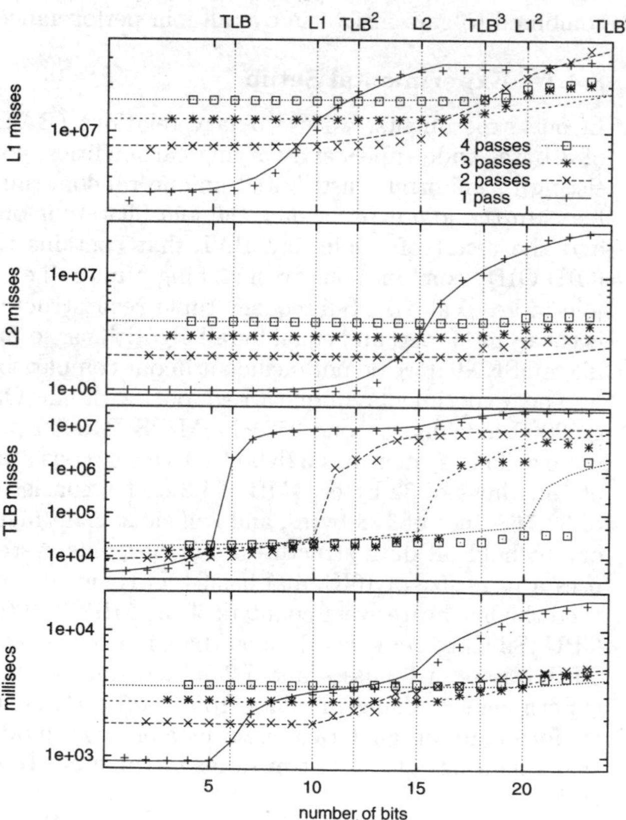

Figure 9: Performance and Model of Radix-Cluster

Finally, we notice that the best-case execution time increases with the number of bits used.

The following model calculates the total execution costs for a radix cluster depending on the number of passes, the number of bits, and the cardinality:

$$T_c(P,B,C) = P * \left(C * w_c + M_{L1,c}\left(\frac{B}{P}, C\right) * l_{L2} + M_{L2,c}\left(\frac{B}{P}, C\right) * l_{Mem} + M_{TLB,c}\left(\frac{B}{P}, C\right) * l_{TLB}\right)$$

with $M_{Li,c}(B_p, C) =$

$$2 * |Re|_{Li} + \begin{cases} C * \dfrac{H_p}{|Li|_{Li}}, & \text{if } H_p \leq |Li|_{Li} \\ C * \left(1 + \log\left(\dfrac{H_p}{|Li|_{Li}}\right)\right), & \text{if } H_p < |Li|_{Li} \end{cases}$$

and $M_{TLB,c}(B_p, C) =$

$$2 * |Re|_{Pg} + \begin{cases} |Re|_{Pg} * \left(\dfrac{H_p}{|TLB|}\right) & \text{if } H_p \leq |TLB| \\ C * \left(1 - \dfrac{|TLB|}{H_p}\right), & \text{if } H_p > |TLB| \end{cases}$$

$|Re|_{Li}$ and $|Cl|_{Li}$ denote the number of cache lines per relation and cluster, respectively, $|Re|_{Pg}$ the number of pages per relation, $|Li|_{Li}$ the total number of cache lines, both for the L1 ($i = 1$) and L2 ($i = 2$) caches, and $|TLB|$ the number of TLB entries.

The first term of $M_{Li,c}$ equals the minimal number of Li misses per pass for fetching the input and storing the output. The second term counts the number of additional Li misses, when the number of clusters either approaches the number of available Li or even exceeds this. $M_{TLB,c}$ is made up analogously. Due to space limits, we omit the term that models the additional TLB misses when the number of clusters exceeds the number of available L2 lines. A detailed description of these and the following formulae is given in [MBK99].

The lines in Figure 9 represent our model for a BAT of 8M tuples. The model shows to be very accurate[4].

The question remaining is how to distribute the number of bits over the passes. The experimental results—not presented here due to space limits (cf. [MBK99])—showed, that the performance strongly depend on even distribution of bits.

[4]On our Origin2000 (250 Mhz) we calibrated l_{TLB} = 228ns, L_{L2} = 24ns, L_{Mem} = 412ns, and w_c = 50ns.

3.4.3 Isolated Join Performance

We now analyze the impact of the number of radix-bits on the pure join performance, not including the clustering cost.

The points in Figure 10 depict the experimental results of radix-join (L1 and L2 cache misses, TLB misses, elapsed time) for different cardinalities. The lower graph ("millisecs") shows that the performance of radix-join improves with increasing number of radix-bits. The upper graph ("L1 misses") confirms, that only cluster sizes significantly smaller than L1 size are reasonable. Otherwise, the number of L1 cache misses explodes due to cache trashing. We limited the execution time of each single run to 15 minutes, thus, using only cluster sizes significantly smaller than L2 size and TLB size (i.e. number of TLB entries * page size). That's why the number of L2 cache misses stay almost constant. The performance improvement continues until the mean cluster size is 1 tuple. At that point, radix-join has degenerated to sort/merge-join. The high cost of radix-join with large cluster-size is explained by the fact that it performs nested-loop join on each pair of matching clusters. Therefore, clusters need to be kept small; our results indicate that a cluster-size of 8 tuples is optimal.

The following model calculates the total execution costs for a radix-join, depending on the number of bits and the cardinality[5]

$$\begin{aligned} &T_r(B,C) = \\ &C * \left\lceil \frac{C}{H} \right\rceil * w_r + C * w'_r + M_{L1,r}(B,C) * l_{L2} \\ &+ M_{L2,r}(B,C) * l_{Mem} + M_{TLB,r}(B,C) * l_{TLB} \end{aligned}$$

with $M_{Li,r}(B,C) =$

$$3 * |Re|_{Li} + C * \begin{cases} \frac{|Cl|_{Li}}{|Li|_{Li}}, & \text{if } |Cl|_{Li} \leq |Li|_{Li} \\ |Cl|_{Li}, & \text{if } |Cl|_{Li} > |Li|_{Li} \end{cases}$$

and $M_{TLB,r}(B,C) =$

$$3 * |Re|_{Pg} + C * \frac{||Cl||}{||TLB||}$$

$|Re|_{Pg}$, $|Re|_{Li}$, $|Cl|_{Li}$, and $|Li|_{Li}$ are as above ($i \in \{1,2\}$), $||Cl||$ denotes the cluster size (in byte), and $||TLB|| = |TLB| * ||Pg||$ denotes the memory range covered by $|TLB|$ pages.

The first term of T_r calculates the costs for evaluating the join predicate—each tuple of the outer relation has to be checked against each tuple in the respective cluster; the cost per check is w_r. The second term represents the costs for creating the result with w'_r denoting the costs per tuple. The left term of $M_{Li,r}$

[5]For simplicity of presentation, we assume the cardinalities of both operands and the result to be the same.

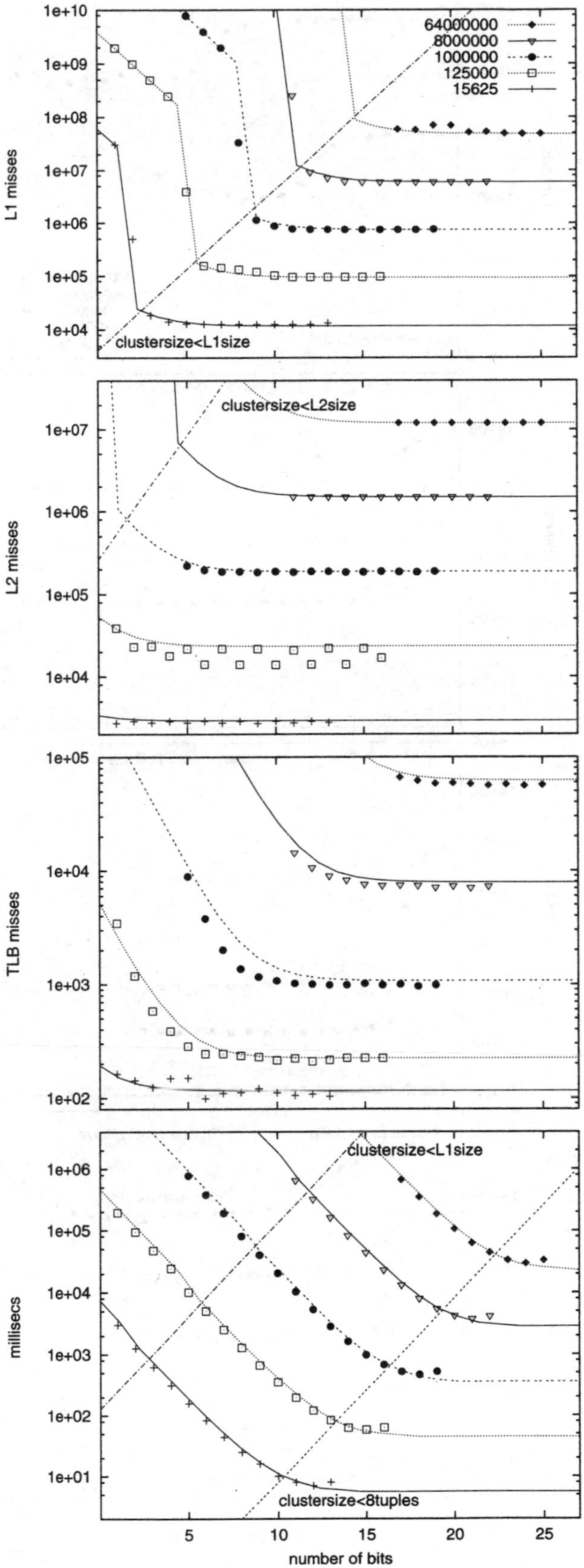

Figure 10: Performance and Model of Radix-Join

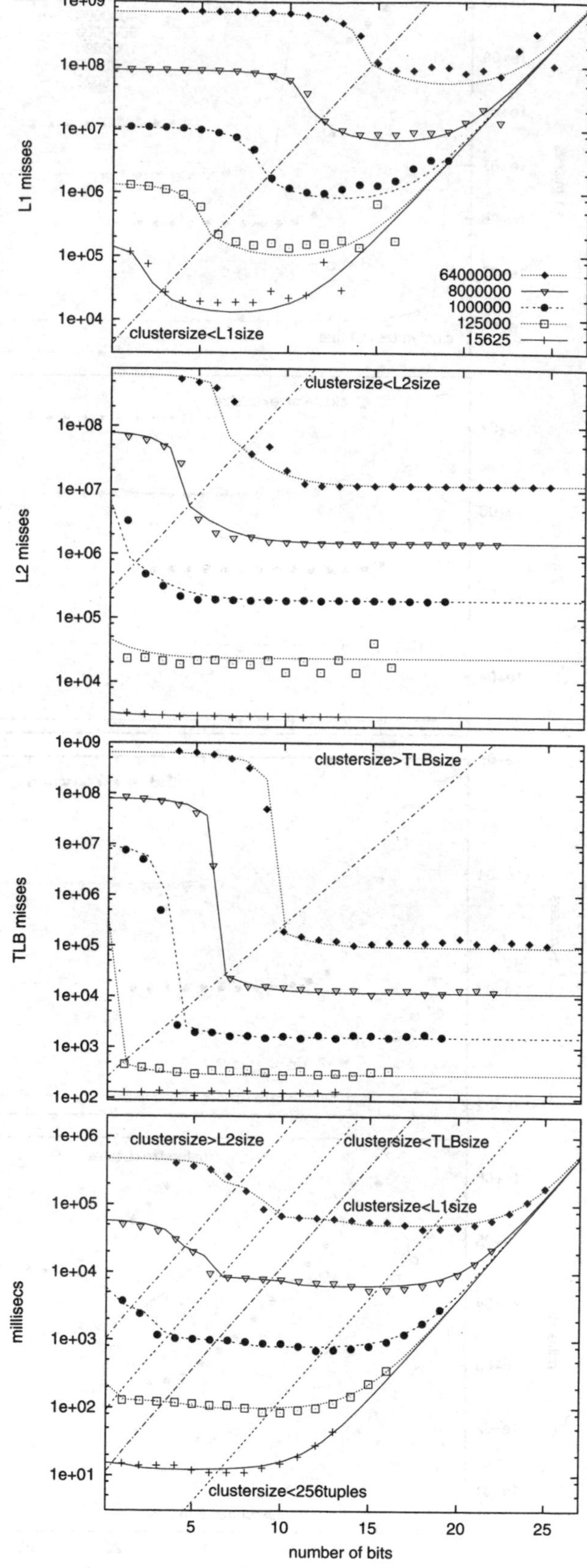

Figure 11: Performance and Model of Partitioned Hash-Join

equals the minimal number of Li misses for fetching both operands and storing the result. The right term counts the number of additional Li misses during the inner loop, when the number of Li lines per cluster either approaches the number of available Li lines or even exceeds this. $M_{TLB,r}$ is made up analogously. The lines in Figure 10 prove the accuracy of our model for different cardinalities ($w_r = 24$ns, $w'_r = 240$ns).

The partitioned hash-join also exhibits increased performance with increasing number of radix-bits. Figure 11 shows that performance increase flattens after the point where the entire inner cluster (including its hash table) consists of less pages than there are TLB entries (64). Then, it also fits the L2 cache comfortably. Thereafter performance decreases only slightly until the point that the inner cluster fits the L1 cache. Here, performance reaches its minimum. The fixed overhead by allocation of the hash-table structure causes performance to decrease when the cluster sizes get too small (200 tuples) and clusters get very numerous.

As for the radix-join, we also provide a cost model for the partitioned hash-join:

$$T_h(B,C) = \\ C * w_h + H * w'_h + M_{L1,h}(B,C) * l_{L2} \\ + M_{L2,h}(B,C) * l_{Mem} + M_{TLB,h}(B,C) * l_{TLB}$$

with $M_{Li,h}(B,C) =$

$$3 * |Re|_{Li} + \begin{cases} C * \frac{||Cl||}{||Li||}, & \text{if } ||Cl|| \leq ||Li|| \\ C * 10 * \left(1 - \frac{||Li||}{||Cl||}\right), & \text{if } ||Cl|| < ||Li|| \end{cases}$$

and $M_{TLB,h}(B,C) =$

$$3 * |Re|_{Pg} + \begin{cases} C * \frac{||Cl||}{||TLB||}, & \text{if } ||Cl|| \leq ||TLB|| \\ C * 10 * \left(1 - \frac{||Li||}{||TLB||}\right), & \text{if } ||Cl|| > ||TLB|| \end{cases}$$

$||Cl||$, $||Li||$, and $||TLB||$ denote (in byte) the cluster size, the sizes of both caches ($i \in \{1,2\}$), and the memory range covered by $|TLB|$ pages, respectively. w_h represents the pure calculation costs per tuple, i.e. building the hash-table, doing the hash lookup and creating the result. w'_h represents the additional costs per cluster for creating and destroying the hash-table.

The left term of $M_{Li,h}$ equals the minimal number of Li misses for fetching both operands and storing the result. The right term counts the number of additional Li misses, when the cluster size either approaches Li size or even exceeds this. As soon as the clusters get significantly larger than Li, each memory access yields a cache miss due to cache trashing: with a bucket-chain length of 4, up to 8 memory accesses per tuple are necessary while building the hash-table and doing the hash lookup, and another two to access the actual tuple. For simplicity of presentation, we omit the formulae for the additional overhead for allocating the hash-table structure when the cluster sizes get very small. The interested reader is referred to [MBK99]. Again, the number of TLB misses is modeled analogously.

The lines in Figure 11 represent our model for different cardinalities (w_h = 680ns, w'_h = 3600ns). The predictions are very accurate.

3.4.4 Overall Join Performance

After having analyzed the impact of the tuning parameters on the clustering phase and the joining phase separately, we now turn our attention to the combined cluster and join cost for both partitioned hash-join and radix-join. Radix-cluster gets cheaper for less radix B bits, whereas both radix-join and partitioned hash-join get more expensive. Putting together the experimental data we obtained on both cluster- and join-performance, we determine the optimum number of B for relation cardinality and join-algorithm.

It turns out that there are four possible strategies, which correspond to the diagonals in Figures 11 and 10:

phash L2 partitioned hash-join on $B = log_2(C * 12/||L2||)$ clustered bits, so the inner relation plus hash-table fits the L2 cache. This strategy was used in the work of Shatdahl et al. [SKN94] in their partitioned hash-join experiments.

phash TLB partitioned hash-join on $B = log_2(C * 12/||TLB||)$ clustered bits, so the inner relation plus hash-table spans at most $|TLB|$ pages. Our experiments show a significant improvement of the pure join performance between phash L2 and phash TLB.

phash L1 partitioned hash-join on $B = log_2(C * 12/||L1||)$ clustered bits, so the inner relation plus hash-table fits the L1 cache. This algorithm uses more clustered bits than the previous ones, hence it really needs the multi-pass radix-cluster algorithm (a straightforward 1-pass cluster would cause cache trashing on this many clusters).

radix radix-join on $B = log_2(C/8)$ clustered bits. The radix-join has the most stable performance but has higher startup cost, as it needs to radix-cluster on significantly more bits that the other options. It therefore is only a winner on the large cardinalities.

Figure 12 compares radix-join (thin lines) and partitioned hash-join (thick lines) throughout the whole bit range, using the corresponding optimal number of passes for the radix-cluster (see Section 3.4.2). The diagonal lines mark the setting for B that belong to the four strategies. The optimal setting for each join algorithm is even beyond these strategies: partitioned hash-join performs best with cluster size of approximately 200 tuples ("phash min") and radix with just 4 tuples per cluster ("radix min") is slightly better than radix 8.

Finally, Figure 13 compares our radix-cluster-based strategies to non-partitioned hash-join ("simple hash") and sort-merge-join. This clearly demonstrates that cache-conscious join-algorithms perform significantly better than the "random-access" algorithms. Here, "cache-conscious" does not only refer to L2 cache, but also to L1 cache and especially the TLB. Further, Figure 12 shows that our radix algorithms improve hash-performance, both in the "phash L1" strategy (cardinalities larger than 250,000 require at least two clustering passes) and with the radix-join itself.

4 Evaluation

In this research, we brought to light the severe impact of memory access on performance of elementary database operations. Hardware trends indicate that this bottleneck remains here for quite some time; hence our expectation that its impact eventually will become deeper than the I/O bottleneck. Database algorithms and data structures should therefore be designed and optimized for memory access from the outset. A sloppy implementation of the key algorithms or 'features' at the innermost level of an operator tree (e.g. pointer swizzling/object table lookup) can become a performance disaster, that ever faster CPUs will not come to rescue.

Conversely, careful design can lead to an order of magnitude performance advancement. In our Monet system, under development since 1992, we have decreased the memory access stride using vertical decomposition; a choice that back in 1992 was mostly based on intuition. The work presented here now provides hard backing that this feature is in fact the basis of good performance. Our simple-scan experiment demonstrates that decreasing the stride is crucial for optimizing usage of memory bandwidth.

Concerning query processing algorithms, we have formulated radix algorithms and demonstrated through experimentation that these algorithms form both an addition and an improvement to the work in [SKN94]. The modeling work done to show how these algorithms improve cache behavior during join processing represents an important improvement over previous work on main-memory cost models [LN96, WK90]. Rather than characterizing main-memory performance on the coarse level of a procedure call with "magical" costs factors obtained by profiling, our methodology mimics the memory access pattern of the algorithm to be modeled and then quantifies its cost by counting cache miss events and CPU cycles. We

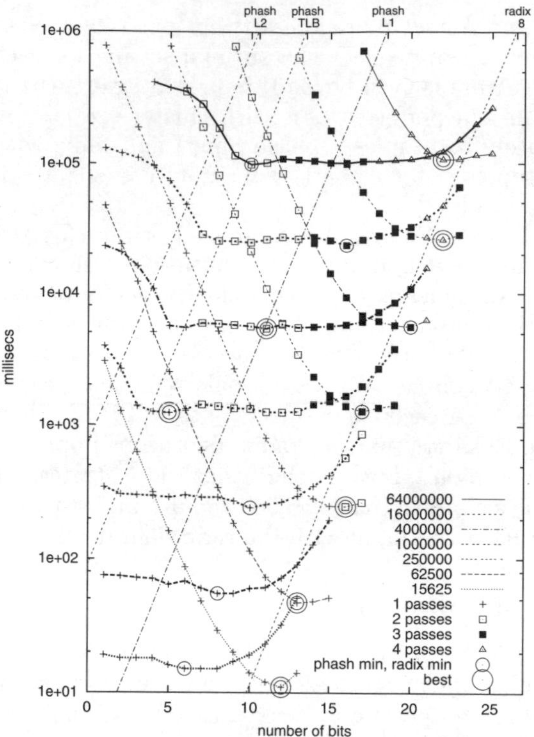

Figure 12: Overall Performance of Radix-Join (thin lines) vs. Partitioned Hash-Join (thick lines)

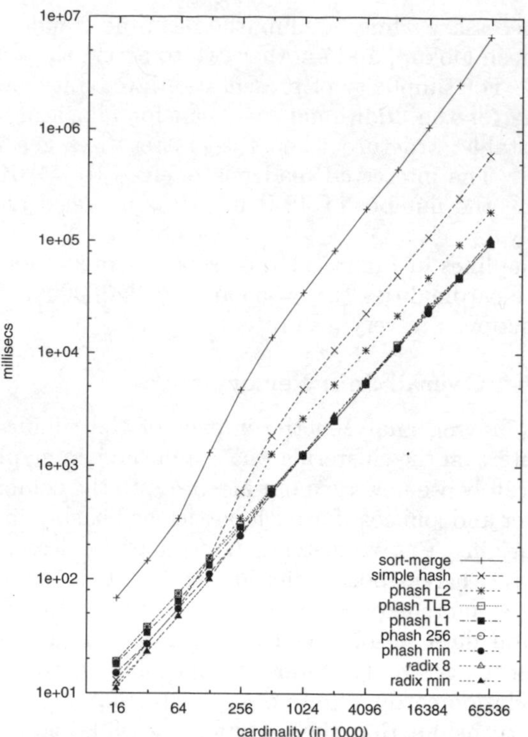

Figure 13: Overall Algorithm Comparison

were helped in formulating these models through our usage of hardware event counters present in modern CPUs.

We think our findings are not only relevant to main-memory databases engineers. Vertical fragmentation and memory access cost have a strong impact on performance of database systems at a macro level, including those that manage disk-resident data. Nyberg et al. [NBC+94] stated that techniques like software assisted disk-striping have reduced the I/O bottleneck; i.e. queries that analyze large relations (like in OLAP or Data Mining) now read their data faster than it can be processed. We observed this same effect with the Data Mining Benchmark [BRK98], where a commercial database product managing disk-resident data was run with a large buffer pool. While executing almost exclusively memory-bound, this product was measured to be a factor 40 slower on this benchmark than the Monet system. After inclusion of cache-optimization techniques like described in this paper, we have since been able to improve our own results on this benchmark with almost an extra order of magnitude. This clearly shows the importance of main-memory access optimization techniques.

In Monet, we use I/O by manipulating virtual memory mappings, hence treat management of disk-resident data as memory with a large granularity. This is in line with the consideration that disk-resident data is the bottom level of a memory hierarchy that goes up from the virtual memory, to the main memory through the cache memories up to the CPU registers (Figure 2). Algorithms that are tuned to run well on one level of the memory, also exhibit good performance on the lower levels (e.g., radix-join has pure sequential access and consequently also runs well on virtual memory). As the major performance bottleneck is shifting from I/O to memory access, we therefore think that main-memory optimization of both data structures and algorithms – like described in this paper – will increasingly be decisive in order to efficiently exploit the power of custom hardware.

5 Conclusion

It was shown that memory access cost is increasingly a bottleneck for database performance. We subsequently discussed the consequences of this finding on both data structures and algorithms employed in database systems. We recommend using vertical fragmentation in order to better use scarce memory bandwidth. We introduced new radix algorithms for use in join processing, and formulated detailed analytical cost models that explain why these algorithms make optimal use of hierarchical memory systems found in modern computer hardware. Finally, we placed our results in a broader context of database architecture, and made recommendations for future systems.

References

[AvdBF+92] P. M. G. Apers, C. A. van den Berg, J. Flokstra, P. W. P. J. Grefen, M. L. Kersten, and A. N. Wilschut. PRISMA/DB: A Parallel Main Memory Relational DBMS. *IEEE Trans. on Knowledge and Data Eng.*, 4(6):541–554, December 1992.

[BQK96] P. A. Boncz, W. Quak, and M. L. Kersten. Monet and its Geographical Extensions: a Novel Approach to High-Performance GIS Processing. In *Proc. of the Intl. Conf. on Extending Database Technology*, Avignon, France, 1996.

[BRK98] P. Boncz, T. Rühl, and F. Kwakkel. The Drill Down Benchmark. In *Proc. of the Int'l. Conf. on Very Large Data Bases*, pages 628–632, June 1998.

[BWK98] P. A. Boncz, A. N. Wilschut, and M. L. Kersten. Flattening an Object Algebra to Provide Performance. In *Proc. of the IEEE Int'l. Conf. on Data Engineering*, Orlando, FL, USA, 1998.

[CK85] G.P. Copeland and S. Khoshafian. A Decomposition Storage Model. In *Proc. of the ACM SIGMOD Int'l. Conf. on Management of Data*, pages 268–279, May 1985.

[htt96] http://www.rambus.com/docs/drtechov.pdf, Rambus Technologies, Inc. *Direct Rambus Technology Disclosure*, 1996.

[htt97] http://www.sldram.com/Documents/SLDRAMwhite970910.pdf, SLDRAM Inc. *SyncLink DRAM Whitepaper*, 1997.

[Knu68] D. E. Knuth. *The Art of Computer Programming*, volume 1. Addison-Wesley, Reading, MA, USA, 1968.

[LC86] T. J. Lehman and M. J. Carey. A Study of Index Structures for Main Memory Database Management Systems. In *Proc. of the Int'l. Conf. on Very Large Data Bases*, August 1986.

[LN96] S. Listgarten and M.-A. Neimat. Modelling Costs for a MM-DBMS. In *Proc. of the Int'l. Workshop on Real-Time Databases, Issues and Applications*, March 1996.

[MBK99] S. Manegold, P. Boncz, and M. Kersten. Database Architecture Optimized for the new Bottleneck: Memory Access. Technical Report INS-R99??, CWI, Amsterdam, The Netherlands, February 1999.

[McC95] J. D. McCalpin. Memory bandwidth and machine balance in current high performance computers. *IEEE Technical Committee on Computer Architecture newsletter*, December 1995.

[MKW+98] S. McKee, R. Klenke, K. Wright, W. Wulf, M. Salinas, J. Aylor, and A. Batson. Smarter Memory: Improving Bandwidth for Streamed References. *IEEE Computer*, 31(7):54–63, July 1998.

[Mow94] T. C. Mowry. *Tolerating Latency Through Software-Controlled Data Prefetching.* PhD thesis, Stanford University, Computer Science Department, 1994.

[NBC+94] C. Nyberg, T. Barclay, Z. Cvetanovic, J. Gray, and D. Lomet. AlphaSort: A RISC Machine Sort. In *Proc. of the ACM SIGMOD Int'l. Conf. on Management of Data*, pages 233–242, May 1994.

[Ron98] Mikael Ronström. *Design and Modeling of a Parallel Data Server for Telecom Applications.* PhD thesis, Linköping University, 1998.

[Sil97] Silicon Graphics, Inc., Mountain View, CA. *Performance Tuning and Optimization for Origin2000 and Onyx2*, January 1997.

[SKN94] A. Shatdahl, C. Kant, and J. Naughton. Cache Conscious Algorithms for Relational Query Processing. In *Proc. of the Int'l. Conf. on Very Large Data Bases*, pages 510–512, September 1994.

[Val87] P. Valduriez. Join Indices. *ACM Trans. on Database Systems*, 12(2):218–246, June 1987.

[WK90] K.-Y. Whang and R. Krishnamurthy. Query Optimization in a Memory-Resident Domain Relational Calculus Database System. *ACM Trans. on Database Systems*, 15(1):67–95, March 1990.

The Persistent Cache: Improving OID Indexing in Temporal Object-Oriented Database Systems

Kjetil Nørvåg
Department of Computer and Information Science
Norwegian University of Science and Technology, Norway
noervaag@idi.ntnu.no

Abstract

In a temporal OODB, an OID index (OIDX) is needed to map from OID to the physical location of the object. In a transaction time temporal OODB, the OIDX should also index the object versions. In this case, the index entries, which we call *object descriptors* (OD), also include the commit timestamp of the transaction that created the object version. The OIDX in a non-temporal OODB only needs to be updated when an object is created, but in a temporal OODB, *the OIDX has to be updated every time an object is updated.* This has previously been shown to be a potential bottleneck, and in this paper, we present the *Persistent Cache* (PCache), a novel approach which reduces the index update and lookup costs in temporal OODBs. We develop a cost model for the PCache, and use this to show that the use of a PCache can reduce the average access cost to only a fraction of the cost when not using the PCache. Even though the primary context of this paper is OID indexing in a temporal OODB, the PCache can also be applied to general secondary indexing, and can be especially beneficial for applications where updates are non-clustered.

1 Introduction

In a transaction time temporal object-oriented database system (TOODB), updating an object creates a new version of the object, but the old version is still accessible. A system maintained timestamp is associated with every object version, usually the commit time of the transaction that created this version of the object.

An important feature of OODBs, is that an object is uniquely identified by an object identifier (OID), and that the object can be accessed via its OID. The OID can be physical, which means that the disk page of the object is given directly from the OID, or logical, which means that an OID index (OIDX) is needed to map from logical OID to the physical location of the object. In a TOODB, logical OIDs is the most reasonable alternative, because an OIDX is necessary anyway to index the object versions. The entries in the OIDX, which we call *object descriptors* (OD), contain administrative information, including information to do the mapping from logical OID to physical address, and the commit timestamp. The OIDX can be quite large. In non-temporal OODBs, a typical size is in the order of 20% of the size of the database itself [2]. This means that in general, only a small part of the OIDX fits in main memory, and that OIDX retrieval can become a bottleneck if efficient access and buffering strategies are not applied.

An important difference between OIDX management in non-temporal and TOODBs, is that with only one version of an object (non-temporal), the OIDX needs only to be updated when a new object is created. This can be done in an efficient append-only operation [2], and we can focus on optimizing OIDX lookups. In a TOODB however, the OIDX must be updated *every time an object is updated.* An object update creates a new object version, without deleting the previous version, hence, a new OD for the new version has to be inserted into the OIDX. The index pages will usually have low locality (the unique part of an OID is usually an integer that will always be assigned monotonic increasing values), and as a result index updates might become a serious bottleneck in a TOODB.

To reduce disk I/O in index operations, the most recently used *index pages* are kept in an *index page buffer*. OIDX pages will in general have low locality, and to increase the probability of finding a certain OD needed for a mapping from OID to physical address, it is also possible to keep the most recently used *index entries* (the ODs) in a separate OD

Proceedings of the 25th VLDB Conference, Edinburgh, Scotland, 1999.

cache, as is done in the Shore OODB [6]. With low locality on index pages, a separate OD cache utilizes memory better, space is not wasted on large pages where only small parts of them will be used. An OD cache reduces the index lookup costs considerably, and can be extended to reduce index update costs as well [10].

However, even when using a "writable" OD cache, OIDX updates are still very costly. In this paper, we present an approach to further reduce the OIDX update costs. Noting that the main reason for the bottleneck against the OIDX is the low locality of entries in the OIDX tree nodes, we use an intermediate *disk resident buffer* between the main memory buffer, and the OIDX itself. We call this the *Persistent Cache* (PCache). The PCache is typically much larger than the available main memory buffer, but smaller than the OIDX itself. The entries in the PCache are managed in an LRU like way, just like a main memory cache. In addition to reducing update costs, the PCache also reduces the lookup costs. The reason for the reduced costs, is the higher locality on PCache pages, compared to the OIDX tree nodes. Higher locality means that less disk operations are necessary to read and write ODs. The PCache-to-OIDX tree writeback can be done very efficiently later. This will be described later in this paper.

In this paper, we describe the PCache in detail, and analyze its performance by the use of cost functions. We will study optimal size of the PCache, and see how buffering of nodes in main memory should be done to optimize the PCache performance. It should also be noted that even though our primary context for this paper is OID indexing, the results are also relevant to entry access cost and index entry caching for general secondary indexes.

The organization of the rest of the paper is as follows. In Section 2 we give an overview of related work. In Section 3 we describe object and index management in TOODBs. In Section 4 we describe the PCache. In Section 5 we develop an the OID access cost model, and in Section 6 we use this cost model to study how different PCache sizes, memory sizes, index sizes, and access patterns affect the performance. Finally, in Section 7, we conclude the paper and outline issues for further research.

2 Related Work

Temporal database systems are in general still an immature technology, and in the case of transaction time TOODBs, we are only aware of one prototype[1] that has temporal OID indexing, POST/C++ [12]. The performance results presented for POST/C++ are only for relatively small databases, where the index fits in main memory, and we expect that with a larger number of objects, the OIDX would be a bottleneck.

The PCache has similarities to LHAM [7], where a hierarchy of indexes is used. One important differences between the PCache and LHAM, is that in LHAM, *all* entries in one level is regularly moved to the next, there are no LRU management, and as such, LHAM only helps in improving write efficiency, not read efficiency.

The cost models in this paper are based on previous work on modeling non-temporal OODBs [9] and temporal OODBs [10], but the models have been extended to include the aspects of the PCache. The buffer and tree models have been compared with simulation results. Detailed results from the simulations with different index sizes, buffer sizes, index page fanout, and access patterns, can be found in [11].

3 TOODB Object and Index Management

We start with a description of how OID indexing and version management can be done in a TOODB. This brief outline is not based on any existing system, but the design is close enough to make it possible to integrate into current OODBs if desired, and it will also be used as a basis for the OID indexing in the Vagabond TOODB.

3.1 Temporal OID Indexing

In a traditional OODB, the OIDX is usually realized as a hash file or a B^+-tree, with ODs as entries, and using the OID as the key. In a TOODB, we have more than one version of some of the objects, and we need to be able to access current as well as old versions efficiently. If access is mostly reading current objects, it is efficient to have two indexes, one with ODs representing the current version of the objects, and one with ODs representing historical objects (i.e., previous versions). The problem with this approach, is that every time a new version is created, we have to update *two* indexes. A second approach, is to use a linked list of versions for each object. If accesses are mostly of the type "get all versions of an object with OID i", this is an efficient alternative. However, access to a particular version, valid at time t, is very costly with this approach, because we have to traverse the object chain.

Our approach to indexing is to have *one* index structure, containing all ODs, current as well as previous versions. While several efficient multiversion access methods exist, e.g., TSB-tree [4] and LHAM [7], they are not suitable for our purpose. We will never have search for a (consecutive) range of OIDs, OID search will always be for *perfect match*, and most of them are assumed to be to the current version. TSB-trees provides more flexibility than needed, e.g., combined key range and time range search, which implies an extra cost, while LHAM can have a high lookup cost when the current version of an object is searched for.

In this paper, we assume one OD for each object version, stored in a B^+-tree. We include the commit time *TIME* in the OD, and use the concatenation of OID and time, *OID*||*TIME*, as the index key. By doing this, ODs for a particular OID will be clustered together in the leaf nodes, sorted on commit time. As a result, search for the current version of a particular OID as well as retrieval of a particular time interval for an OID can be done efficiently.

When a new object is *created*, i.e., a new OID allocated, its OD is appended to the index tree as is done in the case of

[1] Support for versioning exists in most OODBs, but not temporal management, indexing, and operations.

the Monotonic B^+-tree [3]. This operation is very efficient. However, when an object is *updated*, the OD for the new version *has to be inserted into the tree.*

It should be noted that this OIDX is inefficient for many typical temporal queries. As a result, additional secondary indexes can be needed, of which both TSB-tree and LHAM are good candidates. However, *the OIDX is still needed*, to support navigational queries, one of the main features of OODBs compared to relational database systems. Some optimizations are possible to this OIDX, e.g., using variants of nested tree index, but as the PCache is the focus of this paper, we will not elaborate more on this subject here.

3.2 Temporal Object Management

In a non-temporal (one-version) OODB, space is allocated for an object when it is created, and further updates to the object are done in-place. This implies that after an object update, the previous version of the object is not available. The physical location of the new version is the same as the previous version, hence, the OIDX needs only to be updated when objects are created and when they are deleted.

In a TOODB, it is usually assumed that most accesses will be to the current versions of the objects in the database. To keep these accesses as efficient as possible, and benefit from object clustering,[2] the database is partitioned, with current objects in one partition, and the previous versions in the other partition, in the *historical database*. When an object is updated in a TOODB, the previous version is first moved to the historical database, before the new version is stored in-place in the current database. The OIDX needs to be updated *every time an object is updated*. As long as the modified ODs are written to the log before commit, we do not need to update the OIDX itself immediately. This is done in the background, and can be postponed until the second checkpoint after the OD have been written to the log. Index pages will be written to disk either because of checkpointing, or because of buffer replacement.

Not all the data in a TOODB is temporal, for some of the objects, we are only interested in the current version. To improve efficiency, the system can be made aware of this. In this way, some of the objects can be defined as non-temporal. Old versions of these are not kept, and the objects can be updated in-place as in an one-version OODB, and the costly OIDX update is not needed when an object is modified. This is an important point: using an OODB which efficiently supports temporal data management, should not reduce the performance of applications that do not utilize these features.

4 The Persistent Index Entry Cache

The ODs accessed will be almost uniformly distributed over the index leaf nodes. The OD cache makes read ac-

[2]It is also possible that in a TOODB application, a good object clustering includes historical objects as well as current objects. This should be studied further, but does not have any implications to the results studied here, all updates to objects will necessarily necessitate allocations of space for the new object, and an OIDX update.

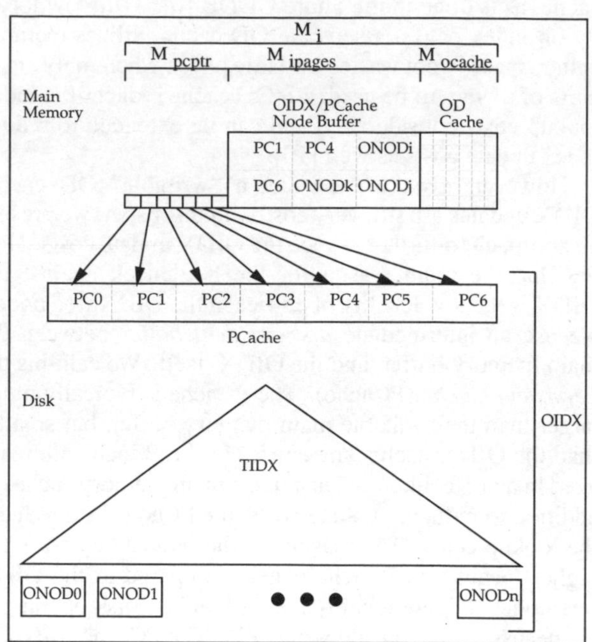

Figure 1: Overview of index, PCache, and index related main memory buffers. PCache nodes PC1, PC4 and PC6, and 3 OIDX nodes (denoted ONOD*n*) are in the buffer.

cesses efficient, but in a database with many objects, most of the ODs that are updated during one checkpoint interval will reside in different leaf nodes. This low locality means that *many leaf nodes have to be updated*. When an index node is to be updated, an installation read of the node has to be done first. With a large index, the access to the nodes will be random disk accesses, and as a result, the installation read is very costly.

To reduce the average access cost, the *persistent cache* (PCache) can be used. The PCache contains a subset of the entries in the OIDX, *the goal is to have the most frequently used ODs in the PCache*. In contrast to the main memory cache (the OD cache), the PCache is persistent, so that we do not have to write its entries back to the OIDX itself during each checkpoint interval. This is actually the main purpose of the PCache: to provide an intermediate storage area for persistent data, in this case, ODs.

The size of the PCache is in general larger than the size of the main memory, but smaller than the size of the OIDX. The contents of the PCache is maintained according to an LRU like mechanism. The result should be high locality on accesses to the PCache nodes, reducing the total number of installation reads, and making checkpointing less costly. Average OIDX lookup cost should also be less than without a PCache.

To avoid confusion, we will hereafter denote the index tree itself as the TIDX, and use OIDX to mean the combined index system, i.e., PCache and TIDX. Thus, when we say an entry is in the OIDX, it can be in the PCache, in the TIDX, or in both. This is illustrated on Figure 1.

4.1 PCache Organization

The index related main memory buffers, the PCache, and the TIDX, are illustrated on Figure 1. The number of nodes in the PCache should be small enough to make it possible to store pointers to all the PCache nodes in main memory. To be able to do the copying of the ODs from the PCache to the TIDX efficiently, the nodes in the PCache should be accessed in the same order as the leaf nodes in the OIDX. Therefore, the nodes in the PCache are range partitioned, each node stores a certain interval of OIDs.

Range-partitioning is vulnerable to skew. To avoid this, the partitioning can be dynamically changed (for each node, we have the OID range boundary in main memory). This is done based on the update access rates on each node. A high update access rate to a node results in a smaller interval being allocated to that node. Because the PCache nodes are frequently accessed, the repartitioning does not represent any extra cost (the repartitioning can be done when neighbor nodes are resident in the buffer).

It is important to note that even though reads of PCache nodes will be random disk accesses, the PCache nodes will be clustered together, so that the random read of PCache nodes will have a small seek time. There will also be several PCache node read requests at any time, so by using an elevator algorithm, the cost of reading from the PCache will be low.

4.2 PCache LRU Management

The PCache nodes are operated similar to an ordinary main memory cache, and when an entry is to be stored in a node in the PCache, one of the existing entries have to be discarded. To provide access statistics, an access table is maintained for each node, with one bit for each entry in the node, and we use the clock algorithm as an LRU approximation. An access bit is set each time an entry is accessed. As for the storage of the access tables, we have several options:

1. The access table of a node could be stored *in the node itself*. A problem with this option, is that when a node is to be discarded from the main memory buffer, and entries have been accessed, the node needs to be written back to disk, even if none of the entries have been changed. This is not desirable.

2. Access tables are maintained in main memory, for each main memory resident node. When a node is discarded, i.e., due to buffer replacement, the table is discarded as well. A problem with the this option, is that until enough accesses have been done to the entries, the bit map is unreliable as a way to approximate LRU, and the "wrong" entries might get discarded.

3. Access tables are maintained in main memory for *all* PCache nodes. One problem with the this approach, is that one table for each node in the PCache is needed, but because the size of each table is small (one bit for each entry in the node), this will not represent a problem as long as the PCache is not too large. If the system crashes, the contents of the access tables will be lost, and wrong caching decisions might be done when the system is restarted. This does only affect *performance* at startup time, the ODs of committed operations are always safe on disk. To reduce the amount of wrong caching decisions at startup time, we store the access table in the node as well when the node is written to disk. Note that this differs from option 1, where the node is *always* written back when it is discarded, even when there are no updates to the ODs stored in the node.

Based on the observations above, we conclude that maintaining access tables in main memory for *all* PCache nodes is the best approach.

In addition to the access tables, each node also contains a table to keep track of the status of the entries with respect to the TIDX. One *dirty* bit is needed for each entry. The dirty bit is set each time an entry is modified or inserted into the node. Only the dirty entries need to be written back to the TIDX, entries not marked as modified can be safely discarded when needed.

4.3 Update Operations

When employing the PCache, inserting ODs resulting from object *updates* are *always* done to the entry in the PCache, never directly to the TIDX. Inserting an OD into a node, implies discarding another OD from the node, based on the LRU strategy. It is preferable to discard a non-dirty entry, so that a synchronous writeback of the dirty entry is avoided. To have a high probability of non-dirty slots in the PCache node, dirty entries in the PCache are regularly copied over to the TIDX itself, asynchronously in the background. This is done efficiently by mostly sequential reading of the PCache nodes, and mostly sequential installation read and subsequent writing of the TIDX nodes.

4.4 Object Creations

Object creations are still applied directly to the TIDX. An OD resulting from an object creation is an efficient append operation into the TIDX. In the case where a new ODs is to be part of the hot set, it will usually be retrieved from the TIDX nodes before they are discarded from the buffer. These ODs will on access be inserted into the PCache.

4.5 Read Operations

Read operations belong to one of two classes: navigational (single object) read, and scan operations.

Single Object Read

Read operations are done by first checking if the entry to be accessed is in the OD cache or the PCache, if not found there, the TIDX itself is searched. The search in the PCache might result in one disk access if the actual node is not in buffer. When using range partitioning, there is only one candidate node, so that at most one disk access will be needed. Accessing the TIDX can result in one or more disk accesses if the TIDX nodes are not in buffer.

When found, either in the PCache or the TIDX, the OD is inserted into the OD cache. If the OD was not already in the PCache, we now have several options, for example:

1. Insert the OD into the PCache immediately. Note that at this point, we are guaranteed to have the candidate PCache node resident in buffer, because we have probed it during the search for the OD. If we manage to get a high hit rate on the PCache, the optimal OD cache size might be quite small in this case. Note that the OD contains, in addition to the entries in the PCache, dirty entries resulted from update operations not yet installed into the PCache.

2. Insert the OD into the PCache only when it is to be discarded from the OD cache. In this way, we get good memory utilization, we do not have to use space for the OD both in the OD cache and in the PCache. However, in this case, we are not guaranteed to have the candidate PCache node resident in buffer, it might have been discarded since it was probed.

3. Never insert the OD into the PCache, only insert entries into the PCache when doing update operations. In this case, we rely on the OD cache to keep the most frequently accessed ODs, and use the PCache to be able to do efficient update of the TIDX. This strategy delays the update of the TIDX, and means that more entries can be collected before batch updating the TIDX.

The best option to choose, depends on access pattern. The possible installation read of option 2 can make it costly, and because ODs retrieved from read operations are not inserted into the PCache in the case of option 3, we only consider option 1 in this paper.

Scan Operations

Scan operations must be treated different from single object read operations, as one single scan operation can make the current contents of the whole PCache to be discarded. The ODs retrieved during a scan operation will in general have less chance of being used again, it is not likely that the whole collection or container to be scanned, represents a hot set. Even if this is the case, it is possible that the number of ODs retrieved during the scan, is larger than the number of ODs that fits in the PCache. In this case, if we do a new scan over the collection/container, we will have a PCache hit probability of 0. This is similar to general buffer management in the case of scan operations.

As a result, scan operations should not update the PCache, but the PCache must be consulted during read, because recently updated ODs from the actual container/collection might reside in the PCache. However, this will not be very costly, because the contents of a physical container cached in the PCache will be clustered in the PCache's pages as well, so that the extra cost of reading the relevant PCache pages is only marginal.

4.6 PCache-to-TIDX Writeback

The update of the TIDX, i.e., writing dirty entries in the PCache to the TIDX, will be done in the background. This is done by reading the PCache, and install the dirty entries of these nodes into the TIDX. This is done in segments, i.e., a number of nodes, and will be mostly sequential reading and writing. The PCache-to-TIDX writeback is a scan operation, and to avoid buffer pollution, nodes accessed during this operation should not affect the rest of the buffer contents, i.e., they should not make other nodes to be removed from the buffer.

The rate of the writeback is a tuning question. By giving it higher priority, i.e., doing more frequent writeback of PCache nodes, the probability of a PCache node being full of dirty entries is less likely. This is important, because it reduces the probability of synchronous writebacks. On the other hand, higher priority to the writeback also means that more of the disk bandwidth will be used for this purpose, because each node contains a smaller number of dirty entries.

All ODs updated since the penultimate checkpoint, and still dirty in the OD cache, needs to be installed into the PCache or TIDX during one checkpoint period. This is not the case with the PCache-to-TIDX writeback. The period between each time the contents of a particular PCache node is written back can be very long, but still short enough to avoid overflow of dirty ODs in the PCache.

4.7 Buffer Considerations

We can have a buffer shared between TIDX nodes and PCache. However, this does not necessarily give optimal performance. In some cases, it might be that TIDX accesses pollutes the buffer, resulting in a low hit rate on PCache nodes. To avoid this, we can use separate buffers, one TIDX buffer, and one PCache buffer. We can also pin a certain number of the upper TIDX levels in memory, this can be advantageous because strict use of LRU is not optimal when buffering nodes of an index tree.

5 Analytical Model

Analytical modeling in database research has mostly focused on I/O costs. This is the most significant cost factor, and in reasonable implementations, the CPU processing should go in parallel with I/O transfer, making the CPU cost "invisible". With increasing amounts of main memory available, this is not necessarily correct, but CPU costs can easily be incorporated into analytic models, and hence we consider it as an orthogonal issue to the one discussed in this paper (though it should be noted, that CPU cost should not affect the qualitative results in this paper). A more important aspect of the increasing amount of main memory, however, is that buffer characteristics become more important, hence, the increased buffer space available must be reflected in the models.

We use a traditional disk model, where the cost of reading a block from disk is the sum of the start up cost T_{start} and the transfer cost T_{transfer}. In our model, the average start up cost is fixed, and is set equivalent to t_r, the time it takes to do one disk revolution. The transfer cost is directly proportional to the block size, and is equivalent to reading disk tracks contiguously, e.g., transfer cost is equal to $\frac{b}{V_s}t_r$, where b is the block size to be transferred, and V_s is the amount of data on one track. Thus, the total time it takes to transfer one block is $T_b(b) = T_{\text{start}} + T_{\text{transfer}} = t_r + \frac{b}{V_s}t_r$. Index costs can be reduced by partitioning the index over several disks. Declustering PCache nodes and TIDX nodes over several disks is straightforward.

The time to read or write a random index page is $T_P = T_b(S_P)$, where S_P is the index page size. In this paper, we do not consider the cost of reading and writing the objects themselves, or log operations. Those costs are independent of the indexing costs, usually done on separate disks, and are issues orthogonal to the ones studied in this paper.

In this paper, we focus on reducing access times. Obviously, the reduced access times comes at the expense of more disk space for the PCache. As disk capacity increases rapidly, with a corresponding decrease in price, we expect that in most cases, using the extra space for the PCache will be worthwhile.

As illustrated on Figure 1, a certain amount of memory, M_{ipages}, is reserved for the index page buffer, i.e., for buffering PCache and TIDX pages, and M_{ocache}, is reserved for the OD cache.

If we assume the size of each OD is S_{od}, and an overhead of S_{oh} bytes is needed for each entry in the OD cache, the number of entries that fits in the OD cache is approximately $N_{\text{ocache}} \approx \frac{M_{\text{ocache}}}{(S_{\text{od}}+S_{\text{oh}})}$. If we use an hash table and a clock algorithm as an LRU approximation, $S_{\text{oh}} \approx 8$ B (B=bytes).

The number of index pages that fits in the buffer is approximately $N_{\text{ibuf}} \approx \frac{M_{\text{ipages}}}{(S_P+S_{\text{oh}})}$. For each PCache page on disk, we need to keep in memory the disk address of the node (4 B), the OID range boundary (4 B), and the LRU access table as described previously. This occupies a total of $M_{\text{pcptr}} = S_{PC}(\frac{S_P/S_{\text{od}}}{8} + 8)$ B, where S_{PC} is the number of PCache nodes.

5.1 Index Entry Access Model

We assume accesses to objects in the database system to be random, but skewed (some objects are more often accessed than others). We further assume it is possible to (logically) partition the range of OIDs into partitions, where each partitions has a certain size and access probability. This is illustrated at the bottom of Figure 2 (note that this is not how it is stored on disk, this is just a model of accesses). We consider a database in a stable condition, with a total of N_{objver} objects versions (and hence, N_{objver} index entries). Note that with the TIDX described in Section 3.1,

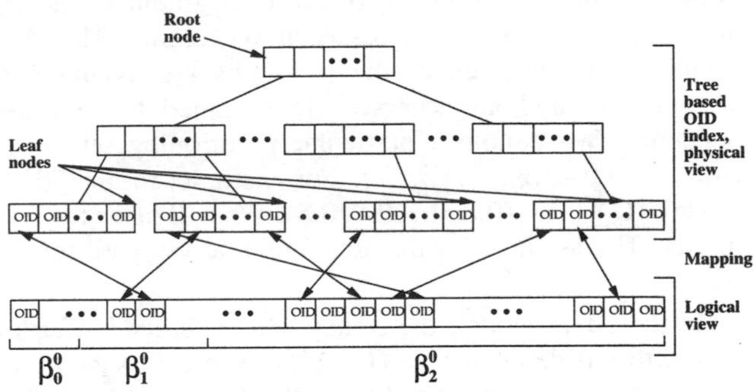

Figure 2: OID index. The lower part shows the index from a logical view, the upper part is as an index tree, which is how it is realized physically. We have indicated with arrows how the entries are distributed over the leaf nodes.

performance is not dependent of the number of existing versions of an object, only the total number of versions in the database.

In many analysis and simulations, the 80/20 model is applied, where 80% of the accesses go to 20% of the database. While this is satisfactory for analysis of some problems, it has a major shortcoming when used to estimate the number of distinct objects to be accessed. When applied, it gives a much higher number of distinct accessed objects than in a real system. The reason is that for most applications, inside the hot spot area (20% in this case), there is an even hotter and smaller area, with a much higher access probability. This is even more important for a temporal database. Most of the accesses will be to a small number of the current versions. With a large number of previous versions, this hot spot area will be much smaller and "hotter" than the one in a typical "traditional" database. This has to be reflected in the model.

5.2 Index Tree Size

If we assume an index tree with space utilization U (typically less than 0.69 for a B$^+$-tree), the number of leaf nodes is $N^0_{\text{tree}} \approx \frac{N_{\text{objver}}}{U\lfloor S_P/S_{\text{od}}\rfloor}$. The fanout F of internal nodes is $F = \lfloor US_P/S_{\text{ie}}\rfloor$, where S_{ie} is the size of an entry in an internal node. The number of levels in the tree is $H = 1+\lceil\log_F N^0_{\text{tree}}\rceil$. The number of nodes at each level in the tree is $N^i_{tree} = \lceil\frac{N^{i-1}_{\text{tree}}}{F}\rceil$ and the total number of nodes in the tree is $N_{\text{tree}} = \sum_{i=0}^{H-1} N^i_{\text{tree}}$.

5.3 Buffer Performance Model

Our buffer model is an extension of the Bhide, Dan and Dias LRU buffer model (BDD) [1]. Due to space constraints, we only present the most important aspects of our model in this paper, but a detailed description can be found in [9].

A database in the BDD model has a size of N data granules (e.g., pages), partitioned into p partitions. Each partition contains a fraction β_i of the data granules, and α_i of the accesses are done to each partition. The distributions *within* each of the partitions are assumed to be uniform, and all accesses are assumed to be independent. We denote a particular partitioning set $\Pi = (\alpha_0, \ldots, \alpha_{p-1}, \beta_0, \ldots, \beta_{p-1})$. For example, for the 80/20 model, $\Pi_{80/20} = (0.8, 0.2, 0.2, 0.8)$. We will in the following use Π_A as short for the actual OD access partitioning set.

In the BDD model, the steady state average buffer hit probability is denoted $P_{\text{buf}}(B, N, \Pi)$, where B is the number of data granules that fits in the buffer. The buffer hit probability for data granules belonging to a particular partition p is denoted $P^p_{\text{buf}}(B, N, \Pi)$. The BDD model can also be used to calculate the total number of distinct data granules accessed after n accesses to the database, $N_{\text{distinct}}(n, N, \Pi)$.

OD Cache Hit Rate

Accesses to the OD cache can be assumed to follow the assumptions behind the BDD model, they are independent and random requests. By applying this model with object entries as data granules, the probability of an OD cache hit is $P_{\text{ocache}} = P_{\text{buf}}(N_{\text{ocache}}, N_{\text{objver}}, \Pi_A)$.

General Index Buffer Model

The BDD LRU buffer model only models independent, non-hierarchical, access. Modeling buffer for hierarchical access is more complicated. Even though searches to the leaf pages can be considered to be random and independent, nodes accessed during traversal of the tree are *not* independent. We have extended the original model to be able to analyze buffer performance in the case of hierarchical index accesses as well [11]. This is based on the observation that *each level* in the tree is accessed with the *same probability* (assuming traversal from root to leaf on every search). Thus, with a tree with H levels, we initially have H partitions. Each of these partitions are of size N^i_{tree}, where N^i_{tree} is the number of index pages on level i in the tree. The access probability is $\frac{1}{H}$ for each partition.

To account for hot spots, we further divide the leaf page partition into p' partitions, each with a fraction of β_{Li} of the leaf nodes, and access probability α_{Li} relative to the other leaf page partitions. Thus, in a "global" view, each of these partitions have size $\beta_{Li} N^0_{\text{tree}}$ and access probability $\frac{\alpha_{Li}}{H}$. In total, we have $p = p' + (H-1)$ partitions. The hot spots at the leaf page level make access to nodes on upper levels non-uniform, but as long as the fanout is sufficiently large, and the hot spot areas are not too narrow, we can treat accesses to nodes on upper levels as uniformly distributed within each level. An example of this partitioning is illustrated to the right on Figure 3, where a tree with $H = 4$ levels and $p' = 2$ leaf page partitions is partitioned into $p = 2 + (4-1) = 5$ partitions.

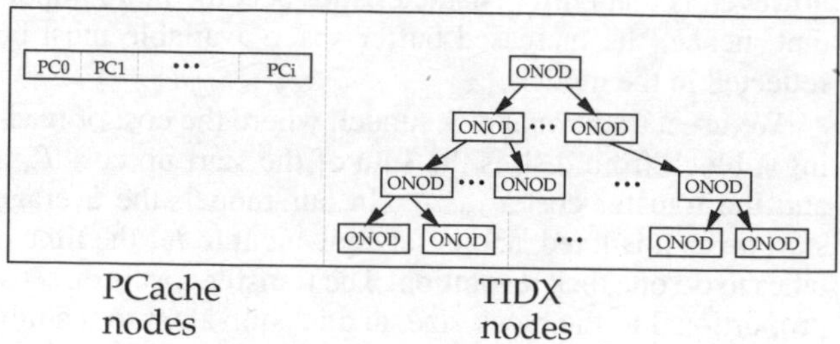

Figure 3: Access partitions.

Index Page Access Model

As noted, we can assume low locality in index pages. Because of the way OIDs are generated, entries from a certain partition are not clustered in the index. This is illustrated in Figure 2, where a leaf node containing index entries contains unrelated entries from different partitions. This means that the access pattern for the leaf nodes is different from the access pattern to the database from a logical view. As described in [11], we can use the initial OD partitioning (the OD access pattern) Π_A as basis for deriving the leaf node access partitioning Π_L.

PCache Hit Rate

We denote the probability that a certain OD is in the PCache as P_{PC}, the actual PCache page might be in memory or on disk.

The number of ODs in each PCache node is $\lfloor \frac{S_P}{S_{\text{od}}} \rfloor$, and with a total of S_{PC} nodes, the number of ODs that fits in the PCache is $N_{PC} = S_{PC} \lfloor \frac{S_P}{S_{\text{od}}} \rfloor$. The probability that a certain OD is in one of the PCache nodes can be approximated to:

$$P_{PC} = P_{\text{buf}}(N_{PC}, N_{\text{objver}}, \Pi_A)$$

PCache and TIDX Buffer Model

When the PCache and the TIDX share the same main memory page buffer, the model has to reflect this. The access probabilities for TIDX nodes and PCache nodes are different, and as a result, in an LRU managed buffer, the hit rate will be different. In the buffer model, we use a partitioning as illustrated on Figure 3. On the figure, the PCache is one partition, and each level in the tree is one partition, with the leaf node partition further divided into two partitions, reflecting the existence of hot spot nodes (nodes belonging to one of the two leaf node partitions need not actually be physically adjacent as on the figure).

Considering the page accesses, all OIDX lookups will access one PCache page, and $(1 - P_{PC})$ of the lookups will also access the TIDX. Each OIDX lookup results on average in $1 + (1 - P_{PC})H$ page accesses. Thus, the total access probability of the PCache is $\alpha_{PC} = \frac{1}{1+(1-P_{PC})H}$, which is the fraction of accessed pages that is part of the PCache partition. The TIDX access probability is $\alpha_{TIDX} = \frac{(1-P_{PC})H}{1+(1-P_{PC})H}$.

The total number of index pages is $S_{PC} + N_{tree}$. The PCache contains $\beta_{PC} = \frac{S_{PC}}{S_{PC}+N_{tree}}$ of these pages, the TIDX contains $\beta_{TIDX} = \frac{N_{tree}}{S_{PC}+N_{tree}}$ of the pages.

The TIDX partitions is further partitioned into p partitions as described above, and we denote the resulting partitioning (Figure 3) as Π_{Shared}. We denote the PCache and TIDX node buffer hit probabilities as:

$$P_{\text{buf\_PC}} = P_{\text{buf}}^{PC}(N_{\text{ibuf}}, S_{PC} + N_{\text{tree}}, \Pi_{\text{shared}})$$

$$P_{\text{buf\_TIDX}} = P_{\text{buf}}^{TIDX}(N_{\text{ibuf}}, S_{PC} + N_{\text{tree}}, \Pi_{\text{shared}})$$

As noted in Section 4.7, it can be advantageous to use separate buffers for the PCache and TIDX. In that case, $N_{\text{ibuf\_PC}}$ buffer pages are reserved for the PCache, and $N_{\text{ibuf_TIDX}}$buffer pages are reserved for the TIDX, so that $N_{\text{ibuf\_PC}} + N_{\text{ibuf\_TIDX}} = N_{\text{ibuf}}$. Denoting the tree partitioning as Π_{Tree}, the corresponding buffer hit probabilities using separate buffers are:

$$P_{\text{buf\_PC}} = \frac{N_{\text{ibuf\_PC}}}{S_{PC}}$$

$$P_{\text{buf\_TIDX}} = P_{\text{buf}}(N_{\text{ibuf\_TIDX}}, N_{tree}, \Pi_{\text{Tree}})$$

5.3.1 OIDX Lookup Cost

Assuming we have the address of all PCache pages in memory, and use a range partitioned PCache, at most one disk access is needed for each PCache lookup. Before a page can be read in, another have to be replaced. A page may contain dirty entries, because all read ODs from the TIDX are inserted immediately. In this case, the PCache page has to be written back. To be able to do this efficiently, we use the following strategy: On disk, we allocate space for more nodes than the number of nodes in the PCache. When we read a page, we at the same time schedule dirty page(s) for writing, to an empty slot near the node(s) to be read. In that way, the extra write cost is only marginal compared to the read. Because we at all times keep the pointers to all PCache nodes in the memory, they can be written back to different places every time.[3] We approximate the lookup cost to:

$$T_{\text{lookup\_PC}} = (1 - P_{\text{buf\_PC}})T_P$$

To access an entry in the TIDX, it is necessary to traverse the H levels from the root to a leaf page. To do this, we need $(1 - P_{\text{buf\_TIDX}})H$ disk accesses. The average cost of an TIDX lookup is:

$$T_{\text{lookup\_TIDX}} = (1 - P_{\text{buf\_TIDX}})HT_P$$

With a probability of P_{ocache}, the OID entry requested is already in the OD cache, but for $(1 - P_{\text{ocache}})$ of the requests, we have to access the PCache. With a probability of P_{PC}, the entry is in the PCache. If not, the TIDX itself has to be accessed. The average cost to retrieve an entry is:

$$T_{\text{lookup}} = (1 - P_{\text{ocache}})(T_{\text{lookup\_PC}} + (1 - P_{PC})T_{\text{lookup\_TIDX}})$$

5.3.2 OIDX Update Cost

We do not need to update the PCache or the index pages in the TIDX immediately after an update has been done. This is done in the background, and can be postponed, increasing the probability that several updates can be done to each index page before they are written back. We calculate the average index update cost as the total index update costs during an interval, divided on the number of updates. In this context, we define the checkpoint interval to be the number of objects that can be written between two checkpoints. The number of written objects, N_{CP}, includes created as well as updated objects. $P_{\text{new}}N_{CP}$ of the written objects are creations of new objects, and $(1 - P_{\text{new}})N_{CP}$ of the written objects are updates of existing objects. We assume that the OD cache is large enough to keep all dirty ODs through one checkpoint interval, and that deleting and compacting pages can be done in background. This means that $N_{CP} < N_{\text{ocache}}$. Using a strategy that write a larger amount of ODs to the log before installing them into the TIDX, is difficult: If we did not keep all ODs not yet installed into the OIDX in the memory, we would have to search the log on each access, to check if the log contained a more recent version than the one in the OIDX.

Creation of New ODs

New object descriptors are created when new objects are created. The number of created objects is $N_{CR} = P_{\text{new}}N_{CP}$. When new objects are created, their ODs are appended to the index (we do not distribute the entries over the old node and the new one when the rightmost nodes are split), and we have clustered updates. As described previously, object creations are done directly to the TIDX, and not to the PCache. This contributes to $N_n^0 = \frac{N_{CR}}{\lfloor S_P/S_{\text{od}} \rfloor}$ created leaf pages. This is a subtree in the index tree, of height H_s, with $S_n = \sum_{i=0}^{H_s-1} N_n^i$ pages. The total cost of creating these object descriptors is the cost of writing S_n index pages to the disk. No installation read is needed for these pages. Assuming that the disk is not too fragmented, these pages can be written in one operation, mostly sequentially:

$$T_{\text{writenew}} = T_b(S_n S_P)$$

Modification of Existing ODs in the PCache

When an object is updated, a new object version is created, and a new OD has to be inserted into the OIDX. The number of updated objects during one checkpoint interval is $N_U = N_{CP} - N_{CR}$.

In general, at least one OD will be inserted into each PCache page (the number of updates in one checkpoint interval is much larger than the number of PCache pages). In this case, the most efficient way to update the PCache is to read sequentially a number of PCache pages, update them,

[3]It is interesting to note that by using this approach, we do things according to the log-structured file system philosophy, which our Vagabond TOODB will be based on [8].

write them back, and continue with the next segment. Assuming that PCache-to-TIDX writeback has high enough priority, we can assume that when inserting a new entry into a PCache node, there is always a non-dirty entry that can be removed. The cost of this is:

$$T_{\text{write\_to\_PC}} = 2T_b(S_{PC}S_P)$$

where S_{PC} is the number of PCache nodes.

PCache-to-TIDX Writeback Cost

The purpose of the PCache-to-TIDX writeback is to always have non-dirty slots in the PCache nodes, where new entries can be inserted. The PCache-to-TIDX writeback runs continuously in the background. The period for each round is ideally so long that each PCache node is almost full of dirty entries when it is processed.

The cost is equal to reading a number of PCache nodes (sequential reading), and writing the dirty entries back to the TIDX. If we assume each PCache node is almost full when we process it, we have fN_{PC} entries to write back in each round, where f is the PCache node dirty fill factor, i.e., the amount of dirty entries in the node. This value should ideally be close to 1, but to avoid delays in normal processing due to overflow of dirty entries in nodes, f should be sufficiently small, we will in the calculations in this paper use a value of 0.90. The number of update objects during each round of PCache-to-TIDX writeback is $N_{SCP} = fN_{PC}$, which we call the *super checkpoint period.*

Updating the index involves a page installation read, where the page where the last (current) version resides is read from disk, if the page is not already in the buffer. The cost of this is $T_{\text{lookup\_TIDX}}$ for each *distinct* object modified. The number of distinct updated objects is:

$$N_{DU} = N_{\text{distinct}}(N_{SCP}, N_{\text{objver}}, \Pi_A)$$

However, as noted in Section 3.2, not all objects in a TOODB are temporal. We denote the fraction of the data accesses going to temporal objects as P_{temporal}. Only updates of these objects alter the OIDX, updates of non-temporal objects will be done in-place. The number of distinct updated temporal objects is:

$$N_{DU}^V = P_{\text{temporal}} N_{DU}$$

The number of leaf pages to be accessed as a part of the installation read:

$$N_m = N_{\text{distinct}}(N_{DU}^V, N_{tree}^0, \Pi_L)$$

If there is space for the new OD in the leaf node of the TIDX, it can be inserted there, and the node can be written back. If there is no space in the node, the node is split, a process done recursively, possibly to the root. If a node is split, the parent node has to be updated as well. Because of the possibility of page splits, determining the update cost is difficult. With sufficiently many entries on each index node, the probability of page split is small enough to be neglected [13]. However, for some pages, there are more than one insertion to that page (possibly generated by several updates to one object during one checkpoint interval, remember that *each update creates a new entry to be inserted into the OIDX*). Thus, we include the page split in our cost functions. According to Loomis [5], the probability of a split in a B$^+$-tree of order m is less than $\frac{1}{\lceil m/2 \rceil - 1}$, so we approximate $P_{\text{split}} \approx \frac{1}{\lceil (S_P/S_{\text{od}})/2 \rceil - 1}$. For each split, the new page needs to be written back, as well as the updated parent node. However, note that there may be several splits affecting one parent node, in this case, it needs only be written back once. The resulting total write back cost is:

$$\begin{aligned} T'_{\text{writeback}} &= (N_m + N_m 2P_{\text{split}})T_P \\ &= N_m(1 + 2P_{\text{split}})T_P \end{aligned}$$

The equation above assumes that there will on average be less than one entry to be inserted in each leaf node. That is the case as long as we use the following optimization: If the checkpoint interval is sufficiently large, it is more efficient to read the complete index, update the index nodes, and write it back (if memory is not large enough, this is done in segments). This will be very efficient, as the reading and writing will be sequential. The cost of this is:

$$T''_{\text{writeback}} = 2T_b(N_{\text{tree}}S_P)$$

giving:

$$T_{\text{writeback}} = \min(N_m T_{\text{lookup\_}TIDX} + T'_{\text{writeback}}, T''_{\text{writeback}})$$

Average Index Update Cost

The average index update cost per object is the total cost of updating the PCache and the PCache-to-TIDX writeback, divided on the number of updated objects:

$$T_{\text{update}} = \frac{T_{\text{writenew}}}{N_{CP}} + \frac{T_{\text{write\_to\_PC}}}{N_{CP}} + \frac{T_{\text{writeback}}}{N_{SCP}}$$

Note that the total PCache-to-TIDX writeback is for one super checkpoint period, while the PCache update and object creating cost is per ordinary checkpoint period.

5.4 OIDX Access Cost Without PCache

In a system with no PCache, the OIDX lookup cost is:

$$T_{\text{lookup}} = (1 - P_{\text{ocache}})T_{\text{lookup\_TIDX}}$$

Without a PCache, we need to write back all ODs to the TIDX each checkpoint interval. This is similar to PCache-to-TIDX writeback, except that we now write back only $N_{CP} - N_{CR}$ entries instead of N_{SCP}, which makes it more difficult to do it efficiently. The average update cost is:

$$T_{\text{update}} = \frac{T_{\text{writenew}}}{N_{CP}} + \frac{T_{\text{writeback\_TIDX}}}{N_{CP}}$$

Set	β_0^0	β_1^0	β_2^0	α_0^0	α_1^0	α_2^0
3P1	0.01	0.19	0.80	0.64	0.16	0.20
3P2	0.001	0.049	0.95	0.80	0.19	0.01
2P8020	0.20	0.80	-	0.80	0.20	-
2P9505	0.05	0.95	-	0.95	0.05	-

Table 1: Partition sizes and partition access probabilities for the partitioning sets used in this study.

where $T_{\text{writeback\_TIDX}}$ is calculated according to the equations used for $T_{\text{writeback}}$, except that $N_{CP} - N_{CR}$ is used instead of N_{SCP} in calculating $N_D U$. When calculating the buffer hit probabilities, the index page buffer is only used for the TIDX, with the absence of a PCache, no memory is used for PCache pointers and tables.

6 Performance Study

We have now derived the cost functions necessary to calculate the average cost of OIDX access under different system parameters and access patterns, with and without the use of a PCache. We will in this section study how different values for these parameters affects the access cost, under which conditions using a PCache is beneficial, and optimal sizes for the PCache. The mix of updates and lookups to the OIDX affects the optimal parameter values, and they should be studied together. If we denote the probability that an operation is a write as P_{write}, the average index access cost is the average of the cost of all index lookup and index update operations:

$$T_{\text{access}} = (1 - P_{\text{write}})T_{\text{lookup}} + P_{\text{write}}T_{\text{update}}$$

Our goal here is to minimize T_{access}. We measure the gain from using a PCache, with optimal parameter values, as:

$$\text{Gain} = 100\left(\frac{T_{\text{access\_noPCache}} - T_{\text{access}}}{T_{\text{access}}}\right)$$

where $T_{\text{access\_noPCache}}$ is the access cost when not using a PCache. In the rest of this paper, we give PCache size as a fraction of the TIDX size.

It is difficult to know what kind of access pattern that will be experienced in TOODBs. It is possible to do predictions based on current access patterns, but we believe that it is quite possible that when support for temporal features become common, application developers can utilize these in new ways. The access patterns used in this paper do not necessarily represent any of these, but we will use them to show that the gain from using the PCache is considerable, under most conditions and access patterns.

We have used four access patterns. The partition sizes and access probabilities are summarized in Table 1 (note that this is the *OID* access pattern Π_A, and not the *index page* access pattern Π_L). In the first partitioning set, we have three partitions, extensions of the 80/20 model, but

Parameter	Value	Parameter	Value
M_{ocache}	0.1 M	N_{objver}	100 mill.
V_s	50 KB	U	0.67
t_r	8.33 ms	N_{CP}	$0.9N_{\text{ocache}}$
S_P	8 KB	P_{new}	0.2
S_{od}	32 B	P_{write}	0.2
S_{oh}	8 B	P_{temporal}	0.8
S_{ie}	16 B		

Table 2: Default parameters.

with the 20% hot spot partition further divided, into a 1% hot spot area, a 19% less hot area, and a 80% relatively cold area. The second partitioning set resembles the access pattern close to what we expect it to be in future TOODBs, with a large cold set, consisting of old versions. The two other sets in this analysis have each two partitions, with hot spot areas of 20% and 5%.

Unless otherwise noted, results and numbers in the next sections are based on calculations using default parameters as summarized in Table 2.[4] Note that in this paper, when we talk about available main memory, we only consider the memory available for index related buffering, M_i. Main memory for object page buffering is orthogonal to this issue.

With the values in Table 2, the ODs would occupy $\approx$ 3.1 GB if stored compactly. Typically, the objects themselves occupies at least four times as much space as the OIDX, if this is reflected in available main memory buffer, $M_i = 50$ MB should imply a total buffer memory of 200-300 MB. In this study, we mainly investigate the index memory interval from $M_i = 1$ MB to $M_i = 50$ MB, as this is the most dynamic area of OIDX access cost, but we will also show how the availability of larger amounts of memory affects performance.

6.1 The Effect of Using a PCache

Figure 4 illustrates the typical cost involved in OIDX access, using the default parameters, but with different index memory sizes M_i. The gain is from 20% to several 100%. We see that the PCache is especially beneficial with relative small index memory sizes compared to the total index size. As the index size increases, the gain decreases (but as we will show in Section 6.4, the gain actually increases again with larger main memory sizes).

6.2 Optimal PCache Size

The optimal PCache sizes are illustrated to the left on Figure 5. With access pattern 2P8020 and 3P1, most of the

[4] Note that even though some of the parameter combinations in the following sections are unlikely to represent the average over time, they can occur in periods, e.g., more write than read operations. It is in situations like this that adaptive self tuning systems would be interesting, when parameter sets differs from the average, which systems traditionally have been tuned against.

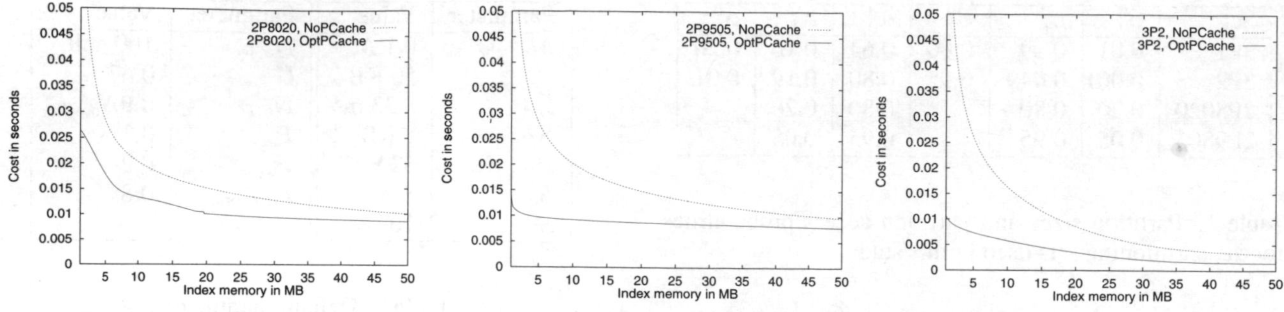

Figure 4: OIDX access cost with and without employing a PCache, with access patterns according to 2P8020, 2P9505, and 3P3.

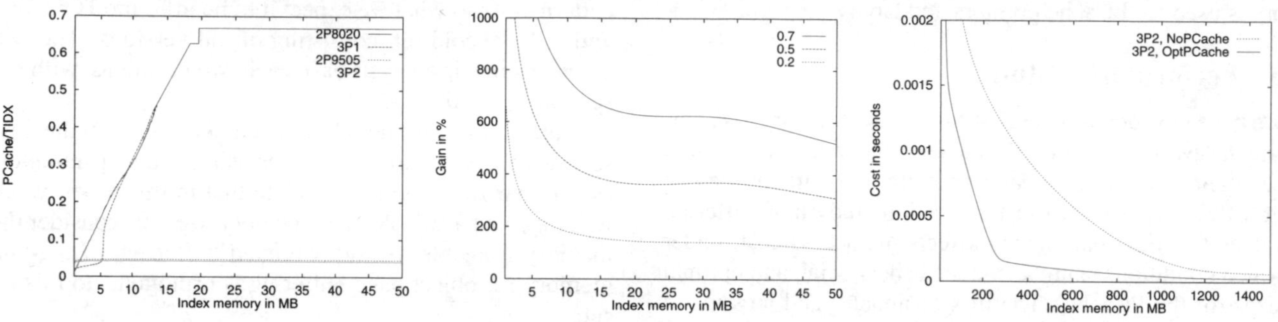

Figure 5: Optimal PCache size for different access patterns to the left. In the middle, the effect of different update ratios P_{write} for access pattern 3P2. To the right, we have the OIDX access cost with and without employing a PCache, employing large index memory sizes.

available index memory, except the memory reserved for the OD cache, is used to store the pointers and LRU tables for the PCache. 2P9505 and 3P2 have more emphasized hot spot ares, in this case, a smaller PCache is optimal, just enough to store the hot spot area.

6.3 The Effect of Different Update Ratios

The main purpose of the PCache is to increase OIDX update performance. This is illustrated very well on the middle subfigure of Figure 5, which shows the gain using different values for P_{write}.

6.4 The Effect of Larger Amounts of Memory

The right subfigure of Figure 5 illustrates that using a PCache is also beneficial when a large main memory buffer is available. The minimum gain here is when $M_i \approx 80$ MB. At that point, the gain is 94%. It then increases again, until $M_i \approx 300$ MB, where the gain is over 600%. After that, the gain from using PCache slowly decreases, with increasing amounts of available main memory.

6.5 The Effect of Different Page Sizes

The page size is an important factor in determining the indexing performance. The optimal page size is a compromise of two contradicting factors. Because of low locality, large page sizes in an OIDX means more wasted space in the index page buffer, and the optimal page size is thus much smaller. However, small pages also results in a higher tree. Even though in most cases upper levels of the index tree will be resident in memory, a tree with smaller page size also needs more space, reducing the buffer hit probability. We can see that there are two strategies for efficiency: Either large pager, which is particularly advantageous for the creation of objects, and small pages, to capture the fact that there is low level of sharing. We have studied optimal page sizes for the different access patterns, with possible page sizes between 2 KB and 64 KB. All shows that a small page size, less than the 8 KB blocks commonly used, is beneficial.

6.6 PCache Using Separate Buffers

We have also done the analysis with separate buffers for the PCache and TIDX. The analysis shows that a cost reduction of a few percent, typically from 2 to 3%, can be found. However, in this case, it is very important with accurate buffer partitioning. This assumes knowledge of current access pattern at all times, something which is difficult in practice. LRU buffer management is in this sense self adaptive, and with only marginal improvement when using separate buffer, we advice against using separate buffers.

7 Conclusions and Future Work

We have in this paper described the PCache, and how it can be used to improve performance in an TOODB by reducing the number of disk operations needed for index maintenance. We have developed cost models which we have used to analyze the improved performance and characteristics of the PCache, under different access patterns, and memory and index sizes. The results show that:

1. The OID indexing cost in a TOODB will be large, but can be reduced by the use of a PCache.

2. The gain from using a PCache can be large.

3. The gain is especially good when using an *optimal* size of the PCache. Having an optimally tuned system is important. Access pattern in a database system is dynamic, and the system should be able to detect this, and tune the size of index page buffer and OD cache size accordingly. The cost models in this paper can be of valuable use for optimizers and automatic tuning tools in TOODBs.

In this paper, we have described several strategies for PCache LRU table storage, and PCache update strategies when doing read operations. These issues are interesting further work. It is possible that by combining several strategies in a dynamic adaptive PCache, performance can be improved even more, and making the system less vulnerable to rapidly changing access patterns and variants of data skew.

This paper described the PCache used to improve OID index in TOODBs. The PCache should also be applicable to general secondary indexing, especially interesting is applications where updates are not clustered, i.e., have low locality.

Acknowledgments

I would like to thank Olav Sandstå and Kjell Bratbergsengen for useful discussions and constructive comments.

References

[1] A. K. Bhide, A. Dan, and D. M. Dias. A simple analysis of the LRU buffer policy and its relationship to buffer warm-up transient. In *Proceedings of the Ninth International Conference on Data Engineering*, 1993.

[2] A. Eickler, C. A. Gerlhof, and D. Kossmann. Performance evaluation of OID mapping techniques. In *Proceedings of the 21st VLDB Conference*, 1995.

[3] R. Elmasri, G. T. J. Wuu, and V. Kouramajian. The time index and the monotonic B$^+$-tree. In A. U. Tansel, J. Clifford, S. K. Gadia, S. Jajodia, A. Segev, and R. Snodgrass, editors, *Temporal databases: theory, design and implementation*. The Benjamin/Cummings Publishing Company, Inc., 1993.

[4] D. Lomet and B. Salzberg. Access methods for multiversion data. In *Proceedings of the 1989 ACM SIGMOD*, 1989.

[5] M. E. Loomis. *Data Management and File Structures*. Prentice Hall, 1989.

[6] M. L. McAuliffe. *Storage Management Methods for Object Database Systems*. PhD thesis, University of Wisconsin-Madison, 1997.

[7] P. Muth, P. O'Neil, A. Pick, and G. Weikum. Design, implementation, and performance of the LHAM log-structured history data access method. In *Proceedings of the 24th VLDB Conference*, 1998.

[8] K. Nørvåg and K. Bratbergsengen. Log-only temporal object storage. In *Proceedings of the 8th International Workshop on Database and Expert Systems Applications, DEXA'97*, 1997.

[9] K. Nørvåg and K. Bratbergsengen. An analytical study of object identifier indexing. In *Proceedings of the 9th International Conference on Database and Expert Systems Applications, DEXA'98*, 1998.

[10] K. Nørvåg and K. Bratbergsengen. Optimizing OID indexing cost in temporal object-oriented database systems. In *Proceedings of the 5th International Conference on Foundations of Data Organization, FODO'98*, 1998.

[11] K. Nørvåg and K. Bratbergsengen. An analytical study of object identifier indexing. Technical Report IDI 4/98, Norwegian University of Science and Technology, 1998. Available from http://www.idi.ntnu.no/grupper/DB-grp/.

[12] T. Suzuki and H. Kitagawa. Development and performance analysis of a temporal persistent object store POST/C++. In *Proceedings of the 7th Australasian Database Conference*, 1996.

[13] J. D. Ullman. *Principles of database and knowledge-base systems*. Computer Science Press, 1988.

Cache Conscious Indexing for Decision-Support in Main Memory

Jun Rao
Columbia University
junr@cs.columbia.edu

Kenneth A. Ross*
Columbia University
kar@cs.columbia.edu

Abstract

We study indexing techniques for main memory, including hash indexes, binary search trees, T-trees, B+-trees, interpolation search, and binary search on arrays. In a decision-support context, our primary concerns are the lookup time, and the space occupied by the index structure.

Our goal is to provide faster lookup times than binary search by paying attention to reference locality and cache behavior, without using substantial extra space. We propose a new indexing technique called "Cache-Sensitive Search Trees" (CSS-trees). Our technique stores a directory structure on top of a sorted array. Nodes in this directory have size matching the cache-line size of the machine. We store the directory in an array and do not store internal-node pointers; child nodes can be found by performing arithmetic on array offsets.

We compare the algorithms based on their time and space requirements. We have implemented all of the techniques, and present a performance study on two popular modern machines. We demonstrate that with a small space overhead, we can reduce the cost of binary search on the array by more than a factor of two. We also show that our technique dominates B+-trees, T-trees, and binary search trees in terms of both space and time. A cache simulation verifies that the gap is due largely to cache misses.

*This research was supported by a David and Lucile Packard Foundation Fellowship in Science and Engineering, by an NSF Young Investigator Award, by NSF grant number IIS-98-12014, and by NSF CISE award CDA-9625374.

Proceedings of the 25th VLDB Conference, Edinburgh, Scotland, 1999.

1 Introduction

As random access memory gets cheaper, it becomes increasingly affordable to build computers with large main memories. The recent "Asilomar Report" ([BBC+98]) predicts "Within ten years, it will be common to have a terabyte of main memory serving as a buffer pool for a hundred-terabyte database. All but the largest database tables will be resident in main memory." But main memory data processing is not as simple as increasing the buffer pool size. An important issue is cache behavior. The traditional assumption that memory references have uniform cost is no longer valid given the current speed gap between cache access and main memory access. So, improving cache behavior is going to be an imperative task in main memory data processing. In this paper, we focus on how to make indexes cache conscious.

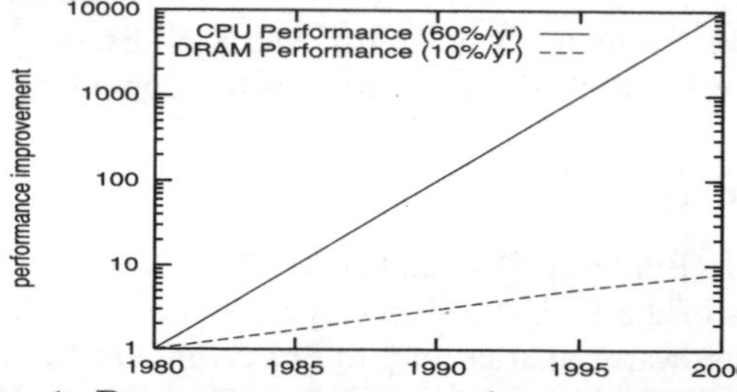

Figure 1: Processor-memory performance imbalance

Index structures are important even in main memory database systems. Although there are no disk accesses, indexes can be used to reduce overall computation time without using too much extra space. With a large amount of RAM, most of the indexes can be memory resident. Past work

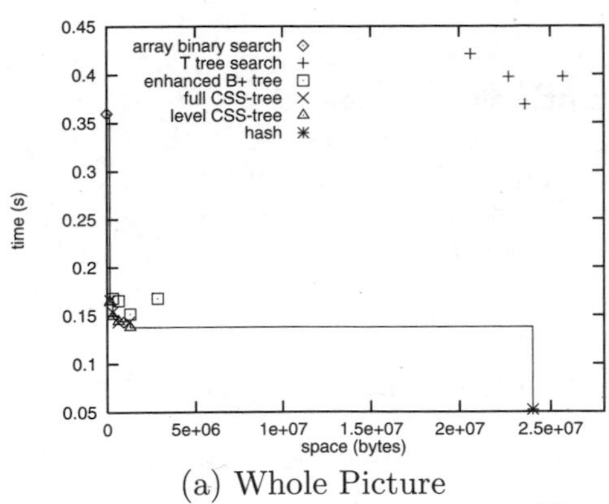

(a) Whole Picture

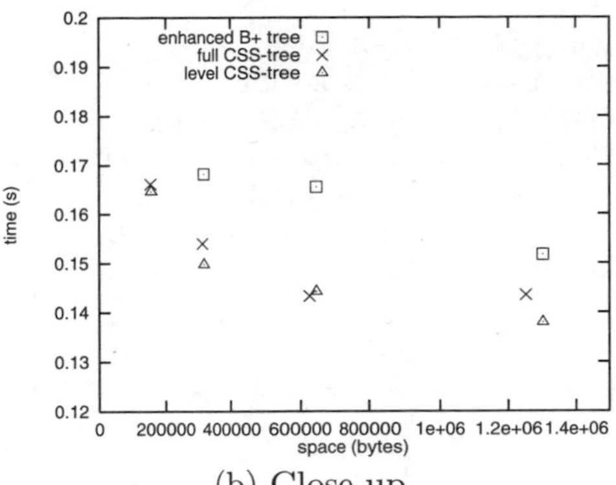

(b) Close-up

Figure 2: Space/time Tradeoffs

on measuring the performance of indexing in main-memory databases includes [LC86b, WK90], with [LC86b] being the most comprehensive on the specific issue of indexing. In the thirteen years since [LC86b] was published, there have been substantial changes in the architecture of computer chips. The most relevant change is that CPU speeds have been increasing at a much faster rate (60% per year) than memory speeds (10% per year) as shown in Figure 1 (borrowed from [CLH98]). Thus, the *relative* cost of a cache miss has increased by two orders of magnitude since 1986. As a result, we cannot assume that the ranking of indexing algorithms given in [LC86b] would be valid on today's architectures. In fact, our experimental results indicate very different relative outcomes from [LC86b] for lookup speed.

Another recent development has been the explosion of interest in On-Line Analytical Processing (OLAP). [Fre95, Fre97] contrasts the requirements of OLAP with OLTP systems and contends that the real performance gains can be obtained by separating the two systems. A dedicated OLAP system can have a much better query performance if we are willing to sacrifice update performance. Commercial systems such as Sybase IQ [Syb97] were designed for such purposes. Thus, typical OLAP workloads are query-intensive, and have infrequent batch updates. For example, a data warehouse for a university, containing all the student records, is probably updated once per day. Census data sets are collected periodically and will remain static for a relatively long period of time. These systems are in the scale of several gigabytes and can already fit in RAM today. Given the current trend, we expect more and more disk-based applications will be moved to main memory in the future. Since updates are batched in those systems, incremental updates of indexes may not be very important. In fact, we may want to rebuild indexes from scratch after a batch of updates, if that leads to faster index searches. In this paper, we focus on such an OLAP environment.

Two important criteria for the selection of index structures are *space* and *time*. Space is critical in a main memory database; we may have a limited amount of space available for precomputed structures such as indexes. Given space constraints, we try to optimize the time taken by index lookups. In a main-memory database there are several factors influencing the speed of database operations. An important factor is the degree of locality in data references for a given algorithm. Good data locality leads to fewer (expensive) cache misses, and better performance.

We study a variety of existing techniques, including hash indexes, binary search on a sorted list of record identifiers, binary trees, B+-trees [Com79], T-trees [LC86a], and interpolation search. We also introduce a new technique called "Cache-Sensitive Search Trees" (CSS-trees). CSS-trees augment binary search by storing a directory structure on top of the sorted list of elements. CSS-trees differ from B+-trees by avoiding storing the child pointers in each node. The CSS-tree is organized in such a way that traversing the tree yields good data reference locality (unlike binary search), and hence relatively few cache misses. CSS-trees also take advantage of the OLAP context to optimize search performance, at the expense of update performance.

We summarize the space/time tradeoffs of various methods in Figure 2. Each point for T-trees, enhanced B+-trees and CSS-trees corresponds to a specific node size (multiple of cache line size). Normally a larger node size means less space but more search time. The stepped line basically tells us what's the optimal searching time for a given amount of space. Our conclusion is that CSS-trees dominate T-trees and enhanced B+-trees in both space and time. There are tradeoffs between space and time for binary search, CSS-trees and hash indices. CSS-trees reasonably balance space and time. We discuss this issue in more detail in Section 7.

2 Main Memory Databases

Main Memory Database Systems: Some past

work on main memory databases has addressed the problems of concurrency, transaction processing and logging [GMS86, LN88, JLRS94], and recovery [Hag86, LC87]. Systems with a significant query-processing component include OBE [WK90], MM-DBMS [LC87], and Starburst [LSC92]. More recently, the TimesTen corporation (formerly the Smallbase project at Hewlett-Packard) has developed a commercial main-memory system, with claims of tenfold speedups over disk-based systems [Sof97]. Most of the systems do not address the issue of cache reference locality.

Data Layout: [AHK85] and others describe the concept of a domain. When data is first loaded into main memory, distinct data values are stored in an external structure, the domain, and only pointers to domain values are stored in place in each column. This has the benefits of: (a) saving space in the presence of duplicates, (b) simplified handling of variable-length fields and (c) pointer comparisons can be used for equality tests. In the main memory database project at Columbia University, we focus on an OLAP main memory database system. We go further than [AHK85] by keeping the domain values in order and associate each value with a domain ID (represented by an integer). As a result, we can process both equality and inequality tests on domain IDs directly, rather than on the original values. Although keeping values in order has extra cost, we expect the data is updated infrequently. Independently, Tandem Inc.'s InfoCharger storage engine [Eng98] has also chosen to keep domain values in sorted order. The use of domains means that many indexes can be built with smaller keys.

Indexing in Main Memory Databases: Although sequential data access is much cheaper in main memory than in disk-based systems, indexing remains very important in main memory databases. First of all, searching an index is still useful for answering single value selection queries and range queries. Next, cheaper random access makes indexed nested loop joins more affordable in main memory databases. Indexed nested loop join is pipelinable, requiring minimal storage for intermediate results and is relatively easy to implement. As a matter of fact, indexed nested loop join is the only join method used in [WK90]. This approach requires a lot of searching through indexes on the inner relations. Last but not least, transforming domain values to domain IDs (as described in the previous section) requires searching on the domain.

A list of record identifiers sorted by some columns provides ordered access to the base relation. Ordered access is useful for range queries and for satisfying interesting orders [SAC$^+$79]. A sorted array is an index structure itself since binary search can be used.

Assumptions: We assume an OLAP environment, so we don't care too much about updates. Our main concerns are the lookup time for an index, and the space required to store the index. There are many applications in this class, as described in Section 1.

3 Cache Optimization on Indexes

In this section, we first describe cache memories and the impact of cache optimization. We then give a survey of the related work. Finally, we analyze the cache behavior of various existing index structures for searching and point out their shortcomings.

Cache memories are small, fast static RAM memories that improve program performance by holding recently referenced data [Smi82]. Memory references satisfied by the cache, called hits, proceed at processor speed; those unsatisfied, called misses, incur a cache miss penalty and have to fetch the corresponding cache block from the main memory.

A cache can be parameterized by capacity, block size and associativity, where capacity is the size of the cache, block size is the basic transferring unit between cache and main memory, and associativity determines how many slots in the cache are potential destinations for a given address reference.

Cache optimization in a main memory database system is similar to main memory optimization in a disk-based system. But the management of the cache is done by the hardware and the database system doesn't have direct control of which block to bring into a cache. This makes cache optimization more subtle.

Typical cache optimization techniques include clustering, compression and coloring [CLH98]. Clustering tries to pack, in a cache block, data structure elements that are likely to be accessed successively. Compression tries to remove irrelevant data and thus increases cache block utilization by being able to put more useful elements in a cache block. This includes key compression, structure encodings such as pointer elimination and fluff extraction. Caches have finite associativity, which means that only a limited number of concurrently accessed data elements can map to the same cache line without causing conflict. Coloring maps contemporaneously-accessed elements to non-conflicting regions of the cache.

Previous research has attacked the processor-memory gap using the above techniques. Wolf and Lam [WL91] exploited cache reference locality to improve the performance of matrix multiplication. LaMarca and Ladner [LL96, LL97] considered the effects of caches on sorting algorithms and improved performance by restructuring these algorithms to exploit caches. In addition, they constructed a cache-conscious heap structure that clustered and aligned heap elements to cache blocks. [CLH98] demonstrated that cache optimization techniques can improve the spatial and temporal locality of pointer-based data structures. They showed improvement on various benchmarks.

In [NBC+94], Nyberg et al. have shown that for achieving high performance sorting, one should focus carefully on cache memory behavior.

Cache conscious algorithms have been considered in database systems also. In [SKN94], the authors suggested several ways to improve the cache reference locality of query processing operations such as joins and aggregations. They showed that the new algorithms can run 8% to 200% faster.

Although cache optimization has been considered on tree-based structures, nobody has looked at the influence of the cache on index structures used in database systems. Some other papers have considered the issue of compact representations of B-tree indexes [CS83, JTR87]. These papers appeared too early to consider cache issues since memory speed wasn't too slow compared with CPU speed. In the rest of this section, we study the cache behavior of various typical index structures used in main memory database systems.

Array Binary Search: The problem with binary search is that many accesses to elements of the sorted array result in a cache miss. We do not get misses for the first references because of temporal locality over many searches. We avoid misses for the last references, due to spatial locality, if many records from the array fit inside a single cache line. However, when the array is substantially bigger than the cache, many of the intervening accesses cause cache misses. In the worst case, the number of cache misses is of the order of the number of key comparisons.

T-Trees: T-Trees have been proposed as a better index structure in main memory database systems. A *T-Tree* [LC86a] is a balanced binary tree with many elements in a node. Elements in a node contain adjacent key values and are stored in order. Its aim is to balance the space overhead with searching time and cache behavior is not considered (thirteen years ago the gap between processor and main memory speeds was not that large). T-Trees put more keys in each node and give the impression of being cache conscious. But if we think carefully, we can observe that for most of the T-Tree nodes, only the two end keys are actually used for comparison (in the improved version [LC86b], only one key is used). This means that the utilization of each node is low. Since the number of key comparisons is still the same, T-Trees do not provide any better cache behavior than binary search.

Another problem with the T-Tree is that it has to store a record pointer for each key within a node. Since most of the time the record pointers won't be needed, essentially half of the space in each node is wasted. Potentially, one could put just RIDs in the T-tree with no keys, but then search is much slower due to indirection.

B+-trees: Although B+-trees were designed for disk-based database systems, they actually have a much better cache behavior than T-trees. In each internal node we store keys and child pointers, but the record pointers are stored on leaf nodes only. Multiple keys are used to search within a node. If we fit each node in a cache line, this means that a cache load can satisfy more than one comparison. So each cache line has a better utilization ratio.

Enhanced B+-trees: In an OLAP environment, we can use all the slots in a B+-tree node (similar to compact B-Trees [CS83] and the ISAM method used in the IBM OS/360 operating system [GR93]) and rebuild the tree when batch updates arrive. We can design the node size to be exactly the same as a cache line and align each node. We can also hard-code the node search since we know all the slots are used. But B+-trees enhanced in these ways still need to store child pointers within each node (even when compact). So for any given node size, only half of the space can be used to store keys.

In the rest of this paper we shall consider only "enhanced B+-trees" as described above; however, we may sometimes use "B+-trees" for brevity.

Hash: Hash indices can also benefit from cache optimization. The most common hashing method is chained bucket hashing [Knu73]. In [GBC98], the authors use the cache line size as the bucket size and squeeze in as many $< key, RID >$ pairs as possible. This can reduce the number of cache misses when scanning through the buckets. Hash indices are fast for searching only if the length of each bucket chain is small. This requires a fairly large directory size and thus a fairly large amount of space. Skewed data can seriously affect the performance of hash indices unless we have a relatively sophisticated hash function, which will increase the computation time. Hash indices do not preserve order. To provide ordered access, an ordered list has to be kept in addition to the hash indices.

4 Cache Sensitive Search Trees

In this section, we present our cache conscious searching methods called CSS-trees. Section 4.1

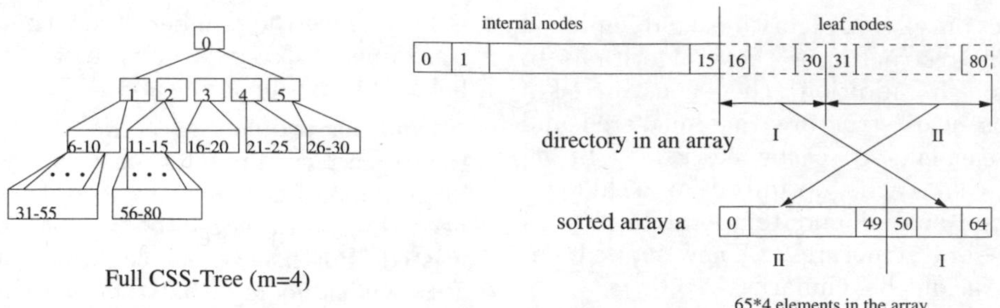

Figure 3: Layout of a full CSS-tree

introduces the concept of "full" CSS-trees. We talk about "level" CSS-trees in Section 4.2.

Suppose that we have a sorted array `a[1..n]` of `n` elements. The array `a` could contain the record-identifiers of records in some database table in the order of some attribute k. `a` could alternatively contain column-k keys from the records in the table, with a companion array holding the corresponding record-identifiers, using some extra space to avoid an indirect reference during the search. `a` could alternatively contain records of a table or domain values.

Binary search of `a` has a serious cache usage problem as described in Section 3. A second problem with binary search is that it requires a calculation to be performed $\log_2 n$ times to find the next element to search. Even if this calculation uses a shift rather than a division by two [WK90], the calculation represents a significant portion of the execution time needed. Nevertheless, binary search has the benefit that no additional space beyond `a` is needed to perform a search. Our goal is to improve upon the search time of binary search without using a significant amount of additional space.

4.1 Full CSS-Trees

We create a search tree with nodes containing exactly m keys. (We'll see how to choose m later.) If the depth of the tree is d, then the tree is a complete $(m+1)$-ary search tree up to depth $d-1$, and at depth d the leaves are filled from left to right. An example tree is shown for $m = 4$ in the left diagram of Figure 3 (the numbers in the boxes are node numbers and each node has four keys). The nodes of a CSS-tree can be stored in an array as shown on the right in Figure 3. Note that we do not need to store explicit pointers to child nodes; the children of a node can be computed from offsets in the CSS-tree array. (The exact formulas are given below.)

Our basic idea is to store a CSS-tree as a directory structure on top of the array `a`. There are two reasons why we expect a traversal of such a tree to be faster than binary search. First, if we choose m such that a node fits in a cache line, then all local searching within a node happens with at most one cache miss. As a result we get at most $\log_{m+1} n$ cache misses for a lookup, unlike binary search which gets up to $\log_2 n$ cache misses. (Even if a node occupies two cache lines, half the time only one cache miss will be generated, while half the time there will be two cache misses.) Second, we can hard-code the traversal within a node, so that calculations needed to find the next node happen $\log_{m+1} n$ times rather than $\log_2 n$ times. (Note that the total number of comparisons is the same.)

Suppose that we number the nodes and keys starting at 0. If we have an internal node numbered b, then it is not difficult to show that the children of that node are numbered from $b(m+1)+1$ to $b(m+1)+(m+1)$. Within the directory, we have m keys per node, so key number i in the directory array maps to node number $\lfloor \frac{i}{m} \rfloor$. As a result, one can find the offset of the first key of the child nodes within the directory array as $(\lfloor \frac{i}{m} \rfloor * (m+1)+1) * m$ through $(\lfloor \frac{i}{m} \rfloor * (m+1)+m+1) * m$.

A subtle point in the structure of a CSS-tree is that we store the leaf nodes in a contiguous array in key order. This conflicts with the natural order of the CSS-tree that stores the nodes from left to right, level by level. The CSS-tree order would split the array, putting the right half of the array (which appears at a higher level than the left half of the array) ahead of the left half of the array. In Figure 3, the natural tree order is to store nodes 16-30 before nodes 31-80. However, when the leaves are stored in a sorted array, nodes 31-80 come before nodes 16-30. Since maintaining a contiguous array in key order is desirable for other purposes, and since the array is given to us without assumptions that it can be restructured, we leave the array in key order. To get to the correct leaves when searching the CSS-tree, we modify the natural search algorithm.

When performing a search, we move from parent to child by recalculating the offset within the directory structure as above. We mark the end of the directory structure (in Figure 3, that's the last key in node 15), and terminate this portion of the search when the computed offset exceeds the endpoint. If the leaves were stored in the natural CSS-tree order, we'd use this offset to look up the directory directly.

However, since the two parts of the leaf nodes are stored in reverse order in a separate array, we need to process this offset further.

The two parts of the leaf nodes are mapped into the sorted array as shown in Figure 3. We use y to denote the boundary of the two parts of the leaf nodes, which is the offset of the first key at the deeper leaf level in the directory array. (In Figure 3 that's the first key in node 31.) Given an offset x of a key in a leaf node, we compare it with y to determine which part of the sorted array to look into. If $x > y$, we find the element at position $x - y$ from the *start* of the sorted array a. Otherwise, we find the element at position $y - x$ from the *end* of a. For example, in Figure 3, the first key in leaf node 30 can be found at the first key in node 64 in the sorted array.

Note that our techniques apply to sorted arrays having elements of size different from the size of a key. Offsets into the leaf array are independent of the record size within the array; the compiler will generate the appropriate byte offsets.

The following lemma tells us how to calculate the node number of the last internal node, and the node number y. Key offsets can be obtained by multiplying these numbers by m.

Lemma 4.1: Let $n = N * m$ be the number of elements in the sorted array a (N is the number of leaf nodes). The total number of internal nodes in a full CSS-tree is $\frac{(m+1)^k-1}{m} - \lfloor\frac{(m+1)^k-N}{m}\rfloor$. The first leaf node in the bottom level is number $\frac{(m+1)^k-1}{m}$. In both formulas, $k = \lceil \log_{m+1}(N) \rceil$.

Notice that CSS-trees are stored in a way similar to heaps. This is possible because of the way we "virtually" split the sorted array. B+-trees can't use the same technique since they require all the leaves to be on the same level.

Building a Full CSS-Tree: To build a full CSS-tree from a sorted array, we first split the sorted array *logically* into two parts (based on Lemma 4.1) and establish the mapping between the leaf nodes and elements in the sorted array. We then start with the last internal node. For each entry in the node, we fill it with the value of the largest key in its immediate left subtree. Finding the largest key in a subtree can be done by following the link in the rightmost branch until we reach the leaf nodes.

Some internal nodes, namely ancestors of the last leaf node at the deepest level, may not have a full complement of keys. In our algorithm, we simply fill in those dangling keys with the last element in the first half of array a. So there may be duplicate keys in some internal nodes. In our searching algorithm, we tune the searching within each node in such a way that the leftmost key will always be found in case of duplicates. So we will never reach the leaf nodes in the deepest level with an index out of the range of the first half of the sorted array.

Although it's difficult to incrementally update a full CSS-tree, it's relatively inexpensive to build such a tree from scratch. Our experiments show that to build a full CSS-tree from a sorted array of twenty-five million integer keys takes less than one second on a modern machine. Therefore, when batch updates arrive, we can afford to rebuild the CSS-tree.

Searching a Full CSS-Tree: Once a full CSS-tree is built, we can search for a key. We start from the root node. Every time we reach an internal node, we do a binary search to find out which branch to go to. We repeat until we reach a leaf node. Finally, we map the leaf node into the sorted array and binary search the node.

All the searches within a node consist of hard-coded *if-else* statements. When doing binary search in the internal nodes, we keep checking whether the keys in the left part are greater than or equal to the searching key. We stop when we find the first slot that has a value smaller than the searching key and then follow the branch on the right. (If such a slot can't be found, we follow the leftmost branch.) In this way, if there are duplicates in a node, we are guaranteed to find the leftmost key among all the duplicates. When there are duplicate keys being indexed, we can return the leftmost match in a fashion similar to B+-trees.

4.2 Level CSS-Trees

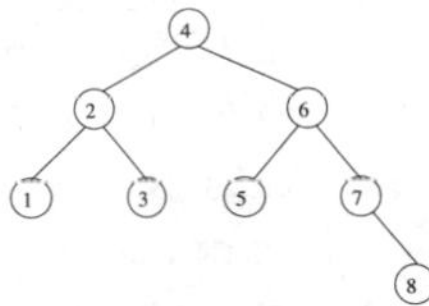

Figure 4: Node with 8 keys

A full CSS-tree with m entries per node will have exactly m keys, i.e., all the entries are fully used. Figure 4 shows the binary search tree of a node with $m = 2^3$ entries. Out of the nine possible branches, seven of them need three comparisons and two of them need four. But if we waste one entry and just put seven keys per node, we will have a full binary search tree and all the branches need three comparisons. This may give us some benefit. So for $m = 2^t$, we define a tree that only uses $m - 1$ entries per node and has a branching factor of m a *level CSS-tree.* A level CSS-tree will be deeper than the corresponding full CSS-tree since now the branching factor is m instead of $m+1$. However, we have fewer comparisons per node. If N is the number of nodes that the elements in the sorted array can form, a

Method	branching factor	# of levels (l)	comparisons per internal node (nComp)	comparisons per leaf node (A_{child})
Binary search	2	$\log_2 n$	1	1
T-trees	2	$\log_2 \frac{n}{m} - 1$	1	$\log_2 m$
enhanced B+-trees	$\frac{m}{2}$	$\log_{\frac{m}{2}} \frac{n}{m}$	$\log_2 m - 1$	$\log_2 m$
Full CSS-trees	$m+1$	$\log_{m+1} \frac{n}{m}$	$(1 + \frac{2}{m+1}) \log_2 m$	$\log_2 m$
Level CSS-trees	m	$\log_m \frac{n}{m}$	$\log_2 m$	$\log_2 m$

Method	Total comparisons	Moving across Level Level	Cache Misses $\frac{mK}{c} <= 1$	Cache Misses $\frac{mK}{c} > 1$
Binary search	$\log_2 n$	$\log_2 n * A_b$	$\log_2 n$	$\log_2 n$
T-trees	$\log_2 n$	$\log_2 n * D$	$\log_2 n$	$\log_2 n$
enhanced B+-trees	$\log_2 n$	$\log_{\frac{m}{2}} \frac{n}{m} * D$	$\frac{\log_2 n}{\log_2 m - 1}$	$\log_{\frac{m}{2}} n((\log_2 \frac{mK}{c}) + \frac{c}{mK})$
Full CSS-trees	$\frac{m+3}{m+1} \log_{m+1} m \log_2 n$	$\log_{m+1} \frac{n}{m} * A_{fcss}$	$\frac{\log_2 n}{\log_2 (m+1)}$	$\log_{m+1} n((\log_2 \frac{mK}{c}) + \frac{c}{mK})$
Level CSS-trees	$\log_2 n$	$\log_m \frac{n}{m} * A_{lcss}$	$\frac{\log_2 n}{\log_2 m}$	$\log_m n((\log_2 \frac{mK}{c}) + \frac{c}{mK})$

Table 1: Time analysis

level CSS-tree has $\log_m N$ levels while a full CSS-tree has $\log_{m+1} N$ levels. The number of comparisons per node is t for a level CSS-tree and $t * (1 + \frac{2}{m+1})$ for a full CSS-tree. So the total number of comparisons for a level CSS-tree is $\log_m N * t = \log_2 N$ and that for a full CSS-tree is $\log_{m+1} N * t * (1 + \frac{2}{m+1}) = \log_2 N * \log_{m+1} m * (1 + \frac{2}{m+1})$. The ratio of the former to the latter is $\frac{(m+1) \log_m (m+1)}{m+3}$. Thus a level CSS-tree always uses fewer comparisons than a full CSS-tree for searching. On the other hand, level CSS-trees may require $\log_m N$ cache accesses and $\log_m N$ node traversals, compared with $\log_{m+1} N$ for full CSS-trees. Whether we obtain a net gain in speed depends upon how time-consuming a comparison operation is compared with node traversals and cache accesses. A level CSS-tree still utilizes most of the data in each cache line. It uses a little more space than a full CSS-tree, but this may be desirable for users who want to trade space for time.

The building of level CSS-trees is similar to that of full CSS-trees. We can also make good use of the empty slot in each node. During the population, we can use that slot to store the largest value in the last branch of each node. We can thus avoid traversing the whole subtree to find the largest element. The searching algorithm of a level CSS-tree is similar to that of a full CSS-tree. The only difference is the calculation of the offset of a child node.

5 Time and Space Analysis

In this section, we analytically compare the time performance and the space requirement for different methods. We let R denote the space taken by a record-identifier, K denote the space taken by a key, P denote the space taken by a child pointer and n denote the number of records being indexed. h denotes a hashing fudge factor (typically about 1.2, meaning that the hash table is 20% bigger than the raw data in the hash table). c denotes the size of a cache line in bytes, and s denotes the size of a node in a T-tree, CSS-tree or enhanced B+-tree measured in cache-lines. We choose typical values as follows: $R = K = P = 4$ bytes, $n = 10^7$, $h = 1.2$, $c = 64$ bytes and $s = 1$.

Time Analysis: To make the analysis easy, in this section we assume that R, P and K are the same. Thus we have a single parameter m, which is the number of slots per node. The size of a node in cache-lines is given by $s = \frac{mK}{c}$.

The first table in Table 1 shows the branching factor, number of levels, comparisons per internal node and comparisons per leaf node for each method. B+-trees have a smaller branching factor than CSS-trees since they need to store child pointers explicitly. The total cost of each searching method has three parts, namely the comparison cost, the cost of moving across levels and the cache miss cost. We show the three costs for each method in the second table in Table 1. We use D to denote the cost of dereferencing a pointer, A_b, A_{fcss}, A_{lcss} to denote the cost of computing the child address for binary search, full CSS-tree and level CSS-tree respectively. First of all, the comparison cost is more or less the same for all the methods. Full CSS-trees have slightly more comparisons than level CSS-trees as we described earlier. Some of the methods find the child node by following pointers and others by arithmetic calculations. The relative cost depends on computation complexity and the hardware. For example, while A_b could be smaller than D, A_{fcss} is likely to be more expensive than D. Nevertheless, methods with a higher branching factor have fewer levels and thus usually have a lower cost of moving across levels. But that doesn't mean the larger the branching factor the better. Too large a node size will increase the cache miss cost, which is probably the most important factor since each cache miss can

Method	Space (indirect)	Typical Value	Space (direct)	Typical Value	RID-Ordered Access
Binary search	0	0 MB	0	0 MB	Y
Full CSS-trees	$\frac{nK^2}{sc}$	2.5 MB	$\frac{nK^2}{sc}$	2.5 MB	Y
Level CSS-trees	$\frac{nK^2}{sc-K}$	2.7 MB	$\frac{nK^2}{sc-K}$	2.7 MB	Y
enhanced B+-trees	$\frac{nK(P+K)}{sc-P-K}$	5.7 MB	$\frac{nK(P+K)}{sc-P-K}$	5.7 MB	Y
Hash table	$(h-1)nR$	8 MB	hnR	48 MB	N
T-trees	$\frac{2nP(K+R)}{sc-2P}$	11.4 MB	$\frac{2nP(K+R)}{sc-2P}+nR$	51.4 MB	Y

Table 2: Space analysis

be an order of magnitude more expensive than a unit computation.

We assume a cold start in the cache. If the node size is smaller than the cache line size, each level has one cache miss. When the node size is larger than the cache line size, we estimate the number of cache misses per node to be $(\log_2 s)+\frac{1}{s} = (\log_2 \frac{mK}{c})+\frac{c}{mK}$ (the total number of cache misses for all the keys adds up to $s*(\log_2 s)+1$ and we divide that by s assuming each cache-line is equally likely to be chosen). The results are summarized in the last two columns of the table. For most reasonable configurations, the number of cache misses is minimized when the node size is the same as cache line size. In the third column, we can see that binary search and T-trees always have a number of misses that are independent of m. B+-trees and CSS-trees have only a fraction of the cache misses of binary search. The fractions for CSS-trees are even smaller than that of B+-trees. So CSS-trees have the lowest values for the cache related component of the cost. As we can see, as m gets larger, the number of cache misses for all the methods approaches $\log_2 n$ (essentially all methods degrade to binary search). There is a tradeoff between full CSS-trees and level CSS-trees. While the latter has slightly more cache misses, it also performs fewer comparisons. It's hard to compare the moving cost of the two since A_{lcss} is cheaper than A_{fcss}. We will show an experimental comparison in Section 6.

To summarize, we expect CSS-trees to perform significantly better than binary search and T-trees in searching, and also to outperform B+-trees. If a bunch of searches are performed in sequence, the top level nodes will stay in the cache. Since CSS-trees have fewer levels than all the other methods, it will also gain the most benefit from a warm cache.

Space Analysis: Table 2 lists the space requirements of the various algorithms. The column "Space (indirect)" describes the space required by the algorithms if the structure being indexed is a collection of record-identifiers that can be rearranged if necessary. In other words, it is acceptable for a method to store record-identifiers internally within its structure, as opposed to leaving the list of record-identifiers untouched as a contiguous list. In this column, we do not count the space used by the record-identifiers themselves since all methods share this space requirement.

The column "Space (direct)" describes the space required by the algorithms if the structure being indexed is a collection of records that *cannot* be rearranged. In other words, it is not acceptable for a method to store the records internally within its structure. In this column, we count the space used by record-identifiers for T-trees and hash tables since record-identifiers would not be necessary with other methods.

All methods other than hash tables support access in RID-order. The formula for Level CSS-trees assumes that $\frac{sc}{K}$ is a power or 2.

6 Experimental Results

We perform an experimental comparison of the algorithms on two modern platforms. We analyze the wall-clock time taken to perform a large number of random successful lookups to the index. We summarize our experiments in this section.

Experimental Setup: We ran our experiments on an Ultra Sparc II machine (296MHz, 1GB RAM) and a Pentium II (333MHz, 128M RAM) personal computer. The Ultra machine has a $< 16k, 32B, 1 >$ (<cache size, cache line size, associativity>) on-chip cache and a $< 1M, 64B, 1 >$ secondary level cache. The PC has a $< 16k, 32B, 4 >$ on-chip cache and a $< 512k, 32B, 4 >$ secondary level cache. Both machines are running Solaris 2.6. We implemented chained bucket hashing, array binary search, interpolation search [Pet57], T-tree, enhanced B+-tree, full CSS-tree and level CSS-tree in C++. We chose to implement all the existing methods ourselves because we are considering them in the context of main memory OLAP environment. Existing implementations won't be optimized for space allocation and cache related issues such as alignment. As a result, we believe our implementation will run faster. Since cache optimization can be sensitive to compilers [SKN94], we also chose two different compilers: one is Sun's native compiler CC and the other is GNU's g++. We used the highest optimization level of both compilers. However, the graphs for different compilers look very similar, so we only report the results for CC. All the keys are integers and are chosen randomly between 0 and 1 million. Each key takes four bytes. The lookup keys are generated in advance to prevent the key generating time from affecting our measurements. We performed 100,000 searches on randomly chosen matching keys. We repeated each test five times and report the minimal time to find the first matching key.

Algorithm Implementation Details: We tried our best to optimize all the searching methods. For methods that can have different node sizes, we implemented specialized versions for selected node size. We allocate a large chunk of memory at the beginning and create all the nodes from that pool to save allocation time. We use logical shifts in place of multiplication and division whenever possible. For T-trees, B+-trees and CSS-trees, we unfold the binary search loop in each internal node by hardcoding all the *if-else* tests to reduce the amount of overhead. The search within a leaf node is also hardcoded. Additionally, once the searching range is small enough, we simply perform the equality test sequentially on each key. This gives us better performance when there are less than 5 keys in the range. Code specialization is important. When our code was more "generic" (including a binary search loop for each node), we found the performance to be 20% to 45% worse than the specialized code.

The sorted array is aligned properly according to the cache line size. For T-trees, B+-trees and CSS-trees, all the tree nodes are allocated at once and the starting addresses are also aligned properly.

We implemented enhanced B+-trees. They use all the slots in each node.[1] Each node is designed to have a prespecified size and all the nodes are aligned properly. We also forced each key and child pointer to be adjacent to each other physically.

We avoid storing the parent pointer in each node of a T-tree since it's not necessary for searching. We implemented the improved version of T-Trees [LC86b], which is a little bit better than the basic version. For each T-tree node, we store the two child pointers adjacent to the smallest key so that they will be brought into the same cache line together. (Most of the time, the improved version checks only the smallest key in each node.)

For the chained bucket hashing, we followed the techniques used in [GBC98] by using the cache line size as the bucket size. Besides keys, each bucket also contains a counter indicating the number of occupied slots in the bucket and the pointer to the next bucket. Our hash function simply uses the low order bits of the key and thus is cheap to compute.

[1]Since there is always one more pointer than keys, for nodes with an even number of slots, we leave one slot empty.

Results: In the first experiment, we test how long it takes to build a CSS-tree. Both building time curves are linear in the size of the sorted array. Level CSS-trees are cheaper to build than full CSS-trees because they don't need to traverse each subtree to find the largest key. We are not claiming that CSS-trees can be built much faster than other index structures. Instead, we want to show that since the absolute rebuilding time is small (less than a second for 25 million keys), we can afford to rebuild CSS-trees periodically. The graph is omitted due to space limitations.

We then measure the searching time for all the algorithms. We first fix the node size and vary the size of the sorted array. We choose the node size to be each of the cache line size of the two levels of cache in the Ultra Sparc (32 bytes and 64 bytes). Figure 5 shows the result on the Ultra Sparc. First of all, when all the data can fit in cache, there is hardly any difference among all the algorithms (except for interpolation search). As the data size increases, we can see that our cache conscious CSS-trees perform the best among all the methods except for hashing. T-tree and binary search are the worst and run more than twice as slow as CSS-trees. The B+-tree curve falls in the middle. Although these searching methods all have to do the same number of key comparisons, they differ on how many of those comparisons cause a cache miss. T-tree search and binary search essentially have one cache miss for each comparison. For CSS-trees, all comparisons within a node are performed with only one cache miss. B+-trees also have one cache miss per node. But since a B+-tree stores half as many keys per node as CSS-trees, it has more levels than a CSS-tree. Although it's hard to discern visually, the level CSS-tree performs slightly better than the full CSS-tree. Across all of our tests we observed that level CSS-trees were up to 8% faster than full CSS-trees. The performance of interpolation search depends on how well the data fits a linear distribution. Although not shown here, we also did some tests on non-uniform data and interpolation search performs even worse than binary search. So in practice, we would not recommend using interpolation search. For B+-trees and the two CSS-trees, the numbers in Figure 5(b) are smaller than that in Figure 5(a). The reason is that the miss penalty for the second level of cache is larger than that of the on-chip cache. B+-trees get more benefit than CSS-trees from having a larger node size. This is because B+-trees always hold half the number of keys per node as CSS-trees and thus its benefit from avoiding extra cache misses is more significant. Although the T-tree has many keys per node, it doesn't benefit from having a larger node size. In this experiment, we chose the hash table directory size to be 4 million. Hashing uses

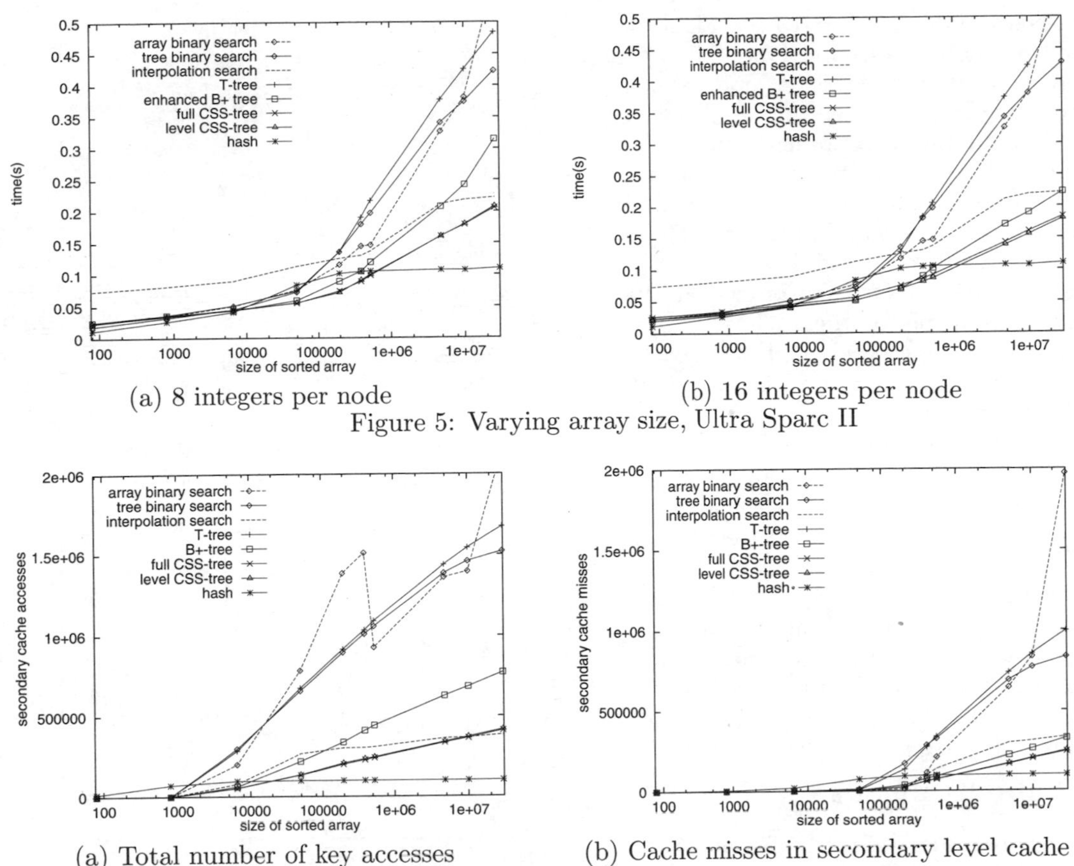

(a) 8 integers per node (b) 16 integers per node

Figure 5: Varying array size, Ultra Sparc II

(a) Total number of key accesses (b) Cache misses in secondary level cache

Figure 6: Ultra Sparc II, 16 integers per node

only one third of the time of CSS-trees. But we have to keep in mind that it's using 20 times as much space.

To compare the number of cache misses, we ran all the searching methods through a cache simulator.[2] Figure 6(a) and 6(b) show the total number of key accesses and the total number of key misses in the secondary level cache in a configuration that matches the Sun Ultra Sparc. As the data set gets larger, a larger proportion of the key accesses are cache misses. B+-trees have approximately 50% more cache misses than CSS-trees. Let's assume that each RAM access takes 180ns.[3] Then enhanced B+-trees take 0.06 seconds to load data from RAM to cache (when there are 25 million keys in the sorted array) and this is about 30% of the total amount of time taken (0.22 seconds). Out of the 0.04 seconds time difference between B+-trees and CSS-trees, about 0.014 seconds is caused by the difference in cache miss penalties. Thus the cache simulation verifies that 30% of the observed performance gap is due to the cache miss behavior. As the speed gap between CPU and RAM widens, this ratio will get higher and the difference between the performance of each method will be even more significant.

The results on the Pentium PC are very similar and are omitted here. In [LC86a, LC86b], the authors reported that T-trees perform better than binary search and B+-trees. Our results show the contrary conclusion. The explanation is that the CPU speed has improved by two orders of magnitude relative to memory latency during the past thirteen years [CLH98].

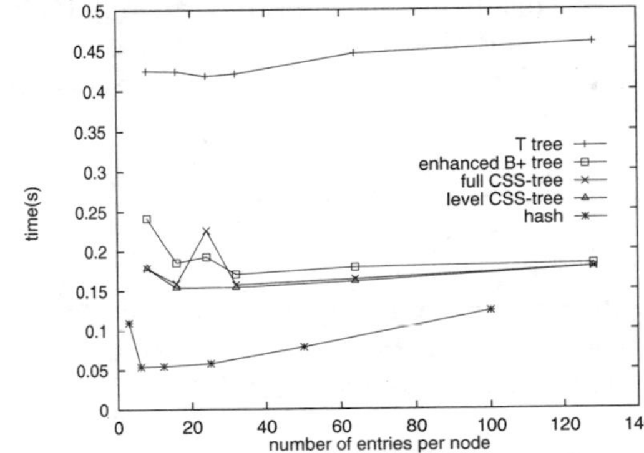

Figure 7: Varying node size, 10 million keys

In our next experiment, we fix the size of the sorted array and vary the node size of T-trees, B+-

[2]We implemented the simulator ourselves and instrumented our code (using `#ifdef SIMULATOR` macros) to log all memory accesses.

[3]We assume the memory has a peak bandwidth of 350MB/s [Inc99]. 64/350M=180ns

trees, full CSS-trees and level CSS-trees. Figure 7 shows the result on the Ultra Sparc. For both CSS-trees, the lowest point is 16 integers per node, which corresponds to the cache line size of the machine. B+-trees have a minimum at 32 integers per node. Although this doesn't quite fit in the time analysis in Section 5, the difference between 16-integers and 32-integers per node is not very significant. There is a bump for full CSS-trees and B+-trees when each node has 24 integers. One reason is that the node size is not a multiple of the cache line size. Thus nodes are not properly aligned with cache line and cause more cache misses. The bumps in full CSS-trees are more dramatic. This is because that the arithmetic computation for the child node is more expensive for $m = 24$ since division and multiplication must be used to compute child nodes instead of logical shifts. We also tested the optimal hash directory size of chained bucket hashing. Each point corresponds to a directory size from 2^{23} to 2^{18} with the leftmost point having the largest directory size. When the directory size has been increased to 2^{23}, the system starts to run out of memory and thus the searching time goes up. T-trees perform much worse on all the node sizes.

7 Space/Time Tradeoffs

An indexing method is measured by the pair (S, T) of space required for the whole index structure (S), and time taken for a single lookup (T). Figure 2 shows the space requirement and searching time for each method.[4] Each point for T-trees, B+-trees and CSS-trees corresponds to a specific node size. Since keeping an ordered RID list is usually necessary, we calculate the space requirement using the formula for "direct" space listed in Table 2. The stepped line basically tells us how to find the optimal searching time for a given amount of space. All the methods on the upper-right side of the line are dominated by some methods on the line. T-trees and B+-trees are both dominated by CSS-trees. Methods on the line have tradeoffs between space and time. On the bottom, we have binary search on the sorted array, which doesn't require any extra space, but uses three times as much time as CSS-trees and seven times as much as hashing. If we invest a little bit of extra space, we can use CSS-trees, which reduce the searching time to one third of binary search. To make another factor of two improvement, we have to pay 20 times as much space as CSS-trees to be able to use hashing. When space is limited, CSS-trees balance the space and time.

We show the breakdown of the cost of enhanced B+-trees and CSS-trees in Figure 8(a). For the time being, the cache miss cost corresponds to a relatively small fraction of the total cost. Given the trend shown in Figure 1, in five years, we expect the CPU to be 10 times faster while the memory speed will be only 1.6 times faster. So the breakdown at that time will probably look like that in Figure 8(b). The cache miss cost will be much more significant. Figure 9 shows the projected space/time tradeoff between B+-trees and CSS-trees in five years. As we can see, the optimal CSS-trees are almost 30% faster than the optimal enhanced B+-trees. In the limit, if cache miss cost dominates the total cost, CSS-trees can be up to 50% faster than enhanced B+-trees. Also, the optimal node size in five years is different from what it is now.

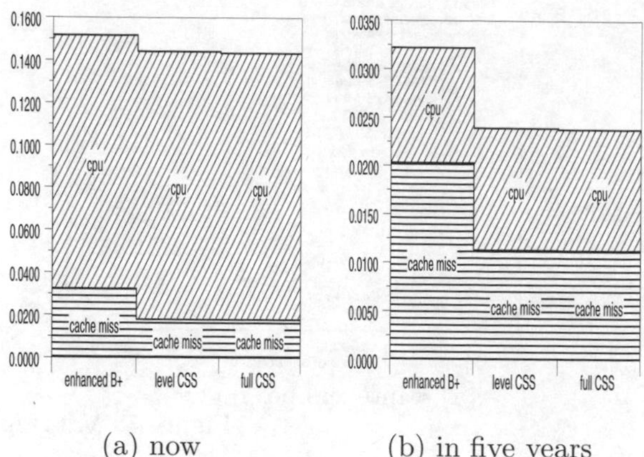

(a) now (b) in five years

Figure 8: Time breakdown (16 integers per node)

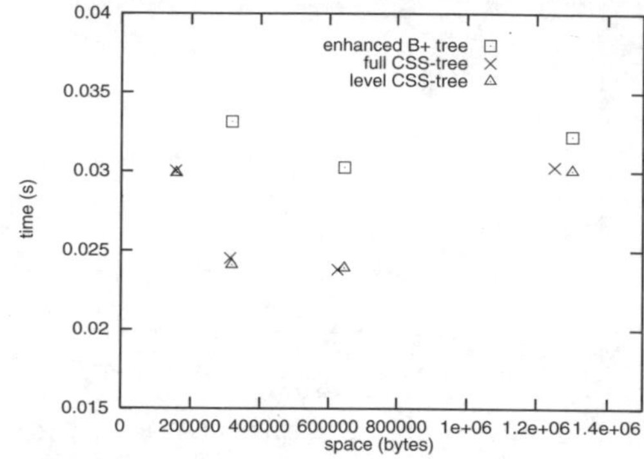

Figure 9: Space/time Tradeoffs (in five years)

8 Conclusion

We studied the cache behavior of various in-memory indexes in an OLAP environment and showed that cache conscious methods such as CSS-trees can improve searching performance by making good use of cache lines. As the gap between CPU and memory speed is widening, we expect the improvement that can be achieved by exploiting the cache will be even more significant in the future. Cache conscious searching behavior is just one step towards efficiently

[4] We present the numbers from searching a sorted array of 5 million elements on an Ultra Sparc II.

utilizing the cache in database systems. We aim to study the effect of cache behavior on other database operations in the future.

Acknowledgment: We thank John Grogan for the implementation of our cache simulator.

References

[AHK85] Arthur C. Ammann, et al. Design of a memory resident DBMS. In *Proceedings of the IEEE COMPCOM Conference*, pages 54–57, 1985.

[BBC+98] Phil Bernstein, et al. The Asilomar report on database research. *ACM Sigmod Record*, 27(4), 1998.

[CLH98] Trishul M. Chilimbi, James R. Larus, and Mark D. Hill. Improving pointer-based codes through cache-conscious data placement. Technical report 98, University of Wisconsin-Madison, Computer Science Department, 1998.

[Com79] D. Comer. The ubiquitous B-tree. *ACM Computing Surverys*, 11(2), 1979.

[CS83] F. Cesarini, et al. An algorithm to construct a compact B-tree in case of ordered keys. *Information Processing Letters*, 17(1):1612–1630, 1983.

[Eng98] InfoCharger Engine. Optimization for decision support solutions (available from http://www.tandem.com/prod_dcs/ifchcgpd/ifchegpd.htm). 1998.

[Fre95] Clark D. French. "One size fits all" database architectures do not work for DDS. In *Proceedings of the ACM SIGMOD Conference*, page 449–450, 1995.

[Fre97] Clark D. French. Teaching an OLTP database kernel advanced data warehousing techniques. In *Proc. IEEE Int'l Conf. on Data Eng.*, 1997.

[GBC98] Goetz Graefe, et al. Hash joins and hash teams in Microsoft SQL server. In *Proceedings of the 24th VLDB Conference*, pages 86–97, 1998.

[GMS86] Hector Garcia-Molina, et al. High perfromance transaction processing with memory resident data. In *Proceedings of the International Workshop on High Performance Transaction Systems*, 1986.

[GR93] Jim Gray, et al. *Transaction processing:concepts and techniques*. The Morgan Kaufmann Publishers, San Francisco, CA, USA, 1993.

[Hag86] R. B. Hagmann. A crash recovery scheme for a memory-resident database system. *IEEE Transactions on Computing*, C-35:839–842, 1986.

[Inc99] Sun Microsystems Inc. Datasheet on memory (available from http://www.sun.com/ microelectronics/datasheets/sme1040/04.html as of feb. 15, 1999). 1999.

[JLRS94] H.V. Jagadish, et al. Dali: A high performance main memory storage manager. In *Proceedings of the 20th VLDB Conference*, 1994.

[JTR87] Wiebren De Jonge, et al. Two access methods using compact binary trees. *IEEE Transactions on Software Engineering*, 13(7):799–810, 1987.

[Knu73] Donald Ervin Knuth. *Sorting and Searching*, volume 3 of *The Art of Computer Programming*. Addison-Wesley, Reading, Massachusetts, USA, 1973.

[LC86a] Tobin J. Lehman and Michael J. Carey. Query processing in main memory database management systems. In *Proceedings of the ACM SIGMOD Conference*, pages 239–250, 1986.

[LC86b] Tobin J. Lehman and Michael J. Carey. A study of index structures for main memory database management systems. In *Proceedings of the 12th VLDB Conference*, pages 294–303, 1986.

[LC87] Tobin J. Lehman and Michael J. Carey. A recovery algorithm for a high performance memory-resident database system. In *Proceedings of the ACM SIGMOD Conference*, pages 104–117, 1987.

[LL96] Anthony LaMarca and Richard E. Ladner. The influence of caches on the performance of heaps. *ACM Journal of Experimental Algorithmics*, 1, 1996.

[LL97] Anthony LaMarca, et al. The influence of caches on the performance of sorting. In *Eighth Annual ACM-SIAM Symposium on Discrete Algorithms*, 1997.

[LN88] K. Li and J. F. Naughton. Multiprocessor main memory transaction processing. In *International Symposium on Databases in Parallel and Distributed Systems*, pages 177–189, 1988.

[LSC92] Tobin J. Lehman, et al. An evaluation of starburst's memory resident storage component. *IEEE Transactions on knowledge and data enginnering*, 4(6):555–566, 1992.

[NBC+94] Chris Nyberg, et al. Alphasort: a RISC machine sort. In *Proceedings of the ACM SIGMOD Conference*, pages 233–242, May 1994.

[Pet57] W. W. Peterson. In *IBM J. Res. & Devel.*, No. 1, pages 131–132, 1957.

[SAC+79] Patricia G. Selinger, et al. Access path selection in a relational database management system. In *Proceedings of the ACM SIGMOD Conference*, pages 23–34, 1979.

[SKN94] Ambuj Shatdal, et al. Cache conscious algorithms for relational query processing. In *Proceedings of the 20th VLDB Conference*, 1994.

[Smi82] Alan J. Smith. Cache memories. *ACM Computing Surverys*, 14(3):473–530, 1982.

[Sof97] TimesTen Performance Software. Main-memory data management technical white paper (available from http://www.timesten.com). 1997.

[Syb97] Sybase Corporation. *Sybase IQ 11.2.1*, 1997.

[WK90] Kyu-Young Whang and Ravi Krishnamurthy. Query optimization in a memory-resident domain relational calculus database system. *ACM Transactions on Database Systems*, 15(1):67–95, 1990.

[WL91] Michael E. Wolf, et al. A data locality optimizing algorithm. *SIGPLAN Notices*, 26(6):30–44, 1991.

Comparing Hierarchical Data in External Memory

Sudarshan S. Chawathe
Department of Computer Science
University of Maryland
College Park, MD 20904
chaw@cs.umd.edu

Abstract

We present an external-memory algorithm for computing a minimum-cost edit script between two rooted, ordered, labeled trees. The I/O, RAM, and CPU costs of our algorithm are, respectively, $4mn+7m+5n$, $6S$, and $O(MN+(M+N)S^{1.5})$, where M and N are the input tree sizes, S is the block size, $m = M/S$, and $n = N/S$. This algorithm can make effective use of surplus RAM capacity to quadratically reduce I/O cost. We extend to trees the commonly used mapping from sequence comparison problems to shortest-path problems in edit graphs.

1 Introduction

We study the problem of comparing snapshots of data to detect similarities and differences between them. Such *differencing* of data has **applications** in version control, incremental view maintenance, data warehousing, standing queries (subscriptions), and change management [Tic85, LGM96, CAW98]. The RCS version control system [Tic85] uses the *diff* program [MM85] to compute and store only the differences between the new and old versions of data that is checked in. As another version control application, consider the process used to merge two divergent versions of a program or document (e.g., the ediff/emerge function in Emacs). The first step consists of comparing the files containing the two versions to determine where and how they differ. These differences are then presented using a graphical interface that allows a user to determine which variant to keep in the merged file.

Proceedings of the 25th VLDB Conference,
Edinburgh, Scotland, 1999.

Differencing algorithms also play a key role in change management systems such as C^3 [CAW98]. Since many databases, especially those on the Web, do not offer change notification facilities, changes must be detected by comparing old and new results of a query. Once changes have been detected in this manner, C^3 uses them to implement standing queries based on the current state as well as the history of the databases being monitored.

We can also use differencing algorithms to reduce the amount of data transmitted over a network in mirroring applications. Popular Web and FTP servers often have dozens of mirror sites around the world. Changes made to the master server need to be propagated to the mirror sites. Ideally, the persons or programs making changes would keep a record of exactly what data was updated. However, in practice, due to the autonomous and loosely organized nature of such sites, there is no reliable record of changes. Further, even if such a record is available, it may be based on a version that is different from the version currently at a certain mirror site. Due to such difficulties, efficient mirroring requires differencing algorithms that compute and propagate only the difference between the version at the master server and that at a mirror site. Similar ideas enable differencing algorithms to improve efficiency in a data warehousing environment [LGM96].

Differencing algorithms are also used to find, mark-up, and browse changes between two or more versions of a document [CRGMW96, CGM97]. Suppose we receive an updated version of an online manual. Again, in the ideal case the new version would highlight the way it differs from the old one. However, for reasons similar to those stated above, in practice we often need to detect the differences ourselves by comparing the two versions. For example, [CAW98] describes experiences in detecting and browsing differences between different versions of a restaurant review database on the Web, while [Yan91] describes the implementation of an application that highlights differences between program versions.

There is a substantial body of prior work on differencing algorithms. The main **distinguishing features** of the work in this paper are the following. (See Section 6 for a detailed discussion.)

- We study algorithms for computing differences between snapshots of **hierarchically structured** data, modeled using rooted, ordered, labeled trees. Our model allows us to accurately capture the hierarchical structure inherent in data such as source code, object class hierarchies, structured documents, HTML, XML, and SGML. For example, an online manual typically has a well-defined hierarchical structure consisting of chapters, sections, subsections, paragraphs, and sentences. Algorithms that take this structure into account produce results that are more meaningful than those that treat their inputs as flat strings.

  While the problem of differencing strings and sequences has been thoroughly studied and admits several efficient solutions, the problem of differencing trees remains challenging. Several formulations of this problem are NP-hard [ZWS95]. In this paper, we study a simple variation that admits efficient solutions.

- We do not assume that the snapshots being differenced are small enough to fit entirely in main memory (RAM); instead, they reside in **external memory** (disk). For example, online manuals for complex machinery, aircrafts, and submarines are tens or hundreds of gigabytes in size, making it impracticable to use main-memory differencing algorithms to compare their versions.

  When data resides in external memory, the number of input-output operations (I/Os), and not the number of CPU cycles, is the primary determinant of running time. Therefore, **external-memory algorithms** use techniques that try to minimize the number of I/Os. A secondary but important consideration is the amount of buffer space required in RAM. See [Vit98] for an overview of external memory algorithms. In this paper, we analyze algorithms based on their I/O, RAM, and CPU costs.

As an illustration of the importance of using an algorithm that is cognizant of the hierarchical structure of data, consider the following example from [Yan91]. Figure 1 depicts depicts fragments of two program versions that are being compared. A sequence comparison program such as the one in[MM85] compares the inputs line-by-line and may result in matching program text as suggested by the solid lines in the figure. Given the nested structure of the program fragment, it is clearly more meaningful to match the inputs as suggested by the dashed lines in the figure. However, the definition of optimality used by most sequence comparison algorithms (based on a longest common subsequence) considers the solution depicted using solid lines more desirable [Mye86]. By modeling the hierarchical structure of programs, tree differencing algorithms are able to produce more meaningful results.

We now present a brief, informal definition of the differencing problem we study in this paper. (See Section 2 for details.) A *rooted, ordered, labeled tree* is a tree in which each node has a label and in which the order amongst siblings is significant. (The label of a node intuitively represents the data content at that node; it is not a unique key or object identifier.) Trees can be transformed using three *edit operations*: (1) We can *insert* a new leaf node at a specified location in the tree. (2) We can *delete* an existing leaf node. (3) We can *update* the label of a node. Note that the restriction that (1) and (2) operate only on leaf nodes means that to delete an interior node, we must first delete all its descendants; similarly, we must insert a node before inserting any of its descendants.

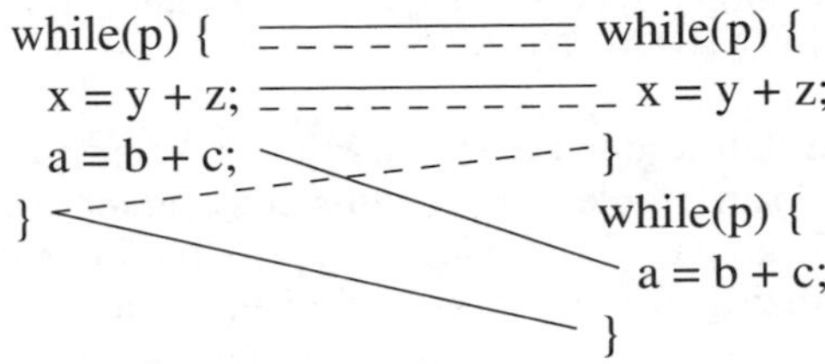

Figure 1: Importance of hierarchical structure

An *edit script* is a sequence of edit operations that are applied in the order listed. We associate a cost with each edit operation and define the *cost of an edit script* to be the sum of the costs of its component operations.

Problem Statement (informal): Given two rooted, ordered, labeled trees A and B, find a minimum-cost edit script that transforms A to B.

Given trees A and B, we can transform one to the other using any of an infinite number of edit scripts. (For example, given any edit script that transforms A to B, we can append to it operations that insert and immediately delete a node, thus generating an infinite number of edit scripts.) This fact motivates the minimum-cost requirement in the problem definition. Another motivation for the minimum-cost requirement is the following: Given two trees that differ only in one node label, the intuitively desirable edit script is one that contains a single update operation. We need to weed out edit scripts that unnecessarily insert, delete, and update nodes. An edit script of minimum cost cannot contain such redundant or wasteful edit operations (since we can obtain another edit script with lower cost by getting rid of the redundancies and inefficiencies).

The two main **contributions** of this paper may be summarized as follows:

- We present an efficient external-memory algorithm for computing the difference (minimum-cost edit script) between two snapshots of hierarchical data (trees). The I/O, RAM, and CPU costs of our algorithm are, respectively, $4mn + 7m + 5n$, $6S$, and $O(MN\sqrt{S})$, where M and N are the input tree sizes, S is the block size, $m = M/S$, and $n = N/S$. To our knowledge, this algorithm is the first external-memory differencing algorithm (for sequences or trees). The $O(mn)$ I/O complexity of our algorithm is optimal over a wide class of computation models due to the $O(mn)$ lower bound for the sequence comparison problem (which is a simple special case of our tree comparison problem) [AHU76, WC76].

- We reduce our tree comparison problem to a shortest path problem in a well-studied graph called the edit graph. This reduction opens the door for generalizing to trees several efficient sequence comparison algorithms that are based on edit graphs (e.g., [MM85, Mye86, WMG90]).

Outline of the paper: In Section 2, we describe our model of trees, edit operations, and edit scripts, followed by the formal problem statement. Section 3 briefly describes edit graphs as they are used for sequence comparison and then presents our modifications that allow them to be used for tree comparison. In Section 4, we present a simple main-memory algorithm for our tree comparison problem. This algorithm illustrates the use of our edit graphs and serves as a basis for our external-memory algorithm. Section 5 first explores a naive extension of our main-memory algorithm for external memory and then presents our main algorithm, *xmdiff*. Related work is discussed in Section 6, followed by the conclusion in Section 7.

2 Model and Problem Statement

Hierarchical data is naturally modeled by trees. In this paper, we focus on *rooted, ordered, labeled trees.* Each node in such a tree has a label associated with it. Informally, we can think of the label of a node as its data value. The children of a node are totally ordered; thus, if a node has k children, we can uniquely identify the ith child, for $i = 1 \ldots k$. There is a distinguished node called the root of the tree. (This feature distinguishes these trees from acyclic graphs, which are also called free trees.)

Formally, a **rooted, ordered, labeled tree** consists of a finite, nonempty set of nodes T and a labeling function l such that: (1) The set T contains a distinguished node r, called the **root** of the tree; (2) The set $V - \{r\}$ is partitioned into k disjoint sets $T_1, \ldots, T_k$, where each T_i is a tree (called the i**th subtree** of T or r); and (3) the label of a node $n \in T$ is $l(n)$ [Sel77]. The root c_i of T_i is called the i**th child** of the node r, and r is called the **parent** of c_i. Nodes in T that do not have any children are called **leaf nodes**; the rest of the nodes are called **interior nodes**.

In the rest of this paper, we use the term trees to mean rooted, ordered, labeled trees. Figure 2 depicts several such trees. The letter next to a node suggests its label. The number next to a node is a node identifier. Note that when we are given two trees to compare, there is, in general, no correspondence between the node identifiers. (In fact, computing such a correspondence is equivalent to computing a minimum-cost edit script for our formulation of the problem.) For example, when we are comparing two versions of a manual, the node identifiers in Figure 2 may represent offsets within the SGML source files for the manuals. Since the source files for the manuals are separate, there is no correspondence between these offsets.

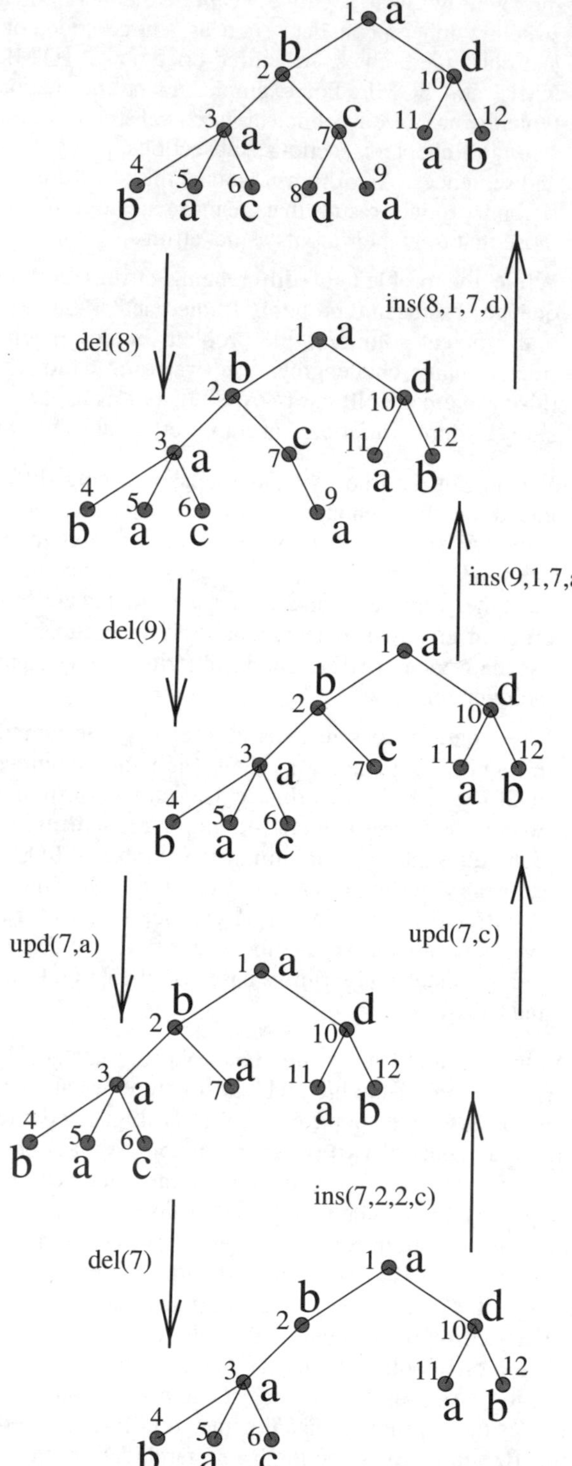

Figure 2: Edit operations on trees

We model changes to trees using the following **tree edit operations**:

Insertion Let p be a node in a tree T, and let $T_1, \ldots, T_k$ be the subtrees of p. Let n be a node not in T, let l be an arbitrary label, and let $i \in [1 \ldots k+1]$. The insertion operation $ins(n, i, p, l)$ inserts the node n as the ith child of p. In the transformed tree, n is a leaf node with label l.

Deletion Let n be a leaf node in T. The deletion operation $del(n)$ results in removing the node n from T. That is, if n is the ith child of a node $p \in T$ with children $c_1, \ldots, c_k$, then in the transformed tree, p has children $c_1, \ldots, c_{i-1}, c_{i+1}, \ldots, c_k$.

Update If n is a node in T and v is a label then the label update operation $upd(n, v)$ results in a tree T' that is identical to T except that in T', $l(n) = v$.

We assume, without loss of generality, that the root of a tree cannot be deleted or inserted.

An **edit script** is a sequence of edit operations. The result of applying an edit script to a tree T is the tree obtained by applying the component edit operations to T, in the order they appear in the script. Consider Figure 2. The downward arrows illustrate the application of the following edit script: $del(8)$, $del(9)$, $upd(7, a)$, $del(7)$. Similarly, the upward arrows illustrate the application of another edit script.

As discussed in Section 1, we formalize the desirability of edit scripts that perform as few and as small changes as possible by defining a cost model for edit scripts. Let $c_i(x)$ and $c_d(x)$ be arbitrary functions return a positive number representing the costs of, respectively, inserting and deleting a node x. Similarly, the cost of updating a label l_1 to l_2 is given by $c_u(l_1, l_2)$. The cost of an edit script is the sum of the costs of its component operations. We can now formally define the problem of **differencing trees** as follows:

Problem Statement: Given two rooted, labeled, ordered trees A and B, find a minimum-cost edit script that transforms A to a tree that is isomorphic to B.

3 Edit Graphs

In this section, we introduce an auxiliary structure, called an edit graph, that we later use in our differencing algorithms. Edit graphs have been used by several efficient algorithms for comparing sequences (equivalently, strings) [Mye86, MM85, WMG90]. In effect, the problem of finding a minimum-cost edit script between two sequences is reduced to the problem of finding a shortest path from one end of the edit graph to the other. Since an edit graph has a very simple and regular structure, this shortest path problem can typically be solved very efficiently. Below, we first explain how edit graphs are used for sequence comparison and then introduce our modifications that permit them to be used for comparing trees.

The **edit graph of two sequences** $A = (A[1]\ A[2] \ldots A[m])$ and $B = (B[1]\ B[2] \ldots B[n])$ is the $(m+1) \times (n+1)$ grid suggested by Figure 3. (Each point where two lines touch or cross is a node in the edit graph.) A point (x, y) intuitively corresponds to the pair $(A[x], B[y])$, for $x \in [1, m]$ and $y \in [1, n]$. In our edit graphs, the origin $(0, 0)$ is the node in the top left corner; the x-axis extends to the right of $(0, 0)$ and the y-axis extends down from $(0, 0)$. There is a directed edge from each node to the node, if any, to its right. Similarly, there is a directed edge from each node to the node, if any, below it. For clarity, these directed edges are shown without arrowheads in the figure. All horizontal edges are directed to the right and all vertical edges are directed down. In addition, there is a diagonal edge from $(x-1, y-1)$ to (x, y) for all $x, y > 0$. For clarity, these edges are omitted in the figure. The edit graph depicted in Figure 3 corresponds to the sequences (strings) $A = ababaccdadab$ and $B = acabbdbbabc$.

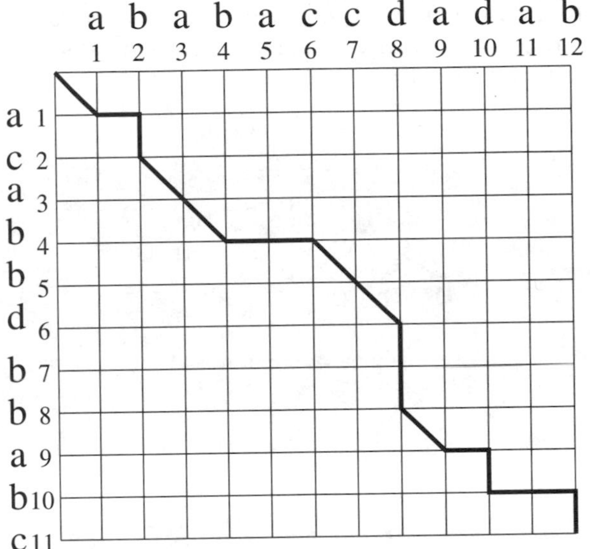

Figure 3: Edit graph for sequence comparison

Traversing a horizontal edge $((x-1, y), (x, y))$ in the edit graph corresponds to deleting $A[x]$. Similarly, traversing a vertical edge $((x, y-1), (x, y))$ corresponds to inserting $B[y]$. Traversing a diagonal edge $((x-1, y-1), (x, y))$ corresponds to matching $A[x]$ to $B[y]$; if $A[x]$ and $B[y]$ differ, such matching corresponds to an update operation.

Edges in the edit graph have **weights** equal to the costs of the edit operations they represent. Thus, a horizontal edge $((x-1, y), (x, y))$ has weight $c_d(a_x)$, a vertical edge $((x, y-1), (x, y))$ has weight $c_i(b_y)$, and a diagonal edge $((x-1, y-1), (x, y))$ has weight $c_u(a_x, b_y)$.

It is easy to show that any min-cost edit script that transforms A to B can be mapped to a path from $(0, 0)$ to (M, N) in the edit graph. Conversely, every path from $(0, 0)$ to (M, N) corresponds to an edit script that transforms A to B. For details, see [Mye86].

For the example suggested in Figure 3, the highlighted path corresponds to the following edit script:

$$del(A[2]), ins(B[2]), del(A[5]), del(A[6]),$$

$upd(A[7], b), del(A[7]), del(A[8]), del(A[10]),$
$ins(B[10]), del(A[11]), del(A[12]), ins(B[11])$

It is easy to verify that applying the above script to A produces B.

In order to use edit graphs to compare trees, we need to modify their definition to incorporate the constraints imposed by the structure of the trees being compared. For example, we must model the constraint that if an interior node is deleted then all its descendants must also be deleted. Before we proceed, we need to define the *ld-pair* representation of a tree.

We define the **ld-pair** of a tree node to be the pair (l, d), where l is the node's label and d is its depth in the tree. We use $p.l$ and $p.d$ to refer to, respectively, the label and depth of an ld-pair p. The **ld-pair representation of a tree** is the list, in preorder, of the ld-pairs of its nodes. In the rest of this paper, we assume that trees are in the ld-pair representation. (A tree can be converted to this representation using a single preorder traversal.)

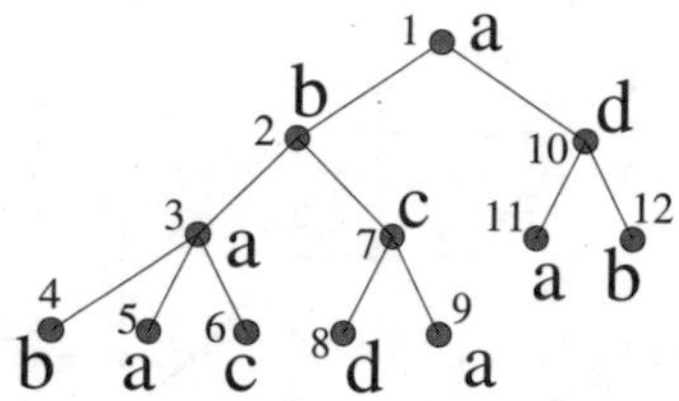

Figure 4: Input tree A

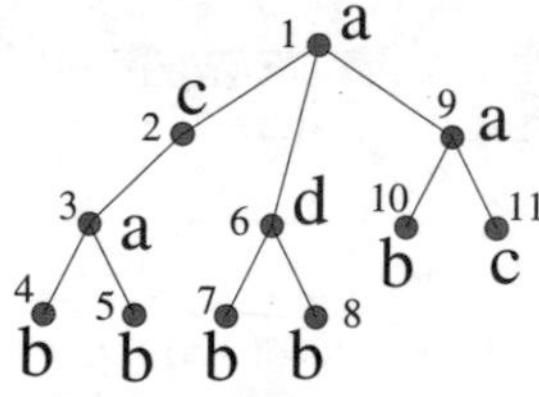

Figure 5: Input tree B

Consider the trees A and B depicted in Figures 4 and 5. The letter next to each node suggests its label and the number next to a node is its preorder rank, which also serves as its identifier. The ld-pair representations of A and B are as follows:

$$\begin{aligned} A &= ((a,0),(b,1),(a,2),(b,3),(a,3),(c,3),(c,2),\\ &\quad (d,3),(a,3),(d,1),(a,2),(b,2)) \\ B &= ((a,0),(c,1),(a,2),(b,3),(b,3),(d,1),(b,2),\\ &\quad (b,2),(a,1),(b,2),(c,2)) \end{aligned}$$

Given a tree (in ld-pair representation) $A = (a_1\ a_2 \ldots a_M)$, we use the notation $A[i]$ to refer to the ith node a_i of tree A. Thus, $A[i].l$ and $A[i].d$ denote, respectively, the label and the depth of the ith node of A.

We define **the edit graph of two trees** A and B to consist of a $(M+1) \times (N+1)$ grid of nodes as suggested by Figure 6. There is a node at each (x, y) location for $x \in [0 \ldots (M+1)]$ and $y \in [0 \ldots (N+1)]$. These nodes are connected by directed edges as follows:

- For $x \in [0, M-1]$ and $y \in [0, N-1]$, there is a diagonal edge $((x,y),(x+1,y+1))$ if and only if $A[x+1].d = B[y+1].d$. (For clarity, these edges are omitted in Figure 6.)
- For $x \in [0, M-1]$ and $y \in [0, N]$, there is a horizontal edge $((x,y),(x+1,y))$ unless $y < N$ and $B[y+1].d > A[x+1].d$.
- For $x \in [0, M]$ and $y \in [0, N-1]$, there is a vertical edge $((x,y),(x,y+1))$ unless $x < M$ and $A[x+1].d > B[y+1].d$.

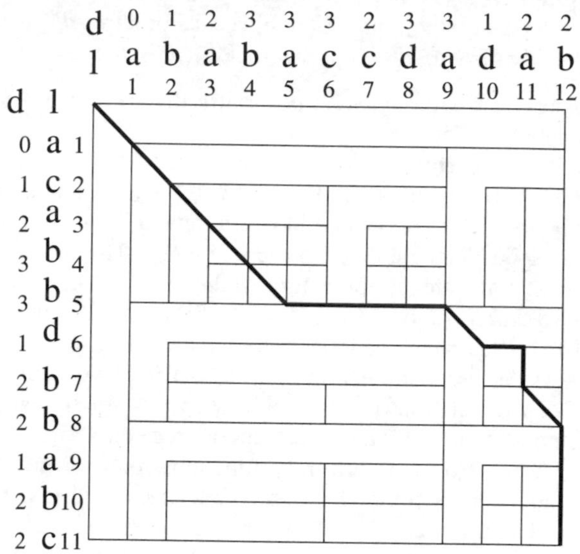

Figure 6: Edit graph for tree comparison

As was the case for sequence edit graphs, horizontal edges represent deletions, vertical edges represent insertions, and diagonal edges represent matching of nodes (with an update operation required if the labels of the matched nodes differ). Similarly, each edge has an edge weight equal to the cost of the corresponding edit operation. However, in contrast to sequence edit graphs, several horizontal and vertical edges are missing from tree edit graphs. Intuitively, the missing vertical edges ensure that once a path in the edit graph traverses an edge signifying the deletion of a node n, that path can only continue by traversing edges that signify the deletion of all the nodes in n's subtree. Similarly, the missing horizontal edges ensure that any path that traverses an edge signifying the insertion of a node n can only continue by traversing the edges signifying insertion of all nodes in n's subtree.

We can show that any min-cost edit script that transforms A to B can be mapped to a path from $(0,0)$ to (M,N) in the tree edit graph; conversely, every path from $(0,0)$ to (M,N) corresponds to an edit script that transforms A to B.

For example, the path indicated using bold lines in Figure 6 corresponds to the following edit script, where $n_1, \ldots, n_4$ are arbitrary identifiers for the newly inserted nodes:

$$\begin{aligned}&upd(2, c), upd(5, b), del(6), del(7), del(8), del(9)\\ &del(11), ins(n_1, 1, 10, b), ins(n_2, 3, 1, a)\\ &ins(n_3, 1, n_2, b), ins(n_4, 2, n_2, c)\end{aligned}$$

4 Differencing in Main Memory

In Section 3, we reduced the problem of computing a min-cost edit script between two trees to the problem of finding a shortest path in the edit graph of those trees. We now use that reduction to present a main-memory algorithm for differencing trees. Given a $(M + 1) \times (N + 1)$ edit graph G, let D be a $(M + 1) \times (N + 1)$ matrix such that $D[x, y]$ is the length of a shortest path from $(0, 0)$ to (x, y) in the edit graph. We call D the **distance matrix** for G.

For notational convenience, let us define the weight of an edge that is missing from the edit graph to be infinity. Consider any path that connects the origin $(0, 0)$ to $n = (x, y)$ in the edit graph. Given the graph's structure, the previous node on this path is either the node to the left of n, the node above n or the node diagonally to the left and above n. Therefore, the distance of n from the origin cannot be greater than that distance for the node to its left plus the weight of the edge connecting the left neighbor to n. Similar relations hold for the top and diagonal neighbors of n, yielding the following recurrence for $D[x, y]$, where $0 < x \le M$ and $0 < y \le N$:

$$\begin{aligned}D[x,y] &= \min\{m_1, m_2, m_3\} \text{ where}\\ m_1 &= D[x-1, y-1] + c_u(A[x], B[y]),\\ &\qquad\qquad \text{if } ((x-1, y-1), (x, y)) \in G\\ &\quad\ \infty, \text{ otherwise}\\ m_2 &= D[x-1, y] + c_d(A[x]),\\ &\qquad\qquad \text{if } ((x-1, y), (x, y)) \in G\\ &\quad\ \infty, \text{ otherwise}\\ m_2 &= D[x-1, y] + c_i(B[x]),\\ &\qquad\qquad \text{if } ((x, y-1), (x, y)) \in G\\ &\quad\ \infty, \text{ otherwise}\end{aligned}$$

This recurrence leads to the following dynamic-programming algorithm for computing the distance matrix D. We call this algorithm mmdiff, for main-memory differencing.

Algorithm mmdiff

Input: Arrays A and B, which represent two trees in ld-pair representation. Thus $A[i].l$ and $A[i].d$ denote, respectively, the label and depth of the ith node (in preorder) of A (and analogously for B). The number of elements in A and B is M and N, respectively.

Output: The distance matrix D where $D[i, j]$ equals the length of the shortest path from $(0, 0)$ to (i, j) in the edit graph of A and B.

Method: Figure 7 presents the pseudocode for a Algorithm mmdiff. All the pseudocode in this paper assumes short-circuit evaluation of Boolean expressions. We initialize D at the origin $(0, 0)$, followed by computation of distances along the top and left edge of the matrix. The nested for loop is a direct implementation of the recurrence for $D[i, j]$. If we assume that the functions c_u, c_d, and c_i execute in constant times α, β, and γ, respectively, the running time of mmdiff is proportional to $1 + \alpha M + \beta N + (\alpha + \beta + \gamma)MN$, or $O(MN)$.

```
D[0, 0] := 0;
for i := 1 to M do
   D[i, 0] := D[i − 1, 0] + c_d(A[i]);
for j := 1 to N do
   D[0, j] := D[0, j − 1] + c_i(B[j]);
for i := 1 to M do
   for j := 1 to N do begin
      m1 := ∞; m2 := ∞; m3 := ∞;
      if (A[i].d = B[j].d) then
         m1 := D[i − 1, j − 1] + c_u(A[i], B[j]);
      if (j = N or B[j + 1].d ≤ A[i].d) then
         m2 := D[i − 1, j] + c_d(A[i]);
      if (i = M or A[i + 1].d ≤ B[j].d) then
         m3 := D[i, j − 1] + c_i(B[j]);
      D[i, j] := min(m1, m2, m3);
   end;
```

Figure 7: Algorithm mmdiff

Once we have computed the distance matrix D, it is easy to recover from it a shortest path from $(0, 0)$ to (M, N). We start at (M, N) and trace the recurrence relation for D backwards. As we traverse horizontal, vertical, and diagonal edges, we emit the appropriate deletion, insertion, and update operation, respectively. Thus, we have the following algorithm for recovering an edit script from the distance matrix. We call this algorithm mmdiff-r (for mmdiff-recovery).

Algorithm mmdiff-r

Input: Arrays A and B representing the input trees (as in Algorithm mmdiff) and the distance matrix D computed by mmdiff.

Output: A min-cost edit script that transforms A to B. (For simplicity of presentation, the insertion and deletion operations only identify the nodes being inserted and deleted. Using the information from the original trees, it is easy to generate an edit script in the syntax of Section 2. Further, insertions of interior nodes are printed after the insertions of their descendants; this ordering is easily fixed.)

Method: Figure 8 presents the pseudocode for Algorithm mmdiff-r. At each iteration of the while loop i and/or j is decremented by one. Thus there are between $\max(M, N)$ and $M + N$ iterations of the while loop, with each iteration performing a constant amount of work. Thus, the running time of mmdiff-r is $O(M + N)$.

```
i := M; j := N;
while (i > 0 and j > 0) do
    if (D[i, j] = D[i − 1, j] + c_d(A[i]) and
            (j = N or B[j + 1].d ≤ A[i].d)) then begin
        print("del" i);
        i := i − 1;
    end;
    else if (D[i, j] = D[i, j − 1] + c_i(B[j]) and
            (i = M or A[i + 1].d ≤ B[j].d)) then begin
        print("ins" j);
        j := j − 1;
    end;
    else begin
        if(A[i].l ≠ B[j].l) then print("upd" i B[j].l);
        i := i − 1; j := j − 1;
    end;
while (i > 0) do begin
    print("del" i);
    i := i − 1;
end;
while (j > 0) do begin
    print("ins" j);
    j := j − 1;
end;
```

Figure 8: Algorithm mmdiff-r

5 Differencing in External Memory

In Section 4, we presented algorithms mmdiff and mmdiff-r to compute a minimum-cost edit distance between two trees in main memory. These algorithms require RAM space for not only the input trees A and B, but also for the distance matrix D. If A and B have sizes M and N, respectively, then the distance matrix D is of size MN, which can be prohibitively large for even modestly sized inputs that fit in RAM. In situations where A and B themselves are too large to fit in RAM, the problem is much worse.

Let us first consider a naive extension of Algorithm mmdiff for external memory. We use two buffers, B_1 and B_2, to read, as needed, the trees A and B, respectively, from disk into RAM. The buffers are exactly large enough to hold one disk block (of size S). As the distance matrix D is computed, we write the distances to a third buffer B_3, also of size S. When B_3 is completely filled, we write it out to disk and overwrite it in RAM. Using a similar buffering scheme, we can adapt the algorithm mmdiff-r, used for recovering the edit script, for external memory. Let us call these buffered version of mmdiff and mmdiff-r **Algorithm bmdiff** and **Algorithm bmdiff-r**, respectively.

Since Algorithm bmdiff computes the distance matrix D in column-major order, each of the $\lceil N/S \rceil = n$ blocks of B is read once for each of the M nodes in A, incurring an I/O cost of Mn. On the other hand, each of the $\lceil M/S \rceil = m$ blocks of A is read exactly once, for an I/O cost of m. Algorithm bmdiff also stores the entire distance matrix, of size MN to disk, incurring an I/O cost of MN/S. Thus the total I/O cost of algorithm bmdiff is $Mn+m+MN/S$, or approximately $2Smn + m$. In addition to space for temporary variables Algorithm bmdiff needs space for only the three buffers B_1, B_2, and B_3, of size S each. Thus the RAM cost of Algorithm bmdiff is $3S$. Other than operations required to read and write disk blocks, Algorithm bmdiff performs the same operations as Algorithm mmdiff. Thus its CPU cost is $O(MN)$. Thus, we may summarize **Algorithm bmdiff's performance** as follows:

I/O	RAM	CPU
$2Smn + m$	$3S$	$O(MN)$

By using techniques similar to those used for computing nested-loop joins in relational databases, it is easy to reduce the I/O cost of reading A and B from Mn to mn. Intuitively, instead of computing the distance matrix in column-major order, we compute it in a blocked manner: When we read in the Ith block of A and the Jth block of B, we compute the entire $S \times S$ submatrix $\{D[i, j] : i \in [SI, (I+1)-1], j \in [SJ, S(J+1)-1]\}$.

However, it is not obvious how we can improve on the I/O cost of storing the distance submatrix itself, which is of size MN/S blocks. As described below, our approach is to avoid storing all of the distance matrix, storing instead only a coarse grid from which the rest of the distance matrix can be quickly computed.

5.1 Computing the Distance Matrix

Consider the $(M+1)\times(N+1)$ distance matrix D suggested by the arrangement of dots in Figure 9, corrsponding to input trees A and B of sizes M and N, respectively. As suggested in the figure, we divide D into a set of overlapping **tiles**. For clarity, the figure alternates the use of solid and dashed lines for marking the tiles. The overlap between neighboring tiles is one item wide.

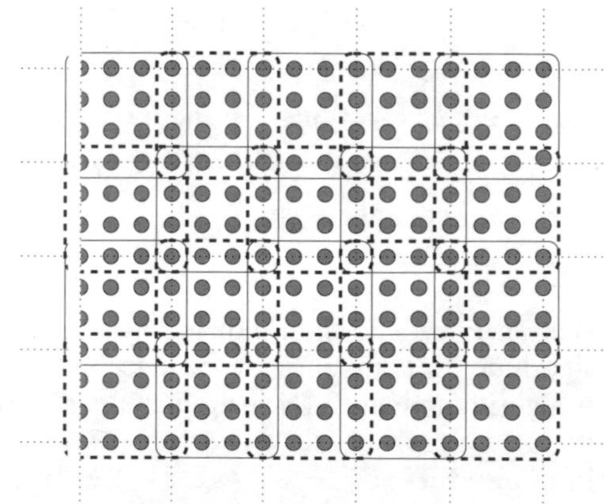

Figure 9: Tiling the distance matrix

More precisely, let $S' = S - 1$. For simplicity in presentation, we shall henceforth assume that M and N are both integral multiples of S', with $M = mS'$ and $N = nS'$. The distance matrix D is then divided into

mn tiles laid out in m columns and n rows. We number these rows and columns of tiles starting with 0, and use the notation (i_b, j_b) to denote the tile in the i_bth column (of tiles) and j_bth row(of tiles). Thus, the tile (i_b, j_b) consists of the following submatrix of the distance matrix D: $\{D[x, y] : x \in [Si_b..S(i_b+1)-1], y \in [Sj_b..S(j_b+1)-1]$.

Our external memory algorithm, called xmdiff (for external memory differencing), is based on the following three key ideas: First, instead of storing the entire distance matrix D, we store only the top and left edges of each of the tiles described above. We call this grid consisting of the tile edges the **distance grid**. Each tile edge is of size S, and there are mn tiles in all. Thus the entire distance grid can be stored using only $2Smn/S = 2mn$ blocks of storage. Referring back to Figure 9, only those entries in the the matrix that are crossed by a dotted line are stored on disk. (Note that for clarity, Figure 9 assumes that the dimension of each tile is only 4×4 items, corresponding to $S = 4$. For such low values of S, our technique does not appear to yield much savings. However, for typical values of S that lie in the hundreds, the savings are substantial.)

Second, given the top and left edges of a tile, we can compute the distance submatrix for the rest of the tile by using the recurrence for D in Section 3. Further, using a few temporary variables, this recurrence allows us to update in-place an array that initially contains the distances for the top (left) edge of a tile to one containing the distances for the bottom (respectively, right) edge.

Third, given the distance grid stored on disk, a shortest path in the edit graph from $(0, 0)$ to (M, N) (and thus the corresponding min-cost edit script that transforms tree A to tree B) can be computed in linear time by working backwards from (M, N), as done in Algorithm mmdiff-r. A straightforward algorithm based on this idea requires $O(S^2)$ RAM as working store. However, we also describe an enhanced version of the algorithm that requires only $O(S)$ RAM.

We assume that the first block of A has a dummy first node, $(0, 0)$. Each successive block has as its first node a copy of the last node from the previous block. The blocks of B are also assumed to be in this format. We also assume that the input sizes M and N are both integral multiples of $S' = (S-1)$, where S is the block size. These assumptions are not necessary for our algorithm; we make them only to simplify the following presentation of the algorithm.

Recall, from Section 3, that we represent a tree using the preorder listing of the ld-pairs of its nodes. These ld-pair sequences are packed densely into disk blocks when the trees are represented on disk. Nodes within a block are arranged at fixed offsets beginning with 0.

Disk blocks are read and written using the function RdBlk and the procedure WrBlk, respectively. RdBlk takes as arguments a file name (which we use to group related blocks) and a block number. Block numbers for each file are separate, and are numbered sequentially beginning with 0. For example, the ith block of a file called A is denoted by $A(i)$ and is read using RdBlk(A, i). The notation for WrBlk is analogous to that used for RdBlk: WrBlk(A,i) writes the buffer A to the ith block of file A. In addition to one dimensional indexing of disk blocks, we also use two-dimensional indexing of the form $D(i, j)$ where the ranges of i and j are fixed and known in advance. Such double indexing of blocks is only a notational convenience. Using a standard row-major encoding of two-dimensional matrices, $D(i, j)$ is equivalent to $D(iN + j)$ where N is the number of different j values. Thus each RdBlk and WrBlk operation requires only a single I/O.

Algorithm xmdiff

Input: Arrays A and B representing the input trees, containing M and N elements, respectively (as in Algorithm mmdiff).

Output: The distance grid (defined above), giving the length of the shortest path from $(0, 0)$ to (x, y) in the edit graph of A and B for all edit graph nodes (x, y) that lie on the edges of tiles of dimension $S \times S$.

Method: Figure 10 lists the pseudocode for Algorithm xmdiff. The first part of the algorithm consists of two for loops which correspond to the first two for loops of Algorithm mmdiff in Figure 7. The first for loop in Figure 10 computes and writes to disk the top row of the distance matrix. Similarly, the second for loop computes and writes to disk the leftmost column of the distance matrix.

The second part of Algorithm xmdiff (the third for loop in Figure 10) corresponds to the nested for loops of Algorithm mmdiff in Figure 7. Each iteration of the inner loop computes the distances in one tile (submatrix) of the distance matrix. Recall that we identify a tile by its tile column and tile row numbers, with numbering starting at 0. The innermost loop computes distances in tile (i_b, j_b). This computation uses, in addition to the appropriate blocks of the input trees A and B, the distances for nodes on the top and left edges of the tile. Due to the overlap of tiles, these edges are the bottom and right edges of some other (previously computed) tiles. The distances for nodes on the bottom and right edges of the tile are then written to disk. By carefully ordering the distance calculations and by using temporary variables (t_a and t_b), we are able to update in place the array D_a, which initially contains the distances for nodes on the top edge, to the distances for nodes in the bottom edge. Similarly, the array D_b initially containing the distances of nodes in the left edge is updated in place to the distances of nodes in the right edge. The tests in the if statements are analogous to those in Algorithm mmdiff.

Analysis

Algorithm xmdiff uses only four buffers in RAM: A, B, D_a, and D_b, each of size S. Thus, the RAM storage requirements are only $4S$ (in addition to the small, constant amount of storage needed for program code and scalar variables).

Let $S' = S - 1$, $m = M/S'$, and $n = N/S'$. The first two for loops of the algorithm make a total of $m + n$ calls to the each of the procedures RdBlk and WrBlk, giving $2(m + n)$ as the I/O cost. In the nested for loops, the first

```
S' := S − 1;
for i_b := 0 to (M/S' − 1) do begin
    A := RdBlk(A, i_b);
    if(i_b > 0) then D_a[0] := D_a[S'];
    else D_a[0] := 0;
    for i := 1 to S' do
        D_a[i] := D_a[i − 1] + c_d(A[i]);
    WrBlk(D_a, i_b, 0);
end;
for j_b := 0 to (N/S' − 1) do begin
    B := RdBlk(B, j_b);
    if(j_b > 0) then D_b[0] := D_b[S'];
    else D_b[0] := 0;
    for j := 1 to S' do
        D_b[j] := D_b[j − 1] + c_i(B[j]);
    WrBlk(D_b, 0, j_b);
end;
for i_b := 0 to (M/S' − 1) do begin
    A := RdBlk(A, i_b);
    D_a := RdBlk(D_a, i_b, 0);
    for j_b := 0 to (N/S' − 1) do begin
        B := RdBlk(B, j_b);
        D_b := RdBlk(D_b, i_b, j_b);
        D_a[0] := D_b[S'];
        for i := 1 to S' do begin
            t_b := D_b[0];
            D_b[0] := D_a[i];
            for j := 1 to S' do begin
                m_1 := ∞; m_2 := ∞; m_3 := ∞;
                if (A[i].d = B[j].d) then
                    m_1 := t_b + c_u(A[i], B[j]);
                if (j = S' or B[j + 1].d ≤ A[i].d) then
                    m_2 := D_b[j] + c_d(A[i]);
                if (i = S' or A[i + 1].d ≤ B[j].d) then
                    m_3 := D_b[j − 1] + c_i(B[j]);
                t_b := D_b[j];
                D_b[j] := min(m_1, m_2, m_3);
            end;
            D_a[i] := D_b[S'];
        end;
        WrBlk(D_a, i_b + 1, j_b);
        WrBlk(D_b, i_b, j_b + 1);
    end;
end;
```

Figure 10: Algorithm xmdiff

two RdBlk statements (for A and D_a) are executed m times. The next two RdBlk statements (for B and D_b) are executed mn times. Finally, the WrBlk statements are executed mn times. Thus, the total number of I/Os in the nested loops of xmdiff is $2m + 4mn$. Combining this number with that for the first two for loops, we conclude that xmdiff makes $4mn + 4m + 2n$ I/Os.

Finally, it is easy to observe that the CPU time is $O(MN)$. Thus, we can summarize **Algorithm xmdiff's performance** as follows, where M and N are the sizes of the input trees, S is the block size, $m = M/(S-1)$, and $n = N/(S-1)$:

I/O	RAM	CPU
$4mn + 4m + 2n$	$4S$	$O(MN)$

5.2 Recovering the Edit Script

Recall, from Figure 8, the Algorithm mmdiff used to recover a minimum-cost edit script in RAM. Using the distance matrix D as a guide, Algorithm mmdiff-r traverses the shortest path from $(0,0)$ to (M,N) backwards, emitting appropriate edit operations along the way. Unlike mmdiff, algorithm xmdiff does not store the entire distance matrix D, making a direct application of the path-recovery algorithm mmdiff-r impossible. However, for each tile (i,j) of the edit graph, xmdiff stores the distances for nodes on its top and left edges in the disk blocks $D_a(i,j)$ and $D_b(i,j)$, respectively. By reading in these blocks and using algorithm mmdiff, the distance matrix for a tile (i,j) can easily be computed at $O(S^2)$ CPU cost (where S is the block-size). Based on these ideas, we have the following:

Algorithm xmdiff-r

Input: Arrays A and B representing the input trees (as in Algorithm mmdiff) and the distance grid computed by xmdiff, stored on disk as D_a and D_b.
Output: A min-cost edit script that transforms A to B (as in Algorithm mmdiff-r).
Method: Figure 11 presents the pseudocode for xmdiff-r. As in algorithm mmdiff-r, we begin at the node (M,N) of the edit graph and move backwards along the shortest path from $(0,0)$ to (M,N). At each iteration of the outer while loop, the current position (i,j) in the edit graph is moved back to either $(i-1,j)$, $(i,j-1)$, or $(i-1,j-1)$ using the if-then-else statement that is very similar to that in algorithm mmdiff-r. Using the boolean variables n_a and n_b, we detect the situation when the current position (i,j) first moves into a new tile in the horizontal and vertical direction, respectively. When n_a is nonzero, (i,j) has just moved to a new tile to the left of the old tile. In this case, we read in the corresponding block of the input file A. Similarly, when n_b is nonzero, we read in the appropriate block of the input file B. In both cases, we read in the top and left edges of the distance matrix for the new tile, (i_b, j_b), into the arrays T and L, respectively. We use T and L to initialize the top and left edges of the complete distance matrix D for the new tile. Recomputation of the

distances in the rest of the matrix D is done in a manner completely analogous to algorithm mmdiff.

Analysis

Each iteration of the outer while loop decrements at least one of i and j; thus, there are at most $M + N$ iterations of that loop. Since i ranges from M down to 1, it follows that n_a is set to 1 for $M/S' = m$ iterations. Similarly, n_b is set to 1 for $N/S' = n$ iterations. Blocks from D_a and D_b are read in whenever one of n_a and n_b is nonzero. In the worst case, this situation can occur $m+n$ times. Thus the I/O cost due to reading D_a and D_b is at most $2(m + n)$. It is easy to observe that each of the m blocks of the input A is read exactly once, for an I/O cost of m. Similarly, the I/O cost incurred in reading the input B is n. Thus, the total I/O cost of algorithm xmdiff-r is $2(m + n) + m + n = 3(m + n)$.

The significant RAM storage requirements of xmdiff-r are due to the arrays A, B, T, and L, and the distance matrix D. The arrays A, B, T, and L are all of size S, the block size. Unfortunately, the distance matrix D is of size S^2. Thus, the total RAM cost is $4S + S^2$.

It is easy to observe that the CPU cost of algorithm xmdiff-r is $O((M + N)S)$. Thus, **Algorithm xmdiff-r's performance** may be summarized as follows:

I/O	RAM	CPU
$3(m+n)$	$4S+S^2$	$O((M+N)S)$

Reducing the RAM cost of xmdiff-r

We can reduce the S^2 RAM space needed to store the distance matrix D as follows. We divide the $S \times S$ distance matrix D into S subtiles of size $\sqrt{S} \times \sqrt{S}$ as suggested by Figure 12. Consider the process of tracing the shortest path backwards through D. We divide this task into stages corresponding to traversing the subtiles. We begin with the subtile in the lower right corner. At the end of each stage, we move to a subtile that is above and/or to the left of the current subtile. At the beginning of the stage corresponding to a subtile, we compute (as before) the distance matrix D, but store distances for only those points that lie in this subtile. Using a technique similar to that used by algorithm mmdiff, this computation can be performed using only a buffer of size S as working storage. Since the size of a subtile is $\sqrt{S} \times \sqrt{S} = S$, the total storage required for the subtile computation is $2S$. Combined with the $4S$ space required to store A, B, T, and L, we have a total RAM cost of $6S$.

The subtile-based enhancement described above results in the distance matrix for each tile being recomputed several times, thus increasing the CPU cost. After each recomputation, the current subtile moves one position to the left and/or up. Thus, the number of subtile computation stages is between $\sqrt{S}$ and $2\sqrt{S}$ (since there are $\sqrt{S}$ subtiles along each dimension of the distance matrix). It follows that the total CPU cost is therefore increased by a factor of at most $2\sqrt{S}$, to $O((M + N)S^{1.5})$.

```
i := M; j := N; S' := S − 1;
n_a := 1; n_b := 1;
while (i > 0 and j > 0) do begin
  i_b := ⌈i/S'⌉ − 1; j_b := ⌈j/S'⌉ − 1;
  i_i := i mod S'; j_i := j mod S';
  if (n_a > 0) then A := RdBlk(A, i_b);
  if (n_b > 0) then B := RdBlk(B, j_b);
  if (n_a > 0 or n_b > 0) then begin
    T := RdBlk(D_a, i_b, j_b); L := RdBlk(D_b, i_b, j_b);
    n_a := 0; n_b := 0;
    D[0..S', 0] := T; D[0, 0..S'] := L;
    for x := 1 to S' do
      for y := 1 to S' do begin
        m_1 := ∞; m_2 := ∞; m_3 := ∞;
        if (A[x].d = B[y].d) then
          m_1 := D[x − 1, y − 1] + c_u(A[x], B[y]);
        if (y = S' or B[y + 1].d ≤ A[x].d) then
          m_2 := D[x − 1, y] + c_i(B[y]);
        if (x = S' or A[x + 1].d ≤ B[y].d) then
          m_3 := D[x, y − 1] + c_d(A[x]);
        D[i, j] := min(m_1, m_2, m_3);
      end;
  end;
  if (D[i_i, j_i] = D[i_i − 1, j_i] + c_d(A[i_i]) and
      (j_i = S' or B[j_i + 1].d ≤ A[i_i].d)) then begin
    i := i − 1;
    if (i mod S' = 0) then n_a := 1;
    print("del" i);
  end;
  else if (D[i_i, j_i] = D[i_i, j_i − 1] + c_i(B[j_i]) and
      (i_i = S' or A[i_i + 1].d ≤ B[j_i].d)) then begin
    j := j − 1;
    if (j mod S' = 0) then n_b := 1;
    print("ins" j);
  end;
  else begin
    i := i − 1; j := j − 1;
    if (i mod S' = 0) then n_a := 1;
    if (j mod S' = 0) then n_b := 1;
    if(A[i_i].l ≠ B[j_i].l) then print("upd" i B[j].l);
  end;
end;
while (i > 0) do begin
  print("del" i);
  if(i mod S' = 0) then A := RdBlk(A, ⌈i/S'⌉ − 1);
  i := i − 1;
end;
while (j > 0) do begin
  print("ins" j);
  if(j mod S' = 0) then B := RdBlk(B, ⌈j/S'⌉ − 1);
  j := j − 1;
end;
```

Figure 11: Algorithm xmdiff-r

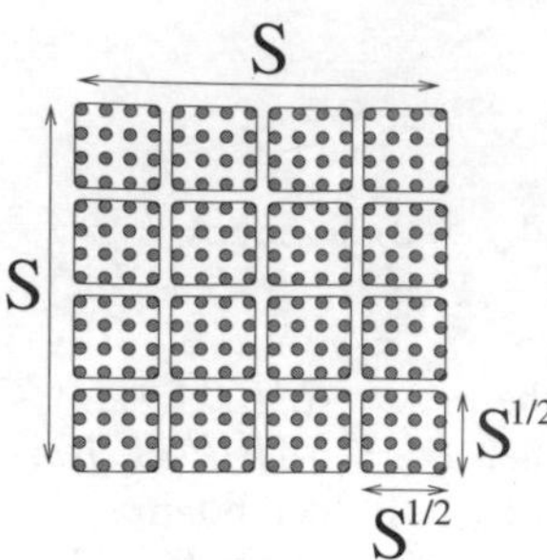

Figure 12: Reducing mmdiff-r's RAM cost

Thus, the **performance of the modified Algorithm xmdiff-r** may be summarized as follows:

I/O	RAM	CPU
$3(m+n)$	$6S$	$O((M+N)S^{1.5})$

Thus, the costs of executing Algorithm xmdiff followed by Algorithm xmdiff-r are as follows:

I/O	RAM	CPU
$4mn+7m+5n$	$6S$	$O(MN+(M+N)S^{1.5})$

Although we have described S to be the block size, our algorithm does not depend on S being equal to the block transfer unit. Another way to interpret the above result is the following: Suppose we have R units of RAM that we can use for our algorithm's buffers. We set $R = 6S$; that is, $S = R/6$. Substituting R for S in our performance results tells us that by increasing the amount of RAM buffer space, we can achieve a quadratic reduction in the significant $4mn$ part of the I/O cost.

6 Related Work

Differencing algorithms have received considerable attention in the research literature, with the problem of comparing sequences receiving the most attention [SK83]. Early sequence comparison algorithms include the classic $O(mn)$ Wagner-Fischer algorithm [WF74], which was shown to be optimal for a wide class of computation models in [AHU76, WC76]. Using the so-called "four Russians" technique, a more efficient $O(nm/\log n)$ algorithm for finite alphabets is presented in [MP80].

More recent work on sequence comparison has focused on improving the expected case running time using output-sensitive algorithms. For example, Myers presents an $O(ND)$ algorithm, where N and D are the sizes of the input and edit script, respectively [Mye86]. (This algorithm forms the basis of the widely used *diff* utility [MM85].) Further improvements are reported in [WMG90]. These algorithms are based on using the special structure of an edit graph.

Our technique for mapping the tree differencing problem to edit graphs, as described in Section 3, allows us to apply the above sequence comparison results to trees. For example, it is relatively straightforward to extend these algorithms in [Mye86] for differencing trees in main memory without any significant increase in running time. However, extending these results to external memory appears more complicated and is part of our continuing work.

Several formulations of the tree comparison problem have also been studied. Early work includes Selkow's recursive algorithm for a simple formulation similar to the one in this paper [Sel77]. More recent work includes [ZS89], which studies ordered trees, and [ZWS95], which studies unordered trees. Most formulations of the tree differencing problem for unordered trees are NP-hard.

There are significant advantages to describing tree differences using not only the three basic edit operations (insert, delete, and update), but also subtree operations such as move, copy, and uncopy. In [CRGMW96], we studied a variation that includes a subtree move operation and described an efficient algorithm that uses simplifying assumptions based on domain characteristics. In [CGM97], we studied a variation that includes subtree copy and uncopy operations in addition to moves. These algorithms are used in the implementation of the C^3 system for managing change in autonomous databases [CAW98].

All the above algorithms are main-memory algorithms; that is, they assume that all input data and working storage resides in RAM. To our knowledge, ours is the first external-memory differencing algorithm. The design of external-memory algorithms based on the problem formulations and ideas in the work described above is a topic for continuing work.

The Unix program *bdiff* implements a sequence comparison algorithm for files that are too large to fit in RAM using a simple wrapper around the standard *diff* algorithm [Mye86]. The bdiff program works by first dividing the input files into segments that fit in RAM, and then running diff on each pair of corresponding (by position in the respective file) segments. This strategy does not guarantee a minimum-cost edit script. In fact, a single inserted line can mislead bdiff into mismatching a large number of other lines.

The problem of computing differences is closely related to the problem of pattern matching (e.g., [WZJS94, WCM+94, WSC+97]). While there are important differences between the two problems, it may be possible to share some of the techniques used by their solutions.

7 Conclusion

We described several applications that are based on comparing two snapshots of data in order to detect the differences between them. We explained the need for external-memory differencing algorithms for both flat (sequence) and hierarchical (tree) data. We modeled hierarchical data using rooted, ordered, labeled trees, and formalized the hierarchical data comparison problem using the idea of a minimum-cost edit script between two trees. We described a method to map this tree comparison problem to a shortest-path problem in a special graph called the tree edit graph. We first presented a main-memory tree differencing algorithm based on the edit graph reduction. Next we discussed its extension to external memory and described problems with a naive extension. We then presented our main algorithm (xmdiff) for efficiently differencing trees in external memory.

As continuing work, we are exploring the use of our edit graph reduction to transfer results from sequence comparison to trees. Preliminary results indicate that while this strategy is relatively easy to use for main-memory algorithms, extending it to external-memory algorithms is more challenging. We are also working on incorporating the algorithm xmdiff into the C^3 change management system and on releasing a public version of the implementation. We also plan to explore the application of our techniques to related problems such as pattern matching and data mining in semistructured data (which is often modeled using trees and graphs).

References

[AHU76] A. Aho, D. Hirschberg, and J. Ullman. Bounds on the complexity of the longest common subsequence problem. *Journal of the Association for Computing Machinery*, 23(1):1–12, January 1976.

[CAW98] S. Chawathe, S. Abiteboul, and J. Widom. Representing and querying changes in semistructured data. In *Proceedings of the International Conference on Data Engineering*, pages 4–13, Orlando, Florida, February 1998.

[CGM97] S. Chawathe and H. Garcia-Molina. Meaningful change detection in structured data. In *Proceedings of the ACM SIGMOD International Conference on Management of Data*, pages 26–37, Tuscon, Arizona, May 1997.

[CRGMW96] S. Chawathe, A. Rajaraman, H. Garcia-Molina, and J. Widom. Change detection in hierarchically structured information. In *Proceedings of the ACM SIGMOD International Conference on Management of Data*, pages 493–504, Montréal, Québec, June 1996.

[LGM96] W. Labio and H. Garcia-Molina. Efficient snapshot differential algorithms for data warehousing. In *Proceedings of the International Conference on Very Large Data Bases*, Bombay, India, September 1996.

[MM85] W. Miller and E. Myers. A file comparison program. *Software–Practice and Experience*, 15(11):1025–1040, 1985.

[MP80] W. Masek and M. Paterson. A faster algorithm computing string edit distances. *Journal of Computer and System Sciences*, 20:18–31, 1980.

[Mye86] E. Myers. An $O(ND)$ difference algorithm and its variations. *Algorithmica*, 1(2):251–266, 1986.

[Sel77] S. Selkow. The tree-to-tree editing problem. *Information Processing Letters*, 6(6):184–186, December 1977.

[SK83] D. Sankoff and J. Kruskal. *Time Warps, String Edits, and Macromolecules: The Theory and Practice of Sequence Comparison*. Addison-Wesley, 1983.

[Tic85] W. Tichy. RCS—A system for version control. *Software—Practice and Experience*, 15(7):637–654, July 1985.

[Vit98] J. Vitter. External memory algorithms. In *Proceedings of the ACM Symposium on Principles of Database Systems*, Seattle, Washington, June 1998.

[WC76] C. Wong and A. Chandra. Bounds for the string editing problem. *Journal of the Association for Computing Machinery*, 23(1):13–16, January 1976.

[WCM+94] J. Wang, G. Chirn, T. Marr, B. Shapiro, D. Shasha, and K. Zhang. Combinatorial pattern discovery for scientific data: some preliminary results. In *Proceedings of the ACM SIGMOD Conference*, pages 115–125, May 1994.

[WF74] R. Wagner and M. Fischer. The string-to-string correction problem. *Journal of the Association of Computing Machinery*, 21(1):168–173, January 1974.

[WMG90] S. Wu, U. Manber, and G.Myers. An $O(NP)$ sequence comparison algorithm. *Information Processing Letters*, 35:317–323, September 1990.

[WSC+97] J. Wang, D. Shasha, G. Chang, L. Relihan, K. Zhang, and G. Patel. Structural matching and discovery in document databases. In *Proceedings of the ACM SIGMOD International Conference on Management of Data*, pages 560–563, 1997.

[WZJS94] J. Wang, K. Zhang, K. Jeong, and D. Shasha. A system for approximate tree matching. *IEEE Transactions on Knowledge and Data Engineering*, 6(4):559–571, August 1994.

[Yan91] W. Yang. Identifying syntactic differences between two programs. *Software—Practice and Experience*, 21(7):739–755, July 1991.

[ZS89] K. Zhang and D. Shasha. Simple fast algorithms for the editing distance between trees and related problems. *SIAM Journal of Computing*, 18(6):1245–1262, 1989.

[ZWS95] K. Zhang, J. Wang, and D. Shasha. On the editing distance between undirected acyclic graphs. *International Journal of Foundations of Computer Science*, 1995.

Mining Deviants in a Time Series Database

H. V. Jagadish
University of Michigan
Ann Arbor, Michigan

Nick Koudas
AT&T Laboratories
Florham Park, NJ 07932

S. Muthukrishnan
AT&T Laboratories
Florham Park, NJ 07932

Abstract

Identifying outliers is an important data analysis function. Statisticians have long studied techniques to identify outliers in a data set in the context of fitting the data to some model. In the case of time series data, the situation is more murky. For instance, the "typical" value could "drift" up or down over time, so the extrema may not necessarily be interesting. We wish to identify data points that are somehow anomalous or "surprising".

We formally define the notion of a deviant in a time series, based on a representation sparsity metric. We develop an efficient algorithm to identify deviants in a time series. We demonstrate how this technique can be used to locate interesting artifacts in time series data, and present experimental evidence of the value of our technique.

As a side benefit, our algorithm are able to produce histogram representations of data, that have substantially lower error than "optimal histograms" for the same total storage, including both histogram buckets and the deviants stored separately. This is of independent interest for selectivity estimation.

Proceedings of the 25th VLDB Conference, Edinburgh, Scotland, 1999.

1 Introduction

Outlier detection has a long history [Cha84] in statistics, and more recently, in data mining. However, the bulk of this work has been concerned with finding outliers in a large set of data, most often with respect to some parametric model in mind. When one deals with time series data, it is not appropriate to ignore the time axis and think of the observed values as an unordered set. As such, standard outlier detection techniques do not carry over easily [KN98].

Consider the data series shown in Figure 1. Point 11 "sticks out" as having a much larger value than neighboring points, and hence may be a deviant worthy of further analysis. Point 4 has a larger value than point 11, but is part of a group (points 4-6) of large-valued points and so is not an interesting outlier (or deviant) in itself[1].

The question then becomes how do we identify points with values that differ greatly from that of surrounding points. Do we consider immediate neighbors only? Do we consider points further away with some

[1] It is reasonable to consider the whole subsequence of points 4-6 for further analysis, since they all have value much higher than typical, and indeed our formulation below will permit this.

X = (38,53,33,390,210,371,46,72,174,47,373,21,30,107,46)

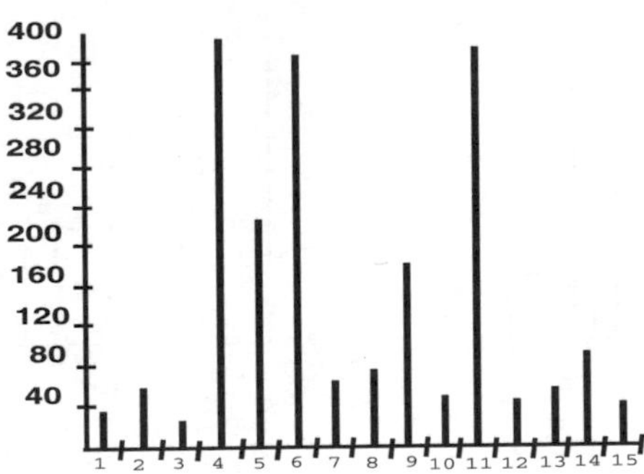

Figure 1: Example Sequence

sort of decreasing weight for distance? How do we deal with cases where a point differs greatly from its left neighbor, but less so from its right neighbor? One can come up with a variety of ad hoc local definitions, each of which gives a different answer, and none of which is conceptually satisfying.

Our proposal is to use the well recognized information theoretic principle of representation length. If the removal of a point P from the time sequence results in a sequence that can be represented more succinctly than the original one (by more than the increment required for explicitly keeping track of P separately), then the point P is a deviant. For succinct, (lossy), representation of series data, we adopt the histogram method, so popular in database literature and practice.

Thus, our problem is to find points in a given time series whose removal from the series results in a histogram representation with lower error than the original, even after the number of buckets has been reduced to account for the separate storage of these deviant points.

The solution to this problem is interesting in itself, and is the focus of the first half of this paper. We show in Section 5, that such identification of deviants can lead to substantial increases in the accuracy of histogramming techniques for the same storage, and only a small additional computational cost. Efficient algorithms for this purpose are developed in Section 4. The proposed algorithms are fast and optimal.

We discuss how to analyze deviants found using these techniques in Section 6. In particular, we develop a simple algorithm to find clusters of deviants. In Section 7, we present a series of experiments performed on real life time series databases, and highlight the utility of the deviant mining algorithms.

We begin with some background and our assumptions in Section 2, followed by the formal definition of a deviant as well as our deviant-finding problem in Section 3.

2 Background

Histogramming techniques are of profound importance in query optimization in relational databases. Accurate estimates of result size of queries are crucial for the choice of execution plan in a relational query optimizer. Histogramming is also invaluable for approximate query answering. There exists a sizeable volume of research on histogramming techniques [IP95, Ioa93, PIHS96, PI97, JKM+98]. We follow these works to define the problem in mathematical terms, and develop a framework within which a solution with general applicability can be described.

We are given a sequence of data points, $X = v_1 v_2 \cdots v_N$ where each v_i, $1 \leq i \leq N$, is an integer drawn from some bounded range. Let S be the set of indices of points in X, thus $S = \{1, 2, \ldots, N\}$. There is great flexibility to the semantics of X. X could represent the sequence of values obtained from the observation of some random variable, i.e., v_i is the value of the random variable at time i. Thus X could represent a stock price over time, the usage (in some time granularity) of an AT&T service, etc. In a different context such as that of query result size estimation, X could represent a frequency vector of an attribute in some relational instance. In this case, i corresponds to an attribute value[2] and v_i to the total number of

[2] We assume that attribute values can be mapped to an integer domain. More general assumptions are possible, but these issues are not important for the main arguments in our paper, so we will assume that the i take values from a dense integer set.

occurrences of i in the attribute instance[3]. Let $D \subseteq S$ be a set containing indices of points in X. We denote as $X - D$ the sequence that results if we remove from X all points with indices in D.

Irrespective of the semantics of vector X, the objective is the same: given some space constraint B, create and store a compact representation of sequence X using at most B storage, denoted H_B, such that H_B is optimal under some notion of error $E_X(H_B)$ defined between X and H_B.

In the process of creating a compact representation for X, several issues arise. We first need to decide on a representation for H_B. Let s_i and e_i be indices of points in X such that $s_i \leq e_i$. The common choice is to collapse the values in the sequence of consecutive points (s_i, e_i) into a single value h_i (typically their average, $h_i = \sum_{j=s_i}^{e_i} v_j$). The value h_i along with (s_i, e_i) (recording the start and the end of the sequence thus collapsed) forms the *bucket* b_i, that is, $b_i = (s_i, e_i, h_i)$. Since h_i is only an approximation for the values in bucket b_i, whenever a bucket is formed an error is induced due to the approximation. We need to choose a way to quantify this error. As is common, we quantify this error using the *Sum Squared Error* (SSE) metric, defined as:

$$F(b_i) = \sum_{j=s_i}^{e_i} (v_j - h_i)^2 \tag{1}$$

Assuming that the space constraint is expressed in buckets, the resulting approximation H_B will consist of B buckets and the total error in the approximation is $E_X(H_B) = \sum_{i=1}^{B} F(b_i)$.[4]

The optimal histogram construction problem is then defined as follows:

[3]Note in particular that the only property of X material to us is that it is an ordered set of values. In this paper, we have focused on time sequences, but all our results are directly applicable also to other ordered sets such as the frequency counts for an attribute value.

[4]Other error functions are possible such as $\max_i F(b_i)$ etc. All our results will hold for any point-wise additive error function $E_X(H_B)$, but we will focus on the specific error function above which is the most common one in the literature.

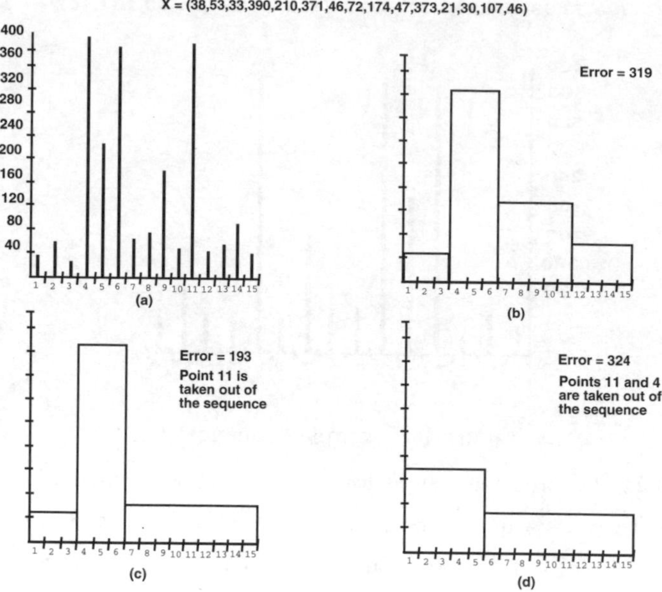

Figure 2: Histogram construction: (a) Original sequence (b) Optimal histogram with 4 buckets (c) Optimal histogram with 3 buckets and point $v_{11} = 373$ removed (d) Optimal histogram with 2 buckets and points $v_4 = 390$ and $v_{11} = 373$ removed.

Problem 1 (Optimal Histogram Construction) *Given a sequence X of length N, a number of buckets B, and an error function $E_X()$, find H_B to minimize $E_X(H_B)$.*

The resulting optimal histogram is the well known `vopt` histogram [IP95]. There exists an efficient algorithm to determine the `vopt` histogram [JKM+98]. This algorithm is based on dynamic programming and it chooses the non overlapping sequences of points that should be collapsed into single values (bucket boundaries), such that the total error metric is minimized.

3 Deviants: Motivation and Definitions

Consider Figure 2(a) which represents a portion of time series extracted from an AT&T data warehouse. Figure 2(b) presents the optimal histogram `vopt` on the sequence in Figure 2(a) using $B = 4$. The approximation in Figure 2(b) has total (sum of squares) error of 319. Assume that we are allowed to remove a point from the sequence and store it separately. This requires two integers, one for the position in the sequence and one for the value of the point. The storage required for one histogram bucket is also two integers: the left boundary and the average value. (Only one boundary needs to be kept since buckets are non-overlapping and adjacent. Without loss of generality, we keep the left boundary.) Thus, we have spent the equivalent of one bucket from our total bucket budget, and we must approximate the remaining sequence with $B-1$ buckets, that is, 3 buckets in this case. One can observe that by removing the point $v_{11} = 373$, the total error of the approximation is reduced to 193 which is an improvement in accuracy of 40%. However, one should be careful about removing the points since not all points in the sequence of Figure 2(a) reduce the total error when they are removed. For example, by removing the point $v_1 = 38$, the total error in the approximation increases (recall that after removing v_1, only 3 buckets are available for the remaining sequence). In the case of a single point removal, one way to determine which point to remove in order to obtain the largest decrease in the total error would be to consider each point in turn and use `vopt` on the remaining sequence; there are a total of N `vopt` executions. Notice that the point causing the largest decrease in error (v_{11}) in this example is not the point that has the maximum value. We refer to points that have this property as *deviants*; these are formally defined below.

Now consider removing two points. In this case, the smallest error one can achieve by removing two points and approximating the resulting sequence with $B-2=2$ buckets is 324. It is achieved by removing points $v_4 = 390$ and $v_{11} = 373$. The total error however is larger than the one with $B = 4$ buckets, so removing two points is not beneficial. In order to determine the pair of points whose removal results in the largest decrease in the total error of approximation, if one were to consider each pair of points and apply `vopt` on the remaining sequence when that pair is removed, the total number of `vopt` executions required is $\binom{N}{2}$. In general, the total number of point sets to consider for removal of "best" k points is $\binom{N}{k}$. By trying to remove additional points, one can verify that no further improvement is possible, with the given bucket budget.

We now formally define the notion of deviants and the problem of finding the optimal ("best") deviants.

Definition 1 *Given a sequence of points X and a number of buckets B, a point set $D \subseteq S$ is a deviant set if and only if $E_X(H^*_B) > E_{X-D}(H^*_{B-|D|})$, where H^*_B is the optimal histogram on X with B buckets (having error $E_X(H^*_B)$) and $H^*_{B-|D|}$ is the optimal histogram on $X-D$ with $B-|D|$ buckets (having error $E_{X-D}(H^*_{B-|D|})$).*

From the preceding discussion, it follows that for a given sequence of points X and a given number of buckets B, there is an optimal deviant set that, if identified, can be used to construct a histogram representation with minimum total error. (In the example above, the optimal number of deviant points is one.) This observation leads to the following optimization problem:

Problem 2 (Optimal Deviant Set) *Given set X and buckets B, identify a set $D \subseteq S$ such that $\forall D', D' \subseteq S, E_{X-D}(H_{B-|D|}) \leq E_{X-D'}(H_{B-|D'|})$.*

4 Algorithms

We are interested in providing an efficient solution to Problem 2. A straightforward solution, that was described earlier, is to examine every possible point set in turn and to compute the optimal histogram on the remaining sequence after that point set has been removed. The computational cost for such an approach would be prohibitive, being exponential in the number of deviants considered. We give a different algorithm which is optimal, and is significantly more efficient. We first develop a solution to the following related problem:

Problem 3 (Optimal κ Deviants) *Given sequence X, a budget of storage B and a non-negative integer κ, identify set $D \subseteq S$ with $|D| = \kappa$ such that $\forall D', D' \subseteq S$, $|D'| = \kappa$, we have*

$$E_{X-D}(H^*_{B-\kappa}) \leq E_{X-D'}(H^*_{B-\kappa}).$$

We are given a sequence X of numbers of total size N. We are also given parameters B, the total storage and κ, the number of deviants. Our goal is to produce a histogram consisting of $B - \kappa$ buckets and κ deviants, so that the total error of the histogram is minimized.

Let (s_i, e_i) denote the starting (leftmost) and ending (rightmost) points respectively in sequence X, of the points contained in bucket b_i. Since some points in the range (s_i, e_i) might be deviants, we have to redefine the error formula given in eqn. (1) for the error induced by the bucket, to account for the points (the deviants) that are removed from the sequence. For bucket $b_i = (s_i, e_i)$, say there is a set T_i of deviants in (s_i, e_i) and $|T_i| = k$. The refined SSE for bucket b_i with these k deviants is denoted $F^{T_i}(s_i \cdots e_i, k)$, and it is defined as:

$$F^{T_i}(s_i \cdots e_i, k) = \sum_{s_i \leq j \leq e_i \; \& j \notin T_i} (v_j - h^{T_i}_{s_i,e_i})^2 \qquad (2)$$

where $h^{T_i}_{s_i,e_i}$ is the average of non-deviants (values at indices not belonging to T_i) within the bucket, that is,

$$h^{T_i}_{s_i,e_i} = \frac{\sum_{j=s_i \;\&\; j \notin T_i}^{e_i} v_j}{e_i - s_i + 1 - k}.$$

The total error of the approximation represented by the histogram and a given set of deviants T is the sum over the buckets of the error in each bucket b_i when the set of deviants $T_i \subseteq T$ that fall within that bucket are removed. Our proposed solution for solving Problem 3 is based on dynamic programming. We first parameterize the error term that we wish to minimize. Let $E(i, j, k)$ represent the error of using j buckets on the sequence v_1 through v_i with k deviants been identified in $[1 \ldots i]$, in the optimal way (therefore, the error is the minimum possible). Using Bellman's equation [Bel54] we can write a recursive expression for $E(i, j, k)$:

$$E(i,j,k) = \min_{1 \leq l \leq i,\; 0 \leq m \leq k} E(l, j-1, m) + F^*(l+1 \cdots i, k-m). \qquad (3)$$

Here, $F^*(a \cdots b, c)$ denotes the minimum error in the bucket $(a \cdots b)$ with c deviants, that is,

$$F^*(a \cdots b, c) = \min_{T| \; T \in \{a,\ldots,b\}, \;\; |T|=c} F^T(a \cdots b, c) \qquad (4)$$

In other words, the equation for $E(i, j, k)$ calculates the error of the optimal strategy with k deviants and j buckets on the sequence $v_1 \cdots v_i$ to be the sum of the errors of the optimal strategy with m deviants and $j-1$ buckets on the sequence $v_1 \cdots v_l$, and that for a single bucket on the sequence $v_{l+1} \cdots v_i$ using $k - m$ (the remaining) deviants. This is appropriately minimized over the choices for the parameters m and l.

The initialization to form the basis of this bootstrapping approach comes from observing that $E(i, 1, m) = F^*(1 \cdots i, m)$, for $1 \leq i \leq N$ and $0 \leq m \leq \kappa$. The remainder of the algorithm uses equation (3) to construct solutions for successively larger number of buckets and number of deviants. After $E(i, j, k)$ has been constructed for $1 \leq i \leq N, 1 \leq j \leq B - \kappa, 0 \leq k \leq \kappa$, the algorithm terminates.

The only piece that still remains unspecified is the computation of $F^*(a \cdots b, c)$ for all possible values of a, b, c. If $c \geq b - a + 1$, clearly $F^*(a \cdots b, c) = 0$. We next show how to efficiently compute $F^*(a \cdots b, c)$ in all the other cases. Recall the definition of F^* from Equation 4, and say the minimum there is reached for the set T^*. (We do not know T^* apriori and it is used only for making the definitions formal.) Define $S^*[a, b, c]$ to be sum of the non-deviant points of the sequence $(v_a \ldots v_b)$ in the solution with error $F^*(a \cdots b, c)$, that is, $S^*[a, b, c] = \sum_{a \leq i \leq b,\; i \notin T^*} v_i$. Similarly, define $SS^*[a, b, c]$ to be the sum of the squares of the non-deviant points in this sequence, that is, $SS^*[a,b,c] = \sum_{a \le i \le b,\, i \notin T^*} v_i^2$. We will again use dynamic programming to compute $S^*[a,b,c]$ and $SS^*[a,b,c]$, and use those to compute $F^*(a \cdots b, c)$ at the same time.

Computing $F^*(a \cdots b, c)$ has two parts, depending on whether b is a candidate deviant point or not. If b is a deviant point in the minimum error solution, we would have to update the parameters as follows:

$$F^*(a \cdots b, c) = F^*(a \cdots b-1, c-1)$$
$$S^*[a,b,c] = S^*[a,b-1,c-1]$$
$$SS^*[a,b,c] = SS^*[a,b-1,c-1]$$

Since b is a deviant point, it is not included in the computation of the error; b is extracted from the sequence. The other case is when b is not a deviant point. In this case, the solution $F^*(a \cdots b-1, c)$ must be adjusted to include v_b. Thus, S^* and SS^* must be updated as $S^*[a,b,c] = S^*[a,b-1,c] + v_b$ and $SS^*[a,b,c] = SS^*[a,b-1,c] + (v_b)^2$. The $F^*(a \cdots b, c)$ value must be updated using the formula obtained by simple algebraic manipulation:

$$F^*(a \cdots b, c) = SS^*[a,b,c] - \frac{S^*[a,b,c]^2}{(b-a+1-c)} \qquad (5)$$

We consider both these cases and calculate the two possible values of F^*. We choose the case that yields the smallest error F^* and the values of F^*, S^* and SS^* are updated as described above depending on the chosen case.

That completes the description of the algorithm *ComputeF** for computing F^* values. These values are stored in a table, which can be looked up whenever needed while computing $E(i,j,k)$'s. That also completes the description of the algorithm for computing $E()$ values. The value $E(N, B-\kappa, \kappa)$ gives the minimum error in the solution to Problem 3. As in all dynamic programming solutions, it is now a standard step to determine a set of κ deviants and the bucket boundaries of the histogram which result in $E(N, B-\kappa, \kappa)$ error of approximation.

Theorem 1 *There is an $O(N^2(B-\kappa)\kappa^2)$ algorithm for solving Problem 3.*

proof. We calculate $S^*[a \cdots b, c]$ for all $1 \le a \le N$, $a+1 \le b \le N$ and $0 \le k \le \kappa$; thus there are $O(N^2\kappa)$ values of $S^*[a \cdots b, c]$ of interest. There are two cases to consider for updating S^* each of which takes $O(1)$ time. Thus, the time taken to calculate all the $S^*[\,]$'s is $O(N^2\kappa)$; the same holds for the $SS^*[\,]$ and $F^*()$ values too. After this precomputation, the value of $F^*(a \cdots b, c)$ for any $1 \le a \le N$, $a \le b \le N$, $0 \le c \le \kappa$, can be retrieved in $O(1)$ time.

We calculate $E(i,j,k)$ for each $1 \le i \le N$, $1 \le j \le B-\kappa$ and $0 \le k \le \kappa$; hence, there are $O(N(B-\kappa)\kappa)$ values of $E(i,j,k)$ of interest in all. Computing each such value using Equation 3 involves considering $O(N\kappa)$ values of $E(l, j-1, m)$ which can be obtained in $O(1)$ time each using the dynamic programming technique, and $O(N\kappa)$ values of $F^*(l+1 \cdots i, k-m)$ which can be obtained in $O(1)$ time each using the precomputation. Thus each $E(i,j,k)$ takes time $O(N\kappa)$ to calculate and the total time taken is $O(N^2(B-\kappa)\kappa^2)$. ∎

Optimal Deviant Set

Using the solution for Problem 3 we can obtain an efficient solution for Problem 2. The simplest approach would be to solve Problem 3 with the number of deviants κ taking values $0, \ldots, B-1$ and the number of buckets taking values $B-\kappa$ for each such choice of κ. This will involve invoking our solution to Problem 3 at most B times. However, we can solve Problem 2 in time that is essentially the time it takes to solve an instance of Problem 3 *once* as follows.

Recall that the algorithm in the previous section finds $E(i,j,k)$ for all $1 \le i \le N$, $1 \le j \le B-\kappa$ and $0 \le k \le \kappa$ in time $O(N^2(B-\kappa)\kappa^2)$. We can extend the algorithm to compute all those values for $1 \le j \le B$ and $0 \le k \le B-1$ so the resulting algorithm takes time $O(N^2B^3)$. We can then read off the minimum error solution amongst $E(i,j,k)$ where $j = B-k$ for all $0 \leq k \leq B-1$. This takes $O(B)$ additional time. Therefore we can conclude the following.

Theorem 2 *There is an $O(N^2B^3)$ time algorithm for solving Problem 2.*

5 Deviant Histogramming

In the previous section, we presented algorithms for finding the optimal κ deviants and for detecting the optimal deviant set in a given sequence X. In fact, our technique gives us a compact representation for X comprising the deviant points, as well as the histogram on the remainder. More precisely, we have κ deviants each stored as a pair of its position i in X and its value v_i, and $B-\kappa$ buckets each stored as a pair of its left endpoint in X and the average of the non-deviant values in that bucket.

This compact representation may be thought of as a histogram in itself, and it will serve the same purposes as a histogram. In this section, we explore its use in selectivity estimation. In particular, we focus on equality queries (other queries such as range queries may also be answered using our compact representation just as it is done with standard histograms). An estimate for an equality query i is obtained as follows. If i is a deviant, we merely return its value v_i and no error is incurred. If i is not a deviant, we determine the bucket to which i belongs and return the value stored with that bucket (recall that this is the average of the non-deviant points that lie within that bucket) as an estimate of v_i.

Here we report experimental results on a number of experiments performed to assess the utility of the proposed algorithm as a histogramming technique. The common method for evaluating selectivity estimation techniques on equality queries is to consider the sum-of-squares metric, namely, $\sum_i(v_i - e_i)^2$ where e_i is the estimate for the point query v_i [IP95]. This is the expected total error on a workload of equality queries if all equality queries are equally likely. Poosala et al [PIHS96] showed that the `vopt` histogram was the optimal histogram for estimating equality queries, provided that one uses a histogram representation without removing any points (deviants). We compare the `vopt` histogram to our histogram wherein our histogram uses the same space as the `vopt` histogram, but it uses a portion of it for storing the deviants and the remainder for the buckets.

We used real data sets extracted from an AT&T data warehouse in our experiments. All data sets consist of 2000 points in a time sequence. Because of proprietary reasons, we are not able to disclose the specific data sets used. However, we do number the data sets in order of increasing skew – data set D4 is close to a skewed (randomized) Zipfian whereas D1 is skewed very little.

In all our experiments, we keep the total space (expressed in buckets) devoted to the histogram fixed, and we vary the number of deviants. With total space B devoted to the histogram and k deviants, $B-k$ buckets are placed in the sequence. (Recall that it takes the same number of bytes to store one deviant point as it does to store a bucket.) The case when $k=0$ is the well known `vopt` histogram.

Figure 3 shows the results for the four data sets, as k is varied, for a representative selection of three values for B, the total storage. For all data sets we see that the error decreases as more storage is devoted, as expected. We also see that identifying and storing deviants separately does help, and in some cases quite substantially. For instance, for data set D3, the error with a storage of 20 is approximately the same as the error with double the storage and no deviants; most of the space is devoted to the deviants in this case. In other words, just by identifying deviants and storing them separately, we are able to decrease error as if we had doubled the storage!

However, most of the curves exhibit a clear minimum indicating that there is a point beyond which devoting additional storage to deviants is not desirable. This minimum represents the "optimal" number of deviants for the specific data set and the storage budget.

As expected, the optimal number of deviants increases (linearly) with the storage budget. Also, more skewed is the distribution of data, greater is the benefit obtained from identifying deviants and larger is the number of deviants at the optimal point. In fact, for a highly skewed data set, D4, the minimum is beyond the right end of the feasible region, indicating that it is best for us to devote almost all of our storage budget to the deviants. (In this case, the optimal solution is an end-biased histogram where we keep the most deviant values rather than the extremal values.)

6 Data Mining with Deviants

Consider an analyst examining a large time series. Instead of manually examining the entire sequence, it would be beneficial to have it automatically tagged for regions (or points) of potential interest. The crucial issues are to define the notion of "interesting" regions in a time series, and to design efficient algorithms for finding such regions.

Deviants have an intriguing combination of local and global property. A purely global approach to finding interesting points in a time series may be to identify points farthest away from the mean of the entire sequence [AAR95]. This approach would find all the extremal points. In contrast, a purely local approach to finding interesting points may be to determine pairs of neighboring points that differ by the largest amount. The MaxDiff [IP95, GMP97] heuristic for histogram construction accomplishes this efficiently. For example, this technique will find all regions with the highest derivative, that is, the slope. While the points determined for the purely local, or the purely global approaches may be of interest, there are instances when one needs a more sophisticated notion of interesting points or regions. An optimal set of deviants combines the local and global aspects naturally: they are local in so far as trying to minimize the deviation from the average within a bucket, and global in trying to minimize the total sum of the errors from the different buckets.

Our overall approach for data mining with deviants is as follows. We first determine a set of deviants in the original time series. We then analyze the set of deviants for useful structure. We discuss these two steps in the following subsections.

6.1 Deviant Sets

One method for obtaining a set of deviants for further analysis would be to choose parameters κ, the number of deviants, and B, the total storage allowed, and use the algorithms in Section 4 to determine an optimal set of deviants. A particular choice of interest for κ would be the optimal number of deviants for a given storage B. Another method would be to choose a small set of values for these parameters and determine the optimal deviant sets for each choice of the parameters. Then one can collate the "consensus" deviant points from the different optimal deviant sets. There are many ways to define the notion of consensus. Here, we adopt the notion exemplified in the following problem.

Problem 4 (Consensus Deviants) *Given sequence X of length N, a non-negative integer κ and parameters k_l, k_m, B_l, B_m, identify the κ most frequently occurring elements in the sets $D_{k,B}$ for $B_l \leq B \leq B_m$ and $k_l \leq k \leq k_m$, where each $D_{k,B}$ is the optimal set of k deviants for sequence X given B buckets of storage.*

It may seem on the face of it that solving Problem 4 requires multiple solutions to Problem 3 for different values of k and B. However, it turns out once again that the solution to Problem 3 already computes all the necessary additional solutions required here, so that only a single run of Problem 3 with a sufficiently large choice of k and B (k_m and B_m respectively) is required. It follows from our results in Section 4 that Problem 4 can be solved in time $O(N^2 B_m k_m^2)$. This method calls for choosing the parameter values k_l, k_m, B_l, B_m appropriately. Since one desires to isolate a few areas of potential interest, keeping κ small and varying k and B over small ranges is recommended. Many other

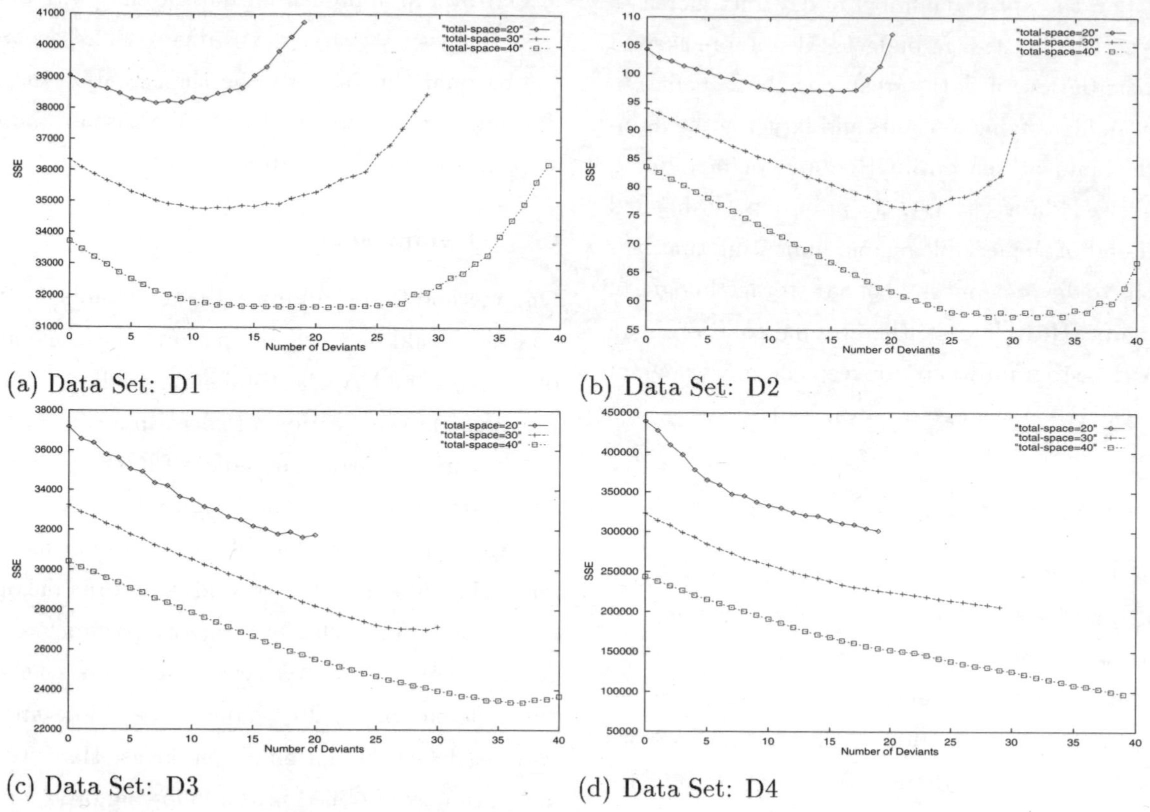

(a) Data Set: D1

(b) Data Set: D2

(c) Data Set: D3

(d) Data Set: D4

Figure 3: Histogram error for increasing number of deviants with fixed total space.

notions of consensus deviant sets can be incorporated into our approach here.

6.2 Deviant Clusters

The individual points in a set of deviants may be of interest by themselves, so they may be considered in isolation. However, from a mining perspective, it is useful to identify properties of groups of deviants in addition to those of individual deviants. More specifically, we consider the clustering of deviants. Since the deviants are derived from the underlying time series, it seems reasonable to consider contiguous segments (intervals) rather than arbitrary subsets of points in the time series, in order to understand the clustering of deviants. We adopt the rather natural notion that an interval is interesting only so far as the number of deviants in it significantly exceeds the "expected" number of deviants, based on uniformly random distribution of the deviants. The significance is controlled by a user-specified parameter δ. More precisely,

Definition 2 *Consider the time series in which κ deviants have been identified. An interval I is a* deviant cluster *if and only if $k \geq \delta|I|\frac{\kappa}{N}$, where k is the number of deviants in I and δ is a user-defined parameter of significance. Furthermore, I is a* maximal deviant cluster *if I is not a proper subset of any other deviant cluster.*

Note that the deviant clusters are not monotonic with respect to the interval size. To explain this further, we consider the example in Figure 4. Say we have identified six deviants and that we are interested in deviant clusters with size between six and twelve points and $\delta = 1$. Note that while $I1$, $I2$ are deviant clusters, $I4$, $I1 \in I4 \in I2$, is not one. Hence $I4$, which has a subset that is a deviant cluster and which is itself contained in a deviant cluster, is not a deviant cluster.

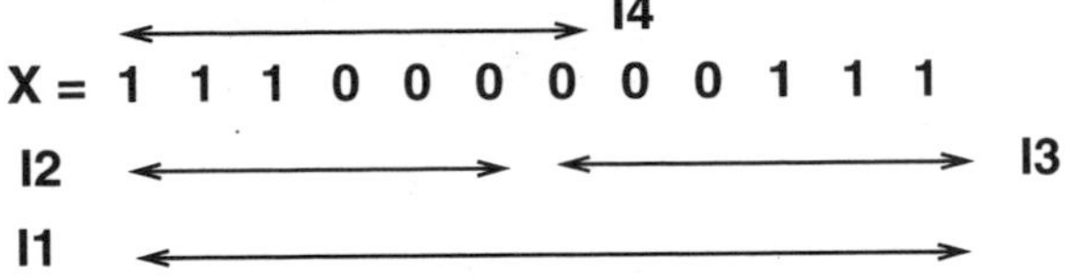

Figure 4: Non monotonicity of clusters.

Note further that while deviant clusters are monotonic with respect to δ, maximal deviant clusters do not have this property. In particular, as δ is decreased, longer intervals may get declared deviant and could subsume shorter intervals that were maximal deviant clusters for smaller values of δ.

6.3 Searching for Deviant Clusters

Given a set of κ deviants for a time series, we present an algorithm to determine the deviant clusters. Rather than return a specified subset of deviant clusters, our algorithm returns *all* maximal deviant clusters (these deviant clusters may overlap). Note that our algorithm can easily output all deviant clusters, not merely the maximal ones, but the output size may be too large for user attention.

Formally, we are given a binary vector $D = d_1 d_2 \ldots d_N$ such that $d_i = 1$ if d_i is a deviant, and it is zero otherwise. The user specifies a δ controlling the significance, as well as L, the minimum size and U, the maximum size of clusters of interest. The goal is to output all maximal deviant clusters of size between L and U.

The algorithm first computes the prefix sum of the number of deviants so that the number of deviants in any interval can be determined efficiently by looking at the prefix sums to the two endpoints of the interval.

The algorithm has two phases. In the first phase, it determines all the deviant clusters of length between L and U. In the first phase, the algorithm iterates over all intervals of interest ($(i, i+j-1)$ for $1 \leq i \leq N-j+1$ and $L \leq j \leq U$) and determines whether the number of deviants in the corresponding interval is above the threshold ($\frac{\delta \kappa j}{N}$), and if it is, it marks the interval as a deviant cluster by setting the array $\texttt{MaxCluster}(i, j)$ to 1. It does not matter in what order the MaxCluster array is evaluated: since deviant clusters are not monotonic, proceeding in increasing values of j (for a given i) does not necessarily help prune the search space.

In the second phase of the algorithm, deviant clusters that are not maximal are removed. The algorithm proceeds by setting $\texttt{MaxCluster}(i, j) = 0$ if there exists a $k > j$, $i + j - k \leq l \leq i$, such that $\texttt{MaxCluster}(l, k) = 1$. (This is because if any such $\texttt{MaxCluster}(l, k) = 1$, then there is a deviant cluster $[l, l+k-1]$ which would contain the cluster $[i, i+j-1]$ that is under consideration.) This is implemented simply by iterating over all values $\texttt{MaxCluster}(i, j)$ for a given i.

Upon termination, the maximal deviant clusters are the intervals i to $i+j-1$ where $\texttt{MaxCluster}(i, j) = 1$. The entire algorithm takes $O(N(U-L))$ time for each of the two phases.

7 Mining Experiments

We implemented a prototype system incorporating these algorithms that is capable of analyzing time series data. The user has to specify the parameters that defines the deviants, the parameter δ for the significance of the cluster density, as well as the minimum and maximum sizes of the clusters (L and U respectively) that are of interest. The system determines the deviants as described in Section 6 and also returns the maximal clusters of deviants meeting these specifications.

We present an exploration of a variety of publicly available data sets ($M1 - M4$ below). In all our experiments, we search for 10 most frequent deviants ($\kappa = 10$) and for choosing consensus deviants, we let k range between 1 and 10, and B between 1 and 40. Larger ranges for k and B are certainly possible. These values, however, provide a nice trade off between performance and the quality of the information obtained, in all our experiments. Figure 5 presents a subset of our results. We keep $\delta * \frac{\kappa}{N} = 0.4$ and search for clus-

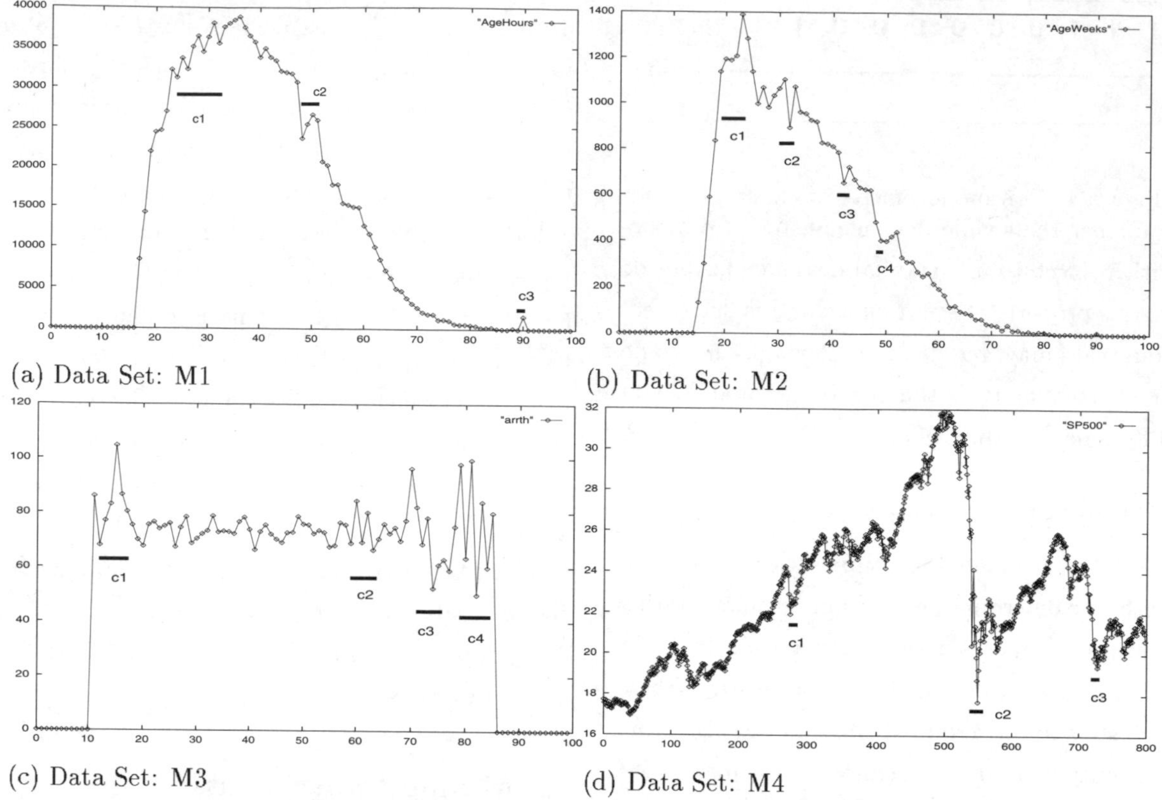

(a) Data Set: M1

(b) Data Set: M2

(c) Data Set: M3

(d) Data Set: M4

Figure 5: Mining for deviant clusters in sample time series.

ters of size between 1 ($L = 1$) and 10 ($U = 10$) points. Note that one can potentially control the number of the clusters identified by changing the values of U and L.

The datasets that we present are described below:

- M1: A time series showing the total number of hours worked by people of a given age in a year, drawn from a census database (available at www.kdnuggets.com).

- M2: A time series showing the total number of weeks worked by people of a given age in a year, drawn from a census database (available at www.kdnuggets.com).

- M3: A times series showing the heart rate of individuals of different ages with arrythmia cases (available at www.ics.uci.edu/~mlean/Machine-Learning.html).

- M4: A time series containing the closing S&P 500 index value each day starting from 1928.

For data set $M1$, we are able to identify the cluster containing points 23 to 30 (labeled $c1$ in Figure 5(a)), the cluster between 48 and 51 (labeled c_2), as well as the cluster at point 91 (labeled c_3). These clusters seem to match our intuitive visual notion of deviant sequences of points in this time series. If the value of δ is decreased, the identified clusters remain the same, but they become larger in size (encompassing more points). Similarly a larger value of δ produces the same, but smaller-sized clusters. Similar observations hold for Figure 5(b) where four clusters are identified (c_1 to c_4). Figure 5(c) is an example of a more "noisy" time series. Again, we can identify clusters corresponding to our intuitive visual notion of the "noisy" parts of the series. Finally, Figure 5(d), presents the results for M4. Curiously, cluster c_2 corresponds to a well known financial disaster in the US economy in 1929.

We leave it to the reader to judge subjectively the quality of deviants we report. Notice that in each of the figures, the reported deviants (clusters) are rarely at the extrema of the functions; hence, deviant points and clusters are not necessarily the global extrema. Also in many cases, such as the datasets M1, M2, and M3 (in Figure 5a-c respectively), no deviants have been identified in the region of the fastest change in the function. Thus, deviants find regions that are not necessarily the local extrema of changes.

8 Conclusion

This work makes two specific contributions. First, we have presented a framework for the formal definition of a deviant point in time series, and demonstrated it to be of data mining value. We have proposed efficient optimal algorithms for the identification and mining of deviant points in a time series database. Second, we have shown how these algorithms can be used to decrease histogram error (or reduce storage for the same error) substantially.

This work raises several important issues for future exploration. Deviant points might have other properties as well, besides clusters, that might be of great mining value. For example, one could extend the framework and algorithms presented in this work, to mine for periodic patterns of deviants. Moreover, since deviants, most likely, will not be exactly periodic, notions of approximate periodicity, in the spirit of [HDY99], could be introduced. In addition, it would be interesting to couple deviants with other attributes as well, towards the design of effective discovery driven exploration tools for time series analysis.

References

[AAR95] A. Arning, R. Agrawal, and P. Raghavan. A Linear Method for Deviation Detection in Large Databases. *KDD*, August 1995.

[Bel54] R. E. Bellman. The Theory of Dynamic Programming. *Bull. Amer Math Soc. Vol 60*, pages 503–516, 1954.

[Cha84] C. Chatfield. *The Analysis of Time Series.* Chapman and Hall, 1984.

[GMP97] P. Gibbons, Y. Mattias, and V. Poosala. Fast Incremental Maintenance of Approximate Histograms. *Proceedings of VLDB, Athens Greece*, pages 466–475, August 1997.

[HDY99] J. Han, G. Dong, and Y. Yin. Effcient Mining of Partial Periodic Patterns in Time Series Databases. *Proceedings of ICDE*, page to appear, March 1999.

[Ioa93] Y. Ioannidis. Universality of Serial Histograms. *Proceedings of VLDB, Dublin Ireland*, pages 256–277, August 1993.

[IP95] Y. Ioannidis and Viswanath Poosala. Balancing Histogram Optimality and Practicality for Query Result Size Estimation. *Proceedings of ACM SIGMOD, San Hose, CA*, pages 233–244, June 1995.

[JKM+98] H. V Jagadish, N. Koudas, S. Muthukrishnan, V. Poosala, K. C. Sevcik, and T. Suel. Optimal Histograms with Quality Guarantees. *Proceedings of VLDB*, pages 275–286, August 1998.

[KN98] E. Knorr and R. Ng. Algorithms for Mining Distance Based Outliers in Large Databases. *Proceedings of VLDB, New York*, pages 392–403, August 1998.

[PI97] V. Poosala and Y. Ioannidis. Selectivity Estimation Without the Attribute Value Independence Assumption. *Proceedings of VLDB, Athens Greece*, pages 486–495, August 1997.

[PIHS96] V. Poosala, Y. Ioannidis, P. Haas, and E. Shekita. Improved Histograms for Selectivity Estimation of Range Predicates. *Proceedings of ACM SIGMOD, Montreal Canada*, pages 294–305, June 1996.

Exploiting Versions for Handling Updates in Broadcast Disks

Evaggelia Pitoura
Department of Computer Science
University of Ioannina
GR 45110 Ioannina, Greece
email: pitoura@cs.uoi.gr

Panos K. Chrysanthis*
Department of Computer Science
University of Pittsburgh
Pittsburgh, PA 15260, U.S.A.
email: panos@cs.pitt.edu

Abstract

Recently, broadcasting has attracted considerable attention as a means of disseminating information to large client populations in both wired and wireless settings. In this paper, we exploit versions to increase the concurrency of client transactions in the presence of updates. We consider three alternative mediums for storing versions: (a) the air: older versions are broadcast along with current data, (b) the client's local cache: older versions are maintained in cache, and (c) a local database or warehouse at the client: part of the server's database is maintained at the client in the form of a multiversion materialized view. The proposed techniques are scalable in that they provide consistency without any direct communication from clients to the server. Performance results show that the overhead of maintaining versions can be kept low, while providing a considerable increase in concurrency.

1 Introduction

While traditionally data are delivered from servers to clients on demand, a wide range of emerging database applications benefit from a broadcast mode for data dissemination. In such applications, the server repetitively broadcasts data to a client population without a specific request. Clients monitor the broadcast channel and retrieve the data items they need as they arrive on the broadcast channel. Such applications typically involve a small number of servers and a much larger number of clients with similar interests. Examples include stock trading, electronic commerce applications, such as auction and electronic tendering, and traffic control information systems.

The concept of broadcast delivery is not new. Early work has been conducted in the area of Teletext and Videotext systems [3, 23]. Previous work also includes the Datacycle project [10] at Bellcore and the Boston Community Information System (BCIS) [13]. In Datacycle, a database circulates on a high bandwidth network (140 Mbps). Users query the database by filtering relevant information via a special massively parallel transceiver. BCIS broadcasts news and information over an FM channel to clients with personal computers equipped with radio receivers. Recently, data dissemination by broadcast has attracted considerable attention ([12], [19]), due to the physical support for broadcast provided by an increasingly important class of networked environments such as by most wireless computing infrastructures, including cellular architectures and satellite networks. The explosion of data intensive applications and the resulting need for scalable means for providing information to large client populations are also motivated by the dramatic improvements in global connectivity and the popularity of the Internet [9, 24].

As such systems continue to evolve, more and more sophisticated client applications will require reading current and consistent data despite updates at the server. In most current research, updates have been mainly treated in the context of caching (e.g., [6], [2], [11], and [16]). In this case, updates are considered in terms of local cache consistency; there are no transactional semantics. Transactions and broadcast were

Proceedings of the 25th VLDB Conference, Edinburgh, Scotland, 1999.

*This work is supported in part by National Science Foundation under grant IRI-9502091 and IIS-9812532.

first discussed in the Datacycle project [10] where special hardware was used to detect changes of values read and thus ensure consistency. The Datacycle architecture was extended in [4] for the case of a distributed database where each database site broadcasts the contents of the database fragments residing at that site. More recent work involves the development of new correctness criteria for transactions in broadcast environments [22] as well as the deployment of the broadcast medium for transmitting concurrency control related information to clients so that part of transaction management can be undertaken by them [5].

In our previous work [18], we proposed and comparatively studied a suite of techniques for ensuring the consistency of client read-only transactions in broadcast environments. In this paper, we propose maintaining multiple versions of items to increase the concurrency of client transactions. Versions are combined with invalidation reports to inform clients of updates and thus ensure the currency of their reads. We assume that updates are performed at the server and disseminated from there. The currency and consistency of the values read by clients is preserved without requiring clients contacting the servers.

We consider three alternative means for storing older versions. One potential storage medium is the air, in which case, older versions are broadcast along with current values. We introduce protocols for interleaving current and previous versions as well as for determining the frequency of broadcasting old versions. A second proposal is maintaining older versions in the client's cache. In this case, garbage collection of old versions is possible since there is local information about active client transactions and their access requirements. Lastly, we exploit the scenario of maintaining part of the server's database at the client in the form of a multiversion materialized view. The novel aspect is that the base relations are on air. Hybrid approaches where older versions are on air, in cache, and in client's main memory or disk are also possible.

Performance results show that the overhead of maintaining older versions can be kept low, while providing a considerable increase in concurrency. For instance, when about 10% of the broadcast items are updated per broadcast, maintaining 5 versions per item increases the number of consistent read-only transactions that successfully complete their operation from 10% (when no versions are maintained) to 80% – 90%. The increase of the broadcast size is around 10% to 15% of the original size depending on the broadcast organization used. For less update-intensive environments, the overhead is considerably smaller.

The remainder of this paper is organized as follows. Section 2 introduces the problem, defines currency and presents two basic approaches for maintaining correctness. Section 3 describes the multiversioning scheme and related issues. Section 4, 5 and 6 discuss keeping

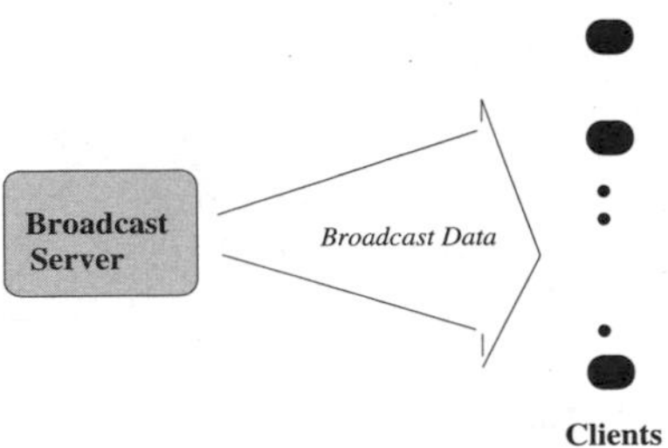

Figure 1: Broadcast architecture

old versions on air, in cache and in a warehouse respectively. Section 7 discusses disconnections and updates, while Section 8 presents our performance model and experimental results. Section 9 concludes the paper.

2 Broadcast and Updates

In a broadcast dissemination environment, a data server periodically broadcasts data items to a large client population (Figure 1). Each period of the broadcast is called a *broadcast cycle* or *bcycle*, while the content of the broadcast is called a *bcast*. Each client listens to the broadcast and fetches data as they arrive This way data can be accessed concurrently by any number of clients without any performance degradation. However, access to data is strictly sequential, since clients need to wait for the data of interest to appear on the channel. We assume that all updates are performed at the server and disseminated from there.

2.1 The Broadcast Model

Clients do not need to listen to the broadcast continuously. Instead, they tune-in to read specific items. Such selective tuning is important especially in the case of portable mobile computers, since they most often rely for their operation on the finite energy provided by batteries and listening to the broadcast consumes energy. However, for selective tuning, clients must have some prior knowledge of the structure of the broadcast that they can utilize to determine when the item of interest appears on the channel. Alternatively, the broadcast can be self-descriptive, in that, some form of directory information is broadcast along with the data. In this case, the client first gets this information from the broadcast and uses it in subsequent reads. Techniques for broadcasting index information along with data are given for example in [15, 11].

The smallest logical unit of a broadcast is called a *bucket*. Buckets are the analog to blocks for disks. Each bucket has a header that includes useful information. The exact content of the bucket header depends on the specific broadcast organization. Information in the header usually includes the position of the bucket in the bcast as an offset from the beginning of the bcast as well as the offset to the beginning of the next bcast. The offset to the beginning of the next bcast can be used by the client to determine the beginning

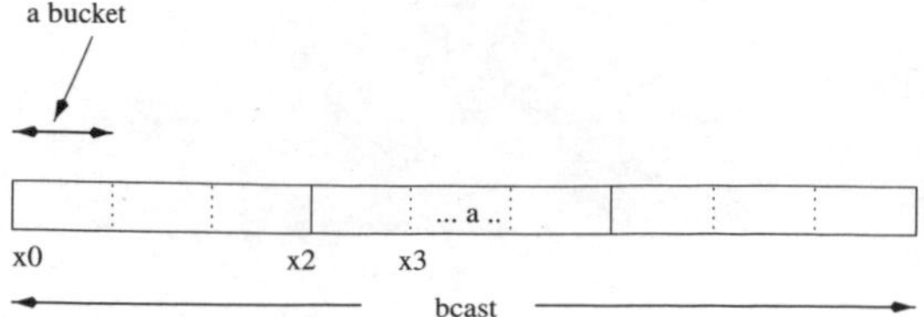

Figure 2: Currency of updates

of the next bcast when the size of the broadcast is not fixed. Data items correspond to database records (tuples). We assume that users access data by specifying the value of one attribute of the record, the search key. Each bucket contains several items.

2.2 Updates and Consistency

During each bcycle, the server broadcasts items from a database. A database consists of a finite set of data items. A database state is typically defined as a mapping of every data item to a value of its domain. Thus, a databases state, denoted DS, can be defined as a set of ordered pairs of data items in D and their values. In a database, data are related by a number of integrity constraints that express relationships of values of data that a database state must satisfy. A database state is consistent if it does not violate the integrity constraints [8].

While data items are being broadcast, transactions at the server may update their values. There are a number of reasonable choices, regarding the currency of data on the broadcast. For example, the values on the broadcast may correspond to current values at the server, that is to the values produced by all transactions so far committed at the server. Alternatively, updates at the server may not be reflected in the bcast immediately but at pre-specified intervals, such as at each bcast or at fractions of the bcast. We call such intervals *currency intervals*. In particular, we assume that, when an item is to appear on the broadcast, the value that will be broadcast is that produced by all transactions committed at the server by the beginning of the current currency interval (which may not be its current value at the server). For uniformity of presentation, when updates are immediately reflected in the bcast, we say that the currency interval is that of an item.

Figure 2 depicts possible currency intervals. The value of data item a depends on which definition of the currency interval is adopted. For instance, the value of a is the value produced by all transactions committed by x_0, x_2, x_3, or just prior to the broadcast of a, if we assume that the currency interval is the whole bcast, three buckets, a bucket, or an item correspondingly.

A client transaction may read data items from different currency intervals. We define the *span* of a client transaction T, $span(T)$, to be the maximum number of different currency intervals from which T reads data. We define the *readset* of a transaction T, denoted $Read\_Set(T)$, to be the set of items it reads. In particular, $Read\_Set(T)$ is a set of ordered pairs of data items and their values that T read. Our correctness criterion for read-only transactions is that each transaction reads consistent data. Specifically, the readset of each read-only transaction must form a subset of a consistent database state [21].

We make no assumptions about transaction management at the server. Our only assumption is that the values broadcast for each item are those produced by *committed* transactions. Since the set of values broadcast during a single currency interval correspond to the same database state, this set is a subset of a consistent database state. Thus, if for some transaction T, $span(T) = 1$, T is correct. However, since, in general, client transactions read data values from different currency intervals, there is no guarantee that the values they read are consistent.

When information about the readset of a transaction is available, query optimization can be employed to reduce the transaction span. One approach is to re-order reads based on the order by which items appear on the broadcast. Another query optimization technique would be to introduce additional reads. Additional reads may be used to execute reads in all control branches of a query; such an approach is cheap in a broadcast environment, since the data are on air anyway. Such query optimization techniques can effectively reduce the span of a transaction but can not guarantee that all values in the readset would belong to the same currency interval, especially when currency intervals are short.

2.3 Invalidation Techniques

A way to ensure the correctness of read-only transactions is to invalidate, e.g., abort, transactions that read data values that correspond to different database states. To achieve this, a timestamp or version number is broadcast along with the value of each data item. This version number corresponds to the currency interval at the beginning of which the item had the corresponding value. Let v_0 be the currency interval at which a transaction performs its first read. For each subsequent read, we test that the items read have versions $v \leq v_0$. If an item has a larger version, the transaction is aborted. We call this method the *versioning* method. Since the values read by each transaction correspond to the database broadcasted at v_0, the versioning method produces correct read-only transactions.

Another way is to broadcast an invalidation report at pre-specified points during the bcast. The invalidation report includes a list with the data items that have been updated since the previous invalidation report was broadcast. Let us assume that an invalidation report is broadcast at the beginning of each currency interval. In addition, at each client, a set $RS(R)$

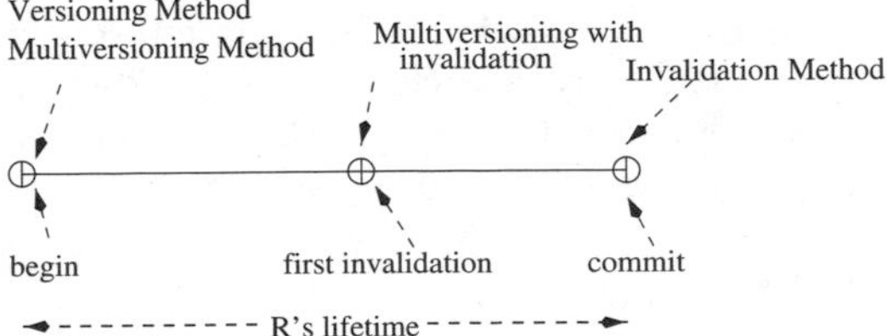

Figure 3: Currency of reads

is maintained for each active transaction R, that includes all data items that R has read so far. The client tunes in at the pre-specified points to read the invalidation reports. A transaction R is aborted if an item $x \in RS(R)$ appears in the invalidation report, i.e., if x is updated[1]. We call this method the *invalidation* method.

Theorem 1 *The invalidation method produces correct read-only transactions.*

Proof. Let c_c be the currency interval during which a committed transaction R performed its last read operation and DS^{c_c} be the database state that corresponds to the currency interval c_c, i.e., the database state at the beginning of c_c. We claim that the values read by R correspond to the database state DS^{c_c}. For the purposes of contradiction, assume that the value of a data item x read by R is different then the value of x at DS^{c_c}, then an invalidation report should have been transmitted for x at the beginning of c_c and thus R should have been aborted. □

With the versioning method, transaction R reads values that correspond to the database state at the beginning of the currency interval at which R performs its first read operation. With the invalidation method, R reads the most current values as of the beginning of the currency interval at which it commits (Figure 3).

There is no need to transmit invalidation reports at the beginning of each currency interval. Instead, invalidation reports may be broadcast more or less frequently. In the latter case, there is an additional requirement, that before committing, each transaction R must read the next invalidation report that will appear in the broadcast. The proof is similar to the proof above. Reading an additional invalidation report is necessary because in this case, items broadcast between invalidation reports do not necessarily correspond to a single database state. With this variation of the invalidation method, a read-only transaction R reads the most current values as of the time of its commitment.

3 Multiversion Schemes

Invalidation methods are prone to starvation of queries by update transactions. To increase the number of read-only transactions that are successfully processed, we propose maintaining multiple versions of data items. Multiversion schemes, where older copies of items are kept for concurrency control purposes, have been successfully used to speed-up processing of on-line read-only transactions in traditional pull-based systems (e.g., [17]).

3.1 The Basic Multiversion Schemes

The basic idea underlying multiversioning is to temporarily retain older versions of data items, so that the number of aborted read-only transactions is reduced. Versions correspond to different values at the beginning of each currency interval and version numbers to the corresponding currency interval. Thus, there is a trade-off between the length of the currency interval and the number of versions: the shorter the currency interval, the greater the number of versions that are created.

Let S_{max} be the maximum transaction span among all read-only transactions. Let v_0 be the currency interval at which R performs its first read operation. During v_0, R reads the most current versions, that is the versions with the largest version number. In subsequent intervals, for each data item, R reads the version with the largest version number v_c smaller than or equal to v_0. If such a version exists, R proceeds, else R is aborted. In the extreme case, in which, all S_{max} most current values for each data item are available, all read-only transactions proceed successfully. We call this scheme *multiversioning.*

Theorem 2 *The multiversioning method produces correct read-only transactions.*

Proof. Let R be a read-only transaction, v_0 the currency interval at which R performs its first read operation and DS^{v_0} be the database state broadcast at this interval. We will show that the values read by R correspond to the database state DS^{v_0} which is consistent and thus R is correct. For any data item $x \in RS(R)$, R reads the version with the largest version number v_c of x, such that $v_c \leq v_0$. This value is the most recent value of x produced by the beginning of the currency interval v_0, that is the value that the item had at DS^{v_0}. □.

In terms of currency, R reads the database state that corresponds to the currency point at v_0 as in the versioning scheme. If invalidation reports are available, we get the following variation of the multiversion method that we call *multiversioning with invalidation* method. Initially, R reads the most current version of each item. Let v_i be the currency interval at which R is invalidated for the first time, i.e., a value that R has read is updated. After v_i, R reads the version with the largest version number v_c such that $v_c < v_i$. If such a version exists, R proceeds, else R is aborted.

[1]A possible optimization is to just mark R as *invalid* if one of its $x \in RS(R)$ appears in an invalidation report and abort R only if it tries to read another data item.

Theorem 3 *The multiversioning with invalidation method produces correct read-only transactions.*

Proof. Let R be a read-only transaction, v_i be the first bcycle during which an item read by R is updated for the first time and DS^{v_i} the database state broadcast at interval v_i. We will show that the values read by R correspond to the database state DS^{v_i-1} which is consistent and thus R is correct. The items that are read before bcycle v_i were not updated prior to v_i thus their values correspond to the database state DS^{v_i-1}. In subsequent bcyles, R reads the version with the largest version number v_c, such that $v_c < v_i$. This value is the most recent value produced before cycle v_i, that is the value that the item had at DS^{v_i-1}. □.

In the multiversioning with invalidation method, R reads the values as of the beginning of the currency interval of its first invalidation v_i, as opposed to the multiversioning method, in which R reads the values that correspond to v_0 (Figure 3). Clearly, multiversioning with invalidation permits better currency than simple multiversioning but at the cost of broadcasting invalidation reports.

3.2 Updates and Caching

To reduce latency in answering queries, clients can cache items of interest locally. Caching reduces the latency of transactions, since transactions find data of interest in their local cache and thus need to access the broadcast channel for a smaller number of times. We assume that each page, i.e., the unit of caching, corresponds to a bucket, i.e., the unit of broadcast. Next, we outline how multiversioning can be used in conjunction with caching.

In the presence of updates, items in cache may become stale. There are various approaches to communicating updates to the clients. Invalidation combined with a form of autoprefetching was shown to perform well in broadcast delivery [2]. The server broadcasts an invalidation report, which is a list of the pages that have been updated. This report is used to invalidate those pages in cache that appear in the invalidation report. These pages remain in cache to be autoprefetched later. In particular, at the next appearance of the invalidated page in the broadcast, the client fetches its new value and replaces the old one. We assume this kind of cache updates in this paper. Other techniques, such as selectively propagating frequently accessed pages [2] that may outperform autoprefetching, should be easily combined with our techniques as well.

To support multiversioning, items in cache also have version numbers. For reading items from the cache, we have to perform the same tests regarding their version numbers as when reading items from the broadcast. To ensure that items in cache are current, the propagation of cache invalidation reports must be at least as frequent as the propagation of invalidation reports for data items. This way, a cached page is either current (i.e., corresponds to the value at the current currency interval) or is marked for auto-prefetch.

3.3 Other Issues

The multiversioning methods can be easily enhanced to handle deletion and insertion of items. When an item is deleted, we create a new version with version number the currency interval, say v, of its deletion and a special field indicating that the item is deleted. A transaction R beginning at v_i with $v_i \geq v$ (or invalidated at v_i if multiversioning with invalidation is used) will read the version with version number v and find out that the item has been deleted. Previous transactions with $v_i < v$ will read versions with smaller version numbers as desired. Similarly, when an item is inserted, we add a version with version number the interval of its insertion.

Another issue is that of the granularity of versions. Instead of maintaining versions of items, it is possible to maintain versions of buckets. Similarly, it is possible to set the invalidation report at the bucket level as well. In this case, to implement the invalidation method, instead of maintaining for each transaction the set of items it has read, we maintain the corresponding set of buckets.

Central to multiversioning is the number of versions maintained per data item. We may always keep the k most current values for each item resulting in a fixed increase in size. Alternatively, we may keep only the different versions of each item during the last k currency intervals and discard older values. In addition, to allocate less space for version numbers, instead of maintaining the absolute number of the currency interval, we can maintain the difference between the current interval and the interval during which the value was updated, i.e., how old the value is. For example, if the current currency interval is interval 30, and the version corresponds to currency interval 27, the version number is set to 3 instead of 27. In this case, $log(S_{max})$ bits are sufficient for version numbers.

Finally, we consider two possibilities for the storage of previous versions. In the *clustering approach*, all versions of the same item are maintained in consequent locations. In the *overflow approach*, older versions are stored separately from the current versions in overflow buckets that are appropriately linked to the current versions.

4 Multiversion Broadcast

With multiversion broadcast, the server, instead of broadcasting the last committed value for each data item, maintains and broadcasts multiple versions for each data item. The number k of older versions that are retained can be seen as a property of the server. In

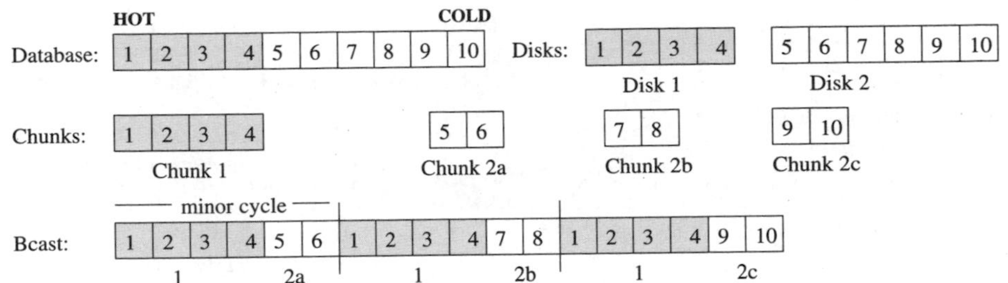

Figure 4: Broadcast disks

this sense, a k-multiversion server, i.e., a server that broadcasts the previous k values, is one that guarantees the consistency of all transactions with span k or smaller. Transactions with larger spans can proceed at their own risk; there is a possibility that they will be aborted. The amount k of broadcast reserved for old versions, can be adapted depending on various parameters, such as the allowable bandwidth, feedback from clients, or update rate at the server.

There are two interrelated problems with multiversion broadcast. The first is how to organize the broadcast, that is where to place the old versions. The other is determining the optimal frequency of transmitting versions. In other words, if we consider a broadcast disk organization [1], where specific items are broadcast more frequently than others (i.e., are placed on "faster disks"), at what frequency should old versions be broadcast?

To describe the broadcast disk organization, we will use an example; for a complete definition of the organization refer to [1]. In a broadcast disk organization, the items of the broadcast are divided in ranges of similar access probabilities. Each of these ranges is placed on a separate disk. In the example of Figure 4, buckets of the first disk $Disk_1$ are broadcast three times as often as those in the second disk $Disk_2$. To achieve these relative frequencies, the disks are split into smaller equal sized units called chunks; the number of chunks per disk is inversely proportional to the relative frequencies of the disks. In the example, the number of chunks is 1 (chunk 1) and 3 (chunks 2a, 2b and 2c) for $Disk_1$ and $Disk_2$ respectively. Each bcast is generated by broadcasting one chunk from each disk and cycling through all the chunks sequentially over all disks. A minor cycle is a sub-bcycle that consists of one chunk from each disk. In the example of Figure 4, there are three minor cycles.

4.1 Clustering

Following the clustering approach, one way to structure the broadcast is to broadcast all versions of each item successively. Thus, older versions of hot items (chunk 1 in Figure 5) are placed along with the current values of hot items on fast disks, while versions of cold data (chunks 2a, 2b and 2c) are placed on slow disks. Consequently, clustering works well when each transaction may access any version of an item with equal probability.

The size of each disk, and thus the size of its chunks, is increased to accommodate old versions. The number of chunks per disk, however, remains fixed. The overall increase in the size of the bcast depends on how the hot data items are related to the items that are frequently updated. The increase is the largest when the hot items are the most frequently updated ones since their versions are broadcast more frequently during each bcycle.

Regarding indexing, items are still broadcast in the same disk and disk chunk, however their relative position inside the chunk changes due to the increase of the chunk size. One approach is to broadcast older versions at a special location inside each chunk, e.g., at the end, and chain them to the current versions.

4.2 Overflow Bucket Pool

With the overflow approach, older versions of items are broadcast at the end of each bcycle. In particular, one or more additional minor cycles at the end of each broadcast is allocated to old versions (Figure 5).

Regarding indexing, the offset of the position of the current value of each item in the broadcast from the beginning of the bcast remains fixed. Thus, the server needs not recompute and broadcast an index at each broadcast cycle. Instead, the client may use a locally stored directory to locate the first appearance of a data item in the broadcast. To locate old versions, since their position in the broadcast is fixed, an index can be broadcast before the minor cycle carrying the overflow bucket pool. A transaction that needs to locate old versions first tunes in to read this index. Alternatively, we can maintain a pointer along with the current version of each item pointing to its older version in the overflow pool. After reading an item, if a transaction needs an older version, it uses the pointer to locate it in the overflow bucket.

In the overflow approach, long-running read-only transactions that read old versions are penalized since they have to wait for the end of the bcast to read such versions. However, transactions that are satisfied with current versions do not suffer from a similar increase in latency. On the contrary, in the clustering approach, the overhead in latency due to the increase in the broadcast size is equally divided among all transactions.

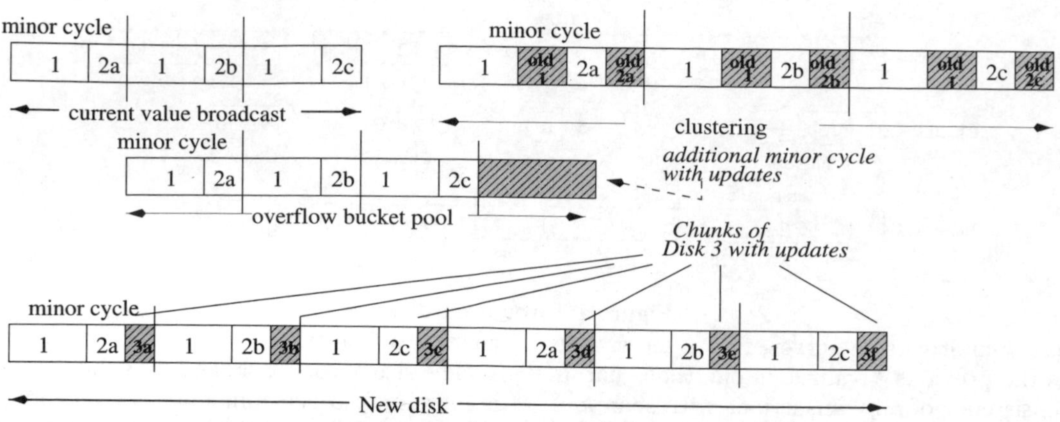

Figure 5: Broadcast disks with multiple versions

A drawback of this approach is that the introduction of the additional minor cycle affects the relative speed of each disk. Another problem is that the space allocated to old versions is fixed; it is a multiple of the size of a minor cycle. To avoid this restriction, older versions can be placed on the slowest disk. In this case, the size of the slowest disk and the size of its chunks are increased to accommodate old versions. Old versions are placed on those chunks of the disk that are broadcast last. Again, the relative speed is affected.

4.3 Old Versions on New Disk

With this approach, a new disk is created to hold any old versions. The relative frequency of the disks with the current versions is maintained, by simply multiplying their frequency by a positive number m, so that the slow disk that carries the old versions is m times slower than the disks with the current versions. For instance, say we have a broadcast organization for the current versions consisting of three disks: $Disk_1$ with speed 4, $Disk_2$ with speed 2, and $Disk_3$ with speed 1. We create a new disk $Disk_4$ where we place the old versions. Assume that we want the current versions to be broadcast three times ($m = 3$) more frequently than old versions. Then, we adjust the relative frequencies of the disks as follows: $Disk_1$ now has speed 12, $Disk_2$ has speed 6, $Disk_3$ has speed 3, and $Disk_4$ has speed 1. With this approach, the size of each bcast is also multiplied by m.

Figure 5 shows yet another example. A new disk $Disk_3$ with 6 chunks is created for the old versions. Current items are broadcast twice ($m = 2$) as frequent as old versions. The relative frequency of the two disks is maintained; items of $Disk_1$ are broadcast three times as frequent as items of $Disk_2$. The resulting bcast is twice the size of the original plus the extra space for the old versions.

To locate older versions of items, pointers may be kept along with their current versions. This approach is adaptive. Old versions are placed on faster disks when there are many long-running transactions and on slower disks when most transactions need current values.

5 Multiversion Caching

In multiversion caching, the client cache is used to provide an alternative storage medium for older versions of data items. A version is associated with each cache entry. When an item is updated at the server, its cache entry is not updated; instead, a new entry is inserted in cache for the new version. Thus, for a data item, there may be multiple entries with different version numbers. We assume that the cache replacement policy is such that, the following always hold:

Page Replacement Invariant: For each data item, the versions cached are the most recent ones.

Then, we can either use the multiversioning method or the multiversioning with invalidation method. It is also possible to avoid broadcasting version numbers along with items. In this case, the version number associated with each cached item is the currency interval during which the item was inserted in the cache. This value is larger than or equal to the currency interval during which the item was actually updated. In this case, we get the following variation of the multiversioning with invalidation method. Until its first invalidation at currency interval say v_i, a transaction R reads items from the broadcast. After v_i, R only reads items from the cache. In particular, R continues operation as long as there are versions in cache with version numbers $v < v_i$, that is versions inserted in cache prior to the invalidation.

With multiversion caching, the effective cache size is decreased, since part of the cache is used to maintain old versions of items. However, for long-running transactions that read old versions, there may be some speed-up, since older versions may be found in cache. Whereas, k (the number of older versions broadcast) in the multiversion broadcast, is a property of the server, in multiversion caching, k (the number of versions kept in cache) is a characteristic of each client. Transactions at different clients may have varying spans. In this case, it is the client's responsibility to adjust the space in cache allocated to older versions, based on the size of its cache, the requirements and types of its read-only transactions, or other local parameters.

5.1 Garbage Collection

Instead of maintaining in cache all k oldest versions, it is reasonable to maintain only the useful ones. A version is *useful* if it may be read by some invalidated transaction. In this case, the page replacement invariant is revised accordingly.

Page Replacement Invariant(revised): for each data item, the versions cached are the most recent useful ones.

We assume that the multiversioning with invalidation method is used, but the same also holds for the simple multiversioning method, if we just consider begin points of transactions in the place of invalidation points. Let $IL=\{R_i, R_{i+1}, \ldots, R_{i+n}\}$ be the set of all active invalidated transactions, that is all transactions for which one of the items they have read was subsequently updated. Let v_{R_j} be the currency interval that corresponds to the database state read by R_j (that is, R_j was invalidated for the first time at $v_{R_j}+1$). Transactions appear in the list in ascending order of invalidation, that is, R_i is the transaction that was invalidated first.

When an item in cache is updated, the version in cache is invalidated and the new value of the item is autoprefetched. Instead of always maintaining the previous version, that is the version in cache with the largest version number v', we maintain this version only if there is a possibility that it will be read, that is, if there is an R_j in IL that may read v'. This can be tested as follows. Recall that $v_{R_{i+n}}$ is the most recent invalidation point. We discard v', if $v_{R_{i+n}} < v'$. This is because in this case v' is not useful: transactions that will be invalidated in future bcycles will read the newly inserted version, while transactions in the current IL will read versions with version numbers smaller than v'.

Furthermore, when a transaction R_m in IL finishes (aborts or commits), for each item x in cache, we delete all versions that were useful only to R_m. In particular,

Condition for Discarding Versions

When a transaction R_m completes its operation, a version of x with version number v_o is discarded, if all three of the following conditions hold:

(1) there is a version of x with version number v such that $v > v_o$ (i.e., v_o is not the current version),

(2) if R_m is not the most recently invalidated transaction (i.e., $m \neq i+n$), then there is a version with version number v_l such that $v_o < v_l \leq v_{R_{m+1}}$, and

(3) if R_m is not the transaction that was invalidated first ($m \neq i$), then $v_o > v_{R_{m-1}}$.

We will show that the above conditions are correct (no useful versions are deleted) and optimal (all non-useful versions are deleted).

Correctness: We will show that it is not possible that any transaction will read v_o. Case (a): For each R_j in IL, with $v_{R_j} > v_{R_m}$, it holds $v_{R_j} \geq v_{R_{m+1}}$, thus R_j would not read v_o but a version $v \geq v_l$ where v_l is the version of Condition (2) above. Case (b): For each R_j in IL, with $v_{R_j} < v_{R_m}$, it holds $v_{R_j} \leq v_{R_{m-1}}$, thus R_j would not read v_o, but from Condition (3) above, it will read an item with version number $v_{R_{m-1}}$ or smaller. Case (c): Since from Condition (1), v_o is not the most recent version, any transaction that will be invalidated in the future will not read v_o but a more current version.

Optimality: We will show that if any of the three conditions does not hold useful versions may be deleted. Case (a): Assume that we delete a version v_o for which there is no version in cache with version number v, such that $v > v_o$, then v_o is the current value and may be read by a transaction invalidated at some future point. Case (b): Assume that we delete a version v_o for which there is no v_l, such that $v_o < v_l \leq v_{R_{m+1}}$, then v_o is useful at least to R_{m+1}. Case (c): Assume that we delete a version v_o, such that $v_o \leq v_{R_{m-1}}$, then R_{m-1} may read v_o.

5.2 Page Replacement

When older versions are maintained in cache, the page replacement policies must be revised. An approach that offers flexibility is to divide the cache space into two parts: one that maintains current versions and one that maintains older ones. In this case, different cache replacement policies can be used for each part of the cache. This approach provides for adaptability, since the percentage of cache allocated to older versions can be adjusted dynamically. The most suitable organization for this approach is overflow buckets with old versions placed on the old version part of the cache.

Another approach is to apply a global policy, that is to replace the page with the overall smallest probability of being accessed without considering version numbers. Clustering works better with this approach. Finally, to maintain the invariant, when a version of item x with version number v is selected for replacement, we must in addition discard from the cache all x's versions with version numbers $v' < v$.

6 Multiversion Warehouse

In this scenario, the client stores the data of interest locally. Data are defined and maintained using views defined over base relations. When the base data are updated the view becomes stale. Updating the view to reflect changes of base data is called view maintenance.

View maintenance is a well known and studied problem (e.g., see [14] for a survey) which is beyond the scope of this paper. Here, we only focus on views in terms of broadcast and versioning.

In the broadcast setting, for scalability reasons, we assume that the server is stateless. In particular, the server cannot maintain any views in lieu of its clients. Furthermore, the server is not aware of the views maintained at its clients. In addition and in contrast to [25], we assume that there is no direct communication from clients to the server. Specifically, the client cannot ask the server to compute the view.

One main advantage of the broadcast model is that the base relations are available to clients without any storage overhead. In fact, the base relations are on air and thus using them to recompute the view is not expensive in terms of communication messages. To maintain the view, we create a client transaction that we call the view maintenance transaction. The view maintenance transaction has two parts: the first part, called view-query, recomputes the view, while the second part, called view-updater, installs the updates in the local view.

The view-query part is executed as a normal client read-only transaction concurrently with any query processing at the client. The view-query recomputes the view to take into account any updates. Depending on the currency requirements, any of the versioning, invalidation or multiversioning methods can be used by the view-query. For instance, if the most-up-to-date values as of the commitment of the view-query are required, then the view-query must use the invalidation method. The view-query can either recompute the view from scratch or use an incremental technique. Furthermore, a locally stored index can be used to speed-up the processing of the query and decrease its span. The view-updater installs the updates at the client. To allow reads at the client to proceed concurrently with the view updater, two versions of data may be kept along the lines of [20].

With this simple view maintenance scheme, the server is not aware of the fact that clients maintain views and thus there is no associated overhead at the server. Furthermore, there is no need to modify the content of the broadcast. An important issue is that of the currency of the locally maintained view that can be decoupled from the currency of the broadcast data. The maintenance transaction may run periodically or when updates occur. In the second case, the invalidation reports can be used to trigger the execution of view maintenance.

7 Related Issues

7.1 Disconnections

In many settings, it is desirable for clients not to monitor the broadcast continuously as for example, in the case of clients carrying portable devices and thus seeking for reducing battery power consumption. Further, access to the broadcast may be monetarily expensive, and thus minimizing access to the broadcast is sought for. Finally, client disconnections are very common when the data broadcast are delivered wirelessly. Wireless communications face many obstacles because the surrounding environment interacts heavily with the signal, thus in general wireless communications are less reliable and deliver less bandwidth than wireline communications. In such cases, clients may be forced to miss a number of broadcast cycles.

In general, versioning frees transactions from the requirement of reading invalidation reports. When there are no versions, a transaction can not tolerate missing any invalidation reports. Furthermore, with multiversioning, client transactions can refrain from listening to the broadcast for a number of cycles and resume execution later as long as the required versions are still on air. In general, a transaction R with $span(R) = s_R$ can tolerate missing up to $k - s_R$ currency intervals in any k-multiversion broadcast. The tolerance of the multiversion scheme to intermittent connectivity depends also on the rate of updates, i.e., the creation of new versions. For example, if the value of an item does not change during m, $m > k$, currency intervals, this value will be available to read-only transactions for more intervals. Multiversion caching further improves tolerance to disconnections. In this case, disconnected operation is supported, since a read-only transaction can proceed without reading data from the broadcast, as long as appropriate versions can be found in cache.

7.2 Update Transactions

While read-only transactions can proceed without contacting the server, update transactions must communicate their updates to the server for certification. Multiversion concurrency control for update transactions is also possible. Actually, it is easy to provide *snapshot isolation* introduced in [7] and supported by a number of databases vendors. To this end, we outline an implementation of the *first-committer-wins* method [7].

Regarding reads, update transactions at the client proceed like read-only transactions; if their reads are invalidated, they are aborted. Regarding updates, values of items updated at the client are maintained locally and transmitted to the server for certification. They are incorporated and included in subsequent broadcast intervals only if certified successfully.

Specifically, a client update transaction T records the currency interval v_{init} during which T performed its first read (or in the case of invalidation reports, the currency interval $v_{inval}-1$, where v_{inval} is the currency interval of T's first invalidation). Further, it records the currency interval v_{commit} in which it completes its operation. When T completes its operation, the client sends to the server the list of items $WS(T)$ written by

T and their values, the commit interval v_{commit}, and the initial interval v_{init}.

At the server, T is certified and committed, if for all transactions T' with v'_{commit} in $[v_{init}, v_{commit}]$ $WS(T) \cap WS(T') = \emptyset$. To perform this test, we simply check the current version numbers of the items written by T.

Snapshot isolation is not equivalent to serializability. For example, it suffers from the write skew anomaly, e.g., two transactions read two items x and y and each modifies one of them resulting in a violated constraint between x and y. However if all update transactions transform the system from one consistent state to another, snapshot isolation will guarantee consistent reads. To ensure serializability (e.g., one-version serializability [8]), stronger tests are required for update transactions, such as also checking their readsets.

8 Performance Evaluation

In this section, we evaluate the performance of multiversion methods with respect to various parameters.

8.1 The Performance Model

Our performance model is similar to the one presented in [1]. The server periodically broadcasts a set of data items in the range of 1 to $NoItems$. We assume a broadcast disk organization with 3 disks and relative frequencies 5, 3 and 1. The client accesses items from the range 1 to *ReadRange*, which is a subset of the items broadcast (*ReadRange* $\leq$ $NoItems$). Within this range, the access probabilities follow a Zipf distribution. The Zipf distribution with a parameter *theta* is often used to model non-uniform access. It produces access patterns that become increasingly skewed as *theta* increases. The client waits $ThinkTime$ units and then makes the next read request.

Updates at the server are generated following a Zipf distribution similar to the read access distribution at the client. The write distribution is across the range 1 to *UpdateRange*. We use a parameter called *Offset* to model disagreement between the client access pattern and the server update pattern. When the offset is zero, the overlap between the two distributions is the greatest, that is the client's hottest pages are also the most frequently updated. An offset of k shifts the update distribution k items making them of less interest to the client. We assume that during each bcycle, N transactions are committed at the server. All server transactions have the same number of update and read operations, where read operations are four times more frequent than updates. Read operations at the server are in the range 1 to $NoItems$, follow a Zipf distribution, and have zero offset with the update set at the server.

The client maintains a local cache that can hold up to $CacheSize$ pages. The cache replacement policy is LRU: when the cache is full, the least recently used page is replaced. When pages are updated, the corresponding cache entries are invalidated and subsequently autoprefetched. The currency interval is a bcast. Table 1 summarizes the parameters that describe the operation at the server and the client. Values in parenthesis are the default.

8.2 Performance Results

Due to space limitations, we only present some representative results to show the applicability of the method. Figure 6 shows the increase of the size of the broadcast using each one of the proposed multiversion broadcast organization schemes. In all experiments, we used the simple multiversion schemes (without invalidation reports). For the clustering approach, the increase depends on the offset. The increase is the maximum when the hot items are the most updated ones (*Offset* = 0), while it is minimum when the frequently updated items are cold and thus their versions are placed on slow disks. For the new disk approach, the size of the broadcast is doubled from the case of no versions. However, the current value of each item appears twice as often as in the no version case, thus, it is as if we had an additional bcycle. The increase shown for this case is only that for broadcasting versions on the slowest disk.

Figure 7 shows the decrease of transactions aborted due to updates. With the overflow pool approach, transactions have to wait for the end of the broadcast to locate old versions, thus their span increases as does their probability of abort. For the new disk approach, since the broadcast size is effectively double the size of the other methods, for the same update rate the updates are 200 and 100 correspondingly. However, these updates appear in the broadcast very late (the currency interval is that of a bcast, thus in this case, it is also two times larger than in the other two). Thus, we pay for the increase in concurrency, by reading less current data.

Regarding caching, using part of the cache space to keep old versions results in a very small increase in concurrency of long running transactions. This is because less space is allocated to current versions and transactions have to read items from the broadcast, thus their span increase and so does their abort rate. Thus, our conclusion is that it is better to keep older versions in secondary memory than in cache. In this case, garbage collection results in a dramatic decrease of the space required to maintain old versions (e.g., for maintaining up to 3 old versions per item in cache, a same size secondary storage is sufficient).

9 Conclusions

Data dissemination by broadcast is an important mode for data delivery in data intensive applications. In this

Server Parameters		Client Parameters	
No of Items Broadcast	1000	ReadRange (range of client reads)	500
UpdateRange	500	theta (zipf distribution parameter)	0.95
theta (zipf distribution parameter)	0.95	Think Time (time between client reads in broadcast units)	2
Offset (update and client-read access deviation)	0 - 250 (100)	Number of reads per quey	5 - 50 (20)
Number of updates at the server	50 - 500 (50)	S (transaction span)	varies
Currency interval	bcast		
Broadcast Disk Parameters		**Cache**	
No of disks	3	CacheSize	125
Relative frequency: Disk1, Disk2, Disk3	5, 3, 1	Cache replacement policy	LRU
No of items per range (disk) Range1, Range2, Range3	75, 175, 750	Cache invalidation	invalidation + autoprefetch

Table 1: Performance model parameters

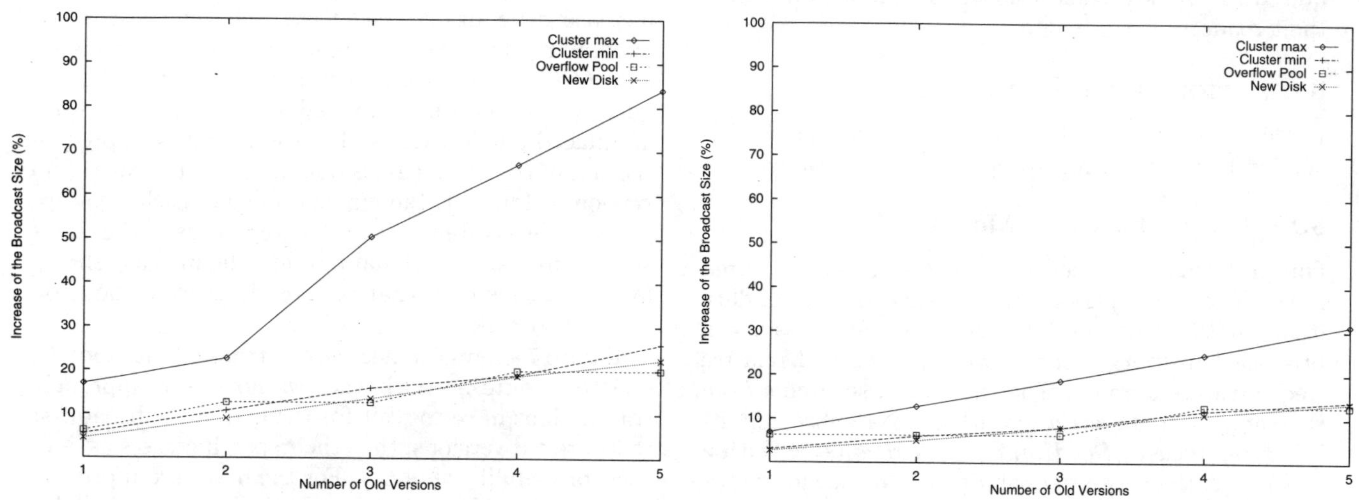

Figure 6: Increase of the broadcast size. For the figure at the left updates are set to 100 per bcast, while for the figure at the right to 50.

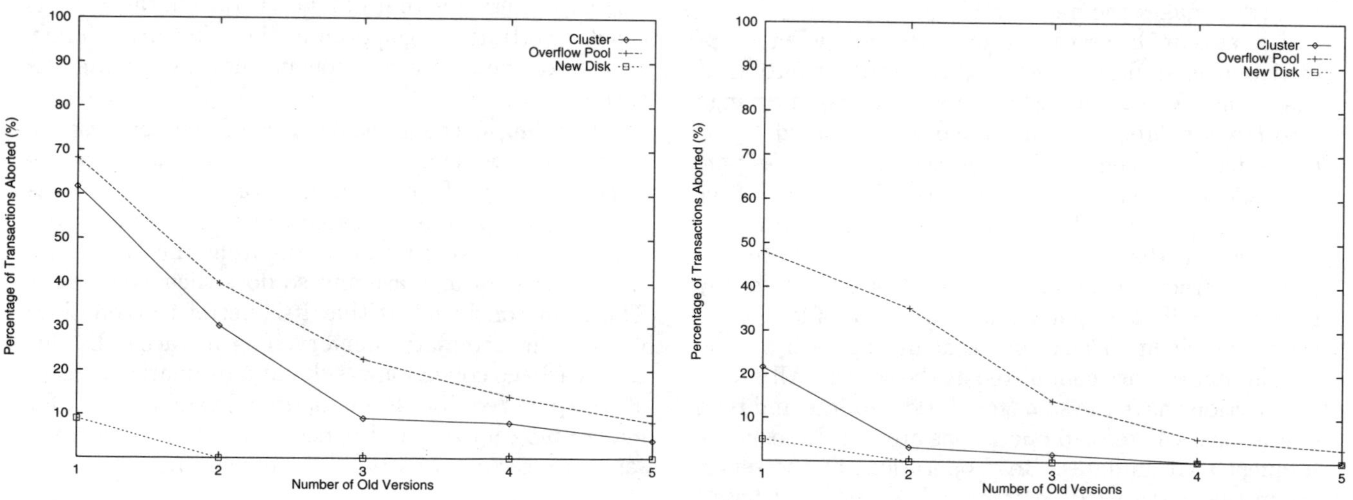

Figure 7: Abort rate. For the figure at the left updates are set to 100 per bcast (in this case, when no versions are maintained, the abort rate is 88.5%) while for the figure at the right the updates are set at 50 per bcast (in this case, when no versions are maintained, the abort rate is 83%).

paper, we propose maintaining multiple versions to increase the concurrency of read-only transactions in the presence of updates. Invalidation reports are also used to ensure the currency of reads. The approach is scalable in that it is independent of the number of clients. Performance results show that the overhead of maintaining versions can be kept low, while providing a considerable increase in concurrency.

References

[1] S. Acharya, R. Alonso, M. J. Franklin, and S. Zdonik. Broadcast Disks: Data Management for Asymmetric Communications Environments. In *Proc. of the ACM SIGMOD Intl. Conf. on Management of Data*, pp. 199–210, 1995.

[2] S. Acharya, M. J. Franklin, and S. Zdonik. Disseminating Updates on Broadcast Disks. In *Proc. of the 22nd Int'l Conf. on Very Large Data Bases*, pp. 354–365, 1996.

[3] A. H. Ammar and J. W. Wong. The Design of Teletext Broadcast Cycles. *Performance Evaluation*, 5(4), 1985.

[4] S. Banerjee and V. O. K. Li. Evaluating the Distributed Datacycle Scheme for a High Performance Distributed System. *Journal of Computing and Information*, 1(1), 1994.

[5] D. Barbará. Certification Reports: Supporting Transactions in Wireless Systems. In *Proc. of the IEEE Int'l Conf. on Distributed Computing Systems*, 1997.

[6] D. Barbará and T. Imielinski. Sleepers and Workaholics: Caching Strategies in Mobile Environments. In *Proc. of the ACM SIGMOD Intl. Conf. on Management of Data*, pp. 1–12, 1994.

[7] H. Berenson, P. Bernstein, J. Gray, J. Melton, E. O'Neil., and P. O'Neil. A Critique of ANSI SQL Isolation Levels. In *Proc. of the ACM SIGMOD Intl. Conf. on Management of Data*, pp. 1–10, 1995.

[8] P. A. Bernstein, V. Hadjilacos, and N. Goodman. *Concurrency Control and Recovery in Database Systems*. Addison-Wesley, 1987.

[9] A. Bestavros and C. Cunha. Server-initiated Document Dissemination for the WWW. *IEEE Data Engineering Bulletin*, 19(3):3–11, 1996.

[10] T. Bowen, G. Gopal, G. Herman, T. Hickey, K. Lee, W. Mansfield, J. Raitz, and A. Weinrib. The Datacycle Architecture. *Communications of the ACM*, 35(12):71–81, 1992.

[11] A. Datta, A. Celik, J. Kim, D. VanderMeer, and V. Kumar. Adaptive Broadcast Protocols to Support Efficient and Energy Conserving Retrieval from Databases in Mobile Computing Environments. In *Proc. of the 13th IEEE Int'l Conf. on Data Engineering*, pp. 124–133, 1997.

[12] M. J. Franklin and S. B. Zdonik. A Framework for Scalable Dissemination-Based Systems. In *Proc. of the OOPSLA Conf.* , pp. 94–105, 1997.

[13] D. Gifford. Polychannel Systems for Mass Digital Communication. *Communications of the ACM*, 33(2):141–150, 1990.

[14] A. Gupta and I. S. Mumick. Maintenance of Materialized Views: Problems, Techniques and Applications. *IEEE Data Engineering Bulletin*, 18(3):3–18, June 1995.

[15] T. Imielinski, S. Viswanathan, and B. R. Badrinanth. Data on Air: Organization and Access. *IEEE Transactions on Knowledge and Data Engineering*, 9(3):353–372, 1997.

[16] J. Jing, A. K. Elmargarmid, S. Helal, and R. Alonso. Bit-Sequences: An Adaptive Cache Invalidation Method in Mobile Client/Server Environments. *ACM/Baltzer Mobile Networks and Applications*, 2(2):115–127, 1997.

[17] C. Mohan, H. Pirahesh, and R. Lorie. Efficient and Flexible Methods for Transient Versioning to Avoid Locking by Read-Only Transactions. In *Proc. of the ACM SIGMOD Intl. Conf. on Management of Data*, pp. 124–133, 1992.

[18] E. Pitoura and P. K. Chrysanthis. Scalable Processing of Read-Only Transactions in Broadcast Push. In *Proc. of the 19th IEEE Int'l Conf. on Distributed Computing Systems*, 1999.

[19] E. Pitoura and G. Samaras. *Data Management for Mobile Computing*. Kluwer Academic Publishers, 1998.

[20] D. Quass and J. Widom. On-Line Warehouse View Maintenance. In *Proc. of the 1997 SIGMOD Intl. Conf. on Management of Data*, pp. 393–404, 1997.

[21] R. Rastogi, S. Mehrotra, Y. Breitbart, H. F. Korth, and A. Silberschatz. On Correctness of Non-serializable Executions. In *Proc. of ACM Symposium on Principles of Database Systems*, pp. 97–108, 1993.

[22] J. Shanmugasundaram, A. Nithrakashyap, R. Sivasankaran, and K. Ramamritham. Efficient Concurrency Control for Broadcast Environments. In *ACM SIGMOD Int'l Conf. on Management of Data*, 1999.

[23] J. Wong. Broadcast Delivery. *Proc. of the IEEE*, 76(12), 1988.

[24] T. Yan and H. Garcia-Molina. SIFT – A Tool for Wide-area Information Dissemination. In *Proc. of the 1995 USENIX Technical Conf.* , pp. 177–186, 1995.

[25] Y. Zhuge, H. Garcia-Molina, J. Hammer, and J. Widom. View Maintenance in a Warehousing Environment. In *Proc. of the 1995 SIGMOD Intl. Conf. on Management of Data*, pp. 316–327, 1995.

Fast Algorithms for Maintaining Replica Consistency in Lazy Master Replicated Databases*

Esther Pacitti
NCE-UFRJ Rio de Janeiro
Brazil
esther.pacitti@inria.fr

Pascale Minet
INRIA Rocquencourt
France
pascale.minet@inria.fr

Eric Simon
INRIA Rocquencourt
France
eric.simon@inria.fr

Abstract

In a lazy master replicated database, a transaction can commit after updating one replica copy at some master node. After the transaction commits, the updates are propagated towards the other replicas, which are updated in separate refresh transactions. A central problem is the design of algorithms that maintain replica's consistency while minimizing the performance degradation due to the synchronization of refresh transactions. We propose a simple and general refreshment algorithm that solves this problem and we prove its correctness. We then present two main optimizations. One is based on specific properties of replicas' topology. The other uses an immediate update propagation strategy. Our performance evaluation demonstrates the effectiveness of this optimization.

1 Introduction

Lazy replication (also called asynchronous replication) is a widespread form of data replication in (relational) distributed database systems [21]. With lazy replication, a transaction can commit after updating one replica copy[1]. After the transaction commits, the updates are propagated towards the other replicas, and these replicas are updated in separate refresh transactions. In this paper, we focus on a specific lazy replication scheme, called *lazy master* replication [10] (also called Single-Master-Primary-Copy replication in [4]). There, one replica copy is designated as the *primary copy*, stored at a *master* node, and update transactions are only allowed on that replica. Updates on a primary copy are distributed to the other replicas, called *secondary copies*. A major virtue of lazy master replication is its ease of deployment [4, 10]. In addition, lazy master replication has gained considerable interest because it is the most widely used mechanism to refresh data warehouses and data marts [5, 21].

However, lazy master replication may raise a consistency problem between replicas. Indeed, an observer of a set of replica copies at some node at time t may see a state I of these copies that can never be seen at any time, before or after t, by another observer of the same copies at some other node. We shall say that I is an *inconsistent* state. As a first example, suppose that two data marts S_1 and S_2 both have secondary copies of two primary copies stored at two different data source nodes[2]. If the propagation of updates coming from different transactions at the master nodes is not properly controlled, then refresh transactions can be performed in a different order at S_1 and S_2, thereby introducing some inconsistencies between replicas. These inconsistencies in turn can lead to inconsistent views that are later almost impossible to reconciliate.

Let us expand the previous example into a second example. Suppose that a materialized view V of S_1, considered as a primary copy, is replicated in data mart S_2. Now, additional synchronization is needed so that the updates issued by the two data source nodes *and* the updates of V issued by S_1 execute in the same order for all replicas in S_1 and S_2.

Thus, a central problem is the design of algorithms that maintain replica's consistency in lazy master replicated databases, while minimizing the performance degradation due to the synchronization of refresh transactions. Considerable attention has been given to the maintenance of replicas' consistency.

*Work partially supported by Esprit project DWQ.

Proceedings of the 25th VLDB Conference, Edinburgh, Scotland, 1999.

[1]From now on, we suppose that replicas are relations.

[2]This frequent situation typically arises when no corporate data warehouse has been set up between data sources and data marts. Quite often, each data mart, no matter how focused, ends up with views of the business that overlap and conflict with views held by other data marts (e.g., sales and inventory data marts). Hence, the same relations can be replicated in both data marts.

First, many papers addressed this problem in the context of lazy group replicated systems, which require the reconciliation of updates coming from multiple primary copies [25, 15, 10, 28]. Some papers have proposed to use weaker consistency criterias that depend on the application semantics. For instance, in the OSCAR system [9], each node processes the updates received from master nodes according to a specific weak-consistency method that is associated with each secondary copy. However, their proposition does not yield the same notion of consistency as ours. In [3, 26, 1], authors propose some weak consistency criterias based on time and space, e.g., a replica should be refreshed after a time interval or after 10 updates on a primary copy. There, the concern is not anymore on fast refreshment and hence these solutions are not adequate to our problem. [2, 19, 24] achieve one-copy serializability of synchronous update transactions in a fully replicated database, which guarantees that all conflicting transactions execute in the same order at all sites. They share in common the use of broadcast primitives (e.g., atomic broadcast in [19, 2], reliable broadcast in [24]), as a basis for their replication protocols. However, their notion of consistency is different from ours. Furthermore [19] studies relaxed notions of consistency such as cursor stability and snapshot isolation and proposes efficient protocols to handle node failures and recovery. In [6], the authors give conditions over the placement of secondary and primary copies into sites under which a lazy master replicated database can be guaranteed to be globally serializable (which corresponds to our notion of consistency). However, they do not propose any refreshment algorithm for the cases that do not match their conditions, such as our two previous examples. Finally, synchronization algorithms have been proposed and implemented in commercial systems, such as Digital's Reliable Transaction Router [4], where the refreshment of all secondary copies of a primary copy is done in a distributed transaction. However, to the best of our knowledge, these algorithms do not assure replica consistency in cases like our second above example.

This paper makes three important contributions with respect to the central problem mentionned before. First, we analyze different types of configurations of a lazy master replicated system. A configuration represents the topology of distribution of primary and secondary copies accross the system nodes. It is a directed graph where a directed arc connects a node N to a node N' if N holds a primary copy of some secondary copy in N'. We formally define the notion of correct refreshment algorithm that assures database consistency. Then, for each type of configuration, we define sufficient conditions that must be satisfied by a refreshment algorithm in order to be correct.

As a second contribution, we propose a simple and general refreshment algorithm, which is proved to be correct for a large class of acyclic configurations (including for instance, the two previous examples). We show how to implement this algorithm using system components that can be added to a regular database system. Our algorithm makes use of a reliable multicast with a known upper bound, that preserves a global FIFO order. Our algorithm also uses a deferred update propagation strategy, as offered by all commercial replicated database systems. The general principle of the algorithm is to make every refresh transaction wait a certain "deliver time" before being executed.

As a third contribution, we propose two main optimizations to this algorithm. First, using our correctness results on configurations types, we provide a static characterization of nodes that do not need to wait. Second, we give an optimized version of the algorithm that uses an immediate update propagation strategy, as defined in [23]. We give a performance evaluation based on simulation that demonstrates the value of this optimization by showing that it significantly improves the freshness of secondary copies.

The rest of this paper is structured as follows. Section 2 introduces our lazy master replication framework, and the typology of configurations. Section 3 defines the correctness criteria for each type of configuration. Section 4 describes our refreshment algorithm, how to incorporate it in the system architecture of nodes, and proves its correctness. Section 5 presents our two main optimizations. Section 6 introduces our simulation environment and presents our performance evaluation. Section 7 discusses some related work. Finally, Section 8 concludes.

2 Lazy Master Replicated Databases

We define a (relational) lazy replicated database system as a set of n interconnected database systems, henceforth called *nodes*. Each node N_i hosts a relational database whose schema consists of a set of pairwise distinct relational schemas, whose instances are called relations. A replication scheme defines a partitioning of all relations of all nodes into partitions, called *replication sets*. A replication set is a set of relations having the same schema, henceforth called *replica copies*[3]. We define a special class of replicated systems, called *lazy master*, which is our framework.

2.1 Ownership

Following [10], the *ownership* defines the node capabilities for updating replica copies. In a replication set, there is a single updatable replica copy, called *primary* copy (denoted by a capital letter), and all the other relations are called *secondary* copies (denoted by lower-case letters). We assume that a node never holds the primary copy and a secondary copy of the

[3] A replication set can be reduced to a singleton if there exists a single copy of a relation in the replicated system.

same replication set. We distinguish between three kinds of nodes in a lazy master replicated system.

Definition 2.1 *(Types of nodes).*

1. *A node M is said to be a* master *node iff :* $\forall m \in M$ *m is a primary copy.*
2. *A node S is said to be a* slave *node iff :* $\forall s \in S$ *s is a secondary copy of a primary copy of some master node.*
3. *A node MS is said to be a* master/slave *node iff :* $\exists ms$ *and* $ms' \in MS$*, such that ms is a primary copy and ms' is a secondary copy.*

Finally, we define the following slave and master dependencies between nodes. A node M is said to be a *master node of* a node S iff there exists a secondary copy r in S of a primary copy R in M. We also say that S is a *slave node of* M.

2.2 Configurations

Slave dependencies define a DAG, called configuration.

Definition 2.2 *(Configuration).*
A configuration *of a replicated system is defined by a directed graph, whose nodes are the nodes of the replicated system, and there is a directed arc from a node N to a node N' iff N' is a slave node of N. Node N is said to be a predecessor of N'.*

In the following, we distinguish different types of configurations. Intuitively, to each configuration will correspond a correctness criteria to guarantee database consistency. In the figures illustrating the configurations, we use integers to represent nodes in order to avoid confusion with the names of the relations that are displayed as annotation of nodes.

Definition 2.3 *(1master-per-slave configuration).*
An acyclic configuration in which each node has at most one predecessor is said to be a 1master-per-slave *configuration.*

This configuration, illustrated in Figure 1(a), corresponds to a "data dissemination" scheme whereby a set of primary copies of a master or master/slave node is disseminated towards a set of nodes. It characterizes for instance the case of several data marts built over a centralized corporate data warehouse.

Definition 2.4 *(1slave-per-master configuration).*
An acyclic configuration in which each node has at most one successor is said to be a 1slave-per-master *configuration.*

This configuration, illustrated in Figure 1(b), corresponds to what is often called a "data consolidation" scheme, whereby primary copies coming from different nodes are replicated into a single node. It characterizes for instance a configuration wherein a data warehouse node (or even, an operational data store node) holds a set of materialized views defined over a set of relations stored by source nodes. In this context, replicating the source relations in the data warehouse node has two main benefits. First, one can take advantage of the replication mechanism to propagate changes from the source towards the data warehouse. Second, it assures the self-maintainability of all materialized views in the data warehouse, thereby avoiding the problems mentioned in [29].

Definition 2.5 *(bowtie configuration).*
An acyclic configuration in which there exist two distinct replicas X_1 and X_2 and four distinct nodes M_1, M_2, S_1 and S_2 such that (i) M_1 holds the primary copy of X_1 and M_2 the primary copy of X_2, and (ii) both S_1 and S_2 hold secondary copies of both X_1 and X_2.

Such configuration, illustrated in Figure 1(c), generalizes the two previous configurations by enabling arbitrary slave dependencies between nodes. This configuration characterizes, for instance, the case of several data marts built over several data sources. The benefits of a replication mechanism are the same as for a data consolidation configuration.

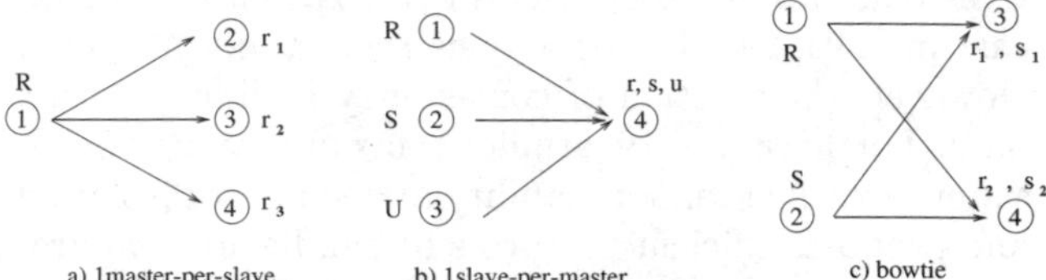

Figure 1: Examples of Configurations

Definition 2.6 *(triangular configuration).*
An acyclic configuration in which there exist three distinct nodes M, MS and S such that (i) MS is a successor of M, and (ii) S is a successor of both M and MS, is said to be a triangular *configuration. Nodes M, MS and S are said to form a* triangle.

This configuration, illustrated in Figure 2(a), slightly generalizes the two first configurations by enabling a master/slave node to play an added intermediate role between a master node and a slave node. This configuration was also considered in [6].

Definition 2.7 *(materialized view).*
A primary copy of a master/slave node MS which is defined as the result of the query over a set of secondary copies of MS is called a materialized view.

Definition 2.8 *(view triangular configuration).*
A derived configuration in which all the primary copies hold by any node MS of any triangle are materialized views of local secondary copies, is said to be a view triangular *configuration.*

This configuration, illustrated in Figure 2(b), characterizes, for instance, the case of two independent data marts defined over the same data warehouse in which one of the data mart replicates some materialized view of the other data mart. Although they overlap, the bowtie and the view triangular configurations are incomparable (none is included into the other).

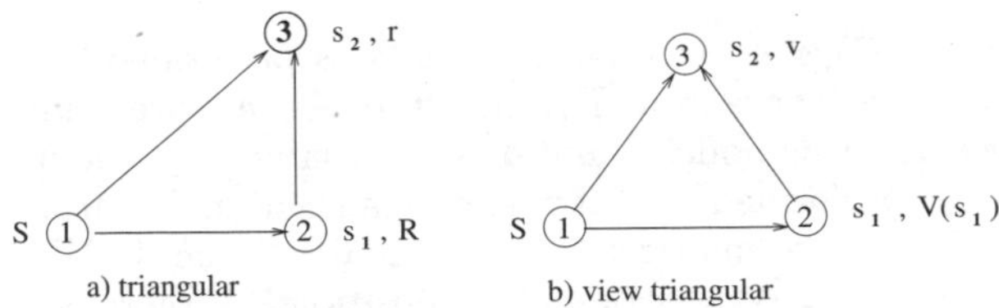

Figure 2: Examples of Configurations

2.3 Transaction Model

The *transaction model* defines the properties of the transactions that access the replica copies at each node. Moreover, we assume that once a transaction is submitted for execution to a local transaction manager at a node, all conflicts are handled by the local concurrency control protocol, in such a way that serializability of local transactions is ensured.

We focus on three types of transactions that read or write replica copies: *update transactions, refresh transactions* and *queries.* All these transactions access only local data.

An update transaction is a local user transaction (i.e., executing on a single node) that updates a set of primary copies. Updates performed by an update transaction T are made visible to other transactions only after T's commitment. We denote T_{R_1,R_k} an update transaction T that updates primary copies R_1, R_k. We assume that no user transaction can update a materialized view.

A refresh transaction associated with an update transaction T and a node N, is composed by the serial sequence of write operations performed by T on the replica copies hold by N. We denote RT_{r_1,r_k} a refresh transaction that updates secondary copies r_1, r_k. Finally, *a query transaction*, noted Q, consists of a sequence of read operations on replica copies.

2.4 Propagation

The propagation parameter defines "when" the updates to a primary copy must be multicast towards the nodes storing its secondary copies. The multicast is assumed to be reliable and to preserve the global FIFO order [18]: the updates are received by the involved nodes in the order they have been multicast by the node having the primary copy.

Following [23], we focus on two types of propagation: *deferred* and *immediate.* When using a *deferred* propagation strategy, the sequence of operations of each refresh transaction associated with an update transaction T is multicast to the appropriate nodes within a single message M, after the commitment of T. When using an *immediate* propagation, each operation of a refresh transaction associated with an update transaction T is immediately multicast inside a message m, without waiting for the commitment of T.

2.5 Refreshment

The *refreshment algorithm* defines: (i) the *triggering parameter* i.e., when a refresh transaction is started, and (ii) the *ordering parameter* i.e., the commit order of refresh transactions.

We consider three triggering modes: *deferred, immediate* and *wait.* The combination of a propagation parameter and a triggering mode determines a specific update propagation strategy. With a *deferred-immediate* strategy, a refresh transaction RT is submitted for execution as soon as the corresponding message M is received by the node. With an *immediate-immediate* strategy, a refresh transaction RT is started as soon as the first message m corresponding to the first operation of RT is received. Finally, with an *immediate-wait* strategy, a refresh transaction RT is submitted for execution only after the last message m corresponding to the commitment of the update transaction associated with RT is received.

3 Correctness Criteria

In this section, we first formally define the notion of a correct refreshment algorithm, which characterizes a refreshment algorithm that does not allow inconsistent states in a lazy master replicated system. Then for each type of configuration introduced in Section 2, we provide criteria that must be satisfied by a refreshment algorithm in order to be correct.

We now introduce useful preliminary definitions similar to those used in [17] in order to define the notion of a consistent replicated database state. We do not consider node failures, which are out of the scope of this paper. As a first requirement, we impose that any committed update on a primary copy must be eventually reflected by all its secondary copies.

Definition 3.1 *(Validity). A refreshment algorithm used in a lazy master replicated system is said valid iff any node that has a copy of a primary copy updated by a committed transaction T is guaranteed to commit the refresh transaction RT associated with T.*

Definition 3.2 *(Observable State). Let N be any node of a lazy master replicated system, the observable state of node N at local time t is the instance of the local data that reflects all and only those update and refresh transactions committed before t at node N.*

In the next definitions, we assume a global clock so that we can refer to global times in defining the notion of consistent global database state. The global clock is used for concept definition only. We shall also use the notation $I_t[N](Q)$ to denote the result of a query transaction Q run at node N at time t.

Definition 3.3 *(Quiescent State). A lazy master replicated database system is in a quiescent state at a global time t if all local update transactions submitted before t have either aborted or committed, and all the refresh transactions associated with the committed update transactions have committed.*

Definition 3.4 *(Consistent Observable State). Let N be any node of a lazy master replicated system D. Let t be any global time at which a quiescent state of D is reached. An observable state of node N at time $t_N \leq t$ is said to be consistent iff for any node N' holding a non-empty set X of replica copies hold by N and for any query transaction Q over X, there exists some time $t_{N'} \leq t$ such that $I_{t_N}[N](Q) = I_{t_{N'}}[N'](Q)$.*

Definition 3.5 *(Correct Refreshment Algorithm for a node N). A refreshment algorithm used in a lazy master replicated system D, is said to be correct for a node N of D iff it is valid and for any quiescent state reached at time t, any observable state of N at time $t_N \leq t$ is consistent.*

Definition 3.6 *(Correct Refreshment Algorithm). A refreshment algorithm used in a lazy master replicated system D, is said to be correct iff it is correct for any node N of D.*

In the following, we define correctness criteria for acyclic configurations that are sufficient conditions on the refreshment algorithm to guarantee that it is correct. Due to space limitation, the proofs of all propositions are omitted and can be found in the long version of this paper [22].

3.1 Global FIFO Ordering

For 1master-per-slave configurations, inconsistencies may arise if slaves can commit their refresh transactions in an order different from their corresponding update transactions. Although in 1slave-per-master configurations, every primary copy has a single associated secondary copy, the same case of inconsistency could occur between the primary and secondary copies. The following correctness criterion prevents this situation.

Definition 3.7 *(Global FIFO order). Let T_1 and T_2 be two update transactions committed by the same master or master/slave node M. If M commits T_1 before T_2, then at every node having a copy of a primary copy updated by T_1, the refresh transaction associated with T_2 can only commit after the refresh transaction associated with T_1.*

Proposition 3.1 *If a lazy master replicated system D has an acyclic configuration which is neither a bowtie nor a triangular configuration, and D uses a valid refreshment algorithm meeting the global FIFO order criterion, then this refreshment algorithm is correct.*

A similar result was shown in [6] using serializability theory.

3.2 Total Ordering

Global FIFO ordering is not sufficient to guarantee the correctness of refreshment for bowtie configurations. Consider the example in Figure 1(c). Two master nodes, node 1 and node 2, store relations $R(A)$ and $S(B)$, respectively. The updates performed on R by some transaction T_R: insert $R(A : a)$, are multicast towards nodes 3 and 4. In the same way, the updates performed on S by some transaction T_S: insert $S(B : b)$, are multicast towards nodes 3 and 4. With the correctness criterion of proposition 3.1, there is no ordering among the commits of refresh transactions RT_r and RT_s associated with T_R and T_S. Therefore, it might happen that RT_r commits before RT_s at node 3 and in a reverse order at node 4. In which case, a simple query transaction Q that computes $(R - S)$ could return an empty result at node 4, which is impossible at node 3. The following criterion requires that RT_r and RT_s commit in the same order at nodes 3 and 4.

Definition 3.8 *(Total order). Let T_1 and T_2 be two committed update transactions. If two nodes commit both the associated refresh transactions RT_1 and RT_2, they both commit RT_1 and RT_2 in the same order.*

Proposition 3.2 *If a lazy master replicated system D that has a bowtie configuration but not a triangular configuration, uses a valid refreshment algorithm meeting the global FIFO order and the total order criteria, then this refreshment algorithm is correct.*

3.3 Master/Slave Induced Ordering

We first extend the model presented in Section 2 to deal with materialized views as follows. From now on, we shall consider that in a master/slave node MS having a materialized view, say $V(s_1)$, any refresh transaction of s_1 is understood to encapsulate the update of some virtual copy $\hat{V}$. The actual replica copies V and v are then handled as if they were secondary copies of $\hat{V}$. Hence, we consider that the update of the virtual copy $\hat{V}$ is associated with:

- at node MS, a refresh transaction of V, noted RT_V,
- at any node S having a secondary copy of v, a refresh transaction of v, noted RT_v.

With this new modeling in mind, consider the example of Figure 2(b). Let $V(A)$ be the materialized view defined from the secondary copy $s1$. Suppose that at the initial time t_o of the system, the instance of $V(A)$ is: $\{V(A : 8)\}$ and the instance of $S(B)$ is: $\{S(B : 9)\}$. Suppose that we have two update transactions T_S and $T_{\hat{V}}$, running at nodes 1 and 2 respectively: T_S: [delete $S(B : 9)$; insert $S(B : 6)$], and $T_{\hat{V}}$: [if exists $S(B : x)$ and $x \leq 7$ then delete $V(A : 8)$; insert $V(A : 5)$]. Finally, suppose that we have the query transaction Q over V and S, Q: [if exists $V(A : x)$ and $S(B : y)$ and $y < x$ then *bool* = *true* else *bool* = *false*], where *bool* is a variable local to Q.

Now, a possible execution is the following. First, T_S commits at node 1 and its update is multicast towards nodes 2 and 3. Then, RT_{s_1} commits at node 2. At this point of time, say t_1, the instance of s_1 is $\{s_1(\vec{B} : 6)\}$.

Then the update transaction $T_{\hat{V}}$ commits, afterwards the refresh transaction RT_V commits. The instance of V is $\{V(A:5)\}$. Then at node 3, RT_v commits (the instances of v and s_2 are $\{v(A:5)\}$ and $\{s_2(B:9)\}$), and finally, RT_{s_2} commits (the instances of v and s_2 are $\{v(A:5)\}$ and $\{s_2(B:6)\}$). A quiescent state is reached at this point of time, say t_2.

However, there exists an inconsistent observable state. Suppose that Q executes at time t_1 on node 2. Then, Q will return a value *true* for *bool*. However, for any time between t_0 and t_2, the execution of Q on node 3 will return a value *false* for *bool*, which contradicts our definition of consistency.

The following criterion imposes that the commit order of refresh transactions must reflect the commit order at the master/slave node.

Definition 3.9 *(Master/slave induced order). If MS is a node holding a secondary copy s_1 and a materialized view V, then any node N_i, $i > 1$, having secondary copies s_i and v_i must commit its refresh transactions RT_{s_i} and RT_{v_i} in the same order as RT_V and RT_{s_1} commit at MS.*

Proposition 3.3 *If a lazy master replicated system D that has a view triangular configuration but not a bowtie configuration, uses a valid refreshment algorithm meeting the global FIFO order and the master/slave induced order criteria then this refreshment algorithm is correct.*

As said before, a configuration can be both a bowtie and a view triangular configuration. In this case, the criteria for both configurations must be enforced.

Proposition 3.4 *If a lazy master replicated system D having both a view triangular configuration and a bowtie configuration, uses a valid refreshment algorithm meeting the global FIFO order, the master/slave induced order and the total order criteria, then this refreshment algorithm is correct.*

4 Refreshment Algorithm

We start this section by presenting the system architecture assumed by our algorithms. Then, we present our refreshment algorithm that uses a deferred update propagation strategy and prove its correctness. Finally we discuss the rationale for our algorithm.

4.1 System Architecture of Nodes

To maintain the autonomy of each node, we assume that four components are added to a regular database system, that includes a transaction manager and a query processor, in order to support a lazy master replication scheme. Figure 3 illustrates these components for a node having both primary and secondary copies. The first component, called *Replication Module*, is itself composed of three sub-components: a Log Monitor, a Propagator and a Receiver. The second component, called *Refresher*, implements a refreshment strategy. The third component, called *Deliverer*, manages the submission of refresh transactions to the local transaction manager. Finally, the last component, called *Network Interface*, is used to propagate and receive update messages (for simplicity, it is not portrayed on Figure 3). We now detail the functionality of these components.

We assume that the *Network Interface* provides a global FIFO reliable multicast [18] with a known upper bound [11]: messages multicast by a same node are received in the order they have been multicast. We also assume that each node has a local clock. For fairness reasons, clocks are assumed to have a bounded drift and to be ε synchronized. This means that the difference between any two correct clocks is not higher than the precision ε.

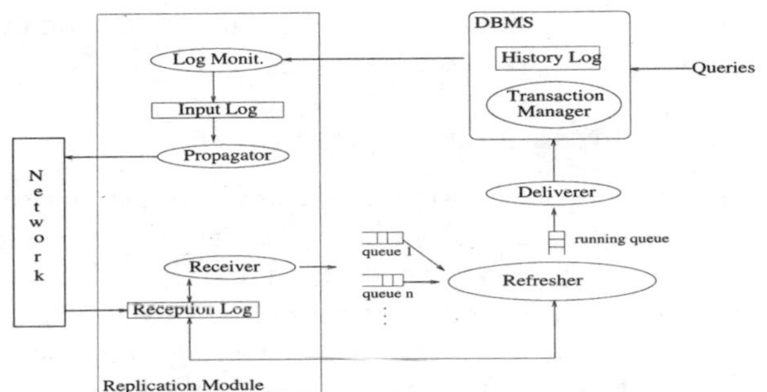

Figure 3: Architecture of a Node

The *Log Monitor* uses *log sniffing* [25, 20] to extract the changes to a primary copy by continuously reading the content of a local History Log (noted H). We safely assume (see Chap. 9 of [16]) that a log record contains all the information we need such as the timestamp of a committed update transaction, and other relevant attributes that will be presented in the next section. Each committed update transaction T has a timestamp (henceforth denoted C), which corresponds to the real time value at T's commitment time. When the log monitor finds a write operation on a primary copy, it reads the corresponding log record from H and writes it into a stable storage, called *Input Log*, that is used by the Propagator. We do not deal with conflicts between the write operations on the History Log and the read operations performed by the Log Monitor.

The *Receiver* implements update message reception. Messages coming from different masters or master/slaves are received and stored into a *Reception Log*. The receiver then reads messages from this log and stores them in FIFO *pending queues*. We denote Max, the upper bound of the time needed to multicast a message from a node and insert it into a pending queue at a receiving node. A node N has as many pending queues $q_1, \ldots q_n$ as masters or master/slaves nodes from which N has a secondary copy. The contents of these queues form the input to the Refresher.

The *Propagator* implements the propagation of update messages constructed from the Log Monitor. Such messages are first written into the *Input Log*. The propagator then continuously reads the *Input Log* and propagates messages through the network interface.

The *Refresher* implements the refreshment algorithm. First, it reads the contents of the pending queues, and based on its refreshment parameters, submits refresh transactions by inserting them into a *running queue*. The running queue contains all ordered refresh transactions not yet entirely executed.

Finally, the *Deliverer* submits refresh transactions to the local transaction manager. It reads the content of the running queue in a FIFO order and submits each write operation as part of a refresh transaction to the local transaction manager. The local transaction manager ensures serializability of local transactions. Moreover, it executes the operations requested by the refresh transactions according to the submission order given by the *Deliverer*.

4.2 Refreshment Algorithm

As described in Section 2, the refreshment algorithm has a triggering and an ordering parameters. In this section, we present the refreshment algorithm in the case of a *deferred-immediate* update propagation strategy (i.e., using an immediate triggering), and focus on the ordering parameter.

```
Deferred-Immediate Refresher
input: pending queues q1...qn
output: running queue
variables:
  curr_M, new_M: messages from pending queues;
  timer: local reverse timer whose state is either active or inactive;
begin
  timer.state = inactive;
  curr_M = new_M = ∅;
  repeat
    on message arrival or change of timer's state to inactive do
      Step 1:
      new_M ← message with min C among top messages of q1, qn;
      Step 2:
      if new_M ≠ curr_M then
        curr_M ← new_M;
        calculate deliver_time(curr_M);
        timer.value ← deliver_time(curr_M) − local_time
        timer.state ← active;
      endif
    on timer.value = 0 do
      Step 3:
      write curr_M into running queue;
      dequeue curr_M from its pending queue;
      timer.state ← inactive;
  for ever
end
```

Figure 4: Deferred-Immediate Refreshment Algorithm

The principle of the refreshment algorithm is the following. A refresh transaction RT is committed at a slave or master/slave node (1) once all its write operations have been done, (2) according to the order given by the timestamp C of its associated update transaction, and (3) at the earliest, at real time $C + Max + \varepsilon$, which is called the deliver time, noted *deliver_time*. Therefore, as clocks are assumed to be ε synchronized, the effects of updates on secondary copies follow the same chronological order in which their corresponding primary copies were updated.

We now detail the algorithm given in Figure 4. Each element of a pending queue is a message that contains: a sequence of write operations corresponding to a refresh transaction RT, and a timestamp C of the update transaction associated with RT. Since messages successively multicast by a same node are received in that order by the destination nodes, in any pending queue, messages are stored according to their multicast order (or commitment order of their associated update transactions).

Initially, all pending queues are empty, and *curr_M* and *new_M* are empty too. Upon arrival of a new message M into some pending queue signaled by an event, the Refresher assigns variable *new_M* with the message that has the smallest C among all messages in the top of all pending queues. If two messages have equal timestamps, one is selected according to the master or master/slave identification priorities. This corresponds to Step 1 of the algorithm. Then, the Refresher compares *new_M* with the currently hold message *curr_M*. If the timestamp of *new_M* is smaller than the timestamp of *curr_M*, then *curr_M* gets the value of *new_M*. Its deliver time is then calculated, and a local reverse timer is set with value *deliver_time* − *local_time*. This concludes Step 2 of the algorithm. Finally, whenever the timer expires its time, signaled by an event, the Refresher writes *curr_M* into the running queue and dequeues it from its pending queue. Each message of the running queue will yield a different refresh transaction. If an update message takes Max time to reach a pending queue, it can be processed immediately by the Refresher.

4.3 Refreshment Algorithm Correctness

We first show that the refreshment algorithm is valid for any acceptable configuration. A configuration is said *acceptable* iff (i) it is acyclic, and (ii) if it is a triangular configuration, then it is a view triangular configuration.

Lemma 4.1 *The Deferred-immediate refreshment algorithm is valid for any acceptable configuration.*

Lemma 4.2 *(Chronological order). The Deferred-immediate refreshment algorithm ensures for any acceptable configuration that, if T_1 and T_2 are any two update transactions committed respectively at global times t_1 and t_2 then :*

- *if $t_2 - t_1 > \varepsilon$, the timestamps C_2 for T_2 and C_1 for T_1 meet $C_2 > C_1$.*
- *any node that commits both associated refresh transactions RT_1 and RT_2, commits them in the order given by C_1 and C_2.*

Lemma 4.3 *The Deferred-immediate refreshment algorithm satisfies the global FIFO order criterium for any acceptable configuration.*

Lemma 4.4 *The Deferred-immediate refreshment algorithm satisfies the total order criteria for any acceptable configuration.*

Lemma 4.5 *The Deferred-immediate refreshment algorithm satisfies the master/slave induced order criteria for any acceptable configuration.*

From the previous lemmas and propositions, we have:

Theorem 4.1 *The Deferred-immediate refreshment algorithm is correct for any acceptable configuration.*

4.4 Discussion

A key aspect of our algorithm is to rely on the upper bound Max on the transmission time of a message by the global FIFO reliable multicast. Therefore, it is essential to have a value of Max that is not overestimated. The computation of Max resorts to scheduling theory (e.g., see [27]). It usually takes into account four kinds of parameters. First, there is the global reliable multicast algorithm itself (see for instance [18]). Second, are the characteristics of the messages to multicast (e.g. arrival laws, size). For instance, in [12], an estimation of Max is given for sporadic message arrivals. Third, are the failures to be tolerated by the multicast algorithm, and last are the services used by the multicast algorithm (e.g. medium access protocol). It is also possible to compute an upper bound Max_i for each type i of message to multicast. In that case, the refreshment algorithm at node N waits until $max_{i \in J}\ Max_i$ where J is the set of message types that can be received by node N.

Thus, an accurate estimation of Max depends on an accurate knowledge of the above parameters. However, accurate values of the application dependent parameters can be obtained in performance sensitive replicated database applications. For instance, in the case of data warehouse applications that have strong requirements on freshness, certain characteristics of messages can be derived from the characteristics of the operational data sources (usually, transaction processing systems). Furthermore, in a given application, the variations in the transactional workload of the data sources can often be predicted.

In summary, the approach taken by our refreshment algorithm to enforce a total order over an algorithm that implements a global FIFO reliable multicast trades the use of a worst case multicast time at the benefit of reducing the number of messages exchanged on the network. This is a well known tradeoff. This solution brings simplicity and ease of implementation.

5 Optimizations of the Refreshment

In this section, we present two main optimizations for the refreshment algorithm presented in Section 4. First, we show that for some configurations, the deliver time of a refresh transaction needs not to include the upper bound (Max) of the network and the clock precision (ε), thereby considerably reducing the waiting time of a refresh transaction at a slave or master/slave node. Second, we show that without sacrificing correctness, the principle of our refreshment algorithm can be combined with immediate update propagation strategies, as they were presented in [23]. Performance measurements, reported in Section 6, will demonstrate the value of this optimization.

5.1 Eliminating the Deliver Time

There are cases where the waiting time associated with the deliver time of a refresh transaction can be eliminated. For instance, consider a multinational investment bank that has traders in several cities, including New York, London, and Tokyo. These traders update a local database of positions (securities held and quantity), which is replicated using a lazy master scheme (each site is a master for securities of that site) into a central site that warehouses the common database for all traders. The common database is necessary in order for risk management software to put limits on what can be traded and to support an internal market. A trade will be the purchase of a basket of securities belonging to several sites. In this context, a delay in the arrival of a trade notification may expose the bank to excessive risk. Thus, the time needed to propagate updates from a local site to the common database must be very small (e.g., below a few seconds).

This scheme is a 1slave-per-master configuration, which only requires a global FIFO order to ensure the correctness of its refreshment algorithm (see proposition 3.1). Since, we assume a reliable FIFO multicast network, there is no need for a refresh transaction to wait at a slave node before being executed. More generally, given an arbitrary acceptable configuration, the following proposition characterizes those slave nodes that can process refresh transactions without waiting for their deliver time.

Proposition 5.1 *Let N a node of a lazy master replicated system D. If for any node N' of D, X being the set of common replicas between N and N', we have:*

- *$cardinal(X) \leq 1$, or*
- *$\forall X_1, X_2 \in X$, the primary copies of X_1 and X_2 are hold by the same node,*

then any valid refreshment algorithm meeting the global FIFO order criteria is correct for node N.

From an implementation point of view, the same refreshment algorithm runs at each node. The behavior of the refreshment algorithm regarding the need to wait or not, is simply conditioned by a local variable. Thus, when the configuration changes, only the value of the variable of each node can possibly change.

5.2 Immediate Propagation

We assume that the Propagator and the Receiver both implement an immediate propagation strategy as specified in [23], and we focus here on the Refresher. Due to space limitations, we only present the *immediate-immediate* refreshment algorithm. We have chosen the *immediate-immediate* version because it is the one that provides the best performance compared with *deferred-immediate*, as indicated in [23].

```
Immediate_immediate Refresher
input: pending queues q1...qn
output: running queue
variables:
  curr_m, new_m: messages from pending queues;
  timer: local reverse timer whose state is either active or inactive;
begin
  timer.state = inactive;
  curr_m = new_m = ∅;
  repeat
    on message arrival or change of timer's state to inactive do
      if m ≠ commit then
        write m into the running queue;
        dequeue m from its pending queue;
      else
        new_m ← commit message with min C
          among top messages of q1...qn;
        if new_m ≠ curr_m then
          curr_m ← new_m;
          calculate deliver_time(curr_m);
          timer.value ← deliver_time(curr_m) − local_time
          timer.state ← active;
        endif
      endif
    on timer.value = 0 do
      write curr_m into running queue;
      dequeue curr_m from its pending queue;
      timer.state ← inactive;
  for ever
end
```

Figure 5: Immediate-Immediate Refreshment Algorithm

5.2.1 Immediate-Immediate Refreshment

We detail the algorithm of Figure 5. Unlike deferred-immediate refreshment, each element of a pending queue is a message m that carries an operation o of some refresh transaction, and a timestamp C. Initially, all pending queues are empty. Upon arrival of a new message m in some pending queue, signaled by an event, the Refresher reads the message and if m does not correspond to a *commit*, inserts it into the running queue. Thus, any operation carried by m other than commit can be immediately submitted for execution to the local transaction manager. If m contains a *commit* operation then *new_m* is assigned with the commit message that has the smallest C among all messages in the top of all pending queues. Then, *new_m* is compared with *curr_m*. If *new_m* has a smallest timestamp than *curr_m*, then *curr_m* is assigned with *new_m*. Afterwards, the Refresher calculates the *deliver_time* for *curr_m*, and timer is set as in the *deferred-immediate* case. Finally, when the timer expires, the Refresher writes *curr_m* into the running queue, dequeues it from its pending queue, sets the timer to inactive and re-executes Step 1.

5.2.2 Algorithm Correctness

Like the deferred-immediate refreshment algorithm, the immediate-immediate algorithm enforces refresh transactions to commit in the order of their associated update transactions. Thus, the proofs of correctness for any acceptable configuration are the same for both refreshment algorithms.

6 Performance Evaluation

In this section, we summarize the main performance gains obtained by an *immediate-immediate* refreshment algorithm against a *deferred-immediate* one. More extensive performance results are reported in [23]. We use a simulation environment that reflects as much as possible a real replication context. We focus on a bowtie configuration which requires the use of a $Max + \varepsilon$ deliver time, as explained in Section 5.2. However, once we have fixed the time spent to reliably multicast a message, we can safely run our experiments with a single slave and several masters.

Our simulation environment is composed of *Master*, *Network*, *Slave* modules and a database server. The Master module implements all relevant capabilities of a master node such as log monitoring and message propagation. The Network module implements the most significant factors that may impact our update propagation strategies such as the delay to reliably multicast a message. The Slave module implements the most relevant components of the slave node architecture such as Receiver, Refresher and Deliverer. In addition, for performance evaluation purposes, we add the Query component in the slave module, which implements the execution of queries that read replicated data. Finally, a database server is used to implement refresh transactions and query execution.

Our environment is implemented on a Sun Solaris workstation using Java/JDBC. We use sockets for inter-process communication and Oracle 7.3 to implement refresh transaction and query processing. For simulation purposes, each write operation corresponds to an UPDATE command submitted to the server.

6.1 Performance Model

The metrics used to compare the two refreshment algorithms is given by the freshness of secondary copies. More formally, given a replica X, which is either a secondary or a primary copy, we define $n(X, t)$ as the number of committed update transactions on X at global time t. We assume that update transactions can have different sizes but their occurence is uniformly distributed over time. Using this assumption, we define the degree freshness of a secondary copy r at global time t as: $f(r,t) = n(r,t)/n(R,t)$. Therefore, a degree of freshness close to 0 means bad data freshness while close to 1 means excellent.

The mean degree of freshness of r at a global time T is defined as: $mean_f = 1/T \int_0^T f(r,t)dt$.

We now present the main parameters for our experimentations summarized in Table 6.1. We assume that the mean time interval between update transactions, noted λ_t, as reflected by the history log of each master, is bursty. Updates are done on the same attribute of a different tuple. We focus on *dense* update transactions, i.e., transactions with a small time interval between each two writes. We define two types of update transactions. Small update transactions have size 5 (i.e., 5 write operations), while long transactions have size 50. We define four scenarios in which the proportion of long transactions, noted *ltr*, is set respectively to 0, 30, 60, and 100. Thus, in a scenario where *ltr* = 30, 30 % of the executed update transactions are long. Finally, we define an abort transaction ratio, noted *abr*, of 0, 5%, 10%, 20%, that corresponds to the percentage of transactions that abort in an experiment. Furthermore, we assume that a transaction abort always occurs after half of its execution.

Table 1: Performance Parameters

Param.	*Definition*	*Values*
λ_t	mean time between Trans.	bursty:200ms
λ_q	mean time between Queries	low:15s
nbmaster	Number of Master nodes	1 to 8
$\|Q\|$	Query Size	5
$\|RT\|$	Refresh Transaction Size	5; 50
ltr	Long Transaction Ratio	0; 30; 60; 100%
abr	Abort Ratio	0; 5; 10; 20%
t_{short}	Multicast Time per record	20ms; 100ms

Network delay is calculated by $\delta + t$, where δ is the waiting time in the input queue of the Network module, and t is the reliable multicast time of a message until its insertion in the pending queue of the Refresher. Concerning the value of t used in our experiments, we have a short message multicast time, noted t_{short}, which represents the time needed to reliably multicast a single log record. In addition, we consider that the time spent to reliably multicast a sequence of log records is linearly proportional to the number of log records it carries. The network overhead delay, δ, is implicity modeled by the system overhead to read from and write to sockets. The *Total propagation time* (noted t_p) is the time spent to reliably multicast all log records associated with a given transaction[4]. Finally, when $ltr > 0$, the value of Max is calculated using the maximun time spent to reliably multicast a long transaction ($50 * t_{short}$). On the other hand, when $ltr = 0$, the value of Max is calculated using the maximun time spent to reliably multicast a short transaction ($5 * t_{short}$). The refresh transaction execution time is influenced by the existence of possible conflicting queries that read secondary copies at the slave node. Therefore, we need to model queries. We assume that the mean time interval between queries is low, and the number of data items read is small (fixed to 5). We fix a 50% conflict rate for each secondary copy, which means that each refresh transaction updates 50% of the tuples of each secondary copy that are read by a query.

To measure the mean degree of freshness, we use the following variables. Each time an update transaction commits at a master, variable *version_master* for that master, is incremented. Similarly, each time a refresh transaction commits at the slave, variable *version_slave*, is incremented. Whenever a query conflicts with a refresh transaction we measure the degree of freshness.

6.2 Experiments

We present three experiments. The results are average values obtained from the execution of 40 update transactions. The first experiment shows the mean degree of freshness obtained for the *bursty* workload. The second experiment studies the impact on freshness when update transactions abort. In the third experiment, we study the effect of an increase in network delay.

We now summarize our major results. As depicted in Figure 6, when $ltr = 0$ (short transactions), the mean degree of freshness is already impacted because on average, $\lambda_t < t_p$[5]. With 2, 4, and 8 masters, the results of *immediate-immediate* are much better than those of *deferred-immediate*, as *ltr* increases. For instance, with 4 masters with *ltr* = 30, the mean degree of freshness is 0.62 for *immediate-immediate* and 0.32 for *deferred-immediate*. In fact, *immediate-immediate* always yields the best mean degree of freshness even with network contention due to the parallelism of log monitoring, propagation, and refreshment.

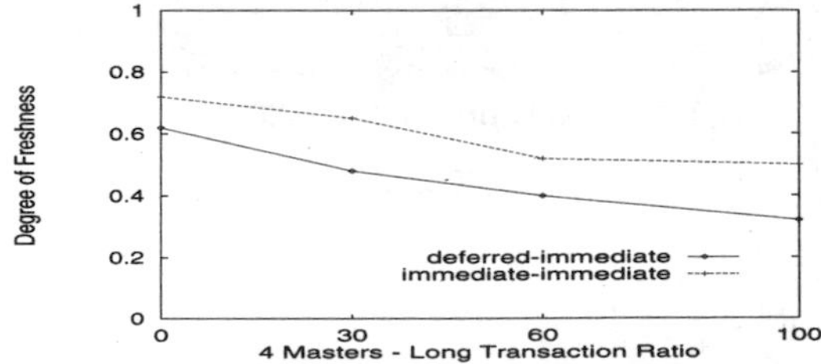

Figure 6: Bursty Workload

With *immediate-immediate*, the mean query response time may be seriously impacted because each time a query conflicts with a refresh transaction, it may be blocked during a long period of time since the propagation time may be added to the refresh transaction execution time. When $\lambda_q >> \lambda_t$, the probability

[4]If n represents the size of the transaction with immediate propagation, we have $t_p = n \times (\delta + t_{short})$, while with deferred propagation, we have $t_p = (\delta + n \times t_{short})$.

[5]Therefore, during T_i's update propagation, $T_{i+1}...T_{i+n}$ may be committed.

of conflicts is quite high. The higher the network delay value, the higher are the query response times in conflict situations. However as also pointed out in [19], we verified that the use of a multiversion protocol on the slave node may significantly reduce query response times, without a significant decrease in the mean degree of freshness.

The *abort* of an update transaction with *immediate-immediate* does not impact the mean degree of freshness since the delay introduced to undo a refresh transaction is insignificant compared to the propagation time. As shown in Figure 7, for $ltr = 0$ and various values of *abr* (5,10,20), the decrease of freshness introduced by update transactions that abort with *immediate-immediate* is insignificant[6]. This behavior is the same for other values of *ltr* (30, 60, 100).

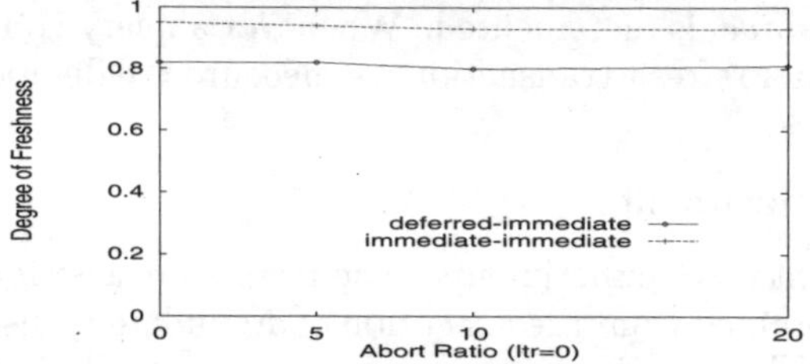

Figure 7: *Abort* Effects

Finally, the improvements brought by *immediate-immediate* are more significant when the network delay to propagate a single operation augments. Figure 8 and Figure 9 compares the freshness results obtained when $\delta = 100ms$ and $\delta = 20ms$. For instance, when $\delta = 20$ and $ltr = 100$ *immediate-immediate* improves 1.1 times better than *deferred-immediate* and when $\delta = 100$, *immediate-immediate* improves 5 times better. This clearly shows the advantages of having tasks being executed in parallel.

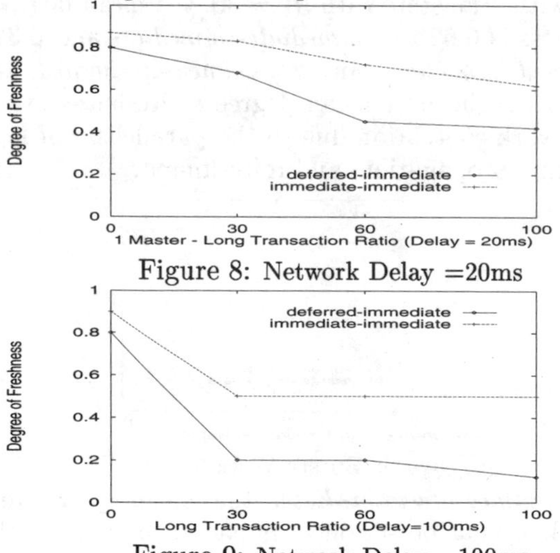

Figure 8: Network Delay =20ms

Figure 9: Network Delay =100ms

7 Related Work

Apart from the work cited in Section 1, the closest work to ours is in [6]. The authors show that for any strongly acyclic configuration a refreshment algorithm which enforces a global FIFO ordering, guarantees a global serializability property, which is similar to our notion of correction. Their result is analogous to our Proposition 3.1. They also propose an algorithm, which assigns, when it is possible, a site to each primary copy so that the resulting configuration is strongly acyclic. However, no algorithm is provided to refresh secondary copies in the cases of non strongly acyclic configurations.

Much work has been devoted to the maintenance of integrity constraints in federated or distributed databases, including the case of replicated databases [7, 13, 8, 17]. These papers propose algorithms and protocols to prevent the violation of certain kind of integrity constraints by local transactions. However, their techniques are not concerned with the consistent refreshment of replicas.

In [25], the authors describe a lazy group replication scheme in which the update propagation protocol applies updates to replicated data in their arrival order, possibly restoring inconsistencies when arrivals violate the timestamp ordering of transactions. The major difference with our work is that they achieve consistency by undoing and re-executing updates which are out-of-order, whereas we do not allow inconsistent database states.

The timestamp message delivery protocol in [15] implements eventual delivery for a lazy group replication scheme [10]. It uses periodic exchange of messages between pairs of servers that propagate messages to distinct groups of master nodes. At each master node incoming messages are stored in a history log (as initially proposed in [20]) and later delivered to the application in a defined order. Eventual delivery is not appropriate in our framework since we are interested in improving data freshness.

The goal of epidemic algorithms [28] is to ensure that all replicas of a single data item converge to the same value in a lazy group replication scheme. Updates are executed locally at any node. Later, nodes communicate to exchange up-to-date information. In our approach, updates are propagated from each primary copy towards its secondary copies.

Formal concepts for specifying coherency conditions in a replicated distributed database have been introduced in [14]. The authors focus on a *deferred-immediate* update propagation strategy and propose concepts for computing a measure of relaxation[7]. Their concept of *version* is closely related to our notion of freshness.

8 Conclusion

In a lazy master replicated system, a transaction can commit after updating one replica copy (primary copy) at some node. The updates are propagated towards

[6]In the worst case, it achieves 0.2.

[7]called *coherency index*.

the other replicas (secondary copies), and these replicas are refreshed in separate refresh transactions.

We proposed refreshment algorithms which address the central problem of maintaining replicas' consistency. An observer of a set of replicas at some node never observes a state which is never seen by another oberver of the same set of replicas at another node.

This paper has three major contributions. Our first contribution is a formal definition of (i) the notion of correct refreshment algorithm and (ii) correctness criteria for any acceptable configuration.

Our second contribution is an algorithm meeting these correctness criteria for any acceptable configuration. This algorithm can be easily implemented over an existing database system. It is based on a deferred update propagation, and it delays the execution of a refresh transaction until its deliver time.

Our third contribution concerns optimizations of the refreshment algorithm in order to improve the data freshness. With the first optimization, we characterized the nodes that do not need to wait. The second optimization uses *immediate-immediate* update propagation strategy. This strategy allows parallelism between the propagation of updates and the execution of the associated refresh transactions.

Finally, our performance evaluation shows that the *immediate-immediate* strategy always yields the best mean degree of freshness for a bursty workload.

References

[1] G. Alonso and A. Abbadi, *Partitioned Data Objects in Distriduted Databases*,Distributed and Parallel Databases, 3(1):5-35, 1995.

[2] D. Agrawal and G. Alonso and A. El Abbadi and I. Stanoi,*Exploiting Atomic Broadcast in Replicated Databases*, EURO-PAR Int. Conf. on Parallel Processing, August 1997.

[3] R. Alonso and D. Barbara and H. Garcia-Molina, *Data Caching Issues in an Information Retrieval System*, ACM Transactions on Database Systems, 15(3):359-384, September 1990.

[4] P.A. Bernstein and E. Newcomer, *Transaction Processing*, Morgan Kaufmann, 1997.

[5] S. Chaudhuri and U. Dayal, *An Overview of Data Warehousing and OLAP Technology*, ACM SIGMOD Record, 26(1), March 1997.

[6] P. Chundi and D. J. Rosenkrantz and S. S. Ravi, *Deferred Updates and Data Placement in Distributed Databases*, Int. Conf. on Data Engineering (ICDE), Louisiana, February 1996.

[7] S. Ceri and J. Widom, *Managing Semantic Heterogeneity with Production Rules and Persistent Queues*, Int. Conf. on VLDB, 1993.

[8] L. Do and P. Drew, *The Mangement of Interdependent Asynchronous Transactions in Heterogeneous Database Environments*, Int. Conf. on Database Systems for Advanced Applications, 1995.

[9] A. Downing and I. Greenberg and J. Peha, *OSCAR: A System for Weak-Consistency Replication*, Int. Workshop on Management of Replicated Data, pages26-30, Houston, November 1990.

[10] J. Gray and P. Helland and P. O'Neil and D. Shasha, *The Danger of Replication and a Solution*, ACM SIGMOD Int. Conf. on Management of Data, Montreal, June 1996.

[11] L. George and P. Minet, *A FIFO Worst Case Analysis for a Hard Real-Time Distributed Problem with Consistency Constraints*, Int. Conf. on Distributed Computing Systems (ICDCS97), Baltimore, May 1997.

[12] L. George and P. Minet, *A Uniform Reliable Multicast Protocol with Guaranteed Responses Times*, ACM SIGPLAN workshop on Languages Compilers and Tools for Embedded Systems, Montreal, June 1998.

[13] H. Gupta and I.S. Mumick and V.S. Subrahmanian, *Maintaining Views Incremently*, ACM SIGMOD Int. Conf. on Management of Data, Washington, DC, May 1993.

[14] R. Gallersdorfer and M. Nicola, *Improving Performance in Replicated Databases through Relaxed Coherency*, Int. Conf. on VLDB, Zurich, September 1995.

[15] R. Goldring, *Weak-Consistency Group Communication and Membership*, PhD Thesis, Univ. of Santa Cruz, 1992.

[16] J.N. Gray and A. Reuter, *Transaction Processing: Concepts and Techniques*, Morgan-Kaufmann, 1993.

[17] P. Grefen and J. Widom, *Protocols for Integrity Constraint Checking in Federated Databases*, Distributed and Parallel Databases, 54,October 1997.

[18] V. Hadzilacos and S. Toueg, *A Modular Approach to Fault-Tolerant Broadcasts and Related Problems*, Technical Report TR 94-1425, Cornell Univ., Ithaca, NY 14853, 1994.

[19] B. Kemme and G. Alonso, *A Suite of Database Replication Protocols based on Group Communication Primitives*, Int. Conf. on Distributed Computing Systems (ICDCS98), Amsterdam, May 1998.

[20] B. Kahler and O. Risnes, *Extending Logging for Database Snapshot Refresh*, Int. Conf. on VLDB, Brighton, September 1987.

[21] T. Özsu and P. Valduriez, *Principles of Distributed Database Systems*, 2nd Edition, Prentice Hall, 1999.

[22] E. Pacitti and P. Minet and E. Simon, *Fast Scheduling Algorithms for Maintaining Replica Consistency in Lazy Master Configurations*, Long Paper, http://www-rodin.inria.fr/~pacitti/public_html/v99l.ps, February 1999.

[23] E. Pacitti and E. Simon and R. de Melo, *Improving Data Freshness in Lazy Master Schemes*, Int. Conf. on Distributed Computing Systems (ICDCS98), Amsterdam, May 1998.

[24] I. Stanoi and D. Agrawal and A. El Abbadi, *Using Broadcast Primitives in Replicated Databases*, Int. Conf. on Distributed Computing Systems (ICDCS98), Amsterdam, May 1998.

[25] S. K. Sarin and C. W. Kaufman and J. E. Somers, *Using History Information to Process Delayed Database Updates*, Int. Conf. on VLDB, Kyoto, August 1986.

[26] A. Sheth and M. Rusinkiewicz, *Management of Interdependent Data: Specifying Dependency and Consistency Requirements*, Int. Workshop on Management of Replicated Data, Houston, November 1990.

[27] K. Tindell and J. Clark, *Holistic Schedulability Analysis for Distributed Hard Real-Time Systems*, Microprocessors and Microprogramming, 40, 1994.

[28] D. B. Terry and M. M. Theimer and K. Petersen and A. J. Demers and M. J. Spreitzer and C. H. Hauser, *Managing Update Conflicts in Bayou, a Weakly Connected Replicated Storage System*, Symposium on Operating System Principles (SIGOPS), Colorado, December 1995.

[29] Y. Zhuge and H. Garcia-Molina and J. L. Wiener, *View Maintenance in a Warehouse Environment*, ACM SIGMOD Int. Conf. on Management of Data, 1995.

Active Views for Electronic Commerce*

S. Abiteboul, S. Cluet, L. Mignet

B. Amann

T. Milo, A. Eyal

INRIA/Verso
Rocquencourt, France

CNAM/CEDRIC
Paris, France

Computer Science Dept.
Univ. of Tel. Aviv

Abstract

Electronic commerce is emerging as a major Web-supported application. In this paper we argue that database technology can, and should, provide the backbone for a wide range of such applications. More precisely, we present here the ActiveViews system, which, relying on an extensive use of database features including views, active rules (triggers), and enhanced mechanisms for notification, access control and logging/tracing of users activities, provides the needed basis for electronic commerce.

Based on the emerging XML standards (DOM, query languages for XML, etc.), the system offers a novel declarative view specification language, describing the relevant data and activities of all actors (e.g. vendors and clients) participating in electronic commerce activities. Then, acting as an application generator, the system generates an actual, possibly customized, Web application that allows users to perform the given set of controlled activities and to work interactively on the specified data in a standard distributed environment.

The ActiveView system is developed at INRIA on top of Java and ArdentSoftware's XML repository.

*Work partially founded by a French Israeli grant.

Proceedings of the 25th VLDB Conference, Edinburgh, Scotland, 1999.

1 Introduction

Internet has revolutionized the electronic publication of data. We should expect to see more and more Internet applications allowing clients to interact on the net notably by sharing data. It is possible to develop such applications today but this is at the cost of intense software developments by sophisticated programmers. We believe that (i) the need for fast application deployment, (ii) the generalization of such applications, and (iii) the often-met requirement of *proving* properties of these applications, will require the use of declarative specifications of applications. The situation is somewhat similar to what lead in the 70's to declarative query languages. Indeed, we believe that declarative query languages and databases form an essential component of the problem. This paper proposes such a specification language (the *ActiveView* language) and discusses how it is supported in the *ActiveView* system.

To illustrate the issues, consider electronic commerce. (Our examples will be based on a Web catalog.) Electronic commerce is emerging as a major Web-supported application. In a nutshell, electronic commerce supports business transactions between multiple parties via the network. This activity has many aspects, including security, authentication, electronic payment, and designing business models [25]. Electronic commerce also requires database support, since it often involves handling large amounts of data (e.g. product catalogs, yellow pages, etc.) and must provide transactions, concurrency control, distribution and recovery. It also involves strong interactions between participants (e.g., customers and vendors) and a control of the sequencing of activities (i.e., workflow management). All these aspects will be addressed by active views.

More generally, the applications we are interested in involve: (i) sharing of data and (ii) some cooperative work by a number of actors connected via the network. These are typical features found also for instance in digital libraries or information manufacturing systems.

We believe that database technology provides the backbone for such applications. Indeed, the ActiveView system can be seen as a *database application generator*. The system enables a *declarative* specification of *certain kinds* of database applications. By declarative, we mean here that there is little (or no program) to write and that the description of the application is in a high level language (or via a graphical user interface). The specification of an application includes definitions of the main actors involved in the application. For each actor, we specify: i)the data and operations available to this particular actor (a *view* mechanism) and these with a sophisticate access control; ii)the activities this actor may be engaged in and the data and operations available in each; ii)some active rules that notably specify the sequencing of activities (a *workflow* component) but also the events this actor wants to be notified of (a *subscription* component) and those that have to be logged (a *tracing* component).

So, the ActiveView language allows to declaratively specify a number of features that are often considered in isolation. A main contribution of this paper is to show how these various aspects may be combined in a simple coherent framework. Active views rely heavily on four key components:

XML : From a data viewpoint, we selected the eXtended Markup Language (XML) [20] as the model for data.[1] All data stored, exchanged or presented to users are XML;

Active rules : Our active rules are rather simple compared to what may be found in the literature [24, 15]. The novelty is in the way they are integrated into a general framework and the way they are used for many purposes (workflow, change control, tracing);

Method calls and notifications : The events that enable active rules are method calls. The system relies on some subscription mechanism that allows views to be notified of certain events;

View management : Views have been quite studied in databases [9, 11]. We build here on our experience with O_2-Views [17], a system developed at INRIA. The views we are considering here are much simpler. The novelty is in the combination with active features.

To see an example, suppose a product is added to the catalog. A notification is issued to all actors that are interested in this event, i.e. a change in the catalog. For instance, vendors may want to always see the most recent version of the catalog. Their specification should thus include an active rule to specify that, when such an event occurs, their view of the catalog should be updated. Observe that both the detection of the event and the maintenance may take advantage of incremental techniques. In particular, if the update affects a portion of the catalog a specific vendor is not interested in, we should avoid updating the view. Furthermore, when a vendor view has to be updated, we want to do it incrementally to avoid re-sending large portions of the catalog on the net.

[1] The Web has so far relied primarily on HTML that emphasizes an hypertext document approach. XML, although originally a document markup language, includes more structure. It is believed that XML will soon be the standard for data exchanges on the Web.

A second contribution consists in the presentation of a system that implements these concepts. A guideline was to follow the standards as much as possible. An ActiveView application is compiled into a running application based on the following environment:

- We use the O_2 XML repository developed by ArdentSoftware [6] and its DOM interface for storing and querying XML data and methods.

- We intend to use the standard query language for XML when available. In the meantime (and in the examples of the present paper), we use a simple language inspired by Lorel [3].

- Each active view session corresponds to a multi-threaded repository client using the Java-DOM binding of the XML repository server. We also use the notification mechanism provided by the O_2 system[2].

- We intend to use for Web interfaces XML documents and XML browsers interacting with the views via Java remote method invocation. Until XML browsers offer the support we need, we use dynamic HTML with embedded Java applets. From a user viewpoint, an application presents a sequence of Web pages containing (modifiable) data and buttons, in a standard manner. The pages may evolve dynamically (e.g., new promotions may appear).

- A running application can be automatically generated from a view specification. We offer flexible means to customize such applications.

We already implemented a first prototype that was supporting only very partially the ActiveView features. The first prototype on top of O_2 was based on ODMG data and OQL. We were lead to XML mostly because a lot of data relevant for Web applications do not have the regular structure of ODMG and because of the (future) existence of many standard tools for XML such as sophisticated editors and browsers. In this paper, we describe the system that we are currently implementing. We mainly focus on the functionalities it provides.

The paper is organized as follows. Section 2 introduces active view applications. Using an example, it illustrates the needs for the various functionalities of our system, presents the data model and query language on which we rely and the architecture of a running application. In Section 3, we show how the data part of the application is specified before considering active features in Section 4. Section 5 discusses the default application generated by the system and different ways to customize it. A more detailed description of the user interface to *ActiveView* is beyond the scope of the present paper.

[2] This mechanism existed already for C++ and we had to adapt it to the Java-O_2 binding.

2 General framework

In this section, we introduce active views. We briefly give some minimum background on XML. Finally, we present the architecture of the system.

2.1 Active views

An ActiveView application allows different users to work interactively on the same data in order to perform a particular set of controlled activities. An electronic commerce application, say, a virtual store, typically involves several types of *actors*, e.g, customers and vendors, and a significant amount of *data*, e.g. the products catalog (typically searched by customers) or the products promotion information (typically viewed by customers and updated by vendors). Each of the actors (i) *views* different parts of the repository data (e.g. a customer can only see his/her own orders and the promotions relevant to his/her category, while vendors may view all the orders and promotions), (ii) performs different *actions*, and (iii) has different *access rights* (e.g. promotions can be updated only by certain vendors). Also, the requirements for *freshness* of data differ. For example, when promotions are updated, we may want to immediately refresh the customers screen with the new data, whereas catalog updates are only propagated to the customer interface when the customer explicitly clicks on a specific "refresh" button.

Each actor typically performs several *activities* during a session. For example, a customer's activities might be *searching* the catalog, *ordering* products and *changing* a passed order. In each of these activities, we expect to show a different Web page to the actor that includes only that part of the data and actions which is useful for the specific activity.

The main contribution of ActiveViews is the declarative specification and automatic generation (by compilation) of Web applications which might else be produced only by large amounts of application specific code. We will first focus on the declarative specification. We will see in Section 5 various ways to customize the application that is automatically generated.

An ActiveView specification is a declarative description of an application which specifies for each kind of actor participating in the application: (i) the available data and operations, (ii) the various activities, and (iii) some active rules. Thus, the general specification of an application has the following form:

ActiveView application application_name

ActiveView actor-kind$_1$ **in application** application_name
 view data specification
 methods definition
 activities specification
 active rules ...
ActiveView actor-kind$_n$ **in application** application_name ...

Such a specification is compiled by the ActiveView system into some actual application that allows the different users to perform the given set of controlled activities, working interactively on the specified data. An ActiveView application may of course use an existing application of the repository and in some ways can also be seen as a means to export to the Web an existing database application in a controlled manner.

```
<catalog>
<name> the catalog </name>
<dept>
    <name> Books </name>
    <item myid="b1">
        <name> Leagues under the sea, J. Verne </name>
        <price> 4.75 </price>
        ....
        <suppliers supps="s1 s2" />
        <seealso otheritems="b2 b3"> Books by the same author </seealso>
    </item>
    <item myid="b2">
        <name> Around the world in 80 Days, J. Verne </name>
        ...
    </item>
....
</dept>
....
</catalogue>
```

Figure 1: The Catalog

We will detail in the following sections the syntax and semantics of the various parts of a view specification. In the remaining of this section, we briefly introduce the XML data model and query language on which the system relies and then give an overview of the architecture of an ActiveView application.

2.2 Data Model and Query Language

XML [23] is emerging as the new standard for data exchange on the Web. Its simplicity, the features and tools that it supports or will soon support (such as dynamic features, query language, sophisticated editors, browsers, etc.) makes it particularly attractive to both end-users and programmers. The database industry has recognized the potential of this new format and many vendors are now extending their technology so as to propose XML repositories (e.g., ArdentSoftware [6], Poet [16], ODI [13]). Given that and the fact that our goal is to support Internet applications such as electronic commerce, we chose this emerging technology as the basis for our work. For lack of space, the presentation of XML, DOM and the XML query language is rather brief. Full definition of XML, DOM, and the query language constructs can be found in [20, 19, 3, 2].

XML : Figure 1 shows an XML document corresponding to the catalog of some electronic commerce application. The `<item>` `</item>` tags are used to delimit the information corresponding to one catalog item, each item consisting of a sequence of tagged fields such as `name`, `price`, etc. Note that items can be given an identifier (e.g., `myid=''b1''`) which can be used to reference them within the document (e.g., in element `seealso`) or in some other documents. As a matter of fact, in our example, each item references a list of supplier elements (see field `suppliers`) that are defined in some other documents of our repository.

An XML document can be typed. This is achieved by means of a Document Type Definition (DTD). Typing is not a mandatory feature in XML, i.e. one can have documents,

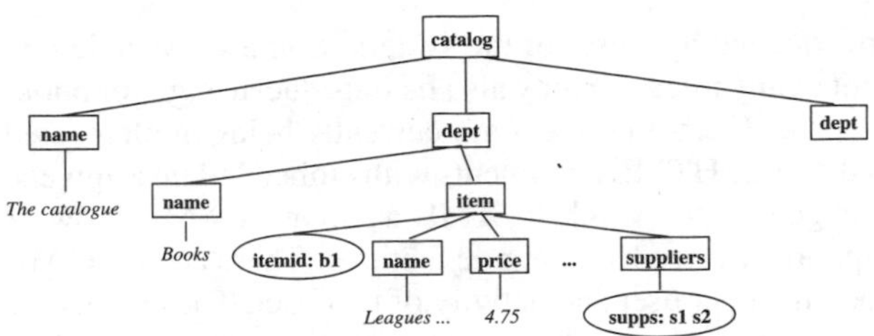

Figure 2: The Dom Representation of the Catalog

or document parts, without an associated DTD. However, since most optimization techniques rely on typing, it is realistic to assume that large XML applications will come with appropriate DTDs. In the sequel, we will denote element type definitions using the `Elem` suffix. For instance, `catalogElem` will denote the type definition associated with the catalog element `<catalog>...</catalog>` of the XML document in Figure 1. Also, we assume that (using XML namespace mechanism if needed) names of element types are unique in our context.

DOM (Document Object Model) provides an API to develop applications using XML data. It gives a uniform way to view and access XML documents. It is a standard and for instance, ArdentSoftware and Poet repositories use DOM interfaces. In DOM, an XML repository is abstractly described as a graph, whose internal nodes represent data elements and whose leaves represent text or attributes. As expected, the parent-child relationship typically represents the component-of relationship. This is illustrated by Figure 2 which shows a partial DOM representation of our catalog. Rectangles and ovals represent, respectively, element and attribute nodes.

The DOM standard basically consists of a collection of classes and methods, providing generic access and update interface for the different kinds of nodes in the graph. For instance, the `getElementsByTagName` method, when applied on an element node, returns all the sub-elements (children) of the node having the given tag name. In the sequel, we assume that the interface of each element type can support a set of methods defined within the XML repository.[3] This feature is essential for most applications, e.g., to define a method on `Dept` element that will allow to update the price of all its items according to some change of VAT.

Query Language : So far, XML does not provide a standard query language. However, there is a major standardization effort in that direction [8, 21, 22]. Our goal here is not to propose a new language or to compete against the up coming standard. Indeed, the ActiveView system will use this standard as soon as it becomes available. In the meantime, we rely on the Lorel language [3] to query DOM graphs.

For example, the following query searches for `Item` elements whose price is less than 50 within the catalog document of Figure 2.

select	i
from	i **in** Catalog.$\star$.Item
where	i.Price $<$ 50

Note that we use the "$\star$" symbol to denote paths of arbitrary length.

The above query constructs a new DOM node whose children are the selected `Item` elements. But what data exactly, besides the nodes corresponding to the selected items, is considered a part of the user's view? Does it include all the DOM graph rooted at these nodes? And what about referenced nodes? (e.g. should the suppliers referenced by the selected items be included or not?)

As observed in [2], it is useful in a distributed environment to provide in the query language means for specifying the exact scope of a query result. Furthermore, as we shall see later, this will also turn to be useful for specifying appropriate access rights for the retrieved data. We follow here the syntax of [2] and add a *with* clause to queries. This extra clause describes, using path expressions, the subgraph reachable from the selected elements to be included in the view. For example, when added to the above query, the clause *with i.name, i.price* specifies that only the `name` and `price` elements of each selected item should be viewed. In general, a *with* clause may contain complex path expressions and introduce new variables. We will see some examples of that in the sequel. Observe that the *with* clause is a nonstandard syntax we are using. We believe that an XML query language will support such a feature, possibly as a separate clause as here or embedded in the *select* clause of the query.

2.3 Architecture of an application

The ActiveView system is based on a three-tier architecture (Figure 3) composed of an (i) O_2 XML repository server and (ii) various repository clients which are communicating with (iii) remote Web user interfaces (standard Java enabled Web browsers). The O_2 XML repository server provides all the usual database features such as persistency, versioning, concurrency control, etc. An active view application (such as the one that will be specified in the next sections) consists of several independent repository clients communicating between them and with the repository server through notifications and the DOM programming interface. As can be noted, there are two kinds of repository clients: a single *active view application manager* for each application, and an *active view* client for each user connected to the system.

The ActiveView application manager consists of a set of modules managing: (i) connection and authentication, (ii) tracing, and (iii) active rules. More precisely:

- The connection/authentication module is in charge of authenticating users and giving them the means to create[4] or quit a view (via the network).

[3]Note in particular that this feature will be supported by the coming release of the ArdentSoftware XML repository.

[4]An active view is started from the Web using a particular URL.

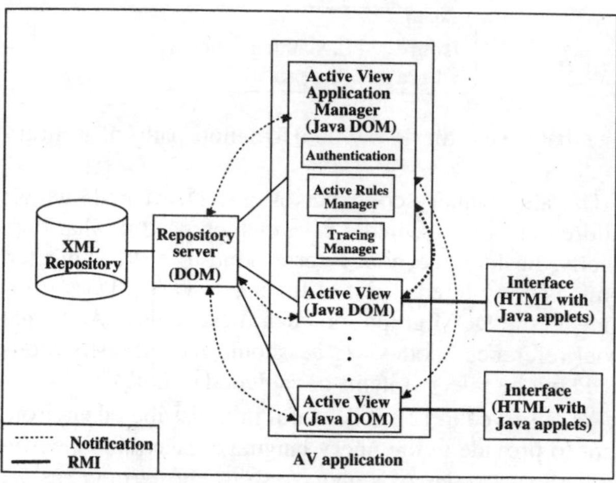

Figure 3: Three-tier Architecture of ActiveViews

- The tracing module keeps a log of specified events. These events are generated by the application or by some views.

- The active rule module manages a programmer-specified set of rules. (We will see their role in the application later on). These rules are fired according to events and may have impact on the repository and on some or all of the active views. They form the essential components to specify a business model.

The last two modules (tracer, rule manager) rely heavily on a stream of notifications managed by the repository server that enables the interaction between views at run time. These notifications are generated according to the views specification. Two kinds of events can be notified: (i) events generated by the repository server after the creation/deletion/update of objects and (ii) user defined events generated by the clients. The notifications mechanism on which we rely has been partially developed by the Verso team at INRIA.

An active view client is basically implemented as an instance of a subclass of a class called *ActiveView*, which is an abstraction of the class used in the actual implementation. This abstract class contains certain instance variables (whose role will be explained later), including in particular the *owner* instance variable that is used for storing information on the user initiating the view. The *ActiveView* class also defines some methods such as transaction/commit/abort to handle a transaction mode, or init/quit/sleep/resume to change the execution state of a view.

Each active view instance has access to the repository as well as to some local data (the instance variables of the view object). It reacts to user commands and may be refreshed according to notifications sent by the server or the application manager. The methods available in a view instance depend on the view specification and the users access rights and may read, update, write, etc. part or the whole the data it sees.

An active view is generally related to an actual Web window opened by a user of the system. Some views independent of any interface may also be introduced, e.g., for bookkeeping. Users interfaces are currently being implemented as dynamic HTML documents with embedded Java applets. Our goal is to switch to XML as soon as XML browser supports the needed dynamic features. There is one HTML document per user and activity of that user. The applets are built on top of an API generated by the system according to the view specification. Although the system generates default interfaces, the application programmer may redefine/customize them using the generated API that captures the semantics of the application.

In principle, the server, clients and interfaces may run on different machines. Typically, the interface is actually on a remote system. The view data is obtained by check-in/check-out, so the propagation of repository updates to the view can be controlled by the programmer. On the other hand, the view and the interface see the same data. In the current prototype, each ActiveView session corresponds to a Java repository client (Figure 3). We are aware that this solution is sufficient for managing simultaneous connections to only a restricted number of users and has to be improved by a more scalable architecture, e.g., based on threads.

3 Data and method specification

As stated in the previous section, an active view application involves several sorts of actors, each with a different view of the system. The specification of each kind of view consists of four parts that define respectively (i) data, (ii) methods, (iii) activities and (iv) active rules. In this section, we illustrate how the viewed data and the methods are specified and discuss related issues. The activities and active rules will be considered in the next section.

3.1 Data specification

An active view has local instance variables and derived ones defined using XML-queries. When specifying derived data, one also specifies the access modes (e.g., read). We illustrate this here using a very simple example in which we consider the interaction of three kinds of users: a set of *Customer*s and *Vendor*s and a single *Dispatcher*. A customer may browse the catalog, pass or modify an order. The dispatcher is in charge of assigning vendors to customers. At any time, there is only one active dispatcher. When someone tries to enter the system as a dispatcher, the person is simply turned down if a dispatcher is already in charge or if the person has not the proper qualification to be dispatcher. A vendor is mainly in charge of some customers and may interact with them, e.g., by offering them new promotions.

Consider first the customer view. A simple mode of importing data to the view is *read*. This is what is achieved for the catalog as follows:

let	catalog : CatalogElem
be	RepCatalog
with	catalog.⋆
mode	**read all**

This essentially imports the root element of the XML repository named *RepCatalog* (in our examples, the repository entry points are prefixed by *Rep*), and, as specified in the *with* statement, all the data in the *RepCatalog* document. That is, the entire DOM tree rooted at *RepCatalog* is imported. The *mode* clause specifies that we can read all we imported. This last statement is in fact not needed since the default on imported data is *read* for everything.

The possible modes beside *read* are *write*, *append*, and *remove*. An example of *append* in the *Vendor* active view is as follows:

let	promos: (PromoElem)*
be	RepPromos
with	promos.⋆
mode	**append** promos

This allows the vendors to see the set of promotions (implicit read) and to append new promotions to it. Removal of promotions from within the view is disallowed. The expression *(PromoElem)** indicates that the view document consists of a sequence of promotion elements[5]. To see a slightly more complex example, suppose vendors are also allowed to update the end-date of promotions. This is specified as follows:

let	promos: (PromoElem)*
be	RepPromos
with	promos.end-date X, promos.⋆
mode	**write** X, **append** promos

The query binds X to promotions *end-dates*. The expression *write X* indicates that these can be modified by vendors.

So far, we have defined only derived variables. Local instance variables are defined in the same way, except that they are not associated with a query specifying their value. Let us illustrate this with the variable *caddy* in the customer view.

local	caddy : (ItemElem)*
mode	**append**, **remove**

As illustrated above, the *with* clause is used to specify which data can be reached (i.e., viewed) from the objects bound to some query variables. Specifying this for each and every variable may be tedious, especially when the same element type is reachable from different variables and we want the same scope and access modes in all cases. One way to simplify the specification is to specify things at the element type level, i.e.. define for a given element type, the data that can be seen or modified when such elements are accessed.

To see an example, remember that the catalog contains references to suppliers. The following instruction, when added to the customer view, specifies that whenever a supplier element is included in the view, its name and full description are also included, in read mode (default), and its evaluations are included in an append mode (i.e., a customer may add his/her own evaluation of the supplier):

element	SupplierElem
with	self.name, self.description.⋆, self.evaluations E
mode	**append** E

3.2 More on read and write

We consider next two issues related to read/write. The first has to do with the materialization of derived instance variables. The second is related to writes and transactions.

An issue is whether the views that we are using are materialized or not (loaded in the client interface). In general, the system must decide whether a derived instance variable of the view is fully computed at initialization time, partially computed only (e.g., two levels of the tree of the query result are materialized), or computed (fully or partly) only when there are specific requests for data it contains.

The current default in the system is that instance variables are fully loaded at the initialization of the view. Also, when we read an instance variable, we read all elements specified by the *with* clause that are contained in the same document. Elements accessible by references to other documents are loaded only upon request. A similar philosophy is followed when reading an element based on an *element* specification. Observe however that certain applications may have some specific different requirements:

1. Consider an application that allows the user to check out a report to work on it at home, disconnected from the repository. Then the system should load the entire report. Suppose the report includes bibliographic citations that are references to some other bibliography document. The system should also load them immediately since the connection may not exist anymore when the user may request to see one of these citations.

2. On the other hand, consider a stock market application. We do not want to load in advance all trading rates since such information becomes rapidly stale. In this case it is better wait until a user explicitly requests a particular trading value before loading it.

To overrule the default, one can use two specific kinds of read modes, namely *deferred read* or *immediate read*. The first instructs the system to load elements only on demand, while the later indicates that elements should be loaded immediately when encountered. The keyword *read* can be replaced by one of these more specific modes anywhere in a view specification. For instance, one may add the keyword *deferred* to the *read* mode in the *Customer* specification of *catalog*. The elements contained in the catalog will then not be loaded at the initialization of the view but only upon explicit request from the customer.

[5]In some cases it is possible to derive the type of an XML query [12]. We will ignore this issue here.

Once some data is materialized and loaded into the client's interface, the user can view it or modify it, according to the specified access modes. Observe that these updates are not propagated to the database until explicitly requested by the user (i.e. by an explicit call to the *write* method that is part of the view interface). We will consider the problem of update propagation in more details later on. For now we only want to highlight the issue of transactions.

By default, a view is not in a transaction mode. Using base methods of the class *ActiveView*, a view can start a transaction and terminate it with an abort or commit. Reads are allowed outside transactions; so by default all reads requested by a view are *dirty*, i.e., no locks are installed. For updates, all updates *from a method call* in the repository issued by a view are required to be within a transaction. If an update is requested as a consequence of some method call and the view is not in transaction mode, an error is raised. The only exception is when the user issues an explicit call to the *write* method mentioned above. In this case, if the view is not already in a transaction, a new transaction is automatically started that lasts for the duration of the *write*.

3.3 Methods

The active view specification also includes definition of the methods available to the user in the given context. For example, assume that the dispatcher (more precisely, the user who is running a dispatcher view) is always aware of the connected customers in need of a vendor and of the active vendors. To support this, the dispatcher view may contain instance variables whose values are computed from the repository and describe the relevant customer and vendor sets. The dispatcher also has a method, namely *assign*, that allows to perform assignments, i.e., assign a customer to vendor. In the view specification, this method is defined as follows:

method	assign(v: Vendor, c: Customer)	**is** v→attend(c)

Note that the implementation of that method is specified in the view. But it essentially consists in calling some method known by the repository. Therefore, the view specification does not contain real code (besides XML queries) and is independent of any particular programming language. The methods in the XML repository may be in Java or C++ or in any language supported by DOM and the particular repository.

When activated by the application dispatcher, the above method will send a message to one specific vendor. This message will entail the execution of some code within the active view corresponding to the vendor (see Figure 3) and, potentially, the vendor interface will be modified. Another, sometimes more interesting way to modify a client interface, is to have it run its own code, independently from the repository server or the active view. In order to do, the ActiveView system allows the declaration of *remote methods*. For instance, one can specify the following remote method in the Vendor view:

remote method	new_customer (c: Customer)

and change the *assign* method to also invoke *new_customer*. Note that the code of the method is not specified. In the default application, it corresponds to a simple *message* with the name of the method as title and the parameters of the method as content. Thus in the default application, the vendor who is assigned to a new customer will receive a message titled "new_customer" with an object *Customer* in it. The visible portion of this object will have to be defined with an *element* statement in the *Vendor* specification. Now, as will be explained in Section 5, this default application is in fact built on top of an API, generated by the application compiler. A programmer desiring to customize the interface has the means to redefine the method *new_customer* which is executed locally when a call is received by the interface.

3.4 Access Rights

It should be stressed that access rights have to be much more sophisticated in the kind of Web applications we are targeting, e.g., electronic commerce applications, than in most standard repository applications. We therefore provide the means to attach an access predicate to any instance variable or method of a view. This predicate may use, for instance, the actual content of the view data and the user identification.

In general, access rights determine the modes of instance variables (e.g., read/write), and determine if methods are active or not. For instance, a customer may be disallowed to submit orders if its approved credit is negative or if he/she is in the group of blacklisted clients. This can be implemented by adding an access control clause to the specification of the method *submit_order*:

method	submit_order() **is** self.owner→pass_order(neworder)
if	(owner→approved_credit() >= 0 **and** !("blacklisted"**in** owner→group))

In the *if* clause, we allow arbitrary XML queries returning a boolean.

Remark : Access right may be quite expensive to check. In many cases, the access rights will depend only the parameters of the initialization procedure of the view. The access rights may then be evaluated once and for all during the initialization of the view. This optimization may result in enormous gains in performance. But observe that it may be difficult to detect that it is indeed the case that some rights depend only on immutable values of the view. So, to indicate to the compiler that access writes have to be computed at initialization only, one can use the clause *static if* instead of *if* to specify the access rights. ◇

To conclude this section, we consider the issue of update propagation.

3.5 Update propagation

In one direction, when a derived attribute is modified in the view and a *write* is requested, we have to propagate the change from the view to the repository. In the other direction, when the repository changes and a *read* is requested for some derived attribute whose value was already previously computed for the view, we have to propagate the changes from the repository to the view. The detection of changes will be considered in Section 4.

Let us consider first the *view update* problem. We touch here upon one critical issue in databases. Most works on view updates have focused on updating views defined by complex relational queries involving joins and projections, e.g., [7]. This is a quite complex problem that we avoid here by an extensive use of objects and simply disallowing updates to views defined by too complex queries.

We maintain a correspondence between the repository and the modifiable portion of the view. In the best cases, an atomic value in the view (say a string) corresponds to an atomic value in the repository and the modification of the value in the view is easily propagated to the repository. In other cases, a view value does not have any exact correspondence in the repository (e.g., it is defined as a selection on some collection). We can still accept the update and propagate it to the repository in some simple unambiguous cases. In many cases, we simply disallow the update through the view unless the application programmer provides a method for it – and in that case, the system is not responsible for correctly propagating the update.

We mention next two important cases where the update is propagated, more on the subject can be found in [1]:

1. Strict correspondence between two collections: this is the case when each element in the repository collection has a corresponding element in the view, e.g., a set of objects and the same set of objects with a different interface specified by the view. Updates to elements are propagated when possible, i.e., when the propagation is defined at the element level. If an element is removed from the collection, we remove it from the corresponding repository collection. If one is inserted, we construct a corresponding element (eventually with a default value) if possible.

2. Partial correspondence between collections: this may happen if the view is obtained by filtering only some elements in a repository collection (and possibly restructuring them). This is a case quite frequent in practice that raises a number of issues. The main difficulty is upon insertion of an element (in the view) to verify that the view element that has been inserted when propagated to the repository actually results in an object that passes the filtering test. If this is not the case, the update is simply rejected.

To illustrate the previous discussion, we consider a definition of *Customer* where a customer may modify his orders by updating an instance variable *myorders* defined in the view:

let	myorders: (MyOrderElem)*	
be	**select**	O
	from	O **in** RepOrders
	where	O.buyer = owner
with	O.*	
mode	**write all except** O.buyer	

A customer may now update the result of a filtering of the entire set of orders, *RepOrders*. The system maintains a correspondence between the elements of *myorders* and those of *RepOrders*, so that an update to such elements can be propagated to the repository. The removal of such an element would result in removing the corresponding element from *RepOrders*. The addition of a new element would result in adding a new order to *RepOrder*. Observe that the customer cannot modify the identity of the buyer who issued a passed order because of *except O.buyer*. However, as it is defined here, the customer may in principle add a new order as if it was issued by another customer by simply putting the description of another customer in the *buyer* field. This could be anticipated using active rules to be defined further.

Let us now consider the *repository update propagation* problem. An issue is the re-computation of some view values when the database changes. Suppose that a user has loaded in a view the catalog and asks to re-read this catalog at some later time. The sequence of updates between the two reads is not available. One may consider using the repository versioning mechanism. It would suffice to compute the Δ between the version the user has and the current version. Clearly, sending a Δ instead of the entire value may result in large saving in communication. Versions are not considered in the ActiveView system for the moment. We will see further how, in some cases, we may have the list of updates and consider directly the incremental maintenance of the view.

4 Active features

The previous section considered the static part of the view definition. We now illustrate how a view can be made active. Note that we touch here a subject in close relation with workflow management. The main difference between our approach and workflows is the importance we give to data specification.

Workflow systems give declarative means for specifying the operations flow, but the data involved is typically described in a very abstract manner, often disconnected from the description of the flow itself. This makes the analysis of the connection between various pieces of information, their sources, and mutual effect of operations on them, very hard. A good example is the newly adopted standard, UML [14], which includes state-charts and activity diagrams for business process modeling but where data objects, whose value are used or determined by the action, are modeled only as parameters of some messages.

Most workflow models available today lack a semantic definition other than the operational definition implied by the tools [10]. The meta-model proposed by the Workflow Management Coalition [18] connects input and output data to activity, but doesn't provide implementation details. Due to lack of concrete guidelines, workflow management system as promoted by industry, uses a process-centric approach. Those models are extended by customized features for modeling and executing applications, but do not have adequate support to satisfy the modeling and correctness requirements of advanced applications [5]. Some of the deficiencies include lack of support to keep track of data dependencies for distributed workflow, lack of support to control concurrent accesses to objects managed by non-transactional activities, insufficient support for recovery etc.

In our system, activities are specified in two steps. First, for each kind of actors (i.e., each view), the programmer declares a set of activities along with the data and methods that can be used in those activities. Then, a set of rules specifies the semantics of the view. Typically, rules specify how to react to certain events. Two particular kinds of rules are of particular importance: (i) notification rules that allow to be notified that certain events took place, and (ii) *tracing rules* that allow to keep a log of some selected events.

We next consider the declaration of activities, the general rules, then the notification and tracing rules.

4.1 Declaring Activities

From end-user viewpoint, each activity corresponds to a hypertext document with some data and buttons. For instance, the activity *search* defined within a customer view will show the catalog, some promotions, a collection of selected items (i.e., a caddy) and some buttons allowing the user to search the catalog, add some items to the caddy, order (i.e., change activity) or quit the application. This is specified as follows:

```
activity   search   includes
           catalog, promotions, caddy
           search(), goto_order(), add_to_caddy(), quit()
```

A default stylesheet is attached to each activity. More generally, an activity declaration has the following form:

```
activity   <activity-name>   includes
           <variable-name>* <method-name>* | all
```

where <variable-name> (resp. <method-name>) denote variables (resp. methods) specified within the view where the activity is being defined. The keyword *all* may be used to specify that all variables and methods of the view are visible.

It should be noted that although a given activity sees only a specific part of the view stated in its definition, *all* the ActiveView data is maintained (at least virtually) by the system. This allows different non consecutive activities to share data, and is in particular useful when a user resumes some activity after having gone temporarily to another one.

4.2 Rules

We consider here very standard active rules. Rules are specified inside a view. If global rules need to be considered in an application, one can clearly add a particular view that does it in the style of the *Dispatcher* of our example application. This provides some modular way of specifying active rules.

The specification of a view may therefore contain some active rules. The rules are processed by a *rule manager*. Rules are expressions of the form:

```
on <event> if <condition> do <action>
```

The components of an active rule are defined as follows:

- the events are (remote) methods calls (e.g., switch of activity), operations on instance variables or objects (i.e., write/read/append/remove) and detection of changes;
- the conditions are XML queries returning a boolean; and
- the actions are (remote) methods calls, operations on instance variables or objects, notifications or traces.

We illustrate active rules with some simple examples. The discussions on variable changes, notifications and traces are postponed to the following sections.

Suppose that when a new order is issued, we want to modify the stock of the store. This may be achieved by a method, say *update-stock*. The following rule in the *Dispatcher* view may be used:

```
on   submit_order(owner,neworder)
do   neworder→update-stock()
```

(An absent *if* clause is assumed to be always true.)

Next, let us consider remote method calls. For instance, suppose that a remote method *missive* has been defined in the *Customer* view and that we want to send a particular welcome-back message to good customers when then start their *search* activity. This can be achieved by defining the following rule:

```
on   goto (owner, activity)
if   activity = Customer::search and "good-customer"
     in owner→group
do   owner→missive("Welcome back.
     We appreciate your business.")
```

Observe that the bindings of *activity* and *owner* in the triggering event is used by the *if* clause.

4.3 Notifications and change monitoring

Notifications are based on remote method calls that can be sent to the interface of a view to notify that certain events (as specified in the previous section) have occurred. An important kind of events are (potential) changes of an instance variable. In the application default interface, the detection of a change for an instance variable (or an object) results in changing the background color for the display of the variable. The notification of other events results in a message being displayed to the user with a "notification" icon. These messages resemble the remote method calls we already discussed. Indeed, notification may be customized in the same manner as remote method calls.

To see an example, suppose all vendors need to be notified of submissions of important orders by customers they are in charge of. This is achieved by the following rule in the *Vendor* view:

on	submit_order(owner,neworder)
if	neworder.amount > 10000 **and** owner **in** MyCustomers
do	**notify-me**

In this statement, the keyword *notify-me* specifies that the particular event must be notified to this view. In some sense, the view is issuing a *subscription* to certain events. Observe that only the views that explicitly subscribe are notified.

Now, let us consider derived instance variable monitoring. It is easy to detect that a repository object has changed. If an instance variable is defined by a complex query, the situation is more intricate. To see an example, consider the instance variable *promos* in the *Customer* view. In order to have the customer be notified of a change in its *promos*, the following rule must be included (*changed_promos* indicates that the variable *promos* has changed):

on	changed_promos	**do**	**notify-me**

The variable *promos* may change if a new promotion that applies to the particular customer is appended or deleted. It may also change if one existing promotion is modified. The view therefore maintains the list of objects whose change may affect the derived data. (In this case, the collection object and each element in the collection.) When such a possible change has been detected, two cases occur:

1. The derived data cannot be maintained incrementally. In this case a notification is issued. Clearly, this may result in false "alarms".

2. The derived data can be maintained incrementally. An incremental evaluation of the changes is performed in the style of [2] to see whether actually changes occurred. No false alarm may occur.

Notification are just warnings. Data can be updated by the user by clicking on a *read* button or, automatically, by a customized user-interface (Section 5). Even when an incremental evaluation has been used and the new value is known by the system, it is sent to the client only when requested. It is possible to include in the view a rule to actually force changes to be sent to the client whenever detected. For instance, one could use the rule:

on	changed_promos	**do**	promos→read()

In this particular case, the derived instance variable is simple enough to be maintainable incrementally. In case (2), such a statement may be costly since each detection of possible change will trigger the full re-computation of the instance variable and its shipping to the client.

Remark : The need to "monitor" instance variables or to "refresh" them when changes occur is encountered in many applications. We therefore provide syntactic shortcuts to specify such features without having to explicitly write the corresponding rules. Instead of using *let <variable>* in the view specification, one may use *let monitored <variable>* or *let fresh <variable>*. This results in generating the appropriate rules to notify changes and eventually (in the case of *fresh*) trigger automatically a read when a change is detected.

4.4 Traces

Typically, database systems provide *logs* that are (i) low level and (ii) difficult or impossible to access. Yet, tracing the run of a business transaction is essential for electronic commerce applications. This may be required for legal reasons, to be able to handle eventual disputes between the participants, or to analyze buying patterns. In ActiveView, events and rules are at the core of the *tracer* module. We explain this next.

In a view specification, in the same manner we request to notify the view of certain events, we can request to *trace* them, i.e., notify the tracer. For instance, we may request to trace all order submissions:

on	submit_order(owner,neworder)	**do**	**trace**

If such a statement is included, the tracer will be notified of the new orders and record them in the repository. The tracer also records the parameters and the time of the event. The log can then be viewed as a partial history of the activity of the application and can be queried. For instance, the following query returns the orders of a particular customer in 1998:

select	O
from	O in Trace.submit_order
where	O.neworder.buyer.name = "J. Doe" **and** O.date = 98

In this query, *Trace* is an entry-point to the XML repository that allows to access traces.

5 Default interface and customization

Compared to traditional database applications, electronic commerce and, more generally, Web applications are evolving very rapidly according to new commercial needs. For this reason, the ActiveView system not only supports the declarative definition of views and activities on the server side, but also a fast exploitation on the end-user side by generating *default user interfaces*. In this section, we briefly discuss the default interface, then various means of customizing the application and its interface.

5.1 Default User-Interface

When a user starts a new active view client by following a URL link, e.g.

http://www.activestore.com/customer,

a default HTML page is displayed and asks for identification information before proposing all possible activities that can be executed by the registered user. For example, all unregistered clients may be able to browse the catalog (activity *search*), but only registered users can also buy the selected products (activity *pay*).

Activities form the basic interface metaphors perceived by end-users (e.g. client) interacting with the ActiveView system. Each activity is represented by a distinct HTML page which displays all accessible variables and methods in form of simple applets/buttons. (As previously mentioned, we intend to move soon to XML and stylesheets.) Applets are necessary to implement active features for calling methods and modifying/monitoring variables by communicating with the system via Java RMI calls (see architecture in Figure 3). Essentially, each variable corresponds to an applet editing the variable value and providing specific buttons for all access modes (read/write/append/remove) defined in the view.

The editing of view variable is an interesting issue. The ActiveView system is based on the XML document model and some XML query language for representing and querying data. This also means that variable values are XML fragments that should be *dynamically* merged into a comprehensive and uniform XML document. Whereas this issue is outside the scope of this paper, we believe that future XML browsers will propose some script language for modifying documents dynamically based on the DOM standard. Observe that a similar mechanism is already existing for HTML browsers in form of the JavaScript language.

View methods are called by simple button clicks. For example, in order to add a product to the caddy, the user calls a method *add_to_caddy* which adds a selected product to the caddy. Observe that this assumes to be able to select a product, e.g., in the catalog, and provide it as argument to *add_to_caddy*.

5.2 Application Customization

As defined so far an ActiveView application includes practically no code besides XML queries. Although we did not insist on that, it is clear that it may call repository methods that are implemented in conventional (DOM compatible) programming languages such as C++ or Java. Such code may be part of database application somewhat independent of the view application itself. View applications can also be customized in various ways at the cost of writing some *view specific* code. For instance, one may want to redefine the authentication procedure or the HTML page layout. Customization is briefly considered next.

Customizing view components : Each Web client interface is communicating with an active view which is an instance of a subclass of class *ActiveView*. For instance, *Customer* is a particular subclass of *ActiveView*. Instances of this class provide the necessary functionalities for logging into the system (init, owner, start_date), choosing among available activities and controlling the view status (quit, transaction, commit, abort, sleep, resume, timeout, see Section 3 for details). The class features also instance variables (i) the kind of the view (e.g. *vendor*, *client*), (ii) the owner, (iii) the date of creation, (iv) the current status (running, asleep), (v) the current activity, and (vi) the list of other available activities.

Customization essentially is possible by creating subclasses and overloading existing method codes. For example, the *init* method is executed when a new user logs into the system (creates a new view instance). It executes a private *authentication* method that verifies (by password or more sophisticated third-party authentication services) the identity of the user and fills in the value of *owner*. Both methods *init* and *authentication* are defined in the class *ActiveView* and may be redefined in a subclass, e.g., *Customer*, by the administrator, for example, to change the access right rule (Section 3), authorization mechanism or add additional preprocessing.

To see another example, consider *timeout*. Since active view applications run over the network there is no means to control the liveliness of a network client. Therefore, view objects come equipped with a simple timeout method that may force a view into *sleep* mode if the view has been inactive for too long. (The "too long" is specified by default.) The application programmer may decide to redefine this method in a particular subclass of *ActiveView* and indeed may also make it take into consideration some values of the view or specific resource parameters (transmit rate, client architecture, ...).

Customizing the interface : One may customize the interface at several levels: presentation, method redefinition or total rewriting of the interface.

Users choose among various activities which correspond (by default) to different HTML and, in the future, XML pages. At the lowest level, it is obviously very easy to modify the presentation of an XML page by simply changing the stylesheet. Note that by doing so, one may hide certain functionalities of the particular activity.

Each interface is attached to a particular activity that specifies the available data and (remote) methods. Each such interface is implemented by an applet that communicates with a remote object that corresponds to that particular *Activity*. For instance, we may have an *Activity:Customer* class. It is possible to redefine the code of some methods of the class. As mentioned in Section 3, remote methods have to be implemented by the user interface. The default behavior of methods, i.e. display the parameters on the screen, can be modified. For instance, when a vendor receives the notification that a new customer is assigned to him/her, the interface might save in a local file the data about this particular customer.

Finally, one may want to completely redefine the interface to some activity, e.g., *Activity:Customer*. The API to the ActiveView system for this activity remains fixed. It is however possible to develop a Java applet (or application) that interacts with the ActiveView system via this particular API.

Acknowledgments

We thank V. Vianu, B. Fordham and Y. Yesha for works with one of the authors [4] that somewhat initiated the present work. The first prototype of the system was implemented by S. Arnoud, M. Bani, R. Dhaou and F. Hubert. V. Aguilera, S. Ailleret, B. Hills, A. Marian and B. Tessier are thanked for their work on the second prototype. We also thank G. Ferran, S. Gamerman, J.C. Mamou (from ArdentSoftware) and A. Sahuguet for discussions on this work. Finally, members of the Verso and Rodin groups at INRIA provided valuable comments, and in particular, S. Amer-Yahia, J. Siméon and A.M. Vercoustre.

References

[1] S. Abiteboul, S. Cluet, and T. Milo. A logical view of structured files. *The VLDB Journal*, 7(2), May 1998.

[2] S. Abiteboul, J. McHugh, M. Rys, V. Vassalos, and J. L. Wiener. Incremental maintenance for materialized views over semistructured data. In *Int. Conf. on Very Large Databases (VLDB)*, New-York, August 1998.

[3] S. Abiteboul, D. Quass, J. McHugh, J. Widom, and J. L. Wiener. The lorel query language for semistructured data. *International Journal on Digital Libraries*, 1(1), April 1997.

[4] S. Abiteboul, V. Vianu, B. Fordham, and Y. Yesha. Relational transducers for electronic commerce. In *ACM SIGACT-SIGMOD-SIGART Symposium on Principles of Database Systems (PODS)*, pages 179–187, New York, USA, 1998.

[5] G. Alonso, D. Agrawal, A. El Abbadi, Mohan. U. Kamath, R. Guenthoer, and C. Mohan. Advanced transaction models in workflow contexts. In *Proc. Int. Conference on Data Engineering*, 1996.

[6] Ardent Software. *http://www.ardentsoftware.fr*.

[7] F. Bancilhon and N. Spyratos. Update semantics of relational views. *ACM Transactions on Database Systems*, 6(4):557–575, 1981.

[8] A. Deutsch, M. Fernandez, D. Florescu, A. Levy, and D. Suciu. Xml-ql: A query language for xml. http://www.w3.org/TR/NOTE-xml-ql/.

[9] A. L. Furtado and M. A. Casanova. Updating relational views. In W. Kim, D.S. Reiner, and D.S. Batory, editors, *Query Processing in Database Systems*. Springer-Verlag, New York, 1985.

[10] M. U. Kamath and K. Ramamritham. Bridging the gap between transaction management and workflow management. In *In NSF Workshop on Workflow and Process Automation in Information Systems, Athens, Georgia*, 1996.

[11] A. M. Keller. Updates to relational databases through views involving joins. In Peter Scheuermann, editor, *Improving Database Usability and Responsiveness*. Academic Press, New York, 1982.

[12] T. Milo and D. Suciu. Type inference for queries on semistructured data. In *ACM Principles of Database Systems (PODS)*, 1999.

[13] Objectstore. *http://www.odi.com*.

[14] OMG. Uml notation guide, version 1.1, 1 september 1997, 1997. http://www.omg.org/techprocess/meetings/schedule/-Technology_Adoptions.htm.

[15] Philippe Picouet and Victor Vianu. Semantics and expressiveness issues in active databases. *Journal of Computer and System Sciences*, 57(3):325–355, December 1998.

[16] Poet. *http://www.poet.com*.

[17] C. Souza, S. Abiteboul, and C. Delobel. Virtual schemas and bases. In *Proc. EDBT, Cambridge*, 1994.

[18] WfMC standards. The workflow reference model, version 1.1, wfmc-tc-1003,19-jan-95, 1995. http://www.aiim.org/wfmc/mainframe.htm.

[19] W3C. Document object model (dom). http://www.w3.org/DOM.

[20] W3C. Extensible markup language (xml) 1.0. http://www.w3.org/TR/REC-xml.

[21] W3C. Extensible stylesheet language (xsl). http://www.w3.org/Style/XSL/.

[22] W3C. The w3c query languages workshop, dec 1998, boston, massachussets. http://www.w3.org/TandS/QL/QL98/cfp.html.

[23] W3C. The word wide web consortium. http://www.w3.org/.

[24] J. Widom and S. Ceri. *Active Database Systems: Triggers and Rules for Advanced Database Processing*. Morgan-Kaufmann, San Francisco, California, 1995.

[25] Yelena Yesha and Nabil Adam. Electronic commerce: An overview. In Nabil Adam and Yelena Yesha, editors, *Electronic Commerce*. Lecture Notes in Computer Science, Springer-Verlag, 1996.

An Adaptive Hybrid Server Architecture for Client Caching Object DBMSs*

Kaladhar Voruganti M. Tamer Özsu
University of Alberta
Edmonton, Canada

Ronald C. Unrau
Cygnus Solutions
Sunnyvale, California

Abstract

Current client-server object database management systems employ either a page server or an object server architecture. Both of these architectures have their respective strengths, but they also have key drawbacks for important system and workload configurations. We propose a new hybrid server architecture which combines the best features of both page server and object server architectures while avoiding their problems. The new architecture incorporates new or adapted versions of data transfer, recovery, and cache consistency algorithms; in this paper we focus only on the data transfer and recovery issues. The data transfer mechanism allows the hybrid server to dynamically behave as both page and object server. The performance comparison of the hybrid server with object and page servers indicates that the performance of the hybrid server is more robust than the others.

1 Introduction

We propose a new hybrid server architecture for client-server object database management systems (ODBMSs) which can dynamically adapt and operate either as a page server or as an object server. Our fundamental thesis is that page servers and object servers are generally preferable under a limited set of system and workload configurations [DFMV90, CFZ94, DFB+96] and adaptive techniques that combine the features of both are likely to respond better to a larger class of system and workload configurations. Moreover, object servers are not as popular as page servers, because previous performance studies have shown that object servers are not scalable with respect to data transfer [DFMV90] and concurrency control/cache consistency algorithms [CFZ94]. In this paper we present new techniques and report performance results that show that objects servers can compete with page servers.

*This research is supported in part by the Natural Sciences and Engineering Research Council (NSERC) of Canada.

Proceedings of the 25th VLDB Conference
Edinburgh, Scotland, 1999

1.1 Background

Object servers and page servers are the two competing data-shipping architectures employed by the existing ODBMSs [DFMV90, CFZ94]. In data-shipping systems, the clients fetch data from the server into their caches and perform some of the database processing locally. Thus, from scalability standpoint, clients help the server from becoming a bottleneck by off-loading some of the work. Prefetching useful data also reduces effective network latency. Figure 1 presents a classification of the different data-shipping ODBMSs according to their data transfer mechanism. In data-shipping object server systems (THOR, Versant), the server responds to client data requests by returning logical objects to the client (the first column in Figure 1). In page server data-shipping systems (ObjectStore, BeSS, O2, SHORE), the server responds to client data requests by returning physical disk pages to the client (the second column in Figure 1). Thus, the granularity of the data transferred from the server to the clients is the key distinguishing factor between object and page servers. The data transfer granularity from the server to the client, in turn, has an impact on buffer management, concurrency control, recovery and pointer swizzling algorithms. These issues are discussed in Section 2.

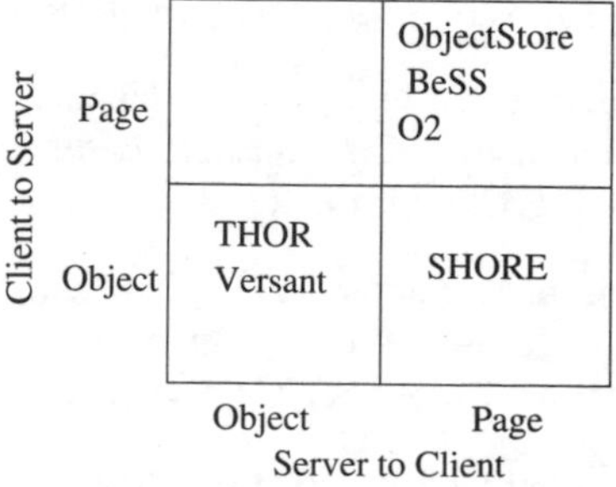

Figure 1: ODBMS Client-Server Architecture Classification According to the Data Transfer Mechanism

1.2 Motivation For Adaptive Hybrid Server

The need for a hybrid client-server architecture was recognized from the very beginning of client-server ODBMS research [DFMV90], because the page server and object server architectures are desirable under different (but overlapping) sets of workloads and system configurations. However, there has been no hybrid server system design that can dynamically change its mode of operation to effectively satisfy the needs of different workloads and system configurations.

Page server systems can outperform object servers when the application data access pattern matches the data clustering pattern on disk (which we refer to in the rest of the paper as good clustering) [DFMV90]. By receiving pages under good clustering, the clients in the page server architecture are able to prefetch useful objects that they will likely use in the future. Prefetching helps to amortize communication costs in page servers. In comparison, object servers incur higher communication overhead since they transfer individual objects from the server to the client [DFMV90]. However, when the data clustering pattern on disk does not match the data access pattern (bad clustering), transferring the entire page from the server to the clients is counter-productive since this increases the network overhead and decreases client buffer utilization. Dual client buffer schemes [KK94, CALM87], which allow the storage of well clustered pages and isolated objects from badly clustered pages help improve client buffer utilization.

Page servers are inefficient for the emerging hybrid function-shipping/data-shipping architectures [KJF96] where, in addition to requesting data from the server, the clients also send queries to be processed at the server. The server processes the queries and returns only the results back to the client. If a query result is spread across multiple disk pages each of which contains only a few objects, then it is very inefficient to send all of the disk pages to the client [DFB+96].

An important study on clustering [TN92] has shown that it is difficult to come up with good clustering when multiple applications with different data access patterns access the same data. Therefore, good clustering cannot be taken for granted and the problem of transferring badly clustered pages is a fundamental issue in page servers.

The data transfer problem of object servers can be resolved by transferring a group of objects rather than a single object from the server to the client (so called grouped object servers). A dynamic object grouping mechanism has been proposed [LAC+96] that makes grouped object servers competitive with page servers with respect to the data transfer mechanism. However, grouped object servers incur higher group forming/breakup overhead than page servers when clustering is good. Thus, there is a need for an architecture which deals with pages when the clustering is good. Cache consistency/concurrency control is still a problem in object servers because they send separate lock escalation messages (for escalating from read lock to write lock) to the server for each object [CFZ94]. Page servers are able to send lock escalation messages at the granularity of a page and are thus able to reduce locking related communication overhead. In order to avoid this problem, object servers typically use optimistic concurrency control algorithms which have no explicit lock escalation messages [LAC+96]. However, the resulting high abort rate is undesirable from performance and usability standpoints [OVU98]. Thus, at present, there does not exist an efficient, low abort concurrency control/cache consistency algorithm for object servers. Object server recovery has been a neglected area, perhaps partially as a result of giving up on object servers due to their perceived problems. Currently there are no published object server recovery algorithms that are comparable, performance-wise, to the page server recovery algorithms [MN94, FZT+92]. Finally, when clients in the object server architecture return updated objects to the server, the server has to re-install these updated objects on their corresponding home page (redo-at-server recovery) before writing the page back to disk. If the server buffer is heavily contended, then the home pages might not be present in the server buffers necessitating installation reads to retrieve the home pages from disk. The proponents of object servers have introduced the notion of a modified object buffer (MOB) [Ghe95] at the server. The MOB stores the updated objects that have been returned by the clients. The MOB helps to intelligently schedule a group of installation reads and thus reduce the installation read overhead. However, in workloads where the clients are updating large portions of a page, it is desirable to return updated pages to the server. Thus, a client-server architecture must be flexible and should allow for the return of updated pages from the client to the server.

1.3 Paper Scope and Contributions

In this paper we propose an adaptive hybrid server architecture which adjusts its behavior between a page and an object server, and is thus able to incorporate the strengths of both page and object servers. The adaptive hybrid server architecture incorporates the following contributions:

1. An adaptive data transfer mechanism that dynamically decides whether to ship pages or objects between the server and the client.

2. A new efficient object server recovery mechanism, which is used by the hybrid server and can also be adopted by existing object server architectures.

3. An efficient, low abort rate cache consistency algorithm for object servers. *Asynchronous avoidance-based cache consistency* (AACC) algorithm [OVU98] for page servers has been shown to have both good performance and and a low abort rate. We adapt AACC for object servers.

We compare the performance of the hybrid server with three other prominent architectures: grouped object servers, page servers that use hardware page faulting, and page servers that use software page handling. The results, reported in Section 5, show that performance-wise the hybrid server architecture is more robust than the others. Besides these results, the performance study is important in its own right for two reasons:

Data Transfer		Cache Consistency				Buffer Management		Recovery		Pointer Swizzling	
Page	Object	Page		Object		Page	Object	Page	Object	Page	Object
		Low Abort	High Abort	Low Abort	High Abort						
[DFVM90] [OS94] [BP95]	[GK94] [LAC+96] [This Paper]	[FC94] [CFZ94] [FCL96] [OVU98]	[AGLM95]	[CFZ94] [This Paper]	[AGLM95]	[KK94] [CALM97]	[Ghe95]	[FZT+92] [MN94] [WD95] [PBJR96]	[KGBW90] [This Paper]	[LLOW91] [WD94]	[LAC+96] [This Paper]

Figure 2: Decade of research into page and object server ODBMSs

1. This is the first multi-user client-server performance study that compares the performance of page servers and grouped object servers. Previous studies either focused on single-user systems [DFMV90, CDN93, LAC+96], or they did not consider grouped object servers [DFMV90, CFZ94].

2. This is the first multi-user client-server performance study that looks at data transfer, buffer management, cache consistency, concurrency control, recovery and pointer-swizzling system components in an integrated manner. Currently, the existing ODBMS products use different combinations of algorithms for these system components, and due to the interaction between them, it is difficult to properly assess the strengths and weakness of the different architectures under a range of important workloads.

1.4 Paper Organization

Section 2 discusses the related work. Section 3 presents the new hybrid server architecture. Section 4 describes the experimental setup and workloads. In Section 5 we present results of our experiments. Section 6 contains a discussion of the experiment results and Section 7 contains our conclusions.

2 Related Work

Figure 2 summarizes the client-server ODBMS research that has been performed over the last decade on topics relevant to this paper. These play a significant role in determining the overall performance of data-shipping client-server ODBMSs. In this section we summarize the research that has been conducted into data transfer, cache consistency, buffer management, recovery and pointer swizzling.

Data Transfer: The initial client-server performance study [DFMV90] identified page server, object server, and file server as the three alternative client-server architectures. A key conclusion was that page servers are desirable when the data access pattern matches the data clustering pattern on disk. This study prompted the development of prefetching techniques for both page and object servers [GK94, LAC+96]. A static hybrid data transfer mechanism has been implemented in Ontos [CDN93] in which, for each object type, the application programmers specify whether they want to deal with objects or pages. In this paper we propose a dynamic hybrid data transfer mechanism which uses run-time information to automatically adapt itself and operate as either a page or an object server. A partial hybrid server architecture in which the server always sends pages to the clients, but the clients can dynamically choose to return either updated pages or updated objects has been proposed [OS94]. This flexibility requires revisions in the concurrency control and recovery mechanisms, but these have not been addressed in the partial hybrid server proposal. Moreover, the study was in favor of architectures that return pages because clients updated a large portion of a page. This increased server buffer utilization and led to their algorithm always returning updated pages if they are present in the client cache. Our performance results show that returning pages is not always desirable. Finally, while dealing with large objects that span multiple pages, it is desirable to be able to transfer only portions of the large object between clients and servers. Both page and object servers have to be modified to ensure that the entire large object is not transferred as a single unit between the server and the client. Our proposal is a full hybrid architecture where both the server and the clients can transfer pages or objects. As discussed in Section 3, our proposal addresses many of the issues raised above.

Cache Consistency: Most of the existing cache consistency research has been conducted within the context of page servers (for an excellent survey see [FCL96]). For most user workloads, invalidation of remote cache copies during updates is preferred over propagation of updated values to the remote client sites. Moreover, caching of read-locks across transactions at the clients is preferred over caching of both read and write-locks [FC94]. It has been shown that adaptive locking algorithms that switch between page level and object level locks are more robust than purely page level locking algorithms [CFZ94]. Cache consistency algorithms have been classified as avoidance-based and detection-based algorithms [FCL96]. Avoidance-based algorithms do not allow for the presence of stale data (data that has been updated and committed by remote clients) in client caches, whereas detection-based algorithms permit clients to have stale data in their caches and abort transactions (*stale cache* aborts) when they have accessed stale data. Client cache consistency algorithms can also be classified according to when the clients send a lock escalation message to the server. Clients can send lock escalation messages in a synchronous, asynchronous or deferred manner [FCL96]. In a previous paper we showed that a new adaptive algorithm, called *asynchronous avoidance-based cache consistency* (AACC), outperforms other leading cache consistency algorithms [OVU98] such as ACBL [CFZ94], which is a synchronous avoidance-based algorithm, and AOCC [AGLM95] which is a deferred detection-based algorithm. AACC is an avoidance-based algorithm, and, therefore, it has a much lower abort rate than AOCC. It uses asynchronous lock escalation messages to have lower blocking overhead than ACBL, and a lower abort rate than deferred avoidance-based algorithms. AACC also piggybacks lock escalation messages while updating data that is not cached at multiple clients to reduce its message handling overhead. Finally, since there currently does not exist a cache consistency algorithm for object servers that provides both high performance and low abort rate we have modified the page-based AACC for object servers.

Pointer Swizzling: The pointer-swizzling research has led to the development of hardware-based and software-based algorithms [WD94]. In the former the page level virtual memory facilities provided by the operating system are used to eagerly swizzle the pointers on a page. In the latter, a function call interface is provided to the client applications to access the pointers. The function code performs residency checks and dereferencing of pointers. In software swizzling, the swizzled pointers usually point to the target object's entry in an indirection data structure (object table). Thus, there is a level of indirection while traversing from the source object to the target object. Page servers can use either the hardware or the software pointer swizzling mechanism, but object servers use only software-based pointer swizzling, since it is inefficient to reserve virtual memory frames at the object level. Currently, most of the hardware pointer swizzling mechanisms store the swizzled in-memory version of the object identifiers on disk [WD94, LLOW91]. Since the in-memory version of an object identifier is usually smaller than the on-disk version, this reduces the size of the objects on disk, which, in turn, leads to fewer disk I/Os (in comparison to the software swizzling algorithms) while reading the objects from disk [WD94]. The second advantage of storing swizzled pointers on disk is that if a client's working set fits completely into its virtual memory address space, then the hardware pointer swizzling mechanism has to swizzle the on-disk version of the object identifier only once during its initial access. Storing of swizzled pointers on disk is an important strength of the hardware swizzling mechanism. However, the hardware pointer swizzling creates problems related to object migration (both between pages and across systems) and deletion, since there is no level of indirection between the source and the target objects. Finally, since the hardware swizzling relies on operating system provided page faulting mechanism, it usually employs page level locking, data transfer, recovery and buffer management mechanisms [LLOW91, BP95] and this has negative performance implications as demonstrated by our performance study.

Recovery: In page servers, clients can send to the server either updated pages (whole-page logging), updated pages and log records [FZT+92, MN94], or log records (redo at server) [WD95]. For page servers, returning both pages and log has been shown, in general, to have the best normal operation performance [WD95]. Existing page server recovery mechanisms use the STEAL/NO-FORCE buffer management policy where the pages on stable storage can be overwritten before a transaction commits, and pages do not need to be forced to disk in order to commit a transaction. STEAL/NO-FORCE is generally regarded as the most efficient buffer management policy, but the published object server recovery proposals [KGBW90] do not use it. The need for an efficient object server recovery algorithm has been identified as an outstanding research problem [FZT+92, MN94]. It has also been shown that for ODBMS workloads, it is not desirable to generate a log record for each update since the same object can be updated multiple times within a transaction. Instead, it is more efficient to perform a *difference* operation at commit time between the before-update and after-update copies of data and to generate a single log record [WD95].

Buffer Management: Buffer management innovations have been made for both page and object servers. Dual buffer management techniques can be utilized by clients in page servers to increase client buffer utilization [CALM87, KK94]. Dual buffering allows buffering both well clustered pages and isolated objects from badly clustered pages. Object servers can use the modified object buffer (MOB) at the server that stores the updated objects that are returned by the clients [Ghe95]. The objects stored in the MOB have to be installed on their corresponding home pages and written back to disk. The MOB allows the server to intelligently schedule installation reads using a low priority process and thus helps to amortize the installation read cost.

3 Adaptive Hybrid Server Design

The fundamental principle of the hybrid server is that it can dynamically adapt and behave as both page and as grouped object server; hence the name *adaptive hybrid server*. The hybrid server architecture that we propose in this paper has the following key components:

Data Transfer: A key feature is the ability to dynamically adapt between sending pages or a group of objects between the server and the client. Both the client and the server have an important role to play to make the adaptive behavior feasible (details are presented in Section 3.1).

Buffer Management: Since clients and the server can receive either pages or objects, both client and server buffers need to be able to handle pages and objects. The client implements a dual buffer manager similar to [KK94] which can manage both pages and objects. The server contains a staging page buffer to store the pages that are requested by the clients, and a modified object/page buffer to store the updated data returned by the clients [Ghe95].

Pointer Swizzling: Since the hybrid server needs to manipulate data at both the object and page level it can use the software pointer swizzling mechanism. However, this leads to an increase in the database size, because the software swizzling scheme stores object identifiers which are larger in size than memory pointers that are stored on disk. Therefore, in order to have the flexibility of manipulating data at an object level while storing memory pointers on disk, the hybrid server architecture uses a hybrid pointer swizzling mechanism. In this technique the source object points to an entry in an indirection structure [BP95] that, in turn, contains a pointer to the target object. The disk version of the object stores the memory pointer from the source object to the indirection structure entry. Once the appropriate part of the indirection structure has been faulted into memory, the target object is brought into memory using DBMS software (similar to the software swizzling mechanisms) as part of an object group or a page. Therefore, unlike the hardware swizzling schemes, operating system page faulting support is not used to bring in data objects and this gives hybrid swizzling the flexibility to manipulate data at both object and page levels. Moreover, unlike the hardware swizzling approach, the level of indirection enables the hybrid pointer swizzling mechanism to avoid object migration/deletion problems, and it also allows for fine-granularity object level locking.

Since the hybrid pointer swizzling approach uses the same techniques and data structures that have been developed by the hardware pointer swizzling algorithms for storing and handling memory pointers [WD94], we are not repeating the details here. The indirection structure is an additional data structure (also present in software swizzling mechanism) that is not used by the hardware pointer swizzling mechanism, but it has to be stored and retrieved from a persistent store. As a minimum, each entry in the indirection structure contains the OID of the target object, a pointer to a structure containing run-time information, and also a pointer to the target object. The indirection structure's pages are under the control of the DBMS.

Recovery: Recovery management and *client-to-server* data transfer are tightly linked because the client can either return both pages and log records, or it can return only log records when the page is not present in the client cache. The server stores both the redo and undo portions of a log record in its log buffer, but it stores only the redo portion of a log record in its MOB. If the client returns only log records then the server uses a redo-at-server recovery mechanism, but if the client returns both pages and log records, then the server dynamically switches and uses the ARIES-CSA [MN94] recovery mechanism. The recovery management details are presented in Section 3.2.

Cache Consistency/Concurrency Control: Since the clients in the hybrid server architecture handle both pages and object groups, the hybrid server should be able to support locking operations at both page and object levels. As discussed in a previous client-server locking performance study [CFZ94], it is very inefficient to send lock escalation messages from the client to the server for each individual object in an object group. Since page servers can perform locking operations at the granularity of a page, they do not incur high lock processing and lock escalation message overheads. In this paper, we adapt the page-based AACC [OVU98] algorithm for object servers. The object servers use the physical disk page itself as the granule of locking when dealing with object groups. It is important to note that this locking arrangement still gives each client the freedom to dynamically form object groups for data transfer. Therefore, there can be situations when the object group size is much smaller than the page level unit of locking. If object groups are allowed to span across multiple pages, then one can incrementally lock only those pages whose objects are accessed. Since our unit of locking is a page, even if the size of the object group is smaller than a page and the page does not exist at the client, we still lock the entire page. The server includes the id of the locking unit (page) along with each object that it sends to the client. If there are conflicts at the page level, then the clients dynamically de-escalate to individual object level locks. The clients maintain locking information at both individual object level and at the page level. The server primarily maintains locking information at the page level, but it also maintains information about objects on pages that are accessed in a conflicting manner by different clients. Thus, the hybrid server can lock data at both page and object levels. A detailed description of AACC along with a performance study that compares it with other cache consistency algorithms can be found in [OVU98].

In this paper, due to space constraints, we only provide the details of the data transfer and recovery mechanism.

3.1 Adaptive Hybrid Data Transfer Mechanism

The data transfer mechanism that is used in our server architecture is hybrid because the granularity of data that is sent from the server to the client and subsequently returned from the client to the server can be either pages or groups of objects. Clients provide hints to the server as to whether to send a page or an object group. If the clients want a group of objects, then they also provide a hint about the size of the object group. If the server notices that its buffers are contended, then the server overrides client hints and sends pages to the clients. The server also informs the client whether the server resources are contended. After performing an update, the client returns a page to the server only if a large portion of the page has been updated and the server is busy, otherwise, the client returns updated objects back to the server. We now discuss the specifics of this mechanism in detail.

Initial Client Request: A client's first request is for an object; it sends an object id to the server and requests the corresponding object. It also initializes the object group size to be equal to the page size and sends this to the server along with the object id.

Request Processing at Server: In servicing the request, the server checks if its disks and buffers are contended (the details are given below):

- If its disks and buffers are contended (server is busy), then the server ignores client's object group size hint and sends back the page on which the requested object resides. In this case, the server does not consider whether the clustering is good or bad. Returning a page during periods of high contention helps the server to reduce the group forming overhead.

- If the server is not busy then it checks the client provided hint to see whether it should return a page or a group of objects back to the client. If the client requested a page, then the server returns the page to the client. If the client requests an object group, then the client specifies the size of the object group. The server partitions the page into *n* equal sized sub-segments whose size is equal to the size of the object group requested by the client [LAC+96]. The server then returns to the client sub-segment in which the requested object resides. The server also determines whether it is busy and piggybacks this information along with other messages.

The server determines that its resources are contended if the disk utilization, and the *page buffer miss ratio* are above their respective thresholds, otherwise it considers itself not busy. Page buffer miss ratio measures the number of server page buffer misses. We empirically determined the disk utilization and the server page buffer miss ratios to be 0.80 and 0.60 respectively. These thresholds were determined by running multiple experiments (not reported in this paper) with different threshold values. For disk utilization values between 0.70 and 0.90, the overall system throughput did not change appreciably. Similarly, the server page buffer miss ratio values between 0.50 and 0.70, the overall system throughput did not change appreciably. Disk utilization needs to be checked because, if the disks are not contended, then the clients can return objects and the installation reads can be performed in the background. Hence, returning objects to the server will not be a problem. Similarly, server page buffer miss ratio is important because if no client read requests are present at the server, then, once again, the installation reads will not be an issue. It is important to note that other heuristics using other system parameters (such as CPU and network utilization) are possible and we are now exploring these.

Client Receives Object Group: If the client receives an object group it registers the objects in the resident object table, and loads the objects in the object buffer. The client determines whether there is a good match between data access and data clustering patterns (i.e, whether the group size is accurate). It determines accuracy by keeping track of the number of objects used in the previously received object groups [LAC+96]. Therefore, if many objects in the previously received object groups have been used, then there is a good match between access and clustering. The object group size is dynamically increased if the data access pattern matches the data clustering pattern, and decreased otherwise. In this paper the object group size varies in increments of 5 objects, where the upper limit of the group size is the number of average objects allowed on a page, and the lower limit is the increment size itself. Each client adjusts the group size using two parameters: *fetch* and *use*. *Fetch* is the number of objects in the object group received by the client, and *use* is the number of objects that have been used for the first time by the client after they are fetched. When an object group of size *N* arrives, the client recalculates these parameter values using exponential forgetting [LAC+96]: $fetch = fetch/2 + N$ and $use = use/2 + 1$. The client decreases the object group size by 5 objects if *use/fetch* is less than the threshold (which is empirically determined to be 0.3) and increases it by 5 objects otherwise. This threshold of 0.3 was determined by running multiple experiments. For threshold values between 0.20 and 0.40, the overall system throughput does not change appreciably. Moreover, if the client determines that the group size is over 30 percent of the page size, then it switches to page request mode for subsequent requests from the server in order to reduce the object group forming/breakup costs. We found that switching from object to page mode for group size values between 25 percent and 35 percent of the page size did not change the overall system performance appreciably.

Client Receives Page: If the client receives a page then it registers the page in the resident page table, and puts the page into its page buffer. The page stays in the client page buffer as long as there is no client buffer contention and the page is well clustered. Otherwise, the client flushes the page and retains only the objects that have been already used by moving them to the object buffer [KK94]. Once again the client determines whether the current object group size (now equal to a page) is accurate in the manner described above. The client switches back to requesting objects if the group size falls below 30 percent of the page size.

Client Returning Updated Data: When a client performs an update, it can return either an updated page or an object. If the server is busy, then the client returns an updated page if the page is present in the client buffer and more than 10 percent of the page has been updated (for a range between 5 and 10 percent, the overall system performance did not change appreciably). Otherwise, the client returns updated objects. The clients do not want to return sparsely updated pages when the server buffers are contended.

Server Receiving Updated Data: After receiving the updated objects/page from the client, the server loads them into its modified buffer, and then flushes them to disk in the background.

3.2 Hybrid Server Recovery Algorithm

Since the hybrid server can behave as either a page server or an object server, its recovery mechanism must be flexible to handle both modes of operation. In this paper we describe a recovery algorithm that meets this requirement. We should note that the algorithm can also be used by pure object servers but the details are not presented in this paper.

Our algorithm is based on the ARIES-CSA recovery algorithm [MN94], which we adapt for hybrid servers. We do not present the details of this algorithm, and instead refer the reader to [MN94]. Similar to ARIES-CSA, our recovery algorithm generates log records at the clients which

	Server->Client	Recovery Client->Server	Cache Consistency	Pointer-Swizzling	Server Buffer	Client Buffer
PageHard	Page	ARIES Logs and Page	Page Level AACC	Hardware	Page/ Modified Page	Page
PageSoft	Page	Redo At Server Logs	Adaptive AACC	Hybrid	Page/ Modified Object	Dual
ObjSrv	Objects	Redo At Server Logs	Adaptive AACC	Hybrid	Page/ Modified Object	Object
HybSrv	Page / Objects	ARIES Or Redo at Server Page/Logs	Adaptive AACC	Hybrid	Page/ Modified Dual	Dual

Figure 3: Systems under comparison

are stored persistently at the server (logs are not stored on local client disks), and the server does not rely on clients for its restart recovery. The transaction rollback operations are performed at the clients. Our algorithm uses the STEAL/NO-FORCE buffer management policy at the server. Clients generate log records by comparing the pre-update copy of the data with the post-update copy of the data. The log generation operation is performed at commit time or when data are flushed from the client buffers. Clients can take checkpoints, and the server can take a coordinated checkpoint which contacts all of the clients for their dirty page table and transaction table information. The server and client failure recovery operations use the standard ARIES 3-pass approach.

3.2.1 Hybrid Server Recovery Issues

The following recovery issues have to be addressed when ARIES-CSA recovery algorithm is extended to hybrid servers:

Absence of pages at the client: The log records generated at the client, the client dirty page table, and the state of a page with respect to the log (PageLSN) all require page level information. Each generated log record contains a log sequence number (LSN). The LSNs are generated and handled in the same manner as in ARIES-CSA. Each page contains a PageLSN, which indicates whether the impact of a log record has been captured on the page. In hybrid servers, objects can exist at the clients without their corresponding pages. Hence, the page level information might not always be available at the clients. The hybrid server passes to the client the PageLSN and the page id information along with every object. After the client receives a group of objects, in addition to creating resident object table (ROT) entries, the client also creates the resident page table (RPT) entry. For each received object, the client stores the PageLSN in the corresponding page entry in the RPT. This allows the client to generate LSNs for the log records corresponding to the page, and also RecLSN values for the page in the dirty page table. RecLSN refers to the log record of the earliest update on the page that is not present on disk. Thus, even though the clients might have only objects and not their corresponding pages in their caches, the clients still keep track of the necessary recovery information for the objects at page level.

Presence of updated objects at the server: The updated objects returned by the clients are stored in the server MOB. The pages corresponding to the updated objects might not be residing in the server page buffer. Therefore, it is necessary to keep track of the state of the updated objects in the MOB with respect to the log records. That is, if a client fails and the server is doing restart processing, then the server needs to know the state of the objects in the MOB in order to correctly perform the redo operations. In page servers, the dirty page table at the server helps to keep track of the pages in the server buffer. Consequently, in addition to the dirty page table, we introduce the notion of a *dirty object table* (DOT) at the server. Each (DOT) entry contains the LSN of both the earliest and the latest (because objects do not contain PageLSN field) log records that correspond to an update on the corresponding object.

Fine-Granularity Locking: In hybrid servers, different objects belonging to a page can be simultaneously updated at different client sites. In centralized systems the LSNs are generated centrally, so the combination of PageLSN and the LSN of the log record is enough to assess whether the page contains the update represented by a log record. In client-server systems, since the clients generate the log record LSNs, two clients can generate the same LSN for log records pertaining to a page. Therefore, the PageLSN alone cannot correctly indicate whether the page contains the update represented by a particular log record. Two of the previous page server recovery solutions do not allow the simultaneous update of a page at multiple client sites [FZT+92, MN94]. A more recent proposal [PBJR96] permits this and requires the server to write a *replacement* log record to the log disk before an updated page is written to data disk. For every client that has performed an update since the last time the page was written to disk, the *replacement* log record contains details (client ID and client specific PageLSN) about the client's update to the page. Thus, the *replacement* log record helps to overcome the problems encountered due to the generation of the same PageLSN value at multiple clients. In our hybrid server solution, we also use the notion of *replacement* log records.

Returning pages or logs to the server: In the hybrid server architecture, clients return either both pages and log records or only log records (redo-at-server recovery). In the latter, the log records have to be installed on their corresponding home pages whereas ARIES-CSA avoids this. Therefore, each log record is classified at the client as a redo-at-server (RDS) log record or a non-redo-at-server (NRDS) log record. At the server, the RDS log record is stored both in the server log buffer and also in the MOB, whereas, the NRDS log record is only stored in the server log buffer. As per the adaptive data transfer algorithm (Section 3.1), if the client decides to return a page to the server, then it generates a NRDS log record, else it generates a RDS log record. When the client returns an NRDS log record to the server, it ensures that the corresponding page is also returned to the server. The client does not return the corresponding page when it sends a RDS log record to the server.

4 Experiment Setup

We compare our hybrid server (HybSrv) architecture with a software-based page server (PageSoft), a hardware-based page server (PageHard), and an object server (ObjSrv). The software-based page server falls under the Page-Object server classification of Figure 1 and is similar to SHORE [CDF+94]. The hardware-based page server falls under the Page-Page server classification, and is similar to ObjectStore [LLOW91] and BeSS [BP95] in that it sends pages in both directions during client-server interaction. The object server architecture falls under the Object-Object server classification and is similar to Versant [Ver98] and Thor [LAC+96]. The existing hardware page server systems [BP95, LLOW91] employ page level data transfer, concurrency control and buffer management. As a representative of these systems PageHard also adheres to these page level restrictions, and these are the key distinguishing features between PageHard and the other architectures. The data transfer mechanism from the server to the client is the key distinguishing factor between PageSoft and ObjSrv. The ability to send pages or objects from the server to the client, and to return pages or objects from the client are the key distinguishing factors between HybSrv and the other architectures (PageSoft, ObjSrv and PageHard). It is important to note that we are only conducting a performance study on the client-server related issues. The overall performance of a system is also affected by other issues such as query processing, query optimization, indexing and others, which are not considered in this paper. We have tried to incorporate the latest advances in cache consistency, pointer swizzling, buffer management and recovery strategies into all of the systems under comparison in this study (refer to Figure 3), ensuring that they all benefit from the same advantages. Therefore, the systems under comparison in this paper are similar but not the same as their commercial/research counterparts.

4.1 Basic System Model

The baseline setup of this performance study is similar to the previous client-server performance studies [DFMV90, CFZ94, WD94, LAC+96, AGLM95, OVU98], which were useful in validating our results. As in the previous performance studies, the input work comes to the clients as a stream of object and page identifiers from a workload generator; it comes to the server from the clients via the network. The number of clients was chosen to ensure that the server and client resources and the network resources do not become a bottleneck, which would prevent us from gaining insights into the different algorithms and architectures. Disks are modeled at the server and not at the clients. The server is responsible for managing data and log disks. A buffer manager, a lock manager, and a recovery manager have been modeled at both the clients and the server. The data buffers use the second chance (LRU-like) buffer replacement algorithm, and the log buffers and modified object buffers use the FIFO buffer replacement policy. The server buffer space is partitioned equally between the page buffer and the MOB. We configured the client dual buffer in a manner similar to the initial dual buffer study [KK94] where the buffer is configured as best as possible, given the application's profile and the total size of the client's buffer. However, in future we plan to use a dynamically configurable dual buffer [CALM87]. The client and the server CPUs have a high priority and a low priority input queue for managing system and user requests respectively [CFZ94]. Each disk has a single FIFO input queue. We use a fast disk I/O rate for installation I/O (because the I/O for the data in the MOB is intelligently scheduled) and a slow disk I/O rate for normal user read operations. The LAN network model consists of FIFO server (separate queues for the server to clients and clients to server interaction) with the specified bandwidth. In order to prevent network saturation, we ran our experiments assuming a 80Mbps switched network. The network cost consists of fixed and variable transmission costs along with the wire propagation cost. Every message has a separate fixed sending and receiving cost associated with it; the size of the message determines the variable cost component of the message.

Cost Type	Description	Value
Client CPU Speed	Instr rate of client CPU	50 MIPS
Server CPU Speed	Instr rate of server CPU	100 MIPS
ClientBuffSize	Per-Client buffer Size	12% DB Size
ClientLogBuffSize	Per-Client Log buffer	2.5% DB Size
ServerBuffSize	Server Buffer Size	50% DB Size
ServerDisks	Disks at server	4 disks
FetchDiskTime	General disk access time	1600microsecs/Kbyte
InstDiskAccessTime	MOB disk I/O time	1000microsecs/Kbyte
FixNetworkCost	Fixed number of instr. per msg	6000 cycles
VariableNetwork Cost	Instr. per msg byte	4 cycles/byte
Network Bandwidth	Network Bandwidth	80Mbps
DiskSetupCost	CPU cost for performing disk I/O	5000 cycles
CacheLookup/Locking	Lookup time for objects/page	300 cycles
Register/Unregister	Instr. to register/unregister a copy	300 cycles
Page Pointer Handling	Pointer Handling Cost Per Page	40000 cycles
DeadlockDetection	Deadlock detection cost	300 cycles
CopyMergeInstr	Instr. to merge two copies of a page	300cycles/object
Pointer Handling	Pointer handling Cost Per Object	1000 cycles/object
Database Size	Size of the Database	2400 pages
PageSize	Size of a page	4K
Object Size	Size of an object	100 bytes
GroupFormCost	Group FormingCost per Object	100 cycles
NumberClients	Client Workstations	12
Indirection Cost	Ptr indirection Cost per Access	15 cycles

Figure 4: System Parameters

Figure 4 lists the costs of the different operations that are considered in this performance study which are similar to the ones used in previous performance studies [CFZ94, AGLM95]. The pointer handling costs represent the overhead associated with handling the memory pointers stored on disk. We assume that the disks contain the swizzled memory pointers. These costs are similar to the ones used in the hardware pointer swizzling study [WD95]. The schemes using the hybrid swizzling approach assume that the indirection structure is well clustered with respect to the objects accessed by each client in its private region.

Since this indirection structure is not present in the hardware swizzling approach, we compensate it by allocating 10 percent more client buffer space. The group forming cost consists of the cost of creating the object group header, the cost of copying the objects from the page, and the cost of determining the objects lock group. The group breakup cost consists of the cost of registering each object in the group into the ROT. The registration cost also includes the cost of loading objects into the client object buffer. We ensured that the type and size of the object identifiers and the object representation mechanism is the same across all of the architectures.

4.2 Workload Model

The multi-user OO7 benchmark has been developed to study the performance of object DBMSs [CDN93]. However, this benchmark is inadequate for client-server concurrency control and data transfer studies. Multi-user OO7 is under-specified for client-server concurrency control/cache consistency studies, because it does not contain data sharing patterns and transaction sizes. It is also under-specified for a data transfer study, because it does not contain the notion of data clustering. Therefore, we borrowed data sharing notions from the previous concurrency control studies [CFZ94, AGLM95], and the data clustering notions from the initial data transfer study (ACOB benchmark) [DFMV90]. We obtained the transaction size and length characteristics from the market surveys performed by the commercial ODBMS vendors [Obj98]. The key findings of their survey is that the majority of the application domains using ODBMSs use short (in terms of time) and small (number of objects accessed) transactions with multiple readers and few updaters operating on each object. Moreover, most of these applications use small objects. We have ensured that our base workloads satisfy these transaction characteristics.

In our workload each client has its own hot region (hotness indicates affinity) and there is a shared common region between all the clients. Each region is composed of a number of base assembly objects. Each base assembly object is connected to 10 complex objects. Each complex object consists of 4 atomic objects. A transaction consists of a series of traversal operations. Each traversal operation consists of accessing a base assembly and all of the complex objects (along with their atomic objects) connected to that base assembly object. The clustering factor indicates how closely the data access pattern matches the data placement on the disk. It is desirable to have good clustering (high clustering factor) because it allows one to easily prefetch useful data and thus reduce the disk I/O and network overhead. We use a similar notion of clustering as was used in the initial page server/object server data transfer study [DFMV90]. When creating the database, the clustering factor determines the location of the complex objects connected to a base assembly object. For each complex object, a random number between 0 and 99 is generated, and if the random number is smaller than the clustering factor, the complex object is placed on the same page as its siblings. Otherwise, the complex object is placed on a different page.

In this study we examine *Private* and *Sh-Hotcold* data sharing patterns [CFZ94, AGLM95]. These two sharing patterns are the most common in ODBMS workloads [CFZ94]. There is no data contention in the *Private* workload, but one encounters read-write and write-write conflicts in the *Sh-Hotcold* workload. In the *Private* workload 80 percent of the traversal operations in a transaction are performed on the client's hot region and 20 percent of the traversal operations are performed on the shared region. Moreover, the clients only update the data in their hot regions. In the *Sh-Hotcold* workload, 80 percent of the traversal operations in a transaction are performed on the client's hot region, 10 percent of the traversal operations are performed on the shared region, and 10 percent of the traversal operations are performed on the rest of the database (including other clients' hot regions). The clients can update objects in all of the regions. Upon accessing an object, the object write probability determines whether the object will be updated. There is a CPU instruction cost associated with the read and write operations. The transaction think time is the delay between the start of two consecutive transactions at the clients. Figure 5 describes the workload parameters used in this study.

Parameter	Setting
Transaction size Private	800 objects
Transaction size Sh-HotCold	200 objects
Clustering Factor	10 to 90 %
Per Client Region	50 pages
Shared Region	50 pages
Object write probability	2% to 30 %
Read access think cost	50 cycles/byte
Write access think cost	100 cycles/byte
Think time between trans	0

Figure 5: Workload Parameters

5 Results of Experiments

In this section we report the performance comparison of the adaptive hybrid server architecture (HybSrv) with the hardware page server architecture (PageHard), the software page server architecture (PageSoft) and the object server architecture (ObjSrv). All of the experiments use the cost and workload settings as described in Figures 4 and 5. In cases where the default values have been changed, it is explicitly specified. The average response time for a single client in seconds (for 50 transaction interval) is the primary performance metric. Data sharing patterns, server and client buffer sizes, data clustering accuracy, and write probability are the key parameters that are varied.

5.1 Large Client and Large Server Buffers

In this setup, (which we call Large/Large) both the client and the server have large buffers. In a large client buffer the entire working set of the client (all of the objects accessed by a particular client) fits in the client's cache. A large server buffer means that a large portion of the working sets of all the clients fit into the server buffer resulting in low disk utilization upon reaching steady state. Due to these conditions, buffer management is not the performance differentiating factor between different architectures. The client buffer is 12 percent of the database size

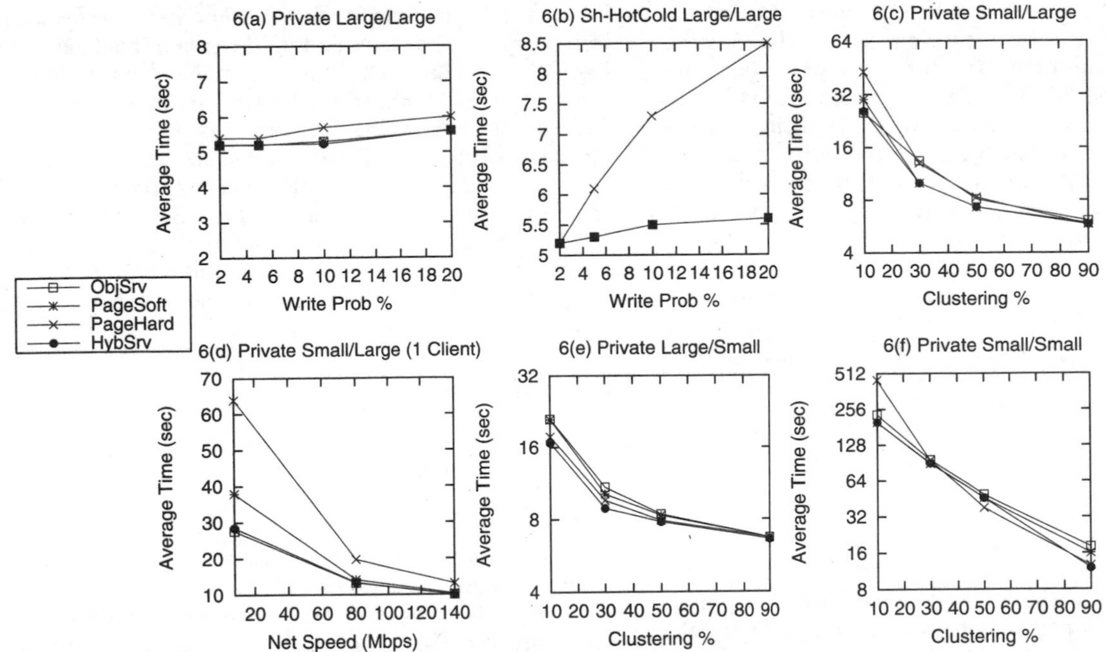

Figure 6: Experiment Results

and the server buffer is 50 percent of the database size and we ran the experiment with 50 percent clustering. In the private workload there is no data contention and, therefore, concurrency control/cache consistency is not an issue. As seen in Figure 6(a), the performance of all of the architectures is quite similar. Our hybrid pointer swizzling mechanism has allowed ObjSrv, PageSoft and HybSrv to successfully compete with PageHard in this workload. Since all the architectures store memory pointers on the disk, pointer swizzling is not an issue. PageSoft, HybSrv and ObjSrv outperform PageHard by a very small margin because they return updated objects instead of updated pages (like PageHard) and thus incur lower network overhead. In the Large/Large buffer case, the server buffer is not heavily contended, therefore, the installation read overhead is minimized for the architectures that return updated objects. For the Large/Large buffer configuration, we also ran the Sh-HotCold workload with the clustering factor fixed at 30 percent (Figure 6(b)). The software page handling architectures outperform PageHard, because they are able to lock data at a finer granularity than PageHard. The hardware page handling mechanisms rely on the operating system provided page protection mechanisms to lock data only at page level. For this experiment we don't present the results for higher clustering percentages, but we noticed that the performance of PageHard improved as the clustering became better because higher page locality leads to fewer page accesses and thus less contention for PageHard. As evident from Figure 6(b), ObjSrv and HybSrv (when it is operating as an object server) are able to successfully compete with PageSoft for the Sh-HotCold workload. This shows that AACC cache consistency algorithm, which was originally designed for page servers, can be successfully extended to object servers.

5.2 Small Client and Large Server Buffers

In this system configuration (referred to as Small/Large) the client's working set does not fit into its cache. This is possible if the size of the working set is very large or if the client buffer is shared by multiple applications. The client buffer is 1.5 percent of the database size and the server buffer is still 50 percent of the database size. We ran the private workload with 10 percent write probability. We varied the clustering factor to see the relationship between clustering and client buffer size. As shown in Figure 6(c), PageHard performs worst during low clustering, because it manages the client cache strictly at page level. Therefore, the clients in PageHard continue to cache badly clustered pages which, in turn, leads to low client buffer utilization. However, the clients in ObjSrv, HybSrv and PageSoft only retain useful objects in their cache. The low buffer utilization in PageHard leads to a higher number of cache misses and this, in turn, degrades PageHard's performance. The second important result is that HybSrv and ObjSrv perform better than PageSoft during bad (10 percent) clustering. Even though HybSrv and ObjSrv incur a higher number of client cache misses, they outperform PageSoft because it transfers badly clustered pages from the server to the client and thus, incurs higher network overhead. The third important result is that HybSrv and PageSoft outperform ObjSrv for 30 to 50 percent clustering because in these architectures when a client caches a page it is able to get more cache hits during subsequent accesses to different regions of the page, whereas the object server (due to its grouping algorithm) has to make multiple requests to the server to get the different portions of the page. However, if over time, the client repeatedly accesses only a particular region of the page, then the object server architecture is more competitive due to the better performance of its grouping algorithm. The adaptive nature of HybSrv allows it to behave as a page server when the clustering is good and like an object server when the clustering is bad and this allows it to be more robust (performance-wise) than page and object servers. We also ran this experiment with slow (8Mbps) and fast (140Mbps) network speeds for a single client. As evident in Figure 6(d), the architectures that send pages from the client to the server suffer even more in the presence of slow networks. This result is important for the popular low bandwidth wireless environments. For the 140 Mbps, we also reduced the software overhead (reduced the variable and fixed network overhead by 50 percent) associated with sending and receiving a message. We found that as the network speed is increased and the software overhead is reduced, the systems that send badly clustered pages are able to close the performance gap.

5.3 Large Client and Small Server Buffers

In Large/Small configuration, the server buffer is small and cannot hold the working sets of the active clients (contended server buffer) but the client buffer is large and it can hold the local working set. It would have been preferable to model the small server buffer case by keeping the server buffer size constant and by increasing the number of clients. However, the memory constraints of our simulator did not allow for this type of modeling. Therefore, by reducing the server buffer size, we are trying to capture the essence of the impact of many clients on the server buffer. We set the client buffer at 12.5 percent of the database size and the server buffer at 3 percent of the database size. We ran the Large/Small experiments for the Private workload configuration. We found that with a write probability of 20 percent, PageHard is beaten by all of the other architectures because PageHard is returning sparsely updated pages to a server whose buffer is highly contended. Therefore, the server consumes valuable buffer space much more quickly (lower server buffer absorption) in PageHard than the schemes that are returning updated objects. However, as we increase the write probability to 30 percent (Figure 6(e)), PageHard and HybSrv are able to beat PageSoft and ObjSrv because PageSoft and ObjSrv return updated objects and the installation read overhead in PageSoft and ObjSrv offsets the gains due to better MOB buffer utilization. Since HybSrv dynamically decides at the client whether to return updated pages or objects, its performance is more robust than the other algorithms.

5.4 Small Client and Small Server Buffers

In Small/Small configuration, the server buffer is small and cannot hold the working sets of the active clients and the client buffer is small and it cannot hold the working set of that particular client. We set the client buffer at 1.5 percent of the database size and the server buffer at 3 percent of the database size. We ran this experiment with 30 percent write probability for Private workload to see whether a small client buffer has any impact on the results presented in the Large/Small buffer case. Figure 6(e) shows that HybSrv, PageSoft and ObjSrv outperform PageHard during low clustering because PageHard has lower client buffer utilization than the other architectures. Moreover, HybSrv and PageSoft outperform ObjSrv because ObjSrv incurs a higher number of client buffer misses due to the object grouping algorithm, and in the Small/Small case (unlike the Small/Large case), a miss in the client buffer also leads to a miss in the server buffer. Since, HybSrv sends pages to the clients when the server is busy, it has similar client buffer hit rate as PageSoft. As the clustering percentage increases, PageHard and HybSrv outperform PageSoft and ObjSrv, because PageHard and HybSrv return updated pages to the server, and, thus, incur fewer installation reads. HybSrv returns pages since it takes into account that the server is busy and a large portion of the page has been updated.

6 Discussion

The integrated performance study has provided us with many interesting insights into ODBMS client-server architectures. A previous client-server recovery study has shown that installation reads can become a problem [WD95] for the redo-at-server recovery mechanisms. However, the combined study of recovery and server buffer management mechanism has shown that the presence of a MOB at the server prevents the degradation of the redo-at-server recovery mechanism during medium-to-low server contention.

Previously [OS94], it was thought that it is better to return an updated page to the server if the page is present at the client. However, we have found that if the server buffer is highly contended, and the page has been sparsely updated, then it is better to return updated objects because this increases the MOB buffer absorption. Another previous study [Ghe95] has shown that is desirable to return updated pages to the server if a large portion of the page has been accessed (high clustering) and updated (high write probability). Our results agree with this study, and we have also found that in addition to clustering and write probability, the server buffer contention level is also a key component which dictates whether it is desirable to return updated pages or objects.

Until now, hardware pointer swizzling systems stored memory pointers on disk to attain good performance [WD94, LLOW91]. However, since the hardware pointer swizzling systems use the operating system provided page handling mechanism, they employ page level locking, data transfer and buffer management mechanisms [LLOW91, WD94]. The combined study of data transfer, pointer swizzling and client buffer management has shown that managing client buffers at strictly page level and always returning updated pages back when the server is busy has a negative impact on the performance of hardware page handling architectures.

Initially, ODBMSs were primarily used by applications, such as computer aided design, which consisted of large transactions with little or no data contention. However, many of emerging application domains such as network management, financial trading and product information management which use ODBMSs use small transactions with read/write locking conflicts [Obj98]. Therefore, hardware page handling architectures that lock data at only page level are increasingly less suitable.

Many techniques we have developed for the hybrid server architecture can be applied to other architectures (to object servers in particular). Lack of an efficient, low aborting cache consistency algorithm, and the absence of a Steal/No-Force recovery algorithm were considered to be two major drawbacks of object servers. Our adaptation of AACC algorithm for hybrid server eliminates one of the problems. The key insight behind this adaptation is that even though the clients in the object server architecture strictly manipulate objects, and pages do not exist in the client cache, the clients can still lock the pages corresponding to the objects. Therefore, we are essentially decoupling the data transfer and concurrency control mechanism for object servers. Previously, this flexibility was only provided to the page servers [CFZ94]. Our adaptation of ARIES-CSA page server recovery to hybrid servers provides a STEAL/NO-FORCE recovery algorithm which can also be used by object servers. The clients in the object server architecture maintain page level recovery information for the objects in the client cache. This, in turn, allows the object servers to use all of the page server recovery techniques. Thus, object servers are now quite competitive with the page server architecture and these adaptations can be pursued by the existing object server architectures.

7 Conclusion

In this paper we presented a new adaptive hybrid server architecture with more robust performance than page or object servers across a spectrum of system configurations and workloads. Our hybrid server uses a new adaptive data transfer mechanism in which the clients and server pass valuable information to each other to dynamically adapt between sending pages or objects between themselves. The paper describes, in detail, the key points of this adaptive data transfer mechanism. An adaptive data transfer method has an impact on data transfer, cache consistency/concurrency control, recovery, and buffer management mechanisms. Each of these system components need to be able to support both page and object server architectures while continuing to operate in an integrated manner. Due to the absence of efficient cache consistency and recovery algorithms for object servers, we have adapted the leading page server cache consistency [OVU98] and recovery [MN94] algorithms for object servers. These adaptations are important in their own right since they can be used by existing object sever architectures. We have also shown that it is possible for architectures to both store swizzled memory pointers on disk while maintaining the flexibility to manipulate data at the clients at object level. In addition to characterizing the behavior of the hybrid server proposal, the performance study and its results that are reported are important for a number of reasons. First of all, this study improves our understanding of the client-server architectures, in particular, it shows that with our new recovery, pointer swizzling and cache consistency adaptations, object servers can compete successfully with page servers. Thus, the belief that object servers are not scalable is no longer valid. Finally, we are now investigating alternative adaptive data transfer heuristics which take varying object size, page size, CPU and network contentions into account.

References

[AGLM95] A. Adya, R. Gruber, B. Liskov, and U. Maheshwari. Efficient Optimistic Concurrency Control Using Loosely Synchronized Cl ocks. In *Proceedings of ACM SIGMOD Conference*, 1995.

[BP95] A. Biliris and E. Panagos. A High Performance Configurable Storage Manager. In *Proceedings of 11th International Conference on Data Engineering*, 1995.

[CALM87] M. Castro, A. Adya, B. Liskov, and Andrew Myers. HAC:Hybrid Adaptive Caching for Distributed Storage Systems. In *Proceedings of ACM Symposium on Operating System Principles*, 1987.

[CDF+94] Michael Carey, D. DeWitt, M. Franklin, N. Hall, and et al. Shoring Up Persistent Applications. In *Proceedings of ACM SIGMOD Conference*, 1994.

[CDN93] M. Carey, D. DeWitt, and J. Naughton. The OO7 Benchmark. In *Proceedings of ACM SIGMOD Conference*, 1993.

[CFZ94] M. Carey, M. Franklin, and M. Zaharioudakis. Fine Grained Sharing in a Page Server OODBMS. In *Proceedings of ACM SIGMOD Conference*, 1994.

[DFB+96] S. Dar, M. Franklin, B.T.Jonsson, D. Srivastava, and M. Tan. Semantic Data Caching and Replacement. In *Proceedings of VLDB Conference*, 1996.

[DFMV90] D. DeWitt, P. Futtersack, D. Maier, and F. Velez. A study of three alternative workstation-server architectures for OODBS. In *Proceedings of VLDB Conference*, 1990.

[FC94] M. Franklin and M. Carey. Client-Server Caching Revisited. In T. Ozsu, U. Dayal, P. Valduriez, editor, *Distributed Object Management*. Morgan Kaufmann, 1994.

[FCL96] M. Franklin, M. Carey, and M. Livny. Transactional Client-Server Cache Consistency: Alternatives and Performance. *ACM Transactions on Database Systems*, 22(4), 1996.

[FZT+92] M. Franklin, M. Zwilling, C.K. Tan, M. Carey, and D. DeWitt. Crash Recovery in Client-Server EXODUS. In *Proceedings of ACM SIGMOD Conference*, 1992.

[Ghe95] S. Ghemawat. *The Modified Object Buffer: A Storage Management Technique for Object-Oriented Databases*. PhD thesis, MIT, 1995.

[GK94] C. Gerlhof and A. Kemper. A Multi-Threaded Architecture for Prefetching in Object Bases. In *Proceedings of EDBT Conference*, 1994.

[KGBW90] W. Kim, J. Garza, N. Ballou, and D. Woelk. Architecture of the ORION Next-Generation Database System. *IEEE TKDE*, 2(1), 1990.

[KJF96] D. Kossmann, B.T. Jonsson, and M. Franklin. A Study of Query Execution Strategies for Client-Server Database Systems. In *Proceedings of ACM SIGMOD Conference*, 1996.

[KK94] A. Kemper and D. Kossmann. Dual-Buffering Strategies in Object Bases. In *Proceedings of VLDB Conference*, 1994.

[LAC+96] B. Liskov, A. Adya, M. Castro, M. Day, and et al. Safe and Efficient Sharing of Persistent Objects in Thor. In *Proceedings of ACM SIGMOD Conference*, 1996.

[LLOW91] C. Lamb, G. Landis, J. Orenstein, and D. Weinreb. The ObjectStore database system. *Communications of the ACM*, 34(10), 1991.

[MN94] C. Mohan and I. Narang. ARIES/CSA: A Method for Database Recovery in Client-Server Architectures. In *Proceedings of ACM SIGMOD Conference*, 1994.

[Obj98] Objectivity. White Paper: Choosing an Object Database. In *www.objectivity.com/ObjectDatabase/WP/Choosing/Choosing.html*, 1998.

[OS94] J. O'Toole and L. Shrira. Hybrid caching for large scale object systems. In *Proceedings of Workshop on Persistent Object Systems*, 1994.

[OVU98] M.T. Ozsu, K. Voruganti, and R. Unrau. An Asynchronous Avoidance-based Cache Consistency Algorithm for Client Caching DBMSs. In *Proceedings of VLDB Conference*, 1998.

[PBJR96] E. Panagos, A. Biliris, H. Jagadish, and R. Rastogi. Fine-granularity Locking and Client-Based Logging for Distributed Architectures. In *Proceedings of EDBT Conference*, 1996.

[TN92] M. Tsangaris and J. Naughton. On the performance of object clustering techniques. In *Proceedings of ACM SIGMOD Conference*, 1992.

[Ver98] Versant. ODBMS. In *http://www.versant.com*, 1998.

[WD94] S. White and D. DeWitt. QuickStore: A high performance mapped object store. In *Proceedings of ACM SIGMOD Conference*, 1994.

[WD95] S. White and D. DeWitt. Implementing Crash Recovery in QuickStore: A Performance Study. In *Proceedings of ACM SIGMOD Conference*, 1995.

Dynamic Load Balancing for Parallel Association Rule Mining on Heterogeneous PC Cluster System

Masahisa Tamura and Masaru Kitsuregawa

Institute of Industrial Science, The University of Tokyo
7-22-1, Roppongi, Minato-ku, Tokyo 106, Japan
{masahisa,kitsure}@tkl.iis.u-tokyo.ac.jp

Abstract

The dynamic load balancing strategies for parallel association rule mining are proposed under heterogeneous PC cluster environment. PC cluster is recently regarded as one of the most promising platforms for heavy data intensive applications, such as decision support query processing and data mining. The development period of PC hardware is becoming extremely short, which results in heterogeneous system, where the clock cycle of CPU, the performance/capacity of disk drives, etc are different among component PC's. Heterogeneity is inevitable. Basically, current algorithms assume the homogeneity. Thus if we naively apply them to heterogeneous system, its performance is far below expectation. We need some new methodologies to handle heterogeneity. In this paper, we propose the new dynamic load balancing methods for association rule mining, which works under heterogeneous system. Two strategies, called candidate migration and transaction migration are proposed. Initially first one is invoked. When the load imbalance cannot be resolved with the first method, the second one is employed, which is costly but more effective for strong imbalance. We have implemented them on the PC cluster system with two different types of PCs: one with Pentium Pro, the other one with Pentium II. The experimental results confirm that the proposed approach can very effectively balance the workload among heterogeneous PCs.

Proceedings of the 25th VLDB Conference, Edinburgh, Scotland, 1999.

1 Introduction

Recently commodity based PC cluster system is regarded as one of the most promising platforms for data intensive applications such as decision support query processing and data mining. The power of PC is superior to the workstation for integer performance and the price of PC is also much lower. The floating-point computational power of workstation is higher than PC but usually it is not necessary for database processing. So far extensive researches on parallel database processing algorithms have been done[6]. Most of RDB vendors have developed engines with parallel extensions. Currently parallel execution option is available for most of RDB products. Parallel engine is essential for large-scale data warehouse and is becoming popular nowadays. Thus combining the above two key trends, namely, parallel database processing on PC cluster would be a most cost-effective solution for large scale data warehousing. Many researches on PC clusters are being undergone. However most of them such as Beowulf machines at JPL and Caltech are targeting scientific applications[3]. We have built 100 node PC cluster system named NEDO-100 for data base applications. We implemented parallel RDB kernel on it. TPC-D benchmark and association rule mining were run on the machine[8, 13] and, it showed sufficiently high performance. We exemplified that the PC cluster can achieve considerably improve cost-performance ratio.

The problem we faced in that project is "heterogeneity." The system we built[8, 13] was completely uniform. However, when we planed to increase the number of nodes, it was extremely difficult to find out the same machines. Since the development period of PC is extremely short, configuration of machines is changing so quickly. The clock speed of CPU, the size of main memory, the capacity and transfer rate of disk drives, all these components are completely different from generation to generation and also different from vendor to vendor . We wanted to increase the number of nodes uniformly, but we could not find out the same PC. Once six months have passed, we have to introduce different type of PCs. Thus heterogeneity is inevitable.

Most of the parallel algorithms developed so far assume the system be uniform. Very few papers address heterogeneity problem[5]. If we apply the parallel algorithm developed for uniform parallel system to the heterogeneous environment, apparently we will see significant performance deterioration. A high performance node can process its allocated task quickly but node with less powerful processor or with low bandwidth disk usually takes longer time to finish. Thus, we have to develop some methodologies to handle these problems, which is the motivation of our research. In near future, the high performance system will be built based on a cluster system, where we will have to face the heterogeneity problem anyway. We picked up data mining as a data intensive application and tried to solve the heterogeneity problem. As the size of database increases, the data mining workload becomes significantly heavy. It is also common that users start from small set of data and gradually increase the size of the data set to be mined. Thus the mining platform can not be uniform but should be heterogeneous PC cluster.

In this paper, we propose run time load balancing algorithms for association rule mining under heterogeneous PC cluster environment. Two strategies named candidate migration and transaction migration are developed. Details on these two will be given in later sections. PCs do not have to communicate each other before the execution in order to normalize the performance among different CPUs and disks etc. During executing data mining, the workload of each node is monitored autonomously and the system performance is controlled to be balanced by migrating candidates/transaction among nodes at runtime.

Section 2 briefly explains the association rule mining and its parallel algorithms. Section 3 introduces the fundamental idea of load balancing for association rule mining. Section 4 describes the detail. Section 5 explains the PC cluster system, and implementation details. Performance evaluation results are given and examined in detail. Section 6 discusses the future work and concludes the paper.

2 Association Rule Mining and Its Parallel Algorithm

2.1 Association Rule

Association rule mining is one of the most well known problems in data mining. Sometime it is also recognized as basket analysis . Its typical application is to find buying pattern in retail databases. An example of an association rule is if a customer buys A and B then 90% of them buy also C . Here 90% is called the *confidence* of the rule. Another measure of a rule is called the *support* of the rule.

Transactions in a retail database usually consist of an identifier and a set of items or itemset. $\{A, B, C\}$ in above example is an itemset. An association rule is an implication of the form $X \Longrightarrow Y$ where X and Y are itemsets, and $X \cap Y = \emptyset$. An itemset X has support s if $s\%$ of transactions contain that itemset, here we denote $s = support(X)$. The support of the rule $X \Longrightarrow Y$ is $support(X \cup Y)$. The *confidence* of that rule can be written as the ratio $support(X \cup Y)/support(X)$.

The problem of mining association rules is to find all the rules that satisfy a user-specified minimum support and minimum confidence, which can be decomposed into two subproblems:

1. Find all combinations of items, called large itemsets, whose support is greater than minimum support.
2. Use the large itemsets to generate the rules.

Since determination of large itemsets from large scale database requires much more processing time, most researches to date have focused on first subproblem. After finding all large itemsets, association rules are derived in straighforward manner.

2.2 Mining Association Rules and Apriori

Here we briefly explain the Apriori algorithm for finding all large itemsets, proposed in [1], since the parallel algorithms we use are based on this algorithm.

In the first pass, support count for each item is incremented by scanning the transaction database. Hereafter we prepare a field named support count for each itemset, which is used to measure how many times the itemset appeared in transactions. Since itemset here contains just single item, each item has a support count field. All items that satisfy the minimum support are picked out. These items are called large 1-itemset. Here k-itemset is defined as a set of k items. The second pass, the 2-itemsets are generated using large 1-itemset that is called the candidate 2-itemsets. Then the support count of the candidate 2-itemsets is incremented by scanning the transaction database. Here support count of the itemset means the number of transactions which contain the itemset. At the end of scanning the transaction data, the large 2-itemsets which satisfy minimum support are determined. The following denotes the k-th iteration, pass k:

1. Generate candidate itemset:
   The candidate k-itemsets are generated using large $(k-1)$-itemsets which were determined in the previous pass. Apriori candidate generation

includes pruning of candidate itemsets that is deleting all of the itemsets in the candidate k-itemset where some of the $(k-1)$-subset of candidate itemsets are not in the large $(k-1)$-itemset.

2. Count support:
The count support for the candidate k-itemsets are incremented by scanning the transaction database.

3. Determine large itemset:
The candidate k-itemsets are checked for whether they satisfy the minimum support or not, the large k-itemsets which satisfy the minimum support are determined. The procedure terminates when the large itemset becomes empty. Otherwise $k := k+1$ and goto 1 .

Thus the large itemsets are derived iteratively by scanning the transaction data several times. Apriori is sequential algorithm. In the next section, we examine parallelization methods of Apriori.

2.3 Parallel Association Rule Mining

J.S.Park, et.al proposed bit vector filtering for association rule mining and naive parallelization of Apriori [2, 9], where every node keeps the whole candidate itemsets and scans the database independently. Communication is necessary only at the end of each pass. Local counts are gathered to a certain node at the end of each pass and are summed up to calculate the global count(=support value). Although this method is very simple and communication overhead is very small, memory utilization efficiency is terribly bad. Since all the nodes have the copy of all the candidate itemsets, it wastes memory space a lot.

In [11] Hash Partitioned Apriori(HPA) was proposed. The candidate itemsets are not copied over all the nodes but are partitioned using hash function. The number of itemsets at second pass is usually extremely high, sometimes three orders of magnitude larger than the first pass in a certain retail transaction database which we examined. If the candidate itemsets are partitioned over all nodes' memory space, we can fully utilize the memory of all the nodes. When the user-specified support is low, the candidate itemsets overflow the memory space and incur a lot of disk I/O. By utilizing whole space through partitioning the candidates over nodes instead of duplication, HPA can minimize the extra I/Os.

Hybrid approach between candidate duplication and candidate partitioning is proposed at [7]. The processors are divided into some number of groups. Within each group, all the candidates are duplicated and among groups, candidates are partitioned. [12] proposes the parallel algorithms for mining generalized association rule, which incorporates the classification hierarchy. All the strategies above were proposed for shared nothing parallel machines. Recently parallel strategies for shared memory machines are also proposed[15, 10]. Distributed algorithms are also proposed[4].

However, the algorithms so far proposed assume homogeneous parallel processing environment. In this paper, we propose dynamic load balancing algorithms for heterogeneous parallel systems, where each node might have different type of CPU, and different kinds of disks, etc.

2.4 Hash Partitioned Apriori:HPA

HPA addresses the problem of main memory overflow caused by large number of candidate itemsets by partitioning those itemsets among nodes using hash function as in the hash join[11]. Although it has to exchange transaction data among nodes, its effective utilization of memory space results in better parallelization gain. And using hash function, HPA eliminates broadcasting of all the transaction data and can reduce the comparison workload significantly. In brief, HPA performs following steps:

1. Generation of k-length candidate itemsets:
At pass k, HPA generates k-length candidate itemsets using large itemsets with length $k-1$ created at previous pass. Then it applies hash function on those itemsets to decide the destination node ID. If the ID is its own, insert it into the hash table. If not, it is discarded.

2. Support counting:
While reading transaction data, each node generates k-itemsets. Itemsets with support less than user specified minimum support are filtered out while k-itemsets are generated from transaction. Applies the same hash function that used in phase 1 to the k-itemset, and derives the destination node ID and setds the k-itemsets to it. For the itemsets received from the other nodes and those locally generated whose ID equals the node's own ID, search the hash table. If hit, increment its support count.

3. Determination of large itemsets with length k:
After processing all transaction data, each node determines large itemsets from its own candidate itemsets. Overall large itemsets for pass k are obtained by accumulating large itemsets from all nodes.

In the following sections, we employ HPA as an underlying parallel algorithm.

3 How to balance load for parallel association rule mining

Before describing the detail algorithms in the next section, we will explain the fundamental idea of load balancing for parallel association rule mining. As described in the previous section of HPA, each node receives the itemsets and probes them against its own hash table. If a node is assigned more candidate itemsets and keeps them as a hash table, it will receive more itemsets from other nodes during counting phase. This means that we can adjust the workload of each node by adjusting the amount of candidate itemsets. If the load of a certain node is higher than the other nodes, we take some of the candidate itemsets from that node and give them to the other nodes. Then the itemsets that are originally directed to that node are now redirected to the new nodes to which the removed itemsets are relocated. Thus the counting workload is migrated from the original node to the other nodes. We name this strategy Candidate Migration. Figure 1 shows the idea.

The workload depends on the itemset. Some itemsets have higher support value, which means those itemsets will receive more counting requests. Thus we have to put weighting factor to each itemset. However real support value is obtained after the execution. So basically the weighting factor is not available before execution. In our approach, we exploit information from the previous pass. Apriori algorithm, as described in section 2.2, consists of several passes. For each pass, transaction database has to be scanned. When we do the load balancing at pass-k, we use the information on the support value of itemset at pass $k-1$. For example, let's consider pass 2, since almost all the time pass 2 is most time consuming. We estimate the support of 2-itemsets at pass 2 using the information on support of 1-itemsets at pass 1. Before the execution of pass 2, the support of 1-itemset is available. We estimate the support of 2-itemset, $support(\{i_1, i_2\})$ by $min(support(\{i_1\}), support(\{i_2\}))$. Here $support(x)$ means the support of itemset x. It can be proved that $support(\{i_1, i_2\}) \leq min(support(\{i_1\}), support(\{i_2\}))$. There might be an error, but much better than not giving any weighting factor. This can be generalized to any pass. Thus we estimate the support of k-itemset by using support of large $(k-1)$-itemsets derived at pass $k-1$ and use it to determine the weighting factor. The details of Candidate Migration algorithm will be given in the next section.

The Candidate Migration is possible if the node still has candidate itemsets to be migrated. The node can transfer the workload by migrating the candidate itemsets. If the skew is high, there arises the case where migrating all the candidates is still not sufficient. In order to handle such situation, we need yet another strategy to migrate workload.

Let's examine the HPA algorithm again in more detail. Each node has two major task. One is to receive the itemset sent from other nodes, probe it against the

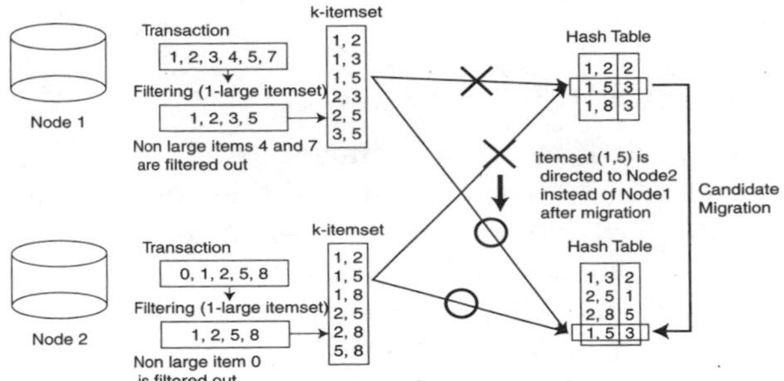

Figure 1: Candidate Migration

hash table and increment the count corresponding to that itemset. The other task is to read the transactions from the disk, generate the itemsets and send them to the nodes determined using hash function. We use the former task for Candidate Migration.

Now we consider the latter task. Actually, the itemset generation from transactions is rather complicated process. Transaction contains the items whose support is less than user defined support. So we can eliminate such itemsets by examining the table of large itemsets derived at the previous pass. This workload could be migrated. The node with heavy workload reads the transactions from the disk and it does not do itemset generation itself but just sends the transactions to the light nodes. We name this strategy Transaction Migration.

Transaction Migration incurs overhead of network transfer for each transaction. On the other hand, no additional overhead is incurred for Candidate Migration. Thus, we put priority to the Candidate Migration. Initially heavy node migrates candidate itemsets only. When there are no candidate itemsets remained to migrate, then it migrates transactions. The algorithm to derive the amount of transactions to be migrated will be given in the next section.

4 Run Time Load Balancing Methods

We propose dynamic load balancing methods during the execution of data mining to cope with the skew in heterogeneous system. In this approach, a coordinator node collects necessary information from all the nodes and controls the distribution of workload.

Support counting for pass k in HPA can be divided into 2 processes. The first process is SEND process which comprises reading transaction data from disks, generating k-itemsets and sending the k-itemsets to destination nodes by applying hash function to the itemsets. The second process is called RECV process since processing node receives the k-itemsets from other nodes then probes its hash table to increase the support counts of candidate itemsets. If the time required by node i for SEND process and RECV process are expressed by ST_i and RT_i respectively, overall

CPU processing time for that node can be formulated by:

$$\Delta T_i = \Delta ST_i + \Delta RT_i \tag{1}$$

Here Δ stands for definite time interval.

If we can estimate the required time for each node's SEND and RECV processes to complete the processing of remaining transaction data, we can obtain the estimated remaining processing time for that node as indicated by following expression.

$$\text{rest}T_i = \text{rest}ST_i + \text{rest}RT_i \tag{2}$$

Each of restT_i, restST_i and restRT_i denotes estimated remaining overall CPU processing time, estimated remaining CPU time for the SEND process and estimated remaining CPU time for RECV process respectively.

Since the goal is to have all nodes complete their job at the same time, our method dynamically controls the load allocated for each node so that every node has the same restT_i.

The skew is defined as follow,

$$skew = \frac{\max(\text{rest}T_i) - \min(\text{rest}T_i)}{\text{avg}(\text{rest}T_i)} \tag{3}$$

$$\begin{cases} skew \le threshold & : no\ skew \\ skew > threshold & : skew\ exists \end{cases} \tag{4}$$

We can judge that the load control is needed if this value exceeds some certain threshold. Here we propose two strategies for balancing the load: Candidate Migration and Transaction Migration.

4.1 Candidate Migration

RECV process can be divided further into 2 subprocesses: (recv1) receives k-itemsets and (recv2) probes the hash table and increment the support count for the corresponding candidate itemsets. If the time for each subprocess are represented by RNT_i and RCT_i respectively, RT_i can be expressed as follow:

$$\Delta RT_i = \Delta RNT_i + \Delta RCT_i \tag{5}$$

Since large scale data mining has to probe large amount of candidate itemsets against hash table, most part of processing time is dominated by (recv2). Thus expression (5) can be reduced to:

$$\Delta RT_i \approx \Delta RCT_i \tag{6}$$

RCT_i itself is proportional to the amount of k-itemsets to receive, thus if we express that amount as RK_i, we can assume:

$$\Delta RCT_i = \alpha_i^1 \Delta RK_i \tag{7}$$

RK_i varies according to the candidate itemsets allocated to that node. RK_i is unknown before execution. But we can estimate RK_i of pass k using the statistics of pass $k-1$ [1]. The support count for a candidate itemset $cand_j = \{t_{j1}, t_{j2}, \ldots, t_{jk}\}$ is always smaller than the least support count of all its subsets[14]. If the support count for an itemset X is defined as S_X, we can define a weighting factor for that candidate itemset as follow:

$$CW_{cand_j} = \min(S_{Lj1}, S_{Lj2}, \ldots, S_{Ljk}) \quad \{L_{j1}, L_{j2}, \ldots, L_{jk}\} \in Sub_j \tag{8}$$

Sub_j denotes a set of all large $(k-1)$-itemsets that are subsets of $cand_j$.

RK_i represents a set of all candidate itemsets in pass k. Then if we represent CD_i as a set of candidate itemsets to be allocated to node i, the weighting factor for that node can be defined as:

$$CV_i = \sum_{j}^{|CD_i|} CW_{cand_j} \qquad cand_j \in CD_i \tag{9}$$

If overall amount of transactions to be read by all nodes is expressed as DR, RK_i is proportional to the product of CV_i and DR. Therefore, expression (7) can be expanded further into:

$$\Delta RCT_i = \alpha_i^1 \alpha_i^2 CV_i \Delta DR \tag{10}$$

From expression (2) we can express restT_i as:

$$\text{rest}T_i = \text{rest}ST_i + \alpha_i^1 \alpha_i^2 CV_i \text{rest}DR \tag{11}$$

On the other hand, during SEND process each node performs following subprocesses: (send1) read transaction data from database (send2) generate k-itemsets (send3) send them to proper nodes. If the time for each subprocesses are represented by SDT_i, SCT_i, SNT_i respectively, ST_i can be expressed as:

$$\Delta ST_i = \Delta SDT_i + \Delta SCT_i + \Delta SNT_i \tag{12}$$

In most cases of large scale data mining, processing time is dominated by (send2). Therefore, we can approximate expression (12) with:

$$\Delta ST_i \approx \Delta SCT_i \tag{13}$$

Since the load for (send2) subprocess depends on the amount of k-itemsets to send and this amount is proportional to DR_i that is the amount of transactions to be processed by node i, we can express SCT_i as:

$$\Delta SCT_i = \alpha_i^3 \Delta DR_i \tag{14}$$

Hence we have expanded expression (2) into:

$$\text{rest}T_i = \alpha_i^3 \text{rest}SK_i + \alpha_i^1 \alpha_i^2 CV_i \text{rest}DR \tag{15}$$

Here SK_i is denotes the amount of k-itemsets for node i to send out.

[1] See the conclusion on the precision of this approach.

Coefficients α_i^1, α_i^2, α_i^3 are determined using statistical information collected during previous interval. Expression (15) indicates that we can adjust restT_i by varying CV_i.

When *skew* defined in (3), (4) excesses *threshold*, Candidate Migration reallocates candidate itemsets among nodes so restT_i of each node becomes equal. In order to do this, Candidate Migration computes CV_i for all nodes using expression (15) and following restriction: $\sum_i^n CV_i$ = constant We can solve these equations if all CV_is are non-negative, it means there is a solution for candidate migration. Derived CV_i's are used to generate allocation plan for each node, sends the plan and instructs all nodes to begin migration process. Otherwise it sets the negative CV_is to zero before creating allocation plan. Here zero means all the candidate itemsets should be migrated to other nodes. There remains no candidate itemsets. In this case we also need Transaction Migration to be described soon.

As for the implementation, candidate migration requires the remapping of hash table. Once the itemset is migrated, new destination address is put onto the entry so that itemsets are appropriately distributed over the nodes. If remapping is done itemset by itemset, it costs a lot of space. We implemented migration based on range of hash entries.

4.2 Transaction Migration

When load is extremely skewed, we can not rely only on workload migration of RECV process. Thus, we propose another load balancing strategy based on the SEND process.

As described before, in most cases of large scale data mining, processing time is dominated by (send2). Since the load for (send2) subprocess depends on the amount of k-itemsets to be sent, we can express SCT_i as:

$$\Delta SCT_i = \beta_i^1 \Delta SK_i \tag{16}$$

Here SK_i is defined as the amount of k-itemsets for node i to send.

Each node in PC cluster has its own partition of transaction data, Transaction Migration sends some part of that transaction data to other nodes and delegates the generation of k-itemsets to those nodes. In order to do this, each node holds a list of destination nodes and their assignment. This list is dynamically updated during execution. This approach can remove the burden of SEND process of heavy nodes to nodes with excessive computing power, thus it can effectively balances the workload.

As mentioned before, the amount of k-itemsets sent to other nodes SK_i is proportional to the amount of k-itemsets generated by that node. Therefore if node j delegates DM_{ij} $(= -DM_{ji})$ k-itemsets generation to node i and the ratio of DM_{ij} against all the transaction data in node j is defined as $TM_{ij}(= -TM_{ji})$ then SK_i can also be expressed like following:

$$\Delta SK_i = \beta_i^2(\Delta DR_i + \sum_{j,j\neq i} \Delta DM_{ij}) \tag{17}$$

$$\Delta DM_{ij} = \begin{cases} TM_{ij}\Delta DR_j & TM_{ij} \geq 0 \\ TM_{ij}\Delta DR_i & TM_{ij} < 0 \end{cases} \tag{18}$$

Then the expression (16) will be:

$$\begin{aligned}\Delta SCT_i &= \beta_i^1\beta_i^2(\Delta DR_i + \sum_{j,j\neq i} \Delta DM_{ij}) \\ &= \beta_i^1\beta_i^2(\Delta DR_i + \sum_{j,j\neq i,TM_{ij}\geq 0} TM_{ij}\Delta DR_j \\ &\quad + \sum_{j,j\neq i,TM_{ij}<0} TM_{ij}\Delta DR_i)\end{aligned} \tag{19}$$

Here coefficients β_i^1, β_i^2 are determined during execution.

Finally we have the restT_i in the following form:

$$\begin{aligned}\text{rest}T_i &= \beta_i^1\beta_i^2(\text{rest}DR_i + \sum_{j,j\neq i,TM_{ij}\geq 0} TM_{ij}\text{rest}DR_j \\ &\quad + \sum_{j,j\neq i,TM_{ij}<0} TM_{ij}\text{rest}DR_i) \\ &\quad + \alpha_i^1\alpha_i^2 CV_i \text{rest}DR\end{aligned} \tag{20}$$

From expression (20), we can also control restT_i by delegating k-itemsets generation of SEND process. If Candidate Migration is not enough to overcome the skew, we can supplement it with Transaction Candidate. First, we compute CV_is as described in previous subsection, substitute them into expression (20). For candidate migration, we can analytically derive the solution, but for transaction migration we use hill-climbing method to determine TM_{ij}. TM_{ij} is distributed to the nodes. Nodes with negative TM_{ij} migrate TM_{ij} parts of transactions to light nodes. $(1 - TM_{ij})$ parts of transactions are processed in an ordinary fashion. Nodes with positive TM_{ij} receive the TM_{ij} parts of transactions from heavy nodes.

4.3 Migration plan derivation

Here we assume a coordinator who derives the global migration plan. Coordinator can run on one of the processing nodes or on a separate node. It determines the Candidate Migration and Transaction Migration plan. As mentioned earlier, since the cost of Candidate Migration is smaller, we put priority to Candidate Migration over Transaction Migration. The derivation process is as follows:

1. Acquisition of workload information and skew detection:
   Coordinator acquires workload information from every nodes and computes skew using expression (3). If skew is detected, it proceeds to the following steps.

2. Migration planning:
   Coordinator makes a plan for Candidate Migration using expression (15). If skew still presents, it also creates another plan for Transaction Migration using expression (20).

3. The execution of migration plan:
   Coordinator sends migration plan to all processing nodes and instructs them to reallocate the load. When Candidate Migration is employed, each node transfers candidate itemsets according to the plan and renews the hash table. It also remakes the destination list of transaction data if Transaction Migration is needed.

The above procedure is periodically invoked. Coordinator checks the skew condition every fixed time interval. The complete load balancing is difficult by any means. Error gradually accumulates. Once it becomes beyond the threshold, the coordinator tries to balance the workload again.

5 Performance Evaluation on PC Cluster

5.1 PC Cluster

We have developed a large scale PC cluster consists of 108 PCs interconnected with 155 Mbps ATM and 10 Mbps Ethernet networks[8, 13]. Initially the PC cluster was made up of 100 PCs with 200 MHz Pentium Pro only and then we have added another 8 nodes but with more powerful 333 MHz Pentium II since the performance of PC hardware had improved dramatically. We implement our load balancing strategies on this heterogeneous system. We create two processes on each node, one handles SEND process and the other takes care of RECV process.

5.2 Experimental Environment and Transaction Dataset

In order to simplify the problem and to show clearly the effectiveness of our approach we have made performance evaluation on a group of four nodes each with different CPU power, disk performance and data distribution as shown in table 1. The datasets that mimic retail sales data are generated using procedure described in [1]. The parameters used are described in table 2. Dataset 1 and dataset 2 have 1 and 1.5 million transactions respectively. In practice, we are force to mine database in various situation, so data distribution is skewed. The dataset 1 amounts to 80MB and it is partitioned into 40MB, 20MB, 10MB and 10MB and allocated to over four nodes. Thus, each nodes has different size of dataset. We put least amount of data to node 4 while employing fast microprocessor in order to artificially generate skew. This is prepared for candidate migration experiments. The dataset 2 is 120MB, and is devided into 80MB,20MB,10MB and 10MB. Apparently experiment with dataset 2 has higher skew than that with dataset 1. This is used for transaction migration experiments. And in all of the experiments, the *skew* value was set to 0.2 [2]. Here we changed the size of data sets, just because the target data set could be different for each data mining applications. Thus uneven data distribution naturally happens in such situations.

	Node 1	Node 2	Node 3	Node 4
Proc.	P.Pro	P.Pro	P.Pro	P.II
Clock	200MHz	200MHz	200MHz	333MHz
Disk	SCSI	SCSI	SCSI	IDE
DataSet1	40MB	20MB	10MB	10MB
DataSet2	80MB	20MB	10MB	10MB

Table 1: Execution environment

	DataSet1	DataSet2
Number of transactions	1000000	1500000
Avg. size of transactions	20	20
Number of items	5000	5000

Table 2: Datasets

5.3 Performance evaluation results

Experiment with Dataset 1 for candidate migration

The numbers of candidate itemsets(C) and large itemsets(L) resulted from data mining of dataset 1 with 0.7% minimum support are shown in table 3. It is known that generally second pass produces the largest amount of candidate itemsets. The execution traces without any load migration are shown in Figure 2. The figure shows four different resource usage: CPU, disk, interconnection network (send/receive). Horizontal axis is elapsed time and vertical axis denotes utilization ratio for CPU and data transfer throughput for disk read and interconnection network. The network throughput is divided into two parts, send throughput and receive throughput.

Since we are activating four nodes, we could show four different traces. But we omit that for Node 3, since the space is limited. The figure shows that each node generates k-itemsets and sends them to destination nodes consecutively. In the first half of second pass Node 1 is too busy with RECV process receiving k-itemsets from other nodes, and could not even afford to read its own transaction data and perform SEND process. On the other hand, Node 4 with more powerful CPU and less data finishes reading its 10MB transaction data in first 40 seconds and spends the rest of time just waiting for incoming k-itemsets from other nodes. Node 2 has more work than Node 4 but

[2] In this case, result of some experiments, we set *skew* 0.2. But we think this parameter's tuning is one of the future works

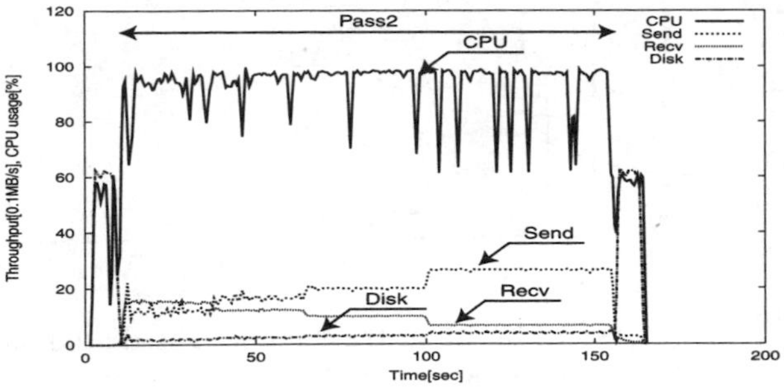

(a)Node1

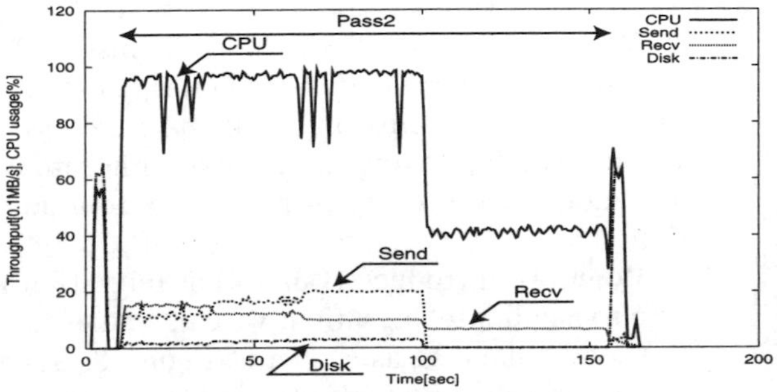

(b)Node2

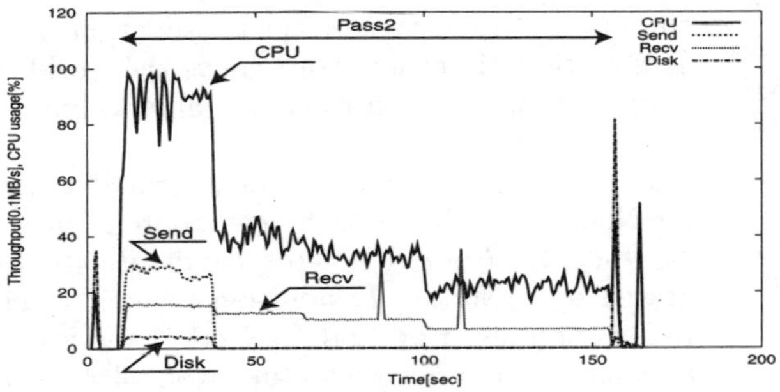

(b)Node4

Figure 2: Execution trace without load balancing (DataSet1)

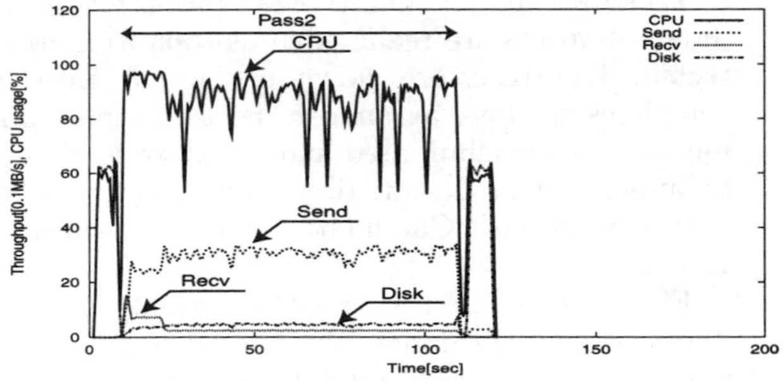

(a)Node1

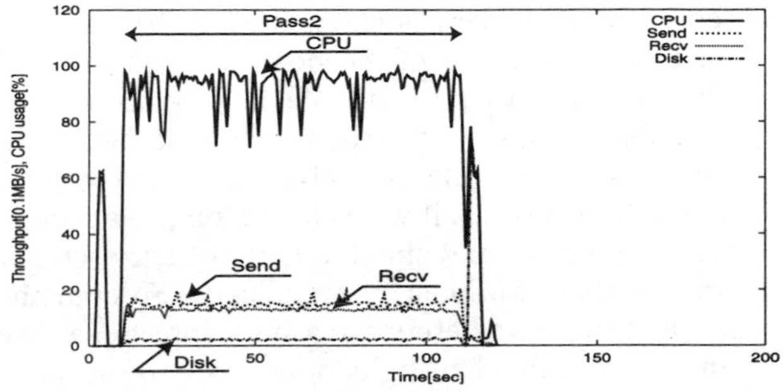

(b)Node2

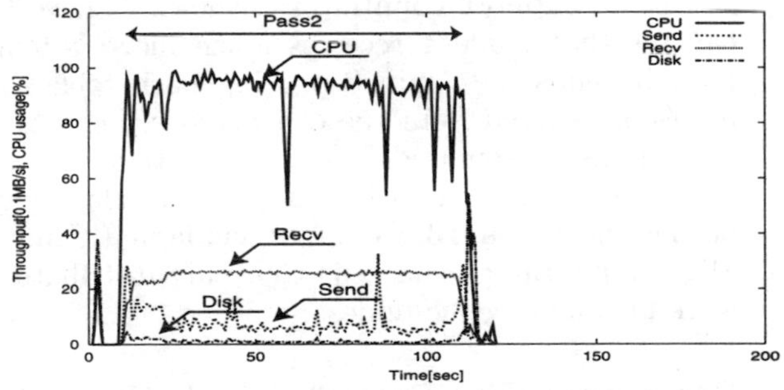

(b)Node4

Figure 3: Execution trace with Candidate Migration (DataSet1)

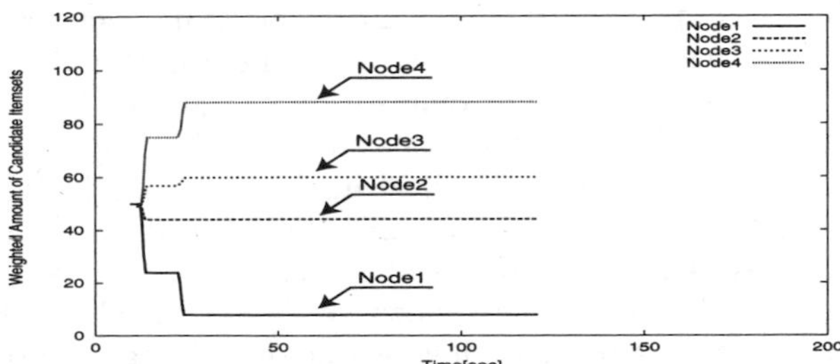

Figure 4: Migration trace for weighted amount of candidate itemsets(DataSet1)

	DataSet1		DataSet2	
	C	L	C	L
Pass 1	5000	989	5000	982
Pass 2	488566	54	481671	51
Pass 3	42	4	38	4
Pass 4	0	0	0	0

Table 3: Number of candidate itemset and large itemset for DataSet1 and DataSet2

it completes reading the transaction data much earlier than Node 1. The total execution time is 164.03 s.

When we apply Candidate Migration strategy, candidate itemsets are reallocated as soon as skew is detected. The traces are shown in Figure 3. Every node completes its task at almost the same time indicating the skew is eliminated and workload is evenly distributed. The processing time is also greatly improved; data mining with Candidate Migration requires only 120.21 s.

Figure 4 shows the trace of weighted candidate itemsets of all the nodes. We can see that Node 1 and Node 2 migrate their candidate itemsets to Node 3 and Node 4. The amount of migrated itemsets gradually increases and finally converged to a certain value. Currently the load skew is checked every 10 seconds. But for first several tens of seconds we should not wait 10 seconds, such a long time. We had better wait longer time for the system to reach certain stable condition, where we can calculate α values in the expression (15) precisely. However, if we wait too long, the nodes with faster processor and small amount of transactions will process their workload very quickly. So even though some of the parameters are a bit imprecise, we should migrate workload to light nodes as early as possible. After that, we can gradually tune the workload by performing additional migration.

During support counting, as shown Figure 3, we can see that Node 4 receives much more k-itemsets than it sends out. Since probing hash table for k-itemsets received from the other nodes precedes that for k-itemsets from node's own transaction data, reading transactions from disk is suppressed. Thus by comparing Figure 2 and 3, we can conclude that Candidate Migration strategy succeeds to evenly distributes the work load among the nodes.

Experiment with Dataset 2 for both candidate migration and transaction migration

We did an experiment with more skewed environment using dataset 2. Result of data mining using dataset 2 and 0.7% minimum support is also shown in table 3. It produces most of candidate itemsets during second pass like dataset 1. Node 1 is becoming the bottleneck of the parallelization as shown in Figure 5. Since the space is limited, we omit the traces of Node 2 and 3, and shows the behavior of only Node 1 and 4. The total execution time is 287.09 s.

By introducing the Candidate Migration, performance can be improved. The burden of workload is dispersed from Node 1 since the candidate itemsets are reallocated to other nodes, which is shown in Figure 6. The processing time is reduced to 198.36 s. However since the load is extremely concentrated at Node 1, as figure 6 shows, Candidate Migration alone can not get rid of that skew completely. Node 4 finishes reading out the transactions from disk at around 125 s. After

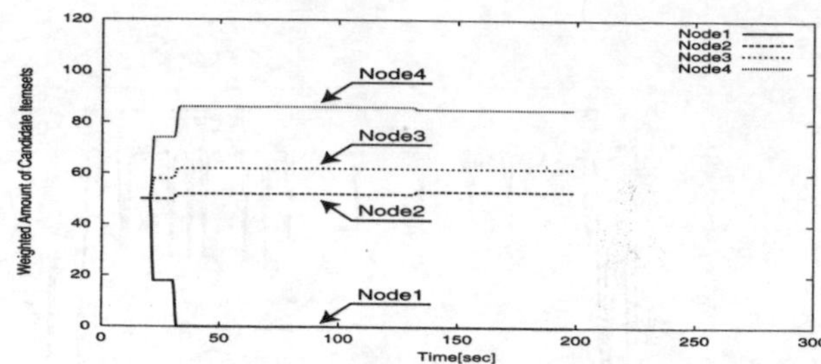

Figure 7: Migration trace for weighted amount of candidate itemsets(DataSet2)

that, it just receives the itemsets from other nodes. Thus the CPU usage goes down between 125 s. to 180 s. We can see that all candidate itemsets of Node 1 has been transferred to other nodes, as shown at figure 7. There remains no candidate itemsets at Node 1. Thus candidate migration cannot migrate workload any more. We need to introduce Transaction Migration.

When we introduce transaction migration in addition to candidate migration, we can achive almost perfect load balancing as shown at Figure 8. Transaction migration works very effectively for highly skewed environment. Node 1 sends its transaction data and delegates the generation of k-itemsets to other nodes. The elimination of skew records processing time of 182.18 s. Transaction Migration can remove the workload skew which Candidate Migration is unable to handle.

Figure 9 shows the trace of amount of weighted candidate itemset and amount of migrated transactions for Node 1 and Node 4. No candidate itemsets is left at Node 1. Node 4 accepts candidate itemsets migrated from Node1. In addition to it, it receives the transaction given by Node 1. Node 1 sends out transactions to the other nodes and Node 4 receives some of the transactions from Node 1.

Experiment for scalability

We have also examined the scalability of our strategies. We scaled up the system by multiplying the configuration we used so far. We used the configuration of a group of 4 nodes as multiplication unit and expanded the system from 4 nodes to 8, 12, 16, 24 and 32 nodes. We retained the composition of the 4 node system as described in table with dataset 1. Namely 8 node system is composed by just duplicating the original 4 node system. 12 node system is by replicating the original system three times and so on.

The results are shown in figure 10. The amount of transaction on each node does not change. So the total volume of transaction increases proportionally as the number of nodes increases. Execution time increases slightly as the number of nodes increases. As the number of nodes increases, the overhead time for synchronization becomes non-negligible. We think this is the

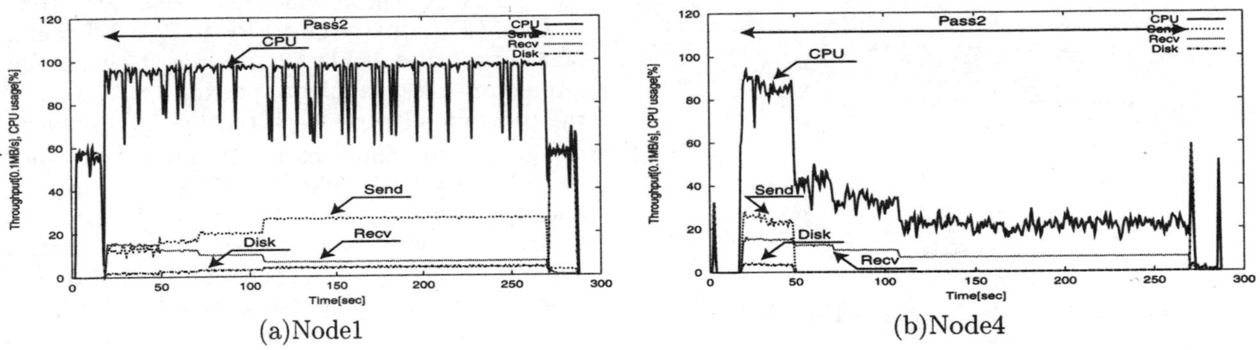

(a)Node1 (b)Node4

Figure 5: Execution trace without any load balancing(DataSet2)

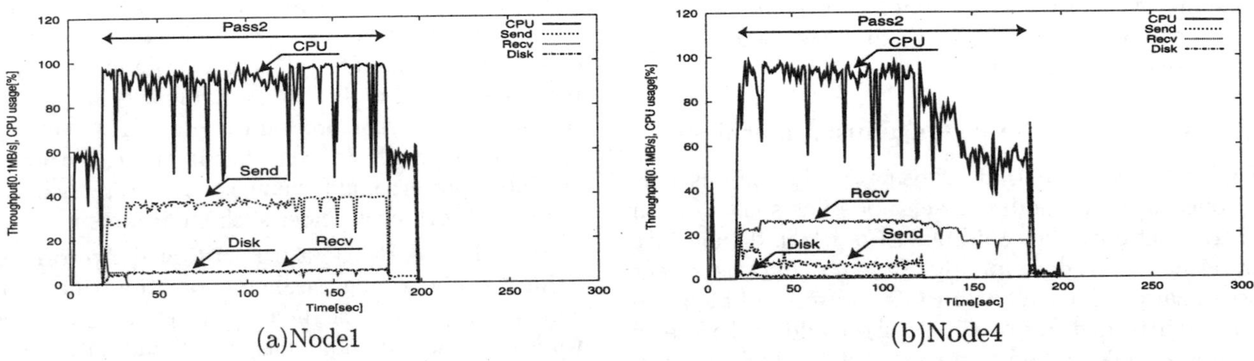

(a)Node1 (b)Node4

Figure 6: Execution trace with Candidate Migration(DataSet2)

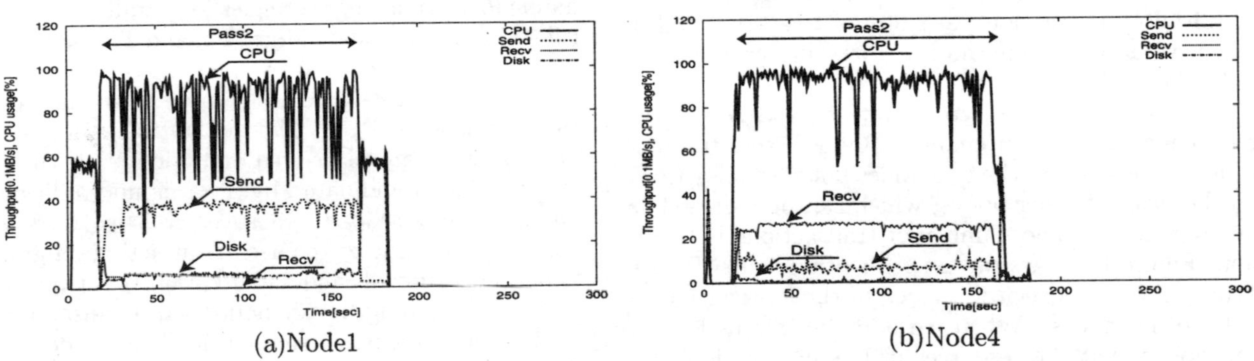

(a)Node1 (b)Node4

Figure 8:Execution trace with both Candidate Migration and Transaction Migration(DataSet2)

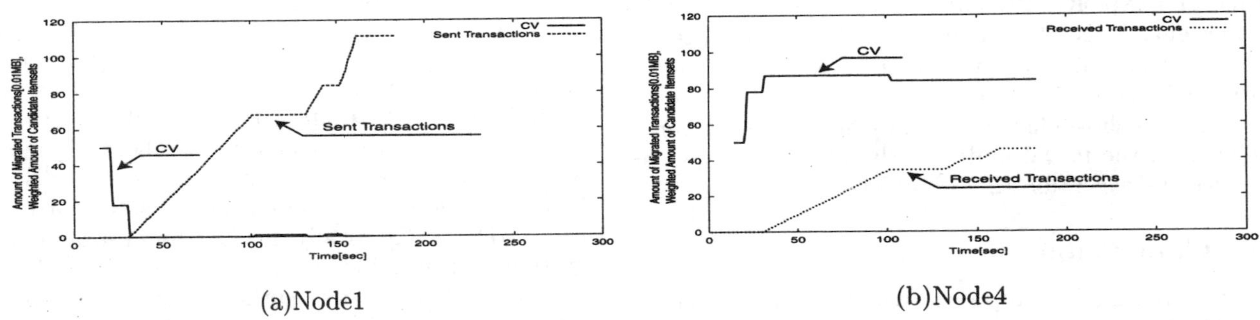

(a)Node1 (b)Node4

Figure 9:Migration trace of weighted candidate itemsets and transactions(DataSet2)

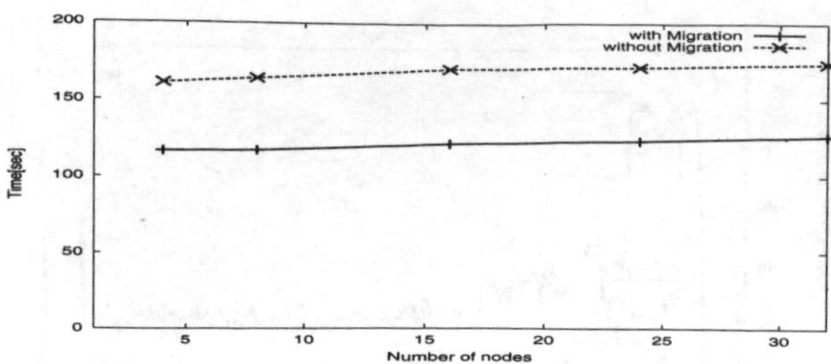

Figure 10: Scale-up results(DataSet1)

reason of slight performance degradation. We will describe this problem as a future extension at the conclusion. We are currently planing to introduce more nodes with 450MHz Pentium II and Xeon and perform larger scale experiment.

Experiment for the use of unused machines

So far we assumed that transaction database is partitioned over the nodes. Each node has some portion of transactions. We could use PC's which do not have transactions for data mining. In real situations, recent organizations have a lot of PC's and some of them are not used from time to time. We could make use of such idle PC's, in addition to the PC's which are originally assigned for data mining. This experiment tries to show how our scheme works in such environments.

Initially transactions are stored over two nodes. Then we add four idle nodes. Here in order to simplify the problem, we use same kinds of PC's. From the machine hardware type point of view, this might be homogeneous environment. But we store transactions on the disks of the two nodes but no transactions on the disks of other nodes, which can be regarded as heterogeneous. The number of transactions is 1 million. Figure 11 shows the experimental results. Figure 11(a) shows the execution trace of the experiment on only initial nodes. When we add the idle nodes, we can not exploit the resources of idel nodes effectively as shown figure 11(b). As you can see from the figure 11(c), by migrating the workload from the initial two nodes to the idle nodes, we can reduce the execution time and exploit CPU and memory resources of idle nodes effectively. And figure 11(d) shows the scale-up result, when initially 4 million transactions are stored over eight nodes, then we add idle nodes from one to sixteen. As shown figure 11(d), by migrating the workload from the initial nodes to the idle nodes, we can reduce the execution time significantly.

6 Conclusion

In this paper, we proposed dynamic load balancing strategies for parallel association rule mining on heterogeneous PC cluster system. Due to the short development period of recent PCs, it is inevitable that the PC cluster system becomes heterogeneous. Different types of CPUs are used from PC to PC. Different kinds of disks are also employed. In order to utilize all the system resources as fully as possible, we have to make the program adaptive to its runtime environment.

Compilation approach has its limitation, since the available resource might be different run by run. In addition, recent softwares have a lot of knobs, that is, tuning parameters, which makes system maintenance so difficult. This problem is pointed out also in Asilomar Report [16]. Thus the system had better adapt itself to the runtime environment autonomously.

In our proposed scheme, the parameters such as performance ratios are not necessary. At run time, the program derives several necessary coefficients by itself. Thus a programmer/compiler does not have to care about them. If we plan to use the unused system resources, say at night, the availability is unforseeable. In some case, other program might enter the system and start to run. So even during the execution, the available power might change. Our approach is designed to work even under such environment.

We adopted HPA(Hash Partitioned Apriori) algorithm for underlying parallel association rule mining. This partitions the candidate itemsets over the nodes, while ordinary methods just copy candidate itemsets all over the nodes. HPA can improve the memory efficiency significantly. We proposed two kinds of dynamic load balancing strategies for parallel association rule mining, Candidate Migration and Transaction Migration. We showed that by changing the allocation of candidate itemsets among the nodes, we can control the workload of PCs. The amount of candidates to be migrated can be derived analytically. If the skew is very high, Candidate Migration is not sufficient to balance the workload. In such case, we introduced yet another strategy named Transaction Migration. Since generation of candidate itemset from transaction is time consuming, heavy nodes send transactions to light nodes to whom itemset generation is delegated. This incurs extra data transmission but is effective to remove the workload skew.

In order to clearly show the effectiveness of our approach, we set up rather simple 4 node cluster with two kinds of PCs and varied the size of dataset for each PC. We demonstrated the feasibility of our approach showing the execution trace. By examining the trace, we confirmed that the proposed scheme effectively works to remove workload inbalance. Candidate Migration works under medium skew environment. If the skew is high and candidate migration can not sufficiently help, the system automatically invokes the Transaction Migration. In addition, we also showed the scalability experiments. We increased the size of the system from 4 nodes to 32 nodes. We found sufficient scalability can be archived

Currently, our algorithm estimates the itemset fre-

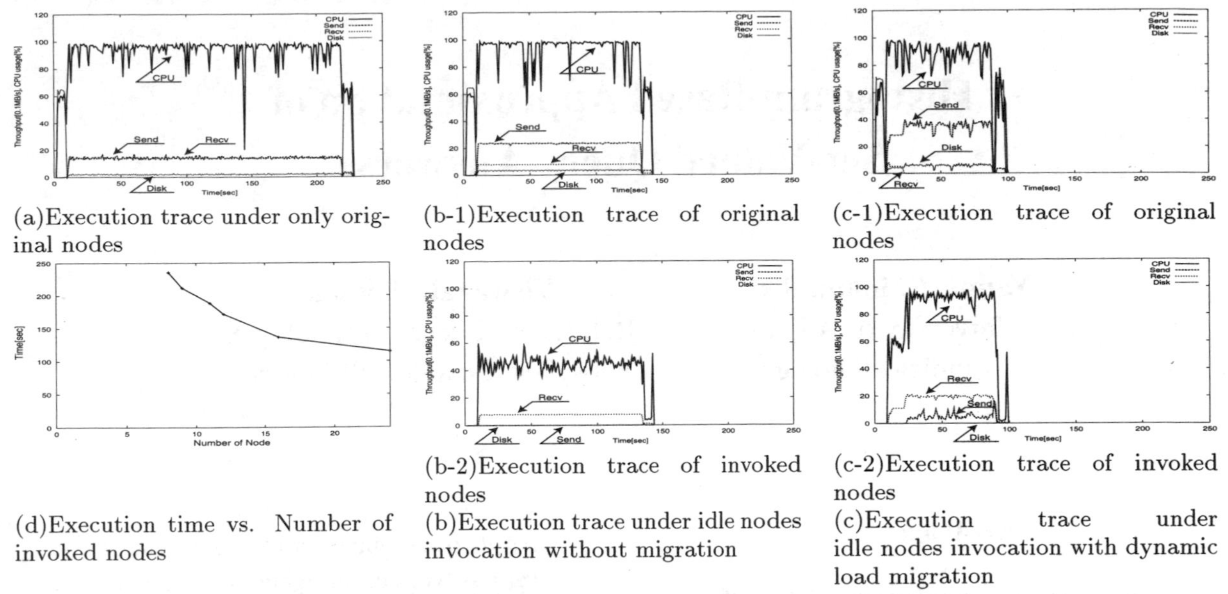

(a)Execution trace under only original nodes

(b-1)Execution trace of original nodes

(c-1)Execution trace of original nodes

(b-2)Execution trace of invoked nodes

(c-2)Execution trace of invoked nodes

(d)Execution time vs. Number of invoked nodes

(b)Execution trace under idle nodes invocation without migration

(c)Execution trace under idle nodes invocation with dynamic load migration

Figure 11: Experiment for the use of unused machines

quency using the support values of the previous pass. Based on this estimated itemset frequency, we derive the relative workload of candidate itemsets and determine the migration plan. Apparently this estimation can not be precise. During execution, we could modify the estimated value by using the runtime statistics. We are now examining the effect of estimation error and also implementing the extended version using runtime learning. Another extension is on the synchronization. In current implementation, the Candidate Migration is performed using barrier synchronization. That is, on migration all the nodes stop and migrate candidate simultaneously. Once migration completes, the system restarts again. If the size of the system becomes large, obviously it incurs a lot of overhead. So asynchronous migration should be employed, which we are going to investigate. And we also plan on implementing our ideas in generalized association rules[12], and sequential patterns. Still remains lots of interesting extensions, such as elimination of coordination nodes. Fully distributed algorithm is more challenging. So far we have focused on heterogeniety of hardware but same approach should work among PC's with different OS's. The number of nodes in our experiments is not necessarily large. The experimental results on 100 node environments is being undertaken, which will be reported in the future paper.

References

[1] Rakesh Agrawal and Ramakrishnan Srikant. "Fast Algorithms for Mining Association Rules". In *Proc. of VLDB* , pp. 487–499, Sep. 1994.

[2] Rakesh Agrawal and John C. Shafer. "Parallel Mining of Associaton Rules". In *IEEE TKDE*, Vol. 8, No. 6, pp. 962–969, Dec. 1996.

[3] *http://cesdis.gsfc.nasa.gov/beowulf/beowulf.html*

[4] D.W. Cheung, J. Han, V.T. Ng, A.W. Fu, and Y. Fu. "A Fast Distributed Algorithms for Mining Association Rules." In *Proc. of PDIS*, pp. 31–42, Dec. 1996.

[5] Hasanat M. Dewan, Mauricio A. Hernandez, Kui W. Mok, Salvatore J.Stolfo "Predictive Dynamic Load Balancing of Parallel Hash-Joins Over Heterogeneous Processors in the Presence of Data Skew." In *Proc. of PDIS*, pp. 40–49, 1994.

[6] D. DeWitt and J. Gray "Parallel Database Systems: The Future of High Performance Database Systems." In *Communications of the ACM*, Vol. 35, No. 6, pp. 85–98, Jun. 1992.

[7] E.-H.Han and G.Karypis and Vipin Kumar "Scalable Parallel Data Mining for Association Rules." In *Proc. of SIGMOD*, pp. 277–288, May. 1997

[8] Masaru Kitsuregawa, Takayuki Tamura, Masato Oguchi "Parallel Database Processing/Data Mining on Large Scale ATM Connected PC Cluster." In *Euro-PDS*, pp. 313–320, Jun. 1997

[9] J.S.Park, M.-S.Chen, P.S.Yu "Efficient Parallel Algorithms for Mining Association Rules" In *Proc. of CIKM*, pp. 31–36, Nov. 1995

[10] S.Parthasarathy and M.J.Zaki and W.Li "Memory Placement Techniques for Parallel Association Mining." In *Proc. of KDD*, pp. 304–308, Aug. 1998

[11] T. Shintani and M. Kitsuregawa "Hash Based Parallel Algorithms for Mining Association Rules". In *Proc. of PDIS*, pp. 19–30, Dec. 1996.

[12] T. Shintani, M. Kitsuregawa "Parallel Mining Algorithms for Generalized Association Rules with Classification Hierarchy." In *Proc. of SIGMOD*, pp. 25–36, 1998.

[13] Takayuki Tamura, Masato Oguchi, Masaru Kitsuregawa "Parallel Database Processing on a 100 Node PC Cluster: Cases for Decision Support Query Processing and Data Mining." In *Super Computing 97::High Performance Networking and Computing*, 1997

[14] Yongqiao Xiao and David W. Cheung "Effect of Data Skewness in Parallel Data Mining of Association Rules ". In *Proc. of PAKDD*, pp. 48–60, Apr. 1998.

[15] M.J.Zaki, S.Parthasarathy, M.Ogihara and W.Li "New Parallel Algorithms for Fast Discovery of Association Rules". Data Mining and Knowledge Discovery, Dec. 1997.

[16] P.Bernstein, M.Brodie, S.Ceri, et.al "The Asilomar Report". Sep. 1998.

Histogram-Based Approximation of Set-Valued Query Answers

Yannis E. Ioannidis* †
University of Athens
yannis@di.uoa.gr

Viswanath Poosala
Bell Labs - Lucent Technologies
poosala@research.bell-labs.com

Abstract

Answering queries approximately has recently been proposed as a way to reduce query response times in on-line decision support systems, when the precise answer is not necessary or early feedback is helpful. Most of the work in this area uses sampling-based techniques and handles aggregate queries, ignoring queries that return relations as answers. In this paper, we extend the scope of approximate query answering to general queries. We propose a novel and intuitive error measure for quantifying the error in an approximate query answer, which can be a multiset in general. We also study the use of histograms in approximate query answering as an alternative to sampling. In that direction, we develop a histogram algebra and demonstrate how complex SQL queries on a database may be translated into algebraic operations on the corresponding histograms. Finally, we present the results of an initial set of experiments where various types of histograms and sampling are compared with respect to their effectiveness in approximate query answering as captured by the introduced error measure. The results indicate that the *MaxDiff(V,A)* histograms provide quality approximations for both set-valued and aggregate queries, while sampling is competitive mainly for aggregate queries with no join operators.

* Partially supported by the members of the Wisconsin database group industrial affiliates program (http://www.cs.wisc.edu/~raghu/dbaffiliates.html) and by the Special Account (*Ειδικος Λογαριασμος*) of the Univ. of Athens under grant 70/4/3244.

† On leave from the Univ. of Wisconsin - Madison. Part of this work was done while the author was visiting Bell Labs.

Proceedings of the 25th VLDB Conference,
Edinburgh, Scotland, 1999.

1 Introduction

The users of a large number of applications pose very complex queries to Database Management Systems (DBMSs), which take a long time to execute. Examples of such applications are decision support, experiment management, etc. Given the exploratory nature of such applications, many of these queries end up producing no result of particular interest to the user. Much wasted time could have been saved if users were able to quickly see an *approximate answer* to their query, and only proceed with the complete execution if the approximate answer indicated something interesting.

It is easy to conceptualize approximating a query answer when that answer is an image; instead of the actual image, a compressed version of it is retrieved. Alternatively, a series of compressed images may be retrieved, each one being less compressed (more accurate) than the previous one, with the last one being the actual image. The key question that we want to answer is how to provide a similar kind of functionality for alphanumeric queries. For ease of presentation, we use the relational model as the underlying environment in this discussion, but the problem and the methodology followed can be applied in more general settings.

Given an SQL query, its answer is a relation, i.e., a (multi)set of tuples (we use the term *set* to mean a *multiset* whenever no confusion arises). Most earlier work in approximate query answering has been dealing with approximating individual values in the results of aggregate queries [1, 6] and does not handle general (non-aggregate) SQL queries. The few instances of past work that have dealt with general queries, have been based on defining approximations as subsets and/or supersets of the actual answer [2]. This is not very useful, however, for many database applications. Much better intuition is given by a set with roughly the same number of tuples as the actual query answer containing values that are approximations of the actual values (e.g., a numeric field having the value 10 instead of 9). This is more apparent when the query result is presented visually, where the analogy to approximating images can be drawn much closer: *a large number of somewhat misplaced points form a more desirable approximation than a small number of the actual points.*

As an example, consider the typical employee relation, and assume that a query asks for the values of the 'salary', 'age', and 'department' attributes. Further assume that the result is to be displayed visually as a set of points (*starfield*) in the salary-age space, each point representing an employee with the corresponding salary and age. The shade of each point represents the corresponding employee's department. A typical display of this information may be as shown in Figure 1.

Consider two approximations to this query answer, as shown in Figures 2 and 3. The first one (Figure 2) is a small subset of the actual answer, e.g., obtained by sample-based query processing aiming at a 20% sample. The second one (Figure 3) is a set with elements close to those of the actual query answer. We believe that, in most cases, users would much rather receive the latter than the former, as it generates a much better feel for the true answer.

The obvious question that arises is how we can obtain query result approximations of the above form. The idea we pursue in this paper is using *histograms* for this purpose. Briefly, we use histograms (in the usual manner) to approximate the data in the database and employ novel techniques to provide approximate answers using SQL queries on the histograms which are stored as relations. A great advantage of taking this route for approximate query answers is that almost all commercial database systems already maintain histograms, so obtaining such approximations does not require any fundamental changes to these systems.

Our contributions are summarized as follows:

- We have defined a novel measure to quantify the error in the approximate answer. Identifying such a measure is essential for any systematic study of approximation of set-valued query answers to take place, because it presents common grounds for comparing multiple techniques. We have shown via a series of examples that this measure provides a satisfactory idea of the quality of an approximation to a general query, while other well known metrics fail to do so.
- We have proposed storing histograms as regular relations in a relational DBMS and appropriately translating regular database queries into equivalent queries on the histograms so that approximate query answers can be obtained using the same mechanism as exact query answers. To this end, we have defined a *histogram algebra* that can be used to express all required queries on histograms, and have implemented its operators in a query processor that we have used for experimentation.
- We have performed an extensive set of experiments comparing various kinds of histograms and sampling with respect to their effectiveness in approximating general query answers. The results point to a specific class of histograms as the most effective overall.

2 Related Work

There are three aspects of this work for which we discuss related work. The first aspect is *approximate query answering*. There has been extensive work on this topic for quite some time now ranging from establishing theoretical foundations [2, 11], to building actual systems (e.g., CASE-DB [12], APPROXIMATE [20]). All these works are based on the subset/superset definition of approximations, which they obtain mostly through partial query processing. Recently, there has been some work on providing approximate answers to *aggregate queries* using precomputed samples [1], histograms [14, 15], and wavelets [19], which does not address general queries. Online aggregation [6] constitutes another style of sampling-based approximate query answering (for aggregate queries) wherein the answers are continuously refined till the exact answer is computed. In contrast to all earlier work, this paper

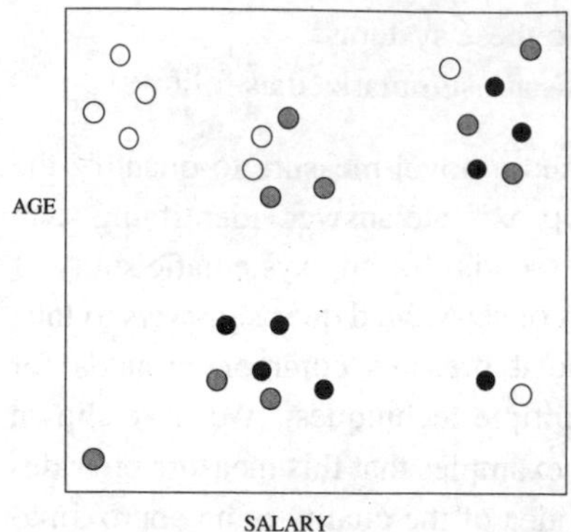

Figure 1: Visual display of query answer

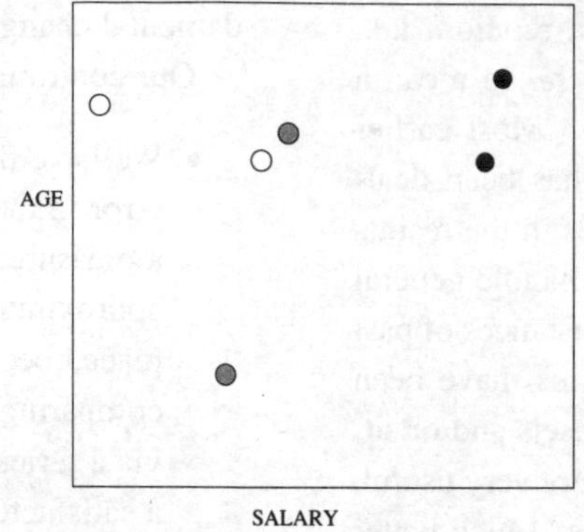

Figure 2: Visual display of approximation of query answer (as a subset)

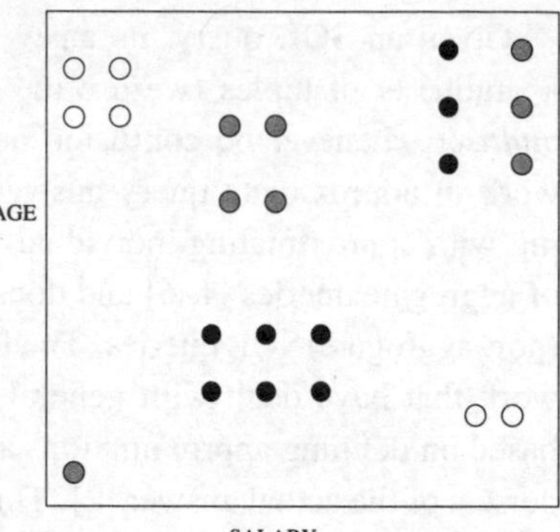

Figure 3: Visual display of approximation of query answer (through value proximity)

deals with producing one approximate query answer to either aggregate or non-aggregate queries.

The second aspect of our work is *statistical techniques*. There has been considerable amount of work in using statistical techniques to approximate data in databases, particularly for selectivity estimation in query optimizers. The three widely studied classes of techniques are *sampling* [10], *parametric techniques* [3] (approximating the data using a mathematical distribution), and *histogram (or non-parametric) techniques* [9, 13, 17]. Of these, histograms are probably the most widely used statistics in commercial database systems (e.g., they are used in the DBMSs of Oracle, Sybase, Microsoft, IBM, etc.), because a) they occupy small amounts of space and do not incur much overhead at estimation time and b) they are particularly suited for accurately approximating the skewed distributions arising in real-life. In our earlier work, we have identified several novel classes of histograms to build on one or more attributes [16, 17] and also proposed techniques for maintaining many of them incrementally up-to-date as the database is updated [5]. However, histograms have not been studied in the context of approximate query answering before.

The third aspect of our work is *quantifying the error in an approximate answer* (a multiset in general). One way to compute this error is to use a known distance metric between two multisets. However, since sets are not embeddable in metric spaces typically, there is very little advanced work in this area. We list three commonly used metrics next. First, it is common to define set-difference based on the cardinality of the symmetric difference between two sets S_1 and S_2, i.e.,

$$dist_{\{\}}(S_1, S_2) = |(S_1 - S_2) \cup (S_2 - S_1)|.$$

This can be generalized for multisets by making each copy count in the multiset difference. Second, for data distributions, there is the approach based on the various distribution moments. If $F_1 = \{f_{11}, \ldots, f_{1n}\}$ and $F_2 = \{f_{21}, \ldots, f_{2n}\}$ represent the frequency sets of two data distributions on a universe of n elements, the family (for $m \geq 1$) of moment-related distances are as follows:

$$dist_{dd}^{(m)}(F_1, F_2) = \frac{1}{n}\left(\sum_{k=1}^{n} |f_{1k} - f_{2k}|^m\right)^{1/m}.$$

Finally, the *Hausdorff distance* is another well known metric for comparing two sets [7]. Briefly, two sets are within *Hausdorff distance* h from each other iff any item in one set is within distance h from some item of the other set.

However, none of these approaches capture proximity between the sets in the way we believe is required for approximate query answering. One of the key limitations of the first two metrics is that they do not take into account the actual values of the set elements. For example, according to these two metrics, the sets $\{5\}$ and $\{100\}$ are at the same distance from the set $\{5.1\}$. On the other hand, the Hausdorff metric ignores the frequency of the elements in the sets. For example, the sets $\{5\}$ and $\{5, 5, 5\}$ are at the same Hausdorff distance (equal to 0) from the set $\{5\}$. In contrast, our error measure strikes a balance between values and frequencies, and is therefore more natural for evaluating approximate answers.

3 Error Measure for Set-Valued Approximate Answers

For queries returning a single numerical answer, there is a straightforward metric for the error of an approximate answer. It is simply the difference between the actual and approximate answers. For queries returning a single tuple containing only numerical fields, one can use the *Euclidean Distance* (square root of the sum of squared differences between the corresponding fields). In this section, we develop a novel and robust measure of the error in an answer to a query returning a *multiset* of tuples or numbers. We have examined many formulas before concluding on the one that we present below. The key criterion in our choice has been capturing as much as possible the nature of approximation implied in approximate query answering, where both the actual values in an answer and their frequencies count.

3.1 Error Formula

Consider two multisets $S_1 = \{u_1, \ldots, u_n\}$ and $S_2 = \{v_1, \ldots, v_m\}$ corresponding to the actual and approximate answers, respectively. Let *dist* be an error metric for the object type of the multiset elements. Based on this, our metric of the error of S_2 with respect to S_1 is computed as follows: first, determine which element in the approximate answer best corresponds to an element in the exact answer and vice versa; then, compute the error by using the *dist* between the objects mapped to each other.

In more detail, consider a complete bipartite graph G_{S_1,S_2} where the two classes of nodes correspond to the elements of the two answers (each element represented by as many nodes as there are copies of it in the answer). Each edge (u_i, v_j) is associated with a cost equal to $dist(u_i, v_j)$. Let C be a *minimum cost edge cover* of G_{S_1,S_2}, i.e., it is a subset of the edges of G_{S_1,S_2} such that (a) for each node, there is at least one edge in C adjacent to the node, and (b) the following expression is minimized:

$$MINCOVER(S_1, S_2) = \sum_{(u_i,v_j)\in C} dist(u_i, v_j). \quad (1)$$

Then, the error in the approximate answer, which we call its *Match And Compare (or MAC) distance* and denote by $MAC^{(l,m)}$ for any power $l \geq 0, m \geq 0$, is:

$$MAC^{(l,m)}(S_1, S_2) = \sum_{(u_i,v_j)\in C} mult^l(u_i, v_j) \times dist[q]^m(u_i, v_j), \quad (2)$$

where for each edge (u_i, v_j) in C such that d_1 edges are incident to u_i and d_2 edges are incident to v_j, the following hold:

$$mult(u_i, v_j) = max(1, max(d_1, d_2) - 1)$$

$$dist[q](u_i, v_j) = \begin{cases} dist(u_i, v_j), \text{if } max(d_1, d_2) = 1 \\ dist(u_i, v_j) + q, \text{otherwise} \end{cases}$$

Essentially, $mult(u_i, v_j)$ captures the extent to which one of u_i or v_j is paired up with multiple elements of the other multiset[1]. By choosing $l = 0$, one can also opt to ignore the effects of multiplicities, e.g., when interested in the set (not multiset) properties of the two answers. Likewise, q (for *q*uantum, any small integer, typically 1), increases the error due to paired up elements whenever this pairing up is not exclusive on both sides.

Figure 4 shows a small set of examples that illustrate *MAC* and the mapping C. We note that many well-known metrics often failed to capture our intuition behind the error in multiset approximation, whereas *MAC* has worked quite satisfactorily.

Some indication of the naturalness of the formula is that it is symmetric (i.e, $MAC(S_1, S_2) = MAC(S_2, S_1)$) and for certain special cases, it reduces to well-accepted specialized distances and error metrics: for singleton answers, *MAC* is the *dist* between their elements; for frequency distributions with the same set of elements appearing in both (and for $q = 1$), *MAC* is closely related to the corresponding moment-related distance raised to the lth power; and for accurate answers, *MAC* is always equal to zero.

It should be noted that this represents a first attempt at evaluating an approximate answer set. In fact, *MAC* has some drawbacks when used as a general set distance metric. It does not satisfy the *triangle inequality* required of general distance metrics, i.e., $MAC(S_1, S_2) + MAC(S_2, S_3)$ may some times be less than $MAC(S_1, S_3)$. The following counter example shows this: S1 = { 1 }, S2 = { 3 }, S3 = { 5,5 }. It follows that *MAC*(S1,S3) = 8 + 2q, which is greater than *MAC*(S1,S2) + *MAC*(S2,S3) = 2 + (4 + 2q). Our attempts to fix this deficiency have revealed that *MAC* will have to be significantly simplified in the process, causing it to face the same problems as the other metrics, i.e., not capturing intuition behind approximate query answering. Another minor problem with *MAC* is that in some cases there may be multiple minimum-cost edge covers resulting in different values for *MAC*. In such cases, one should ideally use the least value of *MAC*.

[1] It can be easily shown that $min(d_1, d_2) = 1$ always. If both degrees are greater than 1, one can drop the edge between the two nodes, resulting in a lower cost edge cover.

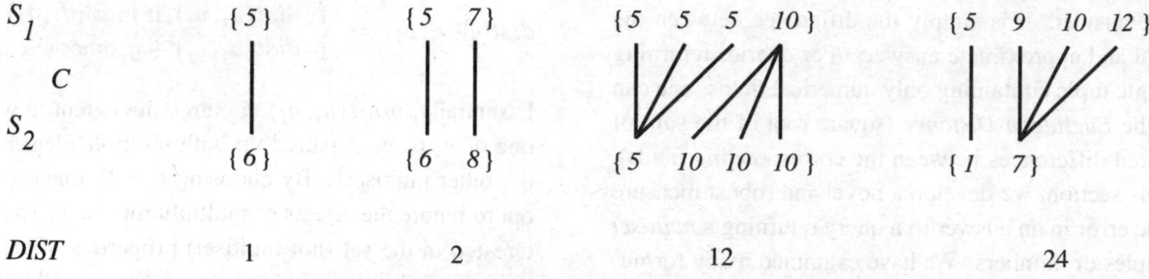

Figure 4: Examples of MAC distances between Answers

3.2 Computation of *MAC*

The difficult part of computing *MAC* is identifying the minimum cost edge cover C between the two answers. For this, we have identified an efficient polynomial time algorithm based on a reduction to the *minimum cost perfect match* problem. The details of this algorithm are given in a related technical report. Here, we present a more efficient heuristic. First, map each element to its closest element in the other set (this is done efficiently by first sorting the two sets). This may result in some surplus edges, i.e., edges that can be removed and still obtain a cover. These are the edges both of whose nodes have degrees greater than 1. Next, go through these edges in decreasing order of their costs (distances) and eliminate each one that remains redundant when it is examined. The complexity of this algorithm is easily seen to be $O(nlogn)$, because of the sorting operations.

4 Histograms

In this section, we give an overview of standard histogram-based techniques for summarizing the data in a database [17, 16]. First, we present some useful definitions.

The *value set* $\mathcal{V}_i$ of attribute X_i of relation R is the set of values of X_i that are present in R. Let $\mathcal{V}_i = \{v_i(k)\text{: } 1 \leq k \leq D_i\}$, where $v_i(k) < v_i(j)$ when $k < j$. The *spread* $s_i(k)$ of $v_i(k)$ is defined as $s_i(k) = v_i(k+1) - v_i(k)$, for $1 \leq i \leq D_i$. (We take $s_i(D_i) = 1$.) The *frequency* $f_i(k)$ of $v_i(k)$ is the number of tuples in R with $X_i = v_i(k)$. The *area* $a_i(k)$ of $v_i(k)$ is defined as $a_i(k) = f_i(k) \times s_i(k)$. The *data distribution* of X_i is the set of pairs $\mathcal{T}_i = \{ (v_i(1), f_i(1)), (v_i(2), f_i(2)), \ldots, (v_i(D_i), f_i(D_i)) \}$. Typically, real-life attributes tend to have *skewed* data distributions, i.e., they may have unequal frequencies and/or unequal spreads.

Example 4.1 The following table shows how each parameter defined above is instantiated for a hypothetical attribute.

Quantity	Data Distribution Element				
Value	10	60	70	90	100
Frequency	100	120	10	80	2000
Spread	50	10	20	10	1
Area	5000	1200	200	800	2000

A *histogram* on an attribute X is constructed by using a *partitioning rule* to partition its data distribution into β (≥ 1) mutually disjoint subsets called *buckets* and approximating the frequencies and values in each bucket in some common fashion. In particular, the most effective approach for values is the *uniform spread* assumption [17], under which the attribute values in a bucket are assumed to be placed at equal intervals between the lowest and highest values in the bucket. The most effective approach for frequencies is to approximate the frequencies in a bucket by their average (*uniform frequency assumption*). In practice, each bucket in a histogram keeps the following information: the total number of tuples that fall in the bucket (*tot*), and for each dimension i, the low and high values (lo_i, hi_i) and the number of distinct values ($count_i$) in that dimension (the subscripts are dropped for single-dimensional histograms). For the purpose of this work, we store histograms as regular relations in the database with each bucket forming a tuple. For ease of explanation in later sections, we also include additional fields: the average spreads along each dimension ($sp_i = \frac{hi_i - lo_i}{u_i - 1}$) and the average frequency for the bucket ($avg = \frac{tot}{u_1 u_2 \ldots u_d}$).

As an example, consider a 3-bucket histogram on the above data with the following bucketization of attribute values: $\{10\}$, $\{60, 70, 90\}$, $\{100\}$. The buckets in this histogram are given below.

tot	*lo*	*hi*	*count*	*sp*	*avg*
100	10	10	1	-	100
210	60	90	3	15	70
2000	100	100	1	-	2000

Conceptually, one can "expand" a histogram into a relation containing the approximate attribute values as its tuples, with each tuple appearing as many times as the approximate frequency of that value. We call this the *approximate relation* (*ApproxRel*) of that histogram. For a 1-dimensional histogram H, its approximate relation can be computed using the following SQL query, called `Expand.sql`[2].

$$\begin{array}{ll} \texttt{SELECT} & (H.lo + I_C.idx * H.sp) \\ \texttt{FROM} & H, I_C, I_A \\ \texttt{WHERE} & I_C.idx \leq H.ct \text{ and } I_A.idx \leq H.avg; \end{array}$$

Here, H is the histogram stored as a relation and I_A, I_C are auxiliary relations, each with a single attribute idx. Relation I_A (resp., I_C) contains the integers $1, 2, .., A$ (resp., $1, 2, .., C$), where A (resp., C) is the largest *average frequency* (resp., *count*) in the buckets of H. Essentially, this query uses I_C to generate the positions of values within each bucket and then uses the *low* and *spread* values of the bucket to compute each of the approximate values, under the uniform spread assumption. Then, it uses I_A to replicate each value based on its frequency.

The approximate distribution captured by the above histogram looks as follows.

Quantity	Data Distribution Element				
Approx. Value	10	60	75	90	100
Approx. Frequency	100	70	70	70	2000

Histograms can also be built on multiple attributes together, by partitioning the joint distribution of the attributes into multi-dimensional buckets and using extensions of the uniform frequency and spread assumptions. It is also possible to *combine* two histograms on different sets of attributes to obtain a single histogram on the union of those two sets by making the *attribute value independence assumption*. Details on multi-dimensional histograms are given elsewhere [16]. In practice, there may be several one- or multi-dimensional histograms maintained on the attributes of a relation R. For simplicity of presentation, we assume that there is a single (multi-dimensional) histogram maintained on the full set of attributes of each relation.

Given the mechanisms of approximation within a histogram, it is clear that the accuracy of the approximation is determined by which attribute values are grouped together into each bucket. Several partitioning rules have been proposed for this purpose. For example, in an *equi-width* histogram, all buckets are assigned value ranges of equal width; in an *equi-depth* histogram, all buckets are assigned the same total number of tuples. In earlier work, we have introduced several new classes of histograms and identified a particular class of histograms, that we call *MaxDiff(V,A)*, which performs the best in estimating the selectivities of most kinds of queries. In a β-bucket *MaxDiff(V,A)* histogram, there is a bucket boundary between two successive attribute values if the difference between the *areas* of these values is one of the $\beta-1$ largest such differences. By avoiding grouping dissimilar frequencies or spreads, the MaxDiff(V,A) histogram ensures that the uniform frequency and spread assumptions do not cause much errors. As an illustration, consider the histogram presented in Example 4.1, which is a MaxDiff(V,A) histogram. Note that it clearly separates the value 10 (skewed attribute value) and the value 100 (skewed frequency) from others.

[2] It is straightforward to generalize it so that it works with a multi-dimensional histogram, but it becomes quite complex without offering any new insight, so we do not present it.

5 Query Processing Using Histograms

In this section, we develop a histogram-based solution to approximate query answering.

First, we define the notion of a *valid approximate answer* to a query using histograms. Let *ApproxRel*(H) be the approximate relation corresponding to a histogram H on relation R (Section 4). The following definition captures the intuition behind an approximate query answer based on histograms.

Definition 5.1 Consider a query Q operating on relations $R_1..R_n$, and let $H_1..H_n$ be corresponding histograms. The *valid approximate answer* for Q and $\{H_i\}$ is the result of executing Q on ApproxRel(H_i) in place of R_i, for $1 \leq i \leq n$.

Next, we present two different ways to provide valid approximate answers.

5.1 Naive Approach

This approach is a direct application of Definition 5.1 and involves two steps: first, compute the approximate relations of all the histograms on the relations in the query (using the `Expand.sql` query given in the previous section); next, execute the query Q on these relations. This approach is clearly impractical because ApproxRel(H_i) may have as many tuples as R_i itself.

5.2 Efficient Approach

First, we formally define a *valid translation* of a query.

Definition 5.2 Consider a query Q operating on relations $R_1..R_n$, and let $H_1..H_n$ be corresponding histograms. A query Q' on these histograms is a *valid translation* of Q if the result of Q' is a histogram whose corresponding approximate relation is identical to the *valid approximate answer* for Q and $\{H_i\}$.

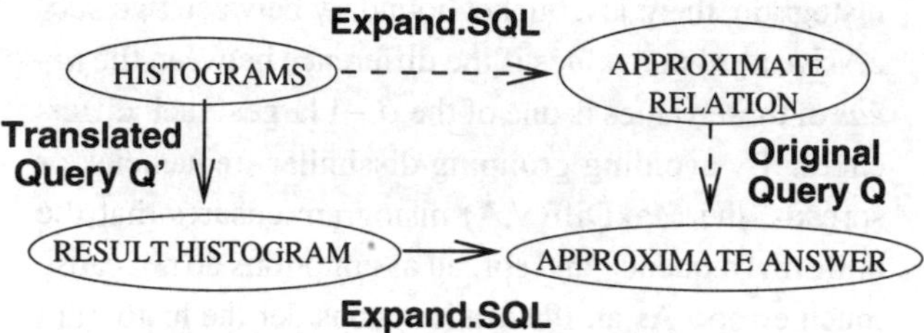

Figure 5: Valid Query Translation

Definition 5.2 is illustrated in the transition diagram of Figure 5. Essentially, Q' is a valid translation of Q when both paths from the HISTOGRAMS node to the APPROXIMATE ANSWERS node generate the same answer. The dashed path in Figure 5 corresponds to the above naive application of Definition 5.1 to obtain a valid query answer. The solid path in the figure, however, suggests the following, much more efficient approach to obtain the same result:

1. Obtain a valid translation Q' of Q
2. Execute Q' on $\{H_i\}$ to obtain a result histogram H_{res}
3. Compute ApproxRel(H_{res}) using `Expand.sql`

Since most of the query processing takes place on small histogram relations, this approach is clearly very efficient.

The last two steps above are straightforward. The rest of this subsection concentrates on the first step and provides valid translations for various query classes. We consider aggregate and non-aggregate SQL queries containing just *Select, From,* and *Where* clauses, but no *nesting, Group-By,* or *Having* clauses. These features can be added in a straightforward manner.

5.2.1 Non-Aggregate Queries

These queries are equivalent to relational algebra expressions involving just *selection, projection,* and *join* operations. A query Q in this category is translated as follows:

1. Construct an operator tree T of *select, project,* and *join* operations that is equivalent to Q.
2. Replace all the base relations in T by their corresponding histograms (that is, histogram relations as described in Section 4 to obtain another tree T'.
3. Starting from the bottom of T', translate each operator into an SQL query that takes the histograms from the operator's children and generates another histogram as output.

Note that, in general, there are many algebraic expressions that may be chosen in step 1 of the translation process, each giving a different valid translation. Although they may differ in cost, these costs are so low that there is no real need to optimize among the algebraic expressions.

The key contribution in the above process is step 3, as it involves valid translations of individual operators, which although not very complex are not completely straightforward either. They are described in detail below. For simplicity, we only deal with one-dimensional histograms (the proof of validity and extensions to multi-dimensional histograms are straightforward and are given elsewhere [8].

1. Equality Selection ($\sigma_{A=c}$): Equality selection is translated into the following query $Q_=$:

`SELECT` $c, c, 1, avg$
`FROM` H
`WHERE` $(c \geq lo)$ and $(c \leq hi)$ and $(mod(c - lo, sp) = 0)$;

2. Range Selection ($\sigma_{A\leq c}$): Range selection is translated into the query $Q_\sigma = Q_a \cup Q_b$, where Q_a and Q_b are given below:

Q_a : `SELECT` $*$
`FROM` H
`WHERE` $hi \leq c$;

Q_b : `SELECT` $lo, lo + sp * \lfloor \frac{c-lo}{sp} \rfloor *$ $count, \lfloor \frac{c-lo}{sp} \rfloor * count, avg$
`FROM` H
`WHERE` $(lo \leq c)$ and $(hi > c)$;

3. Projection (π_A): Projection with duplicate elimination is translated into the following query Q_π:

`SELECT` $lo, hi, count, 1$
`FROM` H;

Projection with no duplicate elimination is just the identity query (i.e., selecting all tuples from the histogram relation with no changes).

4. Equi-Joins ($R_1 \bowtie_{R_1.A=R_2.B} R_2$): Let H_i be the histogram on the joining attribute of R_i, and N_i be the largest count in the buckets of H_i. Join is translated into a sequence of two queries, $Q1_{\bowtie}$ and $Q2_{\bowtie}$[3]. Query $Q1_{\bowtie}$ computes the frequency distribution of the approximate join result by joining the approximate frequency distributions of H_1 and H_2. It assumes the existence of two auxiliary relations of integers I_{N_1} and I_{N_2} defined in the same fashion as I_C described earlier.

```
SELECT   (H1.lo + I_N1.idx * H1.sp) as v, H1.lo as lo1,
         H2.lo as lo2, H1.avg * H2.avg as navg
FROM     H1, H2, I_N1, I_N2
WHERE    (H1.lo + I_N1.idx * H1.sp =
         H2.lo + I_N2.idx * H2.sp) and
         (I_N1.idx <= H1.count) and
         (I_N2.idx <= H2.count);
```

Query $Q2_{\bowtie}$ converts the result of query $Q1_{\bowtie}$ (say, $Q1R$) into a histogram by appropriate grouping.

```
SELECT    min(v), max(v), count(*), navg
FROM      Q1R
Group By  lo1, lo2, navg;
```

Example 5.1 Consider the following SQL query:

```
SELECT  R2.B
FROM    R1, R2
WHERE   R1.A <= 10 and R1.B = R2.B;
```

An equivalent operator tree and the corresponding translation result (a histogram query sequence depicted as nodes in a tree) are shown in Figure 6.

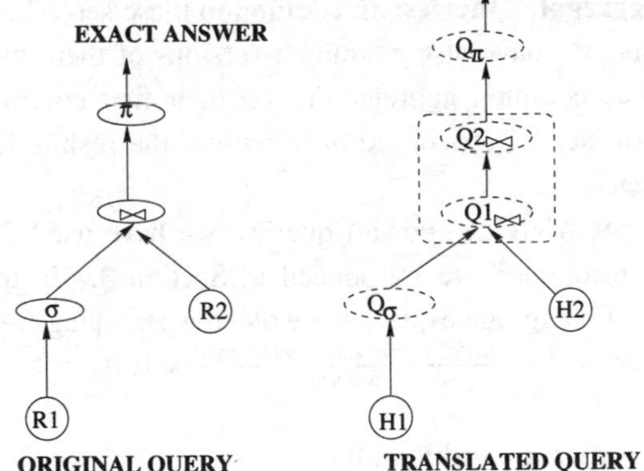

Figure 6: Example Query Translation

5.2.2 Aggregate Queries

In general, an aggregate query Q_{agg} is equivalent to an aggregate computation over some of the attributes in the result of a non-aggregate query Q. Hence, a valid translation for Q_{agg} consists of a valid translation for Q producing a histogram H followed by an aggregate-specific SQL query on H computing a single bucket histogram containing the aggregate value. These queries are given in Table 1 for the most common aggregate operators. Here, *bsum* is the sum of all the attribute values in a bucket as many times as each appears, i.e., $bsum = avg * count * (lo + \frac{sp*(count-1)}{2})$.

[3] In our implementation, we make this scheme more efficient by running another simple query in the beginning to identify overlapping buckets in the histograms and then executing $Q1_{\bowtie}$ and $Q2_{\bowtie}$ for each pair of overlapping buckets.

5.2.3 Computational Complexity of Translated Queries

It can be easily seen that the queries for *selections* and *projections* access just β tuples, where β is the number of buckets in the histogram. This is usually insignificant compared to the number of tuples in the relations. For joins, the translated queries access $u_1+u_2+\beta_1+\beta_2$ tuples, where u_i is the number of distinct attribute values in H_i and β_i is the number of buckets in H_i. The total number of operations is also proportional to this term because this query can be best run using Sort-Merge joins by always storing the histograms and the auxiliary relations in sorted order. The complexity is significantly smaller than the cost of running the original query because u_i is typically much smaller than the cardinality of the corresponding relation.

6 Experiments

We have conducted an extensive set of experiments using AQUA to study the effectiveness of various statistical techniques in providing approximate query answers. Our experiments involve different data sets and queries with set-valued as well as aggregate results. First, we present the testbed.

6.1 Testbed

6.1.1 Approximation Techniques

We have used different classes of histograms to approximate the data. They include the MaxDiff(V,A), Equi-Width, and EquiDepth classes. We call the corresponding approximate answering techniques *MaxDiff*, *Equi-Width*, and *EquiDepth* respectively. We have also studied the traditional uniformity assumption over the entire data, which is equivalent to a histogram with a single bucket. We call this technique *Trivial*. The final technique, which we call *Sampling*, uses sampling to provide approximate answers. Here, a set of samples is

distinct COUNT	SUM	AVG	MAX	MIN
SELECT SUM(*count*) FROM H;	SELECT SUM(*bsum*) FROM H;	SELECT $\frac{\text{SUM}(bsum)}{\text{SUM}(count)}$ FROM H;	SELECT MAX(*hi*) FROM H;	SELECT MIN(*lo*) FROM H;

Table 1: Queries to Compute Aggregate Values from Histograms

collected on each relation in the database and the submitted query is executed on the sample relations, with appropriate scaling of the final result.

In order to ensure a fair comparison among these techniques, we have allocated the same amount of space to each one. We have computed the number of buckets and samples corresponding to a space of s bytes as follows. Consider a relation with d integer attributes. Since each bucket in a d-dimensional histogram stores $(3 * d + 1)$ numbers (Section 4), the number of buckets is $\frac{s}{12*d+4}$ (assuming 4 bytes per number). Similarly, since each sampled tuple contains d numbers, the corresponding sample set contains $\frac{s}{4*d}$ tuples.

6.1.2 Data Sets

We have primarily used a synthetic database that we have created. We have also experimented with the TPC-D benchmark database [18], generated at scale factor of 0.6. Due to lack of space, we focus on our synthetic data, which offers more insights into the performance of various techniques than the TPC-D data, which has mostly uniform and independent attributes. The synthetic data consists of two relations R_1 and R_2; R_1 contains two numerical attributes (A, B), and R_2 consists of a single numerical attribute (A); having additional attributes does not impact our study. The distribution of data in these attributes is described next.

Value Domain: The attribute values were generated from a combination of *Zipf* distributions [21]. The details of all such combinations are given elsewhere [17]; here we describe the two that we chose to present in this paper. The *Cusp-Max* distribution consists of increasing spreads (distances between successive values) followed by decreasing spreads, with the spreads taken from a Zipf distribution. The skew in the spreads is controlled via the z parameter (higher z implies higher skew). The *Uniform* distribution consists of equally spaced values.

Frequency Domain: The frequencies of the different attribute value combinations were also generated based on Zipf distributions with different levels of skew.

The set of values that we have experimented with for all data set parameters is given in Table 2.

Parameter	Values
Value Skew for *Cusp-Max* (z_v)	$0.2 - 3$
Frequency Skew (z_f)	$0 - 3$
Num. Distinct Values per Dimension (u)	$10 - 10K$
Num. Attribute Combinations (U)	$500 - 50K$
Num. Tuples in the Relation (T)	$50K - 500K$

Table 2: Synthetic Data Set Parameters

6.1.3 Queries

Non-Aggregate Queries: The SQL queries used are listed in Table 3. Here, we summarize their key characteristics.

- *Range Queries:* These queries contain a single two-dimensional *range selection* predicate on $R1$. In each experiment, we have used 100 queries with randomly generated values for a and b. These values were chosen from a subset of the entire column range in order to vary the average selectivity of the queries.
- *Projection Queries:* These queries simply project a relation onto one of its attributes, with duplicate elimination.
- *SJ Queries:* These queries contain both *join* and *selection* operations.

Aggregate Queries: In addition to these set-valued queries, we have also examined versions of them that produce common aggregations on their first column. Due to lack of space, we only present the results for *average*.

Error Metrics: For all queries, we have used the *MAC* error measure introduced in Section 3. In the graphs for aggregate queries, we plot the percentage relative error, i.e., $\frac{MAC(=actual-estimate)}{actual} * 100$.

6.2 Experimental Results

Here, we first present the experimental results for different query sets and then provide the explanation for them.

6.2.1 Range Queries

For this set of experiments, the number of tuples in $R1$ was $200K$ and the average selectivity of the queries was approximately 0.15.

Non-aggregate Queries:

Range Query		Projection Query		SJ Query	
SELECT	$R_1.A, R1.B$	SELECT	distinct $R1.A$	SELECT	$R_1.A$
FROM	R_1	FROM	R_1;	FROM	R_1, R_2
WHERE	$(R_1.A \leq a)$ and $(R1.B \leq b)$			WHERE	$(R_1.A = R_2.A)$ and $(R1.B \leq c)$;

Table 3: Non-Aggregate Queries in the Experiment Testbed

Effect of Space: Here, we have fixed the frequency skew of both attributes $R1.A$ and $R2.A$ at $z_f = 0.86$ (which roughly corresponds to the "80-20" rule) and have chosen the value domain as *Uniform*. Figure 7 shows the errors due to various techniques (in log scale on the y-axis) as the space is varied (in log scale on the x-axis). The error for *Trivial* is not given because it is very high (above 4×10^6) and falls out of the range depicted. As expected, the performance of the various techniques improves with increasing space.

Effect of Frequency Skew: For this experiment, we have fixed the space at 400 bytes and have chosen again a *Uniform* value domain. Figure 8 depicts frequency skew (z value) on the X-axis and *MAC* errors (in log scale) on the y-axis.

Aggregate Queries: The errors for *average* are given for varying amounts of space in Figure 9.

Note that *MaxDiff* performs very well under all circumstances.

6.2.2 Projections (with no aggregates)

In Figure 10, we compare the performance of various techniques for the *Cusp-Max* value distribution. The frequency skew is 0 and the values of $R.A1$ range from 0 to 10000. Once again, *MaxDiff* performs the best and *Sampling* performs very poorly.

6.2.3 SJ Queries (with no aggregates)

Here, R_1 and R_2 contain 100000 and 1000 tuples, respectively, and have 500 distinct values each. The range predicate has a selectivity of 10%. The value distributions of R_1 and R_2 are both *Cusp-Max*, with z_v of 0.2 and 1, respectively. The frequency distributions of both relations have a skew of $z_f = 1.5$. The errors in estimating the result set are given in Figures 11 and 12 as functions of space and frequency skew, respectively. Note that *MaxDiff* performs very well for the SJ-queries as well.

6.2.4 Explanation of Results

All of the above results demonstrate a similar pattern in the relative behavior of the techniques studied. In particular, *MaxDiff* performs the best in most circumstances. The reasons are that a) it approximates the *entire* data distribution, and b) it captures the more skewed attribute values with high accuracy using a constant amount of space (1 bucket per such value). In contrast, *Sampling* captures a fraction of the given set precisely and misses the remaining parts completely. Furthermore, it allocates disproportionate amounts of space to the high frequency values. Since our *selection* queries cover the *entire value domain*, many of them contain the low-skewed regions that may not be captured (or even approximated) at all in *Sampling*, resulting in a high error. The problem gets worse for SJ-queries because join of two samples often contains few or no tuples [1]. Some of the sampling-related problems have been addressed elsewhere in a different context [4, 1]. We are currently incorporating these optimizations in our work.

As for the effect of skew, errors due to *Sampling* increase with skew because it allocates more and more samples for the high frequency values. This degrades performance for queries on the remaining regions. On the other hand, *EquiWidth* and *EquiDepth* perform poorly because they do not consider frequency skews much in forming the buckets, unlike *MaxDiff*. Interestingly, *MaxDiff* performs best for extreme values of skew (0 & 3). The reasons are as follows: at high skew values, there are very few "important" values in the relation that need to be captured and histograms are able to do that using a small number of buckets: at low skew values, almost all frequencies are identical and even one or two buckets are enough. For medium values of skew there are sufficient number of distinct frequencies, so that the histogram needs more buckets to accurately approximate the distribution.

6.2.5 Times Taken by Different Approaches

We have measured the times taken by various techniques in answering the SJ queries on a SUN SPARC machine with 250MB of memory and 10GB of disk space. Evaluation of the exact answer for these queries took around 248 seconds (averaged over 30 runs). Table 4 lists the times for different values of space. Note

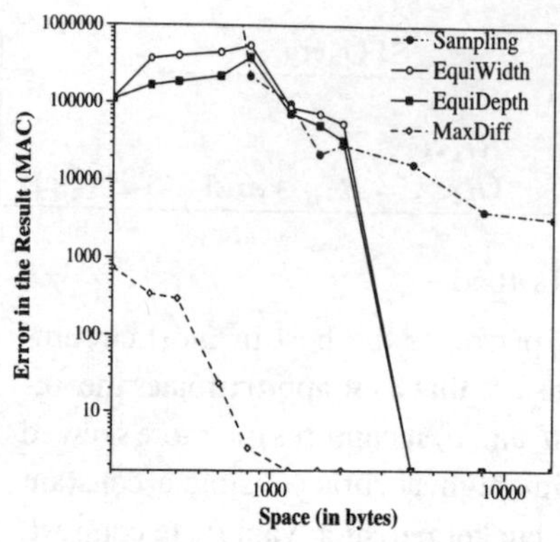

Figure 7: Effect of Space on *MAC* (Range Queries)

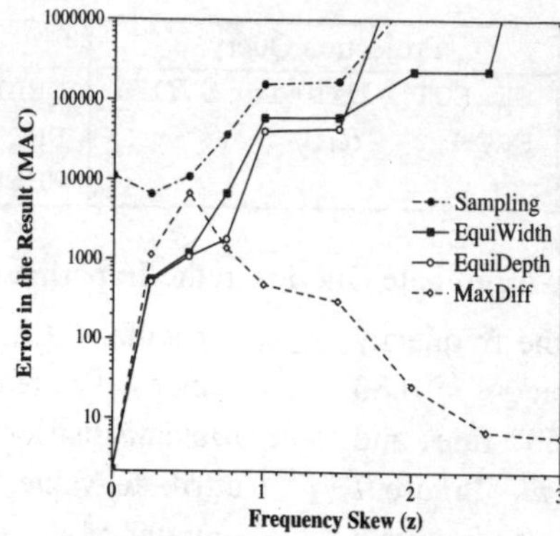

Figure 8: Effect of Frequency Skew on *MAC* (Range Queries)

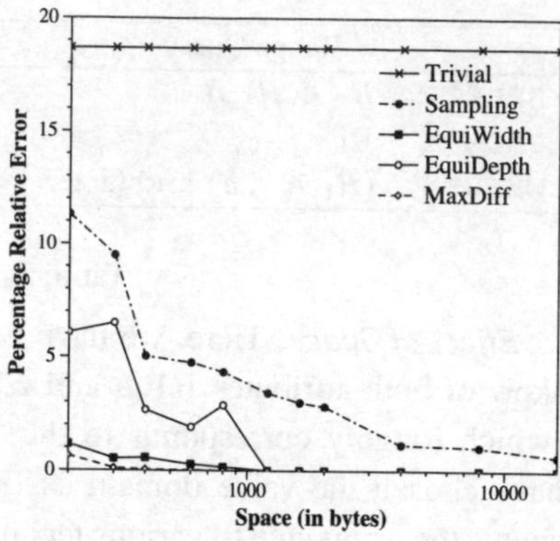

Figure 9: Effect of Space on Estimating Averages (Range Queries)

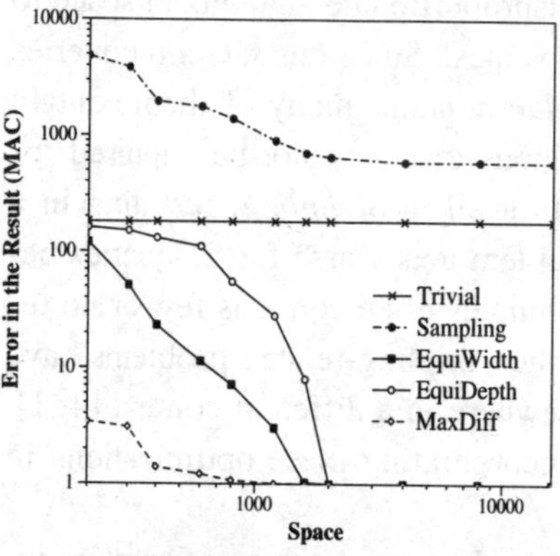

Figure 10: Effect of Space on *MAC* (Projections)

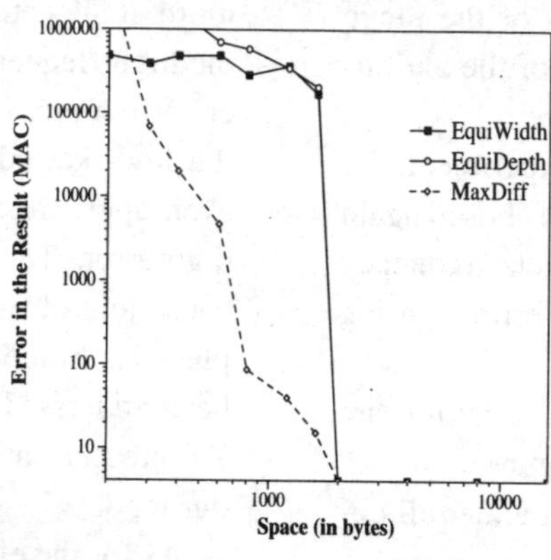

Figure 11: Effect of Space on *MAC* (SJ Queries)

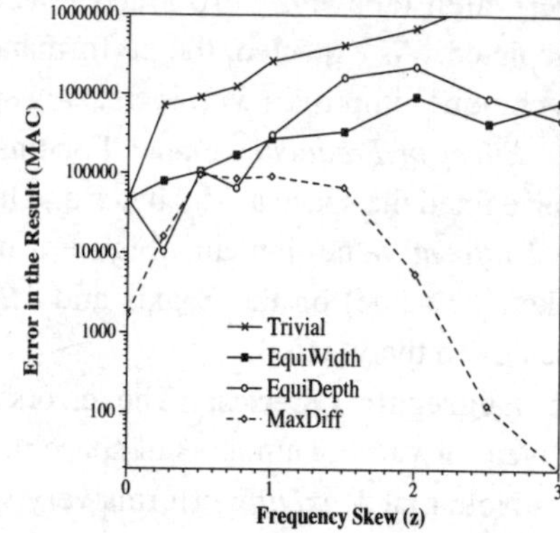

Figure 12: Effect of Frequency Skew on *MAC* (SJ Queries)

Technique	Space (in bytes)					
	50	100	500	1000	2000	4000
Sampling	0.10	0.18	0.72	2.60	5.30	10.30
MaxDiff	0.56	0.82	1.32	3.20	6.10	11.19

Table 4: Times Taken for Answering SJ-Queries (sec)

that *MaxDiff* takes slightly more time than *Sampling*, as join queries on histograms require as many operations as the number of distinct values in the join attributes. Nevertheless, the times are still very small and are insignificant compared to the actual time of execution.

7 Conclusions

Approximate query answering is likely to become an essential tool in applications demanding fast responses, such as on-line decision support systems and interactive data visualization tools. However, the work in this area so far has been limited in its scope. First, it has only considered aggregate queries and has not dealt with queries that return multisets of tuples. Second, sampling has been essentially the only technique used.

In this paper, we have attempted to increase the scope of approximate query answering as follows:

- We have developed a numerical measure (*MAC*) to quantify the quality of an approximate answer to set-valued query. We have demonstrated that this measure is intuitive, reduces to well-known metrics in simple cases, and works well for most instances of answer-sets.
- We have proposed histogram-based techniques for providing approximate answers to general as well as aggregate queries. In this regard, we have devised a histogram algebra for transforming queries on regular relations to queries on histograms.

We believe that the error measure and the histogram algebra form a reasonable first step towards systematically providing approximate query answers for general queries. Furthermore, the results of our experiments indicate that *MaxDiff* histograms answer most kinds of queries very accurately, like in selectivity estimation.

Acknowledgements: The authors would like to thank S. Muthukrishnan for help with the exact algorithm for identifying the minimum cost edge cover.

References

[1] S. Acharya, P. Gibbons, V. Poosala, and S. Ramaswarmy. Join synopses for improving approximate query answers. *Proc. of ACM SIGMOD Conf*, 1999.

[2] P. Buneman, S. B. Davidson, and A. Watters. A semantics for complex objects and approximate queries. In *Proc. 7th ACM SIGMOD-SIGACT Symposium on Principles of Database Systems*, pages 305–314, April 1988.

[3] C. M. Chen and N. Roussopoulos. Adaptive selectivity estimation using query feedback. *Proc. of ACM SIGMOD Conf*, pages 161–172, May 1994.

[4] P. B. Gibbons and Y. Matias. New sampling-based summary statistics for improving approximate query answers. *Proc. of ACM SIGMOD Conf*, 1998.

[5] P. B. Gibbons, Y. Matias, and V. Poosala. Fast incremental maintenance of approximate histograms. *Proc. of the 23rd Int. Conf. on Very Large Databases*, August 1997.

[6] J. M. Hellerstein, P. J. Haas, and H. J. Wang. Online aggregation. In *Proc. ACM SIGMOD Conference on the Management of Data*, pages 171–182, Tucson, AZ, June 1997.

[7] Huttenlocher. Comparing images using the hausdorff distance. *IEEE Transactions on pattern analysis and machine intelligence*, 15(9), September 1993.

[8] Y. Ioannidis and V. Poosala. Histogram-based techniques for approximating set-valued queries. Technical report, Bell Labs, 1998. Contact poosala@bell-labs.com for a copy.

[9] R. P. Kooi. *The optimization of queries in relational databases.* PhD thesis, Case Western Reserve University, Sept 1980.

[10] R. J. Lipton, J. F. Naughton, and D. A. Schneider. Practical selectivity estimation through adaptive sampling. *Proc. of ACM SIGMOD Conf*, pages 1–11, May 1990.

[11] A. Motro. Query generalization: A method for interpreting null answers. In L. Kerschberg, editor, *Expert Database Systems, Proceedings from the First International Workshop*, pages 597–616. Benjamin/Cummings, Inc., Menlo Park, CA, 1986.

[12] G. Ozsoyoglu, K. Du, S. Guruswamy, and W.-C. Hou. Processing real-time non-aggregate queries with timeconstratings in CASE-DB. In *Proc. 8th International Conference on Data Engineering*, pages 140–147, Tempe, AZ, February 1992.

[13] G. Piatetsky-Shapiro and C. Connell. Accurate estimation of the number of tuples satisfying a condition. *Proc. of ACM SIGMOD Conf*, pages 256–276, 1984.

[14] V. Poosala and V. Ganti. Fast approximate answers to aggregate queries on a data cube. *International working conference on scientific and statistical database management*, 1999.

[15] V. Poosala and V. Ganti. Fast approximate query answering using precomputed statistics. *Proc. of IEEE Conf. on Data Engineering*, 1999.

[16] V. Poosala and Y. Ioannidis. Selectivity estimation without the attribute value independence assumption. *Proc. of the 23rd Int. Conf. on Very Large Databases*, August 1997.

[17] V. Poosala, Y. Ioannidis, P. Haas, and E. Shekita. Improved histograms for selectivity estimation of range predicates. *Proc. of ACM SIGMOD Conf*, pages 294–305, June 1996.

[18] Transaction processing performance council (TPC). *TPC-D Benchmark Manual*, 1996.

[19] J. S. Vitter, M. Wang, and B. R. Iyer. Data cube approximation and histograms via wavelets. *CIKM*, pages 96–104, 1998.

[20] S. Vrbsky and J. W. S. Liu. APPROXIMATE: A query processor that produces monotonically improving approximate answers. *IEEE Trans. on Knowledge and Data Engineering*, 5(6), December 1993.

[21] G. K. Zipf. *Human behaviour and the principle of least effort.* Addison-Wesley, Reading, MA, 1949.

Semantic Compression and Pattern Extraction with Fascicles

H.V. Jagadish
U. Michigan, Ann Arbor
jag@cs.uiuc.edu

Jason Madar
U. British Columbia
jmadar@cs.ubc.ca

Raymond T. Ng
U. British Columbia
rng@cs.ubc.ca

Abstract

Often many records in a database share similar values for several attributes. If one is able to identify and group together records that share similar values for some – even if not all – attributes, one can both obtain a more parsimonious representation of the data, and gain useful insight into the data from a mining perspective.

In this paper, we introduce the notion of *fascicles*. A fascicle $F(k,t)$ is a subset of records that have k compact attributes. An attribute A of a collection F of records is *compact* if the width of the range of A-values (for numeric attributes) or the number of distinct A-values (for categorical attributes) of all the records in F does not exceed t. We introduce and study two problems related to fascicles. First, we consider how to find fascicles such that the total storage of the relation is minimized. Second, we study how best to extract fascicles whose sizes exceed a given minimum threshold (i.e., support) and that represent patterns of maximal quality, where quality is measured by the pair (k,t). We develop algorithms to attack both of the above problems. We show that these two problems are very hard to solve optimally. But we demonstrate empirically that good solutions can be obtained using our algorithms.

Proceedings of the 25th VLDB Conference, Edinburgh, Scotland, 1999.

Name	Position	Points	Played Mins	Penalty Mins
Blake	defense	43	395	34
Borque	defense	77	430	22
Cullimore	defense	3	30	18
Gretzky	centre	130	458	26
Konstantinov	defense	10	560	120
May	winger	35	290	180
Odjick	winger	9	115	245
Tkachuk	centre	82	530	160
Wotton	defense	5	38	6

Figure 1: A Fragment of the NHL Players' Statistics Table

1 Introduction

Figure 1 shows part of a table of National Hockey League (NHL) players' statistics in 1996. For each player, his record describes the position he played, the number of points he scored, the number of minutes he was on the ice and in the penalty box. While there are players of almost every possible combination, there are numerous ***subsets having very similar values for many attributes.*** In other words, records in one of these subsets vary considerably only in the other attributes. For example, (i) Cullimore and Wotton belong to a group of defensemen who played, scored and penalized sparingly; and (ii) Borque, Gretzky and Tkachuk belong to another group who played and scored a lot. Identification of such subsets can be the basis for good compression schemes, and can be valuable for data mining purposes.

To do so, the crucial first step is the identification of what we call *fascicles*[1]. A k-dimensional, or k-attributed, *fascicle* $F(k,t)$ of a relation is a subset of records that have k *compact* attributes. An attribute A of a collection F of records is *compact* if the width of the range of A-values (for numeric attributes), or the number of distinct A-values (for categorical attributes) of all the records in F does not exceed t. We refer to t as the compactness tolerance. For instance, in Figure 1, suppose the compactness tolerance imposed on the attributes are: $t_{Position} = 1$ (i.e., exact match is required), $t_{Points} = 10$, $t_{PlayedMins} = 60$ and $t_{PenaltyMins} = 20$.

[1] According to Webster, a fascicle is 1. a small bundle; 2. one of the installments of a book published in parts.

Then Cullimore and Wotton are in a 4-D fascicle with `Position`, `Points`, `Played Mins` and `Penalty Mins` as the compact attributes. Different fascicles may have different numbers and sets of compact attributes.

Now given a fascicle, we can minimize its storage requirement by projecting out all the compact attributes and storing their representative values only once separately. More precisely, suppose we have N records in a relation with n attributes, each requiring b bytes of storage for a total of Nnb bytes. Suppose we are able to find c fascicles, each with k compact attributes projected out, such that they together cover all but N_0 of the records. Then the storage required for a fascicle with cardinality s is $kb + (n-k)bs$. Adding up over all c fascicles, we get $kcb + (n-k)(N-N_0)b$. Thus, in total, we save $(N - N_0 - c)kb$ bytes of storage. If we are able to get small values for N_0 and for c, at least compared to N, then the storage savings would be almost Nkb bytes. Thus, we consider the following problem:

> **[Storage Minimization with Fascicles]** *Find fascicles such that the total storage is minimized.*

Note that existing compression techniques are "syntactic" in the sense that they operate at the byte-level. Compression with fascicles are *"semantic"* in nature in that the tolerance t takes into account the meanings and the dynamic ranges of the attributes. The two styles of compression are orthogonal and can work in tandem. In Section 4.2, we will show experimentally that:

- **(lossless compression mode)** First using fascicles only to re-order the tuples, and then applying normal syntactic compression on the re-ordered relation results in substantially greater compression than applying syntactic compression alone.
- **(lossy compression mode)** First performing lossy compression with fascicles by removing compact attributes, and then applying normal syntactic compression on the remaining attributes can reduce the final compressed size a few times more.

Furthermore, because fascicles are semantic in nature, the contents of the fascicles constitute patterns with legitimate semantic meanings. Provided that the size of a k-D fascicle is not small, the fascicle represents a significant sub-population that more or less agrees on the values of the k attributes. For instance, corresponding to a certain 3-D fascicle, amazingly there are about 25% of NHL players who had little impact on the game, i.e., their `Points`, `Played Mins` and `Penalty Mins` all very low (e.g., Cullimore and Wotton in Figure 1). Such observations are clearly of data mining value.

From a data mining perspective, the quality of a fascicle is measured by two components: t, the compactness tolerance, and k, the number of compact attributes. Given the same compactness tolerance, a fascicle with more compact attributes is of higher quality than another with fewer compact attributes. Similarly, given the same number of compact attributes, a fascicle with a smaller compactness tolerance is of higher quality than another with a larger tolerance. Two fascicles are incomparable if one has more compact attributes but the other has a smaller tolerance. This ordering of fascicles, formalized in Section 5.1, is denoted as $\geq_f$. Now given fascicles $F_1, \ldots, F_u$ all containing record R, we define:

$$Fas(R) \quad = \quad \{F_i \mid \nexists 1 \leq j \leq u : F_j >_f F_i\} \qquad (1)$$

That is, we are only interested in the fascicles with the maximal qualities among $F_1, \ldots, F_u$. Finally, we maximize the set $Fas(R)$ for each record R. Since $Fas(R)$ is a set, maximization is conducted with respect to the well-known Smyth ordering of power sets[20], denoted as $\geq_s$, which will be detailed in Section 5.1. Thus, we have the following problem:

> **[Pattern Extraction with Fascicles]** *Given a minimum size m, find fascicles of sizes $\geq m$, such that for all records R, $Fas(R)$ is maximized with respect to the ordering $\geq_s$.*

In this paper, we will develop algorithms to solve both the storage minimization and pattern extraction problems. These algorithms are strongly related to one another. We will show that these two problems are hard to solve optimally. However, we will demonstrate empirically that our algorithms give good solutions. We will also investigate the effect of various parameter choices.

The outline of the paper is as follows. In Section 2, we describe the basic model of fascicles. In Section 3, we develop two algorithms to solve the storage minimization problem. In Section 4, we present experimental results on semantic compression and storage minimization. In Section 5, to solve the pattern extraction problem, we show how to modify previous algorithms and present empirical results. In Section 6, we discuss related work.

2 Model and Assumptions

Altogether there are three parameters in the fascicle framework. First, there is the compactness tolerance t. Strictly speaking, t should be represented as $\vec{t}$ because, as shown in the earlier NHL example, each attribute should have its own compactness tolerance. We simplify our presentation here by using t instead of $\vec{t}$. Moreover, in practice, more elaborate definitions of compactness are possible. For instance, values of a categorical attribute can be organized in a generalization hierarchy and the compactness tolerance defined in terms of the depth of the hierarchy. For numeric attributes, one could specify compactness based on quantiles rather than actual values. The specific definition of compactness is not central to the algorithms developed here. For ease of discussion, we use the definition given in Section 1.

The second parameter in the fascicle framework is the minimum size parameter m. For storage minimization, the smaller the value of $m \geq 2$, the more fascicles could be found and the larger the potential for minimization. Thus, in principle, m is not a key parameter in the storage minimization problem, although in practice very small fascicles, with only a few records, do result only in small incremental savings in storage. For pattern extraction, however, m plays a more critical role. If the value of m is too small, this indicates that the pattern applies to too small a sub-population. In this setting, m plays a role akin to the support threshold in association rule mining.

Finally, there is the dimensionality parameter k, the number of compact attributes required of a fascicle. In both the storage minimization and pattern extraction problems, k plays a central role. Our algorithms to find fascicles treat k as the main independent variable.

3 Solving the Storage Minimization Problem

In this section, we study the storage minimization problem. We first develop algorithms to find candidate fascicles, and show how to minimize storage by selecting from amongst these candidates.

3.1 The Single-k Algorithm

Below we develop the Single-k algorithm, which finds k-D fascicles for a given value k. Later we show how to extend the Single-k algorithm to form the Multi-k algorithm, which finds fascicles with dimensionalities $\geq k$.

3.1.1 The Basic Approach: a Lattice-based Conceptualization

Consider a lattice consisting of all the possible subsets of records in the given relation. As usual, an edge exists between two subsets S, T if $S \supset T$ and $|S| = |T| + 1$. At the top of the lattice is a single point/set, denoted as $\top$, representing the entire relation. At the bottom of the lattice is a single point $\bot$ representing the empty set. Let n be the total number of attributes in the relation, and k $(0 \leq k \leq n)$ be the number of compact attributes desired in a fascicle. Consider any path $\langle \bot, S_1, S_2, \ldots, \top \rangle$ linking the bottom and top points in the lattice. Trivially, $\bot$ and set S_1, which consists of a single record, are n-D fascicles. By the definition of a fascicle, it is clear that if S is a superset of T, and if S is a j-D fascicle, then T must be an i-D fascicle for some $i \geq j$. This monotonicity property guarantees that for any given value $1 \leq k \leq n$, either $\top$ is itself a k-D fascicle[2], or there must exist two successive sets S_t, S_{t+1} on the path such that: (i) S_t is an i-D fascicle, and (ii) S_{t+1} is a j-D fascicle, with $j < k \leq i$. We call S_t a *tip* set.

[2]If this rather unlikely corner case applies, our problem is trivially solved. To keep our exposition clean, we assume that this corner case does not apply in the sequel. That is, $\top$ is a j-D fascicle for some $j < k$. For all practical purposes, $\top$, consisting of the entire relation, is almost never a j-D fascicle for any $j > 0$, and k is always chosen to be at least one.

To put it in another way, S is a (k-D) tip set if S is a k-D fascicle, and there is an (immediate) parent T of S in the lattice such that T is a j-D fascicle with $j < k$. Within the class of tip sets, there is a subclass that we call *maximal* sets. S is a (k-D) maximal set if S is a k-D fascicle, and for *all* parents T of S in the lattice, T is a j-D fascicle with $j < k$.

Our goal is to find maximal sets. Forming the border analyzed in [16], the set of maximal sets completely characterizes all k-D fascicles. However, given the *huge* size of the lattice space, the entire set of maximal sets is so large that its computational cost is prohibitive. Furthermore, as we will see, we cannot in any case afford to select optimally from a given set of candidate fascicles for the problems we seek to address. It may suffice to compute some, but not all, maximal sets. Below we describe how the Single-k algorithm selects "good" initial tip sets, and eventually grows them to maximal sets.

3.1.2 Choosing Good Initial Tip Sets

Conceptually, to find a tip set, we begin by picking a random record as the first member of a tip set. We then add in a second record at random, and then a third, and so on – until the collection of records is no longer a k-D fascicle. In essence, we are constructing a path $\langle \bot, S_1, S_2, \ldots, S_t \rangle$. We can repeat this process as many times as we wish, each time exploring a different path up the lattice.

Given a relation that does not fit in main memory, each record sampled would require one disk access. To minimize the amount of I/O activity performed, a commonly used technique is "block sampling", where an entire disk page is read into memory and all records on the page are used. We propose to adopt this approach as well, but there is an important difference. In traditional sampling, possible correlations between co-located records can be compensated for by increasing the sample size. In our case, the specific ordering of records in the sample is of critical importance. Increasing the sample size would be of no help at all. For example, suppose that the hockey players relation is stored on disk sorted by `Played Mins`. When we consider successive records, they will very likely have `Played Mins` as a compact attribute, to the potential detriment of other possible compact attributes.

To address these concerns, we read into memory some number b of randomly sampled blocks of the relation. Now we can work purely with the sample of the relation in memory, without paying any attention to block boundaries. From amongst the records in memory, we can choose records based on a random permutation of the records (without physically sorting them). When one tip set is complete, the first record that would render it non-compact is used to start a second tip set, and so on. Once all records in the sampled relation have been considered once, a new random permutation of the records is established, and more tip sets are generated.

Algorithm Single-k
Input: A dimensionality k, number of fascicles P, a buffer of b pages, and a relation R of r pages
Output: P k-D fascicles

{ 1. Divide R into q disjoint pieces, each comprising upto b randomly chosen pages from R, i.e., $q = \lceil r/b \rceil$.
  2. For each piece: /* choosing initial tip sets */
    2.1 Read the piece into main memory.
    2.2 Read the records in main memory to produce a series of tip sets as discussed in Section 3.1.2.
    2.3 Repeat 2.2, each with a different permutation of the records, until P/q tip sets are obtained.
  3. /* growing the tip sets */
    Grow all P tip sets, as discussed in Sections 3.1.3, with one pass over the relation. Output the grown tip sets. }

Figure 2: A Skeleton of the Single-k Algorithm

This process is repeated as many times as desired. All operations are in memory and that no (physical) sorting is required.

Because of the oversampling we perform, it is possible not to work with just a single sample of the relation. Instead, we can produce some tip sets working with the sampled relation described above; when this is done, we can obtain a fresh sample of b completely different pages from the relation on disk, and repeat. Proceeding thus, we can consider the entire relation as q disjoint pieces, where each piece is a random collection of pages.

3.1.3 Growing a Tip Set to a Maximal Set

Tip sets obtained thus far leave two aspects to be desired. First, they are confined to records in one piece of the relation. We seek to "grow" a tip set so that it includes all qualified records from the remaining pieces of the relation. Second, with respect to the conceptual lattice discussed earlier, a tip set may be far from maximal. We seek to make a tip set maximal.

This turns out to be quite easy to do. A tip set obtained thus far has k compact attributes, corresponding to k attribute value ranges (for numeric attributes) or sets of values (for categorical attributes). These in effect specify a k-D selection predicate on the relation. And we can simply evaluate a query that returns all records matching the query, such as by scanning the entire relation one more pass. The newly grown tip set is still a k-D fascicle. We refer to this process as the tip set growing phase.

With respect to maximality, the simple scan above is sufficient for most circumstances. Specifically, if before the growing phase the k compact attribute ranges and values of a tip set are already at the maximum "width" allowed by t, then it is easy to see that after the growing phase, the newly grown tip set has indeed become a maximal set, i.e., it is impossible to add any more record to keep it a k-D fascicle. In the less common circumstances, where before the growing phase there is some compact attribute that still has room to reach the maximum allowable width, maximality can be achieved by expanding the compact range or set dynamically until the maximum width is reached. For lack of space, we omit the details here; see [15] for details and an argument why maximality is guaranteed.

In summary, Figure 2 shows a skeleton of the Single-k algorithm. It is a randomized algorithm that computes k-D fascicles, all of which are maximal sets. Note that the algorithm does not compute all k-D fascicles. In Section 4.6, we will present an alternative algorithm that computes all k-D fascicles, but will show that such an alternative is both ineffective and impractical.

3.2 The Multi-k Algorithm

Recall that for both the storage minimization problem and the pattern extraction problem, we may allow fascicles to vary in their dimensionalities. The Single-k algorithm, however, only produces fascicles with one specified value k. The problem here is that the algorithm may miss out on the opportunities offered by the fascicles with higher values of k. For instance, there could be a fascicle of dimensionality 10 that is a subset of a fascicle (of dimensionality 6) found by the algorithm. The higher dimensionality fascicle, if known and exploited, can clearly lead to additional reduction in storage cost.

One simple way to overcome the above problem is to run the Single-k algorithm repeatedly, each with a different value of k. But different runs of the algorithm share many repetitive operations, including the relation scans. The Multi-k algorithm exploits this sharing to produce fascicles all having dimensionalities $\geq k$.

Recall from the Single-k algorithm how a k-D tip set corresponds to a path $\langle \perp, S_1, S_2, \ldots, S_t \rangle$. Observe that as we move from the beginning of the path to the end of the path, the dimensionality of the corresponding fascicle decreases monotonically. Thus, while the Single-k algorithm constructs a path $\langle \perp, S_1, S_2, \ldots, S_t \rangle$ and obtains S_t as a k-D tip set, the Multi-k algorithm uses exactly the same path to obtain the largest set on the path with dimensionality i, for $i \geq k$.

Let us illustrate this by an example. Suppose there are a total of $n = 12$ attributes in the relation. Suppose $k = 6$, and the path corresponding to a particular 6-D tip set computed by the Single-k algorithm is $\langle \perp, S_1, S_2, \ldots, S_{10} \rangle$. The following table shows the dimensionality of each set on the path:

Set	$\perp$	S_1	S_2	S_3	S_4	S_5	S_6
k	12	12	12	11	11	11	9

Set	S_7	S_8	S_9	S_{10}
k	9	8	6	6

The Multi-k algorithm uses the same path to obtain the tip sets S_2, S_5, S_7, S_8 and S_{10} with dimensionalities 12, 11, 9, 8 and 6 respectively.

To complete the description of the Multi-k algorithm, these tip sets with varying dimensionalities can all go through the same growing phase together to become maximal sets, sharing one relation scan. Thus, Figure 2 presents an accurate skeleton of the Multi-k algorithm, provided that Step 2.2 is modified to implement the procedure discussed in the previous paragraph.

No matter what the available amount of buffer space is, both Single-k and Multi-k read each data page from disk at most twice (i.e., once for Step 2 and once for Step 3). Furthermore Step 3 is a sequential scan. Step 2 requires random pages to be read, but since the specific set of random pages is not material, it is conceivable that clever techniques could choose "random" pages while being aware of disk layout to optimize disk access. This assumes that P is small enough to fit in memory, which is easily achievable as will be shown by the results in Section 4. For a relation R, the main memory computational complexity of both algorithms is $O(P|R|)$.

3.3 Greedy Selection for the Single-k Algorithm

To solve the storage minimization problem, the next step is to select from amongst the candidate fascicles produced by either the Single-k or the Multi-k algorithms. The main complication is that the candidate fascicles may overlap. To proceed, let us consider briefly the "unweighted" version of the above task: find the minimum *number* of candidate fascicles that cover the whole data set. This turns out to correspond to the well-known minimum cover problem [12]. That is, given a collection C of subsets of a finite set S and a positive integer K, is there a subset $C' \subseteq C$ with $|C'| \leq K$ such that every element of S belongs to at least one member of C'? The minimum cover problem is NP-complete. Greedy selection is among the best heuristics that exist for solving the minimum cover problem, and is the basis for our selection algorithms. We discuss first greedy selection for the Single-k algorithm.

To represent the storage savings induced by a fascicle F, it is weighted by $wt(F) = k * |F|$, where k is the dimensionality of F.[3] This weight corresponds to the storage savings induced by F, since there are k fewer attributes to store for each record contained in F. In a straightforward implementation of the greedy selection, we select the candidate fascicle with the highest weight, subtract from all the remaining fascicles records that are in the selected fascicle, and adjust the weights of the remaining fascicles accordingly. Specifically, if A is the selected fascicle, then the adjusted weight of each remaining fascicle F is given by:

$$wt(F/A) \quad = \quad k * |F - A| \tag{2}$$

Then from among the remaining fascicles, we pick the one with the highest adjusted weight, and repeat.

In [15], we give a more optimized implementation of the above greedy selection. The basic idea is not to do weight re-adjustment and re-sorting of the remaining fascicles after each fascicle has been selected. Instead, we pick a "batch" of fascicles $F_1, \ldots, F_u$ so that none of them overlap with each other. At the end of each batch, re-sorting and weight re-adjustment is done only once based on $\cup_{i=1}^{u} F_i$. This saves considerable overhead.

3.4 Greedy Selection for the Multi-k Algorithm

The weight re-adjustment formula is more complicated for the Multi-k algorithm, because the candidate fascicles may have varying dimensionalities. More importantly, as described in Section 3.2, the Multi-k algorithm can generate many pairs of candidates F_1, F_2 such that: (i) $F_1 \subset F_2$, but (ii) $k_1 > k_2$, where k_1 and k_2 are the dimensionalities of the fascicles. If F_2 is selected first, then according to Equation (2), $wt(F_1/F_2)$ becomes 0. However, it is easy to see that even after F_2 is selected, F_1 can still be chosen to provide further storage savings, albeit only to the records contained in F_1. Consider the following example, where $|F_1| = 50$, $k_1 = 8$, $|F_2| = 100$ and $k_2 = 6$. F_2 is selected because its storage savings is 600, as compared with 400 from F_1. However, for the 50 records contained in both F_1 and F_2, they can indeed be compressed further to 8 compact dimensions using F_1. This means an additional savings of $50 * (8 - 6) = 100$ is possible. To reflect this additional savings possibility, we re-adjust the weight of a fascicle in a way more general than in Equation (2):

$$wt(F/A) \quad = \quad \begin{cases} k_F * |F - A| & \text{if } k_F \leq k_A \\ k_F * |F - A| + & \\ \quad (k_F - k_A) * |F \cap A| & \text{otherwise} \end{cases} \tag{3}$$

If the selected fascicle A is of the same or higher dimensionality, then the weight of F is re-adjusted as usual. However, if A is of a lower dimensionality, then the weight of F includes the component $(k_F - k_A) * |F \cap A|$, corresponding to the additional storage reduction of the records in both A and F.

4 Experimental Evaluation for Semantic Compression

4.1 Data Sets used and Experimental Setup

Since we seek to exploit hidden patterns in the data, it is hard to perform any meaningful experiments with synthetic data. We used two very different real data sets for all our experiments:

[3] The value k is the same for all fascicles produced by the Single-k algorithm. As such the multiplication by k can be dropped. However, for easier comparison with Equation (3) later, we show the multiplication explicitly.

	syntactic only	fascicle re-ordering + syntactic	fascicle lossy + syntactic
ascii (gzip)	0.45	0.32	0.14
binary (compress)	0.68	0.51	0.20

Figure 3: Relative Storage: Semantic Compression in Tandem with Syntactic Compression

- **AT&T Data Set**: This data set has 13 attributes describing the behavior of AT&T customers, one per record. Some attributes are categorical (e.g., calling plan subscribed), and others are numeric (e.g., minutes used per month). This is a large data set, of which 500,000 records were extracted randomly and used for the bulk of the experiments.
- **NHL Data Set**: We have already seen a sample of the NHL data set earlier in the paper. For each of about 850 players, there is one record with 12 categorical and numeric attributes describing the position the player played, the minutes played, etc. Among numerous other sites, NHL players statistics can be found in http://nhlstatistics.hypermart.net.

All experiments described in this section were run with both data sets, and produced very similar results. For lack of space, we only show in this section the results from the larger AT&T data set. All experiments were run in a time-sharing environment provided by a 225MHz ultrasparc workstation.

As shown below, the behavior of the algorithms may depend on the choices of values of several parameters: the dimensionality k, the compactness tolerance t, the number P of tip sets, the minimum size m of a fascicle, and the data set size. Unless otherwise stated, the default values are: data set containing 500,000 records, $P = 500$, $m = 8$, [4] and $t = 1/32$, which means that for a numeric attribute A, t is set to be $1/32$ the width of the range of A-values in the data set, and that for a categorical attribute A, t is set to be $\lceil w/32 \rceil$, where w is the total number of distinct A-values in the data set. For most of the categorical attributes in our data sets, w is indeed ≤ 32, which effectively means that we are applying *lossless* compression to categorical attributes with this t value.

Results of interest are runtime, relative storage, and coverage. Runtimes are given in seconds of total time (CPU + I/O). *Relative storage* is defined to be the ratio of the size of the compressed data set to the original size. *Coverage* is defined to be the percentage of records that are contained in some fascicle after the greedy selection.

4.2 The Bottom Line: Semantic Compression with Syntactic Compression

In this experiment we show how storage minimization with fascicles can work in tandem with normal syntactic compression algorithms. We used the unix gzip and compress to compress the ascii and binary versions of the data sets respectively. Figure 3 shows the relative storage figures when (i) fascicles are used only to re-order tuples for subsequent syntactic compression; and (ii) fascicles are used to provide lossy compression on compact attributes, followed by syntactic compression on the remaining attributes.

For both the binary and ascii versions, Figure 3 shows that even if we are to use fascicles simply to re-order tuples (i.e., lossless compression here), the additional savings is considerable (e.g., an additional 30% $\approx$ (0.45-0.32)/0.45). And when we allow acceptable lossiness (as governed by $t = 1/32$ here) in the compact attributes, the additional savings is substantial (e.g., 0.45 versus 0.14, a factor of 3).

4.3 The Effect of P, the Number of Tip Sets

Next we study the effect of the various parameters on the Single-k and Multi-k algorithms. For all the results reported below, we focus on the amount of storage savings produced by fascicles alone. We begin with the internal parameter P, the number of tip sets generated. Figure 4 shows how P affects the relative storage and runtime of the two algorithms. We ran with: $k = 4$, P from 250 to 4000, m from 8 to 8000, and t one of 1/16, 1/32 and 1/48. In terms of storage requirements, we make the following observations:

- Even for as few as $P = 250$ tip sets, for a data set of 500,000 records, both algorithms offer a storage savings of over 30%. This indicates that both algorithms are effective in generating (at least some) good quality candidate fascicles.
- The Single-k algorithm is relatively insensitive to P and gives a relative storage around 0.7 for all values of P with $t = 1/32$ and $m = 8$. With other combinations of t and m, the relative storage changes in a way to be described in Section 4.5. But in all cases, we still get a very flat curve, which is not included in Figure 4(a).
- In contrast, the Multi-k algorithm can be more sensitive to P. For example, with $t = 1/32$ or $1/16$ and $m = 8$, Multi-k becomes more effective in storage reduction with increasing P values. (Here we focus on the shape of the curve; the absolute position of the curve regarding changes in t and m will be discussed in Section 4.5.) This is the case because for the Multi-k algorithm, P corresponds to

[4]Strictly speaking, for storage minimization, the minimum size of a fascicle can be as low as 2. However, to allow some pruning power for the FAP algorithm to be shown in Section 4.6, we arbitrarily set m to a small integer.

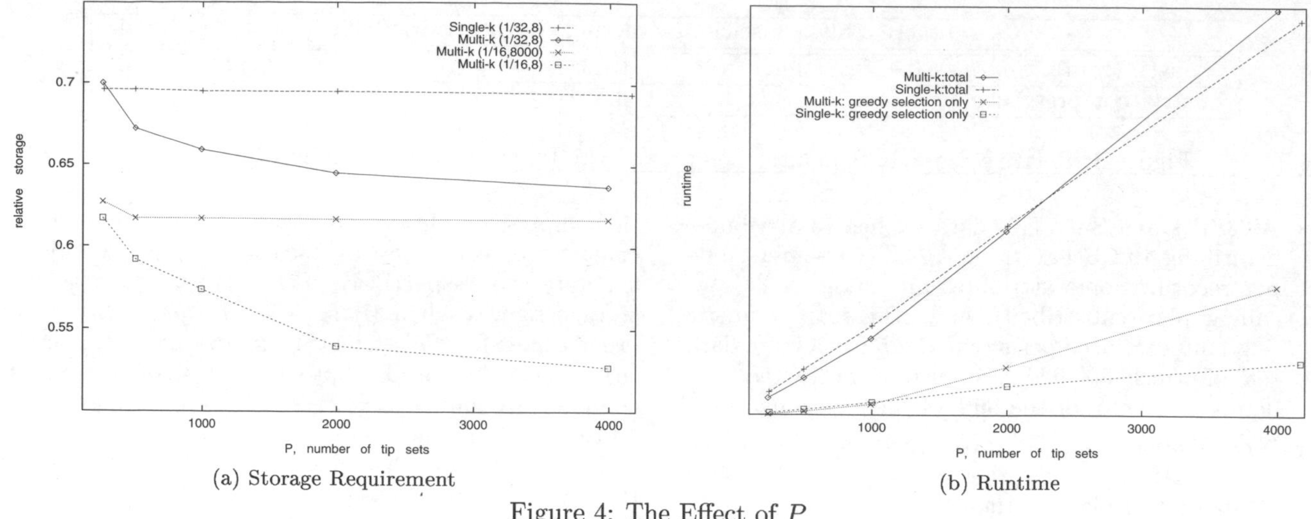

(a) Storage Requirement

(b) Runtime

Figure 4: The Effect of P

the total number of j-D tip sets for all $j \geq k$. For example, among a total of 4,000 tip sets found by Multi-k, there may only be around 500 4-D tip sets (there are 13 attributes). Thus, more tip sets are required for the Multi-k algorithm to stablize in relative storage. However, with $m = 8000$, a situation where there are not many tip sets to begin with, even Multi-k becomes insensitive.

In terms of runtime, Figure 4(b) shows the total time and the fraction of the total time spent on greedy selection for both algorithms with $t = 1/32$ and $m = 8$. (The runtime trends for other combinations are the same.) The total time increases linearly with P, and there is little difference between the two algorithms. But Multi-k takes a lot longer in greedy selection than Single-k does. This is the overhead in conducting the more sophisticated weight re-adjustment shown in Section 3.4.

For the remaining experimentation, because the runtimes of both algorithms increase linearly with P, and the improvement of storage from using a larger P value tails off quickly, we consider $P = 500$ as a reasonable choice for our data sets. And all comparisons of the two algorithms are based on the Multi-k algorithm obtaining exactly the same number P of tip sets as the Single-k algorithm. In previous paragraphs, we have explained how Multi-k would compare if a larger value of P were used. We note in passing that the buffer size used, b, has little effect on the above results, so long as it is not too small (say, a few percent of the data set size).

4.4 The Effect of k, the (Minimum) Dimensionality of Fascicles

Figure 5(a) shows the relative storage provided by both algorithms as k varies from 2 to 12. For the Single-k algorithm, we observe that the storage savings is maximized for an intermediate value of k. When k is small, only a small amount of savings in storage is achieved through compaction – precisely because k is small. As k increases, there are two opposing forces: (i) k itself favors further storage reduction, but (ii) coverage decreases, thereby decreasing the number of records that can be compressed. Figure 5(b) shows the coverage figures as k varies. Initially the k factor dominates the coverage factor, giving a minimum relative storage below 0.5. But as k increases past the optimal value, in this case $k_{opt} = 8$, the drop in coverage dominates.

For the Multi-k algorithm, there is also an optimal value of k. This is the case because as explained in Section 3.4, the greedy selection procedure tends to select first fascicles of the minimum dimensionality. So in this sense, it behaves like the Single-k algorithm. But it differs from the Single-k algorithm in the following ways:

- It is less sensitive to k. This is because even if the input k value is smaller than the actual optimal value, Multi-k algorithm is able to produce candidate fascicles of dimensionality $\geq k$.
- When k is small, observe from Figure 5(a) and (b) that despite having a lower coverage, Multi-k provides better compression than Single-k. This is again due to the former's ability to produce candidate fascicles of dimensionality $\geq k$.
- For larger values of k, however, this ability of Multi-k becomes less important because there are fewer fascicles of dimensionality $\geq k$. At that point, coverage becomes more correlated with relative storage, and Multi-k lags behind Single-k in effectiveness. But this is largely a consequence of our forcing both algorithms to generate the same number P of tip sets. The effectiveness of Multi-k can be improved by running with a larger value of P – at the expense of a larger runtime.

As expected, the runtimes of the algorithms were independent of k (results not included here).

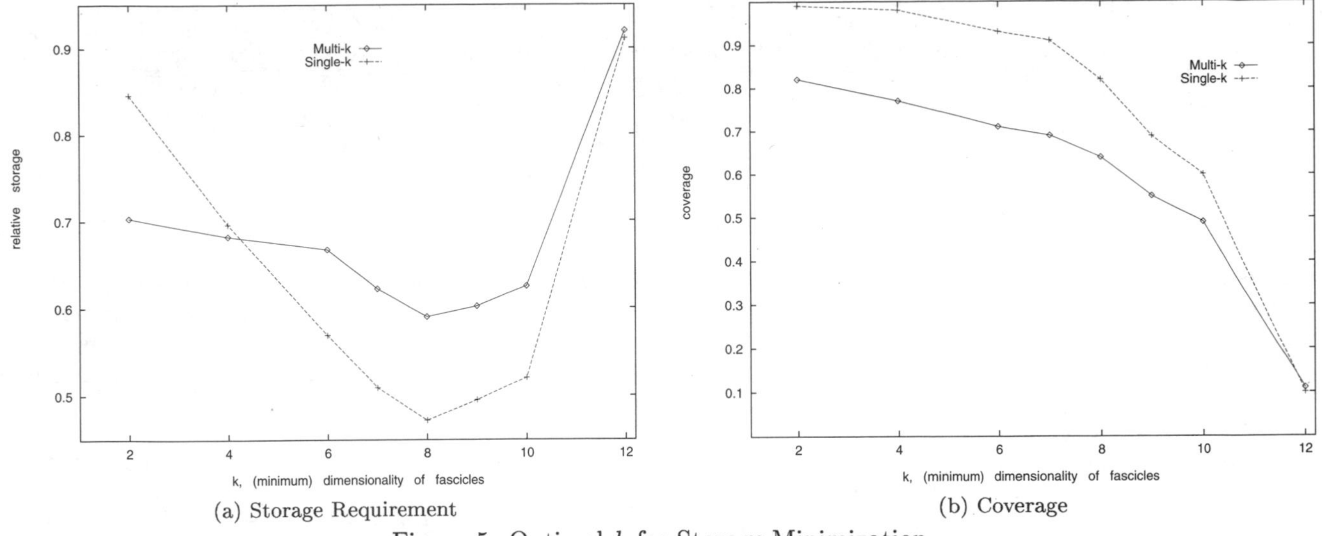

(a) Storage Requirement
(b) Coverage

Figure 5: Optimal k for Storage Minimization

4.5 Miscellaneous Effects and Practitioners' Guide

As t, the compactness threshold, increases, more records qualify to participate in a fascicle, and so there are more opportunities for storage reduction. The k_{opt} value that minimizes storage changes slightly as t varies; for both algorithms, as t increases, larger values of k are desirable. In other words, as we become more forgiving in our lossy compression, it is fruitful and possible to compact more dimensions. As for m, the minimum fascicle size, fewer fascicles can assist in storage minimization when m increases. And the optimal k_{opt} value decreases as m increases. Curves are not presented for lack of space.

Figure 6 shows how the two algorithms scale up with respect to increasing data set size. Both algorithms scale up linearly. While the results shown in the figure are based on $k = 4$, the results generalize to other values of k. The reason why Multi-k runs faster than Single-k is strictly a consequence of our forcing both algorithms to produce the same number of tip sets ($P = 500$ as usual).

In sum, we have shown empirically how the two algorithms behave when the various parameters change, among which P is the most critical. In general, increasing values of P result in both greater computational cost and better compression. However, even fairly small values of P give fairly good results. As a "practitioners' guide", we recommend starting with $P = .001$ of the database size. If one can afford more computational resources, one can pick a larger P. Finally, we recommend the Multi-k algorithm for small values of k, but recommend the Single-k algorithm otherwise.

4.6 Comparison with The FAP Algorithm for Finding All k-D Fascicles

Both the Single-k and Multi-k algorithms selectively find P candidate fascicles for storage minimization. In this section we consider a non-randomized alternative that computes all fascicles.

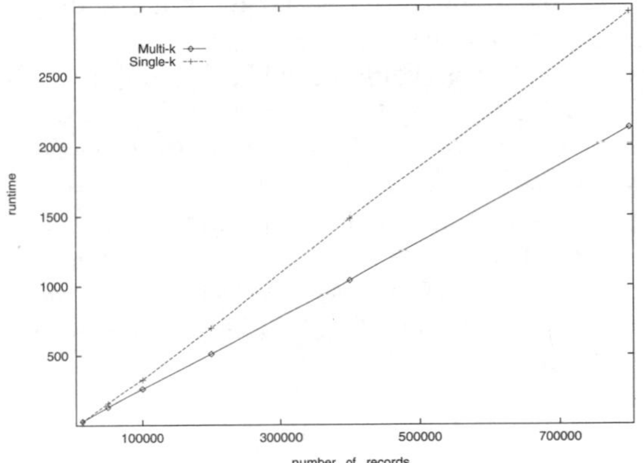

Figure 6: Scalability with respect to Data Set Size

Specifically, we consider an algorithm called *FAP* or *Fascicles through APriori*. As the name suggests, FAP is an adaptation of the well-known Apriori algorithm for association rule mining [2, 3, 13]. Apriori basically performs a bottom-up, level-by-level computation of the underlying lattice space. In the case of FAP for computing all k-D fascicles, the underlying lattice space consists of all possible subsets of attributes. For a given subset of attributes $\{A_1, \ldots, A_u\}$, its "support" is the number of records that form a fascicle with $A_1, \ldots, A_u$ as the compact attributes. This simplified view applies perfectly to categorical attributes. But for numeric attributes, a pre-processing step is necessary to divide the attribute range into bins of width equal to the specified tolerance t. We call this step *pre-binning*. Once pre-binning has been performed, the FAP algorithm computes 1-D fascicles whose support exceed the minimum size parameter m. Then it proceeds to compute 2-D fascicles and so on. The usual pruning strategy applies because the set of records supporting the fascicle monotonically decreases

k	Single-k			FAP		
	Runtime	Relative Storage	Coverage	Runtime	Relative Storage	Coverage
2	3.5	0.846	0.999	13.5	0.848	0.992
3	3.5	0.772	0.988	299.8	0.780	0.967
4	3.4	0.700	0.974	1591.0	0.750	0.846
5	3.4	0.640	0.941	> 2500.0	n/a	n/a

Figure 7: Inappropriateness to Compute All Fascicles for Storage Minimization

in size as the set of compact attributes grows.

Figure 7 compares the FAP algorithm with the Single-k algorithm for computing k-D fascicles, for various values of k. To ensure that FAP terminates in a reasonable amount of time, we used a data set of 1,000 records extracted at random from the AT&T data set.

The difference in runtime performance between Single-k and FAP is truly astonishing. Even for 1,000 records, the time required for FAP for $k \geq 5$ is so large that we did not find it possible to continue running the process on our computer. For $k \leq 4$, Single-k dominates FAP by orders of magnitude. There are two explanations. First, for a given value of k, FAP computes all j-D fascicles for all $1 \leq j \leq k$. This bottom-up strategy is not practical except for very small values of k. Second, particularly for low values of the parameter m, virtually no pruning occurs in the first few passes, resulting in a exponential growth in the number of intermediate candidates. Specifically, if there are u 1-D fascicles, there could be $O(u^2)$ 2-D fascicles, $O(u^3)$ 3-D fascicles, so on, at least for the first several passes.

The only remaining question is whether FAP gives better storage and coverage results, possibly justifying the additional computational cost. Surprisingly, Figure 7 shows that FAP actually did *worse* than Single-k. This is due to the pre-binning step conducted in a fascicle-independent and on a per-attribute basis. In contrast, Single-k (and Multi-k) forms the compact ranges and sets dynamically based on all the attribute values of the current set of tuples under consideration.

5 Solving the Pattern Extraction Problem

Pattern extraction is not as well-defined a problem as storage minimization. There are many different types of patterns one may wish to extract from a data set, and many different possible metrics to assess the quality of the extracted patterns. So we begin this section by defining our pattern extraction task in precise terms. Then we develop an algorithm to carry out the task, which is an extension to the Multi-k algorithm. Finally, we show some empirical results.

5.1 The Pattern Extraction Problem with Fascicles

By definition, a k-D fascicle contains records that more or less agree on the values of the k compact attributes. Given a minimum size m, like the minimum support in association rules, we say that a fascicle is *frequent* if it contains at least m records. Given two (frequent) fascicles F_1, F_2 with dimensionality k_1, k_2 and compactness tolerance t_1, t_2 respectively, we say that:

$$F_1(k_1, t_1) \geq_f F_2(k_2, t_2) \quad \text{iff} \quad k_1 \geq k_2 \text{ and } t_1 \leq t_2 \quad (4)$$

The intuition is that for any fascicle $F_1(k_1, t_1)$, F_1 is automatically a fascicle of the quality pair (k_2, t_2) where $k_2 \leq k_1$ and $t_2 \geq t_1$. For any record R contained in both F_1, F_2 with $F_1 >_f F_2$, we prefer F_1.

For the pattern extraction problem, there is a pre-defined range of dimensionalities $[k_{min}, k_{max}]$ and a series of compactness tolerance $t_1 < \ldots < t_u$. Given these, the ordering in Equation (4) defines a lattice. Figure 8 gives an instance of the quality lattice for pattern extraction from the NHL data set. In this instance, the dimensionality k varies from some minimum (not shown in the figure) to 12, and the compactness tolerance can be 1/8, 1/16 or 1/32 (cf: Section 4.1). In the figure, a directed edge indicates the partial ordering relationship, e.g., (12,1/32) $>_f$ (12,1/16).

The ordering $\geq_f$ defined on fascicles can be extended to give an ordering $\geq_s$ on *sets of fascicles*. To do so, we rely on the well-known Smyth ordering for power sets [20]:

$$\mathcal{S}_1 \geq_s \mathcal{S}_2 \quad \text{iff} \quad \forall F_2 \in \mathcal{S}_2, \exists F_1 \in \mathcal{S}_1 : F_1 \geq_f F_2 \quad (5)$$

For the example in Figure 8, the sets $\mathcal{S}_1 = \{(12, 1/8), (10, 1/16)\}$ and $\mathcal{S}_2 = \{(11, 1/32)\}$ are mutually incomparable. But the set $\mathcal{S}_3 = \{(12, 1/32)\}$ dominates both, i.e., $\mathcal{S}_3 >_s \mathcal{S}_1$, $\mathcal{S}_3 >_s \mathcal{S}_2$.

The Smyth ordering induces equivalence classes of fascicles. Specifically, it is possible to have two sets $\mathcal{S}_1 \geq_s \mathcal{S}_2$ and $\mathcal{S}_2 \geq_s \mathcal{S}_1$ without having $\mathcal{S}_1 = \mathcal{S}_2$. An example are the sets $\{(12, 1/32)\}$ and $\{(12, 1/32), (11, 1/32)\}$. In other words, the equivalence classes induced by $\geq_s$ are not necessarily minimal in the set inclusion sense. This is particularly relevant to our task at hand, because a record R may be contained in many fascicles. To ensure that the final generated fascicles and patterns are of the highest quality, we define $Fas(R)$ given in Equation (1) to ensure that among the set of fascicles all containing R, only the maximal ones with respect to $\geq_f$ can keep R. Hence, putting all the pieces together, the pattern extraction problem we are tackling here is one that given a pre-defined range of dimensionalities $[k_{min}, k_{max}]$ and

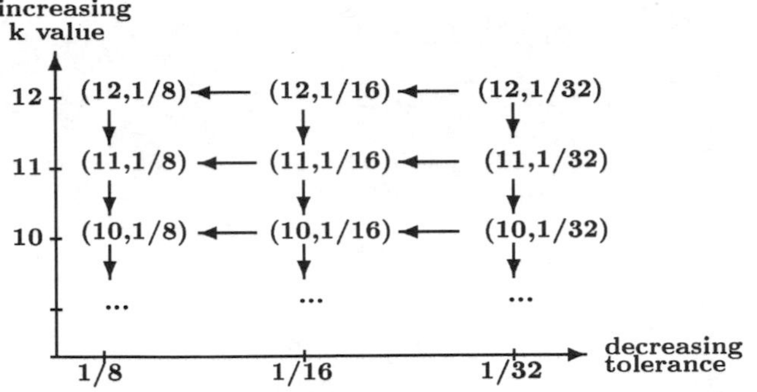

Figure 8: An Example: Pattern Extraction with Fascicles for the NHL data set

a series of compactness tolerance $t_1 < \ldots < t_u$, and a minimum size m, tries to find fascicles of sizes $\geq m$, such that for all records R, $Fas(R)$ is maximized with respect to the ordering $\geq_s$.

There are two important details to note. First, a record R that is contained in both F_1 and F_2 with $F_1 >_f F_2$, does not contribute to the size of F_2. In other words, for F_2 to be frequent, there must be at least m records for which F_2 is a maximal fascicle. Second, one may wonder why bother to maximize $Fas(R)$ for each record R, rather than simply find the fascicles with the maximal qualities. Under this second approach, if we have fascicles of qualities (11,1/16), (10,1/32) and (9,1/32), those of qualities either (11,1/16) or (10,1/32) would be output, but those of quality (9,1/32) would be discarded. Our definition of the problem is strictly more informative than this second approach in that while fascicles of qualities either (11,1/16) or (10,1/32) are output, fascicles F of quality (9,1/32) are also output – provided that there are at least m records for which F is maximal.

5.2 The Multi-Extract Algorithm

5.2.1 Computing Fascicles for all (k,t) Pairs

Like the storage minimization problem, there are two steps in solving the pattern extraction problem. The first step is to find the fascicles. We could simply run the Multi-k algorithm with different values of t. However, it is easy to adapt the Multi-k algorithm to do better. Recall that there is an initial tip set generation phase, followed by a phase to grow tip sets into maximal sets. Iterating the Multi-k algorithm for multiple values of t amounts to running both the generation and the growing phase multiple times. But we can be more efficient by running the generation phase multiple times, but only once for the growing phase. Specifically, we iterate the generation phase (over each piece of the relation read into memory) to produce tip sets for different values of t. This does not require any additional disk I/O. Then we grow all tip sets of varying dimensionalities and compactness tolerance simultaneously in one

Algorithm Multi-Extract

Input: relation R, minimum dimensionality k, minimum size m, a series of tolerance $t_1 < t_2 < \ldots < t_u$, integer P

Output: fascicles F with dimensionality $\geq k$ and containing at least m records for which F is maximal

```
{ 1. ... /* basically the same as in the Single-k algorithm
  2. ...     except for the optimization discussed in
  3. ...     Section 5.2.1 */
  4. /* maximize Fas(R) */
     For all the tip sets F obtained above, process in
     ascending rank:
     4.1 F_rem = F − (∪_{G>F} G), where the G's were frequent
         tip sets obtained in previous iterations of this loop.
     4.2 If |F_rem| ≥ m, output F_rem.
}
```

Figure 9: A Skeleton of the Multi-Extract Algorithm

final scan of the relation. The I/O and main memory complexity remain the same as before.

5.2.2 Maximizing $Fas(R)$

Once candidate fascicles have been generated, the second step for pattern extraction is quite different from that for storage minimization, because for pattern extraction it is fine to have a record put in multiple (frequent) maximal fascicles. To achieve this, we define the *rank* of a fascicle, with respect to the partial ordering given in Equation (4). Given the range of dimensionality $[k_{min}, k_{max}]$ and a series of compactness tolerance $t_1 < \ldots < t_u$, we have the following inductive definition of *rank*:

- (base case) $rank(F(k_{max}, t_1)) = 1$; and
- (inductive case) $rank(F(k,t_i)) = 1 + min\{ rank(F(k+1,t_i)), rank(F(k,t_{i-1}))\}$

For the example given in Figure 8, the series of compactness tolerances is 1/32, 1/16 and 1/8, and the largest dimensionality is 12. Accordingly, all fascicles $F(12,1/32)$ are assigned the top rank, i.e., $rank = 1$. By the inductive case of the definition, all fascicles $F(11,1/32)$ and $F(12,1/16)$ have $rank = 2$. Similarly, all fascicles $F(12,1/8)$, $F(11,1/16)$ and $F(10,1/32)$ have $rank = 3$. From Figure 8, it is easy to see that the rank of $F(k,t)$ corresponds to the length of the shortest path to (k,t) from the root, which is the top pair, e.g., (12,1/32). Also, for any pair of fascicles F_1, F_2 assigned the same rank, it is the case that $F_1 \not\geq_f F_2$ and $F_2 \not\geq_f F_1$.

Having defined the notion of rank, we can now solve the pattern extraction problem by processing fascicles in ascending order of rank. In our example, we first process (12,1/32) fascicles. Then we process all (11,1/32) fascicles and (12,1/16) fascicles, and so on. This order of processing fascicles is captured in Step 4 of the Multi-Extract algorithm shown in Figure 9.

The following formal result ascertains the correctness of the Multi-Extract algorithm. Proof of this lemma can

Fascicles	(12,1/16)	(10,1/12)	(8,1/8)
Population	10%	+ 12.5%	+ 12.5%
Games played [1,82]	[1,5]	([1,79])	([1,82])
Goals Scored [0,50]	[0,0]	[0,3]	[0,3]
Assists [0,80]	[0,2]	[0,5]	[0,5]
Points [0,130]	[0,2]	[0,7]	[0,7]
PlusMinus [-20,40]	[-2,1]	[-2,1]	([-13,8])
Penalty Mins [0,400]	[0,18]	[0,22]	([0,233])
Power Play Goals [0,20]	[0,0]	[0,1]	[0,1]
Short Handed Goals [0,9]	[0,0]	[0,0]	[0,1]
Game winning Goals [0,12]	[0,0]	[0,1]	[0,1]
Game tying Goals [0,8]	[0,0]	[0,0]	[0,1]
Shots [0,400]	[0,8]	[0,23]	[0,25]
Percentage of Goals Scored [0,20]	[0,0]	([0,5])	([0,5])

Figure 10: Descriptions of Sample Patterns in the NHL Data Set. Each column is a fascicle with the attribute ranges given. All attributes are compact except the ones in parentheses.

be found in [15]. The lemma basically shows that Step 4 of Multi-Extract is correct in producing $Fas(R)$ and maximizing $Fas(R)$ for each record R – based on all the candidate fascicles computed in Steps 1 and 3. But the algorithm as a whole is not complete because in Steps 1 and 3 we do not seek to compute all fascicles. The experimental results shown in Section 4.6 convincingly demonstrates that computing all fascicles is computationally prohibitive.

Lemma 1 (Correctness of Multi-Extract) Let $\mathcal{S}$ be the set of candidate fascicles generated in Steps 1 and 3 of Algorithm Multi-Extract. For any record R, let the set of maximal fascicles containing R output by Step 4 be $\mathcal{S}_R = \{F_1, \ldots, F_u\}$. Then: (i) there does not exist a pair F_i, F_j such that $F_i >_f F_j$, $1 \leq i, j \leq u$; and (ii) there does not exist a set $\mathcal{S}' \subseteq \mathcal{S}$ and $\mathcal{S}' \not\supseteq \mathcal{S}_R$ such that $\mathcal{S}' >_s \mathcal{S}_R$. □

5.3 Empirical Results

Below we present the result of applying the Multi-Extract algorithm to the NHL data set. The results from the larger AT&T data set were also interesting. But because we are unable to present these results without divulging proprietary information, we restrict our discussion only to the NHL data set.

Figure 10 shows three fascicles obtained in the NHL data set. Each row describes the range of a particular attribute. The range following the name of the attribute in the first column gives the range of the attribute of the entire data set. The first fascicle has all 12 attributes of the data set as compact attributes and a compactness tolerance of 1/16 of the attribute range. In spite of the stringent requirements, 10% of the players are in this fascicle. These are players who have very limited impact on every aspect of the game. The second fascicle accounts for an additional 12.5% of the population. Compared with the first fascicle, the additional players here could play in a lot more games and have some variations in scoring percentage. Even so, this group still had little impact on the game. The first two fascicles together indicate that almost 1 out of 4 players did next to nothing. Finally, on top of the first two fascicles, there are an additional 12.5% of players whose main contribution appears to be their penalty minutes, as indicated by the dramatic expansion of the range of `Penalty Mins` ([0,22] to [0,233]). The performance of the Multi-Extract algorithm is very similar to that of the Multi-k algorithm, and hence not presented here.

6 Related Work

There are numerous studies on partitioning a data space spanned by a relation or a collection of points, including the studies on clustering (e.g., [17, 21, 6, 1, 10]). Almost all clustering algorithms, with the exception of CLIQUE [1], operate in the original data space, corresponding to row partitioning of a relation. Like CLIQUE, fascicles correspond to both row and column partitioning. CLIQUE is a density based method that finds all clusters in the original data space, as well as all the subspaces. Clusters found by CLIQUE are largest regions of connected dense units, where pre-binning is used to create a grid of basic units. This notion of clusters is fundamentally different from fascicles. Furthermore, the study conducted in [1] does not address the storage minimization problem and the pattern extraction problem analyzed here. Despite all the above differences, the FAP algorithm presented here can be considered a variant of CLIQUE. As shown in Section 4.6, it suffers from the same pitfalls of requiring pre-binning and operating in a bottom-up level-wise computational framework.

One important aspect of fascicles is dimensionality reduction (which leads to compression). In fact, "feature reduction", is a fundamental problem in machine learning and pattern recognition. There are many well-known statistical techniques for dimensionality reduction, including Singular Value Decomposition (SVD) [9] and Projection Pursuit [8]. The key difference here is that the dimensionality reduction is applied to the entire data set. In contrast, our techniques handle the additional complexity of finding different subsets of the data, all of which may permit a reduction on different subsets of dimensions. The same comment extends to FastMap [7], the SVDD technique [14], and the DataSphere technique [11].

The rearrangement of columns in a relation has been shown to affect the compression achieved in previous studies, such as [19, 18]. With fascicles, this idea is carried further since the columns, as well as the number of columns, could be arranged differently for different subsets of tuples.

7 Conclusions and Future Work

Data sets often have approximately repeated values for many attributes. We have taken a first step towards identifying and exploiting such repetition in this paper. We have introduced the notion of a fascicle, which is a subset of records in a relation that have approximately matching values for some (but not necessarily all) attributes, categorical or otherwise. We have presented a family of algorithms to find fascicles in a given relation. We have evaluated how these algorithms behave under different choices of parameters, and shown how fascicles can be used effectively for the tasks of storage reduction and pattern extraction. Given that optimality is hard to obtain for both tasks, our algorithms produce good results.

We believe that the compression aspect of fascicles can provide good support of approximate query answering in the style championed in [4]. The dimensionality reduction aspect of fascicles can find applications in reducing indexing complexity, reverse engineering of schema decomposition, vocabulary-based document classification, and other operations that are exponential in the number of dimensions. Finally, as shown in Section 5, the pattern extraction aspect of fascicles can find applications in any data set that has (approximately) repeated values for many attributes.

As for future work, we believe that fascicles have opened the door to conducting data reduction (and analysis) not on the coarse granularity of the entire data set, but on the fine granularity of automatically identified subsets. As such, it would be interesting to see how the notion of compactness studied here change to other more sophisticated criteria, such as subsets with strong correlation, subsets amenable to SVD, etc.

References

[1] R. Agrawal, J. Gehrke, D. Gunopulos and P. Raghavan. Automatic subspace clustering of high dimensional data for data mining applications. *Proc. 1998 SIGMOD*, pp 94–105.

[2] R. Agrawal, T. Imielinski and A. Swami. Mining association rules between sets of items in large databases. *Proc. 1993 SIGMOD*, pp 207–216.

[3] R. Agrawal and R. Srikant. Fast algorithms for mining association rules in large databases. *Proc. 1994 VLDB*, pp 478–499.

[4] D. Barbará, W. DuMouchel, C. Faloutsos, P. J. Haas, J. M. Hellerstein, Y. Ioannidis, H. V. Jagadish, T. Johnson, R. Ng, V. Poosala, K. A. Ross, K. C. Sevcik. The New Jersey Data Reduction Report. *IEEE Data Engineering Bulletin*, 20, 4, Dec. 1997.

[5] S. Brin, R. Motwani, J. Ullman and S. Tsur. Dynamic itemset counting and implication rules for market basket data. *Proc. 1997 SIGMOD*, pp 255–264.

[6] M. Ester, H.P. Kriegel, J. Sander and X. Xu. A density-based algorithm for discovering clusters in large spatial databases with noises. *Proc. 1996 KDD*, pp 226–231.

[7] C. Faloutsos and K. Lin. FastMap: a Fast Algorithm for Indexing, Data-Mining and Visualization of Traditional and Multimedia Datasets. *Proc. 1995 ACM-SIGMOD*, pp. 163–174.

[8] J.H. Friedman and J.W. Tukey. A Projection Pursuit Algorithm for Exploratory Data Analysis. *IEEE Transactions on Computers*, 23, 9, pp 881–889, 1974.

[9] K. Fukunaga. Introduction to Statistical Pattern Recognition. *Academic Press*, 1990.

[10] S. Guha, R. Rastogi, K. Shim. CURE: an Efficient Clustering Algorithm for Large Databases. *Proc. 1998 ACM-SIGMOD*, pp. 73–84.

[11] T. Johnson and T. Dasu. Comparing massive high-dimensional data sets. *Proc. 1998 KDD*, pp 229–233.

[12] R. Karp. Reducibility among combinatorial problems. *Complexity of Computer Computations*, Plenum Press, 1972, pp 85–103.

[13] M. Klemettinen, H. Mannila, P. Ronkainen, H. Toivonen, and A.I. Verkamo. Finding interesting rules from large sets of discovered association rules. CIKM 94, pp 401–408.

[14] F. Korn, H.V. Jagadish, C. Faloutsos. Efficiently Supporting Ad Hoc Queries in Large Datasets of Time Sequences. *Proc. 1997 ACM-SIGMOD*, pp. 289–300.

[15] J. Madar. *Fascicles for Semantic Compression and Pattern Extraction*, MSc. Thesis, Department of Computer Science, University of British Columbia, 1999.

[16] H. Mannila and H. Toivonen. Level-Wise search and borders of theories in knowledge discovery. *Data Mining and Knowledge Discovery*, 1, 3, pp 241–258.

[17] R. Ng and J. Han. Efficient and effective clustering methods for spatial data mining. *Proc. 1994 VLDB*, pp 144–155.

[18] Ng and Ravishankar. Block-Oriented Compression Techniques for Relational Databases. TKDE, April 1997, pp 314–328.

[19] Olken and Rotem. Rearranging Data to Maximize the Efficiency of Compression. *Proc. 1986 PODS*, pp 78-90.

[20] M. Smyth. Power Domains. *Journal of Computer and System Sciences*, 16, 1, pp. 23–36, 1978.

[21] T. Zhang, R. Ramakrishnan and M. Livny. BIRCH: an efficient data clustering method for very large databases. *Proc. 1996 SIGMOD*, pp 103–114.

Issues in Networked Data Management in the Next Millennium

Michael L. Brodie
GTE Laboratories
brodie@gte.com

Surajit Chaudhuri
Microsoft Research
surajitc@microsoft.com

1. Premise

The next generation of computing will involve vast numbers of devices and humans interacting to achieve organizational, enterprise, and any number of other personal objectives. The explosive growth of the web and the emergence of a new generation of personal gizmos are two extreme examples: the web is a universal publishing platform and the PalmPilot™ is a hand-held database of contact and scheduling information. In the emerging networked world, data will reside not on a few data servers but on millions of servers and devices distributed worldwide in connected and disconnected modes. Conventional database concepts, tools, and techniques apply in the abstract but the networked world will present several discontinuities. Some fundamental database assumptions will no longer apply. What are the data management requirements in the future networked world? What are the current and future requirements and challenges for networked data management? In this industrial session, three industry leaders with major commitments to networked data management will present their views and will respond to questions.

2. A Sampling of Issues

We motivate the discussion among the panelists by raising a few key specific technical issues that are sure to play an important role in the networked data management architectures.

A key requirement in the networked data management is to recognize the inherent *dynamic* nature of the network. Such dynamism requires mechanisms that *make universal plug and play p*ossible. How would such a plug and play architecture be supported? Several issues that need to be addressed in this context are role of *meta-data*, and the inherently difficult aspects of *administration* and models of *data consistency*. The networked data management infrastructure would require support for *novel programming and execution environment*. For example, the gizmos should be able to *auto-install applications* from the network with ease. The support for multiple models for data consistency will need to be complemented by support for *degrees of completeness* in the querying subsystem. Such architectural decisions will impact the nature of *caching strategy* in the network. What are the new sets of tools that we will need in the context of a networked data management? Will there be collateral changes? In particular, can current operating systems adequately support future networked requirements? Finally, we need to consider the effect of XML and other industry initiatives on networked data management.

Panelists, Christopher J. Pound from BT, Rafiul Ahad from Oracle and James Hamilton from Microsoft will express the challenges that they see and help us find answers to these complex technical issues. Dr. Pound expresses the view of a major Telcom operator, a consumer of database technology and a major owner of the networked data management problem. Ahad and Hamilton express the views of major database technology providers with different approaches to the challenges ahead.

Proceedings of the 25th VLDB Conference, Edinburgh, Scotland, 1999.

A Scalable and Highly Available Networked Database Architecture

Roger Bamford, Rafiul Ahad, Angelo Pruscino

Oracle Corporation
500 Oracle Parkway
Redwood Shores, California
U.S.A
rbamford,rahad,apruscin@us.oracle.com

Abstract

The explosive growth of the Internet and information devices has driven database systems to be more scaleable, available, and able to support online, mobile, and disconnected clients while keeping the cost of operations low. This paper presents the concept of Scalable Server that has the above characteristics and that can directly serve applications and data.

1. Introduction

The explosive growth of Internet commerce, combined with the increasing capability of cell phones and handheld information devices has imposed some challenges on the application system architectures. The system must provide near-linear scalability and high availability, it must support online and offline mobile applications, and the cost of operating the system must be low.

For the traditional application deployment, the three-tier client-server application architecture, with thin clients in the first tier, an application server in the middle tier, and a database server in the third tier solved the scalability problem to some degree. By replicating the application server, these systems were able to support more users. There are two basic models of the three-tier architecture. The first model uses a single database server. The second model uses many database servers with one designated as a master and the rest as replicas.

Proceedings of the 25th VLDB Conference, Edinburgh, Scotland, 1999.

The single database server model creates a scalability and availability bottleneck in the database server. A typical approach to solve these problems is to use redundant high-end hardware for the database server. Such a solution is very costly and still has a low threshold for the number of concurrent users it can support. On the other hand, using database replicas create system management overhead as many databases have to be maintained and replicating and reconciling changes in them with the master database is non trivial.

This paper presents an application architecture that is optimized for scalability, availability, and cost of operation for the new breed of online and mobile applications. The architecture is based on the following observations:

1. The price of mid-size server hardware is low and continues to fall.
2. The cost of operations of an application system is directly proportional to the number of independent application and database servers used in the system.
3. The bandwidth of the "last mile" of wireless traffic of the Internet has not increased significantly but the number of wireless/mobile clients of Internet commerce is growing rapidly, resulting in traffic congestion in the last mile.

The architecture consists of a large number of *logically thin clients* served by a single *Scalable Server* (Scalable

Server) either directly (two-tier) or via an application server (three-tier). The clients can operate in, and switch between, both connected and disconnected mode seamlessly. The clients carry a satellite database that contains a subset of data from the server. This database is managed by an ultra-slim DBMS. Both applications and data are transparently downloaded into the client a priori so that it uses less of the available bandwidth during operation. A good deployment strategy will permit clients to operate in a disconnected mode for an extended period of time.

The Scalable Server is a network of inexpensive physical servers that share the same disk storage system. A high speed interconnect among the physical servers is used to keep their states in sync. The client sees the Scalable Server as a single server with a single IP address. By using a Redundant Array of Inexpensive Disks (RAID) for the disk storage and redundant physical servers, the Scalable Server can support high availability. The Scalable Server is operational so long as at least one of the physical servers is running. To support more users without degrading the response time, more physical servers can be added while the system is operating. Thus the Scalable Server supports scalability without downtime and with virtually no administrative overhead. Finally, the Scalable Server presents a single-system view to its users, which simplifies manageability by reducing the complexity of managing a server cluster. Due to this feature, the administrative overhead, and thus the cost of operation, is very low.

Section 2 of this paper presents the Scalable Server architecture in more detail. Section 3 provides an overview of the client technology. Section 4 contains the concluding remarks.

2. Architecture of the Scalable Server

The Scalable Server is responsible for providing highly-available and scalable access to data and applications. The hardware platform of the Scalable Server is a scalable cluster of mid-sized commodity servers sharing storage over a scalable interconnect. On top of this platform the Scalable Server software provides a single-system view for data and applications. At the core of the Scalable Server is an extensible and scalable shared-disk database server running on the platform's commodity single-node operating system. Cluster coordination code in the database server talks across the interconnect to provide lock management and a globally-coherent distributed data cache. Experiments show that over current interconnects this architecture scales linearly with only a slight response time degradation when compared to single-node database. Although it is well-known that single-node database servers have the best base-line performance, the exponential price-performance curve of the hardware and the vulnerability to single component failures makes single-node database servers unsuitable as the core for the Scalable Server.

On top of the database server, the Scalable Server provides scalability, availability, and accessibility services such as event management, single IP appearance, and cluster volume management. Since the application and the database reside on the same computer, special attention is paid to minimizing the cost of the context switch between conventional applications and the database. Our studies show that many of the performance gains of in memory databases can be attributed to their low-overhead (linked-in) connection to the applications. As commodity operating systems such as Windows NT and Linux mature support is expected for light-weight subsystem calls that can provide similar performance gains without loss of fault isolation.

For the new world of Java applications, the Scalable Server provides an integrated Java platform. Thin clients and legacy applications communicate with the applications and data server on the Scalable Server via standard protocols and content representations such as HTTP, FTP, LDAP, IMAP4, IIOP, HTML, and XML. Proprietary protocols are used for SQL data access, queue propagation, replication, and publish/subscribe.

Since all services and libraries required to run the applications are provided by Scalable Server software, and since all inter-node protocols are controlled by the Scalable Server, it is possible to mix-and-match the hardware and operating system when expanding a Scalable Server cluster. In addition, Scalable Server management services provide single point of administration for all components. Combined with the linear hardware price-performance curve, the effect is an economy of scale for total cost of ownership as the workload and Scalable Server grow.

3. Client Technology

As information devices such as cell phones and hand-held devices grow in popularity, businesses are looking for ways to support them as terminals in Internet commerce applications. The problem, however, is the relatively narrow bandwidth of the wireless communication medium used by these devices in the first leg of their communication with the servers. The CPU speed and the memory capacity of these devices are growing at a faster rate than the communication bandwidth. This has prompted a new thinking in client technology to reduce the use of the communication medium and support disconnected clients. This goes beyond the traditional technique of caching.

A popular approach to improving the response time on the client for slow networks is to cache the data on the client side. Caching does improve the performance of the client. However, it has the following limitations:

1. Caching is reactive. The information must be retrieved from the server when the client needs it for the first time. Subsequent access to the same information may not need to access the server.
2. Updating the cached information requires access to the server to update the corresponding information (write-through cache). This is due to the fact that keeping the cached information consistent with the version on the server is a difficult problem to solve when updates to the cache are not immediately written to the server.
3. The validity period of cached information is the minimum of the validity of information items in it. For example, if a browser is caching a Web page that contains several information items in it and one of them changes every minute, then the validity period of the Web page is at most one minute. Even if this information item constitutes a tiny percentage of the total Web page size, the whole Web page must be refreshed if it is used after the validity period of the information item has expired.

In addition to the preceding limitations, caching is only used for data. The application that processes the data can either reside on the server or on the client. Server-resident applications are easier to maintain but require the clients to have continuous connectivity to the server. Thus they cannot be used to support disconnected clients. Permanent installation of applications on the client can result in high cost of application maintenance.

Our approach is to use a small-footprint database management system on the client side and automatically install and update required applications on the client. By selecting the deployment configuration in terms of data and applications needed by each client, this approach can optimally support wireless and disconnected clients without incurring the high cost of maintenance associated with a "fat" client. Changes made by the client application to the client database are synchronized with the Scalable Server. Any conflicts which result from the client and server (or other client) making changes to the same data item are resolved by either built-in conflict resolution methods or user-defined methods on the Scalable Server. Different policies can be easily implemented to resolve conflicts that cannot be resolved by these methods.

1. Concluding Remarks

This paper presents a high-level application architecture that supports scalable and highly available servers and mobile and disconnected clients. Oracle has shipped these types of products for over two years. Oracle8*i* with the Parallel Server option is the latest example of the Scalable Server. It supports a shared-disk cluster of machines that can be extended as needed. A highly scaleable Java virtual machine (VM) and PL/SQL VM are included in the data server for executing Java and PL/SQL stored procedures and triggers. Standard protocols including HTTP and IIOP are supported to access applications running on the data server platform. Release 8.2 improves scalability of the cluster cache and extends scalability and availability services of release 8*i*.

The Oracle8*i* Lite product is designed for mobile and disconnected clients. It consists of two versions of a small footprint DBMS, a data synchronization module, and an application development and deployment environment. One version of the DBMS is a full-featured object-relational DBMS that supports up to 32 concurrent applications. It provides ODBC, JDBC, C, C++, and Java fast path interfaces. The other version of DBMS is a 50KB version for cell phones and information devices. Both versions use the same database format and can replicate to the same server.

The data synchronization module supports both transaction log-based and state-based data synchronization. It can use wireless, dial-up, or a LAN network to communicate with the server, and supports both synchronous and asynchronous replication models.

The application development and deployment environment currently supports easy management of Web-based application development and deployment. It supports a runtime environment that permits one-click installation and update of Web applications and data. It employs a small footprint Web server on the client side that permits both online and offline modes of operation for the Web applications.

Networked Data Management Design Points

James Hamilton

Microsoft SQL Server Development
One Microsoft Way
Redmond, WA
USA
JamesRH@microsoft.com

1. Introduction

Data management in a networked world presents us with some of the same challenges that we've seen in the past, but emphasizes our ability to deal with scale, in that there are several orders of magnitude more database users, and database sizes are rising more quickly than Moore's law. We have considerably less control over the structure of the data than in the past and must efficiently operate over poorly or weakly specified schema.

After more than 30 years of evolution, and substantial commercial success, database technology is more relevant now than ever. We are close to being able to keep all human produced information stored and machine accessible, and to having all devices owned by all people online. These advances will force us towards new client device programming models, and will require much more research in query processing techniques and algorithms, not just on performance, but on returning approximate result sets, new indexing techniques, and support for a multi-tiered caching data management hierarchy. Database administration will move from a job classification to an automatic system performed operation, and there will be dramatic changes in database server architectures.

Proceedings of the 25th VLDB Conference, Edinburgh, Scotland, 1999.

2. The Client DB Environment

International Data Corporation (www.idc.com) estimates the number of US Internet users in 1998 at 51 million and the worldwide count at 131 million. In 2001, they expect the worldwide count to hit 319 million, at which point there will be 515 million connected devices. And, although these estimates seem quite reasonable, the numbers could arguably be substantially higher once we start networking non-standard computing devices such as VCRs, televisions, and other home automation functions. Just surveying my house and counting devices that have memory or internal state that require setting or configuration produces over a hundred count including (often with multiple copies of each): cell phones, water heater, clocks, radios, sprinkler controllers, oven (clock), microwave (clock), watches, televisions, CD players, VCRs, PH controller (fresh water aquarium), wave maker (marine aquarium), aquarium light controllers, home thermostat, desktop computers, laptop computers, several palmtop computers, refrigerator, and many more. Each of these devices requires independent attention to be set, many need to be reset after a power failure, and none of these devices cooperate or feedback today. Just setting all the clocks in the house after a power failure can be a bit painful given that few modern devices don't include a clock these days (VCR, stove, microwave, TV, thermostat, etc.). Instead of having on average, 1 to 2 devices per person connected to the net, we could see several hundred each, yielding a 2 orders of magnitude increase in the number of network-connected devices ranging to upwards of hundreds of billions.

Connecting these devices and having them interoperate and share data is quite compelling. Rather than putting on my home air-conditioning when the house temperature starts to climb it might make sense for the system to observe that I'm not currently in the house and shut off the 4,000 watts of lights over the fish tank and ensure the the tank still receives the appropriate daily photoperiod by putting them back on once the house has returned to a more moderate temperature.

Clearly there are many inhibitors to such interconnection happening in the near future, such as the multiple-hundred million non-networked install base, and the lack of a widely supported appliance interconnection standard. To be successful an existing infrastructure such as power line, radio, or telephone must be exploited rather than requiring that the home be rewired. So, although it won't happen immediately, it appears inevitable that it will happen. Microsoft and a consortium of others have proposed Universal Plug and Play (www.upnp.org) as an appliance interconnection standard. Sony is aggressively supporting IEEE 1394 as a digital appliance interconnection mechanism (www.sel.sony.com/semi/ieee1394wp.html) and they predict that the market for these devices will grow from the current 2 million devices to 460 million units by 2011.

The growth of the network-connected user population, in conjunction with a substantial predicted increase in the number of network-connected devices per user, will lead to 100's of billions of network connected devices. And, of course, the whole point behind network connecting these devices is so they can share data. In effect, each of these devices is a database client in a huge web of interconnected database management systems.

2.1. Is Client DB Size Really the Issue?

Currently, DB footprint has been the dominant issue in discussions of client side database management systems perhaps followed by the implementation language in which the database was written (SIGMOD99, "Honey I shrunk the database: footprint, Mobility, and beyond"). I argue that both features are either irrelevant or rapidly becoming so.

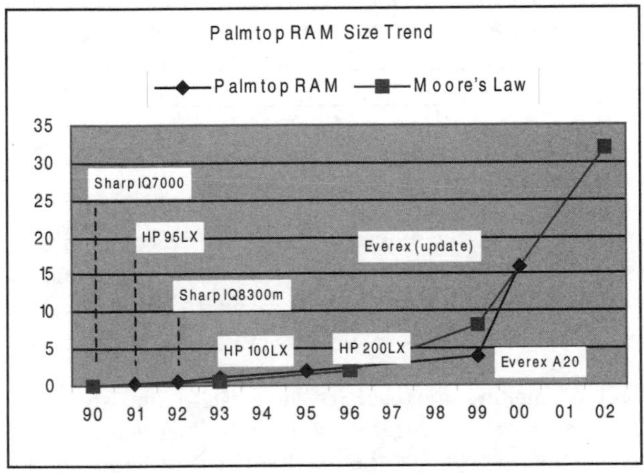

Consider the device resource growth driven by Moore's law. We are very close to having the resources even on the smallest devices to support standard applications and programming infrastructure. In the figure above, I plot the RAM sizes in black of the 5 palmtop devices I've owned over the last 10 years and, in grey , I plot the Moore's law predicted growth.

This data predicts that a commodity price point (under $500) palmtop device will have 32 MB of memory by 2002 and, if the current memory growth rate continues, will have 128 MB before 2005. Since most of these devices exhibit a significant degree of specialization and therefore have less than general system memory resource requirements, it would appear that we are very near to having the memory resources needed to support standard operating systems, database management systems, and applications. Special device specific programming models and database programming interfaces can only be justified when space is unaffordable. Even a year ago this was obviously the case. However, with available memory growing exponentially without increase in price, why would we trade off programmer time to rewrite features a second time in order to save memory resources? Programmer costs are rapidly increasing, and the limiting resource for most software projects is skilled developers. Even saving half of the memory in a more memory efficient implementation cannot justify or recover the additional time and expense of a custom infrastructure.

Saving memory at this cost is unaffordable.

The argument that the database implementation language is important centers around the need to automatically install the application software and database software infrastructure on each client when needed. Obviously this is an important feature but, equally obviously, Java isn't required to achieve this goal. For example, Office 2000 is composed of many components most of which don't need to be installed until needed. When a feature is accessed, it can be automatically installed on the client. As client-side devices evolve, all the data stored on client system should just be a cache of those most recently used applications and data. Nothing should have to be explicitly installed. This is an important attribute of a networked client database-programming infrastructure but it does not dictate that any particular programming language be used.

If database footprint and implementation language aren't the most important attributes of a networked data management infrastructure, then what is? I argue that the number one characteristic will be supporting a programming interface and execution environment that is symmetric with the server tiers. Any program should be able to run on any device, anywhere in the multi-tier computing hierarchy. Different devices will exhibit different performance characteristics, many will be optimized to support a narrow set of features at a given point in time, but every device will support exactly the same programming interface and execution environment. Further, such infrastructures will support automatic installation of both data and applications, in effect just being redundant caches of resources available elsewhere on the network. The distinguishing features of client-side devices should be input/output device support, size, and battery life.

3. Networked DB Design points

3.1. Save Everything for all Time

In "How Much Information Is There In the World" (www.lesk.com/mlesk/ksg97/ksg.html), Michael Lesk argues that we are on the cusp of being able to store all information produced by the human race and never need to delete anything. His argument is based upon summing all the yearly media sales and information sources in the US and then extrapolating to worldwide quantities using GNP ratios:

- Paper sources: less 160 terabytes
- Cinema: less than 166 terabytes
- Images: 520,000 terabytes
- Broadcasting 80,000 terabytes
- Sound: 60 terabytes
- Telephony: 4,000,000 terabytes

These data yield a sum of approximately 5,000 petabytes. Others have estimated the number to be as high as 12,000 petabytes but most estimates appear to agree that the total amount of data produced annually is on the order of thousands of petabytes.

Looking at the worldwide storage production as estimated by Optitek for 1998, we get about 13,000 petabytes leading to the conclusion that annual tape and disk production are on verge of being able to store all human produced data.

At least three database management system related conclusions follow from this data: 1) the amount of online storage is climbing prodigiously fast and it's increasingly network attached, 2) the bulk of the data in the world is unstructured or only weakly structured, and 3) current query techniques and algorithms will perform poorly on a corpus with these composition and size characteristics. Much of the data that is currently without apparent structure will be self-describing (with XML being the most likely mechanism). Query systems will efficiently exploit hidden structure returning less "noise" on each query and allowing efficient joins between data in different data storage systems.

Pre-computed results, summary tables, materialized views, multiple redundant index structures, and detailed distribution and cardinality metadata are all space/query time trade-off that will make sense as our online data sizes rapidly increase.

3.2. DB Administration a Major Deployment Barrier

Server administrative costs dominate both software and hardware costs, and with hardware and software costs continuing to decline, this ratio worsens each year. However, some early research is showing significant promise. Surajit Chaudhuri of Microsoft Research is leading the Autoadmin project (http://www.research.microsoft.com/research/db/AutoAdmin/default.htm) the focus of which is to automate all database administrative activity. Early work on index tuning was published at SIGMOD'98. Essentially, auto administration techniques trade off machine resources to perform database administrative tasks. Given that hardware costs are rapidly trending towards zero while, database administration costs stubbornly remain constant or even climb year-to-year, this is an excellent trade-off. SQL Server 7.0 shipped the first result of this research, the index-tuning wizard. As research activity in this area increases across the industry, we should eventually be able to automatically create and destroy indexes as dictated by query load balanced against update activity and available system resources. Materialized views are another form of redundant data that today require administrative tuning but, over time, should be automatically managed by the system. Another automatic administrative feature demonstrated by Microsoft SQL Server is the automatic computation of data distribution and cardinality statistics as needed by the optimizer. Resource-based administrative decisions are much better made dynamically by the database management system than left to an administrator, partly to avoid the administrative costs, and partly because automatic reconfiguration adapts more quickly and efficiently to changing query loads. Microsoft SQL Server has implemented dynamic memory reconfiguration, and other features such as automatic degree-of-parallelism selection are common in commercial products. So, the industry as a whole is making progress, but it remains perhaps the most important problem we face.

3.3. Affordable Availability

The ubiquity of the Internet allows many companies to make their back office systems directly accessible to customers without sales people as intermediaries. This can dramatically decrease the cost of providing a service and improve the quality of that service, but it has the effect of making the back office system into the front office. There no longer is a layer of service or sales representative between the back office system and the customer, so any interruption of service has immediate negative impact. In addition to this intolerance to unexpected downtime, 24-hour availability requirements make it very difficult to perform periodic offline maintenance and upgrade operations. Paradoxically, database management system size and complexity has been on the increase for years – many systems have grown by at least a factor of two over the last 5 years – at the same time that system availability is becoming increasingly important.

From spending many attempting to build bug free database management systems, it became increasingly clear to me that, as an industry, we do an excellent job of removing functional errors. The bugs that actually get missed tend to be complicated combinations of different operations and sequences of relatively unlikely events. These problems are insidiously difficult to isolate without years of testing and we simply can't wait that long prior to shipping. This class of bug is very difficult to remove but their interesting characteristic is that, if a failed operation is re-run, it's very unlikely that the same sequence of multi-user events will again lead to failure. Typically a failed operation will succeed if it is re-run. Jim Gray has described these bugs Heisenbugs in the talk "Heisenbugs: A Probabilistic Approach to availability" (http://research.microsoft.com/~gray/Talks) and in an earlier paper. Several commercial database management systems exploit characteristics of these bugs to increase system availability. For example, Tandem will attempt to re-run the operation on a surviving process pair and Microsoft Exchange will re-try failed I/O operations. We need to make systems resilient to such failures rather than trying to remove them at great time and development expense.

3.4. Redundant Data, Summary Data, and Metadata

Efficient point access to data, the core of most transaction processing systems, is very close to a solved problem across the industry. TP systems tend to scale with the number of user, number of customers or, in the limit, the number of people on the planet. However, large decision support and data analysis problems are not nearly so well behaved. Database size is growing faster than Moore's law (David Patterson; SIGMOD'98 keynote address) and the amount of data referenced by a single query can be a substantial part of the total database size. While many improvements remain to be made, a couple of factors are working in our favor. Perhaps the most significant is that dramatic increases in the amount of available storage online will allow use of multiple redundant copies of data for more efficient data access. These copies include, for example, mirrored disks where the non-busy member of the pair can support a read while the other member is busy. Also included in this class are index structures and materialized views, which allow query results or sub-results to be stored and automatically maintained. In addition to being able to store redundant copies of data affordably, we'll also continue to allocate larger percentages of the total database size to storing statistics about the data (data distribution and cardinality information), helping the query optimizer choose more efficient query plans.

We need to continue improving indexing and materialized view techniques, and devise other mechanisms to exploit multiple data copies in support of more efficient access. However, as we continue to increase the number of possibilities, we need to recognize that systems are becoming increasingly difficult to tune. These indexing structures and other metadata need to be automatically produced when needed and removed when their cost/benefit is no longer positive for a given systems work load. Leaving the decisions on which structures to add and when to remove them to administrators, as many current systems do, is contributing the scaling problem rather than helping to addressing it.

3.5. Data Structure Matters

Most Internet content is today unstructured text and, as a consequence, search techniques are restricted to simple Boolean search through unstructured text, with the side effect of the search not being particularly selective, and typically returning many irrelevant documents mixed in with the search targets. All of these documents actually do have some structure, but it's typically not explicit. Search products, such as Yahoo, go through and categorize the online corpus but as more and more data is put on-line, this manual approach won't scale. Further, the categorization provided by these search products is fairly limited, typically only categorizing at a high level and not parsing out and representing finer document structure.

There exist many possible solutions to this apparent lack of structure, but XML is emerging as a good mix of simplicity and potential richness to become the structure expression language of the Internet. Database management systems need to support XML data as a first class type and support efficient searching and processing of XML data.

3.6. Approximate answers quickly

Current database management systems have specialized for years in computing the correct answer when queries are posed, however, text search systems have shown for years that an approximate answer computed quite quickly can be more valuable than waiting for the right answer.

Joe Hellerstein has begun to exploit this observation by working on database query processing techniques that produce an approximate answer very quickly and then steadily improve the accuracy of the result. This is a novel approach that is made far more useful by constantly showing both the current approximate answer and the statistical confidence bound on this result. Peter Haas and Hellerstein wrote up this approach and some incremental query processing techniques in "Ripple Joins for online Aggregation" (SIGMOD'99). Also, presented at SIGMOD'99 was "Approximate Computation of Multidimensional Aggregates of Sparse Data Using Wavelets (Jeffrey Vitter and Min Wang).

I believe that these techniques have tremendous potential to fundamentally improve the efficiency of database users working on analytical problems. Clearly, there will always be a place for conventional algorithms that compute the exact answer as quickly as possible, but I can imagine using approximate techniques to explore a search space and form a hypothesis and then an exact technique to prove that an interesting data trend actually does exist.

3.7. Convergence of Data Processing and Data Storage

David Patterson in his SIGMOD 98 keynote address (cs.Berkeley.edu/~patterson/talks) made the case for intelligent disks arguing:

- I/O bus bandwidth is a bottleneck to delivering bandwidth
- Fast switched serial networks can support enormous bandwidth
- Processor/memory interface is a bottleneck to delivering bandwidth
- Growing CPU-DRAM performance gap leading to under-utilized CPUs

And, as a result, we have a new system opportunity in combining CPU, high-speed serial network, and disk together in a single package that, incidentally, was already required by the disk. In fact, the power and chassis requirements of these disks would be largely unaffected.

In the NASD presentation "Put Everything in Future (Disk) Controllers (It's not "if" it's "when?")" (www.research.microsoft.com/~gray/talks) Jim Gray agrees with Patterson's prediction that we will need to move processing power to data sources. Gray goes on to state that these devices should be leveraging commodity parts, including standard operating systems and standard database management systems, rather than special purpose real time kernels and purpose built software. His point is very similar to the one that I made earlier in this abstract when I argued that light-weight client devices (palmtops, etc.) should be built using standard applications, system software and data management infrastructure. Leveraging the existing programming environments and skills is much more important than optimizing for hardware utilization and exploitation.

I agree that programs, data management software, and standard operating system software will be implemented in cyberbricks and this conclusion argues strongly that database management systems will have to be built to support clusters of thousands, rather than existing design points of tens to, at a stretch, hundreds of nodes. And, rather than a cluster only being suitable for very large databases or very large numbers of users, it would become the standard component from which all database management systems would be constructed. The only difference between a small system and a large system would be the number of nodes employed.

4. Conclusion

Managing data in a networked world presents us with some of the same challenges that we've always faced – scale and robustness -- but on a scale several orders of magnitude beyond past experience. XML will bring some structure to what has appeared to be unstructured data and provide a common language for the expression of metadata about the documents and about the corpus as a whole. Even with these expected improvements in document structure, we're expecting huge changes in our handling of weakly structured or unstructured data and we will need to introduce far more schema flexibility to efficiently store and query this data. The sizes of our databases will have grown to the point where the focus has shifted from operational access to data analysis and data mining – some data items may, over the course of their storage lives, only be summarized or aggregated and never directly accessed. A statistically near answer quickly is rapidly becoming much more useful than the "right answer" and, more than ever, we will be trading space for performance in the storage of indexes, statistics, summary tables, etc.

Rather than supporting low end client devices with specially developed applications and data management infrastructure, decreasing device cost and stable to increasing programmer cost will force us to a model where the programming model and infrastructure software is the same across all tiers in the computing hierarchy.

Applications will continue to migrate to the data with servers composed of many cooperating cyberbricks each slice of which is a disk, CPU, memory, network connect component. And, data will continue to replicate to client devices where each client is a large cache of recently accessed data and recently used programs.

"In Cyberspace No One Can Hear You Scream …"

Dr. Christopher J. Pound

British Telecommunications plc.
Enterprise House, 84-85 Adam Street,
Cardiff CF24 2XF
United Kingdom
chris.pound@bt.com

Abstract

As the telecommunications industry endeavours to reinvent itself, the effective management and exploitation of *information*, data delivered in *context*, is now the key weapon in gaining and retaining customers. The data management challenges in an environment of massively growing data volumes and complexity introduced by distributed processing are outlined. A framework and methodology for the management of information is presented and the term *Context Data* is introduced.

1. Introduction

"I have a simple but strong belief. The most meaningful way to differentiate your company from the opposition…is to do an outstanding job with information. How you gather, manage, and use information will determine whether you win or lose…You need a fast flow of good information to streamline processes, raise quality and improve business execution." - Bill Gates[1]

As globalisation takes hold against a backdrop of accelerated convergence of the internet, communications and entertainment industries, an unprecedented wave of mergers and acquisitions amongst telecommunications providers (telcos) is occurring. These telcos are currently endeavouring to reinvent themselves – a future based solely on the transmission of bits (POTS – Plain Old Telephony Services) is no longer tenable. As network bandwidth becomes commoditised, telcos now regard networks as platforms for hosting value-added products and services offering higher margins than simple POTS.

Against this background, arguably the greatest assets that telcos possess are not the physical switches, access and transmission networks comprising copper twisted pairs and optic fibre, but the *information* that these networks and associated systems generate. It is this information that enables telcos to gain competitive advantage by understanding usage patterns and behaviours in order to refine and target product and service offerings to existing and potential customers.

2. *'The Challenge Facing Telcos'*[A]

Telcos generate immense volumes of data e.g. British Telecommunications (BT) currently holds a staggering 60 Terabytes of data on disk (excluding PC's and LAN servers) and 1.9 Petabytes on tape. As complexity increases in the networked world and vast numbers of data-generating devices are introduced, e.g. through growth in mobile computing, data volumes and data distribution are set to explode. The situation is compounded by the fact that most traditional telcos are battling to break free from a legacy of product-centric platforms and systems, where data was viewed and managed as a by-product, in order to satisfy the rapid growth in demand for customer-centric communications solutions. In the spirit of the tagline from Ridley Scott's movie *Alien*: 'In cyberspace no one can hear you scream …'

[A] The views expressed do not necessarily reflect or imply BT policy or strategy.

Proceedings of the 25th VLDB Conference, Edinburgh, Scotland, 1999.

Whilst the volumes of data persisted in the network are relatively low, the volumes of data stored long-term in operational data stores (ODS's) and data warehousing (DW) environments is large e.g. BT collects and stores in excess of one terabyte of raw call data records (CDR's) per month. Telcos have made substantial progress in consolidating data in ODS's to provide a customer-centric view. As e-commerce 'zero latency' channels open up, customers, suppliers and partners are increasingly being provided Internet access to telco ODS and DW data to place orders, view billing data etc. Transaction rates will be high. BT's Customer Service System, which covers PSTN service, experiences 80 million transactions a day, 8 million transactions per peak hour.

As data transmission volumes overtake voice, IP-based networks will increase substantially. The IP equivalent of CDR's will need to be captured (e.g. from WEB-server logs), stored, summarised and analysed in ODS and DW environments. These trends will require technologies that improve the synchronisation of network data (typically held in object databases) with ODS and DW data (typically held in relational databases). Longer-term, distributed DBMS capable of serving both transactional and decision support query access will be required in order to avoid unnecessary data duplication.

Telco networks will increasingly be viewed as an integral part of extended information supply chains. Existing approaches to data management will be replaced by concepts such as subscription to parameter-driven data services with associated data service tariffs. Data consumers will select the quality, accuracy, currency etc. level they are prepared to pay for. The data service will then select the appropriate protocol to deliver the data.

3. *'Data into Information'*

In recognition of the role of information as a key business asset, a framework and methodology has been developed within BT to support the translation of data into information. The requirement was for an environment that promoted the delivery of data accompanied by sufficient contextual detail to enable both business and technical data consumers to translate the data into information. Operational implementation of solutions developed in BT's Marketing Systems environment in 1996 has led to subsequent wider adoption across the business.

3.1 *'The Problem With Meta-data'*

From the outset it was recognised that 'traditional' meta-data, with its emphasis on technical systems definition and description, was too narrow in scope. Furthermore, meta-data management tools and repositories available in the marketplace at the time were firmly aimed at the information systems development professional. Indeed the very term 'meta-data' sounds overly technical and confusion surrounds its precise definition.[2] Furthermore, what is regarded as meta-data by one person may be regarded by another person as data. The word Metadata® has even been trademarked[B] – hence the usage of the hyphenated form 'meta-data' in this paper.

Devlin[2] defined *information* as "data in context". The following example serves to illustrate the range of contextual data that a market analyst may require access to in interpreting a report containing response data from a marketing campaign: descriptive 'look-up' values for 'Standard Industry Classification' code values⁺; definition of 'Region'*; data type and range details for 'Percentage Response'*; business rule used for calculating 'Percentage Response'; data source, accuracy and currency; data quality issues applying to the data analysed; Campaign Brief document; video clip of the TV commercial etc... Where: ⁺ = reference data; * = 'traditional' meta-data.

The technology exists today to access all of these items in a digital form from hyperlinks embedded 'in context' within a WEB-browser delivered report. It is proposed that the term *'Context Data'* is adopted for this class of data and is defined as 'anything that provides meaning to data'. The definition is deliberately open; the key point is that context data is broader in concept than, but can include, 'traditional' meta-data. As with meta-data, context data is perspective-based and multi-tiered: what is regarded as context data by one person may be regarded by another person as data.

3.2 A Framework for Delivering Data in Context

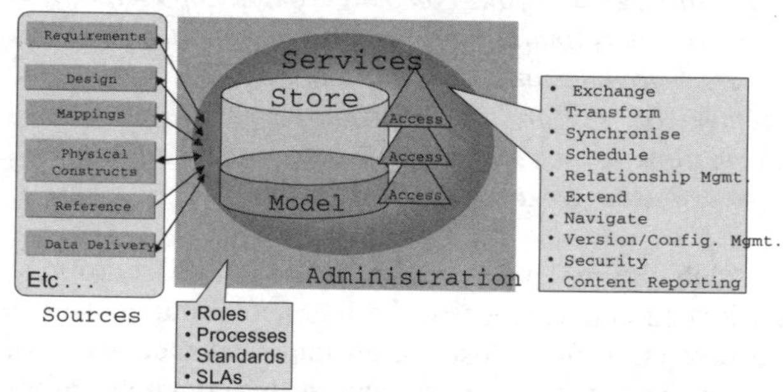

Fig. 1 – Context Data Management Framework

With reference to figure 1, the following principles were adopted during the design and development of the solution:

[B] The mark METADATA® was registered in 1986 in the United States of America Patent and Trademark Office as U.S. Trademark Registration No. 1,409,260 by Megadyne Information Systems; the Metadata Company is the current owner of the trademark. The trademark was granted "Incontestable" status in 1991.

Access via a WEB-browser was a given due to the pervasive use of a corporate intranet within BT. A single 'plain vanilla' user interface was considered inadequate; the user interface must reflect the role and objectives of the information consumer and dynamically adapt to reflect navigation and usage patterns over time.

Sources encompass any potentially relevant digitally available content available to the browser. A survey by the Meta Group in 1997 revealed that between 80% and 95% of large organisation's information was held in an unstructured format. As can be seen from the marketing campaign analysis example given above, access to unstructured context data sources is essential.

The *store*, which architecturally may be physically distributed, is analogous to a traditional meta-data repository and includes a meta-*model* schema / information medol. The *store* contains both context data *content* and *relations*, and has the following characteristics:

- The *content* is minimal, tending to be restricted to 'traditional' meta-data representing entity-relationship models and associated DBMS schemas. The reasons for keeping *store* content minimal are two-fold: (i) the *store* presents a performance bottleneck within the constraints of current technologies; (ii) organisational culture frequently militates against central 'control' of information.
- The *relations* are of two types: (i) *tightly-coupled*, facilitating navigation between instance context data items held *within* the *store* – typically to navigate between meta-data instances within entity-relationship and DBMS schema models; (ii) *loosely-coupled*, to facilitate the linkage of disparate context data sources e.g. a hypertext link from a data item reference embedded within unstructured text to associated data quality, currency and accuracy details applying to the data item but physically stored elsewhere.

A range of *services* are used in order to synchronise, exchange, transform etc. context data between point *sources* via the *store*. This service-based approach facilitates architectural separation between server-side functionality and storage from the browser-based user interface within a component assembly development environment.

The success of the project overall was largely not due, however, to the relatively simple technology deployed – the key proved to be in ensuring that the *administration* environment was in place i.e. roles, responsibilities, standards and Service Level Agreements were clearly defined and adhered to over the long-term. Particular emphasis was placed on ensuring the most appropriate person, irrespective of business or technical organisational alignment, was assigned responsibility for content creation and update. Root-cause analysis of meta-data repository implementation failures across industry revealed that inappropriate assignment of the content creation and update responsibility to the IS Department frequently mitigates against long-term success.

The design framework adopted can be distilled into three dimensions:

- *Functional* areas supported e.g. data definitions, data quality issues, operational metrics …
- *Content* held by system and/or business subject area
- *Role* and objectives of people accessing data in context – a spectrum ranging from knowledge workers 'surfing' context data in a discovery mode, through to data consumers who require the ability to drill-through from data in WEB-delivered reports to associated context data.

3.3 Methodology

The framework outlined above facilitated delivery of the technical solution and population of content to targeted roles via incrementally building outwards along the function / content / role dimensions. A methodological approach, adopting the central tenets of the Dynamic Systems Development Method[3], was evolved which has the following characteristics:

- continuous data consumer involvement during the design, development, testing and deployment phases
- iterative prototyping
- rigorous requirements prioritisation
- time-boxing

Delivery phases of three months duration with fixed end-dates were set. Rigorous prioritisation of requirements by the executive sponsors enabled requirements to be added / modified during a development phase; delivery end-dates were always met as lower priority requirements were rolled-over into subsequent delivery phases.

3.4 Context Data Futures

The following issues will need to be tackled if the context data framework is to be further developed:

Connecting Context Data With DSS / Data Warehouse Data: Although techniques and tools are now available for the sophisticated versioning of context data, in the DSS / data warehousing environment data and context data frequently become disconnected. A DSS table row will generally comprise fragments of data that reflect a long lineage of data merged, spilt and transformed during its passage through multiple source systems. Looking down a DSS column, meta-data is not constant until you get to the level of row-sets where all the rows have a common temporal lineage. Data warehouse designers are not always successful in their attempts to 'normalise'/baseline data in columns to achieve a single column meta-data definition. Although a full history of meta-data versions over time may be available, source systems (typically OLTP) data will have long since been archived / deleted. In other cases, current tools simply do not enable meta-data to be recorded at the row-set level within columns.

Recovering Business Rules from Legacy Information Systems: When analysing the context and lineage of data, gaining an understanding of the business rules that have been applied to the data is crucial. In most cases these business rules are 'locked' in legacy system source code. Techniques and tools to recover these business rules are in their infancy[4].

Versioning and Access Authority Granularity: Techniques and tools have been developed that allow meta-object instance level versioning within current meta-data repositories. Consider the following scenario. In ensuring that the most appropriate people are authorised for content creation and amendment of context data (see above): for 'Product Group', a business person would maintain the meta-object property 'Description', a technical person the meta-object property 'Data Type', whilst different Product Managers may be responsible for 'Allowed Value Descriptions' … by range i.e. person one for code values 1 thru' 20, person two for code values 21 thru' 40, etc. Meta-object property (by range) instance versioning granularity is beyond the capabilities of currently available meta-data repositories, particularly those with relational DBMS engines where *n*-way joins typical of meta-data repository queries impose severe performance penalties.

XML-based Meta-data Standards: Significant progress has been achieved recently in converging meta-data standards. A joint press release issued by the Meta Data Coalition (MDC - which now also maintains the Microsoft produced Open Information Model) and the Object Management Group on 20th April 1999 announced plans for a "co-operative relationship to build consensus on metadata standards" – an initiative that spans all the key commercial vendors of meta-data solutions. It remains to be seen whether full meta-data interoperability will be achieved between the CORBA-based XML Metadata Interchange (XMI) and COM-based XML Interchange Format (XIF) standards. Finally, a gulf still exists between the MDC-OMG axis and the W3C XML Resource Description Framework (RDF) meta-data standards. Work to define RDF schemas is ongoing e.g. concerns surround the relatively simple constraints currently applied to the Dublin Core schema[5].

4. The Challenge Ahead

In a survey of major companies, McKean[6] established that of the major determinants of competency (people / process / organisation / culture / leadership / information / technology) in those who had successfully implemented customer information initiatives, technology only accounted for 10% of the competency determinant total; paradoxically, 82% of historical investment was in technology. The message is clear: IT designers and developers must re-focus their approach and provide solutions that more readily address the constantly changing people / process / organisation / culture / leadership environment that technologies will be embedded in. Of critical importance, investment in IT will be increasingly measured in terms of its impact on improving and exploiting the information assets of companies and organisations – speed to market and improved functionality are no longer sufficient to guarantee long-term survival.

Acknowledgements

I have been fortunate in working with a wide range of people who have contributed to the development of the ideas presented in this paper. Jeff Lee, Nigel Turner, Mike Kellett and Darryl Benjamin at BT and Subhash Chowdary (VIT Inc.), Prof. Keith Jeffery (CLRC Rutherford Appleton Labs.) and James Jonas (Oracle Corp.) have been particularly influential. Thanks are extended to Dr. Mike Revett and Dave Freestone of BT and Dr. Steve McKearney (Bournmouth University) for discussion of VLDB challenges facing the telecoms industry.

References

1 Gates, W. H. & Hemingway, C. 1999. **Business @ The Speed of Thought – Using a Digital Nervous System**, Warner Books, p. 3.

2 Devlin, B. 1997. **Data Warehouse: From Architecture to Implementation**. Addison Wesley Longman, Inc., 432 pp.

3 DSDM Consortium. 1995. **Dynamic Systems Development Method – Version 2**. Tesseract Publishing, Farnham, UK., 240 pp.

4 Shao, J. & Pound, C. J. (in press). Extracting business rules from information systems. *BT Technology Journal.*

5 Jeffery, K. G. An Architecture for Grey Literature in a R&D Context, accepted for publication in **Proceedings GL'99 Conference**, October 1999.

6 McKean, J. 1999. **Information Masters : Secrets of the Customer Race**. John Wiley & Sons Ltd., 287 pp.

Finding Intensional Knowledge of Distance-Based Outliers

Edwin M. Knorr and Raymond T. Ng
Department of Computer Science
University of British Columbia
Vancouver, BC V6T 1Z4 Canada

Abstract

Existing studies on outliers focus only on the *identification* aspect; none provides any *intensional knowledge* of the outliers—by which we mean a *description* or an *explanation* of why an identified outlier is exceptional. For many applications, a description or explanation is at least as vital to the user as the identification aspect. Specifically, intensional knowledge helps the user to: (i) evaluate the validity of the identified outliers, and (ii) improve one's understanding of the data.

The two main issues addressed in this paper are: *what kinds* of intensional knowledge to provide, and *how to optimize* the computation of such knowledge. With respect to the first issue, we propose finding *strongest* and *weak* outliers and their corresponding structural intensional knowledge. With respect to the second issue, we first present a naive and a semi-naive algorithm. Then, by means of what we call *path* and *semi-lattice* sharing of I/O processing, we develop two optimized approaches. We provide analytic results on their I/O performance, and present experimental results showing significant reductions in I/O, and significant speedups in overall runtime.

Proceedings of the 25th VLDB Conference, Edinburgh, Scotland, 1999.

1 Introduction

Knowledge discovery tasks can be classified into four general categories: (a) dependency detection, (b) class identification, (c) class description, and (d) exception/outlier detection. The first three categories of tasks correspond to patterns that apply to many objects, or to a large percentage of objects, in the dataset. Most research in data mining (e.g., association rules and variants [AIS93, BMS97, NLHP98, SBMU98], data clustering [KR90], and classification [AGI+92, BFOS84]) belongs to these three categories. In contrast, the fourth category focuses on only a very small percentage of data objects. While such objects are sometimes ignored or treated as "noise", we note that "one person's noise is another person's signal." In other words, for numerous knowledge discovery applications, the rare events can be more interesting than the common events. Sample applications include the detection of credit card fraud and the monitoring of criminal or suspicious activities (e.g., [TN98]).

1.1 Related Work

Existing approaches to outlier detection can be broadly classified into three categories. The first category is *distribution-based*, which relies on fitting the data with standard statistical models. (See [BL94] for a comprehensive treatment.) However, distribution-based approaches are mainly univariate in nature, and require extensive and expensive testing to find a distribution to fit the data, thus making such approaches unsuitable for most data mining applications.

The second category is *depth-based*, which relies on organizing the data objects in some k-D space. Based on some definition of depth (e.g., [Tuk77]), data objects are organized in layers in the data space, with the expectation that shallow layers are more likely to contain outlying data objects than are the deep layers. Depth-based approaches avoid the aforementioned problem of distribution fitting, and conceptually allow multi-dimensional data objects to be processed. Although there are efficient techniques for 2-D spaces

Player Name	Power-play Goals	Short-handed Goals	Game-winning Goals	Game-tying Goals	Games Played
MARIO LEMIEUX	31	8	8	0	70
JAROMIR JAGR	20	1	12	1	82
JOHN LECLAIR	19	0	10	2	82
ROD BRIND'AMOUR	4	4	5	4	82

Figure 1: NHL Players' Statistics: Outliers Identified

[JKN98, RR96], depth-based approaches do not scale up well with the dimensionality k. Specifically, depth-based approaches are lower bounded in complexity by k-D convex hull computation, i.e., $\Omega(n^{k/2})$, where n is the number of data objects.

The third category is *distance-based.* As we introduced in [KN98],

An object O in a dataset is a DB(p, D)-outlier if at least a fraction p of the other objects in the dataset lies greater than distance D from O.

We showed that the notion of $DB(p, D)$-outliers generalizes many of the distribution-based outliers discussed above, and we developed (i) Algorithm NL with complexity $O(k\ n^2)$—thus, making it far more attractive than the depth-based approaches for k-D datasets with $k \geq 4$; and (ii) Algorithm CELL [1] with a complexity linear on n, and a guarantee of no more than 3 passes over the data. However, the latter Algorithm CELL is exponential on k, and is recommended only for smaller values of k (i.e., $k \leq 4$). In [TN98], we documented a case study that successfully applies the distance-based outlier methodology to a video surveillance situation, in which the dimensionality of the dataset exceeds 20.

1.2 Contributions of This Paper

All the studies on outliers research focus only on *identification*; none is able to provide any *intensional knowledge* of the outliers—by which we mean a *description* or an *explanation* of why an identified outlier is exceptional. For many applications, the description/explanation aspect is at least as vital to the user as the identification aspect. Intensional knowledge helps the user to: (i) evaluate the validity or the credibility of the identified outliers, and (ii) more importantly, improve the user's understanding of the data.

Consider an example based on 1995-96 National Hockey League players' statistics. (Such statistics can be found at http://nhlstatistics.hypermart.net, among many other sites.) For certain parameter values of p and D and a specific choice of a distance function, the four players in Figure 1 are identified as exceptional (among 855 players) in the 5-D space of power-play goals, short-handed goals, game-winning goals, game-tying goals, and games played. Note that the numbers in the table cannot directly pinpoint the strengths

```
MARIO LEMIEUX:
  (i)  An outlier in the 1-D space of Power-play goals
  (ii) An outlier in the 2-D space of Short-handed goals and
       Game-winning goals
       (No player is exceptional on Short-handed goals alone;
        No player is exceptional on Game-winning goals alone.)
ROD BRIND'AMOUR:
  (i)  An outlier in the 1-D space of Game-tying goals
JAROMIR JAGR:
  (i)  An outlier in the 2-D space of Short-handed goals and
       Game-winning goals
       (No player is exceptional on Short-handed goals alone;
        No player is exceptional on Game-winning goals alone.)
  (ii) An outlier in the 2-D space of Power-play goals and
       Game-winning goals
       (But for Power-play goals alone, the current player is
        dominated by another and is not exceptional.)
JOHN LECLAIR:
  (i) An outlier in the 2-D space of Game-winning goals and
      Game-tying goals
      (But for Game-tying goals alone, the current player is
       dominated by another and is not exceptional.)
```

Figure 2: NHL Players' Statistics: Intensional Knowledge Provided

or greatness of these players with respect to all other NHL players. Specifically, the intensional knowledge described in Figure 2 cannot be derived directly from the numbers. While we shall discuss in detail in Section 2 the nature of the provided intensional knowledge, it suffices to say that the additional explanations give new and valuable insights about the dataset in general and about the outliers in particular.

The two main issues addressed in this paper are: *what kinds* of intensional knowledge to provide, and *how to optimize* the computation of such knowledge. Specifically:

- We define in Section 2 two notions of outliers and the corresponding intensional knowledge. The two notions are *strongest* outliers and *weak* outliers. To illustrate, Jaromir Jagr in Figure 2 is: (i) a strongest outlier in the 2-D combination of short-handed goals and game-winning goals, but (ii) only a weak outlier in the 2-D combination of power-play goals and game-winning goals.
- We develop in Section 3, a naive and a semi-naive algorithm for computing strongest and weak outliers and the corresponding intensional knowledge. While the naive algorithm conducts its processing in a bottom-up fashion over an appropriate lattice, the semi-naive algorithm starts at a certain intermediate level of the lattice, and "drills down" to lower levels only if necessary.
- We show in Section 4 that, instead of processing one node of the lattice at a time, it is possible to

[1] In [KN98], Algorithm CELL was called FindAllOutsM or FindAllOutsD for memory or disk-resident versions, respectively. For convenience, we use the name CELL. We deal exclusively with disk-resident data in this paper.

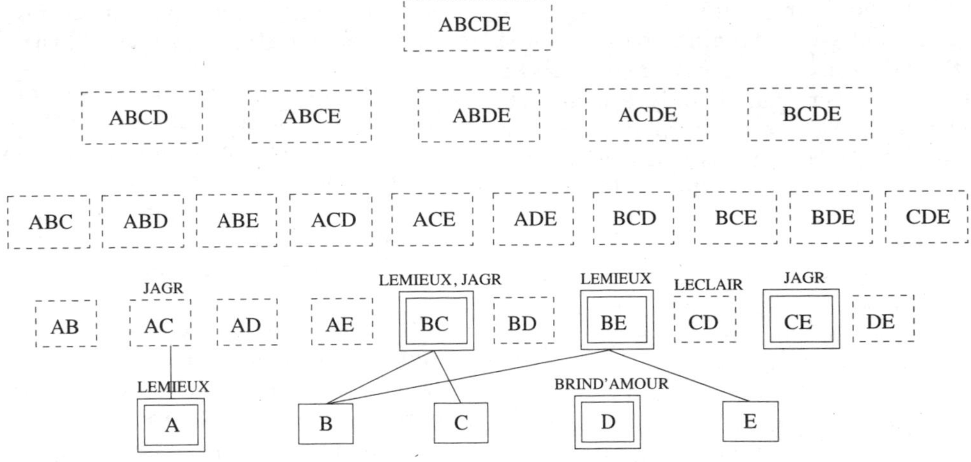

Figure 3: Intensional Knowledge in a Lattice Representation

process nodes in groups, thereby sharing the I/O's among the nodes. We show that effective sharing of I/O's can be achieved in two flavours: a *path* mode and a *semi-lattice* mode. We present analytic results guaranteeing their I/O performance. Finally, we give experimental results showing how much improvement these optimizations can yield.

2 Strongest and Weak Outliers and the Corresponding Intensional Knowledge

In this section, we first introduce the notions of strongest and weak outliers, and show examples. Then, we offer a few justifications of why we opt to work with these notions.

2.1 Definitions

Given an object P which has been identified to be exceptional in some attribute space $\mathcal{A}_P$ (containing possibly many attributes/dimensions), two items of knowledge that would be of interest to the user are:

I. What is the smallest set of attributes to explain why P is exceptional?

II. Is P "dominated" by other outliers?

With respect to question (I), given $\mathcal{A}_P$, we seek to find all the minimal subsets of attributes in which P is exceptional. We have the following definition.

Definition 1 Suppose that P is an outlier in the attribute space $\mathcal{A}_P$. P is a *non-trivial* outlier in $\mathcal{A}_P$ if P is not an outlier in any subspace $\mathcal{B} \subset \mathcal{A}_P$. □

Note that a subspace's points are simply a projection of points of a given/original space onto a subset of its attributes. While question (I) focuses on the examination of P alone, question (II) concerns the evaluation of P against other outliers. With respect to question (II), we seek to find the minimal (sub)sets of attributes in which there is an outlier—*any* outlier, be it P, Q, etc. We have the following definition.

Definition 2 Let $\mathcal{A}_P$ be an attribute space containing one or more outliers. $\mathcal{A}_P$ is called a *strongest outlying space* if no outlier exists in any subspace $\mathcal{B} \subset \mathcal{A}_P$. Furthermore, any P that is an outlier in $\mathcal{A}_P$ is called a *strongest* outlier. □

One reason for why a strongest outlying space $\mathcal{A}_P$ is noteworthy is that this is the first time that $\mathcal{A}_P$ and any of its subspaces contain an outlier. It follows immediately from the above definitions that if P is a strongest outlier, then P must be non-trivial. To completely classify non-trivial outliers, we have the following definition.

Definition 3 Suppose that P is a non-trivial outlier in the attribute space $\mathcal{A}_P$. Then if P is not a strongest outlier, P is called a *weak* outlier. □

In summary, we differentiate among three kinds of outliers: *strongest*, *weak*, and *trivial* outliers. Trivial outliers are the least interesting because they convey no new information than what was already observed or reported for some subspace of the given space.

2.2 NHL Players Example Revisited

According to the above definitions, we can represent the intensional knowledge given in Figure 2 using the lattice shown in Figure 3. This is the attribute lattice formed by the 5 attributes in our example, with the attributes denoted as A, B, C, etc. We use single-lined rectangles to denote attribute spaces that do not contain any outlier; we use double-lined rectangles to denote strongest outlying spaces; and we use dashed rectangles to denote spaces that cannot contain strongest outliers but *may* contain weak outliers. All strongest outliers are shown, but for simplicity, not all weak outliers and not all edges between nodes are shown. We have labelled the nodes of the lattice with the outliers that first appear at a given node (and nowhere below it). Corresponding to Figure 2, Mario Lemieux is a strongest outlier in: the 1-D space of power-play goals (denoted as "A" in the figure), and the 2-D space of short-handed goals and game-winning goals (denoted as "BC"). In the latter space, Jaromir Jagr is also a strongest outlier. However, Jagr is only a weak outlier in the 2-D space "AC" of power-play goals and game-winning goals, because Jagr is being dominated by Lemieux in "A". This example shows that a data object can be a strongest and/or weak outlier in multiple spaces at the same time.

Although this is only a very small example, it is easy to see that such a categorization of outliers conveys far more information to a user than does a single, unqualified list of all outliers for the largest space only. Thus, a user who is not hockey literate can actually see which players dominate which attributes. Even domain experts may be surprised to find players who surface as outliers in unusual combinations of attributes. As our earlier work [KN98] pointed out, outliers need not be those observations which have extreme values. For example, it is quite possible that a player with "average" values is an outlier, simply because that player is so different from the rest of the players in the dataset.

In a very large dataset containing many attributes, there may be many outliers, but some of those outliers may be strongest outliers which noticeably stand out among the larger pool of outliers. Such outliers may get closer scrutiny, as might be the case involving "worst offenders" in a fraud detection application.

2.3 Justification of Our Choices of Intensional Knowledge

Earlier, we pointed out that it is valuable to provide explanations/descriptions about the identified outliers, but explanations can clearly come in many different forms. Below, we discuss why we opt to work with the intensional knowledge associated with strongest and weak outliers.

- First, we hope the NHL example has served to argue that the knowledge corresponding to strongest and weak outliers is intuitive and meaningful to the user, and is otherwise not immediately derivable by just using the values of the attributes in the space $\mathcal{A}_P$.
- Second, the notions of strongest and weak outliers are close in spirit with the subspace clustering problem addressed by Agrawal *et al.* [AGGR98]. They obtain not only the clusters in the original attribute space, but also the clusters in the subspaces. Our work is different from their work in at least two ways. First, we go beyond minimal description length (i.e., non-trivial outliers) and seek to find out whether a non-trivial outlier is dominated by others—in the sense formalized by strongest outliers. Imposing a partial order denoting the dominance or strength of non-trivial outliers is well-suited to our task. Second, finding strongest and weak outliers is computationally different from subspace clustering. The remaining sections of this paper will illustrate why.
- Finally, there are numerous forms of explanations possible. In general, there is the tradeoff between what the explanation says and how long it takes to compute it. For the two reasons given above, we believe that the explanation offered by strongest and weak outliers is meaningful. We will show below that their computation is highly optimizable.

In closing this section, we comment that we can extend the definitions given in Section 2.1 by defining the notion of *top-u* strongest or weak outliers, where we rank strongest or weak outliers P in ascending order of cardinalities of their associated space $\mathcal{A}_P$. That is, we prefer an outlier that can be explained with fewer attributes. The top-u notion, in practice, is particularly natural for weak outliers. This is because, given their nature, weak outliers can be more numerous than strongest outliers. The top-u notion helps to avoid a situation whereby too many outliers are returned than the user cares for, and yet the user is charged for the entire computation. In the remainder of this paper, though, we give algorithms that compute *all* strongest and weak outliers; it should be easy to see how they can be modified to give a top-u list.

3 Two Simpler Algorithms for Finding Strongest and Weak Outliers

In this section, we present a naive algorithm, called UpLattice, for finding all strongest and/or weak outliers. Then, we present a more intelligent algorithm, called JumpLattice. Before doing so, however, we provide a short summary in Section 3.1 of the algorithms developed and evaluated in [KN98] for finding outliers in a particular space. Readers familiar with that paper can skip the summary.

3.1 Background Summary: Algorithms for Finding Outliers in a Particular Space

Given a particular space $\mathcal{A}$, with cardinality (dimensionality) k, we considered in [KN98] primarily two algorithms [2] for finding all outliers in that space. First, there is Algorithm NL, which for a given amount of buffer space, uses a nested loop algorithm to find all outliers. In the worst case, NL checks each pairwise distance between two objects/tuples, and thus has a complexity of $O(k\,n^2)$. See [KN98] for details of the algorithm. Experimental results show that NL is the faster algorithm for $k \geq 5$.

[2] Actually, we evaluated another strategy, which we call Algorithm INDEX, that is based on a multi-dimensional index such as an R*-tree. Because this algorithm is dominated by CELL for small values of k, and by NL for the remaining values of k, we skip that algorithm here.

Second, there is Algorithm CELL, which is based on building an optimized cell structure. The general idea is as follows. Let D be the radius of the local neighbourhood (i.e., the D value selected for $DB(p, D)$-outliers). The k-D space is divided into cells with length equal to $\frac{D}{2\sqrt{k}}$ along each dimension. Each tuple is then quantized (mapped) to an appropriate cell. Because of the carefully chosen size of each cell, we can first eliminate cells, called "red" cells, that contain too many tuples quantized to them, and also those cells which are immediate neighbours of red cells. Thus, very quickly, a significant number of cells—and the large number of tuples they contain—are pruned. What remain are called "white" cells, containing "white" tuples. These are tuples P that require explicit distance calculations with each tuple Q in certain neighbouring cells. This phase, as expected, can require many I/O operations, and makes the algorithm essentially I/O-dominant. While readers are referred to [KN98] for more details, because the focus of this paper is on I/O optimizations, we summarize below the four key phases of I/O operations:

- Phase 1: Make one pass over the entire dataset to quantize the tuples into cells, from which the "non-white" cells are eliminated.
- Phase 2: Read the pages that contain some white tuples P. We call such pages *Class I* pages.
- Phase 3: Read the pages that do not contain any white tuples but contain non-white tuples Q needed by some white tuple P for tuple-by-tuple processing. We call such pages *Class II* pages.
- Phase 4: Repeat Phase 2.

In [KN98], we showed why the above four phases of I/O are all the I/O operations that are needed. Moreover, we have the following performance guarantee.

Lemma 1 ([KN98]) (1) Class I pages and Class II pages are mutually exclusive. (2) The total number of pages read is equal to $M+2M_1+M_2$, where M, M_1 and M_2 are the total number of pages of the entire dataset, of Class I pages, and of Class II pages, respectively. (3) Each page in the dataset is guaranteed to be read at most 3 times. □

In practice, most pages are read only once or twice. The complexity of CELL is $O(c^k\, n)$, and experimental results show that Algorithm CELL is the faster algorithm for $k \leq 4$.

3.2 A Naive Algorithm: Procedure UpLattice

As suggested in Figure 3, the computation of strongest and weak outliers can be conducted over the lattice formed by the attributes. As is done in association rule mining [AIS93], subspace clustering [AGGR98], and functional dependencies detection [HKPT98], a standard algorithmic strategy is to compute or traverse the lattice in a bottom-up, level-wise fashion. That is to say, we first find outliers in the 1-D spaces, then in the 2-D spaces, and so on. This simple algorithm is outlined in Figure 4.

Procedure UpLattice($\mathcal{A}$)

1 Insert into queue Q all the subsets of attribute set $\mathcal{A}$ in ascending order of cardinalities.

2 While Q is not empty {

  2.1 Remove the subset of attributes at the front of Q. Let that be $\mathcal{A}'$.

  2.2 Call Procedure FindOutliersInNode($\mathcal{A}'$).

  2.3 If there is some outlier found above {

    2.3.1 If only strongest outliers are to be found, remove from Q all supersets of $\mathcal{A}'$. } }

Procedure FindOutliersInNode($\mathcal{A}'$)

1 If $|\mathcal{A}'| \leq 4$, call Procedure CELL($\mathcal{A}'$)

2 Else call Procedure NL($\mathcal{A}'$).

Procedure JumpLattice($\mathcal{A}$, k)

1 Insert into Q all the subsets of $\mathcal{A}$ (which have cardinalities $\geq k$) in ascending order of cardinalities.

2 While Q is not empty {

  2.1 Remove the subset of attributes at the front of Q. Let that be $\mathcal{A}'$.

  2.2 Call Procedure FindOutliersInNode($\mathcal{A}'$).

  2.3 If there is some outlier found above {

    2.3.1 If only strongest outliers are to be found, remove from Q all supersets of $\mathcal{A}'$.

    2.3.2 If $|\mathcal{A}'| = k$, call Procedure DrillDown($\mathcal{A}'$).} }

Procedure DrillDown($\mathcal{A}'$)

1 Insert into queue Q the proper subsets of $\mathcal{A}'$ in *descending* order of cardinalities.

2 While Q is not empty {

  2.1 Remove the subset of attributes at the front of Q. Let that be $\mathcal{B}$.

  2.2 Call Procedure FindOutliersInNode($\mathcal{B}$).

  2.3 If $|\mathcal{B}| > 1$ and if no outlier is found in $\mathcal{B}$, remove from Q all *subsets* of $\mathcal{B}$. } }

Figure 4: Skeletons for UpLattice and JumpLattice

There are three aspects worth noting about Procedure UpLattice as shown in the figure. First, it should be clear from Definition 2 that once the space $\mathcal{A}'$ is found to contain some outlier, any superset of $\mathcal{A}'$ cannot contain any strongest outlier. This is the purpose of Step 2.3, and this is one of the few differences between the computation of strongest and weak outliers. Note that if only strongest outliers are sought, and in the very rare event that all strongest outliers appear at level 1, then UpLattice is very efficient. Second, if the skeleton shown in Figure 4 is to find weak outliers, strictly speaking, there should be the additional step to screen out trivial outliers after Step 2. We do not include the step here because all the algorithms considered in this paper differ mainly in how the lattice is traversed or grouped. Thus, Figure 4 only concentrates on this aspect. Third, as summarized in Section 3.1, the sub-procedure FindOutliersInNode($\mathcal{A}'$) chooses between Algorithms CELL and NL, based on the cardinality of $\mathcal{A}'$.

3.3 Procedure JumpLattice

A key problem with Procedure UpLattice is that there could be few outliers (if any) found in the smallest dimensional spaces. In other words, a bottom-up strategy may take a lot of wasted effort before a space containing outliers is encountered. It would be nice to be able to jump to some node in the intermediate levels of the lattice, instead of climbing slowly from the bottom. The advantage is that if there is no outlier in some intermediate level node $\mathcal{A}'$, then none of the remaining $2^k - 2$ non-empty subsets of $\mathcal{A}'$ (where $k = |\mathcal{A}'|$) needs to be considered anymore. Figure 4 shows a skeleton of Procedure JumpLattice. Note that the only differences between JumpLattice and UpLattice are: (i) Step 2.3.2, which deals with the situation when a space $\mathcal{A}'$ of cardinality k contains some outlier, and (ii) the level k at which to begin processing. (Note that JumpLattice is a strict generalization of UpLattice because for $k = 1$, the former is reduced to the latter.) We examine these differences below.

3.3.1 Procedure DrillDown

When the space $\mathcal{A}'$ of cardinality k contains some outlier, what needs to be done, for both strongest and weak outliers, is to consider the proper subsets of $\mathcal{A}'$. This is outlined in Procedure DrillDown in Figure 4. Specifically, subsets $\mathcal{B}$ of $\mathcal{A}'$ are processed one-by-one by calling the same Procedure FindOutliersInNode($\mathcal{B}$). If no outlier is found in $\mathcal{B}$, then the "drill down" can omit the subspaces of $\mathcal{B}$. The fact that no outlier exists in $\mathcal{B}$ suffices to guarantee that no outlier exists in any of its subspaces.

3.3.2 Choice of k for JumpLattice

In the above discussion, we motivated why JumpLattice can be useful. However, if JumpLattice starts with $\mathcal{A}'$ at a level k that turns out to be too high, and $\mathcal{A}'$ *does* contain some outlier, then the subsets of $\mathcal{A}'$ need to be examined. In the case that the task is to find strongest outliers or the top-u strongest/weak outliers, processing $\mathcal{A}'$ can be completely wasteful (i.e., both time consuming and unnecessary) in the event that there is a subset containing an outlier. So the main question is: What should the value of k be? Unfortunately, we do not know of any reliable analysis that can be done to predict an optimal value for every situation. We do, however, offer the following heuristic.

Figure 5 shows the relative amount of (CPU+I/O) time taken to find all outliers in a particular space $\mathcal{A}'$ with all parameters set to identical values, except for the dimensionality $k = |\mathcal{A}'|$ (in effect, running Procedure FindOutliersInNode for varying k). This graph is based on using the best algorithms among those summarized in Section 3.1. The results were experimentally obtained and are representative of numerous other cases. It is clear from the graph that as k increases from 1 to 3, the "marginal cost" is relatively small. However, as k increases to 4 and beyond, the "marginal cost" becomes substantial for each increment in k. Thus, our heuristic is:

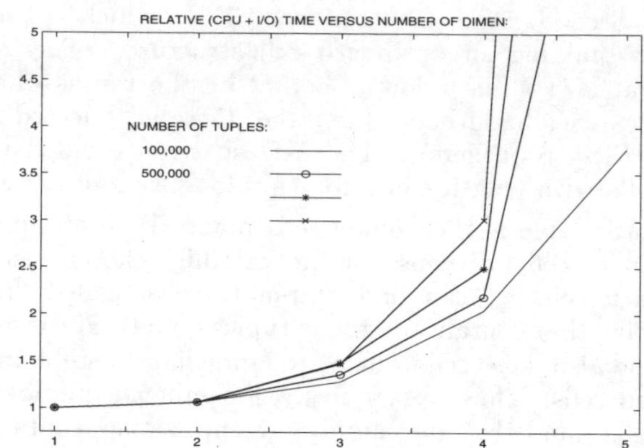

Figure 5: Heuristic Selection of k for JumpLattice

In the absence of any information predicting the value of k, [3] *we pick k to be 3.*

In Section 5, we present experimental results comparing JumpLattice with UpLattice. We will report exclusively the results of JumpLattice with k set to 3. Due to the lack of space, results for other values of k are not shown; however, for the conclusions we want to draw, the results with $k = 3$ are sufficiently representative.

4 Grouped Processing of Multiple Nodes and Performance Analysis

So far, we have considered two ways of processing the nodes in the lattice to find strongest and/or weak outliers, but in both cases, nodes are processed or examined one at a time (i.e., via Procedure FindOutliersInNode). The objective of this section is to show how multiple nodes, suitably selected, can be grouped and processed together. We provide proof of correctness and performance guarantees.

4.1 Grouping Two Nodes Satisfying an Edge Relationship

We begin by considering the simultaneous processing of two nodes/spaces using Algorithm CELL, and later

[3] We only recommend $k = 3$ in the event that no other information is available, and there are indeed situations whereby other values of k could be more beneficial. One example is a situation in which the user runs the algorithms with varying parameter values. Knowing which subspaces contain outliers, given the current set of parameter values, the value of k can be set up more intelligently by comparing the new set of parameter values with the previous set. For example, if the new set of parameter values has the effect of decreasing the number of outliers, then k should be set higher. We do not pursue the issue of incremental processing here, but simply comment on the utility of the general JumpLattice Procedure.

we will generalize this notion to many nodes.

Definition 4 Given two nodes $\mathcal{A}$, $\mathcal{B}$, we say that $\mathcal{A}, \mathcal{B}$ satisfy a (directed) *edge* relationship, denoted as $\langle \mathcal{A}, \mathcal{B} \rangle$, if $\mathcal{A} \supset \mathcal{B}$ and $|\mathcal{A}| = |\mathcal{B}| + 1$. That is, an edge exists between the two nodes in the lattice. □

For the example shown in Figure 3, $\mathcal{A} = \{A, B, C\}$ and $\mathcal{B} = \{A, B\}$ satisfy an edge relationship. Recall from Section 3.1 that Algorithm CELL requires four I/O phases. The task here is to examine how each of the four phases can be extended to process the two nodes simultaneously. During Phase 1 (quantizing the tuples into cells and eliminating "non-white" cells), processing two nodes together is easy, because separate cell structures can be maintained. The situation is, however, very different for the other phases. We carefully consider those phases, below.

4.1.1 Combined Reading of Class I Pages (Phase 2)

By the definition given in Section 3.1, Class I pages are data pages that contain some white tuples. For a given white tuple P, we use the notation $PgI(P)$ to denote the single data page that contains P. For a space $\mathcal{A}$, we use the notation $WT_{\mathcal{A}}$ to denote the set of all white tuples in $\mathcal{A}$. Then, to generalize, we use the notation $PgI(S)$ to denote the set of data pages that contain tuples in the set S, that is, $PgI(S) = \cup_{P \in S} PgI(P)$. The following result identifies a key relationship between white tuples for two nodes satisfying an edge relationship.

Lemma 2 Given the edge relationship $\langle \mathcal{A}, \mathcal{B} \rangle$, it is the case that: P is a white tuple in $\mathcal{B} \Rightarrow P$ is a white tuple in $\mathcal{A}$. □

While details of a proof are left to [KN99], the basic rationale behind this lemma is that the distance between P and any tuple Q grows from $\mathcal{B}$ to $\mathcal{A}$. If there are not enough tuples surrounding P in a fixed-radius local neighbourhood in $\mathcal{B}$, there cannot be enough tuples surrounding P in the same-radius neighbourhood in $\mathcal{A}$. It is easy to see that the converse of the lemma is not true. With the above lemma, we have the following result.

Lemma 3 Given the edge relationship $\langle \mathcal{A}, \mathcal{B} \rangle$, it is the case that: the set of data pages containing white tuples in $\mathcal{B}$ is contained in the corresponding set in $\mathcal{A}$, that is, $PgI(WT_{\mathcal{B}}) \subseteq PgI(WT_{\mathcal{A}})$. □

The rationale behind the above lemma is that from Lemma 2, it is necessary that the set of white tuples in $\mathcal{B}$ is contained in the corresponding set in $\mathcal{A}$, i.e., $WT_{\mathcal{B}} \subseteq WT_{\mathcal{A}}$. The significance of the above lemma is that as far as Phase 2 of Algorithm CELL is concerned, it suffices to read in Class I pages for $\mathcal{A}$ for the processing of *both* $\mathcal{A}$ and $\mathcal{B}$, as summarized below.

Corollary 1 Given $\langle \mathcal{A}, \mathcal{B} \rangle$, the combined set of Class I pages to process both spaces simultaneously is given by: $PgI(WT_{\mathcal{A}} \cup WT_{\mathcal{B}}) = PgI(WT_{\mathcal{A}})$. □

4.1.2 Combined Reading of Class II Pages (Phase 3)

Next, we consider Class II pages. We use the notation $PgII(P, \mathcal{A})$ to denote the set of data pages containing non-white tuples needed to check whether white tuple P is an outlier in $\mathcal{A}$. [4] Then, to generalize, we use the notation $PgII(S, \mathcal{A})$ to denote $\cup_{P \in S} PgII(P, \mathcal{A})$.

Lemma 4 Given the edge relationship $\langle \mathcal{A}, \mathcal{B} \rangle$, it is the case that: $PgII(P, \mathcal{A}) \subseteq PgII(P, \mathcal{B})$, for white tuples P in $\mathcal{B}$ (and therefore in $\mathcal{A}$). □

The rationale behind the lemma is that for checking whether P is an outlier, because the distance between P and any other tuple Q grows from $\mathcal{B}$ to $\mathcal{A}$, there are possibly more tuples Q to be examined in $\mathcal{B}$ than in $\mathcal{A}$ within a fixed-radius neighbourhood. When compared with Lemma 3 for Class I pages, the above lemma points out that—for white tuples P in both $\mathcal{B}$ and $\mathcal{A}$—the containment relationship for Class II pages is *opposite* to that for Class I pages. And as a counterpoint to Corollary 1, we have the following corollary. It says that for Phase 3 of Algorithm CELL, it suffices to read in the Class II pages for $\mathcal{B}$, as well as the Class II pages for all the white tuples in $\mathcal{A}$ but not in $\mathcal{B}$.

Corollary 2 Given $\langle \mathcal{A}, \mathcal{B} \rangle$, the combined set of Class II pages to process both spaces simultaneously is given by: $PgII(WT_{\mathcal{A}}, \mathcal{A}) \cup PgII(WT_{\mathcal{B}}, \mathcal{B}) = PgII(WT_{\mathcal{A}} - WT_{\mathcal{B}}, \mathcal{A}) \cup PgII(WT_{\mathcal{B}}, \mathcal{A}) \cup PgII(WT_{\mathcal{B}}, \mathcal{B}) = PgII(WT_{\mathcal{A}} - WT_{\mathcal{B}}, \mathcal{A}) \cup PgII(WT_{\mathcal{B}}, \mathcal{B})$. □

4.1.3 I/O Performance Guarantee: Number of I/O's Saved

By now, it should be clear that the same four phases of Algorithm CELL, as shown in Section 3.1, are sufficient to simultaneously process two nodes satisfying an edge relationship—so long as the Class I and II pages are modified as given in the previous lemmas. Below, we consider two kinds of I/O performance guarantees for the shared processing. The first guarantee applies to the number of I/O's that can be saved.

Lemma 5 Compared with processing $\mathcal{A}$ and $\mathcal{B}$ separately, grouped processing of $\langle \mathcal{A}, \mathcal{B} \rangle$ saves at least $M + 2M_{1,\mathcal{B}}$ page reads.

Proof Sketch: Recall from Lemma 1 that if we are to process $\mathcal{A}$ and $\mathcal{B}$ separately, the total number of I/O's will be $(M + 2M_{1,\mathcal{A}} + M_{2,\mathcal{A}}) + (M + 2M_{1,\mathcal{B}} + M_{2,\mathcal{B}})$,

[4] For Class I pages, it is not necessary to use the space as a parameter, because regardless of which space we are considering, it is the same data page that contains the tuple P. For Class II pages, however, the space $\mathcal{A}$ may make a difference.

where $M_{1,\mathcal{S}}$ and $M_{2,\mathcal{S}}$ denote the number of Class I and II pages for space $\mathcal{S}$, respectively. Based on the two corollaries above, the total number of I/O's required by the grouped processing of $\langle \mathcal{A}, \mathcal{B} \rangle$ is upper bounded by $(M + 2M_{1,\mathcal{A}} + M_{2,\mathcal{B}} + |PgII(WT_{\mathcal{A}} - WT_{\mathcal{B}}, \mathcal{A})|)$. The last term is upper bounded by $|PgII(WT_{\mathcal{A}}, \mathcal{A})| = M_{2,\mathcal{A}}$. Thus, the total number of I/O's saved is at least $M + 2M_{1,\mathcal{B}}$. □

4.1.4 I/O Performance Guarantee: Reads per Page

The second I/O performance guarantee applies to the number of reads per page.

Lemma 6 When applying CELL to process two spaces $\langle \mathcal{A}, \mathcal{B} \rangle$ simultaneously, each page is guaranteed to be read at most 4 times. □

Recall from Lemma 1 that when CELL is applied to one space only, Class I and Class II pages are mutually exclusive. This is the reason why even though there are four different phases involving I/O, each page is guaranteed to be read at most 3 times. The situation for two spaces satisfying an edge relationship is different, because the combined Class I pages as given in Corollary 1 and the combined Class II pages as given in Corollary 2 are not guaranteed to be mutually exclusive. To see this, let us consider the intersection between $PgI(WT_{\mathcal{A}})$ and $PgII(WT_{\mathcal{A}} - WT_{\mathcal{B}}, \mathcal{A}) \cup PgII(WT_{\mathcal{B}}, \mathcal{B})$ by considering two cases: (a) $PgI(WT_{\mathcal{A}}) \cap PgII(WT_{\mathcal{A}} - WT_{\mathcal{B}}, \mathcal{A})$, and (b) $PgI(WT_{\mathcal{A}}) \cap PgII(WT_{\mathcal{B}}, \mathcal{B})$.

(a) Since (i) $PgI(WT_{\mathcal{A}}) \cap PgII(WT_{\mathcal{A}}, \mathcal{A}) = \emptyset$, and (ii) $PgII(WT_{\mathcal{A}}, \mathcal{A}) \supseteq PgII(WT_{\mathcal{A}} - WT_{\mathcal{B}}, \mathcal{A})$, it is necessary that $PgI(WT_{\mathcal{A}}) \cap PgII(WT_{\mathcal{A}} - WT_{\mathcal{B}}, \mathcal{A}) = \emptyset$. There is mutual exclusion here.

(b) However, for the intersection $PgI(WT_{\mathcal{A}}) \cap PgII(WT_{\mathcal{B}}, \mathcal{B})$, we know that (i) $PgI(WT_{\mathcal{B}}) \cap PgII(WT_{\mathcal{B}}, \mathcal{B}) = \emptyset$, but (ii) $PgI(WT_{\mathcal{A}}) \supseteq PgI(WT_{\mathcal{B}})$. Therefore, it is *not* sufficient to conclude that $PgI(WT_{\mathcal{A}}) \cap PgII(WT_{\mathcal{B}}, \mathcal{B}) = \emptyset$.

The above argument makes it clear that if in fact, for the specific $\mathcal{A}, \mathcal{B}$, there is a page that is read 4 times, the page must belong to the non-empty intersection $PgI(WT_{\mathcal{A}}) \cap PgII(WT_{\mathcal{B}}, \mathcal{B})$. Whenever this intersection becomes empty, Lemma 6 above can be strengthened to give back the three-reads per page guarantee. In any case, it should be noted that the guarantee provided is a very pessimistic worst-case. Experimental results reported in Section 5 will illustrate that in practice, most pages are only needed once or twice.

4.2 Grouping Multiple Nodes Satisfying a Path Relationship

So far, we have shown how to combine the processing of two nodes simultaneously, and we have presented an analysis to show how such grouped processing can be beneficial. Below, we generalize the grouping to multiple nodes and give corresponding analytic results.

Definition 5 Given the nodes/spaces $\mathcal{A}_1, \ldots, \mathcal{A}_w$, we say that these spaces satisfy a (directed) *path* relationship, denoted as $\langle \mathcal{A}_1, \ldots, \mathcal{A}_w \rangle$, if $\langle \mathcal{A}_i, \mathcal{A}_{i+1} \rangle$ satisfies an edge relationship for all $1 \leq i < w$. That is, there is a path in the lattice connecting all the nodes. □

For the example shown in Figure 3, the spaces $\{A, B, C, D\}$, $\{A, B, C\}$, $\{A, B\}$ and $\{A\}$ satisfy a path relationship. The following lemma generalizes the lemmas and corollaries given above for an edge relationship to a path relationship.

Lemma 7 Given the path relationship $\langle \mathcal{A}_1, \ldots, \mathcal{A}_w \rangle$:

- The combined set of Class I pages to process all w spaces simultaneously is given by: $PgI(WT_{\mathcal{A}_1} \cup \ldots \cup WT_{\mathcal{A}_w}) = PgI(WT_{\mathcal{A}_1})$.
- The combined set of Class II pages to process all w spaces simultaneously is given by: $\bigcup_{i=1}^{w} PgII(WT_{\mathcal{A}_i}, \mathcal{A}_i) = PgII(WT_{\mathcal{A}_w}, \mathcal{A}_w) \bigcup_{i=1}^{w-1} PgII((WT_{\mathcal{A}_i} - WT_{\mathcal{A}_{i+1}} - \ldots - WT_{\mathcal{A}_w}), \mathcal{A}_i)$.
- Compared with processing all w spaces separately, grouped processing of $\langle \mathcal{A}_1, \ldots, \mathcal{A}_w \rangle$ saves at least $(w-1)M + 2\sum_{i=2}^{w} M_{1,\mathcal{A}_i}$ page reads.
- When applying CELL to w spaces simultaneously, each page is guaranteed to be read ≤ 4 times. □

There are two interesting comments to make about the last two parts of the above lemma. First, with reference to Lemma 6, the last part says that regardless of how many edges there are on a path, the same worst-case guarantee of at most four-reads per page still applies. This suggests that the longer the path, the more shared I/O is possible and the larger is the saving. Second, the hidden overhead, however, is that the intersection between Class I pages and Class II pages grows as the length of the path increases. In other words, more and more pages are needed four times, instead of three.

4.3 Grouping Multiple Nodes Satisfying a Semi-Lattice Relationship

The generality of the analytic framework presented in Section 4.1 does not stop at the level of path relationships. We now show how to group and process even more nodes together, while preserving the properties and the I/O guarantee shown above.

Definition 6 Given multiple spaces $\mathcal{A}_1, \ldots, \mathcal{A}_w$, we say that these spaces satisfy a *semi-lattice* relationship, if there exists a $\top$-element $\mathcal{A}_i$ for some $1 \leq i \leq w$ such that the entire set $\{\mathcal{A}_1, \ldots, \mathcal{A}_w\}$ consists of all the subspaces of $\mathcal{A}_i$ and nothing else. □

For the example shown in Figure 3, the spaces $\{A, B, C\}$, $\{A, B\}$, $\{A, C\}$, $\{B, C\}$, $\{A\}$, $\{B\}$ and $\{C\}$ satisfy a semi-lattice relationship, with the T-element being the space $\{A, B, C\}$.

Like Lemma 7 is for a path relationship, we can give a general lemma for a semi-lattice relationship. However, we decide to omit the general lemma here because the notation would be too messy for the points we want to make. Instead, we only give results for an instance of a semi-lattice relationship, and point out a few interesting aspects.

Lemma 8 Consider a semi-lattice relationship, with the T-element being the space $\{A, B, C\}$.

- The combined set of Class I pages to process all 7 spaces simultaneously is given by: $PgI(WT_{ABC})$.
- The combined set of Class II pages to process all 7 spaces simultaneously is given by: $PgII(WT_A, A) \cup PgII(WT_B, B) \cup PgII(WT_C, C) \cup PgII(WT_{AB} - WT_A - WT_B, AB) \cup PgII(WT_{AC} - WT_A - WT_C, AC) \cup PgII(WT_{BC} - WT_B - WT_C, BC) \cup PgII((WT_{ABC} - WT_{AB} - \ldots - WT_A - \ldots), ABC)$.
- Compared to processing all 7 spaces separately, semi-lattice grouped processing saves at least $6M + 2M_{1,A} + 2M_{1,B} + 2M_{1,C} + 2M_{1,AB} + 2M_{1,BC} + 2M_{1,AC}$ page reads.
- When applying Algorithm CELL to the 7 spaces simultaneously, each page is still guaranteed to be read at most 4 times. □

It is interesting to note that the "at most four-reads per page" guarantee applies to the path relationship $\langle\{A, B, C\}, \{A, B\}, \{A\}\rangle$, *as well as to* the semi-lattice relationship with $\{A, B, C\}$ being the T-element. The difference, again, is that there are many more pages that need to be read 4 times in the latter relationship.

Finally, it is conceivable that we can simultaneously process multiple semi-lattice relationships. This begs the question: In terms of grouped processing of multiple nodes, where is the limit?

- First, there is the limit on the memory side. Our analysis of grouped processing focuses on I/O, and necessitates that there be sufficient memory space to simultaneously handle multiple nodes. For very large datasets returning many outliers, multiple instances of semi-lattice processing may indeed be problematic.
- Second, there are in fact scenarios where grouped processing of multiple nodes may not be beneficial. To illustrate, this is a good point to tie our discussion back to Procedures JumpLattice and DrillDown shown in Figure 4. Consider the space $\{A, B, C\}$. If *no* outlier is found in $\{A, B, C\}$, DrillDown is never called from JumpLattice, and none of the subspaces needs to be examined. In contrast, if we begin by processing the whole semi-lattice relationship with $\{A, B, C\}$ as the T-element, we will have done more CPU operations and I/O reads (four-reads versus three-reads) than necessary. In Section 5, we will compare these different strategies experimentally.

4.4 Grouped Processing with Algorithm NL

So far in this section, we have focused on grouped processing of multiple nodes using Algorithm CELL. This has been the focus because grouped processing is expected to be prevalent in situations where CELL is the baseline algorithm of choice and when strongest outliers are sought. But in some other situations, it is possible that Algorithm NL would need to be used as well (i.e., for k-D spaces where $k \geq 5$). Then, in those cases, as with CELL, grouped processing of nodes with NL can bring about an efficiency gain. For completeness, we outline how to do that with NL.

Recall that to allow CELL to process multiple nodes simultaneously, we deal with two key issues: (i) how to make the algorithm itself process multiple nodes/spaces (e.g., combined Class I and II pages); and (ii) how to group and select the multiple nodes effectively (e.g., path and semi-lattice relationships). Here, we examine the same two issues for NL. The first issue is conceptually simple. If there is only one space for NL to process, NL keeps for each tuple P a count of the tuples that are within the fixed-radius neighbourhood of P in that space. If there are w spaces for NL to process simultaneously, NL can keep for each tuple P a count for each of the w spaces. Because the w counts are so unrelated to each other (except that they share the same I/O), the second issue of grouping and selecting the w spaces for NL becomes simple as well, unlike the situation for CELL. Theoretically, any w spaces can do. In practice, though, the heuristic of picking the spaces in ascending cardinalities is the most sensible, assuming we wish to find the strongest outliers or the top-u strongest/weak outliers.

5 Experimental Evaluation

5.1 Experimental Setup

Our base dataset is an 855-record dataset consisting of 1995-96 NHL player performance statistics. These statistics include numbers of goals, assists, points, penalty minutes, shots on goal, etc. Since this real-life dataset is quite small, and since we want to test our algorithms on large, disk-resident datasets, we created a number of synthetic datasets mirroring the distribution of statistics within the NHL dataset. Specifically, we determined the distribution of the attributes in the original dataset by using a 10-partition histogram. Then, we generated datasets containing up to 2 million tuples, and whose distribution mirrored that of the base dataset. Each data page held up to 13 tuples.

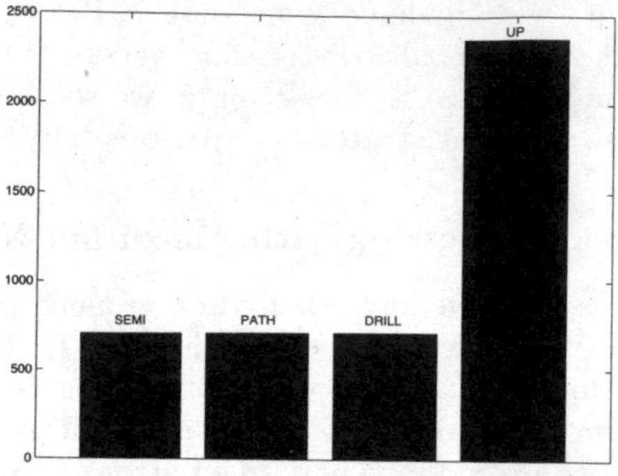

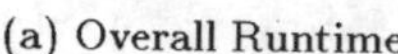

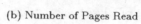

(a) Overall Runtime

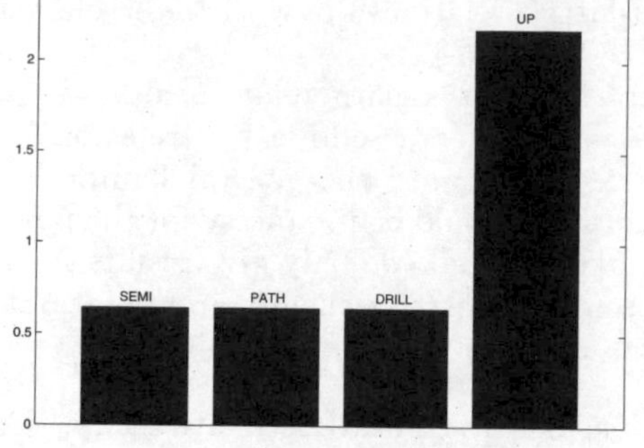

(b) Number of Pages Read

Figure 6: Scenario I: Outliers Found Only in 3-D Spaces

We implemented all four strategies analyzed so far. Specifically, for the results reported below:

- "UP" denotes UpLattice shown in Figure 4.
- "DRILL" denotes JumpLattice using DrillDown to process the subspaces if necessary.
- "PATH" denotes JumpLattice that, instead of calling DrillDown, applies grouped processing of nodes satisfying a path relationship.
- Finally, "SEMI" denotes JumpLattice that applies grouped processing of nodes satisfying a semi-lattice relationship.

Our tests were run on a time-sharing environment provided by a Sun Microsystems Ultra-60 workstation. Unless otherwise indicated, all times shown in this paper are CPU times plus I/O times. Buffer management was done by the operating system. Even though different buffer management strategies may change the reported results in absolute terms, they do not change how the various algorithms compare with one another in relative terms.

5.2 Computing All Strongest Outliers

In the first set of experiments, we focus on the computation of all strongest outliers. The results reported below are based on a 4-dimensional space. We compare the number of I/O operations and the overall runtime required by the four different strategies. As discussed before, the relative performance of the strategies depends on how many outliers are contained in the 3-D space, and in its 2-D and 1-D subspaces. Below, we report on the results of three different scenarios: (I) outliers found only in the 3-D space but not in any of the subspaces, (II) a small number of outliers (e.g., 10) found in some 2-D subspace(s) but not in any of the 1-D subspaces, and (III) a large number of outliers (e.g., 400) found in the 2-D subspaces. Later in this section, we comment on the scenario where all strongest outliers are found at the 1-D level.

Figure 6 shows how the four strategies compare under Scenario (I). Figure 6(a) compares their overall runtimes, and Figure 6(b) shows their total number of pages read for 2 million tuples. UpLattice is the only strategy that does poorly, while the other three give almost identical performance running more than three times faster than, and requiring only about 30% of the I/O's needed by, UpLattice. Thus, Scenario (I) is highly unfavourable to the bottom-up approach taken by UpLattice. Note that there is a strong 1-to-1 correspondence between the overall runtime and the number of pages read, indicating that this is a very I/O dominant job. From now on, we only show the overall runtime figures.

Figures 7(a) and (b) show the overall runtimes of the four strategies under Scenarios (II) and (III), respectively. While UpLattice remains a poor strategy, DrillDown can do worse. Both the path and semi-lattice strategies continue to be best, with relatively little difference between them. Notice that as there are more outliers contained in the 2-D subspaces, the gap between UpLattice and the path and semi-lattice strategies becomes smaller. Eventually, when all 1-D subspaces contain outliers, even the path and semi-lattice strategies deteriorate beyond UpLattice. In practice though, the scenario where all strongest outliers are found in 1-D subspaces, is expected to be rare. For more typical scenarios, it is clear that the path and the semi-lattice strategies are the ones to use.

5.3 Computing Top-u Outliers

The experimental results reported so far pertain to strongest outliers only. In this set of experiments, we compare the performance of the four strategies for computing the top-u non-trivial (i.e., strongest or weak) outliers. Recall that when computing strongest outliers only, once a space is found to contain outliers, none of its superspaces needs to be computed. But when it is necessary to compute the weak outliers also, even the superspaces need to be examined. In general, this scenario favours the path and semi-lattice strategies because of the shared processing.

Figure 8 shows how the overall runtime changes for

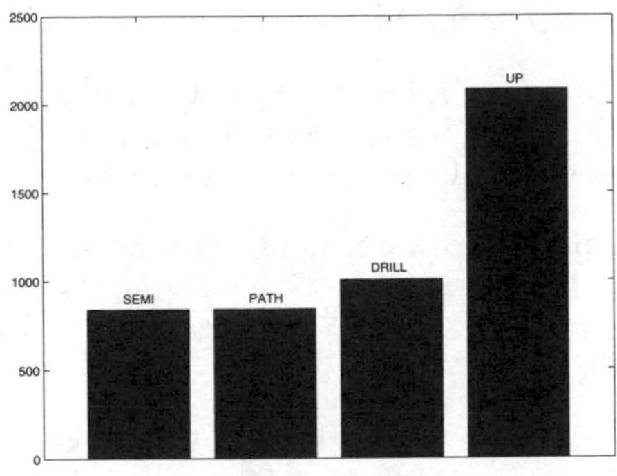

(a) Scenario II

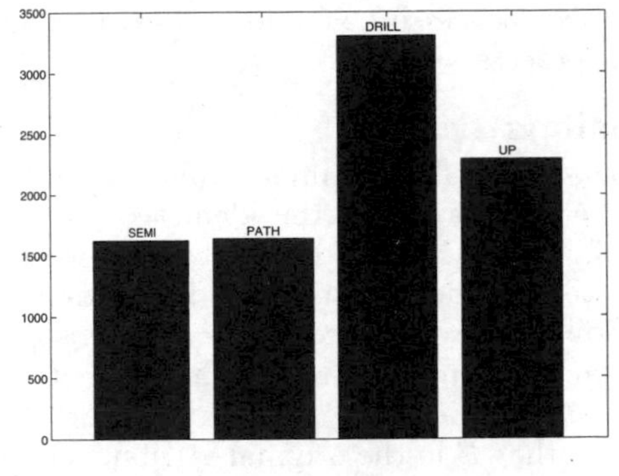

(b) Scenario III

Figure 7: Outliers Found in 2-D Subspaces: Overall Runtime

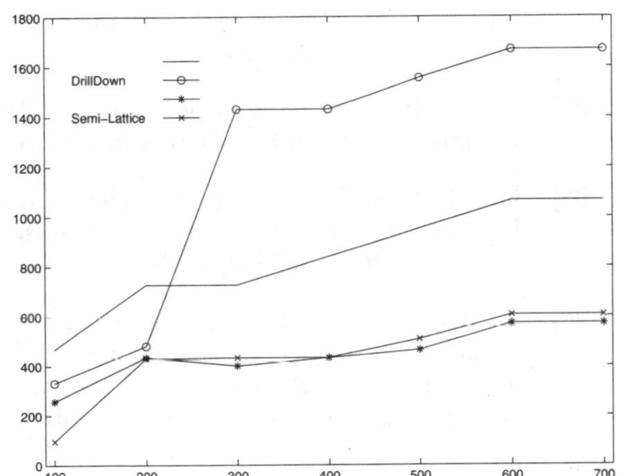

Figure 8: Top-u Strongest and/or Weak Outliers

computing top-u outliers when u varies from 100 to 700, for 500,000 tuples. UpLattice starts off poorly even for small values of u, and remains poor as u increases. DrillDown starts off very well, but quickly degrades to be the worst. Both the path and the semi-lattice strategies are again the winners, with a slight edge being given to the path strategy. The main reason for this difference is: because computation stops once the first u non-trivial outliers are found, the semi-lattice strategy may over-do what is actually needed.

With respect to the four-reads per page guarantee, we provide the following results to give readers an appreciation for the fact that four-reads per page are encountered relatively infrequently in practice. For example, for a 2 million tuple dataset using the semi-lattice strategy, with 4.8 million pages read in all, 0.17 million pages were read exactly once, 1.7 million page were read exactly twice, 0.4 million pages were read exactly three times, and only 13,025 pages were read exactly four times.

In Section 4.3, we pointed out that we can generalize from the path strategy to the semi-lattice strategy, and even further. This leads to the question of how far we can go and where we should stop. The experimental results presented so far indicate that for computing strongest/weak outliers, there appears to be little promise to go beyond the semi-lattice strategy. In fact, between the path and the semi-lattice strategies, we recommend the former. It gives results at least as good as the semi-lattice strategy, and it is simpler in many ways.

5.4 Grouped Processing with Algorithm NL

So far, we have seen how grouped processing pays off in lower dimensional spaces using Algorithm CELL. We now turn our attention to higher dimensional spaces. As mentioned before, Algorithm CELL is the preferred algorithm for $k \leq 4$. Now suppose that a lattice contains two or more unprocessed nodes of cardinality ≥ 5, that more outliers are sought, and that all processing for nodes of cardinality ≤ 4 is complete. Then, we can either use Algorithm NL to process each remaining node on an individual basis, or we can group nodes and thus share I/O's.

Below are some performance results for grouped NL processing, in which seven nodes are processed together—one $k = 6$ node and all six of its $k = 5$ subspaces. For a dataset containing 500,000 tuples, using 25% buffering, individual NL processing on these seven nodes took 24% longer than with grouped NL processing. For this case, grouped processing requires 16 MB of memory, which is almost twice as much memory as each individual case requires. If we were to equate the memory allocations to about 8 MB (by providing only 9% buffering for the grouped case), then individual processing took only about 1% more time than grouped processing. Although we do not make performance guarantees, we observe that grouped NL processing generally yields only modest gains (e.g., 10%). This is due to the fact that the overall time for grouped NL processing is roughly broken down into 95% CPU time and 5% I/O time. Thus, while it is true that I/O operations are reduced significantly, the impact of shared I/O may not be significant overall. In summary, because of simplicity and the somewhat unpredictable nature of finding outlying spaces, we conclude that individual NL processing should be used in place of grouped NL processing.

6 Conclusions

This paper focused on finding intensional knowledge of outliers to help explain why the identified outliers are exceptional. To the best of our knowledge, we are the first to go beyond identification to explanation.

The intensional knowledge considered in this paper is structural in nature. Through the concepts of strongest and weak outliers, our algorithms report, for each identified outlier P in the original attribute space $\mathcal{A}_P$, the minimal subspaces in which P is outlying, and how P compares against other identified outliers with respect to these minimal subspaces. We believe that the reported intensional knowledge is valuable to the user in helping to evaluate the validity of the identification, and in improving the user's understanding of the dataset in general and the outliers in particular.

We presented four strategies for the computation of strongest and weak outliers: UpLattice, JumpLattice with DrillDown, JumpLattice with Path, and JumpLattice with Semi-Lattice. For the latter two strategies, we showed that the kinds of grouped processing they perform are correct, and we presented a detailed analysis on their I/O performance. We provided two I/O performance guarantees: one on the minimum number of I/O's saved, and the other on the maximum number of times a data page has to be read.

The I/O analytic results are confirmed by experimental results. Under various scenarios, grouped processing with the path or the semi-lattice strategies can bring about a 65–75% reduction in I/O operations and overall runtime, when compared with the alternatives. And even though computing intensional knowledge appears to be time-consuming, especially for large and/or high dimensional datasets, our results clearly show that effective sharing of I/O's, via the path or the semi-lattice strategies, can go a long way towards reducing the overall runtime.

References

[AGGR98] R. Agrawal, J. Gehrke, D. Gunopulos, and P. Raghavan. "Automatic Subspace Clustering of High Dimensional Data for Data Mining Applications," *Proc. ACM SIGMOD*, pp. 94–105, 1998.

[AGI+92] R. Agrawal, S. Ghosh, T. Imielinski, B. Iyer, and A. Swami. "An Interval Classifier for Database Mining Applications", *Proc. VLDB*, pp. 560–573, 1992.

[AIS93] R. Agrawal, T. Imielinski, and A. Swami. "Mining Association Rules between Sets of Items in Large Databases", *Proc. ACM SIGMOD*, pp. 207–216, 1993.

[BL94] V. Barnett and T. Lewis. *Outliers in Statistical Data*. John Wiley & Sons, 1994.

[BFOS84] L. Breiman, J. Friedman, R. Olshen, and C. Stone. *Classification and Regression Trees*. Wadsworth International Group, 1984.

[BMS97] S. Brin, R. Motwani, and C. Silverstein. "Beyond Market Basket: Generalizing Association Rules to Correlations", *Proc. ACM SIGMOD*, pp. 265–276, 1997.

[HKPT98] Y. Huhtala, J. Karkkainen, P. Porkka, and H. Toivonen. "Efficient Discovery of Functional and Approximate Dependencies Using Partitions", *Proc. ICDE*, 1998.

[JKN98] T. Johnson, I. Kwok, and R. Ng. "Fast Computation of 2-Dimensional Depth Contours," *Proc. KDD*, pp. 224–228, 1998.

[KR90] L. Kaufman and P. Rousseeuw. *Finding Groups in Data*. John Wiley & Sons, 1990.

[KN98] E. Knorr and R. Ng. "Algorithms for Mining Distance-Based Outliers in Large Datasets," *Proc. VLDB*, pp. 392–403, 1998.

[KN99] E. Knorr and R. Ng. "Finding Intensional Knowledge of Distance-Based Outliers," Technical Report, Dept. of Computer Science, University of British Columbia.

[NLHP98] R. Ng, L. Lakshmanan, J. Han, and A. Pang. "Exploratory Mining and Pruning Optimizations of Constrained Associations Rules", *Proc. ACM SIGMOD*, pp. 13–24, 1998.

[RR96] I. Ruts and P. Rousseeuw. "Computing Depth Contours of Bivariate Point Clouds", *Computational Statistics and Data Analysis*, 23, pp. 153–168, 1996.

[SBMU98] C. Silverstein, S. Brin, R. Motwani, and J. Ullman. "Scalable Techniques for Mining Causal Structures", *Proc. VLDB*, pp. 594–605, 1998.

[TN98] V. Tucakov and R. Ng. "Identifying Unusual People Behavior: A Case Study of Mining Outliers in Spatio-Temporal Trajectory Databases", *Proc. SIGMOD Workshop on Research Issues on Knowledge Discovery and Data Mining*, 1998.

[Tuk77] J. Tukey. *Exploratory Data Analysis*. Addison-Wesley, 1977.

SPIRIT: Sequential Pattern Mining with Regular Expression Constraints

Minos N. Garofalakis
Bell Laboratories
minos@bell-labs.com

Rajeev Rastogi
Bell Laboratories
rastogi@bell-labs.com

Kyuseok Shim
Bell Laboratories
shim@bell-labs.com

Abstract

Discovering sequential patterns is an important problem in data mining with a host of application domains including medicine, telecommunications, and the World Wide Web. Conventional mining systems provide users with only a very restricted mechanism (based on minimum support) for specifying patterns of interest. In this paper, we propose the use of Regular Expressions (REs) as a flexible constraint specification tool that enables user-controlled focus to be incorporated into the pattern mining process. We develop a family of novel algorithms (termed SPIRIT – Sequential Pattern mIning with Regular expressIon consTraints) for mining frequent sequential patterns that also satisfy user-specified RE constraints. The main distinguishing factor among the proposed schemes is the degree to which the RE constraints are enforced to prune the search space of patterns during computation. Our solutions provide valuable insights into the tradeoffs that arise when constraints that do not subscribe to nice properties (like anti-monotonicity) are integrated into the mining process. A quantitative exploration of these tradeoffs is conducted through an extensive experimental study on synthetic and real-life data sets.

1 Introduction

Discovering *sequential patterns* from a large database of sequences is an important problem in the field of knowledge discovery and data mining. Briefly, given a set of data sequences, the problem is to discover subsequences that are *frequent*, in the sense that the percentage of data sequences containing them exceeds a user-specified minimum *support* [3, 11]. Mining frequent sequential patterns has found a host of potential application domains, including retailing (i.e., market-basket data), telecommunications, and, more recently, the World Wide Web (WWW). In market-basket databases, each data sequence corresponds to items bought by an individual customer over time and frequent patterns can be useful for predicting future customer behavior. In telecommunications, frequent sequences of alarms output by network switches capture important relationships between alarm signals that can then be employed for online prediction, analysis, and correction of network faults. Finally, in the context of the WWW, server sites typically generate huge volumes of daily log data capturing the sequences of page accesses for thousands or millions of users[1]. Discovering frequent access patterns in WWW logs can help improve system design (e.g., better hyperlinked structure between correlated pages) and lead to better marketing decisions (e.g., strategic advertisement placement).

As a more concrete example, the `Yahoo!` Internet directory (`www.yahoo.com`) enables users to locate interesting WWW documents by navigating through large *topic hierarchies* consisting of thousands of different document classes. These hierarchies provide an effective way of dealing with the abundance problem present in today's keyword-based WWW search engines. The idea is to allow users to progressively refine their search by following specific *topic paths* (i.e., sequences of hyperlinks) along a (predefined) hierarchy. Given the wide variety of topics and the inherently fuzzy nature of document classification, there are numerous cases in which distinct topic paths lead to different document collections on very similar topics. For example, starting from `Yahoo!`'s home page users can locate information on hotels in New York City by following *either* `Travel:Yahoo!Travel:North America:United States:New York:New York City:Lodging:Hotels` *or* `Travel:Lodging:Yahoo!Lodging:New York:New York Cities:New York City:Hotels and Motels`, where "`:`" denotes a parent-child link in the topic hierarchy. Mining user access logs to determine the most frequently accessed topic paths is a task of immense marketing value, e.g., for a hotel or restaurant business in New York City trying to select a strategic set of WWW locations for its advertising campaign.

The design of effective algorithms for mining frequent sequential patterns has been the subject of several studies in recent years [3, 4, 7, 8, 11, 12]. Ignoring small differences in the problem definition (e.g., form of input data, definition of a subsequence), a major common thread that runs through the vast majority of earlier work is the *lack of user-controlled focus in the pattern mining process*. Typically,

[1] In general, WWW servers only have knowledge of the IP address of the user/proxy requesting a specific web page. However, *referrers* and *cookies* can be used to determine the sequence of accesses for a particular user (without compromising the user's identity).

Proceedings of the 25th VLDB Conference, Edinburgh, Scotland, 1999.

the interaction of the user with the pattern mining system is limited to specifying a lower bound on the desired support for the extracted patterns. The system then executes an appropriate mining algorithm and returns a very large number of sequential patterns, only some of which may be of actual interest to the user. Despite its conceptual simplicity, this "unfocused" approach to sequential pattern mining suffers from two major drawbacks.

1. *Disproportionate computational cost for selective users.* Given a database of sequences and a fixed value for the minimum support threshold, the computational cost of the pattern mining process is fixed for any potential user. Ignoring user focus can be extremely unfair to a highly selective user that is only interested in patterns of a very specific form.

2. *Overwhelming volume of potentially useless results.* The lack of tools to express user focus during the pattern mining process means that selective users will typically be swamped with a huge number of frequent patterns, most of which are useless for their purposes.

The above discussion clearly demonstrates the need for novel pattern mining solutions that enable the incorporation of user-controlled focus in the mining process. There are two main components that any such solution must provide. First, given the inadequacy of simple support constraints, we need a *flexible constraint specification language* that allows users to express the specific family of sequential patterns that they are interested in. For instance, returning to our earlier "New York City hotels" example, a hotel planning its ad placement may only be interested in paths that (a) begin with `Travel`, (b) end in either `Hotels` or `Hotels and Motels`, and (c) contain at least one of `Lodging`, `Yahoo!Lodging`, `Yahoo!Travel`, `New York`, or `New York City`, since these are the only topics directly related to its line of business. Second, we need novel pattern mining algorithms that can exploit user focus by *pushing user-specified constraints deep inside the mining process*. The abstract goal here is to exploit pattern constraints to prune the computational cost and ensure system performance that is *commensurate* with the level of user focus (i.e., constraint selectivity).

We should note that even though recent work has addressed similar problems in the context of association rule mining [9, 10], the problem of incorporating a rich set of user-specified constraints in sequential pattern mining remains, to the best of our knowledge, unexplored. Furthermore, as we will discover later in the paper, pattern constraints raise a host of new issues specific to sequence mining (e.g., due to the explicit ordering of items) that were not considered in the subset and aggregation constraints for itemsets considered in [9, 10]. For example, our pattern constraints do not satisfy the property of *anti-monotonicity* [9]; that is, the fact that a sequence satisfies a pattern constraint does not imply that all its subsequences satisfy the same constraint. These differences mandate novel solutions that are completely independent of earlier results on constrained association rule mining[2] [9, 10].

In this paper, we formulate the problem of mining sequential patterns with *regular expression constraints* and we develop novel, efficient algorithmic solutions for pushing regular expressions inside the pattern mining process. Our choice of regular expressions (REs) as a constraint specification tool is motivated by two important factors. First, REs provide a simple, natural syntax for the succinct specification of families of sequential patterns. Second, REs possess sufficient expressive power for specifying a wide range of interesting, non-trivial pattern constraints. These observations are validated by the extensive use of REs in everyday string processing tasks (e.g., UNIX shell utilities like `grep` or `ls`) as well as in recent proposals on query languages for sequence data (e.g., the Shape Definition Language of Agrawal et al. [1]). Returning once again to our "New York City hotels" example, note that the constraint on topic paths described earlier in this section can be simply expressed as the following RE: `Travel(Lodging|Yahoo!Lodging|Yahoo!Travel|-New York|New York City)(Hotels|Hotels and Motels)`, where "`|`" stands for disjunction. We propose a family of novel algorithms (termed SPIRIT – Sequential Pattern mIning with Regular expressIon consTraints) for mining frequent sequential patterns that also belong to the language defined by the user-specified RE. Our algorithms exploit the equivalence of REs to deterministic finite automata [6] to push RE constraints deep inside the pattern mining computation. The main distinguishing factor among the proposed schemes is the *degree* to which the RE constraint is enforced within the generation and pruning of candidate patterns during the mining process. We observe that, varying the level of user focus (i.e., RE enforcement) during pattern mining gives rise to certain interesting tradeoffs with respect to computational effectiveness. Enforcing the RE constraint at each phase of the mining process certainly minimizes the amount of "state" maintained after each phase, focusing only on patterns that could potentially be in the final answer set. On the other hand, minimizing this maintained state may not always be the best solution since it can, for example, limit our ability to do effective support-based pruning in later phases. Such tradeoffs are obviously related to our previous observation that RE constraints are *not* anti-monotone [9]. We believe that our results provide useful insights into the more general problem of constraint-driven, ad-hoc data mining, showing that there can be a whole spectrum of choices for dealing with constraints, even when they do not subscribe to nice properties like anti-monotonicity or succinctness [9]. An extensive experimental study with synthetic as well as real-life data sets is conducted to explore the tradeoffs involved and their impact on the overall effectiveness of our algorithms. Our results indicate that incorporating RE constraints into the pattern mining computation can some times yield more than an order of magnitude

[2] Due to space constraints, we omit a detailed discussion of earlier work. The interested reader is referred to the full version of this paper [5].

improvement in performance, thus validating the effectiveness of our approach. Our experimentation with real-life WWW server log data also demonstrates the versatility of REs as a user-level tool for focusing on interesting patterns. The work reported in this paper has been done in the context of the $\mathcal{SERENDIP}$ data mining project at Bell Laboratories (`www.bell-labs.com/projects/serendip`).

2 Problem Formulation

2.1 Definitions

The main input to our mining problem is a database of sequences, where each sequence is an ordered list of *elements*. These elements can be either (a) *simple items* from a fixed set of literals (e.g., the identifiers of WWW documents available at a server [4], the amino acid symbols used in protein analysis [12]), or (b) *itemsets*, that is, non-empty sets of items (e.g., books bought by a customer in the same transaction [11]). The list of elements of a data sequence s is denoted by $< s_1\ s_2 \cdots s_n >$, where s_i is the ith element of s. We use $|s|$ to denote the *length* (i.e., number of elements) of sequence s. A sequence of length k is referred to as a k-*sequence*. (We consider the terms "sequence" and "sequential pattern" to be equivalent for the remainder of our discussion.) Table 1 summarizes the notation used throughout the paper with a brief description of its semantics. Additional notation will be introduced when necessary.

Symbol	Semantics
$s, t, u, \ldots$	Generic sequences in the input database
$< s\ t >$	Sequence resulting from the concatenation of sequences s and t
$\lvert s \rvert$	Length, i.e., number of elements, of sequence s
s_i	i^{th} element of sequence s
s_i^*	Zero or more occurrences of element s_i (Kleene closure operator)
$s_i \mid s_j$	Select one element out of s_i and s_j (disjunction operator)
$\mathcal{R}$	Regular expression (RE) constraint
$\mathcal{A}_\mathcal{R}$	Deterministic finite automaton for RE $\mathcal{R}$
$b, c, d, \ldots$	Generic states in automaton $\mathcal{A}_\mathcal{R}$
a	Start state of automaton $\mathcal{A}_\mathcal{R}$
$b \stackrel{s_i}{\rightarrow} c$	Transition from state b to state c in $\mathcal{A}_\mathcal{R}$ on element s_i
$b \stackrel{s}{\Rightarrow} c$	Transition path from state b to state c in $\mathcal{A}_\mathcal{R}$ on the sequence of elements s
C_k	Set of candidate k-sequences
F_k	Set of frequent k-sequences

Table 1: Notation.

Consider two data sequences $s =< s_1\ s_2\ \cdots\ s_n >$ and $t =< t_1\ t_2\ \cdots\ t_m >$. We say that s is a *subsequence* of t if s is a "projection" of t, derived by deleting elements and/or items from t. More formally, s is a subsequence of t if there exist integers $j_1 < j_2 < \ldots < j_n$ such that $s_1 \subseteq t_{j_1}$, $s_2 \subseteq t_{j_2}$, ..., $s_n \subseteq t_{j_n}$. Note that for sequences of simple items the above condition translates to $s_1 = t_{j_1}$, $s_2 = t_{j_2}$, ..., $s_n = t_{j_n}$. For example, sequences $< 1\ 3 >$ and $< 1\ 2\ 4 >$ are subsequences of $< 1\ 2\ 3\ 4 >$, while $< 3\ 1 >$ is not. Srikant and Agrawal [11] observe that, when mining market-basket sequential patterns, users often want to place a bound on the *maximum distance* between the occurrence of adjacent pattern elements in a data sequence. For example, if a customer buys bread today and milk after a couple of weeks then the two purchases should probably not be seen as being correlated. Following [11], we define sequence s to be a *subsequence with a maximum distance constraint of* δ, or alternately δ-*distance subsequence*, of t if there exist integers $j_1 < j_2 < \ldots < j_n$ such that $s_1 \subseteq t_{j_1}$, $s_2 \subseteq t_{j_2}$, ..., $s_n \subseteq t_{j_n}$ *and* $j_k - j_{k-1} \leq \delta$ for each $k = 2, 3, \ldots, n$. That is, occurrences of adjacent elements of s within t are not separated by more than δ elements. As a special case of the above definition, we say that s is a *contiguous* subsequence of t if s is a 1-distance subsequence of t, i.e., the elements of s can be mapped to a contiguous segment of t.

A sequence s is said to *contain* a sequence p if p is a subsequence of s. We define the *support* of a pattern p as the fraction of sequences in the input database that contain p. Given a set of sequences $\mathcal{S}$, we say that $s \in \mathcal{S}$ is *maximal* if there are no sequences in $\mathcal{S} - \{s\}$ that contain it.

A RE constraint $\mathcal{R}$ is specified as a RE over the alphabet of sequence elements using the established set of RE operators, such as disjunction (|) and Kleene closure (*) [6]. Thus, a RE constraint $\mathcal{R}$ specifies a language of strings over the element alphabet or, equivalently, a regular family of sequential patterns that is of interest to the user. A well-known result from complexity theory states that REs have exactly the same expressive power as *deterministic finite automata* [6]. Thus, given any RE $\mathcal{R}$, we can always build a deterministic finite automaton $\mathcal{A}_\mathcal{R}$ such that $\mathcal{A}_\mathcal{R}$ accepts exactly the language generated by $\mathcal{R}$. Informally, a deterministic finite automaton is a finite state machine with (a) a well-defined *start* state (denoted by a) and one or more *accept* states, and (b) deterministic transitions across states on symbols of the input alphabet (in our case, sequence elements). A transition from state b to state c on element s_i is denoted by $b \stackrel{s_i}{\rightarrow} c$. We also use the shorthand $b \stackrel{s}{\Rightarrow} c$ to denote the sequence of transitions on the elements of sequence s starting at state b and ending in state c. A sequence s is *accepted by* $\mathcal{A}_\mathcal{R}$ if following the sequence of transitions for the elements of s from the start state results in an accept state. Figure 1 depicts the state diagram of a deterministic finite automaton for the RE 1^* (2 2 | 2 3 4 | 4 4) (i.e., all sequences of zero or more 1's followed by 2 2, 2 3 4, or 4 4). Following [6], we use double circles to indicate an accept state and > to emphasize the start state (a) of the automaton. For brevity, we will simply use "automaton" as a synonym for "deterministic finite automaton" in the remainder of the paper.

2.2 Problem Statement

Given an input database of sequences, we define a sequential pattern to be *frequent* if its support in the database ex-

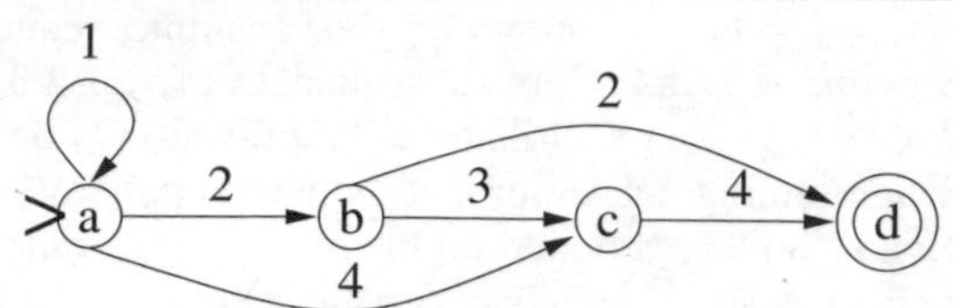

Figure 1: Automaton for the RE 1* (2 2 | 2 3 4 | 4 4).

ceeds a user-specified minimum support threshold. Prior work has focused on efficient techniques for the discovery of frequent patterns, typically ignoring the possibility of allowing and exploiting flexible structural constraints during the mining process. In this paper, we develop novel, efficient algorithms for mining frequent sequential patterns in the presence of user-specified RE constraints. Due to space constraints, the discussion in this paper focuses on the case of *sequences of simple items* with *no maximum distance constraints*. The necessary extensions to handle itemset sequences and distance constraints for pattern occurrences are described in detail in the full version of this paper [5]. The following definitions establish some useful terminology for our discussion.

Definition 2.1 A sequence s is said to be *legal with respect to state* b of automaton $\mathcal{A}_{\mathcal{R}}$ if every state transition in $\mathcal{A}_{\mathcal{R}}$ is defined when following the sequence of transitions for the elements of s from b.

Definition 2.2 A sequence s is said to be *valid with respect to state* b of automaton $\mathcal{A}_{\mathcal{R}}$ if s is legal with respect to b *and* the final state of the transition path from b on input s is an *accept* state of $\mathcal{A}_{\mathcal{R}}$. We say that s is *valid* if s is valid with respect to the start state a of $\mathcal{A}_{\mathcal{R}}$ (or, equivalently, if s is accepted by $\mathcal{A}_{\mathcal{R}}$).

Example 2.1 : Consider the RE constraint $\mathcal{R}$ = 1* (2 2 | 2 3 4 | 4 4) and the automaton $\mathcal{A}_{\mathcal{R}}$, shown in Figure 1. Sequence $< 1\ 2\ 3 >$ is legal with respect to state a and sequence $< 3\ 4 >$ is legal with respect to state b, while sequences $< 1\ 3\ 4 >$ and $< 2\ 4 >$ are not legal with respect to any state of $\mathcal{A}_{\mathcal{R}}$. Similarly, sequence $< 3\ 4 >$ is valid with respect to state b (since $b \stackrel{<3\ 4>}{\Longrightarrow} d$ and d is an accept state), however it is not valid, since it is not valid with respect to the start state a of $\mathcal{A}_{\mathcal{R}}$. Examples of valid sequences include $< 1\ 1\ 2\ 2 >$ and $< 2\ 3\ 4 >$. ∎

Having established the necessary notions and terminology, we can now provide an abstract definition of our constrained pattern mining problem as follows.

- **Given:** A database of sequences $\mathcal{D}$, a user-specified minimum support threshold, and a user-specified RE constraint $\mathcal{R}$ (or, equivalently, an automaton $\mathcal{A}_{\mathcal{R}}$).
- **Find:** All *frequent and valid* sequential patterns in $\mathcal{D}$.

Thus, our objective is to efficiently mine patterns that are not only frequent but also belong to the language of sequences generated by the RE $\mathcal{R}$[3]. To this end, the next section introduces the SPIRIT family of mining algorithms for pushing user-specified RE constraints to varying degrees inside the pattern mining process.

[3] Our algorithms can readily handle a *set* of RE constraints by collapsing them into a single RE [6].

3 Mining Frequent and Valid Sequences

3.1 Overview

Figure 2 depicts the basic algorithmic skeleton of the SPIRIT family, using an input parameter $\mathcal{C}$ to denote a generic user-specified constraint on the mined patterns. The output of a SPIRIT algorithm is the set of frequent sequences in the database $\mathcal{D}$ that satisfy constraint $\mathcal{C}$. At a high level, our algorithmic framework is similar in structure to the general Apriori strategy of Agrawal and Srikant [2]. Basically, SPIRIT algorithms work in passes, with each pass resulting in the discovery of longer patterns. In the kth pass, a set of candidate (i.e., potentially frequent and valid) k-sequences C_k is generated and pruned using information from earlier passes. A scan over the data is then made, during which the support for each candidate sequence in C_k is counted and F_k is populated with the frequent k-sequences in C_k. There are, however, two crucial differences between the SPIRIT framework and conventional Apriori-type schemes (like GSP [11]) or the Constrained APriori (CAP) algorithm [9] for mining associations with anti-monotone and/or succinct constraints.

1. *Relaxing $\mathcal{C}$ by inducing a weaker (i.e., less restrictive) constraint $\mathcal{C}'$ (Step 1).* Intuitively, constraint $\mathcal{C}'$ is *weaker* than $\mathcal{C}$ if every sequence that satisfies $\mathcal{C}$ also satisfies $\mathcal{C}'$. The "strength" of $\mathcal{C}'$ (i.e., how closely it emulates $\mathcal{C}$) essentially determines the degree to which the user-specified constraint $\mathcal{C}$ is pushed inside the pattern mining computation. The choice of $\mathcal{C}'$ differentiates among the members of the SPIRIT family and leads to interesting tradeoffs that are discussed in detail later in this section.
2. *Using the relaxed constraint $\mathcal{C}'$ in the candidate generation and candidate pruning phases of each pass.* SPIRIT algorithms maintain the set F of frequent sequences (up to a given length) that satisfy the relaxed constraint $\mathcal{C}'$. Both F and $\mathcal{C}'$ are used in:
   (a) the candidate generation phase of pass k (Step 6), to produce an initial set of candidate k-sequences C_k that satisfy $\mathcal{C}'$ by appropriately extending or combining sequences in F; and,
   (b) the candidate pruning phase of pass k (Steps 8-9), to delete from C_k all candidate k-sequences containing at least one subsequence that satisfies $\mathcal{C}'$ and does not appear in F.

Thus, a SPIRIT algorithm maintains the following *invariant*: at the end of pass k, F_k is exactly the set of all frequent k-sequences that satisfy the constraint $\mathcal{C}'$. Note that incorporating $\mathcal{C}'$ in candidate generation and pruning also impacts the terminating condition for the **repeat** loop in Step 15. Finally, since at the end of the loop, F contains frequent patterns satisfying the induced relaxed constraint $\mathcal{C}'$, an additional filtering step may be required (Step 17).

Procedure SPIRIT($\mathcal{D}$, $\mathcal{C}$)
begin
1. let $\mathcal{C}'$:= a constraint *weaker* (i.e., less restrictive) than $\mathcal{C}$
2. $F := F_1 :=$ frequent items in $\mathcal{D}$ that satisfy $\mathcal{C}'$
3. $k := 2$
4. **repeat** {
5. // *candidate generation*
6. using $\mathcal{C}'$ and F generate $C_k := \{$ potentially frequent k-sequences that satisfy $\mathcal{C}'$ $\}$
7. // *candidate pruning*
8. let $P := \{s \in C_k : s$ has a subsequence t that satisfies $\mathcal{C}'$ and $t \notin F\}$
9. $C_k := C_k - P$
10. // *candidate counting*
11. scan $\mathcal{D}$ counting support for candidate k-sequences in C_k
12. $F_k :=$ frequent sequences in C_k
13. $F := F \cup F_k$
14. $k := k + 1$
15. } **until** TerminatingCondition(F, $\mathcal{C}'$) holds
16. // *enforce the original (stronger) constraint* $\mathcal{C}$
17. output sequences in F that satisfy $\mathcal{C}$

end

Figure 2: SPIRIT constrained pattern mining framework.

Given a set of candidate k-sequences C_k, counting support for the members of C_k (Step 11) can be performed efficiently by employing specialized search structures, like the *hash tree* [11], for organizing the candidates. The implementation details can be found in [11]. The candidate counting step is typically the most expensive step of the pattern mining process and its overhead is directly proportional to the size of C_k [11]. Thus, at an abstract level, the goal of an efficient pattern mining strategy is to employ the minimum support requirement and any additional user-specified constraints to restrict as much as possible the set of candidate k-sequences counted during pass k. The SPIRIT framework strives to achieve this goal by using two different types of pruning within each pass k.

- *Constraint-based pruning* using a relaxation $\mathcal{C}'$ of the user-specified constraint $\mathcal{C}$; that is, ensuring that all candidate k-sequences in C_k satisfy $\mathcal{C}'$. This is accomplished by appropriately employing $\mathcal{C}'$ and F in the candidate generation phase (Step 6).
- *Support-based pruning*; that is, ensuring that all subsequences of a sequence s in C_k that satisfy $\mathcal{C}'$ are present in the current set of discovered frequent sequences F (Steps 8-9). Note that, even though *all* subsequences of s must in fact be frequent, we can only check the minimum support constraint for subsequences that satisfy $\mathcal{C}'$, since only these are retained in F.

Intuitively, constraint-based pruning tries to restrict C_k by (partially) enforcing the input constraint $\mathcal{C}$, whereas support-based pruning tries to restrict C_k by checking the minimum support constraint for qualifying subsequences. Note that, given a set of candidates C_k and a relaxation $\mathcal{C}'$ of $\mathcal{C}$, the amount of support-based pruning is maximized when $\mathcal{C}'$ is *anti-monotone* [9] (i.e., all subsequences of a sequence satisfying $\mathcal{C}'$ are guaranteed to also satisfy $\mathcal{C}'$). This is because support information for *all* of the subsequences of a candidate sequence s in C_k can be used to prune it. However, when $\mathcal{C}'$ is *not* anti-monotone, the amounts of constraint-based and support-based pruning achieved vary depending on the specific choice of $\mathcal{C}'$.

3.1.1 Pushing Non Anti-Monotone Constraints

Consider the general problem of mining all frequent sequences that satisfy a user-specified constraint $\mathcal{C}$. If $\mathcal{C}$ is anti-monotone, then the most effective way of using $\mathcal{C}$ to prune candidates is to push $\mathcal{C}$ "all the way" inside the mining computation. In the context of the SPIRIT framework, this means using $\mathcal{C}$ *as is* (rather than some relaxation of $\mathcal{C}$) in the pattern discovery loop. The optimality of this solution for anti-monotone $\mathcal{C}$ stems from two observations. First, using $\mathcal{C}$ clearly maximizes the amount of constraint-based pruning since the strongest possible constraint (i.e., $\mathcal{C}$ itself) is employed. Second, since $\mathcal{C}$ is anti-monotone, all subsequences of a frequent candidate k-sequence that survives constraint-based pruning are guaranteed to be in F (since they also satisfy $\mathcal{C}$). Thus, using the full strength of an anti-monotone constraint $\mathcal{C}$ maximizes the effectiveness of constraint-based pruning as well as support-based pruning. Note that this is exactly the methodology used in the CAP algorithm [9] for anti-monotone itemset constraints. An additional benefit of using anti-monotone constraints is that they significantly simplify the candidate generation and candidate pruning tasks. More specifically, generating C_k is nothing but an appropriate "self-join" operation over F_{k-1} and determining the pruned set P (Step 8) is simplified by the fact that all subsequences of candidates are guaranteed to satisfy the constraint.

When $\mathcal{C}$ is *not* anti-monotone, however, things are not that clear-cut. A simple solution, suggested by Ng et al. [9] for itemset constraints, is to take an anti-monotone relaxation of $\mathcal{C}$ and use that relaxation for candidate pruning. Nevertheless, this simple approach may not always be feasible. For example, our RE constraints for sequences do not admit any non-trivial anti-monotone relaxations. In such cases, the degree to which the constraint $\mathcal{C}$ is pushed inside the mining process (i.e., the strength of the (non anti-monotone) relaxation $\mathcal{C}'$ used for pruning) impacts the effectiveness of both constraint-based pruning and support-based pruning in different ways. More specifically, while increasing the strength of $\mathcal{C}'$ obviously increases the effectiveness of constraint-based pruning, it can also have a negative effect on support-based pruning. The reason is that, for any given sequence in C_k that survives constraint-based pruning, *the number of its subsequences that satisfy the stronger, non anti-monotone constraint* $\mathcal{C}'$ *may decrease*. Again, note that only subsequences that satisfy $\mathcal{C}'$ can be used for support-based pruning, since this is the only "state" maintained from previous passes (in F).

Pushing a non anti-monotone constraint $\mathcal{C}'$ in the pattern discovery loop can also increase the computational complexity of the candidate generation and pruning tasks. For candidate generation, the fact that $\mathcal{C}'$ is not anti-monotone means that some (or, all) of a candidate's subsequences may be absent from F. In some cases, a "brute-force" approach (based on just $\mathcal{C}'$) may be required to generate an initial set of candidates C_k. For candidate pruning, computing the subsequences of a candidate that satisfy $\mathcal{C}'$ may no longer be trivial, implying additional computational overhead. We should note, however, that candidate generation and pruning are inexpensive CPU-bound operations that typically constitute only a small fraction of the overall computational cost. This fact is also clearly demonstrated in our experimental results (Section 4). Thus, the major tradeoff that needs to be considered when choosing a specific $\mathcal{C}'$ from among the spectrum of possible relaxations of $\mathcal{C}$ is the extent to which that choice impacts the effectiveness of constraint-based and support-based pruning. The objective, of course, is to strike a reasonable balance between the two different types of pruning so as to minimize the number of candidates for which support is actually counted in each pass.

3.1.2 The SPIRIT Algorithms

The four SPIRIT algorithms for constrained pattern mining are points spanning the entire spectrum of relaxations for the user-specified RE constraint $\mathcal{C} \equiv \mathcal{R}$. Essentially, the four algorithms represent a natural progression, with each algorithm pushing a stronger relaxation of $\mathcal{R}$ than its predecessor in the pattern mining loop [4]. The first SPIRIT algorithm, termed SPIRIT(N) ("N" for Naive), employs the weakest relaxation of $\mathcal{R}$ – it only prunes candidate sequences containing elements that do not appear in $\mathcal{R}$. The second algorithm, termed SPIRIT(L) ("L" for Legal), requires every candidate sequence to be *legal* with respect to some state of $\mathcal{A}_\mathcal{R}$. The third algorithm, termed SPIRIT(V) ("V" for Valid), goes one step further by filtering out candidate sequences that are not *valid with respect to any state of* $\mathcal{A}_\mathcal{R}$. Finally, the SPIRIT(R) algorithm ("R" for Regular) essentially pushes $\mathcal{R}$ "all the way" inside the mining process by counting support only for *valid* candidate sequences, i.e., sequences accepted by $\mathcal{A}_\mathcal{R}$. Table 2 summarizes the constraint choices for the four members of the SPIRIT family within the general framework depicted in Figure 2. Note that, of the four SPIRIT algorithms, SPIRIT(N) is the only one employing an anti-monotone (and, trivial) relaxation $\mathcal{C}'$. Also, note that the progressive increase in the strength of $\mathcal{C}'$ implies a subset relationship between the frequent sequences determined for each pass k; that is,

$$F_k^{SPIRIT(R)} \subseteq F_k^{SPIRIT(V)} \subseteq F_k^{SPIRIT(L)} \subseteq F_k^{SPIRIT(N)}.$$

The remainder of this section provides a detailed discussion of the candidate generation and candidate pruning phases for each of the SPIRIT algorithms. Appropriate terminating conditions (Step 15) are also presented. The quantitative study of the constraint-based vs. support-based pruning tradeoff for the SPIRIT algorithms is deferred until the presentation of our experimental results (Section 4).

Algorithm	Relaxed Constraint $\mathcal{C}'$ ($\mathcal{C} \equiv \mathcal{R}$)
SPIRIT(N)	all elements appear in $\mathcal{R}$
SPIRIT(L)	legal wrt some state of $\mathcal{A}_\mathcal{R}$
SPIRIT(V)	valid wrt some state of $\mathcal{A}_\mathcal{R}$
SPIRIT(R)	valid, i.e., $\mathcal{C}' \equiv \mathcal{C} \equiv \mathcal{R}$

Table 2: The four SPIRIT algorithms.

3.2 The SPIRIT(N) Algorithm

SPIRIT(N) is a simple modification of the GSP algorithm [11] for mining sequential patterns. SPIRIT(N) simply requires that all elements of a candidate sequence s in C_k appear in the RE $\mathcal{R}$. This constraint is clearly anti-monotone, so candidate generation and pruning are performed exactly as in GSP [11].

Candidate Generation. For every pair of $(k-1)$-sequences s and t in F_{k-1}, if $s_{j+1} = t_j$ for all $1 \leq j \leq k-2$, then $< s\ t_{k-1} >$ is added to C_k. This is basically a self-join of F_{k-1}, the join attributes being the last $k-2$ elements of the first sequence and the first $k-2$ elements of the second.

Candidate Pruning. A candidate sequence s is pruned from C_k if at least one of its $(k-1)$-subsequences does not belong to F_{k-1}.

Terminating Condition. The set of frequent k-sequences, F_k, is empty.

3.3 The SPIRIT(L) Algorithm

SPIRIT(L) uses the automaton $\mathcal{A}_\mathcal{R}$ to prune from C_k candidate k-sequences that are not *legal* with respect to any state of $\mathcal{A}_\mathcal{R}$. In our description of SPIRIT(L), we use $F_k(b)$ to denote the set of frequent k-sequences that are legal with respect to state b of $\mathcal{A}_\mathcal{R}$.

Candidate Generation. For each state b in $\mathcal{A}_\mathcal{R}$, we add to C_k candidate k-sequences that are legal with respect to b and have the potential to be frequent.

Lemma 3.1: Consider a k-sequence s that is legal with respect to state b in $\mathcal{A}_\mathcal{R}$, where $b \xrightarrow{s_1} c$ is a transition in $\mathcal{A}_\mathcal{R}$. For s to be frequent, $< s_1 \cdots s_{k-1} >$ must be in $F_{k-1}(b)$ and $< s_2 \cdots s_k >$ must be in $F_{k-1}(c)$. ∎

Thus, the candidate sequences for state b can be computed as follows. For every sequence s in $F_{k-1}(b)$, if $b \xrightarrow{s_1} c$ is a transition in $\mathcal{A}_\mathcal{R}$, then for every sequence t in $F_{k-1}(c)$ such that $s_{j+1} = t_j$ for all $1 \leq j \leq k-2$, the candidate sequence $< s\ t_{k-1} >$ is added to C_k. This is basically a join of $F_{k-1}(b)$ and $F_{k-1}(c)$, on the condition that the

[4]The development of the SPIRIT algorithms is based on the equivalent automaton form $\mathcal{A}_\mathcal{R}$ of the user-specified RE constraint $\mathcal{R}$. Algorithms for constructing $\mathcal{A}_\mathcal{R}$ from $\mathcal{R}$ can be found in the theory literature [6].

$(k-2)$-length suffix of $s \in F_{k-1}(b)$ matches the $(k-2)$-length prefix of $t \in F_{k-1}(c)$ and $b \xrightarrow{s_1} c$ is a transition in $\mathcal{A}_{\mathcal{R}}$.

Candidate Pruning. Given a sequence s in C_k, the candidate generation step ensures that both its prefix and suffix of length $k-1$ are frequent. We also know that in order for s to be frequent, every subsequence of s must also be frequent. However, since we only count support for sequences that are legal with respect to some state of $\mathcal{A}_{\mathcal{R}}$, we can prune s from C_k only if we find a *legal* subsequence of s that is not frequent (i.e., not in F). The candidate pruning procedure computes the set of maximal subsequences of s with length less than k that are legal with respect to some state of automaton $\mathcal{A}_{\mathcal{R}}$. If any of these maximal subsequences is not contained in F, then s is deleted from C_k.

We now describe an algorithm for computing the maximal legal subsequences of a candidate sequence s. Let maxSeq(b, s) denote the set of maximal subsequences of s that are legal with respect to state b of $\mathcal{A}_{\mathcal{R}}$. Then, if we let $t = < s_2 \cdots s_{|s|} >$, a superset of maxSeq($b$, s) can be computed from maxSeq(b, t) using the fact that: (a) maxSeq$(b, s) \subseteq$ maxSeq$(b, t) \cup \{< s_1\ u >: u \in$ maxSeq$(c, t)\} \cup \{s_1\}$, if $b \xrightarrow{s_1} c$ is a transition in $\mathcal{A}_{\mathcal{R}}$; and, (b) maxSeq$(b, s) \subseteq$ maxSeq(b, t), otherwise. The intuition is that for a subsequence $v \in$ maxSeq(b, s), *either* v does not involve s_1, in which case v is a maximal subsequence of t that is legal with respect to b, *or* $v_1 = s_1$ and $< v_2 \cdots v_{|v|} >$ is a maximal subsequence of t with respect to state c. Based on the above observation, we propose a *dynamic programming* algorithm, termed FINDMAXSUBSEQ, for computing maxSeq(b, s) for all states b of $\mathcal{A}_{\mathcal{R}}$ (Figure 3). Intuitively, FINDMAXSUBSEQ works by computing the set maxSeq for successively longer suffixes of the input sequence s, beginning with the suffix consisting of only the last element of s.

More specifically, given an input sequence s and two sets of states in $\mathcal{A}_{\mathcal{R}}$ ($Start$ and End), algorithm FINDMAXSUBSEQ returns the set of all maximal subsequences t of s such that (a) the length of t is less than $|s|$, and (b) t is legal with respect to a state b in $Start$ and if $b \overset{t}{\Rightarrow} c$, then $c \in End$. In each iteration of the for loop spanning Steps 3–17, for each state b in $\mathcal{A}_{\mathcal{R}}$, maximal legal subsequences for the suffix $< s_l \cdots s_{|s|} >$ are computed and stored in maxSeq[b]. At the start of the lth iteration, maxSeq[b] contains the maximal subsequences of $< s_{l+1} \cdots s_{|s|} >$ that are both legal with respect to state b and result in a state in End. Thus, if a transition from b to c on element s_l is in $\mathcal{A}_{\mathcal{R}}$, then the maximal legal subsequences for b comprise those previously computed for $< s_{l+1} \cdots s_{|s|} >$ and certain new sequences involving element s_l. These new sequences containing s_l are computed in the body of the for loop spanning Steps 5–9 and stored in tmpSeq[b]. A point to note is that, since we are only interested in maximal legal subsequences that result in a state in End, we add s_l to tmpSeq[b] only if $c \in End$ (Step 7).

After the new maximal subsequences involving s_l are stored in tmpSeq[b] for every state b of $\mathcal{A}_{\mathcal{R}}$, they are added to maxSeq[b], following which, non-maximal subsequences in maxSeq[b] are deleted (Steps 11–16)[5]. Finally, after maximal legal subsequences for the entire sequence s have been computed for all the states of $\mathcal{A}_{\mathcal{R}}$, only those for states in $Start$ are returned (Step 18).

```
Procedure FINDMAXSUBSEQ(Start, End, s)
begin
1.  for each state b in automaton A_R do
2.      maxSeq[b] := ∅
3.  for l := |s| down to 1 do {
4.      for each state b in automaton A_R do {
5.          tmpSeq[b] = ∅
6.          if (there exists a transition b --s_l--> c in A_R) {
7.              if (c ∈ End) tmpSeq[b] := {s_l}
8.              tmpSeq[b] := tmpSeq[b] ∪{< s_l t >: t ∈ maxSeq[c]}
9.          }
10.     }
11.     for each state b in automaton A_R do {
12.         maxSeq[b] := maxSeq[b] ∪ tmpSeq[b]
13.         for each sequence t in maxSeq[b] do
14.             if (there exists u in maxSeq[b] − {< s_l ··· s_|s| >}
                such that t is a subsequence of u)
15.                 delete t from maxSeq[b]
16.     }
17. }
18. return ∪_{b∈Start} maxSeq[b] - {s} (after
        deleting non-maximal sequences)
end
```

Figure 3: Algorithm for finding maximal subsequences.

To recap, the candidate pruning procedure of SPIRIT(L) invokes FINDMAXSUBSEQ to determine all the maximal legal subsequences of each candidate s in C_k, and deletes s from C_k if any of these subsequences is not frequent. For SPIRIT(L), algorithm FINDMAXSUBSEQ is invoked with $Start$ and End both equal to the set of all states in $\mathcal{A}_{\mathcal{R}}$.

Terminating Condidition. The set of frequent k-sequences that are legal with respect to the start state a of $\mathcal{A}_{\mathcal{R}}$ is empty; that is, $F_k(a)$ is empty.

Time Complexity. Consider the candidate pruning overhead for a candidate k-sequence s in C_k. Compared to the candidate pruning step of SPIRIT(N), which has a time complexity of $O(k)$ (to determine the k subsequences of s), the computational overhead of candidate pruning in SPIRIT(L) can be significantly higher. More specifically, the worst-case time complexity of computing the maximal legal subsequences of s using algorithm FINDMAXSUBSEQ can be shown to be $O(k^2 * |\mathcal{A}_{\mathcal{R}}| * |\text{maxSeq}(s)|)$, where $|\mathcal{A}_{\mathcal{R}}|$ is the number of states in $\mathcal{A}_{\mathcal{R}}$ and $|\text{maxSeq}(s)|$ is the number of maximal legal subsequences for s. To see this, note that the outermost **for** loop in Step 3 of FINDMAXSUBSEQ is executed k times. The time complexity of the first **for** loop in Step 4 is $O(|\mathcal{A}_{\mathcal{R}}| * |\text{maxSeq}(s)|)$,

[5] In Steps 13–15, we have to be careful not to consider $< s_l \cdots s_{|s|} >$ to delete other sequences in maxSeq[b] since we are interested in maximal sequences whose length is *less than* $|s|$.

while that of the second **for** loop in Step 11 is $O(k * |\mathcal{A_R}| * |\text{maxSeq}(s)|)$, since maxSeq[$b$] can be implemented as a trie, for which insertions, deletions, and subsequence checking for k-sequences can all be carried out in $O(k)$ time.

We must point out that the higher time complexity of candidate pruning in SPIRIT(L) is not a major efficiency concern since (a) the overhead of candidate generation and pruning is typically a tiny fraction of the cost of counting supports for candidates in C_k, and (b) in practice, $|\text{maxSeq}(s)|$ can be expected to be small for most sequences. In the worst case, however, for a k-sequence, $|\text{maxSeq}(s)|$ can be $O(2^k)$. This worst case scenario can be avoided by imposing an a-priori limit on the size of maxSeq[b] in FINDMAXSUBSEQ and using appropriate heuristics for selecting *victims* (to be ejected from maxSeq[b]) when its size exceeds that limit.

Space Overhead. SPIRIT(N) only utilizes F_{k-1} for the candidate generation and pruning phases during the kth pass. In contrast, the candidate pruning step of SPIRIT(L) requires F to be stored in main memory since the maximal legal subsequences of a candidate k-sequence may be of any length less than k. However, this should not pose a serious problem since each F_k computed by SPIRIT(L) contains only frequent and legal k-sequences, which are typically few compared to all frequent k-sequences. In addition, powerful servers with several gigabytes of memory are now fairly commonplace. Thus, in most cases, it should be possible to accommodate all the sequences in F in main memory. In the occasional event that F does not fit in memory, one option would be to only store $F_{k-l}, \ldots, F_{k-1}$ for some $l \geq 1$. Of course, this means that maximal subsequences whose length is less than $k - l$ cannot be used to prune candidates from C_k during the candidate pruning step.

3.4 The SPIRIT(V) Algorithm

SPIRIT(V) uses a stronger relaxed constraint $\mathcal{C}'$ than SPIRIT(L) during candidate generation and pruning. More specifically, SPIRIT(V) requires every candidate sequence to be *valid* with respect to some state of $\mathcal{A_R}$[6]. In our description of SPIRIT(V), we use $F_k(b)$ to denote the set of frequent k-sequences that are valid with respect to state b of $\mathcal{A_R}$.

Candidate Generation. Since every candidate sequence s in C_k is required to be valid with respect to some state b, it must be the case that the $(k-1)$-length suffix of s is both frequent and valid with respect to state c, where $b \xrightarrow{s_1} c$ is a transition in $\mathcal{A_R}$. Thus, given a state b of $\mathcal{A_R}$, the set of potentially frequent and valid k-sequences with respect to b can be generated using the following rule: for every transition $b \xrightarrow{s_i} c$, for every sequence t in $F_{k-1}(c)$, add $< s_i\ t >$ to the set of candidates for state b. The set C_k is simply the union of these candidate sets over all states b of $\mathcal{A_R}$.

[6]Note that an alternative approach would be to require candidates to be legal with respect to the start state of $\mathcal{A_R}$. This approach is essentially symmetric to SPIRIT(V) and is not explored further in this paper.

Candidate Pruning. The pruning phase of SPIRIT(V) is very similar to that of SPIRIT(L), except that only valid (rather that legal) subsequences of a candidate can be used for pruning. More specifically, given a candidate sequence s in C_k, we compute all maximal subsequences of s that are valid with respect to some state of $\mathcal{A_R}$ and have length less than k. This is done by invoking algorithm FINDMAXSUBSEQ with $Start$ equal to the set of all states of $\mathcal{A_R}$ and End equal to the set of all *accept* states of $\mathcal{A_R}$. If any of these subsequences is not contained in F, then s is deleted from C_k.

Terminating Condition. The set of frequent k-sequences F_k is empty. Unlike SPIRIT(L), we cannot terminate SPIRIT(V) based on just $F_k(a)$ becoming empty (where a is the start state of $\mathcal{A_R}$). The reason is that, even though there may be no frequent and valid sequences of length k for a, there could still be longer sequences that are frequent and valid with respect to a.

3.5 The SPIRIT(R) Algorithm

SPIRIT(R) essentially pushes the RE constraint $\mathcal{R}$ "all the way" inside the pattern mining computation, by requiring every candidate sequence for which support is counted to be valid (i.e., $\mathcal{C}' \equiv \mathcal{R}$).

Candidate Generation. Since F contains only valid and frequent sequences, there is no efficient mechanism for generating candidate k-sequences other than a "brute force" enumeration using the automaton $\mathcal{A_R}$. The idea is to traverse the states and transitions of $\mathcal{A_R}$ enumerating all paths of length k that begin with the start state and end at an accept state. Obviously, each such path corresponds to a valid k-sequence containing the elements that label the transitions in the path. (The terms "path" and "sequence" are used interchangeably in the following description.)

We employ two optimizations to improve the efficiency of the above exhaustive path enumeration scheme. Our first optimization uses the observation that, if a path of length less than k corresponds to a sequence that is valid but not frequent, then further extending the path is unnecessary since it cannot yield frequent k-sequences. The second optimization involves exploiting *cycles* in $\mathcal{A_R}$ to reduce computation.

Lemma 3.2: Suppose for a path $< t\ u >$ (of length less than k), both t and $< t\ u >$ result in the same state from the start state a. (That is, u corresponds to a cycle in $\mathcal{A_R}$.) Then, if the path $< t\ u\ v >$ obtained as a result of extending $< t\ u >$ with v is to yield a candidate k-sequence, it must be the case that $< t\ v >$ is both frequent and valid. ∎

Consider the generation of candidate k-sequences C_k. Given a path $< t\ u >$ satisfying the assumptions of Lemma 3.2, we only need to extend $< t\ u >$ with sequences v for which $< t\ v >$ belongs to $F_{|<t\ v>|}$ (since the length of $< t\ v >$ is less than k). Due to space constraints, we have omitted the detailed definition of the candidate generation algorithm for SPIRIT(R) and examples of its operation. The interested reader is referred to [5].

Candidate Pruning. A candidate sequence s in C_k can be pruned if a valid subsequence of s is not frequent. The maximal valid subsequences of s can be computed by invoking algorithm FINDMAXSUBSEQ with $Start$ equal to $\{a\}$ and End equal to the set of all accept states of $\mathcal{A_R}$.

Terminating Condition. For some iteration j, sets $F_j, \ldots, F_{j+|\mathcal{A_R}|-1}$ are all empty, where $|\mathcal{A_R}|$ is the number of states in automaton $\mathcal{A_R}$. To see this, consider any frequent and valid sequence s whose length is greater than $j + |\mathcal{A_R}| - 1$. Obviously, s contains at least one cycle of length at most $|\mathcal{A_R}|$ and, therefore, s must contain at least one frequent and valid subsequence of length at least j. However, no valid sequence with length greater than or equal to j is frequent (since $F_j, \ldots, F_{j+|\mathcal{A_R}|-1}$ are all empty). Thus, s cannot be a frequent and valid sequence.

4 Experimental Results

In this section, we present an empirical study of the four SPIRIT algorithms with synthetic and real-life data sets. The objective of this study is twofold: (1) to establish the effectiveness of allowing and exploiting RE constraints during sequential pattern mining; and, (2) to quantify the constraint-based vs. support-based pruning tradeoff for the SPIRIT family of algorithms (Section 3.1).

In general, RE constraints whose automata contain fewer transitions per state, fewer cycles, and longer paths tend to be more *selective*, since they impose more stringent restrictions on the ordering of items in the mined patterns. Our expectation is that for RE constraints that are more selective, constraint-based pruning will be very effective and the latter SPIRIT algorithms will perform better. On the other hand, less selective REs increase the importance of good support-based pruning, putting algorithms that use the RE constraint too aggressively (like SPIRIT(R)) at a disadvantage. Our experimental results corroborate our expectations. More specifically, our findings can be summarized as follows.

1. The SPIRIT(V) algorithm emerges as the overall winner, providing consistently good performance over the entire range of RE constraints. For certain REs, SPIRIT(V) is more than an order of magnitude faster than the "naive" SPIRIT(N) scheme.
2. For highly selective RE constraints, SPIRIT(R) outperforms the remaining algorithms. However, as the RE constraint becomes less selective, the number of candidates generated by SPIRIT(R) explodes and the algorithm fails to even complete execution for certain cases (it runs out of virtual memory).
3. The overheads of the candidate generation and pruning phases for the SPIRIT(L) and SPIRIT(V) algorithms are negligible. They typically constitute less than 1% of the total execution time, even for complex REs with automata containing large numbers of transitions, states, and cycles.

Thus, our results validate the thesis of this paper that incorporating RE constraints into the mining process can lead to significant performance benefits. All experiments reported in this section were performed on a Sun Ultra-2/200 workstation with 512 MB of main memory, running Solaris 2.5. The data sets were stored on a local disk.

4.1 Synthetic Data Sets

We used a synthetic data set generator to create a database of sequences containing items. The input parameters to our generator include the number of sequences in the database, the average length of each sequence, the number of distinct items, and a Zipf parameter z that governs the probability of occurrence, $\frac{1}{i^z}/\Sigma_i \frac{1}{i^z}$, of each item i in the database. The length for each sequence is selected from a Poisson distribution with mean equal to the average sequence length. Note that an item can appear multiple times in a single data sequence.

In addition, since we are interested in a sensitivity analysis of our algorithms with respect to the RE constraint $\mathcal{R}$, we used an RE generator to produce constraints with a broad range of selectivities. Each RE constraint output by the generator consists of *blocks* and each block in turn contains *terms* with the following structure. A term T_i is a disjunction of items and has the form $(s_1 \mid s_2 \mid \cdots \mid s_l)$. Each block B_i is simply a concatenation of terms, $T_1 T_2 \cdots T_m$. Finally, the constraint $\mathcal{R}$ is constructed from blocks and has the form $(B_1 \mid B_2 \mid \cdots \mid B_n)^*$ – thus, every sequence that satisfies $\mathcal{R}$ is a concatenation of one or more sequences satisfying the block constraints. The generic structure of the automaton $\mathcal{A_R}$ for $\mathcal{R}$ is shown in Figure 4. RE constraints with different selectivities can be generated by varying the number of items per term, the number of terms per block, and the number of blocks in $\mathcal{R}$. Note that, in terms of the automaton $\mathcal{A_R}$, these parameters correspond to the number of transitions between a pair of states in $\mathcal{A_R}$, the length of each cycle, and the number of cycles contained in $\mathcal{A_R}$, respectively.

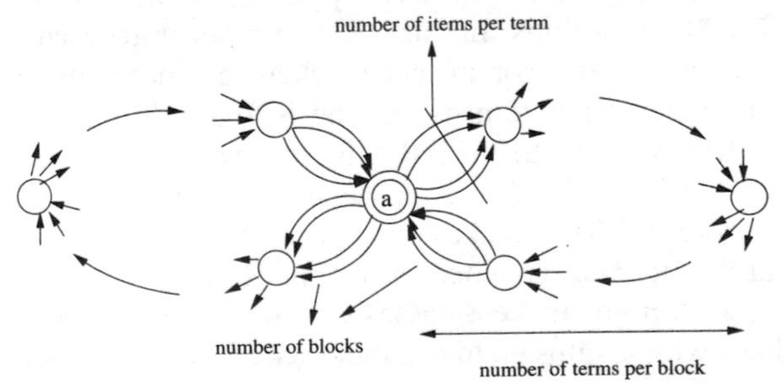

Figure 4: Structure of automaton for RE generation.

The RE generator accepts the maximum number of items per term, the number of terms per block, and the number of blocks as input parameters. In the RE constraint that it outputs, the number of items per term is uniformly distributed between 1 and the maximum specified value.

The items in each term of $\mathcal{R}$ are chosen using the same Zipfian distribution that was used to generate the data set. The RE generator thus enables us to carry out an extensive study of the sensitivity of our algorithms to a wide range of RE constraints with different selectivities.

Table 3 shows the parameters for the data set and the RE constraint, along with their default values and the range of values for which experiments were conducted. The default value of $z = 1.0$ was chosen to model an (approximate) 70-30 rule and to ensure that the item skew was sufficient for some interesting patterns to appear in the data sequences. In each experiment, one parameter was varied with all other parameters fixed at their default values. Once again, due to space constraints, we only present a subset of our experimental results. The full set of results (including scaleup and maximum distance experiments) can be found in [5].

Parameter	**Default**	**Range**
No. of Sequences	10^5	$5 \cdot 10^4 - 2.5 \cdot 10^5$
Avg. Sequence Length	10	
No. of Items	1000	
Zipf Value	1.0	
Max. No. of Items per Term	10	2 – 30
No. of Terms Per Block	4	2 – 10
No. of Blocks	4	2 – 10
Min. Support	1.0	0.5 – 2.0
Max. Distance	2	0 – 15

Table 3: Synthetic data and RE constraint parameters.

4.2 Performance Results with Synthetic Data Sets

Maximum Number of Items Per Term. Figure 5(a) illustrates the execution times of the SPIRIT algorithms as the maximum number of items per term in $\mathcal{R}$ is increased. As expected, as the number of items is increased, the number of transitions per state in $\mathcal{A_R}$ also increases and so do the numbers of legal and valid sequences. Thus, constraint-based pruning becomes less effective and the performance of all SPIRIT algorithms deteriorates as more items are added to each term. As long as the number of items per term does not exceed 15, $\mathcal{R}$ is fairly selective; consequently, constraint-based pruning works well and the SPIRIT algorithms that use $\mathcal{R}$ to prune more candidates perform better. For instance, when the maximum number of items per term is 10, the SPIRIT(N), SPIRIT(L), SPIRIT(V), and SPIRIT(R) algorithms count support for 7105, 1418, 974, and 3822 candidate sequences, respectively. SPIRIT(R) makes only two passes over the data for valid candidate sequences of lengths 4 and 8. The remaining algorithms make 8 passes to count supports for candidates with lengths up to 8, a majority of which have lengths 4 and 5.

However, beyond 15 items per term, the performance of the algorithms that rely more heavily on constraint $\mathcal{R}$ for pruning candidates degenerates rapidly. SPIRIT(R) sustains the hardest hit since it performs very little support-based pruning and its exhaustive enumeration approach for candidate generation results in an enormous number of candidates of length 4. In contrast, since SPIRIT(N) only uses $\mathcal{R}$ to prune sequences not involving items in $\mathcal{R}$, and few new items are added to terms in $\mathcal{R}$ once the number of items per term reaches 15, the execution times for the SPIRIT(N) algorithm hold steady. Beyond 25 items per term, the running times of SPIRIT(L) and SPIRIT(V) also stabilize, since decreases in the amount of constraint-based pruning as $\mathcal{R}$ becomes less selective are counterbalanced by increases in support-based pruning. At 30 items per term, SPIRIT(V) continues to provide a good balance of constraint-based and support-based pruning and, thus, performs the best.

Number of Terms Per Block. The graph in Figure 5(b) plots the running times for the SPIRIT algorithms as the number of terms per block is varied from 2 to 10. Increasing the number of terms per block actually causes each cycle (involving the start state a) to become longer. The initial dip in execution times for SPIRIT(L), SPIRIT(V), and SPIRIT(R) when the number of terms is increased from 2 to 4 is due to the reduction in the number of candidate sequences of lengths 4 and 5. This happens because with short cycles of length 2 in $\mathcal{A_R}$, sequences of length 4 and 5 visit the start state multiple times and the start state has a large number of outgoing transitions. But when $\mathcal{A_R}$ contains cycles of length 4 or more, the start state is visited at most once, thus causing the number of candidate sequences of lengths 4 and 5 to decrease. As cycle lengths grow beyond 4, the number of legal sequences (with respect to a state in $\mathcal{A_R}$) starts to increase due to the increase in the number of states in each cycle. However, the number of valid sequences (with respect to a state in $\mathcal{A_R}$) does not vary much since each of them is still required to terminate at the start state a.

Note that when the number of terms exceeds 6, the number of candidates generated by SPIRIT(R) simply explodes due to the longer cycles. On the other hand, SPIRIT(V) provides consistently good performance throughout the entire range of block sizes.

Number of Blocks. Figure 6(a) depicts the performance of the four algorithms as the number of blocks in $\mathcal{R}$ is increased from 2 to 10. The behavior of the four algorithms has similarities to the "number of items per term" case (Figure 5(a)). The only difference is that, as the number of blocks is increased, the decrease in $\mathcal{R}$'s selectivity and the increase in the number of legal and valid sequences in $\mathcal{A_R}$ are not as dramatic. This is because the number of blocks only affects the number of transitions associated with the start state – the number of transitions for other states in $\mathcal{A_R}$ stays the same. Once again, SPIRIT(V) performs well consistently, for the entire range of numbers of blocks. An interesting case is that of SPIRIT(R) whose execution time does degrade beyond SPIRIT(V)'s, as the number of blocks is increased, but it still manages to do better than SPIRIT(L), even when $\mathcal{R}$ contains 10 blocks. This can be attributed predominantly to the effectiveness of the optimization for cycles in $\mathcal{A_R}$ that is applied during SPIRIT(R)'s candidate generation phase. In general, due to

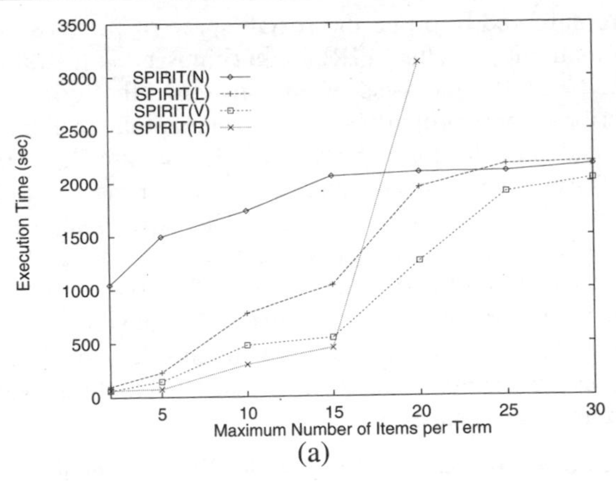

(a)

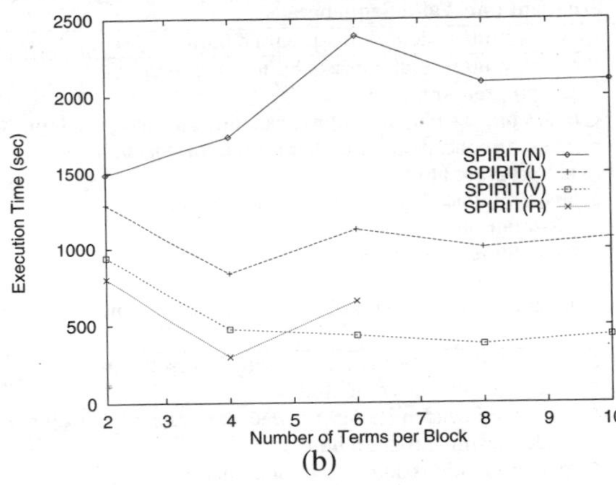

(b)

Figure 5: Performance results for (a) number of items and (b) number of terms.

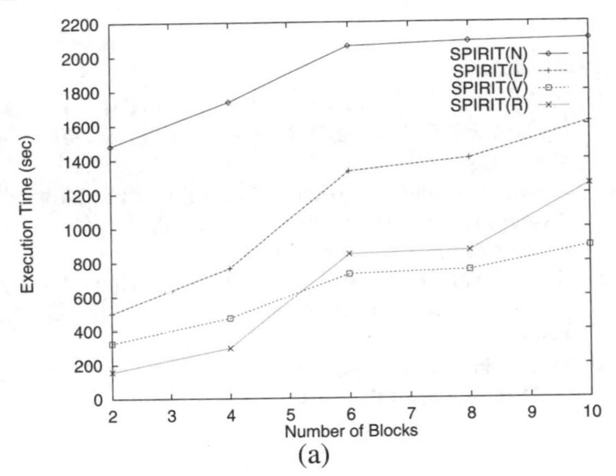

(a)

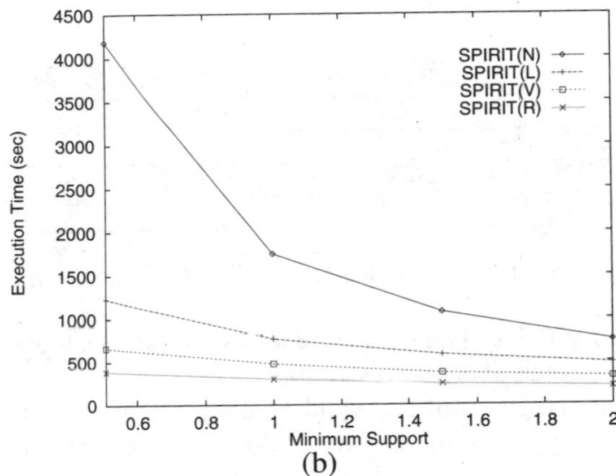

(b)

Figure 6: Performance results for (a) number of blocks and (b) minimum support.

our cycle optimization, one can expect the SPIRIT(R) algorithm to perform reasonably well, even when $\mathcal{A}_{\mathcal{R}}$ contains a large number of cycles of moderate length.

Minimum Support. The execution times for the SPIRIT algorithms as the minimum support threshold is increased from 0.5 to 2.0 are depicted in Figure 6(b). As expected, the performance of all algorithms improves as the minimum support threshold is increased. This is because fewer candidates have the potential to be frequent for higher values of minimum support. Furthermore, note that the running times of algorithms that rely more heavily on support-based pruning improve much more rapidly.

4.3 Real-life Data Set

For our real-life data experiments, we used the WWW server access logs from the web site of an academic CS department[7]. The logs contain the sequences of web pages accessed by each user[8] starting from the department's web site, for the duration of a week. The department's home page contains links to a number of topics, including `Academics`, `Admissions`, `Events`, `General information`, `Research`, `People`, and `Resources`. There are additional links to the university and college home pages to which the CS department belongs, but we chose not to use these links in our RE constraint. Users navigate through the web pages by clicking on links in each page, and the sequences of pages accessed by a user are captured in the server logs.

We used a RE constraint to focus on user access patterns that start with the department's home page (located at `/main.html`) and end at the web page containing information on the M.S. degree program (located at `/academics/ms-program.html`). In addition, we restricted ourselves to patterns for which the intermediate pages belong to one of the aforementioned 7 topics (e.g., `Academics`). Thus, the automaton $\mathcal{A}_{\mathcal{R}}$ contains three states. There is a transition from the first (start) state to the second on `/main.html` and a transition from the second state to the third (accept) state on `/academics/ms-program.html`. The second state has 15 transitions to itself, each labeled with the location of a web page belonging to one of the above 7 topics. We used a minimum support

[7] At the department's request, we do not disclose its identity.

[8] We use IP addresses to distinguish between users.

Size	Frequent and Valid Sequences
2	< /main.html/academics/ms-program.html >
3	< /main.html/general/contacts.html/academics/ ms-program.html >
	< /main.html/general/nav.html/academics/ms-program.html >
	< /main.html/academics/academics.html/academics/ ms-program.html >
	< /main.html/academics/nav.html/academics/ ms-program.html >
	< /main.html/admissions/nav.html/academics/ ms-program.html >
	< /main.html/admissions/admissions.html/academics/ ms-program.html >
4	< /main.html/general/nav.html/general/contacts.html/ academics/ms-program.html >
	< /main.html/academics/nav.html/academics/academics.html/ academics/ms-program.html >
	< /main.html/admissions/nav.html/admissions/ admissions.html/academics/ms-program.html >

Table 4: Interesting patterns discovered in the WWW logs.

Algorithm	Exec. Time (sec)	Candidates	Passes
SPIRIT(N)	1562.8	5896	13
SPIRIT(L)	32.77	1393	10
SPIRIT(V)	16.0.	59	5
SPIRIT(R)	17.67	52	7

Table 5: Execution statistics for the SPIRIT algorithms.

threshold of 0.3%. The number of access sequences logged in the one week data set was 12868.

The mined frequent and valid access patterns are listed in increasing order of size in Table 4. Note that there is a number of distinct ways to access the M.S. degree program web page by following different sequences of links (e.g., via admissions, academics). The execution times and the numbers of candidates generated by the four SPIRIT algorithms are presented in Table 5. As expected, since the RE constraint is fairly selective, both SPIRIT(V) and SPIRIT(R) have the smallest running times. SPIRIT(L) is about twice as slow compared to SPIRIT(V) and SPIRIT(R). The execution time for SPIRIT(N) is almost two orders of magnitude worse than SPIRIT(V) and SPIRIT(R), since it generates a significantly larger number of candidate sequences with lengths between 5 and 9 (almost 4000). We believe that our results clearly demonstrate the significant performance gains that can be attained by pushing RE constraints inside a *real-life* pattern mining task.

5 Conclusions

In this paper, we have proposed the use of Regular Expressions (REs) as a flexible constraint specification tool that enables user-controlled focus to be incorporated into the pattern mining process. We have developed a family of novel algorithms (termed SPIRIT) for mining frequent sequential patterns that also satisfy user-specified RE constraints. The main distinguishing factor among the proposed schemes is the degree to which the RE constraints are enforced to prune the search space of patterns during computation. The SPIRIT algorithms are illustrative of the tradeoffs that arise when constraints that do not subscribe to nice properties (like anti-monotonicity) are integrated into the mining process. To explore these tradeoffs, we have conducted an extensive experimental study on synthetic and real-life data sets. The experimental results clearly validate the effectiveness of our approach, showing that speedups of more than an order of magnitude are possible when RE constraints are pushed deep inside the mining process. Our experimentation with real-life data also illustrates the versatility of REs as a user-level tool for focusing on interesting patterns.

Acknowledgments: We would like to thank Narain Gehani, Hank Korth, and Avi Silberschatz for their encouragement. Without the support of Yesook Shim, it would have been impossible to complete this work.

References

[1] R. Agrawal, G. Psaila, E. L. Wimmers, and M. Zaït. "Querying Shapes of Histories". In *Proc. of the 21st Intl. Conf. on Very Large Data Bases*, September 1995.

[2] R. Agrawal and R. Srikant. "Fast Algorithms for Mining Association Rules". In *Proc. of the 20th Intl. Conf. on Very Large Data Bases*, September 1994.

[3] R. Agrawal and R. Srikant. "Mining Sequential Patterns". In *Proc. of the 11th Intl. Conf. on Data Engineering*, March 1995.

[4] M.-S. Chen, J. S. Park, and P. S. Yu. "Efficient Data Mining for Path Traversal Patterns". *IEEE Trans. on Knowledge and Data Engineering*, 10(2):209–221, March 1998.

[5] M. N. Garofalakis, R. Rastogi, and K. Shim. "SPIRIT: Sequential Pattern Mining with Regular Expression Constraints". *Bell Labs Tech. Memorandum BL0112370-990223-03TM*, February 1999.

[6] H. R. Lewis and C. Papadimitriou. *"Elements of the Theory of Computation"*. Prentice Hall, Inc., 1981.

[7] H. Mannila and H. Toivonen. "Discovering Generalized Episodes Using Minimal Occurrences". In *Proc. of the 2nd Intl. Conf. on Knowledge Discovery and Data Mining*, August 1996.

[8] H. Mannila, H. Toivonen, and A. I. Verkamo. "Discovering Frequent Episodes in Sequences". In *Proc. of the 1st Intl. Conf. on Knowledge Discovery and Data Mining*, August 1995.

[9] R. T. Ng, L. V.S. Lakshmanan, J. Han, and A. Pang. "Exploratory Mining and Pruning Optimizations of Constrained Association Rules". In *Proc. of the 1998 ACM SIGMOD Intl. Conf. on Management of Data*, June 1998.

[10] R. Srikant, Q. Vu, and R. Agrawal. "Mining Association Rules with Item Constraints". In *Proc. of the 3rd Intl. Conf. on Knowledge Discovery and Data Mining*, August 1997.

[11] R. Srikant and R. Agrawal. "Mining Sequential Patterns: Generalizations and Performance Improvements". In *Proc. of the 5th Intl. Conf. on Extending Database Technology (EDBT'96)*, March 1996.

[12] J. T.-L. Wang, G.-W. Chirn, T. G. Marr, B. Shapiro, D. Shasha, and K. Zhang. "Combinatorial Pattern Discovery for Scientific Data: Some Preliminary Results". In *Proc. of the 1994 ACM SIGMOD Intl. Conf. on Management of Data*, May 1994.

A Novel Index Supporting High Volume Data Warehouse Insertions

Christopher Jermaine
College of Computing
Georgia Institute of Technology
jermaine@cc.gatech.edu

Anindya Datta
DuPree College of Management
Georgia Institute of Technology
adatta@cc.gatech.edu

Edward Omiecinski
College of Computing
Georgia Institute of Technology
edwardo@cc.gatech.edu

Abstract

While the desire to support fast, ad hoc query processing for large data warehouses has motivated the recent introduction of many new indexing structures, with a few notable exceptions (namely, the LSM-Tree [4] and the Stepped Merge Method [1]) little attention has been given to developing new indexing schemes that allow fast insertions. Since additions to a large warehouse may number in the millions per day, indices that require a disk seek (or even a significant fraction of a seek) per insertion are not acceptable.

In this paper, we offer an alternative to the B+-tree called the *Y-tree* for indexing huge warehouses having frequent insertions. The Y-tree is a new indexing structure supporting both point and range queries over a single attribute, with retrieval performance comparable to the B+-tree. For processing insertions, however, the Y-tree may exhibit a speedup of 100 times over batched insertions into a B+-tree.

1 Introduction

Efficiency in OLAP system operation is of significant current interest, from a research as well as from a practical perspective. There are two primary options for supporting efficient queries over a huge data warehouse. The first option is to allow the user to pre-define a set of views on the warehouse, where query results are at least partially pre-computed and maintained as data are added to the warehouse. The second option is to compute the results of a query only after it has been issued using indexing and fast algorithms, thereby allowing ad-hoc querying of the warehouse. We focus on the second option in this paper.

Work on processing ad-hoc queries over huge warehouses has resulted in the development of a number of special-purpose index structures, such as Projection Indices in Sybase IQ, Bitmapped Indices (BMI) in Oracle and Bitmapped Join Indices (BJI) in Informix and Red-Brick (see [5] for an excellent treatment of these structures). Together with the regular value-list (B+-tree) index, the various grid-based approaches, and hierarchical, multidimensional structures such as the R-tree (we refer the reader to [8] for a survey of these and other access methods), these structures represent a formidable set of options for indexing large warehouses. However, while significant query processing advantages have resulted from these indices, warehouse refresh performance has suffered, seriously affecting the availability of the warehouse.

Warehouse refreshes differ from standard database insertion in that typically, refresh involves the addition of a number of new rows to a single, central fact table. The smaller dimension tables may also grow, but such growth is usually very slow compared to fact table growth. Usually, indexing in a data warehouse is done on foreign keys in the central fact table. If the number of distinct attribute values for a foreign key is relatively small, this can allow for fast index refresh, with only a few localized index changes required for each insertion. It is in this situation that a BMI is particularly useful, since a refresh of the fact table will result in appends of bits to only a few, already existing bitmaps. However, it is not always the case that the number of distinct foreign key values is small. We now present a case where this quantity is not small, and discuss the implications for index refresh.

1.1 Example

We illustrate the problem of maintaining an index in the face of a high insertion rate with an example drawn from the domain of *call detail record* (CDR) warehousing for telecommunication service providers. CDRs are records that are generated corresponding to every call through a telecommunication network. Such records are approximately 700 bytes

Proceedings of the 25th VLDB Conference, Edinburgh, Scotland, 1999.

in length. The AT&T corporation experiences a call detail growth of around 20 GB/day, which translates to approximately 28 million calls per day [2]. When these records are warehoused, assuming significant aggregation with respect to the detail records accumulated in CDR stores, one can reasonably expect an order of magnitude decrease in the number of stored records. This translates to an average addition of nearly 3 million records per day. If seven years worth of data are maintained, the complete warehouse needs to store approximately 8 billion records.

Now, consider a BMI on some attribute of the central fact table of this warehouse, perhaps on the customer account number. It is not unimaginable that on the order of 10 million distinct account numbers would be found in this particular fact table. A BMI on the customer account number would then be made up of 10 million (very sparse) bitmaps composed of *8 billion bits each*. Clearly, this is likely a prohibitive storage requirement.

Of course, these bitmaps could be compressed, but in such an extreme case, it would probably be preferable to use a value-list index, where instead of a bitmap for each customer account number, a list of pointers to fact table entries is stored. Note that if a compression scheme like RLE [3] were used on the BMI, it would essentially become equivalent to using a value-list index. Because of this, and the prohibitive storage costs associated with using an uncompressed BMI in this warehouse, the value-list index is the primary existing option that we will consider for such a situation throughout this paper. Were a value-list index used instead of a BMI, there are two likely approaches to handling the 3 million insertions per day:

- *Incremental, batch insertion* could be used. Insertions could be batched, so that each edge in the tree need be traversed at most once. We have found that on our system, incremental, bulk insertion (following the algorithm outlined in [6]) into a similar structure, under similar conditions (cf. Section 4) can be accomplished at the sustained rate of 100,000 (*key, ptr*) pairs in slightly more than 41 minutes. This means that insertion of 3 million (*key, ptr*) pairs per day could be expected to take longer than 20 hours to complete. In other words, it would barely be possible to keep up with this insertion rate even if all system resources were devoted to maintenance, 24 hours a day. Even if more hardware were added to combat the problem, one can assume that in the face of ever-increasing warehouse sizes, the problem is bound to recur.

- Or, we could forsake the purely incremental approach and rebuild the index, using the old index as a guide. The LSM-Tree [4] and the Stepped Merge Method [1] are two access methods that use a version of such a rebuild of a B+-tree as their fundamental approach. These methods both have the important advantage that the resulting tree structures can be constructed optimally, with full nodes, and long runs of data can be stored sequentially on disk to allow fast query processing. Also important is the fact that since the new structure can be constructed from fast, sequential scans of the old structure, disk seeks can be minimized during construction, thereby drastically decreasing the average time required per insertion when compared to the value-list index. However, a disadvantage of these methods is that in the case of a skewed insertion distribution, entire nodes must be rewritten, even if only a very few key values need be written to that node. We will discuss these issues more in detail in Section 5.

1.2 An Index Allowing Fast Insertions

In response to these issues, we have developed the *YATS-tree* (*Yet Another Tree Structure*-tree) or *Y-tree* for short. The Y-tree is an exceedingly simple, hierarchical, secondary indexing structure for use in evaluating point and range queries over a single attribute, much like the value-list index. In fact, it can be used to support the same set of secondary indexing applications as the value-list index.

However, in contrast to the value-list index, the Y-tree is designed to allow very fast insertions into a huge database. This is accomplished with the idea of a *single-path, bulk insertion*. In a Y-tree, a set of some small number of insertions (say, 500) are batched and inserted at once into the structure. There are no constraints placed on what key values may be in this set and performance is totally unaffected by the key values a batched insertion set contains. Insertion into the Y-tree is called *single-path, bulk insertion* because regardless of the key values, an insertion of a set of (*key, ptr*) pairs will only require a traversal from the tree root to a *single* leaf node holding a list of record identifiers. In this way, the Y-tree can achieve speed-ups on the order of 100 times over incremental, batch insertion into a value-list index. The daily insertion of 3 million key values into the value-list index described above (that would take nearly the entire day to complete) would take less than 12 minutes were a Y-tree used instead.

There *is* a cost associated with the faster insertion times. The Y-tree can produce slower query response times when compared to the value-list index. For example, when used for evaluation of a point query returning a single (*key, ptr*) pair, the Y-tree is on the order of four times slower than the value-list index (point queries, however, are expectedly rare in a warehousing environment). But as the size of the query result increases, as is the case in standard OLAP queries, the efficiency of the Y-tree increases as well. When used for evaluating range queries returning 1 million such pairs for a large database, the Y-tree is only around 50% slower than an optimally, bulk-constructed value-list index, and can be *nearly three times faster* than a value-list index that has been built incrementally. Depending on certain parameters, a

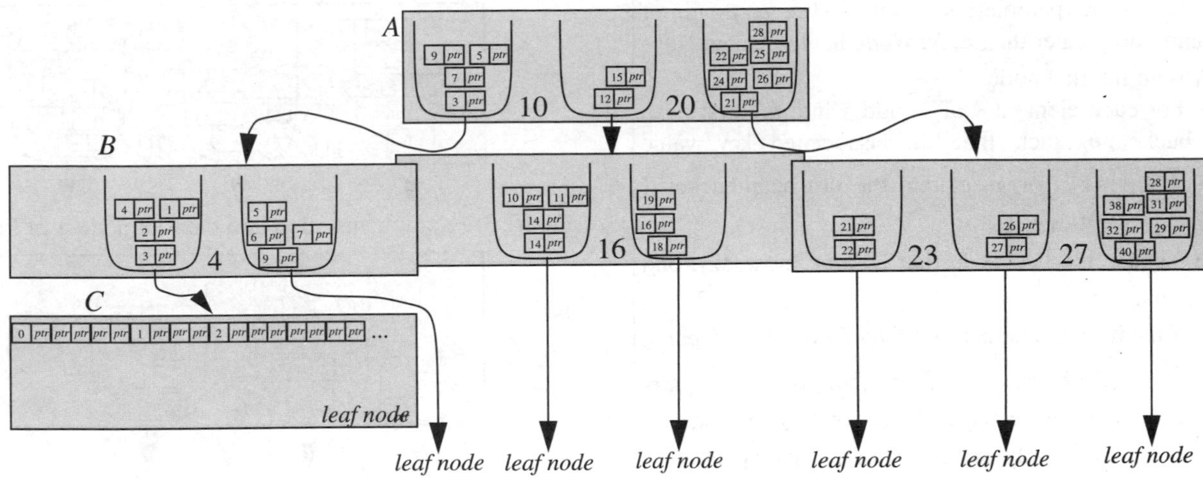

Figure 1: An example Y-tree.

Y-tree may then actually be *preferable* to a value-list index for handling large queries. Combined with the fact that standard, value-list index insertion is virtually unusable for huge, constantly growing databases, we feel that the Y-tree represents an important alternative to the value-list index.

1.3 Paper Organization

This paper is organized as follows. In Section 2, we present the Y-tree structure and the associated algorithms. In Section 3, we present an analytical study of the Y-tree. We compare it to the value-list index, showing that the Y-tree presents a very attractive alternative to the value-list index at query and insertion loads that one would commonly expect in a huge data warehouse. In Section 4, we present experimental results comparing the performance of actual implementations of the two structures. Section 5 presents some related work; we conclude the paper in Section 6.

2 The Y-Tree

The Y-tree is similar in many ways to the value-list index. Like the value-list index, it is a hierarchical structure composed of *leaf nodes* and *internal nodes*:

- *Leaf Nodes*. Assuming that the data are not clustered on disk with respect to the indexed attribute, leaf nodes are simply sets of ordered pairs of the form (*key, ptr-list*) where *key* is a value from the domain of the attribute value to be indexed, and *ptr-list* is a list of RIDs containing that key value. Each leaf node is guaranteed to be at least 50% full at all times. In practice, we have found that a utilization of 65-70% is typical. This much is similar to the classical value-list index.
- *Internal Nodes*. The internal nodes of the Y-tree are quite different from those of the value-list index. Each internal node contains two components, the *pointer-list* and the *heap*. The *pointer-list* is borrowed from the value-list index. It is simply a list of the form:

$$<P_1, K_1, P_2, K_2, ..., P_{f-1}, K_{f-1}, P_f>.$$

The associated *heap* is logically a set of *f buckets*, where *f* is a constant chosen before the structure is constructed. *f* denotes the fanout of the tree. The heap has an associated maximum heap size *h*, which likewise is chosen a priori. Each of the *f* buckets is associated with exactly one pointer to a node lower in the tree, and holds a set of ordered pairs of the form (*key, ptr*). These ordered pairs are identical to those found in the leaf nodes; indeed, they may eventually be moved into leaf nodes from buckets located in internal nodes, as we will describe below.

Logically, then, the Y-tree looks something like what is depicted above in Figure 1. Figure 1 shows a tree constructed with value $f = 3$.

2.1 Insertion Into the Y-tree

The primary goal in designing the Y-tree is to provide for fast insertion while maintaining the functionality of the value-list for indexing quickly evaluating range queries and also point queries. We discuss Y-tree insertion in this section.

2.1.1 Why Insertion Is Fast

Insertion into the Y-tree is very fast because of the two important properties of the Y-tree we describe now. The first property is common to both the Y-tree and the value-list index:

Property 1. The insertion of a (*key, ptr*) pair into the tree results in the reading and writing of nodes on at most one path from root to leaf level in the tree.

The second property is quite different than for a value-list index, and is at the heart of the speed with which insertion into the Y-tree may be accomplished:

Algorithm Insert (parameters *S*: set of (*key, ptr*) pairs of cardinality no greater than *d*, *N: Node* having fanout f_N)

1) If *N* is an internal node:
    2) For each element *s* of *S*, add *s* into the first heap bucket b_i such that the associated key value $K_i \geq s.key$; or, inset into the last heap bucket if there is no such K_i.
    3) Choose the bucket b_j that has the most (*key, ptr*) pairs.
    4) If the heap contains more than $(f_N - 1) \times d$ pairs,
        5) Remove *min* (*d, size*(b_j)) (*key, ptr*) pairs from b_j to create S_{new}, write *N* to disk, and recursively call *Insert* (S_{new}, node pointed to by P_j).
    6) Else, write *N* to disk.
7) Otherwise, *N* is a leaf node:
    8) Simply add *S* to the set of (*key, ptr*) pairs in *N*, then write *N* to disk.

Figure 2: Algorithm to insert *d* (*key, ptr*) pairs into a Y-tree.

Property 2. For a given heap size, there exists some constant *d* such that the cost of inserting *d* (*key, ptr*) pairs into the Y-tree is identical to the cost of inserting a single (*key, ptr*) pair into the tree.

We will elaborate on this property in Section 2.3.2, but the immediate implication of this property is that *d* insertions into the structure may be buffered and inserted *in bulk* into the tree, and that single insertion of *d* pairs *will still result in updates to nodes on only a single path from root to leaf level* in the tree. If *d* is large enough, this has the potential to allow an orders-of-magnitude speedup in time required for insertions into the tree. Also, it is important to note that, as we will describe in a later section, this is quite different (and superior, we argue) to the common method of bulk insertion into a value-list index where a huge number of insertions (perhaps as many as can be fit into main memory) are buffered and a massive update of the tree at one time is performed. In the Y-tree, insertion is still local and incremental. Thus, insertion performance is relatively insensitive to the size of the tree, just as is the case in the classical value-list index. Insertion costs, however, are amortized across insertions of perhaps hundreds of (*key, ptr*) pairs, allowing for a huge speedup.

2.1.2 The Insertion Algorithm

We now describe the algorithm for insertion into the Y-tree, which is quite simple. For the moment, we ignore the issue of full leaf nodes, which may cause node splitting. The algorithm is shown above in Figure 2.

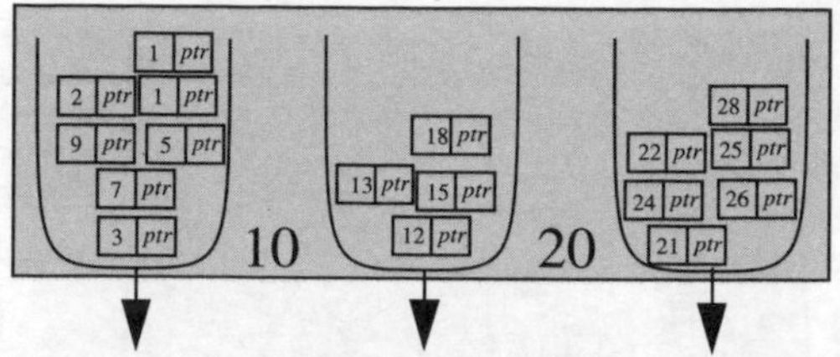

Figure 3: Example insertion into the root node *A* of Figure 1.

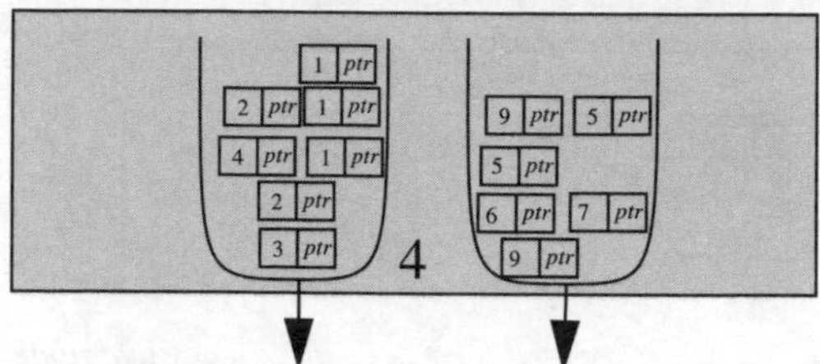

Figure 4: Recursive insertion into node B of Figure 1.

2.1.3 Example Insertion

We now demonstrate the algorithm on the tree of Figure 1, by adding the set *S* = {(1, *ptr*), (1, *ptr*), (2, *ptr*), (13, *ptr*), (18, *ptr*)} to the tree. In this case, *d* = 5. First, *S* is distributed among the buckets of the root node *A*, as shown in Figure 3. Note that the right-most bucket in Figure 3 had more than *d* pairs even *before* the insertion of the set *S*, a state that is indeed possible in practice.

Next, we determine that the leftmost bucket of *A* contains the most pairs. This bucket is then *drained* by removing *d* items from the leftmost bucket of *A*, which are then recursively inserted into the corresponding child node, *B*. Note that the set of *d* pairs drained from a node and recursively inserted into a child node is likely to be different than the set of pairs originally inserted into the node. In our example, after the set of pairs {(1, *ptr*), (1, *ptr*), (2, *ptr*), (5, *ptr*), (9, *ptr*)} has been drained into *B*, *B* will appear as is depicted in Figure 4. Finally, the left bucket of the node *B* will be drained, with the set {(1, *ptr*), (1, *ptr*), (1, *ptr*), (2, *ptr*), (4, *ptr*)} selected and recursively inserted into the proper child, leaf node *C*, of Figure 1.

The reason that a single insertion only follows one path from root to leaf is that at each level of the tree, pairs not following a given path from root to leaf are effectively traded for pairs that do and have been buffered in the heap. The heap within an internal node provides a storage space for items which have been inserted previously but never reached a leaf node. A future insertion will again traverse that internal node, picking up those buffered items and dropping off others en route to a leaf node. By not requiring that the *actual* set of pairs inserted into the tree at that time reach a leaf and instead only requiring that *some* set of pairs of equivalent size reach a leaf, fast insertion can be achieved.

2.2 Node Splits and Queries of the Y-tree

As mentioned previously, when a leaf node becomes full, it must be split. Splits are handled in the same way as in most hierarchical structures. We describe the handling of splits and queries now:

Leaf Node Split: The entries of the leaf node L are partitioned around the median key value k from L. Entries greater than the median key value are placed into a new leaf node, L_{new}. This node is then added to the parent internal node, N_{parent}. The bucket in N_{parent} associated with L is split, with the *(key, ptr)* pairs it contains partitioned around k. Finally, the pointer-list in N_{parent} is updated accordingly.

Internal Node Split: Identical to the leaf node split, except that the node (heap buckets and pointer-list entries) is partitioned around the pointer-list entry $K_{f/2}$.

Queries: Queries to the structure are handled with a simple in-order traversal of the tree. Note that since *(key, ptr)* pairs may be present in buckets in internal nodes, the heaps of internal nodes that are traversed must be searched as well.

2.3 Discussion

In this section, we discuss some of the concerns and practical considerations associated with the use of the Y-tree. In particular, we discuss storage issues and some of the trade-offs involved in choosing values of f and d.

2.3.1 Bucket Growth and Storage

Of practical concern is the amount of heap storage space per internal node that must be allocated to allow a single path, bulk insertion size of d. Not unexpectedly, this requirement scales with f and d:

Theorem 1.3.1. Let n be the number of bytes needed to store a *(key, ptr)* pair. The total *disk* storage required for an internal node heap is at most $(f_N - 1) \times d \times n$, where f_N is the fanout of the node in question.

Proof. The proof is by induction on the number of insertions. Assume that after a previous insertion, there were no more than $max = (f_N - 1) \times d$ *(key, ptr)* pairs in the node. Then, an additional x pairs are inserted into the node such that $0 < x \leq d$. Assume that the node is now overfull by a certain number of pairs o, such that $0 < o \leq d$ (if the node is not overfull, then the node has fewer than *max* pairs after the insert and the theorem trivially holds). In this case, at least one bucket has a minimum of $(max + o)/f_N$ pairs (since to *minimize* the number of pairs in the bucket with the *most* pairs, pairs must be evenly distributed among buckets). Since $o \leq d$, by algebraic manipulation it follows that $o \leq (max + o)/f_N$. Thus, there exists at least one bucket having o or more pairs. After this bucket is drained, the heap again contains fewer than *max* total pairs.

Note the presence of the word *disk* in Theorem 1.3.1. This is important; after a node has been read from disk and the insertion set added, its size while resident in memory may be *greater* than $(f_N - 1) \times d \times n$. However, once it has been drained and written back to disk, Theorem 1.3.1 will again hold. An important related property is the following:

Property 3. While the total heap size is bounded by $(f_N - 1) \times d \times n$ on the upper side for a node N, in practice N will contain $(f_N - 1) \times d$ *(key, ptr)* pairs.

That is, the heaps in all internal levels of the tree tend to fill up quickly; and except immediately after splits occur there is rarely any extra space in a given heap. This implies that there is likely no easy way to decrease the amount of storage space required for an internal node (and increasing the fanout) by somehow making use of some property of the heap.

Also, it is worthwhile to note that there is very little utility in considering the idea of storing the heap for an internal node separately from the pointer-list. This is because both during updates to the structure and during query evaluation, the buckets associated with a node will need to be accessed at the same time as the pointer-list is searched.

2.3.2 Practical Choices of f and d

Choosing f and d is a subjective optimization problem whose choice is balanced by two competing goals: the desire for fast query evaluation times and the desire for fast insertion time. Providing some insight into proper choices of f and d is at the heart of this paper.

We now outline the parameters that can be modified prior to construction of a Y-tree, and briefly describe the costs associated with each:

d: A larger maximum insertion set size typically speeds the insertion rate into the tree.

f: A larger internal node fanout typically decreases query response times and insertion times. However, a high fanout coupled with a large value for d can cause node sizes to become large enough that query evaluation and insertions are slowed.

Node size: Larger internal node sizes typically increase fanout, decreasing query times up to the point where nodes are too large to be read and written quickly. Larger nodes almost always result in faster insertions.

What are typical values of f and d, and typical node sizes? The node size grows proportionally to f and d, so that f = (*Node size* / $(\alpha \times d + \beta)$), where a *(key, ptr)* pair has a size in bytes α and there is some small overhead per bucket β to store pointers, boundaries, and any other information (this quantity is on the order of 12 bytes in a typical implementation). As might be expected from this linear relationship between node size and insertion set size, node sizes in the Y-tree are relatively large. While a value-list index typically uses internal node sizes that are equivalent in size to one disk block (perhaps using larger node sizes for leaf nodes) a Y-tree node may be huge in comparison. Node sizes in the range 8KB to 256KB or even larger are typical. Typical choices of d, the maximum insertion set size, range from 50 to 2500 or larger, with corresponding maximum fanout f from a high value of 100 all the way down to 10, much smaller than for a value-list index. However, as we will argue in subsequent sections, the negative effects that one may expect would be associated with huge node size and small fanout never really materialize, making the Y-tree a natural choice for many database applications.

2.3.3 Handling Very Large Node Sizes

For very fast insertion times, node sizes may be very large: up to a significant fraction of a megabyte. Though it may not be possible to optimize by locating internal node heaps at a location other than with the internal node, a few optimizations are possible when node sizes are particularly large. These optimizations prove especially effective when nodes are too large to fit on a single disk track.

A first optimization is to couple an *end-pointer* with every pointer in the pointer list. Thus, the internal node pointer list becomes as follows:

$<(P_1, end_1), K_1, (P_2, end_2), K_2,..., (P_{f-1}, end_{f-1}), K_{f-1}, (P_f, end_f)>$.

The *end-pointer* denotes an offset from the beginning of the corresponding child node that lets the parent node know exactly how many bytes need be transferred from disk into main memory. When the node corresponding to the end-pointer is a leaf node, the end-pointer points to the last *(key, ptr)* pair in that node. When a leaf is transferred from disk into memory, on average it is only around 70% full (though this percentage varies from 50% to 100%). The end-pointer allows the transfer to be halted at the point where the portion of the node that is in use has been completely transferred. In the case of an internal node, the end-pointer points to the end of the pointer list, so that initially, the entire heap need not be read from disk.

More conventional storage of the end-pointer within the node itself is of less use because of the delay incurred between reading the head of the node, stopping the transfer, and re-sending the request that the remainder of the node be retrieved from the disk. Note that this is a non-issue in the case of a value-list index, where node size is typically equivalent to the system disk block size, and so it makes little sense to access less than an entire node.

The second possible large-node optimization follows immediately from the first. During query evaluation, it is the case that the heap of every internal node encountered must be searched for the existence of *(key, ptr)* pairs meeting the search predicate. However, it is *not* the case that the *entire* heap need be searched; we need only those heap buckets corresponding to the children meeting the search predicate. This fact can be used to our advantage as follows. First, we pack the heap buckets tightly together, and add pointers to the pointer-list to the beginning of each bucket. The disk layout of an internal node, then, resembles the diagram of Figure 5.

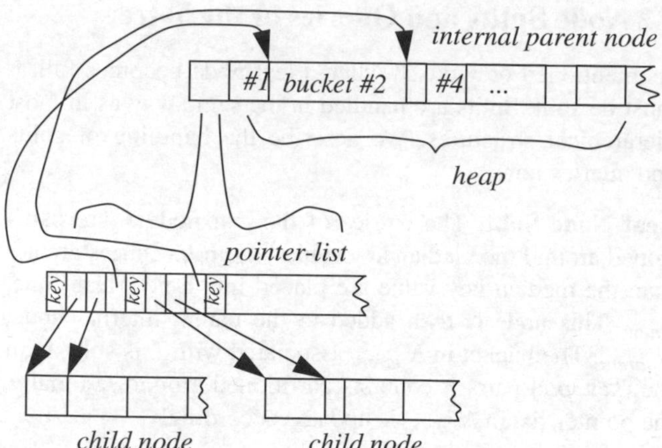

Figure 5: Optimized layout of an internal node for huge node sizes in the Y-tree.

T_{seek}	Average time required to perform a disk seek
T_{trans}	Average time to transfer one *(key, ptr)* pair from disk into main memory
N	Size, in *(key, ptr)* pairs, of a tree node
f	Fanout
d	Insertion set size for the Y-tree
b	Number of insertions batched for value-list index
n	Number of *(key, ptr)* pairs in the tree

Table 1: Notation

In the case where a query over the depicted internal node is encompassed wholly by the range defined by the first and second keys in the node's pointer-list, a short disk seek can be performed to reach the beginning of the second bucket. Then, a scan of that bucket up until the beginning of the third bucket is performed. The corresponding *(key, ptr)* entries from that bucket can then be searched for a match. Particularly in the case of an index over a huge database with very large node sizes, this method can provide a substantial time savings in evaluation of certain types of queries, as we will show in Section 4.

3 The Y-Tree Vs. The Value-List Index

We now offer an analytical comparison of Y-tree and value-list index performance as a preface to Section 4, where we will describe our experimental results. In this section, we will use the notation in Table 1. Also, for the sake of simplicity and brevity, we will assume that the node sizes for both internal nodes and leaf nodes are the same, and that in a leaf node, each key value has a single, unique, associated pointer (as opposed to an associated, varying-sized RID-list as would be expected for an attribute with a small cardinality compared to the overall, fact table size). We will drop this assumption in Section 4.

3.1 Insertions

In our analysis, we will compare Y-tree insertion times to batched, value-list index insertion times using the algorithm outlined in [6]. The advantage of using a batch algorithm for value-list index insertion (as opposed to classical, item by item insertion) is that each edge in the tree is traversed at most once, which can lead to a reduction in total seek time and data transfer time required. In building our analytical model for batched value-list index insertion performance, we assume that the number of nodes read and written is equal to the batched insertion set size. This assumption is justified by the following:

- We assume that the number of leaf level nodes and the number of distinct key values inserted into the trees are large enough that we can assume that every new (*key, ptr*) pair is inserted into a *distinct* leaf node. The rationale for this is as follows. If the structure contains n (*key, ptr*) pairs, there are then approximately $\frac{n}{N_{B+} \times 0.68}$ leaf nodes, assuming an average 68% fill rate. Given the simplifying assumption that each to-be-inserted attribute value has an equal probability of belonging to any given leaf node, then, the expected number of leaf nodes receiving j of the d new (*key, ptr*) pairs (again assuming a 68% fill rate) is: $\binom{d}{j} \times \left(\frac{N_{B+} \times 0.68}{n}\right)^{j-1} \times \left(1 - \frac{N_{B+} \times 0.68}{n}\right)^{d-j}$

  Setting $j = 0$ in the above expression yields the number of leaf nodes receiving none of the d pairs. Thus, the number of distinct leaves expected to receive at least one (*key, ptr*) pair is: $\frac{n}{N_{B+} \times 0.68} \times \left(1 - \left(1 - \frac{N_{B+} \times 0.68}{n}\right)^{d}\right)$

  Using this expression, we can calculate that, for the AT&T example of Section 1, with an insertion set size of one million, we would expect more than 963 thousand distinct leaf nodes to be written. Thus, the savings in terms of leaf level pages *not* written in this example due to batch insert is small (less than 4%). The effect of this is that in a huge database with a large attribute domain, by using batch insertion, we can avoid multiple reads of internal nodes, but *nearly one node* must still be read/written for *each* pair inserted.

- We assume that the cost of accessing internal nodes during a large, batched insert is negligible. If one million different leaf nodes must be read and written, the number of distinct internal nodes which must be traversed in order to reach those leaf nodes will be less than 1/100 of the number of such leaf nodes (assuming a fanout of larger than 100), and will be insignificant.

- We assume that splits occur infrequently enough that they do not contribute significantly to the cost of batched insertion.

Given these assumptions, the cost to batch insert a set of b (*key, ptr*) pairs into a value-list index is simply:

$$b \times (2 \times T_{trans} \times N_{B+} + T_{seek})$$

For a Y-tree, in comparison, inserting b (*key, ptr*) pairs requires that each node on a unique path from root to leaf be read and written. Assuming that an average node is 68% full, since data are held in internal nodes as well, the depth of a Y-tree can be expected to be *at most* $\lceil \log_{0.68 f_Y} n - \log_{0.68 f_Y} N_Y + \log_{0.68 f_Y} 0.68 \rceil$. Since the final term in the above expression will be very small, we ignore it in our analysis for the sake of simplicity. Note that this expression takes into account the fact that the number of pairs in a leaf node (N_Y) is likely to be different and much greater than the fanout of the internal nodes (f_Y). In our analysis, we will also ignore the reduction in the number of leaf nodes due to the fact that data are also present in internal nodes. Assuming that the root node is stored in memory, the cost to insert b pairs is then:

$$\frac{b}{d} \times \lceil \log_{0.68 f_Y} n - \log_{0.68 f_Y} N_Y - 1 \rceil \times (2 \times T_{trans} \times N_Y + T_{seek})$$

3.2 Queries

Querying a value-list index is a simple matter. To evaluate a range query, a single path is traversed from root to leaf, down the tree. When a leaf node is reached, a string of leaf nodes are typically traversed, following pointers, until the end of the range has been reached. The time to process a query returning s (*key, ptr*) pairs, assuming that the root node is resident in memory, is then:

$$\left(\lceil \log_{0.68 N_{B+}} n \rceil - 1 + \left\lceil \frac{s}{N_{B+} \times 0.68} \right\rceil\right) \times (T_{trans} \times N_{B+} + T_{seek})$$

Querying a Y-tree is slightly more complex, since an inorder traversal of the tree must be undertaken in order to answer a range query. In order to produce a simple expression, we ignore the fact that since some of the desired (*key, ptr*) pairs

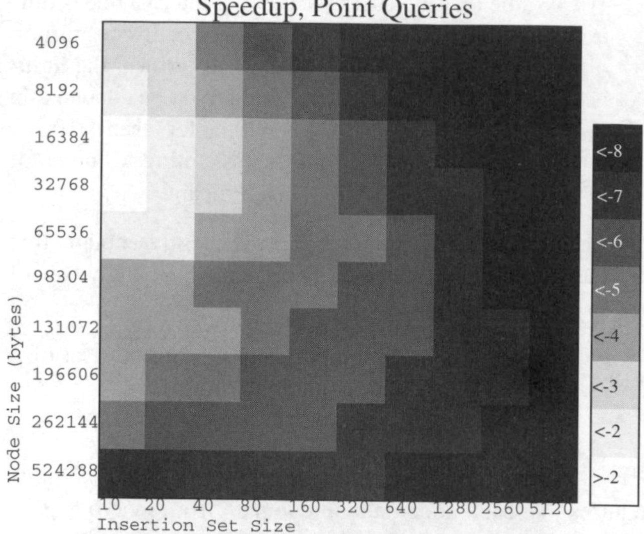

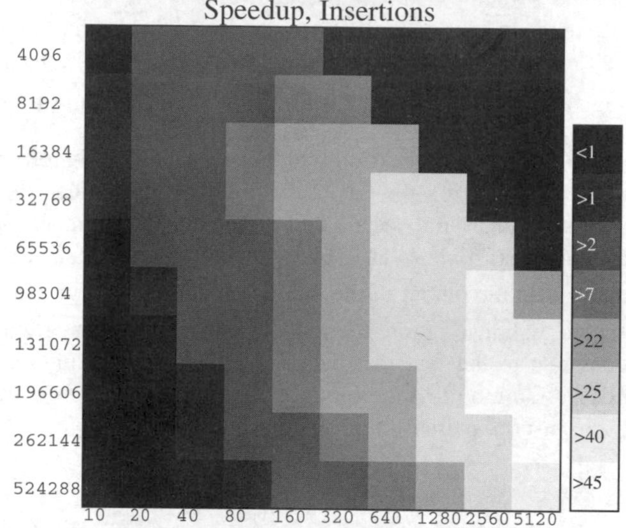

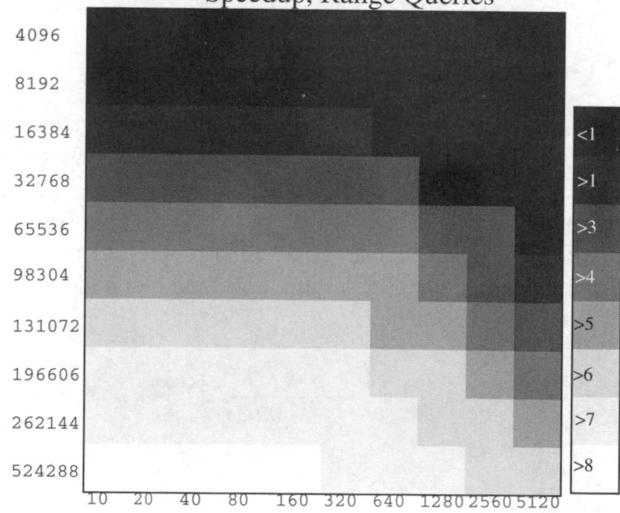

Figure 6: Analytically predicted performance of the Y-tree as compared to a value-list index with a node size of 8KB. The time to write one million (*key, ptr*) pairs to disk is assumed to be ten times the average disk seek time.

will be found in internal nodes, the actual number of leaf nodes that must be processed will be less than for a value-list index having the same leaf node size. Under these assumptions, the time needed to query a Y-tree, assuming that the root node is resident in memory, is then:

$$\left(\sum_{i=0}^{\left\lceil \log_{0.68 f_Y} n - \log_{0.68 f_Y} N_Y \right\rceil - 1} \left\lceil \frac{s}{(f_Y)^i N_Y \times 0.68^{i+1}} \right\rceil\right) \times (T_{trans} \times N_Y + T_{seek})$$

Note again that this expression takes into account the difference between the number of entries in a leaf node and the fanout of an internal node.

3.3 Discussion

Given the algebraic expressions of Sections 3.1 and 3.2, natural questions are: How do these expressions translate into expected query slowdowns and expected insertion speedups for the Y-tree in a typical system? Are the potential query evaluation slowdowns justified by the insertion time speedups?

To help answer these questions, in Figure 6 we plot the analytically expected slowdown and speedup factors for a Y-tree as opposed to an incrementally constructed value-list index for a typical, large, database system. Both indexing structures are assumed to index a table containing 2 billion records. The seek time T_{seek} is assumed to average 10 ms, and the transfer rate T_{trans} is one million (*key, ptr*) pairs per second. In each contoured plot depicted in Figure 6, the Y-tree is compared for a variety of node sizes and insertion set sizes against a value-list index with a node size of 8KB.

The first plot in Figure 6 shows the analytically expected speedup for evaluation of a point query returning a single (*key, ptr*) pair using a Y-tree. Speedup was computed as $(T_{B+} - T_Y) / T_Y$. The plot shows that as one would expect, as insertion set size is increased, the performance of point query evaluation suffers due to the decreased fanout associated with the larger heap that must be stored in each internal node. Perhaps slightly more surprising is the fact that increasing the node size in order to increase the fanout and perhaps deal with a large insertion set size is only effective up to a point. This is due to the fact that doubling, or even increasing the fanout in a tree by an order of magnitude, may have little effect on the actual number of disk seeks required to evaluate a query. Why? The reason is that the depth of a hierarchical structure with an effective fanout f is $\lceil \log_f n \rceil$. Increasing the fanout by the factor y yields a depth of:

$$\lceil \log_{f \times y} n \rceil = \left\lceil \frac{\log n}{\log y + \log f} \right\rceil$$

That is, for a given database size, increasing an already significant fanout by 10 times will have little effect because the log of the factor is only *added* into the divisor on the right-hand side of the above equation. For large node sizes, the gain from the increased fanout is mitigated by the associated increase in node transfer time.

Figure 6(b) shows the expected slowdown for a large, range query returning one million (*key, ptr*) pairs. Performance for evaluation of range queries is arguably more important than point query performance, since range query evaluation is important to join evaluation, which is typically the bottleneck during overall query evaluation. Surprisingly, query evaluation for large ranges is expectedly faster by *nearly an order of magnitude* using a Y-tree when compared to the value-list index. This is due to the typically much larger leaf node size in a Y-tree, which more than compensates for the smaller Y-tree fanout. Moreover, we argue that if any type of incremental insertion algorithm must be used frequently by a value-list index, it is *not* a viable option to increase leaf node sizes to those comparable to the larger Y-tree node sizes in order to speed up processing of large range queries using a value-list index. This is because the time needed to perform insertions will increase proportionally along with the larger node size using the value-list index.

It is also interesting to note that there is little additional cost associated with the inorder traversal of the Y-tree as opposed to simply following pointers along leaf nodes, as is typically done in a value-list index. This is because the number of additional internal nodes that must be accessed is typically tiny when compared to the number of leaf nodes accessed, and thus adds little cost to range query evaluation.

Finally, Figure 6(c) shows the speedup of insertion of one million (*key, ptr*) pairs using a Y-tree as compared to using batched insertion into the value-list index. For the parameters used to produce the plot, speedups of more than 50 times are analytically predicted.

4 Experimental Results

Unfortunately, in order to make an analytical model simple enough to be useful, a number of real-world factors must be left out. In addition to the assumptions described in detail in the previous section, the following factors were also not considered in the analytical model:

- *DBMS caching*. If memory permits, it might be possible to hold entire upper levels of a tree in memory. Or, a FIFO queue of recently-encountered nodes could be maintained.
- *File system issues*. File system caching, buffering performed by the disk, disk fragmentation, location of data on disk, etc., will all affect indexing performance and were ignored by our model.
- *Special, Algorithmic issues*. The effect of the suggested enhancements of Section 2.3.3, for example, was not considered in the model. Also, space can be saved by the simple enhancement of eliminating redundant key values in leaf nodes (this is essentially equivalent to storing pointers to separate RID-lists at the bottom level of the tree, and requiring that the RID-lists be stored sequentially on disk).

Thus, the analytical results present only a very rough estimation for the type of behavior that one might expect to encounter in actual implementations of these structures.

4.1 Scope

In order to overcome these limitations and fully test the practicality of the Y-tree for use in indexing real data, we implemented the following:

1) *An optimal, bulk value-list index loader.* We implemented a bulk loader that builds a packed value-list index at a fill rate of $p\%$, where p is a parameter supplied at index creation time. All leaf nodes are written in sequence to disk, guaranteeing that once a single RID has been located, no seeks need be performed during range query evaluation as all RIDs are read in sequence.

2) *Non-optimal, Y-tree and value-list index bulk loaders.* We also implemented non-optimal loaders, which build trees packed to an *average* fill rate $p\%$, where leaf nodes are not written in sequential order, in order to simulate a tree that had been built incrementally as the data accumulated.

3) *Value-list index and Y-tree insertion and query algorithms.* We implemented Y-tree query and insertion, as well as batched value-list index insertion and the value-list index query algorithm. For these algorithms, root nodes were pinned in main memory, and a FIFO buffer of nodes was maintained (in order to simulate DBMS caching), in addition to the caching provided by the file system.

4.2 Query Processing Experiments

For testing query processing, we ran two sets of experiments, concentrating on queries and insertions, respectively. We constructed a synthetic data set having a single attribute and 200 million rows of data. We believe that even for a larger, real-world application indexing 10 billion or more rows, the results presented here still hold since the larger database size probably equates to only one additional level (if any) in a hierarchical index.

For the query processing experiments, we constructed optimal value-list indexes containing a (*key, ptr*) pair for each row of the data set. We built a series of value-list indexes, one at each of several different node sizes. We constructed optimal value-list indexes (as opposed to our analysis of non-optimal indices in Section 3) since we felt that for a database of that size, the incremental, batched construction that would have led to a non-optimal tree was not a viable option in practice due to the tremendous time that would be required to build such an index (cf. Section 4.3). In other words, no one would build such a huge index incrementally

Average Query Evaluation Time

Node Size	Query Selectivity (# items returned) 0.5e10^{-8} (1)	0.5e10^{-5} (10^3)	0.5e10^{-3} (10^6)
4096B	0.020 sec	0.088 sec	2.85 sec
8192B*	0.018 sec	0.067 sec	6.60 sec
8192B	0.018 sec	0.066 sec	1.36 sec
16384B	0.044 sec	0.068 sec	1.43 sec
32768B	0.048 sec	0.065 sec	1.40 sec

*non-optimal value-list index, provided for comparison

Table 2: Average evaluation times required per query, over 500 trials, for optimal, bulk-loaded, value-list indexes.

Average Query Evaluation Time

Node Size	*d*	Query Selectivity (# items returned) 0.5e10^{-8} (1)	0.5e10^{-5} (10^3)	0.5e10^{-3} (10^6)
16384B	100	0.059 sec	0.065 sec	3.09 sec
32768B	200	0.056 sec	0.064 sec	2.81 sec
65536B	400	0.064 sec	0.064 sec	2.55 sec
98304B	400	0.069 sec	0.057 sec	2.27 sec
196608	800	0.080 sec	0.076 sec	2.13 sec
262144B	1200	0.096 sec	0.098 sec	2.10 sec

Table 3: Average evaluation times required per query, over 500 trials, for Y-trees.

in the real world. Since they would have to build it in bulk, it can be assumed that this would be done optimally.

We also constructed a series of *non-optimal* Y-trees in bulk, to simulate Y-trees that had been constructed incrementally. Thus, we will compare *optimal* value-list indexes with *non-optimal* Y-trees. The Y-trees were constructed at a fill rate of 68%, so nodes averaged 68% full. The Y-trees constructed in this way were typically 2.2GB to 2.5GB in size. The optimal value-list indexes were typically around 65% of this size.

For each tree constructed, at each of several different query selectivities, we ran a batch of 500 queries. At the beginning of each run of 500 queries, the tree node cache was empty, but it was not flushed as the queries were executed. Queries were run at a variety of selectivities.

We summarize the results at several different selectivities and node sizes for value-list indexes above in Table 2. It is useful to note that since each value-list index is constructed optimally, increasing node size past 8KB does little to increase query evaluation efficiency. Since it is the case

Y-Tree Insertion Rates

Node Size (bytes)	*d*	Avg. insert time per key	Speedup
16384	100	0.000958 sec	25 times
32768	200	0.000843 sec	28 times
65536	400	0.000566 sec	42 times
98304	400	0.000576 sec	42 times
196608	800	0.000465 sec	52 times
262144	1200	0.000245 sec	99 times

Table 4: Y-tree insertion speedup vs. batched, incremental insertion into a value-list index having a node size of 4096 bytes.

that once a leaf node has been reached, no more disk seeks are required (due to the value-list index optimality), increasing node size past a certain point is harmful as it leads to longer transfer times for internal nodes. In Table 3, we similarly give the query evaluation times required by the Y-tree for selected combinations of different node sizes and insertion set sizes.

Comparing the two tables, it is clear that there is a significant performance hit taken from using the Y-tree for evaluating point queries, with the Y-tree taking anywhere from three to five times as long. For larger queries (more common in OLAP), however, an incrementally constructed Y-tree may be three times as fast as an incrementally constructed value-list index. With a large node size, the Y-tree is only 56% slower than a 100% full, optimally constructed value-list index with leaf nodes located sequentially on the disk. We believe that the excellent performance for larger queries is important, since larger ranges are of more use during join evaluation.

4.3 Insertion Experiments

For this set of tests, we wished to determine whether, in practice, Y-tree insertion is fast when compared to incremental, batched, value-list index insertion. We now discuss the results of our tests:

Incremental, batched, value-list index insertion. Our first set of tests involved using an *incremental, batched insertion algorithm* on a value-list index that had been constructed using our non-optimal bulk loader to simulate a tree that had been constructed completely incrementally. The tree was loaded so that each node was, on average, filled to 68% of capacity. During our tests, batches of 10,000 (*key, ptr*) pairs were inserted at one time into the tree. Using this method, the fastest insertion rate was achieved at a node size of 4096 bytes, averaging one insert every 0.0246 seconds. While this method avoids many of the pitfalls associated with the massive rebuild, the insertion rate we achieved was painfully slow. At this rate, in order to handle the three million insertions per day without concurrent query processing, more than 20 hours would be required.

The Y-tree. Finally, we tested insertion into the Y-tree. As with our query experiments, we tested the Y-tree at a variety of different node and insertion set sizes. A subset of those results is given in Table 3 above. Clearly, the Y-tree is much faster than the value-list index for processing insertions, with speedups ranging from 25 to nearly 100 over the value-list index.

4.4 Discussion of Experimental Results

The experimental results show that the Y-tree is a viable alternative to the value-list index in practice. Due to the support for very large node sizes, the Y-tree is considerably faster than an incrementally constructed value-list index for large range queries, and is competitive with an optimal value-list index. The primary factor we encountered that limits node sizes in an incrementally constructed value-list index is that with larger node sizes come larger insert times, so frequent insertions place a practical limitation on value-list index node size.

In general, when insertion rates are fully considered, the Y-tree looks more attractive still. Handling three million insertions using a Y-tree may take little longer than 12 minutes, compared with 20 hours or more using a value-list index. If the attribute domain and the database size are both large, a value-list index simply cannot handle such a high, sustained insertion rate, taking 100 times as long. When all of this is considered together, the Y-tree proves to be worth serious consideration as an indexing structure.

5 Related Work

While the subject of database indexing has attracted a huge amount of attention, very few of the proposed methods have dealt specifically with the issue of allowing fast inserts. We briefly discuss two methods that have addressed the insertion problem, and we compare these methods with the Y-tree. Specifically we discuss the *Log-Structured Merge Tree* [4] (LSM-Tree) and the *Stepped Merge Method* [1].

Both of these methods make use of the fact that on a per insertion basis, it is much faster to buffer a large set of insertions and then scan the entire base relation at once (which is organized as a B+-tree[1]), adding new data to the structure. Since the structure can be scanned in this way with a minimum of disk seeks, the average time required per insertion is likely to be much less than would be required were the classical B+-tree insertion algorithm used instead. Both the LSM-Tree and the Stepped Merge Method utilize algorithms that efficiently accept and organize the new data until such a time as they can efficiently be added to the base relation.

The LSM-Tree uses a smaller, secondary tree to buffer insertions and updates as they are issued. An ongoing *rolling merge* process feeds nodes from the smaller tree into the larger tree, where the new nodes are written out to disk as large, multi-page runs of records known as *filling blocks*. These runs are written out log-style, and older versions of nodes are kept on disk as long as is feasible to facilitate easy rollback and recovery, in a manner reminiscent of a log-structured file system [7]. In the more general case, there can be *N* such trees in all, where each tree feeds into a larger tree in a series of rolling merges, with each record eventually reaching the base relation after passing through each tree. The Stepped Merge Method can be viewed as a variation of the LSM-tree, where at each of the *N - 1* levels *K* trees (instead of just one tree) are stored and are merged and propagated to the higher level when they become too large. Because data are written only once at each level, each data insertion may require fewer disk operations than in the LSM-Tree.

In an important way, the LSM-Tree and presumably the Stepped Merge Algorithm are superior to the Y-tree: the data blocks are written to the base relation (the leaf level of the final tree) totally full. This implies that the overall space utilization of these methods would be perhaps 30% greater than for the Y-tree. Also, in the case of the LSM-Tree, if there is only a single, secondary tree (or if there are multiple trees stored on separate disks) and that secondary tree is stored in main memory, then query performance may be substantially better than for the Y-tree. In this case, the LSM-Tree range query performance would be comparable to that of the optimally constructed B+-tree due to the large node size (which would reduce disk seeks during long leaf scans) and high space utilization (which increases the effective fanout).

However, the Y-tree does have some advantages. The Y-tree may exhibit improved query performance over the Stepped Merge Method, since at each level of the structure built by the Stepped Merge Method, *K* trees must be searched during query execution. Unless these trees are stored on separate disks, query evaluation performance may suffer. Since some of the trees at certain levels are likely to be relatively small, placing each on a separate disk may require that many more disk seeks be used in order to maintain query performance than would be needed to simply store the data.

In addition, the Y-tree has at least one important advantage over both of the other methods. Regardless of the insertion pattern, the LSM-Tree and the Stepped Merge Method must eventually merge entire smaller trees with entire larger trees. The Y-tree, on the other hand, can adapt well to certain circumstances such as a small set of "hot" key values. In this

1. In contrast, we have described the Y-tree as primarily a secondary indexing structure, though it could be used as a primary index. Likewise, the LSM-Tree and the Stepped Merge Method could both be used as secondary indices.

case, only hot spots would need to be drained to leaf nodes, whereas the other methods must rewrite an entire leaf node, even if only a single key value must be inserted into that node.

6 Conclusions

In this paper, we have presented a new, secondary index for use in huge, constantly growing data warehousing environments. Our new index, called the *Y-tree*, is fast because of the use of a *single path, bulk insertion*. During a single path, bulk insertion, a set of insertions is processed together (similar to batched insertion into a value-list index) but in contrast to a value-list index, nodes need be written only on a *single path* from root to leaf, regardless of the key values in the insertion set.

We have shown that because of this, the Y-tree is very fast for processing insertions: insertions are processed up to 100 times faster than they can be processed using batch insertion with a value-list index. Furthermore, the Y-tree processes large range queries competitively when compared to an optimally constructed value-list index, and several times faster than an incrementally constructed value-list index. Point query evaluation using a Y-tree is slower, but point queries are infrequent in OLAP applications. We have discussed two alternative indexing methods for supporting fast insertions, the LSM-Tree [4] and the Stepped Merge Method [1], and pointed out at least one advantage of the Y-tree over these other methods: namely, the ability of the Y-tree to adjust well to highly skewed insertion patterns. For these reasons, we believe that the Y-tree offers an attractive alternative to the value-list index for indexing massive, perpetually growing warehouses.

References

[1] H.V. Jagadish, P.P.S Narayan, S. Seshadri, S. Sudarshan, R. Kanneganti. Incremental Organization for Data Recording and Warehousing. In *Proceedings of the 23rd VLDB Conference*.

[2] Personal communication w. K. Lyons, AT&T Corporation, 1998.

[3] M. Nelson. *The Data Compression Book*. M and T Books, New York, 1996.

[4] P. O'Neil, E. Cheng, D. Gawlick, and E. O'Neil. The Log-Structured Merge Tree. *Acta Informatica*, 33:351-385, 1996.

[5] P. O'Neil, D. Quass. Improved Query Performance with Variant Indexes. In *Proceedings of the 1997 ACM SIGMOD Conference*.

[6] K. Pollari-Malmi, E. Soisalon-Soininen, T. Ylonen. Concurrency Control in B-trees with Batch Updates. *IEEE TKDE*, December, 1996.

[7] M. Rosenblum and J. Ousterhout. The Design and Organization of a Log Structured File System. *ACM Trans. on Computer Systems*, 10:1:28-52, 1992.

[8] B. Salzberg. Access Methods. In *Computing Surveys* 28:1, 1996.

Microsoft English Query 7.5
Automatic Extraction of Semantics from Relational Databases and OLAP Cubes

Adam Blum
Microsoft Corp, Redmond, WA. USA
mailto:AdamBlum@microsoft.com

1. What is English Query?

Microsoft English Query (EQ) lets users pose database queries in plain English. To do this, a developer need only define the database semantics, in effect building a conceptual model of the database. EQ provides an *Authoring Tool* that allows the developer to define the set of the entities and relationships in the database along with the database objects that the entities are associated with. Once this model is defined, the *English Query Engine* converts any English question posed in terms of the defined entities and relationships into a SQL statement. The application developer may use this engine, specifically it's a COM automation server, inside her Web, C++, Java, or Visual Basic application. This allows users to ask English questions of arbitrary complexity. These questions can be refined with as many follow-up questions as necessary) to find the information that is of interest.

EQ is a standard part of SQL Server 7.0 and 7.5. This talk explores the internals of a feature in the next release: the *Model Wizard*, which automatically extracts semantics from a database or cube and builds a model. It also describes *Semantic Modeling Format*, an XML grammar that allows any other tool to use the semantic information generated by the Model Wizard. Finally, the talk describes *Author by Example*, an amazing facility that, by analyzing failed questions, gleans additional database semantics that Model Wizard didn't capture.

Proceedings of the 25th VLDB Conference, Edinburgh, Scotland, 1999.

2.0. Model Wizard

The EQ Authoring Tool is easy to use and does not require any programming experience. The developer just needs to know the structure of their database. Still, it can be quite tedious to author semantic models for *very complex databases*. EQ 7.5, in beta test by VLDB99, contains a feature of particular interest to developers using very large relational databases or OLAP cubes. EQ uses a feature called the *Model Wizard* to automatically create the entities and relationships based on the database or cube structure. In effect, Model Wizard automatically extracts the database semantics from the database's tables and fields and the various objects in an OLAP cube: dimensions, levels, measures, properties and facts.

In order to capture as much of the semantics available in the database as possible, EQ has a rich set of heuristics for automatically determining the entities and relationships of a SQL database or OLAP cube. The talk describes these heuristics for both SQL databases, where they achieve approximately 70% capture of relationships that would be created manually, and OLAP cubes, where they automatically capture more than 85% of available relationships.

2.1. SQL Database Heuristics

The SQL database heuristics are divided into rules for creating entities and rules for creating relationships. Creating entities for each table and field is simple enough. Automatically creating relationships is more complex, and is driven by a set of rules, which include rules for creating:

trait phrasings between table and field entities
trait phrasings between table entities and other tables to which it have a join path..
name phrasings between certain field entities and major (table) entities
preposition phrasings between certain fields entities and the table entity

The talk describes these and other relationship creation rules in detail.

OLAP Cube Heuristics

The rules for determining entities and relationships in cubes are much richer. Thus they capture a larger fraction of the available relationships. The semantics of a cube are much more explicit than that of a database, due to the hierarchy of levels in a dimension, and the implied relationships of each of the dimensions and levels to the cube's fact and its various measures. Entities are automatically created for all OLAP dimensions, levels, properties (of levels), measures, and the cube's fact table. The OLAP relationship creation rules can be broken into the following categories:

level to level relationships – Each dimension contains a hierarchy of levels (if there is more than one level) that the Model Wizard exploits to create level to level relationships that reflect the hierarchy (lower level entities are "in" higher level entities which also "have" those lower level entities.) Also, due to the EQ engine's inference capabilities, the number of level to level relationships must be sufficient to be a "minimum spanning set" of the available levels with only one level of inference. This implies some interesting algorithmic challenges for level to level relationship generation that we will describe.

level to dimension relationships – The entity associated lowest level of a dimension is often the identifier or "name entity" of the dimension's entity.

level to fact relationships – Each level's entity is related directly to the entity that is associated with the cube's fact table.

dimension to fact relationships – Each dimension's entity is also related directly to the fact table.

fact to measures relationships – Each fact table "has" each measure that is available for the cube.

3.0. Semantic Modeling Format - Access to EQ Model Information

The Model Wizard Heuristics capture a wealth of semantic information about an OLAP cube or database. The authoring tool allows developers to add semantics that were not automatically captured. Since this information is a set of richly described entities and relationships, this conceptual model is of value for other applications.

EQ externalizes these extracted entities and relationships through an XML document following a grammar known as Semantic Modeling Format (SMF), described here and in the product documentation. SMF lets you either programmatically consume the EQ model or create it via the XML Document Object Model, a W3C standard API for manipulating XML hierarchies.

4.0. Author By Example

Any relationships not automatically created by the Model Wizard can usually be created in response to questions posed to the EQ model. This is possible through the Author By Example Feature. When working in the authoring tool, the developer can pose questions using a testing facility inside the tool. If EQ cannot answer the question directly, the developer can click the *Suggestion* button to invoke *Author By Example,* which will suggest a set of entities and relationships to be created which will allow the question to be answered. Author By Example can also be run in batch over a set of failed questions, for example captured from a Web site that incorporates English Query.

The talk will describe the architecture of Author By Example and how its designed to work to complement the semantic capture capabilities provided by the Model Wizard.

Each of these components will be demonstrated as part of the talk.

The New Locking, Logging, And Recovery Architecture of Microsoft SQL Server 7.0

David Campbell
Microsoft Corporation, Redmond, WA, USA
davidc@microsoft.com

The Microsoft SQL Server storage engine was rearchitected to support row level locking in Version 7.0. This required significant changes throughout the store; from page update primitives, logging and recovery, to access-methods. One interesting engineering aspect of this project was the fact that we kept the system running during the entire transformation of the underlying architecture – a task we liken to transforming a zebra into a cheetah by transplanting one organ at a time. This talk will focus on how real-world pragmatics collided with academic purity and what solutions resulted.

A brief overview of the pre-existing locking, access methods, and recovery systems will be followed by a discussion of the new architecture and how we changed a strictly page based concurrency control and recovery system into a highly concurrent storage system that has significantly better performance and concurrency behavior than its predecessor.

We will discuss:

- How we originally implemented a standard key-range locking architecture as described in the literature, and then had to extend it to process deletes as updates to improve concurrency for a number of real-world workloads.
- How we implemented a multi-granular lock protocol for B-trees that includes both page and row granularity locking, and the benefits and complications that resulted.
- How we added a run-time cost-based optimization scheme to determine the appropriate locking granularity for each access method scan.
- How we changed allocation and index structural modifications from a transaction consistent policy to an action consistent policy where the changes are performed under short-term "system" transactions and how these system transactions are used in a multi-level recovery scheme.
- How we addressed the issue of log reservation for compensation logging of undo actions.
- How we maintained the behavior of prior releases such as minimal logging for bulk update operations including index creation.
- How we instrumented and tested the system to ensure it was ready for production use.

The talk will conclude with a presentation of the lessons learned from this effort.

Proceedings of the 25th VLDB Conference, Edinburgh, Scotland, 1999.

The Value of Merge-Join and Hash-Join in SQL Server

Goetz Graefe
Microsoft, Redmond, WA 98052-6399
GoetzG@Microsoft.com

Abstract

Microsoft SQL Server was successful for many years for transaction processing and decision support workloads with neither merge join nor hash join, relying entirely on nested loops and index nested loops join. How much difference do additional join algorithms really make, and how much system performance do they actually add? In a pure OLTP workload that requires only record-to-record navigation, intuition agrees that index nested loops join is sufficient. For a DSS workload, however, the question is much more complex. To answer this question, we have analyzed TPC-D query performance using an internal build of SQL Server with merge-join and hash-join enabled and disabled. It shows that merge join and hash join are both required to achieve the best performance for decision support workloads.

1.0 Introduction

For a long time, most relational database systems employed only nested loops join, in particular in the form of index nested loops join, and merge join. The general rule of thumb, stated over 20 years ago [Blasgen and Eswaran 1977], is that nested loops join is good if at least one join input is small, and merge join is good for two large inputs. Given that an input is either small or large, who needs more join algorithms?

Some database systems, in particular those that targeted online transaction processing (OLTP) applications, did not even use merge join. All join operations were executed by the nested loops algorithm. The most sophisticated join algorithm sorted the outer input and built an index on the inner input on the fly. Given the very similar disk reference patterns, we call index nested loops join with a sorted outer input a *poor man's merge join.*

Starting in about 1984, hash-based algorithms found intense interest among database researchers [Kitsuregawa et al. 1993, DeWitt at al. 1984, Sacco 1986, Shapiro 1986], and many hash join variants were invented. Product development teams were slow to adopt these new algorithms. Some relational database systems still have not added hash joins to their repertoire. One reason has been that query optimization technology wasn't sufficiently extensible to permit easy integration of a new algorithm.

Given the success of database systems that don't even have merge join, what is the value of hash and merge joins? We believe that the value of these algorithms strongly depends on both the workload and the set of available indexes. Moreover, the most desirable indexes most likely depend on the available algorithms. In other words, any comparison of these algorithms should be based on indexes specifically designed for the workload and the available algorithms.

Choosing the best indexes by hand for a single complex query with any assurance of optimality is hard. For an entire workload consisting of multiple complex queries, it is very, very hard (basically impossible). Such complex workloads require an automated tool to evaluate the alternatives and find an optimal design. SQL Server includes such a tool, called the "index tuning wizard" [Chaudhuri and Narasayya 1998], as well as variants of nested loops join, merge join, and hash join. The tool heuristically explores very many combinations of indexes, and relies on the query optimizer to estimate execution costs for given or collected workload. While the tool might run for minutes or even hours for workloads much more complex than TPC-D, it can design index sets for entire workloads with a reasonable assurance of optimality.

This study relies on the index-tuning wizard to design optimal index sets for a specific workload with complex queries (TPC-D, TPC-H, TPC-R) and for specific combinations of available join algorithms. After establishing a baseline using a small set of indexes, it compares the performance and assesses the value of merge join and hash join using an index set optimized for the entire, complex workload.

Proceedings of the 25th VLDB Conference, Edinburgh, Scotland, 1999.

2.0 Experiment setup and environment

Like many performance studies, ours leaves many parameters and definitions constant for all our experiments. The database is the TPC-D verification database with 100 MB of raw data (scale factor 0.1) [TPC-D]. There are not-null constraints on all columns, a primary key constraint on each table, and all suitable referential integrity constraints are declared and enforced in the database.

All experiments were performed using a desktop PC running Windows NT Server 4.0 and a functionally complete and partially tuned development build of Microsoft SQL Server 7.5. The hardware was a 450 MHz Pentium II CPU, 128 MB of memory, and a single 13.4 GB EIDE disk drive. Other than a minimized instance of Enterprise Manager (the graphical administration tools) and a minimized instance of Query Analyzer (the interactive SQL query tool used to drive the experiments), there are no other applications running on the machine. Each run started with both the I/O buffer and the procedure cache (compiled query plans) empty. The TPC-D queries were run in the order Q1, Q2, ..., Q17, Q13-old, Q18, ..., Q22. SQL Server's memory usage is set to 32 MB in all runs, which is shared among buffer, procedure cache, query memory (sort workspace, hash tables), etc. While the software supports parallel query processing, this feature was not employed in this study because there is only a single CPU. Asynchronous I/O is exploited extensively, including pre-fetching multiple needed records at a time, e.g., in index nested loops join.

The query optimizer plans each query for minimal resource consumption. Its cost functions presume a mostly cold buffer. For an entire workload, this means the query optimizer and the tuning wizard optimize system load or elapsed time of the entire workload. Therefore, these are the measures we report in the experiments below.

Since release 7.0, SQL Server automatically samples the database to create statistics on columns desired by the query optimizer. In order to eliminate the cost of statistics creation, we optimized the entire batch of queries once before running an experiment, and then cleared out both the I/O buffer and the procedure cache before running each set of queries.

Since the product is still under development, we do not report actual elapsed times. All reported performance numbers are scaled to the elapsed time of the entire workload using the most simplistic physical database design studied. Given the improvements in hardware performance, relative numbers serve the purposes of this comparison study just as well as absolute numbers could.

3.0 Effects in a simple database design

The first physical database design we evaluate is particularly simple. The only indexes are those required as part of the primary key definitions as well as indexes on foreign keys and on date columns. All indexes are non-clustered indexes. The purpose of evaluating this design is to establish a baseline for comparison to other physical database designs and demonstrate how important index choices are for any comparative analysis of query evaluation algorithms.

The performance of all TPC-D requests against this physical database design is shown in Table 1, with all times normalized to indicate percentages of the elapsed time of entire run using only nested loops join (see column 1). The columns represent the set of join algorithms available to the query optimizer. Algorithms are named by the abbreviations NLJ, MJ, and HJ. NLJ implies naïve nested loops join, index nested loops join, and poor man's merge join, where applicable. The merge join algorithm is very standard, using a temporary file to generate all matches in many-to-many joins. The hash join is a fairly sophisticated implementation, exploiting bit vector filters, role reversal, recursion for very large inputs, and "teams" of hash operators. The latter technique provides in hash-based query processing most of the long-known benefits of "interesting orderings" in sort-based query processing [Selinger et al. 1979, Graefe et al. 1998].

Table 1 – Performance for the simple physical database design. Results are elapsed time scaled so that NLJ sums to 100.

	NLJ only	NLJ+MJ	NLJ+HJ	All
Query 1	2.85	2.96	1.15	1.18
Query 2	0.16	0.16	0.17	0.27
Query 3	3.41	1.38	0.82	0.83
Query 4	3.35	0.88	0.78	0.79
Query 5	4.39	1.85	0.81	0.80
Query 6	0.73	0.63	0.62	0.63
Query 7	3.85	1.25	0.80	0.80
Query 8	6.28	2.97	0.82	0.83
Query 9	40.34	3.59	1.28	1.33
Query 10	7.01	1.41	1.02	0.99
Query 11	2.55	0.49	0.21	0.21
Query 12	1.29	1.03	0.76	0.76
Query 13	0.30	0.29	0.31	0.30
Query 14	1.12	0.79	0.67	0.67
Query 15	1.54	1.49	1.22	1.25
Query 16	0.17	0.19	0.17	0.16
Query 17	0.40	0.53	0.35	0.35
Query 13 (old)	2.24	0.45	0.41	0.40
Query 18	5.65	3.29	3.26	3.23
Query 19	0.76	0.76	0.71	0.72
Query 20	5.13	5.95	5.85	5.79
Query 21	6.40	10.11	7.44	7.55
Query 22	0.10	0.18	0.09	0.18
Total	100.00	42.61	29.71	30.00

Some observations are immediately obvious from Table 1. By looking at the totals, it is clear that for this fairly restricted index set, SQL Server's old set of query processing algorithms are not sufficient. Adding merge join or hash join gives a 2-fold or 3-fold performance improvement respectively.

Hash join has a substantial advantage over merge join only. In fact, a query processor using only merge join for large inputs is 40% slower than one using hash join (30 vs. 42). Thus, if there are very few indexes in the database, or if the existing indexes don't serve a query very well, hash join has substantial value. In a way, this is not surprising, given that the hash table in a hash join is nothing but an in-memory on-demand index.

A more surprising observation is that the total for the column "NLJ+HJ" is comparable to that for all algorithms. For this query set, Merge-Join does not add anything to a "NLJ+HJ" system.

This is in part due to weaknesses in the beta-quality optimizer and execution engine used in these experiments. Compare the elapsed times for query 2. Clearly, when given a choice, the optimizer wrongly chooses merge join or hash join. Also, query 21 is executed most efficiently using nested loops join.

Nonetheless, the optimizer frequently makes good use of merge join and hash operations. For example, query 1 shows the effectiveness of hash grouping. Queries 3, 4, 5, 7, 8, etc. benefit substantially from the additional join algorithms being available to the optimizer. Query 9 in particular performs very poorly, and it alone accounts for ½ of the difference in the column totals.

4.0 Effects in optimized database designs

The experiment in the previous section compared the performance of the different combinations of available join algorithms on a fixed physical database design. However, it is well known that desirable algorithms and desirable indexes affect each other.

Consider an index set specifically optimized for the entire workload using the index-tuning wizard for and for the query processor including all join algorithms. The index-tuning wizard limits index creation either by the cost of update operations included in the workload or by the available disk space. In our optimization, we did not include update operations but limited the space available for all indexes in the database to twice the data space. Table 2 shows the chosen set of indexes created or retained from the simple database design for the given query set, in addition to retaining non-clustered indexes on all primary keys. Note that there is no index on the "nation" table or the "customer" table, and that there is only a single clustered index in the entire database. Note also that the wizard clearly focuses on creating covering indexes to enable index-only scans.

Table 2 – Indexes as optimized for all algorithms

Table	Clustered	Columns
Region	No	R_RegionKey
Supplier	No	S_SuppKey, S_NationKey
Part	No	P_PartKey
PartSupp	No	PS_PartKey, PS_SuppKey, PS_AvailQty, PS_SupplyCost
Orders	No	O_OrderDate, O_OrderKey, O_CustKey
	No	O_CustKey, O_OrderKey
	No	O_OrderKey, O_OrderStatus
LineItem	Yes	L_ShipDate
	No	L_ShipDate, L_Quantity, L_ExtendedPrice, L_Discount, L_Tax, L_ReturnFlag, L_LineStatus
	No	L_PartKey, L_OrderKey, L_SuppKey, L_Quantity, L_ExtendedPrice, L_Discount
	No	L_OrderKey, L_SuppKey, L_PartKey, L_CommitDate, L_ReceiptDate
	No	L_OrderKey, L_ExtendedPrice, L_Discount, L_ReturnFlag
	No	L_OrderKey, L_Quantity

The performance of all TPC-D requests against this physical database design is shown in Table 3 with all times normalized to the same base line as the previous experiment.

Interestingly, even though the index set was optimized for the query processor with all algorithms, the more limited query processors benefit, too. The most limited query processor using only NLJ improved by a factor of 2.3 (100 to 44.70), whereas the most complete query processor improved only by a factor 1.5 (30 to 19.94). The limited query processor depends most heavily on useful indexes, and the complete query processor degrades gracefully if optimal indexes are missing. Moreover, an improvement of 50% is substantial and worthwhile the cost of running the tuning wizard.

Table 3 – Performance for an optimized physical database design

	NLJ only	NLJ + MJ	NLJ+HJ	All
Query 1	2.59	2.71	0.91	0.96
Query 2	0.09	0.10	0.15	0.16
Query 3	1.67	0.87	0.86	0.88
Query 4	1.54	0.84	0.87	0.82
Query 5	4.36	2.75	0.88	0.88
Query 6	0.10	0.07	0.07	0.08
Query 7	5.40	1.12	0.75	0.76
Query 8	2.27	0.28	0.20	0.20
Query 9	4.58	1.84	1.58	1.58
Query 10	2.60	1.00	0.95	0.87
Query 11	2.03	0.57	0.09	0.09
Query 12	3.31	3.29	1.84	1.83
Query 13	0.26	0.24	0.22	0.21
Query 14	0.35	0.08	0.05	0.05
Query 15	0.26	0.24	0.13	0.12
Query 16	0.18	0.20	0.16	0.16
Query 17	0.04	0.04	0.03	0.03
Query 13 (old)	1.54	0.48	0.40	0.40
Query 18	2.46	1.17	1.15	0.94
Query 19	1.73	1.68	1.67	1.67
Query 20	0.36	0.29	0.24	0.26
Query 21	6.86	6.81	12.28	6.77
Query 22	0.13	0.19	0.10	0.21
Total	44.70	26.85	25.59	19.94

It is also interesting to see that the totals for the query processors using merge join only and hash join only are very similar, although the performance for individual queries is quite varied. For example, queries 5, 11, and 12 benefit significantly from hash joins, whereas query 21 benefits from merge joins. The complete query processor chose the optimal query plan for each of the queries, and its performance is about 25% better than the performance of the query processors using either only merge join or only hash join (20 vs. 25).

5.0 Summary and conclusions

In summary, we found that merge join and hash join are both required to achieve the best performance for decision support workloads. To a surprising degree, careful index design alleviates the problem substantially, but it requires an automated tool for complex workloads. Even then, navigating indexes is not competitive with a query processor that includes a full complement of query evaluation algorithms.

However, a query processor using only nested loops join quite successfully processes only the required records. Thus, nested loops join tends to increase the elapsed time (as reported above), but it also reduces the CPU time. A more complete version of this study will compare both elapsed and CPU times as well as investigate the effectiveness of asynchronous I/O for scanning and fetching.

6.0 References

Blasgen and Eswaran 1977. Mike W. Blasgen, Kapali P. Eswaran: Storage and Access in Relational Data Bases. IBM Systems Journal 16(4): 362-377 (1977).

Chaudhuri and Narasayya 1998: Surajit Chaudhuri, Vivek Narasayya: Microsoft Index Tuning Wizard for SQL Server 7.0. ACM SIGMOD Conference 1998: 553-554.

DeWitt at al. 1984. David J. DeWitt, Randy H. Katz, Frank Olken, Leonard D. Shapiro, Michael Stonebraker, David A. Wood: Implementation Techniques for Main Memory Database Systems. ACM SIGMOD Conference 1984: 1-8.

DeWitt et al. 1993. David J. DeWitt, Jeffrey F. Naughton, J. Burger: Nested Loops Revisited. Proc. Parallel and Distributed Information Systems 1993: 230-242.Graefe et al. 1998. Goetz Graefe, Ross Bunker, Shaun Cooper: Hash Joins and Hash Teams in Microsoft SQL Server. VLDB Conference 1998: 86-97.

Masaru Kitsuregawa, Hidehiko Tanaka, Tohru Moto-Oka: Application of Hash to Data Base Machine and Its Architecture. New Generation Computing 1(1): 63-74 (1983).

Sacco 1986. Giovanni Maria Sacco: Fragmentation: A Technique for Efficient Query Processing. ACM Trans. on Database Systems 11(2): 113-133 (1986).

Selinger et al. 1979: Patricia G. Selinger, Morton M. Astrahan, Donald D. Chamberlin, Raymond A. Lorie, Thomas G. Price: Access Path Selection in a Relational Database Management System. ACM SIGMOD Conference 1979: 23-34.

Shapiro 1986. Leonard D. Shapiro: Join Processing in Database Systems with Large Main Memories. ACM Trans. on Database Systems 11(3): 239-264 (1986).

TPC-D. Transaction Processing Performance Council, www.tpc.org.

Model to Evaluate the Performances of OODBs

Jérôme Darmont [†] Michel Schneider [‡]

Laboratoire d'Informatique (LIMOS)
Université Blaise Pascal – Clermont-Ferrand II
Complexe Scientifique des Cézeaux
63177 Aubière Cedex
FRANCE

[†] *darmont@libd2.univ-bpclermont.fr* [‡] *schneider@cicsun.univ-bpclermont.fr*

Abstract

Performance of object-oriented database systems (OODBs) is still an issue to both designers and users nowadays. The aim of this paper is to propose a generic discrete-event random simulation model, called VOODB, in order to evaluate the performances of OODBs in general, and the performances of optimization methods like clustering in particular. Such optimization methods undoubtedly improve the performances of OODBs. Yet, they also always induce some kind of overhead for the system. Therefore, it is important to evaluate their exact impact on the overall performances. VOODB has been designed as a generic discrete-event random simulation model by putting to use a modelling approach, and has been validated by simulating the behavior of the O_2 OODB and the Texas persistent object store. Since our final objective is to compare object clustering algorithms, some experiments have also been conducted on the DSTC clustering technique, which is implemented in Texas. To validate VOODB, performance results obtained by simulation for a given experiment have been compared to the results obtained by benchmarking the real systems in the same conditions. Benchmarking and simulation performance evaluations have been observed to be consistent, so it appears that simulation can be a reliable approach to evaluate the performances of OODBs.

Keywords: Object-oriented database systems, Object clustering, Performance evaluation, Discrete-event random simulation.

1 Introduction

The needs in terms of performance evaluation for Object-Oriented Database Management Systems (OODBMSs) remain strong for both designers and users. Furthermore, it appears a necessity to perform *a priori* evaluations (before a system is actually built or achieved) in a variety of situations. A system designer may need to *a priori* test the efficiency of an optimization procedure or adjust the parameters of a buffering technique. It is also very helpful to users to *a priori* estimate whether a given system is able to handle a given workload.

The challenge of comparing object clustering techniques motivated us to contribute to OODBMSs performance evaluation. The principle of clustering is to store related objects close together on secondary storage. Hence, when one of these objects is loaded into the main memory, all its related objects are also loaded at the same time. Subsequent accesses to these objects are thus main memory accesses that are much faster than disk I/Os. However, clustering induces an overhead for the system (e.g., to reorganize the database, to collect and maintain usage statistics...), so it is important to gauge its true impact on the overall performances. For this particular problem, *a priori* evaluation is very attractive since it avoids coding inefficient algorithms in existing systems.

Discrete-event random simulation constitutes a traditional approach to *a priori* performance evaluation. Numerous simulation languages and/or environments

Proceedings of the 25th VLDB Conference, Edinburgh, Scotland, 1999.

exist nowadays. They allow the simulation of various classes of systems (computer systems, networks, production systems...). However, the use of simulation is not as widely disseminated as it could be in the database domain. The main difficulty is to elaborate a "good" functioning model for a system. Such a good model must be representative of the performances to evaluate, with the requested precision degree. For this sake, finding out the significant characteristics of a system and translating them into entities in the chosen simulation language often remains a specialist issue. Hence, users must call on consulting or specialized firms, which stretches out study times and costs.

In the field of OODBs, discrete-event random simulation has been chiefly used to validate proposals concerning optimization techniques, especially object clustering techniques. For instance, a dedicated model in PAWS was proposed in [Cha89] to validate a clustering and a buffering strategy in a CAD context. The objective was to find out how different optimization algorithms influence performances when the characteristics of the application accessing data vary, and which relationship exists between object clustering and parameters such as read/write ratio. Discrete-event random simulation was also used by [Dar96, Gay97] in order to compare the efficiency of different clustering strategies for OODBs. The proposed models were coded in SLAM II.

Some other studies use simulation approaches that are not discrete-event random simulation approaches, but are nevertheless interesting. [Che91] conducted simulation to show the effectiveness of different clustering schemes when parameters such as read/write ratio vary. The authors particularly focused on disk drive modelling. The CLAB (*CLustering LAboratory*) software [Tsa92] was designed to compare graph partitioning algorithms applied to object clustering. It is constituted of a set of Unix tools programmed in C++, which can be assembled in various configurations. Yet other studies from the fields of distributed or parallel databases prove helpful, e.g., the modelling methodologies from [Iae95] or the workload models from [He93, Bat95].

These different studies bring forth the following observations.

First, most proposed simulation models are dedicated: they have been designed to evaluate the performance of a given optimization method. Furthermore, they only exploit one type of OODBMS, while various architectures influencing performances are possible (object server, page server, etc.). We advocate a more generic approach that would help modelling the behavior of various systems, implanting various object bases into these systems, and executing various transactions on these databases.

Besides, precision in specifications for these simulation models varies widely. It is thus not always easy to reproduce these models from the published material. Hence, it appears beneficial to make use of a modelling methodology that allows, step by step, analyzing a system and specifying a formalized knowledge model that can be distributed and reused.

Finally, as far as we know, none of these models has been validated. The behavior of the studied algorithm, if it is implemented in a real system, is thus not guaranteed to be the same than in simulation, especially concerning performance results. Confronting simulated results to measurements performed in the same conditions on a real system is a good method to hint whether a simulation model actually behaves like the system it models or not.

Considering these observations, our motivation is to propose a discrete-event random simulation model that addresses the issues of genericity, reusability and reliability. This model, baptized VOODB (*Virtual Object-Oriented Database*), is indeed able to take into account different kinds of Client-Server architectures. It can also be parameterized to serve various purposes, e.g., to evaluate how a system reacts to different workloads or to evaluate the efficiency of optimization methods. Eventually, VOODB has been validated by confronting simulation results to performance measures achieved on real systems (namely O_2 and Texas).

The remainder of this paper is organized as follows. Section 2 introduces our modelling approach. Section 3 details the VOODB simulation model. Section 4 presents validation experiments for this model. We eventually conclude this paper and provide future research directions in Section 5.

2 Modelling approach

In order to clearly identify the interest of a structured approach, let us imagine that a simulation program is directly elaborated from informal knowledge concerning the studied system (Figure 1). Only experts mastering both the system to model and the target simulation language can satisfactorily use such an approach. It is thus only usable for punctual studies on relatively simple systems. The obtained simulation program is not meant to be reusable or later modified, and its documentation is minimal at best.

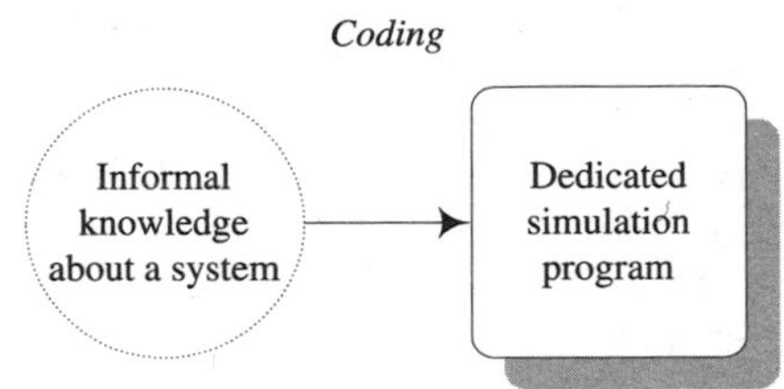

Figure 1: Unstructured approach to simulation

In opposition, a structured approach first consists in translating informal knowledge into an organized knowledge model (Figure 2). This knowledge model rests on concepts close to those of the study domain. It may be more or less formalized, and must enable the systematic generation of a simulation program. This approach helps focusing on the modelled system's properties and to make abstractions of constraints related to the simulation environment. It facilitates feedback to improve simulation quality: it is possible to reconsider functioning hypothesis or detail some pieces by modifying the knowledge model and generating new code. Low-level parameters may be introduced (e.g., mean access time to a disk block). The workload model may be directly included into the knowledge model and may itself incorporate some parameters (e.g., the proportion of objects accessed within a given class). Since long, specialists in simulation worked on defining the principles of such an approach [Sar79, Nan81, Sar91, Bal92, Gou92, Kel97].

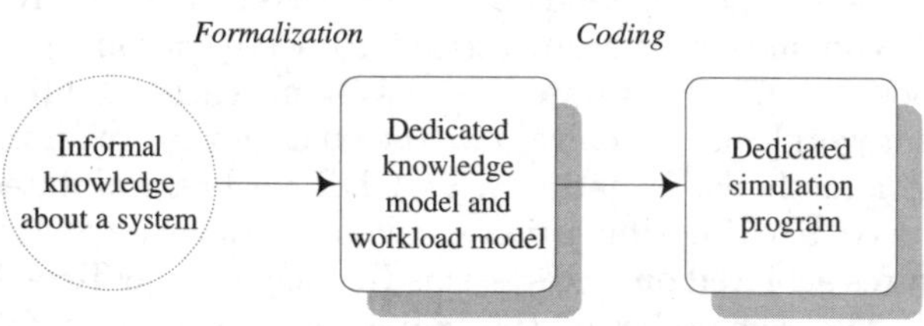

Figure 2: Structured modelling approach

The approach we recommend (Figure 3) is a generic extension to the former approach. Its consists in broadening the study field to take into account a whole class of systems. The knowledge model must hence be tunable (e.g., high-level parameters may help selecting the system's architecture) and modular (some functionalities are included in specific modules that may be added or removed at will). The knowledge model, which is necessarily more complex, must be described in a hierarchical way up to the desired detail level. We used the concepts and diagrams of UML [Rat97] to describe it.

We also propose that the workload model be separately characterized. It is then possible to reuse workload models from existing benchmarks (like HyperModel [And90], OO1 [Cat91] or OO7 [Car93]) or establish a specific model. We chose to incorporate the workload model from the OCB (*Object Clustering Benchmark*) generic benchmark [Dar98]. Thanks to numerous parameters, this workload model can be adapted to various situations (existing benchmark workload, specific application workload...).

The generic simulation program is obtained in a systematic way. Its modular architecture is the result of the two models it is based on. The final simulation program for a specific case study is obtained by instantiation of this generic program. This approach guarantees a good reusability. It is possible after a first simulation experiment to broaden the study specter by changing the parameters' values (especially those concerning the workload), by selecting other modules (for instance, by replacing a clustering module by another), or by incorporating new modules.

3 The VOODB simulation model

3.1 Knowledge model

In our context, the knowledge model describes the execution of transactions in an OODBMS (Figure 4).

Transactions are generated by the *Users*, who submit them to the *Transaction Manager*. The *Transaction Manager* determines which objects need to be accessed for the current transaction, and performs the necessary operations on these objects. A given object is requested by the *Transaction Manager* to the *Object Manager* that finds out which disk page contains the object. Then, it requests the page from the *Buffering Manager* that checks if the page is present in the memory buffer. If not, it requests the page from the *I/O Subsystem* that deals with physical disk accesses. After an operation on a given object is over, the *Clustering Manager* may update some usage statistics for the database. An analysis of these statistics can trigger a reclustering, which is then performed by the *Clustering Manager*. Such a database reorganization can also be demanded externally by the *Users*. The only treatments that differ when two distinct clustering algorithms are tested are those performed by the *Clustering Manager*. Other treatments in the model remain the same, whether clustering is used or not, and whatever the clustering strategy.

The knowledge model is hierarchical. Each of its activities (rounded boxes) can be further detailed, as is illustrated in Figure 5 for the "Access Disk" functioning rule.

The system's physical resources that appear as *swimlanes* in the knowledge model may be qualified as *active resources* since they actually perform some task. However, the system also includes *passive resources* that do not directly perform any task, but are used by the active resources to perform theirs. These passive resources do not appear on Figure 4, but must nevertheless be exhaustively listed (Table 1).

3.2 Evaluation model

3.2.1 Simulator selection

We first selected the QNAP2 (Queuing Network Analysis Package 2nd generation, version 9) discrete-event random simulation software [Sim95] to implement VOODB, because it proposes the following essential features:

- QNAP2 is a validated and reliable simulation tool;

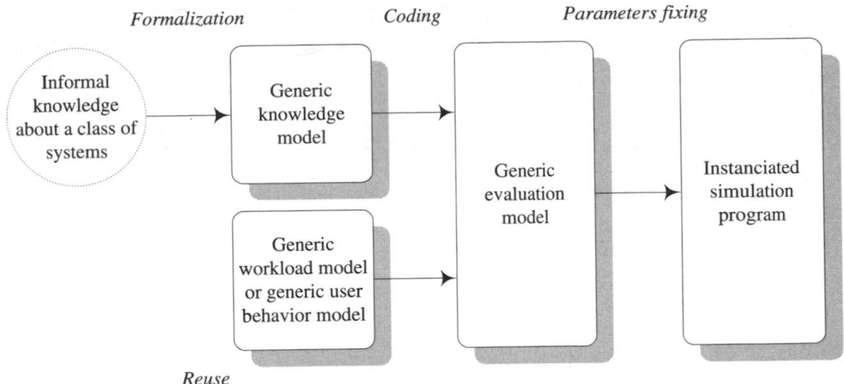

Figure 3: Generic, structured modelling approach

Passive resource
Processor and main memory in a centralized architecture, or *server processor and main memory* in a Client-Server architecture
Clients processor and main memory in a Client-Server architecture
Server disk controller and secondary storage
Database. Its concurrent access is managed by a scheduler that applies a transaction scheduling policy that depends on the multiprogramming level.

Table 1: VOODB passive resources

- QNAP2 allows the use of an object-oriented approach (since version 6);
- QNAP2 includes a full algorithmic language, derived from Pascal, which allows a relatively easy implementation of complex algorithms (object clustering, buffer page replacement, prefetching, etc.).

However, QNAP2 is an interpreted language. The models written in QNAP2 are hence much slower at execution time than if they were written in a compiled language. Therefore, we could not achieve the intensive simulation campaign we intended to. For instance, the simplest simulation experiments (without clustering) were 8 hours long, while the most complex were more than one week long. Thus, we could not gain much insight beyond basic results.

We eventually considered the use of C++, which is both an object-oriented and compiled language. This also allowed us reusing most of the OCB benchmark's C++ code. But the existing C++ simulation packages were either not completely validated, featured much more than we actually needed, and hence were getting as complicated to use as general simulation languages, or were not free. Hence, we decided to design

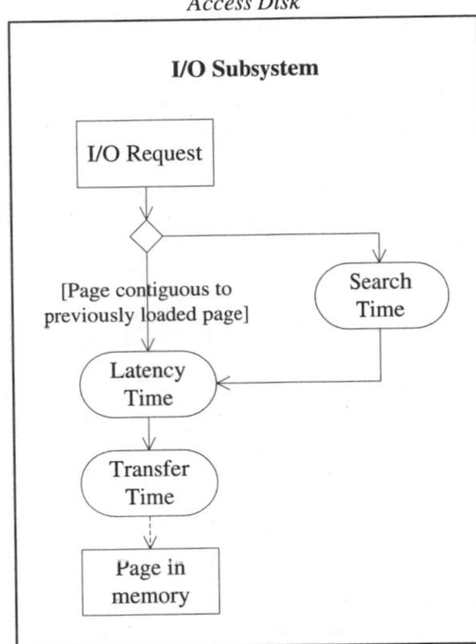

Figure 5: "Access disk" functioning rule detail

our own C++ simulation kernel. It has been baptized DESP-C++ (*Discrete-Event Simulation Package for C++*). Its main characteristics are validity, simplicity and efficiency. DESP-C++ has been validated by comparing the results of several simulation experiments conducted with DESP-C++ and QNAP2. Simulation experiments are now 20 to 1,000 times quicker with DESP-C++, depending on the model's complexity (the more a model is complex, the more QNAP2 performs poorly).

3.2.2 Knowledge model translation

Once the knowledge model is designed, it can be quasi-automatically translated into an evaluation model using any environment, whether it is a general simulation language or a usual programming language. Each entity in the knowledge model appears in the evalua-

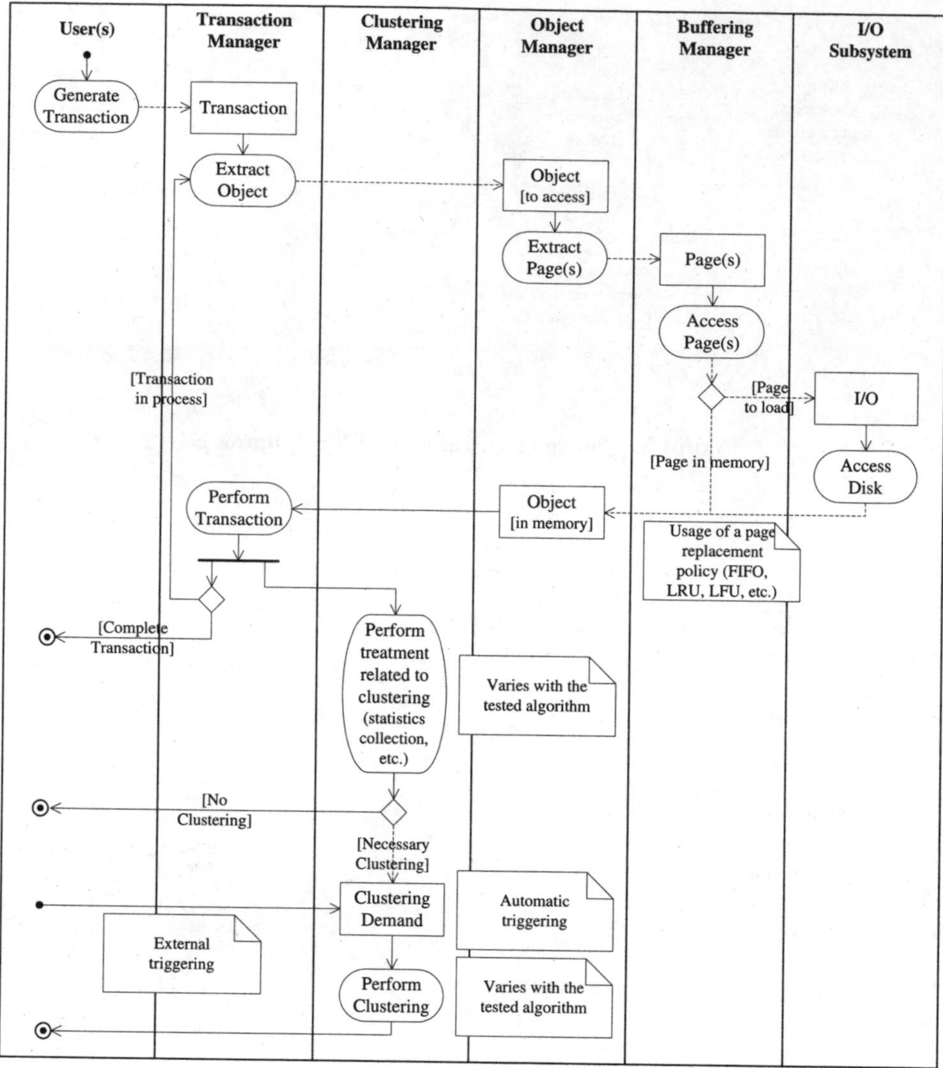

Figure 4: Knowledge model

tion model some way. In an object-oriented environment, resources (active and passive) become instantiated classes, and functioning rules are translated into methods.

More precisely, the translation from the knowledge model to the evaluation model proceeds as follows:

- each active resource (*swimlanes* in Figure 4) becomes a component of the simulation program (i.e., a class);
- each object (square boxes in Figure 4) becomes an interface to these components (i.e., it is used as a parameter in messages between two classes);
- each activity (round boxes in Figure 4) becomes a method within a component.

Passive resources are classes bearing mainly two methods: one to reserve the resource and another one to release it.

Table 2 recapitulates how entities from the knowledge model are translated in QNAP2 and DESP-C++, which both use a resource view (where the demeanor of each active resource is described). Table 2 also provides a translation in SLAM II [Pri86], which uses a transaction view (where the specification concerns the operations undergone by the entities flowing through the system). This is simply to show that the implementation of VOODB with a simulator using the transaction view is also possible.

3.3 Genericity in VOODB

Genericity in VOODB is primarily achieved through a set of parameters that help tuning the model in a variety of configurations, and setting up the different policies influencing the eventual behavior of an instance of the generic evaluation model. VOODB also

Subsystem	Entity	QNAP2 translation	DESP-C++ translat.	SLAM II translation
Workload	(Sub)Transaction	CUSTOMER object	Instance of class Client	SLAM Entity
Physical	Passive resource	RESOURCE STATION object	Instance of class Resource	RESOURCE block
	Active resource	Standard STATION object	Instance of an active resource class inheriting from class Resource	Set of SLAM nodes (ACTIVITY, EVENT, FREE, GOON...)
Control	Functioning rule	PROCEDURE called in the SERVICE clause of an active resource	Method of an active resource class	FORTRAN subroutine called in an EVENT node

Table 2: Translation of the knowledge model entities

benefits from the genericity of the OCB benchmark [Dar98] at the workload level, since OCB is itself tunable through a thorough set of 26 parameters. The parameters defining an instance of the VOODB evaluation model are presented in Table 3. Each active resource is actually associated to a set of parameters. These parameters are normally directly deduced from the studied system's specifications. However, some parameters are not always readily available and have to be worked out from benchmarks or measures (e.g., to determine network throughput or disk performances).

Our generic model allows simulating the behavior of different types of OODBMSs. It is in particular adapted to the different configurations of Client-Server architectures, which are nowadays the standard in OODBs. Our model is actually especially suitable to page server systems (like ObjectStore [Lam91], or O_2 [Deu91]), but can also be used to model object server systems (like ORION [Kim88] or ONTOS [And91]), or database server systems, or even multiserver hybrid systems (like GemStone [Ser92]). The organization of the VOODB components is controlled by the "System class" parameter.

4 Validation experiments

4.1 Experiments scope

Though we use validated tools (QNAP2, or DESP-C++), the results provided by simulation are not guaranteed to be consistent with reality. To check out if our simulation models were indeed valid, we simulated the behavior of two systems that offer object persistence: O_2 [Deu91] and Texas [Sin92]. We compared these results to those provided by benchmarking these real systems with OCB. The objective here was to use the same workload model in both sets of experiments.

In a second step, we seeked to evaluate the impact of an optimization method (the DSTC clustering technique [Bul96], which has been implemented in Texas). We again compared results obtained by simulation and direct measures performed under the same conditions on the real system.

Due to space constraints, we only present here our most significant results. Besides, our goal is not to perform sound performance evaluations of O_2, Texas and DSTC. We just seek to show our simulation approach can provide trustworthy results.

4.2 Experimental conditions

4.2.1 Real systems

The O_2 server we used (version 5.0) is installed on an IBM RISC 6000 43P240 biprocessor workstation. Each processor is a Power PC 604e 166. The workstation has 1 GB ECC RAM. Its operating system is AIX version 4. The O_2 server cache size is 16 MB by default.

The version of Texas we use is a prototype (version 0.5) running on a PC Pentium-II 266 with 64 MB of SDRAM, which operating system is Linux, version 2.0.30. The swap partition size is 64 MB. DSTC is integrated in Texas as a collection of new modules, and a modification of several Texas modules. Texas and the additional DSTC modules were compiled using the GNU C++ (version 2.7.2.1) compiler.

4.2.2 Simulation

Our C++ simulation models were compiled with the GNU C++ (version 2.7.2.1) compiler. They run on a PC Pentium-II 266 with 64 MB of SDRAM, under Windows 95.

In order to simulate the behavior of O_2 and Texas, VOODB has been parameterized as showed in Table 4. These parameters were all fixed up from the specification and configuration of the hardware and software systems we used.

Our simulation results have been achieved with 95% confidence intervals ($c = 0.95$). To determine these intervals, we used the method exposed in [Ban96]. For given observations, sample mean $\bar{X}$ and sample standard deviation σ are computed. The half-interval width h is $h=t_{n-1,1-\alpha/2}.\sigma/\sqrt{n}$, where t is given by the Student t-distribution, n is the number of replications and $\alpha=1-c$. The mean value belongs to

Active resource	Parameter	Code	Range	Default
System	System class	SYSCLASS	{Centralized | Object Server | Page Server | DB Server | Other}	Page Server
	Network throughput	NETTHRU	–	1 MB/s
Buffering Manager	Disk page size	PGSIZE	{512 | 1024 | 2048 | 4096 } bytes	4096 bytes
	Buffer size	BUFFSIZE	–	500 pages
	Buffer page replacement strategy	PGREP	{RANDOM | FIFO | LFU | LRU-K | CLOCK | GCLOCK | Other}	LRU-1
	Prefetching policy	PREFETCH	{None | Other}	None
Clustering Manager	Object clustering policy	CLUSTP	{None | Other}	None
	Objects initial placement	INITPL	{Sequential | Optimized sequential | Other}	Optimized Sequential
I/O Subsystem	Disk search time	DISKSEA	–	7.4 ms
	Disk latency time	DISKLAT	–	4.3 ms
	Disk transfer time	DISKTRA	–	0.5 ms
Transaction Manager	Multiprogramming level	MULTILVL	–	10
	Locks acquisition time	GETLOCK	–	0.5 ms
	Locks release time	RELLOCK	–	0.5 ms
Users	Number of users	NUSERS	–	1

Table 3: VOODB parameters

the $[\bar{X}\text{-}h, \bar{X}+h]$ confidence interval with a probability $c = 0.95$.

Since we wish to be within 5% of the sample mean with 95% confidence, we first performed a pilot study with $n = 10$. Then we computed the number of necessary additional replications n^* using the equation: $n^* = n.(h/h^*)^2$, where h is the half-width of the confidence interval for the pilot study and h^* the half-width of the confidence interval for all replications (the desired half-width).

Our simulation results showed that the required precision was achieved for all our performance criteria when $n+n^* \geq 100$, with a broad security margin. We thus performed 100 replications in all our experiments. In order to preserve results clarity in the following figures, we did not include the confidence intervals. They are however computed by default by DESP-C++.

4.3 Experiments on O_2 and Texas

First, we investigated the effects of the object base size (number of classes and number of instances in the database) on the performances (mean number of I/Os necessary to perform the transactions) of the studied systems. In this series of experiments, the number of classes in the schema (*NC*) is 20 or 50, and the number of instances (*NO*) varies from 500 to 20,000. The workload configuration is showed in Table 5. The other OCB parameters were set up to their default values.

In a second step, we varied the server cache size (O_2) or the available main memory (Texas) in order to study the effects on performances (mean number of I/Os). The objective was also to simulate the system's reaction when the (memory size / database size) ratio decreases. In the case of O_2, the server cache size is specified by environment variables. Our Texas version is implanted under Linux, which allows setting up memory size at boot time. Cache or main memory size varied from 8 MB to 64 MB in these experiments. Database size was fixed (*NC*=50, *NO*=20,000), we reused the workload from Table 5, and the other OCB parameters were set up to their default values.

4.3.1 Results concerning O_2

Database size variation

Figures 6 and 7 show how the performances of O_2 vary in terms of number of I/Os when the number of classes and the number of instances in the database vary. We can see that simulation results are in absolute value lightly different from the results measured on the real system, but that they clearly show the same tendency. The behavior of VOODB is indeed conforming to reality.

Cache size variation

The results obtained in this experiment in terms of number of I/Os are presented in Figure 8. They show that the performances of O_2 rapidly degrade when the database size (about 28 MB on an average) becomes

Parameter	Code	Value for O_2	Value for Texas
System class	SYSCLASS	Page server	Centralized
Network throughput	NETTHRU	$+\infty$	N/A
Disk page size	PGSIZE	4096 bytes	4096 bytes
Buffer size	BUFFSIZE	3840 pages	3275 pages
Buffer page replacement strategy	PGREP	LRU	LRU
Prefetching policy	PREFETCH	None	None
Object clustering policy	CLUSTP	None	DSTC
Objects initial placement	INITPL	Optimized Sequential	Optimized Sequential
Disk search time	DISKSEA	6.3 ms	7.4 ms
Disk latency time	DISKLAT	2.99 ms	4.3 ms
Disk transfer time	DISKTRA	0.7 ms	0.5 ms
Multiprogramming level	MULTILVL	10	1
Locks acquisition time	GETLOCK	0.5 ms	0
Locks release time	RELLOCK	0.5 ms	0
Number of users	NUSERS	1	1

Table 4: Parameters defining the O_2 and the Texas systems within VOODB

Parameter	Val.	Parameter	Val.
COLDN: Number of transactions (cold run)	0	*HOTN:* Number of transactions (warm run)	1000
PSET: Set-oriented access occurrence probability	0.25	*SETDEPTH:* Set-oriented access depth	3
PSIMPLE: Simple traversal occurrence probability	0.25	*SIMDEPTH:* Simple traversal access depth	3
PHIER: Hierarchy traversal occurrence probability	0.25	*HIEDEPTH:* Hierarchy traversal access depth	5
PSTOCH: Stochastic traversal occurrence probability	0.25	*STODEPTH:* Stochastic traversal access depth	50

Table 5: OCB workload definition

greater than the cache size. This decrease in performance is linear. Figure 8 also shows that the performances of O_2 can be reproduced again with our simulation model.

4.3.2 Results concerning Texas

Database size variation

Figures 9 and 10 show how the performances of Texas vary in terms of number of I/Os when the number of classes and the number of instances in the database vary. As is the case with O_2, we can see that simulation results and results measured on the real system lightly differ in absolute value, but that they bear the same tendency.

Memory size variation

Since Texas uses the virtual memory mechanisms from the operating system, we studied the effects of a decrease in available main memory size under Linux. The results obtained in terms of number of I/Os are presented in Figure 11. They show that the performances of Texas rapidly degrade when the main memory size becomes smaller than the database size (about 21 MB on an average). This degradation is due to Texas' object loading policy, which provokes the reservation in memory of numerous pages even before they are actually loaded. This process is clearly exponential and generates a costly swap, which is as important a hindrance as the main memory is small. The simulation results provided by VOODB are still conforming to reality.

4.4 Effects of DSTC on the performances of Texas

We underlined DSTC's clustering capability by placing the algorithm in favorable conditions. For this sake, we ran very characteristic transactions (namely, depth-3 hierarchy traversals) and measured the performances of Texas before and after clustering. We also evaluated clustering overhead. We checked out that the behavior of DSTC was the same in our simulation model and in the real system, by counting the number of created clusters and these clusters' mean size.

This experiment has been performed on a mid-sized database (50 classes, 20,000 instances, about 20 MB on an average). We had also planned to perform this experiment on a large object base, but we encoun-

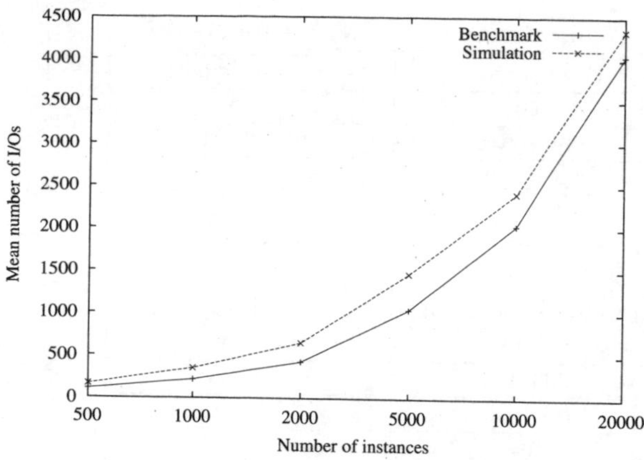

Figure 6: Mean number of I/Os depending on number of instances (O_2 – 20 classes)

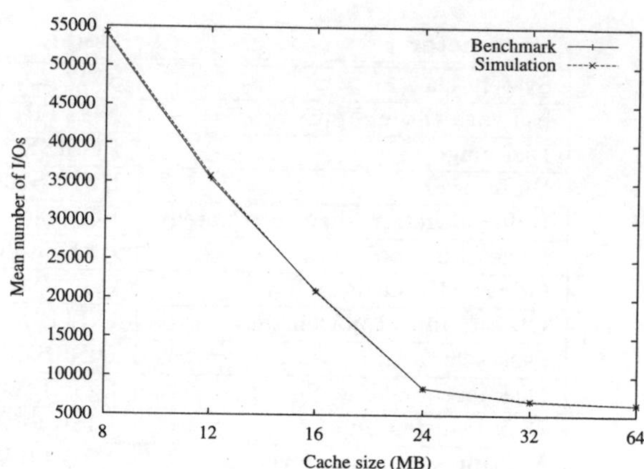

Figure 8: Mean number of I/Os depending on cache size (O_2)

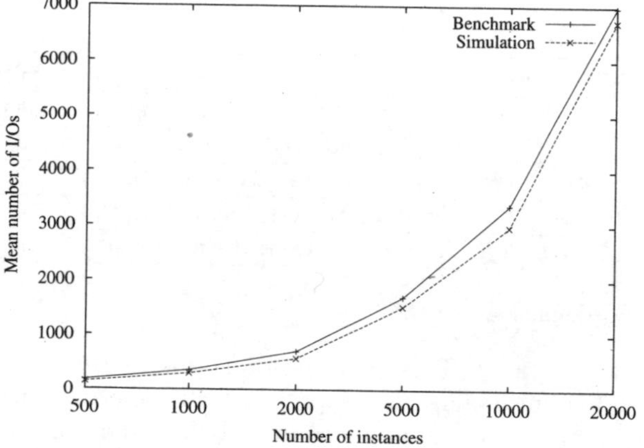

Figure 7: Mean number of I/Os depending on number of instances (O_2 – 50 classes)

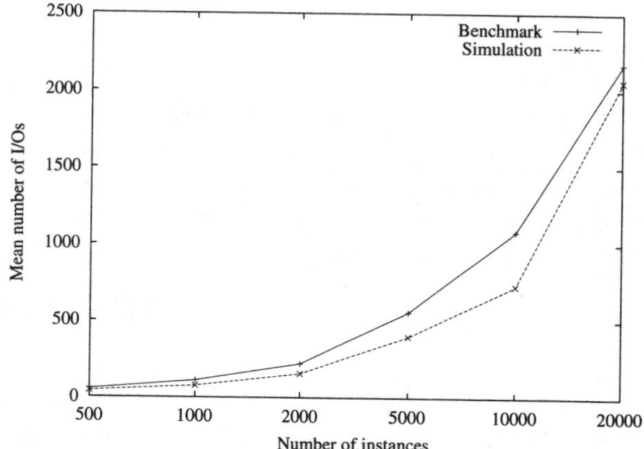

Figure 9: Mean number of I/Os depending on number of instances (Texas – 20 classes)

tered technical problems with Texas/DSTC. To bypass the problems, we reduced the main memory size from 64 MB to 8 MB so that the database size is actually large compared to the main memory size. Then, we reused the mid-sized object base from the first series of experiments. The other OCB parameters were set up to their default values.

Table 6 presents the numbers of I/Os achieved on the real system and in simulation, for the mid-sized database. It shows that DSTC allows substantial performance improvements (performance gain around a factor 5). Clustering overhead is high, though. Furthermore, the simulation results are overall consistent with the performance measurements done on the real system, except concerning clustering overhead, which is far less important in simulation than in reality.

This flagrant inconsistency is not due to a bug in the simulation model, but to a particularity in Texas. Indeed, after reorganization of the database by DSTC, objects are moved on different disk pages. Hence, their OIDs change because Texas uses physical OIDs. In order to maintain consistency among inter-object references, the whole database must be scanned and all references toward moved objects must be updated. This phase, which is very costly both in terms of I/Os and time, is pointless in our simulation models, since they necessarily use logical OIDs.

To simulate DSTC's behavior within Texas in a wholly faithful way, it would have been easy to take this conversion time into account in our simulations. However, we preferred keeping our initial results in order to underline the difficulty to implant a dynamic clustering technique within a persistent object store using physical OIDs. On the other hand, our simula-

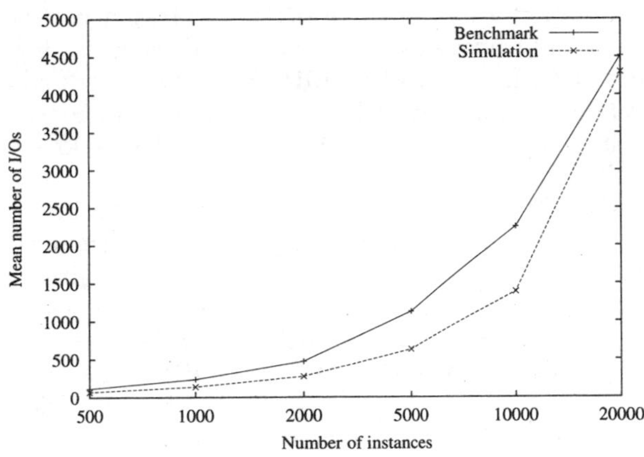

Figure 10: Mean number of I/Os depending on number of instances (Texas – 50 classes)

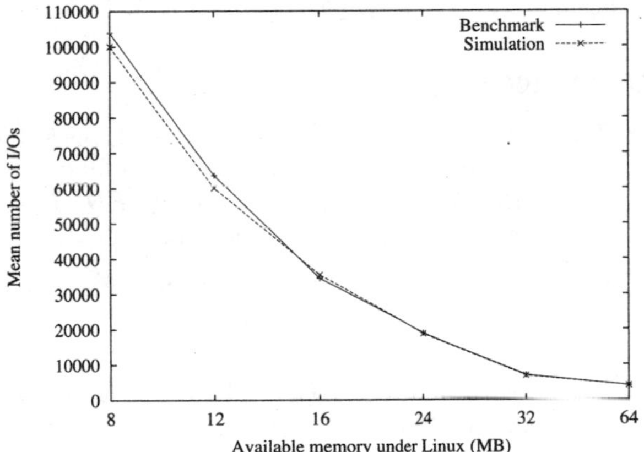

Figure 11: Mean number of I/Os depending on memory size (Texas)

tions show that such a dynamic technique is perfectly viable in a system with logical OIDs.

The number of clusters built by the DSTC method and these clusters' average size are presented in Table 7. We can observe again that there are few differences between the real system's behavior and its simulated behavior with VOODB.

Eventually, Table 8 presents the number of I/Os achieved on the real system and by simulation, for the "large" database. It shows that simulation results are still consistent with performances observed on the real system. Furthermore, the gain induced by clustering is much higher when the database does not wholly fit into the main memory (increase from a factor 5 to a factor of about 30). This result was foreseeable, since the more the memory size is reduced, the more the system must perform page replacements. Unused pages

	Bench.	Sim.	Ratio
Pre-clustering usage	1890.70	1878.80	1.0063
Clustering overhead	12799.60	354.50	36.1060
Post-clustering usage	330.60	350.50	0.9432
Gain	5.71	5.36	1.0652

Table 6: Effects of DSTC on the performances (mean number of I/Os) – Mid-sized base

	Bench.	Sim.	Ratio
Mean number of clusters	82.23	84.01	0.9788
Mean number of obj./clust.	12.83	13.73	0.9344

Table 7: DSTC clustering

hence normally remain only a short time in memory. A good object clustering is thus more useful in these conditions. Clustering overhead is not repeated here, since we reused the object base (in its initial and clustered state) from the first series of experiments.

	Bench.	Sim.	Ratio
Pre-clustering usage	12504.60	12547.80	0.9965
Post-clustering usage	424.30	441.50	0.9610
Gain	29.47	28.42	1.0369

Table 8: Effects of DSTC on the performances (mean number of I/Os) – "Large" base

5 Conclusion

We present in this paper a generic discrete-event random simulation model, VOODB, which is designed to evaluate the performances of OODBs. VOODB is parameterized and modular, and thus can be adapted to various purposes. It allows the simulation of various types of OODBMSs and can capture performance improvements achieved by optimization methods. Such optimization methods can be included in VOODB as interchangeable modules. Furthermore, the workload model adopted in VOODB (the OCB benchmark) can also be replaced by another existing benchmark or a specific workload. VOODB may be used as is (its C++ code is freely available) or tailored to fit some particular needs.

We have illustrated the genericity of VOODB and hinted its validity by setting its parameters to simulate the behavior of the O_2 OODB and the Texas persistent object store. We correlated the simulated performances of both systems with actual performance measures of the real systems (performed with the OCB benchmark), and observed they matched. The effects of the DSTC clustering technique on Texas' performances have also been mimicked by simulation.

VOODB may be used for several purposes. The performances of a single, or several optimization algorithms, may be evaluated in many different conditions. For instance, the host OODB or OS can vary, to see how a given algorithm behaves. Such clustering strategies may also be compared to each other that way. Furthermore, simulation has a low cost, since the different simulated systems (hardware, OS, OODBs) do not need to be acquired. Their specifications are enough. Eventually, we can *a priori* model the behavior of new systems, test their performances, analyze the simulation results, and ameliorate them (and then reiterate the process).

Eventually, VOODB has been obtained through the application of a modelling methodology that led to the design of a generic knowledge model and a generic evaluation model. This approach ensured that the specifications of the simulation models were precise enough for our deeds and that the evaluation model was properly translated from the knowledge model. It is also possible to reuse our knowledge model to produce simulation programs in other simulation languages or environment than QNAP2 or DESP-C++.

The reusability of VOODB may be important in a context of limited publicity. Since benchmarkers can encounter serious legal problems with OODB vendors if they publish performance studies [Car93], it can be helpful to have a tool to perform private performance evaluations.

Future work concerning this study is first performing intensive simulation experiments with DSTC. We indeed only have basic results. It would be interesting to know the right value for DSTC's parameters in various conditions. We also plan to evaluate the performances of other optimization techniques, like the clustering strategy proposed by [Gay97], which has also been implemented in Texas, recently. This clustering technique originates from collaboration between the University of Oklahoma and Blaise Pascal University. The ultimate goal is to compare different clustering strategies, to determine which one performs best in a given set of conditions.

Though simulation may be used in substitution to benchmarking (mainly for *a priori* performance evaluations), it may also be used in complement to benchmarking. For instance, mixed benchmarking-simulation approach may be used to measure some performance criteria necessitating precision by experimentation, and other criteria by simulation (e.g., to determine the best architecture for a given purpose). With such an approach, using the same workload (e.g., OCB) in simulation and on the real system is essential.

The VOODB simulation model could also be improved, in order to include more components influencing the performances of OODBs. For instance, it currently only provides a few basic buffering strategies (RANDOM, FIFO, LFU, LRU-K, CLOCK...) and no prefetching strategy, which have been demonstrated to influence the performances of OODBs a lot, too [Bul96].

VOODB could even be extended to take into account completely different aspects of performance in OODBs, like concurrency control or query optimization. VOODB could also take into account random hazards, like benign or serious system failures, in order to observe how the studied OODB behaves and recovers in critical conditions. Such features could be included in VOODB as new modules.

Eventually, to make reusability easier and more formal, VOODB could be rebuilt as part of a reusable model library, as modular fragments that could be assembled to form bigger models. For this sake, slicing the model into fragments is not enough. The structure and interface of each module must also be standardized and an explicit documentation for every submodel must be provided [Bre98].

References

[And90] T.L. Anderson et al., "The HyperModel Benchmark", *International Conference on Extending Database Technology (EDBT '90)*, Venice, Italy, March 1990, pp. 317-331

[And91] T. Andrews et al., "ONTOS: A persistent database for C++", *Object-Oriented Databases with Applications to CASE, Networks, and VLSI CAD*, Prentice Hall, 1991, pp. 387-406

[Bal92] O. Balci and R.E. Nance, "The simulation model development environment: an overview", *1992 Winter Simulation Conference*, pp. 726-736

[Ban96] J. Banks, "Output Analysis Capabilities of Simulation Software", *Simulation*, Vol. 66, No. 1, January 1996, pp. 23-30

[Bat95] C. Bates et al., "Simulating transaction processing in parallel database systems", *7th European Simulation Symposium (ESS '95)*, Erlanger-Nuremberg, Germany, October 1995, pp. 193-197

[Bre98] A.P.J. Breunese et al., "Libraries of Reusable Models: Theory and Application", *Simulation*, Vol. 41, No. 1, July 1998, pp. 7-22

[Bul96] F. Bullat and M. Schneider, "Dynamic Clustering in Object Database Exploiting Effective Use of Relationships Between Objects", *ECOOP '96*, Linz, Austria, July 1996; *LNCS* Vol. 1098, pp. 344-365

[Car93] M.J. Carey et al., "The OO7 Benchmark", *ACM SIGMOD International Conference on Management of Data*, Washington DC, May 1993, pp. 12-21

[Cat91] R.G.G. Cattell, "An Engineering Database Benchmark", *The Benchmark Handbook for Database Transaction Processing Systems*, Morgan Kaufmann, 1991, pp. 247-281

[Cha89] E.E. Chang and R.H. Katz, "Exploiting Inheritance and Structure Semantics for Effective Clustering and Buffering in an Object-Oriented DBMS", *ACM SIGMOD International Conference on Management of Data*, Portland, Oregon, June 1989, pp. 348-357

[Che91] J.R. Cheng and A.R. Hurson, "Effective clustering of complex objects in object-oriented databases", *ACM SIGMOD International Conference on Management of Data*, Denver, Colorado, May 1991, pp. 22-31

[Dar96] J. Darmont and L. Gruenwald, "A Comparison Study of Clustering Techniques for Object-Oriented Databases", *Information Sciences*, Vol. 94, No. 1-4, December 1996, pp. 55-86

[Dar98] J. Darmont et al., "OCB: A Generic Benchmark to Evaluate the Performances of Object-Oriented Database Systems", *6th International Conference on Extending Database Technology (EDBT '98)*, Valencia, Spain, March 1998; *LNCS* Vol. 1377 (Springer), pp. 326-340

[Deu91] O. Deux et al., "The O_2 System", *Communications of the ACM*, Vol. 34, No. 10, October 1991, pp. 34-48

[Gay97] J.-Y. Gay and L. Gruenwald, "A Clustering Technique for Object Oriented Databases", *8th International Conference on Database and Expert Systems Applications (DEXA '97)*, Toulouse, France, September 1997, *LNCS* Vol. 1308 (Springer), pp. 81-90

[Gou92] M. Gourgand and P. Kellert, "An object-oriented methodology for manufacturing systems modelling", *1992 Summer Computer Simulation Conference (SCSC)*, Reno, Nevada, pp. 1123-1128

[He93] M. He et al., "An Efficient Storage Protocol for Distributed Object-Oriented Databases", *IEEE Parallel and Distributed Processing*, 1993, pp. 606-610

[Iae95] G. Iaezolla and R. Mirandola, "Analysis of two simulation methodologies in performance studies of distributed data bases", *7th European Simulation Symposium (ESS '95)*, Erlanger-Nuremberg, Germany, October 1995, pp. 176-180

[Kel97] P. Kellert et al., "Object-oriented methodology for FMS modelling and simulation", *Int. J. Computer Integrated Manufacturing*, Vol. 10, No. 6, 1997, pp. 405-434

[Kim88] W. Kim et al., "Integrating an object-oriented programming system with a database system", *OOPSLA '88 International Conference*, San Diego, California, September 1988, pp. 142-152

[Lam91] C. Lamb et al., "The ObjectStore Database System", *Communications of the ACM*, Vol. 34, No. 10, October 1991, pp. 50-63

[Nan81] R.E. Nance, *Model representation in discrete event simulation: the conical methodology*, Technical Report CS-81003-R, Department of Computer Science, Virginia Tech, Blacksburg, Va., 1981

[Pri86] A.A.B. Pritsker, *Introduction to Simulation and SLAM II*, Hasted Press (John Wiley & Sons), System Publishing Corporation, 1986

[Rat97] Rational Software Corporation et al., *UML Semantics, version 1.1* and *UML Notation Guide, version 1.1*, September 1997

[Sar79] R.G. Sargent, "Validation of simulation models", *1979 Winter Simulation Conference*, San Diego, 1979, pp. 497-503

[Sar91] R.G. Sargent, "Simulation model verification and validation", *1991 Winter Simulation Conference*, Phoenix, 1991, pp. 37-47

[Ser92] Servio Corporation, *GemStone V. 3.2 Reference Manual*, 1992

[Sim95] Simulog, *QNAP2V9: Reference Manual*, 1995

[Sin92] V. Singhal et al., "Texas: An Efficient, Portable Persistent Store", *5th International Workshop on Persistent Object Systems*, San Miniato, Italy, 1992

[Tsa92] M.M. Tsangaris and J.F. Naughton, "On the Performance of Object Clustering Techniques", *ACM SIGMOD International Conference on Management of Data*, San Diego, California, June 1992, pp. 144-153

DBMSs On A Modern Processor: Where Does Time Go?

Anastassia Ailamaki David J. DeWitt Mark D. Hill David A. Wood

University of Wisconsin-Madison
Computer Science Dept.
1210 W. Dayton St.
Madison, WI 53706
U.S.A.
{natassa,dewitt,markhill,david}@cs.wisc.edu

Abstract

Recent high-performance processors employ sophisticated techniques to overlap and simultaneously execute multiple computation and memory operations. Intuitively, these techniques should help database applications, which are becoming increasingly compute and memory bound. Unfortunately, recent studies report that faster processors do not improve database system performance to the same extent as scientific workloads. Recent work on database systems focusing on minimizing memory latencies, such as cache-conscious algorithms for sorting and data placement, is one step toward addressing this problem. However, to best design high performance DBMSs we must carefully evaluate and understand the processor and memory behavior of commercial DBMSs on today's hardware platforms.

In this paper we answer the question "Where does time go when a database system is executed on a modern computer platform?" We examine four commercial DBMSs running on an Intel Xeon and NT 4.0. We introduce a framework for analyzing query execution time on a DBMS running on a server with a modern processor and memory architecture. To focus on processor and memory interactions and exclude effects from the I/O subsystem, we use a memory resident database. Using simple queries we find that database developers should (a) optimize data placement for the second level of data cache, and not the first, (b) optimize instruction placement to reduce first-level instruction cache stalls, but (c) not expect the overall execution time to decrease significantly without addressing stalls related to subtle implementation issues (e.g., branch prediction).

Proceedings of the 25th VLDB Conference, Edinburgh, Scotland, 1999.

1 Introduction

Today's database servers are systems with powerful processors that overlap and complete instructions and memory accesses out of program order. Due to the sophisticated techniques used for hiding I/O latency and the complexity of modern database applications, DBMSs are becoming compute and memory bound. Although researchers design and evaluate processors using programs much simpler than DBMSs (e.g., SPEC, LINPACK), one would hope that more complicated programs such as DBMSs would take full advantage of the architectural innovations. Unfortunately, recent studies on some commercial DBMSs have shown that their hardware behavior is suboptimal compared to scientific workloads.

Recently there has been a significant amount of effort toward improving the performance of database applications on today's processors. The work that focuses on optimizing the processor and memory utilization can be divided into two categories: evaluation studies and cache performance improvement techniques. The first category includes a handful of recent studies that identified the problem and motivated the community to study it further. Each of these studies presents results from experiments with only a single DBMS running a TPC benchmark on a specific platform. The second category includes papers that propose (a) algorithmic improvements for better cache utilization when performing popular tasks in a DBMS, such as sorting, and (b) data placement techniques for minimizing cache related waiting time.

Although generally the results of these evaluation studies corroborate each other, there are no results showing the behavior of more than one commercial DBMS on the same hardware platform. Such results are important in order to identify general trends that hold true across database systems and determine what problems we must work on to make database systems run faster.

This is the first paper to analyze the execution time breakdown of four commercial DBMSs on the same hardware platform (a 6400 PII Xeon/MT Workstation running Windows NT v4.0). The workload consists of range selections and joins running on a memory resident database, in order to isolate basic operations and identify common trends across the DBMSs. We conclude that, even with these simple queries, almost half of the execution time is spent on stalls. Analysis of the components of the stall time provides more insight about the operation of the cache as the record size and the selectivity are varied. The simplicity of the queries helped to overcome the lack of access to the DBMS source code. The results show that:

- On the average, half the execution time is spent in stalls (implying database designers can improve DBMS performance significantly by attacking stalls).
- In all cases, 90% of the memory stalls are due to:
  - Second-level cache data misses, while first-level data stalls are not important (implying data placement should focus on the second-level cache),

  and
  - First-level instruction cache misses, while second-level instruction stalls are not important (implying instruction placement should focus on level one instruction caches).
- About 20% of the stalls are caused by subtle implementation details (e.g., branch mispredictions) (implying that there is no "silver bullet" for mitigating stalls).
- (A methodological result.) Using simple queries rather than full TPC-D workloads provides a methodological advantage, because results are simpler to analyze and yet are substantially similar to the results obtained using full benchmarks. To verify this, we implemented and ran the TPC-D benchmark on three of the four systems, and the results are substantially similar to the results obtained using simpler queries.

The rest of this paper is organized as follows: Section 2 presents a summary of recent database workload characterization studies and an overview of the cache performance improvements proposed. Section 3 describes the vendor-independent part of this study: an analytic framework for characterizing the breakdown of the execution time and the database workload. Section 4 describes the experimental setup. Section 5 presents our results. Section 6 concludes, and Section 7 discusses future directions.

2 Related Work

Much of the related research has focused on improving the query execution time, mainly by minimizing the stalls due to memory hierarchy when executing an isolated task. There are a variety of algorithms for fast sorting techniques [1][12][15] that propose optimal data placement into memory and sorting algorithms that minimize cache misses and overlap memory-related delays. In addition, several cache-conscious techniques such as blocking, data partitioning, loop fusion, and data clustering were evaluated [17] and found to improve join and aggregate queries. Each of these studies is targeted to a specific task and concentrate on ways to make it faster.

The first hardware evaluation of a relational DBMS running an on-line transaction processing (OLTP) workload [22] concentrated on multiprocessor system issues, such as assigning processes to different processors to avoid bandwidth bottlenecks. Contrasting scientific and commercial workloads [14] using TPC-A and TPC-C on another relational DBMS showed that commercial workloads exhibit large instruction footprints with distinctive branch behavior, typically not found in scientific workloads and that they benefit more from large first-level caches. Another study [21] showed that, although I/O can be a major bottleneck, the processor is stalled 50% of the time due to cache misses when running OLTP workloads.

In the past two years, several interesting studies evaluated database workloads, mostly on multiprocessor platforms. Most of these studies evaluate OLTP workloads [4][13][10], a few evaluate decision support (DSS) workloads [11] and there are some studies that use both [2][16]. All of the studies agree that the DBMS behavior depends upon the nature of the workload (DSS or OLTP), that DSS workloads benefit more from out-of-order processors with increased instruction-level parallelism than OLTP, and that memory stalls are a major bottleneck. Although the list of references presented here is not exhaustive, it is representative of the work done in evaluating database workloads. Each of these studies presents results from a single DBMS running a TPC benchmark on a single platform, which makes contrasting the DBMSs and identifying common characteristics difficult.

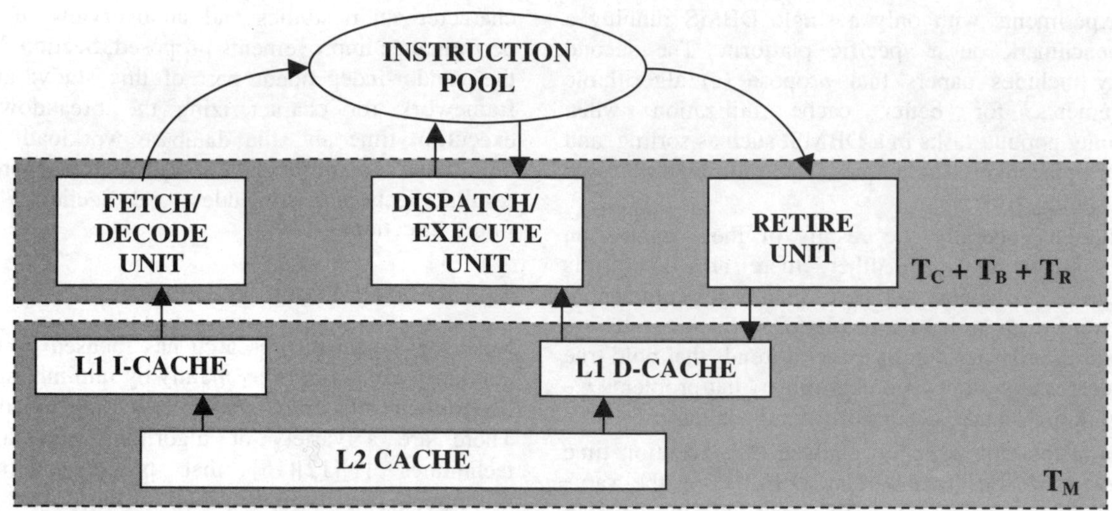

Figure 2.1: *Simplified block diagram of a processor operation*

3 Query execution on modern processors

In this section, we describe a framework that describes how major hardware components determine execution time. The framework analyzes the hardware behavior of the DBMS from the moment it receives a query until the moment it returns the results. Then, we describe a workload that allows us to focus on the basic operations of the DBMSs in order to identify the hardware components that cause execution bottlenecks.

3.1 Query execution time: a processor model

To determine where the time goes during execution of a query, we must understand how a processor works. The pipeline is the basic module that receives an instruction, executes it and stores its results into memory. The pipeline works in a number of sequential stages, each of which involves a number of functional components. An operation at one stage can overlap with operations at other stages.

Figure 3.1 shows a simplified diagram of the major pipeline stages of a processor similar to the Pentium II [6][8]. First, the FETCH/DECODE unit reads the user program instructions from the instruction cache (L1 I-cache), decodes them and puts them into an instruction pool. The DISPATCH/EXECUTE unit schedules execution of the instructions in the pool subject to data dependencies and resource availability, and temporarily stores their results. Finally, the RETIRE unit knows how and when to commit (retire) the temporary results into the data cache (L1 D-cache).

In some cases, an operation may not be able to complete immediately and delay ("stall") the pipeline. The processor tries to cover the stall time by doing useful work, using the following techniques:

- Non-blocking caches: Caches do not block when servicing requests. For example, if a read request to one of the first-level caches fails (misses), the request is forwarded to the second-level cache (L2 cache), which is usually unified (used for both data and instructions). If the request misses in L2 as well, it is forwarded to main memory. During the time the retrieval is pending, the caches at both levels can process other requests.
- Out-of-order execution: If instruction X stalls, another instruction Y that follows X in the program can execute before X, provided that Y's input operands do not depend on X's results. The dispatch/execute unit contains multiple functional units to perform out-of-order execution of instructions.
- Speculative execution with branch prediction: Instead of waiting until a branch instruction's predicate is resolved, an algorithm "guesses" the predicate and fetches the appropriate instruction stream. If the guess is correct, the execution continues normally; if it is wrong, the pipeline is flushed, the retire unit deletes the wrong results and the fetch/decode unit fetches the correct instruction stream. Branch mispredictions incur both computation overhead (time spent in computing the wrong instructions), and stall time.

Even with these techniques, the stalls cannot be fully overlapped with useful computation. Thus, the time to execute a query (T_Q) includes a useful computation time (T_C), a stall time because of memory stalls (T_M), a branch misprediction overhead (T_B), and resource-related stalls (T_R). The latter are due to execution resources not being available, such as functional units, buffer space in the instruction pool, or registers. As discussed above, some of the stall time can be overlapped (T_{OVL}). Thus, the following equation holds:

$$T_Q = T_C + T_M + T_B + T_R - T_{OVL}$$

T_C			**computation time**
T_M			**stall time related to memory hierarchy**
	T_{L1D}		stall time due to L1 D-cache misses (with hit in L2)
	T_{L1I}		stall time due to L1 I-cache misses (with hit in L2)
	T_{L2}	T_{L2D}	stall time due to L2 data misses
		T_{L2I}	stall time due to L2 instruction misses
	T_{DTLB}		stall time due to DTLB misses
	T_{ITLB}		stall time due to ITLB misses
T_B			**branch misprediction penalty**
T_R			**resource stall time**
	T_{FU}		stall time due to functional unit unavailability
	T_{DEP}		stall time due to dependencies among instructions
	T_{MISC}		stall time due to platform-specific characteristics

Table 3.1: *Execution time components*

Table 3.1 shows the time breakdown into smaller components. The DTLB and ITLB (Data or Instruction Translation Lookaside Buffer) are page table caches used for translation of data and instruction virtual addresses into physical ones. The next section briefly discusses the importance of each stall type and how easily it can be overlapped using the aforementioned techniques. A detailed discussion on hiding stall times can be found elsewhere [6].

3.2 Significance of the stall components

Previous work has focused on improving DBMS performance by reducing T_M, the memory hierarchy stall component. In order to be able to use the experimental results effectively, it is important to determine the contribution each of the different types of stalls makes to the overall execution time. Although out-of-order and speculative execution help hide some of the stalls, there are some stalls that are difficult to overlap, and thus are the most critical for performance.

It is possible to overlap T_{L1D} if the number of L1 D-cache misses is not too high. Then the processor can fetch and execute other instructions until the data is available from the second-level cache. The more L1 D-cache misses that occur, the more instructions the processor must execute to hide the stalls. Stalls related to L2 cache data misses can overlap with each other, when there are sufficient parallel requests to main memory. T_{DTLB} can be overlapped with useful computation as well, but a DTLB miss penalty depends on the page table implementation for each processor. Processors successfully use sophisticated techniques to overlap data stalls with useful computation.

Instruction-related cache stalls, on the other hand, are difficult to hide because they cause a serial bottleneck to the pipeline. If there are no instructions available, the processor must wait. Branch mispredictions also create serial bottlenecks; the processor again must wait until the correct instruction stream is fetched into the pipeline. The Xeon processor exploits spatial locality in the instruction stream with special instruction-prefetching hardware. Instruction prefetching effectively reduces the number of I-cache stalls, but occasionally it can increase the branch misprediction penalty.

Although related to instruction execution, T_R (the resource stall time) is easier to overlap than T_{ITLB} and instruction cache misses. The processor can hide T_{DEP} depending on the degree of instruction-level parallelism of the program, and can overlap T_{FU} with instructions that use functional units with less contention.

3.3 Database workload

The workload used in this study consists of single-table range selections and two table equijoins over a memory resident database, running a single command stream. Such a workload eliminates dynamic and random parameters, such as concurrency control among multiple transactions, and isolates basic operations, such as sequential access and index selection. In addition, it allows examination of the processor and memory behavior without I/O interference. Thus, it is possible to explain the behavior of the system with reasonable assumptions and identify common trends across different DBMSs.

The database contains one basic table, R, defined as follows:

create table R (a1 **integer not null,**
a2 **integer not null,**
a3 **integer not null,**
<rest of fields>)

In this definition, <rest of fields> stands for a list of integers that is not used by any of the queries. The relation is populated with 1.2 million 100-byte records. The values of the field a2 are uniformly distributed between 1 and 40,000. The experiments run three basic queries on R:

1. *Sequential range selection:*

```
select avg(a3)
from R
where a2 < Hi and a2 > Lo          (1)
```

The purpose of this query is to study the behavior of the DBMS when it executes a sequential scan, and examine the effects of record size and query selectivity. Hi and Lo define the interval of the qualification attribute, a2. The reason for using an aggregate, as opposed to just selecting the rows, was twofold. First, it makes the DBMS return a minimal number of rows, so that the measurements are not affected by client/server communication overhead. Storing the results into a temporary relation would affect the measurements because of the extra insertion operations. Second, the average aggregate is a common operation in the TPC-D benchmark. The selectivity used was varied from 0% to 100%. Unless otherwise indicated, the query selectivity used is 10%.

2. *Indexed range selection:* The range selection (1) was resubmitted after constructing a non-clustered index on R.a2. The same variations on selectivity were used.

3. *Sequential join:* To examine the behavior when executing an equijoin with no indexes, the database schema was augmented by one more relation, S, defined the same way as R. The field a1 is a primary key in S. The query is as follows:

```
select avg(R.a3)
from R, S
where R.a2 = S.a1          (2)
```

There are 40,000 100-byte records in S, each of which joins with 30 records in R.

4 Experimental Setup

We used a 6400 PII Xeon/MT Workstation to conduct all of the experiments. We use the hardware counters of the Pentium II Xeon processor to run the experiments at full speed, to avoid any approximations that simulation would impose, and to conduct a comparative evaluation of the four DBMSs. This section describes the platform-specific hardware and software details, and presents the experimental methodology.

4.1 The hardware platform

The system contains one Pentium II Xeon processor running at 400 MHz, with 512 MB of main memory connected to the processor chip through a 100 MHz system bus. The Pentium II is a powerful server processor with an out-of-order engine and speculative instruction execution [23]. The X86 instruction set is composed by CISC instructions, and they are translated into up to three RISC instructions (μops) each at the decode phase of the pipeline.

Characteristic	**L1 (split)**	**L2**
Cache size	16KB Data 16KB Instruction	512KB
Cache line size	32 bytes	32 bytes
Associativity	4-way	4-way
Miss Penalty	4 cycles (w/ L2 hit)	Main memory
Non-blocking	Yes	Yes
Misses outstanding	4	4
Write Policy	L1-D: Write-back L1-I: Read-only	Write-back

Table 4.1: *Pentium II Xeon cache characteristics*

There are two levels of non-blocking cache in the system. There are separate first-level caches for instructions and data, whereas at the second level the cache is unified. The cache characteristics are summarized in Table 4.1.

4.2 The software

Experiments were conducted on four commercial DBMSs, the names of which cannot be disclosed here due to legal restrictions. Instead, we will refer to them as System A, System B, System C, and System D. They were installed on Windows NT 4.0 Service Pack 4.

The DBMSs were configured the same way in order to achieve as much consistency as possible. The buffer pool size was large enough to fit the datasets for all the queries. We used the NT performance-monitoring tool to ensure that there was no significant I/O activity during query execution, because the objective is to measure pure processor and memory performance. In addition, we wanted to avoid measuring the I/O subsystem of the OS. To define the schema and execute the queries, the exact same commands and datasets were used for all the DBMSs, with no vendor-specific SQL extensions.

4.3 Measurement tools and methodology

The Pentium II processor provides two counters for event measurement [8]. We used *emon*, a tool provided by Intel, to control these counters. Emon can set the counters to zero, assign event codes to them and read their values either after a pre-specified amount of time, or after a program has completed execution. For example, the following command measures the number of retired instructions during execution of the program *prog.exe*, at the user and the kernel level:

```
emon –C (INST_RETIRED:USER,
         INST_RETIRED:SUP    ) prog.exe
```

Emon was used to measure 74 event types for the results presented in this report. We measured each event type in both user and kernel mode.

Stall time component			Description	Measurement method
T_C			computation time	Estimated minimum based on μops retired
T_M	T_{L1D}		L1 D-cache stalls	#misses * 4 cycles
	T_{L1I}		L1 I-cache stalls	actual stall time
	T_{L2}	T_{L2D}	L2 data stalls	#misses * measured memory latency
		T_{L2I}	L2 instruction stalls	#misses * measured memory latency
	T_{DTLB}		DTLB stalls	Not measured
	T_{ITLB}		ITLB stalls	#misses * 32 cycles
T_B			branch misprediction penalty	# branch mispredictions retired * 17 cycles
T_R	T_{FU}		functional unit stalls	actual stall time
	T_{DEP}		dependency stalls	actual stall time
	T_{ILD}		Instruction-length decoder stalls	actual stall time
T_{OVL}			overlap time	Not measured

Table 4.2: *Method of measuring each of the stall time components*

Before taking measurements for a query, the main memory and caches were warmed up with multiple runs of this query. In order to distribute and minimize the effects of the client/server startup overhead, the unit of execution consisted of 10 different queries on the same database, with the same selectivity. Each time emon executed one such unit, it measured a pair of events. In order to increase the confidence intervals, the experiments were repeated several times and the final sets of numbers exhibit a standard deviation of less than 5 percent. Finally, using a set of formulae[1], these numbers were transformed into meaningful performance metrics.

Using the counters, we measured each of the stall times described in Section 3.1 by measuring each of their individual components separately. The application of the framework to the experimental setup suffers the following caveats:

- We were not able to measure T_{DTLB}, because the event code is not available.
- The Pentium II event codes allow measuring the number of occurrences for each event type (e.g., number of L1 instruction cache misses) during query execution. In addition, we can measure the actual stall time due to certain event types (after any overlaps). For the rest, we multiplied the number of occurrences by an estimated penalty [18][19]. Table 4.2 shows a detailed list of stall time components and the way they were measured. Measurements of the memory subsystem strongly indicate that the workload is latency-bound, rather than bandwidth-bound (it rarely uses more than a third of the available memory bandwidth). In addition, past experience [18][19] with database applications has shown little queuing of requests in memory. Consequently, we expect the results that use penalty approximations to be fairly accurate.
- No contention conditions were taken into account.

T_{MISC} from Table 4.1 (stall time due to platform-specific characteristics) has been replaced with T_{ILD} (instruction-length decoder stalls) in Table 4.2. Instruction-length decoding is one stage in the process of translating X86 instructions into μops.

5 Results

We executed the workload described in Section 3 on four commercial database management systems. In this section, we first present an overview of the execution time breakdown and discuss some general trends. Then, we focus on each of the important stall time components and analyze it further to determine the implications from its behavior. Finally, we compare the time breakdown of our microbenchmarks against a TPC-D and a TPC-C workload. Since almost all of the experiments executed in user mode more than 85% of the time, all of the measurements shown in this section reflect user mode execution, unless stated otherwise.

5.1 Execution time breakdown

Figure 5.1 shows three graphs, each summarizing the average execution time breakdown for one of the queries. Each bar shows the contribution of the four components (T_C, T_M, T_B, and T_R) as a percentage of the total query execution time. The middle graph showing the indexed range selection only includes systems B, C and D, because System A did not use the index to execute this query. Although the workload is much simpler than TPC benchmarks [5], the computation time is usually less than half the execution time; thus, the processor spends most of the time stalled. Similar results have been presented for OLTP [21][10] and DSS [16] workloads, although none of the studies measured more than one DBMS. The high processor stall time indicates the importance of further

[1] Seckin Unlu and Andy Glew provided us with invaluable help in figuring out the correct formulae, and Kim Keeton shared with us the ones used in [10].

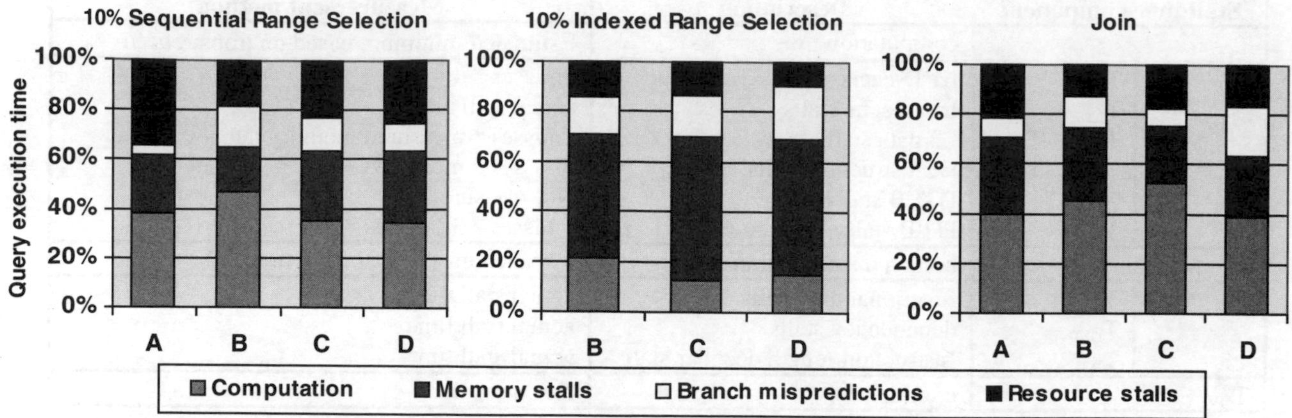

Figure 5.1: *Query execution time breakdown into the four time components.*

analyzing the query execution time. Even as processor clocks become faster, stall times are not expected to become much smaller because memory access times do not decrease as fast. Thus, the computation component will become an even smaller fraction of the overall execution time.

The memory stall time contribution varies more across different queries and less across different database systems. For example, Figure 5.1 shows that when System B executes the sequential range selection, it spends 20% of the time in memory stalls. When the same system executes the indexed range selection, the memory stall time contribution becomes 50%. Although the indexed range selection accesses fewer records, its memory stall component is larger than in the sequential selection, probably because the index traversal has less spatial locality than the sequential scan. The variation in T_M's contribution across DBMSs suggests different levels of platform-specific optimizations. However, as discussed in Section 5.2, analysis of the memory behavior yields that 90% of T_M is due to L1 I-cache and L2 data misses in all of the systems measured. Thus, despite the variation, there is common ground for research on improving memory stalls without necessarily having to analyze all of the DBMSs in detail.

Minimizing memory stalls has been a major focus of database research on performance improvement. Although in most cases the memory stall time (T_M) accounts for most of the overall stall time, the other two components are always significant. Even if the memory stall time is entirely hidden, the bottleneck will eventually shift to the other stalls. In systems B, C, and D, branch misprediction stalls account for 10-20% of the execution time, and the resource stall time contribution ranges from 15-30%. System A exhibits the smallest T_M and T_B of all the DBMSs in most queries; however, it has the highest percentage of resource stalls (20-40% of the execution time). This indicates that optimizing for two kinds of stalls may shift the bottleneck to the third kind. Research on improving DBMS performance should focus on minimizing all three kinds of stalls to effectively decrease the execution time.

5.2 Memory stalls

In order to optimize performance, a major target of database research has been to minimize the stall time due to memory hierarchy and disk I/O latencies [1][12][15][17]. Several techniques for cache-conscious data placement have been proposed [3] to reduce cache misses and miss penalties. Although these techniques are successful within the context in which they were proposed, a closer look at the execution time breakdown shows that there is significant room for improvement. This section discusses the significance of the memory stall components to the query execution time, according to the framework discussed in Section 3.2.

Figure 5.2 shows the breakdown of T_M into the following stall time components: T_{L1D} (L1 D-cache miss stalls), T_{L1I} (L1 I-cache miss stalls), T_{L2D} (L2 cache data miss stalls), T_{L2I} (L2 cache instruction miss stalls), and T_{ITLB} (ITLB miss stalls) for each of the four DBMSs. There is one graph for each type of query. Each graph shows the memory stall time breakdown for the four systems. The selectivity for range selections shown is set to 10% and the record size is kept constant at 100 bytes.

From Figure 5.2, it is clear that L1 D-cache stall time is insignificant. In reality its contribution is even lower, because our measurements for the L1 D-cache stalls do not take into account the overlap factor, i.e., they are upper bounds. An L1 D-cache miss that hits on the L2 cache incurs low latency, which can usually be overlapped with other computation. Throughout the experiments, the L1 D-cache miss rate (number of misses divided by the number of memory references) usually is around 2%, and never exceeds 4%. A study on Postgres95 [11] running TPC-D also reports low L1 D-cache miss rates. Further analysis indicates that during query execution the DBMS accesses private data structures more often than it accesses data in the relations. This

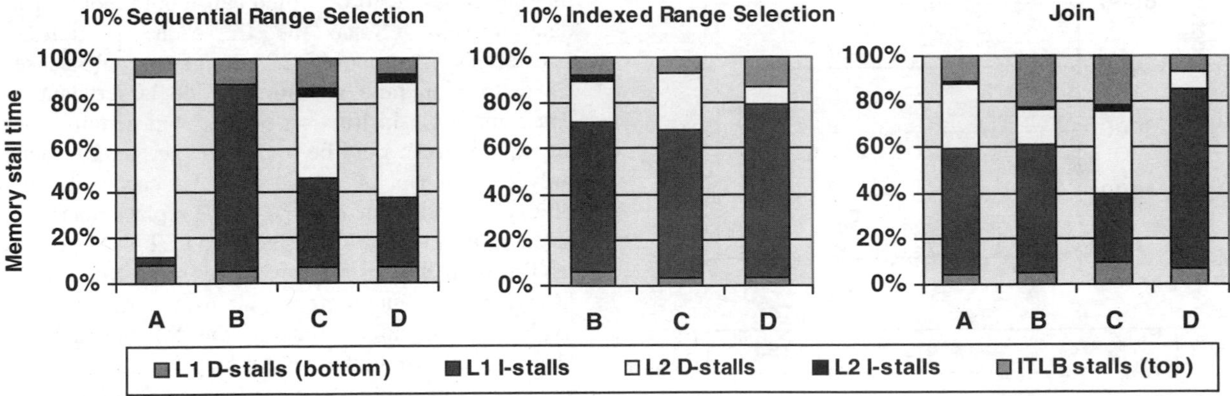

Figure 5.2: *Contributions of the five memory components to the memory stall time (T_M)*

often-accessed portion of data fits into the L1 D-cache, and the only misses are due to less often accessed data. The L1 D-cache is not a bottleneck for any of the commercial DBMSs we evaluated.

The stall time caused by L2 cache instruction misses (T_{L2I}) and ITLB misses (T_{ITLB}) is also insignificant in all the experiments. T_{L2I} contributes little to the overall execution time because the second-level cache misses are two to three orders of magnitude less than the first-level instruction cache misses. The low T_{ITLB} indicates that the systems use few instruction pages, and the ITLB is enough to store the translations for their addresses.

The rest of this section discusses the two major memory-related stall components, T_{L2D} and T_{L1I}.

5.2.1 Second-level cache data stalls

For all of the queries run across the four systems, T_{L2D} (the time spent on L2 data stalls) is one of the most significant components of the execution time. In three out of four DBMSs, the L2 cache data miss rate (number of data misses in L2 divided by number of data accesses in L2) is typically between 40% and 90%, therefore much higher than the L1 D-cache miss rate. The only exception is System B, which exhibits optimized data access performance at the second cache level as well. In the case of the sequential range query, System B exhibits far fewer L2 data misses per record than all the other systems (B has an L2 data miss rate of only 2%), consequently its T_{L2D} is insignificant.

The stall time due to L2 cache data misses directly relates to the position of the accessed data in the records and the record size. As the record size increases, T_{L2D} increases as well for all four systems (results are not shown graphically due to space restrictions). The two fields involved in the query, a2 and a3, are always in the beginning of each record, and records are stored sequentially. For larger record sizes, the fields a2 and a3 of two subsequent records are located further apart and the spatial locality of data in L2 decreases.

Second-level cache misses are much more expensive than the L1 D-cache misses, because the data has to be fetched from main memory. Generally, a memory latency of 60-70 cycles was observed. As discussed in Section 3.2, multiple L2 cache misses can overlap with each other. Since we measure an upper bound of T_{L2D} (number of misses times the main memory latency), this overlap is hard to estimate. However, the real T_{L2D} cannot be significantly lower than our estimation because memory latency, rather than bandwidth, bind the workload (most of the time the overall execution uses less than one third of the available memory bandwidth). As the gap between memory and processor speed increases, one expects data access to the L2 cache to become a major bottleneck for latency-bound workloads. The size of today's L2 caches has increased to 8 MB, and continues to increase, but larger caches usually incur longer latencies. The Pentium II Xeon on which the experiments were conducted can have an L2 cache up to 2 MB [23] (although the experiments were conducted with a 512-KB L2 cache).

5.2.2 First-level cache instruction stalls

Stall time due to misses at the first-level instruction cache (T_{L1I}) is a major memory stall component for three out of four DBMSs. The results in this study reflect the real I-cache stall time, with no approximations. Although the Xeon uses stream buffers for instruction prefetching, L1 I-misses are still a bottleneck, despite previous results [16] that show improvement of T_{L1I} when using stream buffers on a shared memory multiprocessor. As explained in Section 3.2, T_{L1I} is difficult to overlap, because L1 I-cache misses cause a serial bottleneck to the pipeline. The only case where T_{L1I} is insignificant (5%) is when System A executes the sequential range query. For that query, System A retires the lowest number of instructions per record of the four systems tested, as shown in Figure 5.3. For the other systems T_{L1I} accounts for between 4% and 40% of the total execution time, depending on the type of the query and the DBMS. For all DBMSs, the average contribution of T_{L1I} to the execution time is 20%.

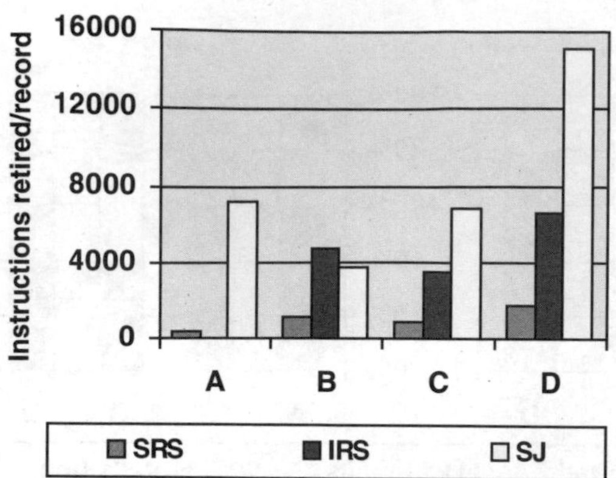

Figure 5.3: *Number of instructions retired per record for all four DBMSs. SRS: sequential selection (instructions/number of records in R), IRS: indexed selection (instructions/number of selected records), SJ: join (instructions/number of records in R)*

There are some techniques to reduce the I-cache stall time [6] and use the L1 I-cache more effectively. Unfortunately, the first-level cache size is not expected to increase at the same rate as the second-level cache size, because large L1 caches are not as fast and may slow down the processor clock. Some new processors use a larger (64-KB) L1 I-cache that is accessed through multiple pipeline stages, but the trade-off between size and latency still exists. Consequently, the DBMSs must improve spatial locality in the instruction stream. Possible techniques include storing together frequently accessed instructions while pushing instructions that are not used that often, like error-handling routines, to different locations.

An additional, somewhat surprising, observation was that increasing data record size increases L1 I-cache misses (and, of course, L1 D-cache misses). It is natural that larger data records would cause both more L1 and L2 data misses. Since the L2 cache is unified, the interference from more L2 data misses could cause more L2 instruction misses. But how do larger data records cause more L1 instruction misses? On certain machines, an explanation would be inclusion (i.e., an L1 cache may only contain blocks present in an L2 cache). Inclusion is often enforced by making L2 cache replacements force L1 cache replacements. Thus, increased L2 interference could lead to more L1 instruction misses. The Xeon processor, however, does not enforce inclusion. Another possible explanation is interference of the NT operating system [19]. NT interrupts the processor periodically for context switching, and upon each interrupt the contents of L1 I-cache are replaced with operating system code. As the DBMS resumes execution, it fetches its instructions back into the L1 I-cache. As the record size varies between 20 and 200 bytes, the execution time per record increases by a factor of 2.5 to 4, depending on the DBMS. Therefore, larger records incur more operating system interrupts and this could explain increased L1 I-cache misses. Finally, a third explanation is that larger records incur more frequent page boundary crossings. Upon each crossing the DBMS executes buffer pool management instructions. However, more experiments are needed to test these hypotheses.

5.3 Branch mispredictions

As was explained in Section 3.2, branch mispredictions have serious performance implications, because (a) they cause a serial bottleneck in the pipeline and (b) they cause instruction cache misses, which in turn incur additional stalls. Branch instructions account for 20% of the total instructions retired in all of the experiments.

Even with our simple workload, three out of the four DBMSs tested suffer significantly from branch misprediction stalls. Branch mispredictions depend upon

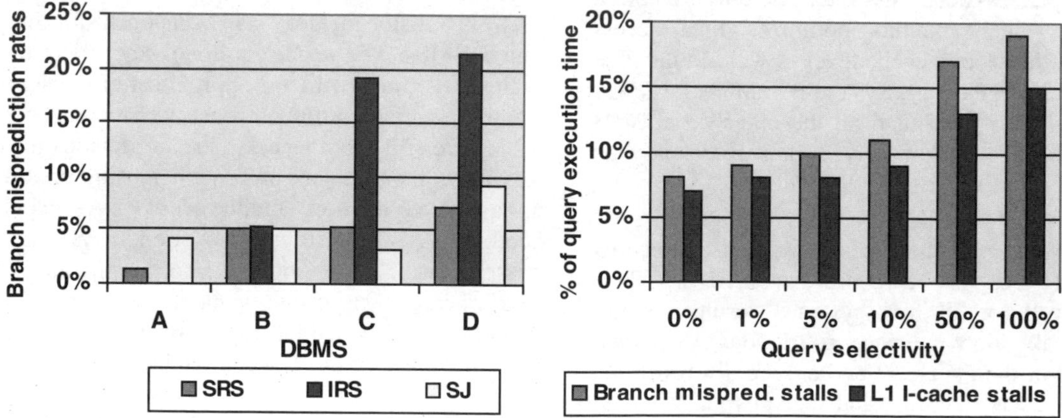

Figure 5.4: *Left: Branch misprediction rates. SRS: sequential selection, IRS: indexed selection, SJ: join. Right: System D running a sequential selection.* T_B *and* T_{L1I} *both increase as a function of an increase in the selectivity.*

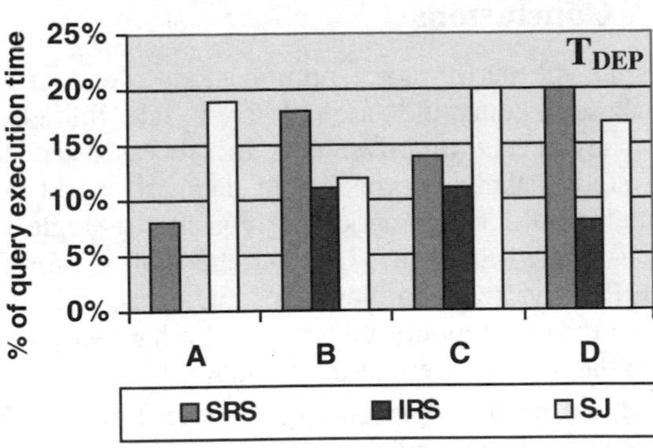

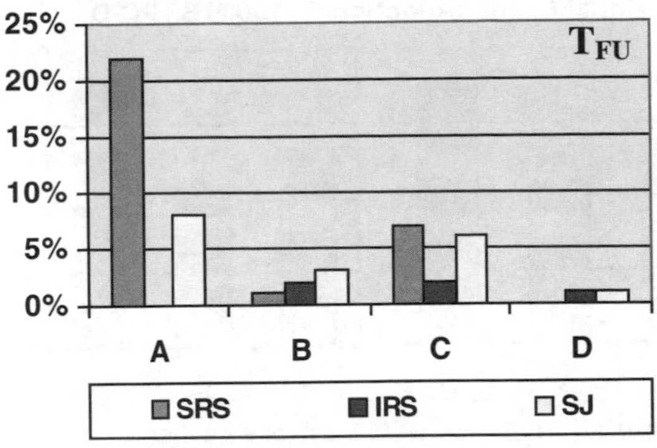

Figure 5.5: *T_{DEP} and T_{FU} contributions to the overall execution time for four DBMSs. SRS: sequential selection, IRS: indexed selection, SJ: join. System A did not use the index in the IRS, therefore this query is excluded from system A's results.*

how accurately the branch prediction algorithm predicts the instruction stream. The branch misprediction rate (number of mispredictions divided by the number of retired branch instructions) does not vary significantly with record size or selectivity in any of the systems. The average rates for all the systems are shown in the left graph of Figure 5.4.

The branch prediction algorithm uses a small buffer, called the Branch Target Buffer (BTB) to store the targets of the last branches executed. A hit in this buffer activates a branch prediction algorithm, which decides which will be the target of the branch based on previous history [20]. On a BTB miss, the prediction is static (backward branch is taken, forward is not taken). In all the experiments the BTB misses 40% of the time on the average (this corroborates previous results for TPC workloads [10]). Consequently, the sophisticated hardware that implements the branch prediction algorithm is only used half of the time. In addition, as the BTB miss rate increases, the branch misprediction rate increases as well. It was shown [7] that a larger BTB (up to 16K entries) improves the BTB miss rate for OLTP workloads.

As mentioned in Section 3.2, branch misprediction stalls are tightly connected to instruction stalls. For the Xeon this connection is tighter, because it uses instruction prefetching. In all of the experiments, T_{L1I} follows the behavior of T_B as a function of variations in the selectivity or record size. The right graph of Figure 5.4 illustrates this for System D running range selection queries with various selectivities. Processors should be able to efficiently execute even unoptimized instruction streams, so a different prediction mechanism could reduce branch misprediction stalls caused by database workloads.

5.4 Resource stalls

Resource-related stall time is the time during which the processor must wait for a resource to become available. Such resources include functional units in the execution stage, registers for handling dependencies between instructions, and other platform-dependent resources. The contribution of resource stalls to the overall execution time is fairly stable across the DBMSs. In all cases, resource stalls are dominated by dependency and/or functional unit stalls.

Figure 5.5 shows the contributions of T_{DEP} and T_{FU} for all systems and queries. Except for System A when executing range selection queries, dependency stalls are the most important resource stalls. Dependency stalls are caused by low instruction-level parallelism opportunity in the instruction pool, i.e., an instruction depends on the results of multiple other instructions that have not yet completed execution. The processor must wait for the dependencies to be resolved in order to continue. Functional unit availability stalls are caused by bursts of instructions that create contention in the execution unit. Memory references account for at least half of the instructions retired, so it is possible that one of the resources causing these stalls is a memory buffer. Resource stalls are an artifact of the lowest-level details of the hardware. The compiler can produce code that avoids resource contention and exploits instruction-level parallelism. This is difficult with the X86 instruction set, because each CISC instruction is internally translated into smaller instructions (μops). Thus, there is no easy way for the compiler to see the correlation across multiple X86 instructions and optimize the instruction stream at the processor execution level.

5.5 Comparison with DSS and OLTP

We executed a TPC-D workload against three out of four of the commercial DBMSs, namely A, B, and D. The workload includes the 17 TPC-D selection queries and a 100-MB database. The results shown represent averages from all the TPC-D queries for each system.

Figure 5.6 shows that the clock-per-instruction breakdown for the sequential range selection query (left) is similar to the breakdown of TPC-D queries (right). The clock-per-instruction (CPI) rate is also similar between the two workloads, ranging between 1.2 and 1.8. A closer look into the memory breakdown (Figure 5.7) shows that

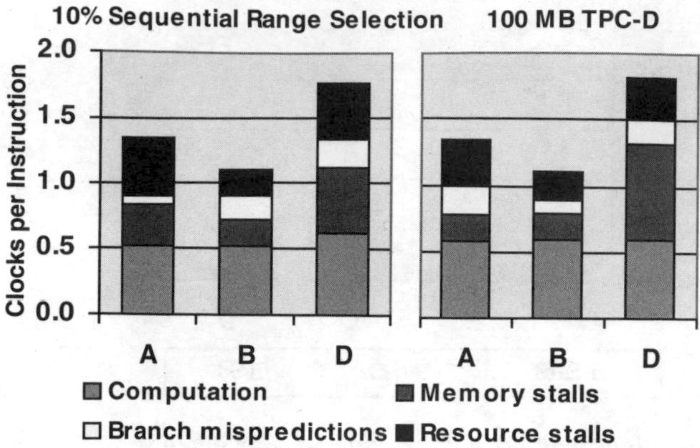

Figure 5.6: *Clocks-per-instruction (CPI) breakdown for A, B, and D running sequential range selection (left) and TPC-D queries (right).*

first-level instruction stalls dominate the TPC-D workload, indicating that complicated decision-support queries will benefit much from instruction cache optimizations.

TPC-C workloads exhibit different behavior than decision-support workloads, both in terms of clocks-per-instruction rates and execution time breakdown. We executed a 10-user, 1-warehouse TPC-C workload against

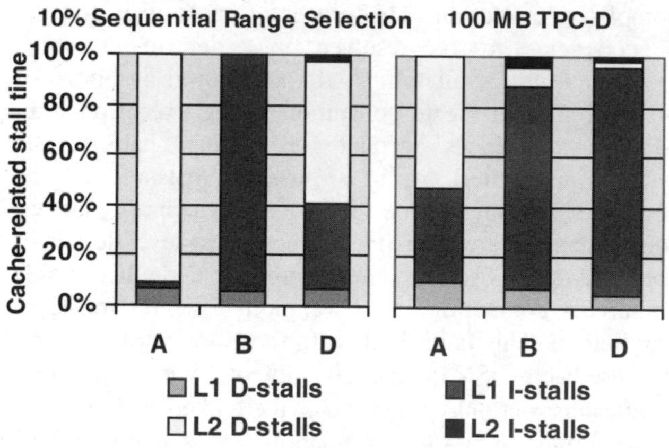

Figure 5.7: *Breakdown of cache-related stall time for A, B, and D, running the sequential range selection (left) and TPC-D queries (right).*

all four DBMSs (results are not shown here due to space restrictions). CPI rates for TPC-C workloads range from 2.5 to 4.5, and 60%-80% of the time is spent in memory-related stalls. Resource stalls are significantly higher for TPC-C than for the other two workloads. The TPC-C memory stalls breakdown shows dominance of the L2 data and instruction stalls, which indicates that the size and architectural characteristics of the second-level cache are even more crucial for OLTP workloads.

6 Conclusions

Despite the performance optimizations found in today's database systems, they are not able to take full advantage of many recent improvements in processor technology. All studies that have evaluated database workloads use complex TPC benchmarks and consider a single DBMS on a single platform. The variation of platforms and DBMSs and the complexity of the workloads make it difficult to thoroughly understand the hardware behavior from the point of view of the database.

Based on a simple query execution time framework, we analyzed the behavior of four commercial DBMSs running simple selection and join queries on a modern processor and memory architecture. The results from our experiments suggest that database developers should pay more attention to the data layout at the second level data cache, rather than the first, because L2 data stalls are a major component of the query execution time, whereas L1 D-cache stalls are insignificant. In addition, first-level instruction cache misses often dominate memory stalls, thus there should be more focus on optimizing the critical paths for the instruction cache. Performance improvements should address all of the stall components in order to effectively increase the percentage of execution time spent in useful computation. Using simple queries rather than full TPC workloads provides a methodological advantage, because the results are much simpler to analyze. We found that TPC-D execution time breakdown is similar to the breakdown of the simpler query, while TPC-C workloads incur more second-level cache and resource stalls.

7 Future Work

Although database applications are becoming increasingly compute and memory intensive, one must measure the I/O factor as well and determine its effects on the time breakdown. Our experiments did not include I/O, but we intend to study that in the near future.

In addition, we intend to compare the behavior of a prototype system with commercial DBMSs, using the same workloads. With a prototype DBMS we will verify the actual cause of major bottlenecks and evaluate techniques for improving DBMS performance.

8 Acknowledgements

We would like to thank NCR for funding this research through a graduate student fellowship, Intel and Microsoft for donating the hardware and the operating system on which we conducted the experiments for this study. This work is supported in part by the National Science Foundation (MIPS-9625558) and Wisconsin Romnes Fellowships. We would also like to thank Seckin Unlu and Andy Glew for their help with the Pentium II counters and microarchitecture, Kim Keeton for her collaboration on the formulae, Babak Falsafi for his invaluable feedback on the paper, and Miron Livny for his suggestions on how to design high-confidence experiments. Last but not least, we thank Jim Gray, Yannis Ioannidis, Hal Kossman, Paul Larson, Bruce Lindsay, Mikko Lipasti, Michael Parkes, and Don Slutz for their useful comments.

9 References

[1] A. C. Arpaci-Dusseau, R. H. Arpaci-Dusseau, D. E. Culler, J. M. Hellerstein, and D. A. Patterson. High-performance sorting on networks of workstations. In *Proceedings of 1997 ACM SIGMOD Conference*, May 1997.

[2] L.A. Barroso, K. Gharachorloo, and E.D. Bugnion. Memory system characterization of commercial workloads. In *Proceedings of the 25th Annual International Symposium on Computer Architecture*, pages 3-14, June 1998.

[3] T. M. Chilimbi, M. D. Hill, and J. R. Larus. Cache-conscious structure layout. In *Proceedings of Programming Languages Design and Implementation '99 (PLDI)*, May 1999.

[4] R. J. Eickemeyer, R. E. Johnson, S. R. Kunkel, M. S. Squillante, and S. Liu. Evaluation of multithreaded uniprocessors for commercial application environments.
In *Proceedings of the 23rd Annual International Symposium on Computer Architecture*, May 1996.

[5] J. Gray. *The benchmark handbook for transaction processing systems*. Morgan-Kaufmann Publishers, Inc., 2nd edition, 1993.

[6] J. L. Hennessy and D. A. Patterson. *Computer Architecture: A Quantitative Approach*. Morgan Kaufman Publishers, Inc., 1996, 2ond edition.

[7] R. B. Hilgendorf and G. J. Heim. Evaluating branch prediction methods for an S390 processor using traces from commercial application workloads. Presented at *CAECW'98,* in conjunction with *HPCA-4*, February 1998.

[8] Intel Corporation. Pentium® II processor developer's manual. Intel Corporation, Order number 243502-001, October 1997.

[9] K. Keeton. Personal communication, December 1998.

[10] K. Keeton, D. A. Patterson, Y. Q. He, R. C. Raphael, and W. E. Baker. Performance characterization of a quad Pentium pro SMP using OLTP workloads. In *Proceedings of the 25th International Symposium on Computer Architecture*, pages 15-26, Barcelona, Spain, June 1998.

[11] P. Trancoso, J.L. Larriba-Pey, Z. Zhang, and J. Torellas. The memory performance of DSS commercial workloads in shared-memory multiprocessors. In *Proceedings of the HPCA conference, 1997*.

[12] P. Å. Larson, and G. Graefe. Memory management during run generation in external sorting. In *Proceedings of the 1998 ACM SIGMOD Conference*, June 1998.

[13] J. L. Lo, L. A. Barroso, S. J. Eggers, K. Gharachorloo, H. M. Levy, and S. S. Parekh. An analysis of database workload performance on simultaneous multithreaded processors. In *Proceedings of the 25th Annual International Symposium on Computer Architecture*, pages 39-50, June 1998.

[14] A. M. G. Maynard, C. M. Donelly, and B. R. Olszewski. Contrasting characteristics and cache performance of technical and multi-user commercial workloads. In *Proceedings of the 6th International Conference on Architectural Support for Programming Languages and Operating Systems*, San Jose, California, October 1994.

[15] C. Nyberg, T. Barklay, Z. Cvetatonic, J. Gray, and D. Lomet. Alphasort: A RISC Machine Sort. In *Proceedings of 1994 ACM SIGMOD Conference*, May 1994.

[16] P. Ranganathan, K. Gharachorloo, S. Adve, and L. Barroso. Performance of database workloads on shared-memory systems with out-of-order processors. In *Proceedings of the 8th International Conference on Architectural Support for Programming Languages and Operating Systems*, San Jose, California, October 1998.

[17] A. Shatdal, C. Kant, and J. F. Naughton. Cache conscious algorithms for relational query processing. In *Proceedings of the 20th* VLDB Conference, Santiago, Chile, 1994.

[18] S. Unlu. Personal communication, September 1998.

[19] A. Glew. Personal communication, September 1998.

[20] T. Yeh and Y. Patt. Two-level adaptive training branch prediction. In *Proceedings of IEEE Micro-24*, pages 51-61, November 1991.

[21] M. Rosenblum, E. Bugnion, S. A. Herrod, E. Witchel, and A. Gupta. The impact of architectural trends on operating system performance. In *Proceedings of the 15th ACM Symposium on Operating System Principles*, pages 285-298, December 1995.

[22] S. S. Thakkar and M. Sweiger. Performance of an OLTP Application on Symmetry Multiprocessor System. In *Proceedings of the International Symposium on Computer Architecture*, 1990.

[23] K. Diefendorff. Xeon Replaces PentiumPro. In *The Microprocessor Report* 12(9), July 1998.

Performance Measurements of Compressed Bitmap Indices

Theodore Johnson
AT&T Labs – Research
johnsont@research.att.com

Abstract

Bitmap indices are commonly used by DBMS's to accelerate decision support queries. A bitmap index is a collection of bitmaps in which each bit is mapped to a record ID (RID). A bit in a bitmap is set if the corresponding RID has property P (i.e., the RID represents a customer that lives in New York), and is reset otherwise. A significant advantage of bitmap indices is that complex logical selection operations can be performed very quickly, by performing bit-wise AND, OR, and NOT operations. Bitmap are also compact representations of densely populated sets. By using bitmap compression techniques, they are also compact representations of sparsely populated sets.

In spite of the great interest in bitmap indices, little has been published about the comparative performance of bitmap compression algorithms (i.e., compression ratios and times for Boolean operations) in a DBMS environment. We have implemented the three main bitmap compression techniques (LZ compression, variable bit-length codes, and variable byte-length codes) and built a generic bitmap index from them. We have tested each of these compression techniques (and their variants) for their compression ratio on a wide variety of synthetic and actual bitmap indices. Because bitmap indices are valuable for complex selection conditions, we evaluate four methods for performing a Boolean operation between compressed bitmaps, including methods that use compressed or partially uncompressed bitmaps directly.

Our results show that the best bitmap index compression technique and the best Boolean operation algorithms strongly depend on the bitmaps being compressed or operated on and the operations being performed. These results are a step towards understanding the space-time tradeoff in *adaptive compressed bitmap indices*, developing a bitmap index design methodology for compressed bitmaps, and optimizing Boolean expression evaluation on compressed bitmaps.

Proceedings of the 25th VLDB Conference, Edinburgh, Scotland, 1999.

1 Introduction

A *bitmap index* is a bit string in which each bit is mapped to a record ID (RID). A bit in the bitmap index is set if the corresponding RID has property P (i.e., the RID represents a customer that lives in New York), and is reset otherwise. One advantage of bitmap indices is that complex selection predicates can be computed very quickly, by performing bit-wise AND, OR, and NOT operations on the bitmap indices. This property of bitmap indices has led to considerable interest in their use in Decision Support Systems (DSS).

In a recent paper, O'Neil and Quass [10] provide an excellent discussion of the architecture and use of bitmap indices. Typically, a bitmap index is created for each unique value of an indexed attribute. Each bitmap is broken into fixed size fragments and stored in an index structure. O'Neil and Graefe [9] show that bitmap indices can be used as join indices for evaluating complex DSS queries on star schemas. O'Neil and Quass [10] point out that bitmap indices not only accelerate the evaluation of complex Boolean expressions, but can also be used to answer some aggregate queries directly. Several DBMS vendors have incorporated bitmap index technology into their products [12, 11].

A problem with using uncompressed (*verbatim*) bitmap indices is their high storage costs and potentially high query costs when the indexed attribute has a high cardinality. Recent research has investigated methods for organizing bitmap indices to solve these problems. O'Neil and Quass [10] proposed *bit-slice* indices, in which a bitmap is created for each binary digit of the range of values of the indexed attribute. Chan and Ioannidis [3] propose *attribute value decomposition*, which generalizes the bit-slice index to use multiple radixes. They present an improved algorithm for making range queries on attribute-value indices, and for optimizing the design of attribute value decomposition indices. Wu and Buchmann [13] propose methods for improving the performance of hierarchy range queries on bit-slice indices.

An alternative method for dealing with the problem of using bitmap indices on high-cardinality attributes is to compress the bitmaps. For example, in a secondary index B-tree each unique key value might be shared by many records in a relation. Oracle uses compressed bitmaps (BBC encoded) to represent these sets of records [11]. A considerable body of work has been devoted to the study of bitmap index compression (see [7]). The use of bitmap compression has many potential performance advantages. Less disk space is required to store the indices, the indices can be read from disk into memory faster, and more indices can be cached in memory. However, the use of bitmap compression can introduce some problems. Performing Boolean operation requires the decompression or interpretation of the compressed bitmap, and this overhead might outweigh any savings in disk space or bitmap loading time. In addition, storing the bitmap in compressed form can make updates more expensive.

Using compression introduces many complications into bitmap index design, but much of the existing bitmap index design research [13, 3] applies to uncompressed bitmaps only. Some of the issues include:

- The compressibility of the bitmap depends strongly on the bit patterns in the bitmap.

- The compressibility of a bitmap depends on the bitmap compression algorithm. Which of the compression algorithms achieves the highest compression depends strongly on the bit patterns in the bitmap.

- There are several options for performing Boolean operations between compressed bitmaps. The default method is to uncompress the both bitmaps, then perform bitwise Boolean operations one word at a time. However other algorithms are possible (including direct operations on the compressed bitmaps) and they might be considerably faster.

Clearly, the best index design depends strongly on the nature of the data being indexed and the types of queries being performed. For bitmap indices on low cardinality attributes, compression might be effective on some but not all of the component bitmaps. For high cardinality attributes, an attribute value decomposed bitmap index [3] is likely to require more storage space than a compressed but non-decomposed bitmap index. However, such an index will evaluate range queries faster than a regular but compressed index if the query mix contains many large range queries. In some cases, it might be appropriate to use the techniques discussed in [13, 3] and compress the resulting bitmaps. But in this case an accurate model of bitmap compression ratios and Boolean operation costs should be used in the design.

A principled design of bitmap indices that makes use of compression requires an understanding of the performance of bitmap compression algorithms and their interaction with evaluating Boolean expressions. In this paper, we present a performance measurement study of several aspects of bitmap index compression, making the following contributions:

- **Evaluate bitmap compression algorithms in a DBMS setting.** We evaluate three representative approaches to bitmap compression: LZ compression using the widely available `zlib` library, variable bit length encoding using the ExpGol algorithm, and variable byte length encoding using the BBC codes. We evaluate these algorithms for their compression ratios on a wide variety of synthetic and actual bitmaps with widely varied selectivities and degrees of clusteredness.

- **Evaluate algorithms for Boolean operations on compressed bitmaps.** In a DBMS setting, one typically uses bitmap indices to evaluate complex selection predicates. For example, "New York, New Jersey, or Connecticut residents who are married, have three to five children, own a house, and work in a different state than their residence". The time to evaluate this expression depends on the time to perform all of the necessary Boolean operations. One option for performing the operations is to decompress each of the bitmaps involved, and then evaluate the expression. However, other algorithms for performing operations between compressed bitmaps are possible, including algorithms that operate directly on the compressed bitmaps. We evaluate the performance of four algorithms for performing Boolean operations on compressed bitmaps using synthetic bitmaps with a wide variety of selectivities and degrees of clusteredness.

The results that we present are necessary for a variety of follow-up research activities, including:

- Developing "adaptive compressed bitmaps" that choose the best compression algorithms for a given bitmap (based on compression ratios, time to perform Boolean operations, or both).

- Developing Boolean expression evaluation optimizers that rearrange the evaluation tree and choose algorithms for performing Boolean operations in order to minimize the total expression evaluation time.

- Developing a theory of optimal compressed bitmap indices similar to that described in [13, 3], but accounting for compression ratios and Boolean operation execution times.

The paper proceeds as follows. In Section 2, we discuss the three bitmap compression techniques evaluated in this paper. In Section 3.1, we evaluate the performance of these bitmap compression algorithms on a variety of synthetic and actual bitmap indices. In Section 3.2, we evaluate four Boolean operator evaluation algorithms using a variety of compression techniques and synthetic bitmaps. In Section 4, we discuss the impact of bitmap compression on bitmap index design. We discuss our conclusions in Section 5.

2 Bitmap Index Compression Algorithms

In our search of the literature, we have found a variety of techniques for compressing bitmap indices. The simplest method is to convert the bitmap into a *Run-Length Encoding* (RLE), which is a list of differences in the positions of successive set bits (Model 204 [8] uses a related method). If four byte integers are used to represent the run lengths, then the RLE representation uses less space than the uncompressed (verbatim) representation if fewer than 1 bit in 32 is set. The representation of run lengths as four-byte integers contains a great deal of redundancy, and typically can be compressed much further. We do not test RLE by itself as one of the encoding methods, but it is a component of the methods we do test.

We settled on three approaches to bitmap index compression as being representative of the methods that can be employed. The first method is to use the widely available LZ compression algorithm, which compresses repeated sequences of symbols. The second method compresses the RLE using variable bit length codes. The third method, the Byte-aligned Bitmap Codes (BBC) uses a variable byte-length representation of the RLE in places where the bitmap is sparse, and transcribes the bitmap where the bitmap is dense (verbatim codes).

In this section, we describe the bitmap index compression techniques used in this study. Each of the compression algorithms accepts a block of bitmap data and returns a block of compressed bitmap codes. By encoding a large bitmap one block at a time and indexing the compressed bitmap blocks, one can uncompress only those bits in a desired range.

2.1 LZ encoding

Lempel-Ziv encoding searches for long repeated strings in a body of text and replaces them with short compression codes. High-quality LZ compression software is easily available, both as the `gzip` file compression tool, and as the `zlib` data compression library [6]. Because LZ software is so readily available, the natural default choice of a compression engine is LZ even though the readily available implementation (`zlib`) is designed for text compression rather than for bitmap compression.

We implemented two variations of LZ bitmap index compression. The first method, *LZ*, compresses the verbatim bitmap, while *LZ-RLE* first converts the bitmap into a RLE representation, then compressed the RLE using LZ.

2.2 ExpGol encoding

A number of variable bit length techniques for compressing the run length encodings of bitmaps have been developed in the Information Retrieval literature. In [7], Moffat and Zobel present a unifying description of many of these coding techniques and a performance comparison of them. We chose the ExpGol code as representative of these techniques, as it is reported to have the best performance of the codes that do not rely on Huffman trees (LZ uses Huffman trees and the ExpGol algorithm has performance competitive with the highest compression algorithms discussed in [7]). The discussion of the ExpGol code we present here is based on the presentation given in [7].

A basic variable bit length representation of integers is a *gamma* code. The gamma code of integer n, $\gamma(n)$ is $\lfloor \log_2(n) \rfloor$ zero bits followed by the least significant $\lfloor \log_2(n) \rfloor + 1$ bits of the binary representation of n. Note that the truncated binary representation of n will always start with a 1. For example, $\gamma(1) = 1$, $\gamma(2) = 010$, $\gamma(3) = 011$, $\gamma(4) = 00100$, and so on. Interpreting a gamma code is done by counting the number of bits from the starting position to the first 1 bit, then copying the truncated binary representation of n to a location where it can be interpreted as an integer.

Fraenkel and Klein [5] have observed that a large class of bitmap encodings can be fit into a simple framework. Let V be a list of positive integers v_i. To encode n, we find the k such that

$$\sum_{j=1}^{k-1} v_j < n \leq \sum_{j=1}^{k} v_j$$

Let

$$d = n - \sum_{j=1}^{k-1} v_j - 1$$

To encode n, we write k in some encoding, followed by d using $\lceil \log_2(d) \rceil$ bits. For example, a γ code encodes k in unary (a string of zero bits followed by a 1 bit) using the following vector: $V = (1, 2, 4, 8, 16, \ldots)$.

Moffat and Zoebel find that the following extension to the ExpGol code gives the best compression. Let b be an integer that is representative of gap lengths in a bitmap. Then, use a gamma code to represent k and set:

$$V = (b, 2b, 4b, 8b, 16b, \ldots)$$

Moffat and Zoebel found that setting b to the median gap length, or to the geometric average of the gap lengths, to be effective. We implemented both approaches (*ExpGol median* and *ExpGol mean*, respectively).

2.3 Byte-aligned Bitmap Codes

Antoshenkov [2, 1] has proposed the use of *Byte-aligned Bitmap Codes* (BBC). The claimed advantage of BBC codes is their speed, since all operations occur locally on full bytes. The BBC encoding algorithm is a 1-pass algorithm, which permits incremental bitmap compression. Antoshenkov proposes logical operations on bitmaps that use only the compressed bitmap codes, which can be substantially faster than operating on uncompressed bitmaps. Finally Antoshenkov shows that his BBC codes achieve better compression than do gamma-delta codes (but there was no comparison to the considerably more efficient ExpGol codes).

BBC codes can be *one-sided* or *two-sided*. We first discuss one-sided codes. Every BBC code consists of two parts, a *gap* and an *ending*. The gap specifies the number of zero bytes that precede the ending. The ending can either be a *bit* (a byte with a single bit set), or it can be a *verbatim* sequence of bitmap bytes. Bit endings are used where the bitmap is sparse, while verbatim endings are used where the bitmap is dense. BBC codes use a clever packing to minimize space use; if the gap is short, a bit code is expressed in one byte. Long gaps are expressed with multi-byte codes. Two-sided codes are similar, except that the gap can be either zero-filled or one-filled.

In the course of our experiments, we found that a few simple modifications to Antoshenkov's encoding scheme resulted in a substantial improvement in space compression. All of the BBC related results in this paper use the improved BBC codes. We do not have space in this paper to discuss the improvements, but will do so in the full paper.

3 Performance

The most important aspects of compressed bitmap performance are the *compression ratio* (size of the compressed bitmap divided by the size of the uncompressed bitmap), and the time required to perform Boolean operations. Secondary performance considerations include the time to uncompress a bitmap, whether the compressed representation can be incrementally updated, storage management issues, and so on. Because of space constraints, we must defer a discussion of these issues to the full paper. However, Figures 7 and 8 illustrate the timne to uncompress.

After performing the experiments, we found that the LZ-RLE algorithm never had the best performance. To avoid cluttering our charts, we do not present LZ-RLE results. We also found that ExpGol Mean and ExpGol Median have nearly identical performance. We present results for ExpGol Mean only, and refer to them as ExpGol.

We built a generic compressed bitmap index to support our experiments. The core of the index is a list of pointers to compressed bitmap blocks, and the associated metadata. Each compressed bitmap block represents a fixed-size block of uncompressed bitmap. The minimal metadata associated with a compressed bitmap block is the length of the block. Additionally, one can store the type of compression used (to support multiple compression methods) and so on. We ran our experiments by generating a test bitmap, compressing and storing the compressed representation in the index, and then operating on the uncompressed representation. Throughout this study, we used 32 Kbyte blocks (which is the size of the compression window in zlib).

All experiments were carried out on a 225 Mhz Ultrasparc. We note that timing measurements are highly dependent on processor architecture and coding optimizations. However, we ported our code to an SGI Challenge and to an Intel Pentium Pro, and obtained nearly identical relative performance. We made efforts to optimize the ExpGol and BBC coding and decoding algorithms (by using pre-computed values, minimizing data copies, etc.) but an extensive tuning effort would probably yield faster code. We used zlib as it was provided. While small differences in execution speed are not significant, we feel that we have captured the relative performance of the algorithms well enough that large differences in execution speed are significant.

3.1 Bitmap Compression Ratio

In this section, we present the compression ratios achieved by the bitmap compression algorithms with a variety of input bitmaps. In our first experiments, we generate uniform random bitmaps as test input. A bit is set with probability p independently of all other bits in the bitmap. This model describes bitmaps that are uncorrelated with the sort attributes of the data set. We refer to the proportion of set bits in the bitmap as the *bit density*, which we represent with the symbol p. In all of the charts, the X axis is the bit density. We generated an 8 Mbyte bitmap (64 Mbits), and compressed in blocks of 32 Kbytes each. We measured the compression ratio to be the size of the compressed bitmap divided by the size of the uncompressed bitmap.

Figure 1 shows the compression ratio of the four compression algorithms as the bit density varies between .0001 and .9999. All of the algorithms achieve a good degree of compression when p is close to zero, but only the two-sided algorithms (LZ and BBC 2s) achieve good compression when p is close to 1. the LZ coding has the best compression on dense bitmaps (roughly, $.2 \leq p \leq .98$). To minimize buffer use, we modified the ExpGol encoders to return a verbatim bitmap instead of an encoded bitmap if the encoded bitmap is larger than the verbatim bitmap. For this reason, their compression ratio is 1 when $p > .2$.

One can expect that many bitmaps are sparse, whether because the indexed attribute has a high cardinality, or because the data distribution is highly skewed. In Figure 2, we compare the compression ratios of the algorithms as p ranges from .0001 to .1. To better illustrate relative compression ratios, we present the size of the compressed bitmap as a multiple of the size of the ExpGol compressed bitmap. The ExpGol algorithms achieve significantly better compression than the other algorithms on sparse bitmaps, for example occupying one third the space of the LZ compressed bitmap when $p = .0001$. The ExpGol algorithms produce a 90% space reduction when $p = .01$, and a 99.8% space reduction when $p = .0001$.

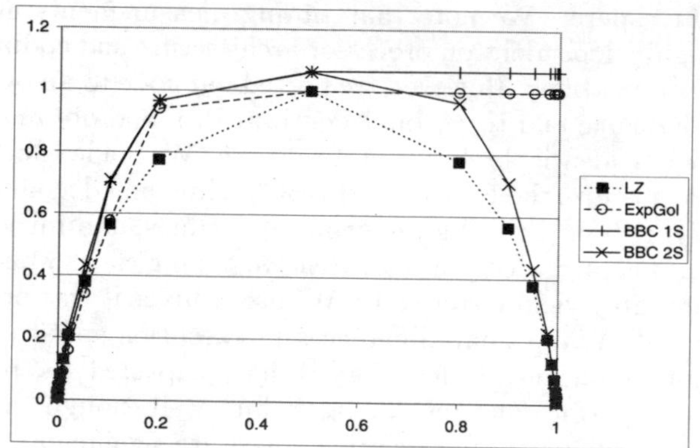

Figure 1: Bitmap compression ratio vs. bit density, uniform random.

If the indexed attribute is correlated with the sort order of the data set, then the bitmap is likely to be bursty. We model this type of burstiness with a *recursive biased distribution* (RBD) [4]. Each bit b_i in the range $i = 0 \ldots 2^l - 1$ is assigned a probability of being set, p_i, and each bit is set or reset independently of the other bits. Given a bias b, we set

$$q_i = b^{ones(i)}(1-b)^{1-ones(i)}$$

where $ones(i)$ is the number of ones in the binary rep-

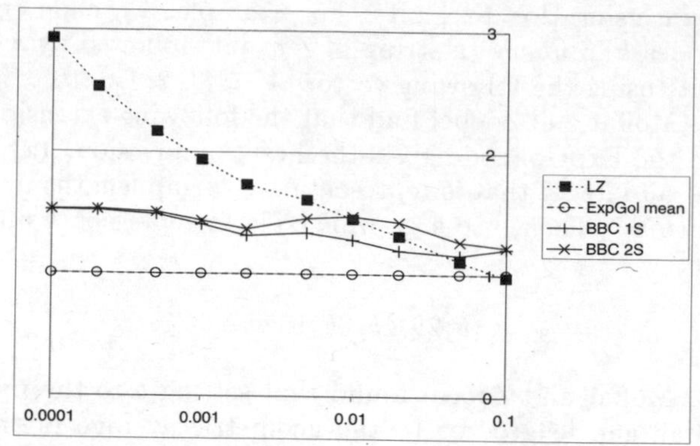

Figure 2: Compression ratio relative to ExpGol vs. bit density, unif. random.

resentation of i. The value q_i represents the chance of receiving a ball in a ball-and-urn model. We throw R balls into the 2^l urns. We compute p_i to be the probability that urn i is non-empty.

We have found that a RBD is a good model of a clustered bitmap [4]. A bias of $b = .5$ produces uniform random bitmaps, while larger biases produce increasingly clustered bitmaps. We generated synthetic data by computing p_i for $i = 0 \ldots 2^l - 1$, repeating this pattern for the entire synthetic bitmap. Then each bit $i + k * 2^l$ is set with probability p_i. We adjusted R to adjust the bit density in the bitmap.

We present the relative compression ratio (Figure 3) for a bias of .8. The charts (and charts for other values of the bias) show that the relative performance of the algorithms has not changed significantly. The compression ratio of LZ and the BBC codes improve relative to ExpGol, with the crossover point moving from a bit density of .1 closer to a bit density of .01. The changes are more accentuated as the bias increases.

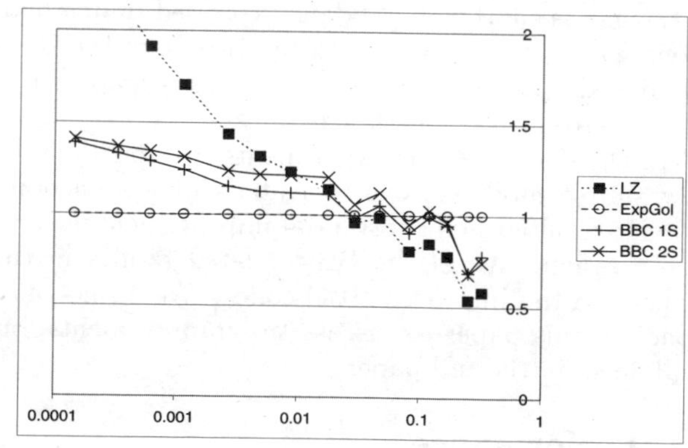

Figure 3: Relative compression ratio vs. bit density, bias=.8

While synthetic data is an excellent tool for the controlled testing of algorithm performance, we also need to evaluate the algorithms using actual bitmap data. We collected data from AT&T data warehouses and generated bitmap indices on the data. In the data set A, the attribute range is 682 values, and the most common value appears in about 28% of the attributes. In the data set B, the attribute range is 50 values, and the the most common value appears in about 13% of the tuples. In data set C, the attribute range is 11 values, and the most common value value occurs in about 80% of the tuples. The indexed attribute is correlated with the sort order of data set A, and is uncorrelated with the sort order of data sets B and C. The data sets were about .5 Mbytes in size each. We catenated the bitmaps to obtain 8 Mbyte bitmaps, for an easier comparison to the results on the synthetic data.

The compression ratio for data set A is shown in Figure 4. The compression performance is excellent, as the BBC 2S encoding of all 682 bitmaps uses 1.04 bits per tuple, while BBC 1S uses 1.5 bits per tuple, ExpGol encoding uses 1.75 bits per tuple, and LZ uses 2.25 bits per tuple. The relative performance of the algorithms is similar to that obtained with a highly biased RBD data set. The data set tends to contains runs of 1's as well as runs of 0's even in low density bitmaps. Because the BBC 2S code can represent runs of 1's succinctly, it is particularly effective at compressing this data set. The ExpGol code obtains the best compression, on the sparse data sets.

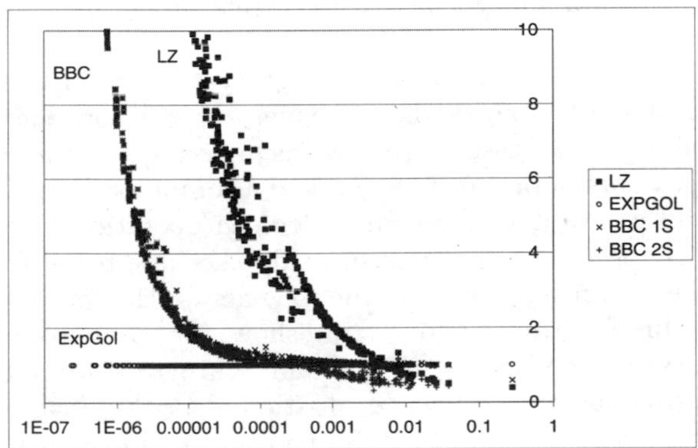

Figure 4: Relative compression ratio vs. bit density, data set A

The compression ratio for data set B is shown in Figure 5. The ExpGol algorithms require about 7.2 bits per tuple, the BBC codes require 8.5 bits per tuple, and LZ requires 8.6 bits per tuple to represent all 50 compressed bitmaps. The relative performance of the compression algorithms is similar to that obtained with uniform random synthetic data.

The compression ratio for data set C is shown in Figure 6. The ExpGol algorithms require about 2.3

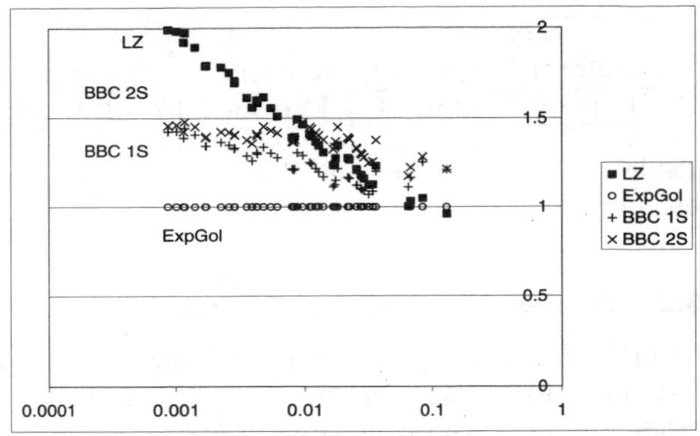

Figure 5: Relative compression ratio vs. bit density data set B

bits per tuple, the BBC codes require 2.5 bits per tuple, and LZ requires 2.3 bits per tuple to represent all 11 compressed bitmaps. The relative performance of the algorithm is similar to that obtained with uniform random synthetic data. The ExpGol algorithm generally obtains the best compression.

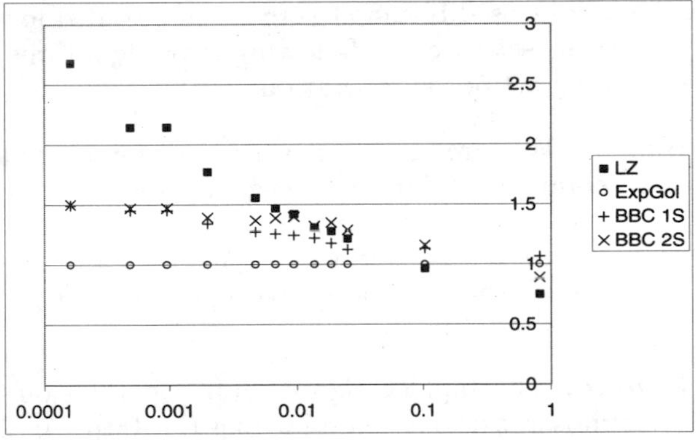

Figure 6: Relative compression ratio vs. bit density data set C

3.1.1 Summary

Existing bitmap compression algorithms can achieve very good compression ratios. As our results indicate, the best compression algorithm depends on the bitmap to be compressed. For dense bitmaps (i.e., density larger than about .1) usually the LZ algorithm will give the best compression, although BBC 2S can work better for clustered dense bitmaps.

For non-dense bitmaps, the choices are more complex. In Table 1 we list the best compression algorithm depending on whether the bitmap is uniform or clustered, sparse or non-sparse. Non-sparse means that the bit density is between .002 and .1, but these boundaries are not precise.

sparse		non-sparse	
uniform	clustered	uniform	clustered
ExpGol	ExpGol	ExpGol	LZ, BBC 2S

Table 1: Best compression algorithms for non-dense bitmaps.

3.2 Boolean Operation Performance

Clearly, compressing bitmap indices confers many performance advantages, including reducing disk space usage and decreasing the time to load the index into memory. The primary advantage of using bitmap indices in the first place is the fast evaluation of complex selection predicates. The overhead of uncompressing the bitmaps before performing the Boolean operations can negate any advantage of using compression.

However, many Boolean operations can be performed using the compressed or partially uncompressed bitmaps. For some operations on some bitmaps, using compressed bitmaps can lead to a speed increase. In these experiments, we assume that a foundset has been partially computed, and we need to perform a Boolean operation between the foundset and a compressed bitmap to create an updated foundset. We investigate the following four algorithms for performing a Boolean operation:

Basic: We are given a verbatim foundset and a compressed bitmap. The bitmap is uncompressed, and the bitwise operations between the two bitmaps are performed. We used the largest possible word size for these operations (e.g., 64 bit words).

Inplace: The Inplace algorithm [8] operates on the foundset without materializing the bitmap. The OR operation is performed by setting bits in the foundset, while the AND operation zeros out inter-bit gaps and perform AND operations between the foundset and the bitmap bits.

Merge: We are given a foundset in RLE format, and a compressed bitmap. We partially uncompress the bitmap into RLE format. Then, it is a simple matter to merge these two lists into an output list while performing the desired Boolean operation. In our implementation, we operate on lists of sorted set bit positions instead of lists of run lengths.

Direct: The Direct algorithm takes a compressed foundset and a compressed bitmap, performs a Boolean operation, and produces a compressed foundset for output. The BBC codes best support this algorithm [2, 1]. The main idea is simple. Each BBC code expresses a gap and an ending.

We scan through the two BBC code blocks keeping track of the current position in the codes. We accumulate an output gap, then an output ending. When the output code is finished (a gap occurs, or the verbatim ending is too long), we create an output BBC code word from the gap and ending description.

The actual implementation is quite complex and contains many special cases. For this reason, we implemented the Direct algorithm only for the BBC 1S code.

We implemented each of the algorithms for two Boolean operations, AND and OR, which can exhibit different performance characteristics. Other Boolean operations can be implemented in a similar fashion, and will have similar performance. For example, OR NOT (e.g. P OR NOT Q) is similar to AND, while XOR and AND NOT are similar to OR. The NOT operation will perform well only on verbatim bitmaps (or on two sided compression codes). However, many NOT operations can be combined with other operations to form operations that can be performed quickly from compressed bitmaps (e.g., the AND NOT and OR NOT operations). It is also possible to compute aggregate functions (e.g., count) on compressed or partially uncompressed bitmap representations. However, we do not address this issue here.

We note that some bitmap compression techniques do not support all of the four Boolean operation algorithms. The LZ encoding supports only the Basic algorithm, and we have implemented the Direct algorithm only for the BBC 1S algorithm.

For our experiments, we generated uniform and clustered bitmaps (where the bias $b = .8$). For each experiment, we assume that we have been given a foundset (in an appropriate form) and a compressed bitmap, and we want to perform a Boolean operation (AND, OR) on them. We measure only the time to perform the operation, not the time to generate the foundset.

In Figures 7 and 8, we show the time to perform an AND operation on an 8 Mbyte compressed bitmap using the Basic evaluation algorithm (the performance charts for the OR operation are identical). In these experiments, we repeatedly fetched a 32 Kbyte block from the foundset, uncompressed a 32 Kbyte block from the compressed bitmap, then performed the Boolean operation, until the entire bitmap was processed. Because we operate on small chunks of data, the bitmaps are cached at the time of the Boolean operation giving a very fast operation time (about .05 seconds). If we had uncompressed the entire bitmap before performing the operation, the overhead would have been significantly larger (about .5 seconds). We ran all of our experiments in this way, on the assumption that one would want to take advantage of cache locality to the greatest extent possible, especially when evaluating complex Boolean predicates.

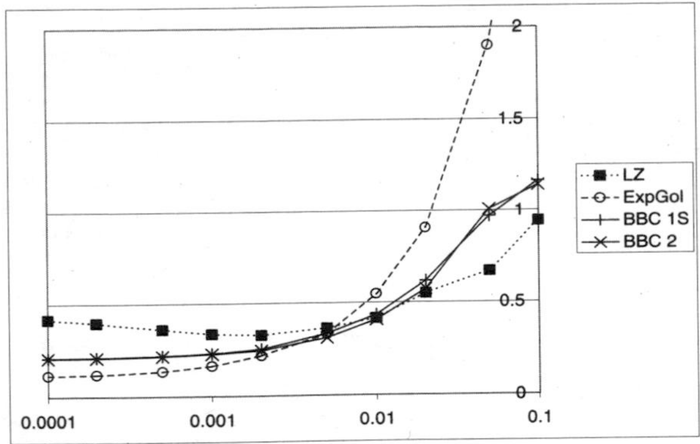

Figure 7: Basic AND operation time (secs) vs. bit density, uniform.

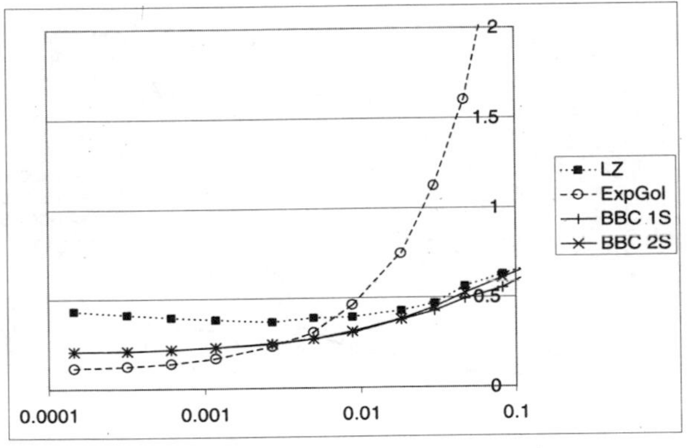

Figure 8: Basic AND operation time (secs) vs. bit density, bias=.8.

We note that these charts also represent the performance of decompressing bitmaps for each of the compression algorithms. We found that the decompression time charts for data sets A, B, and C are similar to those for the synthetic uniform data (B and C) or the biased synthetic data (data set A). To save space, we present timing results for the synthetic data only.

We next examined the performance of the Inplace algorithm, relative to that of the Basic algorithm. In Figures 9 and 10, we show the time to perform an AND operation using uniform and RBD bitmaps. In Figures 11 and 12, we show the time to perform an OR operation. These charts (and also Figures 13 through 16) show the time to perform an operation as a multiple of time for the Basic algorithm with the fastest encoding for the identical bitmap. We use this convention because we are interested in relative performance, and we can tell at a glance whether an evaluation algorithm has better performance than the Basic algorithm.

Performing an Inplace AND operation generally takes about the same amount of time as a Basic AND operation. Although we save on a memory copy, the logic for performing the operation is more complex and therefore slower. However, performing an Inplace OR operation using sparse bitmaps can be significantly faster than the Basic OR operation because only a small fraction of the output bytes must be modified. For a highly clustered bitmap compressed with a BBC code, the Inplace OR is faster than the Basic OR even for fairly dense bitmaps.

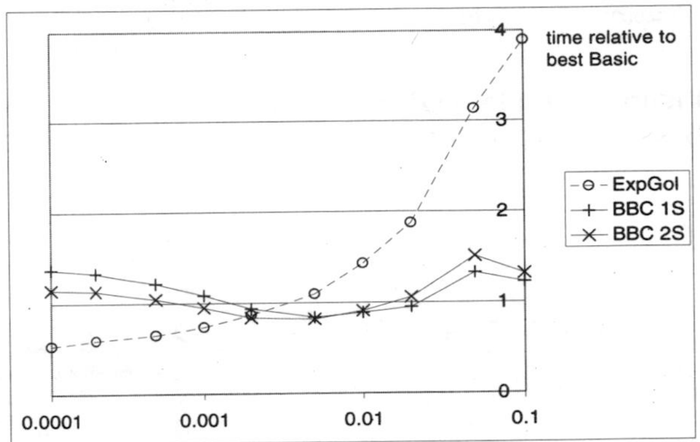

Figure 9: Inplace AND operation time (relative to best Basic) vs. bit density, uniform.

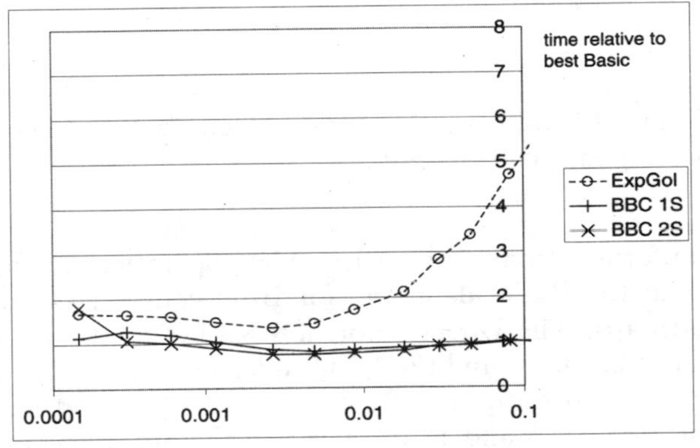

Figure 10: Inplace AND operation time (relative to best Basic) vs. bit density, bias=.8.

Finally, we test the performance of the Merge and the Direct algorithms. The foundset that is operated on has a significant impact on the operation performance (i.e., because the foundset is stored as a list of RLEs). In Figures 13 and 14 we use a uniform random bitmap with $p = .0001$ and show the time to perform an AND operation using uniform and RBD bitmaps. The OR operation is slower (because the result is larger), but the performance is similar. With

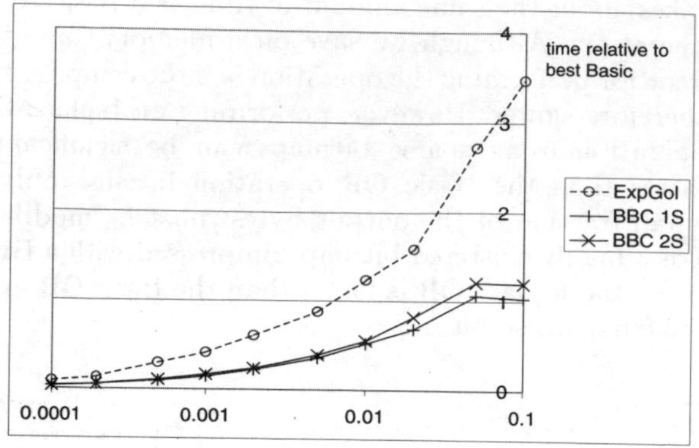

Figure 11: Inplace OR operation time (relative to best Basic) vs. bit density, uniform.

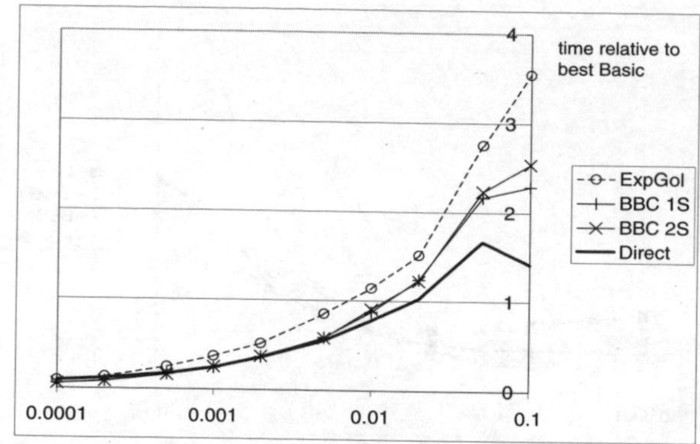

Figure 13: Merge and Direct AND operation (relative to best Basic) vs. bit density, unif. on unif. $p = .0001$.

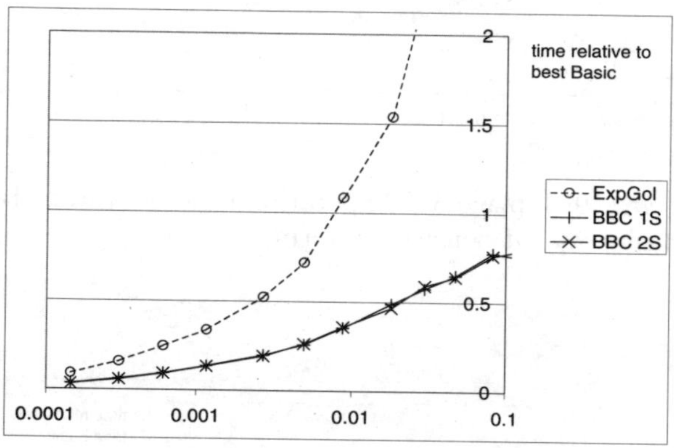

Figure 12: Inplace OR operation time (relative to best Basic) vs. bit density, bias=.8.

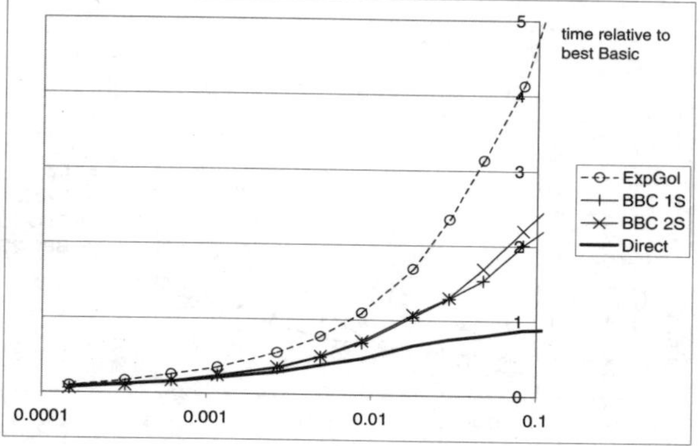

Figure 14: Merge and Direct AND operation (relative to best Basic) vs. bit density, bias=.8 on unif. $p = .0001$.

uniform bitmaps, the RLE AND operation is faster than the Basic algorithm for BBC codes and sparse bitmaps. The Direct algorithm is the fastest on clustered bitmaps, and the BBC codes are faster than the Basic algorithm even for moderately sparse bitmaps. In Figures 15 and 16, we perform the operations on a uniform random bitmap with $p = .1$. In general the operations become considerably slower when using the Merge or Direct algorithms than when using the Basic algorithm.

3.2.1 Summary

The best algorithm for performing an operation depends on the operator, the density of the existing foundset, and the density of the compressed bitmap. The best algorithm to use in each case is listed in Table 2. The computation cost of the algorithms depend on the amount of data touched and also on the complexity of the logic for performing the operation. Because the Basic algorithm is so simple, it performs surprisingly well. However, operations between sparse bitmaps using the Inplace, Merge, or Direct algorithms can occur 50 times faster than using Basic algorithm.

We note that in some cases, Boolean operations can be performed faster with compressed bitmaps than with with a verbatim bitmap. As we noted, the time to perform a Boolean operation between verbatim bitmaps is about .05 seconds in this study. The Merge algorithm is faster if the foundset and the compressed bitmap have a bit density of .001. The Inplace algorithm is faster if the foundset has a bit density of .002 or less.

4 Implications for Index Design

In Sections 3.1 and 3.2, we have seen that the performance of the alternatives for compressing bitmap indices varies considerably with the density of the

operation	foundset type	sparse foundset		non-sparse foundset	
		sparse bmp	non-sparse bmp	sparse bmp	non-sparse bmp
AND	uniform	Merge BBC, Direct	Basic	Inplace ExpGol	Basic
AND	clustered	Merge BBC, Direct	Direct	Basic	Basic
OR	uniform	Inplace BBC	Basic	Inplace BBC	Basic
OR	clustered	Inplace BBC	Basic	Inplace BBC	Basic

Table 2: Best Boolean operation evaluation algorithms.

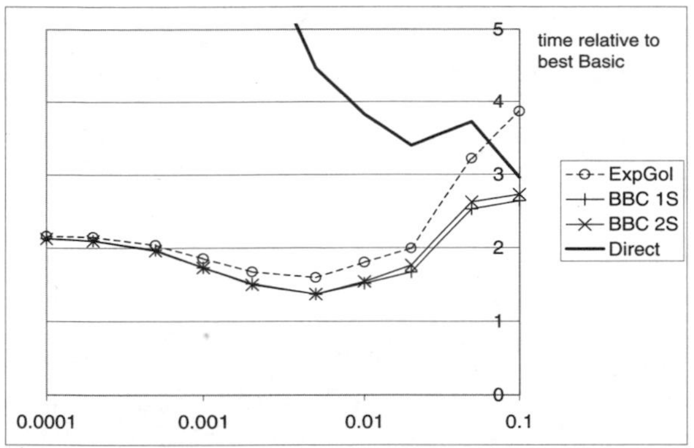

Figure 15: Merge and Direct AND operation time (relative to best Basic) vs. bit density, unif. on unif. $p = .1$.

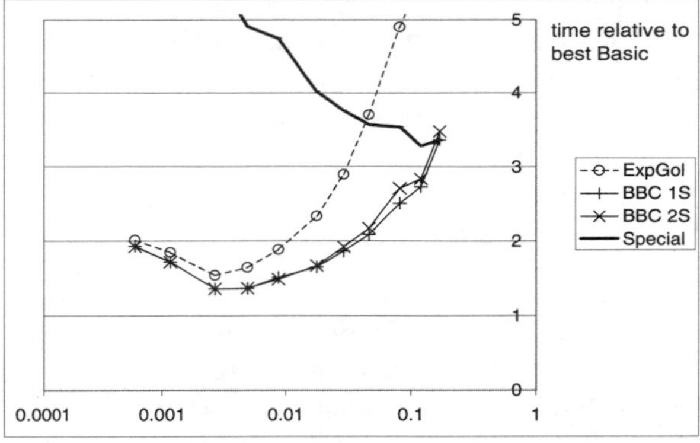

Figure 16: Merge and Direct AND operation time (relative to best Basic) vs. bit density, bias=.8 on unif. $p = .1$.

bitmap, the clusteredness of the bitmap, and the operations to be performed on the bitmaps. In this section, we discuss the implications of our measurement study on bitmap index design.

Indices on Attributes:

When bitmaps are compressed, we can observe that *zeros are cheap*. For example, AT&T data set A has a range of 682 values, but the total size of all 682 compressed bitmaps is slightly more than one bit per tuple. Data set B has a smaller range, but the bitmaps are uncorrelated with the sort position. Still, all fifty bitmaps require less than 8 bits per tuple, comparing favorably with a projection index. This property has been exploited, e.g. in [11]

An efficient bitmap compression algorithm such as ExpGol achieves a compression ratio close to the entropy encoding [7] on uniformly randomly generated bitmaps. On clustered bitmaps, the compression ratios are considerably better, as can be seen in Figures 17 and 18. These figures plot the number of compressed bitmap bits required to represent each set bit in the uncompressed bitmap, for data sets A and B respectively. We use the algorithm with the highest compression for each bitmap. We note that the flat part at the right hand side of Figure 17 is due to the clustering of set bits, which can make ones inexpensive to represent also (in the LZ and 2-sided BBC codes).

Several recent papers have addressed the issue of bitmap index design, with one goal being to minimize space usage. This has been accomplished by reducing the number of bitmaps required to represent a range of values, but increasing their density. However, if the goal of designing a bitmap index on an attribute is *only* to minimize total space use, the bit-slice indices discussed in [10, 13] and the range decomposed bitmaps discussed in [3] are unlikely to significantly reduce total space usage as compared to compressing the per-value bitmaps. An uncompressed bit-slice index (i.e., the most compact range decomposed bitmap index) on data sets A, B, and C will use 10, 6, and 4 bits per tuple, respectively, while the best compression algorithms used 1.04, 7.2, and 2.3 bits per tuple for the collection of per-value bitmaps.

However, an advantage of attribute value decomposed bitmap indices (including bit-slice indices) is the ability to express range queries by accessing only a few bitmaps. Algorithms for extracting ranges from bit-slice or range decomposed indices have been proposed in [10, 13, 3]. Chan and Ioannidis [3] show that at most $4n - 2$ bitmaps must be accessed to evaluate a two-sided range predicates, where n is the number of levels of decomposition. However, n bitmaps must be accessed for equality predicates.

The relative performance of attribute value decomposed bitmap indices versus regular but compressed bitmap indices clearly depends on the query workload. regular indices have the advantage for equality queries, small ranges, or for selecting based on membership in moderate sized non-contiguous sets; but a disadvantage for large range or set membership queries. When the regular bitmap index is compressed, a performance comparison cannot be made only on the basis of the number of bitmaps scanned because the time to load or to perform a Boolean operation on a compressed bitmap is highly data and operation dependent, as charts 7 through 18 show. Given a sample of the bitmap indices and a sample of the workload, it is clear that an estimate of relative performance can be obtained. Unfortunately, a full treatment of this subject is beyond the scope of this paper.

Another dimension of designing bitmap indices on table attributes is the possibility of compressing attribute value decomposed and/or range encoded bitmap indices. This possibility is briefly explored in [3]. However, this subject is made difficult again because of the highly data dependent nature of the size and Boolean operation time of compressed bitmaps. The bitmap index optimization work [13, 3] assumes that each bitmap occupies the same space and requires the same amount of time to perform a Boolean operation. However this assumption clearly does not hold when bitmaps are compressed. Considering just space use, there are two problems. First, attribute value decomposition has the potential to increase space use instead of decreasing space use because of the increased number of set bits. For an example, we decomposed data set B using radixes (5, 10) (which is space-optimal for a 2-level decomposition) without changing the order of the bitmaps and using equality encoding. While the 50 original bitmaps required only 7.15 bits per tuple using the best compression, the 15 bitmaps in radix decomposition form required 9.01 bits per tuple using the best compression. A second problem is that different methods of grouping per attribute-value bitmaps into summary bitmaps will give different compression ratios. For example, by making a few experiments in which we reorder the per attribute-value bitmaps, we adjusted the space use of the attribute value decomposed bitmap from 8.31 bits per tuple to 9.12 bits per tuple.

Boolean Expression Evaluation Plans:

Current work in optimizing Boolean expression evaluation on bitmaps [3, 13] assumes that every Boolean operation on every bitmap requires the same amount of time to execute. However, our experimental results show that this is clearly not the case, and that the method by which the expression is evaluated has a significant effect on performance. For example, one should perform ORs on the sparse bitmaps using the Merge algorithm until the result bitmap becomes dense. Then one should uncompress the result bitmap and use the Inplace or Basic algorithm. It might be possible to rearrange the evaluation order, use multiple result bitmaps, and delay the changeover to the Inplace and Basic algorithms for as long as possible.

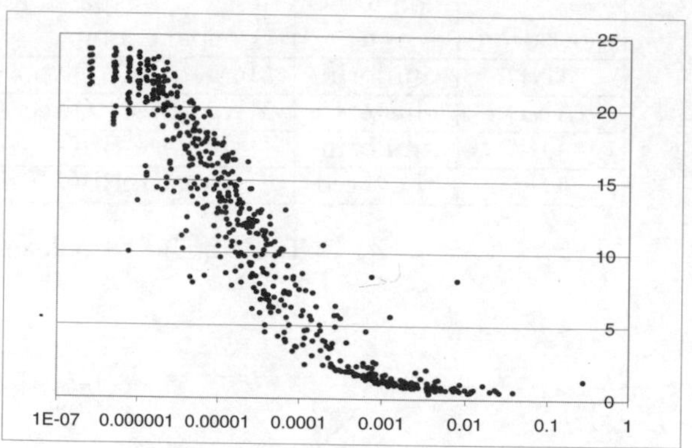

Figure 17: Bits per tuple, data set A

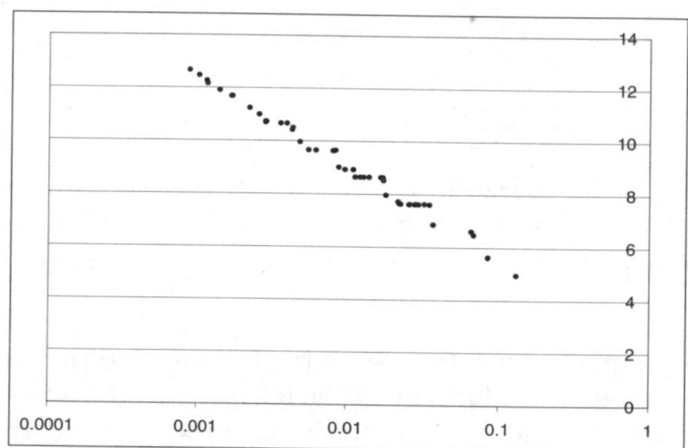

Figure 18: Bits per tuple, data set B

Adaptive Bitmap Compression:

In the previous sections, we have seen that different compression techniques work best on bitmaps with different characteristics. It is easy to design an index structure which can manage multiple compression algorithms (i.e., we built one for the experiments in this paper). Therefore, we have the flexibility to choose the compression algorithm on a bitmap-by-bitmap, or even on a block-by-block basis.

Suppose that we want to minimize compressed bitmap storage. By using the compression algorithm that minimizes space use, we can reduce the space use of the bitmap indices of data set A to .93 bits per tuple (11% space reduction), of data set B to 6.9 bits per tuple (2% space reduction), and of data set C to 2.01 bits per tuple (11% space reduction).

Another goal can be to minimize the time to evaluate a Boolean function of the bitmaps. A full treatment of this issue requires a consideration of the workload and of the typical Boolean expression evaluation plan. For the purpose of an example, we make some simplifying assumptions; that only ExpGol compression is used, that only Inplace evaluation is used, that OR operations occur three times as often as AND operations, and that the bitmaps are uniform. We further assume that the database contains 64 million tuples. For any bitmap, we want to determine whether or not we should compress it.

The time to perform a Boolean operation between the foundset and a bitmap is the sum of the time to load the bitmap from disk and the time to perform the operation once the bitmap is loaded into memory. If the disk transfer rate is 6 Mbytes/sec, then performing an operation with an uncompressed bitmap requires

$$(8 \text{ Mbytes})/(6 \text{ Mbytes/sec}) + .05 \text{ sec} = 1.38 \text{ sec}$$

Evaluating the time to perform an operation with an uncompressed bitmap is similar, but the size and the operation time depend on the bit density. By using the data from Figures 2 and 11, we can determine that any bitmap with a bit density less than .06 should be compressed, all others should be verbatim. If the disk transfer rate is 10 Mbytes/sec, the cutoff is .04.

5 Conclusions

Bitmap indexing has received new attention recently because of its application in OLAP and data warehouses. In many cases, bitmap compression can reduce space usage and possibly Boolean operation evaluation time, and can be a useful adjunct to index design. However, bitmap compression introduces new complications, and its performance has not been studied in a DBMS setting.

In this paper, we present a performance measurement study of algorithms for compressed bitmap indices. We evaluate the compression ratio of representative bitmap compression algorithms on a variety of synthetic and actual bitmap indices. Boolean expression evaluation time depends on the time to perform Boolean operations on the compressed bitmaps (i.e., rather than on the decompression time). For this reason, we evaluate four methods for performing a Boolean operation between a compressed bitmap and a (possibly compressed) foundset. We find that the various compression methods and Boolean operation evaluation algorithms have regions of best performance, which we summarize.

Based on our measurements, we find three areas of future research.

- *Adaptive compressed bitmaps* that choose the best compression scheme for each bitmap.
- Optimizing Boolean expression evaluation plans.
- Accounting for compression in bitmap index design.

Acknowledgements

We'd like to thank Pat O'Neil for his informative discussions concerning compressed bitmap indexes, and for suggesting the use of adaptive compressed bitmaps.

References

[1] G. Antoshenkov. Byte-aligned data compression. U.S. Patent number 5,363,098.

[2] G. Antoshenkov. Byte-aligned bitmap compression. Technical report, Oracle Corp., 1994.

[3] C.-Y. Chan and Y. Ioannidis. Bitmap index design and evaluation. In *SIGMOD '98*, pages 355–366, 1998.

[4] C. Faloutsos and T. Johnson. Accurate block selectivities using the recursive biased distribution. In submission, 1998.

[5] A. Fraenkel and S. Klein. Novel compression of sparse bit-strings – preliminary report. In *Combinatorial Algorithms on Words*, pages 169–183. Springer-Verlag, 1985. NATO ASI Series F.

[6] J.-L. Gailly and M. Adler. Zlib home page. http://quest.jpl.nasa.gov/zlib/.

[7] A. Moffat and J. Zobel. Parameterized compression of sparse bitmaps. In *Proc. SIGIR Conf. on Information Retrieval*, 1992.

[8] P. O'Neil Model 204 Architecture and Performance In *2nd Int. Workshop on High Performance Transactions Systems*, Springer-Verlag Lecture Notes in Computer Science 359, pages 40–59, 1987.

[9] P. O'Neil and G. Graefe. Multi-table joins through bitmapped join indices. *ACM SIGMOD Record*, 24:8–11, 1995.

[10] P. O'Neil and D. Quass. Improved query performance with variant indices. In *SIGMOD '97*, pages 38–49, 1997.

[11] Rdb7: Performance enhancements for 32 and 64 bit systems. http://www.oracle.com/products/servers/rdb/html/fs_vlm.html.

[12] Sybase iq indexes. In *Sybase IQ Administration Guide*, Sybase IQ Release 11.2 Collection, Chapter 5., 1997. http://sybooks.sybase.com/cgi-bin/nph-dynaweb/siq11201/iq_admin/1.toc.

[13] M.-C. Wu and A. Buchmann. Encoded bitmap indexing for data warehouses. In *Int. Conf. on Data Engineering*, pages 220–230, 1998.

Capturing and Querying Multiple Aspects of Semistructured Data

Curtis E. Dyreson
Department of Computer Science
James Cook University, Australia
curtis@cs.jcu.edu.au

Michael H. Böhlen Christian S. Jensen
Department of Computer Science
Aalborg University, Denmark
{boehlen,csj}@cs.auc.dk

Abstract

Motivated to a large extent by the substantial and growing prominence of the World-Wide Web and the potential benefits that may be obtained by applying database concepts and techniques to web data management, new data models and query languages have emerged that contend with web data. These models organize data in graphs where nodes denote objects or values and edges are labeled with single words or phrases. Nodes are described by the labels of the paths that lead to them, and these descriptions serve as the basis for querying.

This paper proposes an extensible framework for capturing and querying meta-data *properties* in a semistructured data model. Properties such as temporal aspects of data, prices associated with data access, quality ratings associated with the data, and access restrictions on the data are considered. Specifically, the paper defines an extensible data model and an accompanying query language that provides new facilities for matching, slicing, collapsing, and coalescing properties. It also briefly introduces an implemented, SQL-like query language for the extended data model that includes additional constructs for the effective querying of graphs with properties.

1 Introduction

The World-Wide Web ("web") is arguably the world's most frequently used information resource. While current web data has little and mostly local structure, web data will likely have far more in the near future. Specifically, the eXtended Markup Language (XML) is expected to replace the Hypertext Markup Language [12, 4]. An XML web page can have a schema of how the data in the page is structured. XML will at best only provide some structure for data since the page-level schemas may (and likely will) vary from page to page. The ability of semistructured data models to accommodate data that lacks a well-defined schema makes them attractive candidates for querying and managing XML data [14, 26]. XML-like representation of web meta-data has also been proposed, cf. the RDF standard [21]. Somewhat unlike database meta-data, web meta-data is typically taken to mean additional information about a document, such as the author, subject, language, or URL. In this paper we use the term 'meta-data' to encompass both database and web meta-data.

Semistructured data models organize data in graphs [8, 14] where each node represents an object or a value, and each edge represents a relationship between the objects or values represented by the edge's nodes. Edges are both directed and labeled. The labels are important because they make nodes *self-describing* in the sense that a node is described by the sequences of labels on paths through the graph that lead to the node [8].

This paper introduces an extensible, semistructured data model that generalizes existing semistructured models. In this model, each label is a set of descriptive *properties*. A property is a kind of meta-data. Typical properties are the name of the edge and the level of security that protects the edge, but any property can be used in a label to describe the nodes that are reachable through that edge.

To exemplify edge labels, consider Figure 1. Part (a) shows a conventional edge that is labeled `employee` and connects nodes `&ACME` and `&joe`. In contrast, part (b) shows the kind of label introduced in this paper. This label is a set of '**property name**: *property value*' pairs. Each pair is collectively referred to as a property. This label has two properties: **name** and **transaction time**. This generalizes existing semistructures since the label in part (a) can be assumed to specify an implicit **name** property, with the value *employee*.

The paradigm of using labels with properties can be recursively applied. For instance, the property **name** in Figure 1(b) could itself be transformed into a label with two properties: **name** and **language**, e.g., English, indicating

Proceedings of the 25th VLDB Conference, Edinburgh, Scotland, 1999.

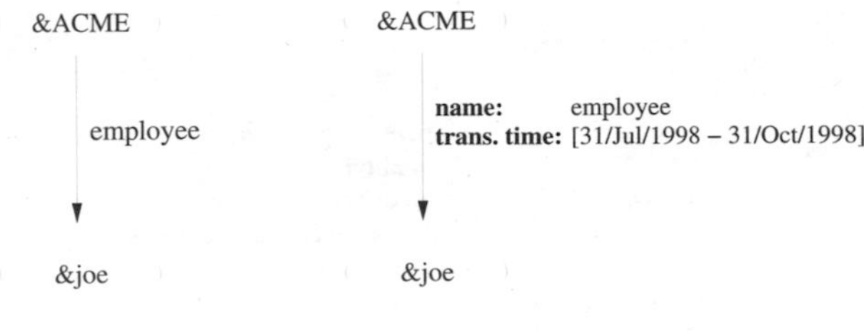

(a) a typical edge (b) a label with properties

Figure 1: The New Kind of Edge Labels

that **name** is an English word. While the recursive nature of labels with properties is theoretically appealing, it is of limited utility since meta-meta-data (and meta-meta-meta-data, etc.) is uncommon in the real-world. So although this framework could capture and query recursively nested properties, we focus exclusively on a single level of meta-data in this paper.

Previous research in semistructured and unstructured data models has focussed on basic issues such as query language design [6, 7, 25, 3, 20], restructuring of query results [13, 2], tools to help naive users query unknown semistructures [16, 17], techniques for improving implementation efficiency [25, 15, 23], and methods for extracting semistructured data from the web [18, 24]. Several well-designed languages have also been presented [6, 3, 20, 13, 14].

Our paper is different, in part, because it treats edge labels as something other than single words or strings. Buneman et al. also propose a semistructured model with complex labels [9]. In their model, key information from objects in the database is added to labels making each path in the database unique. We focus on adding meta-data rather than data to the labels and on the additional operations necessary to manipulate the meta-data in labels. Another paper with augmented labels presents the Chlorel query language for the DOEM data model [10]. DOEM extends OEM with special annotations on edges to record information about updates; in particular, the (transaction) time and kind of update. This permits a history of changes to a semistructure to be maintained. We further extend the scope and power of the annotations on edge labels into a more general framework. Chlorel is a language for querying the extended data model. Chlorel supports a limited kind of temporal query, which lacks both coalescing and collapsing. We believe these operations are important to correctly supporting temporal semantics [5].

The paper is organized as follows. Section 2 motivates the extended semistructured model, arguing the utility of introducing a richer structure for labels. Section 3 presents the extended model. Initially, the format of a database is defined. An important feature is that the set of properties present may vary from label to label. Section 3.2 proceeds to introduce several new or extended query operators to contend with properties in labels. Section 4 incorporates the new query operations into a derivative of the SQL-like Lorel query language [25, 22, 3], called AUCQL, for querying semistructured data with properties. The last section covers future work and summarizes the paper.

The URL `<www.cs.auc.dk/~curtis/AUCQL>` provides an interactive query engine for the example database given in this paper, documentation and examples on using AUCQL, and a freely-available implementation package.

2 Motivation and Background

This section aims to describe the new type of semistructured database proposed, with an emphasis on its background, the underlying design ideas, and its relation to existing semistructures.

2.1 An Example Database

A sample movie database spans semistructured data from a total of six sites. The *Internet Movie Database* site contains a wealth of movie data; *Videotastic* is a monthly, on-line movie industry magazine, portions of which are available only by subscription; the *Haus du Flicks* site charges a fee in e-cash for access to each of its many film clips, the fee being collected by an e-cash broker when a clip is accessed; *Joe Doe* is a Yankee On-line User site devoted to science fiction movies; the site *Horsing Around Movies* has data about R- and NC-18 rated films, portions of which are restricted to web surfers over the age of 18; and the *Internet Archives* site offers movie data collected by a robot that periodically traverses part of the web.

Figure 2 shows a portion of the movie database. Edges are directed arrows, values are given in italics, and objects are depicted as ovals. Most of the semistructure is not shown—many other edges and nodes exist in the complete movie database.

The database models the following pertinent facts. Information about a new movie, *Star Wars IV*, was added to the database on 31/Jul/1998. A review of this movie appeared in the June issue of *Videotastic*, which was made available on 25/May/1988. The review is only available to paid subscribers. *Joe Doe* also has a review of *Star Wars IV*, but since he is a Yankee On-line User, it is deemed to be of *low* quality. *Haus du Flicks* charges $2 dollars for a *Star Wars IV* film clip, but under a deal with *Videotastic*, paid subscribers can get the clip for free in one of the magazine's reviews. Bruce Willis stars in *Star Wars IV*. His misspelled name was corrected on 2/Apr/1997. Finally, *Horsing Around Movies* has data about the NC-18 rated movie, *Color of Night*, which also stars Bruce Willis. Only surfers with an appropriate security clearance are permitted to view this movie.

We will use this sample database for illustration throughout the paper.

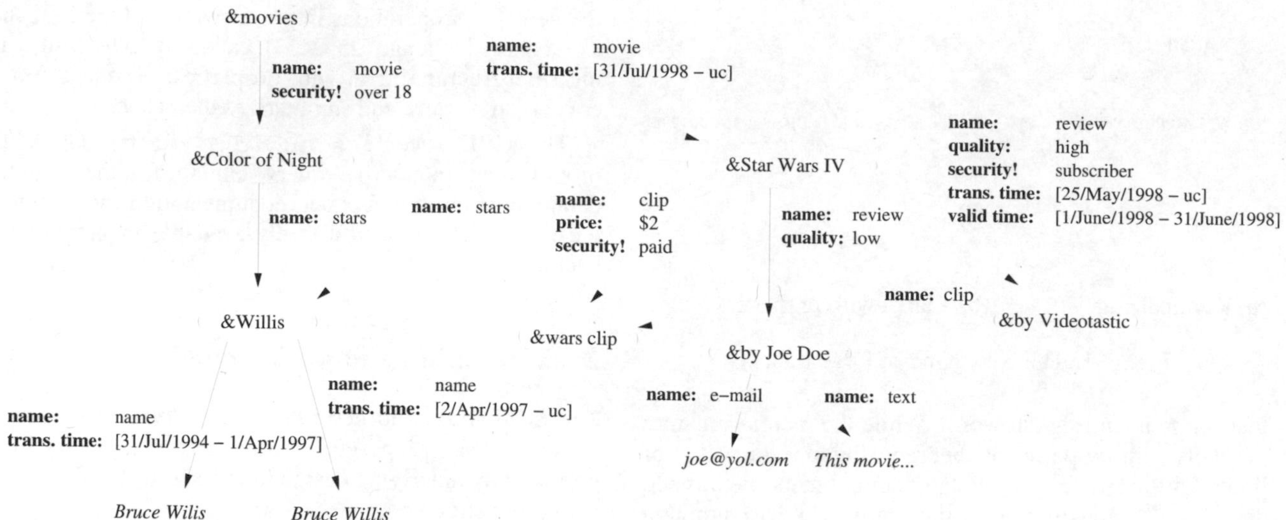

Figure 2: A Web Movie Database

2.2 Sample Properties

The data model presented in this paper is capable of capturing the facts described above, in part by using properties in labels. Labels are the most appropriate locations for properties since nodes are *completely* described by the paths that lead to them. For instance, while the `&Willis` node in Figure 2 has a meaningful internal name, `&Willis`, this name is of *no* importance, and the node may just as easily be called `&foo`. It is only known that `&Willis stars` in a `movie` because there exists an incoming edge labeled `stars`, which in turn is reached after traversing a `movie` edge. Other descriptions of `&Willis`, say as a `father` or as a `person`, would only be available as labels along other paths to the node (not shown in the figure).

The data model is extensible, in that any properties may be used. Below, we discuss a partial list of such properties. None of them are mandatory. Indeed, for most labels, one or more properties may be *missing*.

name: The name is a text description. The domain for names is the set of finite-length strings over some alphabet (e.g., Unicode characters). In general, the value of this property is a set of names. For simplicity, in this paper our examples only use a single name.

security: Some data has security restrictions, which are intended to indicate that only qualifying users are allowed access to the data. The essential ingredient to supporting this kind of security is to provide a method to restrict access to edges in queries. We use required properties for this purpose, as will be discussed further in Section 3.2.2. This paper assumes that security is controlled through Netscape-like *certificates*. So a more descriptive property name would be **security.netscape.read**, but for brevity we have shortened it. Several protocols exist for obtaining and managing these certificates. Once obtained, a certificate or combination of certificates permits access to various services and documents. For clarity, we render a certificate in plain text rather than in its encrypted form. The security is given as a formula built of individual certificates, AND, and OR. For instance a security of `over 18 AND subscriber` would mean that a user needs *both* certificates to access a service; and a security of `over 18 OR subscriber` would mean that either certificate alone would suffice. This is only one possible security property; the extensible data model can support others.

transaction time: The transaction time is the time when the edge is current in the database. It is called transaction time since it is the time interval between the time of the transaction that led to the edge and the time of the transaction that deleted or updated the edge [19]. Edges that are current have a special transaction-time end value, *until changed*, which indicates that the edge is current and will remain so until it is changed (deleted or updated). The special role of transaction time in database modifications is elaborated in Section 3.4.

valid time: The valid time of a database fact indicates when that fact is true in the modeled reality [19]. In our context, the valid-time property thus indicates when that edge reflects the real world. As for transaction time, valid-time timestamps are closed intervals.

price: When data is spread over a network, accessing some data may have substantially greater cost than other data, e.g., in terms of size, time, or money. The price property reflects these differing costs in obtaining data. Multiple price properties can comfortably coexist, but we simply assume that the price is a U.S. dollar amount.

quality: Information on the web arises from many sources, some of which are far more credible than others. For instance, one would commonly rate information from the CNN server as more credible than information from a user's personal home page. The quality property records the quality of the source of the information. We will assume that the quality is an intuitive ranking from *low* to *high*.

The above list only covers properties used in the movie database and does not exclude other properties such as language, Dublin Core tags, or URL space.

2.3 Features of Properties in Labels

Many labels consist of several properties. For example, the two edges from the `&Willis` node shown in Figure 2 have the same value for the **name** property, but different transaction times. The most common property is **name**—only in unusual circumstances will an edge be unnamed.

The ability to accommodate the schema irregularities found in web data is an important feature of a semistructured (or unstructured) data model. In keeping with this requirement, the data model presented in the paper has several features worth mentioning.

One feature is that a property found in one label can be *missing* from other labels. In Figure 2, the transaction time property is in only a few of the labels. Generally, a property is missing because it is *don't care* information, as in, this property is missing because we don't care if it is present, it is not germane to or will not improve the description of the data.

Another feature is that a property can be specified as being *required*. A required property is required to be matched in a query to gain access to nodes below that edge, but otherwise is just like any other property.[1] The **security** property on the edge to `&Color of Night` is a required property (indicated by affixing an '!' to the property name). It is meant to indicate that a user *must* have a matching security clearance, i.e., an appropriate certificate, to traverse that edge. Further details on required properties are presented in Section 3.2.2.

There are few restrictions on the properties in labels. Common properties may be shared by a number of labels. Meta-data is often specified for a bag or container for a collection of objects [21]. Since a label is a set, it can easily be shared, in part or in whole, among a number of labels. In addition, multiple edges may connect the same pair of nodes with overlapping or redundant labels. Requiring labels to contain disjoint descriptions would be an unnecessary restriction.

Multiple properties in a label can capture more data semantics, but they break existing query languages. To take one example, consider the path from `&movies` through `&Star Wars IV` to the misspelled value *Bruce Wilis*. It would be easy to retrieve that path by using an appropriate regular expression over the **name** property in each label (e.g., `movie.stars.name`). While this is a path, it is not a *valid* path since the transaction times of the first and last edges in the path are disjoint: when the first edge in the path was inserted, the final edge was already deleted. So at no time did the two edges coexist in the current database state.

This paper offers a collection of query language operators that support a more correct manipulation of the extended edge labels. Each operator is extensible in the sense that the semantics of properties are not fixed in the data model; rather, the meaning is supplied by a database designer. For instance, to test the validity of a path, the **transaction time** property will be tested quite differently than the **name** property. Several new query operators are also described. *Match* matches a so-called *path regular expression* to the labels along a path in the semistructure. *Collapse* collapses entire paths to single edges that have their labels computed from the labels on each edge in the path. *Coalesce* computes the value of a property which is distributed among a number of different labels on edges between the same pair of nodes. Finally, *Slice* restructures the labels along paths by slicing a portion from selected properties in each label.

2.4 Contrast With Existing Semistructured Data Models

Our proposed model is not the only one capable of representing meta-data; existing semistructured data models with simple string labels can also explicitly capture meta-data. For example, the "property" information in a label could be encoded by splitting an edge into separate *data* and *meta-data* edges, with the properties branching from the end of the meta-data edge. But there are at least two problems with this approach of encoding the meta-data together with the data.

First, meta-data has no special status in such a model, so a query that involves a *wildcard* (which matches any label) may unintentionally access meta-data rather than data. A user could formulate a query that follows only *data* edges, but this is challenging and, we believe, unnecessary. It should not be left to the user to guess how the meta-data is represented in the database and to write queries to explicitly avoid such data.

A second, more fundamental problem, is that *some* of the meta-data has special semantics that must be accounted for in queries. For instance, assume that in a semistructured database with simple string labels, the transaction time for an object is represented as a **ttime** edge from that node. As discussed above, a path is only valid if its edges are concurrent in the database—any other semantics is incorrect. Below we give a Lorel-like query to correctly retrieve only `movie.star.names` that are concurrent (assuming that the INTERSECT operation computes the intersection of two time intervals).

```
SELECT N
FROM movie M, M.star S, S.name N
WHERE NOT_EMPTY(M.ttime INTERSECT
              S.ttime INTERSECT N.ttime)
```

The WHERE clause tests the transaction times of objects along the path to ensure that they are concurrent.

Although a user may explicitly formulate each query to correctly manipulate the transaction time and other properties, such a strategy has several highly undesirable features. First, all properties must be accounted for in all queries.

[1] A required property is similar to the **MUST** keyword in a proposal for privacy meta-data [27].

For example, the query given above is incorrect since it does not correctly handle the security property. Second, the semantics of a property cannot be enforced. For example, a user could simply omit the WHERE clause in the query given above, or test some other condition on transaction time. The query will run to completion and return a result. But since the semantics of the transaction time property has not been observed, the result may include *fictive* paths. Third, naive users cannot formulate queries. A user has to know which properties exist, be familiar with the semantics of those properties, and must appropriately contend with all properties in every query. Fourth, queries become brittle. Even correctly formed queries will have a short shelf-life since adding a new property, or deleting an existing one, can break existing queries.

In summary, it is theoretically possible, but unattractive and beyond the capabilities of users to represent and query properties using an ordinary semistructured database. The extensible data model presented in this paper can be viewed as, and perhaps can even be implemented as, a layer on top of a normal semistructured data model. The layer implements the semantics for each property and correctly translates queries and results between the user and the underlying database.

3 Extending a Semistructured Data Model With Properties

This section first defines a semistructure with properties, then defines the foundation necessary for querying such a semistructure, and finally considers update.

3.1 A Semistructured Model With Properties

A semistructured database, $DB = (V,\ E,\ \&root,\ \Gamma)$, consists of a set of nodes, V, a set of labeled, directed edges, E, a single root node, $\&root$, and a collection of so-called property operations, Γ, that determine the semantics of properties. We also define $ROOTS \subseteq E$ to be the set of edges emanating from $\&root$. (These edges lead to what would normally be considered the roots of the semistructure; the extra level of indirection serves to record the properties of the root nodes.) An edge in E from node v to node w with the label $\mathcal{L}$ is denoted $v \xrightarrow{\mathcal{L}} w$. $\mathcal{L}$ is a *label with properties.*

Definition 3.1 [Label with properties]
A label with properties, $\mathcal{L}$, is a set of m pairs, $\{(p_1\colon x_1),\ (p_2\colon x_2),\ \ldots\ ,\ (p_m\colon x_m)\}$, where (i) each p_i is the *name* of a property, (ii) x_i is a *value* drawn from the property's domain, that is $x_i \in domain(p_i)$, (iii) property operations exist in Γ for each p_i, and (iv) each property name is unique, that is, $\forall i, j(p_i = p_j \Rightarrow i = j)$.

A *required* property, say p_i with value x_i, is denoted $(p_i!\ x_i)$. □

Example 3.2 In Figure 2, an edge connects `&movies` to `&Color of Night`. The label is the set of properties $\{$(**name:** movie), (**security!** over 18)$\}$. The **security** property is a required property. It is intended to limit access to the node to individuals over 18 years of age. □

To accommodate properties in queries, several operations for each property are needed, namely property collapse (*PrCl*), property match (*PrMa*), property coalesce (*PrCs*), and property slice (*PrSl*) (see Section 3.2). These operations determine the semantics of properties and are included in Γ.

Definition 3.3 [Property operations]
For each property p in a label, operations with the following signatures should be present in Γ. For brevity, let T be $domain(p)$.

- $PrCl_p : T \times T \rightarrow T \cup \{undefined\}$
- $PrMa_p : T \times T \rightarrow BOOLEAN$
- $PrCs_p : 2^{T \,\cup\, \{undefined\}} \rightarrow T \cup \{undefined\}$
- $PrSl_p : T \times T \rightarrow T \cup \{undefined\}$ □

These operations collapse, match, coalesce, and slice property values.

New properties may be introduced at any time by registering the appropriate operations with the database. Default semantics are available for the operations, as will be discussed in Section 3.4.2. Table 1 lists operations for one possible implementation of the properties discussed in this paper. The role of the property operations will become clear when querying is considered, next.

3.2 Retrieving Information From Semistructures With Properties

This section extends the information retrieval capability of an ordinary semistructured query language to handle labels with properties. Emphasis is on the query language aspects that are affected by the new labels. These aspects are quite localized, since labels are used only in path regular expressions to traverse paths in the semistructure. There are two parts to the extension. First, when retrieving data, only *valid* paths should be followed, as discussed in Section 2. We define a *Valid* predicate to test whether a path is valid by determining whether the path can be *collapsed* to a single edge with a label that preserves the information content of all the labels along the path. Second, path regular expressions must be generalized to support labels with properties and required properties. This involves redefining how labels are matched in the evaluation of an expression. We conclude by observing that the extension is strictly additive—the extended retrieval mechanism works as expected on a semistructure with simple string labels.

3.2.1 Path Validity

Only some of the paths in the semistructure are *valid*. Intuitively a path is valid if it transits through properties that share some "commonality." This commonality is computed by collapsing the labels on the path.

	name	valid time	security	transaction time	price	quality
$PrMa_p$	=	truth assignment	overlaps	overlaps	$\geq$	$\leq$
$PrCl_p$	concatenation	AND	intersection	intersection	sum	minimum
$PrCs_p$	union	OR	coalesce	coalesce	min	average
$PrSl_p$	semantic error	conjunct elimination	intersection	intersection	> pruning	< pruning

Table 1: Property Operations

Consider the case of a path to a movie star's name. One such path is shown in Figure 3, composed by the solid lines. Intuitively, the path forms a *virtual edge* from `&movies` to *Bruce Willis*. In the figure, the virtual edge is depicted as a dashed line. The virtual edge should have a label that describes it, just like any other edge. This label is determined by collapsing the labels along the path into a single label.

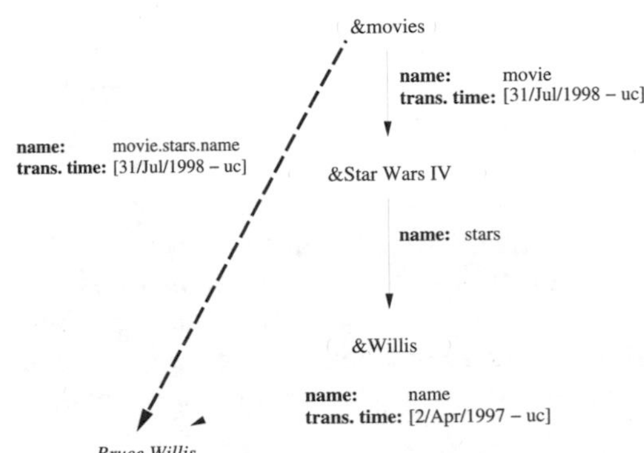

Figure 3: A (Virtual) Edge for the Name of a Movie Star

The operation described below collapses a path by recursively collapsing the labels along the path. A pair of labels is collapsed by determining their common properties. If only one of the labels has some property, that property is propagated to the collapsed label. A missing property in a label is interpreted as "don't care information," meaning that any value of the missing property is acceptable for the label. For properties that appear in both labels, a property-specific collapsing constructor is used to compute the value of the property. This constructor could result in an *undefined* value, which signifies that these labels do not have any commonality for that property. The path is collapsed backwards, that is, from the sink to the source, which effectively means that each collapsing constructor is left-associative.

Definition 3.4 [$ClPt_\Gamma : PATH \rightarrow EDGE$]
Collapse path ($ClPt_\Gamma$) takes a path and computes the label for the virtual edge between the first and last nodes in the path. The operation is extensible in that it depends on the semantics of the properties as given by Γ. Each constructor $PrCl_p$ in Γ is property-specific and is used to collapse a pair of property values for property p. In this operation, required properties are treated the same as other properties.

$$ClPt_\Gamma(v \xrightarrow{\mathcal{L}} w) \triangleq v \xrightarrow{\mathcal{L}} w$$
$$ClPt_\Gamma(v \xrightarrow{\mathcal{L}_1} u \xrightarrow{\mathcal{L}_2} w) \triangleq \; v \xrightarrow{\mathcal{L}} w \text{ where}$$
$$\mathcal{L} = \{(p\colon PrCl_p(x,\, y) \mid (p\colon x) \in \mathcal{L}_1 \;\wedge\; (p\colon y) \in \mathcal{L}_2\} \cup$$
$$\{(p\colon x) \mid (p\colon x) \in \mathcal{L}_1 \;\wedge\; (p\colon y) \notin \mathcal{L}_2\} \cup$$
$$\{(p\colon y) \mid (p\colon x) \notin \mathcal{L}_1 \;\wedge\; (p\colon y) \in \mathcal{L}_2\}$$
$$ClPt_\Gamma(v \xrightarrow{\mathcal{L}_1} u \xrightarrow{\mathcal{L}_2} \ldots \xrightarrow{\mathcal{L}_m} w) \triangleq$$
$$ClPt_\Gamma(v \xrightarrow{\mathcal{L}_1} ClPt_\Gamma(x \xrightarrow{\mathcal{L}_2} \ldots \xrightarrow{\mathcal{L}_m} w)) \qquad \square$$

The collapsing constructor, $PrCl_p$, depends on the semantics of the property. Table 1 suggests constructors for a few common properties. In general, since each property is collapsed independently, the collapse constructor for a property should either be a *mutator*, which transforms one domain value into another, e.g., concatenation, or a *restrictor*, which reduces the extent of the domain value, e.g., time interval intersection.

Example 3.5 The **transaction time** property in the collapsed path in Figure 3 is [31/Jul/1998 - uc]. This is the intersection of the transaction times on the edges on the path. It follows that the value *Bruce Willis* was described in the database as a `movie.stars.name` from 31/Jul/1998 to the current time (until it is changed). Note that this is not an *exclusive* description—a different `movie.stars.name` path (through `&Color of Night`) is current over a slightly longer transaction-time interval. □

To determine if a path is valid, the path is collapsed and then each property is checked to ensure that it is defined.

Definition 3.6 [$Valid_\Gamma : PATH \rightarrow BOOLEAN$]
A path, P, is valid if after collapsing the path, there are no properties with *undefined* values.

$$Valid_\Gamma(P) \triangleq \forall p\, [\, (p{:}undefined) \notin \mathcal{L} \;\wedge$$
$$(p!undefined) \notin \mathcal{L} \;\wedge$$
$$v \xrightarrow{\mathcal{L}} w = ClPt_\Gamma(P)\,] \qquad \square$$

Example 3.7 Consider the path from `&movies` through `&Star Wars IV` to the misspelled value *Bruce Wilis* in Figure 2. When the path is collapsed, the **name** property in the resulting label has the value `movie.stars.name`. The **transaction time** property is *undefined*. The transaction times of the first and last edges in the path are disjoint, so their intersection does not produce a valid transaction time value. Consequently the path is invalid. □

The cost of checking path validity is $\mathcal{O}(n \cdot m)$, where n is the length of the path and m is the number of properties in a label. We expect that m will usually be much smaller than n. Path validity can be checked as a path is matched, as discussed next.

3.2.2 Path *Match*

In this section, we first provide a means of determining whether a user-given *descriptor*, specified in a query, matches a label. The label matching operation is then incorporated into an *Match* operation to match a path regular expression to paths in the semistructure.

Label matching in existing semistructured query languages is straightforward. The descriptor is typically a single word or phrase that is compared, using string comparison, to the label. For example, in the regular expression `(person | employee).name?`, the descriptors, the basic building blocks of the regular expression, are `person`, `employee`, and `name`. During evaluation of this expression, the descriptor `person` would only match a label `person` on an edge. More flexible string comparisons between descriptors and labels are supported in some languages, such as Lorel [3], which reuse the wildcard operator '`%`' from SQL. The descriptor `per%` would match any label that starts with 'per'.

The semantics of label matching is more involved in our model since each label is a set of properties. In addition, string comparison is insufficient because many properties are not strings. These complications are addressed in the label match operation *LaMa*, defined below. In general, operation *LaMa* succeeds if every individual property in the descriptor has a match in the label or is missing from the label. Extra properties in the label are ignored, and different $PrMa_p$ operations are used for different properties, p. Note that the descriptor is a label in the operator definition.

There are three cases to consider. (1) A *required* property in one label is *missing* from the other label. In this case, the match does not succeed. A required property must be present in both labels. (2) A non-required property in one label is *missing* from the other label. In this case, the match succeeds because missing properties are treated as don't care information. (3) The property is present in both labels. The predicate, $PrMa_p$ specific to the property is used to determine if the property values match. Required and non-required properties are treated the same.

Definition 3.8 [$LaMa_\Gamma : LABEL \times LABEL \rightarrow BOOL$] Label $\mathcal{L}$ is matched against label $\mathcal{S}$ as follows. *LaMa* depends on the semantics of the properties as specified in Γ, since properties in the labels are individually matched.

$$\begin{aligned} &LaMa_\Gamma(\mathcal{L},\ \mathcal{S}) \triangleq \\ &\quad \forall p, x[(p!\ x) \in \mathcal{L} \Rightarrow \exists y[(p\colon y) \in \mathcal{S} \wedge PrMa_p(x,y)]] \wedge \\ &\quad \forall p, y[(p!\ y) \in \mathcal{S} \Rightarrow \exists x[(p\colon x) \in \mathcal{L} \wedge PrMa_p(x,y)]] \wedge \\ &\quad \forall p, x, y[(p\colon x) \in \mathcal{L} \wedge (p\colon y) \in \mathcal{S} \Rightarrow PrMa_p(x,y)] \end{aligned}$$ □

The property-specific predicate $PrMa_p$ matches two property values. For example, equality may be used for **name**, and time interval overlaps may be used for **transaction time**. See Table 1.

Example 3.9 The label that follows requires a movie description.

$\mathcal{L}_{movie}$:= {(**name!** movie)}

In Figure 2, there are two labels with a `movie` name property. One describes `&Color of Night`; the other, `&Star Wars IV`.

$\mathcal{S}_c$:= {(**name:** movie), (**security!** over 18)}
$\mathcal{S}_w$:= {(**name:** movie), (**trans. time:** [31/Jul/1998 - uc])}

These labels are matched as follows.

- $LaMa_\Gamma(\mathcal{L}_{movie},\ \mathcal{S}_c) =$ *False*; the required **security**, over 18, is missing from $\mathcal{L}_{movie}$.
- $LaMa_\Gamma(\mathcal{L}_{movie},\ \mathcal{S}_w) =$ *True*; the extra **transaction time** property in $\mathcal{S}_w$ is ignored. □

Operation *LaMa* is the basis for interpreting regular expressions of descriptors. Generally, these regular expressions are interpreted exactly as in other semistructured query languages, and the usual regular expression operations (+, *, ?, |, and . for sequencing) have their usual meaning. The only essential difference between our language and standard semistructured query languages is that the matched path is checked to ensure that it is valid. The following operation extends a set of paths in a semistructure, if the sequence of labels on an extended path matches the regular expression and the entire path is valid.

Definition 3.10 [$Match_{DB} : 2^{PATHS} \times REG \rightarrow 2^{PATHS}$] Let S be a set of starting paths (typically the roots of the semistructure) and X be a regular expression over an alphabet of (extended) labels. Then X is said to match a path in $DB = (V,\ E,\ \&root,\ \Gamma)$ by extending a path in S as follows.

$Match_{DB}(S,\ X) \triangleq \{x \mid x \in M(S,X)\ \wedge\ Valid_\Gamma(x)\}$,
where the matcher, M, is defined as follows.

$$\begin{aligned} M(S,\mathcal{L}) = \{&v_1 \xrightarrow{\mathcal{L}_1} \ldots \xrightarrow{\mathcal{L}_m} v_{m+1} \mid \\ &v_1 \xrightarrow{\mathcal{L}_1} \ldots \xrightarrow{\mathcal{L}_{m-1}} v_m \in S \wedge \\ &v_m \xrightarrow{\mathcal{L}_m} v_{m+1} \in E\ \wedge\ LaMa_\Gamma(\mathcal{L},\mathcal{L}_m)\} \\ M(S,X.Y) &= M(M(S,X),Y) \\ M(S,X*) &= S \cup M(S,X+) \\ M(S,X+) &= M(S,X.X*) \\ M(S,X?) &= S \cup M(X) \\ M(S,X|Y) &= M(S,X) \cup M(S,Y) \end{aligned}$$ □

In the definition, the matcher M extends a path in S by recursively decomposing a path regular expression (the expression unifies with the second argument). The matcher extends a standard semistructured database matcher to use $LaMa_\Gamma$ to match individual labels, as discussed above.

We note that the presence of cycles in the semistructure can lead to an infinite result set, just like matching in any semistructured query language. Consequently, when this operation is implemented, some strategy must be adopted to either break cycles (e.g., node marking is used for Lorel) or otherwise generate a finite result sets (e.g., stop after the first N matches). Which strategy to use is a decision best left to a language designer; AUCQL uses node marking to break cycles.

The cost of *Match* is essentially the same as path matching in a normal semistructured database: at worst the entire semistructure is explored. The path validity can be computed as each path is explored, although it costs an extra factor of $\mathcal{O}(m)$, where m is the number of properties in a label. $LaMa$ is also an $\mathcal{O}(m)$ operation, assuming that the properties in a label are sorted or hashed. So overall, the cost of matching in our framework grows by a factor of the size of each label.

Sometimes only the set of final nodes in a set of paths is desired.

Definition 3.11 [$Nodes : 2^{PATHS} \rightarrow 2^{NODES}$]
Let P be a set of paths.

$$Nodes(P) \triangleq \{w \mid v \xrightarrow{\mathcal{L}_1} \ldots \xrightarrow{\mathcal{L}_m} w \in P\} \qquad \Box$$

Example 3.12 A user is interested in retrieving information about movie stars as of 31/Jul/1998. That set of nodes can be obtained as follows.

$\mathcal{L}_{movie}$:= {(**name!** movie),
(**trans. time:** [31/Jul/1998 - 31/Jul/1998])}
$\mathcal{L}_{stars}$:= {(**name!** stars),
(**trans. time:** [31/Jul/1998 - 31/Jul/1998])}
$\mathcal{L}_{name}$:= {(**name!** name),
(**trans. time:** [31/Jul/1998 - 31/Jul/1998])}

$$Nodes(Match_{DB}(ROOTS,\ \mathcal{L}_{movie}.\mathcal{L}_{stars}.\mathcal{L}_{name}))$$

Recall that *ROOTS* is the set of edges from *&root* to roots in the semistructure. The regular expression in this example is a sequence of descriptors. In each descriptor, the **name** is required (so an edge without a **name** will not match), but the transaction time is not required (an edge that is missing a transaction time is presumed to exist at all transaction times). Properties not mentioned in the descriptor are ignored in the path matching, unless the property is required, in which case the label is not matched.

It is instructive to consider four paths in Figure 2. (1) The path through `&Color of Night` to the misspelled value *Bruce Wilis* is not matched since the required level of **security** (over 18) is missing from the descriptors. The user must have a digital certificate that authenticates her or him as being over 18, and must add that to the first descriptor to match that edge. (2) The path through `&Color of Night` to the value *Bruce Willis* is also not matched for the same reason. (3) The path through `&Star Wars IV` to the misspelled value *Bruce Wilis* matches the regular expression, but is not a valid path (see Example 3.7). (4) The path through `&Star Wars IV` to the value *Bruce Willis* is the only path that both matches the regular expression and is a valid path. □

3.2.3 Backwards Compatibility

Compatibility with current semistructured models is achieved by assuming that the string labels in those models default to **name** properties. Hence our framework can represent any existing semistructured database by modeling it as a database in which every label contains exactly one **name** property.

Using the same default, retrieval queries also remain unchanged. In existing semistructured databases all paths are valid. In our framework, if every label consists of a single **name** property, then all paths are also valid (**name**s are collapsed using string concatenation, which never results in an *undefined* value). In existing semistructured databases, the labels are matched using string comparison, just like in our framework, so path regular expressions match exactly the same paths in both models.

Finally, we observe that our framework seamlessly supports the mixing of data from existing semistructures with data that has richer meta-data since properties can vary from label to label. Hence as much or as little data as desired can be migrated to use the new type of labels.

3.3 Additional Query Operators

In this section we present several query language operators that are useful when querying the information within labels. First, a label restructuring operation, called *Slice*, is given that carves a portion from each label on a path. Next, the previously defined *ClPt* operation is trivially generalized to operate on the result of a *Match*. Finally, a *Coalesce* operation is defined to extract the value of a property that is distributed in several labels.

3.3.1 *Slice*

It is often useful to slice a portion from a property in each label along a path. The most common example is a transaction-time slice, or *rollback*, query that determines the other properties as of a particular transaction time. A path is sliced by slicing each property in a label on the path, and checking whether the resulting path is valid.

Definition 3.13 [$Slice_\Gamma : LABEL \times 2^{PATHS} \rightarrow 2^{PATHS}$]
A descriptor, $\mathcal{L}$, *slices* the labels along each path in a set of paths, P, as follows.

$$\begin{aligned} Slice_\Gamma(\mathcal{L},\ P) \triangleq \{v \xrightarrow{\mathcal{L}'_1} \ldots \xrightarrow{\mathcal{L}'_m} w \mid \\ v \xrightarrow{\mathcal{L}_1} \ldots \xrightarrow{\mathcal{L}_m} w \in P \ \wedge \\ \mathcal{L}'_1 = LaSl_\Gamma(\mathcal{L}, \mathcal{L}_1) \wedge \ldots \wedge \mathcal{L}'_m = LaSl_\Gamma(\mathcal{L}, \mathcal{L}_m) \ \wedge \\ Valid_\Gamma(v \xrightarrow{\mathcal{L}'_1} \ldots \xrightarrow{\mathcal{L}'_m} w) \end{aligned} \qquad \Box$$

A label is sliced property by property. This slicing is complicated by missing properties. Specifically, if a property is missing from the descriptor, but present in the label, it is passed unchanged into the result. A missing property in a label is also missing in the result, except if the descriptor *requires* the property, in which case the property from the descriptor is added to the result. Finally, if the property is both in the label and the descriptor then a property-specific constructor slices the property appropriately and adds it to the result.

Definition 3.14 [$LaSl_\Gamma : LABEL \times LABEL \rightarrow LABEL$]
A label, $\mathcal{L}$, *slices* a label, $\mathcal{S}$, as follows.

$$
\begin{aligned}
&LaSl_\Gamma(\mathcal{L}, \mathcal{S}) \triangleq \\
&\quad \{(p!\ PrSl_p(x, y)) \mid \\
&\qquad (p!\ x) \in \mathcal{L} \wedge ((p{:}\ y) \in \mathcal{S} \vee (p!\ y) \in \mathcal{S})\} \cup \\
&\quad \{(p!\ PrSl_p(x, y)) \mid \\
&\qquad (p!\ y) \in \mathcal{S} \wedge ((p{:}\ x) \in \mathcal{L} \vee (p!\ x) \in \mathcal{L})\} \cup \\
&\quad \{(p{:}\ PrSl_p(x, y)) \mid (p{:}\ x) \in \mathcal{L} \wedge (p{:}\ y) \in \mathcal{S}\} \cup \\
&\quad \{(p!\ y) \mid (p!\ y) \in \mathcal{S} \wedge \neg\exists x[(p{:}\ x) \in \mathcal{L} \vee (p!\ x) \in \mathcal{L}]\} \cup \\
&\quad \{(p!\ x) \mid (p!\ x) \in \mathcal{L} \wedge \neg\exists y[(p{:}\ y) \in \mathcal{L} \vee (p!\ y) \in \mathcal{L}]\} \cup \\
&\quad \{(p{:}\ x) \mid (p{:}\ x) \in \mathcal{L} \wedge \neg\exists y[(p{:}y) \in \mathcal{S} \vee (p!\ y) \in \mathcal{S}]\} \quad \square
\end{aligned}
$$

Recall that $PrSl_p$ is a property-specific constructor that slices a property. Table 1 shows the slicing operators.

Example 3.15 A user is interested in retrieving the other properties about movie stars names as of the current time. That set of paths can be obtained as follows.

$\mathcal{L}_m$:= {(**name!** movie)}
$\mathcal{L}_s$:= {(**name!** stars)}
$\mathcal{L}_n$:= {(**name!** name)}
$\mathcal{L}_{now}$:= {(**trans. time:** [now - now])}
$Slice_\Gamma(\mathcal{L}_{now}, Match_{DB}(ROOTS, \mathcal{L}_m.\mathcal{L}_s.\mathcal{L}_n))$

Note that a $Slice_\Gamma$ with $\mathcal{L}_{now}$ as its first argument differs from a *Match* with that descriptor since the **transaction time** property of every label (that has a transaction time) in the sliced path is [now - now], whereas the **transaction time** property in the matched path would be unchanged from the underlying data. □

3.3.2 *Collapse*

In this section, the $PathCollapse_\Gamma$ operation introduced in Section 3.2.1 is trivially generalized to collapse every path in a set of paths. Typically, $Match_{DB}$ first chooses a set of paths that match some regular expression, then the paths are collapsed, and a property is coalesced from the collapsed paths.

Definition 3.16 [$Collapse_\Gamma : 2^{PATHS} \rightarrow 2^{EDGES}$]
A set of paths, S, is collapsed by collapsing each path independently.

$$Collapse_\Gamma(S) \triangleq \{ClPt_\Gamma(P) \mid P \in S \wedge Valid_\Gamma(P)\} \quad \square$$

The utility of an operation like *Collapse* has been investigated in other semistructured query languages where it has been called "pull-up" [1]. In Lorel, *Collapse* is not an operation at the query language level; rather, it is used in the implementation to compute the value of a *path variable*.

3.3.3 *Coalesce*

Several (virtual) edges may connect a pair of nodes. For example, two edges connect the pair of nodes in Figure 4. The first edge was added when the review began to be developed on 15/Mar/1998. The security was set to restrict the edge to page developers. By 25/May/1998, the edge was publicly released as part of the June issue and so the security was weakened to include paid subscribers.

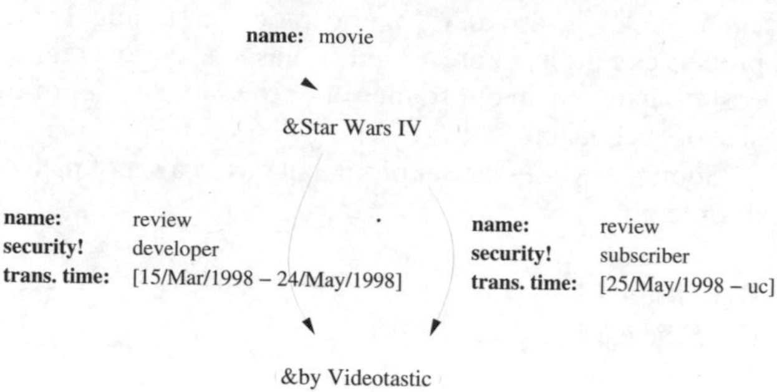

Figure 4: Evolving Information About a Review

When several edges connect a pair of nodes, information about a single property may be distributed among multiple labels. In order to determine the full extent of a property that (conceptually) pertains to a relationship between a pair of nodes, regardless of whether information about that property is distributed among a number of edges, it is advantageous to *coalesce* the property from the set of edges.

Definition 3.17 [$Coalesce_\Gamma : NAME \times 2^{EDGES} \rightarrow VALUE$]
Assume that a set of edges, F, connects the same pair of nodes. F is coalesced for a *single* property, p, as follows.

$$
\begin{aligned}
&Coalesce_\Gamma(p, F) \triangleq PrCs_p(\\
&\quad \{x \mid ((p{:}\ x) \in \mathcal{L} \vee (p!\ x) \in \mathcal{L} \wedge v \xrightarrow{\mathcal{L}} w \in F\})\} \cup \\
&\quad \{\textit{undefined} \mid ((p{:}\ x) \notin \mathcal{L} \wedge (p!\ x) \notin \mathcal{L}) \wedge \\
&\qquad\qquad v \xrightarrow{\mathcal{L}} w \in F\}) \quad \square
\end{aligned}
$$

The $PrCs_p$ operation is a property-specific constructor. Unlike the collapsing constructor, the coalescing constructor does not have to be a restrictor or mutator. Also, the result is not a label, but a single, coalesced value.

Example 3.18 The following strategy can be used to determine the **transaction time** for the review of *Star Wars IV* by *Videotastic*, irrespective of the **security, valid time**, etc. First, find all the paths from a root to the review. Note that this requires a certain level of **security**. Second, collapse each path into a virtual edge. Finally, coalesce the **transaction times** of the virtual edges.

$\mathcal{L}_{movie}$:= {(**name!** movie), (**security:** developer)}
$\mathcal{L}_{review}$:= {(**name!** review), (**security:** developer)}
$E := Collapse_\Gamma(Match_{DB}(ROOTS, \mathcal{L}_{movie}.\mathcal{L}_{review}))$
$Coalesce_\Gamma$(**trans. time**, E)

The result is $\{($&root, (**trans. time:** [15/Mar/1998 - uc]), &by Videotastic$)\}$. The coalesced transaction time property, [15/Mar/1998 - uc], is the union of the two transaction time intervals in Figure 4. □

3.4 Updates

When transaction time is one of the supported properties, special semantics for update should be enforced to accommodate transaction time. In a transaction-time database the database is trusted to enforce these semantics. On the web, no such trusted mechanism is available for updates. However, individual sites or even collections of pages within a site can be archived to correctly support transaction time. Because of the flexibility of our framework, information from pages that support transaction time can be freely mixed with information from pages that do not.

In this section, we describe the constraints that should exist to correctly support transaction time, but leave open the issue of how these constraints are enforced on update. An update can be either at the data level, consisting of a change to an edge, label, or node, or at the meta-data level, consisting of the addition of a property. We discuss each kind of modification in turn.

3.4.1 Data Updates

An edge can be inserted at any time into the semistructure. On insertion, the transaction time of the label on the inserted edge is set to $[\mathit{current\ time} - \mathrm{uc}]$.

Definition 3.19 [Edge insertion]
Let T be the current time. An edge is inserted into a semistructure, $DB = (V,\ E,\ \&root,\ \Gamma)$, as follows.

$$\mathit{Insert}_{DB}(T, v \xrightarrow{\mathcal{L}} w) \triangleq$$
$$(V\ \cup\ \{v,\ w\},\ E\ \cup\ \{v \xrightarrow{\mathcal{L}'} w\},\ \&root,\ \Gamma),$$
where $\mathcal{L}' = \mathcal{L}\ \cup\ \{(\textbf{transaction time: } [T - \mathrm{uc}])\}$. □

Redundant and overlapping labels are permitted on edges, i.e., the data is not stored *coalesced*. Note also that edge insertion inserts nodes if the nodes not already exist in the database. We do not give a separate operation to insert only a node (our focus is on the relevant changes needed to support properties in labels).

Edges are (logically) deleted by terminating their transaction-time interval.

Definition 3.20 [Edge deletion]
Let T be the current time. An edge is deleted from a semistructure, $DB = (V,\ E,\ \&root,\ \Gamma)$, as follows.

$$\mathit{Delete}_{DB}(T,\ v \xrightarrow{\mathcal{L}} w) \triangleq$$
$$(V,\ (E\ -\ \{v \xrightarrow{\mathcal{L}} w\})\ \cup\ \{v \xrightarrow{\mathcal{L}'} w\},\ \&root,\ \Gamma),$$
where the label $\mathcal{L}'$ is exactly the same as $\mathcal{L}$ except in the transaction time property. If $\mathcal{L}$ has a transaction time property, say (**transaction time:** x), then

$$\mathcal{L}' = \mathcal{L} - \{(\textbf{transaction time: } x)\}\ \cup$$
$$\{(\textbf{transaction time: } (x\ \cap\ [\mathrm{beginning} - T]))\}.$$

If the transaction time property is missing from $\mathcal{L}$,

$$\mathcal{L}' = \mathcal{L}\ \cup\ \{(\textbf{transaction time: } [\mathrm{beginning} - T])\}.$$ □

Finally, a node can be (logically) deleted by removing all incoming edges, and an edge modification is modeled as an edge deletion followed by an edge insertion.

Example 3.21 The transactions that created the two edges in Figure 4 are given below. Let

$v :=$ &Star Wars IV,
$w :=$ &by Videotastic,
$\mathcal{L}_1 :=$ $\{$(**name:** review), (**security!** developer)$\}$, and
$\mathcal{L}_2 :=$ $\{$(**name:** review), (**security!** paid subscriber)$\}$.

On 15/Mar/1998, the first edge is inserted:

$$\mathit{Insert}_{DB}(15/\mathrm{Mar}/1998, v \xrightarrow{\mathcal{L}_1} w)$$

On 24/May/1998, the first edge is deleted:

$$\mathit{Delete}_{DB}(24/\mathrm{May}/1998, v \xrightarrow{\mathcal{L}_1} w)$$

On 25/May/1998, the second edge is inserted:

$$\mathit{Insert}_{DB}(25/\mathrm{May}/1998, v \xrightarrow{\mathcal{L}_2} w)$$ □

3.4.2 Adding and Removing Properties

Just as data evolves over time, properties can also be added and (logically) deleted.

A property may be added to a label at any time. For all existing labels, the new property is simply missing. When a label is subsequently inserted or updated, the new property can be used as needed. Each property consists of a unique *name*, a *domain* or type, and four operations: $PrCl_p$ (collapse), $PrMa_p$ (match), $PrSl_p$ (slice), and $PrCs_p$ (coalesce). A database designer adds this information to the semantics of properties, Γ, within *DB*. For most properties, the default semantics for operations given below will suffice.

Definition 3.22 [Default property semantics]
Let t_1 and t_2 be any values for the property.

$$PrCl_p(t_1, t_2) = \lambda t_1\ t_2.\ t_2$$
$$PrMa_p(t_1, t_2) = \lambda t_1\ t_2.\ t_1 = t_2$$
$$PrSl_p(t_1, t_2) = \text{Semantic Error}$$
$$PrCs_p(\{t_1, \ldots, t_n\}) = \text{Semantic Error}$$ □

Two properties are by default collapsed to the second since paths are collapsed top-down, from a root to a leaf. The "closest" or most recent property to a leaf is taken to be the relevant property. Consider a **URL** property that gives the URL at which a datum resides. The URL of the page that contains the datum is more relevant than the URL of a parent page, and this is exactly what is computed by the default collapse constructor. Two properties match only if they are equal. No defaults are provided for and $PrSl_p$ and $PrCs_p$ since no reasonable, general defaults exists. Furthermore, these operations are only invoked by mentioning the property name in an additional, specific query language operation (they are in some sense optional).

A property can be deleted by removing the property semantics from Γ. Although existing labels in the data store will mention the property, the property is ignored in all subsequent operations (except for labels with a required property in the deleted property, which will fail to match any subsequent query). To save space, and remove required properties, the property should also be deleted from each edge, but this might be costly and disruptive.

This simple support for properties can be enhanced by maintaining a history of property insertions and deletions as meta-meta-data. This can be accomplished by using name and transaction time properties within each label in the meta-data. Then previous database states can be queried with the properties available as of that previous state, but this issue of transaction time support for property changes is beyond the scope of this paper.

4 AUCQL

This section offers a brief overview of an SQL-like query language, AUCQL, for querying a semistructured database that has been extended with properties. AUCQL is like Lorel [3], but has additional constructs to permit queries to exploit properties. The focus of this presentation is on the small changes to the SELECT statement to support the extended query language operators discussed in the previous sections. The reader is encouraged to interactively try the AUCQL queries given here, or other queries, at the AUCQL website: <www.cs.auc.dk/~curtis/AUCQL>.

4.1 Variables in AUCQL

The key to understanding AUCQL is understanding the specification and use of variables. Variables in AUCQL are very much like variables in Lorel, the primary difference being that in AUCQL, a variable can range over the result of any of the extended query operators discussed in Section 3.2. Below is an AUCQL (or Lorel) query to find the names of movie stars.

```
SELECT Name
FROM   movie.stars.name Name;
```

(This is not the shortest, or best possible query, but is adequate for the purposes of this discussion.) This query sets up a variable Name that ranges over the terminal nodes of paths that match the regular expression movie.stars.name. In terms of the operations discussed in Section 3.2, the variable has the following meaning.

$\mathcal{L}_m := \{(\textbf{name!}\ \text{movie})\}$
$\mathcal{L}_s := \{(\textbf{name!}\ \text{stars})\}$
$\mathcal{L}_n := \{(\textbf{name!}\ \text{name})\}$
$\texttt{Name} \in Nodes(Match_{DB}(ROOTS,\ \mathcal{L}_m.\mathcal{L}_s.\mathcal{L}_n))$

In fact, in AUCQL, this interpretation can be given explicitly.

```
SELECT Name
FROM NODES(MATCH(roots, (NAME! movie).
     (NAME! stars).(NAME! name))) Name;
```

In AUCQL, a bareword descriptor (e.g., movie) defaults to a required use of the **name** property (e.g., to (NAME! movie)), since that will be the most commonly used property.

4.2 Defaults

Default properties can be set to simplify queries. Once a default is set, that value is used for the property in all subsequent operations. Properties specifically mentioned in an operation override their default values. The syntax for setting defaults is straightforward. Below is an example that retrieves movie stars' names that are current in the semistructure.

```
SET DEFAULT PROPERTY
    (TRANSACTION_TIME: [now-now]);
SELECT movie.star.name;
```

Security is one of the most common default settings. Users can advertise their security certificates in all subsequent queries by setting a default.

```
SET DEFAULT PROPERTY
    (SECURITY: over 18 AND subscriber);
```

5 Summary and Future Work

This paper proposes an extensible framework for capturing more data semantics in semistructured data models. The framework is extensible so that it can incorporate the latest advances in diverse domains, from web security and e-commerce to transaction-time databases. The additional semantics for each domain are captured in enriched labels. The new labels are sets of descriptive properties. The properties used as examples in this paper include transaction time, price, security, quality, and valid time. But the properties do not have to be the same for every database or even for every label within a database since this framework permits missing properties. Support for required properties, to model properties such as security, is also built into the framework.

Several new operations are needed to manipulate labels with properties. *Match* chooses a set of paths from the semistructure that match a user-given path regular expression. *Collapse* combines the properties in labels along a path to create a new label for the entire path. *Slice* slices a portion from each label on a path. Finally, *Coalesce* coalesces a property from a set of edges. These operations are built into the AUCQL query language, an implemented, Lorel-like query language, which is briefly described in this paper.

This work may be extended in a number of directions. Labels can be further extended to include a *set* of labels. This does not greatly increase the modeling power since multiple descriptions of the same relationship can be split into individual labels on a multitude of edges. However, it is essential to storing coalesced labels, which may be of some convenience to the user.

We also need to research translating meta-data in XML, such as RDF [21] or P3P [27], to a set of properties. The translation should be relatively straightforward since there is a clear mapping between paths in an XML data-set and properties: each path maps to a property, the labels along the path collapse to the property's name, while the terminal value of the path is the property's value.

Finally, and perhaps most importantly, the impact of our framework on path indexes must be addressed. We expect that a spatial or (bi)-temporal index can be generalized to index paths through properties in labels, and we plan to investigate this issue in the future.

Acknowledgements

This research was supported in part by a grant from the Nykredit Corporation, by the Danish Technical Research Council through grant 9700780, and by the CHOROCHRONOS project, funded by the European Commission DG XII Science, Research and Development, contract no. FMRX-CT96-0056.

References

[1] S. Aggarwal, I. Kim, and W. Meng. Database Exploration with Dynamic Abstractions. In *DEXA'94*, Sep. 1994.

[2] G. Arocena and A. Mendelzon. WebOQL: Restructuring Documents, Databases, and Webs. In *ICDE'98*, pp. 24–33, Feb. 1998.

[3] S. Abiteboul, D. Quass, J. McHugh, J. Widom, and J. Wiener. The Lorel Query Language for Semistructured Data. *International Journal of Digital Libraries*, 1(1):68–88, 1997.

[4] T. Berners-Lee. Keynote Address. In *WWW7*, Apr. 1998.

[5] M. Böhlen, R. Snodgrass, and M. Soo. Coalescing in Temporal Databases. In *VLDB'96*, pp. 180–191, Sep. 1996.

[6] P. Buneman, S. Davidson, and D. Suciu. Programming Constructs for Unstructured Data. In *DBPL-5*, 1995.

[7] P. Buneman, S. B. Davidson, G. G. Hillebrand, and D. Suciu. A Query Language and Optimization Techniques for Unstructured Data. In *SIGMOD'96*, pp. 505–516, Jun. 1996.

[8] P. Buneman. Semistructured Data. In *SIGMOD/-PODS'97* (tutorial notes), May 1997.

[9] P. Buneman, A. Deutsch, and W.-C. Tan. A Deterministic Model for Semi-structured Data. In *ICDT'99 Workshop on the Web Query Languages*, Jan. 1999.

[10] S. Chawathe, S. Abiteboul, and J. Widom. Representing and Querying Changes in Semistructured Data. In *ICDE'98*, pp. 4–13, Feb. 1998.

[11] S. Castano, M. Fugini, G. Martella, and P. Samarati. *Database Security*. Addison-Wesley, 1994.

[12] D. Connolly, R. Khare, and A. Rifkin. The Evolution of Web Documents: The Ascent of XML. *XML special issue of the World Wide Web Journal*, 2(4):119–128, 1997.

[13] M. Fernandez, D. Florescu, A. Levy, and D. Suciu. A Query Language for a Web-Site Management System. *SIGMOD Record*, 26(3), Sep. 1997.

[14] D. Florescu, A. Levy, and A. Mendelzon. Database Techniques for the World-Wide Web: A Survey. *SIGMOD Record*, 27(3):59–74, Sep. 1998.

[15] M. Fernandez and D. Suciu. Optimizing Regular Path Expressions Using Graph Schemas. In *ICDE'98*, pp. 14–23, Feb. 1998.

[16] R. Goldman and J. Widom. Dataguides: Enabling Query Formulation and Optimization in Semistructured Databases. In *VLDB'97*, pp. 436–445, Sep. 1997.

[17] R. Goldman and J. Widom. Interactive Query and Search in Semistructured Databases. In *the First International Workshop on the Web and Databases*, pp. 42–48, Mar. 1998.

[18] J. Hammer, H. Garcia-Molina, J. Cho, R. Aranha, and A. Crespo. Extracting Semistructured Information from the Web. In *the Workshop on the Management of Semistructured Data* (in association with *SIGMOD'97*), Jun. 1997.

[19] C. S. Jensen and C. E. Dyreson (eds.). *A Consensus Glossary of Temporal Database Concepts - February 1998 Version*. In O. Etzion et al. (eds.), *Temporal Databases: Research and Practice*, LNCS 1399, pp. 367–405. Springer-Verlag, 1998.

[20] B. Ludäscher, R. Himmeröder, G. Lausen, W. May, and C. Schlepphorst. Managing Semistructured Datat with FLORID: A Deductive Object-Oriented Perspective. To appear in *Information Systems*.

[21] O. Lassila and R. Swick. Resource Description Framework (RDF) Model and Syntax Specification. W3C Technical Report, Jan. 1999.

[22] J. McHugh, S. Abiteboul, R. Goldman, D. Quass, and J. Widom. Lore: A Database Management System for Semistructured Data. *SIGMOD Record*, 26(3):54–66, Sep. 1997.

[23] T. Milo and D. D. Suciu. Index Structures for Path Expressions. In *ICDT '99*, Jan. 1999.

[24] S. Nestorov, S. Abiteboul, and R. Motwani. Inferring Structure from Semistructured Data. In *the Workshop on the Management of Semistructured Data* (in association with *SIGMOD'97*), Jun. 1997.

[25] D. Quass, A. Rajaraman, J. D. Ullman, J. Widom, and Y. Sagiv. Querying Semistructured Heterogeneous Information. *Journal of Systems Integration*, 7(3/4):381–407, 1997.

[26] D. Suciu. Semistructured Data and XML. In *FODO'98*, 1998.

[27] W3C. Platform for Privacy Preferences (P3P1.0). W3C Technical Report, Jan. 1999.

Relational Databases for Querying XML Documents: Limitations and Opportunities

Jayavel Shanmugasundaram   Kristin Tufte   Gang He
Chun Zhang   David DeWitt   Jeffrey Naughton

Department of Computer Sciences
University of Wisconsin-Madison
{jai, tufte, czhang, dewitt, naughton}@cs.wisc.edu, ganghe@microsoft.com

Abstract

XML is fast emerging as the dominant standard for representing data in the World Wide Web. Sophisticated query engines that allow users to effectively tap the data stored in XML documents will be crucial to exploiting the full power of XML. While there has been a great deal of activity recently proposing new semi-structured data models and query languages for this purpose, this paper explores the more conservative approach of using traditional relational database engines for processing XML documents conforming to Document Type Descriptors (DTDs). To this end, we have developed algorithms and implemented a prototype system that converts XML documents to relational tuples, translates semi-structured queries over XML documents to SQL queries over tables, and converts the results to XML. We have qualitatively evaluated this approach using several real DTDs drawn from diverse domains. It turns out that the relational approach can handle most (but not all) of the semantics of semi-structured queries over XML data, but is likely to be effective only in some cases. We identify the causes for these limitations and propose certain extensions to the relational model that would make it more appropriate for processing queries over XML documents.

Proceedings of the 25th VLDB Conference, Edinburgh, Scotland, 1999.

1. Introduction

Extensible Markup Language (XML) is fast emerging as the dominant standard for representing data on the Internet. Like HTML, XML is a subset of SGML. However, whereas HTML tags serve the primary purpose of describing how to display a data item, XML tags describe the data itself. The importance of this simple distinction cannot be underestimated – because XML data is self-describing, it is possible for programs to interpret the data. This means that a program receiving an XML document can interpret it in multiple ways, can filter the document based upon its content, can restructure it to suit the application's needs, and so forth.

The initial impetus for XML may have been primarily to enhance this ability of remote applications to interpret and operate on documents fetched over the Internet. However, from a database point of view, XML raises a different exciting possibility: with data stored in XML documents, it should be possible to query the contents of these documents. One should be able to issue queries over sets of XML documents to extract, synthesize, and analyze their contents. But what is the best way to provide this query capability over XML documents?

At first glance the answer is obvious. Since an XML document is an example of a semi-structured data set (it is tree-structured, with each node in the tree described by a label), why not use semi-structured query languages and query evaluation techniques? This is indeed a viable approach, and there is considerable activity in the semi-structured data community focussed upon exploiting this approach [5,14]. While semi-structured techniques will clearly work, in this paper we ask the question of whether this is the only or the best approach to take. The downside of using semi-structured techniques is that this approach turns its back on 20 years of work invested in relational database technology. Is it really the case that we cannot use relational technology, and must start afresh with new techniques? Or can we leverage relational technology to provide query capability over XML documents?

In this paper we demonstrate that it is indeed possible to use standard commercial relational database systems to evaluate powerful queries over XML documents. The key that makes this possible is the existence of Document Type Descriptors (DTDs) [2] (or an equivalent, such as DCDs [4] or XML Schemas [16]). A DTD is in effect a schema for a set of XML documents. Without DTDs or their equivalent, XML will never reach its full potential, because a tagged document is not very useful without some agreement among inter-operating applications as to what the tags mean. Put another way, the reason the Internet community is so excited about XML is that there is the vision of a future in which the vast majority of files on the web are XML files conforming to DTDs. An application encountering such a file can interpret the file by consulting the DTDs to which the document conforms.

Our approach to querying XML documents is the following. First, we process a DTD to generate a relational schema. Second, we parse XML documents conforming to DTDs and load them into tuples of relational tables in a standard commercial DBMS (in our case, IBM DB2). Third, we translate semi-structured queries (specified in a language similar to XML-QL [9] or Lorel [1]) over XML documents into SQL queries over the corresponding relational data. Finally, we convert the results back to XML.

The good news is that this works. A main contribution of this paper is the description of an approach that enables one to take the XML queries, data sets, and schemas so foreign to the relational world and process them in relational systems without any manual intervention. This means that we are presented with a large opportunity: all of the power of relational database systems can be brought to bear upon the XML query problem.

However, the fact that something is possible does not necessarily imply that it is a good idea. Our experience with implementing this system and using it with over 30 different XML DTDs has revealed that there are a number of limitations in current relational database systems that in some instances make using relational technology for XML queries either awkward or inefficient. Relational technology proves awkward for queries that require complex XML constructs in their results, and may be inefficient when fragmentation due to the handling of set-valued attributes and sharing causes too many joins in the evaluation of simple queries. Another contribution of this paper is the identification of those limitations, and a discussion of how they might be removed. It is an open question at this point whether the best approach is to start with relational technology and try to remove those limitations, or to start with a semi-structured system and try to add the power and sophistication currently found in relational query processing systems.

1.1 Related Work

There has been a lot of work developing special purpose query engines for semi-structured data [5,14]. Many of the abstracts submitted to the XML query languages workshop use this approach [18]. Our goal in this paper, however, is to investigate the use of relational database systems to process queries on semi-structured documents. In this sense, our work is similar to the work on STORED [10]. However, our approach differs in important ways. The STORED approach uses a combination of relational and semi-structured techniques to process any semi-structured documents. We begin with the assumption that the document conforms to a schema and store the document entirely within the relational system. Further, we handle recursive queries, address the issue of constructing the result in XML and evaluate the relational approach using real DTDs.

Oracle 8i provides some basic support for querying XML documents using a relational engine [17]. However, the translation from document schemas to relational schemas is manual and not automatic as in our approach. In addition, Oracle 8i does not provide support for semi-structured queries over XML documents and provides only primitive support for converting results to XML.

There has also been work on processing SGML data using an OODBMS [6]. The conclusion was that this is feasible with some extensions to OO query languages. Our work considers a more restricted set of documents (XML, rather than SGML) and considers mapping to the relational model, rather than a general OO model.

Our method of eliminating wild cards and alternations in path expression queries to enable processing by a relational engine bears some similarities to the work on compile time optimization of path expressions in semi-structured query engines [12,15]. Our different focus, however, results in modified techniques.

1.2 Roadmap

The rest of the paper is organized as follows. Section 2 gives an overview of XML documents, schemas and query languages. The algorithms for translating DTDs and XML documents to a relational format and an evaluation of the algorithms using real DTDs are given in Section 3. Section 4 describes the translation of queries over XML documents to SQL queries. Section 5 deals with the conversion of the results to XML. Section 6 concludes by proposing extensions to the relational model that will make it more suitable for processing XML documents.

2. Overview of XML, XML Schemas and XML Query Languages

In this section, we give a very brief overview of XML, XML schemas and XML query languages. Further details can be obtained from the references.

2.1 Extensible Markup Language

Extensible Markup Language (XML) is a hierarchical data format for information exchange in the World Wide Web. An XML document consists of nested element structures, starting with a root element. Element data can be in the form of attributes or sub-elements. Figure 1 shows an XML document that contains information about a book. In this example, there is a book element that has two sub-elements, booktitle and author. The author element has an id attribute with value "dawkins" and is further nested to provide name and address information. Further information on XML can be found in [3,8].

```
<book>
  <booktitle> The Selfish Gene </booktitle>
  <author id = "dawkins">
        <name>
            <firstname> Richard </firstname>
            <lastname> Dawkins </lastname>
        </name>
        <address>
            <city> Timbuktu </city>
            <zip> 99999 </zip>
        </address>
  </author>
</book>
```

Figure 1

```
<!ELEMENT book (booktitle, author)
<!ELEMENT article (title, author*, contactauthor)>
<!ELEMENT contactauthor EMPTY>
<!ATTLIST contactauthor authorID IDREF IMPLIED>
<!ELEMENT monograph (title, author, editor)>
<!ELEMENT editor (monograph*)>
<!ATTLIST editor name CDATA #REQUIRED>
<!ELEMENT author (name, address)>
<!ATTLIST author id ID #REQUIRED>
<!ELEMENT name (firstname?, lastname)>
<!ELEMENT firstname (#PCDATA)>
<!ELEMENT lastname (#PCDATA)>
<!ELEMENT address ANY>
```

Figure 2

2.2 DTDs and other XML Schemas

Document Type Descriptors (DTDs) [2] describe the structure of XML documents and are like a schema for XML documents. A DTD specifies the structure of an XML element by specifying the names of its sub-elements and attributes. Sub-element structure is specified using the operators * (set with zero or more elements), + (set with one or more elements), ? (optional), and | (or). All values are assumed to be string values, unless the type is ANY in which case the value can be an arbitrary XML fragment. There is a special attribute, id, which can occur once for each element. The id attribute uniquely identifies an element within a document and can be referenced through an IDREF field in another element. IDREFs are untyped. Finally, there is no concept of a root of a DTD – an XML document conforming to a DTD can be rooted at any element specified in the DTD. Figure 2 shows a DTD specification, while Figure 1 gives an XML document that conforms to this DTD.

Document Content Descriptors (DCDs) [4] and XML Schemas [16] are extensions to DTDs. For our purposes, the main difference between these and DTDs is that they allow typing of values and set size specification. If DCDs and XML Schemas become standard, the additional information would aid in our translation process; for example, we could create tables with integer attributes where appropriate instead of using just strings. The types in the current DCD proposal are compatible with types supported by current relational systems. More complex types will require object-relational extensions.

2.3 XML Query Languages

```
SELECT X.author.lastname
FROM book X
WHERE X.booktitle = "The Selfish Gene"
```

Figure 3

```
WHERE <book>
            <booktitle> The Selfish Gene </booktitle>
            <author>
                <lastname> $l </lastname>
            </>
        </> IN a.xml, b.xml
CONSTRUCT <lastname> $l </lastname>
```

Figure 4

There are many semi-structured query languages that can be used to query XML documents, including XML-QL [9], Lorel [1], UnQL [5] and XQL (from Microsoft). All these query languages have a notion of path expressions for navigating the nested structure of XML. XML-QL uses a nested XML-like structure to specify the part of a document to be selected and the structure of the result XML document.

Figure 4 shows an XML-QL query to determine the last name of an author of a book having title "The Selfish Gene", specified over a set of XML documents conforming to the DTD in Figure 2. The last names thus selected will be nested within a lastname tag, as specified in the construct clause of the query. Lorel is more like SQL and its representation of the same query is shown in Figure 3. In this paper, we use a combination of XML-QL and Lorel (modified appropriately for our purposes).

3. Storing XML Documents in a Relational Database System

In this section, we describe how to generate relational schemas from XML DTDs. The main issues that must be addressed include (a) dealing with the complexity of DTD element specifications (b) resolving the conflict between the two-level nature of relational schemas (table and attribute) vs. the arbitrary nesting of XML DTD schemas and (c) dealing with set-valued attributes and recursion.

3.1 Simplifying DTDs

In general, DTDs can be complex and generating relational schemas that capture this complexity would be unwieldy at best. Fortunately, one can simplify the details of a DTD and still generate a relational schema that can store and query documents conforming to that DTD. Note that it is not necessary to be able to regenerate a DTD from the generated relational schema. Rather, what is required is that (a) any document conforming to the DTD can be stored in the relational schema, and (b) any XML semi-structured query over a document conforming to the DTD can be evaluated over the relational database instance.

Most of the complexity of DTDs stems from the complex specification of the type of an element. For instance, we could specify an element a as <!ELEMENT a ((b|c|e)?,(e?|(f?,(b,b)*))*)>, where b, c, e and f are other elements. However, at the query language level, all that matters is the position of an element in the XML document, relative to its siblings and the parent-child relationship between elements in the XML document. We now propose a set of transformations that can be used to "simplify" any arbitrary DTD without undermining the effectiveness of queries over documents conforming to that DTD. These transformations are a superset of similar transformations presented in [10].

$(e_1, e_2)^* \rightarrow e_1^*, e_2^*$
$(e_1, e_2)? \rightarrow e_1?, e_2?$
$(e_1|e_2) \rightarrow e_1?, e_2?$

Figure 5

$e_1^{**} \rightarrow e_1^*$
$e_1^*? \rightarrow e_1^*$
$e_1?^* \rightarrow e_1^*$
$e_1?? \rightarrow e_1?$

Figure 6

..., a*, ..., a*, ... → a*, ...
..., a*, ..., a?, ... → a*, ...
..., a?, ..., a*, ... → a*, ...
..., a?, ..., a?, ... → a*, ...
..., a, ..., a, ... → a*, ...

Figure 7

The transformations are of three types: (a) flattening transformations which convert a nested definition into a flat representation (i.e., one in which the binary operators "," and "|" do not appear inside any operator – see Figure 5) (b) simplification transformations, which reduce many unary operators to a single unary operator (Figure 6) and (c) grouping transformations that group sub-elements having the same name (for example, two a* sub-elements are grouped into one a* sub-element - see Figure 7). In addition, all "+" operators are transformed to "*" operators. Our example specification would be transformed to: <!ELEMENT a (b*, c?, e*, f*)>.

The transformations preserve the semantics of (a) one or many and (b) null or not null. The astute reader may notice that we have lost some information about relative orders of the elements. This is true; fortunately, this information can be captured when a specific XML document is loaded into this relational schema (e.g., by position fields in the tuples representing some of the elements.) We now explore techniques for converting a simplified DTD to a relational schema.

3.2 Motivation for Special Schema Conversion Techniques

Traditionally, relational schemas have been derived from a data model such as the Entity-Relationship model. This translation is straightforward because there is a clear separation between entities and their attributes. Each entity and its attributes are mapped to a relation.

When converting an XML DTD to relations, it is tempting to map each element in the DTD to a relation and map the attributes of the element to attributes of the relation. However, there is no correspondence between elements and attributes of DTDs and entities and attributes of the ER-Model. What would be considered "attributes" in an ER-Model are often most naturally represented as elements in a DTD. Figure 2 shows a DTD that illustrates this point. In an ER-Model, *author* would be an "entity" and *firstname, lastname* and *address* would be attributes of that entity. In designing a DTD, there is no incentive to make *author* an element and *firstname, lastname* and *address* attributes. In fact, in XML, if *firstname* and *lastname* were attributes, they could not be nested under name because XML attributes cannot have a nested structure. Directly mapping elements to relations is thus likely to lead to excessive fragmentation of the document.

3.3 The Basic Inlining Technique

The Basic Inlining Technique, hereafter referred to as *Basic*, solves the fragmentation problem by inlining as many descendants of an element as possible into a single relation. However, *Basic* creates relations for every element because an XML document can be rooted at any element in a DTD. For example, the *author* element in Figure 2 would be mapped to a relation with attributes *firstname, lastname* and *address.* In addition, relations would be created for *firstname, lastname* and *address.*

We must address two complications: set-valued attributes and recursion. In the example DTD in Figure 2, when creating a relation for article, we cannot inline the set of authors because the traditional relational model does not support set-valued attributes. Rather, we follow the standard technique for storing sets in an RDBMS and create a relation for author and link authors to articles using a foreign key. Just using inlining (if we want the process to terminate) necessarily limits the level of nesting in the recursion. Therefore, we express the recursive relationship using the notion of relational keys and use relational recursive processing to retrieve the relationship. In order to do this in a general fashion, we introduce the notion of a DTD graph.

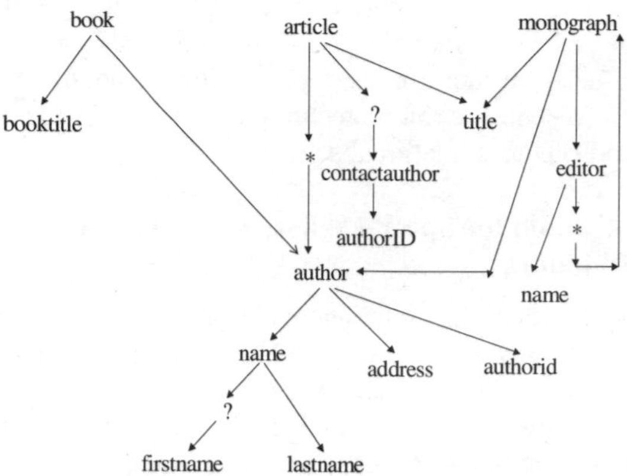

Figure 8

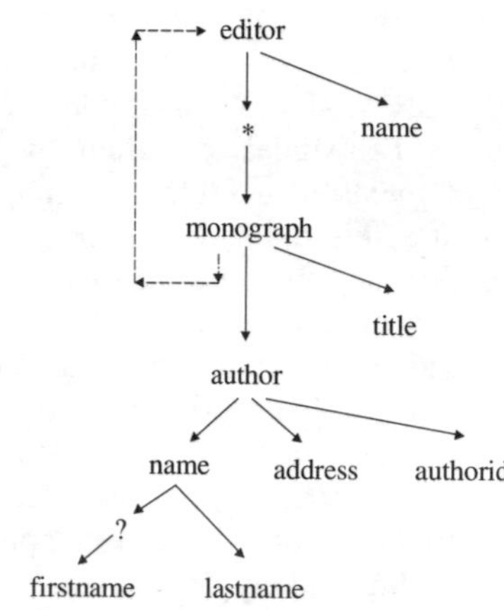

Figure 9

A DTD graph represents the structure of a DTD. Its nodes are elements, attributes and operators in the DTD. Each element appears exactly once in the graph, while attributes and operators appear as many times as they appear in the DTD. The DTD graph corresponding to the DTD in Figure 2 is given in Figure 8. Cycles in the DTD graph indicate the presence of recursion.

The schema created for a DTD is the union of the sets of relations created for each element. In order to determine the set of relations to be created for a particular element, we create a graph structure called the *element graph*. The element graph is constructed as follows.

Do a depth first traversal of the DTD graph, starting at the element node for which we are constructing relations. Each node is marked as "visited" the first time it is reached and is unmarked it once all its children have been traversed.

If an unmarked node in the DTD graph is reached during depth first traversal, a new node bearing the same name is created in the element graph. In addition, a *regular* edge is created from the most recently created node in the element graph with the same name as the DFS parent of the current DTD node to the newly created node.

If an attempt is made to traverse an already marked DTD node, then a *backpointer* edge is added from the most recently created node in the element graph to the most recently created node in the element graph with the same name as the marked DTD node.

The element graph for the *editor* element in the DTD graph in Figure 8 is shown in Figure 9. Intuitively, the element graph expands the relevant part of the DTD graph into a tree structure.

Given an element graph, relations are created as follows. A relation is created for the root element of the graph. All the element's descendents are inlined into that relation with the following two exceptions: (a) children directly below a "*" node are made into separate relations – this corresponds to creating a new relation for a set-valued child; and (b) each node having a backpointer edge pointing to it is made into a separate relation – this corresponds to creating a new relation to handle recursion. Figure 10 shows the relational schema that would be generated for the DTD in Figure 2. There are several features to note in the schema. Attributes in the relations are named by the path from the root element of the relation. Each relation has an ID field that serves as the key of that relation. All relations corresponding to element nodes having a parent also have a parentID field that serves as a foreign key. For instance, the *article.author* relation has a foreign key *article.author.parentID* that joins authors with articles. The XML document in Figure 1 would be converted to the following tuple in the book relation:

(1, The Selfish Gene, Richard, Dawkins,
<city>Timbuktu</city><zip>99999</zip>, dawkins)

The ANY field, address, is stored as an uninterpreted string; thus the nested structure is not visible to the database system without further support for XML (see Section 6). Note that if the author Richard Dawkins has authored many books, then the author information will be replicated for each book because it is replicated in the corresponding XML documents.

While *Basic* is good for certain types of queries, such as "list all authors of books", it is likely to be grossly inefficient for other queries. For example, queries such as "list all authors having first name Jack" will have to be executed as the union of 5 separate queries. Another disadvantage of *Basic* is the large number of relations it creates. Our next technique attempts to resolve these problems.

book (bookID: integer, book.booktitle : string, book.author.name.firstname: string, book.author.name.lastname: string, book.author.address: string, author.authorid: string)

booktitle (booktitleID: integer, booktitle: string)

article (articleID: integer, article.contactauthor.authorid: string, article.title: string)

article.author (article.authorID: integer, article.author.parentID: integer, article.author.name.firstname: string, article.author.name.lastname: string, article.author.address: string, article.author.authorid: string)

contactauthor (contactauthorID: integer, contactauthor.authorid: string)

title (titleID: integer, title: string)

monograph (monographID: integer, monograph.parentID: integer, monograph.title: string, monograph.editor.name: string, monograph.author.name.firstname: string, monograph.author.name.lastname: string, monograph.author.address: string, monograph.author.authorid: string)

editor (editorID: integer, editor.parentID: integer, editor.name: string)

editor.monograph (editor.monographID: integer, editor.monograph.parentID: integer, editor.monograph.title: string, editor.monograph.author.name.firstname: string, editor.monograph.author.name.lastname: string, editor.monograph.author.address: string, editor.monograph.author.authorid: string)

author (authorID: integer, author.name.firstname: string, author.name.lastname: string, author.address: string, author.authorid: string)

name (nameID: integer, name.firstname: string, name.lastname: string)

firstname (firstnameID: integer, firstname: string)

lastname (lastnameID: integer, lastname: string)

address (addressID: integer, address: string)

Figure 10

book (bookID: integer, book.booktitle.isroot: boolean, book.booktitle : string)

article (articleID: integer, article.contactauthor.isroot: boolean, article.contactauthor.authorid: string)

monograph (monographID: integer,monograph.parentID: integer, monograph.parentCODE: integer, monograph.editor.isroot: boolean, monograph.editor.name: string)

title (titleID: integer, title.parentID: integer, title.parentCODE: integer, title: string)

author (authorID: integer, author.parentID: integer, author.parentCODE: integer, author.name.isroot: boolean, author.name.firstname.isroot: :boolean, author.name.firstname: string, author.name.lastname.isroot: boolean, author.name.lastname: string, author.address.isroot: boolean, author.address: string, author.authorid: string)

Figure 11

3.4 The Shared Inlining Technique

The Shared Inlining Technique, hereafter referred to as *Shared*, attempts to avoid the drawbacks of *Basic* by ensuring that an element node is represented in exactly one relation. The principal idea behind *Shared* is to identify the element nodes that are represented in multiple relations in *Basic* (such as the *firstname*, *lastname* and *address* elements in the example) and to share them by creating separate relations for these elements.

We must first decide what relations to create. In *Shared*, relations are created for all elements in the DTD graph whose nodes have an in-degree greater than one. These are precisely the nodes that are represented as multiple relations in *Basic*. Nodes with an in-degree of one are inlined. Element nodes having an in-degree of zero are also made separate relations, because they are not reachable from any other node. As in *Basic*, elements below a "*" node are made into separate relations. Finally, of the mutually recursive elements all having in-degree one (such as *monograph* and *editor* in Figure 8), one of them is made a separate relation. We can find such mutually recursive elements by looking for strongly connected components in the DTD graph.

Once we decide which element nodes are to be made into separate relations, it is relatively easy to construct the relational schema. Each element node X that is a separate relation inlines all the nodes Y that are reachable from it such that the path from X to Y does not contain a node (other than X) that is to be made a separate relation. Figure 11 shows the schema derived from the DTD graph of Figure 8. One striking feature is the small number of relations compared to the *Basic* schema (Figure 10).

Inlining an element X into a relation corresponding to another element Y creates problems when an XML document is rooted at the element X. To facilitate queries on such elements we make use of isRoot fields.

The element sharing in *Shared* has query processing implications. For example, a selection query over all authors accesses only one relation in *Shared* compared to five relations in *Basic*. Despite the fact that *Shared* addresses some of the shortcomings and shares some of

book (bookID: integer, book.booktitle.isroot: boolean, book.booktitle : string, author.name.firstname: string, author.name.lastname: string, author.address: string, author.authorid: string)

article (articleID: integer, article.contactauthor.isroot: boolean, article.contactauthor.authorid: string, article.title.isroot: boolean, article.title: string)

monograph (monographID: integer, monograph.parentID: integer, monograph.parentCODE: integer, monograph.title: string, monograph.editor.isroot: boolean, monograph.editor.name: string, author.name.firstname: string, author.name.lastname: string, author.address: string, author.authorid: string)

author (authorID: integer, author.parentID: integer, author.parentCODE: integer, author.name.isroot: boolean, author.name.firstname.isroot: boolean, author.name.firstname: string, author.name.lastname.isroot: boolean, author.name.lastname: string, author.address.isroot: boolean, author.address: string, author.authorid: string)

Figure 12

the strengths of *Basic*, *Basic* performs better in one important respect – reducing the number of joins starting at a particular element node. Thus we explore a hybrid approach that combines the join reduction properties of *Basic* with the sharing features of *Shared*

3.5 The Hybrid Inlining Technique

The Hybrid Inlining Technique, or *Hybrid,* is the same as *Shared* except that it inlines some elements that are not inlined in *Shared.* In particular, *Hybrid* additionally inlines elements with in-degree greater than one that are not recursive or reached through a "*" node. Set sub-elements and recursive elements are treated as in *Shared.* Figure 12 shows the relational schema generated using this hybrid approach. Note how this schema combines features of both *Basic* and *Shared* – *author* is inlined with *book* and *monograph* even though it is shared, while *monograph* and *editor* are represented exactly once.

So far, we have implicitly assumed that the data model is unordered, i.e., the position of an element does not matter. Order could, however, be easily incorporated into our framework by storing a position field for each element.

3.6 A Qualitative Evaluation of the Basic, Shared and Hybrid Techniques

In this section we qualitatively evaluate our relation-conversion algorithms using 37 DTDs available from Robin Cover's SGML/XML Web page [8]. We did not pose any criterion for selecting DTDs except for availability for easy download and validity. Some DTDs were excluded because they did not pass our XML parser, the IBM alphaWorks xml4j.

3.6.1 Evaluation Metric

Our major concern in evaluating the algorithms is the efficiency of query processing. Our metric is *the average number of SQL joins required to process path expressions of a certain length N.* We use this metric because path expressions are at the heart of query languages proposed for semi-structured data. We are particularly concerned about path expressions because we use a relational database which uses joins to process path expressions.

This subsection logically contains "forward references" to Section 4, in which we describe how SQL queries are generated from semi-structured XML queries. However, the only point from Section 4 that is necessary to understand the results here is that a single semi-structured query could give rise to a union of several SQL queries, and that each of these queries may contain some number of joins. The use of *Basic* vs. *Shared* vs. *Hybrid* determines how many queries are generated, and how many joins are found in each query. Although *Basic* and *Hybrid* reduce the number of joins *per SQL query*, their higher degree of inlining could cause more SQL queries to be generated. For each algorithm, each DTD, and a variable number of path lengths, we make the following measurements:

- The average number of SQL queries generated for path expressions of length N.
- The average number of joins in each SQL query for path expressions of length N.
- The total average number of joins in order to process path expressions of length N (the product of the two previous measurements.)

In Sections 3.6.2 and 3.6.3, we assume that path expressions start from an arbitrary element in the DTD. We relax this assumption in Section 3.6.4.

3.6.2 Evaluation Results for Expression Paths of Length 3

In this section we show the results for path expressions of length 3, which is the longest path length applicable to all 37 DTDs. We shall examine the results for other path lengths in the next section. In the interest of space, we show the results only for a subset of the DTDs and summarize the others.

First we consider whether the *Basic* approach is practical. For 11 of our 37 DTDs, *Basic* did not run to completion because it ran out of virtual memory. The reason for this is that *Basic* generates huge numbers of relations if DTDs have large strongly connected components. We can see this effect clearly on some of the DTDs that *Basic* did run to completion. One 19 node

DTD has a SCC size of 4, and the number of relations created is 204 times as many as created by *Hybrid*, totalling 3462 relations. Due to this severe limitation of *Basic*, we concentrate on the comparisons between *Shared* and *Hybrid*.

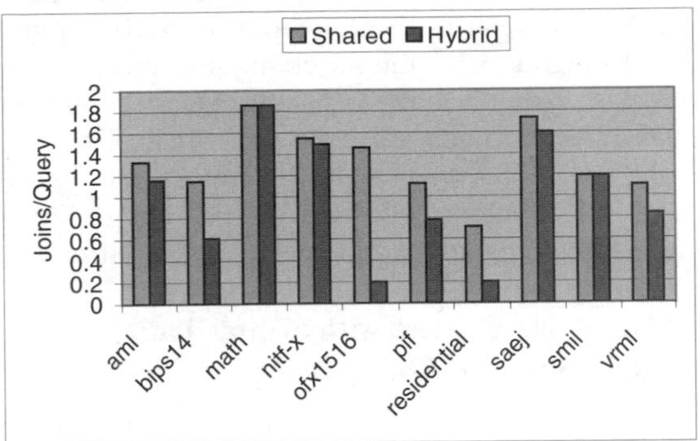

Figure 13

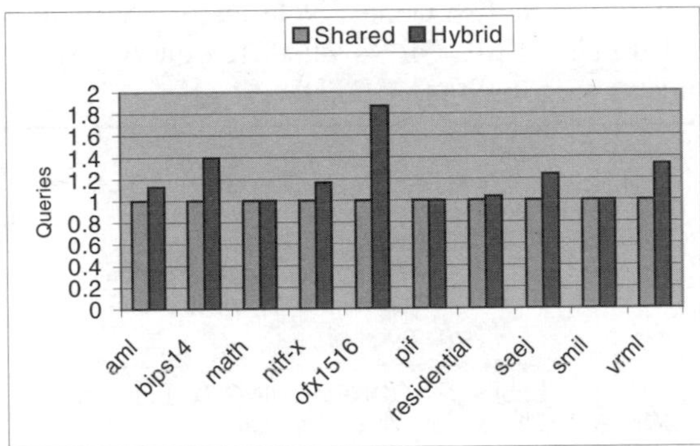

Figure 14

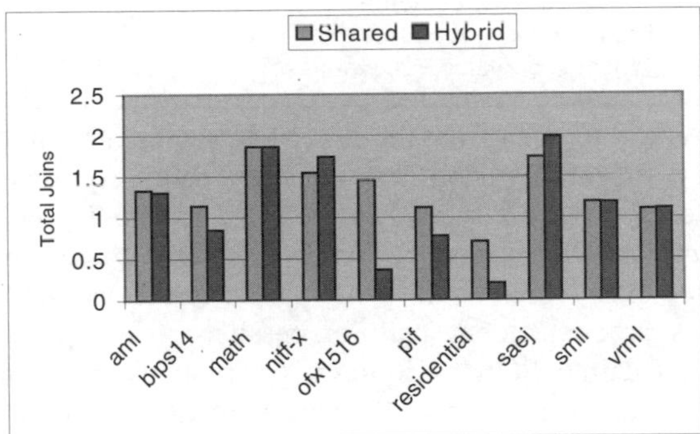

Figure 15

Figures 13, 14 and 15 show results for 10 of the DTDs. As shown in Figure 13, *Hybrid* eliminates a large number of joins for some DTDs, whereas for others, *Hybrid* and *Shared* produce about the same number of joins. Figure 14 shows that for some DTDs, querying over 3-length path expressions using *Hybrid* requires more SQL queries than using *Shared*, while for other DTDs, the number of SQL queries is the same. Note that for any path expression, *Shared* always produces at least the number of joins per SQL query as *Hybrid*, and *Hybrid* always produces at least the number of SQL queries as *Shared*. Figure 15 shows the total number of joins.

Using the average total number of joins required to process path expressions of length 3, we can roughly categorize the 37 DTDs into four groups:

Group 1. DTDs for which *Hybrid* reduces a large percentage of joins per SQL query but incurs a smaller increase in the number of SQL queries. The net result is *Hybrid* requires fewer joins than *Shared*. Example: DTD "ofx1516".

Group 2. DTDs for which *Hybrid* reduces a large percentage of joins per SQL query and incurs a comparable increase in the number of SQL queries. The total number of joins is about the same. Example: DTD "vrml".

Group 3. DTDs for which *Hybrid* reduces some joins per SQL query, but not enough to offset the increase in the number of SQL queries; therefore *Hybrid* generates more joins for a path expression than *Shared*. Example: DTD "saej".

Group 4. DTDs for which both *Shared* and *Hybrid* produce about the same number of joins per SQL query, and about the same number of SQL queries, resulting in approximately the same total number of joins. Example: DTD "math".

Hybrid inlines more than *Shared* in Groups 1, 2 and 3. This reduces the number of joins per SQL query but increases the number of SQL queries. The net increase or decrease in the total number of joins depends on the structure of the DTD. In Group 4, most of the shared nodes are either set nodes or involved in recursion. Since *Shared* and *Hybrid* treat set nodes and recursive nodes identically, there is no significant difference in their performance in Group 4.

	Group 1	Group 2	Group 3	Group 4
Num DTDs	13	2	6	16

The number of DTDs in each group from all 37 DTDs is summarized in the table above. We can infer that in a large number of DTDs (Group 4), most of the shared nodes are either set nodes or recursive nodes.

3.6.3 Results for Path Expressions of Other Lengths

In the previous section, we showed the results for path expressions of length 3. In order to see how the results carry over to other path lengths, let us examine how the number of joins scales with the path length. We found that for almost all the DTDs, the number of joins scales linearly with the path length, the only difference is the scaling factor, which is determined by the structure of the DTD. Furthermore, the gap between the performance of *Shared* and *Hybrid* typically widens when the path lengthens. Figure 16 and Figure 17 show the scaling for two DTDs in group 1 and group 3 respectively.

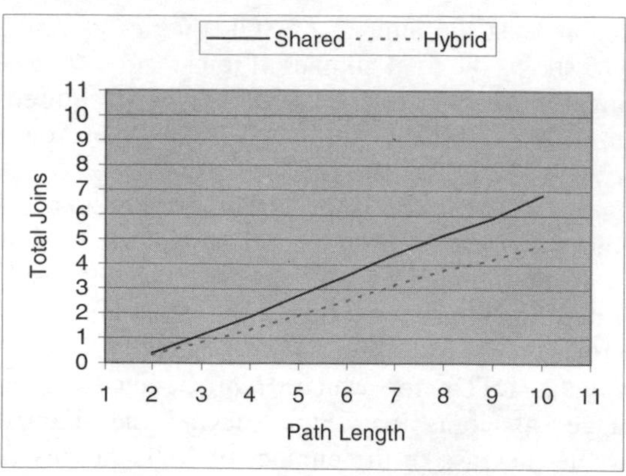

Figure 16

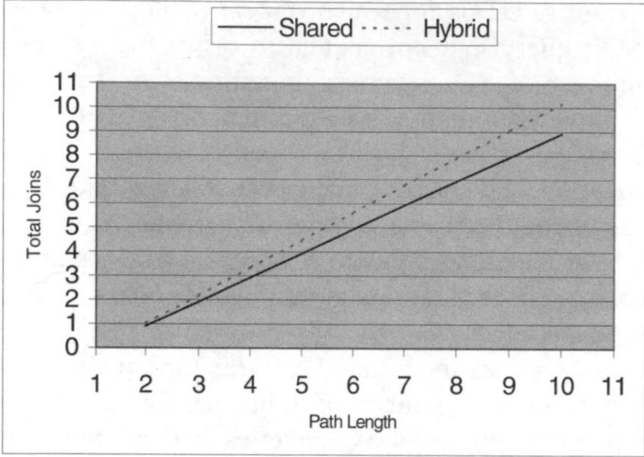

Figure 17

3.6.4 Evaluation Using Path Expressions Starting From the Document Root

So far, we have examined the performance of our algorithms assuming path expressions start from an arbitrary node in the DTD graph. What is different if the path expressions start from the root of a document? The real difference is in the total number of joins. A path expression starting from the root of a document is always converted to one SQL query - therefore the total number of joins is equivalent to the number of joins per SQL query. Since the *Hybrid* algorithm always produces fewer joins per SQL query, it is always better than *Shared* for path expressions that start from the document root.

For DTDs in groups 3 and 4 (the majority of DTDs), both *Shared* and *Hybrid* are practically the same. The main issue is the excessive fragmentation of the DTDs that leads to the number of joins being almost equal to the length of the path expression (Figure 17). This is likely to be very inefficient in the relational model, especially for long path lengths. The main cause of this fragmentation is the presence of set sub-elements. Section 6 includes a proposed extension to alleviate this problem.

4. Converting Semi-Structured Queries to SQL

Semi-structured query languages have a lot more flexibility than SQL. In particular, they allow path expressions with various operators and wild cards. The challenge is to rewrite these queries in SQL exploiting DTD information. In this section, we consider only queries with string values as results. Queries with more complex result formats are dealt with in Section 5. For ease of exposition, we present the translation algorithm only in the context of the *Shared* approach. The generalization to the other approaches is straightforward.

4.1 Converting Queries with Simple Path Expressions to SQL

Consider the following XML-QL query, and an equivalent Lorel-like query, over the DTD in Figure 2 that asks for the first and last name of the author of a book with title "The Selfish Gene". Note that we have slightly extended the XML-QL syntax to query over all documents conforming to a DTD.

```
WHERE <book>
            <booktitle> The Selfish Gene </booktitle>
            <author>
                <name>
                    <firstname> $f </firstname>
                    <lastname> $l </lastname>
                </name>
            </author>
        </book> IN * CONFORMING TO pubs.dtd
CONSTRUCT <result> $f $l </result>
```

```
Select Y.name.firstname,
       Y.name.lastname
From   book X, X.author Y
Where X.booktitle = "Databases"
```

As can be seen from the Lorel-like representation, this query essentially consists of five path expressions, namely, *book*, *X.author*, *Y.name.firstname*, *Y.name.lastname* and *X.booktitle*. Of these path expressions, *book* is the root path expression and the others are dependent path expressions. This query is translated into SQL as follows: (a) first, the relation(s) corresponding to start of the root path expression(s) are identified and added to the from clause of the SQL query, then (b) if necessary, the path expressions are translated to joins among relations (when elements are inlined, joins are not necessary). The SQL query generated in this fashion for the example query above is shown in Figure 18. Note that a join condition has been added to the where clause to link the book and author and a selection (A.parentCODE = 0, where 0 indicates that the parent of the author is a book) is performed on author to make sure that only authors reached through book are considered.

```
Select A."author.name.firstname",
       A."author.name.lastname"
From  author A, book B
Where B.bookID = A.parentID
        AND A.parentCODE = 0
        AND B."book.booktitle" = "The Selfish Gene"
```

Figure 18

4.2 Converting Simple Recursive Path Expressions to SQL

Consider the following XML-QL query that requires the names of all editors reachable directly or indirectly from the monograph with title "Subclass Cirripedia". The corresponding XML-QL query (and an equivalent Lorel-like query) is shown below:

```
WHERE <*.monograph>
                <editor.(monograph.editor)*>
                      <name> $n </name>
                </>
                <title> Subclass Cirripedia </title>
          </> IN * CONFORMING TO pubs.dtd
CONSTRUCT <result> $n </result>
```

```
Select Y.name
From   *.monograph X, X.editor.(monograph.editor)* Y
Where X.title = "Subclass Cirripedia"
```

There are two interesting features about this query. The first is the tag "*.monograph" which states that we are interested in monographs reachable from any path. The second is the tag "editor.(monograph.editor)*" that specifies all editors reachable directly or indirectly from a monograph. The trick in converting this to a least fix-point query such as that supported by IBM DB2 is to determine (a) the initialization of the recursion and (b) the actual recursive path expression. In the example above, the initialization of the recursion is the path expression *.monograph.editor with the selection condition monograph.title = "Subclass Cirripedia" and the recursive path expression is monograph.editor. Each can be converted to a SQL fragment just like a simple path expression. The final query is the union of the two SQL fragments within a least fix-point operator. The query generated in this fashion is shown in Figure 19, in IBM DB2 syntax. Note that the "with clause" is the equivalent of the least fix-point operator in DB2.

```
With Q1 (monographID, name) AS
(Select X.monographID, X."editor.name"
 From monograph X
 Where X.title = "Subclass Cirripedia"
UNION ALL
 Select Z.monographID, Z."editor.name"
 From Q1 Y, monograph Z
 Where Y.monographID = Z.parentID AND
        Z.parentCODE = 0
)
Select A.name
From Q1 A
```

Figure 19

4.3 Converting Arbitrary Path Expressions to Simple Recursive Path Expressions

In general, path expressions can be of arbitrary complexity. For example, we could have a query that asks for all the name elements reachable directly or indirectly through *monograph*. This would be represented in a Lorel-like language as (an equivalent query can be expressed in XML-QL):

```
Select X
From monograph.(#)*.name X
```

We have a general technique that takes path expressions appearing in such queries (in this example "monograph.(#)*.name") and translates them into possibly many simple (recursive) path expressions. SQL queries are then generated for each simple recursive path expression. This notion of splitting a path expression to many simple path expressions is crucial to processing queries having arbitrary path expressions in SQL. The details of the technique are tedious and we omit them here in the interest of space.

Our technique is general enough to handle path expressions with nested recursion (e.g., "(a.(b)*.c)*"). However, relational database systems such as IBM DB2 cannot currently handle these queries because they do not have support for nested recursive queries.

5. Converting Relational Results to XML

In the previous section, we assumed that the results of a query were string values. We relax this assumption in this section and explore how the tabular results returned by SQL queries can be converted to complex structured XML documents. This is perhaps the main drawback in using current relational technology to provide XML querying – constructing arbitrary XML result sets is difficult. In this section we give some examples, using XML-QL as the illustrative query languages because it provides XML structuring constructs.

5.1 Simple Structuring

Consider the query in Figure 20 that asks for the first name and last name of all the authors of books, nested appropriately. Constructing such results from a relational system is natural and efficient, since it only requires attaching the appropriate tags for each tuple (Figure 21).

5.2 Tag Variables

A tag variable is one that ranges over the value of an XML tag. Some queries requiring tag variables in their results are naturally translated to the relational model. Consider the query in Figure 22 that ask for names of authors of all publications, nested under a tag specifying the type of publication. This can be handled by generating a relational query that contains the tag value as an element of the result tuple. Then at result generation

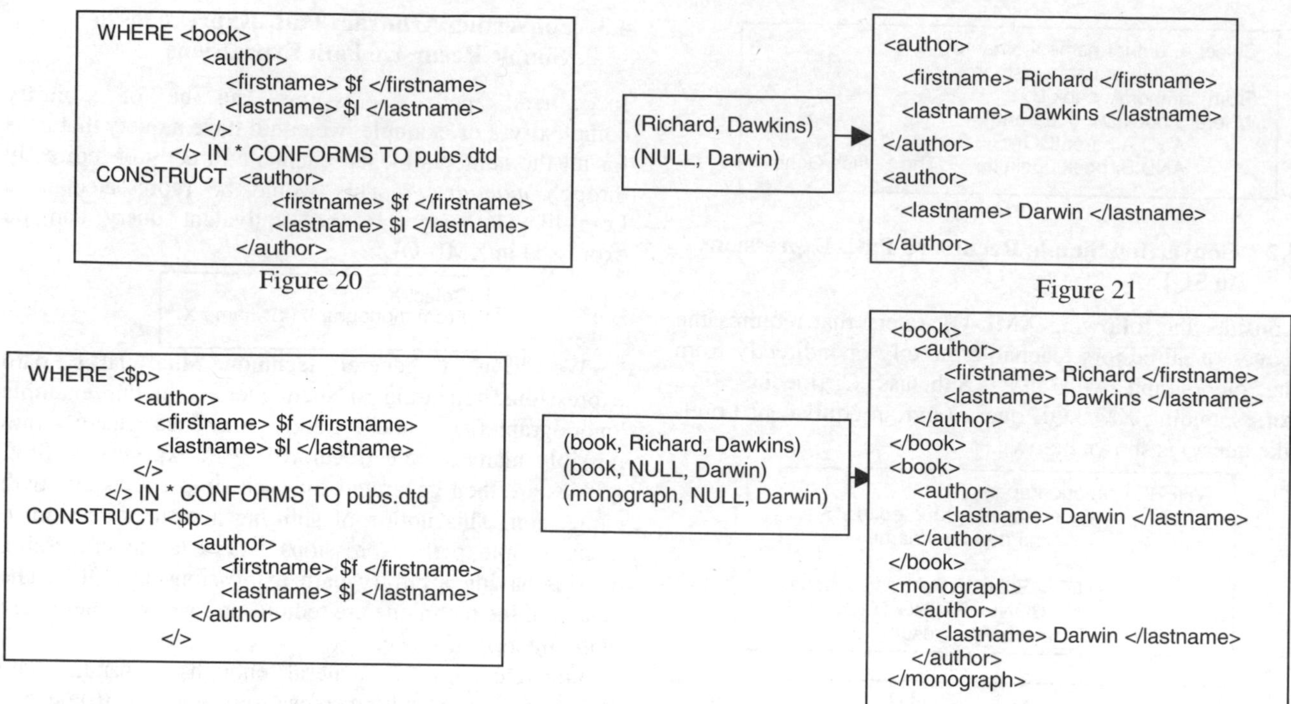

Figure 20

Figure 21

Figure 22

Figure 23

time, the tag attribute in the result tuple can be converted to the appropriate XML tag (Figure 23).

5.3 Grouping

Consider the query in Figure 24 that requires all the publications of an author (assuming an author is uniquely identified by his/her last name) to be grouped together, and within this structure, requires the titles of publications to be grouped by the type of the publication. The relational result from the translation of this query will be a set of tuples having fields corresponding to last name of author, title of publication and type of publication. However, we cannot use the relational group-by operator to group by last name and type of publication because the SQL group-by semantics implies that we should apply an aggregate function to title, which does not make sense. Thus, the options are either (a) have the relational engine order the result tuples first by last name and then by type and scan the result in order to construct the XML document or (b) get an unordered set of tuples and do a grouping operation, by last name and then by type, outside the relational engine. The first approach is illustrated in Figure 25.

Figure 25 illustrates several points. The first is that treating tag variables as attributes in the result relation provides a way of uniformly treating the contents of the result XML document. In this case, we are able to group by the tag variable just like any other attribute. The second observation is that some relational database functionality (hash-based group-by) is either not fully exploited or is duplicated outside.

5.4 Complex Element Construction

Unfortunately, returning tag values as tuple attributes cannot handle all result construction problems. In particular, queries that are required to return complex XML elements are problematic. Consider a query that asks for all article elements in the XML data set, and furthermore assume that an article may have multiple authors and multiple titles. In object-relational terminology, article has two set-valued attributes, authors and titles, corresponding to two set sub-elements in XML terminology.

```
WHERE <book>
        <article> $a </article>
      </> IN * CONFORMS TO pubs.dtd
CONSTRUCT <article> $a </>
```

To create the appropriate result, we must retrieve all authors and all titles for each article. This is difficult to do in the relational model because flattening multiple set-valued attributes into tuple format gives rise to a multi-valued dependency [11] and is likely to be very inefficient when the sets are large, for example, if papers have many authors and many titles. There appears to be no efficient way to tackle this problem in the traditional relational model. One solution would be to return separate relations, each flattening one set-valued attribute and "join" these relations outside the database while constructing the XML document. However, this requires duplication of database functionality both in terms of execution and optimization. This solution would be particularly bad for an element with many set-valued attributes. A related problem occurs when reconstructing recursive elements. We return to these issues in Section 6.

```
WHERE <$p>
        <(title|booktitle)> $t </>
        <author>
            <lastname> $l </lastname>
        </>
    </> IN * CONFORMS TO pubs.dtd
CONSTRUCT <author ID=authorID($l)>
            <name> $l </name>
            <$p ID=pID($p)>
                <title> $t </>
            </>
        </>
```

Figure 24

```
(Darwin, book,  Origin of Species)
(Darwin, book, Descent of Man)
(Darwin, monograph, Subclass
 Cirripedia)
(Dawkins, book, The Selfish Gene)
```

```
<author>
   <name> Darwin </name>
   <book>
      <title> Origin of Species </title>
      <title> The Descent of Man </title>
   </book>
   <monograph>
      <title> Subclass Cirripedia </title>
   </monograph>
</author>
<author>
   <name> Dawkins </name>
   <book>
      <title> The Selfish Gene </title>
   </book>
</author>
```

Figure 25

5.5 Heterogeneous Results

Consider the following XML-QL query that creates a result document having both titles and authors as elements (this is the heterogeneous result). This is easily handled in our approach for translating queries because this query would be split into two queries, one for selecting titles and another for selecting authors. The results of the two queries can be handled in different ways, one constructing title elements and another constructing author elements. The results can then be merged together.

```
WHERE <article>
            <$p> $y </>
      </article> IN * CONFORMING TO pubs.dtd
CONSTRUCT <$p> $y </>
```

5.6 Nested Queries

XML-QL is structured in terms of query blocks and one query block can be nested under another. These nested queries can be rewritten in terms of SQL queries, using outer joins (and possibly skolem function ids) to construct the association between a query and a sub-query. The details are complex and we omit it in the interest of space.

6. Conclusions

With the growing importance of XML documents as a means to represent data in the World Wide Web, there has been a lot of effort on devising new technologies to process queries over XML documents. Our focus in this paper, however, has been to study the virtues and limitations of the traditional relational model for processing queries over XML documents conforming to a schema. The potential advantages of this approach are many – reusing a mature technology, using an existing high performance system, and seamlessly querying over data represented as XML documents or relations. We have shown that it is possible to handle most queries on XML documents using a relational database, barring certain types of complex recursion.

Our qualitative evaluation based on real DTDs from diverse domains raises some performance concerns – specifically, in many cases relatively simple XML queries require either many SQL queries, or require a few SQL queries with many joins in them. It is an open question whether semi-structured query processing techniques can do this kind of work more efficiently. The fact that semi-structured models represent a sequence of joins as a path expression, or handle what is logically a union of queries by using wildcards and "or" operators, does not automatically imply more efficient evaluation strategies.

Our experience has shown that relational systems could more effectively handle XML query workloads with the following extensions:

Support for Sets: Set-valued attributes would be useful in two important ways. First, storing set sub-elements as set-valued attributes [19,21] would reduce fragmentation. This is likely to be a big win because most of the fragmentation we observed in real DTDs was due to sets. Second, set-valued attributes, along with support for nesting [13], would allow a relational system to perform more of the processing required for generating complex XML results.

Untyped/Variable-Typed References: IDREFs are not typed in XML. Therefore, queries that navigate through IDREFs cannot be handled in current relational systems without a proliferation of joins – one for each possible reference type.

Information Retrieval Style Indices: More powerful indices, such as Oracle8i's ConText search engine for XML [17], that can index over the structure of string attributes would be useful in querying over ANY fields in a DTD. Further, under restricted query requirements, whole fragments of a document can be stored as an indexed text field, thus reducing fragmentation.

Flexible Comparisons Operators: A DTD schema treats every value as a string. This often creates the need to compare a string attribute with, say, an integer value, after typecasting the string to an integer. The traditional relational model cannot support such comparisons. The problem persists even in the presence of DCDs or XML

Schemas because different DTDs may represent "comparable" values as different types. A related issue is that of flexible indices. Techniques for building such indices have been proposed in the context of semi-structured databases [14].

Multiple-Query Optimization/Execution: As outlined in Section 4, complex path expressions are handled in a relational database by converting them into many simple path expressions, each corresponding to a separate SQL query. Since these SQL queries are derived from a single regular path expression, they are likely to share many relational scans, selections and joins. Rather than treating them all as separate queries, it may be more efficient to optimize and execute them as a group [20].

More Powerful Recursion: As mentioned in Section 4, in order to fully support all recursive path expressions, support for fixed point expressions defined in terms of other fixed point expressions (i.e., nested fixed point expressions) is required.

These extensions are not by themselves new and have been proposed in other contexts. However, they gain new importance in light of our evaluation of the requirements for processing XML documents. Another important issue to be considered in the context of the World Wide Web is distributed query processing – taking advantage of queryable XML sources. Further research on these techniques in the context of processing XML documents will, we believe, facilitate the use of sophisticated relational data management techniques in handling the novel requirements of emerging XML-based applications.

7. Acknowledgements

Funding for this work was provided by DARPA through Rome Research Laboratory Contract No. F30602-97-2-0247 and NSF through NSF Award CDA-9623632.

8. References

1. S. Abiteboul, D. Quass, J. McHugh, J. Widom, J. Wiener, "The Lorel Query Language for Semistructured Data", International Journal on Digital Libraries, 1(1), pp. 68-88, April 1997.
2. J. Bosak, T. Bray, D. Connolly, E. Maler, G. Nicol, C. M. Sperberg-McQueen, L. Wood, J. Clark, "W3C XML Specification DTD", http://www.w3.org/XML/1998/06/xmlspec-report-19980910.htm.
3. T. Bray, J. Paoli, C. M. Sperberg-McQueen, "Extensible Markup Language (XML) 1.0", http://www.w3.org/TR/REC-xml.
4. T. Bray, C. Frankston, A. Malhotra, "Document Content Description for XML", http://www.w3.org/TR/NOTE-dcd.
5. P. Buneman, S. Davidson, G. Hillebrand, D. Suciu, "A Query Language and Optimization Techniques for Unstructured Data", Proceedings of the ACM SIGMOD Conference, Montreal, Canada, June 1996.
6. V. Christophides, S. Abiteboul, S. Cluet, M. Scholl, "From Structured Documents to Novel Query Facilities", Proceedings of the ACM SIGMOD Conference, Minneapolis, Minnesota, May 1994.
7. G. Copeland, S. Khoshafian, "A Decomposition Storage Model", Proceedings of the ACM SIGMOD Conference, Austin, Texas, May 1985.
8. R. Cover, "The SGML/XML Web Page", http://www.oasis-open.org/cover/xml.html.
9. Deutsch, M. Fernandez, D. Florescu, A. Levy, D. Suciu, "XML-QL: A Query Language for XML", http://www.w3.org/TR/NOTE-xml-ql.
10. Deutsch, M. Fernandez, D. Suciu, "Storing Semi-structured Data with STORED", Proceedings of the ACM SIGMOD Conference, Philadelphia, Pennslyvania, May 1999.
11. R. Fagin, "Multi-valued Dependencies and a New Normal Form for Relational Databases", ACM Transactions on Database Systems, 2(3), pp. 262-278, 1977.
12. M. Fernandez, D. Suciu, "Optimizing Regular Path Expressions Using Graph Schemas", Proceedings of the Fourteenth ICDE Conference, Orlando, Florida, February 1998.
13. Jaeschke, H. J. Schek, "Remarks on the Algebra of Non First Normal Form Relations", Proceedings of the ACM Symposium on Principles of Database Systems, Los Angeles, California, March 1982.
14. J. McHugh, S. Abiteboul, R. Goldman, D. Quass, J. Widom, "Lore: A Database Management System for Semistructured Data", SIGMOD Record, 26(3), pp. 54-66, September 1997.
15. J. McHugh, J. Widom, "Compile-Time Path Expansion in Lore", Workshop on Query Processing for Semistructured Data and Non-Standard Data Formats, Jerusalem, Israel, January 1999.
16. Microsoft Corporation, XML Schema, http://www.microsoft.com/xml/schema/reference/star.asp.
17. Oracle Corporation, "XML Support in Oracle 8 and beyond", Technical white paper, http://www.oracle.com/xml/documents.
18. The Query Languages Workshop (QL'98), http://www.w3.org/TandS/QL/QL98/, December 1998.
19. K. Ramasamy, J. F. Naughton, D. Maier, "Storage Representations for Set-Valued Attributes", Working Paper, Department of Computer Sciences, University of Wisconsin-Madison.
20. T. Sellis, "Multiple-Query Optimization", ACM Transactions on Database Systems, 12(1), pp. 23-52, June 1990.
21. Zaniolo, "The Database Language GEM", Proceedings of the ACM SIGMOD Conference, San Jose, California, May 1983.

Query Optimization for XML*

Jason McHugh, Jennifer Widom
Stanford University
{mchughj,widom}@db.stanford.edu, http://www-db.stanford.edu

Abstract

XML is an emerging standard for data representation and exchange on the World-Wide Web. Due to the nature of information on the Web and the inherent flexibility of XML, we expect that much of the data encoded in XML will be *semistructured*: the data may be irregular or incomplete, and its structure may change rapidly or unpredictably. This paper describes the query processor of *Lore*, a DBMS for XML-based data supporting an expressive query language. We focus primarily on Lore's cost-based query optimizer. While all of the usual problems associated with cost-based query optimization apply to XML-based query languages, a number of additional problems arise, such as new kinds of indexing, more complicated notions of database statistics, and vastly different query execution strategies for different databases. We define appropriate logical and physical query plans, database statistics, and a cost model, and we describe plan enumeration including heuristics for reducing the large search space. Our optimizer is fully implemented in Lore and preliminary performance results are reported.

1 Introduction

The World-Wide Web community is rapidly embracing *XML* as a new standard for data representation and exchange on the Web [BPSM98]. At its most basic level, XML is a document markup language permitting tagged text (*elements*), element nesting, and element references. However, XML also can be viewed as a data modeling language, and a significant potential user population views XML in this way [Mar98]. Fortuitously, work from the database community in the area of *semistructured data* [Abi97, Bun97]—work that significantly predates XML—uses graph-based data models that correspond closely to XML. Thus, research results in the area of semistructured data are now broadly applicable to XML.

*This work was supported by Rome Laboratories under Air Force Contract F30602-96-1-0312 and by the National Science Foundation under grant IIS-9811947.

Proceedings of the 25th VLDB Conference, Edinburgh, Scotland, 1999.

Semistructured data has been defined as data that may be irregular or incomplete, and whose structure may change rapidly or unpredictably. Although data encoded in XML may conform to a *Document Type Definition*, or *DTD* [BPSM98], DTD's are not required by XML. Due to the nature of information on the Web and the inherent flexibility of XML—with or without DTD's—we expect that much of the data encoded in XML will exhibit the classic characteristics of semistructured data as outlined above.

The *Lore* system at Stanford is a complete DBMS designed specifically for semistructured data [MAG+97]. Lore's original data model, the *Object Exchange Model* (*OEM*), is a graph-based data model with a close correspondence to XML. The query language of Lore, called *Lorel* (for *Lore Language*), is an expressive OQL-based language for declarative navigation and updates of semistructured databases. Recently we migrated Lore to a fully XML-based data model, and extended the Lorel query language accordingly. For details see [GMW99]. The results presented in this paper apply directly to the new XML version of Lore.

This paper describes Lore's query processor, with a focus on its cost-based query optimizer. While our general approach to query optimization is typical—we transform a query into a *logical query plan*, then explore the (exponential) space of possible *physical plans* looking for the one with least estimated cost—a number of factors associated with XML data complicate the problem. Path traversals (i.e., navigating subelement and reference links) play a central role in query processing and we have introduced several new types of indexes for efficient traversals through data graphs. The variety of indexes and traversal techniques increases our search space beyond that of a conventional optimizer, requiring us to develop aggressive pruning heuristics appropriate to our query plan enumeration strategy. Other challenges have been to define an appropriate set of statistics for graph-based data and to devise methods for computing and storing statistics without the benefit of a fixed schema. Statistics describing the "shape" of a data graph are crucial for determining which methods of graph traversal are optimal for a given query and database.

Once we have added appropriate indexes and statistics to our graph-based data model, optimizing the navigational *path expressions* that form the basis of our query language does resemble the optimization problem for path expressions in object-oriented database systems, and even to some extent the join optimization problem in relational systems. As will be seen, many of our basic techniques are adapted from prior work in those areas. However, we decided to build a new overall optimization framework for a number of reasons:

- Previous work has considered the optimization of single path expressions (e.g., [GGT96, SMY90]). Our query language permits several, possibly interrelated, path expressions in a single query, along with other query constructs. Our optimizer generates plans for complete queries.
- The statistics maintained by relational DBMS's (for joins) and object-oriented DBMS's (for path expression evaluation) are generally based on single joining pairs or object references, while for accuracy in our environment it is essential to maintain more detailed statistics about complete paths.
- The capabilities of deployed OODBMS optimizers are fairly limited, and we know of no available prototype optimizer flexible enough to meet our needs. Building our own framework has allowed us to experiment with and identify good search strategies and pruning heuristics for our large plan space. It also has allowed us to integrate the optimizer easily and completely into the existing Lore system.

2 Related Work

Lore. Details of the syntax and semantics of Lorel can be found in [AQM+97]. The overall architecture of the Lore system, including the simple query processing strategy we used prior to developing our cost-based query optimizer, can be found in [MAG+97].

Other semistructured databases. The *UnQL* query language [BDHS96, FS98] is based on a graph-structured data model similar to OEM. For query optimization, a translation from UnQL to *UnCAL* is defined [BDHS96], which provides a formal basis for deriving optimization rewrite rules such as pushing selections down. However, UnQL does not have a cost-based optimizer as far as we know. The *Strudel* Web-site management system is based on semistructured data [FFLS97, FFK+99], and query optimization is considered in [FLS98]. In Strudel, semistructured data graphs are introduced for modeling and querying, while the data itself may reside elsewhere in arbitrary format. A key feature of Strudel's approach to query optimization is the use of declarative *storage descriptors*, which describe the underlying data stores. The optimizer enumerates query execution plans, with a cost model that derives the costs of operators from their descriptors. In contrast, Lore data is stored under our control, and the user may dynamically create indexes to provide efficient access methods depending upon the expected queries. Finally, [FLS98] includes detailed experimental results of how large their search space is, but no other performance data is given. In contrast, our experiments focus on the performance of the query plan selected by the optimizer versus other possible query plans.

Some much earlier systems, such as *Multos* [BRG88] and *Model 204* [O'N87], considered problems associated with semistructured data but in very different settings. Multos operated on *complex data objects* which allowed, among other things, sets and pointers to objects of any type. Basic knowledge of the schema was crucial, however, and queries were placed into categories with a fixed set of execution strategies for each category. Lore follows a more traditional and flexible model of query processing. Model 204 was based on self-describing record structures somewhat resembling OEM, but the work concentrated primarily on clever bit-mapped indexing structures to achieve high performance for its relatively simple queries.

Relational databases. As mentioned earlier, at a coarse level the problem of optimizing a Lorel path expression is similar to the join ordering problem in relational databases. However, join ordering algorithms usually rely on statistics about each joining pair, while for typical queries in our environment it is crucial to maintain more comprehensive statistics about entire paths. The computation and storage of our statistics is further complicated by the lack of a schema. In addition, when quantification is present in our queries, the SQL translation results in complex subqueries that many relational optimization frameworks are ill-equipped to handle.

Object-oriented databases. Many of the points discussed in the previous paragraph apply to object-oriented databases as well. There has been some work on optimizing path expressions in an OODBMS context [GGT96]. They propose a set of algorithms to search for objects satisfying path expressions containing predicates, and analyze their relative performance. Our work differs in that we consider many interrelated path expressions within the context of an arbitrary query with other language constructs. We also provide additional access methods for path expressions, and our optimization techniques are implemented within a complete DBMS. Similar comparisons can be drawn between our work and other recent OODB optimization work, e.g., [GGMR97, KMP93, OMS95, SO95, MSOP86, LV91, YM97]. Some recent papers have specified cost models for object-oriented DBMSs, e.g., [BF97, GGT95]. Object-oriented databases typically support object clustering and physical extents, rendering many of these formulas inapplicable in our setting. Work on indexing in OODBs is surveyed in [YM97]; for a discussion of indexing in Lore, please see [MWA+98].

Generalized path expressions. Other recent work, including [FLS98] discussed above, has considered the problem of optimizing the evaluation of *generalized path expressions*, which describe traversals through data and may contain regular expression operators. In [CCM96] an algebraic framework for the optimization of generalized path expressions in an OODBMS is proposed, including an approach that avoids exponential blow-up in the query optimizer while still offering flexibility in the ordering of operations. In [FS98] two optimization techniques for generalized path expressions are presented, *query pruning* and *query rewriting using state extents*. Lore's techniques for handling generalized path expressions are described in [MW99a], but the work of [FLS98, CCM96, FS98] could

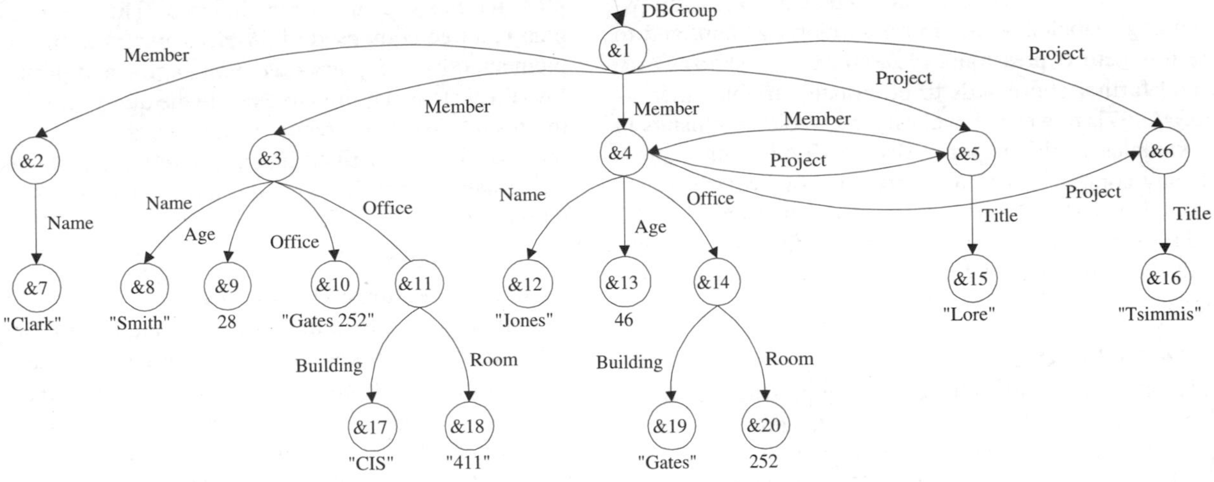

Figure 1: A tiny OEM database

be applicable within our framework.

XML query languages. The *XML-QL* data model and query language [DFF+98] is similar in expressibility to ours, with some extensions specific to the current specification of XML. *XQL* [RLS98] is a simpler query language based on single path expressions and is strictly less powerful than XML-QL, Lorel [AQM+97], StruQL [FFLS97], or UnQL [BDHS96]. To the best of our knowledge no full cost-based query optimizer has been developed for XML-QL or XQL, and the optimization principles presented in this paper should be directly applicable when that task is tackled.

3 Preliminaries

3.1 Data Model

Lore's original data model, *OEM* (for *Object Exchange Model*) [PGMW95], was designed for semistructured data. An example OEM database containing (fictitious) information about the Stanford Database Group appears in Figure 1. Data in OEM is schema-less and self-describing, and can be thought of as a labeled directed graph. The vertices in the graph are *objects*; each object has a unique *object identifier* (oid), such as &5. *Atomic objects* have no outgoing edges and contain a value from one of Lore's basic atomic types such as `integer`, `real`, `string`, `gif`, `java`, `audio`, etc. All other objects may have outgoing edges and are called *complex objects*. Object &3 is complex and its *subobjects* are &8, &9, &10, and &11. Object &7 is atomic and has value "Clark". *Names* are special labels that serve as aliases for single objects and as entry points into the database. In Figure 1, *DBGroup* is a name that denotes object &1.

The correspondence between OEM and XML is evident: OEM's objects correspond to elements in XML, and OEM's subobject relationship mirrors element nesting in XML. The fundamental differences are that subelements in XML are inherently ordered since they are specified textually, and XML elements may optionally include a list of attribute-value pairs. Note that graph structure (multiple incoming edges) must be specified in XML with explicit references, i.e., via *ID* and *IDREF(S)* attributes [BPSM98]. The following XML fragment corresponds to the rightmost `Member` in Figure 1, where `Project` is an attribute of type IDREFS.

```
<Member Project="&5 &6">
   <Name>Jones</Name>
   <Age>46</Age>
   <Office>
      <Building>Gates</Building>
      <Room>252</Room>
   </Office>
</Member>
```

As mentioned earlier, we have migrated Lore to a fully XML-based data model, and extended the Lorel query language accordingly [GMW99]. The primary changes to the model were the introduction of ordered subobjects, attribute-value lists, and *reference* edges in addition to normal subobject edges. Corresponding changes were made to the Lorel query language, although in most cases the queries one uses over an OEM database are identical to those used over a corresponding XML database.

We now introduce two definitions that are useful in the remainder of the paper.

Definition 3.1 (Simple Path Expression) A *simple path expression* specifies a single-step navigation in the database. A simple path expression for a variable or name x and label l has the form $x.l\ y$, and denotes that variable y ranges over all l-labeled subobjects of the object assigned to x. If x is an atomic object, or if l is not an outgoing label from x, then y ranges over the empty set.

Definition 3.2 (Path Expression) A *path expression* is an ordered list of simple path expressions.

Path expressions are the basic building blocks in the Lorel language and describe traversals through the data in a declarative fashion. For example, "`DBGroup.Member x, x.Age y`" says that variable y ranges over all objects that can be reached by starting with the `DBGroup` object, following an edge labeled Member, then following an edge labeled Age. Lorel supports a shorthand to write this path expression as "DBGroup.Member.Age y", and further shorthands to eliminate variables such as y [AQM+97], however for clarity we avoid shorthands in the examples in this paper. Also, a simple path expression may contain a regular expression or "wildcards" as described in [AQM+97]. In general, l in Definition 3.1 could be a component of a generalized path expression, but we have simplified the definition for presentation purposes in this paper.

3.2 Query Language

Lorel is an extension of OQL [Cat94] supporting declarative path expressions for traversing graph data and extensive automatic coercion for handling heterogeneous and typeless data without generating errors [AQM+97]. Although Lorel offers much syntactic sugar over OQL that is convenient in practice (including the shorthands mentioned above), in this paper we write our queries without these syntactic conveniences in order to be very explicit and enable understanding for those familiar with OQL but unfamiliar with Lorel. As a simple example, consider the following query, which asks for all of the young members of the Database Group.[1] The result of the query over the database of Figure 1 is shown.

```
QUERY 1: Select x
         From   DBGroup.Member x
         Where  exists y in x.Age: y<30

RESULT: <Member>
          <Name>Smith</Name>
          <Age>28</Age>
          <Office>Gates 252</Office>
          <Office>
             <Building>CIS</Building>
             <Room>411</Room>
          </Office>
        </Member>
```

3.3 Lore Query Processing

The general architecture of the Lore system is very much like a traditional DBMS [MAG+97]. After a query is *parsed*, it is *preprocessed* to factor out common subexpressions and convert Lorel shorthands into a more traditional OQL form. The *logical query plan generator* then creates a single logical query plan describing a very high-level execution strategy for the query. As we will show in Section 5.1, generating logical query plans is fairly straightforward, but special care was taken to ensure that the logical query plans are flexible enough to be transformed easily into vastly different physical query plans. The "meat" of the query optimizer occurs in the *physical query plan enumerator*. This component uses statistics and a cost model in order to transform the logical query plan into the estimated best physical plan that lies within our search space. The physical query plan is a tree composed of *physical operators* that are implemented by the *query execution engine* and perform the low-level steps required to execute the query and construct the result. We use a recursive *iterator* approach in query processing, as described in, e.g., [Gra93], and we assume the reader is familiar with the basic concepts associated with iterators.

3.4 Lore Indexes

As in a conventional DBMS, indexes in Lore enable fast and efficient access to the data. In a relational DBMS, an index is created on an attribute in order to locate tuples with particular attribute values quickly. In Lore, such a *value index* alone is not sufficient, since often the path to a node is as important as the node's value. Lore contains several indexing structures that are useful for finding relevant atomic values, parents of objects, and specific paths and edges within the database. The *value index*, or Vindex, supports finding all atomic objects with a given incoming edge label and satisfying a given predicate. The *label index*, or Lindex, supports finding all parents of a given object via an edge with a given label. The *edge index*, which we term the Bindex, supports finding all parent-child object pairs connected via a specified label. In addition to these indexes, Lore's *DataGuide* [GW97] provides the functionality of a path index, or Pindex. Details on Lore indexes, including coercion issues addressed by the Vindex, can be found in [MWA+98].

4 Motivation

As in any declarative query language, there are many ways to execute a single Lorel query. Let us consider Query 1 introduced in Section 3.2 and roughly sketch several types of query plans. As we will illustrate, the optimal query plan depends not only on the values in the database but also on the *shape* of the graph containing the data. It is this additional factor that makes optimization of queries over XML data both important and difficult.

The most straightforward approach to executing Query 1 is to fully explore all Member subobjects of DBGroup and for each one look for the existence of an Age subobject of the Member object whose value is less than 30. We call this a *top-down* execution strategy since we begin at the named object DBGroup (the top), then process each simple path expression in a forward manner. This approach is similar to *pointer-chasing* in object-oriented systems, and to nested-loop index joins in relational systems. This query execution strategy results in a depth-first traversal of the graph following edges that appear in the query's path expressions.

Another way to execute Query 1 is to first identify all objects that satisfy the "y < 30" predicate by using an appropriate Vindex if it exists (recall Section 3.4). Once we have an object satisfying the predicate, we traverse backwards through the data, going from child to parent, matching path expressions in reverse using the Lindex. We call

[1] The existential quantification in the Where clause is necessary since a Member object could conceivably have many Age subobjects. A shorthand in Lorel allows simply "where x.Age < 30", which is preprocessed automatically into the query as shown here [AQM+97].

Query: Select x From A.B x where exists y in x.C: y = 5

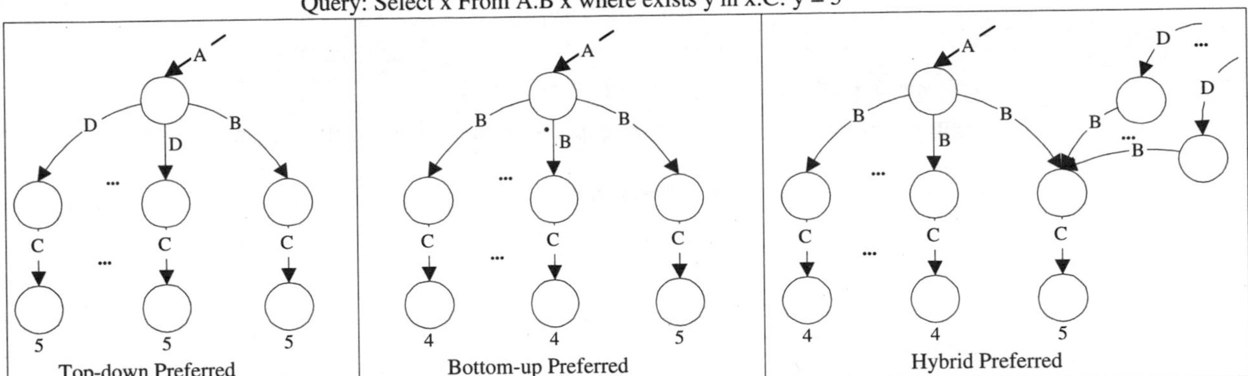

Figure 2: Different databases and good query execution strategies

this query execution strategy *bottom-up* since we first identify atomic objects and then attempt to work back up to a named object. This approach is similar to *reverse pointer-chasing* in object-oriented systems. The advantage of this approach is that we start with objects guaranteed to satisfy the `Where` predicate, and do not needlessly explore paths through the data only to find that the final value does not satisfy the predicate. Bottom-up is not always better than top-down, however, since there could be very few paths satisfying the path expression but many objects satisfying the predicate.

A third strategy is to evaluate some, but not all, of a path expression top-down and create a temporary result of satisfying objects. Then use the Vindex as described earlier and traverse up, via the Lindex, to the same point as the top-down exploration. A join between the two temporary results yields complete satisfying paths. (In fact certain join types do not require temporary results at all.) We call this approach a *hybrid* plan, since it operates both top-down and bottom-up, meeting in the middle of a path expression. This type of plan can be optimal when the fan-in degree of the reverse evaluation of a path expression becomes very large at about the same time that the fan-out degree in the forward evaluation of the path expression becomes very large.

These three approaches give a flavor of the very different types of plans that could be used to evaluate a simple query, one that effectively consists of a single path expression. The actual search space of plans for this simple query is much larger, as we will illustrate in Section 5.4, and more complicated queries with multiple interrelated path expressions naturally have an even larger variety of candidate plans.

To make things even more concrete, suppose we are processing the query "`Select x From A.B x Where exists y in x.C: y = 5`", which is isomorphic to Query 1. In Figure 2 we present the general shape and a few atomic values for three databases, illustrating cases when each type of query plan described above would be a good strategy. The database on the left has only one `A.B.C` path and top-down execution would explore only this path. Bottom-up execution, however, would visit all the leaf objects with value 5, and their parents. The second database has many `A.B.C` paths, but only a single leaf satisfying the predicate, so bottom-up is a good candidate. Finally, in the third database top-down execution would visit all the leaf nodes, but only a single one satisfies the predicate. Bottom-up would identify the single object satisfying the predicate, but would visit all of the nodes in the upper-right portion of the database. For this database, a hybrid plan where we use top-down execution to find all `A.B` objects, then bottom-up execution for one level, then finally join the two results, would be a good strategy.

Each of these three example plans has a substantially different shape from the others, and each is the optimal plan for a particular database. Our primary goal when designing our logical query plans was to create a structure that represents, at a high level, the sequence of steps necessary to execute a query, while at the same time permits simple rules to transform the logical query plan into a wide variety of different physical query plans.

5 Query Execution Engine

5.1 Logical Query Plans

Recall that a single logical query plan is created after the query is preprocessed into a canonical form. Before explaining the logical query plan operators and structure of the plans, we introduce two additional definitions.

Definition 5.1 **(Variable Binding)** During query processing, a variable x in the query is said to be *bound* if an object o has been assigned to x. We also say that *o is bound to x*.

Definition 5.2 **(Evaluation)** During query processing, an *evaluation* of a query plan (or subplan) is a list of all variables appearing in the plan along with the object (if any) bound to each variable.

The goal of query execution is to iteratively generate complete evaluations for all variables in the query, producing the set of query results based on these evaluations.

One major difference between the top-down and bottom-up query execution strategies introduced in Section 4 is the order in which the query is processed. In the top-down approach we handle the `From` clause before the `Where`;

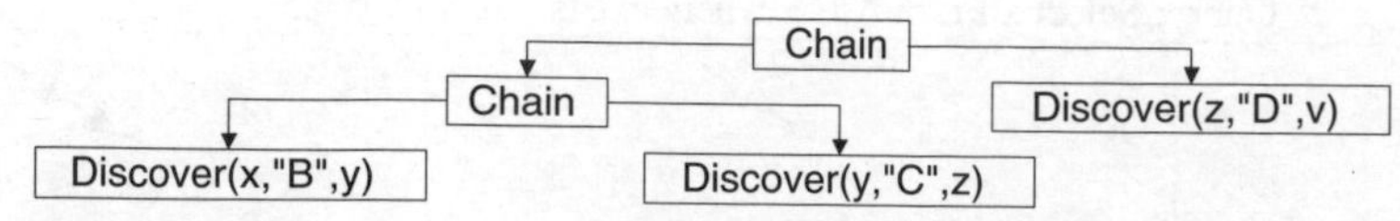

Figure 3: Representation of a path expression in the logical query plan

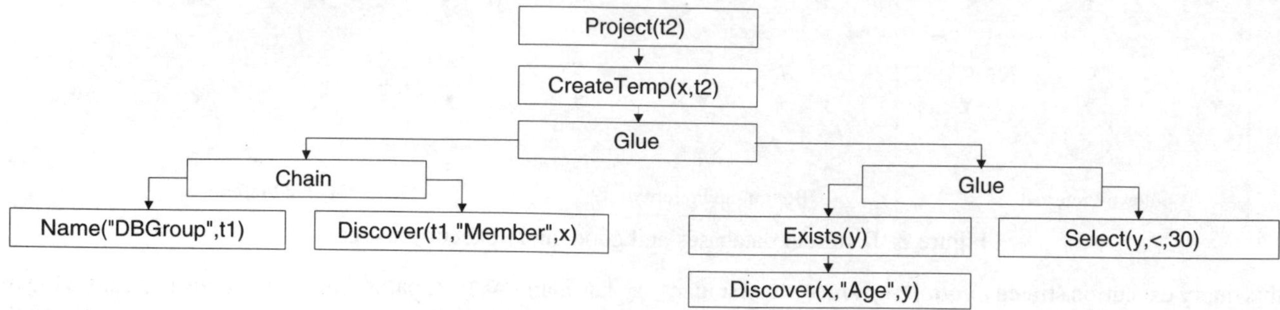

Figure 4: A complete logical query plan

the order is reversed for the bottom-up strategy. Also consider the Where clause of Query 1: "`Where exists y in x.Age:y < 30`". We can break this clause into two distinct pieces: (a) find all `Age` subobjects of `x`, and (b) test their values. In the bottom-up plan we first use the **Vindex** to satisfy (b) and then we use the **Lindex** for (a). In the top-down strategy first we satisfy (a) by finding an `Age` subobject of x, then we test the condition to fulfill (b).

In fact, all queries can be broken into independent components where the execution order of the components is not fixed in advance. We term the places where independent components meet *rotation points*, since during the creation of the physical query plan we can rotate the order between two independent components to get vastly different plans.

In our approach, each logical operator can construct its optimal physical (sub)plan with respect to a set of variables that are already bound elsewhere in the plan. The mechanism by which we store the binding information must also store information about *how* a variable was bound in order for the statistics to accurately estimate the cost and number of results. For example, given the path expression "`x.B y, y.C z`" and assuming that we are following subobjects from variable y to variable z, then the statistics for z will depend on how y was bound. If y was bound via a **Bindex** operator then the number of object bindings for y (number of `C` edges) might be quite different from the case where y was bound by following subobjects from x. Statistics are discussed further in Section 5.3.

A list and description of most of our logical operators is given in [MW99b]. Here we will focus on the *Discover* and *Chain* logical operators used for path expressions. Each simple path expression in the query is represented as a *Discover* node, which indicates that in some fashion information is discovered from the database. When multiple simple path expressions are grouped together into a path expression, we represent the group as a left-deep tree of *Discover* nodes connected via *Chain* nodes. It is the responsibility of the *Chain* operator to optimize the entire path expression represented in its left and right subplans. As an example, consider the path expression "`x.B y, y.C z, z.D v`" (where x is defined elsewhere in the query) which has the logical query subplan shown in Figure 3. The leftmost *Discover* node is responsible for choosing the best way to provide bindings for variables `x` and `y`. The *Chain* node directly above it is responsible for evaluating the path expression "`x.B y, y.C z`" efficiently. This could be done by using the children's most efficient ways of executing their subplans and joining them together, or possibly by using a path index for the entire path expression. The final *Chain* and *Discover* nodes are similar.

Figure 4 shows the complete logical query plan for Query 1. Each rotation point is represented by a *Glue* node that has as its children the two independent subplans. The topmost *Glue* node connects the subplans for the `From` and `Where` clauses. The *Chain* node connects the two components of the path expression appearing in the `From`. The *Exists* node quantifies y. A *Glue* node separates the existential in the `Where` from the actual predicate test, allowing either operation to occur first in the physical query plan. Because the semantics of Lorel requires a set of objects to be returned, the *CreateTemp* and *Project* nodes at the top of the plan are responsible for gathering the satisfying evaluations and returning the appropriate objects to the user.

Space limitations preclude a full description of logical query plans or examples of more complex queries, but the general flavor and flexibility of our approach should be evident. For details please see [MW99b].

5.2 Physical Query Plans

The number of physical query plan operators is large; a list and description of the more common operators appears in [MW99b]. Here we focus on some of the more interesting operators including those used to traverse paths through the data. Recall that our physical query plan operators are iterators: each node in the plan requests a "tuple" at a time from its children, performs some operation on the tuple(s), and passes result tuples to its parent. The "tuples" that our query plans operate over are evaluations (Definition 5.2):

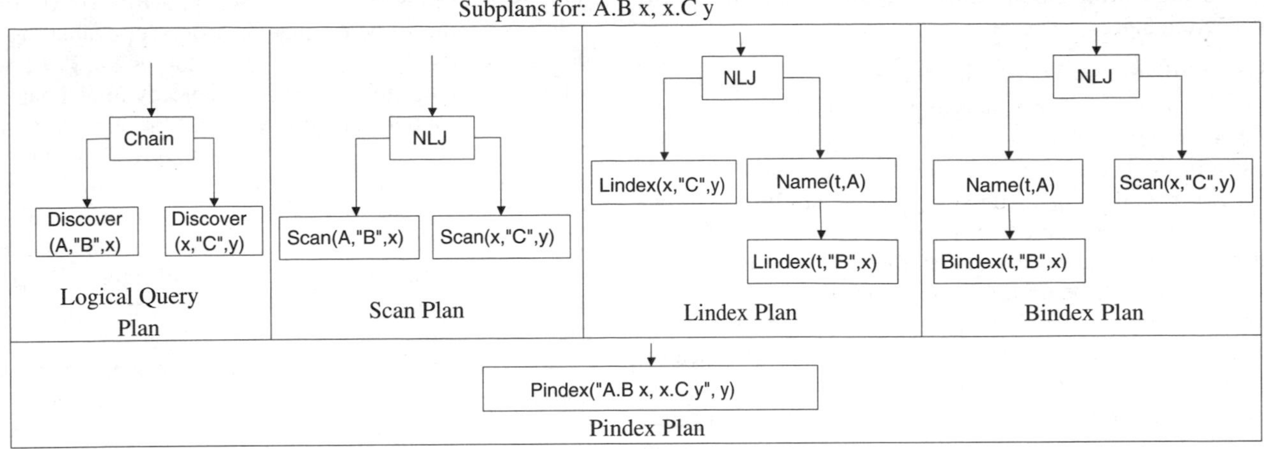

Figure 5: Different physical query plans

vectors of bindings for variables in the query.

In a physical query plan, there are six operators that identify information stored in the database:

1. *Scan*(x, l, y): The *Scan* operator performs pointer-chasing: it places into y all objects that are subobjects of the complex object x via an edge labeled l.
2. *Lindex*(x, l, y): In the reverse of the *Scan* operator, the *Lindex* operator places into x all objects that are parents of y via an edge labeled l. This reverse pointer-chasing operator is implemented in Lore by the link index (Section 3.4).
3. *Pindex*(*PathExpression*, x): Lore maintains a dynamic "structural summary" of the current database called a *DataGuide* [GW97]. The DataGuide also can be used as a *path index*, enabling quick retrieval of oid's for all objects reachable via a given path expression. The *Pindex* operator places into x all objects reachable via the *PathExpression*.
4. *Bindex*(l, x, y): The *Bindex* operator finds all parent-child pairs connected via an edge labeled l. This operator allows us to efficiently locate edges whose label appears infrequently in the database.
5. *Name*(x, n): The *Name* operator simply verifies that the object in variable x is the named object n. (Recall from Section 3.1 that *named objects* are entry points to a Lore database.)
6. *Vindex*(*Op*, *Value*, l, x): The *Vindex* operator accepts a label l, an operator *Op*, and a *Value*, and places into x all atomic objects that satisfy the "*Op Value*" condition and have an incoming edge labeled l.

As an example that uses some of these operators, consider the path expression "`A.B x, x.C y`" (where `A` is a name) and four possible plans as shown in Figure 5. (The optimizer can generate up to eleven different physical plans for this single path expression.) The logical query plan is shown in the top left panel. In the first physical plan, the "Scan Plan", we use a sequence of *Scan* operators to discover bindings for each of the variables, which corresponds to the top-down execution strategy introduced in Section 4. If we already have a binding for y then we can use the second plan, the "Lindex Plan". In this plan we use two *Lindex* operations starting from the bound variable y, and then confirm that we have reached the named object `A`. This corresponds to the bottom-up execution strategy of Section 4. In the "Bindex Plan", we directly locate all parent-child pairs connected via a `B` edge using the *Bindex* operator. We then confirm that the parent object is the named object `A`, and *Scan* for all of the `C` subobjects of the child object. In the "Pindex Plan", we use the *Pindex* operator, which allows us to directly obtain the set of objects reached via the given path expression. Note that several of the plans use a nested-loop join (NLJ) operator without a predicate. These are dependent joins where the left subplan passes bound variables to the right subplan.

Recall the hybrid query execution strategy introduced in Section 4. One subplan evaluates a portion of the query and obtains bindings for a set of variables, say V, and another subplan obtains bindings for another set of variables, say W. Suppose $V \cap W$ contains one variable, but the plans are otherwise *independent*, meaning one does not provide a binding that the other uses (as in the hybrid plan). Then by creating evaluations for both subplans and joining the results on the shared variable, we efficiently obtain complete evaluations. As in relational systems, deciding which join operator to use is an important decision made by the optimizer. (Currently we support nested-loop and hash joins.)

Again space limitations preclude a full description of physical query plans or examples of even remotely complicated queries, although we will visit physical query plans for Query 1 later in Section 5.4. In addition to the basic traversal operators discussed above, we have operators to perform projection and selection, manage temporary results, perform an aggregation operation over a subplan, ensure the existential and universal quantification of a variable, perform set and arithmetic operations between two subplans, and others. For details please see [MW99b]. The physical operators can be combined in numerous ways, producing a vast search space for even relatively simple queries. Our plan enumeration and pruning heuristics will be discussed in Section 5.4.

5.3 Statistics and Cost Model

As with any cost-based query optimizer, we need to establish a metric by which we estimate the execution cost for a given physical query plan or subplan. Lore currently does not enforce any object clustering, so we are limited to using the predicted number of object fetches as our measure of I/O cost, since we cannot accurately determine whether two objects will be on the same page. Despite this rough approximation, experiments presented in Section 6 validate that our cost model is reasonably accurate. Nevertheless, refining and expanding the cost model, especially by increasing our knowledge of the locality of objects on pages (through statistics-gathering and/or actual clustering), is an area where we intend to invest future effort.

5.3.1 Statistics

Our query optimizer must consult statistical information about the size, shape, and range of values within a database in order to estimate the cost of a physical query plan. Initially we stored statistics in the *DataGuide*, but quickly were limited by the fact that we could only store statistics about paths beginning from a named object [GW97]. The optimizer may choose to begin evaluating a path expression anywhere within the path (via the *Bindex* or *Vindex* operator), so we needed more flexible statistics. Our new approach is to store statistics about all possible subpaths (label sequences) in the database up to a length k, where k is a tuning parameter. (Typical object-oriented and relational database systems compute and store statistics for $k = 1$.) We have explored several algorithms for efficiently computing and storing such statistics, but a presentation of these algorithms is outside of the scope of this paper. Regardless of algorithm used, a clear trade-off exists between the cost in time and space for a larger k and the accuracy of the statistics.

The statistics we maintain for every label subpath p of length $\leq k$ include:

- For each atomic type, the total number of atomic objects of that type reachable via p.
- For each atomic type, the minimum and maximum values of all atomic objects of that type reachable via p.
- The total number of instances of path p, denoted $|p|$.
- The total number of distinct objects reachable via p, denoted $|p|_d$.
- The total number of l-labeled subobjects of all objects reachable via p, denoted $|p_l|$.
- The total number of incoming l-labeled edges to any instance of p, denoted $|p^l|$.

As mentioned earlier, our I/O cost metric is based on the estimated number of objects fetched during evaluation of the query. Thus, for example, given an evaluation that corresponds to a traversal to some point in the data, the optimizer must estimate how many objects will bind to the next simple path expression to be evaluated. Consider evaluating the path expression "`A.B x, x.C y`" top-down. If we have a binding for x, then the optimizer needs to estimate the number of `C` subobjects, on average, that objects reached by the path "`A.B x`" have. Alternatively, if we proceed bottom-up with a binding for x, then the optimizer must estimate the average number of parents via a `B` edge for all the `C`'s. We call these two estimates *fan-out* and *fan-in* respectively. The fan-out for a given path expression p and label l is computed from the statistics by $|p| * (|p_l|/|p|_d)$. Likewise, fan-in is $|p| * (|p^l|/|p|_d)$.

Our statistics are most accurate for path expressions of length $\leq k+1$, since for a given k we store statistics about paths of length up to k, and these statistics include information about incoming and outgoing edges to the paths—effectively giving us information about all paths of length $k+1$. Given a path expression of length $k+2$, for maximum accuracy we combine the statistics for two overlapping paths p_1 and p_2 each of length $k+1$.

When estimating the number of atomic values that will satisfy a given predicate, standard formulas such as those given in [SAC+79, PSC84] are insufficient in our semistructured environment due to the extensive type coercion that Lore performs [AQM+97]. Our formulas take coercion into account by combining value distributions for all atomic types that can be coerced into a type comparable to the value in the predicate.

5.3.2 Cost Model

Each physical query plan is assigned a *cost* based upon the estimated I/O and CPU time required to execute the plan. The costing procedure is recursive: the cost assigned to a node in the query plan depends on the costs assigned to its subplans, along with the cost for executing the node itself. In order to compute estimated cost recursively, at each node we must also estimate the number of evaluations expected for that subplan. To decide if one plan is cheaper than another, we first check the estimated I/O cost. Only when the I/O costs are identical do we take estimated CPU cost into account. Again, our cost metric is admittedly simplistic, but it does appear acceptable for the first version of our cost-based optimizer as shown by the performance results in Section 6.

Due to space constraints, our formulas for estimated I/O and CPU cost and number of evaluations are omitted but appear in [MW99b]. As an example, consider the I/O formula for the *Vindex*(*Op*, *Value*, l, x) operator: $BLevel_{l,type1}+$ $Selectivity_1(l,$ Op, $Value)$ $+BLevel_{l,type2}+$ $Selectivity_2(l,$ Op, $Value)$. Here *BLevel* gives the height of the relevant B+-tree index, and the *Selectivity* functions are the formulas to estimate the number of satisfying results given Lore's coercion system. (Because of type coercion, multiple B+-trees need to be accessed during a *Vindex* operation.) As a second example, the I/O cost for the *Lindex*(x, l, y) operator is $2 + Fin_{PathOf(y),l}$, where *Fin* is the fan-in statistic as defined earlier. The *Lindex* is implemented using *extendible*

n: number of simple path expressions	n=3	n=5	n=7
All possible plans/Lore's search space	1458 / 48	2,361,960 / 228	8,035,387,920 / 948

Table 1: Analysis of Search Space Size

hashing, and our cost estimate assumes no overflow buckets. Thus, it requires two page fetches (one for the directory and one for the hash bucket) and one additional page fetch for every possible parent.

5.4 Plan Enumeration

The search space of physical query plans for a single Lorel query is very large. For example, a single path expression of length n can be viewed as an n-way join, where as "join methods" Lore considers pointer-chasing, reverse pointer-chasing, and two different standard relational joins. Furthermore, there may be many interrelated path expressions in a single query, along with other constructs such as set operations, subqueries, aggregation, etc. [AQM+97]. In order to reduce the search space as well as the complexity of our plan enumerator, we use a greedy approach to generating physical query plans. Each logical query plan node makes a locally optimal decision, creating the best physical subplan for the logical plan rooted at that node. The decision is based on a given set of bound variables passed from the node's parent. The key to considering a variety of different physical plans is that a node may ask its child(ren) for the optimal physical query subplan many times, using different sets of bound variables each time. While this greedy approach greatly reduces the search space, it still explores an exponentially large number of physical query plans. Thus, our plan enumerator currently uses the following additional heuristics to further prune the search space.

- The optimizer does not consider joining two simple path expressions together unless they share a common variable. This restriction substantially reduces the number of ways to order the evaluation of simple path expressions. (See [MW99b] for a detailed discussion.)
- The *Pindex* operator is considered only when a path expression begins with a name, and no variable except the last is used elsewhere within the query. The latter requirement is based on the fact that *Pindex* only binds the last variable in its path expression, so other needed variables in the path would have to be discovered by some additional method.
- The `Select` clause always executes last, since in nearly all cases it depends on one or more variables bound in the `From` clause. Also, the physical query plan will always execute either the complete `From` or complete `Where` clause before moving on to the other one.
- The optimizer does not attempt to reorder multiple independent path expressions.

A detailed analysis of our physical query plan search space is provided in [MW99b]. Table 1 gives some examples of how dramatically our heuristics reduce the search space. However, even with our aggressive pruning, Lore still chooses very good plans as we demonstrate in Section 6. For further refinement, we intend to experiment with a final optimization phase in which we can apply transformations directly over the generated physical query plan, such as moving subplans to different locations in the overall plan.

We now discuss how physical plans are produced. As mentioned earlier, each logical plan node creates an optimal physical plan given a set of bound variables. During plan enumeration we track for every variable in the query: (1) whether the variable is bound or not; (2) which plan operator has bound the variable; (3) all other plan operators that use the variable; (4) whether the variable is stored within a temporary result. For instance, the logical query plan node *Discover* for the simple path expression `x.Age y` may be asked to create its optimal plan given that x has already been bound by some other physical operator, in which case it may decide that *Scan* is optimal. However, if y was bound instead then it may decide that *Lindex* is optimal. After a node creates its optimal subplan, the new state of the variables and the optimal subplan are passed to the parent. Note that a logical node may be unable to create any physical plan for a given state of the variables if it always requires some variables to be bound. In this case, "no plan" is returned and a different choice must be made at a higher level in the plan. In [MW99b] we detail how each logical plan node generates its optimal physical subplan.

To illustrate the transformation from a logical plan to a physical plan, let us consider part of the search space explored during the creation of the physical query plan for Query 1, whose logical query plan was given in Figure 4. The topmost *Glue* node (indicating a rotation point) in Figure 4 is responsible for deciding the execution order of its children: either left-then-right or right-then-left. It requests the best physical query plan from the left child and then, using the returned bindings, requests the best physical query plan from the right child. One possible outcome is the physical query plan fragment shown in Figure 6(a). After exploring left-then-right execution order, the topmost *Glue* node considers the right-then-left order. The right child is another *Glue* node which recursively follows the same procedure. Suppose that for this nested *Glue* node, the left-then-right execution order results in the physical subplan shown in Figure 6(b), while the right-then-left execution order results in Figure 6(c). (For details of the *CreateTemp* and *Once* operators please see [MW99b].) Suppose plan (c) is chosen based on a lower estimated cost. The bindings provided by this subplan are then supplied to the left child of the topmost *Glue* node to create the optimal query plan for the left child, which could result in the final subplan shown in Figure 6(d). Notice that in the right subplan for the

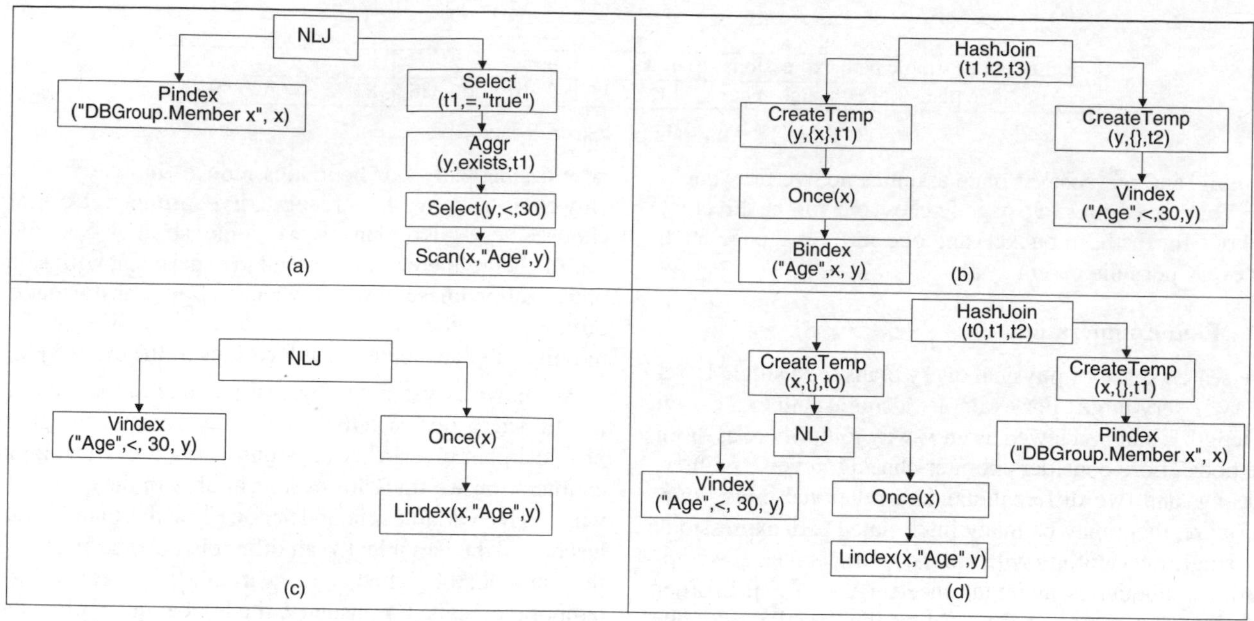

Figure 6: Possible transformations for Query 1 into a physical query plan

topmost *Glue* node, the *Chain* node decided that the *Pindex* operator is the best way to get all "`DBGroup.Member x`" objects within the database, despite the fact that we already have a binding for x. This choice makes sense when the estimated fan-in for x with label `DBGroup` is very high. As a final step the topmost *Glue* node decides which query plan is cheaper, either (a) or (d), and passes that plan to its parent.

6 Performance Results

The query optimization techniques described in this paper are fully implemented and integrated into Lore, including the physical operators, statistics, cost formulas, logical query plan generation, and physical query plan enumeration and selection. The implementation for these components consists of approximately 31,000 lines of C++ code. We also have implemented mechanisms for instructing the optimizer to favor certain types of plans (in order to debug and conduct experiments), and we have built a very useful query plan visualization tool. We now present some preliminary performance results showing that our cost model is reasonably accurate and that the optimizer is choosing good plans. Extensive performance evaluations over a large suite of queries and databases is beyond the scope of this paper.

All of our tests were run on a Sun Ultra 2 with 256 megabytes of RAM. However, Lore was configured to have a small buffer size of approximately 150K bytes, in order to match the relatively small databases used by our initial performance experiments. Each query was run with an initially empty buffer. Over all of the queries in our experiments the average optimization time was approximately 1/2 second.

At the time of this writing we have not located any significant amounts of readily available XML data. What is available consists mostly of small, tree-structured documents usually with cryptic tags or presentational tags borrowed from HTML. Rather than use these small datasets for our experiments we built our own XML database about movies made in 1997, combining information from many sources including the Internet Movie Database (located at `http://www.imdb.com`). The database contains facts about 1,970 movies, 10,260 actors and actresses, plot summaries, directors, editors, writers, etc., as well as multimedia data such as stills and audio clips. The database loaded into Lore is about 5 megabytes. Value, Link, and Edge indexes (recall Section 3.4) account for an additional 8.1 megabytes. The database is semistructured and very cyclic; for example, actors have edges to each movie they appeared in (along with their role in the movie), and movies have edges to all of the actors in the movie. The database graph contains 62,256 nodes and 130,402 edges.

Lore allows us to turn off all pruning heuristics temporarily, in order to create and execute all possible query execution plans within our search space for a single query. Thus, we can evaluate how the chosen plan performs against other possible plans. However, it is infeasible to perform this extensive experiment for large queries, since the number of plans in the search space is very large, and some plans are extremely slow to execute (even if the chosen plan is very efficient). We report on a sample of experiments, again emphasizing that exhaustive performance evaluations are beyond the scope of this paper.

Experiment 1. We begin with an extremely simple query: `Select DB.Movie.Title`. Using exhaustive search Lore produces eleven different query plans, with estimated I/O costs and actual execution times (in seconds) as show in Table 2. In this and subsequent tables the plan chosen by the optimizer when the pruning heuristics are used is marked with a star (*). The first and best plan simply uses Lore's path index to quickly locate all the movie titles. The

Plan #	1*	2	3	4	5	6	7	8	9	10	11
Exec. Time (sec.)	0.36	1.78	2.02	14.44	61.82	67.24	74.09	94.15	250.61	397.18	423.34
Estimated I/O	1975	3944	3944	9853	31918	31918	11823	37827	17742	17733	23855

Table 2: Query execution times

second plan, which is only slightly slower, uses top-down pointer-chasing. The worst plan uses *Bindex* operators and hash joins.

To evaluate the relative accuracy of our cost model, consider the estimated I/O cost against the actual execution time. With some exceptions, the estimated cost accurately reflects the relative execution time for each plan. Since our cost model is still quite simplistic, we are very encouraged by these results. □

Experiment 2. Our second query asks for all movies with a `Genre` subobject having value "Comedy". This turned out to be a "point" query, since many movies don't have a `Genre` subobject and most aren't comedies. Estimated I/O costs again reflected relative execution times fairly accurately, so hereafter we focus only on execution times. Twenty-four plans were considered using exhaustive search. The following table describes some of them, where "Time" is the execution time and "Rank" indicates the plan rank by execution time among all plans considered.

Rank	Time	Description
1*	0.3307	Bottom-up
2	0.3768	*Bindex, Select* then *Lindex*
7	3.3384	Top-down
24	458.58	Full *Bindex*

Since the `Where` clause is very selective, the optimal plan uses a bottom-up strategy: a *Vindex* operator locates all objects having the value "Comedy" and an incoming edge labeled `Genre`. The *Lindex* operator matches the remainder of the path expression in reverse. The second-best plan is only slightly slower. It uses the *Bindex* to locate all `Genre` edges, filters using the "Comedy" predicate, then proceeds bottom-up. The slowest plan uses a poor combination of *Bindex* operators and joins. Top-down evaluation results in the seventh-best plan. □

Experiment 3. In the remaining two experiments we did not execute all possible plans since the queries and space of plans are much larger. Instead, we generated and executed samplying of plans from within our search space. Again, the plan chosen by the optimizer is marked with a star(*). The following results are for a query with two existentially quantified variables in the `Where` clause.

Rank	Time	Description
1	0.33	Bottom-up
2*	3.68	Top-down
3	6.95	Hybrid with *Pindex*
4	7.01	Hybrid with pointer-chasing
5	23.13	*Bindex* and *Vindex* then *Lindex*

Notice that the optimizer chose plan 2, the top-down or pointer-chasing execution strategy, as the best plan. The mistake is due largely to simplistic estimates of atomic value distributions (we have not yet implemented histograms) and of set operation costs. Devoting some effort to improving the optimizer in these areas should lead it to select the optimal plan. □

Experiment 4. Our fourth query selects movies with a certain quality rating. Here too we considered only a sampling of all possible plans.

Rank	Time	Description
1*	0.61	*Bindex* for rating, then *Lindex* up
2	0.89	Bottom-up
3	4.04	Top-down

Since it turns out that quality ratings are fairly uncommon in the database, the optimizer (correctly) chooses to find all ratings via the *Bindex*, then to work bottom-up. □

We have performed many experiments in addition to those reported here, although the ones described are a representative sample. In general, our experiments so far allow us to conclude: (i) our cost estimates are accurate enough to select the best plan in most cases, although some refinements are needed; (ii) execution times of the best and worst plans for a given query and database can differ by many orders of magnitude; and (iii) the best execution strategy is highly dependent on the query and database, indicating that a cost-based query optimizer for XML data is crucial to achieving good performance.

7 Future Work

Extensions to the work presented here are underway, including specific optimization techniques for *branching path expressions*, a query rewrite that moves `Where` clause predicates into the `From` clause, and a transformation that introduces a `Group-By` clause when a large number of paths pass through a small number of objects. We are also considering *partially correlated subplans*, which are similar to correlated subqueries but rely on the bindings passed between portions of the physical query plan rather than on the query itself. In the area of statistics we are considering even more efficient statistics-gathering algorithms, perhaps incorporating some graph sampling. We also plan to gather statistics about the location of objects on disk, with corresponding modifications to the cost formulas to generate more accurate cost estimates.

References

[Abi97] S. Abiteboul. Querying semistructured data. In *Proc. of the International Conference on Database Theory*, pages 1–18, Delphi, Greece, January 1997.

[AQM+97] S. Abiteboul, D. Quass, J. McHugh, J. Widom, and J. Wiener. The Lorel query language for semistructured data. *Journal of Digital Libraries*, 1(1):68–88, April 1997.

[BDHS96] P. Buneman, S. Davidson, G. Hillebrand, and D. Suciu. A query language and optimization techniques for unstructured data. In *Proc. of the ACM SIGMOD International Conference on Management of Data*, pages 505–516, Montreal, Canada, June 1996.

[BF97] E. Bertino and P. Foscoli. On modeling cost functions for object-oriented databases. *IEEE Transactions on Knowledge and Data Engineering*, 9(3):500–508, May 1997.

[BPSM98] T. Bray, J. Paoli, and C. Sperberg-McQueen. Extensible markup language (XML) 1.0, February 1998. W3C Recommendation available at http://www.w3.org/TR/1998/REC-xml-19980210.

[BRG88] E. Bertino, F. Rabitti, and S. Gibbs. Query processing in a multimedia document system. *ACM Transactions on Office Information Systems*, 6(1):1–41, January 1988.

[Bun97] P. Buneman. Semistructured data. In *Proc. of the Sixth ACM SIGACT-SIGMOD-SIGART Symposium on Principles of Database Systems*, Tucson, Arizona, May 1997. Tutorial.

[Cat94] R.G.G. Cattell. *The Object Database Standard: ODMG-93*. Morgan Kaufmann, San Francisco, California, 1994.

[CCM96] V. Christophides, S. Cluet, and G. Moerkotte. Evaluating queries with generalized path expressions. In *Proc. of the ACM SIGMOD International Conference on Management of Data*, pages 413–422, Montreal, Canada, June 1996.

[DFF+98] A. Deutsch, M. Fernandez, D. Florescu, A. Levy, and D. Suciu. XML-QL: A query language for XML, August 1998. Available at http://www.w3.org/TR/NOTE-xml-ql/.

[FFK+99] M. Fernandez, D. Florescu, J. Kang, A. Levy, and D. Suciu. Catching the boat with Strudel: Experiences with a website management system. In *Proc. of the ACM SIGMOD International Conference on Management of Data*, pages 414–425, Seattle, Washington, June 1999.

[FFLS97] M. Fernandez, D. Florescu, A. Levy, and D. Suciu. A query language for a web-site management system. *SIGMOD Record*, 26(3):4–11, September 1997.

[FLS98] D. Florescu, A. Levy, and D. Suciu. Query optimization algorithm for semistructured data. Technical report, AT&T Laboratories, June 1998.

[FS98] M. Fernandez and D. Suciu. Optimizing regular path expressions using graph schemas. In *Proc. of the Fourteenth International Conference on Data Engineering*, pages 14–23, Orlando, Florida, February 1998.

[GGMR97] J. Grant, J. Gryz, J. Minker, and L. Raschid. Semantic query optimization for object databases. In *Proc. of the Thirteenth International Conference on Data Engineering*, pages 444–454, Birmingham, UK, April 1997.

[GGT95] G. Gardarin, J. Gruser, and Z. Tang. A cost model for clustered object-oriented databases. In *Proc. of the Twenty-First International Conference on Very Large Data Bases*, pages 323–334, Zurich, Switzerland, September 1995.

[GGT96] G. Gardarin, J. Gruser, and Z. Tang. Cost-based selection of path expression processing algorithms in object-oriented databases. In *Proc. of the Twenty-Second International Conference on Very Large Data Bases*, pages 390–401, Bombay, India, 1996.

[GMW99] R. Goldman, J. McHugh, and J. Widom. From semistructured data to XML: Migrating the Lore data model and query language. In *Proc. of the 2nd International Workshop on the Web and Databases*, Philadelphia, PA., June 1999.

[Gra93] G. Graefe. Query evaluation techniques for large databases. *ACM Computing Surveys*, 25(2):73–170, 1993.

[GW97] R. Goldman and J. Widom. DataGuides: Enabling query formulation and optimization in semistructured databases. In *Proc. of the Twenty-Third International Conference on Very Large Data Bases*, pages 436–445, Athens, Greece, August 1997.

[KMP93] A. Kemper, G. Moerkotte, and K. Peithner. A blackboard architecture for query optimization in object bases. In *Proc. of the Nineteenth International Conference on Very Large Data Bases*, pages 543–554, Dublin, Ireland, August 1993.

[LV91] R. Lanzelotte and P. Valduriez. Optimization of nonrecursive queries in OODBs. In *Proc. of the Second International Conference on Deductive and Object-Oriented Databases*, pages 1–21, Munich, Germany, December 1991.

[MAG+97] J. McHugh, S. Abiteboul, R. Goldman, D. Quass, and J. Widom. Lore: A database management system for semistructured data. *SIGMOD Record*, 26(3):54–66, September 1997.

[Mar98] M. Marchiori. *Proc. of QL'98 - The Query Languages Workshop*. Boston, MA, December 1998. Papers available online at http://www.w3.org/TandS/QL/QL98/.

[MSOP86] D. Maier, J. Stein, A. Otis, and A. Purdy. Development of an object-oriented DBMS. In *Proc. of the Conference on Object-Oriented Programming Systems, Languages, and Applications*, pages 472–481, Portland, Oregon, November 1986.

[MW99a] J. McHugh and J. Widom. Compile-time path expansion in Lore. In *Workshop on Query Processing for Semistructured Data and Non-Standard Data Formats*, Jerusalem, Isreal, January 1999.

[MW99b] J. McHugh and J. Widom. Query optimization for semistructured data. Technical report, Stanford University Database Group, February 1999. Document is available at ftp://db.stanford.edu/pub/papers/qo.ps.

[MWA+98] J. McHugh, J. Widom, S. Abiteboul, Q. Luo, and A. Rajaraman. Indexing semistructured data. Technical report, Stanford University Database Group, 1998. Document is available at ftp://db.stanford.edu/pub/papers/semiindexing98.ps

[OMS95] M. T. Ozsu, A. Munoz, and D. Szafron. An extensible query optimizer for an objectbase management system. In *Proc. of the Fourth International Conference on Information and Knowledge Management*, pages 188–196, Baltimore, Maryland, November 1995.

[O'N87] Patrick O'Neil. Model 204 architecture and performance. In *Proc. of the Second International Workshop on High Performance Transaction Systems (HPTS)*, pages 40–59, Asilomar, CA, 1987.

[PGMW95] Y. Papakonstantinou, H. Garcia-Molina, and J. Widom. Object exchange across heterogeneous information sources. In *Proc. of the Eleventh International Conference on Data Engineering*, pages 251–260, Taipei, Taiwan, March 1995.

[PSC84] G. Piatetsky-Shapiro and C. Connell. Accurate estimation of the number of tuples satisfying a condition. In *Proc. of the ACM SIGMOD International Conference on Management of Data*, pages 256–276, Boston, MA, June 1984.

[RLS98] J. Robie, J. Lapp, and D. Schach. XML query language (XQL). In *[Mar98]*, 1998.

[SAC+79] P. Selinger, M. Astrahan, D. Chamberlin, R. Lorie, and T. Price. Access path selection in a relational database management system. In *Proc. of the ACM SIGMOD International Conference on Management of Data*, pages 23–34, Boston, MA, June 1979.

[SMY90] W. Sun, W. Meng, and C. T. Yu. Query optimization in object-oriented database systems. In *Database and Expert Systems Applications*, pages 215–222, Vienna, Austria, August 1990.

[SO95] D. D. Straube and M. T. Ozsu. Query optimization and execution plan generation in object-oriented database systems. *IEEE Transactions on Knowledge and Data Engineering*, 7(2):210–227, April 1995.

[YM97] C. Yu and W. Meng. *Principles of Database Query Processing for Advanced Applications*. Morgan Kaufmann, San Francisco, California, 1997.

Context-Based Prefetch for Implementing Objects on Relations

Philip A. Bernstein Shankar Pal David Shutt
Microsoft Corporation
One Microsoft Way, Redmond, WA 98052-6399
{philbe, shankarp, dshutt}@microsoft.com

Abstract

When implementing persistent objects on a relational database, a major performance issue is prefetching data to minimize the number of round-trips to the database. This is especially hard with navigational applications, since future accesses are unpredictable. We propose using the context in which an object is loaded as a predictor of future accesses, where context can be a stored collection of relationships, a query result, or a complex object. When an object O's state is loaded, similar state for other objects in O's context is prefetched. We present a design for maintaining context and using it to guide prefetch. We give performance measurements of its implementation in Microsoft Repository, showing up to a 70% reduction in running time. We describe variations that selectively apply the technique, exploit asynchronous access, and use application-supplied performance hints.

1 Introduction

One way to implement persistent objects is to map them to a relational database system (RDBMS). This approach has two main benefits: it provides persistent object views of existing relational databases; and it allows an RDBMS customer to build new object-oriented databases without introducing a new database engine, which avoids changes to database administration procedures and interoperability problems with existing applications. The approach is even more attractive with object-relational DBMSs, which support more of the desired object functionality in the database engine itself. The main disadvantage of mapping objects to relations is performance, which for many common usage scenarios is well below that of object-oriented database systems (OODBs) that use storage servers designed explicitly for object-oriented access.

An important feature of persistent object implementations (on any kind of storage system) is the ability to load persistent objects as active main memory objects, using the object model of the application environment (e.g., C++, Java, Smalltalk, OMG CORBA, or COM). This minimizes the impedance mismatch between the language and DBMS [11], but creates performance challenges for the database implementation, especially when mapped to an RDBMS rather than a custom storage system.

One major performance problem is that application object models are inherently navigational. That is, objects have references or relationships to other objects, which applications follow one at a time. Caching of recently-accessed objects is helpful to avoid accessing the RDBMS too often. But even with caching, if each access to a non-cached object entails a round-trip to the RDBMS, performance will be unbearably slow.

To get a feeling for the performance penalty of round-trips to an RDBMS, consider the following simple experiment. Define a relational database consisting of one table, whose 100,000 rows are 100 bytes each. Each row has a 16-byte ObjectID column which has a clustered index, three 24-byte string-valued columns, and three 4-byte integer-valued columns. Suppose the application knows which ObjectID values it wants, and it retrieves the rows for 100 randomly selected keys in batches of 1, 20, or 100 rows. Using a warm server cache to factor out the cost of disk accesses, we ran the experiment on an RDBMS product and retrieved 580 rows/second, 2700 rows/second, and 3200 rows/second for batch sizes 1, 20, and 100 respectively.[1] This corresponds to a retrieval time of 170 ms (milliseconds), 37ms, and 31ms for 100 rows.

**Proceedings of the 25th VLDB Conference
Edinburgh, Scotland, 1999**

[1] All experiments in this paper use commodity hardware. The hardware and software configurations are left unspecified, to avoid the usual legal and competitive problems with publishing performance numbers for commercial products. All performance measurements are averages over multiple trials, with more trials for higher variance measurements.

In this case, it is up to 5.5 times faster to get rows (i.e., object states) in a batch of 100 rows rather than a-row-at-a-time.

To minimize the performance penalty of database round-trips, applications often issue a query to identify the objects of interest, and then scan the resulting cursor, one object at a time. This tells the DBMS which objects to retrieve in batch, but often leaves open which pieces of the objects' state are desired, and hence which tables to access. Moreover, for many simple popular navigational patterns, such as following a relationship, it's a nuisance to issue a query. The application programmer would be happier to navigate from one object to the next, accessing the objects as it needs them, letting the DBMS automatically determine what data to prefetch. Programming interfaces for most OODBs, such as the ODMG model [7], satisfy this desire by offering both navigational and query access. But how can the DBMS figure out what to prefetch in response to navigational access? This is the central question addressed by this paper.

Some OODBs use page servers [15]. When accessing an object, the page-oriented OODB (POODB) retrieves the page containing the object, and therefore prefetches other data on the same page. Thus, by clustering data that will be accessed together on the same page, a POODB ensures effective prefetching. That is, the clustering approach amounts to a static prefetching algorithm. Clustering and prefetching are dual problems.[2]

Suppose that whenever a navigational application gets an object O for the first time, it shortly thereafter accesses most of the objects on O's page — the best case for a POODB, whose performance in this case is hard to beat. By comparison, when implementing objects on an RDBMS, there's an additional query processing step to find the same records that the POODB clustered on O's page. Even if the RDBMS clusters the records the same way, it still takes more time to find them and gather them up for transmission to the application than the POODB, which simply ships the page.

Even if the POODB's clustering strategy is optimal for the average workload, access patterns vary and the page-oriented prefetching will make mistakes. Sometimes it will make useless prefetches, where the fetched data isn't subsequently accessed. At other times it will miss prefetch opportunities, because a predictable access pattern hits objects that are mostly on different pages. These mistakes are inherent in the architecture: static clustering of records and page-oriented accesses.

A system that maps objects to an RDBMS (we'll call it an *OMRDB*) probably cannot match the POODB for access patterns that follow the POODB's physical data clustering. However, it may be able to earn back some of that lost performance, in two ways. First, since the OMRDB uses a row server, not a page server, it can prefetch an arbitrary combination of rows. That is, it can use knowledge of recent application behavior to identify combinations of rows worth prefetching, and then use its powerful query processor to find and retrieve those rows in one round-trip, whether or not the data is physically clustered. By contrast, a POODB generally retrieves pages from the server on demand. For a given data layout, both OMRDB and POODB will retrieve the same number of pages. But query-based prefetching allows an OMRDB to prefetch rows before they're referenced, reducing latency. Second, if the density of desired rows on each page is low, then the OMRDB will make better use of client cache than a POODB (since it prefetches only desired rows) and will use less network bandwidth to transfer prefetched rows. Of course, OODBs that use object servers rather than page servers can use this OMRDB tactic, so they too can benefit from the techniques described in this paper.

When prefetching objects, an OMRDB has two related decisions to make: which objects to prefetch and which portions of those objects' state to prefetch. To illustrate our technique, we focus first on the latter question with a simple example (see Figure 1). Suppose an application accesses a relationship R on object O, which returns a set of objects, S. Suppose the state of each object in S is spread across multiple tables. The application may not access all of that state of each object. To avoid prefetching state that the application does not need, the OMRDB delays deciding which state to prefetch. Instead, it simply retrieves the object IDs of the objects in S (making a round-trip to the RDBMS) and waits to see what the application does next. Suppose the application selects an object O′ in S (which is now in application cache) and accesses attribute A in O′. This requires another round-trip. But rather than just retrieving A for O′, the OMRDB retrieves (prefetches) A for all objects in S. This is useful if the application later accesses A for many of those other objects in S, a very common access pattern in workloads we have observed.

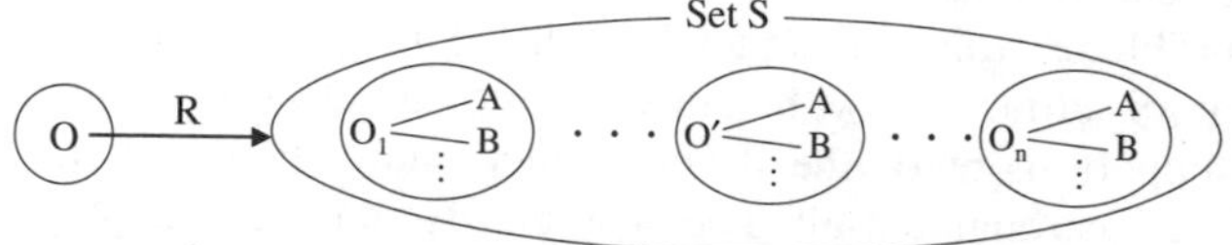

Figure 1 Simple Example of Context-Based Prefetch

Notice that the prefetch decision is based on the application's access pattern — it is not statically determined. O′ could be a member of many collections in the database. The decision to prefetch A for all objects in S is based on the fact that O′ was fetched as part of S, and not

[2] Pointed out to us by Michael Franklin.

some other collection. The OMRDB must remember this fact, to use S as the basis for prefetching A. This is the core idea of our prefetching technique: The OMRDB uses the context in which each object is accessed as a predictor of other objects that will be accessed later.

To implement this approach, the OMRDB creates a *structure context* for each object, which describes the structure in which the object was fetched. Examples of "structures" are stored collections of relationships, query results, and complex objects. When accessing some state of an object O, the OMRDB prefetches the same pieces of the state for other objects in O's structure context, as in the example of accessing O''s attribute A for all objects in O''s structure context S. We call this approach *context-controlled prefetch*. As in the above example, the approach is beneficial whenever all objects in a context undergo similar manipulation.

The rest of the paper is organized as follows. Section 2 summarizes related work on the general problem of implementing OMRDBs efficiently. Section 3 presents the basic mechanisms for context-controlled prefetch. Since the technique is not cost effective in all situations, Section 4 proposes performance hints to selectively enable the optimizations. A summary of our implementation in Microsoft[3] Repository version 2.0 (in Microsoft SQL Server 7.0) is discussed in Section 5. Performance measurements in Section 6 show up to a 3-fold speedup due to these optimizations. Section 7 describes extensions for asynchronous prefetch, lazy loading of objects, and prefetching across paths. Section 8 is the conclusion.

2 Related Work

Although much has been published on the implementation of persistent objects, very little of it uses an RDBMS as the underlying store. Keller *et al.* provide a good overview of the issues [14]. Most papers assume that the set of objects to be retrieved is defined by a query, such as [16, 17, 18, 23], where the issues are running the query efficiently and assembling the objects in the OMRDB, and caching the query result for reuse with later queries [13]. Navigational access is applied to the result of the query, so there's nothing to prefetch. Descriptions of some commercial products that map objects to relations can be found in [19, 22, 24, 27].

Proponents of OODBs have published many white papers to show that their products outperform a similar implementation on RDBMSs, but little of this has made it into the scientific literature. A useful bibliography is [9].

Prefetching architectures based on recent reference behavior are described in [12, 21]. Palmer and Zdonik use pre-analyzed reference traces to guide prefetch [21]. Curewitz, Krishnan and Vitter use compression algorithms to guide page prefetch based on recent reference behavior [12]. Both approaches work when the exact same objects or pages are retrieved again and again. By contrast, our approach works for any reference sequence that conforms to our generic navigational pattern, even the first (and possibly only) time the objects are accessed, and allows application programmers to influence prefetch decisions. The approaches appear to be complementary and could potentially be used in the same system, a possible subject for further investigation.

3 Using Structure Context

3.1 Object Model

To describe details of the approach, we need to define an object model. We choose one that is similar to those in common use, such as the ODMG model [7], COM [26], and UML [3, 25]. The approach is largely insensitive to the details of the model used here. It should work well for any model that groups objects into structures.

Each persistent object has a persistent *state* that consists of attributes. Each attribute value can be a *scalar*, an *object*, or a *set*.

- Each scalar-valued attribute conforms to a *scalar type*, which gives the name of the attribute and its data type, such as string, integer, or Boolean.
- Every object has a scalar-valued ObjectID attribute that uniquely identifies the object.
- Each object-valued attribute is one side of a *binary relationship*. That is, each relationship consists of two objects that refer to each other.
- Each set-valued attribute contains an object of type set, which in turn contains a set of either scalar values or object references. The concept of set is a representative example of a generic structure type. Other structure types would be handled analogously to sets, such as sequence, array, table, or record structure, but we do not consider them here.

Each object conforms to an object type. Each *object type* has a name and a set of attribute types it can contain. Each binary relationship conforms to a *relationship type*, which gives the name of the relationship, the two object types that can be related, and for each of the two object types, the attribute name by which the reference is accessed.

A *class* is a body of code that implements one or more object types. It includes a class factory that produces objects that are instances of the class. It also includes code that implements the usual read and write operations

[3] Microsoft is a trademark of Microsoft Corporation.

on all of the attributes and structures of the object types that the class implements.

3.2 Operations

The set of navigational object-oriented operations that we consider are GetObject, GetAttribute, GetNext, and ExecuteQuery. These are meant to be a representative sample of the kinds of navigational operations found in programming interfaces for persistent object systems.

- GetObject(ObjectID) returns a running copy of the persistent object whose unique identifier is ObjectID.
- O.GetAttribute(AttrName) returns the value of the attribute AttrName from object O. (The notation O.M means execute method M on object O.) The result is a scalar, object, or set, depending on the attribute type. A set has an associated cursor, initially pointing to the set's first element.
- S.GetNext either returns the scalar or object identified by set S's cursor and advances the cursor, or, if the cursor points beyond the end of S, returns Null.
- ExecuteQuery(Q) returns the set of objects that satisfy query Q's qualification (as in OQL [7, 10]).

3.3 Database Schema

An OMRDB maps objects to rows of tables. A class maps to a table whose columns represent its single-valued attributes. Our optimizations are applicable independent of the rules used to map attributes of a class to a particular table. However, for completeness, we give a few details of mappings that are commonly used.

The simplest mapping is to map a class to exactly one table that contains all of the class's attributes. But more complex mappings are also popular. For example, suppose class B inherits from a class A. If both classes are concrete (i.e., have instances), then there are separate tables for B and A. A's columns, which B inherits, may be stored in both A's and B's tables (Figure 2(ii)), or only in A's table (Figure 2(iii), sometimes called "vertical partitioning" [14]). In the latter case, B's state is reconstructed by joining A's and B's tables. If A is abstract, then its columns might only be stored in tables of concrete classes that inherit from it, in which case it has no corresponding table (i.e., in Figure 2, only store Table T_B, sometimes called "horizontal partitioning").

We assume each many-to-many relationship type is represented in a "junction" table. There could be a separate junction table for each relationship type, with columns SourceObjectID and TargetObjectID, or a generic junction table for all relationship types with columns SourceObjectID, RelationshipTypeID, and TargetObjectID. Each one-to-many relationship can be represented either in a

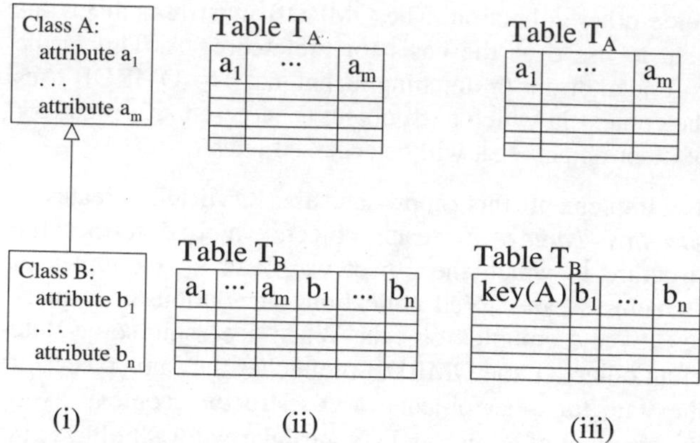

Figure 2 Mapping Classes to Tables

junction table or as a foreign key on the "many side." E.g., if the one-to-many is parent-child, then the foreign key to the parent is stored in the child.

An attribute consisting of a set of scalars can be stored in a table with columns ObjectID, AttributeID (short form of the attribute name), and Value. If the set's maximum cardinality N is known, it could instead be stored as columns of the class's table, such as $AttrName_1$, ..., $AttrName_N$. Since these two table structures are isomorphic to one-to-many relationships and single-valued attributes (respectively), the prefetch scenarios for a set of scalar attributes are isomorphic to those other two cases as well and therefore are not treated further in this paper.

3.4 The Prefetch Pattern

As discussed in Section 1, the main approach is to maintain a structure context (or, more simply, a *context*) for each object, which describes the structure in which the object was loaded, and to use that context to guide later prefetch decisions. In this section, we explain one usage of the approach in detail. We reapply this usage to other operations in the next section.

Consider the following operation sequence:

a. S = O.GetAttribute(R), which returns a set S of objects, which is the value of relationship attribute R.

b. O′ = S.GetNext, which returns an object O′ in S.

c. V = O′.GetAttribute(A), which returns the value V of scalar-valued attribute A of O′.

This is the scenario of Figure 1. Attribute A corresponds to a column of a table, T, containing (some of) the state of O′'s class, C. Unless T is very wide (e.g., has lots of long columns), it costs little more to retrieve all of T's columns that are part of C's state than to retrieve only A. This is because most of the cost is in the disk accesses, which retrieve all of the columns from disk whether or not they are fetched by the OMRDB. Thus, if there is a good chance that some of those columns will be accessed, then it is worth prefetching all of those columns of T for O′. Moreover, since O′ was retrieved via S, if we expect other objects in S to be accessed similarly to O′, then we should prefetch all of those columns of T for all objects in S, not just for O′. This avoids later round-trips to the database for each object in S.

The optimization is illustrated in Figure 3. Table T is shown in Figure 3(i), with relationships, such as R, implemented by a junction table J. Steps (a) and (c) above are illustrated in Figure 3(ii) and (iii) respectively. Notice that step (c) uses the same selection clauses for J as step (a), and then joins with T to get the columns of T for *all* objects in O.GetAttribute(R), not just for O′.

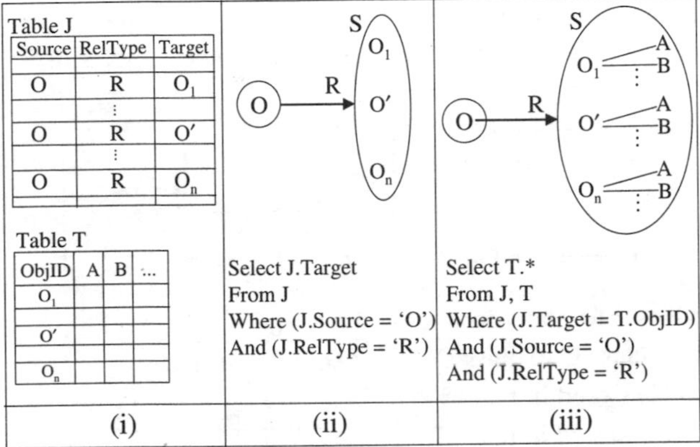

Figure 3 Prefetching Scenario

The experiment in Section 1 suggests this prefetch is profitable if at least 4-5 items in the collection are later accessed (since batch retrieval is 4-5 times the cost of a single-row retrieval). However, the addition of object-level processing reduces the fractional contribution of DB round-trips to total cost. Thus, in our experiments, across a variety of workloads and database profiles, the prefetch is profitable if at least 3 items are subsequently accessed (for our combination of data server, network, etc.). The more items that are accessed, the more round-trips that are saved by the prefetch, hence the greater the benefit.

If objects in S have state in two tables, T and T′, is it worth getting attributes from both of them? Usually not. For example, we extended the experiment in Section 1 by duplicating the table, to model T and T′. Getting 100 rows from both tables in one round-trip added 50% to the execution time over retrieving only from T. So the cost of needlessly getting T′'s columns is high. Also, the benefit is modest, since retrieving those rows from both tables was only 19% slower in two round-trips vs. retrieving the join in one round-trip. Thus, one should only retrieve T′'s columns if they are almost certain to be needed.

Since the technique heavily uses cache, the interactions of prefetching and cache management need careful attention. E.g., if the cache is nearly full or if the data to prefetch is very large, then the prefetch may not work well. We will see other examples of this later.

To generate the SQL query shown in Figure 3(iii), the OMRDB needs the context of O′. The context should include the information that was used to create the set S initially, namely, the object ID of the relationship's source, O, and the relationship name, R. These are the parameters that are needed to construct the SQL query, which retrieves the desired attributes of all objects in the context.

We expect it is worth supporting variations of this pattern where only attribute A or a predefined subset of attributes is retrieved, and not all the attributes of its table. However, as this is only a slight variation of our main idea, we don't consider it further in this paper.

3.5 Case Analysis

We generalize Section 3.4 to other navigational access patterns that suggest future navigational behavior. These suggestions lead naturally to prefetch recommendations, which retrieve the data needed to service the later accesses before those accesses occur. Of course, recent navigational accesses don't guarantee that those later accesses will occur, so prefetch recommendations must be applied selectively, an issue we will discuss in Section 4. For now, we simply describe potentially useful prefetches and how to implement them, for each of the operation types in Section 3.2.

In the following descriptions, we omit the initial test to determine if the requested data is already in cache and therefore does not need to be fetched.

GetObject(ObjectID) – Prefetch some or all of the object's state. Note that to load the object into main memory, the OMRDB only needs to know the object's class (to know what class to instantiate) and that the object exists (to know whether to return an error). Prefetching other object state is optional at this stage. Set the object's context to null, which means it was loaded directly, not as part of a larger structure.

O.GetAttribute(AttrName) – where AttrName is the name of an attribute in O's class. There are six cases to consider, Case (i) – Case (vi) below:

Case (i) If AttrName is a single-valued object reference, and O's context is null, then get the reference to the object from the database. If the object reference is stored as a foreign key in a table containing other attributes of O, then retrieve those other attributes too.

For example, suppose AttrName is a many-to-one relationship R from O's class C to class D (see Figure 4). Suppose C's table T_C(ObjID, A_1, …, A_n, FKey) contains scalar attributes A_1, …, A_n of C and foreign key attribute FKey that contains the object ID of an object in D related via R. Since getting the reference to O_D in D involves accessing the FKey column of O's row in T_C, prefetch the other attributes A_1, …, A_n of that row too.

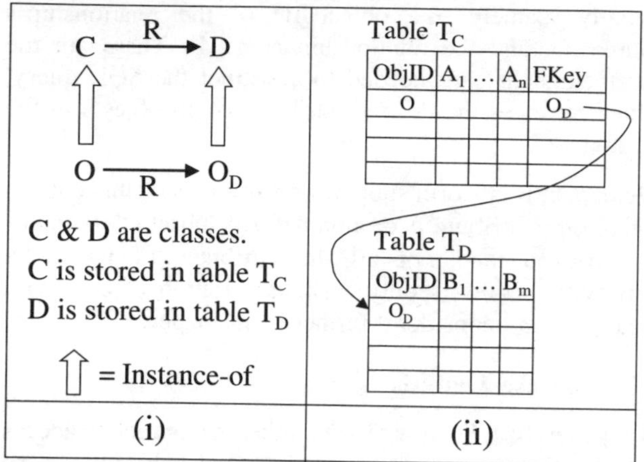

Figure 4 Prefetching Attributes with a Foreign Key

If T_C is indexed on the compound key [ObjID, FKey], rather than just ObjID, then the query processor can get O_D without accessing O's row, making it cheaper to retrieve FKey by itself. If the index on [ObjID, FKey] is non-clustered, this raises the incremental cost of getting A_1, …, A_n, which should therefore be prefetched too only if there's a high probability of subsequent access.

Case (ii) If AttrName is a scalar and O's context is null, then simply retrieve the attribute. As in Case (i), retrieve other attributes of O's state that are in the table containing AttrName's column. Here and in Case (i), prefetching those other attributes is cost-beneficial if some of them are subsequently referenced.

Case (iii) If AttrName is an object reference, and O's context is a set S′, then prefetch the reference for *every* object O′ in S′, not just for O. That is, run one SQL statement that returns the ObjectID value of AttrName for all objects in S′. As in Case (i), if the object references are stored as foreign keys in a table containing other attributes of O′, then retrieve those other attributes too. Prefetching the object reference for other objects in S′ is cost-beneficial if at least several other objects in S′ are subsequently accessed. This case is essentially the same as Figure 4, except that multiple rows of T_C are retrieved (one for each object in S′) instead of just one (for O).

Case (iv) If AttrName is a scalar and O's context is a set of objects, then O.GetAttribute(AttrName) corresponds to step (c) in Section 3.4. Do the prefetch described there and in Figure 3(iii).

Case (v) If AttrName is set-valued and O's context is null, then retrieve the set's content for O, which is a set S of either scalar values or objects. In the latter case, assign S to be the context of each object in S.

If S is a set of objects and the object references are stored as foreign keys in the referenced objects, then retrieve other attributes of the referenced objects stored in the same table as the foreign key. Modifying the example of Figure 4 so that AttrName is a one-to-many (rather than many-to-one) relationship R from O's class C to class D, we get Figure 5, where B_1, … B_m can be retrieved along with objects in D referenced by O. As usual, prefetching those other attributes is cost-beneficial if some of them are referenced later for at least several other objects in S.

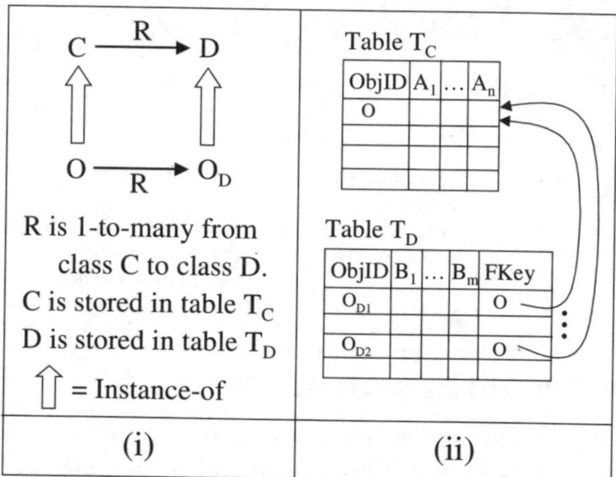

Figure 5 Prefetching Attributes of Referenced Objects

Case (vi) If AttrName is a set (of scalars or objects) and O's context is a set S′, then prefetch the AttrName set for every object in S′. For example, suppose AttrName is a relationship R to a set of objects. Then execute *one* SQL statement that returns a table of <$ObjID_1$, $ObjID_2$> pairs, where $ObjID_1$ denotes an object in S′ and $ObjID_2$ denotes an object referenced by $ObjID_1$ via R, thereby prefetching Object-IDs of members of the R-set of *every* object in S′. This is analogous to Section 3.4, where the scalar attributes of all objects in S′ are prefetched. For the R-set S_i referenced by each $ObjID_{1,i}$ in S′, assign S_i to be the context of each object in S_i. The prefetch is cost-beneficial if those R-sets are accessed for at least several other objects in S′.

Continuing the example of Figure 5, if R is one-to-many from O's class C to class D, and is represented as a foreign key in D's table T_D, then the attributes of objects in D can be prefetched too, modulo the additional cost, depending on whether FKey is part of the compound index on T_D.

ExecuteQuery(Q) – We apply context-based prefetch to the set that results from the execution of a query, just as we do for a set of stored object references in cases (iii) and (iv). We could do this by executing the query, saving the resulting ObjectID's in a set, and sending the ObjectID's to the RDBMS on each prefetch. However, this is inefficient for large query results, and problematic since the query that does the prefetch could exceed the maximum size of a SQL statement or stored procedure call. We could re-execute the query on each prefetch, but this too would be inefficient unless the query is cheap. Therefore, we store the context on the server in a temporary table.

So, assume each session has a temporary table TEMP(SetID, ObjectID) in the DBMS. Associate a unique SetID, s, with the query. Map the query into an Insert statement that appends rows <s, o> to TEMP for each ObjectID o in the result of the query. Execute the Insert and return the ObjectID's of the query result into a set, S, also identified by s.

Creating this context is cost-beneficial if attributes of the objects in S are subsequently accessed, making prefetches of those attributes cost-beneficial, and if the query is too expensive to re-execute to perform the prefetch.

TEMP can be created any time after starting the database session, but no later than the first call to ExecuteQuery.

Like any query result, a query context in TEMP can be used across transaction boundaries only if the application is using read-committed, not repeatable-read, isolation.

S.GetNext – Return the designated element of S. Prefetching was accomplished when S was loaded, i.e., in GetObject(ObjectID) or O.GetAttribute(AttrName).

3.6 Managing Structure Context

Structure context is part of the state of a loaded object. The context's lifetime is governed by that of the object. Thus, when the object is released, the context is deallocated too. This includes context information that is maintained with the object by the OMRDB, typically in main memory. Also, when releasing a set that was the result of an ExecuteQuery, it includes deleting rows of the temporary table containing the cached result of the query. Like any deallocation, the latter can be done lazily and asynchronously with respect to other processing.

Like persistent database tables, the performance characteristics of temporary tables must be carefully analyzed when using them to cache query results. For example, depending on how space is managed, it may be important to preallocate temporary table space. It may or may not be valuable to have an index on SetID, depending on how queries are processed, the size of query results, and how many query results are concurrently active.

Suppose an object is loaded multiple times via different navigational paths. For example, an application might load object O via O′.GetAttribute(AttrName), where AttrName is a set S containing O, and later reload O via GetObject(o), where o is O's ObjectID. In some programming interfaces, the later operation does not return the same loaded object, but rather returns another copy of the same persistent object. If so, then one would expect the two objects to share their cached persistent object state, since they refer to the same object. However, since the two objects were loaded via different paths, they should have different contexts. In the example, the first object's context is S, while the second's is null.

4 Performance Hints

Since the prefetch optimizations of Section 3.5 are not always cost-effective, it is important to be able to enable and disable them. Enabling an optimization is essentially a performance hint to the underlying OMRDB. This general approach of application-supplied hints has been adopted by other object-to-relational mapping systems, such as [20], and in other commercial products [8].

The main optimizations that are worth controlling in this way are the following:

1A. **A**ttributes for **1** object - When accessing an object O, prefetch all of O's scalar attributes.

1R. **R**elationships for **1** object - When accessing an object O, prefetch all of O's references to other objects.

MA. **A**ttributes for **M**any objects - When accessing a scalar attribute A of an object O, prefetch all of the attributes in A's table for all objects in O's set context.

MR. **R**elationships for **M**any objects - When accessing a relationship attribute A of an object O, prefetch the objects related via A for every object in O's set context.

Some contexts are very large — too large to prefetch the attributes or relationships for every object in the context. One could specify a threshold for context size, above which the MA or MR prefetch is disabled. Or, it may be better to stream in the prefetched data in batches. This requires finding a query that retrieves a subset of the data to be prefetched plus a remainder query that identifies the remaining data to be prefetched. This isn't always doable. For example, in MA, to prefetch attribute values for a large unordered set, we would need a column value that partitions the set into non-overlapping subsets.

It is often appropriate to enable a prefetch optimization for an application's entire execution, but sometimes it is not. For example, if an application accesses all members of some sets but only one member of others, MA will speed up accesses to the former and slow down accesses to the latter. Thus, it is beneficial to enable and disable the optimizations dynamically during its execution.

Performance hints can be added as tags in an information model to specify the default prefetch behavior of a class. For example, a class C could be tagged to enable MR but disable MA. Such default behavior can be overridden by the application.

Although prefetch is enabled and disabled dynamically, it is still beneficial to maintain context for each loaded object. This makes it possible to perform context-based prefetch on an object that was loaded when prefetching was disabled. Since maintaining context is cheap, there is little benefit to disabling it, with one possible exception: The result of a query is cached in a temporary table for use as the context of each object in that result. Since adding the result to the temporary table has non-negligible cost, it is probably worth disabling in cases where it is known to be ineffective.

Although the manual control that performance hints offer is worthwhile, it would be even better if the system could automatically decide when to enable and disable prefetching. One approach is to run the application on sample data to generate traces, and then analyze the traces to determine whether each type of optimization is cost effective for a given run. Another approach is to statically analyze the application to predict certain access patterns. For example, a common pattern is to call GetAttribute(R), where R is a relationship that returns a set of object references, and then loop through the result, accessing attributes of each object. In this case, the program would be modified to enable MA before entering the loop. Even finer grained control is possible here, since the exact set of attributes that will be referenced could be made known in the hint, thereby reducing the cost of the prefetch.

A cache control mechanism would also be beneficial, to reduce the amount of prefetching when the OMRDB's cache is stressed. The cache manager could track the amount of free space, for this purpose.

5 Implementation in Microsoft Repository

The prefetch optimizations of Section 3 are implemented in the latest version of Microsoft Repository, whose storage engine is a persistent object layer implemented on top of Microsoft SQL Server. The product's object model, table layout, and API do not include all of the alternatives in Sections 3.1 - 3.3. The differences that are relevant to the prefetch optimizations being considered here are:

- All relationships are currently stored in a single junction table, like Table J in Figure 3(i), not as foreign keys in class-oriented tables.
- The object model is COM, where classes implement interfaces and interfaces have single-valued scalar properties and relationship-valued collections. Each interface's scalar properties are stored in (i.e., are columns of) one table, each of whose rows contain state for an object whose class implements the interface. Each table can store the properties of many interfaces, but a class's interfaces need not all be stored in one table.
- There is an additional method, ObjectInstances, that gets the set of all objects that are instances of either a given class or a class that supports a given interface. Objects that are retrieved by this method have the retrieved set as their context, which is represented by the identity of the class or interface. This is very similar to Case (v) in Section 3.5, O.GetAttribute(AttrName), where AttrName designates a set of object references.
- Each time a persistent object P is loaded, a new COM object is created, which shares its cached state with other COM objects that represent P. The context is stored in the COM object, since each load operation for P may be via a different navigational path and therefore have a different context to guide prefetch.

The object model, table layout, and API are described in detail in [1, 2].

6 Performance Measurements

The prefetch optimizations as implemented in Microsoft Repository have been useful for many customer applications we have tested, so they are frequently enabled — especially MA, which we have found is almost always beneficial. However, it is hard to report on these in a way that bears scientific scrutiny, since each application yields a varying workload that is hard to characterize succinctly. We therefore ran some more controlled experiments to show how the optimizations work in practice.

6.1 Experiment 1 – The 007 Benchmark

A good test to show the benefits of MA is the 007 benchmark [4, 5, 6], since it is a highly regular workload that is representative of many persistent object applications (a brief summary is in the Appendix). We ran the 007 queries and traversals using Microsoft Repository on the medium sized 007 database (225MB). We ran with a cold server cache, to ensure the optimizations are fully penalized for useless prefetches. We did not run 007 structural modifications, since their behavior is not affected by our optimizations.

Queries Q1-Q3 and Q7 are all of the form: retrieve a set of objects (in our case using ExecuteQuery) and access the objects' state. Q8 also accesses state, to form a subquery for each object in an outer query (it retrieves a set of object pairs). So they all benefit from optimization

MA, which prefetches the objects' state in one round-trip based on the cached query result. Figure 6(i) reports the percentage improvement in running time over an execution with no prefetch optimizations enabled (i.e., ((old-new)/old)×100). The benefit varies based on the size of the result and the algorithm for joining the temp table (containing cached query results) with the attribute table at the server. Query Q4 is of the same form as Q1-Q3, but the query plan for the prefetch is sub-optimal, making MA ineffective. None of the queries benefit from 1R or MR, because they don't access any relationships, nor from 1A, because only one attribute of each object is accessed. Query Q5 simply counts the number of objects in the result of a query, so there's no benefit to prefetching properties or relationships.

007 Test	Benefit of MA
Q1	87 %
Q2	17 %
Q3	54 %
Q4	-39 %
Q5	0 %
Q7	73 %
Q8	42 %

(i)

007 Test	Benefit of MA
T1	1 %
T2a	-11 %
T2b	34 %
T2c	31 %
T3a	-12 %
T3b	34 %
T3c	39 %
T6	0 %

(ii)

Figure 6 Benefit of Prefetch in 007

Traversals T1-T6 navigate relationships starting from a root. Like the queries, traversals T2b,c and T3b,c access attributes and therefore benefit from MA. T1 and T6 do not access attributes, so MA has no effect. T2a and T3a access only one object in each collection, so prefetching attributes for all objects is a cost that has no compensating benefit. Thus, MA decreases their performance.

In principle, traversals T1-T3 should benefit from MR, but they actually do not. The traversals visit the entire bill of materials hierarchy of a base assembly, which includes 655,000 atomic parts. This overflows the client cache, causing prefetched objects to be replaced before being accessed. Currently we do not handle this situation very gracefully in that we let the cache overflow. In a future version, we will have a more adaptive algorithm.

6.2 Experiment 2 – XML Export

Another application with a highly regular workload is the XML export utility that ships with the product. We wrote a program that uses the utility to export a set of objects reachable from a root, by doing a breadth-first traversal from the given root and writing them out as an XML stream. We exported a UML model consisting of 3100 objects and 3900 relationships. The execution time was 267 ms with no optimizations, 117ms with 1R enabled, 220ms with MA, and 78ms with both 1R and MA. That is, the execution was 56%, 18%, and 71% faster with optimizations 1R, MA, and 1R+MA, respectively.

1R helps because in UML each object has many relationship types, all of which are accessed, either to export them or determine that they're empty. MA helps because if a relationship is non-empty, then attributes of all related objects are exported. These benefits are nearly independent, in that the benefit of 1R+MA (71%) is nearly the sum of the benefits of 1R and MA (56%+18%=74%).

6.3 Experiment 3 – Measuring MR

To measure the benefits of MR in a controlled setting, we created an object hierarchy stored as relationships in a junction table like Table J of Figure 3(i), with a clustered index on its key (Source, RelType, Target). The hierarchy has a top level fan-out of 100, and a second level fan-out of 20. We traversed the hierarchy by running SQL. The baseline ran a SQL query to get the 100 children of the root followed by a query for each child to get its 20 children. To model MR, we replaced the 100 queries for grandchildren by one query to get all grandchildren. The latter retrieves the same amount of data as the former, but replaces the fixed overhead of 100 queries by that of just one query. The resulting execution time was 71% faster with MR enabled than disabled.

MR is sensitive to the size of the context to which it's applied, since that affects the number of queries it saves. For example, running the previous experiment on a hierarchy with top level fan-out of 20 and second level fan-out of 100, the benefit of MR is only 33%, less than half as much as the previous case. The same amount of data is retrieved as before, but only 20 queries for grandchildren are replaced by one query. This effect also explains, in part, the lack of benefit of MR in 007 traversals, since all the fan-outs are of size 3. In XML, MR actually hurts performance, probably because the contexts are small and the prefetch requires an extra expensive join.

7 Extensions

7.1 Asynchronous Prefetch

To improve response time further, it is desirable to do the minimal work necessary to return from each data access call and prefetch any additional data asynchronously with respect to the call. To some extent, an application can do this manually by reordering its logic so that the OMRDB gets data before the application actually needs it. Beyond this rather crude recommendation, there are two approaches to making the prefetch asynchronous: pipeline the prefetch or prefetch after processing the request.

In the pipelined approach, the OMRDB issues a query to retrieve the requested and prefetched data together. When the first packet arrives from the DB server, the OMRDB starts populating its cache. As soon as the requested data arrives, the OMRDB returns to the application, but it continues processing packets asynchronously until all the prefetched data have arrived.

If the DBMS supports multiple active statements on a database session, then a second application request can be executed while a previous prefetch is still active. Most DBMSs do not support this, since it requires parallel nested transactions so that concurrent SQL statements can be independently backed out. Without this feature, a second session is needed to avoid delaying an application call while a prefetch is tying up the session. In any case, if the application later asks for an item that is still being prefetched, it is blocked.

In the non-pipelined approach, the OMRDB retrieves the requested data plus a subset of data to be prefetched. After receiving this data, it returns to the application and asynchronously issues a query for the remaining data to prefetch. However, as discussed in Section 4, finding a query that retrieves a subset of the data to be prefetched plus a remainder query that gets the remaining data to be prefetched is sometimes infeasible.

In some cases, it is unavoidable to fetch the entire result before returning to the caller. For example, Microsoft Repository stores sequenced collections as rows linked by back pointers [1]. If an application requests an item of the collection other than the first, then all of the collection elements must be loaded into cache for the engine to determine the requested item. This defeats both the pipelined and non-pipelined approaches.

Finally, statistics are needed to determine how much to prefetch. The goal is to fetch only a small amount to avoid delaying the application much by the prefetch, but fetch enough to keep the application busy while the second, asynchronous prefetch is running.

7.2 Prefetching Across Paths

We can extend context-based prefetch to apply to paths of relationships. For example, consider a persistent object base that contains a database schema definition object, which contains table definition objects, each of which contains column definition objects, each of which is related to a data type definition object. When accessing a column of the first table definition, MR will prefetch column definitions of all table definitions. We showed in Section 6.3 that this can yield significant improvements. It may also be beneficial to prefetch the scalar attributes of those column definitions (i.e., Section 3.5, Case (v)) and their relationships to data type definitions (adding another hop to the path). To estimate the benefit, recall in Section 3.4 that getting 100 rows from two identical tables with 100-byte rows in 2 round-trips is 19% slower than getting the join in one round-trip. One could extend the hints of Section 4 to specify when to prefetch across such a path.

An issue with this approach is the representation of the inherently hierarchical result of the prefetch, when a relational query is used. As observed in [17], in a parent-child relationship, when retrieving all the children of a parent, the parent information is repeated for every child due to the normalization inherent in relational queries. Possible solutions are to return the result in a nested table, a tree structure, or an XML stream (that represents the tree structure), all of which require some extension to the underlying RDBMS.

7.3 Lazy Loading of Sets

Suppose O.GetAttribute(AttrName) returns a set, S, of objects (i.e., Case (iv) and Case (vi) in Section 3.5). One could execute GetAttribute by storing only its definition (i.e., "O.GetAttribute(AttrName)") and not its instances in main memory. If S is used only to insert new objects, then the existing state of S never needs to be loaded, a significant optimization. If existing objects in S are retrieved, then its instances can be loaded on the first invocation of S.GetNext.

Suppose it is known that all objects in S are instances of the same concrete class C (rather than different specializations of C). Now even GetNext can avoid loading instances of S, by creating a hollow instance O′ of C. This can be done using only cached type information, without accessing database instances. The state of O′ is populated only when one of its attributes is accessed. At this point, MA kicks in, which retrieves that attribute (and possibly others in the same table) for all objects in S. This prefetch gets the object IDs of all objects in S as a side effect, which allows S finally to be populated with instances. Thus, the initial round-trip to the RDBMS to get the object IDs of objects in S is entirely avoided, leaving only one round-trip to get the attributes of all objects in S, thus halving the number of round-trips in this scenario.

While this benefit is appealing, unfortunately the line of logic to attain it is not quite sound: If S is empty, then S.GetNext should return Null. If this is known to be impossible (e.g., because the set has an enforced integrity constraint saying it has non-zero cardinality), then the technique works fine. Otherwise, if it can return Null, then it is not valid for it to return a hollow instance of C. Therefore, to benefit from this optimization, a change is needed in the programming interface. There are several options: a hint could be issued before the first call to GetNext, to tell the system what attribute(s) to prefetch; the GetNext call itself could optionally include a list of attributes of interest; or the semantics of GetNext could be modified so that the first GetNext on an empty set returns an object and an exception is raised only when attempting to access one of that object's attributes. The use of a hint strikes us as the best of the alternatives.

8 Conclusion

We described a technique for predicting useful prefetches when a navigational object-oriented interface is implemented on a relational DBMS. We presented a design for the technique and measured its performance in a commercial product, Microsoft Repository 2.0. We proposed a number of extensions, some of which would benefit from further work, such as automatically issuing hints to enable the prefetch optimization and prefetching across paths of relationships.

Overall, there has been much published about efficient implementations of persistent objects. Having worked on an implementation of persistent objects on a relational database for the past several years, we feel that the problem of optimizing the performance of such a system is only partially understood and would benefit from much more research. Given the advent of object-relational DBMSs, and the need to offer persistent object interfaces on top, the importance of this problem is growing.

Appendix – Summary of 007

The 007 benchmark is based on a bill-of-materials database. In the medium database, each assembly has 3 sub-assemblies, and so on through 7 levels. Each assembly has also has 3 composite parts, each of which has an associated document and has 200 interconnected atomic parts. The following queries and retrievals are taken from [6], paraphrased to save space:

Q1 – Given 10 random atomic part id's, get the atomic parts (that exist) and the number retrieved.

Q2 – Given a range of dates containing the last 1% of dates in atomic parts, retrieve the atomic parts.

Q3 – Given a range of dates containing the last 10% of dates in atomic parts, retrieve the atomic parts.

Q4 – Given 100 random document titles, for each document, find all base (i.e., level 1) assemblies that use the composite part corresponding to the document. Also return the number of such base assemblies.

Q5– Find all base assemblies that use a composite part whose build date is later than that of the base assembly. Also report the number of base assemblies found.

Q7 – Scan all atomic parts.

Q8 – Find all pairs of documents and atomic parts where the atomic part's document id equals the document's id. Return the number of pairs found.

T1 – Traverse the assembly hierarchy. For each base assembly, visit its unshared composite parts. For each composite part, do a depth first search on its atomic parts. When done, return the number of atomic parts visited.

T2 – Same as T1, but swap attributes x and y for some of the objects:
a. Update one atomic part per composite part.
b. Update every atomic part encountered.
c. Update each atomic part in a composite part four times.

T3 – Same as T2, but update the (indexed) date field.

T6 – Same at T1, but for each composite part, visit only its root atomic part.

Note that there is no Q6, T4, or T5 in 007. Traversals T7 and T8 are omitted because they run very fast and therefore lead to inaccurate (high variance) measurements.

Acknowledgments

We thank Thomas Bergstraesser and Jason Carlson for many stimulating discussions about the performance of Microsoft Repository. We are also very grateful to Jayaram Mulupuru and Daniel Reib for implementing the approaches described in this paper and to Jim Hance and Gary Miao for measuring them, all of which helped uncover many of the detailed problems we addressed.

References

1. Bernstein, P.A., B. Harry, P.J. Sanders, D. Shutt, J. Zander, "The Microsoft Repository," *Proc. 23rd VLDB Conf.*, 1997, pp. 3-12.

2. Bernstein, P.A., T. Bergstraesser, J. Carlson, S. Pal, P.J. Sanders, D. Shutt, "Microsoft Repository Version 2 and the Open Information Model," *Information Systems 24(2),* 1999, to appear.

3. Booch, G., J. Rumbaugh, I. Jacobson, *The Unified Modeling Language User Guide*. Addison-Wesley, Reading, MA, 1998.

4. Carey, Michael J., David J. DeWitt, Jeffrey F. Naughton, "The 007 Benchmark," *Proc. 1993 ACM SIGMOD Conf.*, pp. 12-21.

5. Carey, Michael J., David J. DeWitt, Chander Kant, Jeffrey F. Naughton, "A Status Report on the 007 Benchmark," *Proc. OOPSLA 1994*, pp. 414-426.

6. Carey, Michael J., David J. DeWitt, Jeffrey F. Naughton, "The OO7 Benchmark," technical report, ftp.cs.wisc.edu., Univ. of Wisconson, Jan. 1994.

7. Cattell, R.G.G., D. Barry, D. Bartels, M. Berler, J. Eastman, S. Gamerman, D. Jordan, A. Springer, H.

Strickland, D. Wade. *The Object Database Standard: ODMG 2.0*, Morgan Kaufmann Publishers, 1997.

8. Chang, E. E., Randy H. Katz, "Exploiting Inheritance and Structure Semantics for Effective Clustering and Buffering in an Object-Oriented DBMS," *Proc. 1989 ACM SIGMOD Conf.*, pp. 348-357.

9. Chaudhri, Akmal B., "ODBMS Resources," http://www.soi.city.ac.uk/~akmal/html.dir/resources.html

10. Cluet, S., "Designing OQL: Allowing Objects to be Queried," *Information Sys. 23(5)*, 1998, pp. 279-306.

11. Copeland, G. and D. Maier, "Making SmallTalk a Database System," *Proc. 1984 ACM SIGMOD Conf.*, pp. 316-325.

12. Curewitz, K.M., P. Krishnan, J. S. Vitter, "Practical Prefetching via Data Compression," *Proc. 1993 ACM SIGMOD Conf.*, pp. 257-266.

13. Keller, A., J. Basu, "A Predicate-based Caching Scheme for Client-Server Database Architectures," *VLDB Journal 5(1)*, Jan. 1996, pp. 35-47.

14. Keller, A., R. Jensen, and S. Agrawal, "Persistence Software: Bridging Object-Oriented Programming and Relational Database," *Proc. 1993 ACM SIGMOD Conf.*, pp. 523-528.

15. Lamb, Charles, Gordon Landis, Jack A. Orenstein, Daniel Weinreb, "The ObjectStore System," *CACM* 34(10), 1991, pp. 50-63.

16. Lee, Byung Suk and Gio Wiederhold, "Outer Joins and Filters for Instantiating Objects from Relational Databases Through Views," *IEEE Trans. On Knowledge and Data Eng.* 6(1), 1994, pp. 108-119.

17. Lee, Byung Suk and Gio Wiederhold, "Efficiently Instantiating View-Objects From Remote Relational Databases" *VLDB Journal* 3(3), 1994, pp. 289-323.

18. Mitschang, Bernhard, Hamid Pirahesh, Peter Pistor, Bruce G. Lindsay, and Norbert Sdkamp, "SQL/XNF - Processing Composite Objects as Abstractions over Relational Data," *Proc. 1993 Int'l Conf. On Data Eng.*, pp. 272-282.

19. Ontos, http://www.ontos.com

20. Orenstein, Jack A. and D. N. Kamber, "Accessing a Relational Database through an Object-Oriented Database Interface," *Proc. 21st VLDB Conf.*, 1995, pp. 702-705.

21. Palmer, M. and S. Zdonik, "Fido: A Cache that Learns to Fetch," *Proc. 17th VLDB Conf.*, 1991, pp. 255-264.

22. Persistence Software, http://www.persistence.com

23. Pirahesh, Hamid, Bernhard Mitschang, Norbert Sdkamp, and Bruce G. Lindsay, "Composite-object views in relational DBMS: an implementation perspective," *Information Sys* 19(1), 1994, pp. 69-88.

24. POET Software, POET SQL Object Factory, http://poet.com/factory.htm

25. Rational Software Corp. Unified Modeling Language Resource Center. At http://www.rational.com/uml

26. Rogerson, D. *Inside COM*. Microsoft Press, 1997.

27. RogueWave Software, DBTools.h++, http://www.roguewave.com/products/dbtools/

GHOST: Fine Granularity Buffering of Index

Cheng Hian Goh[†] Beng Chin Ooi Dennis Sim Kian-Lee Tan
Dept. of Computer Science
National University of Singapore

Abstract

Buffering has all along been an important strategy for exploiting the cost/performance ratio of disk versus random-access memory. The buffering of disk pages belonging to a database has been well-studied, but literature that deals specifically with *index* buffering is scarce. This is surprising given the significance of indexes (especially B+-tree like indexes) in modern DBMSs. In this paper, we describe a dual buffering scheme for indexes, called GHOST, in which part of the buffer is used to maintain popularly used "paths" of the B+-tree index, while the remainder is devoted to maintaining a Splay-tree with pointers to leaf pages containing frequently used leaf pages. This scheme allows us to maintain pointers to leaf nodes long after the paths leading to the leaf nodes have been replaced, thus maintaining "ghost" paths to the nodes. In addition to describing the search and maintenance operations for the GHOST buffering scheme, we also conduct a series of experiments in which it is shown that GHOST outperforms the best existing schemes (ILRU and OLRU) by impressive margins for almost all pragmatic query workloads.

1 Introduction

Despite the fact that modern computer systems are equipped with an abundance of main memory, the latter remains a scarce resource with increasingly sophisticated (and large) software and the rapid buildup of huge data sets. In particular, although database servers are now routinely equipped with between 512 MB and 2 GB of main memory, it is not uncommon to find databases consisting of terabytes of data. Moreover, any available memory will have to be fragmented among large numbers of concurrent transactions. For example, at the National University of Singapore, the university database is managed by Oracle 8.05 running on a powerful 4-way V2200 HP machine with 2 GB of memory. Applications range from student result management system, human resource to fund management systems. It has a user base of 26,000 and a database size of about 100 GB. Many of the relations are indexed on attributes that are frequently queried. Despite the powerful configuration and proper database tuning, due to the high number of applications and stored procedures, we have observed that at peak, the memory resources and processors are fully utilized. In short, a good buffer management system that is effective in exploiting differential access speed of main memory (versus disk) remains a key determinant of system performance and throughput.

In the past, a variety of different buffering schemes for pages of a database have been proposed. Early works were adaptations from research in operating systems [7], such as the LRU and its variants [10], the Hot Set model [13], and other mutations (e.g. DBMIN [5]). Interestingly, very few work have been reported on the buffering of database indexes themselves. To the best of our knowledge, only three such schemes have been reported in the literature: the ILRU and OLRU [12], and the extensible buffer mechanism described in [4].

In this paper, we studied the management of buffers for large B+-tree-like indexes. Besides being the most widely used indexing scheme, the B+-tree index [6] has also been shown in recent works to provide superior performance in managing high dimensional data [3, 11]. Our goal is to further improve the performance by minimizing the number of page faults for fetching index pages from large B+-trees. The novelty of our proposal lies in the use of a dual-buffering scheme; specifically, one part of the buffer space is used as an

[†]Deceased on 1 April 1999.

Proceedings of the 25th VLDB Conference, Edinburgh, Scotland, 1999.

ILRU buffer that allows popular paths of the B+-tree to remain in main memory, while the rest is devoted to caching pointers to leaf pages, and are organized into a Splay-tree [14]. This allows previously popular paths of the B+-tree to be evicted from the ILRU buffer, while keeping the pointers to leaf nodes directly, making it appear that "ghost" paths now exist in the main memory buffer.[1]

We also studied the sensitivity of the buffering approach to the proportion of memory devoted to the ILRU buffer (and as a consequence, those available to the Splay tree) and the efficacy of GHOST under different levels of data skew. It is shown that GHOST outperforms existing index buffering schemes by impressive margins under most circumstances, regardless of the amount of memory available and different amount of data skew.

The remainder of this paper is organized as follows. In section 2, we introduce the case for buffer management of indexes and describe briefly the various techniques proposed in the literature. This is followed by a description of the splay tree structure in section 3, and the GHOST strategy for buffer management in section 4. In section 5, we present results of the experimental studies using the proposed buffering scheme under different retrieval patterns, and compare these results to existing buffering strategies. Finally, we summarize our contributions in the last section and describe some work in the pipeline.

2 Buffer Management for Indexes

The management of buffers *for indexes* has received considerably less attention compared to the problem of buffer management in general. Throughout this paper, we assume that a B+-tree index [2] is used. Nonetheless, the analysis and experimental results in this paper can be easily extended to most other hierarchical index structures.

To the best of our knowledge, only two distinct set of works have been reported in the literature [4, 12]; specifically, the replacement policies *ILRU* (Inverse LRU) and *OLRU* (Optimal LRU) proposed in [12], and a more generic *priority-based* approach proposed in [4]. These approaches are described briefly in the next three subsections.

2.1 Inverse LRU (ILRU)

The ILRU replacement policy is formulated with the following observation in mind. Access to index pages involves the traversal of a tree from the root to the leaf pages. Suppose p is the parent page of the set of of children denoted by c. To access a child c_i ($\in c$), p must be first accessed. Hence, the sum of accesses to children in c cannot exceed the total number of accesses to p. Consequently, it is always suboptimal to replace p, if any of the $c_i \in c$ are still in the buffer.

[1]The acronym for the proposed buffering strategy is also a pun on the authors' names.

Let B be the number of buffers allocated for supporting the index, and suppose L is the height of the B+-tree (i.e., the number of traversals needed to reach a leaf node from the root, plus one). It should be clear that whenever $B < L$, the classic LRU policy will perform poorly, since the pages which are nearest to the root will be swapped out first.

The Inverse LRU (ILRU) policy modifies the LRU policy by simply reversing the order in which pages are scheduled for replacement. Hence, when a page p at level i (the root being level 0) is accessed, it is not placed at the top of the LRU stack but at its i-th position: thus, the root will be placed at position 0 (the top of the stack). Index pages being accessed are always appended. In the exceptional situation when the stack has $B < L$ buffers, the currently referenced page at level i ($> B$) is placed at the B-th position. This means that whenever no more buffers are available, the page at position B of the LRU-stack will be replaced. This strategy guarantees that top level pages of a B+-tree always have higher priority compared to those further from the root. As an example, a buffer with $B \geq 2$ is sufficient to keep the root in the buffer at all times.

2.2 Optimal LRU (OLRU)

In the case of the Optimal LRU (OLRU) strategy, the index pages are logically partitioned into L independent regions, each managed by a local LRU stack. The number of buffers allocated to region i is given by T_i and is estimated by Yao's function [15]. There are two distinct cases that need to be considered. If $B \geq T(= \sum_{i=1}^{L} T_i)$ then all of the regions can be given a full allocation. If however $B < T$, then there exists $j \leq L$ such that $\sum_{i=1}^{j-1} T_i < B < \sum_{i=1}^{j} T_i$. In which case, we allocate T_i buffers to regions T_i ($i = 1, 2, \ldots, j-1$) and the remainder $B' = (B - \sum_{i=1}^{j-1} T_i) - 1$ to region j. In other words, three types of regions may exist in the buffer for a given buffer size: *non-deficient* regions where each is allocated the full set of T_i buffers; *coalesced* regions which share a single unallocated buffer; and finally a single *deficient* region that is allocated B' buffers.

Whenever an index page at level i is accessed, it is kept in region i of the buffer (or, in the case of coalesced regions, in the single free buffer). Buffers in a given region are managed using the LRU policy (though a random replacement policy may work equally well). Under the assumption that leaf pages are accessed with the same probability, this allocation is optimal because available buffers are allocated to the index pages according to their reference frequency. Sacco [12] has also shown that similar results can be obtained even if the access probability is skewed (such as when a Zipf distribution is used).

2.3 Priority-Based Index Buffering

In the priority-based buffering scheme proposed in [4], each page in the buffer is assigned a priority value which may be dynamically modified to reflect its "replacement potential" relative to other buffered pages brought into memory. Pages present in the buffer is denoted as either *useful* or *useless*: a buffer page is considered useful if it is to be re-referenced again (in the context of the same query) and useless otherwise. This information is known because of the predictability of the reference pattern. Within each set, the pages can be further assigned priority values based on the level number of the page with reference to the *anchor page* (the index page furthest from the root that contains the entire range of leaf pages required by the query). More specifically, priority values are assigned as follows:

- useful pages are assigned higher priority than useless pages;
- among useless pages, higher priority is assigned to pages nearer to the root (since these are more likely to be accessed in *subsequent* queries);
- among useful pages, higher priority is given to more recently used pages since they will be re-referenced sooner because of the depth-first traversal reference pattern.

Notice that this priority scheme is dynamic since the priority of a page may decrease as the B+-tree is traversed; for example, a useful page (descending from the anchor page) becomes useless after the entire subtree rooted at that page has been traversed.

Under the prescribed priority scheme, the buffer page with the least priority is selected as the victim whenever the buffer runs out of room. This replacement strategy can be understood as a hybrid scheme representing a combination of the LRU and MRU replacement policies. Specifically, useful pages are managed in an LRU manner (favoring pages nearer to the leaf), and useful pages are managed using a MRU policy (favoring pages nearer to the root).

2.4 Discussion

The performance of ILRU and OLRU are compared in a preliminary study reported in [12]. Both schemes are shown to be better than the classic LRU.

We observed that in the case of B+-trees, the priority scheme in [4] does not present a distinct contribution for the following reasons. For key-probes, it degenerates into ILRU since all pages are useless. In the case of range queries, there is no occasion for the index structure to be backtracked (to the anchor node) since adjacent leaf pages are linked. (Note that this is only true for this context; in a more generic tree-based indexed, such as the R-tree [9], the priority scheme will actually behave differently from ILRU.)

3 The Splay-Tree

The Splay tree is a self-adjusting binary search tree introduced in the mid 1980s [14]. It is shown in [14] that although the operations (e.g., search, insert, delete) performed on a Splay tree is not necessarily individually efficient, they are guaranteed to be so over a sequence of operations. In other words, it has been shown that the *amortized cost* of a sequence of operations of a Splay tree is bounded by $O(log\ n)$. This behavior is achieved by a *splaying* operation which allows the Splay tree to be restructured after each operation, so that subsequent operations can be accomplished more cheaply.

The splaying operation consists of a sequence of rotations in such a way that the node containing the key (or a node which would be a neighbor of this key if the latter is not in the tree) ends up being the root of the splay tree. In performing the Splay operation, three cases can be distinguished depending on the node R being accessed and its parent Q and grandfather P (if any).

case 1: Node R's parent is the root.

case 2: *Homogeneous configuration.* Node R is the left child of Q which in turn is the left child of P; or both are right children.

case 3: *Heterogeneous configuration.* Node R is the right child of parent Q which in turn is the left child of P, or vice versa.

Each configuration presents different opportunities for elevating node R to the root. Figure 1 shows the animated rotation associated with each configuration. The abstracted algorithm is given in Figure 2. One readily observed property of the Splay tree is that *the most recently observed key (being searched on or inserted) will float to the top of the tree, while the remainder percolates down to lower parts of the tree.* Because of this property, the search cost for the same node is greatly reduced.

4 The GHOST Index Buffering Scheme

In the classical management of buffers for indexes, it is common to adopt index pages (which includes both internal and leaf pages) as a unit for buffering: i.e., an index page is either in the buffer, or it is not. In this section, we describe a dual-buffering strategy which consists of two different data structures

- a conventional index buffering scheme (in our case, the ILRU scheme) that allows recently used paths in the index to be cached; and
- an appropriate in-memory data structure (in our case, the Splay tree) that allows pointers to leaf

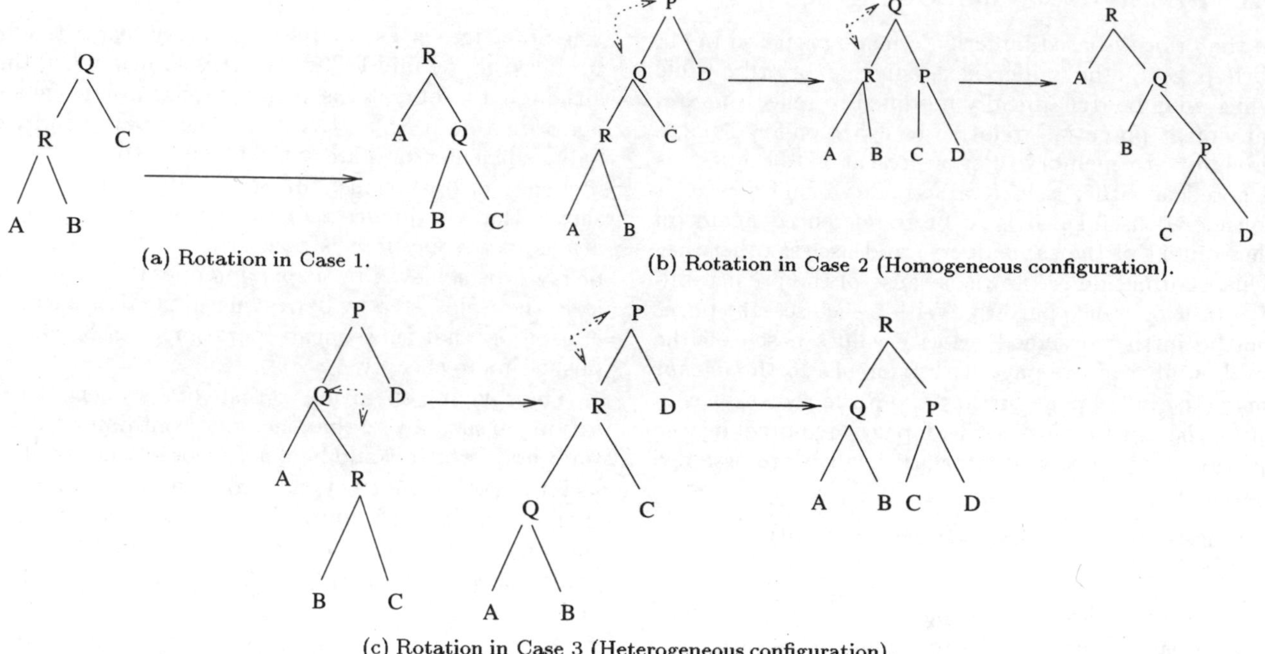

(c) Rotation in Case 3 (Heterogeneous configuration).

Figure 1: Animation of rotations for different Splay cases.

nodes to be stored (accompanied with their respective key ranges).

Notice that in the second case, the leaf node pointers may remain in the main memory even long after the paths have been evicted. This creates the impression that a "ghost" path to the leaf node exists and hence the name of the index buffering scheme.

The proposed dual buffering scheme is motivated by the following observations. As the memory resident data structure stores pointers to leaf nodes, given a fixed amount of memory, it can store more pointers than that under a conventional scheme that stores paths. By retaining as many pointers to frequently accessed leaf nodes as possible, we hope to reduce the access cost to these nodes to only a single page fault. For the conventional scheme, because of the need to store paths, the number of index nodes that can be retained in the main memory is severely limited. On the other hand, purely storing pointers to leaf nodes is not expected to perform well also. This is because in the event of a cache miss, the entirety of the path (from root to the leaf node) has to be accessed. The conventional scheme's ability to retain the path can avoid this. Thus, a dual buffering scheme is expected to be superior. Our experimental study in section 5 confirms these observations.

4.1 Key Data-structures in GHOST

There are three key data structures in GHOST:

- a B+-tree index;
- a ILRU buffer; and
- a mutated Splay-tree.

The B+-tree is a hierarchical index constructed over the data. It is normally too large to be stored in the main memory and relies on some buffering scheme to keep the commonly traversed index records in the cache. The ILRU scheme is chosen because it gives greater priority to the pages of the B+-tree nearer to the root. Furthermore, it is simpler and is reported to yield better performance than schemes that are known.

The ILRU buffer operates exactly as described in [12]. By caching popular (frequently and least recently used) paths in the tree, the ILRU scheme provides a method for caching the paths leading to the data nodes.

Finally, we adopted the Splay tree as our in-memory data structure. The Splay tree used by GHOST differs from the one described earlier in two aspects. First, despite the (relatively) large amount of main memory available, the latter resource is finite. This requires an eviction policy: in our implementation, a leaf node is chosen randomly to make room whenever necessary. Recall that in a Splay tree, data at the leaf nodes are the least recently used, and hence randomly picking a leaf node is a reasonable heuristics. In fact, it is this property that the Splay tree is preferred over other *height-balanced structures* (such as AVL trees [1] and Red-Black trees [8]). There is no mechanism in

Algorithm Splay:

```
while R is not the root
    if R's parent is the root
        rotate R about Q
    else if R is in a homogeneous configuration with its predecessors
        perform a homogeneous splay, first rotate Q about P
        and then R about Q
    else /* R is in heterogeneous configuration with its predecessors */
        perform a heterogeneous splay, first rotate R about Q
        and then about P
```

Figure 2: Splay algorithm.

these structures to facilitate an efficient eviction policy without maintaining additional information. This, however, will consume the already scarce storage resource and hence is expected to be less effective than the Splay tree. Second, the node structure of our Splay tree differs slightly: as shown in Figure 3, ours is laden with a key range as opposed to a single key value, and an additional pointer to a leaf page.

Figure 3 provides a pictorial representation of how the different data structures are related to one another. The figure contains two parts: the top portion shows that the main memory is split into two regions, one for the splay tree and the other for the ILRU; the second portion shows the disk-based B+-tree structure. The B+-tree shown stores the data records at its leaf nodes. As shown, the splay tree buffers store the frequently accessed leaf pages, and the ILRU buffers manage frequently traversed paths (i.e., the internal nodes of the B+-tree). We note that the leaf nodes are not kept at the ILRU buffer. This is because it will be kept in the Splay tree where the search process begins (see the Search algorithm in the next section).

4.2 GHOST operations

As in any data structures, the three primitive operations that have to be addressed are: search, insert, and delete. In our case, we are interested in the effects of these operations and their implications for the GHOST scheme.

Search

Figure 4 describes the algorithm for searching via its search key. There are two cases to consider. The first is when the pointer to the leaf page is in the Splay tree: in which case, only one I/O for fetching the leaf page from disk is needed. Searching the Splay tree will bring the relevant Splay tree node to be the root. This ensures that frequently and permanently used leaf pages have corresponding entries near the top of the Splay tree.

Second, if the required key cannot be found in the Splay tree, the B+-tree will be searched directly. The presence of an ILRU buffer allows popular index pages to be obtained without additional disk I/O.

Algorithm Search(Key)

```
Search Splay tree for a node where the key
        is covered by the key interval
if found, return pointer to leaf page
else (/* not found */)
        Search B+-tree, with the aid of ILRU buffer
            to reduce the amount of I/O
        When the leaf page is found
            create a new node for it
            insert it into the Splay tree
            Return pointer to leaf page.
```

Figure 4: Search algorithm for the GHOST scheme.

Insertion

Insertion of a new data item in a DBMS is preceded by a Search operation. This means that by the time the appropriate node is located, there will be a Splay node entry for the corresponding leaf node in the root of the Splay tree. There are now only two situations to worry about:

- When the boundary values of the leaf node have been changed. For instance, in inserting a data item with key value 96 into a leaf node having key interval [100,145], we are required to update the key range in the Splay tree root to [96,145].
- When the insertion causes a node split in the leaf node. For example, if insertion causes a node split with node A (interval [96,120]) and B [121,145]), the corresponding key interval in the Splay tree will have to be changed to reflect one interval, and a new node is inserted to reflect the other interval.

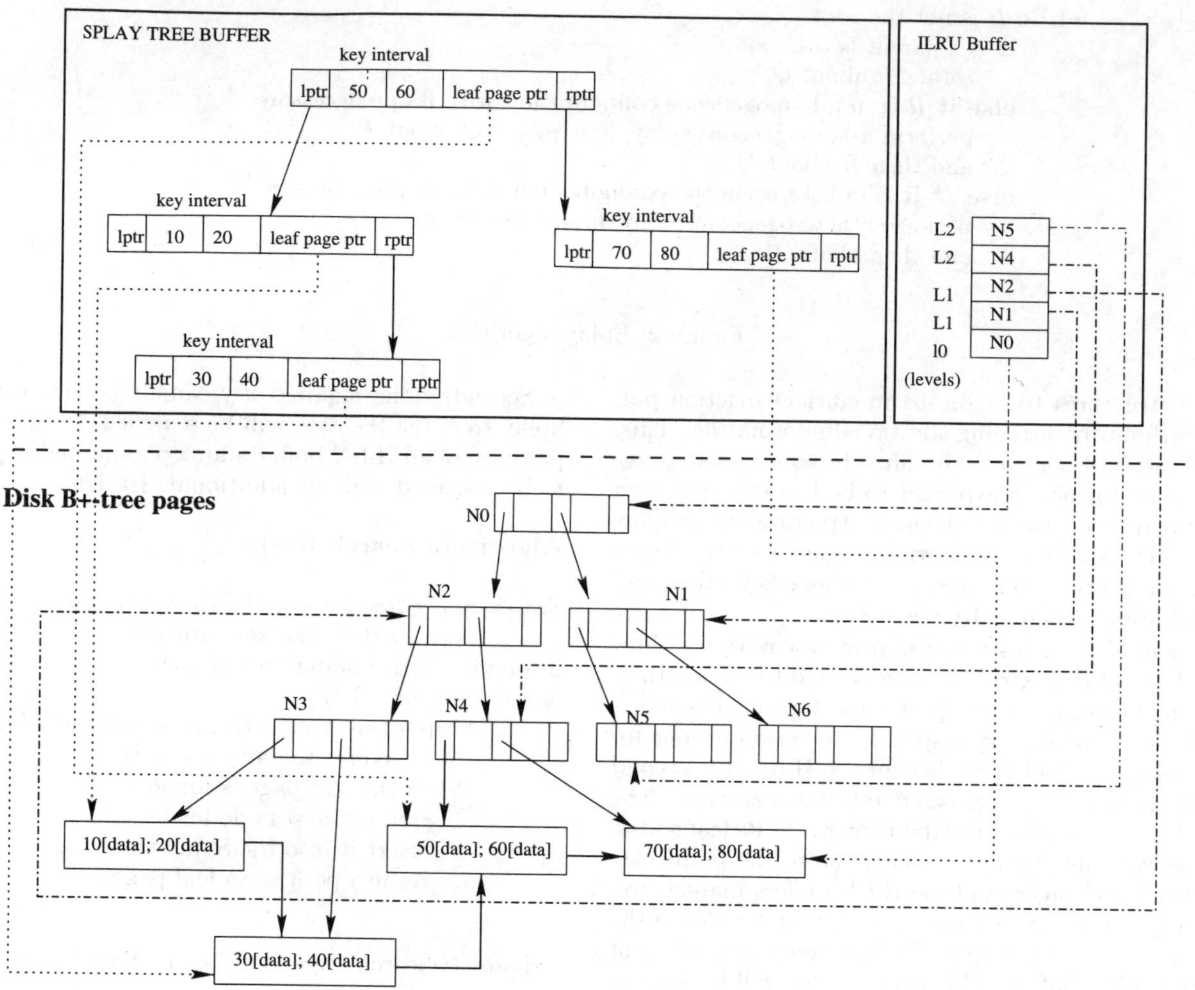

Figure 3: A graphical representation of the GHOST scheme.

Deletion

Like insertion, deletion requires a prior search operation. The situations requiring attention are symmetrical to the ones in Insertion:

- When the deletion causes a change in the key intervals as a result of deleting data items that are boundary key values in the Splay tree nodes. This requires changing the Splay tree nodes to reflect the new ranges.
- When deletion causes two leaf pages to be merged together, thus requiring a change to the key interval of one Splay tree node, while the other can be deleted.

5 Experimental Study

We present in this section an experimental study of the GHOST strategy proposed in this paper. There are two performance metrics. The first is the hit ratio which is defined as the ratio obtained by dividing the number of requests into the number of page faults (i.e., disk I/O operations). The second is the number of disk I/Os missed in a sequence of 500,000 disk queries made.

The data set we used in our experiments consists of 10 million unique integers drawn randomly from the interval $[1..100M]$. These numbers are inserted into a B+-tree at random prior to the conduct of any experiment. Table 1 summarizes the system parameters that are used. We assume that each data record contains 200 bytes and is stored in the leaf of the B+-tree. The resultant B+-tree has four levels with $1, 61, 6868$ and $769, 230$ nodes at levels 1, 2, 3 and 4 respectively.

We experimented with three different types of queries: uniform, skewed-clustered, and skewed-unclustered. The difference among the last two is that while queries are skewed towards certain datapoints,

Parameter	Default Values	Variations
System Parameters		
page size	4K	
buffer size	128 pages	16-1024 pages (or 64K-4M)
percentage of buffers allocated to Splay tree	50%	0-100%
disk pointer size	16 bytes	
data key size	8 bytes	
in-memory pointer	4 bytes	
Splay tree parameters		
size of node	40 bytes	
Database Parameters		
number of records	10 million	
size of record	200 bytes	
Query Parameters		
query type	point	range
query distribution	skewed-unclustered	uniform, skewed-clustered
no. of queries	500,000	

Table 1: Parameters and their values.

the latter's spread of skewness is across a greater range, i.e., the number of "hot" pages is larger for the latter. This behavior is demonstrated in Figure 5. Notice that both data query points in skewed-clustered and skewed-unclustered distributions are identical (Zipf at 0.01), but the latter is randomly scattered.

The first three sets of experiments examine the performance of our proposed buffering scheme, GHOST, against ILRU and OLRU, under different workloads as total available size for index buffering are varied. The priority scheme of [4] will not be examined for reasons highlighted in section 2.4. In the GHOST scheme, 50% of the available memory is devoted to the Splay tree and the remaining is reserved for buffering index nodes under the ILRU strategy.

5.1 Effect of Workloads

Experiment 1

In the first experiment, we examine the performance of different buffering schemes under *uniform workload.* Intuitively, uniform workload is the worst case scenario for the GHOST scheme. This is because, under uniform workload, all records are equally likely to be accessed, and so the benefit of retaining pointers to "frequently" accessed leaf pages (all pages are equally frequently accessed!) significantly reduces. Figures 6(a) and (b) show the results under which total memory size is varied from 16-1024 pages. As expected, the hit-rate under all schemes increases with the buffer size (see Figure 6(a)). Furthermore, we observe that the hit-rate under OLRU and ILRU are roughly the same. While the GHOST scheme performs close to OLRU and ILRU for small buffer sizes (< 128 pages), it is twice as well for large buffer sizes. Figure 6(b) shows the number of cumulative number of page I/Os under each buffering scheme. As is predicted, all the numbers decrease with increasingly larger buffers. However, we observe that when the buffer size is small, the GHOST scheme actually incurs more I/Os (despite its higher hit rate). Upon investigation, we found that this is attributed to the high page fault when there is a cache miss in the Splay tree. For small buffer sizes, the space allocated to the ILRU is too small to be useful. As a result, any cache miss will result in the entirety of the search path being accessed. As the buffer sizes increase, the GHOST scheme's ability to retain more pointers (than the ILRU and OLRU) still pays off and it takes the lead once again.

Experiment 2

Figures 7(a) and (b) show the performance of the three buffering schemes under a skewed-clustered query distribution. Unlike Experiment 1 where the query is uniform (a.k.a. random), we expect queries to be skewed along a given key cluster. This suggests that better performances can be expected. Indeed, the GHOST scheme performs better than the closest contender in both hit rate and total I/O count. For I/O count, the gain is about 25%. This is considered significant since under a clustered skewed distribution all the frequently accessed leaf nodes will be collected in close proximity, which a simple ILRU-type scheme can be expected to perform well as the same paths along the index tree is traversed frequently to reach that data cluster.

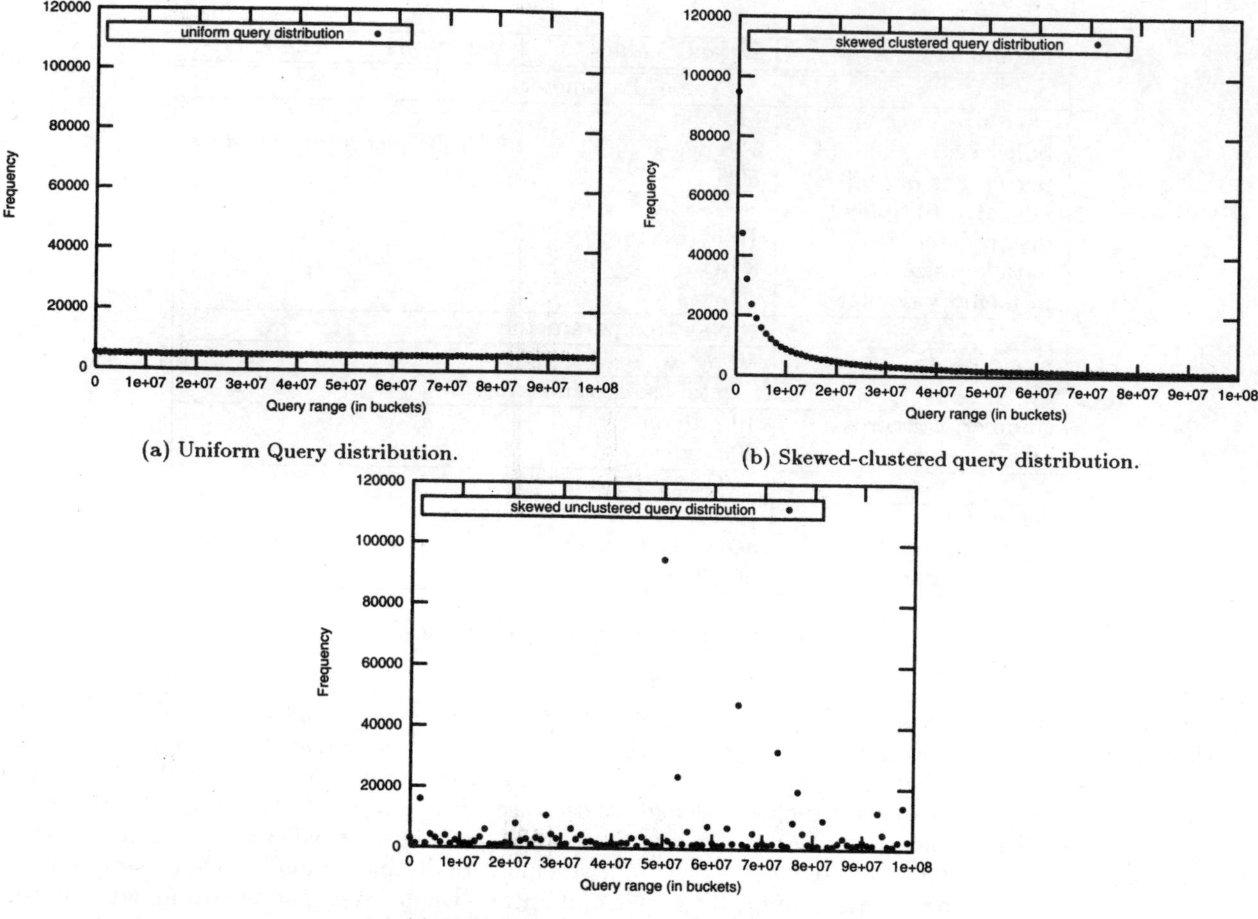

(a) Uniform Query distribution.

(b) Skewed-clustered query distribution.

(c) Skewed-unclustered query distribution.

Figure 5: Different Query workloads and their visual representation.

Experiment 3

In this experiment, we compare the three schemes under skewed-unclustered distribution. Unlike the skewed-clustered distribution, there are now multiple non-contiguous active clusters. As a result, there will be many more such paths and it will become unlikely that all or these paths can be cached. Thus, we can expect the performance of ILRU and OLRU to be poorer. This is confirmed in our result shown in Figure 8. On the other hand, in the GHOST scheme, the problem is corrected through the use of the Splay tree nodes, whose nodes store only pointers to leaf nodes. GHOST outperforms ILRU and OLRU by up to 30% in terms of I/O. The results clearly demonstrate the impressive performance of the GHOST scheme over the rest.

5.2 Effect of Range Queries

We also conducted an experiment to evaluate the relative performance of the three buffering schemes on range queries under a skewed-unclustered workload (skew factor of 0.01). Here, we fixed the total number of memory pages to 256 (i.e., 1 MB of memory), and 50% of the space is allocated to the Splay tree. For a range query with interval $[r1, r2]$, it is evaluated by searching for the leaf node that contains $r1$, and the chain of leaf nodes are followed to retrieve all records whose key values are in the interval. In this experiment, the queries are generated such that it retrieves an average of four leaf nodes. We vary the percentage of range queries from 0% (all point queries) to 100% (all range queries). The result is shown in Figure 9. As shown, the hit ratio is not affected by the percentage of range queries. However, all schemes' I/O counts increase with the percentage of range queries. This is expected since more data are being accessed. The interesting point to note is that the GHOST scheme remains the best scheme, and outperforms the other scheme by up to 20% of the total I/O count. We note that this is lower than the result for point queries. This can be explained as follows. The total I/O count comprises two components: internal nodes and leaf nodes. For all the schemes, the cost to access the leaf nodes are the same and is larger for range queries than point

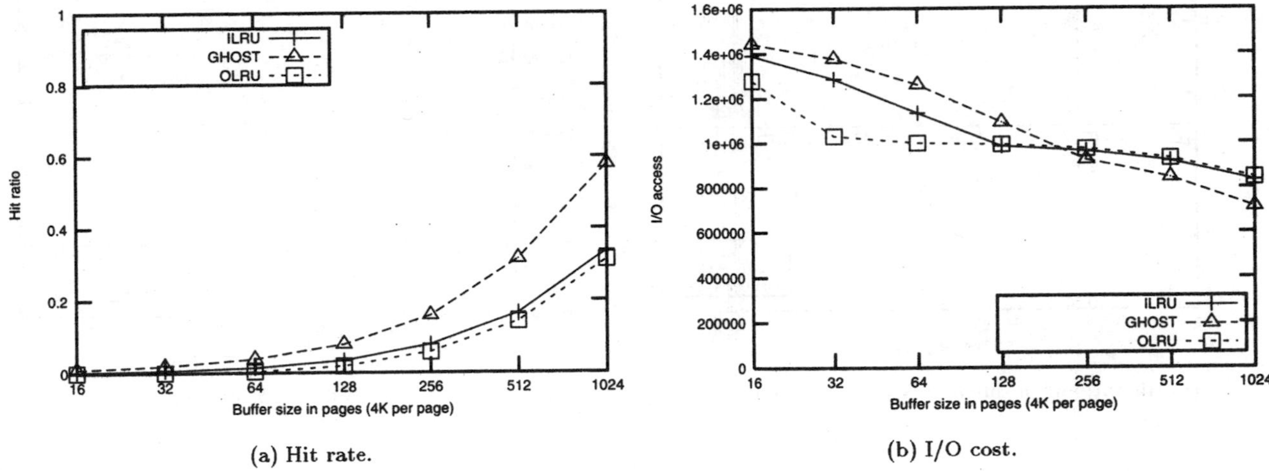

(a) Hit rate. (b) I/O cost.

Figure 6: Query hit rate and page I/O of different buffering schemes under uniform query workloads.

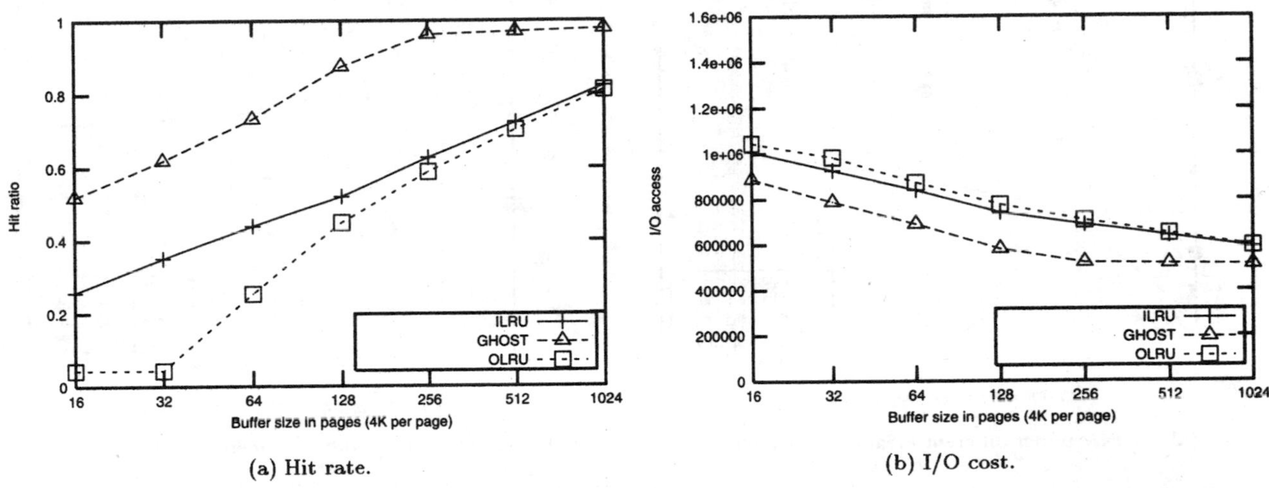

(a) Hit rate. (b) I/O cost.

Figure 7: Query hit rate and page I/O of different buffering schemes under skewed clustered distribution.

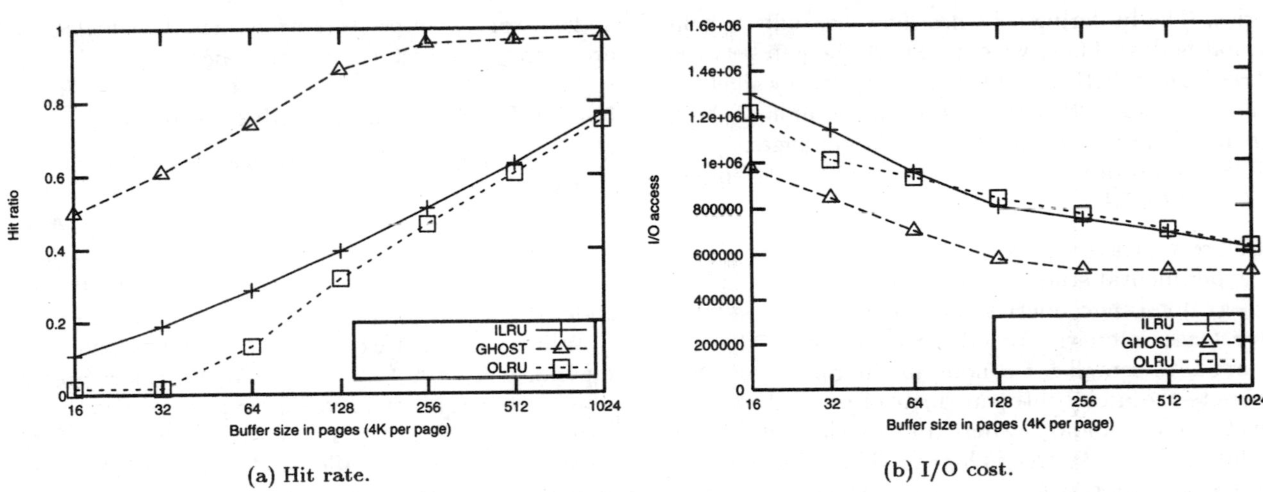

(a) Hit rate. (b) I/O cost.

Figure 8: Query hit rate and page I/O of different buffering schemes under skewed unclustered distribution.

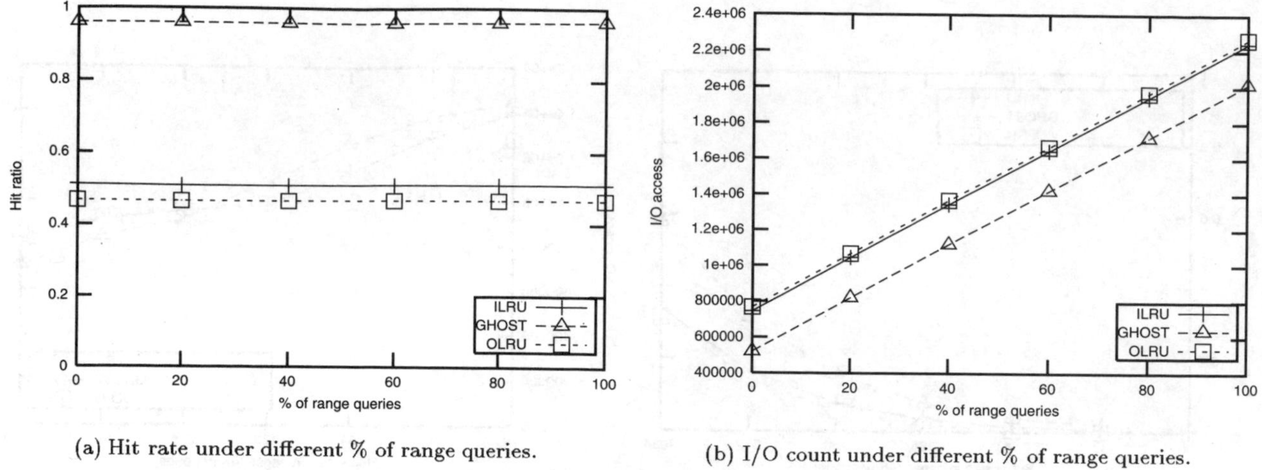

(a) Hit rate under different % of range queries.

(b) I/O count under different % of range queries.

Figure 9: Results for range queries.

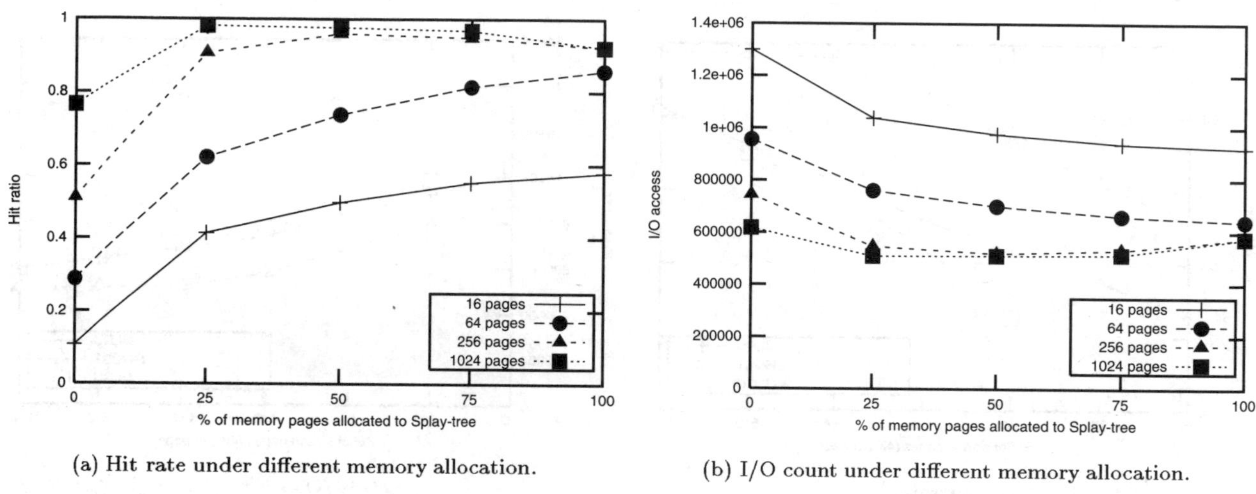

(a) Hit rate under different memory allocation.

(b) I/O count under different memory allocation.

Figure 10: Results under skew unclustered for varying memory allocation and distributions.

queries. The buffering schemes, however, only benefit internal nodes. Thus, we can expect the gap between GHOST, and ILRU and OLRU, to be narrower as the range increases. However, it is uncommon to have large number of range queries with large ranges. Thus, GHOST is a promising alternative buffering scheme to ILRU and OLRU.

Before we leave this section, it is worth noting that the experimental study is based on a naive evaluation strategy for range queries, i.e., it can be considered a worst case scenario for GHOST. In fact, a cleverer scheme is to search for a node in the Splay tree that intersects the query interval (instead of one that contains the left boundary value). In this way, the chances of a hit in the Splay tree is higher. This will, however, requires us to modify the leaf nodes to be chained backward as well as forward. Thus, by hitting a node that is in the middle of a range, we can use the backward and forward pointers to traverse the leaf nodes. We are currently investigating this scheme.

5.3 Effect of Memory Allocation

In the preceding experiments, we have split the total buffer size evenly between the ILRU buffer and the Splay tree. One of our concerns is whether and how GHOST's performance is affected by the allocation of memory between the Splay tree and the ILRU buffer under varying amount of available total memory.

While we do not expect the GHOST scheme to be superior when 100% of the available memory are allocated to the Splay tree, we do conjecture that the performance of GHOST is likely to be better if a larger portion of buffers are allocated. We verify this with an experiment, where we plot the performance metric against different internal allocation under different allocations of total buffer memory. Figure 10 shows our

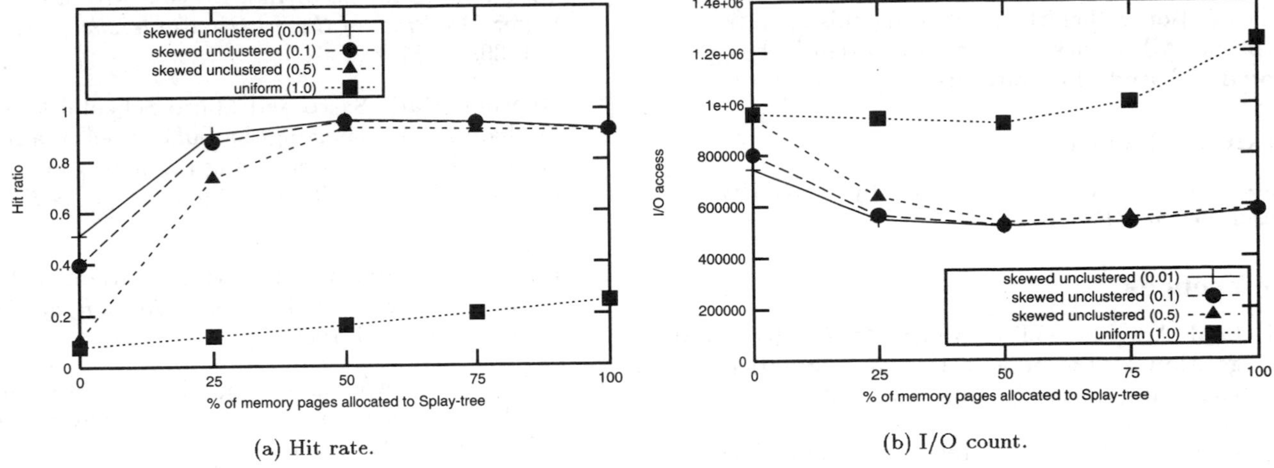

(a) Hit rate.

(b) I/O count.

Figure 11: Results under skew unclustered for varying Zipfian factor.

empirical findings for four different buffer sizes: 16, 64, 256 and 1024 pages. The evidence reveals more then just a simple relation; instead, it suggests that when the total available memory is small (e.g. in the 16-page case), allocating more memory to the Splay tree will give a sharp boost to the performance. This further confirms our result and observation in earlier experiments. On the other hand, with a large buffer size, the performance hits the performance limit rapidly even with small allocations to the Splay tree. We also observe that assigning too much buffer may not be helpful. For very large buffer size, the Splay tree is caching not only frequently accessed pointers, but also those that are not frequently accessed. Pointers in the latter category are often replaced before they are being accessed again, thus caching them only results in fewer space being allocated to the ILRU buffers (which in turn restricted the number of paths being retained in the ILRU buffers). As a result, the overall performance degrades a little.

We also studied the effect of the distribution of queries under the skewed-unclustered workload, i.e., how the value of the zipf factor affects the performance of GHOST. In this experiment, we fixed the total memory at 256 pages. Figure 11 shows the results of this experiment. When the Zipf factor is 1.0, all leaf pages are equally likely to be accessed, i.e., the skewed-unclustered workload degenerates to the uniform workload. In this case, it becomes more beneficial to allocate more memory to the Splay tree. On the other hand, a small Zipf factor means more queries are accessing a certain set of "hot" pages. Our results show that the hit rate and I/O performance improves as the Zipf factor reduces. This is because the chances of finding the pointers to the hot pages in the Splay tree increases with more queries accessing them. However, unlike the uniform workload, we note that we do not need to allocate too much memory to the Splay tree for the same reasons that we have discussed in the previous experiment. In our experiments, it turns out that 50% of the memory allocated to the Splay tree is sufficient to lead to excellent performance.

6 Conclusion

It appears from the preceding discussions and experimentations that the GHOST scheme for index buffering presents a more efficient and robust alternative to other known strategies. The power of our proposed approach centers on the observation that we can store a direct pointer to leaf nodes of a B+-tree without having to buffer the search path of the structure. As a first cut, we have picked the ILRU and Splay tree in our implementation. However, any other buffering mechanisms and data structures having similar properties would have sufficed.

We have experimented with the GHOST scheme under a variety of different workloads, but it has emerged being the best performer in most of the cases. This performance gain is beyond what we have imagined and provides an illustration of the power of the proposed scheme.

Like any deserving piece of work, we are interested in understanding more of its features if not for the time constraints faced. For example, our results show that the optimal allocation of buffers to the Splay tree depends on the workload. This may call for an adaptive approach in dynamic environments where the workload changes. We are currently investigating how to realize such a scheme.

Last but not least, there are a number of policies which we have adopted because of their simplicity. For example, a leaf node of the Splay tree is selected at random for eviction whenever we are out of memory space. There could have been other policies: e.g., pick the node furthest away from the root, or perform a bulk eviction rather than repeating this operation all so often. All of these options are currently being explored and studied empirically.

Acknowledgement

This work is partially supported by University Research Grant RP982694.

References

[1] G.M. Adel'son-Vel'skii and E. M. Landis. An algorithm for the organization of information. *Soviet Mathematics*, 3:1259–1263, 1962.

[2] R. Bayer and C. McCreight. Organization and maintenance of large ordered indexes. *Acta Informatica*, 1(3):173–189, 1972.

[3] S. Berchtold, C. Bohm, and H.-P. Kriegel. The pyramid-technique: Towards breaking the curse of dimensionality. In *Proc. of the ACM SIGMOD Conference*, pages 42–153, 1998.

[4] Chee Yong Chan, Beng Chin Ooi, and Hongjun Lu. Extensible buffer management of indexes. In *Proc. of the 18th VLDB Conference*, pages 444–454, Vancouver, British Columbia, Canada, 1992.

[5] Hong-Tai Chou and David J. DeWitt. An evaluation of buffer management strategies for relational database systems. In *Proc. of the 11th VLDB Conference*, pages 127–141, 1985.

[6] D. Comer. The ubiquitous b-tree. *ACM Computing Surveys*, 11(2):121–137, June 1979.

[7] Wolfgang Effelsberg and Theo Haerder. Principles of database buffer management. *ACM Trans. on Database Systems*, 9(4):560–595, Dec 1984.

[8] L. J. Guibas and R. Sedgewick. A dichromatic framework for balanced trees. In *Proceedings of the 19th Annual IEEE Symposium on Foundations of Coputer Science*, pages 8–21, 1978.

[9] A. Guttman. R-trees: A dynamic index structure for spatial searching. In *Proc. of the ACM SIGMOD Conference*, pages 47–57, 1984.

[10] Elizabeth J. O'Neil, Patrick E. O'Neil', and Gerhard Weikum. The LRU-K page replacement algorithm for database disk bufferin. In *Proc. of the ACM SIGMOD Conference*, pages 297–306, 1993.

[11] Beng Chin Ooi, Cheng Hian Goh, and Kian-Lee Tan. Fast high-dimensional data search in incomplete databases. In *Proc. of the 24th VLDB Conference*, pages 357–367, New York City, NY, 1998.

[12] Giovanni Maria Sacco. Index access with a finite buffer. In *Proc. of the VLDB Conference*, pages 301–309, 1987.

[13] Giovanni Mario Sacco and Mario Schkolnick. A mechanism for managing the buffer pool in a relational database system using the hotset model. In *Proc. of the 8th VLDB Conference*, pages 257–262, 1982.

[14] Daniel D. Sleator and Robert E. Tarjan. Self-adjusting binary search trees. *Journal of the ACM*, 32:652–686, 1985.

[15] S. B. Yao. Approximating block accesses to database organizations. *Communications of the ACM*, 20:260–261, 1977.

Loading a Cache with Query Results

Laura M. Haas
IBM Almaden

Donald Kossmann
University of Passau

Ioana Ursu
IBM Almaden

Abstract

Data intensive applications today usually run in either a client-server or a middleware environment. In either case, they must efficiently handle both database queries, which process large numbers of data objects, and application logic, which involves fine-grained object accesses (e.g., method calls). We propose a wholistic approach to speeding up such applications: we load the cache of a system with relevant objects as a by-product of query processing. This can potentially improve the performance of the application, by eliminating the need to fault in objects. However, it can also increase the cost of queries by forcing them to handle more data, thus potentially reducing the performance of the application. In this paper, we examine both heuristic and cost-based strategies for deciding what to cache, and when to do so. We show how these strategies can be integrated into the query optimizer of an existing system, and how the caching architecture is affected. We present the results of experiments using the Garlic database middleware system; the experiments demonstrate the usefulness of loading a cache with query results and illustrate the tradeoffs between the cost-based and heuristic optimization methods.

1 Introduction

Data intensive applications today usually run in either a middleware or client-server environment. Examples of middleware systems include business application, e-commerce or database middleware systems, while CAD and CAE systems are typically client-server. In either case, they must efficiently handle both database queries, which process large numbers of data objects, and application logic, with its fine-grained object accesses (e.g., method calls). In both architectures, application logic and query processing may be co-resident, and take place on a processor other than that on which the data resides. It is increasingly likely that some or all of the data will be on remote and/or nontraditional data sources that are expensive to access, such as web sources or specialized application systems.

Sophisticated optimization techniques reduce query processing times in these environments, while caching is used to reduce the cost of the application logic by avoiding unnecessary requests to the data sources. Applications often ask queries to identify objects of interest and then manipulate the result objects. Though it is now possible to do chunks of application logic in the query processor, applications still do much of the work themselves. Some applications require user interaction; others desire greater portability and ease of installation (e.g., big business applications such as Baan IV, Peoplesoft 7.5, or SAP R/3). In traditional systems, query processing and caching decisions are made in isolation. While this provides acceptable performance for these systems, it is a disaster for applications using data from the Internet. This query-and-manipulate pattern means that traditional systems access the data twice: once while processing the query, and then again, on the first method call, to retrieve and cache the object. If data is on the Internet, this will be prohibitively expensive. In some cases, the data source may not even be able to look up individual objects; hence this extra round trip is impossible.

In this paper we propose to load the cache with relevant objects as a by-product of the execution of a query. With this technique it is possible to get orders of magnitude improvements for applications that involve both queries *and* methods over expensive-to-access data. However, a naive implementation can do more harm than good. An application today can manually cache query results by explicitly selecting all the data for the object in the query itself. However, this may increase the cost of queries dramatically by forcing them to handle more data. For complex queries this effect may be large enough to more than offset the benefit. Therefore, the decisions of what to cache and when during query execution to do so should be made by the query optimizer in a cost-based manner.

The remainder of this paper is organized as follows. In Section 2, we elaborate on the motivation for our work, and discuss the caching of objects in our environment. While loading a cache with query results is essential when data is expensive or difficult to access, our ap-

Proceedings of the 25th VLDB Conference, Edinburgh, Scotland, 1999.

proach can also be used to speed up applications in traditional two- or three-tier architectures as described above. For ease of exposition we will talk about "middleware" as the site of query processing and caching in the following sections. In a two-tier system, these activities would take place in the client. Section 3 presents alternative ways to extend an optimizer to generate query execution plans that load a cache with query results. We describe two simple heuristics, as well as a more sophisticated cost-based approach. Section 4 discusses our implementation of caching in the Garlic database middleware system, and Section 5 contains the results of performance experiments that demonstrate the need to load a cache with query results and show the tradeoffs of the three alternative ways of extending the query processor. Section 6 discusses related work, and Section 7 concludes the paper.

2 Caching in Middleware

2.1 A Motivating Example

To see why loading the cache with query results is useful, consider this (generic) piece of application code:

```
foreach o, o2, o5 in
        (select r.oid, s2.oid, s5.oid
        from R r, S1 s1, S2 s2, ...
        where ...)
    {...o.method(o2, o5);... }
```

The query in this example is used to select relevant objects from the database. After further analysis and/or user interaction, the method carries out operations on these objects. The query can be arbitrarily complex, involving joins, subqueries, aggregation, etc. The method will involve accesses to certain fields of the object o and possibly to other objects (o_2, o_5) as well. *r.oid* refers to the object identifier of an object of collection *R*; this identifier is used to invoke methods on the object and to access fields of the object. Such a code fragment could be found in many applications. For example, an inventory control program might select all products for which supplies were low (and their suppliers and existing orders). After calculating an amount to order (perhaps with user input), it might invoke a method to order the product.

In a traditional middleware system this code fragment is carried out as follows:

1. the query processor tries to find the best (i.e., lowest cost) plan to execute the query.

2. the query processor executes the query, retrieving the object ids requested.

3. an interpreter executes the method, using the object ids to retrieve any data needed. To speed up the execution of methods that repeatedly access the same objects, the interpreter uses caching. Requests to access objects already in the cache can be processed by the interpreter without accessing the underlying data source(s), and a request to access an object not found in the cache would result in *faulting in* that object.

The key observation is that query processing does not affect caching in traditional systems: if the relevant objects of *R* are not cached prior to the execution of the query, these objects will not be cached as a by-product of query execution and they will have to be faulted in at the beginning of each method invocation. In an environment in which data access is slow, this can be extremely expensive – just as expensive, in fact, as processing the query. Loading the cache with query results avoids this extra cost of faulting in objects by copying the *R* objects into the cache while the query is executed; that is, it seizes the opportunity to copy the *R* objects into the cache at a moment at which the objects must be accessed and processed to execute the query anyway.

2.2 Caching Objects

Our goal is to decrease the overall execution time of applications, such as those described above, that use queries to identify the objects on which they will operate (i.e., on which they will invoke methods). There are many possible ways to accomplish this goal. In this paper, we focus on speeding up method execution, by essentially "pre-caching" the objects that methods will need. This pre-caching is possible in our environment, first, because, in executing the query, the query processor has to touch the needed objects anyway, and second, because in the architectures we consider, some portion of the query processing is done at the same site as that at which the methods are executed. Hence, the query processor has the opportunity to copy appropriate objects into a cache, for the methods to use.

Obviously, it will only be beneficial to cache objects that are subsequently accessed by the application program. Ideally, one would carry out a data flow analysis of the application program [ASU89] in order to determine which objects of the query result are potentially accessed. Unfortunately, such data flow analyses are impossible in many cases due to the separation of application logic and query processing – and interactive applications are totally unpredictable. Thus some heuristic approach to identifying the relevant objects is needed. It is likely that the objects whose oids are returned as part of the query result (i.e., objects of collections whose oid columns are part of the query's `SELECT` clause) are going to be accessed by the application program subsequently (why else would the query ask for oids?)[1]. We refer to such collections as *candidate collections*; these collections are candidates because objects of these collections are likely to be accessed. However, they are not guaranteed to be cached, as it might nevertheless not be cost-effective.

[1] Alternatively, we could assume that the application programmer gives hints that indicate which collections should be cached.

In the applications we are considering, queries and methods run in the same transaction. Hence we are only interested in intra-transaction caching in this paper, and cache consistency is not an issue. Our approach is particularly attractive in environments that do not support inter-transaction caching because transactions start with no relevant objects in the cache. Issues of locking and concurrency control are orthogonal to loading a cache with query results. In a middleware environment, it is often undesirable or impossible to lock data in the sources for the duration of the transaction. Under such circumstances, our approach may cause an application to produce different output; but, in some sense, this output can be seen as better output because our approach guarantees that the methods see the same state of an object as the query.

In this paper, we assume that the granularity of caching is an entire object. (We discuss how an object is defined in Section 4.) To cache the object, the whole object must be present. One may argue that we should only copy those fields of objects that are retrieved as part of the query anyway. However, state-of-the-art caches cache in the granularity of whole objects (e.g., the cache of SAP R/3 [KKM98]). This is necessary for pointer swizzling [Mos92, KK95] and to organize the cache efficiently (i.e., avoid a per attribute overhead in the cache). One may also argue that the granularity of caching and data transfer should be a group of objects or a *page*; caching and data transfer in such a granularity, however, is not possible in systems like Garlic.

A consequence of this approach is that caching during query execution is not free. It introduces additional cost, as no attribute of an object may be projected out before the object is cached, even if the attribute is not needed to compute the query result. This has two implications. First, objects should only be cached if the expected benefit (overall application speedup due to faster execution of methods) outweighs the cost in query execution time. Second, the point in the query execution at which objects are cached will affect the cost and benefit. If caching occurs too early, irrelevant objects may be cached, and might even flood the cache, squeezing out more relevant objects. If caching occurs too late, the intermediate results of query processing will be larger due to the need to preserve whole objects for caching. Consider, for instance, a query that involves a join between R and S and asks for the *oid* of the R objects that qualify: joining only the *oid* column of R with S is cheaper than joining the *whole* R (i.e., *oid* and all other columns) with S, especially if the *oid* column of R fits into main memory and the *whole* R does not. Because caching impacts the size of intermediate results, it should also impact join ordering; for instance, joins that filter out many objects of candidate collections should perhaps be carried out early in a query plan if caching is enabled. Hence, the best way of executing the query may be different depending on whether we are caching objects.

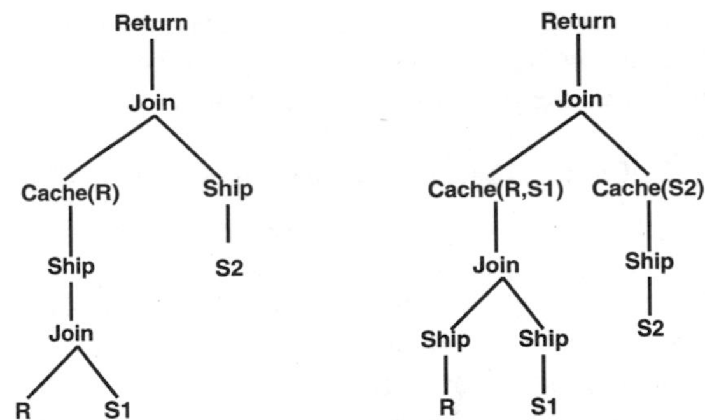

Figure 1: Example Cache Enhanced Query Plans

In summary, our goal is to speed up the execution of methods by caching the objects they need (as indicated by the select list of a query) during execution of that query. The granularity of the cache is an object, and caching objects during query execution incurs costs that can affect the choice of query execution plan. As a result, we will allow the query optimizer to decide what objects to cache, and when.

3 Caching During Queries

In this section, we describe ways to extend the query processor of a middleware system in order to generate plans which cache relevant objects. We introduce a new *Cache* operator which the query optimizer can use to indicate where in a plan objects of a particular collection should be cached. A *Cache* operator copies objects from its input stream into the cache and projects out columns of the input stream which are not needed to produce the query results. A *Cache* operator takes two parameters, one that specifies which objects of the input stream should be copied into the cache, and one that specifies which columns should be "passed through" to the next operator (not projected out). The plans shown in Figure 1 could be produced by the enhanced query optimizer. The *Cache* operator of the first plan copies objects of collection R; the first *Cache* operator of the second plan copies objects of R and S_1 while the second copies S_2 objects. A plan may contain several *Cache* operators if the objects of more than one collection are to be cached; however, it makes no sense to have two *Cache* operators for the same collection in a plan. The *Return* operators pass the query results to the application program. The *Ship* operators pass intermediate query results from a data source to the middleware; since *Cache* operators are always executed by the middleware, all *Cache* operators must be placed somewhere above a *Ship* operator and below the final *Return* operator.

In order to generate such plans, the query optimizer must decide (1) for which collections involved in a query to include *Cache* operators in a query plan, and (2) where to place *Cache* operators in a query plan. We present three approaches. The first two are heuristics which serve as baselines for our study. The third approach is cost-based cache operator placement: this approach is likely to make better decisions (i.e., produce better plans), but increases the cost of query optimization.

3.1 Cache Operators at the Top of Query Plans

The first approach makes the two cache operator placement decisions in the following heuristic way: (1) generate a *Cache* operator for every candidate collection, and (2) place all *Cache* operators high in a query plan. This approach corresponds to what an application could do manually, and is based on the principle that *all* relevant objects (objects which are part of the query result and belong to candidate collections) should be cached during the query and *no* irrelevant objects (those not part of the query result) should be cached. In detail, this approach works as follows:

1. rewrite the `SELECT` clause of a query, replacing all occurances of `oid` by `*`.
2. optimize the rewritten query in the conventional way.
3. include *Cache* operators for the collections whose *oid* columns are requested in the `SELECT` clause of the query, and place those *Cache* operators at the top of the query plan generated in Step 2 (i.e., just below the *Return* operator); remember that *Cache* operators carry out projections so that the right columns for the original query are returned.
4. push down *Cache* operators through *non-reductive* operators. A non-reductive operator is an operator that does not filter out any objects. Examples are *Sort* operators and certain functional joins for which integrity constraints guarantee that all objects satisfy the join predicate(s) (see [CK97] for a formal definition of non-reductive operators).

The push-down of *Cache* operators through non-reductive operators (Step 4) reduces the cost of executing the query and at the same time obeys the principle that only relevant objects are copied into the cache. Suppose, as an example, that a *Cache* operator is pushed below a *Sort*: the cost of the *Sort* is reduced because the *Sort* operator works on *thin* tuples, because the *Cache* operators project out all the columns that were added as part of the rewriting in Step 1. At the same time, no irrelevant objects are copied into the cache because the *Sort* does not filter out any objects.

While pushing down *Cache* operators through non-reductive operators is certainly an improvement, this "caching at the top" approach clearly does not always produce good cache-enhanced plans. Because *Cache* operators impact the size of intermediate results, the placement of *Cache* operators should also impact join ordering; however, the heuristic ignores this interdependency. Furthermore, *Cache* operators high in a plan force lower operators to handle *thick* tuples with high extra cost. The heuristic basically assumes that the extra cost incurred by plans with *Cache* operators is always outweighed by the benefit of these *Cache* operators for (future) method invocations – an assumption which is not always valid, even when data accesses are expensive (Section 5.4).

3.2 Cache Operators at the Bottom of Query Plans

The second approach, "caching at the bottom", makes the following cache operator placement decisions: (1) generate a *Cache* operator for every candidate collection, and (2) place all *Cache* operators low in a query plan. Like the "caching at the top" heuristic, the "caching at the bottom" heuristic assumes that the benefits of *Cache* operators for candidate collections always outweigh the cost incurred by the presence of *Cache* operators. However, the "caching at the bottom" heuristic places *Cache* operators low in query plans, following the principle that columns which are only needed for caching and not to evaluate the query itself should be projected out as early as possible. Thus, the "caching at the bottom" approach affects the cost of other query operators (i.e., joins, group bys, etc.) as little as possible, but it might copy objects into the cache that are not part of the query result and which would be filtered by these other query operators.

In detail, the "caching at the bottom" approach works as follows:

1. optimize the original query in the conventional way.
2. for each leaf node of the resulting plan, if the operator accesses a candidate collection, expand the list of attributes returned to include all the attributes of the objects.
3. place a *Cache* operator for that collection above each such leaf operator.
4. pull up *Cache* operators that sit below pipelining operators (e.g., filters or nested-loop joins).

Cache operator pull-up in the "caching at the bottom" approach is analogous to *Cache* operator push-down in the "caching at the top" approach. Push-down heuristics reduce the cost of a query without increasing the number of *false cache insertions* (adding objects to the cache that do not participate in the query result, hence will not be used later). Pull-up heuristics reduce the number of *false cache insertions* without increasing the cost of a query. Consider as an example a *Cache* operator that sits below a pipeline operator which filters out some of its input tuples. Moving the *Cache* operator above that pipeline operator will reduce the number of objects copied into the cache, without increasing the cost of the pipeline operator because the cost of a pipeline operator does not depend on the width of the tuples it processes.

3.3 Cost-based Cache Operator Placement

It should be clear from the previous two subsections that there is a fundamental tradeoff between "high" and "low" *Cache* operators: the higher a *Cache* operator, the lower the number of *false cache insertions*, and the higher the number of other query operators that sit below the *Cache* operator and operate at increased cost because they must process *thick* tuples. The "caching at the top" and "caching at the bottom" heuristics attack this tradeoff in simple ways; obviously, there are situations in which either one or even both approaches do not find the best place to position a *Cache* operator in a query plan.

In this section, we show how a query processor can make *Cache* operator placement decisions in a cost-based manner. The approach is based on the following extensions:

1. extend the enumerator to enumerate alternative plans with *Cache* operators
2. estimate the cost and potential benefit of *Cache* operators to determine the best plan; the cost models for other query operators (e.g., joins, etc.) need not be changed
3. extend the pruning condition of the optimizer to eliminate sub-optimal plans as early as possible

We describe these three extensions in more detail in the following subsections.

3.3.1 Enumeration of Plans with *Cache* Operators

The implementation of the cost-based placement strategy is integrated with the planning phase of the optimizer. We discuss the necessary changes in the context of a bottom-up dynamic programming optimizer [SAC+79]. Optimizers of this sort generate query plans in three phases. In the first phase, they generate plans for single collection accesses. In the next phase, they generate plans for joins. They first enumerate the two-way joins, using the plans built in the first phase as input. Likewise, they then plan three-way joins, using the plans previously built (for single collections and two-way joins), and so on, until a plan for the entire join is generated. The final phase then completes the plan by adding operators for aggregation, ordering, unions, etc. Each plan has a set of *plan properties* that track what work has been done by that plan. In particular, they record what collections have been accessed, what predicates applied, and what attributes are available, as well as an estimated cost and cardinality for the plan[2]. Each operator added to a plan modifies the properties of that plan to record what it has done. At the end of each round of joins, as well as at the end of each phase, the optimizer *prunes* the set of generated plans, finding plans which have done the same work (have the same properties) and eliminating all but the cheapest.

[2] There are several other properties that are tracked; we only list the most relevant for this paper.

Plan 1: Index Scan - $A_{\mathtt{thick}}$
Plan 2: Index Scan - $A_{\mathtt{thin}}$
Plan 3: Relation Scan - $A_{\mathtt{thick}}$
Plan 4: Relation Scan - $A_{\mathtt{thin}}$
Plan 5: Cache(A) - Ship - Index Scan - $A_{\mathtt{thick}}$
Plan 6: Cache(A) - Ship - Relation Scan - $A_{\mathtt{thick}}$

Figure 2: Plans for Accessing Table A

Only a few changes need to be made to an existing optimizer to allow it to generate plans with *Cache* operators. First, we have to define what a *Cache* operator does to a plan's properties. *Cache* projects out (i.e., does not pass on to higher operators) unneeded attributes, so it changes the attribute property. It also will affect the cost, as discussed in Section 3.3.2 below. Next, the first and second phases must be modified to generate alternative plans with *Cache* operators. In modern dynamic programming optimizers [Loh88, HKWY97], this corresponds to adding one *rule* to each of those phases. In the access phase, in addition to the normal (*thin*) plans for a collection, which select out just the attributes needed for the query, the new rule will also generate plans for getting all the attributes of the objects in the collection (*thick plans*), if the collection is one of those whose *oid* column is selected by the query (i.e., a candidate collection). In addition, the rule will generate extra plans which consist of a *Cache* (and *Ship*) operator above each of the thick plans. Figure 2 shows the six plans that would be generated in phase one of enumeration if the collection access could be done by either scanning the collection or by scanning an index. If *thick* and *thin* coincide (i.e., all columns of A are needed to produce the query result, regardless of caching), only four plans would be enumerated, as Plans 1 and 3 would be identical to 2 and 4, respectively.

Similarly, in the join planning phase, the enumerator must consider possible caching plans in addition to normal join plans. Since there will be a thick plan for each candidate collection, we will automatically get joins with thick result objects. On top of these, we add appropriate *Cache* operators during each round of joining. We can consider caching any subset of *available* candidate collections in a given plan, where *available* means that the plan's properties indicate that that collection has been accessed, that no other *Cache* operator for that collection is present in the plan, and that the full objects are present (it's a thick plan for that collection). This, of course, can cause an exponential explosion in the number of plans that must be considered. For example, Figure 3 shows four basic join plans and five caching plans for a two table join query; actually, even more plans are possible taking into account that more than one join method is applicable and that *Ship* operators can be placed before or after the joins. In Section 3.3.3, we discuss how ag-

Plan 1: Join - Ship - Scan - A_{thick}
- Ship - Scan -B_{thick}
Plan 2: Join - Ship - Scan - A_{thin}
- Ship - Scan -B_{thick}
Plan 3: Join - Ship - Scan - A_{thick}
- Ship - Scan -B_{thin}
Plan 4: Join - Ship - Scan - A_{thin}
- Ship - Scan -B_{thin}
Plan 5: Cache(A) - Join - Ship - Scan - A_{thick}
- Ship - Scan -B_{thick}
Plan 6: Cache(B) - Join - Ship - Scan - A_{thick}
- Ship - Scan -B_{thick}
Plan 7: Cache(A,B) - Join - Ship - Scan - A_{thick}
- Ship - Scan -B_{thick}
Plan 8: Cache(B) - Join - Ship - Scan - A_{thin}
- Ship - Scan -B_{thick}
Plan 9: Cache(A) - Join - Ship - Scan - A_{thick}
- Ship - Scan -B_{thin}

Figure 3: Plans Generated for $A \bowtie B$
A, B are candidate collections

gressive pruning can help control this explosion.

3.3.2 Cost/Benefit Calculation of *Cache* Operators

Since *Cache* operators can only be applied on whole objects, their presence increases the cost of underlying operators (because these underlying operators must work on more data). Further, since *Cache* operators project out the columns not needed for the query result, their properties (other than cost) are the same as a simple (non-caching) thin plan. For example, Plans 2, 4, 5 and 6 in Figure 2 have the same properties, excluding cost. Plans with *Cache* operators have done more work to get to the same point; they can survive, therefore, only if the *Cache* operators have a negative cost. At the beginning of optimization, a potential *benefit* is computed for each collection to be cached. The *cost* of a *Cache* operator is defined as the *actual cost* to materialize its input stream *minus* the estimated *benefit*, or savings, from not faulting in objects in future method invocations. The actual cost of the *Cache* operator is proportional to the cardinality of the input plan, and represents the time to copy objects into the cache, and do the project to form the output stream.

The benefit is considerably trickier to estimate. Fortunately, a reasonably detailed model is possible, and is sufficient for choosing good plans. To compute the benefit of a collection, we need to know how many distinct objects of the collection will be part of the query result. For simplicity, we will refer to this number as the *output* of the collection for this query. We assume that the application will invoke methods on a certain fraction F (e.g. 80 %) of the objects in the query result. The benefit, B, is proportional to the output, O: $B = k \times F \times O$, where k represents the time to fault in the object[3]. k, F, and the output of a collection are constant for a given query; they do not depend on the plan for the query, or when (or if) caching occurs. Thus, the benefit can be computed before planning begins. For complete accuracy, B should include a factor f_1 representing the fraction of the relevant objects not already in the cache; however, the overhead to estimate f_1 is not justified given the accuracy we can achieve for other parts of the formula, so we ignore this factor and assign F a lower value accordingly.

The tricky part is how to estimate the output. One approach is to let the optimizer do it. For this alternative, to find the output of a collection R, the optimizer is asked to plan a modified version of the original query, such that the original select list is replaced by "distinct R.oid". The result cardinality of this query is the required output. Note that since the plan for this modified query is unimportant, the optimizer can use any greedy or heuristic approach it wants to reduce optimization time, as long as it does use its cardinality estimation formulas. However, this approach is still likely to be expensive, especially for large queries in which multiple collections are candidates for caching, as the optimizer will be called once per candidate collection, and then again to plan the actual query. Nor is the result guaranteed to be accurate; it will be only as good as the optimizer's cardinality estimates.

Instead, we devised a simple algorithm for estimating output [HKU99]. This approach has much less overhead and estimates the output of a collection with accuracy close to that of the optimizer for queries where the join predicates are independent. The algorithm takes a query as input, and returns an estimate of the output of each candidate collection for the query. The algorithm essentially emulates the optimizer's cardinality computations, but without building plans. It starts by estimating the effect of applying local predicates to the base collections, using the optimizer formulas. It then heuristically chooses an inner for each join and "applies" the join predicate to the inner's output. The output of a collection is taken to be the minimum value among its initial cardinality, its output after applying the most selective local predicate (if any) and its output after applying the most selective join predicate (if any). The algorithm seems to provide a good compromise between accuracy and overhead, though it needs tuning for joins over composite keys.

3.3.3 Pruning of Plans with *Cache* Operators

At the end of each phase of planning, and at the end of each round of joins, the optimizer examines the plans that have been generated, and "prunes" (i.e., throws away) those which are at least as expensive as some other plan that has equivalent or more general properties. Thin plans are less general (because they make available fewer attributes) than thick ones; hence, although thick plans

[3] k depends on the data source and object. [ROH98] describes how an optimizer can assess the value of this parameter.

are typically more expensive, they will not naturally be pruned in favor of thin plans.

This is good, in terms of ensuring that all possible caching plans are examined. However, as described in Section 3.3.1, it also leads to an exponential explosion in the number of plans. Fortunately, since the *Cache* operator only passes through those attributes needed for the query, it creates thin plans (or at least, thinner plans) that compete with each other. For example, in Figure 2, of the six plans generated for accessing collection A in the first phase of optimization, at most two will survive: one thick plan and one thin plan (if it is cheaper than the thick one). The thin survivor could either be a caching plan (e.g., Plan 6) or an original thin plan (e.g., Plan 2). In the join phase, the maximum number of plans that survives each round is 2^n, where n is the number of candidate collections in this round. So in Figure 3, four plans could survive: one in which both A and B are thick, one in which both are thin, one in which A is thick and B thin, and one in which B is thick and A thin (for example, the survivors might be Plans 1, 2, 6 and 7).

However, under certain conditions we can safely prune a thick plan in favor of a thin – and the sooner we eliminate such plans the better for optimization times. In particular, we can prune the thick plan for a candidate collection A if:

$$Cost_{A_{thin}} \leq Cost_{A_{thick}} + Cost_{A_{CacheBest}} - Benefit$$

where $Cost_{A_{CacheBest}}$ is the minimum actual cost incurred to cache a collection and corresponds to the case where the *Cache* operator sits directly above that join that results in the minimum number of output tuples from the collection. It can be computed before optimization, during the output calculations described in Section 3.3.2. The condition basically says that if we assume the minimal possible cost for caching A (lowest actual cost less constant benefit), and that is still more than the cost of a thin plan for A, then there is no point in keeping the thick plan, as caching A is not a good idea.

3.4 Other Strategies and Variants

In this section, we presented three alternative ways to generate plans with *Cache* operators. These three approaches mark cornerstones in the space of possible strategies for integrating *Cache* operator placement into a query processor. The first two approaches are simple strategies that always place *Cache* operators either at the top or at the bottom of query plans. Neither approach causes much overhead during query optimization, but they are likely to make sub-optimal decisions in many cases. The third approach is a full-fledged, cost-based approach for determining cache operator placement. This approach can be the cause of significant additional overhead during query optimization, but is likely to make good decisions.

We can imagine many approaches that make better decisions than the "caching at the top" and "caching at the bottom" heuristics at the expense of additional overhead, or approaches that are cheaper than "cost-based caching" at the risk of making poor decisions in some cases. We describe here just a few variants:

cost-based Cache operator pushdown: rather than push *Cache* operators down through *non-reductive* query operators only, this variant would push a *Cache* operator down through another operator if the result would be a lower cost plan, using the cost model and cost/benefit calculations for *Cache* operators of Section 3.3.2.

cost-based Cache operator pull-up: *Cache* operator pull-up can also be carried out during post-processing of plans in a cost-based manner, instead of pulling *Cache* operators up only through pipeline operators.

flood-sensitive Cache operator elimination: The "caching at the bottom" variant can be extended in such a way that *Cache* operators that would flood the cache because they are applied to too many objects (according to the cardinality estimates of the optimizer) are eliminated from the plan.

rigorous pruning in cost-based approach: There are several possible variants of the "cost-based caching" approach which more aggressively prune plans, even when it may not be wholly "safe" to do so (in other words, they may discard plans that could be the basis of winning plans later on). These variants reduce the cost of query optimization considerably, at the expense of perhaps missing good plans. For example, one aggressive variant might generalize the pruning condition of Section 3.3.3, and always keep at most one of the alternative plans at the end of the round. A somewhat gentler variant might keep two plans at the end of each round of plan generation: a "pure" thick plan, that is, a plan in which all attributes of all candidate collections of the plan are present, and a "pure" thin plan, that is, a plan in which no attributes not necessary for the original query are present.

4 Implementation Details

We implemented all three cache operator placement strategies described in the previous section and integrated them into the Garlic database middleware system. In this section, we describe the major design choices we made in our implementation.

4.1 Double Caching Architecture

Figure 4 shows the overall design of the cache manager and query execution engine. Our implementation involves a double caching scheme. There is a *primary cache* used by the application, while *Cache* operators load objects into a *secondary cache* during query execution. From the secondary cache these objects are copied into the primary cache when they are first accessed by a method. *Resident object tables* (ROT) in both the primary and secondary cache are used to quickly find an

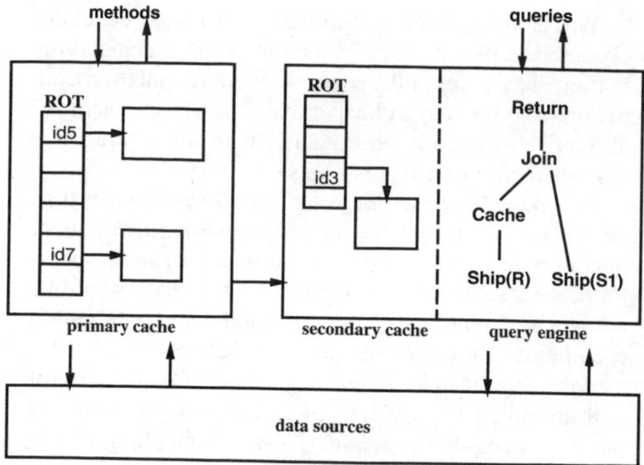

Figure 4: Double Caching Architecture

object in the cache. *Cache* operators only copy objects into the secondary cache that are not present in either the primary or the secondary cache. Thus, they waste as little main memory for double caching as possible and avoid copying objects into the secondary cache multiple times if the input stream of the *Cache* operator contains duplicates. During method invocations, an object is faulted into the primary cache from the data sources if it is not found in the primary or the secondary cache, just as in a traditional middleware system.

The double caching scheme shown in Figure 4 has two important advantages. First, copying objects into a secondary cache, rather than directly into the primary cache, prevents the primary cache from being flooded with query results, thus displacing frequently used objects. Consider, for example, a case in which the query optimizer estimates that the *Cache* operator copies, say, 100 objects; but in fact, the optimizer errs because of outdated statistics and the *Cache* operator would in fact copy millions of objects into the cache. The double caching scheme makes it possible to control and limit the impact of *Cache* operators. Second, the overhead of copying objects into the cache as a by-product of query execution can be reduced in such a double caching scheme. In the primary cache, objects are managed and replaced in the granularity of objects—this is reasonable because individual objects are faulted in and replaced in the primary cache during method invocations. The secondary cache, on the other hand, is organized in chunks; that is, when a *Cache* operator begins execution it will allocate space for, say, 1000 objects in the secondary cache, knowing that it is likely to copy many objects. In other words, the double caching scheme makes it possible to efficiently *bulkload* the cache with relevant objects.

However, the double caching scheme also has some disadvantages: (1) it incurs additional computational overhead in order to copy objects from the secondary cache into the primary cache when the objects are needed; (2) it does waste main memory because after an object has been copied from the secondary into the primary cache, it is cached twice; (3) it requires some (albeit little) tuning effort—this is the flip side of the coin which provides better control over the impact of *Cache* operators. In our experience, the advantages of the double caching scheme outweigh these disadvantages, but, in general, the tradeoffs strongly depend on the kind of application being processed by the middleware system.

4.2 Caching in Middleware for Diverse Sources

Garlic has been designed with an emphasis on handling diverse sources of information, especially sources that do not have traditional database capabilities, though they may offer interesting search and data manipulation capabilities of their own. Loading the middleware cache with query results is particularly attractive for systems like Garlic. First, communicating with some sources may be expensive in Garlic; almost any Web source, for example, will have a highly variable and typically long response time. In such situations, the benefit of *Cache* operators is particularly high (i.e., parameter k is large). Second, some sources are unable to just produce an object given its oid; that is, they do not support the faulting in of objects. Applications that operate on data stored in such data sources *must* load relevant objects as a by-product of query execution; otherwise, such applications simply cannot be executed.[4]

Loading the middleware cache with query results also raises several challenges in this environment. Diverse sources have diverse data. It may not always be practical to cache an entire object. For example, an object may have large and awkward attributes that should only be brought to the middleware if they are really needed. Alternatively, it may be desirable to cache values that are actually computed by methods of a data source because these values are frequently referenced by application programs. So, a flexible notion of "object" is needed. Garlic provides some flexibility in defining objects. Garlic communicates with sources by way of wrappers [RS97]. A wrapper writer must understand the data of a source and describe it in terms of objects. The description can indicate for each attribute (and method) of an object whether it should be part of the cached representation of the object. Garlic has access to this description during query processing, and can use it to decide what attributes and/or methods to include in a thick plan. Ideally, however, we would cache *application objects* which could include data from several collections, possibly from different data sources, and let programmers define such *application objects* for each application program individually. At present we have no mechanism to cache such user-defined application objects, but caching the underlying objects serves the same purpose, by bringing the data needed to construct the application

[4] In such situations, our cost-based approach must be extended to make sure that the winning plan contains a *Cache* operator.

Collection	Base cardinality	Data source
course	12,000	UDB
department	250	UDB
coursesection	50,000	UDB
professor	25,000	UDB
student	50,000	UDB
kids	116,759	UDB
NotesCourses	12,000	Notes
NotesDepartments	250	Notes
WWWPeople	25,000	WWW

Table 1: Test Data Sources and Object Collections

Query	Data sources	Output cardinality
select c.oid from course c where c.deptno<11	UDB	500
select c.oid from NotesCourses c where c.course_dept<11	Notes	500
select p.oid from WWWPeople where p.WWWcategory = 'professor' and p.WWWname like 'professorName15%'	WWW	500

Table 2: Benchmark Queries for Experiment 1

object to the middleware server.

5 Experiments and Results

This section presents the results of experiments that demonstrate the utility (and even, the necessity) of loading a cache with query results by studying the overall running times of applications that involve queries and methods. Next, we look at how query planning time is affected by the three *Cache* operator placement strategies. Finally, we compare the quality of plans produced by the three approaches. We begin with a description of the experimental environment.

5.1 Experimental Environment

The experiments were carried out in the context of the Garlic project, using the double caching architecture described in Section 4.1. For our experiments, we adapted the relational schema and data from the BUCKY benchmark [CDN+97] to a scenario suitable for a federated system. The test data is distributed among three data sources: an IBM DB2 Universal Database (UDB), a Lotus Notes version 4.5 database, and a World Wide Web (WWW) source. The WWW source is populated with data from UDB at the time of query execution using IBM's Net.Data product. The data collections, base cardinalities, and distribution among data sources are shown in Table 1. The Garlic middleware and the UDB and WWW databases run on separate IBM RS/6000 workstations under AIX; the Notes database resides on a PC running Windows NT. All machines are connected by Ethernet. In all experiments, the middleware cache is initially empty.

5.2 Experiment 1: The Value of Caching

The first set of experiments shows the importance of caching in general, and of our *enhanced caching* (loading the cache with query results) in particular. We measured the running times of three simple application programs that initiate the execution of a query and invoke two methods on each object of the query result. The queries used in the three application programs are given in Table 2; they are simple one-table queries against the UDB, Lotus Notes, and WWW databases. For these simple queries, all three *Cache* operator placement strategies presented in Section 3 produce the same plan: *Cache-Ship-Scan*. Each method involves reading the value of one attribute of the object to which the method is bound. The size of the primary and secondary cache are chosen such that all relevant objects fit in both. We ran each application program ten times (beginning with an empty cache each time) and report on the average running times.

	UDB	Notes	WWW
no caching	47.8	22.9	3538.5
traditional caching	22.9	18.2	1762.3
enhanced caching	2.2	12.7	11.9

Table 3: Total Running Time [secs]

Table 3 shows the results. As expected, *enhanced caching* wins in all cases. The gains are particularly pronounced for the WWW application because interaction with the WWW database, as required to fault in objects, is particularly expensive—even if the WWW server is only lightly loaded and has all information available in main memory. The savings in cost are relatively low for the Notes application because faulting in objects from the Notes database is quite cheap so that the cost of query processing dominates the overall cost of the application in this case. In all cases, *traditional caching*, which faults in objects when they are used for the first time as part of a method invocation, beats *no caching* because it saves the cost of interacting with the data sources for the second method invocation.

In this experiment, the application program accesses *all* objects returned by the query; i.e., $F = 1$. For smaller F, the savings obtained by traditional and enhanced caching are less pronounced. As mentioned in Section 3.3.2, the benefit increases linearly with F; in the extreme case, for $F = 0$, no caching and traditional caching have the same running time as enhanced caching (in fact, a little better).

5.3 Experiment 2: Query Planning Times

The next experiment studied the planning times of the three *Cache* operator placement strategies. The two parameters that impact the planning time most are the number of collections involved in the query and the number of candidate collections. Our queries join collections stored in UDB and Notes. We varied the number of collections involved in the query and in all cases, all collections were considered candidate collections. Thus, these queries can be seen as tough cases which are expensive to optimize.

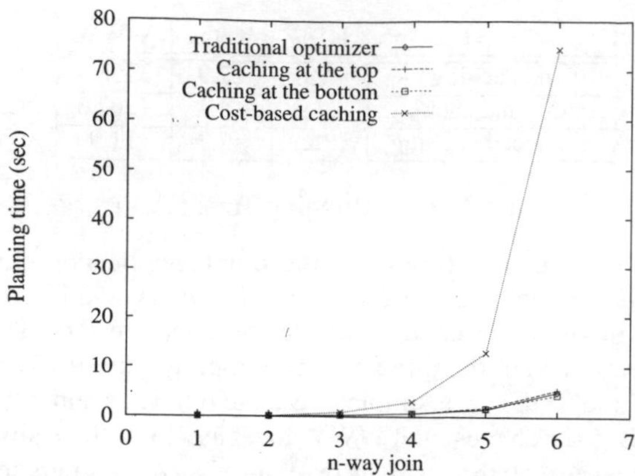

Figure 5: Planning Times for UDB/Notes Queries

Figure 5 shows the resulting planning times for each of the three approaches presented in Section 3. As a baseline, we also show the running time of a traditional optimizer that does not generate plans with *Cache* operators. Again, there are no surprises. The full-fledged cost-based approach becomes prohibitively expensive if there are more than four candidate collections in a query. At this point one of the two heuristics or the variants proposed in Section 3.4 should be used. Up to that point, however, the cost-based approach has negligible overhead and can safely be used. Comparing the "caching at the bottom," "caching at the top," and "traditional optimizer" lines, we see that the two heuristics have virtually no overhead.

5.4 Experiment 3: The Right Caching Decisions

The last set of experiments demonstrates the need to carry out cost-based *Cache* operator placement in certain situations. The experiments show: 1) how a *Cache* operator at the top can increase the cost of the other operators that sit below; 2) the overhead introduced by unnecessarily caching a large number of objects when a *Cache* operator is placed at the bottom; 3) the need to avoid flooding the secondary cache with irrelevant objects; and 4) that it is not always beneficial to have *Cache* operators for all candidate collections, even when accessing slow sources. We used queries over collections from the UDB and WWW databases. The queries and the best execution plan for each query are presented in Figure 6. "Caching at the top" works best for the first query; for the second query, "caching at the bottom" works best; and for the third query, no *Cache* operator at all should be generated. We again measured the total execution time of three simple application programs that each execute one of these queries and invoke one method on each object returned by that query. The method simply reads the value of one attribute. The size of the primary cache was set to 1000 objects which is more than enough to hold all objects involved during method invocations. For the first query (Q1), we studied two configurations for the secondary

	Q1(large)	Q1(med)	Q2	Q3
no caching	405.5	405.5	842.5	129.2
traditional caching	405.5	405.5	842.7	129.9
caching at the top	71.3	71.3	49.8	177.5
caching at the bottom	76.0	415.8	34.9	141.9
cost-based caching	71.4	71.4	35.1	130.7

Table 4: Total Running Time [secs]
size of sec. cache: medium=1000 obj.; large=6000 obj.

cache: (a) *medium*, with a capacity of 1000 objects, and (b) *large*, with a capacity of 6000 objects. We varied the size of the secondary cache for Q1 in order to study the implications of loading the cache with irrelevant objects, in particular for the "caching at the bottom" approach. For the other two queries, a *medium* secondary cache was sufficient in all cases, so we only show the results obtained using such a *medium* secondary cache.

Table 4 shows the results. We can see that the cost-based approach to loading the cache with query results shows the overall best performance, making the right caching decisions in all situations. The "caching at the top" approach, as expected, makes suboptimal decisions for Q2 and Q3, and the "caching at the bottom" approach makes suboptimal decisions for Q1 and Q3. The "caching at the bottom approach" shows particularly poor performance if it floods the secondary cache, so that few relevant objects are loaded as a by-product of executing the query (Q1 with a medium-sized secondary cache). "Caching at the bottom" is never much worse than traditional caching or no caching at all, and it can, therefore, be seen as a *conservative* method of extending today's database systems to load a cache with query results. The "caching at the top" heuristic, on the other hand, is as much as 37% more expensive than traditional caching in our experiments, and could easily be more. In these experiments, traditional caching and no caching show approximately the same performance because every result object is accessed exactly once as part of the method invocations.

6 Related Work

Most work on data processing in distributed systems has focused either on query processing or on caching, and most middleware systems today are built in such a way that query processing does not affect caching and vice versa. For example, SAP R/3 [BEG96, KKM98] is a very popular business administration system that supports the execution of (user and pre-defined) queries and methods, processing applications that involve both as described in Section 2.1. Persistence [KJA93] is a middleware system that enables the development of object-oriented (C++, Smalltalk, etc.) applications on top of a relational database system. That system typically pushes down the execution of queries to the relational database system and executes methods in the middleware using caching. Query processing and caching do not interact in

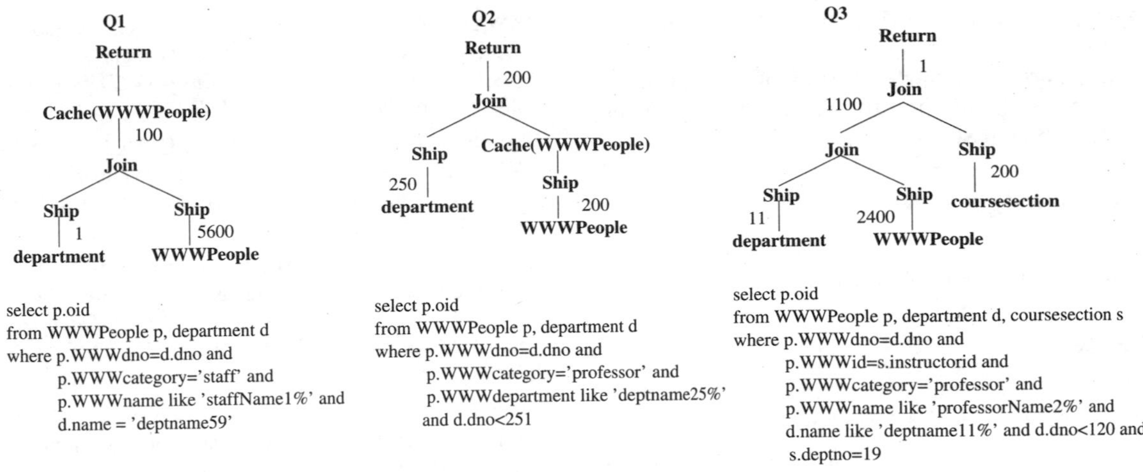
Q1
Return
Cache(WWWPeople)
100
Join
Ship
1
department
Ship
5600
WWWPeople
select p.oid
from WWWPeople p, department d
where p.WWWdno=d.dno and
p.WWWcategory='staff' and
p.WWWname like 'staffName1%' and
d.name = 'deptname59'
Q2
Return
200
Join
Ship
250
department
Cache(WWWPeople)
Ship
200
WWWPeople
select p.oid
from WWWPeople p, department d
where p.WWWdno=d.dno and
p.WWWcategory='professor' and
p.WWWdepartment like 'deptname25%'
and d.dno<251
Q3
Return
1
Join
1100
Join
Ship
11
department
Ship
2400
WWWPeople
Ship
200
coursesection
select p.oid
from WWWPeople p, department d, coursesection s
where p.WWWdno=d.dno and
p.WWWid=s.instructorid and
p.WWWcategory='professor' and
p.WWWname like 'professorName2%' and
d.name like 'deptname11%' and d.dno<120 and
s.deptno=19

Figure 6: Benchmark Queries for Experiment 3

either system, so both would benefit from the techniques presented in this paper.

Database systems that have a *data shipping* architecture naturally load a cache with query results; examples are most object-oriented database systems such as O_2 [D+90]. These systems bring all the base data to the middleware (or client) to evaluate a query and that base data is then cached for subsequent queries and methods, if the cache is large enough. In some sense, data shipping, therefore, corresponds to the "caching at the bottom" approach – however, there is no *Cache* operator pull-up and no way to execute joins at data source(s). This causes data shipping to perform poorly for many types of queries [FJK96].

Another experimental database system that supports query processing and caching is KRISYS. In an early version which was targeted for engineering applications, KRYSIS used queries to load the cache with relevant objects [HMNR95], as proposed in our work. However, that version only supported a variant of the "caching at the top" approach (without *Cache* operator pushdown). In a more recent version [DHM+98], KRYSIS supports predicate-based caching. Predicate-based caching [KB94], like view caching [Rou91] and semantic caching [DFJ+96], makes it possible to cache the results of queries. The purpose of predicate-based caching, however, is to use the cache in order to answer future queries (rather than for methods). Hence, it requires significantly more complex mechanisms for tracking cache contents, and is not geared for the lookup of individual objects.

Two further lines of work are relevant. The first is cache investment [FK97]. Cache investment also extends a query processor to make it cache-aware. Again, however, the purpose of cache investment is to load the cache of the middleware in such a way that future queries (rather than methods) can be executed efficiently. The second related line of work is prefetching [PZ91, CKV93, GK94]. The purpose of prefetching is to bring objects into the cache before they are actually accessed. Prefetching, however, is carried out as a separate process, independent of query processing.

7 Conclusion

In this paper, we showed that caching objects during query execution dramatically speeds up applications that involve both queries and methods in a middleware (or client server) environment. The performance wins that can be achieved by this method are huge; they are particularly high in environments in which interactions with the data sources are very expensive; e.g., data sources on the Internet. In certain scenarios, loading a cache with query results in this way is even necessary; such a situation arises in heterogeneous database environments in which some data sources are not able to respond to requests for individual objects.

To implement our approach we extended the cache manager and the query processor of a middleware system. We used a double caching scheme to reduce the overhead of our approach and to avoid flooding the primary cache with (useless) objects as a by-product of query execution. We explored three alternative ways of extending the query processor: "caching at the top," "caching at the bottom," and "cost-based caching." The first two approaches are simple heuristics which can be easily incorporated in an existing query processor and which typically do not increase query optimization times; however, the "caching at the top" approach can result in substantially increased query execution times, while the "caching at the bottom" approach may cache many useless objects, thereby causing additional overhead and providing no benefit if the cache is too small. The third approach is significantly more complex to implement and increases optimization times of complex queries substantially, but is always able to make the best decisions of the three approaches. Based on these observations, we propose to use the full "cost-based" approach for simple queries that involve no more than four collections and heuristics for more complex queries. In the future, we plan to investigate the tradeoffs of optimization time and application performance for some of the variants described in Section 3.4.

8 Acknowledgements

We thank Mary Tork Roth, Peter Schwarz and Bart Niswonger for their help with this work.

References

[ASU89] A. Aho, R. Sethi, and J. Ullman. *Compiler Construction*, volume II. Addison-Wesley, 1989.

[BEG96] R. Buck-Emden and J. Galimow. *SAP R/3 System, A Client/Server Technology*. Addison-Wesley, Reading, MA, USA, 1996.

[CDN+97] M. Carey, D. DeWitt, J. Naughton, M. Asgarian, J. Gehrke, and D. Shah. The bucky object-relational benchmark. In *Proc. of the ACM SIGMOD Conf. on Management of Data*, pages 135–146, Tucson, AZ, USA, May 1997.

[CK97] M. Carey and D. Kossmann. On saying "enough already!" in SQL. In *Proc. of the ACM SIGMOD Conf. on Management of Data*, pages 219–230, Tucson, AZ, USA, May 1997.

[CKV93] K. Curewitz, P. Krishnan, and J. Vitter. Practical prefetching via data compression. In *Proc. of the ACM SIGMOD Conf. on Management of Data*, pages 43–53, Washington, DC, USA, May 1993.

[D+90] O. Deux et al. The story of O_2. *IEEE Transactions on Knowledge and Data Engineering*, 2(1):91–108, March 1990.

[DFJ+96] S. Dar, M. Franklin, B. Jónsson, D. Srivastava, and M. Tan. Semantic data caching and replacement. In *Proc. of the Conf. on Very Large Data Bases (VLDB)*, pages 330–341, Bombay, India, September 1996.

[DHM+98] S. Deßloch, T. Härder, N. Mattos, B. Mitschang, and J. Thomas. KRISYS: Modeling concepts, implementation techniques, and client/server issues. *The VLDB Journal*, 7(2):79–95, April 1998.

[FJK96] M. Franklin, B. Jónsson, and D. Kossmann. Performance tradeoffs for client-server query processing. In *Proc. of the ACM SIGMOD Conf. on Management of Data*, pages 149–160, Montreal, Canada, June 1996.

[FK97] M. Franklin and D. Kossmann. Cache investment strategies. Technical Report CS-TR-3803, University of Maryland, College Park, MD 20742, May 1997.

[GK94] C. A. Gerlhof and A. Kemper. A multi-threaded architecture for prefetching in object bases. In *Proc. of the Intl. Conf. on Extending Database Technology (EDBT)*, volume 779 of *Lecture Notes in Computer Science (LNCS)*, pages 351–364, Cambridge, United Kingdom, March 1994. Springer-Verlag.

[HKU99] L. Haas, D. Kossmann, and I. Ursu. An investigation into loading a cache with query results. Technical report, IBM Almaden, San Jose, CA, March 1999.

[HKWY97] L. Haas, D. Kossmann, E. Wimmers, and J. Yang. Optimizing queries across diverse data sources. In *Proc. of the Conf. on Very Large Data Bases (VLDB)*, pages 276–285, Athens, Greece, August 1997.

[HMNR95] T. Härder, B. Mitschang, U. Nink, and N. Ritter. Workstation/Server-Architekturen für datenbankbasierte Ingenieuranwendungen. *Informatik – Forschung und Entwicklung*, 10(2):55–72, May 1995.

[KB94] A. Keller and J. Basu. A predicate-based caching scheme for client-server database architectures. In *Proc. of the Intl. IEEE Conf. on Parallel and Distributed Information Systems*, pages 229–238, Austin, TX, USA, September 1994.

[KJA93] A. Keller, R. Jensen, and S. Agrawal. Persistence software: Bridging object-oriented programming and relational databases. In *Proc. of the ACM SIGMOD Conf. on Management of Data*, pages 523–528, Washington, DC, USA, May 1993.

[KK95] A. Kemper and D. Kossmann. Adaptable pointer swizzling strategies in object bases: Design, realization, and quantitative analysis. *The VLDB Journal*, 4(3):519–566, August 1995.

[KKM98] A. Kemper, D. Kossmann, and F. Matthes. SAP R/3: a database application system. Tutorial handouts for the ACM SIGMOD Conference, Seattle, WA, USA, June 1998.

[Loh88] G. Lohman. Grammar-like functional rules for representing query optimization alternatives. In *Proc. of the ACM SIGMOD Conf. on Management of Data*, pages 18–27, Chicago, IL, USA, May 1988.

[Mos92] J. E. B. Moss. Working with persistent objects: To swizzle or not to swizzle. *IEEE Trans. Software Eng.*, 18(8):657–673, August 1992.

[PZ91] M. Palmer and S. Zdonik. FIDO: A cache that learns to fetch. In *Proc. of the Conf. on Very Large Data Bases (VLDB)*, pages 255–264, Barcelona, September 1991.

[ROH98] M. Tork Roth, F. Ozcan, and L. Haas. Cost models DO matter: Providing cost information for diverse data sources in a federated system. In *Proc. of the Conf. on Very Large Data Bases (VLDB)*, Edinburgh, GB, September 1998.

[Rou91] N. Roussopoulos. The incremental access method of view cache: Concepts, algorithms, and cost analysis. *ACM Trans. on Database Systems*, 16(3):535–563, September 1991.

[RS97] M. Tork Roth and P. Schwarz. Don't scrap it, wrap it! A wrapper architecture for legacy data sources. In *Proc. of the Conf. on Very Large Data Bases (VLDB)*, pages 266–275, Athens, Greece, August 1997.

[SAC+79] P. Selinger, M. Astrahan, D. Chamberlin, R. Lorie, and T. Price. Access path selection in a relational database management system. In *Proc. of the ACM SIGMOD Conf. on Management of Data*, pages 23–34, Boston, USA, May 1979.

Building Hierarchical Classifiers Using Class Proximity

Ke Wang Senqiang Zhou Shiang Chen Liew

School of Computing
National University of Singapore
{wangk,zhousenq,liewshia}@comp.nus.edu.sg

Abstract

In this paper, we address the need to automatically classify text documents into topic hierarchies like those in ACM Digital Library and Yahoo!. The existing local approach constructs a classifier at each split of the topic hierarchy. However, the local approach does not address the closeness of classification in hierarchical classification where the concern often is how close a classification is, rather than simply correct or wrong. Also, the local approach puts its bet on classification at higher levels where the classification structure often diminishes. To address these issues, we propose the notion of *class proximity* and cast the hierarchical classification as a flat classification with the class proximity modeling the closeness of classes. Our approach is global in that it constructs a single classifier based on the global information about all classes and class proximity. We leverage generalized association rules as the rule/feature space to address several other issues in hierarchical classification.

1 Introduction

The most successful paradigm for making the mass of information on the Internet comprehensible to every one is by classifying them into topics of hierarchical specificity. Hierarchical classification of this kind has been used in collections of IBM's patent documents (http://www.ibm.com/patents), Library of Congress Catalogue, botanical and animal classification, and Internet search engines such as Yahoo! (http://www.yahoo.com/) and Infoseek (http://infoseek.go.com/) that categorize the content of the World Wide Web. Other applications of hierarchical classification are building directories, bookmarks, email folders, product catalogs, etc. Briefly, in *hierarchical classification*, each training document is a set of terms (i.e., words or phrases) and is labeled by one class (i.e., the topic), where classes are organized by their specificities into an *is-a* hierarchy [1] (i.e., a taxonomy of classes). The task is to construct a classifier that is able to assign classes to new documents within a "small error". As online documents grow in number and size, automatic hierarchical classification becomes a pressing need. This paper examines issues involved in this automation and proposes solutions to them.

Proceedings of the 25th VLDB Conference, Edinburgh, Scotland, 1999.

1.1 The issues

The central issue in document classification is separating *feature* terms that determine the classes of documents from *noise* terms that do not. In the context of hierarchical classification, it was observed that this separation depends on the current location in the class hierarchy [CDAR97, KS97]. An example in [CDAR97] is that "car" and "auto" may be good features at the top level of Yahoo!, but become noises when drilled down to *Recreation* : *Automotive*. To address this context-sensitivity, [CDAR97, KS97] determine feature terms and construct a classifier at each split of the class hierarchy. This approach is *local* in that the construction at each split is based on the local information at that split. However, local approaches do not address some important issues.

I. Bias of misclassification. In hierarchical classification, the concern often is how close a classification is, rather than simply correct or wrong: misclassification into a remote class (e.g., a nephew class) incurs a larger error than into a nearby class (e.g., a sibling

[1] In this paper, a hierarchy is any directed acyclic graph.

class); misclassification at a higher level (e.g., from *Science* to *Recreation*) incurs a larger error than at a lower level (e.g., from *Track_Cycling* to *Unicycling*); misclassification from a general class into a specific class (e.g., from *Recreation* to *Recreation* : *Sports*) incurs a larger error than the other way around. The traditional counting of misclassifications like the *confusion matrix* fails to address this closeness of classification.

II. Target-sensitivity of features. Feature terms should be determined with respect to the target class that they characterize. For example, "car" and "auto" may characterize the target class *Recreation* : *Automotive* but not the target class *Recreation*. We call this the *target-sensitivity*. In comparison, the context-sensitivity in [CDAR97, KS97] addresses the ability of *discriminating the subclasses* at location C, whereas the target-sensitivity addresses the ability of *characterizing the target class* C itself. Indeed, [CDAR97, KS97] score a feature without involving a target class. The lack of target classes often yields weak and non-understandable features.

III. High level structure diminishing. The local approach puts its bet on classification at higher levels, in that errors made at higher levels are not recoverable at lower levels. On the other hand, higher levels are often where the classification structure diminishes, due to the divergence of topics. As mentioned above, features like "car" and "auto" that characterize the lower class *Recreation* : *Automotive* may not characterize the higher class *Recreation*. Consequently, the local approach makes critical decisions (i.e., those at higher levels) based on less reliable information.

IV. Appropriateness of feature spaces. Traditionally, terms (or variables) are considered one at a time in search for features (e.g., information gain [Q93], fisher index [CDAR97], naive Bayes model [KS97], mutual information and χ^2 statistic [YP97]), and co-occurred terms, which are prevailing in document classification, have not been given the first-class consideration. Also, as classification at higher levels is considered, more general terms need to be explored to discover the classification structure. For example, when going up to *Recreation* in Yahoo!, documents may not share specific terms "reading" and "car", but may share general concepts "indoor" and "outdoor".

V. Understandability of classifiers. The local approach needs to make multiple classifications in a row to classify a document. It is difficult to understand the characteristics of a class from multiple classifications. Furthermore, the features at location C in [CDAR97, KS97] are not the characteristics of C, as explained above. In fact, [CDAR97, KS97] has to use the Bernoulli model to tell the class of a given document. In many applications, it is more desirable to tell the characteristics of a class than to tell the class of a given document. Automatic annotation of document clusters by salient keywords is such an example.

The focus of this paper is to address these issues.

1.2 Our approach

First, we introduce *class proximity* to model the closeness of classification. Then, we cast hierarchical classification as non-hierarchical classification where the class proximity models the bias introduced by class specificity. Our approach is *global* in that it constructs a single classifier based on the global information about classes and class proximity. This addresses issues I, III, V. To address issue IV, correlated features at different levels of abstraction will be searched, and a straightforward method cannot deal with the amount of work required. We incorporate an *is-a* hierarchy of terms and leverage generalized association rules [HF95, SA95] as the rule/feature space. A rule/feature has the form $X \rightarrow C$, where X is a set of terms and C is a target class; in a sense, feature X is "owned" by target class C. This approach can generate *all* correlated features at *all* abstraction levels for a large corpus, by benefiting from the work on association rules [HF95, SA95]. This addresses issues II and IV.

To construct a good classifier, however, a crucial step is to rank rules/features with respect to the classification goal, taking into account class proximity and interaction of rules/features (e.g., redundancy and preference of rules/features). We propose two ranking criteria for this purpose. We present an algorithm for selecting a "good" set of rules/features from generalized association rules in one scan of the documents.

Section 2 presents an overview of our approach. Section 3 defines two ranking criteria of rules. Section 4 presents the classifier construction. Section 5 reports the evaluation result. Section 6 remarks on related work and concludes the paper.

2 The overview

This section gives background information about association rules, defines the problem being studied, and outlines our approach.

2.1 Association rules

The problem of mining *association rules* was first studied in [AIS93] in the context of discovering purchase patterns. Let $\mathcal{I} = \{i_1, i_2, \ldots, i_m\}$ be a set of literals, called items. Let $\mathcal{D}$ be a set of transactions, where each transaction T has a unique identifier and is a set of items such that $T \subseteq \mathcal{I}$. A transaction T *contains* an itemset X (i.e., a set of some items in $\mathcal{I}$) if $X \subseteq T$. The *support* of an itemset X, denoted $sup(X)$, is the number of transactions that contain X. An *association rule* has the form $X \rightarrow Y$, where $X \subset \mathcal{I}$, $Y \subset \mathcal{I}$, and $X \cap Y = \emptyset$. The *support* of association rule $X \rightarrow Y$ is

$sup(XY)$. [2] The *confidence* of association rule $X \to Y$ is $sup(XY)/sup(X)$. The problem of mining association rules is to generate all association rules that have support and confidence greater than the user-specified minimum support and minimum confidence.

Association rules were extended to the item space organized into an *is-a* hierarchy in [HF95, SA95], where ancestors (e.g., "clothes") are more general than descendants (e.g., "jacket"). If an item is bought in a transaction, all its ancestors are considered bought in the transaction too. To take this effect into account, the support of an itemset is modified as follows. Let T be a transaction and $Anc(T)$ be the set of items in T plus all their ancestors. The *support* of an itemset X is the number of transactions T such that $X \subseteq Anc(T)$. With these modifications, a *generalized association rule* (or *multi-level association rule* in [HF95]) $X \to Y$ could hold between itemsets X and Y with items from any levels.

2.2 Hierarchical classification

In *hierarchical classification*, we are given: (a) A collection of terms $\mathcal{T}$ (i.e., words or phrases), organized into an *is-a* hierarchy called the *term hierarchy.* (b) A collection of classes $\mathcal{C}$ (i.e., topics), organized into an *is-a* hierarchy called the *class hierarchy.* $\mathcal{T} \cap \mathcal{C} = \emptyset$. (c) A collection of documents $\mathcal{D}$. Each document contains at least one term and exactly one class. Terms and the class in a document can be a non-leaf node in their hierarchies. (d) The *class proximity* $\mathcal{B}(C_i, C_j)$, representing the error made by misclassification from class C_i into class C_j. $\mathcal{B}(C_i, C_j) > 1$ (resp. $\mathcal{B}(C_i, C_j) < 1$) means an error larger than (resp. smaller than) an "usual" misclassification. $\mathcal{B}(C_i, C_i) = 0$ for all classes C_i. The task is to find a set of rules, called a *classifier*, that determines the classes for new documents within a small error. In the traditional classification setting, the term hierarchy and class hierarchy contain only leaf nodes and $\mathcal{B}(C_i, C_j) = 1$ for distinct classes C_i and C_j.

Remarks. The quantitative choice of $\mathcal{B}(C_i, C_j)$, essentially a closeness measure of two members in a family hierarchy, is largely application-dependent. Among others, a natural choice is the shortest distance from C_i to C_j in the class hierarchy, which is the default choice in this paper. In this case the classification problem amounts to minimizing the traversal distance between the true class and the predicted class. In the following discussion, we assume that $\mathcal{B}(C_i, C_j)$ is given as part of the problem specification.

2.3 An optimal classifier

We define some properties to be satisfied by our classifiers. Let X be a set of terms. Let $Anc(X)$ denote the set of terms in X plus all their ancestor terms. Consider classification rule $X \to C$ and document d. We say that $X \to C$ *covers* d if $X \subseteq Anc(d)$. We say that $X \to C$ *classifies* d in a classifier if $X \to C$ covers d and is used to determine the class of d in that classifier. While several rules may cover d, only one rule can classify d. We say $X \to C$ covers or classifies d *correctly* (resp. *wrongly*) if C is identical (resp. not identical) to the class of d.

We shall construct the classifier by selecting a number of generalized association rules to optimize the classification goal. The optimality is defined with respect to a given rule ranking criterion. Some rule ranking criteria will be discussed in Section 3. Given a rule ranking criterion, we like to the following principles to be enforced on any classifier.

Classification Principle. Each document is classified either by a selected rule of highest possible rank, or by some default class. This ensures the best classification of each document as per the rule ranking criterion used.

Selection Principle. A rule is selected if and only if it covers at least one document correctly and no selected rule of higher rank covers that document. This ensures the compactness of the classifier in that every selected rule classifies some document correctly.

An algorithm for selecting the rules according to these principles will be presented in Section 4.

An optimal classifier. Let $Rulelist_s$ be the list of selected rules, ordered by the rule ranking criterion. Let L be any prefix of $Rulelist_s$. The *error* of a rule R in L is the error made by R on the documents that R classifies. The *cutoff error* of L is the sum of the errors of all rules in L plus the error made by the default class for L. The *default class* for L, chosen from the classes of the documents not classified by L, is to minimize the error made by classifying these documents into it. An *optimal classifier* is the shortest prefix L that has the minimum cutoff error. (E.g., $<>$, $< a >$, $< a, b >$, $< a, b, c >$, and $< a, b, c, d >$ are prefixes of $< a, b, c, d >$, but $< b >$ and $< a, c >$ are not.) An example of optimal classifiers is given in Section 4.2.

2.4 The outline of construction

Given a rule ranking criterion, we shall construct an optimal classifier in three steps. Step 1 generates all generalized association rules $X \to C$, where X is a set of terms and C is a class, that satisfy the minimum support and (an optional) minimum ranking criterion specified by the user. This step is similar to mining generalized association rules in [SA95]. However, unlike [SA95], we do not generalize the classes of documents because we are aimed at prediction of classes, and we use a minimum value on the chosen rule ranking criterion instead of the minimum confidence. Step 2 sorts all rules found in Step 1 according to the rule ranking criterion. Step 3 finds the list of selected rules $Rulelist_s$ and computes the cutoff error of every prefix

[2] XY is the shorthand of $X \cup Y$.

of $Rulelist_s$. The shortest prefix of $Rulelist_s$ that has the minimum cutoff error is returned. The rest of the paper focuses on Steps 2 and 3.

3 Ranking rules/features

Each rule $X \to C$ found in Step 1 can be considered as feature X for the target class C. Intuitively, X is a good feature for C if it occurs in many documents from class C and few documents from classes that are dissimilar to C. We propose two ranking criteria, with one emphasizing the accuracy of classifiers, and the other emphasizing both accuracy and simplicity of classifiers. Let $X \to C$ be an association rule. $p(X)$ denotes $sup(X)/|\mathcal{D}|$, $p(XC)$ denotes $sup(XC)/|\mathcal{D}|$, and $p(C|X)$ denotes $p(XC)/p(X)$, where $|\mathcal{D}|$ denotes the number of documents in the document collection $\mathcal{D}$.

3.1 The biased confidence

A natural ranking criterion that emphasizes the classification accuracy is the confidence of rules. Taking the class proximity into account, the *biased confidence*, written as $Conf_{\mathcal{B}}(X \to C)$, is defined as

$$\frac{p(XC)}{p(XC) + \sum_{C_j \neq C} \mathcal{B}(C_j, C)p(XC_j)} \tag{1}$$

In other words, the frequency of misclassifying C_j into C is weighed by the error $\mathcal{B}(C_j, C)$. The further the class C_j is from the predicted class C, the less confident the rule is. Note that $Conf_{\mathcal{B}}(X \to C)$ is in $[0, 1]$ and that if $\mathcal{B}(C_j, C) = 1$ for all $C_j \neq C$, $Conf_{\mathcal{B}}(X \to C)$ degenerates into the usual confidence $Conf(X \to C) = p(XC)/p(X)$.

3.2 The biased J-measure

The second ranking criterion is a modification of the information-motivated J-measure [SG92]. The standard J-measure of rule $X \to C$, written as $J(X \to C)$, is

$$p(X)[p(C|X)\log_2 \frac{p(C|X)}{p(C)} + p(\neg C|X)\log_2 \frac{p(\neg C|X)}{p(\neg C)}]$$

The first term $p(X)$ measures the simplicity of the rule. The term inside the square bracket measures the difference between the posteriori $p(C|X)$ and the priori $p(C)$, thus, the discriminating power of X on the target class C: it has a large value if X has either a positive impact on C, where $p(C|X)$ is larger than $p(C)$, or a negative impact on C, where $p(C|X)$ is smaller than $p(C)$.

To suit our purpose, however, we need to make two modifications to the standard J-measure. First, different non-target classes $C_j \neq C$ need to be distinguished because they have different biases towards the target class C. Second, we like to favor the positive impact of X on C and the negative impact of X on non-target classes C_j; we can do this by replacing + sign for non-target classes with − sign. These modifications yield the *biased J-measure*, written as $J_{\mathcal{B}}(X \to C)$, defined by

$$p(X)[p(C|X)\log_2 \frac{p(C|X)}{p(C)} - \sum_{C_j \neq C} \mathcal{B}(C_j, C)p(C_j|X)\log_2 \frac{p(C_j|X)}{p(C_j)}] \tag{2}$$

We expect that $J_{\mathcal{B}}$ yields a smaller, thus more understandable classifier than $Conf_{\mathcal{B}}$ because it takes into account both simplicity and discriminating power of a rule.

4 Constructing an optimal classifier

We assume that one of the ranking criteria in Equations (1) and (2) is used. Let *Rulelist* be the list of generalized association rules found in Step 1, ranked by the chosen ranking criterion. We construct an optimal classifier by selecting rules from *Rulelist* according to Selection Principle and Classification Principle in Section 2. First, we state two strategies to prune some rules never selected by these principles. Consider two rules $X_1 \to C_1$ and $X_2 \to C_2$. We like to characterize the condition that whenever $X_2 \to C_2$ covers a document, $X_1 \to C_1$ covers that document, that is, X_1 is more general than X_2. We denote this condition by $X_1 \preceq X_2$. The following theorem gives a test of $X_1 \preceq X_2$, whose proof is straightforward.

Theorem 1 *$X_1 \preceq X_2$ if and only if $X_1 \subseteq Anc(X_2)$.*

Pruning Strategy 1 below says that if a general rule is ranked higher than a special rule and if both rules have the same target class, the special rule is never selected. Before constructing a classifier, we can apply Pruning Strategy 1 to prune rules.

Pruning Strategy 1 *Assume that $X_1 \to C$ proceeds $X_2 \to C$ in Rulelist. If $X_1 \preceq X_2$, $X_2 \to C$ will not be selected. (Proof in [WZL99].)*

Strategy 2 below says that if a general rule is ranked higher than a special rule and is selected, the special rule is never selected. After selecting a rule, we can apply Pruning Strategy 2 to prune other rules.

Pruning Strategy 2 *Assume that $X_1 \to C_1$ proceeds $X_2 \to C_2$ in Rulelist. If $X_1 \preceq X_2$ and $X_1 \to C_1$ is selected, $X_2 \to C_2$ will not be selected. (Proof in [WZL99].)*

Our construction makes one scan of the documents and keeps track of how each rule in *Rulelist* classifies documents. This information for each rule R is kept in *R.Clist* and *R.Wlist*, which contain the *(id, Class)* pairs for the documents classified by R correctly and wrongly, respectively. Before all the documents are examined, however, we do not know whether R has the chance to classify a document, as governed by Classification Principle. We adopt a simple strategy: if R is a candidate to classify the current document d, we add $(id, Class)$ for d to $R.Clist$ or $R.Wlist$; we prune the $(id, Class)$ pair from $R.Clist$ or $R.Wlist$ as it becomes known that R has no chance to classify document d.

To illustrate the point, consider two rules $R1$ and $R2$ such that $R1$ proceeds $R2$ in *Rulelist*. Assume that neither rule is selected and that some $(id, Class)$ is contained in $Clist$ or $Wlist$ of both rules. Now the next document id' is examined. Suppose that $R1$ covers document id' correctly and no selected rule of higher rank covers the document. By Selection Principle $R1$ is selected, and by Classification Principle $R1$ is deemed to classify document id. We now know that $R2$ has no chance to classify document id, so we can prune $(id, Class)$ from $Clist$ or $Wlist$ of $R2$.

The construction has two phases. Phase 1 scans the documents and maintains $Wlist$ and $Clist$ of the rules involved. Phase 2 makes selection decisions for those rules not yet selected and compute the cutoff error at each selected rule.

4.1 Phase 1: Scan the database

This phase, shown in Figure 1(a), scans the documents and marks a rule in *Rulelist* once it is known that the rule will be selected according to Selection Principle. For the current document d, we find the first rule R in *Rulelist* that covers d. There are two cases, depending on whether R is marked.

Case 1 (lines 30-70): R is marked. R will classify d. So we add the $(id, Class)$ pair of d to $R.Clist$ (line 50) or $R.Wlist$ (line 70).

Case 2 (lines 80-210): R is not marked. There are two subcases, depending on whether R covers d correctly.

- *Case 2a* (lines 90-110): R covers d correctly. In this case R will be selected according to Selection Principle. We mark R and add the $(id, Class)$ pair of d to $R.Clist$ (lines 100-110). The marking of R, denoted by $Mark(R)$, include the following steps: delete all $(id, Class)$ pairs in $R.Clist$ or $R.Wlist$ from all covering rules of d because they do not have the chance to classify these documents, and apply Pruning Strategy 2 to prune more rules. These implementations will be discussed below.

- *Case 2b* (lines 120-210): R covers d wrongly. Since R has not been marked, all rules that cover d (which must be after R) are candidates for classifying d. So, we add $(id, Class)$ of d to the $Clist$ or $Wlist$ of these rules. However, it is not necessary to consider all such rules: we can stop as soon as any of these rules, say R', was already marked or covers d correctly, whichever comes first in *Rulelist*. The reason is that, by Classification Principle, all rules that come after R' have no chance to classify d. These steps are given in lines 130-210. To simplify the presentation, we assume that a dummy rule at the end of *Rulelist* cover all documents.

Implementation details. At lines 20 and 150, we need to find the rules that cover document d. This operation is similar to the subset function of finding the candidate itemsets contained in $Anc(d)$, implemented by the *hash-tree* in [AIS93, AS94]. For our purpose, we store all rules $X \rightarrow C$ in the hash-tree by treating X as an itemset. Then finding all covering rules $X \rightarrow C$ of document d amounts to finding all itemsets X such that $X \subseteq Anc(d)$. Another implementation concerns with $Mark(R)$ (and line 100 in Phase 2 below) where we need to delete a given $(id, Class)$ pair from the rules whose $Clist$ or $Wlist$ contain the pair. To locate these rules quickly, as a new $(id, Class)$ pair is added, we can chain up the entries for $(id, Class)$ in the order of the rules involved. To delete a $(id, Class)$ pair, we simply scan the chain for the pair and delete its entry from each rule encountered. To delete more than one $(id, Class)$ pair, we combine their scans and delete their entries in one scan.

4.2 Phase 2: Select final rules

Phase 2, shown in Figure 1(b), scans *Rulelist* to select rules and determine the best cutoff point. Consider the current rule R. There are two cases, depending on whether R is marked.

Case 1 (lines 20-60): R is marked. We append R to $Rulelist_s$ (which is initially empty) and remove R from *Rulelist* (line 30). $Remain[C]$ denotes the number of documents in class C that have not been classified by $Rulelist_s$. $Remain[C]$ is updated to reflect that the documents in $R.Clist$ and $R.Wlist$ are now classified by $Rulelist_s$ (lines 40-50). Also, we compute the cutoff error of $Rulelist_s$, done in $CutoffError(R)$ (line 60). The cutoff error is defined as $R.RE + R.DE$, where $R.RE$ is the total error of the rules in $Rulelist_s$ and $R.DE$ is the default error of using some default class on the documents not classified by $Rulelist_s$. The class that minimizes the default error is chosen as the default class, denoted $R.DC$.

Case 2 (lines 80-120): R is not marked. In this case, $R.Clist$ must be empty, as shown in Lemma 1 below. Therefore, we simply remove R from *Rulelist* (line 80). Now R is no longer a candidate to classify the documents in $R.Wlist$, which triggers the marking of more rules (lines 90-120): for each $(id, Class)$ in $R.Wlist$, we find the first rule R' such that $R'.Clist$ or $R'.Wlist$ contains $(id, Class)$. If R' is not found, document id will be classified by a default class. If R' is found, we check whether R' covers document id

```
Phase 1:
for each document d do
   find the first rule R in Rulelist that covers d;
   if R is marked then /* Case 1 */
      if R covers d correctly then
         add (id, Class) of d to R.Clist;
      else
         add (id, Class) of d to R.Wlist;
   else /* Case 2 */
      if R covers d correctly then /* Case 2a */
         add (id, Class) of d to R.Clist;
         Mark(R);
      else /* Case 2b */
         repeat
            add (id, Class) of d to R.Wlist;
            R=the next rule covering d;
         until R is the dummy rule, or R covers d correctly, or R is marked;
         if R is not the dummy rule then
            if R covers d correctly then
               add (id, Class) of d to R.Clist;
            else if R is marked then
               add (id, Class) of d to R.Wlist;
```

(a)

```
Phase 2:
   RE = 0;
for each rule R in Rulelist in the ranked order do
   if R is marked then /* Case 1 */
      append R to Rulelist_s and delete R from Rulelist;
      for each (id, Class) ∈ R.Clist ∪ R.Wlist do
         Remain[Class] = Remain[Class] − 1;
      CutoffError(R); /* compute the cutoff error at R */
   else /* Case 2 */
      delete R from Rulelist;
      for each (id, Class) in R.Wlist do
         find the first rule R' in Rulelist such that (id, Class) is in R'.Clist ∪ R'.Wlist;
         if R' is found then
            if (id, Class) is in R'.Clist and R' is not marked yet then Mark(R');
find the first rule R in Rulelist_s that minimizes the cutoff error R.RE + R.DE;
return the prefix of Rulelist_s ending at R, and the default class R.DC;

CutoffError(R):
   R.DE =the maximum machine value;
   for each class C such that Remain[C] ≠ 0 do
      x_C = Σ_{C'} Remain[C'] × B(C', C); /* the default error of using C as the default class */
      if x_C < R.DE then
         R.DE = x_C and R.DC = C;
   RE = RE + Σ_{(id,Class)∈R.Wlist} B(Class, R.Class); /* R.Class denotes the class in R */
   R.RE = RE;
```

(b)

Figure 1: Step 3

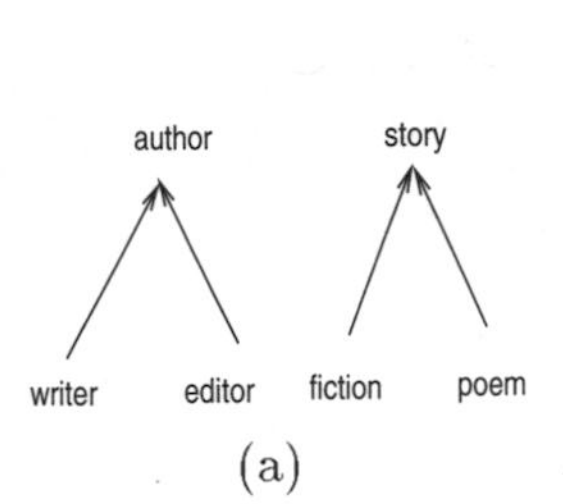

(a)

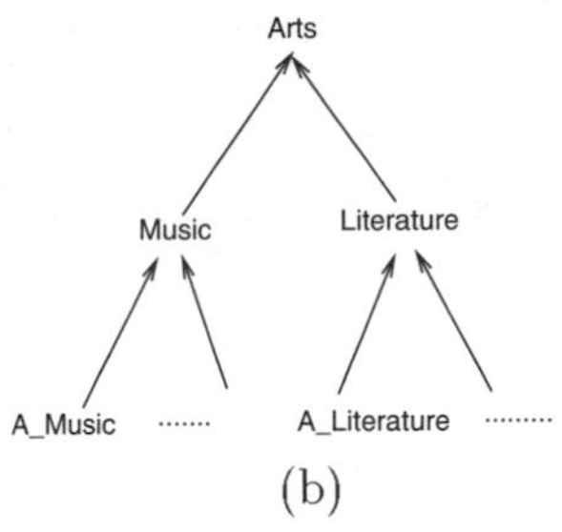

(b)

id	term	class
d1	hall,composer	Music
d2	hall,conductor	Music
d3	hall,States	A_Music
d4	States,book	A_Literature
d5	story,States	A_Literature
d6	hall,fiction,writer	Literature
d7	editor,poem	Literature

(c)

Figure 2: Hierarchical classification

correctly and is not marked yet. If so, we mark R' by calling $Mark(R')$ (line 120).

Finally, the shortest prefix of $Rulelist_s$ that has the minimum cutoff error is returned as an optimal classifier (lines 130-140).

Lemma 1 *In Phase 2, if the current rule R is not marked, R.Clist is empty. (Proof in [WZL99].)*

The following theorem follows from our construction algorithm.

Theorem 2 *(a) The full list $Rulelist_s$ satisfies Classification Principle and Selection Principle. (b) The prefix of $Rulelist_s$ returned by the algorithm is an optimal classifier.*

Example 1 Consider the example in Figure 2, where (a), (b), and (c) give the term hierarchy, the class hierarchy, and the training documents. Assume that $\mathcal{B}(C_i, C_j)$ measures the shortest distance from C_i to C_j in class hierarchy. Suppose that the minimum support is 2. We consider four search strategies: (), (B), (T), and (B,T). T means that term hierarchy is used and B means that class proximity is used in the chosen ranking criterion. For all strategies, the error of a classifier is computed using class proximity.

() Strategy. The term hierarchy is ignored and the usual confidence $Conf$ is used. Only two rules satisfy the minimum support:

R3: States → A_Literature
($Conf$=0.67, *Clist*=d4,d5, *Wlist*=d3(4))
R4: hall D → Music
($Conf$=0.50, *Clist*=d1,d2, *Wlist*=d6(2))

The number following each document id in *Wlist* is the error on that document. For example, the error made on d3 by R3 is 4 because $\mathcal{B}(A\_Music, A\_Literature) = 4$. Both rules are selected because each classifies some documents correctly. To find an optimal classifier, each prefix of $< R3, R4 >$ is considered, shown in Table 1(). For prefix <>, all documents are classified by default class *Literature*, giving the minimum error of 9. For prefix $< R3 >$, the default class for the remaining d1, d2, d6, d7 is either *Music* or *Literature*, giving the minimum default error of 4. Thus, the cutoff error of $< R3 >$ is 8. Finally, the cutoff error of prefix $< R3, R4 >$ is 6, with default class *Literature*. So $< R3, R4 >$ is an optimal classifier.

(B) Strategy. By considering class proximity, R4 is now ranked higher than R3:

R4: hall → Music
($Conf_{\mathcal{B}}$=0.4, *Clist*=d1,d2, *Wlist*=d3(1),d6(2))
R3: States → A_Literature ($Conf_{\mathcal{B}}$=0.33, *Clist*=d4,d5)

Table 1(B) shows the cutoff error for every prefix of $< R4, R3 >$. $< R4, R3 >$ with default class *Literature* is an optimal classifier, where the cutoff error is 3.

(T) Strategy. By considering term hierarchy, five rules now satisfy the minimum support:

R0: author,story → Literature ($Conf$=1, *Clist*=d6,d7)
R1: author → Literature ($Conf$=1, not selected)
R2: story → Literature
($Conf$=0.67, *Wlist*=d5(1), not selected)
R3: States → A_Literature
($Conf$=0.67, *Clist*=d4,d5, *Wlist*=d3(4))
R4: hall → Music ($Conf$=0.50, *Clist*=d1,d2)

By Classification Principle, R1 and R2 do not classify any document correctly, so are not selected, by Selection Principle. Table 1(T) shows the cutoff error for each prefix of selected rules $< R0, R3, R4 >$. $< R0, R3 >$ with default class *Music* is an optimal classifier, where the cutoff error is 4.

(B,T) Strategy. The class proximity changes the relative rank of R3 and R4:

R0: author,story → Literature ($Conf_{\mathcal{B}}$=1, *Clist*=d6,d7)
R1: author → Literature ($Conf_{\mathcal{B}}$=1, not selected)
R2: story → Literature
($Conf_{\mathcal{B}}$=0.67, *Wlist*=d5(1), not selected)
R4: hall → Music ($Conf_{\mathcal{B}}$=0.4, *Clist*=d1,d2, *Wlist*=d3(1))
R3: States → A_Literature ($Conf_{\mathcal{B}}$=0.33, *Clist*=d4,d5)

As before, R1 and R2 are not selected. Table 1(B,T) shows the cutoff error for each prefix of $< R0, R4, R3 >$. $< R0, R4 >$ with default class *A_Literature* is an optimal classifier. The cutoff error is 1. □

From the four strategies considered, (B,T) produces the classifier with the smallest cutoff error. Comparison of (B) with (), and (B,T) with (T), shows that class proximity helps to rank R3 and R4 in an order that produces a small error. Comparison of (T) with (),

prefix	last rule's error	default class	default error	cutoff error
<>	0	Literature	9	9
< *R3* >	4	Music or Literature	4	8
< *R3*, *R4* >	2	Literature	0	6

(): Term hierarchy=off and class proximity=off

prefix	last rule's error	default class	default error	cutoff error
<>	0	Literature	9	9
< *R4* >	3	A_Literature	1	4
< *R4*, *R3* >	0	Literature	0	3

(B): Term hierarchy=off and class proximity=on

prefix	last rule's error	default class	default error	cutoff error
<>	0	Literature	9	9
< *R0* >	0	Music	7	7
< *R0*, *R3* >	4	Music	0	4
< *R0*, *R3*, *R4* >	0			4

(T): Term hierarchy=on and class proximity=off

prefix	last rule's error	default class	default error	cutoff error
<>	0	Literature	9	9
< *R0* >	0	Music	7	7
< *R0*, *R4* >	1	A_Literature	0	1
< *R0*, *R4*, *R3* >	0			1

(B,T): Term hierarchy=on and class proximity=on

Table 1: Four cases of classifier construction

and (B,T) with (B), shows that term hierarchy helps to capture the classification structure at proper concept levels.

5 Experiments

This section evaluates the effectiveness and efficiency of our approach. For effectiveness, we consider the rules, the error, and the size of the classifier constructed. For efficiency, we consider the execution time and the number of document ids kept in memory. To reveal the sources of effectiveness, we consider the following parameters in our approach: the minimum support, class proximity (on or off), term hierarchy (on or off), and ranking criteria (the biased confidence or the biased J-measure). For comparison, we have implemented the fisher index method in [CDAR97, CDI98], a local approach to hierarchical classification by constructing one classifier at each split of the class hierarchy. The traditional classification methods based on a flatten class space are not a good candidate for comparison because they ignore the hierarchical structure of classes. Also, such methods cannot handle tens of thousands of terms, as in our case, because they either assume independence of terms (like the Naive Bayes classification [KS97]) or consider terms one at a time (like decision trees [Q93]). As in Example 1, we use (), (B), (T), (B,T) to represent different search strategies of our approach. (CDAR97,T) and (CDAR97) denote the local approach in [CDAR97] where term hierarchy is turned on and off. All results presented are the averaged result of the 5-fold cross-validation trial [3].

5.1 The data sets

The ACM data set. The ACM Digital Library (http://www.acm.org/dl/toc.html/) is chosen because we can use its classification system to construct both class hierarchy and term hierarchy (see below). Each paper has five logical parts: (a) Title, (b) Categories and Subject Descriptors, (c) General Terms, (d) Abstract, (e) Full Text. Only parts (a) and (b) are compulsory. The classification information is contained in part (b) and is organized into a hierarchy of four levels. An example path in this hierarchy is:

Hardware (B) — level-1 category
 Memory_Structure (B.3) — level-2 category
 Design_Style (B.3.2) — level-3 category
 Cache_Memories — level-4 subject descriptor

Our classification task is determining the level-1 or level-2 category of a paper using Title in part (a) and

[3] In a k-fold cross-validation trial, a data set is partitioned into k buckets of equal size and k runs are performed by using a different bucket each time as the testing set and the remaining buckets as the training set.

subject descriptors in part (b). The level-3 categories are reserved as generalizing concepts of subject descriptors. The fact that the Title part of a paper is chosen by the authors themselves and the subject descriptors are cross-referenced among categories makes the classification task challenging.

The data set was obtained as follows. The class hierarchy consists of the level-1 and level-2 categories. The term hierarchy consists of the level-3 categories and level-4 subject descriptors. For each paper, a document is created to contain its keywords in Title and level-4 subject descriptors in Categories and Subject Descriptors. If the paper has a category of the form X.0 (i.e., the GENERAL subcategory of X), we choose X as the class of the document; otherwise, we choose a majority level-2 category of the paper as the class. After removing the classes with less than 20 documents, we are left with the ACM data set shown in Table 2. The size of training set and testing set is determined by the 5-fold cross-validation trial.

The Sports data set. For the second data set, we choose the *Recreation* : *Sports* hierarchy in Yahoo! (http://dir.yahoo.com/recreation/sports) because its deep class hierarchy well suits the effectiveness study of class proximity. We descend the Sports hierarchy and ignore the classes with less than 20 documents each. Each document corresponds to a page pointed by a link in a Sports page (with the prefix http://dir.yahoo.com/recreation/sports) but outside the Yahoo!'s domain (without the prefix http://dir.yahoo.com/). The document consists of the keywords tagged by this link. We ignore short-cuts and links to non-Sports pages within Yahoo!. This gives us the Sports data set in Table 2. About 90% of the terms occur in no more than 10 documents and many documents contain only such terms. This makes the classification task more challenging than the ACM data set.

For both data sets, the class proximity is the shortest distance between classes in class hierarchy.

number	ACM data	Sports data
documents	26,515	7,550
classes	78	367
terms	14,754	10,747
levels of class hierarchy	2	7
training documents	21,212	6,040
testing documents	5,303	1,510

Table 2: The statistics about data sets

5.2 The result on the ACM data set

The rules/features found. Figure 3 shows a small sample of features found by (CDAR97,T) and rules found by (B,T) (the biased confidence and minimum support of 0.1%). All terms shown are in the processed form where plural and morphological variations are removed by using the standard text processing in IR. For each rule, the first number is the biased confidence and the second is the support.

According to [CDAR97], the features found at location C have a large variance in the subclasses of C, thus, are discriminators of the subclasses. But such features cannot serve as the characteristics of C itself. For example, "visual" appears in 0.55% of the documents under CSO where it was found as a feature, but appears 0.83% of the documents under $Software$ where it was not found as a feature. This is so because "visual" has a large variance in the subclasses of CSO, but not in the subclasses of $Software$. Such features do not fulfill our goal of characterizing CSO. On the other hand, the rules found by (B,T) clearly tell what terms characterize what subclasses of CSO, which is not the case from examining the features at CSO found by (CDAR97,T).

The following discussion refers to Figure 5. The two ranking criteria divide figures into the left column and the right column. The x-axis denotes the minimum support of x% of the training size. The legend in the figure labeled "Size" is uniformly used in all figures.

The error. The two figures labeled "Error" show the total error on the 5,303 testing documents as defined by class proximity. We can see the following points. (a) (B,T) performs the best, in fact, improves upon (CDAT97) and (CDAR97,T) by as much as 75%. (b) Comparing () with (T), (B) with (B,T) reveals that the global approach benefits drastically from term hierarchy, but not much for the local approach. (c) Comparing () with (B), and (T) with (B,T) reveals that class proximity reduces the total error, but only marginally, due to the shallow class hierarchy. (d) The biased confidence yields higher accuracy than the biased J-measure.

Figure 4 shows the distribution of errors according to the distance between the known class and the predicted class, called the *fatalness* of error. The minimum support is 0.1% (of the training size) for our approach. Clearly, (CDAR97) and (CDAR97,T) make far more fatal errors (of distance 3 or 4) than the global approach. Indeed, we observed that 3,624 or 68% and 3,824 or 72% testing documents were wrongly classified at the top level of the class hierarchy by (CDAR97) and (CDAR97,T), respectively, compared to only 21% by (B,T) (the biased confidence). A similar trend was observed for the Sports data set (see below). This confirms the point made in Introduction that high level structures diminish in the local approach.

The count of the usual misclassification is shown in the two figures labeled "Count". We notice that (CDAR97) and (CDAR97,T) make much more misclassifications for the ACM data, i.e., 70%, than for the USPatent data in [CDAR97], i.e., about 25%. This difference is because the ACM data has 78 classes, compared to only 12 classes for the USPatent data.

Best features found by (CDAR97,T):
At Computer_Systems_Organization (CSO):
medium, mainfram, super, attribut, techniqu, comput, stream, multipl, x_mp, embed, apl, train, cyber, oop, win, council, visual, etc.
At Software:
object_oriented_programming, concurrent_programming, classif, processor, featur, techniqu, construct, tool, process, storag, parallel_programming, organiz, compil, file_system, distributed_system, protect, etc.

Best rules found by (B,T):
Under Computer_Systems_Organization (CSO):
vector,stream,processor,parallel → Processor_Architectures (1.00, 22)
multiple_instruction_stream → Processor_Architectures (1.00, 55)
data_flow,architectur → Processor_Architectures (1.00, 30)
internet,architectur → Computer_Communication_Networks (1.00, 67)
mode,atm → Computer_Communication_Networks (1.00, 32)
network,circuit_switching → Computer_Communication_Networks (1.00, 25)
techniqu,model,attribut → Performance_of_Systems (0.94, 65)
Under Software:
program,function,applicative → Programming_Techniques (0.87,52)
object_oriented_programming → Programming_Techniques (0.86,258)
reusable_software → Software_Engineering (0.97,200)
software,methodologie → Software_Engineering (0.92, 55)
programming_environment → Software_Engineering (0.89, 287)
processor,parse → Programming_Languages (1.00, 27)
processor,compiler → Programming_Languages (0.91, 454)
organization,distributed_system → Operating_Systems (1.00, 71)
synchronization,process → Operating_Systems (1.00, 53)

Figure 3: The comparision of features and rules

The size of classifiers. The two figures labeled "Size" show the size of classifiers, which is the number of rules for our approach, and the number of features for (CDAR97,T) and (CDAR97). Clearly, the classifiers produced by (CDAR97,T) and (CDAR97) are much larger, thus, less understandable, than those produced by our approach. The use of term hierarchy has increased the size of classifiers. The biased J-measure yields consistently fewer rules than the biased confidence.

The execution time. The two figures labeled "Time" show the execution time. For our approach, most time was spent on generating association rules. For (CDAR97) and (CDAR97,T), most time was spent on computing the fisher index of terms and determining the cutoff point of the feature list where every prefix of the feature list was examined for each document in the validation set. Our algorithms are much faster than (CDAR97) and (CDAR97,T).

Document ids kept. The two figures labeled "Ids" show the number of document ids kept in *Clist* and *Wlist* in our approach. Recall that the training set has 21,212 documents. Thus, each document id is kept no more than twice. This number drops quickly for a smaller minimum support. We can further reduce this number by keeping *Clist* and *Wlist* only for the rules that are not marked at any time. We omit this detail due to space limitation.

5.3 The result on the Sports data set

For this data set, a similar trend was observed on the size of classifiers, execution time, and number of document ids kept. Also, the remark about the rules and features for the ACM data set is applicable to this data set. The detail can found in [WZL99]. Here we report briefly on the error of classification. As the minimum support varies from 0.02% to 0.5%, the total error of (B) ranges from 2700 to 3700, much smaller than the total error of (CDAR97), which is 5700, and the total error of (), which ranges from 3300 to 5800. (Note that the Sports data set has no term hierarchy.) Again, we observed the trend that (CDAR97) and () more frequently make fatal errors than (B). In fact, 68% of the testing documents were classified wrongly at the top level by (CDAR97), compared to only 37% by (B) (the biased confidence and minimum support of 0.2%). This shows that the global approach based on class proximity indeed achieves the closeness of classification.

6 Concluding remarks

With few exceptions, most work on (supervised) classification ignored the structure of features and classes, e.g., [Q93, SHP95, SOM, YP97]. Recently, hierarchically structured features and hierarchically structured classes were examined in [AAK96] and [CDAR97, KS97], respectively. Related but different topics are

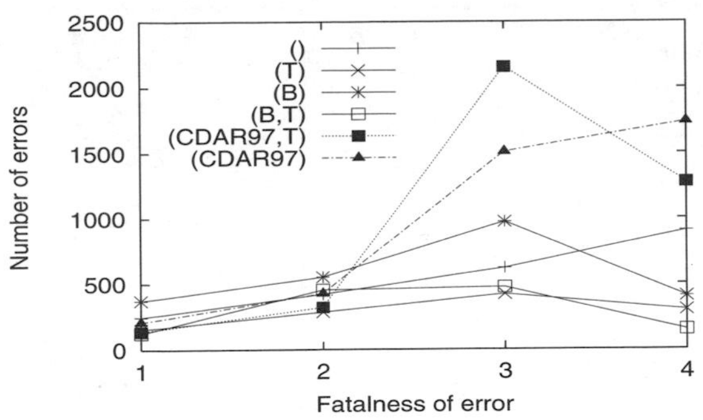

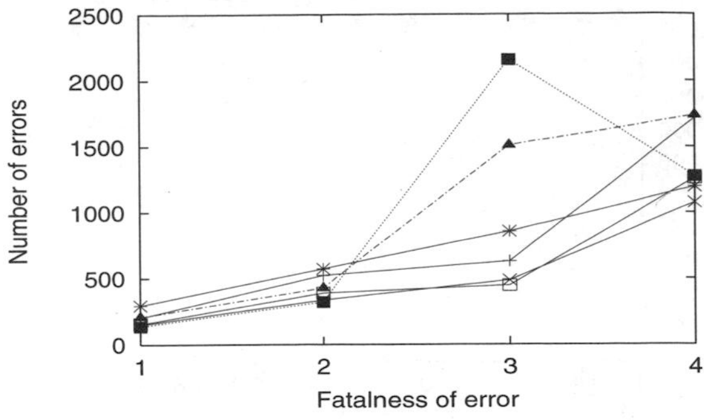

Figure 4: ACM error distribution: biased confidence (left) and biased J-measure (right)

hypertext categorization [CDI98] where some neighbourhood of interconnected documents was explored to enhance the classification accuracy. Association rules [AIS93, AS94, SA95, HF95] were proposed with a different mind set from classification. [LHM98] integrated association rules and classification rules for a relation table, but did not consider hierarchical classification. Also, the algorithm in [LHM98] is rather complex and the database is scanned more than once. Finally, none of these work has considered the notion of class proximity.

This paper makes the following contributions. First, it identifies several important issues in hierarchical classification. Then, it proposes a new approach to hierarchical classification by aiming at the closeness of classification, which is fundamentally different from earlier approaches. The closeness of classification is relevant not only to hierarchical classification, but also to the general setting of classification. For example, classifying *Urgent* emails into *Junk* emails is much more costly than the other way around, and the closeness of classification is useful to minimize misclassification in a way sensible to such applications. Several characteristics make our approach robust and scalable to a large corpus, namely, construction of a global classifier, search for multi-level abstraction and correlation of features, determination of features with respect to target classes, and a single scan of the document database. Experiments have shown encouraging results.

References

[AAK96] H. Almualim, Y. Akiba, S. Kaneda, "An efficient algorithm for finding optimal gain-ratio multiple-split tests on hierarchical attributes in decision tree learning", National Conference on Artificial Intelligence, AAAI 1996, 703-708

[AIS93] R. Agrawal, T. Imielinski, and A. Swami, "Mining association rules between sets of items in large databases", SIGMOD 1993, 207-216

[AS94] R. Agrawal and R. Srikant, "Fast algorithms for mining association rules", VLDB 1994, 487-499

[CDAR97] S. Chakrabarti, D. Dom, R. Agrawal, and P. Raghavan, "Using taxonomy, discriminants, and signatures for navigating in text databases", VLDB 1997, 446-455 (Also see: "Scalable feature selection, classification and signature generation for organizing large text databases into hierarchical topic taxonomies", The VLDB Journal (1998) Vol. 7, No. 3, 163-178)

[CDI98] S. Chakrabarti, B. Dom, and P. Indyk, "Enhanced hypertext categorization using hyperlinks", SIGMOD 1998, 307-318

[HF95] J. Han and Y. Fu, "Discovery of multiple-level association rules from large databases", VLDB 1995, 420-431

[KS97] D. Koller and M. Sahami, "Hierarchically classifying documents using very few words", International Conference on Machine Learning, 1997, 170-178

[LHM98] B. Liu, W. Hsu, and Y. Ma, "Intergrating classification and association rule mining", KDD 1998, 80-86

[WZL99] K. Wang, S. Zhou, S.C. Liew, "Building hierarchical classifiers using class proximity", Technical Report, National University of Singapore, 1999

[Q93] J.R. Quinlan, C4.5: programs for machine learning, Morgan Kaufmann, 1993

[SA95] R. Srikant and R. Agrawal, "Mining generalized association rules", VLDB 1995, 407-419

[SG92] P. Smyth and R. Goodman, "An information theoretic approach to rule induction from databases", IEEE Transactions on Knowledge and Data Engineering, Vol. 4, No. 4, Aug 1992, 301-316

[SHP95] H. Schutze, D.A. Hull, and J.O. Pederson, "A comparison of classifiers and document representations for the routing problem", SIGIR 1995, 229-237

[SOM] Self-organizing map, http://www.cis.hut.fi/nnrc/nnrc-programs.html

[YP97] Y, Yang and J.O. Pederson, "A comparative study on feature selection in text categorization", International Conference on Machine Learning 1997.

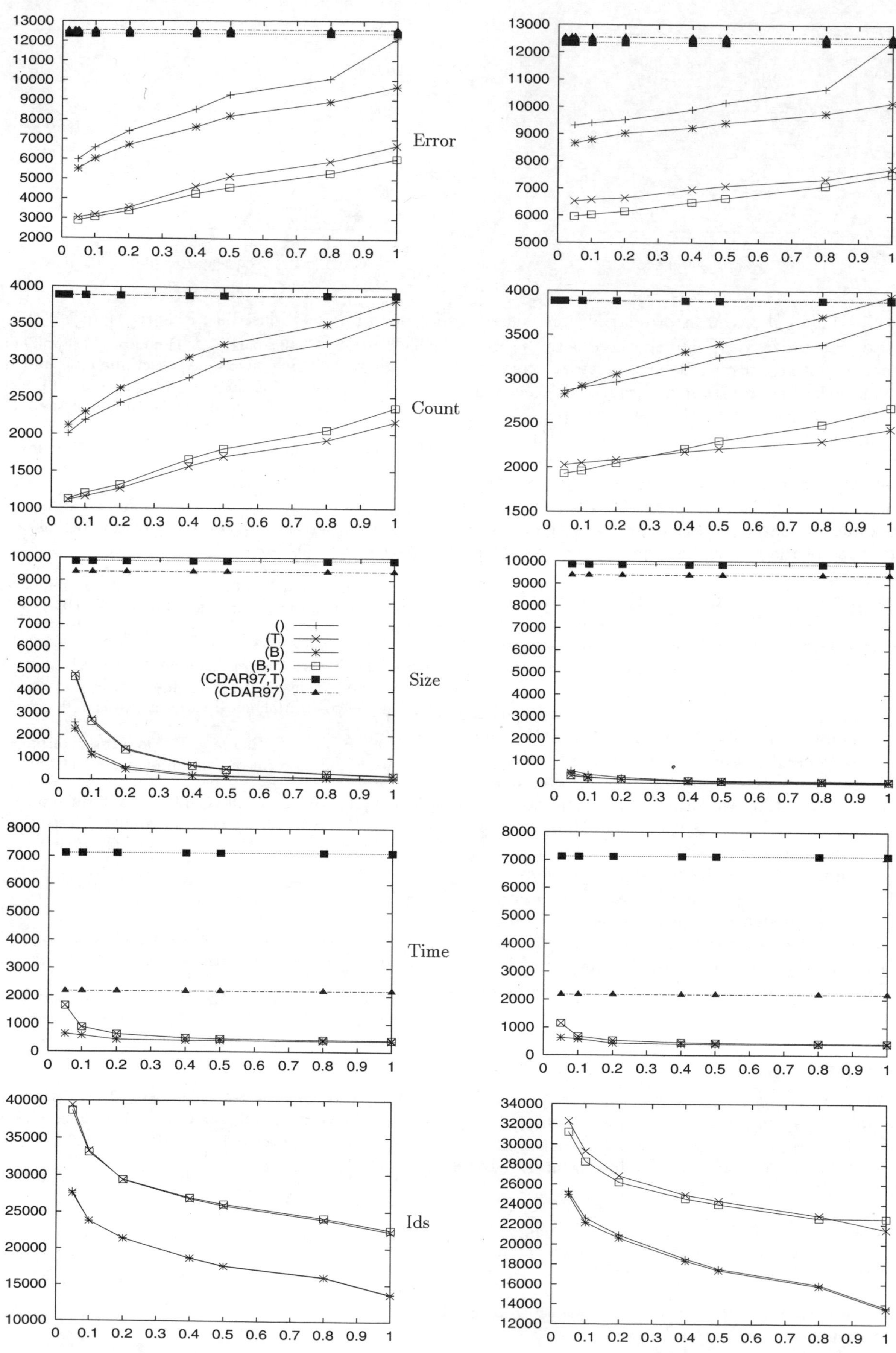

Figure 5: ACM: biased confidence (left) and biased J-measure (right)

Distributed Hypertext Resource Discovery Through Examples

Soumen Chakrabarti[1]
IIT Bombay
soumen@cse.iitb.ernet.in

Martin H. van den Berg[2]
FX Palo Alto Laboratory
vdberg@pal.xerox.com

Byron E. Dom
IBM Almaden
dom@almaden.ibm.com

Abstract

We describe the architecture of a hypertext resource discovery system using a relational database. Such a system can answer questions that combine page contents, metadata, and hyperlink structure in powerful ways, such as "find the number of links from an environmental protection page to a page about oil and natural gas over the last year." A key problem in populating the database in such a system is to discover web resources related to the topics involved in such queries. We argue that that a keyword-based "find similar" search based on a giant all-purpose crawler is neither necessary nor adequate for resource discovery. Instead we exploit the properties that pages tend to cite pages with related topics, and given that a page u cites a page about a desired topic, it is very likely that u cites additional desirable pages. We exploit these properties by using a crawler controlled by two hypertext mining programs: (1) a *classifier* that evaluates the relevance of a region of the web to the user's interest (2) a *distiller* that evaluates a page as an access point for a large neighborhood of relevant pages. Our implementation uses IBM's Universal Database, not only for robust data storage, but also for integrating the computations of the classifier and distiller into the database. This results in significant increase in I/O efficiency: a factor of ten for the classifier and a factor of three for the distiller. In addition, ad-hoc SQL queries can be used to monitor the crawler, and dynamically change crawling strategies. We report on experiments to establish that our system is efficient, effective, and robust.

1 Introduction

There is a growing need for future generations of hypertext search engines that transcend keyword-based search and permit powerful query and discovery by combining predicates on page content, page and hyperlink meta-data, and hyperlink graph structure. Several projects including TSIMMIS[3] [19], WebSQL[4] [26], W3QS[5] [24], WEBL[6] [22], STARTS[7], WHIRL[8], and generalized proximity search [18] have made important advances in the data representation and query optimization for semi-structured and unstructured domains.

Our goal in the Focus project is to go beyond representation and basic querying, to discover properties that combine the topical content of web pages and the linkage relationship between them. We give some examples of such advanced query power:

Citation sociology: Find a topic (other than bicycling) within one link of bicycling pages that is much more frequent than on the web at large. The answer found by the system described in this paper is *first aid.*

Typed link: Find computer science theory faculty who have advised at least one student who has published on database topics.

Spam filter: Find pages that are apparently about database research which are cited by at least two pages about Hawaiian vacations.

Community evolution: Find the number of links from a page about environmental protection to a page related to oil and natural gas over the last year.

The novelty in the examples above is that page content is selected by topics, not keyword matches. In the examples above, the topics are expressed syntactically using simple phrases, but we envisage that in actual use, our system will not depend on the keyword 'bicycling' to select bicycling related pages from the web (many of which might not contain that word) but instead learn to identify bicycling related pages from a set of examples provided by the user. Our goal is to answer such queries while materializing as little of the distributed hypertext repository (in general, the Web) as possible.

In the spirit of Mendelzon and Milo [27], we claim that the traditional self-contained view of a database is not appropriate for answering such questions. The queries above involve small fractions of the web. A standard crawler would waste resources and yet likely to provide stale and incomplete results; the biggest search engines cover 35–40% of the Web today [3].

[1]Work partly done at IBM Almaden
[2]Work done at IBM Almaden

[3]http://www-db.stanford.edu/tsimmis/tsimmis.html
[4]http://www.cs.toronto.edu/~websql/
[5]http://www.cs.technion.ac.il/~konop/w3qs.html
[6]http://www.research.digital.com/SRC/WebL
[7]http://www-db.stanford.edu/~gravano/starts.html
[8]http://whirl.research.att.com/

Proceedings of the 25th VLDB Conference, Edinburgh, Scotland, 1999.

Thus, a large crawl of the web, followed by filtering based on topic (used earlier in a search engine setting [12]) is a poor solution.

This paper deals with the implementation of a novel example-driven, goal-directed data acquisition system. Its goal is to answer a pre-specified set of standing queries continually, not answer interactive queries unless they are contained in the topics crawled to answer the standing queries. Keeping the access costs of the web 'database' in mind, we propose the following problem formulation.

1.1 Problem formulation

We are given a directed hypertext graph G. G is distributed, as is the case for the web, and there is a non-trivial cost for visiting any vertex (web page) of G. There is also a tree-shaped hierarchical topic directory C such as Yahoo!. Each topic node $c \in C$ refers to some pages in G as examples (provided manually). We denote the examples associated with topic c as $D(c)$. These pages can be preprocessed as desired by the system. The user's interest is characterized by a subset of topics $C^* \subset C$ that is marked `good`. No good topic is an ancestor of another good topic. Topics in the subtree of a good topic are called *subsumed* topics. Ancestors of good topics are called `path` topics.

Given a web page q, a measure of relevance $R_{C^*}(q)$ of q w.r.t. C^*, together with a method for computing it, must be specified to the system. C^* will be omitted if clear from the context. In this paper, we will use a probability measure $0 \leq R(q) \leq 1$. By definition, $R_{\{\text{root}\}}(q) = 1 \forall q$. If $\{c_i\}$ are children of c_0, then $\sum_{c_i} R_{c_i}(q) = R_{c_0}(q)$.

The system starts by visiting all pages in $D(C^*)$. In each step, the system can inspect its current set V of visited pages and then choose to visit an unvisited page from the crawl frontier, corresponding to a hyperlink on one or more visited pages[9]. Informally, the goal is to visit as many relevant pages and as few irrelevant pages as possible, i.e., to maximize average relevance. Therefore we seek to find $V \supseteq D(C^*)$ where V is reachable from $D(C^*)$ such that $\sum_V R(v)/|V|$ is maximized.

1.2 Rationale and discussion

The above formulation is primarily for clarity. When G is the web, there is no hope of designing an optimal algorithm, or evaluating practical algorithms against the optimal visited set. Indeed, part of the paper (§3) deals with this non-trivial evaluation problem, measuring various indirect indicators of effectiveness. W.r.t. almost any meaningful C^*, the average relevance of the whole web is extremely small, therefore we expect $|V| \ll |G|$. Thus the system is naturally prevented from visiting and pre-processing the entire web graph, as is attempted by current web crawlers. The user's choice of C^* is a clean way to capture the recall-precision trade-off. Crawlers with very general topics in C^* (such as the root of the topic tree) have large recall whereas topic nodes deep in the topic tree induce high precision.

In a self-contained database, there are, in principle, simple formulations for query by example. There is a universe of n objects U, and given a probe or query object q and a distance measure d, the goal is to find the top $k \ll n$ objects u with the smallest values of $d(q, u)$. Query by Image Content (QBIC) is an example of this paradigm [29].

There are a number of reasons why this model is inadequate for our purposes. The biggest problem is data acquisition. E.g., it is unreasonable to have to acquire and analyze 350 million web pages to decide upon the thirty pages most relevant to the user's interest. Another serious problem is the definition of similarity or relevance. Fairly successful representations and similarity measures have been devised for images, but keyword matches are known to be relatively unreliable for searching text. Third, the diverse styles of hypertext authoring, together with the abundance of pages relevant to broad topics, makes it difficult to completely identify the hyperlinked community from a keyword query response [31].

1.3 Contributions

Our main contribution is the design of a novel example-driven, goal-directed resource discovery system. Our system uses two basic properties of the web: pages cite pages on related topics, and a page that points to one page with a desired topic is more likely than a random page to point to other pages with desired topics. Accordingly, we use two devices: a supervised *classifier* that learns the topic(s) of interest from the user's examples, and then guides the crawler accordingly, and a *distiller*, which runs concurrently with the crawler, identifying nodes in the growing crawl graph that are likely to lead to a large number of relevant pages. (Such pages are not necessarily very relevant in themselves.)

Another contribution is the implementation of the system on a relational database. The three modules, crawler, classifier, and distiller, together with monitoring and administering utilities, run concurrently as clients. The database is not merely a robust data repository, but takes an *active role* in the computations involved in resource discovery (§2.1.3 and §2.2.3). An important aspect of this work is the design of flexible schemes for crawl frontier management, and the representation of the classifier and distiller in a relational framework.

We give experimental evidence that our system is effective at discovering topic-specific web subgraphs. In particular, relevant and high-quality pages are found

[9] But also see §3.2 for more general notions of page visitation.

several links away from the results of keyword searches, establishing the superiority of our approach. We also show how a careful DBMS implementation yields better I/O performance in the classifier and distiller.

1.4 Related work

Although hypertext classification [8] and hyperlink-based popularity analysis (PageRank [5], HITS [23], CLEVER [7] and topic distillation [4]) and similarity search [15] have been studied before, no notion of adaptive goal-directed exploration is evident in these systems. Another important distinction of our system is the integration of topical content into the link graph model. PageRank has no notion of page content[10], and HITS and CLEVER explore the web to a preset radius (typically, 1) from the keyword query response. All involve pre-crawling and indexing the web.

A few systems that gather specialized content have been very successful. Cho et al compare several crawl ordering schemes based on link degree, perceived prestige, and keyword matches on the Stanford University web [13]. Ahoy![11] is a homepage search service based on a crawler specially tuned to locate homepages. Cora[12] is a search engine for computer science research papers, based on a crawler trained to extract such papers from a given list of starting points at suitable department and universities. Information filtering agents such as WebWatcher [20], HotList and ColdList [30], Fish Search [16], Shark Search and Fetuccino [2], and clan search [32] have served a similar purpose. These are special cases of the general example- and topic-driven automatic web exploration that we undertake.

2 Architecture

Our problem formulation in the previous section does not in itself suggest a procedure to attain that goal. If pages of all topics were finely dispersed throughout the web, there would be little hope for finding coherent communities. This, however, is not the case. Most citations are made to semantically related pages. Two rules can be exploited:

Radius-1 rule: Compared to an irrelevant page, a relevant page is more likely to cite another relevant page.

Radius-2 rule: The unconditional probability of a random web page u pointing to a page of a given topic may be quite small. However, if we are told that u does point to one page v of a given topic, this significantly inflates the probability that u has a link to another page of the same topic.

[10] Although Google likely combines PageRank with content-based heuristics.

[11] `http://www.cs.washington.edu/research/ahoy`

[12] `http://www.cora.jprc.com/`

These claims have been demonstrated using corpora such as patents from the US Patent Office and web pages cataloged in Yahoo!. E.g., a page that points to a given first level topic of Yahoo! has about a 45% chance of having another link to the same topic.

In this section we will describe how to exploit these properties. The radius-1 rule is exploited by a **classifier** which makes relevance judgments on pages crawled to decide on link expansion. The radius-2 rule is exploited by a **distiller** which identifies pages with many links to unvisited promising links. The system is built around a **crawler** with dynamically reconfigurable priority controls which are governed by the classifier and distiller.

2.1 Classification

The relevance of each URL fetched is evaluated using a *classifier*. Many different methods for text classification have been studied [1, 6, 14, 17]. Here we will use a Bayesian classifier. This broad family of classifiers have been found to be computationally very inexpensive and yet quite effective for high-dimensional applications such as text. The CMU *World Wide Knowledge Base* project has often used simple Bayesian learning algorithms[13] with good results. Silicon Graphics MineSet includes a Bayesian classifier[14].

2.1.1 Classifier computations

To simplify the exposition, we will propose a simple statistical generative model for documents which has been found to be surprisingly effective. Let classes be denoted c in formulae and `cid` in SQL code. For each term t (from a universe of terms) and each class c, there is a parameter $\theta(c, t)$. (The value of this parameter is unknown and is estimated from the training documents). Terms are denoted as `tid` in formulae. Given numeric values of all θ, a document d is generated as follows. First, a class or topic is chosen using a *prior* distribution. All documents by definition belong to the root of the topic tree; $\Pr[\text{root}] = 1$. Given that we have decided to write a document about internal topic node c_0, we refine the decision by picking a child of c_0: class c_i is picked with probability $\Pr[c_i|c_0]$, whose logarithm[15] is denoted $\texttt{logprior}(c_i)$ later.

Once the (leaf) class node c has been decided, the length of the document is set arbitrarily. (One may also pick the length using a class-conditional distribution, but we keep the model simple.) Having picked the length $n(d)$, we write out the document term after term. Each term is picked by flipping a die with as

[13] `http://www.cs.cmu.edu/afs/cs.cmu.edu/project/theo-11/www/wwkb/`

[14] `http://www.sgi.com/software/mineset/mineset_data.html`

[15] We work in the log domain because the absolute probability is often very small.

many sides as there are terms in the universe. The face corresponding to term t has probability $\theta(c,t)$ of turning up. In the resulting document, the number of occurrences of t is denoted $n(d,t)$ in formulae and freq(d,t) in SQL. The class-conditional probability of generating the document is $\binom{n(d)}{\{n(d,t)\}} \prod_{t \in d} \theta(c,t)^{n(d,t)}$. This is called the Bernoulli or multinomial model for text generation.

During the setup stage, the classifier is *trained* with example documents associated with each node or class in the taxonomy tree. Training is in some sense the opposite of generation: given documents with associated classes, the classifier constructs statistical models for each class and stores these on disk. At each internal node c_0 in the class tree, training involves three steps:

Feature selection: Of all the terms in the universe, a subset $F(c_0)$ is selected. Intuitively, these are terms that provide the maximum *discrimination power* between documents belonging to different subtrees of c_0. Because training data is limited and noisy, accuracy may in fact be *reduced* by including more terms. Feature selection has been studied in detail elsewhere [6].

Parameter estimation: For all internal classes c_0 and all $t \in F(c_0)$, we have to estimate $\theta(c_i,t)$ for each child c_i of c_0 from the training documents. Let $D(c_i)$ be the set of training documents for class c_i. Then $\theta(c_i,t)$ is estimated as:

$$\frac{1+\sum_{d\in D(c_i)} n(d,t)}{\left|\bigcup_{d\in D(c_0)}\{t\in d\}\right| + \sum_{d\in D(c_i)}\sum_{t\in d} n(d,t)} \tag{1}$$

Notice that $\theta(c_i,t) > 0$ for all c_i and t, but for most t, $n(d,t) = 0$ (text data is very sparse). To avoid losing the sparseness, we only store logtheta$(c_i,t) = \log\theta(c_i,t)$, where $\sum_{d\in D(c_i)} n(d,t) > 0$, and logdenom$(c_i)$ = $\log\left(\left|\bigcup_{d\in D(c_0)}\{t\in d\}\right| + \sum_{d\in D(c_i)}\sum_{t\in d} n(d,t)\right)$.

Index construction: In traditional classification, the final indexing table, called BLOB here, is built as a map from (c_0,t), where $t \in F(c_0)$, to a set of records. Each record is for a child c_i of c_0 (all children need not be present), of the form $(c_i,$ logtheta$(c_i,t))$. This structure is shown in Figure 1. c_0 is denoted pcid and c_i are denoted kcid. There is also a TAXONOMY table mapping c_i to logdenom(c_i) and logprior(c_i).

During crawling, each page is subjected to *testing*. The traditional purpose of testing is to assign the document to one or few best-matching classes. A test document d is routed as follows. Suppose the root is denoted c_0. In test mode, d is tokenized, and for each term t an index probe is made with the key (c_0,t). For those $t \in F(c_0)$, a set of c and θ values are retrieved. These are used to update the probability that d was generated from each child of c_0, given it was generated from c_0 (this can be applied recursively from the root using chain rule):

$$\begin{aligned}\Pr[c_i|c_0,d] &= \Pr[d,c_i,c_0]/\Pr[d,c_0]\\ &= \Pr[d,c_i]/\Pr[d,c_0]\\ &= \Pr[c_i|c_0](\Pr[d|c_i]/\Pr[d|c_0]),\end{aligned} \tag{2}$$

because $d\in c_i \Rightarrow d\in c_0$. (See **SingleProbe** in Figure 2 for details.)

The newly evaluated nodes c_i are checked into a pool of nodes to be further expanded. From this pool, the node with highest probability is picked as the new "root" and the above process is repeated. Typically, one may stop after evaluating the highest probability leaf node.

2.1.2 Modifications for resource discovery

In the administration phase, the user has marked a set of classes as good. A simple strategy for resource discovery could be the hard focus rule.

Hard focus rule: Suppose the best leaf class if the current page d is determined to be c^*. If some ancestor of c^* is good, insert the outlinks in d into the crawl frontier.

We won't go into details, but this turns out not to be a good rule; crawls controlled by this rule may *stagnate*, i.e., stop because the entire crawl frontier is found unsuitable for expansion. Manual inspection typically shows that the frontier nodes are quite relevant, but the best *leaf* class is not a descendant of a good class.

Soft focus rule: For queries on the materialized Web subgraph, the hard focus notion may be used to select relevant pages. For data acquisition, however, we are better off evaluating for each document d, the probability that it is good,

$$R(d) \equiv \texttt{relevance}(d) = \sum_{\texttt{good}(c)} \Pr[c|d], \tag{3}$$

and prioritizing page crawls (partly) based on this number. We will report only on the soft focus rule because it is more robust.

2.1.3 I/O efficient implementation

We will first describe the common implementation of the classification, explain why this has poor performance, and give a superior implementation coded directly in SQL. Performance analysis is deferred to §3.

Traditionally, keyword-based near-neighbor search is done using the *inverted file* approach. For classification, we do not need to search for documents by keywords. We can therefore use a more compact inverted file representation, described next.

Keyword indices are constructed by assigning unique ID's to each term (we use t in formulae, tid in SQL) and each document (d in formulae, did in SQL).

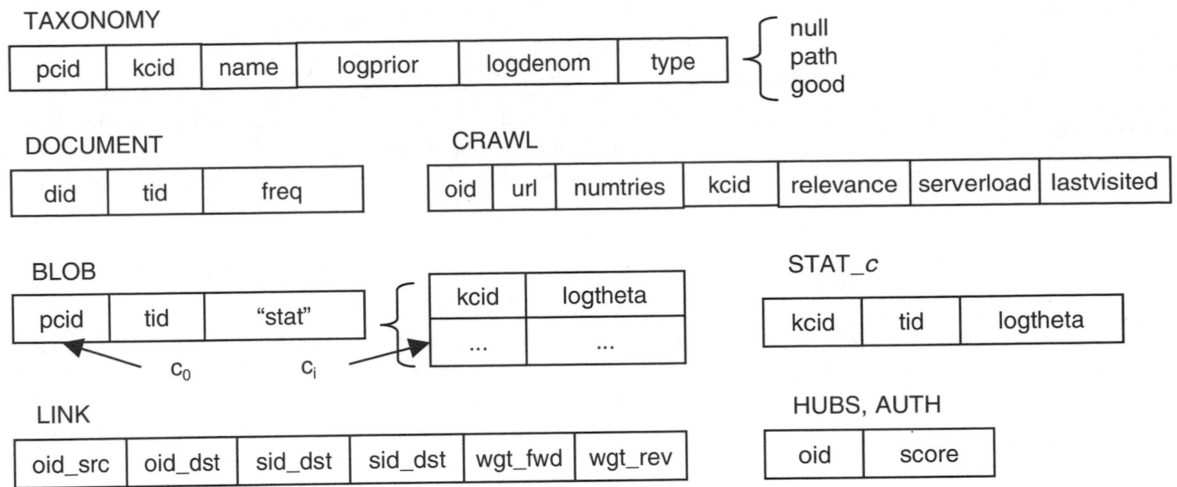

Figure 1: The main DB2 tables used in our system. `TAXONOMY`, `STAT`, `BLOB`, and `DOCUMENT` are used by the classifier. `CRAWL` and `LINK` are used by the crawler. `LINK`, `HUBS` and `AUTH` are used by the distiller. Columns which are not self-explanatory are explained in the text.

In our system we use 32-bit hash codes for terms. For topics (also called classes, denoted c in formulae and `cid` in SQL) we use 16-bit ID's.

Consider internal node c_0 with children $\{c_i\}$. Let $t \in F(c_0)$ be a feature term w.r.t. c_0 (see §2.1 for terminology and notation). The compact inverted file maps (c_0, t) to a sparse vector of θ values, each element being of the form $(c_i, \texttt{logtheta}(c_i, t))$. There is an entry for c_i only if $\sum_{d \in D(c_i)} n(d,t) > 0$. A separate table stores a map from c_i to $\texttt{logdenom}(c_i)$. $\theta(c_i, t)$ can be reconstructed from these numbers.

A key step in classification is to compute $\log \Pr[c_i|c_0, d] = \texttt{logprior}(c_i) + \log \Pr[d|c_i] - \log \Pr[d|c_0]$, where $\log \Pr[d|c_i] = \text{constant} + \sum_{t \in d \cap F(c_0)} \texttt{freq}(d,t) \texttt{logtheta}(c_i, t)$. Note that for a pre-specified C^*, we need to compute $\Pr[c|d]$ only for $c \in C^*$.

The pseudocode using the `BLOB` table (shown in Figure 1) is shown in Figure 2. With regard to disk access, it is similar to any standard keyword indexing engine, and is quite insensitive to the exact math. If, for example, the term distribution is changed from multinomial to Gaussian, θ would be replaced by the mean μ and variance σ, but not much else would change.

For large taxonomies θ cannot be stored entirely in memory. E.g., models derived from about 2100 nodes of Yahoo! and 1.5 GB of text occupy about 350 MB. (As users refine and personalize the taxonomy and ask more queries, this size gets larger.) Consequently most of the classification time is spent in the **PROBE** step. Even with caching, there is little locality of access, because the records are small and most storage managers use page-level caching. A lot of random I/O results, making the classifier disk-bound. The random I/O problem is especially serious in our system because of the multi-threaded crawler. In experimental runs, about thirty threads fetch a total of 5–10 pages a second, a typical web page having 200-500 terms, each term leading to a **PROBE**.

We will now describe a way to classify a large batch of documents using a sort-merge technique, which can be written, with some effort, directly in SQL. The tables needed are shown in Figure 1. The `TAXONOMY` table encodes the relation between parent and child classes in the usual way. Some topics are marked `good` as described earlier; all their ancestors are marked `path`. Nodes marked `null` are not of interest in a particular crawl (but these may be marked otherwise for a different crawl). The `DOCUMENT` table consists of rows of the form $(d, t, \texttt{freq}(d,t))$. Since (d,t) is a key we will refer to this table as $\texttt{freq}(d,t)$. For each internal node c_0 of the taxonomy there is a table $\texttt{STAT\_}c_0$, which stores the map from (c_i, t) to $\texttt{logtheta}(c_i, t)$, where c_i are children of c_0 and only those $t \in F(c_0)$ appear in the table. Note that only `DOCUMENT` has to be populated at crawl time; the rest is precomputed. Populating `DOCUMENT` is part of standard keyword indexing anyway.

Going through the steps in Figure 2, we note that the main step is to evaluate $\sum_{t \in d \cap F(c_0) \cap c_i} \texttt{freq}(d,t) \texttt{logtheta}(c_i, t) - \sum_{t \in d \cap F(c_0), t \notin c_i} \texttt{freq}(d,t) \texttt{logdenom}(c_i)$.

The first sum is an inner join, but the second sum leads to random update I/O. The whole expression is best rewritten (after some trial and error) using one

```
SingleProbe(c_0, d)
For all children {c_i} of c_0
    initialize array of log-probabilities {L[i]}
For each term t ∈ d occurring freq(d,t) times:
    PROBE BLOB with key (c_0, t)
    If t ∉ F(c_0) skip t
    For each (c_i, logtheta(c_i, t)) retrieved:
        L[i] ← L[i] + freq(d,t)logtheta(c_i, t)
    For each c'_i that was missing
        L[i] ← L[i] − freq(d,t)logdenom(c'_i)
Normalize L so that Σ_i e^{L[i]} = 1
For each i
    Assign L[i] ← L[i] + log Pr[c_0|d] + logprior(c_i)
```

Figure 2: Document-by-document classification pseudocode.

```
BulkProbe(c0)
with
   PARTIAL(did, cid, lpr1) as
   (select did, TAXONOMY.kcid,
      sum(freq * (logtheta + logdenom))
      from STAT_c0, DOCUMENT, TAXONOMY
      where TAXONOMY.pcid = c0
      and STAT_c0.tid = DOCUMENT.tid
      and STAT_c0.kcid = TAXONOMY.kcid
      group by did, TAXONOMY.kcid)
   DOCLEN(did, len) as
   (select did, sum(freq) from DOCUMENT
      where tid in (select tid from STAT_c0)
      group by did),
   COMPLETE(did, kcid, lpr2) as
   (select did, kcid, - len * logdenom
      from DOCLEN, TAXONOMY where pcid = c0)
select C.did, C.cid, lpr2 + coalesce(lpr1, 0)
from COMPLETE as C left outer join PARTIAL as P
on C.did = P.did and C.cid = P.cid
```

Figure 3: Hierarchical bulk classification expressed as a ODBC/JDBC subroutine. This is repeatedly called at all `path` nodes in topological order to evaluate the score of the `good` nodes.

inner and one left outer join [11]:

$$\sum_{t \in d \cap F(c_0) \cap c_i} \texttt{freq}(d,t)\Big(\texttt{logtheta}(c_i,t) + \texttt{logdenom}(c_i)\Big) \\ -\texttt{logdenom}(c_i) \sum_{t \in d \cap F(c_0)} \texttt{freq}(d,t).$$

Figure 3 shows a high-level pseudocode for an ODBC/JDBC routine with one parameter c_0 which indicates the node at which bulk evaluation is desired. For simplicity, the code ignores some details such as priors and normalization which are lower order performance concerns.

2.2 Distillation

The purpose of distillation is to identify *hubs*, i.e, pages with large lists of links to relevant resources. A very relevant page without links is only a finishing point in the crawl. In contrast, hubs are good for crawling, and good hubs should be checked frequently for new resource links.

2.2.1 Query-based distillation review

The Web is an example of a *social network*. The edges of a social network can be analyzed to identify pages that are 'central' in some sense [21, 28, 33]. Similar techniques have been applied to the Web graph. Brin and Page [5] model the 'prestige' of a page v as roughly the sum total of the prestige of pages that cite v. If $\mathbf{E}$ is the node adjacency matrix, the prestige of a node is the appropriate component of the dominant eigenvector of $\mathbf{E}$. Kleinberg offers a slightly different model: each node v has both a *hub score* $h(v)$ and an *authority score* $a(v)$; these are estimated by mutual recursion.

Hubs confer prestige to authorities:
$a(v) \leftarrow \sum_{(u,v)\in E} h(u)$ for all v
Total prestige is normalized:
$\Sigma_a \leftarrow \sum_v a(v)$
$a(v) \leftarrow a(v)/\Sigma_a$ for all v
Authorities reflect prestige to hubs [28])
$h(u) \leftarrow \sum_{(u,v)\in E} a(v)$ for all u
Total reflected prestige is normalized:
$\Sigma_h \leftarrow \sum_u h(u)$
$h(u) \leftarrow h(u)/\Sigma_h$ for all u

If $\mathbf{E}$ is the adjacency matrix for E, h and a converge to the dominant eigenvectors of $\mathbf{E}^T\mathbf{E}$ and $\mathbf{E}\mathbf{E}^T$. Pages having large a values are highly popular *authorities*, and pages having large h are good resource lists or *hubs*.

2.2.2 Enhancements for resource discovery

For the purpose of topic-driven discovery, some important enhancements are needed. In the above procedure, each edge is implicitly assumed to have the same importance. Some limitations of this assumption have been described in later work [7, 4], which have assigned various heuristic weights, based on the keyword query, to the edges to improve precision. In our setting there is no query, but there are topics induced by examples, and we wish to model the strength of hyperlinks using the relevance judgment.

To appreciate the model that we will propose, observe that w.r.t. almost any topic, relevant pages refer to irrelevant pages and vice versa with appreciable frequency, owing to the diversity of authorship. Pages of all topics point to Netscape and Free Speech Online. Conversely, bookmark files that are great resources about sports cars may also have links to photography sites.

We will specialize the forward and backward adjacency matrices $\mathbf{E}$ and $\mathbf{E}^T$ into two differently weighted matrices $\mathbf{E}_F$ and $\mathbf{E}_B$. We propose that the weight $\mathbf{E}_F[u,v]$ of edge (u,v) be the probability that u linked to v because v was relevant to the topic, i.e., relevance(v). This has the effect of preventing leakage of endorsement or prestige from relevant hubs to irrelevant authorities. Similarly, we propose that $\mathbf{E}_B[u,v]$ be set to relevance(u), to prevent a relevant authority from transferring prestige to an irrelevant hub. Another effect that has to be corrected for is *inflation* of endorsement. This is done similar to Bharat et al [4].

2.2.3 I/O efficient implementation

Two tables HUBS and AUTH are used to perform distillation. They have the same schema: a 64-bit hashed oid key for the URL (u and v in the formulae before) and a floating point field score representing h and a as per context. The third table involved in distillation is the LINK table, which has six attributes.

oid_src: ID corresponding to source URL, u in previous formulae.

sid_src: The server (represented by IP address) that served u. This is not always fool-proof, because of DNS-based load-balancing, multi-homed hosts, etc., but these aberrations were tolerable.

oid_dst: ID of target URL, or v in formulae.

sid_dst: Server of target URL.

wgt_fwd: Forward iteration edge weight, or $\mathbf{E}_F[u,v]$ in formulae (see §2.2).

wgt_rev: Reverse or backward iteration edge weight, or $\mathbf{E}_B[u,v]$ in formulae (see §2.2).

In past work on distillation, the graphs had few hundred nodes and iterations were done within main memory. An array of links would be traversed, reading and updating the endpoints using node hashes. We estimate that a graph would $|V|$ nodes would need about $336|V|$ bytes of RAM. Large graphs would not fit in memory, which is shared with the classifier and crawler. Furthermore, to keep the crawl persistent and influence the crawler's decisions, we would have to write out the new scores to disk anyway.

A cleaner approach is to write the distillation as another database application, so that depending on the graph size, the database would automatically pick an I/O-efficient execution plan. This also enables running distillation concurrently with the crawler and classifier. Furthermore, distillation can then be triggered by substantial changes in the crawl graph. The code for one iteration of the distiller is shown in Figure 4. Notice how it is asymmetric w.r.t. update of HUBS and AUTH.

3 Experiments

Our prototype crawler is a C++ ODBC/CLI application that was run on a dual-processor 333 MHz Pentium-II PC with 256 MB of RAM and SCSI disk. IBM Universal Database v5 and v5.2 were used. The administration program is a JDBC-based Java applet. Our test machines are connected through a half-duplex 10 MB/s Ethernet through the router to a SOCKS firewall machine. The firewall is connected to the ISP using full-duplex 10 MB/s SMDS over DS3. The ISP connects us to a 622 MB/s OC12 ATM backbone (UUNET High Performance Network). Comparisons between standalone mining and mining written on top of the database were done on a 266 MHz Pentium-II PC with 128 MB or RAM.

3.1 Using a DBMS

We started building our prototype as a C++ application using the file system to maintain crawl state [10]. As we made progress, many services provided by a relational engine became essential. The crawler is multi-threaded; these threads concurrently access the unexplored crawl frontier stored on disk. Few pages on the Web are formally checked for well-formedness, hence all crawlers crash [5]. Keeping all crawl tables and indices consistent by hand amounted to reinventing the wheel.

Robust data storage was the initial reason for using a DBMS, but we quickly realized that we could exploit other features. It became trivial to write ad-hoc SQL queries to monitor the crawler and diagnose problems such as stagnation. In most cases, the queries we asked were not planned ahead of time. Multiple index orders could be implemented on the crawl frontier, and the policy could even be changed dynamically. Such experiments would cost major coding effort in the case of a standalone application.

Gradually we started using the DBMS in more advanced ways. We rewrote the classifier and distiller to maximally exploit the I/O efficiency of sort-merge joins. This increased our discovery rate by almost an order of magnitude. We also used triggers to recompute relevance and centrality scores when the neighborhood of a page changed significantly owing to continued crawling.

3.2 Controlling the crawler

Now we will describe how the scores determined by the classifier and distiller are combined with other per-URL and per-server statistics to guide the crawler. To make the discussion concrete, we give a specific design, but it is important to note the flexibility of the architecture to supporting other policies and designs as well.

There are three numbers associated with each page u: the relevance $R(u)$, the hub score $h(u)$ and the

UpdateHubs	UpdateAuth(ρ)

`delete from HUBS;`
`insert into HUBS(oid, score)`
`   (select oid_src, sum(score * wgt_rev)`
`   from AUTH, LINK`
`   where sid_src <> sid_dst /* avoid nepotism */`
`   and oid = oid_dst`
`   group by oid_src);`
`update HUBS set (score) = score /`
`   (select sum(score) from HUBS)`
	`delete from AUTH;`
	`insert into AUTH(oid, score)`
	`   (select oid_dst, sum(score * wgt_fwd)`
	`   from HUBS, LINK, CRAWL`
	`   where sid_src <> sid_dst`
	`   and HUBS.oid = oid_src and oid_dst = CRAWL.oid`
	`   and relevance > ρ /* filter */`
	`   group by oid_dst);`
	`update AUTH set (score) = score /`
	`   (select sum(score) from AUTH )`

Figure 4: SQL code for distillation to find relevant authorities and hubs. Their scores are used to modify crawl (re)visit priorities.

authority score $a(u)$. $R(u)$ is in the `CRAWL` table, and $h(u)$ and $a(u)$ are the `score` fields in the `HUBS` and `AUTH` tables. Apart from these numbers, we need a few other numbers in the `CRAWL` table to control the crawl. The first is `numtries`, which records the number of times the crawler attempted to fetch the URL u. The second is `serverload`, which is a crude and lazily updated estimate of the number of distinct URL's fetched from the same server as u. Its purpose is to prevent the crawler going depth-first into one or a few sites.

In aggressive discovery mode, the highest priority is seeking out new resources. New work is checked out from the `CRAWL` table in the order

```
(numtries ascending, relevance descending,
    serverload ascending).
```

Occasionally, `HUBS.score` is used to trigger the raising of `relevance` of unvisited pages cited by some of the top hubs. We have not had much experience in crawl maintenance, but lexical orderings such as

```
(lastvisited ascending, HUBS.score descending), or
(numtries descending, AUTH.score descending,
    relevance descending)
```

behaved reasonably, provided timeouts and dead links (very high `numtries`) were picked off separately. In production runs, additional criteria can be useful, for instance, an estimate of the average interval between updates to a page that has already been visited. But notice that the code change would be minimal.

A crawler can use various devices to extend its frontier. Typically, it scans each fetched page for outgoing hyperlink URL's. However, other strategies are also known. E.g., if the URL is of the form `http://`***`host`***`/`***`path`***, the crawler may truncate components of ***`path`*** and try to fetch these URL's. If links could be traversed *backward*, e.g. using metadata at the server [9], the crawler may also fetch pages that point to the page being 'expanded.'

3.3 Evaluation setup

We picked about twenty topics that could be represented by one or few nodes in a master category list derived from Yahoo!, such as gardening, mutual funds, cycling, HIV, etc. On most of these topics, the main performance indicators were comparable, so we present a representative sample of results. We were limited only by experimentation time: we did not want to overload the network and disrupt our firewall. A full-scale crawler never operates through a firewall. Although we had access to machines outside the firewall, we decided to demonstrate the viability of our system by running it inside the firewall and consuming negligible network resources. We ran the crawler with relatively few threads compared to what it can handle. In our opinion, it was more important to study the behavior of the system for many different topics, than study extremely large crawls, although a few crawls were left running for days.

3.4 Harvest rate or precision

By far the most important indicator of the success of our system is the *harvest rate*, or the average fraction of crawled pages that are relevant. We want the crawler to spend most of its time acquiring useful pages, not eliminating irrelevant pages.

Human judgment, although subjective and even erroneous, would be best for measuring relevance. Clearly, even for an experimental crawler that acquires only ten thousand pages per hour, this is impossible. Therefore we use our classifier to estimate the relevance of the crawl graph. This methodology may appear flawed, but is actually not flawed. It is to be noted carefully that we are not, for instance, training and testing the classifier on the same set of documents, or checking the classifier's earlier evaluation of a document using the classifier itself.

Just as human judgment is prone to variation and error [25], we have a statistical program that makes mistakes. Based on such imperfect recommendation, we choose to or not to expand pages. Later, when a page that was chosen is visited, we evaluate its relevance, and thus the value of that decision. Thus we are evaluating not the classifier but the validity and viability of the architecture.

Representative crawls on bicycling starting from the result of topic distillation with keyword search `cycl* bicycl* bike` are studied in Figure 5(a) (standard

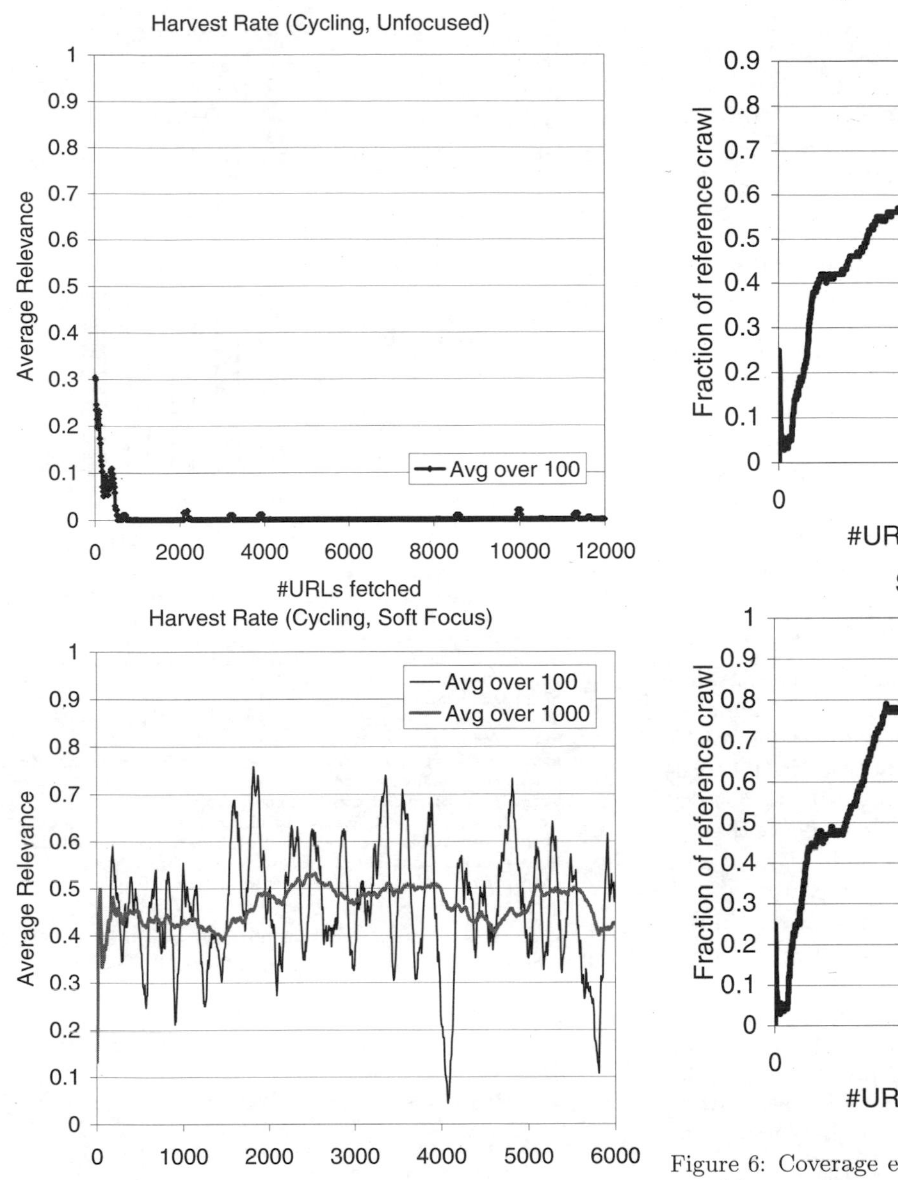

Figure 5: Our system acquires relevant pages at a high harvest rate, whereas a standard crawler starting at the same set of URL's quickly loses its way. The relevance of pages acquired by our system is typically three orders of magnitude higher than a standard crawler.

crawler) and (b) (our system). More extensive experiments with other topics are reported elsewhere [10]. The x-axis shows the number of pages acquired (as a representative of real time). The y-axis shows a moving average of $R(p)$, where p represents pages collected within the window. It is immediately evident that relevant resource discovery does not happen by accident; it has to be done very deliberately. The standard crawler starts out from the same set of dozens of highly relevant links as our crawler, but is completely lost within the next hundred page fetches: the relevance

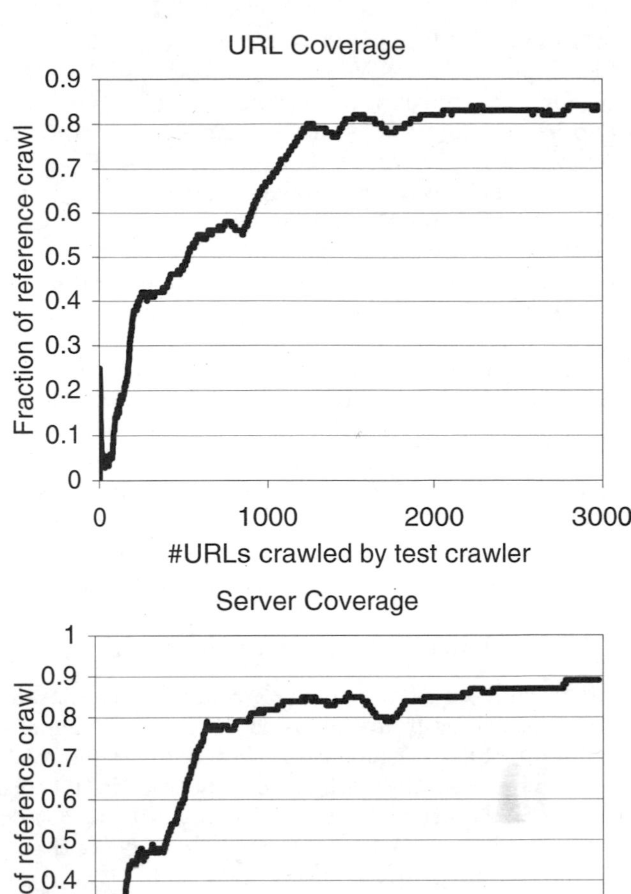

Figure 6: Coverage experiment. A reference crawl is prepared by running our crawler from one start set. Then a disjoint second start set is picked and a test crawl started to see how fast it visits the relevant URL's (a) and web sites (b) visited by the reference crawler.

goes quickly toward zero. In contrast, it is heartening to see that our crawler keeps up a healthy pace of acquiring relevant pages. On an average, every second page is relevant.

3.5 Estimating recall or coverage

For a closed, self-contained data set, precise measurements of recall or coverage can be made. For the web, recall is essentially impossible to assess. However we must produce some reasonable evidence of robust coverage. So we take recourse to the following measurement, similar to Cho et al [13]. We first build a *reference crawl* by selecting a random set S_1

of start URLs from a set of sources, e.g., Yahoo!, Infoseek, and Excite. We run our crawler starting from S_1 for some fixed time (one hour). Then we collect another random set S_2 of start sites from Alta Vista, making sure that $S_1 \cap S_2 = \emptyset$, i.e. the start sets are disjoint. Then we start a separate crawl from S_2, monitoring along time the fraction of the relevant[16] URLs in the reference crawl that are visited by the second test crawl. This ought to give a reasonable feel for how robust the system is. We used a relevance threshold of $\log R(u) > -1$ to include a page u, but the conclusions are not sensitive to this choice. The results are shown in Figure 6(a). It is encouraging to see that within an hour of crawling, the test crawler collects up to 83% of the relevant URLs collected by the reference crawler. It is also important to measure the rate at which *web servers* visited by the reference crawl are visited for the first time by the test crawl; this is shown in Figure 6(b). Within an hour, this number reaches 90%.

3.6 Evidence of large-radius exploration

After one hour of crawling, we collected the top hubs and authorities from the crawl. We list the hubs for cycling in Figure 7 and strongly encourage the reader to follow these links (verified to be accessible on February 22, 1999). How do these compare with traditional topic distillation? We need to provide evidence that we did not unduly help our system by starting it at or near some of the best sites above. To do this, we will plot histograms of the shortest distance (number of links) of the top 100 authorities from the start set. If most of the best authorities are very close to the start set, we cannot claim significant value in the goal-driven exploration. Fortunately, the plots in Figure 7 suggest that this is not the case: excellent resources were found as far as 12–15 links from the start set. Often, there are millions of pages within such distances of any web page. Therefore, our system was performing nontrivial on-line filtering, which was crucial to identifying these resources by crawling only about 6000 pages.

Thus, distillation applied to the goal-directed crawl performs qualitatively better than distillation applied to the result of keyword search, which reconfirms the value of our approach. However, note that superior distillation is just one application of resource discovery. We envisage that a standard search over the corpus, or unsupervised clustering, are likely to be much more satisfying in the scope of the focused corpus. We will explore these in future work.

3.7 Crawl monitoring and tweaking

The ease with which we wrote ad-hoc utilities to monitor the crawler demonstrated the value of using a relational database. We created an applet with a JDBC connection to CRAWL to plot Figure 5 continuously. The query was simply

[16]It does not matter if the irrelevant pages are different.

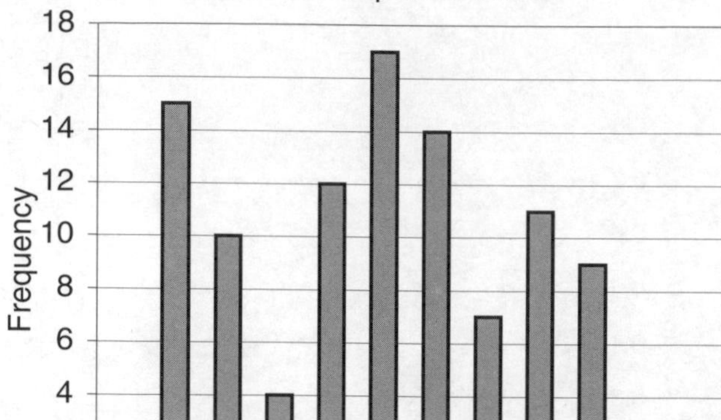


```
http://www.truesport.com/Bike/links.htm
http://reality.sgi.com/billh_hampton/jrvs/links.html
http://www.acs.ucalgary.ca/~bentley/mark_links.html
http://www.cascade.org/links.html
http://www.bikeride.com/links/road_racing.asp
http://www.htcomp.net/gladu/'drome/
http://www.tbra.org/links.shtml
http://www.islandnet.com/~ngs/SVCyclingLinks.html
http://www.novit.no/dahls/Cycling/hotlist.html
http://members.aol.com/velodromes/MajorTaylor/links.htm
http://www.nashville.com/~mbc/mbc.html
http://www.bikindex.com/bi/races.asp
http://www.louisvillebicycleclub.org/links.htm
http://world.std.com/~nebikclb/misc/netresources.html
http://crisny.org/not-for-profit/cbrc/links.htm
http://members.aol.com/velodromes/index.htm
```

Figure 7: Histogram of shortest number of links to the top 100 authorities on cycling and a few top hubs, found after one hour (6000 page fetches). The reader is encouraged to follow these links.

```
select minute(lastvisited), avg(exp(relevance))
from CRAWL
where lastvisited + 1 hour > current timestamp
group by minute(lastvisited)
order by minute(lastvisited).
```

Only one crawl dropped in relevance (mutual funds). To diagnose why, we asked:

```
with CENSUS(kcid, cnt) as
  (select kcid, count(oid) from CRAWL group by kcid)
select kcid, cnt, name from CENSUS, TAXONOMY
  where CENSUS.kcid = TAXONOMY.kcid order by cnt
```

This query immediately revealed that the neighborhood of most pages on mutual funds contained pages on *investment* in general, which was an ancestor of mutual funds. One update statement marking the ancestor good fixed this stagnation problem. Finally, we will give an example of how the distillation program can help the crawler modify its priority to get good pages it was otherwise neglecting. Suppose ψ is the 90th percentile of hub scores. To ask about possibly missed neighbors of great hubs, we write

```
select url, relevance from CRAWL where oid in
  (select oid_dst from LINK
    where oid_src in
```

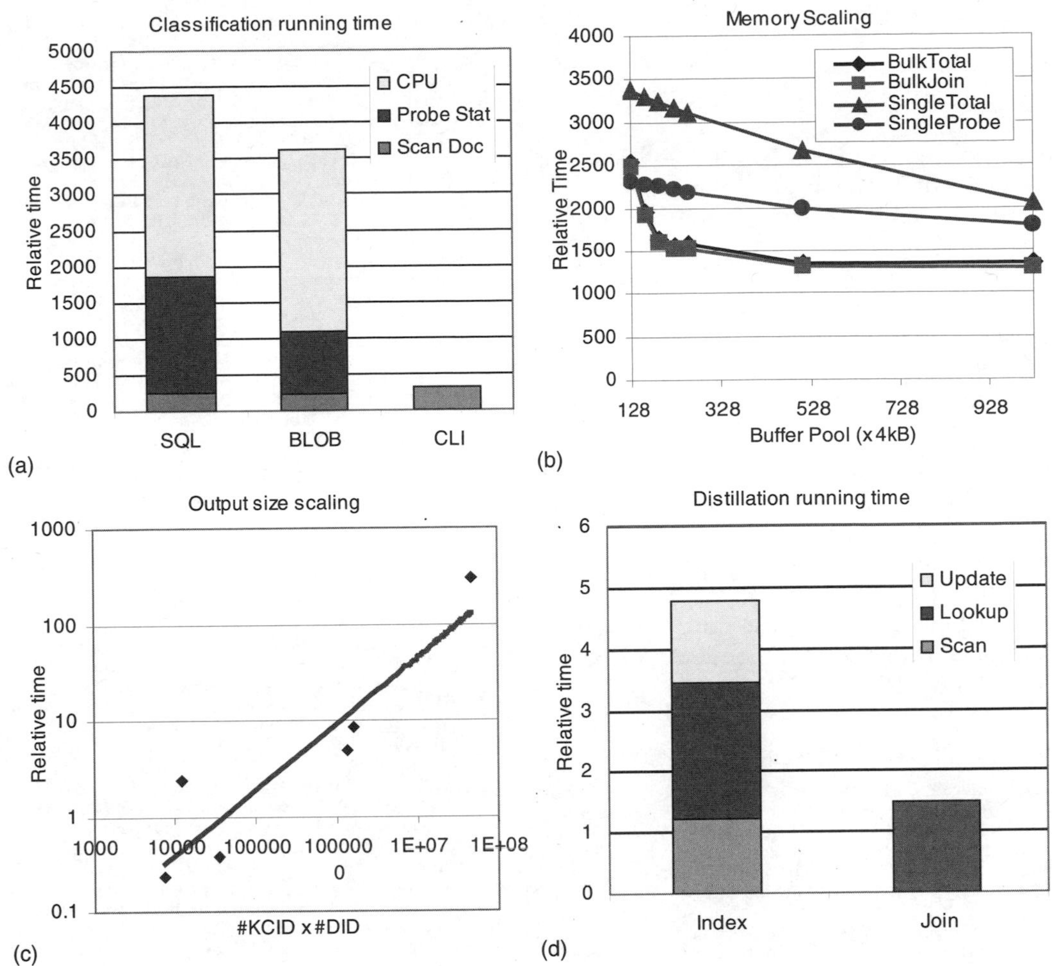

Figure 8: Performance of I/O conscious algorithms against simpler equivalents. (a), (b) and (c) show classification and (d) shows distillation results. (a) shows running time of **SingleProbe** with SQL (left) and BLOB (middle) broken down into CPU time, **PROBE** time, and document scanning time; and **BulkProbe** (marked CLI). (b) shows how **SingleProbe** (BLOB) and **BulkProbe** scale with memory (a smaller dataset was used to collect many data points for **SingleProbe** which is slow). **SingleProbe** shows poor utilization of additional buffer pool whereas **BulkProbe** has better locality. (c) shows that the running time of **BulkProbe** is essentially proportional to output size. (d) compares the running time of naive distillation using sequential link table scan against a better join-based implementation. Time is broken down into scanning of `LINK`, index lookups for `HUBS` and `AUTH` tables, and update of authority and hub scores.

```
      (select oid from HUBS
      where score > ψ)
    and sid_src <> sid_dst)
  and numtries = 0
```

3.8 I/O performance

Figure 8(a) shows the performance of three variants of the classifier. The second bar (BLOB) uses the `BLOB` tables, the first (SQL) and third (CLI) bars don't. The first and second measure **SingleProbe**; the third measures **BulkProbe**. Relative time per document is charted, broken down when appropriate into time for reading `DOCUMENT`, time for computation, and time for probing the statistics. Over an order of magnitude reduction in overall running time is seen using the bulk formulation. Figure 8(b) plots relative running time per document as the buffer pool size is varied, for **SingleProbe** and **BulkProbe**. Because there is little locality, **SingleProbe** shows continual reduction in running time as buffer pool is increased. For much smaller buffer pool size, the running time of **BulkProbe** steeply drops and stabilizes, showing the superior memory usage of the bulk approach. Figure 8(c) shows, for various c_0's and sets of documents $\{d\}$, a scatter of running times against the product $|\{c_i\}||\{d\}|$ (the output size). We see that the bulk algorithm is roughly linear in output size. Figure 8(d) shows the performance of two variants of the distiller: one derived from sequential edge-list walking as in earlier main-memory implementations, the other expressed as a join as in Figure 4. For the former, time is broken down into edge scan, end-vertex index lookup, and score updates. The join approach is a factor of three faster.

4 Conclusion

We have demonstrated that goal-directed web resource discovery is a powerful means to structure web content so that questions combining structured linkage and meta-data with unstructured topic information can be answered efficiently. We have architected such as resource discovery system around a relational database, using it not only as a robust data repository but also as an I/O-efficient hypertext mining engine. It would be interesting to further automate the administration of the system.

Acknowledgements: We are grateful to Global Web Solutions, IBM Atlanta, for partially funding this project. We thank Tom Mitchell, Dan Oblinger and Steve Gates for helpful discussions, Myron Flickner for generously contributing disks and computers, David Gibson for contributing code to the Java user interface, and Sunita Sarawagi, Amit Somani and Kiran Mehta for advice with DB2/UDB.

References

[1] C. Apte, F. Damerau, and S. M. Weiss. Automated learning of decision rules for text categorization. *ACM Transactions on Information Systems*, 1994. IBM Research Report RC18879.

[2] I. Ben-Shaul, M. Herscovici, M. Jacovi, Y. S. Maarek, D. Pelleg, M. Shtalheim, V. Soroka, and S. Ur. Adding support for dynamic and focused search with Fetuccino. In *8th World Wide Web Conference*. Toronto, May 1999.

[3] K. Bharat and A. Broder. A technique for measuring the relative size and overlap of public web search engines. In *Proceedings of the 7th World-Wide Web Conference (WWW7)*, 1998. Online at http://www7.scu.edu.au/programme/fullpapers/1937/com1937.htm; also see an update at http://www.research.digital.com/SRC/whatsnew/sem.html.

[4] K. Bharat and M. Henzinger. Improved algorithms for topic distillation in a hyperlinked environment. In *Proceedings of the 21st International ACM SIGIR Conference on Research and Development in Information Retrieval*, pages 469–477, 1998. Online at http://www.research.digital.com/SRC/personal/monika/papers/sigir98.ps.gz.

[5] S. Brin and L. Page. The anatomy of a large-scale hypertextual web search engine. In *Proceedings of the 7th World-Wide Web Conference (WWW7)*, 1998. Online at http://decweb.ethz.ch/WWW7/1921/com1921.htm.

[6] S. Chakrabarti, B. Dom, R. Agrawal, and P. Raghavan. Scalable feature selection, classification and signature generation for organizing large text databases into hierarchical topic taxonomies. *VLDB Journal*, Aug. 1998. Invited paper.

[7] S. Chakrabarti, B. Dom, D. Gibson, J. Kleinberg, P. Raghavan, and S. Rajagopalan. Automatic resource compilation by analyzing hyperlink structure and associated text. In *Proceedings of the 7th World-wide web conference (WWW7)*, 1998. Online at http://www7.scu.edu.au/programme/fullpapers/1898/com1898.html and at http://www.almaden.ibm.com/cs/people/pragh/www98/438.html.

[8] S. Chakrabarti, B. Dom, and P. Indyk. Enhanced hypertext categorization using hyperlinks. In *SIGMOD*. ACM, 1998. Online at http://www.cs.berkeley.edu/~soumen/sigmod98.ps.

[9] S. Chakrabarti, D. Gibson, and K. McCurley. Surfing the web backwards. In *8th World Wide Web Conference*, Toronto, Canada, May 1999.

[10] S. Chakrabarti, M. van den Berg, and B. Dom. Focused crawling: A new approach to topic-specific resource discovery. In *8th World Wide Web Conference*, Toronto, May 1999.

[11] D. Chamberlin. *A complete guide to DB2 universal database*. Morgan-Kaufmann, 1998.

[12] C. Chekuri, M. Goldwasser, P. Raghavan, and E. Upfal. Web search using automatic classification. In *Sixth World Wide Web Conference*, San Jose, CA, 1996.

[13] J. Cho, H. Garcia-Molina, and L. Page. Efficient crawling through URL ordering. In *7th World Wide Web Conference*, Brisbane, Australia, Apr. 1998. Online at http://www7.scu.edu.au/programme/fullpapers/1919/com1919.htm.

[14] W. W. Cohen. Fast effective rule induction. In *Twelfth International Conference on Machine Learning*, Lake Tahoe, CA, 1995. Online at http://www.research.att.com/~wcohen/postscript/ml-95-ripper.ps and http://www.research.att.com/~wcohen/ripperd.html.

[15] J. Dean and M. R. Henzinger. Finding related pages in the world wide web. In *8th World Wide Web Conference*, Toronto, May 1999.

[16] P. DeBra and R. Post. Information retrieval in the world-wide web: Making client-based searching feasible. In *Proceedings of the First International World Wide Web Conference*, Geneva, Switzerland, 1994.

[17] S. Dumais, J. Platt, D. Heckerman, and M. Sahami. Inductive learning algorithms and representations for text categorization. In *7th Conference on Information and Knowledge Management*, 1998. Online at http://www.research.microsoft.com/~jplatt/cikm98.pdf.

[18] R. Goldman, N. Shivakumar, S. Venkatasubramanian, and H. Garcia-Molina. Proximity search in databases. In *VLDB*, volume 24, pages 26–37, New York, Sept. 1998. Online at http://www-db.stanford.edu/pub/papers/proximity-vldb98.ps.

[19] J. Hammer, H. Garcia-Molina, K. Ireland, Y. Papakonstantinou, J. Ullman, and J. Widom. Information translation, mediation, and mosaic-based browsing in the TSIMMIS system. In *SIGMOD Exhibit*, page 483, San Jose, CA, June 1995. Online at ftp://www-db.stanford.edu/pub/papers/mobie-demo-proposal.ps.

[20] T. Joachims, D. Freitag, and T. Mitchell. WebWatcher: A tour guide for the web. In *IJCAI*, Aug. 1997. Online at http://www.cs.cmu.edu/~webwatcher/ijcai97.ps.

[21] L. Katz. A new status index derived from sociometric analysis. *Psychometrika*, 18(1):39–43, Mar. 1953.

[22] T. Kistler and H. Marais. WebL—a programming language for the web. In *7th World Wide Web Conference*, Brisbane, Australia, 1998. Online at http://www.research.digital.com/SRC/personal/Johannes_Marais/pub/www7/paper.html and http://www.research.digital.com/SRC/WebL.

[23] J. Kleinberg. Authoritative sources in a hyperlinked environment. In *Proc. ACM-SIAM Symposium on Discrete Algorithms*, 1998. Also appears as IBM Research Report RJ 10076(91892), and online at http://www.cs.cornell.edu/home/kleinber/auth.ps.

[24] D. Konopnicki and O. Shmueli. WWW information gathering: The W3QL query language and the W3QS system. *TODS*, 1998. Online at http://www.cs.technion.ac.il/~konop/todsonline.ps.gz.

[25] S. Macskassy, A. Banerjee, B. Davidson, and H. Hirsh. Human performance on clustering web pages: A performance study. In *Knowledge Discovery and Data Mining*, volume 4, pages 264–268, 1998.

[26] A. Mendelzon and T. Milo. Formal models of the web. In *PODS*, Tucson, AZ, June 1997. Online at ftp://ftp.db.toronto.edu/pub/papers/pods97MM.ps.

[27] A. Mendelzon and T. Milo. Formal models of the web. In *PODS*, Tucson, Arizona, June 1997. ACM. Online at ftp://ftp.db.toronto.edu/pub/papers/pods97MM.ps.

[28] M. S. Mizruchi, P. Mariolis, M. Schwartz, and B. Mintz. Techniques for disaggregating centrality scores in social networks. In N. B. Tuma, editor, *Sociological Methodology*, pages 26–48. Jossey-Bass, San Francisco, 1986.

[29] W. Niblack, X. Zhu, J. Hafner, T. Breuel, D. Ponceleon, D. Petkovic, M. Flickner, E. Upfal, S. Nin, , S. Sull, B. Dom, B. Yeo, S. Srinivasan, D. Zivkovic, and M. Penner. Updates to the QBIC system. In *Storage and Retrieval for Image and Video Databases VI*, volume 3312 of *Proceedings of SPIE*, Jan. 1998.

[30] M. Pazzani, L. Nguyen, and S. Mantik. Learning from hotlists and coldlists: Towards a www information filtering and seeking agent. In *Seventh International Conference on Tools with Artificial Intelligence*, 1995. Online at http://www.ics.uci.edu/~pazzani/Publications/Coldlist.pdf.

[31] J. Savoy. An extended vector processing scheme for searching information in hypertext systems. *Information Processing and Management*, 32(2):155–170, Mar. 1996.

[32] L. Terveen and W. Hill. Finding and visualizing intersite clan graphs. In *Computer Human Interaction (CHI)*, pages 448–455, Los Angeles, CA, Apr. 1998. ACM SIGCHI. Online at http://www.research.att.com/~terveen/chi98.htm and http://www.acm.org/pubs/articles/proceedings/chi/274644/p448-terveen/p448-terveen.pdf.

[33] S. Wasserman and K. Faust. *Social Network Analysis*. Cambridge University Press, 1994.

Multi-Dimensional Substring Selectivity Estimation

H. V. Jagadish*
U of Michigan, Ann Arbor
jag@eecs.umich.edu

Olga Kapitskaia
AT&T Labs–Research
olga@research.att.com

Raymond T. Ng
U of British Columbia
rng@cs.ubc.ca

Divesh Srivastava
AT&T Labs–Research
divesh@research.att.com

Abstract

With the explosion of the Internet, LDAP directories and XML, there is an ever greater need to evaluate queries involving (sub)string matching. In many cases, matches need to be on multiple attributes/dimensions, with correlations between the dimensions. Effective query optimization in this context requires good selectivity estimates.

In this paper, we use multi-dimensional count-suffix trees as the basic framework for substring selectivity estimation. Given the enormous size of these trees for large databases, we develop a space and time efficient probabilistic algorithm to construct multi-dimensional *pruned* count-suffix trees directly. We then present two techniques to obtain good estimates for a given multi-dimensional substring matching query, using a pruned count-suffix tree. The first one, called *GNO* (for Greedy Non-Overlap), generalizes the greedy parsing suggested by Krishnan et al. [9] for one-dimensional substring selectivity estimation. The second one, called *MO* (for Maximal Overlap), uses all maximal multi-dimensional substrings of the query for estimation; these multi-dimensional substrings help to capture the correlation that may exist between strings in the multiple dimensions. We demonstrate experimentally, using real data sets, that MO is substantially superior to GNO in the quality of the estimate.

* Supported in part by NSF under grant IDM9877060.

Proceedings of the 25th VLDB Conference, Edinburgh, Scotland, 1999.

1 Introduction

One often wishes to obtain a quick estimate of the number of times a particular substring occurs in a database. A traditional application is for optimizing SQL queries with the *like* predicate (e.g., `name` *like* `jones`). With the growing importance of the Internet, LDAP directory servers, XML, and other text-based information stores, substring queries are becoming increasingly common. Furthermore, in many situations for these applications, a query may specify substrings to be matched on multiple alphanumeric attributes/dimensions. The SQL query ((`name` *like* `mark`) `AND` (`tel` *like* `973360`) `AND` (`mail` *like* `jones`)) is one example. As another example, the LDAP query ([4]) that asks for directory entries in the subtree rooted at the directory entry whose distinguished name (dn) is `dc=research,dc=att,dc=com`, and that match the filter (`tel = *36087*`) can be modeled as a multi-dimensional string matching query (& (`dn = *dc=research,dc=att,dc=com`) (`tel = *973360*`)). The first string component `dn = *dc=research,dc=att,dc=com` matches all the entries in AT&T Research, and the second component `tel = *973360*` specifies a substring match. Often times, the attributes mentioned in these kinds of multi-dimensional queries may be correlated. For the above LDAP example, because of the geographical location of the research labs, people in AT&T Research may have an unexpectedly high probability to satisfy `tel = *973360*`. For such situations, assuming attribute independence and estimating the selectivity of the query as a product of the selectivity of each individual dimension can be grossly inaccurate.

In this paper, we study the problem of multi-dimensional substring selectivity estimation, and make the following contributions:

- We propose a novel generalization of 1-D count-suffix trees [9], referred to as a *k-D count-suffix tree*, as the basic data structure for solving the problem (Section 2). Our trees can handle not only substring matches, but also prefix, suffix and exact matches.

- Given the enormous size of these trees for large databases and for multiple dimensions, it is desirable, and often essential, to try to obtain a compressed representation that satisfies given memory restrictions. To this end, we develop a space and time efficient probabilistic algorithm to construct a k-D *pruned* count-suffix tree without first having to construct the full count-suffix tree (Section 3).

- What we gain in space by pruning a count-suffix tree, we lose in accuracy for estimating the selectivities of those strings that are not completely retained in the pruned tree. Our main challenge, then, is: given a pruned tree, to try to estimate as accurately as possible the selectivity of such strings.

  We develop and analyze two algorithms for this purpose (Section 4). The first algorithm, called *GNO* (for Greedy Non-Overlap), generalizes the greedy parsing suggested by Krishnan et al. for 1-D substring selectivity estimation [9]. The second algorithm, called *MO* (for Maximal Overlap), uses all maximal k-D substrings of the query for estimation, to take advantage of correlations that may exist between strings in the multiple dimensions.

- We present an experimental study, using a real 2-D data set, that compares the accuracy of our two algorithms, GNO and MO, and additionally compares them with the default assumption of attribute independence (Section 5). Our results show the practicality and the superior accuracy of MO, demonstrating that it is possible to obtain freedom from the independence assumption for correlated string dimensions.

1.1 Related Work

1-D suffix tree [18, 11] is a commonly used structure for indexing substrings in a database [9]. One natural generalization of strings is a multi-dimensional matrix of characters. The pattern matching community has developed data structures, also referred to as suffix trees, for indexing sub-matrices in a database of such matrices (see, e.g., [1, 2]). The problem of indexing sub-matrices is clearly a different problem than indexing substrings in multiple correlated dimensions, and the suffix tree developed for the sub-matrix matching problem does not seem applicable to our problem. Our problem, despite its importance, appears to have received much less attention in the literature.

1-D pruned count-suffix trees were studied in [9], and algorithms for the direct construction of the pruned count-suffix tree (i.e., without first constructing the complete count-suffix tree) were proposed. However, those techniques were ad hoc in the sense that no quality guarantees were provided. Our approach of direct construction of a k-D pruned count-suffix tree builds upon the concise sampling technique proposed in [3], provides probabilistic guarantees on the number of false positives and false negatives, and gives *accurate* counts for the substrings in the pruned count-suffix tree.

Histograms have long been used for selectivity estimation in databases [15, 12, 10, 5, 6, 13, 7]. They have been designed to work well for numeric attribute value domains, and one can obtain good solutions to the histogram construction problem using known techniques (see, e.g., [13, 7]). For string domains, and the substring selectivity estimation problem, one could continue to use histograms by sorting substrings based on the lexicographic order, and associating the appropriate counts. However, in this case, a histogram bucket that includes a range of consecutive lexicographic values is not likely to produce a good approximation, since the number of times a string occurs as a substring is likely to be very different for lexicographically successive substrings.

End-biased histograms are more closely related to pruned count-suffix trees [6]. The high-frequency values in the end-biased histogram correspond to nodes retained in the pruned count-suffix tree. The low-frequency values correspond to nodes pruned away. With this approach of estimating the selectivity of substring queries, if α_1 has been pruned, the same (default) value is returned for α_1 and $\alpha_1\alpha_2$, irrespective of the length of α_2.

In spite of the vast literature on histograms, there is very little discussion of histograms in multiple dimensions. A notable exception is the study in [14]. But for the reasons given in the preceding paragraph, this study is not directly applicable to the problem of substring selectivity estimation in multiple dimensions.

A study of 1-D substring selectivity estimation is presented in [9]. Experimental evaluation of various versions of independence-based, child-based and depth-based strategies is given. Among those, a specific version of the independence-based strategies, referred to here as the KVI algorithm, is shown to be one of the most accurate. The GNO algorithm presented here generalizes the KVI algorithm from 1-D to k-D.

In [8], we conducted a formal analysis on 1-D substring selectivity estimation. We compared a suite of algorithms, including KVI and a 1-D version of MO, in terms of the accuracy of their estimates (expressed as log ratios) and their computational complexities. The MO estimation algorithm presented here for k-D strings generalizes the 1-D version analyzed there. As will be shown later, the generalization is not straightforward.

A study of k-D substring selectivity estimation is given in [17]. There are several key differences between that study and the work presented here. First, at a data structure level, k-D substring selectivity estimation in [17] is based on k separate 1-D pruned count-suffix trees and a multi-dimensional array. In our case, the estimation is based on a k-D count-suffix DAG. Second, for constructing pruned data structures, only ad hoc heuristics are considered in [17]. In our case, we develop a space and time efficient probabilistic algorithm. Third, for selectivity estimation, a generalization of the KVI algorithm, as well as child-based and depth-based strategies are developed in [17]. That generalization does greedy parsing independently in each of the k dimensions, using the 1-D pruned count-suffix trees, and computes an estimate for the k-D substring selectivity based on the information in the multi-dimensional array. This technique can be considered as a simple version of the GNO algorithm proposed here. As will be shown later, the MO algorithm proposed here is superior to the GNO algorithm.

2 k-D Structures for Estimation

In this section, we present k-D generalizations of tries and suffix trees for our multi-dimensional estimation problem. To the best of our knowledge, these data structures have not been studied in the literature.

Throughout this paper, we use $\mathcal{A}$, possibly with subscripts, to denote an alphabet for an attribute; and Greek lower case symbols α, β, to denote strings of finite length ≥ 0 in $\mathcal{A}^*$. For simplicity, we do not distinguish between a character in $\mathcal{A}$, and a string of length 1. We use ε to denote the null string.

By a *k-D string*, we mean a k-tuple $(\alpha_1, \ldots, \alpha_k)$, where $\alpha_i \in \mathcal{A}_i^*$ for all $1 \leq i \leq k$. A *k-D substring* of a given k-D string $(\alpha_1, \ldots, \alpha_k)$ is $(\gamma_1, \ldots, \gamma_k)$, such that γ_i is a (possibly empty) substring of $\alpha_i, 1 \leq i \leq k$.

2.1 k-D Count-Tries

In 1-D, a *count-trie* is a trie that does not store pointers to occurrences of the substrings α in the database. Instead, it keeps a count C_α at the node α in the trie. The count C_α can have (at least) two different meanings. First, it can denote the number of strings in the database $\mathcal{D}$ containing α as a substring; we call this *presence*-counting. Second, it can denote the number of occurrences of α as a substring in the database $\mathcal{D}$; we call this *occurrence*-counting. Suppose $\mathcal{D}$ contains only the string `banana`. With the first interpretation, C_{ana} would be 1, but with the second interpretation, C_{ana} would be 2. Both interpretations are obviously useful in different applications. In this paper, our exposition focuses only on presence-counting; all the concepts and techniques presented here carry over easily to occurrence-counting.

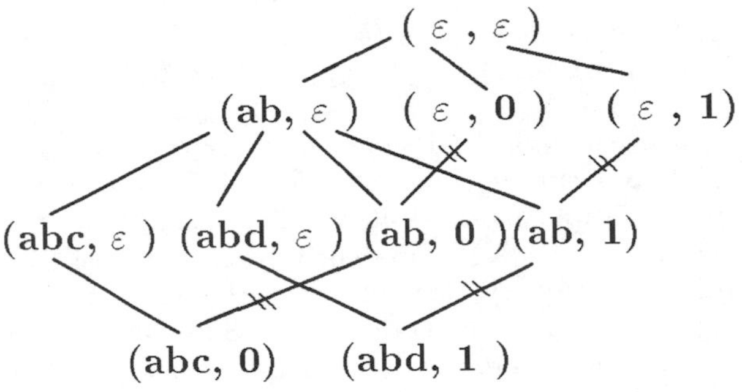

Figure 1: Example 2-D Trie

In k-D, a *count-trie* is a rooted DAG that satisfies the following properties:

- Each node is a k-D string. The root is the k-D string $(\varepsilon, \ldots, \varepsilon)$.
- There is a (directed) edge between two nodes $(\alpha_1, \ldots, \alpha_k)$ and $(\beta_1, \ldots, \beta_k)$ iff:
  - there exists $1 \leq i \leq k$ such that α_i is an immediate prefix of β_i; and
  - for all $j \neq i$, $1 \leq j \leq k$, $\alpha_j = \beta_j$.

By "immediate prefix," we mean that there does not exist another node $(\ldots, \gamma_i, \ldots)$ in the trie, such that α_i is a proper prefix of γ_i, and γ_i is in turn a proper prefix of β_i.

Figure 1 shows the 2-D count-trie for a database with the two 2-D strings $(abc, 0)$ and $(abd, 1)$. The root node $(\varepsilon, \varepsilon)$ and the node (ab, ε) have count $= 2$, while the remaining ones all have count $= 1$.

As is done for standard 1-D tries, a simple optimization can be applied to compress k-D count-tries. For any two nodes connected by an edge, there is no need to store the common prefix twice. In Figure 1, for instance, the node (abd, ε) can simply be stored as (d, ε); we show the prefix in the figure only for clarity.

2.2 k-D Count-Suffix DAGs

In 1-D, a suffix tree [18, 11] is a trie that satisfies the following property: whenever a string α is stored in the trie, all suffixes of α are stored in the trie as well. The same property is preserved for k-D *count-suffix DAGs*, which are k-D count-tries. Specifically:

Property P1: for any k-D string $(\alpha_1, \ldots, \alpha_k)$ in the count-suffix DAG, the k-D strings $(\gamma_1, \ldots, \gamma_k)$ are also in the DAG for *all* (improper) suffixes γ_i of $\alpha_i, 1 \leq i \leq k$.

For example, to make the trie shown in Figure 1 a 2-D count-suffix DAG for $(abc, 0)$ and $(abd, 1)$, we need to add the strings/nodes $(bc, 0)$, (bc, ε), $(c, 0)$, (c, ε), $(bd, 1)$, (bd, ε), $(d, 1)$, and (d, ε), and the corresponding edges.

Just like standard 1-D count-suffix trees, k-D count-suffix DAGs support substring matches. To continue with the simple example above, the query ((attr1 = $*b*$) & (attr2 = $*0*$)) is matched by the node $(bc, 0)$. [1] Similarly, the query ((attr1 = $*ab*$) & (attr2 = $*$)) can be matched by the node (ab, ε). However, it is important to note that count-suffix DAGs cannot handle queries of the forms:

- attr1 beginning with *ab* (i.e., prefix match),
- attr1 ending with *ab* (i.e., suffix match), and
- attr1 matching the string *abc* (i.e., exact match).

Even though in the above example, the node (ab, ε) appears to have handled the prefix query "attr1 beginning with *ab*", it really does not. The reason is that if there is a string (cab, α_2), say, in the database, then according to Property P1 above, (ab, γ_2) for all suffixes γ_2 of α_2 must have been inserted in the DAG. In other words, the count associated with the node (ab, ε) includes not only strings with *ab* as the prefix, but indeed all strings with *ab* as a substring.

It turns out that a simple trick is sufficient to make the count-suffix DAG capable of handling all the variations mentioned above. For each string, we add two special characters: # attached to the beginning, $ appended at the end of the string. As far as insertion into the count-suffix DAG is concerned, these two special characters behave like any other "normal" character in the alphabet. For example, for the 2-D string $(abc, 0)$, we first convert it to $(\#abc\$, \#0\$)$, and then insert all relevant strings based on Property P1 above. As far as querying is concerned, a prefix match to the string "ab" can be specified as a substring match on the (extended) string "#ab" to the count-suffix DAG. Similarly, a suffix match (resp., an exact match) to string "ab" can be specified as a substring match on the string "ab$" (resp., "#ab$").

2.3 Compressed Representation: k-D Count-Suffix Trees

Even though with the simple trick discussed above, we have augmented the query answering capabilities supported by a count-suffix DAG, each query search still begins from the root of the DAG. From this standpoint, a k-D count-suffix DAG is an overkill in the sense that the edges in the DAG allow a search to begin from any node in the DAG (e.g., from $(\varepsilon, 0)$ to $(abc, 0)$ in Figure 1). Thus, to reduce space, we seek to compress a k-D count-suffix DAG into a k-D *count-suffix tree*, while preserving the desired query answering capabilities.

[1] In a trie, the node $(bc, 0)$ is a compressed representation of two nodes $(b, 0)$ and $((b)c, 0)$.

To do so, we first pick a canonical enumeration of the attributes. [2] Without loss of generality, let us assume that the enumeration order is attributes 1 to k. Then for any node $(\alpha_1, \ldots, \alpha_k)$ in the count-suffix DAG, we define the following path from the root to the node as the *canonical path*:

$$(\alpha_{1,1}, \varepsilon, \ldots, \varepsilon), (\alpha_{1,2}, \varepsilon, \ldots, \varepsilon), \ldots, (\alpha_{1,m_1}, \varepsilon, \ldots, \varepsilon),$$
$$(\alpha_1, \alpha_{2,1}, \varepsilon, \ldots, \varepsilon), \ldots, (\alpha_1, \alpha_{2,m_2}, \varepsilon, \ldots, \varepsilon),$$
$$\ldots$$
$$(\alpha_1, \ldots, \alpha_{k-1}, \alpha_{k,1}), \ldots, (\alpha_1, \ldots, \alpha_{k-1}, \alpha_{k,m_k})$$

where for all $1 \leq i \leq k, 1 \leq j < m_i$, $\alpha_{i,j}$ is an immediate prefix of $\alpha_{i,j+1}$, and for all $1 \leq i \leq k$, $\alpha_{i,m_i} \equiv \alpha_i$.

Intuitively, the canonical path of $(\alpha_1, \ldots, \alpha_k)$ corresponds to the path that "completes" first α_1, then α_2 and so on. For example, for the node $(abc, 0)$ in Figure 1, the canonical path from the root passes through the nodes (ab, ε) and (abc, ε). This path is guaranteed to exist already in the DAG.

Finally, to prune a count-suffix DAG to the corresponding count-suffix tree, any edge in the DAG that is not on any canonical path is discarded. In Figure 1, the four edges marked with || are not on any canonical path and are removed to give the count-suffix tree.

As compared with the original count-suffix DAG, the count-suffix tree has the same number of nodes, but fewer edges. Because of the canonical path condition, each node, except for the root, has exactly one parent, [3] reducing the DAG into a tree.

It is important to note that even though we introduce k-D count-suffix trees as pruning the appropriate edges from the corresponding k-D count-suffix DAGs, in practice, a k-D count-suffix tree can be constructed *directly* for a given database, without explicitly constructing the DAG. Effectively, to insert any k-D string, we pick the canonical path as the path for inserting the string into the count-suffix tree.

In the sequel, we use count-suffix trees and suffix trees interchangeably, for simplicity.

3 Construction of Pruned Count-Suffix Trees

3.1 The Necessity of Pruning Nodes

A k-D count-suffix tree compresses the corresponding k-D count-suffix DAG by removing edges not on any canonical path. However, the number of nodes in both structures remain the same. It is obvious that the number of nodes is huge for large databases and for $k \geq 2$.

To be more precise, first consider a 1-D trie. Indexing N strings, each of maximum length L, requires

[2] The choice of the enumeration order turns out to be immaterial from the point of view of selectivity estimation. The only effect it has is on the actual size of the resultant count-suffix tree. Since this is a second order effect, we do not address this issue further in this paper.

[3] In the original DAG, each node may have up to k parents.

at most $N * L$ nodes, assuming no sharing. For a 1-D count-suffix tree, because of all the suffixes, the same database requires $O(N * L)$ strings, each of maximum length L. Thus, the total number of nodes is $O(N*L^2)$.

Now consider a k-D count-trie. Indexing N k-D strings, each of maximum length L, requires $O(L^k)$ possible prefixes for each k-D string, giving a total of $O(N * L^k)$ nodes in the trie. Finally for a k-D count-suffix tree, there are $O(L^k)$ possible suffixes for each k-D string. This gives a grand total of $O(N * L^{2k})$ nodes in the k-D count-suffix tree.

In summary, going from 1 to k dimensions increases the database size by only a factor of k, but it increases the size of the count-suffix tree by a factor of L^{2k-2}. Even in the 1-D case, it has been argued [9, 8] that one cannot afford to store the whole count-suffix tree for many applications and that pruning is required. In the k-D case, the need for pruning becomes even more urgent. [4]

3.2 Rules for Pruning

A tree can be pruned through the use of any well-formulated pruning rule that ensures that when a node is pruned, all its child nodes are pruned as well. In this paper, we consistently use a pruning rule that prunes a node if its count is less than a pruned count threshold $p*N$. (We will shortly be speaking of probabilities of occurrence, and will find it convenient to think of p as the pruned *probability* threshold. If N is the count at the root then, with a frequency interpretation of probability, we get $p * N$ as the corresponding count threshold). The threshold may be fixed a priori, or, for the approximate, probabilistic construction algorithms presented later, the threshold may adjust itself in order to meet given memory restrictions. Since the count associated with any node is guaranteed to be no greater than the count associated with its parent in the tree, our pruning threshold rule is well-formulated.

While the above discusses which nodes to prune, we also have a specific rule that stipulates which nodes *cannot* be pruned, regardless of their counts. These are nodes of the form $(\alpha_1, \ldots, \alpha_k)$ such that for all $1 \leq i \leq k$, the length of α_i is less than or equal to 1. Hereafter, we refer to this as the unit-cube pruning exemption rule. Note that the counts of these nodes are very likely to meet the $p * N$ threshold by themselves. But if they do not, the rule ensures that these nodes are exempted from pruning. The exemption rule is set up to facilitate the selectivity estimation algorithms presented in Section 4.

[4] Because of the dramatic increase in the size of the suffix tree, in practice given k alphanumeric attributes, it is ill advised to blindly build a k-D count-suffix tree. It is expected that some kind of analysis will be carried out, such as correlation testing, to select sub-groups of attributes to be indexed. We do not concern ourselves in this paper on how such a selection can be made.

3.3 Inadequate Ways of Creating Pruned Trees

Given the above rules for pruning, the next question is how exactly to create the pruned count-suffix tree for the given database $\mathcal{D}$. A naive way is to build the full k-D count-suffix tree, and then to apply the pruning rule. For most circumstances, this method is infeasible because the amount of intermediate storage required is tremendous.

Given memory restrictions for creating the pruned tree, we wish to be able to alternate between building and pruning on the fly. An exact strategy to do so is to first form the *completed* database, $comp(\mathcal{D})$, of the given database $\mathcal{D}$ of k-D strings. That is, for each original string $(\alpha_1, \ldots, \alpha_k)$ in $\mathcal{D}$, we form its *completed set* according to Property P1, which is the set $\{(\gamma_1, \ldots, \gamma_k) \mid$ for *all* (improper) suffixes γ_i of α_i for all $1 \leq i \leq k\}$. We then sort (out-of-memory) the completed database $comp(\mathcal{D})$ lexicographically according to the canonical enumeration of the dimensions. Finally, we can simply build the pruned tree by reading in sorted order, and pruning whenever the given memory is exceeded. This strategy, while exact, is in general too prohibitive in cost, because of the sorting involved on a set many times larger than the original database $\mathcal{D}$. Furthermore, as updates are made to the database, there is no obvious incremental maintenance technique.

For most applications, it may be sufficient to construct an *approximate* pruned count-suffix tree. Recently, there has been considerable research activity around the creation of synopsis data structures in a fixed amount of space [3]. In particular, based on the notion of a concise sample, which is "a uniform random sample of the data set such that values appearing more than once in the sample are represented as a value and a count" [3], Gibbons and Matias developed an incremental maintenance algorithm to maintain a concise sample. In the sequel, we refer to this as the GM algorithm.

For a given amount of working memory space, the GM algorithm gives guarantees on the probabilities of false positives and negatives. To be more precise, we wish to find all *frequent* values, i.e., values occurring at least a certain number of times in the data set. Let us use $\mathcal{F}$ to denote the set of all truly frequent values, and $\hat{\mathcal{F}}$ to denote the set of all frequent values reported based on the concise sample. The GM algorithm provides guarantees on the probability of $\alpha \notin \hat{\mathcal{F}}$ given that $\alpha \in \mathcal{F}$ (i.e., false negative), and the probability of $\alpha \in \hat{\mathcal{F}}$ given that $\alpha \notin \mathcal{F}$ (i.e., false positive) [3, Theorem 7]. Thus, one way to create an approximate pruned suffix tree for a given amount of working memory space is to apply the GM algorithm on $comp(\mathcal{D})$.

3.4 A Two-Pass Algorithm

There are, however, two problems with a direct application of the GM algorithm to our task.

Inversions: Recall that for (k-D) count-tries and count-suffix trees, the count associated with a node must not exceed the count associated with a parent. When applied to $comp(\mathcal{D})$, the GM algorithm does not make that guarantee, and it is possible that based on the concise sample, the relative ordering of the count values are reversed. In fact, it is even possible that while a certain node is reported to have a frequency exceeding a given threshold, some of its ancestors are not reported as such, i.e., node $\alpha \in \hat{\mathcal{F}}$ but some of its ancestors $\beta \notin \hat{\mathcal{F}}$.

Inaccurate counts: While the GM algorithm gives probabilistic guarantees on false positives and negatives, it does not provide guarantees on the relative errors of the reported counts (i.e., the error on C_α). As will be clear in our discussion in Section 4 on selectivity estimation, inaccurate counts in the pruned suffix tree may be compounded to give grossly inaccurate estimates for k-D strings not kept in the tree.

To deal with the above two problems, we augment the GM algorithm into the following two-pass algorithm:

1. Pass 1: Construct $comp(\mathcal{D})$ on the fly and apply the GM algorithm.

2. Pass 2: Conduct an extra pass over the original database $\mathcal{D}$ to obtain exact counts for all the strings in $comp(\hat{\mathcal{F}})$.

The second pass of the above algorithm serves two purposes. First, because counts are obtained for $comp(\hat{\mathcal{F}})$, no inversion is possible. Note that in general because of the GM algorithm, the size of $(comp(\hat{\mathcal{F}}) - \hat{\mathcal{F}})$ should not be large compared with the size of $\hat{\mathcal{F}}$. Second, the extra pass over the original database eliminates any possibility of incorrect counts due to the sampling done by the GM algorithm. If the strings in $comp(\hat{\mathcal{F}})$ can all fit in main memory (e.g., $\leq$ 1 million strings), which is achievable for many computer systems these days, the second pass amounts to a single scan of the database.

Thus, in summary, the above two-pass algorithm represents a space- and time-efficient algorithm for constructing a pruned count-suffix tree directly. It gives probabilistic guarantees on false positives and negatives (via the GM algorithm), and at the same time avoids inversions and inaccurate counts. Furthermore, to implement the unit-cube pruning exemption rule mentioned in Section 3.2, the algorithm can simply skip over the strings to be exempted in the first pass, but count them in the second pass.

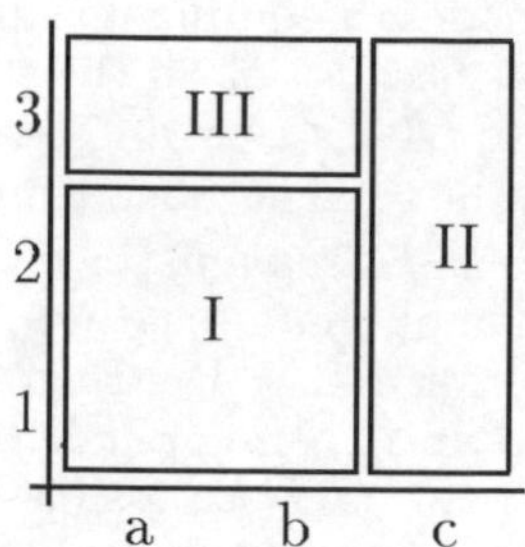

Figure 2: Example 2-D Query with GNO Estimation

When updates $\Delta\mathcal{D}$ are made to the database $\mathcal{D}$, the first pass can be performed in an incremental fashion. Only when there is a change to $\hat{\mathcal{F}}$, is there a need for a pass over $\mathcal{D} \cup \Delta\mathcal{D}$. If there is no change to $\hat{\mathcal{F}}$, then it is sufficient to perform a pass over $\Delta\mathcal{D}$ to update the counts of the existing nodes in the pruned count-suffix tree.

4 k-D Selectivity Estimation Procedures

We now come to the heart of the multi-dimensional substring selectivity estimation problem. Given a k-D query string $q = (\sigma_1, \ldots, \sigma_k)$, where for all $1 \leq i \leq k$ $\sigma_i \in \mathcal{A}_i^*$ (and can be the null string), we use the pruned count-suffix tree to give the selectivity. If q is actually kept in the pruned tree, the exact count C_q can be returned. The challenge is when q is not found, and C_q has to be estimated based on the content of the pruned tree. Below we consider two procedures to do so.

4.1 The GNO Algorithm

Given query q, the GNO (for Greedy Non-Overlap) algorithm applies greedy parsing to q to obtain non-overlapping k-D substrings of q. Before we go into the formal details of the algorithm, we give an example to illustrate the idea.

Consider the 2-D query $(abc, 123)$ shown in Figure 2. The call GNO(abc,123) first finds the longest prefix of abc from the pruned tree, and then from there the longest prefix of 123. In our example, this turns out to be the substring $(ab, 12)$ (rectangle I). Then recursive calls are made to find other substrings to complete the whole query. In our example, the recursive calls are GNO(c,123) and GNO(ab, 3). [5] And as it turns out, the substrings (c,123) (rectangle II) and (ab, 3) (rectangle III) are found in the pruned tree. Then the estimated selectivity is the product of the three selectivities.

[5] Alternatively, the recursive calls can be GNO(c, 12) and GNO(abc, 3). Regardless, in each case, the identified substrings from the pruned tree do not overlap. Experimental results for both alternatives will be presented in Section 5.

Procedure GNO$(\sigma_1, \ldots, \sigma_k)$

1. Find from the pruned tree $(\gamma_1, \ldots, \gamma_k)$ where γ_1 is the longest prefix of σ_1, and given γ_1, γ_2 is the longest prefix of σ_2, and so on.
2. $gno = C_{(\gamma_1,\ldots,\gamma_k)}/N$.
3. If $((\gamma_1, \ldots, \gamma_k)$ equal $(\sigma_1, \ldots, \sigma_k))$, return($gno$).
4. For ($i = 1$; $i \leq k$; i++) {
   4.1 Compute δ_i such that σ_i equal $\gamma_i \delta_i$.
   4.2 If (δ_i not equal null)
   $gno = gno * \text{GNO}(\gamma_1, \ldots, \gamma_{i-1}, \delta_i, \sigma_{i+1}, \ldots, \sigma_k)$.
   }
5. Return(gno).

Figure 3: Pseudo Code of Procedure GNO

Probabilistically, GNO(abc,123) is given by:

$$\begin{aligned} Pr\{(abc, 123)\} &= Pr\{(ab, 12)\} * \\ &\quad Pr\{(c, 123) \mid (ab, 12)\} * \\ &\quad Pr\{(ab, 3) \mid (ab, 12) \& (c, 123)\} \\ &\approx Pr\{(ab, 12)\} * Pr\{(c, 123)\} * \\ &\quad Pr\{(ab, 3)\} \\ &= (C_{(ab,12)}/N) * (C_{(c,123)}/N) * \\ &\quad (C_{(ab,3)}/N) \end{aligned}$$

where N is the count of the root node (i.e., the total number of strings in the database). It is essential to observe that GNO assumes conditional independence *among the substrings*. Note that this is not as simplistic as assuming conditional independence among the attributes/dimensions. For if that were the case, GNO would not have used counts like $C_{(ab,12)}$ from the pruned tree, and would have simply used counts like $C_{(ab,\varepsilon)}$ and $C_{(\varepsilon,12)}$.

A skeleton of the GNO algorithm is given in Figure 3. Step (1) can be implemented by a search of the pruned tree that finds the longest prefix in the order of the dimensions. As usual, the N in Step (2) is the count of the root node.

It should be obvious that in the worst case, GNO searches the pruned tree $O(|\sigma_1| * \ldots * |\sigma_k|)$ times. This brings us back to the unit-cube pruning exemption rule mentioned in Section 3.2. The product $|\sigma_1| * \ldots * |\sigma_k|$ gives the total number of unit-(hyper)cubes for the query. The exemption rule guarantees that the pruned tree has a count for each of the unit-cubes. Depending on the outcome of Step (1), GNO may not need any of the unit-cubes. Strictly speaking, we can do away with the exemption rule, and if a unit-cube is needed but is not found in the pruned tree, we can simply use the prune probability p. We prefer to adopt the exemption rule because in this way, the selectivity of the unit-cube is the most accurate. This accuracy is particularly significant when the actual selectivity is much lower than p, such as for the so-called "negative" queries considered in Section 5.

In terms of formal properties of GNO, the following theorem shows that GNO generalizes the KVI algorithm proposed in [9] and analyzed in [8] for 1-D substring selectivity estimation. In a nutshell, given a 1-D query string σ, KVI(σ) finds the longest prefix γ from the pruned tree, and then makes the recursive call KVI(δ) where $\sigma = \gamma\delta$.

Given a k-D pruned count-suffix tree $\mathcal{T}$, we use the notation $proj(\mathcal{T}, i)$, for some $1 \leq i \leq k$, to denote the subtree of $\mathcal{T}$ such that:

- the set of nodes is given by: $\{\alpha_i \mid$ the node $(\varepsilon, \ldots, \varepsilon, \alpha_i, \varepsilon, \ldots, \varepsilon)$ is in $\mathcal{T}\}$, where α_i can be the null string ε; and
- the set of edges is given by the set of edges in $\mathcal{T}$ connecting only nodes of the form $(\varepsilon, \ldots, \varepsilon, \alpha_i, \varepsilon, \ldots, \varepsilon)$.

For example, the tree shown in Figure 1, when projected on the first dimension, consists of the root node and (ab, ε), (abc, ε) and (abd, ε), and the edges connecting these nodes.

Theorem 4.1 *For any k-D pruned tree $\mathcal{T}$, and k-D query $q = (\varepsilon, \ldots, \varepsilon, \sigma_i, \varepsilon, \ldots, \varepsilon)$, the estimate given by GNO for q using $\mathcal{T}$ is identical to the estimate given by the KVI algorithm for σ_i using $proj(\mathcal{T}, i)$.* ■

4.2 The MO Algorithm: Example

Recall that GNO assumes conditional independence among the substrings. However, it has been observed that complex sequences typically exhibit the following statistical property, called the *short memory property*: if we consider the (empirical) probability distribution on the next symbol a given the preceding subsequence α of some given length, then there exists a length L (the memory length) such that the conditional probability does not change substantially if we condition it on preceding subsequences of length greater than L. Such an observation led Shannon, in his seminal paper [16], to suggest modeling such sequences by Markov chains.

Having said that, we do not intend to determine this magic length L. We believe that determining L is not practical, especially in the presence of updates. However, this points to the fact that there is room for improved estimation accuracy if the overlaps among substrings are taken into consideration. And it is in this aspect that MO tries to excel.

To first illustrate the idea of the MO estimation algorithm, consider again the 2-D query $(abc, 123)$ shown in Figure 2. While GNO finds three 2-D non-overlapping substrings, MO finds overlapping substrings. In Figure 4, to highlight the comparison between MO and GNO, we assume that MO also finds three substrings, corresponding to the ones shown in

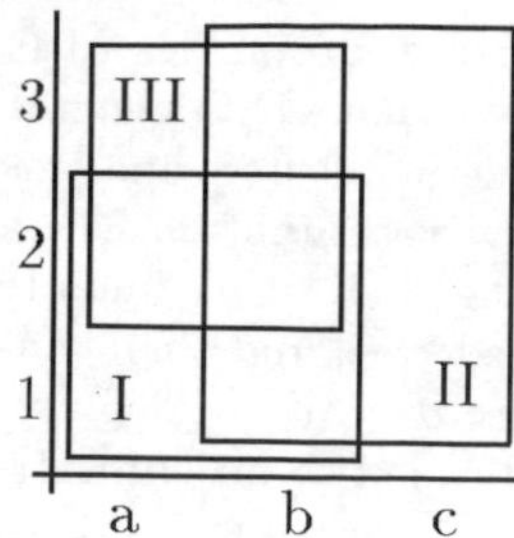

Figure 4: Example 2-D Query with MO Estimation

Figure 2. (In general, MO may find a lot more k-D maximal substrings, i.e., k-D substrings α, β such that α is not a substring of β and vice versa.) While the substring $(ab, 12)$ (rectangle I) remains the same, MO now finds $(bc, 123)$ (rectangle II) and $(ab, 23)$ (rectangle III).

The question now is how to "combine" all these substrings together. Let us begin by considering $(ab, 12)$ and $(ab, 23)$. Probabilistically, we have:

$$\begin{aligned} Pr\{(ab, 123)\} &= Pr\{(ab, 12)\} * \\ &\quad Pr\{(ab, 3) \mid (ab, 12)\} \\ &\approx Pr\{(ab, 12)\} * \\ &\quad Pr\{(ab, 3) \mid (ab, 2)\} \\ &= Pr\{(ab, 12)\} * \\ &\quad Pr\{(ab, 23)\}/Pr\{(ab, 2)\} \end{aligned}$$

Thus, unlike GNO, MO does not assume complete conditional independence among the substrings. Whenever possible, it allows conditioning up to the overlapping substring (e.g., $(ab, 2)$) of the initial substrings under consideration (e.g., $(ab, 12)$ and $(ab, 23)$ here).

Operationally, we can view the above probabilistic argument as a counting exercise. When we take the product of $Pr\{(ab, 12)\}$ and $Pr\{(ab, 23)\}$, we are basically counting rectangles I and III in Figure 4. The problem is that we have "double" counted the rectangle corresponding to substring $(ab, 2)$. To compensate, we divide the product with $Pr\{(ab, 2)\}$.

To continue now by taking into consideration rectangle II, we take the product of the probabilities $Pr\{(ab, 12)\}$, $Pr\{(bc, 123)\}$ and $Pr\{(ab, 23)\}$, basically counting all three rectangles. To compensate for double counting, we divide the product by the three 2-way intersections: (i) $Pr\{(b, 12)\}$ between I and II; (ii) $Pr\{(ab, 2)\}$ between I and III; and (iii) $Pr\{(b, 23)\}$ between II and III.

However, by dividing by the 2-way intersections, we have "over compensated". Specifically, the substring $(b, 2)$ is initially counted three times in the product, but is then dis-counted three times in the division of the three 2-way intersections. To make up, we need to multiply what we have so far with $Pr\{(b, 2)\}$, which is the 3-way intersection between the three initial substrings.

Procedure MO$(\sigma_1, \ldots, \sigma_k)$

1. Find from the pruned tree all the maximal k-D substrings of $(\sigma_1, \ldots, \sigma_k)$. Let these be $\lambda_1, \ldots, \lambda_u$ for some u.
2. Initialize multiset S to $\{\{(\lambda_1, 1, 1), \ldots, (\lambda_u, u, 1)\}\}$, and i to 1.
3. Repeat {
   - 3.1 Initialize multiset S_{new} to $\emptyset$.
   - 3.2 For all $(\alpha, v, w) \in S$ such that w equal i
     - For all $v < j \leq u$ {
     - If $(\alpha \cap \lambda_j$ non-empty)
       - add $(\alpha \cap \lambda_j,\ j,\ i+1)$ to S_{new}.
     - }
   - 3.3 $S = S \sqcup S_{new}$, and $i++$

   } until (S_{new} equal $\emptyset$)
4. Initialize mo to 1.
5. For all $(\alpha, v, w) \in S$ {
   - 5.1 Get count C_α from the pruned tree.
   - 5.2 If (w is an odd integer), $mo = mo * (C_\alpha/N)$
     - Else $mo = mo/(C_\alpha/N)$

   }
6. Return(mo).

Figure 5: Pseudo Code of Procedure MO

4.3 The MO Algorithm: Pseudo Code

The counting exercise illustrated in the above example is generalized in Figure 5, which gives a skeleton of the MO algorithm. Step (1) first finds all the maximal k-D substrings of the query q from the pruned tree. Let these be $\lambda_1, \ldots, \lambda_u$ for some u. Then Steps (2) to (3) find all the non-empty 2-way intersections (i.e., $\lambda_i \cap \lambda_j$), 3-way intersections (i.e., $\lambda_i \cap \lambda_j \cap \lambda_l$), and so on, up to w-way intersections for $w \leq u$. A triple $(\alpha, v, w) \in S$ means that α is a w-way intersection, and λ_v is the highest indexed λ_i participating in this intersection. When computing the $w+1$-way intersections using (α, v, w), the condition "for all $v < j \leq u$" in Step (3.2) ensures that the same λ_j does not participate more than once in the intersection. Note that S and S_{new} have to be multisets, not sets, since duplicate occurrences of the k-D substrings among the λ_i and the various intersections need to be preserved for correctness.

After all the possible intersections among $\lambda_1, \ldots, \lambda_u$ are found, Step (5) of MO computes the final estimate. It obtains the appropriate counts from the pruned count-suffix tree. Note that the suffix tree guarantees that if there are nodes corresponding to α and λ_j, then their non-empty intersection $\alpha \cap \lambda_j$ must have a corresponding node in the tree. Thus, for any (α, v, w) in S, the count C_α can always be obtained from the tree in Step (5.1). Finally, Step (5.2) puts the probability (C_α/N) in the numerator or the denominator depending on whether w is odd or even. That is, if α is a w-way intersection among $\lambda_1, \ldots, \lambda_u$, and w is odd, then the probability appears in the numerator, else in the denominator.

4.4 The MO Algorithm: Properties

A natural question to ask at this point is whether Step (5.2) is "correct". As motivated in the example shown in Figure 4, by "correct", we mean that each substring of query q is counted *exactly* once, i.e., neither over-counting nor over-discounting. We offer the following lemma.

Lemma 4.1 *For any $(\alpha, \_, w)$ in S, representing a w-way intersection, Step (5.2) of MO is correct in that each k-D substring α is counted exactly once.*

Proof sketch. For any w-way intersection α, let us assume, without loss of generality, that α is the intersection of $\lambda_1, \ldots, \lambda_w$. Then: α must have been counted $\binom{w}{1}$ times initially, then dis-counted $\binom{w}{2}$ times due to 2-way intersections, then counted $\binom{w}{3}$ times due to 3-way intersections, and so on. So the total number of times α has been counted and discounted is: $\binom{w}{1} - \binom{w}{2} + \binom{w}{3} - \ldots -(-1)^w \binom{w}{w}$. This can be rewritten as: $(-\sum_{j=1}^{w} (-1)^j \binom{w}{j})$. Now consider the well-known binomial expansion $(1-x)^w = (1 + \sum_{j=1}^{w} (-1)^j \binom{w}{j} x^j)$. By substituting $x = 1$, we get $0 = (1-1)^w = 1 + \sum_{j=1}^{w} (-1)^j \binom{w}{j})$. Hence, $(-\sum_{j=1}^{w} (-1)^j \binom{w}{j}) = 1$. ∎

In [8], for 1-D substring selectivity estimation, we presented a 1-D version of MO. Our analysis indicates that the 1-D version enjoys certain desirable properties and forms the basis for obtaining even more accurate selectivity estimations for 1-D substrings. Thus, to allow all those to carry over, it is important that the k-D MO presented here generalizes the 1-D MO analyzed there. Partly to avoid excessive details, and partly to illustrate the complication in generalizing from 1-D to k-D, we resort to the following example.

Suppose for the query *abcde*, 1-D MO finds three maximal substrings: *abc*, *bcd*, and *cde*. Then 1-D MO, as presented in [8], gives the following estimate:

$$Pr\{abcde\} \approx \frac{C_{abc}}{N} * \frac{C_{bcd}}{C_{bc}} * \frac{C_{cde}}{C_{cd}}$$

On the other hand, the k-D MO procedure shown in Figure 5 gives the following estimate for $Pr\{abcde\}$:

$$\frac{(C_{abc}/N) * (C_{bcd}/N) * (C_{cde}/N) * (C_c/N)}{(C_{bc}/N) * (C_{cd}/N) * (C_c/N)}$$

While it is easy to see that both estimates are identical, we must point out two more subtle details:

- In the k-D MO calculation above, there are terms that cancel off each other, notably (C_c/N). While the (C_c/N) term in the numerator corresponds to the 3-way intersection between the three maximal substrings, the (C_c/N) term in the denominator corresponds to the 2-way intersection between *abc* and *cde*. The point here is that the 3-way intersection of *abc*, *bcd*, and *cde* is exactly the 2-way intersection of the first and the last ones.
- The use of the words "first" and "last" precisely underscore the fact that in 1-D, all the maximal substrings can be *linearly ordered* with respect to the query q. Then it is unnecessary to consider any w-way intersections for $w \geq 3$, and even unnecessary to consider the 2-way intersection between λ_i and λ_j for $j > i+1$. In other words, it is sufficient to just consider 2-way intersections of two successive maximal substrings (e.g., the intersection *bc* between *abc* and *bcd*). The complication in k-D is that there is no linear order to fall back on; λ_i may "precede" λ_j in some dimensions, but vice versa for the other dimensions.

The following results establish that k-D MO is a proper generalization of 1-D MO.

Theorem 4.2 *For any k-D pruned tree $\mathcal{T}$, and k-D query $q = (\varepsilon, \ldots, \varepsilon, \sigma_i, \varepsilon, \ldots, \varepsilon)$, the estimate given by the MO algorithm shown in Figure 5 for q using $\mathcal{T}$ is identical to the estimate given by the 1-D MO algorithm presented in [8] for σ_i using $proj(\mathcal{T}, i)$.* ∎

When the underlying dimensions are independent of each other, the above theorem can be generalized to the following result.

Theorem 4.3 *Suppose the k dimensions are independent of each other, i.e., for all nodes $(\alpha_1, \ldots, \alpha_k)$ in the suffix tree $\mathcal{T}$, $C_{(\alpha_1, \ldots, \alpha_k)}/N = \Pi_{i=1}^{k}(C_{(\varepsilon, \ldots, \alpha_i, \ldots, \varepsilon)}/N)$. Then for any k-D pruned tree $\mathcal{T}'$ of $\mathcal{T}$, and k-D query $q = (\sigma_1, \ldots, \sigma_k)$, the estimate given by k-D MO for q using $\mathcal{T}'$ is equal to the product of the estimates given by 1-D MO for σ_i using $proj(\mathcal{T}', i), 1 \leq i \leq k$.* ∎

Last but not least, let us analyze the complexity of the *MO* algorithm. There are $O(|\sigma_i|^2)$ possible substrings of the 1-D string σ_i. Thus, there are $O(|\sigma_1|^2 * \ldots * |\sigma_k|^2)$ k-D substrings of the k-D string $(\sigma_1, \ldots \sigma_k)$. We check each for presence and maximality in the given pruned count-suffix tree. Hence, in the worst case, Step (1) requires $O(|\sigma_1|^2 * \ldots * |\sigma_k|^2)$ searches of the pruned tree. Step (5) may need another $O(2^u)$ searches of the tree, since in the worst case set S computed in Step (3) may be of size $O(2^u)$. Thus, in terms of worst case complexity, MO is far inferior to GNO. The practical questions, however, are: how much more absolute time is required by MO, and whether the extra runtime gives better accuracy in return. We rely on experimentation to shed light on these questions.

5 Experimental Evaluation

5.1 Experimental Setup

We implemented the algorithms presented in this paper. They were written in C. We paid special attention to ensure that MO is not affected by roundoff errors. Below we report some of the experimental results we collected. The reported results were obtained using a real AT&T data set containing office information about most of the employees. In particular, the reported results are based on two attributes: the last name and the office phone number of each employee. For these two attributes, the un-pruned 2-D count-suffix tree has 5 million nodes. The results reported here are based on a pruned tree that keeps the top 1% of the nodes (i.e., 50,000 nodes) with the highest counts.

Following the methodology used in [9, 8], we considered both "positive" and "negative" queries, and used relative error as one of the metrics for measuring accuracies. Positive queries are 2-D strings that were present in the un-pruned tree or in the database, but that were pruned. We further divided positive queries into different categories depending on how close their actual counts were to the pruned count. Below we use Pos-Hi, Pos-Med, and Pos-Lo to refer to the sets of positive queries whose actual counts were 36, 20 and 4 respectively, where the pruned count was 40. Each of the three sets above consists of 10 randomly picked positive queries. Those were picked to cover different parts of the pruned tree.

To measure the estimation accuracy of positive queries, we give the average relative error over the 10 queries in the set, i.e., (estimated count − actual count)/actual count. Thus, relative error ranges from −100% to infinity theoretically. Because relative error tends to favor under-estimation to over-estimation, we adjust an over-estimated count by the prune count, whenever the former is greater than the latter, i.e., (min(estimated count,prune count) − actual count)/actual count.

While relative error measures accuracy in relative terms, mean squared error, i.e., (estimated count − actual count)^2, measures accuracy in absolute terms. For some of the cases below, we give the square root of the average mean squared error for positive queries. We refer to this as the average mean standard error.

Negative queries are 2-D strings that were not in the database or in the un-pruned tree. That is, if the un-pruned tree were available, the correct count to return for such a query would be 0. To avoid division by 0, estimation accuracy for negative queries is measured using mean standard error as the metric.

	Pos-Hi	Pos-Med	Pos-Lo
MO	(+4%,3.89)	(+16%,10.35)	(-11%,3.38)
GNO	(-98%,35.3)	(-95%,19.13)	(-90%,3.99)

Figure 6: Estimation Accuracy for Positive Queries

5.2 MO versus GNO: Positive Queries

The table in Figure 6 compares the estimation accuracy between MO and GNO. Each entry in the table is a pair, where the first number gives the average relative error, and the second number gives the average mean standard error. For example, the first pair (-98%, 35.3) for GNO indicates that GNO underestimates by a wide margin, and for a "typical" positive query of actual count being 36, GNO estimates the count to be 36 - 35.3 = 0.7. In contrast, MO gives a very impressive average relative error of 4%, and for a "typical" positive query of actual count being 36, MO estimates the count to be 36 + 3.89 = 39.89.

As the actual counts of the positive queries drop, GNO gradually gives better results. This is simply because GNO always under-estimates, but the under-estimation becomes less serious as the actual counts themselves become smaller. On the other hand, no such trend can be said about MO. Sometimes it under-estimates, and other times it over-estimates. But there cannot be any doubt that MO is the winner.

In Section 4.1, we point out that there are many different combinations to make the recursive calls in Step (4.2) of GNO. For 2-D, there are two ways. Besides the version of GNO as shown in Figure 3, we also implemented and experimented with the other version. In general, there are some slight differences in the estimations. But in terms of accuracy, the other version remains as poor.

5.3 MO versus GNO: Negative Queries and Runtime

The mean standard error for negative queries (average over 10 randomly picked ones) is 0.002 for GNO and 0.01 for MO. While GNO is more accurate for negative queries than MO, the accuracy offered by MO is more than acceptable.

By now it is clear that MO offers significantly more accurate estimates than does GNO. The only remaining question is whether MO takes significantly longer to compute than does GNO. For our three sets of positive queries, MO often finds 12–16 maximal 2-D substrings, whereas GNO uses only 3–5 substrings. Consequently, while GNO takes $O(10^{-6})$ seconds to compute, MO usually takes $O(10^{-4})$ seconds (on a 225 MHz machine). Nonetheless, we believe that the extra effort is worthwhile.

	Pos-Hi	Pos-Med	Pos-Lo	Negative
Indep	-23%	-17%	-27%	0.25
MO	+4%	+16%	-11%	0.01

Figure 7: Estimation Accuracy: the Independence Assumption

5.4 MO versus Two 1-D Exact Selectivities

The next question we explore experimentally is as follows. Since we know that a 2-D count-suffix tree is much larger than two 1-D count-suffix trees (i.e., like comparing the product with the sum), there is always the question of: *given the same amount of memory, and in the presence of pruning, would direct 2-D selectivity estimation give more accurate results than using the product of the two 1-D selectivities?* Because it is difficult to get two equal-sized pruned setting, we did the following:

- On the one hand, we used MO on the 2-D pruned tree we have been using so far. This has 50,000 nodes for a total size of 650 Kbytes.
- On the other hand, we used two *un-pruned* 1-D count-suffix trees. In sum, the two trees have more than 160,000 nodes for a total size of 2.3 Mbytes.

Thus, for the latter setting, we used exact 1-D selectivities, without any estimation involved. Essentially, this is an exercise of comparing MO with applying the independence assumption to k-D selectivity estimation. We gave the independence assumption an unfair advantage over MO by allowing the former three times as much space.

Yet, Figure 7 shows that MO compares favorably for both positive and negative queries. For positive queries, the figure only gives the average relative error; and for negative queries, the figure gives the average mean standard error. For easier comparison, the results of MO are repeated in the figure from earlier discussion.

Despite the fact that exact 1-D selectivities are used, and that more space is given to the independence assumption approach, the approach gives less accurate results than 2-D MO. In particular, for negative queries, 2-D MO appears to be far superior. We can attribute this to the unit-cube pruning exemption rule.

The outcome of this comparison is actually somewhat surprising. Initially we expected that the last name attribute of AT&T employees would be quite independent of their office phone numbers. (For instance, office phone numbers and office fax numbers would be far more correlated.) Yet, using MO still gives better results than relying on the independence assumption.

	MO	Indep	GNO
relative error	33%	-57%	-99%

Figure 8: Estimation Accuracy for Large Area Positive Queries

5.5 Accuracy for Large Area Positive Queries

So far, all the positive queries used are "small area", by which we mean that the "area" (i.e., $|\sigma_1| * |\sigma_2|$) covered by $q = (\sigma_1, \sigma_2)$ is between 5 and 12. 2-D strings corresponding to a smaller area tend to be always kept in the pruned tree. Figure 8 shows results for positive queries with "large areas", which is defined to be ≥ 18.

Compared with the small area positive queries, MO becomes less accurate for large area positive queries. One possible explanation is as follows. The larger the area covered by a query, the greater the number of maximal substrings found. Thus, in finding all w-way intersections, w tends to become a larger number than before. Apparently, inaccuracies incurred in the earlier counts are compounded to give a less accurate final estimate. Nonetheless, as compared with the other alternatives, MO is still the best. Finding a way to improve accuracy on large area positive queries is an interesting open problem.

6 Conclusions and Future Work

Queries involving wildcard string matches in multiple dimensions are becoming more important with the growing importance of LDAP directories, XML and other text-based information sources. Effective query optimization in this context requires good multi-dimensional substring selectivity estimates.

We demonstrated, using a real data set, that assuming independence between dimensions can lead to very poor substring selectivity estimates. This argues for the need to develop compact k-D data structures that can capture the correlations between strings in multiple dimensions, and accurate estimation algorithms that can take advantage of such data structures. In this paper, we presented a k-D extension of the pruned count-suffix tree, and described a space- and time-efficient algorithm for the direct construction of the pruned tree, that provides quality guarantees. We formulated an estimation algorithm, MO, that uses all maximal multi-dimensional substrings of the query for estimation; these multi-dimensional substrings help to capture the correlation that may exist between strings in the multiple dimensions. We showed analytically that MO has certain desirable properties, and established empirically the utility of MO for multi-dimensional substring selectivity estimation.

One very interesting open problem is as follows. Given k alphanumeric attributes in the database, the optimization problem is to determine the set of pruned count-suffix trees (possibly with different dimensionalities, possibly with overlapping dimensions) that together satisfy a space constraint, and minimizes some error metric. As far as selectivity estimation is concerned, an interesting open problem is the development of more accurate algorithms for the so-called "large area" queries. One possibility is to use constraints that relate the count of one node to the counts of other nodes in a count-suffix tree. Some of those constraints have been applied to the 1-D substring selectivity estimation problem, and have shown to be able to give more accurate estimates [8]. It would be interesting to see what roles constraints can play in multi-dimensional substring selectivity estimation.

Acknowledgements

We would like to thank Nick Koudas and the anonymous reviewers of the paper, for their suggestions that helped improve the content of the paper.

References

[1] R. Giancarlo. A generalization of the suffix tree to square matrices, with applications. *SIAM Journal on Computing*, 24(3):520–562, 1995.

[2] R. Giancarlo and R. Grossi. On the construction of classes of suffix trees for square matrices: Algorithms and applications. *Information and Computation*, 130(2):151–182, 1996.

[3] P. B. Gibbons and Y. Matias. New sampling-based summary statistics for improving approximate query answers. In *Proceedings of the ACM SIGMOD Conference on Management of Data*, pages 331–342, 1998.

[4] T. Howes and M. Smith. *LDAP: Programming directory-enabled applications with lightweight directory access protocol.* Macmillan Technical Publishing, Indianapolis, Indiana, 1997.

[5] Y. Ioannidis. Universality of serial histograms. In *Proceedings of the International Conference on Very Large Databases*, pages 256–267, 1993.

[6] Y. Ioannidis and V. Poosala. Balancing histogram optimality and practicality for query result size estimation. In *Proceedings of the ACM SIGMOD Conference on Management of Data*, pages 233–244, 1995.

[7] H. V. Jagadish, N. Koudas, S. Muthukrishnan, V. Poosala, K. Sevcik, and T. Suel. Optimal histograms with quality guarantees. In *Proceedings of the International Conference on Very Large Databases*, pages 275–286, 1998.

[8] H. V. Jagadish, R. T. Ng, and D. Srivastava. Substring selectivity estimation. In *Proceedings of the ACM Symposium on Principles of Database Systems*, Philadelphia, PA, June 1999.

[9] P. Krishnan, J. S. Vitter, and B. Iyer. Estimating alphanumeric selectivity in the presence of wildcards. In *Proceedings of the ACM SIGMOD Conference on Management of Data*, pages 282–293, 1996.

[10] R. J. Lipton and J. F. Naughton. Query size estimation by adaptive sampling. In *Proceedings of the ACM SIGACT-SIGMOD-SIGART Symposium on Principles of Database Systems*, March 1990.

[11] E. M. McCreight. A space-economical suffix tree construction algorithm. *J. ACM*, 23:262–272, 1976.

[12] M. Muralikrishna and D. Dewitt. Equi-depth histograms for estimating selectivity factors for multi-dimensional queries. In *Proceedings of the ACM SIGMOD Conference on Management of Data*, pages 28–36, 1988.

[13] V. Poosala, Y. Ioannidis, P. Haas, and E. Shekita. Improved histograms for selectivity estimation of range queries. In *Proceedings of the ACM SIGMOD Conference on Management of Data*, pages 294–305, 1996.

[14] V. Poosala and Y. E. Ioannidis. Selectivity estimation without the attribute value independence assumption. In *Proceedings of the International Conference on Very Large Databases*, pages 486–495, 1997.

[15] P. G. Selinger, M. Astrahan, D. Chamberlin, R. Lorie, and T. Price. Access path selection in a relational database management system. In *Proceedings of the ACM SIGMOD Conference on Management of Data*, June 1979.

[16] C. E. Shannon. Prediction and entropy of printed english. *Bell systems technical journal*, 30(1):50–64, 1951.

[17] M. Wang, J. S. Vitter, and B. Iyer. Selectivity estimation in the presence of alphanumeric correlations. In *Proceedings of the IEEE International Conference on Data Engineering*, pages 169–180, 1997.

[18] P. Weiner. Linear pattern matching algorithms. In *Proceedings of the IEEE 14th Annual Symposium on Switching and Automata Theory*, pages 1–11, 1973.

Evaluating Top-k Selection Queries

Surajit Chaudhuri
Microsoft Research
surajitc@microsoft.com

Luis Gravano
Columbia University
gravano@cs.columbia.edu

Abstract

In many applications, users specify target values for certain attributes, without requiring exact matches to these values in return. Instead, the result to such queries is typically a rank of the "top k" tuples that best match the given attribute values. In this paper, we study the advantages and limitations of processing a top-k query by translating it into a single range query that traditional relational DBMSs can process efficiently. In particular, we study how to determine a range query to evaluate a top-k query by exploiting the statistics available to a relational DBMS, and the impact of the quality of these statistics on the retrieval efficiency of the resulting scheme.

1 Introduction

Internet Search engines rank the objects in the results of selection queries according to how well these objects match the original selection condition. For such engines, query results are not flat sets of objects that match a given condition. Instead, query results are ranked starting from the top object for the query at hand. Given a query consisting of a set of words, a search engine returns the matching documents sorted according to how well they match the query. For decades, the information retrieval field has studied how to rank text documents for a query both efficiently and effectively [13]. In contrast, much less attention has been devoted to supporting such *top-k queries* over relational databases.

As the following example illustrates, top-k queries arise naturally in many applications where the data is exact, as in a traditional relational database, but where users are flexible and willing to accept non-exact matches that are close to their specification. The answer to such a query is a ranked set of the k tuples in the database that "best" match the selection condition.

Example 1: Consider a real-estate database that maintains information like the *Price* and *Number of Bedrooms* of each house that is available for sale. Suppose that a potential customer is interested in houses with four bedrooms, and with a price tag of around \$300,000. The database system should then rank the available houses according to how well they match the given user preference, and return the top houses for the user to inspect. If no houses match the query specification exactly, the system might return a house with, say, five bedrooms and a price tag close to \$300,000 as the top house for the query. ∎

Unfortunately, despite the conceptual simplicity of top-k queries and the expected performance payoff, they are not yet supported by today's relational database systems. This support would free applications and end-users from having to add this functionality in their client code. To provide such support efficiently, we need processing techniques that do not involve full sequential scans of the underlying relations. The challenge in providing this functionality is that the database system needs to handle efficiently top-k queries *for a wide variety of scoring functions*. In effect, these scoring functions might change by user, and they might also vary by application, or by database. It is also important that we are able to process such top-k queries with as few extensions to existing query engines as possible, since today's relational systems are significantly complex and performance sensitive.

As in the case of processing traditional selection queries, one must consider the problem of execution as well as optimization of top-k queries. We assume that the execution engine is a traditional relational engine that supports single as well as possibly multidimensional indexes. Therefore, the key challenge is to *augment the optimization phase* such that top-k selection queries may be compiled into an execution plan that can leverage the existing data structures (i.e., indexes) and statistics (e.g., histograms) that a database system maintains. Simply put, we need to develop new techniques that make it possible to map a top-k query into a traditional selection query. It is also important

Proceedings of the 25th VLDB Conference, Edinburgh, Scotland, 1999.

that any such technique preserves the following two properties: (1) it handles a variety of scoring functions for computing the top-k tuples for a query, and (2) it guarantees that there are no false dismissals (i.e., we never miss any of the top-k tuples for the given query).

In this paper, we undertake a comprehensive study of the problem of mapping top-k queries into execution plans that use traditional selection queries. In particular, we use the database histograms to map a top-k query to a suitable range that encapsulates k best matches for the query. In particular, we study the sensitivity of the mapping algorithms to the following parameters: types of histograms available and their memory budgets, scoring functions, data distribution, and number of query attributes.

The rest of the paper is organized as follows. Section 2 formally defines the problem of querying for top-k matches. Section 3 discusses related work. Section 4 is the core of the paper, and outlines the techniques that form the basis of our approach. Finally, Section 6 presents an experimental evaluation of our approach, using the experimental setting of Section 5.

2 Query Model

In a traditional relational system, the answer to a selection query is a set of tuples. In contrast, the answer to a *top-k query* is an *ordered set* of tuples, where the ordering reflects how closely each tuple matches the given query. This section defines our query model precisely.

Consider a relation R with attributes $A_1, \ldots, A_n$. A top-k query over R simply specifies target values for the attributes in R. Thus, a query is an assignment of values $v_1, \ldots, v_n$ to the attributes $A_1, \ldots, A_n$ of R. In this paper, we will focus on top-k queries on continuous attributes (e.g., `age`, `salary`). Without loss of generality, we will also assume that the values of these attributes are normalized to be real numbers between 0 and 1.

Example 2 : Consider a relation S with two attributes, A_1 and A_2. These attributes have real values that range between 0 and 1. An example of top-10 query over this relation is $q = (0.4, 0.3)$. Such a query asks for the 10 tuples in S that are the closest to the $(0.4, 0.3)$ point, for some definition of proximity, as we discuss below. ∎

Given a top-k query q, the database system with relation R uses some *scoring function Score* to determine how closely each tuple in R matches the target values $v_1, \ldots, v_n$ specified in query q. Given a tuple t and a query q, we assume that $Score(q, t)$ is a real number that ranges between 0 and 1. In this paper, we focus on three important scoring functions, namely *Min*, *Euclidean*, and *Sum*.

Definition 1: *Consider a relation $R = (A_1, \ldots, A_n)$. $A_1, \ldots, A_n$ are real-valued attributes ranging between 0 and 1. Then, given a query $q = (q_1, \ldots, q_n)$ and a tuple $t = (t_1, \ldots, t_n)$ from R, we define the* score *of t for q using any of the following three scoring functions:*

$$Min(q,t) = \min_{i=1}^{n}\{1 - |q_i - t_i|\}$$

$$Euclidean(q,t) = 1 - \sqrt{\sum_{i=1}^{n} \frac{(q_i - t_i)^2}{n}}$$

$$Sum(q,t) = 1 - \sum_{i=1}^{n} \frac{|q_i - t_i|}{n}$$

Example 3 : Consider a tuple $t = (0.3, 0.8)$ in our sample database S from Example 2, and query $q = (0.4, 0.3)$. Then, t will then have a score of $Min(q,t) = \min\{1 - |0.3 - 0.4|, 1 - |0.8 - 0.3|\} = 0.5$ for the *Min* scoring function, a score of $Euclidean(q,t) = 1 - \sqrt{\frac{|0.3-0.4|^2}{2} + \frac{|0.8-0.3|^2}{2}} = 0.64$ for the *Euclidean* scoring function, and a score of $Sum(q,t) = 1 - (\frac{|0.3-0.4|}{2} + \frac{|0.8-0.3|}{2}) = 0.7$ for the *Sum* scoring function. ∎

Figure 1(c) shows the distribution of scores for the *Min* scoring function and query $q = (0.4, 0.3)$. The horizontal plane in the figure consists of the tuples with $z = 0.8$, so what "emerges" above this plane are those tuples with score 0.8 or higher. Note that the tuples with score 0.8 or higher for q are enclosed in a box around q. In contrast, the tuples with score 0.8 or higher for the *Euclidean* scoring function (Figure 1(b)) are enclosed in a circle around q. Finally, the top tuples according to the *Sum* scoring function lie within a rotated box around q (Figure 1(a)). This difference in the shape of the region enclosing the top tuples for the query will have crucial implications on query processing, as we will discuss in Section 4.

A simple variation of the definition of the scoring functions above results from letting the different attributes have different weights. In general, the *Min*, *Euclidean*, and *Sum* functions that we use in this paper are just a few of many possible scoring functions. Our strategy for processing top-k queries can be adapted to handle a wide variety of such functions, as we will discuss. The key property that we ask from scoring functions is as follows:

Property 1: Monotonicity of Scoring Functions: *Consider a relation R and a scoring function Score defined over it. Let $q = (v_1, \ldots, v_n)$ be a top-k query over R, and let $t = (t_1, \ldots, t_n)$ and $t' = (t'_1, \ldots, t'_n)$ be two tuples in R such that $|t'_i - q_i| \leq |t_i - q_i|$ for $i = 1, \ldots, n$. (In other words, t' is at least as close to q as t for all attributes.) Then, $Score(q, t') \geq Score(q, t)$.*

Intuitively, this property of scoring functions implies that if a tuple t' is closer, along each attribute,

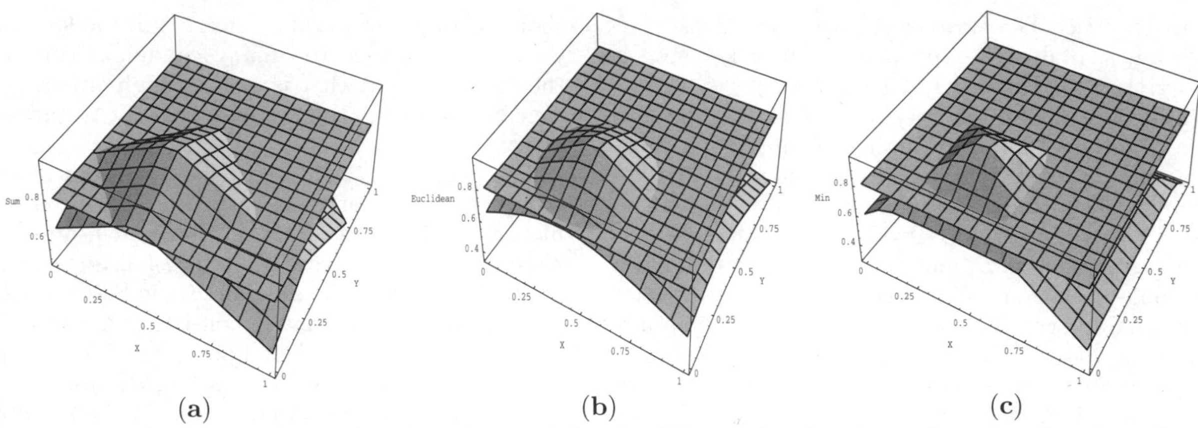

Figure 1: The scores (z axis) for query $q = (0.4, 0.3)$ for the different (x, y) pairs and scoring functions *Sum* **(a)**, *Euclidean* **(b)**, and *Min* **(c)**.

to the query values than some other tuple t is, then, the score that t' gets for the query cannot be worse than that of t. Fortunately, all interesting scoring functions that we could think of satisfy our monotonicity assumptions. In particular, the *Euclidean*, *Min*, and *Sum* scoring functions that we defined above satisfy this property.

A possible SQL-like notation for expressing top-k queries is as follows [3]:

```
SELECT * FROM R
WHERE A1=v1 AND ...  AND An=vn
ORDER k BY Score
```

The distinguishing feature of the query model is in the `ORDER BY` clause. This clause indicates that we are interested in only the k answers that best match the given `WHERE` clause, according to the *Score* function. Section 4 discusses how we will evaluate top-k queries for different definitions of the *Score* function.

3 Related Work

Motro [9] emphasized the need to support approximate and ranked matches in a database query language. He extended the language `Quel` to distinguish between exact and vague predicates. He also suggested a composite scoring function to rank each answer. Motro's work led to further development of the idea of query relaxation that weakens a given user query to provide approximate matches using additional metadata (e.g., concept hierarchies). The querying model for top-k queries that we use in this paper is consistent with Motro's definitions. Our key focus is on exploring opportunities and limitations of efficiently mapping top-k queries into traditional relational queries.

Recently, Carey and Kossman [1, 2] presented techniques to optimize queries that require only top-k matches. Their technique leverages the fact that when k is relatively small compared to the size of the relation, specialized sorting (or indexing) techniques that can produce the first few values efficiently should be used. However, in order to apply their techniques when the scoring function is not based on column values themselves (e.g., as is the case for *Min*, *Euclidean*, and *Sum* as defined in Section 2), we need to first evaluate the scoring function for each database object. Thus, when a query requests the top-k values according to a scoring function like *Min*, their technique would need to first evaluate the *Min* score for every data object. Only after evaluating the score for each object are we able to use the techniques in [1, 2]. Hence, these strategies require a preprocessing step to compute the scoring function itself involving one sequential scan of all the data. In contrast, in this paper we explore techniques that avoid accessing the entire data set.

In [4, 5], Fagin addresses the problem of finding top-k matches for a user query q involving several *multimedia* attributes. Each of these attributes (e.g., an image attribute) is assumed to have a native sub-system that answers top-k queries involving only the corresponding attribute. In the first phase of Fagin's A_0 algorithm, the query processing system obtains a stream L_i of top matches for condition c_i on attribute A_i from the corresponding sub-system. When there are at least k objects in the intersection of all the single-attribute streams L_i, the system is guaranteed to have already accessed k top objects for query q. (These top objects are not necessarily in the intersection of the streams.) The second phase of algorithm A_0 computes the score of each of the retrieved objects, and returns the best k objects. In Section 4.3, we present an adaptation of Fagin's strategy to the case when the top-k query is issued against a relational database system. In [3], we presented an algorithm for processing queries over a multimedia database. Our query model built on Fagin's to also include Boolean conditions to the top-k component of the multimedia queries.

There is a large body of work on finding the nearest-neighbors of a multidimensional data point. Given an n-dimensional point p, these techniques retrieve the k objects that are "nearest" to p according to a given distance metric. The state-of-the-art algorithms (e.g., [7]) follow a multi-step approach. Their key step is identifying a set of points A such that p's k nearest neighbors are no further from p than a is, where a is the point in A that is furthest from p. (A more recent paper [14] further refines this idea.) This approach is conceptually similar to the approach that we follow in this paper (and also in [3]), where we first find a suitable score S, and then we use it to build a relational query that will return the top-k matches for the original query. Our focus in this paper is to study the practicality and limitations of using the information in the *histograms* kept by a relational system for query processing. In contrast, the nearest-neighbor algorithms mentioned above use the data values themselves to identify a cut-off "score."

Finally, references [6, 8] study how to merge and reconcile top-k query results obtained from distributed databases when the databases use arbitrary, undisclosed scoring algorithms.

4 Mapping a Top-k Query into a Traditional Selection Query

This section shows how to map a top-k query q into a relational selection query C_q that any traditional RDBMS can execute. Our goal is to obtain k tuples from relation R that are the best tuples for q according to a scoring function *Score*. Our query processing strategy consists of the following steps:

1. Use statistics on relation R to find a search score S_q (Section 4.1).
2. Build a selection query C_q to retrieve all tuples in R with score S_q or higher for q (Section 4.2).
3. Evaluate C_q over R.
4. Compute $Score(q,t)$ for every tuple t in the answer for C_q.
5. If there are at least k tuples t in the result for C_q with $Score(q,t) \geq S_q$, then output k tuples with the highest scores. Otherwise, choose a lower value for S_q and *restart* the process.

Section 4.3 introduces a related mapping strategy that does *not* follow the five steps above, and is an adaptation of Fagin's A_0 algorithm (Section 3).

4.1 Choice of Search Score S_q

The key step for evaluating a top-k query q is determining score S_q: our algorithm retrieves all tuples t such that $Score(q,t) \geq S_q$. If there are at least k such tuples, then our algorithm above succeeds in finding the top k matches for q. Otherwise, our choice of S_q is too high, and hence the query needs to be *restarted* with a lower value for S_q. Consequently, we should choose a value of S_q that is not too low, so that we do not retrieve too many candidate tuples from the database, but that is not too high either, so that we can obtain the top-k tuples without restarting the query.

Our choice of S_q will be guided by the statistics that the query processor keeps about relation R. In particular, we will assume that we have an n-dimensional histogram H that describes the distribution of values of R. We discuss this issue further in Section 5.2. Until then, we assume that H consists of a series of non-overlapping *buckets*. Each bucket has associated with it an *n-rectangle* $[a_1, b_1] \times \ldots \times [a_n, b_n]$, and stores the number of tuples in R that lie within the n-rectangle, together with other information.

For efficiency, our choice of S_q will be based on histogram H, and not on the underlying relation R itself. More specifically, we choose S_q as follows:

a. Create (*conceptually*) a small, "synthetic" relation R', consistent with histogram H. R' has one distinct tuple for each bucket in H, with as many instances as the frequency of the corresponding bucket.

b. Compute $Score(q,t)$ for every tuple t in R'.

c. Let T be the set of the top-k tuples in R' for q. Output $S_q = \min_{t\in T} Score(q,t)$.

We can conceptually build synthetic relation R' in many different ways. We will study two "extreme" query processing strategies that result from two possible definitions of R'.

The first query processing strategy, *NoRestarts*, results in a search score S_q that is low enough to guarantee that no restarts are ever needed as long as histograms are kept up to date. In other words, Step (5) above always finishes successfully, without ever having to reduce S_q and restart the process. For this, the *NoRestarts* strategy defines R' in a "pessimistic" way: given a histogram bucket b, the corresponding tuple t_b that represents b in R' will be as bad for query q as possible. More formally, t_b is a tuple in b's n-rectangle with the following property:

$$Score(q, t_b) = \min_{t\in T_b} Score(q,t)$$

where T_b is the set of all potential tuples in the n-rectangle associated with bucket b.

Example 4: Consider our example relation S, with two attributes A_1 and A_2, query $q = (0.4, 0.3)$, and the 2-dimensional histogram H shown in Figure 2(a). Histogram H has three buckets, b_1, b_2, and b_3. Relation S has 40 tuples in bucket b_1, 5 tuples in bucket b_2, and 55 tuples in bucket b_3. As explained above, the *NoRestarts* strategy will "build" relation S' based on H by assuming that the tuple distribution in S is

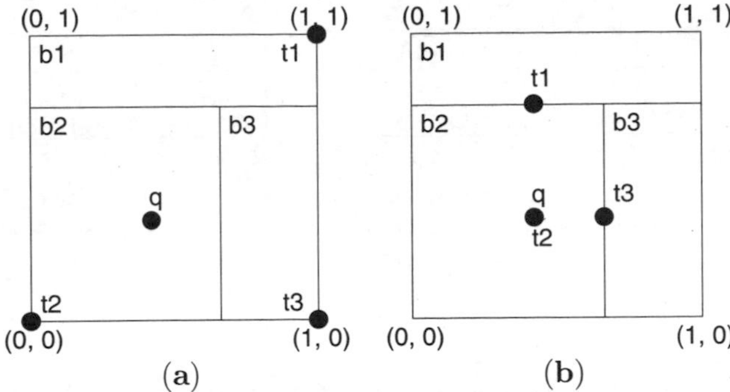

Figure 2: A 3-bucket histogram H and the choice of tuples representing each bucket that strategies *NoRestarts* **(a)** and *Restarts* **(b)** make for query q.

as "bad" as possible for query q. So, relation S' will consist of three tuples (one for each bucket in H) t_1, t_2, and t_3, which are as far from q as their corresponding bucket boundaries permit. Tuple t_1 will have a frequency of 40, t_2 will have a frequency of 5, and t_3 will have a frequency of 55. Assume that the user who issued query q wants to use the *Min* scoring function to find the top 10 tuples for q. Since $Min(q, t_1) = 0.3$, $Min(q, t_2) = 0.6$, and $Min(q, t_3) = 0.4$, to get 10 tuple instances we need the top tuple, t_2 (frequency 5), and t_3 (frequency 55). Consequently, the search score S_q will be $Min(q, t_3) = 0.4$. From the way we built S', it follows that the original relation S is guaranteed to contain at least 10 tuples with score $S_q = 0.4$ or higher for query q. Then, if we retrieve all of the tuples with that score or higher, we will obtain a superset of the set of top-k tuples for q. ∎

Lemma 1: *Let q be a top-k query over a relation R. Let S_q be the search score computed by strategy NoRestarts for q. Then, there are at least k tuples t in R such that $Score(q, t) \geq S_q$.*

The second query processing strategy, *Restarts*, results in a search score S_q that is highest among those search scores that *might* result in no restarts. This strategy defines R' in an "optimistic" way: given a histogram bucket b, the corresponding tuple t_b that represents t_b in R' will be as good for query q as possible. More formally, t_b is a tuple in b's n-rectangle with the following property:

$$Score(t_b, q) = \max_{t \in T_b} Score(q, t)$$

where T_b is the set of all potential tuples in the n-rectangle associated with bucket b.

Example 4: (cont.) The *Restarts* strategy will now build relation S' based on H by assuming that the tuple distribution in S is as "good" as possible for query q (Figure 2(b)). So, relation S' will consist of three tuples (one per bucket in H) t_1, t_2, and t_3, which are as close to q as their corresponding bucket boundaries permit. In particular, tuple t_2 will be defined as q proper, with frequency 5, since its corresponding bucket (i.e., b_2) has 5 tuples in it. After defining the bucket representatives t_1, t_2, and t_3, we proceed as in the *NoRestarts* strategy to sort the tuples on their score for q. For *Min*, we pick tuples t_2 and t_3, and define S_q as $Min(q, t_3)$. This time it is indeed possible for fewer than k tuples in the original table S to have a score of S_q or higher for q, so restarts are possible. ∎

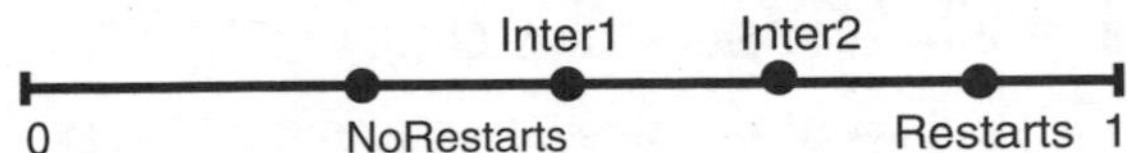

Figure 3: The four strategies for computing the search score S_q.

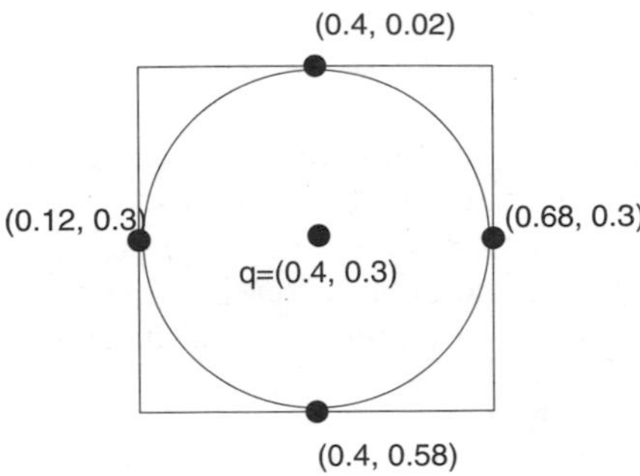

Figure 4: The circle around query $q = (0.4, 0.3)$ contains all of the tuples with *Euclidean* score of 0.8 or higher for q.

The S_q score that *Restarts* computes is the highest score that might result in no restarts in Step (5) of the algorithm above. In other words, using a value for S_q that is higher than that of the *Restarts* strategy will *always* result in restarts. In practice, as we will see in Section 6, the *Restarts* strategy results in restarts in virtually all cases, hence its name.

Lemma 2: *Let q be a top-k query over a relation R. Let S_q be the search score computed by strategy Restarts for q. Then, there are fewer than k tuples t in R such that $Score(q, t) > S_q$.*

In addition to the two extreme score-selection strategies *NoRestarts* and *Restarts*, we will study two other intermediate strategies, *Inter1* and *Inter2* (Figure 3). Given a query q, let S_q be the search score selected by *NoRestarts* for q, and let S'_q be the corresponding score selected by *Restarts*. Then, the *Inter1* strategy will choose score $\frac{2 \times S_q + S'_q}{3}$, while the *Inter2* strategy will choose a higher score of $\frac{S_q + 2 \times S'_q}{3}$. As our experiments will show, *Inter1* and *Inter2* are often the best strategies that we can follow in terms of the efficiency of the resulting techniques.

4.2 Choice of Selection Query C_q

Once we have determined the search score S_q (Section 4.1), the algorithm in Section 4 uses a query C_q to retrieve all tuples t such that $Score(q,t) \geq S_q$, where q is the original top-k query, and *Score* is the scoring function being used. In this section we describe how to define query C_q.

Ideally, we would like to ask our database system to return exactly those tuples t such that $Score(q,t) \geq S_q$. Unfortunately, indexing structures in relational DBMSs do not natively support this kind of predicates, as discussed in Section 3. Our approach is to build C_q as a simple selection condition defining an n-rectangle. In other words, we define C_q as a query of the form:

```
SELECT * FROM R
WHERE (a1<=A1<=b1) AND ...  AND (an<=An<=bn)
```

The n-rectangle $[a_1, b_1] \times \ldots \times [a_n, b_n]$ in C_q should tightly enclose all tuples t in R with $Score(q,t) \geq S_q$.

Example 5 : Consider our example query $q = (0.4, 0.3)$ over relation S, with *Euclidean* as the scoring function. Suppose that our search score S_q is 0.8, as computed by any of the strategies in Section 4.1. Each tuple t with $Euclidean(q,t) \geq 0.8$ lies in the circle around q that is shown in Figure 4. Then, the tightest n-rectangle that encloses that circle is $[0.12, 0.68] \times [0.02, 0.58]$. Hence, the final SQL query C_q is:

```
SELECT * FROM S
WHERE (0.12<=A1<=0.68) AND (0.02<=A2<=0.58)
```

∎

Given a search score S_q, the n-rectangle $[a_1, b_1] \times \ldots \times [a_n, b_n]$ that determines C_q follows directly from the scoring function used, the search score S_q, and the query q.

Example 5: (cont.) Let us assume that the search score for our query $q = (0.4, 0.3)$ is $S_q = 0.8$, as above. We calculate the 2-rectangle that encloses all tuples with 0.8 score or higher by focusing on one attribute at a time. First, consider a tuple $r = (t_1, 0.3)$ that has the same attribute values as query q in all attributes except for maybe attribute A_1. We will compute the range of values that t_1 can have while $Euclidean(q,r) \geq 0.8$. In effect, $Euclidean(q,r) = Euclidean((0.4, 0.3), (t_1, 0.3)) = 1 - \sqrt{\frac{(t_1-0.4)^2}{2}}$. Consequently, $Euclidean(q,r) \geq 0.8$ if and only if $0.12 \leq t_1 \leq 0.68$. Hence, the range of values that attribute A_1 can take is $[a_1, b_1] = [0.12, 0.68]$. Analogously for attribute A_2, $[a_2, b_2] = [0.02, 0.58]$. Putting both pieces together, the final 2-rectangle that encloses all tuples with score 0.8 or higher for q is $[0.12, 0.68] \times [0.02, 0.58]$ (Figure 4). ∎

Score	a'_i	b'_i
Min	$q_i - (1.0 - S_q)$	$q_i + (1.0 - S_q)$
Sum	$q_i - (1.0 - S_q) \cdot n$	$q_i + (1.0 - S_q) \cdot n$
Euclidean	$q_i - (1.0 - S_q) \cdot \sqrt{n}$	$q_i + (1.0 - S_q) \cdot \sqrt{n}$

Table 1: The n-rectangle $[a_1, b_1] \times \ldots \times [a_n, b_n]$ for C_q's selection condition and search score S_q, for different scoring functions, where $a_i = \max\{0, a'_i\}$ and $b_i = \min\{1, b'_i\}$.

Table 1 summarizes how to compute the n-rectangle $[a_1, b_1] \times \ldots \times [a_n, b_n]$ for the three scoring functions from Section 2. The *Min* scoring function presents an interesting property: the region to be enclosed by the n-rectangle is already an n-rectangle. (See Figure 1(c).) Consequently, the query C_q that is generated for *Min* for query q and its associated search score S_q will retrieve only tuples with a score of S_q or higher. This property will result in efficient executions of top-k queries for *Min*, as we will see. Unfortunately, this property does not hold for the *Sum* and *Euclidean* scoring functions (Figures 1(a) and (b)).

4.3 An Alternative Mapping Strategy

This section adapts Fagin's A_0 algorithm (Section 3) to produce a new technique for mapping a top-k query into a traditional relational query. Unlike the Section 4.2 strategies, the selection query resulting from this new mapping is a disjunction, not a conjunction.

Our goal is, again, to build a "one-shot" relational query that avoids restarts whenever possible. We proceed as in strategy *NoRestarts* (Section 4.1) to build a "database" with one tuple representing each bucket in the available n-dimensional histogram. We find the top "tuples" as in the *NoRestarts* strategy. We then compute an n-rectangle $F = [a_1, b_1] \times \ldots [a_n, b_n]$ that encloses these top tuples tightly, and that has been extended so that it is "symmetric" with respect to the given query q. (In other words, $a_i \leq q_i \leq b_i$ and $b_i - q_i = q_i - a_i$, for $i = 1, \ldots, n$.) The tuples matching range $[a_i, b_i]$ are the top tuples for q along attribute A_i. The selection query consists of the disjunction of the $a_i \leq A_i \leq b_i$ conditions. By retrieving all tuples that match *at least one* of these conditions, we retrieve the top tuples for each of the individual attributes. Furthermore, from the way we constructed F, there will be at least k tuples matching all n conditions. As with the original A_0 algorithm, we compute the score for all the one-dimensional matches. The k retrieved tuples having the highest score for q are the final answer to the original top-k query. The correctness of this algorithm follows from that of algorithm A_0 [4]. Due to space constraints, we do not discuss this algorithm any further in this paper.

5 Experimental Setting

We now describe the data sets, histograms, and metrics for the experiments of Section 6.

5.1 Data Sets

Our experiments use a real-world data set as well as synthetic data. The real-world data set is a fragment of US Census Bureau data, and was obtained from the University of California, Irvine archive of machine-learning databases (`ftp://ftp.ics.uci.edu/pub/-machine-learning-databases`). The data set has 45,000 rows. Each row is a record for an individual, with 14 attributes. We picked four continuous attributes that were especially well suited for our top-k query model: `age`, `wage`, `education level`, and `hours of work per week`. We also scaled down the attribute values so that the resulting values ranged between 0 and 1, to simplify our experimental setting. We refer to this database as the *Census database*.

In addition to the Census database, we generated a number of synthetic databases with different data distributions. For this, we wrote a seed program that is capable of generating one-dimensional Zipfian distribution [15] with varying "Z" factors. When this factor is zero, it generates a uniform distribution. Higher values result in higher skew. For an n-dimensional data set, our generation program is parameterized by (1) a vector of n Z values (one for each attribute), $Z_n = < z_1, \ldots, z_n >$; (2) the number of tuples to be generated, N. We created the data corresponding to a Z_n specification as follows. First, we generated a one-dimensional Zipfian distribution of N tuples for attribute A_1 using Z factor z_1. Let us say that for attribute A_1 the value v_1 occurred in N_1 out of the N tuples. We now fill in the value for attribute A_2 for each of these N_1 tuples by generating N_1 values $w_1, \ldots, w_{N_1}$ using a Zipfian distribution with Z factor z_2. At the end of this step, the first two attributes of the original N_1 tuples are filled in with values $(v_1, w_1), \ldots, (v_1, w_{N_1})$. Let us say that this results in N_2 tuples that have v_1 and w_1 as the values for attributes A_1 and A_2, respectively. We then fill in the remaining attribute values $A_3, \ldots, A_n$ for these N_2 tuples in an analogous way as above, using the Z values z_3 through z_n.

For our experiments, we generated databases of 100,000 records with $n = 2$, 3, and 4 attributes. The domain of each attribute is the real numbers between 0 and 1, with a spacing of 0.00001 between attribute values. We varied the Zipfian vectors in the generation of the databases so we obtained databases with a spectrum of skews. More specifically, Section 6 reports experiments for three families of databases, $Z10$, $Z21$, and $Z32$. $Z10$, $Z21$, and $Z32$ represent the skew of databases built using Zipfian vectors $< 1, 0, \ldots, 0 >$, $< 2, 1, \ldots, 1 >$, and $< 3, 2, \ldots, 2 >$, respectively. Table 2 summarizes the synthetic databases for which we report experiments in the next section.

	n		
Data Skew	2	3	4
$Z10$	100,000	100,000	100,000
$Z21$	27,022	52,554	66,426
$Z32$	739	2878	7034

Table 2: The number of distinct tuple values for different data skews and number of attributes n.

5.2 Histograms

As outlined above, we map a top-k query over a table R into a relational selection query. To do this mapping, we exploit the statistics (e.g., histograms) kept by the relational DBMS where relation R resides. One of our goals in this paper is to study the effect on our mapping of the different n-dimensional histogram structures proposed in the literature. These structures rely on an underlying strategy for building one-dimensional histograms. In this paper we focus on the *AVI*, *PHASED*, and *MHIST-p* n-dimensional techniques, with *MAXDIFF* as the underlying one-dimensional strategy [11, 12]. Below we briefly describe these structures. We refer the reader to [11, 12] for a detailed discussion.

Constructing a *MAXDIFF* histogram on an attribute of a relation is logically a two-step process. First, the data values are sorted and, for each distinct value, its frequency of occurrence is calculated. Let the sorted values be $v_1, \ldots, v_n$ with corresponding frequencies $f_1, \ldots, f_n$. We can then define *frequency-gap*$(i) = |f_{i+1} - f_i|$. This function records the difference in frequency of attribute values v_i and v_{i+1}. The bucket boundaries are placed at those attribute values that correspond to the highest values of the *frequency-gap* function. The *MAXDIFF* histogram structure has been shown to have a good trade-off between accuracy and building cost [12]. For the experiments that we report in the next section, we have implemented n-dimensional variants of *MAXDIFF* histograms using the *AVI*, *PHASED*, and *MHIST-p* techniques, as described in [11].

The *AVI* technique for constructing an n-dimensional histogram is to simply assume statistical independence of the one-dimensional attributes. Thus, to determine the fraction of data in an n-dimensional bucket, we multiply the fraction of the data in each one-dimensional projection of the bucket.

The *PHASED* technique for constructing an n-dimensional histogram consists of n steps. In the first step, one of the dimensions is used to partition the dataset into k_1 buckets. In the jth step, each of the buckets obtained at the end of the previous step is divided into k_j buckets along one of the unused dimensions. The order in which dimensions are chosen is determined prior to doing any of the partitioning.

For each dimension (attribute), we compute the variance in the frequency of values on that dimension. We then choose the attributes for partitioning the buckets in descending order of their variance. This order reflects the criticality for separating the values in buckets. This technique for constructing n-dimensional histogram was first used in [10] in the context of equi-depth histogram structures.

The *MHIST-p* technique for constructing an n-dimensional histogram is an adaptation of the *PHASED* approach. More specifically, during the jth step (see the description of *PHASED* above), we determine the bucket in most need of partitioning, and we partition it along the attribute that exhibits the highest variance in frequency within the bucket. The factor p designates the number of buckets into which each bucket is split at every step.

The performance of our mapping techniques (Section 4) depends on the accuracy of the available histograms. The accuracy of a histogram depends in turn on the technique with which it was generated, and on the amount of memory that has been allocated for it. In our experiments, in addition to trying several histogram structures, we also study the effect of varying memory on the accuracy of histograms. We assume throughout that histograms are kept up to date with the data. If histograms are not up to date, then the performance of our techniques might decrease. However, the correctness of the answers produced will remain unaffected, at the expense of a potentially higher number of restarts (Section 4).

5.3 Measuring the Efficiency of the Query Execution Strategies

A top-k query q will typically involve several attributes. We might have indexes available for a number of combinations of the query attributes, and the efficiency of processing the query will be greatly affected by the particular index configuration available. We focus on two configurations: (a) a single-column index exists for every attribute mentioned in the query; or (b) a single n-column index exists, covering all attributes mentioned in the query.

Whenever an n-dimensional index is present, we retrieve exactly as many index "entries" as there are tuples in the n-rectangle defining query C_q, as described in Section 4.2, followed by the actual retrieval of the k top tuples for q. (The index entries provide all the information that we need to decide which k tuples are the ones with the highest score for q.) Alternatively, when only one-dimensional indexes are available, we can intersect one or more indexes to determine the data tuples to be retrieved. When all necessary single-column indexes are present, this strategy results in no redundant retrieval of data tuples, as in the case when an n-dimensional index is available. However, unlike the case with n-dimensional indexes, we must now pay the overhead of the index intersection. The cost of the index intersection can be traded off against the cost of retrieving redundant data tuples (i.e., data tuples that do not belong to the n-rectangle of Section 4.2).

For each top-k query q, we measure the number of objects that match the associated n-dimensional selection query C_q (Section 4.2). In Section 6, we report the average over all queries of the number of tuples retrieved as the fraction of the number of (not necessarily distinct) tuples in the database (*% of tuples retrieved*). This metric reveals the tightness of our mapping of a top-k query into a traditional selection query. A complementary metric is *% of restarts*, the percentage of queries in our workload for which the associated selection query failed to contain the k best tuples, hence leading to restarts. (See Step (5) of the algorithm of Section 4.)

It is important to distinguish between the tightness of the mapping of a top-k query to a traditional selection query, and the efficiency of execution of the latter. The tightness of the mapping depends on the mapping algorithms (Section 4) and on their interaction with the quality of the available histograms. The efficiency of execution of the selection query produced by our mapping algorithm depends in turn on the indexes available on the database and on the optimizer's choice of an execution plan. The cost estimator in an optimizer determines the best access path among the available choices. (These choices include performing a sequential scan of the data.) In this paper, we will not discuss further details of efficient execution of selection queries on databases but rather focus on the problem of mapping top-k queries to selection queries efficiently using histogram structures.

6 Experimental Results

This section presents experimental results for our techniques of Section 4 for evaluating top-k queries. In particular, we study the role of several factors on the efficiency of our strategies, including the size and type of n-dimensional histograms available, the scoring function used in the queries, and the dimensionality and skew of the data sets. Our experiments then involve a large number of parameters, and we tried many different value assignments. For conciseness, we report results on a *default setting* where appropriate. This default setting uses databases built with the $Z21$ (moderate) skew (Section 5.1), the *PHASED* technique for building n-dimensional histograms (Section 5.2), and allocates 5KB per histogram. For each experiment, we generated 100 different queries. Each query was created by picking each attribute value randomly from the $[0, 1]$ range. In the default setting, these queries ask for top 10 tuples (i.e., $k = 10$). We report results for other settings of the parameters as well.

Validity of our General Approach

Our general approach for processing a top-k query q (Section 4.2) is to find an n-rectangle that contains all the top k tuples for q, and use this rectangle to build a traditional selection query. Our first experiment studies the intrinsic limitations of our approach, i.e., whether it is possible to build a "good" n-rectangle around query q that contains all top k tuples and little else. To answer this first question, independent of any available histograms or search-score selection strategies (Section 4), we first scanned the database to find the actual top k tuples for a given query q, and determined a tight n-rectangle T that encloses all of these tuples. We then computed what fraction of the database tuples lies within rectangle T. Table 3 reports these figures. As we can see from the table, the fraction of tuples that lie in this "ideal" rectangle is extremely low, which validates our approach: if the database statistics (i.e., histograms) are accurate enough, then we should be able to find a tight n-rectangle that encloses all the best tuples for a given query, with few extra tuples.

Data Distribution	*Scoring*	n		
		2	3	4
Z10	*Min*	0.01	0.01	0.01
	Sum	0.01	0.01	0.01
	Euclidean	0.01	0.01	0.01
Z21	*Min*	0.03	0.03	0.02
	Sum	0.04	0.02	0.02
	Euclidean	0.04	0.02	0.01
Z32	*Min*	0.38	0.76	0.16
	Sum	0.15	0.05	0.09
	Euclidean	0.10	0.04	0.06

Table 3: The percentage of tuples in the database included in an n-rectangle enclosing the actual top-k tuples for a query ($k = 10$; $N = 100,000$ tuples).

Effect of Multidimensional Histograms

For this experiment, we considered the *AVI*, *PHASED*, and *MHIST*-2 histogram structures (Section 5.2). *AVI* proved to be significantly worse than *MHIST* and *PHASED* since it tended to require restarts in most cases, while retrieving only an extremely low fraction of the database tuples. In effect, the *NoRestarts* strategy of Section 4.1 guarantees no restarts only in the presence of an accurate n-dimensional histogram. *AVI* can only *estimate* the holdings of each n-dimensional bucket by assuming that attributes follow independent distributions. The results for *AVI* were so poor that we omit this histogram structure from the rest of the discussion.

For *PHASED* and *MHIST*, we varied the amount of storage that we allocated for the histograms. Figure 5 shows the effect of this variation for the *Euclidean* scoring function. (The results for *Min* and *Sum* are

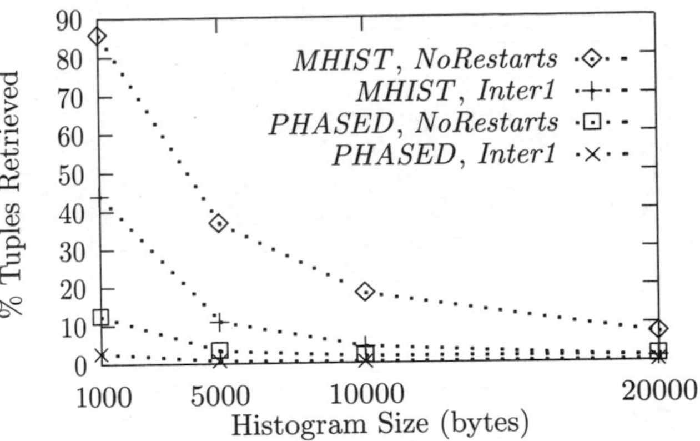

Figure 5: The percentage of tuples retrieved, as a function of the number of bytes dedicated to the n-dimensional histogram (*Euclidean* scoring function; $n = 3$; *Z*21 data distribution).

analogous.) In this figure, we report the results for the *NoRestarts* and the *Inter1* policies of Section 4.1. When we increase the histogram size from 1KB to 5KB, there is a sharp improvement in the efficiency of our technique, as evidenced by the drop in the percentage of tuples retrieved. *PHASED* performs (marginally) better than *MHIST* and therefore for the rest of this section we report results mainly using *PHASED*. Although higher memory allocation clearly increases accuracy, as shown by the figures, we decided to settle on a 5KB budget for each histogram in the rest of this paper.

Effect of Different Scoring Functions

The goal of this experiment is to measure the differences among scoring functions as the data skew and the number of dimensions are varied (Section 5.1). Figure 6 shows that, as the data skew increases, the percentage of tuples retrieved decreases sharply and consistently across all scoring functions. On the other hand, as the number of attributes n is increased (Figure 7), the performance of our techniques drops. Interestingly, the *Min* scoring function copes significantly better with the increase in n than the other scoring functions. As mentioned in Section 4.2, the shape of the region containing the top tuples for a query matches an n-rectangle perfectly, unlike the case for *Sum* and *Euclidean*. The performance of *Euclidean*, though, is better than that of *Sum*. As can be observed from Table 1 and Figures 1(a) and (b), the size of the n-rectangle enclosing the top tuples for *Sum* is much larger than that for *Euclidean* (Sections 4.1 and 4.2).

Effect of the Number of Tuples Requested k

Figure 8 studies the effect of increasing k, the number of tuples requested in a top-k query. As k is increased from 10 to 100, the performance drops. As in the pre-

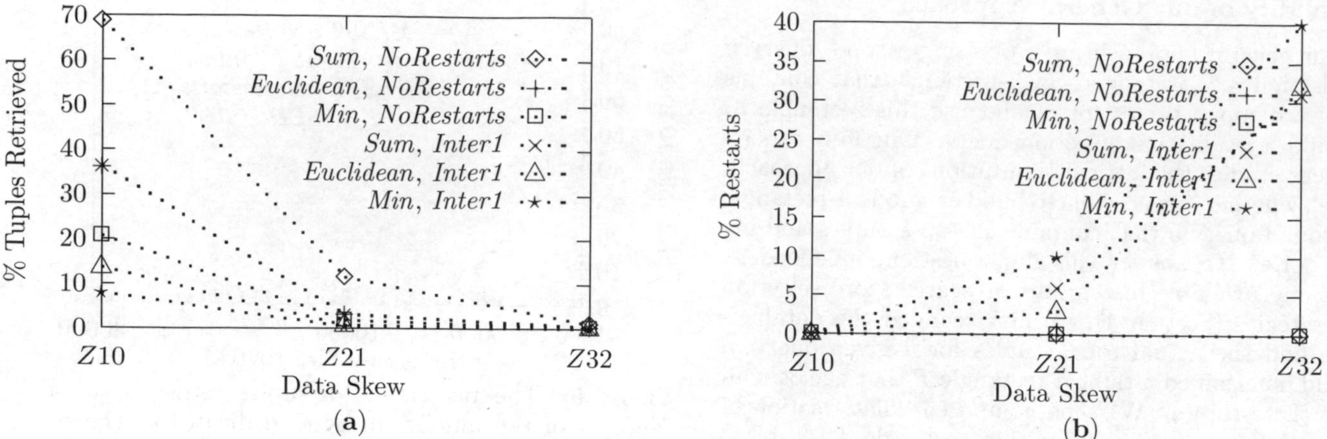

Figure 6: The percentage of tuples retrieved **(a)**, and the percentage of queries that needed restarts **(b)**, for increasing data skew (*PHASED* histogram of 5KB; $n = 3$).

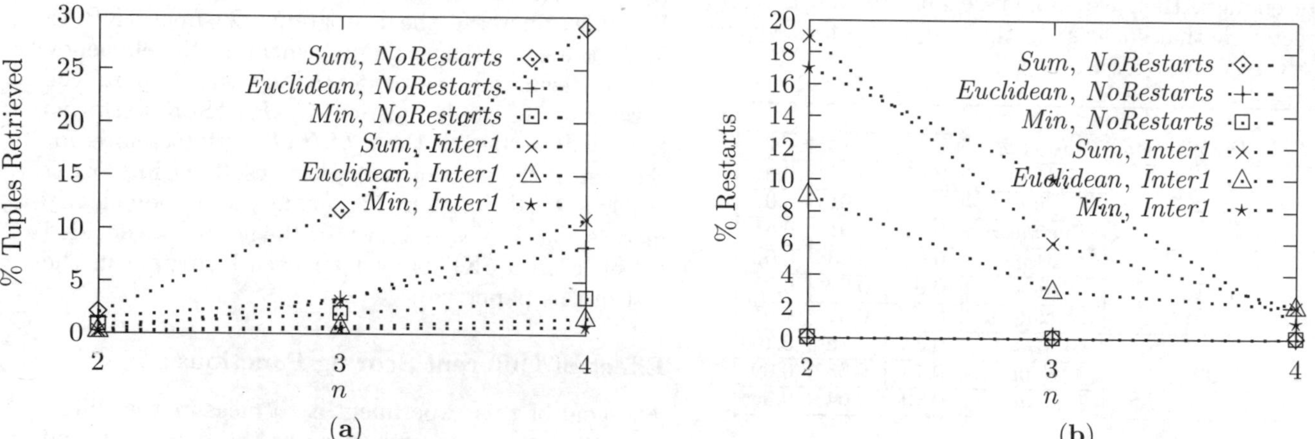

Figure 7: The percentage of tuples retrieved **(a)**, and the percentage of queries that needed restarts **(b)**, as a function of the number of attributes n (*PHASED* histogram of 5KB; $Z21$ data distribution).

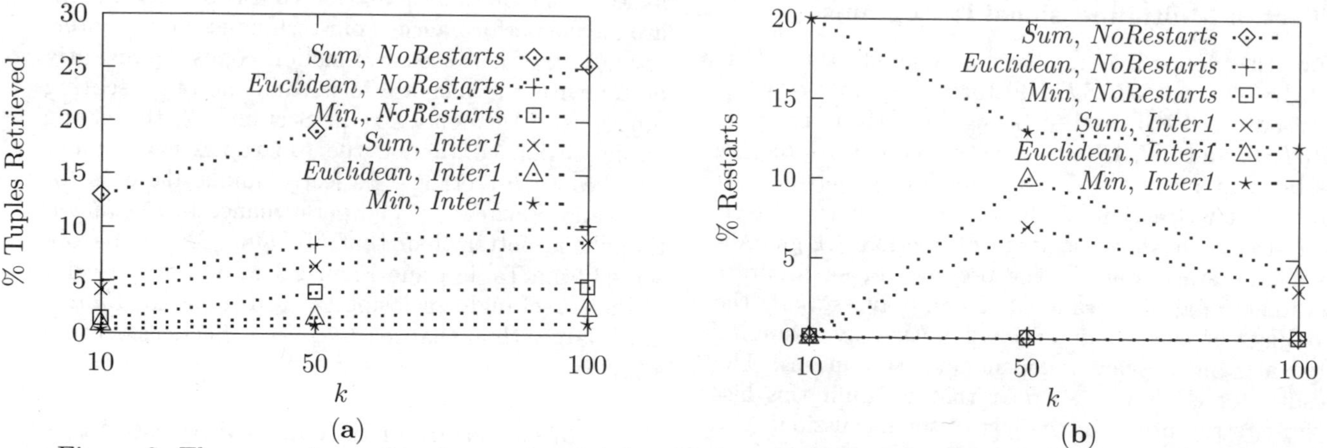

Figure 8: The percentage of tuples retrieved **(a)**, and the percentage of queries that needed restarts **(b)**, for different values of k (*PHASED* histogram of 5KB; $Z21$ data distribution; $n = 3$).

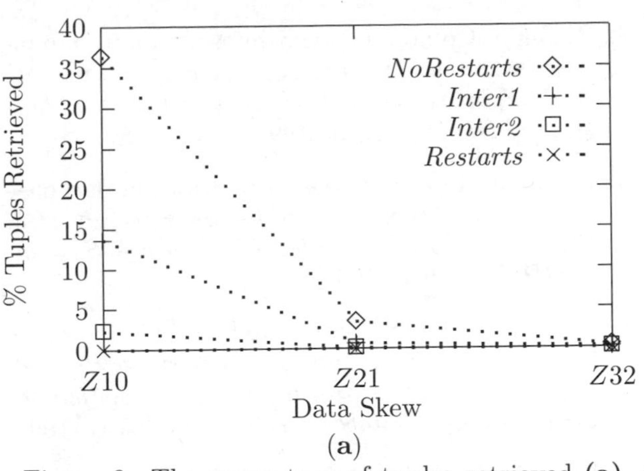

(a)

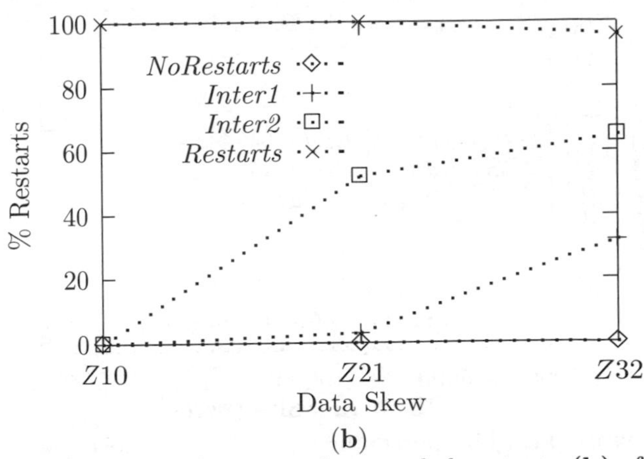

(b)

Figure 9: The percentage of tuples retrieved **(a)**, and the percentage of queries that needed restarts **(b)**, for increasing data skew (*Euclidean* scoring function; *PHASED* histogram of 5KB; $n = 3$).

vious experiment, the percentage of tuples retrieved for *Min* grows the slowest, followed by *Euclidean*. The combination of scoring function *Sum* and the *NoRestarts* strategy performs the worst.

Comparing Query Processing Strategies

Figure 9 compares the relative merits of the query processing strategies of Section 4.1. At low data skews, the *NoRestarts* strategy results in a relatively larger number of matching tuples. However, as skew increases, the performance of *NoRestarts* improves significantly and dominates that of the other strategies, since, by definition, it incurs no query restarts with up-to-date histograms. Strategy *Inter1* proves to be a robust technique, since it maintains good performance for all data skews.

Effect of Using n-Rectangle Queries

As explained in Section 4.2, we process a top-k query q by first finding a score S_q and then finding an n-rectangle that encloses all tuples with a *Score* of S_q or higher. Our goal is for the n-rectangle to have as few "bad" tuples as possible, i.e., as few tuples with *Score* lower than S_q as possible. Figure 10 examines this issue by computing the actual number of tuples t with $Score(q,t) \geq S_q$. In other words, we take the score S_q computed by using a histogram and a query processing strategy (Section 4.1), and we count the tuples in the database with that score or higher. We can then compare these numbers against those in Figure 9(a) to conclude that using n-rectangles for retrieving the database tuples does not result in a major source of inefficiency, since the percentage of tuples in both cases is quite comparable.

Results for the Census Database

Figure 11 shows how our query processing strategies perform on the Census data set (Section 5.1). While none of the strategies resulted in a significant number

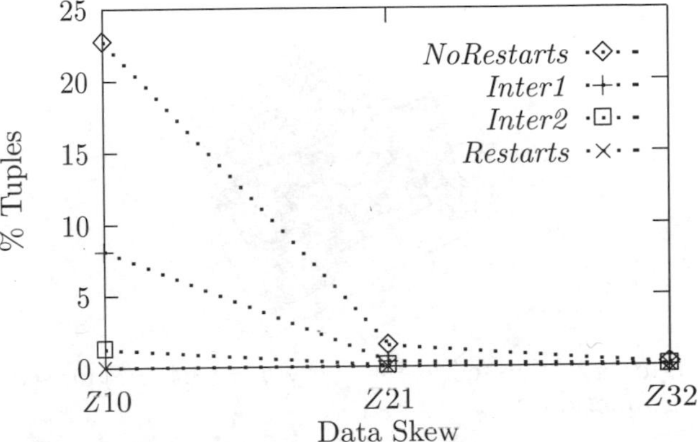

Figure 10: The average number of tuples (as a percentage of N) with score S_q or higher (Step (1) of the Section 4 algorithm) for increasing data skew (*Euclidean* scoring function; *PHASED* histogram of 5KB; $n = 3$).

of restarts (hence we do not show the corresponding plot here), the robustness of strategy *Inter1* for increasing histogram size can be seen clearly. The performance for the different scoring functions is consistent with the results obtained for the synthetic databases described above.

7 Conclusions and Future Work

In this paper, we studied the problem of mapping a top-k query on a relational database to a traditional selection query such that the mapping is "tight," i.e., we retrieve as few tuples as possible. Our mapping algorithms exploit the histogram structures and are able to cope with a wide variety of scoring functions. Our experiments highlighted the effect of different scoring functions, data distributions, as well as histogram-building strategies on the performance of this mapping.

Our focus in this paper has been primarily on queries over continuous attributes. In the future, we will extend our techniques to handle top-k queries over

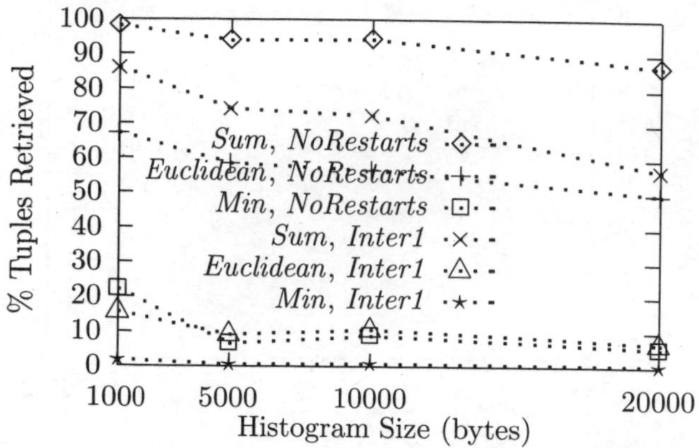

Figure 11: The percentage of tuples retrieved, as a function of the number of bytes dedicated to the histogram (*Census* database; *PHASED* histogram).

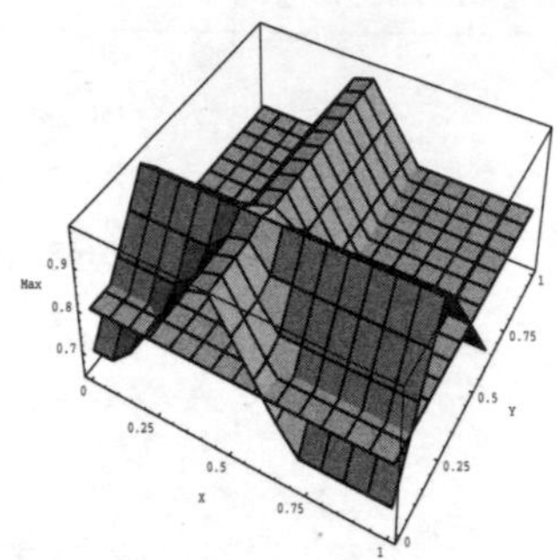

Figure 12: The scores for query $q = (0.4, 0.3)$ for scoring function *Max*.

discrete attributes. Another direction for future work is to explore approaches to support top-k queries with scoring functions (e.g., *Max*) that cannot be mapped tightly to the family of traditional selection queries that we used in this paper (Figure 12).

Acknowledgments

We thank Eugene Agichtein and David Lomet for their useful comments.

References

[1] M. J. Carey and D. Kossmann. On saying "Enough Already!" in SQL. In *Proceedings of the 1997 ACM International Conference on Management of Data (SIGMOD'97)*, May 1997.

[2] M. J. Carey and D. Kossmann. Reducing the braking distance of an SQL query engine. In *Proceedings of the Twenty-fourth International Conference on Very Large Databases (VLDB'98)*, Aug. 1998.

[3] S. Chaudhuri and L. Gravano. Optimizing queries over multimedia repositories. In *Proceedings of the 1996 ACM International Conference on Management of Data (SIGMOD'96)*, June 1996.

[4] R. Fagin. Combining fuzzy information from multiple systems. In *Proceedings of the Fifteenth ACM Symposium on Principles of Database Systems (PODS'96)*, June 1996.

[5] R. Fagin. Fuzzy queries in multimedia database systems. In *Proceedings of the Seventeenth ACM Symposium on Principles of Database Systems (PODS'98)*, June 1998.

[6] L. Gravano and H. García-Molina. Merging ranks from heterogeneous Internet sources. In *Proceedings of the Twenty-third International Conference on Very Large Databases (VLDB'97)*, Aug. 1997.

[7] F. Korn, N. Sidiropoulos, C. Faloutsos, E. Siegel, and Z. Protopapas. Fast nearest neighbor search in medical image databases. In *Proceedings of the Twenty-second International Conference on Very Large Databases (VLDB'96)*, Sept. 1996.

[8] W. Meng, K.-L. Liu, C. Yu, X. Wang, Y. Chang, and N. Rishe. Determining text databases to search in the Internet. In *Proceedings of the Twenty-fourth International Conference on Very Large Databases (VLDB'98)*, Aug. 1998.

[9] A. Motro. VAGUE: A user interface to relational databases that permits vague queries. *ACM Transactions on Office Information Systems*, 6(3):187–214, July 1988.

[10] M. Muralikrishna and D. J. DeWitt. Equi-depth histograms for estimating selectivity factors for multidimensional queries. In *Proceedings of the 1988 ACM International Conference on Management of Data (SIGMOD'88)*, June 1988.

[11] V. Poosala and Y. E. Ioannidis. Selectivity estimation without the attribute value independence assumption. In *Proceedings of the Twenty-third International Conference on Very Large Databases (VLDB'97)*, Aug. 1997.

[12] V. Poosala, Y. E. Ioannidis, P. J. Haas, and E. J. Shekita. Improved histograms for selectivity estimation of range predicates. In *Proceedings of the 1996 ACM International Conference on Management of Data (SIGMOD'96)*, June 1996.

[13] G. Salton and M. J. McGill. *Introduction to modern information retrieval.* McGraw-Hill, 1983.

[14] T. Seidl and H.-P. Kriegel. Optimal multi-step k-nearest neighbor search. In *Proceedings of the 1998 ACM International Conference on Management of Data (SIGMOD'98)*, June 1998.

[15] G. K. Zipf. *Human behaviour and the principle of least effort.* Addison-Wesley, 1949.

Probabilistic Optimization of Top N Queries

Donko Donjerkovic **Raghu Ramakrishnan**

Department of Computer Sciences
University of Wisconsin–Madison
1210 W. Dayton St.
Madison, WI 53706 USA

{donko,raghu}@cs.wisc.edu

Abstract

The problem of finding the best answers to a query quickly, rather than finding all answers, is of increasing importance as relational databases are applied in multimedia and decision-support domains. An approach to efficiently answering such "Top N" queries is to augment the query with an additional selection that prunes away the unwanted portion of the answer set. The risk is that if the selection returns fewer than the desired number of answers, the execution must be restarted (with a less selective filter). We propose a new, probabilistic approach to query optimization that quantifies this risk and seeks to minimize overall cost including the cost of possible restarts. We also present an extensive experimental study to demonstrate that probabilistic Top N query optimization can significantly reduce the average query execution time with relatively modest increases in the optimization time.

1 Introduction

In the multimedia domain, Top N or "Get the best matches" queries are common. The notion of the best match is typically fuzzy, and the cutoff (how many answers to return) is approximate, but the intent is clear. The other area where Top N queries are important is decision support, where users often want to see the high or the low end of some ordered result set. A typical example is "Find the 10 cheapest cars." The importance of Top N queries is underscored by the fact that most major commercial DBMSs include language constructs for expressing such queries. Informix supports `FIRST N`, Microsoft has `SET ROWCOUNT N`, IBM's DB2 has `FETCH FIRST N ROWS ONLY`, and Oracle supports `LIMIT TO N ROWS`.

The simplest way to support Top N queries is to execute the query, sort the result in the desired order, and then discard all but the first N tuples. Computing and sorting a large intermediate result and then discarding most of it is a waste of resources. It was shown [9] that large gains in performance are possible when the database system utilizes the fact that only a certain number of answers are needed.

A Top N query on an attribute X, denoted by Top_N^X, is equivalent to the simple selection query:

$$Top_N^X \equiv \sigma_{X>\kappa} \quad (1)$$

where κ is a *cutoff parameter* determined by N and by the data distribution. Consider the following example query on a table that is neither sorted nor indexed: "List the top 10 paid employees in the sales department". This query translates into: "List the employees from the sales department whose salary is greater than κ", where κ is determined by the distribution of employees' salaries, and must be determined by the optimizer. If κ is too high, we will retrieve less than N employees and therefore will have to restart the query with smaller κ. On the other hand, if κ is too small, the query will unnecessarily run longer. Because restarts involve repetition of work, they are characterized by a large jump in query cost.

How to estimate κ is a nontrivial problem. If the query optimizer had complete knowledge of the data distributions, it could estimate κ exactly, and eliminate restarts. However, because the optimizer's knowledge of data distributions (usually maintained in the form of histograms) is not perfect, it is better to underestimate κ as a guard against restart. The main contribution of this paper is to propose a probabilistic optimization framework that takes into account imprecision in the optimizer's knowledge of data distribution and selectivity estimates. Using probabilistic

Proceedings of the 25th VLDB Conference, Edinburgh, Scotland, 1999.

reasoning, the optimizer arrives at the *expected* cost, and the optimal cutoff parameter is the one that minimizes expected cost. While we apply the probabilistic optimization framework to the problem of estimating cutoffs for Top N queries, the approach clearly has broader applicability to optimization problems in the presence of important parameters (e.g., number of available buffers, number of concurrent queries) that can only be approximately estimated.

The rest of this paper is organized as follows. After reviewing related work, we introduce our probabilistic framework in Section 3. We introduce probabilistic optimization of Top N queries in Section 3. We develop this idea further in Section 4, where we show how to obtain selectivity and cardinality distributions for various kinds of selection predicates, starting with traditional histograms. We then present performance results for Top N queries involving selections and joins in Section 6. Next, in Section 7 we consider two classes of Top N queries that are more complex, involving aggregates and unions. The first class, involving aggregates, shows an interesting and useful connection to the class of Iceberg queries [3]. In Section 8, we then revisit the basic Top N problem formulation and identify two useful variants that can be supported using our techniques. These include an "online" variant in which answers are eagerly returned, together with some confidence bounds that they are indeed in the "top N", and a variant in which the user can specify a probability that returned answers will include all "top N", thereby controlling the time required to compute answers.

2 Related Work

Carey and Kossman [9, 1] proposed a new operator called STOP AFTER N (STOP for short) to terminate computation after the first N results are computed. Large performance gains are possible when the STOP operator is pushed down the plan tree. In contrast, while we can use the STOP operator at the root of the query sub plan, we never push the STOP operator down the plan tree. Instead, we push the equivalent selection (1), using standard techniques for handling selections. Our approach can lead to significantly better plans in some situations, as illustrated in example plans in Fig. 1. Suppose that the best plan found by the STOP pushdown is the one shown in Fig. 1 (a). Obviously, this plan can only be made cheaper by replacing the STOP operator above relation A with the equivalent selection and thus eliminating the sorting, as shown in Fig. 1 (b). Notice that the final SORT is still necessary in both versions because the hash join does not preserve sorting. *All* the implementations of STOP require at least partial sorting of the input stream, and [1] proposes techniques for reducing the sorting cost. In contrast, our approach does not require sorting, except for the final result.

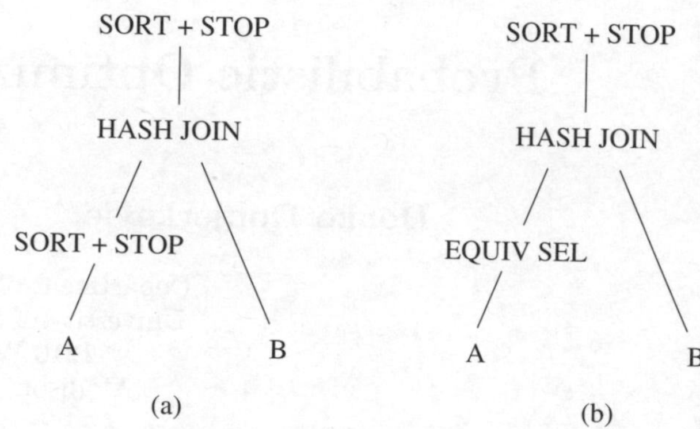

Figure 1: The plan with equivalent selection (b) may be much cheaper to execute.

Technically, the focus of our paper is on a probabilistic framework for optimization, specifically for computing the selection cutoff for Top N queries. This problem is not considered in [9, 1] or other previous work.

A concurrent work [2] has independently suggested that the optimizers should minimize expected cost of a query, and therefore have introduced the probability distributions for certain parameters. However, this work does not deal with Top N queries, which is the focus of our approach.

3 Framework for Probabilistic Query Optimization

Every Top N query is equivalent to a selection query (see Eq. (1)) with a specific cutoff parameter $\kappa = \kappa_{crit}$. Formally, κ_{crit} is defined as the largest cutoff parameter κ that does not cause restart. If complete knowledge of all selectivities and data distributions were available, restarts would never happen since one would always choose $\kappa = \kappa_{crit}$. However, since the optimizer only has approximate knowledge of distributions and selectivities, it is impossible to guarantee that more than N tuples will be eventually retrieved, short of choosing $\kappa = -\infty$. Nonetheless, we can still reason about the likelihood of restart and choose κ accordingly. To enable such probabilistic reasoning, we propose to *generalize selectivity estimates to selectivity probability distributions.*

We consider all selectivities to be random variables and denote a point in this multidimensional probability space as σ and the associated probability as $p(\sigma)$. We then postulate that the optimizers should find a plan with the minimum *expected* value of the cost $C(\sigma)$:

$$E(C) = \sum_{\sigma} C(\sigma)p(\sigma) \tag{2}$$

Even though this work focuses on the random nature of selectivity estimates, our approach applies to other uncertain quantities that enter cost formulas such as allocated memory and connection bandwidths. In fact, the observation that optimizers should minimize expected cost was concurrently made by Chu, Halpern and Seshadri [2] and applied to the problem of memory variability.

At this point we note that, traditionally, optimizers evaluate a cost function for expected values of input parameters $C(E(\sigma))$ in the hope that this is a good approximation for overall expected value of the cost. However, it is well known that the approximation:

$$E(C(\sigma)) \approx C(E(\sigma)) \tag{3}$$

is true *only if* C is a linear function of σ within the range of variability of σ. While most of the cost formulas are not linear, in practice, they are usually well approximated by linear values in the range of variable parameters and consequently, Eq. (3) holds.

Problem of Top N optimization, is a typical example where Eq. (3) does not hold, because the jump in the total cost C due to the restart cost R is within the range of possible cutoff values. If we denote the initial cost by I, and introduce a step function ρ which is 0 when restart does not happen and 1 otherwise, we have:

$$C(\sigma) = I(\sigma) + \rho(\sigma)\,R(\sigma) \tag{4}$$

We note that the selectivity of the cutoff κ is included in the Eq. (4) as one dimension of σ. Also, Eq. (4) assumes that only one restart is possible. Even though multiple restarts could be included in this framework, it would be impractical to optimize for multiple cutoff parameters. Therefore, in our model, restart operation amounts to retrieving the complement of the equivalent selection query, sorting the result and stopping after required number of tuples is returned. Assuming that R is approximately linear in the possible selectivities of κ, we can write:

$$E(C) \approx E(I) + E(R) \sum_{\sigma} \rho(\sigma)\,p(\sigma) \tag{5}$$

$\sum_{\sigma} \rho(\sigma)\,p(\sigma)$ is the probability of restart (r) which can also be written as the probability that fewer than N answers are generated:

$$r = \sum_{n=0}^{N-1} p(n) \tag{6}$$

where $p(n)$ is the probability that the input cardinality to the Top N operator will be n.

Finally, using the traditional approximation (Eq. (3)) the objective function, parameterized by κ becomes:

$$\text{Cost}(\kappa) \approx \text{Init}(\kappa) + r(\kappa)\,\text{Rest}(\kappa) \tag{7}$$

where Init(κ) denotes the traditional cost of processing the query with cutoff parameter κ and Rest(κ) denotes the traditional cost of processing the restart that will complete the answer to the query.

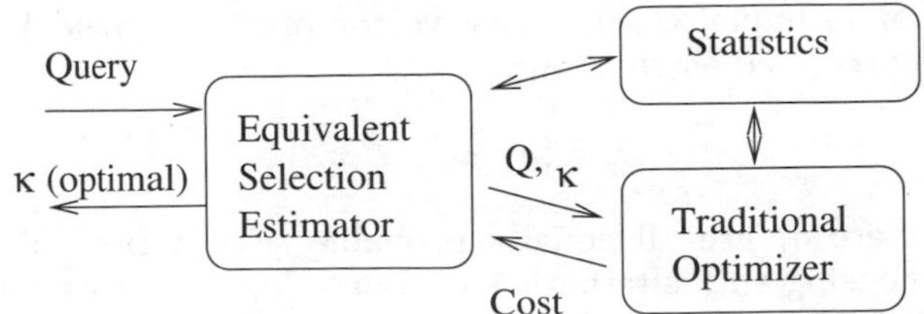

Figure 2: Architecture for incorporating κestimator into a traditional DB system.

A cutoff parameter, κ, is *optimal* if it minimizes the value of the query cost function (Eq. (7)). We restate the problem of optimizing a Top N query as the problem of finding the optimal cutoff parameter κ_{opt} and the associated execution plan. To find the minimum of the cost function (Eq. (7)) we can use a standard function minimization algorithm such as Golden Section Search [15]. The probability of restart is evaluated for every trial κ using Eq. (6).

By using the traditional approximations for expected cost values (Eq. (7)), we are able to reuse the traditional query optimizer for Top N query subtree optimization. The relationship between the equivalent selection (κ) estimator, system statistics and an optimizer are shown in Fig. 2. Equivalent selection (κ) estimator uses Golden Search to find optimal κ, and in the process calls the optimizer repeatedly to evaluate Init(κ) and Rest(κ) and consults the system statistics. For Golden search algorithm, one needs to bound the κ. Initial bound would be the column minimum for the low and the column maximum for the high. Golden search algorithm then successively splits the bound until it becomes sufficiently small.

Init(κ) and Rest(κ) are expensive expressions to evaluate because they require optimization of the query subtree. On the other hand, the best plan for Init(κ) and Rest(κ) are likely not to change for small changes in κ. Consequently, a further approximation would be to find the best plan for these two queries only once. Of course, Init(κ) and Rest(κ) should still be re-evaluated for every trial κ because the cost will change depending on κ even if the plan does not change.

3.1 Probability Distribution Maintenance

In this section we describe how to practically maintain cardinality distributions; the ideas apply to maintaining selectivity distributions as well. In general, a cardinality distribution is completely specified by $(cardinality - value, probability)$ pairs, but maintaining all such pairs is not practical. A simple approximation is to only store a certain number of cardinality values whose associated probabilities are all the same.

For example, a selectivity vector of size η could be represented as an array:

$$\sigma = \{\sigma_1, \sigma_2, \ldots, \sigma_\eta\}$$

where σ_i are all equally probable selectivities. By choosing this alternative we don't have to store individual probabilities, since they are all the same and equal to $1/\eta$. The size of the probability vector (η) is system dependent. A selectivity distribution can be represented in a similar manner.

To find the result of multiplying a cardinality distribution with a selectivity distribution, we just multiply every possible selectivity with every possible cardinality. However, the resulting distribution will have η^2 elements and must be reduced to only η elements; this approximation can be carried out by replacing η neighboring values with their average.

4 Estimating Initial Probability Densities

We have discussed how to propagate cardinality densities through the plan tree, by multiplying the operator selectivity and the input cardinality densities. However, we have not yet addressed the problem of estimating the *initial* cardinality density and the *initial* selectivity density for every predicate in the query; we turn to this next. Database systems usually maintain exact cardinalities for the base tables. Therefore, initial cardinality densities are likely to be single values with probability one. Estimating selectivity densities is much more complex. Keeping in mind that our estimates will be used for optimization purposes only, precision is not of crucial importance, so we choose simplicity as our guiding principle.

We will estimate initial selectivity distributions from histograms. In order for the selectivity distribution to be *consistent* with the traditional (single value) histogram estimate, we require that the expected value of the selectivity distribution coincide with the traditional selectivity estimate. [1] Therefore, we propose to construct a selectivity distribution whose average is equal to the traditional selectivity for a predicate, call it σ. As described in Sec. 3.1, our distribution consists of a set of equally probable cardinality values. Finally, we need to bound our distribution to the left and to the right. Distribution spread reflects the precision of the histogram estimates; the more accurate the histogram is the tighter the bounds.

Summarizing these ideas, we arrive at the generic distribution shown in Fig. 3. Notice that, in general, the left bound (B_L) need not be equal to the right bound (B_R). For example, bounds for a predicate can

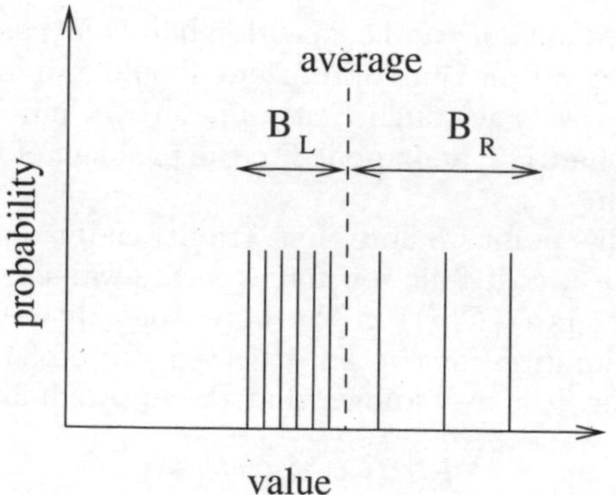

Figure 3: Example of an initial selectivity density.

be asymmetric because a predicate selectivity may not exceed one nor be less than zero. Given the average value (traditional estimate σ from a histogram) and bounds (B_L and B_R) one can easily construct a simple distribution with a certain number of possible values located equi-distantly to the left of the average and the remaining values positioned equi-distantly to the right. Equi-distant positioning is chosen for simplicity, notice that the distance between the left-hand side values may not be the same as the corresponding distance on the right. The total number of values in a selectivity distribution is a predetermined constant (we used 32 in our experiment). Number of values to the left of σ is calculated so that the expected value of all the distribution is equal to σ. In the following sections we will discuss how to estimate the two distribution parameters B_L and B_R for common predicates.

4.1 Estimating the Quality of a Histogram

Distribution parameters B_L and B_R are dependent on the quality of the histogram on the referenced column. Research on histograms has mainly focused on improving their precision [10]. The first paper to introduce the idea of augmenting a histogram with some measure of accuracy is [5]. They suggest maintaining the largest equality selection error within each bucket. This error is determined by comparing histogram estimates to the actual result of an equality selection.

Although the idea of maintaining some error estimates within a histogram is a good one, maintaining per bucket information has the following disadvantages: (1) Per bucket error information will increase the size of the bucket and therefore use space that could otherwise be used to increase histogram precision. (2) Selection errors for range queries will be largely overestimated if they are based on the largest errors per bucket. This is because errors in single values tend to cancel each other, and simply adding them up will greatly overestimate the error.

We propose to maintain the worst-case error for an open-ended range predicate. This has an advantage

[1] Given a predicate, say $X < 100$, its selectivity is estimated from a histogram on the data distribution by adding counts in buckets to the left of the point $X = 100$ and taking the ratio to the total count over all buckets.

of requiring little space, independent of the number of buckets, and it provides good bounds for queries of type *field* $\leq$ *value*. More specifically, let x denote the domain values, $P_{\text{real}}(x)$ denote the cumulative probability distribution of the real data set and $P_{\text{hist}}(x)$ denote the cumulative probability distribution deduced from a histogram. Then, we define ϵ as:

$$\epsilon = \max_{-\infty<x<\infty} | P_{\text{real}}(x) - P_{\text{hist}}(x) | \quad (8)$$

In other words, ϵ is the maximum deviation of the selectivity of the predicate *field* $\leq$ *value* between the histogram and the real data set. We propose to experimentally measure ϵ for each histogram and maintain this value as a part of the system statistics. Notice that a table without a histogram is usually assumed to have uniform distribution that corresponds to the trivial histogram, with only one bucket. Therefore, without the loss of generality, we consider every table to have an associated histogram.

The most precise (and the most expensive) way of measuring ϵ is by sorting the original table and performing the full scan. A much cheaper way is to take a random sample of the original table and measure ϵ from the random sample. The crucial question here is how big a sample is needed in order to estimate ϵ correctly. In general, this depends on the precision of the histogram: the more precise the histogram is, the larger the required sample. Histogram precision in turn depends on the type of the histogram and on the number of buckets β. The most commonly used histogram in current database systems is the equi-depth histogram, and so we present a short analysis for it here. The value of ϵ for an equi-depth histogram is bounded as:

$$\epsilon \leq \frac{1}{\beta} \quad (9)$$

where β is the number of buckets. Also, by the theorem due to Kolmogorov [7] we have:

$$D \leq \frac{\lambda}{\sqrt{s}} \quad (10)$$

where s is the size of the random sample, D is the maximal deviation between the real data set and its sample (Eq. (8)), and λ is a number that depends on the confidence limit. For 80% confidence, $\lambda \approx 1$. So, the pessimistic estimate of D for 80% confidence is:

$$D \approx \frac{1}{\sqrt{s}} \quad (11)$$

To reliably estimate ϵ, D should be much smaller than ϵ, say

$$D \approx \frac{\epsilon}{10}. \quad (12)$$

From formulas (9), (11), and (12) it follows that s can be approximated by:

$$s \geq 100\,\beta^2 \quad (13)$$

We have verified experimentally that the sample size of approximately $100\,\beta^2$ produces satisfactory results. (See Fig. 10).

Notice that ϵ can be calculated at the histogram construction time, using the single sample for both, building the histogram and estimating ϵ. In fact, the required sample size is, for the most cases, of the same order of magnitude. For example, a histogram with 100 buckets ($\beta = 100$) would require a sample of size of 1 million (Eq. (13)). On the other hand, a recent paper on equi-depth histogram construction [13] suggests that for the reasonable values of confidence, data size and deviations from true equi-depth histogram, 0.8 million is the recommended sample size.

4.2 Estimating Selectivity Probability Density for Open Range Selection

From the definition of ϵ (Eq. (8)) and the definition of the cumulative probability density it is clear that the maximal error in the open range selection is ϵ. Therefore, we construct a selectivity density shown in Fig. 3 with the average equal to the selectivity estimate from the histogram and $B_L = B_R = \epsilon$.

4.3 Estimating Selectivity Probability Density for Equality and Closed Range Selection

By knowing ϵ, one can bound the error in an equality selection as well. If one denotes the histogram error in the frequency of a domain value i by Δf_i then the following condition must hold:

$$-\epsilon \leq \sum_{i=-\infty}^{j} \Delta f_i \leq \epsilon \quad (14)$$

for any j element of the value domain. One can express the error in frequency Δf_j as:

$$\Delta f_j = \sum_{i=-\infty}^{j} \Delta f_i - \sum_{i=-\infty}^{j-1} \Delta f_i$$

from which it is seen than Δf_j is bounded as:

$$-2\epsilon \leq \Delta f_j \leq 2\epsilon \quad (15)$$

Following the same argument, it can be shown that the error in the cardinality result R of the closed range query (like $a \leq x \leq b$) is bounded by:

$$-2\epsilon \leq \Delta R \leq 2\epsilon \quad (16)$$

i.e., it is independent of the range. Similar to the open range selection, we construct a selectivity density shown in Fig. 3 with the average equal to the selectivity estimate from the histogram and $B_L = B_R = 2\epsilon$.

4.4 Estimating Selectivity Probability Density for Equi-join Selection

The resulting cardinality of an equi-join (R) can be expressed as:

$$R = \sum_i f_i g_i \qquad (17)$$

where f and g stands for the frequency vectors of the two tables to be joined and i ranges over all domain values in the join columns. Error in R can be obtained by differentiating Eq. (17):

$$\Delta R = \sum_i \Delta f_i \, g_i + \sum_i f_i \Delta g_i \qquad (18)$$

where we have ignored the term $\sum_i \Delta f_i \, \Delta f_j$ because it is small compared to the other terms. This expression can be further simplified by rewriting:

$$f_i = \tilde{f}_i + \Delta f_i \qquad (19)$$
$$g_i = \tilde{g}_i + \Delta g_i \qquad (20)$$

where $\tilde{f}_i$ and $\tilde{g}_i$ stand for the histogram estimate of f_i and g_i respectively. After substituting the above expressions into Eq. (18) and ignoring the terms with two differentials we get:

$$\Delta R \approx \sum_i \Delta f_i \, \tilde{g}_i + \sum_i \tilde{f}_i \Delta g_i \qquad (21)$$

or by noticing that $\tilde{f}$ (and $\tilde{g}$) is constant within a bucket b:

$$\Delta R \approx \sum_b \tilde{g}_b \sum_{j \in b} \Delta f_j + \sum_b \tilde{f}_b \sum_{j \in b} \Delta g_i \qquad (22)$$

Finally, using the bounds from Eq. (16) we obtain:

$$\Delta R \leq 2\epsilon_f \sum_b \tilde{g}_b + 2\epsilon_g \sum_b \tilde{f}_b \qquad (23)$$

From these bounds, we construct a selectivity density shown in Fig. 3 with the average equal to the selectivity estimate from the histogram and $B_L = B_R = \Delta R$.

4.5 Estimating Selectivity Probability Density for Selections on Union

We examine the issues related to Top N queries over unions motivated by the following observations:

1. Many database integration systems, which are expected to have significant presence on the Web, are built as unions over the base tables (see for example [8] and [11]).

2. Top N queries are one of the most common queries in the Web environment. We will then especially be concerned with running a Top N query on a distributed union.

Maximum error in the resulting cardinality ΔR of a selection on union is just the sum of all the component errors ΔR_i.

$$\Delta R = |\Delta R_1| + |\Delta R_2| + \ldots + |\Delta R_n| \qquad (24)$$

From this bounds, we construct a selectivity density shown in Fig. 3 with the average equal to the selectivity estimate from the histogram and $B_L = B_R = \Delta R$.

5 Example

Assume that we want the salaries of top 50 paid employees whose age is less than 40. Selectivities presented in the following table were determined from the system statistics using standard estimation techniques.

Predicate	Selectivity	Max Error
$age < 40$	0.4	0.2
$salary > 100K$	0.1	0.3

Maximal errors for the open range selections was measured and stored with other system statistics. Suppose that the Golden Search technique is currently trying to evaluate the cost function (Eq. (7)) for cutoff $\kappa = 100K$. Assuming that the system is configured with $\eta = 4$, we construct the initial distribution for age predicate, as shown in Fig. 4. Similarly, initial distribution for $salary > 100K$ is shown in Fig. 5. In general, the number of columns to the left of the average η_L and to the right of the average η_R is determined by the following equations:

$$\eta_L B_L = \eta_R B_R$$
$$\eta_L + \eta_R = \eta$$

Result of multiplying these two selectivity distribution, multiplied by the total number of input tuples (1,000), is shown in Fig. 6. From Fig. 6 we conclude that the probability of restart for $\kappa = 100K$ is 75% because 3 out of 4 columns are less than 50. In a similar manner, one would continue with the next iteration of κ and stop when the minimum is bounded with sufficient precision (e.g., 1/10 of the bucket width).

6 Performance Evaluation for Selection and Join Queries

In the following sections, we have applied the ideas developed so far to the optimization of Top N queries on a single table or a join. We compare execution times for the following three algorithms, using average execution time for 15 randomly generated input data sets:

Traditional: Compute all answers, sort, and return the top N.

Naive: Estimate the cutoff parameter for top 1.2 N (20% safety margin) using available system statistics.

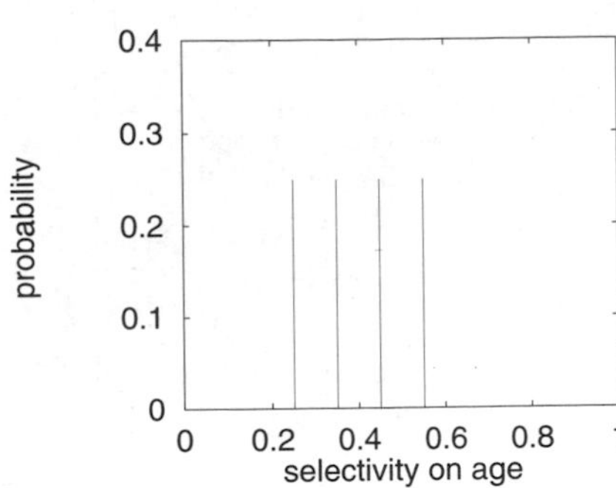

Figure 4: Selectivity distribution of predicate $age < 40$.

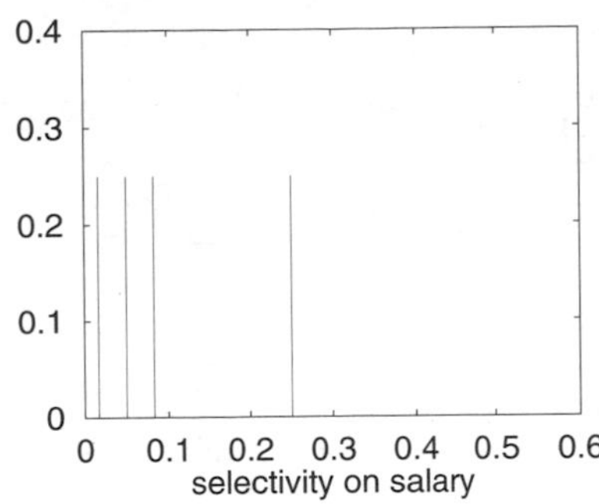

Figure 5: Selectivity distribution of predicate $salary > 100K$.

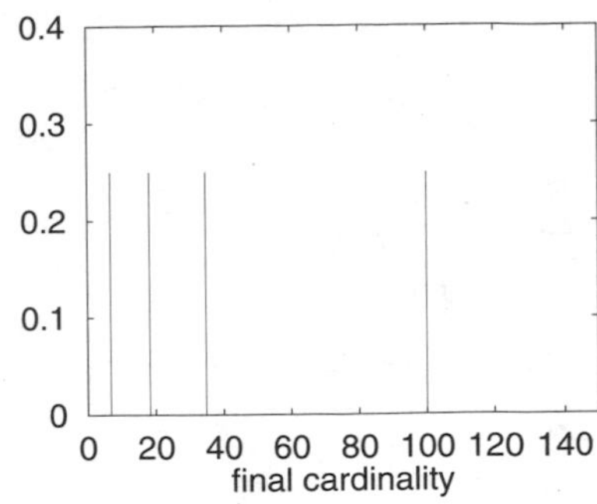

Figure 6: Output cardinality distribution.

Probabilistic: Determine the cutoff parameter probabilistically, using available system statistics (including the measured ϵ).

We varied several parameters: (1) Skew of the underlying data distribution (Zipf parameter[16] Z, by default one). (2) Number of buckets in the histogram. (3) N, the number of tuples selected, by default 1,000. (4) s, the size of the random sample used to estimate ϵ. We fixed the total number of tuples in the data file (100,000), and the total spread of the data, which is approximately equal to the number of distinct values (5,000). We estimated execution times by using standard analytical formulas for cost estimation [12], estimating the cost of a disk I/O as $10ms$ and the CPU cost of a tuple swap (in sorting) as $10\mu s$. Our results show the performance gains to be sufficiently large that the relative merits of our probabilistic approach hold regardless of the approximations inherent in this simple estimation of execution time.

6.1 Top N on a Single Table Selection Query

Consider the query that asks for the Top N employees by salary. Assume that the *Employees* table is neither sorted nor indexed on *salary* field. As suggested by [1], the best plan for this query is probably to use range-partitioning sort. However, the crucial question is how many partitions to materialize. In order to simplify our presentation, we consider only two partitions, one which is materialized and sorted and the other with the rest of the data. (In the terminology of the paper [1] these two partitions are called the winner and the loser, respectively.) In the case of multiple (memory-sized) partitions, there will still be two large groups, one that contains materialized partitions and the other that contains unmaterialized ones. Therefore, our simplified analysis and conclusions would still hold in the more complex multi-partition case. We discuss the parameters varied and the corresponding figures next.

Data Skew: Fig. 7 has the number of histogram buckets fixed to one, implying the uniformity assumption. When data is really uniform ($Z = 0$), the naive and the probabilistic algorithm have the same performance. With a large data skew, uniformity assumption becomes significantly violated and the naive algorithm frequently runs into restarts. Notice that restarts are more expensive that the traditional scan + sort approach. The probabilistic algorithm handles skew gracefully by just becoming more pessimistic in choosing the cutoff.

Number of Buckets: Fig. 8 shows that as the number of buckets increases, the difference between the probabilistic and the naive algorithm becomes less pronounced. This is due to the fact that with a larger number of buckets, the histogram error falls below 20% in which case the naive algorithm will not restart.

Top N selected: Fig. 9 shows that the naive and the probabilistic algorithm converge as N increases. This is because of the fact that eventually the 20% overestimate becomes adequate (conservative), provided that N is large enough. For small N, 20% obviously does not provide enough safety margin.

Sample Size: Fig. 10 shows that the sample size of 100 or more (as predicted by Eq. (13)) is satisfactory for this experiment, and that the performance of the probabilistic algorithm is not sensitive to small variations in the sample size.

6.2 Top N on Equi-Join Queries

Consider an equi-join query of two identical tables that have on average 20 duplicates for each value in the join column, augmented by Top N operator on an independently distributed column. In this section, we compare the performance of naive and probabilistic algorithms on equi-join queries such as this. We used the same data generator as for the selection queries, which implies that the average number of duplicates for a certain attribute value is 20. We discuss the parameters varied and the corresponding figures next.

Data Skew: Fig. 11 shows the increased gap in performance as the data skew increases initially, due to the fact that the naive algorithm runs into restarts. Restarts for the Naive algorithm become more common for increasing skew because the histogram esti-

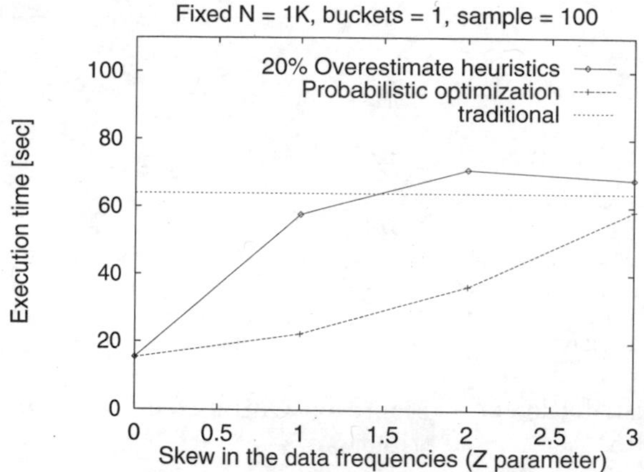

Figure 7: Execution time vs. data skew, using trivial (1 bucket) histogram.

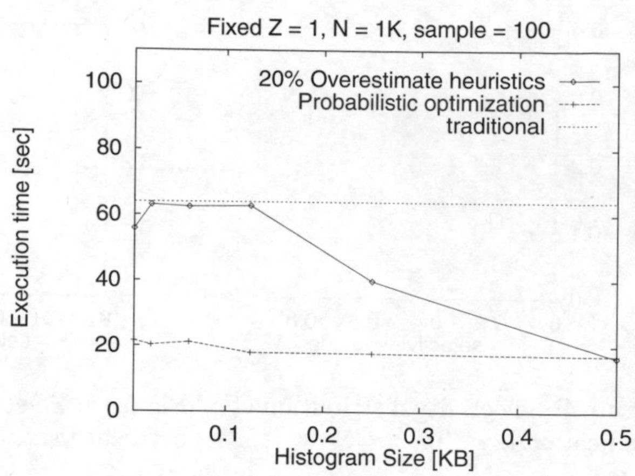

Figure 8: Execution time vs. number of buckets in histogram.

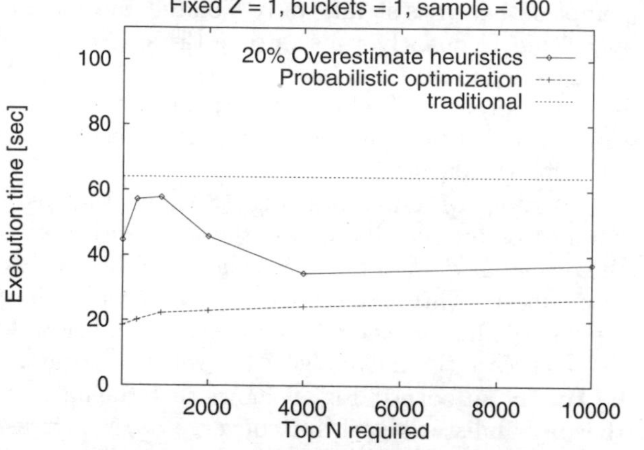

Figure 9: Execution time for different values of Top N selected (in percents of relation size).

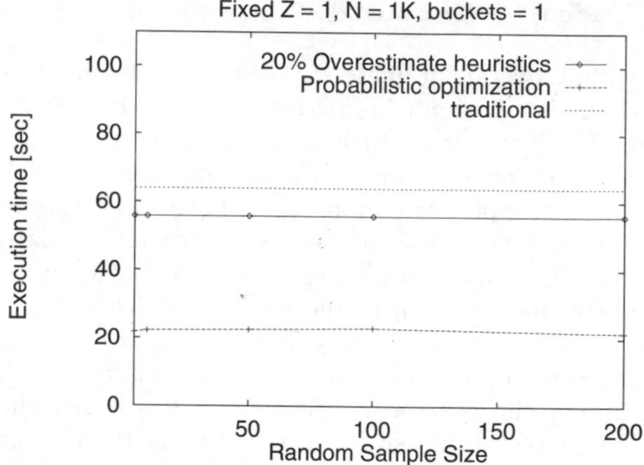

Figure 10: Execution time vs. sample size used to calculate ϵ.

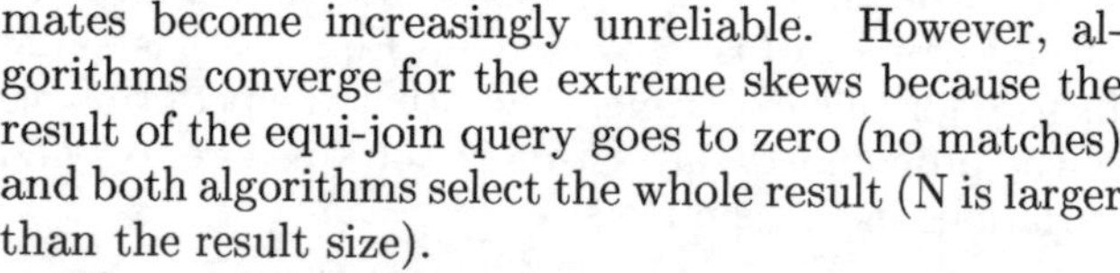

mates become increasingly unreliable. However, algorithms converge for the extreme skews because the result of the equi-join query goes to zero (no matches) and both algorithms select the whole result (N is larger than the result size).

Size of Histogram: Fig. 12 shows that the naive algorithm improves as the histograms become larger, as expected. The probabilistic algorithm improves too but the trend is too small to be visible.

Top N Selected: Fig. 13 shows that the differences between algorithms are less pronounced when larger N is selected, because the 20% overestimate becomes adequate for larger N. The reasoning here is the same as in single table case.

Number of Joins: Fig. 14 shows that the naive algorithm does not work for more than 2 way joins on the test data. The reason for this is twofold. First, the quality of the estimates deteriorates rapidly with the number of joins, thus making the restarts more likely. Second, the punishment for restart skyrockets due to the large join size (100,000 * 20 * 20 tuples for the 3-way join).

In general, join experiments reflect the fact that estimating join selectivity is much more difficult than estimating selectivity of range predicates [4], and consequently, the probabilistic approach is of greater value in this case.

7 Improvements on Some Common Top N Query Evaluations

In this section we consider two cases in which significant additional improvements over the standard Top N query processing are possible: Top N on aggregate queries and Top N over distributed unions.

7.1 Efficient Evaluation of Top N Queries on Aggregates

Consider a Top N aggregate query such as this one asking for the N most common ages among employees:

select age, count(age) **from** Employees emp
group by age **order by** count(age)
stop after N

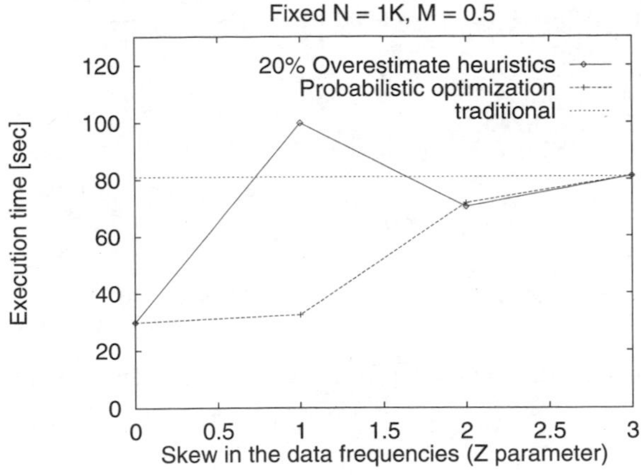

Figure 11: Execution time vs. data skew.

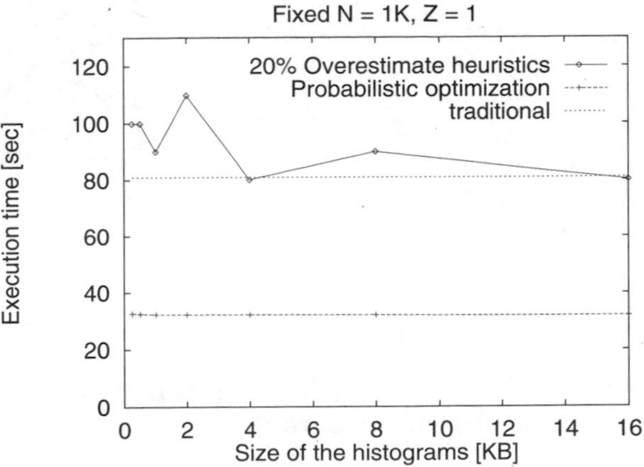

Figure 12: Execution time vs. number of buckets in the histogram.

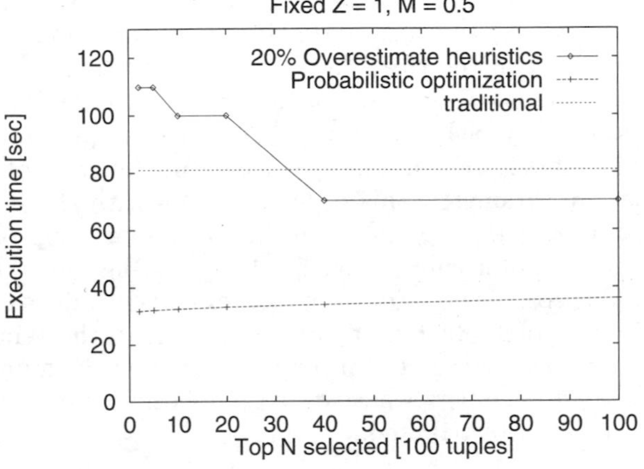

Figure 13: Execution time for different values of Top N selected (in thousand of tuples).

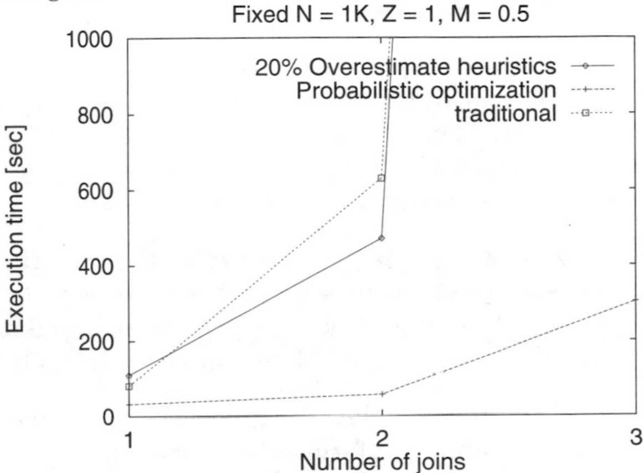

Figure 14: Execution time dependency on the number of joins.

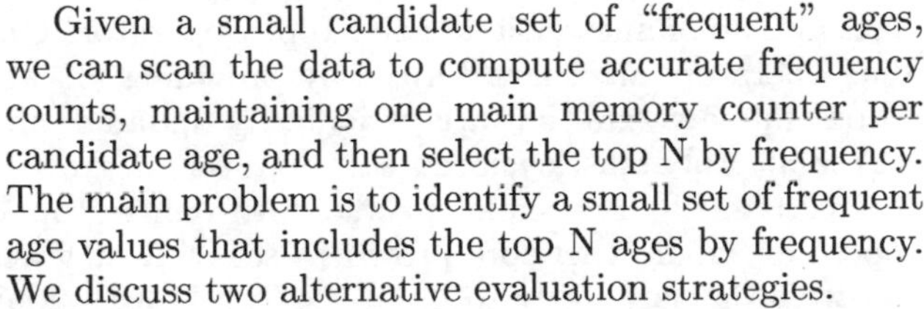

Given a small candidate set of "frequent" ages, we can scan the data to compute accurate frequency counts, maintaining one main memory counter per candidate age, and then select the top N by frequency. The main problem is to identify a small set of frequent age values that includes the top N ages by frequency. We discuss two alternative evaluation strategies.

(I) Reduction to an Iceberg Query: The idea is to replace the Top N operator by the equivalent selection. We need to estimate the cutoff value κ for count(age), then group employees by age and compute the counts above the cutoff. Given the cutoff κ, we can turn the above Top N query into an Iceberg query, allowing us to use the algorithms proposed in [3], as follows: just replace the **stop after** clause with **having** count(age) $> \kappa$. Using this approach, the algorithms of [3] require two full scans of the dataset (one to identify the "frequent" ages, and one to compute their counts), and there is the possibility of additional scans in the case of restart (due to the Top N nature of our main query).

(II) Direct Use of a Histogram: This approach requires a histogram on the Top N attribute (*age* in this example). Let the largest error in equality selection on this histogram be E. Using the histogram, choose an attribute value V that has the smallest frequency F among the N attribute values with the largest frequencies. The actual dataset may have a frequency for value V that is as low as $F-E$. Also, other frequencies in the histogram may be underestimated, and so the candidate set (for inclusion in the Top N) is any value whose histogram frequency is above $F-2E$. The existence of a histogram therefore allows us to identify a candidate set of frequent attribute values that is *conservative*: the top N values by frequency are guaranteed to be here (provided that the error bounds stored with the histogram are accurate!). This eliminates the problem of restart, and further, the candidate set generation is based purely on the histogram. The database is scanned once to count frequencies for each candidate "frequent" attribute value. In Fig. 15 we present experimentally measured number of candidates for the example Top N query on a synthetically

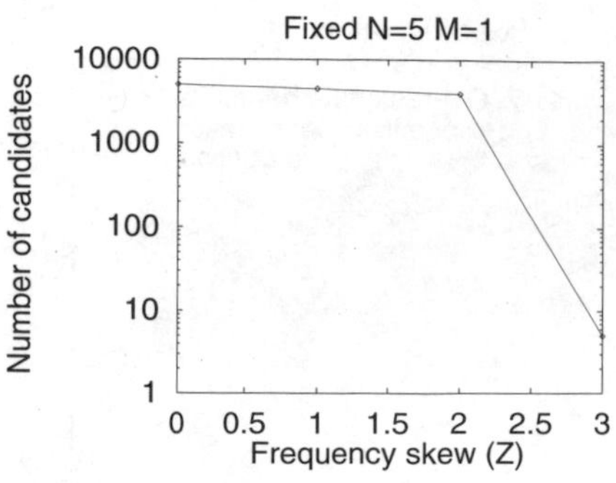

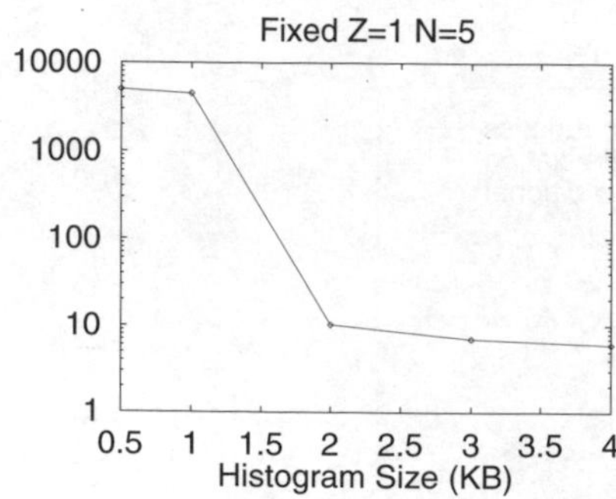

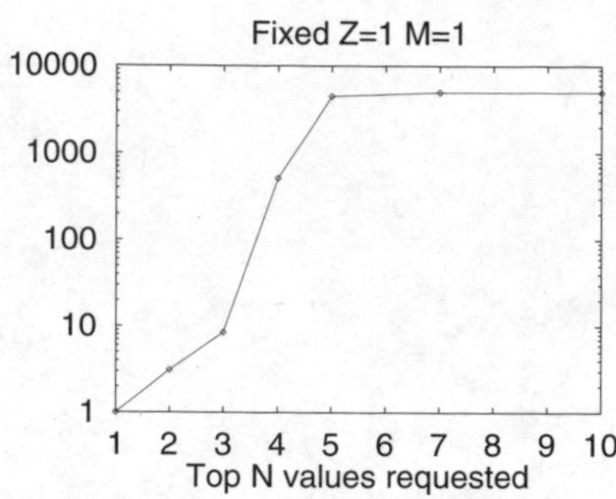

Figure 15: Number of candidates generated by the direct histogram usage as a function of data skew, histogram size, and number of tuples requested.

generated data set. The three graphs in Fig. 15 show expected trends in the effectiveness of the direct histogram alternative, which can be summarized as follows:

1. Number of candidates decreases as the data skew increases. This is expected behavior since it is easier to identify the Top N candidates when there are large differences among frequencies.
2. Number of candidates decreases as the histogram precision (size) increases. This is because the error decreases when the size is increased, making the candidate threshold frequency $F - 2E$ higher.
3. Number of candidates exponentially increases with N (number of tuples requested). This is mainly an artifact of the Zipf distribution, which is exponential.

The conclusion of this section is that the direct histogram method of finding the candidate set is an excellent way to answering Top N queries on aggregates under the circumstances of high skew, large histograms ($> 1KB$), and small N.

7.2 Lazy Evaluation of Top N Over Distributed Unions

In a distributed environment, a Top N query could be run in parallel, ensuring the shortest response time. However, this may unnecessarily waste the computing resources of remote sites. We can reduce resource consumption by waiting to access a new site until it is necessary to do so, at the cost of slowing the execution.

If the user chooses to conserve the resources, what is the proper order of accessing the sites so that the number of accessed sites is minimal? We propose to access the sites in the order of estimated probabilities that they will be useful in answering the query. Suppose that at a certain site S the maximum value for the field of interest is M_S. If M_S is less than the cutoff parameter κ, we will certainly not access the site S. However, even if $\kappa \leq M_S$ there is still a chance that the site S will not be accessed because the κ might be underestimated. The probability of accessing the site S is the probability of restart when $\kappa = M_S$. (The Top N query is translated to selection above the cutoff parameter.) In other words, if $\kappa = M_S$ and no restart occurs than the site S need not be accessed. So, the sites should be accessed in the order of the decreasing probability of being needed. Because the probability of restart is a monotonically decreasing function of the cutoff parameter, this order coincides with the order of decreasing M_S. The benefits of the lazy approach can be potentially large, as shown in Fig. 16. The reduction of the resource usage for certain values of N is due to the fact that one connection to the remote source was saved. In this experiment, we used a union with 20 members whose data are identically but independently distributed.

8 Useful Variants of Top N Queries

8.1 Online Top N with Confidence Estimates

Motivated by the ideas of Online Aggregation [6], we consider an online version of the Top N operator. Online operators are characterized by providing (1) approximate answers that are periodically updated, and (2) some probabilistic guarantees about the (degree of) correctness of the current answers. An online Top N operator should therefore provide a set of N or fewer answers that are likely to be in the Top N list, along with associated probabilities indicating the likelihood that a given answer will be in the final Top N list.

Our probabilistic framework provides the infrastructure to implement such an operator. Consider, for example, a Top N query on a single table. The system will periodically display the current set of tuples that satisfy the cutoff predicate. The probability of a value x not being in the Top N results is the probability of no restart happening when $\kappa = x$. Equivalently, the probability of a selected value x being in the final Top N values is the probability of restart when $\kappa = x$, where the probability of restart is calculated using Eq. (6). These probabilities do not depend on the order in which the data is read.

In the event of restart, while getting all N results

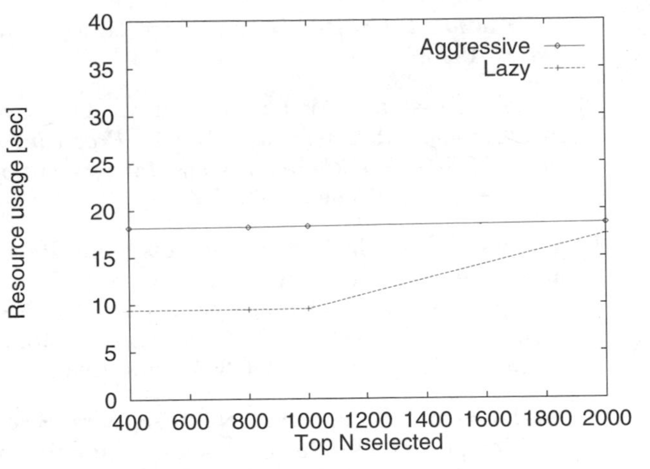

Figure 16: Total resource usage for a union consisting of 20 members with trivial histograms.

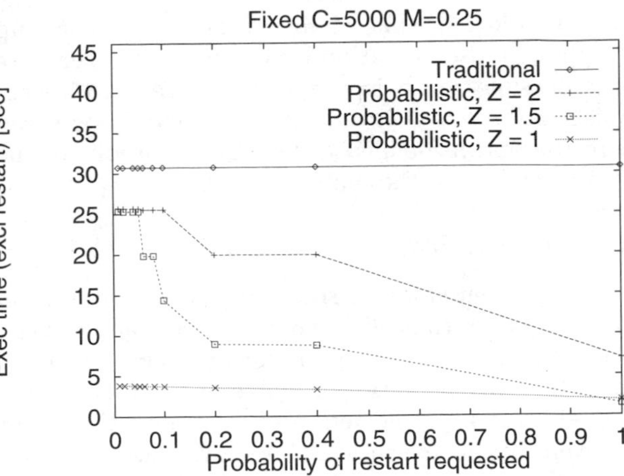

Figure 17: Execution time dependency on user-specified restart probability for single table scans

will take longer, the user at least has a subset of K results which, as of the time restart is initiated, are guaranteed to be the top K. If K is sufficiently close to N, the user may well terminate computation at this point (after all, the choice of N is likely to be rather ad hoc in the first place).

8.2 Fuzzy Top N: An Alternative Formulation of Top N

Top N queries require exactly N answers, and the system has to guarantee N results by restarting the query if necessary. We observe that many times, users may not insist on exactly N answers but may be ready to accept less. We formalize this intuition by allowing a user to specify a bound on the likelihood of restarts. So if a user is willing to accept a small likelihood of restart, the system can compute the cutoff κ more aggressively, and find answers in less time. Of course, as κ is set more and more aggressively, the likelihood of restart increases, and intuitively, the number of answers computed as of the time of restart decreases. So the user indirectly also controls the number of answers that are likely to be computed at the time of restart by directly controlling the bound on the likelihood of restart.

In this formulation of the problem, the cutoff κ is determined solely by p and N (and of course data distribution) but not by the estimated execution time. The desired cutoff is such that it minimizes $|r - p|$ where r is the probability of restart (defined in Eq. (6)) and p is the probability of calculating N or more answers (given by the user). For minimization one can again use the Golden Search technique. After this cutoff is determined, we could just use a traditional optimizer to optimize the query augmented with equivalent selection. This makes it very easy to support Fuzzy Top N in an existing system; all that is needed is a thin layer (using the probabilistic estimation techniques presented here) to augment a query with a cutoff selection predicate.

We have experimentally measured the query execution times (not including restart) for various restart probabilities requested and the skew of the input data. In Fig. 17 we show the results for the single table Top N query for input data files of 100,000 tuples spread over attribute range of 5,000 distinct values. The top 10,000 answers were requested and the histogram size was fixed to 0.25 KB. For comparison, we also include the time for the Traditional alternative which would sort all the data and return first N tuples only. Fig. 17 indicates that for low skews the execution time is not very dependent on the probability of restart. This is due to the fact that a 0.25KB compressed histogram can bound the possible cutoff values well within a small range of attribute values. On the other hand, datasets with high skew require much longer execution time for low values of the probability of restart. This can be explained by the fact that with high skew there are certain attribute values that make up the bulk of the distribution. Selecting such a value ensures no restart with certainty and not selecting it ensures a restart with certainty. When choosing between zero and one, the system chooses zero for small restart probabilities, effectively selecting and sorting large chunks of input data.

9 Future Work

We plan to examine the benefits of the probabilistic optimization for traditional select-project-join queries. Probabilistic query optimization should reduce the average execution time in cases when plan's cost is not a linear function of resources that vary within the non-linear region. Example of such cases are the join cost formula non-linear dependency on the available memory. Another example is the problem of executing queries that refer to relations scattered over a wide-area network [14]. The challenge here is to come up with plans whose execution times are not too sensitive to the possible delays in the network. Yet another example can be found in distributed query processing, where the optimizer has to distribute the jobs to the sites depending on the machine loads.

10 Conclusion

We have presented a new solution to the optimization of Top N queries that offers an interesting, and in some ways simpler, alternative to the approach of [9, 1]. Our extensions to a traditional query optimizer are relatively easy to implement and they show significant improvements in execution times over the naive approach to aggressive pushing of STOP operator. The underlying idea of taking imprecision in estimates into account during query optimization has much wider applicability than just Top N queries.

References

[1] Michael J. Carey and Donald Kossmann. Reducing the braking distance of an sql query engine. In *Proceedings of the International Conference on Very Large Data Bases*, 1998.

[2] P. Seshadri F. Chu, J. Halpern. Least expected cost query optimization: An exercise in utility. In *Proceedings of the International Conference on Very Large Data Bases*, 1999.

[3] Min Fang, Narayanan Shivakumar, Hector Garcia-Molina, Rajeev Motwani, and Jeffrey D. Ullman. Computing iceberg queries efficiently. In *Proceedings of the International Conference on Very Large Data Bases*, pages 299–310, 1998.

[4] Yannis E. Ioannidis and Stavros Christodoulakis. On the propagation of errors in the size of join results. In *Proceedings of ACM-SIGMOD Conference on Management of Data*, 1991.

[5] H.V. Jagadish, Nick Koudas, S. Muthukrishnan, Viswanath Poosala, Ken Sevick, and Torsten Suel. Optimal histograms with quality guarantees. In *Proceedings of the International Conference on Very Large Data Bases*, 1998.

[6] Helen J. Wang Joseph M. Hellerstein, Peter J. Haas. Online aggregation. In *Proceedings of ACM-SIGMOD Conference on Management of Data*, Tucson, Arizona, 1997.

[7] A. N. Kolmogorov. Confidence limits for an unknown distribution function. In *Ann. Math. Statist.*, pages 461–463, 1941.

[8] Alon Levy, Anand Rajaraman, and Joann Ordille. Querying heterogeneous information sources using source descriptions. In *Proceedings of the International Conference on Very Large Data Bases*, 1996.

[9] Donald Kossmann Michael J. Carey. On Saying "Enough Already!" in SQL. In *Proceedings of ACM-SIGMOD Conference on Management of Data*, Tucson, Arizona, 1997.

[10] Viswanath Poosala, Yannis Ioannidis, Peter Haas, and Eugene Shekita. Improved histograms for selectivity estimation of range predicates. In *Proceedings of ACM-SIGMOD Conference on Management of Data*, pages 294–305, June 1996.

[11] Raghu Ramakrishnan and Avi Silberschatz. Scalable integration of data collection on the web. In *Technical Report: CS-TR-98-1376*. University of Wisconsin-Madison, June 1998.

[12] Leonard D. Shapiro. Join processing in database systems with large main memories. In *ACM Transactions on Database Systems*, volume 11, pages 239–264, 1986.

[13] Vivek R. Narasayya Surajit Chaudhuri, Rajeev Motwani. Random sampling for histogram construction: How much is enough? In *Proceedings of ACM-SIGMOD Conference on Management of Data*, pages 436–447, 1998.

[14] Tolga Urhan, Michael J. Franklin, and Laurent Amsaleg. Cost based query scrambling for initial delays. In *Proceedings of ACM-SIGMOD Conference on Management of Data*, pages 130–141, 1998.

[15] Saul A. William H. Press, Brian P. Flannery and William T. Vetterling. *Numerical Recipes in C: The Art of Scientific Computing.* Cambridge University Press, 1993.

[16] G. K. Zipf. *Human Behavior and the Principle of Least Effort.* Addison-Wesley, Reading, MA, 1949.

Combining Histograms and Parametric Curve Fitting for Feedback-Driven Query Result-Size Estimation

Arnd Christian König and Gerhard Weikum
Department of Computer Science,University of the Saarland
P.O. Box 151150, 66041 Saarbrücken, Germany
E-Mail: {koenig,weikum}@cs.uni-sb.de

Abstract

This paper aims to improve the accuracy of query result-size estimations in query optimizers by leveraging the dynamic feedback obtained from observations on the executed query workload. To this end, an approximate "synopsis" of data-value distributions is devised that combines histograms with parametric curve fitting, leading to a specific class of linear splines. The approach reconciles the benefits of histograms, simplicity and versatility, with those of parametric techniques especially the adaptivity to statistically biased and dynamically evolving query workloads.

The paper presents efficient algorithms for constructing the linear-spline synopsis for data-value distributions from a moving window of the most recent observations on (the most critical) query executions. The approach is worked out in full detail for capturing frequency as well as density distributions of data values, and it is shown how result size estimations are inferred for exact-match and range queries as well as projections and grouping. To a large extent, the developed methods can be generalized to multi-dimensional distributions, thus bearing the ability to capture correlations among attributes as well. Experimental studies underline the accuracy of the developed estimation methods, outperforming the best known classes of histograms.

Proceedings of the 25th VLDB Conference, Edinburgh, Scotland, 1999.

1 Introduction

1.1 Deficiencies in the State of the Art

The effectivity of query optimization in database systems critically depends on the system's ability to estimate the costs of different query execution plans as accurately as possible. In most cases, the cost of a plan is dependent on the sizes of intermediate results produced by the query execution. Therefore, accurate estimation of these sizes is crucial to choosing a good plan and properly allocating the necessary resources, especially working memory.

A number of techniques for dealing with this problem have been studied in the literature, almost all of which can be categorized into three major classes: *histogram-based techniques* that capture statistical information about data-value distributions by means of counters for a specified number of data-value buckets, *parametric techniques* that approximate data-value distributions by fitting the parameters of a given type of function (e.g., polynomials of a given maximum degree), and query-specific *sampling* that take samples from the database to statistically estimate the intermediate result sizes for the query at hand (for survey material see [20, 1, 24, 2]). From a generalized perspective, all these approaches can be viewed as constructing an approximate representation, or *synopsis* [11, 9], of the data for the purpose of estimation (or even giving approximative query answers, which is not considered in this paper, however).

With modern OLAP tools and other forms of decision-support query generators, the query optimization takes place within the critical path of the query execution itself (i.e., there is no longer a distinction between the compile-time and run-time of a query). This rules out the relatively expensive sampling on a per query basis. Sampling is still very useful and, in fact, the method of choice for constructing histograms as a query-independent synopsis of the database's data-value distributions [3].

Histograms are traditionally a relatively static representation in that they do not easily adapt themselves to dynamically evolving value distributions (the only exceptional work being the methods for incremental histograms proposed by [10], which, however, need to maintain a "backing sample" in addition to the histogram itself and are thus not exactly light-weight either). Furthermore, a histogram is a statistically unbiased representation in that it is not oriented towards a specific mix of queries and query-input parameters (e.g., the actual parameters used in filter conditions). In practice, however, it is often the case that the current workload bears a statistical bias in the sense that most queries, or the most important or performance-critical queries, refer to specific (ranges of) data values as input parameters. Therefore, it is desirable to express the same bias in the value-distribution representations and to maintain these in a form that can be dynamically adapted to evolving workload patterns with acceptable effort. For example, the representation should be more accurate for value ranges that are frequently referred to by current queries, and may tolerate inaccuracies for the other ranges.

With regard to the mentioned forms of adaptivity, parametric techniques appear to be an intriguing representation of data-value distributions, as they are based on fitting a parameterized curve with observations on data-values frequencies. Thus, these techniques can naturally accommodate biased observations from the actually executed queries, and can be adapted to dynamic shifts in the query patterns relatively easily by recomputing the curve fitting [4]. However, this does not mean that parametric techniques are an adequate representation in the first place. In fact, they seem to be suitable only for data-value distributions that resemble a closed-form distribution such as Zipf or Pareto distributions, whereas they would lead to poor estimations for highly irregular distributions, e.g., with multiple modes (i.e., non-adjacent, very frequent data values such as the top selling product numbers in a table of purchases). Unfortunately, such irregular distributions are typical for many real-life applications. It is only in conjunction with appropriate data-value permutations that many real-life distributions would resemble a closed-form distribution. Capturing the information on the necessary permutation is, however, out of the question from a system's viewpoint, as this would entail the same storage and lookup costs as a full-fledged index. Note in passing that for the same reason, various advanced forms of histograms, most notably, the family of V-optimal histograms that use attribute frequency as sort parameter [24], are not practically viable either.

1.2 Our Approach

So neither histograms nor parametric techniques are satisfactory in all regards; therefore, novel techniques are needed for adaptive result-size estimation in highly dynamic query-processing environments such as modern OLAP applications. In this paper we develop a new approach that combines histograms with parametric fitting into a specific class of *spline-based synopses* of data-value distributions. Such a synopsis is constructed in two steps:

First the active domain of an attribute (or multi-dimensional attribute combination) is divided into a number of buckets each of which represents a contiguous range of data values (multi-dimensional rectangle); a bucket is identified by its lower and upper value bounds (left lower and right upper corner). In contrast to the most simple type of so-called equi-width histograms, we allow the width of the value ranges to vary across buckets; these widths are one of the tunable degrees of freedom. In contrast to the advanced type of V-optimal histograms with attribute frequency as sort parameter, we restrict ourselves to buckets that represent contiguous values (rather than non-adjacent values with similar frequencies) to avoid having to build a full-fledged index for histogram lookups.

Second we represent the value distribution within a bucket as a spline function rather than a flat value. Thus we do not rely on a uniform distribution within a bucket but can capture trends within certain value ranges (e.g., increasing sales figures within a particular time period that corresponds to one bucket of the corresponding date attribute). For tractability, we will restrict ourselves to linear splines for each bucket. In contrast to the kind of representation that is referred to as "spline histograms" in [24], we do not require the splines to be continuous across all buckets. This way we can easily capture "jumps" in attribute value frequencies, for example. As our experimental results will show, this generalization is crucial for high accuracy. So in the one-dimensional case, we need to keep one additional value for each bucket (compared to histograms): in addition to the lower value bound and the frequency (i.e., average frequency in a histogram, and frequency of the lower value bound in our approach), we also store the slope of the linear spline function. The ratio in the memory demand between histograms and spline-based synopses will be taken into account in our experimental comparisons (Section 8).

For adaptivity, the basic idea is to record observations, or *feedbacks*, from a moving window of recent queries and construct a statistically biased representation from these recordings, possibly with focus on particularly important or critical queries (e.g., those that exhibit a large difference between the cost estimation by the optimizer and the actual execution cost). With n recorded observations of say the frequency of an attribute value and a continuous parametric representation with m buckets ($m < n$, and often even $m \ll n$) and k parameters to be fitted for each bucket, this leads to the so-called "knot placement problem" [6] which has been intensively studied in numerical mathematics and is known to have intractable complexity in full generality. Our restriction to linear splines and the relaxation to allow discontinuities at bucket borders render the problem tractable. We will present both optimal fitting algorithms and very efficient, sub-optimal heuristics that allow us to construct the entire synopsis on-the-fly as we obtain new observations from recent queries.

The adaptive representation sketched above is the core of our approach. The actual estimation procedures for the intermediate result sizes of simple selection queries are relatively straightforward. In addition, our representation is also suitable to capture not just the frequencies of data values but also the density of values within the data ranges of the buckets. This way we can represent the sparsity of values (e.g., price values in a fixed-point number domain from $ 0.99 to $ 10,000.00), which is important for estimating the result size of projections and especially grouping operations. Note that this aspect of selectivity estimation has been vastly neglected in the literature. Most prior work, including [24], makes rather simplistic assumptions about data-value densities within buckets, for example, assuming perfectly equi-distant data values. Further note that the data-value density has also a significant impact on the result sizes of range queries and equi-joins over sparsely populated domains. To this end, we will enhance the initial fitting of the bucket-specific values by an additional fitting step that takes into account feedback from range queries. So our approach of spline-based synopses that we pursue in this paper proves to be useful and, in fact, superior to prior methods, for a broad class of estimation problems.

The rest of the paper is organized as follows. Section 2 briefly reviews the state-of-the-art techniques for approximate data synopses and the estimation methods in query optimization. Section 3 introduces architectural assumptions and notation, setting the stage for Section 4, the paper's key section on the construction of spline-based synopses from exact-match query feedback. Section 5 shows how selectivity estimations for range queries are carried based on the spline-based synopses. Section 6 then introduces an additional fitting step to adjust the density values (i.e., number of distinct attribute values) that are kept in the synopses, taking into account additional feedback from range queries and leading to more accurate estimations for range queries. Section 7 shows presents the estimation procedures for projections and grouping queries. Finally, we present experimental results in Section 8 to demonstrate the practical benefits of the developed spline-based synopses. We conclude the paper with a brief discussion of various further extensions, including the treatment of multidimensional distributions and equi-join result sizes.

2 Related Work

Several techniques for dealing with the described problems have been proposed in literature, almost all of which can be categorized in three major classes: *Histogram-based techniques, parametric techniques* and *sampling* (for surveys, see [20, 1, 24]):

Histogram-based Techniques.
Histograms approximate value distributions by grouping attribute values into buckets, and estimating true attribute values and their frequencies based on assuming a uniform distribution within a bucket. Histograms are the most common form of data synopsis in practice and can be found in systems such as DB2, Informix, Ingres, Oracle, Microsoft SQL Server, Sybase and Teradata. The histogram accuracy depends on the type of histogram used: While *V-optimal(F,F)* histograms have been proven optimal for equi-joins and selections [15, 13, 16], they require a list of all attribute values in a bucket, which is impractical in real systems. A good compromise between accuracy and practicability is made by *MaxDiff(V,A)* histograms [24] or *V-optimal* using Sort Parameters other than Frequency [17] . Histograms can be efficiently constructed by sampling-based techniques [25, 10].

Another promising approach are Wavelet-based histograms [21], which so far have only been examined in the context of range queries, however.

Parametric Techniques. Parametric techniques (also known as curve-fitting or regression techniques) approximate value distributions using a mathematical distribution function with a limited number of free parameters. Values for these parameters are then chosen to fit the actual distribution. If the model is a good fit for the distribution, this provides an accurate and compact approximation; however, since the shape of the distribution is usually not known beforehand, this is often not the case.

To overcome this inflexibility, [28, 4] use a general polynomial function and apply least-squares fitting to choose its coefficients. [4] additionally uses query feedback; hereby, the approximation is able to adapt to changes in the value distribution as well as to locality in the actual query parameters, so as to be geared for more accurate estimations for frequently queried values or value ranges.

Sampling. These techniques compute their estimates by collecting and processing random samples of the data. Sampling techniques [12, 3, 7, 19] offer high accuracy and probabilistic guarantees on the quality of the estimation. However, since the sampling itself is typically carried out at the time of the approximation, the resulting overhead prohibits the use of sampling for query optimization. Therefore, in recent works [10, 8] techniques for incremental maintenance of random samples have been developed.

Since our main concern is a compact representation of data, and not its acquisition, we will now concentrate on the properties of parametric and histogram-based techniques, which both offer different advantages. While histograms offer accurate approximation for a wide range of data distributions, parametric techniques are quite limited in the distributions they approximate well. Even when polynomials [4] or rational functions [28] are used, approximation of distributions that exhibit large changes in the frequencies of adjacent attribute values and therefore are not well suited to approximation by means of a continuous function, lead to a degeneration of the approximation (see [4], for example, for the pathological effect of falsely estimating negative selectivities).

However, parametric techniques do have the important advantage of being *adaptive*, i.e. they can adapt to query locality, changes in the data distribution and – by assigning different *weights* to query feedbacks – to the importance of different estimations. While a certain adaptivity to changes in data distribution can be achieved in histograms, too, using techniques for incremental sampling [10, 8], the other forms of adaptivity, to our knowledge, have so far been restricted to parametric techniques.

3 Architectural Assumptions and Notation

3.1 Feedback-driven Architecture

Following the earlier proposals by [4] and, especially, [18] for adaptive selectivity estimation and dynamic re-optimization of query execution plans, we assume that the database system monitors the sizes (i.e., cardinalities in the sense of bags) of intermediate results of the executed queries. Like [18], we do not assume that we can observe all data values in an intermediate result, nor their frequency or density distribution. The rationale for this limitation is that such more insightful observations incur additional run-time overhead that could slow down the underlying database engine. For example, recording the size of a range selection is more or less a byproduct of the query execution with negligible overhead, whereas observing the density of the queried range (i.e., the number of distinct values) or the frequencies of the occurring values may require sorting or, at least, hash tables, and such additional resource consumption would often be out of the question.

Run-time observations, or *feedbacks*, are collected on-the-fly and captured in a suitable form of on-line statistics. In principle, each node in a query's operator tree can provide such feedback. However, we are mostly interested in leaf nodes, which are typically selections, or nodes close to the leaves, including joins that are performed early in the overall execution (e.g., the first join in a many-way join pipeline). The rationale for this consideration is that estimation errors for the early operators are the most troublesome in that they are the biggest factors in the error propagation for the entire execution plan [14]. In this paper, we will focus on feedback from exact-match selections (typically from index lookups, i.e., not necessarily table scans) and range selections. More general notions of feedback are the subject of future work.

Our approach separates the statistical feedback obtained from the executed queries from the approximative synopsis of value distributions that we maintain for selectivity estimations. This allows us to enforce certain filtering and aggregation steps in between the statistics collection and the actual estimations, according to the desired policies and resource allocations. For example, we may want to keep a relatively large number of observations from a moving window of the most recent queries for statistical confidence, but the synopsis should be much more compact. Then we could periodically reconstruct or incrementally maintain the synopsis from the observation window. In both cases the separation of observations and the synopsis serves to smooth out fluctuations.

As mentioned in the introduction, the pursued kind of statistics collection is inherently biased in that it is fed only by the actually executed queries. Sometimes, we may wish to incorporate an additional bias into an approximative synopsis, by focusing on expensive queries (e.g., those whose actually measured run-time costs exceed a certain limit), queries that are especially susceptible to large estimation errors (e.g., those where the difference between estimated and measured run-time costs exceed a certain limit), or simply those queries that are considered particularly important by a human expert (e.g., those which are expected to have a response time below a certain tolerated limit of say 10 seconds). All these forms of bias are readily taken into account by enforcing appropriate filter conditions when statistical observations are used for rebuilding or incrementally updating a synopsis.

3.2 Notation

We adopt the notation used in [24]. Without loss of generality, we consider only countable value domains (i.e., strings and fixed-point numbers, disregarding real numbers) and assume that these domains can be encoded as integers. Thus, we can define the *domain* $\mathcal{D} = \{0, 1, 2, \ldots, N-1\}$ of an attribute X as the set of all possible values of X, and the value set $\mathcal{V} \subset \mathcal{D}, \mathcal{V} = \{v_1, \ldots v_n\}$ is the set of values actually present in the underlying relation $\mathcal{R}$. In the context of this paper, $\mathcal{V}$ is usually observed through the feedback from the executed queries. Therefore, the value set $\mathcal{V}$ may actually be only a subset of the values in relation $\mathcal{R}$ if some value ranges are never touched by the feedback-relevant queries.

The *spread* s_i of v_i is defined as $s_i = v_{i+1} - v_i$

($s_0 = v_1$ and $s_n = 1$). The *density* of attribute X in a value range from a through b, $a, b \in \mathcal{D}$, is the number of unique values $v \in \mathcal{V}$ with $a \leq v < b$. The *frequency* f_i of v_i is the number of tuples in $\mathcal{R}$ of value v_i in Attribute X. The *cumulative frequency* c_i of v_i is the number of tuples $t \in \mathcal{R}$ with $t.X \leq v_i$. The *data distribution* of X is the set of pairs $\mathcal{T} = \{(v_1, f_1), (v_2, f_2), \ldots, (v_n, f_n)\}$. The *cumulative data distribution* of X is the set of pairs $\mathcal{T}^C = \{(v_1, c_1), (v_2, c_2), \ldots, (v_n, c_n)\}$. The *extended cumulative data distribution* of X, denoted by $\mathcal{T}^{C^+}$ is $\mathcal{T}^C$ extended over the entire domain $\mathcal{D}$ by assigning zero frequency to every value in $\mathcal{D} - \mathcal{V}$. For the sake of a simple, uniform notation, we extend $\mathcal{T}$ by an artificial final tuple $(v_{n+1}, 0)$ with $v_{n+1} > v_n$.

4 Linear Splines as an Approximative Synopsis for Value Frequencies

To approximate a given value-frequency distribution $\mathcal{T}$, we partition the (observed) value set $\mathcal{V}$ into m disjoint intervals, henceforth called *buckets*, $b_i = [v_{low_i}, v_{high_i})$ in the following manner, where low_i and $high_i$ denote the *subscripts* of the values from $\mathcal{V}$ (i.e., not the actual values) that form the left and right bounds of the (left-side closed and right-side open) value interval covered by the bucket:

$$\forall i \in \{1, 2, \ldots, m-1\} : high_i = low_{i+1}$$
$$low_1 = 1, high_m = n + 1. \quad (1)$$

Unlike histograms, we approximate the frequency in an interval by a linear function, resulting in a linear spline function [5, 6] over the m buckets. Because our interest is in compact representation of distributions and not in the features more advanced forms of splines offer (smoothness, differentiability), we have chosen simple linear spline functions for this task. In contrast to previous approaches to spline-based histograms [25] we do not approximate $\mathcal{T}^{C^+}$; therefore, we are not faced with the problem of forming approximation that is continuous over all intervals, thereby simplifying the problem of finding the optimal partitioning (see Subsection 4.2).

Using a linear function $f(x) = a_1 \cdot x + a_0$ to approximate the frequencies for the values x in a bucket leads to an improvement in accuracy, depending on the *linear correlation* [26] of the data within a bucket. First, we define $\bar{v}_{[low,high)} := \frac{1}{high-low} \sum_{l=low}^{high-1} v_l$ as the *average attribute value* within $[v_{low}, v_{high})$; analogously, we define the *average frequency* $\bar{f}_{[low,high)} := \frac{1}{high-low} \sum_{l=low}^{high-1} f_l$. The *linear correlation* for interval b_i is then defined as

$$r_{[low_i,high_i)} := \frac{\sum_{l=low_i}^{high_i-1} (v_l - \bar{v}_{[low_i,high_i)})(f_l - \bar{f}_{[low_i,high_i)})}{\sqrt{\sum_{l=low_i}^{high_i-1} (v_l - \bar{v}_{[low_i,high_i)})^2} \sqrt{\sum_{l=low_i}^{high_i-1} (f_l - \bar{f}_{[low_i,high_i)})^2}} \quad (2)$$

For each interval b_i, $r_{[low_i,high_i)} \in [-1, 1]$. In traditional histograms, the frequency in a bucket b_i is approximated by $avg\_f_{[low_i,high_i)}$. Using the least-squares fit as an error metric, this results in the overall error

$$err_{[low_i,high_i)} = \sum_{l=low_i}^{high_i-1} (f_l - \bar{f}_{[low_i,high_i)})^2.$$

In a spline-based synopsis, this error becomes :

$$spline\_err_{[low_i,high_i)} = (1 - r_{[low_i,high_i)}{}^2) \cdot err_{[low_i,high_i)}. \quad (3)$$

Obviously, $spline\_err_{[low_i,high_i)}$ is always less than or equal to $err_{[low_i,high_i)}$. This increase in accuracy is paid for by the fact that each bucket in the spline-based synopsis needs to store one more value than a bucket in a traditional histogram. This trade-off will be further examined by means of experiments in Section 8. Summing the error over all buckets in the synopsis, the overall error becomes:

$$ov\_spline\_err = \sum_{i=1}^{m} \left((1 - r_{[low_i,high_i)}{}^2) \cdot err_{[low_i,high_i)} \right). \quad (4)$$

In the following subsections we will develop algorithms for constructing a spline-based synopsis with m buckets for the n observed data-value frequencies in $\mathcal{T}$, aiming to minimize the overall error according to formula 4. This goal involves identifying the $m-1$ most suitable boundaries between buckets and the fitting for the linear approximation within each bucket. We will present a polynomial but not necessarily highly efficient algorithm for an optimal solution as well as much faster heuristic and thus suboptimal algorithms. All algorithms use the least-squares fitting with a bucket as a basic building block, which is presented in the following Subsection 4.1. The optimal and suboptimal algorithms for the global partitioning are then described in Subsections 4.2 and 4.3.

4.1 Fitting the Frequency Function within a Bucket

For the derivation of this basic building block suppose that the boundaries of a bucket are already fixed. For each bucket $b_i = [v_{low_i}, v_{high_i})$ we need to calculate the linear approximation $frq_i(x) = a_1 \cdot x + a_0$ of the attribute frequency that minimizes the squared error

$$spline\_err_{[low_i,high_i)} = \sum_{l=low_i}^{high_i-1} (frq_i(v_l) - f_l)^2. \quad (5)$$

This definition of the error over a bucket is equivalent to the definition 3 [26]; however, to evaluate formula 3, the coefficients a_1 and a_0, which are the unknowns of the fitting, do not have to be known. We will use this property in Section 4.2.

Using definition 5, finding frq_i becomes a problem of *linear least squares* fitting [26]; i.e. we are fitting the data $(v_l, f_l)_{l=low_i,\ldots,high_i-1}$ via the linear function $frq(x) = \sum_{l=0}^{1} a_l \cdot X_l(x)$ with $X_1(x) = x, X_0(x) = 1$ and the optimal a_1, a_0 to be determined. To do this, we construct a *design matrix* A of $(high_i - low_i) \times 2$ components, which are defined by $A_{l,h} = X_{l-1}(v_h)$, for $l = 1, 2$ and $h = low_i, \ldots, high_i - 1$. Furthermore, we define vector $b = (f_{low_i}, \ldots, f_{high_i-1})^t$. Now the fitting problem can be defined as finding $a = \binom{a_1}{a_0}$, which minimizes

$$spline\_err_i = |A \cdot a - b|^2.$$

This problem can now be solved by Singular Value Decomposition (SVD) [26, 1] in the following way: Let the SVD of A be

$$A = U \times \Lambda \times V^t \quad \text{, with } \Lambda = \begin{bmatrix} s_1 & & \\ & \ddots & \\ & & s_{high_i - low_i} \end{bmatrix}$$

with $s_1, \ldots, s_{high_i - low_i}$ being the singular values of A (i.e., the Eigenvalues of $A \times A^T$). Then a can be expressed as

$$a = \sum_{l=1}^{2} \left(\frac{U_{(i)} \cdot b}{s_i} \right) V_{(i)}$$

, $V_{(i)}$ and $U_{(i)}$ representing the i-th column of V, U. While computing the SVD of the design matrix causes considerable overhead, it is only computed m times, namely, once for each bucket of the final partitioning. Because of formula 3, we are capable of computing the optimal partitioning of $\mathcal{D}$ without calculating the exact frq_i. In addition to frq_i, each bucket b_i stores the number of attribute values contained in b_i. We will refer to this value as the *density* $D_i := high_i - low_i$ of bucket b_i.

4.2 Optimal Partitioning of $\mathcal{V}$

We are now interested in a partitioning such that the overall error (formula 4) is minimized. When arbitrary partitionings and continuous splines of arbitrary degree are considered, this is known as the *optimal knot placement problem* [5], which – due to its complexity – is generally solved only approximatively by heuristic search algorithms (for a detailed discussion, see [6]).

In our case, however, only linear splines are used and only members of $\mathcal{V}$ are candidates for bucket boundaries. Since the value for each $high_i$ is either low_{i+1} or v_{n+1} (see definition 1), we only need to determine the optimal lower bucket boundaries to compute:

$$opt\_err := \min_{\substack{(low_2,\ldots,low_m) \in \mathcal{V}^{m-1} \\ low_1 \le low2 \le \ldots \le low_m}} \sum_{l=1}^{m} (1 - r_{[low_l, high_l)}{}^2) \cdot err_{[low_l, high_l)} \qquad (6)$$

Because the resulting spline function is allowed to be discontinuous over the chosen intervals $b_1, \ldots, b_m$, fitting the data in a bucket can be addressed separately for each bucket b_i. The main improvement in efficiency does, however, result from the fact that the following *principle of optimality* (also known as the Bellman principle) holds for our partitioning problem:

Theorem:

If for $l \ge 2$: $(low_l, low_{l+1}, \ldots, low_m) \in \mathcal{V}^{m-l+1}$ is an optimal partitioning of $[v_{low_{l-1}}, v_{high_m})$ using $m - l + 2$ buckets, then $(low_{l+1}, low_{l+2}, \ldots, low_m) \in \mathcal{V}^{m-l}$ is an optimal partitioning of $[v_{low_l}, v_{high_m})$ using $m - l + 1$ buckets.

Proof:

Because $(low_l, low_{l+1}, \ldots, low_m)$ is optimal, it minimizes

$$E := \sum_{i=l-1}^{m} spline\_err_{[low_i, high_i)}$$

$$= spline\_err_{[low_{l-1}, high_{l-1})} + \sum_{i=l}^{m} spline\_err_{[low_i, high_i)}.$$

Now assume that $(low_{l+1}, \ldots, low_m)$ is not optimal, i.e. there exists a partitioning $(low'_{l+1}, \ldots, low'_m)$ with $\sum_{i=l}^{m} spline\_err_{[low'_i, high'_i)} < \sum_{i=l}^{m} spline\_err_{[low_i, high_i)}$. But then $(low_l, \ldots, low_m)$ is not optimal either, for the partitioning $(low_l, low'_{l+1}, low'_{l+2}, \ldots, low_m)$ results in the overall error $E' = spline\_err_{[low_{l-1}, high_{l-1})} + \sum_{i=l}^{m} spline\_err_{[low'_i, hig'h_i)} < E$.

Because of this property, the problem of finding an optimal partitioning can be seen as a *dynamic programming problem* [27]. This allows us to formulate a recursive redefinition of formula 6: Define

$opt\_err_{low,\bar{m}}$:= the optimal overall error for fitting $[v_{low}, v_n)$ by $\bar{m}$ buckets.

$err_{[low,high)}$:= the approximation error $spline\_err_i$ for bucket $b_i = [v_{low}, v_{high})$.

Trivially, $opt\_err_{i,1} = err_{[i,n)}$. Then the overall error produced by the optimal partitioning is

$$opt\_err_{1,m} = \min_{l \in \{1,2,\ldots,n\}} err_{[1,l]} + opt\_err_{l,m-1}. \qquad (7)$$

By keeping track of the partitioning, this equation can be used to compute an optimal partitioning in $O(m \cdot n^2)$ time, using $O(n^2)$ space. In the experimental section 8, we will refer to this algorithm as $OPTIMAL$.

4.3 Greedy Partitioning

Even if a spline-based synopsis were to be recomputed only occasionally, the cost for computing an optimal partitioning could be unacceptable when n is large. Therefore, we have also developed a greedy method of partitioning of $\mathcal{V}$, which results in a partitioning that is close to optimal while being much more efficient. The key idea is to start out with a large number (e.g., n) of trivial buckets, (e.g., each interval between two adjacent observed data values leads to one bucket), and then gradually merge appropriately chosen adjacent buckets until we arrive at the desired number of m buckets. We will refer to this algorithm as *GREEDY-MERGE*.

In assessing the approximation quality of the buckets in each stage of the algorithm, we exploit the fact that, when merging the data distribution of 2 adjacent buckets $b_1 = [v_a, v_b)$ and $b_2 = [v_b, v_c)$ into one bucket $b' = [v_a, v_c)$, we can compute the resulting $spline\_err_{[a,c)}$ (formula 3) in constant time, if we maintain certain statistics for each bucket $b_i = [v_{low_i}, v_{high_i})$. These statistics are:

$$ff_{[low_i,high_i)} := \sum_{l=low_i}^{high_i-1} f_l^2, \qquad vv_{[low_i,high_i)} := \sum_{l=low_i}^{high_i-1} v_l^2,$$

$$vf_{[low_i,high_i)} := \sum_{l=low_i}^{high_i-1} v_l \cdot f_l, \qquad f_{[low_i,high_i)} := \sum_{l=low_i}^{high_i-1} f_l \quad (8)$$

$$v_{[low_i,high_i)} := \sum_{l=low_i}^{high_i-1} v_l,\ \bar{v}_{[low_i,high_i)} \text{ and } \bar{f}_{[low_i,high_i)}.$$

Now, when merging buckets $b_1 = [v_a, v_b)$ and $b_2 = [v_b, v_c)$ we can recompute these values for the resulting bucket in constant time:

$$\bar{v}_{[a,c)} = \frac{\bar{v}_{[a,b)} \cdot (b-a) + \bar{v}_{[b,c)} \cdot (c-b)}{(c-a)},$$

$\bar{f}_{[a,c)}$ is computed analogously, and the summations are obtained by simply adding the values for each bucket. These values now allow us to compute a bucket's linear correlation $r_{[a,c)}$ in constant time:

$$r_{[a,c)} =$$

$$\frac{vf_{[a,c)} - f_{[a,c)}\bar{v}_{[a,c)} - v_{[a,c)}\bar{f}_{[a,c)} + (c-a)\bar{v}_{[a,c)}\bar{f}_{[a,c)}}{\sqrt{vv_{[a,c)} - 2\bar{v}_{[a,c)}v_{[a,c)} + (c-a)\bar{v}^2_{[a,c)}}\sqrt{ff_{[a,c)} - 2\bar{f}_{[a,c)}f_{[a,c)} + (c-a)\bar{f}^2_{[a,c)}}}$$

$$= \frac{\sum_{l=a}^{c-1} v_l f_l - \bar{v}_{[a,c)} \sum_{l=a}^{c-1} f_l - \bar{f}_{[a,c)} \sum_{l=a}^{c-1} v_l + \sum_{l=a}^{c-1} \bar{f}_{[a,c)}\bar{v}_{[a,c)}}{\sqrt{\sum_{l=a}^{c-1} v_l{}^2 - 2\bar{v}_{[a,c)} \sum_{l=a}^{c-1} v_l + \sum_{l=a}^{c-1} \bar{v}^2_{[a,c)}}\sqrt{\sum_{l=a}^{c-1} f_l{}^2 - 2\bar{f}_{[a,c)} \sum_{l=a}^{c-1} f_l + \sum_{l=a}^{c-1} \bar{f}^2_{[a,c)}}}$$

$$= \frac{\sum_{l=a}^{c-1} (v_l - \bar{v}_{[a,c)})(f_l - \bar{f}_{[a,c)})}{\sqrt{\sum_{l=a}^{c-1} (v_l - \bar{v}_{[a,c)})^2}\sqrt{\sum_{l=a}^{c-1} (f_l - \bar{f}_{[a,c)})^2}}, \text{ corresponding to (2).}$$

Now, the resulting error can easily be computed as

$$spline\_err_{[a,c)} = (1 - r_{[a,c)}{}^2) \cdot (ff_{[a,c)} - 2 \cdot \bar{f}_{[a,c)} \cdot f_{[a,c)} + (c-a) \cdot \bar{f}^2_{[a,c)}).$$

Based on these equations, we can now compute a nearly optimal partitioning using a greedy heuristics in $O(n \log_2 n)$ time. The algorithm partitions $\mathcal{V}$ into $\frac{n}{2}$ trivial buckets and merges the ones that lead to the smallest increase in the overall error, until only m buckets are left (see algorithm 1). The algorithm consists of 2 loops; the **for**-loop has $\frac{n}{2}$ iterations in which the error of merging the trivial buckets is computed, which can be done in constant time. The **repeat**-loop is executed $\frac{n}{2} - m$ times (each repetition reduces the number of buckets by one, there are $\frac{n}{2}$ buckets initially, and m upon termination), and executes 4 different types of operations:

Partition $\mathcal{V}$ into $\frac{n}{2}$ buckets $b_i = [v_{2i-1}, v_{2i+1})$.
for $l = 0$ to $\frac{n}{2}$ **do**
  Compute the $error_{[2l-1,2l+1),[2l+1,2l+3)}$ resulting from merging the buckets b_l and $b_l + 1$ and insert the value into *queue* Q.
end for
repeat
Remove the minimal $error_{[a,b),[b,c)}$ from Q.
Merge the buckets $[a,b)$ and $[b,c)$.
Remove $error_{[a',a),[a,b)}$, $error_{[b,c),[c,c')}$ from Q.
Calculate the error of joining the new bucket with it's left and right neighbor (if exist); insert the resulting $error_{[a',a),[a,c)}$, $error_{[a,c),[c,c')}$ into Q.
until There are only m buckets left.

Algorithm 1: GREEDY-MERGE

1. Removing an item from the *priority queue* Q. We use an implementation of priority queues based on *Fibonacci heaps* [22], allowing the removal of an item in a queue of size n in $O(\log_2 n)$ time.

2. Merging two buckets, requiring constant time.

3. Calculating the error resulting from a merge, requiring constant time.

4. Inserting an item into Q, again requiring $O(\log_2 n)$ time.

Since each operation is carried out no more than three times, computing a greedy partitioning is of complexity $O(n \log_2 n)$.

The initial memory requirement is the space necessary for storing $\frac{n}{2}$ buckets, each of which contains 8 values (the lowest value stored in the bucket and the statistics detailed in definition 8), resulting in storage overhead of $4n$ values. If – due to the size of n – this overhead were not acceptable, one could further reduce the constant by choosing bigger initial buckets; for large n, this would probably not have any significant effect on the approximation quality of the partitioning. Choosing initial buckets of size 2^h leads to a storage overhead of $2^{3-h} \cdot n$ values.

Using a similar approach we developed an additional greedy partitioning-algorithm, which takes the opposite approach: Initially, all tuples are grouped in one bucket. Now, we will compute the split that leads to the greatest reduction in the overall error (formula 4) and execute it, resulting in an additional bucket. This is repeated, until (after $m - 1$ splits)

m buckets remain. Due to space constraints we do not go into more detail here. The algorithm requires $O(m \cdot n \log_2 n)$ time and $O(n)$ space. We will refer to this algorithm as *GREEDY-SPLIT*.

4.4 Running Times

In order to obtain an idea of the algorithms' efficiency in practice, we measured the running times of each partitioning method for different sizes of m and n (the v_i and f_i were choosen randomly, using a uniform distribution). The resulting running times for the partitioning methods *OPTIMAL* (*OPT*), *GREEDY-SPLIT* (*G-S*) and *GREEDY-MERGE* (*G-M*) for execution on a single processor of a *SUN UltraSPARC 4000/5000* (168 MHz) are shown in Table 1.

$n =$	500		1000		4000	
$m =$	10	50	10	50	10	50
OPT	0.59	2.13	2.78	11.04	46.52	191.6
G-S	0.009	0.008	0.019	0.021	0.069	0.068
G-M	0.001	0.007	0.004	0.020	0.042	0.153

Table 1: Running times in seconds

5 Result-Size Estimation for Range Queries

In this section we demonstrate how the spline-based synopsis of data-value distributions can be exploited by the procedure for estimating the intermediate result sizes of queries. Here we restrict ourselves to the estimation problem for simple range queries on a single attribute.

To estimate the result sizes of range queries, it is necessary to estimate the number of tuples whose attribute values for the range condition fall within an interval $[v_a, v_b)$, with $a, b \in \mathcal{D}$ being the query-specific actual parameters. The number of result tuples for such a range query is denoted by $S_{[a,b)}$. In order to account for skewed frequency distributions within a bucket, we need to inspect the spline functions of all buckets that intersect with the query range. This leads to the following estimation: If the query range happens to correspond to the boundaries of a bucket b_i, i.e. $a = low_i$, $b = high_i$, then $S_{[a,b)}$ is estimated by computing the cumulative frequency over the bucket, i.e., the sum of the value frequencies of the bucket, under the assumption that the attribute values that occur in the data and fall into b_i are equidistant within the bucket's spread. The number of values in the bucket, i.e., the bucket's density, is denoted as D_i. This yields the following expression for S^i, which we write instead of S when limited to a single bucket b_i:

$$S^i_{[low_i,high_i)} := \sum_{l=0}^{D_i-1} frq_i\left(low_i + l \cdot \tfrac{high_i-1-low_i}{D_i}\right) \quad (9)$$

$$= \left(\beta_i + \tfrac{\alpha_i\cdot(low_i+(high_i-1))}{2}\right)\cdot D_i + \tfrac{\alpha_i\cdot(low_i-(high_i-1))}{2}.$$

Here the coefficients of the linear spline for b_i are denoted as α_i and β_i rather than a_1 and a_0, respectively, to make the dependency on bucket b_i more explicit. It is important to note that, although we assume an *identical spread* of the attribute values in b_i just like in histograms, our approach is more powerful since it allows us to properly capture a skew in the cumulative tuple distribution *within* each bucket.

For intervals that do not correspond to bucket boundaries, the density D_i needs to be multiplied with the fraction of the bucket covered by the query. If the query interval is completely contained in bucket b_i, i.e. $a \geq low_i, b < high_i$, we define $p_{[a,b),i} := \frac{b-a}{high_i-low_i}$ and obtain

$$S^i_{[a,b)} := \sum_{l=0}^{\lfloor D_j\cdot p_{[a,b),i}\rfloor-1} frq_j\left(a + l \cdot \tfrac{high_j-1-low_j}{D_j\cdot p_{[a,b),j}}\right). \quad (10)$$

This equation can be transformed into the form $S^i_{[a,b]} = \gamma \cdot D_i + \delta$ with constants γ and δ that can be efficiently calculated from a, b, low_i, $high_i$, α_i, β_i, and D_i, but does not involve any summations over D_i. This ensures that the calculation of a range-query selectivity estimation requires only constant time for each bucket. Finally, the result size of range queries for intervals spanning more than one bucket can easily be estimated by partitioning $[v_a, v_b)$ into $[v_a, v_{high_j})$, $[v_{low_{j+1}, high_{j+1}})$, ..., $[v_{low_{j+l-1}}, v_{high_{j+l-1}})$, $[v_{low_{j+l}}, v_b)$ and summing the estimated result sizes obtained by the above formulas:

$$S_{[a,b)} := S^j_{[a,high_j)} + \left(\sum_{h=1}^{l-1} S^{j+h}_{[low_{j+h},high_{j+h})}\right) + S^{j+l}_{[low_{j+l},b)}. \quad (11)$$

6 Improved Fitting of Value Densities

So far the density of a bucket, i.e., the number of distinct values that fall into the bucket's value interval, is simply based on counting the distinct exact-match queries in the observed statistics (see Section 4.1). Once we have formed buckets, we lose the information on the value distribution within a bucket and need to resort to the assumption of equidistant values. This assumption, however, can lead to significant distortions in the result-size estimations for range queries if there is a skew in the actually occurring values. To illustrate this kind of estimation error, consider a simple example with a bucket b_i ranging from $v_{low_i} = 10$ to $v_{high_i} = 20$ with actually observed value-frequency pairs $\{(v_l, f_l) \mid low_i \leq l \leq high_i - 1\} = \{(10,100), (11,90), (12,80), (13,70), (19,10)\}$. So the majority of the observed values lie in the first half of the bucket, and these values are also much more frequent. The spline function that results from the fitting according to Subsection 4.1 is $frq_i(v) = -10v + 200$ (which actually has zero error for the particularly assumed frequencies in this bucket). The density D_i of the bucket simply equals $high_i - low_i = 5$, i.e., the number of observed values. Now suppose that range queries mostly refer to intervals in the first half of the bucket, which may not be surprising at all given that this is where we have observed more data values. (But note that, in general, the distribution of the data does not have to be correlated with the distribution of the actual query parameters.) Then, not taking into account the skew in the value density within the bucket would lead to a significant estimation error for such range queries. For example, the result size of a range query $S_{[10,16)}$ for an interval from 10 through 16 would be estimated as $frq(10) + frq(13) + frq(16) = 100 + 70 + 40 = 210$ based on the equidistant-values assumption and the fact that the query range covers $\frac{3}{5}$ of the bucket interval. The actual result size, however, is $100 + 90 + 80 + 70 = 340$, quite a large deviation from the estimated size.

To rectify the discussed kind of problem, we adjust the density values D_i that are kept for the buckets of a spline-based synopsis by considering additional feedback from range queries. This leads to another fitting problem that aims to minimize the estimation error for range queries. Note, however, that this is addressed as a subsidiary issue which leaves the previously completed fitting of the frequency values (according to Section 4) invariant and only aims to adjust the density values for reducing the estimation error. Again, we are driven by adapting our estimations to the skew in queries, to obtain a more accurate estimation for frequently queried intervals, at the expense of a larger error for less important ones. For this task, we examine a set of query feedbacks from range queries $F := \{([a_j, b_j), size_j), j = 1, \ldots, k\}$ with $size_j = \sum_{\nu | a_j \le v_\nu < b_j} f_\nu$ being the total number of tuples (i.e., counting duplicates) in interval $[a_j, b_j)$. We are interested in finding the optimal D_i, such that

$$\tilde{E} := \sum_{j=1}^{k} (size_j - S_{[a_j,b_j)})^2$$

is minimized where the $S_{[a_j,b_j)}$ are the estimated result sizes for the most recent k observed range queries. Now, $S_{[a_j,b_j]}$ can be rewritten as (cf. formula 9):

$$S_{[a_j,b_j)} = \Big(\sum_{l=0}^{m} \gamma_{j,l} \cdot D_i\Big) + \delta_j \qquad (12)$$

The problem of finding the optimal D_i values that minimize the error $\tilde{E}$ can be formulated as a problem of *linear least squares*. Here, the *design matrix* A holds $k \times m$ components. We define

$$A_{jl} := \gamma_{j,l} \text{ for } j = 1, \ldots, k \text{ and } l = 1, \ldots, m$$

and $b = \begin{pmatrix} size_1 - \delta_1 \\ \vdots \\ size_k - \delta_k \end{pmatrix}$. Now the fitting problem can be defined as finding $a = \begin{pmatrix} D_1 \\ \vdots \\ D_m \end{pmatrix}$ that minimizes $\tilde{E} := |A \cdot a - b|^2$.

We can again compute a using an SVD [26], analogously to Section 4.1. One drawback of this approach is that the space requirement of A and b increase in proportion to the number of query feedbacks k, resulting in considerable overhead when "fitting" long series of query feedbacks. However, since the feedback arrives incrementally, we can use an iterative fitting technique know as the *recursive least squares regression* [29]. For this incremental approach, we only need to maintain two $m \times m$ matrices, as opposed to a $k \times m$ matrix. These matrices are updated with each feedback (for a detailed description of *recursive least squares regression* in the context of database-query feedback, see [4]). Since m (i.e, the number of buckets) is a rather small constant, the resulting overhead for the fitting is affordable.

7 Result-Size Estimation for Projections and Grouping Queries

The density of attribute values, i.e., the number of distinct values within certain ranges, is the decisive information for estimating the result sizes of projections with duplicate elimination. Although such projections themselves are not among the most critical operators as far as query optimization is concerned, implicit projections take place also in grouping and aggregation operators. The latter are definitely among the most important operators in modern decision-support applications. In this section we show how the size of projections in combination with a range-filter condition can be estimated from our approximative synopses.

We denote the number of distinct values that fall into interval $[v_a, v_b)$ by $P_{[a,b)}$. When the query range corresponds to the boundaries of a bucket b_i, $P^i_{[low_i,high_i)}$ is simply approximated by D_i. If $[v_a, v_b)$ is completely contained in b_i, $P^i_{[a,b)} := p_{[a,b),i} \cdot D_i$, where $p_{[a,b),i}$ is the fraction of the bucket's interval covered by the query range (see Section 5). Finally, for intervals spanning multiple buckets, the result-size estimation can be obtained using an partitioning similar to the one employed in formula 11:

$$P_{[a,b)} := P^j_{[a,high_j)} + \Big(\sum_{h=1}^{l-1} P^{j+h}_{[low_{j+h},high_{j+h})}\Big) + P^{j+l}_{low_{[j+l,b)}}.$$

8 Experimental Results

In this section we present experimental results, using synthetic data sets. In order to illustrate the effectiveness of our approach, we compare its accuracy for several estimations problems to histograms proposed in [24, 25].

8.1 Experimental Comparison of the Estimation for Exact-Match Queries

We have experimentally studied the accuracy of several techniques for approximating and estimating the result size of exact-match queries of type $size_i = \{t \in R \mid t.A = v_i\}$. We compared the spline-based synopsis developed in Section 4 to the well-studied *equi-depth* and *equi-width* as well as *MaxDiff(V,A)* [25] and *V-optimal(V,F)* [17] histograms.

Because our technique stores four values per bucket (low value bound, frequency of the low value bound, slope of the frequency curve, and density), whereas traditional histograms store only three (low value bound, average frequency, density), our technique uses only $\frac{3}{4}$ of the buckets of traditional histograms in the experiments. As error measure we again use the squared-error norm: with $size_i$ denoting the actual result size of query i and S'_i the size-approximation, we measure $\sum_i (size_i - S'_i)^2$. We have studied a variety

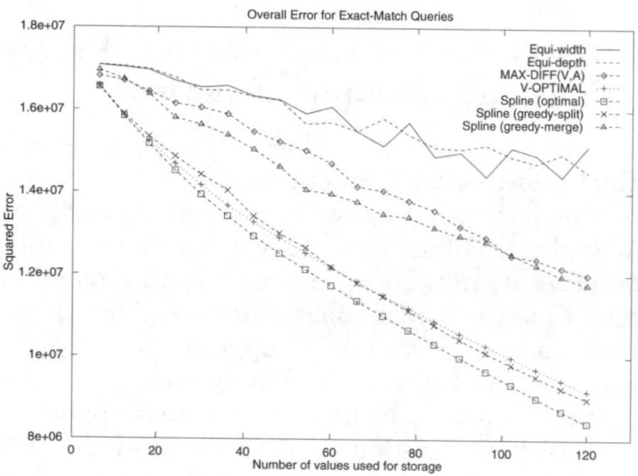

Figure 1: Squared error of various techniques

of data distributions, including the synthetic data sets from earlier studies on histograms, real-life data sets like the NBA database [23], and also completely random data. All of these produced comparable results as far as the estimation accuracy of the studied algorithms is concerned. Here we restrict ourselves to presenting the results for a single synthetic distribution: The value set size is $n = 500$, the domain size is $N = 4096$, and the relation size is $|R| = 10^5$. The data distribution was generated by assigning the individual frequencies randomly, using an uniform distribution. Note that this poses some form of stress test for the various approximation methods, as the data exhibits both highly skewed frequencies and high irregularity. Furthermore, the data distribution exhibits only low linear correlation, thereby minimizing the gain resulting from the use of linear spline approximation. For this experiment, Figure 1 shows the squared error of the various methods under comparison as a function of the number of values that each method can store with a given amount of memory space. So the number of buckets is 1/4 of the number of stored values for the spline-based synopsis, and 1/3 of the number of stored values for the histograms. As the figure shows, the optimal spline-based synopsis performs better than all histograms, while *GREEDY-SPLIT* and *V-optimal* histograms offer comparable accuracy. In data distributions of higher linear correlation, the optimal spline-based synopsis again outperforms all other methods, however, the *GREEDY-SPLIT* and *GREEDY-MERGE* partitioning also surpass the accuracy of all histogram methods. To illustrate the enhanced accuracy of our approach, Figure 2 shows two examples for the fitting of a completely random distribution (i.e., uniformly distributed frequencies) with $n = 30$ different attribute values. Both MaxDiff histograms and the spline-based synopsis adapt themselves to the data in that they choose smaller bucket widths for ranges with high fluctuations. In addition, however, the spline-based synopsis enables us to capture trends within certain ranges of the data, whereas histograms merely reflect average frequencies in these ranges.

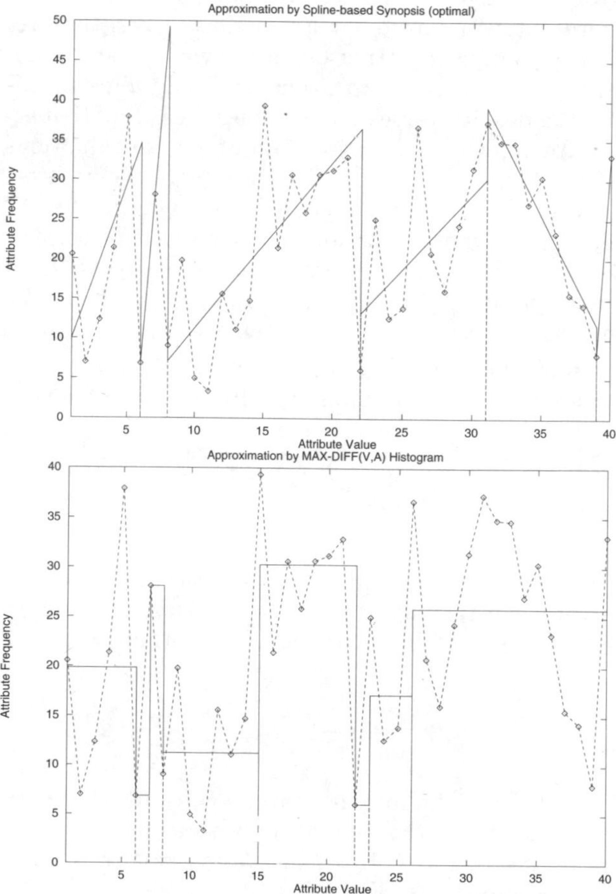

Figure 2: Illustration of approximation quality

8.2 Experimental Comparison of the Estimation for Range-Queries

Using the synthetic data set described in Subsection 8.1, we have also examined the accuracy of the various techniques for estimating the size of range queries, using the techniques of Section 4. We considered the following types:
$A:\{X<b \mid b\in\mathcal{D}\}$, $C:\{a\leq X<b \mid a,b\in\mathcal{D}, a\leq b\}$,
$B:\{X<b \mid b\in\mathcal{V}\}$, $D:\{a\leq X<b \mid a,b\in\mathcal{V}, a\leq b\}$,
$E:\{a\leq X<a+\Delta \mid a\in\mathcal{D}\}$, $F:\{a\leq X<a+\Delta \mid a\in\mathcal{V}\}$
with a, b randomly chosen from the underlying value sets according to a uniform distribution.

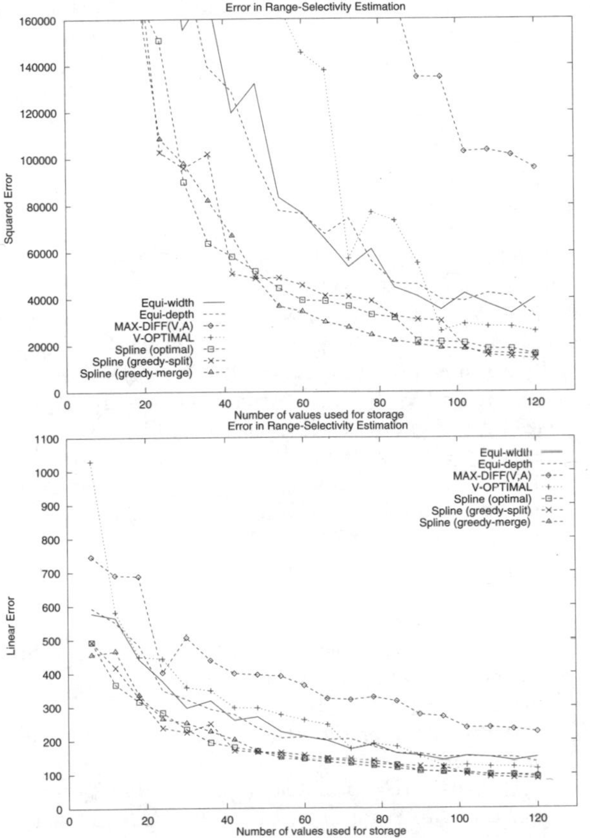

Figure 3: Squared and linear error for range queries

In Figure 3 we show the experimental results for query type A; the experiments for the other query types showed the same qualitative results and are thus omitted here. In order to illustrate that our algorithm – while geared for the least-squares error metric – also results in good estimations with respect to other error metrics, we show the average linear error of a query in addition to the squared error. The *MaxDiff(V,A)* histogram exhibits the worst accuracy in its estimations because of the intricacies of the data set: the data contains many large "jumps" in the frequencies of subsequent attribute values, thereby producing several very small buckets. Interestingly, the optimal partitioning does not always lead to the optimal overall error for range queries; this is due to the fact that the partitioning is initially geared towards minimizing the error for exact-match queries rather than range queries. However, the chart shows that all partitioning techniques for spline-based synopses perform almost equally well, surpassing the histogram-techniques. Again, when using data of higher linear correlation, this trend becomes more clear.

9 Conclusion and Future Work

In this paper we have developed a novel approach to query result-size estimation based on a feedback-driven approximative representation using linear splines that are allowed to be discontinuous across buckets. To the best of our knowledge, this is the first approach that combines the adaptivity with regard to evolving query locality (i.e., actual parameters of the queries) with a very high accuracy of the estimations even in the presence of highly irregular, skewed distributions. In fact, our experimental studies have shown that the spline-based synopses are superior to histograms in terms of accuracy.

The main issue that we have addressed and solved is the fitting of the free parameters of a spline-based synopsis to the observed query feedbacks. This has involved both finding appropriate bucket boundaries – the partitioning problem – and a least-squares regression for each bucket. We have seen that the initial feedback from exact-match queries that we have considered can be enhanced by additional feedback from range queries for an improved fitting of the density value kept in each bucket. However, it has to be noted that there is the unresolvable tension in fitting these values for different query types such as range queries versus projections or grouping/aggregation queries (unless we wanted to keep different synopses for different query types at the expense of more memory space). Our preference for range queries was mostly driven by the observation that estimation errors in the earliest operators typically have the most severe impact as the error propagates through the operator tree.

Extending our technique for spline-based synopses to multiple dimensions (i.e., attribute combinations) is relatively straightforward; however, some open issues remain. When fitting d-dimensional data $\left((v_{i,1},\ldots,v_{i,d}), f_i\right)_{i=1,\ldots,n}$, we partition the data space into a mesh consisting of m^d d-dimensional intervals determined m observed data points. While the approximation of a multidimensional frequency function for each bucket is straightforward (fitting via SVD for $d+1$ coefficients), we are in the process of studying good partitioning techniques that can be computed in acceptable time.

The techniques described in this paper can be further extended to the fitting of feedback generated by equi-join queries. When computing the result size of a join over an interval $b_i=[a,b)$, the decisive factor for an accurate estimation of the join size is the accuracy in estimating the number of joining values t_i from the two relations whose join-attribute values fall into b_i. While a number of heuristics that estimate t_i from the interval's density (i.e., its number of distinct values) have been put forth in the literature, to the best of our knowledge none of these techniques are very accurate for arbitrary distributions of the occurring join-attribute values. An approach that we are pursuing is to exploit feedback from equi-join queries by observing and keeping the number of join tuples within observable value intervals for each pair of frequently joined relations (while resorting to simpler heuristics for infrequent join relations). For a given join with t_i joining values in a join-attribute interval $b_i = [a, b)$, the join result size would be estimated from the value-frequency synopses of the two relations $\mathcal{R}_1, \mathcal{R}_2$ as follows:

$$S_{[a,b)} = \sum_{i=0}^{t_i - 1} frq_i^{\mathcal{R}_1}\left(a + \frac{i}{t_i}(b-a)\right) \cdot frq_i^{\mathcal{R}_2}\left(a + \frac{i}{t_i}(b-a)\right).$$

Our approach would then aim to determine a fitting for the t_i values into a compact synopsis (whose number of buckets is much smaller than that of the observed t values and result sizes). Unfortunately, $S_{[a,b)}$ can not be rewritten as a function that is linear in t_i, thereby making least-squares fitting infeasible. Instead, $S_{[a,b)} = \Lambda \cdot t_i + \Phi + \frac{\Delta}{t_i}$, which can be fit with adequate accuracy using iterative numerical techniques [26].

References

[1] D. Barbará, W. DuMochel, C. Faloutsos, P.J. Haas, J.M. Hellerstein, Y. Ioannidis, H.V. Jagadish, T. Johnson, R. Ng, V. Poosala, K.A. Ross, and K.C. Sevcik. The New Jersey Data Reduction Report. Technical report, 1997.

[2] S. Chaudhuri. An overview of query optimization in relational systems. In *ACM PODS*, pages 34–43, 1998.

[3] S. Chaudhuri, R. Motwani, and V.R. Narasayya. Random sampling for histogram construction: How much is enough? In *Proc. of the ACM SIGMOD Conference*, pages 436–447, 1998.

[4] C.M. Chen and N. Roussoploulos. Adaptive selectivity estimation using query feedback. In *Proc. of the ACM SIGMOD Conference*, pages 161–172, May 1994.

[5] C. de Boor. *A practical guide to splines.* Springer-Verlag, 1978.

[6] P. Dierckx. *Curve and Surface Fitting with Splines.* Monographs on numerical Analysis. Oxford Science Publications, 1993.

[7] S. Ganguly, P.B. Gibbons, Y. Matias, and A. Silberschatz. Bifocal sampling for skew-resistant join-size estimation. In *Proc. of the ACM SIGMOD Conf*, 1996.

[8] P.B. Gibbons and Y. Matias. New Sampling-Based Summary Statistics for Improving Approximate Query Answers. In *Proceedings of the ACM SIGMOD Conference*, 1998.

[9] P.B. Gibbons and Y. Matias. Synopsis data structures for massive data sets. Tech. report, Bell Labs, 1998.

[10] P.B. Gibbons, Y. Matias, and V. Poosala. Fast Incremental Maintenance of Approximate Histograms. In *Proc. of the 23rd VLDB Conference*, 1997.

[11] Phillip B. Gibbons, S. Acharya, Y. Bartal, Y. Matias, S. Muthukishnan, V. Poosala, S. Ramaswamy, and T. Suel. AQUA: System and techniques for approximate query answering. Tech. report, Bell Labs, 1998.

[12] Peter J. Haas. Selectivity and cost estimation for joins based on random sampling. *Journal of Computer and System Sciences*, pages 550–569, 1996.

[13] Y. Ioannidis. Univeratility of Serial Histograms. In *Proceedings of the 19th VLDB Conference*, pages 256–267, December 1993.

[14] Y. Ioannidis and S. Christodoulakis. On the propagation of errors in the size of join results. In *Proc. of ACM SIGMOD Conf.*, pages 268–277, 1991.

[15] Y. Ioannidis and S. Christodoulakis. Optimal Histograms for limiting Worst-Case Error Propagation in the Size of Join Results. In *ACM TODS*, 1993.

[16] Y. Ioannidis and V. Poosala. Balancing Histogram Optimality and Practicality for Query Result Size Estimation. In *Proceedings of the ACM SIGMOD Conference*, pages 233–244, May 1995.

[17] H. V. Jagadish, N. Koudas, S. Mutukrishnan, V. Poosala, K. Sevcik, and T. Suel. Optimal Histograms with Quality Guarantees. In *Proc. of the 24th Int. VLDB Conf.*, pages 275–286, August 1998.

[18] N. Kabra and D.J. DeWitt. Efficient mid-query reoptimization of sub-optimal query execution plans. In *Proceedings of the ACM SIGMOD Conference*, 1998.

[19] Y. Ling and W. Sun. An evaluation of sampling-based size estimation methods for selections in database systems. In *Proc. of the ICDE Conf.*, 1995.

[20] M.V. Mannino, P. Chu, and T. Sager. Statistical Profile Estimation in Databbase Systems. In *ACM Computing Serveys*, 1988.

[21] Y. Matias, J.S. Vitter, and M. Wang. Wavelet-Based Histograms for Selectivity Estimation. In *Proc. of the ACM SIGMOD Conf.*, pages 448–459, 1998.

[22] K. Mehlhorn, S. Näher, and C. Uhrig. LEDA: Library of Efficient Data types and Algorithms. available via ftp:mpi-sb.mpg.de, 1997.

[23] NBA Statistics for the 91-92 Season. available under: ftp:olympos.cs.umd.edu.

[24] V. Poosala. *Histogram-based Estimation Techniques in Database Systems.* PhD thesis, University of Wisconsin-Madison, 1997.

[25] V. Poosala, Y.E. Ioannidis, P.J. Haas, and E.J. Shekita. Improved Histograms for Selectivity Estimation or Range Predicates. In *Proc. of the 1996 ACM SIGMOD Conference on the Management of Data*, pages 294–305. ACM Press, 1996.

[26] W.H. Press, S.A. Teukolsky, W.T. Vetterling, and B.P Flannery. *Numerical Receipes in C, The Art of Scientific Computing.* Cambridge University Press, 1996.

[27] M. Sniedovich. *Dynamic Programming.* Marcel Dekker, Inc., 1992.

[28] W. Sun, Y. Ling, N. Rishe, and Y. Deng. An instant and accurate size estimation method for joins and selections in an retrival-intensive environment. In *Proc. of the ACM SIGMOD Conference*, pages 79–88, 1993.

[29] P. Young. *Recursive Estimation and Time-Series Analysis.* Springer-Verlag, 1984.

Integrating Heterogeneous Overlapping Databases Through Object-Oriented Transformations

Vanja Josifovski
Laboratory for Engineering Databases
Linköping University, Sweden
vanja@ida.liu.se

Tore Risch
Laboratory for Engineering Databases
Linköping University, Sweden
torri@ida.liu.se

Abstract

Integration of data from autonomous and heterogeneous data sources often requires means to mediate and reconcile overlaps and conflicts between the integrated data. It is also desirable that the mediator system stores local data associated with the data from the sources. Achieving acceptable query response time for a mediator system has been a known research problem. This work presents a mediator query processing framework based on a representation of the data mediation and reconciliation by a number of auxiliary system-defined object-oriented (OO) views and overloaded functions (queries). The framework is supported by defining an overloading and late binding mechanism for the OO views through declarative queries. A query over the mediated OO views will have late bound subquery invocations which are transformed into disjunctive query expressions. Consistency and completeness of the queries are guaranteed by expanding the queries with validation subqueries. Performance is improved by type aware query rewrites and selective OID generation in the mediators. Experiments show that the proposed query optimization dramatically improves the query execution time compared to a naive instance-oriented query strategy or partial strategies.

1 Introduction

Modern organizations often need to combine heterogeneous data from different data sources. Tools and infra-structures for *data integration* are required. Data integration using the *wrapper-mediator* architecture [19] with an Object-Oriented (OO) data model is a popular approach to integration of heterogeneous databases [2, 4, 5, 9, 10, 12, 18]. With this approach, the data sources are encapsulated in *wrappers* which interface the data sources using a common query language and a common data model (CDM). The role of the *mediators* is to provide a semantically coherent CDM view of the combined data from the wrapped data sources.

The data and the meta-data (schema) in the sources can have conflicting and overlapping portions. For example, two universities can each have employee databases organized in different ways with corresponding entities bearing different names. Also, there might exist employees employed by both universities. A comprehensive classification of these conflicts can be found in [3]. In this work we will concentrate on a framework for mediating a coherent view of databases in presence of *structural conflicts*, where attributes modeling the same real world property does not match in name and/or value, and *entity overlap conflicts* where there is an overlap of the sets of real-world entities represented by the data in the sources.

In particular, this paper deals with managing OO mediator views defined as unions of real-world entities from other mediators and data sources. Our mediating union views are modeled by a mechanism called *integrated union types* (IUTs) based on OO queries and views. The IUTs model unions of real-world concepts similar to [4, 5], and opposed to unions of type extents from different databases as in [18, 10]. IUTs have *reconciliation* facilities which allow the user to specify how overlaps and conflicts between data from different sources are resolved.

Users and applications using a mediator often need to associate some locally relevant data to the data integrated from the data sources. We call such mediators, permitting local methods and attributes in the OO views, *capacity augmenting mediators.* Capacity augmentation for the IUTs is achieved by making the instances of the IUTs first class objects with their own OIDs that can be used in locally stored attributes and methods as ordinary OIDs.

The data sources are autonomous and can be updated outside the control of the mediators. The system

Proceedings of the 25th VLDB Conference, Edinburgh, Scotland, 1999.

must therefore guarantee the consistency and completeness of queries to the capacity augmented mediators. Our framework for IUTs guarantees that queries to the mediators are consistent and complete when the data sources are updated without any need for a notification mechanism. The queries over the integrated views always return *all* answers that qualify the query condition, and *only* those answers that qualify, based on the *current* state of the data in the data source, regardless of any database state materialized in the mediator.

It is challenging to achieve acceptable performance of OO queries over IUTs, in particular when the integrated extents have overlaps [4, 5]. Such overlaps require outerjoin-based query processing techniques having increased complexity compared to inner joins. Furthermore, queries involving both local and remote data should take advantage of the fast access to local data to improve performance.

This work presents a combination of query processing strategies that significantly improve the performance of queries over IUTs in capacity augmented mediators. The main principles of these strategies are:

1. The IUTs are internally represented as a set of *auxiliary views*, over which the reconciliation is specified by a set of overloaded auxiliary methods (queries).
2. The queries over the IUTs containing outerjoins and reconciliation are translated into late bound queries over the auxiliary views and methods.
3. In order to permit further query rewrites, the late bound queries are translated into disjunctive query expressions. These model the original query by joins and anti-semi-joins which are easier to rewrite and optimize.
4. Novel, type-aware query rewrite techniques remove inconsistent disjuncts and simplify the transformed disjunctive queries.
5. To efficiently support consistent and complete query answers the system uses a novel technique for selective OID generation and validation of the OO view instances, based on declarative queries.
6. Finally, local main-memory indexes created on-the-fly in mediators eliminate repeated accesses to data sources.

Experimental results show that the combination of the above methods has drastically better performance than a naive CORBA-like integration that resolves late binding on an object instance level at run time. The performance is drastically reduced even if only some of the combined optimization methods are relaxed.

2 Background

As a platform for our research we use the AMOS*II* mediator database system [11] developed from WS-Iris [15]. The core of AMOS*II* is an open light-weight and extensible DBMS. AMOS*II* is a distributed mediator system where both the mediators and wrappers are fully functional AMOS*II* servers. For good performance, and since most the data reside in the data sources, AMOS*II* is designed as a main-memory DBMS.

AMOS*II*'s CDM is an OO extension of the DAPLEX [17] functional data model. It has three basic constructs: *objects*, *types* and *functions*. Objects model entities in the domain of interest. An object can be classified into one or more types making the object an *instance* of those types. The set of all instances of a type is called the *extent* of the type. The types are organized in a multiple inheritance, supertype/subtype hierarchy. If an object is an instance of a type, then it is also an instance of all the supertypes of that type; conversely, the extent of a type is a subset of the extent of a supertype of that type (extent-subset semantics). Object attributes, queries, methods, and relationships are modeled by functions.

The non-literal types are divided into *stored*, *derived*, *translated*, and *proxy* types:

- The instances of *stored* types are explicitly stored in the mediator and created by the user.
- The extent of a *derived* type (DT) is a subset of the extents of one or more *constituent* supertypes specified through a declarative query over the supertypes. Its extent is a subset of the *intersection* of the extents of the constituent types. Each DT has an associated *extent function* defining its extent; an *OID generation function* for creating its OIDs; and a *validation function* which for a given DT object checks if the object is still valid, based on the state of the objects of its constituent types and the declarative condition given in the DT definition. The DTs are described in greater detail in [13].
- The *proxy* types represent objects stored in other AMOS*II* servers or in some of the supported types of data sources. In this work we will only use ODBC data sources.

The functions in AMOS*II* are divided by their implementations into four groups. The extent of a *stored* function is physically stored in the mediator (c.f. object attributes). *Derived* functions are implemented by queries in the query language AMOSQL (c.f. views and methods). *Foreign* functions are implemented in some other programming language, e.g. C++ or Java (c.f. methods). To help the query processor, a foreign function can have associated cost and selectivity functions. The *proxy* functions are implemented in other AMOS*II* servers.

The AMOSQL query language is similar to OQL and based on OSQL [16] with extensions of multi-way foreign functions, active rules, late binding, overloading, etc. For example, assuming three stored function *parent*, *name* and *hobby*, the query below retrieves the names of the parents of the persons who have 'sailing' as a hobby:

```
select p, name(parent(p))
from person p
where hobby(p) = 'sailing';
```

The DT definition below defines a type representing persons having 'sailing' as a hobby, and defines a stored function 'yachtType' over this type.

```
create derived type sailors
 subtype of person
  where hobby(person)='sailing'
  properties (yachtType string);
```

The query processing in AMOS*II* first translates the AMOSQL queries into a type annotated *object calculus* representation. For example, the result of the calculus generation phase for the query from the example above is given by the following calculus expression:

$\{ p, nm \mid$
$p = Person_{nil \rightarrow person}() \wedge$
$d = parent_{person \rightarrow person}(p) \wedge$
$nm = name_{person \rightarrow charstring}(d) \wedge$
$'sailing' = hobby_{person \rightarrow charstring}(p)\}$

The first predicate in the expression is inserted by the system to assert the type of variable p. It defines the variable p to be member of the result of the extent function for type the *Person*. In case of a DT, the extent function contains a query defining the extent in terms of predicates over the supertypes. The extent function can be used to generate the extent of a type, as well as to test if a given instance belongs to a type. Therefore, a predicate containing a reference to an extent function is called a *typecheck predicate*. An extent function accesses the *deep extent* of the type, i.e. it includes the extents of all the subtypes. By contrast, the *shallow extent function* considers only the immediate instances of the type. By convention, the shallow extent functions are named by prefixing the type name by the prefix *Shallow*, e.g. $ShallowPerson_{nil \rightarrow Person}()$.

In a second processing phase, the calculus optimizer applies type-aware rewrite rules to reduce the number of predicates. For the example query, this produces the expression below by removing the type check predicate:

$\{ p, nm \mid$
$d = parent_{person \rightarrow person}(p) \wedge$
$nm = name_{person \rightarrow string}(d) \wedge$
$'sailing' = hobby_{person \rightarrow string}(p)\}$

This transformation is correct because p is used in a stored function (e. g. *name*) with an argument or result of type *person*. The referential integrity system of the stored functions constrains the stored instances to the correct type [15].

After the rewrites, queries operating over data outside the mediator are decomposed into distributed subqueries expressed in an *object algebra*, to be executed in different AMOS*II* servers and data sources. The decomposition uses a combination of heuristic and dynamic programming strategies. At each site, a single-site *cost-based optimizer* generates optimized execution plans for the subqueries.

An interested reader is referred to [12] for more detailed description of the data integration features of AMOS*II*, and to [15], [6], [11] [13] and [8] for more comprehensive descriptions of the query processing.

3 Integration Union Types

The integration union types (IUTs) provide a mechanism for defining OO views capable of resolving semantic heterogeneity among meta-data and data from multiple data sources. Informally, while the DTs represent restrictions (selections) and intersections of extents of other types, the IUTs represent reconciled unions of data in one or more mediators or data sources.

The description of the IUTs in this section is from a perspective of a database administrator who models and defines a mediating view used later by the users. From the users' perspective, there is no difference between querying IUTs and ordinary types. The view definition process will be illustrated by an example of a computer science department (CSD) formed from the faculty members of two universities named A and B. The CSD administration needs to set up a database of the faculty members of the new department in terms of the databases of the two universities. The faculty members of CSD can be employed by either one of the universities. There are also faculty members employed by the both universities. The full-time members of a department are assigned an office in the department.

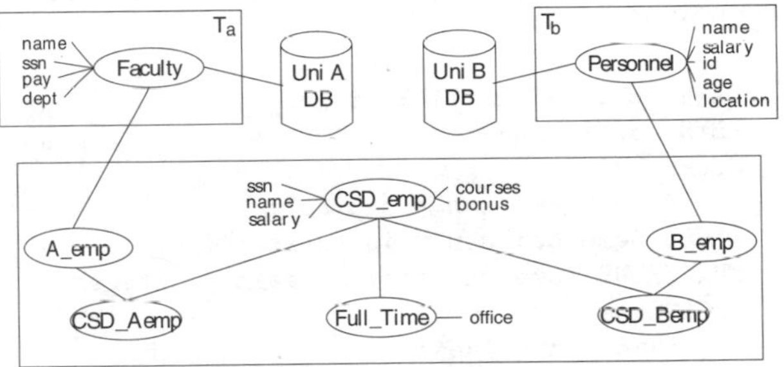

Figure 1: **An Object-Oriented View for the Computer Science Department Example**

One possible system architecture for the data integration problem described above is presented in Figure 1. In this figure, the mediators are represented by rectangles; the ovals in the rectangles represent types; and the solid lines represent inheritance relationships between the types. The two AMOS*II* servers that provide a CDM representation of the data in the sources are labeled T_A and T_B. To distinguish between the wrapper subsystem in AMOS*II*, and an AMOS*II* mediator having a *role* of wrapping some data source(s), the second is named *translator*. The term wrapper will be used to represent the wrapper subsystem.

In T_A, there is a type *Faculty* and in T_B a type *Personnel*. A mediator is setup in the CSD to provide the integrated view. Here, the types *CSD_Aemp* and *CSD_Bemp* are defined as subtypes of the types in the translators:

```
create derived type CSD_Aemp
  subtype of Faculty@Ta fta
    where dept(fta) = ''CSD'';

create derived type CSD_Bemp
  subtype of Personnel@Tb ptb
    where location(ptb) = ''G house'';
```

The system imports the external types, looks up the functions defined over them in the originating mediators, and defines local proxy types and functions with the same signature, but no implementation. In this example, the extents of the DTs are specified as subsets of the extents of their supertypes by using simple selections, but in general the subtyping condition can also contain joins. During the query decomposition process, predicates containing proxy functions are scheduled for execution in the originating mediator.

The IUT *CSD_emp* represents all the employees of the CSD. It is defined over the *constituent types* *CSD_Aemp* and *CSD_Bemp*. *CSD_emp* contains one instance for each employee, regardless of whether it appears in one of the constituent types or in both. There are two kinds of functions defined over *CSD_emp*. The functions on the left of the type oval in Figure 1 are derived from the functions defined in the constituent types. These *reconciled* functions have more than one overloaded implementation, one for each possible combination of constituent types instances, matching an IUT instance. The functions on the right are locally stored functions. Using the data definition facilities of AMOSQL, the type *CSD_emp* can be defined as:

```
CREATE INTEGRATION TYPE csd_emp
  KEYS ssn INTEGER;
  SUPERTYPE OF
    CSD_Aemp ae: ssn = ssn(ae);
    CSD_Bemp be: ssn = id_to_ssn(id(be));
  FUNCTIONS name charstring, salary integer;
    CASE ae
      name = name(ae);
      salary = pay(ae);
    CASE be
      name = name(be);
      salary = salary(be);
    CASE ae, be
      salary = pay(ae) + salary(be);
  PROPERTIES
      courses BAG OF STRING;
      bonus integer;
END;
```

The definition of the *CSD_emp* reveals some details not apparent from the graphical representation of the integration scenario. The first clause defines a set of *keys* and their types. In the example, the key is single valued of type *integer*. For each of the constituent subtypes, a key expression is given to calculate the value of the key from the instances of this subtype. The instances of different constituent types having the same key values will map into a single IUT instance. The key expressions can contain both local and remote functions.

The `FUNCTIONS` clause defines the reconciled functions of *CSD_emp*, derived from the values of the functions over the constituent types. For different subsets of the constituent types, a reconciled function of an IUT can have different implementations specified in the `CASE` clauses. For example, the definition of *CSD_emp* specifies that the *salary* function is calculated as the salary of the faculty member at the university to which it belongs. In the case when she is employed by both universities, the salary is the sum of the two salaries. When the same function is defined for more than one case, the most specific case applies.

Finally, the `PROPERTIES` clause defines the two stored functions over the IUT *CSD_emp*. At any time after the definition of an IUT, the user can add stored or derived functions. The derived functions can be based on any functions already defined in the mediator, regardless whether they are implemented locally or in some other AMOS*II* server.

The IUTs can be subtyped by DTs as any other types. In the example in Figure 1, the type *Full_Time* representing the full time employees is defined as a subtype of the type *CSD_emp*. The locally stored function *office* stores the information about the offices of the full time CSD employees.

4 Modeling and Querying the Integration Union Types

Every instance of an IUT corresponds to either an instance in one of the two constituent types, or to one instance in both of them. Therefore, the extent of an IUT can be divided into three subsets (Figure 2a). Two sets contain the IUT instances corresponding to an instance in a single constituent type. The third set contains the IUT instances corresponding to instances in both constituent types. Since the extent subsets can be defined by declarative queries, we can represent each of them with a DT, named an *auxiliary type* (AT). Three ATs are generated for each IUT, forming an inheritance hierarchy as shown in Figure 2b.

A function f defined over an IUT can have a different implementation for each of these three subsets (i.e. for each `CASE` clause). It can be thus defined for the whole extent of the IUT by being *overloaded* on the ATs. A call to f for an IUT will then result in a late bound function call, to be discussed below.

The ATs are generated by the system and are not visible to the user. Each AT corresponds to a `CASE` clause in the IUT definition. By using the specifications from the `KEYS` clause of the IUT definition, two functions are generated for each constituent type. The overloaded function $key_{CT \rightarrow key\ types}$ calculates the key of an instance of a constituent type CT. The function *Allkeys*`CT`*()* returns all the keys for the type CT. With

a)

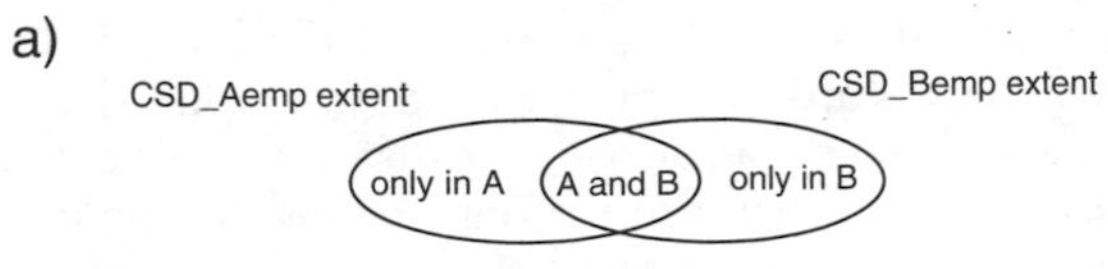

b)

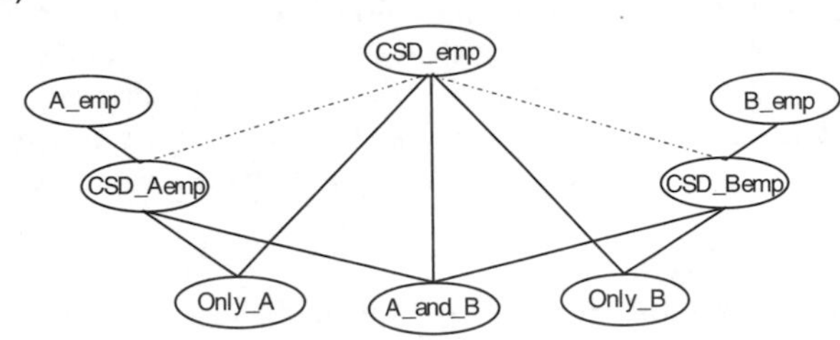

Figure 2: **IUT implementation by ATs**

these functions defined, the AT definitions for the example are:

```
create derived type Only_A
 subtype of CSD_Aemp ae
   where key(ae) not in
         AllkeysCSD_Bemp();

create derived type Only_B
  subtype of CSD_Bemp be
    where key(be) not in
          AllKeysCSD_Aemp();

create derived type A_and_B
  subtype of CSD_Aemp ae, CSD_Bemp be
    where key(ae) = key(be);
```

The first two subtypes represent instances in the anti-semi-joins of the extents of the integrated types, based on the declared keys. The third represents the join of the extents of the integrated types.

Next, the system creates the IUT and makes the ATs its subtypes. The overloaded function resolvents are then defined over the IUT and each of the ATs. The AT resolvents are generated from the *FUNCTIONS* clause in the IUT definition. The resolvent for the IUT itself is defined as *false* since all the instances of the IUT belong to one of the ATs, giving the optimizer a hint to reduce the execution plans.

The extents of the ATs represent mutually exclusive sets of real world entities. The union of these extents forms the extent of the IUT which therefore contains one instance for each entity. From the user's point of view, the only difference between the IUTs and the ordinary types is that no objects can be explicitly created in the IUTs. The extent of the IUTs are completely derived from the extents of the ATs.

4.1 Late Binding Over Derived Types

To process queries over the system-generated OO views having overloaded functions, we developed a novel late binding mechanism for efficient handling of declarative view definitions in a multiple mediators environment. A late bound function call $f(a)$ is first translated into a calculus *late binding operator* (LBO) whose first argument is a tuple of the possible resolvents of f sorted with the least specific type first, and the second argument is a [8]. For functions used when an IUT is modeled by ATs, the late binding calculus expression is:

$$LBO(< f_{iut}, f_{at1}, ..., f_{atn} >, a)$$

where the ATs $at1 \ldots atn$ are subtypes of iut. Based on the types of the argument a, LBO chooses the most-specific resolvent, executes it over the argument, and returns the result(s).

In our previous work, we developed a corresponding algebraic late binding operator for the ordinary types, the Dynamic Type Resolver (DTR) [8]. DTR, as most late binding mechanisms described in the literature (e.g. [7]), processes one tuple at a time and selects the query plan of a resolvent based on the type of a. This mode of processing is not suitable for the IUT queries for the following reasons. First, because the resolvents are functions defined over data in multiple sources, processing a tuple at a time results in calling remote functions in an RPC manner. Second, it requires the instances to have assigned OIDs, leading to OID generation for *all* the instances processed in a query, and not only for the ones requested by the user. Furthermore, such a late binding mechanism assumes that the type information of the argument object is explicitly stored with its OID. By contrast, the ATs are defined *implicitly* by queries, and IUT instances can move from one AT to another dynamically and outside the control of the mediator, based on the state of the data in the sources. Therefore, the use of late binding as above leads into partitioning the query into three separate subqueries: the resolvent function bodies (i.e. the expressions in the `CASE` clauses), the AT subtyping conditions, and the predicate in the query. This separation will prohibit query rewrite techniques to eliminate common subexpressions and other query reduction methods as described in [13] and [6].

In order to overcome these limitations, the LBO is translated into an equivalent disjunctive object calculus predicate, which is then combined and optimized with the rest of the query. AMOS*II* supports multimethods and overloading on all function arguments and the translation algorithm can handle this too. Due to space limitations, here we only present a simplified version of the algorithm that handles overloading on a single argument.

In the translated disjunctive calculus expression every branch (disjunct) is a conjunction of a typecheck for an AT and a call to the overloaded function f corresponding to the AT. The translation algorithm is:

---

generate_lb_calculus(resolvents) − > disjunctive predicate
  result = $\{res \mid\}$; /*empty disjunction predicate */
  while resolvents != ∅ **do**
    head = first(resolvents);

```
  /* the argument type for the head function */
  t_h = arg_type(head);
  if ∄f ∈ resolvents | subtype_of(argtype(f), t_h) then
    result = append(result,
                    ∨{arg = t_h() ∧ res = f_{t_h}(arg)});
  else
    wset = {t_p | subtype_of(t_p, t_h)∧
                  ∄f ∈ resolvents |
                     subtype_of(t_p, argtype(f))}
    for each t_p in wset
     result = append(result,
                     ∨{arg = Shallow_t_p(),
                       res = f_{t_h}(arg)}));
  end if
  resolvents = resolvents - head;
 end while
 return result;
end;
```

First, *append*, and – perform the usual set operations, and *arg_type* returns the argument type of a function. The algorithm traverses the sorted list of resolvents. If the type hierarchy rooted in the argument type of a resolvent does not intersect with the hierarchies of the argument types of some resolvents in the rest of the list, then a conjunction of an ordinary (deep) typecheck and the resolvent call is added as a new disjunct to the result. Otherwise the new disjunct will instead contain a shallow typecheck. Notice that for IUTs there will be no shallow typechecks, because there are never any subtypes of the system-generated ATs. Since the type checks are mutually exclusive, only one resolvent will be evaluated.

To illustrate the translation process we examine the translation of the LBO for the function *salary* over the IUT *CSD_emp*:

$$LBO(< salary_{csd\_emp \to int}, salary_{Only\_A \to int}, salary_{Only\_B \to int}, salary_{A\_and\_B \to int} >, arg)$$

is translated into:

$$\{ s \mid (arg = only\_A_{nil \to only\_a}() \wedge s = salary_{only\_A}(arg)) \vee (arg = only\_B_{nil \to only\_b}() \wedge s = salary_{only\_B}(arg)) \vee (arg = A\_and\_B_{nil \to a\_and\_b}() \wedge s = salary_{a\_and\_b}(arg))\}$$

The expression is a disjunction of only three disjuncts. No disjunct is generated for the first resolvent $salary_{csd\_emp \to int}$ since it is defined as *false*.

After the query normalization, the extent functions of the ATs are expanded by substituting them with their bodies containing the expressions from the CASE clauses of the IUT definition. These expressions in turn reference the extent functions of the constituent types, which are DTs and the expansion continues until no DT extent functions are present. This process makes visible to the query decomposer i) the query selections defined by the user, ii) the conditions in the IUT, and iii) the DT definitions. The query decomposer combines the predicates, divides them into groups of predicates executable in a single mediator or data source, and then schedules their execution. As opposed to dealing with parametric queries over multiple databases, as would have been the case with a tuple-at-the-time implementation of the late binding, the strategy ships and processes data among the mediators and the data sources in bulks containing many tuples. The size of a bulk is determined by the query optimizer to maximize the network and resource utilization. The results in the next section demonstrate how the bulk-processing allows for query processing strategies with substantially better performance than the instance-at-the-time strategies. Furthermore, this strategy allows the optimizer to detect and remove unnecessary OID generations for the instances not in the query result.

4.2 Normalization of Queries Over the Integration Types

If there are disjunctive predicates, we need to normalize the query to disjunctive normal form in order to separate the subqueries for the individual data sources. One drawback of the query normalization is that it duplicates predicates in several different disjuncts of the normalized disjunctive predicate. To avoid some of the unnecessary duplication, we use a query normalization which is aware of the multidatabase environment. The normalization algorithm is based on the principle that as many as possible of the normalization decisions should be delegated to the sites where the predicates are executed. The query decomposer analyzes the elements of a disjunctive predicate and groups together the disjuncts executed in the same mediator or data source capable of processing disjunctions.

Another source of disjunctions in queries over IUTs are the late bound functions from above, which are translated to disjunctions. A full disjunctive normalization would then produce a cross product of the disjuncts in all the late bound IUT functions. For example the query:

```
select salary(e), ssn(e) from csd_emp e;
```

produces the calculus expression:

$$\{ sal, ssn \mid (arg = only\_A_{nil \to only\_a}() \wedge sal = salary_{only\_A}(arg)) \vee (arg = only\_B_{nil \to only\_b}() \wedge sal = salary_{only\_B}(arg)) \vee (arg = A\_and\_B_{nil \to a\_and\_b}() \wedge sal = salary_{a\_and\_b}(arg)) \wedge$$

$$(arg = only\_A_{nil \to only\_a}() \wedge ssn = ssn_{only\_A}(arg)) \vee (arg = only\_B_{nil \to only\_b}() \wedge ssn = ssn_{only\_B}(arg)) \vee (arg = A\_and\_B_{nil \to a\_and\_b}() \wedge ssn = salary_{a\_and\_b}(arg))\}$$

The expression is then normalized into 9 disjuncts, one for each combination of the disjuncts in the two disjunctive predicates above. This expression shows the first two disjuncts:

$$\{ sal, ssn \mid (arg = only\_A_{nil \to only\_a}() \wedge sal = salary_{only\_A}(arg) \wedge arg = only\_A_{nil \to only\_a}() \wedge ssn = ssn_{only\_A}(arg)) \vee$$

$$(arg = only\_B_{nil \to only\_b}() \wedge sal = salary_{only\_B}(arg) \wedge arg = only\_A_{nil \to only\_a}() \wedge ssn = ssn_{only\_a}(arg)) \vee \ldots\}$$

We can see that each disjunct contains two typecheck predicates for the variable *arg*. This will also be the case in the remaining six disjuncts not shown above. Based on the presence of more than one typecheck over the same variable in a conjunctive predicate and on the properties of the type hierarchy, the disjuncts generated by the query normalization can be rewritten into a simpler form or eliminated.

Since an object can have only one most specific type, two typecheck predicates for a single variable of two unrelated types are always rewritten to $false$, and the disjunct is removed. When the types are related, depending on whether the typechecks are deep or shallow, the result of the rewrite is either $false$ or the more specific typecheck predicate.

These rewrite rules eliminate in the example above all six disjuncts in which the typecheck is not performed over the same type (e.g. the second of the two disjuncts shown above). In the remaining three, just a single typecheck is left, transforming thus the query into the following predicate which will be shown to be significantly faster than the original query:

$$
\begin{aligned}
&\{\, sal, ssn \mid \\
&\quad (arg = only\_a_{nil \rightarrow only\_a}() \wedge \\
&\quad sal = salary_{only\_a}(arg) \wedge ssn = ssn_{only\_a}(arg)) \vee \\
&\quad (arg = only\_b_{nil \rightarrow only\_b}() \wedge \\
&\quad sal = salary_{only\_b}(arg) \wedge ssn = ssn_{only\_b}(arg)) \vee \\
&\quad (arg = a\_and\_b_{nil \rightarrow a\_and\_b}() \wedge \\
&\quad sal = salary_{a\_and\_b}(arg) \wedge ssn = ssn_{a\_and\_b}(arg))\}
\end{aligned}
$$

4.3 Managing OIDs for the IUTs

The IUT instances are assigned OIDs when used in locally stored functions. For example, a query giving a bonus of \$1000 to all employees in the department with salary lower than \$1000 can be specified as:

```
set bonus(csde) = 1000 from CSD_emp csde
    where salary(csde) < 1000;
```

In order to manipulate the IUT OIDs we have generalized the framework developed for handling OIDs of DT instances [13] to the IUTs. As noted in the introduction, the DT functionality is modeled with three functions: OID generation function, extent function, and validation function. Next we describe how the system generates each of these functions for the IUTs.

Since an IUT is a supertype of the corresponding ATs, every AT instance is also an instance of the IUT. Each distinct real world entity is always represented by an instance in exactly one of the ATs. Therefore, the extent of an IUT is a non-overlapping union of the extents of the ATs and the extent function of an IUT is a disjunction of the extent functions of its ATs.

The OID generation function assigns an OID to a DT instance. In the case of DTs, the OID generation function is called by the extent function. Since the extent function of an IUT only references the extent functions of its ATs, there is no need for OID generation functions for IUTs. The IUT instances are thus assigned OIDs by the AT OID generation functions.

If the ATs were treated as ordinary DTs, the assignment of OIDs to the AT instances would be made independently of the other ATs of an IUT. On the other hand, due to the nature of the conditions used in the ATs definition, instances 'drift' from one AT to another. For example, let's assume that John Doe is an employee of University A, and also a member of the CSD in the example above. When his bonus is assigned, the system will generate an OID for the instance representing John Doe in the AT *Only_A* and use this OID in the stored function *bonus* to relate John with his bonus. If John now gets an appointment at University B, he still belongs to the *CSD_emp* IUT, but an instance representing him appears in the type *A_and_B*, while the instance in the type *Only_A* is removed. If the newly created instance in *A_and_B* has a different OID from the old instance in *Only_A*, then John cannot be matched with his bonus stored in the database using the old OID.

The example shows that the OID assignment for instances of the ATs must be coordinated, so the instances representing the same real-world entity can move from one AT to another, while preserving their identity. An instance is related to a real world entity through its key, so to solve the problem, the OID assignments of the ATs are controlled by a function storing the generated OIDs along with the keys. When a new AT OID is to be generated, the OID generation function first checks if there is a stored OID with a matching key. If so, it adjusts the type of the stored OID and returns it as result. Otherwise, it generates a new OID. We notice here that, because the selections are pushed to the data sources and due to the OID generation removal mechanism described in [13], only a subset of the whole IUT extent is assigned OIDs in queries containing selections. Very often, queries return literals rather than OIDs of the queried types. In these cases no OIDs are generated at all.

In Section 2 an example was presented on how the typecheck predicate of a variable can be removed from a query when the variable is used in a predicate with a locally stored function of that type. This mechanism, described in greater detail in [15], is extended to apply over the IUTs. An advantage of removing the typecheck is that the costly generation of the IUT extent is not needed, but instead only the already generated OIDs stored in the local function are used. However, when dealing with stored DT or IUT instances, we need to make sure that they are still valid, i.e. that the data sources still contain the corresponding instances.

A straightforward solution to the problem of validating an IUT instance is to test which of the three IUT ATs it belongs to. It is, however, sufficient to validate an IUT instance by testing the existence of a corresponding instance having the same key in one of the two integrated sources; the intersection AT need not be tested. This condition can be expressed by a two-branch disjunctive predicate instead of a three-branch one in the straightforward solution. The gain is due to the fact that we are not interested in exactly which AT an IUT instance belongs to, but if it belongs to *any* of the ATs. As an example we present the calculus representation of the validation function body for the *CSD_emp* type from the example above:

$validate_{csd\_emp}(e) \leftarrow$
$(ssn = skey_{csd\_emp \rightarrow integer}(e) \wedge$
$ssn = ssn_{csd\_a\_emp \rightarrow integer}(csda)) \vee$
$(ssn = skey_{csd\_emp \rightarrow integer}(e) \wedge$
$id = id_{csd\_b\_emp \rightarrow string}(csdb) \wedge$
$ssn = id\_to\_ssn_{string \rightarrow integer}(id))$

The variables *csdb* and *csda* are local variables.

The validation method described above suffices when a query contains only locally stored functions over an IUT, while not containing late bound functions over the same IUT. When a query contains both locally stored and late bound functions, the system needs to determine which AT an IUT instance belongs to, in order to execute the right resolvent. Since an instance can drift between the ATs, the system must determine the AT membership for the IUT instances at query time. In order to do this, a disjunctive predicate similar to the one described earlier in this section is used. The only difference is that here the typecheck predicates are replaced with the corresponding validation predicates.

5 Performance Measurements

The AMOS*II* system with the mediation features described in this paper is implemented on Windows NT. We will present an overview of some experimental results obtained from running the system over 10Mb Ethernet and ISDN networks. The results demonstrate how the techniques presented above drastically reduce the response times.

The experiments are performed for a scenario similar to the running example above. We used two Compaq Professional Workstation 5000 with 200MHz Pentium processors and 64 MB memory, connected through a 10Mb Ethernet network. We also performed the same tests using a 64kb ISDN connection over the public telephone network in Sweden.

One of the workstations hosted an ODBC data source and an associated AMOS*II* system as a translator. For the experiments we used Microsoft Access as a relational data source because of its availability, but the results apply to any other ODBC data source. On the second workstation, another AMOS*II* server represented another data source. To be able to quantify the difference in the times between the processing in AMOS*II* and in the ODBC data source, the data was here stored directly in the AMOS*II*'s main-memory database. The second workstation also hosted the mediator system where the queries were issued. The three AMOS*II* servers just described will be referred to in the rest of this section as T_a (the ODBC translator), T_b (the AMOS*II* storing data locally) and the *mediator* for the AMOS*II* server where the queries are issued.

In the experiments, we scaled simultaneously the tables *Faculty* in the ODBC data source and the extent of the type *Personnel* stored in T_b from 1000 to 30000 tuples (instances). From these tuples, 10% are selected to be members of each of the types *CSD_Aemp* and *CSD_Bemp* (i.e. members of the CSD), which are the constituent types for the integration type *CSD_emp*. Between these two types, we assume that half of the instances are overlapping (represent the same persons), meaning that the size of the extent of the type *CSD_emp* is 15% of the cardinality of the table. For example, when the size of both the *Faculty* table in the ODBC source and the extent of the type *Personnel* in T_b is 30000, there are 3000 instances of each selected as working in the CSD department by the conditions in the definition of the derived types *CSD_Aemp* and *CSD_Bemp*. From each of these two sets of 3000 instances, 1500 appear only in one of these types and 1500 appear in the both constituent types. The extent of integrated type *CSD_emp* therefore has 4500 instances.

The experiments are based on queries over the IUT *CSD_emp*. The queries are simple in order to analyze certain features of the system. Also, we have chosen queries that are the building blocks of most user-specified queries over the IUTs. More specifically the test cases can be divided into i) queries over reconciled IUT functions, and ii) queries calling locally stored functions over the IUT. In the former group we first investigate queries with no selection, exact match, and range selections. Then we present results when more than one function is used in the same query, to investigate the performance impact of the type-aware rewrites. Queries with locally stored functions are investigated in one example. We conclude the tests by comparing the times for some queries over the 10Mb network with the times obtained when the same queries were executed over an ISDN network. Notice that the y-axis in all the graphs represents response time in seconds and the x-axis represents the number of tuples in the test databases. All the measurements are performed with preoptimized queries. Figure 3 shows the execution time of a query retrieving the salaries of the CSD employees. We examine 4 different strategies. The graph on the left shows that the "DTR" strategy using pure late binding on an instance level is by orders of magnitude worse that the remaining three strategies. This strategy, first generates OIDs for all instances in the extent of the type CSD_emp. Then, DTR is executed over each of the OIDs, choosing the resolvent. Finally, the chosen resolvent is executed. The resolvent body also contains predicates to confirm the right AT of the argument, which causes the typecheck to be executed once again before the function value is calculated.

Table 1 shows the percentage of the time spend in the three cooperating AMOS*II* servers, and the network time for each of the examined strategies. For the DTR strategy, the biggest portion of the query execution time is spent in T_a for accessing the relational data

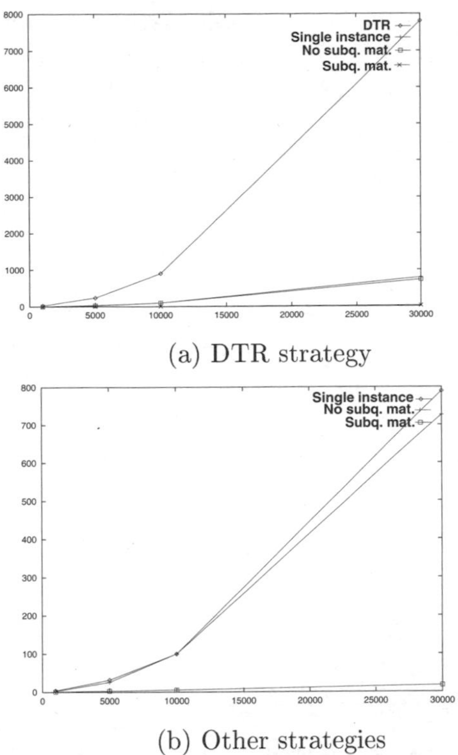

(a) DTR strategy

(b) Other strategies

Figure 3: **select salary(e) from csd_emp e;**

	Time distribution			
	Mediator	T_a	T_b	Net.
DTR	23%	69%	1%	7%
Single instance	5%	80%	3%	12%
No subq. mat.	3%	91%	3%	3%
Subq. mat.	27%	22%	32%	19%

Table 1: **Query execution time distribution**

source. Table 2 presents the number of ODBC calls issued by the data source T_a for the different strategies. The DTR strategy issues by far the most such of calls. The number of calls is a linear function of the data sizes in the sources, but as the data volume grows, each of these calls demands more time, explaining the hyper-linear growth in the query execution time. We can also note that the DTR strategy spends 23% of the time in the mediator. This is due to OID generation, function resolution, and execution of the protocol for shipping instances among different AMOS*II* servers. The OID generation for IUT instances requires that OIDs are generated for the constituent types, which in turn triggers proxy objects generation for the instances imported from the translators. Since the DTR operator is executed over each instance individually, there is a large amount of computation involved.

The lower part of the graph in Figure 3a is enlarged in Figure 3b. Here, we can see the remaining 3 query processing strategies. The uppermost curve represents a strategy in which the late bound function call is substituted by a disjunctive predicate, but the data shipment is still one instance at the time. This type of

	ODBC requests / DB size			
	1000	5000	10000	30000
DTR	251	1251	3001	9017
Single inst.	102	502	1002	3002
No subq. mat.	102	502	1002	3002
Subq. mat.	3	3	3	6

Table 2: **Number of data source accesses**

nested loop join over a network is named bind-join in [10]. Query rewrites eliminate OID generation, duplicate condition evaluations, and run-time function resolution. Also, the number of ODBC calls in T_a is reduced by two thirds. All of this reduces the query execution time by nearly 10 times. Nevertheless, the ODBC calls are still the main factor in the query execution cost. We can also note that the relative network cost has risen to 12%.

The first step into designing a better strategy is to pass the instances in bulks instead of an instance-at-a-time protocol. While this strategy, due to the fast networks used, does not radically improve the result (the next curve in the graph in Figure 3b), it does lower the relative network cost to 3% and makes the final query strategy possible.

The final strategy, which again reduces the response time by a couple of orders of magnitude, is based on the observations that most of the ODBC queries are issued to compute the extents of the ATs which involve anti-semi-joins translated into nested subqueries inside a *not exists* operator. In order to avoid the cost of repeated data access using parametric queries, we execute a single non-parametric query and materialize an index over all the parameter values in T_a. In this example the index contains the *ssn* for the 10% employees of University A who are also in CSD. In this way, we reduce the ODBC requests to one per bulk sent from the mediator to the translator. Being a main-memory based database, AMOS*II* facilitates a very fast index build-up for data sizes which can fit into memory of the translator. For this type of query where the materialized index is used repeatedly, this strategy is clearly advantageous. We can also see that the distribution of the query execution time in the last strategy is balanced evenly among the participating AMOS*II* servers and the network. Note that there is one access to the data source per disjunction branch of the query. Therefore, the skew in the data distribution will not affect the query execution times. The cost of executing a non-parametric query and building an index on-the-fly has to be compared with the cost of completing the query without the index. In the next experiment, we executed a query containing an exact match selection using the same 4 strategies. The DTR strategy is again by far the worst, as shown in Figure 4a. On the other hand, the differences among the other strategies is not as large as in the previous experiment (Figure 4b). Also, here the strategy without index materialization for the nested

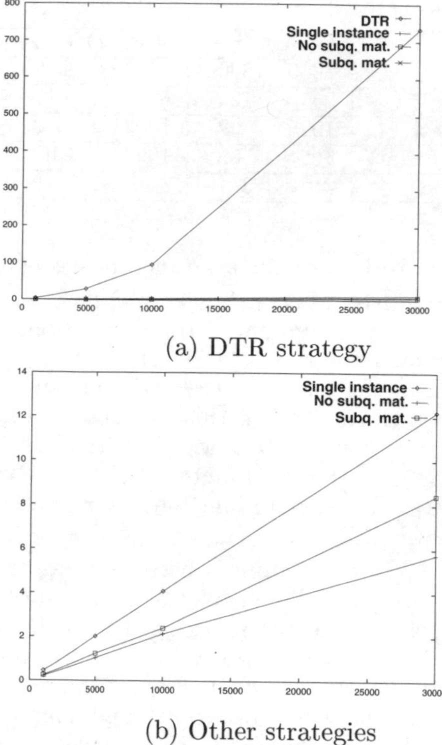

(a) DTR strategy

(b) Other strategies

Figure 4: **select salary(e) from csd_emp e where ssn(e) = 1000;**

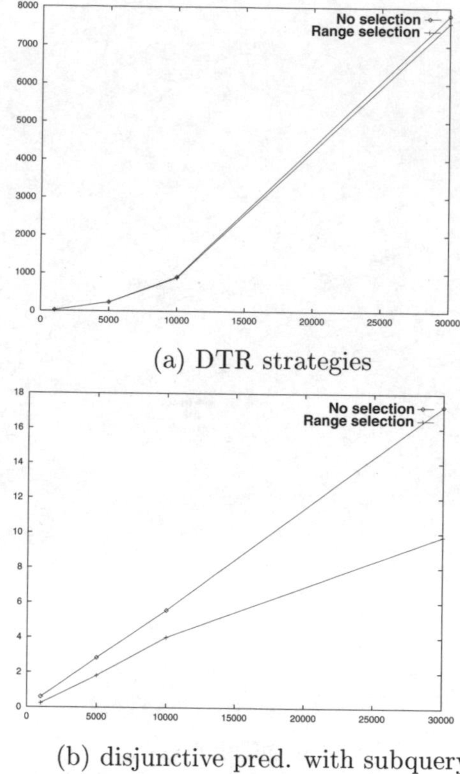

(a) DTR strategies

(b) disjunctive pred. with subquery materialization strategies

Figure 5: **Queries with range selection (salary(e) > 2000)**

subquery performs the best. This is due to the fact that the non-parameterized query used to compute the index has a larger cost than the parameterized query retrieving only the data matching a particular input tuple. In general the index materialization is favorable when: $size(input) * cost(parameterized\ query) > cost(non\ parameterized\ query) + cost(index\ generation)$.

In the next experiment we examine queries with non-equality selections, e.g. range selections. While the DTR strategy is able to apply the selections encapsulated in the DT condition, it is not efficient when the query contains non-equality conditions, since such conditions are then not pushed into the resolvents. In Figure 5a the execution times of a query containing a range selection is compared with the execution times of a query without any selection. It can be seen that the cost is about equal. In Figure 5b, on the other hand, there is clear difference between the execution times of the same queries using disjunctive predicates to model the late binding. This is due to the fact that the selection is pushed in the data sources.

Next, we measure the execution time for queries containing locally stored functions over an IUT. In this experiment, we created a locally stored function *office* over the type *CSD_emp* storing only 15 rows, and then executed a query to retrieve the offices stored in this function. Figure 6a compares the execution times of a naive strategy where the system generates the OIDs for the type extent and then applies the locally stored function with the strategy where the IUT instances of interest are retrieved from the locally stored function and then validated as described previously. Since thc cardinality of a locally stored function is always smaller than the cardinality of the whole type extent, and the validation of an already generated OID is cheaper than a new OID generation, the validation strategy always outperforms the naive strategy.

The graph in Figure 6b demonstrates the speedup obtained by typecheck removal using type-aware rewrites described in the previous section. The query is normalized to a disjunction with 9 branches, 6 of which are removed by the optimizer. The execution times on the other hand show greater than linear speedup and scalability as could be expected from the analysis of the number of the disjunctive branches. This is due to the fact that the 3 remaining branches after the query transformation are single type queries with a selection condition. The rest of the 6 queries are effectively join queries over different ATs. In these cases, the AT extent functions and the extent functions of the constituent types are expanded for both the ATs appearing in the typecheck predicates. The optimizer cannot infer on the basis of these predicates that the whole disjunct will not produce any results. The resulting query execution strategy cannot therefore take advantage of the selections, and ships data proportional to the size of the extents of the constituent types. This leads to execution times with linear growth with the size of the extents, as opposed to the much slower growth of the execution time when the rewrite

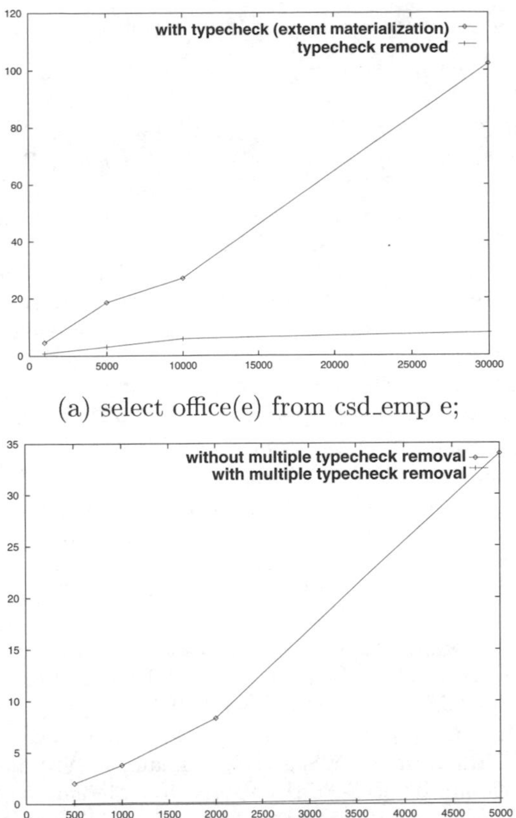

(a) select office(e) from csd_emp e;

(b) select salary(e), name(e) from csd_emp e where name(e)="John";

Figure 6: **a) Queries with locally materialized functions over IUTs. b) Queries calling several derived functions over IUTs.**

rule for removal of the typechecks is applied.

Finally, we briefly compare the execution times obtained over a 10Mb network with the results of the experiments using an ISDN connection over a public telephone network. Keeping all the parameters of the testing the same, the difference in the times can be attributed to the properties of the networks. The graph in Figure 7a shows that when the number of manipulated tuples is low, the results are proportional. However, when the number of shipped tuples increases, as with the query without selection used in Figure 7b, the execution times over ISDN rise faster than over the 10Mb network. Closer examination revealed that ISDN execution times follow the number of bulks sent over the network. We can conclude that the unproportional increase is due to the fact that the message setup time compared to the transmission time per unit is higher in ISDN networks than it is in the 10Mb Ethernet. Probing the network to determine the bulking factor will be a topic of future investigations.

6 Related Work

The research closely related to the work presented in this paper can be divided into roughly two groups: (i)

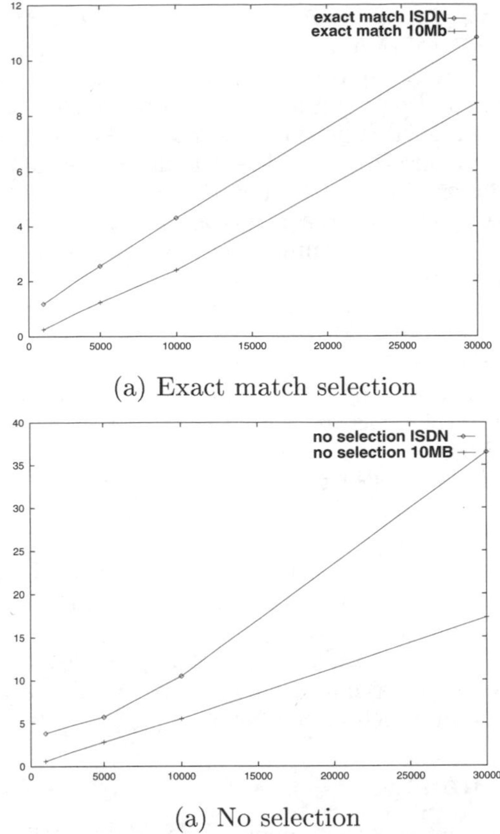

(a) Exact match selection

(a) No selection

Figure 7: **Execution times over 10Mb and ISDN network.**

integration systems that support constructs like the IUT as [5, 4, 14] and (ii) systems that provide basic multidatabase capabilities, but do not provide IUT-like capabilities to deal with overlap and reconciliation (e.g. [10, 18]) so the integration is to be born by the user, using classical select-project-join queries. In the latter, the user needs to simulate the IUT with a series of queries, loosing all the benefits of the coherent view representation and the capacity augmenting features. A comprehensive survey of the data integration field is presented in [2]. Due to space constraints, here we only overview the main differences between our approach and two different query processing strategies used in systems that support integration of overlapping entities in the data sources. A more elaborate comparison of AMOS*II* with other systems for data integration can be found in [12].

In the literature there prevail two overall strategies for processing queries in systems that provide integration of overlapping databases. A representative example of the first group (where also AMOS*II* belongs) is the Multibase system [4]. Here, outer-join based reconciliation is broken into join and anti-semi-join operators. However, there is neither a concept of OIDs, nor capacity augmentation in this system, yielding some of the techniques presented here not applicable. Also, the proposed query rewrites are based on analysis of the query attributes which is more complex than the simple type-based rewrite proposed in this work.

The strategies of the second group are exemplified by the strategy used in the Pegasus [5] system where the reconciliation is performed by a reconciliation operators. These are pushed "upwards" the query tree by the query heuristics, in order to be able to push down joins over small tables through the expensive outerjoin operation. This approach has an advantage of more compact queries in comparison with AMOS*II*. Some disadvantages are that selections based on the reconciled functions are not pushed to the data sources for the anti-semi-join. Also, the whole outer-join needs to be materialized in the mediator before application of the reconciliation operator, preventing streamed execution strategies as used in AMOS*II*. In the experiments above, we can note that the execution times of the queries with selections are about one third of the times without selection, corresponding to the portion of the integrated extents that overlap.

Late binding has been used for data integration in [7], but that system uses instance-level evaluation and no reconciliation facilities.

None of the compared systems provided an extended experimental assessment of the used strategies as the one provided in this work.

7 Summary

We presented a novel framework for data integration based on OO type hierarchies and late binding. Integration union types (IUTs) were introduced to model a coherent view of heterogeneous data in multiple repositories. IUTs allows for resolutions of conflicts in the metadata (e.g. naming, scaling etc.) and for dealing with overlaps in the extents of the integrated types. Furthermore, instances of the IUTs can be assigned OIDs used in locally stored and derived functions.

Each IUT is mapped by the system to a hierarchy of system generated derived types, called auxiliary types (ATs). The ATs represent disjoin parts (a join and two anti-semi-joins) of the outerjoin needed for the data integration. The reconciliation of the attributes of the integrated types is modeled by a system-generated set of overloaded derived functions.

Several novel query processing and optimization technique were developed for efficiently processing queries containing overloaded functions over the system-generated OO views. Queries over such a type hierarchy contain late bound calls. The late bound calls are translated to disjunctive calculus expression which are suitable for application of techniques such as: bulk-oriented processing, type-aware query rewriting, selective OID generation, and dynamic generation of indexes for nested subqueries. The reported measurements compare the impacts of different query processing strategies showing that the combination of these techniques drastically lower the execution times, in some cases by several orders of magnitude.

Our current work includes methods to easily handle non-relational data sources and parallel execution strategies for integration of large number of sources.

References

[1] E. Bertino: A View Mechanism for Object-Oriented Databases. In *3rd Intl. Conf. on Extending Database Technology (EDBT'92)*, Vienna, Austria, 1992.

[2] O. Bukhres, A. Elmagarmid (eds.): Object-Oriented Multidatabase Systems. Pretince Hall, 1996.

[3] M. Garcia-Solaco, F. Saltor, M. Castellanos: Semantic Heterogeneity in Multidatabase Systems. In [2].

[4] U. Dayal, H. Hwang: View Definition and Generalization for Database Integration in a Multidatabase System. *IEEE Trans. on Software Eng.* 10(6), 1984.

[5] W. Du, M. Shan: Query Processing in Pegasus. in [2].

[6] G. Fahl, T. Risch: Query Processing over Object Views of Relational Data. *VLDB Journal*, 1997.

[7] D. Fang, S. Ghandeharizadeh, D. McLeod and A. Si: The Design, Implementation, and Evaluation of an Object-Based Sharing Mechanism for Federated Database System. *9th Intl. Conf. on Data Engineering (ICDE'93)*, Vienna, Austria, 1993.

[8] S. Flodin, T. Risch: Processing Object-Oriented Queries with Invertible Late Bound Functions. *VLDB95*, Zürich, Switzerland, 1995

[9] H. Garcia-Molina, Y. Papakonstantinou, D. Quass, A. Rajaraman, Y.Sagiv, J. Ullman, V. Vassalos, J. Widom: The TSIMMIS Approach to Mediation: Data Models and Languages. *Journal of Intelligent Information Systems (JIIS)* 8(2), 117-132, 1997

[10] L. Haas, D. Kossmann, E. Wimmers, J. Yang: Optimizing Queries across Diverse Data Sources. *VLDB97*, 276-285, Athens Greece, 1997

[11] S. Flodin, V. Josifovski, T. Risch, M. Sköld and M. Werner: *AMOSII User's Guide.* available at *http://www.ida.liu.se/labs/edslab.*

[12] V. Josifovski: Design, Implementation and Evaluation of a Distributed Mediator System for Data Integration. Ph D. Thesis 582, Linköpings universitet, 1999. Available at *http://www.ida.liu.se/labs/edslab.*

[13] V. Josifovski, T. Risch: Functional Query Optimization over Object-Oriented Views for Data Integration. *Journal of Intelligent Information Systems (JIIS)*, 12(2-3), 1999.

[14] E-P. Lim et al: Myriad: Design and Implementation of a Federated Database System. *Software - Practice and Experience*, 25(5), 553-562, 1995.

[15] W. Litwin, T. Risch: Main Memory Oriented Optimization of OO Queries using Typed Datalog with Foreign Predicates. *IEEE TKDE*, 4(6), 517-528, 1992

[16] P. Lyngbaek et al: OSQL: A Language for Object Databases, Tech. Rep., HP Labs, HPL-DTD-91-4, 1991

[17] D. Shipman: The Functional Data Model and the Data Language DAPLEX. *ACM Trans. on Database Systems*, 6(1), 1981.

[18] A. Tomasic, L. Raschid, P. Valduriez: Scaling Access to Heterogeneous Data Sources with DISCO. *IEEE TKDE*, 10(5), 808-823, 1998

[19] G. Wiederhold: Mediators in the Architecture of Future Information Systems. *IEEE Computer*, 1992.

Quality-driven Integration of Heterogeneous Information Systems

Felix Naumann
Humboldt-University of Berlin, Germany
naumann@dbis.informatik.hu-berlin.de

Ulf Leser
Technical University Berlin, Germany
leser@cs.tu-berlin.de

Johann Christoph Freytag
Humboldt-University of Berlin, Germany
freytag@dbis.informatik.hu-berlin.de

Abstract

Integrated access to information that is spread over multiple, distributed, and heterogeneous sources is an important problem in many scientific and commercial domains. While much work has been done on query processing and choosing plans under cost criteria, very little is known about the important problem of incorporating the information quality aspect into query planning.

In this paper we describe a framework for multidatabase query processing that fully includes the quality of information in many facets, such as completeness, timeliness, accuracy, etc. We seamlessly include information quality into a multidatabase query processor based on a view-rewriting mechanism. We model information quality at different levels to ultimately find a set of high-quality query-answering plans.

1 Introduction

Integrated access to information that is spread over multiple, distributed and heterogeneous sources is an important problem in many scientific and commercial domains. For instance, a current list of molecular biology information systems (MBIS) enumerates more than 400 entries [Inf98] of publicly available data sources. These can be both intensionally and extensionally overlapping, replicated, or disjoint. If we are interested in data about human genes, which has many facets, such as related diseases, genomic location, nucleotide sequence etc., we will find many potentially interesting data sources [LLRC98]. Considering them all is expensive and often infeasible.

Therefore, one of the most important tasks of data integration in such a setting is the selection of good data sources. We observed that the main user criterion for selecting sources by hand is not response time, but the expected quality of the data. Clearly, MBIS information sources store data of varying quality. Molecular biology researchers are particularly sensitive to criteria such as *timeliness*, *completeness* or *accuracy of data*. Results become outdated quickly, and the intrinsic imprecision of many experimental techniques leads to fuzzy data, where the degree of fuzziness often varies with the quality standards of the data source. But the result of the integration process is directly influenced by data quality. For example, a large company has reported, that up to 60% of the information integrated to their data warehouse was unusable due to the poor quality of the input data [Orr98].

In this work we describe a data integration system based on a global schema. The contents of data sources are described with respect to this schema in the form of assertions in a top-down fashion. The salient feature of our approach is the tight integration of classical query planning and the assessment and consideration of information quality (IQ). We extend an existing framework for query planning which is based on rules that define the semantic relationship between queries. These rules – and hence queries, not entire sources or relations – are the main targets for quality assessment. This level of granularity is necessary since many information quality criteria can neither be assigned to an entire source nor to single classes.

Proceedings of the 25th VLDB Conference, Edinburgh, Scotland, 1999.

For instance, consider a source that stores data about genes and their location on chromosomes. This source might use two different classes to store the data, one for gene information and one for the location information. We now observe that the gene information is frequently updated, as is the location information for the X chromosome. However, data on locations of genes on the Y chromosome are treated less thoroughly. The timeliness of the data of this source can neither be described with one value for the entire source nor with one value per class. Instead, we want to assign quality measures to *queries*: a high IQ score to queries for X chromosome locations and for gene information, and a low IQ score to queries for Y chromosome locations.

Another example is a source which offers two different interfaces, for instance a simple WWW interface and a direct SQL channel. Logical query planning will consider that the SQL interface might be capable of answering more complex queries than the WWW interface - planning based on information quality will capture the update frequency, accuracy, completeness etc. of the data presented in the two interfaces.

The purpose of our system is to answer a global query by using only queries that are executable by some data source. We use a view rewrite mechanism for this purpose [Les99]. We here improve the logical planning algorithm by adding two steps: First we reduce the overall number of sources in a pre-processing phase, since certain sources are often worse than others in all criteria. We ensure not to lose any source that is unique in some aspect, i.e., the only source storing data about a certain attribute. Filtering sources is important since the planning algorithm inevitably has a time-complexity which is worst-case exponential in the number of rules and hence indirectly in the number of sources. Second, we rank all plans produced in the planning phase by evaluating query-specific and attribute-specific IQ scores following the join-structure of a plan. Eventually we execute plans with the highest information quality until a stop criterion is reached: either some best percentage of plans or until some overall quality threshold is reached.

1.1 Related work.

Despite the fact that there is much research showing the importance of information quality for businesses and users [WS96, Red98], and that many techniques have been proposed to improve and maintain quality of individual information sources [Wan98], we are not aware of any project that tries to use this quality data for structured information integration.

Database interoperability and data integration for molecular biology databases is addressed in a number of projects, such as OPM [CKM+98] or bioKleisli [DOTW97]. Usually these are loose federations in the sense of [SL90], i.e., they do not offer a global unified schema, and no project regards information quality.

Several research projects such as the GlOSS system [GGMT94] or work reported in [FKL97] focussed on the problem of source selection for *text based* information systems. However, selection is typically confined to criteria used in information retrieval systems, such as word-counting measures, or to traditional DBMS criteria such as response time. Within the DWQ project Jeusfeld et al. proposed a quality meta model to store IQ metadata [JQJ98]. However, their approach is guided by data warehouse quality requirements and a data warehouse architecture which is a special case of our mediator architecture.

Our planning method uses a local-as-view approach [Ull97] similar to the Information Manifold [LRO96]. Our notion of query correspondence assertions is an extension to query capability records as described there, in that it combines local-as-view with global-as-view modeling. In [Les98] we presented an improved algorithm for the query planning problem in this framework, which we now enhance with quality considerations.

1.2 Example.

We will use the following example throughout the paper. Our mediator is designed to provide information about genes and is modeled in its global relational schema (see Figure 1). A gene (Gn) is, very roughly speaking, a part of the human genome which is related to some property of humans (see [Rob94] for a thorough discussion on what is a gene from a computer scientist's point-of-view). Genes which are known to be related to a disease (Di) are particularly interesting. We are also interested in the sequence (Se) of a gene, which is essentially a string. Determining a sequence is a complicated and costly process. The quality of the result varies with the institution that carries out the experiments. We store this as its origin (Or). Interesting properties of a sequence, for instance the occurrence of repeats, are stored as annotation (An). Again, the quality of annotation depends highly on the effort that is invested in its analysis and differs from source to source.

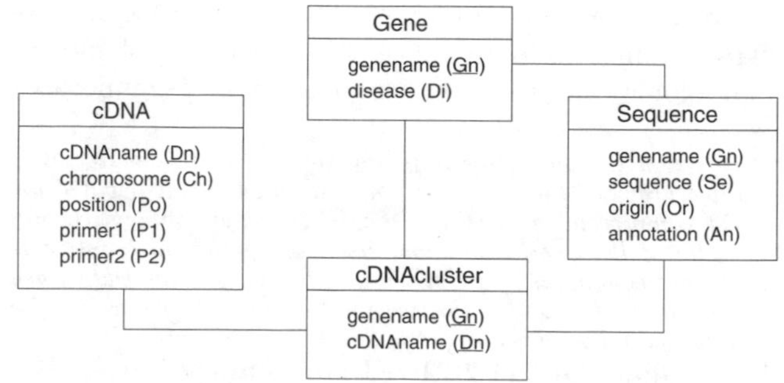

Figure 1: Information model of the mediator.

Most parts of the sequence of a human being do not contain genes. One possibility to find genes is to create pieces of so-called complementary DNA (cDNA). Locating a cDNA on a chromosome requires knowledge of two primers (P1, P2) which are short pieces of its sequence. Different cDNAs are often overlapping. They are therefore clustered into larger sections. cDNAclusters are then related to genes.

The mediator can query the five different sources which are listed below. The sources have overlapping scopes and varying information quality. For their interface relations as exposed by a wrapper see Table 1. Since this work focuses on planning using information quality, we make some simplifications, such as the use of object names as global keys.

- Source S_1 stores sequences which it copies infrequently from other sites, sometimes introducing parsing errors.
- Source S_2 also copies sequence data from other sites, also infrequently updated, but uses more sites and is hence more complete.
- Source S_3 is the WWW server of an institute which does its own sequencing. Sequence data is highly up-to-date, but few annotations are provided. The server is frequently unavailable.
- Source S_4 is a renowned commercial provider of cDNA data. It provides two interfaces: 1. A free WWW server with a slow connection. Only the chromosome location is retrievable. 2. A fast SQL connection through which clients can retrieve all attributes, but there is a charge per query. Primer sequences are available for most of their cDNAs, chromosome positions only some.
- Source S_5 is a directly accessible relational database which stores mapping and sequence data for genes. The schema (not given here) is different from our global schema. The mediator uses two queries: one relates genes and sequences, the other relates genes to their cDNAclusters.

1.3 Structure of this paper.

We describe the logical query planning in Section 2. Section 3 formally introduces information quality as a set of properties, which we classify for use in Section 4. There, we show how IQ plays a decisive role in query processing and leads to high quality results. We conclude in Section 5 and give a brief outlook to future work.

2 Logical Description of Information Sources

Our approach is based on a standard wrapper-mediator architecture (see Figure 2) with the relational model as canonical data model [Wie92]. Each information source is wrapped by one or more source-specific modules, the *wrappers*, which offer a relational export schema and query interface, hiding the particular data model, access path, and interface technology of the source. Wrappers are used by a *mediator* which offers an integrated access through its global schema. In this section we describe the logical planning of user queries. Details can be found in [Les98] and [NLF99].

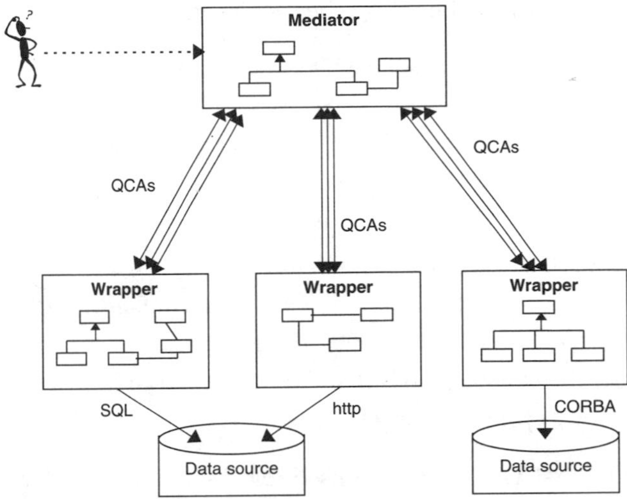

Figure 2: Principal architecture. The content of sources is described with sets of QCAs. Sources can be accessed through one or more interfaces.

To answer queries and to select sources, a mediator must know the content of each source with respect to its own schema. This *semantic knowledge* is defined by an administrator through query correspondence assertions (QCAs), which are set-oriented equations between queries against one wrapper and queries against the mediator schema. We always assume inner-join semantics. A QCA has the general form

$$MQ \leftarrow S_i.v_j \leftarrow WQ$$

where MQ (mediator query) is a conjunctive query against the mediator schema, WQ (wrapper query) is a conjunctive query against the schema of one wrapper and $S_i.v_j$ is a view which must be *safe* in both directions, i.e., variables in the view must appear in both queries. They are called *exported* variables. S_i is the source that is addressed through the QCA; internally, the mediator also bears in memory the wrapper that is used. By defining a QCA, the administrator asserts the intensional equivalence of the results of both MQ and WQ, restricted to the variables appearing in the view.

Example. The following simple QCA describes the

content of S_1:

$$\text{sequence(Gn,Se,Or,An)} \leftarrow S_1.v_1(Gn, Se, Or, An) \leftarrow \text{seq(Gn,Se,Or,An)}$$

Note that this rule does not mean that S_1 is the only source storing sequence data. Others can contribute to the global relation as well.

Describing S_5 requires two QCAs, one for each of the two queries used by the mediator:

gene(Gn,Di), sequence(Gn,Se,-,An)
$\leftarrow S_5.v_1(Gn, Di, Se, An)$
$\leftarrow$ genes(GID,Gn,Di), genepart(GID,PID), part(PID,Se,An)

gene(Gn,-), cDNAcluster(Gn,Dn), cDNA(Dn,Ch,-,P1,P2)
$\leftarrow S_5.v_2(Gn, Dn, Ch, P1, P2)$
$\leftarrow$ clustering(Gn,Dn,CID), cluster(CID,Ch), primers(Dn,P1,P2)

The first QCA could be used for global queries asking for gene sequences, but not for queries asking for the origin of gene sequences, since this attribute is not exported through the view. See Table 1 for the list of QCAs that describe the content of the different sources in our example. □

S_1:	QCA_1	sequence(Gn, Se, Or, An) $\leftarrow S_1.v_1(Gn, Se, Or, An)$ $\leftarrow$ seq(Gn, Se, Or, An)
S_2:	QCA_2	sequence(Gn, Se, Or, An) $\leftarrow S_2.v_1(Gn, Se, Or, An)$ $\leftarrow$ seq(Gn, Se, Or, An)
S_3:	QCA_3	sequence(Gn, Se, Or, An) $\leftarrow S_3.v_1(Gn, Se, Or, An)$ $\leftarrow$ seq(Gn, Se, Or, An)
S_4:	QCA_4	cDNA(Dn, Ch, –, –, –) $\leftarrow S_4.v_1(Dn, Ch)$ $\leftarrow$ www(Dn, Ch)
	QCA_5	cDNA(Dn, Ch, Po, P1, P2) $\leftarrow S_4.v_2(Dn, Ch, Po, P1, P2)$ $\leftarrow$ direct(Dn, Ch, Po, P1, P2)
S_5:	QCA_6	gene(Gn, Di), seq.(Gn, Se, -, An) $\leftarrow S_5.v_1(Gn, Di, Se, An)$ $\leftarrow$ genes(GID, Gn, Di), genepart(GID, PID, -), part(PID, Se, An)
	QCA_7	gene(Gn, -), cDNAcluster(Gn, Dn), cDNA(Dn, Ch, -, P1, P2) $\leftarrow S_5.v_2(Gn, Dn, Ch, P1, P2)$ $\leftarrow$ clustering(Gn, Dn, Cl, P1, P2), cluster(Cl,Ch),primers(Dn,P1,P2)

Table 1: QCAs describing the semantics of the seven possible wrapper queries.

For a given user query against the mediator schema, the mediator tries to find combinations of QCAs that are *semantically contained* [ASU79] in the user query and hence provably compute only correct results. We call such combinations *plans*. In Section 4.2 we describe our algorithm to find all correct plans. The *complete* answer to a user query with respect to the given QCAs is the union over the answers of all correct plans. For instance, the global extension of *sequence* would be the union over the extension of the three "seq"-queries in sources S_1, S_2, and S_3 (Table 1).

However, there can be prohibitively many correct plans. Consider a query asking for the sequence of a specific gene. The mediator detects that S_5 can be used for the *gene* part of the query and S_1, S_2, and S_3 for the *sequence*-part. This already sums up to three different plans. Suppose there were two more sources storing genes, then the number of correct plans would increase to nine. But if the user was, for instance, particularly interested in complete annotation, plans using S_3 are not very promising; if highly up-to-date data is required, S_1 could probably be ignored.

Note that query planning as described here is fundamentally different from classical query optimization for a relational DBMS. Our planning finds plans that are correct, but possibly generate different results, while classical optimization considers plans that all produce the same result.

3 Information Quality for Information Sources

There is no agreed definition or measure for information quality, except such general notions as "fitness for use" [TB98]. In this section we define information quality (IQ) as a set of quality criteria. Information sources and query plans achieve certain IQ scores in each criterion. We aggregate the scores to determine a total IQ score for each source and plan and then rank sources and plans accordingly. Based on this ranking we execute only the best plans over the best sources disregarding the rest.

Wang and Strong have empirically identified fifteen IQ criteria regarded by data consumers as the most important [WS96]. They classified the criteria into "intrinsic quality", "accessibility, "contextual quality", and "representational quality". Their framework has already been used effectively in industry and government. We adapt this set of criteria to our integration model and to the scope of molecular biology information systems. However, we classify the criteria in a different manner to reflect better our planning process.

3.1 IQ Classification.

It is not always sufficient to assign quality scores to entire sources. Since our planning process already uses QCAs and not entire sources as the basic level of correspondence, it is natural to assign IQ scores to QCAs. Furthermore, IQ scores can even apply at an attribute level, as a source may provide high quality information in one attribute, but lower quality in another. Thus, we distinguish three classes of quality criteria:

- **Source-specific criteria** determine the overall quality of an information source. Criteria of this category, for instance reputation, apply to all information of the source, independently of how it is obtained. IQ scores of this class stay unchanged as long as the source itself does not dramatically change.
- **QCA-specific criteria** determine quality aspects of specific queries that are computable by a source. Using this finer granularity, we can e.g. model different response times for different types of queries to the same source.
- **Attribute-specific criteria** assess the quality of an information source in terms of its ability to provide the attributes of a specific user query. The IQ scores for these criteria depend on the attributes specified in the user query, and hence, the scores for these criteria can only be determined at "query time". For instance, we described S_3 as having relatively few annotations attached to the sequences they store. In such cases, we need to define specifically that the completeness of the *annotation* attribute in QCA_3 is not very high.

3.2 IQ Criteria.

We slightly modified the set of IQ criteria by Wang and Strong in [WS96], considering the specific needs of biologists and the specific properties of existing information systems. Some criteria that are not applicable to our area of discourse or data integration model are omitted. We added the two criteria reliability and price, which play a important role for molecular biology information systems. Table 2 on the next page categorizes and summarizes all our criteria. In accordance with our integration and planning process we have found three categories: Source-specific, QCA-specific, and attribute-specific criteria. The criteria of each category are dealt with differently. A more detailed description of each criterion can be found in [NLF99]. As usual, we assume independence of the criteria.

Depending on the application domain and the structure of the available sources, the classification of criteria into the three classes may vary. For instance, if sources charge the same amount of money for each query, the price criterion should be only source-specific. If, on the other hand, a source provides data with different update frequencies, the timeliness criterion should be QCA-specific. Finally, if the information of a source can be partitioned into sets with heavily diverging IQ scores, the QCAs of this source can be split according to this partitioning. Each of the new QCAs will then receive individual IQ scores.

A problem that all projects addressing IQ are facing, is the ability to assign IQ scores in an objective manner. Some of the criteria below can not be measured but are highly subjective, such as source reputation. We suggest user profiles, i.e., sets of IQ scores for all subjective criteria that are set-up once by each user and then used for all of his or her future queries.

4 Finding the Best Sources and Plans

Creating good execution plans for a user query in any DBMS involves a search space of all plans and a cost model to compare plans with one another. Building on this analogy we define the search space in our multidatabase environment as the set of all plans that answer the user query in a semantically correct manner. However, these plans produce extensionally different results as they may involve different sources. Thus, in general more than one plan should be executed to gain a response that is as complete as possible. Due to the heterogeneity of the information sources in quality and cost we expand the traditional cost model to a quality model to valuate the plans.

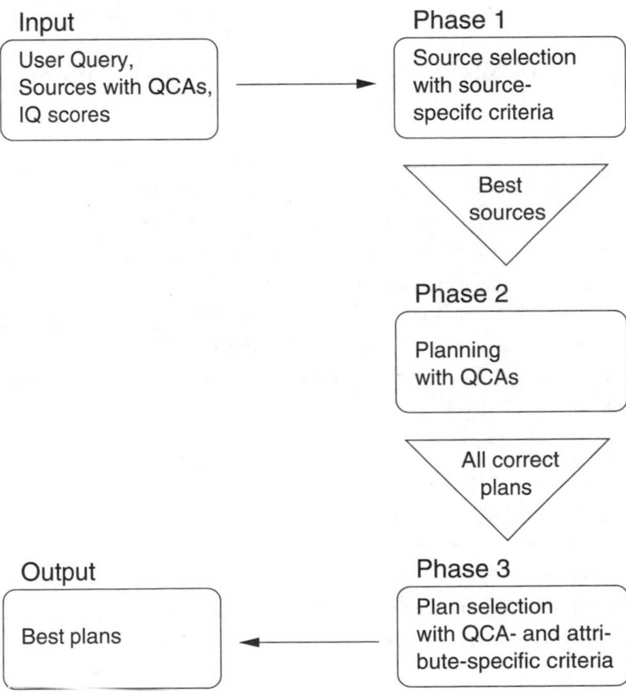

Figure 3: Three-Phase plan selection

To this end, we propose a three-phase approach to quality-driven information integration: In the first phase we reduce computational cost of the second

Class	Criterion	Brief explanation
Source-specific	Ease of understanding	User grade from 1 to 10, based on presentation of the data.
	Reputation	User grade from 1 to 10, based on personal preferences and professional experience.
	Reliability	Ranking from 1 to 10, based on accuracy of experimental method with which the data is produced.
	Timeliness	Update-frequency measured in days.
QCA-specific	Availability	Percentage of time the source is accessible, based on technical equipment and statistics.
	Price	Monetary price of a query in US Dollars. We assume a pay-by-query scheme.
	Representational Consistency	Per-query time consumption of the wrapper (for parsing, translations, etc.), in seconds. The more consistent the presentation of the source, the less work for the wrapper.
	Response Time	Average waiting time for responses, measured in seconds.
	Accuracy	Percentage of objects without data errors such as misspellings, out-of-range values, etc.
	Relevancy	Percentage of real world objects represented in the source. When the total number of real world objects is not known, an approximation can be used.
Attribute-specific	Completeness	Fullness of the relation in each attribute (horizontal fitness). Attributes typically have a certain percentage of `null`-values. Completeness of a QCA is measured as the sum over the percentages of non-`null` values in each attribute, adjusted by a user weighting stating the importance of each attribute. The weighting is specified with the user query.
	Amount	Number of attributes in the response which were not specified in the user query (vertical fitness).

Table 2: Classification of Quality Criteria for MBISs

phase by filtering out low quality sources based on the source-specific IQ criteria, continuing with only the best sources. The second phase uses the QCAs of the remaining sources to generate all correct plans, thus establishing the search space for the last phase. There we explore the entire search space using a quality model for the remaining IQ criteria and choose the best plans for execution. Figure 3 gives an overview of the three phases. For simplicity we do not apply a search strategy to combine Phases 2 and 3, rather we materialize the entire search space in Phase 2 and examine it in Phase 3.

Example. To describe each step in detail we use the example of Section 2. Table 3 gives IQ scores for each QCA and each criterion. We are aware of the difficulties of numerically expressing certain criteria, but since not the absolute IQ scores are of importance but rather their relative values, we believe that our approach is reasonable. □

To find a ranking based on multiple criteria one faces two fundamental problems: (i) The range and units of the IQ scores vary, making it necessary to scale the scores. (ii) The importance of the criteria may vary making it necessary to find a user-specific weighting of the criteria. Several *multiple attribute decision making* methods have been proposed to solve these problems [Nau98]. To find the best sources in Phase 1, we use the "Data Envelopment Analysis" method; to rank the execution plans in Phase 3 we apply the "Simple Additive Weighting" method.

4.1 Phase 1: Source Selection

Our logical planning algorithm can potentially generate an exponential number of plans in the length of the user query and the number of QCAs. Therefore, we thrive to decrease this number before we start planning. For this purpose, we use the source-specific IQ criteria to "weed out" sources that are qualitatively not as good as others. Our goal is to find a certain number or percentage of best sources independently of any user-specific weighting. The mediator performs Phase 1 only once after start-up and does not repeat it until an information source dramatically changes in a source-specific criterion, or until a new information source is added to the system.

To evaluate a large amount of sources in a *general*, user-independent way, we suggest Data Envelopment Analysis (DEA) developed by Charnes et al. as a general method to classify a population of observations [CCR78]. For a more detailed description of DEA for

	S_1	QCA_1	S_2	QCA_2	S_3	QCA_3	S_4	QCA_4	QCA_5	S_5	QCA_6	QCA_7
EoU(grade)	5		7		7		8			6		
Rep.(grade)	5		5		7		8			7		
Reli.(grade)	2		6		4		6			6		
Tim.(days)	30		30		2		1			7		
Av.(%)		99		99		60		80	99		95	95
Pr.(US $)		0		0		0		0	1		0	0
R.C.(sec)		1		1		.5		.7	.2		.7	.7
R.T.(sec)		.2		.2		.2		3	.1		1	1
Ac.(%)		99.9		99.9		99.8		99.95	99.95		99.95	99.95
Relev.(%)		60		80		90		80	80		60	60

Table 3: IQ scores s_{ij} of the 7 QCAs. Scores are partly inferred from the informal description in Section 1.2. Completeness and amount are not contained since they depend on the specific user query.

source selection see [NFS98]. The DEA method avoids the problems of scaling and weighting by defining an efficiency frontier as the convex hull of the unscaled and unweighted vector space of IQ dimensions. Figure 4 shows this vector space for two arbitrary IQ dimensions. Sources on the hull are defined as "good", sources below the hull as "non-good".

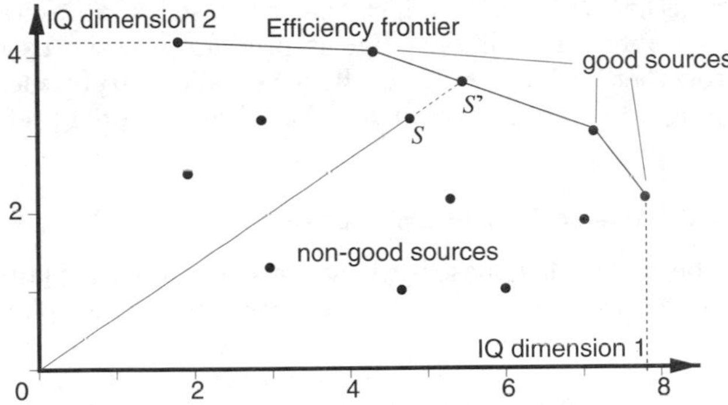

Figure 4: Classifying Sources with Data Envelopment Analysis

Consider the non-good source S in Figure 4. Assuming constant returns to scale, the virtual but realistic source S' is constructed as a convex combination of the two neighboring sources on the efficiency frontier. Clearly the virtual source S' would be better than source S, thus S is non-good.

To determine whether a source is on the frontier or below, we solve the following linear program (LP) once for each information source S_{i_0} with IQ scores s_{ij}. Please note that the variables of the LP are the weightings w_j.

$$\begin{array}{lll} \text{maximize} & & \\ IQ(S_{i_0}) := & \sum_j w_j \cdot s_{i_0 j} & \\ \text{subject to} & & \\ IQ(S_i) \;=\; & \sum_j w_j \cdot s_{ij} & \leq 1 \;\text{ for } i = 1, \dots, n \\ & w_j & \geq \varepsilon > 0 \;\text{ for } j = 1, \dots, 4 \end{array}$$

The result of each LP is the optimal quality score $IQ(S_{i_0})$ of the examined source, which is either 1 (on the frontier = good) or below 1 (below the frontier = non-good). By fine-tuning the ε-parameter we can vary the number of good sources to the desired percentage. The problem of solving such a linear program is of polynomial nature. A common way to solve LPs is the Simplex method, developed by Dantzig [Dan63], which has an exponential worst case complexity but is very efficient on average.

For further planning, we want to completely disregard non-good sources. However, there is a danger of removing a source that has low IQ but is the only source providing a certain attribute of the global schema, e.g., the only source providing chromosome data should be kept for planning, even if its IQ is low. Furthermore we must retain sources that exclusively provide certain extensions of an attribute, e.g., the only source providing data on X chromosomes should be kept, even if its IQ is low and other sources provide chromosome data for other chromosomes. Removing such sources from further consideration would "reduce" the global schema. To avoid suppressing these sources we only weed out non-good sources, whose QCAs are all contained in QCAs of good sources. In this way, the global schema remains intact.

Example. In our example only source S_1 is excluded. All other sources have an IQ score of 1 and will be further considered in the next two phases. □

4.2 Phase 2: Plan Creation

The goal of this phase is to find all combinations of QCAs that obtain semantically correct answers to a given user query. Every QCA defines a view on the global schema. We must find combinations of such views that generate correct tuples. This is equivalent to the problem of answering a query against a schema using only a set of views on the same schema. Levy et al. show that this problem is NP-complete for conjunctive queries and conjunctive view definitions [LMSS95]. In principle, one has to enumerate all combinations of views up to a certain length, and test for each of these whether it is contained in the original query. However, the worst-case exponential behavior of this algorithm only occurs in pathological cases. For instance, Chekuri and Rajaraman show that the problem is polynomial if the *width* of the query is bound [CR97].

In [Les98] we improved the algorithm by Levy et al. [LRO96], but for space limitations we here use a simpler algorithm, similar to the original one.

Example. Imagine a user query UQ asking for all genes of the X chromosome together with their related diseases, sequences, origins, and annotations. We answer this query by joining the gene relation with the sequence relation to obtain origin and annotation. We must also join the gene relation with the cDNA relation to ensure the chromosome-condition:

$$\begin{aligned} &UQ(Gn(100), Di(100), Se(100), Or(30), An(70)) \\ &\quad \leftarrow \text{gene}(Gn, Di), \text{sequence}(Gn, Se, Or, An), \\ &\quad\quad \text{cDNAcluster}(Gn, Dn), \\ &\quad\quad \text{cDNA}(Dn, Ch, \text{-}, \text{-}, \text{-}), Ch =' X'; \end{aligned}$$

□

The user weightings for each attribute are used to reflect how important they are to the user. In the example, the user expresses that he is interested in annotation and not as much in the origin of sequences. The weightings are used to compute the completeness score of plans later on.

First, for each relation of UQ we determine the set of QCAs which contain the relation in their mediator query MQ. We store this set in a *bucket* [LRO96]. We must also check if the QCAs export all necessary attributes, i.e., those that are required in UQ.

In a second step we enumerate the cartesian product of all buckets and check three conditions for each combination: (1) if it is satisfiable, (2) if it is semantically contained in UQ, and (3) whether it can be minimized, i.e., whether certain QCAs are redundant.

Example. For the four relations of UQ we construct the buckets

$$\begin{aligned} \text{bucket(gene)} &= \{QCA_6\} \\ \text{bucket(sequence)} &= \{QCA_2, QCA_3\} \\ \text{bucket(cDNAcluster)} &= \{QCA_7\} \\ \text{bucket(cDNA)} &= \{QCA_4, QCA_5, QCA_7\} \end{aligned}$$

QCA_7 does not occur in bucket(gene) because it does not export the required Di attribute; the same holds for QCA_6 in bucket(sequence) and attribute Or. QCA_1 does not appear in bucket(sequence) since S_1 was deleted from the set of sources in Phase 1.

After enumerating the cartesian product of all buckets and checking the three conditions, we end up with the following plans, each possibly producing a different set of correct tuples for UQ.

$$\begin{aligned} P_1 &= QCA_6 \bowtie QCA_2 \bowtie QCA_7 \bowtie QCA_4 \\ P_2 &= QCA_6 \bowtie QCA_2 \bowtie QCA_7 \bowtie QCA_5 \\ P_3 &= QCA_6 \bowtie QCA_2 \bowtie QCA_7 \\ P_4 &= QCA_6 \bowtie QCA_3 \bowtie QCA_7 \bowtie QCA_4 \\ P_5 &= QCA_6 \bowtie QCA_3 \bowtie QCA_7 \bowtie QCA_5 \\ P_6 &= QCA_6 \bowtie QCA_3 \bowtie QCA_7 \end{aligned}$$

□

A plan is executed by computing the wrapper queries of the QCAs, propagating variables bindings from QCA to QCA as usual. If a WQ is executed, the resulting tuples are temporarily stored in an instance of the mediator schema. Missing values are padded with null or relationship-preserving key values that are generated automatically. The original query UQ is computed on this instance after all results are retrieved.

The mediator also keeps track of the origin of each value. Therefore, for each tuple that is obtained from a source, the mediator stores the name of this source together with the interface that was used in an extra attribute. This information is presented to the user together with the final result, which allows to further judge the information quality based on personal preferences.

4.3 Phase 3: Plan Selection

The goal of this phase is to qualitatively rank the plans of the previous phase and ultimately to restrict plan execution to some best percentage of plans, or alternatively, to as many plans as necessary to meet certain cost- or quality-constraints.

Following the DBMS approach of cost models for query execution plans with a tree-structure, we define a quality model for the tree-structured plans created in Phase 2. Leaves represent QCAs which deliver the base data. Those data are subsequently processed within the inner nodes of the tree, which represent inner join operators performed by the mediator.

Plan selection proceeds in three steps: First the IQ scores of the QCAs are determined (3a). Then the quality model aggregates these scores along tree paths to gain an overall quality score at the root of the tree, which forms the score of the entire plan (3b). Finally, this score is used to rank all plans (3c).

4.3.1 Phase 3.a: QCA Quality.

An IQ vector of length 8 is attached to each QCA, i.e., one dimension for each non-source-specific criterion. QCA-specific criteria have fixed scores for each QCA. They are determined only once or whenever the corresponding source undergoes major changes. The scores of the attribute-specific criteria completeness and amount on the other hand are recalculated for each user-query. The general IQ vector for QCAs is (abbreviated):

$$\begin{aligned} IQ(QCA_i) &:= (s_{i5}, \ldots, s_{i11}) \\ &= (Av, Pr, RC, RT, Ac, Rel, Com(UQ), Am(UQ)) \end{aligned}$$

Example. We determine the following IQ vectors for the QCAs participating in plans P_1 through P_6. The first six elements of each vector are taken from Table 3, the remaining two elements completeness and amount are calculated using the attribute set and attribute weighting of the user query UQ of Section 4.2.

$$\begin{aligned} IQ(QCA_2) &= (99, 0, 1, .2, 99.9, 80, 52.8, 0) \\ IQ(QCA_3) &= (60, 0, .5, .2, 99.8, 90, 49, 0) \\ IQ(QCA_4) &= (80, 0, .7, 3, 99.95, 80, 20, 1) \\ IQ(QCA_5) &= (99, 1, .2, .1, 99.95, 80, 20, 4) \\ IQ(QCA_6) &= (95, 0, .7, 1, 99.95, 60, 48.2, 0) \\ IQ(QCA_7) &= (95, 0, .7, 1, 99.95, 60, 38, 3) \end{aligned}$$

□

Up to this point, each leaf node of each plan-tree is assigned an IQ vector. However, we have no total IQ vectors for the plans yet. These scores are obtained through the quality model in the next phase.

4.3.2 Phase 3.b: Plan Quality.

Corresponding to the idea of *cost models* for DBMSs, we have designed a *quality model* to calculate the total IQ score of a plan. Since we only consider join-operators, a plan is a binary tree with QCAs as leaves and join operators as inner nodes. The IQ vector for an inner join node is calculated as a combination of the IQ vectors of its left and right child nodes l and r, as shown in Equation (1).

$$\begin{aligned} IQ(l \bowtie r) &:= IQ(l) \circ IQ(r) \\ &= (s_{l5} \circ s_{r5}, \ldots, s_{l12} \circ s_{r12}) \end{aligned} \quad (1)$$

Figure 5 shows the plan tree for P_3 with its aggregated IQ vectors. In each criterion the IQ scores s_{ij} are computed with the $\circ$-operator (or "merge function") which is resolved according to Table 4. Since all merge functions in Table 4 are both commutative and associative, a change of the join execution order within a plan has no effect on its IQ score. This is desirable, since the user perceives the quality of the query result and not the quality of how this result is obtained. Furthermore, we do not consider the execution time of joins performed by the mediator since we assume that execution time is dominated by the response times of the sources.

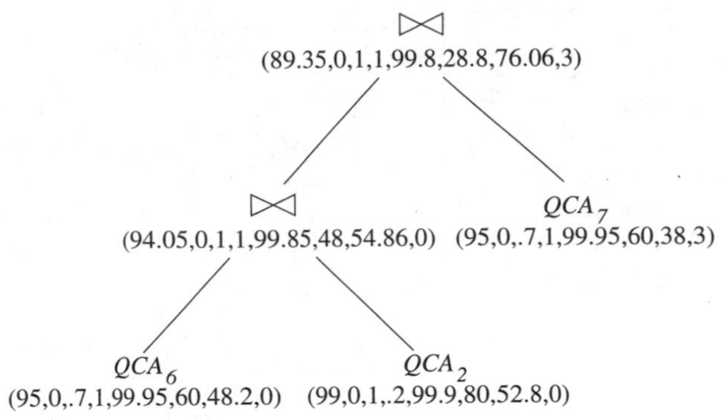

Figure 5: Merging IQ vectors in join nodes in plan P_3

Example. The six plans have aggregated IQ vectors

$$\begin{aligned} IQ(P_1) &= (71.00, 0, 1, 3, 99.75, 23.04, 78.06, 4) \\ IQ(P_2) &= (88.45, 1, 1, 1, 99.75, 23.04, 78.06, 7) \\ IQ(P_3) &= (89.35, 0, 1, 1, 99.80, 28.80, 76.06, 3) \\ IQ(P_4) &= (43.32, 0, .7, 3, 99.65, 25.92, 75.94, 4) \\ IQ(P_5) &= (53.61, 1, .7, 1, 99.65, 25.92, 75.94, 7) \\ IQ(P_6) &= (54.50, 0, .7, 1, 99.70, 32.40, 73.94, 3) \end{aligned}$$

□

Up to this point, the scores are neither scaled nor weighted, making a comparison or ranking of plans impossible.

4.3.3 Phase 3.c: Plan Ranking.

The IQ scores of the vectors must be scaled, weighted, and compared to find a total IQ score for each plan and thus a ranking of the plans. To this end, we use the Simple Additive Weighting (SAW) method. It is one of the simplest but well perceived decision making methods, in that its ranking results are usually very close to results of more sophisticated methods [Nau98]. The method is comprised of three basic steps: scale the scores to make them comparable, apply the user weighting, and sum up the scores for each source.

The IQ scores of the criteria availability, accuracy, relevancy, and completeness are scaled according to Equation (2) below, where $s_j^{\min}$ and $s_j^{\max}$ are the minimum and maximum score in criterion j respectively. The criteria price, representational consistency, response time, and amount are negative criteria, i.e., the higher the score, the worse the quality. Thus, they are scaled according to Equation (3). With these scaling functions all scores are in $[0, 1]$, the best score of any criterion obtains the value 1, and the worst score of any criterion obtains the value 0. This property assures comparability of scores across different criteria and in different ranges.

$$v_{ij} := \frac{s_{ij} - s_j^{\min}}{s_j^{\max} - s_j^{\min}} \quad (2)$$

$$v_{ij} := \frac{s_j^{\max} - s_{ij}}{s_j^{\max} - s_j^{\min}} \quad (3)$$

Criterion	Merge function "∘"	Brief explanation
Availability	$s_{l5} \cdot s_{r5}$	Probability that both sites are accessible.
Price	$s_{l6} + s_{r6}$	Both queries must be payed.
Repr. Consistency	$\max[s_{l7}, s_{r7}]$	Wrapper integrates sources in parallel.
Response Time	$\max[s_{l8}, s_{r8}]$	Both children are processed in parallel.
Accuracy	$s_{l9} \cdot s_{r9}$	Probability that left and right side do not contain an error.
Relevancy	$s_{l10} \cdot s_{r10}$	Probability for join match.
Completeness	$s_{l11} + s_{r11} - s_{l11} \cdot s_{r11}$	Probability that either left or right side has non-`null` value (operations at attribute level).
Amount	$s_{l12} + s_{r12}$	All unnecessary attributes must be dealt with.

Table 4: Merge functions for Quality Criteria

For the weighting step SAW requires a weight-vector $W = (w_1, \ldots, w_m)$ specified by the user such that $\sum_{j=1}^{m} w_j$ equals 1. The weight-vector reflects the importance of the individual criteria to the user. We store the user-specific weight-vectors in a profile. Hence, the inclusion of quality reasoning is completely transparent to a user once the system is set up, i.e., once all QCAs and sources have their IQ scores. The only exception is the possibility to weight specific attributes of a query. However, we believe that most users would appreciate this as a benefit rather than a burden.

For a plan P_i the overall quality score $IQ(P_i)$ is calculated as the weighted sum according to Equation (4):

$$IQ(P_i) := \sum_{j=1}^{m} w_j \cdot v_{ij} \qquad (4)$$

The final IQ score of the plan again is in $[0,1]$ and gives the ranking position of the plan. After the IQ scores for all plans have been calculated, we choose and execute a certain number of best plans.

Example. With the indifferent weighting vector $W = (\frac{1}{8}, \frac{1}{8}, \frac{1}{8}, \frac{1}{8}, \frac{1}{8}, \frac{1}{8}, \frac{1}{8}, \frac{1}{8})$ where all criteria have equal importance, the following IQ scores are obtained (in ranking order):

$$IQ(P_3) = .7663 \qquad (1)$$
$$IQ(P_6) = .697 \qquad (2)$$
$$IQ(P_1) = .5023 \qquad (3)$$
$$IQ(P_2) = .4559 \qquad (4)$$
$$IQ(P_4) = .4429 \qquad (5)$$
$$IQ(P_5) = .3771 \qquad (6)$$

A user preferring quick response time at any price, might specify the weighting $W = (\frac{1}{8}, \frac{0}{8}, \frac{1}{8}, \frac{2}{8}, \frac{1}{8}, \frac{1}{8}, \frac{1}{8}, \frac{1}{8})$ obtaining a ranking of the plans in the order P_3, P_6, P_2, P_5, P_1, P_4. Plan P_1 is ranked lower than before because it includes QCA_4 which has a very high response time. Despite its high price, Plan P_2 is ranked higher than before since it has a low response time. □

With the exception of the completeness criterion, all merge functions decrease the aggregated IQ scores with each additional QCA. Thus, there is a natural tendency favoring short plans, i.e., plans consisting of few QCAs. Not only does this reflect the influence of the criteria, it also conforms to intuition: Biologists will probably not be happy to accept results where the four attributes of the query are generated in four different sources.

The complexity of Phase 3 is linear in the number of considered plans times the maximum length of the plans. This length is in turn bounded by the number of relations in the user query.

5 Conclusion and Outlook

We have proposed a novel method to the well known and important, yet frequently ignored problem of considering information quality in information integration. This problem has not, to our best knowledge, been adequately addressed before. Our results offer a solution to the notorious problem of information overload, based on a filtering of important information with the help of a rich set of quality criteria. Using these criteria quality-driven information integration identifies high quality plans which produce high quality results.

Clearly, the selection of quality criteria is a subjective task. Yet our method is by no way restricted to the criteria we used in this paper. We have described merge functions for each criterion which calculate the quality of the information in a join result. Due to the associativity of these merge-functions, we determine the quality of a result independently of how this result is created. This freedom will allow us to include binding patterns in the QCAs, which often dictate a specific join order. Furthermore, a traditional post-optimization can be performed to find the best join order of the chosen plans without influencing their quality score.

Future work will also include a tighter cooperation of the plan creation phase and plan selection phase: Information quality scores can be used in a branch & bound fashion to dramatically improve planning time. Lifting our current model to a higher level, we plan not only to calculate the quality of plan results, but also the quality of the union of several plans to find the best combination of plans to execute. We believe that the same principles of calculating and merging quality scores apply.

Acknowledgements

This research was supported by the German Research Society, Berlin-Brandenburg Graduate School in Distributed Information Systems (DFG grant no. GRK 316). We also thank Myra Spiliopoulou for many helpful comments.

References

[ASU79] Alfred V. Aho, Yehoshua Sagiv, and Jeffrey D. Ullman. Efficient optimisation of a class of relational expressions. *ACM Transactions on Database Systems*, 4(4):435–454, 1979.

[CCR78] A. Charnes, W.W. Cooper, and E. Rhodes. Measuring the efficiency of decision making units. *European Journal of Operational Research*, 2:429–444, 1978.

[CKM+98] I-Min A. Chen, Anthony S. Kosky, Victor M. Markowitz, Christoph Sensen, Ernest Szeto, and Thodoros Topaloglou. Advanced query mechanisms for biological databases. In *6th Int. Conf. on Intelligent Systems for Molecular Biology*, pages 43–51, Montreal, Canada, 1998. AAAI Press, Menlo Park.

[CR97] Chandra Chekuri and Anand Rajaraman. Conjunctive query containment revisited. In *6th Int. Conference on Database Theory; LNCS 1186*, pages 56–70, Delphi, Greece, 1997.

[Dan63] G.B. Dantzig. *Linear Programming and Extensions.* Princeton University Press, Princeton, NJ, 1963.

[DOTW97] Susan Davidson, G. Christian Overton, Val Tannen, and Limsoon Wong. BioKleisli: A digital library for biomedical researchers. *Int. Journal on Digital Libraries*, 1:36–53, 1997.

[FKL97] Daniela Florescu, Daphne Koller, and Alon Levy. Using probabilistic information in data integration. In *Proc. of the 23rd VLDB Conference*, Athens, Greece, 1997.

[GGMT94] Luis Gravano, Hector Garcia-Molina, and Anthony Tomasic. The effectiveness of GlOSS for the text database recovery problem. In *Proc. of the ACM SIGMOD Conference*, Minneapolis, Minnesota, 1994.

[Inf98] InfoBiogen. DBCat - the public catalog of databases. WWW Page http://www.infobiogen.fr/services/dbcat, Infobiogen, France, 1998.

[JQJ98] M.A. Jeusfeld, C. Quix, and M. Jarke. Design and analysis of quality information for data warehouses. In *Proc. of the 17th Int. Conf. on Conceptual Modeling (ER98)*, Singapore, November 1998.

[Les98] Ulf Leser. Combining heterogeneous data sources through query correspondence assertions. In *Workshop on Web Information and Data Management*, Washington, D.C., 1998.

[Les99] Ulf Leser. Designing a global information resource for molecular biology. In *8th GI Fachtagung: Datenbanksysteme in Buero, Technik und Wissenschaft*, Freiburg, Germany, 1999. to appear.

[LLRC98] Ulf Leser, Hans Lehrach, and Hugues Roest Crollius. Issues in developing integrated genomic databases and application to the human X chromosome. *Bioinformatics*, 14(7):583–690, 1998.

[LMSS95] Alon Y. Levy, Alberto O. Mendelzon, Yehoshua Sagiv, and Divesh Srivastava. Answering queries using views. In *14th ACM PODS*, pages 95–104, San Jose, CA, 1995.

[LRO96] Alon Y. Levy, Anand Rajaraman, and Joann J. Ordille. Querying heterogeneous information sources using source descriptions. In *22th VLDB*, pages 251–262, Bombay, India, 1996.

[Nau98] Felix Naumann. Data fusion and data quality. In *Proc. of the New Techniques & Technologies for Statistics Seminar (NTTS)*, Sorrento, Italy, 1998.

[NFS98] Felix Naumann, Johann Christoph Freytag, and Myra Spiliopoulou. Quality-driven source selection using Data Envelopment Analysis. In *Proc. of the 3rd Conference on Information Quality (IQ)*, Cambridge, MA, 1998.

[NLF99] Felix Naumann, Ulf Leser, and Johann Christoph Freytag. Quality-driven integration of heterogenous information systems. Technical Report 117, Humboldt-Universität zu Berlin, 1999.

[Orr98] Ken Orr. Data quality and systems theory. *Communications of the ACM*, 41(2):66–71, 1998.

[Red98] Thomas C. Redman. The impact of poor data quality in the typical enterprise. *Communications of the ACM*, 41(2):79–82, 1998.

[Rob94] Robert J. Robbins. Representing genomic maps in a relational database. In Sandor Suhai, editor, *Computational Methods in Genome Research*, pages 85–96. Plenum Press, New York, 1994.

[SL90] Amit Sheth and James A. Larson. Federated database systems for managing distributed, heterogeneous and autonomous databases. *ACM Computing Survey*, 22(3):183–236, 1990.

[TB98] Giri Kumar Tayi and Donald P. Ballou. Examining data quality. *Communications of the ACM*, 41(2):54–57, 1998.

[Ull97] Jeffrey D. Ullman. Information integration using logical views. In *6th ICDT*, pages 19–40, Delphi, Greece, 1997.

[Wan98] Richard Y. Wang. A product perspective on Total Data Quality Management. *Communications of the ACM*, 41(2):58–65, 1998.

[Wie92] Gio Wiederhold. Mediators in the architecture of future information systems. *IEEE Computer*, 25(3):38–49, 1992.

[WS96] Richard Y. Wang and Diane M. Strong. Beyond accuracy: What data quality means to data consumers. *Journal on Management of Information Systems*, 12, 4:5–34, 1996.

Physical Data Independence, Constraints, and Optimization with Universal Plans

Alin Deutsch Lucian Popa Val Tannen *

University of Pennsylvania

Abstract

We present an optimization method and algorithm designed for three objectives: physical data independence, semantic optimization, and generalized tableau minimization. The method relies on generalized forms of chase and "backchase" with constraints (dependencies). By using dictionaries (finite functions) in physical schemas we can capture with constraints useful access structures such as indexes, materialized views, source capabilities, access support relations, gmaps, etc.

The search space for query plans is defined and enumerated in a novel manner: the chase phase rewrites the original query into a "universal" plan that integrates all the access structures and alternative pathways that are allowed by applicable constraints. Then, the backchase phase produces optimal plans by eliminating various combinations of redundancies, again according to constraints.

This method is applicable (sound) to a large class of queries, physical access structures, and semantic constraints. We prove that it is in fact complete for "path-conjunctive" queries and views with complex objects, classes and dictionaries, going beyond previous theoretical work on processing queries using materialized views.

1 Introduction

Physical data independence strives to free the query formulation process from needing to know the complex techniques that make the implementation efficient. This is a very desirable property for traditional DBMS and an essential one for information integration systems where the implementations are distributed and hidden. However, traditional DBMS still need techniques for a more radical decoupling of the logical schema from the physical implementation, while in information integration systems most difficulties come from heterogeneity.

There have been several research efforts investigating physical data independence as the central issue [45, 20] or investigating closely related problems [48, 16, 27, 15, 30, 39, 38]. All of them recognize physical data independence as an optimization problem: rewrite a query $Q(\Lambda)$ written against a *logical* schema Λ into an equivalent query *plan* $Q'(\Phi)$ written against a physical schema Φ, given a semantic relationship between Λ and Φ. The question is how to define, broadly but precisely, this relationship and what meaning to give to "equivalent". There are two main approaches to this (see figure 1). The first one is to assume an *abstraction mapping* $\mathcal{A}$ that expresses the instances of the logical schema Λ in terms of those of the physical schema Φ and then

$$\text{define} \quad Q' \stackrel{\text{def}}{=} Q \circ \mathcal{A}$$

and the second one is to assume an *implementation mapping* from Λ to Φ, then

$$\text{solve} \quad X \circ \mathcal{I} =_{\Lambda} Q \quad \text{for } X \quad \text{then define} \quad Q' \stackrel{\text{def}}{=} X$$

(Here $=_{\Lambda}$ means equality in the presence of the constraints of the logical schema Λ). The abstraction mapping approach is the one taken in [20], while the implementation mapping approach is the one taken in [45] and "solving for X" above is related to what is often called "answering queries using views" [30]. The second approach is mathematically and computationally harder but it has a clear advantage from the optimization perspective: the equation $X \circ \mathcal{I} =_{\Lambda} Q$ typically has more than one solution, even more

*Contact: val@cis.upenn.edu, http://db.cis.upenn.edu

Proceedings of the 25th VLDB Conference, Edinburgh, Scotland, 1999.

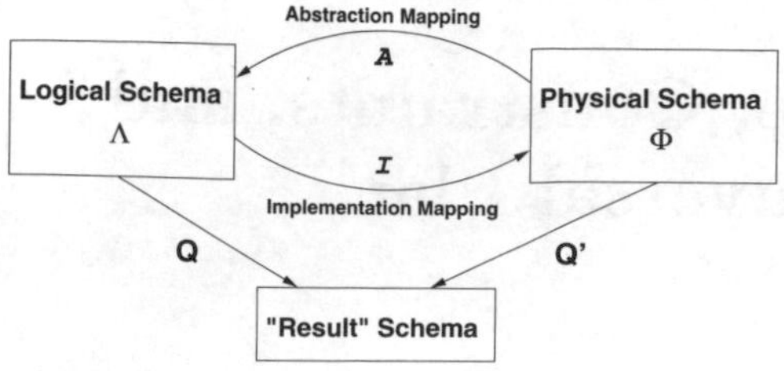

Figure 1: Logical and Physical Schema: two approaches towards rewriting

so because it takes into consideration the *constraints* of the logical schema Λ. In this paper we also take the second approach, but in a richer data model.

The physical data model Both [45] and [20] have some special constructs and types for representing physical structures but the operations on them that can be used in a query plan (e.g., joins or comprehensions) do not explicitly distinguish them from relations/complex values. It is assumed implicitly that the query engine will evaluate the joins and comprehensions over these special constructs in way that takes advantage of their physical efficiency. In constrast, we represent such structures explicitely, mainly using *dictionary* data structures (functions with a finite domain expressible in the language). This is a construct that reflects directly the efficiency of its representation through a fast lookup operation that appears in query plans. It turns out that dictionaries represent in a natural fashion physical structures such as primary and secondary indexes, extent-based representations of OO classes, join indexes [46], path indexes [34], access support relations [28], gmaps [45], etc. The physical level is represented just like the logical level is, with a typed data definition language and with constraints.

Constraints In a previous paper [37] we have generalized the classical relational tableau chase procedure [9] to work for the object-oriented model and dictionaries and for dependencies that capture a large class of semantic constraints including referential integrity constraints, inverse relationships, nested functional dependencies, etc. Moreover, we have shown that classical tableau minimization [14, 5] can be generalized correspondingly, as chasing with "trivial" (always true) constraints [1] In this paper we show that the elements of the implementation mapping (physical access structures, materialized views, etc.) are uniformly captured by the same kind of constraints and that we can use the chase (forwards and backwards) to find the solutions of the equation $X \circ \mathcal{I} =_\Lambda Q$ mentioned above.

Universal plans The constraints that capture the implementation mapping are of two kinds. The first kind apply the chase to the original query introducing explicitly the physical schema structures. Some semantic constraints work in the same way introducing structures that are alternatives to the ones mentioned in the original query. Chasing with these constraints [2] results in a query *plan* that we call *universal* because it is an amalgam of all the query plans allowed by the constraints. In a second phase we chase *backwards* from the universal plan trying to simplify the plan by removing structures, in particular some or all of the structures mentioned in the original query. The soundness of each such *backchase* step relies again on a constraint and we must test if this constraint is implied by the existing ones. This is where the second kind of constraints capturing the implementation mapping are used. This is also where we perform minimization, by testing for trivial constraints.

Applications An important contribution of this work is the systematic procedure for considering *all* alternate plans enabled by indexes and other physical access structures. Conventional relational optimization methods have long relied on ad-hoc heuristics for introducing indexes into a plan. Gmaps [45] have been proposed as an alternative but this work goes beyond gmaps, while for object-oriented data independence it goes beyond the approach of [28]. In fact, we have originally been motivated by our interest in distributed, mediator-based systems [47] for information integration, where it turns out that the techniques presented in [15, 30, 39, 38] are neither general enough nor flexible enough to be adapted to the problems we wish to solve. Moreover, we present our technique in a form that is easy to integrate in the rule-based paradigm [17], and easy to combine with conventional optimization techniques [41] such as selection pushing and join reordering.

Theoretical aspects We prove that our method is complete, i.e., finds the query plans that are minimal in a precise sense, for *path-conjunctive*(PC) queries and physical access structures (implementation mappings). An important restriction is that no constraints beyond those describing the implementation mappings are allowed. Still, PC queries and PC physical structures are more general and expressive than those considered in previous work. The main result of [30] is a particular case of ours.

About the language Our understanding of these results started with a different formalism [3] than the one used in this paper and in fact an efficient internal representation of the queries would be different yet (see [6]). However, to facilitate the presentation, we

[1]In fact, [37] applies the chase to deciding query containment and equivalence under constraints, to constraint derivation and to constraints holding in views.

[2]See [6] for termination of this process

[3]One in which it was easier to see the interaction between queries and constraints and the equivalence laws that govern it [37]

use throughout this paper the well-known syntax of ODMG/ODL and ODMG/OQL [12] (extended with a few constructs) for both logical and physical schema and queries. ODL already has a type of dictionaries $\mathsf{Dict}\langle T_1, T_2\rangle$, with keys of type T_1 and T_2 of type T_2, and OQL already has $M\,[\,k\,]$, the **lookup** operation that returns the entry corresponding to the key k in the dictionary M, provided that M is defined [4] for k. In practice, for dictionaries with set-valued entries, one often assumes the existence of a **non-failing lookup** operation that returns the empty set rather than failing when k is not defined for M. We denote this physical operation by $\mathtt{M}[\![k]\!]$. To this we add the operation $\underline{\mathsf{dom}}\, M$ that returns the **domain** of the dictionary M, i.e., the set of keys for which M is defined and a dictionary construction operation in section 2.

```
Proj: Set<Struct{          class Dept
 string PName;              (extent depts  key DName){
 string CustName;          attribute string DName;
 string PDept;             relationship Set<string> DProjs
 string Budg;}>              inverse Proj(PDept);
primary key PName;         attribute string MgrName;}
foreign key PDept                 foreign key DProjs
 references Dept::DName;            references Proj(PName);
relationship PDept
 inverse Dept::DProjs;
```

Figure 2: The Proj-Dept schema in extended ODMG

An example; logical schema and query Consider the *logical* schema in figure 2. It is written following mostly the syntax of ODL, the data definition language of ODMG, extended with referential integrity (foreign key) constraints in the style of data definition in SQL. It consists of a class Dept and a relation Proj. The schema has referential integrity (RIC), inverse relationship, and key constraints whose meaning can be specified by the following assertions.

(RIC1) $\forall(d \in \mathtt{depts})\ \forall(s \in d.\mathtt{DProjs})$
$\qquad\exists(p \in \mathtt{Proj})\ s = p.\mathtt{PName}$

(RIC2) $\forall(p \in \mathtt{Proj})\ \exists(d \in \mathtt{depts})\ p.\mathtt{PDept} = d.\mathtt{DName}$

(INV1) $\forall(d \in \mathtt{depts})\ \forall(s \in d.\mathtt{DProjs})\ \forall(p \in \mathtt{Proj})$
$\qquad(\ s = p.\mathtt{PName} \Rightarrow p.\mathtt{PDept} = d.\mathtt{DName}\ )$

(INV2) $\forall(p \in \mathtt{Proj})\ \forall(d \in \mathtt{depts})$
$\qquad(\ p.\mathtt{PDept} = d.\mathtt{DName} \Rightarrow$
$\qquad\exists(s \in d.\mathtt{DProjs})\ p.\mathtt{PName} = s\ )$

(KEY1) $\forall(d \in \mathtt{depts})\ \forall(d' \in \mathtt{depts})$
$\qquad(\ d.\mathtt{DName} = d'.\mathtt{DName} \Rightarrow d = d'\ )$

(KEY2) $\forall(p \in \mathtt{Proj})\ \forall(p' \in \mathtt{Proj})$
$\qquad(\ p.\mathtt{PName} = p'.\mathtt{PName} \Rightarrow p = p'\ )$

[4]Otherwise, lookup will fail. We will be careful to avoid this in the case of path-conjunctive queries, see section 5.

Consider also the following OQL query Q that asks for all project names, with their budgets and department names, that have a customer called "CitiBank":

$\underline{\mathsf{select}}\ \underline{\mathsf{distinct}}\ \underline{\mathsf{struct}}(\mathsf{PN} : s, \mathsf{PB} : p.\mathsf{Budg}, \mathsf{DN} : d.\mathtt{DName})$
$\underline{\mathsf{from}}\ \ \mathtt{depts}\ d,\ d.\mathtt{DProjs}\ s,\ \mathtt{Proj}\ p$
$\underline{\mathsf{where}}\ \ s = p.\mathtt{PName}\ \underline{\mathsf{and}}\ \ p.\mathtt{CustName} = \text{"CitiBank"}$

We deal only with set semantics in this paper, thus we omit writing the keyword $\underline{\mathsf{distinct}}$ from now on.

Example continued; physical schema In our approach an OO class must have an extent and is represented as a dictionary whose keys are the oids, whose domain is the extent and whose entries are records of the components of the objects. To maintain the abstract properties of oids we do not make any assumptions about their nature and we invent fresh new base types for them (see Doid for Dept in figure 3; we abused the notation a little by choosing for the dictionary the same name as the class). This representation actually corresponds to the usual semantics of OODB constructs [1]. The syntax of queries and that of query plans are very close: for example, if d is an oid in depts the implicit dereferencing in $d.\mathtt{DName}$ corresponds to the dictionary lookup in $\mathtt{Dept}\,[\,d\,].\mathtt{DName}$. The relation Proj, stored as a table (a set of records), is also part of the physical schema, who therefore is not disjoint from the logical; this is a common situation. In addition, we assume that the following indexes are maintained: a primary index I on the key PName of relation Proj and a secondary index SI on CustName of relation Proj(we could have also added an index between the key DName and the extent of Dept but we don't need it for the example). Both indexes are represented by dictionaries (see figure 3). For example, $\mathtt{I}\,[\,s\,]$ returns the record r in Proj such that $r.\mathtt{PName} = s$. Similarly, $\mathtt{SI}\,[\,c\,]$ gives back the set of records[5] r in Proj such that $r.\mathtt{CustName} = c$. Finally, the physical schema materializes the physical access structure defined by:

(JI) $\quad\underline{\mathsf{select}}\ \underline{\mathsf{struct}}(\mathtt{DOID} : d,\ \mathsf{PN} : p.\mathtt{PName})$
$\qquad\underline{\mathsf{from}}\ \mathtt{depts}\ d,\ d.\mathtt{DProjs}\ s,\ \mathtt{Proj}\ p$
$\qquad\underline{\mathsf{where}}\ \ s = p.\mathtt{PName}$

Note that JI is both a generalized access support relation [28] and a generalized join index [46] since it involves a relation and a class.

Example continued; query plans With this physical schema, with the implementation mapping understood from the partly informal discussion above,

[5]In an implementation this may be a set of record ids rather than a set of records (if SI is not a clustered index), and similarly for the case of the primary index. This would introduce an additional level of indirection that we chose not show here for simplicity of presentation.

$$
\begin{aligned}
\texttt{Dept} &: \mathsf{Dict}\langle\texttt{Doid},\ \mathsf{Struct}\{\mathsf{string}\ \texttt{DName};\ \mathsf{Set}\langle\mathsf{string}\rangle\ \texttt{DProjs};\ \mathsf{string}\ \texttt{MgrName}\}\rangle \\
\texttt{Proj} &: \mathsf{Set}\langle\mathsf{Struct}\{\mathsf{string}\ \texttt{PName};\ \mathsf{string}\ \texttt{CustName};\ \mathsf{string}\ \texttt{PDept};\ \mathsf{string}\ \texttt{Budg}\}\rangle \\
\texttt{I} &: \mathsf{Dict}\langle\mathsf{string},\ \mathsf{Struct}\{\mathsf{string}\ \texttt{PName};\ \mathsf{string}\ \texttt{CustName};\ \mathsf{string}\ \texttt{PDept};\ \mathsf{string}\ \texttt{Budg}\}\rangle \\
\texttt{SI} &: \mathsf{Dict}\langle\mathsf{string},\ \mathsf{Set}\langle\mathsf{Struct}\{\mathsf{string}\ \texttt{PName};\ \mathsf{string}\ \texttt{CustName};\ \mathsf{string}\ \texttt{PDept};\ \mathsf{string}\ \texttt{Budg}\}\rangle\rangle \\
\texttt{JI} &: \mathsf{Set}\langle\mathsf{Struct}\{\texttt{Doid}\ \texttt{DOID};\ \mathsf{string}\ \texttt{PN}\}\rangle
\end{aligned}
$$

Figure 3: The physical schema

and especially with the constraints specified in the logical schema, we give four examples of query plans for the query Q we saw earlier.

(P_0) $\underline{\text{select}}\ \underline{\text{struct}}(\text{PN} : s,\ \text{PB} : p.\text{Budg},\ \text{DN} : \texttt{Dept}[d].\text{DName})$
$\underline{\text{from}}\ \underline{\text{dom}}\,\texttt{Dept}\ d,\ \texttt{Dept}[d].\texttt{DProjs}\ s,\ \texttt{Proj}\ p$
$\underline{\text{where}}\ s = p.\text{PName}\ \underline{\text{and}}\ p.\text{CustName} = \text{"CitiBank"}$

(P_1) $\underline{\text{select}}\ \underline{\text{struct}}(\text{PN} : p.\text{PName},\ \text{PB} : p.\text{Budg},\ \text{DN} : p.\text{PDept})$
$\underline{\text{from}}\ \texttt{Proj}\ p$
$\underline{\text{where}}\ p.\text{CustName} = \text{"CitiBank"}$

(P_2) $\underline{\text{select}}\ \underline{\text{struct}}(\text{PN} : p.\text{PName},\ \text{PB} : p.\text{Budg},\ \text{DN} : p.\text{PDept})$
$\underline{\text{from}}\ \texttt{SI}[\![\text{"CitiBank"}]\!]\ p$

(P_3) $\underline{\text{select}}\ \underline{\text{struct}}(\text{PN} : j.\text{PN},\ \text{PB} : \texttt{I}[j.\text{PN}].\text{Budg},\ \text{DN} : \texttt{Dept}[j.\text{DOID}].\text{DName})$
$\underline{\text{from}}\ \texttt{JI}\ j$
$\underline{\text{where}}\ \texttt{I}[j.\text{PN}].\text{CustName} = \text{"CitiBank"}$

P_0 just introduces the representation of the class as a dictionary and its cost is essentially that of Q, but the other three are potentially significantly better. Depending on the cost model (especially in a distributed heterogeneous system), either one of P_1, P_2, and P_3 may be cheaper than the other two. As we shall see, although they are quite different in nature, our optimization algorithm generates all three.

Overview of the remainder of the paper. In section 2 we describe how we model with constraints physical structures such as primary and secondary indexes, materialized views, access support relations, join indexes, and gmaps. Section 3 presents our optimization algorithm. In section 4 we give two examples of relational scenarios, one on index access paths and one on using materialized views. The completeness results are in section 5. Related work is discussed in section 6.

2 Physical Structures as Constraints

We show here how typical physical access structures captured by constraints. For illustration, we also wish to be able to write down implementation mappings involving dictionaries. OQL does not have an operation that constructs a dictionary so we extend it with the following syntax $\underline{\text{dict}}\ x\ \underline{\text{in}}\ Q \Rightarrow Q'(x)$ denotes the dictionary with domain Q and that associates to an arbitrary key x the entry $Q'(x)$. The notation $Q'(x)$ reflects the fact that Q' is an expression in which the variable x may occur free.

Indexes and classes The operation we just introduced allows us to define explicitly *primary* and *secondary indexes* such as I and SI:

$$\texttt{I} \stackrel{\text{def}}{=} \underline{\text{dict}}\ k\ \underline{\text{in}}\ \Pi_{\texttt{PName}}(\texttt{Proj}) \Rightarrow \underline{\text{element}}(\underline{\text{select}}\ p\ \underline{\text{from}}\ \texttt{Proj}\ p\ \underline{\text{where}}\ p.\text{PName} = k)$$

$$\texttt{SI} \stackrel{\text{def}}{=} \underline{\text{dict}}\ k\ \underline{\text{in}}\ \Pi_{\texttt{CustName}}(\texttt{Proj}) \Rightarrow (\underline{\text{select}}\ p\ \underline{\text{from}}\ \texttt{Proj}\ p\ \underline{\text{where}}\ p.\text{CustName} = k)$$

Here $\Pi_{\texttt{A}}(\texttt{R})$ is a shorthand for the query that projects relation R on A and $\underline{\text{element}}(C)$ is the OQL operation that extracts the unique element of the singleton collection C and fails if C is not a singleton. Luckily, the use of constraints allows us to avoid using this messy operation. Both primary and secondary indexes are completely characterized by **constraints**, eg., for I we use (PI1, PI2) and for SI we use (SI1, SI2, SI3) where

(PI1) $\forall(p \in \texttt{Proj})\ \exists(i \in \underline{\text{dom}}\,\texttt{I})\ i = p.\text{PName}\ \underline{\text{and}}\ \texttt{I}[i] = p$

(PI2) $\forall(i \in \underline{\text{dom}}\,\texttt{I})\ \exists(p \in \texttt{Proj})\ i = p.\text{PName}\ \underline{\text{and}}\ \texttt{I}[i] = p$

(SI1) $\forall(p \in \texttt{Proj})\ \exists(k \in \underline{\text{dom}}\,\texttt{SI})\ \exists(t \in \texttt{SI}[k])\ k = p.\text{CustName}\ \underline{\text{and}}\ p = t$

(SI2) $\forall(k \in \underline{\text{dom}}\,\texttt{SI})\ \forall(t \in \texttt{SI}[k])\ \exists(p \in \texttt{Proj})\ k = p.\text{CustName}\ \underline{\text{and}}\ p = t$

(SI3) $\forall(k \in \underline{\text{dom}}\,\texttt{SI})\ \exists(t \in \texttt{SI}[k])\ \underline{\text{true}}$

Notice that each of (PI1, PI2, SI1, SI2) is an *inclusion* constraint while (SI3) is a *non-emptyness* constraint. In fact, taken together, the pairs of inclusion constraints also state *inverse relationships* between the dictionaries and Proj. Similarly, we can represent the relationship between the class Dept and the dictionary implementing it, Dept, with two constraints. We show one of them (the other is "inverse"):

$(\delta_{\texttt{Dept}})$ $\forall(d \in \text{depts})\ \forall(s \in d.\texttt{DProjs})\ \exists(d' \in \underline{\text{dom}}\,\texttt{Dept})\ \exists(s' \in \texttt{Dept}[d'].\texttt{DProjs})\ d = d'\ \underline{\text{and}}\ s = s'$

Hash tables An interesting extension to this idea are *hash tables*. A hash table for a relation can be viewed as a dictionary in which keys are the results of applying the hash function to tuples in the relation, while the entries are the buckets (sets of tuples). Thus, a hash table can be represented similarly to secondary indexes. A hash table differs from an index because it is not usually materialized, however a hash-join algorithm would have to compute it on the fly. In our framework, we can rewrite join queries into queries that correspond to hash-join plans, provided that the hash-table exists, in the same way we rewrite queries into plans that use indexes. We leave the details out due to lack of space.

Materialized views/Source capabilities Materialized conjunctive or PSJ (project-select-join) views, or cached results of conjunctive/PSJ queries over a relational schema `R` have been used in answering other conjunctive/PSJ queries over `R` [48, 16, 15, 30, 38]. We consider the more general form

$$\mathsf{V} \stackrel{\text{def}}{=} \underline{\mathsf{select}}\ O(\vec{x})\ \underline{\mathsf{from}}\ \vec{P}\ \vec{x}\ \underline{\mathsf{where}}\ B(\vec{x})$$

Here we denote by $\vec{P}\ \vec{x}$ an arbitrary sequence of bindings $P_1\ x_1, \ldots, P_n\ x_n$, by $O(\vec{x})$ we denote the fact that variables $x_1, \ldots, x_n$ can appear in the output record O (and similar for $B(\vec{x})$). Like indexes, such structures can be characterized by constraints, namely:

$$\delta_{\mathsf{V}} \stackrel{\text{def}}{=} \forall(\vec{x} \in \vec{P})\ [\ B(\vec{x}) \Rightarrow \exists(v \in V)\ O(\vec{x}) = v\ ]$$

$$\delta'_{\mathsf{V}} \stackrel{\text{def}}{=} \forall(v \in V)\ \exists(\vec{x} \in \vec{P})\ [\ B(\vec{x})\ \underline{\mathsf{and}}\ O(\vec{x}) = v\ ]$$

Note that δ_{V} corresponds to the inclusion $\underline{\mathsf{select}}\ O(\vec{x})\ \underline{\mathsf{from}}\ \vec{P}\ \vec{x}\ \underline{\mathsf{where}}\ B(\vec{x}) \subseteq \mathsf{V}$ while δ'_{V} corresponds to the inverse inclusion. The two are, in general, constraints *between* the physical and the logical schema.

In our example, `JI` is expressed as such a view and $\delta_{\mathtt{JI}}$ is (we don't show here $\delta'_{\mathtt{JI}}$):

$$(\delta_{\mathtt{JI}})\ \forall(d \in \mathtt{depts})\ \forall(s \in d.\mathtt{DProjs})\ \forall(p \in \mathtt{Proj})$$
$$(\ s = p.\mathtt{PName} \Rightarrow \exists(j \in \mathtt{JI})\ j.\mathtt{DOID} = d\ \underline{\mathsf{and}}\ j.\mathtt{PN} = p.\mathtt{PName}\ )$$

Source capabilities often used in information integration systems can be described by either such materialized views or by dictionaries modeling the binding patterns of [39].

Join indexes [46] were introduced as a technique for join navigation and shown to outperform even hybrid-hash join in most cases with high join selectivity. The technique assumes that tuples have unique, system-generated identifiers called *surrogates* (if the relations have keys, these can be used instead), and that the relations are indexed on surrogates. A join index for the join of relations R and S, denoted J_{RS}, is a precomputed *binary* relation associating the surrogates of R-tuples to surrogates of S-tuples whenever these tuples agree on the join condition. The join is computed by scanning J_{RS} and using the surrogates to index into the relations. We can therefore fully describe a join index by a triple consisting of a materialized binary relation view and two indexes. In our example, the join index for joining `Dept` with `Proj` is `(Dept, I, JI)`.

Access support relations [28, 29] generalize **path indexes** [34, 10, 11] and translate the join index idea from the relational to the object model, generalizing it from binary to n-ary relations. An access support relation (ASR) for a given path is a separate precomputed relation that explicitly stores the oids of objects related to each other via the attributes of the path. As with join indexes, ASRs are used to rewrite navigation style path queries to queries which scan the access support relation, project out the oids of the source and target objects for the path and dereference these oids to access the objects. The oid dereferencing operation is performed implicitly in OQL, which therefore can express this algorithm, but fails to express its join index based relational counterpart because of the lack of explicit dictionary lookup operations. In our approach, access support relations and join indexes are unified using dictionaries both for representing classes with extents and indexes. Analogous to join indexes, we model access support relations for a given path as the materialized relation storing the oids along the path, together with the dictionaries modeling the classes of the source and target objects of the path.

Gmaps [45] specify physical access structures as materialized PSJ views over logical schema. [45] gives a sound (not complete) algorithm for rewriting PSJ queries against the logical schema in terms of materialized gmaps. Our framework subsumes gmaps: PSJ queries alone (in the absence of dictionaries) only approximate index structures with their graph relations (binary relations associating keys to values, which are called *input* respectively *output* nodes in gmap terminology). In contrast, we capture the intended meaning of a general gmap definition using dictionaries:

$$\underline{\mathsf{dict}}\ \vec{z}\ \underline{\mathsf{in}}\ (\underline{\mathsf{select}}\ O_1(\vec{x})\ \underline{\mathsf{from}}\ \vec{P}\ \vec{x}\ \underline{\mathsf{where}}\ B(\vec{x})) \Rightarrow$$
$$\underline{\mathsf{select}}\ O_2(\vec{x}, \vec{z})\ \underline{\mathsf{from}}\ \vec{P}\ \vec{x}\ \underline{\mathsf{where}}\ B(\vec{x})$$

Here O_1, O_2 have flat record type (as outputs of PSJ queries in the original definition). Notice the correlation between the domain and range of the dictionary: they are given by queries which differ only in the projection of the <u>select</u> clause, a limitation resulting from the gmap definition language. We can generalize gmaps by overcoming this limitation and supplying different queries for the domain and range of our dictionaries. Similarly to the case of secondary indexes, we can model this generalized form of gmaps with dependencies.

In the PSJ modeling of gmaps, queries rewritten in

terms of gmaps perform relational joins and don't explicitly express index lookups. Just by looking at the rewritten query, the optimizer cannot decide whether a join should be implemented as such or in an index-based fashion. In other words, PSJ queries used in the gmap approach are not as close to query plans as queries in our language.

3 Optimization

The optimization algorithm starts with a query Q against a logical schema Λ and produces a query plan Q' against the physical schema Φ. Q' will be equivalent to Q under all the constraints and it will be selected according to a cost model. In addition to optimization for physical data independence, the algorithm performs semantic optimizations allowed by the constraints of the logical schema and eliminates superfluous computations (as in tableau minimization [2]).

The algorithm has two main phases: the first one, called the **chase**, introduces all physical structures in the implementation that are *relevant* for Q and rewrites Q to a **universal plan** U that explicitly uses them. The second phase, that we call the **backchase** searches for a minimal plan for Q among the "subqueries" of U. We believe that this is a novel approach. It was in fact inspired by our use of constraints as rewrite rules [37] and it is motivated by the completeness result we prove in section 5. For the following let us denote by D the dependencies on the logical schema and by D' the dependencies between the logical and physical schemas that model the implementation mapping (as we have shown in section 2).

Phase 1: chase. Given a constraint of the form

$$\forall(r_1 \in R_1) \cdots \forall(r_m \in R_m) \; [\, B_1 \;\Rightarrow\; \exists(s_1 \in S_1) \cdots \exists(s_n \in S_n) \;\; B_2 \,]$$

the corresponding *chase step* (in a simplified form) is the rewrite

$$\begin{array}{ll} \underline{\mathsf{select}} & O(\vec{r}) \\ \underline{\mathsf{from}} & \ldots, R_1\, r_1, \ldots, R_m\, r_m, \ldots \\ \underline{\mathsf{where}} & \cdots \;\; \underline{\mathsf{and}} \;\; B_1 \;\; \underline{\mathsf{and}} \;\; \cdots \end{array}$$

$$\Downarrow$$

$$\begin{array}{ll} \underline{\mathsf{select}} & O(\vec{r}) \\ \underline{\mathsf{from}} & \ldots, R_1\, r_1, \ldots, R_m\, r_m, \; S_1\, s_1, \ldots, S_n\, s_n, \ldots \\ \underline{\mathsf{where}} & \cdots \;\; \underline{\mathsf{and}} \;\; B_1 \;\; \underline{\mathsf{and}} \;\; B_2 \;\; \underline{\mathsf{and}} \;\; \cdots \end{array}$$

Example. On our Proj-Dept schema, the logical query Q chases in one step using $\delta_{\mathtt{JI}}$ to the following. Note how new loops and conditions are being added to the ones already existing in Q.

$$\begin{array}{ll} \underline{\mathsf{select}} & \underline{\mathsf{struct}}(\mathsf{PN}: s,\; \mathsf{PB}: p.\mathsf{Budg},\; \mathsf{DN}: d.\mathsf{DName}) \\ \underline{\mathsf{from}} & \mathrm{depts}\; d,\; d.\mathtt{DProjs}\; s,\; \mathtt{Proj}\; p,\; \mathtt{JI}\; j \\ \underline{\mathsf{where}} & s = p.\mathsf{PName} \;\; \underline{\mathsf{and}} \;\; p.\mathsf{CustName} = \text{“CitiBank”} \\ & \;\; \underline{\mathsf{and}} \;\; j.\mathtt{DOID} = d \;\; \underline{\mathsf{and}} \;\; j.\mathsf{PN} = p.\mathsf{PName} \end{array}$$

The *chase phase* consists of applying repeatedly chase steps w.r.t. any applicable constraint from the logical schema and from the characterization of the physical structures (see section 2), i.e. $D \cup D'$. "Applicable" must be defined carefully to avoid trivial loops and to allow for chasing even when the query and the constraint do not match syntactically as easily as we have seen in the simplified form above. We can stop this rewriting anytime and it will still be sound (under the constraints) for a large class of queries, views, indexes and constraints. We show in [37] that the classical relational chase [9] is indeed a particular case of this. We also show that while the chase does not always terminate, it does so for certain classes of constraints and queries, yielding an essentially unique result U whose size is polynomial [6] in that of Q. Sometimes we denote U by *chase*(Q).

Example. We illustrate the first phase of the algorithm on our example. By chasing with δ_{JI}, then with $\delta_{\mathtt{Dept}}$, INV1, SI1 and PI1, U is obtained as follows. None of the other dependencies are applicable.

$$\begin{array}{l} \underline{\mathsf{select}}\; \underline{\mathsf{struct}}(\mathsf{PN}: s, \mathsf{PB}: p.\mathsf{Budg}, \mathsf{DN}: \mathtt{Dept}[d].\mathtt{DName}) \\ \underline{\mathsf{from}}\;\; \mathrm{depts}\; d,\; d.\mathtt{DProjs}\; s,\; \mathtt{Proj}\; p,\; \mathtt{JI}\; j \\ \quad \underline{\mathsf{dom}}\, \mathtt{Dept}\; d',\; \mathtt{Dept}[d'].\mathtt{DProjs}\; s', \\ \quad \underline{\mathsf{dom}}\, \mathtt{SI}\; k,\; \mathtt{SI}[k]\; t,\; \underline{\mathsf{dom}}\; \mathtt{I}\; i \\ \underline{\mathsf{where}}\;\; s = p.\mathsf{PName} \;\; \underline{\mathsf{and}} \;\; p.\mathsf{CustName} = \text{“CitiBank”} \\ \quad\;\; \underline{\mathsf{and}} \;\; j.\mathtt{DOID} = d \;\; \underline{\mathsf{and}} \;\; j.\mathsf{PN} = p.\mathsf{PName} \\ \quad\;\; \underline{\mathsf{and}} \;\; d = d' \;\; \underline{\mathsf{and}} \;\; s = s' \;\; \underline{\mathsf{and}} \;\; p = t \\ \quad\;\; \underline{\mathsf{and}} \;\; p.\mathsf{CustName} = k \;\; \underline{\mathsf{and}} \;\; i = p.\mathsf{PName} \\ \quad\;\; \underline{\mathsf{and}} \;\; p = \mathtt{I}[i] \;\; \underline{\mathsf{and}} \;\; d.\mathsf{DName} = p.\mathsf{PDept} \end{array}$$

For the optimization algorithm, the role of the chase phase is to bring, in a systematic way, all the relevant physical structures into the logical query. For example, chasing with (PI1) and (SI1) adds to the query the accessing of the corresponding primary and secondary index. The result of the chase, U, is the universal plan that holds in one place essentially all possible physical plans expressible in our language. However, U still references elements of the logical schema, and the role of the next phase is to uncover the physical plans.

Phase 2: backchase. The *backchase step* is the rewrite

$$\begin{array}{ll} \underline{\mathsf{select}} & O(\vec{x}, y) \\ \underline{\mathsf{from}} & R_1\, x_1, \ldots, R_m\, x_m,\; R\, y \\ \underline{\mathsf{where}} & C(\vec{x}, y) \end{array}$$

$$\Downarrow$$

[6] This bound could be used a heuristic for stopping the chase when termination is not guaranteed.

$$\underline{\text{select}}\ O'(\vec{x})$$
$$\underline{\text{from}}\ R_1\ x_1, \ldots, R_m\ x_m$$
$$\underline{\text{where}}\ C'(\vec{x})$$

provided that: (1) the conditions C' are implied by C, (2) the equality of O and O' is implied by C, and (3) the following constraint is implied by $D \cup D'$:

$$(\delta)\ \forall(x_1 \in R_1) \ldots \forall(x_m \in R_m)$$
$$[\ C'(\vec{x})\ \Rightarrow\ \exists(y \in R)\ C(\vec{x}, y)\ ]$$

Thus, the purpose of a backchase step is to eliminate (if possible) a **binding** $R\ y$ from the from clause of the query. [7] For any two queries Q and Q' as above such that conditions (1) and (2) are satisfied, we say that Q' is a **subquery** of Q. For computing O' and C' we have a procedure defined for a large class of queries that is sound when it succeeds and that always succeeds for the queries for which the algorithm is complete. The idea is to build a database instance out of the syntax of Q grouping terms in congruence classes according to the equalities that appear in C. Then, we can take C' to be a *maximal* set of equalities implied by C (maximality is needed here for completeness). We can check then by looking at the canonical database whether we can replace O with an equivalent (i.e. in the same congruence class) O' that doesn't depend on y. If we reduce the setting to that of conjunctive relational tableaux, our notion of subquery coincides with the notion of sub-tableau. The only difference is that in our language variables range over tuples rather than over individuals and the equalities (implicit in tableaux!) are explicit.

While the first two conditions ensure that the backchase reduces a query to a subquery of it, condition (3) guarantees that it reduces it to an *equivalent* subquery. This is true because its reverse is just the chase step with constraint (δ) followed by a simplification given by (1) and a replacement of equals given by (2). Sometimes the backchase can apply just by virtue of constraints (δ) that hold in all instances (so-called *trivial* constraints). Relational tableau minimization [2] is precisely such a backchase. To illustrate, if R(A, B) is a relation then query

$$\underline{\text{select}}\ \underline{\text{struct}}(\texttt{A} : p.\texttt{A},\ \texttt{B} : r.\texttt{B})$$
$$\underline{\text{from}}\ \texttt{R}\,p,\ \texttt{R}\,q,\ \texttt{R}\,r$$
$$\underline{\text{where}}\ p.\texttt{B} = q.\texttt{A}\ \underline{\text{and}}\ q.\texttt{B} = r.\texttt{B}$$

rewrites, by backchase, to

$$\underline{\text{select}}\ \underline{\text{struct}}(\texttt{A} : p.\texttt{A},\ \texttt{B} : q.\texttt{B})$$
$$\underline{\text{from}}\ \texttt{R}\,p,\ \texttt{R}\,q$$
$$\underline{\text{where}}\ p.\texttt{B} = q.\texttt{A}$$

[7] We show here a simplified form of backchase. In the case when there are bindings $R_i\ x_i$ depending on the variable y, we need to modify the rule so that either these dependent bindings are eliminated together with $R\ y$ or they can be replaced with bindings that do not depend on y.

It is obvious to see that conditions (1) and (2) are satisfied, while condition (3) is true because the following constraint is trivial:

$$(\delta)\ \forall(p \in \texttt{R})\ \forall(q \in \texttt{R})\ [\ p.\texttt{B} = q.\texttt{A}\ \Rightarrow$$
$$\exists(r \in \texttt{R})\ p.\texttt{B} = q.\texttt{A}\ \underline{\text{and}}\ q.\texttt{B} = r.\texttt{B}\ ]$$

Minimal queries We call a subquery Q_1 of Q_2 a *strict* subquery if Q_1 has strictly fewer bindings than Q_2. We say that a query Q is **minimal** if there does not exist a strict subquery Q' of Q such that Q' is equivalent to Q. In other words, we cannot remove any bindings from Q without losing equivalence. (It turns out that this is a generalization of the minimality notion of [30].) In general, we can think of the backchase as minimization for a larger (than just relational tableaux) class of queries, and under constraints. Trying to see whether (δ) of condition (3) is implied by the existing constraints can actually be done with the chase presented above when constraints are viewed as boolean-valued queries [37]. Again, this is a decidable problem in the case for which the algorithm is complete.

The backchase phase consists of applying backchase steps until this is not possible anymore. Clearly this phase always terminates and the original query must be among those it *could* produce (!), but the obvious strategy for the optimizer is to attempt to remove whatever is in the logical schema but not in the physical schema. For the case in which the algorithm is complete, any query that results from the backchase phase is minimal (as defined above), and, any minimal subquery of a given query Q is guaranteed to be produced by a backchase sequence from Q.

We can now put these together, and add conventional optimization techniques such as "algebraic" rewriting (e.g., pushing selections towards the sources) and cost-based dynamic programming for join reordering [41]. Without elaborating, we mention that by ignoring nesting it is possible to apply these techniques to the queries we consider here.

Algorithm 3.1 (Optimization)
Input: Logical schema Λ with constraints D,
Constraints D' characterizing physical schema Φ,
Cost function $\mathcal{C}$,
Query $Q(\Lambda)$
Output: Cheapest plan $Q'(\Phi)$ equivalent to Q under $D \cup D'$

1. **for each** $U(\Lambda, \Phi) \leftarrow \mathit{chase}_{D,D'}(Q)$
2. **for each** $p(\Phi) \leftarrow \mathit{backchase}_{D,D'}(U)$
3. do cost-based conventional optimization, keep cheapest plan so far p_m
4. $Q' \leftarrow p_m$

The first for loop (chase) enumerates all possible results of chasing (there may be more than one in general). For each such result, the second for loop (backchase) enumerates all possible backchase sequences (again there may be more than one result), each producing a plan p. In step (3) conventional optimization techniques, including mapping into physical operators different than those index-based, are applied to p. If the cost of p is smaller than the current minimum cost plan p_m then update p_m to be p. In step (4) the best query plan p_m is the final result.

The reader can check by backchasing the universal plan U shown previously that P_0, P_1, P_2, and P_3 are obtained as minimal queries in this algorithm. Steps (3) and (4) choose the cheapest plan among them.

Rule-based implementation In an implementation, the conceptual search of algorithm 3.1 can be specified implicitly by configuring a rule-based optimizer ([17, 23]) with the two rewrite rules *chase* and *backchase*, and requesting that the application of the chase rule always takes precedence over that of the backchase rule. Depending on the search strategy implemented by the optimizer, the search space may not be explored exhaustively but rather pruned using heuristics such as in [25, 44].

There is, however, a fundamental difference between our optimization framework and a rule-based optimizer as in Volcano [23]. While in Volcano's optimizer algebraic and physical transformations are mixed and the search is guided by a cost model, steps (1) and (2) of algorithm 3.1 are cost-independent and performed before the phase of (cost-driven) mapping into physical operator trees (other than index-based plans). This is more in the spirit of Starburst optimizer [33] which also had a clear separation between the two kinds of transformations. However, the query rewriting phase in Starburst did not include indexes nor logical constraints, and was heuristics-based.

4 Relational Examples

Our approach extends beyond the relational model, but it also proposes improvements over previous approaches to relational optimization. An important contribution of this work is the *systematic* procedure for considering all alternate plans enabled by indexes, as opposed to the ad-hoc heuristics proposed previously. Consider for example a *logical* schema with one relation R(A, B, C) and a *physical* schema containing secondary indexes SA and SB on attributes A and B of R. Then our algorithm will discover for the logical query

$$\begin{array}{l}\underline{\text{select}}\ r.\text{C}\\ \underline{\text{from}}\ \text{R}\ r\\ \underline{\text{where}}\ r.\text{A} > 5\ \underline{\text{and}}\ r.\text{B} = 20\end{array}$$

the following *index-only access path* plan ([40]):

$$\begin{array}{l}\underline{\text{select}}\ r.\text{C}\\ \underline{\text{from}}\ \underline{\text{dom}}\,\text{SA}\ x,\ \text{SA}[x]\ r_1,\ \text{SB}[\![20]\!]\ r_2\\ \underline{\text{where}}\ x > 5\ \underline{\text{and}}\ r_1 = r_2\end{array}$$

Notice how the scan of R is replaced by a scan of index SA (which can be filtered using condition $x > 5$) interleaved with non-failing lookups in index SB.

Our algorithm considers exhaustively combinations of materialized views, indexes, and semantic constraints, thus generating plans which are not captured in frameworks such as [30]. Assume a *logical* schema with relations R(A, B) and S(B, C), and a *physical* schema that has R and S too (direct mapping!), as well as materialized view $V = \Pi_{\text{A}}(\text{R} \bowtie \text{S})$ and secondary indexes I_{R} and I_{S} on attributes A and B of R and S, respectively. We want to optimize the logical query $Q = R \bowtie S$.

Q itself is a valid plan (modulo join-reordering and various implementations for the join). However, the view V can be used to produce the following equivalent query (again we ignore here the join order):

$$(P)\quad \begin{array}{l}\underline{\text{select}}\ \underline{\text{struct}}(\text{A}: r.\text{A},\ \text{B}: s.\text{B},\ \text{C}: s.\text{C})\\ \underline{\text{from}}\ \ \text{V}\ v,\ \text{R}\ r,\ \text{S}\ s\\ \underline{\text{where}}\ \ v.\text{A} = r.\text{A}\ \ \underline{\text{and}}\ \ r.\text{B} = s.\text{B}\end{array}$$

This is obtained as a first step of the chase phase, by rewriting Q with one of the two constraints characterizing V (namely δ_{V}, see section 2). The techniques used by [30] for answering/optimizing queries using views can also be used to produce query P in a first phase, similar to our chase. Now, if V is small, P can be *implemented*, in a typical relational system, much better than Q because of the two indexes. (V is the only relation that is scanned while the relations R and S are accessed via indexes.) However, in the approach of [30], P is thrown away because Q is a subquery of P, thus P is not minimal. Minimality, in their case as well as in our case, is essential for bounding the search space for optimal plans. The problem in [30] is that Q and P are the only *expressible* plans using the conjunctive relational language. There is no way of expressing and taking advantage of the indexes at the language level. The language used for gmaps in [45] suffers of the same limitation.

Here is how we can overcome this problem and be able to produce a plan that corresponds to the good physical implementation hinted earlier. In our approach, P is still not a minimal plan, thus it will be thrown away, too, in the backchase phase. But the chase phase doesn't stop with P: we can still bring in the two indexes by chasing with constraints relating R and S with, respectively, I_{R} and I_{S}:

$$(U)\quad \begin{array}{l}\underline{\text{select}}\ \underline{\text{struct}}(\text{A}: r.\text{A},\ \text{B}: s.\text{B},\ \text{C}: s.\text{C})\\ \underline{\text{from}}\ \ \text{V}\ v,\ \text{R}\ r,\ \text{S}\ s,\ (\underline{\text{dom}}\ \text{I}_{\text{R}})\ k,\ \text{I}_{\text{R}}[k]\ r',\\ \qquad (\underline{\text{dom}}\ \text{I}_{\text{S}})\ p,\ \text{I}_{\text{S}}[p]\ s'\\ \underline{\text{where}}\ \ v.\text{A} = r.\text{A}\ \ \underline{\text{and}}\ \ r.\text{B} = s.\text{B}\ \ \underline{\text{and}}\ \ k = r.\text{A}\\ \qquad \underline{\text{and}}\ \ r' = r\ \ \underline{\text{and}}\ \ p = s.\text{B}\ \ \underline{\text{and}}\ \ s' = s\end{array}$$

Backchasing twice with the "inverse" constraints relating $\mathtt{I_R}$ and $\mathtt{I_S}$ with, respectively, R and S:

```
select struct(A : r'.A, B : s'.B, C : s'.C)
from   V v, (dom I_R) k, I_R[k] r',
       (dom I_S) p, I_S[p] s'
where  k = v.A and p = r'.B
```

Using the equality $k = v.\mathtt{A}$ and the inclusion constraint $\mathtt{V[A]} \subseteq \mathtt{R[A]}$ that is inferred in our system as a consequence of $\delta_{\mathtt{V}}$, we can backchase one final step and eliminate the loop over dom $\mathtt{I_R}$:

```
select struct(A : r'.A, B : s'.B, C : s'.C)
from   V v, I_R[v.A] r', (dom I_S) p, I_S[p] s'
where  p = r'.B
```

The last transformation replaced a value-based join with a navigation join and the resulting query reflects almost entirely the navigation join implementation hinted earlier, except for the loop over dom $\mathtt{I_S}$. This loop together with the condition $p = r'.\mathtt{B}$ is only a guard that ensures that the lookup of $r'.\mathtt{B}$ into $\mathtt{I_S}$ doesn't fail. It is not redundant, for without it we would lose equivalence (recall that the original query Q never fails). However, using the non-failing lookup, the last query is equivalent to the plan:

```
select struct(A : r'.A, B : s'.B, C : s'.C)
from   V v, I_R[v.A] r', I_S[[r'.B]] s'
```

5 Completeness

We describe first the *path-conjunctive (PC) language* (mainly the one introduced in [37]), after which we give our main theoretical results: the *bounding chase* theorem and the *completeness of backchase* theorem. Completeness of algorithm 3.1 follows immediately from them. These results hold for PC queries when the logical schema has arbitrary classes and (nested) relations, but no constraints, while the physical schema has materialized PC views, but no arbitrary indexes (only dictionaries implementing classes). The two results are a generalization to a richer model of the results of [30].

The path-conjunctive fragment of the ODL / OQL language that we have used so far is defined below. It includes the relational conjunctive queries of [14, 5] but is more general because it includes dictionaries and nested relations.

Paths: $P ::= x \mid c \mid \mathtt{R} \mid P.\mathtt{A} \mid \underline{\mathsf{dom}}\, P \mid P\,[x]$

Path-Conjunctions:

$$B ::= P_1 = P_1' \text{ and } \cdots \text{ and } P_k = P_k'$$

PC Queries: select struct($A_1 : P_1', \ldots, A_n : P_n'$)
from $P_1\, x_1, \ldots, P_m\, x_m$
where B

Here x stands for variables, c denotes constants at base types, and R stands for schema names (relation or dictionary names). The following **restrictions** are imposed on a PC query Q.

(1) Keys of dictionaries, equalities in the where clause, and the expression in the select clause are not allowed to be/contain expressions of set/dictionary type.

(2) A lookup operation can only be of the form $P\,[x]$ with the additional condition that there must exist a binding of the form dom P x[8] in the from clause. The reason for not allowing an arbitrary lookup is mainly technical: all our definitions including query equivalence would need to be extended with explicit null values, and tedious reasoning about partiality. With this restriction a lookup operation never fails.

Restriction (2) implies that we cannot express in the PC fragment navigation-style joins (involving chains of lookup operations). However, these kind of joins can be rewritten as value-based joins (as seen in section 4) and vice-versa provided that certain integrity constraints hold. In the value-based counterpart of a navigation join a chain of lookups is replaced by explicit joins involving equality of oids. Value-based joins are guaranteed not to touch any dangling oids and therefore are easier to reason with them.

Path-conjunctive constraints. *Embedded path-conjunctive dependencies* (EPCDs) defined in [37] are a generalization for the complex value and dictionary model of the relational tgds and egds ([4, 9]). EPCDs play a fundamental role in rewriting of PC queries by chase and they have the logical form:

$$\textit{EPCD: } \forall(x_1 \in P_1)\ldots\forall(x_n \in P_n)\,[\,B_1(\vec{x}) \Rightarrow \exists(y_1 \in P_1')\ldots\exists(y_k \in P_k')\; B_2(\vec{x},\vec{y})\,]$$

P_i and P_i' are paths, while B_1 and B_2 are path-conjunctions (as defined before, with the same restrictions). Each P_i may refer to variables $x_1, \ldots, x_{i-1}$, while P_j' may refer to $x_1, \ldots x_n, y_1, \ldots y_{j-1}$, thus an EPCD is not a first-order formula. A special class of EPCDs are constraints in which there are no existential quantifiers, EGDs. Functional dependencies, like (KEY1) and (KEY2), and the constraints typically involved in conditions (1) and (2) of the backchase step are examples of EGDs.

Main theorems Our assumptions for the rest of this section are that the logical schema contains only relations and classes (no dependencies) and the physical schema contains only (nested) relations (including materialized PC views) and dictionaries implementing class extents (no dictionaries implementing indexes). These restrictions are needed for the completeness result of theorem 5.1 below. We conjecture that the result holds even in the presence of indexes and a certain class of *full* dependencies (introduced

[8] Or, more general, a binding dom P y such that the equality $x = y$ is implied by the conditions in the where clause. This is a PTIME-checkable condition (see [37]).

in [37]).

Completeness follows from the *finiteness* of the space of minimal plans. We provide two upper bounds for this search space: In [6], we show how to generalize to PC queries the upper bound result obtained in [30] for conjunctive relational queries, thus justifying a procedure which enumerates equivalent plans bottom-up by building subsets of at most as many views, relations and classes as the number of bindings in the from clause of logical query Q, combining them by setting appropriate conditions in the where clause, then checking equivalence with Q.

In view of a rule-based implementation however, a top-down enumeration procedure implemented as step-by-step rewriting is better suited, and our algorithm uses a different, novel characterization of the search space of query plans:

Theorem 5.1 (Bounding Chase) *Any minimal plan $Q'(\Phi)$ for logical query $Q(\Lambda)$ is a subquery of the universal plan chase$(Q)(\Lambda, \Phi)$.*

Here *chase*(Q) means the result of chasing Q with the set of all dependencies of the form δ_V (see section 2) associated with the view definitions. Since these are full dependencies(see [37] for definition and theorem), *chase*(Q) exists and is unique.

Theorem 5.1 allows the enumeration of all minimal plans of Q by enumerating those subqueries of *chase*(Q) which mention only the physical schema Φ (as seen in section 3. Conceptually, the enumeration proceeds by first listing the largest subqueries of *chase*(Q) which involve only the physical schema Φ, pruning away those subqueries which are not equivalent to *chase*(Q) and then applying itself recursively to each non-pruned subquery. The equivalence check can be done by unfolding the view definitions. It follows easily from the definition of subqueries that the pruning step doesn't compromise completeness, since whenever a subquery of *chase*(Q) is not equivalent to the latter, neither are its subqueries.

The following theorem states that the desired enumeration and pruning of equivalent subqueries can be implemented in a rule-based optimizer by rewriting with the backchase rule introduced in section 3:

Theorem 5.2 (Complete Backchase) *The minimal equivalent subqueries of a query $Q(\Lambda, \Phi)$ are exactly the normal forms of backchasing $Q(\Lambda, \Phi)$.*

The use of the chase as upper bound for the space of minimal plans leads to an enumeration procedure that remains *sound* even in the presence of constraints on the logical schema and of indexes, which are not dealt with in [30].

Corollary 5.3 (Completeness of algorithm 3.1) *If Λ contains no dependencies and Φ contains no indexes, algorithm 3.1 is complete for PC queries.*

Our algorithm takes exponential time: each chase step is exponential, but in the case of chasing with $\vec{d}_V$, and more generally, as shown in [37], when chasing with arbitrary full dependencies, the chase rule applies only polynomially many times, resulting in a query whose size is polynomial in the size of the chased query. The second phase of algorithm 3.1 preserves the exponential complexity: each backchase step is exponential (is uses the chase to check the applicability of the rule) but it eliminates a binding, so the backchase process always reaches a normal form after at most as many steps as there are bindings in the result of the chase. The NP-completeness results given in [30] for the particular case of answering queries with conjunctive relational views tell us that there is little hope to do better than exponential if we want a complete enumeration.

6 Related work

Relevant work on integrating information systems includes [35, 31, 3, 36]. Arrays, as dealt with in [32] can be formalized as dictionaries, given some arithmetic and operations that produce integer intervals. The maps of [7] and the treatment of object types in [8] are related to our dictionaries. An important difference is made by the operations on dictionaries used here.

The framework that we use for optimization is quite comprehensive as it is possible to represent almost the entire variety of equivalences stated in various papers, beginning with the standard relational "algebraic" optimizations, continuing with OODB optimizations as in the work of Cluet, Zdonik, Maier, Fegaras and others [42, 43, 19, 18], and in fact including the very comprehensive work by Beeri and Kornatzky [8].

Use of referential integrity constraints to eliminate dependent joins is implicit in Orion optimizations [26] and the type-based approach of [19]. This, and the use of precomputed ASR's appear in [28, 29]. Precomputed join indexes are proposed in [46]. An approach to semantic query optimization using a translation into Datalog appears in [13, 24]. The idea of using semantic constraints as rewrite rules is introduced and exploited systematically in [21, 22].

When the physical schema contains only materialized relations, finding an execution plan is a generalization of the problem of answering queries using views ([30], [38]). At the opposite extreme, if the physical schema materializes all relations and classes in the logical schema, the original query is directly executable but the optimizer has to look for (better) execution plans. This is sometimes called the problem of optimizing queries using views [15].

The GMAP approach [45] solves the problem of physical data independence for a special case that is subsumed by our work which applies to a more general class of physical storage structures, queries against the logical schema and dependencies. In contrast to the query plans obtained by our rewriting process, the output of the GMAP rewriting is a family of plans represented by a PSJ query. The burden of choosing a specific plan is shifted on the next phase of the optimizer.

7 What we do *not* do, but we'd like to

- We do not address the problems resulting specifically from the nesting of the queries.
- Our physical data model does not reflect information related to storage organization issues such as paging or clustering.
- By extending the physical data model to include lists, it might be possible to capture in some substantial way algorithms using sorted values.
- We expect that the algorithm proposed here will be used in conjunction with good cost models and good heuristics for pruning the search space, but we have not yet examined how these issues relate to the nature of the algorithm itself. An implementation is under way in order to help us understand these relationships and the feasibility of the whole approach.

Acknowledgements We thank Dan Suciu, Anthony Bonner, Rick Hull and Jerome Simeon for helpful discussions.

References

[1] S. Abiteboul and P. Kanellakis. Object identity as a query language primitive. In *Proceedings of ACM SIGMOD Conference on Management of Data*, pages 159–173, Portland, Oregon, 1989.

[2] Serge Abiteboul, Richard Hull, and Victor Vianu. *Foundations of Databases*. Addison-Wesley, 1995.

[3] S. Adali, K. Selcuk Candan, Y. Papakonstantinou, and V.S. Subrahmanian. Query caching and optimization in distributed mediator systems. In *ACM SIGMOD*, pages 137 - 148, 1996.

[4] A. V. Aho, C. Beeri, and J. D. Ullman. The theory of joins in relational databases. *ACM Transactions on Database Systems*, 4(3):297–314, 1979.

[5] A. V. Aho, Y. Sagiv, and J. D. Ullman. Efficient optimization of a class of relational expressions. *ACM Transactions on Database Systems*, 4(4):435–454, December 1979.

[6] Alin Deutsch and Lucian Popa and Val Tannen. Optimization for Physical Independence in Information Integration Components. Technical report, University of Pennsylvania, 1999.

[7] M. Atkinson, C. Lecluse, P. Philbrow, and P. Richard. Design issues in a map language. In *Proc. of the 3rd Int'l Workshop on Database Programming Languages (DBPL91)*, Nafplion, Greece, August 1991.

[8] Catriel Beeri and Yoram Kornatzky. Algebraic optimisation of object oriented query languages. *Theoretical Computer Science*, 116(1):59–94, August 1993.

[9] Catriel Beeri and Moshe Y. Vardi. A proof procedure for data dependencies. *Journal of the ACM*, 31(4):718–741, 1984.

[10] E. Bertino. *Query Processing for Advanced Database Systems*, chapter A Survey of Indexing Techniques for Object-Oriented Database Management Systems, pages 383–418. Morgan Kauffmann, San Mateo, CA, 1994.

[11] E. Bertino and W. Kim. Indexing techniques for queries on nested objects. *IEEE Trans. on Knowledege and Data Engineering*, 1(2), 1989.

[12] R. G. G. Cattell, editor. *The Object Database Standard: ODMG 2.0.* Morgan Kaufmann, San Mateo, California, 1997.

[13] U. Chakravarthy, J. Grant, and J. Minker. Logic-based approach to semantic query optimization. *ACM Transactions on Database Systems*, 15(2):162–207, 1990.

[14] Ashok Chandra and Philip Merlin. Optimal implementation of conjunctive queries in relational data bases. In *Proceedings of 9th ACM Symposium on Theory of Computing*, pages 77–90, Boulder, Colorado, May 1977.

[15] S. Chaudhuri, R. Krishnamurty, S. Potamianos, and K. Shim. Optimizing queries with materialized views. In *Proceedings of ICDE*, Taipei, Taiwan, March 1995.

[16] C.M. Chen and N. Roussopoulos. The implementation and performance evaluation of the ADMS query optimizer. In *Proceedings of the International Conference on Extending Database Technology*, 1994.

[17] M. Cherniack and S. B. Zdonik. Rule languages and internal algebras for rule-based optimizers. In *Proceedings of the SIGMOD International Conference on Management of Data*, pages ??–??, Montreal, Quebec, Canada, 1996.

[18] S. Cluet. *Langages et Optimisation de requetes pour Systemes de Gestion de Base de donnees oriente-objet.* PhD thesis, Universite de Paris-Sud, 1991.

[19] Sophie Cluet and Claude Delobel. A general framework for the optimization of object oriented queries. In M. Stonebraker, editor, *Proceedings ACM-SIGMOD International Conference on Management of Data*, pages 383–392, San Diego, California, June 1992.

[20] L. Fegaras and D. Maier. An algebraic framework for physical oodb design. In *Proc. of the 5th Int'l Workshop on Database Programming Languages (DBPL95)*, Umbria, Italy, August 1995.

[21] D. Florescu. *Design and Implementation of the Flora Object Oriented Query Optimizer.* PhD thesis, Universite of Paris 6, 1996.

[22] D. Florescu, L. Rashid, and P. Valduriez. A methodology for query reformulation in cis using semantic knowledge. *International Journal of Cooperative Information Systems*, 5(4), 1996.

[23] Goetz Graefe, Richard L. Cole, Diane L. Davison, William J. McKenna, and Richard H. Wolniewicz. Extensible query optimization and parallel execution in Volcano. In Johann Christoph Freytag, David Maier, and Gottfried Vossen, editors, *Query Processing for Advanced Database Systems*, chapter 11, pages 305–335. Morgan Kaufmann, San Mateo, California, 1994.

[24] J. Grant, J. Gryz, J. Minker, and L. Raschid. Semantic query optimization for object databases. In *Proc. of the 13th Int'l. Conference on Data Engineering*, April 1997.

[25] Y. E. Ioannidis and E. Wong. Query optimization by simulated annealing. In Umeshwar Dayal and Irv Traiger, editors, *Proceedings of ACM-SIGMOD International Conference on Management of Data*, pages 9–22, San Francisco, May 1987.

[26] P. Jeng, D. Woelk, W. Kim, and W. Lee. Query processing in distributed orion. In *Proc. EDBT*, Venice, Italy, March 1990.

[27] A.M. Keller and J. Basu. A predicate-based caching scheme for client-server database architectures. In *Proceedings of the International Conference on Parallel and Distributed Information Systems*, 1994.

[28] A. Kemper and G. Moerkotte. Access support relations in object bases. In *Proceedings of ACM-SIGMOD International Conference on Management of Data*, pages 364–374, 1990.

[29] A. Kemper and G. Moerkotte. Advanced query processing in object bases using access support relations. In *Proc. VLDB*, Brisbane, Australia, 1990.

[30] A. Levy, A. O. Mendelzon, Y. Sagiv, and D. Srivastava. Answering queries using views. In *Proceedings of PODS*, 1995.

[31] A. Levy, D. Srivastava, and T. Kirk. Data model and query evaluation in global information systems. *Journal of Intelligent Information Systems*, 1995.

[32] L. Libkin, R. Machlin, and L. Wong. A query language for multidimensional arrays: Design, implementation and optimization techniques. In *SIGMOD Proceedings, Int'l Conf. on Management of Data*, 1996.

[33] Guy M. Lohman, Bruce Lindsay, Hamind Pirahesh, and K. Bernhard Schiefer. Extension to Starburst: Objects, types, functions, and rules. 34(10):94–109, October 1991.

[34] D. Maier and J. Stein. Indexing in an object-oriented dbms. In *Proceedings of 2nd International Workshop on Object-Oriented Database Systems*, pages 171–182, Asilomar, CA, September 1986.

[35] Yannis Papakonstantinou, Hector Garcia-Molina, and Jennifer Widom. Object exchange across heterogenous information sources. In *Proceedings of IEEE International Conference on Data Engineering*, pages 251–260, March 1995.

[36] Yannis Papakonstantinou, Ashish Gupta, and Laura M. Haas. Capabilities-based query rewriting in mediator systems. *Distributed and Parallel Databases*, 6(1), 1998.

[37] Lucian Popa and Val Tannen. An equational chase for path-conjunctive queries, constraints, and views. In *Proceedings of ICDT*, Jerusalem, Israel, January 1999.

[38] X. Qian. Query folding. In *Proceedings ICDE*, pages 48–55, 1996.

[39] A. Rajaraman, Y. Sagiv, and J.D. Ullman. Answering queries using templates with binding patterns. In *Proc. 14th ACM Symposium on Principles of Database Systems*, pages 105–112, 1995.

[40] Raghu Ramakrishnan. *Database Management Systems.* McGraw-Hill, 1998.

[41] P. G. Selinger, M. M. Astrahan, D. D. Chamberlin, R. A. Lorie, and T. G. Price. Access path selection in a relational database management system. In *Proceedings of ACM SIGMOD International Conference on Management of Data*, pages 23–34, 1979. Reprinted in *Readings in Database Systems*, Morgan-Kaufmann, 1988.

[42] G. Shaw and S. Zdonik. Object-oriented queries: equivalence and optimization. In *Proceedings of International Conference on Deductive and Object-Oriented Databases*, 1989.

[43] G. Shaw and S. Zdonik. An object-oriented query algebra. In *Proc. DBPL*, Salishan Lodge, Oregon, June 1989.

[44] M. Steinbrunn, G. Moerkotte, and A. Kemper. Heuristic and randomized optimization for the join ordering problem. *VLDB Journal*, 6(3):191–208, 1997.

[45] O. Tsatalos, M. Solomon, and Y. Ioannidis. The gmap: A versatile tool for physical data independence. In *Proc. of 20th VLDB Conference*, Santiago, Chile, 1994.

[46] P. Valduriez. Join indices. *ACM Trans. Database Systems*, 12(2):218–452, June 1987.

[47] Gio Wiederhold. Mediators in the architecture of future information systems. *IEEE Computer*, pages 38–49, March 1992.

[48] H.Z. Yang and P.A. Larson. Query transformation for psj queries. In *Proceedings of the 13th International VLDB Conference*, pages 245–254, 1987.

On Efficiently Implementing SchemaSQL on a SQL Database System

Laks V. S. Lakshmanan* IIT – Bombay laks@cse.iitb.ernet.in

Fereidoon Sadri UNCG sadri@uncg.edu

Subbu N. Subramanian IBM Almaden subbu@almaden.ibm.com

Abstract

SchemaSQL is a recently proposed extension to SQL for enabling multi-database interoperability. Several recently identified applications for SchemaSQL, however, mainly rely on its ability to treat data and schema labels in a uniform manner, and call for an efficient implementation of it on a *single RDBMS*. We first develop a logical algebra for SchemaSQL by combining classical relational algebra with four restructuring operators – *unfold, fold, split,* and *unite* – originally introduced in the context of the tabular data model by Gyssens et al. [GLS96], and suitably adapted to fit the needs of SchemaSQL. We give an algorithm for translating SchemaSQL queries/views involving restructuring, into the logical algebra above. We also provide physical algebraic operators which are useful for query optimization. Using the various operators as a vehicle, we give several alternate implementation strategies for SchemaSQL queries/views. All the proposed strategies can be implemented *non-intrusively* on top of existing relational DBMS, in that they do not require any additions to the existing set of plan operators. We conducted a series of performance experiments based on TPC-D benchmark data, using the IBM DB2 DBMS running on Windows/NT. In addition to showing the relative tradeoffs between various alternate strategies, our experiments show the feasibility of implementing SchemaSQL on top of traditional RDBMS in a non-intrusive manner. Furthermore, they also suggest new plan operators which might profitably be added to the existing set available to relational query optimizers, to further boost their performance.

*Currently on leave from Concordia Univ., Montreal, Canada. Work performed by this author at IIT–Bombay.

Proceedings of the 25th VLDB Conference, Edinburgh, Scotland, 1999.

1 Introduction

Data warehousing is a technology motivated by decision support applications, which require consolidated high-level information on the OLTP data for the purpose of organizational decision making. A major challenge for this is the integration of data sources that are schematically disparate, in that data values in one source may be modeled as schema (attribute or relation) labels in another. Real examples of such disparity abound (e.g., see [KLK91, LSS97]). As an example, in Figure 1(a), a snap shot of a stock broker's database, the relation names in the ABC brokerage database are stock (ticker) names that could indeed be query-able information. We will use this as a running example in the paper. In an attempt to address this challenge of schematic disparity, researchers have proposed higher-order extensions to relational calculus and SQL that facilitate developing and deploying data warehousing/data integration applications [KLK91, CKW93, Ros92]. SchemaSQL [LSS96] is one such extension to SQL that allows for uniform manipulation of data and schema, and supports: (a) interoperability in a mutlidatabase system and (b) easy specification of various complex queries and computations arising in data warehousing applications.

While SchemaSQL was originally proposed as a language for multi-database interoperability and data warehousing applications, since its proposal, researchers have identified several applications where it can enhance the functionality of a *single* DBMS significantly. These applications include *publishing of relational data on the web* [MTW97, Mil98, KZ95], *techniques for providing physical data independence* [Mil98], *developing tightly coupled scalable classification algorithms in data mining* [WIV98], and *source query optimization in the context of data warehousing*

ABC Brokerage

ibm

date	xge	open	close	low	high
10/01	NYSE	91.43	92.36	90.23	92.38
10/01	TSE	90.06	92.34	90.06	92.78
10/02	LSE	91.78	93.65	91.56	93.86

msft

date	xge	open	close	low	high
10/01	NYSE	86.31	86.79	85.97	86.92
10/01	TSE	85.27	85.20	85.12	85.86
10/02	LSE	86.90	87.35	86.90	87.74

...

...

stock

ticker	busType
ibm	tech
msft	tech
xon	oil
....	...

(a)

```
CREATE   VIEW     X(date, priceType, S) AS
         SELECT   T.date, PT, T.PT
         FROM     -> S, S T, S-> PT, T.xge X, stock U
         WHERE    PT <> date AND PT <> xge AND
                  S <> stock AND S = U.ticker AND
                  U.busType = 'tech'
```

(c)

```
isa(ibm, ticker)              ←
isa(msft, ticker)             ←
isa(hp, ticker)               ←
...
isa(open, priceType)          ←
isa(close, priceType)         ←
...
isa(T.xge, xge)               ←   relVar(S) & isa(S, ticker) &
                                  tupleVar(T, S)
isa(T.date, date)             ←   relVar(S) & isa(S, ticker) &
                                  tupleVar(T, S)
isa(T.PT, price)              ←   relVar(S) & isa(S, ticker) &
                                  colVar(PT, S) & tupleVar(T, S)
                                  isa(PT, priceType)
isa(T.ticker, ticker)         ←   tupleVar(T, stock)
isa(T.busType, busType)       ←   tupleVar(T, stock)
```

(b)

XgeView

NYSE

date	priceType	ibm	msft	...
10/01	open	91.43	86.31	...
10/01	close	92.36	86.79	...
10/02	low	90.23	85.97	...
...	...	...	...	...

TSE

date	priceType	ibm	msft	...
10/01	open	90.06	85.27	...
10/01	low	90.06	85.12	...
10/02	high	92.78	85.86	...
...	...	...	...	...

...

...

(d)

Figure 1: *Example Stock Market Database: (a) ABC brokerage database; (b) Meta-data specs of schema in (a); (c) An example restructuring* SchemaSQL *view against database (a); (d) Materialization of (c).*

[SV98]. Thus there is a clear motivation for realizing an efficient implementation of SchemaSQL on even a *single database system*, and this is the subject of this paper.

Section 1.1 reviews SchemaSQL by examples, while Section 1.2 elaborates on the applications mentioned above, in order to bring out the motivation for our work. [LSS96, Sub97] contain an elaborate exposition of SchemaSQL.

1.1 SchemaSQL by Examples

SchemaSQL extends SQL in the following ways.

(1) While SQL allows only variables ranging over tuples of a fixed relation, SchemaSQL allows variables ranging over relation labels, column labels, tuples in (several) relations, and domain values appearing in relation columns.[1]. E.g., in the query part of the SchemaSQL view definition of Figure 1(c), the declaration '-> S' in the FROM clause (together with the constraint 'S <> stock' in the WHERE clause) says S is a relation label variable that ranges over the relation labels (i.e.the ticker names) ibm, msft, ... in the ABC brokerage; 'S T' says T is a tuple variable that ranges over the tuples in each of the ticker relations; 'S -> PT' says PT is a column label variable that ranges over the column labels of the ticker relations, and 'T.xge X' says X is a domain variable that ranges over the values in the xge column of the ticker relations.

[1] SchemaSQL, as originally proposed for a multi-database system [LSS96], also permits database label variables. Given the single-database focus of this paper, we drop database label variables here.

(2) SQL allows only one type of domain expression, namely tupleVar.attr. In contrast, SchemaSQL allows domain expressions of the form tupleVar.col (e.g., U.ticker and T.PT in Figure 1(c)), relVar (e.g., S), colVar (e.g., PT), and domVar (e.g., X). Note that attr denotes a fixed attribute name, while col may be an attribute name or a column label variable.

(3) The syntax of SchemaSQL permits restructuring views which involve a clear interplay between schema (i.e. relation/column) labels and data. For example, the SchemaSQL view definition in Example 1(c) maps the ABC brokerage database to the view XgeView of Figure 1(d). Corresponding to each exchange '*x*' in the ABC brokerage, XgeView has a relation labeled '*x*'. This is achieved by using the domain variable X in the relation label position in the CREATE VIEW statement. Similarly using the variable S in the column label position generates a column labeled '*t*' in XgeView, for each distinct ticker '*t*' in the input database ABC.

(4) Aggregations more general than the conventional vertical aggregation of SQL can be readily expressed in SchemaSQL: examples include horizontal and rectangular block aggregations [LSS96].

1.2 SchemaSQL in the context of a single database system

Several researchers including Miller [Mil98], Wang et al. [WIV98], and Subramanian and Venkataraman [SV98] have observed the useful functionality that SchemaSQL can bring to a *single* DBMS. Below, we summarize these "killer-apps" that form the basis of their observations.

Database Publishing on the Web: Making information in relational databases Web-available is an important problem in the context of databases and the internet. In [Mil98], Miller makes a compelling argument for the role of SchemaSQL in this context: A web user cannot be expected to know/learn the schema of a data source, which might be quite complex. This necessitates support for 'schema independent querying'. E.g., consider a keyword search interface that permits users to find stocks (tickers) in the ABC brokerage whose price is more than a certain amount on any date. The user may not specify or even care about the price type nor know that tickers appear as relation labels in the database. Under these assumptions, this is a higher-order query on the ABC database. The ability of SchemaSQL to quantify over schema labels can be used to support such schema independent querying required in database publishing environments.

Techniques for Physical Data Independence: An important technique used in indexing architectures for integrating new indexes into a query optimizer is the usage of views for describing the indexes [CKPS95, TSY96]. Conventional techniques (such as [TSY96]) are restricted in that they can only describe indexes that conform to the class of select-project-join views [Mil98]. Miller [Mil98] gives examples of B^+-tree indexes for all subclasses of a class, that can be expressed in SchemaSQL but not in SQL. Besides, she also shows that the optimization of important classes of queries including the *data fusion* queries [YPAG98], ubiquitous on internet databases, can benefit from higher-order views definable *only* in languages like SchemaSQL.

Scalable Classification Algorithms in Data Mining: Classification is a fundamental operation in data mining. The literature abounds with stand-alone algorithms for doing classification on data stored in files [AIS93]. In [WIV98], Wang et al. make a strong case for a tightly coupled implementation of classification algorithms, well integrated with SQL, and give a scalable such algorithm whose operations are expressed using SQL queries. Despite the advantages of tight coupling, they point out that the SQL queries produced by the algorithm are numerous, complex, verbose, and hard to optimize. They also provide a SchemaSQL-based algorithm and show that the resulting queries (and the algorithm) are concise, far fewer, and are readily optimizable w.r.t. database scans. In order to achieve this, they exploit SchemaSQL's ability to quantify over schema labels.

Query Optimization in a Data Warehouse: Optimization using materialized views is a popular and useful technique in the context of traditional database query optimization [BLT86, GMS93, CKPS95, LMSS95, SDJL96] which has been successfully applied for optimizing data warehouse queries [GHQ95, HGW+95, HRU96, GM96, GHRU97]. However, the materialized views considered by *all* of the above works are traditional views expressed in SQL. In [SV98], Subramanian and Venkataraman establish the surprising result that the use of materialized SchemaSQL views involving data/schema restructuring can have an order of magnitude improvement in the execution times of even *traditional* SQL queries. Thus, it is worth expanding the class of views that are candidates for materialization, beyond the class of queries being optimized, in this case from those expressible in SQL to those expressible in SchemaSQL.

The preceding applications demonstrate the need for efficient implementation of SchemaSQL even in the context of an *individual database system*. Given the popularity and extensive use of SQL systems, implementations of SchemaSQL that are *non-intrusive* are particularly attractive: non-intrusive means that the implementation should not require modifications to the SQL engine, in particular, to the set of plan operators used by existing query optimizers.

Contributions: Efficient implementation of SchemaSQL on top of SQL systems with minimal intrusion is the main objective of this paper. To this end, we develop a logical algebra consisting of classical relational algebra together with four restructuring operators – unfold, fold, split, and unite – originally introduced in [GLS96] and simplified and adapted to SchemaSQL setting (Section 3.1). We give an algorithm that can detect whether schema label variables in a given SchemaSQL query are properly constrained and then translate it to an equivalent expression in the logical algebra (Section 3.2). A key idea used by our algorithm is the notion of *meta-data specification*, which can be viewed as an augmentation to system catalog tables, normally maintained in RDBMS. We also provide a physical algebra (Section 4). Using that as a vehicle, we develop several implementation strategies (Section 5). Essentially, the optimizer can choose either to use direct strategies for the logical operators or reduce them to physical operators and use strategies for the latter. We illustrate logical and physical query optimization issues arising with SchemaSQL queries (Section 5.1). None of our strategies requires additions/modifications to the existing set of plan operators used by today's RDBMS. To test the feasibility of our strategies and their relative performance, we conducted a series of experiments based on TPC-D benchmark data, the results of which we report (Section 6). We conclude the paper by summarizing the main results and discussing future work (Section 7). *For lack of space, we only consider single block* SchemaSQL *queries without aggregation in this paper. Details on processing arbitrary* SchemaSQL *queries as well as proofs of various results we present can be found in the full paper [LSS99].* We use the terms queries and views interchangeably for convenience, without causing confusion.

2 Related Work

Several languages have been proposed to deal with schematic disparity in multi-databases. These include (higher-order) logics [KLK91, LSS97, SAB+95], algebras [Ros92, GLS96], and SQL extensions [KKS92, GLRS93, LSS96, GL98]. The work in [LSS96, GL98] is particularly relevant to this paper. Of these, [LSS96], the paper which introduced SchemaSQL, mainly concerns itself with deploying it in the context of multi-database systems and related query processing issues. The approach to query processing in [LSS96] is based on compiling federation queries expressed in SchemaSQL to SQL queries which are then dispatched to component DBMS, answers eventually collected at the server and restructured if necessary before being presented to the user. To a large extent nd-SQL, an offshoot of the SchemaSQL project, has a similar focus, except that it can express a substantially larger class of OLAP queries than SchemaSQL. None of these papers has considered the implementation of SchemaSQL or a variant, on a *single* DBMS.

Miller [Mil98] made powerful observations concerning the value that SchemaSQL can bring to a single DBMS (see Section 1.2). This, together with the SQL/SchemaSQL-based classification algorithm developed by Wang et al. [WIV98], and the work of Subramanian and Venkataraman on query optimization in data warehousing applications [SV98] form a core motivation for our work. Miller calls a schema *first-order* with respect to a set of queries $\mathcal{Q}$, provided all queries in $\mathcal{Q}$ can be expressed in SQL. Intuitively, this means all information of interest (to the queries in $\mathcal{Q}$) is modeled as data. Our notion of "flat schema" (Section 3.1) is similar to that of first-order schema in [Mil98], but a major difference is flatness is an absolute notion, in that it does not depend on the query class being considered. Besides, flat schemas play merely a technical role in query processing in that conceptually we can regard as though all source data is flattened so as to conform to a flat schema before being manipulated further. Miller restricts the integration schema in a federation of databases, or a restructuring schema in a single database, to be first-order. In addition, all sources should be expressed as views of the integration/restructuring schema in the fragment of SchemaSQL that does not use relation label or column label variables. For this setting, she addressed the problem of determining whether an SQL query on the integration/restructuring schema is answerable, as an SQL or SchemaSQL query, over the sources, and provides algorithms to translate the given federation query to a query over the sources.

The main focus of our work is implementing SchemaSQL on a single relational DBMS. In this context, we show that the full-fledged language of SchemaSQL can be implemented as SQL applications with no modification to SQL engines. We also study the issue of optimizing SchemaSQL queries non-intrusively, as well as the feasibility of highly efficient (intrusive) implementation of SchemaSQL.

In [SV98] Subramanian and Venkataraman study the utility of materialized SchemaSQL views for improving the performance of even traditional SQL queries. In this context, they propose algorithms that given an SQL query against the base tables and a set of SchemaSQL views that define the materialized restructured tables, generates alternative queries that exploit the SchemaSQL views. They also propose techniques for incorporating these alternative choices for cost based query optimization. The contributions in [SV98] are complementary to our work in this paper.

3 A Logical Algebra for SchemaSQL

Our approach to implementing SchemaSQL on top of a relational DBMS is based on first transforming SchemaSQL queries into equivalent queries in an extended relational algebra, which are then translated into a physical algebra, consisting of the standard suite of physical operators for relational DBMS, together with new physical operators introduced in Section 4. The logical algebra is the topic of this section. It consists of classical relational algebra augmented with four restructuring operators – *unfold, fold, split,* and *unite*, originally introduced in the context of the tabular algebra, by Gyssens et al. [GLS96]. Our aim in this paper is to develop *practical* and *efficient* strategies for implementing SchemaSQL. With this in mind, we adapt the definitions of the restructuring operators above to our context.

3.1 Restructuring Operators Simplified

We assume infinite pairwise disjoint sets of names $\mathcal{N}$ and values $\mathcal{V}$. We assume that $dom : \mathcal{N} \rightarrow 2^{\mathcal{V}}$ is a partial function such that whenever $dom(N)$ is defined, it associates name N with a non-empty set of values $dom(N) \subset \mathcal{V}$. The following basic notion is needed in the rest of the paper.

Definition 1 (Flat Scheme) A relation scheme $R(A_1, \ldots, A_n)$ is said to be *flat* provided all the entries $R, A_1, \ldots, A_n$ are names. A database scheme is flat if all relation schemes in it are.

The relational model implicitly assumes that schemes are flat. The intuition is that normally one assumes all information of interest is in the values (data). By requiring that no values appear in schema labels, most if not all useful queries against a flat database scheme can be expressed in a first-order query language like SQL. E.g., the relation scheme `stock(ticker, busType)` in Figure 1(a) is flat, assuming all the labels `stock, ticker, busType` are names. However, as the same figure illustrates (e.g., see relations `ibm(date, xge, open, close, low, high), msft(...), ...`), databases corresponding to non-flat schemes *do* get implemented using standard RDBMS.

We next give the intuition behind the restructuring operators.[2] The unfold operator takes a relation over a set of names as input and produces a cross-tab like output which is equivalent in information content to the input, as shown in Figure 2: (a) & (b). The fold operator does the converse. Similarly, the split operator takes a relation as input and produces a set of relations, one for each distinct value of a specified attribute, as output. The labels of the latter relations are set to the said attribute values. This is illustrated in Figure 2: (a) & (c). Finally, unite is the converse of split.

stock	xge	price
att	nyse	91.56
lucent	nyse	89.45
att	tse	92.35
lucent	tse	87.45

(a) Input table close

stock	nyse	tse
att	91.56	92.35
lucent	89.45	87.45

(b) Table uf-close result of UNFOLD$_{\texttt{by xge on price}}$(close)

stock	price
att	91.56
lucent	89.45

(i) table nyse

stock	price
att	92.35
lucent	87.45

(ii) table tse

Result of SPLIT$_{\texttt{by xge}}$(close)

Figure 2: Illustration of operator definitions.

We now give the formal definitions of the four restructuring operators, adapted from [GLS96]. We use the abbreviation $\vec{A}_{i:j}$ to denote the sequence $A_i, ..., A_j$.

Definition 2 (Unfold) Let r be a relation over a scheme $\{\vec{A}_{1:n}\}$, where A_i are names. Then UNFOLD$_{\text{by } A_i \text{ on } A_j}$ (r) is a relation s over the scheme $\{\vec{A}_{1:(i-1)}, \vec{A}_{(i+1):(j-1)}, \vec{A}_{(j+1):n}, u_1, ..., u_m\}$, where $\{u_1, ..., u_m\}$ is the set of distinct values appearing in column A_i of r. The contents of s are defined as $s = \{(\vec{a}_{1:(i-1)}, \vec{a}_{(i+1):(j-1)}, \vec{a}_{(j+1):n}), \vec{v}_{1:m} \mid (\vec{a}_{1:(i-1)}, u_\ell, \vec{a}_{(i+1):(j-1)}, v_\ell, \vec{a}_{(j+1):n} \in r, 1 \leq \ell \leq m\}$.

As an illustration, applying UNFOLD$_{\texttt{by xge on price}}$(close) to the table close of Figure 2(a) produces the table uf-close of Figure 2(b). Note that for unfold, all input column labels must be names.

Definition 3 (Fold) Let r be a relation over the scheme $\{\vec{A}, u_1, ..., u_m\}$, where $\vec{A}$ is a vector of names. Suppose the u_i are values from $dom(B)$, and all entries appearing in columns $u_1, ..., u_m$ of r are elements of $dom(C)$, for some names $B, C \notin \{\vec{A}\}$. Then FOLD$_{\text{by } C \text{ on } B}(r)$ is a relation s over the scheme $S(\vec{A}, B, C)$, defined as $s = \{(\vec{a}, u_i, v_i) \mid \exists$ a tuple $t \in r : t[\vec{A}] = \vec{a}$ & $t[u_i] = v_i\}$.

Fold requires input column labels to be either names or values coming from the domain of a common attribute. The effect of applying fold is to "flatten" the relation over such a scheme. E.g., applying FOLD$_{\texttt{by price on xge}}$(uf-close), where uf-close is the table in Figure 2(b) yields the table close in Figure 2(a).

[2] Each operator can be defined to manipulate a *set* of relations, thus giving closure. For easy exposition, we only show their definition on a single input relation.

```
CREATE VIEW  uf-close   (stock, X) AS
(Q1)         SELECT       stock, T.price
             FROM         close T, T.xge X
CREATE VIEW  close      (stock, xge, price) AS
(Q2)         SELECT     stock, X, T.X
             FROM       uf-close -> X, uf-close T
             WHERE      X <> 'stock'
CREATE VIEW  X          (stock, price) AS
(Q3)         SELECT     stock, price
             FROM       close T, T.xge X
CREATE VIEW  close      (stock, xge, price) AS
(Q4)         SELECT     T.stock, X, T.price
             FROM       -> X, X T
```

Figure 3: SchemaSQL Queries corresponding to the four Restructuring Operators.

Definition 4 (Split) Let r be a relation over a scheme $R(A_1, ..., A_n)$ such that R is a name. Then SPLIT$_{\text{by } A_i}(r)$ is a set of relations obtained as follows. For each distinct value $u \in \pi_{A_i}(r)$, SPLIT$_{\text{by } A_i}(r)$ contains a unique relation u over the scheme $U(\vec{A}_{1:(i-1)}, \vec{A}_{(i+1):n})$, defined as $u = \{t[\vec{A}_{1:(i-1)}, \vec{A}_{(i+1):n}] \mid t \in r$ & $t[A_i] = u\}$.

As an illustration, applying SPLIT$_{\texttt{by xge}}$(close) to the table close in Figure 2(a) produces the two tables 'nyse' and 'tse' in Figure 2(c). Note that split requires the input relation label to be a name.

Definition 5 (Unite) Let $u_1, ..., u_m$ be the set of all relations in a given database, such that each relation label u_i is an element of $dom(B)$, for some fixed name B. Suppose also that they all have a common scheme $\{\vec{A}\}$. Then UNITE$_{\text{by } B|}$Cond(), where Cond is any boolean combination of conditions of the form B relOp const, is a relation r over the scheme $\{B, \vec{A}\}$, defined as $r = \{t \mid \exists \tau \in u_i$, for some u_i where Cond(u_i) : $t[\vec{A}] = \tau[\vec{A}]$ & $t[B] = u_i\}$. When Cond is "true", we omit it.

The operation UNITE$_{\texttt{by xge}}$(), when applied against the database consisting of the tables in Figure 2(c):(i) & (ii), yields the table in Figure 2(a). Note that unlike the preceding operators, unite does not take arguments. It is always implicitly applied against the current state of a database. When so applied, the relation labels in the database are evaluated against the conditions Cond, and those that satisfy them are manipulated by unite.

For further illustration, in Figure 3, we present examples of SchemaSQL queries corresponding to the four operators above, against the database scheme of Figure 2: Q1: UNFOLD$_{\texttt{by xge on price}}$(close); Q2: FOLD$_{\texttt{by price on xge}}$(uf-close); Q3: SPLIT$_{\texttt{by xge}}$(close); and Q4: UNITE$_{\texttt{by xge}}$().

3.2 Translating from SchemaSQL to Extended Algebra

We start with an overview of our translation process. First, we check whether the schema label variables in a given SchemaSQL query are *properly constrained.* Intuitively, this means no column label variable ranges over labels whose attribute types are different, and no relation label variable ranges over relation labels whose schemes are different. E.g., a column label variable ranging over both `date` and `xge` is *not* properly constrained, nor is a relation label variable ranging over both 'ibm' and `stock`. Queries with schema label variables that are not properly constrained are not well-defined. With each schema label L, we can associate an ***attribute type*** as follows. If L is a name, its attribute type is L. If it is a value, then the name A such that $L \in dom(A)$ is said to be its attribute type. Finally, if a schema label variable `V` ranges over a set of schema labels all of whose attribute type is A, we say the attribute type of `V` is A. Essentially, properly constrained column label variables are those that have a well-defined attribute type, while properly constrained relation label variables range over relation labels with an identical scheme. In the full paper [LSS99], we give an algorithm for checking whether a `SchemaSQL` query is well-defined, which at once can also determine the attribute types associated with various labels and label variables.

A key idea used in attribute type detection is *meta-data specification*, expressed in the form of a Datalog program[3]. For instance, for the database scheme of Figure 1(a), the corresponding meta-data specification is given in Figure 1(b). The predicate *isa*(X, `attribute`) indicates the entry X is a value from the domain of `attribute`; predicate *colVar*(X) means X is a column label variable, etc. The facts in the top part of the program say 'ibm', 'msft', etc. have `ticker` as their attribute type. The first rule says whenever `S` is a relation label variable with attribute type `ticker` and `T` is a tuple variable ranging over the tuples in the relations `S`, `T.xge` has `xge` as its attribute type. More interestingly, `T.PT` has `price` as its attribute type, whenever `T` is as above and `PT` is a column label variable with attribute type `priceType`. This idea was inspired by a similar idea, used in [LSS96] for handling semantic heterogeneity in multi-databases.

Once a query is found to be well-defined and the attribute types are detected, the next step is to "flatten" the various relations involved in the query. E.g., if tuple variable `T` ranges over one relation which is in unfolded form. Then we apply a fold operation to this table with relevant parameters. On the other hand, if `T` ranges over many relations which correspond to a split representation, we apply a unite operation to this set of relations. Combinations of the above scenarios may arise and are handled in a similar manner. As a concrete example, in the view definition in Figure 1(c), `T` ranges over many relations whose labels (ibm, msft, ...) are in the range of variable `S`. Thus, a unite operation is called for. However, each of these relations is in unfolded form, so a fold operation is also planned.

After flattening the relevant input relations, the next step is to apply a Cartesian product together with necessary selections and projections. These are identified from the `WHERE` clause and the `SELECT` statement, as usual. Two issues need special attention: (i) if a label variable appears in the relation position in the `CREATE VIEW` statement, the attribute type of that variable should also be included in the project list; (ii) domain expressions that appear in the `SELECT` statement and in the `WHERE` clause need to be modified so that they can be correctly applied as parameters to projection and selection on the Cartesian product of the flattened input tables.

Finally, if necessary an unfold and a split may have to be applied. The parameters for these operations are obtained by query analysis.

Consider a generic `SchemaSQL` query/view Q below.

```
CREATE   VIEW     rel (col1, ..., colk) AS
         SELECT   dom1, ..., domk
(Q):     FROM     decl1, ..., decln
         WHERE    conditions
```

Here, `coli` is either an identifier (i.e. name) or a domain variable, `domi` is a domain expression, and `decli` is a variable declaration.

A concrete example fitting the above template is given in Figure 1(c). It asks "for each tech stock, and for each price type, find the price value on each date and arrange it into one relation per exchange, where each such relation has one column per stock (i.e. ticker)".

Figure 4 gives an algorithm for translating single block `SchemaSQL` queries without aggregation into an expression in the extended algebra described in the preceding section. It invokes the following algorithms: (i) FLATTEN $(r, \mathbf{C})$, an algorithm which takes as input a relation label or variable r and the constraints $\mathbf{C}$ that apply to r (if any), and flattens r as explained above; (ii) *wellDefined*(`Q`, `S`, $\mathbf{C}_\mathtt{S}$), which takes in a `SchemaSQL` query `Q`, a schema label variable `S` in `Q`, and any applicable constraints $\mathbf{C}_\mathtt{S}$ on `S`, and checks whether `S` is properly constrained. Details of these algorithms, suppressed here for lack of space, can be found in [LSS99].

Example 1 (Translating `SchemaSQL` to Algebra) Consider the database scheme and `SchemaSQL` query/view shown in Figure 1(c). This query is clearly well defined. Application of step 3 of the algorithm yields the expression template:

$\text{SPLIT}_{\text{by } splitPar}(\text{UNFOLD}_{\text{by } ufPar1 \text{ on } ufPar2}(\pi_{splitPar, mod(\mathtt{T.date}), mod(\mathtt{PT}), mod(\mathtt{T.PT})}(\sigma_{mod(\mathtt{S})=mod(\mathtt{U.ticker})\ \&\ mod(\mathtt{U.busType})=\text{'tech'}}[\text{FLATTEN}(\mathtt{S}, \{\mathtt{S} \neq \mathtt{stock}\}) \times \text{FLATTEN}(\mathtt{stock}, \text{"}true\text{"})])))$.

In step 4, we can infer that since `X` ranges over the domain of `xge`, splitPar = `xge`. In step 5, we find that since the attribute type of `S` is `ticker` and that of `T.PT` is `price`, *ufPar1* = `ticker`, *ufPar2* = `price`. In step 6, we can identify the parameters for projection

[3]Our methodology and techniques do *not* depend on the specification language. Indeed, the "specification" could well be a C++ program. However, a declarative specification is much easier to read, and we chose Datalog for this reason.

Algorithm *Translate*(Q);
Input: A single block **SchemaSQL** query Q without aggregation;
Output: An expression E in the extended algebra, that is equivalent to Q under multiset semantics.

1. identify $r_1, ..., r_m$, the list of relations or relation label variables appearing in the declarations in the **FROM** clause;

2. for each schema var S {
   //test if query is well-defined;

   identify the set of conditions $\mathbf{C}_S$ of the form S relOp const, in the **WHERE** clause;

   if not wellDefined(Q, S, $\mathbf{C}_S$)

   return(error); }

3. Build the expression:
   //at this point, the attribute types of all schema
   //vars is known from Algorithm wellDefined;
   $E = \text{SPLIT}_{\text{by } splitPar}(\text{UNFOLD}_{\text{by } ufPar1 \text{ on } ufPar2}(\pi_{splitPar, mod(\texttt{dom1}), \ldots, mod(\texttt{domk})}\ \sigma_{mod(\texttt{conditions})}\ [\text{FLATTEN}(r1) \times \cdots \times \text{FLATTEN}(rm)]))$,

   where mod(**domi**), mod(**sc**), *ufPar1*, *ufPar2*, and *splitPar* are determined as follows.

4. if **rel** (in the **CREATE VIEW** statement) is a constant {

   remove the split operation;

   remove the parameter *splitPar* from the project list; }

   else {

   let **rel** be a domain variable **X**, declared to range over the domain of attribute A;
   //A is thus a splitting column;
   then *splitPar* = A; }

5. if no **coli** in the **CREATE VIEW** statement is a domain var

   remove the unfold operation;

   else { //unfold is needed;

   if more than one **col** is a domain var return(error);

   let **coli** be the unique **col** which is a domain var, say X
   obtain the attribute type B of X from algorithm *wellDefined*;

   obtain the attribute type C of **domi** from algorithm *wellDefined*;

   ufPar1 = B; *ufPar2* = C; }

6. for each **domi** {

   if **domi** is of the form **tupleVar.col** {
   find the relation label (variable) **reln** associated with **tupleVar**;

   find the attribute type **attr** of the domain expression **tupleVar.col** from the meta-data specs;

   mod(**domi**) = flat-**reln.attr**, where flat-**reln** refers to the name of the relation obtained by flattening **reln**; }

   if **domi** is of the form **domVar**, declared as **FROM tupleVar.col domVar**, where **tupleVar** and **col** are as above, the treatment is similar to the above;

   if **domi** is of the form **colVar**, declared as **FROM reln-> colVar**, where **reln** is either a relation label or a relation label variable {
   find the attribute type **attr** of **colVar** from algorithm *wellDefined*;

   mod(**domi**) = flat-**reln.attr**, where flat-**reln** refers to the name of the relation obtained by flattening **reln**; }

   if **domi** is of the form **relVar**, declared as **FROM -> relVar** {
   find the attribute type **attr** of **relVar** from algorithm *wellDefined*;

   mod(**domi**) = flat-**relVar.attr**, where flat-**relVar** refers to the name of the relation obtained by flattening **relVar**; }

   replace each domain expression in **conditions** using the same rules as above and set the result to mod(**conditions**); }

Figure 4: Algorithm for translating SchemaSQL queries into extended algebra.

as flat-S.date, flat-S.priceType, flat-S.price. The first three conditions in the **WHERE** clause simply ensure the variables S, PT are properly constrained. We then obtain the modified conditions flat-S.ticker = flat-stock.ticker and flat-stock.busType = 'tech' corresponding to the last two. These may be further simplified to flat-S.ticker = stock.ticker and stock.busType = 'tech'. These two conditions would be parameters for selection. The final algebraic expression obtained by the translation algorithm is:
$\text{SPLIT}_{\text{by } \texttt{xge}}(\text{UNFOLD}_{\text{by } \texttt{ticker} \text{ on } \texttt{price}}(\pi_{\texttt{xge}, \text{flat}-\texttt{S.date}, \text{flat}-\texttt{S.priceType}.\text{flat}-\texttt{S.price}}(\sigma_{\text{flat}-\texttt{S.ticker}=\texttt{stock.ticker} \,\&\, \texttt{U.busType}=\text{'tech'}}[\text{FLATTEN}(\mathsf{S}, \{\mathsf{S} \neq \texttt{stock}\}) \times \texttt{stock})]))$. ■

We have the following result, the proof of which is suppressed for lack of space.

Theorem 1 (Correctness of Algorithm Translate) *Algorithm Translate(Q) always translates a* SchemaSQL *query* Q *into an expression in the extended algebra that is equivalent to it whenever* Q *is well-defined and reports an error otherwise.* ■

4 A Physical Algebra

In this section, we propose some physical operators into which the restructuring operators of Section 3 can be compiled. The advantage is that the compiled expression can be conveniently used for choosing query execution strategies. As mentioned earlier, we are particularly interested in efficient but *non-intrusive* strategies, i.e. those that do not require any modifications or additions to the set of plan operators used by current relational query optimizers. At a conceptual level, an interesting observation that forms the basis of logical to physical algebra transformation is that SchemaSQL, with all its higher-order power, can be essentially reduced to SQL together with looping over attribute domains. For example, $\text{SPLIT}_{\text{by } A}(r)$ can be seen as repeatedly doing the selection $\sigma_{A=a_i}(r)$, $\forall a_i \in \pi_A(r)$.

The first physical operator is called *iterated selection*. It is a generalization of the idea discussed above. It comes in two flavors – *iterated selection by name* and *by value*.

Definition 6 (Iterated Selection) Let r be a relation with scheme $\{A_1, ..., A_n\}$, where A_i are all names, and let $\mathcal{C}$ be a set of conditions of the form A relOp const, or of the form A relOp B, where $A, B \in \{A_1, ..., A_n\}$. Suppose $\{\vec{B}\}$ is a set of attributes such that $\{\vec{B}\} \subseteq (\{\vec{A}\} - \{A_i\})$ and $A_j \in \{\vec{B}\}$, and $\{\vec{C}\}$ is a set of attributes such that $\{\vec{C}\} \subseteq (\{\vec{A}\} - \{A_i, A_j\})$. Then the operators *iterated selection by name*, $iSel_n(r, A_i, \mathcal{C}, \vec{B})$, applied to relation of r, by A_i. subject to conditions $\mathcal{C}$, and *iterated selection by value*, $iSel_v(r, A_i, A_j, \mathcal{C}, \vec{C})$, applied to relation of r, by A_i on A_j, subject to conditions $\mathcal{C}$, are defined as follows.

Iterated Selection by name: $iSel_n(r, A_i, \mathcal{C}, \{\vec{B}\})$: Let $\{a_1, ..., a_k\}$ be the set of distinct A_i-values in $\pi_{A_i}(r)$. Then this operator produces k output tables $rel_{a_p}(\vec{B})$, $1 \leq p \leq k$, such that $rel_{a_p} = \{t[\vec{B}] \mid t \in r \ \& \ t[A_i] = a_p \ \& \ t$ satisfies $\mathcal{C}\}$.

Iterated Selection by value: $iSel_v(r, A_i, A_j, \mathcal{C}, \{\vec{C}\})$: Let $\{a_1, ..., a_k\}$ be the set of distinct A_i-values in $\pi_{A_i}(r)$. Then the operator produces k tables $rel_{a_p}(\vec{C}, a_p)$, $1 \leq p \leq k$, such that $rel_{a_p} = \{t[\vec{C}, A_j] \mid t \in r \ \& \ t[A_i] = a_p \ \& \ t$ satisfies $\mathcal{C}\}$. ■

Remarks: (1) $iSel_n$ intuitively partitions relation r on column A_i (after filtering out tuples violating conditions $\mathcal{C}$), and writes each partition into a separate output table, dropping attributes not in $\vec{B}$, including A_i. The scheme of each output relation produced is set to $\{\vec{B}\}$. Note that the value of attribute A_j is written under column named A_j in the output relations. (2) $iSel_v$ is almost identical to $iSel_n$ except the output scheme of $\texttt{rel}_a$ consists of $\{\vec{C},\ a\}$, so tuples in the partition associated with $\texttt{rel}_a$ are written into this relation, so that all A_j-values are lined up against column 'a'. (3) For the sake of generality, the above definition avoids committing to any implementation strategy. Several strategies will be proposed in the sequel. (4) Like the restructuring operators, the physical operators also can be easily extended to manipulate sets of relations. We focus on applications of these operators to single relations, for clarity. Here is an example of iterated selection.

tabA

stock	price
att	91.56

tabB

stock	price
att	92.35

tabC

stock	xge	price
att	nyse	91.56
lucent	nyse	89.45

tabD

stock	xge	price
att	tse	92.35
lucent	tse	87.45

tabE

stock	nyse
att	91.56
lucent	89.45

tabF

stock	tse
att	92.35
lucent	87.45

Figure 5: Examples for Physical Operators.

Example 2 (Illustrating $iSel_n$ and $iSel_v$) Applying $iSel_n$(`close`, `xge`, {`price` > 90}, {`stock`, `price`}) to the relation `close` in Figure 2(a) yields the two output relations `tabA` and `tabB` of Figure 5. As another example, applying $iSel_v$(`close`, `xge`, `price`, "*true*", {`stock`}) to the same input table as above produces the two tables `tabE` and `tabF` of Figure 5. ■

The second operator is called *iterated projection*. The basic idea is that if an input table contains many column labels $a_1, a_2, ...$ corresponding to values from the domain of some name A, this operator will output projections of the input table on different sets of column labels such that each label a_i ends up in a different projection. Like iterated selection, there are two flavors – corresponding to "by name" and "by value".

Definition 7 (Iterated Projection) Let r be a relation with scheme $\{\vec{A}, a_1, ..., a_m\}$, where As are names, $a_i \in dom(A), 1 \leq i \leq m$, for some name $A \notin \{\vec{A}\}$, and for $1 \leq i \leq m$, all entries in columns a_i are values from $dom(B)$, for some fixed name $B \notin \{\vec{A}\}$, $B \neq A$. Suppose $\mathcal{C}$ is a set of conditions of the form L_1 relOp const, or of the form L_1 relOp L_2, where L_1, L_2 are each, either one of the attributes in $\vec{A}$, or a label a_i, for some $1 \leq i \leq m$. Then the operators *iterated projection by name*, $iProj_n(r, A, B, \mathcal{C})$, and *iterated projection by value*, $iProj_v(r, A, B, \mathcal{C})$, applied to relation of r, by B on A, and subject to conditions $\mathcal{C}$, are defined as follows.

Iterated Projection by name $iProj_n(r, A, B, \mathcal{C})$: This operator produces m output tables $rel_{a_p}(\vec{A}, A, B)$, $1 \leq p \leq m$, such that $rel_{a_p} = \{t[\vec{A}] \cdot `a_p`\cdot t[a_p] \mid t \in r \ \& \ t$ satisfies $\mathcal{C}\}$.

Iterated Projection by value $iProj_v(r, A, B, \mathcal{C})$: This operator produces m output tables $rel_{a_p}(\vec{A}, a_p)$, $1 \leq p \leq m$, such that $rel_{a_p} = \{t[\vec{A}, a_p] \mid t \in r \ \& \ t$ satisfies $\mathcal{C}\}$. ■

Remark: Iterated projection by name and value are similar: the core step involved in each of these operators is projecting r onto each of the column label sets $\{\vec{A}, a\}$, $\forall a \in \{a_1, ..., a_m\}$; in the former case, we also append the corresponding A-value 'a' and re-label column 'a' as B, whereas in the latter we don't. Once again, notice the lack of commitment to any specific implementation strategy.

Example 3 (Illustrating $iProj_n$ and $iProj_v$) Applying $iProj_n$(`uf-close`, `xge`, `price`, "*true*") to the table in Figure 2(b) results in the two tables `tabC` and `tabD` of Figure 5. As another example, applying $iProj_v$(`uf-close`, `xge`, `price`, "*true*") to the same input table results in the tables `tabE` and `tabF` of Figure 5. ■

We next show that each of the four restructuring operators – unfold, fold, split, and unite – can be computed using iterated selection and projection together with classical relational algebraic operations. For a set of relations $\mathcal{R}$ we denote their natural join as $\bowtie(\mathcal{R})$ and their union, whenever their schemes are identical, as $\bigcup(\mathcal{R})$.

Theorem 2 1. Let r be any relation over the scheme $\{\vec{A}\}$ consisting of only names, and let $A_i, A_j \in \{\vec{A}\}$ be any two distinct names in the scheme. Then the output computed by the expressions $\text{UNFOLD}_{\text{by } A_i \text{ on } A_j}(r)$ and $\bowtie(iSel_v(r, A_i, A_j, \text{"}true\text{"}, (\{\vec{A}\} - \{A_i, A_j\})))$ are equivalent.

2. Let r be a relation over the scheme $\{\vec{A}, b_1, ..., b_m\}$, where $\{\vec{A}\}$ is a set of names, $b_1, ..., b_m$ are values from the domain of some name B, and the

entries in columns b_i of r are from the domain of another name C. Then the output computed by the expression $\text{FOLD}_{\text{by } C \text{ on } B}(r)$ and $\bigcup(iProj_n(r, B, C, \text{"true"}))$ are equivalent.

3. Let r be a relation over the scheme $\{\vec{A}\}$, such that $\{\vec{A}\}$ includes two names B, C. Then the output computed by the expressions $\text{SPLIT}_{\text{by } B}(r)$ and $iSel_n(r, B, C, \text{"true"}, (\{\vec{A}\} - \{B\}))$ are equivalent.

4. Let $b_1, ..., b_k$ be relations with the identical scheme $\{\vec{A}\}$, such that $b_1, ..., b_k$ are values from the domain of some name B. Then the output computed by the expression $\text{UNITE}_{\text{by } B}()$ and the expression $\bigcup_{1 \leq i \leq k}(\{`b_i'\} \times \mathbf{rel}_{b_i})$ over the scheme $\{B, \vec{A}\}$ are equivalent. ■

5 Implementation Strategies

We can obtain several implementation strategies for computing SchemaSQL queries by considering ways in which the physical operators introduced in the previous section can be implemented. In addition, we will see that sometimes it makes sense to compute a logical operation such as unfold directly. The exact choice of the operator to be used for query execution and the strategy for the chosen operator should be a cost-based decision made by the query optimizer. While these issues are beyond the scope of the paper, we illustrate by examples that different operators and strategies may lead to efficient executions under different circumstances. Also, for lack of space, we only give strategies for iterated selection by value, iterated projection by name, unfold, and unite. Strategies for other operators are discussed in the full version [LSS99].

Strategies for Iterated Selection:

We give two strategies for iterated selection by name. The first strategy does not involve sorting, while the second strategy incurs an initial sorting overhead.

Strategy *iSel I* **for** $iSel_v$**(rel, By, On, Conditions, ProjList)**:

1. find the set of distinct values $u_1, ..., u_k$ in column By of relation rel, using SELECT DISTINCT ...;
2. for each distinct value found u_i {
   create table tab$_i$(ProjList, u_i) ;
   ```
   INSERT INTO   tab_i
   SELECT        ProjList, On
   FROM          rel
   WHERE         Conditions AND By = u_i }
   ```

Strategy *iSel II* **for** $iSel_v$**(rel, By, On, Conditions, ProjList)**:

1. sort relation rel on the column By;
2. while there are unread blocks {
   - read the next block of tuples from rel;
   - if the By-value of the block, u_i, is new create a new table tab$_i$(ProjList, u_i);
   - project the block on the columns (ProjList, On) and write it into tab$_i$; }

Strategies for Unfold:

Strategies for the unfold operator can be derived by exploiting the equivalence result in Theorem 2. First an iterated selection is performed, then the resulting relations are joined to obtain the unfolded relation. The unfold strategy *unfold I* is obtained by using strategy *iSel I* for the iterated selection, while *unfold II* uses *iSel II*.

It turns out there is a third, direct strategy for the unfold operator.

(Direct) Strategy *unfold III*:

1. find the set of distinct values $u_1, ..., u_k$ in column By of relation rel, using SELECT DISTINCT ...;
2. do CREATE TABLE **uf-rel**(ProjList, $u_1, ..., u_k$);
3. form a partition, say $\langle P_1, ..., P_m \rangle$ of **rel** such that each P_i is a maximal set of tuples which agree on ProjList but disagree on column By;
   //this may be done by sorting on ProjList, By, and using a bitvector
   //representation for the membership of the u_is in each partition;
4. for each cell in the partition, $P_i = \{(\vec{p}, u_1, v_1), ..., (\vec{p}, u_k, v_k)\}$
   write the tuple $(\vec{p}, v_1, ..., v_k)$ into **uf-rel**;

The direct strategy *unfold III* avoids intermediate storage costs for storing the output of iterated selection (unlike Strategies *unfold I* and *unfold II*) as well as the final join cost. However, it incurs a sorting overhead. While it may superficially appear as though Strategy III, implemented judiciously to benefit from block I/O, will always outperform the other strategies, we will show later in the section that expressing a query using the physical operators sometimes allows to exploit unique optimization opportunities. Our non-intrusive implementation of *unfold III* strategy (Section 6) is less efficient than *unfold I* strategy due to the tuple-at-a-time nature of the implementation. But our C++ implementation of *unfold III* turned out to be significantly more efficient.

Strategies for Iterated Projection:

In this paragraph, we give two strategies for iterated projection by name. The first one involves k separate SPJ queries each of which will be used to populate one output table. The second one starts by creating the output tables (schemas); for each input tuple t, it writes the appropriate "piece" of t into the relevant output table. A block-based variant of this strategy can be applied where a block of records is read into memory and processed instead of one tuple, at a time.

Strategy *iProj I* **for** $iProj_n$**(rel, By, On, Conditions, ProjList)**:

1. let $u_1, ..., u_k$ be the column labels of rel that correspond to $dom(B)$;
2. for $(i = 1; i <= k; i++)$
   ```
   CREATE TABLE   tab_i(ProjList, B, C);
   INSERT INTO    tab_i
   SELECT         ProjList, 'u_i', u_i
   FROM           rel
   WHERE          Conditions
   ```

Strategy *iProj II* **for** $iProj_n$**(rel, By, On, Conditions, ProjList)**:

1. let $u_1, ..., u_k$ be the column labels of rel that correspond to $dom(B)$;
2. for $(i = 1; i <= k; i++)$
   - CREATE TABLE tab$_i$(ProjList, B, C);
3. while there are unread tuples {
   - read the next tuple t from rel and test if it satisfies Conditions;
   - write t[ProjList] · 'u_i'·$t[u_i]$ into tab$_i$; }

Strategies for Unite

Strategy *unite I* involves explicit creation of intermediate tables by "padding" each input table u_i by a column whose values are 'u_i'' for all tuples, and then unioning these intermediate tables. Strategy *unite II*, given below, avoids the creation of the intermediate tables.

(Direct) Strategy *unite II*:
let $u_1(\vec{colLabels}), ..., u_k(\vec{colLabels})$ be the set of all relations such that the labels $u_1, ..., u_k \in dom(B)$, for some name B;

1. **CREATE TABLE** unite-rel(B, colL$\vec{a}$bels);
2. for $(i = 1; i <= k; i + +)$ {
   - read each tuple t in relation u_i;
   - write the tuple 'u_i'' $\cdot\, t$ into unite-rel; }

In the following section, we illustrate some query optimization opportunities available to SchemaSQL processing – both at a logical and a physical level. In the full paper [LSS99], we establish several identities among expressions in the logical algebra and also discuss several physical optimizations in detail.

5.1 Query Optimization

To appreciate logical optimization, consider the queries Q5, Q6 given below, expressed against the database of Figure 2. Q5 is a straight projection of uf-close (Figure 2(b)) on column stock. In this case, the translated query $\pi_{\texttt{stock}}(\text{FLATTEN}(\texttt{T}, \text{"true"}))$ is equivalent to $\pi_{\texttt{stock}}(\text{FOLD}_{\text{by price on xge}}(\texttt{uf-close}))$ which in turn is equivalent to $\pi_{\texttt{stock}}(\texttt{uf-close})$. In general, whenever the projectList is disjoint with both the parameter lists of fold, we can push down projection, which in this case ends up removing fold. For Q6, by a similar reasoning, we can show that the translated query can be rewritten into the equivalent query $\pi_{\texttt{stock}}(\sigma_{\texttt{nyse}>90 \vee \texttt{tse}>90}(\texttt{uf-close}))$, which does not involve any restructuring operator. Likewise, there are several opportunities for logical optimization, which are based on operator identities. The decision of when to apply flatten or not should, however be based not only on logical equivalence, but on available indexes and properties of data. Another class of query equivalences have to do with operator commutativity: e.g., unfold and split commute whenever their parameter lists do not overlap.

```
SELECT   T.stock
FROM     uf-close T
         Q5
```

```
SELECT   T.stock
FROM     uf-close -> X, uf-close T
WHERE    X <> stock AND T.X > 90
                  Q6
```

Next we consider physical optimization. Recall the translation of the SchemaSQL query in Figure 1(c) (see Example 1). The resulting expression is depicted as a tree in Figure 6(a).

Now, several execution strategies are possible. One option is to combine Cartesian product with selection and projection (as is done in classical relational optimization), and then apply unfold, followed by split. Clearly, any strategy for join may be used, and any of the proposed strategies for unfold and split may

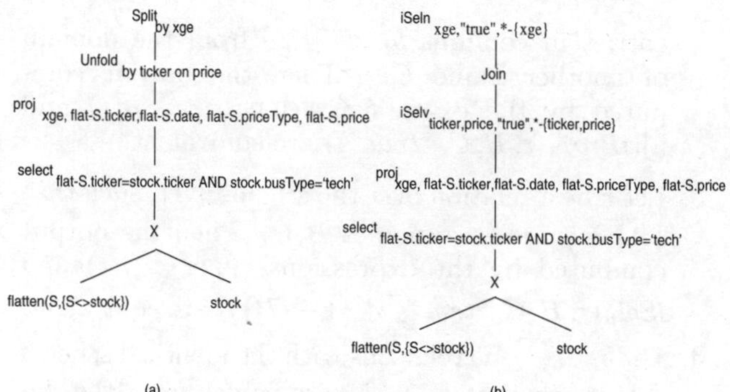

Figure 6: *(a) Operator Tree corresponding to the* SchemaSQL *query in Example 1; (b) Equivalent operator tree employing physical operators, where we use abbreviations: "*-{A}" means all attributes in the scheme except A.*

be used as well. Since the sets of parameters for unfold and split are disjoint, as argued above, the order of these operations can be swapped, leading to a slightly different execution strategy. So far, we have not utilized the physical operators. To do that, we must translate the restructuring operators in the tree into appropriate physical operators. Doing so leads to the tree shown in Figure 6(b).

Now, any of the strategies proposed for the physical operators can be used for computing them. In addition, examining the operators $iSel_v$ and $iSel_n$ in the tree, we notice that the steps needed to perform these operators can be combined. E.g., consider using strategy II for both $iSel_v$ and $iSel_n$. Then instead of first computing $iSel_v$ in full and then (after the join) computing $iSel_n$, the sorts required for these operations can be combined, and we can sort the table generated by projection on the columns ticker, xge. However, the join operation is done on the attributes xge, date, so it makes sense to sort the table on the columns ticker, xge, date, in that order. Now, conceptually, after $iSel_v$, the resulting tables (for different ticker-values) are already sorted on xge, date, and can be joined efficiently. As we join them, we can write the output tuples into different relations corresponding to different xge-values. In fact, even the intermediate output tables corresponding to the application of $iSel_v$ need not be explicitly created and stored. Thus, we can perform the three operations of $iSel_v$, $\bowtie$, and $iSel_n$ in one shot, on the fly.

6 Experiments

We conducted experiments using TPC-D benchmark data [TPC93] on NT workstation running DB2[4]. Our experiments were designed with the following objectives

- To demonstrate the feasibility of non-intrusive implementation of SchemaSQL on an SQL engine.
- To assess relative performance of different non-intrusive strategies.

[4]DB2 is a trademark of IBM.

As a possible indication of the efficiency that may be afforded by an *intrusive* implementation, we also implemented the various operations directly in C++, externally to the DBMS.

6.1 The iterated selection and unite operations

We implemented two non-intrusive strategies for the iterative select, viz., *iSel I* and *iSel II* (Section 5). The non-intrusive implementation of *iSel II* uses SQL ORDER BY facility for the sorting, and a cursor to scan the sorted tuples. We also implemented *unite I* and *unite II* strategies, both non-intrusively. We used the lineItem table in the TPC-D benchmark as a basis for our experiments, which we conducted for varying sizes, while keeping the number of distinct values in the "By" column almost constant. The following table summarizes the timing results. 'Size of table' indicates the number of tuples in the input table (for iSel operations) or output table (for unite operations). 'Number of split tables' indicates the number of tables generated (for iSel operations) or the number of tables united (for unite operations). The experiments show a linear performance for all operations in the range of table sizes we tested. Performance of *iSel I* and *iSel II* are somewhat similar, with *iSel II* becoming less efficient as size of table increases. This may be the result of sorting overhead. Performance of *unite II* is better than that of *unite I* since *unite II* avoids the generation of intermediate tables. Execution times are in seconds.

size	splits	*iSel I*	*iSel II*	*unite I*	*unite II*
2770	326	108	100	176	31
5335	329	132	145	198	36
6712	330	158	180	224	37
14042	333	236	312	334	71
20702	334	281	429	389	101

We also coded, in C++, a direct implementation based on *iSel II* strategy. It differs from *iSel II* in that using a (external) sort-merge sorting algorithm, the generation of output tables is built into the merge phase of the sort-merge algorithm. Hence the C++ implementation avoids storing the sorted table. The performance was surprising: about an oder of magnitude faster than the non-intrusive implementations. Note that the direct C++ implementation avoids significant database overheads such as logging, maintaining the catalog tables, and other similar foot prints. Nevertheless, these experiments suggest that an efficient *intrusive* implementation of SchemaSQL might yield significant benefits. We are currently investigating this hypothesis.

6.2 The unfold and fold operations

We implemented *unfold I* and *unfold III* strategies (Section 5) both non-intrusively. The *unfold II* strategy differs from *unfold I* only in the underlying iSel strategy and its performance can be derived by adding the difference in *iSel I* and *iSel II* to that of *unfold I*. We also implemented two strategies for the fold operation. The following table summarizes the timing results. We used the projection of the TPC-D lineitem table on orderkey, linenumber, extendedprice for these experiments. Since the FD {orderkey, linenumber} $\rightarrow$ extendedprice holds in this table, the number of tuples in the projection is unchanged.

The experiments show a linear performance for all operations in the range of table sizes we tested. In the table below, the columns u-size, uI, and uIII represent the size of unfolded table, unfold I, and unfold III algorithms, respectively. Number of unfolded columns is 7. The relative inefficiency of *unfold III* is attributed to the tuple-at-a-time nature of this non-intrusive implementation. Our C++ implementation of *unfold III* shows a performance improvement similar to that of the iterated select operation: more than an order of magnitude faster. The comments we made regarding the C++ implementation of iterated select are valid here too. In addition, the C++ implementation uses the fstrem library class that performs block I/O. The strategies *fold I* and *fold II* differ in that *fold I* explicitly generates intermediate tables that are UNIONed to produce the folded table, while *fold II* avoids the generation of these intermediate tables (in this respect, they are similar to *unite I* and *unite II*, discussed earlier). Their performance figures reflect the more efficient nature of *fold II*. The parameter 'no. of unfolded columns' refers to the number of column labels which are values that belong to the domain of some name.

size	u-size	*uI*	*uIII*	*fold I*	*fold II*
24146	6000	40	104	41	17
48214	12000	79	210	74	33
60175	15000	89	263	88	48
120515	30000	193	520	182	87
180566	45000	307	801	336	149

7 Summary and Future Work

Efficient implementation of SchemaSQL on a single RDBMS is the main focus of this paper. As mentioned in Section 1, there are several important applications which motivate this. We developed a logical algebra and a physical algebra. We gave an algorithm for translating SchemaSQL queries into equivalent expressions in the logical algebra and established equivalences between logical operators and expressions in the physical algebra. We illustrated several opportunities for optimization at the logical and physical level. We proposed several implementation strategies for the various operators, all of which are non-intrusive in the sense that they require no additions to the plan operators used by existing SQL systems. We conducted a series of experiments based on the TPC-D bench mark data and showed: (i) the feasibility of the various proposed strategies and (b) their relative performances.

In this paper, we confined ourselves to single block SchemaSQL queries without aggregation. In the full paper [LSS99], we address aggregation and nested queries. Our experiments showed the possible promise of intrusive implementations. We are currently investigating this hypothesis. For lack of space, we could only sketch the optimization opportunities available. A comprehensive study of cost-based query optimization as well as development of schema independent indexes for SchemaSQL query processing is a promising direction of work. Many "classical" optimization problems like containment and query answerability using views, acquire a new twist in the SchemaSQL context because of data/schema interplay. We are investigating some of these issues.

Acknowledgements: We would like to thank Keir B. Davis who implemented the operations in C++ and helped with the creation of TPC-D benchmark tables. Lakshmanan's work was supported in part by NSERC (Canada) and Sadri's work was supported by NSF (USA).

References

[AIS93] Agrawal, R., Imielinski, T., and Swami, A. Database Mining: A Performance Perspective. *IEEE TKDE*, 5(6):pp 914-925, 1993.

[BLT86] J.A. Blakeley, P.A. Larson, and F.W. Tompa. Efficiently Updating Materialized Views. *Proc. ACM SIGMOD*, 61–71, May 1986.

[CKPS95] S. Chaudhuri et al. Optimizing Queries with Materialized Views. *ICDE*, March 1995.

[CKW93] Chen W., Kifer M., and Warren D.S. Hilog: A foundation for higher-order logic programming. *Jl. of Logic Prog.*, 15(3):187–230, 1993.

[GHQ95] A. Gupta, V. Harinarayan, and D. Quass. Aggregate Query Processing in Data Warehousing Environments. *VLDB*, 358–369, Sept. 1995.

[GHRU97] H. Gupta et al. Index Selection for OLAP. *ICDE*, May 1997.

[GL98] Gingras F. and Lakshmanan L.V.S. nD-SQL: a multi-dimensional language for interoperability and olap. *VLDB*, 1998.

[GLRS93] Grant, J. et al. Query Languages for Relational Multidatabases. *VLDB Journal*, 2(2): pp 153-171, 1993.

[GLS96] Gyssens, Marc, Lakshmanan, L.V.S., and Subramanian, S. N. Tables as a paradigm for querying and restructuring. In *Proc. ACM Symp. on PODS*, June 1996.

[GM96] A. Gupta and I.S. Mumick. What is the Data Warehousing Problem? Are Materialized Views the Answer. *VLDB*, 1996.

[GMS93] Gupta, A., Mumick, I.S., and Subrahmanian, V.S. Maintaining views incrementally. *ACM SIGMOD*, 1993.

[HGW+95] Hammer, J. et al. The Stanford Data Warehousing Project. *Data Engg Bulletin*, 18(2), June, 1995.

[HRU96] V. Harinaryanan, A. Rajaraman, and J.D. Ullman. Implementing Data Cubes Efficiently. *ACM SIGMOD*, 205–216, May 1996.

[KKS92] Kifer, M., Kim, W., and Sagiv, Y. Querying Object-Oriented Databases. *ACM SIGMOD*, 393-402, 1992.

[KZ95] Krishnamurthy, R., and Zloof, M. RBE: Rendering By Example *ICDE*, 1995.

[KLK91] Krishnamurthy, R., Litwin, W., and Kent, W. Language features for interoperability of databases with schematic discrepancies. *ACM SIGMOD*, 40–49, 1991.

[LMSS95] A.Y. Levy et al. Answering Queries Using Views. *ACM Symp. on PODS*, May 1995.

[LSS93] Lakshmanan L.V.S., Sadri F., and Subramanian I. N. On the logical foundations of schema integration and evolution in heterogeneous database systems. *DOOD '93*, 81–100. LNCS-760, Dec. 1993.

[LSS96] Lakshmanan L.V.S., Sadri F., and Subramanian, I. N. SchemaSQL – a language for querying and restructuring multidatabase systems. *VLDB*, 239–250, Bombay, India, September 1996.

[LSS97] Lakshmanan L.V.S., Sadri F., and Subramanian I. N. Logic and algebraic languages for interoperability in multidatabase systems. *Jl. of Logic Prog.*, 33(2):101–149., November 1997.

[LSS99] Lakshmanan L.V.S., Sadri F., and Subramanian I. N. On An Efficient Implementation of SchemaSQL Technical Report, IIT Bombay, 1999.

[Mil98] Miller R.J. Using Schematically Heterogeneous Structures. *ACM SIGMOD*, 189–200, Seattle, WA, May 1998.

[MTW97] Miller R.J. et al. DataWeb: Customizable Database Publishing for the Web. *IEEE MultiMedia* 4(4): 14-21 (1997).

[Ros92] Ross, K.. Relations with relation names as arguments: Algebra and calculus. *ACM Symp. on PODS*, 346–353, June 1992.

[SAB+95] Subrahmanian, V.S. et al. HERMES: Heterogeneous Reasoning and Mediator System. Tech. report, University of Maryland, College Park, MD, 1995.

[SDJL96] D. Srivastava et al. Answering Queries with Aggregation Using Views. *VLDB*, Sept 1996.

[Sub97] S.N. Subramanian. *A Foundation for Integrating Heterogeneous Data Sources.* PhD Thesis, Department of Computer Science, Concordia University, Montreal, Canada, 1997.

[SV98] S.N. Subramanian and S. Venkataraman. Query Optimization Using Restructuring-Views. IBM Internal Report, 1998. (Submitted for publication.)

[TSY96] O. Tsatalos et al. The GMAP: A Versatile Tool for Physical Data Independence. *VLDB Jl*, 5(2), April 1996.

[TPC93] TPC. TPC Benchmark^{TM} D (Decision Support). Working draft 6.0, Transaction Processing Performance Council, August 1993.

[WIV98] Wang, M. et al. Scalable Mining for Classification Rules in Relational Databases. *Int. Database Engg and Applications Symposium (IDEAS'98)*, Cardiff, Wales, U.K., July 1998.

[YPAG98] Yerneni, R. et al. Fusion Queries Over Internet Databases *EDBT*, pp 57-71, 1998.

Unrolling Cycle to Decide Trigger Termination

Sin Yeung LEE & Tok Wang LING
School of Computing,
National University of Singapore,
Lower Kent Ridge, Singapore 0511, Singapore.
email : jlee@comp.nus.edu.sg, lingtw@comp.nus.edu.sg

Abstract

Active databases have gained a substantial interest in recent years in enforcing database integrity, however, its current implementations suffer many problems such as running into an infinite loop. While deciding termination is an undecidable task, several works have been proposed to prove termination under certain situations. However, most of these algorithms cannot conclude termination if a cyclic execution actually presents during run-time. This is rather limited. The trigger system can still terminate if these cycles can only be executed a finite number of times. Adopting the trigger graph approach, we propose a method to detect if some cycles can only be executed finitely. We then present a cycle-unrolling algorithm to remove those cycles that can only be executed finitely from a trigger graph. Similarly, we present the concept of finitely-updatable predicate to further improve most existing detection methods. Finally, we conclude with an algorithm to detect if a given trigger system will terminate.

Proceedings of the 25th VLDB Conference, Edinburgh, Scotland, 1999.

1 Introduction

Recently, there is an increasing interest in providing rule processing to database systems so that they are capable of automatic updating as well as enforcing database integrity. One of the most popular approaches is to make use of the ECA (Event-Condition-Action) rules [6, 7, 9, 8, 14]. In this active database model, whenever an event occurs, trigger rules with the matching event specifications are triggered, and their associated conditions are checked. For each trigger rule, if its condition is satisfied, then the associated actions of that trigger rule will be executed. These actions may in turn trigger other rules.

While active database systems are very powerful, the way to specify rules is unstructured and its processing is difficult to predict. This is especially true when the action of an ECA rule can falsify the condition of another ECA rule and thus deactivates the second trigger rule. Clearly, the final database state can be highly dependent on the execution order of the set of trigger rules. Furthermore, the set of rules may be triggering each other indefinitely, thus preventing the system from terminating. To illustrate, suppose rule 1 is to increase the salary of an employee if his allowance is increased; while rule 2 is to increase the allowance of an employee from the accounts department if his salary is increased. Intuitively, this pair of rules can reactivate each other ad infinitum if we update the salary of an employee from the accounts department. Such an execution will not terminate.

This non-termination problem makes developing even a small application system a difficult task. Hence, the rule programmer must perform some analysis on the set of trigger rules to predict its behaviour in advance. Although it is undecidable whether the execution of any given set of trigger rules will finally terminate, it is beneficial to have tests to detect the subset of trigger rules which are terminating and those which may not terminate. This can assist the rule programmers so that they need only to verify a smaller subset of the trigger rules.

There are recent works on this termination problem. [1] proposed a method in the context of the Starburst Rule System to detect some definite terminating conditions. This approach makes use of a graph called directed triggering graph proposed in [5]. If the triggering graph constructed has no cycle, then the trigger system will always terminate. This approach is simple but rejects too many terminating situations. In particular, it does not make use of the condition-parts of the trigger rules. As pointed out by later works, many obviously terminating situations cannot be detected.

In [17], the authors suggested some sufficient conditions for trigger termination. However, the method only works for a rather restricted trigger system. For each ECA rule, the condition is a simple query and the action is a simple and single attribute assignment. Deletions and insertions are not considered. This is one of the major drawbacks. [10] proposed a rather different approach. The Event-Condition-Action rules are first reduced to term rewriting systems, then some known analysis techniques for termination are applied. However, it is unclear whether a general trigger database system can always be expressed as a term rewriting system. [4] used an algebraic approach to attack this termination problem for expert database systems. Although the method offers a much stronger solution than [1], the analysis does not involve much on trigger conditions. Later works such as [15, 2, 16, 11] make us of the trigger conditions. To decide if one rule r can actually trigger another rule s, [11] constructs a conjunct based on the trigger conditions of the two rules. If the conjunct is not satisfiable, then the edge between the two rules is removed. On the other hand, [2, 3] augments a trigger graph with an activation graph. An edge is removed unless it is in a cycle and can be re-activated after a self-deactivation [2, 3]. All these analysis are still based on edges in the trigger graph, [13] remedied this problem by considering trigger paths instead of trigger edges so that more terminating situations can now be detected.

However, all these methods suffer from one common drawback — if the trigger system, indeed, has a cyclic execution, none of the previous methods can conclude termination. This is obviously limited. For example, consider the following trigger rules:

Rule 1 : ON insert $a(X,Y)$ IF $(X=1)$
DO insert $a(Y,0)$

Clearly, it is possible that during run-time, rule 1 successfully activates itself several times. Upon closer examination, we see that within this trigger session, after the first insert of the tuple $a(X,Y)$, the system may trigger an insertion of $a(Y,0)$. Thereafter, the insertion of $a(0,0)$ may be triggered. Upon the insertion of $a(0,0)$, the trigger condition is definitely unsatisfied, hence, this trigger session can at most trigger the same rule for three times only. In other words, although the rule causes cyclic execution, the system can still be proven to terminate.

In this paper, we will discuss in more detail the termination problem and propose a method to detect more situations where a given trigger system can be proven to terminate. In our approach, we first translate a trigger system into a graph called *trigger graph* as proposed in [5]. We then present an algorithm to construct a condition to verify if a cycle can only be cycled at most a given finite number. Finally, a graph unrolling method is proposed to remove a given cycle from a given trigger graph. If our method answers affirmatively that the given system always terminates, then the given system can indeed terminate.

2 Trigger Architecture

We assume a general abstract architecture of the underlying active databases that does not depend on any particular architecture. The underlying database can be an active OODB, or just a simple RDB. Each trigger rule takes the following form:

rule_name :: *event* IF *condition*
DO $action_1, \ldots, action_n$

where *rule_name* is the name of the trigger rule. The *event* and $action_i$ in the trigger rules are abstracted to take the following form,

event_name(*variable_list*)

event_name can refer a simple update such as *incr_salary*, or a complex action such as *cascade_delete*. In this paper, we shall use the names $e1$, $e2$, etc in most cases to refer to general events.

condition is a conjunction of positive literals, negative literals and/or evaluable predicates. Any variable which appears in the variable list of any $action_i$ must either appear in the *event* or in the *condition*. Furthermore, in order that the evaluation of *condition* is safe, any variable that appears in any negative literal or an evaluable predicate in *condition* should also appear in either *event* or in a positive literal in *condition*. We shall call those variables that appear in *condition* but not in *event* as *local variables*. Throughout this paper, we will also refer to *event* as *rule_name.*EVENT and *condition* as *rule_name.*COND .

Example 2.1 The following specifies that an increase in an employee's salary should also trigger an increase in the salary of his/her manager by the same amount:

$incr\_salary\_rule$ :: $incr\_salary(EmpID, IncrAmt)$
IF $emp(EmpID, MgrID, Salary)$ DO
$incr\_salary(MgrID, IncrAmt)$ □

As our proposed method is independent of the rule execution order, we do not need to assume any specific model of execution. Our method is equally applicable to trigger systems with rule priority and to those with deferred execution.

3 Activation Formula

[11] introduces the trigger formula, which is a more refined condition to decide if a rule r_1 can trigger another rule r_2. The trigger formula is constructed by conjuncting the trigger conditions of trigger rules r_1 and r_2 in a selective way. If the trigger formula is unsatisfiable, then the corresponding trigger edge between r_1 and r_2 in the trigger graph is removed. If the final graph is acyclic, then the trigger system will terminate. For example, given the following two trigger rules:

r1 :: $e1(X)$ IF $(X>1)$ DO $e2(X)$
r2 :: $e2(X)$ IF $(X<1)$ DO $e1(X)$

[11] constructs the trigger formulae as,

$(X>1) \wedge (X<1)$

This formula is unsatisfiable, therefore, the edge ≪r1,r2≫ is removed from the trigger graph. Since the resultant graph is acyclic, this trigger system will terminate.

A direct generalization is to consider more than one edge by conjuncting more conditions together. If the resultant condition is a contradiction, then the sequence of rules cannot be executed at all. This guarantees termination. For example,

r1 :: $e1(X)$ IF $(X>1)$ DO $e2(X)$
r2 :: $e2(X)$ IF $(X>5)$ DO $e3(X)$
r3 :: $e3(X)$ IF $(X<1)$ DO $e1(X)$

The conjunction of conditions of the rules from the execution sequence ≪r1,r2,r3≫ is

$(X>1) \wedge (X>5) \wedge (X<1)$

which is clearly unsatisfiable. Hence, r1 cannot trigger r3 via r2 during run time.

However, this generalization of conjuncting conditions is far from trivial, there are two major considerations to be handled:

1. Conflict of variables.
   The scope of the variables used in a trigger condition is confined to the rule itself. When the conditions from several trigger rules are conjuncted together, conflict of variables may occur. For example, the variable X of the following two rules belongs to different scope:

   r1 :: $e1(X)$ IF $(X>1) \wedge p(X,Y)$ DO $e2(Y)$
   r2 :: $e2(X)$ IF $(X<1)$ DO $e1(X)$

   Hence, we cannot directly conjunct the trigger conditions of these two rules together. The solution adopted by [11] requires that each variable used in each trigger rule has a different name. This solution has an obvious problem. The variable conflict still occurs if the condition from the same rule appears at least twice in the conjunction. For example, consider another trigger rule:

   r3 :: $e3(X,Y)$ IF $(X>Y)$ DO $e3(Y,X)$

   A simple conjunction of r3 with r3 gives a wrong formula:

   $(X>Y) \wedge (X>Y)$

2. Process to eliminate trigger edges.
   Even if we can prove that a sequence of rules cannot be executed, it is possible that no edge can be removed from the trigger graph. For example, consider the following graph, even if we prove that rule r1 cannot trigger r4 via r2, no edge can be immediately removed from the trigger graph without destroying other cycle. In Section 4, we propose a method to eliminate a path instead of an edge from a trigger graph.

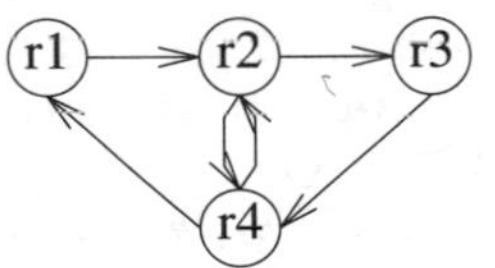

3.1 Predicate Selection Procedure

Our method investigates the conjunction of the trigger conditions in each trigger rule in a given execution sequence. However, as shown in [11], we cannot include every predicate in the trigger conditions, we need a *predicate selection procedure* to select the correct predicates to be included in the conjunction of the trigger conditions. We propose two possible predicate selection procedures:

1. Non-Updatable predicate selection procedure
2. Finitely updatable predicate selection procedure

The first selection procedure is a simplified version of the second selection procedure, and is used for the ease of discussion. The second procedure — finitely updatable predicate selection procedure, will be used in the final termination decision algorithm. Section 5 will discuss the algorithm making use of the latter selection procedure. The two selection procedures are further elaborated as follows:

3.1.1 Non-Updatable predicate procedure

This selection procedure only selects predicates that cannot be updated by any trigger execution. Non-updatable predicates fall into the following categories:

1. Evaluable function
2. Predicate/attribute that is not modified, whether directly or indirectly, by any action of some trigger rules.

Example 3.1 Given a bank database which contains the following relations:

1. *acc(Acc#,Owner,Bal)*
   Acc# is the account number owned by *Owner* with amount *Bal*.
2. *bankcard(Card#,Acc#)*
   The bankcard *Card#* is associated with the account *Acc#*. One account can have many bankcards, but each bankcard can only be associated with one account.

In this database, two trigger rules are specified,

```
// If a bankcard is lost,
// debit into the owner's account
// a service charge of 10 dollars.
```

r1 :: replace_lost_card(*Card#*)
IF *bankcard(Card#,Acc#)*
DO debit(*Acc#*,10)

```
// If an account has insufficient fund
// during debit, alert the owner,
// but allow overdraft.
```

r2 :: debit(*Acc#*,*Amt*) IF *acc(Acc#,Owner,Bal)* $\wedge$ (*Bal* < *Amt*) DO
alert(*Owner*,*Acc#*,'Overdraft')

The trigger events update the databases in the following ways:

1. The event *replace_lost_card* will issue a new bankcard to its owner. It will not update the relations *acc* and *bankcard*.
2. The event *debit* is to update the *Bal* of *Owner*'s account in the relation *acc*.
3. The event *alert* does not update the database.

Note that all these information can be easily extracted from the SQL implementation.

Now consider the following formula,

bankcard(Card#,Acc#) $\wedge$ *acc(Acc#,Owner,Bal)* $\wedge$ (*Bal* < 10)

the predicate (*Bal* < 10), is a non-updatable predicate because it is an evaluable function. The predicate *bankcard(Card#,Acc#)* is another non-updatable predicate as no trigger action updates the relation *bankcard*. On the other hand, the predicate *acc(Acc#,Owner,Bal)* is an updatable predicate as it can be updated by the action *debit* in trigger rule r1. Therefore, using our non-updatable predicate selection procedure, the formula

bankcard(Card#,Acc#) $\wedge$ *acc(Acc#,Owner,Bal)* $\wedge$ (*Bal* < 10)

is modified to be,

bankcard(Card#,Acc#) $\wedge$ (*Bal* < 10)

As the variable *Bal* appears once in the above condition, *Bal* < 10 is trivially satisfiable. Now, the final condition is simplified to,

bankcard(Card#,Acc#) □

3.1.2 Finitely Updatable predicate procedure

In practice, it is unlikely to include many predicates in the conjunction of the trigger conditions, as relations/objects are often targets of update. The *finitely-updatable predicate selection* is therefore an improvement on it. Instead of including only predicates which are not updated by any trigger action, this predicate selection procedure includes predicates that are not updated indefinitely by any trigger action. However, to decide which predicate is updated only finitely is as hard as the original termination problem. In this case, we need to incorporate a much more complex incremental algorithm for termination detection. We will discuss this further in Section 5. Meanwhile, to clarify the basic concept, we employ the non-updatable predicate selection procedure as our default predicate selection procedure.

3.2 Construction of Activation Formula

Definition 3.1 Given an execution sequence $\ll r_1, \ldots, r_n \gg$, an *activation formula* $F_{act}(\ll r_1, \ldots, r_n \gg)$ is a necessary condition for rule r_1 to eventually trigger rule r_n via rules $r_2, \ldots, r_{n-1}$. □

Example 3.2 Consider the following trigger rules,

r1 :: $e1(X,Y)$ IF $X > 3$ DO $e2(X,Y)$
r2 :: $e2(X,Y)$ IF $X < 1$ DO $e1(X,Y)$

An activation formula of path ≪r1,r2≫ is $(X > 3) \wedge (X < 1)$. Events such as $e1(4,2)$ cannot trigger another event $e1$ via the trigger sequence r1,r2. Note that since an activation formula gives only the necessary condition, it is not necessarily unique. Another weaker activation formula is $(X < 1)$. □

The following algorithm computes an activation formula for a given execution sequence $\ll r_1, \ldots, r_n \gg$:

Algorithm 3.1 Given an execution sequence $\ll r_1, \ldots, r_n \gg$, and a predicate selection procedure *PSP*, we compute an activation formula, $F_{act}(\ll r_1, \ldots, r_n \gg)$ as follows,

1. We first compute an intermediate condition C as follows, This C will be transformed into

$F_{act}(\ll r_1, \ldots, r_n \gg)$ at the final step.

2. When $n = 1$, C is set to r_1.COND
3. Otherwise, let C be $F_{act}(\ll r_2, \ldots, r_n \gg)$ subject to the selection procedure *PSP*, and let σ be the substitution unifier between the event of rule r_2 and the triggering action of rule r_1. We perform the following steps,
   i) Rename any local variable in C that also appears in r_1 to another name to avoid name conflict.
   ii) C is set to r_1.COND $\wedge\, C\,\sigma$
4. To compute the final $F_{act}(\ll r_1, \ldots, r_n \gg)$, apply the predicate selection procedure *PSP* to remove any unwanted predicates in the formula C. □

Example 3.3 Consider the following three trigger rules,

r1 :: $e1(X,Y)$ IF $(X>1)$ DO $\{e2(X,0), e3(1,Y)\}$
r2 :: $e2(X,Y)$ IF TRUE DO $e1(Y,X)$
r3 :: $e3(X,Y)$ IF $X \neq Y$ DO $e2(X,Y)$

The trigger graph of these rules is as follows,

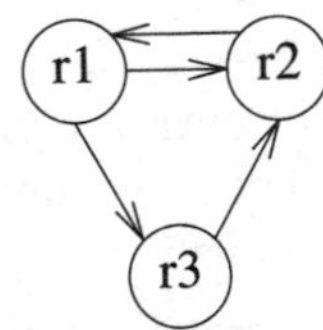

Subject to the non-updatable predicate selection procedure, the activation formula for $F_{act}(\ll r_1, r_2, r_1 \gg)$ can be computed as follows,

1. First, we compute $F_{act}(\ll r_2, r_1 \gg)$, which requires to compute $F_{act}(\ll r_1 \gg)$.
2. Now, $F_{act}(\ll r_1 \gg)$ is actually the condition of rule r1 after removing any updatable predicate. This gives the formula $(X>1)$.
3. To compute $F_{act}(\ll r_2, r_1 \gg)$, we first observe that $\{X/Y, Y/X\}$ is the substitution σ between the event of r_1, $e1(X,Y)$, and the matching action of r_2, $e1(Y,X)$. Applying the algorithm, we have
   TRUE$\wedge\,(X>1)\{X/Y, Y/X\}$
   After simplification and elimination of any updatable predicate, we have $(Y>1)$.
4. Finally, to compute $F_{act}(\ll r_1, r_2, r_1 \gg)$, $\{X/X, Y/0\}$ is the substitution σ between the $e2(X,Y)$, and the matching action $e2(X,0)$. We compute C to be,
   $(X>1) \wedge ((Y>1)\{X/X, Y/0\})$
   It can be simplified to FALSE. In other words, the activation formula of the execution sequence from r_1, to r_2, and then back to r_1 is not possible. □

Definition 3.2 An execution sequence $\ll r_1, \ldots, r_n \gg$ where r_i's are trigger rules which are not necessarily distinct, is an *activable path* subject to a predicate selection procedure *PSP* if the activation formulae $F_{act}(\ll r_1, \ldots, r_n \gg)$ subject to *PSP* is satisfiable. Otherwise, the sequence is a *non-activable path.* □

Example 3.4 From Example 3.3, the path ≪r2,r1≫ is an activable path. The path ≪r1,r2,r1≫ is a non-activable path. □

Definition 3.3 A *cycle* is denoted by $[\![r_1, \ldots, r_n]\!]$ where r_i's are not necessarily distinct. It indicates the cyclic execution that rule r_1 triggers r_2, which then triggers r_3 and so on until r_n, which triggers back r_1. □

Example 3.5 In Example 3.3, [[r1,r2]], [[r1,r3,r2]] and [[r1,r2,r1,r3,r2]] are three different cycles. □

Definition 3.4 The *k*-execution sequence ($k \geq 1$) of a cycle $[\![r_1, \ldots, r_n]\!]$ is denoted as $[\![r_1, \ldots, r_n]\!]^k$. It is the execution sequence if the cycle loops itself for k times. It can be represented by an execution sequence which is defined recursively as follows,

1. $[\![r_1, \ldots, r_n]\!]^1$ is the execution sequence $\ll r_1, \ldots, r_n, r_1 \gg$.
2. $[\![r_1, \ldots, r_n]\!]^k$ is the concatenation of the execution sequence $\ll r_1, \ldots, r_n \gg$ with $[\![r_1, \ldots, r_n]\!]^{k-1}$. □

Example 3.6 $[\![r_1]\!]^1$ represents the execution sequence $\ll r_1, r_1 \gg$. $[\![r_1, r_2]\!]^2$ represents the execution sequence $\ll r_1, r_2, r_1, r_2, r_1 \gg$. □

Definition 3.5 A cycle $[\![r_1, \ldots, r_m]\!]$ contains another cycle $[\![s_1, \ldots, s_n]\!]$ if and only if the execution sequence $[\![r_1, \ldots, r_m]\!]^1$ contains the execution sequence $[\![s_1, \ldots, s_n]\!]^1$. □

Example 3.7 The cycle $[\![r_1, r_2, r_1, r_3]\!]$ contains the cycle $[\![r_1, r_2]\!]$. However, the cycle $[\![r_1, r_2]\!]$ does not contain the cycle $[\![r_1]\!]$ as the execution sequence $\ll r_1, r_2, r_1 \gg$ does not contain the execution sequence $\ll r_1, r_1 \gg$. □

Definition 3.6 A cycle in a graph is a *prime cycle* if it does not contain any other cycle. □

Example 3.8 The cycle $[\![r_1, r_2, r_1, r_3]\!]$ contains the cycles $[\![r_1, r_2]\!]$ as well as $[\![r_1, r_3]\!]$, hence, it is not a prime cycle. On the other hand, both $[\![r_1, r_2]\!]$ and $[\![r_1, r_3]\!]$ are prime cycles. □

Definition 3.7 A cycle $[\![r_1, \ldots, r_n]\!]$ is a *k*-cycle ($k \geq 0$) if

1. $[\![r_1, \ldots, r_n]\!]^{k+1}$ is not an activable path, and
2. if $k \geq 1$, then $[\![r_1, \ldots, r_n]\!]^k$ is an activable path. □

Note that if $[\![r_1, \ldots, r_n]\!]$ is a 0-cycle, it simply means that $\ll r_1, \ldots, r_n, r_1 \gg$ is a non-activable path. If a cycle is a *k*-cycle, then it can only be repeated at most *k* times.

Using this definition, the following algorithm can decide if a given cycle Γ is a k-cycle.

Algorithm 3.2 Given a cycle Γ in a trigger graph G, and an integer k, we decide if Γ is a k-cycle by the following steps:

1. Construct the k-execution sequence Γ^k of the cycle Γ and the $(k+1)$-execution sequence $\Gamma^{(k+1)}$ of the cycle Γ.
2. Apply Algorithm 3.1 to construct $F_{act}(\Gamma^k)$ and $F_{act}(\Gamma^{(k+1)})$.
3. If $F_{act}(\Gamma^k)$ is satisfiable but $F_{act}(\Gamma^{(k+1)})$ is not satisfiable, then return "Γ is a k-cycle."
4. Otherwise, return that "Γ is not a k-cycle." □

Theorem 3.1 Given a trigger graph G, and if each prime cycle is a 0-cycle, then the trigger system can terminate. □

Example 3.9 Consider the following five rules:

r1 :: $e1(X,Y)$ IF $X>1$ DO $\{e2(X,Y), e3(X,Y)\}$
r2 :: $e2(X,Y)$ IF $Y<1$ DO $e1(Y,X)$
r3 :: $e2(X,Y)$ IF $X<2$ DO $e3(X,Y)$
r4 :: $e3(X,Y)$ IF $X<Y$ DO $e4(Y+1,X)$
r5 :: $e4(X,Y)$ IF $X<Y$ DO $e1(X,Y)$

Its trigger graph can be described as:

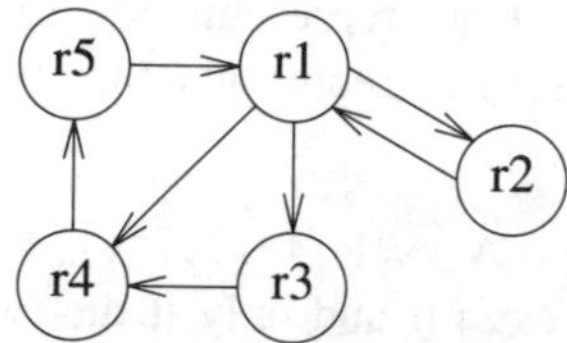

From the graph, we can see that there are three prime cycles: Γ_1:⟦r1,r2⟧, Γ_2:⟦r1,r4,r5⟧ and Γ_3:⟦r1,r3,r4,r5⟧. Note that there are many different cycles such as ⟦r1,r2,r1,r2,r1,r4,r5⟧, but it is not a prime-cycle. It contains three prime cycles: Γ_1,Γ_1 and Γ_2.

Each of the three prime cycles contains at least one non-activable path. For instance, the cycle ⟦r1,r2⟧ contains a path ≪r1,r2,r1≫. This path is non-activable because its activation formula F_{act}(≪r1,r2,r1≫), which can be computed by Algorithm 3.1 to be

$$(X>1)\wedge(Y<1)\wedge(Y>1)$$

is clearly not satisfiable. Since each of the three prime cycles contains at least one non-activable path, all the three cycles are 0-cycle. From Theorem 3.1, this trigger system can always terminate. □

Theorem 3.1 covers many terminating cases detected by previous methods. A natural extension is to ask if every prime cycle is a k-cycle for some finite k, does it imply that the system can always terminate? Unfortunately, the answer is only partially true, as stated in the followings:

Definition 3.8 Given a trigger graph G, its cycles can be *partitioned hierarchically*, if and only if for any two different cycles Γ_1 and Γ_2 in G, whenever Γ_1 can reach Γ_2, it implies that Γ_2 cannot reach Γ_1. □

Theorem 3.2 Given a trigger system, if its prime cycles can be partitioned hierarchically, and all of its prime cycle is a k-cycle for some finite k, then the trigger system can terminate. □

In general, however, the above theorem is false if cycles cannot be partitioned hierarchically. Every prime cycle is some k-cycle for some finite k alone does not imply that the system can always terminate, even if k is as small as 1. This can be illustrated by the following example:

Example 3.10 Consider the following trigger system:

r1 :: $e1(X,Y)$ IF $X<Y$ DO $\{e1(Y,X), e2(Y,X)\}$
r2 :: $e2(X,Y)$ IF $X>Y$ DO $e1(Y,X)$

There are two prime cycles — ⟦r1⟧ and ⟦r1,r2⟧. Note that these two cycles cannot be partitioned hierarchically. The first cycle can reach the second cycle, and the second cycle can also reach the first cycle. Now, both prime cycles are only 1-cycles, however, the trigger system may not necessarily terminate. The non-prime cycle ⟦r1,r1,r2⟧ can be executed without termination. □

To handle this problem, we propose a new method which attempts to remove any k-cycle found in the trigger graph. If every cycle can be removed, then the trigger system can terminate. This differs from all the previous works [1, 17, 2, 11, 18, 3, 13] in that they are aiming to prove that no cycle actually exists in the trigger graph. Our method, however, aims to prove that every cycle in the trigger graph is only finitely executable.

4 Cycle removal by cycle-unrolling method

To prove that every cycle in the trigger graph is only finitely executable, we propose to remove each finitely executable cycle from a given trigger graph. If all finitely executable cycles can be removed from the graph, then we can conclude that the trigger system can terminate.

In order to remove a finitely executable cycle from a trigger graph, we propose a *cycle unrolling* method. The main idea of this method is to unroll the given cycle by multiplicating the nodes inside the given cycle and break the cycle. For example, if a cycle ⟦r_1,r_2,r_3⟧ is proven to be a 2-cycle, then the very definition of a 2-cycle implies that the path P, ≪$r_1,r_2,r_3,r_1,r_2,r_3,r_1,r_2,r_3,r_1$≫ is not an activable path. In this case, we can unroll the cycle by replacing it with a path that does not contain the non-activable path P. This idea is summarized in the following diagram:

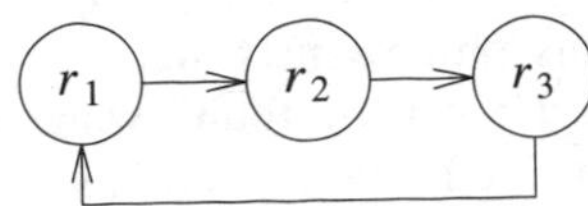

The above 2-cycle ⟦r1,r2,r3⟧ is unrolled to

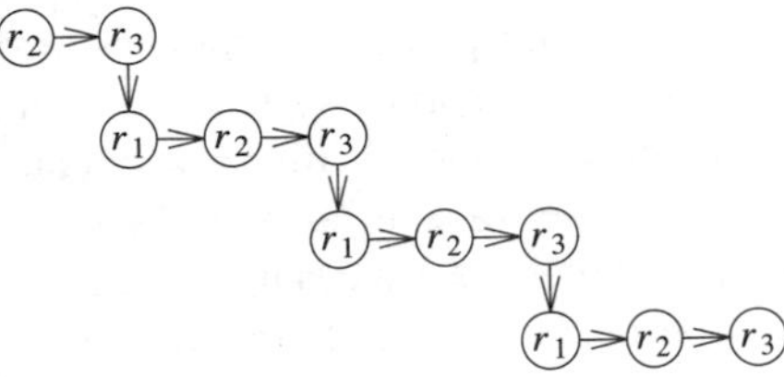

Figure 4.1

There are some points about figure 4.1 that we would like to mention:

1. There are extra duplicated copies of r_2 and r_3 at the front. This is so because the execution sequence $\ll r_2,r_3,r_1,r_2,r_3,r_1,r_2,r_3,r_1,r_2,r_3 \gg$ may be an activable path as it does not contain the non-activable path *P*. As no activable path should be lost during the unroll operation, we need to include an extra copy of the cyclic nodes except the first node (r_1).
2. After the unroll operation, the cycle $[\![r_1,r_2,r_3]\!]$ is allowed to loop twice as the execution sequence $\ll r_1,r_2,r_3,r_1,r_2,r_3,r_1 \gg$ is in the modified graph. Furthermore, this cycle is correctly denied to loop thrice as the non-activable path *P* is missing from the modified graph.

We call the above mentioned operation, which replaces a *k*-cycle Γ in a trigger graph G with a non-cyclic path, the unroll operation $unroll(G,\Gamma,k)$. This operation can be defined formally as follows,

Definition 4.1 The operation $unroll(G,\Gamma,k)$ where G is a trigger graph, Γ is a cycle in G and k is a positive integer generates a new graph G such that

1. The *k*-execution sequence Γ^k can be represented in the new graph G , but
2. Γ^{k+1} cannot be represented in the new graph G , and
3. all other paths in G which do not contain the sequence Γ^{k+1} are represented in G . □

The following gives a formal algorithm on how the operation $unroll(G,\Gamma,k)$ can be implemented:

Algorithm 4.1 *(Cycle unroll algorithm)* Consider a trigger graph G and a *k*-cycle Γ $[\![r_1, \ldots, r_n]\!]$ where $n \geq 1$ The operation $unroll(G,\Gamma,k)$ is done as follows,

1. *(Duplicate the cyclic path)* Duplicate the path $\ll r_1, \ldots, r_n \gg$ for $k+1$ times, we denote $r_i^{(0)}$ as the original node r_i, and we denote $r_i^{(j)}$ $(1 \leq j \leq k+1)$ as the jth copy of the node r_i. Furthermore, for each j from 0 to k, add the edge $\ll r_n^{(j)}, r_1^{(j+1)} \gg$.
2. *(Allow any iteration of the cycle to exit.)* For each outgoing edge $\ll r_i^{(0)}, t \gg$ of node $r_i^{(0)}$, except the edge $\ll r_n^{(0)}, r_1^{(0)} \gg$ and the edges $\ll r_i^{(0)}, r_{i+1}^{(0)} \gg$ where $1 \leq i \leq n-1$, insert the edge $\ll r_i^{(j)}, t \gg$ in the graph for each j from 1 to $k+1$.
3. *(Allow any incoming edge to go into the cycle.)* For each in-coming edge $\ll t, r_1^{(0)} \gg$ of node $r_1^{(0)}$, insert the edge $\ll t, r_1^{(1)} \gg$ in the graph.
4. *(remove the node $r_1^{(0)}$ to break the cycle.)* Remove the node $r_1^{(0)}$ from the graph, and its attached edges from the graph. □

Example 4.1 Given the trigger graph in Figure 4.2, assume that we have proven that the cycle ⟦r1,r2⟧ is a 1-cycle, in another words, the execution sequence ≪r1,r2,r1≫ is activable, but the sequence ≪r1,r2,r1,r2,r1≫ is not. We can remove this cycle by our unroll algorithm, Algorithm 4.1.

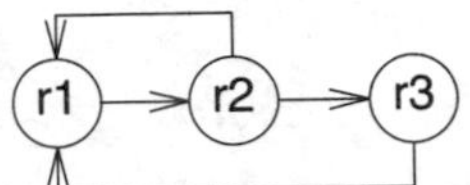

Figure 4.2

In the first step of the algorithm, we duplicate the path ≪r1,r2≫: ≪r1$^{(1)}$,r2$^{(1)}$≫ and ≪r1$^{(2)}$,r2$^{(2)}$≫. We also denote the original r1 as r1$^{(0)}$ and original r2 as r2$^{(0)}$. Furthermore, the algorithm connects the last node of each cyclic path duplication to the first node of the next duplication. In this example, we add the edge ≪r2$^{(0)}$,r1$^{(1)}$≫ and ≪r2$^{(1)}$,r1$^{(2)}$≫. The resultant graph is in figure 4.3(i).

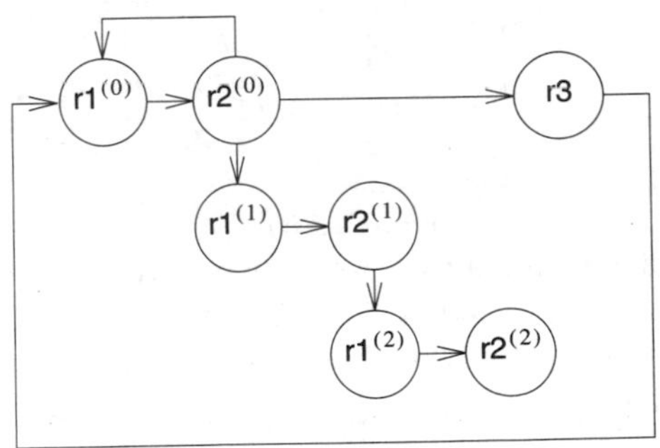

Figure 4.3(i)

In step 2, we add all the outgoing edges to provide exit from the cycle. In this example, since ≪r2,r3≫ was an edge in the original graph, we insert two new edges: ≪r2$^{(1)}$,r3≫ and ≪r2$^{(2)}$,r3≫. The resultant graph will be in Figure 4.3(ii).

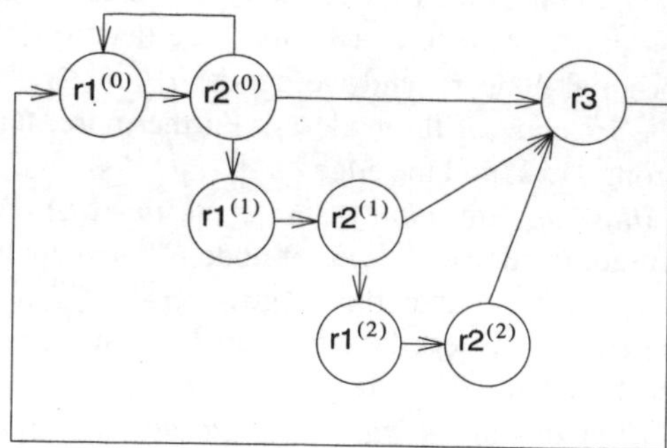

Figure 4.3(ii)

In step 3, all the incoming edges which were originally to $r1^{(0)}$ are now duplicated to point also to $r1^{(1)}$. In this example, since $\ll r3, r1^{(0)} \gg$ is the only incoming edge to $r1^{(0)}$, we add the edge $\ll r3, r1^{(1)} \gg$ to the graph. This gives Figure 4.3(iii).

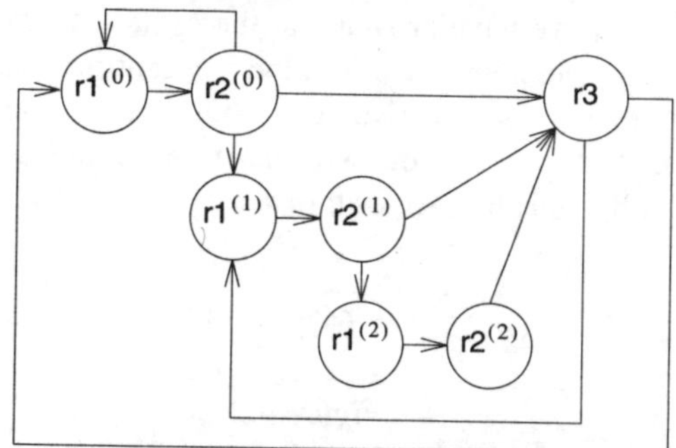

Figure 4.3(iii)

The final step of the algorithm requires us to remove the node $r1^{(0)}$. The resultant graph is as in Figure 4.3(iv).

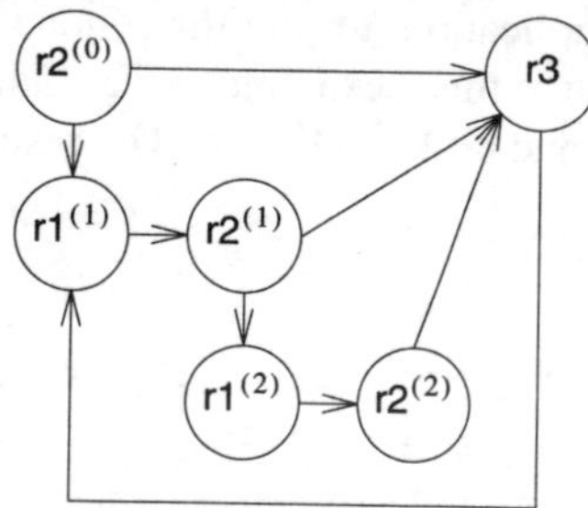

Figure 4.3(iv)

Now there remains only two prime cycles — $[\![r1^{(1)}, r2^{(1)}, r3]\!]$ and $[\![r1^{(1)}, r2^{(1)}, r1^{(2)}, r2^{(2)}, r3]\!]$. The original cycle $[\![r1, r2]\!]$ has been successfully removed. □

Repeatedly of applying Algorithm 4.1 to remove cycles from a trigger graph, if it terminates, can decide trigger termination. However, this repetition process, per se, does not necessarily terminate for two different reasons:

1. After application of Algorithm 4.1, we can generate new prime cycle of longer cyclic length. In the previous example, when the prime cycle $[\![r1, r2]\!]$ of length 2 is removed, a new prime cycle $[\![r1^{(1)}, r2^{(1)}, r1^{(2)}, r2^{(2)}, r3]\!]$ of length 5 is introduced. In theory, this process may not terminate. Longer and longer cycle can be found when some smaller cycles are merged. In the previous example, the node r2 of the 1-cycle $[\![r1, r2]\!]$ is duplicated and merged into the cycle $[\![r1, r2, r3]\!]$ to generate a new longer cycle $[\![r1^{(1)}, r2^{(1)}, r1^{(2)}, r2^{(2)}, r3]\!]$. In practical systems, this merging process is unlikely to be too complex. For a terminating system, it is unlikely that a longer prime cycle is still an activable path. Hence, we propose to set up a threshold value, D_{MAX}, which denotes the maximum number of times a node can be duplicated. If termination cannot be proven after a node has participated in Algorithm 4.1 for D_{MAX} times, then we stop without drawing any conclusion.
2. To decide if a cycle is a k-cycle for a finite value of k is itself also undecidable. To make our algorithm terminate, we need another threshold, K_{MAX}, to limit the value of k.

With these two thresholds in mind, we can now apply Algorithm 4.1 to construct a new termination decision algorithm as follows,

Algorithm 4.2 Given a trigger system *TS*, and two threshold values D_{MAX} and K_{MAX}, we decide if *TS* terminates by the following steps,

1. Construct a trigger graph G for *TS*.
2. Remove any node which is not inside any cycle in the current trigger graph.
3. Remove any edge $\ll s,t \gg$ if its activation formula is unsatisfiable.
4. If the graph is acyclic, then conclude "Terminate" and exit the algorithm.
5. Pick up one of the smallest prime cycles in the current trigger graph. If this cycle contains a node that has been duplicated for D_{MAX} times, then return "May not terminate" and exit the algorithm.
6. Apply Algorithm 3.2 to decide if the chosen cycle is a k-cycle where $0 \le k \le K_{MAX}$. If not, then return "May not terminate" and exit the algorithm.
7. Otherwise, remove this cycle according to Algorithm 4.1. The new graph is now the current trigger graph. Repeat step 2. □

Example 4.2 Given the following trigger sets,

r1 :: $e1(X,Y)$ IF $(X>Y)$ DO $e2(Y,1)$
r2 :: $e2(X,Y)$ IF $b(X,Y)$
DO $\{e3(X,Y), e1(X,Y)\}$
r3 :: $e3(X,Y)$ IF $X<1$ DO $e1(X,Y)$

We assume no event updates the relation b. In addition, we assume K_{MAX} to be 4, and D_{MAX} to be 4. We now apply Algorithm 4.2 to decide if the set of rules will terminate. The first step is to construct a trigger graph as in Figure 4.4(i).

In step 2, we eliminate any node which is not inside any cycle. No such node is found from the current graph. Similarly, no edge can be removed at step 3.

In step 5 of Algorithm 4.2, we pick one of the smallest cycles — $[\![$r1,r2$]\!]$ in the graph. It is not a 0-cycle. The activation formula of the path ≪r1,r2,r1≫ is

$$(X>Y) \wedge b(Y,1) \wedge (1>Y)$$

It is satisfiable. However, it is a 1-cycle. The activation formula of the path ≪r1,r2,r1,r2,r1≫ is

$$(X>Y) \wedge b(Y,1) \wedge (Y>1) \wedge b(1,1) \wedge (1>1)$$

and it is unsatisfiable. Therefore, we have proven that the cycle $[\![$r1,r2$]\!]$ is a 1-cycle. From step 7, we apply Algorithm 4.1 to remove this cycle. The new graph is shown in figure 4.4(ii):

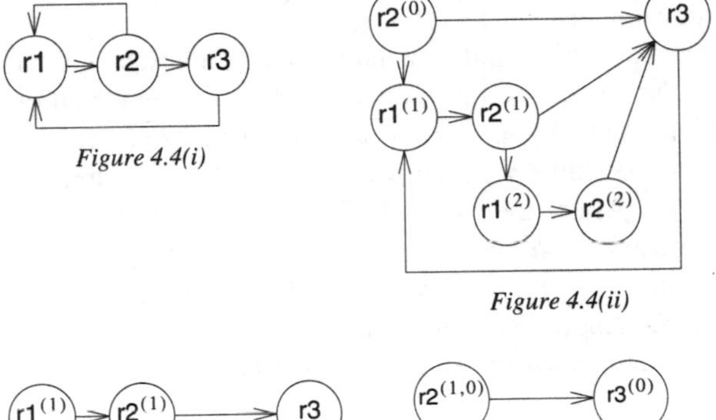

Figure 4.4(i)

Figure 4.4(ii)

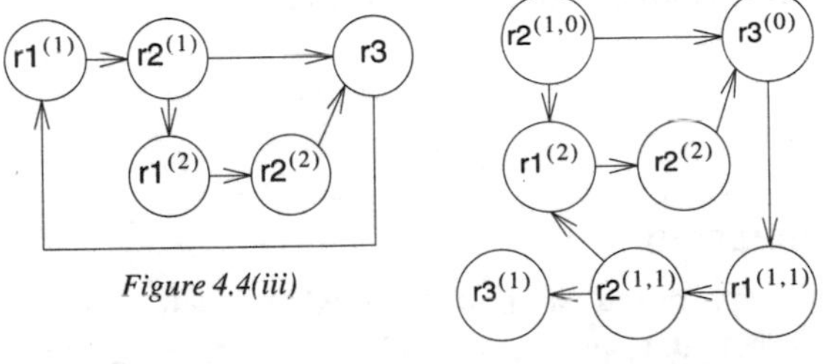

Figure 4.4(iii)

Figure 4.4(iv)

We now repeat step 2. Since the node r2$^{(0)}$ is not inside any cycle in the current trigger graph, it can be removed. The new graph is shown in Figure 4.4(iii). Next, we consider the cycle $[\![$r1$^{(1)}$,r2$^{(1)}$,r3$]\!]$. Without much difficulty, we can prove that it is a 0-cycle, for its activation formula is

$$(X>Y) \wedge b(Y,1) \wedge (Y<1) \wedge (Y>1)$$

is unsatisfiable. This cycle is unroll. The new graph is shown in Figure 4.4(iv). Clearly, r3$^{(1)}$ and r2$^{(1,0)}$ can be removed. Now, there remains only one last cycle: $[\![$r1$^{(1,1)}$,r2$^{(1,1)}$,r1$^{(2)}$,r2$^{(2)}$,r3$^{(0)}$$]\!]$. This cycle is another 0-cycle that can be removed after unrolling. Since there is no more cycle in the transformed graph, we have proven that this system can always terminate. Note that existing works [2, 11, 13] cannot draw the same conclusion. □

5 Complexity of Algorithm 4.2

In this section, we will discuss the complexity of our method.

Theorem 5.1 For any trigger system, if its termination can be detected using existing methods such as [11], then Algorithm 4.2 can also detect termination with the same time complexity at step 4 without any cycle unrolling. □

Lemma 5.1 For a k-cycle Γ in a trigger graph G, assume it shares nodes with p other cycles, then the number of cycles after $unroll(\Gamma,G,k)$ increases at most by $p(k+2)-1$. □

Putting p to be zero, we arrive the following lemma,

Lemma 5.2 For any trigger system such that the cycles in the corresponding trigger graph can be partitioned hierarchically, i.e., for any two different cycles Γ_1 and Γ_2 in the corresponding trigger graph, if Γ_1 can reach Γ_2 implies that Γ_2 cannot reach Γ_1, each *unroll* operation will decrease the number of cycles in the trigger graph by one. □

Theorem 5.2 Given a trigger system of n nodes that can be partitioned hierarchically, Algorithm 4.2 determines its termination with only $O(nK_{MAX})$ evaluations of trigger conditions. □

Theorem 5.3 Given a trigger system such that all its cycle is a 0-cycle, the unroll operation is similar to the path-splitting operation in [13]. Hence, our method can cover the cases detected by [13] with the same time complexity. Note that as stated in [13], considering path (and thus cycle) instead of edge to detect termination is NP-complete. □

Finally, we have an analysis for the general cases as follows,

Theorem 5.4 Given a trigger graph G with p prime cycles, the number of times that operation *unroll* needed to be done before its termination is at most

$$(K_{MAX}+2)^{D_{MAX}}p$$ □

Although our method can decide much more terminating cases which cannot be detected using existing methods, the worst case run-time complexity of this method is exponential. Despite that, our method, in practice, is still an effective method for the following reasons:

1. Any termination case that can be detected by methods [1, 11] can also be detected within the first

four steps of Algorithm 4.1 with the same time complexity.

2. For any method that detects all our termination cases, it is unavoidable that it must be at least NP-complete as stated in [13].
3. Worst case performance only appears in some artificially designed cases. In practice, our method still performs reasonably well.

6 Finitely-updatable predicate

One of the limitations of using non-updatable predicates is that usually very few predicates can be used in an activation formula. To include more predicates in the activation formula, and thus detect more termination conditions, we propose to use a more powerful predicate selection procedure during the computation of activation formula. The idea is to take not only non-updatable predicate, but also finitely updatable predicate. As described in Section 3.1.2, a finitely-updatable predicate is a predicate which can be updated only finitely during a trigger session. Since to decide exactly the set of finitely-updatable predicates is as hard as to prove trigger termination, we can only approximate this set by maintaining a set of predicates which are definitely finitely-updatable, but we have no conclusion on those predicates that are not in the set. The following algorithm describes how to incorporate finitely-updatable predicates in our termination decision algorithm, as well as other existing methods.

Algorithm 6.1 Given a trigger graph, we detect termination by the following steps,

1. Initialize the set of finitely updatable predicates S to be the set of predicates that are not updated by any action of any trigger rule.
2. Treat every element in S as if it is not updated by the trigger system, apply any existing termination detection method to decide termination.
3. If termination is proven, report "termination" and exit.
4. Otherwise, we mark the following rules as possibly infinitely execution rules:
   i) Rules that are in any unresolved cycle, i.e., cycle which has not been proven to terminate, and
   ii) rules that are reachable from some unresolved cycles in the trigger graph.

   Let T be the set of predicates that are updated by some actions of some possibly infinitely execution rules. We update S to contain all other predicates used in the databases except those in T.
5. If any new element is introduced into S, then repeat the process from step 2.
6. Otherwise, S is unchanged. Exit the process and report "no conclusion". □

The following example demonstrates how [11] can be improved with the finitely-updatable predicate concept:

Example 6.1 Given the following three trigger rules in an OODB environment:

r1 :: $incr\_salary(EMP1)$ IF $EMP1 \neq me$
DO $incr\_salary(me)$

r2 :: $e2(EMP2)$ IF $EMP2.salary > 1000$
DO $e3(EMP2)$

r3 :: $e3(EMP3)$ IF $EMP3.salary < 1000$
DO $e2(EMP3)$

Since the *salary* property of an EMPLOYEE class can be updated by rule r1, [11] will not make use of any predicate that used the attribute "salary". The "qualified connecting formula" of the edge ≪r2,r3≫ is therefore a simple TRUE. Hence, [11] can only conclude that the rules set may not terminate.

On the other hand, our concept of finitely-updatable predicate improves this situation. Using the activation formula, ≪r1,r1≫ is not an activable path, and hence it can only be finitely executed. The salary is only updated finitely. After the set of finitely updatable set is incrementally refined, we return to step 2 of Algorithm 6.1 and apply [11]. We improve [11] to construct a more useful formula,

$$(EMP2.salary > 1000) \wedge (EMP2 = EMP3) \wedge (EMP3.salary < 1000)$$

As this formula is unsatisfiable, termination therefore is detected. □

7 Conclusion

We have proposed a new method to detect more termination situations for an ECA-rule active database model. Although our algorithm cannot find the exact answer for all cases, it gives much stronger sufficient conditions than previous works. Our methods can isolate rules that might give rise to non-terminating execution. This means that our methods can be incorporated into an interactive tool for the specification of active database rules.

In comparison with other existing methods, we have shown that we can cover most of the termination situations which other existing methods have covered. For example, if recent works such as [11] conclude that there is no cycle in a trigger graph, then our methods can also conclude the same result with the same efficiency.

Furthermore, our methods detect far more terminating cases. Once a cyclic execution actually exists in a trigger system, existing methods will conclude that an infinite loop may occur. No other attempt is done to further examine the cycle. Our method, however, introduces the concept of *k*-cycle and allows a finite looping of the given set of trigger rules.

In future, we would also like to investigate any other possible means to detect more terminating situations. So far, our method does not assume any execution model. We would therefore like to extend the analysis techniques to incorporate additional features of active databases such as rule priorities, different execution mode of the actions as well as more complex events augmented with temporal elements.

REFERENCE

[1] A.Aiken, J.Widom and J.M.Hellerstein, "Behaviour of database production rules: Termination, confluence, and observable determinism", *Proc ACM SIGMOD International Conf on the Management of Data*, 59-68, 1992.

[2] E.Baralis, S.Ceri and S.Paraboschi, "Run-Time Detection of Non-Terminating Active Rule Systems", *DOOD*, 38-54, 1995.

[3] E.Baralis, S.Ceri and S.Paraboschi, "Compile-time and runtime analysis of Active Behaviors", *IEEE Transactions on Knowledge and Data Engineering,* Vol 10, No. 3, May/June 1998, pp 353-370.

[4] E.Baralis and J.Widom, "An Algebraic Approach to Rule Analysis in Expert Database Systems", *20th VLDB Conf*, 475-486, Sept 12-15, 1994.

[5] S.Ceri and J.Widom, "Deriving Production Rules for Constraint Maintenance", *Proc 16th VLDB Conf*, 566-577, Brisbane, 1990.

[6] U.Dayal, "Active Database Systems", *Proc 3rd International Conf on Data and Knowledge Bases,* Jerusalem Israel, June 1988.

[7] Dennis R.McCarthy and U.Dayal, "The Architecture of An Active Database Management System", *Proc ACM SIGMOD International Conf on the Management of Data* Vol 18, Number 2, 215-224, June 1989.

[8] O.Diaz, N.Paton and P.Gray, "Rule management in object-oriented databases: A uniform approach", *Proc 17th International Conf on VLDB,* Barcelona, Spain, September 1991.

[9] S.Gatzin, A.Geppert and K.R.Dittrich, "Integrating Active Concepts into an Object-Oriented Database System", *Proc 3rd International Workshop on database programming languages,* Nafplion, 1991.

[10] A.P.Karadimce and S.D.Urban, "Conditional term rewriting as a formal basis for analysis of active database rules", *4th International Workshop on Research Issues in Data Engineering (RIDE-ADS'94)*, February 1994.

[11] A.P.Karadimce and S.D.Urban, "Refined Trigger Graphs: A Logic-Based Approach to Termination Analysis in an Active Object-Oriented Database", *ICDE'96*, 384-391.

[12] T.W.Ling, "The Prolog Not-Predicate and Negation as Failure Rule", *New Generation Computing*, 8, 5-31, 1990.

[13] S.Y.Lee and T.W.Ling, "A Path Removing Technique for Detecting Trigger Termination", *EDBT*, 341-355, 1998.

[14] M.Stonebraker and G.Kemnitz, "The POSTGRES Next-Generation Database Management System", *CACM*, 34(10), 78-93, Oct 1991.

[15] H.Tsai and A.M.K.Cheng, "Termination Analysis of OPS5 Expert Systems", *Proc of the AAAI National Conference on Artificial Intelligence*, Seattle, Washington, 1994.

[16] T.Weik and A.Heuer. "An algorithm for the analysis of Termination of Large Trigger Sets in an OODBMS", *Proceedings of the International Workshop on Active and Real-Time Databases Systems*, Skovde, Sweden, June 1995.

[17] L.Voort and A.Siebes, "Termination and confluence of rule execution", *Proc 2nd International Conf on Information and Knowledge Management*, Nov 1993.

[18] D.Zimmer, A.Meckenstock and Rainer Unland, "Using Petri Nets for Rule Termination Analysis", *Proc of Workshop on Databases: Active and Real-Time*, Rockville, Maryland, November 1996.

User-Defined Table Operators: Enhancing Extensibility for ORDBMS

Michael Jaedicke
SFB342, Technische Universität München, Germany
jaedicke@in.tum.de

Bernhard Mitschang
IPVR, University of Stuttgart, Germany
Bernhard.Mitschang@informatik.uni-stuttgart.de

Abstract

Currently parallel object-relational database technology is setting the direction for the future of data management. A central enhancement of object-relational database technology is the possibility to execute arbitrary user-defined functions within SQL statements. We show the limits of this approach and propose user-defined table operators as a new concept that allows the definition and implementation of arbitrary user-defined N-ary database operators, which can be programmed using SQL or Embedded SQL (with some extensions). Our approach leads to a new dimension of extensibility that allows to push more application code into the server with full support for efficient execution and parallel processing. Furthermore it allows performance enhancements of orders of magnitude for the evaluation of many queries with complex user-defined functions as we show for two concrete examples. Finally, our implementation perception guarantees that this approach fits well into the architectures of commercial object-relational database management systems.

1. Introduction

Object-relational DBMS (ORDBMS) are the next great wave ([36], [7]). They have been proposed for all applications that need both complex queries and complex data types. Since the data volumes that come along with new data types like satellite images, videos, CAD objects, etc. are gigantic and the queries are complex, parallel database technology is essential for many of these applications. As commercial ORDBMS are based on matured parallel RDBMS, these systems are well positioned to cope with large data volumes.

But being able to handle large data volumes efficiently in parallel is not sufficient to process complex queries with short response times. For queries that apply complex algorithms to the data and especially for those that correlate data from several tables, it is essential to enable an efficient and completely parallel evaluation of these algorithms within the DBMS. However, extensions of object-relational execution systems are currently limited to user-defined functions that are invoked by built-in database operators. This concept does not provide the necessary flexibility.

Our main contribution in this paper is to propose a new approach to *user-defined database operators.* The main goals of our design were to provide extensibility with respect to new database operators, and to ensure that the design fits well to the existing technology. Especially, it should be possible to integrate the technology into current commercial ORDBMS without a major change of the system architecture. Though some ORDBMS components must be extended no component must be rewritten from scratch. Furthermore, we considered full support for parallel execution and ease of use for developers of new operators as crucial requirements.

In contrast to previous work our approach is to allow tables as arguments for user-defined routines and to allow the manipulation of these input tables by SQL DML commands in the body of these routines. Moreover, these routines are internally used as new database operators. One could at first expect that such an extension would lead to an increased complexity with respect to the development of such routines. But this is not the case, since the body of these new routines can be implemented similar to embedded SQL programs. This is a widely used programming concept.

The rest of this paper is organized as follows. We review today's concept for user-defined functions and discuss the limits of this concept in Section 2. Section 3 introduces and discusses user-defined table operators as an approach to make database systems extensible by new operators. We discuss a spatial join and an aggregation as examples of new operators in Section 4. Finally,

Proceedings of the 25th VLDB Conference, Edinburgh, Scotland, 1999.

we discuss the related work in Section 5 and provide our conclusions in Section 6.

2. User-Defined Functions in ORDBMS

In this Section we provide the basic concepts and definitions that are used in this paper. We will focus on the concepts relevant to our query processing problem and refer the reader to the literature for the general concepts of relational ([12], [11]) and object-relational query processing ([36], [8]). After an introduction to user-defined functions in Section 2.1, we discuss the problem that we address here in Section 2.2.

2.1. User-Defined Functions and Predicates

Every RDBMS comes with a fixed set of built-in functions. These functions can be either scalar functions or aggregate functions. A *scalar function* can be used in SQL queries wherever an expression can be used. Typical scalar functions are arithmetic functions like + and * or `concat` for string concatenation. A scalar function is applied to the values of some columns of a row of an input table. In contrast, an *aggregate function* is applied to the values of a single column of either a group of rows or of all rows of an input table. A group of rows occurs, if a GROUP-BY clause is used. Therefore aggregate functions can be used in the projection part of SQL queries and in HAVING clauses.

In ORDBMS it is possible to use a *user-defined function* (**UDF**) at nearly all places where a system provided built-in function can appear in SQL92. Thus there are two subsets of UDFs: user-defined scalar functions (**UDSF**s) and *user-defined aggregate functions* (**UDAF**s). A UDSF that returns a boolean value and is used as a predicate in the search condition of SQL commands is a *user-defined predicate* (**UDP**). Finally, some ORDBMS [18] offer the possibility to write *user-defined table functions* (**UDTF**s), which can have (scalar) arguments of a column data type and return a table. UDTFs can be used as a table expression in SQL commands. We use the term *user-defined routines (***UDR**s*)* as a generic term for UDFs, UDTFs, and other kinds of user-defined operations like the user-defined table operators that we define later in Section 3.

2.2. Limitations of Current ORDBMS with Respect to New Database Operators

It is a well-known fact that new complex join operators can increase performance for certain operations like spatial joins [31], etc. by orders of magnitude. But, as we have already pointed out in [22], it is currently not possible for developers of database extensions to implement efficient user-defined join algorithms in current commercial ORDBMS. In fact, one cannot implement any new database operators. UDFs cannot be used to implement new operators, as they are invoked by built-in database operators. The limitation of UDTFs is obviously that - although they can produce an entire output table - they can only have scalar arguments. UDTFs are helpful in accessing external data sources [10] etc., but cannot be used to implement a new database operator like a new join algorithm. We propose a new solution for this problem in the next Section.

3. User-Defined Table Operators: UDRs with Table Arguments

When we review the existing concepts for UDRs from a more abstract point of view, we can observe the following: there are routines that operate on a tuple and produce a tuple (UDSFs), there are routines that are called for each tuple of a set of tuples and produce an aggregate value (UDAFs), and finally there are routines that operate on a tuple and return a table (UDTFs). So obviously there is something missing: namely routines that operate on one or more tables (and have possibly additional scalar parameters) and can return a tuple or a table. We want to point out that the argument tables (input tables) for this kind of routines are not restricted to be base tables. They can be intermediate results of a query as well as base tables, table expressions, or views. We call these routines *user-defined table operators* (UDTOs), since they can be used to define and implement new N-ary database operators. This classification is expressed in Table 1. As one can observe, UDTOs increase the orthogonality of SQL.

Table 1: A classification of user-defined routines based on their parameter types

		output parameter types	
		scalar	table
input parameter types	scalar	UDSF	UDTF (UDTO)
	table(s)	UDAF (UDTO)	UDTO

In the following we will explain, how UDTOs can be defined and how their processing can be integrated into parallel object-relational execution engines based on the traditional query processing framework [12]. However, we will first define a generalization relationship for row types. This will allow the application of a given UDTO to a broad range of tables, as we will see later.

3.1. A Generalization Relationship for Row Types

A row type $R = (R_1, R_2, \dots, R_N)$ is a structured type that consists of N attributes. Each of these attributes has a data type R_i. We define that a row type $S = (S_1, S_2, \dots, S_K)$ is a *subtype* of R, if $N \le K$ and there is a mapping $f: \{1, \dots, N\} \rightarrow \{1, \dots, K\}$ such that $R_i = S_{f(i)}$ and $f(i) \neq f(j)$ for all $1 \le i, j \le N$. In other words, S comprises all attributes of R, but may contain additional attributes with arbitrary data types. The order of the attributes in R and S is not important. We say also that R is a *supertype* of S. Please note that each table has an associated row type.

We want to point out that this generalization relationship between subtypes is completely different from the supertable/subtable concept which describes a collection hierarchy and is

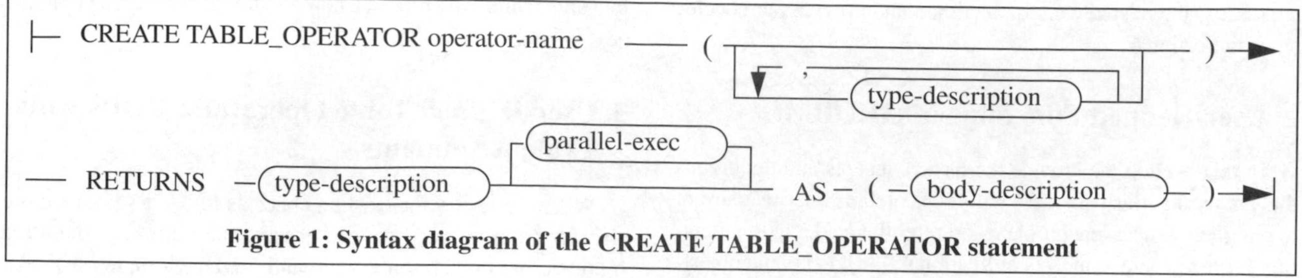

Figure 1: Syntax diagram of the CREATE TABLE_OPERATOR statement

already available in some ORDBMS [19]. As we will describe in the next Subsection, UDTOs can be defined in such a way that they are applicable to all tables whose row types are subtypes of the row types of the corresponding formal parameter input tables of the UDTO.

3.2. Defining UDTOs

3.2.1. Underlying Concept

The basic idea of this approach is easy to understand: the effect of a UDTO can be viewed as a mapping from a set of input tables to a result table or a single result tuple. This is very similar to the effect of a new algebraic operator. One fundamental difference is that a user-defined operator usually does not need to have base tables as input, but tables that represent intermediate results. It also produces an intermediate result table that can be processed further. Based on these observations, we propose to implement UDTOs by means of an extended version of embedded SQL. To enable this we propose the following extensions to user-defined routines: the definition of N input tables and a single output table is permitted and SQL DML commands in the body of this routine are allowed to refer to these input tables.

Generally speaking, a new UDTO can be sequentially executed as follows: All input tables are first materialized. That means they can be furtheron accessed in a similar way as permanently stored base tables. Then the UDTO is executed using these input tables. The UDTO produces and materializes the output table that represents the result of the UDTO and that can be processed further. Of course, the input tables cannot be manipulated and the only SQL command that is permitted for the manipulation of the output table is the INSERT command. Later, we will describe optimizations of this basic execution scheme that will allow a much more efficient execution in many cases. Moreover, in Section 3.4 we will describe how UDTOs can be processed in parallel.

We distinguish two kinds of UDTOs that differ in the implementation of their body: *procedural UDTOs* and *SQL macros.* A procedural UDTO is a UDTO whose body contains procedural statements with embedded SQL statements. As for UDSFs one can implement the body of a procedural UDTO in a programming language (with embedded SQL) compile it, put it into a library and register it with the DBMS. On the other hand, if the body of a UDTO consists of a single INSERT statement or just a RETURN statement we call this UDTO a SQL macro. This kind of UDTO has some similarity to views, but the UDTO can refer to the formal input tables of the UDTO and is therefore not limited to references to base tables or views.

3.2.2. Language Extensions

Obviously, ORDBMS must provide a statement to create UDTOs. We describe the CREATE TABLE_OPERATOR statement in the syntax diagram shown in Figure 1 (we use | to denote beginning and end of a definition; terms in small ovals are described in additional syntax diagrams or in the text). After the name of the table operator the argument list and the return type are described. The repeated use of table arguments enables the definition of N-ary table operators. The parallel execution option allows to specify how the table operator can be executed in parallel (we will refer to parallelization later in Section 3.4). Finally, the body of the routine follows. Please note, that we have not shown other options in Figure 1, which are useful for other purposes like query optimization but which are beyond the scope of this paper.

In Figure 2 we present the type description including input and output tables. Each table is described by specifying the name and data type for each column. In Figure 2 the term 'datatype' should denote all allowed data types for columns, including user-defined types. We will explain the notation `tablename.+` later.

We do not provide a syntax diagram for the description of the body, because we allow here embedded SQL program code or a single INSERT statement - with some extensions of SQL. We try to use SQL/PSM as procedural language in our examples, but our concept is not limited to a particular procedural language. That means that all procedural languages like C, C++, Java or COBOL can be used. In addition, proprietary APIs or other techniques like database programming laguages (see for example [2]) could be used instead of the traditional embedded SQL.

3.2.3. Introductory Examples

In the following we give some definitions of UDTOs. These examples are extremely simple and they are *not* intended to demonstrate the usefulness of the UDTO approach (cf. Section 4). They only serve to illustrate the concepts and the syntax. We will refer to these examples also later in Section 3.3 when we discuss the application of UDTOs.

Example 1: the UDTO `minimum`

In the first example we create a UDTO that computes the minimum for a table with an integer column:

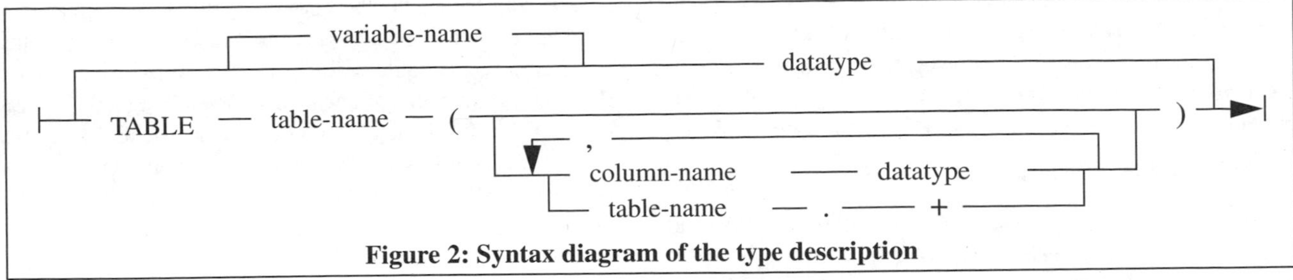

Figure 2: Syntax diagram of the type description

```
CREATE TABLE_OPERATOR minimum
(TABLE Input (number INTEGER))
RETURNS INTEGER
AS {
RETURN(SELECT MIN(value)
       FROM Input)
};
```

This example demonstrates how a new aggregation operator can be defined. Of course there are many aggregate functions (like MIN, MAX, and SUM) that should be programmed by the usual iterator paradigm, since this allows to compute multiple aggregates in a single pass over the input table. In case of aggregations, there is usually no output table, but only an aggregate value.

Before we present further examples, we first introduce the following extensions of SQL within the body of UDTOs: First, all SQL DML statements can read the input tables in the same manner as base tables. Especially, an input table can be read by several different SQL statements. Second, tuples can be appended to the output table by INSERT commands. With these extensions, we can define our next example.

Example 2: the UDTO `has_job`

This UDTO performs a restriction of the input table and does some decoding. Let us assume that a table `employees (emp_no, job)` has been defined with an integer column `job` that is used to code the job of the employees. We assume that the names of the jobs and their codes are stored in a table `jobcodes (code, jobname)`. The UDTO `has_job` selects the name for a given code from the table `jobcodes` and selects then all jobs from the input table with this code. This UDTO is created as follows:

```
CREATE TABLE_OPERATOR has_job
(TABLE Input (job INTEGER), jname VARCHAR)
RETURNS TABLE Output (job INTEGER)
AS {
INSERT INTO Output
SELECT I.job
FROM Input AS I, jobcodes AS C
WHERE  I.job = C.code AND
       C.jobname = jname
};
```

Please note that the database can be fully accessed from within the body of the UDTO. In our example the table `jobcodes` is accessed. This supports information hiding, since the accessed objects are not visible to the user of the UDTO. All side effects of a UDTO evaluation belong to the associated transaction. That is the UDTO is executed within the same transaction as the statement that invokes it.

So far UDTOs can be applied reasonably only to tables that match the row types of the corresponding formal parameter tables *exactly*. For example, the UDTO `has_job` can be applied to a table with a single INTEGER column. Of course, it is desirable to allow the application of a UDTO to a more general class of tables. Our goal is to allow all tables as input tables whose row types are subtypes of the row types of the formal input table of the UDTO. The UDTO operates then only on attributes that appear within the formal input table. All additional columns which may be present in the actual input tables are neglected or can be propagated to the output table, if this is desired (*attribute propagation*).

Therefore developers of UDTOs must have the possibility to determine that the additional columns of an actual input tuple have to be appended to the output tuple. We denote these additional columns by the expression `table_name.+` (the '+' denotes only the *additional* columns. By contrast, *all* columns are usually denoted by the '*' in SQL). That means, an expression like `table_name.+` has to be replaced by all additional columns of the corresponding input table `table_name`, which are present in the actual argument table, but not in the formal argument table of the UDTO. For example, if the actual argument table that is bound to the input table `input1` has one additional column, then `input1.+` represents exactly this column. We permit also a table variable instead of a table name in combination with '+'. Normally all additional columns of the input tables will be appended to the output table. These additional columns have to appear also in the definition of the output table (that is the row type of the formal output table is then a supertype of the row type of the actual output table).

We can now redefine the UDTO `has_job` with attribute propagation as follows (changes are in bold face):

```
CREATE TABLE_OPERATOR has_job
(TABLE Input (job INTEGER), jname VARCHAR)
RETURNS
TABLE Output (job INTEGER, Input.+)
AS {
INSERT INTO Output
SELECT I.job, I.+
FROM Input AS I, jobcodes AS C
WHERE  I.job = C.code AND
       C.jobname = jname
};
```

As the example shows, we have to define the columns of each input table, but only those columns that are needed within the routine's body should be defined. The expression `I.+` appends all additional columns to the output. This allows the application of the UDTO `has_job` as a restriction operator, because a subset of the rows of the input table is returned. The specification of the output table contains the term '`Input.+`' to enable type checking.

3.2.4. Row Identification

Finally, we want to propose here an extension that allows to implement UDTOs more efficiently. Within the body of a UDTO it can be necessary to have access to a unique identifier for each row of an input table (cf. Section 4.1 for an example). To support this, we introduce the special column data type ID for the type description of table columns that are UDTO arguments. The special type ID means that the column contains a unique identifier for each row of an input table. Note that an ID can be either a primary key or an internal identifier like a row identifier or a reference type as proposed in SQL3. Such an ID can always be generated automatically by the DBMS (this can be viewed as a kind of type promotion for row types). An ID column could also be created explicitly in the body of the UDTO by the developer, but if it is defined as a column of an input table, the DBMS can use an already existing identifier as an optimization. In general, it is not useful to append a column value of type ID explicitly to the output table. In case the primary key is used internally to represent the ID, the system does this automatically, if the '+' option has been specified in the projection list of the subquery of the INSERT statement.

3.3. The Different Usages of UDTOs

In this Subsection, we will describe two ways in which UDTOs can be used: first they can be used explicitly by programmers within SQL commands. This allows to augment the functionality of SQL in arbitrary ways. Second, UDTOs can be used to augment the implementation of database operations which involve UDFs. In this case the query optimizer has the task to use the UDTO during the plan generation whenever the use of this UDTO leads to a cheaper query execution plan. We discuss these two applications now in greater detail.

3.3.1. Augmentation of SQL

The explicit usage of UDTOs in SQL statements allows to extend the functionality of SQL by arbitrary new set operations, or to say it in other words: UDTOs make object-relational query processing universal in the sense that the set of database operations becomes extensible. For example, over time a lot of special join operations have appeared: cross join, inner join, anti-join, left, right, and full outer join, union join, etc. Moreover, other operations like recursion or more application specific ones (for data mining, etc.) have been proposed. UDTOs allow developers to define a parallelizable implementation for such operators. These operators can then be invoked in SQL commands by application programmers, as we explain in the following.

A UDTO that returns a table can be used in all places within SQL commands where a table expression is allowed. Moreover, UDTOs with two input tables can be written in infix notation to allow an easy integration into the current SQL command syntax. For example, one could define a UDTO named ANTI_JOIN. Then one can write the following expression in a FROM clause: Table1 ANTI_JOIN Table2. In this case, conceptually, the UDTO is evaluated within the FROM clause. This means that conceptually the Cartesian product of the output table of the UDTO and of all other tables, views, and table expressions in the FROM clause is computed. In addition, UDTOs can also be written in infix notation between two SELECT blocks like the usual set operations (UNION, INTERSECT, EXCEPT).

To allow the application of UDTOs to base tables and views whose row type is a subtype of the row type of the formal input table, we propose the following syntax to bind columns of the actual input table to columns of the formal input table. The programmer can specify an ordered list of columns from a given table (or view) that is bound to the corresponding columns in the parameter list of the UDTO. For example the expression TO1 (T1 USING (C_1, C_2, ..., C_N)) describes that the columns named C_1, C_2, ..., C_N of table T1 are bound to the N columns of the formal input table parameter of the UDTO TO1. The keyword USING is optional and can be left out. This notation can also be used, if binary UDTOs are written in infix notation (it can be seen as a generalization of the ON clause for traditional join expressions). If input tables are given as table expressions then the columns of the resulting table are bound to the columns of the formal input table in exactly the order in which these columns appear in the SELECT clause of the table expression.

The following statements illustrate this syntax. The first query invokes the UDTO `has_job` with a base table; the second query invokes it with a table expression:

```
SELECT *
FROM has_job(employees USING (job),'manager')
```

```
SELECT * FROM has_job(
    (SELECT job, emp_no FROM employees),
    'manager' )
```

3.3.2. Augmentation of the Implementation of UDFs

In this Subsection we describe how UDTOs can be used to improve the performance for queries with UDFs. A very important usage of UDTOs is to define more efficient database operators that can be used by the query optimizer during the plan generation. While there might be some relational queries that can be enhanced by UDTOs, the move to object-relational query processing with UDFs creates a need for UDTOs as we have already outlined in Subsection 2.2. The reason is that UDTOs allow to implement database operations that involve UDFs sometimes more efficiently than in current ORDBMS, where a built-in database operator invokes the UDF.

UDTOs provide a different implementation technique for operations involving UDFs compared to the traditional iterator-based approach for UDF evaluation. For example, a UDSF can be used as a UDP in a *join*, i.e. in a restriction involving attributes from different tables on top of a Cartesian product. In this case, a UDTO will often allow a more efficient implementation. The rea-

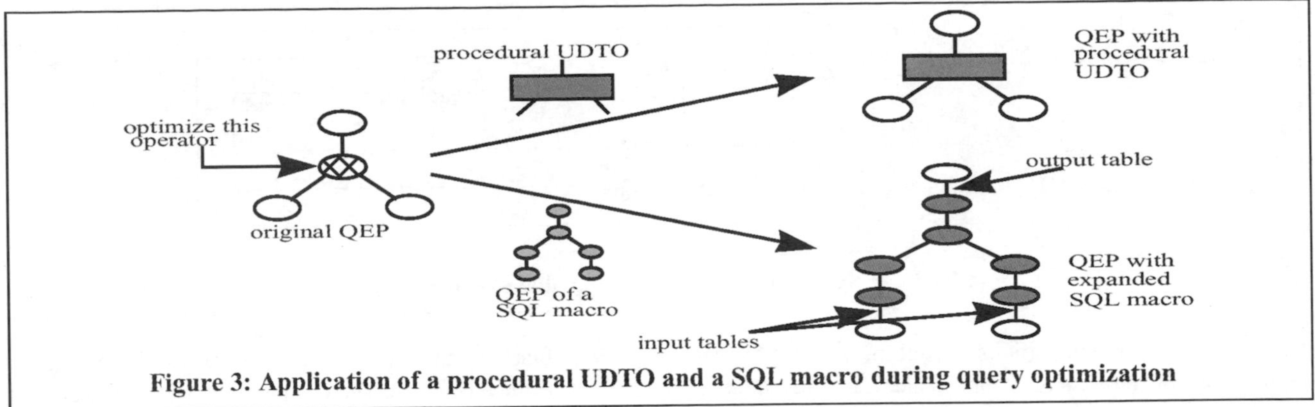

Figure 3: Application of a procedural UDTO and a SQL macro during query optimization

son is that normally the UDP will be evaluated by a nested-loops join operator which has quadratic complexity. By contrast there might be implementation methods with much lower complexity. Therefore joins are an important application of UDTOs, where performance enhancements of orders of magnitude are possible (often because nested-loops joins can be replaced by hash- or sort-merge-based join algorithms; cf. Section 4.1). Furthermore, UDTOs might sometimes be useful as aggregation, restriction, or projection operators. For example, in case of UDAFs it can be useful to provide an implementation by means of a UDTO, since this allows access to the whole input table for the aggregation (cf. Section 4.2 for an example).

The query optimizer has the task to decide when a UDTO should be used. In a rule- and cost-based query optimizer ([13], [15], [25]) this means the following: there must be a rule that generates a plan with the UDTO as an alternative implementation. Such a rule has to be specified by the developer. This is not difficult because the UDTO is always associated with a specific UDF for which it implements a specific database operator (for example a join that has exactly this UDF as join predicate). Hence, the developer must tell the query optimizer only that the UDTO can be used to evaluate the UDF. For this purpose, the CREATE FUNCTION statement that is used to register UDFs with the DBMS can be extended. The statement should include the possibility to specify that a UDTO can be used as an implementation for a specific operation such as a join. For example one could extend the CREATE FUNCTION statement as follows:

```
ALLOW <UDTO-name> AS
(JOIN | RESTRICTION | PROJECTION |
        AGGREGATION) OPERATOR
```

The relationship between the UDF and the UDTO is stored in the system tables and can be used by the query optimizer. The query optimizer has to be extended by general rules that can do these transformations for arbitrary UDFs. The optimizer uses information from the system tables to decide whether the transformation is possible for a given UDF. Please note, that for some functions like a UDAF, the UDTO might be the only implementation. In this case the UDTO is mandatory to execute the UDF.

Let us assume that we want to create a UDP `has_job` for the UDTO that we have introduced in Section 3.2. Then one can register this UDP with the UDTO `has_job` as restriction operator:

```
CREATE FUNCTION has_job (INTEGER, VARCHAR)
RETURNS BOOLEAN
ALLOW has_job AS RESTRICTION OPERATOR ...
```

After this registration the query optimizer considers the UDTO `has_job` as an implementation for the restriction with the UDP `has_job` in the following query:

```
SELECT *
FROM employees AS E
WHERE has_job(E.job, 'manager')
```

Figure 3 illustrates how a traditional database operator that invokes a UDF is replaced by a UDTO. First the operator has to be identified in the original query execution plan (QEP). Then the optimizer replaces this operator either by a procedural UDTO or by a SQL macro. Because the body of a SQL macro consists essentially of a QEP we can simply replace the operator by this QEP (*SQL macro expansion*). However the QEP of the SQL macro has to be modified so that it fits to the comprising QEP. For example, proper attribute propagation has to be considered. The result of this SQL macro expansion is a traditional QEP, which can be further optimized and evaluated as usual. Especially, the materialization of input and output tables can be avoided.

3.4. Parallel Processing of Procedural UDTOs

Nowadays new operators would not be a concept of great use, if these operators could not be executed in parallel. That's why we will discuss the parallel execution of UDTOs in this Subsection. Please note that all SQL DML commands within the body of UDTOs of the implementation are parallelizable as usual. If the UDTO is a SQL-macro, i.e. a single SQL statement, the complete UDTO can be parallelized automatically by the DBMS. In the more general case of a UDTO that is implemented by embedded SQL, the developer must specify how a parallel execution can be done, if it is possible at all.

We provide a method that allows to specify, if an operator can be executed with data parallelism and, should the occasion arise, how the operator can be processed. Applying data parallelism means that one or more of the input tables of an operator are split

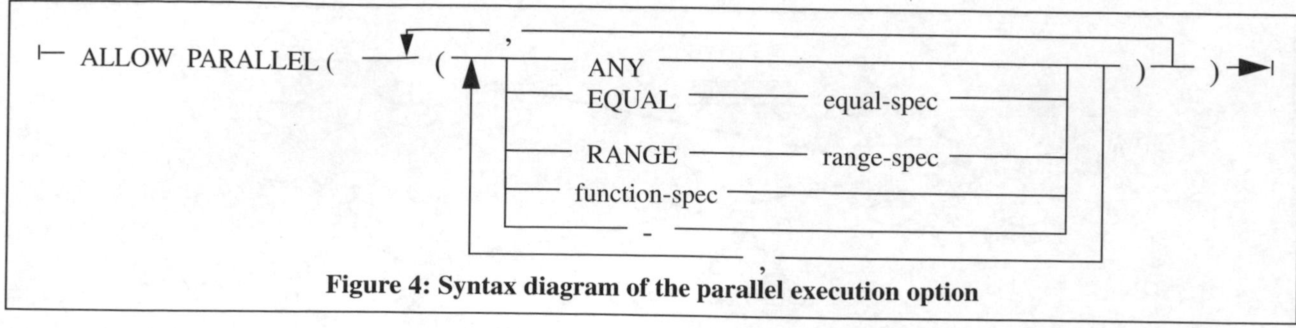

Figure 4: Syntax diagram of the parallel execution option

horizontally into several partitions by means of a suitable partitioning function. If one or more input tables can be partitioned but not all, the other input tables are replicated. Then the operator is executed once for each partition with the following input tables: if the argument table is partitionable, the respective partition of this table is used. If the argument table is not partitioned, then the complete, replicated table is used as an argument. This means that N instances of the operator are executed in parallel if one or more input tables are split into N partitions. Hence, the degree of parallelism is N. In this case, the final result is computed by combining the N intermediate output tables by means of a union (without elimination of duplicates). If no input table is partitioned, the operator is executed without data parallelism - that is sequentially. There can be several possibilities for the parallelization of an operator, depending on which input tables are partitioned and depending on how this partitioning is done.

Hence we must describe the set of all combinations of partitioning functions that can be used to partition the input tables of a given UDTO. We permit different partitioning functions for different tables, but all partitioned input tables must have the same number of partitions. Therefore the partitioning functions must have a parameter that allows to specify the number of generated partitions. This parameter enables the optimizer to set the degree of parallelism for a given UDTO. In some cases, it may be also necessary to specify that exactly the same partitioning function has to be used for some or all input tables. For example, this is needed for equi joins in relational processing.

In [21] we have already proposed the following classes of partitioning functions:

1. ANY: the class of all partitioning functions. Round-robin and random partitioning functions are examples of this class which belong to no other class. All partitioning functions that are not based on attribute values belong only to this class.
2. EQUAL (column name): the class of partitioning functions that map all rows of the input table with equal values in the selected column into the same partition. Examples of EQUAL functions are partitioning functions that use hashing.
3. RANGE (column name): the class of partitioning functions that map rows, whose values of the specified column belong to a certain range, into the same partition. Obviously there must be a total order on the data type of the column (for further details see [21]).

In addition to these three partitioning classes we have proposed that a special user-defined partitioning function can be specified, too. Based on these considerations we have developed the parallel execution option in the CREATE TABLE_OPERATOR statement that allows to specify *all* parallel execution schemes which are possible for a new operator. For operators that have multiple input tables there can be many possibilities. But since we doubt that there will be many complex operators with more than two input tables in practice, we have not tried to optimize the description for this special case. The syntax diagram for this option is shown in Figure 4.

If the partitioning class is not ANY, we have to specify the columns to which the partitioning function should be applied. The same is necessary, if a specific partitioning function must be used. We have left out these details in Figure 4. If no partitioning is possible for a given input table, this is denoted by '-' (in case of parallel processing, this input table is replicated).

In the following, we will describe some examples of parallel execution schemes for familiar (relational) operations: a restriction, a nested-loops join, a hash join, and a merge join. To simplify the examples, we have left out the column specifications of the input and the output tables and the bodies of the operators.

```
CREATE TABLE_OPERATOR restriction
(TABLE Input1(..))
RETURNS TABLE Output1(...)
ALLOW PARALLEL ((ANY))
AS { ... };
```

By specifying the class ANY in the ALLOW PARALLEL option, we have specified that all partitioning functions can be used to partition the input table for the restriction operator that is defined in this example.

```
CREATE TABLE_OPERATOR nested_loops
(TABLE Input1(...), TABLE Input2(...))
RETURNS TABLE Output1(...)
ALLOW PARALLEL ((ANY,-), (-,ANY))
AS { ... };
```

```
CREATE TABLE_OPERATOR hash_join
(TABLE Input1(...), TABLE Input2(...))
RETURNS TABLE Output1(...)
ALLOW PARALLEL
(    (EQUAL pf1(Column_List),
      EQUAL pf1(Column_List)),
     (ANY,-), (-,ANY) )
AS { ... };
```

```
CREATE TABLE_OPERATOR merge_join
(TABLE Input1(...), TABLE Input2(...))
RETURNS TABLE Output1(...)
ALLOW PARALLEL
     (   (EQUAL pf1(Column_List),
          EQUAL pf1(Column_List)),
         (ANY,-), (-,ANY) )
AS { ... };
```

The options for the three join algorithms specify that if one table is replicated, the other table can be partitioned with any partitioning function. In addition, the hash join can be parallelized with the partitioning scheme `(EQUAL pf1(Column_List), EQUAL pf1(Column_List))` that means both input tables are partitioned with the *same* partitioning function `pf1`. The same holds for the merge join, if we restrict it to the computation of equi joins. If we want to use the merge join for more general join predicates - for example an interval join (to execute a predicate like 'x <= y + k or x >= y - k' more efficiently) - then we need a partitioning with a function of class `RANGE(k)`, that is the option should be `ALLOW PARALLEL (RANGE(k) pf1(Column_List), RANGE(k) pf1(Column_List))`. The parameter k could be an argument of this join operator (The corresponding UDP would be used as follows: `interval_join(table1.x, table2.y, k)`).

3.5. Extension to Multiple Output Tables

We can provide even more extensibility, if we allow multiple output tables for UDTFs: one application could be to return a set of tables perhaps holding complex objects that are linked via OIDs. This is something like pushing Starburst's XNF ([27], [33]) into the middle of SQL commands. Using such a UDTO at the top of a query would allow for composite objects as result, which might be interesting for querying XML data ([3], [4]), for example. Internally, the top operator of queries has to be extended, to allow the direct output of several tables as a result of a query. Another use of multiple output tables could be to support a nesting of complex UDTOs. The output tables of one UDTO can then serve as input tables for other UDTOs.

UDTOs with multiple output tables can be used within the FROM clause of queries but not in the WHERE clause, since they do not return a table expression. The renaming of the result tables and their columns should be allowed. UDTOs with multiple output tables can be evaluated in the same manner as UDTOs with a single output table, but they produce multiple output tables. These output tables can be processed further. The result tables in case of a parallel evaluation are obtained by a union of all corresponding partial result tables.

4. Applicability and Expressive Power of the UDTO Concept

The broad applicability and the high expressive power of the UDTO concept can be easily assessed by means of example scenarios. We present the realization of complex operations in two different processing scenarios: one is the well-known spatial join and the other refers to a complex aggregation as needed in OLAP, for example.

4.1. Computing a Spatial Join

In our first example we use the UDTO concept to define a spatial join based on the partition-based spatial merge-join (PBSM) algorithm [31]. Thus we show that the UDTO concept allows among other things a much more elegant implementation than the multi-operator method [22], which we have demonstrated using the same example scenario. We consider the following polygon intersection query (that searches for all gold deposits intersecting lakes) as a concrete example of a spatial join:

```
SELECT*
FROM Lakes as L, Gold_Deposits as G
WHEREoverlaps(L.poly_geometry,
G.poly_geometry)
```

The predicate `overlaps (polygon, polygon)` returns `TRUE`, if the two polygons overlap geometrically and `FALSE` otherwise. In order to define a UDTO for `overlaps` based on the PBSM algorithm [31] we create the following UDFs:

- `bbox(polygon)`:
  This UDSF creates and returns a bounding box (minimum bounding rectangle) for a given polygon.
- `bbox_overlaps(bbox1, bbox2)`:
  This UDP returns TRUE, if both bounding boxes overlap.
- `exact_overlaps(polygon1, polygon2)`:
  This UDP returns TRUE, if the exact geometries of the input polygons overlap.
- `bucket_no(bbox)`:
  This UDTF divides the spatial universe into B equally sized rectangular regions called buckets. Then it computes and returns all buckets, which the input bounding box intersects. Please note that this is a table function. That is it returns a table with a single column of type integer.

With these UDFs we are prepared to create the UDTO `overlaps`. This operator uses three techniques to improve the efficiency of the join algorithm. First, it uses a simple filter-and-refine scheme [30]. The filtering step uses bounding boxes as approximations of the polygons. This means that we test whether the bounding boxes overlap, before we check whether the exact geometries overlap. Second, spatial partitioning is used. This allows to join only the corresponding buckets. Third, the exact geometry is eliminated to reduce the data volumes of the input tables of the join. For the refinement the exact geometry is retrieved. This results in the implementation of the overlaps pred-

```
CREATE TABLE_OPERATOR overlaps
(TABLE Input1(id1 ID, poly1 POLYGON), TABLE Input2(id2 ID, poly2 POLYGON))
RETURNS TABLE Output1(poly1 POLYGON, Input1.+, poly2 POLYGON, Input2.+)
AS {
INSERT INTO Output1
WITH    Temp1(id, bbox, bucket) AS
        (SELECT id1, bbox(poly1), bucket FROM Input1, TABLE(bucket_no(bbox(poly1))) AS B(bucket)),
        Temp2(id, bbox, bucket) AS
        (SELECT id2, bbox(poly2), bucket FROM Input2, TABLE (bucket_no(bbox(poly2))) AS B(bucket))
SELECT  poly1, Input1.+, poly2, Input2.+
FROM    (SELECT DISTINCT Temp1.id AS id1, Temp2.id AS id2 FROM Temp1, Temp2
         WHERE Temp1.bucket = Temp2.bucket AND
         bbox_overlaps(Temp1.bbox,Temp2.bbox)) AS Temp3, Input1, Input2
WHERE   Temp3.id1 = Input1.id1 AND Temp3.id2 = Input2.id2 AND
        exact_overlaps(Input1.poly1, Input2.poly2)
};

CREATE FUNCTION overlaps (POLYGON, POLYGON) RETURNS BOOLEAN
ALLOW overlaps AS JOIN OPERATOR ...
```

Figure 5: Definition of a SQL macro as join operator for the UDP overlaps

icate by means of a new join operator that shown in Figure 5. We discuss this implementation in the following.

The subqueries in the WITH clause generate two temporary tables with the bounding boxes and the bucket numbers for spatial partitioning. Since the UDTF `bucket_no` is used in the FROM clause with a correlated tuple variable, the Cartesian product with the corresponding tuple is generated, that is we replicate the tuple for each intersecting bucket and append the bucket number (a single polygon can intersect several buckets [31]). This allows later on to join the temporary tables on the bucket number (`Temp1.bucket = Temp2.bucket` in the innermost SELECT query). Thus the function `bbox_overlaps` is only evaluated on the Cartesian product of all polygons within the same bucket. Next, duplicate candidate pairs, which might have been introduced by the spatial partitioning, are eliminated. Finally, in the outermost SELECT statement, the UDF `exact_overlaps` is processed on the exact polygon geometries that are fetched from the input tables using an equi join on the unique values of the ID columns.

We want to add some remarks on this example. The UDTO `overlaps` is a SQL macro and can be parallelized automatically. Thus there is no need to specify an option for parallel execution. In order to process the join with data parallelism the bucket number would be selected as a partitioning column due to the equi join on the bucket number. Therefore no specific user-defined partitioning function is needed for parallel processing, as the usual partitioning functions can be applied to the bucket number which is an INTEGER value. Please note, that if the join on the bucket number is done via a hash join with linear complexity, the overall complexity of the UDTO is still linear. This is *much* better than the quadratic complexity of the Cartesian product that has to be used, if no UDTO is provided.

We did measurements with a prototypical implementation of a spatial join with a similar SQL macro and observed an improvement by a factor of 238 for a table with 10 000 polygons. Moreover, we could achieve a speedup of 2.5 for the plan with the SQL macro on a four processor SMP (cf. [23] for a detailed discussion).

A final but important point concerns the function `bucket_no` that in effect does a spatial partitioning. Actually this function is too simple for practice. The reason is that it is crucial for the performance of the algorithm to find a suitable partitioning of the spatial universe. The spatial universe is the area which contains all polygons from both relations. The task is to find a suitable partitioning of the spatial universe into buckets such that each bucket contains roughly the same number of polygons (or at least the differences are not extreme). This task is very difficult, because it should ideally take the following parameters into account: the number of polygons in each input table, their spatial location, their area, the number of points per polygon and their spatial distribution. For traditional relational queries the optimizer tries to use more or less sophisticated statistics that are stored in the system tables to estimate value distributions, etc. In the same manner one could now use such meta data from (user-defined) catalog tables to compute parameters for the spatial partitioning. However, the fundamental problem with this approach would be that the input tables do not correspond to base relations and may have therefore different value distributions (as usual there might be also the problem that the statistics might not be up to date). A more sophisticated approach would be to analyze the polygons in the input tables by extracting statistics on the bounding boxes and to use these statistics to derive an appropriate spatial partitioning. UDTOs provide full support for this method (cf. [24] for the extended example). Therefore UDTOs support *run-time optimization* that takes the actual content of the input tables into account.

4.2. Computing the Median: an Aggregation Operator

In this Section we will show how a complex aggregation operation can be implemented in a clean and efficient way as a proce-

```
SELECT MIN(Age)
FROM Persons AS P
WHERE
(SELECT Ceiling((COUNT(*)+1/2)
 FROM Persons)
<=
(SELECT COUNT(*) FROM Persons AS R
 WHERE R.Age <= P.Age)
```

Figure 6: Computing the median in SQL

dural UDTO. As a concrete example, we consider the `Median` aggregate function that computes the $\lceil (N+1)/2 \rceil$ largest element of a set with N elements. A query finding the median of a set is not very intuitively expressible in SQL92. For example, the simple query to select the median of the ages of certain persons could be formulated as shown in Figure 6. Of course one would prefer a query using a UDAF `Median` as shown in Figure 7. This query

```
SELECT Median(P.Age)
FROM Persons AS P
```

Figure 7: Computing the median with a UDTO

is not only easy to write, but will also run more efficiently (orders of magnitude for a large input table), because the `Median` function can be implemented with lower complexity than the SQL statement in Figure 6. For example, in our UDTO the median is simply computed by fetching values from the sorted input table, until the position of the median is reached. This position is first determined by counting the input table. Here are the statements to create the UDTO `median` and the corresponding UDAF:

```
CREATE TABLE_OPERATOR median
(TABLE Input1(value INTEGER))
RETURNS INTEGER
AS {
DECLARE count, cardinality,
                median_pos, result INTEGER;
SET count = 1;
SELECT COUNT(*) FROM Input1 INTO cardinality;
SET median_pos = ceiling ((cardinality + 1) / 2);
F1:  FOR result AS
        SELECT * FROM Input1 ORDER BY value ASC
     DO
     IF (count = median_pos) THEN
        LEAVE F1;
     SET count = count + 1;
END FOR;
RETURN result;
};

CREATE AGGREGATE Median (INTEGER)
RETURNS INTEGER
ALLOW median AS AGGREGATION OPERATOR ...
```

This example demonstrates how SQL DML statements and procedural statements can be mixed in the body of a UDTO. While this implementation does not use the most efficient algorithm known to compute the median, the algorithm is easy to implement based on SQL and allows a computation for arbitrary large data sets, as it does not rely on explicit intermediate data storage in main memory. Moreover, both embedded SQL queries can be evaluated in parallel as usual. That means that the optimizer can automatically decide to perform the sort operation for the ORDER BY clause in parallel. This example shows again, how our technique can enable a parallel execution of complex user-defined operators. This is a significant progress compared to other approaches. Implementing the median as an aggregate function based on the usual iterator paradigm for UDAFs is much more difficult as we have already pointed out in [21]. Using a first prototypical implementation of procedural UDTOs in an ORDBMS, we computed the median on a table with 20 000 tuples and measured an improvement by a factor of 2550 by means of a UDTO (cf. [23] for details).

5. Related work

User-Defined Functions (UDFs) have attracted increasing interest of researchers as well as the industry in recent years (see e.g. [1], [9], [16], [17], [26], [28], [29], [34], [35], [36]). However, most of the work discusses only the non-parallel execution of UDFs, special implementation techniques like caching, or query optimization for UDFs. In [32] support for the parallel implementation of UDFs in the area of geo-spatial applications is discussed. It is remarked that in this area complex operations are commonplace. Also special new join techniques [31] and other special implementation techniques have been proposed, but no framework for extensibility that allows the integration of such special processing in parallel ORDBMS was mentioned.

An approach that offered extensibility by means of new database operators and that is superior in functionality to our approach is that of the EXODUS project [6]. In EXODUS new operators could be programmed with the E programming language. However, the EXODUS approach differs from our approach fundamentally, since the goal of EXODUS was not to provide a complete DBMS. Rather the goal was to enable the semi-automatic construction of an application specific DBMS. Thus EXODUS was a database software engineering project providing software tools for DBMS construction by vendors. By contrast our approach allows to extend a complete ORDBMS by third parties like independent software vendors. We believe that our approach to program new operators with embedded SQL statements provides more support for parallel execution and fits well into current system architectures. In addition, developers can use a familiar technique to program UDTOs. UDTOs are less flexible than built-in database operators, because they cannot be applied to tables with arbitrary row types. However, they fit perfectly to UDFs. Hence they are the ideal concept to support database extensions for class libraries by third parties as well as application specific extensions. See [14] for a formal approach to the specification of database operations.

In [34] E-ADTs are proposed as a new approach to the software architecture of ORDBMS. An ORDBMS is envisioned as a collection of E-ADTs (enhanced ADTs). These E-ADTs encapsulate the complete functionality and implementation of ADTs. We believe that this is an interesting approach that is in general more ambitious than UDTOs. In contrast to the E-ADT approach, UDTOs fit very well into the architectures of current commercial ORDBMS. Thus UDTOs leverage existing technology. Moreover, UDTOs are designed to support parallel execution.

We have already mentioned that SQL macros can be viewed as a generalization of views [37]. The difference is that views can refer only to existing base tables and other views, but not to the results of subqueries or table expressions and that views cannot have parameters. As we have described, SQL macros can be used to implement database operations with UDFs more efficiently. Hence, SQL macros differ in their functionality from views.

In [21] we proposed a framework for parallel processing of user-defined scalar and aggregate functions in ORDBMS. We introduced the concept of partitioning classes there to support the parallel execution of user-defined scalar and aggregate functions. In this paper we have generalized this work to enable data parallelism for N-ary user-defined table operators. In [22] we proposed the multi-operator method to allow the implementation of complex UDFs like parallel join algorithms for UDPs. However, we view UDTOs in the form of SQL macros as the more appropriate implementation technique. Moreover, procedural UDTOs are a much more powerful concept than the multi-operator method.

6. Summary, Conclusions and Future Work

In this paper we have proposed UDTOs as a novel approach to extensibility with regard to the execution engine and the query optimizer of ORDBMS. While current user-defined functions are used within the traditional database operators, our approach allows to develop user-defined database operators.This technology will provide a new dimension of extensibility for ORDBMS.

We have presented the following core issues of UDTOs:

- the possibility to define M input tables and N output tables for a user-defined routine
- the access to and the manipulation of these tables by means of SQL commands that are embedded into procedural code (procedural UDTOs) or by means of a single SQL statement (SQL macro)
- attribute propagation to allow the application of UDTOs to a broad range of input tables based on a generalization relationship between row types
- a method to specify parallel execution schemes for UDTOs and the general algorithm for their parallel processing
- the explicit application of UDTOs within SQL and their use as high performance implementations for operations involving UDFs.

We believe that the possibility to define new operators is very promising, especially since the SQL-based implementation technique is in our view elegant and easy to understand for developers. In addition, sophisticated optimization technology can be used to produce high-quality plans that are automatically fine tuned to the estimated data volumes.

With regard to SQL macros the UDTO approach is similar to pushing views into the middle of SQL statements. SQL macros allow to push code into a new operator, where it is defined once (e.g. in a DBMS class library) and available for general use in SQL. Hence only a single definition has to be maintained. This eases the task of the application programmer, makes it less error-prone, improves the declarative character of SQL DML commands and enhances the readability. Moreover, SQL macros can always be completely integrated into the query execution plans of SQL statements by macro expansion. As a consequence, the usual parallelization techniques can be used.

The concept of procedural UDTOs is much more powerful, because one can execute a query on the input tables and use a procedural language like SQL PSM to implement complex code. This is especially of interest in combination with an API that is provided for the development of DBMS class libraries by some ORDBMS ([19], [20]). This offers the possibility to implement new algorithms like join algorithms, for example. Moreover, our approach supports data parallelism for these new database operators. Besides being able to define parallel processing schemes by specifying allowed partitioning functions, the possibility to use SQL goes a long way towards enabling as much parallelism as possible, since all embedded SQL statements can be processed automatically in parallel. An additional advantage of our SQL-based approach to the implementation of UDTOs is that query optimization can be fully exploited.

Areas of future work are optimization issues for UDTOs and case studies for their application in other scenarios: promising areas of interest are OLAP, data mining, image analysis, time series processing, genome analysis, or querying XML, for example. Moreover, if several SQL statements are used in the body of the UDTO, multi-query optimization techniques could be beneficial. First results can be found in [24].

Currently, an implementation of UDTOs in MIDAS [5], a prototype of a parallel ORDBMS, is under way. The core extensions have been completed and in a future paper [23] we will report on this effort and describe implementation concepts for UDTOs. As we have mentioned, first measurements demonstrated performance improvements of orders of magnitude by means of UDTOs.

Acknowledgments

We gratefully acknowledge the help of our master student Sebastian Heupel with the implementation and his comments on the draft of this paper which helped us to improve the presentation. We also acknowledge the cooperation with the complete MIDAS team and the valuable comments from the referees.

7. References

[1] Antoshenkov, G., Ziauddin, G.: Query Processing and Optimization in Oracle Rdb. VLDB Journal 5(4): 229-237 (1996).

[2] Bancilhon, F., Buneman, P. (Eds.): Advances in Database

Programming Languages. ACM Press / Addison-Wesley 1990, ISBN 0-201-50257-7, Papers from DBPL-1, September 1987, Roscoff, France.

[3] Beech, D.: Position Paper on Query Languages for the Web, Oracle Corp., http://www.xml.com/xml/pub/Guide/Query_Languages.

[4] Bosworth, A. et al.: Microsoft's Query Language 98 Position Paper, Microsoft Corp., http://www.xml.com/xml/pub/Guide/Query_Languages.

[5] Bozas, G., Jaedicke, M., Listl, A., Mitschang, B., Reiser, A., Zimmermann, S.: On Transforming a Sequential SQL-DBMS into a Parallel One: First Results and Experiences of the MIDAS-Project, Proc. of 2nd Int. Euro-Par Conf., LNCS 1123, Springer, 1996.

[6] Carey, M. J., DeWitt, D.J., Graefe, G., Haight, D. M., Richardson, J. E., Schuh, D. T., Shekita, E. J., Vandenberg, S. L.: The EXODUS Extensible DBMS Project: An Overview, in: Zdonik, S., Maier, D. (eds.): Readings in Object-Oriented Databases, Morgan-Kaufmann, 1990.

[7] Carey, M. J., Mattos, N., Nori, A.: Object-Relational Database Systems: Principles, Products, and Challenges (Tutorial). SIGMOD 1997: 502.

[8] Chamberlin, D.: A Complete Guide to DB2 Universal Database, Morgan Kaufman Publishers, San Francisco, 1998.

[9] Chaudhuri, S., Shim, K.: Optimization of Queries with User-defined Predicates. VLDB 1996: 87-98.

[10] Deßloch, S., Mattos, N.: Integrating SQL Databases with Content-Specific Search Engines. VLDB 1997: 528-537.

[11] DeWitt, D., Gray, J.: Parallel Database Systems: The Future of High Performance Database Systems, In: CACM, Vol.35, No.6, 85-98, 1992.

[12] Graefe, G.: Query Evaluation Techniques for Large Databases. Computing Surveys 25(2): 73-170 (1993).

[13] Graefe, G.: The Cascades Framework for Query Optimization. Data Engineering Bulletin 18(3): 19-29 (1995).

[14] Güting, R. H.: Second-Order Signature: A Tool for Specifying Data Models, Query Processing, and Optimization, SIGMOD Conference 1993: 277-286.

[15] Haas, L. M., Freytag, J.C., Lohman, G. M. , Pirahesh, H.: Extensible Query Processing in Starburst. SIGMOD 1989: 377-388.

[16] Hellerstein, J. M., Stonebraker, M.: Predicate Migration: Optimizing Queries with Expensive Predicates. SIGMOD 1993: 267-276.

[17] Hellerstein, J. M., Naughton, J. F.: Query Execution Techniques for Caching Expensive Methods. SIGMOD 1996: 423-434.

[18] IBM DB2 Universal Database SQL Reference Version 5, Document Number S10J-8165-00, 1997: 441-453.

[19] Illustra User's Guide, Illustra Information Technologies, Inc., 1995.

[20] Informix Universal Server, DataBlade API Programmer's Manual Vers. 9.12, Informix Software Inc., 1997.

[21] Jaedicke, M., Mitschang, B.: On Parallel Processing of Aggregate and Scalar Functions in Object-Relational DBMS, SIGMOD 1998: 379-389.

[22] Jaedicke, M., Mitschang, B.: The Multi-Operator Method for the Efficient Parallel Evaluation of Complex User-Defined Predicates, Technical Report, to appear 1999.

[23] Jaedicke, M., Zimmermann, S., Nippl, C., Mitschang, B.: The Implementation of User-Defined Table Operators in MIDAS, (submitted) 1999.

[24] Jaedicke, M.: New Concepts for Parallel Object-Relational Query Processing, Ph.D. Thesis, University of Stuttgart, 1999.

[25] Lohman, G. M.: Grammar-like Functional Rules for Representing Query Optimization Alternatives. SIGMOD 1988: 18-27.

[26] Mattos, N., Deßloch, S., DeMichiel, L., Carey, M.: Object-Relational DB2, IBM White Paper, July 1996.

[27] Mitschang, B., Pirahesh, H., Pistor, P., Lindsay, B. G., Südkamp, N.: SQL/XNF - Processing Composite Objects as Abstractions over Relational Data. ICDE 1993: 272-282

[28] O'Connell, W., Ieong, I.T., Schrader, D., Watson, C., Au, G., Biliris, A., Choo, S., Colin, P., Linderman, G., Panagos, E., Wang, J., Walters, T.: Prospector: A Content-Based Multimedia Server for Massively Parallel Architectures. SIGMOD 1996: 68-78.

[29] Olson, M. A., Hong, W. M., Ubell, M., Stonebraker, M.: Query Processing in a Parallel Object-Relational Database System, Data Engineering Bulletin, 12/1996.

[30] Orenstein, J. A.: A Comparison of Spatial Query Processing Techniques for Native and Parameter Spaces. SIGMOD Conf. 1990: 343-352.

[31] Patel, J. M., DeWitt, D. J.: Partition Based Spatial-Merge Join. SIGMOD Conf. 1996: 259-270.

[32] Patel, J., Yu, J. Kabra, N., Tufte, K., Nag, B., Burger, J., Hall, N., Ramasamy, K., Lueder, R., Ellman, C., Kupsch, J., Guo, S., DeWitt, D. J., Naughton, J.: Building A Scalable GeoSpatial Database System: Technology, Implementation, and Evaluation, SIGMOD 1997: 336-347.

[33] Pirahesh, H., Mitschang, B. Südkamp, N., Lindsay, B. G.: Composite-Object Views in Relational DBMS: An Implementation Perspective. EDBT 1994: 23-30.

[34] Seshadri, P., Livny, M., Ramakrishnan, R.: The Case for Enhanced Abstract Data Types. VLDB 1997: 66-75.

[35] Stonebraker, M.: Inclusion of New Types in Relational Data Base Systems. ICDE 1986: 262-269.

[36] Stonebraker, M., Brown, P., Moore, D.: Object-Relational DBMSs, Second Edition, Morgan Kaufmann Publishers, 1998.

[37] Stonebraker, M.: Implementation of Integrity Constraints and Views by Query Modification. SIGMOD Conf. 1975: 65-78.

Optimal Grid-Clustering: Towards Breaking the Curse of Dimensionality in High-Dimensional Clustering

Alexander Hinneburg
hinneburg@informatik.uni-halle.de

Daniel A. Keim
keim@informatik.uni-halle.de

Institute of Computer Science, University of Halle
Kurt-Mothes-Str.1, 06120 Halle (Saale), Germany

Abstract

Many applications require the clustering of large amounts of high-dimensional data. Most clustering algorithms, however, do not work effectively and efficiently in high-dimensional space, which is due to the so-called "curse of dimensionality". In addition, the high-dimensional data often contains a significant amount of noise which causes additional effectiveness problems. In this paper, we review and compare the existing algorithms for clustering high-dimensional data and show the impact of the curse of dimensionality on their effectiveness and efficiency. The comparison reveals that condensation-based approaches (such as BIRCH or STING) are the most promising candidates for achieving the necessary efficiency, but it also shows that basically all condensation-based approaches have severe weaknesses with respect to their effectiveness in high-dimensional space. To overcome these problems, we develop a new clustering technique called *OptiGrid* which is based on constructing an optimal grid-partitioning of the data. The optimal grid-partitioning is determined by calculating the best partitioning hyperplanes for each dimension (if such a partitioning exists) using certain projections of the data. The advantages of our new approach are (1) it has a firm mathematical basis (2) it is by far more effective than existing clustering algorithms for high-dimensional data (3) it is very efficient even for large data sets of high dimensionality. To demonstrate the effectiveness and efficiency of our new approach, we perform a series of experiments on a number of different data sets including real data sets from CAD and molecular biology. A comparison with one of the best known algorithms (BIRCH) shows the superiority of our new approach.

Proceedings of the 25th VLDB Conference, Edinburgh, Scotland, 1999.

1 Introduction

Because of the fast technological progress, the amount of data which is stored in databases increases very fast. This is true for traditional relational databases but also for databases of complex 2D and 3D multimedia data such as image, CAD, geographic, and molecular biology data. It is obvious that relational databases can be seen as high-dimensional databases (the attributes correspond to the dimensions of the data set), but it is also true for multimedia data which - for an efficient retrieval - is usually transformed into high-dimensional feature vectors such as color histograms [SH94], shape descriptors [Jag91, MG95], Fourier vectors [WW80], and text descriptors [Kuk92]. In many of the mentioned applications, the databases are very large and consist of millions of data objects with several tens to a few hundreds of dimensions.

Automated clustering in high-dimensional databases is an important problem and there are a number of different clustering algorithms which are applicable to high-dimensional data. The most prominent representatives are partitioning algorithms such as CLARANS [NH94], hierarchical clustering algorithms, and locality-based clustering algorithms such as (G)DBSCAN [EKSX96, EKSX97] and DB-CLASD [XEKS98]. The basic idea of *partitioning algorithms* is to construct a partition of the database into k clusters which are represented by the gravity of the cluster (k-means) or by one representative object of the cluster (k-medoid). Each object is assigned to the closest cluster. A well-known partitioning algorithm is CLARANS which uses a randomised and bounded search strategy to improve the performance. *Hierarchical clustering algorithms* decompose the database into several levels of partitionings which are usually represented by a dendrogram - a tree which splits the database recursively into smaller subsets. The dendrogram can be created top-down (divisive) or bottom-up (agglomerative). Although hierarchical clustering algorithms can be very effective in knowledge discovery, the costs of creating the dendrograms is prohibitively expensive for large data sets since the algorithms are usually at least quadratic in the number of data objects. More efficient are ***locality-based clustering algorithms*** since they usually group neighboring data elements into clusters based on local conditions and therefore allow the clustering to be performed in one scan of the database. DBSCAN, for example, uses a density-based notion of clusters and allows the discovery of arbitrarily shaped clusters. The basic idea is that for each point of a cluster the density of data points in the neighborhood has to exceed some threshold. DBCLASD also works locality-based but in contrast to DBSCAN assumes that the points inside of the clusters are randomly distributed, allowing DBCLASD to work without any input parameters.

A problem is that most approaches are not designed for a clustering of high-dimensional data and therefore, the performance of existing algorithms degenerates rapidly with increasing dimension. To improve the efficiency, optimised clustering techniques have been proposed. Examples include Grid-based clustering [Sch96], BIRCH [ZRL96] which is based on the Cluster-Feature-tree, STING which uses a quadtree-like structure containing additional statistical information [WYM97], and DENCLUE which uses a regular grid to improve the efficiency [HK98]. Unfortunately, the curse of dimensionality also has a severe impact on the effectiveness of the resulting clustering. So far, this effect has not been examined thoroughly for high-dimensional data but a detailed comparison shows severe problems in effectiveness (cf. section 2), especially in the presence of noise. In our comparison, we analyse the impact of the dimensionality on the effectiveness and efficiency of a number of well-known and competitive clustering algorithms. We show that they either suffer from a severe breakdown in efficiency which is at least true for all index-based methods or have severe effectiveness problems which is basically true for all other methods. The experiments show that even for simple data sets (e.g. a data set with two clusters given as normal distributions and a little bit of noise) basically none of the fast algorithms guarantees to find the correct clustering.

From our analysis, it gets clear that only condensation-based approaches (such as BIRCH or DENCLUE) can provide the necessary efficiency for clustering large data sets. To better understand the severe effectiveness problems of the existing approaches, we examine the impact of high dimensionality on condensation-based approaches, especially grid-based approaches (cf. section 3). The discussion in section 3 reveals the source of the problems, namely the inadequate partitioning of the data in the clustering process. In our new approach, we therefore try to find a better partitioning of the data. The basic idea of our new approach presented in section 4 is to use contracting projections of the data to determine the optimal cutting (hyper-)planes for partitioning the data. If no good partitioning plane exist in some dimensions, we do not partition the data set in those dimensions. Our strategy of using a data-dependent partitioning of the data avoids the effectiveness problems of the existing approaches and guarantees that all clusters are found by the algorithm (even for high noise levels), while still retaining the efficiency of a grid-based approach. By using the highly-populated grid cells based on the optimal partitioning of the data, we are able to efficiently determine the clusters. A detailed evaluation 5 shows the advantages of our approach. We show theoretically that our approach guarantees to find all center-defined clusters (which roughly spoken correspond to clusters generated by a normal distribution). We confirm the effectiveness lemma by an extensive experimental evaluation on a wide range of synthetic and real data sets, showing the superior effectiveness of our new approach. In addition to the effectiveness, we also examine the efficiency, showing that our approach is competitive with the fastest existing algorithms (BIRCH) and (in some cases) even outperforms BIRCH by up to a factor of about 2.

2 Clustering of High-Dimensional Data

In this section, we discuss and compare the most efficient and effective available clustering algorithms and examine their potential for clustering large high-dimensional data sets. We show the impact of the curseof dimensionality and reveal severe efficiency and effectiveness problems of the existing approaches.

2.1 Related Approaches

The most efficient clustering algorithms for low-dimensional data are based on some type of hierarchical data structure. The data structures are either based on a hierarchical partitioning of the data or a hierarchical partitioning of the space.

All techniques which are based on partitioning the data such as R-trees do not work efficiently due to the performance degeneration of R-tree-based index structures in high-dimensional space. This is true for algorithms such as DBSCAN [EKSX96] which has an almost quadratic time complexity for high-dimensional data if the R*-tree-based implementation is used. Even if a special indexing techniques for high-dimensional data is used, all approaches which determine the clustering based on near(est) neighbor information do not work *effectively* since the near(est) neighbors do not contain sufficient information about the density of the data in high-dimensional space (cf. section 3.2), which means that algorithms such as the k-means or DBSCAN algorithm do not work effectively on high-dimensional data.

A more efficient approach is BIRCH (Balanced Iterative Reducing and Clustering using Hierarchies) which uses a data partitioning according to the expected cluster structure of the data [ZRL96]. BIRCH uses a hierarchical data structure called CF-tree (Cluster Feature Tree) which is a balanced tree for storing the clustering features. BIRCH tries to build the best possible clustering using the given limited (memory) resources. The idea of BIRCH is store similar data items in the node of the CF-tree and if the algorithm runs short of main memory, similar data items in the nodes of the CF-tree are condensed. BIRCH uses several heuristics to find the clusters and to distinguish the clusters from noise. Due to the specific notion of similarity used to determine the data items to be condensed BIRCH is only able to find spherical clusters. Still, BIRCH is one of the most efficient algorithms and needs only one scan of the the database (time complexity $O(n)$), which is also true for high-dimensional data.

On low-dimensional data, space partitioning methods which in general use a grid-based approach such as STING (STatistical INformation Grid) [WYM97] and WaveCluster [SCZ98] are of similar efficiency (the time complexity is $O(n)$), but better effectiveness than BIRCH (especially for noisy data and arbitrary-shape clusters) [SCZ98]. The basic idea of STING is to divide the data space into rectangular cells and store statistical parameters (such as mean, variance, etc.) of the objects in the cells. This information can then be used to efficiently determine the clusters. WaveCluster[SCZ98] is a wavelet-based approach which also uses a regular grid for an efficient clustering. The basic idea is map the data onto a multi-dimensional grid, apply a wavelet transformation to the grid cells, and then determine dense regions in the transformed domain by searching for connected components. The advantage of using the wavelet transformation is that it automatically provides a multiresolutions representation of the data grid which allows an efficient determination of the clusters. Both, STING and WaveCluster have only been designed for low-dimensional data. There is no straight-forward extention to the high-dimensional case. In WaveCluster, for example, the number of grid cells grows exponentially in the number of dimensions (d) and determining the connected components becomes prohibitively expensive due to the large number of neighboring cells. An approach which works better for the high-dimensional case is the DENCLUE approach [HK98]. The basic idea is to model the overall point density analytically as the sum of influence functions of the data points. Clusters can then be identified by determining density-attractors and clusters of arbitrary shape can be easily described by a simple equation based on the overall density function. DENCLUE has been shown to be a generalization of a number of other clustering algorithm such as k-means and DBSCAN [HK99], and it also generalizes the STING and WaveCluster approaches. To work efficiently on high-dimensional data, DENCLUE uses a grid-based approach but only stores the grid-cells which contain data points. For an efficient clustering, DENCLUE connects all neighboring populated grid cells of a highly-populated grid cell.

2.2 Comparing the Effectiveness

Unfortunately, for high-dimensional data none of the approaches discussed so far is fully effective. In the following preliminary experimental evaluation, we briefly show that none of the existing approaches is able to find all clusters on high-dimensional data. In the experimental comparison, we restrict ourselves to the most efficient and effective algorithms which all use some kind of aggregated (or condensed) information being stored in either a cluster-tree (in case of BIRCH) or a grid (in case of STING, WaveCluster, and DENCLUE). Since all of them have in common that they condense the available information in one way or the other, in the following we call them condensation-based approaches.

For the comparison with respect to high-dimensional data, it is sufficient to focus on BIRCH and DENCLUE since DENCLUE generalizes STING and WaveCluster and is directly applicable to high-dimensional data. Both DENCLUE and BIRCH have a similar time complexity, in this preliminary comparison we focus on their effectiveness (for a detailed comparison, the reader is referred to section 5). To show the effectiveness problems of the existing approaches on high-dimensional data, we use synthetic data sets consisting of a number of clusters defined by a normal distribution with the centers being randomly placed in the data space.

In the first experiment (cf. Figure 1), we analyse the percentage of clusters depending on the percentage of noise in the data set. Since at this point, we are mainly interested in getting more insight into the problems of clustering high-dimensional data, a sufficient measure of the effectiveness is the percentage of correctly found clusters. Note that BIRCH is very sensitive to noise for higher dimensions for the realistic situation that the data is read in a random order. If however the data points belonging to clusters are known a-priori (which is not a realistic assumption), the cluster points can be read first and in this case, BIRCH provides a much better effectiveness since the CF-tree does not degenerate as much. If the clusters are inserted first, BIRCH provides about the same effectiveness as grid-based approaches such as DENCLUE. The curves show how critical the dependency on the insertion order becomes for higher dimensional data. Grid-based approaches are in general not sensitive to the insertion order.

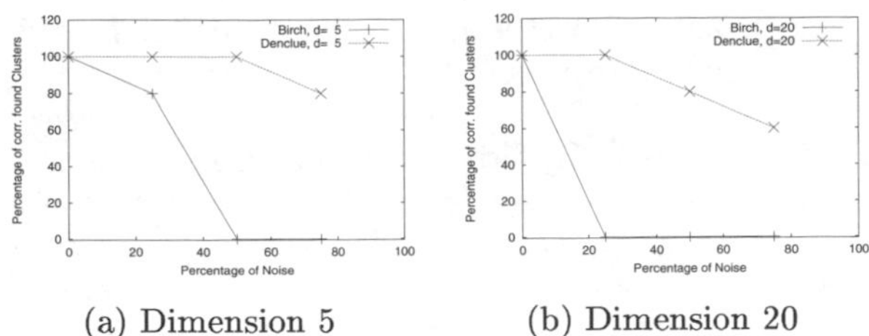

(a) Dimension 5 (b) Dimension 20

Figure 1:
Comparison of DENCLUE and Birch on noisy data

The second experiment shows the average percentage of clusters found for 30 data sets with different positions of the clusters. Figure 2 clearly shows that for high dimensional data, even grid-based approaches such as DENCLUE are not able to detect a significant percentage of the clusters, which means that even DENCLUE does not work fully effective. In the next section, we try to provide a deeper understanding of these effects and discuss the reasons for the effectiveness problems.

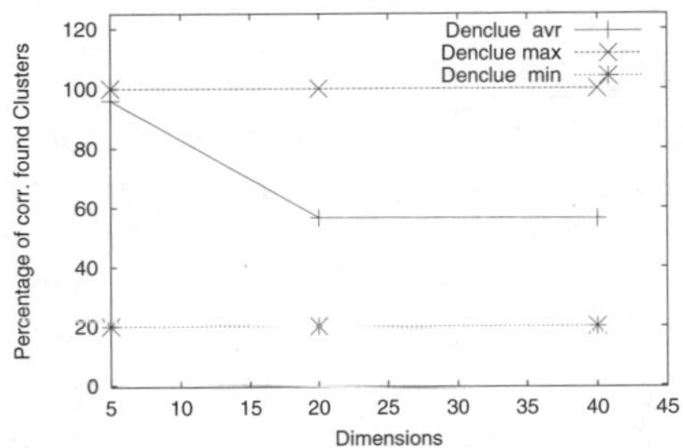

Figure 2: Effects of grid based Clustering (DENCLUE)

2.3 Discovering Noise in High-Dimensional Data

Noise is one of the fundamental problems in clustering large data sets. In high-dimensional data sets, the problem becomes even more severe. In this subsection, we therefore discuss the general problem of noise in high-dimensional data sets and show that it is impossible to determine clusters in data sets with noise correctly in linear time (in the high-dimensional case).

Lemma 1 (Complexity of Clustering)
The worst case time complexity for a correct clustering of high-dimensional data with noise is superlinear.

Idea of the Proof:
Without loss of generality, we assume that we have $O(n)$ noise in the database (e.g., 10% noise). In the worst case, we read all the noise in the beginning which means that we can not obtain any clustering in reading that data. However, it is also impossible to tell that the data we have already read does not belong to a cluster. Therefore, in reading the remaining points we have to search for similar points among those noise points. The search for similar points among the noise points can not be done in constant time ($O(1)$) since we have $O(n)$ noise points and in high-dimensional space, an $O(1)$ access to similar data in the worst case (based on techniques such as hashing or histograms) is not possible even for random noise (cf. section 3 for more details on this fact). The overall time complexity is therefore superlinear. □

The lemma implies that the clustering of data in high-dimensional data sets with noise is an inherently non-linear problem. Therefore, any algorithm with linear time complexity such as BIRCH can not cluster noisy data correctly. Before we introduce our algorithm, in the following we provide more insight into the effects and problems of high-dimensional clustering.

3 Grid-based Clustering of High-dimensional Spaces

In the previous section, we have shown that grid-based approaches perform well with respect to efficiency and effectiveness. In this section, we discuss the impact of the "curse of dimensionality" on grid-based clustering in more detail. After some basic considerations defining clustering and a very general notion of multidimensional grids, we discuss the effects of different high-dimensional data distributions and the resulting problems in clustering the data.

3.1 Basic Considerations

We start with a well known and widely accepted definition of clustering (cf. [HK98]). For the definition, we need a density function which is determined based on kernel density estimation.

Definition 2 (Density Function)
Let D be a set of n d-dimensional points and h be the smoothness level. Then, the **density function** $\hat{f^D}$ *based on the kernel density estimator K is defined as:*

$$\hat{f^D}(x) = \frac{1}{nh} \sum_{i=1}^{n} K\left(\frac{x - x_i}{h}\right)$$

Kernel density estimation provides a powerful framework for finding clusters in large data sets. In the statistics literature, various kernels K have been proposed. Examples are square wave functions or Gaussian functions. A detailed introduction into kernel density estimation is beyond the scope of this paper and can be found in [Sil86],[Sco92]. According to [HK98], clusters can now be defined as the maxima of the density function, which are above a certain noise level ξ.

Definition 3 (Center-Defined Cluster)
A center-defined cluster for a maximum x^* of the density function $\hat{f}^D$ is the subset $C \subseteq D$, with $x \in C$ being density-attracted by x^* and $\hat{f}^D(x^*) \geq \xi$. Points

$x \in D$ are called outliers if they are density-attracted by a local maximum x_o^* with $\hat{f}^D(x_o^*) < \xi$.

According to this definition, each local maximum of the density function which is above the noise level ξ becomes a cluster of its own and consists of all points which are density-attracted by the maximum. The notion of *density-attraction* is defined by the gradient of the density function. The definition can be extended to clusters which are defined by multiple maxima and can approximate arbitrarily-shaped clusters.

Definition 4 (Multicenter-Defined Cluster)
A multicenter-defined cluster for a set of maxima X is the subset $C \subseteq D$, where

1. *$\forall x \in C\ \exists x^* \in X : f_B^D(x^*) \geq \xi$, x is density-attracted to x^* and*

2. *$\forall x_1^*, x_2^* \in X : \exists$ a path $P \subset F^d$ from x_1^* to x_2^* above noise level ξ.*

As already shown in the previous section, grid-based approaches provide an efficient way to determine the clusters. In grid-based approaches, all data points which fall into the same grid cell are aggregated and treated as one object. In the low-dimensional case, the grid can be easily stored as an array which allows a very efficient access time of $O(1)$. In case of a high-dimensional grid, the number of grid cells grows exponentially in the number of dimensions d which makes it impossible to store the grid as a multi-dimensional array. Since the number of data points does not grow exponentially, most the grid cells are empty and do not need to be stored explicitly, but it is sufficient to store the populated cells. The number of populated cells is bounded by the number of non-identical data points.

Since we are interested in arbitrary (non-equidistant, irregular) grids, we need the notion of a cutting plane which is a (d-1)-dimensional hyperplane cutting the data space into the grid cells.

Definition 5 (Cutting Plane)
A **cutting plane** *is a $(d-1)$-dimensional hyperplane consisting of all points y which fulfil the equation $\sum_{i=1}^{d} w_i y_i = 1$. The cutting plane partitions $\mathbb{R}^d$ into two half spaces. The decision function $H(x)$ determines the half space, where a point $x \in \mathbb{R}$ is located:*

$$H(x) = \begin{cases} 1 & , \sum_{i=1}^{d} w_i x_i \geq 1 \\ 0 & , else \end{cases}$$

Now, we are able to define a general notion of arbitrary (non-equidistant, irregular) grids. Since the grid can not be stored explicitly in high-dimensional space, we need a coding function c which assigns a label to all points belonging to the same grid cell. The data space S as well as the grid cells are defined as right semi-opened intervals.

Definition 6 (Multidimensional Grid)
A **multidimensional grid** *G for the data space S is defined by a set $H = \{H_1, \ldots, H_k\}$ of $(d-1)$-dimensional cutting planes. The coding function $c^G : S \longrightarrow \mathbb{N}$ is defined as follows:*

$$x \in S,\ c(x) = \sum_{i=1}^{k} 2^i \cdot H_i(x).$$

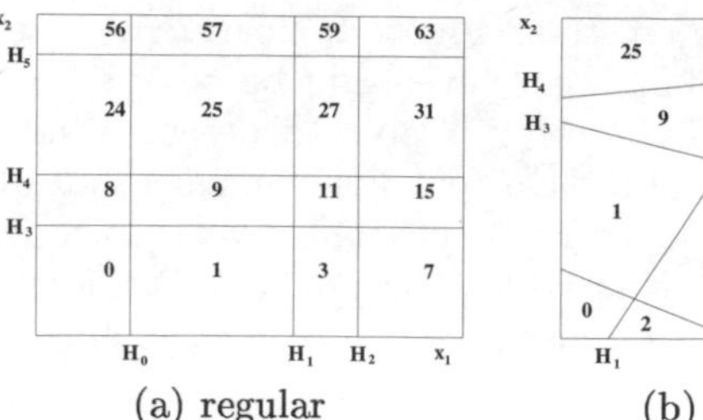

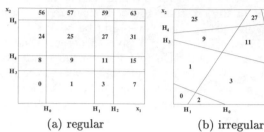

(a) regular (b) irregular

Figure 3: Examples of 2-dimensional Grids

Figure 3 shows two examples of two-dimensional grids. The grid in figure 3a shows a non-equidistant regular (axes-parallel cutting planes) grid and 3b shows a non-equidistant irregular (arbitrary cutting planes) grid. The grid cells are labeled with value determined by the coding function according to definition 6. In general, the complexity of the coding function is $O(k \cdot d)$. In case of a grid based on axes parallel hyperplanes, the complexity of the coding function becomes $O(k)$.

3.2 Effects of Different Data Distributions

In this section, we discuss the properties of different data distributions for an increasing number of dimensions. Let us first consider uniformly distributed data. It is well-known, that uniform distributions are very unlikely in high-dimensional space. From a statistical point of view, it is even impossible to determine a uniform distribution in high-dimensional space a-posteriori. The reason is that there is no possibility to have enough data points to verify the data distribution by a statistical test with sufficient significance. Assume we want to characterize the distribution of a 50-dimensional data space by an grid-based histogram and we split each dimension only once at the center. The resulting space is cut into $2^{50} \sim 10^{14}$ cells. If we generate one billion data points by a uniform random data generator, we get about 10^{12} cells filled with one data point which is about one percent of the cells. Since the grid is based on a very coarse partitioning (one cutting plane per dimension), it is impossible to determine a data distribution based on one percent of the cells. The available information could justify a number of different distributions including a uniform distribution. Statistically, the number of data points is not high enough to determine the distribution of the data. The problem is that the number of data points can not grow exponentially with the dimension, and therefore, in high-dimensional space it is generally impossible to determine the distribution of the data with sufficient statistical significance. (The only thing which can be verified easily is that the projections onto the dimensions follow a uniform distribution.) As a result of the sparsely filled space, it is very unlikely that data points are nearer to each other than the average distance between data points, and as a consequence, the difference between the distance to the nearest and the farthest neighbor of a data point goes to zero in high-dimensional space (see [BGRS99] for a recent theoretical proof of this fact).

Now let us look at normally distributed data. A normal distribution is characterized by the center point (expected value) and the standard deviation (σ). The distance of the data points to the expected point follows a Gaussian curve but the direction from the expected point is randomly chosen without any preference. An important observation is that the number of possible directions from a point grows exponentially in the number of dimensions. As a result, the distance among the normally distributed data points increases with the number of dimensions although the distance to the center point still follows the same distribution. If we consider the density function of the data set, we find that it has a maximum at the center point although there may be no data points very close to the center point. This results from the fact that it is likely that the data points slightly vary in the value for one dimension but still the single point densities add up to the maximal density at the center point. The effect that in high dimensional spaces the point density can be high in empty areas is called the *empty space phenomenon* [Sco92].

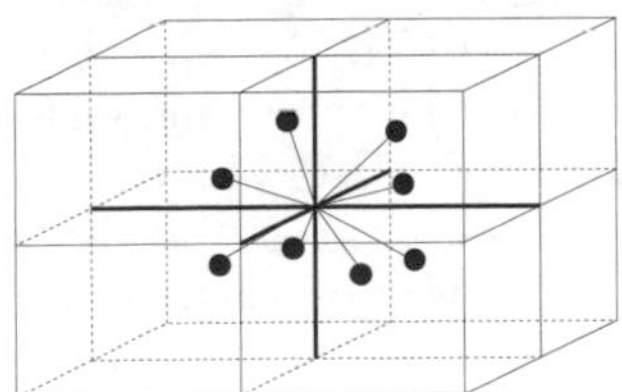

Figure 4:
Example Scenario for a Normal Distribution, $d = 3$

To illustrate this effect, let us consider normally distributed data points in $[0, 1]^d$ with $(0.5, \ldots, 0.5)$ as center point and a grid based on splitting at 0.5 in each dimension. The number of directions from the center point now directly corresponds to the number of grid cells which is exponential in d (2^d). As a consequence, most data points will fall into separate grid cells (Figure 4 shows an example scenario for $d = 3$). In high dimensions, it is unlikely that there are any points in the center and that populated cell are adjacent to each other on a high-dimensional hyperplane which is again an explanation of the high inter-point distances.

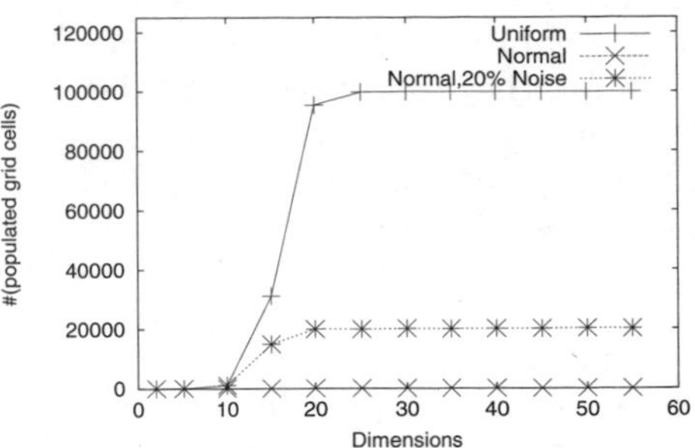

Figure 5:
#(Populated Grid Cells) for Different Data Distributions

To show the effects of high-dimensional spaces on grid-based clustering approaches, we performed some interesting experiments based on using a simple grid and counting the number of populated grid cells containing different numbers of points. The resulting figures show the effects of different data distributions and allow interesting comparisons of the distributions. Figure 5 shows the total number of populated cells (containing at least one data point) depending on the dimensionality. In the experiments, we used three data sets consisting of 100000 data points generated by a uniform distribution (since it is impossible to generate uniform distributions in high-dimensional space we use a uniformly generated distribution of which the projections are at least uniformly distributed), a normal distribution containing 5 clusters with $\sigma = 0.1$ and centers uniformly distributed in $[0, 1)^d$ and a combination of both (20% of the data is uniformly distributed). Based on the considerations discussed above, it is clear that for the uniformly distributed data as many cells as possible are populated which is the number of available cells (for $d \leq 20$) and the number of data points (for $d \geq 25$). For normally distributed data, the number of populated data points is always lower but still increases for higher dimensions due to the many directions the points may vary from the center point (which can not be seen in the figure). The third data set is a combination of the other two distributions and converges against the percentage of uniformly distributed data points (20000 data points in the example).

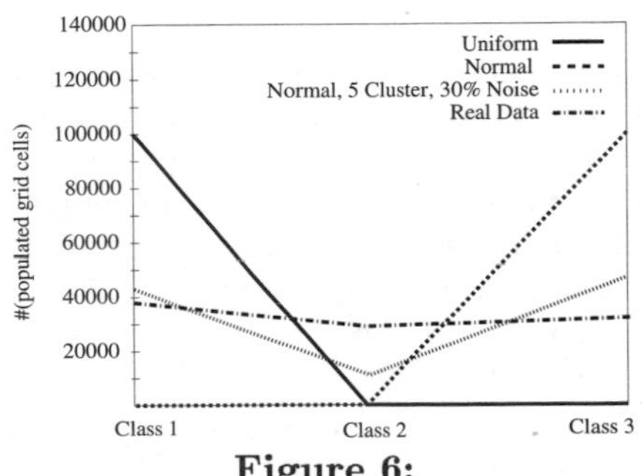

Figure 6:
#(Populated Grid Cells) for Molecular Biology Data

It is now interesting to use the same approach for a better understanding of real data sets. It can be used to analyse and classify real data sets by assessing how clustered the data is and how much noise it contains. Figure 6 shows the results for a real data set from a molecular biology application. The data consists of about 100000 19-dimensional feature vectors describing peptides in a dihedral angle space. In figure 6, we show the number of data points which fall into three different classes of grid cells. Class one accounts for all data points which fall into grid cells containing a small number of data points (less than 2^4), class two those which contain a medium number of data points (between 2^4 and 2^8 data points), and class three those which contain a large number of data points (more than 2^8 data points). We show the resulting curves for uniformly distributed data, normally distributed data, a combination of both, and the peptide data. Figure 6 clearly shows that the peptide data corresponds neither to uniformly nor to normally distributed data, but can be approximated most closely by a combination of both (with about 40% of noise). Figure 6 clearly shows that the peptide data sets contains a significant portion of noise (corresponding to a uniform distribution) but also contains clear clusters (corresponding to the normal distribution). Since real data sets may contain additional structure such as dependencies between dimensions or extended clusters of arbitrary shape, the classification based on counting the grid cells of the different population levels can not be used to detect all properties of the data and completely classify real data sets. However, as shown in Figure 6 thc approach is powerful and allows to provide interesting insights into the properties of the data (e.g., percentage of noise and clusters). In examining other real data sets, we found that real high-dimensional data is usually highly clustered but mostly also contains a significant amount of noise.

3.3 Problems of Grid-based Clustering

A general problem of clustering in high-dimensional spaces arises from the fact that the cluster centers can not be as easily identified (by a large number of almost identical data points) as in lower dimensional cases. In grid-based approaches it is possible that clusters are split by some of the (d-1) dimensional cutting planes and the data points of the cluster are spread over many grid cells. Let us use a simple example to exemplify this situation. For simplification, we use a grid where each dimension is split only once. In general, such a grid is defined by d '$(d-1)$-dimensional hyperplanes which cut the space into 2^d cells. All cutting planes are parallel to $(d-1)$ coordinate axes. By cutting the space into cells, the naturally neighborhood between the data points gets lost. A worst case scenario could be the following case. Assume the data points are in $[0,1]^d$ and each dimension is split at 0.5. The data points lie on a hyper sphere with small radius $\epsilon > 0$ round the split point $(0.5, 0.5, \ldots, 0.5)$. For $d > 20$, most of the points would be in separate grid cells despite the fact that they form a cluster. Note that there are 2^d cells adjacent to the split point. Figure 4 tries to show this situation of a worst case scenario for a three-dimensional data set. In high-dimensional data, this situation is likely to occur and this is the reason for the effectiveness problems of DENCLUE (cf. Figure 2).

An approach to handle the effect is to connect adjacent grid cells and treat the connected cells as one object. A naive approach is to test all possible neighboring cells of a populated cell whether they are also populated. This approach however is prohibitively expensive in high-dimensional spaces because of the exponential number of adjacent neighbor grid cells. If a grid with only one split per dimension is used, all grid cells are adjacent to each other and the number of connections becomes quadratic in the number of grid cells, even if only the $O(n)$ populated grid cells are considered. In case of finer grids, the number of neighboring cells which have to be connected decreases but at the same time, the probability that cutting planes hit cluster centers increases. As a consequence, any approach which considers the connections for handling the effect of splitted clusters will not work efficiently on large databases, and therefore another solution guaranteeing the effectiveness while preserving the efficiency is necessary for an effective clustering of high-dimensional data.

4 Efficient and Effective Clustering in High-dimensional Spaces

In this section, we propose a new approach to high-dimensional clustering which is efficient as well as effective and combines the advantages of previous approaches (e.g, BIRCH, WaveCluster, STING, and DENCLUE) with a guaranteed high effectiveness even for large amounts of noise. In the last section, we discussed some disadvantages of grid-based clustering, which are mainly caused by cutting planes which partition clusters into a number of grid cells. Our new algorithm avoids this problem by determining cutting planes which do not partition clusters.

There are two desirable properties for good cutting planes: First, cutting planes should partition the data set in a region of low density (the density should be at least low relative to the surrounding region) and second, a cutting plane should discriminate clusters as much as possible. The first constraint guarantees that a cutting plane does not split a cluster, and the second constraint makes sure that the cutting plane contributed to finding the clusters. Without the second constraint, cutting planes are best placed at the borders of the data space because of the minimal density there, but it is obvious that in that way clusters can not be detected. Our algorithm incorporates both constraints. Before we introduce the algorithm, in the following we first provide some mathematical background on finding regions of low density in the data space which is the basis for our optimal grid partitioning and our algorithm *OptiGrid*.

4.1 Optimal Grid-Partioning

Finding the minima of the density function $\hat{f}^D$ is a difficult problem. For determining the optimal cutting plane, it is sufficient to have information on the density on the cutting plane which has to be relatively low. To efficiently determines such cutting planes, we use contracting projections of the data space.

Definition 7 (Contracting Projection)
A contracting projection for a given d-dimensional data space S and an appropriate metric $\|\cdot\|$ is a linear transformation P defined on all points $x \in S$

$$P(x) = Ax \quad with \quad \|A\| = \max_{y \in S}\left(\frac{\|Ay\|}{\|y\|}\right) \leq 1 .$$

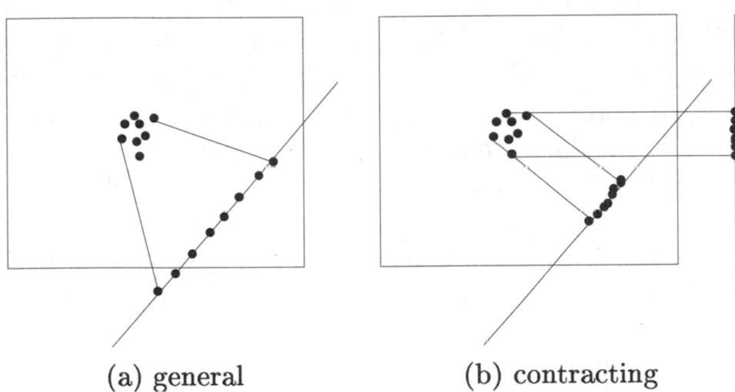

(a) general (b) contracting

Figure 7: General and Contracting Projections

Now we can proof a main lemma for the correctness of our algorithm, which states that the density at a point x' in a contracting projection of the data is an upper bound for the density on the plane, which is orthogonal to the projection plane.

Lemma 8 (Upper Bound Property)
Let $P(x) = Ax$ be a contracting projection, $P(D)$ the projection of the data set D, and $\hat{f}^{P(D)}(x')$ the density for a point $x' \in P(S)$. Then,

$$\forall x \in S \text{ with } P(x) = x' : \hat{f}^{P(D)}(x') \geq \hat{f}^D(x) .$$

Proof: First, we show that the distance between points becomes smaller by the contracting projection P. According to the definition of contracting projections, for all $x, y \in S$:

$$\|P(x) - P(y)\| = \|A(x-y)\| \leq \|A\| \cdot \|x-y\| \leq \|x-y\|$$

The density function which we assume to be kernel based depends monotonically on the distance of the data points. Since the distance between the data points becomes smaller, the density in the data space S grows. □

The assumption that the density is kernel based is not a real restriction. There are a number of proofs in the statistical literature that non-kernel based density estimation methods converge against a kernel based method [Sco92]. Note that Lemma 8 is a generalization of the Monotonicity Lemma in [AGG+98]. Based on the preceeding lemma, we now define an optimal grid-partitioning.

Definition 9 (Optimal Grid-Partioning)
For a given set of projections $P = \{P_0, \ldots, P_k\}$ and a given density estimation model $\hat{f}(x)$, the **optimal l grid partitioning** *is defined by the l best separating cutting planes. The projections of the cutting planes have to separate significant clusters in at least one of the projections of P.*

The term *best separating* heavily depends on the considered application. In section 5 we discuss several alternatives and provide an efficient method for normally distributed data with noise.

4.2 The OptiGrid Algorithm

With this definition of optimal grid-partitioning, we are now able to describe our general algorithm for high-dimensional data sets. The algorithm works recursively. In each step, it partitions the actual data set into a number of subsets if possible. The subsets which contain at least one cluster are treated recursively. The partitioning is done using a multidimensional grid defined by at most q cutting planes. Each cutting plane is orthogonal to at least one projection. The point density at a cutting planes is bound by the density of the orthogonal projection of the cutting plane in the projected space. The q cutting planes are chosen to have a minimal point density. The recursion stops for a subset if no good cutting plane can be found any more. In our implementation this means that the density of all possible cutting planes for the given projections is above a given threshold.

OptiGrid(data set D, q, *min_cut_score*)

1. Determine a set of contracting projections $P = \{P_0, \ldots, P_k\}$
2. Calculate all projections of the data set $D \rightarrow P_0(D), \ldots, P_k(D)$
3. Initialize a list of cutting planes $BEST\_CUT \leftarrow \emptyset$, $CUT \leftarrow \emptyset$
4. FOR i=0 TO k DO
   (a) $CUT \leftarrow$ Determine best_local_cuts($P_i(D)$)
   (b) $CUT\_SCORE \leftarrow$ Score best_local_cuts($P_i(D)$)
   (c) Insert all cutting planes with a score $\geq$ *min_cut_score* into $BEST\_CUT$
5. IF $BEST\_CUT = \emptyset$ THEN RETURN D as a cluster

6. Determine the q cutting planes with highest score from $BEST\_CUT$ and delete the rest
7. Construct a Multidimensional Grid G defined by the cutting planes in $BEST\_CUT$ and insert all data points $x \in D$ into G
8. Determine clusters, i.e. determine the highly populated grid cells in G and add them to the set of cluster C
9. Refine(C)
10. FOREACH Cluster $C_i \in C$ DO OptiGrid(C_i, q, min_cut_score)

In step 4a of the algorithm, we need a function which produces the best local cutting planes for a projection. In our implementation, we determine the best local cutting planes for a projection by searching for the leftmost and rightmost density maximum which are above a certain noise level and for the $q-1$ maxima in between. Then, it determines the points with a minimal density in between the maxima. The position of the minima determines the corresponding cutting plane and the density at that point gives the quality (score) of the cutting plane. The estimation of the noise level can be done by visualizing the density distribution of the projection. Note that the determination of the q best local cutting planes depends on the application. Note that our function for determining the best local cutting planes adheres to the two constrains for cutting planes but additional criteria may be useful.

Our algorithm as described so far is mainly designed to detect center-defined clusters (cf. step 8 of the algorithm). However, it can be easily extended to also detect multicenter-defined clusters according to definition 4. The algorithm just has to evaluate the density between the center-defined clusters determined by OptiGrid and link the clusters if the density is high enough.

The algorithm is based on a set of projections. Any contracting projection may be used. General projections allow for example the detection of linear dependencies between dimensions. In cases of projections $P : \mathbb{R}^d \rightarrow \mathbb{R}^{d'}$, $d' \leq 3$ an extension of the definitions of multidimensional grid and cutting planes is necessary to allow a partitioning of the space by polyhedrons. With such an extension, even quadratic and cubic dependencies which are special kinds of arbitrary shaped clusters may be detected. The projections can be determined using algorithms for principal component analysis, techniques such as FASTMAP [FL95] or projection pursuit [Hub85]. It is also possible to incorporate prior knowledge in that way.

4.3 Complexity

In this section, we provide a detailed complexity analysis and hints for an optimized implementation of the OptiGrid algorithm. For the analysis, we assume that the data set D contain N $d-$dimensional data points. Frist, we analyse the complexity to the main steps. The first step takes only constant time, because we use a fixed set of projections. The number of projections k can be assumed to be in $O(d)$. In the general case, the calculation of all projections of the data set D may take $O(N \cdot d \cdot k)$, but the case of axes parallel projections $P : \mathbb{R}^d \rightarrow \mathbb{R}$ it is $O(N \cdot k)$.

The determination of the best local cutting planes for a projection can be done based on 1-dimensional histograms. The procedure takes time $O(N)$. The whole loop of step 4 runs in $O(N \cdot k)$.

The implemention of the multidimensional grid depends on the number of cutting planes q and the available resources of memory and time. If the possible number of grid cell n^G, i.e $n^G = 2^q$, does not exceed the size of the available memory, the grid can be implemented as an array. The insertion time for all data points is then $O(N \cdot q \cdot d)$. If the number of potential grid cells becomes to large, only the populated grid cells can be stored. Note that this is only the case, if the algorithm has found a high number of meaningful cutting planes and therefore, this case only occurs if the data sets consists of a high number of clusters. In this case, a tree or hash based data structure is required for storing the grid cells. The insertion time then becomes to $O(N \cdot q \cdot d \cdot I)$ where I is the time to insert a data item into the data structure which is bound by $minq, logN$. In case of axes parallel cutting planes, the insertion time is $O(N \cdot q \cdot I)$. The complexity of step 7 dominates to complexity of the recursion.

Note that the number of recusions depends on the data set and can be bounded by the number of clusters $\#C$. Since q is a constant of our algorithm and since the number of clusters is a constant for a given data set, the total complexity is between $O(N \cdot d)$ and $O(d \cdot N \cdot logN)$. In our experimental evaluation (cf. 5), it is shown that the total complexity is slightly superlinear as implied by our complexity lemma 1 in section 2.3.

5 Evaluation

In this section, first we provide a theoretical evaluation of the effectiveness of our approach and then, we demonstrate the efficiency and effectiveness of OptiGrid using a variety of experiments based on synthetic as well as real data sets.

5.1 Theoretical Evaluation of the Effectiveness

A main point in the OptiGrid approach is the choice of the projections. The effectiveness of our approach depends strongly on the set P of projections. In our implementation, we use all projections d $P : \mathbb{R}^d \rightarrow \mathbb{R}$ to the d coordinate axes. The resulting cutting planes are obviously axes parallel.

Let us now examine the discriminative power of axes parallel cutting planes. Assume for that purpose two clusters with same number of points. The data points of both clusters follow an independent normal distribution with standard deviation $\sigma = 1$. The centers of both clusters have a minimal distance of 2σ. The worst case for the discrimination by axes parallel cutting planes is that the cluster centers are on a diagonal of the data space and have minimal distance. Figure 8 shows an example for the 2-dimensional case and the L_1-metric. Under these conditions we can prove that the error of partitioning the two clusters with axes parallel cutting plane is limited by a small constant in high-dimensional spaces.

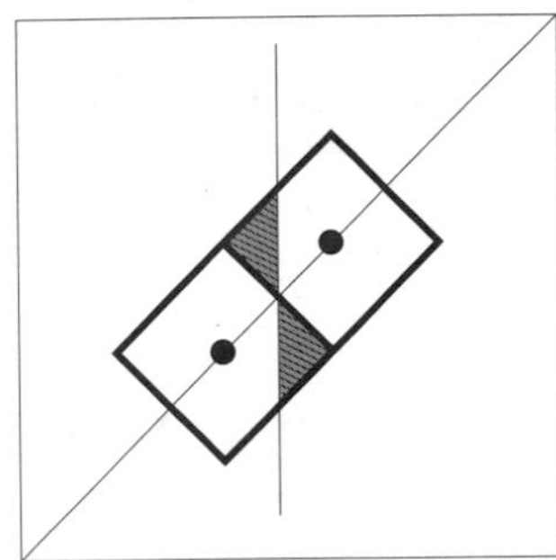

Figure 8:
Worst case for partitioning Center-defined Clusters

Lemma 10 (Error-Bound)
Using the L_1-metric, two d-dimensional center defined clusters approximated by two hyper spheres with radius 1 can be partitioned by an axes parallel cutting plane with at most $(1/2)^{d+1}$ percent wrongly classified points.

Proof: According to the density of the projected data, the optimal cutting plane is in middle between the two clusters but axes parallel. Figure 8 shows the worst case scenario for which we estimate the error. The two shaded regions in the picture mark the wrongly classified point sets. The two regions form a d-dimensional hypercube with an edge length $e = \frac{\sqrt{d}}{2}$. The maximal error can be estimated by the fraction of the volume of the clusters and the volume of the wrongly classified point sets.

$$error_{max} = \frac{V_{bad}}{V_{cluster}} = \frac{(1/2 \cdot \sqrt{d})^d}{2(\sqrt{d})^d} = (1/2)^{d+1} .$$

The error bound for metrics L_p, $p \geq 2$ is lower than the bound for the L_1 metric. □

Note that in higher dimensions the error bound converges against 0. An important aspect however is that both clusters are assume to consist of the same number of data points. The split algorithm tends to preserve the more dense areas. In case of clusters with very different numbers of data points the algorithm splits the smaller clusters more than the larger ones. In extreme cases, the smaller clusters may then be rejected as outliers. In such cases, after determining the large clusters a reclustering of the data set without the large clusters should be done. Because of the missing influence of the large clusters the smaller ones now becomes more visible and will be correctly found.

An example for the first steps of partitioning a two-dimensional data set (data set DS3 from BIRCH) is provided in Figure 9. It is interesting to note that regions containing large clusters are separated first. Although not designed for low-dimensional data, OptiGrid still provides correct results on such data sets.

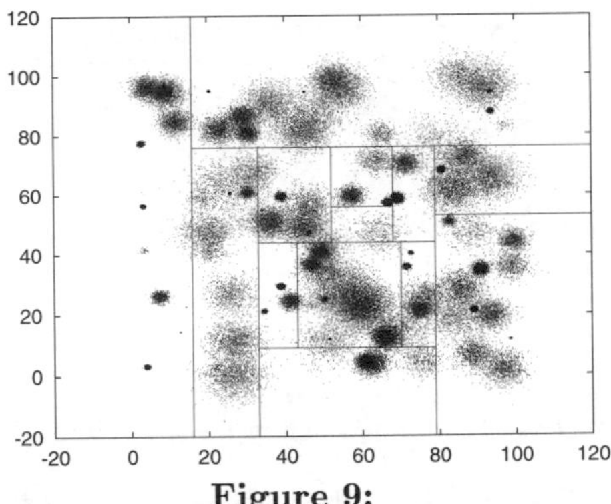

Figure 9:
The first determined cut planes of OptiGrid (q=1)

5.2 Experimental Evaluation of Effectiveness and Efficiency

In this section, we provide a detailed experimental evaluation of the effectiveness and efficiency of OptiGrid. We show that BIRCH is more effective and even slightly more efficient than the best previous approaches, namely BIRCH and DENCLUE.

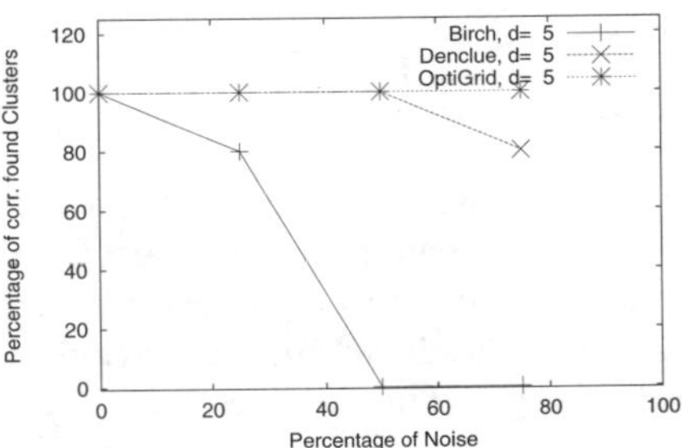

(a) Dimension 5

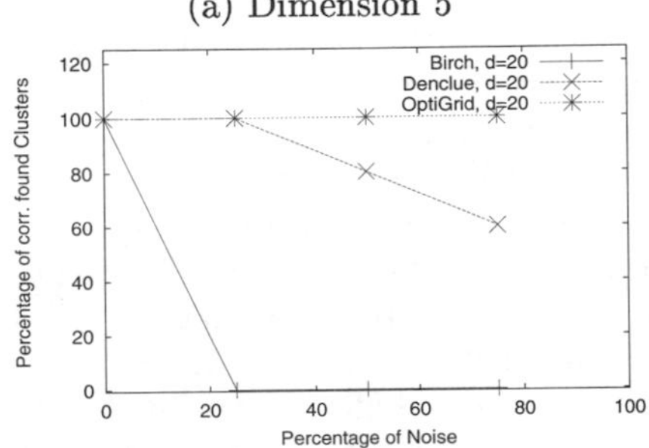

(b) Dimension 20

Figure 10: Dependency on the Noise Level

The first two experiments showing the effectiveness of OptiGrid use the same data sets as used for showing the problems of previous BIRCH and DENCLUE in subsection 2.2. As indicated by the theoretical considerations, OptiGrid provides a better effectiveness than BIRCH and DENCLUE. Figure 10a shows the percentage of correctly found clusters for $d = 5$ and 10b shows the same curves for $d = 20$. OptiGrid correctly determines all clusters in the data sets, even for very large noise levels of up to 75%. Similar curves result for $d > 20$.

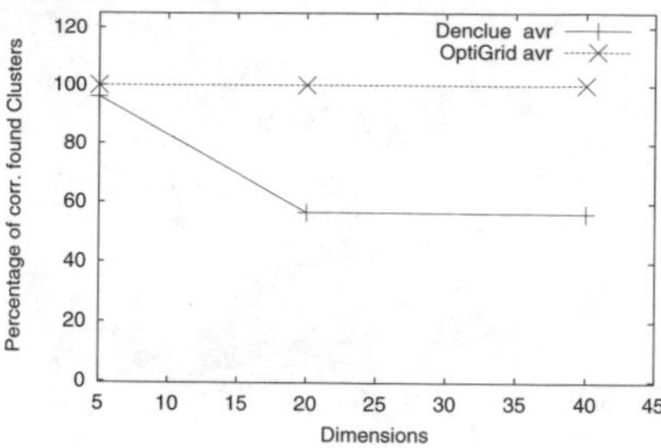

Figure 11: Dependency on the Dimensionality

The second experiments show the average percentage of correctly found clusters for data sets with different cluster centers (cf. figure 2). Again, OptiGrid is one hundred percent effective since it does not partitions clusters due to the optimal grid-partitioning algorithm.

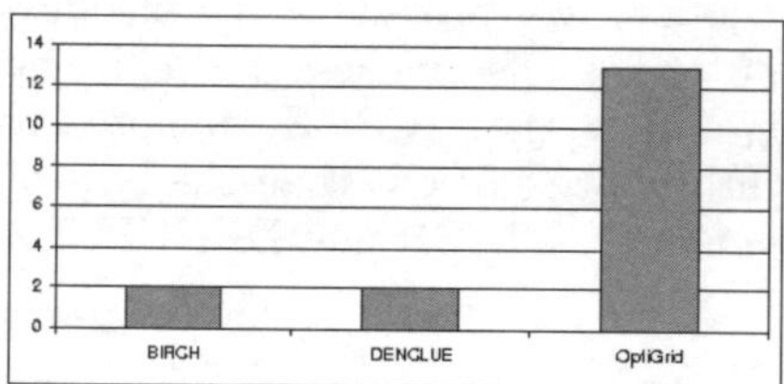

Figure 12:
Effectiveness on Real Molecular Biology Data

For the comparison with real data, we used two data sets which have been previously used in evaluating high-dimensional clustering algorithms [HK98]. The first data set results from an application in the area of molecular biology. The data used for our tests comes from a complex simulation of a very small but flexible peptide. (The time for performing the simulation took several weeks of CPU-time.) The data generated by the simulation describes the conformation of the peptide as a 19-dimensional point in the dihedral angle space [DGRJS97]. The simulation was done for a period of 50 nanoseconds with two snapshots taken every picosecond, resulting in about 100000 data points. The purpose of the simulation was to determine the behavior of the molecule in the conformation space. Due to the large amount of high-dimensional data, it is difficult to find, for example, the preferred conformations of the molecule. This, however, is important for applications in the pharmaceutical industry since small and flexible peptides are the basis for many medicaments. The flexibility of the peptides, however, is also responsible for the fact that the peptide has many intermediate conformations which causes the data to contain large amounts of noise (about 40 percent). In identifying clusters in this data set, OptiGrid turned out to be much more effective than DENCLUE and BIRCH (cf. figure 12). Both BIRCH and DENCLUE are able to find 2 clusters while OptiGrid determines 13 clusters (with a comparable efficiency). Describing the consequences of the identified structure in the data is beyond the scope of this paper, but has an important applications in the pharmaceutical industry.

The second real data set is polygonal CAD data which is transformed into 11-dimensional feature vectors using a Fourier transformation. The number of data points used in the experiments is 36000. In this experiment, OptiGrid and DENCLUE found the same number of clusters but BIRCH did not provide any clustering results. In this case, however, OptiGrid was about 10 times faster than DENCLUE.

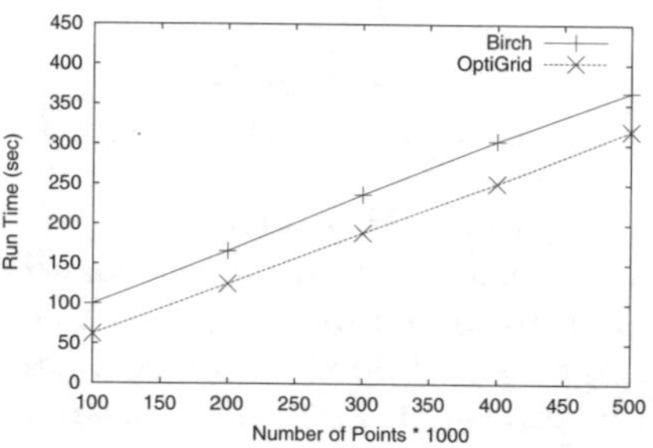

Figure 13: Performance Comparison

Although the previous experiments have shown that the three approaches are incomparable with respect to their effectiveness, in the following we still compare their efficiency. In the comparison, we use synthetic data sets with $d = 40$, 25% noise, and an increasing number of data points ($N = 100000$ to $N = 500000$). Figure 13 shows the resulting performance values for OptiGrid and BIRCH. It is clear that both algorithms are have about the same dependency on the number of data points N(i.e. slightly superlinear in N) but OptiGrid is about 50 seconds faster than BIRCH. This results in a factor of about 2 for $N = 100000$ and a factor of about 1.4 for $N = 500000$). Note that the times measured for BIRCH do not contain the time needed for the clustering phase (phase 4 in BIRCH). The real performance advantage of OptiGrid is therefore even higher.

6 Conclusions

In this paper, we propose a new approach to clustering in large high-dimensional databases with noise. We discuss the weaknesses of previous approaches and provide some interesting insights into the problems of clustering high-dimensional data. We formally introduce multidimensional grids and show that the complexity of a correct clustering of high-dimensional data sets with noise is superlinear in the number data points. We then provide a new algorithm which is fully effective, i.e. is able to correctly determine all clusters, but at the same time is very efficient. The new approach is based on an optimal grid-partitioning which uses a number of projections to determine the optimal cutting planes. In the experiments, we show that our approach avoids all the effectiveness problems of previous approaches and in some cases, it is even more efficient compared to the most efficient known approach (BIRCH). Due to the promising results of the experimental evaluation, we believe that our method will have a noticeable impact on the way clustering of high-dimensional data will be done in the future. Our plans for future work include an application and fine tuning of our method for specific applications and an extension to other projections.

References

[AGG+98] R. Aggrawal, J. Gehrke, D. Gunopulos, P. Raghavan: *'Automatic Subspace Clustering of High Dimensional Data for Data Mining Applications'*, Proc. ACM SIGMOD Int. Conf. on Managment of Data, pp. 94-105, 1998.

[BGRS99] Beyer K., Goldstein J., Ramakrishnan R., Shaft U.: *'When is nearest neighbor meaningful? '*, Proc. 7nd Int. Conf. on Database Theory (ICDT), 1999.

[DJSGM97] X. Daura, B. Jaun, D. Seebach, W.F. van Gunsteren A.E. Mark: *'Reversible peptide folding in solution by molecular dynamics simulation'*, submitted to Science (1997)

[EKSX96] Ester M., Kriegel H.-P., Sander J., Xu X.: *'A Density-Based Algorithm for Discovering Clusters in Large Spatial Databases with Noise'*, Proc. 2nd Int. Conf. on Knowledge Discovery and Data Mining, AAAI Press, 1996.

[EKSX97] Ester M., Kriegel H.-P., Sander J., Xu X.: *'Density-Connected Sets and their Application for Trend Detection in Spatial Databases'*, Proc. 3rd Int. Conf. on Knowledge Discovery and Data Mining, AAAI Press, 1997.

[EKX95] Ester M., Kriegel H.-P., Xu X.: *'Knowledge Discovery in Large Spatial Databases: Focusing Techniques for Efficient Class Identification'*, Proc. 4th Int. Symp. on Large Spatial Databases, 1995, in: Lecture Notes in Computer Science, Vol. 951, Springer, 1995, pp. 67-82.

[FL95] Faloutsos C., Lin K.D.: *'FastMap: A ast Algorithm for Indexing,Data-Mining and Visualisation of Traditional and Multimedia Datasets'*, Proc. ACM SIGMOD Int. Conf. on Managment of Data, 1995.

[FH75] Fukunaga K.,Hostler L.D.: *'The estimation of the gradient of a density function, with application in pattern recognation'*, IEEE Trans. Info. Thy. 1975, IT-21, 32-40

[HK98] Hinneburg A., Keim D.A.: *'An Efficient Approach to Clustering in Large Multimedia Databases with Noise'*, Proc. 4rd Int. Conf. on Knowledge Discovery and Data Mining, AAAI Press, 1998.

[HK99] Hinneburg A., Keim D.A.: *'A General Approach to Clustering in Large Multimedia Databases with Noise'*, submitted to the Knowledge Discovery and Data Mining Journal.

[Hub85] Huber P.J.: *'Projection Pursuit'*, The Annals of Statistics, Vol. 13, No.2, 1985, pp. 435-474.

[Jag91] Jagadish H. V.: *'A Retrieval Technique for Similar Shapes'*, Proc. ACM SIGMOD Int.Conf. on Management of Data, 1991, pp. 208-217.

[Kuk92] Kukich K.: *'Techniques for Automatically Correcting Word in Text'*, ACM Computing Surveys, Vol. 24, No. 4, 1992, pp. 377-440.

[MG95] Methrotra R., Gray J. E.: *'Feature-Index-Based Similar Shape retrieval'*, Proc. of the 3rd Working Conf. on Visual Database Systems, 1995.

[MN89] Mehlhorn K., Naher S.: *'LEDA, a libary of efficient data types and algorithms'*, University of Saarland, FB Informatik, TR A 04/89.

[NH94] Ng R. T., Han J.: *'Efficient and Effective Clustering Methods for Spatial Data Mining'*, Proc. 20th Int. Conf. on Very Large Data Bases, Morgan Kaufmann, 1994, pp. 144-155.

[Sch96] Schikuta E.: *'Grid clustering: An efficient hierarchical clustering method for very large data sets'*, Proc. 13th Conf. on Pattern Recognition, Vol. 2, IEEE Computer Society Press, pp. 101-105.

[Sco92] Scott D.W.: *'Multivariate Density Estimation'*, Wiley & Sons 1992.

[Sil86] Silverman B.W.: *'Density Estimation'*, Chapman & Hall 1986.

[SCZ98] Sheikholeslami G., Chatterjee S., Zhang A.: *'WaveCluster: A Multi-Resolution Clustering Approach for Very Large Spatial Databases'*, Proc. 24th VLDB Conference, 1998.

[SH94] Shawney H., Hafner J.: *'Efficient Color Histogram Indexing'*, Proc. Int. Conf.on Image Processing, 1994, pp. 66-70.

[WW80] Wallace T., Wintz P.: *'An Efficient Three-Dimensional Aircraft Recognition Algorithm Using Normalized Fourier Descriptors'*, Computer Graphics and Image Processing, Vol. 13, 1980.

[WYM97] Wang W., Yang J., Muntz R.: *'STING: A Statistical Information Grid Approach to Spatial Data Mining'*, Proc. 23rd Int. Conf. on Very Large Data Bases, Morgan Kaufmann, 1997.

[XEKS98] Xu X., Ester M., Kriegel H.-P., Sander J.: *'A Nonparametric Clustering Algorithm for Knowlege Discovery in Large Spatial Databases'*, will appear in Proc. IEEE Int. Conf. on Data Engineering, 1998, IEEE Computer Society Press.

[ZRL96] Zhang T., Ramakrishnan R., Linvy M.: *'BIRCH: An Efficient Data Clustering Method for very Large Databases'*, Proc. ACM SIGMOD Int. Conf. on Management of Data, ACM Press, 1996, pp. 103-114.

Similarity Search in High Dimensions via Hashing

ARISTIDES GIONIS * PIOTR INDYK† RAJEEV MOTWANI‡
Department of Computer Science
Stanford University
Stanford, CA 94305
{gionis,indyk,rajeev}@cs.stanford.edu

Abstract

The nearest- or near-neighbor query problems arise in a large variety of database applications, usually in the context of similarity searching. Of late, there has been increasing interest in building search/index structures for performing similarity search over high-dimensional data, e.g., image databases, document collections, time-series databases, and genome databases. Unfortunately, all known techniques for solving this problem fall prey to the "curse of dimensionality." That is, the data structures scale poorly with data dimensionality; in fact, if the number of dimensions exceeds 10 to 20, searching in k-d trees and related structures involves the inspection of a large fraction of the database, thereby doing no better than brute-force linear search. It has been suggested that since the selection of features and the choice of a distance metric in typical applications is rather heuristic, determining an approximate nearest neighbor should suffice for most practical purposes. In this paper, we examine a novel scheme for approximate similarity search based on hashing. The basic idea is to hash the points from the database so as to ensure that the probability of collision is much higher for objects that are close to each other than for those that are far apart. We provide experimental evidence that our method gives significant improvement in running time over other methods for searching in high-dimensional spaces based on hierarchical tree decomposition. Experimental results also indicate that our scheme scales well even for a relatively large number of dimensions (more than 50).

*Supported by NAVY N00014-96-1-1221 grant and NSF Grant IIS-9811904.

†Supported by Stanford Graduate Fellowship and NSF NYI Award CCR-9357849.

‡Supported by ARO MURI Grant DAAH04-96-1-0007, NSF Grant IIS-9811904, and NSF Young Investigator Award CCR-9357849, with matching funds from IBM, Mitsubishi, Schlumberger Foundation, Shell Foundation, and Xerox Corporation.

Proceedings of the 25th VLDB Conference, Edinburgh, Scotland, 1999.

1 Introduction

A similarity search problem involves a collection of objects (e.g., documents, images) that are characterized by a collection of relevant features and represented as points in a high-dimensional attribute space; given queries in the form of points in this space, we are required to find the nearest (most similar) object to the query. The particularly interesting and well-studied case is the d-dimensional Euclidean space. The problem is of major importance to a variety of applications; some examples are: data compression [20]; databases and data mining [21]; information retrieval [11, 16, 38]; image and video databases [15, 17, 37, 42]; machine learning [7]; pattern recognition [9, 13]; and, statistics and data analysis [12, 27]. Typically, the features of the objects of interest are represented as points in $\Re^d$ and a distance metric is used to measure similarity of objects. The basic problem then is to perform indexing or similarity searching for query objects. The number of features (i.e., the dimensionality) ranges anywhere from tens to thousands. For example, in multimedia applications such as IBM's QBIC (Query by Image Content), the number of features could be several hundreds [15, 17]. In information retrieval for text documents, vector-space representations involve several thousands of dimensions, and it is considered to be a dramatic improvement that dimension-reduction techniques, such as the Karhunen-Loéve transform [26, 30] (also known as principal components analysis [22] or latent semantic indexing [11]), can reduce the dimensionality to a mere few hundreds!

The low-dimensional case (say, for d equal to 2 or 3) is well-solved [14], so the main issue is that of dealing with a large number of dimensions, the so-called "curse of dimensionality." Despite decades of intensive effort, the current solutions are not entirely satisfactory; in fact, for large enough d, in theory or in practice, they provide little improvement over a linear algorithm which compares a query to each point from the database. In particular, it was shown in [45] that, both empirically and theoretically, *all* current indexing techniques (based on space partitioning) degrade to linear search for sufficiently high dimensions. This situation poses a serious obstacle to the future development of large scale similarity search systems. Imagine for example a search engine which enables content-based image retrieval on the World-Wide Web. If the system was to index a significant fraction of the web, the number of images to index would be at least of the order tens (if not hundreds) of million. Clearly, no indexing method exhibiting linear (or close to linear) dependence on the data size could manage such a huge data set.

The premise of this paper is that in many cases it is not necessary to insist on the *exact* answer; instead, determining an *approximate* answer should suffice (refer to Section 2 for a formal definition). This observation underlies a large body of recent research in databases, including using random sampling for histogram estimation [8] and median approximation [33], using wavelets for selectivity estimation [34] and approximate SVD [25]. We observe that there are many applications of nearest neighbor search where an approximate answer is good enough. For example, it often happens (e.g., see [23]) that the relevant answers are *much* closer to the query point than the irrelevant ones; in fact, this is a desirable property of a good similarity measure. In such cases, the approximate algorithm (with a suitable approximation factor) will return the same result as an exact algorithm. In other situations, an approximate algorithm provides the user with a time-quality tradeoff — the user can decide whether to spend more time waiting for the exact answer, or to be satisfied with a much quicker approximation (e.g., see [5]).

The above arguments rely on the assumption that approximate similarity search can be performed much faster than the exact one. In this paper we show that this is indeed the case. Specifically, we introduce a new indexing method for approximate nearest neighbor with a truly sublinear dependence on the data size even for high-dimensional data. Instead of using space partitioning, it relies on a new method called *locality-sensitive hashing (LSH)*. The key idea is to hash the points using several hash functions so as to ensure that, for each function, the probability of collision is much higher for objects which are close to each other than for those which are far apart. Then, one can determine near neighbors by hashing the query point and retrieving elements stored in buckets containing that point. We provide such locality-sensitive hash functions that are simple and easy to implement; they can also be naturally extended to the *dynamic* setting, i.e., when insertion and deletion operations also need to be supported. Although in this paper we are focused on Euclidean spaces, different LSH functions can be also used for other similarity measures, such as dot product [5].

Locality-Sensitive Hashing was introduced by Indyk and Motwani [24] for the purposes of devising main memory algorithms for nearest neighbor search; in particular, it enabled us to achieve worst-case $O(dn^{1/\epsilon})$-time for approximate nearest neighbor query over an n-point database. In this paper we improve that technique and achieve a significantly improved query time of $O(dn^{1/(1+\epsilon)})$. This yields an approximate nearest neighbor algorithm running in sublinear time for any $\epsilon > 0$. Furthermore, we generalize the algorithm and its analysis to the case of *external memory*.

We support our theoretical arguments by empirical evidence. We performed experiments on two data sets. The first contains 20,000 histograms of color images, where each histogram was represented as a point in d-dimensional space, for d up to 64. The second contains around 270,000 points representing texture information of blocks of large aerial photographs. All our tables were stored on disk. We compared the performance of our algorithm with the performance of the Sphere/Rectangle-tree (SR-tree) [28], a recent data structure which was shown to be comparable to or significantly more efficient than other tree-decomposition-based indexing methods for spatial data. The experiments show that our algorithm is significantly faster than the earlier methods, in some cases even by several orders of magnitude. It also scales well as the data size and dimensionality increase. Thus, it enables a new approach to high-performance similarity search — fast retrieval of approximate answer, possibly followed by a slower but more accurate computation in the few cases where the user is not satisfied with the approximate answer.

The rest of this paper is organized as follows. In Section 2 we introduce the notation and give formal definitions of the similarity search problems. Then in Section 3 we describe locality-sensitive hashing and show how to apply it to nearest neighbor search. In Section 4 we report the results of experiments with LSH. The related work is described in Section 5. Finally, in Section 6 we present conclusions and ideas for future research.

2 Preliminaries

We use l_p^d to denote the Euclidean space $\Re^d$ under the l_p norm, i.e., when the length of a vector $(x_1, \ldots x_d)$ is defined as $(|x_1|^p + \ldots + |x_d|^p)^{1/p}$. Further, $d_p(p, q) =$

$||p-q||_p$ denotes the distance between the points p and q in l_p^d. We use H^d to denote the *Hamming metric space* of dimension d, i.e., the space of binary vectors of length d under the standard Hamming metric. We use $d_H(p,q)$ denote the *Hamming distance*, i.e., the number of bits on which p and q differ.

The nearest neighbor search problem is defined as follows:

Definition 1 (Nearest Neighbor Search (NNS)) *Given a set P of n objects represented as points in a normed space l_p^d, preprocess P so as to efficiently answer queries by finding the point in P closest to a query point q.*

The definition generalizes naturally to the case where we want to return $K > 1$ points. Specifically, in the *K-Nearest Neighbors Search (K-NNS)*, we wish to return the K points in the database that are closest to the query point. The approximate version of the NNS problem is defined as follows:

Definition 2 (ϵ-Nearest Neighbor Search (ϵ-NNS)) *Given a set P of points in a normed space l_p^d, preprocess P so as to efficiently return a point $p \in P$ for any given query point q, such that $d(q,p) \leq (1+\epsilon)d(q,P)$, where $d(q,P)$ is the distance of q to the its closest point in P.*

Again, this definition generalizes naturally to finding $K > 1$ approximate nearest neighbors. In the *Approximate K-NNS* problem, we wish to find K points $p_1, \ldots, p_K$ such that the distance of p_i to the query q is at most $(1+\epsilon)$ times the distance from the ith nearest point to q.

3 The Algorithm

In this section we present efficient solutions to the approximate versions of the NNS problem. Without significant loss of generality, we will make the following two assumptions about the data:

1. the distance is defined by the l_1 norm (see comments below),
2. all coordinates of points in P are positive integers.

The first assumption is not very restrictive, as usually there is no clear advantage in, or even difference between, using l_2 or l_1 norm for similarity search. For example, the experiments done for the Webseek [43] project (see [40], chapter 4) show that comparing color histograms using l_1 and l_2 norms yields very similar results (l_1 is marginally better). Both our data sets (see Section 4) have a similar property. Specifically, we observed that a nearest neighbor of an average query point computed under the l_1 norm was also an ϵ-approximate neighbor under the l_2 norm with an average value of ϵ less than 3% (this observation holds for both data sets). Moreover, in most cases (i.e., for 67% of the queries in the first set and 73% in the second set) the nearest neighbors under l_1 and l_2 norms were *exactly* the same. This observation is interesting in its own right, and can be partially explained via the theorem by Figiel et al (see [19] and references therein). They showed analytically that by simply applying scaling and random rotation to the space l_2, we can make the distances induced by the l_1 and l_2 norms almost equal up to an arbitrarily small factor. It seems plausible that real data is already randomly rotated, thus the difference between l_1 and l_2 norm is very small. Moreover, for the data sets for which this property does not hold, we are guaranteed that after performing scaling and random rotation our algorithms can be used for the l_2 norm with arbitrarily small loss of precision.

As far as the second assumption is concerned, clearly all coordinates can be made positive by properly translating the origin of $\Re^d$. We can then convert all coordinates to integers by multiplying them by a suitably large number and rounding to the nearest integer. It can be easily verified that by choosing proper parameters, the error induced by rounding can be made arbitrarily small. Notice that after this operation the minimum interpoint distance is 1.

3.1 Locality-Sensitive Hashing

In this section we present locality-sensitive hashing (LSH). This technique was originally introduced by Indyk and Motwani [24] for the purposes of devising main memory algorithms for the ϵ-NNS problem. Here we give an improved version of their algorithm. The new algorithm is in many respects more natural than the earlier one: it does not require the hash buckets to store only one point; it has better running time guarantees; and, the analysis is generalized to the case of secondary memory.

Let C be the largest coordinate in all points in P. Then, as per [29], we can embed P into the Hamming cube $H^{d'}$ with $d' = Cd$, by transforming each point $p = (x_1, \ldots x_d)$ into a binary vector

$$v(p) = \text{Unary}_C(x_1) \ldots \text{Unary}_C(x_d),$$

where $\text{Unary}_C(x)$ denotes the unary representation of x, i.e., is a sequence of x ones followed by $C-x$ zeroes.

Fact 1 *For any pair of points p, q with coordinates in the set $\{1 \ldots C\}$,*

$$d_1(p,q) = d_H(v(p), v(q)).$$

That is, the embedding preserves the distances between the points. Therefore, in the sequel we can concentrate on solving ϵ-NNS in the Hamming space $H^{d'}$. However, we emphasize that we *do not* need to actually *convert* the data to the unary representation, which could be expensive when C is large; in fact, all our algorithms can be made to run in time *independent* on C. Rather, the unary representation provides us with a convenient framework for description of the algorithms which would be more complicated otherwise.

We define the hash functions as follows. For an integer l to be specified later, choose l subsets $I_1, \dots, I_l$ of $\{1, \dots, d'\}$. Let $p_{|I}$ denote the projection of vector p on the coordinate set I, i.e., we compute $p_{|I}$ by selecting the coordinate positions as per I and concatenating the bits in those positions. Denote $g_j(p) = p_{|I_j}$. For the preprocessing, we store each $p \in P$ in the bucket $g_j(p)$, for $j = 1, \dots, l$. As the total number of buckets may be large, we compress the buckets by resorting to standard hashing. Thus, we use two levels of hashing: the LSH function maps a point p to bucket $g_j(p)$, and a standard hash function maps the contents of these buckets into a hash table of size M. The maximal bucket size of the latter hash table is denoted by B. For the algorithm's analysis, we will assume hashing with chaining, i.e., when the number of points in a bucket exceeds B, a new bucket (also of size B) is allocated and linked to and from the old bucket. However, our implementation does not employ chaining, but relies on a simpler approach: if a bucket in a given index is full, a new point cannot be added to it, since it will be added to some other index with high probability. This saves us the overhead of maintaining the link structure.

The number n of points, the size M of the hash table, and the maximum bucket size B are related by the following equation:

$$M = \alpha \frac{n}{B},$$

where α is the memory utilization parameter, i.e., the ratio of the memory allocated for the index to the size of the data set.

To process a query q, we search all indices $g_1(q), \dots, g_l(q)$ until we either encounter at least $c \cdot l$ points (for c specified later) or use all l indices. Clearly, the number of disk accesses is always upper bounded by the number of indices, which is equal to l. Let $p_1, \dots, p_t$ be the points encountered in the process. For Approximate K-NNS, we output the K points p_i closest to q; in general, we may return fewer points if the number of points encountered is less than K.

It remains to specify the choice of the subsets I_j. For each $j \in \{1, \dots, l\}$, the set I_j consists of k elements from $\{1, \dots, d'\}$ sampled uniformly at random with replacement. The optimal value of k is chosen to maximize the probability that a point p "close" to q will fall into the same bucket as q, and also to minimize the probability that a point p' "far away" from q will fall into the same bucket. The choice of the values of l and k is deferred to the next section.

Algorithm Preprocessing
Input A set of points P,
  l (number of hash tables),
Output Hash tables $\mathcal{T}_i$, $i = 1, \dots, l$
Foreach $i = 1, \dots, l$
  Initialize hash table $\mathcal{T}_i$ by generating
  a random hash function $g_i(\cdot)$
Foreach $i = 1, \dots, l$
  Foreach $j = 1, \dots, n$
    Store point p_j on bucket $g_i(p_j)$ of hash table $\mathcal{T}_i$

Figure 1: Preprocessing algorithm for points already embedded in the Hamming cube.

Algorithm Approximate Nearest Neighbor Query
Input A query point q,
  K (number of appr. nearest neighbors)
Access To hash tables $\mathcal{T}_i$, $i = 1, \dots, l$
  generated by the preprocessing algorithm
Output K (or less) appr. nearest neighbors
$S \leftarrow \emptyset$
Foreach $i = 1, \dots, l$
  $S \leftarrow S \cup \{$points found in $g_i(q)$ bucket of table $\mathcal{T}_i\}$
Return the K nearest neighbors of q found in set S
/* Can be found by main memory linear search */

Figure 2: Approximate Nearest Neighbor query answering algorithm.

Although we are mainly interested in the I/O complexity of our scheme, it is worth pointing out that the hash functions can be efficiently computed if the data set is obtained by mapping l_1^d into d'-dimensional Hamming space. Let p be any point from the data set and let p' denote its image after the mapping. Let I be the set of coordinates and recall that we need to compute $p'_{|I}$. For $i = 1, \dots, d$, let $I_{|i}$ denote, in sorted order, the coordinates in I which correspond to the ith coordinate of p. Observe, that projecting p' on $I_{|i}$ results in a sequence of bits which is monotone, i.e., consists of a number, say o_i, of ones followed by zeros. Therefore, in order to represent p'_I it is sufficient to compute o_i for $i = 1, \dots, d$. However, the latter task is equivalent to finding the number of elements in the sorted array $I_{|i}$ which are smaller than a given value, i.e., the ith coordinate of p. This can be done via binary search in $\log C$ time, or even in constant time using a precomputed array of C bits. Thus, the total time needed to compute the function is either $O(d \log C)$ or $O(d)$, depending on resources used. In our experimental section, the value of C can be made very small, and therefore we will resort to the second method.

For quick reference we summarize the preprocessing

and query answering algorithms in Figures 1 and 2.

3.2 Analysis of Locality-Sensitive Hashing

The principle behind our method is that the probability of collision of two points p and q is closely related to the distance between them. Specifically, the larger the distance, the smaller the collision probability. This intuition is formalized as follows [24]. Let $D(\cdot,\cdot)$ be a distance function of elements from a set S, and for any $p \in S$ let $\mathcal{B}(p,r)$ denote the set of elements from S within the distance r from p.

Definition 3 *A family $\mathcal{H}$ of functions from S to U is called (r_1, r_2, p_1, p_2)-sensitive for $D(\cdot,\cdot)$ if for any $q, p \in S$*

- *if $p \in \mathcal{B}(q, r_1)$ then $\Pr_{\mathcal{H}}[h(q) = h(p)] \geq p_1$,*
- *if $p \notin \mathcal{B}(q, r_2)$ then $\Pr_{\mathcal{H}}[h(q) = h(p)] \leq p_2$.*

In the above definition, probabilities are considered with respect to the random choice of a function h from the family $\mathcal{H}$. In order for a locality-sensitive family to be useful, it has to satisfy the inequalities $p_1 > p_2$ and $r_1 < r_2$.

Observe that if $D(\cdot,\cdot)$ is the Hamming distance $d_H(\cdot,\cdot)$, then the family of projections on one coordinate is locality-sensitive. More specifically:

Fact 2 *Let S be $H^{d'}$ (the d'-dimensional Hamming cube) and $D(p,q) = d_H(p,q)$ for $p, q \in H^{d'}$. Then for any r, $\epsilon > 0$, the family $\mathcal{H}_{d'} = \{h_i : h_i((b_1, \ldots, b_{d'})) = b_i, \text{ for } i = 1, \ldots, d'\}$ is $\left(r, r(1+\epsilon), 1 - \frac{r}{d'}, 1 - \frac{r(1+\epsilon)}{d'}\right)$-sensitive.*

We now generalize the algorithm from the previous section to an *arbitrary* locality-sensitive family $\mathcal{H}$. Thus, the algorithm is equally applicable to other locality-sensitive hash functions (e.g., see [5]). The generalization is simple: the functions g are now defined to be of the form

$$g_i(p) = (h_{i_1}(p), h_{i_2}(p), \ldots, h_{i_k}(p)),$$

where the functions $h_{i_1}, \ldots, h_{i_k}$ are randomly chosen from $\mathcal{H}$ with replacement. As before, we choose l such functions $g_1, \ldots, g_l$. In the case when the family $\mathcal{H}_{d'}$ is used, i.e., each function selects one bit of an argument, the resulting values of $g_j(p)$ are essentially equivalent to $p_{|I_j}$.

We now show that the LSH algorithm can be used to solve what we call the (r,ϵ)-Neighbor problem: determine whether there exists a point p within a fixed distance $r_1 = r$ of q, or whether all points in the database are at least a distance $r_2 = r(1+\epsilon)$ away from q; in the first case, the algorithm is required to return a point p' within distance at most $(1+\epsilon)r$ from q. In particular, we argue that the LSH algorithm solves this problem for a proper choice of k and l, depending on r and ϵ. Then we show how to apply the solution to this problem to solve ϵ-NNS.

Denote by P' the set of all points $p' \in P$ such that $d(q, p') > r_2$. We observe that the algorithm correctly solves the (r,ϵ)-Neighbor problem if the following two properties hold:

P1 If there exists p^* such that $p^* \in \mathcal{B}(q, r_1)$, then $g_j(p^*) = g_j(q)$ for some $j = 1, \ldots, l$.

P2 The total number of blocks pointed to by q and containing only points from P' is less than cl.

Assume that $\mathcal{H}$ is a (r_1, r_2, p_1, p_2)-sensitive family; define $\rho = \frac{\ln 1/p_1}{\ln 1/p_2}$. The correctness of the LSH algorithm follows from the following theorem.

Theorem 1 *Setting $k = \log_{1/p_2}(n/B)$ and $l = \left(\frac{n}{B}\right)^\rho$ guarantees that properties* **P1** *and* **P2** *hold with probability at least $\frac{1}{2} - \frac{1}{e} \geq 0.132$.*

Remark 1 *Note that by repeating the LSH algorithm $O(1/\delta)$ times, we can amplify the probability of success in at least one trial to $1-\delta$, for any $\delta > 0$.*

Proof: Let property **P1** hold with probability P_1, and property **P2** hold with probability P_2. We will show that both P_1 and P_2 are large. Assume that there exists a point p^* within distance r_1 of q; the proof is quite similar otherwise. Set $k = \log_{1/p_2}(n/B)$. The probability that $g(p') = g(q)$ for $p \in P - \mathcal{B}(q, r_2)$ is at most $p_2^k = \frac{B}{n}$. Denote the set of all points $p' \notin \mathcal{B}(q, r_2)$ by P'. The expected number of blocks allocated for g_j which contain *exclusively* points from P' does not exceed 2. The expected number of such blocks allocated for all g_j is at most $2l$. Thus, by the Markov inequality [35], the probability that this number exceeds $4l$ is less than $1/2$. If we choose $c = 4$, the probability that the property P2 holds is $P_2 > 1/2$.

Consider now the probability of $g_j(p^*) = g_j(q)$. Clearly, it is bounded from below by

$$p_1^k = p_1^{\log_{1/p_2} n/B} = (n/B)^{-\frac{\log 1/p_1}{\log 1/p_2}} = (n/B)^{-\rho}.$$

By setting $l = \left(\frac{n}{B}\right)^\rho$, we bound from above the probability that $g_j(p^*) \neq g_j(q)$ for all $j = 1, \ldots, l$ by $1/e$. Thus the probability that one such g_j exists is at least $P_1 \geq 1 - 1/e$.

Therefore, the probability that both properties P1 and P2 hold is at least $1 - [(1 - P_1) + (1 - P_2)] = P_1 + P_2 - 1 \geq \frac{1}{2} - \frac{1}{e}$. The theorem follows. □

In the following we consider the LSH family for the Hamming metric of dimension d' as specified in Fact 2. For this case, we show that $\rho \leq \frac{1}{1+\epsilon}$ assuming that $r < \frac{d'}{\ln n}$; the latter assumption can be easily satisfied by increasing the dimensionality by padding a sufficiently long string of 0s at the end of each point's representation.

Fact 3 *Let* $r < \frac{d'}{\ln n}$. *If* $p_1 = 1 - \frac{r}{d'}$ *and* $p_2 = 1 - \frac{r(1+\epsilon)}{d'}$, *then* $\rho = \frac{\ln 1/p_1}{\ln 1/p_2} \le \frac{1}{1+\epsilon}$.

Proof: Observe that

$$\rho = \frac{\ln 1/p_1}{\ln 1/p_2} = \frac{\ln \frac{1}{1-r/d'}}{\ln \frac{1}{1-(1+\epsilon)r/d'}} = \frac{\ln(1 - r/d')}{\ln(1-(1+\epsilon)r/d')}.$$

Multiplying both the numerator and the denominator by $\frac{d'}{r}$, we obtain:

$$\begin{aligned} \rho &= \frac{\frac{d'}{r}\ln(1-r/d')}{\frac{d'}{r}\ln(1-(1+\epsilon)r/d')} \\ &= \frac{\ln(1-r/d')^{d'/r}}{\ln(1-(1+\epsilon)r/d')^{d'/r}} = \frac{U}{L} \end{aligned}$$

In order to upper bound ρ, we need to bound U from below and L from above; note that both U and L are negative. To this end we use the following inequalities [35]:

$$(1-(1+\epsilon)r/d')^{d'/r} < e^{-(1+\epsilon)}$$

and

$$\left(1 - \frac{r}{d'}\right)^{d'/r} > e^{-1}\left(1 - \frac{1}{d'/r}\right).$$

Therefore,

$$\begin{aligned} \frac{U}{L} &< \frac{\ln(e^{-1}(1-\frac{1}{d'/r}))}{\ln e^{-(1+\epsilon)}} \\ &= \frac{-1+\ln(1-\frac{1}{d'/r})}{-(1+\epsilon)} \\ &= 1/(1+\epsilon) - \frac{\ln(1-\frac{1}{d'/r})}{1+\epsilon} \\ &< 1/(1+\epsilon) - \ln(1-1/\ln n) \end{aligned}$$

where the last step uses the assumptions that $\epsilon > 0$ and $r < \frac{d'}{\ln n}$. We conclude that

$$\begin{aligned} n^{\rho} &< n^{1/(1+\epsilon)} n^{-\ln(1-1/\ln n)} \\ &= n^{1/(1+\epsilon)}(1-1/\ln n)^{-\ln n} = O(n^{1/(1+\epsilon)}) \end{aligned}$$

□

We now return to the ϵ-NNS problem. First, we observe that we could reduce it to the (r,ϵ)-Neighbor problem by building several data structures for the latter problem with different values of r. More specifically, we could explore r equal to r_0, $r_0(1+\epsilon)$, $r_0(1+\epsilon)^2, \ldots, r_{max}$, where r_0 and r_{max} are the smallest and the largest possible distance between the query and the data point, respectively. We remark that the number of different radii could be further reduced [24] at the cost of increasing running time and space requirement. On the other hand, we observed that in practice choosing only *one* value of r is sufficient to produce answers of good quality. This can be explained as in [10] where it was observed that the distribution of distances between a query point and the data set in most cases does not depend on the specific query point, but on the intrinsic properties of the data set. Under the assumption of distribution invariance, the same parameter r is likely to work for a vast majority of queries. Therefore in the experimental section we adopt a fixed choice of r and therefore also of k and l.

4 Experiments

In this section we report the results of our experiments with locality-sensitive hashing method. We performed experiments on two data sets. The first one contains up to 20,000 histograms of color images from COREL Draw library, where each histogram was represented as a point in d-dimensional space, for d up to 64. The second one contains around 270,000 points of dimension 60 representing texture information of blocks of large large aerial photographs. We describe the data sets in more detail later in the section.

We decided not to use randomly-chosen synthetic data in our experiments. Though such data is often used to measure the performance of *exact* similarity search algorithms, we found it unsuitable for evaluation of *approximate* algorithms for the high data dimensionality. The main reason is as follows. Assume a data set consisting of points chosen independently at random from the same distribution. Most distributions (notably uniform) used in the literature assume that all coordinates of each point are chosen independently. In such a case, for any pair of points p, q the distance $d(p,q)$ is sharply concentrated around the mean; for example, for the uniform distribution over the unit cube, the expected distance is $O(d)$, while the standard deviation is only $O(\sqrt{d})$. Thus almost all pairs are approximately within the same distance, so the notion of approximate nearest neighbor is not meaningful — almost *every point* is an approximate nearest neighbor.

Implementation. We implement the LSH algorithm as specified in Section 3. The LSH functions can be computed as described in Section 3.1. Denote the resulting vector of coordinates by $(v_1, \ldots, v_k)$. For the second level mapping we use functions of the form

$$h(v_1, \ldots, v_k) = a_1 \cdot v_1 + \cdots + a_d \cdot v_k \bmod M,$$

where M is the size of the hash table and $a_1, \ldots, a_k$ are random numbers from interval $[0 \ldots M-1]$. These functions can be computed using only $2k-1$ operations, and are sufficiently random for our purposes, i.e., give low probability of collision. Each second level bucket is then directly mapped to a disk block. We assumed that each block is 8KB of data. As each coordinate in our data sets can be represented using 1 byte, we can store up to $8192/d$ d-dimensional points per block. Therefore, we assume the bucket size $B = 100$ for $d = 64$ or $d = 60$, $B = 300$ for $d = 27$ and $B = 1000$ for $d = 8$.

For the SR-tree, we used the implementation by Katayama, available from his web page [28]. As above, we allow it to store about 8192 coordinates per disk block.

Performance measures. The goal of our experiments was to estimate two performance measures: speed (for both SR-tree and LSH) and accuracy (for LSH). The speed is measured by the number of disk blocks accessed in order to answer a query. We count all disk accesses, thus ignoring the issue of caching. Observe that in case of LSH this number is easy to predict as it is clearly equal to the number of indices used. As the number of indices also determines the storage overhead, it is a natural parameter to optimize.

The error of LSH is measured as follows. Following [2] we define (for the Approximate 1-NNS problem) the *effective error* as

$$E = \frac{1}{|Q|} \sum_{\text{query } q \in Q} \frac{d_{LSH}}{d^*},$$

where d_{LSH} denotes the distance from a query point q to a point found by LSH, d^* is the distance from q to the closest point, and the sum is taken of all queries for which a nonempty index was found. We also measure the (small) fraction of queries for which no nonempty bucket was found; we call this quantity *miss ratio*. For the Approximate K-NNS we measure separately the distance ratios between the closest points found to the nearest neighbor, the 2nd closest one to the 2nd nearest neighbor and so on; then we average the ratios. The miss ratio is defined to be the fraction of cases when *less than* K points were found.

Data Sets. Our first data set consists of 20,000 histograms of color thumbnail-sized images of various contents taken from the COREL library. The histograms were extracted after transforming the pixels of the images to the 3-dimensional CIE-Lab color space [44]; the property of this space is that the distance between each pair of points corresponds to the perceptual dissimilarity between the colors that the two points represent. Then we partitioned the color space into a grid of smaller cubes, and given an image, we create the color histogram of the image by counting how many pixels fall into each of these cubes. By dividing each axis into u intervals we obtain a total of u^3 cubes. For most experiments, we assumed $u = 4$ obtaining a 64-dimensional space. Each histogram cube (i.e., color) then corresponds to a dimension of space representing the images. Finally, quantization is performed in order to fit each coordinate in 1 byte. For each point representing an image each coordinate effectively counts the number of the image's pixels of a specific color. All coordinates are clearly non-negative

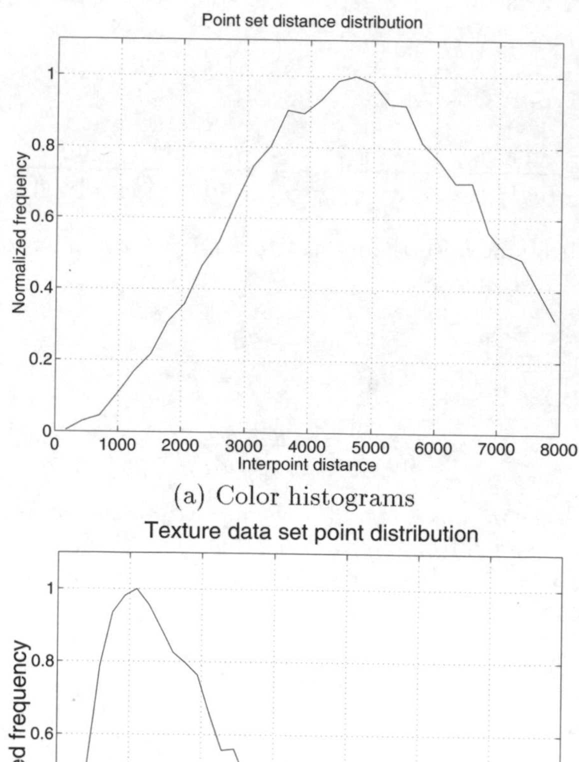

(a) Color histograms

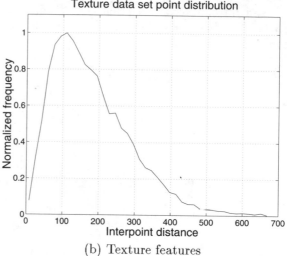

Texture data set point distribution

Normalized frequency

Interpoint distance

(b) Texture features

Figure 3: The profiles of the data sets.

integers, as assumed in Section 3. The distribution of interpoint distances in our point sets is shown in Figure 3. Both graphs were obtained by computing all interpoint distances of random subsets of 200 points, normalizing the maximal value to 1.

The second data set contains 275,465 feature vectors of dimension 60 representing texture information of blocks of large aerial photographs. This data set was provided by B.S. Manjunath [31, 32]; its size and dimensionality "provides challenging problems in high dimensional indexing" [31]. These features are obtained from Gabor filtering of the image tiles. The Gabor filter bank consists of 5 scales and 6 orientations of filters, thus the total number of filters is $5 \times 6 = 30$. The mean and standard deviation of each filtered output are used to constructed the feature vector ($d = 30 \times 2 = 60$). These texture features are extracted from 40 large air photos. Before the feature extraction, each airphoto is first partitioned into non-overlapping tiles of size 64 times 64, from which the feature vectors are computed.

Query Sets. The difficulty in evaluating similarity searching algorithms is the lack of a publicly available database containing typical query points. Therefore, we had to construct the query set from the data set itself. Our construction is as follows: we split the data set randomly into two disjoint parts (call them S_1 and S_2). For the first data set the size of S_1 is 19,000 while the size of S_2 is 1000. The set S_1 forms a database of images, while the first 500 points from S_2 (denoted by Q) are used as query points (we use the other 500 points for various verification purposes). For the second data set we chose S_1 to be of size 270,000, and we use 1000 of the remaining 5,465 points as a query set. The numbers are slightly different for the scalability experiments as they require varying the size of the data set. In this case we chose a random subset of S_1 of required size.

4.1 Experimental Results

In this section we describe the results of our experiments. For both data sets they consist essentially of the following three steps. In the first phase we have to make the following choice: the value of k (the number of sampled bits) to choose for a given data set and the given number of indices l in order to minimize the effective error. It turned out that the optimal value of k is essentially independent of n and d and thus we can use the same value for different values of these parameters. In the second phase, we estimate the influence of the number of indices l on the error. Finally, we measure the performance of LSH by computing (for a variety of data sets) the minimal number of indices needed to achieve a specified value of error. When applicable, we also compare this performance with that of SR-trees.

4.2 Color histograms

For this data set, we performed several experiments aimed at understanding the behavior of LSH algorithm and its performance relative to SR-tree. As mentioned above, we started with an observation that the optimal value of sampled bits k is essentially independent of n and d and approximately equal to 700 for $d = 64$. The lack of dependence on n can be explained by the fact that the smaller data sets were obtained by sampling the large one and therefore all of the sets have similar structure; we believe the lack of dependence on d is also influenced by the structure of the data. Therefore the following experiments were done assuming $k = 700$.

Our next observation was that the value of storage overhead α does not exert much influence over the performance of the algorithm (we tried α's from the interval $[2, 5]$); thus, in the following we set $\alpha = 2$.

In the next step we estimated the influence of l on E. The results (for $n = 19,000$, $d = 64$, $K = 1$) are shown on Figure 4. As expected, one index is not sufficient to achieve reasonably small error — the effective error can easily exceed 50%. The error however decreases very fast as l increases. This is due to the fact that the probabilities of finding empty bucket are independent for different indices and therefore the probability that all buckets are empty decays exponentially in l.

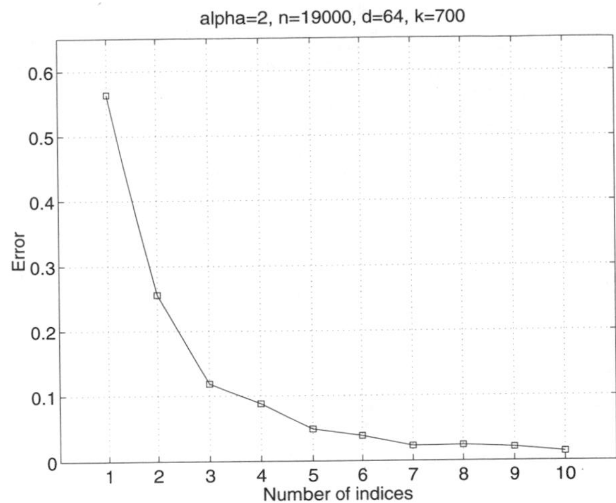

Figure 4: Error vs. the number of indices.

In order to compare the performance of LSH with SR-tree, we computed (for a variety of data sets) the minimal number of indices needed to achieve a specified value of error E equal to 2%, 5% , 10% or 20%. Then we investigated the performance of the two algorithms while varying the dimension and data size.

Dependence on Data Size. We performed the simulations for $d = 64$ and the data sets of sizes 1000, 2000, 5000, 10000 and 19000. To achieve better understanding of scalability of our algorithms, we did run the experiments twice: for Approximate 1-NNS and for Approximate 10-NNS. The results are presented on Figure 5.

Notice the strongly sublinear dependence exhibited by LSH: although for small $E = 2\%$ it matches SR-tree for $n = 1000$ with 5 blocks accessed (for $K = 1$), it requires 3 accesses more for a data set 19 times larger. At the same time the I/O activity of SR-tree increases by more than 200%. For larger errors the LSH curves are nearly flat, i.e., exhibit little dependence on the size of the data. Similar or even better behavior occurs for Approximate 10-NNS.

We also computed the miss ratios, i.e., the fraction of queries for which no answer was found. The results are presented on Figure 6. We used the parameters from the previous experiment. On can observe that for say $E = 5\%$ and Approximate 1-NNS, the miss ratios are quite high (10%) for small n, but decrease

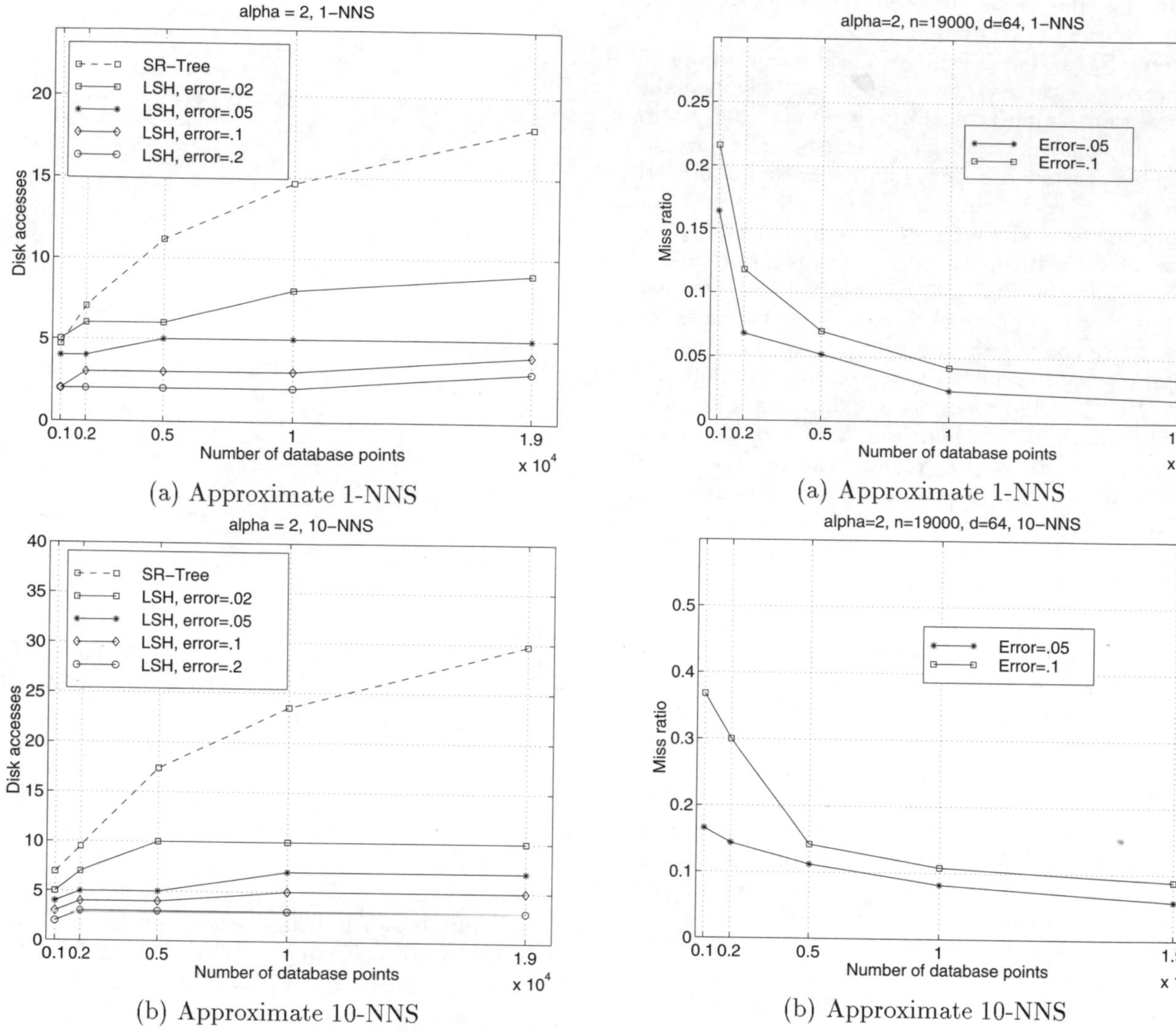

Figure 5: Number of indices vs. data size.

Figure 6: Miss ratio vs. data size.

to around 1% for $n = 19,000$.

Dependence on Dimension. We performed the simulations for $d = 2^3, 3^3$ and 4^3; the choice of d's was limited to cubes of natural numbers because of the way the data has been created. Again, we performed the comparison for Approximate 1-NNS and Approximate 10-NNS; the results are shown on Figure 7. Note that LSH scales very well with the increase of dimensionality: for $E = 5\%$ the change from $d = 8$ to $d = 64$ increases the number of indices only by 2. The miss ratio was always below 6% for all dimensions.

This completes the comparison of LSH with SR-tree. For a better understanding of the behavior of LSH, we performed an additional experiment on LSH only. Figure 8 presents the performance of LSH when the number of nearest neighbors to retrieve vary from 1 to 100.

4.3 Texture features

The experiments with texture feature data were designed to measure the performance of the LSH algorithm on large data sets; note that the size of the texture file (270,000 points) is an order of magnitude larger than the size of the histogram data set (20,000 points). The first step (i.e., the choice of the number of sampled bits k) was very similar to the previous experiment, therefore we skip the detailed description here. We just state that we assumed that the number of sampled bits $k = 65$, with other parameters being: the storage overhead $\alpha = 1$, block size $B = 100$, and the number of nearest neighbors equal to 10. As stated above, the value of n was equal to 270,000.

We varied the number of indices from 3 to 100, which resulted in error from 50% to 15% (see Figure 9 (a)). The shape of the curve is similar as in the previous experiment. The miss ratio was roughly

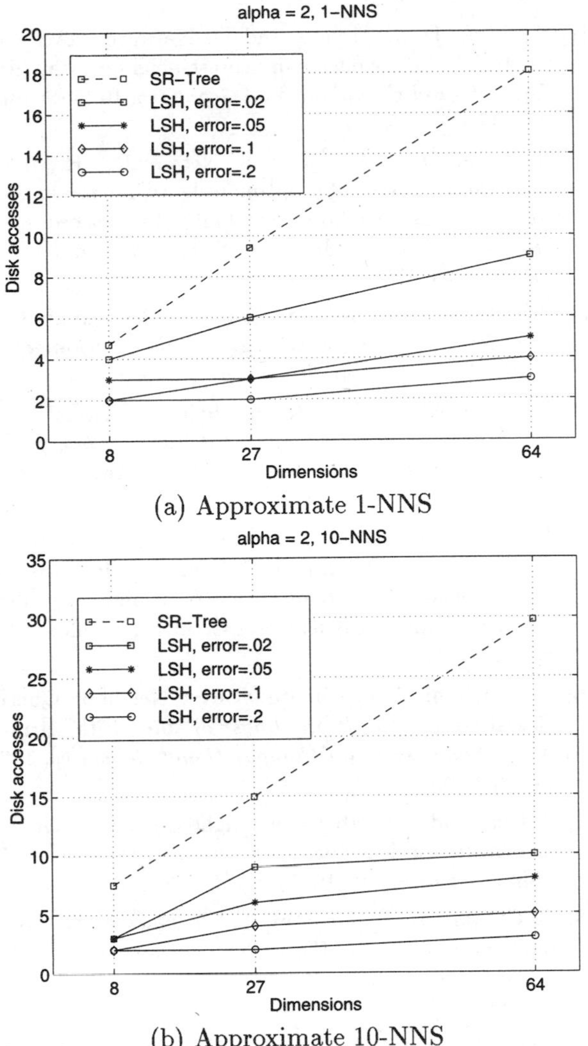

(a) Approximate 1-NNS

(b) Approximate 10-NNS

Figure 7: Number of indices vs. dimension.

4% for 3 indices, 1% for 5 indices, and 0% otherwise.

To compare with SR-tree, we implemented that latter on random subsets of the whole data set of sizes from 10,000 to 200,000. For $n = 200,000$ the average number of blocks accessed per query by SR-tree was 1310, which is one to two orders of magnitude larger than the number of blocks accessed by our algorithm (see Figure 9 (b) where we show the running times of LSH for effective error 15%). Observe though that an SR-tree computes exact answers while LSH provides only an approximation. Thus in order to perform an accurate evaluation of LSH, we decided to compare it with a modified SR-tree algorithm which produces *approximate* answers. The modification is simple: instead of running SR-tree on the whole data set, we run it on a randomly chosen subset of it. In this way we achieve a speed-up of the algorithm (as the random sample of the data set is smaller than the original set)

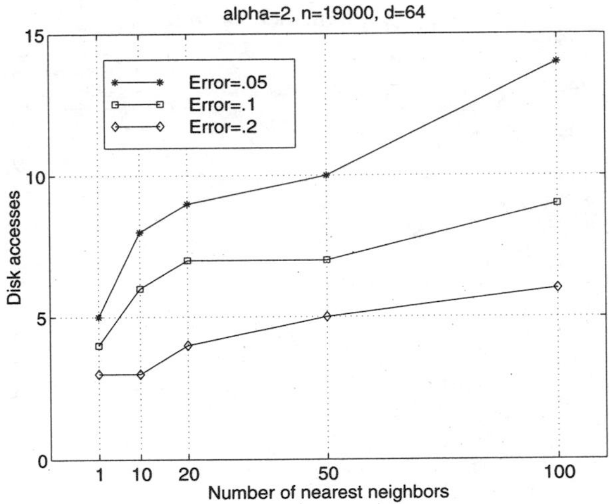

Figure 8: Number of indices vs. number of nearest neighbors.

while incurring some error.

The query cost versus error tradeoff obtained in this way (for the entire data set) is depicted on Figure 9; we also include a similar graph for LSH.

Observe that using random sampling results in considerable speed-up for the SR-tree algorithm, while keeping the error relatively low. However, even in this case the LSH algorithm offers considerably outperforms SR-trees, being up to an order of magnitude faster.

5 Previous Work

There is considerable literature on various versions of the nearest neighbor problem. Due to lack of space we omit detailed description of related work; the reader is advised to read [39] for a survey of a variety of data structures for nearest neighbors in geometric spaces, including variants of k-d trees, R-trees, and structures based on space-filling curves. The more recent results are surveyed in [41]; see also an excellent survey by [4]. Recent theoretical work in nearest neighbor search is briefly surveyed in [24].

6 Conclusions

We presented a novel scheme for approximate similarity search based on locality-sensitive hashing. We compared the performance of this technique and SR-tree, a good representative of tree-based spatial data structures. We showed that by allowing small error and additional storage overhead, we can considerably improve the query time. Experimental results also indicate that our scheme scales well to even a large number of dimensions and data size. An additional advantage of our data structure is that its running time is

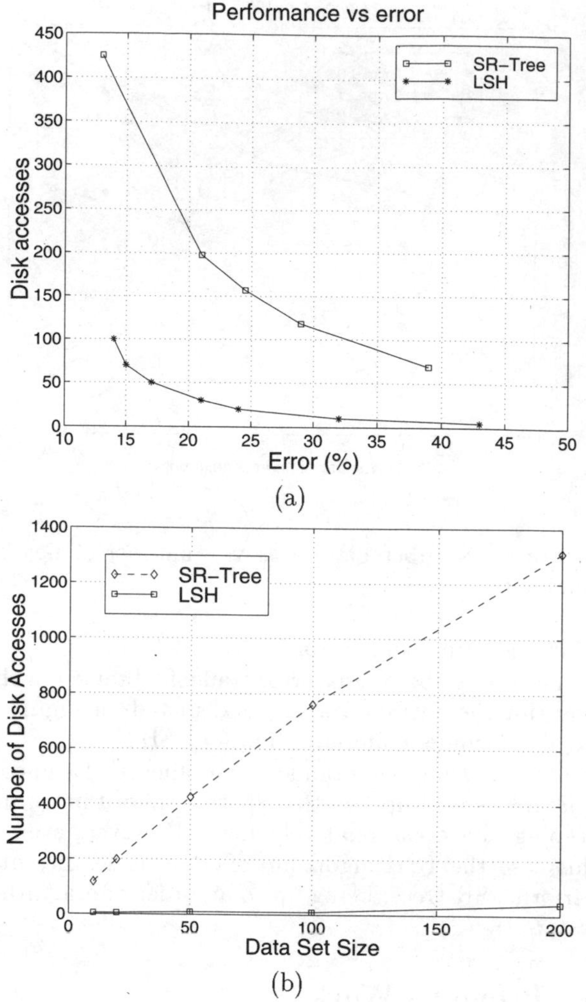

Figure 9: (a) number of indices vs. error and (b) number of indices vs. size.

essentially determined in advance. All these properties make LSH a suitable candidate for high-performance and real-time systems.

In recent work [5, 23], we explore applications of LSH-type techniques to data mining and search for copyrighted video data. Our experience suggests that there is a lot of potential for further improvement of the performance of the LSH algorithm. For example, our data structures are created using a randomized procedure. It would be interesting if there was a more systematic method for performing this task; such a method could take additional advantage of the structure of the data set. We also believe that investigation of *hybrid* data structures obtained by merging the tree-based and hashing-based approaches is a fruitful direction for further research.

References

[1] S. Arya, D.M. Mount, and O. Narayan, Accounting for boundary effects in nearest-neighbor searching. *Discrete and Computational Geometry*, 16 (1996), pp. 155–176.

[2] S. Arya, D.M. Mount, N.S. Netanyahu, R. Silverman, and A. Wu. An optimal algorithm for approximate nearest neighbor searching, In *Proceedings of the 5th Annual ACM-SIAM Symposium on Discrete Algorithms*, 1994, pp. 573–582.

[3] J.L. Bentley. Multidimensional binary search trees used for associative searching. *Communications of the ACM*, 18 (1975), pp. 509–517.

[4] S. Berchtold and D.A. Keim. High-dimensional Index Structures. In Proceedings of SIGMOD, 1998, p. 501. See `http://www.informatik.uni-halle.de/ keim/SIGMOD98Tutorial.ps.gz`

[5] E. Cohen. M. Datar, S. Fujiwara, A. Gionis, P. Indyk, R. Motwani, J. D. Ullman. C. Yang. Finding Interesting Associations without Support Pruning. Technical Report, Computer Science Department, Stanford University.

[6] T.M. Chan. Approximate Nearest Neighbor Queries Revisited. In *Proceedings of the 13th Annual ACM Symposium on Computational Geometry*, 1997, pp. 352-358.

[7] S. Cost and S. Salzberg. A weighted nearest neighbor algorithm for learning with symbolic features. *Machine Learning*, 10 (1993), pp. 57–67.

[8] S. Chaudhuri, R. Motwani and V. Narasayya. "Random Sampling for Histogram Construction: How much is enough?". In *Proceedings of SIGMOD'98*, pp. 436–447.

[9] T.M. Cover and P.E. Hart. Nearest neighbor pattern classification. *IEEE Transactions on Information Theory*, 13 (1967), pp. 21–27.

[10] P. Ciaccia, M. Patella and P. Zezula, A cost model for similarity queries in metric spaces In *Proceedings of PODS'98*, pp. 59–68.

[11] S. Deerwester, S. T. Dumais, T.K. Landauer, G.W. Furnas, and R.A. Harshman. Indexing by latent semantic analysis. *Journal of the Society for Information Sciences*, 41 (1990), pp. 391–407.

[12] L. Devroye and T.J. Wagner. Nearest neighbor methods in discrimination. *Handbook of Statistics*, vol. 2, P.R. Krishnaiah and L.N. Kanal, eds., North-Holland, 1982.

[13] R.O. Duda and P.E. Hart. *Pattern Classification and Scene Analysis*. John Wiley & Sons, NY, 1973.

[14] H. Edelsbrunner. *Algorithms in Combinatorial Geometry*. Springer-Verlag, 1987.

[15] C. Faloutsos, R. Barber, M. Flickner, W. Niblack, D. Petkovic, and W. Equitz. Efficient and effective querying by image content. *Journal of Intelligent Information Systems*, 3 (1994), pp. 231–262.

[16] C. Faloutsos and D.W. Oard. A Survey of Information Retrieval and Filtering Methods. Technical Report CS-TR-3514, Department of Computer Science, University of Maryland, College Park, 1995.

[17] M. Flickner, H. Sawhney, W. Niblack, J. Ashley, Q. Huang, B. Dom, M. Gorkani, J. Hafner, D. Lee, D. Petkovic, D. Steele, and P. Yanker. Query by image and video content: the QBIC system. *IEEE Computer*, 28 (1995), pp. 23–32.

[18] J.K. Friedman, J.L. Bentley, and R.A. Finkel. An algorithm for finding best matches in logarithmic expected time. *ACM Transactions on Mathematical Software*, 3 (1977), pp. 209–226.

[19] T. Figiel, J. Lindenstrauss, V. D. Milman. The dimension of almost spherical sections of convex bodies. *Acta Math.* 139 (1977), no. 1-2, 53–94.

[20] A. Gersho and R.M. Gray. *Vector Quantization and Data Compression.* Kluwer, 1991.

[21] T. Hastie and R. Tibshirani. Discriminant adaptive nearest neighbor classification. In *Proceedings of the First International Conference on Knowledge Discovery & Data Mining*, 1995, pp. 142–149.

[22] H. Hotelling. Analysis of a complex of statistical variables into principal components. *Journal of Educational Psychology*, 27 (1933). pp. 417–441.

[23] P. Indyk, G. Iyengar, N. Shivakumar. Finding pirated video sequences on the Internet. Technical Report, Computer Science Department, Stanford University.

[24] P. Indyk and R. Motwani. Approximate Nearest Neighbor – Towards Removing the Curse of Dimensionality. In *Proceedings of the 30th Symposium on Theory of Computing*, 1998, pp. 604–613.

[25] K.V. Ravi Kanth, D. Agrawal, A. Singh. "Dimensionality Reduction for Similarity Searching in Dynamic Databases". In *Proceedings of SIGMOD'98*, 166 – 176.

[26] K. Karhunen. Über lineare Methoden in der Wahrscheinlichkeitsrechnung. *Ann. Acad. Sci. Fennicae*, Ser. A137, 1947.

[27] V. Koivune and S. Kassam. Nearest neighbor filters for multivariate data. *IEEE Workshop on Nonlinear Signal and Image Processing*, 1995.

[28] N. Katayama and S. Satoh. The SR-tree: an index structure for high-dimensional nearest neighbor queries. In *Proc. SIGMOD'97*, pp. 369–380. The code is available from `http://www.rd.nacsis.ac.jp/~katayama/homepage/research/srtree/English.html`

[29] N. Linial, E. London, and Y. Rabinovich. The geometry of graphs and some of its algorithmic applications. In *Proceedings of 35th Annual IEEE Symposium on Foundations of Computer Science*, 1994, pp. 577–591.

[30] M. Loéve. Fonctions aleastoires de second ordere. *Processus Stochastiques et mouvement Brownian*, Hermann, Paris, 1948.

[31] B. S. Manjunath. Airphoto dataset. `http://vivaldi.ece.ucsb.edu/Manjunath/research.htm`

[32] B. S. Manjunath and W. Y. Ma. Texture features for browsing and retrieval of large image data. *IEEE Transactions on Pattern Analysis and Machine Intelligence, (Special Issue on Digital Libraries)*, 18 (8), pp. 837-842.

[33] G.S. Manku, S. Rajagopalan, and B.G. Lindsay. Approximate Medians and other Quantiles in One Pass and with Limited Memory. In *Proceedings of SIGMOD'98*, pp. 426–435.

[34] Y. Matias, J.S. Vitter, and M. Wang. Wavelet-based Histograms for Selectivity Estimations. In *Proceedings of SIGMOD'98*, pp. 448–459.

[35] R. Motwani and P. Raghavan. *Randomized Algorithms.* Cambridge University Press, 1995.

[36] M. Otterman. Approximate matching with high dimensionality R-trees. M.Sc. Scholarly paper, Dept. of Computer Science, Univ. of Maryland, College Park, MD, 1992.

[37] A. Pentland, R.W. Picard, and S. Sclaroff. Photobook: tools for content-based manipulation of image databases. In *Proceedings of the SPIE Conference on Storage and Retrieval of Image and Video Databases II*, 1994.

[38] G. Salton and M.J. McGill. *Introduction to Modern Information Retrieval.* McGraw-Hill Book Company, New York, NY, 1983.

[39] H. Samet. *The Design and Analysis of Spatial Data Structures.* Addison-Wesley, Reading, MA, 1989.

[40] J. R. Smith. Integrated Spatial and Feature Image Systems: Retrieval, Analysis and Compression. Ph.D. thesis, Columbia University, 1997. Available at `ftp://ftp.ctr.columbia.edu/CTR-Research/advent/public/public/jrsmith/thesis`

[41] T. Sellis, N. Roussopoulos, and C. Faloutsos. Multidimensional Access Methods: Trees Have Grown Everywhere. In *Proceedings of the 23rd International Conference on Very Large Data Bases*, 1997, 13–15.

[42] A.W.M. Smeulders and R. Jain, eds. *Image Databases and Multi-media Search.* Proceedings of the First International Workshop, IDB-MMS'96, Amsterdam University Press, Amsterdam, 1996.

[43] J.R. Smith and S.F. Chang. Visually Searching the Web for Content. *IEEE Multimedia* 4 (1997): pp. 12–20. See also `http://disney.ctr.columbia.edu/WebSEEk`

[44] G. Wyszecki and W.S. Styles. *Color science: concepts and methods, quantitative data and formulae.* John Wiley and Sons, New York, NY, 1982.

[45] R. Weber, H. Schek, and S. Blott. A quantitative analysis and performance study for Similarity Search Methods in High Dimensional Spaces. In *Proceedings of the 24th International Conference on Very Large Data Bases (VLDB)*, 1998, pp. 194-205.

What can Hierarchies do for Data Warehouses?

H. V. Jagadish*
U of Michigan, Ann Arbor
jag@eecs.umich.edu

Laks V. S. Lakshmanan†
IIT, Bombay
laks@cse.iitb.ernet.in

Divesh Srivastava
AT&T Labs–Research
divesh@research.att.com

Abstract

Data in a warehouse typically has multiple dimensions of interest, such as location, time, and product. It is well-recognized that these dimensions have hierarchies defined on them, such as "store-city-state-region" for location. The standard way to model such data is with a star/snowflake schema. However, current approaches do not give a first-class status to dimensions. Consequently, a substantial class of interesting queries involving dimension hierarchies and their interaction with the fact tables are quite verbose to write, hard to read, and difficult to optimize.

We propose the SQL($\mathcal{H}$) model and a natural extension to the SQL query language, that gives a first-class status to dimensions, and we pin down its semantics. Our model permits structural and schematic heterogeneity in dimension hierarchies, situations often arising in practice that cannot be modeled satisfactorily using the star/snowflake approach. We show using examples that sophisticated queries involving dimension hierarchies and their interplay with aggregation can be expressed concisely in SQL($\mathcal{H}$). By comparison, expressing such queries in SQL would involve a union of numerous complex sequences of joins. Finally, we develop an efficient implementation strategy for computing SQL queries, based on an algorithm for hierarchical joins, and the use of dimension indexes.

* Supported in part by NSF under grant IDM9877060.
† Currently on leave from Concordia University, Canada.

Proceedings of the 25th VLDB Conference, Edinburgh, Scotland, 1999.

1 Introduction

Two key aspects of OLAP queries are aggregation and dimension hierarchies. Aggregations can involve multiple `GROUP BY`s as in `CUBE`, `ROLLUP`, and `DRILLDOWN` [8], or multiple levels of granularity [5, 20]. Several algorithms have been proposed for the efficient implementation of these queries (see, e.g., [8, 5, 9, 1, 23, 19, 20]). In contrast, work on dimension hierarchies has been sparse (see Section 1.2 for details). Dimension hierarchies arise naturally and are central to a large class of useful OLAP queries. In fact, `ROLLUP` and `DRILLDOWN` queries make sense only if there are dimension hierarchies with more than one level. This paper is a study of hierarchy in a data warehouse.

1.1 Contributions

We make the following contributions in this paper.

- We identify some key weaknesses (pertaining to modeling and query language) of the standard star/snowflake schemas, for common OLAP applications (Section 2).
- We propose a model for data warehouses, called the SQL($\mathcal{H}$) data model, which naturally extends the relational data model of SQL, by giving a first-class status to the notion of dimension hierarchies (Section 3).
- We present a simple but powerful extension to SQL, called the SQL($\mathcal{H}$) query language, which allows a user to regard dimension hierarchies as fundamental objects in themselves and express many useful OLAP queries concisely (Section 4).

  We show that a direct approach to expressing many SQL($\mathcal{H}$) queries in SQL will lead to an explosion in the size of the SQL query. This situation is analogous to the `CUBE` operator: even though `CUBE` is expressible in SQL, it is far less concise and harder to optimize.
- Finally, we develop algorithms that enable the direct computation of SQL($\mathcal{H}$) queries, and show that they lead to a significant speedup compared with the evaluation of the equivalent SQL queries (Section 5).

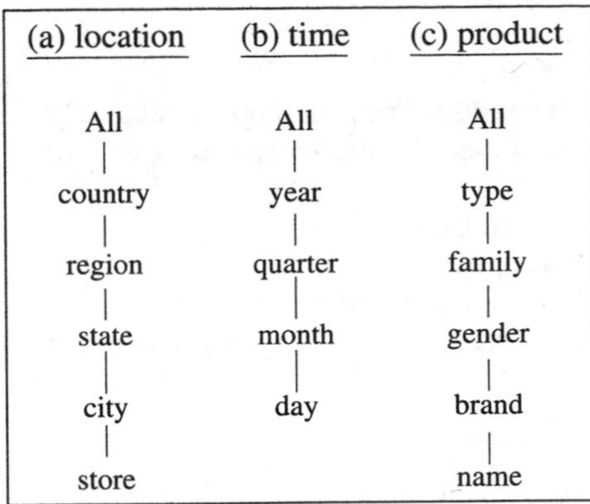

Figure 1: Dimension Hierarchies

1.2 Related Work

There has been a substantial amount of work on the general topic of data warehousing and OLAP (see, e.g., [22, 6]). For the sake of relevance and brevity, we discuss only those works that have addressed the issue of modeling and querying dimension hierarchies here.

Lehner [14] studies modeling issues in large scale OLAP applications and makes a case for heterogeneity arising within and across levels.

The well-known **CUBE** operator was extended by Baralis et al. [2] to deal with multiple aggregations on a data warehouse with hierarchical dimensions. The main issue they addressed was handling the redundancies among **GROUP BY**s arising from the presence of functional dependencies in dimensions. For example, if `zip` $\rightarrow$ `state` holds in dimension `location`, then any aggregation grouped by `zip, state` should yield the same result as one grouped by `zip` alone. This forms the basis for an optimization for computing the so-called hierarchical **CUBE** that they introduce.

Neither of the above two works addresses the technical issues in modeling or querying dimension hierarchies, two novel aspects of our contributions.

On the theoretical side, Cabibbo and Torlone [3] propose a model for multi-dimensional databases. Hurtado et al. [10] build on that model, and address the issue of maintaining materialized views on a data warehouse against updates to dimensions; this issue is completely orthogonal to the objective of this paper. Their models give a first-class status to dimensions, but only insofar as the model is concerned. Their assumption of explicit availability of rollup functions between successive levels of a dimension hierarchy suggests that query evaluation in their model is more likely to resemble that in the snowflake schema model.

2 Motivation

A typical data warehouse consists of *dimensions*, such as `location`, `time` and `product`, and *measures*, such as **dollarAmt** and **quantitySold**, being gauged as a function of the dimensions. The standard way to model and store such data is by means of the *star schema* [12, 6]. In the star schema model, there is a separate *dimension table* for information related to each dimension, and one or more *fact tables* that relate dimension values to measure values.

Star schemas do not model dimension hierarchies very well. They require the complete information associated with a dimension hierarchy to be represented in a single table, even when different levels of the hierarchy have different properties. To mitigate this, the *snowflake schema* was proposed [12, 6], which is obtained by normalizing the star schema, with respect to the various attribute dependencies. Intuitively, each level of a dimension hierarchy is typically represented in a separate table.

While the snowflake schema removes some of the shortcomings of the star schema, it continues to have severe limitations in its support for modeling hierarchies, and for concisely expressing many useful classes of OLAP queries. These limitations are discussed in the next two subsections. In the sequel, by the "traditional approach to data warehousing", we mean modeling data warehouses using snowflake schemas, and querying them using SQL or its extensions, including those with the **CUBE** operator and its variants.

2.1 Limitations on Query Support

Hierarchies enrich the semantics of data in a warehouse and correspondingly enhance the class of interesting and meaningful queries one can pose against it. It is important to be able to express such queries intuitively and concisely, and optimize them effectively. Since hierarchies are not given a first-class status in SQL, even very simple OLAP queries have to be expressed using complex sequences of joins, perhaps together with unions. This makes queries verbose and hard to read. It also makes an implementation of these queries very inefficient.

We now illustrate the above limitations on querying with an example. For the purpose of this example, we temporarily assume that a snowflake schema is adequate for modeling real-life dimension hierarchies, and focus on the limitations of conventional SQL for expressing natural OLAP queries against such a schema. In the next subsection, we shall revisit the modeling issue.

Example 2.1 [A Simple Data Warehouse] Figure 2 shows a data warehouse consisting of a fact table and several dimension tables. The fact table `sales` represents the dollar-sale-amount measure corresponding to the three dimensions: `product, location, time`. (Note the use of the auxiliary `Id` attributes for realizing the hierarchy using a snowflake schema.) We

```
fact table: sales(storeId, prodId, timeId, dollarAmt).
dimension tables:
  location: locn1(storeId, manager, cityId), locn2(cityId, city, manager, stateId),
        locn3(stateId, state, manager, regId), locn4(regId, region, manager, ctryId),
        locn5(ctryId, country, manager).
  time: time1(timeId, day, mthId), time2(mthId, month, qtrId),
        time3(qtrId, quarter, yrId), time4(yrId, year).
  product: prod1(prodId, name, ptfgbId), prod2(ptfgbId, brand, ptfgId),
        prod3(ptfgId, gender, ptfId), prod4(ptfId, family, ptId), prod5(ptId, type).
```

Figure 2: Data Warehouse with Snowflake Schema

(Q1): find location(s) managed by 'john smith'.
(Q2): find the total sales of each location (at any level of the hierarchy) in the NE region of USA.
(Q3): find the total sales of each location (at any level of the hierarchy) that grossed a total sale over $100,000.
(Q4): for each location that grossed a total sale over $100,000, give a breakdown of the sales by its immediate sub-locations.
(Q5): find each location that grossed a total sale over $100,000, and immediate sub-locations that contributed < 10% to the gross value.
(Q6): find the products that performed poorly (grossed less than $1000) in at least one sub-location of every location that grossed over $100,000 dollars (over all products).

Figure 3: OLAP Queries against Snowflake Schema

will refer to the example queries in Figure 3 throughout the paper.[1]

Query Q1 can be expressed using the following SQL query:

```
SELECT storeId
FROM   locn1
WHERE  manager = john.smith
       UNION
       ...
       UNION
SELECT ctryId
FROM   locn5
WHERE  manager = john.smith
```

Depending on the number of levels of the location hierarchy, this can be somewhat tedious. Queries Q2 and Q3 are quite similar. We illustrate how to express query Q3 in SQL:

```
SELECT   locn1.storeId, SUM(dollarAmt)
FROM     locn1, sales
WHERE    locn1.storeId = sales.storeId
GROUP BY locn1.storeId
HAVING   SUM(dollarAmt) > 100000
         UNION
         ...
         UNION
SELECT   locn5.ctryId, SUM(dollarAmt)
FROM     locn5, locn4, locn3, locn2, locn1,
         sales
WHERE    locn5.ctryId = locn4.ctryId AND
         locn4.regId = locn3.regId AND
         locn3.stateId = locn2.stateId AND
         locn2.cityId = locn1.cityId AND
         locn1.storeId = sales.storeId
GROUP BY locn5.ctryId
HAVING   SUM(dollarAmt) > 100000
```

[1] We assume all the Id attributes have compatible domains.

Queries Q4 and Q5 are about as complex to express in SQL, except that they both involve a nested subquery with each of the five single block sub-queries in Q3 above. Query Q6 makes use of the SQL contains predicate, and is very complex to express in SQL. *Note that, in all cases, the SQL queries need to be level sensitive.* ▮

2.2 Limitations on Modeling

We now return to the modeling issue. The snowflake schema, while more flexible than the star schema, still has two key modeling limitations.

- Each dimension hierarchy has to be *balanced*, i.e., the length of the path from the root to any leaf of the hierarchy must be the same.
- All nodes at any one level of a dimension hierarchy have to be *homogeneous*, i.e., they must possess the same set of attributes.

There are many real-life examples where neither of these assumptions is valid.

For example, in the location dimension, stores in USA and in Monaco are forced to be classified in a similar fashion, although it is natural to have a five level hierarchy of store-city-state-region-country for the USA stores, and only a two level hierarchy of store-country for the Monaco stores. Indeed, depending on the geographical distribution of a given enterprise, even within a single country (say USA), dissimilar hierarchies for different regions may be appropriate, since there may be, e.g., many stores in the north-east and fewer in the south.

Snowflake schemas allow for heterogeneity across levels. This enables, e.g., `city` to have the attribute `population`, while `state` may have both `population` and `capital`. However, there can also be considerable heterogeneity within a level, and the snowflake schema offers poor support for modeling such situations. For example, in the `product` dimension, if pants and shirts are at the same level of the dimension hierarchy, they are forced to have the same set of attributes in a snowflake schema, which is quite unnatural: the attribute `inseam` for pants is not applicable to shirts, and the attribute `collarSize` is not applicable to pants.

We conclude this section by noting that the traditional approach does not give a first-class status to the notions of dimension and dimension hierarchies and instead requires explicit manipulation of the set of tables that represent dimension information. Besides, it imposes unrealistic restrictions on the way dimensions can be modeled via such tables.

3 The SQL($\mathcal{H}$) Data Model

Our approach for modeling dimension hierarchies is to (potentially) have an *arbitrary set* of tables for each level in the dimension hierarchy, with no table straddling levels. This SQL($\mathcal{H}$) approach is more flexible than the star or snowflake schemas, and does not require that the dimension hierarchies represented in this fashion be balanced or be homogeneous: (i) Different nodes at the same level of the dimension hierarchy (e.g., ties, pants) could be in different tables, and (naturally) have heterogeneous sets of attributes; (ii) Different "sibling" subtrees in a dimension hierarchy may have different heights, allowing for structural heterogeneity.

Intuitively, we want to treat a *hierarchy* as a tree, where each node corresponds to a tuple over some set of attributes. We want to regard the hierarchy as being based on a special, hierarchical, attribute, in that tables corresponding to all levels share this attribute.

We need a few definitions for formalizing the notion of a dimension.

Definition 3.1 [Hierarchical Domain] A *hierarchical domain* is a non-empty set $\mathcal{V}_\mathcal{H}$ such that it satisfies the following conditions:

1. The only predicates defined on this domain are $=, <, <=, <<, <<=$.
2. The equality predicate $=$ has the standard interpretation of syntactic identity.
3. The predicate $<$ is interpreted as a binary relation over $\mathcal{V}_\mathcal{H}$ such that the graph $G_<$ over the nodes $\mathcal{V}_\mathcal{H}$, with an arc from u to v exactly when $u < v$ holds, is a tree.
4. The predicate $<<$ is interpreted as the transitive closure of (the relation that interprets) $<$.
5. For two elements $u, v \in \mathcal{V}_\mathcal{H}$, $u <= v$ (resp., $u <<= v$) holds iff either $u < v$ or $u = v$ (resp., $u << v$ or $u = v$). ∎

Intuitively, $\mathcal{V}_\mathcal{H}$ is an abstract data type corresponding to hierarchies. The predicate $<$ corresponds to the child/parent relationship: $u < v$ holds iff u is a child of v according to the tree represented by $<$. Similarly, $u << v$ holds iff u is a (proper) descendant of v. We stress that we do not assume any specific implementation of hierarchical domains. For the results and techniques developed in this paper to be applicable, all we require is that the implementation of $\mathcal{V}_\mathcal{H}$ support tests based on the predicates $=, <, <<$, etc.[2] As an example, one way to implement the `location` hierarchy shown in Figure 4 is to represent the location ids as lists of (attribute, value) pairs, as in `country=USA`, `country=USA/region=NE`, `country=USA/region=NE/state=NJ`, etc. As another example, the time ids in the `time` hierarchy can be represented as lists of values, as in `1999`, `1999/2`, etc. Here, the representation indicates ancestors and descendants.

Whenever the domain of an attribute A is a hierarchical domain, we say that A is a *hierarchical attribute* or that A's type is hierarchical. We refer to $dom(A)$ as hierarchical values and sometimes as nodes.

Definition 3.2 [Hierarchy Schema] A *hierarchy schema* is a triple $\mathbf{H} = (G, \mathcal{A}, \sigma)$ such that: (i) G is a rooted DAG, with the root being a special node *All*; (ii) $\mathcal{A}$ is an attribute set, containing a unique hierarchical attribute A_h; and (iii) $\sigma : G \rightarrow 2^\mathcal{A}$ is a function that assigns each node $u \in G$ an attribute set $\sigma(u) \subseteq \mathcal{A}$, such that $\forall u \neq All, A_h \in \sigma(u)$, and $\sigma(All) = \emptyset$. All nodes of G, except *All*, are required to share the unique hierarchical attribute A_h. ∎

As an example, consider the `location` hierarchy (see Figure 1). Let the attributes associated with this hierarchy be {`locId, manager, city, state, region, country`}, and suppose `locId` is the hierarchical attribute. Then the attribute sets associated with the successive nodes from the bottom up are {`locId, manager`}, {`locId, city, manager`}, {`locId, state, manager`}, {`locId, region, manager`}, {`locId, country, manager`}, and {} for the node *All*. Notice that `locId` simultaneously plays the role of `storeId`, `cityId`, `stateId`, `regId` and `ctryId`, and allows for tests of appropriate child/parent and descendant/ancestor relationships among hierarchy nodes.

[2] Preferably efficiently!

Definition 3.3 [Hierarchy] A *hierarchy (instance)* corresponding to a hierarchy schema $\mathbf{H} = (G, \mathcal{A}, \sigma)$ is a collection of tables $\mathcal{H}$, satisfying the following conditions: (i) each table $r \in \mathcal{H}$ corresponds to a unique node $u \in G$, $u \neq All$, and r is a table over $\sigma(u)$; (ii) for any table $r \in \mathcal{H}$ and any two hierarchical values $x, y \in \pi_{A_h}(r)$, neither $x << y$ nor $y << x$ holds;[3] (iii) whenever two tables $r, s \in \mathcal{H}$ correspond to a pair of nodes $u, v \in G$ such that v is a parent (resp., ancestor) of u, then $\forall$ tuples $t_r \in r : \exists t_s \in s : t_r[A_h] < t_s[A_h]$ (resp., $\forall t_r \in r : \exists t_s \in s : t_r[A_h] << t_s[A_h]$). ▮

The first condition says that in a tabular representation of a hierarchy, all tuples in a given level that are represented in one table are over the same attribute set. The second condition essentially says that no table can straddle hierarchy levels. The third condition says that for every tuple in a child (descendant) table, there must correspond a tuple in the parent (ancestor) table such that the hierarchical values in these two tuples are related by the child/parent (descendant/ancestor) relationship. It can be seen that our notion of hierarchy closely corresponds to the notion of hierarchy schema and instance as defined in [3, 10]. The main difference is that we do not assume that nodes (levels) in a hierarchy schema are necessarily named (although our examples show such names, for convenience).

We are now ready to formalize the notion of a dimension.

Definition 3.4 [Dimension] A *dimension schema* $D(\mathbf{H})$ is a name D (called the dimension name) together with a hierarchy schema $\mathbf{H} = (G, \mathcal{A}, \sigma)$. We refer to the attributes $\mathcal{A}$ as the attribute set associated with dimension D.

A *dimension instance* $D(\mathcal{H})$ over a dimension schema $D(\mathbf{H})$ is a dimension name D together with a hierarchy instance $\mathcal{H}$ of $\mathbf{H}$. ▮

Consider the hierarchy schema associated with dimension `location`, described above. An instance of this schema might consist of the tables `loc1`, ..., `loc5` (see Figure 4). Note the difference with the representation of this dimension using the five tables `locn1`–`locn5` in Figure 2. It is important to realize that in each table `loc`i, $1 \leq i \leq 5$, `locId` must be a key. The definition of a dimension instance permits having an arbitrary set of tables (subject to the conditions mentioned). So, in addition to the top-level country table, by introducing separate hierarchy nodes for various countries in the `location` hierarchy of Figure 1, we can have a set of four tables for locations inside USA, perhaps just three tables for locations inside Canada, and only one for those in Monaco. Alternatively, the table `loc1` can contain the tuples for all store locations in USA, Canada and Monaco.[4] Similarly, in the case of dimension `product`, one can have different tables for pants and shirts, even if they are at the same level of the `product` dimension hierarchy, thus permitting modeling of heterogeneous and unbalanced hierarchies with ease.

[3]Note that consequently, neither $u < v$ nor $v < u$ can hold.

[4]In this case, the hierarchy node corresponding to `loc1` may have multiple parents, i.e., the hierarchy schema graph is a DAG.

Definition 3.5 [Data Warehouse Schema] We define a *data warehouse schema* (DW schema) in the SQL($\mathcal{H}$) model as a set of dimension schemas $D_i(\mathbf{H}_i)$, with associated hierarchical attributes A_h^i, $1 \leq i \leq k$, together with a set of fact table schemas[5] of the form $f(A_h^{j_1}, ..., A_h^{j_n}, B_1, ..., B_m)$, where $D_{j_1}, ..., D_{j_n}$ are a subset of the dimensions $D_1, ..., D_k$, and $B_j, 1 \leq j \leq m$, are additional attributes, including the measure attributes. ▮

Recall that each dimension schema itself is composed of a collection of table schemas corresponding to that dimension. As an example, a DW schema corresponding to the data warehouse of Example 2.1 is shown in Figure 4. While the schemas for `location` and `time` closely correspond to the hierarchies shown in Figure 1, for illustrative reasons, we have chosen to make the schema for `product` heterogeneous and unbalanced. For instance, the top level *All* (not shown) of `product` is divided into "formal" and "casual",[6] which are then subdivided using quite different criteria. Notice the considerable heterogeneity in the structure and contents of the `product` dimension hierarchy shown in the figure, compared with that in Example 2.1. An instance of this DW schema would consist of tables over the various table schemas in the figure, subject to the conditions in Definition 3.5.

4 The SQL($\mathcal{H}$) Query Language

The SQL($\mathcal{H}$) model for a data warehouse is consistent with the relational model in that it is possible to query it using standard SQL. In particular, SQL queries continue to have their standard semantics against our extended model for data warehouses.[7] However, to take full advantage of the extended model, we propose simple but powerful extensions to SQL, which exploit the fact that dimensions and their associated hierarchies have a first-class status in the SQL($\mathcal{H}$) model. For simplicity of exposition, we present these extensions in a stage-wise manner.

4.1 Single Block SQL($\mathcal{H}$) Queries

For single block queries, our extensions are of two types.

`DIMENSIONS` clause: We introduce a new `DIMENSIONS` clause in SQL($\mathcal{H}$) queries, where dimension names

[5]Following standard practice (e.g., [6]), we let a DW schema contain one or more fact tables.

[6]We assume all products are clothes.

[7]To perform star and snowflake joins, additional join attributes need to present in the dimension and the fact tables.

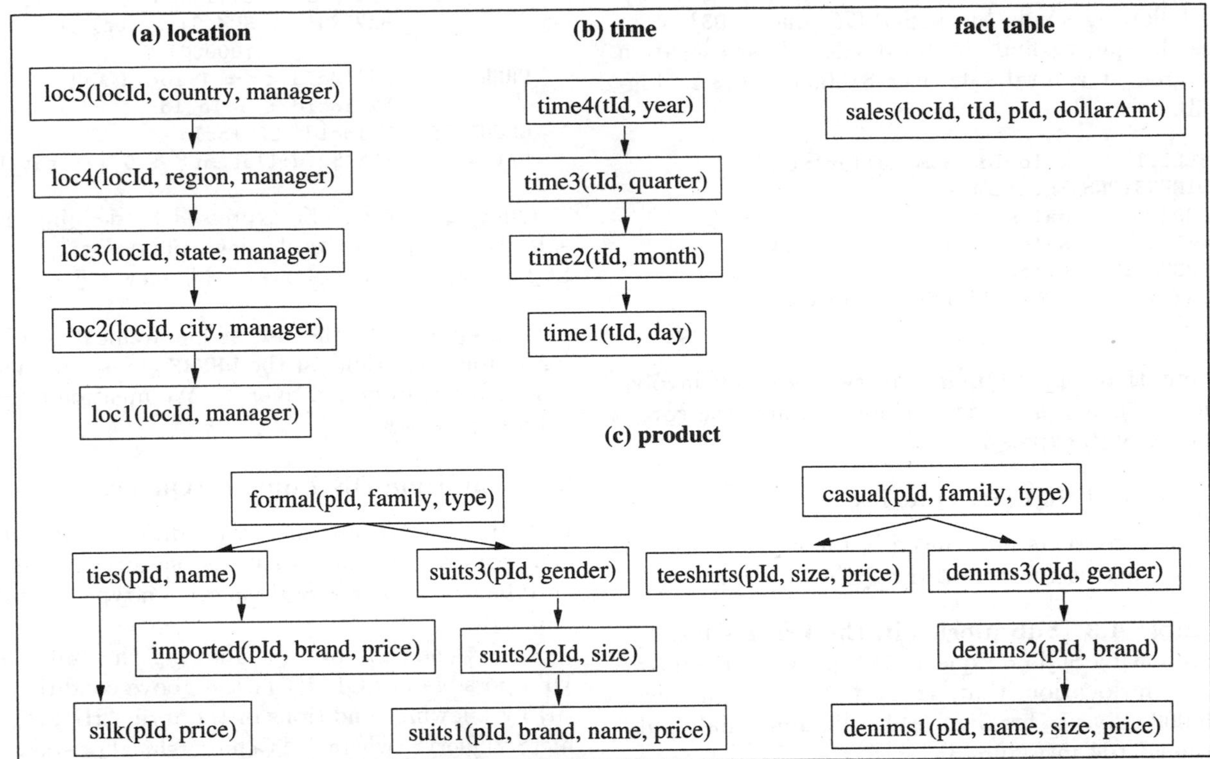

Figure 4: Data Warehouse Schema in the SQL($\mathcal{H}$) Model: Three Dimension Hierarchies and a Fact Table

of interest to the query can be listed, just like tables of interest are listed in the **FROM** clause.

Just as a table R mentioned in the **FROM** clause implicitly declares a tuple variable ranging over R, each dimension name D mentioned in the **DIMENSIONS** clause implicitly declares a dimension variable ranging over that dimension.

Hierarchical predicates: In SQL, domain expressions (DE) of the form $T.A$, T a tuple variable and A an attribute, can be used in various clauses including **SELECT, WHERE, HAVING, GROUP BY**. DEs can be compared with other DEs or with values of a compatible type, using the standard comparison operators $=, <=, <, >, >=, <>$.

In SQL($\mathcal{H}$), we extend the class of domain expressions to include those of the form $V.A$, where V is a dimension variable and A is an attribute associated with the relevant dimension. Such DEs can participate in comparisons just as in SQL.

We also extend domain expressions to include *hierarchical domain expressions* (HDEs), which are of the form $W.A_h$, where W is a tuple variable or a dimension variable and A_h is a hierarchical attribute. A HDE can be compared with another HDE or with a value of a compatible type using the hierarchical predicates $=, <, <=, <<, <<=$. $A < B$ means that A is a child of B in the hierarchy; $A << B$ means that A is a (proper) descendant of B in the hierarchy. The operators $<=$ and $<<=$ correspond to non-proper children and descendants, respectively.

To appreciate the power of these two simple constructs, we present a few examples below.

Example 4.1 [Dimensional Selection]
The following single block SQL($\mathcal{H}$) query, `Q1'`, captures the query "find location(s) managed by john smith" (`Q1` in Figure 3).[8]

```
SELECT      L.locId
DIMENSIONS  location L
WHERE       L.manager = john.smith
```

Note the simplicity of `Q1'` compared with the corresponding SQL expression.

Here, `L` is a dimension variable that ranges over the heterogeneous set of tuples in any of the tables associated with dimension `location`. One can drop the dimension variable `L` from this query. In this case, the attribute **manager** in the **WHERE** clause would implicitly refer to dimension `location`. As in SQL, when there is ambiguity, attributes must be preceded by table names or dimension names (or their aliases). ∎

[8] In general, we shall use the primed versions of query names, `Q1'`, `Q2'`, etc. in the text to indicate the SQL($\mathcal{H}$) expressions corresponding to queries `Q1`, `Q2`, etc.

Example 4.2 [Hierarchical Joins/Aggregation] The following single block SQL($\mathcal{H}$) query, `Q3'`, captures the query "find the total sales of each location that grossed a total sale over $100,000" (`Q3` in Figure 3).[9]

```
SELECT      L.locId, SUM(dollarAmt)
DIMENSIONS  location L
FROM        sales
WHERE       sales.locId <<= L.locId
GROUP BY    L.locId
HAVING      SUM(dollarAmt) > 100000
```

Note that the SQL($\mathcal{H}$) query does not involve (unions of) long sequences of joins, unlike the corresponding SQL expression. ∎

4.2 Nested SQL($\mathcal{H}$) Queries

Our two constructs introduced in the previous section are also very useful in nested SQL($\mathcal{H}$) queries.

Example 4.3 [Subqueries in the `WHERE` Clause] The following SQL($\mathcal{H}$) query, `Q4'`, captures the query "for each location that grossed a total sale over $100,000, give a breakdown by its immediate sub-locations" (`Q4` in Figure 3).

```
SELECT      L1.locId, L2.locId, SUM(dollarAmt)
DIMENSIONS  location L1 L2
FROM        sales
WHERE       sales.locId <<= L1.locId AND
            L2.locId < L1.locId AND
            L1.locId in (
               SELECT      L.locId
               DIMENSIONS  location L
               FROM        sales S
               WHERE       S.locId <<= L.locId
               GROUP BY    L.locId
               HAVING      SUM(S.dollarAmt) >
                           100000)
GROUP BY    L1.locId, L2.locId
```
∎

Example 4.4 [Subqueries in the `FROM` Clause] The following SQL($\mathcal{H}$) query, `Q5'`, captures the query "find each location that grossed a total sale over $100,000, and its immediate sub-locations that contributed to < 10% of the gross value" (`Q5` in Figure 3).

```
SELECT      T.locId, L2.locId
DIMENSIONS  location L2
FROM        sales S2,
            (SELECT      L1.locId,
                         SUM(dollarAmt) AS total
            DIMENSIONS  location L1
            FROM        sales S1
            WHERE       S1.locId <<= L1.locId
            GROUP BY    L1.locId
            HAVING      SUM(S1.sales) >
                        100000) T
WHERE       S2.locId <<= T.locId AND
            L2.locId < T.locId
GROUP BY    T.locId, L2.locId
HAVING      SUM(S2.dollarAmt) < 0.1*T.total
```

Query `Q5` can also be expressed by defining the result of query `Q3'` as a table view, and defining a regular SQL query that makes use of this view. ∎

In keeping with the use of hierarchical predicates for simple conditions in the `WHERE` clause, we also allow their use in nested queries. We mention two such extensions below.

The condition DE θ qual setQuery:

In SQL, one can use such a condition, where θ is a comparison operator, "qual" is one of *all, any*, and "setQuery" is a unary SQL query of a type compatible with DE.

We extend this by: (i) allowing the full class of DEs possible in SQL($\mathcal{H}$) in the above condition, and (ii) by allowing conditions of the form "HDE θ_h qual hierSetQuery", where θ_h is a hierarchical predicate and "hierSetQuery" is an SQL($\mathcal{H}$) query returning a set of hierarchical values from the same domain as HDE.

The `contains` predicate:

In SQL, one can express conditions involving universal quantifiers using expressions of the form "sqlQuery1 **`contains`** sqlQuery2", where "sqlQuery1" and "sqlQuery2" are SQL queries of the same type (and hence over the same number of attributes). The semantics of this condition is a test as to whether the result of "sqlQuery1" is a superset of that of "sqlQuery2".

In SQL($\mathcal{H}$), we additionally allow conditions of the form "hierSqlhQuery1 θ_h **`contains`** hierSqlhQuery2", where both "hierSqlhQuery1" and "hierSqlhQuery2" are SQL($\mathcal{H}$) queries returning a set of hierarchical values from the same domain, and θ_h is as before. The semantics of this condition is a test as to whether for every hierarchical value u in the result of "hierSqlhQuery2", there is a hierarchical value v in the result of "hierSqlhQuery1", such that $v\ \theta_h\ u$ holds.

Example 4.5 [Hierarchical `contains`] The following SQL($\mathcal{H}$) query, `Q6'`, captures the query "find the products that performed poorly (i.e., grossed less than $1000) in at least one sub-location of every location that grossed over $100,000 dollars (over all products)" (`Q6` in Figure 3).

```
SELECT      P.pId
DIMENSIONS  product P
WHERE       (SELECT      L1.locId
             DIMENSIONS  location L1
```

[9] The more natural query "find the *lowest* level locations, and their sales, among locations that grossed a total sale over $100,000" can also be easily expressed in SQL($\mathcal{H}$), though not as a single block query.

```
FROM          sales S1
WHERE         S1.pId <<= P.pId AND
              S1.locId <<= L1.locId
GROUP BY      L1.locId
HAVING        SUM(S1.dollarAmt) <
              1000)

<<= contains

(SELECT       L2.locId
DIMENSIONS    location L2
FROM          sales S2
WHERE         S2.locId <<= L2.locId
GROUP BY      L2.locId
HAVING        SUM(S2.dollarAmt) >
              100000)
```
■

4.3 Semantics of SQL($\mathcal{H}$) Queries

In this section, we define the semantics of single block SQL($\mathcal{H}$) queries.

Before we pin down the semantics, there is an issue to settle. The SQL($\mathcal{H}$) model supports two kinds of first-class objects: *tables* (corresponding to the fact tables) and *dimensions* (with their hierarchies). Even though for practical considerations, dimensions may be realized using a set of tables, they do have a first-class status in the query language, as illustrated in the preceding sections. Thus the input to an SQL($\mathcal{H}$) query consists of both tables and dimensions. If so, what should be the type of the output? In principle, both queries that produce tables as output (like conventional SQL) and those that produce dimensions (i.e., a set of tables that realize them) as output are meaningful. Indeed, we anticipate applications for both types of queries.

The various SQL($\mathcal{H}$) queries presented earlier in this paper all produce tables as output. The following variant of query `Q1'` is an example of an SQL($\mathcal{H}$) query that produces a dimension as an output.

```
SELECT       L.*
DIMENSIONS   location L
WHERE        L.manager = john.smith
```

The result in this case is a hierarchy instance, where each table is a subset of the corresponding table in the input, corresponding to the condition `L.manager = john.smith`.

For lack of space, in this paper, we confine ourselves to SQL($\mathcal{H}$) queries that produce tables as output. A natural restriction on SQL($\mathcal{H}$) queries to ensure that the result is a table is that the **SELECT** clause contain only: (a) the hierarchical **Id** attributes (e.g., **locId**), (b) dimension attributes that appear in every table of the dimension (e.g., **manager**), and (c) aggregates of measure attributes (e.g., **SUM(dollarAmt)**). We refer to such queries as *uniform* SQL($\mathcal{H}$) queries.

Consider a generic uniform SQL($\mathcal{H}$) query:

```
Q: SELECT      domExpList, aggList
   DIMENSIONS  dimList
   FROM        fromList
   WHERE       whereConditions
   GROUP BY    groupbyList
   HAVING      haveConditions
```

An important question is the following. A tuple variable (implicit or explicit) in SQL ranges over the set of tuples in the associated table. If so, what exactly does a dimension variable range over?

> We propose that a dimension variable should range over the set of nodes in the hierarchy associated with the dimension instance.

Given that each hierarchy (instance) node corresponds to a tuple, this means that a dimension variable ranges over a heterogeneous set of tuples corresponding to the various nodes in its associated hierarchy. While this is quite unlike the case with tuple variables (which always range over homogeneous sets of tuples in a given table), we shall show that uniform SQL($\mathcal{H}$) queries are always well-defined and "well-typed".

Following the notation used in [13], we define the semantics of a uniform SQL($\mathcal{H}$) query Q as a function

$$Q : \mathcal{D} \rightarrow \mathcal{R}$$

from input databases $\mathcal{D}$ to tables $\mathcal{R}$ over the output scheme of the query. For a database $\mathbf{D} \in \mathcal{D}$, let $\mathcal{T}_D$ denote the set of all tuples appearing in any table in $\mathbf{D}$, including fact and dimension tables. Let τ be the set of tuple variables in Q and η the set of dimension variables in Q. Define an *instantiation* as a function $\imath : (\tau \cup \eta) \rightarrow \mathcal{T}_D$, that maps each tuple variable to a tuple in the appropriate (fact) table,[10] and each dimension variable to a tuple in some table associated with that dimension. For each condition **cond** appearing in the **WHERE** clause, a notion of satisfaction is defined as follows. Let $\imath(X)[A]$, X being a tuple/dimension variable, denote the restriction of the tuple $\imath(X)$ to the attribute A.

- if **cond** is of the form $T.A\ \theta$ opnd, where T is a tuple variable, A is an attribute, and opnd is either a DE or a value of the appropriate type, then $\imath$ satisfies **cond** iff $\imath(T)[A]$ stands in relationship θ to $\imath$(opnd).[11] This is exactly the same as for SQL.

- if **cond** is of the form $V.A\ \theta$ opnd, where V is a dimension variable, then $\imath$ satisfies **cond** iff $\imath(V)$ is mapped to a tuple in a dimension table for which attribute A is defined, and further $\imath(V)[A]$ stands in relationship θ to $\imath$(opnd).

[10] Recall that there might be more than one fact table.
[11] We assume $\imath(c) = c$, for every constant value c.

- if cond is of the form $W.A_h\ \theta_h$ opnd, where W is a tuple or a dimension variable and A_h is a hierarchical attribute, then $\imath$ satisfies **cond** iff $\imath(V)[A_h]$ is a θ_h-relative of $\imath$(opnd), according to the hierarchical domain of A_h.

Let $\mathcal{I}_Q$ denote the set of all instantiations that satisfy the conditions **whereConditions**. Then a tuple assembly function can be defined as

$$tuple_Q(\imath) = \bigotimes_{\text{“}X.A\text{”} \in \mathbf{domExpList}} \imath(X)[A]$$

Here, the predicate "$X.A$" $\in$ **domExpList** indicates the condition that the attribute denotation $X.A$ literally appears in the list of domain expressions **domExpList** in the **SELECT** statement. The symbol $\otimes$ denotes concatenation. For an instantiation $\imath$, $tuple_Q(\imath)$ thus produces a tuple over the attributes listed in the **domExpList** part of the **SELECT** statement. If Q is a query without aggregation (i.e. **aggList**, **GROUP BY** clause, and **HAVING** clause are empty), then the result of the query is captured by the function

$$Q(\mathbf{D}) = \{tuple_Q(\imath) \mid \imath \in \mathcal{I}_Q\}$$

Handling aggregation is done in the obvious manner, using an appropriately defined equivalence relation, just as is done for SQL. The following result is straightforward.

Proposition 4.1 *Let Q be any legal uniform SQL($\mathcal{H}$) query over a DW schema $\mathbf{S}$. Then Q is well-typed, in the sense that it maps every instance $\mathbf{D}$ of $\mathbf{S}$ to a table over the output scheme of Q.*

Proof: Follows from the semantics of SQL($\mathcal{H}$) queries given above. ∎

5 Direct Evaluation of SQL($\mathcal{H}$) Queries

We present algorithms for the efficient evaluation of SQL($\mathcal{H}$) queries in this section. The two key challenges that we need to address, over standard SQL evaluation, are: (a) dealing with dimension selection conditions, such as "`L.manager = john.smith`" (in query **Q1'**), and (b) dealing with hierarchical joins, such as the one between `location` and **sales** using the predicate "`S.locId <<= L.locId`" (in queries **Q2'** and **Q3'**). We describe our solution for dealing with dimension selections in Section 5.1, and present an efficient approach for hierarchical joins in Sections 5.2 and 5.3.

5.1 Selections and Dimension Indexes

Database indexes available in current database systems, such as B-tree indexes [7], hash indexes [15] and bitmap indexes [16, 4], retrieve tuples of a *single table* with specified values for one or more attributes.

Since dimensions are represented by a set of heterogeneous tables, selection conditions in SQL($\mathcal{H}$) queries implicitly range over tuples in *multiple tables*. For example, "**L.locId <<= country=USA/region=NE**" in query **Q2'** will be satisfied by tuples corresponding to states, cities, and individual stores, which are all represented in different tables. Again, the condition "**L.manager** = `john.smith`" on the `location` dimension in query **Q1'** could be satisfied at any level of the dimension hierarchy. Using conventional (single table) indexes, determining all nodes in a dimension hierarchy that match a given condition would require access to multiple (possibly large number of) indexes, and can be quite inefficient.

Our solution to the problem of efficiently dealing with dimension selections involves construction of indexes, called *dimension indexes*, on (one or more) attributes of a single dimension. Since multiple dimension tables may share an attribute (e.g., the **locId** and the **manager** attributes are shared by all tables in the `location` dimension), dimension indexes are inherently multi-table indexes. Instead of associating the set of tuples in a single table with a keyvalue, dimension indexes (conceptually) associate a set of (table, tuple) pairs with a keyvalue. When multiple tuples in a single table match a keyvalue, factoring out the table can result in a potential for compression. Dimension indexes can be organized as B-trees, hash indexes, bitmap indexes, or any standard index structure.

Dimension indexes are similar, in spirit, to join indexes [21] which typically associate attribute values and tuples of two tables, and their generalizations. However, join indexes (as the name suggests) have been used only to support join processing, not multi-table selections.

5.2 Hierarchical Joins

Star joins have been used to denote the join of a fact table with multiple dimension tables, represented using a star schema. The star join conditions typically include selection conditions on the dimension tables as well. The specialized nature of star schemas makes join indexes especially attractive for OLAP queries [17, 6].

Different flavors of bitmap join indexes have been proposed to efficiently deal with star joins [17, 18]. In its simplest form [17], a bitmap join index is a bitmap index on the fact table T based on a single attribute A of a (star schema) dimension table V.

> The bitmap join index is useful precisely when the OLAP query specifies a selection condition on attribute A of dimension table V, and a join condition between the fact table T and the dimension table V.

For example, one can maintain a bitmap join index on the **sales** fact table based on the attribute **state** in the `location` dimension. Thus, the index entry for **NJ** is a bitmap that identifies the tuples in the **sales** table that correspond to stores whose state is **NJ**. This index entry can be used, e.g., in a star join OLAP query that specifies the selection condition "**location.state = NJ**" and the join condition "**location.storeId = sales.storeId**".

Modeling limitations of star schemas have led to snowflake schemas for data warehouses. However, there has not been much research reported in enhancing star join algorithms to efficiently perform snowflake joins. The approach of [17], of using bitmap join indexes, while applicable, is not as efficient for snowflake joins as in the case of star joins. To see why, consider the following query, which is one of the three subqueries in the SQL expression of Query **Q2**, using the snowflake schema of Figure 2.

```
SELECT   locn1.storeId, SUM(dollarAmt)
FROM     locn1, locn2, locn3, locn4, locn5,
         sales
WHERE    locn5.country = USA AND
         locn4.state = NE AND
         locn5.ctryId = locn4.ctryId AND
         locn4.regId = locn3.regId AND
         locn3.stateId = locn2.stateId AND
         locn2.cityId = locn1.cityId AND
         locn1.storeId = sales.storeId
GROUP BY locn1.storeId
```

Note that there is *no* join condition between the fact table (**sales**) and any of the dimension tables on which selection conditions have been specified (**locn4** and **locn5**). Multiple bitmap join indexes (between tables corresponding to successive levels of the dimension hierarchy) would have to be built to support the above sequence of joins in an SQL query evaluation engine. Clearly, this approach is considerably less efficient for snowflake joins than in the case of star joins. For snowflake joins to have comparable efficiency to star joins, bitmap transitive join indexes could be built for this task. However, using them effectively would require the SQL query evaluation engine to have a detailed knowledge of the representation of dimension hierarchies as tables, and a substantial change to the query processing strategies.

Modeling dimension hierarchies using the SQL($\mathcal{H}$) model not only results in conceptual simplicity and elegance, but also allows for computational efficiency that is comparable to the use of bitmap join indexes for star joins. Our solution involves the use of a star join style algorithm for *hierarchical joins*, i.e., joins that use hierarchical predicates. The SQL($\mathcal{H}$) query **Q2'** can be expressed as follows, using the DW schema of Figure 4.

```
SELECT     L.locId, SUM(dollarAmt)
DIMENSIONS location L
FROM       sales
WHERE      sales.locId <<= L.locId AND
           L.locId <<= country=USA/region=NE
GROUP BY   L.locId
```

Note that the hierarchical join condition *is* between the fact table (**sales**) and the dimension on which a selection condition has been specified (**location**). Given a bitmap join index on the **sales** table based on the pair of attributes **country** and **region** of dimension **location**, *the hierarchical join could be performed as efficiently as the star join.* We next examine how bitmap join indexes that enable hierarchical joins can be constructed efficiently.

5.3 Bitmap Join Indexes for Hierarchical Joins

The bitmap join index used in computing the star join, as described in [17], is based on the assumption that the join between the fact table and the dimension table is an *equality join*. In SQL($\mathcal{H}$) queries, many different join predicates, such as $=, <, <=, <<, <<=$, can be used. To efficiently support each of these predicates between the **Id** attribute of the dimension and the corresponding attribute of the fact table, different bitmap join indexes may be needed. The choice of which ones are created depends on the predicates used in the anticipated query workload.

In this section, we present an efficient algorithm, called **ComputeBitmapHJoinIndex**, for computing a $(<<=, =)$-bitmap join index, which could be used for hierarchical join computation when the hierarchical predicate $<<=$ is used in the join condition between the fact table and the dimension (e.g., **sales.locId <<= L.locId**), and the equality predicate ($=$) is used in the selection condition on a dimension attribute (e.g., **L.manager = john.smith**). This algorithm is loosely based on the I/O efficient algorithm for computing hierarchical semijoins for querying network directories [11].

Let T denote the fact table, V the dimension, and A the dimension attribute on which the $(<<=, =)$-bitmap join index needs to be constructed. The resulting (uncompressed) bitmap join index would have $\mid A \mid$ bit-vectors, each with $\mid T \mid$ bits. A naive algorithm would compute this index as follows, assuming a total ordering on the VId attribute of the dimension and a total ordering on the tuple identifiers (RID's) of the fact table.

- First, allocate a 2-d bit-array VT with $\mid V \mid$ rows and $\mid T \mid$ columns, with each bit initialized to 0.[12]

  Examine each pair of (T tuple, V tuple). If $T.VId <<= V.VId$, set bit $VT[V.VId][T.RID] = 1$.

- Next, allocate a 2-d bit-array AT with $\mid A \mid$ rows and $\mid T \mid$ columns, with each bit initialized to 0.

[12] Zeroing out of an entire array of bits can be done very efficiently in most systems, and is not counted in our cost analysis.

```
Algorithm ComputeBitmapHJoinIndex (T, V, A) {
  T denotes the fact table, with | T | tuples.
  V denotes the dimension, with | V | tuples
      in the various tables of dimension V.
  A denotes V's attribute, with | A | values.
  Let VId denotes the join attribute of T and V.
  Let L denote the leaf nodes of dimension V, and
      | L | denote the number of such nodes.

  /* Phase 1: scan the fact table and build a
      bitmap index on T.VId */
  Let LT be a bit-array with | L | rows and
      | T | columns, initialized to 0's.
  for each tuple in T with tuple identifier T.RID
    LT[T.VId][T.RID] = 1

  /* Phase 2: use the tree structure of VId's domain
      to build a complete hierarchy bitmap */
  Let V_s be a preorder traversal of the VId's in V.
  Let VT be a bit-array with | V | rows and
      | T | columns, initialized to 0's.
  /* stack S identifies (parent, child) pairs */
  Initially stack S is empty.
  node v_l = firstElement(V_s).
  repeat {
    if (stack S is empty)
      push v_l on top of stack S.
      v_l = nextElement(V_s).
    else {
      let v_t be the node at the top of the stack S.
      if (v_l < v_t) /* is v_l a child of v_t? */
        push v_l on top of stack S.
        v_l = nextElement(V_s).
      else {
        if (v_t is a leaf node)
          VT[v_t] = LT[v_t]
        pop stack.
        if (stack S is not empty) {
          let v_b be the node at the top of S.
          /* bit-wise OR with child's bitmap */
          VT[v_b] = VT[v_b] || VT[v_t].
        }
      }
    }
  } until (all nodes in V_s have been processed
      and stack S is empty).

  /* Phase 3: build bitmap join index on A values */
  Let AT be a bit-array with | A | rows and
      | T | columns, initialized to 0's.
  /* many V tuples may have the same A value */
  for each tuple in V
    if (V.A = val)
      AT[val] = AT[val] || VT[V.VId].
}
```

Figure 5: Computing a (<<=, =)-Bitmap Join Index

Examine each V tuple. If $V.A = val$, set $AT[val] = AT[val] \quad || \quad VT[V.VId]$, where $AT[val]$ and $VT[V.VId]$ represent bit-vectors of $| T |$ bits, and "||" is the bit-wise OR.

The naive algorithm scans $O(| V | * | T |)$ tuples, performs $| V | * | T |$ bit-level operations, and $| V |$ bit-vector operations. The overall cost is dominated by the cost of scanning tuples.

We describe Algorithm **ComputeBitmapHJoinIndex**, and analyze its computational complexity. In the first phase, the fact table tuples are scanned once, and a bitmap index on the VId attribute of the fact table T is constructed. In the second phase, the algorithm takes advantage of the hierarchical structure of the VId domain, and (recursively) computes bitmaps for parent nodes in the VId domain based on the bitmaps of their children nodes. (The leaf-level bitmaps are identical to the bitmaps constructed in Phase 1.) In this phase, each node's bit-vector is touched precisely once, without accessing any tuple in any table. In the third phase, the desired (<<=, =)-bitmap join index is constructed on fact table T based on the A attribute of dimension V. Algorithm **ComputeBitmapHJoinIndex** scans each fact table tuple and dimension table tuple exactly once, at the cost of a few more bit-vector operations than the naive algorithm.

Theorem 5.1 *Algorithm* **ComputeBitmapHJoinIndex** *correctly computes the (<<=, =)-bitmap join index. Further, it scans* $| V | + | T |$ *tuples, performs* $| T |$ *bit-level operations, and* $2* | V |$ *bit-vector operations.* ∎

Bitmap join indexes for other hierarchical predicates can be constructed just as efficiently.

6 Conclusions

By recognizing dimensions and dimension hierarchies as a first class construct in the context of a relational data warehouse, and reflecting this through suitable enhancements to SQL, we have demonstrated the considerable benefits that can be derived, both in ease of query expression and in computational efficiency of query evaluation.

Giving dimension hierarchies a first class status in the SQL($\mathcal{H}$) model permitted flexible modeling of structural and schematic heterogeneity, situations often arising in practice that cannot be modeled satisfactorily using the star/snowflake schemas. To take full advantage of the SQL($\mathcal{H}$) model, we proposed two key extensions to the SQL($\mathcal{H}$) query language: a novel **DIMENSIONS** clause, and the use of hierarchical predicates in conditions. The ease of expression of a large variety of OLAP queries is testimony to the power of these simple constructs. Finally, we complemented our extensions to the query language and data model with an algorithm for the efficient construction of a family of bitmap join indexes. These indexes enable the efficient computation of hierarchical joins, in the same way that bitmap indexes are instrumental in the efficient computation of star joins.

Our work establishes the foundations for further research in the important area of hierarchies in data warehouses.

References

[1] S. Agarwal, R. Agrawal, P. M. Deshpande, A. Gupta, J. F. Naughton, R. Ramakrishnan, and S. Sarawagi. On the computation of multidimensional aggregates. In *Proceedings of the International Conference on Very Large Databases*, pages 506–521, 1996.

[2] E. Baralis, S. Paraboschi, and E. Teniente. Materialized view selection in a multidimensional database. In *Proceedings of the International Conference on Very Large Databases*, 1997.

[3] L. Cabibbo and R. Torlone. Querying multidimensional databases. In *Proceedings of the 6th DBPL Workshop*, pages 253–269, 1997.

[4] C.-Y. Chan and Y. Ioannidis. Bitmap index design and evaluation. In *Proceedings of the ACM SIGMOD Conference on Management of Data*, pages 355–366, 1998.

[5] D. Chatziantoniou and K. A. Ross. Querying multiple features of groups in relational databases. In *Proceedings of the International Conference on Very Large Databases*, pages 295–306, 1996.

[6] S. Chaudhuri and U. Dayal. An overview of data warehousing and OLAP technology. *SIGMOD Record*, 26(1):65–74, Mar. 1997.

[7] D. Comer. The ubiquitous B-tree. *ACM Computing Surveys*, 11(2):121–137, 1979.

[8] J. Gray, A. Bosworth, A. Layman, and H. Pirahesh. Datacube : A relational aggregation operator generalizing group-by, cross-tab, and subtotals. In *Proceedings of the IEEE International Conference on Data Engineering*, pages 152–159, 1996. Also available as Microsoft Technical Report MSR-TR-95-22.

[9] V. Harinarayan, A. Rajaraman, and J. D. Ullman. Implementing data cubes efficiently. In *Proceedings of the ACM SIGMOD Conference on Management of Data*, pages 205–216, 1996.

[10] C. Hurtado, A. Mendelzon, and A. Vaisman. Maintaining data cubes under dimension updates. In *Proceedings of the IEEE International Conference on Data Engineering*, 1999.

[11] H. V. Jagadish, L. V. S. Lakshmanan, T. Milo, D. Srivastava, and D. Vista. Querying network directories. In *Proceedings of the ACM SIGMOD Conference on Management of Data*, Philadelphia, PA, June 1999.

[12] R. Kimball. *The data warehouse toolkit.* John Wiley, 1996.

[13] L. V. S. Lakshmanan, F. Sadri, and I. N. Subramanian. SchemaSQL – A language for querying and restructuring multidatabase systems. In *Proceedings of the International Conference on Very Large Databases*, pages 239–250, 1996.

[14] W. Lehner. Modeling large scale OLAP scenarios. In *Proceedings of the International Conference on Extending Database Technology*, 1998.

[15] W. Litwin. Linear hashing: A new tool for file and table addressing. In *Proceedings of the International Conference on Very Large Databases*, pages 212–223, 1980.

[16] P. O'Neil. Model 204 architecture and performance. In *Proceedings of the 2nd International Workshop on High Performance Transaction Systems*, Lecture Notes in Computer Science, No. 359, pages 40–59, 1987.

[17] P. O'Neil and G. Graefe. Multi-table joins through bitmapped join indices. *SIGMOD Record*, 24(3):8–11, Sept. 1995.

[18] P. O'Neil and D. Quass. Improved query performance with variant indexes. In *Proceedings of the ACM SIGMOD Conference on Management of Data*, pages 38–49, 1997.

[19] K. A. Ross and D. Srivastava. Fast computation of sparse datacubes. In *Proceedings of the International Conference on Very Large Databases*, pages 116–125, 1997.

[20] K. A. Ross, D. Srivastava, and D. Chatziantoniou. Complex aggregation at multiple granularities. In *Proceedings of the International Conference on Extending Database Technology*, 1998.

[21] P. Valduriez. Join indices. *ACM Trans. Database Syst.*, 12(2):218–246, June 1987.

[22] J. Widom. Research problems in data warehousing. In *Proceedings of the Fourth International Conference on Information and Knowledge Management (CIKM)*, pages 25–30, Baltimore, MD, Nov. 1995.

[23] Y. Zhao, P. M. Deshpande, and J. F. Naughton. An array-based algorithm for simultaneous multidimensional aggregates. In *Proceedings of the ACM SIGMOD Conference on Management of Data*, pages 159–170, 1997.

O-O, What Have They Done to DB2?

Michael Carey
Don Chamberlin
Srinivasa Narayanan
Bennet Vance
IBM Almaden Research Center

Doug Doole
Serge Rielau
Richard Swagerman
IBM Toronto Laboratory

Nelson Mattos
IBM Database Technology Institute
Santa Teresa Laboratory

Abstract

In this paper, we describe our recent experiences in adding a number of object-relational extensions to the DB2 Universal Database (UDB) system as part of a research and development project at the IBM Almaden Research Center. In particular, we have enhanced DB2 UDB with support for structured types and tables of these types, type and table hierarchies, references, path expressions, and object views. In doing so, we have taken care to design and implement the extensions in such a way as to retain DB2's ability to fully optimize queries and (in our next step) to support business rules and procedures through the provision of constraints and triggers. We describe each of the SQL language extensions that we have made, discuss the key performance tradeoffs related to the design and implementation of these features, and explain the approach that we ended up choosing (and why). Most of the features described here are currently shipping as part of Version 5.2 of the DB2 UDB product. We end this paper with a summary of the current status of our work and a discussion of what we plan to tackle next.

1 Introduction

The introduction of the relational model [6] revolutionized the information systems world by providing a simple, high-level data model and the foundation for declarative query interfaces. Relational database systems, with their separation of the logical schema (tables) from the underlying physical schema (storage and index structures), together with their support for alternative views of a given logical schema, have been very successful in providing a high level of data independence that has led to significant productivity gains for both application programmers and end users. The past 15–20 years of research in the database area, initiated by the relational revolution, have brought us to an era where most modern relational database systems offer efficient query optimization and execution strategies, excellent levels of multiuser performance and robustness through well-tuned buffer and transaction management subsystems, view facilities for alternative conceptual schemas and flexible authorization, and native business logic support through the provision of declarative constraints, triggers, and stored procedures [12]. Finally, the declarative nature and set-orientation of relational query languages laid a natural foundation for research on parallelization of database operations; as a result, parallel relational database systems have become what is by far the most significant commercial success story in the area of parallel computing [7].

Despite this success story, the world has continued to place ever-increasing demands on database technology. One reason for this is the appearance of interesting new data types (text, images, audio, video, spatial data) and applications wishing to use database systems to manage them in large quantities. A second reason is the mismatch between the complexity of modern enterprises and the spartan simplicity of the relational model: enterprises have entities and relationships (versus tables), variations within a given kind of entity (versus the homogeneity of relational tables), and both single- and multi-valued attributes (versus relational normalization rules). A third reason is commercial growth in applications that wish to use database systems to manage large quantities of highly complex interrelated data objects, including

Proceedings of the 25th VLDB Conference, Edinburgh, Scotland, 1999.

CAD/CAM systems, web servers, and digital libraries, to name a few. This has led the research community to look for new solutions, particularly through "objects," for the past decade or so [1]. In particular, this growth has led relational database system researchers and vendors to look at the option of adding object-oriented extensions to the relational model and its query languages. As a result, relational database systems are evolving into *object-relational* database systems that provide such features as an extensible type system, inheritance, support for complex objects, and rules [13].

IBM's DB2 Universal Database system, IBM's version of DB2 for Unix, NT, Windows, and OS/2 platforms (both serial and parallel), has been making the transition into an object-relational database system since the debut of DB2 Version 2 for Common Servers in 1995. DB2 V2 incorporated various new technologies developed in the context of the Starburst research project at IBM Almaden [8]. In terms of object-relational extensions, DB2 V2 included significant new features in the areas of user-defined column types (UDTs, also referred to as "distinct types"), user-defined functions (UDFs), and triggers. The DB2 Universal Database (UDB) System, which became available as DB2 Version 5 in late 1997, added new support for utilizing these features on parallel platforms by merging DB2 V2 with DB2 Parallel Edition, a previously separate product for MPP hardware platforms. In addition, DB2 UDB includes a set of "extenders" for dealing with commonly interesting new data types including text, image, and audio; these extenders currently use a mix of UDTs, UDFs, and triggers to provide their functionality.

For about two years now, the OSF ("Object Strike Force") project, a joint effort between the IBM Almaden Research Center and the IBM Database Technology Institute, has been working to add another dimension of object-relational functionality to DB2 UDB. In particular, we have been extending UDB with support for user-defined structured types with inheritance, tables and subtables of these types, object ids and references, path expressions, and object views. This support made its public debut in DB2 UDB Version 5.2 in September of 1998, and more is coming. In adding these features to UDB, we have taken care to ensure that our extensions provide a step forward in UDB's data modeling and data manipulation functionality without dictating a corresponding step backward in terms of its performance or the provision of advanced features such as automatic query optimization, constraints, or triggers [14, 10]. Our end goal is to evolve UDB into a strong platform for general-purpose complex object management. In this paper, we share some of the experiences that we have had so far in the process. We describe the SQL extensions that we have made, discuss some performance tradeoffs that we have faced in the design and implementation of these extensions, and discuss particular choices that we made (and why) in adding these features to UDB at Almaden. Our hope is that this paper will be of interest to database students and practitioners; it should also be of interest to researchers interested in monitoring commercial progress in the area of object-relational databases. In addition, we have been heavily involved in reshaping the SQL99 (known as SQL3 until recently) standard over the past 1–2 years, and the bulk of our DB2 extensions are SQL99-compliant; thus, this paper also provides a look at the object model and query facilities in SQL99 as it stands today.

The remainder of this paper is organized as follows: In the next few sections, we discuss our SQL language extensions; we start with our basic DDL extensions, turn to the associated DML extensions, and then turn to advanced features such as object views, constraints, and triggers. Throughout, we discuss the design considerations that led us to make the choices that we made. Following the language sections, the next section of the paper discusses how we approached the implementation of certain key object features. Again, we attempt to share some of the reasoning that led to the choices that we ended up making. Finally, the last two sections of the paper discuss where we are with UDB today, roughly how the resulting system compares to other vendors' offerings, and lists some new features that we are either currently exploring or planning to explore.

2 Basic SQL Data Definition Language Extensions

We have extended SQL's data definition language (DDL) into object-oriented (O-O) territory by adding a number of features commonly found in O-O database systems. In this section we describe our extensions by example, using a very simple university database.

One of the fundamental features that we have added to UDB is a facility that allows users to define structured types via a new **create type** statement. Two basic entity types in a university schema are people (Person_t) and departments (Dept_t). University people come in various flavors, such as university employees (Emp_t) and students (Student_t). Within employees, there may again be various flavors; let's suppose that there are just regular employees and professors (Prof_t). Let's assume that each employee works in a department, and that each department is managed by an employee. (We ignore the many other relationships that might exist among these types to keep the example simple.) Figure 1(a) shows the resulting entity and relationship types graphically.

Our O-O extensions to SQL's DDL enable the user to directly translate the entities and relationships above into a set of structured types and subtypes with references. In UDB, these type definitions would be

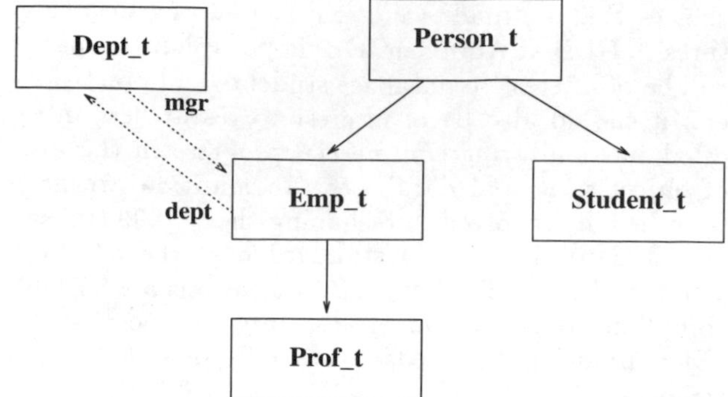

(a) Schematic of university entities and relationships

```
create type Person_t as (
    name Varchar(40), birthyear Integer
) mode db2sql;

create type Emp_t under Person_t as (
    salary Integer
) mode db2sql;

create type Prof_t under Emp_t as (
    rank Varchar(10), specialty Varchar(20)
) mode db2sql;

create type Student_t under Person_t as (
    major Varchar(20), gpa Decimal(5,2)
) mode db2sql;

create type Dept_t as (
    name Varchar(20), budget Integer,
    headcnt Integer, mgr Ref(Emp_t)
) mode db2sql;

alter type Emp_t add attribute dept Ref(Dept_t);
```

(b) DDL statements to create the university types

Figure 1: A structured-type hierarchy

specified (filling in their attribute details) as shown in Figure 1(b). The first statement creates the type Person_t with attributes name and birthyear.[1] The next statement creates the type Emp_t as a subtype of Person_t, adding the attribute salary. Looking ahead for a moment, the final data definition statement in Figure 1(b) adds a second additional attribute, dept, to the type Emp_t. This attribute is a *reference* attribute that refers to (i.e., uniquely identifies) an object of type Dept_t; its definition is deferred until after the type Dept_t is defined because the types Emp_t and Dept_t refer to one another (creating a circularity which the **alter type** statement breaks). The data definition statement following the creation of Emp_t creates type Prof_t as a subtype of Emp_t, adding rank and specialty attributes; an instance of type Prof_t will thus have a total of six attributes: name, birthyear, salary, dept, rank, and specialty. The fourth statement defines one last subtype of Person_t, namely Student_t. These four structured types, Person_t, Emp_t, Prof_t, and Student_t, together form the Person_t *type hierarchy*. The final type definition in the figure defines the type Dept_t. Note that this type also contains a reference attribute, mgr, which references an object of type Emp_t.

[1] The clause **mode db2sql** can be ignored; it protects UDB Version 5.2 applications from future changes that could occur in the SQL99 standard before it is finalized and published in late 1999.

```
create table person  of Person_t
             (ref is oid user generated);
create table emp     of Emp_t     under person
             inherit select privileges;
create table prof    of Prof_t    under emp
             inherit select privileges;
create table student of Student_t under person
             inherit select privileges;
create table dept    of Dept_t
             (ref is oid user generated,
              mgr with options scope emp);

alter table emp alter column dept add scope dept;
```

Figure 2: DDL for creating a table hierarchy

Given these types, we now need places to store their instances. Like rows in the relational world, typed objects reside in tables defined within a DB2 database. UDB supports a variation of the SQL **create table** statement that creates a *typed table*. To store instances of subtypes, one creates typed *subtables* as well; one can create multiple typed tables of a given type if desired. To provide homes for objects of the types defined above, we could write the table definitions of Figure 2.

The first definition in Figure 2 creates a typed table (or object table) named person that can hold Person_t objects. Object table definitions are required to specify a column name that can be used to refer to the object id of their contained objects; thus, the person table will appear to have three columns, an *object id* column called oid (the name specified in the **ref is** clause of the table definition) plus one column for each attribute of Person_t (name and birthyear). The phrase **user generated** tells the system that the object id values for objects in this table will be provided by the user when objects are initially inserted into the table.[2] Object id values must be unique within the table plus all of its supertables and subtables; the system enforces this requirement at insert time. Object id values can only be provided at insert time, when an object is initially created; the object id associated with an existing object is considered immutable and is thus not updatable.

The next three definitions create *subtables* of the

[2] The alternative would be **system generated**, in which case the system would be expected to automatically generate an object id for each inserted row.

person *root table*; emp and student are immediate subtables of person, and prof is a subtable of the emp table. Subtables inherit the columns of their supertables, so no object id column is specified in those definitions; they inherit their oid column from the root table person. Each subtable's type must be an immediate subtype of its supertable's type, and a given table can have only one subtable of any particular type. The person table and subtables in the figure, taken together, form the person *table hierarchy* and are closely related by the "substitutable" DML behavior that we will describe in the next section. They are also managed as a unit for certain purposes, e.g., when certain administrative commands and utilities are invoked (against the root table). For most purposes, a good mental model for a table hierarchy is to think of its root table (e.g., person) as essentially being a heterogeneous collection of objects of its underlying type (e.g., Person_t objects) and subtypes thereof (e.g., Emp_t, Prof_t, and Student_t objects). The clause **inherit select privileges** in each subtable creation statement tells the system that users who hold select privileges on the root table (person) when the subtables are created should be granted those same initial privileges on the subtables. The final table creation statement above creates a separate typed table named dept to hold Dept_t objects; it too has an object id column that we have chosen to call oid.

One other data definition feature that is very important in our SQL DDL extensions is the notion of reference *scope*. The **create table** statement for the dept table contains a clause of the form "mgr **with options scope** emp". This clause tells the system that the Emp_t objects referred to from the reference column mgr of the dept table will reside in the emp table or any subtable thereof, e.g., the prof table in our example. (The **with options** clause is a new addition to the **create table** statement in UDB. It is needed to provide an opportunity to specify any table-specific properties for columns that arise from attributes of the table's type; reference scopes are a very important example of such a property.) Similarly, the last DDL statement in the figure, the **alter table** statement, tells the system that Dept_t objects referred to from the reference column dept of the emp table (and its subtables) will reside in the dept table.

Scope information is used by the system when processing queries involving the dereference operator (->) discussed in the next section. As we will discuss later, scope information is used both for performance reasons, to facilitate query optimization, and for authorization reasons, to allow static authorization checking for queries that involve dereferences. It should be noted that scopes are not a substitute for referential integrity; scopes simply provide information (for dereferencing) about the intended target table of a reference column. Referential integrity (i.e., prevention of dangling references) can be supported for reference columns via UDB's pre-existing referential integrity enforcement facilities, which work for columns of any type. Scopes and referential integrity have been kept orthogonal to allow users to choose whether or not to pay the performance price of referential integrity; some applications inherently ensure it, making any extra checking overhead redundant and undesirable. In the future, we plan to infer scopes from referential integrity constraints (but not vice versa) when possible for reference columns.

3 SQL Data Manipulation Language Extensions

The DDL extensions just described have a set of corresponding DML extensions. In particular, the basic SQL DML statements—**insert**, **select**, **update**, and **delete**—have been extended to deal with typed table hierarchies, and path expression support has been added to the language to enable convenient and natural traversal of object references (a la GEM [16]). The **insert** statement, when applied to a table or subtable, creates a new typed object in the specified table or subtable and initializes its attributes using the values provided by the **insert** statement. The **select**, **update**, and **delete** statements, when applied to a table or subtable, operate on the requested attributes from the target table or subtable *and all of its subtables*—that is, they treat subtable rows as being *substitutable* for supertable rows. If the all-columns operator, *, is specified, the returned attributes are those defined at the targeted table or subtable's level of the table hierarchy. Similarly, all columns mentioned by name in a query that targets an object table or subtable must be defined at (or above) the targeted table's level of the type hierarchy. For path expressions, an arrow operator analogous to that of C++ is provided, and path expressions involving one or more uses of this operator can appear just about anywhere a value expression is permitted in SQL. Finally, we have also added features to SQL to facilitate the manipulation of objects based on their runtime type. These features are best illustrated via a series of examples.

To add a new Emp_t object to the database with oid o100, name Smith, birth year 1968, and salary $65,000, assigning the new employee to work in the CS department, we would use an SQL **insert** statement to create the employee in the emp subtable of the person table:

```
insert into emp (oid, name, birthyear, salary, dept)
  values (Emp_t('o100'), 'Smith', 1968, 65000,
          (select oid from dept where name = 'CS'));
```

The object id for the object created above is provided by typecasting a Varchar constant into a **Ref**(Emp_t) value (because references are strongly typed). The cast is accomplished using a cast function that the system automatically generates when a new structured type is created; again, the system will check to ensure that the newly inserted object has an object id that is unique within the person table hierarchy. Finally, notice that the new employee's department reference is obtained using a subquery that selects the object id of the desired department.

As mentioned above, the **select**, **update**, and **delete** statements all operate on table hierarchies in a manner that is based on the principle of substitutability (or equivalently, on the mental model of heterogeneous collections of objects). Thus, for example, we could select the oid, name, birth year, salary, and department reference of employees of all types (i.e., Emp_t and/or Prof_t objects) born after 1970 who earn more than $50,000 per year via the following query:

```
select  E.*
from    emp E
where   E.birthyear > 1970 and E.salary > 50000;
```

Similarly, we could change the birth year for the person (who might happen to be a regular person, an employee, a professor, or a student) whose oid is o200 to be 1969 via an **update** statement:

```
update person P
set     P.birthyear = 1969
where   P.oid = Person_t('o200');
```

Since this statement targets the person table, it can only mention columns defined at the person level of the table hierarchy (e.g., it cannot mention Emp_t, Student_t, or Prof_t columns). Finally, we could delete all employees (both regular and professors) who earn too much money via:

```
delete from emp E where E.salary > 500000;
```

Of course, to execute these statements, the user must have the proper SQL authorizations. UDB requires explicit authorization on the statement's target subtable; to perform a **delete** on the emp table, the user would have to hold the **delete** privilege there. It is possible (and sometimes desirable) to grant different privileges at different levels of a table hierarchy. As a result, the person table creator might grant a full set of privileges to some user, but that user will not be able to explicitly operate on the emp subtable by virtue of holding person privileges. Instead, the emp subtable creator would have to decide which privileges to give out in order to protect the attributes (e.g., salary) introduced at the emp level of the person table hierarchy.

UDB's support for path expressions greatly simplifies queries that select attributes from a set of related objects by permitting relationships to be explicitly traversed using the dereference operator ->. For example, to find the employee name and salary, as well as the corresponding department name and budget, for all employees who work in departments that have budgets that exceed $150,000 per person, we could simply say:

```
select  E.name, E.salary, E.dept->name,
        E.dept->budget
from    emp E
where   E.dept->budget > 150000 * E.dept->headcnt;
```

In the case where a qualifying employee has no department (because its dept reference attribute is null or dangling), the path expression yields null (a la GEM [16], and unlike OQL [5], which would raise a user-unfriendly runtime exception). Path expressions are similar in this regard to left outer joins. As another example of how path expressions can simplify a query, we could find the names of all of the employees whose manager's manager is Jones, which would require writing a five-way join query in the absence of path expression support, by simply saying:

```
select  E.name
from    emp E
where   E.dept->mgr->dept->mgr->name = 'Jones';
```

In addition to the aforementioned extensions, UDB also makes it possible to restrict a query's attention to objects of a particular type (or types) and to inquire about an object's type. For example, to select the oid, name, birth year, salary, and department reference of employees who are *exactly* of type Emp_t (i.e., objects that reside in the emp table, not a subtable of emp) and who work in a department with a budget of more than $10M, we could say:

```
select  E.*
from    only(emp) E
where   E.dept->budget > 10000000;
```

We expect this to be the most commonly used form of type restriction, which is why it has a special syntax (**only**). For more general cases, UDB supports a *type predicate* in its dialect of SQL. The type predicate compares the runtime data type of a structured type instance (obtained by **deref**erencing a reference value) with a list of types and returns true if its runtime type is one of those in the list. As an example, we could use a type predicate to select the oid, name, and birth year of people born before 1965 who are either of type Student_t or else exactly of type Person_t:[3]

```
select  P.*
from    person P
where   P.birthyear < 1965 and
        deref(P.oid) is of (Student_t, only Person_t);
```

Finally, one other SQL extension that UDB provides is the ability to query the **outer** union of a table hierarchy. For example, the next query selects the type name, object id, and all possible attributes of the lucky employee whose oid is o013. By all possible attributes, we mean all attributes that an employee object *might* have (as an instance of Emp_t or its subtype Prof_t) depending on its runtime type. The **outer** union returns

[3]The reader can think of this example's type predicate as "... **and** P **is of** (Student_t, **only** Person_t) ...", which is the syntax we would have preferred. Unfortunately, we were unable to find a way to make this nicer syntax acceptable in the full context of SQL99.

null values for inapplicable attributes (e.g., for employees who are not professors, rank and specialty will be null). Duplicate attribute names within the hierarchy, if they arise, can be disambiguated using SQL's **from** clause column renaming feature (**as**). The example query is:

```
select  type_name(deref(E.oid)), E.*
from    outer(emp) E
where   E.oid = Emp_t('o013');
```

The type_name function is similar to the type predicate, but instead of testing the runtime type of an object, it returns the runtime type name. (There is also a type_schema function that returns the name of the schema in which the runtime type resides, and a type_id function that returns the type's database-specific internal id.) Given an object id, this form of query is especially useful for obtaining all of the data associated with the referenced object, including its runtime type, through a single call to a dynamic query API like ODBC or JDBC.

4 Advanced SQL Data Definition Language Extensions

As described in the introduction, relational database systems have a number of advanced features that users have come to rely on for providing alternative views of their base data and expressing business rules and logic. As argued in [14, 10], object-relational database systems must fully support such features, as otherwise they will be a step backwards in some important ways. This section describes how UDB addresses this requirement (plus several other DDL requirements).

4.1 Object Views and View Hierarchies

In relational databases, views are virtual tables whose contents are defined by a query; to a user's application or query, a view looks just like a table. In UDB, we support *object views* and *object view hierarchies* that provide this same transparency and flexibility for users of typed tables and table hierarchies. In particular, we support the creation of typed object views, and these views can either be root views or subviews of other object views. The body of an object view is a query whose select list is type-compatible with the declared type of the view. As prescribed in a seminal paper on views of object databases [9], UDB supports networks of object views that reference one another to form view schemas. UDB's object view facility was influenced by the Garlic object-centered view concept [4], which in turn was influenced by prior work on object views.

Again, we will explain this UDB feature using an example. Suppose that we wished to construct a set of interrelated object views that could be shown to users instead of the base tables and subtables defined earlier. Further suppose that we only wished to include non-academic employees and well-funded departments

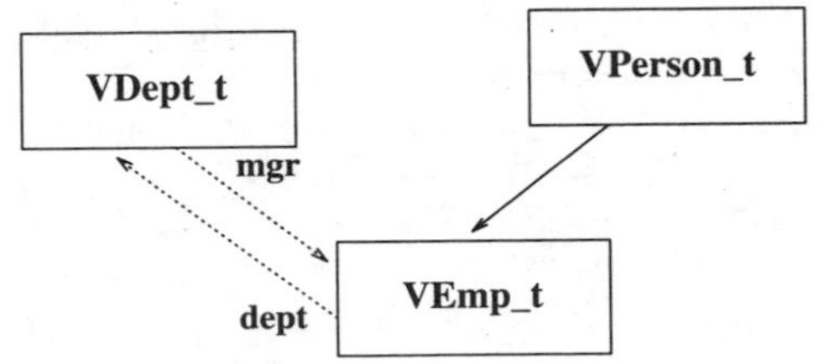

(a) Schematic of view entities and relationships

```
create type VDept_t as (
    name Varchar(20)
) mode db2sql;

create type VPerson_t as (
    name Varchar(40)
) mode db2sql;

create type VEmp_t under VPerson_t as (
    dept Ref(VDept_t)
) mode db2sql;

alter type VDept_t add attribute mgr Ref(VEmp_t);
```

(b) DDL statements for creating the view types

Figure 3: A hierarchy of view types

(those with a budget greater than $1M) in our views. UDB's object views are based on the same type system as its regular object tables. Figure 3(a) depicts a set of view types, and Figure 3(b) gives a set of type definitions to create these view types. Except for the missing attributes, these look similar to our previous type definitions. It is important to notice, however, that these types are interrelated among themselves: the dept attribute of type VEmp_t is of type **Ref**(VDept_t), and the mgr attribute of type VDept_t is of type **Ref**(VEmp_t).

Given these type definitions, we can create the desired object view hierarchy as shown in Figure 4. The first two object view definitions are similar. Each defines a typed view in much the same way that typed tables were defined earlier, and then each provides a query that selects the appropriate set of view objects. Note that objects in an object view have object ids that are created by typecasting their base object ids to be view object ids. (The intermediate cast to Varchar is required because a reference to one type cannot be cast to be a reference to an unrelated type without violating strong reference typing.) The third definition creates a subview vemp of the object view vperson. The query associated with the subview selects the same first two columns as its parent view (subtyping the object id appropriately), extending them with the additional attribute that VEmp_t instances have as compared to VPerson_t objects. In UDB V5.2, all object views in an object view hierarchy are required to be defined over the same underlying table or table hierarchy, with the same column being used as the basis

```
create view vdept of VDept_t mode db2sql
    (ref is oid user generated)
    as select VDept_t(Varchar(oid)), name,
              VEmp_t(Varchar(mgr))
       from   only(dept)
       where  budget > 1000000;

create view vperson of VPerson_t mode db2sql
    (ref is oid user generated)
    as select VPerson_t(Varchar(oid)), name
       from   only(person);

create view vemp of VEmp_t mode db2sql
    under vperson inherit select privileges
    (dept with options scope vdept)
    as select VEmp_t(Varchar(oid)), name,
              VDept_t(Varchar(dept))
       from   only(emp);

alter view vdept alter column mgr add scope vemp;
```

Figure 4: DDL for creating a view hierarchy

for the view's object id column, and the sets of objects identified by the body (query) of each view/subview are required to be disjoint. These rules are enforced by UDB at subview definition time to ensure that the contents of views/subviews in a view hierarchy have the same logical properties as do tables/subtables in a table hierarchy. Finally, note that reference columns of object views are scoped, just like reference columns of object tables, and that their scopes can be other object views. (The dept column of the vemp view has vdept as its scope in our example, and the reference column vdept.mgr has vemp as its scope).

Once defined, object views can be queried, used in path queries, and even updated if their defining **select** statements are of an updatable nature (which they are in our example). For instance, the following query finds the names and department names of view employees who work in a view department whose name starts with D; professors will not be considered due to the nature of the vemp view definition, and departments with small budgets will be filtered by the vdept view definition (thereby making references to such departments behave like dangling references, returning null values in the context of the query's path expressions). Because of the scopes given in the view definitions, the SQL expression dept->name is a path expression that follows references from vemp.dept to get the corresponding vdept.name values:

```
select  E.name, E.dept->name
from    vemp E
where   E.dept->name like 'D%';
```

Type predicates can be used with object views as well, as shown by the following query for finding the names of Scottish people who are regular (i.e., non-professorial) employees of the university:

```
select  P.name
from    vperson P
where   deref(P.oid) is of (only VEmp_t) and
        P.name like 'Mc%';
```

While our example showed object views of object tables, it is important to note that UDB's object view facilities can also be used to create object views and view hierarchies out of existing relational (i.e., non-object) tables. This provides an important migration path for users who have legacy relational data but wish to begin exploiting object-relational modeling in new applications. To provide even better support for such users, we have recently added (but not yet shipped) a new clause, **ref using**, that can be added to a **create type** statement to direct UDB to use a specified data type to represent object ids for that type and its subtypes. This is useful when creating object views of legacy tables, as different tables often use different primary key types. We have also recently relaxed some of the V5.2 restrictions on object view definitions (e.g., so that view hierarchies can be defined over multiple legacy tables).

4.2 Constraints, Triggers, and Other Features

As mentioned earlier, it is important that support for constraints and triggers be extended to the object-relational world as well. To be consistent with the inheritance model that table hierarchies imply, such features must be definable on tables or subtables within a hierarchy and they must be inherited by any subtables of the table upon which they are defined. In UDB, support is provided for defining **not null** and **unique** constraints, as well as for providing **default** values and defining indexes, on tables in a table hierarchy. One can define a **not null** constraint on a column at the point in the table hierarchy where it first appears (i.e., when defining the subtable that introduces the column into the hierarchy), and **default** values and non-unique indexes can be specified for columns at that same point. UDB also supports **unique** constraints and unique indexes (but presently only permits them to be defined on the root table of a table hierarchy). In all cases, these features are implicitly inherited by subtables; the corresponding columns of subtables are thus subject to the same rules and indexing. For example, if the emp subtable in our original person table hierarchy included a **not null** constraint on its dept column, this constraint would also be enforced for rows of its prof subtable.

Support for more general constraint and trigger inheritance is presently under development at IBM Almaden. We have **check** constraints working on table hierarchies, and **foreign key** constraints are in progress. As an example, it is now possible for the emp subtable in our person table hierarchy to include the constraint "**check** (salary > 0)" to ensure salary validity, and it will be possible shortly to have a constraint of the form "**foreign key** (dept) **references** dept(oid)" to maintain referential integrity for employees' department references. Once defined, these constraints are inherited and enforced for prof as well as emp rows. Similarly, if the dept table had the constraint "**foreign key** (mgr) **references** emp(oid)", UDB would ensure that every department has a corresponding manager who is an employee (or some subtype thereof, of course, but not just a person or a student). Again, we remind the reader that scope clauses do not make such referential integrity constraints redundant—**scope** clauses provide reference target table information, but they do not by themselves tell the system to actively prevent dangling references.

We are currently working on trigger inheritance at Almaden as well. A trigger defined on a supertable will be automatically inherited by its subtables and then fired whenever a triggering modification occurs to either the table upon which it is defined or to any of that table's subtables. (It is worth noting that type predicates can be used to limit this behavior in those—rare, we believe—cases where inheritance by subtables is not the trigger definer's desire; of course, the same technique can be used to limit inheritance of check constraints if so desired.)

5 Implementation Issues

In this section, we provide a high-level summary of some of the key design tradeoffs, considerations, and decisions that we faced while designing and implementing these new UDB object-relational extensions. The main principles that guided our thinking and decision-making were:

1. Performance of all features needs to be at least as good as their relational equivalents.

2. The design must be amenable to future work on schema- and instance-level type migration.

3. The bulk of the initial UDB changes should be in the query compiler if possible.

4. Structured type instances must eventually be storable in columns as well as rows of tables.

The first principle almost goes without saying—we felt it would be unacceptable to offer "cool new object-relational features" that caused customer applications to perform worse than equivalent relational solutions. The second principle was a result of looking ahead at some "must have" functionality that we did not have time to deliver in our first release, but which we knew would be critical in the not-too-distant future. The third consideration was motivated by a desire to localize our changes as much as possible, at least initially, and to get as much functionality "for free" as we could. Essentially, we wanted UDB's indexing mechanisms, query rewrite technology, query optimizer and supporting statistics, parallel query execution algorithms, and so on, to work for data in table hierarchies with as few changes as possible. The fourth principle was another future thought; we wanted to avoid making any decisions that would somehow preclude structured type column values in the long run.

5.1 Representing Table Hierarchies

An early question that we faced was how to physically represent table hierarchies. In light of our third design principle, we seriously considered three possible storage alternatives. (We refer the interested reader to [15, 11] for other analyses of storage options for systems with type hierarchies.) Note that in each case, the implementation decision would be invisible to end users; e.g., regardless of UDB's internal storage method, users would see our example person table and its emp, prof, and student subtables as separate (but related) typed tables.

One approach that we considered was the *hierarchy table* approach, where each table hierarchy (as a whole) corresponds to one physical implementation table under the covers; this table contains the union of the columns required to store rows of any subtable in the hierarchy. For example, the hierarchy table for the person table hierarchy would contain a type tag column (to distinguish among rows of different subtables), an object id column, the name and birthyear columns for person rows, the additional salary and dept columns for emp rows, the rank and specialty columns for prof rows, and the major and gpa columns for student rows. Any given row would have a type tag indicating whether it is a Person_t, Emp_t, Prof_t, or Student_t row, and the inapplicable columns for a given row would simply contain null values.

The second approach that we considered was *vertical partitioning*. This approach would have one physical "delta table" for each table in the table hierarchy. The physical person table would contain a type tag and and object id plus the person name and birthyear attribute values. The physical emp table would have an object id column plus just the additional ("delta") attributes of employees, i.e., salary and dept. The physical prof table would contain three columns, an object id plus rank and specialty. The physical student table would contain three columns as well, namely, oid, major, and gpa. With this approach, an object of type Prof_t would be physically spread over the person, emp, and prof delta tables (with its parts being linked by their oids).

The final table hierarchy storage option that we considered using was *horizontal partitioning*. This approach would also utilize one physical table for each table in the table hierarchy, but in this case each physical table would contain all of the columns for rows of that table of the table hierarchy. For example, the prof table would have a total of six columns: oid, name, birthyear, salary, dept, rank, and specialty. No type tag column would be needed since all the instances of each type present in the table hierarchy would be stored together in a separate physical table; the type of each row is implied by the particular storage table that it resides in.

After studying the pros and cons of the three alternatives, we rejected the vertical partitioning approach because of the joins required to fully materialize a row of a subtable—we were afraid that they would make query performance unacceptable, violating our first guiding principle. (Similar reasoning caused GEM's designers to reject this alternative as well [15].) In addition to query performance concerns, we anticipated problems supporting multi-column constraints and multi-column indexes under the vertically partitioned scheme. For example, a simple check constraint involving both inherited and non-inherited columns could not be checked without extending UDB to do joins during constraint checking; teaching UDB's storage manager to index columns split across multiple tables would have been even more of a challenge.

We also rejected the horizontal partitioning approach for UDB, though not as quickly. One reason for rejecting horizontal partitioning was the difficulty that would arise in checking the uniqueness of user-provided object id values (or other unique-constrained columns) across subtables within a table hierarchy, as we would have to ensure their uniqueness across multiple physical tables. Perhaps more seriously, we were also concerned about the costs that this approach would imply for small lookups or joins of table hierarchies. For example, without a multi-table indexing method, a simple query to find the person named Codd would imply four physical lookups (person, emp, prof, student). Similarly, a query to find pairs of people born in the same year, joining person with itself, would internally require either joining two four-way unions or performing all individual pairwise joins of the four underlying physical tables and unioning the results. We were worried that such situations would be fairly common and would lead to poor query performance, again violating our first guiding principle.

As a result of this analysis, we settled on the hierarchy table approach for storing table hierarchies in UDB. We were convinced that the hierarchy table alternative would provide the best initial performance with the fewest problems and restrictions. Since each row contains all attributes (both inherited and non-inherited), no joins are needed to assemble object instances for queries or constraints; indexing combinations of inherited and non-inherited columns poses no problem either. Since all objects in a table hierarchy live in the same physical table, it is easy to properly enforce unique constraints on oids and user-specified columns. A query that selects an object from a table hierarchy maps to a simple lookup in one index on the hierarchy table, and a query that joins a pair of hierarchies together maps to a simple two-way physical join—which nicely satisfies both our first and third design principles. The hierarchy table approach also simplifies the migration issues that are the focus of our second design principle—migrating an object from one type to another within a table hierarchy becomes a simple type tag update under the covers, and modifying a type can be accomplished at the physical level via an **alter table** operation on the affected hierarchy tables. Thus, the hierarchy table approach provided an expedient path to having a fully functional first implementation of table hierarchies that met our design goals. The main downside of the approach is its potential tuple width, as the width of a hierarchy table's rows is a function of the size of the hierarchy rather than of its individual types. However, null values can be represented efficiently in modern data managers [12], and UDB already handles nulls efficiently for variable-length columns (which tend to be the largest columns), so this drawback seemed less serious than those of the other storage approaches.

To quantify some of the tradeoffs discussed above, we have conducted a small set of preliminary experiments comparing the hierarchy table approach to the horizontal and vertical partitioning alternatives. We constructed a three-level type hierarchy with a root type, two subtypes of the root, and two subtypes of each intermediate type (yielding seven types in all). We constructed a corresponding table hierarchy with 40,000 rows of each type; the overall database contained 280,000 rows and constituted approximately 64MB of data. The root type had an integer attribute plus a 200-byte padding attribute; each additional subtype added another integer attribute to those of its supertype. We stored this data using UDB V5.2's implementation approach (the hierarchy table) as well as in sets of relational tables modeled after the other two alternatives. The integer attributes and oid attributes were all indexed, the data was loaded top down by type, and we gathered optimizer statistics for all three approaches before running our tests.

Figure 5 shows the results from running seven different queries of interest against our test database. The test platform was an IBM ThinkPad 770 machine with 128MB of memory running DB2 Version 5.2 under Windows NT. Space precludes a careful analysis of all of the queries and results; hopefully the reader will find them fairly self-explanatory. The root-level queries operate on the root of the table hierarchy and access rows of the root table and all subtables, while the leaf-level queries operate on a leaf table and access its rows only. From the results, it is evident that vertical partitioning pays a price due to joins for the leaf queries, while horizontal partitioning pays a price due to unions for the join queries. The sums of the times at the bottom of the table, while not especially meaningful in absolute terms, suggest that the hierarchy table approach has the most stable overall performance characteristics.

Query	Hierarchy Table	Vertical Partitioning	Horizontal Partitioning
1. count all rows (root)	1.70 sec	1.92 sec	2.16 sec
2. select 1 row (root)	0.27	0.26	0.25
3. select 1 row (leaf)	0.20	0.25	0.18
4. select 1 row and join (root)	0.22	0.27	24.48
5. select 1 row and join (leaf)	0.20	0.33	1.98
6. join all rows (root)	22.75	15.54	86.72
7. join all rows (leaf)	8.51	39.63	8.87
sum of 1–7	33.85 sec	58.20 sec	124.64 sec

Figure 5: Performance comparison of storage alternatives

5.2 References and Path Expressions

One of the major facets of our UDB extensions is support for references and path expressions. Semantically, a path expression is similar to a subquery. For example, consider:

```
select  E.name, E.dept->name
from    emp E
where   E.salary > 90000;
```

If the system knows that the scope of emp.dept is the dept table, this is essentially equivalent to:

```
select  E.name, (select D.name
                 from  dept D
                 where D.oid = E.dept)
from    emp E
where   E.salary > 90000;
```

The subquery, like the corresponding path expression, returns the name of the matching department if there is one, returning null otherwise.

As we mentioned earlier, UDB requires a reference to have a scope if it is dereferenced. One reason for this was the (lack of) performance observed for unscoped references in the BUCKY benchmark [2]. In particular, when a path expression appears in a predicate, knowing the target table for a reference enables the system to fully optimize the query as a join rather than performing naive pointer-chasing. (The latter is what happened to a target system of the BUCKY work; it is also how many object database systems process queries in the absence of type extents or path indices.) By simply requiring references to be scoped, we avoid this problem and ensure that we will be able to answer users' queries efficiently (a la guiding principle number one). In addition, scope information enables us to check authorizations statically for path queries, as we can always identify the tables involved in a query at compile time rather than waiting until runtime to (more slowly, on a row-by-row basis) check whether or not the user has the appropriate authorizations.

It is worth noting that having scopes at the schema level allows reference values to be kept relatively small in size and simplifies the implementation of user-defined references. With scopes, stored reference values do not need to contain table names—they must simply contain enough information to uniquely identify a row within a given table hierarchy, with query compilation ensuring (via an internal type-tag predicate) that only rows of the targeted table/subtables are actually picked up by a dereference operation. Keeping references small is beneficial for keeping the size of complex object-relational databases reasonable. Not storing type or subtable information in references has another very important advantage as well—it means that UDB will have no trouble efficiently supporting type migration (e.g., promoting a Person_t object to be an Emp_t), whereas systems that place such information in references will have to track down all affected references (if that is even possible) and update their target type or subtable indicators.

Given scope information, a possible approach for implementing path expressions would be to simply translate each one internally into an independent subquery. However, there are several problems with this approach. First, it is inefficient, particularly in cases where there are similar path expressions in a given query (e.g., if a number of dept attributes had been requested in the path query above). Second, if the query is run at a non-serializable level of consistency (e.g., cursor stability), independent subqueries could produce surprising results in the face of concurrent updates. As a result, we first translate path expressions internally into a special form of shared subqueries. UDB's query rewrite component then translates these shared subqueries into outer joins when possible; moreover, it rewrites them into inner joins in many cases, such as when a given path appears in the query's **where** clause. From there, UDB's query optimizer is free to consider all of its usual join orders, join methods, parallel execution options, and so on.

Also on the topic of references, UDB V5.2 supports only user-generated object id values, though we have prototyped system-generated object ids as well. There are several reasons for our decision to ship user-generated object ids first. One factor was a series of discussions with a UDB customer who wanted to migrate from an object mapping layer that they had implemented on top of a pure relational system to exploit the (then) forthcoming UDB object support. That customer already had a number of existing "legacy" objects, with existing ids that appeared externally in operating system files as well as in databases. The prospect of being forced to re-identify all of their legacy objects posed a problem for them. Another consideration was our desire to support the efficient initial loading of object-relational data in cases where the user has a convenient way to generate object ids outside of UDB. In the BUCKY benchmark, the object-relational load times were an order of magnitude worse than relational load times [2] because each object that contains system-generated references had to be connected (joined) to the objects that it refers to, and these connections cannot be finalized until their object ids have been generated by creating the objects themselves. In contrast, user-generated object ids allow the loading of data from files—including references—into typed tables at full relational speeds. A related consideration was database creation in external object caches. We wanted to provide efficient support for applications where a graph of objects is created externally, in a cache, and then handed to the system. If the only way to generate object ids is for the system to do it as objects are inserted, this process becomes messy (e.g., one must topologically sort the cached object graph) and/or expensive (because one must backpatch object references between objects after insertion). UDB will of course support system-generated object ids as well in the future, but we have come to believe that user-generated object ids are in fact preferable in a number of common situations.

6 Relationship to Other Work and Systems

As alluded to earlier, our work has been influenced by a number of previous papers and systems (too numerous to cite and do justice to here). The seminal work on GEM [16, 15] heavily influenced our model for path expressions as well as some of our thinking with respect to hierarchy storage. We were also heavily influenced by past experiences in the University of Wisconsin EXODUS project [3] as well as those from a number of other projects from the same era [1] and by various "manifestos" on next-generation database system requirements [14, 10].

It is also appropriate to compare UDB to other vendors' systems; we do so very briefly here. Both Informix and Oracle offer object-relational features as well. Informix supports user-defined structured types and hierarchies of tables; however, to the best of our knowledge, Informix does not yet include support for references, path expressions, or object views. Oracle 8 supports user-defined structured types and object views, but does not provide any support for inheritance or table/view hierarchies. Informix and Oracle 8 both provide degrees of support for methods, nesting of structured types, and collection-valued attributes, features not yet provided in the released version (V5.2) of UDB. Some of the unique aspects of UDB are its support for user-generated object ids, its aggressive approach to scopes and consequently to path query optimization, and its unique support for object views including view hierarchies. Method and nested structured type support for UDB are working in the lab (specifically, IBM's Santa Teresa Laboratory), and we are currently exploring collection type support at IBM Almaden.

7 Status and Future Plans

Most of the object-relational features that have been covered in this paper are available today in Version 5.2 of the DB2 UDB product. These features include structured types, object tables, type and table hierarchies, references, path expressions, and object views and view hierarchies. These features are available on all supported V5.2 platforms, which include a wide variety of operating systems (most common variants of Unix, NT, Windows95, and OS/2) and a variety of serial and parallel (SMP and MPP) hardware platforms. Thus, DB2 UDB now provides a solid initial foundation for the management of complex object data.

We are currently extending this work in several ways. As mentioned earlier, we have check constraints working on table hierarchies and are completing our work on referential integrity and triggers for table hierarchies. Near-term things that we plan to address next include type migration, type evolution, and system-generated oid support. Other topics of current interest include support for collection types, e.g., collection-valued attributes a la ODMG [5], and ways to connect object-relational data to the web using XML or extensions thereof.

Acknowledgments

The authors wish to thank a number of IBM researchers and DB2 UDB developers who helped in one way or another to make tables of objects a reality. Hugh Darwen and Stefan Dessloch provided consulting on various SQL99 language design issues. Cheryl Greene has been a source of moral support and guidance. Discussions with Peter Schwarz, Ed Wimmers, and Jerry Kiernan influenced our thinking on object views. Hamid Pirahesh, Bobbie Cochrane, Richard Sidle, George Lapis, Cliff Leung, Jason Sun, and others helped us to understand and exploit the existing UDB query processing infrastructure; they also made minor extensions to simplify our task. Gene Fuh, Brian Tran, and Michelle Jou made contributions as part of the DBTI team. Paul Bird provided expertise on a number of technical issues. Walid Rjaibi and Calisto Zuzarte made the changes necessary to educate the UDB optimizer statistics utilities about table hierarchies. Leo Lau added table hierarchy support to UDB's data exchange utilities. CM Park, Carlene Nakagawa, and Raiko Nitzsche helped significantly with system testing. Finally, discussions with our Berkeley friends Mike Stonebraker, Joe Hellerstein, and Mehul Shah helped to improve the presentation.

References

[1] M. Carey and D. DeWitt. Of objects and databases: A decade of turmoil. In *Proceedings VLDB Conference, Mumbai (Bombay), India*, pages 3–14, 1996.

[2] M. Carey, D. DeWitt, J. Naughton, et al. The BUCKY object-relational benchmark. In *Proceedings SIGMOD Conference, Tucson, Arizona*, pages 135–146, 1997.

[3] M. Carey, D. DeWitt, and S. Vandenberg. A data model and query language for EXODUS. In *Proceedings SIGMOD Conference, Chicago, Illinois*, pages 413–423, 1988.

[4] M. Carey, L. Haas, P. Schwarz, et al. Towards heterogeneous multimedia information systems: The Garlic approach. In *Proceedings IEEE RIDE-DOM Workshop, Taipei, Taiwan*, pages 124–131, 1995.

[5] R. Cattell, editor. *The Object Database Standard: ODMG 2.0.* Morgan Kaufmann, 1997.

[6] E. Codd. A relational model of data for large shared data banks. *Commun. ACM*, 13(6):377–387, 1970.

[7] D. DeWitt and J. Gray. Parallel database systems: The future of high performance database systems. *Commun. ACM*, 35(6):85–98, 1992.

[8] L. Haas et al. Starburst mid-flight: As the dust clears. *IEEE Transactions on Knowledge and Data Engineering*, 2(1):143–160, 1990.

[9] S. Heiler and S. Zdonik. Object views: Extending the vision. In *Proceedings ICDE, Los Angeles, California*, pages 86–93, 1990.

[10] W. Kim. Object-oriented database systems: Promises, reality, and future. In *Proceedings VLDB Conference, Dublin, Ireland*, pages 676–687, 1993.

[11] B. Nixon et al. Implementation of a compiler for a semantic data model: Experiences with Taxis. In *Proceedings SIGMOD Conference, San Francisco, California*, pages 118–131, 1987.

[12] R. Ramakrishnan. *Database Management Systems.* McGraw-Hill, 1997.

[13] M. Stonebraker. *Object-Relational Database Systems: The Next Great Wave.* Morgan Kaufmann, 1996.

[14] M. Stonebraker et al. Third-generation database system manifesto. *ACM SIGMOD Record*, 19(3):31–44, 1990.

[15] S. Tsur and C. Zaniolo. An implementation of GEM – supporting a semantic data model on a relational back-end. In *Proceedings SIGMOD Conference, Boston, Massachusetts*, pages 286–295, 1984.

[16] C. Zaniolo. The database language GEM. In *Proceedings SIGMOD Conference, San Jose, California*, pages 207–218, 1983.

High Level Indexing of User-Defined Types

Weidong Chen*, Jyh-Herng Chow, You-Chin (Gene) Fuh, Jean Grandbois[1]
Michelle Jou, Nelson Mattos, Brian Tran, Yun Wang

IBM Santa Teresa Laboratory
[1]Environmental System Research Institute

Abstract

To support emerging database applications, object-relational databases leverage the mature relational database technology and allow users to introduce application-specific types and methods. Tables in a database may now contain such objects as geographical shapes, images, and text documents. To realize the full potential of object-relational databases, efficient querying and searching of user-defined objects must be supported. This paper presents a high level framework for indexing of user-defined types with user-defined predicates. It is orthogonal to the low level access methods that are supported. It is unique in providing direct user control over the transformation from a user-defined type into an abstract domain of index key values, the generation of search keys of a user-defined predicate with bound search arguments, and the execution of a user-defined predicate. The high level framework has been implemented in IBM DB2 Universal Database. Its generality, usability, and performance have been demonstrated in different application domains, where indices on user-defined objects can be fully integrated with SQL queries and exploited by the query compiler.

*Contact author: Weidong Chen, IBM Santa Teresa Laboratory, 555 Bailey Ave, Room C347, San Jose, CA 95141. Phone: (408) 463-2443. Fax: (408) 463-3834. Email: cwd@us.ibm.com. On sabbatical leave from Southern Methodist University.

Proceedings of the 25th VLDB Conference, Edinburgh, Scotland, 1999.

1 Introduction

Emerging database applications require scalable management of large quantities of complex data together with traditional business data and flexible querying capabilities for business intelligence. Such applications are called *universal applications* [25]. Object-relational databases have been developed to support universal applications. They leverage the mature relational database technology, which provides scalability, reliability, and recovery. More importantly object-relational databases enable users to introduce application-specific types and methods into a database. Tables in a database may now contain such user-defined objects as geographical shapes, images and semi-structured text documents.

The business value of complex data cannot be fully realized unless efficient search and querying can be provided on user-defined objects together with the traditional business data. Unfortunately existing commercial databases are rather primitive in their support for access and indexing of user-defined objects. B-trees [3, 9] often serve as the sole indexed access method (although Informix [18] does provide a second indexed access method in the form of R-trees [15]). Indexing is also limited in that that an index can be created only on table columns whose data types are understood by the access methods and that an indexed scan of a table can exploit only those predicates that are understood by the access methods. For example, when B-tree is the sole indexed access method, only columns of built-in types can be indexed and only relational operators can be exploited during an indexed scan of a table. Several different approaches have been investigated to provide extensibility in access and indexing.

One approach is to support extensible indexing through query rewriting. Normally a separate entity manages the special access methods and indexing on complex data which the database engine is unaware of. A user query involving predicates on complex data is transformed into a different query by taking into consideration the access methods and indexing specific to complex data. The indices may be stored in a relational database or in external files. For example, in a typical geographical information system (GIS) such as ESRI's SDE [10] a spatial data engine supplies a set of proprietary spatial functions and predicates and uses a relational database to store both user tables and *side tables* representing the spatial indices. Spatial predicates in a user query are converted by the spatial data engine into joins with and predicates on the *side tables*. The resulting query is then given to the relational database for optimization and execution.

The query rewriting approach does not require modifications to the database engine, which is normally not an option for application developers. When the underlying database does not support indexing on complex data, the query rewriting approach offers an excellent solution to build advanced spatial applications with good performance. However, a tighter integration of spatial indexing with the database engine can provide even better performance. This calls for enhancing the database engine with extensible access and indexing of complex data.

A better approach to extensible access and indexing is through user-defined access methods and user-defined indexing that are tightly integrated with the database engine. Stonebraker [24, 25] introduced user-defined access methods by describing an interface for implementing a new access method. Users specify functions for opening a scan of an index, getting the next record in a scan, inserting a record, deleting a record, replacing a record and closing a scan. These functions are called by the database engine at appropriate places when executing a query plan.

User-defined access methods have the performance advantage due to the tight integration of access methods with the database engine. However, experiences have shown that it is extremely difficult for application developers to define a new access method. The reason is that a new access method has to interface with several low level components of a database engine, including lock manager for locking on index objects, log manager for recovery, and buffer manager for page management. Few people possess such an intimate knowledge of the internals of a database engine, other than the database developers themselves, to be able to write an access method effectively. Extensive changes to low level components of a database engine are always a risky proposition that is not taken lightly in the context of real world applications of a mature database product.

Researchers have extended the concept of "search" in a user-defined access method in the form of generalized search trees [16]. The notion of a search key is generalized to a user-defined predicate that holds for every datum below the key in a search tree. Users define six key methods that are invoked during the top-down search and insertion/deletion of generalized search trees. This has been further extended in [1] to allow more powerful searches such as nearest-neighbor and ranked search.

Indexing aims to provide efficient search and querying of data using some underlying indexed access method. The purpose of user-defined indexing is to extend indexing capabilities to data types and predicates that may not be directly supported by the underlying indexed access methods. In [24], Stonebraker introduced a mechanism (called *extended secondary indices* in [20]) that allows users to apply existing access methods such as B-trees to new data types. In the case of B-trees, an *operator class* can be defined that provides a list of user-defined operators and specifies the correspondence between the user-defined operators and the standard relational operators for B-trees. Users can specify an operator class when creating an index on a table column of a new data type.

The mechanism of extended secondary indices in [24] is generalized in [20] so that predicates that cannot be mapped neatly to comparison operators can also be used for indexed scan of a table. For instance, one may want to index on keywords occurring in titles of books. Their idea is to introduce another operator that is applied to values of a column to generate index key values, e.g., an operator that returns a list of keywords occurring in a given string. The result of the operator can be a list of values that can be compared. The introduction of this operator essentially provides a logical separation between values of a table column to be indexed, e.g. the title of a book in a table books, and the corresponding index keys, e.g., keywords occurring in the title of a book.

This paper focuses on user-defined indexing and presents a high level framework of indexing for user-defined types. It generalizes extended secondary indices in [24, 20] in two aspects. First, we provide user control over "search" in indexing that maps a predicate with search argument into search ranges used by an underlying access method for indexed scan of a table. Such mapping is no longer limited to a single search range based upon a relational operator. For a user-defined predicate, users can provide their own method of generating possibly multiple search ranges based upon the search arguments of the predicate. Second, we provide user control over the execution of possibly expensive user-defined predicates using a multi-stage procedure.

As a generalization of extended secondary indices in [24, 20], our framework allows users to concentrate on the semantics of applications and user-defined predicates without being concerned with low level details of locking, recovery, buffer management or balanced search tree updates. It is tightly integrated with the database engine. It enhances the value of the underlying access methods, built-in or user-defined, in a database system by supporting indexing on new data types and indexed scans using new predicates. The multi-stage evaluation of expensive predicates provides an implementation framework for filtering with approximate predicates [23].

The proposed framework has been implemented in IBM DB2 Universal Database. Its generality, ease-of-use and performance advantage have been demonstrated in several different domains of applications including, among others, spatial databases [26] and indexing [8] on structured XML (Extensible Markup Language) documents [27].

The rest of this paper is organized as follows. Section 2 revisits the implicit assumptions that are "hard-wired" in existing database systems that make them inadequate for indexing on user-defined objects. Section 3 presents our high level framework for direct user control over indexing of user-defined types. Section 4 demonstrates its application in two different domains. Section 5 concludes the paper.

2 "Hard-Wired" Indexing

B-trees are arguably the most popular indexed access method in relational databases [3, 9]. Existing database systems are heavily "hard-wired" to support only B-tree indexing on primitive data with relational operators. This section reviews the implicit assumptions that have been made and examines the consequent limitations for indexing of user-defined types.

With B-trees often as the built-in indexed access method, most database systems support primitive indexing that is limited by the B-tree indexed access method. Indices are defined by specifying the table name, the set of index columns, the sort order, and the unique constraint of an index, e.g.,

```
CREATE TABLE employee(empno Char(6),
                      name Char(20),
                      title Char(20),
                      salary Integer);
CREATE INDEX salary_index on employee(salary ASC);
```

When a tuple is inserted into a table, the values of all index columns are concatenated to form the index key that is used to traverse the B-tree for the insertion of the new index entry. Similarly when a tuple is deleted, the index key is used to identify the index entry for deletion.

Once an index is created for a table, subsequent queries can take advantage of the indexed access path provided by the index:

```
SELECT name, salary
FROM employee
WHERE salary > 50000;
```

Existing database systems make several implicit assumptions in their indexing support due to the use of B-trees as the built-in indexed access method. First, an index is created on the values of table columns directly. The index key is the concatenation of the values of the index columns. Clearly this is not acceptable for user-defined objects, which can be large binary objects or text documents that are not appropriate as index key values. Even if all the index columns have built-in types, users may want to create an index on some values *derived* from the values of the index columns, e.g., compensation level based upon the salary or keywords in the title of a book [20].

Second, a total order is assumed over the domain of index key values. An indexing search is restricted by a *single* range of index key values. For example, the predicate *salary* $>$ *50000* maps trivially to the range $(50000, \infty)$. This is not sufficient for a user-defined predicate that may bound a search in more than one dimension, e.g., within a certain distance from a specific location.

Third, for index exploitation, which exploits any available indices for efficient query execution, only simple predicates of relational operators are considered by query optimizers. In a spatial database, a predicate such as *distance(location, point(10,10))* $\leq$ *5* may limit the search space of *location* within the circle centered at *(10, 10)* and with radius *5*. Query compilers need to be able to recognize user-defined predicates and know how to derive the corresponding search space in order to exploit any index of user-defined types for efficient query execution.

3 High Level Indexing of User-Defined Types

Our framework of high level indexing of user-defined types sits on top of the underlying access methods in a database system. It provides direct user control over index maintenance, search key generation for user-defined predicates and efficient predicate execution through filtering. This section describes the main components of the framework and its implementation in IBM DB2.

3.1 Index Maintenance

Index maintenance deals with the update of an index when tuples are inserted, deleted, or updated in a table. Existing database systems often treat the value of an index column directly as its index key, i.e., the mapping from values of an index column to index keys is the trivial identity mapping. To untie index keys from the values of an index column, we allow a user-defined *key transform*. Given the value of an index column, the key transform returns one or more index key values. Therefore a key transform is in general a table function that returns a table as its result. Each row in the result table forms an index key.

The introduction of key transforms brings several fundamental benefits. First of all, the domain of index keys is logically separated from the domain of values for an index column. Since an index column can be of any user-defined type, its values may be large objects

(LOBs) or structurally rich text documents, among other things. It is impossible to store them directly in an index. Nevertheless, an index can still be created on them using index keys derived by the key transform.

Second, even if the values of an index column are all of built-in types, using index keys derived by a key transform can have some nice properties that are not satisfied by indexing on the index column values directly. For example, a high dimensional space can be mapped to a linear ordered space such that multidimensional clustering is preserved and reflected in the one-dimensional clustering [2, 19]. Distance preserving transformations have been successfully used to index high dimensional data in many applications, such as time sequences [12] and images [11]. In [4], a new indexing method was proposed for high dimensional data spaces that can be implemented through a mapping to a one dimensional space. Key transforms allow the implementation of these new indexing methods on top of existing access methods such as B-trees.

Third, from an abstract interpretation point of view, index keys can be viewed as abstractions of the corresponding values of index columns and are simpler and/or occupy less space [8]. For spatial applications, index keys often represent approximations of spatial objects, such as z-values in [21] or minimum bounding boxes (MBRs) in R-trees [15]. Depending upon the abstraction defined by the key transform, the more information that is stored in an index, the more filtering that can be done by indexed search, thus offering a tradeoff between indexing cost and search efficiency.

Fourth, a single value of an index column can be mapped to a number of index keys using a table function as a key transform. The relationship between values of an index column and index keys is no longer one-to-one, but many-to-many, e.g., z-transform [21] and keywords in a book title [20]. Different values of an index column can have the same index key, and one value of an index column can have multiple index keys associated with it.

The idea of key transforms has been explored in [20] for keyword searching in textual databases. We are using the same idea as one of the building blocks for our framework of high level indexing of user-defined types.

3.2 User-Defined Predicates

Existing database systems support simple predicates of relational operators for which the corresponding search ranges can be easily determined based on the operators and the bound arguments. To provide extensible indexing over user-defined objects, two issues have to be tackled. First, a user-defined type may or may not support the standard relational comparisons. Even if it does, these relationships may not translate directly to search ranges over index keys. In addition, users may want to search based upon application-specific predicates other than relational comparisons, such as *overlap* and *within* in spatial databases.

Second, a predicate or condition defined by a user can be an arbitrary condition representing some complicated relationship among different objects. When such a user-defined predicate is used to exploit any existing index for efficient query execution, the rich semantics of user-defined predicates requires sophisticated computation of the corresponding search ranges to be used for the indexed scan of table. This is an efficiency issue as the complete range of index keys is always a logical candidate for search.

Example 3.1 Consider the following example:

```
CREATE TABLE customer(name varchar(20),
                      id integer, ...,
                      xyloc location);
...
CREATE INDEX locationIdx on customer(xyloc);
...
SELECT * FROM customer
WHERE within(xyloc, circle(...));
```

The search region is the minimal rectangular box (called minimal bound box), containing the circle in the WHERE clause. To capture the search region accurately, one might use two B-tree indexes, one on the X coordinate and the other on the Y coordinate of a location, for executing the query. We believe that an extensible mechanism is needed to provide user control over how the search region is determined given an arbitrary search condition.

□

For extensible indexing with user-defined predicates, we want to represent the corresponding search region as closely as possible and introduce the concept of *search methods*. Each search method is a user-defined function that given a semantic relation over user-defined objects and one of its search patterns, returns a *set* of search keys.

A search method computes the set of search keys over which the possible search targets can be found. For the query in Example 3.1, a search method can be defined for the semantic relationship *within* where the first operand is the search target and the second operand is the search argument. Assuming that an index key is a fixed size grid cell intersecting with an object, the search method can return the minimal set of grid cells that covers the circle given in the search argument.

A search method in general is only an approximation for the semantic relation r in the sense that every search target participating in the relation r with search arguments must have an index key among those returned by the search method. For instance, every geometric object that is *within* the circle given in the search argument must have a grid cell that is in the set of search keys generated by the search method.

However, a search method may not be accurate in the sense that some objects with an index key among those returned by the search method may not satisfy r with the search arguments. In other words, it may produce false hits. Therefore it is necessary in general to evaluate r for every object that is found using the index keys from a search method.

3.3 Index Exploitation

Index exploitation is performed by query optimizers in order to utilize any index for efficient query execution. Traditionally query optimizers have been able to exploit only simple relational operators for indexing since the corresponding search range can be easily determined. For index exploitation with user-defined predicates, the query compiler must be able to recognize them and find the relevant search methods to use. The definition of a user-defined function is extended to specify whether it can be used as a predicate and if so, what search method to use when certain operands are search arguments. (See Section 3.4 for details of the syntax of predicate specifications.)

For the query in Example 3.1, suppose that `within` has been defined as a predicate that has an associated search method when the second operand is a search argument. The query compiler can choose an index scan over a table scan to retrieve records from table `customer` for two reasons. One is that there is an index on `xyloc` attribute. The other is that the query compiler recognizes that the second operand of `within` is bound and `within` is a predicate with a search method when the second operand is a search argument. The index scan will use the corresponding search method to generate a set of search keys, which represents the minimal set of grid cells covering the circle in the second operand. The set of search keys will be used by the underlying access method to retrieve the relevant records from table `customer`.

3.4 Implementation and Predicate Filtering

The high level framework of indexing of user-defined types has been implemented in IBM DB2. Besides index maintenance, user-defined predicates and index exploitation, the implementation also provides user control over multistage evaluation of user-defined predicates through filtering. This avoids the potentially expensive evaluation of user-defined predicates and reduces both I/O and CPU costs.

Figure 1 shows the syntax for index extensions with the associated key transform and search methods. The semantic relation corresponding to a search method is not explicitly specified. The CREATE INDEX EXTENSION statement defines a parametric index extension. A parametric index extension is instantiated when an index is created on a table using CREATE INDEX statements. The parameters of an index extension can be used to specify, for example, the number of layers and the size of a grid cell in a multi-layer grid index.

The key aspects of an index extension include the key transform function (indicated by *<key transform invocation>*) and the associated search methods. Each search method contains a search key producer function (indicated by *<search key producer>*) that computes the set of search keys given search arguments and an index filter function (indicated by *<index filter>*) used inside the index component.

The user control over the index filter is a powerful concept. It provides early filtering using the index keys. This avoids the I/O cost of retrieving data that obviously do not satisfy the search criteria since data will not be retrieved from the disk using an index scan until the index keys are determined. This also makes it possible for users to combine multiple indexing mechanisms in a single search by plugging an index filter that performs additional search, e.g., using an external search engine.

Figure 2 shows the syntax of user-defined functions that can serve as predicates. Each predicate specification indicates an optional filter function, and the associated search methods for different search patterns. The data filter aims to reduce the potentially expensive evaluation of the predicate by filtering out records that do not satisfy the predicate using simpler and cheaper operation. In *<exploitation rule>*, the parameters following WHEN KEY indicate the search argument.

The optional keyword EXACTLY following AS PREDICATE requires a little explanation. When an index scan using a predicate is executed, the corresponding search method, which is a user-defined function, is invoked. It computes a set of search keys for the search target using the search arguments. The search keys are sent to the underlying access methods to retrieve the relevant records. The index filter associated with the search method is applied, if there exists one, before the records are retrieved from the disk. The relational data manager then applies the data filter associated with the predicate specification. Finally all records that pass through the data filter are evaluated using the predicate.

When the index filter and the data filter provide only an approximation to the predicate, e.g., in spatial applications, the final step of predicate evaluation is necessary. However, in other applications such as document search, the filters may compute *exactly* the set of all answers that satisfy the predicate. The final step of predicate evaluation should not be carried out in this case. The keyword EXACTLY indicates such a situation.

Figure 3 shows the architecture of the implementation in DB2. It can leverage any underlying access methods that are available. The rectangular boxes represent places where user-defined functions can be

```
<create index extension> ::=
        CREATE INDEX EXTENSION <header> <index maintenance> <index search>
<header> ::= <indexExtensionName> ( { <parmName> <parmType> }+ )
<index maintenance> ::=
        WITH INDEX KEYS FOR ( { <colName> <colType> }+ ) /* index columns */
        GENERATED BY <key transform>
<index search> ::=
        WITH SEARCH METHODS FOR INDEX KEYS
        ( { <colName> <colType> }+ ) {<search method>}+
<search method> ::=
        WHEN <searchmethodName> USING ( { <colName> <colType> }+ ) /* search arguments */
        RANGE THROUGH <search key producer>
        CHECK WITH <index filter>

<create index> ::=
        CREATE [UNIQUE] INDEX <indexName> ON <tableName>
        ( { <colName> [ASC | DESC ] }+ )
        USING <indexExtensionName> ( { <constant> }+ )
```

Figure 1: Syntax for index extensions, where N^+ specifies one or more occurrence of N, with the separator ',' when appropriate.

```
<create function> ::=
        CREATE FUNCTION <functionName> { <parmName> ] <dataType> }+
        <predicate specification>+
<predicate specification> ::=
        AS PREDICATE [EXACTLY]
        [ FILTER BY <data filter> ]
        [ <index exploitation> ]
<index exploitation> ::=
        SEARCH BY INDEX EXTENSION <indexExtensionName> <exploitation rule>*
<exploitation rule> ::=
        WHEN KEY ( { <paramName> }+ ) /* search target */
        USE <searchmethodName> ( { <paramName> }+ )
```

Figure 2: Syntax for user-defined predicates and their associated search methods

plugged in to support user-defined search.

The key transform is invoked in the index manager for index maintenance, when tuples are inserted/deleted/updates in a table. The query compiler utilizes specifications of user-defined predicates for index exploitation. During a search based upon a user-defined predicate, the corresponding search method is invoked by the relational data manager to generate a set of search keys.

For retrieval based upon a user-defined predicate, two filters are included in the architecture. The purpose is to avoid potentially expensive evaluation of user-defined predicates. Users can specify simpler and cheaper functions to be applied as filters before predicate evaluation. The index filter filters out records before they are retrieved from the disk into buffers inside the relational data manager. The data filter in the relational data manager presents another chance of cost efficient filtering before expensive predicates are evaluated.

4 Indexing for GIS Applications

In traditional geographical information systems (GISs), indexing on spatial data is provided through a set of proprietary APIs. When a query involves searching on spatial data, the spatial predicates are transformed for index exploitation, and the resulting query is then sent to the database for optimization and evaluation. The lack of integration of spatial indexing with the database engine leads to integrity issues and performance hits. Our framework of high level indexing makes it possible to have spatial indexing within a database and still take advantage of the special search methods that have been developed in GISs.

For example, suppose that the following user-defined types have been created:

```
CREATE TYPE envelop
AS (xmin int, ymin int, xmax int, ymax int);

CREATE TYPE shape AS (gtype varchar(20),
                      mbr envelop,
                      numpart sint,
                      numpoint sint,
                      geometry BLOB(1M))
                      NOT INSTANTIABLE;

CREATE TYPE point UNDER shape;
CREATE TYPE line UNDER shape;
CREATE TYPE polygon UNDER shape;
```

where **shape** serves a supertype for various subtypes

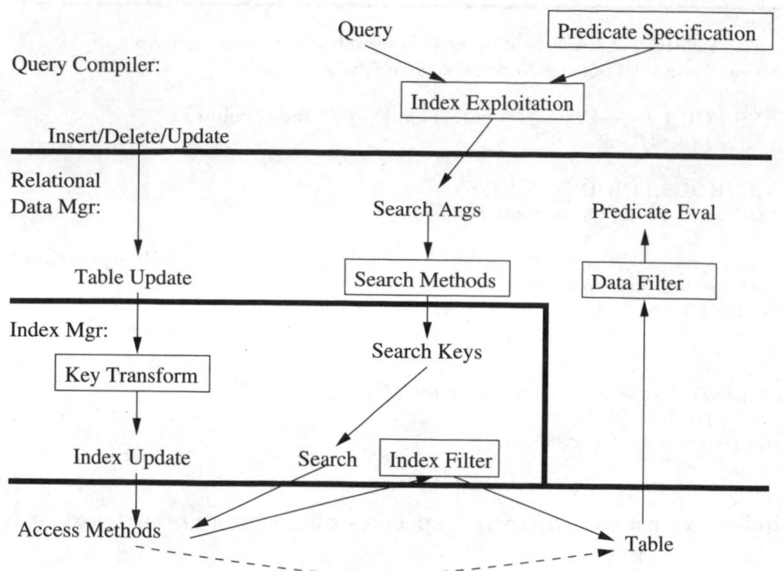

Figure 3: Implementation of high level indexing of user-defined types

such as lines and polygons. Two tables have been defined in the database, one storing the information about schools and the other containing the information on households and their income information.

```
CREATE TABLE schools AS (name varchar(20),
                         district varchar(20),
                         address varchar(20),
                         area shape
                         PRIMARY KEY (name, district));
CREATE TABLE households AS (address varchar(20),
                            annualincome int,
                            location shape);
```

The following query tries to compute the average annual income of all households inside the attendance area of a specific school:

```
SELECT avg(h.annualincome)
FROM houses h, schools s
WHERE s.name = 'Armstrong Elementary' AND
      s.district = 'Highland Park' AND
      within(h.location, s.area);
```

To allow efficient execution of this query, we need to (a) create an index extension incorporating user-defined key transform and search methods for **shape**; (b) create an index on table **households** using the index extension; and (c) specify predicates for **within** and the associated search methods.

The following statement defines an index extension over type **shape**. It uses a multilayer grid index for shapes.

```
CREATE INDEX EXTENSION
       gridshape(levels varchar(20) FOR BIT DATA)
WITH INDEX KEYS for (sh shape)
GENERATED BY gridkeys(
       levels, sh..mbr..xmin, sh..mbr..ymin,
               sh..mbr..xmax, sh..mbr..ymax)
WITH SEARCH METHODS FOR INDEX KEYS
       (level int, gx int, gy int,
        xmin int, ymin int, xmax int, ymax int)
WHEN search_within USING (area shape)
     RANGE THROUGH gridrange(
           levels, area..mbr..xmin, area..mbr..ymin,
                   area..mbr..xmax, area..mbr..ymax)
     CHECK WITH checkduplicate(
           level, gx, gy, xmin, ymin, xmax, ymax,
           levels, area..mbr..xmin, area..mbr..ymin,
                   area..mbr..xmax, area..mbr..ymax)
WHEN search_contain USING (loc shape)
     RANGE THROUGH gridrange(
           levels, loc..mbr..xmin, loc..mbr..ymin,
                   loc..mbr..xmax, loc..mbr..ymax)
     CHECK WITH mbroverlap(
           xmin, ymin, xmax, ymax,
           loc..mbr..xmin, loc..mbr..ymin,
           loc..mbr..xmax, loc..mbr..ymax);
```

The index extension definition specifies the function for key transform, **gridkeys** and two search methods. (DB2 uses the double dot notation for accessing attributes of objects of user-defined types.) One is for searching within a specific area, and the other is for finding shapes that contain a specific location. Both search methods use the same function, **gridrange**, to generate a set of index keys for potential search targets. Each search method has its own filtering function. All the functions that are mentioned may be user-defined functions, whose definitions are omitted here.

We are now ready to create an index on the **location** column of table **households**:

```
CREATE INDEX houselocIDX ON households(location)
       USING gridshape('10 100 1000');
```

The parameter indicates three levels of different grid cell sizes.

For index exploitation, we need to define predicates and their associated search methods. The following specification indicates that **within** should be viewed as a predicate.

```
CREATE FUNCTION within(s1 shape, s2 shape)
                RETURNS int
LANGUAGE C ... EXTERNAL NAME '/lib/gislib!within'
AS PREDICATE
FILTER BY mbrwithin(s1..mbr..xmin, s1..mbr..ymin,
                    s1..mbr..xmax, s1..mbr..ymax,
                    s2..mbr..xmin, s2..mbr..ymin,
                    s2..mbr..xmax, s2..mbr..ymax)
SEARCH BY INDEX EXTENSION gridshape
   WHEN KEY (s1) USE search_within(s2)
   WHEN KEY (s2) USE search_contain(s1);
```

The last three lines indicate that searching based upon predicates of `within` will be done using an index extension `gridshape`. When the first argument `s1` is the search target, use search method `search_within` with `s2` as the search argument. When the second argument `s2` is the search target, use search method `search_contain`. The query compiler is able to generate a plan that takes advantage of the access path provided by the index on `location` of table `households`. The key transform, search key producer, and filtering functions will be called automatically at appropriate places.

5 Performance

Our framework of high level indexing of user-defined types extends the expressive power and integrated optimization of SQL queries to user-defined types. This section presents some preliminary performance measurements for GIS applications using the existing GIS architecture and our integrated approach.

The existing GIS architecture is represented by SDE 3.0.2 on DB2 UDB Version 5 from ESRI [10], which uses a spatial data engine external to the database for spatial optimization. Given a table with business data and a column of spatial attributes, SDE introduces a new *feature table* to represent spatial data and a new index to process spatial queries. The feature table contains an id column as the primary key and all the spatial attributes and the geometric shapes. The spatial column in the original table (called *business table*) is replaced by an id column that is a foreign key for the feature table.

In addition to the feature table, SDE maintains a spatial index table, which uses a three level grid based index method in our example. The spatial index table contains the feature-id (which is a foreign key for the feature table) and the indexing information such as the location of the lower left grid cell and the feature's minimum bounding rectangle (MBR).

When processing a spatial search query, SDE uses the spatial index table and the feature table to compute a list of (ids of) candidate shapes that satisfy the spatial predicate. The computed list of candidate shapes is then used to retrieve data from the business table by applying the remaining predicates in the WHERE clause of the spatial search query. Currently SDE handles the join between the business table and the feature table itself by executing different queries.

Our integrated approach of high level indexing of user-defined types is implemented in DB2 Spatial Extender.

We use the census block data for the state of Kentucky, which has 137173 polygons, with an average of 31 points per polygon. The table `kentuckyBlocks` has a column `boundary` of spatial type `POLYGON`, in addition to other attributes such as the name and the total population. Each polygon represents an area, containing as few as 4 points and as many as 3416 points.

```
CREATE TABLE kentuckyBlocks
      (name varchar(20), ..., boundary POLYGON)
```

The following queries represent some typical operations in GIS applications:

- *loading*: including raw data loading through a sequence of SQL insert statements and the maintenance of spatial indices;
- *region queries*: for three predefined regions in different locations, with the sizes of the answer sets being 3155, 2387 and 1457 respectively;
- *point queries*: 100 random point searches, simulating users pointing at a polygon during spatial browsing;
- *region queries with attributes*: same as *region queries* except that non-spatial attributes such as the name and the total population are also fetched in addition to the spatial data.
- *fetch all*: measuring how fast data can be pumped out of a database.

All queries were run on the IBM RS6000/J40 server and during off hours to minimize variations due to other users and processes. The GIS client programs are run on the same machine as the server. The measurements of query execution time (rounded to seconds) are shown in Table 1. Data loading was run once while the rest of the queries are run 3 times and the averages are shown.

In both *loading* and *fetch all*, we are processing the entire table and the integrated approach is about 4 times faster. In the case of *loading*, an insert statement for a row in the integrated approach becomes three insert statements in the GIS approach, one for the business table, one for the feature table, and one for the spatial index table. In the case of *fetch all*, since the GIS approach handles the join between the business table and the feature table by itself, it is executing a separate query against the feature table repeatedly, once for each set of data retrieved from the business table.

For *region queries* without non-spatial attributes, the integrated approach is about 2.5 times faster than the GIS approach, but is about 3 times faster for *region queries* with non-spatial data. The difference is that the latter case involves the access of the business table. The GIS approach performs very well for *point queries.*

Overall, the results show that our integrated approach of high level indexing of spatial data has a much better performance. This shows the value of enhancing the database engine for extensible indexing of complex data.

6 Related Work and Conclusion

Universal applications involving both complex queries and complex data demand strong and flexible indexing support on non-traditional data such as geographical information and structured documents. Indexing of user-defined types with user-defined predicates is crucial to meeting the demands of modern database applications.

Different approaches make different tradeoffs when it comes to implementing indexing of user-defined types. The query rewriting approach transforms queries involving user-defined predicates into joins with special index tables that the database engine is not aware of. It does not require modification to the database engine, but at the same time, the database engine will not be able to take full advantage of the special indexing for query optimization.

One can also implement application-specific access methods. There is no shortage of special access methods for spatial or multidimensional data [13]. Generalized search trees have also been developed [1, 16] for user-defined access methods. They have the advantage of providing direct support for application-specific searches. Unfortunately, only B-trees [3, 9] and R-trees [15] have found their way into commercial database systems. One of the reasons is that an implementation of a new access method or a generic search tree is a huge undertaking since it interacts closely with low level components of the database engine such as concurrency control, lock manager and buffer manager. Reliability is of paramount importance for a mature database product, which often discourages extensive changes to low level components of the database engine. In addition applications are requiring new datatypes and more advanced searches like nearest neighbor for spatial data [22] or regular path expressions for semi-structured data [14]. It is expected that the access methods supported by a database system will not always match the growing needs of applications.

Our framework of high level indexing of user-defined types generalizes extended secondary indices in [24, 20]. It is tightly integrated with the database engine, especially with the index manager and query optimizer. It is orthogonal to the underlying access methods and can take advantage of any special access methods whenever they are available. Our main contribution is not in developing a new access method or a special search algorithm, but rather in providing a framework in which users have direct control over index maintenance, index exploitation, index filtering and predicate evaluation.

More specifically, users can define their own key transforms. The idea of key transforms is not new, e.g., transforming a geometric object into an MBR for R-trees [15] or into a set of z-values [21]. Following [24, 20], we give the power to users to decide what abstractions or approximations to use as index keys for a user-defined type.

Users can define their own search key producers for different search patterns of arbitrary predicates. Although search key producers are not sufficient by themselves to support advanced searches such as ranked and nearest neighbor (which require direct support from the underlying access methods), they bridge the semantic gap between user-defined predicates and the limited access methods that are available.

Users can define their own filters to avoid expensive predicate evaluation. Multistage predicate evaluation has been explored in [5, 6]. Researchers have also investigated query optimization issues with expensive predicates [7, 17] and with filtering using approximate predicates [23]. Our contribution is in integrating multistage evaluation of predicates with the database engine, especially the index manager, thus providing an implementation framework where approximate predicates can be utilized effectively for efficient query execution. As we have shown, the index filter is a powerful technique that makes it possible to avoid the I/O cost of retrieving useless data into the memory buffer. Furthermore, it offers an interesting mechanism to combine multiple indexing mechanisms in a single search, e.g., structured search with external full-text indexing.

The tight integration with the database engine means that it is possible for query compiler to exploit user-defined predicates in the *standard* framework of query optimization. This means that the full querying capabilities of SQL, including multiple predicates in a WHERE clause, aggregate functions, subqueries and recursion, are now available for universal applications through DB2.

References

[1] P.M. Aoki. Generalizing "search" in generalized search trees. In *IEEE Intl. Conference on Data Engineering*, pages 380–389, 1998.

[2] R. Bayer. The universal B-tree for multidimensional indexing. Technical Report I9639, Technische Universität München, Munich, 1996.

[3] R. Bayer and E.M. McCreight. Organization and maintenance of large ordered indices. *Acta Informatica*, 1(3):173–189, 1972.

Queries	Loading	Region Queries			Region Queries w/Attr			Point Queries	Fetch All
		R1	R2	R3	R1	R2	R3		
GIS	3012	19	14	8	20	15	9	10	731
Integrated	706	8	5	3	8	5	3	8	170

Table 1: Performance measurements of spatial queries

[4] S. Berchtold, C. Böhm, and H.-P. Kriegel. The pyramid-technique: Towards breaking the curse of dimensionality. In *ACM SIGMOD Conference on Management of Data*, pages 142–153, 1998.

[5] T. Brinkhoff, H.-P. Kriegel, and R. Schneider. Comparisons of approximations of complex objects used for approximation-based query processing in spatial database systems. In *IEEE Intl. Conference on Data Engineering*, pages 40–49, 1993.

[6] T. Brinkhoff, H.-P. Kriegel, R. Schneider, and B. Seeger. Multi-step processing of spatial joins. In *ACM SIGMOD Conference on Management of Data*, pages 197–208, 1994.

[7] S. Chaudhuri and K. Shim. Optimization of queries with user-defined predicates. In *Intl. Conference on Very Large Data Bases*, pages 87–98, 1996.

[8] J.-H. Chow, J. Cheng, D. Chang, and J. Xu. Index design for structured documents based on abstraction. In *Proceedings of the 6th International Conference on Database Systems for Advanced Applications*, pages 89–98, April 1999.

[9] D. Comer. The ubiquitous b-tree. *ACM Computing Surveys*, 2(11):121–137, 1979.

[10] ESRI. Environmental System Research Institute (ESRI). Home page http://www.esri.com.

[11] C. Faloutsos, R. Barber, M. Flickner, J. Hafner, W. Niblack, D. Petkovic, and W. Equitz. Efficient and effective querying by image content. *Journal of Intelligent Information Systems*, 3:231–262, 1994.

[12] C. Faloutsos, M. Ranganathan, and Y. Manolopoulos. Fast subsequence matching in time-series databases. In *ACM SIGMOD Conference on Management of Data*, pages 419–429, May 1994.

[13] V. Gaede and O. Günther. Multidimensional access methods. *ACM Computing Surveys*, 30(2):170–231, 1998.

[14] R. Goldman and J. Widom. DataGuides: Enabling query formulation and optimization in semistructured databases. In *Intl. Conference on Very Large Data Bases*, pages 436–445, 1997.

[15] A. Guttman. R-trees: A dynamic index structure for spatial searching. In *ACM SIGMOD Conference on Management of Data*, pages 47–57, 1984.

[16] J.M. Hellerstein, J.F. Naughton, and A. Pfeffer. Generalized search trees for database systems. In *Intl. Conference on Very Large Data Bases*, pages 562–573, 1995.

[17] J.M. Hellerstein and M. Stonebraker. Predicate migration: Optimizing queries with expensive predicates. In *ACM SIGMOD Conference on Management of Data*, pages 267–276, May 1993.

[18] Informix. Informix DataBlade Products, 1997. http://www.informix.com.

[19] H.V. Jagadish. Linear clustering of objects with multiple attributes. In *ACM SIGMOD Conference on Management of Data*, pages 332–342, May 1990.

[20] C.A. Lynch and M. Stonebraker. Extended user-defined indexing with application to textual databases. In *Intl. Conference on Very Large Data Bases*, pages 306–317, 1988.

[21] J.A. Orenstein and F. Manola. PROBE spatial data modeling and query processing in an image database applications. *IEEE Transactions on Software Engineering*, 14(5):611–629, May 1988.

[22] N. Roussopoulos, Kelley S., and F. Vincent. Nearest neighbor queries. In *ACM SIGMOD Conference on Management of Data*, pages 71–79, 1995.

[23] N. Shivakumar, H. Garcia-Molina, and C.S. Chekuri. Filtering with approximate predicates. In *Intl. Conference on Very Large Data Bases*, pages 263–274, 1998.

[24] M. Stonebraker. Inclusion of new types in relational data base systems. In *IEEE Intl. Conference on Data Engineering*, pages 262–269, February 1986.

[25] M. Stonebraker and P. Brown. *Object-Relational DBMSs: Tracking the Next Great Wave*. Morgan Kaufmann Publishers, Inc., 1999.

[26] Y. Wang, G. Fuh, J.-H. Chow, J. Grandbois, N.M. Mattos, and B. Tran. An extensible architecture for supporting spatial data in RDBMS. In *Proceedings of Workshop on Software Engineering and Database Systems*, 1998.

[27] *Extensible Markup Language (XML)*, 1997. http://www.w3.org/TR/WD-xml-lang.

Implementation of SQL3 Structured Types with Inheritance and Value Substitutability

You-Chin (Gene) Fuh, Stefan Dessloch, Weidong Chen*, Nelson Mattos, Brian Tran
Bruce Lindsay[1], Linda DeMichiel[2], Serge Rielau[3], Danko Mannhaupt

IBM Santa Teresa Laboratory, [1]IBM Almaden Research Center
[2]Sun Microsystems, [3]IBM Toronto Laboratory

Abstract

SQL3 has introduced structured types with methods and inheritance through value substitutability. A column of a structured type in a relation may contain values of the structured type as well as values of its subtypes. Integrating structured types with the existing database engine raises some interesting challenges. This paper presents the DB2 approach to enhance the IBM DB2 Universal Database (UDB) with SQL3 structured types and inheritance. It has several distinctive features. First, values of structured types are represented in a self-descriptive manner and manipulated only through system generated observer/mutator methods, minimizing the impact on the low level storage manager. Second, the value-based semantics of mutators is implemented efficiently through a compile-time copy avoidance algorithm. Third, values of structured types are stored inline or out-of-line dynamically. This combines the usability and flexibility with the performance of inline storage. Experimental results demonstrate that the DB2 approach is more efficient in query execution compared to alternative implementations of structured types.

*Contact author: Weidong Chen, IBM Santa Teresa Laboratory, 555 Bailey Ave, Room C347, San Jose, CA 95141. Email: cwd@us.ibm.com. On sabbatical leave from Southern Methodist University.

Proceedings of the 25th VLDB Conference, Edinburgh, Scotland, 1999.

1 Introduction

The relational model [3] has revolutionized the information system world by providing a simple, high-level data model and a declarative query interface. The value-based, declarative nature of the relational model offers high level data independence where the physical organization of the data, including storage and index structures, is separated from the logical schema (or tables) of the data. This has led to modern relational database systems with expressive SQL queries, sophisticated query optimization and execution strategies.

Emerging database applications require scalable management of large quantities of new and complex data together with traditional business data and flexible and efficient querying capabilities for business intelligence. To meet the market demands, object-relational databases have evolved and incorporated various "object" features into the relational database technology, such as user-defined structured types, methods and inheritance [7]. These concepts have been included in the SQL3 standard [6].

A structured type in SQL3 consists of a name, a set of attributes, and a set of methods. Attributes of a structured type are accessed and mutated only through system generated observer and mutator methods. Structured types can be nested and one structured type may be a subtype of another. Inheritance is achieved through a principle called *value substitutability* in the sense that values of subtypes are accepted wherever values of their supertypes are valid.

There are two main places to store values of structured types in an object-relational database: rows in a table and values inside a table column. Given a structured type, a table of that type can be created, where each attribute of the structured type becomes a column of the typed table. Each row of a typed table corresponds to a value of the type. A hierarchy of tables can be defined over a type hierarchy so that standard table operations such as SELECT, UPDATE, and DELETE can be applied to a target table as well as its subtables. This exhibits a form of inheritance where subtables inherit columns from the supertable and operations on the supertable are applicable automatically to all rows in the subtables. The design and the implementation of typed tables in DB2 UDB, including table hierarchies, references, path expressions, and object views, have been addressed in [1].

Values of structured types can also be stored in table columns. A column of a structured type in a table may contain values of the structured type as well as its subtypes, which can be of different sizes. A main challenge of integrating structured types with the existing database engine is to minimize the impact on low level components inside the database engine, and at the same time to support efficient access and manipulation of attribute values of possibly nested structured types with inheritance.

This paper describes our approach to enhance the DB2 UDB with structured types and inheritance through value substitutability. The main contributions are as follows. First, values of structured types are represented in a self-descriptive manner that can be manipulated only through system generated observer and mutator methods. This minimizes the impact on the low level storage manager and provides efficient access and manipulation of structured typed values. Second, the value-based semantics of mutator methods is implemented efficiently through a compile-time copy avoidance algorithm. Third, values of structured types are stored inline or out-of-line dynamically depending upon their sizes. This combines the flexibility of subtyping and nesting of structured types with the performance advantage of inline storage. It should be mentioned that this paper focuses only on the basic infrastructure for supporting structured types within the database engine. Other important issues such as indexing and query optimization involving structured types will be dealt with in a separate paper.

The rest of this paper is organized as follows. Section 2 reviews SQL3 structured types, methods and inheritance. Section 3 discusses several different techniques of implementing structured types and describes the design rationale of our DB2 approach. Section 4 gives a simple compile-time inferencing mechanism that avoids making unnecessary copies of objects for mutator method invocations. Section 5 presents a dynamic mechanism for inline or out-of-line storage of values of structured types. Section 6 compares our DB2 approach with various alternative implementations of structured types and provides performance results on real data sets. Section 7 concludes with a brief summary and some issues for further investigation.

2 SQL3 Structured Types and Inheritance

This section reviews structured types, methods and inheritance in the SQL3 standard [6]. We illustrate these concepts through examples.

2.1 Structured Types with Observers and Mutators

Consider a simple structured type for address:

```
CREATE TYPE Address
AS (street Char(30),
    city   Char(20),
    state  Char(2),
    zip    Integer
   ) NOT FINAL;
```

Every structured type comes with a set of observer/mutator methods for accessing and updating the values of its attributes. For **Address**, the following methods are generated automatically by the system:

- observers: each attribute has a corresponding observer method that returns the value of the attribute given a value of the structured type.

  ```
  Address.street -> Char(30)
  Address.city -> Char(20)
  Address.state -> Char(2)
  Address.zip -> Integer
  ```

  The single-dot notation is for method invocation and is left-associative.

- mutators: each attribute has a corresponding mutator method for updating the value of the attribute.

  ```
  Address.street(Char(30)) -> Address
  Address.city(Char(20)) -> Address
  Address.state(Char(2)) -> Address
  Address.zip(Integer) -> Address
  ```

The implementation of structured types is completely encapsulated in the sense that direct access to its attributes is restricted to observer/mutator methods only.

Values of structured types can be constructed using the "new" notation followed by invocations of the mutators to fill in the attribute values, e.g.,

```
NEW Address().street('555 Bailey Ave')
             .city('San Jose')
             .state('CA')
             .zip(95141)
```

It is also possible for users to define their own constructors (with or without arguments) whose names are the same as the type name.

Structured types can be nested or can be subtypes of one another. For instance, one may define another structured type `ContactInfo` that has an attribute of type `Address`:

```
CREATE TYPE ContactInfo
AS (postal_addr Address,
    home_phone Char(10),
    work_phone Char(10),
    email      Char(20),
    fax        Char(10)
   ) NOT FINAL;
```

Tables can be defined that have columns of structured types, e.g.,

```
CREATE TABLE AddressBook
       (name     Char(30),
        addrinfo ContactInfo);
```

Table **AddressBook** can be modified using the standard insert/update/delete statements:

```
INSERT INTO AddressBook
VALUES ('Mr.J.Smith',
        NEW ContactAddr()
         .postal_addr(
            NEW Address()
             .street('555 Bailey Ave')
             .city('San Jose')
             .state('CA')
             .zip(95141))
        .home_phone('6502347568')
        .work_phone('4084635678')
        .email('jsmith@us.ibm.com')
        .fax('4084631234'));
UPDATE AddressBook
SET addrinfo.postal_addr.street =
    '123 Almaden Way'
WHERE name = 'Mr.J.Smith';
```

In the update statement above, we are updating the street address for Mr. J. Smith. The semantics of the update statement is equivalent to the following statement:

```
UPDATE AddressBook
SET addrinfo =
     addrinfo.postal_addr(
       addrinfo.postal_addr.street(
                  '123 Almaden Way'))
WHERE name = 'Mr.J.Smith';
```

where the right hand side contains two mutator invocations, one nested inside another. It should be mentioned that mutator methods in SQL3 [6] have a value-based semantics in the sense that they do not have any side effects and simply return values as results. Therefore they cannot be used directly to update a column of a structured type in a table. Instead such a table can be updated only through the standard insert/update/delete statements.

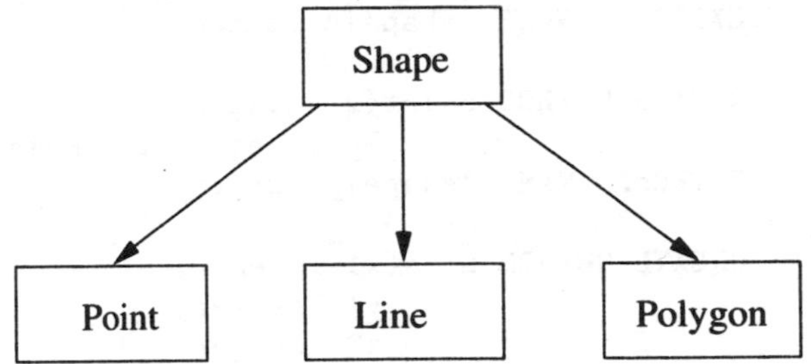

Figure 1: A type hierarchy of shapes

2.2 Inheritance and Value Substitutability

A structured type can be a subtype of another structured type. The subtype inherits attributes and behavior (methods) from its supertypes. Figure 1 shows a simple hierarchy of shapes.

These types can be defined using the CREATE TYPE statement:

```
CREATE TYPE Rectangle
AS (xmin Float,
    ymin Float,
    xmax Float,
    ymax Float
   ) NOT FINAL;

CREATE TYPE Shape
AS (length              Float,
    area                Float,
    mbr                 Rectangle,
    numOfPoints         Integer,
    geometry            Blob(1m)
   ) NOT FINAL
METHOD distance(s Shape) RETURNS Float
       LANGUAGE C ...

CREATE TYPE Point UNDER Shape NOT FINAL
METHOD Point(x Integer, y Integer)
       RETURNS Point LANGUAGE C ...

CREATE TYPE Line UNDER Shape NOT FINAL
METHOD Line(x1 Integer, y1 Integer,
            x2 Integer, y2 Integer)
       RETURNS Line LANGUAGE C ...

CREATE TYPE Polygon UNDER Shape NOT FINAL
METHOD Polygon(p1 Point, p2 Point,
               p3 Point, p4 Point)
       RETURNS Polygon LANGUAGE C ...
```

Each structured type may contain a list of method specifications. In the example above, we have a method for computing the distance between two shapes, and a constructor for each of the subtypes of **Shape**. The implementation of a method is created using a **CREATE METHOD** statement, e.g.,

```
CREATE METHOD distance(s Shape) for Shape
```

```
EXTERNAL NAME 'shape!distance';

CREATE METHOD Point(x Integer,
                    y Integer) for Point
EXTERNAL NAME 'shape!point';

CREATE METHOD Line(x1 Integer,
                   y1 Integer,
                   x2 Integer,
                   y2 Integer) for Line
EXTERNAL NAME 'shape!line';

CREATE METHOD Polygon(p1 Point,
                      p2 Point,
                      p3 Point,
                      p4 Point)
                      for Polygon
EXTERNAL NAME 'shape!polygon';
```

Values of structured types can be used wherever system predefined types can occur in SQL, including table columns and function/method parameters, e.g.,

```
CREATE TABLE real_estate_info
AS (price    Decimal(9,2),
    owner    Char(40),
    property Shape);

INSERT INTO real_estate_info
VALUES (100000, 'Mr.S.White',
        NEW Point(4,4));

INSERT INTO real_estate_info
VALUES (400000, 'Mr.W.Green',
        NEW Line(5,5,7,8));

INSERT INTO real_estate_info
VALUES (150000, 'Mrs.D.Black',
        NEW Polygon(NEW Point(4,4),
                    NEW Point(6,12),
                    NEW Point(12,12),
                    NEW Point(14,4)));
```

Each row of real_estate_info can have a property shape of a different subtype. This is called *value substitutability*, where a column of a structured type can contain values of the type as well as values of all its subtypes.

The principle of *value substitutability* applies not only to table columns but also to function and method parameters. Values of subtypes can be passed to parameters of their supertypes in functions and methods. When a method is invoked, dynamic dispatch is needed to determine the method body to be executed when there is method overriding. In the following query,

```
SELECT owner, price
FROM real_estate_info
WHERE property.distance(Line(10,10,20,20))
      <= 5;
```

if the subtypes of Shape define their own distance methods, the execution of the query will cause the invocation of a different method for each property value at run time, depending upon the specific shape of each property.

3 Implementation of Structured Types in IBM DB2

We have been implementing structured types with inheritance and method support in the SQL3 standard [6] in the IBM DB2. This section discusses the design rationale of supporting table columns of structured types and presents a self-descriptive representation of values of structured types.

3.1 Design Rationale

From an implementation point of view, there are several different options for integrating values of structured types into table columns. One option is to use some existing datatype to represent values of structured types. Since values of structured types can be of different sizes, due to subtyping and variable-sized attributes, one might use variable-length binary characters or binary large objects. Access and manipulation of structured types can be achieved using user-defined functions and methods. For example, the concept of distinct types in IBM DB2 [2] or opaque abstract data types in Informix [5] can be used to implement this approach. However, since an invocation of a user-defined function or method is an expensive operation, this approach can cause significant overhead for runtime query execution.

Another implementation possibility is to expand a table column of a structured type into multiple columns, one for each attribute of the type. While this may provide efficient access, it becomes complicated for nested structured types or subtypes when every attribute of a structured type is expanded into a separate column. This approach also makes it difficult to support inheritance and value substitutability since subtypes may have additional attributes and values of a subtype can appear anywhere values of its supertypes are valid.

Still another implementation option is to use a separate *side table* to store values of structured types. This approach has been used in geographic information systems such as ESRI's SDE [4]. A difference for structured types would be that the database engine will be aware of such side tables and may be able to optimize queries involving these side tables. Nevertheless the side tables are normally hidden from users, who access attributes of structured types through regular tables that contain other business data. This means that access and manipulation of attributes of a structured type inside a table column require extra joins with the side table, increasing the cost of query optimization and execution.

We have three design goals for the representation and manipulation of values of structured types: (a) to minimize the impact of structured types on the low level storage manager; (b) to support efficient access and manipulation of structured types; and (c) to allow arbitrary nesting and subtyping of structured types.

Our representation of structured types is completely opaque to the storage manager, which sees only a sequence of bytes for a value of a structured type. The representation of structured types is encapsulated and can be accessed or manipulated only through a small set of operations, minimizing the impact of structured types on low level components.

The direct access and manipulation of structured types is possible only through builtin operations for observer/mutator methods, avoiding the extra overhead of user-defined functions. The representation of structured types is self-descriptive and carries its own meta information so that it can be operated upon at run time without requiring any extra information. This also makes it easier to change the representation of structured types for future enhancements.

Values of structured types can be of variable sizes for several reasons. First, the concept of *value substitutability* means that values of subtypes can appear wherever values of supertypes are valid. Subtypes often have attributes in addition to those inherited from supertypes. Second, values of structured types can be mutated, constructing new values of different sizes. Third, a structured type may have attributes that are large objects (called LOBs). To accommodate the variable sizes of values of structured types and to support mutations efficiently, we allow values of structured types to be stored in a non-linearized format in memory. When values of structured types are stored in tables on the disk, the same representation is used except that values of attributes of a structured type will be in a linearized format as they are written to the disk. The use of the same representation avoids any extra conversions when values of a structured type are moved between the disk and the memory.

3.2 Self-Descriptive Representation of Structured Types

Given a structured type, a minimum value of the type (i.e., with all attributes set to null) consists of a fixed-size header, an attribute pointer array, and an attribute type array. The fixed-size header contains, among other things, the following fields:

- length: the total length of the structured typed value;
- type id of the structured type;
- the total number of attributes including inherited ones, which also indicates the size of the attribute pointer array and the attribute type array in the variable-length part of the structured type header;

It should be mentioned that the length field of a structured type value may not be exactly the number of bytes that it currently occupies in memory. A structured typed value may contain empty spaces inside when the new value of an attribute after mutation has a shorter length. If it is stored in a non-linearized form, the value of the length field may be less than the minimum length of the structured type in the linearized form due to the padding spaces required for alignment.

The variable-size part of a structured type header contains two arrays, one indicating the values of all the attributes and the other indicating the type of each attribute. The size of both arrays is the number of attributes in the structured type.

- attribute pointer array: each element points to the value of the corresponding attribute. A value zero indicates a null attribute value.
- attribute type array: each element indicates whether the corresponding attribute is of a base type, a structured type, or a large object type, and in case of a large object type, what kind of large object it is.

An attribute value of a base type or a large object type consists of a length field and a data field. If an attribute is of a structured type, the attribute value is represented in the same manner.

From an implementation perspective, when a user invokes an observer or a mutator method to access or mutate the attribute value of a structured typed value, the observer or mutator invocation is converted into an invocation of a builtin operation. Several builtin functions have been introduced for direct access and manipulations of structured types, including:

- three observer operations based upon the three categories of attributes: `adt_observe_base`, `adt_observe_lob` and `adt_observe_adt`. For base or large object attributes, the attribute value or a large object descriptor is copied into an output buffer. No output buffer is needed when observing an attribute of a structured type inside another structured type.
- three mutator functions based upon the three categories of attributes: `adt_mutate_base`, `adt_mutate_lob` and `adt_mutate_adt`. They mutate values of structured types *in place*. To implement the value-based semantics of mutator methods, there is also a builtin `adt_copy` function, which will be discussed in the next section.

Since values of structured types can be accessed and manipulated by users using the system generated observer and mutator methods and invocations of observer and mutator methods are converted into invocations of the builtin operations above, these builtin functions provide the only internal interface through which values of structured types can be accessed or mutated. Therefore any future changes in the representation of structured types can be localized to these builtin operations.

4 Copy Avoidance for Mutators

In SQL3 [6], mutator methods have no side effect and return values as results. However, our implementation uses builtin functions that update values of structured types *in-place*. A naive way to ensure the correctness with respect to the value-based semantics of mutator methods is to precede each mutator invocation with a copying operation so that mutation always takes place on a new copy. However, it leads to too many unnecessary copies of structured typed values. Consider the table **AddressBook** in Section 2.1 and the INSERT statement there:

```
INSERT INTO AddressBook
VALUES ('Mr.J.Smith',
        NEW ContactInfo()
        .postal_addr(
           NEW Address()
           .street('555 Bailey Ave')
           .city('San Jose')
           .state('CA')
           .zip(95141))
        .home_phone('6502347568')
        .work_phone('4084635678')
        .email('jsmith@us.ibm.com')
        .fax('4084631234'));
```

It has five mutator invocations for type **ContactInfo** and four mutator invocations for type **Address**, leading to five potential copies of **ContactInfo** values (including five copies of **Address** values inside) plus four potential copies of **Address** values. The excessive number of copies of structured typed values and the potentially large size of these values can cause significant performance overhead.

We have developed a simple compile-time algorithm that traverses a parse tree and determines when a copy operation is needed for a mutator method invocation.

When an SQL query is compiled, parse trees for invocations of the observer/mutator methods are transformed into parse trees for invocations of the builtin operations. Specifically,

- An invocation of the "NEW" notation is transformed into a call to the builtin function **adt_constructor** for constructing a new value of a structured type with all attributes set to null;
- A call to an observer method is transformed into a call to **adt_observe_base**, **adt_observe_lob** or **adt_observe_adt**, depending upon the type of the corresponding attribute;
- A call to a mutator method is transformed into a call to **adt_mutate_base**, **adt_mutate_lob** or **adt_mutate_adt**, depending upon the type of the corresponding attribute.

The copy avoidance algorithm for mutator methods is based upon the following observations:

- Expressions such as column references, which refer to values in a shared space by all transactions such as the buffer pool, cannot be mutated in-place. This also avoids the direct update of a table through mutator methods, which the SQL3 standard prohibits. Instead tables with columns of structured types can be updated only through the standard INSERT, DELETE and UPDATE statements.
- All other occurrences of expressions represent values that are used only once in an observer/mutator method invocation. Therefore if the incoming argument can be mutated safely in-place, the result can also be mutated safely in-place.
- Any call to a constructor results in a new value that can be mutated safely in-place.

The algorithm is implemented by associating, with each node in a parse tree, a **mutation_safe** flag that is initialized to **false**.

- If the parse tree node references a table column, set the flag to **false**;
- If the operation in the parse tree node is **adt_constructor**, set the flag to **true**;
- If the operation in the parse tree node is an observer (**adt_observe_{base,lob,adt}**), set the flag to the flag of the parse tree node for the subject of the observer method;
- If the operation in the parse tree node is a mutator (**adt_mutate_{base,lob,adt}**), then set the flag to **true** if the flag for the parse tree node of the subject of the mutator is true. Otherwise, insert an **adt_copy** function for the subject of the mutator and set the flag for the mutator operation to **true**.

5 Dealing with Variable Length Attributes and Subtyping

When values of a structured type are stored in the memory, they may not be in a linearized format in the sense that all attribute values may not follow after one another or follow immediately after the header. When they are stored in tables on the disk, they are linearized when they are written to the disk. Because of subtyping and variable length attributes such as large objects, values of a column of a structured type can have drastically different sizes. It may not be possible to store all of them inline since the size of the record buffer for a row in a table is often limited by the page size. On the other hand, it is not wise to store *all* of them out-of-line like large objects as accessing large objects in a separate storage space is more expensive. Our approach is to store values of structured types inline or out-of-line dynamically depending upon their actual sizes. In addition, large object attributes inside a structured type can also be stored inline whenever possible.

To provide some control by the user over the inline storage of structured typed values in a table column, we have introduced a new column option named INLINE LENGTH that can be specified for a structured typed column when a table is created. The value of INLINE LENGTH is an integer that represents a number of bytes. Column values whose size is larger than the inline length will be stored outside the table, in the form of a large object.

Inline Storage of Large Object Attributes

Structured types are often used to encapsulate large objects, e.g., to manage image and textual documents, together with other attributes and with methods. It is important to handle large object attributes inside structured types efficiently. While large objects often have a large maximum size, large object values in an application may have drastically different sizes. For example, a geometry large object may contain only a single point, a small polygon, or a large bitmap for an area. In general, large objects are represented by descriptors that indicate where the data are actually stored, usually in a separate tablespace. Therefore chasing large object descriptors to the actual data is an expensive operation.

To avoid these problems, We store *small* values of large object attributes of structured types in an *inline* fashion under two situations:

- If the size of a large object descriptor is larger than the size of the actual data, we always store its value *inline*.

- If the inline length specified for a table column can accommodate the inline representation of a large object attribute in a value of a structured type, then store the large object attribute *inline*. This decision is made based upon a "first-come first-serve" basis. For instance, if a value of a structured type contains two large object attribute values inside, the one that is encountered first may be stored inline, while the other large object value may have to be stored out-of-line and is represented by a large object descriptor.

Turning Values of Structured Types into Large Objects

Values of structured types are stored inline whenever possible. However, it is possible that even if every large object inside a value of a structured type is represented by a large object descriptor, the resulting size still exceeds the maximum size of the record buffer of a row. If that is the case, we turn the value of the structured type itself into a large object. The corresponding large object descriptor is then stored inline. Notice that there may still be large object values stored inline inside the value of the structured type when the size of the large object value is less than the size of a large object descriptor. This kind of "lobification" is applied to values of structured types that are not nested inside other values.

6 Performance Comparison

This section reports some preliminary performance results comparing several alternative implementations of structured types. All the queries are run using IBM DataJoiner 2.1.2 on a server machine.

We use a table for the census block data for the state of Kentucky with 137173 rows. The table has 10 columns of builtin types and one column of a structured type (called `polygon`). The type `polygon` has 13 attributes, one of which is a binary large object storing all points in the polygon.

```
CREATE TYPE Polygon
AS (srid int, numpoints int,
    geometry_type smallint,
    xmin double, ymin double,
    xmax double, ymax double,
    zmin double, zmax double,
    area double, length double,
    anno_text varchar(256),
    points blob(1m)) NOT FINAL;

CREATE TABLE census
(name varchar(20), rowid int,
 a1 decimal, a2 decimal, a3 decimal,
 a4 decimal, a5 decimal, a6 decimal,
 a7 decimal, a8 decimal, shape Polygon);
```

Several alternative implementations of structured types are considered:

- VARCHAR: The type of column `shape` is changed to `varchar(3930) for bit data`; Its values are truncated if necessary in this case. While the varchar representation has the advantage of inline storage, its size limitation is a serious shortcoming for representing values of structured types.

- BLOB: The type of column **shape** is changed to **blob(1m)**. Compared to VARCHAR, the BLOB representation has a much larger maximum size. However, the actual data for **shape** will be stored out-of-line, separate from the rest of the data in the table.

- SIDE TABLE: Column **shape** is eliminated and all values of the column are stored in a separate side table. Column **rowid** serves as the foreign key linking the side table to the original table containing other business data.

- FLAT TABLE: Column **shape** is expanded into multiple columns, one for each attribute of type **Polygon**. The difference from SIDE TABLE is that all attributes of the structured typed column **shape** are stored in the *same* table with other business data, avoiding the extra join in the SIDE TABLE representation.

Attributes of structured types are accessed by using builtin functions in DB2, user-defined functions in the VARCHAR or BLOB approach, or regular table column access in the SIDE TABLE or FLAT TABLE approach. User-defined functions can be either fenced or unfenced. If a user-defined function is fenced, it will be executed in a process or address space that is separate from that of the database manager. In general a function running as fenced will not perform as well as a similar one running as unfenced. Indexing is not used.

The following queries for the IBM DB2 approach and their corresponding variants for alternative implementations of structured types are executed:

- QALL — retrieve all attributes (except the annotation text) of column **shape** of the entire table (with 137173 records) :

```
SELECT shape.srid, shape.numpoints,
       shape.geometry_type,
       shape.xmin, shape.xmax,
       shape.ymin, shape.ymax,
       shape.zmin, shape.zmax,
       shape.area, shape.length,
       shape.points
FROM   census
```

- QSCALAR1 — retrieve some scalar attributes of column **shape** using a predicate on business data:

```
SELECT shape.numpoints,
       shape.xmin, shape.ymin,
       shape.area
FROM   census
WHERE  a1 = 0
```

The query result contains 45417 records.

- QBLOB — retrieve the binary large object attribute of column **shape** using a predicate on column **rowid**:

```
SELECT shape.points
FROM   census
WHERE  rowid < 30001
```

The query result contains 30000 records.

- QSCALAR2 — retrieve some scalar attributes of column **shape** using a predicate on column **rowid**:

```
SELECT shape.numpoints,
       shape.xmin, shape.ymin,
       shape.area
FROM   census
WHERE  rowid < 10001
```

The query result contains 10000 records.

- QCOUNT1 — count the number of records using an equality predicate on an attribute of a structured type:

```
SELECT count(*)
FROM   census
WHERE  shape.numpoints = 100
```

- QCOUNT2 — count the number of records using a complex predicate on attributes of a structured type:

```
SELECT count(*)
FROM   census
WHERE  (shape.length
         between 1 and 200) and
       (shape.numpoints
         between 10 and 100)
```

For all queries except QSCALAR1 that has a dependency on the business data, there are two versions for the SIDE TABLE approach. One version involves column **rowid** in the main table and a join with the side table. The other version does not involve a join and, instead, retrieves data from the side table directly. The latter version assumes that the query optimizer is intelligent enough to avoid the join. This may not be trivial since users pose queries using the main table, unaware of the side tables being used to store values of structured types. The sole N/A entry in the table is for the case where the join with the side table cannot be avoided.

Table 1 shows the sum of the CPU time and synchronous I/O time (in seconds) for all the queries in different approaches.

For the first four queries, the access of attributes of structured types occurs in the SELECT clause. In the

Queries	Qall	Qscalar1	Qblob	Qscalar2	Qcount1	Qcount2
DB2	96.4	17.2	27	10.1	6.7	7.4
varchar (unfenced)	160	24.01	30.1	11.1	11.3	13
varchar (fenced)	320	33	35.5	16	29	60
blob (unfenced)	520	70	32.3	15.9	59	107
blob (fenced)	740	108	44.8	25.4	81	178
side table (w/join)	320.3	24.04	33.8	14.2	9.7	9.5
side table (w/o join)	159	N/A	29.7	10.1	4.3	4.1
flat table	182	18.1	29.56	11.8	5.6	6.7

Table 1: Performance measurements of retrieval of attributes of structured types

VARCHAR approach, even though all values of structured types are stored inline (and truncated in some cases), the overhead of invoking user-defined functions is much higher than that of executing builtin operations. The reason is that builtin operations are part of the database engine and do not require extra environment setup or protection to be run. When the number of such invocations increases (from QSCALAR2 to QALL), the relative performance of the VARCHAR approach to DB2 deteriorates. The use of fenced user-defined functions adds even more overhead. The BLOB approach is similar to VARCHAR except that all binary large objects are stored out-of-line and have to be retrieved and materialized for the invocation of user-defined functions.

The DB2 approach performs better than the side table approach for two reasons. First, the SIDE TABLE approach requires an extra join, which is normally the case since users access attributes of structured types in side tables from business tables and the side tables are hidden from users. Second, binary large object attributes inside a structured type can be stored inline whenever possible in the DB2 approach, while binary large objects inside a regular table column are stored out-of-line. When the extra join is eliminated *manually* in the SIDE TABLE approach and in the FLAT TABLE approach, DB2 still retains its performance advantage for queries QALL and QBLOB due to its dynamic inline/out-of-line storage of binary large object attributes in structured types and holds its ground for the access of scalar attributes in queries QSCALAR1 and QSCALAR2.

For the two count queries, the access of attributes of structured types occurs in the WHERE clause. The DB2 approach still performs better than the SIDE TABLE approach with join. However when the join is eliminated manually, the direct access of structured types in the side table (without going through the original table of business data) is more efficient. Similarly the FLAT TABLE approach also performs better in this case. The reason is that our attribute access is performed by builtin operations, but predicates involving observer/mutator methods are not pushed down deep enough into the database engine by the query optimizer.

7 Conclusion

We have presented an implementation of SQL3 structured types with inheritance in DB2. Its salient features include: (a) encapsulation of the implementation of structured types, minimizing the impact on low level components of the database engine; (b) compile-time copy avoidance algorithm for efficient implementation of the value-based semantics of mutator methods; and (c) dynamic inline/out-of-line storage of LOB attributes inside structured types and of structured types themselves. For future work, we intend to investigate further the performance and query optimization issues of structured types.

Acknowledgment

The authors thank Michael Carey for his detailed comments on an an early draft of this paper and thank the anonymous referees for their feedback on this paper.

References

[1] M. Carey, D. Chamberlin, S. Narayanan, B. Vance, D. Doole, S. Rielau, R. Swagerman, and N.M. Mattos. O-O, what have they done to DB2? In *Intl. Conference on Very Large Data Bases*, September 1999.

[2] D. Chamberlin. *A Complete Guide to DB2 Universal Database.* Morgan Kaufmann Publishers, Inc., 1998.

[3] E.F. Codd. A relational model of data for large shared data banks. *Communications of ACM*, 13(6):377–387, June 1970.

[4] ESRI. Environmental System Research Institute (ESRI). Home page http://www.esri.com.

[5] Informix. Informix DataBlade Products, 1997. http://www.informix.com.

[6] ISO Final Draft International Standard (FDIS) Database Language SQL – Part 2: Foundation (SQL/Foundation), February 1999.

[7] M. Stonebraker and P. Brown. *Object-Relational DBMSs: Tracking the Next Great Wave.* Morgan Kaufmann Publishers, Inc., 1999.

Generating Call-Level Interfaces for Advanced Database Application Programming[1]

U. Nink, T. Härder, N. Ritter

University of Kaiserslautern

P.O. Box 3049, 67653 Kaiserslautern, Germany

e-mail: nink/haerder/ritter@informatik.uni-kl.de

Abstract

It has always been a hard problem to provide application programming interfaces (API) for database systems without sacrificing some advantages of either the database management system or of the programming languages. Various approaches have been proposed. We discuss APIs with respect to SQL3 and its object-relational extensions as well as to object-oriented programming languages. We argue that generated call-level interfaces (CLI) are better suited than classical CLIs and language embeddings to couple database languages to object-oriented programming languages. Profiting from code generation and early binding of type information, generated CLIs improve the pros of embeddings while obviating the cons of classical CLIs. We propose an architecture for generated CLIs consisting of a cache module, a generated run-time system, and a compiler that generates parts of the (generated) CLI. The partial generation is specified using a configuration language to describe application-specific early binding of type information corresponding to data models, schemas, and queries. With this approach, we can control the sharing of database type information for application programs as well as the deferrable adaptation of applications to different needs by extending interfaces and by replacing implementations.

1 Introduction

Database management systems (DBMS) store and manage large sets of shared data whereas application programs perform the data processing tasks, e. g., to run the business of a company. Often, these programs are written in various programming languages (PLs) embodying different type systems. Thus, DBMSs should be "multi-lingual" to serve the application requests. This is typically achieved by providing a DBMS and its database language (DBL), like SQL2, with an own type system. To access the database (DB), a DBL/PL-coupling called database API (DB-API or API for short) is required.

1.1 DBL/PL-Couplings

The main problem of coupling DBLs and PLs is the impedance mismatch between them, resulting from differences in the type systems or programming models. While, for example, relational DBMSs offer a quite simple and flat data model, programming languages provide many helpful type constructors for the design of complex information models. Furthermore, relational DBMSs support set-oriented, declarative queries (n-set-oriented queries), while PLs are typically navigational, that is, the programmer has to manually follow links between single objects or iterate collections of objects.[2]

Another aspect is that software technology is changing rapidly. Thus, for APIs it is important to exploit approved and stable base concepts, which, additionally, are flexible enough to be adapted to a changing system environment. The paradigm of object-orientation comprises a set of concepts fulfilling these requirements. It has not only considerably influenced application development, but it also forms "a new great wave in the database ocean" - the object-relational wave [23]. What can be observed here is, as the data models are coming closer, the differences seem to vanish more and more. The most important concepts on both sides are references and abstract data types. References allow, similar to pointers, to directly model (n:m)-relationships between object types. Thus, complex object support is also needed at the API. Abstract data types (ADT) allow to define interfaces and to hide their implementations; modeling of ADTs is done with user-defined types (UDT) in object-relational DBMSs (ORDBMS) and with classes and interfaces in OOPLs. ADTs allow for the extension of the type system without extending the underlying grammar. Thus, many needed extensions for a coupling can be implemented through ADTs and obviate grammar extensions.

1. This work has been supported by the German Science Foundation (DFG) as part of the Sonderforschungsbereich (SFB) 501 "Development of Large Systems with Generic Methods".

Proceedings of the 25th VLDB Conference, Edinburgh, Scotland, 1999

2. Extensions in OOPLs support a restricted form of querying (evaluation of simple search arguments on collections: 1-set-oriented queries). Nevertheless, applications still tend to be navigational.

Different couplings have been proposed in the past [9, 13, 14, 15]. Programmers seem to prefer simple interfaces based on well-known concepts in the context of application programming; CLIs, e. g. JDBC [5, 7], have always been accepted best, since they can be combined with the use of standard compilers. API developers, on the other hand, seem to prefer solutions that lead to more elegant interfaces (embedded DBLs, e. g. eSQL or SQLJ [19]); most often precompilers or extended compilers were used to reach this goal.

In order to access the DB via the API, some preparation tasks are needed; each DB statement has to be compiled, optimized, and bound to the data structures (as described in the DB schema). The pure CLI approach essentially considers the DB statement as a string to be passed to the DBMS at run time. Therefore, (most of) the tasks preparing the DB access are to be deferred until run time. Hence, DB access involves additional overhead burdening the response time. Since binding of DB operations (to DB schema information) is "late", DB schema changes can be adjusted until the latest time possible. Hence, data independence is preserved to a maximum degree. In contrast, embedded DBLs shift all preparation tasks to compile time which improves run-time performance and enables more choices to react to errors. On the other hand, early binding makes compiled programs depending on DB schema changes. Hence, such an approach increases data dependence.

1.2 Our Goal

We want to show that by following a generative approach, we are able to 'equip' CLIs with the advantages of embeddings. Thus, we can provide APIs which combine the best of both worlds, i. e., are efficient, have strong typing and early error handling, as well as a high degree of data independence. These APIs that optimally couple DBLs like SQL3 [10, 11] to OOPLs like Java [1] or C++ [21] are *configurable* specializations of CLIs, named ***generated call-level interfaces***.

Such a generative approach allows to properly adapt the API to the application's needs. We will see that especially the selection of suitable binding times (early, late) for interfaces and implementations of API functions and the choice of an adequate pointer swizzling strategy for DB objects cached at the client side are crucial issues in that concern.

In the following, we will first introduce CLIs before we sketch a running example to explain the concepts. Afterwards, the mapping of SQL's data model into data models of OOPLs is discussed. We contrast late binding to early binding and introduce *virtual late binding* as an interesting compromise. Furthermore, the integration of the different programming models on both sides of the API is explored. Then, we introduce a configuration language that allows to specify the adaptation of the API to different needs. Finally, we step through a sample program again contrasting binding times.

2 Generated Call-Level Interfaces

In this section, we want to detail the notion of generated CLIs and introduce our approach. The first subsection identifies important concepts to improve CLIs and defines generated CLIs. Afterwards, we discuss our generative approach, especially by emphasizing the configurability of the API.

2.1 Preconditions and Definition

Many advantages of language extensions like embeddings can also be achieved for CLIs. But, the distance between the concepts of the database language and those of the host language is an important factor for a successful coupling. The following concepts of advanced database languages narrow the gap to programming languages.

- An extensible type system exists for data modeling (collections, user-defined types, and user-defined functions).
- A surrogate concept is the basis for identification and referencing of database objects.
- References between database objects (often as set-valued reference attributes) allow for the direct modeling of (n:m)-relationships.

Regarding OOPLs, we identify the following concepts that allow to improve CLIs.

- Extensible type systems support the definition of user-defined ADTs through interfaces and classes that can be used very similar to built-in data types. Thus, database objects can be treated like programming language objects.
- Encapsulation by using interfaces allows for the replacement of underlying classes and, in consequence, the choice between equivalent implementations with different characteristics.
- Polymorphism and subtyping provide a compromise between pure early and pure late binding and, therefore, open a spectrum of gradual early binding which we also call polymorphic binding.

Code generation is needed to introduce early binding of type information and especially, the early binding of application developer knowledge to certain type information. This leads us to the following definition [16].

Definition: *A generated or early-bound call-level interface (gCLI) is a CLI introducing early binding of type information usually by code generation at compilation time of schemas, queries or applications.*

We propose a specialized compiler to support the provision of early bindings and the necessary code generation. But, in contrast to embeddings, such a CLI compiler is decoupled from the OOPL compiler in order to reduce dependencies. The CLI compiler is based on the database language, that is, it extends the database language compiler (like storage structure languages as part of database languages) or analyzes the database language compiler's output (meta-data, dictionary data).

2.2 Architectural Overview

Figure 1 gives an architectural overview of our approach. At the left-hand side, we see the components needed during run time of an application program: the application program itself, a generated run-time system (gRTS), a cache module, as well as the DBS.

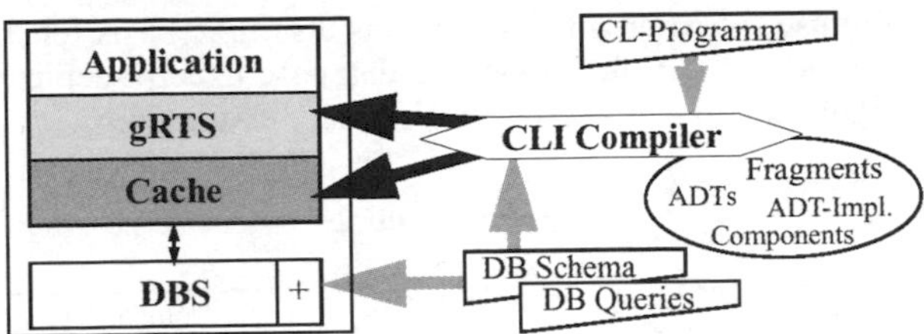

Figure 1: Architectural Overview

Location transparency for access to database objects through the client is provided by the cache module. It supports communication with the DBS, abstraction of object mapping, and (set-oriented) access to DB objects.

Operations of the API are implemented by the gRTS. It contains the operational semantics of the API and provides late-bound and, optionally, early-bound interfaces implemented on top of the cache module. By the gRTS, application programmers get interfaces for database access and session control (transactions). In addition, they can use cursors or iterators to work with the instances. A dictionary provides meta-data access and may be accessible by the programmer, too.

The CLI compiler (see figure 1, right-hand side) produces fragments of the gRTS and the cache module. It performs early binding of type information and allows for the replacement of equivalent (early-bound) implementations (e. g., classes that implement interfaces). In the following, we discuss the task of the CLI compiler in more detail.

2.3 The CLI Compiler

Specifications of the application programmer in a configuration language resulting in a configuration program are analyzed by the CLI compiler to produce early bindings for type information specific to schemas and queries. The generated code extends the core run-time system. As figure 1 shows, the CLI compiler may choose from a pool of code fragments, interfaces, implementations, and ready-to-use components. In addition, it refers to meta-data (DB schema, DB queries) in order to generate type- and query-specific functions. The '+' in figure 1 represents extensions that are needed to manage configuration data. In the following, we discuss the influences of the CLI compiler on cache module and gRTS. Let us start with the cache module.

Access and Object Mapping: These methods support object access based on database object identifiers (OID) and corresponding local identifiers (LID) in virtual memory (pointer, reference) [22] as well as the mapping between OIDs and LIDs. Access through OIDs is location transparent but not as efficient as access through LIDs which omits residency checks and/or reservation checks of referenced objects. In order to speed up access to objects tailored implementations of operations in the run-time system may be generated by the CLI compiler.

The following components (of the cache module) can optionally be configured. To support application-oriented prefetching and pointer swizzling [12], specific control mechanisms are implemented in the run-time system while the basic mechanisms belong to the cache module. Therefore, the following two components cross borders.

Prefetching: If the application knows in advance which objects are needed in the future when calling certain methods of the API, it is useful to early bind this knowledge. Thus, this knowledge can effectively be exploited, to prefetch needed objects in a single step. The CLI compiler can translate this knowledge into additional code for method bodies calling corresponding fetch operations.

Pointer Swizzling: If the application knows in advance, which references between objects are often dereferenced (say more than 2 times), it is useful to early bind this knowledge in order to trigger reference transformation (pointer swizzling [22]). Since dereferencing has to know if references are swizzled or not, a swizzling check is needed, which is also called *lazy-if*. Similar to location transparency we provide reference transparency, which allows for automatic dereferencing of OIDs and LIDs. Again, the CLI compiler may produce efficient implementations that omit the swizzling check in the run-time system.

Before listing the gRTS functions, which can be adapted via the CLI compiler, we want to mention that the gRTS is divided into an external layer and an internal layer. Application programmers use the external layer while API implementers use the internal layer to build the external layer. Each layer is divided into late-bound and early-bound interfaces. At each layer, the decision which kind of interface to use is important for the implementation of the next higher layer (external layer or application, respectively) because of the different syntax. The CLI compiler can either let interfaces reuse existing generic (late-bound) implementations or generate more efficient implementations that use generated (early-bound) interfaces. The following gRTS components can be configured.

Session Control: Local savepoints on the client including all cached database objects and current cursor states are based on the conversion of objects into byte streams and vice versa. This conversion may either occur in a generic method or using generated conversion methods for the various object types.

Database Access: In addition to the generic query class "SQL.gCLI.Query" that can handle query results of arbitrary select statements, each query may be represented by a generated specialized query class "SQL.gCLI.Generated.Query<name>"[3]. An easy thing to do is the early binding of column names of the result set. More work has to be done in order to early bind complex-object structures. We come back to this point later.

3. Queries must be named in this case. The name may be specified in the configuration program.

Result Construction: Also based on conversion of byte streams and virtual memory objects, result construction, too, either occurs in a generic way or has to take replaceable storage structures for objects, indices, and collections into account.

Instances: Besides replaceable storage structures for instance collections, attribute collections, and set-valued attributes the CLI compiler can optionally configure type specific indices for such collections. The CLI compiler produces corresponding code that, for instance, knows if an index is available or not for the current operation.

Dictionary: The dictionary itself is rather generic in nature. But since our object types provide (replicated) methods for meta-data access, these methods can be optimized. Instead of asking the dictionary in the body of the method, it is possible to hardwire known meta-data in advance (like the name of an object type).

Cursor/Iterator: In our architecture this is the most interesting module for the CLI compiler. The CLI compiler can generate statements containing meta-data as constants into method bodies. Attribute access, for instance, can be accelerated by such an optimization since it saves the dictionary lookup at run time. Other configurations may affect prefetching and pointer swizzling. Since method calls trigger prefetching actions or transformation actions, the CLI compiler can also generate code into the method bodies calling predefined or generated actions.

The outline of our approach given in this section is meant to prepare the following discussions. We will start these discussions by introducing a simple application scenario, which will serve as a running example.

3 Example

Developed for the evaluation of ODBMSs the OO7 benchmark [4] is also a candidate for discussing ORDBMSs. Since we do not deal with measurements here, but concentrate on concepts, we narrow our view to a small part of the benchmark which we name *MicroOO7*.

The OO7 benchmark defines a database schema with several entity types. The assembly hierarchy, which we skip here, manifests assembling of composite parts (`CompositePart`) given by a design library.

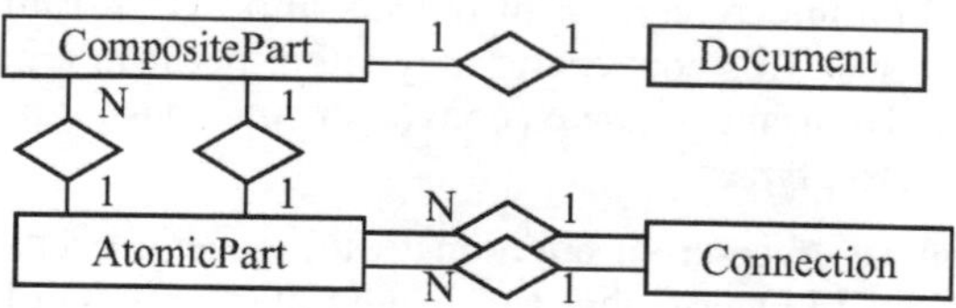

Figure 2: MicroOO7 Schema (ER diagram)

Each `CompositePart` is associated with a describing `Document` and contains a set of `AtomicParts` that are interrelated by explicit `Connection` instances (see figure 2). A CompositePart has exactly one such Document, and each Document belongs to exactly one CompositePart. A CompositePart has a number of AtomicParts (a benchmark parameter), one of which is marked as the root. Each AtomicPart is connected with a fixed number of AtomicParts (also a benchmark parameter). Each such link is represented by a Connection that carries additional attributes.

Figure 3 shows how a complex object of the OO7 benchmark might look like in the database. The entities are represented using row types whereas relationships are modeled by reference attributes. Thus, the instantiated vertices become references in an SQL3 database[4].

We use the MicroOO7 schema as a sample basis for the discussion of API functions; the database excerpt depicted in figure 3 will be used to explain query evaluations.

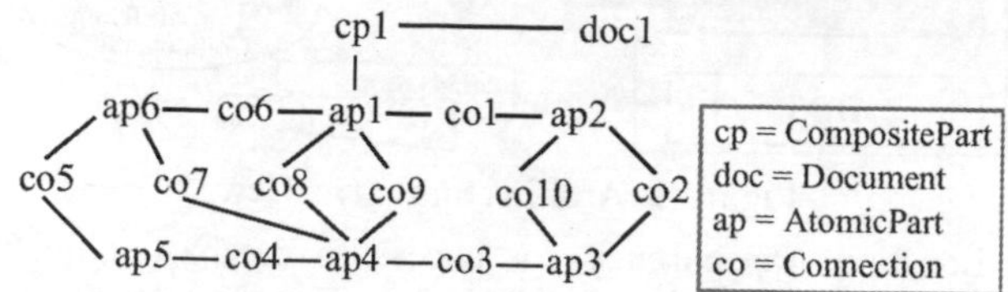

Figure 3: MicroOO7 Complex Object

4 Mapping SQL's Data Model

Now we discuss general aspects of the ADT concept that is found in most advanced data models. Afterwards, we discuss the mapping of SQL concepts.

4.1 General Aspects of ADTs

The concept of ADTs is very important for the DBL/PL-coupling because of its strong encapsulation. ADTs define interfaces which may have several (replaceable) implementations. In OOPLs ADTs are implemented using classes. Some OOPLs like Java allow to explicitly distinguish between interfaces and implementations (interfaces and classes). In order to exploit the ADT concept for mapping, we can to distinguish three cases. First, a seamless coupling can be reached if the concept of ADTs is similar in DBL and PL; thus, DB-ADTs can be mapped to PL-ADTs. Second (sets of) DB-operations are mapped to PL-ADTs. Third, DB-types are mapped to PL-ADTs; for example, for row types the mapping may specify column or attribute access methods with different degrees of early binding for method signatures and their implementations.

4.1.1 Interfaces of ADTs

In the following, we discuss different degrees of early binding for interfaces. Operations or methods constitute the interface of a class (including observer functions and mutator functions for attributes). Thus, the binding of an interface may be reduced to binding corresponding operations. To explain the main idea, we concentrate on attribute read access for row types. Starting discussions with generic solutions independent of row type and attribute we proceed with type-specific and attribute-specific solutions.

4. Due to simplicity, we omit corresponding SQL3 data definition statements. An intuitive understanding of the schema structures is sufficient to follow the discussions in the subsequent sections.

A generic mapping defines a signature for a method `GetAttribute` of the class Row that is capable of reading arbitrary attributes of rows of arbitrary row types. Below we give the definition of the signature and the usage of the method.

```
// as method of class Row
Attr GetAttribute(String rowtype,
String attribute, String attrtype)
{...}
// usage:
value = comp_part.GetAttribute(
"CompositePart", "buildDate", "Integer");
```

The result `value` is of type `Attr`, which is an attribute container for values of all possible attribute types. The current row `comp_part` is of type Row and allows to call the method `GetAttribute` by using the dot-notation. The first parameter `rowtype` of type `String` contains the name of the row type of the current row. The second parameter `attribute` of type `String` specifies the name of the wanted attribute. The third parameter `attrtype` of type `String` is to specify the name of the expected attribute type.

A disadvantage of this approach is that the correctness of the parameter values can only be determined at run time. Another disadvantage is that later calls of type-specific operations on the attribute value demand for explicit type casting.

With the following signature more type information is bound early. Two differences are obvious. First, instead of specifying the attribute type by a string, an output parameter `value` of the attribute's type (Integer) is used. Second, `void` indicates that no return value is delivered.

```
// as method of class Row
void GetAttribute(String rowtype,
String attribute, Integer value)
{...}
// usage:
comp_part.GetAttribute("CompositePart",
"buildDate", value);
```

A disadvantage is the need for implementing one method per attribute type. And still, the consistency of the attribute type and the names for row type and attribute must be checked at run time.

The parameter for the name of the row type may be omitted in an alternative signature, if the name can be implicitly determined. This is easily implementable with an OID containing a hint to the row type. The OID can be part of the row. Unfortunately, this does not avoid the run-time checks, but, at least, it simplifies the interface as is shown below.

```
// as method of class Row
void GetAttribute(String attrname,
Integer value)
{...}
// usage:
comp_part.GetAttribute("buildDate", value);
```

A further improvement is possible by defining attribute access methods for concrete row types. We map the row type `CompositePart` to a subclass of Row named `CompositePart`.

```
// as method of class CompositePart
void GetAttribute(String attribute,
Integer value)
{...}
// usage:
comp_part.GetAttribute("buildDate", value);
```

As a second possibility, the name of the corresponding generated class can be determined dynamically by reusing Java [1] concepts in two ways. First, since Java provides run-time type information (RTTI) for all objects in a dictionary, the name of the class of a given object may easily be found out at run time via the dictionary interface (Java Reflection API). Second, the `GetAttribute` method of `CompositePart` overwrites the inherited method of Row and, therefore, knows which row type is evaluated.

This scope reduction requires schema-specific code generation. The row type must be mapped to a separate class. On the other hand, method evaluation is more efficient, since less (generic) parameters have to be checked.

The overwritten method for attribute read access enables the application to switch from using the inherited method to using the new overwritten method without changing application code. If the parameter for the class name is part of the method's signature, as is with the first two signatures given in this subsection, it must also be part of the overwritten method's signature.

A maximum of performance can be reached by also avoiding the check of the attribute's name and type.

```
class CompositePart ...{ ...
Integer GetBuildDate() {...} }
// usage:
value = comp_part.GetBuildDate();
```

Here, the number of methods to be generated is proportional to the number of attributes in the class. But, the code calling this method is short. Moreover, the correctness of the call can completely be checked at compile time.

4.1.2 Implementations of ADTs

Principally, binding type information for implementations is independent of binding type information for corresponding interfaces. Possible combinations will be discussed in the next subsection.

We again start with the most generic solution for attribute read access. A global procedure expects the name of a class, the name of the attribute to be retrieved, and an object containing the specified attribute.

```
value = GetAttribute("CompositePart",
"buildDate", comp_part);
```

Since the compiler has no clue about the correctness of the call, all checks have to be performed at run time. Therefore, the body of the method implements the following actions.

- Ask the dictionary if the class name exists.
- Check if the given object `comp_part` is an instance of the given class.
- Ask the dictionary if the attribute name exists in the schema and if it belongs to the identified class.
- Determine or check (if given by another parameter) the type of the attribute and write the type information into

the attribute container `value`. Alternatively, leave the type open and delegate the determination of the type to the application programmer.

- Determine the storage location of the attribute[5]. Read and return the corresponding value.

Obviously, the above implementation is rather costly at run time. The optimization goal of attribute read access is to reduce overhead of the these actions or even to avoid costs completely. JDBC reduces overhead of attribute access through a binding mechanism at run time. The application programmer has to explicitly bind columns to variables in the programming language. This way, the main costs are shifted to the call of the function that does the binding. Thus, the performance of consecutive access is increased. We want to do something similar, but automatically at compile time and without preprocessing application code. Therefore, a CLI compiler generates a CLI. To enhance such an API, we have identified two main principles of optimization.

Introducing types and constants corresponding to schema-specific and query-specific type information *reduces the scope of evaluation* of methods at run time. This type-oriented scope reduction heavily depends on the features of the type systems of host programming languages. Especially row types and their columns are ideally suited for the generation of the corresponding types and constants of a host programming language. In contrast to simple strings, generated constants firmly restrict possible values at the type level (column names of row types, for instance). The corresponding generated types narrow the scope to certain row types and certain column types each as a whole. Constraints on row types and column types as well as accepted values at the instance level (when used as parameter types, for example) may be encapsulated. Thus, a generated body of a method exploiting generated types and constants already assumes some preconditions to be fulfilled when the evaluation of the method begins. In consequence, the body of such a method is easier to code and will perform better than generic methods.

Avoiding or improving search is based on replication. While indices are usually used to improve the performance of database queries, many operations of an API are navigational and, therefore, either do not use queries at all or only use simple index lookups. Especially for fine-grained operations, it is often beneficial to improve the index lookup itself. This is because lookups may cost more than the rest of an operation due to the evaluation of the hash function of the index[6]. Improving index lookup may be done by replicating index data into the class of, the object of, or the body of a given method. Instead of asking the index, the replicated value is read. On the other hand, replicated values are to be kept consistent with the index. This means that changing a value may require an index update as well as the update of the replicated value (double update).

These two principles may be applied at different degrees to optimize our example of attribute read access. Skipping the intermediate approaches that have defined methods for class `Row` we now discuss only the most advanced solution using a generated class `CompositePart`. In comparison with the actions to be executed by a generic method (see beginning of this subsection), the list of tasks to be performed by the generated version looks as follows:

- *There is no need to ask* the dictionary if the class name exists in the schema, because the existence has already been checked at compile time.
- *There is no need to check* if the given object `comp_part` is an instance of the given class, because this instantiation check is automatically done by the runtime system of the host programming language[7].
- *There is no need to ask* the dictionary if the attribute name exists in the schema and if it belongs to the identified class, because this has already been checked at compile time, too.
- *There is no need to determine or check* the type of the attribute, because this check, too, has already been done at compile time. *Do not write* any type information anywhere, because the result type exactly matches the attribute type.
- *There is no need to determine* the storage location of the attribute, because it has already been identified at compile time. Read and return the value of the attribute using the access information generated as part of the code of the body. Depending on the storage it may be necessary to type-cast the value to the given return type.

Obviously, this implementation is much more efficient than the generic version. In addition, it is type-safe. On the other hand, the implementation overhead is higher due to code generation. Application compilation takes longer, especially if the generated code has to be regenerated and compiled. Data independence is decreased, because schema-specific or query-specific type information gets part of the grammar of the API.

4.1.3 Interfaces and Implementations

Regarding binding of interfaces and binding of implementations two main aspects can be identified.

- Different degrees of early binding may coexist because of method overloading (as has already been shown in the previous subsections).
- The spectrum of gradual early bindings is orthogonally applicable to interfaces as well as to implementations as to be shown next. To concentrate on the major issue, we, again, only discuss the end points of the spectrum (early and late).

Some combinations of interfaces and implementations seem to be better than others. But this depends on applica-

5. The current object and additional access information that the dictionary has delivered for the checked names are used for the determination. The attribute may, for instance, be accessible through an index into an array of all attributes of the object or through the name of an instance variable defined for the class.

6. Remember that CPU costs are more important for locally executable operations than I/O costs.

7. Of course, a fully static solution avoiding all run-time checks is even more efficient, but it is not quite handy.

tion needs. The most common combinations are generic interfaces with generic implementations and early-bound interfaces with early-bound implementations (a shown previously). But, two other possibilities exist.

A generic interface can have an early-bound implementation that exploits early-bound type information. An example is the replacement of the generic dictionary lookup for a name of a row type by a generated switch statement (case statement) that embodies all possible names of the current schema as constants.

On the other hand, an early-bound interface may have a generic implementation ignoring the early-bound information given by its interface. This fourth combination may prototypically reuse an existing generic method feeding its generic parameters.

We identify the following four rules of thumb for the usefulness of combinations.

- Generic interfaces and implementations (combination L/L) are beneficial w. r. t. implementation overhead, application compilation, and data independence.
- The replacement of a generic implementation by a generated one (L/E) raises implementation overhead and application compilation times, but improves performance [16]. Data independence may stay at the same level when regeneration, compilation, and code replacement are automated.
- Early-bound interfaces and implementations (E/E) are most efficient. In addition, they improve error handling. On the other hand, implementation overhead and application compilation times are increased, and data independence is decreased.
- The combination of early-bound interfaces and generic implementations (E/L) considerably simplifies the prototypical API design or extension. Calls to such an interface are type-safe. Furthermore, an optimized implementation may substitute generic code at any time.

We think that the combination of generic interfaces and early-bound implementations embodies a high potential for optimization in SQL environments. We name this combination ***virtual late binding***, since early binding of implementations is hidden from the application programmer.

4.2 Mapping SQL Concepts

After having introduced the major principals, we proceed with discussing the mapping of SQL concepts.

4.2.1 Generic Mapping

Of course, we cannot discuss all concepts of SQL3 here, so we concentrate on a few that are most important following the top-down access sequence in applications:

- handling SQL statements;
- iterating result sets;
- accessing single rows of query results;
- accessing single fields of a row.

SQL Statements. A generic class `Query` allows to handle arbitrary SQL statements. An instance of `Query` represents a concrete statement. The constructor of the class accepts the statement as string. A call of the method `compile()` triggers compilation of the statement by the DML compiler. To evaluate the statement the method `execute()` is to be performed. The result set is accessible when the evaluation has finished (or earlier in case of asynchronous execution and early delivery of partial result sets).

Iterating Result Sets. A cursor or iterator mechanism is needed to identify a single row for subsequent access. For a detailed discussion of different cursor concepts see [16]. We think that it is a good approach to provide exactly one instantiated cursor as part of `Query`. Such a built-in cursor is most efficient since it assumes that there are no other cursors, and, therefore, does not have to care for keeping several cursor spheres consistent. If more than one cursor is needed or wanted, additional cursors can explicitly be instantiated from a special class `Cursor`. These cursors know about each other and about the existence of the built-in cursor, and, thus, cannot invalidate states of other cursors, respectively. They provide comfortable access sacrificing performance.

Accessing Single Rows. Usually, cursors are positioned to a specific row, in order to access that row. Rows are represented by instances of `Row`. Several methods allow for the manipulation of single rows: `toString()`, `set()`, `copy()`, `delete()` and so forth. Each of these methods may be parameterized to be "shallow" or "deep".

An explicit "fetch into host variables", as supported by JDBC, is not needed. The fetch is implicit and hidden, as supported by the new SQLJ. A call to one of the methods mentioned above automatically involves a dereferencing of the current row. The dereferencing is used as the event to trigger the fetch of SQL data[8].

Accessing Single Fields. A row type specified in a table or query definition consists of fields each representing a pair of field name and data type. The generic class `Row` for row types must be able to handle arbitrary query results with arbitrary numbers of fields (represented by `Field`).

According to the SQL standard, user-defined types implicitly define observer and mutator functions. In analogy, we define access methods to columns of row types for the binding to the host language. In contrast to the SQL binding mechanisms, our approach avoids the need for explicitly binding columns to host variables by the application programmer. A generic method `getField(int)` or `getField(String)` of such a class allows to access all fields by index (depending on the definition sequence) or by name (depending on their names in the table definition[9]). If the table structure is defined by a UDT, then

8. In C++ the dereferencing operator "->" can be overwritten in order to implement a smart pointer that fetches a row if it is not already cached. Since Java does not allow to overwrite the dot-operator, this action has to be implemented in the body of the methods mentioned above or by introducing an indirection using a descriptor (like the Java Reference Class).

9. The initialization of such names occurs at query execution time. In case of compiled queries, the association of names and access information may be stored in the database at compile time. In consequence, the association is only read and does not need to be constructed at query execution time.

getField behaves like getAttribute of the UDT (see below) avoiding the indirection through field.

Several data types are to be distinguished: predefined types, collection types, reference types, locator types, and user-defined data types. User-defined types are schema elements, that is, they are part of a DB schema.

Predefined types include numeric types, string types, the boolean type, datetime types, and interval types. There are always two possibilities to map these types to Java, our representative of OOPLs. Either database types are mapped to predefined Java types or to user-defined Java classes. In the first case it is necessary that the predefined types on both sides are equivalent (range of values, precision) or are at least compatible. Such a mapping is most efficient, but usually provides poor control of value modifications. The second case, mapping to classes, allows for the encapsulation of database types. This approach is not as efficient as the first one, but provides better control of changes, automatic maintenance of constraints (NOT NULL, restrictions like for date), and new operations, which are not available on the server. In addition, polymorphism and subtyping can be exploited, thus, enabling the generic Field to hold any predefined type.

Collection types are mapped to Collection. The only currently proposed collection type is "array". SQL arrays are either mapped to the predefined type constructor "[]" or to Array as subtype of Collection. The former case is, again, faster than the latter case, but provides poor control. C++ offers the concept of templates to realize the latter case. In Java we exploit polymorphism and restrict the element types by their common supertype Element representing all possible element types. The Java approach saves code in the API implementation, but is slower since the exact type of an element has to be determined at run time.

Reference types are mapped to Ref hiding physically stored values (database reference, virtual memory reference). The API implementation may choose between two interfaces implemented by the cache. The first interface already delivers location transparency simplifying the API code above. The second interface forces the API implementation itself to provide location transparency. This interface is harder to use but allows for application-specific optimization. In analogy to the location of objects, it is possible to reach swizzling transparency. In consequence, the API implementation can choose between existing swizzling strategies or can implement an application-specific strategy.

Locator types are used to hide transferring of very large data values or of parts of these values[10]. Locators provide location transparency of SQL data in the absence of explicit references (see reference types above). Moreover, locators are used to handle UDTs. This is the only SQL way to work with user-defined types in the APIs.

10. The standard differentiates between several kinds of locators and their features which we do not discuss here.

User-defined types are schema elements. Therefore, we need a generic UDT to handle arbitrary UDTs. A UDT can be distinct or structured. A *distinct* UDT is based on exactly one predefined type (its base type). Distinct types support strong typing, that is, argument and parameter types of routines must be the same. A method getValue() returns the value of such a field. A *structured* UDT defines a list of attributes and may be subject to inheritance. To generically access those attributes, a method getAttribute() is needed accepting at least a description of the wanted attribute's name (see section 4.1.1).

4.2.2 Generated Mapping

In order to introduce early binding of type information, we have to generate classes specific to schema and query type information.

SQL Statements. Given an SQL statement with name "Parts", a generated class QueryParts allows to handle exactly this SQL statement. An instance of QueryParts represents that statement. The constructor of the class does not need to receive the statement as a string, because it is known at compile time. Calling the method compile() is optional, since the query has already been compiled. Nevertheless, it is useful to support recompilation in the case that preconditions on which the current query execution plan is based on have changed. To evaluate the statement the method execute() is needed. The result set is accessible when the evaluation has finished (or earlier in case of asynchronous execution and early delivery of partial result sets).

Iterating Result Sets. A cursor or iterator mechanism is still needed to identify a single row for later access. The initially instantiated cursor as part of QueryParts knows about the usage of the result set specified by the application programmer. In consequence, cursor operations like "next" are viewed as events and trigger actions, say, prefetching or swizzling of SQL data.

Accessing Single Rows. After having positioned a cursor to a specific row, this row can be accessed. Rows are represented by instances of class RowParts. This class encapsulates the row type implicitly given by the compiled query. Query-specific methods allow for the type-safe manipulation (setting, copying) of corresponding rows. The implicit dereferencing on method invocation may be used to control fetching of fields.

Accessing Single Fields. The generated class RowParts for the given row type of the compiled query can only handle query results with the specified number and names of fields (class FieldX represents a field with name 'X'; the name scope is the package resulting by code generation for the given query).

For each field 'X' a generated method getX() allows access to the field named 'X'. The result type of the method maps the data type of the field.

Predefined types are not affected at all from early binding at the interface. Collection types, reference types, and locator types are independent of the DB schema, too. User-defined names that could be early bound do not exist in their context. But, we can generate specialized methods for the data type 'Y' "behind" a collection type, a reference type, or an locator type. The containing fields provide access methods that deliver "collection of Y", "reference to Y", or "locator for Y" respectively. In consequence, the application programmer can perform save type-casting, and coding profits from type safety.

User-defined types are schema elements and, therefore, have names that can be bound early. In addition to the generic `UDT` we generate a specialized `UDT AtomicPart` that can handle instances of AtomicPart only. For each attribute 'x' of AtomicPart we generate an access method `getx()`. If 'x' is of type 'y' then this method returns a value of the type that maps 'y'.

5 Integration of Programming Models

Different programming models exist on both sides of the coupling of database languages to programming languages. The following aspects have to be discussed:

Kind: SQL3 is n-set-oriented and programming languages like Java, C++, and C are navigational. Adding collections and search over single collections with simple search predicates (SSP) to programming languages, they become 1-set-oriented. Nevertheless, the programming model of the coupling is neither purely n-set-oriented nor navigational or 1-set-oriented. Both styles are available. Most often, the result of n-set-oriented operations like SQL queries is examined with navigational or 1-set-oriented operations. We name this combination *semi-set-oriented.*

Location transparency: Knowing the location of data supports efficient manipulation. Hiding the location of data supports easy coding. Our solution is to provide location transparency to the application programmer. Underneath, optimization may orthogonally occur. Different interfaces with and without location transparency are only internally visible.

Flexible functionality: Different applications have different needs. Thus, it is useful to allow for the configuration of APIs. A browser application does not need early binding at the interface, for instance. Therefore, it should at least be possible to switch support for early binding of the interface. The same argument holds for optimizing applications that use late-bound interfaces. The possibility to switch between late-bound and early-bound implementations of interfaces allows for the optimization of the application without application source code changes.

Decoupled query processing: Queries may be instantly evaluated or evaluation may be deferred. Deferred evaluation demands for the decoupling of query compilation and query execution. This decoupling may be local, inside the same transaction, or global, perhaps spanning different processes. The last case is important for design applications. To support this kind of decoupling we need persistent queries, i. e., storing and maintaining query information in the database. Additionally, it must be possible to find compiled queries at run time, to optionally recompile them, and to execute them. Besides saving the compilation overhead at run time, the generated code for handling such queries and their results inside an application is checked at compile time.

Result set processing: Cursors or iterators are needed to process result sets. As mentioned before, we distinguish flat cursors and nested cursors which support iteration at different levels of abstraction and navigational access at each level (access from nested cursors to flat cursors, for instance). It is useful to have 1-set-oriented operations with cursors. However, the more query functionality the cursor is equipped with, the more server code replication is required at the client.

Dictionary access: Browser applications need dictionary access. Furthermore, in our opinion, any application may profit from dictionary access. Since many operations of the API use dictionary information, dictionary access is mandatory in our architecture.

6 The Configuration Language

The CLI compiler is based on the database language and, optionally, based on a configuration language, which decouples API generation from application development. With a configuration program it is possible to introduce different degrees of early binding and to optimize the application program.

To reduce the overhead of early binding especially for fine-grained operations like attribute access, we prefer a type-oriented instead of a value-oriented approach. In a type-oriented approach types are configured and, thus, all of their values or instances share the same strategy. In a value-oriented approach, the strategy implemented for values or instances depends on their values or states respectively. Value orientation demands for run-time checking and strategy migration in case of value or state changes.

As we have learned from several projects, a configuration language should only depend on DBL concepts and on the methods provided with the API. Thus, configuration becomes implementation independent and portable. In addition, code generation primarily extends the bodies of methods of the API, since these are viewed as events.

In the following, we want to introduce our configuration language. Terminal symbols are written in capitals. We use the following meta-symbols of an extended BNF:

```
#    end of grammar rule
[]   option
{}   choice
[]+  many times, at least once
[]*  many times, optional
```

A configuration program (cl_program) consists of configuration blocks. A configuration block may be a type control block or a query control block (type_cntrl_block or query_cntrl_block). We concentrate on query control blocks here.

```
cl_program ::=
    BEGIN [query_cntrl_block |
    at_cntrl_block]+ END #
query_cntrl_block ::=
    DEFINE_QUERY name AS sql_query
     [BINDING binding ;]
     [SWIZZLING swizzling ;]
     [query_rule ;]*
    END_QUERY #
```

If a query control block is specified, then the generic query class is specialized. The result, the generated query class, contains the name of the query. The AS clause contains the definition of an SQL statement.

The BINDING clause determines the degree of binding for the (nested) cursor of the query result type.

```
binding ::= LATE|VIRTUAL_LATE|EARLY #
```

LATE, the default, corresponds with a late-bound interface using a late-bound implementation. Access uses a dictionary mapping node names and attribute names to node cursors and attribute offsets.

VIRTUAL_LATE means virtually late binding, that is, a late-bound interface on top of an early-bound implementation. Access omits dictionary lookup by testing names against constants contained in the method's body. It is possible to switch from LATE to VIRTUAL_LATE without changing application code.

EARLY demands for the generation of an access method per node and attribute. Node names and attribute names are used to define the names of these methods. The above mentioned tests may be omitted.

Of course, more degrees than shown here can be defined in order to fine-tune applications.

As an example for the use of API method calls as events to trigger optimizing actions we concentrate on pointer swizzling. First, we have to globally decide if pointer swizzling is to be done and if so, which of the both extreme strategies is to be used.

```
swizzling ::= NONE|LAZY|EAGER #
```

NONE, the default, means that no pointer swizzling should take place for query result. Thus, chasing references costs as much as a dictionary lookup.

LAZY means that a reference is swizzled when it is first dereferenced. The advantage is that only those references get swizzled that are really needed[11]. On the other hand, dereferencing the same reference later has the additional cost of asking, whether the current reference is swizzled or not (lazy-if).

EAGER means that references are swizzled before they are dereferenced. Most often swizzling is done when instances are loaded and mapped into virtual memory. The advantage is that the lazy-if is saved, because it is always known in advance that references are swizzled. On the other hand, usually more references are swizzled than needed.

Obviously, there are situations where no strategy fits best. In these situations it may be reasonable to swizzle certain portions of data at certain events. In addition, performance can benefit from programmer knowledge about which references are dereferenced (more than once perhaps) or which event (call to a method) leads to dereferencing such references. In order to support such dynamic swizzling decisions, we propose simple event-action rules.

```
query_rule ::=
    ON query_event DO query_action #
```

An event is defined to be a call to the methods of the query class.

```
query_event ::= exec_event|co_event #
exec_event ::= EXECUTE|RESTORE #
co_event ::=
    FIRSTCO|NEXTCO|PREVIOUSCO|
    OPENNESTEDCURSOR #
```

By query_granule it is specified, which references are to be swizzled.

```
query_action ::= qswizzle_action #
qswizzle_action ::=
    SWIZZLE [query_granule] #
query_granule ::= {CURRENT|ALL} #
```

CURRENT means to swizzle the current object under control, which is a result set in case of an exec_event and a single complex object in case of an co_event. ALL can be used to trigger swizzling of all objects at the next higher level; in case of an co_event all complex objects in the query result get swizzled.

We extended the grammar to capture fine-grained objects like the nodes in a complex object and even single attributes, though the overhead increases substantially. Technically, the class for the complex-object cursor delivers the corresponding events, that is methods (not shown in the grammar above). In general, optimization cannot compensate the implied overhead if the targets to be optimized are too fine-grained. But, in some cases it may nevertheless be beneficial. For very large fields like BLOBs, for instance, selective allocation of main memory and piecewise fetching can significantly increase economic memory usage and processing speed.

7 Sample Program

To see how the discussed concepts apply to application programs we proceed with a brief example based on the query over our sample database (see figure 3). The resulting program compiles and executes a query and does some navigation through the query result. We use this sample scenario to further discuss each of the three main degrees of binding: late, early, and virtual late.

Before going into details, we want to mention that we have chosen an example dealing with complex objects. Currently, SQL3 gives only some basic support for complex objects by means of references and collection types. In order to, at one hand, give some idea of the potential of our approach, and, at the other hand, motivate our opinion that SQL3 needs better complex object support than currently offered (and that current object-relational DBMSs need better data management support at the client side) [3, 8, 6, 20], the query in our example goes beyond the capa-

11. An ideal solution would swizzle only those references that are at least used twice to amortize the swizzling overhead.

bilities of SQL3. We assume that in the FROM clause of a SELECT statement a complex structure can be specified which corresponds to a graph, where the nodes represent base tables and the vertices represent referencing columns. Furthermore, we assume that corresponding instances (complex objects) can be delivered by the DBMS as units and that nested cursor structures can be generated by the CLI compiler serving for traversing and manipulating complex objects (as well as the contained elementary objects, respectively). Due to space limitations, we cannot detail this aspect and have to refer to a long version of this paper [17].

7.1 The LATE Binding

The late-bound interfaces are always provided. Only the corresponding class definitions must be imported.

```
import COAPI.*;
```

The Java package COAPI contains the definitions of all interfaces and classes of the API to handle complex objects. The most important ones are `Query` and `NestedCursor` that control inter-complex-object operations and intra-complex-object operations, respectively.

First, an instance representing the query is instantiated.

```
SQLQuery myQuery = new SQLQuery("
      SELECT ALL
      FROM CompositePart - AtomicPart -
            Connection
      WHERE CompositePart.type='type002';");
```

A call of the method `compile` delivers the query string to the DML compiler of the DBMS.

```
myQuery.compile();
```

The name of the query or the name of the application is used to decouple compilation from execution.

A call of the method `execute` asks the DBMS to evaluate the query. A corresponding transaction is opened.

```
myQuery.execute();
```

Internally, the name of the query is used to parameterize the query execution. The result set (or only the set of representatives depending on the configuration) is shipped to the client and stored in an object buffer in the application's main memory. The result-set cursor is initially opened.

Assume, we want to position the cursor on the first element of the result set.

```
myQuery.firstCO();
```

To step into the complex object at the current position, we open a nested cursor and position it (at the first level) to the first "CompositePart" node and (at the second level) to the first corresponding "AtomicPart" node, and there set the value of attribute "x".

```
SQLNestedCursor co =
    myQuery.openNestedCursor();
co.first("CompositePart").first("AtomicPart");
co.setAttribute("AtomicPart", "x", someInt);
```

Of course, a design step will do a lot more than setting an attribute. But this simple example suffices to illustrate the basic principals, and we proceed to the end of the program by performing the `checkin` of the internally recorded changes.

```
myQuery.checkin();
```

Besides propagating changes, the checkin operation also closes the transaction.

7.2 The EARLY Binding

The early-bound interfaces and implementations are only generated on demand. Some steps have to be taken to prepare their usage in an application.

First, we give a little configuration program that defines lazy pointer swizzling (SWIZZLING LAZY) for all applications bound to the API. It defines a query named "demo" (DEFINE_QUERY) and causes the system to bind early (BINDING EARLY) and to generate an optimizing rule for pointer swizzling of results of the given query (ON ...).

```
BEGIN
SWIZZLING LAZY;
DEFINE_QUERY demo AS
      SELECT ALL
      FROM CompositePart - AtomicPart -
        Connection
      WHERE CompositePart.type = 'type002';
      BINDING EARLY;
      ON EXECUTE DO SWIZZLE ALL;
    END_QUERY;
END
```

This configuration program is input to the CLI compiler which extracts the query, passes it to the DML compiler for compilation, stores resulting meta-data, and generates additional code for the API.

Now we come back to the application using the generated interfaces and classes. First, we have to import the Java interfaces and classes again.

```
import COAPI.Generated.*;
```

Then we instantiate the representative of the query. The name of the query becomes part of the interface name.

```
SQLQuery_demo myQuery = new SQLQuery_demo();
```

Compilation (if needed) and execution of the query stay the same as in the case of late binding (see section 7.1).

```
myQuery.compile();
myQuery.execute();
```

Next, we set the result-set cursor to the first element.

```
myQuery.firstCO();
Stepping into the complex object looks
   like the following.
SQLNestedCursor_demo co =
   myQuery.openNestedCursor();
co.first_CompositePart().first_AtomicPart();
co.AtomicPart().set_x(someInt);
```

Obviously, all strings that have to be used with the late binding are integrated into type names and method names and, therefore, can be checked at compile time.

Checkin is performed in the same way as in the case of late binding.

```
myQuery.checkin();
```

7.3 The VIRTUAL_LATE Binding

The virtual late binding is generated on demand. For that purpose, a configuration program is needed.

```
BEGIN
SWIZZLING LAZY;
DEFINE_QUERY demo AS
      SELECT ALL
      FROM CompositePart - AtomicPart -
        Connection
      WHERE CompositePart.type = 'type002';
      BINDING VIRTUAL_LATE;
      ON EXECUTE DO SWIZZLE ALL;
    END_QUERY;
END
```

Note that the only clause that has changed w.r.t. to the configuration program given in the previous subsection is the BINDING clause. The application program remains similar to the solution with the late binding. As the only difference it does not have to contain the query definition, because it is already part of the configuration program.

A disadvantage of this approach is that only one query is supported. If several queries are to be supported, it is possible to extend the API by context switches using the class loader of Java. A switch to another query implies loading of the corresponding class that implements the stable interface. Then, only the instantiation of the query representative changes. But, different queries can still be used only sequentially. If the results of several queries are to be processed simultaneously, the API must be able to mix query-specific type information within a single class or to provide specializations for each query. This, in turn, implies changes to all statements that use the types `Query` and `NestedCursor`, because the programmer must then use the specializations instead of the superclasses.

8 Conclusions

We have introduced generated CLIs as a configurable specialization of classical CLIs. The central idea to become better than classical CLIs like JDBC or language embeddings like SQLJ is the possibility to choose single or many different binding times out of a spectrum of binding times for database types and operations when mapping them to object-oriented programming languages like Java or C++.

Early binding improves application performance and early error handling. As an import advantage over SQLJ, our solution enables not only schema-specific type information but also query-specific type information to be bound early. By optionally using code generation only for mission-critical paths, the compilation overhead is controllable. An intermediate binding, the virtual late binding, avoids a higher degree of data dependence. This binding substantially enhances performance of generic interfaces like JDBC or ODBC [16].

We have shown that extensions to SQL3 like support for complex objects open a new dimension for early binding of type information. Extending the FROM clause by directed graphs of referencing types in the database allow for generating efficient and type-safe inter- and intra-complex-object operations. Furthermore, we have proposed an architecture for the implementation of generated CLIs that is based on three main components: a cache, a generated run-time system representing the implementation of the operations of the interface, and a CLI compiler. The cache provides location transparency. The run-time system represents an adaptable implementation of the interface operations. The CLI compiler parses a configuration program that contains statements for the application-specific adaptation of the generated run-time system.

Acknowledgments. We would like to thank A. Lambert for his extensive implementation effort.

References

[1] Arnold, K., Gosling, J.: The Java Programming Language. Addison-Wesley. 1996

[2] Atkinson, M., Morrison, R.: Orthogonally Persistent Object Systems. VLDB Journal 4:3. 319-401. 1995

[3] Chamberlin, D.D., Cheng, J.M., DeMichiel, L.G., Mattos, N.M.: Extending Relational Database Technology for New Applications. IBM Syst. Journal 33:2. 264-279. 1994

[4] Carey, M.J., DeWitt, D.J., Naughton, J.F.: The OO7 Benchmark. SIGMOD Record 22:2. 12-21. 1993

[5] Geiger, K.: Inside ODBC. Microsoft Press.1995

[6] Gesmann, M.: Parallel Query Processing in Complex-Object Database Systems (in German). Shaker. 1997

[7] Hamilton, G., Cattell, R.G.G., Fisher, M.: JDBC[tm] Database Access with Java[tm] - A Tutorial and Annotated Reference. Comp. & Eng. Publ. Group. The Java Series. 1997

[8] Härder, T., Meyer-Wegener, K., Mitschang, B., Sikeler, A.: PRIMA - A DBMS Prototype Supporting Engineering Applications. Proc. 13th Int. VLDB Conf. 433-442. 1987

[9] Härder, T., Rahm, E.: Database Systems - Concepts and Techniques of Implementation (in German). Springer. 1999

[10] ISO: Final Committee Draft (FCD), Database Language SQL - Part 1: SQL/Framework. 1998.

[11] ISO: Working Draft, Database Language SQL - Part 2: SQL/Foundation. 1998

[12] Kemper, A., Kossmann, D.: Adaptable Pointer Swizzling Strategies in Object Bases. Proc. 9th Int. Conf. on Data Engineering. 155-162. 1993

[13] Lacroix, M., Pirotte, A.: Comparison of Database Interfaces for Application Programming. Information Systems 8:3. 217-229. 1983

[14] Mitschang, B.: Query Processing in DBMS - Design and Implementation Concepts (in German). Vieweg. 1994

[15] Neumann, K.: Coupling of Programming Languages and Database Languages (in German). Informatik-Spektrum 15:4. 185-194. 1992

[16] Nink, U.: Coupling Design Databases with Object-Oriented Programming Languages (in German). Shaker. 1999

[17] Nink, U., Härder, T., Ritter, N.: Generating Call-Level Interfaces for Advanced Database Application Programming, Internal Report, SFB 501, Univ. of Kaiserslautern, 1999

[18] Nink, U., Ritter, N.: Database Application Programming with Versioned Complex Objects. Proc. Conf. on Advanced Database Systems (BTW'97). Informatik aktuell. Springer. 172-191. 1997

[19] Oracle White Paper: SQLJ: Embedded SQL in Java. 1997

[20] Schöning, H.: Query Processing in Complex-Object Database Systems (in German). Dt. Universitäts-Verlag. 1993

[21] Stroustrup, B.: The C++ Programming Language. Addison-Wesley. 1992

[22] Suzuki, S., Kitsuregawa, M., Takagi, M.: An Efficient Pointer Swizzling Method for Navigation Intensive Applications. Int. Workshop on Persistent Object Systems (POS). Springer. 79-95. 1995

[23] Stonebraker, M., Brown, P., Moore, D.: Object-Relational DBMSs - The Next Great Wave. Morgan Kaufmann. 1998

PM3: An Orthogonally Persistent Systems Programming Language – Design, Implementation, Performance

Antony L. Hosking
hosking@cs.purdue.edu

Jiawan Chen
chenj@cs.purdue.edu

Department of Computer Sciences
Purdue University
West Lafayette, IN 47907-1398
U.S.A.

Abstract

PM3 is an orthogonally persistent extension of the Modula-3 systems programming language, supporting persistence by reachability from named persistent roots. We describe the design and implementation of the PM3 prototype, and show that its performance is competitive with its non-orthogonal counterparts by direct comparison with the SHORE/C++ language binding to the SHORE object store. Experimental results, using the traversal portions of the OO7 benchmark, reveal that the overheads of orthogonal persistence are not inherently more expensive than for non-orthogonal persistence, and justify our claim that orthogonal persistence deserves a level of acceptance similar to that now emerging for automatic memory management (i.e., "garbage collection"), even in performance-conscious settings. The consequence will be safer and more flexible persistent systems that do not compromise performance.

1 Introduction

PM3 is an extension of the Modula-3 systems programming language [Cardelli et al. 1991] that supports *orthogonal persistence* [Atkinson and Morrison 1995], which manifests itself as a model of persistence by reachability from designated persistent roots. Persistent storage is viewed as a transparent extension of the Modula-3 dynamic allocation heap; all heap-allocated data are potentially persistent. The merits of orthogonal persistence have been argued for many years, yet performance-conscious implementations of persistence have been lacking. Indeed, most implementations of orthogonally persistent programming languages have relied on an execution model that involves interpretation by a virtual machine, rather than compilation to native code. This trend continues today with Java.

In contrast, persistent extensions of systems programming languages have traditionally shunned orthogonal persistence as too expensive, or perhaps too difficult to implement. The primary reason for this is its implied reliance on garbage collection to effect *persistence by reachability*. Yet garbage collection is now gaining in acceptance, even in the systems programming realm. Evidence for this comes not just from the increased level of research activity related to garbage collection [ISMM 1998], but also from the commercial success in the C++ market of garbage collector vendors such as Chicago's Geodesic Systems. In this paper, we lay to rest the notion that orthogonal persistence is a luxury that a "real" systems programming language cannot afford.

We organize the remainder of the paper as follows. Section 2 more precisely defines what we mean by the term *orthogonal persistence* and outlines its advantages for programmers of large persistent applications, while also considering the performance problems it poses. Section 3 discusses related work in the area of persistent programming languages. In Section 4 we describe our design and implementation of PM3, followed in Section 5 by a description of our experimental framework for comparison of PM3 with SHORE/C++, our experimental results, and their detailed implications. Section 6 summarizes our conclusions and points towards future research directions.

2 Orthogonal persistence

Orthogonally persistent object systems [Atkinson and Morrison 1995] provide an abstraction of permanent data storage that hides the underlying storage hierarchy of the hardware platform (fast access volatile storage, slower access stable secondary storage, even slower access tertiary storage, etc.). This abstraction is achieved by binding a programming language to an object store, such that persistent objects will automatically be cached in volatile memory for manipulation by applications and updates propagated back

Proceedings of the 25th VLDB Conference, Edinburgh, Scotland, 1999

to stable storage in a fault-tolerant manner to guard against crashes. The resulting *persistent programming language* and object store together preserve *object identity*: every object has a unique persistent identifier (in essence an address, possibly abstract, in the store), objects can refer to other objects, forming graph structures, and they can be modified, with such modifications visible in future accesses using the same unique object identifier.

In defining *orthogonal* persistence Atkinson and Morrison [1995] cite three design principles that are desirable in any persistent programming language design, enabling the full power of the persistence abstraction:

1. *Persistence independence*: the language should allow the programmer to write code independently of the persistence (or potential persistence) of the data that code manipulates. From the programmer's perspective access to persistent objects is *transparent*, with no need to write explicit code to transfer objects between stable and volatile storage.
2. *Data type orthogonality*: persistence should be a property independent of type. Thus, an object's type should not dictate its longevity.
3. *Persistence designation*: the way in which persistent objects are identified should be orthogonal to all other elements of discourse in the language. Neither the method nor scope of its allocation, nor the type system (e.g., the class inheritance hierarchy), should affect an object's longevity.

The advantages that accrue through application of these principles to the design of persistent programming languages are many. Persistence independence allows programmers to focus on the important problem of writing correct code, regardless of the longevity of the data that code manipulates. Moreover, the code will function equally well for both transient and persistent data.

Data type orthogonality allows full use of data abstraction throughout an application, since a type can be applied in any programming context. This permits the development of programming systems based on rich libraries of useful abstract types that can be applied to data of all lifetimes.

Finally, persistence designation gives every data item the right to the full range of persistence without requiring that its precise longevity be specified in advance. Again, this aids programming modularity since the producer of data need not be concerned with the ultimate degree of longevity to which a consumer might subject that data. In sum, orthogonal persistence promotes the programming virtues of modularity and abstraction; both are crucial to the construction of large persistent applications.

2.1 Practicalities

Complete persistence independence typically cannot be achieved, and even if it can, it may not be desirable, since one usually wants to offer a degree of control to the programmer. For example, in using a transaction mechanism one must generally specify at least the placement of transaction boundaries (begin/end). Nevertheless, a language design would not be transparent if it required different expression for the usual manipulation of persistent and non-persistent objects; i.e., for operations such as method invocation, field access, parameter passing, etc.

Similarly, perfect type orthogonality may not be achievable and may not even be desirable. For example, some data structures refer to strictly transient entities (e.g., open file channels or network sockets), whose saving to persistent storage is not even meaningful (they cannot generally be recovered after a crash or system shutdown). Whether thread stacks and code can persist is a trickier question. In many languages these objects are not entirely first class, and supporting persistence for them may also be challenging to implement. Thus, perfect type orthogonality, in the sense that any instance of any type can persist, is not so desirable as that any instance of any type *that needs to persist* can persist.

The principle of persistence designation means that any allocated *instance* of a type is potentially persistent, so that programmers are not required to indicate persistence at object allocation time. Languages in which the extent of an object can differ from its scope usually allocate objects on a heap, where they are retained as long as necessary. Deallocation of an object may be performed explicitly by the programmer, or automatically by the system when it detects that there are no outstanding references to the object. This can be determined by a *garbage collector* [Jones 1996] by computing the transitive closure of all objects reachable (by following references) from some set of system roots. In systems that support garbage collection, persistence designation is most naturally determined by *reachability* from some set of known *persistent* roots.

2.2 Performance

Orthogonal persistence exacerbates problems of performance by unifying the persistent and transient object address spaces such that *any* given reference may refer to either a persistent or transient object. Since every access (read or write) might be to a persistent object, they must all be protected by an appropriate *barrier*. Thus, the persistence *read barrier* ensures that an object is resident in memory, and faults it in if not, before any read operation can proceed. Similarly, the persistence *write barrier* supports efficient migration of updates back to stable storage, either when updated objects are replaced in volatile memory or during explicit stabilization of the persistent store, by maintaining a record of which objects in volatile memory are dirty. In general the read and write barriers can subsume additional functionality, such as negotiation of locks on shared objects for concurrency control.

The read and write barriers may be implemented in hardware or software. Hardware support for barriers, utilizing the memory management hardware of the CPU, is usually implemented via the virtual memory protection primitives of the underlying operating system [Appel and Li 1991; Lamb et al. 1991; Singhal et al. 1992; Wilson and Kakkad 1992; White and DeWitt 1994], though the cost of fielding the resulting protection traps in some operating systems can be expensive [Hosking and Moss 1993]. In the absence of hardware-based solutions, or because of the performance shortcomings, barriers can be implemented in software. Typically, the language compiler or interpreter must arrange for appropriate checks to be performed explicitly before each operation that may access or update a persistent object. Alternatively, some languages (such as C++) support overloading of access operations to include the checks. These explicit software barriers can represent significant overhead to the execution of any persistent program, especially if written in an orthogonally persistent language where every access might be to a persistent object.

There are several approaches to mitigating these performance problems. *Pointer swizzling* [Moss 1992] is a technique that allows accesses to resident persistent objects to proceed at volatile memory hardware speeds by arranging for references to resident persistent objects to be represented as direct virtual memory addresses, as opposed to the persistent identifier format by which they are referenced in stable storage. A read barrier may still be necessary to ensure that a given reference is in swizzled format before it can be directly used. Unnecessary software barriers can also be eliminated by taking advantage of language execution semantics and compile-time program analysis and optimization.[1]

3 Related work

The notion of orthogonal persistence has a long history [Atkinson and Buneman 1987], traced through the development of persistent programming languages such as PS-Algol [Atkinson et al. 1982; Atkinson et al. 1983; Atkinson et al. 1983] and Napier88 [Morrison et al. 1990; Dearle et al. 1990], and extensions to existing languages such as Smalltalk [Kaehler and Krasner 1983; Kaehler 1986; Straw et al. 1989; Hosking 1995] and Java [Atkinson et al. 1997; Atkinson et al. 1996]. It is important to note that all of these persistent languages rely on support for persistence from an underlying virtual machine, implemented as an abstract bytecode interpreter. While dynamic translation (i.e., "just-in-time" JIT compilation) can improve performance in these systems, neither performance nor features for systems programming were a design goal. On the other hand, abstraction of the execution engine as a virtual machine can more easily permit orthogonal persistence of active execution states (i.e., threads); certainly Napier88, Smalltalk and Tycoon [Matthes and Schmidt 1994] are noteworthy for this capability.

Performance-conscious persistent programming languages have historically almost exclusively been based upon C++, which at its outset was hostile to ideas of automatic storage management on the grounds that it compromised performance. Hence, most C++-based persistence extensions have adopted models of persistence that violate orthogonality in one or more dimensions. In E [Richardson and Carey 1987; 1990] and SHORE/C++ there is a distinction between database types and standard C++ types; only database types can persist. O++ [Agrawal and Gehani 1989; 1990] and Texas [Singhal et al. 1992; Wilson and Kakkad 1992], along with several commercial offerings [Lamb et al. 1991], adopt a different approach, requiring designation of persistence at allocation time. Indeed, the object database standard for C++ persistence defined by the Object Data Management Group (ODMG) is not orthogonal [Alagić 1997]. Until our own work [Hosking and Novianto 1997; Hosking and Chen 1999] we are unaware of any attempt to bring orthogonal persistence into the C++ domain. This is not to say that C++ itself will not succumb to orthogonal persistence. In fact, we are also exploring this possibility through extension of Texas with persistence by reachability, by marrying a garbage collector to Texas's portable run-time type descriptors [Kakkad et al. 1998] to obtain accurate information on the location of references stored in the heap.

It is worth noting that orthogonal persistence can be supported without redesign and reimplementation of the programming language if one is prepared instead to layer support for persistence into the operating system. Several experimental projects have taken this approach: support for persistence is targeted explicitly in Grasshopper [Dearle et al. 1994; Rosenberg et al. 1996] and Mungi [Elphinstone et al. 1997; Heiser et al. 1998], but the rudiments are there in other experimental operating systems such as Opal [Chase et al. 1994; Chase et al. 1992], among others. Of course, our interest here focuses on efficient support for orthogonal persistence on stock operating systems.

4 PM3: Orthogonally persistent Modula-3

To serve as a platform for research into compiler support for orthogonally persistent programming languages we have designed and implemented an extension of the Modula-3 programming language [Cardelli et al. 1991] that supports orthogonal persistence.

Modula-3 is a modern, portable, systems programming language in the Algol family, whose other representatives include Pascal, Ada, Modula-2, and Oberon. Modula-3 also adopts selected features from the BCPL family of languages (C and C++ are the current specimens) in order to provide support for low-level systems programming, while retaining a strong type system that avoids dangerous and machine-dependent features. Modula-3 also supports threads (lightweight processes in a single address space), exception handling and information-hiding features such as objects, interfaces, opaque types and generics. Provision for garbage collection recognizes the high degree of safety afforded by automatic storage reclamation, which is achievable even in open runtime environments that allow interaction with non-Modula-3 code.

Modula-3 is *strongly-typed*: every expression has a unique type, and assignability and type compatibility are

[1] [Richardson 1990; Hosking and Moss 1990; 1991; Moss and Hosking 1995; Hosking 1995; 1997; Hosking et al. 1999; Nystrom 1998; Nystrom et al. 1998; Brahnmath 1998; Brahnmath et al. 1999]

```
INTERFACE Transaction;
EXCEPTION
  TransactionInProgress;
  TransactionNotInProgress;
TYPE
  T <: Public;
  Public = OBJECT METHODS
    begin()
      RAISES { TransactionInProgress };
      (* Starts (opens) a transaction.
         Raises TransactionInProgress if
         nested transactions are not
         supported. *)
    commit()
      RAISES { TransactionNotInProgress };
      (* Commits and closes a transaction *)
    chain()
      RAISES { TransactionNotInProgress };
      (* Commits and reopens transaction;
         retains locks if possible *)
    abort()
      RAISES { TransactionNotInProgress };
      (* Aborts and closes a transaction *)
    checkpoint()
      RAISES { TransactionNotInProgress };
      (* Checkpoints updates, retains locks
         and leaves transaction open *)
    isOpen(): BOOLEAN;
      (* Returns true if this transaction
         is open, otherwise false *)
  END;
END Transaction.
```

Figure 1: The Transaction interface

defined in terms of a single syntactically specified subtype relation, written <:. There are specific subtype rules for ordinal types (integers, enumerations, and subranges), references and arrays.

A *traced* reference type REF *T* refers to heap-allocated storage (of type *T*) that is automatically reclaimed by the garbage collector whenever there are no longer any references to it.[2] The type REFANY contains all references. The type NULL contains only the reference value NIL. Object types are also reference types. An *object* is either NIL or a reference to a data record paired with a set of procedures (*methods*) that will each accept the object as a first argument. Every object type has a supertype, *inherits* the supertype's representation and implementation, and optionally may extend them by providing additional fields and methods, or overriding the methods it inherits with different (but type-correct) implementations. This scheme is designed so that it is (physically) reasonable to interpret an object as an instance of one of its supertypes. That is, a subtype is guaranteed to have all the fields and methods defined by its supertype, but possibly more, and it may override its supertype's method implementations with its own.

4.1 Design

Persistence in PM3 is achieved by allowing traced references to refer not only to transient data, but also to persistent data. Allocated storage persists by virtue of its reachability by following traced references from the roots of named PM3 databases. The PM3 implementation is responsible for automatic caching of persistent data in memory, and for automatic mediation of accesses to cached data

[2]Modula-3 also supports *untraced* references to storage allocated in a separate heap that is not subject to garbage collection; untraced storage must be deallocated explicitly.

```
INTERFACE Database;
FROM Transaction IMPORT
  TransactionInProgress,
  TransactionNotInProgress;
EXCEPTION
  DatabaseExists;
  DatabaseNotFound;
  DatabaseOpen;
PROCEDURE Create(name: TEXT)
  RAISES { DatabaseExists,
           TransactionInProgress };
PROCEDURE Open(name: TEXT): T
  RAISES { DatabaseNotFound, DatabaseOpen,
           TransactionInProgress };
TYPE
  T <: Public;
  Public = OBJECT METHODS
    getRoot(): REFANY
      RAISES { TransactionNotInProgress };
    setRoot(object: REFANY)
      RAISES { TransactionNotInProgress };
  END;
END Database.
```

Figure 2: The Database interface

to enforce concurrency control.

Persistence functionality is introduced by way of the new library interfaces *Transaction* and *Database*; their essentials are presented in Figures 1 and 2. They are similar to their namesakes from the ODMG standard [Cattell et al. 1997], with databases and transactions abstracted as Modula-3 objects. Each named database has a distinguished root, from which other persistent data can be reached. Databases can be shared by multiple users and operating system processes, with locking and concurrency control enforcing serializability of transactions. Unlike the ODMG transaction model, we do not necessarily enforce isolation between threads executing in the same virtual address space, though we do require that a thread execute in at most one transaction at any time, and that it enter a transaction before attempting to interact with a database. The design permits transactions to nest, though our current implementation does not. We are also exploring extended semantics for combining transactions and threads in PM3, along the lines of the Venari transaction model for ML [Haines et al. 1994].

4.2 Implementation

The current PM3 implementation is based on the Digital (now Compaq) Systems Research Center's version 3.6 Modula-3 compiler, runtime system and libraries (all written in Modula-3). The compiler is a loosely-coupled frontend to the GNU C compiler, and generates efficient optimized native code. It also produces compact, executable type descriptors for heap-allocated data, in support of both garbage collection and persistence. The PM3 Modula-3 compiler is essentially unchanged from the original; it generates code that is *exactly* the same as that generated by the non-persistent Modula-3 compiler. Instead of explicit compiler-generated read and write barriers, our current implementation relies on the operating system's virtual memory primitives, triggering fault handling routines in the PM3 runtime system to retrieve objects, note updates, and obtain locks.

The PM3 runtime system manages the volatile heap,

supporting allocation of space for new and cached persistent data, and garbage collection to free unreachable space. Since PM3 persistence designation is by reachability, stabilization of the persistent store on transaction commit is driven by the garbage collector, on which we have focused the bulk of our effort so far. We have extended the existing incremental, generational, mostly-copying garbage collector [Bartlett 1988; 1989] to manage both transient objects and resident persistent objects, and to compute the reachability closure for mostly-copying stabilization. Heap objects, whether persistent or transient, have the same size and layout as the original non-persistent Modula-3 implementation. In short, heap objects are clustered into heap pages, which are some small multiple of the virtual memory page size. On the SPARC heap pages are 8K bytes. These are the unit of transfer between volatile memory and stable storage, and the unit of management of persistent data in the volatile heap. Pages are also currently the unit of locking for concurrency control, but we plan also to investigate object-level locking along the lines of Carey et al. [1994]. Stabilization copies newly-persistent objects from the transient pages of the heap into persistent pages, which are then committed to the object store. See Hosking and Chen [1999] for the precise details of the stabilization algorithm.

4.2.1 Pointer swizzling

Each database is treated as a distinct virtual address space: an array of pages bounded by the address range of the hardware platform. Each database has a distinguished root object, at a known address in its address space. The runtime system simply maps pages from any number of open databases into the volatile heap as references to the (persistent) objects on those pages are *discovered*. Requesting the root object of a database is one way to discover a reference; another way is to fault in a page containing references to other persistent pages. Naturally, when a reference is discovered it must be swizzled to point to a mapped (though not necessarily resident) page in the volatile heap; mappings are created on demand as references are swizzled. All mapped but non-resident pages are protected from access using the virtual memory protection primitives. Thus, any access to a protected page in the heap will trap and trigger a page fault: the heap page is unprotected, the data is read into it from the corresponding mapped database page, all references within the heap page are discovered and swizzled, the access is resumed and execution proceeds. As execution proceeds, volatile heap page frames are reserved in a "wave-front" just ahead of the most recently faulted and swizzled pages, guaranteeing that the application will only ever see virtual memory addresses [Singhal et al. 1992; Wilson and Kakkad 1992].

We also track updates to persistent data by protecting heap pages from writes. On the first write to the page we set a dirty bit for it, unprotect the page and resume the write.

Note that at any point in time an application can address only as much persistent data as can be mapped into its virtual address space. Data from multiple databases can be mapped at the same time. However, there is no restriction on the total volume of unmapped persistent data. Cross-database references are also permitted.

4.2.2 Persistent storage

The current PM3 implementation uses the University of Wisconsin's SHORE object repository [Carey et al. 1994] as a simple transactional page server. Each page is described in the SHORE data language (SDL) as a single SHORE text object, with simple read and write access implemented via the SHORE/C++ binding. Concurrency control and recovery support are inherited directly from SHORE, with the PM3 runtime system acquiring read locks on pages as they are faulted and write locks on first update. We also support interaction with a version of the GRAS3 [Kiesel et al. 1995; Baumann 1997] transactional page server that permits nested transactions, and which is implemented purely in Modula-3.

4.2.3 Types and metadata

To ensure type safety each persistent object must also store some representation of its type. The type is used to locate pointers within the object when it is swizzled, and for run-time type checking. Rather than store a full type descriptor, we take advantage of Modula-3's implementation of structural type equivalence, which computes a characteristic 64-bit fingerprint for every type that can be mapped to its descriptor at run time. Every database contains an index for the fingerprints of all the objects in the database; each object is stored with the key of its type's fingerprint entry in this index. This approach also means that we can avoid storing object methods (i.e., code) in the persistent store. Instead, objects are reunited with their methods as their contents are swizzled. The advantage of this is that we can continue to use traditional file-based program development tools such such compilers, assemblers, linkers and loaders. In the future, persistence-aware development tools that operate on code stored in the database will allow a tighter integration of code with data.

The type index is one example of metadata stored in every database. All metadata in PM3 is implemented as Modula-3 data structures, and stored transparently using the existing mechanisms for orthogonal persistence. This sleight of hand derives from our stabilization algorithm, which permits metadata to be treated just like other orthogonally persistent data. We believe PM3 to be unique among persistent programming languages in that it is implemented entirely in Modula-3, with explicit I/O only to read/write persistent pages from/to the page server.

5 Experiments

We compare the performance of the traversal portions of our PM3 implementation of the OO7 benchmark [Carey et al. 1993] against the SHORE/C++ implementation of OO7 distributed with SHORE. The traversal portions of

Modules	1
Assembly levels	7
Subassemblies per complex assembly	3
Composite parts per base assembly	3
Composite parts per module	500
Atomic parts per composite part	20
Connections per atomic part	3
Document size (bytes)	2000
Manual size (bytes)	100000
Total composite parts	500
Total atomic parts	10000

Table 1: Small OO7 database configuration

OO7 are numbered T1 through T9, though we do not present results for all of them here.

5.1 The OO7 benchmark

The OO7 benchmarks [Carey et al. 1993] are an accepted test of object-oriented database performance. They operate on a synthetic design database, consisting of a keyed set of *composite parts*. Associated with each composite part is a *documentation* object consisting of a small amount of text. Each composite part consists of a graph of *atomic parts* with one of the atomic parts designated as the *root* of the graph. Each atomic part has a set of attributes, and is connected via a bi-directional association to several other atomic parts. The connections are implemented by interposing a separate connection object between each pair of connected atomic parts. Composite parts are arranged in an *assembly* hierarchy; each assembly is either made up of composite parts (a *base* assembly) or other assemblies (a *complex* assembly). Each assembly hierarchy is called a *module*, and has an associated *manual* object consisting of a large amount of text. Our results are all obtained with the *small* OO7 database, configured as in Table 1.

5.2 Hardware

Our experiments were run under Solaris 2.5.1 on a 170MHz Sun SPARCstation 5, with 64M bytes RAM. The processor implementation is the Fujitsu TurboSPARC, with direct-mapped instruction and data caches of 16K bytes apiece. Both caches are virtually-addressed, guaranteeing consistent performance regardless of the virtual-to-physical page mapping. This means that elapsed time measurements obtained on this platform are not subject to jitter relating to variations in page mappings from one process incarnation to the next. The local disk is a SUN0535 SCSI disk of 535M bytes.

Since we were uninterested in measuring network latencies both the SHORE server and the client were run on the same machine. This results in much improved client-server communication, with communication through shared memory where possible, and also more fully exposes the underlying overheads of the salient persistence mechanisms of interest to us.

5.3 Software

We use release 1.1.1 of SHORE as the underlying object store for PM3. SHORE objects are lighter-weight than a Unix file, but still more heavyweight than the typical fine-grained data structures coded in ordinary programming languages. For example, a SHORE object may be extended with a variable-sized heap, in which variable-sized components (e.g., strings, variable arrays, sets) of its value can be stored. The heap can also contain dynamic values that do not have independent identity; these may be linked together with *local references*, which are stored on disk as offsets from the start of the heap, but are swizzled in memory to actual memory addresses. SHORE also provides a variety of *bulk* types, including sets, lists and sequences.

The SHORE/C++ language binding allows methods for objects defined in the SHORE data language to be implemented in C++. An application, such as the SHORE/C++ implementation of the OO7 benchmark which we measure, is created as follows. First, one must write a description of the application's types in the SHORE data language (SDL), which the SDL compiler processes to create corresponding type objects as metadata in the SHORE repository. The SDL compiler also generates a set of C++ class declarations and special-purpose function definitions from the SDL types, in the form of a C++ header file. This header file is included in both the C++ source files that supply the implementation of the methods declared for each SDL type, and in source files that manipulate instances of those types. Some SDL types (e.g., integers) correspond directly to C++ types. Others, such as sets and object references (i.e., SHORE object identifiers) are represented in C++ using template classes (i.e., parameterized C++ types). C++ overloading features make SHORE object references appear to behave like ordinary C++ pointers, though with slower performance due to the software read and write barriers built into the overloaded operations.

Our PM3 implementation of OO7 is a direct transliteration of the SHORE/C++ implementation, but with the OO7 types implemented directly in Modula-3. Where the benchmark specifies the use of an index, we used a transparently persistent B+-tree coded in Modula-3. Moreover, the PM3 compiler is based on the same GNU compiler version 2.7.2 used to compile SHORE/C++ programs. Thus, we can directly compare the performance of PM3 with the SHORE/C++ binding. Both versions of OO7 were compiled with optimization turned on (i.e., gcc -O2). The PM3 Modula-3 compiler was also invoked with a flag that disables runtime checks on indexing arrays out of bounds and to catch certain type errors, so as to give a fairer comparison with C++.

We took great care to match the SHORE/C++ implementation as closely as possible, including using the same C library random number generator and initializing it with the same seed so as to generate the same sequence of random numbers used to build the OO7 benchmark database and to drive the benchmark traversals.

5.4 Results

The results were obtained from runs on the small OO7 benchmark database, which is small enough to fit entirely in main memory, including copies being cached in both the server and the client. We report the elapsed time in seconds broken down into three components: user and system CPU time in the client, plus other remaining elapsed time which we charge to interactions with the server for data transfer, concurrency control, etc. (identified in the figures as user, system and server, respectively). As in the original specification of OO7 [Carey et al. 1993] we obtain results for traversals running both "cold" and "hot". A cold traversal begins with no data cached anywhere in the client or the server, nor in the operating system's file system buffers (this is achieved by reading from a very large file in such a way as to flush the buffers of any useful data). The cold traversal is then followed immediately by four successive iterations of the exact same query, with the results from the middle three taken as the hot measure. We ran the successive iterations in two modes: as a single transaction committing only after the last iteration (one), and as a sequence of chained transactions (many). The result for the last iteration is omitted so that the overhead of commit processing is not included in the single-transaction hot times.

In contrast to the original OO7 specification, we report the *sum* of the results for the three hot traversals. The reason for this is that PM3's incremental garbage collector induces random variable behavior from one hot iteration to the next, which would otherwise be obscured by averaging.

5.4.1 Traversal T1: Raw traversal speed

Traverse the assembly hierarchy. As each base assembly is visited, visit each of its referenced unshared composite parts. As each composite part is visited, perform a depth-first search on its graph of atomic parts. Return a count of the number of atomic parts visited when done.

This is a test of raw pointer traversal speed. Figure 3(a) shows the cold T1 results. PM3 outperforms SHORE/C++ in both the traversal without commit (one) and the traversal with commit (many), despite the overhead for PM3 of the virtual memory page protection traps, as measured by the system CPU time, and the cost of swizzling as part of the user CPU time. PM3 fields 385 protection traps to fault 296 pages. The difference of 89 protection traps is due to the use of page protection primitives to implement barriers for PM3's incremental and generational garbage collector. Implementing barriers in PM3 with explicit checks instead would remove most of the system overhead for cold traversals, though they would add some to the user overhead; the compiler can attack this by optimizing away many checks if they are redundant [Cutts and Hosking 1997; Brahnmath 1998; Brahnmath et al. 1999].

SHORE/C++ fetches 41 594 objects into the client-side cache for a total of approximately 3M bytes, compared to PM3's 296 objects (the heap pages) for approximately 2.4M bytes. This demonstrates the compactness of PM3's object representation compared to SHORE/C++.

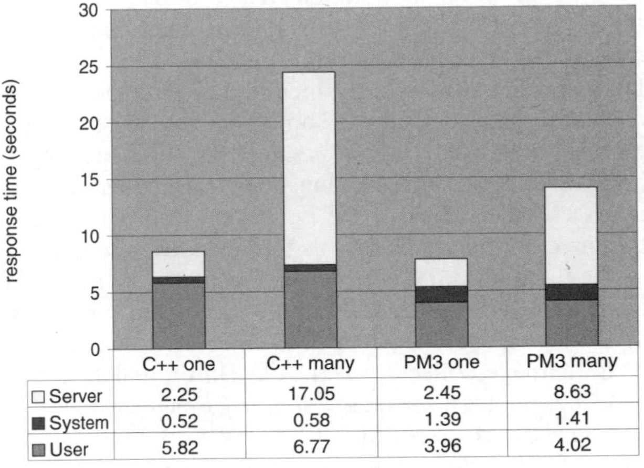

	C++ one	C++ many	PM3 one	PM3 many
□ Server	2.25	17.05	2.45	8.63
■ System	0.52	0.58	1.39	1.41
▨ User	5.82	6.77	3.96	4.02

(a) Cold

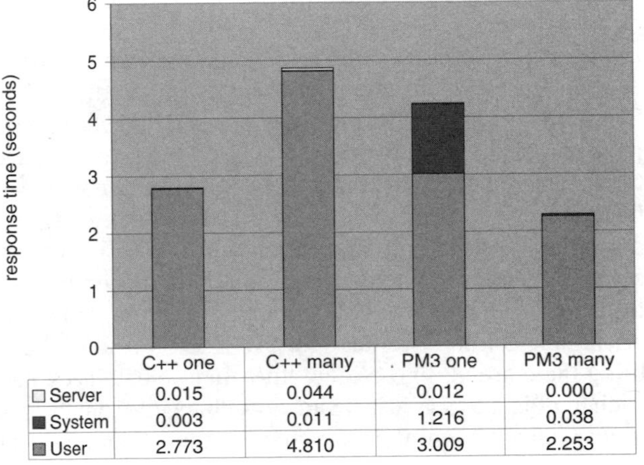

	C++ one	C++ many	PM3 one	PM3 many
□ Server	0.015	0.044	0.012	0.000
■ System	0.003	0.011	1.216	0.038
▨ User	2.773	4.810	3.009	2.253

(b) Hot: 3 iterations

Figure 3: Traversal T1

Despite T1 being a read-only traversal, SHORE still imposes overhead for commits, as revealed in the results which include commit processing (many). The server overhead is higher for SHORE/C++ than PM3 since the cold commit requires a separate client-server communication request for each object in the client-side cache (41 594 versus 296); hot chained commits do not pay this overhead. We assume an explanation as follows: on first chained commit the client must communicate the state (clean or dirty) of any objects it is caching into the next transaction; subsequent chained commits need only update the server with any differences in status from the previous commit (in this case none).

The hot T1 results appear in Figure 3(b). Here, the benefits of client caching are apparent for both SHORE/C++ and PM3. Run in a single transaction, sandwiched between the cold and last iteration, total elapsed time for

PM3 for the three hot iterations (PM3 one) is slower than for SHORE/C++ (C++ one). Indeed, there is noticeable system overhead to field protection traps (225 in fact) related to read barriers for the incremental garbage collector; each of these also results in some non-trivial user-charged garbage collector overhead, as well as contaminating the hardware caches and slowing down subsequent memory accesses. Inspection of the individual results for each of the three hot iterations reveals that response times for two of the three PM3 hot iterations are actually *faster* than the fastest SHORE/C++ hot iteration – 0.89s and 0.72s versus 0.93s, respectively – when PM3 is able to run with little or no garbage-collector overhead. Unfortunately, the last PM3 hot iteration includes a major garbage collection resulting in a response time of 2.6s. We could have turned off garbage collection for the experiments, but since the swizzling and faulting mechanisms are integrated with the garbage collector we felt it would be inappropriate to ignore its impact.

When the iterations are run as separate chaining transactions (many), the client caching is apparent for both SHORE/C++ and PM3 since they are able to cache all objects across the chaining commits into successive transactions. The hot commits impose negligible server-side overhead since the clients determine that no updates have occurred and restrict communication with the server only to signal the commit; nor are they subject to the communication overhead noted for cold commits. There is significant client-side commit overhead for SHORE/C++, almost doubling the elapsed time. Again, the client must check each cached object to see if its status has changed from the previous chained commit, in which case it must communicate that fact to the server; there are simply more objects cached for SHORE/C++ than heap pages for PM3.

At first glance it might seem strange that the total elapsed time for the three PM3 many hot traversals, which include commits, is less than that for the PM3 one and SHORE/C++ hot traversals, which operate without commits. This is explained once again by considering garbage collection overhead. Since a heap stabilization involves a full heap garbage collection (to compute the reachability closure), commits leave the heap in a clean state for the next iteration so that it can proceed without additional traps and processing overhead due to incremental collection. With no updates occurring, no write protection traps are encountered, and the garbage collector can very quickly decide that heap stabilization is trivial; hence also is the commit. Indeed, none of the three PM3 many hot traversals is faster than the fastest PM3 one hot traversal.

As in the original OO7 paper we henceforth omit reporting results for read-only traversals run as a sequence of chained transactions, and report only the cold and hot times for read-only traversals run as a single transaction; the effect of client caching across transaction boundaries is duplicated in every operation of the benchmark.

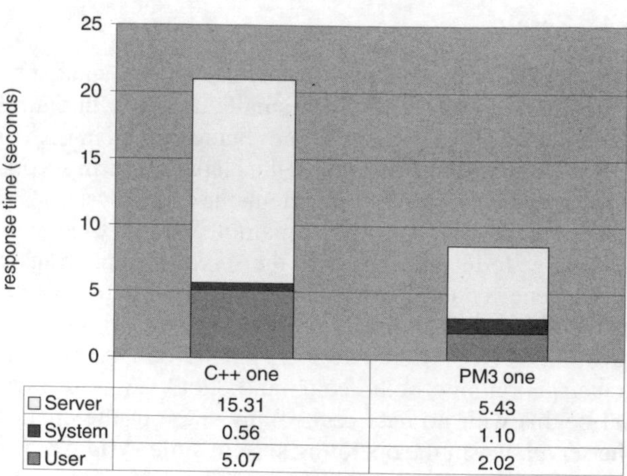

(a) Cold

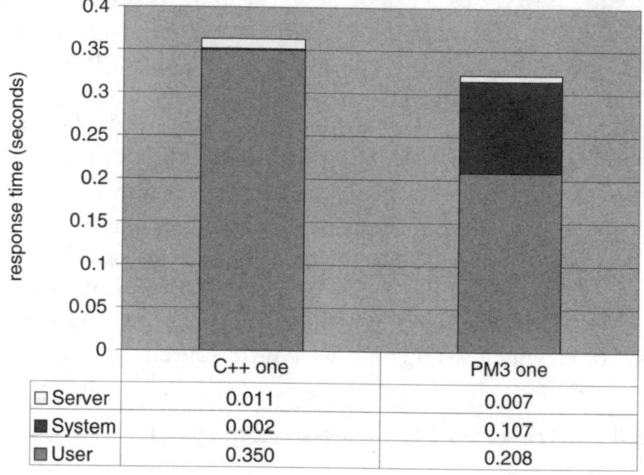

(b) Hot: 3 iterations

Figure 4: Traversal T6

5.4.2 Traversal T6: Sparse traversal speed

Traverse the assembly hierarchy. As each base assembly is visited, visit each of its referenced unshared composite parts. As each composite part is visited, visit the root atomic part. Return a count of the number of atomic parts visited when done.

Carey et al. [1993] intended this traversal to provide insight into the costs and benefits of a full swizzling approach, since it is sparse and follows only a small fraction of swizzled references; one expects full swizzling to be penalized for expending swizzling effort to little or no benefit.[3] However, our elapsed time results do not tell the expected story. For the cold T6 traversal (Figure 4(a)) PM3 appears to pay little user-level swizzling penalty, though the system overhead to field the read barrier traps remains.

[3]One might suspect this to be the reason for ODI's withdrawal from the original OO7 study, since their faulting and swizzling strategy is similar to ours.

The truth of the matter turns out to be related to clustering. SHORE/C++ fetches 41 346 objects (3M bytes) versus PM3's 158 heap pages (1.2M bytes). That SHORE/C++ fetches almost as many objects and as much data for this sparse traversal as for the dense T1 traversal suggests extremely poor clustering. PM3 does much better because its promotion into persistent pages of objects discovered to be persistent during stabilization, via what amounts to breadth-first search [Cheney 1970], yields much better clustering [Schkolnick 1977]. Only an orthogonally persistent system has sufficient flexibility to place objects by reachability, instead of at allocation time, since placement is decoupled from allocation and deferred instead until commit time when the heap is stabilized via reachability.

The hot results (Figure 4(b)) again reveal the superiority of full swizzling for hot operations, with PM3 markedly outperforming SHORE/C++ on the user component. In this case, SHORE/C++ suffers from the overhead of having to issue 5468 paired pin/unpin operations for each access to an object in the cache; PM3 accesses incur no such overhead. Overall, PM3 only just edges out SHORE/C++ because of incremental garbage collection overheads, as revealed by the system component.

5.4.3 Traversal T2: Updates

Repeat traversal T1, but update objects during the traversal. There are three types of update patterns in this traversal. In each, a single update to an atomic part consists of swapping its (x, y) attributes. The three types of updates are:

A *Update one atomic part per composite part.*
B *Update every atomic part as it is encountered.*
C *Update each atomic part in a composite part four times.*

When done, return the number of update operations that were actually performed.

Since these are update traversals the cold traversals with commit are more interesting than without, as presented in Figure 5(a). Again, despite the overhead of trap-driven read barriers, PM3 exhibits superior cold performance. Both SHORE/C++ and PM3 display higher server overhead for the dense update T2B and T2C traversals than the sparse update T2A. Despite the compactness of the PM3 object representation it incurs slightly higher server overhead for the dense updates because of the need to consult a SHORE index for each updated page to map its PM3 page identifier to its corresponding SHORE identifier.

Figure 5(b) presents results for the hot T2 traversals without commits (one), showing the raw overhead to update the objects. The trap-based write barrier poses significant overhead to PM3 for the sparse update T2A traversal, with PM3 just edging out SHORE/C++. For the denser T2B traversals the overhead to PM3 of each trap is amortized over more updates, for significantly faster response than for SHORE/C++. With T2C PM3 is a definite winner since it pays the same trap overhead as for T2B, while SHORE/C++ incurs overhead on every update, even if to a part that has already been updated.

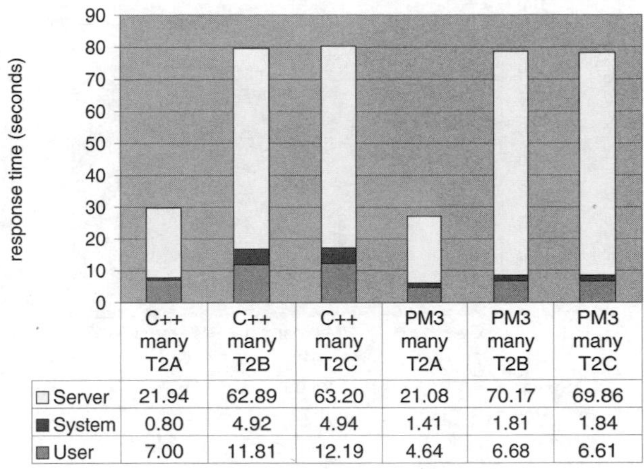

	C++ many T2A	C++ many T2B	C++ many T2C	PM3 many T2A	PM3 many T2B	PM3 many T2C
□ Server	21.94	62.89	63.20	21.08	70.17	69.86
■ System	0.80	4.92	4.94	1.41	1.81	1.84
■ User	7.00	11.81	12.19	4.64	6.68	6.61

(a) Cold

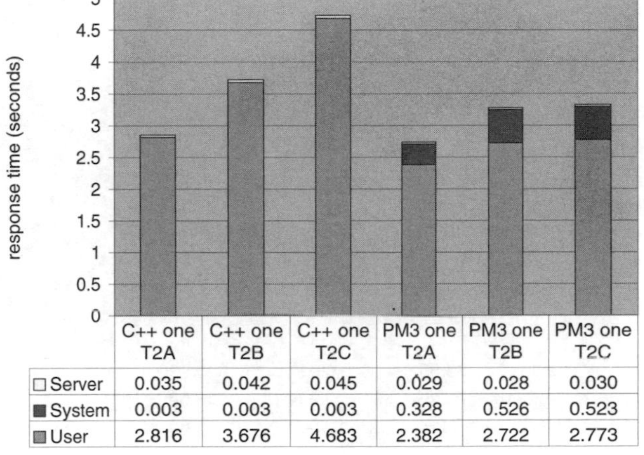

	C++ one T2A	C++ one T2B	C++ one T2C	PM3 one T2A	PM3 one T2B	PM3 one T2C
□ Server	0.035	0.042	0.045	0.029	0.028	0.030
■ System	0.003	0.003	0.003	0.328	0.526	0.523
■ User	2.816	3.676	4.683	2.382	2.722	2.773

(b) Hot: 3 iterations

Figure 5: Traversal T2

5.4.4 Traversal T3: Indexed field updates

Repeat traversal T2, except that now the update is on the date field, which is indexed. The specific update is to increment the date if it is odd, and decrement the date if it is even.

Figure 6 gives results for T3. It turns out SHORE/C++ uses indexes that are centralized on the server so every indexed update requires interaction with the server, at very high cost. In fact, the overhead is so high that we were only able to run SHORE/C++ for the sparse T3A; for our configuration of SHORE the dense indexed updates result in the log overflowing and the transaction aborting. In contrast, our indexes for Modula-3 are implemented natively as orthogonally persistent B+-trees so their pages can be cached and updated at the client. PM3 wins on all 3 indexed traversals. Keeping the index at the server may permit more concurrency, so perhaps the comparison in this instance is not entirely fair. Nevertheless, the difference in performance is staggering.

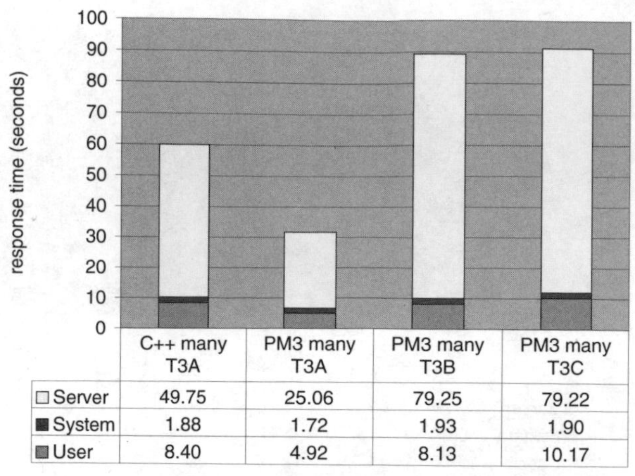

(a) Cold

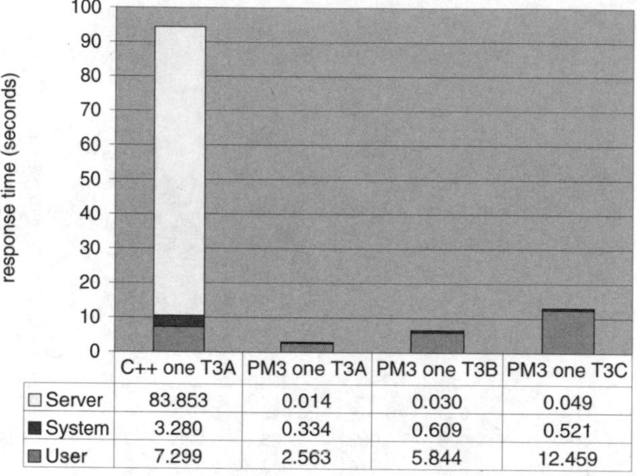

(b) Hot: 3 iterations

Figure 6: Traversal T3

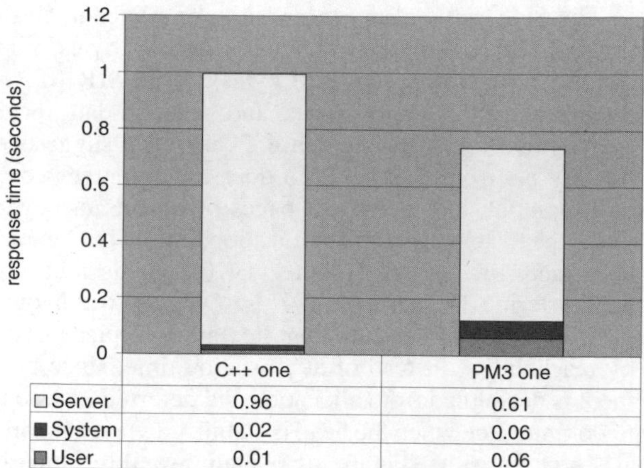

(a) Cold

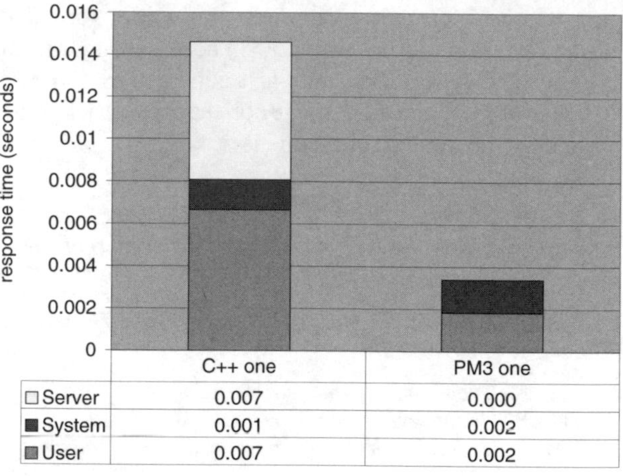

(b) Hot: 3 iterations

Figure 7: Traversal T9

5.4.5 Traversal T9: Operations on manual

Traversal T9 checks the manual object to see if the first and last character in the manual object are the same.

The results for the read-only T9 traversal presented in Figure 7 are for traversals without commits. The cold query results are somewhat inconclusive, mostly because the query accesses so little data in the small OO7 database (there is only one manual) as to be subject to spurious variations in system behavior. For example, the cold SHORE/C++ query incurs 17 virtual memory page faults requiring physical I/O to PM3's one, which accounts for a significant fraction of the server component for SHORE/C++ in Figure 7(a). The client CPU overheads seem more trustworthy, reflecting the high cost of PM3's trap-based read barrier and full swizzling when accessing so little data. For the hot iterations (Figure 7(b)), the high server component for SHORE/C++ results from its receiving a message from the server on each iteration. The cause of this anomaly can only be related to the difference in the underlying representation of the manual object. In PM3, a manual is simply a "large" heap object stored as a sequence of not-necessarily contiguous pages, although these pages are retrieved and mapped contiguously into the PM3 heap. For SHORE/C++ the manual is a large SHORE object, stored contiguously.

5.4.6 Traversals omitted

We have omitted several traversals in addition to those omitted in the original OO7 study Carey et al. [1993], notably traversals T8 (an operation on the manual) and CU (cached update). Unfortunately, we were unable to get the SHORE/C++ T8 traversal to run without crashing, and so could not obtain a comparison. In the case of CU, its goals are amply covered by the results for the other traversals as we have presented them here; nor does it contradict them. In all other cases, while the results for both SHORE/C++ and PM3 are available they do not provide further insights.

6 Conclusions and future work

We have demonstrated through implementation and experimentation that PM3, an orthogonally persistent systems programming language, can provide performance that is highly competitive with its non-orthogonal peers. Thus, the superior software engineering support that orthogonal persistence provides should not be withheld simply on the basis of prejudice against its reachability-based approach. In fact, there is no technical reason why more accepted systems programming languages such as C++ cannot be retrofitted with orthogonal persistence, as opposed to the non-orthogonal realizations of persistence currently imposed on them.

Our future work with PM3 will address the one remaining thorny issue in our results – the overhead of trap-based barrier implementations – by introducing explicit software barriers and using the compiler to optimize away any that are redundant. We also plan to explore the integration of buffer management with volatile heap management, disk garbage collection and extended transaction support.

Acknowledgments

This research is supported in part by the National Science Foundation under Grant No. CCR-9711673 and by gifts from Sun Microsystems, Inc. We thank Tony Printezis and the anonymous referees, whose comments spurred several improvements to this presentation.

References

AGRAWAL, R. AND GEHANI, N. H. 1989. ODE (Object Database and Environment): The language and the data model. In Proceedings of the ACM International Conference on Management of Data (Portland, Oregon, May). *ACM SIGMOD Record 18,* 2 (June), 36–45.

AGRAWAL, R. AND GEHANI, N. H. 1990. Rationale for the design of persistence and query processing facilities in the database language O++. See Hull et al. [1990], 25–40.

ALAGIĆ, S. 1997. The odmg object model: does it make sense? In Proceedings of the ACM Conference on Object-Oriented Programming Systems, Languages, and Applications (Atlanta, Georgia, Oct.). *ACM SIGPLAN Notices 32,* 10 (Oct.), 253–270.

APPEL, A. W. AND LI, K. 1991. Virtual memory primitives for user programs. In Proceedings of the ACM International Conference on Architectural Support for Programming Languages and Operating Systems (Santa Clara, California, Apr.). *ACM SIGPLAN Notices 26,* 4 (Apr.), 96–107.

ATKINSON, M., CHISOLM, K., AND COCKSHOTT, P. 1982. PS-Algol: an Algol with a persistent heap. *ACM SIGPLAN Notices 17,* 7 (July), 24–31.

ATKINSON, M. P., BAILEY, P. J., CHISHOLM, K. J., COCKSHOTT, P. W., AND MORRISON, R. 1983. An approach to persistent programming. *The Computer Journal 26,* 4 (Nov.), 360–365.

ATKINSON, M. P. AND BUNEMAN, O. P. 1987. Types and persistence in database programming languages. *ACM Comput. Surv. 19,* 2 (June), 105–190.

ATKINSON, M. P., CHISHOLM, K. J., COCKSHOTT, W. P., AND MARSHALL, R. M. 1983. Algorithms for a persistent heap. *Software: Practice and Experience 13,* 7 (Mar.), 259–271.

ATKINSON, M. P., DAYNÈS, L., JORDAN, M. J., PRINTEZIS, T., AND SPENCE, S. 1996. An orthogonally persistent Java. *ACM SIGMOD Record 25,* 4 (Dec.), 68–75.

ATKINSON, M. P., JORDAN, M. J., DAYNÈS, L., AND SPENCE, S. 1997. Design issues for persistent Java: A type-safe object-oriented, orthogonally persistent system. See Connor and Nettles [1997], 33–47.

ATKINSON, M. P. AND MORRISON, R. 1995. Orthogonally persistent object systems. *International Journal on Very Large Data Bases 4,* 3, 319–401.

BARTLETT, J. F. 1988. Compacting garbage collection with ambiguous roots. Research Report 88/2, Western Research Laboratory, Digital Equipment Corporation. Feb.

BARTLETT, J. F. 1989. Mostly-copying garbage collection picks up generations and C++. Technical Note TN-12, Western Research Laboratory, Digital Equipment Corporation. Oct.

BAUMANN, R. 1997. Client/server distribution in a structure-oriented database management system. Tech. Rep. AIB 97-14, RWTH Aachen, Germany.

BRAHNMATH, K., NYSTROM, N., HOSKING, A. L., AND CUTTS, Q. 1999. Swizzle barrier optimizations for orthogonal persistence in Java. In *Proceedings of the Third International Workshop on Persistence and Java* (Tiburon, California, August 1998), R. Morrison, M. Jordan, and M. Atkinson, Eds. Advances in Persistent Object Systems. Morgan Kaufmann, 268–278.

BRAHNMATH, K. J. 1998. Optimizing orthogonal persistence for Java. M.S. thesis, Purdue University.

CARDELLI, L., DONAHUE, J., GLASSMAN, L., JORDAN, M., KALSOW, B., AND NELSON, G. 1991. Modula-3 language definition. In *Systems Programming with Modula-3,* G. Nelson, Ed. Prentice Hall, Chapter 2, 11–66.

CAREY, M. J., DEWITT, D. J., FRANKLIN, M. J., HALL, N. E., MCAULIFFE, M. L., NAUGHTON, J. E., SCHUH, D. T., SOLOMON, M. H., TAN, C. K., TSATALOS, O. G., WHITE, S. J., AND ZWILLING, M. J. 1994. Shoring up persistent applications. See SIGMOD [1994], 383–394.

CAREY, M. J., DEWITT, D. J., AND NAUGHTON, J. F. 1993. The OO7 benchmark. In Proceedings of the ACM International Conference on Management of Data (Washington, DC, May). *ACM SIGMOD Record 22,* 2 (June), 12–21.

CAREY, M. J., FRANKLIN, M. J., AND ZAHARIOUDAKIS, M. 1994. Fine-grained sharing in a page server OODBMS. See SIGMOD [1994], 359–370.

CATTELL, R. G. G., BARRY, D., BARTELS, D., BERLER, M., EASTMAN, J., GAMERMAN, S., JORDAN, D., SPRINGER, A., STRICKLAND, H., AND WADE, D., Eds. 1997. *The Object Database Standard: ODMG 2.0.* Morgan Kaufmann.

CHASE, J. S., LEVY, H. M., FEELEY, M. J., AND LAZOWSKA, E. D. 1994. Sharing and protection in a single-address space operating system. *ACM Trans. Comput. Syst. 12,* 4 (Nov.), 271–307.

CHASE, J. S., LEVY, H. M., LAZOWSKA, E. D., AND BAKER-HARVEY, M. 1992. Lightweight shared objects in a 64-bit operating system. In Proceedings of the ACM Conference on Object-Oriented Programming Systems, Languages, and Applications (Vancouver, Canada, Oct.). *ACM SIGPLAN Notices 27,* 10 (Oct.), 397–413.

CHENEY, C. J. 1970. A nonrecursive list compacting algorithm. *Commun. ACM 13,* 11 (Nov.), 677–678.

CONNOR, R. AND NETTLES, S., Eds. 1997. *Proceedings of the Seventh International Workshop on Persistent Object Systems* (Cape May, New Jersey, May 1996). Persistent Object Systems: Principles and Practice. Morgan Kaufmann.

CUTTS, Q. AND HOSKING, A. L. 1997. Analysing, profiling and optimising orthogonal persistence for Java. In *Proceedings of the Second International Workshop on Persistence and Java* (Half Moon Bay, California, Aug.), M. P. Atkinson and M. J. Jordan, Eds. Sun Microsystems Laboratories Technical Report 97-63, 107–115.

DEARLE, A., CONNER, R., BROWN, F., AND MORRISON, R. 1990. Napier88—A database programming language? See Hull et al. [1990], 179–195.

DEARLE, A., DI BONA, R., FARROW, J., HENSKENS, F., LINDSTRÖM, A., ROSENBERG, J., AND VAUGHAN, F. 1994. Grasshopper: An orthogonally persistent operating system. *Computer Systems 7,* 3 (Summer), 289–312.

DEARLE, A., SHAW, G. M., AND ZDONIK, S. B., Eds. 1990. *Proceedings of the Fourth International Workshop on Persistent Object Systems* (Martha's Vineyard, Massachusetts, Sept.). Implementing Persistent Object Bases: Principles and Practice. Morgan Kaufmann, 1991.

ELPHINSTONE, K., RUSSELL, S., HEISER, G., AND LIEDTKE, J. 1997. Supporting persistent object systems in a single address space. See Connor and Nettles [1997], 111–119.

HAINES, N., KINDRED, D., MORRISETT, J. G., NETTLES, S. M., AND WING, J. M. 1994. Composing first-class transactions. *ACM Trans. Program. Lang. Syst. 16,* 6 (Nov.), 1719–1736.

HEISER, G., ELPHINSTONE, K., VOCHTELOO, J., RUSSELL, S., AND LIEDTKE, J. 1998. The Mungi single-address-space operating system. *Software: Practice and Experience 28,* 9 (July), 901–928.

HOSKING, A. L. 1995. Lightweight support for fine-grained persistence on stock hardware. Ph.D. thesis, University of Massachusetts at Amherst. Available as Computer Science Technical Report 95-02.

HOSKING, A. L. 1997. Residency check elimination for object-oriented persistent languages. See Connor and Nettles [1997], 174–183.

HOSKING, A. L. AND CHEN, J. 1999. Mostly-copying reachability-based orthogonal persistence. In *Proceedings of the ACM Conference on Object-Oriented Programming Systems, Languages, and Applications* (Denver, Colorado, Nov.).

HOSKING, A. L. AND MOSS, J. E. B. 1990. Towards compile-time optimisations for persistence. See Dearle et al. [1990], 17–27.

HOSKING, A. L. AND MOSS, J. E. B. 1991. Compiler support for persistent programming. Tech. Rep. 91-25, Department of Computer Science, University of Massachusetts at Amherst. Mar.

HOSKING, A. L. AND MOSS, J. E. B. 1993. Protection traps and alternatives for memory management of an object-oriented language. In Proceedings of the ACM Symposium on Operating Systems Principles (Asheville, North Carolina, Dec.). *ACM Operating Systems Review 27,* 5 (Dec.), 106–119.

HOSKING, A. L. AND NOVIANTO, A. P. 1997. Reachability-based orthogonal persistence for C, C++ and other intransigents. In *Proceedings of the OOPSLA Workshop on Memory Management and Garbage Collection* (Atlanta, Georgia, Oct.). http://www.dcs.gla.ac.uk/~huw/oopsla97/gc/papers.html.

HOSKING, A. L., NYSTROM, N., CUTTS, Q., AND BRAHNMATH, K. 1999. Optimizing the read and write barriers for orthogonal persistence. In *Proceedings of the Eighth International Workshop on Persistent Object Systems* (Tiburon, California, August 1998), R. Morrison, M. Jordan, and M. Atkinson, Eds. Advances in Persistent Object Systems. Morgan Kaufmann, 149–159.

HULL, R., MORRISON, R., AND STEMPLE, D., Eds. 1990. *Proceedings of the Second International Workshop on Database Programming Languages* (Salishan Lodge, Gleneden Beach, Oregon, June 1989). Morgan Kaufmann.

ISMM 1998. *Proceedings of the ACM International Symposium on Memory Management* (Vancouver, Canada, Oct.). ACM.

JONES, R. 1996. *Garbage Collection: Algorithms for Automatic Dynamic Memory Management.* Wiley. With a chapter by R. Lins.

KAEHLER, T. 1986. Virtual memory on a narrow machine for an object-oriented language. In Proceedings of the ACM Conference on Object-Oriented Programming Systems, Languages, and Applications (Portland, Oregon, Sept.). *ACM SIGPLAN Notices 21,* 11 (Nov.), 87–106.

KAEHLER, T. AND KRASNER, G. 1983. LOOM—large object-oriented memory for Smalltalk-80 systems. In *Smalltalk-80: Bits of History, Words of Advice,* G. Krasner, Ed. Addison-Wesley, Chapter 14, 251–270.

KAKKAD, S. V., JOHNSTONE, M. S., AND WILSON, P. R. 1998. Portable run-time type description for conventional compilers. See ISMM [1998], 146–153.

KIESEL, N., SCHÜRR, A., AND WESTFECHTEL, B. 1995. GRAS, a graph-oriented (software) engineering database system. *Information Systems 20,* 1, 21–52.

LAMB, C., LANDIS, G., ORENSTEIN, J., AND WEINREB, D. 1991. The ObjectStore database system. *Commun. ACM 34,* 10 (Oct.), 50–63.

MATTHES, F. AND SCHMIDT, J. W. 1994. Persistent threads. In *Proceedings of the International Conference on Very Large Data Bases* (Santiago, Chile, Sept.). Morgan Kaufmann, 403–414.

MORRISON, R., BROWN, A., CARRICK, R., CONNOR, R., DEARLE, A., AND ATKINSON, M. P. 1990. The Napier type system. In *Proceedings of the Third International Workshop on Persistent Object Systems* (Newcastle, New South Wales, Australia, Jan. 1989), J. Rosenberg and D. Koch, Eds. Workshops in Computing. Springer-Verlag, 3–18.

MOSS, J. E. B. 1992. Working with persistent objects: To swizzle or not to swizzle. *IEEE Trans. Softw. Eng. 18,* 8 (Aug.), 657–673.

MOSS, J. E. B. AND HOSKING, A. L. 1995. Expressing object residency optimizations using pointer type annotations. In *Proceedings of the Sixth International Workshop on Persistent Object Systems* (Tarascon, France, Sept. 1994), M. Atkinson, D. Maier, and V. Benzaken, Eds. Workshops in Computing. Springer-Verlag, 3–15.

NYSTROM, N., HOSKING, A. L., WHITLOCK, D., CUTTS, Q., AND DIWAN, A. 1998. Partial redundancy elimination for access path expressions. Tech. Rep. 98-044, Department of Computer Sciences, Purdue University. Oct. Submitted for publication.

NYSTROM, N. J. 1998. Bytecode level analysis and optimization of Java classes. M.S. thesis, Purdue University.

RICHARDSON, J. E. 1990. Compiled item faulting: A new technique for managing I/O in a persistent language. See Dearle et al. [1990], 3–16.

RICHARDSON, J. E. AND CAREY, M. J. 1987. Programming constructs for database implementations in EXODUS. In Proceedings of the ACM International Conference on Management of Data (San Francisco, California, May). *ACM SIGMOD Record 16,* 3 (Dec.), 208–219.

RICHARDSON, J. E. AND CAREY, M. J. 1990. Persistence in the E language: Issues and implementation. *Software: Practice and Experience 19,* 12 (Dec.), 1115–1150.

ROSENBERG, J., DEARLE, A., HULSE, D., LINDSTRÖM, A., AND NORRIS, S. 1996. Operating system support for persistent and recoverable computations. *Commun. ACM 39,* 9 (Sept.), 62–69.

SCHKOLNICK, M. 1977. A clustering algorithm for hierarchical structures. *ACM Trans. Database Syst. 2,* 1 (Mar.), 27–44.

SIGMOD 1994. *Proceedings of the ACM International Conference on Management of Data* (Minneapolis, Minnesota, May). *ACM SIGMOD Record 23,* 2 (June).

SINGHAL, V., KAKKAD, S. V., AND WILSON, P. R. 1992. Texas, an efficient, portable persistent store. In *Proceedings of the Fifth International Workshop on Persistent Object Systems* (San Miniato (Pisa), Italy, Sept.), A. Albano and R. Morrison, Eds. Workshops in Computing. Springer-Verlag, 11–33.

STRAW, A., MELLENDER, F., AND RIEGEL, S. 1989. Object management in a persistent Smalltalk system. *Software: Practice and Experience 19,* 8 (Aug.), 719–737.

WHITE, S. J. AND DEWITT, D. J. 1994. QuickStore: A high performance mapped object store. See SIGMOD [1994], 395–406.

WILSON, P. R. AND KAKKAD, S. V. 1992. Pointer swizzling at page fault time: Efficiently and compatibly supporting huge address spaces on standard hardware. In *Proceedings of the 1992 International Workshop on Object Orientation in Operating Systems* (Paris, France, Sept.). IEEE Computer Society, 364–377.

Cost Models DO Matter: Providing Cost Information for Diverse Data Sources in a Federated System *

Mary Tork Roth† Fatma Özcan‡ Laura M. Haas§

IBM Almaden Research Center, San Jose CA 95120

Abstract

An important issue for federated systems of diverse data sources is optimizing cross-source queries, without building knowledge of individual sources into the optimizer. This paper describes a framework through which a federated system can obtain the necessary cost and cardinality information for optimization. Our framework makes it easy to provide cost information for diverse data sources, requires few changes to a conventional optimizer and is easily extensible to a broad range of sources. We believe our framework for costing is the first to allow accurate cost estimates for diverse sources within the context of a traditional cost-based optimizer.

1 Introduction

Increasingly, companies need to be able to interrelate information from diverse data sources such as document management systems, web sites, image management systems, and domain-specific application systems (e.g., chemical structure stores, CAD/CAM systems) in ways that exploit these systems' special search capabilities. They need applications that not only access multiple sources, but that ask queries over the entire pool of available data as if it were all part of one virtual database. One important issue for such federated systems is how to optimize cross-source queries to ensure that they are processed efficiently. To make good decisions about join strategies, join orders, etc., an optimizer must consider both the capabilities of the data sources and the costs of operations performed by those sources. Standard database optimizers have built-in knowledge of their (sole) store's capabilities and performance characteristics. However, in a world where the optimizer must deal with a great diversity of sources, this detailed, built-in modeling is clearly impractical.

Garlic is a federated system for diverse data sources. Garlic's architecture is typical of many heterogeneous database systems, such as TSIMMIS [PGMW95], DISCO [TRV96], and HERMES [ACPS96]. Garlic is a query processor [HFLP89]; it optimizes and executes queries over diverse data sources posed in an extension of SQL. Data sources are integrated by means of a *wrapper* [RS97]. In [HKWY97, RS97], we described how the optimizer and wrappers cooperate to determine alternative plans for a query, and how the optimizer can select the least cost plan, assuming it has accurate information on the costs of each alternative plan. This paper addresses how wrappers supply information on the costs and cardinalities of their portions of a query plan and describes the framework that we provide to ease that task. This information allows the optimizer to compute the cost of a plan without modifying its cost formulas or building in knowledge of the execution strategies of the external sources. We also show that cost-based optimization *is* necessary in a heterogeneous environment; heuristic approaches that push as much work as possible to the data sources can err dramatically.

Our approach has several advantages. It provides sufficient information for an optimizer to choose good plans, but requires minimal work from wrapper writers. Wrappers for simple sources can provide cost information without writing any code, and wrappers for more complex sources build on the facilities provided to produce more accurate information as needed. Our framework requires few changes to a conventional bottom-up optimizer. As a result, in addition to examining the full space of possible plans, we get the benefits of any advances in optimizer technology for free. The framework is flexible enough to accommodate a broad range of sources easily, and does not assume that sources conform to any particular execution model. We believe that our framework for costing is the first to allow accurate cost estimates for diverse sources within the context of a traditional cost-based optimizer.

The remainder of the paper is structured as follows. Sec-

*This work was partially supported by DARPA contract F33615-93-1-1339.

†torkroth@almaden.ibm.com

‡fatma@cs.umd.edu; current address: Department of Computer Science, University of Maryland; partial funding provided by Army Research Laboratory contract DAAL01-97-K0135.

§laura@almaden.ibm.com

Proceedings of the 25th VLDB Conference, Edinburgh, Scotland, 1999.

tion 2 discusses the traditional approach to costing query plans. In Section 3, we present a framework by which these costing techniques can be extended to a heterogeneous environment. Section 4 shows how a set of four wrappers with diverse capabilities adapt this framework to provide cost information for their data sources. In Section 5, we present experiments that demonstrate the importance of cost information in choosing good plans, the flexibility of our framework, the accuracy it allows, and finally, that it works – the optimizer is able to choose good plans even for complex cross-source queries. Section 6 discusses related work, and in Section 7 we conclude with some thoughts about future directions.

2 Costing in a Traditional Optimizer

In a traditional bottom-up query optimizer [SAC+79], the cost of a query plan is the cumulative cost of the operators in the plan (plan operators, or *POPs*). Since every operator in the plan is the root of a subplan, its cost includes the cost of its input operators. Hence, the cost of a plan is the cost of the topmost operator in the plan. Likewise, the cardinality of a plan operator is derived from the cardinality of its inputs, and the cardinality of the topmost operator represents the cardinality of the query result.

In order to derive the cumulative costs and cardinality estimates for a query plan, three important cost numbers are tracked for each POP: *total cost* (the cost in seconds to execute that operator and get a complete set of results), *re-execution cost* (the cost in seconds to execute the POP a second time), and *cardinality* (the estimated result cardinality of the POP). The difference between total and re-execution cost is the cost of any initialization that may need to occur the first time an operator is executed. For example, the total cost of a POP to scan a temporary collection includes both the cost to populate and scan the collection, but its re-execution cost includes only the scan cost.

The total cost, re-execution cost, and cardinality of a POP are computed using *cost formulas* that model the runtime behavior of the operator. Cost formulas model the details of CPU usage and I/O (and in some systems, messages) as accurately as possible. A special subset of the formulas estimates predicate selectivity.

Cost formulas, of course, have variables that must be instantiated to arrive at a cost. These include the cardinality of the input streams to the operator, and *statistics* about the data to which the operator is being applied. Cardinality of the input streams is either computed using cost formulas for the input operators or is a statistic if the input is a base table. Hence, statistics are at the heart of any cost-based optimizer. Typically, these statistics include information about collections, such as the base cardinality, and about attributes, such as information about the distribution of data values. A traditional optimizer also has statistics about the physical system on which the data is stored, usually captured as a set of constant weights (e.g., CPU speed, disk transfer rate, etc.).

Figure 1 summarizes this flow of information. At the core

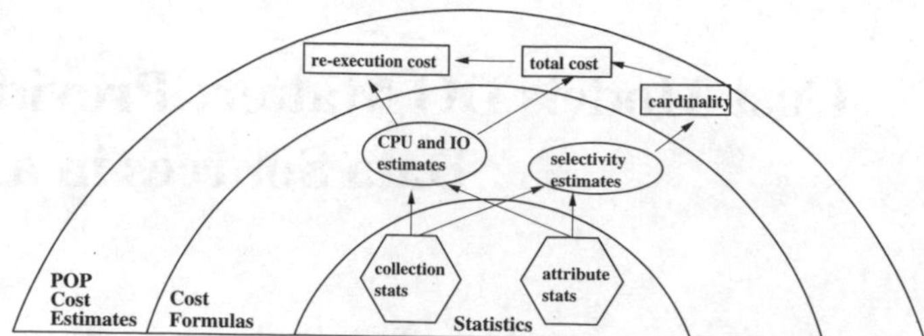

Figure 1: Traditional ost-based optimization

is a set of statistics that describe the data. At the next layer, these statistics feed cost formulas to compute selectivity estimates, CPU and I/O costs. Finally, in the outer layer, operator costs are computed from the cost formulas, and these operator costs ultimately result in plan costs.

3 Costing Query Plans in a Heterogeneous Environment

This section focuses on the process of costing query plans in a heterogeneous environment. Two significant challenges in adapting a traditional cost-based optimizer to a heterogenous environment are first, to identify *what* additional information is required to cost the portions of a query plan executed by remote sources, and second, *how* to obtain such information. Section 3.1 addresses the *what*, by introducing a framework for wrappers to provide information necessary to extend traditional plan costing to a heterogeneous environment. Section 3.2 addresses the *how*, by describing a default adaptation of the framework and facilities that a wrapper may use to compute cost and cardinality information for its data source.

3.1 A Framework for Costing in a Heterogeneous Environment

While the flow of information from base statistics to plan operator costs described in Section 2 works well in a traditional (relational) environment, it is incomplete for a heterogeneous environment. Given the diversity of data sources involved in a query, it is impossible to build cost formulas into the optimizer to compute the costs of operations performed by those data sources. Furthermore, since the data sources are autonomous, a single strategy cannot be used to scan the base data to gather and store the statistics the optimizer needs to feed its formulas. Clearly, a cost-based optimizer cannot accurately cost plans without cooperation from wrappers. In this section, we describe what information is needed from wrappers to extend cost-based optimization to a heterogeneous environment.

3.1.1 Cost Model

The first challenge for an optimizer in a heterogeneous environment is to integrate the costs of work done by a remote data source into the cost of the query plan. In Garlic, the portions of a query plan executed by data sources are encapsulated as PUSHDOWN POPs. Such POPs show up as leaves of the query plan tree. As a result, total cost, re-execution cost, and result cardinality are all that is needed to integrate the costs of a PUSHDOWN POP into the cost of the query plan.

Fortunately, these three estimates provide an intuitive level of abstraction for wrappers to provide cost information about their plans to the optimizer. On one hand, these estimates give the optimizer enough information to integrate the cost of a PUSHDOWN POP into the cost of the global query plan without having to modify any of its cost formulas or understand anything about the execution strategy of the external data source. On the other hand, wrappers can compute total cost, re-execution cost, and result cardinality in whatever way is appropriate for their sources, without having to comprehend the details of the optimizer's internal cost formulas.

3.1.2 Cost Formulas

Wrappers will need cost formulas to compute their plan costs, and most formulas tailored to the execution models of the built-in operators will typically not be appropriate. On the other hand, some of the optimizer's formulas may be widely applicable. For example, the formula to compute the selectivity of a set of predicates depends on the predicates and attribute value distributions, and not on the execution model. Wrappers should be able to pick from among available cost formulas those that are appropriate for their data sources, and if necessary, develop their own formulas to model the execution strategies of their data sources more accurately.

Additionally, wrappers may need to provide formulas to help the optimizer cost new built-in POPs specific to a heterogeneous environment. For example, traditional query processors often assume that all required attributes can be extracted from a base collection at the same time. In Garlic, wrappers are not required to perform arbitrary projections in their plans. However, they must be able to retrieve any attribute of an object given the object's id. If a wrapper is unable to supply all requested attributes as part of its plan, the optimizer attaches a FETCH operator to retrieve the missing attributes. The retrieval cost may vary greatly between data sources, and even between attributes of the same object, making it impossible to estimate using standard cost formulas. Thus, to allow the optimizer to estimate the cost of this FETCH operator, wrappers are asked to provide a cost formula that captures the *access cost* to retrieve the attributes of its objects.

As another example, wrappers are allowed to export methods that model the non-traditional capabilities of their data sources, and such methods can be invoked by Garlic's query engine. Methods may be extremely complex, and their costs may vary greatly depending on the input arguments. Again, accurately estimating such costs using generic formulas is impossible. Wrappers are asked to provide two formulas to measure a method's costs: *total method cost* (the cost to execute the method once), and *re-execution method cost* (the cost to execute the method a second time). These formulas provide an intuitive level of abstraction for the wrapper, yet give the optimizer enough information to integrate method invocation costs into its operator costs.

3.1.3 Statistics

Both the optimizer and the wrappers need statistics as input to their cost formulas. In a heterogeneous environment, the base data is managed by external data sources, and so it becomes the wrapper's task to gather these statistics. Since wrappers provide the cost estimates for operations performed by their data sources, the optimizer requires only *logical* statistics about the external data. Statistics that describe the physical characteristics of either the data or the hardware of the underlying systems are not necessary or even helpful; unless the optimizer actually models the operations of the data sources, it would not know how to use such statistics.

A traditional optimizer's collection statistics include base cardinality, as well as physical characteristics (such as the number of pages it occupies), which are used to estimate the I/O required to read the collection. In a heterogeneous environment, the optimizer still needs base cardinality statistics to compute cardinality estimates for its operators.

For attributes, optimizers typically keep statistics that can be used to compute predicate selectivity assuming a uniform distribution of values, and some physical statistics such as the average length of the attribute's values. More sophisticated optimizers keep detailed distribution statistics for oft-queried attributes. In a heterogeneous environment, an optimizer still needs some attribute statistics in order to compute accurate cardinality estimates. In Garlic, wrappers are asked to provide uniform distribution statistics (number of distinct values, second highest and second lowest values). They may optionally provide more detailed distribution statistics, and the optimizer will make use of them. Physical statistics such as average column length are not required, although they may be helpful to estimate the cost to operate on the data once it is returned to Garlic. If not provided, the optimizer estimates these costs based on data type.

Not only are these statistics needed for the optimizer's formulas, but wrappers may need them as input to their private cost formulas. In addition, wrappers may introduce *new* statistics that only their cost formulas use. Such statistics may be for collections, attributes, or methods. For example, the cost formulas a wrapper must provide to estimate the total and re-execution costs of its methods are likely to require some information as input. Thus, as with cost formulas, the set of statistics in a heterogeneous environment must be extensible.

To summarize, Figure 2 shows the extended flow of information needed for an optimizer in a heterogeneous environment. White objects represent information that is produced and used by the optimizer. Objects with horizontal lines (e.g., the formula to compute predicate selectivity) are provided by the optimizer and made available to the wrappers. Those with vertical lines are provided by the wrappers, and used by both the optimizer and the wrappers. Statistics and cost formulas shown shaded in gray are introduced by and available only to wrappers. The outer circle shows that wrappers are asked to report the total cost, re-execution cost, and result cardi-

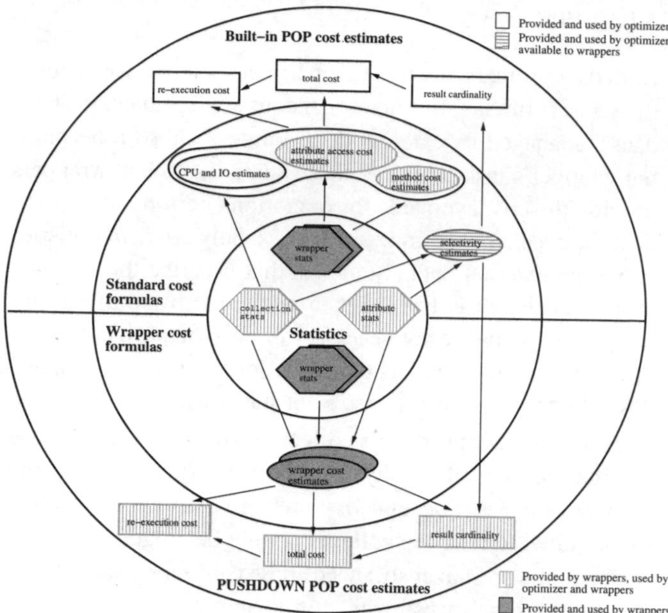

Figure 2: Heterogeneous cost-based optimization

nality for their plans. Armed with this information, the optimizer can combine the costs of PUSHDOWN POPs with the costs of built-in POPs to compute the cost of the query plan. In the next circle, wrappers are asked to provide formulas to compute attribute access costs and method costs. In addition, they can make use of some existing cost formulas, and add new formulas to model the execution strategies of their data sources. Finally, in the inner circle, wrappers are asked to provide the basic statistics about their collections and the attributes of their objects that the optimizer needs as input to its formulas. They may also compute and store statistics that are required by their own formulas.

3.2 Completing the Framework

Figure 2 shows how our framework extends the traditional flow of cost information to include wrapper input at all levels. To make it easy to provide such information (particularly for simple data sources), the framework also provides a default cost model, default cost formulas, and a facility to gather statistics. The framework is completely flexible; wrappers may use any of the defaults provided, or choose to provide their own implementations.

3.2.1 Extending the Cost Model

As described in Section 3.1.1, a wrapper's first job is to report total cost, re-execution cost, and result cardinality for its plans. To make this task as easy as possible, the framework includes a default cost model which wrappers can use to model the execution strategies of their data sources. Wrappers can take advantage of this cost model, or, if it is not sufficient, replace it with a cost model of their own.

The default cost model was designed with simple data sources in mind. We chose this approach for two important reasons. First, simple data sources have very basic capabilities. They can iterate over the objects in their collections, and perhaps apply basic predicates. They do not perform joins or other complex SQL operations. This limited set of capabilities often means that their execution strategy is both straightforward and predictable. These characteristics make it easy to develop a general purpose cost model. Second, an important goal of Garlic is to ensure that writing a wrapper is as easy as possible. If the default cost model is complete enough to model very basic capabilities, then wrapper writers for simple data sources need not provide *any* code for computing costs.

	Cost Model
P1	$plan\_total\_cost = reset\_cost + advance\_cost \times ((result\_cardinality + 1)/BLOCK\_SIZE)$
P2	$plan\_reexecution\_cost = plan\_total\_cost - reset\_cost$
P3	$plan\_result\_cardinality = \prod_{i=1}^{n} BASE\_CARD_i \times applied\_predicates\_selectivity$

Table 1: Default cost model estimates for wrapper plans

The default cost model is anchored around the execution model of a runtime operator. Regardless of whether a runtime operator represents a built-in POP or a PUSHDOWN POP, its work can be divided into two basic tasks[1]: *reset*, which represents the work that is necessary to initialize the operator, and *advance*, which represents the work necessary to retrieve the next result. Thus, the total cost of a POP can be computed as a combination of the reset and advance costs. As shown in Table 1, the default model exploits this observation to compute the total and re-execution costs of a wrapper plan.

(P1), the formula to compute the total cost of a plan, captures the behavior of executing a PUSHDOWN POP once. The operator must be reset once, and advanced to retrieve the complete result set (plus an additional test to determine that all results have been retrieved). *BLOCK_SIZE* represents the number of results that are retrieved at a time. Default formulas to compute reset and advance costs are described in Section 3.2.2 below. The re-execution cost (P2) is computed by factoring out the initialization costs from the total cost estimate. Since PUSHDOWN POPs are leaf POPs of the query plan tree, the result cardinality estimate (P3) is computed by multiplying the cross product of the n collection base cardinalities accessed by the plan by the selectivity of the applied predicates. As described in Section 3.2.3, *BASE_CARD* is the basic collection cardinality statistic, and $applied\_predicates\_selectivity$ can be computed using the standard selectivity formula provided by the optimizer.

3.2.2 Extended Cost Formulas

Our framework provides default implementations of all the cost formulas wrappers need to supply (including those intro-

[1] Our model actually has three tasks; we are omitting discussion of the bind task to simplify exposition. *Bind* represents the work needed to provide the next set of parameter values to a data source, and can be used, for example, to push join predicate evaluation down to a wrapper. However, simple sources typically don't accept bindings, as they cannot handle parameterized queries. Our relational wrapper does accept bindings, and provides cost formulas to calculate their cost.

	Cost formula
F1	$access\_cost(A) = AVG\_ACCESS\_COST_{max} + (n-1) \times OVERHEAD \times AVG\_ACCESS\_COST_{max}$
F2	$method\_total\_cost_i = AVG\_TOTAL\_METH\_COST_i$
F3	$method\_reexecution\_cost_i = AVG\_REEX\_METH\_COST_i$
F4	$reset\_cost = AVG\_RESET\_COST_c$
F5	$advance\_cost = AVG\_ADVANCE\_COST_c$

Table 2: Default cost formulas

duced in Section 3.1.2) as well as those needed by the default cost model of Section 3.2.1. These formulas are summarized in Table 2, and we will describe each formula in greater detail below. They rely on a new set of statistics, and Section 3.2.3 describes how these statistics are computed and stored.

(F1) is the default definition of the attribute access cost formula. A represents a set of n attributes to be retrieved by a FETCH POP. Typically there is a significant charge to retrieve the first attribute, but only an incremental charge to retrieve additional attributes once the first attribute has been retrieved. $AVG\_ACCESS\_COST_i$ is a new attribute statistic that measures the cost to retrieve attribute i, and $AVG\_ACCESS\_COST_{max}$ is the most expensive attribute retrieved by the FETCH. $OVERHEAD$ is a constant multiplier between 0 and 1 that represents the additional cost to retrieve an attribute, assuming that the most expensive attribute in A has already been retrieved. Wrappers may adjust this value as appropriate.

(F2) and (F3) represent the default definitions provided by the framework for the optimizer's method cost formulas. $AVG\_TOTAL\_METH\_COST$ and $AVG\_REEX\_METH\_COST$ are new statistics that represent measures of the average total and re-execution costs to invoke a method. This information is similar to the information standard optimizers keep for user-defined functions [Cor97]. These statistics are extremely simple, and do not, for example, take into account the set of arguments that are passed in to the method. As we will illustrate in Section 4.2, wrappers that use methods to export the nontraditional capabilities of a data source may provide new definitions that match the execution strategy of their underlying data source more accurately, including any dependency on the method's arguments.

Formulas (F4) and (F5) are the default cost formulas used by the default cost model to compute plan costs. For simple wrappers with limited capabilities, computing average times over the range of queries that the data source supports may often be sufficient to obtain accurate cost estimates. The default cost formulas to compute plan costs use this approach. While these formulas are admittedly naive, in Section 5.2 we show that they work remarkably well for the simple data sources in our experiments. Since simple wrappers typically do not perform joins, the reset and advance costs are computed to be the average reset and advance costs of the single collection c accessed by the plan. AVG_RESET_COST and $AVG\_ADVANCE\_COST$ are new collection statistics that represent measures of the average time spent initializating and retrieving the results for queries executed against a collection.

If these default cost formulas are not sufficient for a particular data source (and they won't be for more capable sources), a wrapper writer may provide formulas that more accurately reflect the execution strategy of the data source. In fact, our framework for providing cost formulas is completely extensible; wrappers may use the optimizer's predicate selectivity formulas, any of the default formulas used by the default cost model, or add their own formulas. Wrapper-specific formulas can feed the formulas that compute operator costs and cardinalities, and their implementations can make use of the base statistics, and any statistics wrappers choose to introduce.

Category	Statistic	Query template
Collection	BASE_CARD	select count(*) from collection
	AVG_RESET_COST*, AVG_ADVANCE_COST*	select c.OID from collection c
Attribute	NUM_DISTINCT_VALUES	select count(distinct c.attribute) from collection c
	2ND_HIGH_VALUE	select c.attribute from collection c order by 1 desc
	2ND_LOW_VALUE	select c.attribute from collection c order by 1 asc
	AVG_ACCESS_COST*	select c.attribute from collection c
Method	AVG_TOTAL_METH_COST*, AVG_REEX_METH_COST*	select c.method(args) from collection c

Table 3: Statistics generated by update_statistics facility

3.2.3 Gathering Statistics

As described in Section 3.1.3, both the standard cost formulas and wrapper-provided cost formulas are fueled by statistics about the base data. Garlic provides a generic *update_statistics* facility that wrappers can use to gather and store the necessary statistics. The update_statistics facility includes a set of routines that execute a workload of queries against the data managed by a wrapper, and uses the results of these queries to compute various statistics. Wrappers may use this facility "as-is", tailor the query workload to gain a more representative view of the data source's capabilities and data, or augment the facility with their own routines to compute the standard set of statistics and their own statistics.

Table 3 describes the default query workloads that are used to compute various statistics. From the table, it should be clear how the standard statistics are computed. However, the calculations for the newly introduced statistics (marked with an asterisk) bear further description. For collections, the default cost model described in Section 3.2.1 relies on statistics that measure the average time to initialize and advance a wrapper operator. These measures are derived by executing a workload of single-collection queries defined by the wrapper writer (or DBA) that characterizes the wrapper's capabilities. For example, for a simple wrapper, the workload may contain a single simple "`select c.OID from collection c`" query, executed multiple times. Running averages of the time spent in reset and advance

Wrapper	Code	Cost model	Cost formulas	Statistics
ObjectStore	0	default	default	default
Lotus Notes	0	default	default	default
QBIC	700	default	replaces method cost, reset, advance formulas	added method statistics
Relational	400	default	replaces reset, advance formulas	added collection statistics

Table 4: Wrapper adaptations of framework

of the wrapper's runtime operator are computed for this workload of queries, and those measures are stored as the *AVG_RESET_COST* and *AVG_ADVANCE_COST* statistics. Note that these times include network costs, so the plan cost formulas do not have to consider network costs explicitly.

To compute the new attribute statistic *AVG_ACCESS_COST* (used by the default cost formula to compute attribute access cost), a single query which projects the attribute is executed, and the optimizer is forced to choose a plan that includes a `FETCH` operator to retrieve the attribute. This query is executed multiple times, and a running average of the time spent retrieving the attribute is computed, including network costs.

For the new method statistics, a workload of queries which invoke the method with representative sets of arguments (supplied by the wrapper writer) is executed multiple times. Running averages are computed to track the average time (including network costs) to execute the method both the first time, and multiple subsequent times. These averages are stored as the *AVG_TOTAL_METH_COST* and *AVG_REEX_METH_COST* statistics, respectively.

4 Wrapper Adaptations of the Framework

Figure 2 shows how our framework enables wrapper input in each concentric circle. In this section, we describe how a set of wrappers have adapted this framework to report cost information about their data sources to the optimizer. These wrappers represent a broad spectrum of capabilities, from the very limited capabilities of our complex object repository wrapper to the very powerful capabilities of our wrapper for relational databases. Table 4 summarizes how these different wrappers adapted the framework to their data sources, as well as the number of lines of code involved in the effort.

4.1 Simple Data Sources

We use ObjectStore as a repository to store complex objects, which Garlic clients can use to bind together existing objects from other data sources. This wrapper is intentionally simple, as we want to be able to replace the underlying data source without much effort. This wrapper will only generate plans that return the objects in the collections it manages, i.e., it will only produce plans for the simple query "`select c.OID from collection c`". The optimizer must append Garlic POPs to the ObjectStore wrapper's plans to fetch any required attributes and apply any relevant predicates. Because of its simplicity, the wrapper uses the default cost model to compute its plan costs and cardinality estimates, and uses the update_statistics facility "as-is" to compute and store the statistics required to fuel the default formulas, as well as those used by the optimizer to cost the appended Garlic POPs. We will see in Section 5.2 that the default model is indeed well-suited to this very basic wrapper.

We also implemented a more capable wrapper for Lotus Notes databases. It can project an arbitrary set of attributes and apply combinations of predicates that contain logical, comparison and arithmetic operators. It cannot perform joins. We have observed that the execution strategy for Lotus Notes is fairly predictable. For any given query with a set of attributes to project and set of predicates to apply, Lotus will retrieve each object from the collection, apply the predicates, and return the requested set of attributes from those objects that survive the predicates.

We intended to demonstrate with this wrapper that only a few modifications by the wrapper were needed to tailor the default cost model to a more capable wrapper. However, as we will show in Section 5.2, we discovered that although the wrapper for Lotus Notes is much more capable than the ObjectStore wrapper, the behavior of its underlying data source is predictable enough that the simple default cost model is still suitable. The wrapper writer was only required to tailor the workload of queries used to generate the *AVG_RESET_COST* and *AVG_ADVANCE_COST* collection statistics so that they more accurately represented the data source's capabilities. We used a simple workload of queries; techniques described in [ZL98] might do a better job of choosing the appropriate sample queries.

4.2 Data Sources with Interesting Capabilities

QBIC [N+93] is an image server that manages collections of images. These images may be retrieved and ordered according to features such as average color, color histogram, shape, texture, etc. We have built a wrapper for QBIC that models the average color and color histogram feature searches as methods on image objects. Each method takes a sample image as an argument, and returns a "score" that indicates how well the image object on which the method was invoked matched the sample image; the lower the score, the better the match. These methods may be applied to individual image objects via the Garlic method invocation mechanism. In addition, the QBIC wrapper will produce plans that apply these methods to all image objects in a collection, and return the objects ordered from best match to worst match. It can also produce plans that return the image objects in an arbitrary order. It does not apply predicates, project arbitrary sets of attributes, or perform joins.

Both the average color feature searches and color histogram feature searches are executed in a two-step process by the QBIC image server. In the first step, an appropriate 'color value' is computed for the sample image. In the second step, this value is compared to corresponding pre-computed

Feature	$sample\_eval\_cost$	$comparison\_cost$
Average color	$AVG\_COLOR\_SLOPE \times sample\_size + AVG\_COLOR\_INTERCEPT$	$AVG\_COLOR\_COMPARE$
Color histogram	$AVG\_HISTOGRAM\_EVAL$	$HISTOGRAM\_SLOPE \times (number\_of\_colors) + HISTOGRAM\_INTERCEPT$

Table 5: QBIC wrapper cost formulas

values for the images in the scope of the search. In our implementation, the scope is a single object if the feature is being computed via method invocation, or all objects in the collection if the feature is being computed via a QBIC query plan. For each image in the collection, the relationship between the sample image's color value and the image's color value determines the score for that image. Hence, the cost of both feature searches can be computed using the following general formula:

$$search\_cost = sample\_eval\_cost + m \times comparison\_cost$$

In this formula, $sample\_eval\_cost$ represents the cost to compute the color value of the sample image, $comparison\_cost$ represents the cost to compare that value to a collection image object's corresponding value, and m is the number of images in the scope of the search.

In an average color feature search, the color value represents the average color value of the image. The execution time of an average color feature search is dominated by the first step and depends upon the x-y dimensions of the sample image; the larger the image, the more time it takes to compute its average color value. However, the comparison time is relatively constant per image object. The first entry in Table 5 shows the formulas the wrapper uses to estimate the cost of an average color feature search. AVG_COLOR_SLOPE, $AVG\_COLOR\_INTERCEPT$, and $AVG\_COLOR\_COMPARE$ are statistics the wrapper gathers and stores using the update_statistics facility. The wrapper uses curve fitting techniques and a workload of queries with different sizes for the sample image to compute both the AVG_COLOR_SLOPE and $AVG\_COLOR\_INTERCEPT$ statistics. $AVG\_COLOR\_COMPARE$ represents the average time to compare an image, and an estimate for it is derived using the same workload of queries.

In a color histogram feature search, the color value represents a histogram distribution of the colors in an image. In this case, the execution time is dominated by the second step. For the typical case in which the number of colors is less than six, QBIC employs an algorithm in which the execution time of the first step is relatively constant, and the execution time of the second step is linear in the number of colors in the sample image. The second entry of Table 5 shows the formulas the wrapper uses to compute the cost of color histogram searches. $AVG\_HISTOGRAM\_EVAL$, $HISTOGRAM\_SLOPE$, and $HISTOGRAM\_INTERCEPT$ are new statistics, and $number\_of\_colors$ represents the number of colors in the sample image. Again, the wrapper uses curve fitting and a workload of queries with different numbers of colors for the sample image to compute $HISTOGRAM\_SLOPE$ and $HISTOGRAM\_INTERCEPT$. It uses the same workload of queries to compute an average cost for $AVG\_HISTOGRAM\_EVAL$.

The wrapper uses these formulas to provide both method cost estimates to the optimizer and to compute the costs of its own plans. The effort to provide these formulas and compute the necessary statistics was about 700 lines of code.

4.3 Sophisticated Data Sources

Our relational wrapper is a "high-end wrapper"; it exposes as much of the sophisticated query processing capabilities of a relational database as possible. Clearly, the default formulas are not sufficient for this wrapper. Vast amounts of legacy data are stored in relational databases, and we expect performance to be critically important. The time invested in implementing a more complete cost model and cost formulas for a relational query processor is well-worth the effort.

However, decades of research in query optimization show that modelling the costs of a relational query processor is not a simple task, and creating such a detailed model is not within the scope of this paper. We believe that an important first step is to implement a set of formulas that provide reasonable ball-park cost estimates, as such estimates may be sufficient for the optimizer to make good choices in many cases. With this goal in mind, for the relational wrapper, we chose to use the default cost model, and implement a very simple set of formulas to compute the reset and advance costs that use an oversimplified view of relational query processing:

$$reset\_cost = prep\_cost$$
$$advance\_cost = execution\_cost + fetch\_cost$$

In these formulas, $prep\_cost$ represents the cost to compile the relational query, $execution\_cost$ represents the cost to execute the query, and $fetch\_cost$ represents the cost to fetch the results. At a high level, $prep\_cost$ and $execution\_cost$ depend on the number of collections involved in the query, and $fetch\_cost$ depends on the number of results. The relational wrapper used curve fitting techniques and the update_statistics facility to compute and store cost coefficients for these formulas. The total number of lines to implement this was less than 400.

While this is an admittedly naive implementation, the estimates produced by this formula are more accurate than those from the default model, and provide the optimizer with accurate enough information to make the right plan choices in many cases. However, we do not claim that our implementation is sufficient for the general case. We believe many of the techniques applied in [DKS92] and the approaches of more recent work of [ZL98] could be adapted to work within the context of the relational wrapper, and present an interesting area of research to pursue.

5 Experiments and Results

In this section, we describe the results of experiments that show that the information provided by wrappers through our

	Query	Pushdown join time (secs)	Garlic join time (secs)	Card
Q1	**select** p.id, p1.id **from** professor p, professor p1 **where** p.id < p1.id **and** p.status = p1.status **and** p.aysalary > 115000 **and** p1.aysalary > 115000	369.47	1550.52	605401
Q2	**select** p.id, p1.id **from** professor p, professor p1 **where** p.id < p1.id **and** p.status < p1.status **and** p.aysalary > 115000 **and** p1.aysalary > 115000	6332.14	1766.11	2783677

Table 6: A comparison of execution times for 2 join queries

framework is critical for the optimizer to choose quality execution plans. Without wrapper input, the optimizer can (and will) choose bad plans. However, with wrapper input, the optimizer is able to accurately estimate the cost of plans. As with any traditional cost-based optimizer, it may not always choose the optimal plan. However, for most cases, it chooses a good plan and avoids bad plans.

We adapted the schema and data from the BUCKY benchmark [C+97] to a scenario suitable for a federated system. We used only the relational schema, distributed it across a number of sources, and added to it a collection of images representing department buildings. We developed our own set of test queries that focus on showing how the optimizer performs when data is distributed among a diverse set of data sources. The test data is distributed among four data sources: an IBM DB2 Universal Database (UDB) relational database, a Lotus Notes version 4.5 database, a QBIC image server, and an ObjectStore version 4.0 object database. For the experiments, the query engine executed on one machine, the UDB database, QBIC image server, and ObjectStore database all resided on a second server machine, and the Notes server resided on a third machine. All were connected via a high-speed network. When an execution plan included a join, we limited the optimizer's choices to nested loop join and push-down join. This did not affect performance, and allowed us to illustrate the tradeoffs in executing a join in Garlic or at a data source without having to consider countless alternative plans. It should be noted that Garlic is an experimental prototype, and as such, the Garlic execution engine is slower than most commercial relational database product engines. However, it is significantly faster than Notes. Hence, we believe our test environment is representative of a real world environment in which some sources are slower and some faster than the middleware, and hence, is a fair testbed for our study.

5.1 The Need for Wrapper Input

This first set of experiments addresses the need for cost-based optimization in an extensible federated database system. It has been suggested [ACPS96, EDNO97, LOG93, ONK+96, SBM95] that heuristics that push as much work as possible to the data sources are sufficient. Consider the two queries

ID	Department predicate	Professor predicate	Cardinality
Q3	dno < 1	id = 101	0
Q4	dno < 51	id = 101	50
Q5	dno < 101	id = 101	100
Q6	dno < 151	id = 101	150
Q7	dno < 201	id = 101	200
Q8		id < 102	250
Q9		id < 103	500
Q10		id < 105	1000
Q11		id < 107	1500
Q12		id < 109	2000

Table 7: UDB professorxdepartment predicates

defined in Table 6. (Q1) finds all pairs of similarly ranked professors that make more than $115,000 a year. (Q2) finds, for all professors that make at least $115,000 a year, the set of professors of a lower rank that also make at least $115,000 a year. The professor collection is managed by the relational wrapper. There are two obvious plans to execute these queries: push both the join and the predicate evaluation down to the UDB wrapper, or push the predicate evaluation down to the wrapper but perform the join in Garlic. Table 6 also shows the result cardinality and execution times for these 2 plans. In (Q1), the equi-join predicate on status restricts the amount of data retrieved from the data source, so the pushdown join is a better plan. However, in (Q2), the join predicates actually increase the amount of data retrieved from the data source, so it is faster to execute the join in Garlic. These queries represent two points in a query family that ranges from an equi-join (p.status = p1.status) to a cross product (no predicate on status). At some point in this query family, there is a *crossover point* at which it no longer makes sense to push the join down. The crossover point depends on different factors, such as the amount of data, the distribution of data values, the performance of both query engines, network costs, etc. Cost-based optimizers use such information to compare plan alternatives to identify where such crossover points exist, while heuristic approaches can only guess.

5.1.1 Working without wrapper input

The previous example motivated the need for cost-based optimization in a federated system by showing that pushing down as much work as possible to the data sources is not always a winning strategy. In this experiment, we show that accurate information is crucial for a cost-based optimizer to identify crossover points. For this set of experiments, we chose a family of queries over the UDB department and professor collections. To control result cardinality, we used a cross product with local predicates (shown in Table 7) on each table.

To predict plan costs accurately, a cost-based optimizer depends heavily on the availability and accuracy of statistics. If statistics are not available, the optimizer uses default values for these parameters. Without accurate information, the optimizer will sometimes choose a good plan, and sometimes it will not. In our environment, in the absence of wrapper input,

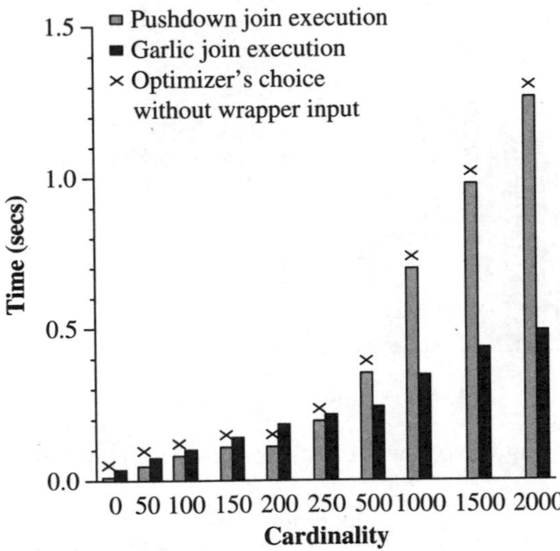

Figure 3: Optimizer choices without wrapper input

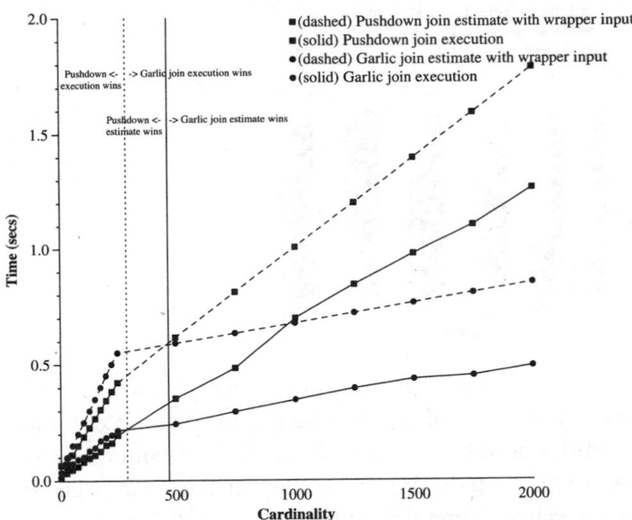

Figure 4: Optimizer estimates with statistics

the optimizer's parameters have been tuned to favor pushing as much work down to the data sources as possible.

For the set of queries in Table 7, the crossover point at which it makes sense to execute the join in Garlic occurs between queries (Q8) and (Q9), or when the result cardinality is between 250 and 500. Figure 3 shows the execution times for executing these queries with both the pushdown join and Garlic join plans. For each query, an x marks the plan that was chosen by the optimizer. Since the optimizer does not have the benefit of wrapper input, it relies on its defaults, and favors the pushdown join plan in all cases. With only default values, the cardinalities of the base collections look the same, and all local predicates (e.g., d.dno < 101 or p.id < 102) have the same selectivity estimates. Without more accurate information, the optimizer cannot easily discriminate between plans.

5.1.2 Working with wrapper input

Consider the same set of queries, only this time with input from the UDB wrapper, using the cost model and formulas described in Section 4.3. Figure 4 shows both the optimizer's estimates and the execution times for both the pushdown and Garlic join plans. The graph shows that while the optimizer's estimates differ by 10% to 45% from the actual execution costs, the wrapper input allows the optimizer to compare the *relative* cost of the two plans. Keep in mind that the cost formulas implemented by the UDB wrapper are fairly naive; if the wrapper writer invested more effort in implementing cost formulas reflecting the execution strategies of UDB, the optimizer's estimates would be more accurate.

Now instead of favoring the pushdown plan in all cases, the optimizer recognizes a crossover point in which it makes sense to execute the join in Garlic. The vertical dotted line on the graph shows the actual crossover point. The vertical solid line on the graph shows the optimizer's estimate of the crossover point. The area between the two lines represents the range in which the optimizer may make the wrong choice. Since we didn't have a data point in this area of the graph, we ran further experiments to identify the range more accurately. These experiments used a few more predicates to allow us to control the result cardinality more precisely. We found that the execution crossover point is at cardinality = 251, and the optimizer identifies the crossover point in the 278-298 range. Thus, the range in which the optimizer will make the wrong choice is between 251 and at most 298. In this narrow range, the execution times of the plans are so close that the wrong plan choice is not significant.

5.2 Adaptability of the Framework

In the previous section, we showed that wrapper input is critical for the optimizer to choose good plans. In this section, we show that our framework makes it easy for wrappers to provide accurate input. We look at 3 wrappers in particular: ObjectStore, Notes, and QBIC.

5.2.1 Wrappers that Use the Default Cost Model

As described in Section 4.1, the ObjcctStore wrapper is our most basic wrapper and uses the default cost model without modification. [ROH99] shows the optimizer's estimates and actual execution times for a set of queries that exercise the wrapper's capabilities. The experiments show that the defaults are well suited for the ObjectStore wrapper; the optimizer's estimates differ from the actual execution time by no more than 10%.

Recall that although Notes is a more capable wrapper, the Notes wrapper also uses the default cost model, formulas, and statistics. Again, [ROH99] shows that for a set of queries that exercise the wrapper's capabilities, the optimizer's estimates are "in the ballpark", ranging from a 13% to 40% difference from the actual execution time. For the experiments with more complicated queries, the optimizer's estimates are off by more than 30%. Further analysis showed that a significant percentage of this difference can be attributed to result cardinality underestimates, which were off by 21% for both of these queries. Such inaccuracies are not unusual for cost-

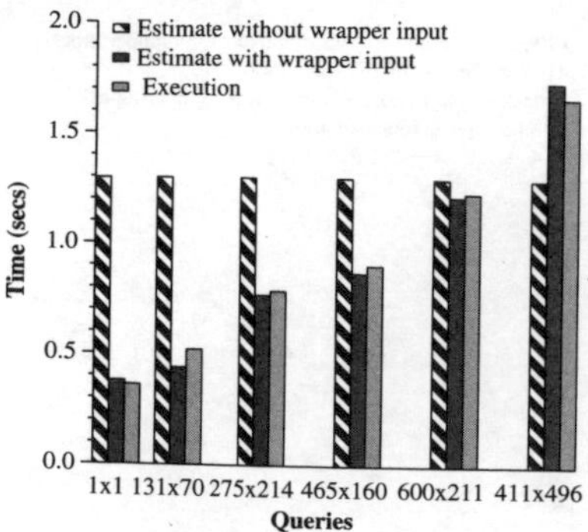

Figure 5: QBIC avg color query plan

based optimizers, and are the result of imperfect cost formulas and deviations in the data from the distribution assumptions. To make up the difference between the estimate and the actual execution time that cannot be attributed to inaccurate result cardinality estimates, the wrapper writer could provide formulas that model the predicate application strategy of Lotus Notes more accurately. However, we do not believe such effort is necessary. Analysis to be presented in section 5.3 shows that even for this more capable wrapper, the default cost formulas provide estimates that are close enough for the optimizer to choose good plans in most instances.

5.2.2 Wrappers with Interesting Capabilities

For data sources with unusual capabilities, such as QBIC, the default model is not sufficient. As described in Section 4.2, the execution time for an average color search depends on the size of the sample image. Figure 5 shows optimizer estimates and actual execution times for a family of average color queries with increasingly larger predicate images. The x-axis shows the size of the sample image. The first bar for each query represents the optimizer's cost estimate without wrapper input, the second bar shows the optimizer's cost estimate with wrapper input, and the third bar shows the actual execution time.

Without wrapper input, the optimizer has no knowledge of how much an average color search costs, nor is it aware that the cost depends on the size of the sample image. Thus, it must rely on default estimates, which can in no way approximate the real cost of the search or the plan. However, with wrapper input, the optimizer's estimates do reflect the dependency on the image predicate size, and its estimates are extremely accurate, with most being within 4% of the actual cost. An analysis of color histogram queries yields similar results. As we will see in Section 5.3, such input from wrappers with unusual capabilities is crucial for the optimizer to choose good plans when data from that source is joined with data from other sources.

5.3 Cross-Repository Optimization

Our final experiment shows that our framework provides sufficient information for the optimizer to choose good plans for complex queries. For this experiment, we used the query template given in Table 8 to generate a query family. The

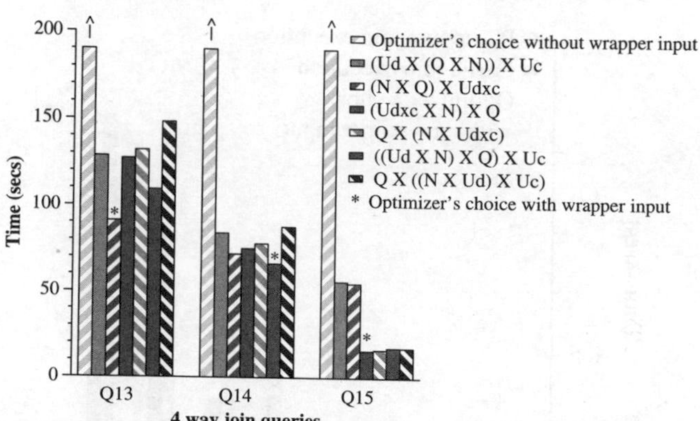

Figure 6: 4-way cross-repository join queries

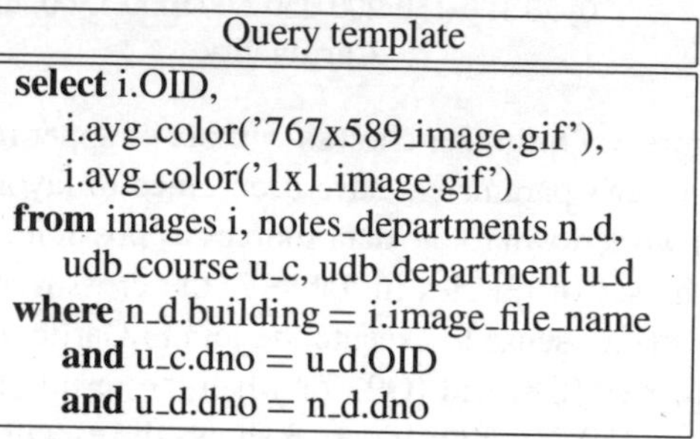

Query template
select i.OID, i.avg_color('767x589_image.gif'), i.avg_color('1x1_image.gif') **from** images i, notes_departments n_d, udb_course u_c, udb_department u_d **where** n_d.building = i.image_file_name **and** u_c.dno = u_d.OID **and** u_d.dno = n_d.dno

Table 8: 4-way join query template

query template is a 4-way join between the department and course collections managed by the UDB wrapper, the Notes department collection, and the QBIC image collection. To generate the family, we added predicates on the UDB department collection and the UDB course collection that control the cardinality of the results. These predicates and the result cardinalities are shown in Table 9. The queries also contain 2 average color image searches, one of which is for a 1x1 image (cheap), while the other is for a 767x598 image (expensive).

The number of possible plans for executing this query family is over 200. However, a large number of these plans are clearly bad choices, as they would require computing large cross-products. We enumerated and forced the execution of the 20 most promising plans, including the ones the optimizer itself selected. In any plan, the optimizer is forced to push one average color search down and evaluate the other by method invocation because the QBIC wrapper returns plans that execute only one search at a time.

Figure 6 shows the execution time of 7 plans for each query. The first bar represents the plan the optimizer chose without statistics or wrapper input. The other 6 bars are representative plans from the set that we analyzed. The plans are

ID	Predicates	Card
Q13	u_d.budget < 10000000 and u_c.cno < 102	456
Q14	u_d.budget < 6000000 and u_c.cno < 102	258
Q15	u_d.budget < 2000000 and u_c.cno = 102	23

Table 9: 4-way join query predicates

denoted by the order in which the joins are evaluated. A collection is identified by the first character of the wrapper that manages it. The UDB collections are further marked by the first character of each collection. An upper case X indicates that the join was done in Garlic, and a lower case x indicates the join was pushed down to the UDB wrapper. A * over a bar indicates that the optimizer, working with wrapper input, chose the corresponding plan.

For all three queries, the optimizer picked the best plan of the alternatives we studied, and, we believe, of all possible plans. Note that this may not happen in general; the purpose of a cost-based optimizer is not to choose the optimal plan for every query, but to consistently choose good plans and avoid bad ones.

The graph once again reinforces the assertion that wrapper input is crucial for the optimizer to choose the right plan. Without wrapper input, the optimizer chose the same plan for all three queries, which was to push the join between the UDB collections down to the UDB wrapper, join the result of that with the Notes department collection, and join that result with the image collection. Without information from the QBIC wrapper about the relative costs of the two image searches, it arbitrarily picked one of them to push down, and the other to perform via method invocation. In this case, the optimizer made a bad choice, pushing the cheap search of the 1x1 image down to the QBIC wrapper, and executing the expensive search via method invocation on the objects that survive the join predicates. This plan is a bad choice for all three queries, with execution times well over 1000 seconds.

When the optimizer was given input from the QBIC wrapper about the relative cost of the two average color searches, it chose correctly to push the expensive search down to the QBIC wrapper and perform the cheap search via method invocation. This is true for all plans we looked at for all queries, and brings the execution times for all of our sample plans to under 200 seconds.

This experiment also shows that pushing down as much work as possible to the data sources does not always lead to the best plan. For (Q13) and (Q15), the best plan did in fact include pushing the join between the UDB collections down to the UDB wrapper. However, for (Q14), the best plan actually split these two collections, and joined UDB department with Notes department as soon as possible. In this plan, the predicate on the UDB department collection (u_d.budget $<$ 6000000) restricted the number of UDB department tuples by 50%. Joining this collection with the Notes department collection first also reduced the number of tuples that needed to be joined with the image collection by 50%. For (Q13), the UDB department predicate (u_d.budget $<$ 10000000) was not as restrictive. In this case, it would have only reduced the number of tuples that needed to be joined with the image collection by 9%, which was not a significant enough savings to make this alternative attractive. Instead, it was better to group UDB department and UDB course together and push the join down to the UDB wrapper.

For (Q15), the UDB department predicate is even more restrictive, filtering out over 90% of the tuples. In this case, it is a good idea to use it to filter out both the Notes department tuples and UDB course tuples as soon as possible. Thus, the two best plans push the join between the UDB collections down to the wrapper, and immediately join the result with Notes. The two worst plans failed to take advantage of this. Plan 2 in the figure arranged these collections out of order, and plan 3 joined the entire Notes department collection with QBIC image before the join with the UDB collections.

These experiments show that cost-based optimization is indeed critical to choose quality execution plans in a heterogeneous environment. Using our framework, wrappers can provide enough information for the optimizer to cost wrapper plans with a sufficient degree of accuracy. By combining such cost information with standard cost formulas for built-in operators, traditional costing techniques are easily extended to cost complex cross-source queries in a heterogeneous environment.

6 Related Work

As federated systems have gained in popularity, researchers have given greater attention to the problem of optimizing queries over diverse sources. Relevant work in this area includes work on multidatabase query optimization [LOG93, DSD95, SBM95, EDNO97, ONK$^+$96] and early work on heterogeneous optimization [Day85, SC94], both of which focus on approaches to reduce the flow of data for cross-source queries, and not on estimation of costs. More recent approaches [PGH96, LRO96] describe various methods to represent source capabilities. Optimizing queries with foreign functions[CS93, HS93] is related, but these papers have focused on optimization algorithms, and again, not on estimating costs. [UFA98] describes orthogonal work to incorporate cost-based query optimization into query scrambling.

Work on frameworks for providing cost information and on developing cost models for data sources is, of course, highly relevant. OLE DB [Bla96] defines a protocol by which federated systems can interact with external data sources, but it does not address cross-source query optimization, and presumes a common execution model. The most complete framework for providing cost information to date is Informix's DataBlades [Cor97] architecture. DataBlades integrates individual tables, rather than data sources, and the optimizer computes the cost of an external scan using formulas that assume the same execution model as for built-in scans.

Various approaches have been proposed to develop cost models for external data sources. These approaches can be grouped into four categories: calibration [DKS92, GST96], regression [ZL98], caching [ACPS96], and hybrid techniques [NGT98]. The calibration and regression approaches typically assume a common execution model for their sources (which doesn't work for heterogeneous federations), but may be useful in developing wrapper cost models for particular sources. Both [ACPS96] and [NGT98] deal with diverse data sources, but neither approach employs standard dynamic programming optimization techniques.

7 Conclusion

We have demonstrated the need for cost-based optimization in federated systems of diverse data sources, and we presented a complete yet simple framework that extends the benefits of a traditional cost-based optimizer to such a federated system. Our approach requires only minor changes to traditional cost-based optimization techniques, allowing us to easily take advantage of advances in optimization technology. Our framework provides enough information to the optimizer for it to make good plan choices, and yet, it is easy for wrappers to adapt. In the future, we intend to continue testing our framework on a broad range of data sources. We would like to add templates to support classes of data sources that share a common execution model, and test our framework for how well it handles object-relational features such as path expressions and nested sets.

8 Acknowledgements

We thank Peter Haas, Donald Kossmann, Mike Carey, Eugene Shekita, Peter Schwarz, Jim Hafner, Ioana Ursu and Bart Niswonger for their help in preparing this paper, and V.S. Subrahmanian for his support.

References

[ACPS96] S. Adali, K. Candan, Y. Papakonstantinou, and V. S. Subrahmanian. Query caching and optimization in distributed mediator systems. In *Proc. of the ACM SIGMOD Conf. on Management of Data*, pages 137–148, Montreal, Canada, June 1996.

[Bla96] J. Blakely. Data access for the masses through ole db. In *Proc. of the ACM SIGMOD Conf. on Management of Data*, Montreal, Canada, June 1996.

[C+97] M. Carey et al. The bucky object-relational benchmark. In *Proc. of the ACM SIGMOD Conf. on Management of Data*, pages 135–146, Tucson, Arizona, US, May 1997.

[Cor97] Informix Corporation. Guide to the virtual table interface. Manual, 1997.

[CS93] S. Chaudhuri and K. Shim. Query optimization in the presence of foreign functions. In *Proc. of the Conf. on Very Large Data Bases (VLDB)*, pages 529–542, Dublin, Ireland, 1993.

[Day85] U. Dayal. Query processing in a multidatabase system. In W. Kim, D. S. Reiner, and D. S. Batory, editors, *Query Processing in Database Systems*, pages 81–108. Springer, 1985.

[DKS92] W. Du, R. Krishnamurthy, and M.-C. Shan. Query optimization in heterogeneous DBMS. In *Proc. of the Conf. on Very Large Data Bases (VLDB)*, pages 277–291, Vancouver, Canada, 1992.

[DSD95] W. Du, M.-C. Shan, and U. Dayal. Reducing multidatabase query response time by tree balancing. In *Proc. of the ACM SIGMOD Conf. on Management of Data*, pages 293–303, San Jose, CA, USA, May 1995.

[EDNO97] C. Evrendilek, A. Dogac, S. Nural, and F. Ozcan. Multidatabase query optimization. *Distributed and Parallel Databases*, 5(1):77–114, 1997.

[GST96] G. Gardarin, F. Sha, and Z.-H. Tang. Calibrating the query optimizer cost model of IRO-DB, an object-oriented federated database system. In *Proc. of the Conf. on Very Large Data Bases (VLDB)*, pages 378–389, Bombay, India, September 1996.

[HFLP89] L. Haas, J. Freytag, G. Lohman, and H. Pirahesh. Extensible query processing in starburst. In *Proc. of the ACM SIGMOD Conf. on Management of Data*, pages 377–388, Portland, OR, USA, May 1989.

[HKWY97] L. Haas, D. Kossmann, E. Wimmers, and J .Yang. Optimizing queries across diverse data sources. In *Proc. of the Conf. on Very Large Data Bases (VLDB)*, Athens, Greece, August 1997.

[HS93] J. M. Hellerstein and M. Stonebraker. Predicate migration: Optimizing queries with expensive predicates. In *Proc. of the ACM SIGMOD Conf. on Management of Data*, pages 267–276, Washington, DC, USA, May 1993.

[LOG93] H. Lu, B.C. Ooi, and C.H. Goh. Multidatabase query optimization: Issues and solutions. In *Proc. of the Intl. Workshop on Research Issues in Data Engineering: Interoperability in Multidatabase Systems*, pages 137–143, 1993.

[LRO96] A. Levy, A. Rajaraman, and J. Ordille. Querying heterogeneous information sources using source descriptions. In *Proc. of the Conf. on Very Large Data Bases (VLDB)*, pages 251–262, Bombay, India, September 1996.

[N+93] W. Niblack et al. The QBIC project: Querying images by content using color, texture and shape. In *Proc. SPIE*, San Jose, CA, USA, February 1993.

[NGT98] H. Naacke, G. Gardarin, and A. Tomasic. Leveraging mediator cost models with heterogeneous data sources. In *Proc. IEEE Conf. on Data Engineering*, Orlando, Florida, USA, 1998.

[ONK+96] F. Ozcan, S. Nural, P. Koksal, C. Evrendilek, and A. Dogac. Dynamic query optimization on a distributed object management platform. In *Proc. of the International Conference on Information and Knowledge Management (CIKM)*, pages 117–124, Rockville, MD, USA, 1996.

[PGH96] Y. Papakonstantinou, A. Gupta, and L. Haas. Capabilities-based query rewriting in mediator systems. In *Proc. of the Intl. IEEE Conf. on Parallel and Distributed Information Systems*, Miami, Fl, USA, December 1996.

[PGMW95] Y. Papakonstantinou, H. Garcia-Molina, and J. Widom. Object exchange across heterogeneous information sources. In *Proc. IEEE Conf. on Data Engineering*, pages 251–260, Taipeh, Taiwan, 1995.

[ROH99] M. Tork Roth, F. Ozcan, and L. Haas. Cost models do matter: Providing cost information for diverse data sources in a federated system. *IBM Technical Report RJ10141*, 1999.

[RS97] M. Tork Roth and P. Schwarz. Don't scrap it, wrap it! A wrapper architecture for legacy data sources. In *Proc. of the Conf. on Very Large Data Bases (VLDB)*, Athens, Greece, August 1997.

[SAC+79] P. Selinger, M. Astrahan, D. Chamberlin, R. Lorie, and T. Price. Access path selection in a relational database management system. In *Proc. of the ACM SIGMOD Conf. on Management of Data*, pages 23–34, Boston, USA, May 1979.

[SBM95] S. Salza, G. Barone, and T. Morzy. Distributed query optimization in loosely coupled multidatabase systems. In *Proc. of the Intl. Conf. on Database Theory (ICDT)*, pages 40–53, Prague, Czech Republic, January 1995.

[SC94] P. Scheuermann and E. I. Chong. Role-based query processing in multidatabase systems. In *Proc. of the Intl. Conf. on Extending Database Technology (EDBT)*, pages 95–108, Cambridge, England, March 1994.

[TRV96] A. Tomasic, L. Raschid, and P. Valduriez. Scaling heterogeneous databases and the design of DISCO. In *Proc. of the Intl. Conf on Distributed Computing Systems (ICDCS)*, Amsterdam, The Netherlands, 1996.

[UFA98] T. Urhan, M. J. Franklin, and L. Amsaleg. Cost based query scrambling for initial delays. In *Proc. of the ACM SIGMOD Conf. on Management of Data*, pages 130–141, Seattle, WA, USA, June 1998.

[ZL98] Q. Zhu and P. Larson. Solving local cost estimation problem for global query optimization in multidatabase systems. *Distributed and Parallel Databases*, 6:1–51, 1998.

Active Storage Hierarchy, Database Systems and Applications – Socratic Exegesis

Felipe Cariño Jr.
FileTek. Inc.
360 N. Sepulveda Blvd, Suite 1080
El Segundo, CA 90245
FCARINO@filetek.com

William O'Connell
IBM Toronto Laboratory
1150 Eglinton Avenue East
Toronto, Ontario M3C 1H7
BOCONNEL@ca.ibm.com

John Burgess
FileTek, Inc.
9400 Key West Avenue
Rockville, MD 20850
JGB@filetek.com

Joel Saltz
Computer Science Department
University of Maryland College Park, MD 20742
Joint Appointment with
Johns Hopkins University Medical
saltz@hyena.cs.umd.edu

Panel Abstract

This panel addresses a very important area that is often neglected or overlooked by database systems, database applications developers and data warehouse designers, namely storage. We propose to inform, discuss and debate the use of *"Active Storage Hierarchy"* in database systems and applications. By active storage hierarchy we mean a database system that uses all storage media (i.e. optical, tape, and disk) to store and retrieve data and not just disk. We will examine, discuss and debate how active storage compares and/or complements what is known in the database research community as *"Active Disks"* [RGF 98] and other emerging disk-centric storage paradigms. The presentations and analysis will span current real products, emerging technology to active (and visionary) research in several related areas, like storage technology, storage systems, federated databases and database system uses of storage.

Panel Format

- Overview of Storage Technology, Current and Future Commercial Products.
- Overview of Database Research and Commercial Database Product Plans
- Overview and sample case studies of current and emerging applications that do and/or will in the future exploit cost-effective storage hierarchy.
- Discussion and debate on feasibility and future (visionary) use of storage systems in database applications.

Proceedings of the 25th VLDB Conference, Edinburgh, Scotland, 1999.

Why This Panel?

Figure 1 shows the storage hierarchy, capacity, performance and cost-benefit tradeoffs. The importance of storage cost and performance can be seen by projected future database applications sizes (see Table1). A panel discussion and debating point will be that even if visionary disk-based research and proposals [RGF 98] [UAS 99] [Gray 98] become reality and commercially viable, then projected disk storage costs may/will require the use of the complete active storage hierarchy (i.e. tape, optical, disk, and so on).

Enabling and Emerging Technologies

There are several existing, evolving and emerging technologies (and products) that when combined and integrated will open the door to "new" uses and applications.

1. The first obvious one is storage itself. An exegesis of storage technologies (commercial or research work) will provide a foundation to discuss future storage uses. A key new storage evolution is the emergence and deployment of Storage Area Network (SAN) technology across enterprises. A major database challenge will be to integrate data sources and provide the same transparent access to data regardless where the data is stored. They can operate on SANs just like they operate on direct attached disks, so the question is will SANs enable new database architectures.
2. The second major panel item is how real commercial database systems currently exploit storage. StorHouse/Relational Manager (RM) [CB 99] approach (see Figure 2) is to store data on active storage and issue queries that retrieve data directly from data on all storage types. We will describe how the major database vendors utilize what is commonly referred to as Hierarchical Storage Management (HSM).
3. The third major (large storage) technology enabler is the emergence and deployment of object/relational databases. As Table 1 shows these applications will require orders of magnitude more storage than current application utilize.
4. Federated databases systems (like DataJoiner) present another interesting opportunity or alternative to the StorHouse/RM direct approach. With respect to large applications that require cost-effective storage (again a discussion point), then federating data sources or moving inactive or large objects to lower-cost storage may be essential to deploy applications. The panel will discuss how federated data sources can exploit storage options.

Panel Discussion & Debating Points

1. The panel will be informative in that we will get major storage vendors to come and/or share their product capabilities and future plans.
2. We plan to have the major database vendors represented or present their product plans in this area. Partisan and parochial interests and instincts of commercial vendors always makes for lively (informative) discussion.
3. The panel will also describe emerging federated, object/relational, legacy and atomic data applications that currently under-utilize storage options (another discussion and debate point).
4. Finally, leading academic researchers will provide their vision of the future.

Panelists

Panel organizers plus industrial and researchers have been invited to participate.

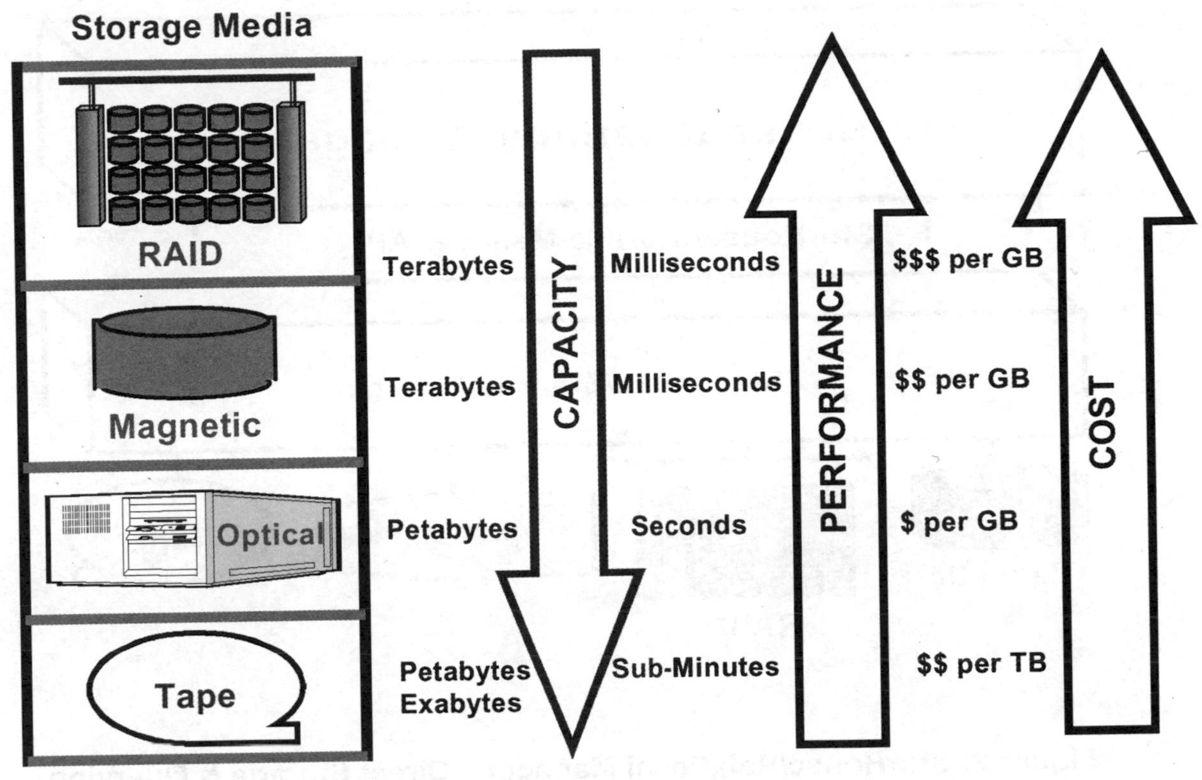

Figure 1: Storage hierarchy - Capacity, Performance and Cost-benefit Tradeoffs

Database Size	Application
Terabyte 10^{12} bytes	*National Retail Point Sale Data*
Petabyte 10^{15} bytes	*Text and Images Product Descriptions*
Exabyte 10^{18} bytes	*National Medical Insurance Records*
Zettabyte 10^{21} bytes	*Spatial and Terrestrial Data*
Yottabyte 10^{24} bytes	*Large Video Archives*

Table 1: Database Sizes for Diverse Applications

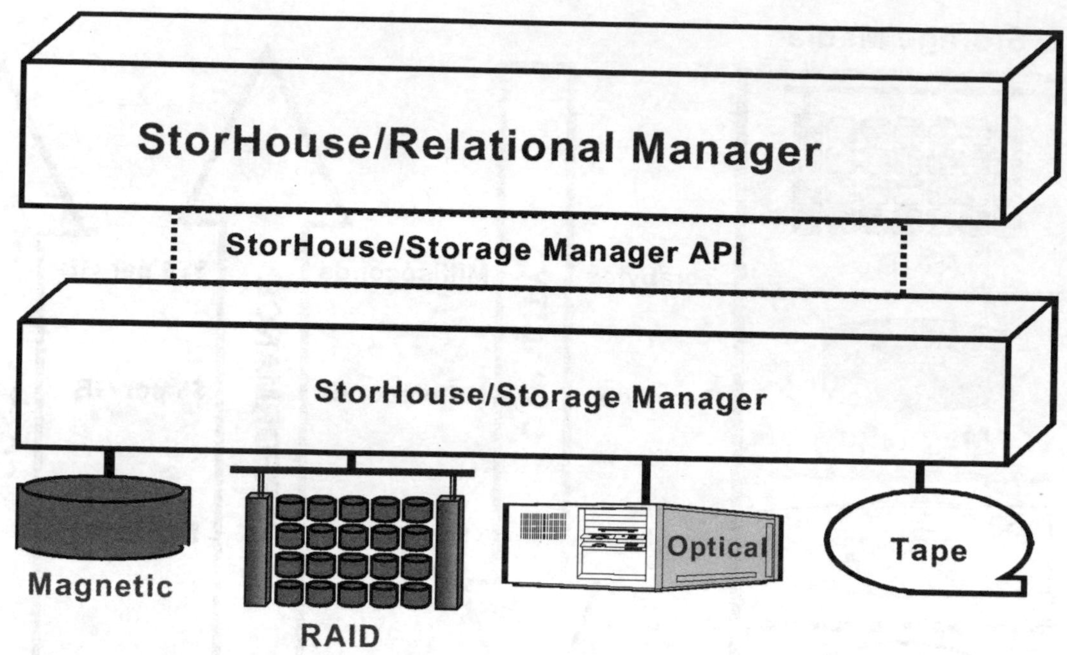

Figure 2: StorHouse/Relational Manager – Direct Storage & Querying

References

[AUS98] Acharya, A., Uysal, M. and Saltz, J., "Structure and Performance of Decision Support Algorithms on Active Disks", UCSB TRCS98-28, October 1998.

[AUS99] Acharya, A., Uysal, M. and Saltz, J., "Active Disks: Programming Model, Algorithms and Evaluation", ASPLOS-VIII.

[BG 88] Bitton, D. and Gray, J., "Disk Shadowing", VLDB 1988.

[CB 99] Cariño, F. and Burgess, J., "Lost in Active Storage Space - New Frontier for IT Managers", To Appear in Intelligent Enterprise Magazine August 1999.

[Gray98] Jim Gray's 10-year best VLDB paper [DG 88] keynote address at VLDB '98.

[RGF98] Erik Riedel, Garth Gibson and Christos Faloutsos, "Active Storage For Large-Scale Data Mining and Multimedia, VLDB 1998.

Data-Driven One-to-One Web Site Generation for Data-Intensive Applications*

Stefano Ceri Piero Fraternali Stefano Paraboschi

Dipartimento di Elettronica e Informazione
Politecnico di Milano
Piazza Leonardo da Vinci 32, I-20133 Milano, Italy
{ceri,fraterna,parabosc}@elet.polimi.it

Abstract

A data-driven approach can be fruitfully used in the specification and automatic generation of data-intensive Web applications, i.e., applications which make large amounts of data available on the Web. We present a multi-level architecture based on orthogonal abstractions for the definition of the structure, derivation, navigation, composition, and presentation of Web sites; then we show how these ingredients are used in *Torii*, a tool environment for the specification and automatic generation of Web sites, currently developed in the context of a large Esprit project.

By means of design tools, specifications are collected in a design repository, which is next used for Web page generation. This dynamic, data-centered approach opens up opportunities for personalizations: each user can be mapped to an individual hypertextual view of the Web site (called *site view*), and business rules may be used to change site views, both statically and dynamically. We argue that personalization of Web access (also called *one-to-one Web delivery*) is naturally supported by the proposed data-driven approach, and is at the same time a key ingredient of the Web applications of the near future.

*We acknowledge the support of ESPRIT Project 28771 W3I3, MURST Project Interdata, CNR-CESTIA, and the HP Internet Philanthropic Initiative.

Proceedings of the 25th VLDB Conference, Edinburgh, Scotland, 1999.

1 Introduction

The integration between Web applications and DBMS technology is subject to continuous and fast evolution; a variety of new technologies are being developed and brought to the market. Tools like Microsoft's Active Server Pages, Allaire's Cold Fusion, and many others, greatly simplify the implementation of integrated Web-DBMS sites. However, these technological advances are not matched by parallel efforts in data abstraction and modeling. Although in the community of database research it has been widely accepted that the "Web changes everything" [4], little effort has been devoted so far to adapt data design methods to the use of the Web as the fundamental data interface.

This paper is concerned with extending the classical data-centric approach to database application design by incorporating Web-related concepts into it. This effort can also be seen specularly from the viewpoint of Web design methods and tools, as an attempt at making them aware of data design aspects.

This methodological approach is well suited to the category of *data-intensive Web applications*, i.e., those Web sites whose primary purpose is to present a large amount of content to a variety of possible users. With respect to traditional database applications, data-intensive Web sites, have the following differences:

- Simpler functional requirements: typically a data-intensive Web site must offer a generic user the possibility to browse a large collection of data, in a way that fulfills some application-specific goal (e.g., in electronic commerce, showing to each user exactly those goods that he will most likely purchase). Sophisticated interaction control is not normally necessary, because the flow of activities is determined by the user via browsing.
- Simpler transactional requirements: in most

cases, it is sufficient to offer high-performance read-only access, and write access is reduced to a few standard operations on a well-delimited fraction of the data (e.g., in electronic commerce, the addition of items to the users' shopping cart).

- Focus on interface organization and ease of navigation: users must immediately grasp the way in which the site is structured, be offered a rich variety of navigation options, and be always confronted with a carefully crafted and appealing presentation of the information.

- Support of *one-to-one* Web delivery [11]: each user must have the impression of interacting with the application by means of a dedicated interface, specifically tailored to his needs and preferences. One-to-one delivery not only requires identifying users and their preferences, but also tracking their interaction with the application and updating the interface dynamically to reflect any improved understanding of the user's needs, typically by means of reactive mechanisms (such as the so-called business rules).

- Support of *multi-device output generation*: with the availability of the Internet on such diverse devices as cellular phones and digital television, content delivery must be automatically tuned to different output languages (e.g., HTML, HDML [13], ATVEF [1]) and rendition capabilities.

We claim that current database and Web design methods and tools are insufficient for coping with the development of highly personalized and dynamic data-intensive Web sites, and that new design abstractions are in order, supported by adequate tools. This paper is concerned with Torii, a tool environment for the specification and automatic generation of Web sites [1]. Torii is developed as part of the W3I3 (Web-based Intelligent Information Infrastructure) Project[2], whose goal is to develop the abstractions, technologies, methods, and tools to support one-to-one data-intensive Web applications.

[1]Torii, an ancient Finnish word, is the signpost that in medieval Scandinavia was used to indicate the Market Place, i.e. the place in the village were people met to chat and exchange goods.

[2]W3I3 is a 3 Million Euro Project of the Esprit IV Framework, sponsored at 50% by the EU. The W3I3 Consortium includes Politecnico di Milano as technology provider, TXT Ingegneria Informatica from Italy as software integrator, Digia (Digital Information Architects) from Finland as responsible of interface design and exploitation. The W3I3 Consortium also includes two pilot users with huge Web applications: OTTO Versand from Germany, the world's largest mail order company, and KPN Research from the Netherlands, the research branch of the major telecom company of Holland.

1.1 Related Work

The Torii proposal builds on the vast body of research that has been devoted to data design techniques, tools, and methods [3], and to the similar approaches developed for hypermedia applications [10, 12]. In fact, in the software industry most of the major data development projects are conducted by first giving an abstract representation of the data content (also called a "conceptual schema"), and then mapping such content to a logical and physical representation [3]. The availability of an abstract, implementation-independent schema is useful not only during design, but also for maintenance, quality assessment, and reverse engineering of data-intensive applications. We expect that a similar, high-level approach to data design for industrial applications will soon characterize the development of data-intensive Web sites. Indeed, several recent projects, namely Araneus [2], Autoweb [9], WebArchitect [12], and Strudel [7], have proceeded along this direction.

In particular, Araneus starts from the description of the content and then derives and/or integrates Web sites; with respect to Araneus, Torii adds to Web modeling the dimensions of presentation design, user modeling, customization and business rules. Strudel proposes a novel way of developing Web sites based on the declarative specification of the site's structure and content by means of queries. In Strudel, the specification of navigation is not orthogonal to structure and presentation, because navigable links and index collections are specified together. An in-depth comparison of Autoweb, Araneus, and Strudel appears in [5].

1.2 Comparison with Commercial Tools

The Torii system fits into the broad market of tools for designing a Web application. We give a concise classification of them, and indicate their main merits and limitations.

- *Visual HTML editors* and *site managers* (like, e.g., NetObject's Fusion, Macromedia's Dreamweaver and Microsoft's FrontPage) concentrate on HTML production and do not support the integration of large amounts of data.

- *HTML-DB integrators* (like, e.g., Microsoft's Active Server Pages (ASP) and Cold Fusion) provide a way to scale the dimension of a site by producing HTML pages dynamically from database content, but are implementation-level tools and do not address conceptual modeling and site customization.

- *Web application generators* (like, e.g., Oracle Designer 2000 Web Generator and Hyperwave) start from conceptual modeling and produce the Web site automatically, but have limitations in the expressiveness of the concepts available to the designer for structuring a Web site. They do not provide a description of user-oriented site views, nor business rules.

- *Rule-driven Web site generators* use rules extensively for matching content to users. The most relevant product in this class is Broadvision (http://www.broadvision.com), which is very powerful in matching content to users based on profile information, transaction history, session behavior, and other data. Broadvision does not support the separation between structural, composition, navigation, and presentation aspects, therefore Broadvision rules apply mostly to content delivery and not to the other aspects of a Web site's delivery.

For a thorough review of the state of the practice of commercial tools for Web design, we refer the reader to [8].

1.3 Outline of the Paper

The main research objective of W3I3 is to rise the level of abstraction of a site's specification, by enriching and refocusing the classical models for database and hypertext design; in Section 2 we will show how Torii supports the five orthogonal dimensions of structure, derivation, navigation, page composition, and presentation. We will discuss in Section 3 how Torii supports personalization, by introducing both a declarative approach, based on data derivation, and a reactive approach, based on business rules. Then, in Section 4 we will describe the implementation of the Torii system, and show that Torii introduces important novelties with respect to the predecessor Autoweb. Finally, we will discuss in Section 5 some preliminary experiences of use of Autoweb, Torii's predecessor, so as to justify the most important decisions that were taken in Torii.

2 Support of Orthogonal Abstractions in Torii

Modeling Web sites according to the Torii approach and tools consists of specifying five orthogonal perspectives: structure, derivation, navigation, page composition, and presentation. This multi-level organization has been motivated in [5]. We here give emphasis to the innovative features of the Torii system.

2.1 A Multi-Level Architecture

The Torii architecture is an extension of the classical multi-level architecture of database systems.

- The *Physical Level* describes the low-level organization of data. Torii will use standard relational technology for implementing this layer, for reasons of availability, standardization and efficiency.

- The *Structural Level* describes the high-level organization of data using the Entity-Relationship model, with the additional notion of "target", which describes how concepts should be aggregated within applications.

- The *Derivation Level* denotes how new concepts can be derived from the concepts of the structural schema. It is analogous to the definition of views commonly found in database applications.

- The *Composition Level* describes how the concepts of the structural schema are mapped to Web pages. Composition-level constructs, called *site views*, group related pages, which fulfill common user requirements; they are analogous to different external schemas of the same database.

- The *Navigation Level* describes the way in which relationships among data should be translated into hypertextual links.

- The *Presentation Level* is responsible of defining the appearance of Web pages, independently of the language used for page construction (HTML, XML, etc.).

All the above levels are associated both with graphic and textual descriptions: each concept is first provided graphically by using the Torii WYSIWYG interface and then mapped to its textual form. The complete XML syntax of Torii models can be found in [6], while a preliminary description of the user interface is given in [14]. We next describe each level separately, except the physical level, which is automatically generated by the Torii system.

2.2 Structural Model

The structural model of Torii defines the organization of the structured data which is used by the application; it is independent from the data models used by the data sources, where such content is stored. The model is based on the classical Entity-Relationship model, and uses the concepts of *entity, attribute*, and *relationship*. All relationships are binary and have no attributes. The model also supports classical *generalization hierarchies*. Properties with multiple or structured values constitute *components* and correspond to the classical part-of relationship. Each entity instance, or object, has an *object identifier*, and each relationship and component has *cardinality constraints* (min and max values). In addition, concepts of the structural model are clustered into *targets*; each target represents an application object of the real world, that may be represented by means of several concepts of the structural schema.

Torii offers two important predefined targets, *Profile* and *Metadata*, whose structure is described by means of the Torii structural model. The *Profile* target contains information regarding users and groups. For each user, we collect identification information (identifier, email address), login history, group membership, and trace information (the URLs of pages accessed at given times). Groups are associated to site views, i.e., to collections of pages which constitute a Web site.

```
<TARGET id="Profile" entryEntity="User">
 <ENTITY id="User">
  <ATTRIBUTE id="UID" type="Number"/>
  <COMPONENT id="Trace" minCard="0" maxCard="N">
    <ATTRIBUTE id="URL" type="Url"/>
    <ATTRIBUTE id="TraceTime" type="Time"/>
  </COMPONENT>
  ...
 </ENTITY>

 <ENTITY id="Group">
  ...
 </ENTITY>
</TARGET>
```

Profiles can be specialized for each application context. For instance, a specialization of the entity *User* in the context of electronic commerce is indicated below. Customers provide their name, age, sex, birthday, and purchase preferences, and are classified by the system (e.g., according to the wealth of their district). The system tracks automatically their last purchases (at most ten).

```
<ENTITY id="Customer" superEntity="User">
  <ATTRIBUTE id="Name" type="String"/>
  <ATTRIBUTE id="BirthDate" type="Date"/>
  <COMPONENT id="PurchasePreferences" minCard="0"
             maxCard="10">
    <ATTRIBUTE id="ProductType" type="String"/>
    <ATTRIBUTE id="Rank" type="Number"/>
  </COMPONENT>
  ...
</ENTITY>
```

In a similar manner, the *Metadata* target enriches objects with information concerning their creator, the modification and usage pattern, their validity, and possibly some user or group-specific access right specification. Also in the case of metadata, it is possible to introduce specializations to reflect the needs of a specific application. Metadata are reachable from the concepts of the structural schema by means of an implicit *Meta* relationship, that is assumed between each concept and the corresponding meta-information.

2.3 Derivation Model

Derivation is the process of defining as many conceptual views of the data as needed to support the various interfaces required by the different users of the Web application. Torii permits the definition of derived attributes, components, relationships, and entities.

The derivation is based on Torii-DL (Derivation Language), whose syntax and semantics are defined in [6]. The language supports path expressions, used for traversing relationships and for accessing components. A predefined *Self* variable represents the entity for which a derived element is being defined. An *ISA* predicate allows checking for membership of instances in a sub-entity.

Path expressions, variable declarations and the management of components are inspired by OQL, embedded within a restricted syntax that permits an efficient and simple translation to the underlying relational model. Each derived concept is translated into a view on the relational database managing the data.

In the example below, a derived attribute is added to entity *Book*, to add a "New" icon to the books which have been introduced into the system by less than 45 days.

```
<ATTRIBUTE id="NewIcon" type="Image"
   value="'icons/new.gif'
          where Self.Meta.Created > Sysdate-45"/>
```

Another derived attribute presents a *Special Offer* if the user accessing the data is member of the *Best Customers* group[3].

```
<ATTRIBUTE id="Special Offer" type="Number"
   value="Price*0.8
          where User.OfGroup.Name='Best Customers'/>
```

2.4 Composition Model

Composition is the process of specifying the content of each page; pages may be associated to an entire target, or to a specific entity within a target, or to a specific component within an entity. In order to preserve coherence between the structural and composition schemas, a page cannot arbitrarily intermix information coming from multiple targets; however, by means of derivation it is possible to extend the information content of a target with derived attributes, components, and relationships, computed on the basis of other related targets.

Conversely, each concept may be described by means of multiple pages; this feature allows the designer to represent the information on the same real-world object in different ways for serving the needs of different users. A complete personalized view of the application (called a *site view*) is constructed for a class of users, by defining a set of user-specific pages and the connections between them. The same concept of the structural model can be mapped to multiple pages belonging to the same site view.

The definition of a page for a target, entity, component, or collection of the structural schema requires:

[3]In both examples of derived attributes, the value is null if the predicate is false; we anticipate that Torii' style sheets, describing the presentation aspects of a given Web page, automatically omit to generate those regions corresponding to null attributes, and rearrange automatically the surrounding regions. Thus, derived attributes whose value is null are automatically "removed" from a given page.

- The mapping between structure and page content. By default, all attributes, components, and relationships of a given target, entity, or component are included into the page (including the derived ones), but the designer may explicitly exclude some of them to tailor the content of a page to the requirements of a class of users.
- The choice of the collections to be included in the page. This aspect is discussed in Section 2.5.2.
- The choice of the pages that are reachable from the page currently being defined, by means of relationships or components. This process is recursive, and is completed when all page references are resolved.

All of the above steps are optional and have default rules; in this way, composition modeling can be entirely skipped, e.g., for Web applications that present a single site view, offer a single page for each concept of the structural model, and do not need any form of personalization.

2.5 Navigation Model

Navigation is the fundamental access paradigm of Web applications: pages are visited by following links connecting anchors to destination pages. A fundamental assumption of Torii is that most navigable links between pages in data-intensive Web sites correspond to conceptual connections in the structural model, i.e., reflect the semantic organization of the site expressed in its structural schema; these are called *contextual navigations*, to denote the fact that the navigation occurs from a given object to a related object in the given semantic context. However, some other *non-contextual* navigations may occur, which enable the user to access other objects regardless of the current semantic context. Coherently with this assumption, Torii navigation modeling requires the specification of two complementary, but orthogonal, aspects: *object traversal* and *non-contextual data access.*

2.5.1 Object traversal

Object traversal specifies how relationships and components of the structural schema are used to navigate from one concept to a related concept. Navigation semantics is straightforward when moving from one page to exactly another page, e.g., following a one-to-one relationship. However, in many cases Torii applications need to support *one-to-many navigation*, e.g., from an entity to the elements of a component, or to a set of entities connected by an n-ary relationship.

For the sake of abstraction, in the following we call *navigable container* any set of related items that must be navigated as a result of a user request. The operational semantics of container navigation is defined by the designer, who establishes the *navigation mode* of the container by considering five independent dimensions:

- *Filtering*: enables the definition of filter predicates that select a subset of the objects of the container.
- *Indexing*: presents representative information of each selected element of the container within an index, enabling a further selection by the user.
- *Showing*: indicates how many selected objects are presented on the same page.
- *Sorting*: defines the order in which the selected objects of the container are presented.
- *Browsing*: indicates the possibility of scrolling from one element of the container to another one, e.g., to the next or previous one.

By assembling different values for the above dimensions, the designer customizes the navigation modes which are most suitable for the application. In addition, Torii supports a rich collection of *predefined navigation modes* which correspond to the choices along the above dimensions which are most commonly used together:

- *Index*, with two variants of location (*detached* and *embedded*); it offers no browsing. A *detached index* may have a filter, producing the *filtered index* mode, also without browsing. The filter is retained for repeated searches.
- *Guided tour*, which presents the objects in a sequence which can be browsed using all the available browsing commands. A variant, the *indexed guided tour*, adds a detached index, so as to enable an initial jump into an arbitrary position of the sequence.
- *Show all*, which presents the elements of a container contiguously, one after the other, either embedded in the same page (*embedded show all*) or detached in a separate page (*detached show all*).

The default modes are summarized in Table 1; when the designer does not provide a navigation mode for a container, the mode *detached index* is the default navigation mode, except for components, whose default is the *embedded show all* mode.

Figure 1 shows the pages that correspond to five different ways of navigating the relationship between an author and his books. Figure 1.a illustrates the *detached index* mode: by clicking on the *AuthorToBook* link, an index of books is presented and after selecting one entry, a specific book is displayed. Figure 1.b illustrates the *guided tour* mode: by clicking on the *AuthorToBook* link, the first book (in descending order of year) is shown and commands are available to

	Sorting	Filtering	Indexing	Showing	Browsing
Detached index	Yes	No	Detached	One	No
Filtered index	Yes	Detached	Detached	One	No
Embedded index	Yes	No	Embedded	One	No
Guided tour	Yes	No	No	One	Yes
Indexed guided tour	Yes	No	Detached	One	Yes
Show all	Yes	No	No	All	No
Show random	No	No	No	All	No

Table 1: Synopsis of the most common navigation modes

scroll the books of the same author. Figure 1.c illustrates the *filtered index* mode: by clicking on the *AuthorToBook* link, a form is presented in a separate page to filter the books to be seen (by publisher and year), then an index of the books that satisfy the filtering condition is presented from which a specific book can be accessed. Figure 1.d illustrates the *detached showall* mode: by clicking on the *AuthorToBook* link, all books are presented together in a new page. Finally, Figure 1.e illustrates the *embedded showall* mode: all books are presented together on the same page of their author.

2.5.2 Non-contextual Data Access

Collections are sets of objects which are meaningfully grouped together; they can be collectively accessed from a user regardless of the current context [4]. Collections can be used to access a Torii application from "outside" (e.g., from the home page); however, they can also be used to move freely within an application. For instance, when a page represents a specific course, the page can include the collections of all courses, of the offered degrees, or even of the services offered by the university. A collection could enclose advertising material reachable from a given page but not related to the page's content.

Enclosing a collection in a page means to add a navigation option anchored to the collection's name. If the collection has a singleton element, that element is immediately shown after activating the link. Otherwise, the collection acts in the same way as a container, and the same mechanisms described for object traversal are applicable for selecting and reaching individual elements of the collection from the collection's name. Torii collections can be hierarchically structured to form collections of collections, and their member objects may be defined *intensionally*, i.e., by means of Torii-DL expressions, or *extensionally*, i.e., by explicit enumeration.

2.6 Presentation Model

Presentation is concerned with the look and feel of Web pages, in particular with the design of the general page layout, with the placement of specific pieces of information on the page, and with the selection of graphical resources like backgrounds, icons and animations.

The basic unit of presentation is the page; each page is associated to one or more *style sheets*, each specifying a different way of presenting the page instances on the screen. Style sheets are formally expressed in XML and can be defined visually by means of suitable WYSIWYG tools.

The style sheet language contains the following elements:

- A sublanguage to define metric spaces, i.e., regions of the screen which can host the presentation of a page. Presently, such regions are bidimensional, but the style sheet language is open to the description of multidimensional metric spaces.
- A sublanguage to define the internal structure of screen regions. Such language is based on an extended notion of grid, enabling overlapping regions and flexibly defined multispan regions.
- A sublanguage to define presentation panels, i.e., the content associated to each screen region. Panels are recursively constructed from atomic elements, which permit the insertion into a page of either language-dependent pieces of content (e.g., HTML text), or of content extracted from the database (e.g., an attribute, a component, or an outgoing relationship). If the content of a given conceptual element is null, the corresponding region is not generated, and surrounding regions are automatically rearranged. The goal of this sublanguage is to allow the designer to define panels at a varying degree of granularity and completeness, to enable the construction of reusable style sheet libraries.

A *default* page style is generated for each page, based on a very simple layout. The screen is separated into five predefined regions by means of a grid. The upper region contains the page header; the left region contains icons enabling non-contextual navigation; the two regions immediately below the header contain icons enabling contextual navigation, respectively on components and relationships; finally, the

[4]In hypertexts and hypermedia, collections are also called "indexes"; we avoid this term which is already quite overloaded.

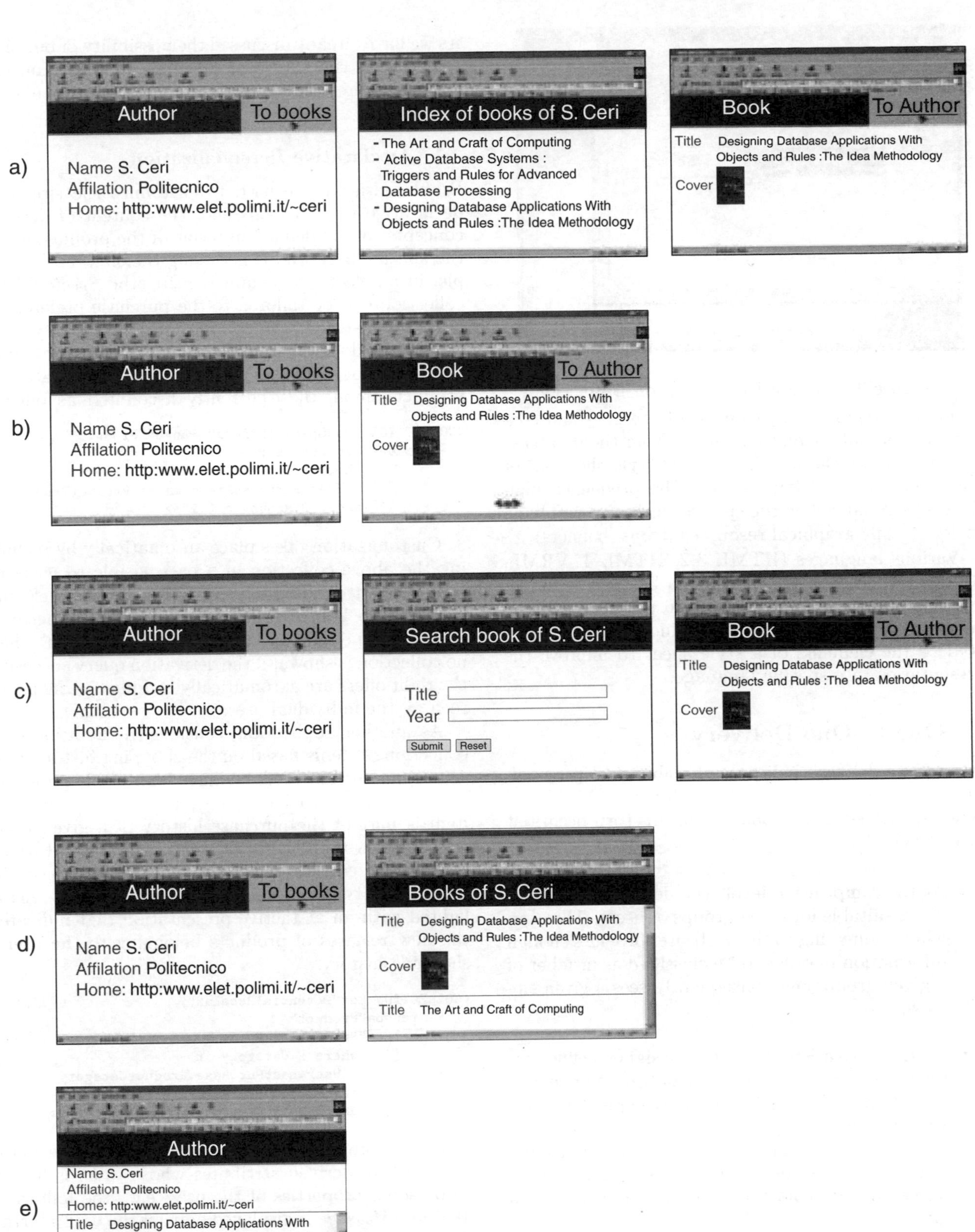

Figure 1: Examples of Navigation Modes

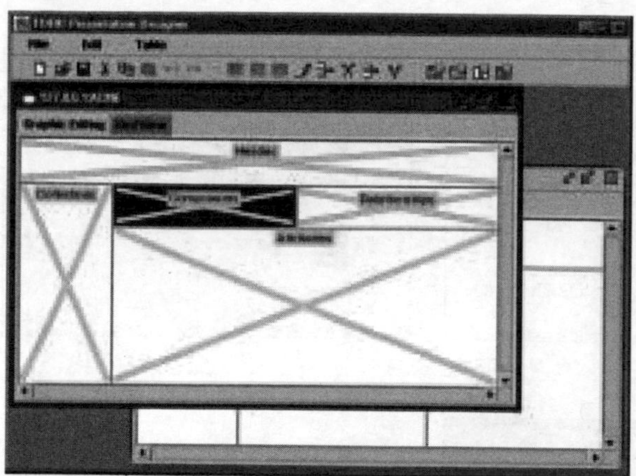

Figure 2: The Torii Presentation Designer

lower right region occupies most of the page and contains the actual content extracted from the database. Figure 2 shows the interface of the style sheet editor operating on the default style. The predefined panels are personalized on the specific entity by supplying entity-specific graphical resources (icons, banners).

Various languages (HTML 3.2, HTML 4, VRML, ATVEF [1], HDML [13], etc.) can be used to implement the presentation pages. Torii provides optional language-dependent attributes, which can be associated to the elements of a style sheet to improve the presentation in a specific language.

3 One-to-One Delivery

One-to-one delivery indicates the ability of personalizing a Web site so as to offer each user a "dedicated view" of the site. Personalization in Torii occurs at three levels.

- At the composition level: the designer builds site views suitable for given groups of users. The user, when connecting to the Web site, provides enough information in order to be classified as member of a given group, and consequently sees a given site view.

- At the derivation level: the designer defines intensional concepts (e.g., attributes, components, collections) whose definition may depend on user-specific data and metadata. In this way, customization is declaratively specified by the designer, and then the runtime page generator computes and presents the information specific to a given user.

- At the business rule level: the designer writes business rules to handle personalization. Typically, business rules manipulate user-specific information, and this results in a change of the site's organization or presentation.

As we have already discussed the possibility of building distinct site views for each group of users, we concentrate on the remaining two options, which are the most innovative.

3.1 Declarative Personalization

Profile data can be used to customize the site in a declarative way. To this end, the content of derived concepts can be defined in terms of the profile data of the specific user who is accessing the site. For example, in an electronic commerce site, the *SpecialOffers* collection can be tailored to the purchase preferences of the user, stored in the profile data of the entity *Purchaser*. To do so, it is sufficient to define a derivation query that looks up user profile data to select matching products among those currently discounted, as follows:

```
<COLLECTION id="SpecialOffers" range="Product"
    value="Product as P
          where P.Type in
            User.PurchasePreferences.ProductType
          and P.Discount > 0.2"/>
```

Customization takes place automatically by including the above collection in a page visible to users of type *Purchaser*. If the query fails (e.g., because the user has no known purchase preferences or because there is no special offer matching his preferences), then no collection is shown; if the derivation query succeeds, the right offers are automatically included in the pages seen by the individual user.

As another application, consider the addition of a collection of items based on the shopping history. Assume that certain products have high resale potential (e.g., books, magazines, CDs); then, when one such item is part of the purchase history of a given user, we collect in the *PotentialResales* collection all items of the same category which were added to the site in the last thirty days. The collection can then be highlighted with an attractive presentation that indicates the new releases of products belonging to the user's shopping history.

```
<COLLECTION id="PotentialResales"
      range="Product"
      value="Product as P
            where P.Category in
              User.LastPurchase.ProductCategory
            and P.ProductResalePotential = 'Y'
            and P.Meta.Created > Sysdate - 30"/>
```

Even more simply, personalization can take place by means of derived attributes whose value is linked to personal properties of the user; e.g., the following *WelcomeMessage* is displayed only on the user's birthday. Style sheets may associate to the welcome message any kind of visualization, generated only if the attribute is not null.

```
<ATTRIBUTE id="WelcomeMessage"
    value="'Special welcome in your birthday!'
          where User.Birthday = Sysdate"/>
```

3.2 Business Rules

Business rules are specified according to the well-known event-condition-action paradigm: they are triggered by a given event, once triggered the condition is considered, and if the condition is true then the action is executed. Rules have tuple-level granularity, therefore each elementary data change event is followed by the triggering of the rules related to it. Rules triggered by the same event may be prioritized; a priority is a positive number, and higher numbers denote higher priorities.

Events considered by rules are classified as *click-stream* and *data change* events. The former include the start and end of a session and each new page access. When the event is a new page being accessed, the event may be specified as relative to a specific entity, denoted by its name.

Conditions evaluate predicates or queries over the database. The condition is satisfied if the predicate is true or the query result is not empty; bindings produced in the evaluation of the condition are available for the execution of the action. Conditions may be missing, in which case the action is always executed. In the evaluation of conditions, special variables are associated to the triggering event. In particular:

- When the event is a clickstream event, the variable *User* denotes the user who performed the clickstream action.
- When the event is a page access, a variable associated to the event is bound to the given entity instance being accessed.
- When the event is a data change, variables *Old* and *New* denote, respectively, the values of the entity instance before or after the operation.

Actions performed by rules include adding or dropping elements from collections, executing simple data updates, sending mail to users or assigning them a given site view.

We next present several examples of business rules, classified according to the specific application being performed by them. A precise characterization of the syntax and semantics of rules can be found in [6].

3.2.1 Rules for User Classification

These rules are focused on assigning a given view to the current user. The condition is typically a predicate on the current user; the action is an assignment of the (current) site view. Rules are executed in priority order, but as soon as one of them assigns a site view to the current user, this value cannot be further updated within the session. The two rules below assign suitable site views to users who classify respectively as kids or as frequent purchasers; the former criterion is predominant, as indicated by the rules' priority.

```
<RULE id="ClassifyKid">
    <EVENT eventType="SessionStart"/>
    <CONDITION predicate="User.Age < 12"/>
    <ACTION action="Assign(SiteView,'SV-KIDS')"/>
    <PRIORITY value="100"/>
</RULE>

<RULE id="ClassifyFrequent">
    <EVENT eventType="SessionStart"/>
    <CONDITION
       predicate="User.LastLogin - Sysdate < 10"/>
    <ACTION action="Assign(SiteView,'SV-FREQ')"/>
    <PRIORITY value="50"/>
</RULE>
```

The advantage of using business rules instead of a static grouping of users and assignment of site views to groups lies in the higher dynamicity and ease of evolution.

3.2.2 Rules for Managing User-Defined Collections

Business rules may be used for managing user-specific information, so as to increase the information about the user and thereby enable current or future personalizations. The following rule adds to the user-defined collection *User.VisitedBook* the book currently being visited.

```
<RULE id="AddToVisitedBooks">
    <EVENT eventType="newpage(Book as B)"/>
    <ACTION action="add(User.VisitedBooks,B)"/>
</RULE>
```

The following two rules add to (drop from) the collection *Group.Chatline*, associated to each group, the user who is starting (ending) a session. On the basis of this information, newsgroup management software may be used to enable conversation among these users so as to facilitate their on-line exchange of information and mutual advice about possible purchases.

```
<RULE id="AddToActiveUsers">
    <EVENT eventType="SessionStart"/>
    <ACTION action="add(Group.Chatline,User)"/>
</RULE>

<RULE id="DropFromActiveUsers">
    <EVENT eventType="SessionEnd"/>
    <ACTION action="drop(Group.Chatline,User)"/>
</RULE>
```

3.2.3 Rules for Pushing Information to the Users

A typical example of push technology in electronic commerce is concerned with providing a user with information about new purchase opportunities. The following rule reacts to the insertion of a new entity *Book* by sending a message to all users who are interested in the book topics, provided that they accept e-mail notifications.

```
<RULE id="NewRelevantBook">
  <EVENT  eventType="Insert(Book)"/>
  <CONDITION
    query="user as U where U in new.Topics.InterestedIn
                       and U.Solicitable = 'Y'"/>
  <ACTION
    action="SendMsg(To:U.address,
                Text:'This book is now available in our
                      electronic store:'+new.Title)"/>
</RULE>
```

3.2.4 Rules for Metadata Management

Although less likely, rules may as well change meta-information [5]. For instance, the following rule increments the number of visitors of the pages of given books.

```
<RULE id="CheckDBTextbooks">
    <EVENT eventType="newpage(Book as B)"/>
    <CONDITION
       predicate="B.Gender = 'Database Textbooks'"/>
    <ACTION action="Increment(B.Meta.Visitors)"/>
</RULE>
```

4 Architecture

The architecture of the Torii system has been conceived to meet the following goals:

- Runtime performance: the system must be able to support high loads.
- Evolvability: due to the inherent dynamicity of the Web standards and technologies, the system architecture must facilitate product evolution. The basic requirements are the porting to different software platforms (Microsoft IIS/ASP, Java servlets), code generation in different Web languages (HTML 3 and 4, XML, ATVEF, HDML), and support for data feeds from heterogeneous legacy databases.
- Adherence to open and commercial standards: to capitalize on existing software and reduce development and maintenance efforts, the architecture is based on well established architectural, data storage, and content formatting standards (SQL, XML 1.0 [16], DOM [15], Java and Corba 2.0).

The experience with the Autoweb system proved inadequate with respect to most of the above objectives:

- Autoweb has a monolithic CGI-server structure, with an active process managing all the phases of page generation. The runtime engine does not benefit from data integration and parallelization capabilities provided by industrial platforms (e.g., application servers).

[5] In principle, business rules can change arbitrary information, including the data content, but this application is not envisioned by the users of the W3I3 Consortium.

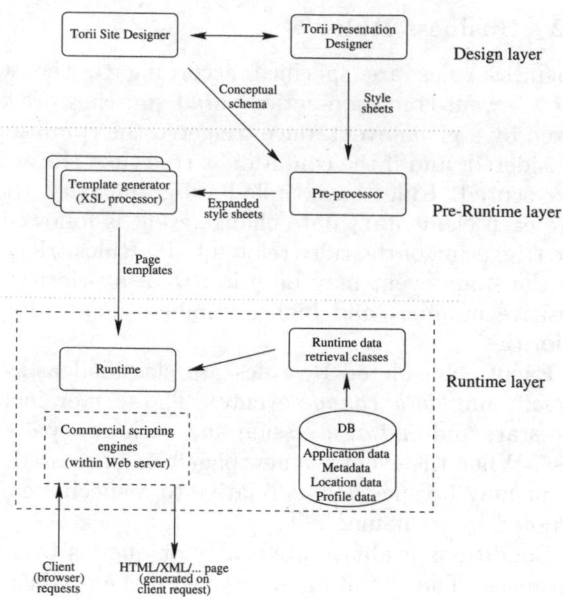

Figure 3: Architecture of the Torii system

- Service requests are serialized by the Autoweb server, which strongly limits performance for heavily loaded systems.
- The monolithic structure results in a tightly integrated piece of software, which proves difficult to manage in view of possible evolution of the design methodology, layout generation strategies, and underlying technologies.
- Autoweb caches output pages to enhance the runtime performance; this technique must be reconsidered in a scenario in which pages are personalized on a per-user or a per-group basis.

Due to these observations, the Torii system is based on a completely different architecture, illustrated in Figure 3. Generally speaking, the Torii architecture consists of three main layers:

- The design layer includes the tools for modeling Web applications; the output of the design layer is a Torii application, coded in the Torii modeling language.
- The pre-runtime layer comprises a chain of code generators that transform the Torii application into an intermediate representation suitable for processing on top of commercial Web-database systems.
- The runtime layer consists of an interpreter for converting page templates into actual application pages. The main functionality of the runtime layer is to merge application data into page templates to obtain the fully instantiated final application pages.

In addition, the Torii architecture includes a repository storing the following data:

- Application data: the actual content delivered by the application to the users. It is further subdivided into structured application data (e.g., database tuples, valid XML documents), and semi-structured and unstructured application data (e.g., image files, HTML pages).

- Metadata: information about the conceptual schema of the application, as defined by the conceptual design.

- Location data: information about the mapping between the Torii conceptual schema and the physical data structures that host the application data (e.g., external databases).

- Profile data: information about users and groups, used to customize a site. User data are managed according to privacy legislation and must be disclosed to owners on demand.

4.1 The Design Tools

The design layer consists of two major components:

- Torii Site Designer: permits the definition of a Torii application and manages a project repository containing the schemas of the defined Torii applications.

- Torii Presentation Designer: deals with the specific aspect of presentation specification, by letting the designer define in a visual way presentation models and style sheets to be used in a Torii application (see Figure 2).

¿From the architectural standpoint, the Torii Design Environment is a multi-user client server application, sitting on top of a project repository structured as a collection of DOM objects. The user interface permits the visual editing of Torii schemas, which are translated in real-time into a DOM representation, so that both the graphical and XML specifications are available to the designer. A dual-interface to persistence permits to store DOM objects either as XML files or database objects.

4.2 The Pre-Runtime and Runtime Environments

The output of the design tools is the input of a chain of transformations operated by the Torii Pre-Runtime and Runtime environments, which ends with the actual application page in the chosen delivery language.

The transformation process is clearly divided into two steps:

- The Pre-Runtime environment pre-processes the Torii presentation styles by unfolding all the implicit information (e.g., type information about the concept to which the style sheet is applied) to obtain a fully instantiated, language independent, specification of the layout, which is then turned into a language and platform dependent page template. Such template is complete, except for the actual data content, which is replaced by suitable calls to the runtime data retrieval classes.

- The Torii data retrieval classes are installed in a commercial engine, which is used to merge application data into templates to produce the actual page sent to the browser.

The Pre-Runtime processors are coded as a library of Java classes which permits the unfolding of presentation styles based on application metadata, plus a set of XSL programs (style sheets, in the XSL terminology) which map pre-processed XML presentation styles into code in the language of choice. With this architecture, adding a new output language does not require coding a new compiler, but simply writing a new XSL program that does the mapping.

The page generation process is illustrated in Figure 3. It is worth noticing that the architectural solutions adopted are flexible enough to guarantee the effortless reconfiguration of the page generation process, which is the base for tracking technology changes.

The requirement for performance clearly pushes in the direction of anticipating as much processing as possible before runtime, but also clashes with the need of serving content dynamically and on the base of the knowledge dynamically accumulated about the user. This tension is the major architectural challenge faced in Torii, and we have solved it by carefully designing the distribution of responsibilities among the different components of the model and of the system.

5 Experiences

Torii is at its infancy, but the predecessor Autoweb system is operational since the end of 1996 and has been used in several projects, both in the industry and in university.

These experiences have proven that a data-driven approach to Web Site design is very useful, offering the following advantages:

- The modeling concepts of the structural model constitute a design notation which can be used also by non-technical people, like graphic designers and content producers.

- Data quality improves, because the Web content needs to adapt to a rigid format; this is especially important when content is highly volatile, as in distance learning applications.

- The approach yields to a dramatic reduction of prototyping times; once the structure schema is in place, a default Web site is already ready to run.

- Maintenance and evolution are dramatically improved, because changes in the structural model can be automatically or semi-automatically propagated to the implementation. This benefit is fundamental, because even model-driven design does not always fully reflect requirements, and requirements change during or after application delivery.

- The decision to provide a high-level model of presentation, which is automatically translated into physical pages, enforces presentation consistency and coherence.

Further experiences of use will be collected through the development of two pilot applications of the industrial partners of the W3I3 Consortium. Otto Versand, which already makes a fraction of its revenues through a large Web site offering a selection of its mail-order catalogs, will experiment the use of Torii to add one-to-one functionality and more effective management and evolution facilities to its application. KPN Research, which manages HetNet, a Web-based network with about one million subscribers in the Netherlands, will use Torii to develop an application acting as an intermediary between service providers and customers, and to offer personalized access and facilitated service location to HetNet subscribers.

6 Conclusions

In this paper, we have argued that data-centric abstractions - already quite popular in database design - are applicable, with very strong potentiality, to data-intensive Web applications. The rationale of this argument is that data-intensive Web applications have a very simple control pattern (e.g., if compared to the nontrivial applications of databases); as such, a fully automatic development of the Web application is quite feasible, even from very rich specifications. We have also shown the very many orthogonal dimensions along which such specifications are needed in order to develop effective Web sites for a variety of users, with different needs.

This approach presents substantial advantages, because implementation and prototyping are immediate, and operation, maintenance and reengineering are greatly facilitated. In addition, the availability of a data-centric repository storing all information about Web site generation, together with the data content, opens up new opportunities to one-to-one Web generation, in the form of data derivations or of business rules operating on the repository itself. The power and novelty of applying both declarative queries and business rules for handling personalizations has been shown by means of several examples.

Presently, the design of the ToriiSoft Environment is completed, and the prototypes of Torii tools are at various stages of design and implementation; some of the innovative features of Torii are already supported by its predecessor project Autoweb, which is operational.

References

[1] Advanced television enhancement forum specification (ATVEF), Feb. 1999. available at http://www.atvef.com.

[2] P. Atzeni, G. Mecca, and P. Merialdo. To Weave the Web. In *Proc. 23rd VLDB*, pages 206–215, Athens, Greece, Aug. 26-29, 1997.

[3] C. Batini, S. Ceri, and S. Navathe. *Conceptual Database Design.* Benjamin Cummings, Menlo Park CA, 1993.

[4] P. Bernstein et al. The Asilomar report on database research. *ACM Sigmod Record*, 27(4):74–80, Dec. 1998.

[5] S. Ceri, P. Fraternali, and S. Paraboschi. Design principles for data-intensive web sites. *ACM Sigmod Record*, 28(1):84–89, Mar. 1999.

[6] S. Ceri, P. Fraternali, and S. Paraboschi. Specification of W3I3 models. Technical Report W3I3PAP2, W3I3 Esprit Project n. 28771, Feb. 1999.

[7] M. F. Fernandez, D. Florescu, A. Y. Levy, and D. Suciu. Catching the boat with Strudel: Experiences with a web-site management system. In *Proc. Sigmod'98*, pages 414–425, Seattle, June, 1998.

[8] P. Fraternali. Tools and approaches for developing data-intensive web applications: A survey. *ACM Comput. Surv.*, 1999. To appear.

[9] P. Fraternali and P. Paolini. A conceptual model and a tool environment for developing more scalable and dynamic Web applications. In *Proc. EDBT'98*, pages 421–435, Valencia, Spain, March, 1998.

[10] T. Isakowitz, E. A. Stohr, and P. Balasubramanian. RMM: a methodology for structured hypermedia design. *Communications of the ACM*, 38(8):34–44, 1995.

[11] D. Peppers and M. Rogers. *Enterprise One to One: Tools for Competing in the Interactive Age.* Currency-Doubleday, 1997.

[12] K. Takahashi and E. Liang. Analysis and Design of Web-based Informations Systems. In *Proc. Sixth Int. WWW Conf.*, Santa Clara, California, 1997.

[13] Unwired Planet Inc. Handheld device markup language (HDML) specification, Apr. 1997.

[14] M. K. Uusitalo. Specification of tools user interface. Technical report, W3I3 Esprit Project n. 28771, Feb. 1999.

[15] World Wide Web Consortium. Document Object Model (DOM) level 1 specification. Oct. 1998.

[16] World Wide Web Consortium. Extensible Markup Language (XML) 1.0. Feb. 1998.

Optimization of Run-time Management of Data Intensive Web Sites

Daniela Florescu
INRIA Rocquencourt, France
Daniela.Florescu@inria.fr

Alon Levy
University of Washington, Seattle
alon@cs.washington.edu

Dan Suciu
AT&T Labs – Research
suciu@research.att.com

Khaled Yagoub
PRISM Versailles, France
khaled.yagoub@prism.uvsq.fr

Abstract

An increasing number of web sites have their data extracted from relational databases. Several commercial products and research prototypes have been moving in the direction of declarative specification of the sites' structure and content. Specifically, the entire site is specified using a collection of queries describing the site's nodes (corresponding to web pages and the data contained in them) and edges (corresponding to the hyperlinks). Given this paradigm, an important issue is *when* to compute the site's pages. Two extreme approaches, with obvious drawbacks, are (1) to precompute the entire site in advance, and (2) to evaluate on demand all the queries necessary to construct a given page. We consider the problem of automatically optimizing the run-time management of declaratively specified web sites. In our approach, given a declarative site specification and constraints on the application, an efficient run-time evaluation policy is automatically derived. An evaluation policy specifies which data to compute at a given browser request. We describe several optimizations that can be used in run-time policies, focusing mostly on optimizations that exploit the *structure* of the web site. We evaluate experimentally the impact of these optimizations on a web site derived from the TPC/D database. Finally, we describe a heuristic-based optimization algorithm which compiles a declarative site specification into a run-time policy that incorporates the proposed optimizations.

1 Introduction

The World Wide Web (WWW) has been proven to be an excellent medium for businesses to disseminate information. As a result, the ability to populate web sites with content derived from large databases has become the key to building enterprise web sites. Tools addressing this problem range from low-level CGI-bin scripts to more sophisticated tools provided by most major DBMS vendors, that enable embedding SQL queries in HTML templates.

In parallel, a new paradigm for building and maintaining web sites based on declarative specifications has arisen in the research community [9, 3, 7, 2, 20]. Two main features underlie this paradigm. First, a declarative specification is based on a logical model of the web site, that captures the content and structure of the web site and is meant to be independent of its graphical presentation. Second, the logical model of the site is defined as a view, in some declarative language, over the data underlying the site. Web-site management systems based on declarative representations have been shown to provide good support for common tasks which are otherwise tedious to perform, such as automatic site updates, site restructuring, creation of multiple versions of a site from the same data, and specification and enforcement of integrity constraints [10].

An example of this paradigm, which is the focus of this paper, is the case where web sites' content is derived from large relational databases. We model web sites as graphs whose nodes represent pages in the web site or data items associated with pages, and the links in the graph represent either hyperlinks between pages or association of data with pages in the site. The structure of the web site is defined *intensionally* by a site schema, which can be regarded as a hyperlink view defined over the relational database.

A critical issue that arises when sites' contents are populated from large databases is when to compute the pages in the site [21] and/or the corresponding nodes in the logical model. One approach is to materialize the site completely, i.e., evaluate all the database queries in the site definition, and compute the complete site before users browse it. Unfortunately, this approach has several obvious drawbacks. First, precomputation cannot be applied to sites with forms (since the inputs are only known at run-time). Second, materializing the site would imply an important space overhead, often even greater than duplicating the entire database, since the same information in the database

Proceedings of the 25th VLDB Conference, Edinburgh, Scotland, 1999.

can appear in multiple web pages. Finally, propagating updates from the database to the web site is costly once the site has been materialized.

A second extreme approach (deployed by commercial tools for extracting content of web sites from databases) is to precompute only the root(s) of a web site, and when a page is requested, to issue to the database a set of parameterized queries that extract the necessary data. The main disadvantage of this approach is that some queries may be too expensive to evaluate at run-time, which is unacceptable given the interactive nature of web access. Furthermore, evaluating queries at run-time may result in repeated computation. An obvious repetition occurs when multiple browsers request the same page. A second, more interesting observation, is that successive queries issued by a single browser share much of their computation.

Multiple requests for the same web page could conceivably be treated by web caching techniques. However, these solutions have two problems. First, current caching techniques do not cache dynamically generated pages. Second, even if caching techniques are extended (e.g., by server-side caching for dynamically generated pages), the granularity of an entire HTML page is too coarse. Clearly, in order to develop optimizations based on sharing of computation in query sequences, a deeper semantic analysis of the web-site structure is required.

Currently, since response time is the main priority, web site builders end up hardwiring optimizations into the design of their sites. Such hardwiring is a labor intensive task which needs to be repeated whenever changes are made to the site's structure. This paper considers the problem of automatically optimizing the run-time behavior of the dynamic evaluation of declarative web sites. We describe a framework, where a declarative specification is compiled into a run-time policy. The policy decides which actions to perform and which queries to evaluate depending on the browsing history. Run-time policies are able to express several traditional optimizations, such as view materialization and data caching, and novel optimizations that depend on the structure of the web site, such as optimization under preconditions and lookahead computation. In a sense, the distinction between the declarative specification of the web site and the run-time policy is analogous to the distinction between a declarative query and a query execution plan in a traditional database. As in the latter context, we automatically compile the declarative specification into an "optimal" run-time policy which is "equivalent" to the declarative specification, using a global cost model, statistics on the database and browsing patterns.

As a first cut, a possible approach to our problem is to consider the set of parameterized queries that are executed against the database as a particular workload, and to apply some of the existing techniques aimed at optimizing a given workload. Such techniques have been considered in various contexts, such as view materialization [24, 13, 12, 14, 6], index selection, data caching [16, 15, 8], multiple query optimization [23], and reuse of query invariants [17, 22].

However, none of the above techniques exploit a key aspect of our context, namely the structure of the web site. The structure of a web site imposes a *topology* over the possible navigational paths through the site and therefore on the set of queries in the workload. More precisely, at each point in the site, while issuing new queries to the database, we have an additional valuable information about the *past* queries issued to the database (which we call the browsing context), as well as extra information about the likelihood of possible *future* queries that may be executed. In this paper, we show that exploiting this structure leads to significant savings over and above the application of the known techniques mentioned above. As a consequence, our techniques are also useful beyond web-site management, for contexts in which the application imposes an analyzable topology on the workload of queries (e.g. SQL queries embedded in programming languages or trigger chains).

In summary, we make the following contributions.

- We describe a framework for automatic compilation of web-site specifications. The framework distinguishes between a declarative specification of the structure and content of a web site, and a run-time policy governing the computation of the web site. The formalism for describing run-time policies can encompass traditional optimizations as well as novel ones specific to our context.
- We describe several optimization techniques for speeding up the run-time behavior of web sites. One class of optimizations includes precomputing a set of views and caching results of certain computations. The second class of optimizations exploits the structure of the web site and includes (1) simplification of queries based on known preconditions, and (2) lookahead computation, i.e., computing more data than is immediately needed for use in nodes that are likely to be visited subsequently. We evaluate the impact of these optimization techniques on a web site derived from the TPC/D data, and show that each of them, even in isolation, yields significant speedups.
- Based on our experiments, we describe a set of guidelines for constructing an algorithm for compiling declarative specifications into run-time policies. We show that applying these guidelines in our experimental setting produced high-quality run-time policies.
- We describe the implementation of STRUDEL-R system[1], which embodies the ideas described in the paper.

The paper is organized as follows. Section 2 describes declarative web-site management systems and different run-time management techniques. Section 3 formally defines the problem we consider in the paper. Section 4 describes several optimization techniques and evaluates their impact. Section 5 formally defines run-time policies, and Section 6 describes the compilation methodology. Finally, Section 7 describes the implementation of STRUDEL-R, and then we conclude with related work.

2 Declarative specification of web sites

We begin by describing the general architecture of declarative web-site management systems, as embodied in the STRUDEL-R system. We note that the key architectural aspects of the STRUDEL-R are common to other systems for declarative web-site management [2, 3, 20, 7]. STRUDEL-R is based on a logical representation of a web site, called a *site graph*, which is independent of its graphical presentation or of the underlying data management systems. The site graph models the pages in the web site, the links between them, and the data associated with each page. A

[1] STRUDEL-R is a derivative of the STRUDEL system [9] where the content is derived from a single relational database system, as opposed to multiple external semi-structured data sources.

site graph in STRUDEL-R is defined intensionally, via a *site schema*. Applying the site schema to a particular instance of the database results in a site graph. The site graph computed by the above procedure can be converted into a browsable web site by applying HTML templates to each of the nodes in the graph.

The STRUDEL-R system contains two components. The site graph generator applies the intentional definition of the site schema to the underlying data and produces (fragments of) the site graph. The HTML generator applies HTML templates to nodes in the site graph, resulting in browsable HTML pages. In the rest of this section we describe site graphs and site schemas. The details of the HTML templates [9] are not relevant to our discussion.

2.1 Site graphs

A site graph is a directed, rooted, labeled graph. There are two types of nodes in the site graph: internal nodes corresponding to web pages, and leaf nodes corresponding to data values. [2] An edge between two internal nodes, called a *ref arc*, models a hyperlink, or the nesting of page components; an edge from an internal node to a leaf, called a *data arc*, models data values to be displayed on the page. Every arc l in the site graph is labeled with a string $label(l)$, and with a string $anchor(l)$: $label(l)$ is the name of the relationship between the two nodes (e.g., "Region"), while $anchor(l)$ is the string shown on the HTML link corresponding to the arc (e.g., the name of the region "Europe").

In STRUDEL-R pages are classified into a small number of relatively homogeneous collections [9]: for example nodes corresponding to customers form a collection, while those corresponding to suppliers another. We refer to the collections of pages in a web site as *site collections*. Each internal node can be uniquely identified by a term of the form $F(a_1, \ldots, a_n)$, where F is the collection's name, and $a_1, \ldots, a_n$ are data items from the database: such an expression is called a Skolem term, and $n \geq 0$ is the collection's arity. We can always model a highly specialized node as a collection with one member, e.g., the root collection *Root* is of arity 0 and has a single member: *Root*().

2.2 Site schemas

A site schema is a directed, rooted, labeled graph G, whose nodes are partitioned into internal nodes and leaf nodes. There is one internal node for each site collection F, and that node is labeled by a Skolem term of the form $F(X_1, \ldots, X_n)$ ($F(\bar{X})$, in short), where F is a site collection name and $X_1, \ldots, X_n$ are variables. The root is labeled by a 0-arity Skolem function: in this paper it will always be *Root*(). Leaf nodes are labeled with single variables and correspond to data items. As before we classify edges into ref arcs and data arcs.

A ref arc between two internal nodes $F_1(\bar{X}_1)$ and $F_2(\bar{X}_2)$ in the site schema is labeled by a query specifying the conditions needed for the existence of an arc between instances of F_1 and F_2 in the site graph. Similarly a data arc between $F_1(\bar{X}_1)$ and Y has a query specifying the conditions needed

[2]To simplify the exposition, our discussion does not include the formalisms needed to model forms in HTML pages, as well as the internal structure within a page. However, we note that extending site specifications to include the above features is relatively straightforward.

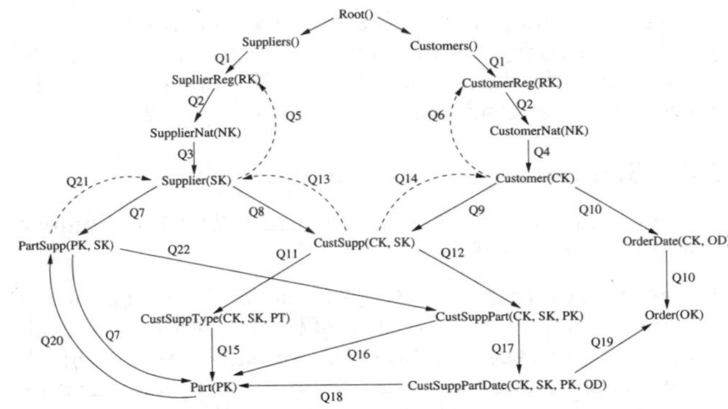

Figure 1: The site schema for the TPC/D example. For clarity, we omitted the data arcs, the anchors and the labels.

for the existence of a corresponding arc in the site graph. In this paper we use the notation of conjunctive queries (corresponding to select-project-join queries in SQL) of the form:

$$q(\bar{X}) : -e_1(\bar{X}_1), \ldots, e_m(\bar{X}_m),$$

where $e_1, \ldots, e_m$ are relations in the database and $\bar{X}, \bar{X}_1, \ldots, \bar{X}_m$ are tuples of variables or constants. We denote all variables in q by $Vars(q)$, and call the variables in $\bar{X}$ *distinguished* variables. Thus, arcs in the site schema are labeled as follows.

- **Ref Arcs:** an arc from $F_1(\bar{X}_1)$ to $F_2(\bar{X}_2)$ is labeled by a triple: $(q, anchor, label)$, where: (a) q is a conjunctive query whose distinguished variables are $\bar{X}_1 \cup \bar{X}_2$, (b) *anchor* is either a string or one of the distinguished variables of q, and (c) *label* is a constant string associated with the arc.
- **Data arcs:** an arc from $F(\bar{X})$ to Y is labeled by a pair: $(q, label)$, where q and *label* have the same meaning as above and $\bar{X} \cup \{Y\}$ are distinguished variables of q.

Example 2.1 We use the following example throughout the paper and in our experiments. Suppose we want to produce a browsable version of the data contained in the TPC/D benchmark. The database contains information about products, customers, and orders. A simplified version of the TPC/D schema is given below.

Part(partkey, name, brand, type, size)
Supplier(suppkey, name, address, nationkey, phone)
PartSupp(partkey, suppkey, availqty, supplycost, comment)
Customer(custkey, name, address, nationkey, phone)
Nation(nationkey, name, regionkey, comment)
Region(regionkey, name, comment)
Lineitem(orderkey, linenumber, partkey, suppkey, quantity)
Order(orderkey, custkey, orderstatus, totalprice, orderdate)

The site schema shown in Figure 1 provides the following organization of the data. The root node has two links to suppliers (Suppliers()) and customers (Customers()). Both suppliers and customers are grouped by geographical region (e.g., SupplierReg(RK)), and inside each region by nationality (e.g., SupplierNat(NK)). Suppliers and customers have further links to detailed information about orders. Specifically there is one page for each customer-supplier pair (CustSupp(CK,SK)) where the customer ordered from the supplier: that page can be accessed from both the supplier and customer pages. From here there are further links to pages detailing orders placed by that customer to that supplier. Of course, in designing the web site, we also add links back to facilitate navigation. The definitions of the queries in the site schema are given in Figure 2.

2.3 Semantics of site schemas

A site schema G and a database instance D define a unique site graph $G(D)$ as follows.

- **Create ref arcs:** let $l = (q, anchor, label)$ be an arc from $F_1(\bar{X}_1)$ to $F_2(\bar{X}_2)$. Let $q(D)$ be the result of evaluating q over the database D. For each tuple $\bar{a} \in q(D)$, we define $\bar{a}_1$ and $\bar{a}_2$ as restrictions of $\bar{a}$ to the variables $\bar{X}_1$ and $\bar{X}_2$, respectively. Then, $G(D)$ contains a link between $F_1(\bar{a}_1)$ and $F_2(\bar{a}_2)$, labeled *label* and whose anchor is the value of the variable *anchor* in the tuple $\bar{a}$. We note that if the nodes $F_1(\bar{a}_1)$ and $F_2(\bar{a}_2)$ were not in the site graph, then they are added as a side effect of inserting the arc.
- **Create data arcs:** let l be a data arc in G between the nodes $F(\bar{X})$ and Y, labeled by $(q, label)$. For each $\bar{a} \in q(D)$ we define $\bar{a}_1$ and a_2 as projections of $\bar{a}$ on $\bar{X}$ and Y, respectively. Then, $G(D)$ contains a link between $F(\bar{a}_1)$ and a_2, labeled *label*.
- **Root node:** the root node in $G(D)$ is *Root*().
- **Eliminate unreachable nodes:** any node in the site graph that is not reachable from the root is removed.

2.4 Strategy for site graph evaluation

There are many strategies for computing the site graph. The semantics described above provide a natural method to compute the entire site graph in advance of browsing. We refer to it as the *static* evaluation strategy.

An alternative strategy is to expand the site graph *dynamically*, starting from the root and computing the nodes in the site graph only upon request. We recall that each web page corresponds to a node $F(\bar{a})$ is the site graph. Therefore, an HTTP request for a given page translates into a request for a node of the form $F(\bar{a})$. To construct that page we need to compute all the data appearing in the page as well as all the outgoing HTML links. Formally, this translates into the following procedure.

Given a site schema G and a database instance D, in order to produce the node $F(\bar{a})$, the dynamic algorithm proceeds as follows:

- **Create ref arcs:** let $l(q, anchor, label)$ be an arc from $F(\bar{X})$ to $F_1(\bar{X}_1)$. Let $q(D)$ be the result of evaluating $q \wedge (\bar{X} = \bar{a})$ over the database D. For each tuple $\bar{b} \in q(D)$, we define $\bar{b}_1$ to be the projection of $\bar{b}$ on $\bar{X}_1$. Then, $G(D)$ contains a link between $F(\bar{a})$ and $F_1(\bar{b}_1)$, labeled *label* and whose anchor is the value of the variable *anchor* in the tuple $\bar{b}$.
- **Create data arcs:** let $l = (q, label)$ be a data arc from $F(\bar{X})$ to Y. For each tuple $\bar{b} \in q(D)$ we define b_1 to be the projection of $\bar{b}$ on Y. Then, $G(D)$ contains a link between $F(\bar{a})$ and b_1, labeled *label*.

Starting at *Root*() and applied repeatedly (e.g., in depth first order), this procedure eventually computes the entire site graph. It is important to note that this graph is provably isomorphic to the site graph given by the static computation, assuming that the database is not changing during the computation.

3 Problem definition

The static and the dynamic evaluation algorithms represent two extreme strategies, with obvious advantages and disadvantages. The goal of our work is to automatically find an optimal intermediate strategy for a given web site, that combines pre-computation, caching and dynamic evaluation of the requested data. The optimal strategy is expressed as a *run-time policy*, which specifies which data to precompute or cache and which actions to execute at each page request, depending on the history of the browsing.

In this section we set up a general framework for studying run-time policies and formally define the optimization problem we consider.

3.1 Inputs to the optimization problem

3.1.1 Statistics on browsing patterns

To evaluate a particular run-time policy, it is necessary to know the characteristics of the browsing patterns. Therefore, we assume that we have access to the following statistics:

- **Node probability distribution**: let $F_1, \ldots, F_n$ be the set of internal nodes in the site schema. We assume the availability of the probability distribution $(p_1, \ldots, p_n)$, where p_i is the probability that a request for a page on the site (from any user) will be for an instance of F_i.
- **Arc probability distribution**: for internal node F in the site schema, with the set of successors $F_1, \ldots, F_m$, we assume the availability of the probability distribution $(l_0, l_1, \ldots, l_m)$, where l_i is the probability that a user will request a page of type F_i after viewing a page of type F, and l_0 is the probability that a user does not follow one of F's children (i.e., either stops browsing or goes back to a predecessor page).
- **Value probability distribution**: for each internal node F in the site schema, let $(F(\bar{a}_1), \ldots, F(\bar{a}_s))$ be its instances in the site graph. We assume that we have the probability distribution $(r_1, \ldots, r_s)$, where r_j is the probability that a request for a page of F will be for $F(\bar{a}_j)$.
- **Context probability distribution**: since in our framework the actions to evaluate a specific node depend on the browsing history leading to that point, we assume that there exists an integer k, such that for every internal node F and and a path $P = F_1, \ldots, F_l$ in the site schema where $F_l = F$ and $l \leq k$, we can obtain the probability that, given a request for an instance of F, it was made after following the path P.

The statistics above can be obtained in several ways. One possibility is to analyze the web site log and another is for the web site administrator to estimate them based on knowledge of the application. It is important to emphasize that, since these statistics (except for the value probability distribution) concern the site schema, they are independent of database updates.

3.1.2 Application constraints

Clearly, the choice of an optimal run-time strategy depends on specific constraints of the given application. In our framework, we identify the following measures associated with a given web site:

Q1(RK, RN) :- Region(RK, RN, _)
Q2(NK, RK, NN) :- Nation(NK, **RK**, NN, _)
Q3(SK, SN, NK) :- Supplier(SK, SN, _ ,**NK**, _)
Q4(CK, CN, NK) :- Customer(CK, CN, _, **NK**, _)
Q5(SK, RK, RN) :- Supplier(**SK**, _, _, NK, _), Nation(NK, _, RK, _), Region(RK, RN, _)
Q6(CK, RK, RN) :- Customer(**CK**, _, _, NK, _), Nation(NK, _, RK, _), Region(RK, RN, _)
Q7(PK, SK, PN) :- Part(PK, PN, _, _, _), PartSupp(PK, **SK**, _, _, _)
Q8(CK, SK, CN) :- Customer(CK, CN, _, _, _), LineItem(OK, _, _, **SK**, _), Order(OK, CK, _, _, _)
Q9(CK, SK, SN) :- Supplier(SK, SN, _, _, _), LineItem(OK, _, _, SK, _), Order(OK, **CK**, _, _, _)
Q10(OK, CK, OD) :- Order(OK, **CK**, _, _, **OD**)
Q11(CK, SK, PT) :- LineItem(OK, _, PK, **SK**, _), Order(OK, **CK**, _, _, _), Part(PK, _, _, PT, _)
Q12(CK, SK, PK, PN) :- LineItem(OK, _, PK, **SK**, _), Order(OK, **CK**, _, _, _), Part(PK, PN, _, _, _)
Q13(CK, SK, SN) :- Supplier(**SK**, SN, _, _, _), LineItem(OK, _, _, SK, _), Order(OK, **CK**, _, _, _)
Q14(CK, SK, CN) :- Customer(**CK**, CN, _, _, _), LineItem(OK, _, _, **SK**, _), Order(OK, CK, _, _, _)
Q15(CK, SK, PK, PN, PT) :- LineItem(OK, _, PK, **SK**, _), Order(OK, **CK**, _, _, _), Part(PK, PN, _, **PT**, _)
Q16(CK, SK, PK, PN) :- LineItem(OK, _, PK, **SK**, _), Order(OK, **CK**, _, _, _), Part(**PK**, PN, _, _, _)
Q17(CK, SK, PK, OD) :- LineItem(OK, _, PK, **SK**, _), Order(OK, **CK**, _, _, OD), Part(**PK**, _, _, _, _)
Q18(CK, SK, PK, PN, OD) :- LineItem(OK, _, PK, **SK**, _), Order(OK, **CK**, _, _, **OD**), Part(**PK**, PN, _, _, _)
Q19(CK, SK, PK, OK, OD) :- LineItem(OK, _, PK, **SK**, _), Order(OK, **CK** _, _, **OD**), Part(PK, _, _, _, _)
Q20(PK, SK, SN) :- PartSupp(**PK**, SK, _, _, _), Supplier(SK, SN, _, _, _)
Q21(SK, PK, SN) :- Supplier(**SK**, SN, _, _, _), PartSupp(**PK**, SK, _, _, _)
Q22(CK, SK, PK, CN) :- Customer(CK, CN, _, _, _), LineItem(OK, _, **PK**, **SK**, _), Order(OK, CK, _, _, _)

Figure 2: Queries labeling the arcs in the site schema in Figure 1. The attribute names in boldface are bound variables in the dynamic evaluation.

- *size(WS)*: the size of the (possibly) materialized HTML pages plus the size of the (possibly) precomputed or cached data;
- *age(WS)*: every data item I shown in the web site depends on a set of data items $dep(I)$ in the database. The age of a web site denotes the maximum difference between the timestamp of a data item I in the web site and the timestamp of a data item in $dep(I)$.
- *wait(WS)*: the maximum estimated cost of all the database operations needed to compute a web page.

We assume that a given web site has a set of given parameters (S, A, W) such that we have the following constraints: $(size(WS) < S, age(WS) < A, wait(WS) < W)$, specifying that we should not exceed space S, the maximum waiting time should be at most W, and the web site freshness should be at least A.

3.2 Cost model

Among the evaluation strategies that satisfy the above constraints, our goal is to find the strategy minimizing the waiting time for expanding an instance of a node in the site schema, weighted by the probability of requesting that node. Formally, we denote by $wait_{RP}(F(\bar{X}))$ the average time for executing the queries needed for expanding a node of type $F(\bar{X})$ in a run-time policy RP. Let $F_1, \ldots, F_n$ be the set of internal nodes in the site schema. The cost formula that we use to estimate the efficiency of a specific run-time policy RP for a web site is:

$$cost(RP) = \sum_{i=1}^{n} p_i \times wait_{RP}(F_i) \qquad (1)$$

3.3 Equivalence of run-time policies

Ideally, our optimization algorithm should choose among *equivalent* run-time policies, i.e., policies that produce identical site graphs. However, equivalence of site graphs is tricky to define when the underlying data is updated concurrently with the site graph expansion. In this work, we consider a weak equivalence condition, by imposing an age constraint of k time units on the site. In this case, we are assured that all the data associated with a given page is computed on snapshots within k time units from one another.

4 Optimization techniques for web-site management

In order to develop a meaningful formalism for specifying run-time policies, we first need to consider which optimizations such a formalism should capture. In this section we describe several techniques for optimizing the dynamic evaluation of web sites, and validate their utility. The first class of optimizations includes precomputation of materialized views and dynamic caching of data. The second class is more specialized for our context, and exploits the structure of the web site in order to reformulate the queries in the site definition and to determine useful caching policies.

We evaluate the impact of our optimizations on the STRUDEL-R system. Our experiments were performed on a web site derived from the TPC/D benchmark. The experiments were run on a TPC/D database at scale factor 1, resulting in a database of 1.84GB. We used the Oracle DBMS Version 7.3.2 and a dedicated Ultra Sparc I machine (143 MHz and 128MB of RAM), running SunOS Release 5.5. The indexes on the database were manually tuned for performance before applying our optimizations.

Our experiments measure the average time for the database operations needed to expand a node in the site graph. The numbers are generated as a result of running 100 independent browsing sequences of length at most 20. The browsing sequences are generated by choosing the next web page randomly using a uniform distribution over the emanating links. Note, however, that since our experiments report speedups per node in the site schema, as opposed to the global utility of a run-time policy, the uniform distribution does not bias the results. The experiments report only the running times for the nodes affected by the proposed optimization and are all presented on a logarithmic scale.

4.1 Query simplification under preconditions

The first optimization we consider is a query rewriting technique that exploits the knowledge about the path used to reach a given node. When evaluating a parameterized query with a particular input, we can often simplify the query if we know which previous query produced the input. For example, assume the user requests the node $F_2(\bar{a}_2)$ after visiting $F_1(\bar{a}_1)$, and q_0 is the query on the corresponding arc between F_1 and F_2 in the site schema. According to the semantics, the tuple $(\bar{a}_1, \bar{a}_2)$ is in the result set of q_0. In order to expand $F_2(\bar{a}_2)$ we have to evaluate all the queries labeling the outgoing arcs from the node F_2 in the site schema, with the additional selection $\bar{X}_2 = \bar{a}_2$. Let q be one of those queries. In some cases the query $q \wedge (\bar{X}_2 = \bar{a}_2)$ can be simplified given that we know that the tuple $(\bar{a}_1, \bar{a}_2)$ is in the result set of q_0 (i.e., some conjuncts will be removed from the query). The following example illustrates this optimization, which we call *simplification under preconditions.*

Example 4.1 Consider a request for an instance of the node CustSuppPart(CK,SK,PK) in Figure 1. In order to expand this node we have to compute the following query. In the rest of the paper we note in bold the variables which are bound in the evaluation of the queries.

Q16(CK,SK,PK,PN) :- Order(OK,**CK**,_,_,_),
Part(**PK**,PN,_,_,_), LineItem(OK,_,**PK**,**SK**,_)

We observe that one way we could have reached this node is from CustSupp(CK,SK) via the edge Q12. To be more precise, the values binding the variables CK, SK, PK should be in the answer set of the query:

Q12(CK,SK,PK,PN) :- Part(**PK**,PN,_,_,_),
Order(OK,**CK**,_,_,_), LineItem(OK,_,**PK**,**SK**,_)

Based on this knowledge, it is possible to expand the instance of the CustSuppPart(CK,SK,PK) node by computing the following simpler query:

Q16'(CK,SK,PK,PN) :- Part(**PK**,PN,_,_,_)

Query simplification under preconditions is a form of query rewrite. Unlike traditional query rewriting techniques, this rewriting cannot be done manually by the person writing the queries for the site specification. For example, the user cannot manually replace Q16 in Figure 1 with Q16' for several reasons. First, this query is not safe for the static evaluation (since some variables in the head do not occur in the body). Second, we may not use this query even during dynamic evaluation if the time between page requests exceeds the age limit of the site. In that case we need to use the original query Q16. Third, the correctness of this rewrite depends on the user's browsing context. When there are multiple paths to a node in the site schema, we obtain different rewritings of the query depending on the path traversed.

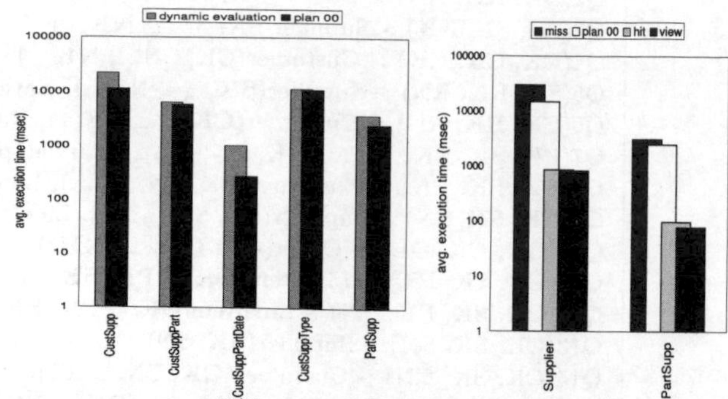

Figure 3: The left graph shows the speedups obtained from query simplification under preconditions. The right graph shows the running times of data caching (hits or misses), view materialization and the original queries.

When query simplification under preconditions modifies the query, it always reduces the running time. Figure 3 (left) shows the running times for the naive dynamic runtime policy versus the policy where all queries are simplified under preconditions (this plan is referred to as Plan 00 in the figures). As we can see, we obtain up to a 4 fold speedup in performance (for the node CustSuppPartDate). The figure shows all the nodes that benefited from query simplification under preconditions. In subsequent experiments, we always compare the additional optimizations to the plan obtained after applying query simplification under preconditions.

4.2 View materialization

Another way to speed up the web-site's performance is to precompute materialized views. The problem is to decide which set of views $\mathcal{V}$ to materialize in order to optimize the evaluation of the parametrized queries involved in the run-time of the web site. The problem of choosing a set of materialized views for a given query workload has received significant attention in the recent literature [24, 13, 12, 14, 6].

Two issues are important when deciding which views to materialize. First, it is essential to choose simultaneously the views *and* their respective indexes. Second, we need to consider views with outerjoins. In order to simultaneously optimize two queries q_1 and q_2 which have a common subquery q_3 (i.e., $q_1 = q_3 \wedge q_1'$ and $q_2 = q_3 \wedge q_2'$), it is attractive to materialize the outerjoin of the queries q_3, q_1' and q_2', i.e., materialize the expression $(q_3 ⟕ q_1') ⟕ q_2'$. In this case, the materialized result can be reused in both q_1 and q_2[3].

Example 4.2 As an example, assume we decide to materialize the following view with an index on the attribute SK:

V(CK,SK,PK,CN) :- Order(OK,CK,_,_,_),
LineItem(OK,_,PK,SK,_), Customer(CK,CN,_,_,_)

The view V can be used in answering the queries Q14, Q8 and Q22. We measured considerable speedup rates for the

[3]We note that algorithms for rewriting queries using views are actually simpler when joins are replaced by outerjoins.

respective nodes: 32 for PartSupp nodes and 18 for Supplier nodes. However, the additional space needed for the view and the indexes is around 600M (27% of the size of the original database).

4.3 Data caching

View materialization decreases query response time, but comes at the expense of significant space overhead and high maintenance costs. An alternative strategy is to cache at run-time the result of parameterized queries executed so far [8, 16] and reuse the result if the same computation is requested again. In this way we can store less data and still obtain significant speedups in certain cases. Furthermore, it is often cheaper to periodically invalidate data in a cache than to pay the cost of view maintenance.

Therefore, our optimization algorithm stores the result of certain parameterized queries in particular relations called *cache functions*. Formally, a cache function f is a pair $(q_f, input(f))$, where q_f is a conjunctive query and the input variables $input(f)$ are a subset of the distinguished variables of q_f. The function encodes a mapping $\bar{a} \mapsto S$, where $\bar{a}$ is a binding for $input(f)$, and S is the set of tuples in the answer of q_f whose projection on $input(f)$ is $\bar{a}$.

In our system, cache functions are implemented as tables in the DBMS, with the same schema as their corresponding view q_f. At run-time, the corresponding table is initialized to be empty, and tuples from q_f are inserted whenever q_f is evaluated with new bindings for the input variables. We impose the following invariant on the contents of a cache function: *for any constant $\bar{a}$, either the cache function does not contain any tuples from q_f whose projections on $input(f)$ is $\bar{a}$, or it contains all such tuples.*

An important question is how functions are used at run-time. Assume that we have a cache function $f = (q_f, input(f))$ stored in a table T and a query q to be executed. Let q' be the equivalent reformulation of q that uses the view q_f and let q'' be obtained by replacing the occurrence of q_f in q' by T. The result of the queries q and q'' are identical if and only if all the needed values for computing q'' are cached in T. Therefore, before computing q' we first need to check whether the needed values are cached, and if not, we compute them before submitting q''. In order to guarantee that we can perform this check, we limit the ways in which functions can be used. Specifically, we require that for any occurrence of T in q'', the variables corresponding to input variables of the cache function are also bound variables in q (and consequently in q''). If at least one of the queries that have to be evaluated in order to expand a certain type of node can benefit from a cache function, we say that the cache is used in this node.

Finally, an important difference between materialized views and cache functions concerns their maintenance policy. Here we assume that views are periodically updated, while functions are not. Instead, expired or invalidated tuples are simply dropped from a function.

Example 4.3 As we saw in Example 4.2, the view V significantly improved performance but at the price of high space overhead. Suppose that instead of V we want to maintain a semantically equivalent cache function, updated while expanding an instance of a node Supplier(SK) and used in the node PartSupp(PK,SK). For simplicity, we mark in bold the input variables of the cache function.

F(SK,CK,PK,CN) :- Customer(CK,CN,_,_,_),
LineItem(OK,_,PK,**SK**,_), Order(OK,CK,_,_,_)

Assume we store the content of the cache function in the table T. The query Q22' bellow is equivalent to the query Q22, in the case where the binding for the variable SK given in Q22 is cached in T.

Q22'(CK,SK,PK,CN) :- T(**SK**,CK,**PK**,CN)

At run-time, when we compute Q22', we first check to see if the given value for SK occurs in the cached input values in T. If we have a hit, we return the set of associated values for the variables PK,CK,CN, from which we selected the ones corresponding to the desired value of PK. In the case of a miss, we first compute the function's body with the additional binding for SK, insert the result in the table T, and then proceed as before.

The utility of caching

Figure 3 (right) illustrates the utility of caching. For each node in the figure we compare the average cost of computing the node in four cases: (1) using a view for one of the outgoing arcs, (2) using an equivalent cache function and assuming a hit, (3) similar to (2), but assuming a miss, and (4) no views or functions. Clearly, the time for case (1) is the lowest because no checks are needed. Case (2) provides speedup factors of 25 and 17 compared to case (4). Most interestingly, the overhead of case (3) compared to case (4) is relatively low (a slowdown of 2%) due to the extra cache check and update.

Choosing which functions to cache and how much memory to allot to each cache is an optimization problem with two constraints: (1) the size of the cache should be sufficiently large so that the hit rate guarantees better performance than no caching at all, and (2) the size of the cache should be much less than the size of the materialized view as to make caching the more attractive option.

Given estimates on the costs of evaluating the query in each of the cases described above, we can use the value probability distribution to estimate the minimal cache size that will yield savings. Specifically, suppose we denote the cost of evaluating a query with no caching by $c_{regular}$, the cost of evaluating a query with a cache hit by $c_{hit}(\mathbf{f})$, and the cost of evaluating a query with a cache miss by $c_{miss}(\mathbf{f})$. In the first step, we use the following formula to derive the minimum value of the hit ratio $\tau(\mathbf{f})$ that will yield savings for the cache $\mathbf{f}$:

$$\tau(\mathbf{f}) \times c_{hit}(\mathbf{f}) + (1 - \tau(\mathbf{f})) \times c_{miss}(\mathbf{f}) < c_{regular} \quad (2)$$

Given the minimum value of $\tau(\mathbf{f})$ and the value probability distribution (see Section 3), we can derive the minimum amount of memory M such that if we allot to the cache less than M we are guaranteed that we cannot achieve the required hit ratio. We assume that there exists a module in the system responsible for periodically removing items from the cache such that the hit ratio is maintained above the necessary threshold, the size of the cache does not exceed the limit and the age constraints are satisfied. The key for such a module is the use of the value probability distribution.

Up to this point we have only considered caching local to a particular node, i.e., a cache is updated in the same node in which it is used. In addition, the cache functions always concerned one of the queries on the arcs in its entirety. In the next section we extend the idea of caching to exploit the structure of the web-site definition. In particular, (1) a cache function can be updated in one node in the site and the result can be used in multiple nodes, and (2) a cache can be defined as a subquery or a superquery of a query appearing on an arc.

4.4 Lookahead computation

The key idea behind lookahead computation is to modify the definition of cache functions such that a query computed in a node F can be used later in one or more of F's descendants in the site schema. We describe two types of lookahead computations: *conservative* and *optimistic* lookahead. Intuitively, conservative lookahead represents the minimal amount of work that would have been done anyway at F and can be reused as much as possible in subsequent requests. In contrast, optimistic lookahead introduces additional computation that would not be needed at F, but is deemed to be useful for future nodes.

Conservative lookahead

Consider the expansion of an instance of the node CustSuppPart(CK,SK,PK) in our example, where we need to compute the following query:

Q17(CK,SK,PK,OD) :- Order(OK,**CK**,_,_,OD),
LineItem(OK,_,**PK**,**SK**,_), Part(**PK**,_,_,_,_)

In a subsequent click of the same user, we might have to expand an instance of a node CustSuppPartDate(CK,SK,PK,OD), with the same bindings for the variables CK,SK,PK. In order to do this, we need to compute the query Q19:

Q19(CK,SK,PK,OK,**OD**) :- Order(OK,**CK**,_,_,**OD**),
LineItem(OK,_,**PK**,**SK**,_), Part(**PK**,_,_,_,_)

Assume we updated a cache function for Q17 with inputs CK, SK and PK. As we can see, much of the computation performed for the function for Q17 is also useful for Q19. However, if we simply cache the result of Q17, we cannot use it unchanged for Q19 because Q17 projected out the attribute OK. Conservative lookahead would define a function with the same subgoals (since the subgoals of Q17 and Q19 are identical) and whose head includes all the attributes needed for both Q17 and Q19.

More generally, consider two consecutive arcs in the site schema, $F_1(\bar{X}_1) \longrightarrow F_2(\bar{X}_2) \longrightarrow F_3(\bar{X}_3)$, where the arcs are labeled with the queries q and q', respectively. We want to define a function in the first node and use it in the second. We want to update a cache while expanding the node F_1 and use it while expanding F_2. The cache f will have as body the intersection: $body(f) = body(q) \cap body(q')$. The distinguished variables of f include (1) all variables in f which are distinguished in q or q', and (2) all variables in f which also occur in $q-f$ or in $q'-f$, where the difference denotes the set difference of the subgoals of the respective queries. $input(f)$ are defined to be those variables of f that occur in $\bar{X}_1$. The cache f will be updated while expanding $F_1(\bar{X}_1)$. It can be used at node $F_2(\bar{X}_2)$ only if $input(f) \subseteq \bar{X}_2$; otherwise we cannot use it (because of the constraint we imposed on cache usability in Section 4.3).

The previous technique can be extended to a set of arcs that form a tree in the site schema. In this way, a cache updated at the root of the tree can be used in its descendants. By applying this technique to the set of nodes CustSupp, CustSuppType, CustSuppPart and CustSuppDate, we obtain the following cache function, updated in the node CustSupp and used in all the others.

F(CK,SK,PK,OD,OK,PN,PT) :- Order(OK,**CK**,_,_,OD),
LineItem(OK,_,PK,**SK**,_), Part(PK,PN,_,PT,_)

Optimistic lookahead

Optimistic lookahead performs while expanding a certain node an additional computation that may be usable for expanding later nodes. For example, consider the expansion of an instance of a node Customer(CK), where we need to compute the following query:

Q9(CK,SK,SN) :- Supplier(SK,SN,_,_,_), Order(OK,**CK**,_,_,OD),
LineItem(OK,_,PK,SK,_)

In a subsequent request, we might need to expand an instance of the node CustSupp(CK,SK). In order to do so, we need to compute the query:

Q12(CK,SK,PK,PN) :- Part(PK,PN,_,_,_), Order(OK,**CK**,_,_,_),
LineItem(OK,_,PK,**SK**,_)

Suppose we want to use a cache function for Q9 that also performs all the necessary computation for query Q12. To do this, we define a function that includes the common subgoals of Q9 and Q12, but also performs an outerjoin with the other subgoals of Q9 and Q12 that are not in the intersection. Specifically, we would define a cache function as follows:

F(CK,SK,PK,PN,SN) :- ((Order(OK,**CK**,_,_,_) $\bowtie$
LineItem(OK,_,PK,SK,_)) $⟕$ Part(PK,PN,_,_,_)) $⟕$
Supplier(SK,SN,_,_,_)

This cache is defined in the node Customer but can also be used in the rewriting of one of the queries of the node CustSupp. Note that in node Customer we do a join with Part that is not necessary there, but that will drastically reduce the cost of computing CustSupp.

More generally, consider two consecutive arcs in the site schema, $F_1(\bar{X}_1) \longrightarrow F_2(\bar{X}_2) \longrightarrow F_3(\bar{X}_3)$, where the arcs are labeled with the queries q and q', respectively. We want to update a cache in the first node that also performs the computation necessary for the second node. Let q_0 be the intersection of the bodies of q and q'. The cache f will have as body the expression $(q_0 ⟕ (q - q_0)) ⟕ (q' - q_0)$, where the difference denotes the set difference of the subgoals of the respective queries.. The distinguished variables are the union of the distinguished variables of q and q'. $input(f)$ are defined to be those variables of f that occur in $\bar{X}_1$. The cache f will be updated at node $F_1(\bar{X}_1)$. It can be used at node $F_2(\bar{X}_2)$ only if $input(f) \subseteq \bar{X}_2$: otherwise we cannot use it.

As with conservative lookahead, we can generalize optimistic lookahead to trees in the site schema. For example, the cache function shown above can also be used in the evaluation of the queries needed for the nodes CustSuppType, CustSuppPartDate, CustSuppPart and CustSupp.

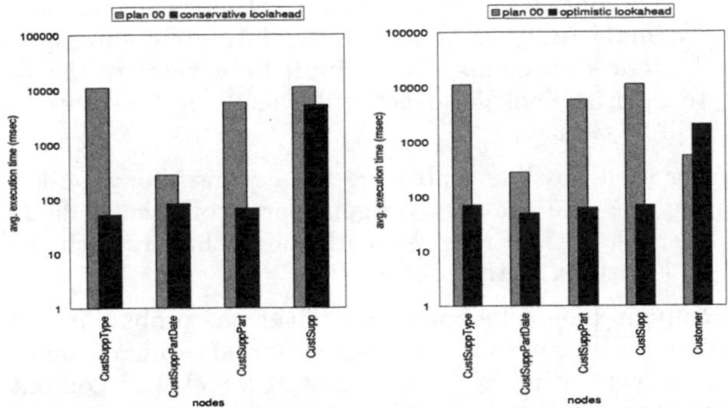

Figure 4: The left graph shows the benefits of conservative lookaheads performed in the node CustSupp. The right graph shows the benefits of optimistic lookahead performed at the node Customer.

The utility of lookaheads

Figure 4 shows the experimental results concerning lookahead computations. The first graph shows the speedups obtained by using conservative lookahead. We observe that the cost of computing CustSupp was not affected, while the speedups obtained for its descendants ranged from factors of 3 to 210. The second graph shows the results for optimistic lookahead. We observe that the node Customer that has a more expensive computation was slowed down by a factor of 3.7, while the speedups for its descendants varied from 5 to 161.

We end this section by noting that lookahead computations benefit from specific patterns in the structure of web sites. However, these patterns occur quite frequently in web sites because they correspond to a natural hierarchical organization of data.

5 Run-time management

After the discussion of possible optimizations in the previous section, we are now in a position to formally define run-time policies that encompass the different optimizations that we presented so far. To define run-time policies we first describe run-time schemas, which are the sets of views and caches over which the run-time policies are expressed.

5.1 Run-time schema

The run-time schema consists of a set of precomputed views $\mathcal{V}$ and a set of dynamically maintained functions $\mathcal{F}$, formally defined as follows.

- $\mathcal{V}$ is a set of view specifications, where a view specification is formally defined as a quadruple (N_V, Q_V, I, age_V), where N_V is the name of the database table storing the view, Q_V is a select-project-join-outerjoin expression defining the view, I is a set of indices on the view N_V and age_V is the maximum allowed difference between a data item in the view and the raw data.

- $\mathcal{F}$ is a set of cache function specifications, where a function specification is formally defined as a quintuple $(N_F, Q_F, Input_F, max\_size_F, min\_hit_F, age_F)$, where N_F is the name of the database table storing the function, Q_F is a select-project-join-outerjoin expression defining the function, $Input_F$ is a set of distinguished variables of Q_F which are inputs to the function, max_size_F is the maximum allowed size for the dynamically maintained table, age_F is the maximum allowed difference between a data item in the function and the raw data, and min_hit_F is the minimum hit ratio acceptable for the function.

5.2 Run-time policy

The run-time policy tells the system what to compute at every page request, i.e., how to use the run-time schema and data in order to compute the requested HTML page. There are several points to note about run-time policies. First, the action that the policy specifies does not depend only on the origin and destination of the hyperlink being followed, but may also take into consideration the path (or parts thereof) used to get to the origin. Hence, the actions in a run-time policy are parameterized by *contexts*, which we define below. The second point to note is that there are two types of possible actions: *query actions*, which specify how to obtain the data needed, and *update actions*, specifying when to update the dynamically maintained functions, and with which inputs.

Contexts are used to formalize the dependence of actions in the run-time policy on the previously visited nodes in the site graph. Formally, a path $[F_1, \ldots, F_n]$ in the site schema G is called the *context* of a request for a node $F(\bar{a})$ if $F = F_n$ and the previously requested nodes of the same user were of the form $[F_1(\bar{a}_1), \ldots, F_{n-1}(\bar{a}_{n-1})]$. A run-time policy fixes the maximum length of the contexts that are maintained at run-time. An action parameterized by a specific context is called a *rule*.

A run-time policy P_G for a site schema G is a directed graph, isomorphic to the graph of G, and whose nodes are labeled with the same Skolem terms as in G. In addition, nodes are labeled with set of update rules, and the arcs are labeled with sets of query rules. An *update rule* associated with a node F is a triple (H, f, ψ), where H is a possible context for the node F, f is the name of a given function and $\psi : Input_f \rightarrow \bar{X}$ is a mapping from the input variables of the function to the set of variable $\bar{X}$, which describes how to obtain input values for the function from the current binding of $\bar{X}$. A *query rule* associated with an arc $F_1(\bar{X}_1) \rightarrow F_2(\bar{X}_2)$ is a pair (H, q), where H is a possible context for the node F_1, and q is the parametrized query to be executed in order to obtain all the outgoing links of a node of type F_1 to nodes of the type F_2.

In order to facilitate inspection and manual construction of run-time policies in our work, we developed a language for describing run-time schemas and policies. We illustrate run-time policies with this language [11] in Figure 5.

5.3 Run-time algorithm

The execution engine of the web-site management system interprets the run-time policy. Execution proceeds in a similar fashion to the dynamic approach, with a few notable differences. Suppose the user requests an instance of the node $F(\bar{X})$ with a binding $\bar{X} = \bar{a}$ and a context $[F_1, \ldots, F_k]$ where $F_k = F$ (k is a constant depending on the run-time policy). We proceed in two steps:

1. Execute any update action (H, f, ψ) associated with the node F whose history H is a suffix of $[F_1, \ldots, F_k]$.

```
/* Run-time schema definition */
define view V as
   SELECT o.custkey l.suppkey, l.partkey,
   FROM LineItem l, Order o
   WHERE l.orderkey=o.orderkey
 max age = 2 hours
 define index on suppkey
define cache function T as
   SELECT o.custkey,l.suppkey,p.partkey,p.name,s.name
   FROM LineItem l, Order o, Supplier s
   WHERE l.orderkey=o.orderkey and s.suppkey=l.suppkey
 input custkey
 max size = 1M
 min hit ratio=0.3
 max age = 20min
/* Run-time policy for the node CustSupp */
 Node CustSupp(CK, SK)
   /* check and (eventually) update the cache */
   if context [Customer,CustSupp]
      update T with custkey → CK
 Link to CustPartType(CK,SK,PT)
   if context [Customer,CustSupp] compute
      SELECT f.custkey, f.suppkey, p.name, p.type
      FROM T f, Part p
      WHERE f.custkey=CK and f.suppkey=SK and
            f.partkey=p.partkey
   else compute
      SELECT v.custkey, v.suppkey, p.name, p.type
      FROM V v, Part p
      WHERE v.custkey=CK and v.suppkey=SK and
            v.partkey=p.partkey
```

Figure 5: Fragments of a run-time schema and policy for our running example.

Specifically, if $\psi(\bar{a})$ is not in the cache of f, we compute q_f with bindings $\bar{a} \circ \psi$ and add the result to the cache.

2. For each arc l outgoing from F we select the rule (H, q) with the most specific context matching $[F_1, \ldots, F_k]$ (i.e., for which there is no longer suffix of $[F_1, \ldots, F_k]$ matching another rule). We evaluate the query q with the binding $\bar{a}$.

5.4 Correctness of a run-time policy

Clearly, we need to impose constraints on run-time policies in order for them to be faithful to the declarative site definition. As we discussed earlier, updates to the database complicate the notion of correctness of a web site. We aim to formalize a minimal notion of correctness here: *given that the materialized views and cache functions are taken from the same snapshot of the database, then applying the dynamic evaluation strategy to that snapshot will produce the same result as invoking the run-time policy.*

The conditions are the following. Consider a link in the site definition $F_1(\bar{X}_1) \to F_2(\bar{X}_2)$ labeled with a query q. Suppose the corresponding link in the run-time policy is labeled by the pairs $(h_1, q_1), \ldots, (h_n, q_n)$, where the h_i's are contexts. The following conditions have to be satisfied:

- For each i, $1 \leq i \leq n$, q_i is an equivalent rewriting of q using the views and the functions under the preconditions implied by h_i (note that in this definition functions are used as view definitions).
- If one of the q_i's uses a cache function f, then the node F in the run-time policy includes a update action for f. The update action in the node F does not necessarily imply that the appropriate values are computed at F. Indeed, they may be computed elsewhere in the site (e.g., using lookahead computations), but the check is still necessary.
- For each possible context H for a request for a node of type F_1 and for each outgoing arc from the node F_1, there it exists a rule (h_i, q_i) labeling this arc such that h_i is a suffix of the context H.

Finally, it should be noted that given the probability distributions on contexts (see Section 3) and estimates on the cost of evaluating SQL queries, it is possible to compute the average waiting time for a request for an instance of a node F in the site schema for a given run-time policy. Hence, we can now compute the global cost of a run-time policy according to Formula 1 in Section 3.

6 Compiling site definitions

The ultimate goal of our work is to automatically compile a declarative site definition into an efficient run-time policy. We have shown that various optimizations can significantly improve the behavior of a web site. In section 5 we showed how to formalize the compilation problem as a search in a space of run-time policies. An important observation is that, in order to obtain the optimal run-time policy, it suffices to consider a finite number of policies.[4]

Given the number of parameters involved and the size of the resulting search problem, finding a compilation algorithm that is both efficient and produces high quality run-time policies is a problem in its own right. We now describe a set of heuristics to partition the search problem into manageable steps that are each relatively well understood. The steps that we describe are inspired by the results of our experiments. In our experiments, applying these heuristics provided significant improvement over the naive dynamic evaluation approach. Hence, we argue that our steps (which can be embodied by a collection of algorithms) provide a proof of the viability of automatic compiling of web-site specifications.

The steps are the following:

1. Apply query simplification under preconditions to all the nodes in the site schema.
2. Detect the set of *sensitive* nodes in the site schema: (1) the nodes whose average cost is above the acceptable limit on waiting time, and (2) the nodes with relatively high cost and probability of access. Let $q_1, \ldots, q_n$ be the parameterized queries on the arcs outgoing from the chosen nodes.
3. Apply a view materialization selection algorithm to $q_1, \ldots, q_n$, with the size and freshness constraints imposed by the web site. This step results in a set of views to materialize. In this step we can apply an exhaustive transformational algorithm similar to the one described in [24].
4. If a view V was a good candidate for improving performance in the previous step but was not chosen because of space or freshness constraints, consider including in the

[4] The crux of the claim is that it suffices to consider only a finite number of run-time schemas because there are only a finite number of views or functions that can be maintained and still be useful in a run-time policy.

run-time schema functions of the form (V, Inp), where Inp is a subset of the arguments of V.

5. For each such function which is usable for expanding a node F, consider applying conservative and optimistic lookahead optimizations, for all the subtrees rooted at F. The decision on which subtrees to consider should take into account the probability of visiting the descendants, given that the user visited F.

Figure 6 shows the results of applying these steps in two scenarios. In the upper figure we alloted enough space for the web site to be able to materialize a sizeable view (we allowed an additional 1GB to the original size of the database). In the lower figure we only alloted an additional 10MB. In the first case the run-time schema included the materialized join between Order and LineItem with 4 indexed columns. The view is used in almost all the nodes, and as a result, all the queries in the site ran in less than 8 seconds, and all but three in less than 400 milliseconds. In the second case the run-time policy includes a conservative lookahead in the node Supplier (which benefits the node PartSupp), and an optimistic lookahead computation in the node Customer which benefits the nodes CustSupp, CustSuppType, CustSuppPart and CustSuppDate. The running times of all the other nodes are comparable with that of the previous run-time policy. This example highlights the savings obtained purely by exploiting the structure of the web site, with very little memory overhead.

7 Implementation

The STRUDEL-R system[11] is implemented and fully operational, though the compiler from declarative specifications to run-time policies is relatively simple. The queries in the site definitions are given in SQL, and are allowed to contain selections, projections, joins, and outerjoins. Run-time policies are expressed in the language described in the previous section [11]. We note that it is also possible for a web site administrator to directly specify a particular desired run-time policy, bypassing STRUDEL-R's compiler.

A browsing session starts with a simple request for a root of the web site, which is precomputed. In order to employ our run-time policies, when an HTML page is served to the browser, the outgoing links (within the same site) are implemented as calls to a CGI-bin script. The script take as input the node in the site schema, the bindings for the variables associated with the node and the browsing context. It first calls the HTML generator, which in turn calls STRUDEL-R's execution engine with the same parameters. The execution engine follows the specification of the run-time policy. In doing so, certain functions can be updated. Finally, the result (the data contained in the page and information about the outgoing links) is sent back to the HTML generator which delivers the final page. The request, as well as all the statistics associated with it (utility of caches, response time, cardinality of resulting data, etc) are recorded in the web site trace.

In order to perform our experiments we also implemented a browser simulator. The input to this module is a set of probability distributions, as described in section 3. The simulator bypasses the HTML generator and calls the execution engine directly. Given a node in the site graph, the simulator randomly chooses the next node to request, according to the given probability distribution.

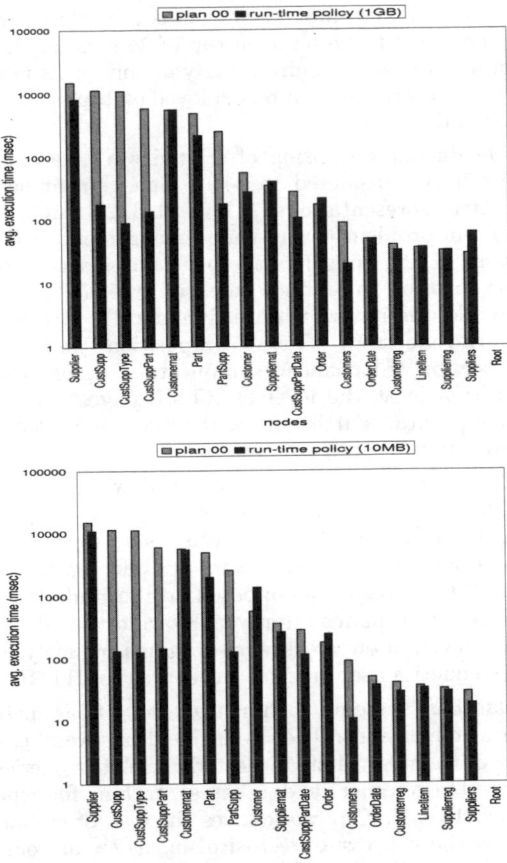

Figure 6: Results of two run-time policies. The upper graph shows a run-time policy in which 1GB of additional memory were provided, and the lower graph shows a policy when only 10MB was provided.

The system is implemented in Java, and all the database connections are done through Oracle's JDBC driver.

8 Conclusions and related work

Commercial products for constructing web sites from large databases and recent research prototypes are clearly moving in the direction of declarative specification of the structure and content of web sites. A critical issue that immediately arises is when to compute parts of the site. Currently, web site designers manually optimize site design in order to achieve reasonable performance, and this is a very labor intensive activity.

This paper described several techniques for optimizing the run-time behavior of web sites, and a framework in which declarative site specifications can be automatically compiled into run-time policies which incorporate these optimizations. Broadly speaking, many optimizations are easy to achieve if we have unlimited space. However, we have shown that, even with limited additional space, we can obtain order-of-magnitude speedups by exploiting the structure of the web site. We described a heuristic based algorithm for compiling a declarative web site definition into a run-time policy, which already yielded much better performance in our experiments. The problem of developing compilation algorithms that are both efficient and produce high-quality run-time policies clearly deserves significant further research. Finally, another important note about our framework and implementation is that they were purposely designed to be built on top of an existing database system and did not require modifying any of its internals. In fact, our prototype can be deployed on top of any JDBC compliant database.

To begin our discussion of related work, several other systems have considered web-site management based on declarative representations [7, 2, 4, 20, 3, 25] but none considered the problem of run-time management of the site. The work of [25] considers the problem of decomposing a site specification to produce an entire tree of HTML pages into smaller chunks which are dynamically invoked when pages are requested. This decomposition can also result in our version of lookahead computation, though their decomposition is at the level of HTML pages and not the underlying data. Furthermore, they do not perform their decomposition w.r.t. a cost function.

A large body of work is concerned with caching web documents (e.g., [5]). The work in [19] extends the idea to prefetching of pages based on statistics on web site browsing patterns. However, this work considers caches at the level of HTML pages, as opposed to the underlying content. The performance improvements and the added flexibility achieved in our work were obtained by analyzing the database queries that produce the content of HTML pages.

In database systems, caching the result of parameterized computations has also been considered in several contexts such as data integration [1], nested correlated queries (implemented in commercial databases), caching for expensive methods [16, 15]. Our work takes the idea of caching further into the context of web-site management: our decisions of what to cache are based on cost estimates, and we do not necessarily cache exactly the computation specified by the parameterized input, but possibly only parts of it or larger computations. In addition, our caching decisions are based on the structure of the web site.

As stated early on, there has been a significant amount of work that tries to optimize workloads of queries on DBMS. This work took the form of selecting views to materialize (and their indexes) (e.g., [24, 13, 12, 14, 6]), multiple query optimization [23] and index selection. All these techniques are of course applicable to our context, since a dynamically generated web site can be viewed as a workload of parameterized queries. However, in our context we can perform additional optimizations because of the known structure of the web site. Also, our application is different in that it has new age and time limit constraints, and because queries in the workload are considered in succession, not in parallel.

Finally, a related body of work uses invariants for query execution [22] (in the context of nested correlated queries) and [17] in the context of optimizing recursive trigger calls. In the latter work, the authors compile the code of the triggers depending on the context of the calls, which are similar to our simplification under preconditions.

Acknowledgments

The authors are thankful to Zack Ives, Ioana Manolescu, Rachel Pottinger, Eric Simon, Ken Ross and Alain Pirotte for many insightful comments on this paper.

References

[1] S. Adali, K. Candan, Y. Papakonstantinou, and V. Subrahmanian. Query caching and optimization in distributed mediator systems. In *SIGMOD*, 1996.

[2] G. Arocena and A. Mendelzon. WebOQL: Restructuring documents, databases and Webs. In *ICDE*, 1998.

[3] P. Atzeni, G. Mecca, and P. Merialdo. To weave the Web. In *VLDB*, 1997.

[4] P. Atzeni, G. Mecca, and P. Merialdo. Design and maintenance of data-intensive Web sites. In *EDBT*, 1998.

[5] M.-L. S. B. Chidlovskii, C. Roncancio. Semantic cache mechanism for heterogeneous Web querying. In *WWW8*, 1999.

[6] E. Baralis, S. Paraboschi, and E. Teniente. Materialized views selection in a multidimensional database. In *VLDB*, 1997.

[7] S. Cluet, C. Delobel, J. Simeon, and K. Smaga. Your mediators need data conversion. In *SIGMOD*, 1998.

[8] S. Dar, M. J. Franklin, B. Jonsson, D. Srivastava, and M. Tan. Semantic data caching and replacement. In *VLDB*, 1996.

[9] M. Fernandez, D. Florescu, J. Kang, A. Levy, and D. Suciu. Catching the boat with Strudel: Experiences with a Website management system. In *SIGMOD*, 1998.

[10] D. Florescu, A. Levy, and A. Mendelzon. Database techniques for the World Wide Web: A survey. *SIGMOD Record*, 27(3):59–74, 1998.

[11] D. Florescu, A. Levy, D. Suciu, and K. Yagoub. Run-time management of data intensive Web-sites. INRIA Technical report RR-3684, 1999.

[12] H. Gupta. Selection of views to materialize in a data warehouse. In *ICDT*, 1997.

[13] H. Gupta, V. Harinarayan, A. Rajaraman, and J. D. Ullman. Index selection for OLAP. In *ICDE*, 1997.

[14] H. Gupta and I. S. Mumick. Selection of views to materialize under a maintenance cost constraint. In *ICDT*, 1999.

[15] J. M. Hellerstein and J. F. Naughton. Query execution techniques for caching expensive methods. In *SIGMOD*, 1996.

[16] A. Kemper, C. Kilger, and G. Moerkotte. Function materialization in object bases: Design, Realization, and Evaluation. *TKDE*, 6(4):587–608, 1994.

[17] F. Llirbat, F. Fabret, and E. Simon. Eliminating costly redundant computations from SQL trigger executions. In *SIGMOD*, 1997.

[18] T. Nguyen and V. Srinivasan. Accessing relational databases from the World Wide Web. In *SIGMOD*, 1996.

[19] T. Palpanas and A. Mendelzon. Web prefetching using partial match prediction. Technical report CSRG-376. Departement of Computer Science, University of Toronto, 1998.

[20] P. Paolini and P. Fraternali. A conceptual model and a tool environment for developing more scalable, dynamic, and customizable Web applications. In *EDBT*, 1998.

[21] B. Proll, W. Retschitzegger, H. Sighart, and H. Starck. Ready for prime time - pre-generation of Web pages in tiscover. In *WebDB Workshop, in conj. with SIGMOD*, 1999.

[22] J. Rao and K. A. Ross. Reusing invariants: A new strategy for correlated queries. In *SIGMOD*, 1998.

[23] T. K. Sellis. Multiple-query optimization. *TODS*, 1988.

[24] D. Theodoratos and T. Sellis. Data warehouse design. In *VLDB*, 1997.

[25] M. Toyama and T. Nagafuji. Dynamic and structured presentation of database contents on the Web. In *EDBT*, 1998.

Extracting large-scale knowledge bases from the web*

Ravi Kumar Prabhakar Raghavan Sridhar Rajagopalan Andrew Tomkins

IBM Almaden Research Center

Abstract

The subject of this paper is the creation of knowledge bases by enumerating and organizing all web occurrences of certain subgraphs. We focus on subgraphs that are signatures of web phenomena such as tightly-focused topic communities, webrings, taxonomy trees, keiretsus, etc. For instance, the signature of a webring is a central page with bidirectional links to a number of other pages. We develop novel algorithms for such enumeration problems. A key technical contribution is the development of a model for the evolution of the web graph, based on experimental observations derived from a snapshot of the web. We argue that our algorithms run efficiently in this model, and use the model to explain some statistical phenomena on the web that emerged during our experiments. Finally, we describe the design and implementation of Campfire, a knowledge base of over one hundred thousand web communities.

1 Overview

The subject of this paper is the creation of knowledge bases by enumerating and organizing all web occurrences of chosen subgraphs. For example, consider enumerating all *cliques* of size four or more, where a clique is a set of web pages each of which links to all the others. Each such clique could represent an alliance between the creators of these pages: business partners, *keiretsus*, members of a family, etc. If we could enumerate all cliques on the web, then organize and annotate them into a usable structure, we would have created a knowledge base of all such alliances—patent as well as latent—as evident in the link structure of the web. More generally, we consider the creation of knowledge bases from an analysis of the web graph using the following paradigm: (1) identify a *signature* subgraph that is likely to arise in every element to be represented in the knowledge base; (2) devise a method for enumerating every instance of this subgraph in the web graph; (3) reconstruct, from each enumerated subgraph, the associated element of the knowledge base; and (4) annotate and index the elements to make the knowledge base usable. In the example above, step (1) could consist of identifying a clique of size four as likely to be present in every keiretsu (say); step (2) would require an efficient method for enumerating cliques of size 4; step (3) would require assembling all pages in a keiretsu given the portion represented by the 4-clique; and step (4) could consist of extracting and indexing statistically significant keywords from the assembled pages.

While the first of these steps is specific to the elements that will populate the knowledge base, the other three share some common challenges that will be our focus here. Foremost among these challenges: enumerating subgraphs on large graphs is, in the worst case, infeasible—from a complexity-theoretic as well as practical standpoint. Clearly, we must exploit the fact that the web is not a "worst-case" graph. To this end, we develop a stochastic model of the web graph that exhibits good agreement with statistics from the web, and show that a traditional random graph model could not exhibit such agreement. We develop an algorithmic paradigm for subgraph enumeration problems, run a concrete instance on the web, and show that its good performance is predicted by our web graph model. We describe the ongoing Campfire project, in which we enumerate, annotate, and index over 100,000 web communities generated using our methods.

Locally dense regions and communities. We begin with the following motivating example:

Example 1 *Consider the set of web pages that point to both* `www.boeing.com` *and* `www.airbus.com`*. There are more than two thousand such pages on today's web, including personal pages, aircraft museums, vendors, legal services, and so forth. Almost all of these pages represent some type of resource list of airplane manufacturers. The subgraph induced by these thousand pages, and the pages they point to, has a specific form: a number of resource lists*

*IBM Almaden Research Center, 650 Harry Road, San Jose, CA 95120. Email: {ravi, pragh, sridhar, tomkins}@almaden.ibm.com

Proceedings of the 25th VLDB Conference, Edinburgh, Scotland, 1999.

all point to some subset of a set of resources, in this case Boeing, Airbus, and dozens of other aircraft manufacturers. Moreover, pages within the subgraph frequently—but not always—cross-reference each other. (*See Figure 1.*)

A knowledge base containing all structures such as the one in Figure 1—aircraft manufacturers, long distance phone companies, US national parks, etc.—would clearly be of tremendous value. This motivates the definition of structures we call *bipartite cores:* a bipartite core in a graph consists of two (not necessarily disjoint) sets of nodes L and R, such that every node in L links *to* every node in R. Note that links from R to L, or within R or L, may or may not be present.

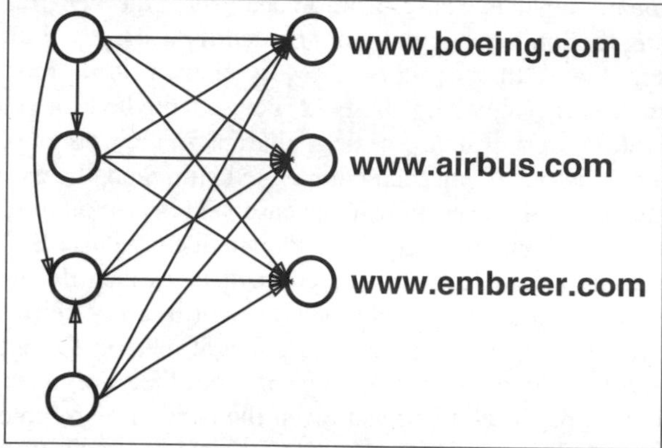

Figure 1: A bipartite core.

Indeed, one may envision building knowledge bases from enumerations of many different interesting structures—bipartite cores, cliques, *webrings* (which manifest themselves as star-shaped graphs with bidirectional links on the spokes), pages in a hierarchically organized website, or newsgroups and newsgroup discussion threads (which manifest themselves as bidirectional paths). The reasons for doing so include: (1) Such knowledge bases represent a better starting point for deeper analyses and mining than raw web data. Indeed, this is the goal of the Campfire project. (2) Structure can be used more effectively for searching and navigation. For instance, an agent responsible for searching a database containing dense bipartite graphs could pay more attention to text surrounding the relevant links, for their annotative value. (3) Fine-grained structures provide a basis for targeted market segmentation. (4) Studying these enumerated structures over time gives us insight into the sociological evolution of the web.

Challenges and approaches. From an algorithmic perspective, the naive "search" algorithm for enumeration suffers from two fatal problems. First, the size of the search space is far too large—using the naive algorithm to enumerate all bipartite cores with two web pages pointing to three pages would require examining approximately 10^{40} possibilities on a graph such as the web with 10^8 nodes. Second, and more practically, the algorithm requires random access to edges in the graph, which implies that a large fraction of the graph must effectively reside in main memory to avoid the overhead of seeking a disk on every edge access.

Although these obstacles appear insurmountable, we exploit additional structure latent in the web graph. For instance, the average number of links out of a page is small. However, the web is not a *random* sparse graph—it is a sparse graph containing many structures (*cliques* for instance) that arise only in far denser random graphs. The reason the web contains these structures is that, despite its overall sparseness, *local regions of the web are dense*. We propose novel algorithms that exploit this structure of the web graph to overcome these challenges.

To understand the performance of our algorithms, we develop a stochastic model for "web-like" graphs. The model exhibits two desirable properties: (1) it agrees with a number of statistical observations about the web graph, and (2) it is a useful tool in algorithm design, suggesting both explanations for the performance of our algorithms, and future directions for other efficient web analyses.

Here is a preview of a key technical element of our stochastic web graph model: intuitively, *new pages are created by borrowing random fragments of existing pages.*

Guided tour of this paper. In Section 2 we detail a number of measurements we have made of a snapshot of the web graph; these include the distribution of in- and out-degrees of nodes, and the numbers of bipartite cores. In Section 3 we motivate and develop our stochastic model for the web graph. We give analyses showing that our model—besides being a plausible high-level process for the creation of the web graph—explains our measurements from Section 2 in ways that traditional random graph models could not. Section 4 describes our three main algorithms: the elimination/generation paradigm for subgraph enumeration, an extension of a link-based web search algorithm for extending bipartite cores into communities, and an index extraction algorithm. In Section 5 we give some results of the Campfire project on organizing web communities.

1.1 Related previous work

Link analysis. A number of web search projects have used links to enhance the quality and reliability of the search results; see for instance HITS [19], its variants [5, 9, 10], and Google [6]. The connectivity server [4] also provides a fast index to linkage information on the web. Dean and Henzinger [12] combine heuristic improvements from [5] and [10] and apply these to the problem of finding related pages on the web.

Sociometrics. Statistical analysis of the structure of the academic citation graph has been the subject of much work in the Sociometrics community. As we discuss below, Zipf distributions seem to characterize web citation frequency. Interestingly, the same distributions have also been observed for citations in the academic literature. This fact, known as *Lotka's law*, was demonstrated by Lotka in 1926 [23]. Gilbert [16] presents a probabilistic model explaining Lotka's law, which is similar in spirit to our proposal, though different in details and application.

Data mining. Traditional data mining research (see for instance Agrawal and Srikant [1]) focuses largely on algorithms for finding association rules and related statistical correlation measures in a given dataset. However, efficient methods such as *a priori* [1] or even more general methodologies such as query flocks [29], do not scale to the numbers of "items" (pages) in the web dataset. This number is currently around four hundred million, which is two to three orders of magnitude more than the number of items in a typical market basket analysis. Further, the graph-theoretic structures we seek could correspond to association rules with very small support and confidence. Our conviction that these structures are interesting comes from additional insight about the web graph, rather than from traditional support and confidence measures.

In the case of bipartite cores, the relation we are interested in is co-citation. Co-citation is effectively the join of the web citation relation with its transpose, the web "cited by" relation. The size of this relation is potentially much larger than the original citation relation. Thus, we need methods that work with the original, without explicitly computing the co-citation relation.

The work of Mendelzon and Wood [25] is an instance of structural methods in mining. They argue that the traditional SQL query interface to databases is inadequate in its power to specify several structural queries that are interesting in the context of the web. We note that this is not the case here. The signature graphs we are interested in are relatively easy to specify in SQL.

Enumerating bipartite cores. In recent work [20] we reported enumerating over 200,000 bipartite cores from a snapshot of the web. The contributions reported in that paper were: (1) a special case of the algorithmic paradigm introduced here; (2) preliminary statistical observations about the web that we extend and explain here, using the web graph model developed in this paper; and (3) A random sampling experiment showing that barely 5% of the cores arose coincidentally. The large scale and high quality of such enumerated structures provides a compelling basis for building knowledge bases out of them. A number of these results, including Kleinberg's HITS algorithm [19], are discussed in the survey paper [21].

Henzinger *et. al.* [17] study algorithmic and memory bottleneck issues in related graph computations from a theoretical perspective, primarily to derive impossibility results. For a survey of database techniques on the web and the relationships between them, see Florescu, Levy, and Mendelzon [13].

2 Measurements of the web graph

In this section we describe a set of measurements generated from a crawl of the web from 1997, provided by Alexa, Inc. As our primary focus is the linkage patterns between pages,

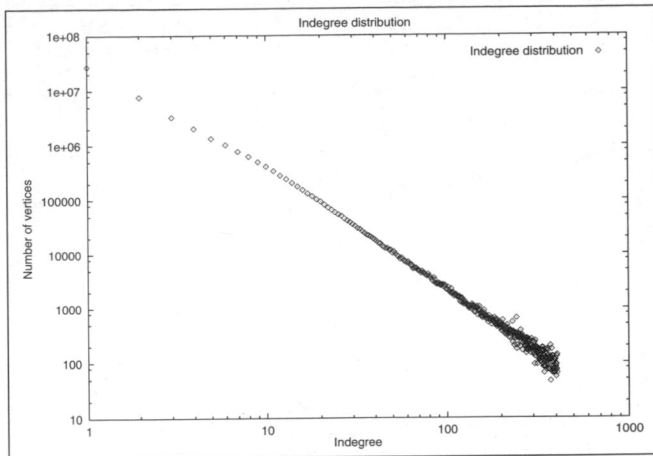

Figure 2: In-degree distribution.

we consider only the interconnection patterns of hyperlinks, and abstract away the textual content of each page. We view each page as a node of a directed graph, and each hyperlink as a directed edge. These measurements provide crucial insights for our web graph model (Section 3) as well as in our efficient enumeration algorithms (Section 4).

In-degree. We say that a hyperlink is an *out-link* of its source page, and an *in-link* of its destination page. We call the number of out-links and in-links of a page the *out-degree* and *in-degree* of the page, respectively. We begin by counting the in-degree of each page. Since the average out-degree is around eight, and since each edge contributes equally to the total in- and out-degree, the average in-degree must also be around eight. Our interest is in understanding not just the average, but the complete distribution of in-degrees. Figure 2 shows a log-log plot of the number of pages that have in-degree i as a function of i. The linearity of the curve indicates that the distribution is an inverse polynomial. Fitting an inverse polynomial to the data we find the probability that a page has i in-links to be roughly proportional to $i^{-2.1}$. We will also refer to inverse polynomial distributions as *Zipfian distributions* [30].

An important characteristic of Zipfian distributions is that they have high probability of deviating significantly from the mean. Thus, although the mean in-degree of a page is about 8, there is a significant probability that a page will have 1000 in-links (for example, approximately 100K pages on the web have $\geq$ 1000 in-links).

Out-degree. Our next observation concerns the roughly Zipfian distribution of out-degrees in the web graph. Figure 3 shows a log-log distribution of i versus the number of pages that have out-degree i. This curve also follows a Zipfian distribution. Fitting an inverse polynomial to the data, we note that a random web page has out-degree i with probability approximately $i^{-2.38}$.

$C_{i,j}$ counts.

In Section 1 we described bipartite cores, which consist of two sets of pages L and R, such that every page in L links *to* every page in R. If L contains i pages, and R contains j pages, we refer to the core as a $C_{i,j}$.

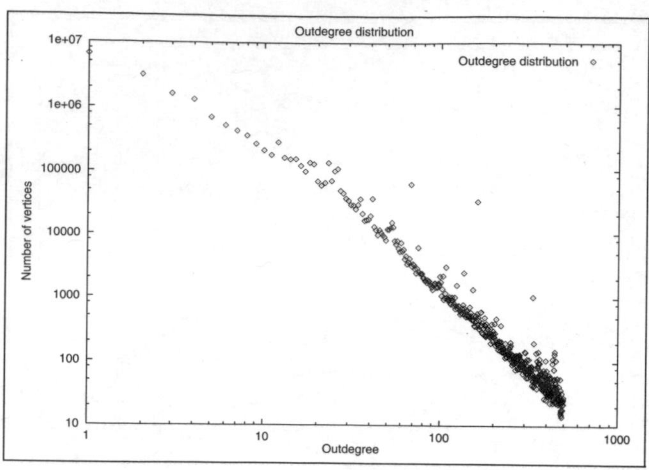

Figure 3: Out-Degree distribution.

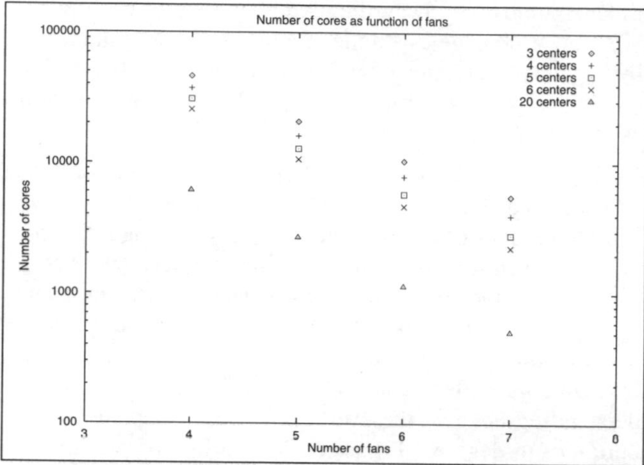

Figure 4: Number of $C_{i,j}$'s as a function of i.

During the exhaustive enumeration [20] of bipartite cores, we created a subgraph of the web consisting of all pages remaining after the algorithm prunes away all nodes of degree less than four. We enumerated all $C_{i,j}$'s in the resulting graph, for all $i \in \{2, \ldots, 7\}$ and $j \in \{3, \ldots, 20\}$. We now analyze the trends in that dataset. We begin by looking at the dependence of the number of $C_{i,j}$'s on i. Figure 4 shows a number of curves representing fixed values of j and four values of i—we display only counts for $i \geq 4$ since the pruning removed nodes of degree less than 4. To avoid clutter, we show values of j ranging from 3 to 6, and 20—intermediate values have the same form. As the figure shows, the number of $C_{i,j}$'s drops exponentially as a function of i, in this range.

Next, Figure 5 shows the curves representing fixed values of i for various values of j. The graph shows a log-log plot with linear behavior. Fitting an inverse polynomial to the data, the number of $C_{i,j}$'s as a function of j drops as j^{-c}, where the value of c is between 1.09 and 1.4.

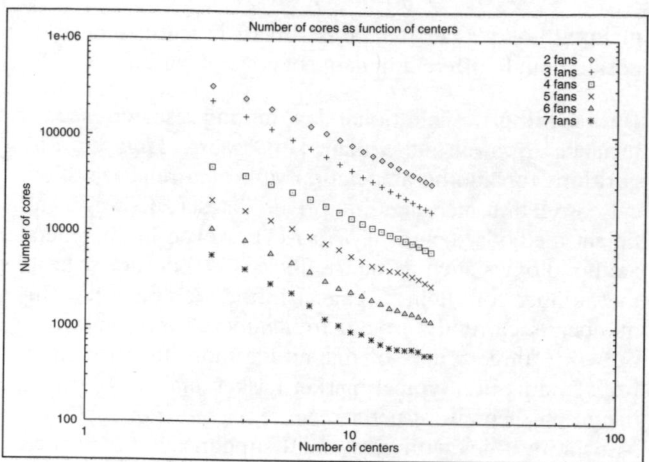

Figure 5: Number of $C_{i,j}$'s as a function of j.

3 Models for web-like graphs

In this section we present our model for web-like graphs, motivated by the following goals:

1. Understand various structural properties of the web graph—in- and out-degrees, neighborhood structures, etc. Of particular interest to us is the distribution of web structures that are signatures of the components of a knowledge base (e.g., the bipartite cores we are interested in).

2. Perform a more realistic analysis of algorithms on the web graph—this is of particular interest because worst case analysis of many algorithms is particularly pessimistic and unrealistic when applied to the web graph.

3. Predict properties of the web graph based on the model—this is of interest because it can lead to better algorithmic and structural insight.

We seek to model the linkage structure of the web graph. In particular, our models do not describe textual content

We begin with a discussion of the properties such a model should have, and then present a general framework for a class of graph models called *copying models*. Next, we give a simple concrete instance of a copying model, and analyze the concrete model to predict the parameters measured in Section 2. We show that measurements and predicted behavior exhibit strong agreement.

3.1 Desiderata for a web graph model.

1. *Simplicity*: It should have a succinct and fairly natural description.

2. *Plausibility*: It should be rooted in a plausible macro-level process for the creation of content on the web. We cannot hope to model the detailed behavior of the many users creating web content. Instead, we only desire that the aggregate formation of web structure be captured well by our graph model. Thus, while the

model is described as a stochastic process for the creation of individual pages, we are really only concerned with the aggregate consequence of these individual actions. Therefore we seek a model that is plausible at this aggregate level.

3. *Topics and communities*: It should provide structure corresponding to the strongly-linked "topics" that have emerged on the actual web, *but* it should not do so by requiring some *a priori* static set of topics that are part of the model description—the evolution of interesting topics and communities should instead be an emergent feature of the model.[1] Such a model has several advantages:
   - *Viability*: It is extremely difficult to characterize the set of topics on the web; thus it would be useful to draw statistical conclusions without such a characterization.
   - *Dynamism*: The set of topics reflected in web content has proven to be fairly dynamic. Thus, the shifting landscape of actual topics will need to be addressed in any topic-aware model of time-dependent growth.
4. *Statistics*: We would like the model to reflect many of the structural phenomena we have observed in the web graph. These include:
   (a) *Zipfian distributions*: A Zipfian distribution [30] for the number of links *to* a web page; in particular, the number of pages with i in-links is well-approximated [20] by $1/i^2$. A similar phenomenon has been observed in the study of scholarly citations [11, 23], and is the basis of studies in the sociology of scientific communities [16].
   (b) *Locally dense globally sparse structure*: Although the web graph is relatively sparse (the average number of links out of a page is roughly 7.2), the graph contains well over one hundred thousand bipartite cores with at least six nodes in them, even after mirrors are deleted. This is because the web graph, though globally sparse, has many locally dense regions.
5. *Evolution:* We should capture the phenomenon that the web graph has nodes and edges appearing and disappearing with time.

Interestingly and unfortunately, Items 3, 5, and all the criteria of Item 4, fail to hold for traditional models [7] of random graph theory. For instance, traditional random graph models would predict in- and out-degrees that are Poisson distributed, rather than the significantly heavier-tailed Zipfian distributions we have observed. It is easy to extend traditional random graph models to capture evolution, but this has not been addressed primarily because in standard models it is unlikely that interesting mathematical phenomena arise from evolution.

[1]In particular, we avoid models of the form "Assume each node is some combination of topics, and add an edge from one page to another with probability dependent on some function of their respective combinations."

3.2 Intuition for our models

Items 1 and 2 of the desiderata listed above ask that our model encapsulate a simple, plausible notion of content creation on the web. Our notion is based on the following intuition:

- some page creators on today's web may create content and link to other sites without regard to the topics that are already represented on the web, but
- *many* page creators will be drawn to existing topics of interest to them, and will link to pages within some of these existing topics.

Consider a user intent on creating a page about recreational sailing. Like most content creators, this user would probably wish to incorporate some links that would be of interest to potential visitors to the page. In order to gather together such links, the user would probably begin to browse around, perhaps using the many excellent resource lists[2] already available about recreational sailing, and choosing links based on his or her particular preferences within the topic. In the end, the resulting page would be another resource list about the topic, albeit one with a new personal spin.

We draw two lessons from this example: first, if a number of users have created links to a page, a new user will be more likely to link to that page than to a random page (partly because the page is probably of higher quality, and partly because the page is easier to find). And second, a user who has added a link to a sailing page is more likely to add another sailing link than an arbitrary link. Or said another way, if a user links to a page, and some existing resource list also links to that page, the user may link to something else appearing on the resource list.

Rephrasing these observations in purely graph-theoretic terms:

1. A new page is more likely to link to pages with higher in-degree.
2. A new page is more likely to link to two pages that co-occur on some resource list than to two random pages.

We therefore propose the following intuition for a simple process of link creation, which results in behavior obeying the previous observations: *A new page adds links by picking an existing page, and copying some links from that page to itself.*

[2]by *Resource lists* we mean pages that collect links on one or more topics, ranging in scope from a carefully-researched node of `Yahoo` to the small personal page of an individual who has collected several links about lateen-rigged sailing vessels.

We reiterate that this process is *not* meant to reflect individual user behavior on the web; rather, it is a local procedure which in aggregate works well in describing page creation on the web. The model also implicitly captures topic creation as follows: First, a few scattered pages begin to appear about the topic. Then, as users interested in the topic reach critical mass, they begin linking these scattered pages together, and other interested users are able to discover and link to the topic more easily. This creates a "locally dense" subgraph around the topic of interest. Furthermore, copying is a powerful mechanism for giving rise to bipartite cores: an author creates a resource list, and others create pages pointing to many pages on this resource list.

This intuitive view summarizes the process from a page-creator's standpoint; we now recast this formulation in terms of a random graph model.

3.3 A class of graph models

We model the web as an evolving graph, in which nodes and edges appear and disappear with time. Our models are described by four stochastic processes—*creation* processes $\mathcal{C}_v$ and $\mathcal{C}_e$ for node- and edge-creation, and *deletion* processes $\mathcal{D}_v$ and $\mathcal{D}_e$ for node- and edge-deletion. These processes are discrete-time processes. Each process is a function of the time step, and of the current graph.

Consider, for instance, the following node creation and deletion process: at time step t, independent of all earlier events, create a node with probability $\alpha_c(t)$. We could have a similar model with parameter $\alpha_d(t)$ for node deletion. Deleting a node also deletes all its incident edges. Clearly, we would tailor these probabilities to reflect the growth rates of the web and the half-life of pages respectively.

We present edge processes ranging from simple to complex to model the web with increasing fidelity. At this stage, we state a complex model we believe to be largely realistic. In Section 3.4, we show that even a greatly simplified process induces a Zipf distribution on in-degrees.

At each step we choose (possibly by random sampling) a node v to add edges out of, and a number of edges k that will be added to v. With probability β we add k edges from v to nodes chosen independently and uniformly at random. With probability $1-\beta$, we choose another vertex u, at random, and *copy* k edges from u to v. That is, after choosing a node u at random, create k (directed) edges (v, w) such that (u, w) is a random edge incident at u. One might reasonably expect that much of the time, u will not have out-degree larger than k; if the out-degree of u exceeds k we pick a random subset of size k. If on the other hand the out-degree of u is less than k we first copy the edges out of u, then pick another random node u' to copy from, and so on until we have enough edges. Such a copying process is not unnatural, and consistent with the qualitative intuition at the beginning of this section.

As a simple example of an edge deletion process, at time t, delete a random edge with probability $\delta(t)$.

3.4 The α and (α, β) models

We illustrate these ideas with a very simple special case that captures destination copying. We show that even in this simple case, the induced in-degree distribution is Zipfian. A node is created at every step. Nodes and edges are never deleted, so the graph keeps on growing. This corresponds to setting $\alpha_c(t)$ to 1, and $\alpha_d(t)$ and $\delta(t)$ to 0.

We now concentrate on the edge creation process. As each node comes into being, with probability $\alpha \in (0,1)$ it adds an edge to itself, and with probability $1-\alpha$ it picks a random edge and copies the edge onto itself, i.e., choose a random edge (u, w) created earlier and add the edge (v, w).

We now argue that the in-degree distribution of nodes in the α model is Zipfian.

Let $p_{i,t}$ be the fraction of nodes at time t with in-degree i. Assume t is sufficiently large that $p_{i,t} = p_{i,t+1}$. Then at time t there are $t \cdot p_{i,t}$ nodes with in-degree i, and at $t+1$ there are $(t+1) \cdot p_{i,t+1}$ such nodes. Therefore the probability that an additional node has in-degree i at time $t+1$ is $(t+1)p_{i,t} - tp_{i,t} = p_{i,t}$. The probability that a node with in-degree $i-1$ garners the single new edge is $(1-\alpha)(i-1)tp_{i-1,t}$, and the probability that a node with in-degree i gains the new edge and therefore becomes in-degree $i+1$ is $(1-\alpha)(it)p_{i,t}$. It must be the case that:

$$\begin{aligned}
(1-\alpha)(i-1)tp_{i-1,t} - (1-\alpha)(it)p_{i,t} &= p_{i,t} \\
(1-\alpha)i(p_{i-1,t} - p_{i,t}) &= p_{i,t} \\
(1-\alpha)i\frac{dp_{i,t}}{di} &= -p_{i,t} \\
(1-\alpha)\frac{dp_{i,t}}{p_{i,t}} &= -\frac{di}{i} \\
(1-\alpha)\ln p_{i,t} &= -\ln i \\
p_{i,t} &= 1/i^{\frac{1}{(1-\alpha)}}.
\end{aligned}$$

As an example, set $\alpha = 1/2$. In this process, each new edge flips a fair coin, and on heads points to the newest page, but on tails points to the destination of a uniformly-chosen random in-link. This process will then have an in-degree distribution given by $1/i^2$, following our observations of the web.

Now, consider an extension to the α model yielding the (α, β) model. Each time a new page arrives, a single edge is added as follows. The process flips two independent coins with probabilities α and β of coming up heads. The new edge (u, v) is built as follows:

The "destination" v is set based on the α coin: if it comes up heads, v is the newest page, and otherwise, v is the destination of a random link. The "source" u is set based on the β coin: if it comes up heads, u is the newest page, and otherwise, u is the source of a random link.

Since the original α model chooses edge destinations without reference to edge sources, the in-degree distribution of the (α, β) model will also be given by $p_{i,t} = 1/i^{\frac{1}{(1-\alpha)}}$. And since the same analysis applies if we flip the definition of "source" and "destination," the out-degree distribution q is given by $q_{i,t} = 1/i^{\frac{1}{(1-\beta)}}$ for large enough t.

For example, setting $\alpha = .52$ and $\beta = .58$, the model generates a graph with the following properties:

1. Pr[A node has in-degree i] $\longrightarrow i^{-2.1}$.
2. Pr[A node has out-degree i] $\longrightarrow i^{-2.38}$.

Both of these values match the web.

3.5 Resource list copying for bipartite cores

The (α, β) model of Section 3.4 induces Zipfian in- and out-degrees, but edges are added one at a time. In the general framework of Section 3.3, a model with more topic focus would copy several links from the same resource list. In this section, we explore the impact of copying multiple links on $C_{i,j}$ formation.

Recall that a $C_{i,j}$ is a bipartite core whose set L contains i nodes, and whose set R contains j nodes. We will refer to the elements of L as *fans*, and the elements of R as *centers*. In [20] it is shown that the web contains over 133,000 $C_{3,3}$ cores. We consider first a traditional random graph model, showing that such a model will not predict this large number of $C_{3,3}$'s. Next, we show that our model will in fact predict such a large number.

Example 2 *Let* $n = 100,000,000 = 10^8$, *and consider a traditional random graph model where every link is independently present with probability* 10^{-7} *(so that the average out-degree is 10, somewhat higher than reality). A 6-tuple of nodes* $L = \{a, b, c\}$ *and* $R = \{x, y, z\}$ *forms a* $C_{3,3}$ *if all nine edges from* L *to* R *are present, an event occurring with probability* $(10^{-7})^9 = 10^{-63}$. *There are approximately* $n^6/720 = 10^{47}/72$ *ways of choosing such 6-tuples. Thus the expected number of* $C_{3,3}$*'s is approximately*

$$10^{-63} \times 10^{47}/72 < 10^{-17} \ll 1,$$

Turning this calculation around, we can compute how large an out-degree an average page must have in the traditional random graph model, in order for 133,000 $C_{3,3}$*'s to arise in the web: roughly 1200, a number that is again inconsistent with the web.*

A similar calculation with our model yields an expected number of roughly 100,000 $C_{3,3}$'s. Consider the model of Section 3.3, with no deletion processes; thus we allow the copying of a random subset of links from a resource list. We omit the details, but the key idea is the following: the probability that a and b both copy the same 3 links from a single resource list c is $\Omega(1/n^2)$ even though the out-degree of a node is a small constant independent of n. When they both copy the same 3 links from the same source, a $C_{3,3}$ results. There are some technicalities that stand in the way of this being a mathematically provable statement; chief of these is the fact that in the early stages of copying, we may attempt to copy from a resource list that does not have 3 links to copy. However, in the "steady state" this should not be a significant effect; proving this rigorously remains an interesting open direction in random graph theory.

4 Algorithms

We identify three steps in the construction of a knowledge base of communities on the web: (i) efficiently enumerating the subgraphs (i.e., cores) of interest; (ii) collecting additional web pages related to each enumerated core to build a community; and (iii) extracting statistically significant information from each such community, leading to a searchable index of these communities. Accordingly in this section we describe three algorithms that we view as central to each of these steps: (i) the *elimination/generation* paradigm for efficient subgraph enumeration on web-scale graphs, using a relatively lean computational infrastructure; (ii) an extension of Kleinberg's HITS algorithm [19] that can take as input only a set of URL's present in a core (and no query terms), to produce authoritative web pages on the community centered around this core; and (iii) a method for extracting statistically significant index terms with which to index such communities. Note that the first and the third steps are generic to building indexable knowledge bases of communities from subgraph enumeration. The second is specified in terms of bipartite cores for concreteness, although the reader may readily see its extension to other subgraphs.

4.1 Enumerating cores

An algorithm in the elimination/generation paradigm performs a number of sequential passes over the web graph. The graph is stored as a binary relation on disk, and thus is not available for random access. During each pass, the algorithm writes a modified version of the dataset to disk for the next pass. It also collects some metadata in main memory which serves as state during the next pass. Passes over the data are interleaved with sort operations, which change the order in which the data is scanned, and constitute the bulk of the processing cost. During each pass over the data, *elimination* and *generation* operations are interleaved. The details are given below:

Elimination. There are often easy necessary (though not sufficient) conditions that have to be satisfied in order for a node to participate in a subgraph of interest to us. Consider for instance the problem of enumerating cliques of size four. We can prune any node whose in-degree or out-degree—*at any stage of the process*—is less than 4 (the significance of this will become apparent below). Consider next the example of $C_{4,4}$'s. Any node with in-degree 3 or smaller cannot participate on the right side of a $C_{4,4}$. Thus, edges which are directed into such nodes and the nodes themselves can be pruned from the graph. Likewise, nodes with out-degree 3 or smaller cannot participate on the left side of a $C_{4,4}$. We refer to these necessary conditions as *elimination filters*.

Generation. Generation is a counterpoint to elimination. Nodes that barely qualify for potential membership in an interesting subgraph can easily be established as either belonging to such a subgraph or not. Consider again the example of a $C_{4,4}$. Let u be a node of in-degree exactly

4. Then, u can belong to a $C_{4,4}$ *if and only if* the 4 nodes that point to it have a neighborhood intersection of size at least 4. It is possible to test this property relatively cheaply. We define a *generation filter* to be a procedure that identifies barely-qualifying nodes, and for all such nodes, either outputs a subgraph or proves that such a subgraph cannot exist.

If the test embodied in the generation filter is successful, we have identified an interesting subgraph. Furthermore, regardless of the outcome, this node can be marked for pruning since all potential interesting subgraphs containing it have already been enumerated.

Similar schemes can be developed for other structures.

Example 3 *Consider enumerating all subgraphs in which four web pages all point to one another. Then, any node with fewer than three links out of it can be eliminated. Likewise, any node with fewer than three links into it can be eliminated. Thus, the elimination filter for such an enumeration finds nodes with fewer than three in-links or out-links. The generation filter finds nodes with exactly three in-links or out-links, and checks to see whether the resulting set of four nodes, namely the original and the three adjacent nodes, is a clique. Notice that the generation filter is substantially cheaper in this case since there is no exhaustive enumeration of subsets of size* 4 *required as would have been the case if the in and out degrees had each been substantially larger than* 3.

Note that if edges appear in an arbitrary order, it is not clear that the elimination filter can be easily applied. If, however, the edges are sorted by source (resp. destination), it is clear that the elimination filter can be applied to the out-links (resp. in-links) in a single scan.

The generation filter is slightly more complicated to implement efficiently. We first explain how this can be done in 3 sub-passes over the data, in the setting of Example 3 above. In the first sub-pass, we construct a list of nodes with in-degree or out-degree 3, along with their in- or out-neighborhoods. We assume that this list fits in main memory during the second sub-pass; if not we can break the second sub-pass into several phases, each processing a main memory-sized chunk of candidates. In the second sub-pass, we verify that each node in the neighborhood points to all other nodes in the neighborhood. At the end of the second sub-pass we output all the interesting subgraphs, and in the third sub-pass, we delete all the candidate nodes.

Notice that the first and the third passes can be overlapped with the preceding and subsequent elimination filtering pass. Thus, the effective cost of the generation filter is just one pass over the data. Also, note that even the first round of the elimination/generation paradigm will eliminate a large fraction of the destination nodes in the graph (see Example 4 for details).

After one elimination/generation phase, the remaining nodes have fewer neighbors than before in the residual graph, which may present new opportunities during the next pass. We can continue to iterate until we do not make significant progress. Depending on the filters, one of two things could happen: either we repeatedly remove nodes from the graph until nothing is left or after several passes, the benefits of elimination/generation "tail off" as fewer and fewer nodes are deleted at each phase. If for instance our elimination filter were "delete all nodes with fewer than 100 in-links from `.com` pages", we will eliminate almost all pages on the web. On the other hand if the elimination filter were "delete all nodes with fewer than 3 out-links", we will reach a fixed point at which repeated elimination passes do not reduce the size of the residual graph substantially (though this may not happen after the first such pass).

Why should such algorithms run fast? We make a number of observations about their behavior:

1. The in/out-degree of every node drops monotonically during each elimination/generation phase.

2. During each generation test, we either remove a node u from further consideration (by developing a proof that it can belong to no instance of the subgraph of interest), or we output a subgraph that contains u. Thus, the total work in generation is linear in the size of the graph plus the number of subgraphs enumerated, assuming that each generation test runs in constant time. This is the case if we are enumerating a constant-sized subgraph; thus our algorithm is *output sensitive*.

3. As shown in Example 4 below, elimination phases rapidly eliminate most nodes in the web graph. A complete mathematical analysis of iterated elimination is beyond current techniques, but the example below shows that just the first elimination phase by itself is quite powerful.

Example 4 *Consider the enumeration of $C_{3,3}$'s. By the inverse quadratic law for in-degrees, eliminating nodes on the basis of in-degree prunes away any node with in-degree $\leq$ 2. As described in Section 2, out-degrees also have a (different) Zipfian distribution, and we can prune away any node with out-degree $\leq$ 2. Finally, applying a generation phase means that we also remove nodes with in/out-degree* equal *to 3. From simple calculations with the corresponding probabilities (noting for instance that $\sum_i 1/i^2 = \pi^2/6$), we determine that these elimination/generation steps would account for nearly 90% of the nodes in just the first iteration. Further iterations are less dramatic—both in theory and in practice.*

It is thus clear that the insights from our measurements and model drive the efficiency of the elimination/generation paradigm. A more mathematically precise analysis of the running time of elimination/generation in our model appears to be beyond the reach of current random graph theory, and is a worthwhile goal.

4.2 From cores to communities

We now describe an extension of Kleinberg's HITS [19], to expand a core $C_{i,j}$ into its surrounding community. For brevity we only detail the novel aspects of our extension; the reader is referred to [19] for details on the basic HITS algorithm. To make our description succinct, we use the notation $p \rightarrow q$ to denote that a web page p has a hyperlink to a web page q.

Given a query, the basic HITS algorithm assembles a small set of pages $\mathcal{R}$ (the *root set*) using a traditional text-based search engine and then constructs $\mathcal{R}'$ (the *expanded set*) by adding all pages that points to or is pointed to pages in the root set. I.e., $\mathcal{R}' = \mathcal{R} \cup \{p \mid p \rightarrow q, q \in \mathcal{R}\} \cup \{q \mid p \rightarrow q, p \in \mathcal{R}\}$. Each page p is associated with a pair of scores $h(p), a(p)$ which are initially set to 1. The algorithm iteratively updates these scores as $h(p) = \sum_{p \rightarrow q} a(q)$ and $a(p) = \sum_{q \rightarrow p} h(q)$, (after appropriate normalization). The top-scoring pages based on $a(\cdot)$ (resp. $h(\cdot)$) are termed "authorities" (resp. "hubs").

In our case, we have no text query; instead we have a core $C_{i,j}$. Since there is no query, the root set $\mathcal{R}$ is constructed using the following rule: the root set consists of (i) the core $C_{i,j}$, (ii) all pages pointed to by the nodes in L and (iii) all pages that point to at least two nodes in R. I.e.,

$$\mathcal{R} = L \cup \{p \mid q \rightarrow p, q \in L\} \cup$$

$$R \cup \{p \mid p \rightarrow q_1, p \rightarrow q_2, q_1, q_2 \in R\}.$$

We apply the basic HITS algorithm to this root set (making the assumption that the community around the core overlaps significantly with the root set). The result is a set of authoritative sources of information for that community, together with a set of hubs that collect together and annotate these authoritative pages.

4.3 Extracting index terms

Having enumerated the cores and run the generalized HITS algorithm above to expand each core into a full community, we must extract from each community index terms to build the knowledge base, and a summary that can be used to identify the contents of the community.

We make the following observation: the title of a page is likely to contain terms describing the page. Using this heuristic, we implement the following algorithm for identifying keywords that are useful for both indexing and summarization:

1. Extract the titles of all web pages in a community (which comprises the top 50 hubs and 50 authorities as returned by the algorithm of Section 4.2)
2. Eliminate stop words (e.g., articles, "html", "home", "page", "web", etc.)
3. Rank the resulting terms by frequency across the entire set of pages
4. Return the top ten most frequent words

We use the resulting set of 10 terms to index the community, and build a search utility against this index.

We are investigating more sophisticated strategies for the future. For instance, anchortext—the text in the vicinity of the "href" tags at the tails of hyperlinks—often represents a description of the contents of the linked-to page. Thus, anchortext of good hubs around links pointing to good authorities may be important for generation of index terms and summaries. We also plan to use phrase extraction techniques instead of simple keyword extraction.

5 Campfire: a knowledge base of communities

In this section we describe Campfire, a knowledge base of communities. We spell out the details of our experimental setup and give some examples of the communities indexed in Campfire.

5.1 Experimental setup

The communities in the Campfire knowledge base were constructed from a 1997 crawl of the web. In addition to extracting cores from the tape, we also extracted the state of `Yahoo` at the time of the crawl. As a reference point, `Yahoo` contained slightly over 16,000 topics in this crawl.

The trawling algorithms were run on a PC with a 333 MHz Intel Pentium II processor. The machine had 256M of main memory and a SCSI chain with multiple disk drives. The cost of running the trawling algorithm has two major components: (i) the data cleaning portion, and (ii) the pruning-based mining algorithm.

Since 2 mirrored copies of a page would generate a spurious $C_{3,j}$, we removed mirrors using the shingling method of Broder et al [8]. Our algorithm shingles 3100 pages/second. This implies that the entire set of potential fan pages (2 Million pages in our case) are shingled in about 10 minutes. Eliminating duplicates (pages which have the same shingle) runs at about the same speed (about 3000 pages/second). Thus, initial data cleaning takes only about half an hour. The major cost in the pruning step is in sorting the edge data. There are 60M edges in the dataset after shingling. The time to sort the edge set is 5 minutes per pass (on average). Our algorithms make 30 passes over the data (for i, j = 3, 3) in the worst case. The total time to trawl all $C_{3,3}$ cores was about 1.5 hours.

Having enumerated the cores, we then expanded them into communities using the algorithm of Section 4.2. To construct the root set, we augmented the fans and centers by following links on today's web. However, since the cores date back to 1997, and the half-life of a web page is of the order of a few weeks, many of these fans and centers no longer exist. Therefore, we only expanded those cores at least half of whose fans were still alive on today's web. For example, in the case of $C_{4,j}$ cores, 41% passed this test. Interestingly, the fraction of centers that are still alive is around 54%, suggesting that centers might have a higher half-life than fans. Running HITS typically expands a core into a community of between 100 and 4000 pages, with the average around 1300. The number of hyperlinks between these pages varies from 200 to 15000, with the average around 3500. Parsing each page takes a few milliseconds, but running the expansion algorithm takes between 2 and 10 seconds.

The final task is to index these communities. To accomplish this, we run the index term extraction algorithm on each of these communities. Given that we already have a parsed version of these pages, running this algorithm takes under a millisecond for each page. Using the keywords extracted, we index each community into Campfire.

5.2 Sample communities

We now provide 5 sample communities automatically generated by expanding $C_{4,j}$ cores. We present the top five hubs and authorities of each community along with indexing keywords, and a brief (manually-generated) annotation for the benefit of the reader. A more detailed list of pages can be found at `www.almaden.ibm.com/cs/k53/campfire.html`

To validate our conclusions further, we conducted the following experiment on the extracted communities. We took a random sample of about 100 communities and manually applied our resource compilation tools [10] to generate, for each community, a high-quality set of relevant pages. We then computed the overlap between these carefully-compiled resource lists and their counterparts in Campfire. The average overlap of sites was around 60%, suggesting that the quality and purity of communities extracted by our algorithm is fairly high.

6 Further directions

Our work raises a number of interesting directions and questions.

1. What are other instances of subgraph structures (possibly in conjunction with text patterns) that can be used to build valuable knowledge bases?

2. Our web graph model leads to very different areas for further investigation:

   (a) What are the dominant modes of content creation that different kinds of users exhibit, and how can these be reconciled (in an aggregate sense) with our model?

   (b) We have only scratched the surface of the rigorous mathematical analysis of our graph model (in contrast to the analysis of simpler, more traditional random graph models). Explicating the structure of graphs generated by our model is far more challenging than these traditional models, but a worthwhile goal in being able to predict the evolution of the web graph.

3. We have given illustrative examples and some general principles for devising elimination/generation algorithms for several interesting subgraph structures. Are there systematic ways for developing elimination/generation algorithms for any web subgraph enumeration problem? How do we exploit the interplay between the nature of the web graph and the elimination/generation phases? What are systematic techniques for tuning this methodology for given resource constraints?

4. In Campfire, we have a knowledge base built from web communities by extending the cores we enumerate from the web. We have not elicited significant semantic content (beyond extracting title words and indexing them for text search). Are there new paradigms for annotating and organizing these knowledge atoms in ways that are more valuable to users?

References

[1] R. Agrawal and R. Srikant. Fast Algorithms for mining Association rules. *Proceedings of VLDB*, Sept, 1994, Santiago, Chile.

[2] G.O. Arocena, A.O. Mendelzon, G.A. Mihaila, Applications of a Web query language, *Proc. 6th International World Wide Web Conference*, 1997.

[3] A.E. Bayer, J.C. Smart, G.W. McLaughlin, Mapping intellectual structure of scientific subfields through author co-citations, *J. American Soc. Info. Sci.*, 41(1990), pp. 444–452.

[4] K. Bharat, A. Broder, M.R. Henzinger, P. Kumar, and S. Venkatasubramanian. The connectivity server: fast access to linkage information on the web. *Proceedings of WWW7*, Brisbane, Australia, April, 1998.

[5] K. Bharat and M.R. Henzinger. Improved Algorithms for Topic Distillation in a Hyperlinked Environment. *Proceedings of ACM SIGIR*, 1998.

[6] S. Brin and L. Page, The Anatomy of a Large-Scale Hypertextual Web Search Engine. *Proceedings of the 7th World-wide web conference (WWW7)*, 1998.

[7] B. Bollobás, *Random Graphs*, Academic Press, 1985.

[8] A. Broder, S. Glassman, M. Manasse and G. Zweig. Syntactic clustering of the Web. In *Proceedings of the Sixth International World Wide Web Conference*, April 1997, pages 391-404.

[9] S. Chakrabarti, B. Dom, D. Gibson, J. Kleinberg, P. Raghavan and S. Rajagopalan. Automatic Resource Compilation by Analyzing Hyperlink Structure and Associated Text, *Proceedings of the 7th World-wide web conference (WWW7)*, 1998.

[10] S. Chakrabarti, B. Dom, S. Ravi Kumar, P. Raghavan, S. Rajagopalan, and A. Tomkins. Experiments in Topic Distillation. SIGIR workshop on hypertext information retrieval, 1998.

[11] H.T. Davis. The Analysis of economic time series., Principia press, 1941.

[12] J. Dean and M.R. Henzinger. Finding related pages in the World Wide Web. *Proceedings of the 8th WWW conference*, 1999.

[13] D. Florescu, A. Levy and A. Mendelzon. Database Techniques for the World-Wide Web: A Survey. SIGMOD Record 27(3): 59-74 (1998).

[14] E. Garfield, Citation analysis as a tool in journal evaluation, *Science*, 178(1972), pp. 471–479.

[15] E. Garfield, The impact factor, *Current Contents*, June 20, 1994.

[16] N. Gilbert. A simulation of the structure of academic science. *Sociological Research Online*, 2(2), 1997.

[17] M.R. Henzinger, P. Raghavan, and S. Rajagopalan. Computing on data streams. *AMS-DIMACS series,* special issue on computing on very large datasets, 1998.

[18] M.M. Kessler, Bibliographic coupling between scientific papers, *American Documentation*, 14(1963), pp. 10–25.

[19] J. Kleinberg, Authoritative sources in a hyperlinked environment, *Proc. ACM-SIAM Symposium on Discrete Algorithms*, 1998. Also appears as IBM Research Report RJ 10076(91892) May 1997.

[20] S. Ravi Kumar, P. Raghavan, S. Rajagopalan and A. Tomkins. Trawling emerging cyber-communities automatically. In *Proceedings of the 8th World-wide web conference*, 1999.

[21] J.M. Kleinberg, S. Ravi Kumar, P. Raghavan, S. Rajagopalan and A. Tomkins. The web as a graph: measurements, models and methods. Invited paper in *Proceedings of the Fifth Annual International Computing and Combinatorics Conference,* 1999.

[22] R. Larson, Bibliometrics of the World Wide Web: An exploratory analysis of the intellectual structure of cyberspace, *Ann. Meeting of the American Soc. Info. Sci.*, 1996.

[23] A.J. Lotka. The frequency distribution of scientific productivity. Journal of the Washington Academy of Sciences. 16, p.317, 1926.

[24] M. Marchiori, The Quest for Correct Information on the Web: Hyper Search Engines, *The 6th International World Wide Web Conference (WWW6)*, 1997.

[25] A. Mendelzon and P. Wood. Finding Regular Simple Paths in Graph Databases. SIAM J. Comp. 24(6), 1995, pp. 1235-1258.

[26] P. Pirolli, J. Pitkow, R. Rao, Silk from a sow's ear: Extracting usable structures from the Web, *Proc. ACM SIGCHI Conference on Human Factors in Computing*, 1996.

[27] E. Rivlin, R. Botafogo, B. Shneiderman, Navigating in hyperspace: designing a structure-based toolbox, *Communications of the ACM*, 37(2), 1994, pp. 87–96.

[28] E. Spertus, ParaSite: Mining structural information on the Web, *Proc. 6th International World Wide Web Conference*, 1997.

[29] D. Tsur, J. Ullman, S. Abiteboul, C. Clifton, R. Motwani, S. Nestorov, and A. Rosenthal. Query Flocks: A Generalization of Association Rule Mining. *Proceedings of ACM SIGMOD*, 1998.

[30] G.K. Zipf. Human behaviour and the principle of least effort. New York: Hafner, 1949.

AUTHORITIES	HUBS
www.midnightbeach.com/hs	user.pa.net/~rtregl/schools.html
www.home-school.com	larch-www.lcs.mit.edu:8001/~raymie/linklist.html
www.comenius.org/chnpage.htm	www.phonet.com/bsimon/educ-nat.html
users.aol.com/WERHSFAM/humor.html	home.sol.no/~hunwww/Elinker.htm
www.sound.net/~ejcol/confer.html	www.thefamily.net/educational.html
indexing keywords: *homeschool homeschooling school education resource*	

Homeschooling.

AUTHORITIES	HUBS
www.netimages.com/~chile	www.chetbacon.com/hotlinks.html
www.webring.org/cgi-bin/webring?list&ring=chile	bigsun.wbs.net/homepages/g/g/h/gghosey/links.html
www.firegirl.com	www.bizkid.com/food.htm
www.azstarnet.com/~coriel	www.catechnologies.com/cuisinesites.html
www.chilegod.com	allison.clark.net/pub/yoda
indexing keywords: *hot food sauce chile cooking recipes spicy peppers*	

Hot and spicy foods.

AUTHORITIES	HUBS
manufacture.com.tw	www.aunet.com.tw/steel.htm
www.rack.com.tw	www.commerce.com.tw/c/metal
www.mold.net.tw	www.acer.net/search/ee.htm
www.pack.com.tw	www.hinet.net/source/business/steel/3.htm
www.or.com.tw	www.hinet.net/source/business/steel/1.htm
indexing keywords: *taiwan corporation products international machinery*	

Taiwanese machine shops.

AUTHORITIES	HUBS
www.eren.doe.gov	www.physic.ut.ee/~janro/ab.html
www.doe.gov	www.csmi.com/oaatweb/links.htm
www.epri.com	www.azstarnet.com/~dcat/Rec_list.htm
www.epa.gov	www.beasley.com.au/news.htm
www.ashrae.org	wwwvms.utexas.edu/~whcii/energy/bldglnks.htm
indexing keywords: *energy wind renewable sustainable*	

Sustainable energy resources.

AUTHORITIES	HUBS
cancer.med.upenn.edu	www.allny.com/health/oncology.html
wwwicic.nci.nih.gov	micf.mic.ki.se/Diseases/c4.html
www.cancer.org	www.medmark.org/onco/onco.html
www.nci.nih.gov	www.meds.com/cancerlinks.html
www.nlm.nih.gov	www.mic.ki.se/Diseases/c4.html
indexing keywords: *cancer breast oncology*	

Cancer.

Aggregation Algorithms for Very Large Compressed Data Warehouses

Jianzhong Li
Dept. of Computer Science
Heilongjiang University
P. R. China

Doron Rotem
Lawrence Berkeley National Laboratory
Berkeley, CA 94720
USA

Jaideep Srivastava
Dept. of Computer Science
University of Minnesota
Minneapolis

Abstract

Many efficient algorithms to compute multidimensional aggregation and Cube for relational OLAP have been developed. However, to our knowledge, there is nothing to date in the literature on aggregation algorithms on compressed data warehouses for multidimensional OLAP. This paper presents a set of aggregation algorithms on very large compressed data warehouses for multidimensional OLAP. These algorithms operate directly on compressed datasets without the need to first decompress them. They are applicable to data warehouses that are compressed using variety of data compression methods. The algorithms have different performance behavior as a function of dataset parameters, sizes of outputs and main memory availability. The analysis and experimental results show that the algorithms have better performance than the traditional aggregation algorithms.

1. Introduction

Decision support systems are rapidly becoming a key to gaining competitive advantage for businesses. Many corporations are building decision-support databases, called *data warehouses*, from operational databases. Users of data warehouses typically carry out on-line analytical processing (OLAP) for decision making.

There are two kinds of data warehouses. One is for relational OLAP, called *ROLAP data warehouse* (RDW)[2,3,4]. The other one is for multidimensional OLAP, called *MOLAP data warehouses* (MDW) [5,6,7]. RDWs are built on top of standard relational database systems. MDWs are based on multidimensional database systems. A MDW is a set of *multidimensional datasets*. In a simple model, a multidimensional dataset in a MDW consists of *dimensions* and *measures*, represented by $R(D_1, D_2, ..., D_n; M_1, M_2, ..., M_k)$, where D_i's are dimensions and M_j's are measures.

The data structures in which RDWs and MDWs store datasets are fundamentally different. RDWs use relational tables as their data structure. That is, a "cell" in a logically multidimensional space is represented as a tuple with some attributes identifying the location of the cell in the multidimensional space and other attributes containing the values of the measures of the cell. By contrast, MDWs store their datasets as multidimensional arrays. MDWs only store the values of measures in a multidimensional space. The position of the measure values within the space can be calculated by the dimension values.

Multidimensional aggregation and Cube[1] are the most common operations for OLAP applications. The aggregation operation is used to "collapse" away some dimensions to obtain a more concise dataset, namely to classify items into groups and determine one value per group. The Cube operation computes multidimensional aggregations over all possible subsets of the specified dimensions.

Computing aggregation and the Cube are core operations on RDWs and MDWs. Methods of computing single aggregation and the Cube for RDWs have been well studied. In [11], a survey of the single aggregation algorithms for relational database systems is presented. In [1], some rules of thumb are given for an efficient

Proceedings of the 25th VLDB Conference, Edinburgh, Scotland, 1999.

implementation of the Cube for RDWs. In [12] and [13], algorithms are presented for deciding what group-bys to pre-compute and indexing for RDWs. In [14] and [15] , a Cubetree storage organization for RDW aggregation views is presented. In [16] , fast algorithms for computing the Cube operator for RDWs are given. These algorithms extend sort-based and hash-based methods with several optimizations.

Aggregation pre-computing is quite common in statistical databases[17]. Research in this area has considered various aspects of the problem such as developing a model for aggregation computations[18], indexing pre-computed aggregations[19], and incrementally maintaining them[20].

While much work has been done on how to efficiently compute aggregation and the Cube for RDWs, to the best of our knowledge, there is only one published paper on how to compute the Cube for MDWs[10], and there is no published work on how to compute single multidimensional aggregation for MDWs.

MDWs present a different challenge in computing aggregation and the Cube. The main reason for this is the fundamental difference in physical organization of their data. The multidimensional data spaces in MDWs normally have very large size and a high degree of *sparsity*. That has made data compression a very important and successful tool in the management of MDWs. There are several reasons for the need of compression in MOLAP data warehouses. The first reason is that a multidimensional space created by the cross product of the values of the dimensions can be naturally sparse. For example, in an international trade dataset with dimensions exporting country, importing country, materials, year and month, and measure amount, only a small number of materials are exported from any given country to other countries. The second reason for compression is the need to compress the descriptors of the multidimensional space. Suppose that a multidimensional dataset is put into a relational database system. The dimensions organized in tabular form will create a repetition of the values of each dimension. In fact, in the extreme, but often realistic case that the full cross product is stored, the number of times that each value of a given dimension repeats is equal to the product of the cardinalities of the remaining dimensions. Other reasons for compression in MDWs come from the properties of the data values. Often the data values are skewed in some datasets, where there are a few large values and many small values. In some datasets, data values are large but close to each other. Also, sometimes certain values tend to appear repeatedly.

There are many data compression techniques applicable for MDWs [8,9]. A multidimensional dataset can be thought of as being organized as a multidimensional array with the values of dimensions as the indices of the array. The rearrangement of the rows and columns of the array can result in better clustering of the data into regions that are highly sparse or highly dense. Compression methods that take advantage of such clustering can thus become quite effective.

Computing multidimensional aggregation and Cube on compressed MDWs is a big challenge. Since most large MDWs must be compressed for storage, efficient multidimensional aggregation and Cube algorithms working directly on compressed data are important.

Our goal is to develop efficient algorithms to compute multidimensional aggregation and Cube for compressed MDWs. We concentrate on single multidimensional aggregation algorithms for compressed MDWs. This paper presents a set of multidimensional aggregation algorithms for very large compressed MDWs. These algorithms operate directly on compressed datasets without the need to first decompress them. They are applicable to a variety of data compression methods. The algorithms have different performance behavior as a function of dataset parameters, sizes of outputs and main memory availability. The algorithms are described and analyzed with respect to the I/O and CPU costs. A decision procedure to select the most efficient algorithm, given an aggregation request, is also given. The analysis and experimental results show that the algorithms compare favorably with previous algorithms.

The rest of the paper is organized as follows. Section 2 presents a method to compress MDWs. In section 3, description and analysis of the aggregation algorithms for compressed MDWs are given. Section 4 discusses the decision procedure that selects the most appropriate algorithm for a given aggregation request. The performance results are presented in section 5. Conclusions and future work are presented in section 6.

2. Compression of MDWs

This section presents a method to compress MDWs. Each dataset in a MDW is first stored in a multidimensional array to remove the need for storing the dimension values. Then, the array is transformed into a linearized array by an array linearization function. Finally, the linearized array is compressed by a mapping-complete compression method.

2.1 Multidimensional Arrays

Let $R(D_1, D_2, ..., D_n; M_1, M_2, ..., M_m)$ be an n-dimensional dataset with n dimensions, $D_1, D_2, ..., D_n$, and m measures, $M_1, M_2, ..., M_m$, where the cardinality of the ith dimension is d_i for $1 \le i \le n$. Using the *multidimensional array method* to organize R, each of the m measures of R are first stored in a separate array. Each dimension of R is used to form one dimension of each of these n-

dimensional arrays. The dimension values of R are not stored at all. They are the indices of the arrays which are used to determine the position of the measure values in the arrays. Next, each of the n-dimensional arrays is mapped into a *linearized array* by an array linerization function.

Assume that the values of the ith dimension of R is encoded into $\{0, 1, ..., d_i-1\}$ for 1? i? n. The *array linerization function* for the multidimensional arrays of R is

$$LINEAR(x_1, x_2, ..., x_n)=x_1d_2d_3...d_n+x_2d_3...d_n+... +x_{n-1}d_n +x_n$$
$$= (...(x_1d_2+ x_2)d_3+...)d_{n-2}+x_{n-2})d_{n-1}+x_{n-1})d_n+x_n.$$

In each of the m linearized arrays,the position where the measure value determined by array indices $(i_1, i_2, ..., i_n)$ is stored is denoted by $LINEAR(i_1, i_2, ..., i_n)$.

Let $[X]$ be the integer part of X. The *reverse array linerization function* of the multidimensional array of R is

$$R\text{-}LINEAR(Y) = (y_1, y_2, ..., y_n),$$

where, $y_n=Y \bmod d_n$, $y_i=[...[Y/d_n]...]/d_{i+1}] \bmod d_i$ for $2\leq i\leq n-1$, $y_1=[[... [[Y/d_n]/d_{n-1}]...]/d_3]/d_2]$. For a position P in a linearized array, the dimension values $(i_1, i_2, ..., i_n)$ determining the measure value in position P, is $R\text{-}LINEAR(P)$.

2.2 Data Compression

The linearized arrays that store multidimensional datasets normally have high degree of sparsity and need to be compressed. It is desirable to develop techniques that can access the data in their compressed form and can perform logical operations directly on the compressed data. Such techniques (see [8]) usually provide two mappings. One is *forward mapping,* it computes the location in the compressed dataset given a position in the original dataset. The other one is *backward mapping*, it computes the position in the original dataset given a location in the compressed dataset.

A compression method is called *mapping-complete* if it provides forward mapping and backward mapping. Many compression techniques are mapping-complete, such as header compression [21] and chunk-offset compression [10]. The algorithms proposed in this paper are applicable to all the MDWs that are compressed by any mapping-complete compression method. To make the description of the algorithms more concrete, we assume that the datasets in the MDWs have been stored in a linearized array, each of which has been compressed using the header compression method[21].

The header compression method is used to suppress sequences of missing data codes, called *constants*, in linearized arrays by counts. It provides an efficient access to the compressed data by forward and backward mappings with I/O and CPU costs of $O(\log_2\log_2S)$, where S is the size of the header, using interpolation search[22]. This method makes use of a *header* that is a vector of counts. The odd-positioned counts are for the unsuppressed sequences, and the even positioned counts are for suppressed sequences. Each count contains the cumulative number of values of one type at the point at which a series of that type switches to a series of the other. The counts reflect accumulation from the beginning of the linearized array to the switch points. In addition to the header file, the output of the compression method consists of a file of compressed data items, called the *physical file*. The original linearized array, which is not stored, is called the *logical file*. Figure 1 shows an example. In the figure, *LF* is the logical file, *0*'s are the suppressed constants, *v*'s are the unsuppressed values, *HF* is the header and *PF* is the physical file.

3. Multidimensional Aggregation Algorithms

In this section, we assume that datasets in MDWs are stored using the compressed multidimensional arrays method presented in section 2. Without loss of generality we assume that each dataset has only one measure.

Let $R(D_1, D_2, ..., D_n; M)$ be a multidimensional dataset. A *dimension order* of R, denoted by $D_{i_1}D_{i_2}...D_{i_n}$, is an order in which the measure values of R are stored in a linearized array by the array linearization function with D_{i_j} as the jth dimension. Different dimension orders leads to different orders of the measure values in the linearized array. In the following discussion, we assume that R is stored initially in the order $D_1D_2...D_n$.

The input of an aggregation algorithm includes a dataset $R(D_1, D_2, ..., D_n; M)$, a *group-by dimension set* $\{A_1, A_2, ..., A_k\}\subseteq\{D_1, D_2, ..., D_n\}$ and an aggregation function F. The output of the algorithm is a dataset $S(A_1, A_2, ..., A_k; F(M))$, where the values of $F(M)$ are computed from the measure values of R by the aggregation function F. In the rest of the paper, we will use the following symbols for the relevant parameters:

d_i: the cardinality of the dimension D_i of R.

N: the number of data items in the compressed linearized array of R.

N_{oh}: the number of data items in the header of R.

N_r: the number of data items in the compressed linearized array of S.

H_{rh}: the number of data items in the header of S.

B: the number of data items of one memory buffer or one disk block.

3.1. Algorithm G-Aggregation

3.1.1 Description

G-Aggregation is a "general" algorithm in the sense that it can be used in all situations. The algorithm performs a multidimensional aggregation in two phases. In phase one, called *transposition phase*, it transposes the

LF: $v_1\, v_2\, 0\,0\,0\,0\,0\,0\,0\,0\,0\, v_3\, v_4\, v_5\, v_6\, v_7\, 0\,0\, v_8\, v_9\, v_{10}\, 0\,0\,0$
HF: $2 \quad 9 \quad 7 \quad 11 \quad 10 \quad 14$
PF: $v_1\, v_2\, v_3\, v_4\, v_5\, v_6\, v_7\, v_8\, v_9\, v_{10}$

Figure 1.

dimension order of the input multidimensionaldataset R into a favorable dimension order so that the aggregation can be easily computed. For example, let $R(A, B, C, D; M)$ be a 4-dimensional dataset that is stored in a linearized 4-dimensional array in the dimension order *ABCD*. Assume that $\{B,C\}$ is the group-by dimension set. The dimension order *BCAD* and *BCDA* are favorable dimension orders for computing the aggregation with group-by dimension set $\{B,C\}$. In phase two, called *aggregation phase*, the algorithm computes the aggregation by one scan of the transposed R. Figure 2 illustrates the algorithm. For expository purposes, we use the relational form in Figure 2. In reality, the algorithm works directly on the compressed linearized array of R.

The *transposition phase* assumes that W buffers are available. Data from the compressed array (physical file) is read into the buffers. For each data item in a buffer, the following is done: (i) backward mapping is performed to obtain the logical position in the logical file, (ii) the dimension values of the item are recovered by the reverse array linearization function, and (iii) a new logical position of the item in the transposed space is computed using the array linearization function. This new logical position, called a "tag", is stored with the data item in the buffer. An internal sort is performed on each of these buffers with respect to the tags of the data items. The sorted data items in these buffers are next merge-sorted into a single run and written to disk along with the tags. This process is repeated for the rest of the blocks in the physical file of R. The runs generated and their tags are next merged using the W buffers. A new header file is constructed for the transposed compressed array in the final pass of the merge sequence. Also, the tags associated with the data items are discarded in this pass. The file produced containing the (shuffled) data items is the new transposed compressed linearized array. The *aggregation phase* scans the transposed array once, and aggregates the measure values for each combined values of the group-by dimensions one by one.

To transpose the compressed multidimensional array of R, G-Aggregation reads, writes and processes the run files (of the same size as that of the original compressed file) $\left\lceil \log_W \left\lceil \frac{N}{B} \right\rceil \right\rceil$ times in the transposition phase. To perform the final aggregation, another scan is needed. In each of the two phases, each of the original and transposed header files are read once. If the aggregation is performed as early as possible, the size of the run files will be reduced and the I/O and CPU costs will be reduced dramatically. To improve the algorithm, we perform aggregation and merge at the same time. With such "early" aggregation, run files will be smaller than the original file, and the cost for creating and reading the transposed header file is deleted.

The improved G-Aggregation assumes that $W+2$ buffers, each of size B, are available. One buffer is used for input and another for output. W buffers are used as aggregate and merge buffers, denoted by *buffer*[j] for $1 \le j \le W$. Let $R(D_1, D_2, \ldots, D_n; M)$ be the operand, and $\{A_1, A_2, \ldots, A_k\} \subseteq \{D_1, D_2, \ldots, D_n\}$ be the group-by dimension set.

The improved G-Aggregation also consists of two phases. The first phase generates the sorted runs of R in the order $A_1A_2\ldots A_k$. Every value v in each run is a local aggregation result of a subset of R with an identification tuple of the group-by dimension values $(a_1, a_2, \ldots, a_k)$ as its tag. To generate a run, the algorithm reads as many blocks of the compressed linearized array of R as

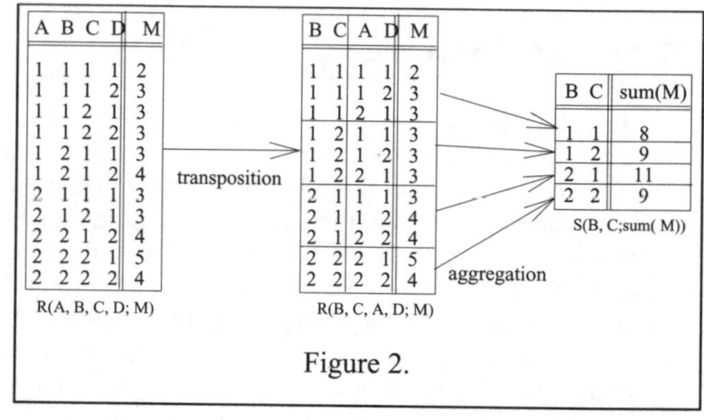

Figure 2.

possible, sorts them in the order $A_1A_2\ldots A_k$, locally aggregates them and fills the W buffers with the locally aggregated results. For each *buffer*[j], the algorithm reads an unprocessed block of the compressed linearized array of R to the input buffer. For each data item v in the input buffer the following is done: (i) backward mapping is performed to obtain the logical position in the logical file; (ii) the dimension values $\{x_1, x_2, \ldots, x_n\}$ of v are recovered using the reverse array linearization function, and (iii) the values $\{a_1, a_2, \ldots, a_k\}$ of the group-by dimensions $\{A_1, A_2, \ldots, A_k\}$ (called a "tag") are selected from $\{x_1, x_2, \ldots, x_n\}$ and then stored with v in the input buffer. An internal sort is performed on the data items in the input buffer with respect to the tags of the data items. The sorted data items, each of which is in the form (v, *tag*) in the input buffer, are next locally aggregated and stored to *buffer*[j]. The process is repeated until *buffer*[j] is full. When all the W buffers are full, all the data items in the W buffers are locally aggregated and merged in order of their tags, and written to disk to form a sorted run. The whole process is repeated until all runs are generated.

In the second phase, the sorted runs generated in phase one are aggregated and merged using W buffers. A new header file is constructed for the compressed array in the final pass of the aggregation and merge sequence, and the tags associated with the data items are discarded. The final compressed file produced is the compressed linearized array of the aggregation result. Figure 3 describes the main steps of the algorithm.

3.1.2 Analysis

We first analyze the I/O cost of G-Aggregation. In phase one, $\lceil N/B\rceil+(\lceil N_0/B\rceil-1)+\lceil N_{oh}/B\rceil$ disk block accesses are needed to read the original compressed linearized array of R, read the original header file and write the sorted runs to disk (the last block is kept in memory for use in the second phase). Here N_0 ($\leq N$) is the number of data items in all the runs generated in this phase. In phase two, $\log_W S$ passes of aggregation and merge are needed. Let N_I be the number of data items in the output of the Ith pass for 1? I? $\log_W S$. Obviously, $N_r=N_{\log_W S}$. A buffering scheme is used so that in the odd (even) pass, disk block reading is done from the last (first) block to the first (last) block. One block can be saved from reading and writing by keeping the first or last block in memory for use in the subsequent pass. In the last pass, we need to build and write the result header file. Thus,

$$\lceil N_r/B\rceil+(\lceil N_0/B\rceil-1)+\sum_{i=1}^{\lceil \log_W S\rceil-1} 2(\lceil N_i/B\rceil-1)+\lceil N_{rh}/B\rceil$$

disk accesses are required in the phase. In summary, the I/O cost of G-Aggregation is

Iocost(G-Aggregation)=$\lceil N/B\rceil+\lceil N_{oh}/B\rceil+\lceil N_r/B\rceil+\lceil N_{rh}/B\rceil+$

$$\sum_{i=0}^{\lceil \log_W S\rceil-1} 2(\lceil N_i/B\rceil-1).$$

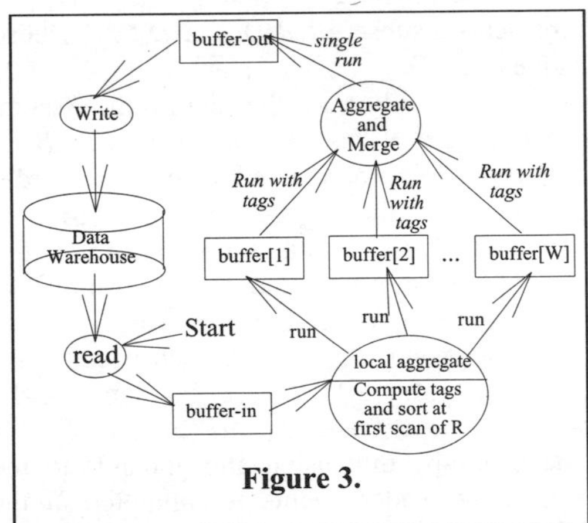

Figure 3.

From the algorithm, $N_r\leq N_0\leq N$ and $N_r\leq N_I\leq N_{I-1}$. The average value of N_0 is $\frac{(N-N_r+1)(N+N_r)}{2(N-N_r+1)}=\frac{N+N_r}{2}$. The average value of N_I is $\frac{(N_{i-1}-N_r+1)(N_{i-1}+N_r)}{2(N_{i-1}-N_r+1)}=\frac{N_{i-1}+N_r}{2}$.

Solving the recursive equation $N_I=\frac{N_{i-1}+N_r}{2}$, we have $N_I\leq\frac{1}{2^{i+1}}(N_r+N)+N_r$. Thus, on the average,

$$\sum_{i=0}^{\lceil \log_W S\rceil-1} 2(\lceil N_i/B\rceil-1)\leq \sum_{i=0}^{\lceil \log_W S\rceil-1} 2\frac{N_i}{B}\leq$$

$$2\sum_{i=0}^{\lceil \log_W S\rceil-1}\left(\frac{1}{2^{i+1}}\frac{N+N_r}{B}+\frac{N_r}{B}\right)\leq 2\left(\frac{N+N_r}{B}+\lceil \log_W S\rceil\frac{N_r}{B}\right).$$

Since $S\leq\left\lceil\frac{N}{BW}\right\rceil$, the average value of Iocost(G-Aggregation) is

AIOcost(G-Aggregation)=$O(\lceil N/B\rceil+\lceil N_{oh}/B\rceil+\lceil N_r/B\rceil+\lceil N_{rh}/B\rceil+2(\frac{N+N_r}{B}+\frac{N_r}{B}\left\lceil\log_W\left\lceil\frac{N}{BW}\right\rceil\right\rceil))$.

Next, we analyze the CPU cost of G-Aggregation. Let N_I be the same as above for $0\leq I\leq \log_W S$. In the first phase, for each value in the compressed linearized array of R, we need to perform a backward mapping and a reverse array linearization. A backward mapping requires one computation because we scan the array and header from the beginning. A reverse array linearization operation requires $2(n-1)$ divisions and subtractions. Thus, $2N(n-1)+N$ computations are needed for the backward mapping and reverse array linearization in this phase. $N-N_0$ computations are needed for the local aggregations in this phase. There are also $\lceil N/B\rceil$ blocks, each with size B, to sort. To sort a block with size B requires $B\log_2 B$ computations. Thus, $\lceil N/B\rceil B\log_2 B$ computations are required to sort the $\lceil N/B\rceil$ blocks. The N_0 output data items of the first phase are generated by merging W buffers. Generating a data item requires at most $\log_2 W$ computations. Therefore, the total number of CPU operations for the first phase is $2Nn-N_0+\left\lceil\frac{N}{B}\right\rceil B\log_2 B+N_0\log_2 W$. In the second phase, the algorithm performs $\log_W S$ iterations. The Ith iteration involves the aggregating and merging of $\left\lceil\frac{S}{W^{i-1}}\right\rceil$ runs into $\left\lceil\frac{S}{W^{i}}\right\rceil$ and output N_I data items. In the Ith iteration, $N_{I-1}-N_I$ aggregations are needed. The N_I output data items are generated by merging W buffers. Each data item requires at most $\log_2 W$ computations. In the final iteration, the N_r computations are needed to compute the result header counts. Therefore, the number of computations required by the second phase is

$$\sum_{i=1}^{\lceil \log_W S \rceil}((N_{i-1}-N_i)+N_i \log_2 W)+N_r = N_0+\sum_{i=1}^{\lceil \log_W S \rceil} N_i \log_2 W .$$

We can show that the the average value of CPUcost(G-Aggregation) is

$$\text{ACPUcost(G-Aggregation)}=O(2Nn+\left\lceil \frac{N}{B} \right\rceil B\log_2 B +$$

$$(N+2N_r+N_r\left\lceil \log_W \left\lceil \frac{N}{BW} \right\rceil \right\rceil)\log_2 W).$$

3.2 Algorithm M-Aggregation

3.2.1 Description

This algorithm is superior to G-Aggregation in case the aggregation result fits into memory. M-Aggregation computes aggregation by only one scan of the compressed linearized array of the operand dataset R. It reads blocks of the compressed linearized array of R one by one. For each data item v in the compressed linearized array of R, the following is done: (I) backward mapping is performed to obtain v's logical position; (ii) the dimension values of v, $(x_1, x_2, \ldots, x_d)$, are recovered by the reverse array linearization function from the logical position of$v$, and the values $(a_1, a_2, \ldots, a_k)$ of thc group-by dimensions are selected from $(x_1, x_2, \ldots, x_d)$; (iii) if there is a w that is identified by $(a_1, a_2, \ldots, a_k)$ in the output buffer, aggregate v to w using aggregation function, otherwise insert$v$ with $(a_1, a_2, \ldots, a_k)$ as a tag into the output buffer using hash method. Finally, the algorithm builds the new header file and writes the output buffer to the result file discarding the tags. M-Aggregation is described as follows.

3.2.2 Analysis

M-Aggregation requires one scan of the original compressed linearized array of R, and a writing of the resulting file. Also, the reading of the original header file and writing of the new header file are needed. The total I/O cost is

$$\text{IOcost(MAggregation)}=\lceil N/B \rceil+\lceil N_r/B \rceil+\lceil N_{oh}/B \rceil+\lceil N_{rh}/B \rceil.$$

The CPU cost of M-Aggregation is, for each data item in the compressed linearized array of R, the cost of performing a backward mapping, a reverse array linearization, a hashing computation, and an aggregation or memory operation (move data to output buffer), and the cost for computing the result header counts. As discussed in 3.1.2, a backward mapping requires only one computation. All the backward mappings for all data items in the compressed linearized array of R requires N computations. All the reverse array linearizations for all data items require $2N(n-1)$ computations. Steps (8) and (9) require N hash computations. Computing the result header counts requires N_r computations. The algorithm requires N-N_r aggregation and N_r memory operations also. Thus, CPU cost of the algorithm is at most

$$\text{CPUcost(M-Aggregation)}= 2Nn+Nh+N_r,$$

where h is the number of computations needed by a hashing computation.

3.3 Algorithm Prefix-Aggregation

3.3.1 Description

This algorithm takes advantage of the situation where

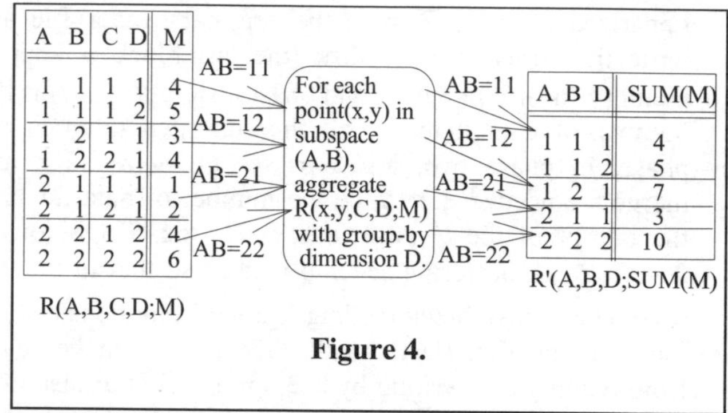

Figure 4.

the group-by dimension set contains a prefix of the dimension order $D_1D_2\ldots D_n$ of the operand dataset $R(D_1, \ldots, D_n; M)$. It performs aggregation in main memory by one scan of the compressed linearized array of R. It requires a memory buffer large enough to hold each portion of the resulting compressed linearized array for each "point" in the subspace composed by the prefix.

In rest of the paper, $R(D_1, \ldots, D_k, a_{k+1}, \ldots, a_{k+p}, D_{k+p+1}, \ldots, D_n; M)$ represents a subset of $R(D_1, \ldots, D_n; M)$ whose dimension values on $\{D_{k+1}, \ldots, D_{k+p}\}$ are $\{a_k, \ldots, a_{k+p}.\}$. We use an example to illustrate the algorithm. Assume that the operand dataset R has four dimensions A, B, C and D, and is stored in a compressed array in the order $ABCD$. Let us consider the aggregation with group-by dimension set $\{A, B, D\}$ that contains a prefix, AB, of the dimension order of R. Figure 4 shows an example of computing the aggregation with group-by dimension set $\{A, B, D\}$. For each "point" (a, b) in the subspace (A, B) of R, namely (1,1), (1,2), (2,1) or (2,2) in Figure 4, the algorithm performs the aggregation on$R(a, b, C, D; M)$ with D as the group-by dimension and appends to the result file. The new header counts is computed at the same time. This is the partial result of the aggregation under the fixed "point" (a, b). All partial results are concatenated to form the final aggregation result. The reason is that the subspace (A, B) is stepped through in the same order as the original R, i.e., the rightmost index is varying the fastest. Prefix-Aggregation is as follows.

3.3.2 Analysis

Prefix-Aggregation requires the reading of the original compressed array of R, and writing of the resulting file. Also, the reading of the original header file and writing of the new header file are needed. The total I/O cost is

$$\text{IOcost(Prefix-Aggregation)}= \lceil N/B \rceil + \lceil N_r/B \rceil + \lceil N_{oh}/B \rceil + \lceil N_{rh}/B \rceil .$$

The CPU cost of Prefix-Aggregation is, for each data item in the compressed linearized array of R, the cost for performing a backward mapping, a reverse array linearization, a comparison (step (9)) and an aggregation or a memory operation (move data to output buffer), and the cost of computing new header counts. Thus, the CPU cost of Prefix-Aggregation is at most

$$\text{CPUcost(Prefix-Aggregation)}=N(2n+1)+N_r.$$

3.4 Algorithm Infix-Aggregation

3.4.1 Description

This algorithm takes advantage of the situation where the set of group-by dimensions is an infix of the dimension order $D_1D_2...D_n$ of the operand $R(D_1, D_2, ..., D_n; M)$. Let $\{D_{t+1}, D_{t+2}, ..., D_{t+k}\}$ be the group-by dimensions, and D be the size of the subspace composed by D_1, D_2, ..., and D_t, denoted by $(D_1, D_2, ..., D_t)$. Obviously, $D_{t+1}D_{t+2}...D_{t+k}$ is an infix of the order $D_1D_2...D_n$. For each "point" $(a_1, ..., a_t)$ in $(D_1, ..., D_t)$, there is a sorted run, $R(a_1, ..., a_t, D_{t+1}, D_{t+2}, ..., D_n; M)$ in the order $D_{t+1}D_{t+2}...D_{t+k}$. $R(D_1, D_2, ..., D_n; M)$ is the connection of D such runs. The algorithm merges the D runs in order of $D_{t+1}D_{t+2}...D_{t+k}$ and perform aggregation at the same time. Figure 5 shows an example how the algorithm aggregates with group-by dimension set $\{C, D\}$ on $R(A, B, C, D, E; M)$. To perform the aggregation, R is first partitioned into 4 sorted runs, $R(1,1, C, D, E; M)$, $R(1,2, C, D, E; M)$, $R(2,1, C, D, E; M)$ and $R(2,2, C, D, E; M)$. Then all the runs are projected to $R(C, D; M)$ without removing repeated values. Finally, the projected runs are aggregated and merged to generate the aggregation result.

Infix-Aggregation assumes W buffers, each with size B, are available. If $W \geq D$, the algorithm becomes a main memory algorithm and requires only one scan of the compressed linearized array of R.

Infix-Aggregation is slower than Prefix-Aggregation when $W<D$ but not as memory intensive as Prefix-Aggregation. It requires $\log_W D$ passes to merge the D runs, where each pass merges W runs into one run. While the runs are merged, local aggregations are performed at the same time. When all the runs are merged into one run, the aggregation result is generated. In the algorithm, $R(a_1, a_2, ..., a_{t-1}, D_t, D_{t+1}, ..., D_{t+k}; M)$ represents the run for a "point" $(a_1, a_2, ..., a_t)$ in the subspace $(D_1, D_2, ..., D_t)$. The start position of the run $R(a_1, a_2, ..., a_t, D_{t+1}, D_{t+2}, ..., D_n; M)$ in the compressed linearized array of R can be computed by the following algorithm.

Using interpolation search[22] in step (2) and backward mapping, The I/O cost of the algorithm is at most $2\log_2\log_2 N_h$, and the CPU cost of the algorithms is at most $2\log_2\log_2 N_h+4(n-1)$, where N_h is the number of data items in *header*.

Infix-Aggregation starts by first computing the start positions of the D runs in the compressed linearized array of R. Then, it computes the aggregation in $\log_W D$ iterations. In the first iteration, it partitions the D runs into $\lceil D/W \rceil$ groups, each with W runs, and aggregates and merges each group into one sorted run in the order $D_{t+1}D_{t+2}...D_{t+k}$. For the jth group ($1 \leq j \leq \lceil D/W \rceil$), the algorithm reads as many blocks of each run in the jth group as possible, locally aggregates them by aggregation function F, and fills the local aggregation results in one of the W buffers. When all the W buffers are filled, the local aggregation results in the W buffers are aggregated and merged further and are appended to the jth new run. The process is repeated until all the data items in all runs of the jth group have been aggregated and merged into the jth new run. After the first iteration, the D runs are merged into $\lceil D/W \rceil$ sorted runs in the order $D_{t+1}D_{t+2}...D_{t+k}$. In the following iteration i^{th} iteration in general, the algorithm partitions the $\left\lceil \frac{D}{W^{i-1}} \right\rceil$ runs produced in the $(i-1)^{th}$ iteration

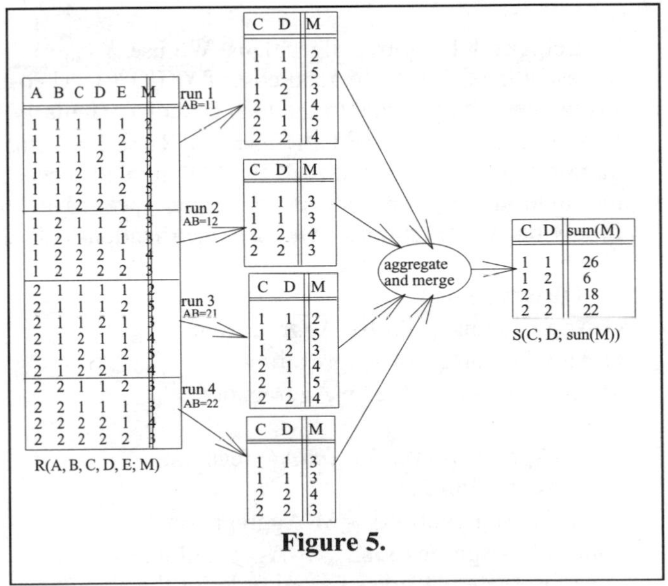

Figure 5.

into $\left\lceil \frac{D}{W^i} \right\rceil$ groups, each with W runs.

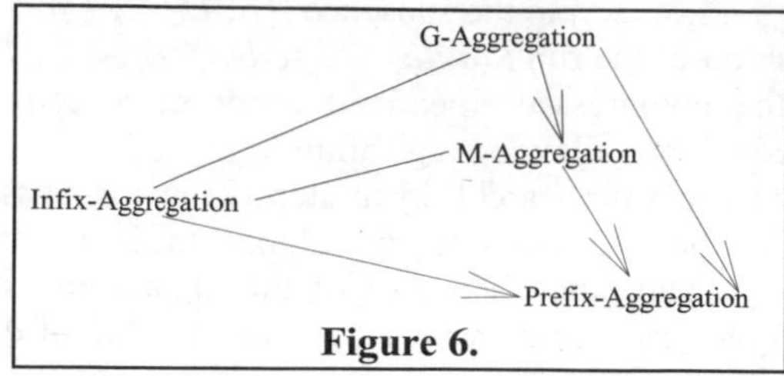

Figure 6.

Full analysis is omitted due to lack of space. We can show that the average value of CPUcost(Infix-Aggregation) is

$$\text{ACPUcost(Infix-Aggregation)} = O(2Nn + 2D\log_2\log_2 N_{oh} + 4D(n-1) + (N + N_r + N_r\lceil \log_W D \rceil)\log_2 W).$$

4. Comparisons of Algorithms and Selection Procedure

Let X and Y be two algorithms. We use $X \geq_{cost} Y$ to represent the fact that the total cost of X (I/O + CPU costs) is greater than or equal to the total cost of Y. Similarly $X \geq_{CPU} Y$ denotes that the CPU costs of X are larger than that of Y. From the analysis of the I/O and CPU costs of the algorithms proposed in the paper, we have the following observations. All the justifications of the observations are presented in [23].

Observation 1.

G-Aggregation $\geq_{cost}$ Prefix-Aggregation,
G-Aggregation $\geq_{cost}$ M-Aggregation ,
M-Aggregation $\geq_{cost}$ Prefix-Aggregation,
and
Infix-Aggregation $\geq_{cost}$ Prefix-Aggregation.

Observation 2.

If Infix-Aggregation $\geq_{CPU}$ M-Aggregation,
then Infix-Aggregation $\geq_{cost}$ M-Aggregation.

Observation 1 gives partial order of the algorithms in terms of I/O and CPU cost. According to the partial order, Prefix-Aggregation and M-Aggregation have better performance. However, these two algorithms require more memory. Further more, Prefix-Aggregation places special requirements on the group-by dimensions.

Figure 6 presents the order determined by observation 1. Each directed edge expresses a relation "$\geq_{cost}$". A dashed edge between two algorithms represents no cost domination relation can be determined between the two.

Below, a general decision procedure is given which is based on the order graph in Figure 8. In the procedure, α represents "the group-by dimension set contains a infix of the dimension order of the operand", β represents "the size of the aggregation result is not greater than the size of the available memory", γ presents " the group-by dimension set contains a prefix of the dimension order of the operand ", and η presents " available memory satisfies the requirement of Prefix-Aggregation ". Also A= Infix-Aggregation $\geq_{cost}$ G-Aggregation; **B**=Condition of Observation 2; **C**= Infix-Aggregation $\geq_{cost}$ M-Aggregation

5. Experimental Results

To examine the performance of the aggregation algorithms in practice, all the four aggregation algorithms have been implemented. The logical disk block size is 4k bytes.

To compare with the aggregation algorithms in relational database systems, we also implemented the sort and hash based traditional aggregation algorithms[11] in relational database systems. The experimental results show that our algorithms have much better performance than the traditional aggregation algorithms.

There are four factors that affect the performance of the aggregation algorithms. The *first one* is data density, namely the fraction of the cells in a multidimensional space actually containing valid data. The *second one* is compression ratio, this is affected by the number of dimensions and the size of the extra storage space required by compression methods. In the header compression method, the extra storage space is the header size. The *third one* is size of the available memory. The *last one* is dimension size, namely the number of elements in each dimension.

We conducted experiments to investigate the effect of the four factors on the performance of the algorithms. In the experiments, datasets were randomly generated, and stored using the compressed multidimensional array method for our algorithms and relational tables for the traditional aggregation algorithms. In each experiment, we randomly generated 10 aggregation operations, and then let each algorithm perform all the 10 operations, and we took the average execution time of the 10 operations as the final execution time of the algorithm. In the rest of this section, G, M, Infix and Prefix denote the G-Aggregation, M-Aggregation, Infix-Aggregation and Prefix-Aggregation. Sort and Hash denote the sort and hash based relational aggregation algorithms, and "$X>Y$" means "the execution time of algorithm X is greater than that of Y".

5.1. Performance Related to Number of Valid Data Entries

In these experiments, the benchmark dataset scheme consists of 15 dimensions and one measure. The data types of all dimensions are 4-byte integer. The data type of the measure is 4-byte float number. We randomly generated 4 versions of the benchmark with 1,000,000, 5,000,000, 10,000,000 and 20,000,000 valid data entries. The header size of each dataset is 50% of the dataset size. The aggregation result size of each dataset is 20% of the dataset size. Since M, Infix and Prefix have special requirements on aggregation dimensions and memory size, five sets of experiments were conducted.

In the first set of experiments, available memory size is fixed at 640K bytes. The memory size and the aggregation operations performed in this set of experiments satisfy the requirements of Prefix. Figure 7 presents the execution times of the algorithms while the number of data entries varies from 1,000,000 to 20,000,000. The figures indicate that Hash>Sort>G >Prefix, namely Prefix is the fastest algorithm and Hash is the slowest one. The figures also show that the larger the dataset size is the larger the ratio of the execution times of Sort and Hash to the execution time of G or Prefix. The reason is that the I/O cost of Sort and Hash increases much faster than that of G and Prefix when the operand

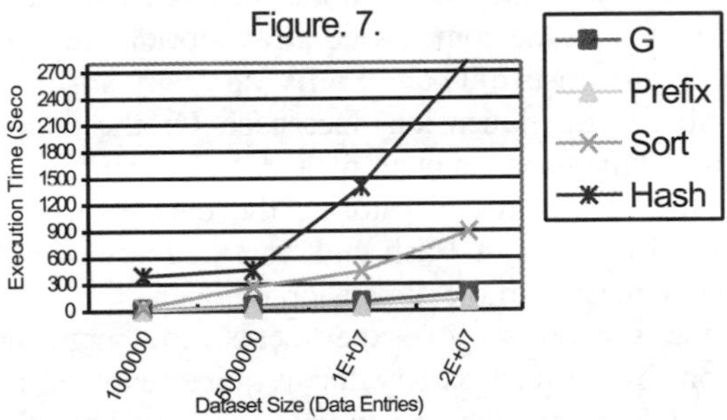

Figure. 7.

dataset size increases. In the figures, we also see that all the execution times have a big jump at the data entry number 5,000,000. It is because that the available memory size can hold the whole aggregation result when the dataset size smaller than 5,000,000.

In the second set of experiments, available memory size is fixed at 640K bytes for G, Infix and Sort, and the aggregation operations performed satisfy the requirements of Infix. In order to get the aggregation results in accept time using Hash algorithm, the available memory size is set to 20% of the aggregation result size for Hash. Figure 8 presents the execution times of the algorithms while the data entry number varies from 1,000,000 to 20,000,000. The figures indicate that Hash>Sort>G >Infix.

In the third set of experiments, available memory size is the size of the maximum aggregation result, 125M bytes, namely 20% of the maximum dataset size 20,000,000, so that all the aggregation results fit in memory. Figure 9 presents the experiment results. It indicates that all the execution times are smaller than the first and second sets of experiments. The reason is that large available memory makes all algorithms faster. The figure also shows Sort>Hash>G >M when the data entry number is greater than 5,000,000. In the figures, we see that the execution times of G are smaller than the

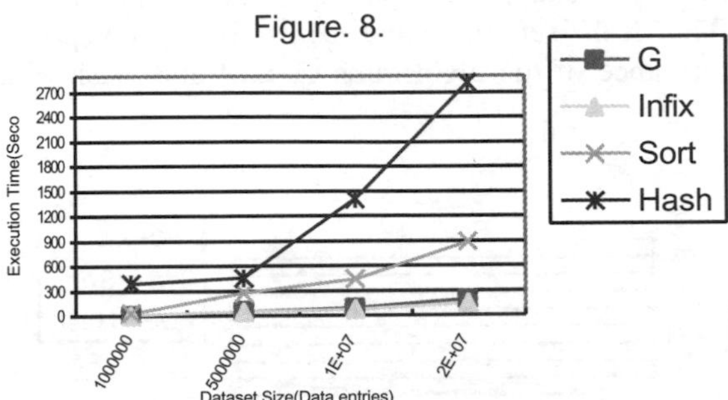

Figure. 8.

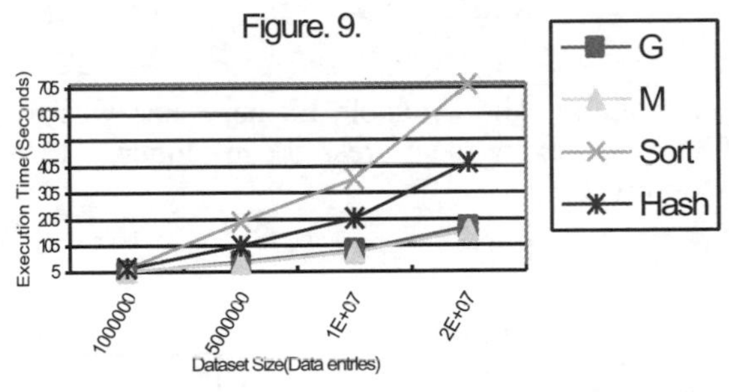

Figure. 9.

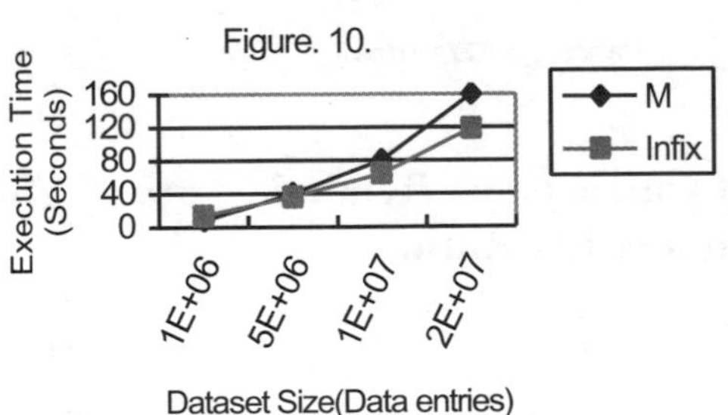

Figure. 10.

execution times of M when the data entry number is smaller than 5,000,000. It is because that when the dataset fit in memory M spends more CPU time for hashing computation.

The fourth set of experiments is to study the performance of the algorithms M, Infix and Prefix in case of the aggregation results fitting in memory. The parameters are the same as in the third set experiments. Figure 10 presents the comparisons of M and Infix, and figure 11 presents the comparison of M and Prefix.

The fifth set of experiments is to compare the performance of the algorithms G, Sort and Hash without

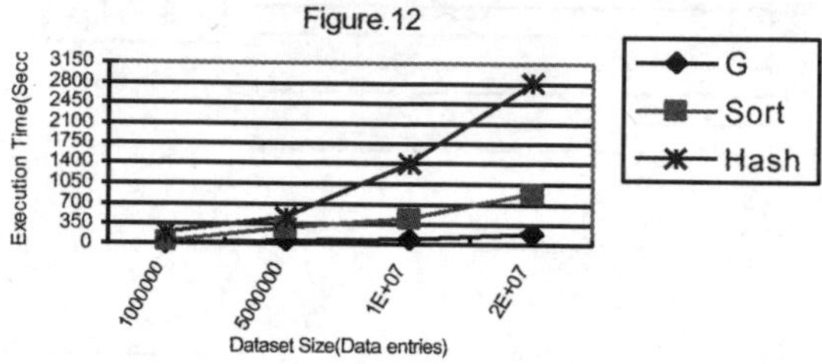

any restriction. The available memory size was fixed at 640K. The experiment results in Figure 12 show Hash>Sort>G.

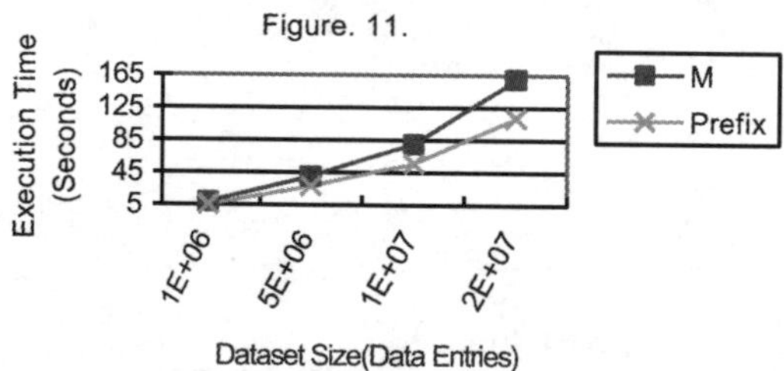

5.2. Performance Related to Data Compression Ratio

We first conducted experiments to study the performance of the algorithms while the dataset size is fixed and the dimension number, which has great effect on the compression ratio, varies. For the experiments, the dimension number of the operand datasets was varied from 2 to 20, the number of data entries was fixed at 10,000,000 data entries, each with 64 bytes, and the aggregation result size was kept at 2,000,000 data entries. Similar to section 5.1, we conducted five sets of experiments to meet the requirements of Prefix, Infix and

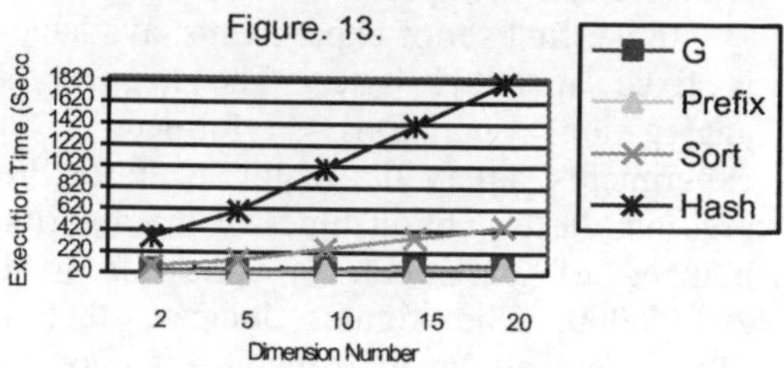

M. In the first two sets of experiments, the available memory size is fixed at 12.5M bytes.

In the first set of the experiments, the aggregation operations performed satisfy the requirements of Prefix. Figure 13 presents the experiment results. This figure shows that the execution times of G and Prefix increase very slowly while the dimension number increases. The reason is that the dimension number of a dataset does not effect the size of the compressed array storing the dataset so that the I/O costs of G and Prefix vary very small when the number of the dimensions increases. On the opposite, when the dimension number of a dataset increases, the size of the relational table storing the dataset increases. Thus, the I/O costs of Hash and Sort increase very fast with the increasing of the dimension number.

In the second set of experiments, the aggregation operations performed satisfy the requirements of Infix. Figure 14 presents the experiment results. This figure shows that the execution times of Sort and Hash still increase much faster than Infix and G with the same reason in the first set of experiments.

In the third set of experiments, To meet the requirement of M, memory size is fixed at 125M bytes to hold the aggregation result. Figure 15 presents the experiment results. The figure shows that the execution times of Sort and Hash increase much faster than M and

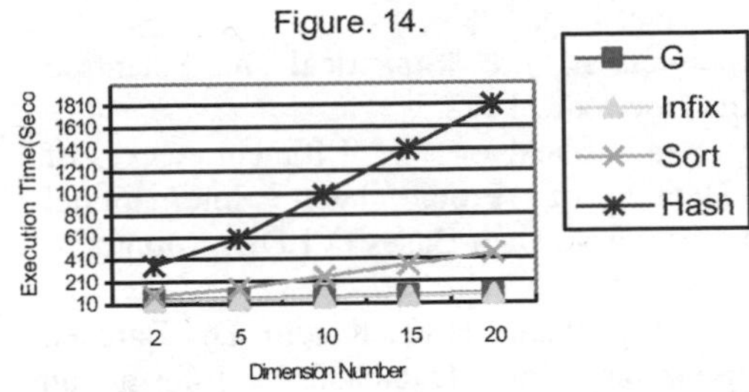

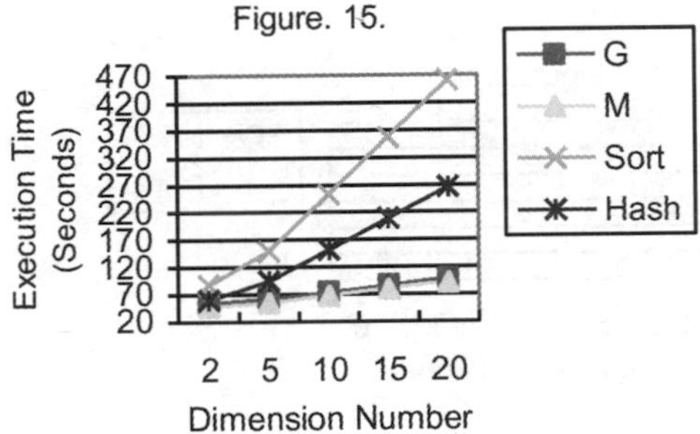

G, the performance of M is only a little better than G in case of aggregation results fitting in memory, and Hash is fast than Sort when available memory size is large enough.

The fourth set of experiments is to study the performance of the algorithms M, Infix and Prefix in case of the aggregation results fitting in memory. The parameters are the same as in the third set experiments. Figure 16 presents the comparison of M and Infix, and figure 17 presents the comparison of M and Prefix.

In the fifth set of experiments, memory size is fixed at 12.5M bytes. Figure 18 presents the experiment results. The figure indicates that the execution times of G increase much slowly than Sort and Hash.

Similar to the above four sets of experiments, we also conducted five sets of experiments to study the performance of the aggregation algorithms while the header size, which also has effect on compression ratio, varies. The experiment results show that the execution times of Sort and Hash kept at the same while the header size increases because that the header size has no effect on the relational table, and the header size has little effect on the performance of G, M, Prefix and Infix. The details of the experiments see [23].

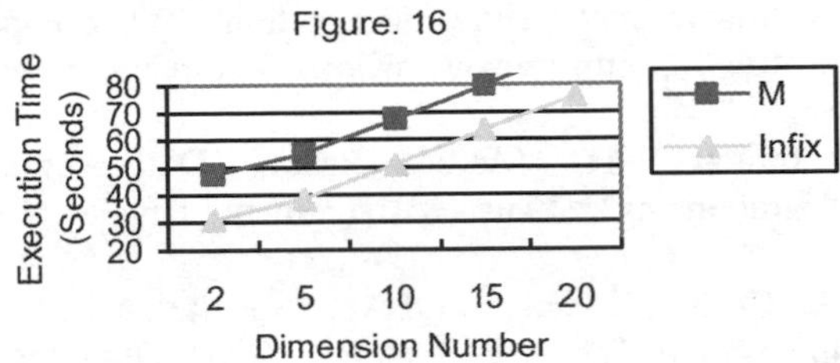

6. Summary and Conclusion

In this paper, a collection of aggregation algorithms was described and analyzed. These algorithms operate directly on compressed datasets in MDWs without the need to first decompress them. The algorithms are applicable to MDWs that are compressed using mapping complete compression methods. A decision procedure is also given to select the most efficient algorithm based on aggregation request, available memory, as well as the dataset parameters. The analysis and experimental results show that the algorithms have better performance than the traditional aggregation algorithms.

In conclusion, direct manipulation of compressed data is an important tool for managing very large data warehouses. Aggregation is just one (and important) such operation in this direction. Additional algorithms will be needed for OLAP operators on compressed multidimensional data warehouses. We are currently working on other operators such as searching, Cube, and other higher level OLAP operators on compressed MDWs.

Acknowledgement

This work was funded by the Department of Energy, Office of Energy Research, Office of Computational and Technology Research, Division of Mathematical Information and Computational Sciences under contract DE-AC03-76SF00098.

References

[1]. Gray, J., Chaudhuri, S., Bosworth, A., et al, "Data Cube: A Relational Aggregation Operator Generalizing Group-by, Cross-tables and Sub-totals", Data Mining and Knowledge Discovery, Vol.1, No.1, 29-53, 1997.

[2] Yazdani, S. and Wong, S., "Data Warehousing with Oracle", Prentice-Hall, Upper Saddle River, N.J.,

1997.

[3] Gupta, V. R., "Data Warehousing with MS SQL Server Unleashed", Sams, Englewood Cliffs, N. J., 1977.

[4] Chatziantonian, D. and Ross, K, "Querying Multiple Features in Relational Databases", Proc. of VLDB, 1996.

[5] Arbor Sofware, "The Role of Multidimensional Database in a Data Warehousing Solution", White Paper, Arbor Software, http://www. arborsoft.com/papers/ware TOC.html

[6] Inmon, W.H., "Multidimensional Databases and Data Warehousing", Data Management Riview, Feb. 1995.

[7] Colliat, G, "OLAP, Relational and Multidimensional Databases Systems", SIGMOD Record, Vol.25, No.3, 1996.

[8] Bassiouni, M.A., "Data Compression in Scientific and Statistical Databases", IEEE Transactions on Software Engineering, Vol. SE-11, No. 10, 1985.

[9] Roth, M. A. and Van Horn, S.J., "Database Compression", SIGMOD RECORD, Vol.22, No.3, 1993.

[10] Zhao, Y., Deshpande, P.M., and Naughton, J.F., "An Array-Based Algorithm for Simultaneous Multidimensional Aggregations", In Proc. of the ACM-SIGMOD Conference, 1997.

[11] Graefe, G., "Query Evaluation Techniques for Large Databases", ACM Computing Surveys, 25(2), 1993.

[12] Harinarayan, V., Rajaraman, A., and Ullman, J. D., "Implementing Data Cube Efficienly", In Proc. of the 1996 ACM-SIGMOD Coference, 1996.

[13] Gupta, H., Harinarayan, V., Rajaraman, A., and Ullman, J.D, "Index Selection for OLAP", In Proc. of the International Conference on Data Engineering, Binghamton, UK, April, 1997.

[14] Kotidis, Y. and Roussopoulos, N., "An Alternative Storage Organization for ROLAP Aggregation Views Based on Cubtrees", In Proc. of ACM-SIGMOD Conference, pp. 249-258, 1998.

[15] Roussopoulos, N., Kotidis, Y., and Roussopoulos, M, "Cubtree: Organization of and Bulk Incremental Updates on the Data Cube", In Proc. of ACM-SIGMOD Conference, pp. 89-99, 1997.

[16] Agarwal, S, Agrawal, R., Deshpande, P.M., et al, "On the Computation of Multidimensional Aggregations", In Proc. of the 22nd VLDB Conference, India, 1996.

[17] Shoshani, A., "Statistical Databases: Characteristics, Problems and Some Solutions", In Proc. Of the Eighth International Conference on Very Large Data Bases (VLDB), Mexico City, Mexico, 1982.

[18] Chen, M.C. and McNamee, L.P., "The Data Model and Access Method of Summary Data Management", IEEE Transactions on Knowledge and Data Engineering, 1(4), 1989.

[19] Srivastava, J., Tan, J.S.E., and Lum, V.Y., "TBSAM: An Access Method for Efficient Processing of Statistical Queries", IEEE Transactions on Knowledge and Data Engineering, 1(4), 1989.

[20] Michalewicz, Z., ed. "Statistical and Scientific Databases", Ellis Horwood, 1992.

[21] Eggers, S. and Shoshani, A., "Efficient Access of Compressed Data", In Proc. 1980 International Conference on Very Large Data Bases (VLDB), Montreal, Canada, Sept, 1980.

[22] Li, Jianzhong, Wang, H.K., Rotem, D. "Batched International Searching on Databases", Information Sciences (An International Journal). 1989. Vol.48.

[23] Li, Jianzhong, Rotem, Doron, and Srivastava, Jaideep, "Aggregation Algorithms for Very Large Compressed Data Warehouses", Technique Report, http://www.lbl.gov/~rotem/paper/aggr.ps.

Figure. 17.

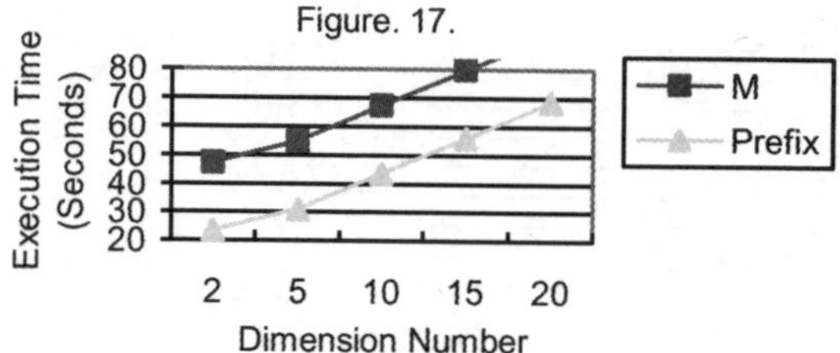

Figure. 18

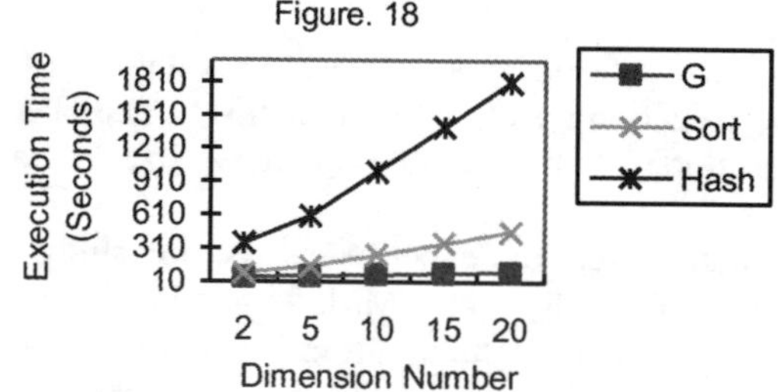

Extending Practical Pre-Aggregation in On-Line Analytical Processing

Torben Bach Pedersen
Kommunedata
DK–8200 Århus N, Denmark
tbp@kmd.dk

Christian S. Jensen Curtis E. Dyreson
Department of Computer Science
Aalborg University, DK–9220 Aalborg Øst, Denmark
{csj,curtis}@cs.auc.dk

Abstract

On-Line Analytical Processing (OLAP) based on a dimensional view of data is being used increasingly for the purpose of analyzing very large amounts of data. To improve query performance, modern OLAP systems use a technique known as *practical pre-aggregation*, where *select* combinations of aggregate queries are materialized and re-used to compute other aggregates; full pre-aggregation, where all combinations of aggregates are materialized, is infeasible. However, this re-use of aggregates is contingent on the dimension hierarchies and the relationships between facts and dimensions satisfying stringent constraints, which severely limits the scope of practical pre-aggregation. This paper significantly extends the scope of practical pre-aggregation to cover a much wider range of realistic situations. Specifically, algorithms are given that transform "irregular" dimension hierarchies and fact-dimension relationships, which often occur in real-world OLAP applications, into well-behaved structures that, when used by existing OLAP systems, enable practical pre-aggregation. The algorithms have low computational complexity and may be applied incrementally to reduce the cost of updating OLAP structures.

1 Introduction

On-Line Analytical Processing (OLAP) systems aim to ease the process of extracting useful information from large amounts of detailed transactional data and have gained widespread acceptance in traditional business applications as well as in new applications such as health care. These systems generally offer a dimensional view of data, in which measured values, termed facts, are characterized by descriptive values, drawn from a number of dimensions; and the values of a dimension are typically organized in a containment-type hierarchy. A prototypical query applies an aggregate function, such as average, to the facts characterized by specific values from the dimensions.

Fast response times are required from these systems, even for queries that aggregate large amounts of data. The perhaps most central technique used for meeting this requirement is termed *pre-aggregation*, where the results of aggregate queries are pre-computed and stored, i.e., materialized, for later use during query processing. Pre-aggregation has attracted substantial attention in the research community, where it has been investigated how to optimally use pre-aggregated data for query optimization [6, 3] and how to maintain the pre-aggregated data when base data is updated [18, 23]. Further, the latest versions of commercial RDBMS products offer both query optimization based on pre-computed aggregates and automatic maintenance of the stored aggregates when base data is updated [28].

The fastest response times may be achieved when materializing aggregate results corresponding to all combinations of dimension values across all dimensions, termed *full* (or eager) pre-aggregation. However, the required storage space grows rapidly, to quickly become prohibitive, as the complexity of the application increases. This phenomenon is called *data explosion* [25, 20] and occurs because the number of possible aggregation combinations grows rapidly when the number of dimensions increase, while the sparseness of the multidimensional space decreases in higher dimension levels, meaning that aggregates at higher levels take up nearly as much space as lower-level aggregates. In some commercial applications, full pre-aggregation takes up as much as 200 times the space of the raw data [20]. Another problem with full pre-aggregation is that it takes too long to update the materialized aggregates

Proceedings of the 25th VLDB Conference, Edinburgh, Scotland, 1999.

when base data changes.

With the goal of avoiding data explosion, research has focused on how to select the best subset of aggregation levels given space constraints [10, 8, 30, 1, 26] or maintenance time constraints [9], or the best combination of aggregate data and indices [7]. This approach is commonly referred to as *practical* (or partial or semi-eager [4, 10, 27]) pre-aggregation. Commercial OLAP systems now also exist that employ practical pre-aggregation, e.g., Informix MetaCube [12] and Microsoft Decision Support Services (Plato) [17].

The premise underlying the applicability of practical pre-aggregation is that lower-level aggregates can be *re-used* to compute higher-level aggregates, known as summarizability [15]. Summarizability occurs when the mappings in the dimension hierarchies are *onto* (all paths from the root to a leaf in the hierarchy have equal lengths), *covering* (only immediate parent and child values can be related), and *strict* (each child in a hierarchy has only one parent); and when also the relationships between facts and dimensions are many-to-one and facts are always mapped to the lowest levels in the dimensions [15]. However, the data encountered in many real-world applications fail to comply with this rigid regime. This motivates the search for techniques that allow practical pre-aggregation to be used for a wider range of applications, the focus of this paper.

Specifically, this papers leverages research such as that cited above. It does so by showing how to transform dimension hierarchies to obtain summarizability, and by showing how to integrate the transformed hierarchies into current systems, transparently to the user, so that standard OLAP technology is re-used. Specifically, algorithms are presented that automatically transform dimension hierarchies to achieve summarizability for hierarchies that are non-onto, non-covering, and non-strict. The algorithms have low computational complexity and are thus applicable to even very large databases. The algorithms can also be used to contend with non-summarizable relationships between facts and dimensions and may be modified to accommodate incremental computation, thus minimizing the maintenance cost associated with base-data updates [22].

To our knowledge, this work is the first to present algorithms to automatically achieve summarizability for non-covering and non-onto hierarchies. The research reported here is also the first to demonstrate techniques and algorithms for achieving summarizability in non-strict hierarchies. The integration of the techniques into current systems, transparently to the user, we believe is a novel feature. The only past research on the topic has been on how to manually, and not transparently to the user, achieve summarizability for non-covering hierarchies [24].

The next section presents a real-world clinical case study that exemplifies the non-summarizable properties of real-world applications. Section 3 proceeds to define the aspects of a multidimensional data model necessary for describing the new techniques, and defines also important properties related to summarizability. Section 4 presents algorithms that transform dimension hierarchies to achieve summarizability and discusses how the algorithms may be applied to non-summarizable relationships between facts and dimensions. Section 5 demonstrates how the techniques may be integrated into current systems, and Section 6 summarizes and points to topics for future research.

2 Motivation—A Case Study

The case study concerns patients in a hospital, their associated diagnoses, and their places of residence. The data analysis goal is to investigate whether some diagnoses occur more often in some areas than in others, in which case environmental or lifestyle factors might be contributing to the disease pattern. An ER diagram illustrating the underlying data is seen in Figure 1.

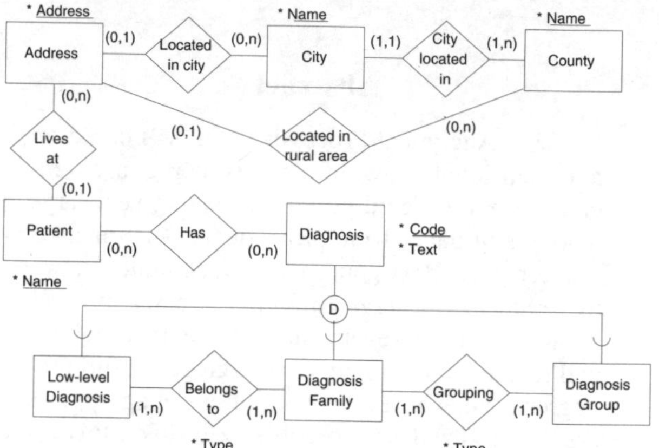

Figure 1: ER Schema of Case Study

The most important entities are the *patients*, for which we record the name. We always want to count the number of patients, grouped by some properties of the patients. Thus, in multidimensional terms, the patients are the *facts*, and the other, describing, entities constitute the *dimensions*.

Each patient has a number of *diagnoses*, yielding to a *many-to-many* relationship between facts and the diagnosis dimension. When registering diagnoses of patients, physicians use different levels of granularity, ranging from very precise diagnoses, e.g., "Insulin dependent diabetes during pregnancy," to more imprecise diagnoses, e.g., "Diabetes," which cover wider ranges of patient conditions. To model this, the relationship from Patient to diagnoses is to the supertype "Diagnosis," which then has three subtypes, corresponding to different levels of granularity, the *low-level diagnosis*, the *diagnosis family*, and the *diagnosis group*. Examples of these are "Insulin dependent diabetes during pregnancy," "Insulin dependent diabetes," and "Diabetes," respectively. The higher-level diagnoses are both (imprecise) diagnoses in their own right, but also serve as groups of lower-level diagnoses, i.e., a diagnosis family consists of 5–20 related low-level diagnoses and a diagnosis group consists of 5–20 related diagnosis families.

Each diagnosis has an alphanumeric code and a descriptive text, which are specified by some standard, here the World Health Organization's International Classification of

Diseases (ICD-10) [29], or by the physicians themselves. In the hierarchy determined by the WHO, one lower-level item belongs to exactly one higher-level item, leading to a *strict*, *covering* hierarchy. In the user-defined hierarchy, one lower-level item may belong to zero or more higher-level items, e.g., the family "Diabetes during pregnancy" may belong to both the "Diabetes" and "Other pregnancy related diseases" groups. Thus, the user-defined hierarchy is *non-strict* and *non-covering*.

We also record the addresses of the patients. If the address is located in a city, we record the *city*; otherwise, if the address is in a rural area, we record the *county* in which the address is located. A city is located in exactly one county. As not all addresses are in cities, we cannot find all addresses in a county by going through the "City located in" relationship. Thus, the mapping from addresses to cities is *non-covering* w.r.t. addresses. For cities and counties, we record the name. Not all counties have cities in them, so the mapping from cities to counties is *into* rather than *onto*.

In order to exemplify the data, we assume a standard mapping of the ER diagram to relational tables and the use of surrogate keys, named *ID*, with globally unique values. The three subtypes of the Diagnosis type are mapped to a common Diagnosis table, and because of this, the "Belongs to" and "Grouping" relationships are mapped to a common "Grouping" table. The resulting tables with sample data are shown in Table 1 and will be used in examples throughout the paper.

If we apply pre-aggregation to the data from the case study, several problems occur. For example, if the counts of patients by City are pre-computed and we use these for computing the numbers of patients by county, an incorrect result will occur. In the data, the addresses "123 Rural Road" and "1 Sandy Dunes" (one of them is the address of a patient) are not in any city, making the mapping from City to County not *covering* w.r.t. addresses.

Next, if the counts of patients by Low-Level Diagnosis are pre-computed and we use these for computing the total count of patients, an incorrect result again ensues. First, patients only with lung cancer are not counted, as lung cancer is not present at the level of Low-Level Diagnosis; the mapping from Low-Level Diagnosis to Diagnosis Family is *into*. Second, patients such as "Jim Doe" only have higher-level diagnoses and will no be counted; the fact-to-dimension mapping has *varying granularity*. Third, patients such as "Jane Doe" have several diagnoses and will be counted several times; the relationship between facts and dimensions is *many-to-many*. Fourth, Low-Level diagnoses such as "Insulin dependent diabetes during pregnancy" are part of several diagnosis families, which may also lead to "double" counting when computing higher-level counts; the dimension hierarchy is *non-strict*.

These problems yield "non-summarizable" dimension hierarchies that severely limit the applicability of practical pre-aggregation, leaving only full pre-aggregation, which requires huge amounts of storage, or no pre-aggregation, which results in long response times for queries.

ID	Name
1	John Doe
2	Jane Doe
3	Jim Doe

Patient

PatientID	DiagID	Type
1	9	Primary
2	5	Secondary
2	9	Primary
3	11	Primary

Has

PatientID	AddressID
1	50
2	51
3	52

LivesAt

ID	Address
50	21 Central Street
51	34 Main Street
52	123 Rural Road
53	1 Sandy Dunes

Address

ID	Code	Text	Type
4	O24	Diabetes during pregnancy	DF
5	O24.0	Ins. dep. diab. during pregn.	LLD
6	O24.1	Non ins. dep. diab. during pregn.	LLD
9	E10	Insulin dependent diabetes	DF
10	E11	Non insulin dependent diabetes	DF
11	E1	Diabetes	DG
12	O2	Other pregnancy related diseases	DG
13	A1	Cancer	DG
14	A11	Lung cancer	DF

Diagnosis

ParentID	ChildID	Type
4	5	WHO
4	6	WHO
9	5	User
10	6	User
11	9	WHO
11	10	WHO
12	4	WHO
13	14	WHO

Grouping

CityID	CountyID
20	30
21	31

CityLocatedIn

ID	Name
20	Sydney
21	Melbourne

City

AddressID	CityID
50	20
51	21

LocatedInCity

ID	Name
30	Sydney
31	Melbourne
32	Outback

County

ID	Name
52	31
53	32

LocatedInRuralArea

Table 1: Tables for the Case Study

The properties described above are found in many other real-world applications. Many-to-many relationships between facts and dimensions occur between bank customers and accounts, between companies and Standard Industry Classifications (SICs), and between students and departments [14, 15]. Non-strict dimension hierarchies occur from cities to states in a Geography dimension [24] and from weeks to months in a Time dimension. In addition, hierarchies where the change over time is captured are generally non-strict. The mapping from holidays to weeks as well as organization hierarchies of varying depth [11] offer examples of "into" mappings. Non-covering relationships exist for days-holidays-weeks and for counties-cities-states, as well as in organization hierarchies [11].

Even though many real-world cases possess the properties described above, current techniques for practical pre-aggregation require that facts are in a many-to-one relationships to dimensions and that all hierarchies are strict, onto, and covering.

3 Data Model Context and Concepts

This section describes the aspects of a multidimensional data model that extend practical pre-aggregation. The full model is described elsewhere [21]. Next, the data model context is exploited for defining properties of hierarchies relevant to the techniques.

The particular data model has been chosen over other multidimensional data models because it quite naturally captures the data described in the case study and because it includes explicit concepts of dimensions and dimension hierarchies, which is very important for clearly presenting the techniques. However, the techniques are also applicable to other multidimensional or statistical data models, as will be discussed in Section 5.

3.1 A Concrete Data Model Context

For each part of the model, we define the *intension* and the *extension*, and we give an illustrating example.

An *n-dimensional fact schema* is a two-tuple $\mathcal{S} = (\mathcal{F}, \mathcal{D})$, where $\mathcal{F}$ is a *fact type* and $\mathcal{D} = \{\mathcal{T}_i, i = 1, .., n\}$ is its corresponding *dimension types*.

Example 1 In the case study from Section 2, *Patient* is the fact type, and *Diagnosis*, *Residence*, and *Name* are the dimension types. The intuition is that *everything* that characterizes the fact type is considered to be *dimensional*.

A dimension type $\mathcal{T}$ is a four-tuple $(\mathcal{C}, \leq_{\mathcal{T}}, \top_{\mathcal{T}}, \bot_{\mathcal{T}})$, where $\mathcal{C} = \{\mathcal{C}_j, j = 1, .., k\}$ are the *category types* of $\mathcal{T}$, $\leq_{\mathcal{T}}$ is a partial order on the $\mathcal{C}_j$'s, with $\top_{\mathcal{T}} \in \mathcal{C}$ and $\bot_{\mathcal{T}} \in \mathcal{C}$ being the top and bottom element of the ordering, respectively. Thus, the category types form a lattice. The intuition is that one category type is "greater than" another category type if members of the former's extension logically contain members of the latter's extension, i.e., they have a larger value size. The top element of the ordering corresponds to the largest possible value size, that is, there is only one value in it's extension, logically containing all other values.

We say that $\mathcal{C}_j$ *is a category type of* $\mathcal{T}$, written $\mathcal{C}_j \in \mathcal{T}$, if $\mathcal{C}_j \in \mathcal{C}$.

Example 2 Low-level diagnoses are contained in diagnosis families, which are contained in diagnosis groups. Thus, the *Diagnosis* dimension type has the following order on its category types: $\bot_{Diagnosis}$ = *Low-level Diagnosis* < *Diagnosis Family* < *Diagnosis Group* < $\top_{Diagnosis}$. Other examples of category types are *Address*, *City*, and *County*. Figure 2, to be discussed in detail later, illustrates the dimension types of the case study.

A *category* C_j of type $\mathcal{C}_j$ is a set of *dimension values* e. A *dimension* D of type $\mathcal{T} = (\{\mathcal{C}_j\}, \leq_{\mathcal{T}}, \top_{\mathcal{T}}, \bot_{\mathcal{T}})$ is a two-tuple $D = (C, \leq)$, where $C = \{C_j\}$ is a set of categories C_j such that $Type(C_j) = \mathcal{C}_j$ and $\leq$ is a partial order on $\cup_j C_j$, the union of all dimension values in the individual categories. We assume a function $Pred : C \mapsto 2^C$ that gives the set of immediate predecessors of a category C_j. Similarly, we a assume a function $Desc : C \mapsto 2^C$ that gives the set of immediate descendants of a category C_j. For both *Pred* and *Desc*, we "count" from the category $\top_{\mathcal{T}}$ (of type $\top_{\mathcal{T}}$), so that category $\top_{\mathcal{T}}$ is the ultimate predecessor and category $\bot_{\mathcal{T}}$ (of type $\bot_{\mathcal{T}}$) is the ultimate descendant.

The definition of the partial order is: given two values e_1, e_2 then $e_1 \leq e_2$ if e_1 is logically contained in e_2. We say that C_j is a category of D, written $C_j \in D$, if $C_j \in C$. For a dimension value e, we say that e is a dimensional value of D, written $e \in D$, if $e \in \cup_j C_j$.

The category of type $\bot_{\mathcal{T}}$ in dimension of type $\mathcal{T}$ contains the values with the smallest value size. The category with the largest value size, of type $\top_{\mathcal{T}}$, contains exactly one value, denoted $\top$. For all values e of the dimension D, $e \leq \top$. Value $\top$ is similar to the *ALL* construct of Gray et al. [5]. When clear from the context, we refer to a category of type $\top_{\mathcal{T}}$ simply as a $\top$ category, not to be confused with the $\top$ dimension value.

Example 3 In our *Diagnosis* dimension we have the following categories, named by their type. The numbers in parentheses are the ID values from the Diagnosis table in Table 1. *Low-level Diagnosis* = {"Insulin dependent diabetes during pregnancy" (5), "Non insulin dependent diabetes during pregnancy" (6)}, *Diagnosis Family* = {"Diabetes during pregnancy" (4), "Insulin dependent diabetes" (9), "Non insulin dependent diabetes" (10), "Lung cancer" (14)}, *Diagnosis Group* = {"Diabetes" (11), "Other pregnancy related diseases" (12), "Cancer" (13)}, and $\top_{Diagnosis} = \{\top\}$. We have that *Pred*(*Low-level Diagnosis*) $=$ {*Diagnosis Family*}. The partial order $\leq$ is obtained by combining the WHO and user-defined hierarchies, as given by the Grouping table in Table 1. Additionally, the top value $\top$ is greater than, i.e., logically contains, all the other diagnosis values.

Let F be a set of facts, and $D = (C = \{C_j\}, \leq)$ a dimension. A *fact-dimension relation* between F and D is a set $R = \{(f, e)\}$, where $f \in F$ and $e \in \cup_j C_j$. Thus R links facts to dimension values. We say that fact f is *characterized by* dimension value e, written $f \leadsto e$, if $\exists e_1 \in D\ ((f, e_1) \in R \wedge e_1 \leq e)$. We require that $\forall f \in F\ (\exists e \in \cup_j C_j\ ((f, e) \in R))$; thus, all fact maps to at least one dimension value in every dimension. The $\top$ value is used to represent an unknown or missing value, as $\top$ logically contains all dimension values, and so a fact f is mapped to $\top$ if it cannot be characterized within the particular dimension.

Example 4 The fact-dimension relation R links patient facts to diagnosis dimension values as given by the Has table from the case study, so that $R = \{$("John Doe" (1), "Insulin dependent diabetes" (9)), ("Jane Doe" (2), "Insulin dependent diabetes during pregnancy" (5)), ("Jane Doe" (2), "Insulin dependent diabetes" (9)), ("Jim Doe" (3), "Diabetes" (11))$\}$. Note that facts may be related to values in higher-level categories. We do not require that e belongs to $\bot_{Diagnosis}$. For example, the fact "John Doe" (1) is related to the diagnosis "Insulin dependent diabetes" (5), which belongs to the *Diagnosis Family* category. This feature will be used later to explicitly capture the different granularities in the data. If no diagnosis was known for patient "John Doe" (1), we would have added the pair ("John Doe" (1),$\top$) to R.

A *multidimensional object* (MO) is a four-tuple $M = (\mathcal{S}, F, D, R)$, where $\mathcal{S} = (\mathcal{F}, \mathcal{D} = \{\mathcal{T}_i\})$ is the fact schema, $F = \{f\}$ is a set of *facts* f where *Type*$(f) = \mathcal{F}$, $D = \{D_i, i = 1,..,n\}$ is a set of *dimensions* where *Type*$(D_i) = \mathcal{T}_i$, and $R = \{R_i, i = 1,..,n\}$ is a set of fact-dimension relations, such that $\forall i((f,e) \in R_i \Rightarrow f \in F \wedge \exists C_j \in D_i(e \in C_j))$.

Example 5 For the case study, we get a three-dimensional MO $M = (\mathcal{S}, F, D, R)$, where $\mathcal{S} = ($*Patient*, $\{$*Diagnosis, Name, Residence*$\})$ and $F = \{$"John Doe" (1), "Jane Doe" (2), "Jim Doe" (3)$\}$. The definition of the diagnosis dimension and its corresponding fact-dimension relation was given in the previous examples. The Residence dimension has the categories *Address* ($= \perp_{Residence}$), *City*, *County*, and $\top_{Residence}$. The values of the categories are given by the corresponding tables in Table 1. The partial order is given by the relationship tables. Additionally, the only value in the $\top_{Residence}$ category is $\top$, which logically contains all the other values in the Residence dimension. The Name dimension is simple, i.e., it just has a *Name* category ($= \perp_{Name}$) and a $\top$ category. We will refer to this MO as the "Patient" MO. A graphical illustration of its schema is seen in Figure 2. Because some addresses map directly to counties, County is an immediate predecessor of Address.

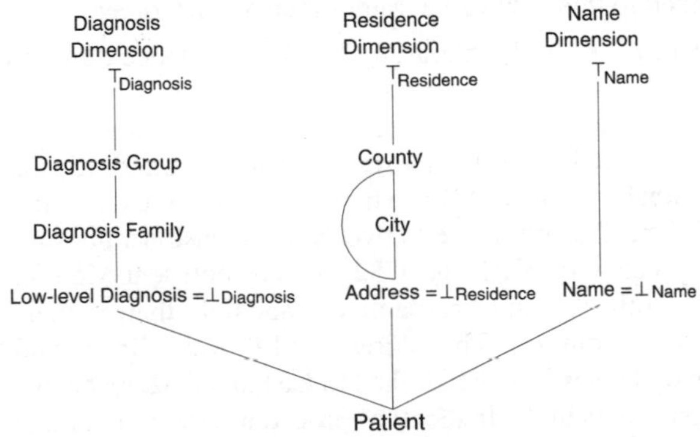

Figure 2: Schema of the Case Study

The facts in an MO are objects with *value-independent identity*. We can test facts for equality, but do not assume an ordering on the facts. The combination of dimension values that characterize the set of facts of an MO do *not* constitute a "key" for the fact set. Thus, several facts may be characterized by the same combination of dimension values. But, the facts of an MO *is* a set, and an MO does not have duplicate *facts*.

3.2 Hierarchy Properties

In this section important properties of MOs are defined, which will be used in the following sections to state precisely what problems the proposed algorithms solve. The first important concept is *summarizability*, which intuitively means that higher-level aggregates may be obtained directly from lower-level aggregates.

Definition 1 Given a type T, a set $S = \{S_j, j = 1,..,k\}$, where $S_j \in 2^T$, and a function $g : 2^T \mapsto T$, we say that g is *summarizable* for S if $g(\{\{g(S_1),..,g(S_k)\}\}) = g(S_1 \cup ..\cup S_k)$. The argument on the left-hand side of the equation is a multiset, i.e., the same value may occur multiple times.

Summarizability is important as it is a condition for the flexible use of pre-computed aggregates. Without summarizability, lower-level results generally cannot be directly combined into higher-level results. This means that we cannot choose to pre-compute only a relevant selection of the possible aggregates and then use these to (efficiently) compute higher-level aggregates on-the-fly. Instead, we have to pre-compute the all the aggregate results of queries that we need fast answers to, while other aggregates must be computed from the base data. Space and time constraints can be prohibitive for pre-computing all results, while computing aggregates from base data is often inefficient.

It has been shown that summarizability is equivalent to the aggregate function (g) being *distributive*, all paths being *strict*, and the mappings between dimension values in the hierarchies being *covering* and *onto* [15]. These concepts are formally defined below. The definitions assume a dimension $D = (C, \leq)$ and an MO $M = (\mathcal{S}, F, D, R)$.

Definition 2 Given two categories, C_1, C_2 such that $C_2 \in Pred(C_1)$, we say that the mapping from C_1 to C_2 is *onto* iff $\forall e_2 \in C_2(\exists e_1 \in C_1\ (e_1 \leq e_2))$. Otherwise, it is *into*. If all mappings in a dimension are onto, we say that the dimension hierarchy is *onto*.

Mappings that are into typically occur when the dimension hierarchy has varying height. In the case study, there is no low-level cancer diagnosis, meaning that some parts of the hierarchy have height 2, while most have height 3. It is thus not possible to use aggregates at the Low-level Diagnosis level for computing aggregates at the two higher levels. Mappings that are into also occur often in organization hierarchies.

Definition 3 Given three categories, C_1, C_2, and C_3 such that *Type*$(C_1) <$ *Type*$(C_2) <$ *Type*(C_3), we say that the mapping from C_2 to C_3 is *covering with respect to* C_1 iff $\forall e_1 \in C_1\ (\forall e_3 \in C_3\ (e_1 \leq e_3 \Rightarrow \exists e_2 \in C_2\ (e_1 \leq e_2 \wedge e_2 \leq e_3)))$. Otherwise, it is *non-covering with respect to* C_1. If all mappings in a dimension are covering w.r.t. any category, we say that the dimension hierarchy is *covering*.

Non-covering mappings occur when some of the links between dimension values skip one or more levels and map directly to a value located higher up in the hierarchy. In the case study, this happens for the "1 Sandy Dunes" address, which maps directly to "Outback County" (there are no cities in Outback County). Thus, we cannot use aggregates at the City level for computing aggregates at the County level.

Definition 4 Given an MO $M = (\mathcal{S}, F, D, R)$, and two categories C_1 and C_2 that belong to the same dimension $D_i \in D$ such that $Type(C_1) < Type(C_2)$, we say that the mapping from C_1 to C_2 is *covering with respect to* F, the set of facts, iff $\forall f \in F\ (\forall e_2 \in C_2\ (f \rightsquigarrow_i e_2 \Rightarrow \exists e_1 \in C_1\ (f \rightsquigarrow_i e_1 \wedge e_1 \leq_i e_2)))$.

This case is similar to the one above, but now it is the mappings between facts and dimension values that may skip one or more levels and map facts directly to dimension values in categories above the bottom level. In the case study, the patients can map to diagnoses anywhere in the Diagnosis dimension, not just to Low-level Diagnoses. This means that we cannot use aggregates at the Low-level Diagnosis Level for computing aggregates higher up in the hierarchy.

Definition 5 Given two categories, C_1 and C_2 such that $C_2 \in Pred(C_1)$, we say that the mapping from C_1 to C_2 is *strict* iff $\forall e_1 \in C_1\ (\forall e_2, e_3 \in C_2\ (e_1 \leq e_2 \wedge e_1 \leq e_3 \Rightarrow e_2 = e_3))$. Otherwise, it is *non-strict*. The hierarchy in dimension D is *strict* if all mappings in it are strict; otherwise, it is *non-strict*. Given an MO $M = (\mathcal{S}, F, D, R)$ and a category C_j in some dimension $D_i \in D$, we say that there is a *strict path* from the set of facts F to C_j iff $\forall f \in F(f \rightsquigarrow_i e_1 \wedge f \rightsquigarrow_i e_2 \wedge e_1 \in C_j \wedge e_2 \in C_j \Rightarrow e_1 = e_2)$. (Note that the paths to the $\top_{\mathcal{T}}$ categories are always strict.)

Non-strict hierarchies occur when a dimension value has multiple parents. This occurs in the Diagnosis dimension in the case study where the "Insulin dependent diabetes during pregnancy" low-level diagnosis is part of both the "Insulin Dependent Diabetes" and the "Diabetes during pregnancy" diagnosis families, which in turn both are part of the "Diabetes" diagnosis group. This means that we cannot use aggregates at the Diagnosis Family level to compute aggregates at the Diagnosis Group level, since data for "Insulin dependent diabetes during pregnancy" would then be counted twice.

Definition 6 If the dimension hierarchy for a dimension D is *onto*, *covering*, and *strict*, we say that D is *normalized*. Otherwise, it is *un-normalized*. For an MO $M = (\mathcal{S}, D, F, R)$, if all dimensions $D_i \in D$ are normalized and $\forall R_i \in R\ ((f, e) \in R_i \Rightarrow e \in \bot_D)$ (, i.e., all facts map to dimension values in the bottom category), we say that M is *normalized*. Otherwise, it is *un-normalized*.

For normalized hierarchies and MOs, all mappings are summarizable, meaning that we can pre-aggregate values at any combination of dimension levels and safely re-use the pre-aggregated values to compute higher-level aggregate results. Thus, we want to normalize the dimension hierarchies and MOs for which we want to apply practical pre-aggregation.

4 Transformation Techniques

This section describes how dimensions can be transformed to achieve summarizability. Transforming dimensions on their own, separately from the facts, results in well-behaved dimensions that can be applied in a number of different systems or sold to third-party users. In addition, it is discussed how to apply the presented algorithms to non-summarizable fact-dimension relations. The transformation of the dimension hierarchies is a three-step operation. First, all mappings are transformed to be *covering*, by introducing extra "intermediate" values. Second, all mappings are transformed to be *onto*, by introducing "placeholder" values at lower levels for values without any children. Third, mappings are made *strict*, by "fusing" values together. The three steps are treated in separate sections. None of the algorithms introduce any non-summarizable properties, so applying each once is sufficient.

In general, the algorithms take as input a set of tables R_{C_1,C_2} that specifies the mapping from dimension values in category C_1 to values in category C_2. The input needs not contain all pairs of ancestors and descendants—only direct parent-child relationships are required. If there are non-covering mappings in the hierarchy, we have categories C, P, H such that $\{P, H\} \subseteq Pred(C)$ and $Type(P) < Type(H)$. In this case, the input must also contain $R_{P,H}$ tables that map P values to H values.

4.1 Non-Covering Hierarchies

The first algorithm renders all mappings in a dimension hierarchy covering w.r.t. any category. When a dimension value is mapped *directly* to another value in a category higher than the one immediately above it in the hierarchy, a new intermediate value is inserted into the category immediately above, and the two original dimension values are linked to this new value, rather than to each other.

Example 6 In the hierarchy for the Residence dimension, two links go from Address directly to County. The address "123 Rural Road" (52) is in "Melbourne County" (31), but not in a city, and the address "1 Sandy Dunes" (53) is in "Outback County" (32), which does *not* have any cities at all. The algorithm inserts two new dimension values in the City category, **C31** and **C32**, which represent Melbourne and Outback county, respectively, and links them to their respective counties. The addresses "123 Rural Road" and "1 Sandy Dunes" are then linked to **C31** and **C32**, respectively. This occurs in the first call of procedure MakeCovering (on the Address category; the procedure is given below). When MakeCovering is called recursively on the City, County, and $\top$ categories, nothing happens, as all mappings are already covering. The transformation is illustrated graphically in Figure 3. The dotted lines show the "problematic" links, and the bold-face values and thick lines show the new dimension values and links.

In the algorithm, C is a *child* category, P is a *parent* category, H is a "*higher*" category, L are the non-covering *links* from C to H, and N are the "higher" dimension values in L. The $\bowtie$ operator denotes natural join. The algorithm works as follows. Given the argument category C (initially the bottom category) in line 1, the algorithms goes through all C's parent categories P (line 2). For each parent category P, it looks for predecessor categories H of C

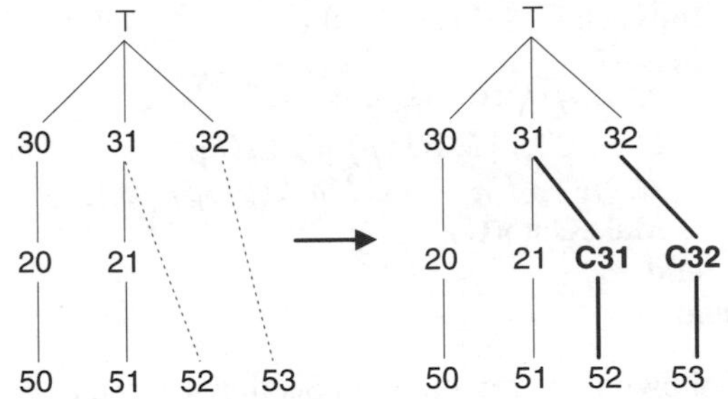

Figure 3: Transformations by MakeCovering

that are "higher" in the hierarchy than P (line 4). If such an H exists, there might be links in the mapping from C to H that are not available by going through P. Line 6 finds these "non-covered" links, L, in the mapping from C to H by "subtracting" the links that *are* available by going through P from *all* the links in the mapping from C to H. Line 7 uses L to find the dimension values N in H that participate in the "non-covered" mappings. For each value in N, line 8 inserts a corresponding marked value into P; these marked values represent the N values in P. The marked values in P are then linked to the original values in H (line 9) and C (line 10). Line 12 contains a recursive call to the algorithm on P, thus fixing mappings higher up in the hierarchy. The algorithm terminates when it reaches the $\top$ category, which has no predecessors.

(1) **procedure** MakeCovering(C)
(2) **for** each $P \in Pred(C)$ **do**
(3) **begin**
(4) **for** each $H \in Pred(C)$ where $Type(H) > Type(P)$ **do**
(5) **begin**
(6) $L \leftarrow R_{C,H} \setminus \Pi_{C,H}(R_{C,P} \bowtie R_{P,H})$
(7) $N \leftarrow \Pi_H(L)$
(8) $P \leftarrow P \cup \{Mark(h) \mid h \in N\}$
(9) $R_{P,H} \leftarrow R_{P,H} \cup \{(Mark(h), h) \mid h \in N\}$
(10) $R_{C,P} \leftarrow R_{C,P} \cup \{(c, Mark(h)) \mid (c,h) \in L\}$
(11) **end**
(12) MakeCovering(P)
(13) **end**
(14) **end**

All steps in the algorithm are expressed using standard relational algebra operators. The *general* worst-case complexity of join is $\mathcal{O}(n^2)$, where n is the size of the input. However, because the input to the algorithm are hierarchy definitions, the complexity of the join in the algorithm will only be $\mathcal{O}(n \log n)$. Thus, all the operators used can be evaluated in time $\mathcal{O}(n \log n)$, where n is the size of the input. The *Mark* operation can be performed in $\mathcal{O}(1)$ time. The inner loop of the algorithm is evaluated at most once for each link between categories, i.e., at most $k^2/2$ times, where k is the number af categories (if all categories are directly linked to all others). Thus, the overall big-$\mathcal{O}$ complexity of the algorithm is $\mathcal{O}(k^2 n \log n)$, where k is the number of categories and n is the size of the largest participating R_{C_1,C_2} relation. The worst-case complexity will not apply very often; in most cases, the inner loop will only be evaluated at most k times.

The algorithm inserts new values into the P category to ensure that the mappings from P to higher categories are summarizable, i.e., that pre-aggregated results for P can be directly combined into higher-level aggregate results. The new values in P mean that the cost of materializing aggregate results for P is higher for the transformed hierarchy than for the original. However, if the hierarchy was not transformed to achieve summarizability, we would have to materialize aggregates for G, and perhaps also for higher level categories. At most one new value is inserted into P for every value in G, meaning that the extra cost of materializing results for P is never greater than the cost of the (otherwise necessary) materialization of results for G. This is a very unlikely worst-case scenario—in the most common cases, the extra cost for P will be much lower than the the cost of materializing results for G, and the savings will be even greater because materialization of results for higher-level categories may also be avoided.

The correctness argument for the algorithm has two aspects. First, the mappings in the hierarchy should be *covering* upon termination. Second, the algorithm should only make transformations that are semantically correct, i.e., we should get the same results when computing results with the new hierarchy as with the old. The correctness follows from Theorem 1 and 2, below. As new values are inserted in the P category, we will get aggregate values for both the new and the original values when "grouping" by P. Results for the original values will be the same as before, so the original result set is a *subset* of the result set obtained with the transformed hierarchy.

Theorem 1 Algorithm MakeCovering terminates and the hierarchy for the resulting dimension D' is covering.

Proof: By induction in the height of the lattice [22].

Theorem 2 Given dimensions D and D' such that D' is the result of running MakeCovering on D, an aggregate result obtained using D is a subset of the result obtained using D'.

Proof: Follows easily from Lemma 1 [22].

Lemma 1 For the dimension $D' = (C', \leq')$ resulting from applying algorithm MakeCovering to dimension $D = (C, \leq)$, the following holds: $\forall e_1, e_2 \in D$ ($e_1 \leq' e_2 \Leftrightarrow e_1 \leq e_2$) (there is a path between any two original dimension values in the new dimension hierarchy iff there was a path between them in the original hierarchy).

Proof: By induction in the height of the lattice [22].

We see that the original values in the hierarchy are still linked to exactly the same original values as before, as stated by Lemma 1, although new values might have been inserted in-between the original values. Thus, when evaluating a query using the transformed hierarchy, the results for the original values will be the same as when using the original hierarchy.

Assuming only the original result set is desired, results for the new values must be excluded, which is easy to accomplish. The new, "internal" values are marked with "mark = internal", whereas the original values have "mark = original". In order to exclude the new, internal values from the result set, the equivalent of an SQL HAVING clause condition of "mark = original" is introduced into the original query.

4.2 Non-Onto Hierarchies

The second algorithm renders all mappings in hierarchies onto, i.e., all dimension values in non-bottom categories have children. This is ensured by inserting placeholder values in lower categories to represent the childless values. These new values are marked with the original values, making it possible to map facts to the new placeholder values instead of to the original values. This makes it possible to only map facts to the bottom category.

Example 7 In the Diagnosis dimension, the "Lung cancer" diagnosis family (ID = 14) has no children. When the algorithm (given shortly) reaches the Diagnosis Family category, it inserts a placeholder value (**L14**) into the Low-level Diagnosis category, representing the "Lung cancer" diagnosis, and links it to the original value. Facts mapped to the "Lung cancer" value may then instead be mapped to the new placeholder value. Using this technique we can ensure that facts are mapped only to the Low-level Diagnosis Category. A graphical illustration of the transformation is given in Figure 4. The bold-faced value **L14** is the new value inserted, and the thick line between 14 and **L14** is the new link inserted.

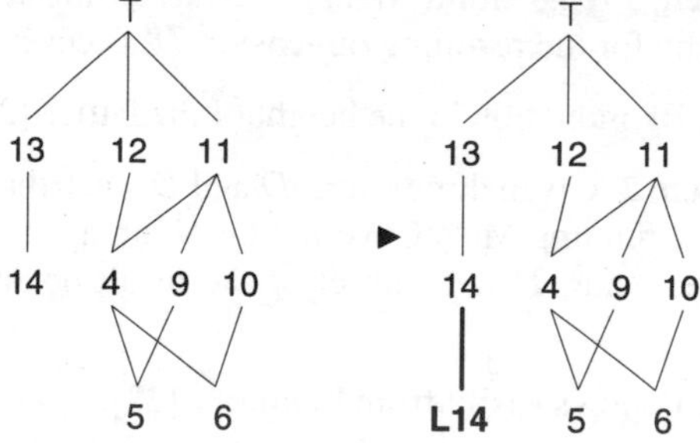

Figure 4: Transformations by MakeOnto

In the algorithm that follows, P is a *parent* category, C is a *child* category, and N holds the parent values with *no* children. The algorithm works as follows. Given a category P (initially the $\top$ category) in line 1, the algorithm goes through all categories C that are (immediate) descendants of P (line 2). For each C, line 4 finds the values N in P that have *no* children in C, by "subtracting" the values *with* children in C from the values in P. For each "childless" value in N, lines 5 and 6, respectively, insert into C a placeholder value marked with the parent value, and links the new value to the original. MakeOnto is then called recursively on C (line 7). The algorithms terminates when it reaches the $\bot$ category, which has no descendants.

(1) **procedure** MakeOnto(P)
(2) **for** each $C \in Desc(P)$ **do**
(3) **begin**
(4) $N \leftarrow P \setminus \Pi_P(R_{C,P})$
(5) $C \leftarrow C \cup \{Mark(p) \mid p \in N\}$
(6) $R_{C,P} \leftarrow R_{C,P} \cup \{(Mark(p), p) \mid p \in N\}$
(7) MakeOnto(C)
(8) **end**
(9) **end**

Following the reasoning in Section 4.1, we find that the overall big-$\mathcal{O}$ complexity is $\mathcal{O}(k^2 n \log n)$, where k is the number of categories and n is the size of the largest participating R_{C_1,C_2} relation. However, the complexity will be $\mathcal{O}(kn \log n)$ for the most common cases.

The MakeOnto algorithm inserts new values into C to ensure that the mapping from C to P is summarizable. Again, this means that the cost of materializing results for C will be higher for the transformed hierarchy than for the original. However, if the new values were not inserted, we would have to materialize results for P, and perhaps also higher categories, as well as C. At most one value is inserted in C for every value in P, meaning that the extra cost for C is never greater than the cost of materializing results for P. As before, this is a very unrealistic scenario, as it corresponds to the case where *no* values in P have children in C. In most cases, the extra cost for C will be a small percentage of the cost of materializing results for P, and the potential savings will be even greater because pre-aggregation for higher-level categories may be avoided.

As before, the correctness argument for the algorithm has two aspects. First, the mappings in the hierarchy should be *onto* upon termination. Second, the algorithm should only make transformations that are semantically correct. The correctness follows from Theorems 3 and 4, below. Again, the result set for the original values obtained using the original hierarchy will be a subset of the result set obtained using the transformed hierarchy. The results for the new values can be excluded from the result set by adding a HAVING clause condition.

Theorem 3 Algorithm MakeOnto terminates and the hierarchy for the resulting dimension D' is onto.

Proof: By induction in the height of the lattice [22].

Theorem 4 Given dimensions D and D' such that D' is the result of applying algorithm MakeOnto to D, an aggregate result obtained using D is a subset of the result obtained using D'.

Proof: Follows easily from the observation that "childless" dimension values are linked to new placeholder values in lower categories in one-to-one relationships, meaning that data for childless values will still be counted exactly once in aggregate computations that use the new dimension.

4.3 Non-Strict Hierarchies

The third algorithm renders mappings in hierarchies strict, meaning that "double-counting" will not occur. Non-strict

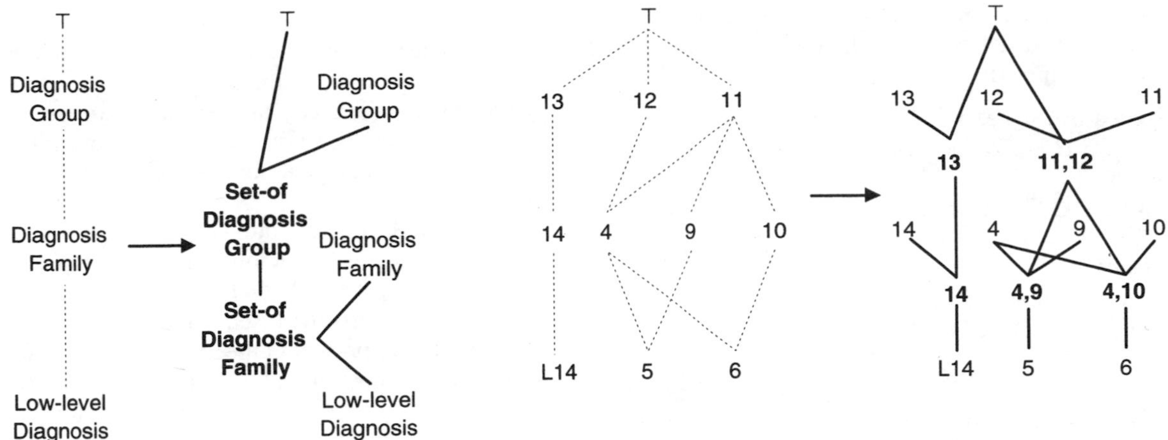

Figure 5: The Diagnosis Dimension Schema and Instance Before and After MakeStrict

hierarchies occur when one dimension value has several parent values.

The basic idea is to "fuse" a set of parent values into one "fused" value, then link the child value to this new value instead. The fused values are inserted into a new category in-between the child and parent categories. Data for the new fused category may safely be re-used for computation of higher-level aggregate results, as the hierarchy leading up to the new category is strict.

The fused value is also linked to the relevant parent values. This mapping is by nature non-strict, but this non-strictness is not a problem, as we prevent aggregate results for the parent category from being re-used higher up in the hierarchy. This is done by "unlinking" the parent category from its predecessor categories.

The categories higher up are instead reached through the fused category. This means that we can still get results for any original category, while being able to apply practical pre-aggregation throughout the hierarchy. In pre-aggregation terms, the "unlinking" of the parent categories means that we must prevent results for including this category from being materialized—only "safe" categories may be materialized. This should be given as a constraint to the pre-aggregation system that chooses which levels of aggregation to materialize.

We note that the algorithm does not introduce more *levels* in the hierarchy, only more categories, and that the number of "safe" categories in the result is the same as the number of original categories. This means that the complexity of the task of selecting the optimal aggregation levels to materialize is unaffected by the algorithm.

Example 8 The result of running the algorithm on the Diagnosis dimension is seen in Figure 5. Because of the non-strictness in the mapping from Low-level Diagnosis to Diagnosis Family, and from Diagnosis Family to Diagnosis Group, two new category types and the corresponding categories are introduced. The third picture indicates the argument to the algorithm; and, in addition, its dotted lines indicate the links deleted by the algorithm. The fourth picture gives the result of applying the algorithm; here, the bold-face values and thick lines indicate the values and links inserted by the algorithm (note that all lines are thick, as no original links remain).

In the first call of the algorithm, the three Low-level Diagnosis values—"(low-level) Lung cancer" (L14); "Insulin dependent diabetes during pregnancy" (5); and "Non insulin dependent diabetes during pregnancy" (6)—are linked to the three new fused values—"(low-level) Lung cancer" (**14**); "Diabetes during pregnancy, Insulin dependent diabetes" (**4, 9**); and "Diabetes during pregnancy, Non insulin dependent diabetes" (**4, 10**)—and these are in turn linked to "Lung Cancer" (14); "Diabetes during pregnancy" (4); "Insulin dependent diabetes" (9); and "Non insulin dependent diabetes" (10). The these latter four values in the Diagnosis Family category are un-linked from their parents, as the Diagnosis Family category is "unsafe."

When called recursively on the Set-of Diagnosis Family category, the algorithm creates the new fused values "Cancer" (**13**) and "Diabetes, Other pregnancy related diseases" (**11, 12**) in the Set-of Diagnosis Group category. These new values are linked to the values "Cancer" (13), "Diabetes" (11), and "Other pregnancy related diseases" (12) in the Diagnosis Group category, and to the $\top$ value; and the values in the Diagnosis Group category are un-linked from their parents. Note the importance of having a $\top$ value: the values not linked to $\top$ are exactly the unsafe values, for which aggregate results should not be re-used.

The algorithm assumes that all paths in the dimension hierarchy have equal length, i.e., all direct links are from children to their immediate parents. This is ensured by the MakeCovering and MakeOnto algorithms. In the algorithm that follows, C is a *child* category, P is a *parent* category, G is a *grandparent* category, N is the *new* category introduced to hold the "fused" values, and $\bowtie$ denotes natural join.

The algorithm takes a category C (initially the $\perp$ category) as input. It then goes through the set of immediate parent categories P of C (line 2). Line 4 tests if there is non-strictness in the mapping from C to P *and* if P has any parents. If this test fails, there is no problem as aggregate results for P can either be safely re-used or are guaranteed not be re-used; and the algorithm is then invoked recursively, in line 20.

(1) **procedure** MakeStrict (C)
(2) **for** each $P \in Pred(C)$ **do**
(3) **begin**
(4)   **if** $(\exists e_1 \in C\, (\exists e_2, e_3 \in P\, (e_1 \leq e_2 \wedge e_1 \leq e_3$
$\wedge\, e_2 \neq e_3))) \wedge Pred(P) \neq \emptyset$ **then**
(5)   **begin**
(6) $N \leftarrow CreateCategory(2^P)$
(7) $R_{C,N} \leftarrow \{(e_1, Fuse(\{e_2 \mid (e_1, e_2) \in R_{C,P}\}))\}$
(8) $N \leftarrow \Pi_N(R_{C,N})$
(9) $R_{N,P} \leftarrow \{(e_1, e_2) \mid e_1 \in N \wedge e_2 \in Unfuse(e_1)\}$
(10) $Pred(C) \leftarrow Pred(C) \cup \{N\} \setminus \{P\}$
(11) $Pred(N) \leftarrow \{P\}$
(12)   **for** each $G \in Pred(P)$ **do**
(13)   **begin**
(14) $R_{N,G} \leftarrow \Pi_{N,G}(R_{N,P} \bowtie R_{P,G})$
(15) $Pred(N) \leftarrow Pred(N) \cup \{G\}$
(16) $Pred(P) \leftarrow Pred(P) \setminus \{G\}$
(17)   **end**
(18)   MakeStrict(N)
(19)   **end**
(20)   **else** MakeStrict(P)
(21) **end**
(22) **end**

If the test succeeds, the algorithm creates a new fused category. First, an empty category N with domain 2^P is created in line 6. The values inserted into this category represent *sets* of values of P. For example. the value "**1, 2**" represents the set consisting of precisely $1, 2$. Values in C are then linked to new, fused values, representing their particular *combination* of parents in P (line 7). The new values are constructed using a Fuse function that creates a distinct value for each combination of P values and stores the corresponding P values along with it.

The resulting links are used in line 8 to insert the fused values into their category N, and an "Unfuse" function, mapping fused values from N into the corresponding P values, is used in line 9 to map the values in N to those in P. In line 10, N is included into, and P is excluded from, the sets of predecessors of C. The set of predecessors of N is set to P in line 11, meaning that the new category N resides in-between C and P in the hierarchy.

For each grandparent category G, the algorithm links values in N to values in G, in line 14; it includes G in the predecessors of N, in line 15; and it excludes G from the predecessors of P, in line 16, thereby also deleting the links from P to G from the hierarchy. The exclusion of the G categories from the predecessors of P means that aggregate results for P will not be re-used to compute results for the G categories.

In the end, the algorithm is called recursively on the new category, N. Note that the test for $Pred(P) \neq \emptyset$ in line (4) ensures that the mapping from N to P will not be altered, as P now has *no* predecessors.

Following the reasoning in Section 4.1, we find that the overall big-$\mathcal{O}$ complexity is $\mathcal{O}(pnk \log n \log k)$, where p is the number of immediate parent and children categories in the dimension type lattice, n is the size of the largest mapping in the hierarchy, and k is the maximum number of values fused together. For most realistic scenarios, p and k are small constants, yielding a low $\mathcal{O}(n \log n)$ complexity for the algorithm.

The MakeStrict algorithm constructs a new category N and inserts fused values into N to achieve summarizability for the mapping from N to P and from N to G. The algorithm only inserts the fused values for the combinations that are actually present in the mapping from C to P. This means that the cost of materializing results for N is never higher than the cost of materializing results for C. This is a worst-case scenario—for the most common cases, the cost of materializing results for N will be be close to the cost of materializing results for P. However, without the introduction of N, we would have to materialize results not only for P, but also for G and *all* higher-level categories. Thus, the potential savings in materialization costs are very high.

Considering correctness, the mappings in the hierarchy should be *strict* upon termination, and the algorithm should only make transformations that are semantically correct. More specifically, it is acceptable that some mappings be non-strict, namely the ones from the new, fused categories to the unsafe parent categories that do *not* have predecessors in the resulting hierarchy, meaning that aggregate results for these categories will not be re-used.

The correctness follows from Theorems 5 and 6, below. When evaluating queries we get the same result for original values as when evaluating on the old hierarchy. The values that are deleted by the algorithm were not linked to any facts, meaning that these values did not contribute to the results in the original hierarchy. As all the new values are inserted into new categories that are unknown to the user, the aggregate result obtained will be the same for the original and transformed hierarchy. We do not need to modify the original query.

Theorem 5 Let D' be the dimension resulting from applying algorithm MakeStrict on dimension D. Then the following hold: Algorithm MakeStrict terminates and the hierarchy for the dimension D'', obtained by removing unsafe categories from D', is strict.

Proof: By induction in the height of the lattice [22].

Theorem 6 Given dimensions D and D' such that D' is the result of applying algorithm MakeStrict to D, an aggregate obtained using D' is the same as that obtained using D.

Proof: Follows from Lemma 2 [22].

Lemma 2 For the dimension $D' = (C', \leq')$ resulting from applying algorithm MakeStrict to dimension $D = (C, \leq)$, the following holds. $\forall e_1, e_2 \in D\ (e_1 \in C_1 \wedge Safe(C_1) \wedge e_1 \leq' e_2 \Leftrightarrow e_1 \leq e_2)$ (there is a path between an original dimension value in a safe category and any other original dimension value in the new dimension hierarchy iff there was a path between them in the original hierarchy).

Proof: By induction in the height of the lattice [22].

4.4 Transforming Fact-Dimension Relations

The algorithms from the previous sections may also be applied to the relationships between facts and dimensions. The basic idea is to view the facts as the bottom granularity in the lattice. The inputs to the algorithms then are the facts F, the $R_{F,C}$ tables that describe the mappings from facts to dimension values, and the C and R_{C_1,C_2} tables that describe the dimension categories and the mappings between them.

Only the covering and strictness properties are of concern for the fact-dimension relationships. An *into* mapping from facts to dimension values means that not all dimension values in the bottom category have associated facts, which does not affect summarizability. The MakeCovering and MakeStrict algorithms may be applied to render relationships summarizable (see [22] for a detailed coverage).

First, facts may be mapped *directly* to dimension values in categories higher than the $\perp$ category. This mapping to values of *mixed* granularities means that not all facts will be accounted for when materializing aggregate results for lower categories. The MakeCovering algorithm rectifies this situation. Second, relationships between facts and dimension values may be many-to-many. This means that the hierarchy, with the facts as the bottom category, is non-strict, leading to possible double-counting of facts. The Makestrict algorithm addresses this problem.

In the case study, the mapping between patients and diagnoses is of mixed granularity and also many-to-many: a patient may have several diagnoses, each of which which may belong to any of the levels Low-Level Diagnosis, Diagnosis Family, and Diagnosis Group.

5 Architectural Context

The overall idea presented in this paper is to take unnormalized MOs and transform them into normalized MOs that are well supported by the practical pre-aggregation techniques available in current OLAP systems. Queries are then evaluated on the transformed MOs. However, we still want the users to see only the original MOs, as they reflect the users' understanding of the domain. This prompts the need for means of handling both the original and the transformed MOs. This section explores their coexistence.

A current trend in commercial OLAP technology is the separation of the front-end presentation layer from the back-end database server. Modern OLAP applications consist of an OLAP client that handles the user interface and an OLAP server that manages the data and processes queries. The client communicates with the server using a standardized application programming interface (API), e.g., Microsoft's OLE DB for OLAP [16] or the OLAP Council's MDAPI [19]. The architecture of such a system is given to the left in Figure 6.

This separation of client and server facilitates our desire to have the user see the original MO while queries are evaluated against the transformed MO. Studies have shown that queries on a data warehouse consist of 80% *navigational*

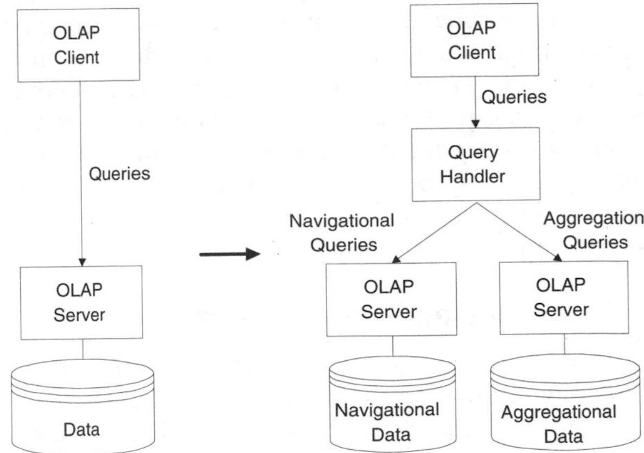

Figure 6: Architecture of Integration

queries that explore the dimension hierarchies and 20% *aggregation* queries that summarize the data at various levels of detail [13]. Examples of navigational and aggregation queries are "Show me the Low-Level Diagnoses contained in the Insulin-Dependent Diabetes Diagnosis Family" and "Show me the count of patients, grouped by Diagnosis Family," respectively. The navigational queries must be performed on the *original* MO, while the aggregation queries must be performed on the *transformed* MO. This is achieved by introducing an extra "Query Handler" component between the client and the server. The OLAP client sends a query to the query handler, the primary task of which is to determine whether the query is a navigational query (internal to a dimension) or an aggregation query (involving the facts). Navigational queries are passed to one OLAP server that handles the original (navigational) data, while aggregation queries are passed to another OLAP server that manages the transformed (aggregation) data. This extended architecture is seen to the right in Figure 6.

The OLAP server for navigation data needs to support dimension hierarchies which have non-summarizable properties, a requirement not yet supported by many commercial systems today. However, relational OLAP systems using snow-flake schemas [13] are able to support this type of hierarchies, as are some other OLAP systems, e.g., Hyperion (Arbor) Essbase [11]. If the OLAP system available does not have sufficiently flexible hierarchy support, one solution is to build a special-purpose OLAP server that conforms to the given API. This task is not as daunting as it may seem at first because only *navigational* queries need to be supported, meaning that multidimensional queries can be translated into simple SQL "lookup" queries.

We note that the only data needed to answer navigational queries is the hierarchy definitions. Thus, we only need to store the fact data (facts and fact-dimension relations, in our model) once, in the aggregational data, meaning that the overall storage requirement is only slightly larger than storing just the aggregational data. Navigational queries are evaluated on the original hierarchy definitions and do not need to be re-written by the query handler.

As described in Section 4, aggregation queries need to

be re-written slightly by adding an extra HAVING clause condition to exclude results for the new values inserted by the transformation algorithms. This can be done automatically by the query handler, giving total transparency for the user. Even though the added HAVING clause conditions are only necessary for the covering and onto transformations, they can also be applied to hierarchies transformed to achieve strictness; this has no effect, but simplifies the query rewriting.

6 Conclusion and Future Work

Motivated by the increasing use of OLAP systems in many different applications, this paper provides transformation techniques for multidimensional databases that leverage the performance-enhancing technique known as practical, or partial or semi-eager, preaggregation, making this technique relevant to a much wider range of real-world applications.

Current pre-aggregation techniques assume that the dimensional structures are *summarizable*. Specifically, the mappings in dimension hierarchies must be *onto*, *covering*, and *strict*; the relationships between facts and dimensions must be many-to-one, and facts must be mapped to the lowest categories in dimensions. The paper presents transformation techniques that render dimensions with hierarchies that do not satisfy these properties summarizable. The transformations have low, practical computational complexity, they may be implemented using standard relational database technology, and the paper also describes how to integrate the transformed hierarchies in current OLAP systems, transparently to the user. The algorithms may also be applied to the cases of non-summarizable relationships between facts and dimensions, which also occur often in real-world applications, and the algorithms can be modified to incrementally maintain the transformed hierarchies when the underlying data is modified [22].

Several directions for future research appear promising. The current techniques render the entire dimension hierarchies summarizable; extending the techniques to consider only the parts that have been selected for preaggregation appears attractive and possible. Another direction is to take into account the different types of aggregate functions to be applied, leading to local relaxation of the summarizability requirement. For example, *max* and *min* are insensitive to duplicate values, which relaxes summarizability.

References

[1] E. Baralis et al. Materialized View Selection in a Multidimensional Database. In *Proc. of VLDB*, pp. 156–165, 1997.

[2] E. F. Codd. Providing OLAP (on-line analytical processing) to user-analysts: An IT mandate. E.F. Codd and Assoc., 1993.

[3] S. Dar et al. Answering SQL Queries Using Views. In *Proc. of VLDB*, pp. 318–329, 1996.

[4] C. E. Dyreson. Information Retrieval from an Incomplete Data Cube. In *Proc. of VLDB*, pp. 532–543, 1996.

[5] J. Gray et al. Data Cube: A Relational Aggregation Operator Generalizing Group-By, Cross-Tab and Sub-Totals. *Data Mining and Knowledge Discovery*, 1(1):29–54, 1997.

[6] A. Gupta et al. Aggregate Query Processing in Data Warehousing Environments. In *Proc. of VLDB*, pp. 358–369, 1995.

[7] H. Gupta et al. Index Selection for OLAP. In *Proc. of ICDE*, pp. 208–219, 1997.

[8] H. Gupta. Selection of Views to Materialize in a Data Warehouse. In *Proc. of ICDT*, pp. 98–112, 1997.

[9] H. Gupta and I.S. Mumick. Selection of Views to Materialize Under a Maintenance-Time Constraint. In *Proc. of ICDT*, pp. 453–470, 1999.

[10] V. Harinarayan et al. Implementing Data Cubes Efficiently. In *Proc. of SIGMOD*, pp. 205–216, 1996.

[11] Hyperion Corporation. Hyperion Essbase OLAP Server. <www.hyperion.com/downloads/essbaseolap.pdf>. Current as of May 20, 1999.

[12] Informix Corporation. MetaCube ROLAP Option for Informix Dynamic Server. <www.informix.com/answers/english/pdf_docs/metacube/4189.pdf>. Current as of May 20, 1999.

[13] R. Kimball. *The Data Warehouse Toolkit*. Wiley Computer Publishing, 1996.

[14] R. Kimball. Help with Multi-Valued Dimension. *DBMS Magazine*, 11(9), 1998.

[15] H. Lenz and A. Shoshani. Summarizability in OLAP and Statistical Data Bases. In *Proc. of SSDBM*, pp. 39–48, 1997.

[16] Microsoft Corporation. OLE DB for OLAP Version 1.0 Specification. Microsoft Technical Document, 1998.

[17] Microsoft Corporation. OLAP Services White Paper. <www.microsoft.com/sql/70/whpprs/olapoverview.htm>. Current as of May 20, 1999.

[18] I. S. Mumick et al. Maintenance of data cubes and summary tables in a warehouse. In *Proc. of SIGMOD*, pp. 100–111, 1997.

[19] The OLAP Council. *MDAPI Specification Version 2.0*. OLAP Council Technical Document, 1998.

[20] The OLAP Report. *Database Explosion*. <www.olapreport.com/DatabaseExplosion.htm>. Current as of May 20, 1999.

[21] T. B. Pedersen and C. S. Jensen. Multidimensional Data Modeling for Complex Data. In *Proc. of ICDE*, 1999. Extended version available as TimeCenter TR-37, <www.cs.auc.dk/TimeCenter>, 1998.

[22] T. B. Pedersen et al. Extending Practical Pre-Aggregation in On-Line Analytical Processing. TR R-99-5004, Comp. Sci. Dept., Aalborg University, <www.cs.auc.dk/~tbp/articles/R995004.ps>, 1999.

[23] D. Quass and J. Widom. On-Line Warehouse View Maintenance for Batch Updates. In *Proc. of SIGMOD*, pp. 393–404, 1997.

[24] M. Rafanelli and A. Shoshani. STORM: A Statistical Object Representation Model. In *Proc. of SSDBM*, pp. 14–29, 1990.

[25] A. Shukla et al. Storage Estimation for Multidimensional Aggregates in the Presence of Hierarchies. In *Proc. of VLDB*, pp. 522–531, 1996.

[26] D. Theodoratos and T. Sellis. Data Warehouse Configuration. In *Proc. of VLDB*, pp. 126–135, 1997.

[27] J. Widom. Research Problems in Data Warehousing. In *Proc. of CIKM*, pp. 25–30, 1995.

[28] R. Winter. Databases: Back in the OLAP game. *Intelligent Enterprise Magazine*, 1(4):60–64, 1998.

[29] World Health Organization. *International Classification of Diseases (ICD-10)*. Tenth Revision, 1992.

[30] J. Yang et al. Algorithms for materialized view design in a data warehousing environment. In *Proc. of VLDB*, pp. 136–145, 1997.

Hierarchical Cubes for Range-Sum Queries

Chee-Yong Chan **Yannis E. Ioannidis*** †

Department of Computer Sciences
University of Wisconsin-Madison
{cychan,yannis}@cs.wisc.edu

Abstract

A range-sum query sums over all selected cells of an OLAP data cube where the selection is specified by ranges of contiguous values for each dimension. An efficient approach to process such queries is to precompute a prefix cube (PC), which is a cube of the same dimensionality and size as the original data cube but with a prefix range-sum stored in each cell. Using a PC, any range-sum query can be evaluated at a cost that is independent of the size of the sub-cube circumscribed by the query. However, a drawback of PCs is that they are very costly to maintain. Recently, a variant of prefix cubes called Relative Prefix Cubes (RPC) has been proposed to alleviate this problem.

In this paper, we propose a new class of cube representations called Hierarchical Cubes, which is based on a design framework defined by two orthogonal dimensions. Our results show that a particular cube design called the Hierarchical Band Cube (HBC) is the overall winner: it not only has a significantly better query-update tradeoff than previous approaches, but it can also be more effectively buffered.

*Partially supported by the National Science Foundation under Grant IRI-9157368 (PYI Award) and the members of the Wisconsin database group industrial affiliates program (http://www.cs.wisc.edu/~raghu/dbaffiliates.html).

†Author's present address: Department of Informatics, University of Athens, Hellas (Greece).

Proceedings of the 25th VLDB Conference, Edinburgh, Scotland, 1999.

1 Introduction

Aggregation is a common and computation-intensive operation in on-line analytical processing systems (OLAP), where the data is usually modeled as a multidimensional data cube, and queries typically involve aggregations across various cube dimensions. Conceptually, an n-dimensional data cube is derived from a projection of $(n+1)$ attributes from some relation R, where one of these attributes is classified as a *measure attribute* and the remaining n attributes are classified as *dimensional attributes.* Each dimension of the data cube corresponds to a dimensional attribute, and the value in each cube cell is an aggregation of the measure attribute value of all records in R having the same dimensional attribute values.

Various forms of precomputation techniques [5, 8, 13] and indexing methods [3, 6, 7, 9, 10, 11, 12] have been proposed to expedite processing of OLAP queries. In this paper, we propose a new precomputation technique for a class of OLAP queries called *range-sum queries.*

A **range-sum query** sums over all selected cells of an OLAP data cube where the selection is specified by ranges of contiguous values for each dimension. An example of a range-sum query over a data cube C with schema $(A_1, A_2, \ldots, A_n, M)$ is as follows:

SELECT	**SUM** $(C.M)$
FROM	C
WHERE	$l_1 \leq C.A_1 \leq h_1$
and	$l_2 \leq C.A_2 \leq h_2$
and	....
and	$l_n \leq C.A_n \leq h_n$

We refer to range-sum queries with $l_i = 0$ for $1 \leq i \leq n$ as **prefix range-sum queries.**

The most direct approach to evaluate a range-sum query is to use the data cube itself, but the disadvantage of this approach is that the number of cells that need to be accessed is proportional to the size of the sub-cube defined by the query. Recently, a more efficient approach to compute range-sum queries was proposed using a **prefix cube** (PC) [5] which costs

C	0	1	2	3	4	5	6	7
0	3	5	1	2	2	4	6	3
1	7	3	2	6	8	7	1	2
2	2	4	2	3	3	3	4	5
3	3	2	1	5	3	5	2	8
4	4	2	1	3	3	4	7	1
5	2	3	3	6	1	8	5	1
6	4	5	2	7	1	9	3	3
7	2	4	2	2	3	1	9	1

(a) Data Cube

P	0	1	2	3	4	5	6	7
0	3	8	9	11	13	17	23	26
1	10	18	21	29	39	50	57	62
2	12	24	29	40	53	67	78	88
3	15	29	35	51	67	86	99	117
4	19	35	42	61	80	103	123	142
5	21	40	50	75	95	126	151	171
6	25	49	61	93	114	154	182	205
7	27	55	69	103	127	168	205	229

(b) Prefix Cube

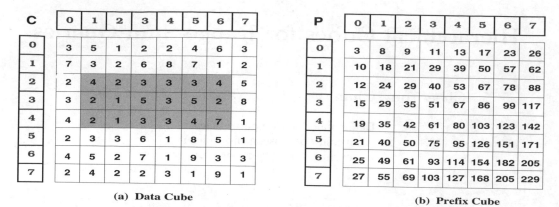

Figure 1: Example of an 8×8 Data Cube C and its Prefix Cube $\mathcal{P}$.

at most 2^n cell accesses to evaluate each range-sum query, where n is the dimensionality of the data cube. However, maintaining a prefix cube is very expensive because a single cell modification in the data cube can affect a large number of cells in the prefix cube. For applications where the data cubes are dynamic and are of very large size, having both fast query response as well as efficient cube maintenance is critical. More recently, a variant of the prefix cube approach called **relative prefix cube** (RPC) [4] has been proposed to try to balance the query-update tradeoff between the data cube and prefix cube approaches.

In addition to the above approaches, which provide precise answers to range-sum queries, a method that provides approximate answers for high-dimensional, sparse data cubes has recently been proposed as well [14].

In this paper, our focus is on data cube designs that provide precise answers for range-sum queries. We make the following contributions:

- We propose a new class of cube representations called **hierarchical cubes**. This new class of cubes is based on a design framework that is defined by two orthogonal dimensions. By varying the options along each dimension, various cube designs with different query-update tradeoffs can be generated. In particular, we present two new cube designs called *hierarchical rectangle cubes* (HRC) and *hierarchical band cubes* (HBC), which are generalizations of the existing cube designs.

- We demonstrate analytically that both HRC and HBC have significantly better query-update tradeoff than earlier approaches, for both expected-case as well as worst-case performances.

- We also analyze the effect of buffering on the tradeoff among the various classes of precomputed cubes. Our results show that HBC can be more effectively buffered than the other classes of precomputed cubes; by using a moderate amount of main-memory for buffering, HBC can become as query-efficient as the most query-efficient approach without incurring its high update-cost.

Note that all the techniques developed for range-sum queries can be applied to any binary operator for which there exists an inverse operator; other applicable aggregation operators include COUNT, AVERAGE, ROLLING-SUM, and ROLLING-AVERAGE [5].

We conclude this section with some preliminaries. Let C be a n-dimensional data cube of size $D_1 \times D_2 \times \cdots D_n$, where D_i is the cardinality of the ith dimension. For simplicity and without loss of generality, let the domain of the ith dimension be $\{0, 1, \cdots, D_i - 1\}$. We use the generic term **precomputed cube** to refer to a cube belonging to any of the classes of precomputed cubes (i.e., data cube, PC, RPC, HRC, and HBC). We denote a range-sum query by $(l_1 : h_1, l_2 : h_2, \cdots, l_n : h_n)$ and a prefix range-sum query by $(h_1, h_2, \cdots, h_n)$. Given two cells $x = (x_1, x_2, \cdots, x_n)$ and $y = (y_1, y_2, \cdots, y_n)$ in an n-dimensional cube, we say that **x precedes y**, denoted by $x \preceq y$, if and only if $x_i \leq y_i$ for $1 \leq i \leq n$.

For ease of presentation, we use only 2-dimensional cube examples to illustrate the various classes of precomputed cubes, and use the notational convention (x, y) to denote a cube cell in row x and column y.

The rest of this paper is organized as follows. Section 2 presents related work on precomputed cubes for processing range-sum queries. In Section 3, we present a new class of precomputed cubes called *hierarchical cubes*. Section 4 introduces three metrics for comparing the space, update, and query costs of the various classes of precomputed cubes, and presents an analytical comparison of their tradeoffs. In Section 5, we consider the effect of buffering on the query-update tradeoff of precomputed cubes. Finally, we summarize our results in Section 6. Due to space constraints, all analytical results are omitted in this paper but are available elsewhere [2].

A	0	1	2	3	4	5	6	7
0	3	8	9	11	2	6	12	15
1	10	18	21	29	10	21	28	36
2	12	24	29	40	13	27	38	48
3	15	29	35	51	16	35	48	66
4	4	6	7	10	3	7	14	15
5	6	11	15	24	4	16	28	30
6	10	20	26	42	5	26	41	46
7	12	26	34	52	8	30	54	60

(a) Relative-Prefix Array A

O	0	1	2	3	4	5	6	7
0	0	0	0	0	11	0	0	0
1	0				18			
2	0				29			
3	0				40			
4	15	14	20	36	77	19	32	50
5	0				14			
6	0				32			
7	0				42			

(b) Overlay Box O

Figure 2: Example of a Relative Prefix Cube for the Data Cube in Figure 1.

2 Related Work

This section presents two classes of precomputed cubes for processing range-sum queries, namely, prefix cube (PC) and relative prefix cube (RPC).

2.1 Prefix Cubes (PC)

The **prefix cube** of a data cube C, denoted by $\mathcal{P}$, is a cube of the same dimensionality and size as C such that each cell $x = (x_1, x_2, \cdots, x_n)$ in $\mathcal{P}$ stores the result of the prefix range-sum $(x_1, x_2, \cdots, x_n)$; i.e., $\mathcal{P}[x] = \sum_{i_1=0}^{x_1} \sum_{i_2=0}^{x_2} \cdots \sum_{i_n=0}^{x_n} C[i_1, i_2, \cdots, i_n]$. The PC approach exploits the property that any range-sum query can be evaluated in terms of at most 2^n appropriate prefix range-sum queries. Therefore, by precomputing all possible prefix range-sums, the evaluation cost of a range-sum query using a PC is no more than 2^n cell accesses. However, the update cost of the PC is high since every modification of a single data cube cell u affects the set of cells $\{c : u \preceq c\}$ in the PC.

For example, Figure 1 shows an 8×8 data cube and its prefix cube. Evaluating the range-sum query indicated by the shaded region in Figure 1 using the data cube C requires 18 cell accesses. On the other hand, processing the same query using the prefix cube $\mathcal{P}$ is given by $\mathcal{P}[4,6] - \mathcal{P}[4,0] - \mathcal{P}[1,6] + \mathcal{P}[1,0]$ which accesses only 4 cells. The disadvantage, of course, is that updating, for example, cell $C[1,2]$ requires updating cells $\mathcal{P}[i,j]$ for $1 \leq i \leq 7$, $2 \leq j \leq 7$. Details of the prefix cube can be found elsewhere [5].

2.2 Relative Prefix Cubes (RPC)

An approach that has recently been proposed to balance the query-update tradeoff between the data cube and prefix cube is the **relative prefix cube** (RPC) [4]. An RPC consists of two components: (1) a *relative-prefix array* $\mathcal{A}$ and (2) an *overlay box* $\mathcal{O}$. The relative-prefix array $\mathcal{A}$ is similar to a prefix cube $\mathcal{P}$ except that it is partitioned into a number of disjoint sub-cubes of equal size such that each sub-cube is organized as a local prefix sub-cube. By structuring the single, large prefix cube into a collection of smaller prefix sub-cubes, $\mathcal{A}$ limits the effect of an update propagation to a local sub-cube thereby reducing its update-cost.

However, evaluating a prefix range-sum query using only the relative-prefix array $\mathcal{A}$ has a worst-case cost proportional to the number of sub-cubes in $\mathcal{A}$. To improve the worst-case query evaluation cost, the RPC approach also precomputes additional information in a second component called the overlay box. Conceptually, the overlay box $\mathcal{O}$ is a cube of the same dimensionality as $\mathcal{A}$ that is partitioned into a number of sub-boxes (of the same dimensionality as each sub-cube) such that there is one sub-box in $\mathcal{O}$ associated with each sub-cube in $\mathcal{A}$ containing additional precomputed values in some cells.

Figure 2 shows an example of a RPC (for the same data cube in Figure 1) where the relative-prefix array is partitioned into four 4×4 sub-cubes. The cost of evaluating a prefix range-sum query using a RPC is between 1 and $(n+2)$ cell accesses; specifically, it requires access to one cell in $\mathcal{A}$ and at most $(n+1)$ cells in $\mathcal{O}$. For example, using the RPC in Figure 2, the prefix range-sum query $(5,6)$ is evaluated as $\mathcal{A}[5,6] + \mathcal{O}[4,4] + \mathcal{O}[5,4] + \mathcal{O}[4,6]$.

3 Hierarchical Cubes

In general, we can characterize a precomputed cube X by the way it maps each of its cells to a collection of cells in the data cube, i.e., each cell value in X is a sum over some subset of cell values in the data cube. We refer to each mapped collection of data cube cells as a **mapped region**. For the data cube, the mapped region for each cell v is simply $\{v\}$, while for the prefix cube, the mapped region for each cell v is $\{c : c \preceq v\}$.

In this section, we present a new class of precomputed cube designs called *hierarchical cubes* that require the same space as the data cube but provide better query-update tradeoff than all earlier approaches. This new class is based on a hierarchical organization of the precomputed cube cells, and its design space is characterized by two orthogonal dimensions[1]:

1. **Cube decomposition**
   This dimension organizes the precomputed cube cells into a hierarchical structure.

2. **Cube mapping**
   This dimension defines a mapping from each precomputed cube cell to a particular subset of cells in the data cube by taking into account the hierarchical organization of the precomputed cube cells.

By varying the options along each dimension, various precomputed cube designs with different query-update tradeoffs can be generated.

3.1 Cube Decomposition

The cells in a cube can be organized into a hierarchical structure by decomposing each dimension of the cube. Such decomposition has previously been applied to the design of bitmap indexes [1]. We first introduce the notion of decomposition and then explain how it defines a hierarchical structure on the cube cells.

3.1.1 Decomposition Technique

Consider an attribute A with cardinality D (i.e., $domain(A) = \{0, 1, \cdots, D-1\}$). Given a sequence of m positive integers $B = < b_m, b_{m-1}, \cdots, b_2, b_1 >$ (where $b_m = \left\lceil D / \prod_{i=1}^{m-1} b_i \right\rceil$), an integer $v \in Domain(A)$ can be decomposed into a sequence of m **component values** $V = < v_m, v_{m-1}, \cdots, v_2, v_1 >$ as follows:

$$v = v_m \left(\prod_{j=1}^{m-1} b_j \right) + \ldots + v_i \left(\prod_{j=1}^{i-1} b_j \right) + \ldots + v_2 b_1 + v_1. \quad (1)$$

Each component value v_i is a base-b_i digit (i.e., $0 \leq v_i < b_i$). We refer to B as a **base-sequence** and V as the **B-decomposition of v**.

For example, consider $D = 24$ and $v = 22$. Since $22 = 3(6)+4 = 1(3)(4)+2(4)+2$, therefore, $< 3, 4 >$ is the $< 4, 6 >$-decomposition of v, and $< 1, 2, 2 >$ is the $< 2, 3, 4 >$-decomposition of v. Thus, by varying the base-sequence, different decompositions of an attribute value can be obtained.

3.1.2 Hierarchical Organization of Cube Cells

We now explain how the cells in an n-dimensional data cube can be organized into a hierarchical structure by applying a (possibly different) base-sequence to each dimensional attribute of the cube. Let m denote the length of the longest base-sequence among the n base-sequences. Base-sequences that are shorter than m are padded with base numbers of value 1 so that all the n base-sequences have the same length of m. Given this, let $\mathcal{B}_i = < b_{i,m}, b_{i,m-1}, \cdots, b_{i,1} >$ denote the base-sequence that is used to decompose the ith dimensional attribute, for $1 \leq i \leq n$; and $p_{i,j}$ denote $\prod_{k=1}^{j} b_{i,k}$ for $1 \leq i \leq n$ and $1 \leq j \leq m$. For notational convenience, let $p_{i,0} = 1$. A data cube that is decomposed using length-m base-sequences has **height** m.

The set of n base-sequences $\{\mathcal{B}_1, \mathcal{B}_2, \cdots, \mathcal{B}_n\}$ recursively partitions the data cube, organizing its cells in a forest as follows:

1. The data cube is first partitioned into $\prod_{i=1}^{n} b_{i,m}$ sub-cubes each of size $\prod_{i=1}^{n} p_{i,m-1}$. The **rank** of each sub-cube is equal to m. The smallest cell in each sub-cube[2] is made a root in the forest at level m.

2. Each rank-k sub-cube S ($1 < k \leq m$) is partitioned into $t = \prod_{i=1}^{n} b_{i,k-1}$ rank-(k-1) sub-cubes each of size $\prod_{i=1}^{n} p_{i,k-2}$. The smallest cell in one of these t sub-cubes is the same as the smallest cell (denoted by c) in the sub-cube S and is already in the forest under construction. The smallest cell in each of the remaining $(t-1)$ sub-cubes becomes a child of c in the forest at level $k-1$.

3. Each rank-1 sub-cube consists of only one cell which is a leaf in the forest at level 1.

We denote the parent of a cell v by **parent(v)**. If $c = (c_1, c_2, \cdots, c_n)$ is a level-k cell with $k < m$, then $parent(c) = (p_1, p_2, \cdots, p_n)$, where $p_i = c_i - (c_i \bmod b_{i,k})$, for $1 \leq i \leq n$. The level of a cell v is denoted by **level(v)**, where $1 \leq level(v) \leq m$.

Figure 3 shows an example of cube decomposition for an 8×8 data cube. In Figure 3(a), the data cube is decomposed with the base-sequence $< 2, 2, 2 >$ for each dimension, which partitions the data cube into four 4×4 rank-3 sub-cubes. Each rank-3 sub-cube is further partitioned into four 2×2 rank-2 sub-cubes

[1] We note that the design framework defined here for data cubes is similar to that defined for the design space of bitmap indexes [1]. In fact, both design spaces can be abstracted into a more general framework, but a discussion of this is beyond the scope of this paper.

[2] The *smallest cell* in a sub-cube S refers to the cell in S that precedes all other cells in S; the smallest cell is unique due to the rectangular structure of the sub-cube.

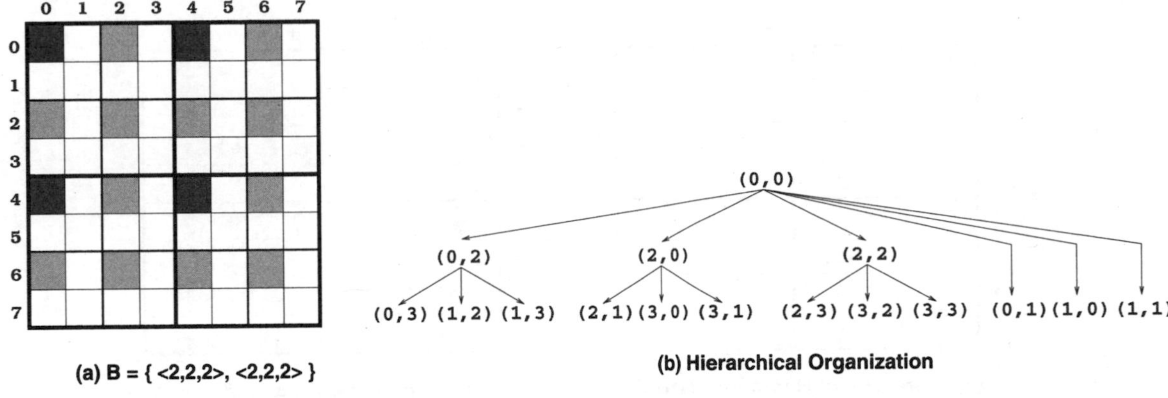

Figure 3: Example of Cube Decomposition.

Cell v	Cube Mappings	
	Hierarchical Rectangle (HR)	Hierarchical Band (HB)
Root cell	$\{v\}$	$\{c : c \preceq v\}$
Non-root cell	$\{c : parent(v) \preceq c \preceq v\}$	$\{c : c \preceq v\} - \{c : c \preceq parent(v)\}$

Table 1: Two Cube Mappings based on Hierarchical Organization of Cube Cells.

each of which consists of 4 cells. Figure 3(b) shows the hierarchical organization for the upper-left rank-3 sub-cube in Figure 3(a). The root cell is $(0,0)$ which is the parent cell of three level-2 cells ($(0,2)$, $(2,0)$, and $(2,2)$) and three level-1 cells ($(0,1)$, $(1,0)$, and $(1,1)$); and each level-2 cell is the parent cell of three level-1 cells (e.g., $(2,2)$ is the parent cell of cells $(2,3)$, $(3,2)$, and $(3,3)$).

Given a cell c in a cube X, let $\lambda(\mathbf{c})$ denote the "largest" descendant cell[3] of c in X; i.e., for any descendant cell c' of c in X, $c' \preceq \lambda(c)$. For example, in Figure 3(a), $\lambda((0,0)) = (3,3)$, $\lambda((4,2)) = (5,3)$, and $\lambda((6,3)) = (6,3)$.

3.2 Cube Mappings

Based on the hierarchical organization of cube cells, we present two cube mappings, **hierarchical rectangle (HR)** mapping and **hierarchical band (HB)** mapping, defined in Table 1. Each mapping is defined in terms of two cases depending on whether the cell being mapped is a root cell or not. Figure 4 illustrates these two cube mappings on an 8×8 cube that is decomposed with the base-sequence $< 2,4 >$ for each dimension. For HR mapping, the mapped region for a root cell r contains only r itself, and the mapped region for a non-root cell c is the "rectangle" of cells defined by $parent(c)$ and c. For HB mapping, the mapped region for a root cell r contains all the cells preceding r and including r itself, and the mapped region for a non-root cell c is an "angular band" of cells defined by the difference between two regions: (1) the cells preceding c and including c itself, and (2) the cells preceding $parent(c)$ and including $parent(c)$ itself.

[3]A cell x is an **ancestor cell** of a cell y (or equivalently, y is a **descendant cell** of x) if either x is a parent cell of y; or x is a parent cell of some cell z, and z is an ancestor cell of y.

We refer to precomputed cubes based on the HR mapping as **hierarchical rectangle cubes (HRC)**, and to those based on the HB mapping as **hierarchical band cubes (HBC)**. Figure 2(a) shows an example of an HRC decomposed with $< 2,4 >$ for each dimension, and Figure 5 shows an example of an HBC decomposed with $< 2,2,2 >$ for each dimension.

3.3 Design Space

Figure 6 shows the design space of precomputed cubes defined by the two dimensions. Along the cube decomposition dimension, we have the various base-sequences to decompose the dimensional attributes of the precomputed cube. Note that each dimensional attribute can be decomposed with a different base-sequence. Along the cube mapping dimension, we have the two mappings, HR and HB. By combining different options along these two dimensions, various data cube designs with different query-update tradeoffs can be obtained.

Interestingly, both data cubes and prefix cubes turn out to be special cases of HRC and HBC, respectively; this occurs when each dimensional attribute A_i of the cube is decomposed with the base-sequence $< D_i >$ so that all the cube cells are root cells (see Table 1 also). Furthermore, the relative-prefix array component of RPC (i.e., RPA) is just a HRC with a height of 2.

3.4 Hierarchical Rectangle Cubes (HRC)

In this section, we present algorithms for constructing, querying, and updating an n-dimensional HRC $\mathcal{H}$ for the case when $\mathcal{H}$ is not a data cube.

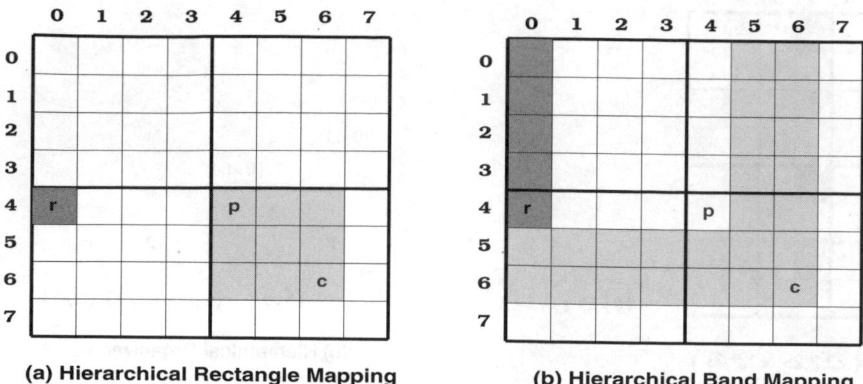

Figure 4: Example of Cube Mappings on an 8×8 cube decomposed with $< 2, 4 >$ for each dimension. Cells r and p are root and $p = parent(c)$.

H	0	1	2	3	4	5	6	7
0	3	5	6	2	13	4	10	3
1	7	15	13	20	26	37	34	39
2	9	12	26	1	40	14	65	10
3	1	17	6	22	14	33	21	39
4	19	16	23	19	80	23	43	19
5	2	21	8	33	15	46	28	48
6	6	24	42	32	34	40	102	23
7	2	30	8	42	13	54	23	47

Figure 5: Example of a HBC for the Data Cube in Figure 1.

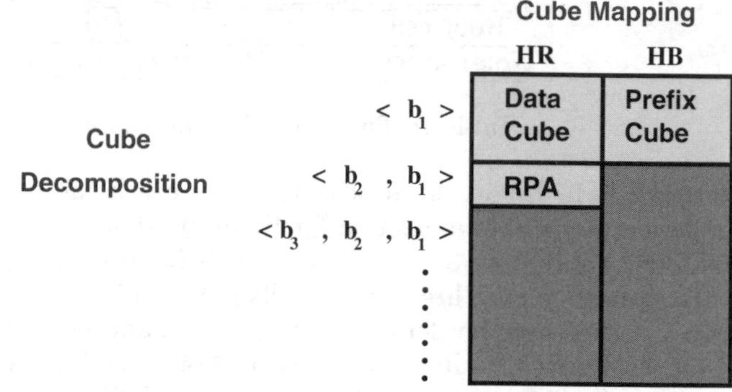

Figure 6: Design Space for Precomputed Cubes.

3.4.1 Construction Algorithm

The construction algorithm for an HRC $\mathcal{H}$ is similar to that for PC except that the prefix range-sum in each cell of $\mathcal{H}$ is computed locally with respect to the cell's parent rather than with respect to the cell $(0, 0, \cdots, 0)$ [5].

3.4.2 Query Algorithm

Figure 7 shows the algorithms for evaluating a range-sum query using an HRC $\mathcal{H}$. Algorithm **Rewrite-LocalRSQ** rewrites a range-sum query Q into a collection of local range-sum queries, with one local range-sum query for each rank-2 sub-cube in $\mathcal{H}$ that overlaps with Q. Algorithm **RewriteLocalPRSQ** rewrites a range-sum query Q into a collection of local prefix range-sum queries by first invoking Algorithm **RewriteLocalRSQ** to obtain a set of local range-sum queries (step 1), and then further rewriting each local range-sum query into a collection of local prefix range-sum queries (steps 2 to 4); Q^+ (Q^-) contains all the local prefix range-sum queries whose results are to be added (subtracted) for the answer to Q. The details for step 4 can be found elsewhere [5].

Algorithm **HRC-Query** is the main algorithm to evaluate a range-sum query Q using $\mathcal{H}$. In step 1, it invokes Algorithm **RewriteLocalPRSQ** to rewrite Q into a collection of local prefix range-sum queries $Q^+ \cup Q^-$. For each $q \in Q^+ \cup Q^-$, if q corresponds to a root or leaf cell in $\mathcal{H}$, then q can be evaluated by accessing the cell $\mathcal{H}[q]$. Otherwise, q needs to be evaluated in terms of a collection of local prefix range-sum queries; the additional rewriting for q is performed in steps 2 to 9. Note that if $\mathcal{H}$ has a height of 2, then steps 2 to 9 are omitted.

3.4.3 Update Algorithm

Figure 8 shows the algorithm to maintain an HRC $\mathcal{H}$ in response to a single-cell update in the data cube C. By definition of HRC, the update of a single data cube cell u can affect only the cells in the rank-m sub-cube S in $\mathcal{H}$ that contains u. The root cell in S is identified in step 1, and it needs to be updated only if it corresponds to cell u (steps 2 and 3). Steps 4 to 7 of the algorithm handle updates to the non-root cells in S and are based on the property that a non-root cell c in S is affected by the update of cell u if and only if

$parent(c) \preceq u \preceq c$.

3.5 Hierarchical Band Cubes (HBC)

In this section, we present algorithms for constructing, querying, and updating an n-dimensional HBC $\mathcal{H}$.

3.5.1 Construction Algorithm

Figure 9 shows a 2-stage algorithm for constructing a HBC from a data cube C. In the first stage (step 1), the prefix cube of C is constructed (an algorithm for this can be found in Section 3.3 in [5]). In the second stage (steps 2 to 5), the HBC is derived from the constructed prefix cube by adjusting the values of the non-root cells. On an implementation note, the order in which the cells are modified should exploit the physical clustering of the cells to minimize I/O.

3.5.2 Query Algorithm

Figure 10 shows the algorithms for evaluating a range-sum query using an HBC. Algorithm **EvaluatePRS-Query** evaluates a prefix range-sum query Q using an HBC $\mathcal{H}$. By the definition of HB mapping (Table 1), the answer is a summation of at most m cell values. Algorithm **HBC-Query** is the main algorithm to evaluate a range-sum query using an HBC. Similarly to PC and HRC, the range-sum query is first rewritten into a collection of prefix range-sum queries $Q^+ \cup Q^-$ (step 2).

3.5.3 Update Algorithm

An update of a data cube cell u affects a cell c in an HBC $\mathcal{H}$ if and only if the value in cell c is derived using the value in cell u. The following two properties are true for HBC $\mathcal{H}$:

(P1) The update of u affects c if and only if (1) none of the ancestor cells of c are affected by the update of u, and (2) $u \preceq c$.

(P2) If $u \not\preceq \lambda(c)$, then none of the descendant cells of c (including c) are affected by the update of cell u.

Property (P1) follows from the definition of HB mapping (Table 1), and property (P2) is a corollary of property (P1). Their proofs are given elsewhere [2].

Algorithm RewriteLocalRSQ $(\mathcal{H}, \beta, \mathcal{Q})$
Input: $\mathcal{H}$ is an n-dimensional HRC with height m.
$\beta = \{B_1, B_2, \cdots, B_n\}$ is a set of base-sequences; each $B_i = < b_{i,m}, \cdots, b_{i,2}, b_{i,1} >$.
$\mathcal{Q} = (l_1 : h_1, l_2 : h_2, \cdots, l_n : h_n)$ is a range-sum query.
Output: T is a set of local range-sum queries such that $\mathcal{Q} = \sum_{q \in T} q$.
1) Let $\mathcal{S} = \{S_1, S_2, \cdots, S_k\}$ be the set of all the rank-2 sub-cubes in $\mathcal{H}$ that overlap with $\mathcal{Q}$.
2) $T = \{\}$;
3) **for each** sub-cube $S_i \in \mathcal{S}$ **do**
4) $Q_i = (x_1 : y_1, x_2 : y_2, \cdots, x_n : y_n)$, where $x_j = \max\{l_j, a_j\}$, $y_j = \min\{h_j, a_j + b_{j,1} - 1\}$ and $a = (a_1, a_2, \cdots, a_n)$ is the smallest cell in S_i;
5) $T = T \cup \{Q_i\}$;
6) **return** T;

Algorithm RewriteLocalPRSQ $(\mathcal{H}, \beta, \mathcal{Q})$
Input: $\mathcal{H}$ is an n-dimensional HRC with height m.
$\beta = \{B_1, B_2, \cdots, B_n\}$ is a set of base-sequences; each $B_i = < b_{i,m}, \cdots, b_{i,2}, b_{i,1} >$.
$\mathcal{Q} = (l_1 : h_1, l_2 : h_2, \cdots, l_n : h_n)$ is a range-sum query.
Output: $Q^+ \cup Q^-$ is a collection of local prefix range-sum queries such that $\mathcal{Q} = \sum_{q \in Q^+} q - \sum_{q \in Q^-} q$.
1) T = **RewriteLocalRSQ**$(\mathcal{H}, \beta, \mathcal{Q})$;
2) $Q^+ = \{\}$; $Q^- = \{\}$;
3) **for each** $q \in T$ **do**
4) Rewrite q into a combination of local prefix range-sum queries, and update Q^+ and Q^-;
5) **return** (Q^+, Q^-);

Algorithm HRC-Query $(\mathcal{H}, \beta, \mathcal{Q})$
Input: $\mathcal{H}$ is an n-dimensional HRC with height m.
$\beta = \{B_1, B_2, \cdots, B_n\}$ is a set of base-sequences; each $B_i = < b_{i,m}, \cdots, b_{i,2}, b_{i,1} >$.
$\mathcal{Q} = (l_1 : h_1, l_2 : h_2, \cdots, l_n : h_n)$ is a range-sum query.
Output: The answer to $\mathcal{Q}$.
1) (Q^+, Q^-) = **RewriteLocalPRSQ**$(\mathcal{H}, \beta, \mathcal{Q})$;
2) **for each** $q \in Q^+$ **do**
3) **if** $(1 < level(q) < m)$ **then**
4) $p = parent(q)$;
5) $Q' = (p_1 : q_1, p_2 : q_2, \cdots, p_n : q_n)$;
6) T = **RewriteLocalRSQ**$(\mathcal{H}, \beta, Q')$;
7) $Q^- = Q^- \cup T - \{q\}$;
8) Repeat steps (2) to (7) with Q^+ & Q^- interchanged;
9) $S = Q^+ \cap Q^-$; $Q^+ = Q^+ - S$; $Q^- = Q^- - S$;
10) **return** $\sum_{q \in Q^+} \mathcal{H}[q] - \sum_{q \in Q^-} \mathcal{H}[q]$;

Figure 7: Algorithms to Evaluate a Range-Sum Query using an HRC.

Figure 11 shows the algorithm to maintain an HBC in response to a single-cell update in the data cube C; its correctness is based on properties (P1) and (P2). Property (P2) is used in step 1 (step 6) to select root cells (child cells) that are either affected by the update of u, or whose descendant cells are affected by the update of u. Property (P1) is used in step 3 to decide whether or not a cell in $\mathcal{H}$ is affected by the update of u. An implementation of this update algorithm should exploit the physical clustering of the cells in $\mathcal{H}$ to order the sequence of cell updates so as to minimize I/O.

Algorithm HRC-Update $(\mathcal{H}, u, \delta)$
Input: $\mathcal{H}$ is an HRC to be updated.
u is a cell in the data cube that has been modified.
δ is the difference between the new and old values of cell u.
Output: $\mathcal{H}$, an updated HRC.
1) let r be the root cell in $\mathcal{H}$ such that $r \preceq u \preceq \lambda(r)$;
2) **if** $(r = u)$ **then**
3) Update cell r with δ;
4) $S = \{c \mid r = parent(c),\ r \preceq u \preceq c\}$;
5) **for each** $p \in S$ **do**
6) Update cell p with δ;
7) $S = S \cup \{c \mid p = parent(c),\ p \preceq u \preceq c\} - \{p\}$;
8) **return** $\mathcal{H}$;

Figure 8: Algorithm to Update an HRC.

Algorithm HBC-Construct (C, β)
Input: C is an n-dimensional data cube.
$\beta = \{B_1, B_2, \cdots, B_n\}$ is a set of base-sequences; each $B_i = < b_{i,m_i}, \cdots, b_{i,2}, b_{i,1} >$.
Output: $\mathcal{H}$, a hierarchical band cube of C.
1) Construct the prefix cube of C and call it $\mathcal{H}$;
2) $L = \max\{m_1, m_2, \cdots, m_n\}$;
3) **for** i = 1 **to** L-1 **do**
4) **for each** level-i cell $v \in \mathcal{H}$ **do**
5) $\mathcal{H}[v] = \mathcal{H}[v] - \mathcal{H}[parent(v)]$;
6) **return** $\mathcal{H}$;

Figure 9: Algorithm to Construct an HBC from a Data Cube.

4 Precomputed Cube Comparison

4.1 Performance Metrics

This section presents three performance metrics, namely, space-cost, query-cost, and update-cost, for comparing the tradeoffs among the various classes of precomputed cubes.

Let X denote a precomputed cube. The **space-cost** of X, denoted by $Space(X)$, is the total number of cells (i.e., values) in X. The **expected query-cost** (**worst query-cost**) of X, denoted by $E_{query}(X)$ ($W_{query}(X)$), is the expected (highest) number of cells in X that are accessed to answer a range-sum query. The **expected update-cost** (**worst update-cost**) of X, denoted by $E_{update}(X)$ ($W_{update}(X)$), is the expected (highest) number of cells in X that need to be updated in response to a single cell modification in the data cube. $E_{query}(X)$ ($E_{update}(X)$) assumes a uniform distribution over the collection of all possible range-sum queries (single-cell updates in the data cube).

Algorithm EvaluatePRSQuery $(\mathcal{H}, \mathcal{Q})$
Input: $\mathcal{H}$ is an HBC.
$\mathcal{Q}$ is a prefix range-sum query.
Output: sum, the answer to $\mathcal{Q}$.
1) $sum = \mathcal{H}[\mathcal{Q}]$;
2) **while** ($\mathcal{Q}$ is a non-root cell) **do**
3) $\mathcal{Q} = parent(\mathcal{Q})$;
4) $sum = sum + \mathcal{H}[\mathcal{Q}]$;
5) **return** sum;

Algorithm HBC-Query $(\mathcal{H}, \mathcal{Q})$
Input: $\mathcal{H}$ is an HBC.
$\mathcal{Q}$ is a range-sum query.
Output: sum, the answer to $\mathcal{Q}$.
1) $Q^+ = \{\}$; $Q^- = \{\}$;
2) Rewrite $\mathcal{Q}$ into a combination of prefix range-sum queries, and update Q^+ and Q^-;
3) $sum = 0$;
4) **for each** $q \in Q^+$ **do**
5) $sum = sum +$ **EvaluatePRSQuery** $(\mathcal{H}, q)$;
6) **for each** $q \in Q^-$ **do**
7) $sum = sum -$ **EvaluatePRSQuery** $(\mathcal{H}, q)$;
8) **return** sum;

Figure 10: Algorithms to Evaluate a Range-Sum Query using an HBC.

4.2 Comparison of Query-Update Tradeoff

In this section, we compare the performance of RPC, HRC, and HBC based on analytical results for the space-, query-, and update-cost metrics defined in the

Algorithm HBC-Update $(\mathcal{H}, u, \delta)$
Input: $\mathcal{H}$ is an HBC to be updated.
u is a cell in the raw data cube that has been modified.
δ is the difference between the new and old values of cell u.
Output: $\mathcal{H}$, an updated HBC.
1) $S = \{c \mid c$ is a root cell in $\mathcal{H},\ u \preceq \lambda(c)\}$;
2) **for each** $p \in S$ **do**
3) **if** $(u \preceq p)$ **then**
4) Update cell p with δ;
5) **else**
6) $S = S \cup \{c \mid p = parent(c),\ u \preceq \lambda(c)\}$;
7) $S = S - \{p\}$;
8) **return** $\mathcal{H}$;

Figure 11: Algorithm to Update an HBC.

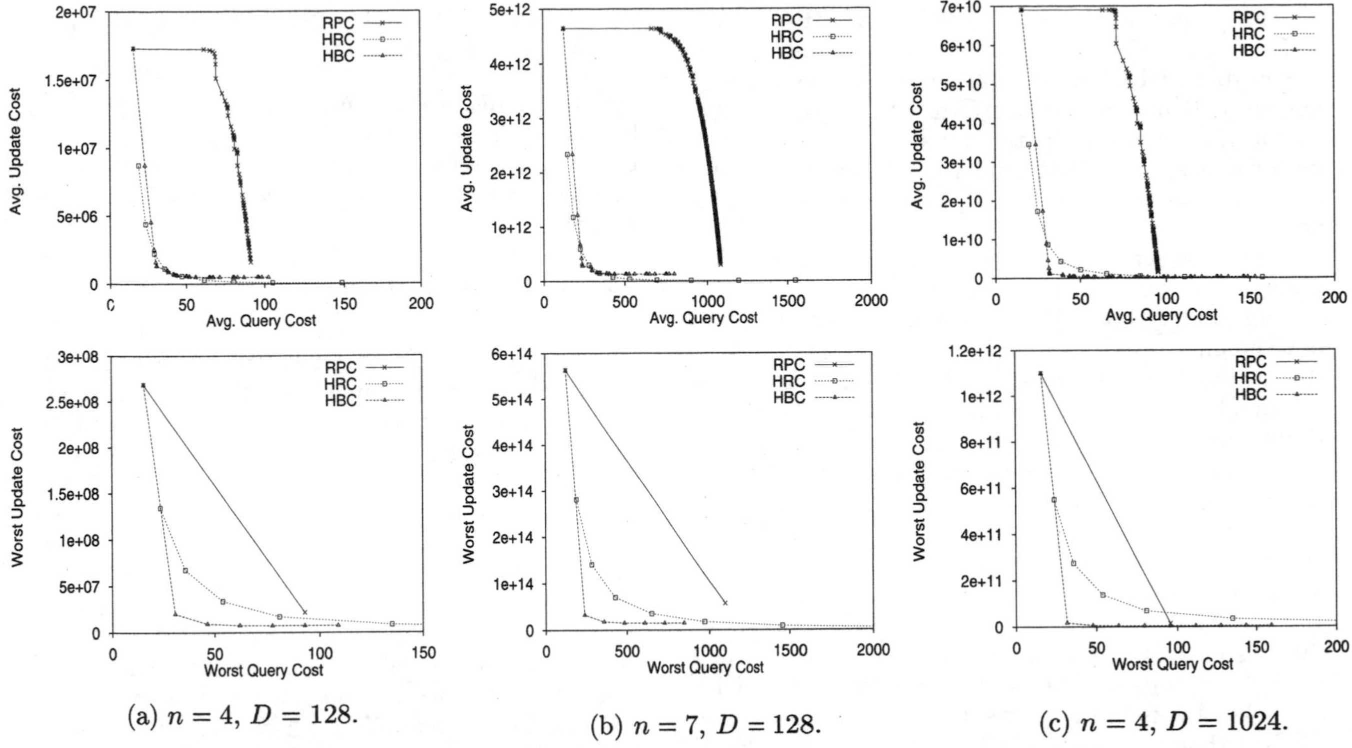

(a) $n = 4$, $D = 128$. (b) $n = 7$, $D = 128$. (c) $n = 4$, $D = 1024$.

Figure 12: Comparison of Average- and Worst-Case Query-Update Tradeoff.

previous section. Analytical formulae for these metrics are given elsewhere [2]. In terms of space cost, both HRC and HBC have the same space requirement as the data cube C, while RPC requires more space than these (for the cells in the overlay box).

We focus on comparing just the query-update tradeoff among the various classes of precomputed cubes using *optimal query-update tradeoff graphs* (for both expected-case as well as worst-case) defined as follows. Let S denote the set of all precomputed cubes that belong to the same class, say X, and have the same values for n and D. A cube $s \in S$ has *optimal expected-case query-update tradeoff* if there does not exist another cube $s' \in S$ that satisfies all of the following conditions: (1) $E_{query}(s') \leq E_{query}(s)$, and (2) $E_{update}(s') \leq E_{update}(s)$, and (3) at least one of the above inequalities is strict. The corresponding points in a query-cost/update-cost diagram constitute the *optimal expected-case query-update tradeoff graph* for X. The *optimal worst-case query-update tradeoff cubes* for X and their graphs are defined similarly in terms of $W_{query}()$ and $W_{update}()$. A cube of class X that has optimal tradeoff, whether in the expected case or the worst case, is called **optimal X** for short, when no confusion arises.

We generated precomputed cubes for the various classes (i.e., RPC, HRC, and HBC) by varying the number of cube dimensions ($2 \leq n \leq 7$), and the size of each cube dimension. For simplicity, we consider data cubes with equal sized dimensions; i.e., data cubes with $D_i = D$ (for $1 \leq i \leq n$) with $D = 128, 512, 1024$. For a given n and D, all possible RPCs are generated by enumerating all combinations for the dimensions of the sub-cube/overlay box. For HBCs, we consider only cubes for which each base-sequence $B_i = < b_{i,m}, b_{i,m-1}, \cdots, b_{i,1} >$ satisfies the property that $b_{i,m} \geq b_{i,m-1} \geq \cdots \geq b_{i,1}$ because initial experiments with $D = 128$ showed that only these are optimal.

For HRCs, we consider only HRCs with height equal to 2. The analysis for the more general class of HRCs is more complex and is part of our future work. Note that for every HRC X with a height of k, $k > 2$, there exists an HRC Y with a height of 2 that has the same dimensionality and size for its rank-2 sub-cubes as X. In terms of update-cost, Y is more efficient than X: although the mapped regions for their leaf cells are equivalent, the mapped regions for the non-leaf-and-non-root cells in X are larger, while the mapped regions for each of the non-leaf cells in Y (i.e., root cells) consists of only a single value. In terms of query-cost, the comparison is less clear since neither X nor Y is a clear winner.

Figure 12 compares both the expected-case and worst-case query-update tradeoff for three cases: (a) $n = 4$ and $D = 128$, (b) $n = 7$ and $D = 128$, and (c) $n = 4$ and $D = 1024$. The top leftmost point in each graph (i.e., the most query-efficient and least update-efficient cube design) corresponds to the prefix cube which is a special case of both RPC and HBC.

In terms of the expected-case query-update performance, both HRC and HBC have comparable tradeoff, and they significantly outperform RPC by up to a factor of 10. In terms of the worst-case query-update performance, both HRC and HBC again have better tradeoff than RPC, with HBC being clearly the winner.

With respect to how query cost is traded off for update cost by each cube design, we have observed the following. For RPCs, the update-cost decreases but the query-cost increases as the number of cells in the overlay box decreases. For HRCs, this happens as the number of rank-2 subcubes increases. For HBCs, things are more complicated. Let $N_i(H)$ denote the total number of level-i cells in a HBC H. For the expected-case, an optimal HBC X with a height of x is more query-efficient but less update-efficient than an optimal HBC Y with a height of y if either (1) $x < y$, or (2) $x = y$, and $N_k(X) < N_k(Y)$ for some $k \geq 1$, and $N_i(X) = N_i(Y)$ for $1 \leq i < k$. For the worst-case, there is exactly one optimal HBC with a height of i for $1 \leq i \leq log_2(D)$ such that the optimal HBC with a height of k is more query-efficient but less update-efficient than the optimal HBC with a height of $(k+1)$ for $1 \leq k < log_2(D)$.

5 Effect of Buffering

5.1 Performance Metrics

One important result from the previous section (Figure 12) is that PC is the most query-efficient but also the least update-efficient precomputed cube. In particular, the query-cost is one cell access per prefix range-sum query evaluation, which implies a worst-case evaluation cost of 2^n cell accesses per range-sum query evaluation, where n is the number of dimensions in the data cube. In this section, we explore the effect of buffering on the performance of the various precomputed cubes; specifically, we examine how each class of precomputed cubes can achieve, with appropriate buffering, the same worst-case query-efficiency as PC but without incurring the high update cost of PC. We compare the *memory-update tradeoff* of the various classes of precomputed cubes, which involves the following two metrics for each class X:

1. Memory: the minimum number of cells in X that need to be buffered so that X achieves the same worst-case query-cost as PC (i.e., access at most 2^n non-buffered cells per range-sum query evaluation). We denote this metric by $MinCell(X)$.

2. Update: the expected number of non-buffered cells in X that need to be updated in response to a single cell modification in the data cube, assuming a uniform distribution over the collection of all $\prod_{i=1}^{n} D_i$ potential single-cell updates. We refer to this metric as the *expected buffered update-cost of* X and denote it by $B_{update}(X)$.

In other words, for each precomputed cube X, we are interested in determining both the cost (in terms of buffer space) as well as the benefit (in terms of the improved update cost) of buffering X for it to become as query-efficient as PC.

5.2 Buffering Strategies

We briefly explain the buffering strategy for each class of precomputed cubes X for the metric $MinCell(X)$. Let Q denote a range-sum query. For an RPC $\mathcal{R}$, each prefix range-sum query evaluation accesses exactly one cell in $\mathcal{A}$ and at most $(n+1)$ cells in $\mathcal{O}$. It follows that for RPC to have the same worst-case query efficiency as PC, at least all the cells in $\mathcal{O}$ need to be buffered.

For an HRC $\mathcal{H}$, Q is rewritten into σ local range-sum queries, where σ is the number of rank-2 subcubes that overlapped with Q; each local range-sum query is in turn evaluated in terms of at most 2^n local prefix range-sum queries. Thus, in the worst case, at most $\sigma 2^n$ cells are accessed, of which at most 2^n of them are *non-outer cells*[4]. Therefore, at least all the outer cells in $\mathcal{H}$ need to be buffered for it to be equally query-efficient as PC.

For an HBC $\mathcal{H}$, each prefix range-sum query evaluation accesses exactly one root-level cell and at most one cell for each non-root level. Since HBC has the property that the number of level-i cells decreases with i, buffering all the non-leaf cells incurs the least amount of buffer space for $\mathcal{H}$ to achieve the same worst-case query-efficiency as PC.

In addition to comparing the cost and benefit of buffering each class of precomputed cubes for it to attain the same query-efficiency as PC, we are also interested in examining how buffering benefits PC in terms of reducing its update-cost. Since each cell in a PC is equally likely to be accessed, a good buffering scheme is to buffer those cells that are more likely to be updated so as to reduce the update-cost of PC. A reasonably good buffering strategy for PC is to buffer it in units of *layers*. Consider a prefix cube $\mathcal{P}$ with each dimension of size D. The cells in $\mathcal{P}$ can be partitioned into D disjoint *layers* such that a cell $(c_1, c_2, \cdots, c_n)$ belongs to *layer* k of $\mathcal{P}$, $0 \leq k < D$, if and only if $\max\{c_1, c_2, \cdots, c_n\} = k$. A cell in layer k is generally more likely to be updated than a cell in layer $(k-1)$. We consider the effect of buffering $\mathcal{P}$ in terms of k outermost layers[5], $1 \leq k \leq D$. Let $L_{space}(\mathcal{P}, k)$ denote the total number of cells in the k outermost layers of $\mathcal{P}$, and $L_{update}(\mathcal{P}, k)$ denote the expected number of

[4]A cell $c = (c_1, c_2, \cdots, c_n)$ in a rank-2 subcube S of an HRC $\mathcal{H}$ is an *outer cell* if $\exists\ 1 \leq j \leq n$, such that $c_j = \max\{s_j | s \in S, s = (s_1, s_2, \cdots, s_n)\}$; otherwise, c is an *non-outer cell.*

[5]Note that the k outermost layers refer to layers $(D-k)$, $(D-k+1)$, $\cdots$, $(D-1)$.

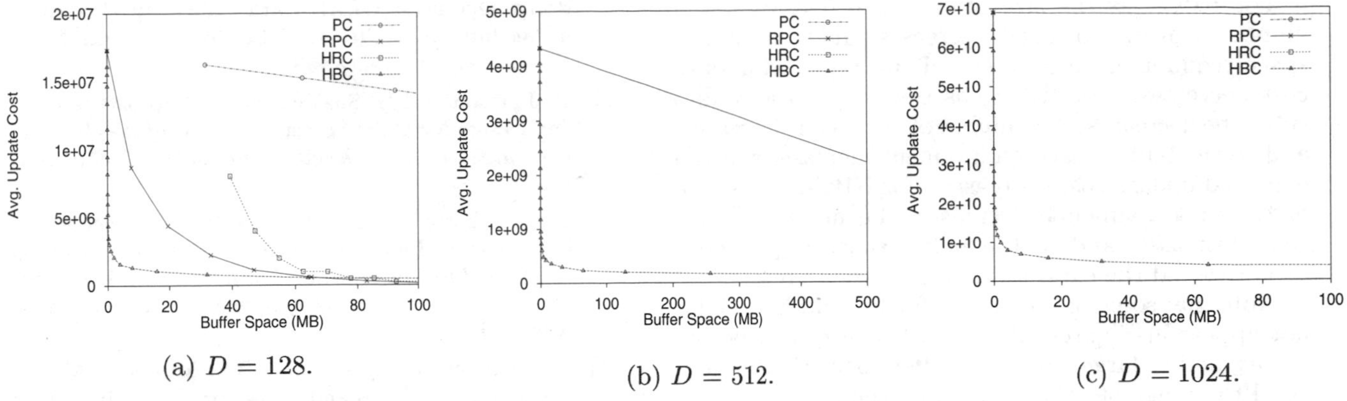

(a) $D = 128$. (b) $D = 512$. (c) $D = 1024$.

Figure 13: Comparison of Average-Case Memory-Update Tradeoff, $n = 4$.

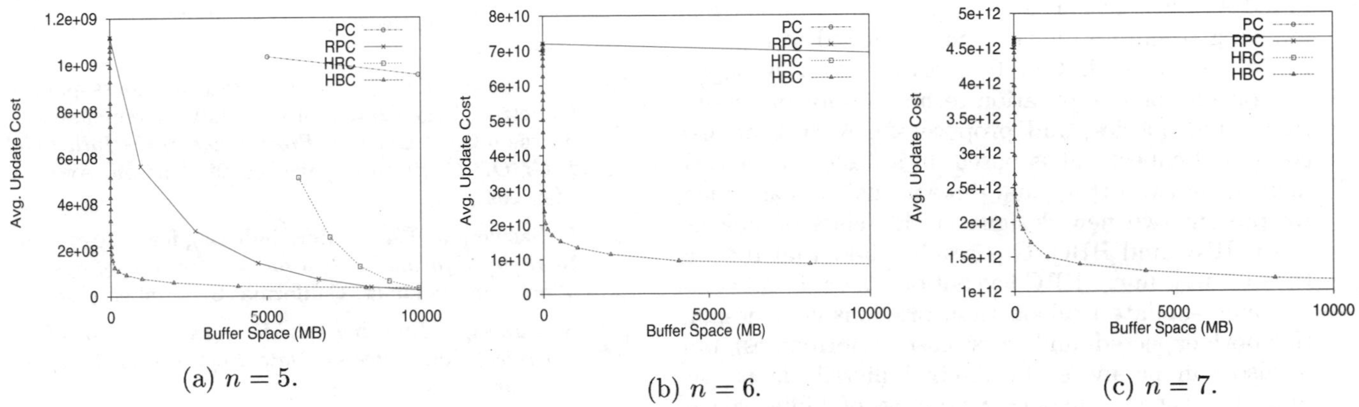

(a) $n = 5$. (b) $n = 6$. (c) $n = 7$.

Figure 14: Comparison of Average-Case Memory-Update Tradeoff, $D = 128$.

non-buffered cells in $\mathcal{P}$ that need to be updated in response to a single cell update in the data cube when the k outermost layers of $\mathcal{P}$ are buffered. Analytical results for $B_{update}(X)$, $MinCell(X)$, $L_{space}(\mathcal{P}, k)$, and $L_{update}(\mathcal{P}, k)$ are given elsewhere [2].

5.3 Comparison of Memory-Update Tradeoff

In this section, we compare the various classes of precomputed cubes using *optimal expected-case memory-update tradeoff graphs*, which are defined similarly as the optimal expected-case query-update tradeoff graphs in Section 4.2, but in terms of $MinCell()$ and $B_{update}()$. For a PC $\mathcal{P}$, the optimal expected-case memory-update tradeoff graph is defined in terms of $L_{space}(\mathcal{P}, k)$ and $L_{update}(\mathcal{P}, k)$ with k being varied from 1 to D. Both $MinCell(X)$ and $L_{space}(\mathcal{P}, k)$ are expressed in units of MB of buffer space by assuming that each cell takes 4 bytes of memory.

As in Section 4.2, precomputed cubes are generated by varying the number of cube dimensions ($2 \leq n \leq 7$) and the size of each cube dimension ($D = 128, 512, 1024$). We consider all possible RPCs and the subclass of HRCs with height 2. Recall from the previous section that the buffering strategy for HBC buffers all the non-leaf cells. Since the number of leaf cells in an HBC and the update cost for them are dependent on the size of the rank-2 subcube but independent of the total number of levels in the HBC, it suffices to consider only the subclass of HBCs with height 2 as well for the memory-update tradeoff comparison in this section.

Figure 13 compares the optimal expected-case memory-update tradeoff for $n = 4$ and $D \in \{128, 512, 1024\}$; the graphs for $D = 128$ and $5 \leq n \leq 7$ are shown in Figure 14. They indicate that HBC has a significantly better memory-update tradeoff than the other classes of precomputed cubes, particularly for large values of n or D. For example, when $n = 4$ and $D = 128$ (Figure 13(a)), the expected update-cost of PC (without buffering) is about 17×10^6. Using a buffer space of 8 KB, HBC reduces this cost by a factor of 2.5 to 8×10^6; by increasing the buffer space to 1 MB, the expected update cost is improved by a factor of almost 7 to 2.5×10^6. Thus, with a moderate amount of buffer space, HBC can become as query-efficient as PC but with a significant improvement over its update-cost.

For RPCs, as the size of sub-cube decreases, the number of overlay box cells increases, and so the buffer space requirement increases and the expected update cost decreases. For HRCs, as the size of the rank-2 sub-cube decreases, the number of outer cells increases, and so the buffer space requirement increases and the expected update cost decreases. For HBCs, as the size of the rank-2 subcube decreases, the number of leaf cells decreases, and so the buffer space requirement increases and the expected update cost decreases.

Note that some of the graphs for PC and HRPC did not appear in Figures 13 and 14 because their points correspond to large values of buffer space that are beyond the range of values shown on the x-axis.

6 Conclusions

Aggregation computation is an important operation in OLAP systems, and several precomputation and indexing techniques have been developed to expedite processing of such OLAP queries. In this paper, we consider precomputation techniques for processing range-sum queries, and propose a new class of precomputed cubes that is based on a design framework defined by two orthogonal dimensions. In particular, we present two new designs in this class of alternatives: HRC and HBC. Our results show that HBC is the overall winner. HBC has not only significantly better query-update tradeoff than previous cube designs (for both expected- and worst-case performances), but it also can be more effectively buffered; in particular, by using a moderate amount of buffer space, HBC can achieve the same query-efficiency as the most query-efficient solution, but with a significantly reduced update-cost.

As part of our future work, we plan to verify our analytical results experimentally, and also to characterize the optimal tradeoff points (e.g., the graph knee) for HBC.

References

[1] C.Y. Chan and Y.E. Ioannidis. Bitmap Index Design and Evaluation. In *Proceedings of the Intl. ACM SIGMOD Conference*, pages 355–366, Seattle, Washington, June 1998.

[2] C.Y. Chan and Y.E. Ioannidis. Hierarchical Cubes for Range-Sum Queries. Computer Sciences Dept., University of Wisconsin-Madison, February 1999. http://www.cs.wisc.edu/~cychan/hc.ps.

[3] R. Earle. Method and Apparatus for Storing and Retrieving Multi-Dimensional Data in Computer Memory. U.S. Patent No: 05359725, October 1994.

[4] S. Geffner, D. Agrawal, A. Abbadi, and T. Smith. Relative Prefix Sums: An Efficient Approach for Querying Dynamic OLAP Data Cubes. In *Proceedings of the 15th Intl. Conference on Data Engineering*, pages 328–335, Sydney, Australia, March 1999.

[5] C.T. Ho, R. Agrawal, R. Megiddo, and R. Srikant. Range Queries in OLAP Data Cubes. In *Proceedings of the Intl. ACM SIGMOD Conference*, pages 73–88, Tucson, Arizona, May 1997.

[6] T. Johnson and D. Shasha. Some Approaches to Index Design for Cube Forest. *Bulletin of the Technical Committee on Data Engineering*, 20(1):27–35, March 1997.

[7] G. Moerkotte. Small Materialized Aggregates: A Light Weight Index Structure for Data Warehousing. In *Proceedings of the Intl. Conference on Very Large Data Bases*, pages 488–499, New York City, New York, August 1998.

[8] I.S. Mumick, D. Quass, and B.S. Mumick. Maintenance of Data Cubes and Summary Tables in a Warehouse. In *Proceedings of the Intl. ACM SIGMOD Conference*, pages 100–111, Tucson, Arizona, May 1997.

[9] P. O'Neil and D. Quass. Improved Query Performance with Variant Indexes. In *Proceedings of the Intl. ACM SIGMOD Conference*, pages 38–49, Tucson, Arizona, May 1997.

[10] N. Roussopoulos, Y. Kotidis, and M. Roussopoulos. Cubetree: Organization of and Bulk Incremental Updates on Cube Data. In *Proceedings of the Intl. ACM SIGMOD Conference*, pages 89–99, Tucson, Arizona, May 1997.

[11] B. Salzberg and A. Reuter. Indexing for Aggregation. In *High Performance Transaction Processing Systems Workshop*, Asilomar, California, September 1995.

[12] S. Sarawagi. Indexing OLAP Data. *Bulletin of the Technical Committee on Data Engineering*, 20(1):36–43, March 1997.

[13] J.R. Smith, V. Castelli, A. Jhingran, and C.-S. Li. Dynamic Assembly of Views in Data Cubes. In *Proceedings of the ACM SIGACT-SIGMOD-SIGART Symposium on Principles of Database Systems*, pages 274–283, Seattle, Washington, June 1998.

[14] J.S. Vitter and M. Wang. Approximate Computation of Multidimensional Aggregates of Sparse Data Using Wavelets. In *Proceedings of the Intl. ACM SIGMOD Conference*, pages 193–204, Philadelphia, Pennsylvania, June 1999.

Implementation of Two Semantic Query Optimization Techniques in DB2 Universal Database

Qi Cheng[1] Jarek Gryz[2] Fred Koo[1] Cliff Leung[3] Linqi Liu[2,4]
Xiaoyan Qian[1] Bernhard Schiefer[1]

IBM[1] Toronto

Department of Computer Science[2] York University, Toronto

IBM[3] Almaden

Daedalian Systems Group Inc.[4] Toronto

Abstract

In the early 1980's, researchers recognized that semantic information stored in databases as integrity constraints could be used for query optimization. A new set of techniques called *semantic query optimization* (SQO) was developed. Some of the ideas developed for SQO have been used commercially, but to the best of our knowledge, no extensive implementations of SQO exist today.

In this paper, we describe an implementation of two SQO techniques, Predicate Introduction and Join Elimination, in DB2 Universal Database. We present the implemented algorithms and performance results using the TPCD and APB-1 OLAP benchmarks. Our experiments show that SQO can lead to dramatic query performance improvements. A crucial aspect of our implementation of SQO is the fact that it does not rely on complex integrity constraints (as many previous SQO techniques did); we use only referential integrity constraints and check constraints.

Proceedings of the 25th VLDB Conference, Edinburgh, Scotland, 1999.

1 Introduction

Relational database systems became the predominant technology for storing, handling, and querying data only after a great improvement in the efficiency of query evaluation in such systems. The key factor in this improvement was the introduction and development of query optimization techniques. The traditional types of optimization, however, exploit to a limited extent the semantic information about the stored data. In the late 1970's and early 1980's, researchers [1, 7, 8, 9, 17] recognized that such information could be used for further query optimization, and developed a new set of techniques called *semantic query optimization* (SQO). SQO uses the integrity constraints associated with the database to improve the efficiency of query evaluation. The techniques most often discussed in literature included the following:

1. Join Elimination: A query may contain a join for which the result is known a priori, hence, it need not be avaluated. (For example, for some queries involving a join between two tables related through a referential integrity constraint).
2. Join Introduction: It may be advantegeous to add a join with an additional relation, if that relation is relatively small compared to the original relations as well as highly selective. (This is even more appealing if the join attributes are indexed).
3. Predicate Elimination: If a predicate is known to be always true it can be eliminated from the query.
4. Predicate Introduction: A new predicate on an indexed attribute may allow for a more efficient access method. Similarly, a new predicate on a join attribute may reduce the cost of the join.
5. Detecting the Empty Answer Set: If the query predicates are inconsistent with integrity constraints, the query does not have an answer.

Example 1. Consider the following two queries (both asked against the TPCD [19]). The first query illustrates the technique of Join Elimination.

$\mathcal{Q}_1$: **select** p_name, p_retailprice, s_name, s_address
from tpcd.lineitem, tpcd.partsupp, tpcd.part, tpcd.supplier
where p_partkey = ps_partkey and s_suppkey = ps_suppkey and ps_partkey = l_partkey and ps_suppkey = l_suppkey and l_shipdate between '1994-01-01' and '1996-06-30' and l_discount $\geq$ 0.1
group by p_name, p_retailprice, s_name, s_address
order by p_name, s_name;

The following referential integrity constraints (parent-child) have been defined in TPCD: **part-partsupp** (on partkey), **supplier-partsupp** (on suppkey), **partsupp-lineitem** (on partkey and suppkey). Given the referential integrity constraints, the intermediate join with **partsupp** can be eliminated from the query, since the tables **part** and **lineitem** can be joined directly. We show in Section 3 that this transformation improves query performance.

The next query illustrates the technique of Predicate Introduction.

$\mathcal{P}_1$: **select** sum(l_extendedprice * l_discount) as revenue
from tpcd.lineitem
where l_shipdate $\geq$ date('1994-01-01') and l_shipdate $<$ date('1994-01-01')+1year and l_discount between $.06 - 0.01$ and $.06 + 0.01$ and l_quantity $<$ 24;

Since the following check constraint, **l_shipdate $\leq$ l_receiptdate**, has been defined for TPCD, a new predicate, **l_receiptdate $\geq$ date('1994-01-01')**, can be added to the **where** clause in the query without changing its answer set. Now, if the only index on **lineitem** table is a clustered index in which *l_receiptdate* is a major column, a new, potentially more efficient evaluation plan is available for the query. Indeed, we show in Section 4, that the use of this new plan leads to an improved query performance.

The SQO techniques discussed in literature were designed to be a part of a two-stage optimizer. In the first step, queries that are logically equivalent - with respect to the semantics of the database (that is, the stored set of integrity constraints) - to the original query, are generated. In the second step, these queries are submitted to the traditional optimizer which generates access plans for all of them and the query with the lowest estimated evaluation cost is chosen and submitted for evaluation. Since the number of equivalent queries generated in the first phase could be large (in general, exponential in the number of integrity constraints that relate semantically to the query), heuristics were necessary to limit their number [1, 7, 16]. Although several different techniques for SQO have been developed, only simple prototypes have been built. To the best of our knowledge, no extensive, commercial implementations of SQO exist today.[1] There are several reasons why SQO has never caught up in the commercial world. The most prominent one is the fact that SQO was in many cases designed for deductive databases [1, 7, 8] and because of this association, SQO might not appear useful for relational database technology. Second, at the time when SQO techniques were being developed, the relative CPU and I/O speeds were not as dramatically different as they are now. The savings in query execution time (dominated by I/O) that SQO could provide was not worth the extra CPU time necessary to optimize a query semantically. (The analysis presented in [16] shows that the cost of semantic optimization could become comparable to the query execution cost.) Last, it has been usually assumed that many integrity constraints have to be defined for a given database if SQO is to be useful there. Otherwise, only few queries could be optimized semantically. However, this is not the case in most real life databases; except for keys, foreign keys, and check constraints, very few integrity constraints are ever defined. Indeed, many of the integrity constraints considered in early days of SQO are not expressible in most commercial database systems, even today !

We have always believed, however, that many of the SQO techniques could provide an effective enhancement to the traditional query optimization. We show in this paper that this is indeed the case. We developed versions of two SQO techniques: Join Elimination (JE) and Predicate Introduction (PI). Significant portions of these technologies have been implemented in a prototype version of IBM DB2 Universal Database (UDB). We hope that this work will provide valuable lessons for future implementations of SQO.

The paper is organized as follows. Section 2 provides a brief overview of the DB2 UDB optimizer and the general assumptions for the implementation. The algorithms and performance results for Join Elimination and Predicate Introduction constitute Sections 3 and 4 respectively. The paper concludes in Section 5.

[1]This is not to say that *no* semantic information is used for optimization (e.g. the information about keys is routinely used to remove the DISTINCT operator from queries). However, the extent to which semantic information is used in that way is far from what the designers of SQO envisioned.

2 Overview of the Implementation

In traditional database systems, query optimization typically consists of a single phase of processing in which an efficient access plan is chosen for executing a query. In Starburst DBMS [6], on which DB2 UDB is based, the query optimization phase is divided up into *query rewrite optimization* and *query plan optimization* phases; each concentrates on different aspects of optimization. The query rewrite phase transforms queries to other semantically equivalent queries. This is also commonly known as the query modification phase, applying rewrite heuristics. The query plan optimization phase determines the join order, join methods, join site in a distributed database, and the method for accessing each input table.

After an input query is parsed and converted to an intermediate form called *query graph model* (QGM), the graph is transformed by the Query Rewrite Engine [13, 14] into a logically equivalent but more efficient form using heuristics. Query rewrite is a rule based system. Such a system permits keeping the range of optimization methods open-ended, considerably reducing the effort it usually takes to extend the optimization range as user needs evolve. For example, it is important to be able to add a new query rewrite rule into the system without having to modify the existing rules or to have an explanation of how the rule system arrives at the solution for a given query. The growing list of rewrite rules implemented in this system includes predicate pushdown, subquery to join transformation, magic sets transformation, handling of duplicates, merging of views and decorrelating complex subqueries [2, 10, 11, 12, 13]. Rules can be grouped into rule classes for higher efficiency, better understandability and more extensibility. Such grouping of query rewrite rules can help the query rewrite system to converge to a fixpoint faster. Furthermore, each rule class uses a particular control strategy that specifies how rules in the class are selected to fire. An important aspect of the implemented rule based system is its efficiency: experimental results show [14] that less than 1% of the query execution time is spent on the query rewrite phase.

Some of the optimization techniques already present in DB2 UDB optimizer use information about integrity constraints to transform queries, hence implement a form of "semantic" query optimization. The following examples illustrate two such techniques.

Example 2. This example illustrates a simple rule that allows eliminating the DISTINCT keyword. Let Q be a query in TPCD schema:

Q: **select** DISTINCT nationkey, name
from tpcd.nation;

Since nationkey is a key for the relation nation, the DISTINCT keyword can be eliminated, thus avoiding a potentially expensive sorting.

Q': **select** nationkey, name
from tpcd.nation;

Example 3. This example illustrates the use of functional dependencies to optimize the order operation [18].

Q: **select** shipdate, commitdate
from tpcd.lineitem
order by shipdate, commitdate;

Assume that there is a functional dependency **shipdate** $\rightarrow$ **commitdate.**[2] Thus, for a given value of **shipdate**, there is only one value of **commitdate**. Hence, Q can be rewritten into the following query:

Q': **select** shipdate, commitdate
from tpcd.lineitem
order by shipdate;

Again, after this transformation a potentially expensive sorting operation is avoided.

The design of the query rewrite engine is ideal for the implementation of SQO. Each of the SQO techniques represents a transformation of a query that can be stated as a condition-action rule. This is exactly how transformation rules are implemented in the query rewrite engine. The only restriction that was forced on us as a result of the design of the DB2 optimizer was as follows. Since only a single query can be passed from the query rewrite engine to the plan optimization phase, we could not assume that the plan optimizer would be able to choose the best query from a set of *several* semantically equivalent queries. The disadvantage of this is that the *single* query generated through SQO had to be guaranteed to be better than the original query (this assumption need not be made when there were several candidate queries, since the original query was among them). The advantage of this approach is, however, that less time had to be spent on SQO, so we would not encounter the problem of spending more time on optimization than query execution [16].

The decision to implement JE and PI, out of the choices of SQO techniques, was based on two factors. Our initial experiments with SQO [5], in which we tested all known SQO techniques by rewriting queries by hand, indicated that both JE and PI provided consistent optimization. In addition to this, however, they

[2]This FD is only assumed for the sake of the example; it does not hold in TPCD.

were also the most practical to implement. The transformations they provided relied only on check constraints and referential integrity constraints. Thus, we did not need to change the support mechanism for integrity constraints in DB2 UDB. Moreover, since almost all database systems support these types of integrity constraints, JE and PI can be potentially implemented in other DBMSs.

3 Join Elimination

3.1 Implementation

The Join Elimination (JE) technique discussed in SQO literature was often presented in two different versions [1]. In the first version, the join under consideration is known to be empty (by reasoning over the set of integrity constraints), hence any further join with its result would also be empty. In the second version, if it could be proved by reasoning over the set of integrity constraints that the join is redundant (as in query Q_1 of Example 1) it can be eliminated from the query. Although, JE in its first version is likely to provide very good optimization, we did not think that it was very practical. First, it is cumbersome to express in SQL as an integrity constraint the fact that the join of two tables (possibly with selects) is empty. Second, it is unlikely that such integrity constraints would be stored, since their verification would be costly.

Thus, we concentrate only on the second version of JE and consider the case where redundant joins are discovered through reasoning over referential integrity (RI) constraints. The most straightforward application of our technique is the elimination of a relation (hence a join) where the join is over the tables related through an RI constraint (we refer to such joins as *RI joins*) and the primary key table is referenced only in the join.

Example 4. Assume that the view **Supplier_Info** has been defined over TPCD schema and the query Q has been asked against that view:

create view Supplier_Info (n, a, c) as
select s_name, s_address, n_name
from tpcd.supplier, tpcd.nation
where s_nationkey = n_nationkey;

Q: **select** s_n, s_a
from Supplier_Info;

Since there is an RI constraint between **supplier** and **nation** on *nationkey*, then every tuple from the **supplier** relation necessarily joins with some tuple in the **nation** relation. Also, no attributes are selected or projected from the **nation** relation. Hence, the query can be rewritten into an equivalent form as Q':

Q': **select** s_n, s_a
from tpcd.supplier;

Q' avoids the join computation, so its evaluation can be more efficient.

Note that even if the user knows that the query Q can be rewritten as Q', he may not be able to do so, since he may only have access to the view. Thus, even such simple optimizations have to be performed within the DBMS. Redundancy in RI joins is likely to occur in environments where views are defined with large number of such joins, for example, in data warehousing with a star schema. But it can also appear in ordinary queries if they are not written by a programmer, but are automatically generated, e.g. by GUIs in query managers where hand optimization is impossible.

The JE algorithm we implemented handles not only the removal of explicit RI joins, but also redundant joins that can be inferred through reasoning over the joins explicitly stated in the query and the RIs defined for the database (query Q_1 of Example 1 was transformed in this way). The algorithm has the following steps:

1. Column equivalence classes are built via transitivity from all join predicates in the query. That is, if $A = B$ and $B = C$ are in the query, we can infer $A = C$. All three columns, A, B, C are then in a single equivalence class.
2. All tables in the **from** clause of the query that are related through RI joins are divided into two groups: R group (removable tables) and N group (non-removable tables). The necessary condition for a table to belong to the R group is that it is a parent table for some RI (such tables need to satisfy other conditions as well, their full description, however, is beyond the scope of this paper).
3. All tables in the R group (that is, redundant joins) are eliminated from the query.
4. Since foreign key columns may be nullable, an 'IS NOT NULL' predicate is added to foreign key columns of all tables whose RI parents have been removed and which, in fact, permit nulls.

We present a few examples of the types of transformations that can be performed by the algorithm.

Example 5. For each query specified below we present an optimized query generated by the algorithm and three graphs describing the join structures. The nodes in each graph represent attributes and the edges represent joins between these attributes. The top graph shows the joins explicitly stated in the query. The middle graph shows all the joins that can be inferred from the first graph (that is, all equivalence classes induced by the explicit joins). The RI joins are distinguished from other joins by arrows (from the child to the parent, that is, N:1). The bottom graph shows the structure of the joins after the redundant joins have been eliminated by the algorithm.

• **Query 1**

Let the query be $\mathcal{Q}_1$ of Example 1. The graphs describing the structure of the joins of the query are shown in Figure 1.

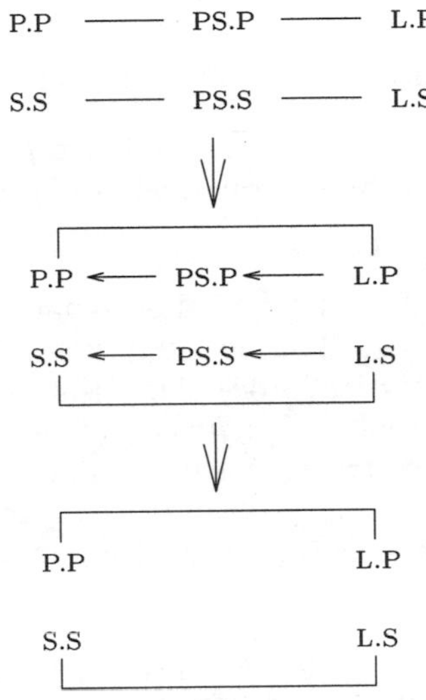

Figure 1: Join graphs for query $\mathcal{Q}_1$.

Thus, $\mathcal{Q}_1$ can be optimized into $\mathcal{Q}_1'$.

$\mathcal{Q}_1'$: **select** p_name, p_rctailprice, s_name, s_address
from tpcd.lineitem, tpcd.part, tpcd.supplier
where p_partkey = l_partkey and
s_suppkey = l_suppkey and
l_shipdate between '1994-01-01' and
'1996-06-30' and l_discount ≥ 0.1
group by p_name, p_retailprice, s_name,
s_address
order by p_name, s_name;

We tested $\mathcal{Q}_1$ and $\mathcal{Q}_1'$ in TPCD database of size 100MB in the same environment as described in Section 4. Execution time for the original query $\mathcal{Q}_1$ was 58.5s and for the optimized query $\mathcal{Q}_1'$ 38.25s (a saving of 35%). Since the database was relatively small, the query was CPU bound. We expect that the optimization would be even more prominent for a large database since the I/O cost was reduced by 67% (from 4631 to 1498 page reads).

• **Query 2**

Consider another query in TPCD.

$\mathcal{Q}_2$: **select** ps_partkey as partkey,
avg(ps_supplycost) as supplycost
from tpcd.supplier, tpcd.partsupp,
tpcd.customer, tpcd.orders
where s_suppkey = ps_suppkey and
s_suppkey = c_custkey
and c_custkey = o_custkey and
o_totalprice ≥ 100
group by ps_partkey
order by 2
fetch first 200 rows only;

The join graph for $\mathcal{Q}_2$ is shown in Figure 2 (since *s_suppkey = ps_suppkey* and *c_custkey = o_custkey* are RI joins, they are marked with arrows in the middle graph). The query can be simplified to a single join as indicated in the bottom graph.

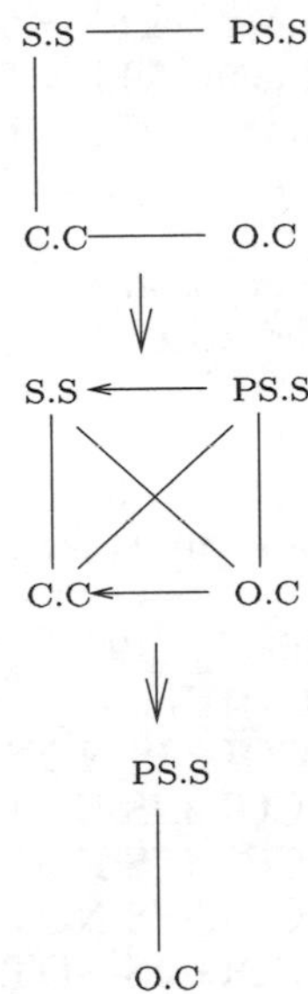

Figure 2: Join graphs for query $\mathcal{Q}_2$.

Thus, the query becomes:

$\mathcal{Q}_2'$: **select** ps_partkey as partkey,
avg(ps_supplycost) as supplycost
from tpcd.partsupp, tpcd.orders
where ps_suppkey = o_custkey and
o_totalprice ≥ 100
group by ps_partkey
order by 2
fetch first 200 rows only;

We tested Q_2 and $Q_2^{'}$ in the same environment as Q_1. The execution time for Q_2 was 6331.64s and for $Q_2^{'}$, 79.33s, for a saving of 99%.

- **Query 3**

Consider the following view defined over a star schema (for brevity, we use "..." to indicate sequences of attributes). Cube1Fact is a fact table, each of the Cube1Dim2–Cube1Dim6 is a dimension table, and each of the joins is an RI join (the schema is described in more detail in Section 3.2):

```
create view olapmain_starview
        ("Measure","Scenario","Channel_label",
        "Customer","Product", "1996", "1995Q3",
        "1995Q4","1996Q1","1996Q2","1996Q3",
        "1996Q4", "199606YTD", "199501",...,
        "199512", "199601",...,"199612") AS
select  T2.Membername, T3.Membername,
        T4.Membername, T5.Membername,
        T6.Membername, F.AN1,...,F.AN32
from    Cube1Fact F, Cube1Dim2 T2,
        Cube1Dim3 T3, Cube1Dim4 T4,
        Cube1Dim5 T5, Cube1Dim6 T6
where   T2.RelmemberId = F.COL2 AND
        T3.RelmemberId = F.COL3 AND
        T4.RelmemberId = F.COL4 AND
        T5.RelmemberId = F.COL5 AND
        T6.RelmemberId = F.COL6;
```

Let Q_3 be a query that uses this view. After the view is replaced with its definition, Q_3 can be simplified into $Q_3^{'}$.

```
Q3: select "1996", "199606YTD"
    from   olapmain_starview;

Q3': select "1996", "199606YTD"
     from   Cube1Fact
     where  F.COL2 IS NOT NULL and
            F.COL3 IS NOT NULL and
            F.COL4 IS NOT NULL and
            F.COL5 IS NOT NULL and
            F.COL6 IS NOT NULL;
```

3.2 Performance Results

The JE technique described above has been implemented in a prototype DB2 UDB installed as part of an OLAP Server. The DB2 OLAP Server is an Online Analytical Processing server that can be used to create a wide range of multidimensional planning, analysis, and reporting applications. DB2 OLAP Server uses the Essbase OLAP engine developed by Hyperion Solutions Corporation. However, DB2 OLAP Server replaces the integrated, multidimensional data storage used by Arbor with a relational storage management, and stores data in the relational data storage using a star schema.

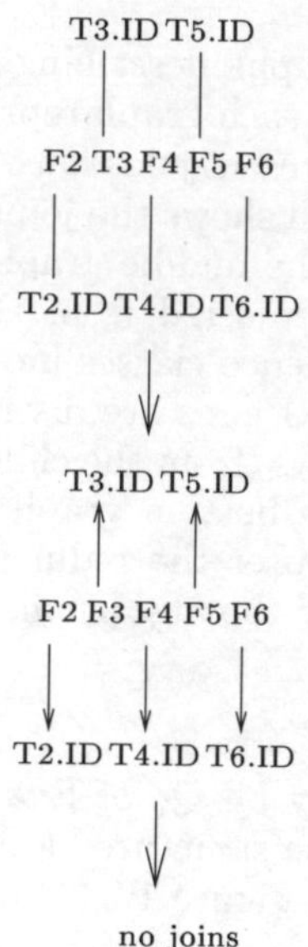

Figure 3: Join graphs for query Q_3.

We used the APB-1 OLAP Benchmark [3] schema for the experiments. The benchmark simulates a realistic on-line analytical processing business situation that exercises server-based software. The logical benchmark database structure is made up of six dimensions: time, scenario, measure, and three aggregation dimensions that define the database size (product, customer, and channel).

When an APB-1 OLAP Benchmark database is created using DB2 OLAP Server, it generates a set of relational tables represented as a star schema. The dimension tables (1-6) are: *Time, Measure, Scenario, Channel, Customer, and Product.* One of the dimensions, in our case *Time*, is chosen as the so-called anchor dimension and is joined with the fact table (hence we refer to the result of that join as the fact table). The attributes of the fact table indicate the sales in a given period of time: *199502* stores the sales value for February of 95, *1996Q1* for the first quarter of 96, etc.

In addition, DB2 OLAP Server creates and manages a number of views that simplify SQL application access to the multidimensional data. One of them, *olapmain_starview* (defined in Query 3 of Example 5), is particularly interesting from our point of view since it joins the fact table with five dimension tables (2–6). All of the joins in the view are RI joins. The sizes of the dimension tables (1–6) are respectively: 86, 15, 16, 12, 1001, 10001 rows. The fact table has 2.4 million rows.

We ran the experiments on DB2 OLAP Server in-

Queries		$\mathcal{J}_1$	$\mathcal{J}_2$	$\mathcal{J}_3$	$\mathcal{J}_4$	$\mathcal{J}_5$	$\mathcal{J}_6$	$\mathcal{J}_7$	$\mathcal{J}_8$	$\mathcal{J}_9$	$\mathcal{J}_{10}$
Execution Time (s)	Original	98.2	576.2	11.3	12.5	504.3	586.4	523.5	5.6	5.2	4.7
	Optimized	9.7	23.9	10.9	11.4	167.2	231.0	268.5	4.9	5.1	4.3

Table 1: Performance Results for Join Elimination

stalled in Windows NT Server 4.0 on a 4-way Pentium II Xeon 450 with 4GB of memory. Each of the queries below was run at least 5 times; execution times are averages over all runs. We designed the queries to involve other operations than just the joins in the view to make them more realistic. Queries $\mathcal{J}_1$ and $\mathcal{J}_2$ allowed elimination of all five dimension tables, queries $\mathcal{J}_3$ and $\mathcal{J}_4$ allowed elimination of four dimension tables, queries $\mathcal{J}_5$ and $\mathcal{J}_6$ allowed elimination of three dimension tables, queries $\mathcal{J}_7$ and $\mathcal{J}_8$ allowed elimination of two dimension tables, and queries $\mathcal{J}_9$ and $\mathcal{J}_{10}$ allowed elimination of one dimension table. We also tested queries from which no joins could be eliminated; no deterioration of performance due to extra optimization step was observed.

```
J1: select  count("1996Q1")
    from    olapmain_starview;

J2: select  sum("199501") as "199501",
            sum("199502") as "199502",
            sum("199503") as "199503",
            sum("199601") as "199601",
            sum("199602") as "199602",
            sum("199603") as "199603"
    from    olapmain_starview;

J3: select   "199606", "199605"
    from     olapmain_starview
    where    channel_label = 'EQ086DVOCPQS'
             and "199606"< "199605"
    order by "199606" , "199605";

J4: select  count("199604") as "199604"
            count("199605") as "199605",
            count("199606") as "199606"
    from    olapmain_starview
    where   measure = 'Dollar Sales'
            and "199604" > 5000.0
            and "199605" > 5000.0
            and "199606" > 5000.0;

J5: select  sum("1995Q4") as "1995Q4"
    from    olapmain_starview
    where   scenario = 'Actual'
            and measure = 'Inventory Units';

J6: select   measure, sum("199606") as total
    from     olapmain_starview
    where    scenario = 'Actual'
    group by measure
    order by measure;

J7: select   channel_label,
             sum("199606") as "199606",
             sum("199506") as "199506"
    from     olapmain_starview
    where    scenario = 'Actual'
             and measure = 'Dollar Sales'
    group by channel_label
    order by "199606", "199506";

J8: select   scenario,
             sum("1996Q2") - sum("1996Q1")
             as change
    from     olapmain_starview
    where    measure = 'Dollar Sales'
             and customer = 'VB8NRNCDLNPT'
    group by scenario
    order by change;

J9: select  sum("1995Q4") as "1995Q4",
            sum("1996Q1") as "1996Q1",
            sum("1996Q2") as $
    from    olapmain_starview
    where   scenario = 'Actual'
            and channel_label = 'VDWRDK3K574X'
            and customer = 'Y8AJBH5KL5LE'
            and measure = 'Dollar Sales';

J10: select   customer,
              avg("1996Q1") as "1996Q1"
     from     olapmain_starview
     where    scenario = 'Actual'
              and measure = 'Dollar Sales'
              and customer = 'VB8NRNCDLNPT'
     group by customer
     order by "1996Q1";
```

The amount of savings provided by the optimization in each of the tested queries is a function of many factors (the selectivity of the predicates, relative cost of the eliminated join versus other operations in a query, the size of the output, etc.). Hence, the optimization ranges from 2% (query $\mathcal{J}_9$) to 96% (query $\mathcal{J}_2$). Nevertheless, for all experiments JE provided consistent optimization for tested queries and for many of them the optimization was substantial. Another point we need to stress here is that for most of the queries the saving in execution time came from reducing the CPU cost, not the I/O (because the dimension tables were small and fit in memory). We expect that we can achieve even more prominent optimization for strictly I/O bound queries.

4 Predicate Introduction

4.1 Implementation

The idea of Predicate Introduction (PI) was discussed in literature as two different techniques: index introduction and scan reduction. The idea behind the index introduction is to add a new predicate to a query if there is an index on the attribute named in the predicate [1, 7, 9, 17] (query $\mathcal{P}_1$ of Example 1 illustrates this transformation). The assumption here is that retrieval of tuples using an index is more efficient than their sequential processing. In general, this assumption is not always true. Thus, the general rule was either accompanied by heuristics [9] or several queries were generated which were then subject to the cost evaluation by the plan optimizer [1]. As we stated in Section 2, we did not have a ready option in our design to get feedback from the plan generator in query rewrite engine. Hence, we needed to restrict the use of PI to situations that would guarantee improvement in the efficiency of query evaluation. Surprisingly, the range of such restrictions had to be more stringent than we expected.

The second use of PI is for table scan reduction. The idea here is to add a predicate to reduce the number of tuples that qualify for a join. As we show later in this section, this provides substantial optimization for all types of join. The problem with scan reduction is, however, that it is not common: it is unlikely that there will be any check constraints or predicates with inequalities about join columns. The example below illustrates scan reduction.

Example 6. $\mathcal{S}_1$ is a query asked against the TPCD database. Given the fact that the check constraint **l_receiptdate ≥ l_shipdate** holds in TPCD, two new predicates *l2.l_receiptdate > date ('1998-07-01')* and *l1.l_commitdate > date ('1998-07-01')* can be added to the query, thus reducing the number of tuples of **l1** and **l2** that qualify for a join.

$\mathcal{S}_1$: **select** sum(l1.l_extendedprice * l1.discount)
    as revenue
from tpcd.lineitem as l1, tpcd.lineitem as l2
where l1.l_commitdate = l2.l_receiptdate and
    l2.l_shipdate > date('1998-07-01') and
    l2.l_discount between 0.06 − 0.01 and
    0.06 + 0.01 and l2.l_quantity < 24;

Our implementation of PI included also another SQO technique discussed in the literature: detecting an empty query answer set. The idea behind this technique is to check whether the set of logical consequences of the set of query predicates and check constraints is consistent. Consider the following example.

Example 7. Let $\mathcal{E}$ be a query asked against the TPCD database:

$\mathcal{E}$: **select** sum(l_extendedprice * l_discount)
    as revenue
from tpcd.lineitem
where l_shipdate > date('1994-01-01') and
    l_receiptdate < date('1994-01-01')

The query itself does not contain a contradiction. However, given the fact that the check constraint **l_shipdate ≤ l_receiptdate** holds in TPCD, the query cannot return any answers. Thus, it does not need to be evaluated.

We should note that DB2 UDB already implements a version of predicate introduction [4]. The exisiting theorem prover generates a transitive closure over all equality predicates. The result of this operation is used to provide the optimizer with a choice of additional joins that may be considered to select the best access plan for the query. In addition, query rewrite will also derive additional local predicates based on transitivity implied by equality predicates. This may lead to scan reduction. The current system does not, however, take into account check constraints.

The PI algorithm we implemented has two main components: a theorem prover and a filter. The input to the theorem prover is the set of all check constraints defined for a database and the set of all predicates in a query. Its output is the set of all non-redundant formulas derivable from the input set. These formulas represent new predicates that can be added to the query; they are of the form A *op* B, where A and B are attribute names or constants and *op* is one of the following: $>$, $<$, $\geq$, $\leq$.[3] Clearly, only a few of the new predicates are useful for optimization. The role of the filter is to find them. Our goal in designing heuristics rules for the filter was to *guarantee* that any new predicate added to the query will allow the optimizer to find only better access plans than the ones available for the original query. The sketch of the algorithm is presented below.

Let $\mathcal{N}$ be the set of new predicates computed by the theorem prover.

1. If $\mathcal{N}$ is inconsistent (as in Example 7) an appro-

[3] This set does not include '=' since DB2 UDB already handles reasoning over predicates with equality.

Queries		$\mathcal{P}_1$	$\mathcal{P}_2$	$\mathcal{P}_3$	$\mathcal{P}_4$	$\mathcal{P}_5$
Estimated Cost (internal units)	Original	54031	113316	108676	128342	195098
	Optimized	18308	11222	69623	35974	133665
Execution Time (s)	Original	13.5	24.9	25.1	46.4	56.5
	Optimized	5.4	4.9	58.3	38.6	98.3

Table 2: Performance Results for Index Introduction

priate flag is raised and the query is not evaluated.

2. Else, for each predicate A *op* $B \in \mathcal{N}$, it is added to the query if one of the following holds
   a. A or B is a join column
   b.
      - A is a constant, and
      - B is a major column of an index, and
      - no other index on B's table can be used in the plan for the original query

Case 1 of the algorithm handles the discovery of inconsistency in the query. Case 2.a allows for scan reduction. The most important part of the algorithm, Case 2.b introduces an index to the query. Our approach is conservative: we introduce a new predicate to the query if this allows the plan optimizer to use an index (not available before) and this new plan does not preempt the use of another, potentially better plan. Thus, we insist that there is no other index available for the optimizer on the table with the new predicate. Our experiments show that without appropriate enhancements in the query optimizer, even this policy may not be sufficiently restrictive.

4.2 Performance Results

The PI technique described above has been implemented as a prototype in DB2 UDB installed in AIX on machine JRS/6000 Model 590H with 512MB of memory. We used 100MB TPCD Benchmark [19] database for our experiments. The queries we present below are a representative sample of many test cases we considered. As before, each of the queries was run at least five times and the timing results are averages over these runs.

• Detecting an Empty Answer Set

The performance results for this technique were, of course, trivial: query execution time was essentially 0 in each case.

• Index Introduction

Our initial conjecture about when index introduction is useful was as follows: the attribute of the new predicate must be a major column (prefix of the search key) of a clustered index, and no such index is otherwise available for the table of that attribute. A sample set of queries on which we tested this conjecture is presented below.

$\mathcal{P}_1$:
```
select sum(l_extendedprice * l_discount)
       as revenue
from   tpcd.lineitem
where  l_shipdate >= date('1994-01-01') and
       l_receiptdate < date ('1994-01-01')+1 year
       and l_discount between .06 - 0.01
       and .06 + 0.01 and l_quantity < 24;
```

$\mathcal{P}_2$:
```
select 100.00 * sum
       (case
          when p_type like 'PROMO%'
          then l_extendedprice * (1 - l_discount)
          else 0
       end)
       / sum(l_extendedprice * (1 - l_discount))
       as promo_revenue
from   tpcd.lineitem, tpcd.part
where  l_partkey = p_partkey and
       l_shipdate >= date('1998-09-01') and
       l_shipdate < date('1998-09-01')+1 month;
```

$\mathcal{P}_3$: same as $\mathcal{P}_2$ except for the indicated lines which are replaced with:

```
l_shipdate >= date('1995-09-01') and
l_shipdate < date('1995-09-01')+1 month;
```

$\mathcal{P}_4$:
```
select l_orderkey,
       sum(l_extendedprice * (1 - l_discount))
       as revenue, o_orderdate, o_shippriority
from   tpcd.customer, tpcd.orders, tpcd.lineitem
where  c_mktsegment = 'BUILDING'
       and c_custkey = o_custkey
       and l_orderkey = o_orderkey and
       o_orderdate < date ('1998-03-15') and
       l_shipdate > date ('1998-03-15')
group by l_orderkey, o_orderdate, o_shippriority
order by revenue desc, o_orderdate
fetch  first 10 rows only;
```

$\mathcal{P}_5$: same as $\mathcal{P}_4$ except for the indicated lines which are replaced with:

	Data Reads		Index Reads		CPU Cost	Estimated Number
	Physical	Logical	Physical	Logical	(s)	of Qualifying Tuples
Original Query	21607	22439	12	26	21.9	20839
"Optimized" Query	10680	286516	2687	288326	55.9	12618

Table 3: Comparison of the Evaluation Costs for $\mathcal{P}_3$.

o_orderdate < date ('1995-03-15') and
l_shipdate > date ('1995-03-15')

We created a clustered index with the search key <l_receiptdate, discount, quantity, extendedprice> for the table **lineitem**. Since the major column of the index, *l_receiptdate*, is not used in any of the queries, this index is not used in query evaluation. However, since the check constraint *l_receiptdate* $\geq$ *l_shipdate* is defined in TPCD for the table **lineitem** and each of the queries contain a predicate of the form *l_shipdate* $\geq$ *DATE*, we may add a new predicate *l_receiptdate* $\geq$ *DATE* to each of the queries. Now, a potentially better access plan is available for query evaluation. Indeed, as Table 2 shows, cost estimates generated by the optimizer indicate that the availability of the new predicate should uniformly improve query execution time. Surprisingly, it did not happen: for queries $\mathcal{P}_3$ and $\mathcal{P}_5$ execution time grew with the addition of the new predicate.

In retrospect, there is a simple explanantion for this deterioration. Consider queries $\mathcal{P}_2$ and $\mathcal{P}_3$. The query plan generated for both of the original queries (that is, without predicate introduction) used table scan to retrieve qualifying tuples from the **lineitem** table. The introduction of a new predicate (*l_receiptdate* $\geq$ *date ('1998-09-01')* for $\mathcal{P}_2$ and *l_receiptdate* $\geq$ *date ('1995-09-01')* for $\mathcal{P}_3$), allows the optimizer to use the index. Indeed, the new plan for both queries uses the index to get directly to the tuples within the specified range of *l_receiptdate*. This requires traversing the index leaves in the range of the predicate and retrieving all tuples pointed to by these leaves. (It is often stated in database textbooks that for a range search with a clustered index, it is sufficient to retrieve the first tuple in the range and then scan the rest of the table. For this approach to work, however, the table has to be perfectly sorted at all times. This is often impractical, hence not implemented in DB2 UDB.) What makes the difference between the performance of the two queries is the size of that range: 2% of the tuples fall within the range of *l_receiptdate* $\geq$ *date ('1998-09-01')* and 48% are within the range of *l_receiptdate* $\geq$ *date ('1995-09-01')*. The second range is so large that a simple table scan would be a better plan. Using an index instead involves a large overhead in locking and unlocking index pages. Indeed, I/O cost (number of physical page reads) for $\mathcal{P}_3$ does go down (see Table 3), but the CPU cost increases even more.

So far, we identified two possible reasons why the optimizer may have chosen a more expensive access plan for the query. One is that the cost model underestimates the cost of locking and unlocking index pages. The second, more interesting reason, is the computation of a filter factor for the query.[4] Since a new predicate is added to the query the filter factor of the predicates of the original query is multiplied by the filter factor of *l_receiptdate* $\geq$ *date ('1995-09-01')*. The estimated number of qualifying tuples goes down (see Table 3) and the optimizer chooses an index scan as the best access plan. However, the number of qualifying tuples does *not* decrease in the optimized query, since the query is semantically equivalent to the original one. The problem, of course, is the correlation between *shipdate* and *l_receiptdate*: the filter factor of a conjunction of the predicates with these two attributes is *not* a product of their individual filter factors. This is an important lesson for any implementation of query rewrite involving addition or removal of predicates with correlated attributes.

Queries		$\mathcal{P}_3$	$\mathcal{P}_5$
Execution Time (s)	Original	21.3	52.2
	Optimized	10.9	45.6

Table 4: Performance Results for Index Introduction (modified algorithm)

Once we discovered that our initial conjecture about the usefullness of predicate introduction was incorrect, we needed to restrict it further. Thus, we modified the algorithm so that a new predicate is added to a query only if it contains a major column of an index and a scan of that index is sufficient to answer the query (that is, no table scan is necessary). To verify our hypothesis, we created an index <receiptdate, discount, quantity, extendedprice, shipdate, partkey, suppkey, orderkey> and ran the queries $\mathcal{P}_3$ and $\mathcal{P}_5$ again. As expected, the use of the index-only plan improved the execution time of the original query. The addition of a major column of that index to the query improved

[4] A filter factor of a predicate (also called a reduction factor) is the proportion of tuples in a relation satisfying the predicate.

that even more. The results are presented in Table 4.

• **Scan Reduction**

Since the only check constraint available to us[5] was *l_receiptdate* ≥ *l_shipdate*, we had to test queries involving a join with at least one of these attributes. (The queries are admittedly not very meaningful.) The only difference between the two queries is the range of qualifying tuples (much larger in the second query).

$\mathcal{S}_1$: **select** sum(l1.l_extendedprice * l1.discount) as revenue
from tpcd.lineitem as l1, tpcd.lineitem as l2
where l1.l_commitdate = l2.l_receiptdate and l2.l_shipdate > date('1998-07-01') and l2.l_discount between 0.06 − 0.01 and 0.06 + 0.01 and l2.l_quantity < 24;

$\mathcal{S}_2$: **select** sum(l1.l_extendedprice * l1.discount) as revenue
from tpcd.lineitem as l1, tpcd.lineitem as l2
where l1.l_commitdate = l2.l_receiptdate and l2.l_shipdate > date ('1996-07-01') and l2.l_discount between 0.06 − 0.01 and 0.06 + 0.01 and l2.l_quantity < 24;

Because of the check constraint, we may add a new predicate *l2.l_receiptdate > date ('1998-07-01')* to $\mathcal{S}_1$ (similarly for $\mathcal{S}_2$) thus limiting the number of tuples that qualify for the join. As shown in Table 5, this provides consistent optimization for the four tested types of join: index nested loops, sort-merge, nested loops, and hash join.

For INL we defined the index <receiptdate, discount, quantity, extendedprice, shipdate, partkey, suppkey, orderkey>. The index was explicitly dropped for all other joins.

Although the results of our experiments were very promising, we could not design more meaningful queries for scan reduction in TPCD. This technique is applicable only when there exist check constraints defined over join attributes of a relation or there are predicates with inequality over join attributes.

5 Conclusions

We developed algorithms for two SQO techniques, Join Elimination (JE) and Predicate Introduction (PI), and implemented siginificant portions of these technologies as a prototype in DB2 UDB. The implementation process and performance analysis provided us with several insights about SQO and query optimization in general. The most important outcome of our work is the experimental evidence which shows that SQO can provide an effective enhancement to the traditional query optimization. This is particularly striking in the case of JE for which our experiments delivered consistent optimization for all tested queries. Although our implementation of JE was geared towards OLAP environment (in which, we believe, JE can be particularly useful), a few experiments we performed in TPCD were also very promising. The algorithm for JE that we developed handles not only the removal of explicit RI joins, but all redundant joins that can be inferred through reasoning over the query and the RIs defined for the database. We showed on several examples that such inferred joins can be difficult to discover and optimize by hand.

What is novel about our implementation of JE is that it does not depend on the existence of complex integrity constraints. The use of semantic reasoning about referential integrity constraints, which are common in both OLTP as well as OLAP workloads, can lead to dramatic performance improvements for typical queries in these workloads. Moreover, our implementation of JE does not depend on intricate and often unavailable cost information. This makes JE easy to implement and efficient to execute.

Our experiments with PI showed that this technique can be very useful in detecting, by reasoning over integrity constraints, when a query's answer set is empty. The use of PI for index introduction delievered good performance improvements when it was sufficiently restricted. To *guarantee* such improvements, however, these restrictions had to be rather severe, thus limiting the applicability of the technique. Nevertheless, the implementation of PI was very useful for us as an experience. The ramifications of adding or removing a predicate from a query turned out to be more complex than we originally predicted. In particular, the estimate of a filter factor in the optimized query has to take into account the fact that semantically related attributes are likely to be statistically correlated.

There is yet another lesson we learned from this work. We found the necessity of having to generate a single query by the rewrite engine constraining. The conditions used to activate rules that produce such a query are not based on database statistics (this comes into play only at the access plan generation phase) hence have to be sufficiently general to work for all databases. Many rewrites useful for a *particular* database can be missed. (The implementation of magic sets [15] as a cost-based optimization technique proved to be much more successful than as a heuristic rewrite technique.) Thus, we advocate establishing a two-way communication between the two phases of the query optimization, so that the plan generator can provide query rewrite

[5] DB2 does not yet support check constraints across multiple tables.

Query		$\mathcal{S}_1$				$\mathcal{S}_2$			
Join Method		INL	SM	NL	Hash	INL	SM	NL	Hash
Execution Time (s)	Original	107.2	107.5	107.8	107.6	270.8	250.0	250.0	250.3
	Optimized	37.4	52.9	54.3	52.9	218.5	209.3	209.4	209.3

Table 5: Performance Results for Scan Reduction

engine with a feedback on which transformations are useful and which are not. This change will increase the complexity of the design of the optimizer, but we believe it can dramatically increase the effectiveness of the rewrites, in particular, those based on SQO.

Acknowledgements

We would like to thank Jennifer Crawford and Cheryl Greene from IBM Toronto Lab for their help with this project and Parke Godfrey and Renée Miller for helpful comments on the paper.

This research was supported by Center for Advanced Studies, IBM Toronto and NSERC (Grant 216748-98).

References

[1] U. Chakravarthy, J. Grant, and J. Minker. Logic-based approach to semantic query optimization. *ACM TODS*, 15(2):162–207, June 1990.

[2] S. Chaudhuri and K. Shim. Including group-by in query optimization. In *Proc. of VLDB*, pages 354–366, 1994.

[3] OLAP Council. APB-1 OLAP Benchmark Release II, November 1998. (www.olapcouncil.org).

[4] IBM DB2 Universal Database. *Administration Guide.* 1998. Version 5.2 S10J-8157-01.

[5] J. Gryz, L. Liu, and X. Qian. Semantic query optimization in DB2: Initial results. Technical Report CS-1999-01, Department of Computer Science, York University, Toronto, Canada, 1999.

[6] L.M. Haas et al. Starburst Mid-Flight: As the Dust Clears. *IEEE TKDE*, pages 143–160, March 1990.

[7] M.T. Hammer and S.B. Zdonik. Knowledge-based query processing. *Proc. 6th VLDB*, pages 137–147, October 1980.

[8] M. Jarke, J. Clifford, and Y. Vassiliou. An optimizing PROLOG front-end to a relational query system. In *SIGMOD*, pages 296–306, 1984.

[9] J.J. King. Quist: A system for semantic query optimization in relational databases. *Proc. 7th VLDB*, pages 510–517, September 1981.

[10] A.Y. Levy, I. Mumick, and Y. Sagiv. Query optimization by predicate move-around. In *Proc. of VLDB*, pages 96–108, 1994.

[11] I. Mumick and H. Pirahesh. Implementation of magic sets in Starburst. In *Proc. SIGMOD*, 1994.

[12] G. Paulley and P. Larson. Exploiting uniqueness in query optimization. In *Proceedings of ICDE*, pages 68–79, 1994.

[13] H. Pirahesh, J. M. Hellerstein, and W. Hasan. Extensible/rule based query rewrite optimization in Starburst. In *Proc. SIGMOD*, pages 39–48, 1992.

[14] H. Pirahesh, T. Y. C. Leung, and W. Hasan. A rule engine for query transformation in Starburst and IBM DB2 C/S DBMS. In *Proc. ICDE*, pages 391–400, 1997.

[15] S. Seshadri et al. Cost-based optimization for magic: Algebra and implementation. In *SIGMOD*, pages 435–446, 1996.

[16] S. Shekar, J. Srivastava, and S. Dutta. A formal model of trade-off between optimization and execution costs in semantic query optimization. In *Proc. 14th VLDB*, pages 457–467, Los Angeles, CA, 1988.

[17] S.T. Shenoy and Z.M. Ozsoyoglu. Design and implementation of a semantic query optimizer. *IEEE Transactions on Knowledge and Data Engineering*, 1(3):344–361, September 1989.

[18] D. Simmen, E. Shekita, and T. Malkems. Fundamental techniques for order optimization. In *Proceedings of SIGMOD*, pages 57–67, 1996.

[19] Transaction Processing Performance Council, 777 No. First Street, Suite 600, San Jose, CA 95112-6311, www.tpc.org. *TPC Benchmark^{TM} D*, 1.3.1 edition, February 1998.

High-Performance Extensible Indexing

Marcel Kornacker*

U. C. Berkeley
marcel@cs.berkeley.edu

Abstract

Today's object-relational DBMSs (ORDBMSs) are designed to support novel application domains by providing an extensible architecture, supplemented by domain-specific database extensions supplied by external vendors. An important aspect of ORDBMSs is support for extensible indexing, which allows the core database server to be extended with external access methods (AMs). This paper describes a new approach to extensible indexing implemented in Informix Dynamic Server with Universal Data Option (IDS/UDO). The approach is is based on the *generalized search tree*, or GiST, which is a template index structure for abstract data types that supports an extensible set of queries. GiST encapsulates core database indexing functionality including search, update, concurrency control and recovery, and thereby relieves the external access method (AM) of the burden of dealing with these issues. The IDS/UDO implementation employs a newly designed GiST API that reduces the number of user defined function calls, which are typically expensive to execute, and at the same time makes GiST a more flexible data structure. Experiments show that GiST-based AM extensibility can offer substantially better performance than built-in AMs when indexing user-defined data types.

1 Introduction

Efficient search tree access methods are crucial for any database system. In traditional relational database management systems, B^+-trees [Com79] suffice for queries posed on the standard SQL data types. Today's extensible object-relational database management systems (ORDBMSs) are being deployed to support new applications such as dynamic web servers, geographic information systems, CAD tools, multimedia and document libraries, sequence databases, fingerprint identification systems, biochemical databases, *etc.* For these applications, new kinds of access methods are required.

Broadly speaking, the research community has responded by developing novel search trees to support each new application. For example, a recent survey article [GG98] describes over 50 alternative index structures for spatial indexing alone. Some of this specialized work has had fundamental impact in particular domains. However, only two or three structures developed since the B^+-tree have enjoyed any significant industrial acceptance.

The reason for this is the fundamental complexity and cost involved in developing access methods (AMs) and integrating them into database servers. Designing an AM for use in a commercial ORDBMS requires a very good understanding of concurrency and recovery protocols; integrating an AM into a database server requires a great deal of familiarity with such central components as the lock and log managers. The commercial state of the art in access method extensibility, exemplified by IDS/UDO's Virtual Index Interface [Inf98b] and Oracle's Extensible Indexing Interface [Ora98] and illustrated in principle in Figure 1 (a), does not reduce this complexity. Essentially, these interfaces represent the access method as an iterator data structure; the query executor calls this interface directly to retrieve tuples from the index. An interface like that allows extensibility, but does not reduce the implementation effort of an external AM when compared to a built-in one, if identical levels of concurrency, robustness and integration are desired.[1] As a result, few if any database extension vendors have undertaken the daunting task of implementing a custom-designed, high-quality access method for any of the popular ORDBMSs.

This paper describes the implementation in IDS/UDO of an alternative approach to access method extensibility. This approach is based on the *generalized search tree* (GiST, originally proposed in [HNP95]), a template search tree

*This work was done while the author was a summer intern at Informix Corp.

Proceedings of the 25th VLDB Conference, Edinburgh, Scotland, 1999.

[1]The advantage of such an iterator interface is that existing external retrieval engines can easily be interfaced to the database system.

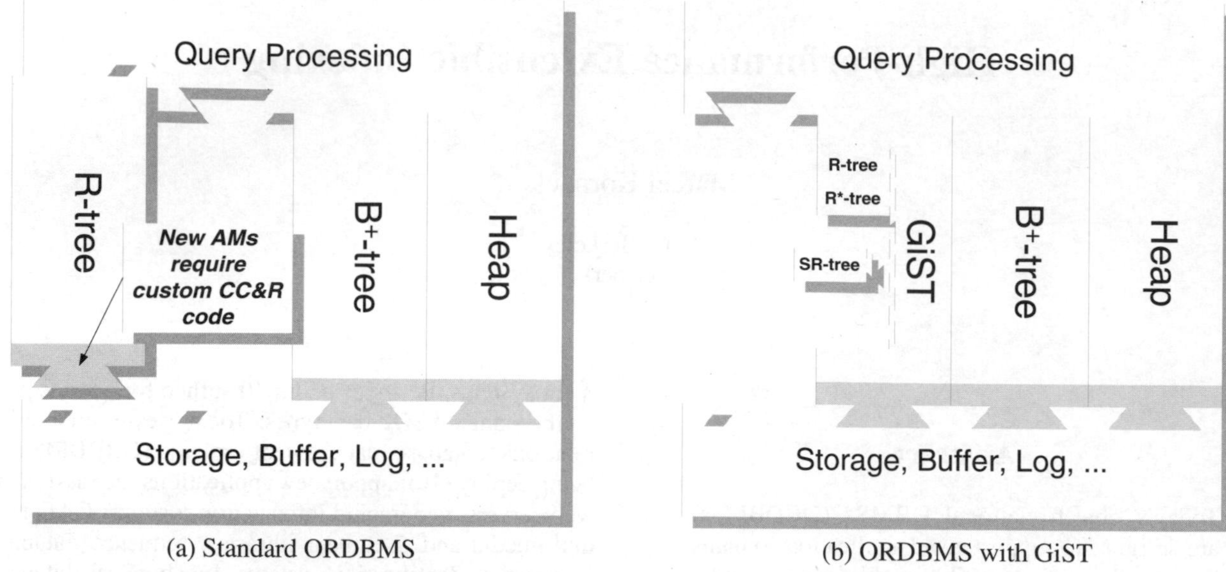

(a) Standard ORDBMS

(b) ORDBMS with GiST

Figure 1: Access method interfaces – the database extender's perspective.

structure that is easily extensible in both the data types it can index and the query types it can support. GiST encapsulates core indexing functionality such as search and update operations, concurrency and recovery. The GiST interface, like the existing extensibility interfaces, defines a set of functions for implementing an external AM. However, the GiST interface raises the level of abstraction, only requiring the AM developer to implement the semantics of the data type that is being indexed and those operational properties that distinguish a particular AM from other tree-structured AMs. An AM extension based on this interface typically needs only a small percentage of the (tens of) thousands of lines of code required for a full access method implementation. The level of abstraction offered by the interface relieves the AM developer of the burden of understanding concurrency and recovery protocols and the corresponding components of the database servers. Instead, it is the ORDBMS vendor who implements the concurrency and recovery protocols within GiST, using the existing, low-level extensibility interface to add GiST to the database server (illustrated in Figure 1 (b)). Given that database extension vendors tend to be *domain knowledge* experts rather than *database server* experts, this approach to access method extensibility should result in much higher-quality access methods at substantially reduced development cost for the extension vendor. For the ORDBMS vendor, implementing GiST is no more complex than implementing any other fully integrated AM.

A key ingredient of ORDBMSs is the ability to call user-defined functions (UDFs) that are external to the database server. Since the reliability of the server must not be compromised, it must take precautionary steps to insulate itself from malfunctioning UDFs. In IDS/UDO, a UDF is executed in the same address space as the server, but calling a UDF still involves some overhead: installation of a signal handler to catch segmentation violations and bus errors,[2] allocation of additional stack space, if necessary, and checking of parameters for NULL values. This makes a UDF call considerably more expensive than a regular function call. In Oracle and DB2, UDFs can be executed in a separate address space, which even adds to the cost. When dividing the full functionality of an AM between the database server and an external extension module, as GiST does, UDF calls become inevitable, which can become a performance problem. To address this issue, the original GiST interface was redesigned to reduce as much as possible the number of UDF calls. The new interface is also more flexible, giving external AMs the option of customizing how data is stored on index pages.

The remainder of this paper is structured as follows: Section 2 gives an overview of the GiST data structures; Section 3 describes how the GiST concept was implemented in IDS/UDO and gives examples that highlight some of the features; Section 4 describes some of the concurrency and recovery implementation issues that would arise in a typically ORDBMS and Section 5 compares the performance of GiST-based R-trees with their built-in counterparts in IDS/UDO.

2 Generalized Search Tree Overview

A GiST is a balanced tree which provides "template" algorithms for navigating the tree structure and modifying the tree structure through page splits and deletes. Like all other (secondary) index trees, the GiST stores *(key, RID)* pairs in the leaves; the RIDs (record identifiers) point to the corresponding records on the data pages. Internal pages contain *(predicate, child page pointer)* pairs; the predicate evaluates

[2]These mechanisms are specific to Unix. On Windows NT, similar mechanisms are used.

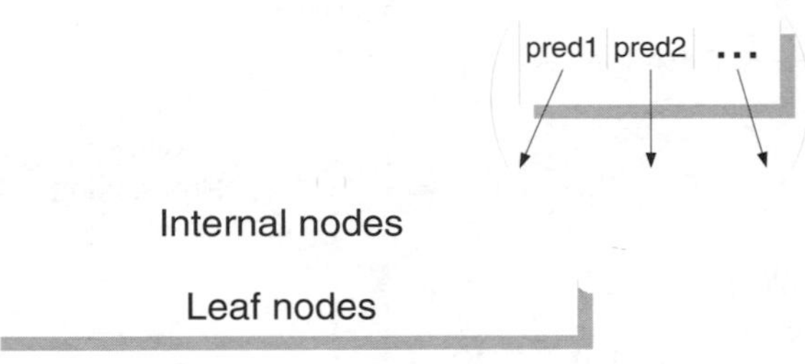

Figure 2: Sketch of a database search tree.

to true for any of the keys contained in or reachable from the associated child page. Figure 2 illustrates this organization, which captures the essence of a tree-based index structure: a hierarchy of predicates, in which each predicate holds true for all keys stored under it in the hierarchy. A B$^+$-tree [Com79] is a well known example with those properties: the entries in internal pages represent ranges which bound values of keys in the leaves of the respective subtrees. Another example is the R-tree [Gut84], which contains bounding rectangles as predicates in the internal pages. The predicates in the internal pages of a search tree will subsequently be referred to as subtree predicates (SPs).

Apart from these structural requirements, a GiST does not impose any restrictions on the key data stored within the tree or their organization within and across pages. In particular, the key space need not be ordered, thereby allowing multidimensional data. Moreover, the pages of a single level need not partition or even cover the entire key space, meaning that (a) overlapping SPs of entries at the same tree level are allowed and (b) the union of all SPs can have "holes" when compared to the entire key space. The leaves, however, partition the set of stored RIDs, so that exactly one leaf entry points to a given data record.

A GiST supports the standard index operations: SEARCH, which takes a predicate and returns all leaf entries satisfying that predicate; INSERT, which adds a *(key, RID)* pair to the tree; and DELETE, which removes such a pair from the tree. It implements these operations with the help of a set of external functions supplied by the access method developer. This set of external functions, which forms the GiST interface, encapsulates the semantics of the data domain to be indexed and the organization of predicates within the tree; a specific implementation of this interface is an *AM extension*. The combination of generic Gist algorithms for search, insert and delete operations and the AM extension constitutes a fully functional AM.

The following overview outlines the generic algorithms and the role of the AM extension within those algorithms. To show the extent to which the GiST interface was redesigned, the GiST interface functions mentioned here are those of the original GiST design. The redesigned interface and a descriptions of the its functions in the context of the generic algorithms are the topic of the next section.

SEARCH

In order to find all leaf entries satisfying the search qualification, we recursively descend *all* subtrees for which the parent entry's predicate is consistent with the search qualification. Interpretation of the search qualification and its evaluation against data stored in the tree is handled by the interface function *consistent()*, which takes a query predicate and a page entry as arguments and returns true if the entry matches the predicate.

INSERT

Given a new *(key, RID)* pair, we must find a single leaf to insert it on. Note that, unlike B-trees, GiSTs allow overlapping SPs, so there may be more than one leaf where the key could be inserted. We traverse a single path from root to leaf, using as the guiding principle for selecting the next child pointer to follow an *insertion penalty*. This is supplied by the *penalty()* interface function, which takes the new key and a page entry as arguments and returns the corresponding penalty (a numerical value). Conceptually, the AM extension is presented with the new key and an SP and computes a penalty value that typically reflects how much the SP needs to be expanded to accomodate the new key. At each traversed index page, the entry with the smallest insertion penalty is chosen for further traversal. The insertion penalty expresses the AM extension's insertion strategy, i.e., which path is taken when locating the target leaf.

If the target leaf overflows as a result of the insertion, it is split; if the parent also overflows, the splitting is carried out recursively. The *pick_split()* interface function determines the split strategy by specifying which of the entries on a page move to the new right sibling page during a split.

If the leaf's ancestors' predicates do not include the new key, they must be expanded, so that the path from the root to the leaf reflects the new key. The *union()* interface function computes the expanded predicate as the union of the old SP and the new key. Like page splitting, expansion of predicates in parent entries is carried out recursively until we find an ancestor page whose predicate does not require expansion.

DELETE

In order to find the leaf containing the key we want to delete, we again traverse multiple subtrees as in SEARCH. Once the leaf is located and the key is found on it, we remove the *(key, RID)* pair and, if possible, shrink the ancestors' SPs. The *union()* interface function computes the contracted SP as the union of all the entries on the corresponding page.

Although the GiST abstraction prescribes algorithm for search and update operations, the AM designer still has full control over clustering, page utilization and the subtree predicates, which are the performance-relevant structural characteristics of an index. The insertion and split strategies of an AM extension, expressed by the interface functions *penalty()* and *pick_split()*, determine where predicates are placed and how they are moved around; they control page utilization and clustering. The subtree predicates, which greatly influence the performance of search operations, are not interpreted by the GiST algorithms directly; to GiST, they are only sequences of bytes. The AM extension determines the semantics of those predicates and communicates this through the GiST interface functions *consistent()* and *union()*.

3 GiST-Based Index Extension Architecture

When implementing a GiST-based AM extension architecture in a commercial-strength ORDBMS, several issues need to be addressed:

- The existing form of datatype extensibility needs to be retained: In some ORDBMSs, the built-in AMs are extensible in the type of data they can index. For example, a B-tree can be made to work with character strings and user-defined data. It is only required that the data type to be indexed has some particular characteristics (such as a defined total order in the case of a B-tree). In order for an AM to index this new data type, the data type implementor need only provide a set of functions that express the particular characteristics required by the AM (in the B-tree example, this would be a comparison function). This kind of datatype-extensible indexing is already a standard feature in currently at least two ORDBMSs (Informix and Oracle), and it is desirable that a GiST-based extension architecture retain this feature.
- UDF calls are expensive and need to be used judiciously: A high number of calls to AM extension UDFs can have a negative impact on the performance of index operations and make the case for extensible indexing less compelling. The original GiST interface as specified in [HNP95] interacts with the AM extension on a per-page entry basis, which results in a large number of UDF calls. A commercial-strength GiST implementation should reduce this overhead.
- Customizable intra-page storage format: The original GiST design assumed that index pages are organized like an unordered collection of data items (page entries are independent of one another and can be inserted and removed without maintaining any particular order on the page). While this is very general, it precludes optimization of the intra-page data layout, which can be used to compress the data or simplify its access. The B-tree is the most well-known AM that takes advantage of customized intra-page data layout: the page entries are ordered within a page to avoid full scans for lookups. Additionally, internal pages compress interval predicates by storing only the right interval boundary (and using the left neighbor's predicate as the left interval boundary). A GiST-based approach to AM extensibility should not preclude customized page layouts.

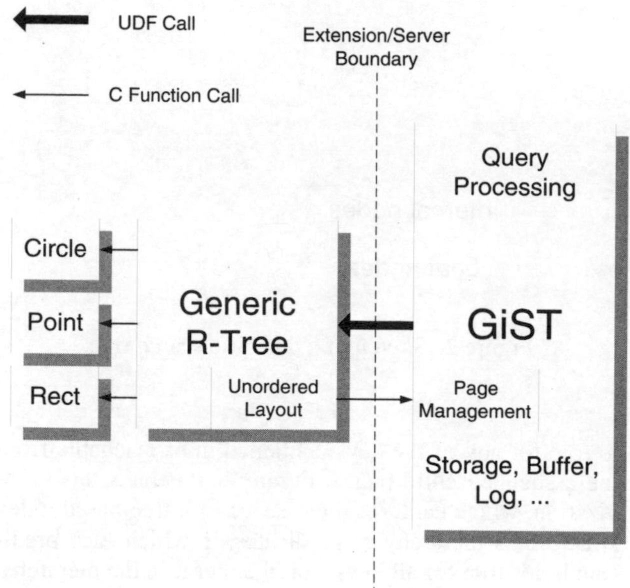

Figure 3: Example of an R-tree in the GiST AM extension architecture

3.1 Architecture Overview

In the IDS/UDO GiST-based AM extension architecture, the full functionality of an AM is divided up into three components: the GiST core inside the database server and the AM extension and a data type adapter in the external database extension module. Figure 3 shows the example of an R-tree extension in this architecture.

GiST Core

The generic GiST algorithms, including the concurrency and recovery protocols, are implemented in the GiST core. It is part of the database server and interacts with the AM extension via the redesigned *GiST interface*, which consists of 11 functions that each AM extension needs to implement. Compared to the original GiST interface, which encapsulates data semantics and the split and insertion strategies, this interface also encapsulates the layout of index pages: the generic GiST algorithms update pages and extract information from them solely through GiST interface functions calls. All of these function calls into the AM extension are executed as UDFs, so that the database server is insulated against failures in the AM extension. In order to reduce the number of UDF calls, the *consistent()* and *penalty()* functions of the original interface have been converted into functions that operate on one entire page instead of individual page entries.

To allow AM extensions to implement customized page layouts, the GiST core exports a GiST-specific page management interface as part of the standard server API (SAPI, see [Inf98a]). This interface is a very thin layer on top of the server-internal page management interface. The latter implements a standard slotted page organization and includes functions to add, update, remove and read page entries, along with various locking and logging options, as well as functions to create and free pages. In contrast, the exported, GiST-specific interface is greatly simplified, being stripped off all logging and locking-related functions and parameters. Furthermore, no page creation and deletion are possible and the target page of each function is implicit (it is the currently "active" page in the tree, i.e., the page that is being traversed, inserted into, etc.). These restrictions do not limit the AM developer's page layout design, but they reduce the potential for doing unwanted damage (since logging, locking and page creation and deletion are handled by the core GiST algorithms, not the AM extension, exposing this functionality to the AM would have no benefit). Also, calls to SAPI functions from the AM extension execute as regular C function calls within the server address space, so there is no need to "ship" the currently active page to the AM extension; copy overhead is therefore avoided. ORDBMSs that execute UDFs outside the server address space could employ careful mapping of address space regions to obtain the same effect.

AM Extension

The AM extension implements the GiST interface and resides in an extension module outside the database server. The AM extension itself specifies an interface, the *extension interface*, that encapsulates the behavior of the data it can index. This interface contains all the functions needed for the supported query operators and to implement the split and insertion strategies. For example, the B-tree extension's interface specifies a comparison function, which is needed to support range queries and perform insertions. The R-tree extension's interface specifies a minimum of seven functions: four of those (namely *overlap()*, *contains()*, *equal()* and *within()*) implement the corresponding search operators, while the other three (*(union()*, *size()* and *intersect()*) are used in the implementations of the split and insertion strategies.

An extension's interface is implemented for every datatype to be indexed by a *datatype adapter* module. For performance reasons, calls by the AM extension to the adapter module are executed as regular C function calls. Since the AM extension functions themselves are called as UDFs, the database server is still insulated from failures in any of the external functions.

The AM extension implements its desired page layout using the GiST-specific page management interface exported by the server. Due to the modular nature of the architecture, user-defined page layouts can be implemented as libraries and reused within other AM extensions (indicated in Figure 3 for the R-tree extension). A standard page layout, which implements the original GiST unordered page layout, is available for AM extensions that do not require customization.

In the current implementation, the B-tree extension occupies about 500 lines of code, excluding comments. The R-tree extension occupies around 800 lines of C code, 150 of which are calls to the unordered page layout and could have been generated automatically. The unordered page layout library is fairly small itself, taking up only about 600 lines of code.

Datatype-specific AM adapter

This user-defined component implements an AM extension's interface for a particular datatype. Typically, datatype adapters are fairly small: our B-tree/integer adapter consists of a 10-line comparison function. An R-tree adapter for simple geospatial objects occupies less than 300 lines of code.

3.2 GiST Interface

The functions of the GiST interface are summarized in Table 1. To provide context, I will go through each index operation chronologically, explaining each interface function as it is called by the generic algorithm.

Each of the GiST interface functions requires as a parameter a pointer to the datatype adapter module, through which the AM extension calls the datatype-specific functions. The GiST core obtains this pointer by calling a UDF that is registered with the database for the specific AM extension/datatype combination. The adapter itself is an array of pointers to functions that implement the AM extension's interface.

SEARCH

To guide tree traversal, the generic search algorithm calls the *search()* function, which, given the currently traversed page, returns the slot indices of those entries that match the query descriptor. For leaf pages, the matching items' heap pointers and predicates—extracted with the *get_key()* function—are returned to the query executor. For internal pages, the child pointers are extracted from the matching items and stored on a stack for future traversal. The query descriptor is assembled by the parser and passed as a parameter into the *search()* function, which then uses SAPI functions to extract the operator and the qualification constants. These server interface calls can involve catalog lookup overhead, which the AM extension may want to avoid incurring for each traversed page. The *begin_scan()* function, called before traversal begins, gives the AM extension an opportunity to extract and store the necessary information from the query descriptor, which is then passed into the *search()* function (as the *state_ptr* parameter). When the search operation is finished, *end_scan()* is called to free up the data allocated in *begin_scan()*.

INSERT

The insertion operation begins by traversing the tree from the root to the insertion target leaf, at each page on the path picking as the next subtree to traverse the child pointer of

Function	Input Parameters	Output Parameters	Purpose
insert()	predicate, heap_ptr, adapter		insert (*predicate, heap_ptr*) entry on page
remove()	slots[], num_slots, adapter		remove items corresponding to *slots[]* from page
update_pred()	slot_num, key, adapter		update predicate part of entry on internal page
begin_scan()	query_descr, adapter	state_ptr	transform query descriptor into AM-specific format
search()	query_descr, state_ptr, adapter	matches[], num_matches	return slot indices of matching items on page
end_scan()	state_ptr, adapter		deallocate data allocated in *begin_scan()*
get_key()	slot_num, adapter	key	extract single entry's predicate from page
pick_split()	adapter, orig_SP	right_entries[], num_right, left_SP, right_SP	determine which entries of a page are to be moved to the new right sibling page and compute the SPs for the resulting left and right page
find_min_pen()	new_key, adapter	slot_num	find page entry with smallest insertion penalty on internal page
union()	SP, is_valid_SP, new_key, adapter	SP, SP_changed	compute a page's SP
eq_op()	adapter		returns AM-specific equality operator number

Table 1: GiST interface summary

the minimum-penalty entry returned by the *find_min_pen()* interface function. At the leaf, the *insert()* interface function physically adds the new item to the leaf page, or signals an overflow, at which point a split is performed. To perform the split, the *pick_split()* function returns the slot numbers of the entries to move to the new right sibling, along with the new SPs for the left and right page produced by the split. The split is then installed in the parent: the old SP for the left page is updated via *update_pred()* and a new entry for the new right page is inserted into the parent with the *insert()* function. Recursive splitting due to parent page overflows are handled in the same way. The actual splitting of the original target page is performed by creating the new right sibling as an exact copy of the page and then removing the unnecessary entries from both pages with the *remove()* interface function. After the split has been completed, the insertion of the new data item can be re-attempted.

If the target page does not overflow, the insertion proceeds without a page split, but must check after calling *insert()* whether the target leaf's SP needs to be updated. This is achieved with a call to the *union()* interface function, which computes the new SP, given the old one and the new item, and also indicates whether the SP has changed. If it has changed, it is installed in the corresponding entry in the parent page with the *update_pred()* interface function. If this causes the parent's SP to change, the SP updates are performed recursively.

DELETE

There are two scenarios for a delete operation. If it is preceded by a search operation in the same index, the leaf that holds the item to be deleted has already been located, and the deletion of the item can be performed immediately via the *remove()* interface function. If an initial lookup of the target item is necessary, it is performed like a search operation for an equality operator. The query descriptor is assembled using the operator number returned by the *eq_op()* interface function.

The next two sections sketch the implementations of two particular AMs to illustrate the flexibility of the GiST interface.

3.3 Example: GiST-Based B-Trees

The B-tree extension implements a sorted page layout, which it maintains during *insert()* calls with the help of the datatype-specific comparison function. The *remove()* function compacts the slots after deleting the requested entry from a page. The *search()* and *find_min_pen()* functions perform a binary search, again using the datatype-specific

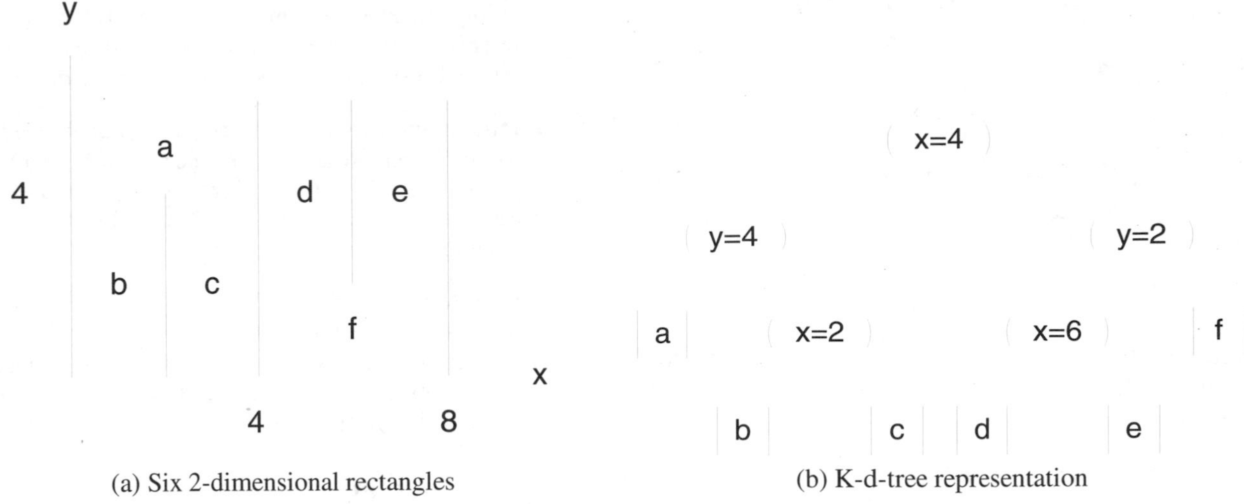

(a) Six 2-dimensional rectangles

(b) K-d-tree representation

Figure 4: K-d-tree example

comparison function, to locate the range of entries that match the query descriptor or to find the entry for the subtree that is appropriate for the new key.

B-trees partition the data space at each level of an index and therefore an insertion never causes an SP to expand. As a result, the *union()* function only indicates that the SP has not changed. In a simple B-tree extension, the *get_key()* function would only return a pointer to the predicate stored on the page. For B-trees that support prefix compression for string keys, the *get_key()* function would need to assemble in a private buffer the full string predicate of the entry from the entries on the page and return a pointer to that buffer. The *update_pred()* function simply overwrites an entry's predicate with the new data; in the case of prefix compression, the new predicate is compared to neighboring page entries to determine the compressed predicate.

Predicates in internal pages store only the right boundary of the interval they represent. The rightmost entry of a page carries a 0-length predicate to signal ∞, which requires the extension's binary search routine to filter out such predicates before calling the datatype's comparison function.

3.4 Example: K-d-tree Page Layout

The k-d-tree [Ben75] is a multidimensional binary search tree that is very efficient for storing iso-oriented rectangles that partition a given space. They are used in hB-trees [LS90], a multidimensional point access method that partitions the data space, as the page layout on non-leaf pages. Figure 4 shows an example of six rectangles in 2-dimensional space and their k-d-tree representation. By organizing rectangles into a tree structure, sides that are common to multiple rectangles need only be stored once, resulting in space savings. On the other hand, each rectangle in a k-d-tree needs to refer to the nodes on its path to reconstruct its coordinates. A simple, unstructured page layout cannot map this hierarchical structure efficiently into a sequence of page entries (it could extract every rectangle from the tree and store each one as a separate page entry with its full set of coordinates, but the advantages of the k-d-tree data structure in terms of compression and searching would be lost).

A k-d-tree page layout can be implemented by mapping each node of the k-d-tree onto a page entry. Internal node entries have four components: the coordinate value, two pointers to child nodes (with pointers being stored as slot indices) and one pointer back to the parent node. The root node entry is assigned slot 0 on every page, and is stored similarly to internal nodes, but without the parent pointer. Leaf node entries represent data rectangles, which are stored as a parent pointer and a heap pointer—the predicate data can be recovered from the ancestor nodes. Figure 5 illustrates this for the left branch (representing data rectangles a, b and c) of the k-d-tree shown in Figure 4.

The *search()* function traverses the k-d-tree and returns the slot indices of the matching k-d-tree leaf node page entries. The *get_key()* function, given a slot index of a k-d-tree leaf entry, can reconstruct the corresponding rectangle by traversing the tree from the leaf to the root. The *insert()* function adds a new rectangle to the tree by creating a new k-d-tree leaf entry and an entry for the required new internal k-d-tree node. The *remove()* function reverses this process, removing both the k-d-tree leaf and internal node page entries. Both update functions must be careful not to alter the existing slot assignment, otherwise they will invalidate the k-d-tree child node pointers stored in the other page entries.

Since a k-d-tree partitions the data space, SPs do not expand and the *union()* function signals that to the caller. For the same reason, a new key can only go into one specific subtree, which the *find_min_pen()* function finds by traversing the k-d-tree. If the split strategy is to bisect the k-d-tree at the root, the *pick_split()* function traverses the

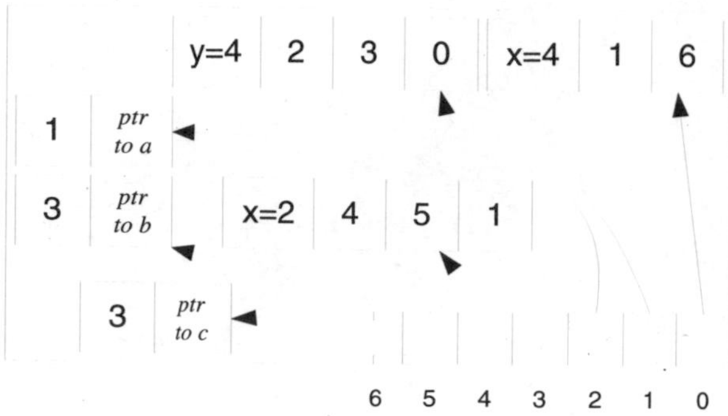

Figure 5: Example of k-d-tree page layout (root: slot 0, internal nodes: slots 1 and 3, leaf nodes: slots 2, 4 and 5)

right subtree of the root and returns the slot indices of its *leaf* nodes, together with SPs for the left and right page of the split, which can be constructed from the root.

3.5 Summary

The redesigned GiST AM extension architecture addresses all three issues mentioned at the beginning of this section:

- Datatype extensibility: By separating the external portion of an AM into an AM extension and a datatype adapter, full datatype extensibility of GiST-based, user-defined AMs can be achieved.
- UDF call overhead: By changing the level of abstraction of the GiST interface from a call-per-entry interface as in the original GiST specification to a call-per-page interface, the number of UDF calls required by index operations is reduced significantly.
- Page layout customization: A further advantage of the call-per-page interface is that it hides the details of the page layout from the GiST core, allowing the AM extension to customize page layout via the SAPI page management interface. This additional flexibility does not necessarily come at the price of an increased implementation effort for the AM developer, because page layout functionality can be separated into libraries and re-used across AM extensions.

Furthermore, it has a number of additional advantages over the current state-of-the-art iterator-style AM extension interfaces:

- AM development is greatly simplified. The above-mentioned B-tree and R-tree extensions were written and debugged in a matter of hours rather than weeks or months. Also, page layout code can be reused across AMs very easily, because it is separated from concurrency and logging considerations. With custom locking and logging protocols intermixed with page layout functionality, such reuse is normally not possible.
- AM stability is improved, because an AM extension is implemented in terms of a (relatively) stable GiST interface and need not rely on interfaces to server-internal services, such as the lock and log manager.
- Intricate concurrency and recovery protocols need only be implemented and tested once, which greatly improves reliability (and oftentimes performance, because externally-developed AMs tend to have somewhat less efficient protocols).
- Despite part of an AM being outside the server, the indices generated by that AM are still fully integrated into the DBMS, with all the advantages: integrated storage management, backup and recovery, support for SQL isolation semantics, built-in concurrency.

4 Implementation Issues

The implementation of the GiST AM extension architecture in IDS/UDO includes concurrency control and recovery. Despite the changes to the GiST interface in the IDS/UDO implementation, the implemented protocols follow mostly what is described in [KMH97]; only in some cases did they need to be adapted. This section describes the implementation details of the protocols.

4.1 Concurrency Control

The locking protocol that allows search and update operations to execute concurrently in the tree is an adaption of the B-link tree technique. All the pages at each level are chained together via links to their right siblings; the addition of this rightlink allows traversing operations to compensate for missed splits by following rightlinks. For this strategy to work, a traversing operation must be able to (1) detect a page split and (2) determine when to stop following rightlinks (a page can split multiple times, in which case the traversing operation must follow as many rightlinks as there are missed page splits). To this end, every page is extended with a sequence number (PSN) in addition to the rightlink. During a page split, a global counter variable is incremented and its new value assigned to the original page's PSN. The new right sibling page receives the original page's old rightlink and PSN. A traversing operation can now detect a split by memorizing the global counter value when reading the parent entry and comparing it with the PSN of the current page. If the latter is higher, the page must have been split and the operation follows the current page's rightlink until it sees a page with a PSN less than or equal to the one originally memorized.

A key component is the global counter variable used to generate page sequence numbers. The counter needs to be incremented atomically and needs to be recoverable in order for split detection to work after a crash. The original paper advocates using the log sequence number of the most recently written log record as a system-global counter variable. This design choice is not possible in IDS/UDO, so instead each index is equipped with an anchor page that holds an index-global counter, among other things. Update operations only consist of simple increment operations, which results in a short critical section around the update and therefore keeps contention low. Making the counter variable recoverable involves writing log records; to amortize the cost of a log write, we only log every 100th increment. This logging is done in advance of the actual increments, so that the logged value nevers falls behind any actual PSN in the index. Putting the counter variable "inside" the index simplifies the implementation considerably, because no changes to server-internal data structures and their recovery are necessary. So far, the degree of concurrency that this allows seems to be adequate.

4.2 Recovery

The GiST logging protocol supports high-concurrency transactional update operations on the index trees by separating them into their content-changing (item insertion and deletion at the leaf level) and structure-modifying parts (page splits, parent entry updates, page deletions). The content change is logged as part of the initiating transaction, whereas the structure modification is logged as an individually committed atomic unit of work (also referred to as atomic actions [LS92] or nested top actions [MHL+92] in the literature). This protocol is not affected by the API change in the IDS/UDO implementation, except for a small detail. When redoing or undoing a leaf insertion or deletion operation, it is not sufficient to perform a simple insertion or deletion of a single page entry, because the AM extension might implement these operations as a sequence of calls to the page interface. Instead, the recovery process must call the AM extension's *insert()* and *remove()* functions.

5 Performance Measurements

A comparison of GiST-based R-trees with the built-in R-trees available in IDS/UDO 9.2 shows that GiST-based AMs not only enjoy software engineering benefits, but can also offer *higher* performance than built-in AMs with datatype extensibility. As mentioned in Section 3.1, the built-in R-tree can be used to index any datatype by supplying datatype-specific functions that implement the query operators and some additional functions needed for splitting and insertion (namely *size()* and *union()*). These datatype-specific functions are provided by the extension module that implements the user-defined type and execute as UDFs. The performance comparison involves individual search and insert operations on a three-level R-tree, which were executed on a Sun machine with a 167MHz UltraSparc CPU. The timings were obtained with the quantify profiling tool, and show the number of cycles needed for full SQL SELECT and INSERT statements.

Extensibility functionality—both AM and datatype extensibility—involves additional cost in comparison to purely hardwired AMs. This cost consists of:

- function descriptor setup: Before calling a UDF, a handle to it must be obtained, which can involve a catalog lookup and permissions checking.
- UDF call overhead: The cost of a single UDF call in IDS/UDO, which is executed in the same address space as the database server, is around 1350 cycles for the test scenario described in this section. In other ORDBMS, a UDF call might involve a context switch and interprocess communication, which would make it far more expensive.

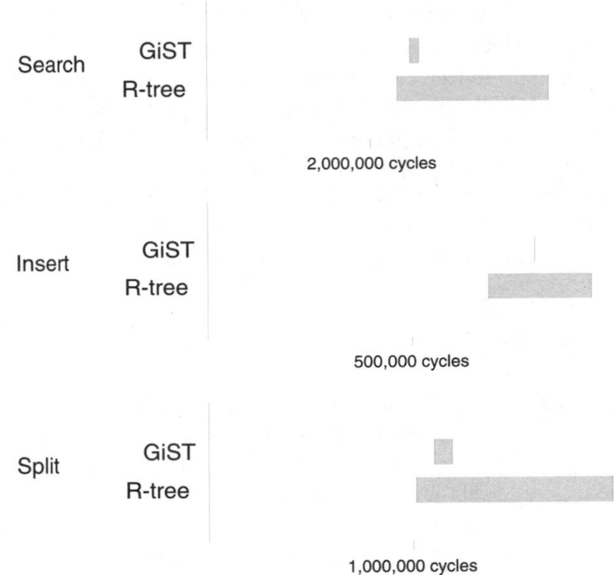

Figure 6: Comparison of GiST-based and built-in R-trees (shaded portion indicates UDF call overhead)

The total execution times, excluding time spent in operating system calls, for three different operations is shown in Figure 6. The operations are: a select with a rectangle containment qualification that retrieves only a single rectangle, but traverses 78 pages in the tree; an insert operation; an insert operation that causes the leaf page to split.

When the built-in R-tree executes a search, it calls the *rectangle_contains()* UDF for every entry on the traversed leaf pages (the *rectangle_overlaps()* UDF for entries on traversed internal pages), resulting in a total of 1359 UDF calls. In contrast, the GiST-based R-tree only calls the *search()* UDF once for every *page* it traverses, requiring only 80 UDF calls (78 plus 2 for *begin_scan()* and *end_scan()*). During the insertion of a new item, the built-in R-tree makes 182 UDF calls, most of these while checking the traversed internal pages for the best subtree to insert in. The GiST-based R-tree subsumes those calls into a single call to the *find_min_pen()* UDF per page, and thereby reduces the total number of calls to only four (two to *find_min_pen()*, one to *insert()* and one to *union()*). When the insertion causes the leaf page to split, the performance gap widens even more: the built-in B-tree makes 704 UDF calls, most of those to find out how to split the page, whereas the GiST-based R-tree only needs 66 UDF calls, 56 of these during the split to extract and insert keys on the new right page.

In all three scenarios, the high number of UDF calls in the built-in R-tree causes it to perform substantially worse than the GiST-based R-tree, resulting in performance losses between 14 and 40 percent. The built-in R-tree has a slight advantage when it comes to function descriptor setup (it uses fewer UDFs, which explains why performance of both AMs is not identical when UDF call overhead is subtracted), but this cannot make up for the large number of UDF calls.

6 Summary

This paper presents a GiST-based approach to extensible indexing implemented in IDS/UDO. The GiST abstraction allows a clean separation of the functionality of an AM into generic tree search and update algorithms as well as generic concurrency and recovery protocols; the AM-specific code, which consists of data domain-specific code and split and insertion strategies, resides in an extension module outside the database server. This has two advantages, that have previously not been realized together: (1) the AM developer need not be concerned with the internals of the database server in general and with the intricacies of concurrency and recovery protocols in particular, (2) the AM is tightly integrated into the database from an operational point of view, offering the same high degree of concurrency and reliability as built-in AMs. The savings in implementation time of new AMs using this architecture are substantial: the B-tree and R-tree extensions are both below 1000 lines of C code, and were written and debugged in a matter of hours rather than weeks or months.

The IDS/UDO implementation of this approach features a GiST interface that allows the external AM developer to take full control of the internal layout of index pages. Additionally, this interface also reduces UDF calling overhead, which can degrade the performance of datatype-extensible AMs. On average, an insert or search operation will only make one UDF call per visitited page. With built-in datatype-extensible AMs, this number can be much higher. A comparison of GiST-based and built-in R-trees in IDS/UDO demonstrates this effect: although the built-in R-tree has lower initial setup cost, the large number of UDF calls reduces performance between approximately 14 and 40 percent for single insertion and search operations in comparison to the GiST-based R-tree.

Acknowledgement

Paul Aoki made valuable contributions to the introduction of this paper and was generally willing to discuss ideas related to this work. Out of the many people at Informix who facilitated this work, I especially want to thank David Ashkenas, Paul Brown, Toni Guttman, Scott Lashley, Kumar Ramayer and Robert Uleman. My thanks also to the anonymous reviewers, who pointed out items that needed clarification.

References

[Ben75] L. Bentley, J. Multidimensional binary search trees used for associative searching. *Communications of the ACM*, 18(9):509–517, September 1975.

[Com79] D. Comer. The Ubiquitous B-Tree. *ACM Computing Surveys*, 11(4):121–137, 1979.

[GG98] Volker Gaede and Oliver Günther. Multidimensional Access Methods. *ACM Computing Surveys*, 30(2), 1998.

[Gut84] A. Guttman. R-Trees: A Dynamic Index Structure for Spatial Searching. In *Proc. ACM SIGMOD Conf.*, pages 47–57, June 1984.

[HNP95] J. Hellerstein, J. Naughton, and A. Pfeffer. Generalized Search Trees for Database Systems. In *Proc. 21st Int'l Conference on Very Large Databases (VLDB), Zürich, Switzerland*, pages 562–573, September 1995.

[Inf98a] Informix Corp. *Universal Server DataBlade API Programmer's Manual, Version 9.12*, 1998.

[Inf98b] Informix Corp. *Virtual Index Interface Guide*, 1998.

[KMH97] M. Kornacker, C. Mohan, and J. Hellerstein. Concurrency and Recovery in Generalized Search Trees. In *Proceedings of the ACM-SIGMOD International Conference on Management of Data, Tucson, Arizona*, pages 62–72, May 1997.

[LS90] D. Lomet and B. Salzberg. The hB-Tree: A Multiattribute Indexing Method with Good Guaranteed Performance. *ACM TODS*, 15(4):625–685, December 1990.

[LS92] D. Lomet and B. Salzberg. Access Method Concurrency with Recovery. In *Proc. ACM SIGMOD Conf.*, pages 351–360, 1992.

[MHL+92] C. Mohan, D. Haderle, B. Lindsay, H. Pirahesh, and P. Schwarz. ARIES: A Transaction Recovery Method Supporting Fine-Granularity Locking and Partial Rollbacks Using Write-Ahead Logging. *ACM TODS*, 17(1), March 1992.

[Ora98] Oracle Corp. *All Your Data: The Oracle Extensibility Architecture*, November 1998.

Online Dynamic Reordering for Interactive Data Processing

Vijayshankar Raman Bhaskaran Raman Joseph M. Hellerstein
University of California, Berkeley
{rshankar,bhaskar,jmh}@cs.berkeley.edu

Abstract

We present a pipelining, dynamically user-controllable reorder operator, for use in data-intensive applications. Allowing the user to reorder the data delivery on the fly increases the interactivity in several contexts such as online aggregation and large-scale spreadsheets; it allows the user to control the processing of data by dynamically specifying preferences for different data items based on prior feedback, so that data of interest is prioritized for early processing. We describe an efficient, non-blocking mechanism for reordering, which can be used over arbitrary data streams from files, indexes, and continuous data feeds. We also investigate several policies for the reordering based on the performance goals of various typical applications. We present results from an implementation used in Online Aggregation in the Informix Dynamic Server with Universal Data Option, and in sorting and scrolling in a large-scale spreadsheet. Our experiments demonstrate that for a variety of data distributions and applications, reordering is responsive to dynamic preference changes, imposes minimal overheads in overall completion time, and provides dramatic improvements in the quality of the feedback over time. Surprisingly, preliminary experiments indicate that online reordering can also be useful in traditional batch query processing, because it can serve as a form of pipelined, approximate sorting.

1 Introduction

It has often been noted that information analysis tools should be interactive [BM85, Bat79, Bat90], since the data exploration tasks they enable are often only loosely specified. Information seekers work in an iterative fashion, starting with broad queries and continually refining them based on feedback and domain knowledge (see [OJ93] for a user study in a business data processing environment). Unfortunately, current data processing applications such as decision-support querying [CD97] and scientific data visualization [A+96] typically run in batch mode: the user enters a request, the system runs for a long time without any feedback, and then returns an answer. These queries typically scan large amounts of data, and the resulting long delays disrupt the user's concentration and hamper interactive exploration. Precomputed summaries such as data cubes [G+96, Z+97] can speed up the system in some scenarios, but are not a panacea; in particular, they provide little benefit for the ad-hoc analyses that often arise in these environments.

The performance concern of the user during data analysis is not the time to get a complete answer to each query, but instead the time to get a reasonably accurate answer. Therefore, an alternative to batch behavior is to use techniques such as Online Aggregation [H+97, H+98] that provide continuous feedback to the user as data is being processed. A key aspect of such systems is that users perceive data being processed over time. Hence an important goal for these systems is to *process interesting data early on*, so users can get satisfactory results quickly for interesting regions, halt processing early, and move on to their next request.

In this paper, we present a technique for reordering data on the fly based on user preferences — we attempt to ensure that interesting items get processed first. We allow users to dynamically change their definition of "interesting" during the course of an operation. Such online reordering is useful not only in online aggregation systems, but also in any scenario where users have to deal with long-running operations involving lots of data. We demonstrate the benefits of online reordering for online aggregation, and for large-scale interactive applications like spreadsheets. Our experiments on sorting in spreadsheets show decreases in response times by several orders of magnitude with online reordering as compared to traditional sorting. Incidentally, preliminary experiments suggest that such reordering is also useful in traditional, batch-oriented query plans where multiple operators interact in a pipeline.

Proceedings of the 25th VLDB Conference, Edinburgh, Scotland, 1999.

The Meaning of Reordering
A data processing system allows intra-query user control by accepting preferences for different items and using them to guide the processing. These preferences are specified in a value-based, application-specific manner: data items contain values that map to user preferences. Given a statement of preferences, the reorder operator should permute the data items at the source so as to make an application-specific *quality of feedback* function rise as fast as possible. We defer detailed discussion of preference modeling until Section 3 where we present a formal model of reordering, and reordering policies for different applications.

1.1 Motivating Applications

Online Aggregation

Online Aggregation [H+97, H+98] seeks to make decision-support query processing interactive by providing approximate, progressively refining estimates of the final answers to SQL aggregation queries as they are being processed. Reordering can be used to give users control over the rates at which items from different groups in a GROUP BY query are processed, so that estimates for groups of interest can be refined quickly.[1]

Consider a person analyzing a company's sales using the interface in Figure 1. Soon after issuing the query, she can see from the estimates that the company is doing relatively badly in Vietnam, and surprisingly well in China, although the confidence intervals at that stage of processing are quite wide, suggesting that the Revenue estimates may be inaccurate. With online reordering, she can indicate an interest in these two groups using the Preference "up" and "down" buttons of the interface, thereby processing these groups faster than others. This provides better estimates for these groups early on, allowing her to stop this query and drill down further into these groups without waiting for the query to complete.

Another useful feature in online aggregation is fairness — one may want confidence intervals for different groups to tighten at same rate, irrespective of their cardinalities. Reordering can provide such fairness even when there is skew in the distribution of tuples across different groups.

Scalable Spreadsheets

DBMSs are often criticized as being hard to use, and many people prefer to work with spreadsheets. However, spreadsheets do not scale well; large data sets lead to inordinate delays with "point-and-click" operations such as sorting by a field, scrolling, pivoting, or jumping to particular cell values or row numbers. MS Excel 97 permits only 65536 rows in a table [Exc], sidestepping these issues without solving them. Spreadsheet users typically want to get some information by browsing through the data, and often don't use complex queries. Hence usability and interactivity are the main goals, and delays are especially annoying.

[1] User preferences can be passed from the interface to the DBMS by calling UDFs in auxiliary queries [H+97].

Stop	Preference	Nation	Revenue	Interval
●	▲▼ 2	China	80005.28	4000.45
●	▲▼ 1	India	35010.24	3892.76
●	▲▼ 1	Japan	49315.90	700.52
●	▲▼ 3	Vietnam	10019.78	1567.88
Confidence: 95%	2% done			

select avg(revenue), nation from sales, branches
where sales.id = branches.id group by nation

Figure 1: Relative speed control in online aggregation

This is unlike a DBMS scenario, where users expect to wait for a while for a query to return.

We are building [SS] a scalable spreadsheet where sorting, scrolling, and jumping are all instantaneous from the user's point of view. We lower the response time as perceived by the user by processing/retrieving items faster in the region around the scrollbar – the range to which an item belongs is inferred via a histogram (this could be stored as a precomputed statistic or be built on the fly [C+98]). For instance, when the user presses a column heading to re-sort on that column, he almost immediately sees a sorted table with the items read so far, and more items are added as they are scanned. While the rest of the table is sorted at a slow rate, items from the range being displayed are retrieved and displayed as they arrive.

Imprecise Querying: With reordering behind it, the scrollbar becomes a tool for fuzzy, imprecise querying. Suppose that a user trying to analyze student grades asks for the records sorted by GPA. With sorting done online as described above, the scrollbar position acts as a fuzzy range query on GPA, since the range around it is filled in first. By moving the scrollbar, she can examine several regions without explicitly giving different queries. If there is no index on GPA, this will save several sequential scans. More importantly, she need not pre-specify a range — the range is implicitly specified by panning over a region. This is important because she *does not know in advance what regions may contain valuable information*. Contrast this with the ORDER BY clause of SQL and extensions for "top N" filters, which require a priori specification of a desired range, often followed by extensive batch-mode query execution [CK97].

Sort of Sort

Interestingly, we have found that a pipelining reorder operator is useful in batch (non-online) query processing too. Consider a key/foreign-key join of two tables R and S, with the foreign key of R referencing the key of S. If there is a clustered index on the key column of S, a good plan would be to use an index-nested-loops join algorithm. Taking advantage of the clustered index, the DBMS might insert a sort operator on R before the join, so that each leaf of the index is fetched at most once. Unfortunately, since sort is a blocking operator, this plan forfeits the pipelined par-

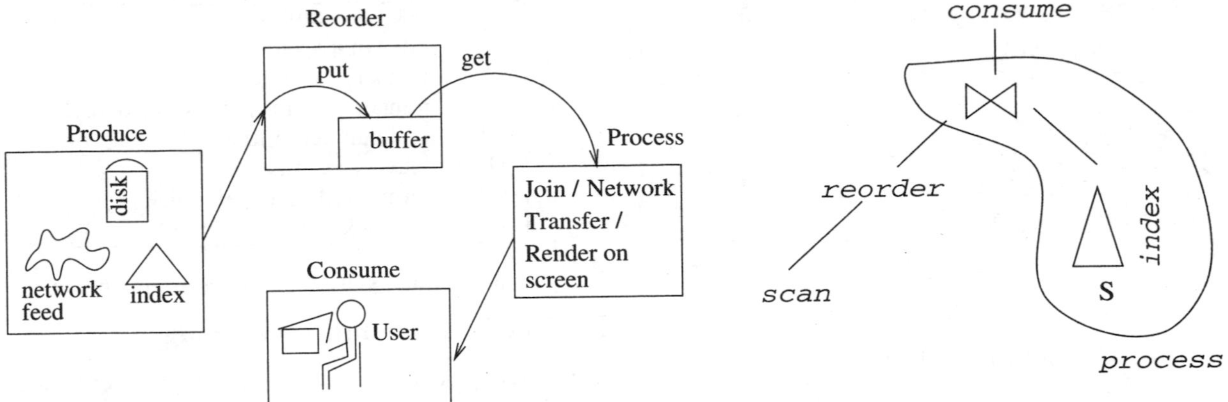

Figure 2: Data flow model for the reordering

Figure 3: Reorder in plan trees for online aggregation

allelism that is available in index-nested-loops join. Note that sorting is used as a performance enhancement to batch up index lookups; total ordering is *not* needed for correctness. Hence we can use a pipelining, best-effort reorder operator instead to gain most of the benefit of sorting, without introducing a blocking operation into the query pipeline. Not only is the resulting query non-blocking (and hence potentially interactive), but the overall completion time may be faster than if we had sorted, since (a) we need not do a complete sort, and (b) opportunities exist for pipelined parallelism (e.g. if the index for S is on a separate disk from R). We have started experimenting with this idea by inserting reorder operators into traditional query plans, and present preliminary results in Section 5.3.

Organization of the paper

We present our technique for reordering in Section 2. In Section 3 we describe several policies for reordering, and corresponding quality of feedback functions that are suited for different applications. We then discuss disk management issues for the reordering algorithm in Section 4. We present performance results for different applications in Section 5. We discuss related work in Section 6, and conclude with some avenues for future work in Section 7.

2 Best Effort Online Reordering

Since our aim is interactivity, the reordering must not involve pre-processing or other overheads that will increase runtime. Instead, we want a "best effort" reordering that runs concurrently with the processing, with negligible overhead. Figure 2 depicts our scheme of inserting a reorder operator into a data flow, which we divide into four stages as described below.

Produce – this may be a disk scan, an index scan, or a data feed from a network or sensor.

Reorder – this reorders the items according to the dynamically changing preferences of the consumer.

Process – this is the set of operations done by the application, and it could involve query plan operators in a DBMS, sending data across a slow network, rendering data onto the screen in data visualization, etc.

Consume – this captures the user think-time, if any — it is important mainly for interactive applications such as spreadsheets or data visualization.

Since all these operations can go on concurrently, we exploit the difference in throughput between the produce stage and the process or consume stages to permute the items: *while the items taken out so far are being processed/consumed,* reorder *can take more items from* produce *and permute them.*

Figure 3 shows a sample data flow in a DBMS query plan. Reorder is inserted just above a scan operator on the table to be reordered, and the processing cost is the cost of the operators above it in the plan tree.

2.1 The Prefetch and Spool (P&S) technique for reordering

Reorder tries to put as many interesting items as possible onto a main-memory buffer, and process issues requests to get an item from the buffer. When Process issues a get operation, Reorder decides which item to give it based on the performance goal of the application; this is a function of the preferences, and will be formally derived for some typical applications in Section 3.1.

The user preferences that indicate interest may be at the granularity of either an individual item or a group of items, depending on the application. Even in the former case, we can divide the items into groups based on a histogram, and reorder at the granularity of a group — process continually gets the best item from the best group on buffer[2]. Reorder strives to maintain items from different groups at different ratios on the buffer based on the preferences and the reordering policy. We derive these ratios in Section 3.2.

The *P&S* algorithm for reordering uses the time gap between successive gets from the buffer (which may arise due to processing or consumption time) to maintain the correct ratios of different groups on the buffer. It has two phases, as shown in Figure 4. In Phase 1 it continually scans the input, trying to maintain the appropriate ratio of items in the buffer by *spooling* uninteresting items to an auxiliary

[2] When process issues a get operation, it is reorder that chooses the item to give out. The decision of which item to give out is made by reorder and is transparent to process

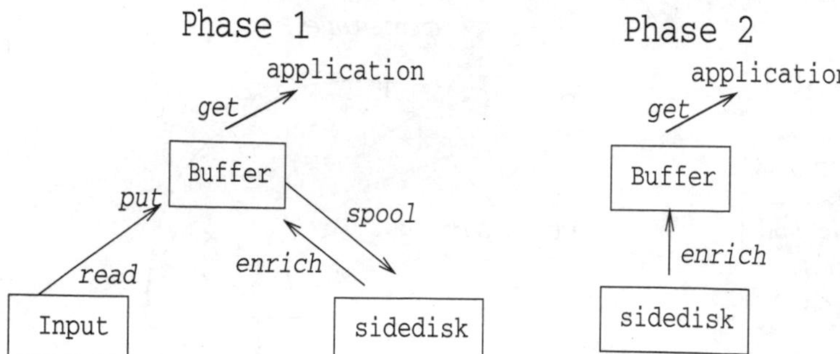

Figure 4: Reordering by Prefetch & Spool

side-disk. It spools out items from the group that has the highest difference between the ratio of items actually on the buffer and the ratio desired. In the common case where `produce` is reading data from a disk, `reorder` does sequential I/Os, and so can often go much faster than the stages down the data flow. If `reorder` finds it has spooled some interesting items to the side-disk (as will happen if the user changes their definition of "interesting" midway), it may have to read them back from the side-disk to *enrich* the buffer. Again, it reads items from the group that has the highest difference between the ratio of items desired, and what is actually on the buffer. Phase 1 completes when the input is fully consumed. In Phase 2, it directly reads items from the side-disk to fill the buffer with needed items. If `produce` is a continuous network feed, Phase 1 never finishes. `Reorder` in this situation will still have to spool out uninteresting items to the side-disk, assuming that the feed rate is faster than the `process` rate.

2.2 Index Stride

We have so far assumed that `reorder` cannot control the order in which data is provided by `produce`. However, if there is an index on the columns that determine the preference for a tuple (the group-by columns in the case of online aggregation), we can use the index to retrieve items at different rates based on the ratio we want in the buffer. We open one cursor for each group and keep filling the buffer with items from that group whose ratio is less than what is needed. This approach — Index Stride — was described in [H+97]. However even if such an index exists, it is may not be clustered. We will see later that despite doing perfect reordering, Index Stride often does worse than regular *P&S* because of random I/Os into the index of `produce`.

As Figure 4 shows, *P&S* is a fairly simple algorithm. It continually "juggles" data between the buffer and the side-disk, to ensure that it has interesting data to give when `process` asks. The details lie in choosing a reordering policy based on the performance goals, and in managing data in memory and on side-disk so as to optimize the enrich and spool operations. We tackle these issues in the next two sections.

i	index of a tuple
j	index of a group
g	number of groups
n	number of items processed so far
N	total number of items
DP	delivery priority
UP	normalized user preference
F	feedback function

Table 1: Notation used in the reordering model

3 Policies for online reordering

What exactly do we want to achieve by reordering a data set? Given an input stream $t_1, t_2, \ldots t_N$, we want to output a "good" permuted stream $t_{\pi_1}, t_{\pi_2}, \ldots, t_{\pi_N}$. Consider the following example. If the user divides data items into groups and is twice as interested in group A as in group B, one good output permutation will be "AABAABAAB...". This sequence corresponds to several possible permutations of the actual tuples, since many tuples fall into each group. Similarly, the permutation "BAABAABAA..." is also just as good. In general, there will be several equivalently good permutations, and our goal is to output some permutation from a good equivalence class.

For each prefix of length n of an output permutation $t_{\pi_1} t_{\pi_2} \ldots t_{\pi_N}$, consider an application-specific *quality of feedback* function (henceforth this will called the *feedback function*) $F(UP(t_{\pi_1}), UP(t_{\pi_2}), \ldots, UP(t_{\pi_n}))$. This function captures the value of the items in the prefix, and models their "interestingness" to the user. $UP(t_i)$ is the *user preference* for item t_i. Since the goal is to improve feedback in the early stages, the goodness of the output permutation is given by *the rate at which the feedback function rises as the number of items processed n goes from 1 to N*. We try (we can only try since the reordering is best-effort) for an output permutation π, such that for any $n, 1 \leq n \leq N$, the prefix $t_{\pi_1}, t_{\pi_2}, \ldots, t_{\pi_n}$ of π maximizes $F(UP(t_{k_1}), UP(t_{k_2}), \ldots, UP(t_{k_n}))$ over all n-element subsets $\{k_1, \ldots k_n\}$ of $\{1, 2, \ldots N\}$

We describe in Section 3.1 how to set F for different applications based on their performance goals. The choice of F dictates the choice of the item that `reorder` gives out when `process` issues a `get`; it gives out the item that will increase F the most.[3] This in turn dictates the ratio of items from various groups that `reorder` should try to maintain in the buffer. We describe how this is derived in Section 3.2.

3.1 Performance Goals and Choice of Items to Remove from the Buffer

Consider the data flow model of Figure 2. When `process` issues a `get`, `reorder` decides which item to give via a *delivery priority* mechanism. This priority for an item is

[3] We can do only a local optimization since we know neither the distribution of items across different groups in the input to be scanned, nor the future user preferences. Our aim is to maximize the feedback early on, and not the overall feedback.

computed dynamically based on how much the feedback F will change if that item is processed. Reorder gives out the item in the buffer with the highest delivery priority (which may not be the highest priority item overall). Note that the delivery priority is not the same as the user preference. The user preference depends on the user interest whereas the delivery priority depends on the feedback function. In fact, for the first two metrics given below, in steady state, assuming that the most interesting group will always be available on buffer, the delivery priority for all the groups will be equal. We proceed to outline some intuitive feedback functions for different applications. The notation we use is summarized in Table 1.

Confidence metric: Average weighted confidence interval

In online aggregation, the goal is to make the confidence intervals shrink as fast as possible. One way to interpret user preferences for different groups is as a weight on the confidence interval. The feedback function is the negative of the average weighted confidence interval (we take the negative since a small confidence-interval width corresponds to high feedback). Almost all the large-sample confidence intervals used in online aggregation (see [Haa97] for formulas for various kinds of queries) are of the general form: (Variance of the results seen so far)/ (number of items seen so far)$^{1/2}$. Hence $1/\sqrt{n_j}$ is a good indicator of the confidence interval for a group j. After n items are processed, the feedback function we want to rise as fast as possible is

$$F = -\sum_{j=1}^{g} UP_j/\sqrt{n_j} \text{ given that } n_1 + \cdots + n_g = n$$

The application chooses items for processing such that F rises as fast as possible. If we process an item from group j, $\Delta(n_j) = 1$ and so F increases by the first derivative $UP_j/{n_j}^{1.5}$. Hence, to process the group which will increase F the most, we set a delivery priority of $DP_j = UP_j/{n_j}^{1.5}$. Each time we process an item from a group, the group's delivery priority decreases. Also, we always process an item in the buffer with the highest priority. Hence this acts a negative feedback, and at steady state, assuming that the highest priority item is always present on buffer, all the delivery priorities will be equal.

Rate metric: Preference as rate of processing

A simple alternative is that items from each group be processed at a rate proportional to its preference. This is primarily a functional goal in that it directly tells reorder what to do. However, it may be useful in applications such as analysis of feeds from sensors, where we want to analyze packets from different sources at different rates based on preferences; if the user finds the packet stream from one sensor to be anomalous, he may want to analyze those packets in more detail. We want the number of items processed for a group to be proportional to its preference, and the feedback function to maximize is the negative of the net deviation from these proportions:

$$F = -\sum_{j=1}^{g}(n_j - nUP_j)^2 \text{ given that } n_1 + \cdots + n_g = n$$

At any given time we want to process the group that will make this deviation decrease the most. If we process an item from group t, $\Delta n_t = \Delta n = 1$. Hence F increases by the first derivative, $-\Delta(\sum_{j=1}^{g}(n_j - nUP_j)^2)$
$= -\sum_{j=1}^{g} 2(n_j - nUP_j)(\Delta n_j - \Delta nUP_j)$
$= 2(nUP_t - n_t)(1 - UP_t) + \sum_{j \neq t} 2(nUP_j - n_j)(0 - UP_j) = 2(nUP_t - n_t) - 2\sum_{j=1}^{g}(nUP_j - n_j)UP_j$
For F to rise fastest, we must process a group t which will cause the above expression to be maximum. Hence the delivery priority is set as $DP_j = nUP_j - n_j$, since the second term of the previous expression is the same for all groups. As in the previous metric, at steady state, assuming that the highest priority group is always available in the buffer, all the delivery priorities will be equal. It can be easily seen that the priorities are in fact 0. The deviation of the delivery priorities from 0 is a measure of how bad the reordering is.

Strict metric: Enforcing a rigid order

When we use a reorder operator in a traditional query plan instead of a sort operator, the goal is a sorted permutation. This can be achieved by assigning monotonically decreasing user preferences for each item from the one that is desired to be the first until the last item. After n items have been processed, the feedback function we want to maximize is

$$F = \sum_{i=1}^{n} UP_i$$

By processing an item n_i, F increases by UP_i. To make this rise fastest, we set the delivery priority to be $DP_i = UP_i$. That is, we always process the item with the highest user preference on buffer. We also use this metric for the spreadsheets application, with the preference for a range of items decreasing with its distance from the range being displayed (this is inferred from the scrollbar position).

3.2 Optimal Ratio on Buffer

Since reorder always gives out to process the highest delivery priority item in buffer, the delivery priority functions derived above directly dictate the ratio of items from different groups that reorder must maintain in the buffer. These ratios in turn determine the buffer replacement policy for reorder.

Confidence metric: At steady state, all the DP_j's are equal. Hence for any two groups j_1 and j_2, $UP_{j_1}/(n_{j_1}\sqrt{n_{j_1}}) = UP_{j_2}/(n_{j_2}\sqrt{n_{j_2}})$, and the ratio of items from any group j must be $UP_j^{2/3}/(\sum_{t=1}^{g} UP_t^{2/3})$.

Rate metric: As explained before, at steady state all DP_j's are 0. Since $DP_j = nUP_j - n_j$, the ratio of items from group j is UP_j. Indeed, the goal is to have the processing rate be proportional to preference.

Strict metric: If DP_i is UP_i, there is no specific ratio — the reorderer tries to have the highest preference item, then the next highest, and so on.

3.3 Handling Preference Changes

In the discussion so far we have not considered dynamic changes in the preferences. After a preference change, we can either express the feedback F as a goal over the items to be delivered subsequently, or as a goal that "remembers history", and is expressed over all the items previously delivered as well. Correspondingly, we can compute delivery priorities either based only on items processed since the last preference change, or on all the items that have been processed since the initiation of the data flow.

For the Confidence metric we want to remember history because the confidence interval is defined in terms of the total number of items seen so far. Hence we re-calculate the delivery priorities based on the new user preferences taking into account all the items that have been processed. This results in a rapid spurt in the processing for a group whose preference is increased — not only is the new preference high, but also we must compensate for not having processed enough items from that group (commensurate with the new preferences) earlier. By contrast, the Rate metric corresponds to the user's request for immediate change in the relative processing rates. Hence, we calculate the delivery priorities based on the number of items processed since the last preference change ($DP_j = n'UP_j - n'_j$, where n' is the number of items processed since the last preference change). The user preferences determine the rate at which tuples from different groups are processed between consecutive preference changes. This is not an issue with the Strict metric; the priorities are independent of the number of items processed.

4 Disk management while reordering

The goal of `reorder` is to ensure that items from different groups are maintained in the buffer in the ratios desired by the application, as derived in Section 3.2. There are four operations which alter the set of items in the buffer: scanning from the input, spooling to the side-disk, enrichment from the side-disk, and `get`'s by the application (Figure 4). The ratios in the buffer are maintained by (a) evicting (spooling) items from groups that have more items than needed, and (b) enrichment with items from the group that is most lacking in the buffer. In essence the buffer serves as a preference-based cache over `produce` and the side-disk. We always strive to maintain some items in the buffer, even if they are not the most interesting ones; the presence of uninteresting items in the buffer may arise, for instance, if the user preferences during Phase 1 are very different from the data distribution across different groups. By guaranteeing the presence of items in the buffer, the `process` stage never has to wait for the `reorder` stage, and the overhead for introducing `reorder` into a data flow is minimized. In addition to the buffer, some memory is required for buffering I/O to and from the side-disk. The amount of memory needed for I/O buffers depends on the data organization on the side-disk, so we defer this discussion until after discussing our treatment of the side-disk.

4.1 Management of Data on Side-Disk

Since we want to process interesting items and give good feedback to the user early on, we must make Phase 1 as fast as possible and postpone time-consuming operations as long as possible. Another reason to finish Phase 1 quickly is that during Phase 1 we cannot control the order of values appearing from `produce` if preferences change; whereas in Phase 2 we know the layout of data on the side-disk and can enrich the buffer with items that best satisfy preferences at a given time. To speed up Phase 1, we want a data layout on side-disk that makes spooling go fast even at the expense of enrichment, because we mainly do spooling in Phase 1 and enrichment in Phase 2.

Graefe [Gra93] notes a duality between sorting and hashing. Hashing initially does random I/Os to write partitions, and later does sequential I/Os to read partitions. Sorting first writes out runs with sequential I/Os, and later uses random I/Os to merge the runs. Unfortunately, neither scheme is appropriate for reordering. Hashing into partitions is undesirable because the random I/Os in Phase 1 slow down spooling. Writing out sorted runs to disk is infeasible for two reasons. First, enrichment of the buffer with items from a particular group would involve a small, random I/O from each run, especially when the cardinality of the group is low. Second, dynamically-changing user preferences drive the decision of what we spool to or enrich from side-disk, meaning that the distribution of values to different spooled runs would be non-uniform.

To achieve the best features of both sorting and hashing, we decided to lay out tuples on the side-disk as fixed size *chunks* of items, where all the items in a chunk are from the same group. Spooling is done with only a sequential write, by appending a chunk to a sequential file of data on the side-disk. Enrichment is done via a random read of a chunk of that group which is most lacking in the buffer. Intuitively, this approach can be viewed as building an approximately clustered index (with only sequential I/Os) on the side-disk, concurrent with the other processing.[4]

Returning to the main-memory layout described earlier, in Phase 1 we require an I/O buffer for each group to collect items into chunks. We also need a in-core index of pointers to chunks for each group to quickly find chunks corresponding to a group.

4.2 Total Ordering

We have so far assumed that the reordering is done at the granularity of a group. However in some applications, such as the reorder operators in batch query processing, our goal is a total ordering on the individual items. We tackle this by dividing the data into groups based on an approximate

[4] We also tried out writing out items as packed runs on the side-disk, where the ratio of items in these runs is determined by current user preferences. With this method, ideally, with no preference changes, we never have to do any random I/Os — we keep appending runs to the side-disk in Phase 1, and keep reading runs in Phase 2. However we found that this method leads to severe fragmentation of items from sparse groups, and that the packing of items into runs is useless if the preference changes. This results in several small, random I/Os.

```
select o_orderpriority, count(*) from order
where o_orderdate >= '10/10/96' and
      o_orderdate < '10/10/96' + 90
and exists (select * from lineitem
            where  l_orderkey = o_orderkey and
                   l_commitdate < l_receiptdate)
group by o_orderpriority
```

Figure 5: TPC-D Query 4

Group	A	B	C	D	E
Preference at the start	1	1	1	1	1
Preference after 1000 tuples processed (T0)	1	1	1	5	3
Preference after 50000 tuples processed (T1)	1	1	3.5	0.5	1

Figure 6: Changes in User Preferences

histogram. This histogram need not be accurate since we only want a best effort reordering. We want the number of groups to be as high as possible (this number is limited by the amount of memory we can allocate for the I/O buffers storing the chunks), so that the size of a group is small, and we do a "fine granularity" reordering that can distinguish between the priorities of small batches of tuples. The re-orderer ensures a good ratio of items from different groups in the buffer, and the application removes for processing the best item in the buffer. Our experiments show that this technique is surprisingly successful, since these applications need only an approximate ordering.

5 Experimental Results

We present results that show the usefulness of reordering in online aggregation and in scalable spreadsheets. The aim is to study a) the responsiveness of the rate of processing to dynamic changes in preference, b) the robustness of reordering to different data distributions and `processing` costs, and c) the overhead in overall completion time due to reordering. We also present promising initial results that show the advantage of using `reorder` operators in traditional batch query plans. We scale up all results involving Informix systems by an undisclosed factor to honor privacy commitments while still allowing comparative analysis of algorithms (hence time is expressed in abstract "chronons").

5.1 Online Aggregation

We have implemented our algorithms for reordering in the context of Online Aggregation in Informix Dynamic Server with Universal Data Option (UDO)[5]. The goal of reordering is to shrink the confidence intervals for the interesting

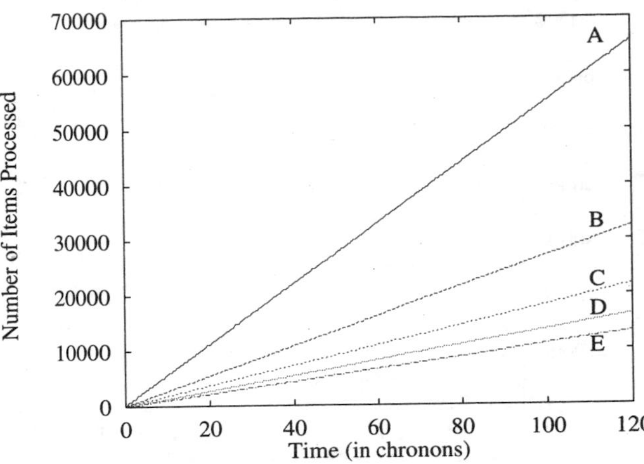

Figure 7: Performance of sequential scan, *Rate* metric

groups quickly. We test the responsiveness and robustness of the reordering by varying a number of parameters:

`Data distribution:` To study the effect of skew in the data distribution across different groups, we test with Zipf and uniform distributions.

`Processing Rate:` We study a TPC-D query (Q4, see Figure 5), modifying it by adding and removing filters and tables to generate index-only joins (where we only need to look at the index of the inner table), index-nested-loop joins, and single table queries. We do not present results for queries with multiple joins because we see experimentally that even one join suffices for good reordering; more joins only make reordering easier by reducing the processing rate. In [H+] we present experiments involving reordering with other `process` operators such as non-flattenable subqueries and ripple joins[6].

`Preference Change Model:` We look at preference changes in Phase 1 and Phase 2, under the Confidence and Rate performance metrics from Section 3.

`Algorithm used:` We compare *P&S*, Index Stride, and a simple sequential scan (no reordering).

Due to space constraints we do not give exhaustive results along all dimensions. We show only results that illustrate salient features of the algorithms and indicate the trade-offs involved. We use the TPC-D *dbgen* program to generate data of different distributions, with a scale factor of 0.1. For our experiments we clustered the data in random order, so as to give statistically correct estimates for the aggregates [Haa97].[7]

Rate Metric, Index-Only Join, Zipf distribution: Our first experiment uses a low processing cost query: *select avg(o_totalprice), o_orderpriority from order where exists (select * from lineitem where l_orderkey = o_orderkey) group by o_orderpriority*. We have removed filters from TPC-D Q4 to make it an index-only join with Order as the outer relation. Order has 150000 tuples. There are five

[5]We ran all experiments on a 200 MHz UltraSPARC machine running SunOS 5.5.1 with 256MB RAM. We used the Informix Dynamic Server with Universal Data Option version 9.14 which we enhanced with online aggregation and reordering features. We chose a chunk size of 200KB for all our experiments. This is reasonable because the number of groups is typically small, and so the I/O buffer (whose size is chunk size × number of groups) is not very big. We used a separate disk for the side-disk, and the size of our buffer was 2MB (including the I/O buffer)

[6]Ripple joins are specialized join algorithms for online aggregation that are efficient yet non-blocking [HH99]

[7]Note that *P&S* preserves the randomness properties of the data within a given group.

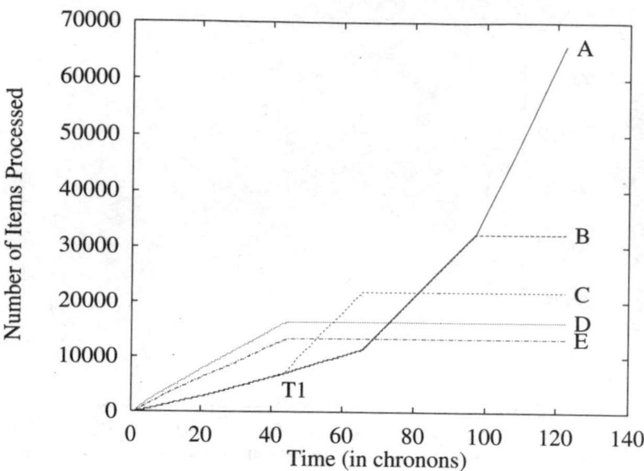

Figure 8: Performance of *P&S*, with *Rate* metric.

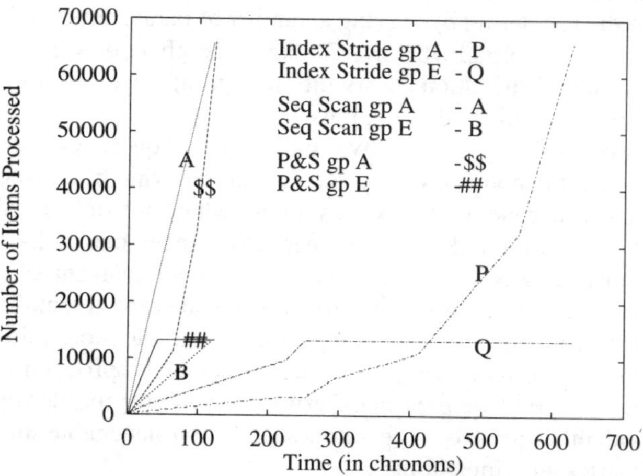

Figure 9: Comparison of different algorithms for processing groups A and E

groups which we will call A, B, C, D, and E for brevity, and we use a Zipf distribution of tuples, in the ratio $1{:}\frac{1}{2}{:}\frac{1}{3}{:}\frac{1}{4}{:}\frac{1}{5}$ respectively.

Figure 6 shows our preference change model, which involves one change at time T0 in Phase 1 (this is not seen in most graphs because it occurs too early), and one change at time T1 in Phase 2. Since Phase 1 ends at about 40000 tuples in most cases, this separately tests our ability to reorder in both phases. We give high preferences to the low cardinality groups to stress the reorderer.

Figures 7 and 8 show the number of tuples processed for each group for sequential scan and *P&S* with the Rate metric. Despite the low processing cost and the high-preference groups being rare, the reordering of *P&S* is quite responsive, even in Phase 1. *P&S* has finished almost all tuples from the interesting groups D and E by 44 chronons while sequential scan takes 120 chronons, *almost 3 times longer*. *P&S* imposes little (2%) overhead in completion time.

Figure 9 compares the number of tuples processed for the largest group (A) and the smallest group (E) for different algorithms. The tuples of interesting group E are processed much faster for *P&S* than for other methods, while for the highest cardinality (and least interesting) group A, sequential scan produces items faster than *P&S*. Index Stride does very poorly because of many random I/Os (it has a 427% completion time overhead).

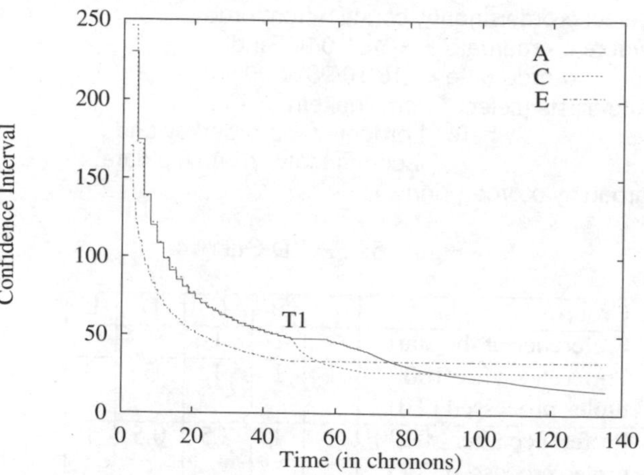

Figure 10: Confidence intervals of different groups for *P&S*. We plot only groups A, C, and E to avoid cluttering the graph. The curve for group B overlaps that of A, and the curve of D is similar to that of E.

To test the effect of reordering on groups with extremely small cardinalities, we added a new group F with 70 tuples, and gave it a constant preference of 2. While Index Stride finished all items from group F in 0.9 chronons, *P&S* took 41.6 chronons and the sequential scan took 111.2 chronons. Index Stride easily outperforms both *P&S* and sequential scan for this outlier group because *P&S* can only provide as many tuples of F as it has scanned. This advantage of Index Stride is also reported in [H+97].

Confidence Metric, Index-Only Join, Zipf distribution: We then removed group F and repeated the previous experiment with the Confidence metric. Figure 10 shows the shrinking of the confidence intervals for different groups for *P&S*. We see that with *P&S* the confidence intervals shrink rapidly for the interesting groups (D,E, and later C), even when they have low cardinalities. In contrast, with a sequential scan, the intervals for D and E shrink more slowly than those for the other groups because D and E have low cardinality (we omit the graph to save space).

Rate Metric, Index-Only Join, Uniform distribution: We now look at the effect of changing the distribution and the processing rates. We first repeat the previous experiment with the Rate metric and a uniform data distribution across different groups. To save space, we do not plot graphs but instead give in Table 2 the delivery priorities of different groups after 30000 tuples are processed and after 60000 tuples are processed. Recall that for the rate metric these priorities capture the deviation in the number of tuples processed from the number that should have been processed. After 30000 tuples are processed, the deviations are $A = -0.64$, $B = 0.36$, $C = 0.36$, $D = -0.18$,

Dist.bn	Proc. Rate	Algor--ithm	Deviation at 30000 tuples processed A	B	C	D	E	Deviation at 60000 tuples processed A	B	C	D	E	Ovhd.
Zipf	Small	*P&S*	−1098	−1097	−1097	27	3266	−0.18	−0.18	0.36	Fin	Fin	2.2
Zipf	Small	IS	0.09	0.09	0.09	0.27	−0.54	−0.27	−0.27	0.54	Fin	Fin	423
Uniform	Small	*P&S*	−0.64	0.36	0.36	−0.18	0.09	−0.88	0.55	0.33	Fin	Fin	2.4
Zipf	Large	*P&S*	−0.64	0.36	0.36	−0.18	0.09	−0.65	0.35	0.23	0.05	Fin	1.1
Zipf	Tiny	*P&S*	−5075	−4785	−2772	8507	4124	−2016	−1571	2170	−860	2278	2.6
Zipf	Tiny	IS	0.64	−0.36	−0.36	0.18	−0.09	0	0	0	Fin	Fin	626

Table 2: Deviation of number of tuples processed of groups A,B,C,D,E, from desired values. A value of Fin for a group means that it has been exhausted. IS = Index Stride. Ovhd. = percentage completion time overhead

and $E = 0.09$ — this is almost an exact reordering. In contrast the deviations after 30000 tuples are processed for the Zipf distribution of the earlier experiment are much higher: $A = -1098.64$, $B = -1097.64$, $C = -1097.64$, $D = 27.09$, and $E = 3266.82$. The uniform distribution is easier to reorder since interesting groups are plentiful. The deviations after 60000 tuples have been processed are very small in both cases; reordering is easy in Phase 2 since we can directly read the needed chunks off the side-disk.

Rate Metric, Index Join, Zipf distribution: We next change the distribution back to Zipf and increase the processing cost: we reintroduce a filter to force an explicit join of Order and Lineitem. The new query is *select o_orderpriority, count(*) from order where exists (select * from lineitem where l_orderkey = o_orderkey and l_commitdate < l_receiptdate) group by o_orderpriority*. The reordering is much better even with the Zipf distribution: the deviations after 30000 tuples are processed are only −0.64, 0.36, 0.36, −0.18, and 0.09. This is because there is more time to reorder between consecutive `gets` of the data by `process`.

Rate Metric, Single Table Query, Zipf distribution: Next, to stress our reorderer, we form a minimal-`process` query by removing Lineitem: *select o_orderpriority, count(*) from order group by o_orderpriority*. Figure 11 shows that the reordering is relatively ineffective in this case. Groups D and E are processed infrequently, since we can never spool to the side-disk and can only reorder within the buffer. This affirms that we can reorder effectively only when the `processing` rate is less than the `produce` rate (*i.e.* the `processing` cost is more than the `produce` cost). Here the only cost is that of the input scan — there is no processing save the addition to the Count aggregate. As Table 2 shows, Index Stride works very well, but it has a huge completion time overhead of 626% — random I/Os have a high penalty since the processing cost is low.

Rate Metric, Original TPC-D Query, Zipf distribution: Finally we add back all the filters and tables, and run the complete TPC-D query given in Figure 5. Due to a low-selectivity filter on the Order table, very few tuples (5669) are handled by the reorderer. Figure 12 shows that *P&S* performs very well. The change at 1000 tuples processed is seen on this graph (T0) since the total number of tuples processed is small. Interestingly, with the predicate applied on Order, E becomes a more frequent group than D.

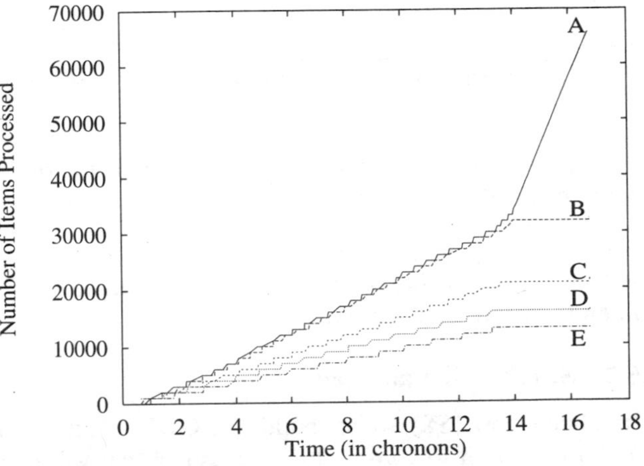

Figure 11: Rate of processing with the *Rate* metric for *P&S*, single table query

Discussion

Our experiments show that reordering by *P&S* is quite responsive to dramatic preference changes even with skewed distributions and low processing-cost queries such as index-only joins; interesting groups are processed much earlier than others even if they have low cardinalities. If the distribution is not too skewed, or the processing cost is higher (even one join suffices), or preferences are changed in Phase 2, we see that the reordering is virtually perfect, with small overheads for completion time. Index Stride has a very high overhead because of random I/Os, but works well for extremely low cardinality "outlier" groups. The reordering in the case of single-table queries is not good because of the low processing cost. However, note that joins are common in decision support queries — for example, 15 out of 17 TPC-D queries involve joins.

As the outlier group case shows, reordering is intrinsically difficult when the preferred groups are extremely rare. We could use a non-clustered index to fetch tuples from the most preferred groups alone (this is a hybrid of *P&S* and Index Stride), but this will involve many random I/Os. Alternatively, we can store tuples from these rare groups in a separate table, and have a clustered index on the group-by column on this table — this is similar to a partial index [Sto89], except that these tuples are now clustered separately and therefore one avoids multiple random I/Os. The challenge lies in automatically deciding which values of which column(s) to treat in this manner, taking into ac-

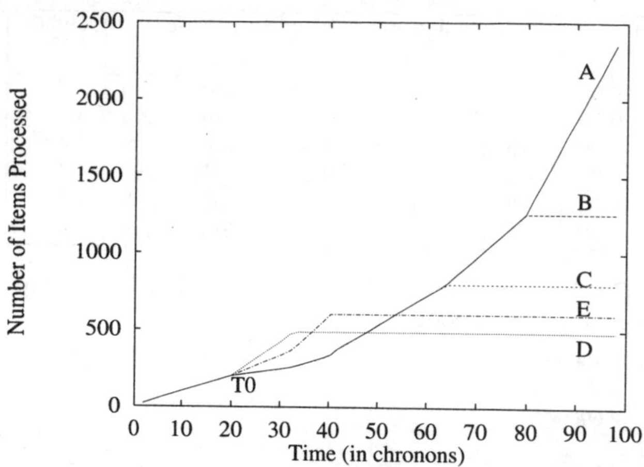

Figure 12: Rate of processing with the *Rate* metric for *P&S*, original TPC-D query:

Operation	Number of tuples accumulated in range being panned over	Time Taken
Sort started	500	2.1 secs
User Thinking	5 seconds	
Short Jump	1000 1500	25.5 msecs 2.4 secs
User Thinking	10 seconds	
Random Jump	2500 5000	263 msecs 21.9 secs
Phase 2 has begun		
Short Jump	2500 5000	6.9 msecs 13.5 msecs
Random Jump	2500 5000	139 msecs 201 msecs

Figure 13: Scalable Spreadsheet: Latencies for various user actions

count the frequency of queries that will use this table, as well as the cardinality of tuples in the different groups. We intend to address this in future work.

5.2 Scalable Spreadsheets

In related work [SS], we are building a GUI widget toolkit, and are using it to construct a spreadsheet that will be as interactive as a regular spreadsheet, but will scale up to large data sizes. An integral component of this spreadsheet is the online reordering library we have implemented, which provides immediate responses for operations such as sorting and pivoting. We have completed the reordering facility for sorting and present results which show that the system can respond almost instantaneously to operations such as scrolling and "jumping" while concurrently sorting the contents of the spreadsheet.

For our experiment, we used a table of 2,500,000 records of 100 bytes each (250MB total). The sort was issued on a 4 byte column, and we modeled a uniform distribution of values for this column in the table. We assume that we have a pre-computed equidepth histogram on that column, though it could be computed on the fly if we sample the data [C+98]. For `reorder` we chose a chunk size of 50KB in order to amortize the costs of random I/Os to enrich in Phase 2, and have an I/O buffer of 25MB. As explained in Section 4.2, we divided the data into the maximum number of groups possible, which is $25\text{MB}/50\text{KB} = 500$ in this case; correspondingly, we divide the range of the key values into 500 groups based on the histogram, and use this partitioning to decide which group any given tuple belongs to. Therefore, each range has $2500000/500 = 5000$ tuples. Since our goal is to sort, we reorder using the Strict metric of Section 3: the preference for different ranges decreases monotonically with their distances from the range the user is currently looking at (the exact values of the preferences assigned do not matter for the Strict metric).

Note that this is an application where the data can be `consumed` multiple times since the user may view the same portion of the spreadsheet many times. Hence the buffer is really only a cache of what is stored on the side-disk. Currently we have an additional in-memory display cache (1.5MB) to store the items that were recently panned over by the user. If we were to do this in a client-server setting where the user is seeing a spreadsheet on a client node and the data is on a separate server, then we believe that we could use multi-level caching schemes to avoid repeatedly sending the same data to the client [A+97].

To place the timings in our experiment in perspective, we sorted a 250MB file with 100 byte records using the UNIX `sort` utility. This took 890.4 seconds (we used a separate disk for the temporary files in order to avoid giving `reorder` any unfair advantage). We studied the following scenario (the timings are summarized in Figure 13): The user starts off by issuing a command to sort by a field, and we immediately start displaying the tuples of the topmost range – within 2.1 seconds, we have output 500 tuples, which is already enough to fill the screen. The user then analyzes the data in this range for 5 seconds, after which he makes a short jump (we model scrolls as short jumps to adjacent ranges) to the next range. As we see in the table, we are able to give 1000 tuples of this range almost at once (25 milliseconds), by enrichment from the side-disk – we have exploited the time the user spent analyzing the previous range to sort more items and so we can respond quickly. After this initial spurt of items in the desired range, we have exhausted all that is available on side-disk, and settle down to fetch more items at the sequential read bandwidth — the next 500 tuples in this range take around 2 seconds.

The user looks at this data for 10 seconds and then makes a random jump to a new location. We see again that `reorder` (in 263 milliseconds) immediately provides 2500 items by enrichment before settling down to sequential read bandwidth (giving 5000 tuples, which is the total size of that range, takes 21.9 seconds). By this time, `reorder` has scanned the entire input and moved into Phase 2. All subsequent latencies are in milliseconds — a short jump (scroll) to a nearby range is about 20 times faster than jumping to a random location because the nearby range has a higher preference.

The above scenario clearly illustrates the advantage of online reordering in a scalable spreadsheet — *most operations have millisecond latencies with* `reorder`*, whereas a blocking sort take 15 minutes!*

5.3 Sort of Sort

With the *Strict* metric, one could view `reorder` as an approximate, pipelining sort operator. As sketched in Section 1.1, best-effort reordering can be exploited in query plans involving "interesting orders" used for performance enhancements.

Although our focus is on user-controlled reordering, we have performed initial experiments to validate our intuitions, comparing the insertion of sort versus reorder operators into a few query plans in UDO. We consider a key-foreign key join of two tables R and S, where the foreign key of S references the key of R. R has 10^5 rows and S has 10^6 rows, each of size 200 bytes. S has a clustered index on the join column, but rows of R are clustered randomly (the join column values are uniformly distributed). A direct index nested loops join of R and S took 3209.6 chronons because it performed several random I/Os. Adding a sort operator before the join reduced the total time taken for the query to 958.7 chronons, since the sort batches index lookups into runs of similar values, resulting in at most one I/O per leaf page of the index.

We then replaced the sort operator with a `reorder` operator, using the *Strict* metric, with a chunk size of 25KB (we chose this so as to amortize the cost of a random I/O over a reasonably large chunk). We used a I/O buffer size of 2.5MB. This means that the number of groups we could support was 2.5MB/25KB = 100 (recall that we want the number of groups to be as high as possible so that we can do a fine granularity reordering). Hence, we divided the range of join column values into 100 groups for the reordering, and used a pre-computed equidepth histogram on the join column values of table R to identify the group to which each value belongs. The time required for the join with `reorder` is 899.5 chronons, which is even better than the time required for the traditional join by sorting. The 6% improvement in completion time occurs because we spool out fewer tuples to disk — the process stage directly `gets` 12.1% of the tuples from the buffer. We are able to do this because we only do a fuzzy, approximate reordering. This suffices because the only purpose of the sorting is to batch up tuples of R that match similar rows of S together. However, the biggest gain by using `reorder` instead of sort is that the plan has become non-blocking. This can allow us to exploit pipelined parallelism (if we have a parallel DBMS) and also allow interactive estimation techniques such as online aggregation. If we consider the rate at which output tuples are delivered, a plain index-nested-loops join delivers 311.6 tuples/chronon, and adding `reorder` increases the rate to 1111.7 tuples per chronon.

6 Related Work

There has been some recent work on making data analysis interactive by providing approximate answers to queries early on [HH99, GM98]. Reordering complements this by allowing users to improve the quality of approximation based on interest.

Algorithmically, our reorder operator is most similar to the unary sorting and hashing operators in traditional query processing [Gra93]. However our performance and usability goals are quite different, which leads to a different implementation. Logically our operator does not correspond to any previous work in the relational context, since it is logically superfluous – ordering is not "supposed" to matter in a strict relational model.

Our focus on ordering was anticipated by the large body of work on ranking in Information Retrieval [vR75]. In more closely related work, there have been a few recent papers on optimizing "top N" and "bottom N" queries [CK97], and on "fast-first" query processing [AZ96]. These propose enhancing SQL with a stopping condition clause which the optimizer can use to produce optimal plans that process only those parts of the data that are needed for output. However in these papers, the user is required to specify *a priori* what portions of the data he is interested in, and does not have any dynamic control over the processing. Our work on spreadsheets can be viewed as an extension of this, where the user can dynamically specify what portions of the data interest him by moving a scrollbar, *after* seeing partial results.

7 Conclusions & Future Work

Interactive data analysis is an important computing task; providing interactive performance over large data sets requires algorithms that are different than those developed for relational query processing. We have described the benefits of dynamically reordering data at delivery in diverse applications such as online aggregation, traditional query processing, and spreadsheets. A main advantage of reordering is that the user can dynamically indicate what areas of the data are interesting and speed up the processing in these areas at the expense of others. This, when combined with continual feedback on the result of the processing, allows the user to interactively control the processing so that he can extract the desired information faster.

We have developed a framework for deriving the nature of the desired reordering based on the performance goals of an application, and have used this to come up with reordering policies in some typical scenarios. We have designed and implemented a reordering algorithm called *P&S*, which implements these ideas in a responsive and low-overhead manner. *P&S* is relatively simple, leveraging the difference between processing rate and data production. We have integrated *P&S* with a commercial DBMS, and are using it as a core component in the development of a scalable spreadsheet. For online aggregation, a single join above the reorder operator is sufficient for good reordering. Our simulation experiments with spreadsheet scrolling and sorting scenarios show that we can provide almost immediate — on the order of milliseconds — responses to sort operators that would otherwise take several minutes, by preferentially fetching items in the range under the scrollbar. Inserting reorder operators into standard query plans in place of sort operators is promising; initial results show that we are able to convert blocking plans into pipelines while actually reducing the completion time.

This paper opens up a number of interesting avenues for further work that we intend to explore.

Other feedback functions appear to be appropriate for applications that process real-time data such as stock quotes, since recent items are more important than earlier ones, and this must considered when calculating delivery priorities.

We have looked at reordering data delivery to meet the dynamic preferences of a single user. When online reordering is used in applications such as broadcast disks [A+97], we need to consider the aggregate preferences from several users, and the reordering policy needs to be chosen suitably.

In graphical data visualization ([A+96]), large volumes of information are presented to the user as a picture or map over which he can pan and zoom. Fetching this data from the disk and rendering it onto the screen typically takes a long time. It makes sense to fetch more data points from the region the user is currently panning over and a small region around it, so that these portions can be rendered in greater detail / higher resolution. Here the user interest is inferred based on mouse position, and this is a two-dimensional version of the spreadsheet problem.

A pipelining best-effort reorder operator appears to be substitutable for regular sort operators at other places in query plans. For instance, it can replace a sort operator that is designed to reuse memoized values of a correlated subquery or expensive user-defined function [HN96, S+96]. Here, online reordering amounts to computing the set of variable bindings on the fly, possibly with some duplication.

Acknowledgments

We would like to thank all the members of the CONTROL project at Berkeley for many useful discussions. The idea of using reordering in general query plans was suggested by Surajit Chaudhuri. Discussions with Miron Livny were useful in understanding the limits of best-effort reordering in meeting performance goals. Paul Aoki, Ron Avnur, Mehul Shah, Mike Stonebraker, and our anonymous referees gave several detailed comments on drafts of this paper. We want to thank Informix Corporation for allowing us access to their source code. Satheesh Bandaram and Kathey Marsden helped us with the programming on UDO. Computing and network resources were provided through NSF RI grant CDA-9401156. This work was supported by a grant from Informix Corp., a California MICRO grant, NSF grant IIS-9802051, and a Sloan Foundation Fellowship.

References

[A+96] A. Aiken et al. Tioga-2: A direct-manipulation data visualization environment. In *ICDE*, 1996.

[A+97] S. Acharya et al. Balancing push & pull for data broadcast. In *SIGMOD*, 1997.

[AZ96] G. Antoshnekov and M. Ziauddin. Query processing and optimization in Rdb. *VLDB Journal*, 1996.

[Bat79] M. Bates. Information search tactics. *Journal of the American Society for Information Science*, 30(4):205–214, 1979.

[Bat90] M. Bates. *User Interface Design*, chapter The Berry-Picking Search. Addison-Wesley, 1990.

[BM85] D. Blair and M. Maron. An evaluation of retrieval effectiveness for a full-text document retrieval system. *CACM*, 1985.

[C+98] S. Chaudhuri et al. Random sampling for histogram construction. In *SIGMOD*, 1998.

[CD97] S. Chaudhuri and U. Dayal. Data warehousing and OLAP for decision support. In *SIGMOD*, 1997.

[CK97] M. Carey and D. Kossman. On saying "Enough Already" in SQL. In *SIGMOD*, 1997.

[Exc] *Microsoft Excel 1997 – Online Help.*

[G+96] J. Gray et al. Data Cube: A relational aggregation operator generalizing group-by, cross-tab, and sub-totals. In *ICDE*, 1996.

[GM98] P. Gibbons and Y. Matias. New Sampling-Based Summary Statistics for Improving Approximate Query Answers. In *SIGMOD*, 1998.

[Gra93] G. Graefe. Query evaluation techniques for databases. *ACM Computing Surveys*, 1993.

[H+] J. M. Hellerstein et al. Informix under Control: Online query processing. *submitted for publication.*

[Haa97] P. Haas. Large-sample and deterministic confidence intervals for online aggregation. In *SSDBM*, 1997.

[HH99] P. Haas and J. M. Hellerstein. Ripple joins for Online Aggregation. In *SIGMOD*, 1999.

[H+97] J. M. Hellerstein, P. J. Haas, and H. J. Wang. Online Aggregation. In *SIGMOD*, 1997.

[H+98] J. M. Hellerstein et al. Interactive Data Analysis with CONTROL. To appear, *IEEE Computer*, 1999.

[HN96] J. M. Hellerstein and J. Naughton. Query execution techniques for caching expensive methods. In *SIGMOD*, 1996.

[OJ93] V. O'day and R. Jeffries. Orienteering in an information landscape: how information seekers get from here to there. In *INTERCHI*, 1993.

[S+96] P. Seshadri et al. Cost based optimization for Magic. In *SIGMOD*, 1996.

[SS] V. Raman et al. Scalable Spreadsheets for Interactive Data Analysis. In ACM Workshop on *DMKD*, 1999.

[Sto89] M. Stonebraker. The case for partial indexes. In *SIGMOD Record*, 18(4):4–11, 1989.

[vR75] C. van Rijsbergen. *Information Retrieval*. Butterworths, 1975.

[Z+97] Y. Zhao et al. An array-based algorithm for simultaneous multidimentional aggregates. In *SIGMOD*, 1997.

What do those weird XML types want, anyway?

Steven J. DeRose

Brown University and Inso Corporation

Providence, RI

USA

Steven_DeRose@Brown.edu

XML tries to bring to natural language documents ("texts" for short), some of what databases have had for decades: explicit structure whose properties can be known; independence of data and structure from reporting (which we foreigners call "formatting"); various kinds of isolation; and so on. But the data buried in those XML elements is weird stuff: deep hierarchies, arbitrary and unpredictable orderings and repetitions, a painful number of atomic types, and enough aggregates to make one's head hurt.

Among the larger problems for dealing with such data is that it has an infuriating combination of the properties of "structured" database data and "unstructured" natural language. I find these labels a bit misleading, so let's cash them out in a little more detail. Databases pin down data types, field sizes and the like, but "meaning" is often conveyed merely by the mnemonics of field names. Both "isbn" and "phone" are likely of the same data type, so have the same structure at one level; but of course distinguishing them makes a difference to querying. Object-oriented databases build more "meaning" in, partly via methods, but this "operational" meaning does not always map cleanly to the kinds of operations humans wish to perform.

In contrast, marked-up text has weak structure in the sense of data typing, but much more indication of the "structure" of interest to users exploring a huge information space. It seems to the document world that "phone-number-ness" has as much claim to being structural information, as does "10-digit numeric field". Texts also include highly structured information such as bibliographies (as well as long undifferentiated prose sections). So we quickly hit a terminological disconnect: what's structure in one world, is un-structure in the other; hence the compromise term "semi-structured," which probably satisfies no one completely.

I'll mention only in passing, various other typological differences in "structure". The order of objects is a fundamental part of the information in documents, though not in the most common database algebras: re-ordering the paragraphs of Hamlet fundamentally changes the structure present, in a way that re-ordering the fields of a relation simply does not. Likewise, documents abound with recursive partitions, or aggregates: any character in Hamlet's soliloquy is just as much a part of Scene 1, of Act 3, etc.

As a practical example of the messy phenomena of text, when I was first preparing for this talk I thought it would make sense to read some of the prior proceedings. After a *lot* of creative searching at Amazon and at LC, I found 18 volumes (including near-duplicates for 1990 and 1994, so really 16). Thus a recall of 64% (my IR friends would be upset if I didn't get "recall" or "precision" in here somewhere):

Very large data bases: proceedings / International Conference on Very Large Data Bases. 1977: Data base; v. 9, no. 2; 1977: SIGMOD record ; v. 9, no. 4.

Proceedings of the 25th VLDB Conference, Edinburgh, Scotland, 1999.

Notes: Title from cover. Vols. for 1983 and 1985 have solely the name of the conference as the title. Subtitle varies.

Proceedings of the ... International Conference on Very Large Data Bases.

Systems for large data bases: proceedings of the 2nd International Conference on Very Large Date [sic] Bases.

Very Large Data Bases: Proceedings International Conference on Very Large Data Bases / Published 1981.

Very Large Data Bases: 8th Intl Conference on Very Large Data Bases Mexico City, Mexico / Published 1982.

Proceedings VLDB 83 / Published 1983.

Very Large Data Basis Conference Proceedings: Singapore 84 (VLDB-84) Paperback / Published 1984.

Very Large Data Bases: Proceedings, 11th International Conference on Very Large Data Bases / Published 1985.

Very Large Data Bases: Proceedings, 12th International Conference on Very Large Data Bases / Published 1986.

Proceedings of the Thirteenth International Conference on Very Ĺarge Data Bases, Brighton, England, 1987 Peter M. Stocker, William Kent (Editor) / Published 1987.

Proceedings of the Fourteenth International Conference on Very Large Data Bases François Bancilhon, David J. DeWitt (Editor) / Published 1988.

Proceedings VLDB 89 International Conference on Very Large Data Bases / Published 1989.

Very Large Data Bases: 16th International Conference on Very Large Data Bases / Proceedings: August 13-16, 1990, Brisbane, Australia Dennis McLeod, *et al.* / Published 1990.

Very Large Data Base Conference Proceedings 1991 (#Vl91) / Published 1990 Proceedings of the Seventeenth International Conference on Very Large Data Bases: September 3-6, 1991: Barcelona (Catalonia, Spain) Guy M. Lohman, *et al.* / Published 1992.

Very Large Data Bases, '92: Proceedings of the 18th International Conference on Very Large Data Bases, August 23-27, 1992 Vancouver, Canada Li-Yan Yuan (Editor) / Published 1992.

Proceedings 19th International Conference on Very Large Data Bases / Published 1994.

Proceedings 19th International Conference on Very Large Data Bases : August 24th-27th 1993, Dublin, Ireland Rakesh Agrawal, *et al.* / Published 1994.

Proceedings of the 20th International Conference on Very Large Data Bases: 20th VLDB Conference September 12-15, 1994 Santiago-Chile (#Vl94) Jorge Bocca / Published 1994.

Proceedings of the International Conferences on Very Large Databases Held in Zurich, Switzerland: VLDB-95 / Published 1998.

Proceedings of the International Conferences on Very Large Databases Held in Bombay, India / Published 1996.

Proceedings of the Twenty-Fourth International Conference on Very Large Databases: New York, NY, USA 24-27 August 1998 (24th Conf) / Published 1998.

These are all obvious to us as humans (1983 is my favourite), but the variety of detail is astonishing (the more so because it is not unusual). Many of the nastiest problems of retrieval in large, but especially heterogeneous, text bases are hinted at here. Morphology ("database" vs. "databases" vs. "data base" vs. "data bases"). Alternate descriptions ("11th" vs. "1985" vs. "85"); different representations of the same data type ("24" vs. "24th" vs. "twenty-fourth"). Structural issues (dates within title vs. in publication date; different dates in both); missing or incomplete data (editors, authors, "*et al.*", locations); and much more.

A system smart enough to do this retrieval right in a single attempt, and to understand the internal structure of this data (that we humans perceive so readily), would go far towards meeting the retrieval needs of text base users and scholars. Oh, it should also catch the years I never was able to locate.

So far, this should be familiar turf. But note that text aggregates have another very annoying property: the data they serve to partition and label must also be treated as a contiguous whole for some purposes. "The text" spans partition (or "element", as we say in XML-land) boundaries, almost but not quite arbitrarily. Speech boundaries in a play usually imply larger discourse boundaries, but there are plenty of cases where one speaker picks up another's sentence -- and these phenomena are typically important. Even at the lowest levels, the boundaries are never sure. Many of the most important, most studied (for our purposes, most queried) texts have come to us in unsure or variant forms. Faithful representations note structure even within words: <sic corr="affect">effect</sic> is an obvious case, and one just as well marked up <sic corr="a">e</sic>ffect. So far, search and retrieval algorithms available to the text-computing user do not deal well with aggregates.

Even determining "the text" to index or query on is hard. A naive understanding of mark up says that what's between the pointy-brackets is meta data, and what's not, is content. But then how should queries involving "affect" and "effect" treat examples such as those just shown? Worse, how should queries operate around textual discontinuities such as footnotes? Should not the words adjacent to a footnote on each side be a phrase? Hypertext links add to the complexity because they can express content sequence and hierarchy, cross-reference, and many other relationships, but in pre-XLink Web technology we cannot say anything definitive *about* what they are saying.

I'll digress to suggest that some of these problems seem a consequence of a wholly inadequate model of text that has become entrenched in the word-processor world and influenced much thinking since. Word-processors typically view documents not as ordered hierarchies, but as lists of paragraphs (at best, some paragraphs may be styled with mnemonics such as "H1"). Aggregates for the most part do not exist: chapters, sections, even lists. This directly leads to bizarre behavior like the list-numbering anomalies of popular systems. Even a slight concession to structure would solve myriad problems. HTML slightly addresses this weakness, as well as various mechanical pains such as the need to parse binary hash rather than just characters. XML promises much more, as more meaningful tag-sets become standard in various genres and domains and as authors and software begin to make better use of them. C's oversimplification that a string is merely an array also didn't help (and seems to have led to more system vulnerabilities than just about anything else).

To resume, a further problem documents bring to the fore is polysemy of many kinds. At first it seems that at the bottom we hit something more tractable then multi-level aggregates: characters. Yet even these are not so simple: "12" and "B" and "0x'0b" and "twelve" and "dose" are all numbers, and people want them kept just that way, yet to compare equal...sometimes. "the ides of March" is a date (and a discontiguous one at that).

At the same level are problems of what logicians call "definite description", where multiple descriptors refer to the same object -- sometimes. Pronouns have of course received some treatment, but time-variant descriptions seem little addressed. Saying "I want to meet the Mayor" may be clear today, but next year when there is a new mayor it becomes ambiguous. Dealing with such "de dicto, de re" ambiguities in texts deserves a few IR and/or database dissertations.

A few levels up, we hit plays on language that may often be critical to understanding the text. A wonderful little book called "Oddities and Curiosities of Words and Literature" (C. C. Bombaugh, out of print but fairly easy to find used), gives many examples where text plays "structure" against "content", such as a 2-column letter of recommendation that reads entirely differently down the columns versus across. A more familiar case is "She went to Essex; she had always liked Essex", where the very ambiguity of "Essex" as place or person, is critical to understanding the text.

And finally, most pernicious of all is that even the best-intentioned, most thoroughly edited and analyzed texts, can only express some of the desired structures. This is of course no reason not to use the structure that *is* there; I am astonished by the number of recent papers where the system actively discards structural information that is there to start with, and then boasts of brilliant AI or heuristics to re-generate some portion of it. The reason is obvious: not all texts have any useful structural information available, and one wants to be inclusive. Yet discarding it when you have it, seems to me as absurd as building a database that cannot use field or object names,, but responds to queries by doing its best to guess which fields are phone numbers, first or last names, etc, on the ground that not all data is broken down just so.

Such phenomena are hard to manage; yet benefits of the traditional database strengths are desperately needed, for all the familiar reasons. Analysts commonly state that 90% of corporate data is in documents, not databases; But however much there may be, it is nowhere near so accessible or manageable.

How can we access this data in more useful ways, more akin to what we (after decades of hard work) can take for granted with databases? Too much of that data languishes in GIF files, bizarre formats, or, not much better, "plain text" where you can't tell the title from the colophon. What kinds of queries apply to XML data structures, and what new opportunities do they present? What can we expect from data a few years from now, and what can we hope to do with it once we have it?

In XML and SGML history the literary scholars discover and solve problems an average of 3 years before industrial users, so they give us a glimpse into the future. Structuring texts can make a difference toward making this truly enormous database called the Web, or ideally called human literature, all it might become.

XML is only step one (or perhaps step 3, following SGML and HTML): it gets rid of the most mechanical, mundane level of parsing and character set incompatibilities. But this does not solve the real problems: it merely clears away the ground cover that hides them. When we couldn't even read each other's files due to proprietary binary word-processor formats, it was hard to notice that even if we could, the documents didn't contain the information most useful to use for any task *other* than formatting. Now we are moving past that first hurdle, and the issues of schemas, semi-structured and semi-ambiguous data, hyperlinking, and retrieval in the face of all these, can come to the fore.

Web-crawlers are obviously not going to cut it, even if enhanced with the best of the capabilities I hope for. I used to say that crawlers were typically 6 months behind (audiences were aghast). I have new news: They no longer even try to keep up. I was wiring my house for Ethernet, and wanted some basic information -- I couldn't find it on the Web. So I got a tutorial from my faithful sysadmin, and then wrote it up and put it on my Web page. Several months later I thought to try searching for it: no luck. So I manually submitted the URL: a few days later a stream of e-mail responses to the page began poring in. Asking around, I discovered that only about 37% of the Web is indexed by even the largest crawlers.

I think the way forward with such data is to integrate tightly the quite different powers of structural algebras and natural language statistics; of "markup" and "content"; of links and hierarchies; in short, of language and data. Yet, although I think structured documents (what many called "semi-structured") is where it's at, and where the power for future retrieval lies, this very large database we called the Web also poses a painfully mundane problem that needs entirely different solutions; but that is another talk.

Bibliography

Abiteboul, Serge et al. 1997. "Querying Documents in Object Databases." In *International Journal on Digital Libraries* 1(1): 5–19.

Agosti, Maristelle and Alan Smeaton. 1996. *Information Retrieval and Hypertext.* Boston: Kluwer Academic Publishers. ISBN 0-7923-9710-X.

André, Jacques, Richard Furuta, and Vincent Quint (eds). 1989. *Structured Documents.* Cambridge: Cambridge University Press. ISBN 0-521-36554-6.

Bishop, Ann Peterson. 1997. "Digital Libraries and the Disaggregation of Knowledge: An Investigation of the Use of Journal Article Components by Researchers." National Synchronization Meeting. Digital Library Initiative, Pittsburgh PA, June 5.

Coombs, James H., Allen H. Renear, and Steven J. DeRose. 1987. "Markup Systems and the Future of Scholarly Text Processing." *Communications of the Association for Computing Machinery* 30 (11): 933-947.

Gibson, David, Jon Kleinberg, and Prabhakar Raghavan. 1998. "Inferring Web Communities from Link Topology." In *Proceedings of Hypertext '98,* Pittsburgh, PA. Association for Computing Machinery Press.

Hall, Wendy, Hugh Davis, and Gerard Hutchings. 1996. *Rethinking Hypermedia: The Microcosm Approach.* Boston: Kluwer Academic Publishers. ISBN 0-7923-9679-0.

Hitchcock, S. et al. 1997. "Citation Linking: Improving Access to Online Journals." In *Proceedings of ACM Digital Libraries '97.* New York: The Association for Computing Machinery.

Myaeng, Sung Hyon, Dong-Hyun Jang, Mun-Seok Kim, and Zong-Cheol Zhoo. 1998. "A Flexible Model for Retrieval of SGML Documents." Pp. 138-145 in SIGIR '98: Proceedings of the 21st Annual International ACM SIGIR Conference on Research and Development in Information Retrieval. W. Bruce Croft et al. (eds). Melbourne Australia, August 24-28. NY: ACM Press.

Simons, Gary F. 1997. "Using Architectural Forms to Map SGML Data Into an Object-Oriented Database. In Proceedings of *SGML/XML '97.* Washington, D.C., December 7–12: 449–460. Sponsored by the Graphic Communications Association (GCA) and Co-sponsored by SGML Open.

Subramanian, Bharathi, Theodore W. Leung, Scott L. Vandenberg, and Stanley B. Zdonik. 1995. "The AQUA Approach to Querying Lists and Trees in Object-Oriented Databases." Presented at the International Conference on Data Engineering, Taipei, Taiwan. Available from the authors.

Tajima, Keishi, Yoshiaki Mizuuchi, Masatsugu Kitagawa, and Katsumi Tanaka. 1998. "Cut as a Querying Unit for WWW, Netnews, and E-mail." In *Proceedings of Hypertext 98.* Pittsburgh: June 20–24: 217–224. New York: ACM Press.

Trigg, Randall H. "Guided Tours and Tabletops: Tools for Communicating in a Hypertext Environment." In ACM Transactions on Office Information Systems, 6.4 (October 1988): 398-414.

Zamir, Oren and Oren Etzioni. 1998. "Web Document Clustering: A feasibility demonstration." In SIGIR '98.

Industrial Panel on Data Warehousing Technologies: Experiences, Challenges, and Directions

Moderator: Umeshwar Dayal

Hewlett-Packard Laboratories
1501 Page Mill Road
Palo Alto, CA 94304
USA
Dayal@hpl.hp.com

Panel Description

Data warehousing is an essential element of decision support systems, which have become the largest growing segment of the database industry. Many products and services are now available, and all of the leading database vendors now have commercial offerings in these technologies. Very large (multi-terabyte) data warehouses are being built and successfully deployed in the telecommunications, financial, retail and other industries, and are now routinely being used for on-line analytical processing and other decision support applications. Many organisations are deriving major operational benefits from the use of data warehousing solutions.

However, serious technological challenges remain in scaling to very large or very complex warehousing applications; and in providing tools for building, deploying and maintaining warehousing solutions through the whole operational chain, starting from the backend processes for extracting, transforming, cleaning and loading data into the warehouse, to the front-end tools for data analysis and mining. Next generation applications such as e-commerce or e-business pose additional challenges.

Proceedings of the 25th VLDB Conference, Edinburgh, Scotland, 1999.

This panel brings together representatives from data warehousing technology vendors and solution integrators to present their views on the following topics:

- Current and future data warehousing requirements from customers
- Real-world data warehousing scenarios
- Scalable architectures for data warehousing
- Lessons learnt from deploying data warehousing solutions
- Technology directions: what are vendors doing to meet requirements
- What problems should the research community be working on?

Panelists

- Ray Roccaforte, Oracle Corporation
- Bob Walker, Informix
- Thomas Zurek and Markus Sinnwell, SAP Business Information Warehouse

Data Warehousing Has More Colours Than Just Black & White

Thomas Zurek
Email: Thomas.Zurek@sap-ag.de

Markus Sinnwell
Email: Markus.Sinnwell@sap-ag.de

SAP Business Information Warehouse
P.O. Box 1461
61985 Walldorf
Germany

Abstract

Data warehouses are frequently described to be orthogonal to operational database systems. In this paper, we show that such a point of view is often misleading as a data warehouse (a) often has to share structures and issues with the OLTP systems that are linked to the data warehouse and (b) serves as an infrastructure element to support other tools for strategic management. We describe how data warehousing requirements evolve in that context.

1 Introduction

Since the advent of data warehousing in the early 1990s, many (marketing and research) papers, books, brochures etc. have been written on the topic. A lot of them argue that data warehouses (DW) are somewhat othogonal to the traditional operational database (ODB) systems. To that end, many contrasting pairs of expressions have been cited in order to underpin that notion:

- transactional vs. analytical processing
- operational vs. informational processing
- application-oriented vs. subject-oriented
- predictable retrieval vs. ad-hoc retrieval
- OLTP vs. OLAP
- detailed vs. summarised data
- normalised vs. denormalised data

See [Chaudhuri and Dayal, 1997], [Anahory and Murray, 1997], [Berson and Smith, 1997], [Bontempo and Zagelow, 1998] or the many industrial white papers that you find at locations like [DataWarehouse.com, 1999] or [DW-Institute, 1999].

In this paper, we will not argue against these 'black & white' patterns; they certainly focus on important issues. They also clarify to the non-expert what the ideal distribution of tasks between ODBs and DWs should look like. In this paper however, we will abandon the prototypical situation and turn to real-world-scenarios of data warehousing. There, many of the patterns that are mentioned above look more colourful rather than just 'black & white'.

The background of this paper is as follows. In 1998, SAP released the *Business Information Warehouse (BW)* [SAP, 1997], a complete standard solution for data warehousing. In March 1999, it had been delivered at over 400 customer sites worldwide. During that year, we were able to watch many customer projects, their approaches, their requirements and especially the way in which they perceived data warehousing as the technology that can possibly and hopefully resolve some of their business problems. In this paper, we will summarise some of this experience, particularly with respect to those patterns above.

The remainder of this paper is organised as follows. In section 2, we describe the typical environment that is created through enterprise resource planning (ERP) systems and that is the base of our discussion. In section 3, we discuss four data warehousing issues that do not match the general, orthogonal patterns that should distinguish DW and ODB systems. Finally, the paper is concluded in section 4.

Proceedings of the 25th VLDB Conference, Edinburgh, Scotland, 1999.

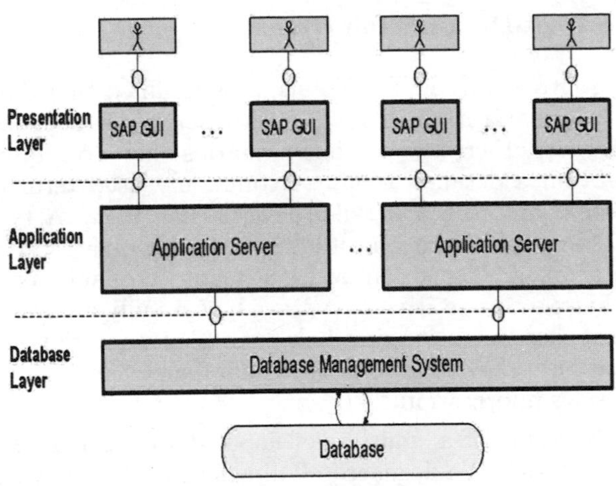

Figure 1: The three-tier client-server architecture as employed by R/3.

2 ERP-Environments

2.1 ERP-Systems

In order to understand a user's point of view on data warehousing, one has to look at the state of ODB data management. In this section we want to focus on the particular sector of enterprise resource planning (ERP) systems. The latter constitute a considerable part of the wider OLTP market.

A typical ERP-system, such as SAP's R/3 product, integrates a wide number of business applications that cooperate over a single database. Typical business applications are financial accounting (FI), controlling (CO), sales and distribution (SD), materials management (MM), production planning (PP), plant maintenance (PM) etc. Many of these applications share data. For instance, objects such as *customer orders* or *articles* play major roles in SD, CO, PP and many more. The major benefit of an integrated ERP-system is that all these applications can cooperate over the same database. In that way, one matches the natural fact that an object (like *order*) passes several departments (application areas). Ideally, every application could run on its own, private server. In summary, this motivates a three-tier client-server architecture (see figure 1). Someone who uses such an integrated system might wonder why something like a data warehouse is required: the central database theoretically provides opportunities for cross-application data analysis and reporting. And in fact, most of these systems provide (at least statical) querying facilities, even across several systems. Thus, this widely cited argument in favour of a data warehouse might fade away in front of some users.

2.2 ERP & Data Warehousing

Figure 2 shows an example of data warehousing in an ERP-environment. There are tools for planning, such

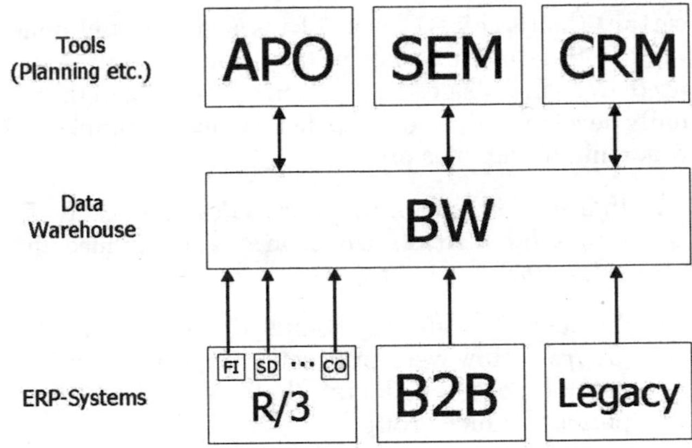

Figure 2: Data warehousing in an ERP-environment.

as SAP's APO (advanced planning & optimisation) or SEM (strategic enterprise management) products, and for CRM (customer relationship management). In practice there are many more such tools. They are all based on anlytical information about the state of the company and its businesses. Such information is provided by a data warehouse system which itself is linked to many sources of operational data, such as R/3, B2B (business-to-business procurement) or legacy systems.

In such a context, a data warehouse (a) provides not only powerful staging and OLAP engines for consolidated data extraction and integrated reporting, respectively, and (b) serves as an infrastructure element to support further tools for strategic management. Below, we will discuss some of the services that a DW might provide for those tools.

3 Non-Standard Data Warehousing Requirements

In order to show the wide (colourful) spectrum of data warehousing we now dive into some issues that go beyond *slicing*, *dicing* and the traditional black & white patterns that we mentioned in section 1. Those issues have come up with many of our customers. We will try to show the motivation of such requirements.

Realignment

The term *realignment* is used to refer to structural changes in the data warehouse. They might – but do not necessarily imply – changes to the data schema. Realignment plays an important role in data warehousing as such systems are tuned towards fast reporting which is achieved by fixing and precomputing certain portions of the data. Any changes can impose major reorganisations of the underlying data. We would like to look at one issue that is likely to affect a major overhaul of certain structure in a data warehouse, namely ***hierarchies***.

Hierarchical relationships are frequently used in OLAP. They are used to summarise information on certain (hierarchical) levels of interest. Simply imagine the time hierarchy of year – month – day that is used to look at sales figures on a yearly, monthly or daily level, respectively. Other typical examples for reporting hierarchies are:

1. In a sales scenario, there are *sales regions* divided into *sales districts* which are again divided into *sales offices.*
2. *Products* are usually bundled to form *product groups.* However, product groups itself can be considered as products[1] that form part of a superior product group.
3. *Cost centres* usually match the organisational structure of a company with departments being divided into several (sub-) departments that consist of several groups. Here, there is no fixed depth of the hierarchy as some departments might have a deep organisational structure while others might not.

These examples show a number of problems with respect to realignment; such problems do not exist in static and simple examples as the one of the time hierarchy:

- All these hierarchies might change regularly: the sales organisation (1.) or the cost centre (3.) hierarchies are likely to change frequently due to reorganisations within the company. This can trigger major reorganisations within the data warehouse if the hierarchical changes are to be applied to historical data as well. The latter situation is not rare as data warehousing data is frequently used for planning purposes (e.g. to improve organisational structures).
- Many hierarchies do not have a fixed number of levels. Usually, each level is represented as a column within the table that describes a dimension of a multidimensional data cube. This solution does not work when the number of levels is not known in advance. Workarounds comprise the use of recursive levels as in the product hierarchy (2.). There, a product group can be considered as a product. However, this moves the problem to query processing where the recursive definition has to be resolved.
- Originally, many of the hierarchies are defined and maintained in the OLTP systems. Cost and profit centre hierarchies, for example, are exposed to frequent[2] changes. Many customers expect to synchronise the OLTP and the OLAP hierarchies.

[1] Just imagine software products like word processing, spreadsheet, drawing, database etc. programs being sold individually as well as part of a software package.

[2] Monthly changes are not rare. In extreme cases, we have seen daily and weekly changes.

Level-of-Detail (Line Items)

In contrast to OLTP-systems, it is assumed that data is *summarised* when loaded into a data warehouse. However, there are various scenarios that do require data on a detailed level. A commonly used term to refer to data on a detailed level is *line item.* A typical example for a line item is an order or a receipt. In areas of intense competition, many companies only achieve a competitive advantage by carefully analysing their customers' buying habits (basket analysis). To that end, they require detailed data such as the point of sales information.

In terms of a multidimensional data schema, this translates into a degenerated dimension with many entries. In turn, this creates query processing problems as many star query processing techniques cannot be applied in such a case.

Updates

Another assumption that is frequently cited to be a distinguishing characteristic between DW and ODB management is that data is read-only, i.e. it is never updated. Unfortunately, this is not true as we describe in the following two scenarios.

Many companies regularly evaluate the quality of their services. A prominent example is that of customer order being delivered on time. In that context, orders are classified to be *open, delivered, billed* or *closed.* Now, a controller might want to see how many customers do not receive any items within two weeks. To answer this query, it is necessary to already hold those orders in the DW whose state is *open.* However, this implies that – later, when the state changes to *delivered, billed* and *closed* – updates in the DW are required.

A second example arises in the context of planning tools being used in conjunction with a DW. Many of those tools are based on the kind of data that is found in a DW, i.e. summarised, aggregated on certain (e.g. hierarchical) levels, cleansed and scrubbed. Those tools start to plan on that kind of data in order to project sales, revenue etc. figures to the future. Afterwards, one usually wants to compare planned versus actual data. To that end, the plan data is pushed back into the data warehouse. This is not a particular problem. However, planning is an iterative process: initially, crude estimates are created and then those estimates are subsequently refined. Translated into database management terms this means that a certain portion of the fact table data (i.e. the part representing the plan data) is subsequently updated. This, in turn, imposes a considerable burden on (query) performance enhancing techniques in the data warehouse such as the maintenance of materialised views.

Frequency of Data-Uploads

An OLTP system processes many writing transactions each second. In contrast to that, the writing operations in a DW are concentrated on certain windows with no or few reading operations, such as weekends or nights. This is again a result of a data warehouse creating redundant, precomputed data portions (e.g. denormalised schemas or materialised views) that allow fast reporting possibilities.

Frequently, it is not easy for a user to accept that inserting new data into a DW requires major efforts. While some users simply regard a data warehouse as a reporting tool (that should be synchronised with the OLTP systems) there is a whole bunch of scenarios that require an upload frequency that is well below a daily interval. A prominent example is again planning on top of historic data (provided by a DW) and subsequently refining that plan data.

One can think of various mechanisms to support such processes without destroying the existing data warehousing mechanisms. However, from a conceptual point of view, this concedes that, in such scenarios, DW data has to be much more up to date and that the actuality of data is not necessarily as a distinguishing factor between OLTP and DW as it is often assumed.

Predictable vs. Ad-Hoc Retrieval

Many companies have sets of standard reports that are run daily, weekly or monthly to determine key (company) performance indicators. Very often, such indicators have been well defined (and refined) by those companies over many years. Those standard reports are the result of this process.

Ad-hoc reporting is certainly an issue, especially with respect to data mining. However, it is only one part of OLAP beside the sets of standardised queries.

4 Conclusions

In this paper, we have discussed and motivated certain issues of data warehousing that contrast the black & white patterns that are frequently cited to show that DW and ODB systems are somehow orthogonal. We argue that in real-world scenario the orthogonality often disappears as there is a need to bridge the gap between the prototypical DW and ODB systems.

References

Anahory, S. and Murray, D. (1997). *Data Warehousing in the Real World.* Addison-Wesley, 1st edition.

Berson, A. and Smith, S. (1997). *Data Warehousing, Data Mining & OLAP.* McGraw-Hill.

Bontempo, C. and Zagelow, G. (1998). The IBM Data Warehouse Architecture. *Communications of the ACM*, 41(9):38–48.

Chaudhuri, S. and Dayal, U. (1997). An Overview of Data Warehousing and OLAP Technology. *SIGMOD Record*, 26(1).

DataWarehouse.com (1999). DataWarehouse.com – White Papers. http://www.datawarehouse.com.

DW-Institute (1999). Data Warehousing Institute – White Papers. http://www.dw-institute.com.

SAP (1997). Business Information Warehouse – Technology. White Paper. available via http:// www.sap-ag.de / products / bw / index.htm.

SAP (1998a). Advanced Planner and Organizer. White Paper. available via http:// www.sap-ag.de / products / apo / index.htm.

SAP (1998b). R/3 System. White Paper. available via http:// www.sap-ag.de / products / r3 / index.htm.

SAP (1999). SAP Customer Relationship Management Initiative. White Paper. available via http:// www.sap-ag.de / crm / index.htm.

Curio: A Novel Solution for Efficient Storage and Indexing in Data Warehouses

Anindya Datta
College of Computing.
Georgia Institute of Tech.
adatta@cc.gatech.edu

Krithi Ramamritham
Computer Science Dept.
Indian Institute of Technology, Bombay
krithi@cse.iitb.ernet.in

Helen Thomas
College of Computing.
Georgia Institute of Tech.
adatta@cc.gatech.edu

1 Introduction

Data warehousing and *On-Line Analytical Processing* (OLAP) are becoming critical components of decision support as advances in technology are improving the ability to manage and retrieve large volumes of data. *Data warehousing* refers to "a collection of decision support technologies aimed at enabling the knowledge worker (executive, manager, analyst) to make better and faster decisions" [1]. OLAP refers to the technique of performing complex analysis over the information stored in a data warehouse. It is often used by management analysts and decision makers in a variety of functional areas such as sales and marketing planning. Typically, OLAP queries look for specific trends and anomalies in the base information by aggregating, ranging, filtering and grouping data in many different ways [8]. Efficient query processing is a critical requirement for OLAP because the underlying data warehouse is very large, queries are often quite complex, and decision support applications typically require interactive response times.

Proceedings of the 25th VLDB Conference, Edinburgh, Scotland, 1999.

Two main approaches for fast OLAP query processing have emerged:

1. *Precomputation Strategies.* This approach relies on *summary tables*, derived tables that house precomputed or "ready-made" answers to queries [1]. This has been, by far, the most explored area in the context of data warehouses [3].

2. *Ad-hoc Strategies.* This approach to fast OLAP query processing supports ad-hoc querying by using fast access structures on the base data such as *B^+-tree indexes*, *bitmapped indexes* [7], *bit-sliced indexes* [8] and *projection indexes* [8].

However, in these and other index structures proposed for OLAP, a separate set of indices or access structures is typically maintained in addition to the base data. Given the large size of data warehouses, storage is a non-trivial cost, and so is the additional storage requirement due to the index structures. This is especially true given that data and storage maintenance costs are often up to seven times as high per year as the original purchase cost [11]. Hence, a terabyte-sized system, with an initial media cost of \$100,000, could cost an additional \$700,000 for every year it is operational.

Curio, a data repository and OLAP query server, provides a potential solution to this problem. Curio is based on a novel design technique that allows fast access to data, yet *does not require indexes* [6]. Hence, Curio provides drastically improved performance for ad-hoc queries, while *simultaneously* reducing the storage costs associated with warehousing. We briefly describe the underlying positional indexing techniques behind Curio and report results from a performance comparison with several leading commercial relational warehousing products in terms of query performance. We demonstrate the improved query performance of Curio over a specific product reported here, namely Oracle [9].

2 The Positional Indexing Approach

We now present an example to motivate the need for efficient storage and retrieval in data warehousing environments. Figure 1 contains a simple warehouse *star schema* [5], which models the 10-year history of the sales of an automobile manufacturer with dealerships located around the globe and is intended to support marketing and strategic decision-making.

In conventional database design, one envisions a set of relations or table structures, and a separate set of indices or access structures. In a relational system, tables would be stored "as-is": each table would be represented as a series of records partitioned over a chain of data blocks linked by *block pointers*. In addition to the base tables, for retrieval efficiency, index structures would typically be defined. More specifically, the `SALES` table will likely be indexed on each of its four dimensional attributes. A large number of indexing schemes have been proposed in the literature. Among these, four index types have been shown in [8] to be particularly appropriate for data warehousing/OLAP and they are indeed used in both commercial and research systems. These structures are *"standard" B^+-tree indexes*, *bitmapped B^+-tree indexes*, *projection indexes*, and *bit-sliced indexes*. While these structures have indeed improved query performance, they have imposed a significant space penalty. Certain schemes, such as the standard B^+-tree and bitmapped B^+-tree, incur much more storage overhead than others due to the nature of their structure. It is not uncommon for a standard or bitmapped B^+-tree index on a single column of a table to be 50 to 100% of the size of the table itself.

Curio is based on the notion of vertically partitioning a table into sets of attributes. By applying this idea, we can divide the `SALES` table in figure 1, into five smaller tables, as shown in figure 2. The new schema is then composed of 5 vertical partitions: one for each of the dimensional attributes (i.e., `SALES.TimeStamp`, `SALES.PoS ID`, `SALES.Profile ID` and `SALES.Product ID`), and one for the remaining columns from the original, i.e, the business metrics of the `SALES` table (i.e., `Tax`, `Discount` and `Status`). Each of these partitions can be considered a positional index. The resulting database size is essentially the same as the size of the raw data in the original database configuration. However, we can now utilize the separate dimensional columns of the partitioned fact table as *both elements of and indexes onto* that table. In terms of storage cost, the indexing is free. This indexing is made possible by a mapping that exists between the positional index and the original or reduced table such that one can easily associate the elements of a record in the positional index and the reduced table.

The ideas presented here have been extended to develop several additional proprietary data structures and algorithms that allow efficient join and aggregation operations.

3 Performance Evaluation of Curio

We now present selected results from a performance study, which compares the query processing speeds of Curio with those of several existing RDWMS products. We report the results for 3 specific products: Oracle (version 8.0.5) [9], Red Brick Warehouse (version 5.1.5) [10], and DB2 Universal Database (version 5.0) [4]. All tests were performed on a Windows NT machine having a single 300 MHz Intel Pentium processor and 64 MB of RAM. The queries used in this experiment are based on a star schema similar to the one shown in Figure 1. For each RDWMS product, indexes were built *only on those columns used in the test queries*, thus providing a significant advantage for the above mentioned products in terms of storage requirements. Typically, in a warehouse environment, indexes would be built on most (if not all) attributes, incurring significant additional storage overhead. Where possible, we used specialized indexes to give the other products as much of an advantage as possible. For example, bitmapped indexes were used in Oracle and star indexes in Red Brick.

The data for the schema were randomly gener-

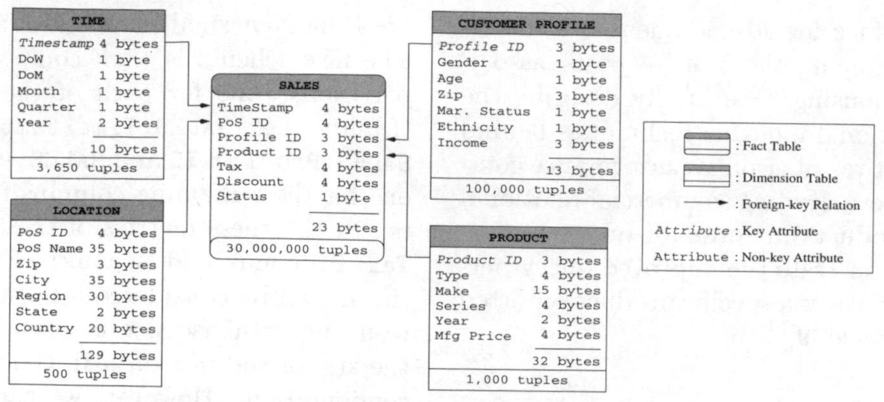

Figure 1: A Simple Warehouse Star Schema

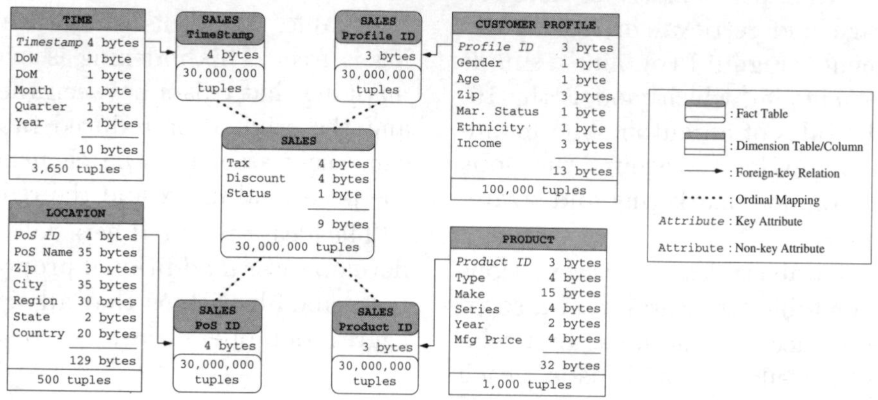

Figure 2: Example Warehouse Schema with Vertical Partitioning Index Scheme

ated and loaded into each RDWMS using their respective bulk load utilities. Three database sizes were considered in this experiment: 0.25 GB, 0.5 GB, and 1 GB. Database size here refers to the size of the raw data, and thus does not include any overhead that may be added once the data is loaded.

For each of the queries, we provide a plot of the response times for each RWDMS at each of the 3 data size levels. The results for all tests are presented using bar charts. The numbers above each bar for Red Brick, DB2, and Oracle are ratios of the performance compared to that of Curio. Two queries are shown in Figure 3, a 2-way join (Figure 3A) and a 4-way join (Figure 3B). Curio displays a remarkable peformance advantage over all other products, and this advantage increases with the query complexity. Two aggregation queries are shown in Figure 4, a 2-way join with 1 `GROUP BY` column (Figure 4A) and a 4-way join with 3 `GROUP BY` columns (Figure 4B). The performance advantage of Curio is similar, but on a greater scale.

4 Conclusion

We have presented Curio, an efficient OLAP query engine and data repository based on a simple data storage and indexing scheme. Clearly, one of the main advantages of this approach lies in the fact that essentially indexing is provided "for free". Our demonstration at VLDB shows that Curio is highly effective in reducing storage requirements while also delivering excellent query performance. To this end we demonstrate its superior performance with a set of typical OLAP queries and compare the run-times under Curio against a leading commercial relational warehousing product.

References

[1] S. Chauduri and U. Dayal. An overview of data warehousing and OLAP technology. *SIGMOD Record*, 26(1):65–74, March 1997.

[2] International Data Corp. Data warehousing tools: 1998 worldwide markets and trends, report 17622, 1998.

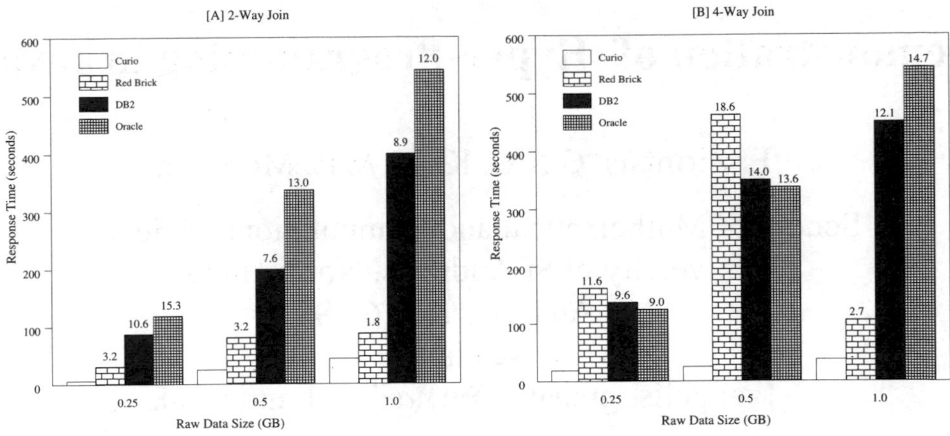

Figure 3: Response Times for Non-Aggregation Queries

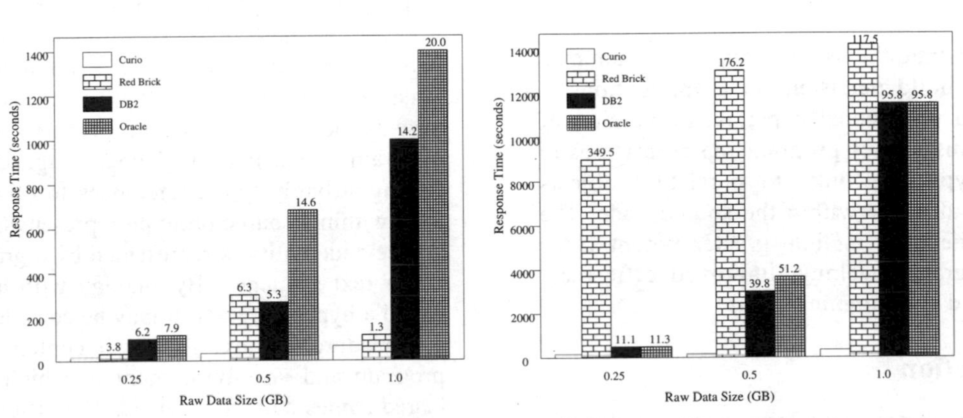

Figure 4: Response Times for Aggregation Queries

[3] V. Harinarayan, A. Rajaraman, and J.D. Ullman. Implementing data cubes efficiently. In *Proc. ACM SIGMOD*, pages 205–216, Montreal, Canada, June 4-6 1996.

[4] IBM Corp. Db2 universal database version 5.0 for windows nt, 1997.

[5] R. Kimball. *The Data Warehouse Toolkit*. J. Wiley & Sons, Inc., first edition, 1996.

[6] Muninn Technologies, LLC. Curio: A novel solution for efficient storage and indexing in data warehouses. White Paper, URL: `http://www.muninn.com`, 1999.

[7] P. O'Neil. Model 204 architecture and performance. In *2nd Intl. Workshop on High Performance Transaction Systems (HPTS)*, volume 359 of *Springer-Verlag Lecture Notes on Computer Science*, pages 40–59. Springer-Verlag, Asilomar, CA, 1987.

[8] P. O'Neil and D. Quass. Improved query performance with variant indexes. In *Proc. ACM SIGMOD Intl. Conf. on Management of Data*, pages 38–49, Tucson, AZ, May 13-15 1997.

[9] Oracle Corp. Oracle8 enterprise edition release 8.0.5 for windows nt, 1998.

[10] Red Brick Systems. Red brick warehouse version 5.1 for windows nt, 1998.

[11] D. Simpson. Corral your storage management costs. *Datamation*, pages 88–93, April 1997.

Demonstration of Hyper-Programming in Java™

E. Zirintsis, G.N.C. Kirby & R. Morrison

School of Mathematical and Computational Sciences
University of St Andrews, North Haugh
St Andrews KY16 9SS
Scotland
{vangelis, graham, ron}@dcs.st-and.ac.uk

Abstract

We demonstrate the use of a hyper-programming system to build persistent Java applications in PJama, an orthogonally persistent version of Java™. This allows program representations to contain type-safe links to persistent objects embedded directly within the source code. The potential benefits include greater potential for static program checking, improved efficiency, and reduced programming effort.

1. Introduction

Persistent programming languages were developed in an effort to reduce the burden on the application programmer of organising the transfer of long-term data between volatile program storage and non-volatile storage [1]. Previously, application data to be retained between activations had to be written explicitly to a database or file system, and later read in again to the application space. This flattening and rebuilding of data structures involved a significant programming overhead, and an increased intellectual effort since the programmer had to keep track of a three-way mapping between program representation, database/file representation and real world. The introduction of orthogonally persistent languages meant that any program data could be made persistent simply by identifying it as such, with all transfers between memory hierarchy layers handled transparently.

The treatment of source programs as strongly typed persistent objects, which is made possible by the use of a Persistent Object System (POS) or Object Oriented Database as the support platform, permits a new approach to program construction. Hyper-programming involves storing strongly typed references to other persistent objects within a source program representation [2]. Thus the source code entity is represented by a graph rather than a linear text sequence. By analogy with hyper-text this is called a hyper-program. It may be considered as similar to a procedure closure, in that it contains both a textual program and an environment in which non-locally declared names may be resolved. The difference is that with a hyper-program the environment is explicitly constructed by the programmer, who specifies persistent objects to be bound into the hyper-program at construction time.

Figure 1 shows an example hyper-program, comprising a class definition containing two links. The first is to a class, *Person*, while the second is to an object that is an instance of that class. As illustrated by the link to the class, a hyper-programming system may support linking to non-first-class entities for convenience.

persistent store

hyper-program

```
class X {
   ...
   ...
   Person p = [ ] ;
   ...
}
```

class — object — object — object

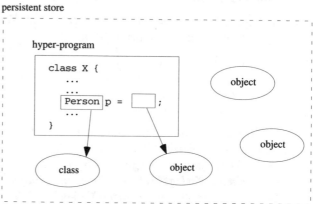

Figure 1. Example hyper-program

Proceedings of the 25th VLDB Conference, Edinburgh, Scotland, 1999.

The support of hyper-program construction techniques by a POS provides a number of potential advantages:

- Program succinctness: textual descriptions of the locations and types of persistent components used by the program may be replaced by simple embedded references.
- Increased execution efficiency: checking of the validity of specified access paths to other components is factored out when they are embedded directly in the source program. Checking of type consistency may be performed at compilation time rather than execution time.
- Reliable access to components: where a textual description of a component is replaced by a direct reference, the underlying referential integrity of the POS ensures that the component will always be accessible by the program. By contrast, where a textual description is used it may become invalid by the time the program executes, even if it was valid at the time the program was constructed.
- Complete closure representations: it is possible to fully represent code fragments that refer to existing values within their closure. This is not possible with purely textual representations, since the identities of those values may be significant.

2. Summary of Demonstration

Hyper-Program Composition and Viewing

The demonstration shows a prototype hyper-programming system [3] based on the PJama [4] persistent version of Java™.

Figure 2 shows an example of the hyper-programming user interface. It provides two tools: an editor in which hyper-programs are composed, together with an object/class browser that is used to locate persistent objects for linking. The browser is also used in conjunction with the editor for viewing hyper-programs: when the programmer clicks on a link in the editor, a representation of the corresponding linked entity is displayed in the browser.

The top window shows a hyper-program under construction in the editor. The body of the *main* method contains links to a static method, *Person.marry*, and to two instances of class *Person*. The lower window shows the object browser, currently displaying details of one of the object instances in the left pane, and the object's class in the right pane.

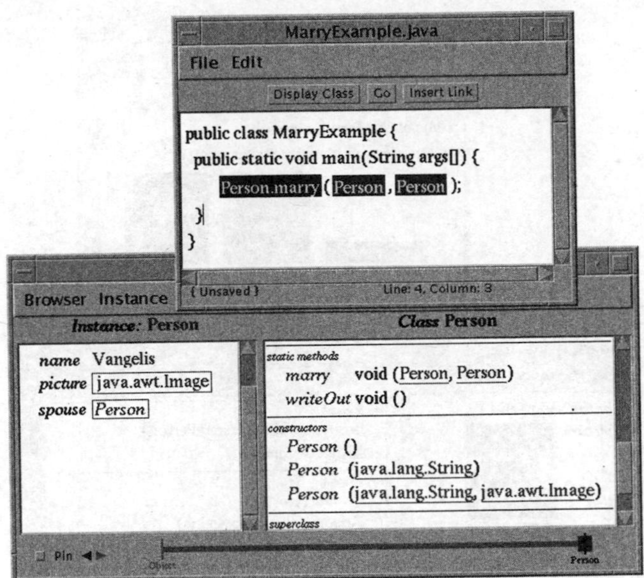

Figure 2. Hyper-programming user interface

The following activities are illustrated during the demonstration:

- locating persistent objects using the object/class browser;
- composing a hyper-program, including inserting hyper-links;
- viewing the hyper-linked entities in a hyper-program using the object/class browser;
- compiling and executing a hyper-program;
- dynamic invocation of object methods using the object/class browser;
- customisation of the editor and object/class browser displays, as described in the next section.

Customisation

By default, the editor displays hyper-links as textual labels. It is also possible to customise the display style on a per-object or per-class basis, achieved via user calls to a customisation API. The object/class browser can be similarly customised. Figure 3 shows an example in which both editor and browser have been customised to display instances of classes *Person* and *java.awt.Image* using an appropriate bitmap.

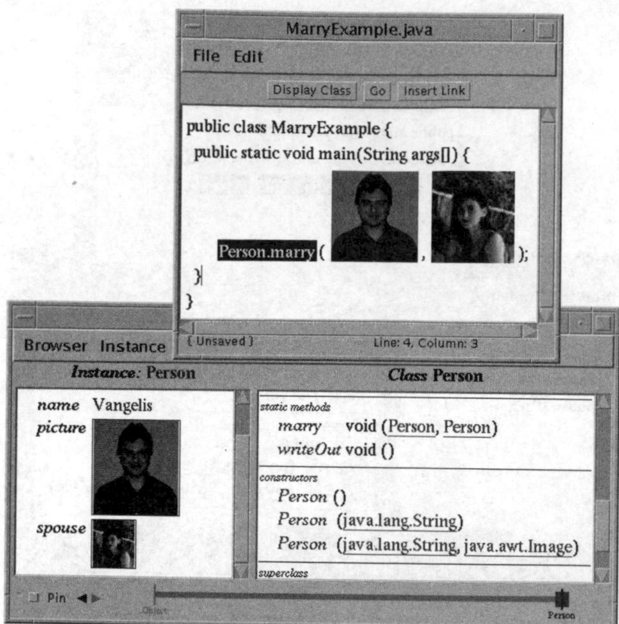

Figure 3. Example customisation

3. Design and Implementation Issues

The major issue in building hyper-programming systems concerns the semantics of the hyper-links, such as:

- what can a hyper-link refer to?
- what guarantees can be made about a hyper-link's referent data?
- how are hyper-links typed and when does type-checking occur?

The degrees of freedom regarding what a hyper-link can refer to depend upon the programming language semantics and the measure of open-ness in the system. Normally hyper-links will be able to refer to all first class language values. Second class entities not in the value space, such as classes or types, may also be conveniently hyper-linked depending on the flavour of the language. Update may be accommodated through hyper-links by linking to locations, which may or may not be first class values. More interesting is the extent to which hyper-links may refer to values created independently of the system, such as Web pages and DCOM objects. Furthermore the open-ness of the system can be extended by making the hyper-program representation open for other tools to manipulate.

In Java not all denotable values are first class values, for example methods, and there is no simple production rule to capture this in the syntactic definition. We define the denotable values that can be hyper-linked in Java as: objects; classes; interfaces; arrays; array elements; static members; non-static members; and constructors. Furthermore, links may be made to both values and locations that contain values (such as fields and array elements) where appropriate.

Table 1 shows the Java denotable values that can be hyper-linked in the hyper-programming prototype, and the corresponding syntactic productions [5].

Hyper-link To	Production
class	ClassType
primitive type	PrimitiveType
interface	InterfaceType
array type	ArrayType
object	Primary
primitive value	Literal
(static) field	FieldAccess
(static) method	Name
constructor	Name
array	Primary
array element	ArrayAccess

Table 1. Java hyper-links and productions

Referential integrity in a hyper-programming system means that once a hyper-link is established it is guaranteed by the system to exist and to be the same value when the hyper-link is executed. While this guarantee may be provided by a strongly typed persistent object store, it may also be expensive to provide in a distributed system. Variations therefore include the hyper-link being valid but not necessarily referring to the original value, and the hyper-link referring to a copy of the original. This may only be a problem where object identity is important such as in sharing semantics. A hyper-program may therefore display a range of failure modes from not failing to failure from the hyper-link being no longer valid.

The final issue is how hyper-links are typed, if at all. Assuming that they are, the interesting aspect of type checking is that the contract between the program and the referenced value may now take on a different agreement procedure. Instead of the program asserting the type of the hyper-link and the type checking system ensuring that the hyper-link has the correct type when it is used, the reverse may be used. That is the hyper-link knows its own type and therefore when it is used the program can be made to conform to this type. Statically this removes the need for type specifications for hyper-links in hyper-programs and dynamically it means that the program may be in error rather than the hyper-link.

4. Current research: hyper-code

Current research is directed at refining the concept of hyper-program to remove all distinctions between multiple program forms.

The goal is to maximise simplicity for the programmer. A single, uniform, program representation is presented at all stages of the software process. Since this

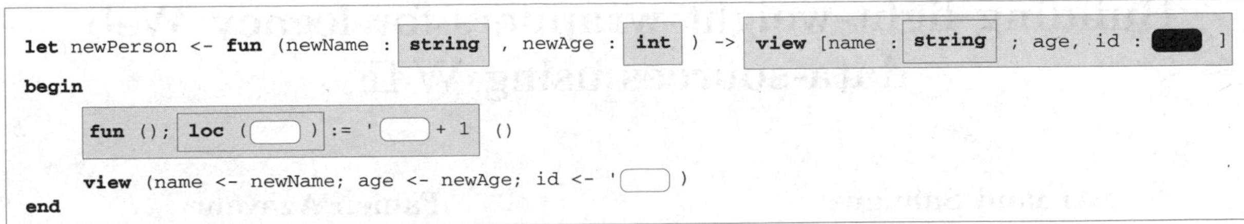

Figure 4. Hyper-code example

representation must be suitable for programs with closure, by implication it must be a form of hyper-program that can represent links to persistent values directly. To distinguish it from existing prototypes we refer to this representation as *hyper-code* [6].

The demonstrated PJama hyper-program system falls short of this goal in several respects. Different representations are used for creating new values and browsing existing values: new values are created by writing hyper-program source definitions, while existing values are displayed graphically in the object/class browser. Secondly, full representations are not provided for all existing values, in particular it is not possible to view method source code.

The hyper-code system will address these deficiencies by retaining all source code in the persistent store, and by providing the same single representation of values at all stages of the software process. As a consequence the distinction between editor and object browser will disappear: all programmer interaction with the system will take place via a single unified hyper-code editor. This will support a small set of simple operations that can be composed orthogonally to achieve all programming activities:

evaluate : this executes a selected fragment of hyper-code. If any result is produced this is returned as a further fragment of hyper-code.
explode : this expands a selected fragment of hyper-code to show more detail, while retaining the identities of any values referred to.
edit : this encompasses conventional editing facilities.

Implementation of this scheme in any particular language involves mapping the operations to the syntax of the language, and designing an appropriate hyper-code representation that can be used both to define new programs and represent existing values, in all possible cases. Figure 4 shows a simple example in ProcessBase [7, 8] in which the definition of a procedure *newPerson* contains various hyper-links, both exploded and unexploded. The exploded links, denoted by grey boxes, show detail of the linked entities in the form of more hyper-code.

5. Further Information

Further details of the hyper-program and hyper-code projects are available, with related publications, at the St Andrews web site:

`http://www-ppg.dcs.st-and.ac.uk/`

6. References

[1] Atkinson, M.P., Bailey, P.J., Chisholm, K.J., Cockshott, W.P. & Morrison, R. "An Approach to Persistent Programming". Computer Journal 26, 4 (1983) pp 360-365.

[2] Kirby, G.N.C., Connor, R.C.H., Cutts, Q.I., Dearle, A., Farkas, A.M. & Morrison, R. "Persistent Hyper-Programs". In **Persistent Object Systems**, Albano, A. & Morrison, R. (ed), Springer-Verlag (1992) pp 86-106.

[3] Zirintsis, E., Dunstan, V.S., Kirby, G.N.C. & Morrison, R. "Hyper-Programming in Java". In **Advances in Persistent Object Systems**, Morrison, R., Jordan, M. & Atkinson, M.P. (ed), Morgan Kaufmann (1999).

[4] Atkinson, M.P., Daynès, L., Jordan, M.J., Printezis, T. & Spence, S. "An Orthogonally Persistent Java™". ACM SIGMOD Record 25, 4 (1996) pp 68-75.

[5] Gosling, J. & McGilton, H. "The Java™ Language Environment: A White Paper". Sun Microsystems, Inc (1995).

[6] Connor, R.C.H., Cutts, Q.I., Kirby, G.N.C., Moore, V.S. & Morrison, R. "Unifying Interaction with Persistent Data and Program". In **Interfaces to Database Systems**, Sawyer, P. (ed), Springer-Verlag (1994) pp 197-212.

[7] Warboys, B.C., Balasubramaniam, D., Greenwood, R.M., Kirby, G.N.C., Mayes, K., Morrison, R. & Munro, D.S. "Instances and Connectors: Issues for a Second Generation Process Language". In **Lecture Notes in Computer Science 1487**, Gruhn, V. (ed), Springer-Verlag (1998) pp 137-142.

[8] Morrison, R., Balasubramaniam, D., Greenwood, M., Kirby, G.N.C., Mayes, K., Munro, D.S. & Warboys, B.C. "ProcessBase Reference Manual (Version 1.0.4)". Universities of St Andrews and Manchester (1999).

Building light-weight wrappers for legacy Web data-sources using W4F

Arnaud Sahuguet
Department of Computer and Information Science
University of Pennsylvania
sahuguet@saul.cis.upenn.edu

Fabien Azavant
École Nationale Supérieure des Télécommunications
Paris, France
fabien.azavant@enst.fr

1 Introduction

The Web has become a major conduit to information repositories of all kinds. Today, more than 80% of information published on the Web is generated by underlying databases (however access is granted through a Web gateway using forms as a query language and HTML as a display vehicle) and this proportion keeps increasing. But Web data sources also consist of stand-alone HTML pages hand-coded by individuals, that provide very useful information such as reviews, digests, links, etc. As for the information that also exists in underlying databases, the HTML interface is often the only one available for many would-be clients.

1.1 A need for HTML wrappers

As soon as we want to go beyond the basic mode of a *browsing human*, for example to achieve Web-awareness among services (services taking advantage of one another) or inter-operability (between Web sources and legacy databases or among Web sources themselves), we need software applications and these need to access HTML data. HTML was really designed to display information to a human user, so applications need **HTML wrappers** that can make the content of HTML pages directly available to them.

The purpose of the World-Wide Web Wrapper Factory (W4F) toolkit that we propose to demonstrate here is the rapid design, generation, and integration in applications of such wrappers. Specifically, W4F's key features are: fully declarative specifications, light-weight components, rapid development, robustness, direct integration into Java programs and re-usability.

Proceedings of the 25th VLDB Conference, Edinburgh, Scotland, 1999.

This work is presented at an interesting time because of the on-going emergence of XML as a more application-friendly standard for Web pages. Some people have already argued that there is no more need for HTML wrappers because data sources will soon serve XML documents. In fact, there already are countless HTML pages on the Web and the information that many of them contain will have to be displayed in XML in a relatively near future. This demonstration will show that our W4F toolkit, among other things, is an efficient instrument for facilitating the migration from HTML to XML.

More generally, we believe light-weight HTML wrappers are currently indispensable for Web inter-operation and Web information integration. In particular, such wrappers turn out to be also an excellent testbed for the construction of smarter customized applications for e-commerce, digital libraries, etc.

1.2 Outline of the demonstration

To keep our demonstration focused, we will show how to build a wrapper for the the Internet Movie Database (IMDb) and create a *gateway* to serve these HTML pages as XML documents. First we will explain how to specify what information to extract from HTML pages using our wysiwyg extraction wizard and our extraction language. Then we will display and test the wrapper using our visual interface. The next step will be to define an XML mapping for the extracted information. Finally, we will deploy the wrapper as a standard CGI-based Web interface that serves transparently and on-the-fly HTML pages as XML documents with their corresponding DTD.

However, we hope that the demonstration will argue for the effectiveness of the toolkit on any Web data source and for a broader range of applications.

2 The W4F toolkit in a nutshell

W4F (World-Wide Web Wrapper Factory) is a toolkit to generate Web wrappers. Our wrappers consist of three independent layers: retrieval, extraction and mapping. The **retrieval layer** is in charge of fetching the HTML content from a Web data source. From the user's point of view it means to provide the location of the document. The **extraction layer** extracts the information from the document. It is important here to note that we can extract complex structures and not just atomic elements from the page. The user provides extraction rules to identify relevant pieces of information. The **mapping layer**'s role is to specify how to export the data.

A wrapper processes a Web source in the following way, as presented in Figure 1. An HTML document is first retrieved from the Web according to one or more retrieval rules. Once retrieved, the document is fed to an HTML parser that constructs a corresponding parse tree. Extraction rules are then applied on the parse tree and the extracted information is stored in our internal format.
Finally, information is mapped to structures exported by the wrapper to the upper-level application, according to mapping rules.

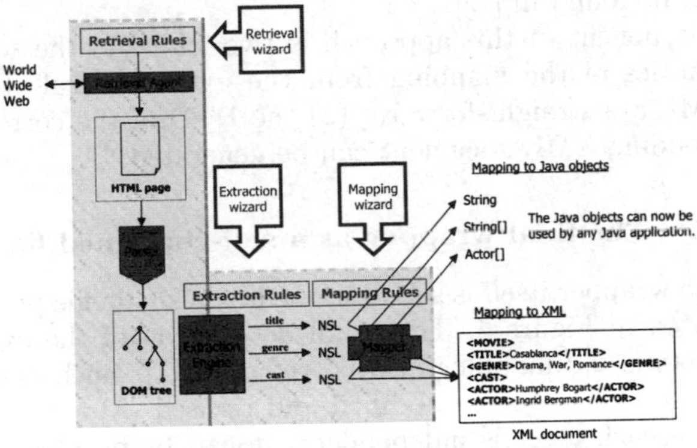

Figure 1: W4F information flow.

For the construction of the wrapper per-se, the toolkit provides a compiler that generates Java classes from a specification file, as well as some wizard applications to assist in the design of the wrapper layers.

2.1 HEL: HTML Extraction Language

A key feature of the toolkit is the HTML Extraction Language (HEL[11]) that permits a declarative specification of information extraction. HEL is a DOM-centric [13] language where an HTML document is represented as a labeled graph. It comes with two ways to navigate the tree. The first one follows the hierarchy of the document, implied by tags. This navigation is extremely useful in table-based documents for instance. The second one follows the flow of the document, i.e. a depth-first traversal of the document tree which corresponds to the way a document is read by a human. Using both navigation styles, most structures can be easily identified as extraction paths. To the best of our knowledge, HEL is the only language that captures both *dimensions* of a document.

The language also offers conditions and extraction features based on regular expressions à la Perl (like `match` and `split`). The first allow the definition of robust extraction rules where conditions are resolved at run-time, on a per document basis. The second permit to capture a finer granularity inside the document.

Moreover, the language has been designed to extract complex structures from HTML documents and not just isolated pieces. For instance, the language can extract *as a whole* a movie with its title, genre and cast (see Figure 3, using the "#" operator, a record constructor in a sense). The implicit structure of the document does not have to be reconstructed from scratch but is extracted as is.

2.2 NSL, our internal data-model

Another interesting aspect is that the extracted information is stored using an anonymous and language neutral representation called NSL *nested string lists* (NSL), the data-type defined by $NSL = null + string + listof(NSL)$. NSL can represent complex structures (unlimited level of nesting) and then be mapped easily to the desired data structure. The user can take advantage of an automatic mapping to Java base types (`String`, `int`, `float`, etc. and their array extensions); he can also provide his own Java classes by writing a valid constructor that consumes the NSL; finally he can specify XML mappings using the XML declarative specification. Some new mapping extensions are to be included in future releases of the toolkit.

3 The demonstration

The demonstration will go through the various steps of the building and deployment of a wrapper. As *advertised* in the introduction, we want to "wrap" the Internet Movie Database. IMDb is the biggest information repository about movies and is freely available. Its underlying information system is a big file system[1] that serves HTML pages.

3.1 Building a wrapper, step by step

Building a wrapper consists of the following steps:

1. define each layer (retrieval, extraction, mapping)
2. test
3. refine
4. compile the wrapper into a Java class
5. include the Java class as part of an application

The toolkit provides wizards to help the user write, test and refine the definition of the wrapper.

[1] See http://www.imdb.com/interfaces#plain for more details.

3.2 Defining extraction rules using the extraction wizard

The most critical part of the design of the wrapper is the definition of extraction rules. The role of the extraction wizard (see Figure 2) is to help the user write such rules. Instead of forcing the user to mess up with the HTML code, W4F adopts an annotation approach.
For a given HTML document, the wizard feeds it into W4F and returns the document to the user with some invisible annotations (the document appears exactly as the original).

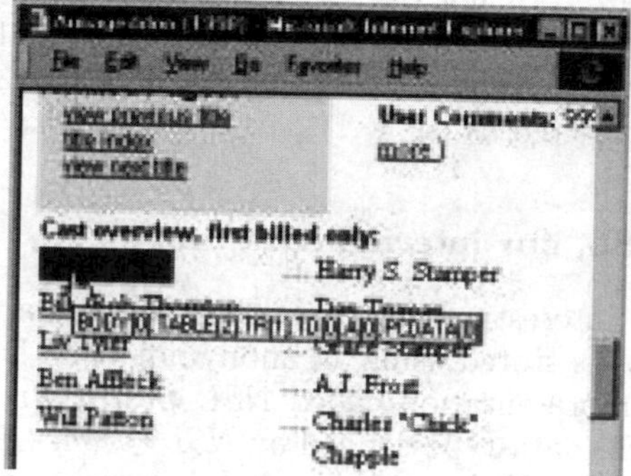

Figure 2: the extraction wizard.

On Figure 2, when the user points to "Bruce Willis", the corresponding text element gets highlighted and the canonical[2] extraction rules pops-up. Even if the wizard is not capable of providing the best extraction rule, it is always a good start. Compare what is returned by the wizard and what we actually use in our wrapper (figures 2 and 4).

3.3 Testing

Figure 3 presents the wizard (a Java applet here) that assists the user when writing and testing the wrapper. The applet layout represents the 3-layer architecture of the wrapper.

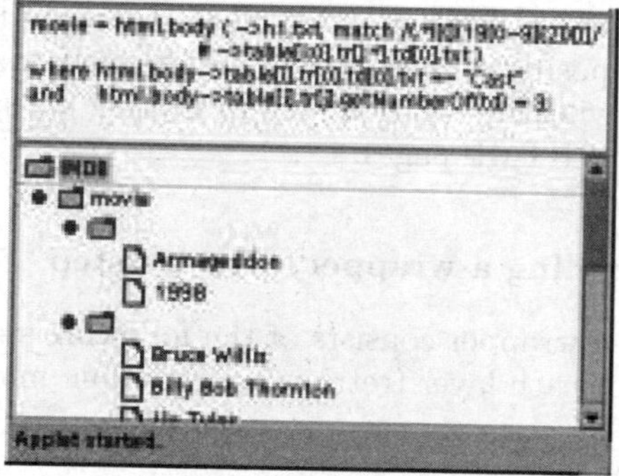

Figure 3: a visual view of a wrapper with its 3 layers.

The top layer (not presented on the screen shot) represents the location of the Web source.

[2]By canonical we mean that it uses only hierarchy based navigation.

The middle layer displays the extraction rule – expressed in the HEL language – to be applied on the retrieved HTML page. In this example, the rule will extract the title, the year and the cast of the movie (list of actors).
The bottom layer represents the structure of the information extracted as an NSL data-structure. This is the default mapping exported by the toolkit.

3.4 Refining with a mapping to XML

The NSL structure extracted from the HTML pages can be used as is – the toolkit provides printing methods – or can be mapped to other data structures. For our target application, we can take advantage of a declarative specification for an XML mapping (see figure 4). This XML mapping is very close to the corresponding extraction rule (it can be seen as an annotation of the extraction or a template). Strings indicate tag or attributes names; dots indicate tag nesting; "#" indicate concatenation; "*" indicates lists; "^" indicates that the value as to be used as an attribute of the parent tag. The full details of the XML mapping can be found in [12].
The benefit of this approach is two-fold: (1) the semantics of the mapping from the extraction-rule to XML are straight-forward; (2) the DTD of the corresponding XML document can be generated.

3.5 The final wrapper as a self-contained file

The wrapper itself is self described by a single file presented in Figure 4. For a full description of the extraction and mapping syntax, refer to [11]. Such files can later be copied, modified and re-used. Moreover, since each layer is independent, it can be developed separately and replaced later on.

```
EXTRACTION_RULES ::
movie = html.body(
  ->h1.txt, match/(.*?) [(]/                                    // title
# ->h1.txt, match/.*?[(]([0-9]+)[)]/                            // year
# ->td[i:0].a[*].txt                                            // list of genre
# ->table[ii:0].tr[jj:*].td[0].txt, match/(\S+)\s(.*)/  // first, last name
                 )
where html.body->td[i].b[0].txt = "Genre"
and   html.body->table[ii].tr[0].td[0].txt =~ "Cast"
and   html.body->table[ii].tr[jj].getNumberOf(td) = 3;
}

XML_MAPPING ::
movie_XML_template = .Movie ( .TITLE^
                   # .YEAR^
                   # .CATEGORIES*.Genre
                   # .ACTORS*.Actor ( .FN # .LN )
                          );
```

Figure 4: `IMDB.w4f`, the wrapper description file.

The wrapper description file `IMDB.w4f` is then compiled into a Java class `IMDB.class` (less than 5 kb)[3] that can be used as a stand-alone application or integrated into another Java application.

For the XML-Gateway service, the only thing we have to do is to make the wrapper available as a CGI

[3]The footprint of the entire W4F package is less than 200kb.

script. The result of the migration from HTML to XML is presented in Figure 5.

```
<?xml version="1.0" encoding="ISO-8859-1"?>
<!DOCTYPE W4F_DOC [
  <!ELEMENT W4F_DOC (MOVIE)>
  <!ELEMENT MOVIE (CATEGORIES,ACTORS)>
  <!ATTLIST MOVIE
     TITLE CDATA #IMPLIED
     YEAR CDATA #IMPLIED>
  <!ELEMENT CATEGORIES (GENRE)*>
  <!ELEMENT GENRE (#PCDATA)>
  <!ELEMENT ACTORS (ACTOR)*>
  <!ELEMENT ACTOR (FN,LN)>
  <!ELEMENT FN (#PCDATA)>
  <!ELEMENT LN (#PCDATA)>
]>
<W4F_DOC>
  <MOVIE TITLE="Armageddon" YEAR="1998">
    <CATEGORIES>
      <GENRE>Action</GENRE>
      <GENRE>Sci-Fi</GENRE>
      <GENRE>Thriller</GENRE>
    </CATEGORIES>
    <ACTORS>
      <ACTOR> <FN>Bruce</FN> <LN>Willis</LN> </ACTOR>
      <ACTOR> <FN>Billy</FN> <LN>Bob Thornton</LN>
...
```

Figure 5: the XML document generated on-the-fly.

4 Conclusion

Wrapper construction is a key issue in the implementation of mediator-based architectures. And with more and more data sources being available on the Web, it is important to have a convenient framework to build, test and deploy such wrappers in order to make the content of Web sources directly available to applications.

In this demonstration, by using the W4F toolkit we have managed to build quickly a wrapper for a large HTML-based Web data source and deploy it as a gateway that serves on-the-fly these pages as XML documents.

The main contributions of W4F are: (1) Wrappers are split into 3 separate layers. (2) The description of a wrapper is fully declarative. (3) Entire structures can be extracted from HTML pages and not just single "atomic" pieces. (4) The toolkit comes with visual wizards to help the user define extraction rules and test the wrapper before deployment. (5) Generated wrappers are ready to be integrated in any Java application.

Compared to other approaches [8, 9], we do not use a grammar-based approach for extraction but rely on the DOM object-model, which gives us for free some wysiwyg visual tools like [1].

With rich features like hierarchical and flow-based navigations, conditions and nested constructs, our extraction language is more expressive and robust than [6, 2]. Unlike [3], we do not try to query the Web but simply extract structure from Web information sources: querying is the concern of the application.

In W4F, we do not address problems that are specific to mediators but we believe that our wrappers can be easily included into existing integration systems like TSIMMIS [7], Kleisli [5], Garlic [10], etc. W4F is already used by the K2 [4] mediation system.

The toolkit is freely available from the Penn Database Research Group web site [4]. On-line examples of W4F applications (including the wrapper presented here) can be found at the same location.

References

[1] Brad Adelberg. NoDoSE – A Tool for Semi-Automatically Extracting Semi-Structured Data from Text. In *Proc. of the SIGMOD Conference*, Seattle, June 1998.

[2] Charles Allen. WIDL: Application Integration with XML. *World Wide Web Journal*, 2(4), November 1997.

[3] Gustavo Arocena and Alberto Mendelzon. WebOQL: Restructuring Documents, Databases, and Webs. In *Proc. ICDE'98*, Orlando, February 1998.

[4] Johnatan Crabtree, Scott Harker, and Val Tannen. K2. http://www.cbil.upenn.edu:8089/K2/k2web?page=home.

[5] Susan Davidson, Christian Overton, Val Tannen, and Limsoon Wong. Biokleisli: A digital library for biomedical researchers. *Journal of Digital Libraries*, 1(1):36–53, November 1996.

[6] Jean-Robert Gruser, Louiqa Raschid, M. E. Vidal, and L. Bright. Wrapper Generation for Web Accessible Data Sources. In *COOPIS*, 1998.

[7] J. Hammer, H. Garcia-Molina, J. Cho, R. Aranha, and A. Crespo. Extracting Semistructured Information from the Web. In *Proceedings of the Workshop on Management of Semistructured Data. Tucson, Arizona*, May 1997.

[8] Gerald Huck, Peter Fankhauser, Karl Aberer, and Erich J. Neuhold. JEDI: Extracting and Synthesizing Information from the Web. In *COOPIS*, New-York, 1998.

[9] G. Mecca, P. Atzeni, P. Merialdo, A. Masci, and G. Sindoni. From Databases to Web-Bases: The ARANEUS Experience. Technical Report RT-DIA-34-1998, Universita Degli Studi Di Roma Tre, May 1998.

[10] Mary Tork Roth and Peter Schwartz. A Wrapper Architecture for Legacy Data Sources. Technical Report RJ10077, IBM Almaden Research Center, 1997.

[11] Arnaud Sahuguet and Fabien Azavant. W4F, 1998. http://db.cis.upenn.edu/W4F.

[12] Arnaud Sahuguet and Fabien Azavant. Web Ecology: Recycling HTML pages as XML documents using W4F. In *WebDB'99*, 1999.

[13] World Wide Web Consortium (W3C). The Document Object Model, 1998. http://www.w3.org/DOM.

[4] http://db.cis.upenn.edu/W4F

XML repository and Active Views Demonstration

S. Abiteboul, V. Aguilera,
S. Ailleret, B. Amann,
S. Cluet, B. Hills,
F. Hubert, A. Marian,
L. Mignet, B. Tessier.
A.M. Vercoustre

INRIA/Verso
Rocquencourt, France

J.C. Mamou, C. Souza

ArdentSoftware
Denver, Colorado

T. Milo

Computer Science Dept.
Univ. of Tel. Aviv

1 Overview

The goal of this demonstration is to present the main features of (i) Axielle, an XML repository developed by Ardent Software [3] on top of the O_2 object-oriented DBMS and (ii) the ActiveView system which has been built by the Verso project at INRIA [1] on top of Axielle.

The demonstration is based on a simple electronic commerce application which will be described in Section 2. Electronic commerce is emerging as a major Web-supported application. It involves handling and exchange of data (e.g. product catalogs, yellow pages, etc.) and must provide (i) database functionalities (query language, transactions, concurrency control, distribution and recovery) for the efficient management of large data volumes and hundreds of users as well as (ii) standard data storage and exchange formats (e.g. XML, SGML) for the easy integration of existing software and data.

The ActiveView system combined with the Axielle XML repository enables a fast deployment of electronic commerce applications based on a new high-level *declarative* specification language (AVL), advanced database technology (object-oriented data model, XML query language, notifications), Web standards (HTTP, HTML) and other Internet compliant technologies (Java, RMI).

The prime motivations for building on the emerging XML technology are that XML will be a standard for exchanging semi-/structured information over the Internet and will be supported by many software components in form of compilers, import/export filters, query interfaces and sophisticated editors and browsers. Besides the usage of an XML repository, the ActiveView system integrates a number of other modern database technology:

XML Views: Typically, in electronic commerce application there exists different kinds of users who access data with different points of view depending on their access rights and on the nature of the activity they are presently involved in. These aspects of ActiveViews are built on our experience with O_2-Views [5], a system we developed at INRIA. Roughly speaking, we modified O_2Views by (i) considering XML data and query languages and (ii) adding sophisticated access and update facilities.

Active databases: An active database is a database that can respond to certain *events* according to certain *triggers*. Very sophisticated active mechanisms have been proposed with modest success in industry. (Some database systems provide limited triggering mechanisms.) Electronic commerce applications are, by nature, very active, e.g., when a new order is received a number of actions may have to be started. We introduce active features in a somewhat minimal way based on a notification mechanism and a rule manager.

Although we primarily target electronic commerce applications, our approach can obviously be applied to

Proceedings of the 25th VLDB Conference, Edinburgh, Scotland, 1999.

a wide range of other applications involving (i) sharing of data and (ii) cooperation of a number of actors connected via a network.

2 Demonstration

2.1 A Simple E-Commerce Application

The demonstrated electronic commerce application involves several types of *actors*, i.e. a customer, a vendor, a dispatcher. It also manages a significant amount of *data* :

- a products catalog provided by CAMIF, a French company specialized in mail-order business,
- a list of promotions information (typically viewed by customers and updated by vendors),
- the list of current customers and available vendors (used by the dispatcher).

Each of the actors *view* different parts of the data (e.g. each of the customers can see only their own orders and the promotions relevant to their class, while vendors view all the orders and promotions), each may perform different *actions* on the data, and have different *access rights* (e.g. promotions can be updated only by certain vendors). Also, the *'freshness'* of data may differ, e.g. when promotions are updated, the customers screen is immediately updated by the new data, while refresh of catalog portions viewed by customers are deferred until explicit requests.

The activity of each of the actors consists of several *sub-tasks*, e.g. a customer can *search* the catalog, *order* some selected item, *change* an existing order. Observe that each of these sub-tasks requires only part of the data and actions available for the given actor, and that the same piece of data can be used in several not necessarily consecutive sub-tasks, e.g. the *search* task queries catalog while the *order* and *change order* activities use the orders list and add, or update, resp., elements to the list.

Finally, actions performed by an actor in a certain task may initiate other tasks of the same actor (e.g. a 'perform search' action in the customer's *search* subtask may query the catalog and then move the customer to the *order* sub-task where he can view the selected items and order them), or effect other actors (e.g. when a vendor updates a promotion, the screen of the relevant customers is refreshed). The system may also want to log some of the actors operations, providing a *trace* for later analysis.

2.2 Demonstration Architecture

The ActiveView system uses Ardent Software's XML repository that provides all the usual database features such as persistency, versioning, concurrency control, etc. All data stored, exchanged and viewed by users are XML data which are accessed by a standard DOM [6] API. The system is based on a client/server architecture. An Active View application consists of several independent clients communicating among themselves and with the repository server through notifications. Clients are programmed in Java and communicate with the server using the DOM interface.

Figure 1 shows the various components of the demonstrated application (obviously, several such applications may run simultaneously on the same server).

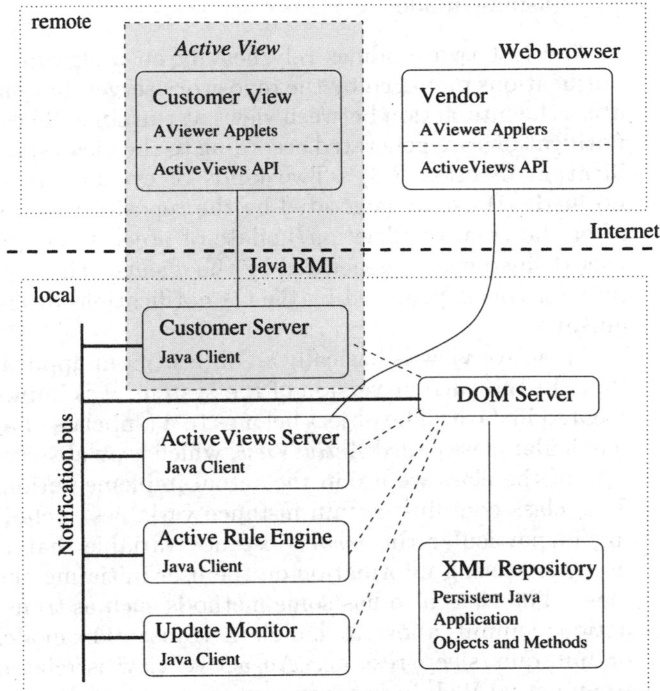

Figure 1: Demonstration Architecture

The active view application manager consists of a set of modules managing: (i) connection and authentication, (ii) tracing, (iii) update propagation and (iv) active rules. More precisely:

1. The connection/authentication module is in charge of authenticating users and giving them the means to create[1] or quit a view (via the network). Whereas we currently use a simple internal authentication mechanism, the integration of external authentication services is straightforward and outside the scope of the demonstration.
2. The update monitor propagates update events generated by the XML repository. Essentially, it transforms primitive update events (modification of a DOM node) into higher-level events concern-

[1] An active view is started from the Web using a particular URL. The system provides a form asking for the name of the system, the name of the view application, and the type of the view.

ing the modification of query results (views) and XML documents used by other components.

3. The tracing module keeps a log of specified events. These events are generated by the application or by some views.

4. The active rule module manages a programmer-specified set of rules. These rules are fired according to events and may have impact on the repository and on some or all of the active views. They form the essential components to specify a business model.

The last two modules rely heavily on a stream of notifications managed by the repository server that enables the interaction between views at run time. These notifications are generated according to the views specification (Section 2.3). Two kinds of events can be notified: (i) events generated by the repository server after the creation/deletion/update of objects and (ii) user defined events generated by the clients. The support for this is provided by the O_2 notifications mechanism.

An active view is basically an object of our application. In the current version of the system, it is implemented in Java. The object belongs to a (subclass of a) particular class called *ActiveView*, which is an abstraction of the class we use in the actual implementation. This class contains certain instance variables, including in particular the *owner* instance variable that is used for storing information on the user initiating the view. The class also has some methods such as transaction/commit/abort to handle a transaction mode, or init/quit/sleep/resume. An active view is related to an actual Web browser opened by a user of the system. Some views independent of any interface may also be introduced, e.g., for bookkeeping. An active view has access to the repository as well as to some local data (the instance variables of the view object). It reacts to user commands and may be refreshed according to notifications sent by the server or the view manager. The methods available on a view depend on the users access rights and may allow him/her to read, load, write, etc. part or the whole the data it sees.

The demonstrated user interfaces are implemented as HTML documents with embedded Java applets (see Figure 2). Our goal is to switch to XML as soon as XML browser supports the needed dynamic features. By default, for each activity and user there exists one HTML page. The embedded applets are built on top of an API generated by the system according to the view specification. Although the system generates default interfaces, the application programmer may redefine/customize them using the generated API that captures the semantics of the application.

The repository server, the active views and the corresponding interfaces run on different machines. Typically, the interface corresponds actually to some Web browser on any PC connected to the Internet. The view data is obtained by check-in/check-out, so repository changes are not in general immediately propagated to the view although they can be propagated, if specified by the programmer. On the other hand, the view and the interface see the same data.

2.3 Specification Language and Application Generator

The above application can be specified in the high-level ActiveView Language (AVL) [1] we have defined for describing electronic commerce applications. Acting as an application generator, the Active View system can then generate an actual application that captures the semantics of the above specification and allows the different users to work interactively on the specified data for performing the given set of controlled activities.

AVL specifications are given to a compiler that uses information stored in the repository to generate: (i) an Active View manager (unique per application), (ii) a set of active views, and (iii) users interfaces. An Active View specification is a declarative description of applications of the above nature. It specifies, for each of the actor types participating in the application,

1. the data and operations available to this particular actor and these with a sophisticate access control. The specification of the view is based on AVQL, a query language for XML we have implemented in the spirit of Lorel [2] and XML-QL [4].

2. the kinds of activities this actor may be engaged in and the subset of data and operations available in each;

3. some active rules that notably specify the sequencing of activities (a *workflow* component) but also the events this actor wants to be notified of (a *subscription* component) and those that have to be logged (a *tracing* component).

References

[1] S. Abiteboul, B. Amann, S. Cluet, A. Eyal, L. Mignet, and T. Milo. Active views for electronic commerce. In *Int. Conf. on Very Large DataBases (VLDB)*, Edinburgh, Scotland, September 1999.

[2] S. Abiteboul, D. Quass, J. McHugh, J. Widom, and J. L. Wiener. The Lorel query language for semistructured data. *International Journal on Digital Libraries*, 1(1), April 1997.

[3] Ardent Software. *http://www.ardentsoftware.com.*

[4] A. Deutsch, M. Fernandez, D. Florescu, A. Levy, and D. Suciu. Xml-ql: A query language for xml. http://www.w3.org/TR/NOTE-xml-ql/.

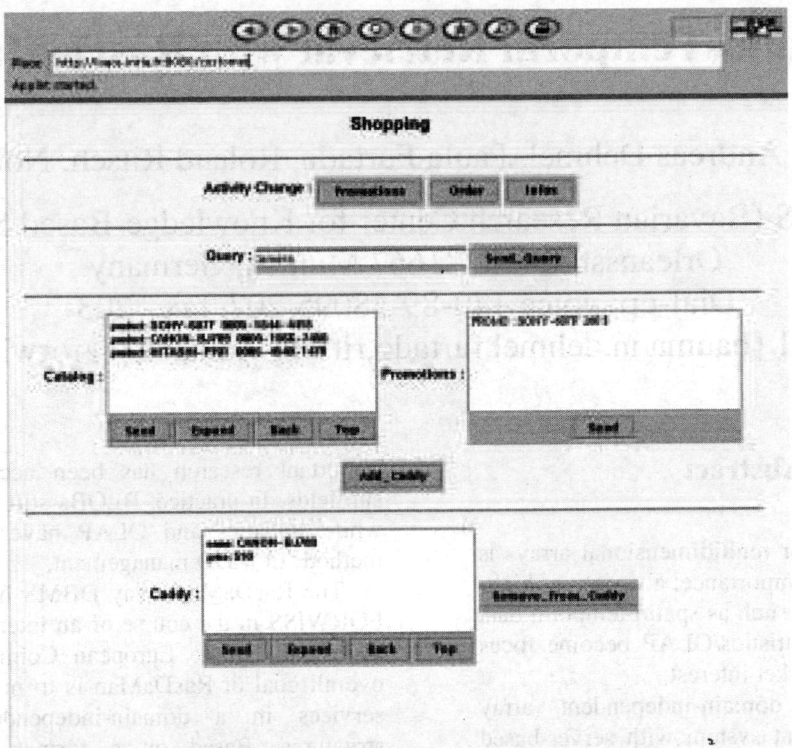

Figure 2: Example: The client user interface

[5] C. Souza, S. Abiteboul, and C. Delobel. Virtual schemas and bases. In *Proc. EDBT, Cambridge*, 1994.

[6] W3C. Document Object Model (DOM). http://-www.w3.org/DOM.

Spatio-Temporal Retrieval with RasDaMan

Peter Baumann, Andreas Dehmel, Paula Furtado, Roland Ritsch, Norbert Widmann

FORWISS (Bavarian Research Center for Knowledge-Based Systems)
Orleansstr.34, D-81667 Munich, Germany
Dial-up: voice +49-89-48095-207, fax - 203
E-Mail {baumann,dehmel,furtado,ritsch,widmann}@forwiss.de

Abstract

Database support for multidimensional arrays is an area of growing importance; a variety of high-volume applications such as spatio-temporal data management and statistics/OLAP become focus of academic and market interest.

RasDaMan is a domain-independent array database management system with server-based query optimization and evaluation. The system is fully operational and being used in international projects. We will demonstrate spatio-temporal retrieval using the rView visual query client. Examples will encompass 1-D time series, 2-D images, 3-D and 4-D voxel data. The real-life data sets used stem from life sciences, geo sciences, numerical simulation, and climate research.

1. System Overview

Arrays of arbitrary size and dimension, so-called Multidimensional Discrete Data (MDD), appear in a multitude of database applications; natural sciences, OLAP and statistics, and multimedia comprise but a few representative fields. It is estimated that the larger part of digital data stored worldwide belongs to the MDD category. Nevertheless, MDD are not comprehensively understood by database research as of today, although important research has been accomplished in several subfields. In practice, BLOBs still prevail in multimedia, while statistics and OLAP have developed their own methods of MDD management.

The RasDaMan array DBMS has been developed by FORWISS in the course of an international project partly sponsored by the European Commission [Bau97]. The overall goal of RasDaMan is to provide classic database services in a domain-independent way on MDD structures. Based on a formal algebraic framework [Bau99], RasDaMan offers a query language [Bau98a], which extends SQL-92 [ISO92] with declarative MDD operators, and an ODMG 2.0 conformant programming interface [Cat96]. Server-based query evaluation provides several optimization techniques and a specialized storage manager. The latter combines MDD tiling with spatial indexing and compression whereby an administration interface allows to change default strategies for application-driven database tuning [Fur99]. Array sets resulting from queries are delivered in the client's main memory format or in some a data exchange format as selected by the application.

Research on array data management in DBMSs usually focuses on particular system components, such as storage of multidimensional data [Sar94], or query language [Mar97]. RasDaMan, on the other hand, is a fully implemented and operational generic array DBMSs. This makes it a unique opportunity to study all aspects of multidimensional data management in a holistic way, thereby augmenting focused research done elsewhere.

In [Bau98b] RasDaMan has been demonstrated in combination with the object-oriented database system O2 [Ban92]. This time, RasDaMan will be coupled with Oracle, thereby showing the interoperability capabilities with both relational and object-oriented systems and giving insight into the interworking of RasDaMan and Oracle. Additionally, advanced physical storage tuning, including various array decomposition techniques and transparent compression, will be demonstrated the first time.

Proceedings of the 25th VLDB Conference, Edinburgh, Scotland, 1999.

1.1 Conceptual Model

The conceptual model of RasDaMan centers around the notion of an n-D array (in the programming language sense) which can be of any dimension, size, and array cell type (for the C++ binding, this means that valid C++ types or structs are admissible). Each dimension's lower and upper bound can be fixed at data definition time, or can be left variable. Type definition is done through the RasDaMan definition language, RasDL, which is based on ODMG ODL.

The RasDaMan query language, RasQL, consists of MDD primitives embedded in ODMG's OQL; as usual, a SELECT statement returns a homogeneous set of items. Array expressions can be used in the SELECT part to modify the selected elements, and they can be used in the WHERE part to search for arrays with particular properties. The expressive power of RasQL allows to state operations up to the complexity of the Discrete Fourier transformation [Bun93]. Recursive operations (such as determinants or matrix inversion) are not supported to obtain a language which is safe in evaluation. Nevertheless, this enables a wide range of statistical, imaging, and OLAP operations. The underlying array algebra is described in detail in [Bau99].

1.2 Storage Management

RasDaMan employs a storage structure for MDD which is based on the subdivision of an MDD object into arbitrary tiles, i.e., possibly non-aligned subarrays, combined with a spatial index to accelerate access to the tile subset affected by a query. A choice of different tiling strategies under control of the database administrator or an application programmer serves to accommodate different query patterns. Support of arbitrary tiling is one of the distinguishing features of RasDaMan. The tiling strategies supported lead to performance increases of access operations to MDD objects, as they allow tuning of tiling to different types of retrieval. The following tiling strategies have been implemented: directional tiling which optimizes accesses along given dimension categories, tiling according to areas of interest which optimizes access to a given set of query regions, and statistical tiling which optimizes access given the statistics of access to an MDD object. These reflect different application requirements regarding types of access. The underlying tiling algorithms minimize the amount of data read for the most frequent accesses, thus reducing execution time. In [Fur99] these algorithms are described and performance comparisons against other tiling strategies are presented which are based on measurements on 3-D data cubes with different tile sizes. Average performance increases of 200% have been observed compared to the performance of regular tiling.

1.3 Query Processing

Demands on Array Query Processing (AQP) differ essentially from the ones on standard Relational Query Processing.(RQP): With RQP, tuples are very small compared to relation size and operations on single tuples (e.g., string comparison) are very inexpensive wrt. CPU costs. The main effort has to be spent on processing large sets of tuples. In contrast, single MDD objects already can reach the scale of Gigabytes, and MDD operations, such as consolidation in OLAP datacubes, become extremely complex and time consuming.

On the logical level, RasDaMan applies a specialized rewriting heuristic based on about 150 algebraic transformation rules derived from MDD operations, relational operations, and their combinations to construct optimized expressions wrt. evaluation performance and memory usage. Examples for such rules are "pull out disjunctions while aggregating cell values of an MDD using logical or" and "push down geometric operations to the expressions' leaves". The latter rule ensures that just the minimal amount of data necessary to compute the result of the query branch is read from the storage manager. Further, the query tree is searched for common MDD subexpressions. Beyond conventional subexpression matching, the spatial domains are checked for overlapping regions which have to be loaded and computed only once. The choice of physical algorithms, finally, is driven by indexing and tiling information. For instance, if an operation does not prescribe any particular tile inspection sequence, iteration order will be chosen corresponding to storage order. The tile-based execution strategy pipelines the execution process on the level of tiles whenever possible in order to reduce memory requirements for intermediate results and to obtain a high pipelining degree. Due to associativity and commutativity of most cell operations, there is a huge potential for parallelization which will be incorporated in future versions of RasDaMan.

1.4 Architecture

The RasDaMan API consists of *RasQL* and the C++ Raster Library (*RasLib*) which serves for the integration of the MDD type into the C++ language. To make MDD persistent, RasDaMan follows the ODMG-2.0 standard through providing a smart pointer which behaves like a normal C++ pointer capable of managing transient and persistent data in a transparent way.

The cross-platform client-server architecture is realized through standard remote procedure calls. The server architecture consists of the modules *Query Evaluator*, *Index Manager*, *Catalog Manager*, and *Tile Manager*. The *Query Evaluator* parses the query and builds an operator based query tree. Then query optimization takes place in two steps. First, algebraic query rewriting is done, then physical optimization based on tiling and clustering information takes place. The

Query Evaluator is tile-based, operations on MDD items are decomposed into operations on tiles. To identify the tiles involved in a query and to calculate the costs to retrieve them, the *Index Manager* is consulted. The *Catalog Manager* takes care of schema information specified through RasDL. The final execution plan is evaluated by retrieving tile sets from the *Tile Manager* and applying elementary image operations, e.g. spatial or induced operations, on them. An interface layer between RasDaMan modules and the base DBMS, the *Storage Management Interface*, is responsible for the storage and access to all data in persistent storage. This prepares RasDaMan for easy portability between different base DBMSs and storage systems. RasDaMan is implemented in C++ and runs under several Unix versions as well as Windows NT; heterogeneous client/server environments are supported. The server interfaces with the object-oriented DBMS O2 and with relational systems.

2 Demonstration

We will demonstrate RasDaMan using the visual frontend rView, a C++ RasDaMan client, to interactively submit RasQL queries and display result sets containing 1-D to 3-D data. The system will run in a client/server environment with a Unix server and a Unix or Windows NT client. Demonstration will rely on the following data sets: 1-D time series, a 2-D Digital Elevation Model (DEM), 3-D volume CAT scans, a 3-D movie clip, the 3-D Visible Human [Nat90], a 3-D thermal flow simulation result, and a 4-D climate data set. If Internet access can be provided, wide-area queries to our Munich server will be shown.

2.1 RasQL Operations Overview

Demonstration will start by showing sample retrieval, thereby introducing basic RasQL concepts. Queries will encompass both search and array manipulation operations; examples will range from 1-D to 4-D, showing in particular how cross-dimensional queries work.

2.2 Effectivity of query optimization

Next, selected queries will serve to demonstrate the effect of several algebraic rewriting rules. This allows to discuss how they contribute to overall performance.

2.3 Tiling strategies

Finally, implications of physical data organization will be presented. To this end, a sample 3-D volume tomogram and an animation sequence is stored with different tiling strategies. A particular administrator tool allows to visually inspect the tiling of MDD instances. Queries such as sub-cube extraction and cuts along the three different space axes clearly indicate strengths and weaknesses of particular tiling schemata. Various tiling strategies should be offered as a database tuning tool similar to indexes on tables in relational DBMS for optimal query performance.

References

[Ban92] F. Bancilhon, C. Delobel, P. Kanellakis: *Building an Object-Oriented Database System.* Morgan Kaufmann Publishers, San Mateo, CA, 1992.

[Bau97] P. Baumann, P. Furtado, R. Ritsch, N. Widmann: Geo/Environmental and Medical Data Management in the RasDaMan System. *Proc. of the VLDB'97 Conference*, Athens, Greece, 1997.

[Bau98a] P. Baumann: *The RasDaMan Array Algebra.* RasDaMan Technical Report for012, FORWISS, 1998.

[Bau98b] P. Baumann, A. Dehmel, P. Furtado, R. Ritsch, N. Widmann: The Multidimensional Database System RasDaMan. *Proc. ACM SIGMOD'98*, Seattle, USA 1998, pp. 575 - 577.

[Bau99] P. Baumann: An Algebra for Domain-Independent Multidimensional Array Management in Databases. RasDaMan Technical Report for016, 1999.

[Bun93] P. Buneman: The Discrete Fourier Transform as a Database Query. *Technical Report MS-CIS-93-37/L&C 60*, University of Pennsylvania, 1993.

[Cat96] R. Cattell: *The Object Database Standard: ODMG-93.* Morgan Kaufmann Publishers, 1996.

[Fur99] P. Furtado, P. Baumann: Storage of Multidimensional Arrays Based on Arbitrary Tiling. *Proc. ICDE'99*, Sidney - Australia 1999.

[ISO92] The International Organization for Standardization (ISO): *Database Language SQL.* ISO 9075, 1992(E), 1992.

[Mar97] A. P. Marathe, K. Salem: A Language for Manipulating Arrays. *Proc. of VLDB'97 Conference*, Athens, Greece, 1997.

[Nat90] National Library of Medicine (US) Board of Regents: *Electronic Imaging: Report of the Board of Regents.* US Department of Health and Human Services, Public Health Service, National Institutes of Health, NIH Publication 90-2197, 1990.

[Sar94] S. Sarawagi, M. Stonebraker: Efficient Organization of Large Multidimensional Arrays. *Tenth Int. Conf on Data Engineering*, pp. 328-336, Houston, Feb. 1994.

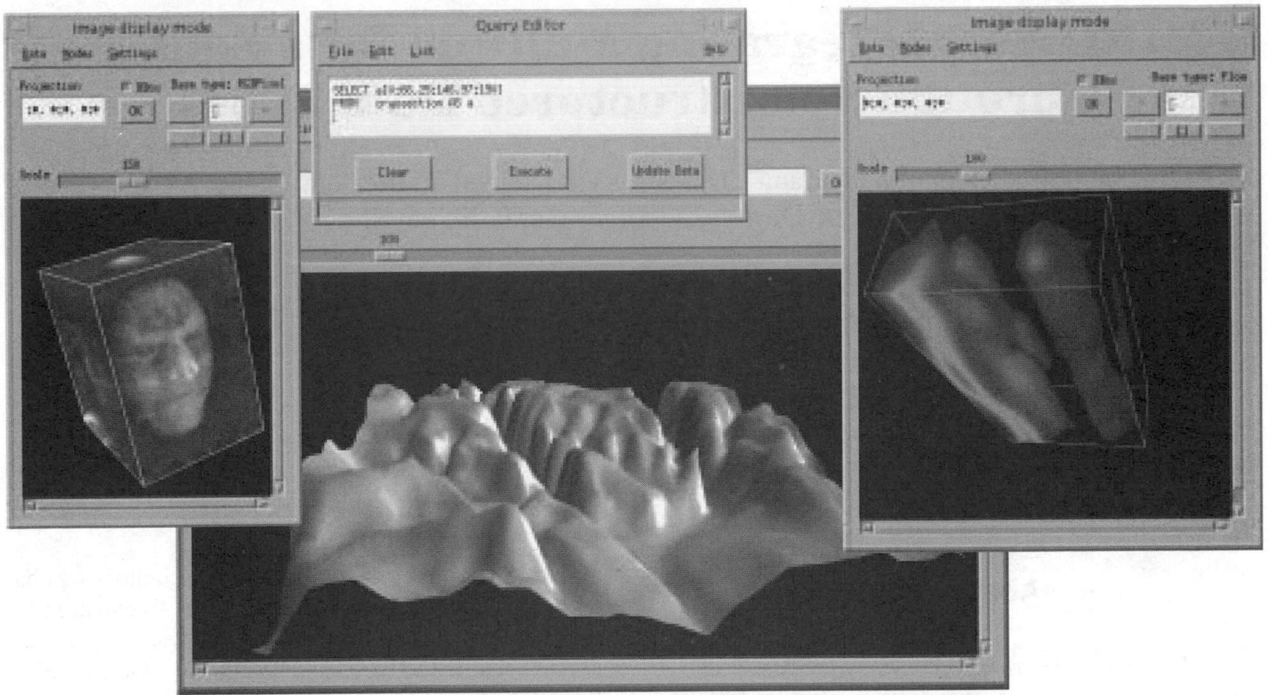

Figure 1: Sample MDD visualization using rView. The image to the top left shows a volume rendering of a section of the Visible Human obtained with the query displayed to its right. Top right and background images visualize a climate data set and a DEM of the Grand Canyon, respectively.

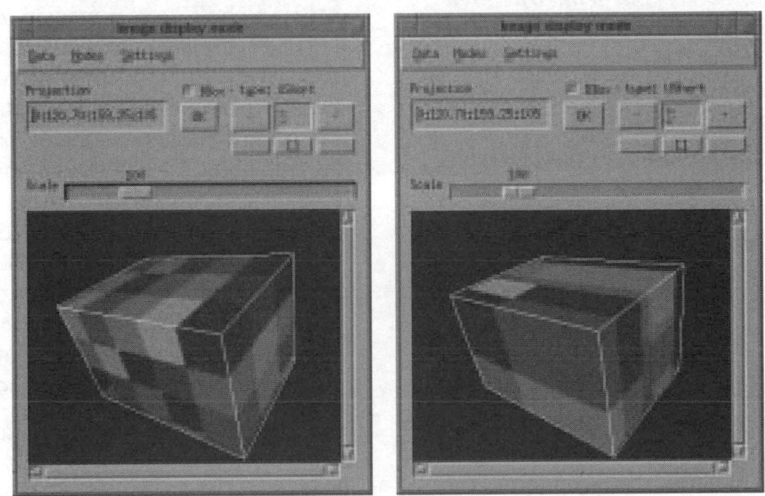

Figure 2: Visualization of different tiling strategies of a3-D movie sequence with rView: regular tiling (left) and areas of interest resulting in nonaligned tiles (right).

MIROWeb: Integrating Multiple Data Sources Through Semistructured Data Types

Luc Bouganim, Tatiana Chan-Sine-Ying, Tuyet-Tram Dang-Ngoc,
Jean-Luc Darroux, Georges Gardarin, Fei Sha

MIROWeb Research Group, PRiSM Laboratory
University of Versailles Saint-Quentin
78035 Versailles Cedex, France
<Firstname>.<name>@prism.uvsq.fr

Abstract

The MIROWeb Esprit project has developed a unique technology to integrate multiple data sources through an object-relational model with semistructured data types. It addresses the problem of integrating irregular Web sources and regular relational databases through a mediated architecture based on a hybrid model, supporting relational, object and semistructured features. The project data exchange format is XML, the new standard of the Web, and the pivot language is XMLQL, a query language based on XML templates from AT&T. The demonstration will show the data warehousing approach for mediation, based on Oracle 8 and a semistructured cartridge developed in the project for supporting XML and XMLQL queries.

1. Introduction

Most distributed heterogeneous DBMSs adopt the so-called mediation architecture to federate multiple data sources. They integrate data from multiple heterogeneous sources and provide users with uniform integrated views of data. While the first generation of mediators was based on the relational model, the second was founded on some variations of the object model. It was illustrated by projects as IRO-DB [1], DISCO [2], Garlic [3] and Information Manifold [4]. A new generation, under development, uses a semistructured data model for dealing with the heterogeneity of the data sources. TSIMMIS [5] and YAT [6] are good representatives of this new trend.

Capitalizing on the previous IRO-DB experience, MIROWeb [7] uses a mediation architecture based on the object-relational model enhanced with a semistructured data type. With this approach, sources are modeled as tables with possibly semistructured attributes. Instances of those attributes are modeled as labeled directed graphs. Atomic objects are stored in object-relational tables. They contain values from one of the primitive object-relational types such as integer, real, string or user defined data types. They can be referenced as graph leaves of semistructured instances. This powerful yet simple model gives MIROWeb the capability of supporting both structured and non-structured data. It also greatly simplifies the development of source wrappers.

The choice of the object-relational model extended with semistructured objects as pivot model requires the use of a powerful object-relational DBMS at the mediator layer to integrate the data. The MIROWeb mediator is based on Oracle 8 which acts as the integration platform. Oracle 8 has been extended with a semistructured data type through the development of a Java cartridge to support semistructured objects.

To query semistructured objects, two solutions at least were possible: either build specific methods inside SQL3 or use a new query language more general than SQL3. MIROWeb retains the second alternative and chooses XMLQL [8] as pivot query language. Thus, any query

Proceedings of the 25th VLDB Conference, Edinburgh, Scotland, 1999.

exchanged between clients and mediators are XMLQL queries. Answers are XML documents. At the source layer, tables and complex objects (*e.g.,* HTML files) are translated in tables with XML attributes. At the mediator layer, XML documents are stored in tables with semistructured attributes. The mediator receives XMLQL queries from clients, decomposes them in XMLQL queries addressed to wrappers or in SQL queries for Oracle 8. Results are loaded in and processed by Oracle 8 extended with the semistructured cartridge. They are then transformed in XML to be sent to clients.

The demonstration will show the MIROWeb project in action on a toy integrated database. The database is derived from multiple sources: relational data, XML data and HTML files. Using the wrappers and loaders, the data will be loaded in Oracle 8 and its semistructured component. Then, through the user interfaces, we will browse and query the data in a uniform way using XMLQL.

2. System Architecture

As most mediation systems, MIROWeb is composed of three layers: client, mediator, and source. The client provides a *Query Browser* and a *Java API*. The mediator is based on Oracle 8. It includes the *Message Manager* to handle client-server protocols, the *Query Decomposer* and the *Semistructured Cartridge*. The system architecture is shown in Figure 1.

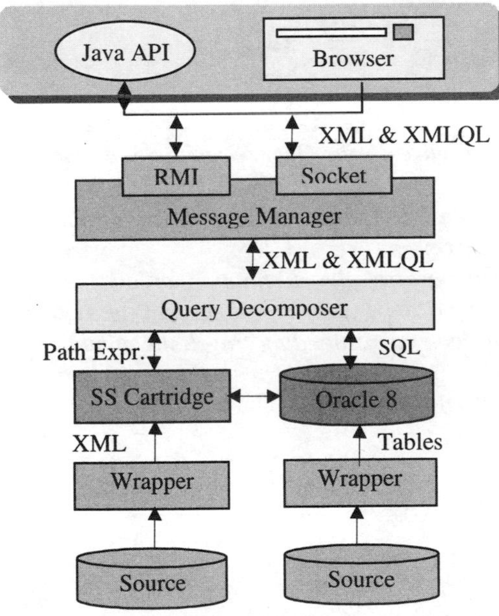

Figure 1: Overview of the MIROWeb System

The *Query Browser* is a graphical interface to browse through virtual XML documents from any starting label chosen by the user. To avoid errors, a list of accessible labels is fetched from the mediator dictionary, which contains a metadata structure similar to *dataguide* [9]. The user can choose a root, develop the hierarchy, formulate selection and join predicates, select projection nodes and submit the resulting XMLQL query.

The *Java API* is invoked by a client Java program through an extended JDBC interface to fetch data from the database. Basic extensions of JDBC are provided and allow to send an XMLQL query to the mediator and to navigate through the resulting XML document.

The *Message Manager* handles the client-server dialog. The clients communicate with the server via sockets or RMI. The message manager handles the two protocols. It also parses the query and delivers it to the query decomposer in an internal representation.

The *Query Decomposer* is responsible for decomposing queries into SQL queries for structured data and method calls to the Java cartridge to handle semistructured data at the mediator layer. The type of data (*e.g.,* semistructured or relational) and its status (*e.g.,* from which data source) is given by the dictionary through the dataguide. Queries are decomposed according to the referenced data type (semistructured or relational). When returned, results are recomposed as a unique XML document according to the query graph.

The *Semistructured Cartridge* implements semistructured objects within Oracle 8. From an external point of view, semistructured objects are seen as XML documents. Internally, they are modeled as labeled directed graph. However, our modeling is slightly different from data models such as OEM[10]. We distinguish two types of links: a link originated and targeted within the same object is called an *aggregation link,* and a link between different objects is called an *association link.* When assembling an object, only links of aggregation type are considered as relevant. This information is particularly important to model XML documents, which include M to N relationships (*i.e.,* association links). In addition, we introduce an optional order of edges among those going out from a given node. The order is simply memorized through an ordinal number. This is important to memorize and retrieve XML document items in the correct order.

In the current version of the system, all integrated data are first loaded within Oracle 8 in a data warehouse approach, then queried through the user interfaces. Storing the data is the responsibility of the mediator administrator through the wrappers and data loader. Later, it should be done on demand, at least partly.

3. Demonstration

We now introduce a typical scenario which will be demonstrated at the conference. Semistructured (XML) real data are loaded within Oracle 8 using a specific database wrapper allowing to generate and rename metadata (*i.e.,* tags). Three data sources are first loaded in the mediator as tables with semistructured attributes. Then, the demonstration focuses on the browser and the mediator. It shows how XMLQL queries are formulated, then sent to the server, decomposed and processed either through the SQL engine or through the semistructured cartridge. In the following, we describe four typical steps of the demonstration.

The Control Panel

A user can access MIROWeb with his Internet Browser, going to the URL providing our services. Then, the MIROWeb Java applet is launched in the browser, and begins with a Control Panel (see Figure 2) where the user must be authenticated by giving *login* and *password*.
Once the user is authenticated, the dictionary window is shown.

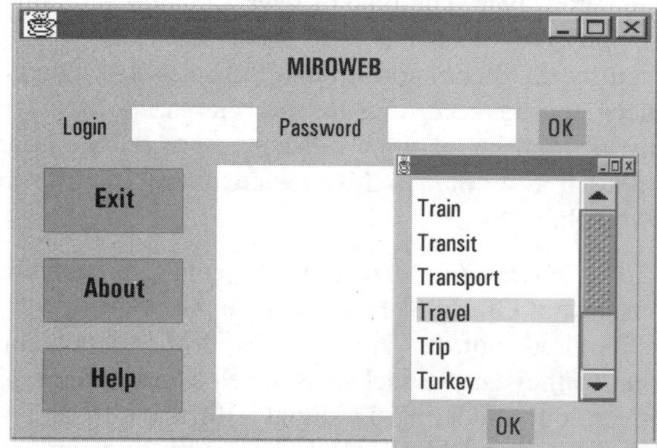

Figure 2: The Control Panel and the Dictionary

The dictionary

The Java applet first fetches all the labels which can be provided to the user. The labels are metadata from which the user wants to later start his query. These labels are generated from the *dataguide* built on the server as part of the dictionary, and sent to the client browser which parses and displays them as a list of labels. In our example (see Figure 2) the user has chosen the label *Travel.*

The Query Specification

MIROWeb is designed such that the user formulates queries graphically (see Figure 3). Specific buttons are provided to help the user.

- **Attribute**: clicking on this button switch to the attribute mode (default mode). In this mode, if the user clicks on a node (folder), then it will open/close it, connecting to the server if necessary to provide the next level of the opened folder. If the user clicks on a leaf, then an input form will appear on the screen, where the user can provide restrictions on the selected attribute. Filling it with a value means that the user wants this attribute correspond to the entered value. Strings, operators signs will be introduced. And filling it with a star (*) means that the user wants this value to exist, but does not care about the precise value.
- **New Root**: by clicking on this button and choosing a node, the user selects a new starting label for his query.
- **Projection**: in the projection mode, user can select/deselect attributes to be shown at result time.
- **Submit**: this button is used to submit the request to the server, and so the user will pass to the next step.

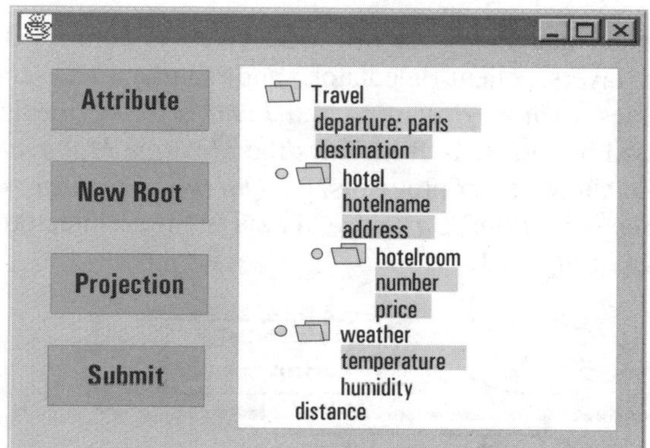

Figure 3: The Query Specification

In our example (see Figure 3), the user has formulated the following query:
select the departure, the destination of all the travels starting from "Paris" with the name and address of the hotel(s) for each corresponding travel, the number(s) and price(s) of each room of each hotel matching, and the weather temperature.

The Query Result

The query result (see Figure 4) is then generated by the server and sent to the client browser which displays it visually as a tree. As we can see on the screenshot, every matching result is represented as a node which can be opened if the user wants details on its content.

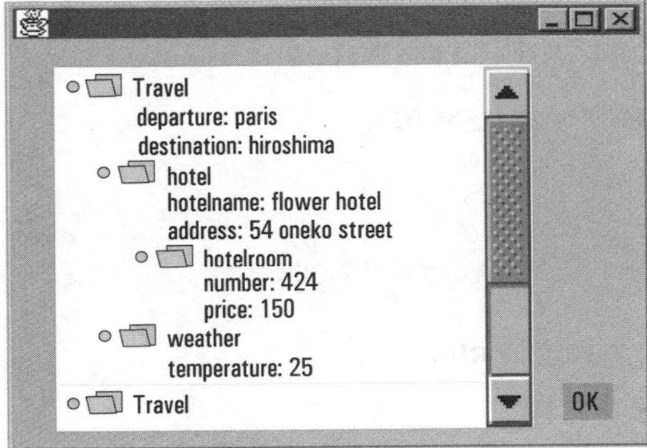

Figure 4: The Query Result

4. Conclusion

The development of MIROWeb shows a number of important points about the integration of data sources based on an hybrid object-relational semistructured model: (i) Object-relational systems can support quite efficiently semistructured objects based on a cautious implementation of graphs in tables using both clustering and indexing. (ii) From a user viewpoint, it is easy to browse through integrated data seen as XML virtual documents that can be queried on tags and contents. (iii) XML and XMLQL are appropriate and complementary exchange format and query language for heterogeneous irregular data. More than its power, the beauty of XMLQL is its homogeneity with XML, making queries as easy to transfer as documents. (iv) Decomposing XMLQL queries according to a repository giving the tag types and localization in SQL or XMLQL queries is possible. We have developed a special technology for that. (v) Developing intelligent wrappers capable of translating any source in a table with semistructured columns is quite easy. Furthermore, the wrappers can be intelligent enough to unify the tags based on a common directory. This last point requires further investigation.

5. Acknowledgments

We would like to thank Dana Florescu, Peter Fankhauser, Henri Laude and Patrick Valduriez for their help within the design of the MIROWeb system. Our research was sponsored by Esprit Project N° 25208.

6. References

[1] G. Gardarin, B. Finance, P. Fankhauser, W. Klas: "IRO-DB: A Distributed System Federating Object and Relational Databases", *In book "Object Oriented Multibase Systems: A Solution for Advanced Applications"*, Chap. 1, O. Bukhres and A. Elmagarmid Editors, 1994.

[2] A. Tomasic, L. Raschid and P. Valduriez: "Scaling Heterogeneous Databases and the Design of Disco". *Int. Conf. on Distributed Computing Systems*, Hong Kong, 1996.

[3] M.J. Carey and all: "Towards Heterogeneous Multimedia Information Systems: The Garlic Approach", *IEEE Workshop on Research Issues in Data Engineering (RIDE-95)*, Taipei, 1995.

[4] A. Levy, A. Rajaraman and J. Ordille: "Querying Heterogeneous Information Sources Using Source Descriptions". *Int. Conf. On VLDB,* Bombay, 1996.

[5] S. Chawathe, H. Garcia-Molina, J. Hammer, K. Ireland, Y. Papakonstantinou, J. Ullman and J. Widom: "The TSIMMIS Project: Integration of Heterogeneous Information Sources". In *Proc. of 10th Anniversary Meeting of the Information Processing Society of Japan*, Tokyo,1994.

[6] S. Cluet, C. Delobel, J. Simeon and K. Smaga: "Your Mediators Need Data Conversion!". *Int. Conf. on Management of Data ACM SIGMOD*, Seattle, 1998.

[7] P. Fankhauser, G. Gardarin and M. Lopez: "Experiences in Federated Databases: From IRO-DB to MIRO-Web". *Int. Conf. on VLDB*, New York, 1998.

[8] A. Deutsh, M. Fernandez, D. Florescu, A. Levy and D. Suciu: "XML-QL: A Query Language for XML". *Submission to the WWW Consortium*, 1998.

[9] R. Goldman, J. Widom: "DataGuides: Enabling Query Formulation and Optimization in Semistructured Databases". *Int. Conf. on VLDB*, Athens, 1997.

[10] Y. Papakonstantinou, H. Garcia-Molina and J. Widom: "Object Exchange Across Heterogeneous Information Sources". *Int. Conf. on Data Engineering*, Taipei, 1995

Aqua: A Fast Decision Support System Using Approximate Query Answers

Swarup Acharya   Phillip B. Gibbons   Viswanath Poosala

Information Sciences Research Center
Bell Laboratories
600 Mountain Avenue
Murray Hill NJ 07974

Abstract

Aqua is a system for providing fast, approximate answers to aggregate queries, which are very common in OLAP applications. It has been designed to run on top of any commercial relational DBMS. Aqua precomputes *synopses* (special statistical summaries) of the original data and stores them in the DBMS. It provides approximate answers (with quality guarantees) by rewriting the queries to run on these synopses. Finally, Aqua also incrementally keeps the synopses up-to-date as the database changes.

1 Motivation

Traditional query processing has focused solely on providing exact answers to queries, in a manner that seeks to minimize response time and maximize throughput. However, in large data recording and warehousing environments, providing an exact answer to a complex query can take minutes, or even hours, due to the amount of computation and disk I/O required.

There are a number of scenarios in which an exact answer may not be required, and a user may prefer a fast, approximate answer. For example, during some drill-down query sequences in ad-hoc data mining, initial queries in the sequence are used solely to determine what the interesting queries are. An approximate answer can also provide feedback on how well-posed a query is. Moreover, it can provide a tentative answer to a query when the base data is unavailable. Another example is when the query requests numerical answers, and the full precision of the exact answer is not needed, e.g., a total, average, or percentage for which only the first few digits of precision are of interest (such as the leading few digits of a total in the millions, or the nearest percentile of a percentage).

Motivated by these concerns, we have developed the Approximate QUery Answering (Aqua) system. Aqua is a system designed to provide fast, approximate answers to aggregate as well as set-valued queries. The work is tailored to data warehousing environments. Our goal is to provide an estimated response in orders of magnitude less time than the time to compute an exact answer, by avoiding or minimizing the number of accesses to the base data.

2 Architecture

Aqua is designed as a module that sits on top of any SQL-compliant DBMS managing a data warehouse. Aqua precomputes statistical summaries on the relations in the warehouse. Currently, the statistics take the form of various types of samples and histograms, and are stored as regular relations inside the warehouse; they are also incrementally maintained up-to-date as the base data is updated.

Aqua answers user queries using the pre-computed summaries. Approximate answers are provided by rewriting the user query over the summary relations and executing the new query. The rewriting involves suitably scaling the results of certain operators within the query. Finally, the

Proceedings of the 25th VLDB Conference, Edinburgh, Scotland, 1999.

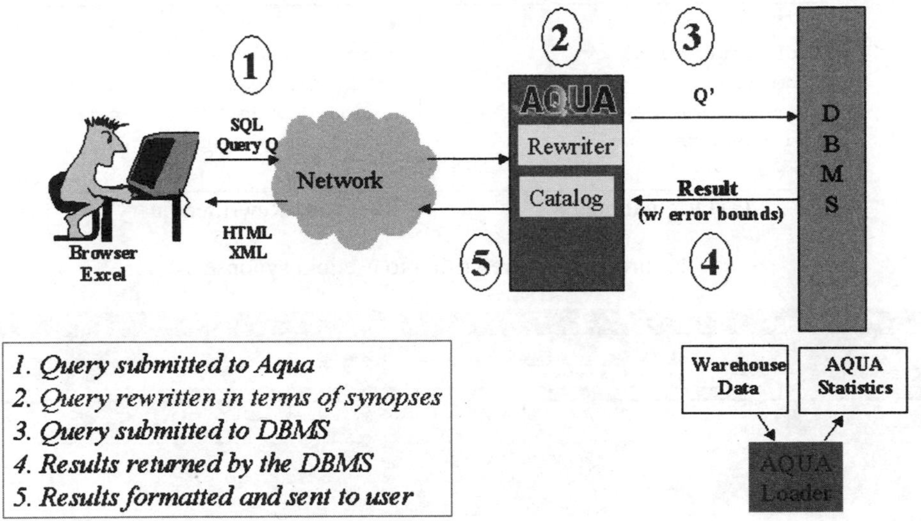

Figure 1: The Aqua architecture.

query and the approximate answer are analyzed to provide guarantees on the quality of the answer, and report error bounds. The high-level architecture of Aqua is depicted in Figure 1, along with the steps taken during query processing. As new data arrives, Aqua maintains the synopses up to date, with few or no accesses to the original data.

3 Aqua Technical Results and Operational Details

There are several technical problems arising in answering approximate queries. We have identified and solved a few of them, and incorporated the solutions into Aqua. Many of these results appear in [GMP97, GM98, AGPR99]. The key features of Aqua are as follows:

- Novel incremental maintenance techniques for keeping histograms and samples up-to-date in the presence of database updates.
- Improved error bounds based on a novel subsampling scheme.
- Strategies for allocating space among various summary statistics.
- Biased samples for improving the accuracy for queries with group-by operations.
- Improved sampling techniques (concise and counting samples) that use less space than traditional samples.

We have shown that schemes for providing approximate answers to multi-table queries that rely on using random samples of base relations alone suffer from serious disadvantages. We have developed an approach, which we call *join synopses*, that overcomes these disadvantages. We have shown both theoretically and empirically that join synopses provide highly-accurate answers and tighter confidence bounds than sampling from base relations.

In a recent work [AGP99], we demonstrate the drawback of uniform samples to effectively answer *group-by* queries, a key component of drill-down and roll-up analysis in OLAP. We propose new biased sampling techniques to address this handicap. Incorporation of these techniques into Aqua have shown their utility in making group-by queries significantly more accurate in practice.

As an illustration of query processing in Aqua, we present a key component, the query rewrite process using a simple example (details in [AGPR99]). Figure 2 gives an example of this rewriting that takes into account join synopses. The query is based on the schema for the TPC-D benchmark. When the query is submitted to Aqua, it identifies the join being computed in the query and rewrites the query to refer to the appropriate join synopsis. Specifically, the table names `lineitem` and `order` are replaced by the Aqua table names `bs_lineitem` and `js_order`. In this example, the resulting join synopsis is a 1% sample of the join between `lineitem` and `order`, so the `sum` aggregate in the select clause is scaled by 100. The rewritten query submitted to the warehouse is shown in Figure 2(b). (Calculation of error bounds is not shown here for simplicity.)

Aqua also provides a web-based interface to allows users to pose queries. A screenshot of the interface is

```
select sum(l_quantity)
  from lineitem, order
  where l_orderkey = o_orderkey
  and o_orderstatus = F
```

(a) Original query

```
select 100*sum(l_quantity)
  from bs_lineitem, js_order
  where l_orderkey = o_orderkey
  where o_orderstatus = F
```

(b) Rewritten query

Figure 2: Query rewriting to use join synopses.

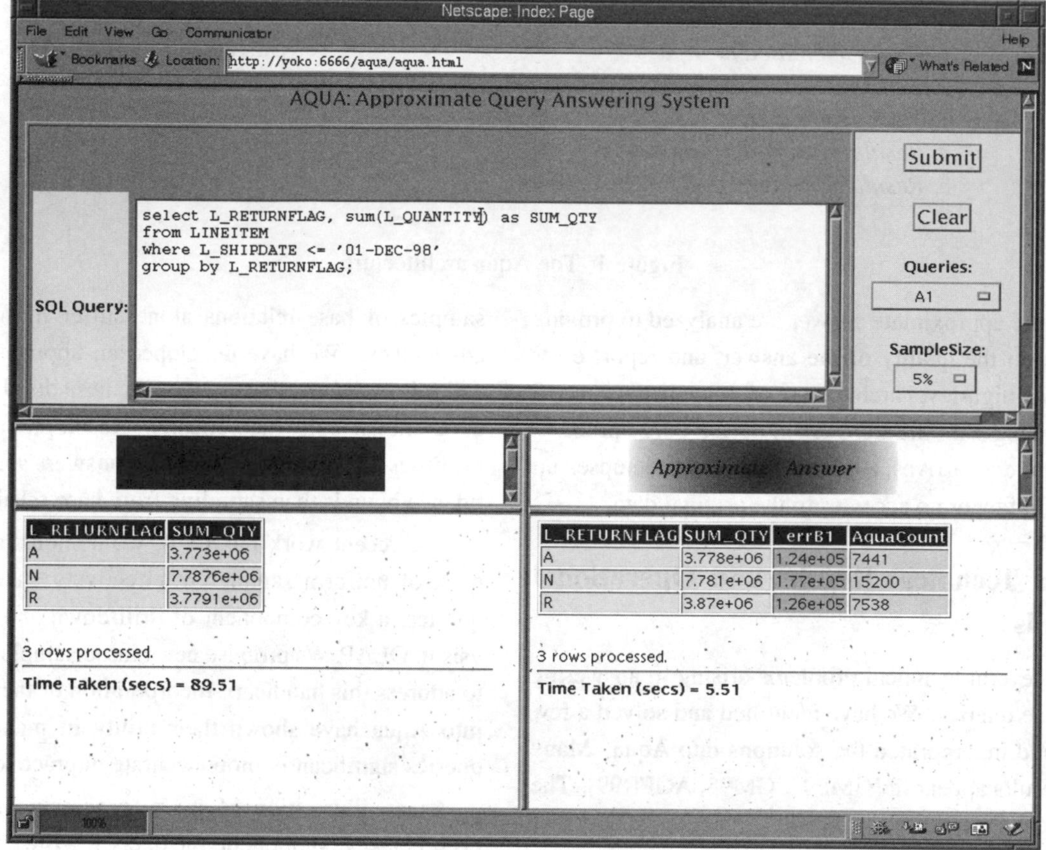

Figure 3: Aqua user interface

shown in Fig 3. It shows the actual answer and the approximated answer generated by Aqua for a simplified version of Query $Q1$ of the TPC-D suite along with the running times. The results are for a 0.1 scalefactor TPC-D database (100 MB). The approximate answer window also shows the error bound calculated for each group (errB1), along with a count of the tuples used to generate the estimate (AquaCount).

4 Related Work

Statistical techniques have been applied in databases for more than two decades now, but primarily inside a query optimizer for selectivity estimation. However, the application of statistical techniques to approximate query answering has started receiving attention only very recently. Hellerstein *et al.* [HHW97] proposed a framework for approximate answers of aggregation queries called *Online Aggregation*, in which the base data is scanned in random order at query time and the approximate answer is continuously updated as the scan proceeds. Unlike Aqua, this work involves accessing the base data at query time, thus being more costly; but at the same time, this approach provides the fully accurate answer gradually. Other systems support limited on-line aggregation features; e.g., the Red Brick system supports running COUNT, AVG, and SUM. Since the scan order used to produce these aggregations is not random, the accuracy can be quite poor. In the *Approximate* query processor, developed by Vrbsky and Liu [VL93], an approximate answer to a set-valued query is any superset of the exact answer that is a subset of the cartesian product. Recently, Ioannidis and Poosala have developed a robust numerical measure for computing the error in an approximate set-valued query answer and also provided histogram-based techniques for answering complex queries [IP99]. There has also been some work on using histograms and wavelets to approximate the data cube for providing approximate answers to aggregate queries [PG99, VWI98].

5 Details of the Demo

The main focus of the demo will be on the ability of Aqua to provide quick and high-quality approximate answers to queries of varying complexities. The data warehouse will consist of the popular TPC-D benchmark data loaded into a commercial DBMS. The queries include many of the benchmark queries as well as some generated by us, chosen to demonstrate the benefits of various statistical techniques in Aqua. In particular, we will show that join synopses outperform base samples for queries with joins and that biased samples outperform uniform samples for group-by queries. We will also show some of the key features of the Aqua front-end, such as the ability to execute a query using any one of the available sets of statistics.

Acknowledgments

The authors acknowledge the contribution of Sridhar Ramaswamy in the initial design and development of the Aqua prototype.

References

[AGP99] S. Acharya, P. B. Gibbons, and V. Poosala. Congressional samples for approximate answering of group-by queries. Technical report, Bell Laboratories, Murray Hill, New Jersey, February 1999.

[AGPR99] S. Acharya, P. B. Gibbons, V. Poosala, and S. Ramaswamy. Join synopses for approximate query answering. In *Proc. of ACM SIGMOD Conf*, June 1999.

[GM98] P. B. Gibbons and Y. Matias. New sampling-based summary statistics for improving approximate query answers. *Proc. of ACM SIGMOD Conf*, pages 331–342, June 1998.

[GMP97] P. B. Gibbons, Y. Matias, and V. Poosala. Fast incremental maintenance of approximate histograms. *Proc. of the 23rd Int. Conf. on Very Large Databases*, pages 466–475, August 1997.

[HHW97] J. M. Hellerstein, P. J. Haas, and H. J. Wang. Online aggregation. In *Proc. ACM SIGMOD International Conf. on Management of Data*, pages 171–182, May 1997.

[IP99] Y. Ioannidis and V. Poosala. Histogram-based techniques for approximating set-valued query-answers. *Proc. of the 25rd Int. Conf. on Very Large Databases*, September 1999.

[PG99] V. Poosala and V. Ganti. Fast approximate answers to aggregate queries on a data cube. *International working conference on Scientific and Statistical Database Management*, July 1999.

[VL93] S. V. Vrbsky and J. W. S. Liu. Approximate—a query processor that produces monotonically improving approximate answers. *IEEE Trans. on Knowledge and Data Engineering*, 5(6):1056–1068, 1993.

[VWI98] J. S. Vitter, M. Wang, and B. R. Iyer. Data cube approximation and histograms via wavelets. *Proc. of the CIKM*, pages 96–104, 1998.

The Mirror MMDBMS architecture

Arjen P. de Vries Mark G.L.M. van Doorn Henk M. Blanken Peter M.G. Apers

Centre for Telematics and Information Technology
University of Twente
The Netherlands

1 Introduction

Handling large collections of digitized multimedia data, usually referred to as multimedia digital libraries, is a major challenge for information technology. The Mirror DBMS is a research database system that is developed to better understand the kind of data management that is required in the context of multimedia digital libraries (see also URL http://www.cs.utwente.nl/~arjen/mmdb.html). Its main features are an integrated approach to both content management and (traditional) structured data management, and the implementation of an extensible object-oriented logical data model on a binary relational physical data model. The focus of this work is aimed at design for scalability.

2 Query processing

The query facilities of the Mirror DBMS rely on the **Moa Object Algebra** [BWK98]. Moa constitutes an object data model and query algebra, designed to be used at the logical level of a DBMS. It has been implemented on top of the Monet extensible database management system. The Moa data model is based on the principle of 'structural object-orientation'. Structures, such as tuple and (multi-)set, define complex data types out of the simple base types. The base types, such as integer and string, are inherited from the underlying physical database. This way, Moa introduces the notion of **data independence** into the world of object-oriented databases: the translation from the logical data model into a different physical model (Monet supports a binary relational data model) provides an excellent basis for algebraic query optimization, and allows often for set-at-a-time processing of complex query expressions.

The Moa kernel provides the tuple (or record) structure, and the multi-set structure. The resulting data model is equivalent to what is generally known as the NF^2 algebra. However, Moa object algebra is more than 'just' an implementation of NF^2 algebra. It is an *open* complex object system, supporting extensibility of structures. Thus, new structures can be added to the system, similar to the well-known principle of base type extensibility in object-relational database systems. Obviously, this enables the definition of new generic structures, such as lists. A more interesting use for structural extensibility is however the definition of *domain specific structures.*

3 Content management

The prototype implementation of our database system demonstrates the particular application of Moa's extensibility in the domain of multimedia information retrieval. An information retrieval (IR) model consists of three parts: a document and query representation scheme, a ranking function which determines to which extent a document is relevant to a query, and a query formulation model [WY95]. Documents and queries are usually represented by its terms. The `CONTREP` Moa structure supports the ranking scheme known as the inference network retrieval model. This retrieval model is the basis of the successful IR system InQuery. It allows flexible modeling of the combination of evidence originating from different sources. We have adapted this text retrieval model to handle also multimedia information retrieval [dV98]. New structures in Moa, supported by new probabilistic operators at the physical level, provide an efficient implementation of the inference network retrieval model.

To illustrate the use of these extensions, we model a traditional digital library of (manually) annotated images using these Moa structures. Assume that an image is identified by its URL, and its textual annotation is indexed using the inference network retrieval model:

```
define TraditionalImgLib as
```


Proceedings of the 25th VLDB Conference, Edinburgh, Scotland, 1999.

```
SET<
  TUPLE<
    Atomic<URL>:   source,
    CONTREP<Text>: annotation
>>;
```

Ranking the images with respect to a query is then performed with the following query, in which `query` refers to a set of query terms, and `stats` is a structure that represents global statistics of the whole collection:[1]

```
map[sum(THIS)](
  map[getBL(THIS.annotation,
    query, stats)]( TraditionalImgLib ));
```

Because these query expressions can be combined with 'normal' relational operators (such as `select` or `join`), the resulting system is an efficient integration of information and data retrieval. This way, it is possible to refer to both structure and content of multimedia data in a single query (see also [dVW99]).

4 Distributed architecture

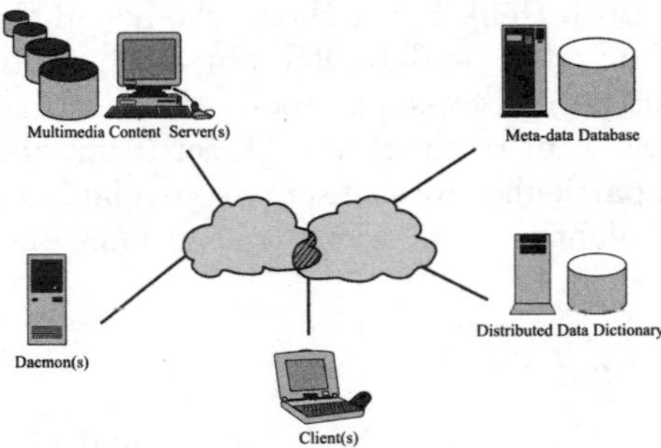

Figure 1: The distributed architecture

Another aspect of our design is related to more practical issues for the creation and maintenance of a multimedia digital library. A digital library involves several more or less independent parties, including human annotators, software to extract meta data automatically, and owners of multimedia footage [dVEK98]. Hence, we believe that a digital library can only be a success if it follows the model of the web. We use an open distributed architecture instead of a monolithic database system, cf. figure 1 [dVB98]. The notion of a 'daemon' abstracts from the various techniques for meta data extraction and query formulation. Using CORBA, we allow distribution of operations, establishing independence between the management of meta data and the parties that create these meta data.

5 The demo system

In the Mirror architecture, the retrieval *application* is not integrated in the database system itself, unlike in most 'multimedia databases' found in literature. The Mirror DBMS provides the basic functionality for probabilistic inference, multimedia data types, and feature extraction techniques, just like traditional database systems provide the basic functionality to build administrative applications. In this section, we describe an example image retrieval application, using the functionality provided by the Mirror DBMS. The underlying philosophy of this application has been inspired by theories from cognitive psychology, in particular Paivio's dual coding theory [EK95]. Aspects of its design are similar in spirit to both the Viper [SMMR99] and the FourEyes [MP97] image retrieval systems.

5.1 Our prototype environment

The digital library constructed for the demo consists of images collected by a simple web robot. Some of the images in the library are annotated with text. One of the daemons segments the images. Several feature extraction daemons independently create feature representations of the image segments. At the moment of writing, we have implemented two color histogram daemons. In addition, we use the four reference implementations of texture algorithms provided by the MeasTex framework (see URL http://www.cssip.elec.uq.edu.au/~guy/meastex/meastex.html). These feature spaces are then clustered using the public domain clustering package AutoClass [CS95]. Furthermore, we have thesaurus daemons that are interactively used during query formulation. The Mirror DBMS implements the meta data database (see figure 1), which contains the content representations. The media server is a web server.

5.2 The example application

The data model of the image library can be specified by the application programmer as:

```
define ImageLibrary as
SET<
  TUPLE<
    Atomic<URL>:   source,
    Atomic<Text>:  annotation,
    Atomic<Image>: image
>>;
```

Next, the daemons in the prototype environment start to work on this schema. Like the example in section 3, the text annotations are indexed and represented as `CONTREP` structures. The images are segmented, and feature representations are extracted from the segments, creating the following (internal) intermediate schema:

```
SET<
  TUPLE<
    Atomic<URL>: source,
    CONTREP<Text>: annotation,
```

[1] For further details about the query language and the structural extensions, refer to [dV98] and [dVW99]

```
SET<
  TUPLE<
    Atomic< Image >: segment,
    Atomic< Vector >: RGB,
    Atomic< Vector >: Gabor,
    ...
  >
  >: image_segments
>>;
```

The feature spaces are clustered with AutoClass, to obtain a representation of the image content that can be queried using the CONTREP structure. We further use the identified clusters as if they are words in text retrieval; they become the basic blocks of 'meaning' for multimedia information retrieval. This results in the following internal schema, which corresponds to the original ImageLibrary schema:

```
define ImageLibraryInternal as
SET<
  TUPLE<
    Atomic<URL>: source,
    CONTREP<Text>: annotation,
    CONTREP<Image>: image
>>;
```

Of course, the clusters in the image content representation (such as 'gabor_21') are not suited for interaction with the users of the digital library. Therefore, we automatically construct a thesaurus, associating words in the textual annotations to the clusters in the image content representation. An interesting aspect of this approach, is that this thesaurus can be considered an implementation of Paivio's dual coding theory. Following the observation used in PhraseFinder [JC94], an association thesaurus can be seen as measuring the belief in a *concept* (instead of in a document) given the query. Thus, the domain specific Moa structures that model IR query evaluation, can also be used for query formulation using the thesaurus.

Querying the digital image library now takes place as follows. First, the user enters an initial (usually textual) query. Next, we use the thesaurus to select clusters from the image content representations that are relevant to this initial query. Assuming that the result is a Moa expression called query, we then retrieve images from the digital library as follows:

```
map[sum(THIS)](
  map[getBL(THIS.image,
    query, stats)]( ImageLibraryInternal ));
```

The results of this query are shown to the user. The user may provide relevance feedback for these images; this relevance feedback is used to improve the current query. A problem for the current retrieval system is that the thesaurus sometimes associates words in the annotations to irrelevant clusters, or AutoClass identifies clusters of little semantic value. To alleviate these problems, we are investigating machine learning techniques to adapt the thesaurus and the content representation, using the relevance feedback across query sessions.

As we demonstrated, the multimedia querying process is expressed in Moa expressions. The Mirror DBMS provides the primitives for managing the images and its meta data, as well as the probabilistic inference required during the interaction with the user. New feature models, different clustering algorithms, or different query modification techniques, can easily be added or modified. Hence, a variety of multimedia retrieval systems can be implemented by simply changing the sequence of Moa expressions issued in the Mirror DBMS.

6 Acknowledgments

This demo could never have been created without the Moa kernel, designed and implemented mainly by Annita N. Wilschut and Jan Flokstra. Erik van het Hof has implemented the open distributed architecture of figure 1. Both Henk Ernst Blok, who added the LIST structure to Moa, and Roelof van Zwol, contributed significantly in discussions about the system design. Finally, we want to thank the Monet team, and Peter Boncz in particular, for the support, explanations, and all those nightly hours spent tracing bugs and fixing them.

References

[BWK98] P. Boncz, A.N. Wilschut, and M.L. Kersten. Flattening an object algebra to provide performance. In *Fourteenth International Conference on Data Engineering*, pages 568–577, Orlando, Florida, February 1998.

[CS95] P. Cheeseman and J. Stutz. Bayesian classification (AutoClass): Theory and results. In *Advances in Knowledge Discovery and Data Mining*. AAAI Press, 1995.

[dV98] A.P. de Vries. Mirror: Multimedia query processing in extensible databases. In *Proceedings of the fourteenth Twente workshop on language technology (TWLT14): Language Technology in Multimedia Information Retrieval*, pages 37–48, Enschede, The Netherlands, December 1998.

[dVB98] A.P. de Vries and H.M. Blanken. Database technology and the management of multimedia data in Mirror. In *Multimedia Storage and Archiving Systems III*, volume 3527 of *Proceedings of SPIE*, pages 443–455, Boston MA, November 1998.

[dVEK98] A.P. de Vries, B. Eberman, and D.E. Kovalcin. The design and implementation of an infrastructure for multimedia digital libraries. In *Proceedings of the 1998 International Database Engineering & Applications Symposium*, pages 103–110, Cardiff, UK, July 1998.

[dVW99] A.P. de Vries and A.N. Wilschut. On the integration of IR and databases. In *Database issues in multimedia; short paper proceedings, international conference on database semantics (DS-8)*, Rotorua, New Zealand, January 1999.

[EK95] M.W. Eysenck and M.T. Keane. *Cognitive Psychology. A student's handbook*, chapter Mental representation. Lawrence Erlbaum Associates, 3 edition, 1995.

[JC94] Y. Jing and W.B. Croft. An association thesaurus for information retrieval. Technical Report 94-17, University of Massachusetts, 1994.

[MP97] T.P. Minka and R.W. Picard. Interactive learning using a "society of models". *Pattern Recognition*, 30(4), 1997.

[SMMR99] D. McG. Squire, W. Müller, H. Müller, and J. Raki. Content-based query of image databases, inspirations from text retrieval: inverted files, frequency-based weights and relevance feedback. In *The 11th Scandinavian Conference on Image Analysis*, Kangerlussuaq, Greenland, June 1999. To appear.

[WY95] S.K.M. Wong and Y.Y. Yao. On modeling information retrieval with probabilistic inference. *ACM Transactions on Information Systems*, 13(1):38–68, January 1995.